collect.com

BUSINESS REPLY MAIL
FIRST CLASS MAIL   PERMIT NO. 50   DUBUQUE, IA

POSTAGE WILL BE PAID BY ADDRESSEE

ANTIQUE TRADER
ONLINE PRICE GUIDE
PO BOX 1050
DUBUQUE, IA 52004-1050

ANTIQUE TRADER

BUSINESS REPLY MAIL
FIRST CLASS MAIL   PERMIT NO. 12   IOLA, WI

POSTAGE WILL BE PAID BY ADDRESSEE

ANTIQUE TRADER
700 EAST STATE STREET
IOLA, WI 54945-9984

Antique Trader®

Antiques & Collectibles

2002 PRICE GUIDE

Kyle Husfloen

Published by
Antique Trader Books, A Division of

**krause
publications**

700 E. State Street • Iola, WI 54990-0001
Telephone: 715/445-2214
www.krause.com

Please, call or write us for our free catalog of antiques and collectibles publications.
Our toll-free number to place an order or obtain a free catalog is 800-258-0929 or
please use our regular business telephone, 715-445-2214.

ISBN: 0-87349-223-4

Printed in the United States of America

A WORD TO THE READER

Welcome to the *Antique Trader Antiques & Collectibles Price Guide 2002*. This is our eighteenth annual edition and continues the tradition begun over thirty years ago when Antique Trader first began producing special price guides back in 1970. Now into a new century and millennium we're proud to offer our latest comprehensive pricing guide to the vast and fascinating world of collecting.

A hallmark of our price guides has always been to provide detailed and accurate listings highlighted with numerous quality photographs. Our 2002 edition carries on that tradition and offers a comprehensive overview of the current collecting marketplace. We've included over 18,000 individual listings illustrated by over 4,000 photographs, a very high percentage for a guide of this type. In addition to the photographs many of our ceramics and glass categories also include a sketch of signatures or trademarks found on those pieces. Also of great value to the reader are the hundreds of brief introductory notes we include for categories listed. All of these factors make the *Antique Trader Antiques & Collectibles Price Guide* one of the most detailed and informative references in the field of collecting.

We have always included extensive pricing sections on major segments of collecting such as Ceramics, Glass and Furniture but we go far beyond those areas today. The world of collecting has grown and expanded to such an extent in the past thirty years that keeping up with all the new trends is a daunting task.

However, in each of our guides we strive to include listings for new or unusual fields of collecting, along with timely information which will prove invaluable to collectors, dealers and appraisers. For instance, in this year's volume we have separate pricing sections on such diverse collectibles as Halloween Collectibles, British Invasion 45 Records, Dog Collectibles, Ice Skating Collectibles, Mardi Gras Memorabilia, Casino Chips and, under the heading of "Kitchenwares," such items as Cow Creamers, Cookie Cutters and Trivets. There are many other special sections too numerous to list here. Of course, we haven't forgotten the more traditional collecting topics so in our 900 pages we offer you, the reader, the single best guide to all things collectible.

With each new edition the editors and staff of our price guide work diligently to provide the most accurate and up-to-date information possible and do our best to provide detailed indexing and cross-referencing to help you find the special information you are seeking. We're also pleased to note that our list of Special Contributors continues to grow and the expertise of these authorities brings even more depth and scope to our price listings. I want to offer special thanks to all of these people and organizations for their efforts and you can find out more about them in our complete listing of names and addresses on the following pages.

As noted, we are especially pleased with the abundance of black and white illustrations included this year and, as an added bonus, we also provide a spe-

4

cial 16 page full-color supplement, both eye-catching and informative. We draw our illustrations from numerous sources and they are also listed below.

Readers of a guide such as ours can enjoy the vast amount of detailed information provided here, however, they should always remember that this book should only be used as a *guide* to pricing. Many of the pieces listed here were sold through auctions and private sales around the country and it is important to remember that regional factors can sometimes influence what a piece may sell for in a particular market. Also, factors such as rarity and condition are of paramount importance when noting what a particular item sold for at any given time. Our detailed descriptions will be of help to you in understanding these pricing variations and it is also important to keep in mind that a majority of the values listed here are for "retail replacement" costs, in other words the price a particular piece might bring at a specialized auction, show or shop where an enthusiastic buyer is on hand. There will always be market variations in the field of antiques and collectibles and the prospect of finding an unexpected treasure at a bargain price is one of the exciting aspects of this collecting hobby.

Antique Trader Antiques & Collectibles Price Guide follows a basically alphabetical format for most of our categories. However, we have arranged the larger categories of Ceramics, Furniture and Glass into their own subcategories where each specific type or maker will be listed alphabetically within that section. Check our comprehensive INDEX at the back of this guide if you have a question as to where your special item may be listed.

Finally, please remember that although our descriptions, prices and illustrations have been double-checked and every effort has been made to ensure accuracy, neither the editor, pub-

lisher or contributor can assume responsibility for any losses that might be incurred as a result of consulting this guide, or of typographical or other errors.

Although a majority of our photographs are provided by our Special Contributors and the auctioneers and galleries listed below, a number of photographers have contributed pictures to this volume including: E.A. Babka, East Dubuque, Illinois; Stanley L. Baker, Minneapolis, Minnesota; Johanna Billings, Danielsville, Pennsylvania; Donna Bruun, Galena, Illinois; Herman C. Carter, Tulsa, Oklahoma; Susan N. Cox, El Cajon, California; J.D. Dalessandro, Cincinnati, Ohio; Ruth Eaves, Marmora, New Jersey; Susan Eberman, Bedford, Indiana; Scott Green, Manchester, New Hampshire; Jeff Grunewald, Chicago, Illinois; Vance Hall, Wichita, Kansas; Charles Hippler, Monticello, Illinois; Robert G. Jason-Ickes, Olympia, Washington; Dorothy Kamm, Port St. Lucie, Florida; Marlyn Margulis, Cherry Hill, New Jersey; Louise Paradis, Sparta, Wisconsin, and David H. Surgan, Brooklyn, New York;

For other photographs, artwork, data or permission to photograph in their shops, we sincerely express appreciation to the following auctioneers, galleries, museums, individuals and shops: Albrecht Auction Service, Vassar, Michigan; Alderfers, Hatfield, Pennsylvania; American Social History and Social Movements, Tucker, Georgia; Antiquorum, New York, New York; Charlton Hall Galleries, Columbia, South Carolina; Frank Chiarenza, Newington, Connecticut; Christie's, New York, New York; Collector's Auction Service, Oil City, Pennsylvania; Collector's Sales & Services, Pomfret Center, Connecticut; Copake Country Auction, Copake, New York; Daniel Auction Company, Sylvester, Georgia; DeFina Auctions, Austenburg, Ohio; William

Doyle Galleries, New York, New York; DuMouchelles, Detroit, Michigan; John Fontaine Gallery, Pittsfield, Massachusetts; Garth's Auctions Inc., Delaware, Ohio; Glass-Works Auctions, East Greenville, Pennsylvania; Green Valley Auctions, Mt. Crawford, Virginia.

Also to Vicki Harmon, San Marcos, California; the Gene Harris Antique Auction Center, Marshalltown, Iowa; Kenneth S. Hays & Associates, Louisville, Kentucky; the late William Heacock, Marietta, Ohio; International Toy Collectors Association, Athens, Illinois; Michael Ivankovich Antiques & Auctions, Doylestown, Pennsylvania; Jackson's Auctions, Cedar Falls, Iowa; Lang's Sporting Collectibles, Raymond, Maine; Leland's Auctions, New York, New York; Jim Ludescher, Dubuque, Iowa; J. Martin, Mt. Orab, Ohio; Mastro Fine Sports Auctions, Oakbrook, Illinois; Ross McCall Auctioneers, Onawa, Iowa; Randall McKee, Kenosha, Wisconsin; McMasters Doll Auctions, Cambridge, Ohio; Dr. James Measell, Marietta, Ohio; William Morford Auctions, Cazenovia, New York; Gary Metz's Muddy River Trading Company, Salem, Virginia; Richard Opfer Auctioneering, Inc., Timonium, Maryland; Pacific Glass Auctions, Sacramento, California; Past Tyme Pleasures, San Ramon, California; David Rago Arts & Crafts, Lambertville, New Jersey; Jane Rosenow, Galva, Illinois; Skinner, Inc., Bolton, Massachusetts; Slawinski Auction Company, Felton, California; Sotheby's, New York, New York; Stanton's Auctioneers, Vermontville, Michigan; Michael Strawser, Wolcottville, Indiana; Temples Antiques, Eden Prairie, Minnesota; Town Crier Auction Service, Burlington, Wisconsin; Tradewinds Antiques, Manchester-by-the-Sea, Massachusetts; Treadway Gallery, Cincinnati, Ohio and Lee Vines, Hewlett, New York.

We hope everyone who consults the *Antique Trader Antiques & Collectibles Price Guide* will find it the most accurate and informative guide to the ever-changing world of collecting.

The staff of this guide welcomes all letters from readers, especially those of constructive critique, and we make every effort to respond personally.

- Kyle Husfloen, Editor

Special Category Contributors

Architectural Items
Recycling the Past
381 N. Main Street
Barnegat, NJ 08005
(609) 660-9790
fax: (800) 878-3251
e-mail: salvage-
matt@yahoo.com
www.recyclingthep-
ast.com

Baby Mementoes
Teethers
Marcia Hersey
Author of *Collecting Baby
Rattles and Teethers
Identification and Value
Guide*

Bottle Openers
John Stanley
P.O. Box 64
Chapel Hill, NC 27514
(919) 419-1546
fax: (425) 795-8874
e-mail: jfo@mind-
spring.com

Casino Chips
Greg Susong
P.O. Box 654
Wellington, KS 67152
fax: (316) 326-3893
e-mail:
greg@chipguide.com

Cat Collectibles
Cat Collectors
P.O. Box 150784
Nashville, TN 37215
(615) 297-7403
fax: (615) 383-1359
e-mail: musiccity-
kitty@yahoo.com

Character, Radio & Television Collectibles
Dana Cain
5061 S. Stuart Court
Littleton, CO 80123
(303) 347-8252
e-mail: dana.cain@world-
net.att.net

Children's Books
Children's Books 1900-1920
Children's Books 1920s - 1950s
Little Golden Books
School Primers - 20th Century
Michael J. Goldberg
823 SE 25th Ave.
Portland, OR 97214
(503) 238-1977
e-mail: emjaygee@ine-
tarena.com

Children's Valentines
Kerra Davis
925 Bud Street
Blackshear, GA 31516
(912) 449-6494

Cookbooks
Kerra Davis
925 Bud Street
Blackshear, GA 31516
(912) 449-6494

Corkscrews
John Stanley
P.O. Box 64
Chapel Hill, NC 27514
(919) 419-1546
fax: (425) 795-8874
e-mail: jfo@mind-
spring.com

Cow Creamers
LuAnn Riggs
1486 Moonridge Ct.
Upland, CA 91784
e-mail: st-ark-
bucks@netwebb.com or
st-ark-bucks@world-
net.att.net

Dog Collectibles
Jane D. Swanson
10290 Hill Road
Erie, IL 61250
(309) 659-2166
e-mail: jane.swan-
son@ararental.org

Fraternal Order Collectibles
Masonic, Shrine, Order of the Easten Star
Bobbie Zucker Bryson
1 St. Eleanoras Lane
Tuckahoe, NY 10707
e-mail: napkin-
doll@aol.com

Games & Game Boards
Alex Malloy
P.O. Box 38
So. Salem, NY 10590
(203) 438-0396
fax: (203) 438-6744
e-mail: alexmal-
loy@aol.com

Garden Fountains & Ornaments
Recycling the Past
381 N. Main Street
Barnegat, NJ 08005
(609) 660-9790
fax: (800) 878-3251
e-mail: salvage-
matt@yahoo.com
www.recyclingthep-
ast.com

Halloween Collectibles
Ellen Bercovici
5118 Hampden La.
Bethesda, MD 20814
(301) 652-1140

Heintz Art Metal Shop Wares
David Surgan
328 Flatbush Ave.,
Suite 123
Brooklyn, NY 11238
(718) 638-3768

Ice Skating Collectibles
Bob Hudovernik
P.O. Box 49
Cascade, WI 63011
(920) 564-2913
e-mail: Manda-
layBE@aol.com

Japanese Woodblock Prints
Sandra Andacht, Sandra Andacht Inc.
P.O. Box 94
Little Neck, NY 11363
(718) 229-6593
e-mail: Orienta-lia@aol.com

Kewpie Collectibles
Jody Cooper
(805) 647-1464
e-mail: jlcooper@west.net

International Rose O'Neill Club
P.O. Box 668
Branson, MO 65616
3-Mail: agdc1@aol.com

Kitchenwares

General
Carol Bohn
501 Mark St.
Miffinburg, PA 17844
(717) 966-1198

Cast-Iron Items
Marion Grammer
1708 SW 19th Drive
Boynton Beach, FL 33426
e-mail:
mgrammr@aol.com

Coffee Mills
Mike White
P.O. Box 483
Fraser, CO 80442
(970) 726-0448
e-mail:
mwhite483@rkymt-nhi.com
web page: rkymt-nhi.com/grinder

Cookie Cutters
Ruth Capper
1167 Teal Road
Dellroy, OH 44620
(330) 735-2839

Hallmark Cookie Cutters
Kerra Davis
925 Bud Street
Blackshear, GA 31516
(912) 449-6494

Egg Timers, Pie Birds & String Holders
Ellen Bercovici
5118 Hampden La.
Bethesda, MD 20814
(301) 652-1140

Juice Reamers, Napkin Dolls & Range Salt & Pepper Shakers
Bobbie Zucker Bryson
1 St. Eleanoras Lane
Tuckahoe, NY 10707
e-mail: napkin-doll@aol.com

Laundry Room Items

Clothes Sprinkler Bottles
Ellen Bercovici
5118 Hampden La.
Bethesda, MD 20814
(301) 652-1140

Irons
Jimmy & Carol Walker
P.O. Box 68
Waelder, TX 78959-0068

Mardi Gras Memorabilia
Arthur Hardy Enterprises, Inc.
602 Metairie Road, Suite C
Metairie, LA 70005-4009
(504) 838-61111
fax: (504) 838-0100
e-mail: mardi-hardy@aol.com

Nutcrackers
Marion Grammer
1708 SW 19th Drive
Boynton Beach, FL 33426
e-mail:
mgrammr@aol.com
Photos by Don Melchoir
DMFJR@prodigy.net

Nutting (Wallace)
Michael Ivankovich
P.O. Box 1536
Doylestown, PA 18901
fax: (215) 345-6692

Phonographs
Mike Ellingson
1412 2nd Ave., S.
Fargo, ND 58103
e-mail: mikelling-son@webtv.net

Pinback Buttons
Michael J. Goldberg
823 SE 25th Ave.
Portland, OR 97214
(503) 238-1977
e-mail: emjaygee@ine-tarena.com

Plant Waterers
Bobbie Zucker Bryson
1 St. Eleanoras Lane
Tuckahoe, NY 10707
e-mail: napkin-doll@aol.com

Political & Campaign Items
Bobbie Zucker Bryson
1 St. Eleanoras Lane
Tuckahoe, NY 10707
e-mail: napkin-doll@aol.com

Print Artists - Early 20th Century
Michael Ivankovich
P.O. Box 1536
Doylestown, PA 18901
fax: (215) 345-6692

Radios
Harry Poster
P.O. Box 1883
S. Hackensack, NJ 07606

Records - British Invasion
Michael J. Goldberg
823 SE 25th Ave.
Portland, OR 97214
503-238-1977
e-mail: emjaygee@ine-tarena.com

Ribbon Dolls
Bobbie Zucker Bryson
1 St. Eleanoras Lane
Tuckahoe, NY 10707
e-mail: napkin-doll@aol.com

School House Collectibles
Kerra Davis
925 Bud Street
Blackshear, GA 31516
(912) 449-6494

Scottish Tartenware
Ellen Bercovici
5118 Hampden La.
Bethesda, MD 20814
(301) 652-1140

Scouting Items
C. Cuhaj
Box 433
Iola, WI 54945
(718) 445-5666
e-mail:
cuhajg@yahoo.com

Sewing Adjuncts
Beth Pulsipher
Prairie Home Antiques
240 N. Grand
Schoolcraft, MI 49087
(616) 679-20962

Television Sets
Harry Poster
P.O. Box 1883
S. Hackensack, NJ 07606
(201) 794-9606
fax: (201) 794-9553
e-mail: hposter@world-
net.att.net

Toothpick Holders
Judy Knauer
1223 Spring Valley Lane
West Chester, PA 19380
(610) 431-3477
e-mail:
winkjk@netaxs.com

Trivets
Marion Grammer
1708 SW 19th Drive
Boynton Beach, FL 33426
e-mail:
mgrammr@aol.com

Toys

Toy Buildings
Patty Cooper
e-mail: garden-
mont@aol.com

Fisher-Price Toys
Kerra Davis
925 Bud Street
Blackshear, GA 31516
(912) 449-6494

Hot Wheels
Paul M. Provencher
Spring Garden House
20115 Woodfield Road
Gaithersburg, MD 20882-
1229
(301) 948-2858
e-mail: ppro@white-
metal.com
http://whitemetal.com

Pedal Cars
Richard D. Friz
P.O. Box 472
Peterborough, NH 03458
(603) 563-8155
e-mail: joshdick-
mad@monadnet.com

Toy Soldiers
Jim Trautman
R.R. 1
Orton Ontario, Canada
L0N 1N0
(519) 855-6077
e-mail: emjaygee@ine-
tarena.com

Ceramics

American Painted Porcelain
Dorothy Kamm
P.O. Box 7460
Port St. Lucia, FL 34985-
7460
(561) 465-4008
e-mail: dor-
othy.kamm@usa.net

Bauer
Steven R. Soukup
P.O. Box 7662
15459 Wyandotte St.
Van Nuys, CA 91406
e-mail:
soukup@dfhaia.com

Blue & White Pottery
Steven E. Stone
18102 East Oxford Dr.
Aurora, CO 80013
fax: (303) 969-2737

Chintz
Jane Fehrenbocher
600 Columbia St.
Pasadena, CA 91105
e-mail: chintz4u@aol.com

Clarice Cliff
Carole A. Berk
4918 Fairmont Ave.
Bethesda, MD 20814
(800) 382-2413 or (301)
656-0355
e-mail: cab@carole-
berk.com
http://www.carole-
berk.com

Doulton, Royal Doulton
Reg Morris
7360 Martingale
Chesterland, OH 44026

Florence Ceramics
Rita Bee, Editor
Florence Collector Club
Newsletter
(909) 683-1485
e-mail: AR2Bee@aol.com

Flow Blue
Vivian Kramer
Cobblestone Antiques
Spring, TX 77379
(281) 251-0660
e-mail: jimnviv@aol.com

Hall China
Steve Cagle & Dave Peri-
ord
e-mail: slcagle@aol.com

Harker Pottery
Don & Neva Colbert
69565 Crescent Rd.
St. Clairsville, OH 43950-
9350
(740) 695-2355
e-mail: colbert@1st.net
http://users.1st.net/col-
bert/harker/harker/htm

Haviland
Nora Travis
P.O. Box 6008
Cerritos, CA 90701
(714) 521-9283

Hull Pottery
Joan Gray Hull
1376 Nevada S.W.
Huron, SD 57350-3135
(605) 352-1685

Hummel Figurines
Dean A. Genth
Miller's Hallmark & Gift
Gallery
Northedge Mall
1322 North Barron St.
Eaton, OH 45320
(513) 456-4151

Ironstone
General, all-white
Dieringer's Arts &
Antiques
P.O. Box 536
Redding Ridge, CT 06876
fax: (203) 938-8378
e-mail:
Dieringer1@aol.com

Lefton
Loretta DeLozier
P.O. Box 50201
Knoxville, TN 37950-0201
(865) 539-2140
e-mail: Lefton-
Lady@aol.com
Author: *Collector's Encyclopedia of Lefton China (Books I & II)*

McCoy
Craig Nissen
P.O. Box 223
Grafton, WI 53024-0223
(414) 377-7932
e-mail:
McCoyCN@aol.com

Morton Potteries
Burdell Hall
210 W. Sassafras Dr.
Morton, IL 61550-1254
(309) 263-2988
e-mail: bnb-
hall@mtco.com

Noritake
Tim Trapani
145 Andover Place
West Hempstead, NY
11552-1603
(516) 292-8355 or (718)
464-9009
fax: (718) 464-8448
e-mail: ttrapani@aol.com
President: Noritake Collectors' Society

Shelley
Mannie Banner
6412 Silverbrook W.
W. Bloomfield, MI 48322

Torquay
J. Wucherer
Transitions of Wales, Ltd.
P.O. Box 1441
Brookfield, WI 53008

Uhl Pottery
Lloyd Martin
1582 Gregory Lane
Jasper, IN 47546

Warwick
Donald C. Hoffmann
1291 N. Elmwood Dr.
Aurora, IL 60506
(630) 859-3435

Willow Wares
Jeff Siptak
P.O. Box 41312
Nashville, TN 37204
(615) 383-7855
fax: (615) 269-7123
e-mail: Willow-
Ware@aol.com

Glass

Amberina
Louis O. St. Aubin, Jr.
Brookside Antiques
New Bedford, MA

Carnival Glass
Bruce Dooley
2571 7th Ave.
Sweetwater, NJ 08037
(609) 965-2535

Crown Milano
Louis O. St. Aubin, Jr.
Brookside Antiques
New Bedford, MA

Cut Glass
Vance Hall
A Touch of Glass, Ltd.
9107 Autumn Chase
Wichita, KS 67206
(316) 634-2220

Milk Glass
Frank Chiarenza
National Milk Glass Collectors Society
80 Crestview
Newington, CT 06111-2405
(860) 666-5576

Pattern
Iris Cottage Interiors
Andrea & Alan Koppel
Rt. 295 & County Rt. 5
P.O. Box 254
Canaan, NY 12029
(518) 781-4379

Tim Timmerman
11655 S.W. Allen Blvd.,
#31
Beaverton, OR 97005
(U.S. Coin pattern)

Rose Bowls
Johanna S. Billings
P.O. Box 244
Danielsville, PA 18038-0244
e-mail: bankie@concentric.net
Author: *Collectible Glass Rose Bowls*

Wall Pocket Vases
Bobbie Zucker Bryson
1 St. Eleanoras Lane
Tuckahoe, NY 10707
e-mail: napkin-
doll@aol.com

ABC PLATES
Ceramic

6 1/4" d., birds, "Nightingale," center brown transfer-print of a bird w/polychrome enamel trim, molded alphabet border, back marked "E.M. & Co.," 19th c. (imperfections).. **$110**

8 1/2" d., adult activities, "Chairs to Mend," center transfer-printed scene of a man carrying chairs, molded alphabet border, 19th c. **220**

Tin

"Who Killed Cock Robin" ABC Plate

7 3/4" d., embossed scene in center w/"Who Killed Cock Robin...," embossed alphabet border (ILLUS.) **121**

ADVERTISING ITEMS

Thousands of objects made in various materials, some intended as gifts with purchases, others used for display or given away for publicity are now being collected. Also see various other categories and Antique Trader Advertising Price Guide.

Calendars

1891 Butchers Supply Calendar

Butchers supply, 1891, "Gus Becht Butchers Supply - St. Louis," bright colored graphic of bull's head, full calendar pad, litho by Gast, St. Louis & New York, unused condition, framed, 10 x 14" (ILLUS.).. **$1,045**

"Squeezers" Playing Cards Calendar

Card company, 1899, "Consolidated Card Co.," die-cut cardboard, depicting a clown holding fanned-out playing cards marked "Squeezers" w/"The N.Y. Consolidated Card Co. - 222 to 228 West 16th St. New York - Sole Owners & Makers of 'Squeezer Playing Cards'" marked on lower body, foldout marked "The N.Y. Consolidated Card Co's. Playing Cards - 1899 - Playing Card Novelties" measures 5 1/2 x 6" (ILLUS.) **413**

Clothing store, 1919 "Browning, King & Co.," celluloid pocket-type, center oval depicts small nude baby flanked by a man in a soldier's uniform & one in sailor's uniform, marked at the top "'I Want My Clothes' And It's Gotta Be A Uniform'," the bottom marked "Browning, King Co. - A National Institution," 2 1/4 x 3 3/4 .... **55**

1913 Winchester Calendar

Firearms, 1913, "Winchester," half-length portrait of bearded hunter w/gun on shoulder, by noted artist Robert Robinson, bands top & bottom, November page only, American Litho, New York, dry-mounted, few wrinkles (ILLUS.) **935**

1928 Remington Calendar

Firearms, 1928, "Remington," showing older gentleman cleaning gun, seated before fireplace w/a dog sitting on a rug near his master, by Henry Watson, 14 calendar pages, top 2" glued to mat board, 15 x 27" (ILLUS.)................................ **660**

Gunpowder, 1917, "Hercules Powder," lithograph scene of two wild turkeys in wooded setting, three months displayed, framed under glass, image 33 1/2" h. **275**

1907 Grand Union Tea Co. Calendar

Tea company, 1907, "Grand Union Tea Co., Brooklyn, NY," die-cut, large colorful scene of small girl wearing a white dress, red shoes & large red hat, seated & holding a small puppy, litho by Sackett & Wilhelms, professionally framed, overall 14 x 32" (ILLUS.).. **385**

1908 Grand Union Tea Co. Calendar

Tea company, 1908, "Grand Union Tea Co.," rectangular die-cut, large scene of young girl w/doll standing before a china cabinet & near a small table set for tea, flanked at the bottom by months of the year, minor ding top center, 11 x 29" (ILLUS.) **440**

Clocks

Electric

Vernors Soda Advertising Clock

Beverage company, "Vernors," round, wall-mount, glass dome w/metal case marked "Drink Vernors - deliciously different" above head of bearded man, 19 1/2" d. (ILLUS.) **145**

Dr. Pepper Clock

Soft drinks, "Dr. Pepper," 1930s Deco style, red & black w/gold trim & "Drink Dr. Pepper 5¢" (ILLUS.).................................... **5,750**

Pepsi-Cola Clock

Soft drinks, "Pepsi-Cola," wall-mount, glass front, large blue numbers on white light-up background, center logo, working condition, one of the hands slips, ca. 1940s, by Telechron, 15" d. (ILLUS.)............. **209**

Key-wind

Sidney Advertising Clock

Tin and hardware company, "John H. Hough - the Leader in Tinware - Hardware - Stoves & Ranges," wooden wall-type, rectangular case shelf & drawer, arched top w/advertising, corner spire finials, Sidney Clock Co. (ILLUS.) **6,000**

Display Cabinets

Diamond Dyes Counter Display Cabinet

Fabric dyes, "Diamond Dyes," wood w/embossed tin lithographed outdoor scene of children playing, stairway w/ornate railing & large home in background, 9 x 15 1/2 x 24 1/2" (ILLUS.) **1,925**

Fabric dyes, "Putnam Dyes," lower left corner w/scene of man on horseback, red & blue lettering reading "Putnam Fadeless Dyes - Tints - To Dye Use Boiling Water - To Tint Dip in Warm Water," 8 x 15 x 19" **154**

Tobacco, "Sweet Cuba," lithographed tin, square store bin w/slanted lid marked "Sweet Cuba Fine Cut" & front marked 5¢ w/product package shown, 8 x 8 x 10" (minor dings & scrapes) **182**

Dr. Daniels' Medicine Cabinet

Veterinary products, "Dr. Daniels' Warranted Veterinary Medicines," wood, front-opening w/embossed tin lithographed front panel showing the doctor & various remedies w/list of prices at bottom (ILLUS.) **6,710**

Display Figures & Displays

Western Super-X Shells Sign

Cartridges, "Western Super-X Shells," die-cut cardboard, stand-up type, shows cutaway shell near box of shells, birds, cloudy sky & hunters in background, marked "15 to 20 Yards More Range - New Seal-tite Wads - Progressive Burning Powder," 11 x 21" (ILLUS.) **644**

American Field Counter Sign

Clothing & accessories, "American Field Hunting Garments," die-cut cardboard w/jump-out model of mallard, hunter in background, ca. 1940-50, 14 x 16" (ILLUS.) **138**

Black Cross Teas Countertop Sign

Food, "Black Cross Teas," embossed cardboard, stand-up type, figure of young girl wearing large pink bonnet holding sign reading "'Oh You Black Cross - The Widlar Co.'" & showing box marked "Black Cross Pure Selected Teas," few minor scrapes, 7 1/4 x 16" (ILLUS.) **204**

Varnish, "Ohio Varnish Co.," cardboard, marked "Floor Enamel for any surface - Interior or Exterior - Chi-Namel Product," w/interior & exterior scene of person using the product, color samples attached, ca. 1920-30s, 12 x 18" (few minor scuffs) **66**

Display Jars & Containers

Brother Jonathan Store Bin

Chewing tobacco, "Brother Jonathan Chewing Tobacco," metal store size bin depicting caricature of Brother Jonathan seated in a tobacco field (ILLUS.) **6,050**

Soap, "Fairbanks Fairy Soap," wooden shipping container w/paper label on inside cover, center design of large red rose supporting a winged woman in white, marked "Fairbanks - The Soap of the Century - Pure - White - Floats - For the Toilet, Bath & Fine Laundry Use," 8 x 15 x 16".. **358**

Pinback Buttons

Cartridges, "Peter's Cartridges," celluloid, scene of clouds w/duck flying through letter P, by Bastian Bros., Rochester, New York, 3/4" d.. **63**

Cartridges, "Peters Shells," celluloid, litho by Whitehead & Hoag, white w/red shell pictured w/"Shoot Peters Shells," 7/8" d.......... **65**

Signs & Signboards

Cardboard

Cigars, "Free Lance Cigars," w/string hanger, embossed cigar label insert, marked "Smoke a 5¢ Free Lance Cigar and be Convinced," 9 1/2 x 11".................................... **55**

Framed Kis-Me Gum Die-cut Sign

Gum, "Kis-Me Gum," die-cut, lithographed in color, profile of a young woman w/dark hair fashioned in a bun, lacy ruffled collar over red dress w/a border of arching pink & red roses, advertising above & below portrait, framed (ILLUS.) **2,000**

Soft drink, "Squirt," double-sided die-cut oval, string hanger, yellow, red & green, depicts two monkeys holding a bottle & marked "Why Monkey? Drink Squirt," dated 1941, 7 1/2 x 9 1/2".................................. **77**

Paper

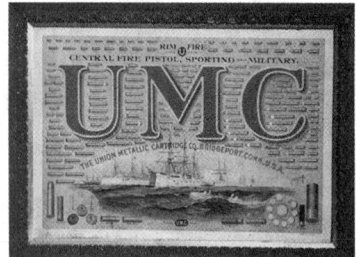

Union Metallic Cartridge Co. Cartridge Board Sign

Cartridges, "Union Metallic Cartridge Co.," showing various shell casings & scene of battleships in background w/smaller boat in waves in foreground & marked "Rim Fire - Central Fire Pistol, Sporting and Military UMC - The Union Metallic Cartridge Co. Bridgeport, Conn. U.S.A.," ca. 1898, framed (ILLUS.)................................ **4,125**

Cartridges, "Winchester Shells," colorful woodland scene depicting bird, titled "Cock of the Woods," ca. 1905, overall 15 x 25" (top & bottom bands missing, 3" tear mid left at tail feathers to edge, uneven tear on bottom edge) **836**

Sanita Malt Coffee Poster

Coffee, "Sanita Malt Coffee," rectangular, depicts two young children sitting at a table, marked "Both of us drink only Sanita Malt Coffee," metal bands at top & bottom, framed, 10 x 14 1/2" (ILLUS.)................ **187**

Stetson Hats Lithograph

Hats, "Stetson Hats - naturally- - -," color lithograph of cattle roundup, four cowboys wearing Stetson hats, near mint condition, 17 x 22 (ILLUS.) **77**

New York Sunday Journal Poster

Newspaper magazine, "New York Sunday Journal," 1898, rectangular, scene of sailboat on water featuring the Yellow Kid comic strip character, w/"Around the World with the Yellow Kid - in the Great New York Sunday Journal" w/"The Yellow Kid Sails Jan 17" at the bottom (ILLUS.)... **4,950**

Mayo's Plug Linen Poster

Tobacco, "Mayo's Plug - Light and Dark," rectangular, linen, yellow w/black lettering & image of rooster w/blue, green & black feathers, standing on brown boxes w/labels, 17 3/4 x 30" (ILLUS.)........................ **770**

Tin

Merita Bread Sign

Bread, "Merita Bread," lithographed, colorful scene of the Lone Ranger on Silver above a loaf of bread w/"It's Enriched - Buy Merita Bread" in black & red lettering at the bottom (ILLUS.) **5,750**

Cigars, "A.K. Walch's Cigars," rectangular, lithographed, red w/white lettering reading "Smoke A.K. Walch's 'Good Company' 3¢ Cigars - 4 for 19 cts. - Have No Equal - Have You Tried The Silver Quarter 5¢ Cigar? - If Not, Why Not! - A.K. Walch, Phila, Pa.," 7 1/2 x 13 3/4"................. **204**

Clothing, "Duxbak," mounted over cardboard, shows birds in air over water, marked "Duxbak Serviceable Clothes For Life in The Open - 'Sheds water like a Duck's Back'," 15 x 18 1/2" (minor rust bottom edge).. **330**

Small Lithographed Rev-O-Noc Sign

Sporting goods, "Rev-O-Noc Sporting Goods," rectangular, lithographed over cardboard w/scenes of baseball, golf, fishing & hunting, marked in upper left corner "H.S.B. & Co. Rev-O-Noc" & upper right corner "Fire Arms - Sporting Goods - Fishing Tackle" (ILLUS.).............. **2,970**

Tea company, "McCormick's Tea," orange, black & yellow, dated "1936" w/lithograph scene of a house on one side, front w/teapot & marked "Banquet - McCormick's Orange Pekoe Tea," 1 lb., 3 3/4 x 6".. **44**

Five Brothers Plug Tobacco Sign

Tobacco, "Five Brothers Plug - Toothsome as Honey," lithographed tin over cardboard, featuring adorable black bear cubs on red background w/yellow lettering (ILLUS.) **6,050**

Trade

Figural Pacific Butcher's Supply Co. Sign

Butcher's supply company, "Pacific Butcher's Supply Co., San Francisco, CAL," cast-iron dimensional sign w/figural saw, cleaver & knife supporting a figural steer, front plate marked "Gloekler's Patent June 25, 1889," original old paint, 12 lbs., 20 x 24 1/2" (ILLUS.) **1,210**

Locks, "Independent Lock Co., Fitchburg, Mass," cast metal, large hanging figural key, 20 lbs., 1 x 1 1/2 x 28" **371**

Other

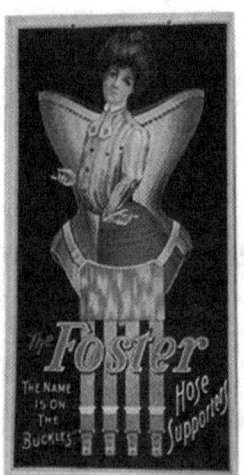

Foster Hose Supporters Sign

Clothing & accessories, "The Foster Hose Supporters," celluloid w/string hanger, litho by E.F. Pulver Co., Rochester, New York, depicts a corset w/hose supporters w/figure of a woman superimposed, black background (ILLUS.) **550**

Yellow Kid Sign

Gum, "Yellow Kid Bubble Chewing Gum," celluloid, yellow, blue & red, center depicts figure marked "YK" bordered by "There is only one - Yellow Kid - Big Bubble Chewing Gum," promoting popular early comic character, Bastian Bros., slight scratch, 8" d. (ILLUS.) **43**

Whiskey, "Claymore Scotch Whiskey," copper spittoon, marked "J.R. Grant & Son Ltd, London," nice patina, 3 x 4" **77**

Soda Fountain Collectibles

Fan pull, "Dr. Pepper," two-sided cardboard, features Patricia White & autumn leaves, marked "Drink Dr. Pepper - Good For Life!," 8 1/4" l. (ILLUS. left) **2,640**

Dr. Pepper Fan Pulls

Fan pull, "Dr. Pepper," two-sided cardboard, shows a young woman w/large hat & gloves, seated in director's chair & holding bottle, marked "Drink Dr. Pepper - Good For Life!," 8 1/4" l. (ILLUS. right) ... **1,870**

Thermometers

Boots & shoes, "Finn & Feather Boots & Shoes," rectangular embossed tin litho, white w/red lettering, 4 1/2 x 14" **110**

Coffee, "Golden Sun Coffee," rectangular, porcelain by Beach, Coshocton, white w/black lettering reading "Golden Sun Coffee is Always Good" above graphic of product package & "Buy Coffee of Your Grocer Only" at bottom, ca. 1915, 2 3/4 x 11 1/2" (minor dings at edge) **385**

Flour, "David Harum Flour," rectangular, wood marked "David Harum Flour - David Harum Feed," dated 1937, 3 x 12" **66**

Medicine, "Lash's Kidney Bitters," rectangular, wood, by American Mfg. Concern, Jamestown, New York, 5 1/4 x 21"................. **523**

Medicine, "Nature's Remedy," rectangular, porcelain, black w/white & red lettering reading "NR To-Night - Tomorrow Alright - Nature's Remedy Tablets" at top & "Come In - If you get it here It's good," edge dings, glass tube broken, 7 x 27"......... **176**

Soft drink, "Double Cola," rectangular, tin, green w/yellow trim, marked "Drink Double Cola - You'll like it better," 5 x 17" **138**

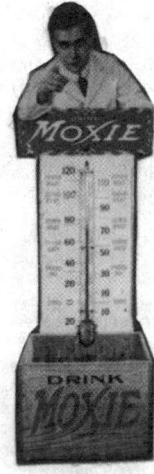

Moxie Outdoor Thermometer

Soft drink, "Moxie Soda," metal over wood, outdoor-type, man at top w/sign reading "Drink Moxie," box at bottom containing miniature bottles also marked "Drink Moxie," 38" h. (ILLUS.) **6,930**

Strawberry Growers Thermometer

Strawberry plant growers, "Waller Bros.," rectangular w/round top, metal w/bunch of red strawberries & green leaves at top, thermometer on left side & marked "Waller Bros. - Judsonia Ark. The Honest Strawberry Plant Growers," few minor scrapes, 6 x 15" (ILLUS.)................................. **248**

Miscellaneous Items

F.O. Stone Baking Co. Blotter

Blotter, "F.O. Stone Baking Co.," rectangular celluloid giveaway dated 1915, by Whitehead & Hoag, scene of Santa in sleigh pulled by reindeer, Christmas greeting in upper right corner, 3 x 7 3/4" (ILLUS.) **77**

Compass, "Dave Cook Sporting Goods Co. - corner 1601 Larimer St., Denver, Colorado," celluloid, lithograph by Parisian Novelty, Chicago, Illinois, working condition, 1 3/4" d. **66**

Doll, "Miss Flaked Rice," printed stuffed cloth w/hand-made cotton dress in a blue print, early 20th c., 23 1/2" h. (wear, a couple of holes) **248**

Crystal White Soap Door Push

Door push, "Crystal White Soap," rectangular, metal, blue w/white lettering reading "Come In - Crystal White - The Billion Bubble Soap," minor scrapes, 3 1/2 x 8 3/4" (ILLUS.)...................................... **259**

Door push, "Fleischmann's Yeast," rectangular, lithographed tin by Haeusermann, New York, depicts a bread figure w/apron & chef's hat, marked "Eat Bread" at top &

"Made with Fleischmann's Yeast" at bottom, 3 1/4 x 9" **99**

George Long Dust Pan

Dust pan, "George Long, Vanderbilt, Mich.," embossed tin, blue w/gold trim, bright colorful lithograph center scene of couple, scalloped top w/floral medallions, minor scuff marks, 8 3/4 x 9" (ILLUS.) **55**

B.I. Barlow Ice Pick

Ice pick, "B.I. Barlow - Gold Field, Nev" on four-sided wood handle also reading "Ice and Fuel, Beverage, Flowers and Cereals" & phone number, near mint, rare (ILLUS.) **140**

Bee Hive Overalls Mirror

Mirror, "Bee Hive Overalls," pocket-type oval, celluloid by Whitehead & Hoag, Newark, NJ, shows woman wearing overalls & marked "Bee Hive Overalls Best Maid - Made by Bittner, Hunsicker &

Co., Allentown, PA," ca. 1910, mirror broken, 1 3/4 x 2 3/4" (ILLUS.) **286**

Berry Bros. Celluloid Mirror

Mirror, "Berry Bros. Varnished," pocket-type oval celluloid by J.B. Carroll, Chicago, colorful scene of young boy wearing overalls & straw hat pulling a wooden wagon w/red wheels holding a dog, 1 3/4 x 2 3/4" (ILLUS.) **154**

Mirror, "Buckwalter Stove Co.," pocket-type oval celluloid w/graphic of black & silver cooking stove on green ground & marked "An Enameled Range Beautifies and Modernizes Your Kitchen," distributor's name at bottom, few minor scratches, 1 3/4 x 2 3/4" **99**

Mirror, "Oliver Typewriter," pocket-type oval celluloid w/photo of young girl & typewriter, image by Photo Jewelry, Chicago, Illinois, 2 x 2 3/4" (minor scratches) **44**

Needle case, "Coca Cola," shows bottle & glass of cola & young woman holding a glass of cola w/bottle nearby, ca. 1924, overall excellent condition, 2 x 3" **55**

King's Powder Oil Painting

Oil painting, "King's Powder 'Quickshot'," gunpowder, original oil on canvas, scene of hunter near water in background, duck he has shot falling in the foreground, ca. 1890, in original ornate frame, unsigned, professionally cleaned & revarnished, overall 24 x 32" (ILLUS.) **10,010**

Ribbon, "Shaker Cloak E.J. Neale & Co., Mount Lebanon, N.Y.," woven silk, rectangular w/a floral bordered reserve depicting a Shaker building & the inscription on the front w/a view of a cloaked woman on the back, 19th c., 3 x 7 1/2" **259**

Meredith Diamond Club Whiskey Jug

Whiskey jug, "Meredith Diamond Club," ceramic, bulbous ovoid body w/cylindrical neck, grey w/blue lettering, marked "Meredith's Diamond Club Pure Rye Whiskey - Expressly for Medicinal Use - East Liverpool, Ohio," KT & K Pottery Co., 7 1/2" h. (ILLUS.) **66**

ARCHITECTURAL ITEMS

In recent years the growing interest in and support for historic preservation has spawned a greater appreciation of the fine architectural elements which were an integral part of early building, both public and private. Where, in decades past, structures might be razed and doors, fireplace mantels, windows, etc., hauled to the dump, today all interior and exterior details from unrestorable buildings are salvaged to be offered to home restorers, museums and even builders who want to include a bit of history in a new construction project.

Building finial, copper, square steeple-form w/ball finial, verdigris patina, 19th c., 25" sq., 40" h. (dents) **$863**

Building ornament, Ellis Auditorium, terra cotta, from Elvis's high school **395**

Building ornament, finial, marble, original, 14" h. w/6 3/4" d. base.................................... **225**

Carnegie Mellon Frieze

Building ornament, large terra cotta frieze designed for the old Carnegie Mellon bank in Philadelphia from where it was removed, 8' l., 3' h. (ILLUS.)....................... **2,695**

Building ornament, terra cotta chimney square, blocks originally from old Philadelphia building, 8 x 8" sq................................. **56**

Building ornament, terra cotta corbels, from building in Philadelphia, 31 x 18" h. **395**

Carved Limestone Capitals

Building ornaments, limestone, large carved capitals, from great hotel outside of Philadelphia, Pennsylvania, some have minor damage, 36 x 34" h., 8" thick, ea. (ILLUS.)... **1,800**

Commercial Bronze Doors

Commercial doors, bronze, no glass, inner panels measure 19 x 67 1/2", 58 x 84" h., pr. (ILLUS.) **1,275**

Large Cupola

Cupola, large & exquisite, originally graced a barn on the Campbell Soup Family Estate outside of Philadelphia, Cabrini College now occupies this site, 6' x 21" h. (ILLUS.)... **2,500**

Door arch, cut limestone door arch & keystone from Philadelphia, 97" l., 25" h. **250**

Downspout, tin, flared crimped half-round rim on funnel-shaped body, decorated w/cut-out ten-pointed star, 19th c., 9 1/2 x 13 1/2"... **288**

Drive gates, large set of drive gates from Brooklyn, New York, ca. early 1900s, 118 x 61" h., the set **2,650**

Arched Entry Door

Entry door, arched, pine, 35 1/2 x 96" h. (ILLUS.)... **295**

Entry door, oak core, veneered, beveled glass intact, dentil molding, 36 x 84" h. **395**

Entry door, oak veneer, exterior, features a shelf w/decorative carving and decorative letter slot, 36 x 89" h.............................. **475**

Entry door, pine, four raised panels, 32 x 78" h.. **195**

Entry door, pine, two raised panels, beveled glass intact, 36 x 83 1/4" h. **325**

Entry door, solid oak, exterior, w/two inlaid panels, beveled glass intact, dentil shelf surrounds the panel, 29 1/2 x 83" h. **225**

Exterior Entry Door

Entry door, solid oak, exterior, w/two inlaid panels & colored glass surrounding the center glass, glass intact, ca. 1860s,

small crack on the clear center glass pane, 28 x 79 1/2" h. (ILLUS.)...................... **250**

Entry door, solid oak, exterior, w/two inlaid panels & nine glass panes completely intact, brass hardware including kick plate, door handle & keyhole, ca. 1910, 36 x 80" h. **195**

Entry door, solid oak, has one raised mail slot, w/intact beveled glass window, front has exquisite hand-carved shelf w/decorative keyhole/doorknob plate, ca. 1850s, 39 x 83 1/2" h., 2 1/4" deep **450**

Entry door, solid oak, w/matching transom, both w/beveled leaded glass, door has one raised panel & features dentil molding under the window ledge, ca. 1900s, door window 29 x 49" h., transom an additional 14" h., leaded glass 35" w., 9 1/2" h.. **1,895**

Entry doors, double, pine, features two raised decorative panels, raised bull's-eye motif, ca. 1880s, 42 1/2 x 86 1/2" h., pr.. **300**

Entry doors, double, pine, w/two raised panels, 50 x 88" h. **375**

Finial, tin, found along the roof line of old Philadelphia brownstone, 8 1/2" w., 45" l., 18" from wall **175**

Fireplace mantel, carved pine, George II-Style, the rectangular narrow top shelf above foliate, egg-and-dart & dentillated borders, above the frieze carved in the center w/a basket of flowers, flanked by flowering foliate scrolls, the molded opening flanked by leaf-tip carved brackets surmounted by flowerheads above ribbon-tied floral swags, England, 14 x 66", 47 1/4" h..................................... **3,900**

Fireplace surround, tile, composed of seventeen Minton ceramic enameled tiles of the seasons & other subjects in browns, yellow & pale blue, England, late 19th c., 37 x 43".. **3,795**

Flat iron gate, 30 x 13" h. **75**

French Interior Doors

French doors, interior, pine, 15 lights per door, 58 x 90" h., pr. (ILLUS.) **375**

Gable ends, wood, Victorian design, from a West Virginia home, 9' l., 3' h., pr.................. **600**

Garden set: table, four chairs; wrought iron, white, table 29 x 26" h., chairs 39 x 20" square, 5 pc. set.. **975**

Gates, cast iron, opens & separates in middle, removed from the Vaudeville Theater in Ashbury Park, New Jersey, ca. 1930s, 6 x 9', the set **3,750**

Interior door, solid oak, w/two recessed panels, comes from a seminary in Mahwah, New Jersey, 36 x 80" h. **300**

Interior door, solid walnut, four inlaid panels w/molding, 34 1/2 x 82" h. **175**

Mantel, 60 1/4 x 53" h., 9 3/4" deep **400**

Oak Mantel

Mantel, oak, 60 1/2 x 50 1/8" h., 12" deep (ILLUS.) **495**

Tiger Oak Mantel

Mantel, tiger oak, w/Ionic columns, 60 x 52" h., 12" d. (ILLUS.) **500**

Pediment, oak, from closet, 68 l., 10" h., 4" deep **245**

Pocket doors, solid maple, this pair of doors has six recessed panels & brass hardware, original finish, glass replacement, 60 x 82 1/2" h., pr. **675**

Post finial, a large pineapple upright atop an upright cluster of curl-tipped long leaves above a round socle base, dark green repaint, mold number on base, late 19th c., 20 1/2" h. **220**

Figural Owl Roof Ornament

Roof ornament, model of an owl, full-bodied molded zinc bird, standing on a hemispherical form, w/glass eyes, hinged head, painted brown, split on base, reinforcement, paint loss, dents, 19th c., 27 3/4" h. (ILLUS.) **2,875**

Roof ornament, tin & sheet iron, a star & crescent, molded five-point star above a sphere above a crescent w/round cutouts, resting on a larger sphere, mounted on a hollow tapering shaft, attributed to the Crescent Mfg. Co., Rutland, Vermont, late 19th c., 50" h. (corrosion, four bullet holes) **978**

Window arches, cut limestone, from Philadelphia, eight stones & two keystones, 63" d., pr. **475**

Painted Brown & Silver Window Grate

Window grate, cast iron, painted brown & silver, 30 1/2 x 26" h. (ILLUS.) **75**

Window grate, cast-iron verticals, w/wrought iron, painted black, 26 x 17 1/4" h. **85**

Window grate, cast-iron verticals w/wrought-iron & cast-iron medallion, painted white, 46 1/2 x 23 1/4" h. **125**

Window grate, cast-iron verticals w/wrought-iron, painted grey & brown, 33 1/2 x 21 1/4" h. **95**

Window grate, cast-iron verticals & wrought finials, painted black w/silver finials, 30 1/2 x 26" h. **95**

Window Grate w/Cast Medallion

Window grate, wrought-iron w/cast medallion, painted black, 28 x 32" h. (ILLUS.) **175**

Window grate, wrought-iron w/metal flowers, painted black, 32 3/4 x 25" h. **95**

Window Grate with Metal Flowers

Window grate, wrought-iron w/metal flowers, painted white, 21 1/2 x 17" h.
(ILLUS.)... **65**
Window valances, painted wood, a rectan-
gular board w/a scalloped bottom edge
supporting a narrow flat crestrail mounted w/a long pierced scrolling crest, old
worn brownish green paint on one, other
shows earlier pumpkin color beneath,
19th c., 39 3/4" l., pr. (small edge chips &
cracks)... **440**

ART DECO

*Interest in Art Deco, a name given an art movement
stemming from the Paris International Exhibition of
1925, continues to grow today. This style flowered in the
1930s and actually continued into the 1940s. A mood of
flippancy is found in its varied characteristics - zigzag
lines resembling the lightning bolt, sometimes steps,
often the use of sharply contrasting colors such as black
and white and others. Look for prices for the best examples of Art Deco design to continue to rise. Also see
JEWELRY, MODERN.*

Art Deco Busts

Busts, porcelain, female heads w/blond
coiled hair covered w/an ethnic sash decorated w/a scrolling floral pattern,
stamped "Roman, made in Italy," mid-
20th c., 8 1/4" h., pr. (ILLUS.)...................... **$288**

Art Deco Car Hood Ornament

Car hood ornament, stylized figure of a
draped woman w/outstretched arm, pale
topaz glass w/threaded disk base, raised
on a later cylindrical black stand w/light,
attributed to Etling, ca. 1927, France,
stress cracks, glass 11" h., overall
14 1/4" h. (ILLUS.) **1,150**
Clock, electric desk-type, rectangular black
glass clock face w/chrome Arabic numerals & etched leaf & scallop decoration on
the chrome rectangle in the center, General Electric, ca. 1930s, impressed
marks on back, 7 1/2" l., 5 5/8" h. (wear
on chrome) **173**

Art Deco Clock Garniture

Clock garniture, mantel-type, marble, diamond-shaped clock w/matte silvered
metal face signed "Uteau" & "Bordeaux,"
set into a marble frame on rectangular
marble standard flanked by two gilt-metal
seated female figures w/outstretched
hands holding a bird, all raised on a rectangular platform of striated white & black
marble, together w/two marble garnitures
w/geometric decoration, ca. 1935,
France, chips, separation, cracks, clock
12 1/2" h., garniture 7 3/4" h., the three-
piece set (ILLUS. of part).............................. **489**
Cocktail shaker, cov., cylindrical, a red
Bakelite knob on the sterling silver spout
above a tapered black amethyst glass
body decorated w/silver overlay scenes
of stylized deer in a landscape, impressed sterling mark, possibly
Rockwell, ca. 1925, 15 3/4" h. (minor
wear) **173**

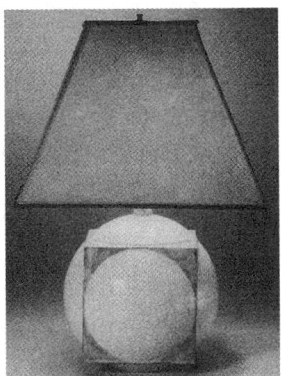

Art Deco Table Lamp

Lamp, table model, two-socket fixture w/slender metal standard above ceramic base designed as a sphere within a cube, cream & grey crackle glaze, impressed "Editions Etling" within a triangle, "Marcel Guillard" & "J. Martin" on base, metal-framed ochre paper shade, ca. 1927, Paris, France, minor chips, 16 1/2" h. (ILLUS.).. **690**

Mirror, vanity-type, a stepped-arch glass w/black reverse-painting & radiating mirror panels at each side, engraved linear & beveled highlights, silvered metal geometric fittings, ca. 1925, 22 x 38".................. **460**

Mirrors, wall-type, wooden crest w/stylized doves among flowers & leaves over an elongated hexagonal frame, fleur-de-lis sides, one w/antique gold finish, the other silvered, 44 1/2 x 56", pr. (wear to finish & mirrors)... **1,725**

Smoking stand, bronze-patinated metal, figural, an eagle finial on a tray w/removable covered match canister, two ashtrays & a small lighter amber dome, the tray decorated w/raised images of Presidents Washington & Lincoln & American landmarks, the tray supported by a figure of the Statue of Liberty on a round, stepped base, ca. 1930s, 27 1/2" h. (minor wear to patina) **230**

Tea set: cov. teapot, cov. coffeepot, creamer & open sugar bowl; silver plate, each piece of stepped cylindrical form w/stepped & canted feet, the coffeepot w/a taupe-colored finial, teapot w/black composition finials & handle, Wm. Hutton & Sons & J. Dixon & Sons, Sheffield, England, ca. 1930, coffeepot 6 1/4" h., the set (wear, replaced teapot handle) **288**

Vase, blown glass, swelled cylindrical body tapering slightly to a short widely flaring neck, translucent opal, engraved & etched w/two stylized nude women supporting a polished disk, etched initials "A.N.B." at bottom of decoration, "Gray...(illegible)" around polished pontil, possibly Gray-Stan, England, ca. 1930, 10" h. (minor staining)...................... **259**

Wall sconces, mixed metal, elongated shield-shaped, embossed overlapped

circles at top, etched linear decoration on white metal, beveled mirrors, brass brackets, double candleholders & studs........ **518**

ART NOUVEAU

Art Nouveau's primary thrust was between 1890 and 1905, but commercial Art Nouveau productions continued until about World War I. This style was a rebellion against historic tradition in art. Using natural forms as inspiration, it is primarily characterized by undulating or wave-like lines and whiplashes. Many objects were made in materials ranging from glass to metals. Figural pieces with seductive maidens with long, flowing hair are especially popular in this style. Interest in Art Nouveau remains high, with the best pieces by well known designers bringing strong prices. Also see JEWELRY, ANTIQUE.

Art Nouveau Andirons

Andirons, bronze & glazed stoneware, uprights w/large scrolled flame-form finials, supported by twisted vines atop paneled standards above an arched & scroll-pierced undulating foot, blackish brown patina, in the manner of Hector Guimard, ca. 1900, 21 3/4" h., pr. (ILLUS.) **$16,100**

Box, cov., domed square cover on a broad shouldered four paneled box of rust brown shaded to colorless cased glass, Art Nouveau acid-etched decoration w/textured surface, gilt highlights, early 20th c., script gilt mark "H 57" on base, 4" h. **345**

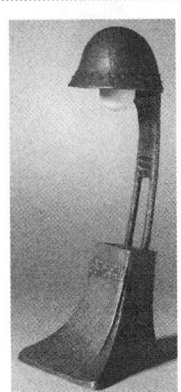

Art Nouveau Desk Lamp

Lamp, desk-type, bronze helmet-shaped & textured shade w/raised leafy vine border, flattened bar & double rod shaft on a flared base w/front band of raised petal decoration, early 20th c., 13 7/8" h. (ILLUS.)... **863**

Art Nouveau Figural Lamp

Lamp, gilt bronze, figure of semi-nude female w/long flowing hair, arms raised, hem of long skirt forms base, inscribed "G. Flamand," (1895-1925), France, 23 1/2" h. (ILLUS.)....................................... **8,625**

Lavabo, brass, corner fitting w/embossed figural dogs at splashback corners, curvilinear decoration, spigot at center, ending in a round basin w/stylized woven strap border, early 20th c., 13 1/2 x 14", 19" h. (dents).................................... **230**

Figural Art Nouveau Mirror

Mirror, dressing table-type, filigree floral base supporting female figure w/raised arms, swivel mirror w/beveled edge, gold paint, 22" h. (ILLUS.) **440**

Vase, round bulbous form raised on five shaped square feet, decorated w/raised bellflowers & leafy gilt swags on a speckled buff colored ground w/gilt highlights, early 20th c., Austria, 4" h., 7 3/4" d.............. **431**

AUDUBON PRINTS

John James Audubon, American ornithologist and artist, is considered the finest nature artist in history. About 1820 he conceived the idea of having a full color book published portraying every known species of American bird in its natural habitat. He spent years in the wilderness capturing their beauty in vivid color only to have great difficulty finding a publisher. In 1826 he visited England, received immediate acclaim, and selected Robert Havell as his engraver. "Birds of America," when completed, consisted of four volumes of 435 individual plates, double-elephant folio size, which are a combination of aquatint, etching and line engraving. W. H. Lizars of Edinburgh engraved the first ten plates of this four volume series. These were later retouched by Havell who produced the complete set between 1827 and early 1839. In the 1840s, another definitive work, "Viviparous Quadrupeds of North America," containing 150 plates, was published in America. Prices for Audubon's original double-elephant folio size prints are very high and beyond the means of the average collector. Subsequent editions of "Birds of America," especially the chromolithographs done by Julius Bien in New York (1859-60) and the smaller octavo (7 x 10 1/2") edition of prints done by J. T. Bowen of Philadelphia in the 1840s, are those that are most frequently offered for sale.

Anyone interested in Audubon prints needs to be aware that many photographically-produced copies of the prints have been issued during this century for use on calendars or as decorative accessories, so it is best to check with a print expert before spending a large sum on an Audubon purported to be from an early edition.

American Avocet - Plate CCCXVIII, hand-colored etching, engraving & aquatint by Robert Havell, Jr., London, 1827-38, framed, 22 1/4 x 31 3/4" (margin discoloration, remains of double-sided tape in margins, laid down).................................... **$1,380**

American Goldfinch

American Goldfinch, Plate 33, hand-colored etching, engraving & aquatint by Robert Havell, London, 1827-38, framed, laid down on card, 12 1/4 x 19 3/4", (ILLUS.) **2,530**

American Ptarmigan. White-tailed Grous - Plate CCCXVIII) hand-colored etching, engraving & aquatint by Robert Havell, Jr., London, 1827-38, 25 5/8 x 38 1/4" (stitch holes along disbound edge, minor light- & mat stain) **7,475**

Black Vulture or Carrion Crow - Plate CVI, hand-colored etching, engraving & aquatint by Robert Havell, Jr., London, 1827-38, framed, 25 1/8 x 37 5/8" (mottled foxing, sheet edges slightly darkened) **5,750**

Brant Goose - Plate CCCXCI, hand-colored etching, engraving & aquatint by Robert Havell, Jr., London, 1827-38, framed, 25 1/4 x 37 3/4" (light- & mat stain, foxing, few edge nicks, two strips of tape staining at top edge) **4,312**

Broad-winged Hawk

Broad-Winged Hawk - Plate XCI, hand-colored etching, engraving & aquatint by Robert Havell, Jr., London, 1827-38, framed, few short tears in margins, 25 1/4 x 38" (ILLUS.) **8,050**

Buffel-Headed Duck - Plate CCCXXV, hand-colored etching, engraving & aquatint by Robert Havell, Jr., London, 1827-38, framed, 25 1/8 x 38 1/8" (minor discoloration in margins, few faint foxing specks, repaired tear in right corner) **6,900**

Cayenne Tern - Plate CCLXXIII, hand-colored etching, engraving & aquatint by Robert Havell, Jr., London, 1827-38, framed, 25 5/8 x 38" (stitch holes along disbound edge) **9,775**

Chuck-Will's Widow - Plate 52, hand-colored etching, engraving & aquatint by Robert Havell, London, 1827-38, framed, 25 7/8 x 38 1/2" (minor light- & mat stain, soiling in margins, few edge nicks) **17,250**

Common American Wildcat - Plate I, hand-colored lithograph by J.T. Bowen, Philadelphia, ca. 1843, 21 3/8 x 27 1/4" (minor light-stain, few nicks in edges) **11,500**

Eider Duck - Plate 405, hand-colored lithograph by J. Bien, New York, ca. 1859-60, framed, 26 1/2 x 38 7/8" (mottled foxing,

repaired loss in lower left corner, repaired tear in lower right, pale mat stain in margins, minor edge soiling, backed w/wove paper) **2,300**

Golden-Winged Woodpecker - Plate XXXVII, hand-colored etching, engraving & aquatint by Robert Havell, Jr., London, 1827-38, 25 7/8 x 37 5/8" (light-stain, scattered soiling in margins, few small nicks at edges, backed) **6,900**

Goosander - Plate CCCXXXI, hand-colored etching, engraving & aquatint by Robert Havell, Jr., London, 1827-38, framed, 25 3/4 x 38 3/4" (sheet edges darkened, few small fox marks) **19,550**

Great American Cock Male - Plate 1, hand-colored etching, engraving & aquatint by Robert Havell, Jr., London, 1827-38, 26 1/2 x 39 1/2" (light-stain, scattered foxing, numerous short, repaired tears at edges, backed w/Japan) **54,625**

Great American Hen & Young

Great American Hen & Young - Plate VI, hand-colored etching & aquatint by W.H. Lizars, repaired tear, light- & mat stain, scattered foxing, numerous short margin tears, 26 3/8 x 39 3/4" (ILLUS.) **40,250**

Green Heron - Plate CCCXXXIII, hand-colored etching, engraving & aquatint by Robert Havell, Jr., London, 1827-38, laid down on card, 25 x 26 3/8" (minor timestaining, occasional foxing, staining at upper edge) **5,750**

Greenshank - Plate CCLXIX, hand-colored etching, engraving & aquatint by Robert Havell, Jr., London, 1827-38, laid down on card, 20 7/8 x 27" (staining in corner, other minor defects) **1,754**

Harlequin Duck - Plate CCXCVII, hand-colored etching, engraving & aquatint by Robert Havell, Jr., London, 1827-38, framed, 25 1/8 x 37 3/4" (scattered foxing, pale mat stain, two small repaired tears) **2,875**

Hooded Merganser

Hooded Merganser - Plate CCXXXII, hand-colored etching, engraving & aquatint by Robert Havell, Jr., London, 1823-38, framed, pale mottled foxing, light damp stain in lower edge, 24 7/8 x 29 3/4" (ILLUS.)............................. **4,025**

Iceland or Jer Falcon

Iceland or Jer Falcon - Plate CCCLXVI, hand-colored etching, engraving & aquatint by Robert Havell, London, 1827-38, frame, margins trimmed, pale mat stain, 25 1/4 x 37 1/8" (ILLUS.)............................ **90,500**

Mississippi Kite - Plate CXVII, hand-colored etching, engraving & aquatint by Robert Havell, London, 1827-38, framed, 22 x 27 1/2" (few specks of foxing, laid down).. **2,300**

Mocking Bird (The) - Plate XXI, hand-colored etching, engraving & aquatint by Robert Havell, Jr., London, 1823-38, 26 x 37 3/4" (light-stain, few small nicks & edge losses) **18,400**

Moose Deer: Old Male and Young - Plate LXXVI, hand-colored lithograph by J.T. Bowen, Philadelphia, ca. 1845, framed, 21 7/8 x 28" (few repaired edge tears, slight discoloration) **3,162**

Pileated Woodpecker - Plate CXI, hand-colored etching, engraving & aquatint by Robert Havell, Jr., London, 1827-38, framed, 26 3/4 x 38 3/8" (light- & mat stain, few short repaired margin tears, minor damp staining, laid down) **21,850**

Polar Bear

Polar Bear - Plate XCI, hand-colored lithograph by J.T. Bowen, Philadelphia, ca. 1845, minor light-stain, few soft creases at corners, 21 3/4 x 27 1/2" (ILLUS.) **8,625**

Purple Martin - Plate 22, hand-colored, engraving & aquatint by Robert Havell, Jr., London, 1827-38, 24 5/8 x 38" (light- & mat stain, scattered foxing) **4,600**

Red-Breasted Merganser - Plate CCCCXII, hand-colored etching, engraving & aquatint by Robert Havell, Jr., London, 1827-38, unframed, 25 x 38"............ **4,070**

Red-Cockaded Woodpecker - Plate CCCLXXXIX, hand-colored etching, engraving & aquatint by Robert Havell, Jr., London, 1827-38, framed, 25 1/4 x 38" (minor light- & mat stain, scattered specks of foxing, repaired tear in right margin) **1,955**

Scolopaceus Courlan - Plate CCCLXXVII, hand-colored etching, engraving & aquatint by Robert Havell, Jr., London, 1827-38, laid down on card, 24 1/2 x 37" (stained, tears in margins, small loss at upper right corner) **1,495**

Smew or White Nun - Plate CCCXLVII, hand-colored etching, engraving & aquatint by Robert Havell, Jr., London, 1827-38, framed, 24 5/8 x 29 1/4" (light- & mat stain, few scratches, few small fox marks) **2,300**

Whip-Poor-Will - Plate 82, hand-colored etching, engraving & aquatint by Robert Havell, Jr., London, 1827-38, framed, 25 1/4 x 31" (light- & mat stain, scattered specks of foxing, horizontal crease, repaired tears at ends).............................. **6,900**

White Ibis - Plate CCXXII, hand-colored etching, engraving & aquatint by Robert Havell, Jr., London, 1823-38, framed, 25 1/4 x 37 7/8" (red slightly faded, isolated fox mark, pale mat stain in margin, stitch holes along disbound edge)............ **21,850**

White-Fronted Goose - Plate 380, hand-colored lithograph by J. Bien, New York, 1860, framed, 23 1/2 x 36 7/8" (some minor creasing, few stains in margins) **1,955**

Wild Turkey - Plate 287, hand-colored lithograph by J. Bien, New York, ca. 1859-60, framed, 24 3/4 x 36" (light-stain, scratches, mottled discoloration, water stains in lower portion, top mat affixed to sheet) **4,600**

AUTOGRAPHS

As usual, the sampling of autographs that follows, all actual sales from reputable auction houses - selected for their representative nature and price - attempts to list only persons not given in previous editions so that annual purchasers of this volume may build up a large cross-sampling of typical values.

Standard terminology includes: ALS - "Autograph Letter Signed" (body of letter in secretarial hand), DS - "Document Signed," and PS - "Photograph Signed." Sizes given are approximations. "Octavo" means roughly 7 x 9", "quarto" means roughly 12 x 14" and "folio" means roughly 11 x 14".

Adams, John (1735-1826), 2nd U.S. president, clipped signature on vellum, some damage, no size or date given.................... **$475**

Adams, Samuel (1722-1803), Declaration of Independence signer, DS, military commission appointing a captain, dated 29 May 1794, 1 pg., 12 x 15" 1,300

Anderson, Robert (1805-71), Union general remembered for surrendering Ft. Sumter, PS, carte-de-visite portrait in uniform, no year, 2 1/2 x 4"............................ 950

Arthur, Chester (1830-86), 21st U.S. president, DS, pre-presidential piece as customs collector swearing in a clerk, dated 29 June 1875, 1 pg., quarto.......................... 300

Astor, John Jacob (1763-1848), influential early financier & fur trader, LS, requests an appointment for a relative, some damage, dated 12 August 1834, no size or pages given.. 400

Audubon, John James (1785-1851), influential ornithologist, clipped signature, no date, 1 x 4"... 400

Balzac, Honore de (1799-1850), prolific French novelist, ALS, requests an appointment, no date, 1 pg., 6 x 8" 600

Bankhead, Tallulah (1902-68), film & stage star, PS, no date, 6 x 8" 480

Barrymore, Ethel (1879-1959), stage actress from the famed acting dynasty, PS, portrait in costume, no date, framed, 10 x 13".. 475

Bartok, Bela (1881-1945), Hungarian composer & pianist, PS, no date or size given, some damage 2,200

Baruch, Bernard M. (1870-1965), financier & advisor to presidents, collection of two ALSs and six LSs, concerning financial matters, 1921 to 1931, octavo, total 26 pp.. 600

Beauregard, P.G.T. (1818-93), Confederate general, DS, membership certificate in the Association of the Army of Tennessee, rather worn, dated 15 July 1880, no size given, 1 pg.. 800

Beckett, Samuel (1906-89), Nobel Prize-winning Irish playwright, ALS, thanks a correspondent for his letter, dated 19 April 1981, 1 pg., 3 x 5" 225

Begin, Menachem (1913-92), Nobel Prize-winning Israeli prime minister, LS, concerns Israel's relations w/Germany, dated 22 November 1966, 1 pg., quarto 400

Benton, Thomas Hart (1889-1975), regional artist & muralist, original sketch of Benton w/Uncle Sam & journalist Leonard Lyons, dated 24 May 1964, 1 pg., octavo...... 750

Bernstein, Leonard (1918-90) conductor & prolific composer, PS, dated 28 July 1957, 11 x 14".. 750

Bierce, Ambrose (1842-1914), author & journalist who disappeared in Mexico, ALS, regards publication of his collected works, no date, 1 pg., quarto.......................... 900

Bogart, Humphrey (1899-1957), American film actor, DS, release permitting his image to be usd in ads selling Schwinn bicycles, dated 31 January 1947, 1 pg., quarto 800

Bormann, Martin (1900-45), Nazi henchman, LS, requests a document from fellow Nazi Heinrich Himmler, dated 25 December 1941, 1 pg., quarto 300

Brahms, Johannes (1833-97), German composer & pianist, ALS, thanks sender for a Bach work, dated March 1859, 4 pp., octavo.. 3,500

Brandeis, Louis (1856-1941), U.S. Supreme Court justice & universiity namesake, ALS, mentions Palestine, dated 20 November 1933, 1 pg., octavo...................... 500

Bronte, Charlotte (1816-55), English author of "Jane Eyre," rare ALS, regards a gift & mentions her sisters, dated 21 April 1844, 2 pp., octavo 13,000

Browning, Robert (1812-89), British poet who married Elizabeth Barrett, ALS, discusses a photo, dated 12 July 1869, 2 pp., octavo.. 1,100

Brynner, Yul (1920-85), actor, best known for his role in "The King and I," PS, dated 1976, 10 x 14".. 120

Buchanan, James (1791-1868), 15th U.S. president, free-franking signature on envelope, no date, framed, 2 1/2 x 5" 475

Burns, George (1896-1996), Oscar-winning comedian & husband of Gracie Allen, PS, unusual inscription mentioning Bing Crosby, no date, 8 x 10" 500

Byron, George Gordon (1788-1824), English poet of the Romantic movement, signature on envelope addressed in his hand to poet Robert Southey, dated 28 November 1814, no size given 950

Cagney, James (1899-1986), versatile film actor who could play gangsters & hoofers, PS, portrait from "Mr. Roberts," no date, quarto.. 130

Callas, Maria (1923-77), American operatic soprano, scarce PS, no date, octavo............ 650

Calloway, Cab (1907-92), Big Band leader remembered for "Minnie the Moocher," PS, no date, 8 x 10"................................ 200

Capp, Al (1909-79) famed "Li'l Abner" cartoonist, PS, creased, no date, quarto 75

Capra, Frank (1897-1991), film director remembered for "It Happened One Night" & other sentimental classics, PS, no date, 11 x 14".. 80

Carrera, Primo (1906-67), heavyweight boxing champ from Italy, PS, no date, 8 x 10".. 225

Caruso, Enrico (1873-1921), legendary Italian tenor, signed self-caricature, no date, 1 pg., 6 x 8".................................... 1,500

Cezanne, Paul (1839-1906), French Impressionish artist, rare ALS, good content to an art critic, dated 5 February 1895, 1 pg., octavo 4,500

Chaliapin, Feodor (1873-1938), Russian opera singer, PS, dated 1924, 6 x 8" 225

Chandler, Raymond (1888-1959), dectective novelist & creator of Philip Marlowe, rare LS, tells agent his days in Hollywood are numbered, dated 14 June 1956, 2 pp., quarto 1,800

Chrysler, Walter P. (1875-1940), auto manufacturer, LS, encourages his son in his studies, dated 28 November 1925, 1 pg., no size given 400

Clay, Henry (1777-1852), powerful senator known as "The Great Compromiser," ALS, sends thanks for supporting his presidential bid, dated 12 April 1849, 1 pg., quarto **500**

Cleveland, Groover (1837-1908), 22nd and 24th U.S. president, signed "Executive Mansion" card, dated 26 October 1885, 3 x 4 1/2".............. **300**

Cody, William F. "Buffalo Bill" (1846-1917), buffalo hunter turned famed "Wild West" entertainer, scrace PS, some damage, dated 1898, 4 x 6" **1,000**

Cole, Nat "King" (1919-65), singer & bandleader, PS, publicity photo portrait, some damage, no date, quarto **180**

Dandridge, Dorothy (1923-65), singer & actress, PS, no date, framed, 8 x 10" **350**

DeGaulle, Charles (1890-1970), French military leader in World War II & French president, scarce ALS, as president sends a check, dated 16 January 1963, 1 pg., octavo **500**

Doenitz, Karl (1891-1980), Third Reich naval head & Hitler's successor, DS, typescript of his famed radio broadcast to the German people near war's close, dated 7 December 1974, 1 pg., quarto **400**

Ellington, "Duke" (1899-1974), Big Band leader and prolific composer, PS, no date, quarto **200**

Fillmore, Millard (1800-74), 13th U.S. president, DS, ship's papers co-signed by Daniel Webster, some damage, dated 29 November 1851, 1 pp., folio **1,000**

Fitzgerald, Ella (1918-96), jazz singer reknowned for improvisational "scat" singing, PS, no date, 11 x 14" **375**

Flaubert, Gustave (1821-80), French novelist of "Madame Bovary," ALS, declines an invitation, dated 16 January (no date), 1 pg., octavo **450**

Ford, Gerald R. (born 1913), 38th U.S. president, scarce ALS, thanks friends for a gift, dated 15th December 1984, 1 pg., quarto, framed w/PS **550**

Garrett, Pat (1850-1908), lawman known for killing Billy the Kid, rare ADS, certified he has delivered a subpoena, dated 20 October 1881, 1 pg., quarto **1,800**

Gates, Horatio (1728-1806), American commander in the Revolutionay War, ALS, recommends a surgeon for military duty, dated 12 November 1776, 1 pg., quarto **1,200**

George III, King (1738-1820), British monarch during the American Revolutionary War, clipped signature, no date, 4 x 4" vellum **110**

George V, King (1865-1936), British monarch, PS, some damage, dated 1930, framed, 4 x 5 1/2" **400**

Getty, J. Paul (1892-1976), founder of Getty Oil Company, ALS, excellent personal content to his mother, dated 7 June 1932, 8 pp., octavo **2,500**

Ginsburg, Allen (1926-97), controversial Beat poet, PS, shown in 1972 Democratic political convention, dated 19 August 1993, 8 x 10" **225**

Goodman, Benny (1909-86), Big Band leader & clarinetist, PS, some damage, no date, 7 x 9" **50**

Greenaway, Kate (1846-1901), British children's book illustrator, original ink & watercolor, no date or size, framed **2,000**

Guiteau, Charles (1844-82), assassin of President Garfield, two signatures (one smeared), no dates, each 2 x 3" **450**

Haley, Bill (1927-81), musician known as the "Father of Rock 'n Roll," PS, some damage, no date, quarto **350**

Hammerstein, Oscar II (1895-1960), popular Broadway lyricist who worked w/Richard Rodgers, DS, agreement regarding film version of "Oklahoma," dated 1 July 1954, 2 pp., quarto **350**

Harding, Warren G. (1865-1923), 29th U.S. president, PS, no date, 9 x 11 1/2" **275**

Harrison, Benjamin (1833-1901), 23rd U.S. president, DS, promissary note for $13,000, dated 31 December 1900, 1 pg., quarto **400**

Hayes, Rutherford B. (1822-93), 19th U.S. president, DS, authorizes Secretary of State to affix U.S. seal to a warrant, dated 5 June 1879, 1 pg., quarto **700**

Hendrix, Jimi (1942-70), pioneering electric guitarist, signature, no date, 3 1/2 x 5" card, w/publicity photograph **650**

Hitchcock, Alfred (1899-1980), noted suspense film director, PS, some damage, no date, 8 x 10" **400**

Horowitz, Vladimir (1904-89), Russian pianist, PS, portrait performing, dated 5 November 1988, 11 x 14" **325**

Joyce, James (1882-1941), Irish author, rare ALS, seeks teaching job for brother, dated 8 April 1937, 2 pp., octavo **3,000**

Keller, Helen (1880-1968), blind & deaf author/lecturer, LS, some damage, thanks dancer Martha Graham for a performance, dated 11 February 1941, 1 pg., quarto **850**

Key, Francis Scott (1779-1843), author of the "Star Spangled Banner," ALS, political matters, dated 30 November 1832, 1 pg., quarto **800**

Langtry, Lillie (1852-1929), actress known as "The Jersey Lily," PS, cabinet card portrait, no date, 4 1/2 x 7" **550**

Lanza, Mario (1921-59), opera singer & actor, DS, film contract w/Warner Brothers for "Serenade," dated 4 January 1955, 2 pp., quarto **650**

Lewis, Sinclair (1885-1951), Nobel Prizewinning American novelist, LS, sends an autograph, dated 12 October 1931, 1 pg., quarto **200**

Lind, Jenny (1820-87), Victorian coloraturo soprano known as the "Swedish Nightingale," ALS, declines an invitation, no date, 4 pp., octavo **200**

Lombard, Carole (1908-42), film star & wife of Clark Gable, PS, no date, framed, 4 x 6" **380**

Longfellow, Henry Wadsworth (1807-82), popular poet, ALS, declines a writing proposal, dated 26 April 1851, 3 pp., no size given **300**

Madison, James (1751-1836), 4th U.S. president, DS, land grant, some damage, dated 3 May 1815, 1 pg., folio vellum **325**

Mansfield, Jayne (1932-67), actress known for dizzy blonde roles, PS, no date, 8 x 10" 240

Marshall, Thurgood (1908-93), first black U.S. Supreme Court justice, PS, no date, 4 1/2 x 6 1/2" 275

McClellan, George B. (1826-85), Union Civil War general & presidential candidate, PS, carte-de-visite portrait in uniform, no date, 2 1/2 x 4" 1,000

Mix, Tom (1880-1940), silent film star in more than 400 Westerns, PS, no date, 13 1/2 x 17 1/2" 350

Monroe, James (1758-1831), 5th U.S. president, DS, land grant, dated 31 May 1824, 1 pg., folio vellum 550

Morris, Robert (1734-1806), Declaration of Independence signer & important financier, LS, regards paying for a shipment of tobacco, some damage, dated 25 July 1787, 1 pg., 7 x 8" 550

Moses, Anna "Grandma" (1860-1961), folk painter, PS, dated 1958, octavo 525

Nast, Thomas (1840-1902), political cartoonist, PS, cabinet card portrait, some damage, dated 8 July 1872, 4 x 6" 750

Onassis, Jacqueline Kennedy (1929-94), First Lady, PS, shows her unpacking in the White House, no date, 6 x 9" 800

Paderewski, Ignace (1860-1941), Polish pianist & statesman, PS, cabinet card portrait, some damage, no date, 4 x 6"......... 325

Parker, Dorothy (1893-67), witty journalist & author, DS, typescript of essay, dated 1935, 3 pp., quarto 1,000

Pavlova, Anna (1881-1931), celebrated Russian dancer, PS, ballerina pose, dated 10 December 1916, octavo, framed 575

Polk, James K. (1795-1849), 11th U.S. president, clipped signature, no date, 1 x 3 1/2"... 275

Rachmaninoff, Sergei (1874-1943), Russian composer & pianist, PS, dated 1934, 8 x 10" 1,250

Salinger, J.D. (born 1919), reclusive American writer, rare LS, some damage, about using his magazine stories, dated 17 December 1975, 1 pg., quarto 2,400

Stowe, Harriet Beecher (1811-96), author of "Uncle Tom's Cabin," ANS, regards paying an account, dated 4 January 1865, 1 pg., 5 x 7".............................. 350

Taylor, Zachary (1784-1850), 12th U.S. president, DS, appoints a naval midshipman, dated 26 September 1849, 1 pg., 8 x 11"... 1,200

Thomas, George H. (1816-70), Union general, PS, carte-de-visite portrait, some damage, no date, 2 1/2 x 4" 800

Villa, "Pancho" (1877-1923), Mexican bandit & revolutionary, LS, some damage, military matters, dated 13 May 1914, 1 pg., octavo.. 1,100

Webster, Noah (1758-1843), dictionary author, ALS, some damage, concerns a package of books, dated 8 March 1796, 1 pg., quarto 550

Zanuck, Darryl (1897-1972), film producer & studio founder, LS, good content to a noted critic, dated 17 May 1951, 3 pp., quarto 500

AUTOMOBILE LITERATURE

Book, "Rambler Family Album," covers Hudson & American Motors cars, 431 photos of cars built between 1897 & 1962 ..... **$62**

Hudson owner's manual, 1948 35

Hudson owner's manual, 1955 38

Hudson owner's manual, "Hudson Terraplane," 1936 44

Pamphlet, "Edsel," 1958 33

AUTOMOBILES

1965 Chevrolet Impala Super Sport

Chevrolet, 1965 Impala Super Sport, two-door hard top, white w/red interior, V8 engine, automatic transmission, 31,000+ miles, professionally restored (ILLUS)..... **$5,225**

Mercedes Benz, 1971, 280 SL model, all-original, two tops, fuel-injected six-cylinder engine, automatic transmission, 91,000 original miles................................ **17,050**

1957 Mercedes-Benz 190SL Roadster

Mercedes-Benz, 1957 190SL Roaster, silver, white-wall tires (ILLUS.) **16,000**

Packard, 1928 Club Sedan, Series 533, six-cylinder engine, fine interior, rebuilt motor, transmission, clutch, brakes & radiator, very nice condition **17,600**

1989 Porsche 911 Targa

Porsche, 1989 911 Targa, near mint, 22,000 miles (ILLUS.)................................. **38,500**

Studebaker, 1936 Dictator 3A, new brakes & hood ornament, spare engine & transmission, rear fenders, radiator, four extra wheels & tires, many small miscellaneous parts, runs well **2,860**

AUTOMOTIVE COLLECTIBLES

Also see: Antique Trader Advertising Price Guide.

Horn, 1912 Model T, fine condition **$110**
License plate, New Jersey, 1915, w/tags **150**
Speedometer, 1912 Model T, w/new brass
   cable **83**

AVIATION COLLECTIBLES

Booklet, "Guide to Commercial Aviation,"
   1922, paper covers, French & English
   text covering air routes between Paris,
   Brussels & Amsterdam, photos of
   planes, pilots & air views of cities, colorful
   cover w/stylized airplane above a map of
   the region covered, detailed information,
   76 pp., 7 1/4 x 10 1/4" (slight wear, slight
   spine separation, small stain at top of
   cover) **$88**
Booklet, souvenir for a reception & banquet
   for the crew of the monoplane Bremen in
   honor of the first successful non-stop
   flight westward across the Atlantic on
   May 9, 1928, image of plane & map on
   the cover, photos of the three crew members inside w/the listing of the program &
   menu, 5 1/2 x 7" (some cover soiling).............. **28**

BABY MEMENTOES

Carriage, painted wood & oil cloth, the carriage bed w/a narrow wood framework enclosed by delicate spindled sides, front
   end w/an oilcloth folding hood, a very long
   slender handle, raised on a spring undercarriage w/wooden-spoked wheels, the
   front two slightly larger than the rear two,
   early red & brown repaint w/white line trim,
   Zoar, Ohio, late 19th - early 20th c.,
   21 1/2 x 41 1/2", 36" h. (damage & resto-
   rations to oil cloth) **$990**
Carriage, woven wicker, a deep & wide seat
   compartment w/high sides w/tightly woven thick serpentine upper borders over
   pairs of large swelled inverted teardrop
   panels centered by a cornucopia-form
   half-round pocket on each side, high S-
   scrolled woven wicker front footrest,
   raised on high scrolled metal springs on
   four large wire-spoked wheels, ca. 1890,
   45" l., 33" h. **672**
Rattle, sterling silver, figural Teddy bear rat-
   tle attached to a mother-of-pearl teething
   ring, early 20th c., bear 2 7/8" h. **86**

Teethers

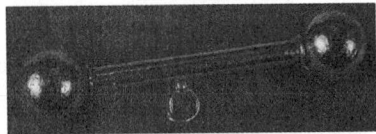

Gold Teether

Gold, narrow rod w/knobbed ends in a modified dumbbell shape, w/ring for chain or
   cord, India, ca. 1900, 2 7/8" (ILLUS.)............. **700**

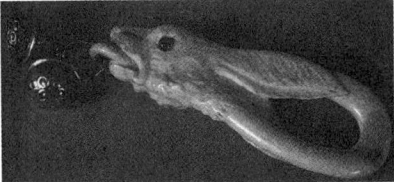

Coral & Gold Teether

Gold, very fine brightwork, whistle tip, thick
   coral handle, hallmark identified Nicholas
   Dunee, England, George III era, 1775,
   5 1/2" (ILLUS.) **7,000**

Carved Ivory Teether

Ivory, carved jester face in profile, fixed
   balls once held blue ribbons & small ivory
   beads, England, late 19th c., 4 1/2"
   (ILLUS.) **450**

Carved Ivory Teether w/Silver Bells

Ivory, handle-shaped w/rabbit's head & two
   silver bells, England, ca. 1900-10, 4"
   (ILLUS.) **600**

Ivory Teether

Ivory, narrow rod w/knobbed ends in a modified dumbbell shape, India, ca. 1900,
   2 3/4" (ILLUS.) **80**

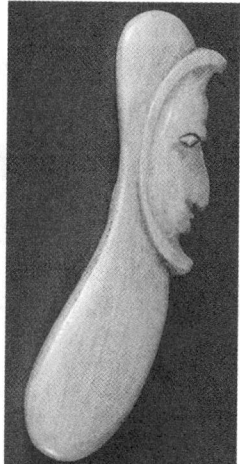

Carved Ivory Teether

Ivory, patinated, man-in-the-moon profile, U.S., ca. 1910, 3 3/4" (ILLUS.)...................... **100**

Carved Scrimshaw Teether

Ivory or bone, scrimshaw, carved in shape of a saw, may have been part of a set, U.S., New England, ca. 1850s, 3 3/4" (ILLUS.).. **120**

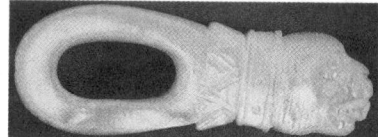

Carved Mother-of-Pearl Teether

Mother-of-pearl, carved in shape of baby's hand at one end w/loop opening as a handle at the other end, U.S., ca. 1920-30, 3 1/2" (ILLUS.)... **130**

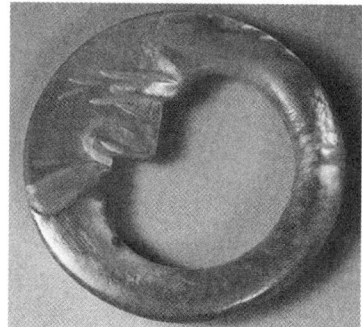

Carved Mother-of-Pearl Teether

Mother-of-pearl, carved man-in-the-moon face on pearl ring, U.S., ca. 1915-20, 2 1/2" d. (ILLUS.).. **100**

Silver Teether

Silver, figure of little girl reading a book marked "ABC" & "XYZ," two silver bells attached, she is mounted atop a nipple-shaped ivory teether, Kate Greenaway storybook character, no marks, England, ca. 1900, 3" (ILLUS.) **600**

Silver Teether

Silver, spaniel dog head w/one bell attached, ivory carved teething stick & ring, England, ca. 1920s, 4 1/2" (ILLUS.).............. **800**

Coral & Vermeil Teether

Vermeil, geometric brightwork design, whistle tip, thick coral handle, no maker's mark, England, ca. 1810, 3 1/2" (ILLUS.) **1,400**

Scrimshaw Teething Sticks

Whalebone, scrimshaw teething sticks, lightly incised, meant to be hung across cradle where they could jingle or be pulled down by the baby, U.S., New England, ca. 1850s, 4 1/2" (ILLUS.).......... **1,000**

BANKS

Pottery

Model of a cottage, roof w/coleslaw trim in orange, green & yellow, chimney in center, on rectangular base w/floral trim, 5 3/4" h. (minor enamel wear on flowers & several flakes at rim of base).................. **$110**

Still

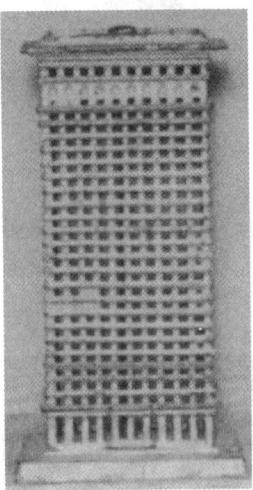

Woolworth Tower Bank

1040 Building - "Woolworth Building," cast iron, Kenton Mfg. Co., 1915, 2 5/8 x 3 1/8 x 8 1/8" h., W. 386 (ILLUS.).. **1,320**

115 Grant (U.S.) Bust, cast iron, J.M. Harper, ca. 1905, 5 3/4" h. (some wear, screw replaced) **2,300**

1181 Building - Domed "Bank," cast iron, building w/mesh sides & solid domed roof, A.C. Williams Co., 1899, 1 3/4 x 2 1/4 x 3 5/8" h. (W. 423) **125**

136 Washington, George - Washington (hollow base), cast iron, standing figure of Washington, American-made, ca. 1970, 6 3/8" h. **75**

Oregon Battleship Bank

1450 Battleship - "Oregon" (small), cast iron, J. & E. Stevens Co., 1891-1906, 4 7/8" l., 3 7/8" h., W. 144 (ILLUS.) **413**

Stiff-legged Elephant Bank

469 Elephant - Stiff-legged Elephant, cast iron, Harris Toy Co., ca. 1904, 3 1/2 x 4 5/16" (ILLUS.) **303**

Tally Ho Bank

535 Horse - "Tally Ho," cast iron, horse head framed by horseshoe w/fox hunt items, Chamberlain & Hill, England, 4 1/2" h., 4 3/16" l., (W. 168), pristine (ILLUS.) **204**

Blackpool Tower Bank

Blackpool Tower, cast iron, Chamberlain & Hill, England, ca. 1908, 2 7/8 x 4 3/8 x 7 3/8" (ILLUS.) **220**

BARBERIANA
Barber Bottles

Rare & Colorful Barber Bottle

Canary yellow flashed w/ruby red, Hobnail patt., bulbous body tapering to a tall ringed neck w/stopper, lower body in canary w/the neck & upper half flashed in red, rolled lip, pontiled base, ca. 1890, 6 1/8" h. (ILLUS.) **$3,410**

Canary yellow, Hobnail patt., squatty bulbous body tapering to a tall slender neck w/hobs, tooled lip, polished pontil, ca. 1900, 6 5/8" h. **253**

Clear opalescent, Seaweed patt., squared tapering body w/slender neck & molded rim, ca. 1900, 8 1/4" h. **176**

Clear opalescent, swirled Stripe patt., cylindrical w/tall neck & rolled mouth, smooth base, ca. 1900, 9" h. **143**

Cobalt blue, brilliantine-style, short cylindrical form w/two rows of pressed Thumbprint panels, shoulder tapering to cylindrical neck w/tooled mouth & stopper, smooth base, ca. 1900, 3 1/2" h. **1,100**

Cobalt blue, bulbous base tapering to a tall cylindrical neck, decorated w/central colored band trimmed w/white enamel blossoms & scrolls, bands of white dots & scrolls above & below band, ca. 1900, 7 7/8" h. **77**

Cobalt blue, ovoid body tapering to a lady's leg neck w/rolled rim, enameled w/scattered white, yellow & orange stylized blossoms, base pontil, ca. 1900, 8 1/4" h. **110**

Cranberry opalescent, Hobnail patt., bulbous base w/tall slender ringed neck w/tooled lip, pontiled base, early 20th c., 8" h. **165**

Opalescent Seawood Pattern Bottle

Cranberry opalescent, Seaweed patt., gently tapering cylindrical body w/tall neck & rolled rim, polished pontil, ca. 1900, 8 3/4" h. (ILLUS.) **468**

Cut-overlay, ruby cut to clear, a stepped club-form body w/a tall slender neck & flared rim, cut around the base w/narrow stepped arches below a band of punties w/a shoulder band of cut icicle design w/further punties & bands cut around the neck, ca. 1900, polished pontil, 7 1/4" h. **413**

Emerald green, bulbous ovoid body w/ringed base tapering to a ringed & swelled neck w/rolled lip, decorated w/vertical bands of small stylized enameled blossoms in white, yellow & blue, pontiled base, 7 3/4" h. (few spots of interior haze) **154**

Personalized Barber Bottle

Decorated milk glass, ringed slightly tapering cylindrical body w/a curved shoulder & tall slender ringed neck w/original pewter screw cap, colored ground decorated in the front w/a large flower-bordered reserve w/owner's name above a pair of large crossed American flags, W.T. & Co. mark on base, ca. 1900, 9 1/2" h. (ILLUS.) **1,210**

Hair Tonic Barber Bottle

Fiery opalescent milk glass, slightly tapering cylindrical form w/a tall slender neck & rolled lip, polished pontil, h.p. large water grist mill scene framed by trees, marked "Hair Tonic" above, applied mouth, pontiled base, ca. 1900, 8 7/8" h. (ILLUS.).. **605**

Frosted emerald green, ovoid body tapering to a lady's leg neck w/rolled rim, Art Nouveau floral silver overlay decoration around the sides, pontiled base, ca. 1900, 7 7/8" h..................................... **660**

Green, bright optic ribbed design enameled w/scattered enameled blossoms in white, yellow & orange, cylindrical body tapering at the shoulder to a tall slender neck w/rolled lip, smooth base, ca. 1900, 8 3/4" h... **385**

Mary Gregory Barber Bottle

Mary Gregory-type, deep cobalt blue decorated w/a white enamel figure of a boy playing tennis, bulbous ovoid body tapering to a tall lady's leg neck w/tooled mouth, smooth base, ca. 1900, 7 7/8" h. (ILLUS.) **264**

Rare Brilliantine Barber Bottle

Purple, brilliantine-type, slender cylindrical tapering ringed body w/a ringed neck & flared rim w/stopper, smooth base, ca. 1900, 4 1/4" h. (ILLUS.) **495**

Ruby flashed & etched, ovoid body tapering to a tall slender neck w/tooled lip, ruby etched to frosted clear w/a running stag in forest scene, delicated etched scroll bands around base & neck, probably Bohemia, late 19th c., 7 7/8" h................. **176**

Spatter, deep ruby swirled w/white splotches, bulbous base w/conical sides tapering to a tall slender waisted neck w/tooled mouth, polished pontil, ca. 1900, 7 3/4" h. **132**

Turquoise blue, bulbous melon-lobed base in the Coin Spot patt., tall slender neck w/rolled lip, smooth base, ca. 1900, 6 7/8" h... **105**

Turquoise blue opalescent, Fern patt., slender ovoid body tapering to a tall slender neck w/rolled rim, polished pontil, ca. 1900, 8 1/4" h. **143**

Turquoise blue opalescent, Seaweed patt., squared body tapering to tall cylindrical neck w/rolled rim, polished pontil, ca. 1900, 8 3/8" h. **209**

White porcelain, square body tapering to a rounded shoulder & tall slender slightly flaring neck, colorful floral decoration below "Witch Hazel," ca. 1900, 8 7/8" h............. **55**

Mugs

General

Bust portrait of a pretty Victorian lady, enclosed in an arched reserve, the border band w/the name in gold, gilt trim, ca. 1900, 3 1/2" h. **275**

Eagle & roses, a large spread-winged eagle at the top above an arched banner w/the gold name, cluster of roses & blossoms across the bottom front, ca. 1900, 3 1/2" h.. **165**

Landscape, an oval vignette scene of a landscape w/a small cottage among large trees, color sprig of flowers on back, script name in arched white band above the scene, company stamp mark on base, ca. 1900, 3 7/8" h. (ILLUS. top next page)... **330**

Shaving Mug with Landscape Scene

Owl in tree, rebus-type, color scene of a large owl perched on a bare branch w/a large full moon in the background, name in gold across the top, ca. 1900, 3 1/2" h....... **198**

Shaving Mug with Man's Portrait

Portrait of man, central oval reserve enclosing the bust portrait of a man w/moustache wearing a dress suit, ornate gilt scrolls above oval & colorful floral sprigs at sides, further floral sprigs on back, no name given, Kansas City decorator's mark, ca. 1900, 4" h. (ILLUS.)......... **2,310**

Winter landscape, a continuous design of a small cottage in a snow-covered landscape, two small birds on a branch in the foreground, name around bottom in gold, ca. 1900, 3 7/8" h. **110**

Fraternal Order

Brotherhood of Locomotive Firemen, large h.p. color image of a locomotive w/name in gold across top, letters "B. of

L.F." on engine tender, ca. 1900, 3 3/4" h... **825**

Odd Fellows Fraternal Shaving Mug

Odd Fellows, h.p. design of Odd Fellow emblem above an open Bible crossed by a sword, gilt leafy scrolls flank design, name across top in gold, ca. 1900, 3 1/2" h. (ILLUS.)................................. **88**

Odd Fellows, large h.p. image of locomotive & coal car w/Odd Fellows emblem on door of locomotive, name in gold across the top, ca. 1900............................... **176**

Occupational

Artist, h.p. artist's palette & brushes, name in worn gold across the top, base stamped "Eugene Berninghaus Cincinnati, Ohio - Climax (chair)," ca. 1900 3 1/2" h.. **176**

Baker, wide h.p. scene of a baker putted bread in a large oven, table & barrels in front of oven, name in gold across the top, base stamped "Royal China International," ca. 1900, 3 5/8" h. **242**

Rare Barber Shop Scene Mug

Barber, h.p. detailed barber shop scene w/barbers, customer, mug rack, furniture & mirrors, name in gold across top, Koken & W.G. & Co. Limoges marks on base, ca. 1900, 3 7/8" h. (ILLUS.) **4,510**

Bartender, h.p. barroom scene w/bartender & two customers, bottles & kegs shown, name in gold across top, colorful sprigs of flowers down the sides, Haviland & Co. base mark, ca. 1900, 3 7/8" h. 330

Baseball player, h.p. full-length image of a baseball pitcher ready to throw the ball, worn gold name across top, W.G. & Co., Limoges, France on base, ca. 1900, 3 7/8" h. **2,090**

Bricklayer, h.p. color scene of five brick masons at work on a wall, name in gold across the bottom, ca. 1900, 3 5/8" h. 660

Butcher, h.p. large bull's head flanked by crossed saws & tools, name in gold across bottom, ca. 1900, 3 5/8" h. 77

Carpenter, h.p. scene of a carpenter standing sawing a board in front of his tool-covered workbench, name in gold across top, W. G. & Co., Limoges, France base mark, ca. 1900, 4" h. 440

Detailed Coal Miner's Mug

Coal miner, detailed h.p. scene of miner leaving shaft in mule-drawn cart (ILLUS.).. **3,520**

Cobbler, h.p. scene of a cobbler standing working on a shoe w/bench to one side & shoes scattered on floor, name in gold across top, ca. 1900, 3 3/4" h. (professional rim repair above decoration) 330

Druggist, h.p. mortar & pestle framed by gilt leafy vines above the name in gold, T. & V. Limoges, France mark on base, ca. 1900, 3 5/8" h. 165

Early Fireman's Shaving Mug

Fireman, h.p. scene of a racing horse-drawn steam fire engine, name below in gold, ca. 1900, 3 3/4" h. (ILLUS.) **1,073**

Mail wagon driver, h.p. scene of an enclosed mail wagon w/driver pulled by two horses, worn gold name around top, late 19th c., 4" h. 963

Photographer's Occupational Mug

Photographer, h.p. scene of a photographer w/large camera shooting a picture of a standing young man w/top hat next to a seated young woman, ca. 1900, 3 5/8" h. (ILLUS.) **2,090**

Policeman, h.p. three-quarters length portrait of an early policeman holding a billy club, name in gold across top, ca. 1900, 3 7/8" h. 908

Printer, color scene of a hand holding a printer's type set block, name in gold across top, ca. 1900, 3 1/2" h. 242

Railroadman, h.p. large red caboose marked on the side "C.B. & Q.," name in gold across bottom, ca. 1900, 3 5/8" h. (gilt redone) 209

Tailor's Occupational Shaving Mug

Tailor, h.p. scene of a tailor seated working at a bench surrounded by parts of a man's suit, name in gold across top, gilt scroll trim, ca. 1900, 3 7/8" h. (ILLUS.) 825

Trolley car driver, h.p. scene of an electric trolley w/front & rear conductors & six riders, name in gold around the top, T. & V. Limoges, France mark on base, ca. 1900, 3 5/8" h. **495**

Mustache Cups

Cup & saucer, china, hand-painted, applied mustache guard, marked "Trademark" (on applied sticker), overglaze-purple, England or USA, ca. 1863+ (England), 1876+ (USA) **250-275**

Cup & saucer, china, hand-painted, applied mustache guard, unmarked, country unknown, ca. 1875-1885........................ **140-150**

Cup & saucer, china, hand-painted, applied mustache guard, unmarked, country unknown, ca. 1885-1890........................ **110-120**

Cup & saucer, china, hand-painted, applied mustache guard, unmarked, country unknown, ca. 1870-1880........................ **150-165**

Cup & saucer, china, hand-painted Art Deco design, applied mustache guard, marked "Hand Painted Nippon" & green "M" in Wreath mark (Morimura Bros., importer), underglaze-green, Japan, ca. 1891-1921...................................... **275-300**

Cup & saucer, china, hand-painted & decal, applied mustache guard, country unknown, ca. 1870-1880 .... **125-150**

Cup & saucer, china, hand-painted & decal, applied mustache guard, marked "R" (pierced by arrow), "Made in Germany," overglaze-red, ca. 1920s **125-135**

Cup & saucer, china, hand-painted & decal, unmatched saucer, applied mustache guard, unmarked, country unknown, ca. 1880-1890............................. **60-65**

Cup & saucer, china, hand-painted & decals, applied mustache guard, marked "J&C" (Jaeger & Co.), "Malmaison," underglaze-bluish green, "Germany," overglaze-red, ca. 1902 .... **150-175**

Cup & saucer, china, hand-painted & decals, applied mustache guard, marked "R. C. Sanssouci" (Philip Rosenthal & Co." underglaze-green, "Germany, 2338/56," overglaze-lavender, ca. 1901-1910.. **150-175**

Cup & saucer, china, hand-painted & decals, applied mustache guard, marked "Royal Bayreuth, Pt., Germany," overglaze-gold, ca. 1902 .... **110-125**

Cup & saucer, china, hand-painted & decals, applied mustache guard, marked "Three Crown China, Germany," ca. 1892-1910..................................... **150-175**

Cup & saucer, china, hand-painted & decals, applied mustache guard, unmarked, country unknown, ca. 1865-1875.. **160-180**

Cup & saucer, china, hand-painted & decals, modified pedestal, applied mustache guard, marked "R. C., Iris, Bavaria, Philip Rosenthal & Co.," overglaze-green, ca. 1901-1910 .... **200-225**

Cup & saucer, china, hand-painted & decals, rare salmon color, wishbone handle, applied mustache guard, marked "TM" (intertwined) "1885," underglaze-black, country unknown, ca. 1885+ **150-175**

Haviland Limoges Mustache Cup & Saucer

Cup & saucer, china, hand-painted, elaborate & delicate floral design, applied gold handle, applied & gold decorated mustache guard, Haviland Limoges, marked "CFH/GDM," France, ca. 1891-1900 (ILLUS.) **275-300**

Cup & saucer, china, hand-painted, gold wishbone handle, applied mustache guard, marked "Elite/L, France" (Limoges), underglaze-green, signed & dated, ca. 1900-1903 .... **275-300**

Cup & saucer, china, hand-painted (possibly over stencil), applied mustache guard, marked w/red Oriental characters, Oriental, country unknown, ca. unknown **300-325**

Cup & saucer, china, hand-painted rare fruit & flower design, applied mustache guard, marked "Rosenthal," crown & "Hand-Painted," Germany, ca. 1907-1920 .... **280-300**

Cup & saucer, china, hand-painted rare geometric design, applied recessed mustache guard, unmarked, country unknown, date unknown **250-300**

Cup & saucer, china, hand-painted, rare pearl yellow & deep purple lustre, applied decoration, applied mustache guard, marked "Germany" in red, ca. 1891-1900 .... **145-165**

Cup & saucer, china, hand-painted, rare tree design, applied mustache guard, marked "ES" (Erdman Schlegelmilch), "Depon" (registered), "3352," overglaze-brown, Germany, ca. 1891-1900 .... **295-310**

Cup & saucer, china, hand-painted shamrocks, lustre, basketweave design, split twig handle, applied mustache guard, marked "Belleek, Co. Fermanagh, Ireland," second black mark, printed, ca. 1891-1926................... **1,100-1,300**

Cup & saucer, china, hand-painted & signed, applied mustache guard, unmarked, country unknown, ca. 1875-1885 .... **125-150**

Cup & saucer, china, hand-painted to mold, applied mustache guard, unmarked, country unknown, ca. 1850-1860 .... **175-200**

Cup & saucer, china, hand-painted & transfer, applied mustache guard, marked "Limoges, France," w/bird, underglaze-green, marked "GD&C" (G. Demartine & Co.), "Limoges, France," overglaze-green, ca. 1891-1904 .... **275-325**

Cup & saucer, china, hand-painted & transfer, applied mustache guard, unmarked, country unknown, ca. 1860-1870....... 125-135

Cup & saucer, china, hand-painted & transfer, ornate handle, applied mustache guard, marked "R" (pierced by arrow), "Made In Germany," overglaze-red, ca. 1920s..... 175-200

Cup & saucer, china, hand-painted, unmatched saucer, applied mustache guard, unmarked, country unknown, ca. 1880-1890..... 70-75

Cup & saucer, china, hand-painted unusual color, applied mustache guard, cracks in cup, unmarked, country unknown, ca. 1880-1890..... 40-110

Cup & saucer, china, hand-painted, unusual thundermug shape, rectangular handle, applied mustache guard w/deep apron, unmarked, France, ca, 1870-1880 175-200

Cup & saucer, china, hand-painted, unusual weave design, applied mustache guard, marked "Manufactured In Germany," overglaze-brown, ca. 1891-1900 175-200

Cup & saucer, china, hand-painted wedding band design, applied mustache guard, marked "P K Silesia" & eagle, underglaze-dark green, Germany, ca. 1880-1890..... 110-130

Cup & saucer, china, hand-painted wedding band design, applied mustache guard, marked "H&Co." (Haviland & Company), "L" (Limoges), underglaze-green, "Haviland & Co. Limoges," overglaze-blue, France, ca. 1876-1889..... 300-325

Cup & saucer, china, hexagonal, hand-painted unusual design, hexagonal pedestal, applied mustache guard, marked "M. Z." (Moritz Zdekauer, Altrohlau), "Austria," underglaze-green, ca. 1900 ... 175-200

Cup & saucer, china, left-handed, hand-painted, rare cherry design, applied mustache guard, marked "Austria," ca. 1892+ 450-500

Mustache Cup & Saucer w/Red Cherries

Cup & saucer, china, left-handed, hand-painted rare red cherries design, marked "Austria," ca. 1891-1918 (ILLUS.)..... 400-500

Cup & saucer, china, left-handed, hand-painted & transfer, rare fruit & nut design, applied mustache guard, unmarked, country unknown, ca. 1880-1890 800-900

Cup & saucer, china, left-handed, transfer design, applied mustache guard, un-marked, country unknown, ca. 1880-1890 700-750

Cup & saucer, china, miniature, hand-painted, question mark handle, applied mustache guard, marked "Rose Crown," overglaze-gold, country unknown, ca. 1880-1890, rare 400-450

R.S. Prussia Mustache Cup & Saucer

Cup & saucer, china, outstanding hand-painted rare tree branch design w/butterflies & berries, continues inside cup as well as on applied mustache guard, early "ES" (Erdmann Schlegelmilch), Germany, ca. 1891-1900 (ILLUS.)..... 295-310

Cup & saucer, china, pink pattern design, half-scissors handle, applied mustache guard, marked "Royal Worcester, England," overglaze, pink, ca. 1889...... 275-325

Cup & saucer, china, presentation-type, hand-painted, rare pansy design, half scissors handle, applied mustache guard, unmarked, Germany, ca. 1895-1900 120-130

Cup & saucer, china, presentation-type, hand-painted, unique gold handle, applied mustache guard, marked "Elite/L, France" (Limoges), underglaze-green, signed & dated, ca. 1900-1903 275-300

Cup & saucer, china, rare heart-shaped, hand-painted & transfer, wishbone handle, applied mustache guard, rare "RS" (Reinhold Schlegelmilch) wing mark, "Germany," overglaze-reddish brown, pre-World War I 1,100-1,300

Cup & saucer, china, rare square shape, hand-painted, applied mustache guard in corner of cup, unmarked, country unknown, ca. 1880-1883...... 225-275

Cup & saucer, china, rare square shape, hand-painted, pearlescent lustre, ornate handle, four-footed, applied mustache guard, unmarked, country unknown, ca. 1875-1885..... 225-250

Cup & saucer, china, seashell-shape, hand-painted, very deep saucer, applied mustache guard, unmarked, country unknown, ca. 1880-1890...... 175-200

Cup & saucer, china, square, hand-painted, unusual use of color, applied mustache guard, unmarked, country unknown, ca. 1880-1890...... 300-325

Cup & saucer, china, transfer design, unmatched saucer, applied mustache guard, marked "Three Crown China, Germany," underglaze-black, ca. 1891-1920.. 85-90

Miscellaneous

Barber pole, painted wood, a tall slender columnar form w/a large turned ball finial & two double ring-turned bands around the center, remnants of original red, white & blue spiraled painting, 19th c., 72" h. (wear)... **523**

Barber pole, painted wood, tall cylindrical pole w/turned narrow band at the center, the top w/a double ball finial, worn spiral stripes in old polychrome repaint, deteriorated base w/added stand, 19th c., 81" h. **688**

Barber pole, turned & painted wood, a heavy column turned at the top w/a large rounded knob above a section of turned rings flanking a baluster section at the top of a heavy gently tapering column, worn red & white repaint, tin cover on top, 76" h. (filled age cracks & chips on base)...... **550**

Early Oak Shaving Mug Rack

Shaving mug rack, oak, tall upright case w/a scroll-carved crest on the crestrail above the narrow flared cornice above a frieze band above 35 compartments for mugs, ca. 1900, 8 x 41", 45" h. (ILLUS.) **908**

Rare Shaving Paper Glass Vase

Shaving paper vase, fiery opalescent milk glass decorated w/a large colorful reserve w/frolicking cherubs, framed by scrolls & florals, wide baluster-form body w/flared, polished rim, smooth base, ca. 1900, 7 3/4" h. (ILLUS.)............................... **4,070**

BARBIE DOLLS & COLLECTIBLES

At the time of her introduction in 1959, no one could have guessed that this statuesque doll would become a national phenomenon and eventually the most famous girl's plaything produced.

Over the years, Barbie and her growing range of family and friends have evolved with the times, serving as an excellent mirror on the fashion and social changes taking place in American society. Today, after over 40 years of continual production, Barbie's popularity goes on unabated among both young girls and older collectors. Early and rare Barbies can sell for remarkable prices and it is everyone's hope to find mint condition "#1 Barbie."

Dolls

Allan Doll and Box

Allan, painted red hair, pink lips, straight legs, redressed in striped knit shirt, tan pants, black wire stand, near mint w/box, box age discolored & w/some wear & damage (ILLUS.)... **$95**

Barbie, "1920s Flapper Barbie," The Great Eras Collection, Second Edition, No. 4062, dated 1993, never removed from box (back side of box creased along edge) **85**

Barbie, "American Girl Barbie," ash blonde hair w/plastic cover, gold lips w/faint tint of orange, finger & toe paint, bent legs, wearing original one-piece swimsuit, wrist tag, Exlusivie Fashions Book 1, aqua open-toed shoes in cellophane bag, in box w/gold wire stand, mint-near mint... **800**

Barbie, "American Girl Barbie," ash brown hair, repainted bright pink lips, nostril paint, finger & toe paint, bent legs, wearing original one-piece swimsuit, in box w/gold wire stand, Exclusive Fashion by Mattel Book 1 & aqua open-toed shoes in cellophane bag, near mint (box slightly age discolored, slightly worn & w/other minor damages) **975**

Barbie, "American Girl Barbie," titian hair, beige lips, finger paint, wearing original one-piece swimsuit, near mint (eyebrows slightly faded) **475**

Barbie, "Barbie as Eliza Doolittle in My Fair Lady," No. 15500, wearing Embassy Ball gown, 1995, never removed from box (back left side of box creased, upper back left box corner creased) **35**

Barbie, "Barbie as Rapunzel," Children's Collector Series First Edition, No. 13016, dated 1994, never removed from box, price sticker on upper right front of box **20**

Barbie, "Bubblecut Barbie," brunette hair, red lips, nostril paint, finger & toe paint, straight legs, original white striped swimsuit, wrist tag, pearl earrings, in box w/black wire stand, cardboard neck & leg inserts, pink cover Barbie-Ken booklet in cellophane bag w/white-rimmed glasses w/blue lenses, black open-toed shoes, near mint in box **375**

Bubblecut Barbie in Box

Barbie, "Bubblecut Barbie," white ginger hair, beige lips w/a touch of orange, finger & toe paint, straight legs, wearing black & white striped swimsuit, in box w/black wire stand, face slightly darker than body, hair smells of cigarette smoke, minor fading, stain & chip off lower leg, box age discolored & worn (ILLUS.) **370**

Barbie, "Circus Star Barbie," limited edtion, No. 13257, dated 1994, never removed from box **55**

Barbie, "Color Magic Barbie," yellow blonde hair w/blue barrette & original plaid nylon headband, pink lips, nostril paint, finger paint, bent legs, wearing plaid Color Magic dress, near mint **525**

Barbie, "Evening Sophisticate Barbie," Classique Collection designed by Robert Best, No. 19361, 1997, never removed from box **30**

Barbie, "Fashion Queen Barbie," painted brunette hair w/blue band, coral lips, nostril paint, finger & toe paint, straight legs, wearing original gold & white one-piece swimsuit, matching hat, pearl earrings, black open-toed shoes, white plastic wig stand w/brunette, titian & blonde wigs, near mint (blue headband loose, yellow tape stains on wig stand) **185**

Barbie, "Feelin' Groovy Barbie," Billy Boy Limited Edition, No. 3421, dated 1986, never removed from box **155**

Barbie, "Happy Holidays Barbie,"Special Edition, No. 1703, red gown w/silver accents, never removed from box, 1988 .... **400**

Barbie, "Jeweled Splendor Barbie," FAO Schwarz Signature Collection, No. 14061, dated 1995, never removed from box w/cardboard shipping box **100**

Barbie, "Living Barbie," brunette hair, pink lips, cheek blush, bendable arms & legs, wearing original one-piece swimsuit w/orange net cover-up, wrist tag, clear plastic stand, in box w/box insert, near mint (wrist tag creased, box discolored & damaged) **200**

Barbie, "Malibu Barbie," blonde hair w/attached plastic sunglasses & clear plastic band, pink lips w/painted teeth, bent legs, wearing original light blue nylon swimsuit, wrist tag, yellow terrycloth towel, in plastic bag, never removed from package, made in Japan **145**

Barbie, "Mardi Gras Barbie," American Beauties Collection, No. 4930, dated 1987, never removed from box **35**

Barbie, "Montgomery Ward's Anniversary Barbie," 1972, Ponytail Barbie w/brunette hair in original set, red lips, straight legs, wearing original black & white knit swimsuit, white open-toed shoes taped to her feet, wrist tag, mint **355**

Fine No. 1 Ponytail Barbie

Barbie, "No. 1 Ponytail Barbie," brunette hair in ponytail, red lips, finger & toe paint, original black & white striped swimsuit, near mint in original box (ILLUS.) **8,700**

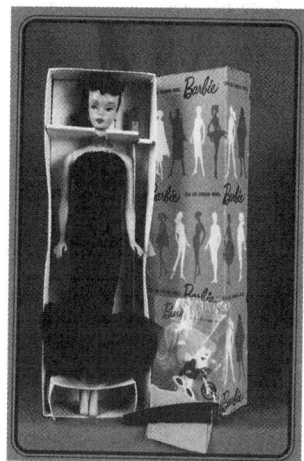

No. 4 Ponytail Barbie in Costume

Barbie, "No. 4 Ponytail Barbie," dressed in Solo in the Spotlight outfit, brunette hair in original top knot, red lips, eyeshadow, finger & toe paint, straight legs, gold loop earrings, black sequin dress w/tulle & flower accents, black nylon gloves, #1 light navy blue open-toed shoes w/holes, four-strand bead choker, pink scarf, microphone on stand, pink cover Barbie booklet in cellophane bag w/white-rimmed glasses w/blue lenses, in box w/black pedestal stand, cardboard neck-microphone & foot insert, near mint (ILLUS.) **4,100**

Barbie, "No. 5 Ponytail Barbie," yellow blonde hair in original ponytail w/top & bottom rubberbands, red lips, nostril paint, oily face, finger & toe paint, straight legs, wearing black & white striped swimsuit, pearl earrings, in box w/black wire stand, white-rimmed glasses w/blue lenses & black open-toed shoes in cellophane booklet bag, cardboard foot insert, near mint in box **450**

Barbie, "No. 5 Ponytail Barbie," yellow blonde hair, red lips, nostril paint, finger & toe paint, straight legs, wearing original black & white striped swimsuit, very good condition, no box (small amount of green discoloration on both ears, two earring holes in right ear, left eyebrow faded, lower right leg bends outward) **115**

Barbie, "No. 6 Ponytail Barbie," brunette hair in original top knot, coral lips, finger & toe paint, straight legs, wearing red nylon swimsuit, pearl earrings, in box w/gold wire stand, Exclusive Fashions Book 2, near mint (strands of hair loose, small split & green discoloration on one ear, box age discolored & worn w/name written on lower front, booklet age discolored w/small stain on back) **370**

Barbie, "Queen of Hearts," Bob Mackie designed Seventh Limited Edition, No. 12046, dated 1994, never removed from box w/cardboard shipping box **185**

Barbie, "Royal Barbie," International Series, No. 1601, dated 1979, never removed from box (box slightly age discolored & worn) **125**

Barbie, "Scottish Barbie," International Series, No. 3263, dated 1980, never removed from box (box slightly age discolored & worn) **75**

Barbie, "Serenade in Satin," Barbie Couture No. 17572, 1996, never removed from box **75**

Barbie, "Swan Lake Barbie," First in Series of Barbie Musical Ballerina Dolls, No. 1648, dated 1991, never removed from box w/cardboard shipping box **70**

Barbie, "Swirl Ponytail Barbie," brunette hair in original set w/yellow ribbon, beige lips, finger & toe paint, wearing red nylon swimsuit, wrist tag, in box w/cardboard box insert, gold wire stand, red open-toed shoes, Exclusive Fashions Book 1, near mint (top of bangs loose, face & arms slightly darker than body, box age discolored & worn) **410**

Barbie, "Twist 'n Turn Barbie," brunette hair, pink lips, cheek blush, rooted eyelashes, finger paint, bent legs, wearing No. 1453 Flower Wower print dress, wrist tag, clear plastic stand, near mint, no box **205**

Barbie, "Winter Princess Barbie," Limited Edition, No. 10655, dated 1993, never removed from box (box slightly scuffed) **145**

Barbie, Ken & Midge Gift Set

Barbie, Ken & Midge, "Barbie, Ken & Midge On Parade Gift Set," near mint in original box w/costumes & accessories (ILLUS.) **1,760**

Christie, "Live Action Christie," black hair, brown lips, rooted eyelashes, bendable arms & legs, wearing two-piece print pants w/fringe accent & matching skirt w/fringe trim, near mint (several light colored areas on torso) **135**

Christie, "Malibu Christie," The Sun Set, black hair w/plastic head wrap & attached plastic sunglasses, brown lips, bent legs, wearing red nylon swimsuit, white terrycloth towel, never removed from package (cardboard backing age discolored & creased)................................ **190**

Francie, "Twist 'n Turn Francie," brunette hair w/brown string attached to both sides of head, pink lips, rooted eyelashes, bent legs, wearing No. 1207 Floating In dress, very good condition **95**

Ken, brunette flocked hair, beige lips, straight legs, wearing red swim trunks w/white stripe, in box w/black wire stand, cork sandals w/red straps, cardboard neck & foot inserts, near mint in box **70**

Ken, brunette flocked hair, beige lips, straight legs, wearing red & white striped jacket, red swim trunks, cork sandals w/red straps, yellow terrycloth towel, light blue cover Barbie-Ken booklet, black wire stand, no box, near mint (faint ink stain on back of right leg, jacket & booklet age discolored) **110**

Ken, painted brunette hair, beige lips, straight legs, wearing gold corduroy pants, diamond pattern knit sweater, black shoes, black wire stand, near mint, no box (white paint dot above left eyebrow, small stain on back of pants) **50**

Ken Doll with Box

Ken, painted brunette hair, beige lips, straight legs, wearing red swim trunks w/white stripe, striped jacket, cork sandals w/red straps, in box w/black wire stand & Exclusive Fashions Book 4, box aged discolored & slightly worn & mended (ILLUS.) **65**

Midge, blonde hair, pink lips, finger & toe paint, straight legs, wearing No. 978 Let's Dance print dress w/ribbon waistband & sash, black open-toed shoes, black wire stand, near mint, no box **65**

Midge, brunette hair, pink lips, finger & toe paint, straight legs, wearing No. 978 Let's Dance dress, black open-toed shoes, near mint (several indentations in torso, tag slightly frayed) **75**

Midge, titian hair, pink lips, finger & toe paint, straight legs, wearing two-piece chartreuse & orange swimsuit, black wire stand, near mint in box (inseams slightly frayed on swimsuit, box discolored & slightly worn, small box edge tear) **85**

Skipper, "Malibu Skipper," The Sun Set, blonde hair w/plastic head wrap, twist-n-turn, bent legs, wearing two-piece orange nylon swimsuit, never removed from box (box age discolored & slightly worn)... **85**

Skipper, "Pose 'n Play Skipper," blonde hair in original set w/blue ribbon ties, pale pink lips, bendable arms & legs, wearing one-piece blue & white outfit w/button accents, no box, near mint (clothing & ribbons age discolored) **55**

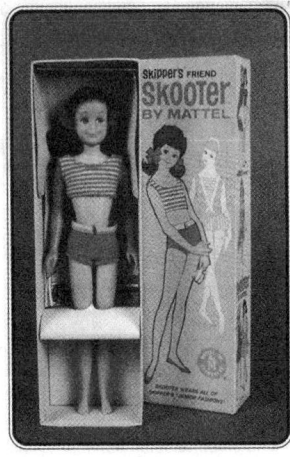

Skooter Doll in Box

Skooter, brunette hair w/replaced red vevlet ribbon, pink lips, straight legs, wearing original two-piece red & white swimsuit, in box w/gold wire stand, gold cover Skipper-Skooter-Ricky booklet, cardboard box liner, near mint, box age discolored & worn (ILLUS.)... **90**

Skooter, red hair w/original red ribbons, pink lips, cheek blush, straight legs, wearing No. 1935 Learning to Ride outfit including yellow jodhpurs, black & white jacket w/button accents, black plastic riding cap, near mint **85**

Clothing & Accessories

Accessory pak, Barbie set w/white-rimmed glasses w/blue lenses & gold glitter, white nylon short gloves, pairs of open-toed shoes including orange, red, white & clear w/gold glitter, three-strand pearl choker w/two pearl drops, matching bracelet & drop earrings, white hanger stapled to cardboard backing, yellow cover booklet, paper Barbie-Midge label on lower left cellophane corner w/$1.00 printed price sticker, never removed from package **260**

Accessory set, "Color Coordinates," No. 1832, Barbie outfit, includes clutch purses w/button closure in hot pink, orange, powder blue, yellow & red w/coordinating open-toed shoes, dark blue cover Ken-Barbie-Midge #4 booklet, paper label, never removed from package, (cardboard back age discolored) **120**

Accesssory pak, "Purse Pak," Barbie item, red velveteen clutch purse w/button closure, black vinyl clutch purse w/button closure, woven basket w/flowers, white hanger stapled to cardboard backing, dark blue cover booklet, paper Barbie-Midge label on lower left cellophane corner w/.80 printed price sticker, dated 1962, never removed from package (cardboard backing slightly discolored, edges slightly worn) 35

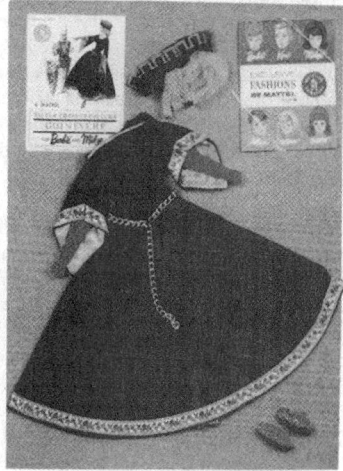

Barbie's Austin Healy Auto

Automobile, Barbie's Austin Healy, peach plastic w/turquoise interior, silver plastic accessories, by Irwin, near mint, small scuffs & discolored spots on silver trim, plastic window scuffed (ILLUS.) 90

Clothing set, "All That Jazz," No. 1848, Barbie outfit, striped jacket w/button accents, gold foil belt w/yellow plastic closure, matching dress w/pleated skirt, beige sheer nylon stockings, orange bow shoes, near mint (small stain on front of jacket sleeve) 305

Clothing set, Barbie Fur Fashion from France, dark & white fur long coat w/'snakeskin' belt, sleeves & matching cap, dated 1979, mint in box (box damaged & worn) 30

Clothing set, "Bride's Dream," No. 947, Barbie set, white wedding gown w/ribbon bow accent & cardboard bodice form, white tulle veil w/pearl headband, long white nylon gloves, white open-toed shoes, blue nylon garter w/flower accents, flower bouquet w/ribbon streamers, pearl necklace, near mint (tag slightly frayed on gown, necklace loosely strung) 80

Clothing set, "Can You Play?," No. 1923, Skipper outfit, red & blue dress w/red polka dot trim, matching red polka dot panties & head scarf w/ties, red flap shoes in small cellophane bag, white plastic ball in small cellophane bag, red & white jump rope w/plastic handles, Fashions & Play Accessories booklet, never removed from box (box age discolored & worn) 90

Clothing set, "Check the Suit," No. 1794, Barbie outfit, pink & yellow knit jacket w/button accents, matching pants w/vinyl waistband & attached buckle, yellow knit sleeveless shirt, yellow high tongue shoes, yellow Barbie hanger, near mint (buckle discolored on pants) 35

Clothing set, "Club Meeting," No. 1672, Barbie outfit, turquoise jacket w/ribbon & flower accents, matching sheath dress w/print bodice w/glitter accents, turquoise pointed-toe shoes, The World of Barbie Fashions Book 3," never removed from box (booklet age discolored, box in poor condition) 320

Clothing set, "Day 'n Night," No. 1723, Barbie Sew-Free Fashion-Fun, never re-

moved from box (box slightly discolored & worn)... 50

Clothing set, "Dream-Ins," No. 1867, Barbie outfit, fuchsia furry robe w/ribbon & lace trim & ties, short nightie w/lace & ribbon straps & ties, Barbie hanger, mint 50

Clothing set, "Fun Runners," No. 3372, Skipper outfit, yellow nylon sleeveless shirt, denim pants, red & white print scarf, red belt w/buckle & red plastic sunglasses in small plastic bag, white tennis shoes in small plastic bag, dated 1971, never removed from package (edges of cardboard backing slightly worn) 25

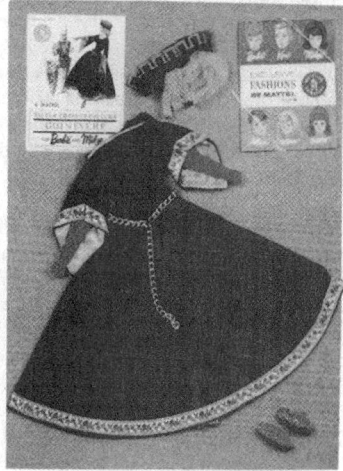

Barbie "Guinevere" Clothing Set

Clothing set, "Guinevere," No. 0873, navy velveteen gown w/embroidered trim & attached chain belt, red nylon armlets, felt hat w/gold trim & attached snood & neckstrap, red & gold brocade shoes, Theatre program, Exclusive Fashion Book 3, attached to cardboard backing w/cellophane sleeve, never removed from cardboard, booklet & program slightly discolored, top string on booklet loose (ILLUS.) 180

Clothing set, "Hiking Holiday," No. 1412, Ken outfit, green knit sweater, beige shorts, white cotton socks, brown shoes, near mint (socks & shorts slightly age discolored)... 55

Clothing set, "In Training," No. 780, Ken outfit, white cotton shirt & briefs, red & white shorts, two black plastic dumbbells, "How to Build Muscles" book, pink cover Barbie booklet, paper label, never removed from box (slight wear & discoloration on box) 35

Clothing set, Ken, "Tuxedo," No. 787, black jacket w/boutonniere & button closure, black pants, white shirt w/button accents, black socks & shoes, burgundy cummerbund & bow tie, white flower corsage, booklet, never removed from box (box slightly worn & discolored)............................. 110

Clothing set, "Land & Sea," No. 1917, Skipper outfit, blue denim jacket w/cord drawstring & red stitching, matching short pants & cap, red & white striped knit shirt, white flat shoes in small cellophane bag, red plastic sunglasses, white cover Skipper booklet, never removed from box (box slightly age discolored & worn) **110**

Clothing set, Lingerie Pak, Barbie set w/blue bra, panties & slip, pink plastic mirror, blue open-toed scuffs w/pompons, white hanger stapled to cardboard backing, blue cover booklet, paper Barbie-Midge label on lower left cellophane corner, never removed from package **120**

Clothing set, "Lovely 'n Lavender," No. 3358, Barbie Best Buy Fashions, pale pink long robe w/fur collar & lace trim, matching short nightgown, pink open-toed shoes, white plastic pitcher & cup, never removed from box (cardboard backing age discolored & worn) **85**

Clothing set, "Open Road" No. 985, Barbie outfit w/beige jacket w/toggle buttons & braided attachments, beige short-sleeved sweater, striped pants, straw hat w/attached red chiffon scarf, cork wedgies w/red uppers, red-rimmed glasses w/blue lenses, Mattel Road Map, near mint **135**

Clothing set, Pedal Pushers, Barbie Pak, blue sleeveless shirt w/yellow stitching & cardboard form, matching shorts, one yellow soft flat shoe **50**

Clothing set, "Plantation Belle," No. 966, Barbie outfit w/pale pink dress w/lace trim, white nylon petticoat w/tulle trim & bow accent, woven straw hat w/pink brim, bow accent & flowers, on cardboard hat form, matching purse w/bead & sequin design, pink pearl necklace & bracelet, pink open-toed shoes, near mint **185**

Clothing set, "Pretty Traveler," No. 1706, Barbie Sew-Free Fashion-Fun, never removed from box (box slightly discolored & worn) **40**

Clothing set, "Rare Pair," No. 1462, Barbie outfit, pink & yellow knit dress w/button accents, matching jacket, yellow nylon stockings on cardboard insert, yellow high tongue shoes, Barbie hanger, Living Barbie and Skipper booklet, paper label, never removed from box (box age discolored & damaged) **105**

Clothing set, Ricky, "Lights Out," No. 1501, light blue robe w/matching belt & scuffs, yellow two-piece pajamas w/button accents & "h" on pocket, booklet, cellophane, never removed from carton **35**

Clothing set, Satin Pants, Barbie Pak, rose-colored satin pants w/pale pink open-toed shoes w/silver glitter, white hanger stapled to cardboard backing, light blue cover booklet, paper Barbie label on lower left cellophane corner w/perforated price sticker missing, cardboard & paper discolored, small split on right & bottom right side seams (ILLUS. top next column) **80**

Barbie Pak with Satin Pants

Clothing set, "Saturday Matinee," No. 1615, Barbie outfit, tweed jacket w/button accents & fur trim, matching sheath, skirt & hat, gold foil purse w/fur trim, chain handle & flower accent, brown open-toed shoes, short brown nylon gloves, near mint (small amount of foil lifted on purse) **550**

Clothing set, Scoop-neck Playsuit, Barbie Pak item, black & white print suit, red belt w/buckle, three-charm bracelet, white hanger stapled to cardboard backing, light blue cover booklet, paper Barbie label on lower left cellophane corner w/1.00 printed price sticker, dated 1962, never removed from package (cardboard backing & stickers very age discolored, backing faded, metal belt buckle discolored, side of paper label loose) **90**

Clothing set, "Seein' the Sights," No. 1421, Ken outfit, red & black tweed jacket w/button closure, black pants, white short sleeve shirt w/button accents, red cotton socks, black shoes, red cover The World of Barbie Fashion and Playthings booklet, paper label, never removed from box **240**

Clothing set, "Skater's Waltz," No. 1629, Barbie set w/pink leotard dress w/attached skirt, beige pantyhose on cardboard form, pink fur mittens & collars w/braid ties, white ice skates in small cellophane bag, Exclusive Fashion Books 2, "1629" written on lower right box **215**

Clothing set, Skipper, "Loungin' Lovelies," aqua long robe w/lace & ribbon trim, two-piece aqua pajamas w/lace trim, matching scuffs, booklet, never removed from package (soiled dot on robe, large section of cellophane missing) **45**

Clothing set, Skipper, "Quick Changes!," No. 1962, orange, pink & blue knit sweater w/button closures, orange & blue pleated skirt, blue sleeveless shirt w/zipper closure, pink knit socks w/orange tassel, hot pink ankle boots, cellophane,

cardboard box label stapled to upper right cardboard backing & cellophane, never removed from carton (booklet missing, lower edge of cellophane torn) **105**
Clothing set, "Smasheeroo," No. 1860, Barbie outfit, red striped dress w/button accents & chain belt, yellow plush jacket w/striped lining, matching hat, yellow diamond pattern stockings on cardboard forms, near mint (stitching on top of stocking loose) **60**
Clothing set, "Sorority Tea," No. 1703, Barbie Sew-Free Fashion Fun, never removed from box (box slightly discolored & worn) **30**
Clothing set, "Suburban Shopper," No. 969, Barbie set w/striped sundress w/flower design, straw hat w/ribbon band, cardboard hat form, pink plastic telephone w/metal dial, white open-toed shoes, near mint **85**
Clothing set, "Sunflower," No. 1683, Barb-toe shoes, pink & blue dangle earrings, two pink bracelets, near mint (metal on earrings discolored) **125**

BASEBALL MEMORABILIA

Baseball was named by Abner Doubleday as he laid out a diamond-shaped field with four bases at Cooperstown, New York. A popular game from its inception, by 1869 it was able to support its first all-professional team, the Cincinnati Red Stockings. The National League was organized in 1876 and though the American League was first formed in 1900, it was not officially recognized until 1903. Today, the "national pastime" has millions of fans and collecting baseball memorabilia has become a major hobby with enthusiastic collectors seeking out items associated with players such as Babe Ruth, Lou Gehrig, and others who became legends in their own lifetimes. Though baseball cards, issued as advertising premiums for bubble gum and other products, seem to dominate the field there are numerous other items available.

Baseball Autographed Banjo Skin

Banjo skin, signed by 31 members of the 1926 Philadelphia Athletics team below

the inscription "Philadelphia Athletics - 1926 - Fort Meyers - Florida," signed at spring training, shows wear, w/letter of authenticity (ILLUS.) **$1,763**
Banner, printed cloth, rectangular, white glossy ground printed in dark blue & red "Souvenir of 1961 World Series - Cincinnati Reds - New York Yankees," w/team logos, wide golden fringe at bottom, excellent condition, 9 1/2 x 16" **1,093**
Base, original game-used canvas sack w/leather ties on one side, printed "Brooklyn Dodgers National Association," 1930s **843**
Baseball, 1930 New York Yankees team-signed, official American League Barnard ball, signed by 22 members of the 1929 Yankees team, glue-mounted on a walnut-stained wooden stand w/Babe Ruth signature showing at top, w/letter of authenicity **2,115**
Baseball, 1961 New York Yankees team signed, signed by 37 members of the 1961 World Series Champions, clean w/a small gouge on one side panel, letter of authenticity **2,585**
Baseball, autographed by Harry Heilmann & Birdie Tebbetts, fair signature **452**
Baseball, Babe Ruth-signed, Wilson Official League Ball, flawlessly signed in blue ink, near mint, w/letter of authenticity **14,688**
Baseball, early 'lemon peel' style ball, primitive hand-sewn leather, 1850s **713**
Baseball, Roger Maris-signed, MacGregor branch, boldly signed on the sweet spot, near mint, w/letter of authenticity **940**
Baseball, signed by Ty Cobb, official American League Harridge ball, signed & personalized by Cobb, dated 9/30/49, near mint, w/letter of authenticity **3,055**
Baseball cap, Hank Aaron game-worn model, solid navy blue Atlanta Braves cap, late 1960s - early 1970s, size 7 1/4, signed by Aaron in black marker on bill..... **4,710**
Baseball card, Babe Ruth, 1933 Goudey series, No. 149, red ground, near mint **48,897**
Baseball card, Benny Bengough, 1933 Goudey series, No. 1, red ground, near mint.. **48,703**
Baseball card, Jimmy Foxx, 1933 Goudey series, No. 154, near mint........................ **8,967**
Baseball card, Joe DiMaggio rookie card, 1934 Zeenut series, black & white image of DiMaggio swinging, printed in the bottom right "Coast League - J. DeMaggio (sic) - Seals," signed by DiMaggio in black Sharpie, excellent....................... **3,061**
Baseball card, Lou Gehrig, 1933 Goudey series, No. 92, blue ground (small white dot on background)................................. **10,500**
Baseball card, Lou Gehrig 1933 Goudey series, No. 92, excellent (slight border discoloration on front, small smudge near upper right on back)................................ **1,058**
Baseball card, Mickey Mantle, 1956 Topps series, No. 135, near mint....................... **2,527**
Baseball card, Napoleon Lajoie, 1933 Goudey series, No. 106, near mint **53,130**

Baseball glove, early Workman style crescent glove, leather w/crescent-shaped padded palm, original brass button on the strap, lined w/wool batting & well stitched, printed w/former owner's name, ca. 1890s 1,252

Baseball glove, leather, owned by Joe DiMaggio, a Joe DiMaggio model by the Hutch Company of Cincinnati, Ohio, given away by DiMaggio at spring training in 1948, shows moderate to heavy use, w/letter of provenance 11,163

Bat, 1961 New York Yankees black model, Hillerich & Bradsby model commemorating the 1961 World Series Champion team, features the names of 37 members of the team, 35" l. (light nicks, scratches, paint flecks) 1,293

Bat, Babe Ruth game-used model, Hillerich & Bradsby Co., Babe Ruth trademark, 1920s, 41 oz., 34" l. 26,021

Bat, limited edition Louisville Slugger 125 Signature Model autographed on the barrell by Joe DiMaggio in bold blue Sharpie, numbered on the barrell "Limited Edition 396/1941," 36" l. 1,880

Miniature Louisville Slugger Bat

Bat, miniature, advertising-type, a chromolithographed label for the "Louisville Slugger Bats" centered by a color bust portrait of J. Honus Wagner, early 20th c., 14" l. (ILLUS.) 825

Bat, Pete Rose game-used model, Adirondack, Pete Rose trademark & signed in black Sharpie "Pete Rose Hit King 4256," 1970s, 35" l. 9,620

Bat, Rogers Hornsby game-used model, Hillerich & Bradsby Co., Hornsby trademark, 1920s 19,364

Bat, Ty Cobb game-used model, Hillerich & Bradsby Model 125, Ty Cobb trademark, a gift from Cobb in 1925, inscribed in silver "Given to me in 1925 by Ty Cobb - Joe Sewell," 34 1/2" l. 79,810

Bat, Zack Wheat game-used model, Hillerich & Bradsby Co., Zack Wheat trademark, early 1920s, 34" l. (repaired cracked handle) 4,333

Check, personal check signed by Christy Mathewson, name printed at left edge, dated "Jan. 29, 1923," near mint 7,938

China place setting: cup, saucer & dinner plate; white w/each piece printed in red & blue w/a pennant below an arch of five stars, reads "Brooklyn 1952 Dodgers - National League Champions," bottom marked "With Sincere Appreciation from the Dodgers, National League Champions 1952," presentation set, the set 672

Cigarette silk, silk printed w/portrait of Ty Cobb, w/packaging back, from Old Mill Cigarettes, 1911, near mint 817

Club membership card & pin, Dizzy Dean, 1936, in original mailer 35

Joe DiMaggio Driver's License

Driver's license, Joe DiMaggio's Florida driver's license, issued March 19, 1986, signed "Joe Paul DiMaggio" (ILLUS.) 11,750

Roger Maris Novelty Figure

Figure, Roger Maris, souvenir miniature bobbing head-type, wearing black & white Yankees uniform & holding bat, on round base w/decal marked "Roger Maris" in gold, w/original box w/cover label marked "Mr. Home Run," early 1960s, 5" h., slightest loss to facsimile signature decal on base, box torn on bottom (ILLUS. of figure & box) 843

Figurine, bisque, full-figure of a young Victorian baseball batter in full uniform, finely painted details, Heubach, Germany, ca. 1880s, 13" h. (restored bat) 1,346

Flannel, 1969 Hank Aaron game-used road flannel, size 40, signed by Aaron on the right tail 24,079

Glove, leather, Thurman Munson catcher's mitt, Rawlings "Wingtip" model, written on back in black marker "15 Munson," w/heavy use, w/letter of provenance.......... 2,820

Invitation, official printed invitation for the opening of Comiskey Park, Chicago on February 15, 1910, league logo at the top & black & white engraving of the stadium at the bottom, w/original black envelope, framed.. 6,346

Jacket, Cincinnati Reds 1950s spring warm-up model, satin, size 40, near mint 974

Jersey, 1940s Detroit road jersey, flannel, worn by Birdie Tebbetts, signed by Tebbetts in black Sharpie **1,814**

Letter, two-page handwritten letter from Lou Gehrig to a young fan giving advice on the fundamentals of playing first base, written in pencil on 6 x 9 1/2" stationery of the Noel Hotel, Nashville, Tennessee, undated, w/letter of authenticity **12,925**

Lithograph, color cabinet size image of George Davis, bust portrait in uniform facing left, on cardboard mount, ca. 1889-93, near mint **5,963**

Life Magazine Signed by Joe DiMaggio

Magazine, "Life", August 1, 1949, black & white cover photo of Joe DiMaggio, authographed by DiMaggio (ILLUS.) **225**

Magazine, "Life," July 30, 1965, Mickey Mantle cover **20**

"Safe at Home" Movie Poster

Movie poster, "Safe at Home," Columbia Pictures, 1962, starring Mickey Mantle &

Roger Maris, color images of the two ball players & other members of the cast w/credits, linen-backed, 41 x 61" (ILLUS.) **635**

Mug, hand-painted porcelain, cylindrical w/flaring base & loop handle, decorated w/a running baseball player in red, green & pink against blue sky & green grass, base marked "M.Z. Austria," ca. 1900, 5" h. **348**

Photograph, 1946 Detroit Tigers, jumbo sized black & white shot of the team, signed by 28 team members, near mint, 11 x 14" **2,553**

Photograph, original black & white group shot showing Babe Ruth & Lou Gehrig in their "Bustin' Babes" & "Larrupin' Lous" uniforms, surrounded by young boys from St. Marys school, from their 1927 post-season tour, signed by Ruth & Gehrig, near mint, 8 x 10" **13,893**

Photograph, Roger Maris autographed black & white wire photo, showing Maris connecting w/his 61st home run in 1961, signed in black Sharpie, 8 x 10" **1,530**

Pillow cover, silk, large square printed for the 1907 Detroit Tigers, a central large black & white image of a growling tiger head holding crossed pennants w/"Detroit '07" above three images, two players & manager Hugie Jennings, each full-length figure marked with his name, "Wild Bill" Donovan, "Wee-e-e-ah" Jennings & Ty Cobb, The Great and Only, near mint, 18 x 20" **2,447**

Pinback button, Brooklyn Dodgers Ebbets Field souvenir, round, printed to look like a baseball w/blue & red lettering "Our Bums - 1947," first year for Jackie Robinson, near mint, 2" d. **746**

Pinback button, celluloid, produced for the 1910 World Series, printed in the form of a baseball in blue & red on white, marked "Athletics - World 1910 Series - Cubs," near mint **455**

Pocket watch, 1952 Yankees World Championship model, silver Whitnauer watch presented to players & front office executives to commemorate the Yankees fourth consecutive World Series title, silver-dollar size, near mint **3,261**

Postcard, jumbo-size, black & white photo of Jackie Robinson wearing a suit & seated next to a microphone to broadcast his NBC radio show, unused, 1950s, near mint, 5 1/2 x 7 1/2" **201**

Rare Pittsburgh Pirates Postcard

Postcard, white stock w/black printing & an applied yellow felt banner reading "Pittsburgh," background reads "The Pirates - 1909 - Champions of the World...," near mint (ILLUS.) **725**

Rare Early Spalding's Guide Poster

Poster, advertising-type, lithographed in black, white & red, "Spalding's Official Base Ball Guide - 1885 - For Sale Here" w/a full-length image of an early baseball batter, near mint, 17 1/4 x 22 1/8" (ILLUS.)... **5,604**

Press pin, enameled metal, 1916 Brooklyn Dodgers World Series type, round metal w/an embossed gold center baseball, printed in black "Brooklyn," a white & blue enamel border band w/"World Series - 1916," near mint **4,746**

Press pin, enameled metal, 1920 Brooklyn Dodgers, round button w/a central gold baseball w/"Brooklyn" framed by a red enamel band w/"World Series - 1920" **2,910**

Program, 1921 World Series, printed paper, cover printed w/oval reserves w/bust portraits of John McGraw & Miller Huggins, also printed in red, black & white on a grey ground "Giants vs Yankees - 1921 - Worlds Championship Series - Polo Grounds," excellent...................................... **1,236**

1958 Yankees Championship Ring

Ring, 1958 New York Yankees championship ring, 14k gold set w/a diamond in the

round top, a ring around the top w/raised wording "New York Yankees World Champions," each side w/the Yankee logo & the date "1958," original owner's name engraved inside (ILLUS.) **4,700**

Brooklyn Dodgers Salt & Pepper

Salt & pepper shakers, ceramic, white cylindrical form w/side handle & metal lid, colored decal of the Brooklyn Dodgers 'Bum' logo above "Dodgers," 1950s, near mint, pr. (ILLUS.).. **421**

Season pass, 1891 Cincinnati Reds, printed paper card w/signatures, reverse w/a list of the eight National League teams that year, near mint... **789**

Sheet music, "Oh! You - Babe Ruth! - The 1921 World Series Song," black & red type on white w/a large three-quarters length photo of Babe Ruth **731**

Very Rare Ruth Advertising Display

Sign, counter display-type, tri-fold color-printed cardboard, "Old Gold Cigarettes," central panel w/a large color image of Babe Ruth swinging a bat w/endorsement by Ruth, left side panel w/picture of a pack & "Smoother and Better," right panel w/slogan "Not a cough in a carload," green ground w/orange, black & yellow printing, 1930s, excellent condition, 38 x 52" (ILLUS.) **32,766**

Stereocard, rectangular cardboard w/orange ground, mounted w/a sepia two-part photo of an early baseball team, inscribed in ink along border "Pine Tree B.B.C., Fall Team of '77," reverse lists other photos available from the Belfast, Maine photographer, 1877, 4 x 7" **383**

Team photo, 1961 New York Yankees, black & white image signed by team members of the World Champion team, mounted w/two blue plaques w/gold lettering, w/letter of authenticity, 15 1/2 x 19 1/2" **1,763**

Trade card, 1869 photo card of the Cincinnati Red Stockings, first all-professional baseball team, group photo of the team w/their names below & "Red Stocking B.B. Club of Cincinnati," reverse w/advertising for a New York City sports equipment company, 3 1/4 x 4 1/2" **12,329**

Tumbler, cylindrical clear glass printed in blue & white w/"Brooklyn Dodgers" & the 'Bum' team logo, 1950s, mint **201**

World Series ticket, 1938 Game 3 ticket at Yankee Stadium, excellent condition w/slight paper loss on the reverse, a number 4 written in pencil on reverse, 2 3/4 x 7 1/2" **940**

Wristwatch, 1948 All-Star Game model, a Lord Elgin commemorating the 1948 All-Star Game played in St. Louis, 14k gold, made by the I.W.C. Company w/Speidel band, engraved on the back "All Star Game St. Louis July 13, 1948," face somewhat dirty, working **588**

Yearbook, 1946 Negro League edition, full-length photo of Jackie Robinson holding bat on cover against a red ground, titled "Negro Baseball - 1946 Yearbook," featured articles listed on the cover include "Records - All-America Team - East-West Game - World Series - Crashing the Majors," excellent **611**

BASKETS

The American Indians were the first basket weavers on this continent and, of necessity, the early Colonial settlers and their descendants pursued this artistic handicraft to provide essential containers for berries, eggs and endless other items to be carried or stored. Rye straw, split willow and reeds are but a few of the wide variety of materials used. The Nantucket baskets, plainly and sturdily constructed, along with those made by specialized groups, would seem to draw the greatest attention to this area of collecting.

"Buttocks" basket, miniature, woven splint, 11-rib construction w/bentwood handle w/Eye of God design, 3" h. plus handle (some damage) **$55**

"Buttocks" basket, woven splint, 23-rib construction, wide wrapped rim, bentwood handle, 6" l., 3" h. plus handle **138**

"Buttocks" basket, miniature, woven splint, 18-rib construction w/bentwood handle, center band w/over-weaving, 3 1/2" w., 3 1/2" h. including handle **165**

"Buttocks" basket, woven splint, 20-rib construction, deep rounded sides w/a wrapped rim, bentwood handle, good old worn patina, 7 1/2" d., 4" h. plus handle (some wear & damage) **165**

"Buttocks" basket, woven splint, 26-rib construction, bentwood handle, center band w/over-weaving, 6" w., 4 1/2" h. including handle **330**

Small "Buttocks" Basket

"Buttocks" basket, woven splint, 54-rib construction, bentwood handle, minor damage at handle, 5 3/4" w., 5 1/4" h. (ILLUS.) **578**

"Buttocks" basket, woven splint, 14-rib construction w/eye of God design at ends of bentwood handle, good patina, 11 1/2" l. (minor breaks) **138**

"Buttocks" basket, woven splint, 28-rib construction, two-tone brown & natural finish, Woodland Indian origin, 11 x 12 1/2", 6" h. plus bentwood handle **523**

Large "Buttocks" Basket

"Buttocks" basket, woven splint, 28-rib construction, minor wear, 12 3/4 x 19 1/2", 6" h. (ILLUS.) **193**

"Buttocks" basket, woven splint, 30-rib construction, bentwood handle, wide rim & center band w/decorative over-weaving, 7" w, 6 1/2" h. including (minor damage at edge of handle) **303**

"Buttocks" basket, woven splint, 34-rib construction, light patina, 12 x 14", 7" h. plus bentwood handle (minor damage) **193**

"Buttocks" basket, woven splint, 30-rib construction, dark original alligatored finish, tightly woven, 9 x 11", 8" h. **193**

"Buttocks" basket, woven splint, 24-rib construction, wide low bentwood center handle, good patina, 14 x 16", 8" h. plus handle **220**

"Buttocks" basket, woven splint, 26-rib construction, bentwood handle, deep rounded sides, good color, 13 x 15", 9" h. plus handle (splint breaks) **110**

"Buttocks" basket, woven splint, 36-rib construction, good color, 15 x 19", 10 h. plus bentwood handle **220**

"Buttocks" basket, woven splint, 28-rib construction, bentwood handle, good color, 12 3/4" l., 12 1/2" h. plus handle **248**

Large Painted "Buttocks" Basket

"Buttocks" basket, tightly woven splint, 28-rib construction, wide wrapped rim & arched bentwood handle, old bluish green exterior paint, minor paint wear, a couple of splint breaks in base, 14 1/4 x 16 3/4", 13 3/4" h. (ILLUS.) **1,293**

Fine Quality "Buttocks" Basket

"Buttocks" basket, finely woven splint, 64-rib construction, brown & red weaving stripes, w/twisted twig handle, 14 x 20", 15" h. (ILLUS.) **165**

Cheese basket, woven splint, hexagonal honeycomb design w/wrapped round rim, good color, 22 1/2" d., 7 1/2" h. (few breaks, one repair) **270**

Field basket, woven splint, carved notched handles on a rounded form w/square base, late 19th c., 25" d., 14" h. **345**

Gathering basket, woven splint, rectangular base w/slightly flaring woven sides w/a wrapped rim & small bentwood end rim handles, nice patina, 8 x 16", 6" h. **275**

Gathering basket, woven splint, deep slightly tapering round sides w/a flat base, wide wrapped rim w/angled bentwood handle, natural finish, carved handle, 14 3/4" h. (slightly misshapen) **105**

Gathering basket, woven splint, wide deep round sides w/a wrapped rim, high bentwood handle, good patina, 15 3/8" d., 15" h. (minor cracks in splints) **138**

Gathering basket, woven splint, round deep sides w/wrapped ring & swivel bentwood handle, dark brown varnish finish, 16" d., 7 1/2" h. (well-executed repairs in base) **193**

Goose feather gathering basket, cov., woven splint, deep cylindrical sides w/wide

domed cover & high arched bentwood handle, old red paint, found in New England, 15" d., 8" h. **715**

Half-basket, woven splint, 11-rib construction, oblong half-round form w/wrapped rim & bentwood handle from end to end, green paint, 9" l., 4 1/2" h. plus handle **220**

Rare Leather Key Basket

Key basket, decorated leather, the tapered oval form w/sides embossed w/stars, diamonds, hearts & running vines along w/the name "N.C. Dann" within a rectangular border, the bottom also inscribed w/a six-point star & concentric circles, the stationary leather handle w/applied leather hearts, the interior in red leather, minor rim wear, probably Richmond, Virginia, ca. 1830, 5 1/4 x 7 1/8", 7 1/4" h. (ILLUS.) **21,450**

Unusual Kettle-shaped Basket

Market basket, woven splint w/whip-wrapped rim & bentwood handle, kettle-shaped, minor damage & worn yellow paint, 13 1/2" d., 8" h. plus handle (ILLUS.) **550**

Market basket, woven splint, a wide rounded bottom w/upright sides, oval bentwood rim band & wooden base, high arched center bentwood handle, old dark green paint, 11 x 16", 13 1/4" h. (areas of paint wear, few splint breaks)......................... **165**

"Melon" basket, tightly woven splint, 20-rib construction, two bluish green stained lines along the bottom, bentwood handle, 6 1/2" h. (small breaks)..................................... **83**

"Melon" basket, tightly woven splint, 18-rib construction, flat base, wrapped rim, slender bentwood handle, 7 1/4" h. **165**

"Melon" basket, woven splint, 16-rib construction, deep half-round form w/wrapped rim & bentwood end-to-end handle, medium patina, 13" l., 9" h. plus bentwood handle (minor wear).. **275**

"Melon" basket, woven splint, 20-rib construction in radiating design, arched bentwood handle, good brown patina, 10 1/2" h. **83**

"Melon" basket, woven splint, 16-rib construction, tightly woven over the flat bentwood staves, arched bentwood handle, 13 1/2" h. (two short sections of splint missing)... **176**

Nantucket Basket

Nantucket basket, woven splint, round w/wooden swing handle & brass ear assembly, 20th c., America, minor break on rim, 9 5/8" d., 5 1/4" h. (ILLUS.) **748**

Nantucket basket, finely woven splint, round w/carved swing handle & turned wooden base, Massachusetts, early 20th c., 10 1/2" d., 9" h. **2,070**

Nantucket basket, finely woven splint & cane, early large rectangular form, double-wrapped rim, two side handles & three wooden runners on base, 19th c., 19 1/2 x 30", 11 1/2" h. **748**

Nantucket purse basket, finely woven splint, oval, hinged wooden lid, swing handle, lid w/inscribed ivory oval w/ship design on a walnut oval, ivory pin & knobs, impressed marks of Mike Kane, 1974, 6 1/2 x 7 3/4", 5 1/4" h. **978**

Nantucket purse basket, finely woven splint, oval, the flat wooden lid decorated w/a walnut medallion & whale's tooth within an inscribed whaling scene, ivory pin, knobs & latch, branded mark of S.G. Gibbs, 8 1/4 x 11 1/4", 7" h. **1,035**

Nantucket purse basket, finely woven splint, round w/footring & deep sides

w/wrapped rim w/ivory fitting, hinged domed cover center w/a plaque w/a carved ivory design of two flying sea gulls, impressed label "Made by Wm. & J. Reis - 1973 Nantucket Island," 7 1/2 x 10 1/2", 7 1/2" h. plus swivel bentwood handle............ **825**

Nantucket purse basket, finely woven splint, oval, flat wooden lid decorated w/ivory whale on a walnut oval medallion, swing handle, ivory pin & knobs, impressed mark of Wm. T.J. Reis, 20th c., 6 3/4" h... **3,565**

Nantucket purse basket, woven splint, tightly woven deep oval form w/a hinged low domed cover centered by an oval wood medallion w/a relief-carved ivory whale, turned ivory pegs & angled arched bentwood handle, ivory closure, natural finish, cloth-lined, 7 x 9 3/4", 10" h. plus handle **330**

Nantucket sewing basket, finely woven splint, round, flat wooden lid w/a round wooden button on the lid w/ebony whale decoration, hasp & ebony latch pin closure, fabric-lined interior, by Jose Formoso Reyes, mid-20th c., 10 1/4" d., 6" h. (one pin detached)............................. **3,450**

Storage basket, cov., woven splint, square base w/upright rounded sides & rim w/a fitted domed cover, the checkered design decorated w/blue & red geometric potato stamp designs, 5" d., 4" h. (few breaks in cover) **935**

Storage basket, woven splint, round base w/flaring lower body & rounded upper body w/a narrow wrapped round rim, finely woven w/traces of early newspapers dated to 1834, 12 1/2" d., 7 1/2" h. (minor small breaks) **248**

Storage basket, cov., woven splint, squared form w/a fitted cover, 19th c., 12 1/2" w., 11" h. (wear, minor loss) **345**

Storage basket, cov., woven splint, the wide woven bands nicely decorated w/potato stamped designs, 14 x 19", 11" h. (some wear & breaks)......................... **413**

New England Indian Baskets

Storage basket, woven splint cylindrical w/alternating blue & natural staves & blue, natural & yellow weft, New England

Indian, 19th c., 14 1/4" d., 11 1/2" h.
(ILLUS. top) **575**

Storage basket, woven splint, rectangular
w/fitted flat cover, the sides decorated
w/alternating blue & natural splints w/cir-
cle & dot potato stamp decoration, New
England Indian-made, wear, splitting on
some edges, 19th c., 15 1/2 x 22", 13" h.
(ILLUS. bottom) **1,955**

Storage basket, woven splint, a square
base w/canted sides on the lower half below a central band of geometric loops below the tapering upper section, wrapped
round rim w/bentwood handle, natural
w/stained salmon & black weaving,
13 3/4" h. (few splint breaks) **358**

Storage basket, woven splint, a square
bottom below wide swelled rounded
sides & a double-wrapped round rim,
high bentwood handle, painted dark
green, 19th c., 13" d., 14" h. (some
breaks on base, wear) **345**

Storage basket, woven rye straw, swollen
oval form composed of woven coils of rye
straw, probably Pennsylvania, 18" h.
(losses) **316**

Utility basket, woven splint, round base
w/upright round sides & wrapped rim,
bentwood swing handle, partial ink inscription on handle including "Glouster -
1932," good patina, 10" d., 6 3/4" h. plus
handle **468**

Utility basket, woven splint, square base
w/deep rounded sides & wrapped round
rim w/high arched bentwood handle,
good patina, 8 3/4" h. **275**

Utility basket, woven splint, a square base
below high upright rounded sides w/a
round wrapped rim & bentwood handle,
9" h. **83**

Utility basket, woven splint, kettle-shaped,
9" d., 6" h. plus bentwood handle **825**

Utility basket, woven splint, rectangular w/a
double-wrapped rim w/a band of red dyed
splint beneath the rim, carved wooden rim
handles, attributed to Albra Lord, Lovell,
Maine, early 20th c., 9 1/2 x 12 3/4" (mi-
nor losses on the bottom) **201**

Utility basket, woven splint, rectangular
bottom w/upright sides & oblong
wrapped rim, watercolor designs in red,
blue & yellow, 13" l. **248**

Utility basket, woven splint, round
w/square base, floral painted splint
bands in blue & red & yellow on rim &
base, blue-painted accent bands, 19th c.,
13 1/2" d., 6" h. (minor breaks) **345**

Utility basket, woven splint, semicircular
fishing creel-shaped, the front woven
with what appears to be oak ribs w/five
brown & green leather panels, the center
panel depicts a potted tulip flanked by the
initials "BB," the side panels w/potted tulips & corner panels w/tulip heads, top
edges wrapped in leather, top hinges
back & locks w/a pine wedge, applied
handle woven in a diamond pattern
w/matching green & brown leather, back
is sloped w/leather border & three ap-

plied undecorated brown leather
panels, ca. 1860, probably Pennsylva-
nia, 14 x 20", 13 1/2" h. (ILLUS. below) **6,325**

Unusual Leather Decorated Basket

Utility basket, woven splint, round
w/carved loop handles, square base, yellow & brown painted decorative bands,
19th c., 13 3/4" d., 7 3/4" h. (minor wear) **173**

Utility basket, woven splint, square base
w/deep rounded sides & a wrapped
round rim w/small bentwood end rim han-
dles, 16" d., 12 1/2" h. plus handles **110**

BILLIKENS

*The Billiken originated in 1908 when his character
was the winner of a design contest. He was originally
promoted as "The God of Things as They Ought To Be,"
and while this was very clever, it is probably also the
reason that his popularity was limited to just a few
years. He was also referred to as the God of Good Luck.*

*Most dated Billiken items are from 1908 through
1910. A wide variety of items were made, but the most
popular were probably the doll, the cast-iron bank and a
wide variety of postcards.*

*Later Billiken was adopted as the mascot of the Royal
Order of Jesters. He has also been a popular character
in Alaska for many years and is often carved in ivory
there.*

*The Billiken doll was reissued in the late 1980s and
the 4" cast-iron bank has been widely reproduced. Some
reproduction postcards and thimble holders are also
known.*

Items marked with an asterisk (*) have been reproduced.

Billiken Cast-Iron Still Bank

*Bank, cast iron, figure of a seated Billiken, marked "Good Luck," Patent No. 39603, 4" h. (ILLUS.) **$85**
Bank, ceramic, figural Billiken **35**
Bank, metal, seated Billiken w/church window background, 8" h. **145**

Billiken Brass Belt Buckle

Belt buckle, brass, squared frame w/embossed flowers & a seated Billiken in the center (ILLUS.) **60**

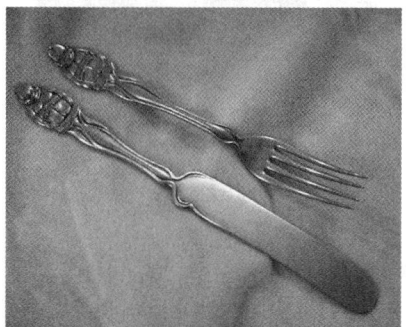

Decorative Billiken Brooch

Brooch, brass, oblong domed form w/embossed scrolls flanking the central figure of a seated Billiken (ILLUS.) **75**
Candy container, glass, seated figural Billiken, bronze/gold paint, 4" h. **125**
*Doll, composition, Horsman, early 20th c......... **300**

Figural Billiken Inkstand

Inkstand, thin rectangular base w/a brass seated figural Billiken next to a square clear glass inkwell w/hinged metal lid, base 6 3/4" l. (ILLUS.) **320**
Knife, table-type, silver plate, figural Billiken handle, 7 1/2" l. (ILLUS. bottom with fork) **40**
Pin, sterling silver, figural Billiken, Pairpoint Mfg. Co., 3/4" h.. **75**

Porcelain Billiken Plate

Plate, porcelain, transfer-printed color picture of a Billiken in the center above a poem, gold trim in the border, 7" d. (ILLUS.) **75**
Plate, porcelain, transfer-printed color picture of a Billiken in the center above a poem, blue trim in the border, 8" d. **85**
*Postcards, depending on design & condition, each... **5-45**
Sheet music, "The Billiken Man Song" **18**
Spoon, silver plate, figural Billken handle, Queen City Silver Co., 5 1/4" l. **45**
Tape measure, figural Billiken, 2" l.................... **370**

Billiken Figural Toothpick Holder

Toothpick holder, silver plate, figural seated Billiken next to a large urn-form vase

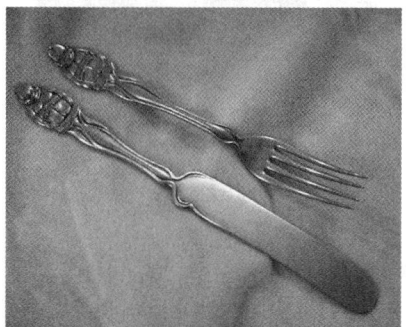

Early Billiken Fork & Knife

Fork, silver plate, figural Billiken handle, 6 1/2" l. (ILLUS. top) **40**

engraved "Billiken," Queen City Silver Co. (ILLUS.) **125**

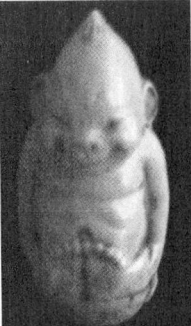

Celluloid Roly-Poly Billiken Toy

Toy, celluloid, figural roly-poly type, 2" h. (ILLUS.).. **120**
Watch fob, sterling silver, figure of Billiken advertising Dr. Pepper.. **85**

BIRDCAGES

Although probably not too many people specialize in just collecting birdcages, many who keep birds as pets enjoy keeping them in old or antique cages. The shiny brass birdcages widely produced earlier in this century by firms such as Hendryx are also popular decorative accent pieces in the homes of antiques lovers who may use them to hold a fern or potted plant rather than a live bird. Note that the very large and elaborate cages produced in the 19th century are the ones which today bring the highest prices on the collecting market. Readers should also be aware that a great many antique-style wooden and wire birdcages are currently on the market as simply decorative accessories but they might fool the unwary buyer in the antiques market.

Rare Battleship-shaped Birdcage

Pine & wire, constructed to resemble a battleship w/turrets, crow's nest, lifeboat-shaped feeders & pilot house above oblong cage ship, painted white, 20th c. (ILLUS.).. **$1,725**
Tin, a wide conical top above closely fitted vertical bar sides fitted w/a small hinged door, flat bottom, old blue repaint, 14" d., 20" h. plus small ring handle (several bars loose).. **220**
Wire & painted wood, large model of a house, the rectangular form w/central peaked roof issuing four projecting ga-

bles w/chimneys flanked by four iron wire turrets above a conforming framework set w/cylindrical & corkscrew-twisted iron wire alternating w/ring- and baluster-turned columns, w/one long end centering an arched door, the short ends fitted w/glazed windows & doors all enclosing an interior set w/perches, on a conforming base, worn white & red paint, late 19th - early 20th c., 13 x 21 3/4", 21" h. **2,990**

Tramp Art Birdcage

Wood, carved & painted pine "Tramp Art" house form, a three-storied rustic turreted house w/shuttered windows & a central clock tower, decorated w/handsawed birds & flowers, dated 1909, 8 3/4 x 31", 28 1/2" h. (ILLUS.) **1,035**
Wood & wire, architectural-style, a three-section building w/a tall pointed dome central turret above an arched portico at the base, center section flanked by lower compartments w/Gothic arch pointed roof framing, each side w/arched window designs, dry brown paint w/dark grey on the windows, 19th c., 11 1/2 x 27 1/4", 33 1/2" h. **440**

Victorian Cottage-form Birdcage

Wood & wire, carved & painted, modeled as a Victorian Gothic Revival cottage w/tall central tower w/scrollwork trim on the roof, lower central double doors w/scrollwork trim, removable carved acanthus leaf base, very minor imperfections, 19th c., 15 3/4 x 20 1/4", 19 1/4" h. (ILLUS.) **1,380**

Wood & wire, jigsaw-cut frame. painted in red & blue in the form of an Eastlake-style Victorian house w/gingerbread trim, wire sides, mortise & tenon & nailed construction, late 19th - early 20th c., 13 1/4 x 18", 18 1/4" h. (minor paint loss, wear)... **345**

Wood & wire, ornate folk art-style structure w/ornate pierced & carved square corner columns w/peaked turrets flanking the half-round roof composed of fanned pieces pierced w/bands of small hearts & bars, wire front, back & sides, old worn white paint, 19th c., 13 1/2 x 18", 15 1/2" h. (some damage) **330**

Wood & wire, painted house-form in green w/a grand entrance, front porch, bay windows, dormers & a cupola, trimmed w/red painted wooden buttons, knobs & perches, late 19th - early 20th c., 18 x 19 1/2", 21" h. (some paint loss) **230**

Continental Wooden Birdcage

Wood & wire, painted structure w/central tower surmounted by a carousel flanked by turrets, the central cage w/perches & outset rounded turrets on a rusticated base w/central steps, 19th c., losses, 15 x 33", 41" h. (ILLUS.) **1,955**

BLACK AMERICANA

Over the past decade or so, this field of collecting has rapidly grown and today almost anything that relates to Black culture or illustrates Black Americana is considered a desirable collectible. Although many representations of African-Americans, especially on 19th and early 20th century advertising pieces and housewares, were cruel stereotypes, even these are collected as poignant reminders of how far American society has come since the dawning of the Civil Rights movement, and how far we still have to go. Other pieces related to this category will be found from time to time in such categories as Advertising Items, Banks, Character Collectibles, Kitchenwares, Cookie Jars, Signs and Signboards, Toys and several others. For a complete overview of this subject see Antique Trader Books' Black Americana Price Guide *with a special introduction by Julian Bond.*

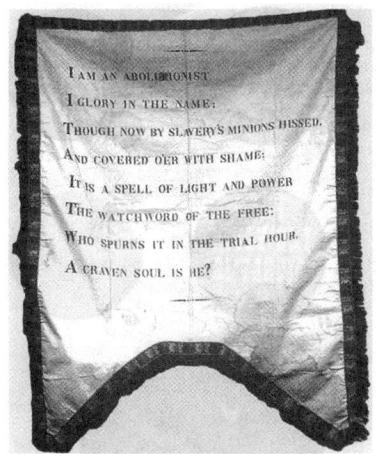

Rare Early Abolitionist Banner

Banner, Abolitionist, glazed cotton fabric w/a hand-sewn multicolored woven wool border w/braid trim & stenciled wording, some corrections in the wording made w/appliqued fabric, Abolitionist message on each side, some yellowing, water stains, ca. 1840s, 44 x 54" (ILLUS.)......... **$5,849**

Book, "Scotts Official History of the American Negro in the World War," by Emmett J. Scott, 1919, red cloth covers w/gold lettering, review of participation in World War I, ex-library, 512 pp. (stain, edge wear, spine loose, first page detached).......... **55**

Booklet, "The Lincoln Settlement - 1915," promotional item for a Brooklyn, New York, settlement house for colored families, 8 pp., 3 1/2 x 5 1/2" (some cover discoloration).. **67**

Bust of a Blackamoor, terra cotta w/polychrome paint w/glass bead jewelry, Europe, 19th c., 8" h.. **690**

Carte de Visite of Slave Children

Carte de visite, "Our Protection - Rosa, Charley, Rebecca - Slave Children from New Orleans," photo of light-skinned emancipated slave children, backmark of Charles Paxson, New York, circulated to promote Northern support for the war & the education of colored people in the Department of the Gulf, each child wrapped in a large American flag, 1864, slight soiling & foxing (ILLUS.) **216**

Louis Armstrong Concert Program

Concert program, "Louis Armstrong and His Concert Group - Satchmo The Great," photo of laughing Armstrong on the cover, autographed & inscribed by Armstrong, well-illustrated, slight soiling on the front & back, 20 pp., 9 x 12" (ILLUS.) **133**

Document, Kentucky will noting disposing of slaves, dated February 27, 1842, two-sided, original folds, 7 1/2 x 12" **105**

Document, slave bill of sale from the Republic of Texas, dated November 18, 1840, lists two slaves for sale, "Big Peter & Rose," matted & framed (folds, stains, three tape stains at top) **330**

Doll, stuffed cloth, an African-American woman in hand- and machine-stitched cloth wearing a purple, tan, red & green print long dress, a broad striped shoulder sash, a matching turban & flat woven hat, foil & bundles of cloth form her arm bands & necklace, embossed brass earrings, 15 3/4" h. (hat starting to unravel) **193**

Staffordshire Little Eva & Uncle Tom

Figure group, Staffordshire china, Little Eva & Uncle Tom, figures seated under a large arching leafy tree trunk, applied sanded leafy trim, polychrome highlights, 19th c., 4" w., 6" h. (ILLUS.) **440**

Flyer, printed paper, "What The Poll Tax Means," long rectangular form, notes inequity of the poll tax system, produced by the National Committee to Abolish Poll Tax, 1943, 6 pp., open to 8 1/2 x 11" **138**

Figural Humidor

Humidor, cov., figural half-length African American man wearing a green jacket, red scarf & yellow striped vest & smoking a cigarette, majolica, unmarked, hands & face unglazed except for eyes & lips w/worn red repaint, edge chips, 10 3/4" h. (ILLUS.) **605**

"Black Gold" Movie Lobby Card

Movie lobby cards, from the movie "Black Gold" by Norman Studios, all-colored cast, photos of various characters on each card in sepia tone rotographs, ca. 1920s, some w/soiling, stains, foxing & one w/top corner tear, each 11 x 14", set of 8 (ILLUS. of one) **263**

Movie lobby cards, "Regeneration," produced by Norman Studios, with two photo scenes from the movie & "With An All Colored Cast - Romance in the South Seas," sepia tone rotographs, each 11 x 14", set of 8 (some soil, stains, fox spots, tack holes & small tears) **204**

Cabinet Photo of Cockfight

Photograph, cabinet card-size, group of African-American cockfighting enthusiasts pose w/their prize roosters, ca. 1920s, near mint, 5 x 6 1/2" (ILLUS.) **144**

Louis Armstrong Signed Photograph

Photograph, half-length portrait of Louis Armstrong, promotional glossy from Associated Booking Corp., inscribed in green ink, "To Trudy Boyce, From Louis Armstrong," photo & signature excellent to mint condition, 8 x 10" (ILLUS.) **994**

Emancipation Proclamation Pinback

Pinback button, "Emancipation Exposition - New York City 1913," bust photo of elderly Frederick Douglas in the center, multicolored image on gold, celebrates the 50th Anniversary of the Emancipation Proclamation, near mint, 3/4" d. (ILLUS.) **446**

Pinback button, "Fight Discrimination - Defend the Bill of Rights," celluloid, blue & white w/American Labor Party emblem in the top center, late 1940s, 1 1/4" d. **154**

Pinback button, "Free The Scottsboro Boys," lithographed tin w/blue wording on white, 7/8" d. **167**

"Remember Brownsville" Pinback

Pinback button, "Remember Brownsville - Discharged Without Honor," celluloid in cream printed in blue w/wording & a row of soldiers representing the 25th Colored Infantry blamed wrongly for a 1906 shooting in Brownsville, Texas, light foxing, 1 1/4" d. (ILLUS.) **977**

Pinback button, "The March For Freedom - Aug. 28, 1963 - Washington, D.C.," celluloid, blue & white printing, light soil, 3 3/8" d. **331**

Rare Scottsboro Boys Pinback Button

Pinback button, "The Nine Negro Boys of Scottsboro - Shall Not Die! - Negro and White Workers Unite! - Scottsboro United Front Defense," celluloid printed in black & red on cream, w/a group photo of the nine Scottsboro Boys, 1930s, 1 1/4" d. (ILLUS.) **5,590**

Poem, carbon copy of typed Lanston Hughes poem "Peace Conference in an American Town," text differs from published version, Hughes' big signature at the bottom, 8 1/2 x 11" (small tears on edge, slight foxing) **440**

Poster, "Write-In For President Dick Gregory - Mark Lane/Vice President," blue & white w/large photo bust portrait of Gregory, 1968, from Philadelphia, 22 x 28".......... **88**

Ring, silver, figural three-quarters view bust portrait of John Brown, ca. 1859, heavy weight (worn on raised areas).................... **1,210**

Official Joe Louis Scrapbook

Scrapbook, "Official Souvenir Scrap Book - World's Heavyweight Champion - Joe Louis," cream cover w/half-length photo of Louis, brown ink on interior, many photos of Louis in various pursuits, pasted-on ad on back from an African-American beer distributor, cover slightly soiled, 44 pp., 7 x 10" (ILLUS.) **399**

Slave tax badge, copper, diamond-shaped, stamped "Charleston 1831 No 218 Servant," Charleston, South Carolina, early 19th c., 2" sq. (wear, some surface cleaning, traces of glue on back, tag number may be a restrike) **1,725**

Slavery document, bill of sale listing "five negros by names of Molly, Betty, Rosena, Chloe and Hagar," sold in Charleston, South Carolina for $1,450, dated January 23, 1835, one page, 8 1/2 x 13" (old repairs, minor paper loss) **220**

Stereoview card, photo of a group of 14 little African-American boys above the caption "Florida, the Land of Flowers & Tropical Scenery," reverse label "Productions of St. Augustine," orange mat (some spots, light foxing, mount edge wear) **33**

Tintype, carte-de-visite-size, image of an African-American gentleman, standing full-length w/his hat on a pedestal, mid- to late 19th c. **50**

Tintype, sixth plate image of Civil War African-American soldier depicted standing w/musket & various accouterments, image gold highlighted to kepi insignia, belt buckle & buttons, exhibits solarization, housed in leatherette case w/split hinge (ILLUS. top next column) **605**

Tintype of Civil War Soldier

Token, round copper, for the Liberia-American Colonization Society, the obverse w/a black man w/a tree of liberty, ship on sea behind, reverse dated 1837, 1¢ value, & "Founded AD 1816," 1 1/8" d. (some wear) **182**

Token, round white metal, "Am I Not a Man and a Brother?," obverse w/an image of a kneeling slave, reverse w/inscription "Whatsoever ye would that men should do to you, do ye even so to them," 1 1/4" d. (one dark spot on reverse).............. **367**

BOOK ENDS

Bronze, architectural asymmetrical stepped geometric elements on a rectangular platform, verdigris patina, post-World War II, 4 x 6 1/2", 4 1/2" h., pr...................... **$144**

Bronze, free-form tri-corner shape w/dark patina, indistinctly signed "Anbork," Eastern Europe, mid-20th c., 3 6/8 x 6 1/2", 2 1/8" h., pr. (minor wear) **75**

Figural Elephant Book Ends

Bronze, figural elephants, one standing w/trunk down, the other w/front legs, head & trunk raised, both mounted on wooden brackets w/metal plaque reading "ARY BITTER, Sculp. Sousse Fres. ed PARIS," Ary Jean-Léon Bitter (1883-1960), taller book end 11" h., pr. (ILLUS.) **5,700**

Bronzed metal, model of a doorway
w/arched classic style transom & flanking
columns, half-round steps in the front,
Handel, early 20th c., pr. 550-600
Cast metal, curvilinear abstract form of two
figures, late 19th c., 7 1/2" h., pr. 115
Copper & tile, copper-framed square tiles
of a sailing ship, raised linear decoration
in blue, brown & green on a matte ochre
ground, mounted on a rectangular base,
marked w/the windmill stamp of Dirk Van
Erp, San Francisco, dark brown
patina, ca. 1915, 4" h., pr. (minor stress
to one seam) 1,267
Gilt-bronze, Bookmark patt., shaped arch
top over square panel of gilt, relief-deco-
rated w/framed vegetation & shield elements, stamped "Tiffany Studios New
York 1056," early 20th c., 4 3/4 x 4 7/8",
6 1/2" h., pr. 920
Ivory & brass, each depicting a scene of a
diety riding a wave & viewing a smaller
figure, ca. 1890, 7 1/4" w., 8" h., pr. 532

BOTTLE OPENERS

*Before the turn of the century, the crown cap for bot-
tled drinks was invented and immediately there was a
need for a bottle cap remover or bottle opener.*

*There are many variations of openers, some in com-
bination with other tools, others are utilitarian with
fancy handles. Perhaps the most important type of bottle
opener today is the figural bottle opener. There are 22
classifications or types of figural bottle openers, with
Type 1 being the most important and sought after by collectors. Figures for openers include people, animals,
birds, pretzels, keys, etc. Wall-mount openers are mostly
faces of people or animals with the opener located in or
near the mouth.*

*The important early producers (ca. 1940-50) of iron
and pot-metal (zinc) figural openers were Wilton Products, John Wright Inc., Gadzik Sales and L & L Favors.
Figural openers were made primarily as souvenirs from
vacation spots around the country.*

*Today, new original figural openers are produced in
limited numbered editions and sold to collectors. Manufacturers such as Reynolds Toys have produced over 40
different figural bottle opener editions since 1988.*

*There are two clubs for bottle opener collectors: Fig-
ural Bottle Opener Collectors (F.B.O.C.) and Just For
Openers (J.F.O.). J.F.O. is a club primarily for beer
opener collectors, but includes collectors of figural
openers, corkscrews and can openers.*

*The numbers used at the end of the entries refer to
Figural Bottle Openers Identification Guide, a new book
printed by F.B.O.C.*

*Bottle Openers By TypeType 1—Figural bottle open-
ers, free-standing or in natural position or wall-
mounted, the opener an integral part of the figure.Type
2—Figural openers with corkscrew, nut-cracker, or nutcracker, etc.Type 3—Figural openers, three-dimensional
on both sides but do not stand.Type 4—Figural openers
with loop openers an integral part of design.Type 5—
Figural openers with a loop inserted in the casting process. The loop or opener is not part of the casting pro-
cess.Type 6—Same as Type 5 with an added can
punch.Type 7—Same as Type 5 with an added corkscrew
or lighter.Type 8—Flat, back not three-dimensional,
loop part of casting.Type 9—Same as Type 8, loop*

*inserted in the casting process.Type 10—Same as Type 8
with a corkscrew.Type 11—Openers are coin or medallion shape, one- or two-sided, with an insert or cast integral loop opener. (These are very common.)Type 12—
Figural stamped openers, formed by the stamping process (steel, aluminum, or brass).Type 13—Extruded
metal openers.Type 14—Johnny guitars or figural holders. Johnny Guitars are figures made of wood, shells,
string, etc.; they have a magnet that holds a stamped
steel (Type 12) opener; figural holders or display holders are cast holders that have a clip that holds one or
two cast figural openers.Type 15—Church keys with a
figure riveted or cast on the opener. Some do not have a
punch key.Type 16—Figural church-key openers with
corkscrew.Type 17—Decorated church-key openers
(church-key loop or wire loop openers with names and
jewels attached).Type 18—Base opener (opener molded
in bottom as integral part).Type 19—Base opener added
(opener added to bottom by brazing or soldering).Type
20—Base-plate opener (opener screwed in base of figure).Type 21—Wooden openers/Syroco openers (metal
insert, cast stamped or wire type).Type 22—Knives,
hatchets, scissors, etc., with openers.*

*RarityA—Most Common, B—Difficult, C—Very diffi-
cult, D—Very hard to find, E—Rare to Very Rare (few
known).*

Bar mounted, opener, mounts w/two thumb
screws, "Never Chip," opener attached to
large bracket place, Vaughan, 5" w.,
O-11 .... $60-75

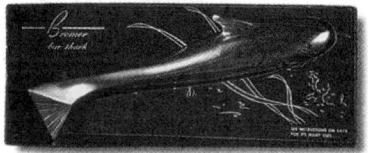

"Bar Shark" Figural Bottle Opener

Figural, "Bar Shark," aluminum, packaging
says "Body - used as an ice cracker;
Nose - used as a muddler; Mouth - used
for opening bottles; Tail - for removing
push collar caps; Fin - for breaking cello-
phane wrap on neck of bottle;" Bremmer
Mfg. Co., Milwaukee, Wisconsin, 7", R-5
(ILLUS.) 100-125
Figural, "Bar Trivet," opener, cast iron, ad-
vertising type, "Schlitz," Japan, pat. no.
134873 & 499791, 4 3/4", R-12 20-25
Figural, baseball cap, w/cap lifter insert in
base, "Rheingold, 1963 Award," marked
"Loyal Prod NYC Bottle Opener," 3 3/4",
R-9 100-150
Figural, dog, cap lifter, brass, embossed
w/"Sun Shine Beer," American design
patent 79,877 issued to M.D. Avillar, November 12, 1929, 5", R-10...................... 100-150
Figural, football helmet, w/cap lifter insert in
bottom, "Budweiser," marked "Taiwan,"
2 3/4", R-16 5-8
Figural, guitar, cap lifter, pewter, advertis-
ing type, embossed "Hard Rock," made
for 1998 debut of Hard Rock Beer, 4",
R-20... 25-30
Figural, hawk's head, "Spirit of the Hawk,"
bronze, beak is the cap lifter, limited edi-

tion of 50, Mendocino Brewing Co. Hopland, California, 2 1/2", R-13 .... **20-25**

Figural, Indian, free-standing, 3-D, feather form cap lifter, produced in aluminum, brass & magnesium, 4 3/4", R-3 .... **20-50**

Figural, Indian, free-standing, 3-D, feather form cap lifter, top hinged to expose lighter, 5", R-4 .... **250-300**

Pretzel Cap Lifter

Figural, pretzel, cast iron, 2 7/8" R-7 (ILLUS.) **60-75**

Figural, shark, cap lifter, plastic, advertising type, "Bud Light," 3 1/4", R-17 .... **5-8**

Figural, snowboard, cap lifter, advertising type, "Bud Light," marked "WB Enterprises Pat Des 3851, steel, 3 1/2", China, R-24 .... **3-5**

Figural, wall-mounted cap lifter, brass, depicts brewmaster w/mug of beer, opener marked "Copyright Mr Lanc., PA. 6 1/4," embossed w/"Sprenger Brewing Co., Lancaster, PA.," R-6 .... **300-400**

Figural, wall-mounted cap lifter, painted cast iron, depicts brewmaster w/mug of beer, opener marked "Copyright Mr Lanc., PA. 6 1/4," embossed w/"Sprenger Brewing Co., Lancaster, PA.," R-6 .... **400-600**

Figural Indian Cap Lifter

Figural Indian, red plastic w/metal cap lifter on back, 4 1/2", R-1 (ILLUS.) **10-15**

Novelty, "Bar Boy," includes cap lifter, folding corkscrew, ice masher & jigger, "the six-in-one appliance," Tempro Incorporated, New Haven, Connecticut, N-64 (ILLUS. top next column) **75-100**

Novelty, bartender's tool w/cap lifter, corkscrew, jigger, ice cracker & drink recipe viewer included, 6 1/2", N-19 .... **40-50**

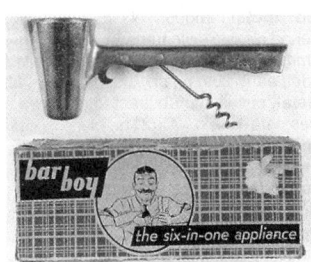

"Bar Boy"

Novelty, cap lifter, bullet end contains a pencil which reverses & is inserted into the handle for use, marked G. Felsenthal & Sons, Chicago, 4 5/8", N-29 .... **20-50**

Novelty, cap lifter & can piercer on a fishing lure, American patent 2,986,812 issued to William Arter, Jr. & Robert J. Clouthier, June 6, 1961, Heddon Company, includes box labeled "The Growler," 3 3/4", N-32 ..... **30-40**

Novelty, cap lifter & can piercer, wood baseball bat shape, 12", N-13 .... **30-50**

Novelty, cap lifter & lighter, remove round end cap to expose lighter, "Redlite, Pat. 1,820,131, Made in U.S.A., B & B., St. Paul, Minn." on the lighter end, American patent 1,820,131 issued for the lighter to Howard L. Fischer, August 25, 1931, 6 1/2", N-12 .... **40-50**

Novelty, cap lifter on shoe horn, "Pat. Apl. For," shown in a 1961 Handy Walden catalog w/slightly different design shown in a 1971 Vaughan catalog, 3 3/8", N-11 ...... **10-25**

Novelty, cap lifter on single knife blade, "Derby Duke," "Bassett U.S.A. Patd. 2,779,098," American patent 2,779,098 issued to Edward J. Pocoski & William G. Hennessy, January 1, 1957, 2 1/4", N-3 ..... **3-15**

Knife & Fork w/Cap Lifter

Novelty, cap lifter, stainless knife & fork slide together in plastic handle for storage, cap lifter on fork, marked "Pat. Pend Made in U.S.A.," both knife & fork marked "Stainless," 7 1/2", N-39 (ILLUS.) **15-25**

Novelty, cap lifter w/bowling pin-shaped handle, American design patent 153,349 issued to Oscar Galter, April 12, 1949, 2 1/2", N-2 .... **10-12**

Novelty, cap lifter w/cylindrical handle, "Drink Dixie Beer," developed to satisfy demands of local bartenders in New Orleans area who were not happy w/the short handle of the N-2 cap lifter, 4 3/4", N-88 .... **15-20**

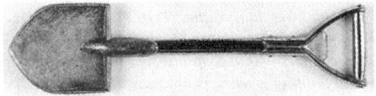

Cap Lifter w/Ice Scoop

Novelty, cap lifter w/ice scoop, shovel-shaped, "Japan," 7 1/8", N-91 (ILLUS.) **20-25**

Novelty, cap lifter w/knife blade, bottle-shaped, "Obermeyer Solingen, Germany," 3 5/8", N-80.. **75-100**

Cap Lifter w/Meat Cleaver & Tenderizer

Novelty, cap lifter w/meat cleaver & tenderizer, "Stainless Steel Japan," included in box labeled "Burnco 'George Washington's' Cheese Hatchet," 5 1/2", N-71 (ILLUS.) **35-45**

Novelty, cap lifter w/Prest-O-Lite key, watch fob, 2 1/2", N-78 .... **100-125**

Novelty, cap lifter w/screwdriver, cap lifter says "Pabst Blue Ribbon," ca. 1939, 3", N-1, pr. **40-50**

Novelty, cap lifter w/sliding cigar cutter & Prest-O-Lite key, "Pat. 10.12.09," American patent 936,678 issued to John L. Sommer, October 12, 1909, 3", N-7 .... **100-125**

Novelty, fishing lure w/cap lifter, "Sport Pal," "Fishing - 7 Uses": wrench, bottle opener, first aid kit, scale, scaler, screwdriver, and tape measure, 7 1/4", N-69 ... **20-25**

Novelty, knife w/cap lifter built into handle, single blade, "Etched P. Co., L.I.C., N.Y. Org. Schrade Bport, CT.," 3", N-4 .... **30-60**

Novelty, knife w/cap lifter, corkscrew, cigar cutter, file blade & single knife blade, bottle shape, "Griffon Cutlery Works, Germany, 3 1/4", N-6...................................... **150-200**

Novelty, knife w/cap lifter formed in handle, single blade, "B&B St. Paul," 3", N-35 .... **25-30**

Novelty, knife w/cap lifter on bolster of two blade knife, boot-shaped w/ivory handles, "Utica Cutlery, Utica, N.Y.," 3 1/4", N-5......... **75-90**

Novelty, knife w/cap lifter, three cutting blades, file blade & scissors, "Made by Bertram, Germany Rostfrei," 3 1/8", N-92......... **75-100**

Novelty, knife w/folding cap lifter/can piercer, one master blade, "Prov. Cut. Co. Prov. R.I. U.S.A.," 3", N-95 .... **35-40**

Novelty, knife w/master blade & cap lifter blade, bottle shape, "Lunawerk, Solingen, Germany," 3", N-48 .... **75-90**

Novelty, knife w/master blade & cap lifter blade, copper handles, Dolphin Cutlery, New York, 3 1/2", N-44............................. **100-125**

Novelty, knife w/master blade, file blade, cap lifter blade & ornate handles, "Eka, Eskilstuna," Eskilstuna is the cutlery center of Sweden, 2 1/8", N-74 .... **75-90**

Novelty, knife w/pen blade & cap lifter blade, shaped like a sack of malt, Paul A. Henckels, Germany, 2 1/8", N-59 .... **40-50**

Novelty, knife w/three blades, cap lifter on one blade w/screwdriver tip, 2 3/8", N-18..... **10-15**

Mechanical Pencil w/Cap Lifter

Novelty, mechanical pencil, w/cap lifter, 5 1/2", N-67 (ILLUS.) **40-50**

Novelty, money clip w/cap lifter, 2 3/4", N-46.. **30-40**

Novelty, opener for malt cans, advertises "Anheuser Busch, Budweiser Malt," "Pat. Appld., 5 1/2", N-21..................................... **40-50**

Wall mounted, cap lifter, bronze, hawk's head, "Mendocino," 2 3/4" w., O-13 .... **20-25**

Wall mounted, cap lifter, enameled, mounts w/four screws, Erickson Company, Des Moines, Iowa, 2 1/8" w., O-2........ **10-25**

Wall mounted, cap lifter, enameled, mounts w/three screws, probably made by Erickson Company, Des Moines, Iowa, 2 5/8" w., O-6.. **30-50**

Cap Lifter w/Bin

Wall mounted, cap lifter, metal & plastic, bin catches caps, Brown & Bigelow, St. Paul, Minnesota, 2 5/8" w., O-7 (ILLUS.) .. **15-20**

Cap Lifter Mounted in Cap Catcher

Wall mounted, cap lifter, mounted inside metal crown cap catcher, 5 1/2" w., 9" t., O-17 (ILLUS.) **20-25**

Wall mounted, cap lifter, mounts w/four screws, American patent 1,711,678 issued to Thomas Harding of Newark, New Jersey, May 7, 1929, also covered by Canadian patent 289,495, J.L. Sommer Mfg. Co., 2" w., O-8 .... **30-40**

Wall mounted, cap lifter, mounts w/two screws, side walls, "Walden Cambridge 38 Mass.," 1 3/8" w., O-16 .... **15-20**

Wall mounted, cap lifter, mounts w/two screws, "Starr," trademarked as "Starr X," American patent 2,033,088 issued to Raymond M. Brown, November 2, 1943, in 1946 advertisement we learn that Starr is "The World's Best Opener. Eliminate loss of bottles and contents. Prevent danger to the public. Have long life,"

Brown Manufacturing Co., Inc., Newport News, Virginia, 2 3/4" w., O-5 .... **5-7**

Wall mounted, cap lifter, "No-Chip," Model #163, mounts w/two screws, Vaughan, 2 7/8" w., O-1 .... **40-50**

Toothed Cap Lifter

Wall mounted, cap lifter, toothed, mounts w/two or three screws, Protector Mfg. Co., 4" w., O-18 (ILLUS.) **100-125**

BOTTLES

Bitters

(Numbers with some listings below refer to those used in Carlyn Ring's For Bitters Only.)

Acorn & Beggs Dandelion Bitters

Acorn Bitters, square w/beveled corners, tooled top, bright golden amber, Western (ILLUS. left) **$325**

Fine Allen's Congress Bitters Bottle

Allen's (William) Congress Bitters, semi-cabin w/pointed side panels, applied sloping collar mouth, smooth base, ca. 1855-70, deep emerald green, 10 1/2" h. (ILLUS.) **2,860**

American Stomach Bitters Bottle

American Stomach Bitters Rochester, N.Y., rectangular w/arched paneled sides, tooled mouth, smooth base, amber, ca. 1900, 8" h. (ILLUS.) **105**

Angostora Bitters (around shoulder), sample size, round w/tooled mouth, "Angostora Bitters" on base, deep Prussian blue, 4 3/8" h. (chip on base rim, small bruise on neck) **61**

Appentine Bitters (under) Geo. Benz & Sons, St. Paul, Minn., sample size, w/"Pat. Nov. 23, 1897" on base, square w/tooled mouth, scrolls along sides of label panel, 95% original paper labels on three sides, w/contents, amber, 3 1/2" h. **523**

Appetine Bitters Bottle

Appetine Bitters (below) Geo. Benz & Sons - St. Paul Minn., square w/paneled sides surrounded by ornate scrolling, tooled mouth, smooth base marked "Pat. Nov. 23 1897," deep reddish amber, faint iridescent bruise on inside of lip, ca. 1900, 8 1/4" h. (ILLUS.) **303**

**Atwood's - Jaundice Bitters - Moses At-
woods - Georgetown - Mass,** twelve-
sided, applied mouth, base pontil, deep
bluish aqua, 6 1/4" h. (tiny shoulder flake)....... **154**

Bavarian Bitters Bottle

Bavarian Bitters - Hoffheimer Brothers,
square w/beveled corners, applied sloping collar mouth, smooth base, olive
green, ca. 1880, 7 1/4" h. (ILLUS.)............. **1,218**

Beggs - Dandelion Bitters - Chicago, Ill,
square, tooled top, amber (ILLUS. right
with Acorn Bitters) **60**

**Bennet's Celebrated Stomach Bitters -
Jos. N. Souther & Co. Sole Proprietors, San Francisco,** square, amber,
9" h. (semi-cloudy, bubbled in one corner)...... **468**

**Bicknell's (Dr. Geo-W.) - Tonic - Stomach
- Bitters,** square w/applied sloping collar
mouth, ca. 1875-85, golden amber,
9 1/2" h. (small chip on corner of base) **66**

**Bishop's (Dr.) Wa-Hoo Bitters - Wa-Hoo
Bitter Co. - New Haven Conn.,** rectangular semi-cabin, applied mouth, medium yellowish amber, 10 1/4" h. (tiny flake
off edge of lip) **600**

**Bolivar (General) Bitters (around shoul-
der),** footed drum shape w/tall neck &
tooled mouth, 7-Up green, 6 1/2" h. **400**

Botanic Bitters Bottle

**Botanic (design of sphinx) Bitters -
Herzberg Bros - New York,** rectangular
w/arched paneled sides & beveled corners, applied sloping double collar
mouth, smooth base, golden yellow
amber, ca. 1880, some light stain,
9 3/4" h. (ILLUS.)... **2,200**

Bourbon Whiskey & Greeley's Bitters

Bourbon Whiskey Bitters, barrel-shaped
w/rings above & below center band, applied top, smooth base, medium raspber-
ry puce, tiny flake on lip (ILLUS. left) **500**

**Brown's Celebrated Indian Herb Bitters -
Patented Feb. 11 1868,** figural Indian
Queen, ground lip, medium to light amber, much original gold paint on lip,
12 1/4" h. **550**

**Brown's Celebrated Indian Herb Bitters -
Patented Feb. 11, 1868,** figural Indian
Queen, rolled lip, yellow amber,
12 1/8" h. (tiny flake edge of base)................. **675**

**Burgundy Bitters - Trade (motif of shield
w/three fleur-de-lis) Mark Registered -
Manfgd By R.P. Burwell,** round, tooled
mouth, medium amber, 8 1/4" h. (some
light scratching) **94**

Burton's Ginger Wine Bitters, sample
size, square, tooled mouth, aqua,
4 1/8" h. (overall stain) **385**

Canton (five-point star) Bitters, round
w/lady's leg neck, applied mouth, medi-
um amber, 12 1/4" h. **440**

**Cognac Bitters Steinfeld Sole Agent For
The U.S.A.,** round, applied sloping double collar mouth, deep yellowish olive
green, 11 1/8" h. **1,450**

**Constitution Bitters - Seward & Bentley
Buffalo NY - AMS-2 1864,** rectangular,
applied top, amber, 9 1/4" h. **2,000**

Dandelion Bitters

Dandelion Bitters Trade (design of dandelion) Mark, cylindrical w/rings base & shoulder, tooled mouth, smooth base, medium amber, two flat chips off top of lip, minor ground imperfections, ca. 1900, 7 1/4" h. (ILLUS.) 440

DeAndries (Dr.) - Sarsaparilla Bitters - E.M. Rusha New Orleans, rectangular w/paneled sides, applied sloping collar mouth, amber, 10" h. (very light inside stain) 1,595

DeWitts Stomach Bitters Chicago, oval, strap sided, amber, pint, 7 1/2" h. 60

DeWitts Stomach Bitters Chicago, square, tooled top, amber, quart, 9 1/4" h. 40

Didier's - Bitters, rectangular w/beveled shoulders, tooled mouth, honey amber, 7 7/8" h. 165

Sample Size Digestine Bitters

Digestine Bitters, sample size, rectangular w/tooled mouth, smooth base, golden amber, ca. 1900, 3 1/2" h. (ILLUS.) 578

Digestine (diamond & scroll motif) Bitters P.J. Bowlin Liquor Co. Sole Proprietors St. Paul, Minn., rectangular w/beveled corners, rounded shoulders & stepped neck base, tooled mouth, golden amber, 8 1/4" h. 358

Doyle's - Hop - Bitters - 1872, semi-cabin, words around sides of sloping shoulder, square w/paneled sides w/raised clusters of hop berries & leaves, applied sloping double collar mouth, medium yellow olive or citron, 9 5/8" h. (minor inside stain) 585

Drake's (S T) - 1860 - Plantation - Bitters - Patented - 1862, no "X," cabin-shaped, six-log, golden yellowish amber, 10" h. (D-103) 176

Drake's (S T) - 1860 - Plantation - X - Bitters - Patented - 1862, cabin-shaped, four-log, applied sloping collar mouth, ca. 1862-70, yellow olive, 10 1/8" h., D-110 (small chip edge of lip) 880

Drake's (S T) - 1860 - Plantation - X - Bitters - Patented - 1862, cabin-shaped, six-log, applied sloping collar mouth, yellow amber, 10" h. (D-105) 330

Two Drake's Bitters Bottles

Drake's (S T) - 1860 - Plantation - X - Bitters - Patented - 1862, cabin-shaped, six-log, deep red chocolate, 10" h., D-105 (ILLUS. right) 120

Drakes (arabesque) - Plantation (arabesque) - Bitters - Patented 1862, cabin-shaped, six-log, three-tier roof, square, applied sloping collar mouth, smooth base, ca. 1865-75, light golden amber w/some olive, 9 7/8" h., D-102 (ILLUS. left) 1,200

Eagle Angostura Bark Bitters (around shoulder) sample size, footed globe shape, tooled mouth, amber, 4" h. 303

Eagle Angostura Bark Bitters - Eagle Liqueur Distilleries (around shoulder), footed globe shape, tooled mouth, "Patented Feb. 4th 1902" on base, medium amber, 7" h. (few minor spots of outside stain) 55

Ferra Quina Bitters D.P. Rossi Dogliana Italia & S.F. Cal., sample size, square w/paneled sides, lady's leg neck, tooled mouth, golden amber, 3 3/4" h. 176

Ferra Quina Stomach Bitters Blood Maker Dogliani Italia D.P. Rossi 1400 Du-Pont Str. S.F. Sole Agent U.S.A. and Canada, square w/paneled sides & lady's leg neck, tooled top, amber, quart, 9" h. 50

Fisch's (Doctor) Bitters - W.H. Ware Patented 1866, figural fish, applied top, reddish amber, 10" l. 240

Fish (The) Bitters - W.H. Ware, Patented 1866, figural fish, applied top, reddish amber, 11 1/2" h. 250

Fish (The) Bitters - W.H. Ware, Patented 1866, figural fish, applied top, tobacco amber w/light olive hue, 11 1/2" h. (hint of interior haze) 600

Frank's (Sol) - Panacea Bitters - Frank Hayman & Rhine - Sole Proprietors - New York, lighthouse-shaped, applied sloping double collar mouth, deep amber, 10" h. 1,375

Dr. Gilbert's Stomach Bitters

Gilbert's (Dr.) Rock and Rye Stomach Bitters, square w/paneled sides, tooled lip, smooth base, brilliant teal blue, ca. 1885, 7 5/8" h. (ILLUS.) **2,420**

Gilbert's Sarsaparilla - Bitters - N.A. Gilbert & Co. - Enosburgh Falls, VT., octagonal, applied mouth, medium amber, 8 3/4" h. (slight chip edge of label panel, small chip off lip) **253**

Globe Bitters Bottle

Globe Bitters Byrne Bros & Co. New York - Globe Bitters Manufactured Only by Byrne Bros & Co. New York, cylindrical w/stepped, ringed neck & applied mouth, smooth base, medium amber, professionally cleaned, ca. 1870, 10 3/4" h. (ILLUS.) **770**

Golden Seal Bitters (inside vines), rectangular, applied sloping collar mouth, golden amber, 9" h. (very tiny bruise on lip) **385**

Great Tonic (The) - Dr. Caldwell's - Herb Bitters, triangular, applied top, graphite pontil, amber, 12 3/4" h. **250**

Greeley's Bourbon Bitters, barrel-shaped w/ten rings above & below center band, applied top, smooth base, mossy green, very crude, couple of flakes on top (ILLUS. right with Bourbon Whiskey Bitters) **850**

Greeley's Bourbon Whiskey Bitters, barrel-shaped, ten rings above & below center band, applied mouth, reddish puce, 9 3/8" h. (G-102) **585**

Hagan's Bitters Bottle

Hagan's - Bitters, triangular, applied sloping collar mouth, smooth base, medium amber, 9 7/8" h. (ILLUS.) **413**

Rare Hall's Bitters Barrel-form Bottle

Hall's Bitters, barrel-shaped, applied mouth, smooth base, ca. 1855-65, deep reddish amber, 9 1/2" h. (ILLUS.) **4,400**

Hall's Bitters - E.E. Hall New Haven - Established 1842, barrel-shaped, applied mouth, smooth base, amber, 9 1/8" h. (few minor spots of inside stain) **220**

Hartwig - Kantorowicz - Nache - Berlin, case gin-form w/paneled sides, applied sloping double collar mouth, medium olive green, 11" h. **330**

Hartwig Kantorowicz Posen Germany (on paper labels), sample size square case gin-form, applied rim, part of main label missing, milk glass, 3 3/4" h. (ILLUS. right with Lohengrin Bitters) **110**

Hellman's - Congress Bitters - St. Louis, Mo., square, applied sloping collar mouth, deep amber, 8 7/8" h. (cleaned) **254**

Hepatic Bitters - Dr. A.S. Russell & Co., square, applied top, amber, 8 3/8" h. **198**

Herb (H.P.) Wild Cherry Bitters, Reading, Pa., cabin-shaped, square w/cherry tree motif & roped corners, tooled mouth, yellow amber, 10 1/8" h. **935**

Herkules Bitter - AC (monogram) - 1 Quart, ball-shaped, tooled mouth, deep 7-Up green, 7 1/2" h. **1,320**

Herkules Bitter - AC (monogram) - 4 Fl. Oz., sample size, ball-shaped, tooled mouth, deep 7-Up green, 4 1/4" h. **1,375**

Highland Bitters and Old Scotch Tonic, barrel-shaped. ten ribs above & below center band, applied mouth, deep amber, 9 5/8" h. **1,820**

Holtzermann's - Patent - Stomach - Bitters, cabin-shaped, two-roof, smooth logs, applied sloping collar mouth, medium amber shaded to yellowish amber, 9 1/2" h. **2,255**

Hopkins (Dr. A.S.) - Union Stomach Bitters - F.S. Amidon, Sole Prop. - Hartford, Conn U.S.A., sample size, rectangular w/paneled sides, tooled mouth, ca. 1880-1900, medium amber, 4 1/8" h. **495**

Hops & Malt Bitters (on four roof panels) - Hops & Malt Trade (sheaf of grain) Mark Bitters, sample size, square semicabin, tooled mouth, golden yellow amber, 3 5/8" h. **440**

Hostetter's (Dr. J.) Stomach Bitters, square w/rounded shoulder, applied top, smooth base, deep olive green, very crude (ILLUS.) **300**

Jewitt's Celebrated Bitters

Jewitt's (Dr. Stephen) - Celebrated Health Restoring Bitters - Rindge, N.H., rectangular w/wide beveled corners, rounded shoulder, applied mouth, pontil, yellow w/amber & olive tone, ca. 1850, shallow chip on base, smaller shallow chips on side of base, 7 1/4" h. (ILLUS.) **1,540**

Johnson's Calisaya Bitters Bottle

Johnson's Calisaya Bitters - Burlington Vt, square w/paneled sides, applied sloping collar mouth, smooth base, reddish amber, ca. 1880, 9 3/4" h. (ILLUS.) **440**

Hostetter's Stomach Bitters

Kelly's Old Cabin Bitters Bottle

Kelly's Old Cabin Bitters - Patented 1863, cabin-shaped, applied mouth, smooth base, ca. 1863-70, medium amber, 9 1/8" h. (ILLUS.).. **1,980**

Kelly's Old Cabin Bitters Bottle

Kelly's Old Cabin Bitters - Patented 1863 (on roof), two-roofed log cabin-shaped, applied sloping collar mouth, smooth base, yellowish olive, tiny professionally repaired hole in one base corner, ca. 1865, 9 1/4" h. (ILLUS.)......................... **3,520**

Kimball's Jaundice Bitters Bottle

Kimball's Jaundice - Bitters - Troy. N.H., rectangular w/beveled corners, applied sloping collar mouth, iron pontil, medium yellowish amber, pinhead flake on edge of lip, ca. 1850, 7" h. (ILLUS.)......................... **633**

Ko-Hi Bitters Bottle

Ko-Hi Bitters - Koehler & Hinrichs St. Paul, flask-shaped w/ribbing at base & shoulder, tooled mouth, smooth base, medium amber, some light inside haze, tiny base flake, ca. 1900, 9" h. (ILLUS.)........ **242**

Koch's (Dr. Med.) Universal Magen Bitters, square, two sides w/overall fine waffle design, applied sloping collar mouth, medium yellowish olive green, Germany, 8" h. **578**

Langley's (Dr.) Root & Herb Bitters, cylindrical, paneled sides, applied mouth, medium golden amber, 5 7/8" h. **66**

Lawrence's (Dr.) Wild Cherry Family Bitters - Newark, N.J. U.S.A., sample size, square, tooled mouth, medium amber, 5 5/8" h. **303**

Litthauer Stomach Bitters - Invented 1864 - By Joseph Loewenthal, case gin-form, tooled mouth, Germany, clear w/amethystine tint, 7" h. **105**

Dr. Loew's Stomach Bitters

Loew's (Dr.) Celebrated Stomach Bitters
Nerve Tonic - The Loew & Sons Co
Cleveland, rectangular w/paneled sides
& spiral-twist neck, tooled mouth, smooth
base, medium yellowish green, ca. 1880,
9 3/8" h. (ILLUS.)... 330

Loew's (Dr.) Celebrated Stomach Bitters
& Nerve Tonic - The Loew & Sons Co.
Cleveland, O., sample size, square
w/paneled sides, ribbed shoulder & spiral-twisted neck w/tooled mouth, light yel-
lowish green, 3 7/8" h. 303

Loew's (Dr.) Celebrated Stomach Bitters
& Nerve Tonic - The Loew & Sons Co.
Cleveland, O., sample size, square
w/paneled sides, ribbed shoulder & spiral-twisted neck w/tooled mouth, aqua,
3 3/4" h. (small bruise inside edge of lip)....... 468

Lohengrin & Hartwig Bitters Bottles

Lohengrin Bitters Adolph & Marcus Von
Buton Germany (on full paper labels),
square case gin-form w/applied top, milk
glass (ILLUS. left)... 120

Mampe - (Carl) - design of elephant - Berlin, sample size, square w/tall neck &
tooled mouth, medium amber, 2 1/4" h. 242

McKeever's Army Bitters, drum-shaped
w/graduated bubble design on top steeply
sloping shoulder, crudely applied top, amber, 10 1/2" h. (flat chip along top ridge)...... 1,200

Sample Size Morning Star Bitters

Morning (star) Bitters Inceptum 5869 -
Patented - 5869, sample size, triangular
w/slanted ribbing on the shoulder, tooled
mouth, smooth base, yellow w/olive
tone, ca. 1880, some faint stain, few
scratches, 5" h. (ILLUS.)............................. 2,200

Moulton's Oloroso Bitters Trade mark
(design of pineapple), round w/tall neck
& applied sloping double collar mouth,
deep bluish aqua, long string of unmelted
sand grains & impurities, 11 1/2" h. 770

National Bitters Ear of Corn Bottle

National Bitters, figural ear of corn, applied
mouth, smooth base, deep strawberry
puce, ca. 1870, 12 12" h. (ILLUS.)............. 2,035

National Bitters - Patent 1867, figural ear
of corn, "Patent 1867" on base, applied
mouth, light golden yellow, 12 5/8" h. 990

New York Hop Bitters Company (below
large American flag), square semi-cabin, applied sloping collar mouth, deep
bluish aqua, 9 7/8" h. 242

Newman's Golden Fruit Bitters, cylindrical, applied sloping collar mouth, medi-
um amber, 10 3/4" h. 440

O.K. Plantation Bitters Bottle

O.K. Plantation - Patented 1863 (on shoulder), triangular w/paneled sides & shoulders, applied sloping collar mouth, smooth base, deep strawberry puce, ca. 1870, 11" h. (ILLUS.)............................ **3,850**

Old Hickory Celebrated Stomach Bitters - J. Grossman New Orleans, LA, sample size, square, tooled mouth, medium amber, 4 1/2" h. (cleaned) **88**

Old Homestead Wild Cherry Bitters

Old Homestead Wild Cherry Bittters - Patent, cabin-shaped, applied sloping collar mouth, smooth base, medium apricot puce, ca. 1870, pinhead base flake, 9 3/8" h. (ILLUS.)...................................... **5,500**

Old Sachem - Bitters - and - Wigwam Tonic, barrel-shaped, ten-rib, applied mouth, ca. 1855-70, amber, 9 1/2" h. **523**

Old Sachem - Bitters - and - Wigwam Tonic, barrel-shaped, ten-rib, applied mouth, smooth base, ca. 1855-70, medium strawberry puce, 9 1/4" h. **1,540**

Penn's Pony Bitters, H.W. Long M.D. & Co., Philadelphia, PA," oval w/indented panels, tooled mouth, amber, 9" h. **275**

Petzold's (Dr.) Genuine German Bitters Incept. 1862 - Pat'd 1884 (on shoulder), oval w/seventeen side ribs, tooled top, medium amber, 7 3/4" h. **176**

PHD & Co. (monogram on shoulder) - Sazerac Aromatic Bitters (on base), round w/lady's leg neck & applied mouth, yellow amber w/olive tone, 10 1/8" h. (tiny polished chip on side of lip)..................... **413**

Pineapple figural, embossed diamond-shaped panel, applied top, light amber, 8 7/8" h... **190**

Pineapple figural - W. & Co. N.Y. (in small diamond), embossed diamond-shaped panel, applied double collar mouth, base pontil, deep olive or forest green, 8 3/8" h... **3,520**

Roback's (Dr. C.W.) - Stomach Bitters - Cincinnati, O., barrel-shaped, applied sloping collar mouth, smooth base, ca. 1860-70, medium yellow amber w/olive tone, 9 3/8" h. (small open bubble on an upper ring)... **358**

Roberg's (Victor) - Prussian Bitters," square case gin-form, "H. Hexe Bremen" on base, applied sloping collar mouth, honey amber, ca. 1875-85, 10 1/8" h. **688**

Root's (John) Bitters - Buffalo, N.Y. - 1834 - 1834, rectangular, applied top, bluish green nearly turquoise, 10 1/4" h.... **3,200**

John Root's Bitters Bottle

Root's (John) Bitters - Buffalo, N.Y. - 1834 - 1834, square semi-cabin w/paneled sides & shoulders, applied mouth, smooth base, medium bluish green, ca. 1870, small chip on side of lip, minor outside stain, 10 1/8" h. (ILLUS.)................... **825**

Royal Italian Bitters Registered (design of shield, crown, spears & drapery) Trade Mark A.M.F. Gianelli Genova, round, tall slender form w/applied mouth, purple amethyst, 13 5/8" h. **743**

Russ' St. Domingo Bitters - New York, square, applied sloping collar mouth, ginger ale color, ca. 1870-80, 10" h. (very light inside haze) **1,210**

Russell (Doctor) Angostura Bitters, round, applied top, amber, 7 3/4" h................. **30**

Schroeder's Bitters - Established 1845 - Louisville and Cincinnati, sample size, round w/lady's leg neck, tooled mouth, amber, 5 1/8" h. **413**

Schroeder's Bitters - Louisville, KY, round w/lady's leg neck, "S.B. & G" on base, tooled mouth, 9" h. **358**

Seaworth Lighthouse Bitters Bottle

Seaworth Bitters Co Cape May New Jersey, lighthouse-shaped, tooled mouth, smooth base, medium amber, ca. 1890, 6 3/8" h. (ILLUS.)... **3,300**

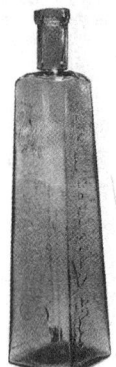

Sherry Iron Co. Bitters Bottle

Sherry Iron Co (The) Stockton Cal Sherry and Iron - The Standard Tonic (with monogram), square tall tapering form w/applied top, yellowish green, small flake on lip, slight interior dirt, 11 1/4" h. (ILLUS.).. **1,300**

Simon's Centennial Bitters - Trade Mark, bust of George Washington on pedestal, applied double collar mouth, reddish amber to amber, 10" h. **1,815**

Simon's (Dr.) - Indian Bitter, sample size, round w/tooled mouth, bright yellowish green, 5 1/4" h. **880**

Sims (Dr.) Anti-Constipation Bitters, square w/beveled corners, tooled mouth, medium amber, 7" h... **165**

Smiths Druid Bitters Bottle

Smiths Druid Bitters (below) B.T. 1865 S.C., barrel-shaped w/ten ribs above & below center band, applied mouth, smooth base, root beer amber, ca. 1865, 9 3/8" h. (ILLUS.).. **1,540**

Smyrna Stomach Bitters

Smyrna Stomach Bitters - Prolongs Life Dayton Ohio, square w/wide shoulder, short lady's leg neck, tooled mouth, smooth base, medium amber, ca. 1890, 9" h. (ILLUS.) **176**

Snyder's Celebrated Bitter Cordial

Snyder's - Celebrated Bitter Cordial - H.G. Leisenring & Co. Philada. Pa., square w/paneled sides, applied sloping double collar mouth, smooth base, amber, ca. 1880, 9 5/8" h. (ILLUS.) **138**

Solomons' Strengthening Bitters

Solomons' Strengthening & Invigorating Bitters - Savannah Georgia, square w/paneled sides, applied sloping collar mouth, smooth base, cobalt blue, ca. 1880, small open bubble across several panels in shoulder, some outside stain, 9 3/4" h. (ILLUS.) **578**

Soule (Dr.) - Hop - Bitters - 1872 (on shoulders), square semi-cabin w/embossed hop flowers & leaves design on one side, applied sloping double collar mouth, yellow olive, 9 3/4" h. (some minor stain on one label panel & corner) **523**

Steketee's Blood Purifying Bitters, square w/beveled corners, tooled mouth, golden amber, 6 5/8" h. **198**

Suffolk Bitters Figural Pig Bottle

Suffolk Bitters - Philbrook & Tucker Boston, figural pig, applied double collar mouth, smooth base, golden amber, ca. 1870, 10 1/4" l. (ILLUS.) **633**

Swan Bitters - McFarland Bro's, Meadville, PA, square, applied top, amber, lightly cleaned, 9 1/2" h. **140**

Tompkins' (Dr.) Vegetable Bitters, rectangular, tooled mouth, medium teal blue, variant w/letters peened out, mold recut, 9" h. **688**

Varena's (Dr.) - Japan Bitters, rectangular, paneled sides, tooled mouth, medium amber, 9 1/8" h. **110**

Vigo Bitters - F.C. Altmaier & Co. Chicago, square, tooled top, amber **40**

W.C. Bitters Brobst & Rentschler Reading, PA, barrel-shaped w/three rings above & below center band, tooled mouth, medium amber shading to yellowish amber in shoulders, 10 3/4" h. **550**

Wahoo - & - Calisaya - Bitters - Jacob Pinkerton - Y!! - O.K. - I.M. - Y!!!, semi-cabin w/paneled sides, applied sloping collar mouth, ca. 1865-75, medium amber, 9 3/4" h. **550**

Wallace's Tonic Stomach Bitters - Geo. Powell & Co., Chicago, IL, square, applied top, in-the-making inside lip flaw, amber, 9" h. **50**

Wampoo Bitters - Blum Siegel & Bro. New York, square, paneled sides, applied sloping double collar mouth, olive yellow, 10" h. (shallow chip underside of collar) **633**

Wampoo Bitters - Blum Siegel & Bro. New York, square, paneled sides, applied top, amber, 9 5/8" h. **90**

Warner's Safe Tonic Bitters (design of safe) Rochester, N.Y., oval, tooled mouth, smooth base, medium amber, ca. 1890, 7 1/2" h. (ILLUS. top next column) **688**

Wheeler's (Dr.) Tonic Sherry Wine Bitters - Established 1848 (inside shield) - Boston, square w/roped corners, applied sloping collar mouth, deep bluish aqua, 9 1/2" h. **3,080**

Warner's Safe Tonic Bitters

Wheeler's Genuine Bitters, oval, applied sloping collar mouth, deep bluish aqua, 8 7/8" h.. **72**

Wryghte's Bitters - London - Wryghte's Bitters - London, rectangular, outward rolled mouth, base pontil, cleaned, deep olive green, 5 3/4" h..................................... **853**

Yerba Buena - Bitters, S.F. Cal., flask-shaped, applied sloping double collar mouth, medium amber, 8 1/4" h. **121**

Young America Stomach Bitters

Young America - Stomach Bitters - P. Rindskupf & Bro, rectangular w/beveled corners, applied sloping collar mouth, smooth base, medium golden amber, ca. 1880, 9 1/4" h. (ILLUS.) **605**

Youngs (Dr.) Wild Cherry Bitters, Brooklyn, N.Y., rectangular w/paneled sides, tooled mouth, medium amber, 8 1/4" h. **132**

Zingari Bitters Bottle

Zingari Bitters - F. Rahter, cylindrical w/lady's leg neck, applied mouth, smooth base, golden yellow amber, shallow chip on side of lip, ca. 1885, 11 7/8" h. (ILLUS.) **2,200**

Figurals

Ear of Corn Figural Bottle

Ear of corn, smooth base, applied mouth, open area on reverse for paper label, ca. 1870-80, amber, 9 3/4" h. (ILLUS.).......... **220**

French Bear & Shield Bottle

Bear, sitting up w/shield in front, marked "Distrie Mercator Sa - Anvers Belgiouc - Depose," smooth base, tooled mouth, applied face, olive green, French, ca. 1880-1910, 9 3/4" h. (ILLUS.).................. **303**

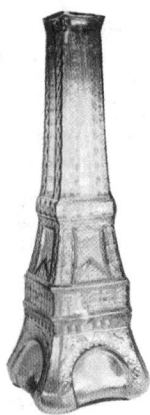

French Eiffel Tower Bottle

Eiffel Tower, base pontil, tooled mouth, straw yellow w/slight amber tone, French, ca. 1890-1910, 14 5/8" h. (ILLUS.) **220**

Bunker Hill Monument Bottle

Bunker Hill Monument, rolled lip, smooth base, tall cologne-type, teal green, ca. 1860, 12" h. (ILLUS.)............................. **1,725**

Figural Cigar Bottle

Cigar, amber, tooled mouth, 5 1/4" l. (ILLUS.)... **60**

Coachman, wide oval base, applied mouth, "Van Dunck's Genever Trade Mark Ware & Schmitz," deep reddish amber, American, ca. 1885-95, 8 3/4" h. (thin open bubble on one arm)................................... **99**

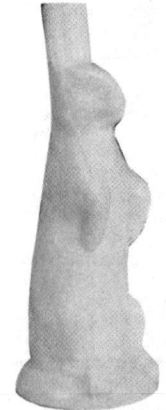

Rare Milk Glass Rabbit Bottle

Rabbit, sitting up, smooth base, ground lip, milk glass, American or European, ca. 1880-1910, 7" h. (ILLUS.)..................... **6,325**

Santa Claus in Chimney Bottle

Santa Claus in chimney, tooled lip, amber, 5 1/2" h. (ILLUS.)... **130**

Flasks

Flasks are listed according to the numbers provided in American Bottles & Flasks and Their Ancestry *by Helen McKearin and Kenneth M. Wilson.*

Early Blown Chestnut Flask

Chestnut, kicked-up pontil, applied string at mouth, deep green, late 18th c., base wear, small chip under area where top applied, 6" h. (ILLUS.) **$300**
Chestnut, sixteen broken ribs swirled to the left, attributed to Mantua, Ohio, early 19th c., aqua, 5 1/8" h. **358**
Chestnut, sixteen broken ribs swirled to the right, deep violet blue, 4 1/2" h. (wear, short neck w/rough lip w/grinding)................. **495**
GI-102 - "Jeny. Lind (sic)" above bust wearing broad bertha collar within wreath - View of Glasshouse below "Glass (star) Factory," vertically ribbed sides, applied sloping collar mouth, calabash, bluish aqua, qt. **121**
GI-114 - Classical draped bust of Byron facing right - Classical draped bust of Scott

facing left, tooled lip, pontil, deep yellow-ish olive green, 1/2 pt. **176**

Rare Washington - Bust Flask

GI-23 - Washington bust facing right w/no inscription - Classical bust facing right below "Baltimore X Glass. Works.," sheared lip, pontil, medium yellow green, qt. (ILLUS.)... **4,070**
GI-3 - Bust of Harrison in uniform facing left below "Wm. H. Harrison" - Log cabin flying American flag above plow & cider barrel, horizontal beading w/vertical medial rib at edges, sheared lip, pontil, greenish aqua, pt. **650**
GI-31 - "Washington" above bust - "Jackson" above bust, bright olive green, pt. **200**
GI-33 - "Washington" above bust facing left - "Jackson" above bust facing left, bars on lapels of coats missing, sheared lip, pontil, yellowish amber, pt. **209**
GI-34 - Washington bust portrait obverse - Jackson bust portrait reverse, Coventry, Connecticut Glass Works, olive amber, 1/2 pt., 5 1/2" h. **230**

Rare Washington - Taylor Flask

GI-37 - Washington bust below "The Father of His Country" - Taylor bust below "Gen Taylor Never Surrenders" below upper band w/"Dyottville Glass Works Philada," smooth edges, sheared lip, pontil, medium to deep grape amethyst, qt. (ILLUS.).. **4,730**

GI-38 - Washington bust below "The Father of His Country" - Taylor bust below "Gen Taylor Never Surrenders" above panel w/"Dyottville Glass Works Philada," smooth edges, applied square collar, aqua, pt. 80

GI-39 - Washington bust below "The Father of His Country" - Taylor bust below "Gen Taylor Never Surrenders," smooth edges, sheared lip, pontil, deep bluish green, qt. 743

GI-39 - Washington bust below "The Father of His Country" - Taylor bust below "Gen Taylor Never Surrenders," smooth edges, sheared lip, pontil, golden yellow amber, qt. 1,870

GI-40c - Washington bust below "The Father of His Country" - Taylor bust below "Gen Taylor Never Surrenders" w/arc of tiny beads connecting inscription, smooth edges, sheared lip, pontil, deep bluish green, qt. 303

GI-41 - Washington bust below "The Father of His Country" - Taylor bust below "Gen Taylor Never Surrenders," smooth edges, sheared lip, pontil, deep olive green, 1/2 pt. 3,080

GI-42 - Washington bust below "The Father of His Country" - Taylor bust below "A Little More Grape Captain Bragg, Dyottville Glass Works, Philad.a," smooth edges, sheared lip, open pontil, aqua, qt. (bubbles in shoulder) 80

Green Washington - Taylor Flask

GI-42 - Washington bust below "The Father of His Country" - Taylor bust below "A Little More Grape Captain Bragg, Dyottville Glass Works, Philad.a," smooth edges, sheared lip, open pontil, brilliant emerald green, qt. (ILLUS.) 375

GI-46 - Washington bust below "The Father of His Country" - Taylor bust below "Gen. Z. Taylor," sheared lip, pontil, light bluish green, qt. 253

GI-54 - Washington bust without queue - Taylor bust in uniform, applied mouth, pontil, light to medium bluish green, qt. 440

GI-69 - Jackson bust facing right below Masonic arch & above fleur-de-lis in oval re-serve below "Andrew Jackson" - American Eagle w/shield facing left below seven stars in oval reserve surrounded by "Wheeling - Knox & McKee," sheared lip, pontil, smooth edges, greenish aqua, pt. (epoxy repair to one base corner) 798

GI-71 - Taylor bust (facing left) w/"Rough and Ready" below - Ringgold bust (facing left) w/"Major" in semicircle above bust & "Ringgold" below bust, tooled lip, pontil, heavy vertical ribbing, smoky clear, pt. 193

Taylor - Ringgold Flask

GI-71 - Taylor bust (facing left) w/"Rough and Ready" below - Ringgold bust (facing left) w/"Major" in semicircle above bust & "Ringgold" below bust, heavy vertical ribbing, light pink amethyst, shallow lip flake, pt. (ILLUS.) 1,100

GI-73 - Taylor bust facing left below "Genl. Taylor" - Washington Monument, Baltimore without statue, "Fells Point" above & "Balto" below, sheared lip, pontil, pale greenish aqua, pt. 138

GI-75 - Taylor bust facing right wearing uniform, "Zachery Taylor" above & "Rough & Ready" below - Tall corn stalk below "Corn For The World," smooth edges, sheared lip, pontil, brilliant dark green, pt. . 3,600

GI-90 - Lafayette bust facing right below "General La Fayette," "Republican Gratitude" in border band - American Eagle facing left w/shield below "E. Pluribus Unum" & above oval reserve w/twenty-one pearls & "T.W.D.," border band w/"Kensington Glass Works Philadelphia," tooled lip, pontil, aqua, pt. 303

GI-99 - "Jenny Lind" above bust - View of Glasshouse w/"Glass Works" above & "Huffsey" below, calabash, smooth sides, broad sloping shoulder, emerald green, qt. (ILLUS. top next page) 950

GII-10 - American Eagle w/"W. Ihmsen's" above & "Glass" below in oval frame - Sheaf of Rye w/"Agriculture" above & farm implements below, vertically ribbed edges, tooled lip, open pontil, light bluish green, pt. 1,375

Philadelphia," tooled lip, pontil, pale
aqua, 1/2 pt. **303**

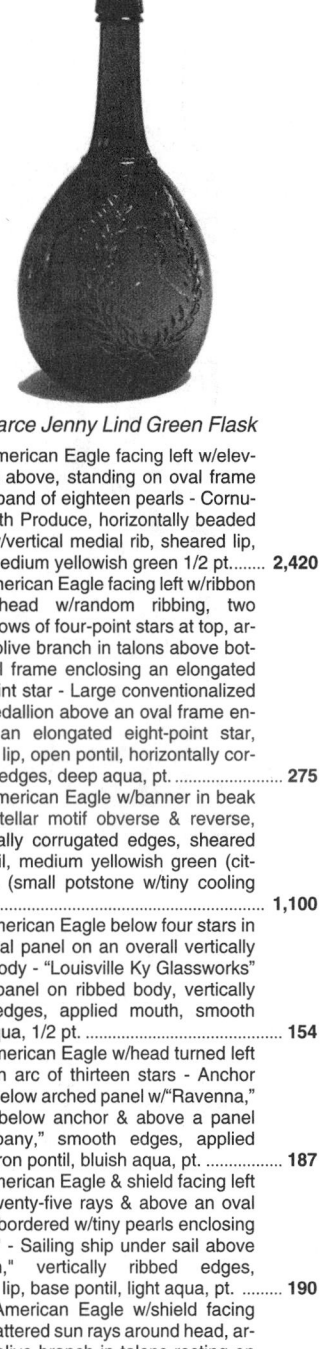

Scarce Jenny Lind Green Flask

American Eagle & Flag Flask

GII-11 - American Eagle facing left w/eleven stars above, standing on oval frame w/inner band of eighteen pearls - Cornucopia with Produce, horizontally beaded edges w/vertical medial rib, sheared lip, pontil, medium yellowish green 1/2 pt....... **2,420**

GII-24 - American Eagle facing left w/ribbon above head w/random ribbing, two arched rows of four-point stars at top, arrows & olive branch in talons above bottom oval frame enclosing an elongated eight-point star - Large conventionalized floral medallion above an oval frame enclosing an elongated eight-point star, sheared lip, open pontil, horizontally corrugated edges, deep aqua, pt. **275**

GII-26 - American Eagle w/banner in beak above stellar motif obverse & reverse, horizontally corrugated edges, sheared lip, pontil, medium yellowish green (citron), qt. (small potstone w/tiny cooling line)... **1,100**

GII-33 - American Eagle below four stars in small oval panel on an overall vertically ribbed body - "Louisville Ky Glassworks" in oval panel on ribbed body, vertically ribbed edges, applied mouth, smooth base, aqua, 1/2 pt. **154**

GII-37 - American Eagle w/head turned left below an arc of thirteen stars - Anchor w/rope below arched panel w/"Ravenna," "Glass" below anchor & above a panel w/"Company," smooth edges, applied mouth, iron pontil, bluish aqua, pt. **187**

GII-42 - American Eagle & shield facing left below twenty-five rays & above an oval reserve bordered w/tiny pearls enclosing "T.W.D." - Sailing ship under sail above "Franklin," vertically ribbed edges, sheared lip, base pontil, light aqua, pt. **190**

GII-43 - American Eagle w/shield facing right, scattered sun rays around head, arrows & olive branch in talons resting on an oval frame w/band of small pearls around "T.W.D.," border w/"E Pluribus Unum One of Many" - Cornucopia w/Produce, border w/"Kensington Glass Works

GII-48 - American Eagle facing left w/shield on breast above a plain oval panel - Furled American Flag w/nineteen stars below "Coffin & Hay." & above "Hammonton," oval border panels, sheared lip, pontil, ca. 1830, medium bluish green, qt. (ILLUS.) **2,420**

GII-52 - American eagle facing left w/large shield, stars above & crossed olive branches below - American flag furled above "For Our Country," sheared neck, open pontil, aqua, pt. **130**

GII-54 - American Eagle facing left on large shield, sunrays around head - U.S. flag furled above standard above "For Our Country," sheared lip, open pontil, light aqua, pt. (some lip roughness) **80**

GII-60 - American Eagle in oval beaded medallion - "Liberty" in scroll above beaded medallion around leafy tree, tooled mouth, pontil, light appled green, 1/2 pt. **2,090**

GII-62 - American Eagle below "Liberty" - inscription in five lines "Willington - Glass - Co - West, Willington - Conn.," smooth edges, brilliant emerald green, pt. **425**

GII-63 - American Eagle below "Liberty" - inscription in five lines "Willington - Glass - Co - West Willington - Conn.," smooth edges, yellowish olive green, 1/2 pt. **160**

GII-64 - "Liberty" above American Eagle w/shield facing left on leafy branch - "Willington - Glass - Co - West Willington - Conn," smooth sides, applied mouth, smooth base, deep olive green, pt. **220**

GII-73 - American Eagle w/head turned right & standing on rocks - Cornucopia w/produce & X to the left, vertically ribbed edges, sheared neck, open pontil, solid green, pt. (minor interior haze)....................... **140**

GII-81 - American Eagle above oval inscribed "Granite - Glass Co." obverse - reverse the same except inscription "Stoddard - NY," narrow vertical edge rib, sheared lip, pontil, deep yellowish amber, pt. (some highpoint wear) **209**

GII-86 - American Eagle above oval obverse & reverse, vertically ribbed edges, sheared lip, pontil, yellowish amber, 1/2 pt. **143**

American Eagle & Frame Flask

GII-91 - American Eagle facing left above large oval frame obverse & reverse, applied rim band, smooth base, brilliant emerald green, small flake of side of lip, qt. (ILLUS.)... 600

GII-101 - American Eagle w/shield & banner facing left above oval frame enclosing "Pittsburgh PA" - American Eagle w/shield & banner facing left above plain oval frame, applied mouth, smooth base, aqua, qt. 55

GII-105 - American Eagle above oval obverse & reverse, w/"Pittsburgh, PA" in oval on obverse, narrow vertical rib on edges, medium yellowish amber, pt. (some highpoint wear, tiny flake off base edge)) 99

Eagle with "Pittsburgh, PA" in Panel

GII-106 - American eagle w/shield facing left, holding banner, above oval panel w/"Pittsburgh PA" obverse - same on reverse w/plain panel, applied ring top, smooth base, ca. 1860, dark olive green, pt. (ILLUS.) 231

GIII-11 - Cornucopia with Produce w/compound leaf on stem protruding from left -

Urn with Produce, tooled lip, pontil, yellow w/olive tone, 1/2 pt................................. 83

GIII-12 - Cornucopia with Produce in a broken-up design - Urn in unusual form w/seven vertical bars with Produce in a broken-up design, sheared lip, pontil, yellow olive w/amber tone, 1/2 pt. (highpoint wear) 88

GIII-4 - Cornucopia with Produce - Urn with Produce, vertically ribbed edges, plain lip, pontil, dark olive green, pt. 83

GIII-7 - Cornucopia with Produce - Urn with six bars filled with Produce, vertically ribbed sides, sheared lip, pontil, medium olive green, 1/2 pt. (some highpoint wear) 83

GIII-7 - Cornucopia with Produce - Urn with six bars filled with Produce, vertically ribbed sides, tooled lip, pontil, olive amber, 1/2 pt. 99

Masonic - American Eagle Flask

GIV-1 - Masonic Emblems - American Eagle w/ribbon reading "E Pluribus Unum" above & "P" (old-fashioned J) below in oval frame, sheared lip, open pontil, light bluish green, pt. (ILLUS.) 275

GIV-32, Masonic Arch over Farmer's Arms - American Eagle facing right below "Zanesville" & above oval reserve w/"Ohio" above "J. Shepard & Co." w/reversed "S," aqua, pint, 6 3/8" h. (interior ring, wear, broken blister) 385

GIV-32 - Masonic arch, pillars & pavement enclosing Farmer's Arms w/sheaf of rye & implements - American Eagle & shield facing right below "Zanesville" & above oval frame enclosing "Ohio" above "J. Shepard (S reversed) & Co.," tooled mouth, pontil, bluish aqua, pt. 413

GIV-39 - Shield enclosing clasped hands above compass & square surrounded by five small five-pointed stars, an arch of stars & "Union" above shield & olive branches below - American Eagle flying right w/a long banner in its beak above a small oval frame enclosing "H & S," applied wide collar flat mouth, smooth base, teal bluish green shading to slightly darker color at shoulder & base, qt. 2,750

GV-9 - Horse pulling loaded cart & no inscription - Large American Eagle with shield lengthwise, no stars, tooled lip, pontil, olive green w/hint of amber, pt. 275

GVI-2 - Baltimore Monument above "Balto." - Sloop sailing to the right w/"Fells" above & "Point" below, vertically ribbed edges, sheared lip, pontil, medium pinkish amethyst, 1/2 pt. (U-shaped piece missing in lip)....................... 358

GVI-3 - Balitmore Monument below "Baltimore" - "Liberty & Union," sheared lip, open pontil, smooth edges, aqua, pt............. 231

GVI-4 - "Baltimore" below monument - "Corn For The World" in semicircle above ear of corn, smooth edges, applied mouth, smooth base, aqua, qt. 143

GVIII-8 - Sunburst w/twenty-eight triangular sectioned rays obverse & reverse, center raised oval w/"KEEN" reading from top to bottom on obverse & "P & W" on reverse, sheared lip, open pontil, medium yellowish amber, pt. 440

GVIII-9 - Sunburst w/twenty-nine triangular sectioned rays, obverse & reverse, center raised oval w/"KEEN" in reverse on obverse & w/"P & W" on reverse w/twenty-nine rays, olive green, pt. 550

GVIII-10 - Sunburst w/twenty-nine triangular sectioned rays, center raised oval w/"Keen" reading from top to bottom on obverse & reverse, tooled lip, pontil, deep yellowish amber, 1/2 pt. (shallow flake off edge of one side rib) 330

GVIII-25 - Sunburst in oval form w/twenty-four rays & center five-petal flower motif obverse & reverse, five vertical side ribs, tooled lip, pontil, pale aqua, 1/2 pt................. 220

GVIII-27 variant - Sunburst w/sixteen rays obverse & reverse, rays converging to a definite point at center & covering entire side of flask horizontally, smooth edges, sheared lip, open pontil, light green, 1/2 pt. ....÷....................................... 275

GVIII-29 - Sunburst in small sunken oval w/twelve rays obverse & reverse, panel w/band of tiny ornaments around inner edge, sides around panels w/narrow spaced vertical ribbing, light bluish green, 3/4 pt. 223

GIX-2 - scroll w/large inverted heart-shaped frame formed by medial & inferior scrolls & containing a large six-point star w/a similar star above frame, sheared lip, open pontil, bluish green, qt. 100

GIX-6 - Scroll w/two large stars above "Louisville KY" w/the "e" flowing into scroll above - Scroll w/two large stars above "Glassworks," sheared mouth, iron pontil, aqua, qt. 303

GIX-8 - Scroll w/eight point star at top & in medial space above lower space w/"Louisville" - similar obverse w/"Glass Works" in lower space, sheared lip, pontil, light bluish green, pt. 523

GIX-8 - Scroll w/eight point star at top & in medial space above lower space w/"Louisville" - similar obverse w/"Glass Works" in lower space, sheared lip, red iron pontil, light apple green, pt. 550

Sapphire Blue Scroll Flask

GIX-10 - scroll w/eight-point star at top & upper center, tooled lip, iron pontil, ca. 1850, deep sapphire blue, pt. (ILLUS.)................. **2,200**

Teal Blue Scroll Flask

GIX-10 - scroll w/eight-point star at top & upper center, tooled lip, pontil, ca. 1850, medium teal blue, pt. (ILLUS.) **1,320**

GIX-10 - Scroll w/six-point stars, a small one in upper space & medium sized one in lower space obverse & reverse, medial scrolls nearly touch, vertical medial rib, citron, pt. 550

GIX-10 - Scroll w/six-point stars, a small one in upper space & medium sized one in lower space obverse & reverse, medial scrolls nearly touch, vertical medial rib, medium yellow olive, pt. 880

GIX-10 - Scroll w/six-point stars, a small one in upper space & medium sized one in lower space obverse & reverse, medial scrolls nearly touch, vertical medial rib, light to medium cornflower blue, pt. 1,540

GIX-10 - Scroll w/six-point stars, a small one in upper space & medium sized one in lower space obverse & reverse, medial scrolls nearly touch, vertical medial rib, bright yellow amber, pt. 1,705

GIX-10 - Scroll w/six-point stars, a small one in upper space & medium sized one in lower space obverse & reverse, medial scrolls nearly touch, vertical medial rib, deep teal blue, pt. **2,145**

GIX-11 - Scroll w/six-point stars, a small one in upper space & medium sized one in lower space obverse & reverse, vertical medial rib, applied mouth, medium to deep amber, pt. (tiny flakes at lip & on medial rib) **231**

GIX-11 - Scroll w/six-point stars, a small one in upper space & medium sized one in lower space obverse & reverse, vertical medial rib, applied mouth, clear, pt. **385**

GIX-11 - Scroll w/six-point stars, a small one in upper space & medium sized one in lower space obverse & reverse, vertical medial rib, sheared lip, pontil, light bluish green, pt. **825**

GIX-11 - Scroll w/six-point stars, a small one in upper space & medium sized one in lower space obverse & reverse, vertical medial rib, applied mouth, pontil, dark emerald or forest green, pt. **1,980**

GIX-13 - Scroll w/seven point star at top & in medial space above lower space w/"Louisville" - similar obverse w/"Glass Works" in lower space, tooled lip, pontil, greyish aqua clambroth, pt. **413**

GIX-20 - Scroll with large oval ornament at top above central eight-point star, a large six-petal flower at bottom center obverse & reverse, sheared lip, pontil, yellowish green, pt.. **1,375**

GIX-38 - Scroll with eight-petaled flower at top above large pearl w/a large fleur-de-lis motif at the bottom - Scroll with flower & two pearls above scroll frame w/"BP & B," tooled mouth, pontil, bluish aqua, 1/2 pt. **440**

GX-6 - Cannon framed by "Genl Taylor Never Surrenders" in oval - Grapevine frame around "A Little More Grape Capt Bragg," vertically ribbed sides, sheared lip, pontil, copper color, 1/2 pt. (lightly cleaned) **1,650**

GX-12 - Stout man wearing derby standing w/cane behind him & arguing w/a seated man wearing a derby & leaning on an umbrella - Grotesque head w/large full face & elaborate headdress, smooth edges, sheared lip, pontil, pale greenish aqua, 1/2 pt. **187**

GX-18 - Spring Tree (leaves & buds) - Summer Tree, smooth edges, applied sloping double collar mouth, open pontil, light to medium yellow-olive, qt.............................. **1,870**

GX-19 - Summer Tree - Winter Tree, smooth edges, applied double collar mouth, pontil, bright yellowish olive green, qt. (several shallow chips on base edge)............................ **908**

GX-22, Log cabin below arch of nine five-pointed stars - American Flag above "Hard Cider" over barrel & plow, aqua, pint, 6 1/2" h. (wear, minor stain & damage) **935**

GXI-8 - "For Pike's Peak" above a miner w/tools above oblong frame enclosing "Old Rye" - American Eagle above oval frame enclosing "Pittsburgh PA," applied mouth, smooth base, green aqua, qt. **176**

GXI-35 - "For Pike's Peak" above prospector w/tools & cane standing on oblong

frame - American Eagle w/pennant above frame "Ceredo," applied mouth, smooth base, greenish aqua, pt. **154**

GXII-6 - Clasped Hands above oval frame all inside large shield, below thirteen stars & flanked by laurel branches obverse - American Eagle flying right w/plain shield & banner above plain oval frame reverse, applied mouth, smooth base, lightly cleaned, medium yellowish green, qt. (two minor base chips) **633**

GXII-29 - Clasped hands above oval, all inside large shield w/"Union" above - American Eagle w/shield w/bars & long banner in beak, applied mouth, smooth base, medium golden amber, 1/2 pt. **231**

GXIII-4 - Hunter facing left wearing flat-top stovepipe hat, short coat & full trousers, game bag hanging at left side, firing gun at two birds flying upward at left, large puff of smoke from muzzle, two dogs running to left toward section of rail fence - Fisherman standing on shore near large rock, wearing round-top stovepipe hat, V-neck jacket, full trousers, fishing rod held in left hand w/end resting on ground, right hand holding large fish, creel below left arm, mill w/bushes & tree in left background, calabash, edged w/wide flutes, open pontil, applied sloping collar mouth, golden amber, qt. **248**

GXIII-4 - Hunter facing left wearing flat-top stovepipe hat, short coat & full trousers, game bag hanging at left side, firing gun at two birds flying upward at left, large puff of smoke from muzzle, two dogs running to left toward section of rail fence - Fisherman standing on shore near large rock, wearing round-top stovepipe hat, V-neck jacket, full trousers, fishing rod held in left hand w/end resting on ground, right hand holding large fish, creel below left arm, mill w/bushes & tree in left background, calabash, edged w/wide flutes, open pontil, medium copper puce, qt............. **385**

GXIII-8 variant - Sailor dancing a hornpipe on an eight-board hatch cover, above a long rectangular bar w/"Chapman" - Banjo player sitting on a long bench above a long rectangular bar w/"Balt. MD," smooth edges, open pontil, aqua, 1/2 pt. **154**

GXIII-15 - U.S. Army officer in full-dress uniform standing at attention facing left & holding rifle w/bayonet upright - Large eleven-petal daisy, four wide vertical side ribs, applied sloping collar mouth, iron pontil, deep bluish aqua, calabash, qt. **330**

GXIII-19 - "Flora Temple" above figure of a horse over "Harness Trot 219 3/4" above "Oct. 15, 1859" - plain reverse, applied shoulder handle, applied mouth, medium copper puce, qt.. **578**

GXIII-23 - "Flora Temple" above figure of a horse over "Harness Trot 219 3/4" - plain reverse, no handle, applied mouth, smooth edges, medium bluish green or teal, pt. **330**

GXIII-30, Duck swimming to left below "Will You Take A Drink?," & "Will A (duck)" w/"Swim?" below the duck, plain reverse, aqua, half-pint, 6" h. (worn, scratched w/stain) **220**

GXIII-60 - Anchor w/upper banner enclosing "Spring Garden" & lower banner enclosing "Glassworks" above long narrow panel - Log Cabin & leafless tree above a long narrow panel, applied mouth, smooth base, bluish aqua, pt. 132

GXV-20 - "Geo. W. Robinson" in an arc & "Main St. W. V.A" in a reverse arc on obverse, plain reverse, strapside flask, smooth base, applied mouth, aqua, 1/2 pt....... 187

Pitkin, thirty-two broken ribs swirled to the right, sheared lip, pontil, medium bluish green, 6 3/4" h. 440

Pitkin, twenty-four broken-ribs swirled to the left, sheared lip, medium emerald green, ca. 1780-1810, 7" h. (some scratching, mostly on edges)......................... 330

Inks

Barrel-shaped, horizontal ringed form w/central neck, embossed "S.I. Comp," tooled mouth, smooth base, aqua, ca. 1880, 2 1/8" h. (two pinhead flakes on side of lip) 99

Barrel-shaped, horizontal ringed form w/central neck, embossed "S.I. Comp," tooled mouth, smooth base, milk glass, ca. 1880, 2 1/4" h. (tiny spot of roughness on one stave) 176

Barrel-shaped, horizontal w/ringed ends on tab feet, short cylindrical neck at top center, light sapphire blue, marked "Pat. Oct. 17 1865".. 170

Barrel-shaped, upright ringed form w/central neck, embossed around middle "W.E. Bonney," tooled mouth, smooth base, aqua, 2 3/4" h............................. 77

Cathedral, master-size, six Gothic arch panels w/three embossed at the bottom "CA - RT - ER," cobalt blue, ABM lip, smooth base marked "Carter's," ca. 1920, 6 1/4" h. 242

Cone-shaped, aqua, marked "Wood's Black Ink Portland," rolled lip, pontil, ca. 1850, 2 1/2" h. 242

Cone-shaped, cobalt blue, rolled lip, open pontil, ca. 1850, 2 1/2" h. 825

Cone-shaped, greenish aqua, embossed "J.J. Butler Cinct. Ohio," rough sheared lip, pontil, ca. 1850, 2 3/8" h. 285

Cone-shaped, medium bluish green, rolled lip, open pontil, ca. 1850, 2 3/8" h. 154

Cone-shaped, yellow olive, "X" on base pontil, sheared lip, ca. 1850, 2 3/8" h............. 330

Early Green Conical Ink Bottle

Conical, deep emerald green, sheared lip, pontil, ca. 1850, 2 3/8" h. (ILLUS.) 633

Rare E. Waters Ink Bottle

Cylindrical, aqua, ribbed neck & flared applied lip, open pontil, embossed "E. Waters Troy. NY" (ILLUS.) 700

Cylindrical, aqua, rounded lobed shoulder centered by short neck w/flattened applied lip, "E. Waters Troy NY" around sides, open pontil, ca. 1850, 3 1/2" h. 550

Master Size Harrison's Columbian Ink

Cylindrical, master size, cobalt blue, "Harrison's Columbian Ink," applied disc-type mouth, iron pontil, ca. 1850, shallow chip off shoulder edge, some light dullness, 7" h. (ILLUS.) 798

Cylindrical, master size, deep olive green, applied sloping collar mouth w/pour spout, base pontil, 95% front & back paper labels reading "Ink - Maynard & Noyes Boston," ca. 1850, 7 1/2" h........................ 358

Cylindrical, master size, medium cobalt blue, angled shoulder & short neck w/rolled lip, smooth base, 97% original paper label reading "Continental Ink Beautiful Violet, Philadelphia," ca. 1870, 4 1/2" h. 275

Labeled "Carter's" Master Ink Bottle

Cylindrical, master size, medium green, "Carter's" on shoulder, tooled mouth, smooth base, 99% original paper labels on front & back, ca. 1890, 6 1/8" h. (ILLUS.).. **209**

Rare Early Labeled Master Ink

Cylindrical, master size, medium olive green, applied sloping double collar mouth, pontil, 99% original label for "Superior Blue-Ink Manufactured by Goodwin & Leonard Lowell, Mass., Warrented Permanent," ca. 1845, 9" h. (ILLUS.)............. **715**

John Baker Master Ink Bottle

Cylindrical, master size, olive amber, labeled "Finest Jet Black Ink Prepared By John Baker," applied mouth, pontil, 70% original label, ca. 1850, 6" h. (ILLUS.)........... **605**
Cylindrical w/angled shoulder, aqua, shoulder embossed "J.J. Butler Cin.O.," mold markings "E" reversed & "S" on pontil, rolled lip, ca. 1850, 2 5/8" h. **154**
Eight-sided w/central neck, aqua, "Harrison's - Columbian - Ink," applied flaring mouth, pontil, "Patent" on shoulder, 90% original paper label, ca. 1850, 3 1/8" h. (ILLUS. top next column) **385**
Eight-sided w/central neck, aqua, rolled lip, pontil, embossed "Harrison' Columbian Ink," ca. 1845-55, 2 1/2" h. (light inside stain) **165**

Harrison's Columbian Ink with Label

Figural, figures of Ma & Pa Carter, porcelain w/original paint, heads form stoppers on cylindrical bodies, "Carter Inx" on the reverse, "Made in Germany" on the base, ca. 1910, 3 5/8" h., pr. (tiny base rim chips) **154**
Figural, model of a seated dog, clear pressed glass, hinged at metal collar, original red painted tongue & black lips & eyes, smooth base, American, ca. 1920, 3 3/4" h. **121**
Figural, model of a thistle, pewter, an upright thistle blossom w/hinged flat lid w/quill hole raised on a short stem supported by two large flattened leaves, American, ca. 1900, 2 3/4" h. **83**

Carter's Clover Pattern Ink Bottle

Hexagonal, deep cobalt blue, each panel w/a clover design, ABM lip, smooth base w/"Carter's," ca. 1930, 2 7/8" h. (ILLUS.) **171**
Semi-cabin w/beveled corners, deep bluish aqua, embossed "J.J. Butler Cin.," rolled lip, pontil, lightly cleaned, ca. 1850, 2 3/4" h. **110**

Rare Cut-overlay Teakettle Ink

Teakettle, cut-overlay paneled sides in cobalt blue cut to clear, angled base spout
w/original brass neck & hinged cap,
ca. 1880, 1 5/8" h. (ILLUS.) **963**

Fine Majolica Decorated Ink

Teakettle, majolica, tapering hexagonal
form w/angled side spout w/original
brass neck ring & hinged cap, light blue
glaze, top w/detailed scene of woman &
children, lightly molded diamond lattice
design in panels, original gold trim,
ca. 1880, 2 5/8" h. (ILLUS.) **605**

Fine Art Glass Teakettle Ink

Teakettle, tapering hexagonal form w/short
base spout, polished lip & pontil, clear alternating w/blue & white twisted looping
throughout, ca. 1880, 1 3/4" h. (ILLUS.) **688**

Decorated Mint Green Teakettle Ink

Teakettle, tapering octagonal sides
w/domed top & angled base spout
w/original brass neck ring & hinged cap,
opalescent mint green w/blue & gold
enamel trim, ca. 1880, 2 5/8" h. (ILLUS.) **578**

Sapphire Blue Teakettle Ink Bottle

Teakettle, tapering rib-cut sides, curved
base spout w/original brass neck ring,
deep sapphire blue, ca. 1880, 2" h.
(ILLUS.) **385**
**Teakettle-type fountain inkwell w/neck
extending up at angle from base,** black
amethyst, tapering octagonal sides
above short flared octagonal base,
ground lip, smooth base, original brass
neck ring & hinged lid, ca. 1880, 2 1/4" h. **358**
**Teakettle-type fountain inkwell w/neck
extending up at angle from base,** cobalt blue, eight-sided w/concave panels
divided by narrow ribs, ground lip,
smooth base, original brass neck ring &
hinged lid, ca. 1880-90, 2" h. **633**
**Teakettle-type fountain inkwell w/neck
extending up at angle from base,** jade
green to clear cut-overlay glass, tapering
cylindrical sides cut w/an overall drape
design, sunburst cut in base, ground lip,
original brass neck ring, ca. 1885, 2" h.
(metal cap missing).. **633**
**Teakettle-type fountain inkwell w/neck
extending up at angle from base,** white
porcelain w/gold band trim, melon-lobed
shape w/blossom-form cap, probably
Europe, ca. 1875-95, 3" h. **385**
Turtle-form, paneled sides, light teal green,
embossed letters on panels "J - & - I - E -
M," ground lip, smooth base, ca. 1880,
1 3/4" h. **176**
Twelve-sided w/central neck, aqua, em-
bossed around panels "Butlers Ink Cincinnati," rolled lip, pontil, ca. 1850,
2 3/8" h. (light outside stain) **143**

Early Crude Umbrella Ink Bottle

Umbrella (8-panel cone shape), deep yellowish amber, rolled lip, open pontil,
crude, ca. 1850, 2 1/4" h. (ILLUS.)................. **275**

Early Amethyst Umbrella Ink Bottle

Umbrella (8-panel cone shape), medium grape amethyst, rolled lip, smooth base, ca. 1860 (ILLUS.) **1,430**

Labeled Umbrella Ink Bottle

Umbrella (8-panel cone shape), yellowish olive green, tooled mouth, 99% paper label for "Unoco Fast Black Writing Ink," ca. 1870, 2 7/8" h. (ILLUS.) **248**

Umbrella-type (6-panel cone shape), aqua, rounded sides w/rolled lip & open pontil, embossed "Waters - Ink - Troy N.Y.," ca. 1845-55, 2 5/8" h. (light inside haze) **743**

Umbrella-type (8-panel cone shape), dark amber, burst top w/bent neck (light interior residue) **70**

Umbrella-type (8-panel cone shape), deep reddish amber, sheared lip, pontil, ca. 1850, 2 3/8" h. **253**

Umbrella-type (8-panel cone shape), golden amber shading to yellow at base, rolled lip, smooth base, ca. 1860-70, 2 5/8" h. **159**

Umbrella-type (8-panel cone shape), light cobalt blue, reversed "77" on smooth base, tooled mouth, ca. 1870, 2 3/4" h. (small area of roughness polished on lip) **209**

Umbrella-type (8-panel cone shape), light green, rolled lip, open pontil, crude **160**

Umbrella-type (8-panel cone shape), medium bluish green, rolled lip, open pontil, ca. 1850, 2 1/2" h. (some light stain) **94**

Umbrella-type (8-panel cone shape), medium olive green, sheared lip, pontil, ca. 1850, 2 5/8" h. **264**

Umbrella-type (8-panel cone shape), medium yellowish amber, tooled mouth, smooth base, ca. 1870-85, 2 1/2" h. **105**

Umbrella-type (8-panel cone shape), olive green w/amber tone, sheared lip, pontil, ca. 1850, 2 1/4" h. **198**

Umbrella-type (12-panel cone shape), medium green, rolled lip, pontil, ca. 1850, 1 7/8" h. **209**

Medicines

Black Gin For the Kidneys - Wm. Zoeller - Pittsburgh, PA, square w/beveled corners, medium orangish amber, 9 1/8" h. **154**

Buckhout's (E.A.) Dutch Liniment (design of standing man) - Prepared at Mechanicville Saratoga Co. N.Y., flattened rectangle w/rounded shoulders &

rolled lip, pontil, ca. 1845-55, aqua, 4 7/8" h. **578**

By A.A. Cooley Hartford, Con, oval, sheared lip, open pontil, olive green, ca. 1850, 4 5/8" h. **660**

Coxe (Dr. E.J.) New Orleans - Southern Cough Syrup, cylindrical w/side panel, applied sloping collar mouth, smooth base, ca. 1850-60, aqua, 7 3/8" h. **688**

Craig's Kidney & Liver Cure Company, oval, medium amber, applied double collar mouth, smooth base, ca. 1890, 9 5/8" h. **187**

Elmore's (Dr.) Rheumative-Goutaline 105 William St, N.Y. - The Only Remedy For Rheumatic Diseases - Best Remedy fo Dyspepsia & Kidney Liver Bladder Blood Disorders, square w/beveled corners, applied sloping collar mouth, smooth base, medium amber, ca. 1880, 9 5/8" h. **330**

Folger's (Doctor Robt. B.) Olosaonian - New York, rectangular w/deeply beveled corners, applied sloping collar mouth, pontil, bluish aqua, ca. 1850, 7 1/4" h. **77**

Gun Wa's Chinese Remedy - Warranted Entirely Vegetable and Harmless, square, applied double collar mouth, smooth base, ca. 1880, golden yellow w/amber tone, 8 1/8" h. **440**

Kier's (S.M.) - Petroleum - Pittsburgh, PA, rectangular w/paneled sides, applied top, open pontil, deep aqua, ca. 1850, 6 1/2" h. **130**

Lake's (H.) Indian Specific, rectangular w/paneled sides & beveled corners, bluish aqua, applied mouth, pontil, ca. 1850, 8 1/4" h. **1,320**

Log Cabin - Cough and Consumption - Remedy, three-sided w/flat back, tooled lip, smooth base marked "Pat. Sept.6.87," amber, ca. 1890, 7" h. **132**

Log Cabin - Extract - Rochester, N.Y., three-sided w/flat back, chocolate amber, "Patd Sep 6 - 1887" on smooth base, tooled mouth, 6 1/2" h. **132**

Log Cabin - Extract - Rochester, N.Y., three-sided w/flat back, medium amber, "Patd Sep 6 - 1887" on smooth base, tooled mouth, 99% original paper label, 6 3/8" h. **259**

Lucina Cordial or Elixir of Love, rectangular w/beveled corners, delicate flared lip, aqua, ca. 1850, 6" h. **650**

Lyon's Powder - B. & P. N.Y., cylindrical, rolled lip, pontil, dark amethyst, ca. 1850, 4 1/4" h. **121**

Lyon's Powder - B. & P. N.Y., cylindrical, rolled lip, pontil, grape amethyst, ca. 1850, 4 3/8" h. (minor outside stain) **264**

M'Lean's Strengthening Cordial, oval, applied mouth, pontil, deep bluish aqua, ca. 1850, 9 1/8" h. **330**

Peruvian Syrup, cylindrical w/applied mouth, pontil, 95% original paper label w/"Peruvian Syrup...," ca. 1850, 9 3/8" h. **165**

Phelps Arcanum Worcester Mass., recessed paneled cylinder, ca. 1830-45, olive amber, 8 1/2" h. (minor mold imperfection in base) **1,380**

Phelps (Dr.) - Arcanum - Genuine, hexagonal, ca. 1830-45, deep olive green,
8 1/4" h. (chips to collar & base, mold
roughness) 3,450
Pratt's Abolition Oil for Abolishing Pain,
rectangular w/paneled sides, flared lip,
smooth base, aqua, 6 3/4" h. (slight inte-
rior stain) 60
Rohrer's - Expectoral Wild Cherry Tonic
- Lancaster, PA, tapering square w/rope
corners, applied sloping double collar
mouth, iron pontil, medium golden
amber, ca. 1860, 10 1/2" h. 468
Rushton & Aspinwall New-York - Com-
pound Chlorine Tooth Wash, square,
wide flattened flared lip, pontil, medium
shading to deep yellowish amber,
ca. 1840, 6" h. (two chips in lip) 5,060
Shaker Fluid Extract of Valerian, rectan-
gular w/paneled sides, thin flared rim,
open pontil, aqua, 3 1/2" h. 88
Swaim's - Panacea - Philada, paneled cyl-
inder, applied sloping double collar, brilliant yellowish olive, lightly cleaned,
ca. 1830-40, 8" h. 500
Swift's Syphilitic Specific, strap-side flask
form, applied double collar mouth,
smooth base, ca.1875, cobalt blue,
9 1/2" h. 798
True Daffy's Elixir - True Daffy's Elixir,
rectangular w/widely beveled corners,
applied mouth, pontil, England, ca. 1845,
medium olive green, 4 3/8" h. 853
U.S.A. - Hosp. Dept., cylindrical w/applied
double collar, smooth base w/"S.D.S.,"
yellow w/amber tone, ca. 1860, 9 1/4" h. 743
Umatilla Indian Hogah - Campbell & Lyon
- Detroit, MI, rectangular w/paneled
sides, rolled rim, aqua, 9" h. 70
Vaughn's (Dr. G.C.)Vegetable Lithontrip-
tic Mixture, square w/paneled sides, applied top, smooth base, medium bright
aqua, ca. 1850, 6 1/4" h. 100
Warner's Safe Cure (motif of safe) Frank-
furt Main, oval w/applied blob mouth,
smooth base, medium reddish amber,
9 1/2" h. 330
Warner's Safe Cure (motif of safe) Lon-
don, sample size, oval, tooled lip,
smooth base, bright yellowish green,
4 1/2" h. 660
Warner's Safe Rheumatic Cure (motif of
safe) - Rochester, N.Y., oval, tooled
mouth, smooth base, late 19th c., medi-
um amber, 9 1/2" h. 77
Wishart's (L.Q.C.) - Pine Tree Tar Cordial,
Phila. - Patent (design of pine tree)
1859, square w/beveled corners, applied
sloping collar, medium bluish green,
10 1/4" h. 154
Wishart's (L.Q.C.) - Pine Tree Tar Cordial,
Phila. - Patent (design of pine tree)
1859, square w/beveled corners, applied
sloping collar, medium bluish green,
10 1/4" h. 154
Wishart's (L.Q.C.) - Pine Tree Tar Cordial,
Phila. - Patent (design of pine tree)
1859, square w/beveled corners, applied
sloping collar, medium green, 7 7/8" h. 171

Wishart's (L.Q.C.) - Pine Tree Tar Cordial,
Phila. - Patent (design of pine tree)
1859, square w/beveled corners, applied
sloping collar, smooth base, 99% original
paper label & contents, ca. 1859-70, me-
dium amber, 9 5/8" h. 413
Wishart's (L.Q.C.) - Pine Tree Tar Cordial,
Phila. - Patent (design of pine tree)
1859, square w/beveled corners, applied
sloping collar, smooth base, ca. 1859-70,
deep teal green, 9 5/8" h. 440
Wishart's (L.Q.C.) - Pine Tree Tar Cordial,
Phila. - Patent (design of pine tree)
1859, square w/beveled corners, applied
sloping collar, smooth base, very
crude, ca. 1859-70, deep yellowish
green, 7 7/8" h. 1,073
Wishart's (L.Q.C.) - Pine Tree Tar Cordial,
Phila. - Patent (design of pine tree)
1859, square w/beveled corners, variant
w/two rivet circles on one of the beveled
corners, applied deep emerald green,
9 5/8" h. (inside shoulder haze) 330

Mineral Waters, Sodas & Sarsaparillas

Abel (C.) & Co. St. Louis Mo Soda Water,
ten-sided w/tall neck & applied top,
Hutchinson stopper-type, graphite pontil,
aqua, very crude.. 70
Artesian Spring Co. "AS" (monogram)
Ballston N.Y. - Ballston Spa Lithia
Mineral Water, cylindrical w/applied
sloping double collar, smooth base,
ca. 1865-75, bluish green, pt. 165
Babb & Co San Francisco Cal, cylindrical
w/tall neck & tooled mouth, Hutchinson
closure-type, graphite pontil, light green,
ca. 1850s (uncleaned)..................................... 160

Ten-pin & Cylindrical Soda Waters

Barothy & Cooks Aerated Waters Chicago, ten pin-shape w/applied top, deep
aqua, tiny chip on base, bright aqua
(ILLUS left) 220
Batelle (M.M.) Brooklyn N.Y. - This Bottle
Is Never Sold Union Glass Works, cylindrical w/applied blob top, iron pontil,
teal green, ca. 1845-55, 7 3/8" h. (overall
dullness & some scratches) 66

Bay City Soda Water Co San Francisco Cal., cylindrical w/tapering shoulder & applied top, gravitating stopper-type, light green, ca. 1870s (small flake on front base) 160

Belfast (The) Soda Water Ginger Ale Co. San Francisco Cal., cylindrical w/tall neck & tooled applied top, Hutchinson closure-type, ca. 1880, deep aqua 70

Bigelow & Co Springfield Mass., cylindrical w/applied sloping collar mouth, original metal closure, smooth base, medium green, ca. 1860-70, 7 1/4" h. (pinhead flake off lip) 66

Blount Springs Natural Sulphur Water - Trade BS (monogram) Mark, cylindrical w/tall neck & applied mouth, smooth base, cobalt blue, ca. 1865-75, qt. 209

Burt (W.H.) San Francisco, cylindrical w/applied blob top, iron pontil, emerald green, ca. 1852 (uncleaned, minor case wear)... 150

Cal Lemonade & Seltzer Water Co S.F. Cal. - star enclosing "CL," cylindrical tall form w/short neck & tooled neck, Hutchinson stopper-type, ca. 1900, aqua...... 550

Casey (Owen) Eagle Soda Works Sac City, cylindrical w/applied blob top, ca. 1870, cobalt blue (ILLUS. right with Empire Soda) 90

Champion Spouting Spring Saratoga. N.Y. - Champion Water, cylindrical w/tall neck & applied sloping double collar mouth, smooth base, ca. 1865-75, aqua, pt. (cleaned) 221

Chase & Co Mineral Water San Francisco Cal., cylindrical w/tall neck & applied lip, emerald green, ca. 1850s (uncleaned, minor case wear).. 190

Chase & Co Mineral Water San Francisco, Stockton & Maryville Cal., cylindrical w/tall neck & applied lip, graphite pontil, emerald green, ca. 1850s (uncleaned, minor case wear, slight interior haze)... 325

Clarke & Co. (dot & line below "o") New York, cylindrical w/applied double collar mouth, pontil, olive green, ca. 1850-60, pt....... 187

Clarke & Co. New York, cylindrical w/applied double collar mouth, pontil, medium emerald green, ca. 1855-75, pt. (shallow flake off side of lip) 132

Clarke (John) - New York (around shoulder), cylindrical w/tall neck & applied sloping double collar mouth, pontil, deep yellowish olive green, ca. 1860, qt. 143

Clarke & White - (C) - New York, cylindrical w/applied sloping double collar mouth, ca. 1860-75, deep forest green, qt.................... 40

Clarke & White - (C) - New York, cylindrical w/applied sloping double collar mouth, ca. 1860-75, deep olive green, pt......... 60

Cleminshaw (C.) - Troy. N.Y., eight-sided w/applied blob top, "C.C." on smooth base, aqua, ca. 1855-70, 7 1/4' h. (shallow open bubble on one corner) 77

Congress & Empire Spring Co. Columbian Water Saratoga, N.Y., cylindrical w/applied double collar mouth, smooth base, grass green, ca. 1870, pt. (ILLUS. top next column)................................. 908

Congress & Empire Spring Bottle

Congress & Empire Spring Co. Hotchkiss' Sons (CW monogram) New York Saratoga N.Y., cylindrical w/applied sloping double collar mouth, smooth base, ca. 1860-70, medium olive green, 1/2 pt. 209

Congress & Empire Water Bottle

Congress & Empire Spring Co. Hotchkiss' Sons - E - New York Saratoga, N.Y. - Congress Water, cylindrical w/applied double collar mouth, smooth base, emerald green, ca. 1870, pt. (ILLUS.) 242

Congress Water (on shoulder), cylindrical w/applied sloping double collar mouth, ca. 1865-75, deep emerald green, qt.............. 150

Congress Water (on shoulder), cylindrical w/applied sloping double collar mouth, smooth base, ca. 1865-75, olive green, qt. (tiny chip off base) 330

Crystal Spring Co. Soda Bottle

Crystal Spring Co. Saratoga Springs N.Y., cylindrical w/applied double collar mouth, smooth base, medium bluish green, shallow flake off inside of lip, ca. 1870, pt. (ILLUS.) 743

Crystal Spring Water C.R. Brown Saratoga Springs N.Y., cylindrical w/applied sloping double collar mouth, smooth base, ca. 1865-75, deep emerald green, pt. (faint bruise inside of lip)........................ 1,100

Cudworth (A.W.) San Francisco Cal., cylindrical w/a tall neck & applied top, Hutchinson stopper-type, graphite pontil, deep emerald green (uncleaned) 160

Deep Rock Spring Oswego. N.Y., cylindrical w/applied sloping double collar, smooth base, medium teal blue, ca. 1870-80, pt. 413

Eel River Valley Soda Works Springville, Cal., cylindrical w/short neck & tooled mouth, Hutchinson closure-type, ca. 1890-1900, greenish aqua 180

Empire Soda & Casey Eagle Sodas

Empire Soda Works San Francisco - Frank S. Waldo, cylindrical w/applied top, aqua (ILLUS. left) 90

Excelsior Spring Saratoga N.Y., cylindrical w/applied sloping double collar mouth, smooth base, ca. 1860-70, deep teal blue, pt. 215

Franklin Spring Mineral Water Ballston Spa Saratoga Co. N.Y., cylindrical w/applied sloping double collar mouth, smooth base, ca. 1865-75, emerald green, pt. 385

Gardner (John H.) Sharon Springs N.Y. - Sharon Sulphur Water, cylindrical w/applied sloping double collar mouth, smooth base, medium bluish green, ca. 1865-75, pt. (small flake on side of lip)...... 231

Geyser Spring - Saratoga Springs - State of New York - The Saratoga Spouting Spring, cylindrical w/applied sloping double collar, ca. 1865-75, aqua, pt., 7 3/4" h. (cleaned) 130

Golden Gate, cylindrical w/applied blob top, graphite pontil, dark teal blue, uncleaned, ca. 1855 (ILLUS. top next column) 275

Hassinger & Petterson 15th Street St. Louis, eight-sided w/tall neck & applied top, Hutchinson stopper-type, graphite pontil, aqua, very crude 100

Golden Gate Mineral Water Bottle

Hawthorne Spring Saratoga, NY, cylindrical w/applied double collar mouth, emerald green, pt. (tiny chip off collar, small chip off lip) 100

Highlander Ginger Ale, Redwood City, Cal., cylindrical w/crown top, aqua (some minor dirt) 30

Highrock Congress Spring- 1767- (design of a rock), C. & W. Saratoga N.Y., cylindrical w/applied sloping double collar mouth, smooth base, deep emerald green, ca. 1865-75, pt. 468

Highrock Congress Spring (design of a rock), C. & W. Saratoga N.Y., cylindrical w/applied sloping double collar, smooth base, ca. 1865-75, deep teal blue, pt. (some minor scratches, pinhead size potstone) 204

Highrock Congress Spring (design of a rock), C. & W. Saratoga N.Y., cylindrical w/applied sloping double collar, smooth base, ca. 1865-75, yellow olive, pt. 253

Highrock Congress Spring (design of a rock), C. & W. Saratoga N.Y., cylindrical w/applied sloping double collar, smooth base, ca. 1865-75, emerald green, pt. (some minor scratches)................................. 259

Highrock Congress Spring (design of a rock), C. & W. Saratoga N.Y., cylindrical w/applied sloping double collar, smooth base, ca. 1865-75, yellowish amber, pt. 264

Highrock Congress Spring Bottle

Highrock Congress Springs (design of rock) C.& W. Saratoga, N.Y., cylindrical w/applied double collar mouth, smooth base, deep teal blue, ca. 1870, some minor outside scuffs & inside stain, pt. (ILLUS.)... **330**

Kiefer's City Bottling Works Indianapolis, ten-sided w/short neck & applied lip, Hutchinson stopper-type, aqua, very crude (uncleaned) **70**

Kimball & Co., cylindrical w/tall neck & tooled mouth, Hutchinson closure-type, graphite pontil, dark cobalt blue, California, ca. 1850s (uncleaned) **190**

L & V, cylindrical w/tall neck & applied top, graphite pontil, dark emerald green, California, ca. 1852-57 (uncleaned, some interior dirt) **110**

Latterne (P.) - Mineral Water - Cincinnati, ten-sided w/applied sloping collar mouth, iron pontil, aqua, ca. 1845-55, 7 1/2" h. (lightly cleaned) **110**

Early Lynch & Clarke Bottle

Lynch & Clarke New York, cylindrical w/applied sloping double collar mouth, pontil, olive amber, ca. 1850, pt. (ILLUS.)...... **413**

Lynch & Clarke New York, cylindrical w/high shoulder & applied sloping double collar mouth, pontil, ca. 1850, deep olive amber, qt. (small chip off underside of neck)...........:.. **413**

Lynde & Putnam Mineral Waters San Francisco Cala. Union Glass Works, Philad., cylindrical w/tall neck & applied top, Hutchinson stopper-type, graphite pontil, cobalt blue (uncleaned, minor exterior scratching, light interior haze) **275**

Lynde & Putnam Mineral Waters San Francisco Cala. Union Glass Works, Philad., cylindrical w/tall neck & crude applied top, Hutchinson stopper-type, graphite pontil, emerald green (cleaned)....... **220**

Martinelli's Soda Works M.S., cylindrical w/long neck & applied lip, Hutchinson stopper-type, aqua, California, ca. 1875-85 .... **40**

Mayfield Soda Works, cylindrical w/crown top, aqua, very crude (hint of haze) **50**

Mineral Waters, cylindrical w/applied mouth, pontil, deep cobalt blue, ca. 1845-55, 7 1/4" h. (some light outside stain) **121**

Mooney (M.) Visalia, cylindrical w/short neck & applied top, Hutchinson stopper-

type, aqua, California, ca. 1872-81 (minor haze)... **70**

Nash & Sutton Cobalt Blue Bottles

Nash (H.) & Co Root Beer Cincinnati, cylindrical paneled sides w/sloping neck to applied flat rim, iron pontil, cleaned, cobalt blue (ILLUS. right) **1,000**

Rare Early California Soda Bottle

Neyman & Drake Mok Hill Union Glass Works Philad.a, cylindrial tapering to an applied blob top, iron pontil, rare early California original, 1850s, few scratches & other imperfections, dark teal blue (ILLUS.) **1,600**

Norris (B.D.) Titusville PA., cylindrical w/short neck & deep applied top, deep aqua, chip on left front (ILLUS. right with Barothy & Cooks bottle) **110**

Pavilion & United States Spring Co. - P - Saratoga N.Y. - Pavilion Water, cylindrical w/applied sloping double collar mouth, smooth base, ca. 1860-80, deep yellow olive, pt. **198**

Pearson Bros., Placerville - P, cylindrical w/short neck & tooled wide mouth, Hutchinson closure-type w/inside floating ball & sealer, ca. 1890-1900, aqua **70**

Pearson's Soda Works, cylindrical w/short neck & tooled mouth, Hutchinson closure-type, from California, ca. 1890-1900, aqua **50**

Quaker Springs I.W. Meader & Co. Saratoga Co. N.Y. - Old Saratoga Spring Water, cylindrical w/applied double collar mouth, smooth base, emerald green, ca. 1865-80, pt. **2,090**

Saratoga Seltzer Spring Bottle

Sarastoga Seltzer Spring Co. (design of spouting bottle) Saratoga, N.Y. - S.S.S., cylindrical w/applied double collar mouth, smooth base, emerald green, faint bruise on edge of lip, ca. 1870, pt. (ILLUS.). **2,640**

Saratoga (A) Spring Co NY, cylindrical w/tall neck & applied sloping double collar, ca. 1855-65, dark olive amber, pt. (tiny bruise on shoulder, some minor scratches) **121**

Saratoga (A) Spring Co NY, cylindrical w/tall neck & applied sloping double collar, ca. 1866-89, emerald green, qt. (some scratches, some interior stain) **60**

Saratoga Red Spring, cylindrical w/applied sloping double collar, smooth base, ca. 1865-75, emerald green, original contents w/cork & wire closure, pt. **105**

Saratoga (star) Spring, cylindrical w/applied double collar mouth, smooth base, ca. 1865-75, medium yellowish amber, pt. **231**

Saratoga (star) Spring, cylindrical w/tall neck & applied double collar mouth, smooth base, ca. 1865-75, deep olive green, qt. **143**

Saratoga (star) Spring, cylindrical w/tall neck & applied double collar mouth, smooth base, ca. 1865-75, emerald green, pt. **495**

Saratoga Vichy Spouting Spring - V - Saratoga N.Y., cylindrical w/applied sloping double collar mouth, smooth base, ca. 1865-75, aqua, 1/2 pt. (overall inside & outside stain) **66**

Saratoga Vichy Spouting Spring - V - Saratoga N.Y., cylindrical w/applied sloping double collar mouth, smooth base, ca. 1865-75, medium amber, pt. **495**

Saratoga Vichy Water Saratoga. N.Y., cylindrical w/applied sloping double collar mouth, smooth base, ca. 1870-80, amber, qt. **121**

Star Spring Co. (design of star) Saratoga, N.Y., cylindrical w/applied sloping double collar mouth, smooth base, deep reddish amber, ca. 1865-75, pt. **143**

Star Spring Co. (design of star) Saratoga, N.Y., cylindrical w/applied sloping double collar, smooth base, ca. 1865-75, deep yellowish amber, pt., 7 3/4" h. **165**

Sutton (I.) & Co Covington, KY, cylindrical paneled sides w/sloping neck to applied flat rim, iron pontil, cleaned, cobalt blue (ILLUS. left with Nash Root Beer) **500**

Taylor & Co. Soda Waters San Francisco, Eureka, cylindrical w/tall neck & applied blob top, Hutchinson stopper-type, graphite pontil, sapphire blue, ca. 1850s (some wear, some interior haze) **220**

Two Dr. Townsend's Bottles

Townsend's (Dr.) - Sarsaparilla - Albany, N.Y., square w/applied top, graphite pontil, crude, dark green, 9 1/4" h. (ILLUS.) **500**

Townsend's (Dr.) - Sarsaparilla - Albany, N.Y., square w/applied top, graphite pontil, crude, teal blue, 9 1/4" h. (ILLUS. left) **700**

Townsend's (Dr.) - Sarsaparilla - Albany, N.Y., square w/beveled corners & applied sloping collar, ca. 1845-55, yellowish olive green w/amber tone, 9 7/8" h. (partial open bubble near one panel base) **198**

Triton Spouting Springs - T - Saratoga, N.Y. - Triton Water, cylindrical w/applied sloping double collar mouth, smooth base, bluish aqua, ca. 1865-80, pt. (tiny potstone in neck) **853**

Tweddles & Twedles Soda Bottles

Tweddles Celebrated Sold or Mineral Waters 38 Portland Street New York, cylindrical w/tall neck & applied top, graphite pontil, deep bluish green (ILLUS. left) 240

Twedles Celebrated Sold or Mineral Waters 38 Portland Street New York, cylindrical w/tall neck & applied top, graphite pontil, crude w/ overall bubbles, lightly cleaned, dark bluish green (ILLUS. right with Tweddles) 1,600

Union Glass Works Philada A.W. Rapp New York - Mineral Waters - R - This Bottle Is Never Sold, cylindrical w/applied sloping collar mouth, iron pontil, deep cobalt blue, ca. 1845-55, 7 5/8" h. (faint bruise inside lip) 413

Rare Union Spring Soda Water Bottle

Union Spring Saratoga, N.Y., cylindrical w/applied double collar mouth, smooth base, emerald green, ca. 1870, pt. (ILLUS.) 3,190

Vichy Water Hanbury Smith, cylindrical w/applied sloping double collar mouth, smooth base, golden yellow amber w/olive tone, ca. 1875-85, pt. 143

W.H.H. Chicago, cylindrical w/short neck & tooled mouth, Hutchinson stopper-type, "H" on the base, cobalt blue (slight lip roughness, cleaned) 70

W.H.H. Chicago III. - W.H. C.C. & Co., cylindrical w/paneled mug base & short neck w/tooled mouth, Hutchinson stopper-type, ice blue 120

Walter's Napa County Soda (horseshoe motif) - Mineral Water From Walter's Soda Springs, cylindrical tall form w/short neck & tooled mouth, Hutchinson stopper-type, ca. 1890, aqua 50

Washington Lithia Well Mineral Water, Ballston Spa, N.Y., cylindrical w/applied sloping double collar, smooth base, ca. 1865-80, aqua, pt. 303

Washington Lithia Well Mineral Water, Ballston Spa, N.Y. (variant w/wording in straight lines), cylindrical w/applied sloping double collar, smooth base, ca. 1865-80, aqua, pt. (shallow small bruise inside lip) 330

Washington Spring Co. (bust of Washington) Ballston Spa N.Y. - C, cylindrical w/rounded shoulder, applied sloping double collar mouth, smooth base, emerald green, ca. 1865-75, pt. 1,650

Washington Spring - Saratoga - N.Y., cylindrical w/rounded shoulder, applied sloping double collar mouth, smooth base, grass green, pt. 220

G.W. Weston Mineral Water Bottle

Weston (G.W.) & Co. Saratoga. N.Y., cylindrical w/applied sloping double collar mouth, smooth base, deep olive green, ca. 1860, pt. (ILLUS.) 154

Williams & Severance San Francisco, Cal. Soda and Mineral Waters, cylindrical w/applied blob top, iron pontil, dark green, ca. 1852-54 uncleaned, some case wear) 200

Yoakum (Jesse) Clifton, Ariz., cylindrical w/crown top, aqua (minute flake off neck, some interior haze) 80

Peppersauces

Aqua, Cathedral-type, four-sided, Gothic arch panels, applied top, open pontil, 10 3/4" h.(small open bubble on one column) 300

Aqua, Cathedral-type, four-sided, Gothic arch panels, applied top, smooth base 110

Deep bluish aqua, Cathedral-type, six-sided, plain Gothic arch panels below tapering double-arch shoulder panels, applied double collar mouth, open pontil, 10 5/8" 231

Cathedral-type Peppersauce Bottle

Light to medium green, four-sided Cathedral-type, two graduated Gothic arch panels on each side, applied double collar mouth, open pontil, ca. 1855, tiny flake off top of lip, 8 5/8" h. (ILLUS.) **204**

Pickle Bottles & Jars

Aqua, eight-sided w/tulip petal design around the shoulder, applied top, graphite pontil, two areas for slug plates, 10 1/2" h... **300**

Aqua, four-sided Cathedral-type, four Gothic arches, ringed wide applied neck, smooth base, ca. 1855-65, 11 1/2" h. **190**

Aqua, four-sided Cathedral-type, four Gothic arches w/crosshatching in three panels, ringed wide drippy applied neck, smooth base, ca. 1855-65, 7 1/2" h. **170**

Rare Marked Pickle Bottle

Aqua, four-sided Cathedral-type, panel marked "Wendell & Espey Phila," rolled lip, pontil, ca. 1855, 7 5/8" h. (ILLUS.) **660**

Aqua, six-sided Cathedral-type, applied top, smooth base, some interior stain (ILLUS. below right) **160**

Bluish aqua, four-sided Cathedral-type, four Gothic arches, ringed wide applied neck, smooth base, ca. 1855-65, 9" h. **220**

Bluish aqua, six-sided Cathedral-type w/Gothic windows, rolled lip, iron pontil, ca. 1855-1865, 13" h. (slight inside stain) **413**

Two Cathedral-type Pickle Bottles

Clear, six-sided Cathedral-type, applied top, smooth base marked "M.G. Co." (ILLUS. left) **220**

Deep aqua, four-sided Cathedral-type, four Gothic arches, ringed wide applied neck, smooth base, ca. 1855-65, 7 1/4" h. **300**

Large Cathedral-type Pickle Bottle

Deep aqua w/a hint of green, four-sided Cathedral-type, rolled lip, smooth base, ca. 1855, 11 1/4" h. (ILLUS.) **440**

Greenish aqua, four-sided Cathedral-type, four Gothic arches, ringed wide applied neck, open pontil, ca. 1855-65, 8 3/4" h. **325**

Medium to greenish aqua, four-sided Cathedral-type, four Gothic arches, ringed wide applied neck, smooth base, ca. 1855-65, 11 1/2" h. **300**

Poisons

Rare Small Amber Poison Bottle

Amber, eight-sided w/line of diamond points at each beveled corner, marked w/"skull & crossbones - Poison - Jacobs - Bichloride - Tablets - skull & crossbones - Poison," tooled mouth, smooth base, lightly cleaned, ca. 1900, 3 3/8" h. (ILLUS.) **1,210**

Amber, eight-sided w/tooled mouth & smooth base, "design of skull & crossbones - Poison - Jacobs - Bichloride - Tablets - design of skull & crossbones - Poison," ca.1900, 2 1/4" h. **908**

Amber, triangular w/rounded back, "Poison - Poison," tooled lip, smooth base, 99% original paper label on back, neck & cork, partial pill contents, ca. 1900, 8 1/4" h............. **94**

Very Rare Skull-form Poison Bottle

Cobalt blue, figural skull, marked on smooth base "Poison - Pat. Appl'd For - Pat. June 26th 1894," tooled mouth, ca. 1900, 4 1/8" h. (ILLUS.) **2,475**

Cobalt blue, oval w/diamond hobnails on front w/"Poison," tooled lip, "Davis & Geck, Inc. - Brooklyn, N.Y. U.S.A." on smooth base, ca. 1900, 3 1/8" h. (two hobnails w/roughness, professional repair on lip) **825**

Cobalt blue, six-sided w/horizontal ribbing & four panels w/"Poison," tooled rim, 4 1/2" h. **40**

Cobalt blue, triangular w/tooled top, "Owl Poison - The Owl Drug Co.," one-wing owl on side, 2 7/8" h. (slight interior stain) **90**

Medium green, six-sided w/tooled mouth, "Gift! - design of skull & crossbones - Gift! - Gitflasche," smooth base w/"250," Germany, ca. 1910-20, 6 1/2" h. **440**

Poison Bottle in Four Languages

Medium green, square w/overall thumbprint design, marked "Vorsicht! (skull & crossbones) Gift! - Attenzione! (skull & crossbones) Veleno!," ABM lip, smooth base, Germany, ca. 1920, 9" h. (ILLUS.) **963**

Medium yellowish green, six-sided w/ABM lip, smooth base, "design of skull & crossbones - Poison - Gift - Velend - design of skull & crossbones," Germany, ca. 1910-25, 8 3/8" h. **330**

Whiskey & Other Spirits

Beer, "Angel's Brewery & Soda Works, Ernst Hubler Prop.," amber, stopper w/wire bell , California, qt. (wire bell partially broken)... **70**

Beer, "Buffalo Br'g. Co. Sac. Cal.," cylindrical w/tall neck & applied rim, yellowish amber, 1/2 pt... **80**

Beer, "Cervelli 1615 Francisco Street S.F.," cylindrical w/tall neck & tooled rim, amber, 1/2 pt....................................... **110**

Beer, "Consumers   Bottling Co." above large monogram over "Redwood City," cylindrical w/tall neck w/tooled rim, amber, pt. **70**

Beer, "Enterprise" above large monogram over "Brewing Co. S.F.," cylindrical w/tall neck & blob top, deep amber, pt................... **160**

Beer, "Enterprise Brewing Co. San Francisco" in oval around a large monogram, cylindrical w/tall swelled neck & applied top, dark amber, 1/2 pt. (small chip on base)... **150**

Beer, "Fredericksburg Bottling Co. S.F." in ring w/shield & monogram above "This Bottle Not To Be Sold," cylindrical w/tall neck, green, qt... **50**

Beer, "Kenison (A.W.) Co. Auburn, Cal.," cylindrical w/wide tall neck & tooled rim, reddish amber, 1/2 pt. **60**

Beer, "Minahan (Daniel) Vallejo Cal.," amber w/original wire & porcelain stopper, qt. **40**

Beer, "Postel (C.D.)" above crossed sheaf of wheat & shovel over "S.F. Cal.," cylindrical w/tall neck w/drippy applied rim, amber, qt. **1,000**

Beer, "Schnerr (C.) & Co. Sacramento Cal.," cylindrical w/tall neck & tooled rim, dark amber, 1/2 pt............................. **140**

Case gin, free-blown square tapering shape w/small crude applied top, open pontil, 18th c., olive green............................... **90**

Case gin, free-blown tall slender square tapering shape w/applied flared lip, large open pontil, Dutch, ca. 1770-90, deep olive amber, 10" h. **110**

Case gin, free-blown tall slender square tapering shape w/applied flared lip, open pontil, Dutch or English, ca. 1770-90, deep olive green, 9" h. **132**

Two Case Gin Bottles

Case gin, square sharply tapering form w/seal on shoulder marked "AVH," applied top, dark green, 10 1/2" h. (ILLUS. left) **70**

Case gin, square tapering form, marked "Avan Hoboken Rotterdam" w/a marked "AVH" seal on two sides, applied top, smooth base, very crude, dark green, 11" h. (ILLUS. right) 50

Wide-mouthed Case Gin Bottle

Case gin, wide square tapering form w/a wide rolled mouth, improved pontil, dark olive green, 10 1/2" h. (ILLUS.)..................... 850

Gin, "Bininger (A.M.) & Co. No. 19 Broad St. N.Y. - Old London Dock - Gin," square w/beveled corners & applied top, smooth base, dark amber, qt....................................... 160

Gin, "Bininger (A.M.) & Co. No. 19 Broad St. N.Y. - Old London Dock - Gin," square w/beveled corners & applied top, smooth base, dark yellowish olive green, qt., 9 3/4" h. 275

Gin, "Gin Cocktail S.M. & Co. N.Y." (on applied shoulder seal), conical w/optic ribbing, applied neck band to seal, applied body, pontil, golden yellow amber, American, ca. 1855-65, 10" h. (tiny shallow open bubble on back) 605

Schnapps, "Hanks (J.H.) Sinera Aromatica Azulejo," rectangular w/short neck & applied top, smooth base, Mexican or South American, 19th c., olive green 110

Schnapps, "Rudolph's - Schiedam - Aromatic Schnapps," square w/beveled corners, applied sloping double collar mouth, smooth base, deep olive green, ca. 1865-75, 9 7/8" h. 220

Schnapps, "Udolpho Wolfe's Aromatic Schnapps, Schiedam," sample size, rectangular w/beveled corners, tooled mouth, smooth base, complete original label & foil neck seal, olive green, ca. 1880-90, 3 3/4" h. 154

Schnapps, "Von Thofen's - Aromatic - Scheidam Schnapps," square w/short neck & applied rim, graphite pontil, medium emerald green, pt., 8" h. (minor interior haze)......... 210

Spirits, cylindrical w/tall neck w/applied string lip, applied seal on shoulder w/"Loop - 1777," pontil-scarred base, olive green, England, 10 3/8" h. 908

Spirits, cylindrical w/tall neck w/double collar neck, pontil-scarred base, seal on front w/"W. Leman - Chard - 1771," shoulder w/"Patent," base marked "H.

Rickett's Glass Works Bristol," dark olive green, England, 11 1/8" h. 385

Spirits, free-blown bulbous bladder-form body tapering to a tall neck w/applied string lip, large seal on side w/"INO - Hawkins - 1741," pontil-scarred base, England, ca. 1741, olive amber, 7 1/8" h. (chip out of lip string) 4,730

Spirits, free-blown globular body w/a wide shoulder centered by a tall tapering neck w/applied lip ring, large crude gloppy seal on the shoulder w/"W.I.S." above a globe design, pontil scarred base, medium olive green, England, ca. 1660-1670, 8 7/8" h. (overall heavy etching & wear).... 9,625

Spirits, globular free-blown form w/tall neck & rolled rim, twenty-four ribs swirled to the left, Zanesville, Ohio, early 19th c., amber, 8 1/2" h. (minor scratches, tiny broken bubble).. 495

Spirits, mold-blown club-form w/twenty-four ribs swirled to the right, applied mouth, pontil, bluish aqua, ca. 1820-35, Midwestern, 8 1/4"h. 132

Spirits, squatty bulbous free-blown onion-form w/tall tapering neck w/tooled rim & laid-on ring w/pontil, light lime green, Holland, 18th c., 7 1/2" h. 140

Whiskey, "Ambrosial - B.M. & E.A.W. & Co." on seal, chestnut flask-shaped w/applied mouth, handle & seal, open pontil, ca. 1855-65, medium amber, 8 5/8" h............. 110

Whiskey, "Bininger (A.M.) & Co. - 19 Broad St. - New York," cylindrical w/wide sloped shoulder to short neck w/applied double collar mouth & small strap handle, smooth base, golden amber, ca. 1855-65, 8" h.. 358

Whiskey, "Bininger's (clock face) Regulator 19 Broad St. New York," round flat shape w/faint clock face, applied double collar mouth, open pontil, ca. 1855-65, golden amber, 5 7/8" h. 990

Whiskey, "Bonanza Bourbon J. Renz Sold Agent S.F.," cylindrical w/tall neck & applied top, amber, ca. 1880s (light interior stain, small star on reverse shoulder)........ 2,700

Whiskey, "Booz's (E.G.) Old Cabin Whiskey - 120 Walnut St. Philadelphia" (on roof), "1840 - E.G. Booz's Old Cabin Whiskey" (on sides), cabin-shaped, applied sloping collar mouth, smooth base, amber, ca. 1855-70, 7 1/2" h................ 4,070

Whiskey, "Carroll's (Jimmy) O.K. Capitol Whisky 66 Market & 4099-18th Sts," flask-shaped, light amethyst, ca. 1900, pt. (light stain) 40

Whiskey, "Casper Whiskey Made by Honest North Carolina People," cylindrical w/ribbed shoulder & neck w/tooled mouth, smooth base, tiny flake off edge of base, cobalt blue, ca. 1900, 12 1/8" h. (ILLUS. top next page) 385

Whiskey, "Chestnut Grove Whiskey, C.W.," chestnut flask-shaped w/applied neck handle, applied mouth, pontil, reddish amber, 8 7/8" h. 132

Blue Casper Whiskey Bottle

Whiskey, "Choice Old Cabinet KY Bourbon" in ring above "Crane Hastings Sole Agents San Francisco," cylindrical w/tall neck & applied top, golden amber **1,000**

Whiskey, "Crown Cocktail Ready To Drink," cylindrical w/tall neck & tooled top, dark amber, fifth (very small pressure ding on right base) **100**

Whiskey, "Cutter (J.F.) Extra Old Bourbon" centering a star in shield flanked by "Trade Mark," cylindrical w/tall neck w/applied lip, deep chocolate amber (minor case wear, small ding on base) **110**

Whiskey, "Cutter (J.H.) Old Bourbon A.P. Hotaling & Co.," shoo-fly flask-shaped w/tooled lip, bright amber (small imperfection on base) **750**

Whiskey, "Cutter (J.H.) Old Bourbon A.P. Hotaling & Co. Sole Agents" in circle centered by a crown, "A No. 1" on reverse shoulder, cylindrical w/tall neck & tooled rim, bright yellow amber w/touch of olive (small pressure ding on base) **120**

Whiskey, "Cutter (J.H.) Old Bourbon Bottled by A.P. Hotaling & Co." in circle centered by a crown, "A No. 1" on shoulder, cylindrical w/tall neck & tooled rim, yellowish amber **40**

Whiskey, "Cutter (J.H.) Old Bourbon (design of crown) E. Martin & Co Sole Agents," cylindrical w/tall neck & applied sloping double collar mouth, smooth base, ca. 1870s, golden yellow amber, 11 5/8" h. (ILLUS. top next column) **330**

Whiskey, "Cutter (J.H.) Whisky" within ring w/"C.Tynan - Salinas, Cal.," flask-shaped, clear, 1/2 pt. **110**

Whiskey, "Cutter OK Whiskey" in circle above "J. H. Cutter Old Bourbon" above crown over barrel flanked by "Trade Mark," "C. P. Moorman Manufacturer Louisville, KY" at bottom, cylindrical w/tall neck & tooled rim, amber **50**

J.H. Cutter Old Bourbon Bottle

Whiskey, "Davy Crockett Pure Old Bourbon" in ring around "Hey, Grauderholz & Co., S.F. Sole Agents," cylindrical w/tall neck & tooled mouth, ca. 1900, medium to deep amber, 12" h. (crude) **50**

Whiskey, "Duffy Crescent" inside crescent moon & rooster, "Saloon 204 Jefferson Street Louisville, KY," figural pig, ground lip, smooth base, clear, 1870-80, 7 5/8" l. . **1,705**

Whiskey, "Good Old Bourbon - In A Hogs" w/arrow, figural pig, ca. 1885-1900, medium amber shading to a deeper red amber, 6 3/4" l. **385**

Whiskey, "Lovejoy & Co. Honolulu T.H.," w/central monogram, cylindrical w/tall neck & tooled lip, golden amber **275**

Early J. Moore Western Whiskey

Whiskey, "Moore (J.) Old Bourbon E. Chielovich & Co Sole Agents (design of antlers)," cylindrical w/tall neck & applied collar top, Western, mid-1870s, dark amber (ILLUS.) **2,000**

Whiskey, "Newman's Richelieu Kearny, Market & Geary Sts.," pumpkin seed flask-shaped, clear, 1/2 pt............. 275

Whiskey, "Old Bourbon Castle Whiskey - F. Chevalier & Co., Sole Agents," cylindrical w/tall neck & tooled lip, bright medium amber, 12" h................. 100

Whiskey, "Old Dundalk Malt Whiskey - Hugh Casey Proprietor Sacramento, Cal.," flattened flask-type w/ringed tooled neck, clear, 8 1/4" h. (some interior haze)....... 50

Whiskey, "Oullahan (Edward) Pioneer Liquor House Stockton, Cal.," flask-shaped, embossed bear, clear, 1/2 pt. (etching, cleaned, little pressure ding on front lip 70

Whiskey, "P.M.S.S. & Co Bottles by A. P. Hotaling Co San Francisco Cal," cylindrical w/tall neck & applied drippy top, ca. 1890, brilliant reddish orange (ILLUS. right w/"United We Stand...") 2,600

Whiskey, "Perrine's - Apple - Ginger - Phila" on roof, "Perrine's (design of apple) Ginger," cabin-shaped w/ropetwist corners, tooled mouth, smooth base, medium amber, ca. 1885-95, 9 3/4" h........... 209

Whiskey, "Phoenix Old (motif of spread-winged phoenix) Trade Mark (above) Bourbon Naber, Alfs & Brune San Francisco Sole Proprts," flask-form w/tooled mouth & smooth base, amber, ca. 1895, 6 3/8" h................. 303

Whiskey, "Phoenix Whiskey" in ring above & below flying phoenix bird, "Nabor Alfs & Brune, San Francisco, Cal" around bottom, cylindrical w/tall neck & tooled mouth, amber, 11 3/4" h................. 252

Whiskey, "Rothenberg (S.B.) & Co. Old Judge Kentucky Bourbon," w/picture of the judge drinking, cylindrical w/tall tapering neck w/applied collar, amber, fifth........... 250

Whiskey, "Smokine - Imported and Bottled By Alfred Andersen & Co. The Western Importers Minneapolis, Minn. Winnepeg. Man. - Smokine," log cabin-shaped, tooled mouth, smooth base, reddish amber, ca. 1885-95, 5 1/4" h........... 242

Whiskey, "Something Good "In A Hog's" (pointing hand) - He Won't Squeal - Pat. W. (on belly)," figural pig, tooled mouth, smooth base, clear, ca. 1885-95, 4 1/8" l........ 88

Whiskey, "Spruance Stanley & Co. (inside horseshoe) Wholesale Liquor Dealers San Francisco Cal," cylindrical w/tall neck & applied sloping double collar mouth, smooth base, ca. 1895, deep reddish amber, 11 5/8" h..................... 143

Whiskey, "Taylor & Loyall (star) Fine Liquors Norfolk, VA," cylindrical w/applied mouth, smooth base, medium orange amber, ca. 1880, lightly cleaned, 11 1/2" h. (ILLUS. top next column) 385

Whiskey, "Teakettle Old Bourbon" around design of teakettle above "--- San Francisco," cylindrical w/tall neck & tooled lip, medium to light amber...................... 700

Taylor & Loyall Fine Liquors Bottles

Whiskey, "Treadwell Whiskey San Francisco," squat cylindrical form w/tall neck w/tooled rim, amber, fifth (hint of stain) 30

Two Rare Western Whiskey Bottles

Whiskey, "United We Stand Old Bourbon Whisky Wilmerding & Co SF Cal - W & Co," cylindrical w/long neck & crude drippy top, cleaned, area of crazing on reverse upper neck, ca. 1878-83, amber (ILLUS. left)................. 2,000

Whiskey, "Van Beil (N.) 88 Chamber St. New York" (on applied seal), cylindrical w/tall neck & applied sloping double collar mouth, shoulder seal, smooth base, yellow w/slight olive tone, ca. 1865-75, 11 5/8" h. 358

Whiskey, "Van Bergen & Co. (N.) Gold Dust Kentucky Bourbon" inside ring, further wording around outside of ring, cylindrical w/tall neck & applied top, medium to deep aqua (cleaned)..................... 1,000

Whiskey, "Wilson Fairbank & Co Sole Agents - Old Bourbon Whiskey For Medicinal Purposes," square w/paneled sides, tooled crude lip, smooth base, aqua (small flake where neck applied) **110**

Flask-form Whiskey Bottle

Whiskey, "Wormser Bros. San Francisco," flask-shaped w/applied double collar mouth, smooth base, some content etching, ca. 1867-72, medium amber, pt., 8 1/2" h. (ILLUS.) **358**

Wine, "Star Wine Co. Wholesale & Family Wines & Liquors Los Angeles Cal.," tall conical shape paneled above & below the central inscribed band, tooled top, amber, 1/2 gal. **450**

Wine, "Sutter Home Wine and Dist. Co. Cal," around monogram, cylindrical w/tall neck & tooled rim, light amber **40**

BOXES

Band box, cov., tall oval shape w/fitted flat cover, worn original wallpaper covering in a floral design in green, white & beige on a wooden base, lined w/old newspapers & labeled "Band Boxes made by Hannah Davis, Jaffery, N.H.," early 19th c., 14 3/4" l. **$715**

Band box, oval wallpaper-covered cardboard, deep sides w/flat fitted cover, a Napoleon design paper in shades of green & white w/touches of gilt, on a yellow ground, paper Hannah Davis label, includes a reprinted booklet about Davis, New Hampshire, ca. 1830, 19" l., 16 1/2" h. (imperfections) **403**

Bride's box, cov., oval bentwood w/laced seams, original salmon ground w/blue borders & yellow & white stripes, white, green & blue flowers around base, cover w/a scene of a courting couple w/a German inscription, 19th c., 12 1/4 x 18 3/4", 7" h. (faded ground, some wear & edge damage, base missing laces & bottom) **798**

Bride's box, oval bentwood, painted & decorated pine, the flat top decorated in original red & polychrome w/a scene of two hunters standing in the center of a landscape w/their rifles & a dog, polychrome florals around the sides, wood-burned initials in the bottom "K.E.," Europe, 19th c., 18" l. (repairs, old touch-up, colors on top & base vary slightly) **1,320**

Bride's box, oval bentwood w/laced seams, the flat fitted cover w/original painted landscape w/yellow, white & tan buildings w/trees in the background, the sides of cover & base in white, red, salmon & yellow flowers & foliage, Europe, 19th c., 12 x 18", 8" h. (edge wear) **2,200**

Candle box, painted pine, primitive rectangular construction w/a sliding lid w/tab handle, worn old red paint, 8" l. plus handle **413**

Candle box, pine, rectangular w/slide-lid, one-board sides w/a chamfered lid, square nail construction, mellow refinishing, 19th c., 10 1/2 x 20", 7 5/8" h. (slight damage along lid channels, one nail missing) **220**

Document box, painted poplar, rectangular hinged top w/molded edges above a dovetailed case on a narrow molded base, opens to till w/lock, original floral decoration on a green ground, yellow & black accent striping, 8 1/4 x 16", 6 3/4" h. (wear, green paint slightly faded, age cracks in till) **688**

Document box, painted wood, low domed hinged cover decorated w/an urn of flowers, bees & swags, the sides w/flowers, all on a mustard yellow old repainted ground, red-painted interior, w/a lock, 19th c., 7 1/2 x 10 1/2", 4 5/8" h. **220**

Doughnut box, cov., bentwood, deep round sides on molded round base & w/a flat board top w/angled wood hand grip, decorated w/black graining on a dark red ground, faint stenciled red, black & yellow flowers on each side within beaded frame w/invected corners, two metal tabs lock cover in place, attributed to Ohio, 19th c., 11 1/2" d., 8 1/4" h. (two splits in body, edge damage on cover) **385**

Glass Box with Bulldog on Cover

Glass box, metal mounts w/hinged cover, round, leaded glass paperweight-style domed top over painted head of French bulldog, 19th c., France, 2" d. (ILLUS.) **1,955**

Hat box, oval bentwood, deep sides w/steel nails & wooden pegs, flat fitted cover, pine base & lid, mellow refinishing, 19th c., 11 1/4 x 14 1/2", 10" h. (few pegs missing) **193**

Jewelry box, cov., carved wood, heart-shaped, flat top & base w/beveled edges, the upright sides & top chip-carved w/poinsettia-like flowers, inside of the cover incised w/a heart & initials, old mustard yellow paint around the middle w/old alligatored varnish overall, 9 x 9 1/2", 4 1/2" h. (minor edge damage, replaced hinges) **303**

Letter box, brass-mounted marble, the arched hinged cover fitted w/heavy brass mounts, opening to divided compartments, England, ca. 1870, 4 3/4 x 9", 6" h. **616**

Pantry box, cov., round bentwood, cylindrical w/lapped seam, flat fitted cover, wire bail handle w/wood grip, old cream yellow paint, 9" d., 5 1/2" h. (minor paint wear, age crack in paper-covered bottom) **468**

Pipe box, hanging-type, carved & painted pine, the backboard carved at the top w/a heart pierced w/a hanging hole, concave top edges above the tall box w/a small bottom drawer w/a brass pull, old red paint, early 19th c., 5 x 5 1/4", 15 3/4" h. (losses, wear) **3,105**

Pipe box, hanging-type, painted pine, an upright square box w/molded base & concave-cut rim below a tall fan-shaped backboard w/large hanging hole, dark brown paint, New England, 18th c., 5 1/4 x 6", 16 1/2" h. (wear, losses) **3,335**

Pipe box, painted pine, the narrow backboard w/arched crest w/round hanging tab flanked by tapering scroll-cut sides & front around the tall box w/a small drawer at the base, red paint w/shield, wreath & a monogrammed "B" in green, red, blue & yellow, red & yellow linear outlines, New England, early 19th c., 15" h. (losses) **2,875**

Salt box, cov., hanging-type, poplar, an arched & stepped back crest w/a hanging hole above a hinged slant lid over the dovetailed rectangular box w/an inlaid star on the front w/a center circle of bird's-eye maple, varnish finish, 5 3/4 x 8 1/2", 9 7/8" h. (varnish wear, minor damage) **495**

Storage box, bentwood, deep round sides w/lapped seams on the base & a finger lappet on the fitted flat cover, square nail construction & square brass tacks decorating cover, 19th c., 18 1/4" d., 13 1/4" h. **220**

Storage box, oval bentwood, finger lappet construction w/iron tacks, flat fitted top w/single finger lappet, old varnish finish, Hersey-type, Hingham, Massachusetts, 6 1/2" l. **495**

Storage box, oval bentwood, wide single lappet w/steel tack on base & thin single lappet on fitted flat cover, worn natural varnish finish, 6" l. **99**

Storage box, painted bentwood, oval w/single finger lappet on base & flat lid, copper tacks, old worn green paint, C. Hersey-type, 4 3/4" l. **578**

Storage box, painted & decorated pine, rectangular hinged domed cover w/wire staple hinges above the flat sides, original brown ground decorated w/striping, flowers & birds in outlined panels in red & white, 19th c., 10" l. (wear & minor edge damage) **1,980**

Storage box, painted & decorated pine, rectangular low domed cover above the flat sides, original orangish red ground w/yellow striping & large stylized flowers in red, white, green & mahogany, wire & tin hinges & tin hasp, attributed to Heinrich Bucher, first half 19th c., 9 3/8" l. (some edge damage) **7,700**

Storage box, painted & decorated pine, rectangular top w/a central rectangular landscape scene w/mountains, a lake & buildings, additional polychrome floral decoration, original dark painted ground w/grey & red striping, matching decoration on lid interior also inscribed "To Jennie," 19th c., 9 7/8" l. (lock removed) **974**

Storage box, painted & decorated pine, rectangular w/high domed top centered by a shaped bail handle, original black paint w/blue edge striping & stenciled decoration in red & silver w/free-hand red & yellow flowers on the lid, lock w/hasp, New England, probably Massachusetts, early 19th c., 6 1/2 x 10", 5" h. (minor edge wear) **5,225**

Storage box, painted & decorated poplar, rectangular top decorated w/a sailing ship w/the American flag, the dovetailed base decorated w/gold, red & black striping & foliage decoration on the original blue ground w/worn yellowed varnish, w/lock & key, attributed to Baltimore, early 19th c., 7 1/2" l. **3,300**

Storage box, painted & decorated, rectangular hinged lid above the dovetailed base, decorated w/original overall brown vinegar decoration of random designs on a green ground w/gesso beneath, wrought-iron end handles, initials "H.C.L." integrated into design on the front, paper label in brown ink on one end reads "Jon--Aldrick, Brattleboro," 19th c., 13 x 32", 12 1/2" h. (one bail handle missing, edge wear) **440**

Storage box, painted pine, rectangular w/dovetailed construction, interior w/a sliding panel opening to a compartment & a drawer below, painted green, New England, early 19th c., 17 3/4 x 34", 18" h. **460**

Storage box, painted wood, nearly square upright form w/fitted flat cover, square nail construction w/hand planing marks, old blue paint, 19th c., 8 5/8 x 9 1/2", 9 1/8" h. **220**

Storage box, painted wood, rectangular w/sliding lid, painted in an overall argyle diamond design in shades of red, black, brown & yellow, 19th c., 6 x 12", 6 3/4" h. (wear) **1,610**

Storage box, round bentwood, painted, finger lappet seams w/iron tacks, old dark green paint, faint branded label "___Murdock Jr.," 5 1/8" h., 9 7/8" d. (minor edge damage) **440**

Storage box, round bentwood, the base w/a single wide finger lappet, the fitted flat cover w/a single narrow finger lappet, old dark green paint, 8" d. **495**

Storage box, wallpaper-covered, oval upright sides w/flat fitted cover, blue w/white & dark blue basketweave design, tan band around cover w/burgundy dots, partial newspaper lining, 3 1/2 x 6", 3" h. (minor edge wear, small flakes) **688**

Tool box, curly maple, a rectangular lift top w/a heavy molded edge above a well w/a heavy molded rim band & fitted w/a removable nail carrier, a molded base w/a long narrow drawer w/a wooden knob at the front bottom, the top w/a large applied quatrefoil panel in the center, very good wood figure, 9 1/2 x 19 3/4", 10" h. **825**

Wall box, painted pine, a slanted hinged lid on an upper compartment, open lower compartment, painted dark red, early 19th c., 6 3/4 x 13 3/4" (minor split, wear)...... **489**

Wall box, painted wood, the tall hanging tab w/a rounded top above slanted top edges over round-topped sides flanking two slant-fronted open compartments, painted brown, 19th c., 5 1/2 x 9 3/8", 24" h. (wear, scratches) **2,070**

BREWERIANA

Beer is still popular in this country but the number of breweries has greatly diminished. More than 1,900 breweries were in operation in the 1870s but we find fewer than 40 major breweries supply the demands of the country a century later, although micro-breweries have recently sprung up across the country.

Advertising items used to promote various breweries, especially those issued prior to prohibition, now attract an ever growing number of collectors. The breweriana items listed are a sampling of the many items available.

Also see: Antique Trader Advertising Price Guide.

Backbar display, "Altes Golden Lager Beer," white chalkware, molded as an upright round disk w/writing above a narrow rectangular base w/a round indent at the right end holding an amber bottle of the product, printed in red & gold, 1950s, 11 x 11 1/2" (some corner chips) **$95**

Backbar figure, "Blatz Beer," metal & plastic, seated banjo player w/barrel body beside a large model of a Blatz beer bottle, upright back w/sign across the top reading "It's Draft-Brewed - Blatz," colorful, 1950s (some scuffs to bottle label).................... **87**

Backbar figure, "Cooper's Beer," figural chalk standing bartender w/towel over one arm & holding up a large bottle of beer in front, 1940s, 7 x 15" (lots of wear, chips, missing bottle labels)............................ **150**

Miller High Life Beer Bar Figure

Backbar figure, "Miller High Life Beer," hard rubber figure of a standing girl wearing a large round red hat & short flaring red skirt w/blue & yellow trim, high-top black boots, flaring rectangular red & white base, 1930s, some overall scratches, 6" h. (ILLUS.) **115**

Neuweiller Beer Backbar Figure

Backbar figure, "Neuweiler Beer - Ale," molded plastic figure of an older bartender holding up glass of beer, printed in yellow, black, white, red & pink, 1950s, some worn & chipped paint, 8 1/2 x 12" (ILLUS.) **77**

Backbar light, "Schmidt Beer," model of a covered wagon, metal, wood & cloth, wooden wagon & wheels w/a cloth cover in white printed in red "Schmidt" above a blue banner printed "The brew that grew with the Great Northwest," electric light inside, cord extends from base, 1950s, 10 x 17" (cloth yellowed w/some stains) **102**

Bank, "Metz Beer," ceramic, barrel-shaped, tan glaze, embossed "Premium Metz Beer," 1950s, 6 1/2" h. (light crazing & some small base rim chips) **25**

Beer can, "Fitzgerald's Pale Ale," cone-top crown closure type, cylindrical, oblong front label printed in red w/white & black design, an emblem at the top above "Fitzgerald's Pale Ale," address in white border band, white ground, 1940s, 12 oz. (rub mark between faces, ding in shoulder) **125**

Gluek's Beer Can

Beer can, "Gluek's Beer," cone-top crown closure type, cylindrical, printed w/a squared label reading "Gluek's" in blue on a white band flanked by dark blue bands w/"Beer" in white below, all within a thin red border, narrow red base band printed in white "Gluek Brewing Company," 1940s, 12 oz., few tiny humidity spots on spout (ILLUS.) **96**

Beer can, "Hanley's Lager Beer," cone-top w/crown closure type, cylindrical sides, fine black on silver check ground, central red oval w/small reclining lion above white wording "Hanley's Extra Dry Lager Beer," cigarette lighter in neck, 1940s, 12 oz. (few dings in spout) **377**

Rare Hudephol Chevy Ale Can

Beer can, "Hudepohl Chevy Ale," cone-top crown closure type, cylindrical, silver ground w/round front label w/wavy border enclosing a pale blue ground w/dark blue, red & white wording, narrow wavy blue & red stripes around the shoulder & base, 1940s, 12 oz., small scattered scratches (ILLUS.) **726**

Beer can, "Jung Pilsener Beer," cone-top crown-closure stype, cylindrical, silver ground w/a large green hop leaf on the front printed in white & black "Jung Pilsener Beer," 1940s, 12 oz. (rusty rim, small rust spot on one face) **227**

Milwaukee Club Beer Can

Beer can, "Milwaukee Club Beer," cone-top, low profile-type, black background w/wide yellow stripe w/black lettering, reads "Keg Beer Flavor - Milwaukee Club Beer," minor scratches in black, 1930s (ILLUS.) **507**

Beer can, "Neuweiler's Pilsener Beer," cone-top, high-profile style, yellow ground w/ornate silvery blue, red & black design, minor nicks, tiny scratches, 1940s (ILLUS. right w/Piel's can) **1,000**

Beer can, "Pacific Lager Beer," cone-top, low profile-style, dark blue upper portion w/white wording, narrow bluish green lower band w/white waves & small sailing boat, 1930s (overall small rust spots, lacquered) **75**

Rare Piel's and Neuweiler's Cans

Beer can, "Piel's Special Light Beer," cone-top, low-profile style, red ground w/silver oval ribbon reserve enclosing black & red wording, few small nicks, some minor dings, 1930s (ILLUS. left w/Neuweiler's can) **427**

Beer can, "Schmidt's First Premium Lager Beer," cone-top, high-profile style, colorful printing, 1940s (some small nicks & scratches) **187**

Schlitz Beer Cab Light

Cab light, "Schlitz Beer," reverse-painted glass & metal, a flat arched glass plate w"Schlitz" in red on a gold ground, set upright in a rectangular silvered metal base, 1930s, some oxidation on the base, few rust spots on rear cover, 7 1/2 x 13" (ILLUS.)........................ **406**

Cigar box, "Budweiser Perfecto Cigars," wooden, w/labels, 1910, 5 1/2 x 9 1/4" (warped lid, tears, wear, grime on paper)........ **28**

Dart board, "Pabst Blue Ribbon," Masonite printed in color, square, cartoon caricatures of Hitler & Tojo in upper corners, the remainder of the board printed in color w/a deck of playing cards laid out in rows, "Pabst Blue Ribbon" banner across the top, blue borders w/white printing including "Poker - Black Jack" at the bottom, made w/dart holes, 1940s, 18" sq. (some soiling & water stains, dinged corners) **58**

Hamm's Bear Decanter

Decanter w/stopper, "Hamm's Beer," ceramic figural Hamm's bear in black & white, colored Hamm's label at front, head forms stopper, like new, 1972 (ILLUS.).. **37**

Foam scrapper holder, "Ballantine Ale - Beer," plastic, a cylindrical tumbler above a flaring short conical base printed w/wording, 1950s, 7" h. (overall light scuffs & scratches mostly on tumbler) **29**

Letterhead, "Lebanon Valley Brewing Company," 1945, one sheet (creases, staple holes)... **10**

Letterhead, "Terre Haute Brewing Co.," letter dated 1906, one sheet (creases, staple holes)... **20**

Early Brewery Match Safe

Match safe, "Scheidt (Adam) Brewing Co.," silver plated brass, flattened rectangular form w/rounded corners & hinged lid, stamped scroll border, inscribed "Adam Scheidt Brewing Co. (w/logo) Norristown, Pa.," worn plating around edges, some dents, early 1900s (ILLUS.)............................. **36**

Promotional set, "Piel's Light Beer," boxed, three compartments, two holding six round coasters & center one w/a metal bottle opener, 1940s, the set (overall light wear & slight yellowing)....................................... **6**

Hamm's Beer Bear Radio

Radio, "Hamm's Beer," stuffed cloth Hamm's bear in black & white w/red tongue, Hamm's cloth label on his chest, radio inside works, 16" h. (ILLUS.).................. **60**

Sign, "Blatz Beer," color-printed tin, rectangular, white ground printed in color w/a banner reading "Take Home" above "draft-brewed Blatz - Milaukee's Finest Beer," 1950s, 8 1/4 x 14" (some paint chips at edges, screw holes, few scratches)................ **105**

Sign, "Budweiser Beer," electric, model of a large man's pocket watch, gold-colored watch frame w/white dial w/Arabic numerals, printed in red in the center "Budweiser" over small yellow wording "King of Beers," 1950s, 19" d. (some wear & scuffs on gold) **82**

Sign, "Burger Beer," lighted reverse-painted glass in tin frame, upright diamond-shaped sign attached to narrow rectangular electric platform, signed w/color crest at top above oval border around "Burger" above "Beer," 1950s, 10" sq. (frame spotted) **95**

Sign, "Champagne Velvet Beer," rectangular plastic in color, shows hands forming letters "C-V" above "Signal For CV - Champagne Velvet...," embossed amber bottle on the right edge, 1950s, 9 3/4 x 12 1/4" (some soiling, a few scuffs) **105**

Sign, "Drewrys Old Stock Ale," color-printed composition, rectangular w/rounded corners, brown wood-grained ground printed in pale yellow & red, white oval surrounding a color image of a bottle in the center, printed across the bottom "For those who appreciate The Finest Ale," 1940s, 10 1/2 x 16 1/2" (minor edge dings & soiling, small chips at top of bottle).......... **95**

Sign, "Falls City Beer," plastic, rectangular, assorted blocks around the border showing various sporting scenes printed in white on a yellow, green on blue ground, red, white & black central oval w/"Falls City Beer" w/a yellow block at the bottom center printed in black "Year 'Round Favorite!," 1960s, unused, 15 x 21" **50**

Sign, "Gold Crown Beer," color-printed tin over cardbard, rectangular, gold lettering on a black ground at the right, a narrow red band w/black logo on the left, 1940s, 7 x 14 3/4" (some scratches & scuffs, sticker residue) **47**

Hamm's Preferred Stock Beer Sign

Sign, "Hamm's Preferred Stock Beer - Fully Aged," color-printed embossed tin, rectangular, in red, white, blue, black & yellow, few small rust spots & light scuffs, 17 3/4 x 23 3/4" (ILLUS.)................................. **435**

Sign, "Happy-Peppy Beer," rounded starburst wood sign composed of wedges of wood glued together & printed in red, white & black w/advertising & cartoon figure of walking 1930s man in tuxedo

(some wood splits, some discolored spots) **225**

Hudepohl Beer Tin Sign

Sign, "Hudepohl Beer," color-printed tin over cardboard, rectangular, a mottled pale yellow ground printed w/"Ask For Gold Old Hudepohl Beer - Cincinnati, Ohio" in silver, black & red, a color image of the bottle at the center, only minor scuffs, 1930s, 9 x 13" (ILLUS.) **460**

Sign, "Kingsbury Pale Beer," color-printed cardboard, self-framed w/border of crossed logs surrounding a color picture of two birds, titled at top "Bobwhite Quail," marked at bottom edge "Kingsbury Pale Beer," 1950s, 17 x 20" (very minor creases) **38**

Sign, "McGovern Pilsener Beer," color-printed cardboard, large image of a kicking mule, framed, 1940s, 10 x 13" (slight yellowing & a few stains)................................. **22**

Sign, "Minnesota City Brewery Bock Beer," lithographed paper in color w/a scene of a Cavalier blowing a horn while riding on a ram leaping over a beer barrel, light wear & stains, framed, ca. 1900, 25 x 37" **622**

Sign, "Rainier Beer - Bock," printer's mock-up lithograph, design for imprinting on standard lithograph, color design w/a large ram head in center left w/a sandwich & large foaming mug of beer in the front right, "Rainier Beer" in red at top & "Bock" in large pale green letters at the bottom, one-of-a-kind, framed, 24 x 29"........ **219**

Sign, "Redtop Beer," vacuum-formed plastic printed in color, rectangular, name in top reserve above lower reverse w/"Bright - Refreshing - Flavor - bottles....cans," 1950s... **50**

Sign, "Steinhaus Beers," color printed tin over cardboard, rectangular, brown woodgrain background printed in silver, red & black "Steinhaus Beers - For Fine Flavor - Pilsener and Lager," 1930s, 9 x 13" (few scratches)................................. **201**

Signs, "Old German Premium Lager," rectangular, reverse-painted glass restroom signs, one w/brand name & "For Men" w/cartoon of man, the other w/"For Women" w/cartoon of woman, like new, 1950s, pr. **72**

Altes Lager & Arrow Beer Knobs

Tap knob, "Altes Lager," plastic w/enamel insert, green w/dark green & white insert, 1950s (ILLUS. left) 66

Tap knob, "Arrow Beer," chrome w/printed enamel insert, red & white insert, 1930s, small hairline in insert, bubbles in chrome (ILLUS. right w/Altes Lager knob).................... 35

Tap knob, "English Lad," black Bakelite w/enamel insert, 1930s (minor wear & scratches) 437

McCoy & Michelob Beer Tap Knobs

Tap knob, "McCoy Beer,"chrome w/enamel insert, insert w/red & black wording on white, reads "It's the real McCoy," light wear, 1940s (ILLUS. left) 110

Tap knob, "Michelob Beer," Bakelite w/enamel insert, black knob w/red insert w/center gold band w/"Michelob" in white, 1940s, wear, small chips to rim (ILLUS. right w/McCoy knob) 60

P.O.C. & Pabst Beer Tap Knobs

Tap knob, "P.O.C. Beer," Bakelite w/printed metal insert, black knob w/white insert & red wording, 1940s, small spots on insert, wear (ILLUS. left) 100

Tap knob, "Pabst Breweries," chrome w/enamel insert, red, white & blue insert w/blue maple leaf & "B" in center surrounded by "Pabst Breweries," 1930s, light wear (ILLUS. right with P.O.C. knob)........ 28

Tap knob, "Rainier," black Bakelight w/a white enamel disk w/red wording, 1940s (few small cracks in white).............................. 140

Tap knob, "(Star) Pilsener Special," chrome w/red, white & blue enamel insert w/a

blue star & red & blue wording, overall light scratches, few small rim dings, Star Union Company, Peru, Illinois. ca. 1940s (ILLUS. right with Walter's knob).................. 155

Walter's and Star Pilsener Tap Knobs

Tap knob, "Walter's Pilsener Beer," black Bakelite w/red & white enamel insert, lists both Wisconsin & Colorado breweries, minor wear, few small spots on face, 1940s (ILLUS. left) 147

Toy, "Budweiser Beer," HO scale railroad reefer car, plastic, applied weathering, 1970s (some wear to print)............................... 27

Toy, "Coors Beer," HO scale railroad reefer car, plastic, 1970s 21

Tray, "Beverwyck Brewing Co.," rectangular w/rounded corners, large central color scene of a large, fancy brewery building in reds, browns & yellow w/name above factory "Beverwyck Brewing Co., Albany, N.Y.," dark green border band w/yellow wording "Beverwyck Famous Lager," 1910s, 12 1/4 x 17 1/4" (many small chips, overall spots & wear) 557

Tray, "Bucyrus Brewing Co.," pre-Prohibition, rectangular w/rounded corners, wood-grained ground, the center w/a color printed standing portrait of a Dutch girl holding a tray of beer, blue apron & red bodice w/white bonnet, gold letters in border read "Ehrenpreis - Bucyrus Brewing Co. - "Brownie" - The Quality Brews," 10 x 13" (some spots & rim chips)................. 150

Cardinal Beer Tray

Tray, "Cardinal Beer," porcelain pie tin-shaped, white ground printed in red wording "Drink Cardinal Beer - Costs 25% More to Brew, But Worth More - Standard Brewing Co. of Scranton, PA," narrow dark green border band, minor front scratches, some small back chips, slighly yellowed, 1940s, 12" d. (ILLUS.) **195**

Congress Beer Tray

Tray, "Congress Beer," round pie tin-shaped, printed at the interior top w/a small oval reserve w/a picture of the U.S. Capital above "Congress Beer" in gold & red all on a pale blue ground, gold border w/black wording "Haberle - Congress Brewing Co. - Syracuse, N.Y.," several nicks, 1930s, 13" d. (ILLUS.) **181**

Derby Cream Ale Tray

Tray, "Derby Cream Ale," round, large center center of two horse heads, one black & one brown, racing neck & neck, white background, light blue border band printed in red "Derby Cream Ale - Brilliant and Export Ales.," printed in small letters under the horse heads "National Brewing Co., Syracuse, N.Y.," 1930s, overall scratches, rim chips, 12" d. (ILLUS.) **328**

Dutch Club Beer Tray

Tray, "Dutch Club Beer," scene in the center of a blond Dutch boy holding out a tray w/beer steins, pale yellow & blue, dark blue border, 1940s, minor nicks & scratches, 12" d. (ILLUS.) **110**

Tray, "Eagle Brewing Co.," square w/rounded corners, color center half-length portrait of a pretty turn-of-the-20th-century lady w/brown hair wearing a pale blue gown & holding up a glass of beer against a dark ground, black border band printed in gold "The Eagle Brewing Co. - Ales - Lager - Utica, N.Y. - Both Phones 645," 1910s, 13" w. (overall chips & scuffs) **293**

Tray, "Ehret's (Geo.) Extra," oval, oval black central reserve printed in red & gold w/a six-point star w/monogram above "New York," wide red oval ring printed in gold & black "Geo. Ehret's Extra - Hell Gate Brewery," black outer border band printed w/clusters of wheat along each side & w/a small red star at the top & bottom end, early 1900s, 13 1/2 x 16 1/2" (wear on black, small overall nicks, rim chips) **155**

Tray, "Frontenac Breweries Limited," serving-type, round, large central color scene of the brewery w/"Frontenac - Canada's Best" in gold, upright border band printed "Frontenac Breweries Limited - Montreal," 1930s, 12" d. (minor overall scratches) **120**

Goebel Beer Tray

Tray, "Goebel Beer," round pie tin-shaped, center color scene of a German man wearing a red vest & white shirt seated at a table holding a mug of beer w/the bottle in front, border printed in gold & green w/wheat & hop vines, center reads "Goebel Beer - Detroit, U.S.A.," overall wear, some scuffs, few small spots, 1910s, 12" d. (ILLUS.) **372**

Tray, "Golden Drops Lager Beer," pre-Prohibition, rectangular w/rounded corners, center color scene of Cavaliers sitting & standing around a tavern table drinking, red arch above scene reads "Decidedly Different," green lettering below scene reads "Two Rivers Beverage Co. - Twin Rivers, Wisconsin," wide light green border band w/white wording "Golden Drops Lager Beer," 10 x 13" (minor nicks, few small dings) **165**

Tray, "Hanley's Ale," center w/black ground, printed w/a large black & white bulldog reclining above gold & red word "Hanley's" above ""Peerless Ale" in red, white & black," location of brewery in small white letters at the bottom, narrow red border band w/gold working, 1930s, 12" d. (minor spots & marks) **67**

Tray, "Horse Head Beer & Ale," round, central large brown horse head on a pale yellow ground titled "Champion Don Juan," dark green border band w/yellow wording, 1940s, 12" d.. **162**

Tray, "Kaier's Beer," oval, colorful large central image of large cut roses in red, pink & white w/green & yellow leaves, border band of hop vines, printed in small black letters in the center bottom "Kaier's - Beer, Ale & Porter. - Bottled and Pasteurized at Brewery," early 1900s, 13 1/2 x 16 1/2" (wear, rim chips, few scratches, light dent in rim) **222**

Tray, "Monarch Ale," pre-Prohibition, round, overall dark woodgrain background w/a large printed bottle of the product in the center in color, 12" d. (few scattered chips) **257**

Tray, "National Brewery - St. Louis, Mo." rectangular w/rounded corners, color lithographed metal w/large central scene & picture of a bottle, 10 x 13 3/4", ca. 1900 (few small nicks & spots) **330**

Tray, "National Brewing Co.," round, center w/pale yellow ground centered by a large blue dot under a large red star overprinted in white script "National Brewing Co.," maroon border printed in yellow "Brilliant Ale - Porter and India Pale," 1930s, 12" d. (light overall scratches) **251**

Tray, "Old Reading Beer," round, colorful center scene of a cartoon-style barkeeper holding a mug of beer high above a begging brown & white dog, red, yellow & white wording on a dark blue ground, dark red border band w/yellow wording "Reading Brewery Inc. - Reading, PA," 1930s, 13" d. (few rim scuffs) **122**

Tray, "Oneida Brewing Co.," porcelain pie tin-shaped, round w/center standing black & white portrait of "Chief Shenandoah," black band w/white wording "Oneida Brewing Co. - Ales & Porter - Utica, N.Y.," 1930s, 12" d. (few chips) **466**

Tray, "Pacific Beer," pre-Prohibition, round, a color scene of a snow-capped peak w/a lakeside landscape in the foreground, wide pale yellow border printed in brown "Pacific Beer - Best East or West - Pacific Brewing & Malting Co. - Tacoma," brown border band, back packing slip dated 1912, 12" d. (few rim chips, some light web crackling overall) **140**

Tray, "Robinson's (E.) Sons Brewery," round pie tin-shaped, large color center scene of a large brewery in red, yellow, green, etc., red border band printed in gold "E. Robinson's Sons - Pilsener Bot-

Robinson's Sons Brewery Tray

tled Beer," 1910s, wear & rim chips, few chips on inside rim, 13" d. (ILLUS.) **401**

Tray, "Seipp's Extra Pale Beer," pre-Prohibition, round, colorful center scene of two pretty young woman seated next to each other in a garden surrounded by yellow roses w/a bottle & glass of the beer in the left foreground, wording around the border, 12" d. (overall nicked & spotted) **196**

Tray, "Stegmaier's Beer - Ale Porter," round pie tin-shaped, central scene of a red brewery building scene below the large red wording all on a pale yellow ground, small black wording along lower inner rim "Stegmaier Brewing Co. - Wilkes-Barre, PA," outer border of wheat & hops printed in black on yellow, red border bands, 1910s, 12 1/2" d. (some rust & wear spots) **213**

Sunrise Beer Tray

Tray, "Sunrise Beer," round, large center scene w/a large rising sun over a lake w/a green & yellow field w/scattered green fields in the foreground, bottle of the product in the front right, printed in red "Sunrise Beer - Brightens Every Day," red border band, 1930s, few minor scratches & chips, 12" d. (ILLUS.) **182**

BUTTER MOLDS & STAMPS

Acorn mold, round, a large acorn beside a large curved leaf within a carved ropetwist border, dark patina, 4 5/8" d. **$138**

Acorn stamp, round w/a central radiating cluster of three large acorns alternating w/three large oak leaves, border carved w/name "J. Ozanne, Houguette," soft patina, 5 1/4" d. **83**

Acorn & thistle stamp, carved w/a large acorn below a large thistle head, each flanked by leaf clusters, narrow zipper-cut border, soft finish, screw-in handle, 3 7/8" d. (ILLUS. right w/cow and thistle stamps) **138**

Acorns stamp, a pair of large nuts suspended side by side from a twig w/two large carved oak leaves above & two on the side, soft, slightly shiny finish, 3 5/8" d. (short age crack)................ **110**

Cow at fence mold, round, stylized animal standing w/head over a rail fence, a triple sprig branch above, ropetwist-carved border, scrubbed finish, 4 1/4" d. **220**

Cow mold, round, stylized standing cow w/a serrated long leaf in front & above the animal, ropetwist-carved border, dark patina, 4 7/8" d. **220**

Cow stamp, deeply carved standing cow facing right, an arched stalk of grain above it, zipper-cut border, scrubbed finish, 4 3/8' d. (age cracks) **165**

Three Carved Butter Stamps

Cow stamp, round w/a standing stylized animal under an arching tree & on a ground of graduated bands, bold notch-cut border, screw-in handle, 4 3/8" d. (ILLUS. left) **110**

Cow stamp, small rectangular thin block carved w/a standing cow w/eight small triple-leaf sprigs around the edges, worn, 3 1/2 x 4 7/8" (minor age cracks).................. **193**

Cow & tree stamp, round w/crudely carved cow under arched tree, finely notched border band, turned handle, scrubbed finish, 4 1/2" d. (age cracks) **165**

Eagle stamp, deeply carved stylized short-necked bird w/large shield at breast, narrow wings & radiating tail feathers, good patina, prominent turning rings, 3" d. **275**

Eagle Butter Print

Eagle stamp, round w/stylized eagle w/cross-hatched feathers, surrounded by stars, one piece handle, good patina, minor age crack, 4 1/4" d. (ILLUS.) **770**

Eagle stamp, stylized long-necked bird w/shield on breast, thin wings & radiating tail feathers, flanked by a leaf sprig on each side, 3 3/4" d. **193**

Fish stamp, rectangular lollipop-style, dark patina w/scratch marks, 3 1/4" w., overall 8 1/4" l.............................. **193**

Flower Butter Print

Flower stamp, round, flower surrounded by leaves, one piece handle, good patina, minor edge damage, 4 3/8" d. (ILLUS.)........ **110**

Flower stamp, round w/deep floral carving resembling mums, one-piece handle, 4 1/4" d. (worm holes & small hole in middle)...................... **550**

Flower stamp, round w/slender-stemmed blossom w/three petals above a curved pair of thin leaves above a curved pair of wide leaves, smaller leaves below, notched rim band, handle on top, scratched numbers on the back, 3 3/4" d. **193**

Heart & leaf "lollipop" stamp, curly maple, round top chip-carved w/straight feathered leaves radiating from the center & alternating w/feathered hearts, good patina, lightly scrubbed finish, 8 3/4" l. (age crack in back)...................... **330**

Pomegranate mold, round, a round lobed fruit w/a pointed topnotch flanked by long serrated leaves, case impressed "Patd. Apr 17, 1866," 3 3/4" d. **110**

Prince of Wales Feathers, a central crest enclosed by a wide feathered ring border, varnished w/dark brown paint or thick stain on back, screw-in handle, 3 1/4" d.............................. **110**

Sheep mold, round, standing stylized animal flanked by slender leaf sprigs, carved ropetwist border, 2 3/4" d. (refinished, two filled age cracks) **413**

Thistle mold, round, large bulbous thistle head w/feathery top above a pair of long slender serrated leaves, carved ropetwist border, 4 7/8" d. (old edge damage) **105**

Thistle mold, round, large realistic thistle blossom flanked by large, wide thistle leaves, 3 1/4" d. (wear, minor edge chips).. **138**

Thistle stamp, carved in the center w/a large thistle head w/feathered top, flanked by pairs of large & small leaves, leaf-cut border band, good patina, minor edge wear, 4 1/2" d. (ILLUS. center w/cow and acorn & thistle stamps)................ 165

Tulip stamp, stylized carved blossom above a round sunburst, fine notched border band, turned handle, scrubbed finish, 3 1/4" d. 358

CANDLESTICKS & CANDLEHOLDERS

English Candlestick with Bell

Candleholder, wrought-iron, table model, an arched low tripod base w/penny feet supporting a very slender upright pointed rod fitted w/an adjustable flat cross-arm w/square brackets & fitted at each tip w/a candle socket w/drip tray, 22 1/4" h. $770

Candlestick, brass, a dished saucer base centering a short spiral-twist standard supporting a cylindrical socket, polished, early, 6 1/4" h. (minor dents, old solder on threads of base) 220

Candlestick, brass, hand-hammered, a flared rim on an egg-shaped candlecup, slender shaft ending in a bulbed cone on a disk base, incised mark of Jarvie, Chicago, early 20th c., 11" h. (spotting) 431

Candlestick, taper jack-type, a small round reticulated base w/three hearts, cast handle on base, slender shaft wrapped w/an old wax taper below the top crossbar & urn finial, England, late 18th - early 19th c., 5" h. 770

Candlestick, brass, a round dished base centered by a domed support for the columnar shaft w/flared rim & side push-up knob, England, late 18th - early 19th c., 6 3/4" h. 385

Candlestick, brass, a round ringed & domed foot below the solid knob- and ring-turned shaft w/a wide center drip pan, tall cylindrical socket, late 18th - early 19th c., 7 3/8" h. (minor dents)............... 1,100

Candlestick, brass, ring-turned & stepped domed base w/a ring-turned & tapering columnar shaft below the tall cylindrical socket, polished, 19th c., 8 1/2" h.................. 248

Candlestick, brass, round domed base w/flat top centered by a baluster-turned stem & tall cylindrical socket, Spain, probably 18th c., 8 3/4" h. 550

Candlestick, brass, a square platform base raised on small peg feet, a conical lower shaft tapering to a flaring ring-turned upper shaft supporting the tall ring-turned candle socket, single-piece shaft, early, 9" h. 248

Candlestick, brass, Queen Anne-style, a round slightly domed scalloped foot centering a very slender shaft topped by a compressed knob below the cylindrical socket w/flared rim, w/push-up, England, 18th c., 9 3/8" h. (repair to rim) 275

Candlestick, brass, a flaring paneled & stepped base below the slender trumpet-form standard w/base & top rings below the cylindrical ringed socket, copper-colored patina w/traces of silver plating, 19th c., 9 1/2" h. 220

Candlestick, brass, a wide flat-bottomed dished base w/low upright sides centering a tall slender ring-turned shaft w/an open yoke suspending a bell below the tall knobbed cylindrical socket w/flared rim, England, 12 1/2" h. (ILLUS.)................... 495

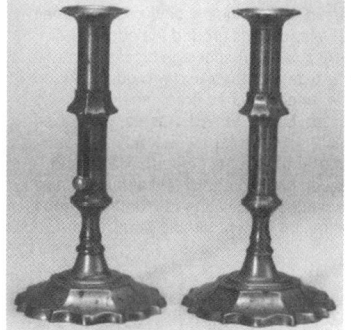

Early Dutch Brass Candlesticks

Candlesticks, brass, a domed, stepped round base below the ring- and knob-turned standard centered by a wide disk-form drip tray, tall ring-turned cylindrical shaft, Holland, 18th-19th c., minor battering, 7 1/2" h., pr. (ILLUS.) 385

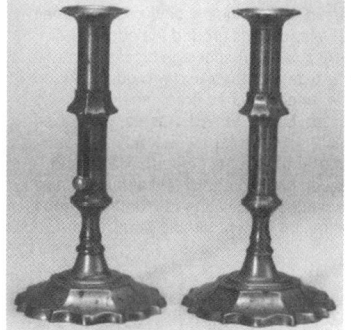

Early English Brass Candlesticks

Candlesticks, brass, a flaring petal-form rounded base supporting a ringed graduated shaft w/a side candle ejector knob & a tall cylindrical socket w/flared rim, one ejector knob missing, minor dents, England, mid-18th c., 8 1/4" h., pr. (ILLUS.)................ 1,380

Candlesticks, brass, a stepped domed round foot below a small double-knop stem supporting a tall cylindrical shaft bulbed at the bottom & w/a flared rim, w/push-ups, 19th c., 8" h., pr........................ **220**

Candlesticks, brass, a tall open double spiral-twist standard w/a tall slender ringed socket w/flattened rim, on a wide round dished foot w/flared sides, Europe, late 19th c., 18 1/4" h., pr. **460**

Candlesticks, brass, flaring domed & stepped octagonal base below the tapering knob-turned standard & waisted cylindrical socket, early, 9" h., pr. **660**

Candlesticks, brass, "King of Diamonds" patt., a squared foot w/beveled corners supporting a tall knob- and ring-turned shaft w/a bulbous diamond pattern central knob, tall cylindrical socket w/flattened rim, w/push-ups, England, late 19th c., 12 1/2" h., pr. **495**

Candlesticks, brass, "Prince of Diamonds" patt., a squared domed foot below the tall shaft w/ringed sections above & below the central bulbous diamond patterned section, a tall cylindrical socket w/flared rim, w/pushups, marked "The Diamond Prince," England, 19th c., 11 7/8" h., pr....... **448**

Candlesticks, brass, "Princess of Diamonds" patt., a squared domed foot below the tall shaft w/ringed sections above & below the central bulbous diamond patterned section, a tall cylindrical socket w/flared rim, w/pushups, marked "The Diamond Princess," England, 19th c., pr. **448**

Candlesticks, brass, Queen Anne-style, a round scalloped base below the slender ring-turned shaft w/a tall cylindrical socket w/flattened rim, England, 18th c., 7 1/2" h., pr.. **1,870**

Candlesticks, brass, "Queen of Diamonds" patt., a squared domed foot below the tall shaft w/ringed sections above & below the central bulbous diamond patterned section, a tall cylindrical socket w/flared rim, w/pushups, marked "The Queen of Diamonds," England, 19th c., 11 1/4" h., pr......... **644**

Candlesticks, brass, round tapering foot below a baluster- and ring-turned shaft w/a tall cylindrical socket w/flattened rim, original pushups, 19th c., 12" h., pr............... **275**

Candlesticks, brass, rounded stepped & domed foot w/scalloped edge tapering to a tall slender paneled & ring-turned shaft below the tall ring socket w/a removable scalloped bobeche, France, late 18th - early 19th c., 9 5/8" h., pr. **1,650**

Candlesticks, brass, tapering baluster-form fluted shaft, domed paneled square base w/dentil borders, 19th c., 9 5/8" h., pr. (small base loss, wear)............................. **403**

Candlesticks, bronze, a cylindrical socket on a slender upper shaft above a figural seahorse shaft, on a round disk foot w/concentric ridges, green patina, one signed & dated by E.T. Hurley, 1916, Kentucky, 10 3/4" h., pr. **2,530**

Candlesticks, bronze, a flared bobeche inserted into an urn-form socket held in a

three-prong bulbed standard over a swirled round foot, dark brown patina, impressed mark of Tiffany Studios, No. 1213, 16 3/4" h., pr. (minor wear).............. **1,955**

Candlesticks, sterling silver, each in the form of a Doric column w/a chased, reeded stem, the shoulder beaded w/embossed rosette band, on a square stepped base, Gorham Mfg. Co., Providence, Rhode Island, 1908, 8 3/4" h., set of 4..... **1,725**

Candlesticks, wrought-iron, wedding ring hogscraper-type, round base & cylindrical shaft w/brass ring, mid-19th c., 13 1/4" h., pr. (corrosion) **4,025**

Chamberstick, brass, a shallow round dished base w/upright finger loop handle at the side, a cylindrical shaft w/candle ejector knob & a flared flattened socket rim, 19th c., 4 3/4" h. **275**

Chamberstick, silver plate, round w/an embossed scalloped rim w/repoussé roses & foliate designs, a C-scroll edge handle, Tiffany & Co., New York, late 19th - early 20th c., 2 1/4" h. **86**

Wall sconce, tin, round reflector pan w/radiating small mirrored segments, cylindrical socket w/fluted edge bobeche, American, second quarter 19th c., 10" d., 11" h. (wear, corrosion, minor imperfections)........ **2,185**

Wall sconces, tin, the extended back plate w/a fluted round top, single candle socket in the half-round tray base, 19th c., 3 1/4" w., 9 1/2" h., pr. (minor corrosion)....... **978**

CANDY CONTAINERS

Airplane, "Liberty Motor," clear glass, replaced propeller, all other tin original **$800**

Airplane, "T.M.A. 44," replaced propeller & closure **140**

Automobile, embossed "Pat ap'ld for Limousine," original closure, 85% green, black & grey repaint, no dots between door panels **125**

Automobile, "West Spec. Co. Limousine," original green wheels, yellow taxi closure . **1,800**

Baseball Player w/Bat, original closure, 60% paint, letter 'D' on shaft **650**

Bell, "Fancy School Hand Bell," original closure. **140**

Boat, "U.S.N. Dreadnaught," original closure. **224**

Bottle carrier, holds six empty bottles, no closure, packed by Tarson Products, Chicago, Illinois **1,000**

Buddy Bank **220**

Building, Village Railroad Station w/insert, replaced clip, green shingle roof................... **280**

Bus, embossed "Victory Glass Co.," no paint, no closure **1,000**

Camera on Tripod, original tripod, head, string & metal ring on lens, no picture on replaced closure **350**

Carpet Sweeper, embossed "Dolly Sweeper," original closure, all original, 95% paint **575**

Cash Register, original closure (very small
& minor chip on ledge above drawer) 500

Chicken on Round Base, large chicken,
replaced closure 300

Coach, embossed "Esther Overland Limited," original closure & wheels (chips
around axle openings & couplers 500

Delivery truck, embossed "Bakery,"wheel
flanges 100% (small chip behind bottom
of grill) 1,650

Ear of Corn 110

Elephant, embossed "G.O.P.," original clo-
sure, no paint 200

Fanny Farmer Lighthouse Candy Box 140

Felix the Cat, no closure, left hand has fin-
gers, 25% paint 600

Fire Engine Ladder Truck, traces of paint,
replaced closure 250

Flossie Fisher's Bed, tin frame w/original
glass panel w/partial contents, George
Borgfeldt Co. label attached 3,200

Hot Doggie, blue, original closure 900

Iron, embossed "Flat Iron," original closure,
80% gilding, ... 600

Jack O'Lantern, "Pop Eyed," original clo-
sure & bail, 15% paint..................................... 700

Jackie Coogan, original closure, 40% paint...... 700

Lamp, embossed "Inside Ribbed Base," all
original, base marked "Pat. Apld. For" 130

Lamp, Monkey, original closure, all original
& complete 550

"Lawn Swing," amethyst, original closure,
all original tin 400

Locomotive, embossed "Stough's Patent
115533," no closure 950

Locomotive, embossed "Two Stacker #23,"
original closure.. 300

Luggage, suitcase w/bail handle, original
closure, w/decal of two ladies seated on
bench.. 260

Man on Motorcycle, w/sidecar, original clo-
sure, traces of paint 450

Mounted Policeman, original closure, 50%
paint 2,100

Parlor car, "New York Central" marked
above windows, "Parlor Car" below windows, amethyst coke glass, original clo-
sure (minor chips on coupler)........................ 225

"Pumpkin Head Policeman," original clo-
sure, 85% paint, no bail.................................. 1,900

"Pumpkin Head Witch," w/bail, original
closure, 90% paint... 1,100

"Purse," souvenir, ruby-flashed panel
w/"Morrison, Wis," original closure 625

Rabbit Family, replaced closure, 85% paint...... 750

Rabbit Mother & Daughter, original clo-
sure, no paint 700

**Rabbit with Feet Together, Round Nose
#2,** original closure 675

Radio, embossed "12,'" replaced closure,
no paint 160

Santa bottle 330

Santa Claus by Square Chimney, original
closure, 10% paint... 170

Santa Claus in Banded Coat, replaced clo-
sure, some repaint 160

"Spark Plug," replaced closure, some re-
paint.. 125

Table, original closure, ruby-flashed top
w/"Paw Paw, Mich." (slight roughness
under table top edge) 700

Tank, embossed "World War I,"original clo-
sure, 75% paint.. 190

Truck, embossed "Gasoline," no closure....... 1,700

Washing machine, pressed glass, painted
pink. closure embossed "Little Miss
Washing Machine," Marx Toys 190

Watch, all-glass including painted face, flat
bottom w/strap & fob embossed w/five-
point star, original closure (strap torn) 800

Wild Willie Western Cowboy 700

CANES & WALKING STICKS

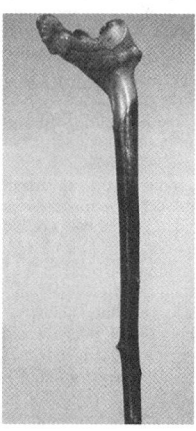

Carved Applewood Cane

Carved applewood cane, figurehead-style
carved handle in the form of a female
nude w/draped waist sash & scroll embellishments, exposed knot at the top of
the bark-covered tapering shaft
w/clipped twigs, varnished natural surface, w/stand, America, ca. 1875,
35 3/4" l. (ILLUS.)..................................... **$1,035**

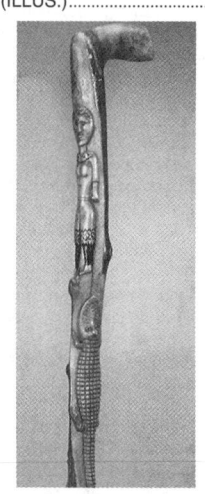

Carved Applewood Figural Cane

Carved applewood figural cane, bark covered tapering shaft w/high relief carvings of a woman, squirrel, alligator, rabbit, hunting dog, frog, pelican, snake & turtle, highlighted w/jeweled & glass eyes, green & black coloring, w/stand, Southern United States, early 20th c., minor paint wear, 37" l. (ILLUS.) **1,150**

Carved Ash Figural Cane

Carved ash figural cane, copper doorknob mounted on tapering shaft carved w/a naked man climbing above two snakes wrapped around the shaft & the initials "FW," brass cuff at tip, w/stand, America, 19th c., 36 1/8" l. (ILLUS.) **431**

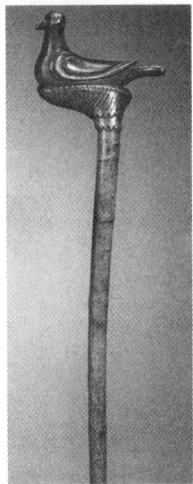

Carved Cane w/Figural Handle

Carved cane w/figural handle, w/carved bird on roost over a tapering shaft, old varnished surface, no stand, attributed to "Schtockschnitzler" Simmons, ca. 1870-1910, 41 3/4" l. (ILLUS.) **2,415**

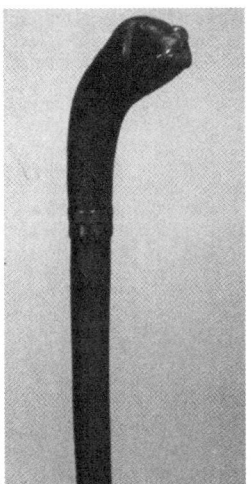

Carved Figural Cane

Carved figural cane, the head of a dog w/bared teeth & spike collar, old varnished surface, no stand, attributed to "Schtockschnitzler" Simmons, ca. 1870-1910, Pennsylvania German, Berks County, Pennsylvania, late 19th - early 20th c., 34" l. (ILLUS.) **546**

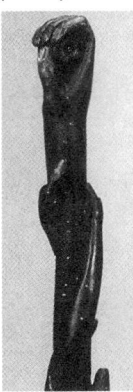

Carved Figural Walking Stick

Carved figural wood cane, a carved hand holding an apple on cane w/snakes, a lizard & a frog climbing the shaft, w/stand, 19th c., imperfections, 32 5/8" l. (ILLUS.) **690**

Carved ivory & ebonized wood cane, carved elephant ivory petite cane of a floral chain & bead design, slender handle 9 1/2" l & 2/3" across top is elaborately & intricately carved w/twisting columns of descending beads & floral roping, ebonized shaft w/1/4" gold-plated collar & 1" horn ferrule, ca. 1890, European, 36" l...... **1,064**

Carved ivory & ebony cane, carved elephant ivory bust depicting finely detailed Dr. Watson, of Sherlock Holmes fame, glass eyes, short beard & moustache, smoking a pipe & wearing a jaunty feathered hat, thick ebony shaft w/1/3" silver collar & 1" brass ferrule, late 19th - early 20th c., England.. **1,964**

Carved ivory, silver & ebonized wood walking stick, the round handle of carved elephant ivory w/a silver child's face on each of the flat sides, one smiling & happy, the other frowning & sad w/an applied silver bee under the chin of sad child, ebonized shaft w/1 1/4" silver collar & 7/8" horn ferrule, ca. 1900, England, 36" l... **896**

Figural Walking Stick

Carved ivory & wood walking stick, the carved elephant ivory handle molded in the shape of the head of Robert Baden-Powell, founder of the Boy Scout movement, depicting Powell wearing his Scouting hat & uniform, coconut wood shaft w/3/4" brass ferrule, ca. 1905, England, 38 1/2" l. (ILLUS.) **1,810**

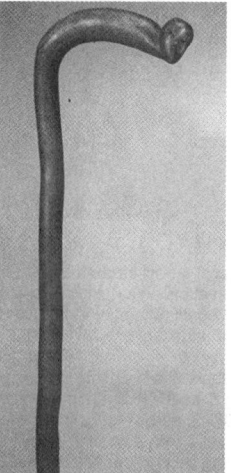

Carved Maple Bentwood Figural Cane

Carved maple bentwood figural cane, handle terminating in the head of a bald man, no stand, probably Iroquois, early to mid-19th c., 33 3/4" l. (ILLUS.) **431**

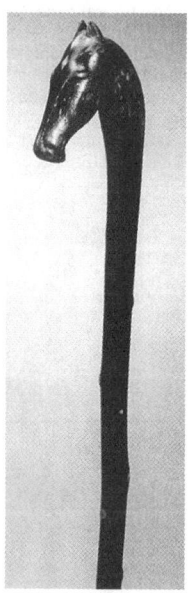

Carved & Painted Buck Thorn Cane

Carved & painted buck thorn cane, w/horse & head top, brown head & black shaft, no stand, America, 19th c., 36 1/8" l. (ILLUS.).. **1,265**

Carved & Painted Burl Figural Cane

Carved & painted burl figural cane, the black-painted knob handle over burl carved w/birds, dog & man's face on shaft, old varnished surface, no stand, American, late 19th - early 20th c., paint wear, 33 1/2" l. (ILLUS.)................................. **345**

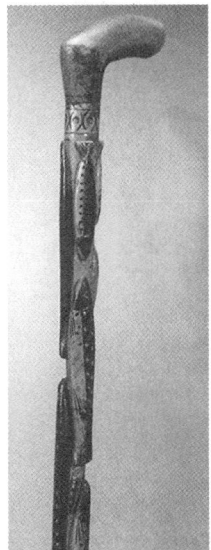

Carved & Painted Figural Cane

Carved & painted figural cane, handle on tapering shaft decorated w/branded band over polychrome trout & bait carved in high relief above chip & foliate carving, w/stand, probably Michigan, dated 1900, very minor wear, 35 3/8" l. (ILLUS.) **1,380**

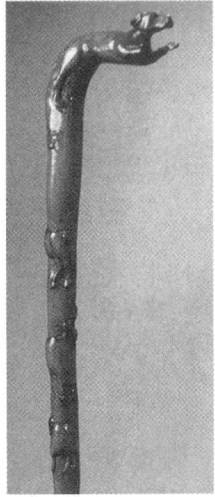

Carved & Painted Figural Wood Cane

Carved & painted figural wood cane, handle in the form of a full-bodied leaping dog on tapering shaft w/carved initials "PSL" over renderings of a horse, bull, ram, pig, mule, goat, dog, rooster, chicken, duck & goose, traces of red paint, varnished, "Bally Carver," no stand, Pennsylvania German, Berks County,

late 19th - early 20th c., dog w/front leg loss, 36 1/2" l. (ILLUS.) **805**

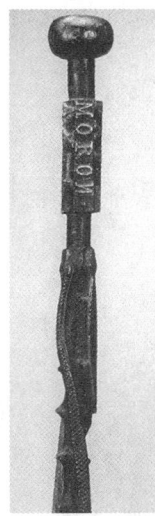

Carved & Painted Logger's Cane

Carved & painted logger's cane, knob handle on twisted spiny shaft w/faceted personalized cuff "To Pat Moronay," & symbolic logging and drinking carvings over beaver, reptile & wrap-around snake carvings in high relief, original black, green, yellow & white surface, New York, 19th c., 34" l. (ILLUS.).............. **3,335**

Carved & Painted Wood Cane

Carved & painted wood cane, fiddles encircling cane shaft, old red & black paint & varnish, w/stand, possibly Arkansas, ca. 1900, loss to top of shaft & handle, 34 3/4" l. (ILLUS.) **1,955**

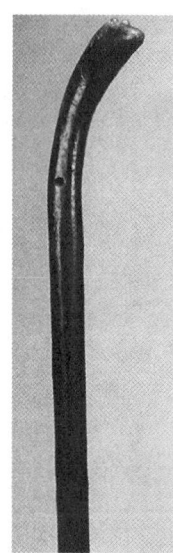

Carved & Painted Wood Snake Head Cane

Carved & Painted Wood Hound Cane

Carved & painted wood hound cane,
spotted dog form handle continuing to tapering shaft, original white, brown & red paint w/ink, inscribed "Rollin Cooper, Wells, VT.," w/stand, 19th c., minor paint wear, cracking, 35 3/4" l. (ILLUS.).................. **546**

Carved & painted wood snake head cane, black painted head w/glass eyes & traces of green paint continuing to shaft drilled for tether & tapering to metal cuff, America, late 19th - early 20th c., 35 1/2" l. (ILLUS.)... **115**

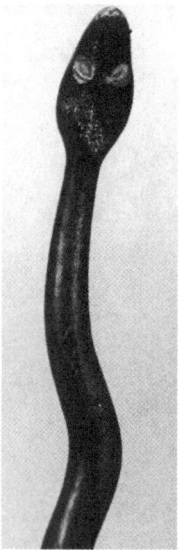

Carved & Painted Wood Walking Stick

Carved & Painted Wood Snake Cane

Carved & painted wood snake cane,
head-shaped handle continuing to tapering full-bodied shaft terminating w/ball tip, original black & red paint surface, w/stand, America, late 19th c., 32" l. (ILLUS.).. **978**

Carved & painted wood walking stick,
carved dog's head knob handle on tapering shaft decorated w/climbing figures above a four-legged creature & a snake all carved in high-relief, carved spiral tip, old green, black & red paint, probably American Indian, Mide Society, Great Lakes, 19th c., no stand, minor paint wear, 32 7/8" l. (ILLUS.).................................. **575**

Carved Head Wooden Walking Stick

Carved & painted wood walking stick,
knob carved in the form of a black woman's head w/kerchief, eyes closed, mouth
smiling, traces of dark paint, above a figure leaning on a pedestal, w/stand, probably New York, 19th c., 35 3/4" l.
(ILLUS.).. **2,300**

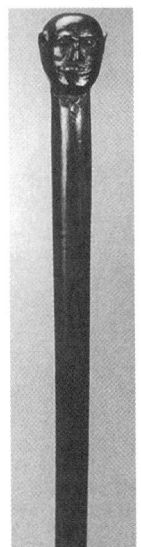

Carved Rosewood Figural Walking Stick

Carved rosewood figural walking stick,
carved head of a black man on cane
w/slim-tapered shaft, w/stand, America,
late 19th - early 20th c., 35 5/8" l.
(ILLUS.).. **1,265**

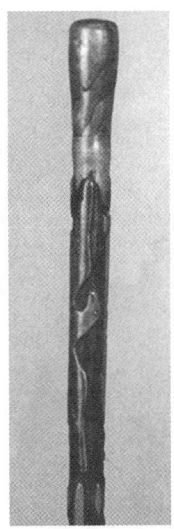

Carved & Stained Patriotic Walking Stick

**Carved & stained patriotic wood walking
stick,** top of knob handle inset w/copper
G.A.R. token, tapering shaft carved
w/various symbols w/scratch & ink detailing, brass tack eyes, original brown
stained surfaces, no stand, attributed to
Charles W. Teale, 1817-95, Bath, New
York, 19th c., minor wear, missing cuff,
34 1/4" l. (ILLUS.)....................................... **2,070**

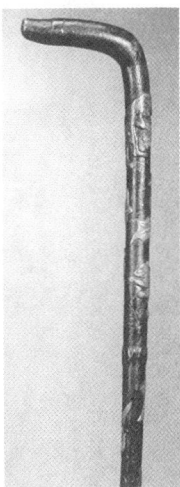

Carved & Stained Wood Cane

Carved & stained wood cane, w/hound
handle, heart, bear, squirrel, eagle &
shield & sheaf of wheat carvings, probably Pennsylvania, ca. 1880, 35 1/4" l.
(ILLUS.) **863**
Carved whale ivory & whalebone cane,
an L-shaped handle w/three baleen
spacers on a whalebone shaft, engraved
at the top "J. M. C.," 19th c., 35 1/2" l. **403**

Carved whalebone & ivory walking stick,
ring-turned octagonal handle & space
above diamond-, spiral- and ring-turned
section continuing to a round shaft, 19th c.,
37" l. (handle loose, warping)........................ **1,783**

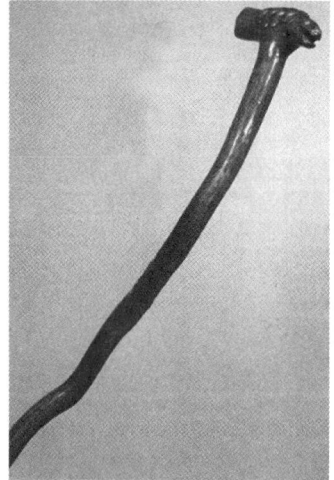

Carved Wood Branch Cane

Carved wood branch cane, the top carved
w/a hand, a dog's head & face, old var-
nish, America, late 19th c., 32" l. (ILLUS.)...... **345**

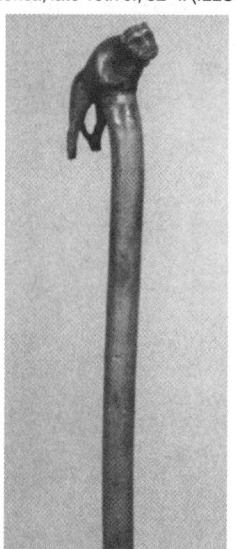

Carved Wood Monkey Cane

Carved wood cane, carved full-bodied
monkey mounted on a knotted tapering
shaft, natural surface, w/stand, America,
19th c., 34 1/8" l. (ILLUS.)................................ **690**

Carved wood cane, twining snakes around
shaft, Adam & Eve heads form finial, dark
patination, w/stand, America, 19th c.,
wood checked from top down, finial
6 3/4" h. (ILLUS. top next column) **805**

Carved Wood Snakes Cane

**Carved wood figural "automation" walk-
ing stick,** the handle carved as a realistic
cat's head w/inlaid glass eyes, pointed
wears & pink-painted nose, a lever behind the neck pushes his bright red
tongue out of his mouth, smooth silver
collar, thick malacca shaft, Germany,
ca. 1890, 36 1/2" l. **1,320**

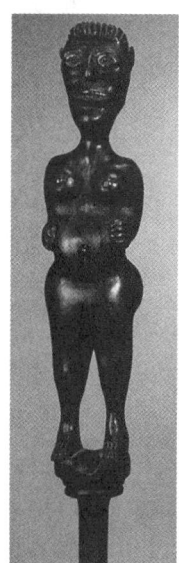

Carved Wood Figural Walking Stick

Carved wood figural Walking Stick, full
figure of a black woman, old dark varnish,
w/stand, Georgia, late 19th - early 20th c.,
chip on right ear, 36" l. (ILLUS.)................... **2,300**

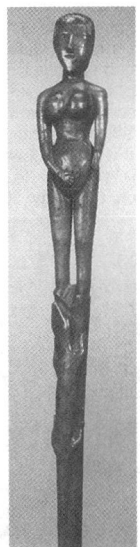

Carved Wood Figural Walking Stick

Carved wood figural walking stick, w/an alligator climbing the shaft towards a nude figure of a woman, old varnished surface, no stand, possibly Michigan, late 19th - early 20th c., 36 5/8" l. (ILLUS.) **1,150**

Carved Wood Dog Walking Stick

Carved wood figural walking stick, carved knob handle in the form of a full-bodied seated male dog, on tapering shaft, old varnished surface, w/stand, Pennsylvania, 19th c., 34 3/4" l. (ILLUS.)...... **920**

Carved wood figural walking stick, egg-shaped finial on cane w/stylized graduated frogs spiraling up the shaft, medium brown varnish, w/stand, America, 19th c., 36 1/4" l. **431**

Carved wood walking stick, decorated w/multiple carved animal heads & reptile bodies w/glass eyes, silver top w/engraved presentation inscription dated 1846, 35" l. (some glass eyes missing) **288**

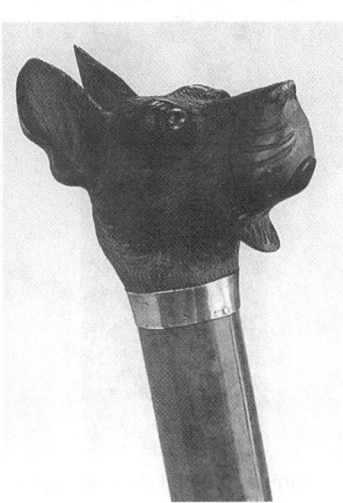

Figural Dog Head Walking Stick

Carved wood walking stick, the handle carved in dark wood in the shape of a realistic dog's head w/large upright ears & inlaid glass eyes, the lower jaw hinged & revealing a red tongue & white teeth, used to hold a glove or scarf, sterling silver collar, thick malacca shaft w/horn ferrule, ca. 1890, 36 1/2" l. (ILLUS.).............. **880**

Cigarette lighter cane, malacca crook & shaft w/a 4" l. decorated & gold-plated hinged compartment w/a small unmarked cartouche near the top, slide catch opens a door to a fold-out gold-plated "Ronson Delight" cigarette lighter, early 20th c., 34 1/2" l................................. **5,500**

Ebony walking stick, wooden shaft w/gold-plated hexagonal top w/foliate decoration & engraved presentation, "Presented to JAs. E. Pinkham by his friends of Weave Room No. 4 on his retiring from the employ of the York Co., Saco, July 1854," Maine, 36 1/2" l.. **173**

Glass cane, the crook handle of ruby glass w/a thin white stripe in a twisted design blending into the squared shaft, twisted again about 5" from end finishing w/tapered point, ca. 1890, America, 40" l............ **448**

Mother-of-pearl, silver & hardwood cane, the large square "L" handle of sterling silver, classic Art Deco design of elaborate scrolling chased w/mythical bird on top & decorated w/six large open panels of mother-of-pearl, marked "sterling" & initialed "E.T.T.," figured hardwood, perhaps chestnut, shaft carved to simulate bamboo, 1 1/2" smooth band marked "sterling" 7 1/2" down the shaft, 1 1/2" white metal & iron ferrule, ca. 1920, America, 35" l. **728**

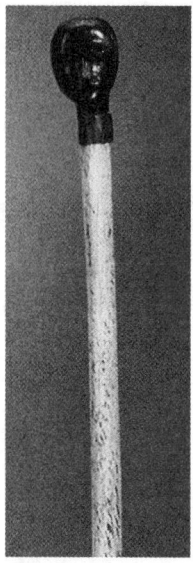

Narwhal & Wood Walking Stick

Narwhal & carved wood figural walking stick, knob handle of carved & ebonized wood in the form of a woman's head joined by copper riveted brass cuff to a tapering narwhal bone shaft, w/stand, New England, ca. 1820-40, 34 3/8" l. (ILLUS.).. **2,185**

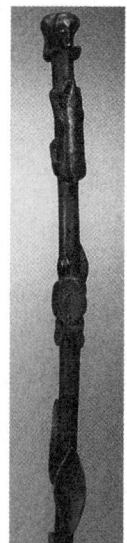

Polychrome Carved Figural Cane

Polychrome carved figural cane, w/ram's head handle over bear, turtle, snake, wildcat & stylized leafage, old brown, red-brown & black paint, no stand, Sioux Nation, ca. 1880, wear, imperfections, 36 7/8" l. (ILLUS.).. **3,450**

Porcelain & ebonized wood walking stick, the porcelain handle molded in the shape of a lady's head wearing a large brim hat w/turned-up sides & covered w/a floral scarf, underside of hat is light green w/top & scarf decorated w/flowers in shades of red, blue, orange & light green, ebonized wood shaft w/thin gold-plated collar & 1" horn ferrule, ca. 1850, perhaps Meissen, Germany, 36" l. **504**

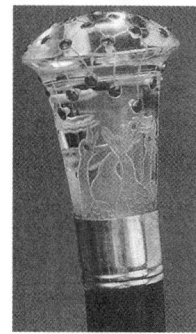

Etched & Jeweled Rock Crystal Walking Stick

Rock crystal & ebonized wood walking stick, the tapering cylindrical rock crystal handle w/a low domed top decorated w/acid etching & inlaid w/40 facted rubies encased in gold rims, ten long-necked geese w/very tiny round emerald eyes, carved & acid-etched at base, silver collar on ebonized shaft w/1" horn ferrule, ca. 1900, perhaps French, 34 1/2" l. (ILLUS.).. **7,560**

Silver Overlay Walking Stick

Rock crystal, silver overlay & ebonized wood walking stick, tapering cylindrical handle of clear rock crystal overlaid w/finely crafted silver festoons of ribbons, flowers & vines, slight tint of gilt remaining, heavy ebonized hardwood shaft w/7/8" horn ferrule, tiny French hallmarks, ca. 1900, French, 34" l. (ILLUS.) **647**

Wooden cane, the handle carved w/a double head of a man & monkey, well-carved features w/inlaid eyes, man w/beard & collar, plain stick shaft, good patina, 38 1/4" l. **660**

CANS & CONTAINERS

The collecting of tin containers has become quite popular within the past several years. Air-tight tins were first produced by hand to keep food fresh and, after the invention of the tin-printing machine in the 1870s, containers were manufactured in a wide variety of shapes and sizes with colorful designs. Also see: ADVERTISING, AUTOMOTIVE COLLECTIBLES, COCA-COLA COLLECTIBLES and TOBACCIANA and Antique Trade Advertising Price Guide.

Black powder shells, Winchester Repeater two-piece box, marked "15 Winchester 24 ga. Repeater Grade Paper Shot Shells Loaded with Black Powder," label dated 1903, 2 1/2 x 3 1/2 x 3 1/2".................. **275**

Kellogg's Rice Krispies Box

Colgate's Baby Talc Tin

Baby powder, Colgate's tin w/screw top, ivory w/gold top, center oval w/image of baby on both sides, marked "Colgate's Baby Talc," minor surface scratches & small ding, 1 1/4 x 2 1/4 x 6" (ILLUS.) **$110**

Cereal, Kellogg's Rice Krispies cardboard box, front depicts outdoor scene w/young girl and her toys & dolls lined up behind her w/"Ladybug - Ladybug" marked in the upper left corner, "Rice Krispies" on the top & "Kellogg's Rice Krispies"at the bottom, dated 1940, 2 1/2 x 5 x 7" (ILLUS.) **149**

Parrot and Monkey Baking Powder Tin

Baking powder, Parrot and Monkey tin w/paper label in red w/colored scene of a monkey & a parrot on tree branches & marked in white & black letters "Parrot and Monkey Baking Powder" by the "Sea Gull" Specialty Co., Baltimore & New Orleans, full container, unopened, minor paper tears, 2 1/2 x 5" (ILLUS.) **55**

Possum Cigar Tin

Cigars, Possum Cigar tin, red w/white possum depicted & marked "Possum - Am Good and Sweet," same image on reverse, minor dings & scratches, 5 x 5" (ILLUS.) **204**

Cigars, War Eagle Cigar tin, red w/image of eagle in flight clutching American shield on both sides & marked in white letters "War Eagle - Cigars - 2 for 5¢," 5 x 5" **88**

Astor House Coffee Tin

Coffee, Astor House Coffee 1 lb. tin w/screw top, black & white w/scene of large building, & marked "Astor House Brand - Coffee," original lustre, 4 x 6 1/4" (ILLUS.).. **187**

Coffee, Beech Nut Coffee key wind sample tin by American Can, red w/black & white lettering, 2 1/2 x 3 1/4", 4 oz............................. **55**

Blanke's "Happy Thought Coffee" Tin

Coffee, Blanke's "Happy Thought Coffee" tin, figural trunk form, tan w/black lettering, minor scrapes, 4 1/2 x 4 1/2 x 9" (ILLUS.).. **77**

Coffee, Bueno Coffee 1 lb. tin w/slip lid, black & silver w/gold top, marked "Bueno Coffee - Walker-Smith Co., Brownwood Texas," litho by LaCrosse Can, Wisconsin, 4 x 5 1/4" **231**

Coffee, Dining Room Coffee 1 lb. tin w/screw top, litho by Passaic Metalware, N.J., yellow & black, marked on both sides "Progess Dining Room Coffee - Roasted and Packed by American Food Co., Newark, N.J.," 4 x 6".................... **165**

Coffee, Golden West Coffee 2 lb. keywind tin, red w/black band around base, both sides depict young girl w/neckerchief & Western-type hat, packed by Closset & Devers, Portland, OR., dated 1927, 5 x 7" (ILLUS. top next column) **152**

Golden West Coffee Tin

Coffee, Heart's Delight Coffee 1 lb. tin, blue w/red heart depicted in center w/"Heart's Delight" above & "Coffee - packed by Scoville, Brown & Co., Wellsville, N.Y." below, 4 1/4 x 6" **88**

Loyl Coffee Tin

Coffee, Loyl Coffee 1 lb. tin w/screw top, w/splendid spread-winged eagle & clouds against blue background & marked "Loyl Coffee - Roasted and Packed For (illegible)," litho by Passaic Metal Ware, N.J., same image on reverse, 4 x 6" (ILLUS.) **275**

Coffee, Perfect Coffee 1 lb. tin w/screw top, white w/black cover, red lettering above logo w/"A.H. Perfect & Company" in black letters below, dated 1923, 4 x 6" (minor scrapes)... **77**

Coffee, WGY Coffee 1 lb. tin w/screw top, litho by Continental Can, Passaic, N.J., both sides w/image of table set w/coffeepot & cup & saucer, blue, tan, black & white, 4 x 6" (minor scrapes near bottom) **132**

Cookies, Nabisco "Barnum's Animals" cardboard box w/cloth handle, red & yel-

low w/scene of caged animals,
ca. 1940s, 1 3/4 x 2 1/2 x 5" **44**
Corset, Royales Corsets cardboard box
w/brightly colored tropical water scene
w/seated woman & lion pictured in center, litho by J. Goosens, Bruxelles,
ca. 1870-80, 3 x 3 x 15 3/4" **99**

Hazard Gunpowder Tin

Gunpowder, Hazard "Indian Rifle Gunpowder" round 1/4 lb. tin w/colorful lithograph
of Native American w/headdress carrying
a rifle in wooded scene w/mountain in
background w/"Indian Rifle Gunpowder"
above & "Hazard Powder Com. N.Y." below, back marked "FFFG," CA. 1890,
1 x 2 1/2 x 2 7/8" (ILLUS.)............................... **660**
Jar Rings Roundup Jar Rings box, black
w/yellow lettering & scene of cowboy on
horseback in center w/red border reading
"Roundup Grocery C.," same image on
reverse, full box, 3 x 3 x 1 1/4" (minute
tear on back side).. **132**
Oil, Simoniz Graphite Oil tin w/screw-on
top, red & yellow litho by Continental Can
depicts a witch seated on a large fish,
marked "Penetrating Graphite Oil - Stops
Squeaks - Lubricates Springs - Dissolves
Rust - The Simoniz Company, Chicago,
USA," 2 x 6"... **77**
Oysters, Christy's Oysters 1 gal. tin, blue &
red graphic showing man at ship's wheel
& marked "Christy's Choice Quality Oys-
ters," 6 3/4 x 7".. **77**

Monadnock Peanut Butter Tin

Oysters, Lady Adams Oysters tin w/early
paper litho showing a large oyster on the
front w/"Lady Adams Oysters - packed
expressly for Mebius & Drescher Co.,
Sacramento, Cal." & directions for use on
back, unopened, 2 3/4 x 4 1/4" **88**
Peanut butter, FI-NA-ST Peanut Butter 1 lb.
tin w/bail handle, red w/image of man
wearing white jacket on both sides,
3 1/2 x 3 3/4" (minor scrapes & blemishes) **83**
Peanut butter, Monadnock Peanut Butter 1
lb. tin w/bail handle, litho by Canco, red
w/gold scrolls flanking white ground
w/center oval mountain lake scene &
marked "1 Lb. Net Monadnock Brand
Peanut Butter - Distributed by The Hol-
brook Grocery Co. Keene, N.H.," same
image on reverse, 3 1/2 x 3 3/4" (ILLUS.
bottom previous column)................................ **198**

Bomb-Buster Popcorn Tin

Popcorn, Bomb-Buster tin w/paper label
showing a pan w/popping kernels of
corn, yellow, white & black, 2 1/2 x 5"
(ILLUS.) **66**
Popcorn, Popeye Popcorn tin by American
Can Co., red, white & blue w/image of
Popeye on front & marked "Popeye
Brand White Hulless Pop Corn" & dated
"1949 King Features," 2 x 3 x 4 3/4" **77**
Powder tin, Dupont Schuetzen Smokeless
Powder 1 lb. tin w/paper label, green &
gold, man in suit of armor holding gun de-
picted, 1 1/4 x 4 x 5 3/4" (some discolor-
ation) **67**

Sailor's Brand Salmon Tin

Salmon, Sailor's Brand Alaska Pink Salmon
tin w/paper label, lithograph of sailor
smoking pipe on front, large salmon on

reverse w/"Alaska Packers Assoc., Loring, Alaska," by Mutual Label, San Francisco, California, tear bottom of sailor's shoulder, minor tears, 3 x 4 1/2" (ILLUS.)...... **231**

Fairbank's "Gold Dust" Tin

Scouring powder, Fairbank's "Gold Dust" tin, red, white & black, depicts two small black children & marked "Fairbank's Gold Dust Scouring Cleanser" & "Free Sample," dated 1931, 2 x 2 3/4" (ILLUS.)............. **110**

Selby Air Rifle Shot Container

Shot powder, Selby Air Rifle Shot cardboard tube w/brass cap, twist top to dispense, 3/4 x 3" (ILLUS.)............................. **165**

Sears "Sport Loads" Shotgun Shells Box

Shotgun shells, Sears "Sport Loads" two-piece box w/image of flying goose marked "25 Sport Loads 12 ga. Xtra-Range Shotgun Shells Smokeless Powder," 2 1/2 x 4 x 4" (ILLUS.) **198**

Spice, Amocat Spice tin, red, both sides w/center oval scene of a house near water, hills in background, marked "Net Weight - 2 Ounces - Amocat Brand - Ginger," West Coast Grocery, Tacoma, Washington, litho by American Can Co., 1 x 2 x 3".. **132**

Spice, Golden Drip, 2 ozs., Empire Distributing Co., tin litho, gold w/"Golden Drip" in black.. **30-60**

Spice, Golden Key, 4 ozs., round, yellow, skeleton key & "Golden Key" in white........ **25-55**

Spice, Grand Prize, 2 ozs., Empire Distributing Company, tin litho, ivory w/four bands of dark blue w/"Grand Prize" on one blue band, red prize ribbon & "spices" written in red.......................... **25-55**

Spice, H & H, 2 ozs., The Harnit & Hewitt Co., green rectangular label w/Art Deco marking, company name on banner at bottom **30-60**

Spice, H & K, 1 1/2 ozs., Hanley & Kinsella Coffee & Spice Co., tin top & bottom, cardboard body, wrap-around paper label, red w/four ivory bands, man wearing turban holding tray w/coffee pot, sugar bowl & cup in blue circle **30-65**

Hazel Spice Tin

Spice, Hazel, 2 ozs., Geo. Rasmussen Co., tin top & bottom, cardboard body, wrap-around paper label (ILLUS.) **75-125**

Spice, Hoosier Poet, 1 1/2 ozs., M. O'Connor & Co., tin top & bottom, cardboard body, paste-on paper label, distinguish gentleman w/wire rimmed glasses, green fields, trees & dirt road **30-60**

Spice, Hostess, 2 1/2 ozs., Paul D. Newton & Co., Inc., red, four ladies seated at table w/waiter standing by in oval at center of tin... **95-225**

Spice, Hub City, 1 1/2 ozs., Hub City Jobbing Co., tin litho, black & red w/outline of state of Wisconsin in gold, red circle in center of state w/"Hub City" **30-60**

Spice, Iris, 1 1/4 ozs., Smart & Final Iris Co., tin litho, black & white w/purple iris on green stem **10-30**

Spice, K-W-G, 2 ozs., Kansas Wholesale Grocery Co., light yellow & gold w/green wreath & light blue ribbon, "K-W-G" in red lettering across wreath, tin litho **30-65**

King Crop Spice Tin

Spice, King Crop, 2 ozs., Lawndale Wholesale Grocery Co., tin litho (ILLUS.)......... **125-225**

Spice, KO-WE-BA, 1 oz., Kothe-Wells & Bauer Co., tin top & bottom, cardboard body, wrap-around paper label, white w/two men leading camels, red diamond shape at top w/"KO-WE-BA" & butterfly in it...................... **20-45**

Spice, L-C-B, 1 1/2 ozs., Lyle C. Brown Supply Co., white w/"L-C-B" in red & gold band at top & bottom, head of bulldog in blue circle in center of tin, other lettering is black... **15-35**

Spice, Leadway, 2 ozs., Leadway Foods, ivory & red w/dark blue arrow pointed down w/band major in full dress, "Leadway" in black letters w/red arrow through letters on ivory stripe.................................... **35-65**

Little Boy Blue Spice Tin

Spice, Little Boy Blue, 1 1/2 ozs., Lansing Wholesale Grocery Co., tin litho (ILLUS.).. **45-70**

Spice, Maison Royal, 1 oz., Food Trading Corp. of America, tin litho, white & red w/bridge spanning river w/outline of city behind **10-45**

Spice, McCannon's, 3 1/4 ozs., McConnon & Co., yellow, green & black w/black person dressed in white wearing red turban leading pack camel, two palm trees & red sun w/sand under foot, all on yellow background, tin top & bottom, cardboard body, wrap-around paper label **25-55**

McCormick Spice Tin

Spice, McCormick, 7/8 oz., McCormick & Co., Inc., tin litho (ILLUS.).......................... **15-45**

Spice, Millar, 2 ozs., E.B. Millar & Co., tin top & bottom, cardboard body, wrap-around paper label, white w/three red flowers, green stems & leaves **25-50**

Spice, Mohican, 2 ozs., The Mohican Company, tin litho, red & black, Indian in full head dress within white circle trimmed in light blue & red in center of tin **100-150**

Spice, Monarch, 1 1/2 ozs., Reid, Murdoch & Co., ivory background w/lion head in center, lettering in black **45-80**

Spice, National, 1 1/2 ozs., Geo. Rasmussen Co., round w/capitol building in center & American flag to right, "National" is red, white & blue... **55-100**

Spice, Old Judge, 4 ozs., David G. Evans Coffee Co., background colors are red & yellow, brown & yellow owl sitting on green branch in blue circle in center of tin, tin top & bottom, cardboard body, wrap-around paper label **20-45**

Spice, Old Manor, 2 ozs., Coffee Industries, Inc., red w/manor house in white & green trees on yellow background in center of tin, white lettering, tin litho **25-55**

Pilot Spice Tin

Spice, Pilot, 1 1/2 ozs., General Grocer Co. (ILLUS.) **50-100**

Spice, Pine Hills, 1 oz., Schultz Brothers Co., orange hill w/green pine trees & grass at top w/light yellow sky, black lettering, tin top & bottom, cardboard body, wrap-around paper label **25-50**

Spice, Radio, 1 1/2 ozs., McKnight-Keaton Grocery Co., yellow w/black band & "Radio" in white, white band at bottom w/company name in red 25-55

Spice, Red Label, 4 ozs., S.S. Pierce Co., red w/eagle on top of white bordered shield, lion on each side, tin litho 30-65

Spice, Red Plume, 1 1/2 ozs., The C. Callahan Co., red tin w/green paste on paper label, w/red plume & black lettering 15-35

Spice, Red Ribbon, 1 1/2 ozs., J.M. Steiner, Inc. tin litho, white w/red ribbon tied in bow in center of tin, "Red Ribbon" in red, other lettering is light blue 25-55

Royal Crown Spice Tin

Spice, Royal Crown, 2 ozs., Albert Paper & Products Co., tin top & bottom, cardboard body, wrap-around paper label (ILLUS.)...................... 45-95

Spice, Silver Sea, 1 1/2 ozs., The Koenig Coffee Co., dark blue & yellow w/sailing ship in full sails on choppy sea in circle at center of tin, tin litho.................................... 25-55

Spice, Stickney & Poor's, 2 ozs., tin litho, yellow w/sailing ship in full sails riding on blue sea 25-55

Spice, Stuart's Handy, 2 ozs., Stuart Products, Inc., tin litho 60-90

Spice, Sunny Rose, 3 ozs., Sunny Rose Stores, red lettering, pure spices in large blue circle & red band at bottom w/company name, tin litho.................................... 25-55

Spice, Telmo, 1 1/2 ozs., Franklin MacVeagh & Co., white, "Telmo" in white lettering on red band across tan circle, tin top & bottom, cardboard body, wrap-around paper label 15-35

Spice, Time O'Day, 2 ozs., Jordan Stevens Co., clock w/Roman numerals in center of tin, green band at top w/"Time O'Day" in ivory lettering, bottom of tin is ivory w/red & black lettering, tin litho 30-65

Spice, Triangle Club, 1/4 lb., Montgomery Ward & Co., green & white striped background w/red triangle, white lettering across triangle, tin top & bottom, cardboard body, wrap-around paper label 35-65

Spice, Trumpet, 2 ozs., H.P. Coffee Co., red, gold trumpet w/blue cord attached, tin top & bottom, cardboard body, wrap-around paper label 25-55

Uncle William Spice Tin

Spice, Uncle William, 1 1/2 ozs., Marshall Canning Co., tin top & bottom, cardboard body, wrap-around paper label (ILLUS.) 100-150

University Spice Tin

Spice, University, 1 oz., Eisner Grocery Company, tin litho (ILLUS.) 35-65

Spice, Van Roy, 3 1/2 ozs., The Van Roy Coffee Co., red & black, half sun w/rays in red background, white lettering in black background, tin top & bottom, cardboard body, wrap-around paper label........ 45-75

Spice, Wards, 3 3/4 ozs., The Ward Co., round, tin litho, palm trees & two sailboats on calm sea, green mountain & white clouds in background 15-35

White Villa Spice Tin

Spice, White Villa, 1 oz., White Villa Grocers, Inc., tin litho (ILLUS.) 25-50

"Baby Mine" Talcum Powder

Talcum powder, "Baby Mine" Talcum tin by American Product, Cincinnati, blue w/scene of small baby seated & playing w/toys, marked "Baby Mine Nursey Powder," 1 x 2 x 5" (ILLUS.)..................................... **385**

Violet Talcum Powder Tin

Talcum powder, Violet Talcum Powder tin, black & gold w/portrait of lady w/upswept hair & markedPerfumed Talcum Powder - Violet," top w/same portrait & marked "Violet Talcum Powder," litho by American Stopper Co., Brooklyn, N.Y., 2 x 6" (ILLUS.)... **160**

Talcum powder, Ward's Talcum Powder tin by Bullock Ward Co., Chicago, Illinois, pictures baby on front, 1 1/2 x 2 1/2 x 4" (some scratches)... **154**

Tobacco, Himyar Tobacco Tin, scene of man on white horse & marked "Himyar Cigarette Tobacco," intact w/cigarette papers under tax stamp, same image on reverse, 5 1/4 x 6 1/2", 14 oz. **121**

J.J. Bagley Chewing Tobacco Tin

Tobacco, J.J. Bagley & Co. Chewing Tobacco "Fast Mail" tin w/paper label showing an early train engine (ILLUS.).............. **2,420**

Niggerhair Smoking Tobacco Tin

Tobacco, Niggerhair Smoking Tobacco tin, gold & black w/bail handle, pictures African American w/ear & nose rings on both sides, by Leiderdoft Co., Milwaukee, The American Tobacco Co. Successor, 5 1/2 x 6 1/2" (ILLUS.)..................................... **231**

CAROUSEL FIGURES

The ever popular amusement park merry-go-round or carousel has ancient antecedents but evolved into its most colorful and complex form in the decades from 1880 to 1930. In America a number of pioneering firms, begun by men such as Gustav Dentzel, Charles Looff and Allan Herschell, produced these wonderful rides with beautifully hand-carved animals, the horse being the most popular. Some of the noted carvers included M. C. Illusions, Charles Carmel, Solomon Stein and Harry Goldstein.

Today many of the grand old carousels are gone and remaining ones are often broken up and the animals sold separately as collectors search for choice examples. A fine reference to this field is Painted Ponies, American Carousel Art, *by William Mannas, Peggy Shank and Marianne Stevens (Zon International Publishing Company, Millwood, New York, 1986).*

Looff Carousel Goat

Goat, running position, carved wood, raised front legs, head down, deeply carved fur, simple trappings decorated w/three wood medallions to the front of strap, finished in black & white w/maroon straps, outside row, ca. 1885, Looff, American, 60" l. (ILLUS.).. **$7,475**

Charles Looff Carousel Horse

Horse, outside row jumper, carved w/an open jaw, raised forelegs, eagle-carved saddle & bridle inset w/glass jewels, long horse hair tail, good paint, Charles I.D. Looff, Brooklyn, New York, late 19th c., 56" l., 56" h. (ILLUS.)................................... **7,200**

Horse, outside row prancer, carved & painted, w/a flowing mane & double eagle-back saddle, white, green, yellow & grey over earlier pink paint, areas of separation at seams, Gustav Dentzel, Pennsylvania, ca. 1900-10, 57" l., 58" h. (ILLUS. top next column) **10,350**

Gustav Dentzel Carousel Horse

Horse, probably second row figure, cantle carving behind the saddle & flowing mane, painted in grey & pink over old pale blue paint, by Charles Looff, early 20th c., 65" l., 48" h. (areas of separation at seams).. **3,738**

Dentzel Carousel Horse

Horse, prancing position, carved wood, outside row stander, full mane, tucked head, ribbons & tassles decorating the saddle blanket, twin eagle heads at saddle cantle, ca. 1900, Dentzel, American, 59" l. (ILLUS.) **13,800**

Horse, galloping position, carved & painted wood figure in racing pose w/head lunging forward, forelegs up & hind legs back, detailed windswept mane & cropped tail, decorative jeweled bridle & saddle painted in shades of green, yellow & red, mounted on steel bar w/wooden base, horseshoes stamped "C.W. Parker, Leavenworth, Kansas, number 37," ca. 1917, 69" l., 37" h. (ILLUS. top next page) **8,050**

Galloping Carousel Horse

CARPET BALLS

Glazed china spheres, about 3 1/2" in diameter, are commonly called "carpet balls" by collectors who seek them. Originally made for a popular 19th century game called "bowls," these balls were rolled at a smaller ball called a "jack." Because the game could be played indoors on the carpet or taken out to the lawn, the ceramic balls were fired two or more times after the design was applied to ensure their durability.

Three Decorative Carpet Balls

Black, bluish green & white, a bold plaid
   design w/black stripes & bluish green
   bands, wear, 3" d. (ILLUS. left) **$121**
Blue & white, an overall design of small
   free-hand concentric circles, 3 1/8" d.
   (minor wear) **176**
Blue & white, overall star-like designs, 3" d. **143**
Red & black, light swirled red background
   decorated w/pairs of intersecting black
   pinstripes, 2 1/2" d. **99**
Red & white, overall bold star design, 3" d.
   (ILLUS. center) **242**
Red & white, overall star-like designs, 3" d.
   (minor wear) **99**
Yellow & white, overall crossed thin yellow
   stripes on white, minor wear, 3" d.
   (ILLUS. right) **198**

CASINO CHIPS

The ranks of casino chip collectors have grown dramatically over the last few years. With the proliferation of riverboat and Indian gaming throughout the country, more and more people are being drawn to the fascination of collecting these miniature works of art. Casino chips come in many varieties. They are best described by denomination, color, mold design and manufacturer.

Atlantic City Casinos

Boardwalk Regency $100 Chip

Boardwalk Regency, Atlantic City, New
   Jersey, $100, black, house mold, two
   pink/red/blue edge inserts (ILLUS.) **$800**

Golden Nugget $25 Chip

Golden Nugget, Atlantic City, New Jersey,
   $25, green, house mold, eight yellow
   edge inserts (ILLUS.) **550**

Playboy Casino Chips

Playboy Casino, Atlantic City, New Jersey,
   $2.50, pink, Bud Jones mold, no edge in-
   serts, olive bunnies (ILLUS.) **1,500-1,600**

Resorts International $5 Chip

Resorts International, Atlantic City, New Jersey, $5, red, hat & cane mold, three blue/peach/white edge inserts, Baccarat (ILLUS.)... **3,500-4,000**

The Brighton $25 Chip

The Brighton, Atlantic City, New Jersey, $25, green, house mold, six white edge inserts (ILLUS.).................................. **1,500-1,700**

European Casinos

5000 Casino Lago Maggiore Chip

5000 Casino Lago Maggiore, Italy, 80 x 50mm., ca. pre-World War II (ILLUS.).. **200**

Casino Palais de la Mederterranee Chip

Casino Palais de la Mederterranee, Nice, France, 62 x 44mm., ca. 1950s (ILLUS.) **150**

Curzon House Club Chip

Curzon House Club, London, England, 125 x 90mm., ca. 1970s (ILLUS.).................. **250**

Kursaal Oostende Chip

Kursaal Oostende, Belgium, 140 x 95mm., ca. 1980s (ILLUS.).................. **250**

Illegal Clubs

B&B Club Chip

B&B Club, Hot Springs, Arkansas, no denomination, black, arodie mold, three white edge inserts (ILLUS.) **30**

Belvedere Club Association $1 Chip

Belvedere Club Association, Hot Springs, Arkansas, $1, pink, T mold, no edge inserts (ILLUS.)... **15**

Benny's Restaurant Chip

Benny's Restaurant, Lake Charles, Louisiana, no denomination, orange, hub mold, no edge inserts (ILLUS.) **10**

Choctaw Club of Louisiana Chip

Choctaw Club of Louisiana, New Orleans, Louisiana, no denomination, red, crest & seal mold, no edge inserts (ILLUS.)............... **150**

Club Greyhound Chip

Club Greyhound, Jeffersonville, Indiana, no denomination, black, hub mold, no edge inserts (ILLUS.)....................................... **40**

Floridian Casino $50 Chip

Floridian Casino, Miami, Florida, $50, blue, crest & seal mold, no edge inserts (ILLUS.).. **200**

Indiana Club Chip

Indiana Club, Jeffersonville, Indiana, no denomination, black, T mold, no edge inserts (ILLUS.)...................................... **10**

Kentucky Club Chip

Kentucky Club, Jeffersonville, Indiana, no denomination, yellow, small key mold, no edge inserts (ILLUS.).. **250**

Playtorium Club $5 Chip

Playtorium Club, Newport, Kentucky, $5, yellow, small key mold, three green edge inserts (ILLUS.)... **35**

Roman Pools Casino $25 Chip

Roman Pools Casino, Miami, Florida, $25, green, hub mold, no edge inserts (ILLUS.) **20**

The Vapors $5 Chip

The Vapors, Hot Springs, Arkansas, $5, green, diamond mold, three blue edge inserts (ILLUS.).. **15**

Indian Casinos

Apache Nugget Casino $1 Chip

Apache Nugget Casino, Dulce, New Mexico, $1, white, Langworthy mold, green edge inserts (ILLUS.)................................... **15-20**

Big Bucks Casino $1 Chip

Big Bucks Casino, Cloquet, New Mexico, $1, white, Langworthy mold, three black edge inserts (ILLUS.).................................. **20-30**

Casino Sandia, Albuquerque, New Mexico, $1, gray, dash A mold, no edge inserts....... **5-10**

Cocapah Casino $1 Chip

Cocapah Casino, Yuma, Arizona, $1, blue, hat & cane mold, no edge inserts (ILLUS.)... **25-35**

Desert Diamond Casino $5 Chip

Desert Diamond Casino, Tucson, Arizona, $5, red, Chipco mold, dark center variety (ILLUS.) **50-75**

Harrah's Casino $5 Chip

Harrah's Casino, Skagit Valley, Washington, $5, red, reverse hat & cane mold, four blue/pink/gray edge inserts, Grand Opening (ILLUS.) **15-20**

Indian Head Gaming Center $1 Chip

Indian Head Gaming Center, Warm Springs, Oregon, $1, blue, reverse hat & cane mold, two green & two pink edge inserts (ILLUS.)... **5-10**

Kings Club $5 Chip

Kings Club, Brimley, Michigan, $5, red, Langworthy mold, three white edge inserts (ILLUS.)... **20-25**

Lummi Casino $5 Chip

Lummi Casino, Bellingham, Washington, $5, purple, Chipco mold, 2nd Anniversary (ILLUS.) **25-35**

Mill Bay Casino $2.50 Chip

Mill Bay Casino, Manson, Washington, $2.50, pink, reverse hat & cane mold, two blue - green edge inserts (ILLUS.) **25-50**

Muckleshoot Indian Casino $20 Chip

Muckleshoot Indian Casino, Auburn, Washington, $20, yellow, reverse hat & cane mold, three blue & three purple edge inserts (ILLUS.)................................. **30-50**

Ohkay Casino $1 Chip

Ohkay Casino, San Juan Pueblo, New Mexico, $1, blue, Langworthy mold, three white edge inserts (ILLUS.) **5-10**

Oneida Casino $25 Chip

Oneida Casino, Green Bay, Wisconsin, $25, green, Bud Jones mold, four split white edge inserts (ILLUS.) **50-75**

Regency Resort Casino, Mole Lake, Wisconsin, $5, red, clover mold, no edge inserts... **15-20**

San Felipe Casino $2 Chip

San Felipe Casino, San Felipe, New Mexico, $2, pink, Chipco mold (ILLUS.) **75-100**

Seven Cedars Casino Chip

Seven Cedars Casino, Sequim, Washington, no denomination, white, reverse hat & cane mold, 1995 Grand Opening souvenir (ILLUS.).. **10-15**

The Mill Casino, Coos Bay, Oregon, $1, white, Chipco mold... **5-10**

Nevada Casinos

Del Webb's Primadonna $5 Chip

Del Webb's Primadonna, Reno, Nevada, $5, red, hat & cane mold, three pink/gray edge inserts (ILLUS.)............................... **600-800**

Stardust Casino $100 Chip

Stardust Casino, Las Vegas, Nevada, $100, "no cash value", purple, house mold, three blue edge inserts (ILLUS.) **500**

Tropicana Chip

Tropicana, Las Vegas, Nevada, no cash value, pink/gray, house mold, no edge inserts (ILLUS.)... **50-75**

Ultra New Town Tavern $1 Chip

Ultra New Town Tavern, Las Vegas, Nevada, $1, blue, hat & cane mold, three purple/white edge inserts (ILLUS.)....................... **15**

Riverboats

Bayou Caddy's Jubilee $5 Chip

Bayou Caddy's Jubilee, Lakeshore, Mississippi, $5, red, Chipco mold, Grand Opening commemorative (ILLUS.)............. **15-20**

Boomtown Belle Casino $100 Chip

Boomtown Belle Casino, Harvey, Louisiana, $100, black, reverse hat & cane mold, four yellow & four white edge inserts, original issue (ILLUS.) **100-125**

Casino Magic $25 Chip

Casino Magic, Bay St. Louis, Mississippi, $25, green, Chipco mold, 1st bet chip (ILLUS.) **30-40**

Casino Queen .50 Chip

Casino Queen, E. St. Louis, Illinois, .50, mustard colored, house mold w/four green edge inserts (ILLUS.) **10-15**

Circus Circus

Circus Circus, Robinsonville, Mississippi, $5, red, Bud Jones mold, four blue edge inserts (ILLUS.).. **10-15**

Copa Casino, Gulfport, Mississippi, no cash value, purple, unicorn mold, tournament chip **10-20**

Diamond Jo Casino .25 Chip

Diamond Jo Casino, Dubuque, Iowa, .25, blue, hat & cane mold, no edge inserts (ILLUS.).. **5-10**

Diamond Lady Casino $25 Chip

Diamond Lady Casino, Bettendorf, Iowa, $25, green, hat & cane mold, six green edge inserts (ILLUS.)................................ **75-125**
Dubuque Casino Belle, Dubuque, Iowa, $5, multicolored, Chipco mold, New Years 1992 commemorative **35-45**
Emerald Lady, Burlington, Iowa, $2.50, pink, hat & cane mold, two teal edge inserts.. **40-60**

Emerald Queen $5 Chip

Emerald Queen, Tacoma, Washington, $5, red, reverse hat & cane mold, two purple & two blue edge inserts, Grand Opening (ILLUS.).. **5-10**

Gold Shore Casino Chip

Gold Shore Casino, Biloxi, Mississippi, roulette, any color, hat & cane mold (ILLUS.) **8-12**

Grand Victoria $5 Chip

Grand Victoria, Rising Sun, Indiana, $5, red, reverse hat & cane mold, two green & two peach edge inserts (ILLUS.) **50-75**

Harrah's $5 Chip

Harrah's, Kansas City, Missouri, $5, red, reverse hat & cane mold, three brown & three lavender edge inserts, Grand Opening (ILLUS.) **20-30**

Harrah's $1 Token

Harrah's, Shreveport, Louisiana, $1, color stickered token (ILLUS.) **20-30**

Harrah's Colored Token

Harrah's, Tunica, Mississippi, $1, yellow, colored token (ILLUS.) **15-25**

Hollywood Casino, Aurora, Illinois, $1, white, Bud Jones mold, four split teal edge inserts.. 90-110

Isle of Capri "1995" Chip

Isle of Capri, Vicksburg, Mississippi, $2.50, pink, Chipco mold, "1995" (ILLUS.).............. 5-10
Isle of Capri Casino, Biloxi, Mississippi, $100, black, hat & cane mold, six gold & six purple edge inserts 125-150

Lady Luck $1 Chip

Lady Luck, Bettendorf, Iowa, $1, white, Chipco mold (ILLUS.) 5-10
Lady Luck, Biloxi, Mississippi, .25, colored tokens... 4-8

Lighthouse Point $100 Chip

Lighthouse Point, Greenville, Mississippi, $100, black, reverse hat & cane mold, two white & two gray edge inserts (ILLUS.)... 100-125
Mississippi Belle II, Clinton, Iowa, .25, brown, hat & cane mold, no edge inserts.... 5-10
Par-A-Dice Casino, East Peoria, Illinois, $2.50, pink, hat & cane mold, three brown/white edge inserts 8-12
President Casino, Tunica, Mississippi, $25, green, reverse hat & cane mold, four blue/white edge inserts.................... 100-150

River City Crescent City Queen $2.50 Chip

River City Crescent City Queen, New Orleans, Louisiana, $2.50, peach, reverse hat & cane mold, two green edge inserts, uncancelled (ILLUS.) 15-20

Sam's Town $25 Chip

Sam's Town, Kansas City, Missouri, $25, green, reverse hat & cane mold, four orange/blue/orange edge inserts (ILLUS.) ... 50-75

Showboat Casino $100 Chip

Showboat Casino, East Chicago, Indiana, $100, black, reverse hat & cane mold, three gray/white/red edge inserts (ILLUS.) 125-150

Silver Eagle .50 Chip

Silver Eagle, East Dubuque, Illinois, .50, yellow, Bud Jones mold, w/four blue edge inserts (ILLUS.)..................................... 5-10

Silver Eagle Roulette Chip

Silver Eagle, East Dubuque, Illinois, roulette, any color, Bud Jones mold, 12 white edge inserts (ILLUS.) **10-20**

Sioux City Sue $25 Chip

Sioux City Sue, Sioux City, Iowa, $25, green, Bud Jones mold, four orange edge inserts (ILLUS.)................................ **75-100**
Splash Casino, Tunica, Mississippi, $1, white, hat & cane mold, two blue edge inserts... **20-25**

Star Casino $25 Chip

Star Casino, New Orleans, Louisiana, $25, green, hat & cane mold, four yellow & four purple edge inserts (ILLUS.) **100-125**

Treasure Bay .25 Chip

Treasure Bay, Tunica, Mississippi, .25, yellow, Bud Jones mold, no edge inserts (ILLUS.).. **200**

CASTORS & CASTOR SETS

Castor bottles were made to hold condiments for table use. Some were produced in sets of several bottles housed in silver plated frames. The word also is sometimes spelled "Caster."

Individual Breakfast Caddy Set & Castor Set

Breakfast caddy, footed oval silver plate base w/overhead handle, bird finial, individual shaker w/original top, salt, egg cup & openwork silver plate napkin ring, dated 1892, Aurora, the set, 7 1/2" h. (ILLUS. left) .. **$225**
Castor set, a pedestal-based silver plate frame holding seven clear bottles w/cut panels, one w/engraving, the frame w/a round scalloped base, the upper support ring w/convex circles & flared compartments w/drops beneath, late 19th c. (one bottle mismatched, stoppers missing, minor chips)... **259**
Castor set, eight matching rib- and ring-cut clear cylindrical bottles w/stoppers & jars w/silver tops, fitted in a sterling silver frame w/an oval footed tray base w/loop support rings & a central handle w/scalloped loop top grip, frame w/London, England hallmarks for 1811-12, matching markings on jar fittings, 9" h., the set (one jar lid repaired w/replaced finial) **1,045**

George III Castor Set

Castor set, five-bottle, George III, cut glass w/unmarked lids, fitted in a center-handled silver plate frame pierced w/scrolling foliage between bands of engraved guilloché, beaded rim & stem, mahogany base raised on three ball & claw feet, Robert Hennell, ca. 1777, London, England, 8 3/4" h. (ILLUS.) **978**

Castor set, four-bottle, clear engraved glass w/original tops, in fitted square silver plate frame w/shell feet, center handle in a pierced cross-form design, 19th c., Meriden, 10" h., the set (ILLUS. right w/breakfast caddy set) **125**

Castor set, six-bottle, frosted cut to clear bottles w/original closures, ornate silver plate frame w/a round low platform base w/an angled Greek key border on medallion feet w/portraits or Egyptian lion heads, a center tall handle w/triangular grip, frame marked "Rogers & Bro., Waterbury, Ct.," ca. 1880, 14" h. (one bottle mismatched) **248**

Barley Pattern Pickle Castor

Pickle castor, clear glass Barley patt. cylindrical insert, in ornate silver plate frame w/high domed cover & tongs, 19th c., 10 1/4" h. (ILLUS.) **200**

Pickle castor, cranberry Hobnail patt. cylindrical insert, silver plate footed holder w/simple arched handle & fork **550**

Pickle castor, cranberry Inverted Thumbprint patt. glass cylindrical insert enameled w/large white blossoms & green & white leaves, silver plate marked Homan frame w/round base & tall ornate pierced squared handle & tongs, domed silver plate cover **660**

Pickle castor, cranberry Inverted Thumbprint patt. insert in a tapering gourd-form finely gilded overall w/spiraling flowers & vines, ornate Tufts silver plate frame w/high arched handle, cover & tongs **660**

Pickle castor, cranberry opalescent Reverse Swirl patt. barrel-shaped glass insert, ornate silver plate frame w/flaring round base & tall squared handle, cover & tongs **825**

Pickle castor, spangled glass waisted cylindrical molded swirl glass insert w/yellow, white & maroon spatter & silver mica flecks, in an ornate silver plate frame w/high domed cover & tongs **330**

CAT COLLECTIBLES

Tabby Cat Ashtray

Ashtray, cat on red clay pipe w/brown high glaze, tabby cat w/red bow sits on pipe stem, cold paint accents, no marking (ILLUS.) **$45-50**

Ashtray, ceramic cat w/metal top, push down on handle & the butts drop down out of sight until you clean it out, still works, near mint, no crazing, scratches or chips, 4 1/2" around, 4 1/2" to top of handle/knob (silver plating has some wear) **40**

Vintage Black Cat Head Ashtray

Ashtray, vintage black cat head, smoke escapes from cat's nose, cold paint red ears, nose, green eyes are very bright w/no wear, stamped "109," incised w/what appears to be an "N" in a circle on bottom, very good condition, approx. 3 1/2" (ILLUS.) **20-30**

Bank, black cat w/red cold painted ears, mouth, white eyebrows, rhinestone eyes **45**

Kliban Cat Bank

Bank, Kliban cat, black & white stripes, w/red tennis shoes, by Sigma (ILLUS.) **50**

Box purse, Enid Collins "Sophistikits," mahogany, three cats decorated w/clear & green plastic "jewels," hand-decorated w/black plastic handle w/gold accent latch that opens to show small round mirror, original tag, by Collins of Texas, copyright 1967 (three "jewels" missing).......... **80**

Brass Cat Business Card Holder

Business card holder, brass, cat sitting in front of fireplace that serves as back of card holder, English, 2 1/2" (ILLUS.)............... **30**

Calendar, Chessie, 1947, featuring Chessie & her kittens made famous as the symbol of the Chesepeake Railroad **75**

Candy dish, Chessie, kitten asleep w/pillow & blanket, label attached, Fenton, 4 x 8", depending on age & color............................ **40-60**

Cigarette lighter, black cat/kitten, cat sitting on a book beside a lamp, pull chain on the lamp lights the lighter, lighter does spark, pottery part is in excellent condition, 1950s, 5 7/8" t. (two tone shade is mildly scratched & worn) **30-45**

Cookie jar, cat, redware pottery w/a high gloss glaze over the black paint, hand-painted in the cold paint over the glaze & has white lined green eyes, white whiskers & a red bow, ears & mouth, base contains the number "845," Shafford, no chips, cracks, crazing or repairs, 6 1/4" t. to the tip of its bow w/an opening diameter of 4" (few very minor flakes to the red paint on the top bow) **50**

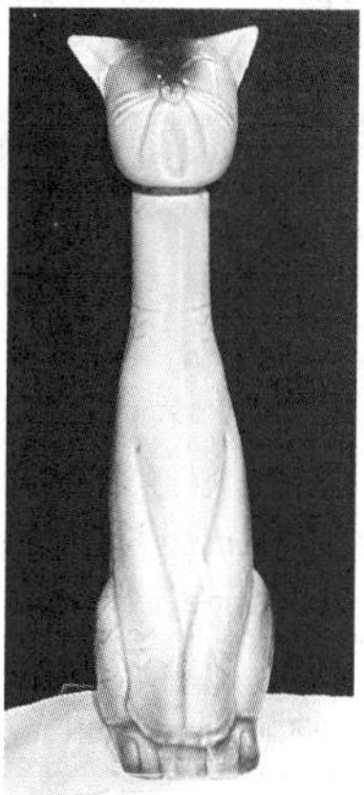

Sitting Cat Decanter

Decanter, bottle shaped like sitting cat, beige & brown glaze, cork intact, marked "Germany," light crazing, 10" (ILLUS.)............. **35**

Woman w/Cat Decanter

Decanter, bottle shaped like woman w/cat, unusual, red clay w/black glaze & near perfect cold painted accents, marked "Japan" 9" (ILLUS.) **50-60**

Dish, enameled blue w/green Deco-style cats, signed, nearly 7" **45**

Bovano Enameled Copper Plate Dish

Dish, enameled copper plate, Bovano, w/black cat, handcrafted Cheshire, Connecticut, 3" (ILLUS.)... **30**

Dish, enameled copper plate, Bovano, w/black, green & red cats, handcrafted Cheshire, Connecticut, 6" **55**

Doorstop, cast iron, black cat, all original paint, Hubley, good condition, 1930s, 4 x 10" (minimal loss to silver paint facial features)... **300**

Cat Figurine

Figurine, cat, bronze, cold painted, Austrian, moderate paint loss in spots, 1 1/2 x 2 1/2" (ILLUS.) **110**

Figurine, cat, ceramic, for Walt Disney Productions, Figaro, small, pouncing or begging, Brayton Laguna **110**

Crouching Cat Figurine

Figurine, cat, ceramic, large, crouching position, stylized orange-red body w/brown face & ears, matte finish, Brayton Laguna, late '50s or early '60s (ILLUS.) **250-350**

Figurine, cat, ceramic, "Mimi," on pedestal w/hat, shawl, boots, name on bottom of base, Brayton Laguna **100**

Goldscheider Cat Figurine

Figurine, cat, porcelain, long gray hair, pink nose, gold eyes, stamp marked "Made in Austria," "Goldscheider," "Wien," signed on tail, 6 x 13" (ILLUS.) **250-350**

Figurine, ceramic black cat, Deco-style, w/dried reed collar, whiskers, Austria **50**

Standing Cat Figurine

Figurine, ceramic, Hannibal, standing cat w/arched back, Kay Finch, excellent condition, no nicks or crazing, just over 10" (ILLUS.) **450-500**

Figurine, ceramic, Sylvac cat, striped tail, England, 13" **120**

Figurine, green porcelain cat, China, 8" **20**

Figurine, "Pity Kitty," ceramic, big green eyes, orange tabby, by Gig **25**

Figure of Large Cat

Figurine, white clay cat w/free-standing forelegs, seated on oval base w/molded rope twist design, running brown glaze, wear & flakes, 10 1/4" l. base, 11 1/4" h. (ILLUS.) **935**

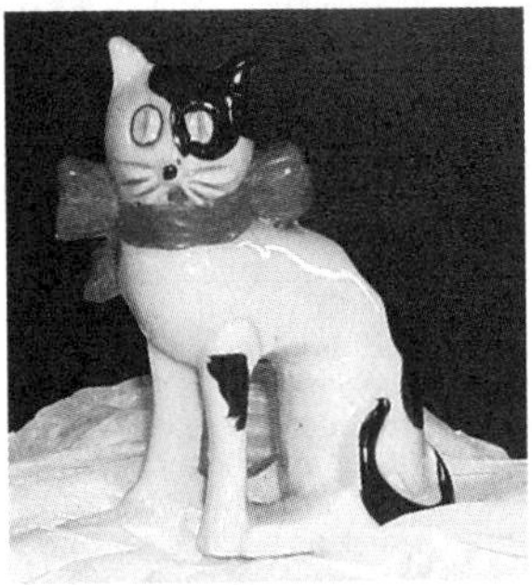

Porcelain Cat Figurine

Figurine, white porcelain cat w/black spots, orange bow, green eyes, marked "Japan" in red, 4 1/2" (ILLUS.) **30**

Three Kitten Figurines

Figurines, ceramic, three pink kittens, "See No Evil," "Hear No Evil," "Speak No Evil," Kay Finch, the set (ILLUS.) **400-450**

Figurines, tall bisque Siamese cats, rhinestone collars, handpainted features, blue eyes, 12, 17", pr. (minimal paint loss) **75-85**

Lamp, black cat, bisque, cat's back is arched, mouth open & has huge glass eyes that glow orange when lit, Germany, probably 1920s or '30s, over 10"

(original electrical cord has some fraying,
minor flaking around eyes) **850**
Lamp/ashtray, ceramic, w/black cat sitting
on top of ashtray that serves as base for
lamp, cat's back is arched, good condi-
tion, approx. 22" h. (needs to be rewired).. **50-60**
Lighter, white cat, ceramic, marked
"Japan," 3 1/2" h. **15-25**

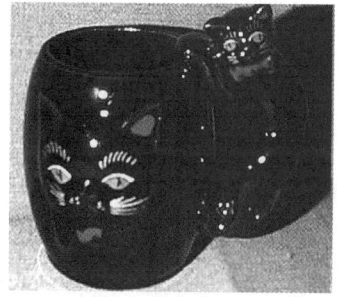

Mug w/Black Cat Handle

Mug, black cat for a handle, hard to find especially in good condition, cold hand-
painted details, Shafford, some cold
paint loss, 4 1/2" h. (ILLUS.)......................... **50-65**
Music box, cat standing behind cheese
waiting for mouse to rise from inside
cheese as music plays "I will wait for
you," handpainted, marked Otagiri, 1979........ **36**
Oil & vinegar cruets, boy & girl cats, red
clay pottery w/a high gloss black paint &
cold handpainted details, both have red
collars, ears & mouths, white whiskers &
claws, the girl cat cruet has closed painted white eyes in the shape of a V (vinegar), the boy cat cruet, has wide open
green eyes in the shape of an O (oil),
heads remove & corks are intact, Shafford labels intact, mint condition, no
chips, cracks, crazing or repairs, both
around 8" h., pr. **45-60**

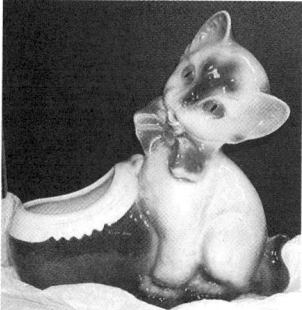

Cat by Shoe Planter

Planter, ceramic, cat by shoe, not marked,
Royal Copley (ILLUS.)..................................... **75**
Plate, cat design, Imari porcelain w/scal-
loped edge, raised relief of cat sitting on
carpet in center of plate w/blue background & flowers, Japanese, late 1800s-
early 1900s, no chips, oval 9 x 11" (some
crazing, minor wear to gilding on edges)....... **700**

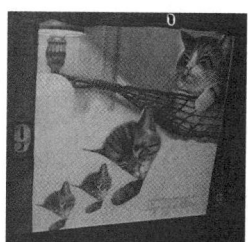

Chessie, Peake & Kittens

Print, Chessie, Peake & the kittens, vintage
frame & glass, titled "Peake, Too, Pre-
pares to Sleep Like a Kitten" (ILLUS.) ... **100-130**
Print, Currier & Ives, "My Dear Little Pet,"
curly haired girl w/kitten wearing blue rib-
bon, hand tinted... **100-125**
Print, tabby kitten, w/artist's printed signa-
ture, Clare Turlay Newberry, children's
author & illustrator, dated 1958........................ **35**
Purse, Enid Collins "Copy Cats," features
two white cats w/big turquoise blue glit-
tery rhinestone eyes sitting beside a flowerpot amidst a starry background, wood
is a light blonde color, copyright 1965,
approx. 6 1/2 x 12" not including handles
(minor damage to one corner underside)........ **55**
Salt & pepper shakers, ceramics, gingham
dog & calico cat, Brayton Laguna, pr......... **50-75**
Scarf, silk, Chessie & kittens, sleeping pose . **40-45**
Set of figurines: conductor, drummer, clar-
inet, trumpet, trombone, accordion, cello,
tuba, flute & singer; cat band, bronze,
hand-painted, excellent detailing in casting, Austrian, 20th c., no damage or repair, set of 10 (light paint loss mostly due
to age).. **700**
Store display, Cat's Meow Village dealer's
sign **75**
Stuffed cat, jewel eyes, rhinestone collar,
good condition, 1950s, approx. 12" h. **55-60**
Stuffed cat, Krazy Kat, black & white, orange ribbon around neck matches bottom of feet, stands upright, made by
George Herman, New York, early 1900s,
good condition (some restitching on cen-
ter seam) **250**

Black Cat Tape Measure

Tape measure, black cat, cold paint features, red ears, red bow tie, yellow eyes,
tape measure "tongue," pincushion
"back," thimble on tail (ILLUS.) **40**

Teapot, ceramic, cat, double spout, separated on inside, wicker handle, Shafford, excellent condition, no chips or cracks, near perfect cold paint, 5 1/2" (minor loss to eyelashes & bow) **250-300**

Toy, Krazy Kat on scooter, tin litho, black & white cat w/"Krazy Kat" on tail on yellow scooter w/green wheels (minimal paint loss) **450**

Wall hanging, ceramic, plaster, cat, green, rhinestone eyes, marked "1962, 764R," Universal Statuary Corp. **25**

Wall hanging, metal, cats, brown w/gold collars, marked Sexton USA, 13 1/2", 14 1/2", 20", set of three............................ **45-55**

Wall pocket, Siamese cat & pink basket, excellent condition.. **50-60**

CERAMICS

ALSO SEE: Antique Trader Ceramics Price Guide, 3rd Edition.

American Painted Porcelain

During the late Victorian era American artisans produced thousands of hand-painted porcelain items, including tableware, dresser sets, desk sets, and bric-a-brac. These pieces of porcelain were imported and usually bear the marks of foreign factories and countries. To learn more about identification, evaluation, history, and appraisal, the following books and newsletter by Dorothy Kamm are recommended: American Painted Porcelain: Collector's Identification & Value Guide, Comprehensive Guide to American Painted Porcelain, and Dorothy Kamm's Porcelain Collector's Companion.

Berry spoon holder, pierced handles, decorated w/two clusters of blackberries, light blue border, burnished gold rim & handles, marked "Bavaria," ca. 1894-1914, 4 5/8 x 10" **$35**

Bonbon Decorated with Currants

Bonbon, round w/gold upright ring handles, decorated w/clusters of currants on a multicolored ground, an inner border band w/gilded outlines of spider webs & currant clusters, burnished gold rim, signed "I.A. Johnson, 1915" & marked "UNO-IT - Favorite - Bavaria," 6 3/8" d. (ILLUS.).. **40**

Bouillon cup & saucer, decorated w/a curvilinear geometric design in burnished gold outlined in dark blue, burnished gold rims & handles, marked "T & V - Limoges - France," ca. 1892-1907 .... **30**

Bowl, 7 1/2" d., cereal, decorated w/a border design of daisy clusters on an ivory ground, light blue border & burnished gold rim, marked "HR - Hutschenreuther - Selb - Bavaria," ca. 1905-18 .... **22**

Bowl, 8 3/4" w., square fruit-type, decorated on the interior w/geraniums on a polychrome ground, on the exterior w/scrolls on a graduated green ground, burnished gold rim, ca. 1880-1900 .... **70**

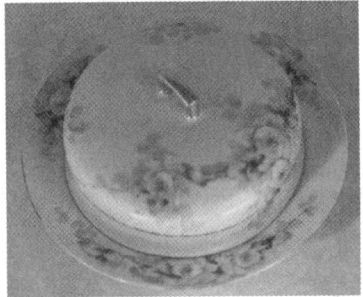

Early Painted Butter Dish

Butter dish, cover & liner, decorated on the domed cover & dished base w/clusters of pink roses & greenery on a pale pink & green ground, burnished gold rim & handle, signed "R.O. BRIGGS, AUSTIN, IL (?)," marked w/crowned double-headed eagle & "MZ - Austria," 1884-1909 (ILLUS.) **75**

Butter tub, round, decorated w/forget-me-nots on an ivory ground, burnished gold rim & handles, signed "Tossy," marked "T & V - Limoges - France," ca. 1892-1917 (no pierced insert) **45**

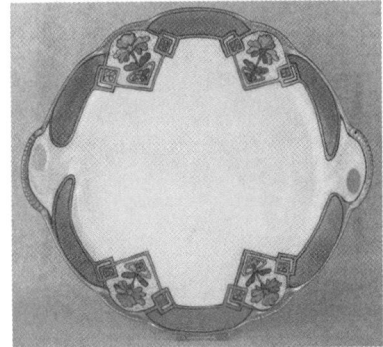

Cake Plate with Floral Panels

Cake plate, pierced rim handles, scalloped edge, decorated w/a four-panel design w/conventional-style flowers in each panel, burnished gold border outlines, dotted grounds & rim, signed w/illegible cipher & marked "HR - Charlotte - Bavaria," ca. 1887+, 9 1/8" d. (ILLUS.)............................ **55**

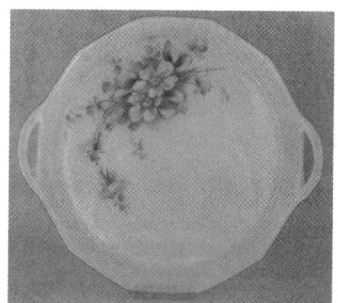

Individual Cake Plate with Wild Roses

Cake plate or cookie tray, individual size, paneled sides, open handles, decorated w/a cluster of pink wild roses on a multi-colored pastel ground, signed "R.J.'30" (ILLUS.).. 22

Chocolate cup & saucer, decorated w/yellow primrose on a shaded yellow brown ground, burnished gold rims, cup base & handle, signed "A. Brown," marked "Haviland - Limoges - France," ca. 1894-1931 30

Chocolate pot, cov., decorated w/cluster of pink roses on a pastel polychrome ground, burnished gold knob & handle, signed "M.H. Dorothy," marked "GDA - France," ca. 1900-41 150

Coffeepot, cov., decorated w/a conventional-styled dandelion design, burnished gold rims, spout interior, upper lip & handles, signed "M. Lamour," marked "J. & C. Bavaria," ca. 1902, 10" h. 175

Cracker & cheese dish, decorated w/a conventional Chinese-style floral design, an opal lustre ground, burnished gold borders & rims, illegible signature, marked w/a wreath & star & "R.S. Tillowitz - Silesia," ca. 1920-38, 8 1/2" d................ 105

Cracker jar, cov., decorated w/white wild roses on a pastel polychrome ground w/burnished gold handles, signed "A.S.S.," marked "Royal" & wreath w/"O. & E.G.," 1898-1918............................ 62

Creamer & open sugar bowl, decorated w/yellow roses on a light green border band, burnished gold borders, rims, base rims & handles, creamer marked w/a bird & "C. T. - Altwasser - Silesia," marked marked "KPM," ca. 1909-1930, pr. 35

Cup, after dinner size, decorated w/panels of Japanese-style medallions in antique green & bright gold on a dull red ground, signed "MA 12/92" (no saucer) 12

Breakfast Cup & Saucer with Clover

Cup & saucer, breakfast-size, decorated w/a clover design on a light blue ground, burnished gold rims & handle, signed "A. H. h.," ca. 1880s-90s (ILLUS.) 45

Cup & saucer, decorated w/pink roses on a pastel polychrome ground, opal lustre interior, burnished gold rims & handle, marked "Favorite - Bavaria," ca. 1908-18, the set...................................... 25

Fern pot, decorated w/pink wild roses on a graduated green ground, signed "B.E. Miehling 99," marked "Elite" in a shield & "Limoges - France," 1899, 7 1/2" d., 4 3/4" h. 175

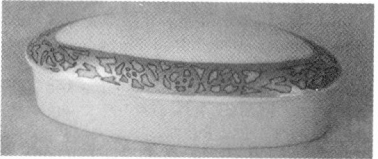

Decorated Hairpin Box

Hairpin box, cov., oval, decorated w/a conventional-style rose, leaf & stem borders on a burnished gold ground, ivory top, light blue base, marked "Favorite - Bavaria," ca. 1908-1915, 1 1/2 x 4 1/2", 1 3/4" h. (ILLUS.)............................... 30

Gold-decorated Hair Receiver

Hair receiver, cov., squatty round form on three gold curved legs, decorated w/a conventional rose design in burnished gold, burnished gold rim & feet, signed "Ferver," ca. 1900-10, 3 7/8" d., 3 1/4" h. (ILLUS.) 50

Handkerchief box, cov., decorated w/peach-tinged yellow roses on a pastel polychrome ground, signed "WSO - 1913," marked "D. & Co. - France," 5 1/4" sq., 3" h. 65

Honey dish, on three ball feet, decorated w/pink clover & wheat sheaves, light grey border, white enamel trim, burnished gold rim, marked "Bavaria," ca. 1891-1914, 7 1/8" d. 35

Ice cream bowl, decorated w/a winter scene w/burnished gold border & rim, signed "F.L. Hey," marked "CFH - GDM," ca. 1920-30, 6 3/4 x 10 5/8", 2 3/16" h.. 112

Jelly tray, round, individual size, decorated w/a conventional border design in greens, blue, yellow & burnished gold, outlined in black, burnished gold rim & handles, signed "LMC," marked "Made in Japan," ca. 1925, 7 1/8" d. 30

Lobster or shrimp salad bowl, decorated w/border clusters of seashells & seaweeds, white enamel trim, pale polychrome ground colors on exterior, burnished gold rim, marked "H and Co. - Limoges - France," ca. 1888-1896, 7 3/4 x 10 1/2" 100

Luncheon set: 7 1/2" d. plate & cup & saucer; decorated in a conventional style floral border w/white enameled flower centers & burnished gold rims & handle, marked "Germany," ca. 1914-18, the set 35

Mayonnaise bowl & underplate, decorated w/clusters of forget-met-nots on a pale blue border, ivory ground, burnished gold rims & feet, signed "AG," marked "Stouffer," 1906-1914, bowl 4 1/2" d., underplate 5 7/16" d., 2 pcs. 24

Muffin dish, cov., round, decorated w/pink wild roses & greenery on a pastel polychrome ground, burnished gold rim & handles, signed "E. Starer," marked "J & C - 'Louise' - Bavaria," ca. 1902, 9 1/4" d., 4" h. 325

Mug, decorated w/colorful yellow & yellowish red gooseberries on a polychrome ground, marked w/a crown & two shields w/"Vienna - Austria," ca. 1900-15, 4 3/4" h. 55

Mustard jar w/attached underplate & cover, decorated w/conventional style waterlilies on a light blue & burnished gold ground, burnished gold handle & rims, marked "D. & Co. - France," ca. 1879-1900, 3" h. 40

Napkin ring, decorated w/forget-me-nots, white enamel trim & burnished gold rims, signed "Luken," ca. 1895-1926, 2" d. 20

Napkin ring, half moon-shape, decorated w/a purple columbine on an ivory ground, ca. 1880-1915, 2 1/2" w. 15

Olive dish, ring-handled, decorated w/heliotrope w/etched & burnished gold border & burnished gold handle, marked "T & V - Limoges - France," ca. 1892-1907, 7 3/8" d. 40

Decorated Orange Cups

Orange cups, footed, decorated w/designs of orange blossoms on light blue & yellow grounds, embellished w/white & yellow enamel, burnished gold rim, base band, foot & prongs, signed "CKI," marked "T & V - France - Deposé," ca. 1900-15, 3 1/4" d., 2 3/4" h., pr. (ILLUS.) 100

Pitcher, 9 3/4" h., claret-type, decorated w/a conventional Art Nouveau-style floral design outlined in gold, burnished gold handle & edges, signed "V.B. Chase," ca. 1890-1914 50

Pitcher, 5 3/4" h., lemonade-type, decorated w/clusters of purple grapes on an ivory ground, antique green beaded handle & border band at top, ca. 1900-16 200

Pitcher & underplate, 3 3/8" h. pitcher, 5 1/4" d. plate, milk-type, decorated w/conventionalized orange blossoms w/burnished gold borders, rims, spout & handle, signed "J.M. Cliffe, 11/28" & marked "Japan," the set 30

Tulip-decorated Plate

Plate, 8 1/4" d., decorated w/large red tulips & green leaves on a shaded rust to cream ground w/burnished gold rim, marked w/a bird & "Altwasser - Germany," ca. 1909-34 (ILLUS.) 45

Poppy-decorated Plate

Plate, 8 3/4" d., decorated w/large orange poppies & green leaves on a shaded green ground, burnished gold rim, stamped on bottom "J. Lycett - St. Louis, Mo. - The Odean," ca. 1900-15 (ILLUS.) 50

Plate, 5 1/4 x 9 1/2", salad-type, crescent-shaped, decorated w/multicolored sweet peas on a pale violet & green ground, burnished gold rim, ca. 1900-24 .... **42**

Hand-painted Pomade Jar

Pomade jar, cov., small cylindrical form, decorated w/a conventional geometric design in baby blue & burnished gold outlined in brown, marked "W. G. & Co. - Limoges - France," ca. 1901, 2 1/2" d., 1 1/2" h. (ILLUS.)................................ **35**

Punch cups, decorated w/clusters of forget-me-nots, opal lustre interiors, burnished gold stems & rims, marked w/"Royal," a wreath & "O. & E.G.," 1898-1918, 4" h., set of 5 .... **112**

Salt dips, cauldron-shaped, decorated w/pink roses on a pale blue & yellow ground, burnished gold rims & ball feet, signed "P. Putzki," marked w/a crown double-head eagle & "MZ - Austria," ca. 1884-1909, set of 6.................................. **105**

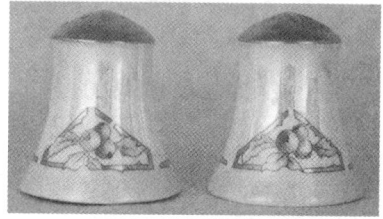

Decorated Nippon Porcelain Shakers

Salt & pepper shakers, decorated w/delicate panels of conventional-style hawthorne berries & leaves on an opal lustre ground, burnished gold tops & branch-shaped borders, signed "A.E.F.," marked "Noritake Nippon," 1914-21, 2 1/2" h., pr. (ILLUS.).. **35**

Sherbet, decorated w/daisies on an ivory ground, mother-of-pearl lustre interior, burnished gold border, rim & foot, signed "M. Paddock," marked "Epiag - Czechoslovakia," ca. 1920-39, 3 1/8" h. **30**

Soup plates, flanged rim decorated w/three clusters of seashells & seaweeds on a very pale polychrome ground, burnished gold rims, signed "ALB," marked "H. & Co. - Haviland - Limoges - France," 1876 - 1879, 9" d., pr. **40**

Sugar shaker, decorated w/Art Nouveau-style florals & squiggling border band in burnished gold, burnished gold pierced top, signed "E.C.R.," ca. 1905-15, 2 3/4" d., 4 1/2" h.............................. **35**

Syrup jug, cov., decorated w/pink & ruby roses on a polychrome ground, burnished gold handle, knob & rims, opal lustre spout interior, marked "ADK - France," ca. 1891-1910, 4" h. (missing underplate) **30**

Table top centerpiece, decorated w/a cluster of daisies on a pastel polychrome ground, burnished gold rim, signed "E. Miller," marked "T & V - Limoges - France," ca. 1892-1907, 11 5/8" d. **90**

Toast set: plate & cup; 9 3/16 w. plate decorated w/conventional-style strawberries on an ivory ground, opal lustre cup interior, burnished gold borders, rims & handle, ca. 1925-30, 2 pcs. **40**

Toothpick holder, decorated w/double violets on a pastel ivory & green ground, burnished gold rim, signed "Wats" & "Pitkin & Brooks Studio," marked "T & V - Limoges - France," 1903-10, 2 3/4" h. **25**

Tumbler, decorated w/ruby roses on a polychrome ground, burnished gold rim, illegible signature, marked "La Seynie - PP - Limoges - France," ca. 1903-17, 3 3/8" h. **22**

Vase, 7" h., bulbous base tapering to a tall slender neck, two-handled, decorated w/pink & yellow roses on a pastel polychrome ground, burnished gold rim, accents & handle, ca. 1900-20............................. **45**

Bauer

The Bauer Pottery was moved to Los Angeles, California from Paducah, Kentucky, in 1909, in the hope that the climate would prove beneficial to the principal organizer, John Andrew Bauer, who suffered from severe asthma. Flowerpots, made of California adobe clay, were the first production at the new location, but soon they were able to resume production of stoneware crocks and jugs, the mainstay of the Kentucky operation. In the early 1930s, Bauer's colorfully glazed earthen dinnerwares, especially the popular Ring-Ware pattern, became an immediate success. Sometimes confused with its imitator, Fiesta Ware (first registered by Homer Laughlin in 1937), Bauer pottery is collectible in its own right and is especially popular with West Coast collectors. Bauer Pottery ceased operation in 1962.

Bauer Mark

Baking dish, cov., individual, Ring-Ware patt., green or yellow, 4" d., each.................. **$40**

Batter bowl, Ring-Ware patt., green, 1 qt. **125**

Ring-Ware Beater Pitcher

Beater pitcher, Ring-Ware patt., red, 1 qt. (ILLUS.).. **85**

A Variety of Bauer Ring-Ware Pieces

Bowl, berry, 5 1/2" d., Ring-Ware patt., delphinium (ILLUS. far left) **30**
Bowl, berry, 5 1/2" d., Ring-Ware patt., yellow....... **25**
Bowl, soup, cov., 5 1/2" d., lug handles, Ring-Ware patt., orange, green, ivory or cobalt blue, each **90**
Bowl, 13" d., Cal-Art line, green **35**
Bowl, 15" d., wide low sides, white & brown speckled glaze, No. 149................................... **95**
Butter dish, cov., round, Ring-Ware patt., red...... **155**
Cake plate, Monterey patt., yellow..................... **185**
Candleholders, spool-shaped, Ring-Ware patt., jade green, pr.. **130**
Casserole, cov., individual, Ring-Ware patt., cobalt blue, 5 1/2" d. **300**
Casserole, cov., individual, Ring-Ware patt., ivory, 5 1/2" d. **300**
Casserole, cov., individual, Ring-Ware patt., orange/red, 5 1/2" d. **200**
Coffee carafe, cov., Ring-Ware patt., copper handle, delph blue..................................... **250**
Coffee carafe, cov., Ring-Ware patt., copper handle, orange/red..................................... **150**
Console set: bowl & pr. of three-light candlesticks; Cal-Art line, pink, semi-matte finish, 3 pcs. **145**
Cookie jar, cov., Monterey Moderne patt., chartreuse... **100**

Monterey Midget Creamer

Creamer, midget, Monterey patt., orange/red (ILLUS.) **20**
Creamer & cov. sugar bowl, Ring-Ware patt., ivory, pr. **150**
Creamer & cov. sugar bowl, Ring-Ware patt., orange, pr. **75**
Cup & saucer, demitasse, Ring-Ware patt., yellow **125**
Cup & saucer, Ring-Ware patt., yellow (ILLUS. third from right w/bowl) **45-50**
Flowerpot, Ring-Ware patt., cobalt blue.............. **45**
Flowerpot, Speckleware, flesh pink, 8 1/4" d., 6 1/2" h.. **40**
Gravy boat, Monterey Moderne patt., pink **40**
Gravy boat, Ring-Ware patt., burgundy **145**
Mixing bowl, Atlanta line, No. 24, cobalt blue.. **100**
Mixing bowl, nesting-type, Ring-Ware patt., No. 18, chartreuse **75**
Mixing bowl, nesting-type, Ring-Ware patt., No. 36, ivory.. **55**
Mug, barrel-shaped, Ring-Ware patt., jade green or yellow, each **150**

Bauer Oil Jar

Oil jar, No. 100, orange, 16" h. (ILLUS.)........ **1,000**
Oil jar, No. 100, cobalt blue, 22" h.................. **1,700**
Oil jars, No. 100, white, 12" h., pr................... **3,000**
Pie plate, Ring-Ware patt., green **45**
Pitcher, Ring-Ware patt., orange, 1 qt. **85**
Pitcher, Ring-Ware patt., delph blue, 2 qt. **200**
Pitcher, cov., jug-type, ice water, Monterey patt., turquoise... **325**
Pitcher, water, w/ice lip, Monterey patt., green **125**
Planter, model of a swan, chartreuse, medium **95**
Plate, 5" d., bread & butter, Ring-Ware patt., green (ILLUS. center front w/bowl) **15**
Plate, salad, 7 1/2" d., Ring-Ware patt., yellow (ILLUS. center front w/bowl)...................... **30**
Plate, 9" d., Ring-Ware patt., grey **65**
Plate, 10 1/2" d., dinner, Ring-Ware patt., cobalt or delph blue, each............................... **95**
Plate, 10 1/2" d., dinner, Ring-Ware patt., jade green, orange or yellow, each................. **85**
Plate, chop, 12" d., Ring-Ware patt., burgundy **150**
Plate, chop, 12" d., Ring-Ware patt., white..... **230**
Plate, chop, 14" d., Ring-Ware patt., yellow..... **125**
Plate, chop, Monterey Moderne patt., yellow **45**

Plate, grill, Monterey Moderne patt., char-
treuse 35
Plate, luncheon, Ring-Ware patt., yellow
(ILLUS. center back w/bowl) 40
Punch bowl, Ring-Ware patt., three-footed,
cobalt blue, 14" d.. 850
Punch bowl, Ring-Ware patt., three-footed,
jade green, 14" d. 550
Punch cup, Ring-Ware patt., delph, cobalt
blue, green, yellow or burgundy, each............. 35
Relish dish, divided, Ring-Ware patt., co-
balt blue 195
Salt & pepper shakers, beehive-shaped,
Ring-Ware patt., orange/red, pr. 60
Salt & pepper shakers, Ring-Ware patt.,
black, pr. (ILLUS. back, second from left
w/bowl) 85
Sugar bowl, cov., demitasse, Ring-Ware
patt., burgundy.. 60
Sugar shaker, Ring-Ware patt., jade green...... 350
Syrup pitcher, Ring-Ware patt., cobalt blue...... 285
Teapot, cov., Ring-Ware patt., burgundy,
2-cup size 325
Teapot, cov., Ring-Ware patt., yellow,
2-cup size 125
Tumbler, Ring-Ware patt., green, large
(ILLUS. second from right w/bowl) 45-65
Tumbler, Ring-Ware patt., delphinium,
small (ILLUS. far right w/bowl) 40
Vase, 4 1/4" h., bulbous, Fred Johnson Art-
ware line, jade green 65
Vase, 8" h., Hi-Fire line, deep trumpet-
shaped form w/widely flaring sides fluted
on the exterior, yellow...................................... 90

Matt Carlton Line Vase

Vase, 8" h., ovoid base w/widely flared rim,
twist shoulder handles, orange, Matt Car-
lton Artware line (ILLUS.)................................. 650
Vase, 10 1/2" h., cylindrical, Ring-Ware
patt., delph blue 95
Vase, 13" h., ovoid base w/widely flared rim,
twist shoulder handles, jade green, Matt
Carlton Artware line 1,200
Vase, 24" h., Rebekah, tall slender baluster-
form w/loop handles near the short flaring neck, jade green, Matt Carlton Art-
ware line (ILLUS.) 2,500

Large Rebekah Vase

Belleek

*Belleek china has been made in Ireland's County
Fermanagh for many years. It is exceedingly thin porce-
lain. Several marks were used, including a hound and
harp (1865-1880), and a hound, harp and castle (1863-
1891). A printed hound, harp and castle with the words
"Co. Fermanagh Ireland" constitutes the mark from
1891. Belleek-type china also was made in the United
States last century by several firms, including Ceramic
Art Company, Columbian Art Pottery, Lenox Inc., Ott &
Brewer and Willets Manufacturing Co. Also see LENOX.*

American Belleek

Jars
**Ceramic Art Company (CAC palette
mark),** dresser jar, hand-decorated w/gold
paste roses & stripes, 3 1/2" d., 5" h.............. $150
Lenox (palette mark), condiment jar & cover, tapering hexagonal form w/domed
cover, white ground w/blue jewel beading
w/gold paste swags, sterling finial,
4 1/2" w., 5 1/2" h.. 270
Ott and Brewer (sword & crown mark),
cracker jar & cover, hand-decorated
w/gold paste flowers & gold handles,
5" d., 7" h... 400

Tankards
**Ceramic Art Company (CAC palette
mark),** tankard, h.p. grapes, leaves &
vines w/heavy gold accents, artist-signed
"Nosek," dated "1905," 14 1/2" h. 900
Lenox (palette mark), tankard, h.p. grapes,
leaves & vines, embossed handle
trimmed in gold, 14" h. 625
Willets (serpent mark), tankard, h.p.
grapes, leaves & vines on light green matte
ground, artist-signed "Fisher," 11 1/4" h. 625
Willets (serpent mark), tankard, h.p. scene
of a monk holding a pipe, brown matte
ground, artist-signed "AST," 13 3/4" h. 800

Toothpick Holders
Lenox (palette mark), toothpick
holder, h.p. ravens sitting on pine
branches, straight sides, 2 1/4" h. 140

Bennington

Bennington wares, which ranged from stoneware to parian and porcelain, were made in Bennington, Vermont, primarily in two potteries, one in which Captain John Norton and his descendants were principals, and the other in which Christopher Webber Fenton (also once associated with the Nortons) was a principal. Various marks are found on the wares made in the two major potteries, including J. & E. Norton, E. & L. P. Norton, L. Norton & Co., Norton & Fenton, Edward Norton, Lyman Fenton & Co., Fenton's Works, United States Pottery Co., U.S.P. and others.

The popular pottery with the mottled brown on yellowware glaze was also produced in Bennington, but such wares should be referred to as "Rockingham" or "Bennington-type" unless they can be specifically attributed to a Bennington, Vermont factory.

Book flask, binding marked "Departed Spirits," Flint Enamel glaze, 5 5/8" h. (minor edge wear) **$468**

Bottle, figural coachman, mottled running Rockingham glaze, 1848-49 marks, 10" h. (chips, spide crack in base)................. **385**

Butter churn, stoneware, elongated ovoid body w/eared handles & molded rim, cobalt blue slip-quilled floral spray decoration, impressed mark of E. & L.P. Norton, 4 gal., brown-glazed cover & wooden dasher, 1861-81, 17 1/2" h. (chips) **575**

Candlestick, ringed columnar form w/heavy socket ring & flaring round base, overall motted brown Flint Enamel glaze, hairline in foot & line around flange of base, probably manufacturing defect, 7 3/4" h. **385**

Crock, stoneware, cylindrical w/molded rim & eared handles, slip-quilled cobalt blue decoration of a recumbent stag in a landscape w/shrubs, fences & a tree, impressed "J. & E. Norton - Bennington VT - 2," mid-19th c., 2 gal., 10 3/4" d., 9 1/4" h. **5,460**

Bisque

Bisque is biscuit china, fired a single time but not glazed. Some bisque is decorated with colors. Most abundant from the Victorian era are figures and groups, but other pieces from busts to vases were made by numerous potteries in the U.S. and abroad. Reproductions have been produced for many years so care must be taken when seeking antique originals

Bisque Seated Dutch Boy

Bust of a young boy, holding a letter, 8" h. .. **$138**

Figure group, a young boy & girl standing on a rockwork base, he holding a fishing pole up in one hand & another projecting out while the girl ties the fishing line to it, fine detailing & delicate coloring, marked by Heubach, 8 1/2" h. **165**

Figure of a Dutch boy, seated w/one hand on knee, orange jacket, yellow pants, grey hat & shoes, black & white neck scarf, unmarked, 3 1/2 x 5 1/2", 6" h. (ILLUS.) **195**

Bisque Dutch Girl Figure

Figure of a Dutch girl, seated pose w/hands on her knees, wearing a white bonnet over light brown hair, tinted face & arms, blue dress w/white bodice & trim on sleeves & at waist, unmarked, 3 1/2 x 5", 6 1/2" h. (ILLUS.)........................... **195**

Figure of young girl, w/cat on a swing, 5 3/4" h.. **110**

Figures, a male & female w/gilt & yellow enamel trim, he standing holding a fishing net, she holding a small keg, Germany, late 19th c., 28" h., pr. **920**

French Skating Figures

Figures of a lady & man, each in 18th c. costume, wearing ice skates & depicted in skating pose, each on a shaped platform base, France, late 19th c., facing pair, minor restorations, 28" h., pr. (ILLUS.) **2,070**

Blue & White Pottery

The category of blue and white or blue and grey pottery includes a wide variety of pottery, earthenware and stoneware items widely produced in this country in the late 19th century right through the 1930s. Originally marketed as inexpensive wares, most pieces featured a white or grey body molded with a fruit, flower or geometric design and then trimmed with bands or splashes of blue to highlight the molded pattern. Pitchers, butter crocks and salt boxes are among the numerous items produced but other kitchenwares and chamber sets are also found. Values vary depending on the rarity of the embossed pattern and the depth of color of the blue trim; the darker the blue, the better. Some entries refer to several different books on Blue and White Pottery. These books are: Blue & White Stoneware, Pottery & Crockery *by Edith Harbin (1977, Collector Books, Paducah, KY);* Stoneware in the Blue and White *by M.H. Alexander (1993 reprint, Image Graphics, Inc., Paducah, KY); and* Blue & White Stoneware *by Kathryn McNerney (1995, Collector Books, Paducah, KY).*

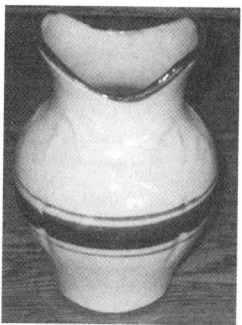

Bow Tie Blue-banded Brush Vase

Brush vase, embossed Bow Tie (Our Lucile) patt., w/narrow blue bands, 5 1/2" h. (ILLUS.) **225**

Miniature Bean Pot and Coffeepot

Bean pot, miniature, cov., wide blue band, souvenir-type (ILLUS. left) **$225**

Peacock Berry Bowl

Bowl, 4 1/2" d., 2 1/4" h., berry, embossed Peacock patt. (ILLUS.) **325**
Bowl, 4 1/2" d., 2 1/2" h., berry, plain w/pale blue rim band **55**

Grape Ware Pattern Bowls

Bowl, 8" d., embossed Grape Ware patt. (ILLUS. left) **225**
Bowl, 9 1/2" d., 5" h., embossed Currants and Diamonds patt. **230**
Bowl, 10" d., embossed Grape Ware patt. (ILLUS. right) **275**

Printed Wildflower Brush Vase

Brush vase, printed Wildflower patt., tapering cylindrical form, printed designs inside, 5" h. (ILLUS.) **300**
Butter crock, cov., embossed Daisy and Trellis patt., 6" d., 4" h. **175**
Butter crock, cov., embossed Daisy and Waffle patt., 7" d., 6 3/4" h. **235**

Two Blue & White Butter Crocks

Butter crock, cov., embossed Daisy patt., Red Wing, 3 1/2" h. (ILLUS. right) **395**

Eagle Butter and Salt Crocks

Butter crock, cov., embossed Eagle patt., 6" d., 6" h. (ILLUS. right) **700**
Butter crock, cov., embossed Good Luck (Swasitka) patt., 6 1/4" d., 5 1/4" h. **150**
Butter crock, cov., embossed Indian patt., 3 lb. **700**
Butter crock, cov., embossed Leaf Flemish patt., 8" d., 7" h. **200**
Butter crock, cov., plain **125**
Butter crock, cov., printed Cows patt., 6 1/2" d., 5" h. **195**
Butter crock, cov., Western Stoneware Co., advertising "Compliments of J. Mueller," 4 1/4" h. (ILLUS. left w/Daisy patt. crock) **295**
Canister, cov., Diffused Blues patt., 5 3/4" d., 6 1/2" h. **175**

Printed Dutch Scene Sugar Canister

Canister, cov., printed Dutch Scene patt., "Sugar," 5 1/2 to 6" h. (ILLUS.) **450-650**

Barley & Blank Wildflower Canisters

Canister, cov., printed Wildflower patt., "Barley," "Cornstarch" or "Grape Nuts," Barley 5 3/4" h., each (ILLUS. of Barley, left)............. **500**
Canister, cov., printed Wildflower patt., "Beans," "Oatmeal" or "Peas," 5 1/2 to 6 1/2", each **325**
Canister, cov., printed Wildflower patt., blank title (ILLUS. right w/Barley) **475**

Tall Wildflower Butter Canister

Canister, cov., printed Wildflower patt., "Butter," tall w/flared rim, 5 3/5" h. (ILLUS.) **350**
Canister, cov., printed Wildflower patt., "Crackers" or "Tobacco," 5 1/2 to 6 1/2" h., each.. **600**
Canister, cov., printed Wildflower patt., "Sugar," 5 1/2 to 6 1/2" **250**

Embossed Grape Ware Canister

Canister, embossed Grape Ware patt., "Pepper," 3 3/8" h. (ILLUS.)............................ **400**

Robinson Sugar Canister

Canister, cov., embossed Robinson patt., "Sugar" (ILLUS.) **275**

Embossed Flying Bird Casserole

Casserole, cov., embossed Flying Bird patt., 9 1/2" d. (ILLUS.).................................... **600**
Chamber pot, cov., embossed Beaded Rose patt., two sizes made, large 9 1/2" d., 6" h. **250**
Chamber pot, open, embossed Bowtie (Our Lucile) patt., 11" d., 6" h. **165**
Coffeepot, miniature, cov., wide blue band, souvenir-type (ILLUS. right w/bean pot)........ **300**

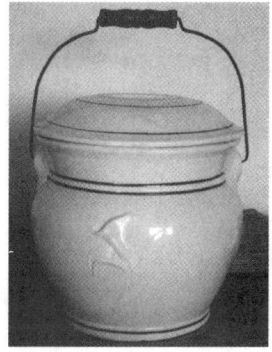

Red Wing Lily Pattern Combinette

Combinette, embossed Lily patt., Red
Wing (ILLUS.) **250-300**
Cookie jar, cov., Brickers patt., 8" d., 8" h. **475**

Rare Anchovies Storage Crock

Crock, anchovies storage-type, swelled cylindrical form, three blue bands around
top & bottom, stenciled on the side "A.
Rensch & Co. - Anchois (sic) Mustard
(over a fish) - Toledo, O.," impressed on
the bottom "Burley, Winter & Co. -
Crooksville, O.," 10 1/2" h. (ILLUS.) **575**
Cup, embossed Paneled Fir Tree patt.,
3" d., 3 1/2" h. **175**
Cuspidor, embossed Basketweave and
Morning Glory (Willow) patt., 7 1/2" d.,
5 1/2" h. **185**
Ewer, printed Wildflower patt., 10 1/2" h.
(ILLUS. right) **325**

Printed Wildflower Ewers

Ewer, printed Wildflower patt., 6 1/2" h.
(ILLUS. left) **225**
Ewer, printed Wildflower patt., 8 1/2" h.
(ILLUS. center) **295**

Wildflower Ewer and Basin Set

Ewer & basin, printed Wildflower patt.,
stenciled designs inside the ewer & the
basin, basin 15" d., ewer 11" h., the set
(ILLUS.) **650**

Embossed Cosmos Jardiniere

Jardiniere, embossed Cosmos patt., 6" h.
(ILLUS.) **800**
Mug, embossed Apple Blossom patt., 5" h........ **275**

Printed Dutch Scene Mug

Mug, printed Dutch Scene mug, boy on one
side, girl on the other, 4 1/4" h. (ILLUS.) **275**
Pitcher, embossed Beaded Rose patt.,
large, 10" h. **425**

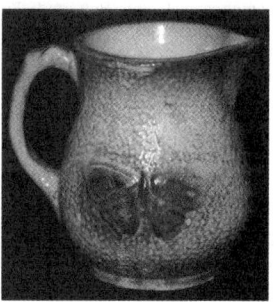

Small Embossed Butterfly Pitcher

Pitcher, embossed Butterfly patt., 4 3/4" h.
(ILLUS.)... **600**
Pitcher, embossed Butterfly patt., 9" h. **345**

Chrysanthemum Pitchers & Salt Box

Pitcher, embossed Chrysanthemum patt.,
8" h. (ILLUS. right)... **225**
Pitcher, embossed Chrysanthemum patt.,
9 1/2" h. (ILLUS. left) **275**

Daisy and Nautilus Pitchers

Pitcher, embossed Daisy patt., Brush-Mc-
Coy, 7" h. (ILLUS. left)..................................... **425**

Dutch Boy and Girl Kissing Pitcher

Pitcher, embossed Dutch Boy and Girl
Kissing patt., Brush-McCoy Pottery Co.,
9" h. (ILLUS.) **265**
Pitcher, embossed Flying Bird patt., 9" h.,
6" d. **825**
Pitcher, embossed Grape Cluster on Trellis
patt., four sizes, 5" to 9 1/2" h., depend-
ing on size, each **165-245**
Pitcher, embossed Grape Cluster on Trellis
patt., squat body, 2 pt. **400**
Pitcher, embossed Grape Cluster on Trellis
patt., squat body, 3 pt. **425**
Pitcher, embossed Grape Cluster on Trellis
patt., squat body, 5 pt. **475**
Pitcher, embossed Lincoln Head patt., sev-
eral sizes, depending on size **900**

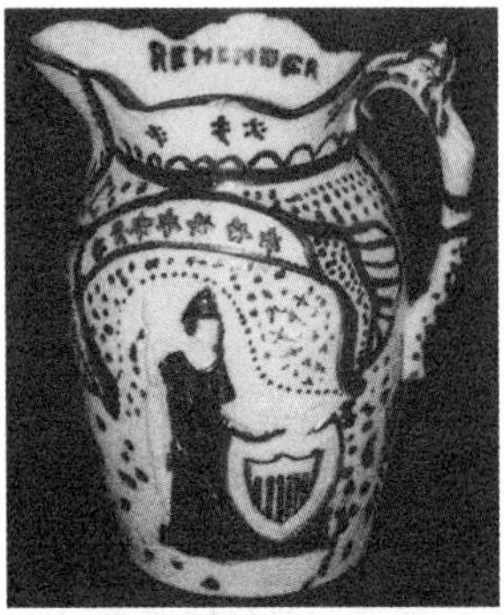

Rare Remember Pitcher

Pitcher, embossed Remember patt., molded figure of Columbia standing beside an
American shield, "Remember" on the in-
terior rim (ILLUS.).. **1,500**
Pitcher, embossed Rose on Trellis patt.,
8 3/4" h.. **375**
Pitcher, embossed Scroll and Leaf patt.,
w/advertising, 7" h. **410**

Embossed Stag Pattern Pitcher

Pitcher, embossed Stag patt., 9" h.
(ILLUS.) **650-850**

Embossed Windy City Pitcher

Pitcher, embossed Windy City patt.,
8 1/2" h. (ILLUS.)... **300**
Pitcher, miniature, Diffused Blues w/souve-
nir markings in gold lettering, each **325**
Pitcher, printed Cattail patt. 5 3/4" h. **275**
Pitcher, printed Conifer Tree patt., 5" h........... **250**

Pitcher, printed Nautilus patt., 8 1/2" h. (ILLUS. right with Daisy pitcher) **325**

Pitcher, printed Wildflower patt., tall w/long spout, five stencils per side, 8 1/2" h. **400**

Bulbous Wildflower Pitcher

Pitcher, printed Wildflower patt., bulbous body, 10 3/4" h. (ILLUS.).................................. **425**

Blue & White Stupid Pattern Pitcher

Pitcher, Stupid patt., Diffused Blues, 8" h., 6" d. (ILLUS.) **475**

Pitcher, side-pour, molded bands, w/advertising, Western Stoneware, each................... **400**

Ramekin or nappy, embossed Peacock patt., 4" d. **300**

Roaster, cov., printed Wildflower patt., 12" d., 8 1/2" h. **345**

Salt box, cov., embossed Apricot patt., 5 3/4" d., 5" h. **250**

Salt box, cov., embossed Blocks patt., 6 1/2" d., 6 3/4" h.. **175**

Salt box, cov., embossed Butterfly patt., 5 3/4" d., 5 3/4" h.. **275**

Salt box, cov., embossed Chrysanthemum patt., 4 1/4" h. (ILLUS. front w/pitchers) **210**

Salt box, cov., embossed Grape and Basketweave patt., 6" d., 4" h. **235**

Salt box, cov., embossed Grape and Lattice patt., 6 3/4" d., 6 1/2" h. **400**

Salt crock, cov., hanging-type, embossed Eagle patt., 6" d., 4" h. (ILLUS. left w/Eagle butter crock).. **600**

Wildflower Advertising Salt Crock

Salt crock, open, hanging-type, printed Wildflower patt., printed advertising "Your Credit Is Good - Freed Furniture & Carpet Co.," 6" d., 4 1/2" h. (ILLUS.) **450**

Miniature Inscribed Slop Jar

Slop jar, miniature, souvenir-type, one side inscribed "Mar. 29.05," other side inscribed "J.A. Wells" (ILLUS.).......................... **425**

Soap dish, embossed Beaded Rose patt., 4 3/4" d.. **150**

Stein, embossed Windy City patt., 5 1/2" h....... **165**

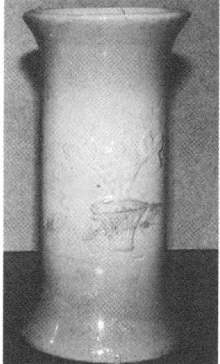

Wicker Basket and Bouquet Vase

Vase, 11" h., embossed Wicker Basket and Bouquet patt. (ILLUS.)` **300**

Water cooler, cov., embossed Cupid patt., w/spigot, 5 gal... **725**

Water cooler, cov., embossed Elk and Polar Bear patt., w/spigot, 9 1/2" d., 14" h. **825**

Wildflower Water Cooler and Base

Water cooler, cov., printed Wildflower patt., w/spigot & base, 3 gal. (ILLUS.) **2,225**

Blue & White Polar Jug

Water jug, Polar jug, footed flat-sided moon-shape w/short cylindrical top spout, 9 3/4" d., 10" h. (ILLUS.) **650**

Other Colors

Yellowware Pitchers

Pitcher, embossed Grape patt., 10" h. (ILLUS. left) **395**
Pitcher, embossed Willow patt., yellowware, 9" h. (ILLUS. right) **300**

Canton

This ware has been decorated for nearly two centuries in factories near Canton, China. Intended for export sale, much of it was originally inexpensive blue-and-white hand-decorated ware. Late 18th and early 19th century pieces are superior to later ones and fetch higher prices.

Basket & undertray, flaring oval basket w/reticulated sides, on an matching oval undertray, 19th c., 10 1/4" l., 3 3/4" h., 2 pcs. (minor edge chips) **$805**
Basket & undertray, oval basket w/deep slightly flared reticulated sides, on a matching undertray, 19th c., 7 1/2 x 8 3/4", 2 pcs. (glaze imperfections) **575**
Creamer, helmet-shaped w/angled branch handle, 4" h. **495**
Fruit basket & undertray, deep oval reticulated basket w/gently flaring sides & flanged rim, in a deep matching undertray w/reticulated flanged rim, 19th c., basket 8 5/8" l., 4 1/2" h., undertray 9 7/8" l., 2 pcs. **1,150**
Hot water plate, rounded slightly paneled rim, edge spout opening, 19th c., 9 1/2" d. **303**
Pitcher, 4 1/2" h., jug-form w/double twisted strap handle, 19th c. **605**
Platter, 11 1/2" l., oblong w/canted corners, 19th c. **413**
Platter, 11 1/2 x 14 1/2", oblong w/cut corners, well-and-tree-type, cloud borders, 19th c. **1,210**
Platter, 16 7/8" l., 13 3/4" w., oblong w/canted corners, 19th c. **748**
Platter, 14 3/4 x 17 7/8" oval, 19th c., (minor imperfections) **1,093**
Platter, 17 x 21 1/8", oblong w/wide cutcorners, 19th c. (minor glaze irregularities) **1,840**
Serving bowl, oblong octagonal form, 11 x 13 1/2" **880**
Serving dish, cov., footed oval form w/snout-shaped handles, 19th c., 8 3/4 x 10", 6" h. (chip) **805**
Tureen, cov., footed oblong body w/animal head end handles, 10 x 12", 8" h. **1,540**
Tureen, cov., rectangular w/rounded corners, flared base, the cover decorated w/a leaf-shaped knop, boar's head end handles, 19th c., 13" l., 8 1/2" h. (minor small firing cracks) **1,955**
Vegetable bowl, open, oblong w/cut corners, 9 3/4 x 11 1/2" **605**
Vegetable dish, cov., almond-shaped w/flanged rim, low domed cover w/pine cone finial, 10 1/4" l. (chips) **385**
Vegetable dish, cov., rectangular shaped form, 19th c., 7 1/2 x 8 3/4", 4 1/2" h. (small rim nick) **345**

Carlton Ware

The Staffordshire firm of Wiltshaw & Robinson, Stoke-on-Trent, operated the Carlton Works from about 1890 until 1958, producing both earthenwares and porcelain. Specializing in decorative items like vases and teapots, they became well known for their lustre-finished wares, often decorated in the Oriental taste. The trademark Carlton Ware was incorporated into their printed mark. Since 1958, a new company, Carlton Ware Ltd., has operated the Carlton Works at Stoke.

Cracker jar, cov., footed bulbous ovoid form w/short waisted neck fitted w/a silver plate rim, cover & swing bail handle, decorated around the sides w/a transfer-printed colorful peony design, 7" h. **$115**

Carlton Ware Pitcher

Pitcher, 6 3/4" h., 5" d., "Rouge Royale," footed ovoid body w/large rim spout & long squared gold handle & gold ringed foot, the body w/a deep rouge iridescent ground decorated w/a large flying bird in gold, yellow, green, pink, blue & orange against an ornate gilt foliate ground, mother-of-pearl interior (ILLUS.) **595**
Potpourri jar, cov., wide ovoid body w/a fitted domed cover, deep yellow ground decorated on each side & the top of the cover w/cartouche-shaped reserves showing Oriental buildings & people in colored enamels against a black satin ground, gold borders, 7 1/2" d., 9 3/4" h. **425**
Toast holder, Art Deco-style, black & orange edged wedges w/loop handles on a yellow-glazed ground, 2 1/2 x 6 1/2", 2 1/4" h. **144**
Vase, 8 1/4" h., 7 3/4" d., flaring foot & tall wide trumpet-form body w/angled loop handles below the rim, a gilt decoration of an Oriental landscape w/a pagoda & gilt borders on a dark green ground **275**

Catalina Island Pottery

The Clay Products Division of the Santa Catalina Island Co. produced a variety of wares during their brief ten-year operation. The brainchild of chewing-gum magnate, William Wrigley, Jr., owner of Catalina Island at the time, and his business associate D. M. Retton, the plant was established at Pebbly Beach, near Avalon in 1927. Its two-fold goal was to provide year-round work for the island's residents and building material for Wrigley's ongoing development of a major tourist attraction at Avalon. Early production consisted of bricks and roof and patio tiles. Later, art pottery, including vases, flower bowls, lamps and home accessories were made from a local brown-based clay and, about 1930, tablewares were introduced. These early wares carried vivid glazes but had a tendency to chip readily and a white-bodied,

more chip-resistant clay, imported from the mainland, was used after 1932. The costs associated with importing clay eventually caused the Catalina pottery to be sold to a California mainland competitor in 1937. These wares were molded and are not hand-thrown but some pieces have hand-painted decoration.

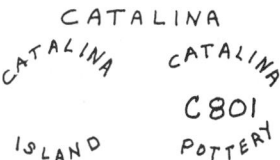

Catalina Island Pottery Marks

Ashtray, figural bear, Monterey brown glaze **$475**
Ashtray, figural fish, decorated 175
Ashtray, model of a baseball glove 950
Ashtray, figural goat, 4" w. 495
Book ends, figural monk, pr. 650
Book ends, Monterey brown glaze, pr. 600
Bowl, 7 1/2" d., Starlight 160
Candelabrum, three-light, pr. 295
Candleholder, low 90
Casserole, cov., rope edge 125
Charger, Mexican scene, 11 1/2" d. 650
Charger, relief-molded swordfish, Descanso green glaze, 14" d. 600
Coaster 75
Coffee server, cov. 150
Console bowl, fluted 225
Creamer, rope edge 75
Creamer, 6" h. 250
Cup, demitasse 45
Cup & saucer, rope edge 45
Custard cup 45
Flower frog, model of a pelican 250
Flower frog, model of a stork, 7" h. 295
Flowerpot, 4 1/2" h. 95
Indian bowl, rare 475
Model of clamshell, Pearly white glaze 300
Model of cowboy hat 175
Mug, 6" h. 55
Pipe holder, Mexican peon, painted over glaze 475
Planter, model of a cactus, Cat-Lina 475
Plate, Moorish design decoration 425
Plate, 8 1/2" d., salad, rope edge 28
Plate, 10 1/2" d., dinner, rope edge 32
Plate, 11 1/4" d., painted desert scene 550
Plate, chop, 13 1/2" d., rope edge 95
Plate, 14" d., submarine garden decoration .. **1,250**
Salt & pepper shakers, figural Senorita & Peon, pr. 140
Salt & pepper shakers, gourd-shaped, pr. 75
Salt & pepper shakers, model of cactus, pr. 95
Salt & pepper shakers, model of tulip, pr. 75
Shot tumbler, nude figure, 3 1/4" h. 325
Sugar bowl, cov., rope edge 55
Tea tile, 8" w. 295
Teapot, cov., rope edge 195
Tile, Spanish design, 6 x 6" sq. 150
Tumbler 50
Vase, trophy-type, Toyon red 395
Vase, 7 1/4" h., sawtooth edge 175
Vase, 9" h., experimental multicolored glaze 800

Vase, 10" h., fluted 225
Vase, 10" h., Pearly white glaze 195
Vinegar bottle w/stopper, gourd-shape 165
Wall pocket, basketweave design, 9" l. 375
Wall pocket or vase, seashell form, white
clay 350

Chinese Export

Large quantities of porcelain have been made in China for export to America from the 1780s, much of it shipped from the ports of Canton and Nanking. A major source of this porcelain was Ching-te-Chen in the Kiangsi province but the wares were also made elsewhere. The largest quantities were blue and white. Prices fluctuate considerably depending on age, condition, decoration, etc.

CANTON and ROSE MEDALLION export wares are listed separately

Coffeepot, cov., blue Nanking patt., footed
bulbous ovoid body tapering to a small
neck fitted w/a domed flanged cover
w/fruit finial, short shaped rim spout & applied entwined strap handle, gilt trim,
9 1/8" h. (small flakes on cover) **$1,045**
Dish, Famille Rose palette, irregular wide
rounded & lobed form, shallow w/flared
rim, floral-decorated rim band, interior
w/scattered designs of figures, fish, Chinese characters, etc., 19th c., 11 1/4" l. 825
Plate, 9" d., scalloped edge, made for the
Continental market w/polychrome & gilt
armorial decoration, late 18th c. (minor
edge chips) 633
Platter, 11 1/2" l., oval, blue Fitzhugh patt.,
19th c. 385
Platter, 13 7/8" l., rectangular w/deeply an-
gled corners, blue Nanking patt., orange
peel glaze, 19th c. 770
Platter, 14 1/2" l., oval, flanged rim, gilded
"A" in circle mark, 19th c. (spot of rim re-
pair) 633
Platter, 15 5/8'" l., oval, green Fitzhugh
patt., 19th c. 1,725
Platter, 16 1/8" l., 13 3/8" w., blue Nanking
patt., oblong w/beveled corners, 18th c.
(rim chips) 575
Platter, 16 1/2" l., oval, blue & white Nanking
patt., w/pierced oval insert, 19th c., 2 pcs. 440
Platter, 16 1/2" l., 13 1/2" w., blue Nanking
patt., oblong w/canted corners, late 18th c.
(glaze bubbles, minor rim chips) 690
Platter, 20" oval, blue Fitzhugh patt., 19th c. 805
Platter, 20 1/2" l., oval w/cut corners, blue &
white Nanking patt., painted w/a monogram within a shield w/lion crest & Latin
motto, early 19th c. 978
Punch bowl, armorial, footed, rounded
flared sides, decorated w/scroll band,
spearhead & floral border, coat of arms &
floral sprays, ca. 1790, 10 1/4" d.,
4 1/4" h. 1,064
Teapot, cov., cylindrical w/h.p. polychrome
& gilt eagle w/wings down & shield decoration, entwined strap handle, 19th c.,
5 3/4" h. (chips, hairline, scratches) 690
Tray, blue Nanking patt., oval w/wide flared
& reticulated border & shallow center
w/landscape scene, 19th c., 10 3/4" l. 495

Tureen, decorated w/spearhead band, coat
of arms & floral sprays, pineapple finial &
bent twig handles, 13 1/2" l., 11" h. 532
Tureen, cov., flared pedestal foot below
oval form w/rounded sides, twisted twig
handles, domed cover w/blossom finial,
decorated in green & gold designs on
cream ground, 14" l., 11 1/2" h. 3,360
Vegetable bowl, cov., Famille Rose palette, footed rectangular form w/notched
corners & stepped domed cover w/fruit
finial, heavy gilt trim, orange peel glaze,
9 1/2" l. 1,045
Vegetable dish, cov., blue Fitzhugh patt.,
rectangular w/notched corners, stepped
domed cover w/large fruit finial, trimmed
in gilt, 19th c., 9 1/2" l. 825
Vegetable dish, cov., blue "Nanking" patt.,
almond-shaped w/flanged rim, low
domed cover w/pine cone finial, 19th c.,
10 3/4" l. (edge chips) 330
Vegetable dish, open, blue Nanking patt.,
oval w/slightly scalloped flanged rim on
flaring sides, orange peel glaze, 19th c.,
11 1/2" l. 275

Chintz China

*There are over fifty flower patterns and myriad col-
ors from which Chintz collectors can choose. That is not
surprising considering companies in England began
producing these showy, yet sometimes muted, patterns in
the early part of this century. Public reception was so
great that this production trend continued until the
1960s.*

Bowl, Sweet Pea patt., Crown shape, Royal
Winton **$750**
Butter pat, Sunshine patt., Royal Winton 135
Cheese dish, cov., Summertime patt.,
Dane shape, Royal Winton 350
Compote, open, oblong shallow shaped
bowl on a flaring rectangular pedestal
base, Queen Anne patt., Royal Winton 225
Creamer & cov. sugar bowl, Chintz patt.,
Old Cottage shape, Royal Winton, pr. 250
Gravy boat & undertray, Sunshine patt.,
Royal Winton, 2 pcs. 295
Mustard jar, cov., footed barrel shape, Tri-
umph patt., Royal Winton 155
Pitcher, 3" h., jug-form, miniature milk-
type, Chelsea patt., Globe shape, Royal
Winton 110
Trivet, round, Silverdale patt., Royal Winton 95

Clarice Cliff Designs

*Clarice Cliff was a designer for A. J. Wilkinson, Ltd.,
Royal Staffordshire Pottery, Burslem, England when
they acquired the adjoining Newport Pottery Company
whose warehouses were filled with undecorated bowls
and vases. About 1925 her flair with the Art Deco style
was incorporated into designs appropriately named
"Bizarre" and "Fantasque" and the warehouse stock-
pile was decorated in vivid colors. These hand-painted
earthenwares, all bearing the printed signature of
designer Clarice Cliff, were produced until World War II
and are now finding enormous favor with collectors.*

*Note: Reproductions of the Clarice Cliff "Bizarre"
marking have been appearing on the market recently.*

Clarice Cliff Mark

Bowl, 7 1/2" d., 3 1/8" h., "Forest Glen" patt., a thin footring below the deep upright round sides curved around the base, a variation w/an orange & brown sky produced in Delicia runnings, mottled orange interior, marked, ca. 1936 (glaze flaking around rim) **$288**

Bowl, 8 3/8" d., 3 1/2" h., round w/deep upright sides, "Keyhole" patt., a geometric design in yellow, black & green, stamped marks, ca. 1929 (glaze wear) **374**

Candleholders, figural, modeled as a kneeling woman w/her arms raised high holding the candle socket modeled as a basket of flowers, My Garden patt., orange dress & polychrome trim, marked, 7 1/4" h., facing pr. **575**

Various Clarice Cliff Items

Candleholders, Fantasque line, cylindrical form w/flared base & rim, Melon patt., decorated w/a band of overlapping fruit in predominantly orange glaze w/yellow, bluish green & brown outline, stamped on base "Hand Painted Fantasque by Clarice Cliff Wilkinson Ltd. England," ca. 1930, minor glaze nicks, two small firing cracks to inside rim of one, 3 1/4" h., pr. (ILLUS. front) **1,380**

Candlestick, loop-handled, Tonquin patt., red **30**

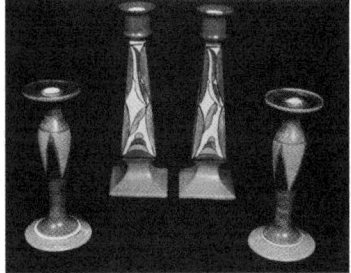

Two Pairs of Clarice Cliff Candlesticks

Candlesticks, slender baluster-form shaft above a disk foot & w/a wide flattened rim, painted w/bold geometric designs in blue, orange & green, Delecia Citrus patt., brightly painted fruits on a cream ground pr. (ILLUS. left & right) **2,500**

Candlesticks, squared pedestal foot supporting a tall square tapering shaft & cylindrical socket w/flared rim, decorated in bold geometric designs in orange, cream, green, blue & yellow, pr. (ILLUS. center) **2,900**

Clarice Cliff Figural Centerpiece

Centerpiece, "Bizarre" ware, model of a stylized Viking longboat, raised on trestle supports & w/a frog insert, glazed in orange, yellow, brown & black on a cream ground, printed factory marks, ca. 1925, restored, 15 3/4" l., 9 5/8" h., 2 pcs. (ILLUS.) **1,500**

Rare Crest Pattern Charger

Charger, large round dished form, Crest patt., three large Japanese-style crests in gold, blue, rust red, black & green on a mottled green ground (ILLUS.) **12,000**

Charger, "Taormina" patt., round, decorated w/large stylized trees on a cliff top w/the sea in the distance in tones of orange, yellow, green & blue, marked, 17" d. (minor crazing) **1,093**

Coffee service: cov. coffeepot, creamer, open sugar bowl, five cake plates & six cups & saucers; Ravel patt., creamer & sugar w/pointed conical bodies supported by buttress legs, other serving pieces w/flaring cylindrical bodies, marked, coffeepot 6" h., the set **1,100**

Condiment set: two jars w/silver-plated lids & a small open bowl fitted in a silver-plated frame w/a looped center handle; each piece h.p. w/stylized red & blue flowers on an ivory ground, marked, tray 4 1/2 x 5", the set (small chip on one piece).............. **523**

Cracker jar, cov., "Celtic Harvest" patt., spherical footed body decorated w/embossed fruit & sheaves of wheat, chromed metal cover, 6 1/2" h. (chrome wear).............. **173**

Jam jar, cov., cylindrical body, Melon patt., decorated w/a band of overlapping fruit, predominantly orange w/yellow, blue & green w/brown outline, ca. 1930, restoration to rim & side, marked, 4" h. (ILLUS. top right w/candleholders).............. **690**

Pitcher, 5 1/8" h., "Fantasque" line, squared base w/flattened spherical sides, Autumn (Balloon Trees) patt. in blue, yellow, green, orange, black & purple, stamped on base "Registration Applied For Fantasque Hand Painted Bizarre by Clarice Cliff Newport Pottery England," ca. 1931, minor glaze bubbles & nicks (ILLUS. center right w/candleholders).............. **920**

Vase, 9" h., 4 3/4" d., "Bizarre" ware, baluster-shaped, Original Bizarre patt., a wide middle band of multicolored triangles flanked by a dark blue rim band & yellow & orange base bands, No. 264, ink mark (minor wear).............. **2,500**

Vase, 9 1/2" h., 6 1/2" d., "Bizarre" ware, Isis shape, ovoid body tapering to a wide, flat rim, decorated in the Melon patt., bold stylized abstract fruits in dark red, blue, orange, green & yellow around the middle flanked by wide dark orange bands, ink mark.............. **3,200**

Vase, 12 1/4" h., gently flaring conical body on a wide round foot, molded in bold relief w/green & yellow budgie birds on a leafy branch against a light blue shaded to cream ground.............. **410**

Clarice Cliff Crocus Vase

Vases, 8" h., "Bizarre" ware, footed ovoid body w/flared rim, Crocus patt., orange, blue & purple crocuses, green, brown & yellow bands, small glaze chip, marked, pr. (ILLUS. of one).............. **690**

Copeland & Spode

W. T. Copeland & Sons, Ltd., have operated the Spode Works at Stoke, England, from 1847 to the present. The name Spode was used on some of its productions. Its predecessor, Spode, was founded by Josiah Spode about 1784 and became Copeland & Garrett in 1843, continuing under that name until 1847. Listings dated prior to 1843 should be attributed to Spode.

Copeland & Spode Mark

Bust of Music, parian, a young woman w/a laurel wreath in her hair, waisted circular socle, impressed title & Copeland mark, ca. 1874, 13 1/2" h. (shallow chip to flower in her hair).............. **$518**

Dessert plates, each finely decorated in raised paste gilding w/a different exotic bird perched on rockwork or branches detailed in turquoise & white enamel, within a scalloped gilt-edged rim, painted by C.B. Brough, printed Copeland-Spode mark, artist-signed, retailer's mark, ca. 1884, 8 1/4" d., set of 10 (some slight rubbing).............. **5,700**

Dessert service: footed oval dish, eleven dessert plates; each piece of festoon-embossed shape, each finely painted w/two panels of oranges alternating w/two panels of different colorful flowers reserved on a pierced border richly decorated w/raised paste gilding, green printed "Spode Copeland's China England" & retailer's mark, ca. 1937, the set.............. **7,800**

Dinner service: sixteen 10" d. plates, eight 7" d. plates, ten 6" d. plates, ten 5" d. bowls, sixteen cups & saucers & one extra saucer, 13" l. platter, 10" l. oval vegetable dish (hairline); "India Tree" patt., each piece marked "Copeland Spode England India Tree," 20th c., the set.............. **690**

Figure of St. Filomena, parian, standing w/a lamp & staff, Copeland, late 19th c., 26" h. (losses).............. **748**

Pitcher, 8 1/4" h., 'Chicago' design, stoneware, decorated w/molded medallions & vignettes depicting the early history of Chicago in white on a matte blue ground, impressed "Copeland England - Copeland Late Spode, England" & "Chicago Pitcher - Designed by Frank E. Burley, Edition Delux, Burley & Co., Chicago," late 19th c.............. **460**

Tea set: cov. 8 3/4" h. teapot, cov. 5" h. sugar bowl & 4" h. creamer; Shanghai patt., the set.............. **146**

Cybis

Though not antique, fine Cybis porcelain figures are included here because of the great collector interest.

They are produced in both limited edition and non-numbered series and thus there can be a wide range available to the collector.

Cybis Marks

Bear, brown **$225**
Burro, "Fitzgerald," No. 632, 1964, 7" h. **175**
Carousel Pony, "Sugarplum," No. 651,
    1981, 12" h. **875**
Little Match Girl, No. 4067, 1983, 5 3/4" h. **350**
Little Princess, No. 457, 1968-1970, 10" h. **550**
Raccoon, "Raffles," No. 636, 1965, signed,
    7 1/2 x 9" **170**
Sea King's Steed (The), "Oceania," 1977,
    limited edition, 14 1/2" h. **985**

Czechoslovakian

Czechoslovakia did not exist until the end of World War I in 1918. The country was put together with parts of Austria, Bohemia and Hungary as a reward for the help of the Czechs and the Slovaks in winning the war. In 1993 Czechoslovakia split and became two countries: the Czech Republic and the Slovak Republic. Items are highly collectible because the country was in existence only 75 years. For a more thorough study of the subject, refer to the following books: Made in Czechoslavakia Books 1 and 2 by Ruth A. Forsythe; Czechoslavakian Glass & Collectibles Books I and II by Dale & Dian Barta and Helen M. Rose and Czechoslovakian Perfume Bottles and Boudoir Accessories by Jacquelyne Y. Jones North.

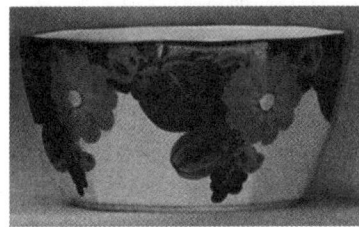

Art Deco Bowl

Baby plate, divided, white w/colorful nursery rhyme scene of Humpty Dumpty in
    each section, 7 1/4" d. **$125**
Bank, figural, model of a pear, shaded yellow & peach, green stem finial, Erphila,
    5 1/4" h. **75**
Basket w/overhead handle, cream ground w/figural blue bird by handle, 4 1/2" h. **48**
Basket w/overhead handle, yellow basketweave exterior w/band of flowers at
    rim, 5 1/4" h. **38**
Basket w/overhead handle, purple, tan & blue, majolica, Eichwald, 7 1/2" h. **185**
Basket w/overhead handle, flared foot, center portrait decoration within narrow band of white & rust dots & similar band at rim, band of white & rust hearts on foot w/blue & rust leaf design on overhead

handle & side handles, rust ground, Amphora, 12" h. **350**
Book ends, figural mountain climbers in tan, green & brown on grey rock form
    base, 6 1/4" h., pr. **125**
Bowl, 4'" l., oval, handled, green ground **165**
Bowl, 4 1/4" d., flower & fruit decoration in red, green, brown & blue on yellow ground, (Peasant Art Industries), P.A.I. (ILLUS.) **225**

Art Deco Style Covered Box

Box, cov., center band of Art Deco style painted under glaze flowers & fruit in red, blue & green on cream ground, cover decorated w/flowers & fruit, button finial, P.A.I., 5" h. (ILLUS.) **260**
Candleholder, hanging-type, flattened oblong form w/pink, blue & green floral design on black ground, bulbous base holding candle socket, black w/blue & red center medallion, orange trim, majolica,
    9" h. **95**
Canister, cov., "Coffee," border design w/single pink rose & gold trim on white
    ground, 7 1/2" h. **45**
Canister, cov., "Coffee," red ground w/slip floral decoration in yellow, blue, lavender & green & black on white ground,
    7 1/2" h. **75**
Cookie jar, cov., cylindrical w/rattan-wrapped swing handle, Silhouette patt., Erphila, 7 1/2" h. **175**
Creamer, footed bulbous body, blue shading to brown, figural moose head forms spout, antlers form rim, 3 1/4" h. **45**
Creamer, tan & brown, 3 1/2" h. **20**
Creamer, figural, model of a duck, green, brown & yellow, 4" h. **60**
Creamer, figural, model of a parrot, orange,
    4 1/2" h. **55**
Creamer, figural, model of a sitting cow, tail forms handle, brown, 4 1/2" h. **65**
Creamer, figural, model of a walking cow, tail forms handle, brown, 6" h. **125**
Creamer & cov. sugar bowl, figural, model of a strawberry, shaded red w/green handles, strawberry finial on sugar bowl cover, 4" h., pr. **100**
Dinner set: service for eight together w/all serving pieces; Eden patt., octagonal shape w/floral border & center scene of exotic birds on branches, the set **650**
Dish, cov., oval, blue w/figural tan & blue duck w/yellow bill on cover, 3" h. **75**

Dish, cov., figural, model of a crab, red, 3 1/2" 50

Dish, cov., figural, model of a potato, brown w/yellow butter pat-shaped finial, 4 1/4" h. 65

Egg cup, Chintz patt. 80

Figure of woman, 1920's lady, light green, 11 1/2" h. 350

Flower frog, figural, model of a parrot on a stump, blue & yellow, 5 1/2" h. 40

Flower frog, figure of nude standing on a turtle, 10 1/2" h. 375

Jardiniere, cylindrical body w/side ring handles, decorated w/airbrushed blue & red cherries, Erphila, 4 1/4" h. 85

Lamp base, footed wide bulbous base w/shoulder tapering to flaring cylindrical neck w/tapering domed top, center decorated w/wide tan & gold checked band flanked by narrow bands of pink roses & oval white medallion w/vase filled w/pink roses, green ground, 5 1/2" h. 85

Lamp base, tapering cylindrical body w/flaring foot, decorated overall w/Art Deco type blue, red & yellow flowers & fruit, wide black band at top & narrow red & black band at foot, Peasant Art Industries, 7 1/2" h. 225

Lamp base, "World," spherical body w/flaring foot, relief-molded countries in shades of blue on mottled yellow ground, Amphora, 9 1/2" h. 650

Lamp base, tapering cylinder above wide cylindrical base w/Art Deco style floral decoration, yellow ground, black disk foot, Peasant Art Industries, 10" h. 385

Lamp base, footed baluster-form body, dark blue lustre, 12 1/2" h. 250

Model of a dog, bulldog, sitting, wearing collar, white w/brown trim, 7" h. 450

Model of a Horse

Model of a horse, blue w/white trim, 4" h. (ILLUS.) 75

Model of a parrot, blue & green, on white globe pedestal, 8 1/2" h. 275

Model of Pheasant

Model of a pheasant, orange, blue, yellow & grey, on white oblong base, 4 1/2" h. (ILLUS.) 150

Model of a zebra, standing w/neck & head thrust backward, brown & grey w/dark green curly mane & tail, 6 1/2" h. 150

Napkin ring, figural, sitting girl, pink & green w/yellow bonnet, Erphila, 4" h. 45

Pipe holder, figural Chinese man, yellow & brown, 4 1/4" h. 50

Pitcher, 6" h., figural woman, red & white 85

Pitcher, 6 1/2" h., decorated w/scene of couple w/sheep, brown ground 85

Pitcher, cov., 7" h., bulbous body w/flattened side w/large loop handle from rim to base, fruit & flower decoration, P.A.I. 295

Art Deco Style Ram Goat Pitcher

Pitcher, 8 1/2" h., figural Art Deco style ram goat, yellow w/red & black trim, horn forms handle (ILLUS.) 650

Plate, dinner, 9 1/2" d., red lobster & crab design on border, white ground 35

Salt box, cov., border design w/single pink rose, gold trim on white ground, 6" h. 95

Salt & pepper shakers, figural, model of a lobster, red, 2 1/2" h., pr. 25

Salt & pepper shakers, figural, "Bashful Boy & Girl," brown & white, 3 1/4" h., pr. 30

Sauceboat, figural, model of a lobster, red, 3 1/4" h. 55

Snack plate w/cup, diamond-shaped, 8 1/4" plate w/cup well, blue & tan luster, the set 55

Sugar bowl, cov., figural, model of a swan, neck forms spout, C-scroll handle, button finial, white w/red bill, 3 1/4" h. 75

Teapot, creamer & cov. sugar bowl, stacking-type, decorated overall w/red, green & blue flowers on white ground, 5 1/2" h. 275

Tile, h.p. cottage scene, brown & tan, 6" sq. 45

Urns, portrait decoration, blue & gold, 7" h., pr. 270

Vase, 5 1/2" h., slightly swelled cylindrical body w/flared rim, angled D-form shoulder handles, decorated w/bust portrait of woman on brown ground (ILLUS. top next page) 40

Vase, 5 1/2" h., tapering cylindrical form w/cupped rim, flanked by black C-form angled handles, yellow luster finish .. 15

Vase, 7" h., bulbous ovoid body, decorated w/multicolored flowers & geometric designs, white ground, blue rim, Amphora 200

Small Portrait Vase

Vase, 7 1/2" h., fan-shaped, blue, white & orange paisley type design 235

Vase, 7 1/2" h., footed bulbous base w/wide tapering neck w/flared rim, flower & fruit motif, green ground, P.A.I. 165

Vase, 8" h., footed, slender ovoid body w/flared rim flanked by scrolled handles, Silhouette patt., scene of girl w/sheep, Erphila 95

Vase, 8 1/2" h., figural bust of Madonna & Child, white ground 175

Vase, 9" h., bulbous ovoid body w/figural King Tut handles, decorated w/band depicting colorful Egyptian scene, cream ground 500

Vase, 10" h., six-sided tapering form w/flared foot & rim, slip-decorated design in orange & blue 325

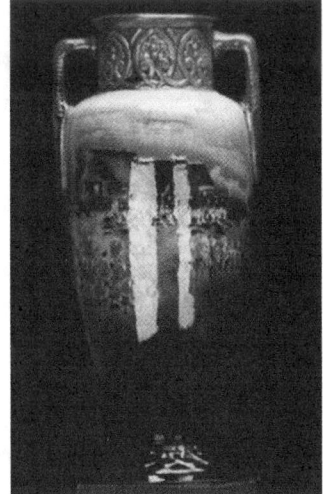

Large Scenic Vase

Vase, 10 1/4" h., footed ovoid body tapering slightly to wide cylindrical neck, angled handles from shoulder to rim, decorated w/sunset scene of house w/colorful garden in foreground, brown & tan (ILLUS.) 145

Vase, 11 1/4" h., waisted cylindrical body, decorated w/scene of storks near water,

tan, black, brown, orange & light blue, tan ground w/dark green C-form handles, Amphora 400

Wall pocket, figural, red, orange, white & blue bird beside brown birdhouse in tan Y-shaped branch, 6" h. 60

Wall pocket, figural white, yellow & blue bird w/white seashell, luster finish, 6" h. 70

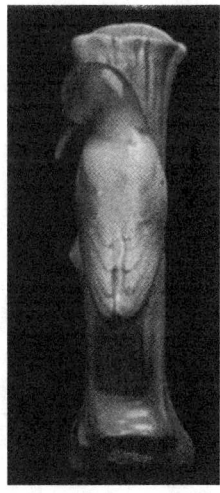

Wall pocket with Woodpecker

Wall pocket, figural, woodpecker in tan, orange, yellow & blue on side of tan tree branch, 6 1/2" h. (ILLUS.) 70

Wall pocket, conical, decorated w/large red flower w/yellow center, green leaves, white ground, 7" h. 85

Wall pocket, conical, fruit & flower decoration on green ground, P.A.I., 8" h. 125

Wall pocket, Amphora portrait-type, 8 1/2" h. 250

Watering can, decorated w/lavender flowers on white ground, 4 1/2" h. 45

Watering can, orange flowers & green leaves on white ground, 7" h. 145

Dedham & Chelsea Keramic Art Works

Dedham & Chelsea Keramic Art Works Marks

This pottery was organized in 1866 by Alexander W. Robertson in Chelsea, Massachusetts, and became A. W. & H. Robertson in 1868. In 1872, the name was changed to Chelsea Keramic Art Works and in 1891 to Chelsea Pottery, U.S.A. About 1895, the pottery was moved to Dedham, Massachusetts, and was renamed Dedham Pottery. Production ceased in 1943. High-fired colored wares and crackle ware were specialties. The rabbit is said to have been the most popular decoration on crackle ware in blue.

Since 1977, the Potting Shed, Concord, Massachusetts, has produced quality reproductions of early Dedham wares. These pieces are carefully marked to avoid confusion with original examples.

Dedham Turtle Pattern Bowl

Bowl, 7 1/2" d., 2 1/2" h.,Turtle patt., flat rim, several small chips to edge, ink stamp mark (ILLUS.)................................ **$660**

Bowl w/spoon, 5 3/8" d., 2 1/8" h., cereal, Rabbit patt., Chinese spoon w/rabbit decoration, both w/ink stamp mark, the set 413

Centerpiece bowl, Rabbit patt., ink stamp mark, 3 x 12" (peppering to glaze) 523

Cup & saucer, Rabbit patt., ink stamp mark, cup 2 1/4" h. 193

Dish, oyster shell-shaped, decorated w/a free-hand painted blue rabbit, blue ink stamp mark, 4 1/2" w. 193

Oyster dishes, modeled as an oyster half-shell w/a small molded blue-glazed pearl, ink stamp mark, 4 1/2" l., pr. 660

Dedham Plates

Plate, 6" d., Horse Chestnut patt. border, blue mark & one foreshortened rabbit, early 20th c. (ILLUS. right)............................... **173**

Plate, breakfast, 8 3/8" d., Iris patt., pre-1932, blue stamp mark & impressed rabbit mark, East Dedham, Massachusetts....... **144**

Plate, 6 1/4" d., Lily patt., central lily decoration w/"o" mark on stem, decorated by Maude Davenport, blue mark & one foreshortened rabbit, early 20th c. (ILLUS. left)... **1,150**

Plate, 7 1/2" d., Crab patt. **575**

Plate, 8 1/2" d., Crab patt. **374**

Plate, 8 1/2" d., Duck patt........................ **230**

Plate, 8 1/2" d., Lobster patt. (rim glaze imperfection) **345**

Plate, 10" d., dinner, Rabbit patt., decorated by Maude Davenport, ink stamp mark (small glaze nick on edge of rim).................. **303**

Plate, 10" d., Horse Chestnut patt. **86**

Plate, 10 1/4" d., Cloverleaf patt., rim w/experimental greenish glaze on molded cloverleaf design, interior blue accent band w/circular greenish glazed dots, Chelsea Keramic Art Works cipher mark, ca. 1891 ..... **920**

Table service: six Crab patt. plates, one Crab patt. bowl, four Lobster patt. plates, three Lobster patt. serving platters & four Rabbit patt. ashtrays; stamped mark, ca. 1920s, the set..................................... **5,520**

Azalea Pattern Tureen

Tureen, cov., Azalea patt., blue stamp, 9 1/2" d., 5 3/4" h. (ILLUS.)............................ **920**

Vase, 5 3/4" h., terra cotta, classical urn-form w/two applied leaf-form handles, ca. 1880, impressed Chelsea Keramic Art Works cipher (firing cracks to base & handles).. **633**

Vase, 8" h., 6 1/2" d., pilgrim flask-form, flattened round form w/a short tapering cylindrical neck, raised on four short peg feet, the lower half carved in high-relief w/an ivory hunting dog in a field against a blue ground, by Hugh Robertson, die-stamped & initialed (small chips on feet).. **4,125**

Delft

In the early 17th century Italian potters settled in Holland and began producing tin-glazed earthenwares, often decorated with pseudo-Oriental designs based on Chinese porcelain wares. The city of Delft became the center of this pottery production and several firms produced the wares throughout the 17th and early 18th century. A majority of the pieces featured blue on white

designs, but polychrome wares were also made. The
Dutch Delftwares were also shipped to England and
eventually the English copied them at potteries in such
cities as Bristol, Lambeth and Liverpool. Although still
produced today, Delft peaked in popularity by the mid-
18th century.

Bowl, 10" d., 5 3/4" h., footed, tapering
sides w/wide flat rim, polychrome floral
design, monogram mark, England (minor
wear & chips on base)............................... **$2,200**

Charger, round w/wide flanged rim, scattered colored floral clusters in the Faza-
ckerly palette, Liverpool, England, 18th
c., 13 1/2" d. (edge chips, spider crack) **715**

Dry drug jar, ovoid body, h.p. in blue w/a
cherub & shell label inscribed
"U:AEGYPTIAC:," ca. 1730, England,
7 1/8" h. (large chip to foot, some craz-
ing) **1,150**

Dry drug jar, ovoid body, h.p. in blue w/an
angel's head & ribbon label inscribed
"V:POPULNEU" above the initials
"i.G.," ca. 1680, London, 7 7/8" h.
(cracks & some cracking & flaking of sur-
face glaze) **2,070**

Flower brick, rectangular, h.p. blue floral
decoration, England, mid-18th c., 5" l.
(rim & edge chips, glaze loss) **374**

Mantel garniture set: two covered baluster-form vases w/domed covers & two
trumpet-form tall vases; each w/a scal-
lop-framed blue-decorated landscape
cartouche, England, 18th c., cov. vases
10" h., other vases 8" h., the set (rim
chips & glaze flakes, repaired chips
throughout, glaze wear & rim restora-
tions).. **1,725**

Plate, 8 3/4" d., polychrome decoration,
painted in the center in blue, red & green
w/a dolphin spouting a spray of water
flanked by two distant ships, within a border of concentric blue lines & a blue &
white checkered band at the rim,
England, ca. 1730 (typical minor glaze
loss at rim).. **2,760**

Puzzle jug, bulbous body inscribed in blue
"Here Gentlemen Come try your Skill - I'll
hold a wager if you will - That you don't
drink this liqr all - Without you spill or let
some fall," flanked by stylized flowering
plants beneath a cylindrical neck pierced
w/a pattern of hearts & flowers, ca. 1760,
probably Liverpool, 7 1/2" h. (two spouts
missing & some restored-over glaze flak-
ing to the rim) **1,150**

Derby & Royal Crown Derby

*William Duesbury, in partnership with John and
Christopher Heath, established the Derby Porcelain
Works in Derby, England about 1750. Duesbury soon
bought out his partners and in 1770 purchased the
Chelsea factory and six years later, the Bow works.
Duesbury was succeeded by his son and grandson. Robert Bloor purchased the business about 1814 and managed successfully until illness in 1828 left him unable to
exercise control. The "Bloor" Period, however, extends
from 1814 until 1848, when the factory closed. Former
Derby workmen then resumed porcelain manufacture in*

*another factory and this nucleus eventually united with a
new and distinct venture in 1878 which, after 1890, was
known as Royal Crown Derby.*

*A variety of anchor and crown marks have been used
since the 18th century.*

Derby & Royal Crown Derby Marks

Royal Crown Derby Coffee Set

Candlestick, 'Birds in Branches' style,
modeled w/two figural birds, one w/or-
ange & purple plumage, the other pale
yellow, each perched among branches of
white blossoms below a foliate-molded
candle socket, ca. 1765, 9 3/8" h. (minor
chips & repair)..................................... **$3,162**

Coffee set: cov. 10 3/4" h. coffeepot, hot
milk pitcher, twenty large egg cups, twenty small cake plates, twenty coffee cups
& saucers, a lozenge-shaped dish, a two-
handled oval tray & two two-handled
serving dishes; decorated w/floral reserves, blue & gilt trim borders, decorated by A. Gregory & gilt by G.W. Darling-
ton, artist-signed, gilt printed factory
marks, Royal warrant & Tiffany & Co.,
New York retailer's mark, impressed
"DERBY," ca. 1907-09, the set (ILLUS. of
part) **57,500**

Royal Crown Derby Desk Set

Creamer, helmet-shaped, flattened rim & naturalistically colored twig handle, painted on the front w/a bouquet of summer flowers & on the back w/honeysuckle, w/floral sprigs on the rim & foot, ca. 1760, 5 1/8" h. (tiny chips) **1,265**

Desk set, rectangular tray set on paw feet & mounted w/pen tray & three covered pots, domed covers w/pointed finials, floral decoration, early 19th c., red factory mark, tray 8 1/2" l., the set (ILLUS. bottom previous page) **1,035**

Dessert dish, lozenge-shaped, the central oval panel painted w/two huntsmen & hounds within a gilt frame & a wide gilt foliate border at the lobed rim, probably painted by William Cotton, ca. 1815, crowned crossed batons & D in iron-red, painted initial I or number 7, 11 1/4" l. (slight rubbing) **1,380**

Crown Derby Dessert Plate

Dessert plates, eleven 9 1/4" d. plates & three footed 9 1/2" plates, each painted w/different foliate sprays, last quarter 19th c., wear, the set (ILLUS. of one) **2,415**

Figure group, 'Tithe Pig,' modeled w/the farmer's wife offering her baby to the black-clad parson, in lieu of the piglet held by her husband, all standing before a leafy tree on a grassy mound base w/a further piglet, a basket of eggs & a wheat sheaf, ca. 1770, 7 1/4" h. (some minor chips & restoration, fine hairline in base) **862**

Jar, cov., globular form, floral decoration in colored enamels & gilt, ca. 1890, 12" h. **1,150**

Model of peacock, the colorful bird on a base w/colorful foliage, factory marks, 20th c. (minor chip) **230**

Plates, 8 3/4" d., shaped scalloped rim w/a cobalt blue band & gilt floral decoration, the center h.p. w/birds in landscapes, artist-signed by Charles Harris, Royal Crown Derby, ca. 1898, set of 12 .... **3,738**

Platters, 13 1/2" l., oval, King's patt., painted in an Imari palette w/a central flowering prunus tree, peonies & other flowers within an elaborate foliate scroll border, ca. 1825, crowned crossed batons & D marks in iron-red, number 36 in underglaze-blue & incised 13, pr. (some rubbing to the gilding at the rim edges) **690**

Teapot, cov., globular form, painted in bright colors w/two Oriental figures seated beside a table, the reverse w/a figure walking between two large vases, the small domed cover painted w/a butterfly & vases within an iron red & gilt chain link border, 5 3/8" h. (cracks between body & handle terminals, handle possibly re-affixed, tiny chips to foot rim) **3,737**

Vase, 8 1/4" h., bottle-form, enamel & gilt-decorated w/fruits, flowers & foliage, ca. 1887 .... **403**

Vase, cov., footed bottle-shaped form w/tall cylindrical neck w/fitted cylindrical cap-type cover, Imari-style decoration, ca. 1800, 10 1/4" h. **728**

Doulton & Royal Doulton

John Doulton, the founder, was born in 1793. He became an apprentice at the age of twelve to a potter in south London. Five years later he was employed in another small pottery near Lambeth. His two sons, John and Henry subsequently joined their father in 1830 in a partnership he had formed by the name of Doulton & Watts. Watts retired in 1864 and the partnership was dissolved. Henry formed a new company that traded as Doulton & Co.

In the early 1870s the proprietor of the Pinder bourne Co., located in Burslem, Staffordsire, offered Henry a partnership. The Pinder Bourne Co. was purchased by Henry in 1878 and became part of the Doulton & Co. in 1882.

With the passage of time the demand for the Lambeth industrial and decorative stoneware declined whereas demand for the Burslem manufactured and decorated bone china wares increased.

Doulton & Co. was incorporated as a limited liability company in 1899. In 1901 the company was allowed to use the word "Royal" on its trademarks by Royal Charter. The well known "lion on crown" logo came into use in 1902. In 2000 the logo was changed on the company's advertising literature to one showing a more stylized lion's head in profile.

Today Royal Doulton is one of the world's leading manufacturers and distributors of premium grade ceramic tabletop wares and collectibles. The Doulton Group comprises Minton, Royal Albert, Caithness Glass, Holland Studio Craft and Royal Doulton. Royal Crown Derby was part of the group from 1971 until 2000 when it became an independent company. These companies market collectibles using their own brand names.

Royal Doulton Mark

Animals & Birds

Bird, Bullfinch, blue & pale blue feathers, red breast, HN 2551, 1941-46, 5 1/2" h. **$325**

Cat, Persian Cat, seated, black & white, HN
999, 1930-85, 5" h. **115**

Cat, seated animal, red "Flambé" glaze,
1920-96, 4 1/2" h. **100**

Cat, seated animal, red "Flambé" glaze,
1977-96, 11" h. **525**

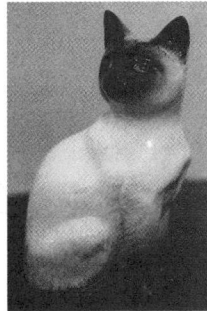

Siamese Cat

Cat, Siamese, seated, glossy cream &
black, DA 129, 4" h. (ILLUS.) **25**

Cat, Siamese Cat, standing, cream & black,
HN 2660, 1960-85, 5" h. **115**

Dog, Airedale Terrier, Ch. 'Cotsford Top-
sail,' standing, dark brown & black, light
brown underbody, HN 1024, 1931-68,
4" h. **250**

Dog, Alsatian, 'Benign of Picardy,' dark
brown, HN 1117, 1937-68, 4 1/2" **225**

Dog, American Great Dane, light brown,
HN 2602, 1941-60, 6 1/2" h. **625**

Dog, Boxer, Champion 'Warlord of Maze-
laine,' golden brown coat w/white bib, HN
2643, 1952-85, 6 1/2" h. **125**

Dog, Bulldog, HN 1044, brown & white,
1931-68, 3 1/4" h. **210**

Dog, Bulldog, HN 1047, standing, brown &
white, 1931-38, 3 1/4" **165**

Dog, Bulldog, HN 1074, standing, white &
brown, 1932-85, 3 1/4" **165**

Dog, Bulldog, K 1, seated, tan w/brown
patches, 1931-77, 2 1/2" **95**

Dog, Bulldog Puppy, K 2, seated, tan
w/brown patches, 1931-77, 2" **85**

Dog, character dog yawning, white
w/brown patches over ears & eyes, black
patches on back, HN 1099, 1934-85,
4" h. **85**

Dog, Chow (Shibu Ino), K 15, golden, 1940-
77, 2 1/2" **110**

Dog, Cocker Spaniel, Ch. 'Lucky Star of
Ware,' black coat w/grey markings, HN
1021, 1931-68, 3 1/2" h. **165**

Dog, Cocker Spaniel, golden w/dark brown
patches, HN 1187, 1937-69, 5" **125**

Dog, Cocker Spaniel, liver & white, 1931-
60, HN 1002, 6 1/2" h. **575**

Dog, Cocker Spaniel, 'Lucky Star of Ware,'
black coat w/grey markings, HN 1020,
1981-85, 5" **165**

Dog, Cocker Spaniel, seated, K9A, golden
brown w/black highlights, 1931-77,
2 1/2" h. **80**

Dog, Cocker Spaniel w/ Pheasant, seated,
white coat w/dark brown markings, red,
brown & green pheasant, HN 1062,
1931-68, 3 1/2" **175**

Dog, Cocker Spaniel w/Pheasant, seated,
white coat w/dark brown markings, red &
brown pheasant, HN 1029, 1931-68,
3 1/2" h. **175**

Dog, Cocker Spaniel, white w/black mark-
ings, HN 1078, 1932-68, 3" h. **165**

Dog, Cocker Spaniel, white w/black mark-
ings, HN 1109, 1937-85, 5" **140**

Dog, Cocker Spaniel, white w/light brown
patches, HN 1037, 1931-68, 3 1/2" **175**

Dog, Collie, Ch. 'Ashstead Applause,' dark
& light brown coat, white chest, shoulder
& feet, HN 1057, 1931-60, 7 1/2" h. **750**

Dog, Collie, dark & light brown coat, white
chest, shoulders & feet, HN 1059, 1931-
85, 3 1/2" **175**

Dog, Collie, dark & light brown coat, white
chest, shoulders & feet, medium, HN
1058, 1931-85, 5" h. **185**

Dog, Dalmatian, 'Goworth Victor,' white
w/black spots, black ears, HN 1113,
1937-85, 5 1/2" **225**

Dog, Dalmatian, 'Goworth Victor,' white
w/black spots, black ears, HN 1114,
1937-68, 4 1/4" **325**

Dog, Doberman Pinscher Ch. 'Rancho Do-
be's Storm,' black w/brown feet & chin,
HN 2645, 1955-85, 6 1/4" **155**

Dog, Dog of Fo, Flambé, RDICC, 1981,
5 1/4" h. **175**

Dog, English Setter, Ch. 'Maesydd Mustard,' off-white coat w/black highlights,
HN 1051, 1931-68, 4" h. **220**

Dog, English Setter, 'Maesydd Mustard,' off
white coat w/black highlights, HN 1050,
1931-85, 5 1/4" h. **145**

Dog, English Setter w/pheasant, grey
w/black markings, reddish brown bird,
yellowish brown leaves on base, HN
2529, 1939-85, 8" h. **475**

Dog, Foxhound, K 7, seated, white w/brown
& black patches, 1931-77, 2 1/2" **110**

Dog, French Poodle, HN 2631, white
w/pink, grey & black markings, 1952-85,
5 1/4" h. **175**

Dog, Great Dane, 'Rebeller of Ouborough,'
light brown, HN 2562, 191-52, 4 1/2" **750**

Dog, Greyhound, standing, golden brown
w/dark brown markings, cream chest &
feet, HN 1065, 1931-55, 8 1/2" h. **1,150**

Dog, Greyhound, white w/dark brown
patches, HN 1077, 1932-55, 4 1/2" **625**

Dog, Irish Setter, Ch. 'Pat O'Moy,' reddish
brown, HN 1054, 1931-60, 7 1/2" h. **725**

Dog, Irish Setter, 'Pat O'Moy,' reddish
brown, HN 1055, 1931-85, 5" **140**

Dog, Labrador, 'Bumblikite of Mansergh,'
black, HN 2667, 1967-85, 5 1/4" **145**

Dog, Labrador, standing, black, DA 145,
1990-present, 5" h. **48**

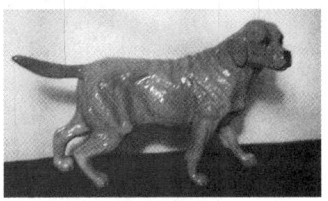

Golder Labrador

Dog, Labrador, standing, golden, DA 145, 1990-present, 5" h. (ILLUS.) **48**

Dog, Pekinese, Ch. 'Biddee of Ifield,' golden w/black highlights, HN 1012, 1931-85, 3" **100**

Dog, Rough-haired Terrier, Ch. 'Crackley Startler,' white w/black & brown markings, HN 1014, 1931-85, 3 3/4" h. **165**

Dog, Scottish Terrier, Ch. 'Albourne Arthur,' black, HN 1015, 1931-60, 5" **305**

Dog, Scottish Terrier, Ch. 'Albourne Arthur,' black, HN 1016, 1931-85, 3 1/2".................... **175**

Dog, Sealyham, Ch. 'Scotia Stylist,' white, HN 1031, 1931-55, 4"..................................... **405**

Dog, Springer Spaniel, 'Dry Toast,' white coat w/brown markings, HN 2517, 1938-55, 3 3/4".. **175**

Dog, Springer Spaniel, white w/black markings, HN 1078, 1932-68, 3" **135**

Dog, St. Bernard, lying, brown & cream, K 19, 1940-77, 1 1/2 x 2 1/2" **110**

Dog, Wire Fox Terrier, K 8, seated, white w/brown & black patches, 1931-77, 2 1/2".. **85**

Dog, Airedale Terrier, K 5, 1931-55, 1 1/4 x 2 1/4" **225**

Dog, Bull Terrier, K 14, lying, white, 1940-59, 1 1/4 x 2 3/4" **325**

Dog, Scottish Terrier, seated, black & white, K 18, 1940-77, 2 1/4 x 2 3/4"........................ **150**

Dog, Irish Setter, Ch. 'Pat O'Moy,' HN 1056, 1931-68, 6" l., 4" h. **225**

Dog, Cocker Spaniel w/ Pheasant, seated, white coat w/black markings, HN 1137, 1937-66, 6 1/2 x 7 3/4" **435**

Dogs, Cocker Spaniels sleeping, white dog w/brown markings & golden brown dog, HN 2590, 1941-69, 1 3/4" h. **110**

Dogs, Terrier Puppies in a Basket, three white puppies w/light & dark brown markings, brown basket, HN 2588, 1941-85, 3" h. **115**

Duck, Drake, standing, green, brown & white, HN 807, 1923-77, 2 1/2" h. **95**

Duck, Drake, standing, white, HN 806, 1923-68, 2 1/2" h. **95**

Elephant, trunk in salute, grey w/black, HN 2644, 1952-85, 4 1/4"..................................... **175**

Horse, Punch Peon, Chestnut Shire, brown w/black mane & black & white markings on legs, HN 2623, 1950-60, 7 1/2" h. **795**

Horses, Chestnut Mare and Foal, chestnut w/white stockings, fawn-colored foal w/white stockings, HN 2522, 1938-60, 6 1/2" h. **625**

Kitten, licking hind paw, brown & white, HN 2580, 2 1/4".. **75**

Kitten, looking up, tan & white, HN 2584, 1941-85, 2" **75**

Shetland Pony

Kitten, on hind legs, light brown & black on white, HN 2582, 1941-85, 2 3/4"..................... **75**

Kitten, sleeping, brown & white, HN 2581, 1941-85, 1 1/2" **75**

Monkey, Langur Monkey, long-haired brown & white coat, HN 2657, 1960-69, 4 1/2" h. **225**

Penguin, grey & white w/black tips, K 22, 1940-68, 1 3/4", ... **150**

Pony, Shetland Pony (woolly Shetland mare), glossy brown, DA 47, 1989 to present, 5 3/4" (ILLUS. bottom previous column) **45**

Salmon, curved leaping pose, printed mark, 1940-50, 12" h. **431**

Tiger, crouching, brown w/dark brown stripes, HN 225, 1920-36, 2 x 9 1/2"............. **525**

Tiger on a Rock, brown, grey rock, HN 2639, 1952-92, 10 1/4 x 12" **1,250**

Character Jugs

Anne Boleyn

Anne Boleyn, large, D 6644, 7 1/4" h. (ILLUS.) **85**

Anne of Cleves

Anne of Cleves, large, D 6653, 7 1/4" h. (ILLUS.) **85**

Antony & Cleopatra, large, D 6728, 7 1/4" h... **125**

Aramis

Aramis, large, D 6441, 7 1/4" h. (ILLUS.).......... **115**
Aramis, miniature, D 6508, 2 1/2" h. **45**

'Ard of 'Earing

'Ard of 'Earing, large, D 6588, 7 1/2" h.
(ILLUS.)... **1,500**

'Arriet

'Arriet, large, D 6208, 6 1/2" h. (ILLUS.)............ **185**
'Arriet, tiny, D 6256, 1 1/4" h. **175**
'Arry, large, D 6207, 6 1/2" h. **185**
'Arry, tiny, D 6255, 1 1/2" h. **175**
Athos, small, D 6452, 3 3/4" h. **60**
Auld Mac, miniature, D 6253, 2 1/4" h. **45**
Auld Mac "A", large, D 5823, 6 1/4" h. **85**

Bacchus

Bacchus, large, D 6499, 7" h. (ILLUS.) **95**
Bacchus, miniature, D 6521, 2 1/2" h. **50**
Baseball Player, small, D 6878, 4 1/4" h. **120**

Beefeater

Beefeater, large, D 6206, 6 1/2" h. (ILLUS.) **85**
Beefeater, small, D 6233, 3 1/4" h....................... **90**
Ben Franklin, small, D 6695, 4" h. **90**

Blacksmith

Blacksmith, D 6571, large, 7" h. (ILLUS.)......... **140**
Bootmaker, small, D 6579, 4" h............................ **70**
Busker (The), large, D 6775, 6 1/2" h. **125**
Buzfuz, small, D 5838, 4" h. **110**
Cap'n Cuttle, mid, D 5842, 5 1/2" h. **175**
Capt Ahab, large, D 6500, 7" h. **145**
Capt Ahab, small, D 6506, 4" h............................ **65**

Capt Henry Morgan

Capt Henry Morgan, large, 6 3/4" h.
(ILLUS.) **95**
Capt Henry Morgan, miniature, 2 1/4" h. **55**

Capt Hook

Capt Hook, large, D6597, 7 1/4" h (ILLUS.). **575**
Capt Hook, small, D 660, 4" h. **350**
Cardinal (The), small, D 6033, 3 1/2" h. **65**
Cardinal (The), tiny, D 6258, 1 1/2" h. **210**

Catherine Howard

Catherine Howard, large, D 6645, 7" h.
(ILLUS.)... 165

Catherine of Aragon

Catherine of Aragon, large, D 6643, 7" h.
(ILLUS.)... 120

Catherine Parr

Catherine Parr, large, D 6664, 6 3/4" h.
(ILLUS.)... 190
Cavalier (The), large, D 6114, 7" h..................... 135
Cavalier (The), small, D 6173, 3 1/4" h............... 60
City Gent, large, D 6815, 7" h. 150
Cliff Cornell, large, variation 2, dark blue
suit, red tie w/cream polka dots, 9" h. 300

Cliff Cornell Toby Jugs

Cliff Cornell, large, variation No. 1, light
brown suit, brown & cream striped tie,
9" h. (ILLUS. left) 450
Cliff Cornell, large, variation No. 3, dark
brown suit, green, black & blue designed
tie, 9" h. (ILLUS. right) 300
Cliff Cornell, small, variation No. 1, light
brown suit, brown & cream striped tie,
5" h. 1,500
Cliff Cornell, small, variation No. 2, blue
suit, 5" h. 3,500

Cliff Cornell, small, variation No. 3, dark
brown suit, 5" h. 300
Clown w/red hair (The), large, D 5610,
7 1/2" h. 2,600

Clown with White Hair

Clown w/white hair (The), large, D 6322,
7 1/2" h. (ILLUS.)... 1,200
Collector (The), large, D 6796, 7" h.................. 175
Davy Crockett & Santa Anna, large, D
6729, 7" h. 150
Dick Turpin, horse handle, large, D 6528,
7" h. 100
Dick Turpin, horse handle, miniature, D
6542, 2 1/4" h. 60
Dick Turpin, miniature, D 6128, 2 1/4" h........... 45
Dick Turpin, pistol handle, small, D 5618,
3 1/2" h. 55
Dick Turpin "A", pistol handle, D 5485,
6 1/2" h. 130
Dick Whittington, large, D 6375, 6 1/2" h........ 400

Don Quixote

Don Quixote, large, D 6455, 7 1/4" h.
(ILLUS.) 110
Drake, small, D 6174, 3 1/4" h............................. 65
Falconer (The), miniature, D 6547, 2 3/4" h. 55
Falconer (The), small, D 6540, 3 3/4" h. 60

Falstaff

Falstaff, large, D 6287, 6" h. (ILLUS.) **110**
Farmer John, large, D 5788, 6 1/2" h. **135**
Farmer John, small, D 5789, 3 1/4" h. **65**
Fat Boy, mid, D 5840, 5" h. **175**
Fat Boy, miniature, D 6139, 2 1/2" h. **60**

The Fortune Teller

Fortune Teller (The), large, D 6497,
6 3/4" h. (ILLUS.) **550**
Fortune Teller (The), small, D 6503,
3 3/4" h. **330**
Friar Tuck, large, D 6321, 7" h. **425**
Gaoler, small, D 6577, 3 3/4" h. **70**

The Gardener

Gardener (The), large, D 6630, 7 3/4" h.
(ILLUS) **160**
General Gordon, large, D 6869, 7 1/4" h. **215**
Genie, large, D 6892, 7" h. **225**
George Washington, large, D 6669,
7 1/2" h. **165**

George Washington

George Washington and George III, large,
D 6749, 7 1/4" h. (ILLUS. of Washington
side) **175**

Gladiator

Gladiator, large, D 6650, 7 3/4" h. (ILLUS.) **650**
Gladiator, small, D 6553, 4 1/4" h. **395**
Gone Away, miniature, D 6545, 2 1/2" h. **60**
Gone Away, small, D 6538, 3 3/4" h. **55**
Granny, large, D 5521, 6 1/4" h. **95**
Granny, miniature, D 6520, 2 1/4" h. **60**

Groucho Marx

Groucho Marx, large, D 6710, 7" h.
(ILLUS.) **135**

The Guardsman

Guardsman (The), large, D 6568, 6 3/4" h.
(ILLUS.) **95**

Gulliver

Gulliver, large, D 6560, 7 1/2" h. (ILLUS.)......... **825**
Gulliver, miniature, D 6566, 2 1/2" h. **395**
Gunsmith, small, D 6580, 3 1/2" h. **65**

Hamlet

Hamlet, large, D 6672, 7 1/4" h. (ILLUS.) **165**
Happy John "A", large, D 6031, 8 1/2" h............ **95**

Henry V

Henry V, embossed flag, large, variation
    No. 1, D 6671, 7 1/4" h. (ILLUS.).................... **205**

Henry V, flag decal, large, variation No. 3, D
    6671, 7 1/4" h. **140**

Henry VIII

Henry VIII, large, D 6642, 6 1/2" h. (ILLUS.) **105**

Izaac Walton

Izaac Walton, large, D 6404, 7" h. (ILLUS.) **95**

Jane Seymour

Jane Seymour, large, D 6646, 7 1/4" h.
    (ILLUS.) **115**
Jarge, small, D 6295, 3 1/2" h. **135**

Jester, seated, medium, D 6910, 5" h.............. **175**
Jester, small, D 5556, 3 1/8" h. **90**
Jockey, large, D 6625, 7 3/4" h. **275**
John Barleycorn, small, D 5735, 3 1/2" h. **55**
John Doulton, small, two o'clock, D 6656,
4 1/4" h.. **50**

John Peel

John Peel, large, D 5612, 6 1/2" h. (ILLUS.)...... **125**
John Peel, tiny, D 6259, 1 1/4" h. **200**
John Shorter, small, D 6880, 4 1/4" h. **165**

Johnny Appleseed

Johnny Appleseed, large, D 6372, 6" h.
(ILLUS.).. **260**
Juggler (The), large, D 6835, 6 1/2" h. **155**
King Charles I, large, D 6917, 7" h. **375**

The Lawyer

Lawyer (The), large, D6498, 7" h. (ILLUS.)....... **115**
Lawyer (The), small, D 6504, 4" h. **60**
Leprechaun, large, D 6847, 7 1/2" h.................. **145**
Little Mester Museum Piece, large, D
6819, 6 3/4" h... **165**

Lobster Man, large, D 6617, 7 1/2" h. **90**
London 'Bobby' (The), large, D 6744, 7" h. **103**
Long John Silver, miniature, D 6512,
2 1/2" h.. **50**

Lord Nelson

Lord Nelson, large, D 6336, 7" h. (ILLUS.)....... **380**

Louis Armstrong

Louis Armstrong, large, D 6707, 7 1/2" h.
(ILLUS.) **200**

Lumberjack

Lumberjack, large, D 6610, 7 1/4" h.
(ILLUS.) **90**
Macbeth, large, D 6667, 7 1/4" h. **135**

Mad Hatter

Mad Hatter, large, D 6598, 7 1/4" h.
(ILLUS.).. **175**
Mark Twain, small, D 6694, 4" h......................... **135**
Mephistopheles, large, w/verse, D 5757,
7" h. **2,750**
Mephistopheles "A", small, two-faced,
w/verse, D 5758, 3 3/4" h.............................. **950**

Merlin

Merlin, large, D 6529, 7 1/4" h. (ILLUS.) **90**
Merlin, small, D 6536, 3 3/4" h. **50**
Mine Host, miniature, D 6513, 2 1/2" h............... **60**
Mr. Micawber, mid, D 5843, 5 1/2" h................. **165**

Mr. Pickwick

Mr. Pickwick, large, D 6060, 5 1/2" h.
(ILLUS.) **185**
Mr. Pickwick, tiny, D 6260, 1 1/4" h. **165**
Mr. Quaker, large, D 6738, 7 1/2" h. **650**
Neptune, small, D 6552, 3 3/4" h.......................... **55**

Night Watchman

Night Watchman, large, D 6569, 7" h.
(ILLUS.) **95**
North American Indian, small, D 6614,
4 1/4" h.. **50**
Old Charley, large, D 5420, 5 1/2" h................... **95**

Old King Cole

Old King Cole, large, D 6036, 5 3/4" h.
(ILLUS.) **275**
Old Salt, large, D 6551, 7 1/2" h. **105**

Paddy

Paddy, large, D 5753, 6" h. (ILLUS.).................. **110**
Paddy, tiny, D 6145, 1 1/4" h. **75**

Parson Brown

Parson Brown "A", large, D 5486, 6 1/2" h.
(ILLUS.)... **125**
Pearly King, large, D 6760, 6 3/4" h. **125**
Pearly Queen, large, D 6759, 7" h.................... **115**
Pied Piper, large, D 6403, 7" h........................... **125**
Poacher (The), variation 2, large, D 6429,
7" h. **175**

Punch & Judy Man

Punch & Judy Man, large, D 6590, 7" h.
(ILLUS.)... **750**
Queen Victoria, small, D 6913, 3 1/2" h............ **165**
Red Queen (The), large, D 6777, 7 1/4" h. **135**

The Ringmaster

Ringmaster (The), large, D 6863, 7 1/2" h.
(ILLUS.).. **175**

Rip Van Winkle

Rip Van Winkle, large, D 6438, 6 1/2" h.
(ILLUS.) **100**

Robin Hood

Robin Hood, 2nd version, large, D 6527,
7 1/2" h. (ILLUS. left) **105**
Robin Hood, 2nd version, small, D 6234,
3 1/4" h. (ILLUS. right)...................................... **65**

Robinson Crusoe

Robinson Crusoe, large, D 6532, 7 1/2" h.
(ILLUS.) **120**
Robinson Crusoe, miniature, D 6546,
2 3/4" h.. **55**
Romeo, large, D 6670, 7 1/2" h. **105**
Ronald Reagan, large, D 6718, 7 3/4" h. **750**

Sairey Gamp

Sairey Gamp, large, No. 5451, 6 1/4" h.
(ILLUS.).. **85**
Sairey Gamp, tiny, D 6146, 1 1/4" h..................... **80**
Sam Johnson, large, D 6289, 6 1/4" h. **325**

Sam Weller

Sam Weller, large, D 6064, 6 1/2" h.
(ILLUS.).. **325**
Sam Weller, tiny, D 6147, 1 1/4" h........................ **75**
Sancho Pança, large, D 6456, 6 1/2" h. **125**

Santa Claus w/Doll & Drum Handle

Santa Claus, doll & drum handle, large, D
6668, 7 1/2" h. (ILLUS.).................................... **148**

Santa Claus with Plain Handle

Santa Claus, plain handle, large, D 6704,
7 1/2" h. (ILLUS.)... **165**

Scaramouche

Scaramouche, large, first version, D 6558,
7" h (ILLUS.). **900**
Simon the Cellarer, large, D 5504, 6 1/2" h. **110**
Simon the Cellarer, small, D 5616,
3 1/2" h.. **60**

Simple Simon

Simple Simon, large, D 6374, 7" h.
(ILLUS.) **495**
Sir Francis Drake, large, D 6805, 7" h. **225**

Sir Thomas More

Sir Thomas More, large, D 6792, 6 3/4" h.
(ILLUS.).. **215**

The Sleuth

Sleuth (The), large, D 6631, 7" h. (ILLUS.)....... **105**

St. George

St. George, large, D 6618, 7 1/2" h.
(ILLUS.).. **350**
Tam O'Shanter, miniature, D 6640,
2 1/2" h. **85**
Toby Philpots, large, D 5736, 6 1/4" h. **120**

Tony Weller

Tony Weller, large, D 5531, 6 1/2" h.
(ILLUS.).. **145**
Touchstone, large, D 5613, 7" h. **245**
Town Crier, large, D 6530, 7" h. **245**

Ugly Duchess

Ugly Duchess, large, D 6599, 6 3/4" h.
(ILLUS.) **650**
Uncle Tom Cobbleigh, large, D 6337, 7" h. **550**

Veteran Motorist

Veteran Motorist, large, D 6633, 7 1/2" h.
(ILLUS.) **165**

The Walrus & Carpenter

Walrus & Carpenter (The), large, D 6600,
7 1/4" h. (ILLUS.).. **195**

Shakespeare

William Shakespeare, large, D 6689,
7 3/4" h. (ILLUS.).. **150**
Winston Churchill, style 1, large, D 6907,
Union Jack & bulldog handle, 7" h. **325**

Yachtsman

Yachtsman, large, D 6626, 8" h. (ILLUS.)......... **145**

Figurines

Abdullah, HN 2104, multicolored, 1953-62....... **425**
Ace (The), HN 3398, white, 1991-95................. **210**
Adele, HN 2480, flowered white dress,
1987-92.. **175**
Affection, HN 2236, purple, 1962-94............... **150**
Afternoon Tea, HN 1747, pink & blue,
1935-82.. **500**
Ajax, HN 2908, red, green & gold, 1980, lim-
ited edition of 950.. **600**
Alexandra, HN 2398, patterned green
dress, yellow cape, 1970-76.......................... **280**
Alison, HN 2336, blue & white, 1966-92 .... **200**
Amy, HN 3316, blue & rose, Figure of the
Year series, 1991 .... **950**
An Old King, HN 2134, purple, red, green &
brown, 1954-92.. **425**
Anna, HN 2802, purple & white, Kate
Greenaway Series, 1976-82.......................... **250**
Anne Bolelyn, HN 3232, red & grey, 1990,
limited edition of 9,500 .... **475**
April, HN 2708, white dress w/flowers,
Flower of the Month series, 1987 .... **245**
Aragorn, HN 2916, tan, 1981-84 .... **175**
Artful Dodger, M 55, black & brown, Dick-
ens Miniatures Series, 1932-83 .... **85**
As Good As New, HN 2971, blue, green
and tan, 1982-85 .... **160**
Ascot, HN 2356, green dress w/yellow
shawl, 1968-95 .... **200**

The Auctioneer

Auctioneer (The), HN 2988, black, grey &
brown, 1986, R.D.I.C.C Series (ILLUS.)........ **295**
August, HN 3165, white & blue dress
w/poppies, Flower of the Month Series,
1987 .... **255**
Autumn Breezes, HN 2131, orange, yellow
& black, 1990-94 (ILLUS. top next page)...... **275**
Autumn Breezes, HN 2147, black & white,
1955-71.. **425**
Autumntime, HN 3231, golden brown,
R.D.I.C.C. Four Seasons Series (Style
Four), 1989.. **250**
Babie, HN 1679, green dress, 1935-92 .... **105**
Ballad Seller, HN 2266, pink, 1968-73............. **375**

Autumn Breezes

Balloon Man (The), HN 1954, black & grey, 1940 to present 350

Balloon Seller (The), HN 583, green shawl, cream dress, 1923-49 1,150

Basket Weaver (The), HN 2245, pale blue & yellow, 1959-62 500

Beachcomber, HN 2487, matte, purple & grey, 1973-76 275

Beat You To It, HN 2871, pink, gold & blue, 1980-87 425

Bedtime

Bedtime, HN 1978, white w/black base, 1945-97 (ILLUS.) 85

Bedtime Story, HN 2059, pink, white, yellow & blue, 1950-98 450

Belle, HN 2340, green dress, 1968-88 85

Belle O' the Ball, HN 1997, red & white, 1947-79 400

Bernice, HN 2071, pink & red, 1951-53 995

Biddy, HN 1513, red dress, blue shawl, 1932-51 275

Bill Sykes, M 54, black & brown, 1932-81 80

Blacksmith of Williamsburg, HN 2240, white shirt, brown hat, 1960-83 375

Blithe Morning, HN 2065, red dress, 1950-73 325

Bo Peep, HN 1811, orange dress, green hat, 1937-95 150

Bonnie Lassie, HN 1626, red dress, 1934-53 515

Boy from Williamsburg, HN 2183, blue & pink, 1969-83 225

Bride (The), HN 2166, pale pink dress, 1956-76 250

Bride (The), HN 2873, white w/gold trim, 1980-89 175

Bride (The), HN 3284, style 4, white, 1990-97 225

Bridesmaid, M 30, pink & lavender, 1932-45 300

Bridesmaid (The Little), HN 2196, white dress, pink trim, 1960-76 155

Bridesmaid (The Little), M 12, multicolor gown, 1932-45 295

Bridget, HN 2070, green, brown & lavender, 1951-73 325

Broken Lance (The), HN 2041, blue, red & yellow, 1949-75 650

Bunny, HN 2214, turquoise, 1960-75 225

Bunny's Bedtime, HN 3370, pale blue, pink ribbon, 1991, RDICC Series, limited edition of 9,500 225

Buttercup, HN 2309, green dress w/yellow sleeves, 1964-97 210

Buz Fuz, M 53, black & red, 1932-83 80

Camellia, HN 2222, pink, 1960-71 350

Captain Cook, HN 2889, black & cream, 1980-84 500

Captain Cuttle, M 77, yellow & black, 1939-82 80

Captain (The), HN 2260, black & white, 1965-82 300

Carolyn, HN 2112, white & green flowered dress, 1953-65 475

Carpet Seller (The), HN 1464, (hand open), green & orange, 1929-? 315

Carpet Seller (The), HN 1464A, (hand closed), green & orange, 1931-69 275

Carpet Seller (The), HN 2776, Flambé, 1990 to present 225

Catherine, HN 3044, white, 1985-96 65

Catherine of Aragon, HN 3233, green, blue & white dress, 1990, limited edition of 9,500 525

Charlotte

Charlotte, HN 3813, brown figure, ivory
dress, 1996-97 (ILLUS.)................................ 285
Chief (The), HN 2892, gold, 1979-88.............. 265
Child from Williamsburg, HN 2154, blue
dress, 1964-83... 265
China Repairer, HN 2943, blue, white &
tan, 1983-88.. 175
Chloe, HN 1765, blue, 1936-50........................ 475

Christmas Parcels

Christmas Parcels, HN 2851, black, 1978-
82 (ILLUS.).. 235

Cissie

Cissie, HN 1809, pink dress, 1937-93
(ILLUS.).. 175
Claire, HN 3209, red, 1990-92........................ 215
Claribel, HN 1951, red dress, 1940-49............ 425
Clarinda, HN 2724, blue & white dress,
1975-81.. 210
Coachman, HN 2282, purple, grey & blue,
1963-71.. 625
Cookie, HN 2218, pink & white,1958-75........... 215
Coralie, HN 2307, yellow dress, 1964-88........ 175
Cup O' Tea, HN 2322, dark blue & grey,
1964-83.. 315
Curly Locks, HN 2049, pink flowered
dress,1949-53... 265
Daffy Down Dilly, HN 1712, green dress,
1935-75.. 405
Dainty May, M 67, pink skirt, blue over-
dress, 1935-49... 625
Daisy, HN 3805, ivory & gold, Charleston
series, 1996-97 (ILLUS. top next column)...... 285
Darling, HN 1319, white w/black base,
1929-59.. 225

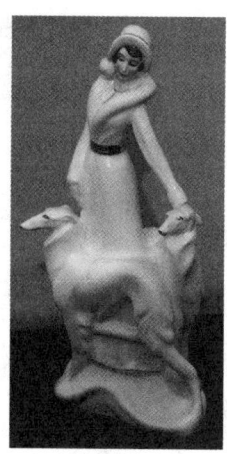

Daisy

Darling, HN 1985, white nightshirt, 1946-97 95
David Copperfield, M 88, black & tan, Dick-
ens Miniatures Series, 1949-83.................... 85
Deborah, HN 2701, green & white, 1983-84 215
Delight, HN 1772, red dress, 1936-67.............. 265
Diana, HN 1986, red, 1946-75.......................... 250
Discovery, HN 3428, matte white, 1992........... 375
Duchess of York (The), HN 3086, cream,
1986, limited edition of 1,500 1,450
Duke of Edinburgh (The), HN 2386, black
& gold, 1981, limited edition of 1,500............ 500
Dulcie, HN 2305, blue, 1981-84...................... 220
Easter Day, HN 1976, white dress, blue
flowers, 1945-51... 525
Easter Day, HN 2039, multicolored, 1949-
69.. 500
Eliza, HN 2543, gold, Haute Ensemble Se-
ries, 1974-79.. 405
Eliza, HN 3179, red & lilac, 1988-92................. 200

Ellen

Ellen, HN 3816, ivory & light blue dress,
1996-97 (ILLUS.).. 285
Elyse, HN 2429, blue dress, 1972-95 225

Fond Farewell

Fortune Teller

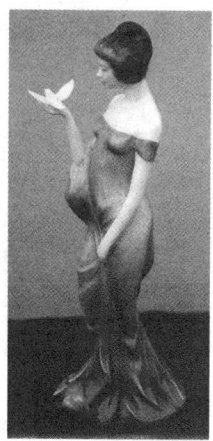

Harmony

Honey, HN 1909, pink, 1939-49 .... **525**
Hornpipe (The), HN 2161, blue jacket, blue
& white striped trousers, 1955-62 .... **900**

The Huntsman

Huntsman (The), HN 2492, grey coat,
cream pants, black hat & boots, 1974-79
(ILLUS.) **325**
Ibrahim, HN 2095, brown & yellow, 1952-55 ...... **700**
Innocence, HN 2842, red, 1979-83 .... **225**
Invitation, HN 2170, pink, 1956-75 .... **215**
Irene, HN 1621, pale yellow dress, 1934-51 ...... **550**
Isadora, HN 2938, lavender, 1986-92 .... **350**
Ivy, HN 1768, pink hat, lavender dress,
1936-79 .... **135**
Jack, HN 2060, green, white & black, 1950-
71 .... **235**
Jacqueline, HN 2001, pink dress, 1947-51 ...... **800**
Jane, HN 2806, yellow dress, 1983-86 .... **225**
Jane, HN 3260, green, blue & yellow, 1990-
95 .... **275**
Janet, HN 1537, red dress, 1932-95 .... **150**
Janet, M 69, pale green skirt, green over-
dress, 1936-49 .... **495**
Janet, HN 1916, pink & blue, 1939-49 .... **350**
Janice, HN 2022, green dress, 1949-55 .... **715**
Jennifer, HN 2392, blue dress, 1981-92 .... **295**

Jester (A), HN 2016, pink, purple & orange,
1949-97 .... **325**
Jill, HN 2061, pink & white, 1950-71 .... **250**
Joan, HN 2023, blue, 1949-59 .... **225**
Joker (The), HN 2252, white, 1990-92 .... **250**
Judge (The), HN 2443, red & white, 1972-
76 .... **250**
Judge (The), HN 2443A, (gloss), red &
white, 1976-92 .... **260**
Judith, HN 2089, red & blue, 1952-59 .... **405**
Judith, HN 2278, yellow, 1986-89 .... **275**
Julia, HN 2705, gold, 1975-90 .... **265**
June, HN 2991, lavender & red, 1988-94 .... **235**
Karen, HN 1994, red dress, 1947-55 .... **450**
Karen, HN 2388, style two, red & white,
1982 to present **475**
Kate, HN 2789, white dress, 1978-87 .... **200**
Kathleen, HN 3100, purple, cream & pink,
1986 .... **300**
Katrina, HN 2327, red, 1967-69 .... **475**
Kelly, HN 2478, white w/blue flowers, 1985-
92 .... **220**
Kirsty, HN 3213, red, 1988-97 .... **150**
Ko-Ko, HN 2898, yellow & blue, 1980-85 .... **650**
L'Ambitieuse, HN 3359, rose & pale blue,
1991, RDICC, limited edition of 5,000 .... **350**
La Sylphide, HN 2138, white dress, 1954-
65 .... **475**
Lady April, HN 1958, red dress, 1940-49 .... **360**
Lady Betty, HN 1967, red, 1941-51 .... **450**
Lady Charmian, HN 1948, green dress, red
shawl, 1940-73 .... **320**
Lady of the Georgian Period (A), HN 41,
gold & blue, 1914-38 .... **1,900**

Lambing Time

Lambing Time, HN 1890, light brown,
1938-80 (ILLUS.) **300**
Last Waltz, HN 2315, apricot dress, 1967-
93 .... **220**
Laura, HN 2960, pale blue & white w/yellow
flowers, 1984-94 .... **300**
Laura, HN 3136, dark blue & white, 1988 .... **300**
Lavinia, HN 1955, red dress, 1940-79 .... **145**
Lawyer (The), HN 3041, grey & black,
1985-95 .... **225**
Leading Lady, HN 2269, blue & yellow,
1965-76 .... **325**

Legolas, HN 2917, cream & tan, Middle Earth Series, 1981-84.................................. **175**

Lights Out, HN 2662, blue trousers & yellow spotted shirt, 1965-69.............................. **325**

Lilac Time, HN 2137, red, 1954-69 .... **400**

Lily, HN 1799, green & blue, 1936-49............... **550**

Lisa, HN 2394, yellow & lilac, 1983-90............ **200**

Little Boy Blue, HN 2062, blue, 1950-73......... **200**

Lizzie, HN 2749, green, white & red, 1988-91 .... **190**

Lobster Man (The), HN 2317, blue, grey & brown, 1964-94...................................... **275**

Lorna, HN 2311, green dress, apricot shawl, 1965-85 .... **260**

Love Letter, HN 2149, pink & blue dress, 1958-76 .... **500**

Lucy Locket, HN 524, yellow dress, 1921-49 .... **700**

Lynne, HN 2329, green dress, 1971-96............. **225**

Madonna of the Square, HN 2034, light green-blue, 1949-51 .... **1,100**

Make Believe

Make Believe, HN 2225, blue dress, 1962-88 (ILLUS.)....................................... **180**

Margaret, HN 1989, red & green, 1947-49....... **500**

Marguerite, HN 1928, pink dress, 1940-49....... **450**

Marie, HN 1370, style two, purple dress, 1930-88... **95**

Marietta, HN 1341, black & red, 1929-49 ...... **1,650**

Marjorie, HN 2788, blue & white dress, 1980-84... **375**

Mary, HN 3375, blue & white, Figure of the Year Series, 1992 .... **650**

Mary Had a Little Lamb, HN 2048, lavender, 1949-88.. **150**

Mary, Mary, HN 2044, pink, Nursery Rhymes Series, 1949-73 .... **225**

Masque, HN 2554, (hand holds wand of mask), blue, 1973-82................................... **325**

Master (The), HN 2325, green & brown, 1967-92... **225**

Maxine, HN 3199, pink & purple, 1989-90......... **215**

Mayor (The), HN 2280, red & white, 1963-71 .... **450**

Maytime, HN 2113, pink dress w/blue scarf, 1953-67.. **400**

Melissa, HN 2467, purple & cream, 1981 to present... **225**

Melody, HN 2204, blue & peach, 1957-62 .... **350**

Mendicant (The), HN 1365, brown, 1929-69 .... **325**

Meriel HN 1931, pink dress, 1940-49............ **1,650**

Michelle, HN 2234, green, 1967-94 .... **185**

Midinette, HN 2090, blue dress, 1952-65........ **395**

Midsummer Noon, HN 2033, pink, 1949-55 ..... **750**

Minuet, HN 2019, white dress, floral print, 1949-71.. **400**

Miss Demure, HN 1402, lavender & pink dress, 1930-75... **250**

Miss Fortune, HN 1897, blue & white shawl, pink dress, 1938-49..................... **1,600**

Miss Muffet, HN 1936, red, 1940-67............... **200**

Modesty, HN 2744, white, 1987-91................... **225**

Monica, HN 1467, flowered purple dress, 1931-95.. **175**

Monica, M 66, shaded pink skirt, blue blouse, 1935-49.. **700**

Mr. Micawber, HN 1895, brown, black & tan, 1938-52... **450**

Mr. Micawber, M 42, yellow & black, 1932-83 .... **80**

Mr. Pickwick, HN 1894, blue, tan & cream, Dickens Series, 1938-42..................... **475**

Mrs. Bardell, M 86, green, 1949-82 .... **80**

My Love, HN 2339, white w/red rose, 1969-97 .... **325**

Newsboy, HN 2244, green, brown & blue, 1959-65.. **625**

Newsvendor, HN 2891, gold & grey, 1986, limited edition of 2,500 .... **260**

Nicola, HN 2839, flowered lavender dress, 1978-95.. **350**

Nina, HN 2347, matte blue, 1969-76 .... **200**

Ninette, HN 2379, yellow & cream, 1971-97 ..... **325**

Noelle, HN 2179, orange, white & black, 1957-67.. **450**

Old Country Roses

Old Country Roses, HN 3692, red, 1995-99 (ILLUS.).. **360**

Old King Cole, HN 2217, brown, yellow & white, 1963-67... **695**

Old Meg, HN 2494, blue & grey matte finish,
1974-76.. 250
Olga, HN 2463, turquoise & gold, 1972-75........ 315
Oliver Twist, M 89, black & tan, Dickens
Miniatures Series, 1949-83.............................. 80
Omar Khayyam, HN 2247, brown, 1965-83...... 250
Once Upon a Time, HN 2047, pink dotted
dress, 1949-55.. 475
Orange Lady (The), HN 1953, light green
dress, green shawl, 1940-75.......................... 315
Orange Vendor (An), HN 1966, purple
cloak, 1941-49... 1,050
Owd Willum, HN 2042, green & brown,
1949-73.. 265
Paisley Shawl, HN 1392, white dress, red
shawl, 1930-49.. 475
Paisley Shawl, M 4, green dress, dark
green shawl, black bonnet w/red feather
& ribbons, 1932-45... 450
Pamela, HN 3223, style two, white & blue,
1989-89.. 250
Pantalettes, HN 1362, green & blue,
1929-38.. 600
Pantalettes, M 16, red skirt, red tie on hat,
1932-45.. 400
Parisian, HN 2445, blue & grey, matte
glaze,1972-75.. 250
Partners, HN 3119, black, blue & grey,
1990-92.. 300
Paula, HN 3234, white & blue, 1990-96............. 250
Pauline, HN 2441, peach, 1984-1989................ 250
Pearly Boy, HN 2035, reddish brown,
1949-59.. 250
Pearly Boy, HN 20352, (hands clasped),
red jacket, 1949-59... 250
Pearly Girl, HN 1483, red jacket, 1931-49 350
Pecksniff, HN 2098, black & brown,
1952-67.. 400
Peggy, HN 2038, red dress, green trim,
1949-79.. 135
Penelope, HN 1901, red dress, 1939-75........... 400
Penny, HN 2338, green & white dress,
1968-95.. 130
Pensive, HN 3109, white w/yellow flowers
on skirt, 1986-88... 250
Pied Piper (The), HN 2102, brown cloak,
grey hat & boots, 1953-76.............................. 395
Piper (The), HN 2907, green, 1980-92.............. 375
Polka (The), HN 2156, pale pink dress,
1955-69.. 465
Polly, HN 3178, green & lavender, 1988-91...... 325
Polly Peachum, HN 550, red dress,
1922-49.. 495
Polly Peachum, M 21, red gown, 1932-45........ 650
Premiere, HN 2343, (hand holds cloak),
green dress, 1969-79...................................... 250
Pride & Joy, HN 2945, brown, gold & green,
RDICC, 1984 (ILLUS. top next column) 325
Priscilla, M 24, red, 1932-45.............................. 600
Promenade, HN 2076, blue & orange,
1951-53... 1,650
Prue, HN 1996, red, white & black, 1947-55...... 550
Puppetmaker, HN 2253, green, brown &
red, 1962-73.. 500
Queen Anne, HN 3141, green, red & white,
1989, Queens of the Realm Series, limit-
ed edition of 500... 425
Queen Elizabeth I, HN 3099, red & gold,
1987, Queens of the Realm Series, limit-
ed edition of 5,000.. 550

Pride & Joy

Queen of the Ice, HN 2435, cream, En-
chantment Series, 1983-86 225
Rachel, HN 2919, gold & green, 1981-84......... 265
Rebecca, HN 2805, pale blue & lavender,
1980-96.. 425
Regal Lady, HN 2709, turquoise & cream,
1975-83.. 250
Rosabell, HN 1620, red & green, 1934-38..... 1,450
Rosamund, M 32, yellow dress tinged
w/blue, 1932-45.. 750

Rosemary

Rosemary, HN 3698, mauve & yellow,
1995-97 (ILLUS.)... 375
Rowena, HN 2077, red, 1951-55 650
Sabbath Morn, HN 1982, red, 1945-1959 350
Sailor's Holiday, HN 2442, apricot jacket,
1972-79.. 315
Sairey Gamp, HN 2100, white dress, green
cape, 1952-67.. 550
Salome, HN 3267, red, blue, lavender &
green, 1990, limited edition of 1,000.......... 1,100
Sam Weller, M 48, yellow & brown, 1932-81 80

Samwise, HN 2925, black & brown, Middle
Earth Series, 1982-84 .... **450**
Sandra, HN 2275, gold, 1969-97 .... **163**
Sara, HN 2265, red & white, 1981-97 .... **150**
Schoolmarm, HN 2223, 1958-81 .... **375**
Secret Thoughts, HN 2382, green 1971-88...... **275**
Sharon, HN 3047, white, 1984-95 .... **150**

The Shepherd

Shepherd (The), HN 1975, light brown,
1945-75 (ILLUS.) **350**
Shore Leave, HN 2254, 1965-79 .... **325**
Silks and Ribbons, HN 2017, green, red &
white dress, 1949 to present **345**
Simone, HN 2378, green dress, 1971-81 .... **195**
Sir Edward, HN 2370, red & grey, 1979,
limited edition of 500 .... **550**
Skater (The), HN 3439, red, 1992-97 .... **325**

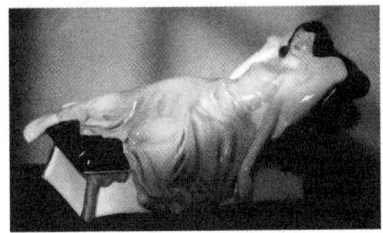

Sleeping Beauty

Sleeping Beauty, HN 3079, green, 1987-
89 (ILLUS.) **275**
Sleepyhead, HN 2114, 1953-55 .... **1,850**
Soiree, HN 2312, white dress, green over-
skirt, 1967-84 .... **200**
Solitude, HN 2810, cream, blue & orange,
1977-1983 .... **375**
Sophie, HN 3257, blue & red, 1990-92 .... **250**
Southern Belle, HN 2229, red & cream,
1958-97 .... **250**
Spring, HN 2085, 1952-59 .... **465**
Spring Flower, HN 1807, green skirt, grey-
blue overskirt, 1937-59 .... **450**
Spring Morning, HN 1922, green coat,
1940-73 .... **325**
Spring Morning, HN 1922, pink & blue,
1940-73 .... **325**

Spring Walk

Spring Walk, HN 3120, blue, 1990-92
(ILLUS.) **325**
St. George, HN 2051, 1950-85 .... **625**
St. George, HN 2067, purple, red & orange
blanket, 1950-76 .... **2,250**
Stiggins, M 50, black suit, 1932-1982 .... **80**
Stop Press, HN 2683, brown, blue & white,
1977-81 .... **250**
Summer, HN 2086, red gown, 1952-59 .... **575**
Summer's Day, HN 2181, 1957-62 .... **400**
Summertime, HN 3137, white & blue, 1987,
RDICC Series **250**
Sunday Morning, HN 2184, red & brown,
1963-69 .... **475**
Susan, HN 2952, blue, black & pink, 1982-
93 .... **350**
Suzette, HN 2026, 1949-59 .... **450**
Sweet Anne, HN 1330, red, pink & yellow
skirt, 1929-49 .... **350**
Sweet Anne, HN 1496, pink & purple dress
& hat, 1932-67 .... **375**
Sweet April, HN 2215, pink dress, 1965-67 ..... **550**
Sweet Dreams, HN 2380, multicolored,
1971-90 .... **225**
Sweet Lavender, HN 1373, green, red &
black, 1930-49 .... **1,050**

Thanks Doc

Sweet Seventeen, HN 2734, white w/gold
trim, 1975-93 .... **250**
Sweet Sixteen, HN 2231, 1958-65 .... **325**
Sweet Suzy, HN 1918, 1939-49 .... **1,250**
Sweet & Twenty, HN 1298, red & pink
dress, 1928-69 .... **450**
Sweeting, HN 1935, pink dress, 1940-73 .... **250**
Teatime, HN 2255, 1972-95 .... **275**
Teresa, HN 1682, red and brown, 1935-49 ... **1,250**
Thanks Doc, HN 2731, white & brown,
1975-90 (ILLUS. bottom previous page) **275**
This Little Pig, HN 1793, red robe, 1936-95 ...... **150**
Tiny Tim, HN 539, black, brown & blue,
1922-32 .... **80**
Tootles, HN 1680, pink, 1935-75 .... **115**
Top O' The Hill, HN 1833, green & blue
dress, 1937-71 .... **400**

Top 'O The Hill

Top 'O The Hill, HN 2126, mauve & green,
1988, miniature (ILLUS.) **150**
Town Crier, HN 2119, 1953-76 .... **350**
Toymaker (The), HN 2250, brown & red,
1959-73 .... **500**
Treasure Island, HN 2243, 1962-75 .... **225**
Tumbler, HN 3183, pink & yellow, 1989-91 ...... **225**
Tuppence a Bag, HN 2320, green dress,
blue shawl, 1968-95 .... **250**
Uriah Heep, HN 554, black jacket & trou-
sers, 1923-39 .... **450**
Valerie, HN 2107, red gown w/white apron,
1953-95 .... **150**
Vanity, HN 2475, red, 1973-1992 .... **175**
Veneta, HN 2722, green & white, 1974-81 .... **200**
Veronica, HN 3205, style 3, white & pink,
1989-92 .... **200**
Victoria, HN 2471, patterned pink dress,
1973 to present **400**
Victorian Lady (A), HN 728, red skirt, pur-
ple shawl, 1925-52 .... **525**
Victorian Lady (A), M 1, red-tinged dress,
light green shawl, 1932-45 .... **550**
Virginia, HN 1693, yellow dress, 1935-49 .... **1,750**
Wendy, HN 2109, blue dress, 1953-95 .... **100**
Willy-Won't-He, HN 2150, red, green, blue
& white, 1955-59 .... **250**
Windflower, M 79, blue & green, 1939-49 .... **1,650**

Winter, HN 2088, shaded blue skirt, 1952-
59 .... **425**
Winter's Walk (A), HN 3052, pale blue &
white, 1987-95 .... **250**

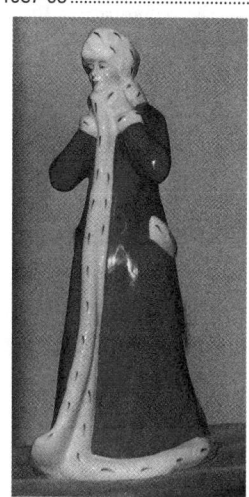

Wintertime

Wintertime, HN 3060, 1985, RDICC
(ILLUS.) **350**
Wizard (The), HN 2877, blue w/black &
white hat, 1979 to present **525**
Writing, HN 3049, flowered yellow dress,
1986, limited edition of 750, Gentle Arts
Series **1,650**
Young Dreams, HN 3176, pink, 1988-92 .... **250**
Young Master, HN 2872, purple, grey &
brown, 1980-89 .... **325**
Yvonne, HN 3038, turquoise, 1987-92 .... **225**

Miscellaneous

Pitcher, 5 1/2" h., brightly colored rose design on a salmon pink background, angled handle, mottling on the collar & base
rim, gold trim, Doulton, Burslem, artist-
signed **110**
Pitcher, 5 1/2" h., stoneware, bulbous form,
the tan ground incised w/playful cats, the
shoulder & neck glazed w/cobalt blue
strapwork, decorated by Hannah Barlow,
impressed Doulton Lambeth mark, late
19th c. **920**
Pitcher, 9" h., stoneware, bulbous ovoid
body tapering to a cylindrical neck
w/pinched spout, C-form handle, the upper half w/a dark brown glaze over a tan
glaze on the lower half, lower half applied
w/white relief designs including a windmill, dogs chasing deer, men drinking,
etc., Model No. 6859, Doulton, Lambeth
mark, late 19th c. **116**
Plates, 10 1/4" d., each w/a central rosette,
the border elaborately gilded & enameled
in the Art Nouveau style w/displaying
peacocks, spade ornaments & trailing
berried branches, the outer paneled blue
border gilded w/beaded flowers, dated
1902, retailed by Tiffany & Co., New
York, set of 4 .... **2,300**

Tyg (three-handled drinking vessel), waisted cylindrical shape decorated w/applied figures & animals in relief, Sheffield silver rim band marked "Maypin and Webb," Doulton, Lambeth, late 19th - early 20th c., 4 3/4" d., 6 1/2" h. **193**

Florence Ceramics

"Cinderella and Prince Charming"
Figure Group

Some of the finest figurines and artwares were produced between 1940 and 1962 by the Florence Ceramics Company of Pasadena, California. Florence Ward began working with ceramics following the death of her son, Jack, in 1939.

Mrs. Ward had not worked with clay before her involvement with classes at the Pasadena Hobby School. After study and first-hand experience, she began production in her garage, using a kiln located outside the garage to conform with city regulations. The years 1942-44 were considered her "garage" period.

In 1944 Florence Ceramics moved to a small plant in Pasadena, employing fifty-four employees and receiving orders of $250,000 per year. In 1948 it was again necessary to move to a larger facility in the area with the most up-to-date equipment .The number of employees increased to more than 100. Within five years Florence Ceramics was considered one of the finest producers of semi-porcelain figurines and artwares.

Florence created a wide range of items including figurines, lamps, picture frames, planters and models of animals and birds. It was her extensive line of ladies in beautiful gowns and gentlemen in fine clothes that gave her the most pleasure and was the foundation of her business. Two of her most popular lines of figurines were inspired by the famous 1860 Godey's Ladies' Book and by famous artists from the Old Master group. In the mid-1950s two bird lines were produced for several years. One of the bird lines was designed by Don Winton and the other was a line of contemporary sculpted bird and animal figures designed by the well-known sculptor, Betty Davenport Ford.

There were several unsuccessful contemporary artwares lines produced for a short time. The Driftware line consisted of modern free-form bowls and accessories. The Floraline is a rococo line with overglazed dec-

oration. The Gourmet Pottery, a division of Florence Ceramics Company, produced accessory serving pieces under the name of Scandia and Sierra.

Florence products were manufactured in the traditional porcelain process with a second firing at a higher temperature after the glaze had been applied. Many pieces had overglaze paint decoration and clay ruffles, roses and lace dipped in slip prior to the third firing.

Florence Marks

Bank, figural, model of a dog standing w/left paw across body w/"Ford" advertising under left paw & right paw on top of head, head turned slightly to left, glossy grey w/black highlights, in-mold mark "Florence Ceramics Pasadena, California" & copyright symbol, 6 3/4" h. **$100-125**

Bell, anniversary, applied pink Dresden-type flowers on white ground w/gold trim, 4 1/2" h. **75-100**

Casserole, cov., Scandia line, satin white, w/metal frame, 2 1/2 qt. **30-40**

Chip 'n dip, leaf-shaped, Sierra patt., white, 9 1/4 x 14" h. **25-35**

Cornucopia-vase, pink shading to grey, w/pink rose at base, 7 3/4" h. **50-75**

Dealer sign, figural, woman dressed in pink w/left hand on top & right hand on side of a white sign inscribed "Florence Pasadena California," 7" h. **500-600**

Dish, Driftwood line, model of two leaves, pale green, marked "Florence Ceramics Inc. Pasadena, California," 3 1/2 x 9" **20-30**

Figure group, "Cinderella & Prince Charming," dancing couple on raised base, both in white Renaissance period costume, white w/gold trim & gold tiara on her blonde hair, he holds a silver slipper behind her back in his right hand, 11 3/4" h. (ILLUS.) **3,000-5,000**

"The Christening" Figure Group

Figure group, "The Christening," woman w/peacock blue dress trimmed in lace at neck, sleeves & front of dress holding an infant in a long white christening dress, articulated fingers, 8 1/2" h. (ILLUS.)..... **700-800**

"Grandmother and I" Figure Group

Figure group, two women sitting at a round table covered w/a white tablecloth w/a teapot on it , the older woman sitting on a white chair holding a teacup in her right hand, wearing a violet dress w/lace trimmed cuffs & collar, the young woman dressed in a pink dress w/lace trim at the neck & a bow tied in the back, holding a teacup in her left hand, 6 3/4" h. (ILLUS.)... **1,500-2,000**

"Story Hour" Figure

Figure group, "Story Hour," seated mother & girl, woman reading book held in left hand, rose dress w/lace at neck, roses in her hair, girl w/blonde hair w/right arm on bench, ruffled lace short-sleeved white dress w/blue & pink trim, small boy dressed in blue shirt & pants & standing near girl 8" l., 6 3/4" h. (ILLUS.) **800-900**

Figure of a ballerina, "Marcella," standing w/right foot pointed in front of left leg, arms w/elbows slightly bent & pointed downward, pink tutu, applied roses in brown hair, 7" h. **150-200**

Figure of a boy, "Little Don," standing w/a grey cat at right side w/both arms extended outward, red pants & shirt w/ruffled lace trim, white cummerbund & shoes, from the Old Master group, Francisco Goya's "Don Manuel Osorio," 7 3/4" h. (ILLUS. top next column) **750-850**

Figure of a boy, "Mike," standing w/head thrown back & arms straight up & back w/palms up, 6 1/2" h. **200-250**

Florence "Little Don" Figure

Figure of a boy, "Peter," standing w/legs apart & holding a package in his right hand, white jacket, shirt & shoes, pale blue pants & hat, brown hair, 5 1/2" h. **100-125**

Figure of a boy, "Sandy," standing w/feet slightly apart, left hand holding an inner tube, right arm bent w/hand on hip, brown hair, navy swimsuit w/polka dots, navy shoes, 7 1/2" h. **350-400**

Figure of a boy, standing w/dog seated at his left leg, Colonial white clothes w/gold trim, white shoes w/gold buckles, 6" h... **200-250**

Figure of a choir boy, head down & tilted slightly to left, looking at songbook held in left hand, white & black attire, inkstamp mark, 5 1/2" h. **90-100**

Figure of a choir boy, looking upward, holding a song book, white & royal red attire, inkstamp mark, 5 1/2" h................... **100-125**

Figure of a girl, "Blondie," standing w/feet slightly apart, sand pail in right hand & left arm bent w/hand holding shovel to shoulder, black bathing suit w/yellow polka dots & matching scarf tied around blonde hair, 7 1/2" h.. **350-400**

Figure of a girl, young blonde girl seated & holding a bird in her hands, white dress & shoes w/grey trim & hat, 5" h. **100-150**

Figure of a Godey woman, "Abigail," full-skirted dress, cape & bonnet w/green bow tied under chin, 8 1/4" h. **150-200**

Figure of a Godey woman, "Annabelle," standing w/right arm bent & holding a white dove in hand, left arm in outward position, brown hair, white long full jacket w/gold trim, large white hat, articulated fingers, 8 3/4" h. (ILLUS. top next page).. **350-400**

Figure of a Godey woman, "Delia," beige dress w/long sleeves, green hat & ribbon tied under chin, holding a muff, 7 1/2" h. **75-125**

Figure of a Godey woman, "Delia," beige dress w/long sleeves, green hat & ribbon tied under chin, left hand showing at muff, 7 1/2" h. **250-300**

"Annabelle" Figure

Figure of a Godey woman, "Genevieve," standing w/head bent slightly, dark green hat, purse & dress, pink coat w/heart-shaped buttons & white trim, 8 1/4" h. **150-200**

"Georgette" Figure

Figure of a Godey woman, "Georgette," royal red dress w/full skirt, long sleeves w/lace & gold trim, large white bonnet w/lace & flower trim, holding a hatbox in left hand, articulated fingers, 10 1/4" h. (ILLUS.)... **325-400**

Figure of a Godey woman, "Irene," grey dress w/gold trim, flower in upswept hair, right hand holding muff near face, 6" h. **50-75**

Figure of a Godey woman, "Lillian," long pink jacket, white collar, hat & purse, 7 1/4" h.. **75-125**

Figure of a grandmother, "Memories," sitting in a white wing chair w/gold trim, reading a book, white dress w/gold trim, white lace shawl around shoulders, 6 1/2" h. (ILLUS. top next column) **750-800**

"Memories" Figure

Figure of a man, "Edward," black top hat, grey suit w/green trimmed vest, sitting in grey & purple chair, 7" h. **250-350**

Figure of a man, "Eugene," standing w/gloved hands touching the shoulders, green suit, triangular hat, 9" h. **250-300**

Figure of a man, "Leading Man," standing w/right leg in front of left, royal red knee-britches, white stockings w/gold-trimmed shoes, knee-length coat w/lacy jabot at neck, left arm bent at elbow & raised upward, left arm extended outward holding a scroll, 10 1/2" h. **250-350**

Figure of "Louis XV"

Figure of a man, "Louis XV," standing wearing pink knee-length britches, royal red coat w/lacy jabot at neck, white stockings & black shoes, left arm bent at elbow & raised upward holding a gold package, scroll-molded base, 12 1/2" h. (ILLUS.) **350-450**

Figure of a man, "Martin," white trousers & tie, rose & royal red knee-length coat w/cape & top hat, standing w/right hand on hip, left hand resting on a walking stick, 9" h. **175-225**

Figure of a man, "Rhett," standing w/right hand on vest, left hand in pocket, white ruffled shirt trimmed in red, knee-length coat & top hat, 9" h. **175-225**

Figure of a man, "Victor," holding white top hat in right hand, white trousers & shirt, royal red jacket w/tails & long swirling white cape, 9 1/2" h. **175-225**

"Adeline" Figure

Figure of a woman, "Adeline," brown hair w/applied roses in both sides of hair, green off-the-shoulder full pleated dress, holding a pink shawl wrapped around her lower arms, 9" h. (ILLUS.)...................... **250-300**

Figure of a woman, "Amber," brown hair, pink ruffled long dress & large bonnet , right arm bent & holding a pink parasol at right shoulder, left arm extended w/fingers touching her dress, articulated fingers, 9 1/4" h.. **400-500**

Figure of a woman, "Anita," standing w/right arm bent, palm extended near waist, left arm almost straight down at side, gold brocade long dress w/short sleeves & fitted waist, articulated fingers, 15" h. **900-1,200**

Figure of a woman, "Ann," teal dress, bonnet tied beneath chin, basket on her left arm, 6" h. **50-75**

Figure of a woman, "Ava," dirndl-type dress w/brown skirt & tan peasant blouse, left hand on hip & right arm raised & holding a large green basket on her head, 6" h. **250-350**

Figure of a woman, "Betsy," green skirt & long jacket w/tight bodice, ruffled floral trim & long sleeves, hands in muff, 7 1/2" h.. **75-100**

Figure of a woman, "Carmen," dancer w/head slightly turned & tilted to left, right arm bent w/fingers touching black hair, left arm across body at waist, ruffled lace short-sleeved white dress w/red & gold trim, 12 1/2" h...................................... **900-1,200**

Figure of a woman, "Charmaine," holding a parasol, ruffled green dress, large hat w/flowers, 8 1/2" h. **250-350**

Figure of a woman, "Clarissa," full-sleeved jacket & long swirled & pleated skirt, wearing a bonnet & holding a muff in right hand, left arm bent, articulated fingers, 7 3/4" h... **150-200**

Figure of a woman, "Claudia," ruffled dress w/lace trim, shawl on shoulders, large hat, bouquet in left hand, 8 1/2" h. **150-200**

Figure of a woman, "Colleen," standing w/head slightly turned to left, right hand behind back & left arm to the front, green dress w/white collar, bonnet w/ribbon tied under chin, 8" h. **150-200**

"Cynthia" Figure

Figure of a woman, "Cynthia," standing w/left arm extended slightly backward, head turned slightly to left, right hand holding large white hat trimmed w/flowers, aquamarine overdress w/white underskirt, lacy jabot at neck & lace cuffs, articulated fingers, 9 1/4" h. (ILLUS.)..... **450-550**

"Darlene" Figure

Figure of a woman, "Darlene," standing w/head tilted, brown hair w/curls & roses at neck, green dress, white underskirt, white lace trim on bodice & extending to bottom of dress, right arm bent & holding an open parasol at right shoulder, left arm at waist, articulated fingers, 8 1/4" h. (ILLUS.) **400-500**

Figure of a woman, "Delores," royal red dress w/white collar & hat w/floral trim, holding a parasol, 8" h............................ **150-200**

Figure of a woman, "Denise," off-the-shoulder white dress w/gold trim extending down the dress front, violet overskirt, brown hair w/roses, both arms bent at waist w/right hand holding a closed fan, articulated fingers, 10" h. **500-600**
Figure of a woman, "Eugenia," fuchsia dress, 9" h. **325**

"Fair Lady" Figure

Figure of a woman, "Fair Lady," standing on scrolled base decorated w/roses & gold trim, rose dress w/ornate white lace trim panel in front of dress, rose trim at bodice, upswept brown hair w/roses, right hand raised, articulated fingers, 11 1/2" h. (ILLUS.)............................ **1,400-1,500**
Figure of a woman, "Gibson Girl," white dress w/gold trim, lace & gold trim at cuffs & bodice, large white hat w/gold & floral trim, 10" h. **175-225**
Figure of a woman, "Jenette," green full-skirted dress w/peplum, white collar, flower at neck, left hand holding green hat w/bow, right hand holding parasol, 7 3/4" h. **175-200**
Figure of a woman, "Julie," pink dress w/long ruffled sleeves, white collar w/ruffled edge & hat, roses in hair, right hand holding a white purse trimmed in gold, 7 3/4" h. **100-125**
Figure of a woman, "Laura," pink dress w/applied roses on skirt, white collar w/gold trim, pink hat w/roses, both hands holding hat ribbons near chin, 7 1/2" h. **150-175**
Figure of a woman, "Linda Lou," green skirt & hat, dark green jacket w/peplum, holding a bouquet near her head, 7 3/4" h. (ILLUS. top next column) **150-175**
Figure of a woman, "Louise," beige dress & hat, green trim ribbon at neck & gloves, left hand at shoulder, right arm extended & holding a green parasol, 7 1/4" h. **75-125**
Figure of a woman, "Mary," grey dress, lacy jabot at neck, seated in an armchair w/foot on small footstool, 7 1/2" h. **450-550**
Figure of a woman, "Nancy," teal dress, left hand holding a large hat at her side, right hand touching shoulder, 6 3/4" h. **150-175**

"Linda Lou" Figure

Figure of a woman, "Princess," royal red w/flower trim at neck, large bow tied to right side of waist w/ruffle extending down the dress front, left hand holding fan, roses in hair, articulated fingers, 10 1/4" h. **400-500**
Figure of a woman, "Rita," dress w/ruffled skirt & bodice, holding skirt out at both sides, early garage period, 9 1/2" h. **125-150**

"Rosalie" Figure

Figure of a woman, "Rosalie," moss green dress w/lace ruffle at the off-the-shoulder neckline, brown hair w/roses, holding skirt at each side, articulated fingers, 9 1/2" h. (ILLUS.).................................... **350-450**
Figure of a woman, "Tess," light green dress w/lace ruffle at neckline, large hat, holding edge of skirt up over shoe, 7" h. **350-450**
Figure of a woman, "Vivian," wearing a bonnet w/ribbon tied on left side of neck, full-skirted dress w/long sleeves, right hand holding a parasol overhead, left hand holding a lace hankie, 9 3/4" h. **175-250**
Figure of an angel, w/yellow hair, arms bent across upper body, part of angel's wings showing, white robe w/gold trimmed rope sash, cuffs & collar, gold & brown ribbon sticker, 7" h. **75-90**

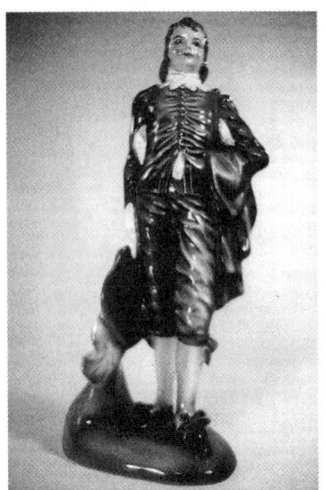

Figure of "Blueboy"

Figures, "Blueboy" & "Pinkie," figure of man standing on base, blue pants & coat w/white trim, white stockings, holding plumed hat in right hand, woman standing on base, wearing white dress w/rose trim & hat w/loose ribbon, right arm behind back, left arm held in front of body, 12" h., pr. (ILLUS. of Blueboy) **600-750**

Figures of "Dot" & "Bud"

Figures, "Bud" & "Dot," standing w/legs apart, "Bud" w/hands on guns at side, brown hair, white chaps, blue shirt, red neckerchief, black hat, vest, boots & gloves, "Dot" w/right hand on gun at side, left hand holding a doll, brown hair, blue skirt, red neckerchief, black hat, vest & boots, 7 1/2" h., each (ILLUS.) **350-400**

Figures, "John Alden" & "Priscilla," he dressed in dark grey kneebritches, light grey coat, shoes & large brim hat & holds a gun, she dressed in light grey skirt & cap, white apron, gloves & bonnet tied under the chin & holds books, both w/gold trim, 9 1/4 & 7 1/4" h., pr............. **375-425**

Flower holder, figural, "Patsy," wearing tiered & ruffled white dress w/pink floral trim, pink scarf in blonde hair, standing in front of square white relief-molded rock wall flower holder, 6" h. **45-50**

Flower holder, figural, "Jerry," white suit trimmed in blue, pink tie, holding a white bass fiddle trimmed w/gold, 8" h............ **125-150**

Flower holders, figural, Chinese boy & girl, boy holding a vase in left hand, girl holding a fan in her right hand, white w/gold trim, 7 3/4" h., pr. **75-100**

Head vase, "Violet," brunette hair, moss green bodice & large hat, 7" h. **125-150**

Lamp base, figural, "Delia," eggshell dress, hardwood base, 7 1/2" h. **250-300**

Lamp base, figural, Oriental man & woman, polished brass base, 7 3/4" h................. **250-300**

Lapel pin, figural bust of woman w/brown hair, grey hat & ribbon tied under chin, 2 1/4" h.. **250-300**

Model of a bird, "Cardinal," flying position w/head turned slightly to left, mounted on a stump w/flowers around base, designed by Don Winton, 4 3/4" h. **275-350**

Model of a fox, on base, running position w/back legs & tail up, head turned to side, brown & white porcelain bisque, designed by Betty Davenport Ford, Model No. B-13, 9 x 16"..................................... **375-450**

Model of a High Button Shoe

Model of a high button shoe, white w/lace & gold trim, small applied pink rose buttons, 5" h. (ILLUS.) **125-150**

Picture frame, white w/lace trim, 2 x 3"....... **75-100**

Picture frame, white w/roses & lace trim, 4 x 5"... **125-175**

Picture frame, white w/Dresden-type flowers, 5 x 7" **175-225**

Planter, model of a swan, neck up & head bent downward, designed by Don Winton, 7 x 7 x 12"... **225-275**

Wall plaque, cameo-type, irregular dark grey edge fading gradually to light grey at center, relief-molded bust of man w/black hat & tie, Model P7, 7 1/4" h................... **100-150**

Wall plaque, rectangular, pink frame w/brown design, 1860 "Godey's Ladies' Book" figure holding a muff, Model P1, 6 1/4 x 9"... **100-150**

Flow Blue

Flow Blue ironstone and semi-porcelain was manufactured mainly in England during the second half of the 19th century. The early ironstone was produced by many of the well known English potters and was either transfer-printed or hand-painted (Brush stroke). The bulk of the ware was exported to the United States or Canada.

The "flow" or running quality of the cobalt blue designs was the result of introducing certain chemicals into the kiln during the final firing. Some patterns are so "flown" that it is difficult to ascertain the design. The transfers were of several types: Asian, Scenic, Marble or Floral.

The earliest Flow Blue ironstone patterns were produced during the period between about 1840 and 1860. After the Civil War Flow Blue went out of style for some years but was again manufactured and exported to the United States beginning about the 1880s and continuing through the turn of the century. These later Flow Blue designs are on a semi-porcelain body rather than heavier ironstone and the designs are mainly florals. See: Antique Trader CERAMICS PRICE GUIDE, VOLUME III.

Hong Kong Platter

Platter, 18" l. (ILLUS.) **675**

Indian Tree (Unknown, probably English, probably early-Victorian, ca. 1845)

Indian Tree Plate

Plate, 8" d. (ILLUS.) **40**

Abbey (George Jones & Sons, ca. 1900)

Abbey Dinner Plate

Plate, dinner, 10 1/2" d. (ILLUS.) **$135**

Amoy (Davenport, dated 1844)
Coffeepot, cov., large **1,395**
Platter, 20" l. **2,000**

Asiatic Pheasants (John Meir & Son, ca. 1865)
Butter dish w/insert **495**
Butter pat **60**

Cashmere (Francis Morley, ca. 1845)
Coffeepot, cov., octagonal, 9 1/2" h. **1,925**
Plate, 8 1/4" w., paneled, set of 13 (one w/spider crack, one w/flake) **935**
Plate, 10 1/4" d., paneled, set of 4 .... **715**
Soup plate w/flanged rim, 10 3/4" w., scalloped edges, set of 7 .... **1,375**

Cashmere (Morley & Ashworth, ca. 1859-62)
Platter, 13 3/4 x 17", scalloped edge **880**

Glenwood (Johnson Bros., ca. 1900)
Teapot, cov. **695**

Hong Kong (Charles Meigh, ca. 1845)
Pitcher, water **950**

La Francais (French China Co., ca. 1890)
Butter pat, scenic decoration **22**
Creamer **65**
Cup & saucer **35**
Serving bowl, paneled **150**

Lorne (W.H. Grindley, ca. 1900)
Dinner service: six 10" d. dinner plates, ten 9" d. luncheon plates, thirteen cups & ten saucers, one each sauce dish, gravy boat & cov. vegetable dish; each marked, the set (minor stains, several chips) **1,210**

Lorne Platter

Platter, 18" l. (ILLUS.) **500**

Manilla (Podmore, Walker & Co., ca. 1845)
Plate, 9 3/4" d. 195
Relish dish 325
Serving bowl 250

Matlock (F. Winkle & Co., ca. 1890)

Matlock Covered Vegetable Dish
Vegetable dish, cov., 7 x 11 1/2", 5 1/2" h.
(ILLUS.).. 195

Nankin (Davenport, ca. 1850)
Teapot, cov. 995

Non Pareil (Burgess & Leigh, ca. 1891)
Vegetable bowl, open 150

Osborne (Ridgways, ca.1905)
Vegetable bowl, open, small.............................. 140

Pearl (Upper Hanley Potteries, ca. 1904)
Gravy boat 65

Shanghae (J. Furnival, ca. 1860)
Relish dish 265
Teapot, cov. 1,095

Strawberry (J. Furnival, Brushstroke, ca. 1850)
Plate, 8" d. 135

Sutherland (Royal Doulton, ca. 1905+)
Gravy boat, cov. 245

Tonquin (W. Adams & Son, ca. 1845)
Teapot, cov. 1,095

Touraine (Henry Alcock, ca. 1898 & Stanley Pottery, ca. 1898)
Creamer 283

Touraine Luncheon Plate
Plate, luncheon, 9" d. (ILLUS.) 95
Sugar bowl, cov. 435

Touraine Waste Bowl
Waste bowl (ILLUS.) 200

Virginia (John Maddock & Sons, ca. 1891)
Butter pat 50

Virginia Pitcher
Pitcher, water, 9" h. (ILLUS.).............................. 375

Waldorf (New Wharf Pottery, ca. 1892)
Creamer 338
Serving bowl, round 175

Warwick (Podmore Walker & Co., ca. 1850)
Jardiniere 525

Fulper

The Fulper Pottery was founded in Flemington, New Jersey, in 1805 and operated until 1935, although operations were curtailed in 1929 when its main plant was destroyed by fire. The name was changed in 1929 to Stangl Pottery, which continued in operation until July of 1978, when Pfaltzgraff, a division of Susquehanna Broadcasting Company of York, Pennsylvania, purchased the assets of the Stangl Pottery, including the name.

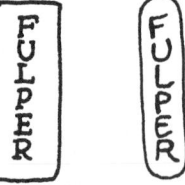

Fulper Marks

Book ends, figural, "Roman Mausoleum" model, bold classical doorway w/peaked roof over fan light above the door which stands ajar, sheer mottled ivory & white matte glaze w/clay showing through, rectangular ink mark, 5 1/2" w., 6" h., pr. (small chip & restoration to corner of one).... **$605**

Bowl, 10" d., 6" h., deep rounded sides, the slightly rounded shoulder tapering to a wide, flat molded mouth, decorated w/molded thistles & branches & covered in an ivory to Chinese blue flambé glaze, rectangular ink mark (rim chip & hairline)...... **523**

Bowl, 11 1/2" d., 6 1/2" h., footed, deep flaring sides, interior covered in Flemington green glaze, exterior in Famille Rose glaze, unmarked... **825**

Bulb bowl, shallow round body w/wide closed rim, glossy streaked brown, blue & green glaze interior, glossy & matte dark blue & rose exterior, early 20th c., faint vertical Fulper stamp, 9 1/4" d., 2 1/4" h.. **144**

Center bowl, figural, "Ibis" model, three stylized birds w/wings spread support the wide shallow bowl w/incurved sides, Flemington Green flambé exterior & brown flambé over mustard matte exterior, rectangular ink mark, 11" d., 5 3/4" h. **935**

Doorstop, model of a cat, reclining animal facing viewer, tail curled along the body, creamy ground w/streaky brown cat's-eye flambé glaze, ink racetrack mark, 9" l., 6" h. **1,045**

Flower frog, figural, modeled as an Indian maiden seated in a canoe perched on a rocky outcrop, in green, mahogany, & brown matte glazes, unmarked, 7" l., 4" h. (small flat bottom chip, probably in the making)... **520**

Flower frog, model of a medieval castle on grassy base, brown & green matte glaze, early ink mark, 5 x 5" (a few minor nicks to edges)... **440**

Flower frog, figural, a penguin standing atop a large rocky outcrop base w/flower holes, the bird in cream, brown & blue matte glazes w/brown matte glaze on the base, rectangular ink mark, 7" h. **303**

Flower frog, figural, frog on lily pad, mirrored green & caramel flambé glaze, vertical inkstamp rectangle mark, 7" d. **220**

Urn, small round pedestal foot supporting a large bulbous ovoid body w/a wide rounded shoulder to a short wide flat mouth flanked by small loop handles, fine ochre, mahogany & pale blue flambé glaze over textured body, raised racetrack mark, 9" d., 9" h. **935**

Urn, tall slender classical form w/wide shoulders & a short neck w/widely rolled rim, upright scroll-tipped handles from the shoulder to the rim, overall Mirror Black glaze on a "hammered" body, rectangular ink mark, 5 1/2" d., 11" h. **495**

Urn, Chinese-form, footed tapering bulbous ovoid body w/a tall cylindrical neck & flared rim, small squared loop shoulder handles, overall Mirror Black glaze over a

"hammered" body, raised racetrack mark, 8" d., 11" h. (reglued handle tip)...... **1,045**

Urn, footed baluster-form, shoulder tapering to cylindrical neck w/molded rim, flanked by scrolled handles, covered in a glossy & matte Chinese blue flambé glaze, rectangular ink mark, 11 1/4" h., 5 3/4" d........... **715**

Vase, 3" h., squatty bulbous body tapering gently to a closed rim, overall dark purple & mottled blue matte glaze, vertical stamped mark... **176**

Vase, 4 1/2" h., swelled cylindrical body w/an angled shoulder to a short, wide cylindrical neck, green over blue to red overall drip glaze, unmarked......................... **176**

Vase, 4 1/2" h., 4 1/2" d., footed, lobed bell pepper-shaped, w/small closed mouth, blue over Famille Rose flambé glaze, rectangular ink mark **660**

Vase, 5" h., wide half-round lower body w/an angled center shoulder below the wide tapering neck w/flat rim, squared curled C-scroll handles from rim to shoulder, overall purple & blue mottled matte glaze, stamped vertical mark **231**

Vase, 5 1/4" h., 6 3/4" d., footed spherical body w/incurved rim, light blue to elephant's breath flambé glaze, ink racetrack mark.. **385**

Vase, 5 1/2" h., 4 1/2" d., bulbous ovoid body tapering to a wide short flared rim, dark mirrored green & blue flambé glaze, raised mark **330**

Vase, 6 1/4" h., 8 1/2" d., footed spherical body w/short wide cylindrical neck, three loop handles, matte Wisteria glaze, incised racetrack mark **385**

Vase, 6 1/2" h., 8" d., wide bulbous body w/angled shoulder handles, purple & blue crystalline glaze, impressed racetrack mark... **275**

Vase, 6 3/4" h., ovoid body w/cream flambé over Wisteria glaze, raised vertical mark **303**

Vase, 6 3/4" h., 4"' d., footed cylindrical body w/rolled rim, incised vertical ribbed bands, covered w/a rich, flowing brown matte finish, impressed mark **3,080**

Vase, 7" h., wide gently tapering cylindrical body w/a rounded bottom edge & closed flat rim, cat's-eye flambé glaze, impressed vertical mark (minor grinding chips to base) **248**

Vase, 7 1/4" h., 5" d., wide gently tapering cylindrical body w/a rounded bottom edge & closed flat rim, cat's-eye flambé glaze, ink racetrack mark.............................. **385**

Vase, 7 1/2" h., baluster-form w/rolled neck rim, fine purple crystalline glaze over grey & salmon, stamped vertical mark **605**

Vase, 7 1/2" h., 5 1/2" d., bulbous ovoid body tapering to a short trumpet neck, overall frothy matte Wisteria glaze, ink racetrack mark.. **358**

Vase, 7 1/2" h., 5 1/2" d., gourd-form, bulbous ovoid shouldered body w/a short tapering cylindrical neck w/flared rim, curved integral handles from rim to shoulder, Leopard Skin crystalline glaze, ink racetrack mark.. **825**

Vase, 8" h., 6" d., baluster-form w/a wide flat molded mouth, covered in a frothy matte Cucumber glaze, incised racetrack mark.. 468

Vase, bud, 8 1/4" h., slender slightly tapering square form raised on a low angled square foot, glossy & matte Chinese blue flambé glaze, rectangular ink mark 275

Vase, 8 1/2" h., squatty bulbous base w/tall tapering cylindrical neck, four buttressed handles, cat's-eye flambé glaze, ink racetrack mark 440

Vase, 8 1/2" h., wide bulbous body w/short wide cylindrical neck flanked by four buttress handles to the shoulder rim, Wisteria matte glaze, raised racetrack mark (hairline to one handle) 1,100

Vase, bud, 8 1/2" h., 3" d., slender baluster-form w/very slender trumpet neck, Leopard Skin crystalline glaze in shades of green, cream & brown, rectangular ink mark.. 1,430

Vase, 9 1/2" h., baluster-form, Leopard Skin crystalline glaze, incised racetrack mark....... 523

Vase, 10" h., compressed bulbous base tapering to tall cylindrical neck w/flat rim flanked by angular loop buttress handles, covered in fine Copperdust crystalline to green flambé glaze, raised racetrack mark.. 715

Vase, 10" h., 7 1/2" w., Pilgrim flask-form, an oval foot supporting an upright round flattened disk body tapering to a short cylindrical neck w/flared rim, S-scroll shoulder handles, fine curdled green, Mirror Black, blue & ivory flambé glaze, rectangular ink mark 1,045

Vase, 10 1/2" h., footed wide bulbous body, the wide shoulder tapering to a short cylindrical neck, Mirror Black flambé glaze, raised racetrack mark 1,870

Vase, 12" h., large classic baluster-form body w/flaring rim covered in a Rouge flambé glaze, raised racetrack mark 715

Vase, 12" h., raised & flared neck on a tall ovoid body, ochre rim & sparse cobalt blue crystals on a periwinkle blue ground, vertical black ink stamp mark, ca. 1915........ 633

Vase, 12 1/2" h., bulbous ovoid body w/four shoulder handles, collared neck w/flat rim, Chinese blue flambé over Famille Rose glaze, vertical die-stamped race track mark (one handle reglued)................... 715

Vase, 12 1/2" h., footed bulbous ovoid body w/short cylindrical neck w/molded rim, loop shoulder handle, Leopard Skin crystalline glaze, incised racetrack mark 2,530

Vase, 12 3/4" h., 7 3/4" d., bullet-shaped body w/two ring handles, covered in textbook Cucumber & Leopard Skin crystalline glaze, ink racetrack mark...................... 3,850

Vase, 16 1/4" h., tall slightly expanding cylindrical body w/short molded rim, covered in a frothy Moss to Rose glaze, ink racetrack mark 1,540

Vase, 17 1/2'" h., 9" d., floor-type, tall baluster-form w/a short rolled neck, mirrored Flemington Green flambé glaze, incised racetrack mark (burst bubble near base) 495

Vase, footed, wide bulbous base tapering to short wide cylindrical neck, large loop handles from mid section to rim, matte purple & blue glaze, black vertical Fulper in lozenge mark 460

Gaudy Dutch

This name is applied to English earthenware with designs copied from Oriental patterns. Production began in the 18th century. These copies flooded into this country in the early 19th century. The incorporation of the word "Dutch" derives from the fact that it was the Dutch who first brought the Oriental wares into Europe. The ware was not, as often erroneously reported, made specifically for the Pennsylvania Dutch.

Creamer, Double Rose patt., 3 3/4" h. $495
Cup & saucer, Dahlia patt., cup 2 1/4" h., saucer 5 1/2" d. 7,975
Cup & saucer, handleless, Butterfly patt. (wear, stains, chips, hairlines, close mismatch) 275
Cup & saucer, handleless, Carnation patt., cup 2 1/2" h., saucer, 5 1/2" d. (imperfections).. 468
Cup & saucer, handleless, Double Rose patt., cup 2" h., saucer 5 1/2" d..................... 578
Cup & saucer, handleless, Dove patt., cup 2 1/2" h., saucer 5 1/2" d. (imperfections) 495
Cup & saucer, handleless, Grape patt., cut 2 1/2" h., saucer 5 3/4" d. (minor imperfections) 495
Cup & saucer, handleless, Oyster patt., cup 2 1/4" h., saucer 5 1/2" d. 468
Cup & saucer, handleless, Single Rose patt. (cup stained & crazed, saucer w/small rim repair, wear to both) 330
Cup & saucer, handleless, Single Rose patt. (stains, minor wear) 534
Cup & saucer, handleless, Sunflower patt., cup 2 1/2" h., saucer 5 1/2" d. (imperfections).. 715
Cup & saucer, handleless, Urn patt., cup 2" h., saucer 5 1/4" d. 550
Plate, 10" d., Carnation patt. 1,265
Plate, 7 1/2" d., Double Rose patt., framed, a gift from Max Hess.................................... 605
Plate, 7 1/2" d., Dove patt. 523
Plate, 7 1/2" d., Oyster patt. 578
Plate, 7 1/2" d., Single Rose patt. 495
Plate, 8" d., Single Rose patt. 440

Urn Pattern Plate

Plate, 8" d., Urn patt. 715
Plate, 8 1/4" d., Carnation patt............................. 935
Plate, 8 1/4" d., Urn patt., wear & scratches
  (ILLUS. bottom previous page) 743
Plate, 9 1/4" d., Grape patt................................. 440
Plate, 9 3/4" d., Sunflower patt. (imperfec-
  tions).. 825
Plate, 10" d., Oyster patt.,............................... 1,540
Plate, 10" d., Single Rose patt.,.......................... 935
Plate, 10" d., Urn patt....................................... 935
Soup plate w/flanged rim, Double Rose
  patt., 10" d. 1,760
Soup plate w/flanged rim, Single Rose
  patt., 10" d. 1,495
Soup plate w/flanged rim, Zinnia patt., im-
  pressed "Riley" on underside, 10" d. 4,675
Sugar bowl, cov., Sunflower patt., shell
  handles, 5 1/2" h. (damage on lid)............... 770
Tea set: child's, cov. teapot, creamer, cov.
  sugar bowl, two cups & saucers, two
  waste bowls & two plates; Wagon Wheel
  patt., 11 pcs. (imperfections) 523
Teapot, cov., Single Rose patt, 5 1/2" h.
  (restoration on spout) 1,045
Teapot, cov., Single Rose patt, 6" h. (chip
  on spout).. 1,210
Teapot, cov., Urn patt., 6 1/4" h. 825
Teapot, cov., War Bonnet patt., 7" h.
  (chipped spout).. 4,400
Waste bowl, Sunflower patt., 6 1/2" d............... 495

Gaudy Welsh

This is a name for wares made in England for the American market about 1830 to 1860, with some examples dating much later. Decorated with Imari-style flower patterns, often highlighted with copper lustre, it should not be confused with Gaudy Dutch wares whose colors differ somewhat.

Bowl, 10 1/4" d., 5 1/2" h., footed, molded
  arched panel designs w/floral decoration
  in underglaze-blue w/red & green enamel
  & lustre trim (wear, hairline & some
  enamel touch-up w/recoating)...................... $165
Compote, 8 1/4" d., 4"h., open, round bowl
  w/molded designs & painted interior in a
  Grape patt., underglaze-blue, red &
  green w/lustre trim (minor wear &
  scratches) 358
Pitcher, 6 1/8" h., footed squatty bulbous
  body w/a wide gently flared neck & wide
  arched spout, high arched loop handle,
  decorated in red & green w/pink & copper
  lustre trim in the Llanberis patt., first half
  19th c. 220
Punch bowl, flared & paneled low pedestal
  foot supporting a wide bowl w/deep
  slightly flared sides, the exterior molded
  w/oblong panels each w/an individual
  fruit cluster, the interior decorated in
  polychrome w/the Grape IV patt., mid-
  19th c., 10" d., 5 7/8" h. (minor flakes
  w/chips on foot) 880
Teapot, cov., Grape I patt., footed boat-
  shaped deep body w/a flaring upswept
  neck & domed fitted cover w/button finial,
  swan's-neck spout, upswept angled loop
  handle, underglaze-blue, red, green
  enamel & pink lustre trim, ca. 1830 (mi-

nor wear, some painted-over spout
  chips)... 770

Gouda

While tin-enameled earthenware has been made in Gouda, Holland since the early 1600s, the productions of modern factories are attracting increasing collector attention. The art pottery of Gouda is easily recognized by its brightly colored peasant-style decoration with some types having achieved a "cloisonné" effect. Pottery workshops located in, or near, Gouda include Regina, Zenith, Plazuid, Schoonhoven, Arnhem and others. Their wide range of production included utilitarian wares, as well as vases, miniatures and large outdoor garden ornaments.

Gouda Pottery Marks

Clock garniture, circular clock mount
  w/painted ceramic face supported by four
  ceramic arms on a baluster-shaped body
  & flared base, together w/two candleholders of similar form, all decorated
  w/Art Nouveau style flowers in glossy
  glaze of pink, purple, blue, green & tan,
  signed "Zuid Holand" & w/impressed
  house & "R" on base, early 20th c., clock
  20 1/2" h., candleholders 16 3/4" h., 3
  pcs. (repairs to candleholder base).......... $2,875
Lamp base, footed wide squatty bulbous tapering base w/a wide shoulder centering
  a tall cylindrical neck w/small domed cap,
  decorated around the sides w/floral &
  leaf designs & linear & dot decorative
  bands, glazed in shades of blue, rust,
  green & mustard yellow on a shaded
  green & brown ground, two socket metal
  fixture, mounted on a circular patinated
  metal base w/impressed Greek key
  design, ca. 1937, 13 1/4" h. (minor rim
  nick)... 546
Vase, 7 3/4" h., raised rim on oval body ta-
  pering to base, decorated w/central band
  w/upside down stylized tulip blossoms in
  blue, green & cream on a green ground,
  painted marks include Holland 091/1............ 173
Vase, 4 1/8" h., 3 1/2" d., two-handled, footed bulbous form, decorated w/stylized
  flowers in blue, gold, rust, tan & black on
  off-white ground, bands in shades of
  green on rim, black interior, foot & han-
  dles 95
Vase, 7 3/8" h., bulbous, nearly spherical
  body w/shoulder tapering to short cylindrical neck w/wide flared rim, handles
  from shoulder to rim, decorated w/color-
  ful Art Nouveau flowers, blue, tan &
  cream on dark green to black ground,
  marked "Made in Zuid Holland" on bottom in black slip & incised "18," also
  marked w/small house & "W" in black slip 770

Grueby

Some fine art pottery was produced by the Grueby Faience and Tile Company, established in Boston in 1891. Choice pieces were created with molded designs on a semi-porcelain body. The ware is marked and often bears the initials of the decorators. The pottery closed in 1907.

GRUEBY

Grueby Pottery Mark

Book ends, upright square form, "The Pines," decorated w/a polychrome cuenca designs of two large trees in the foreground & hills in the distance, in shades of green, blue & brown, designed by Addison Le Bouthillier, mounted in fine period hammered copper frames, 6" sq., pr.. **$8,800**

Bowl-vase, spherical form w/flared raised rim, repeating raised leaf design decorating the sides, mustard yellow matte glaze, impressed mark & label on base, 7" h. (small rim chip) **4,600**

Model of a scarab, matte green glaze, early 20th c., Boston, impressed pottery mark & partial paper label, 2 3/4" w., 4" l. **633**

Tile, square, depicting a row of four stylized white & brown penquins on a white iceberg on green water against a pale blue sky, unmarked, 4" sq. (minor chip, fleck to back edge) **935**

Tile, square, from the Dreamworld Mansion, Scituate, Massachusetts, decorated in cuenca w/a frieze of ivory horses on a green path against a pale blue sky, signed "RE" in glaze, 1902, 6" sq. **1,870**

Vase, 3 1/4" h., 5" d., narrow footring below the wide squatty bulbous body tapering to a wide short neck w/rolled rim, leathery matte green glaze, stamped circular mark **990**

Vase, 4" h., 5 1/4" d., squatty bulbous wide body tapering to a short, wide cylindrical neck, leathery matte green glaze, stamped ciruclar Faience mark **990**

Vase, 5 1/2" h., 3 3/4" d., wide ovoid body w/wide lightly embossed panels, fine leathery matte green glaze, circular stamp mark **1,430**

Vase, 6" h., 3 1/4" d., a thin footring below a squatty bulbous base tapering to a tall cylindrical body, flowing matte green glaze, stamped circular mark **935**

Vase, 7 1/4" h., 8 1/4" d., wide bulbous compressed form w/the wide angled upper half centered by a short, wide cylindrical neck, the body decorated w/a continuous design of tall slender excised stylized leaves, mottled matte green glaze, by Wilhelmina Post, circular stamp mark.. **6,050**

Vase, 8" h., 4 1/2" h., gently swelled cylindrical form w/a three-lobed rim, tooled & applied full-length wide leaves alternating w/small buds, covered in a rich leathery matte green glaze, Faience stamp (restored chips at rim)................. **1,760**

Vase, 10" h., 6" d., tall ovoid form w/molded flat mouth, full-length tooled & applied oblong leaves under a curdled ochre glaze, circular stamp mark & "RE" (glaze miss on side, minor chips under tips of two leaves) **3,850**

Hall China

Founded in 1903 in East Liverpool, Ohio, this still-operating company at first produced mostly utilitarian wares. It was in 1911 that Robert T. Hall, son of the company founder, developed a special single-fire, lead-free glaze which proved to be strong, hard and nonporous. In the 1920s the firm became well known for their extensive line of teapots (still a major product) and in 1932 they introduced kitchenwares followed by dinnerwares in 1936 and refrigerator wares in 1938.

The imaginative designs and wide range of glaze colors and decal decorations have led to the growing appeal of Hall wares with collectors, especially people who like Art Deco and Art Moderne design. One of the firm's most famous patterns was the "Autumn Leaf" line, produced as premiums for the Jewel Tea Company. For listings of this ware see "Jewel Tea Autumn Leaf."

Helpful books on Hall include, The Collector's Guide to Hall China *by Margaret & Kenn Whitmyer, and* Superior Quality Hall China - A Guide for Collectors *by Harvey Duke (An ELO Book, 1977).*

Hall Marks

Cookie jar, cov., Owl, brown glaze.................. **$120**
Pitcher, jug-type, Plaza shape, Chinese red **135**
Teapot, cov., Adele shape, olive green............. **200**
Teapot, cov., Apple shape, black w/gold decoration.. **95**
Teapot, cov., Art Deco style, Adele shape, olive green... **200**
Teapot, cov., Benjamin shape, warm yellow **100**
Teapot, cov., Blue Garden patt., morning set... **400**
Teapot, cov., Damascus shape, blue................ **175**
Teapot, cov., Danielle shape, maroon **175**

Orange Poppy Doughnut Shape Teapot

Teapot, cov., Doughnut shape, Orange
Poppy patt. (ILLUS.) 400
Teapot, cov., Hollywood shape, silver lustre decoration 325
Teapot, cov., Hook Cover shape, yellow 65
Teapot, cov., Illinois shape, maroon w/gold decoration 175
Teapot, cov., Illinois shape, yellow 325
Teapot, cov., Lipton shape, yellow 60
Teapot, cov., Radiance shape, Acacia patt. 225
Teapot, cov., Regal shape, apple green, gold decoration w/rhinestones 125

Hampshire Pottery

Hampshire Pottery was made in Keene, New Hampshire, where several potteries operated as far back as the late 18th century. The pottery now known as Hampshire Pottery was established by J. S. Taft shortly after 1870. Various types of wares, including Art Pottery, were produced through the years. Taft's brother-in-law, Cadmon Robertson, joined the firm in 1904 and was responsible for developing over 900 glaze formulas while in charge of all manufacturing. His death in 1914 created problems for the firm and Taft sold out to George Morton in 1916. Closed during part of World War I, the pottery was later reopened by Morton for a short time and manufactured white hotel china. From 1919 to 1921, mosaic floor tiles became the main production. All production ceased in 1923.

J.S.T.&CO.
KEENE.N.H.

HAMPSHIRE

Hampshire
Pottery

Hampshire Marks

Bowl, 5 1/2" d., 2 3/4" h., wide low bulbous incurved sides, matte green glaze, signed "Hampshire Pottery L2/1 - M (within) O," designed by Cadmon Robertson $173
Bowl-vase, low sides decorated w/repeating petals & leaves in low-relief, matte two-tone blue glaze highlighted w/strands of pale blue, impressed & incised marks, No.132, designed by Cadmon Robertson, 6" d., 3" h. 546
Bowl-vase, wide bulbous tapering form w/a wide rounded shoulder centering a short molded mouth, overall green matte glaze, embossed mark, 3 1/2" h. 308
Inkwell, low cylindrical form, the flat top pierced w/pen holes centering the small round cap w/button finial, w/liner, smooth matte green glaze, impressed mark, 3 1/2 x 4" 385

Lamp base, ovoid form, decorated w/alternating bud on stem & lotus leaves in relief under a dark matte blue glaze, raised on a carved Oriental-style wood base, green glass & brass finial, modeled by Cadmon Robertson, impressed "Hampshire Pottery 42" w/a Robertson cipher, ca. 1910, 19 1/4" h. (minor glaze bursts) 575
Lamp base, squatty wide bulbous gourdform lobed form on small flat feet, the wide shoulder centered by a short wide cylindrical neck mounted w/electric fittings complete w/a cap & period silk-lined wicker shade, impressed mark on base, base 11" d., 6 1/2" h. 1,320
Vase, 2 1/2" h., 5 1/2" d., squatty bulbous form tapering to a wide flat mouth, incised geometric design under a matte green glaze, marked on the base & w/the cipher of "M" as tribute to Cadmon Robertson's wife, Emoretta, early 20th c. 345
Vase, 2 7/8" h., flattened square form w/inverted rim, brown over green curdled matte glaze, designed by Cadmon Robertson, impressed mark, artist's cipher & No. 149 on base (glaze burst at rim) 288
Vase, 4 7/8" h., footed compressed bulbous base w/wide cylindrical neck & flat rim, shaded matte green & mauve glaze, by Cadmon Robertson, Keene, New Hampshire, early 20th c., impressed "Hampshire Pottery 155" & "M" within an O cipher 345
Vase, 5" h., 6" d., wide bulbous ovoid body w/wide closed rim, fine overall dark blue & green matte glaze, impressed mark 413
Vase, 6 1/2" h., Arts & Crafts style shouldered cylindrical body w/flat rim, decorated w/relief-molded tulips & leaves, matte green glaze, impressed "Hampshire Pottery," "33" & M inside an O 605
Vase, 6 7/8" h., swelled cylindrical body w/narrow shoulder & rolled rim, three impressed columns around body, mottled matte mauve glaze over light green, by Cadmon Robertson, Keene, New Hampshire, early 20th c., incised "Hampshire Pottery 157" & "M" within O cypher 748
Vase, 7" h., expanding cylinder w/rounded shoulder, relief-molded leaf decoration, thick feathered blue & white matte glaze, impressed "Hampshire Pottery" 660
Vase, 7 1/2" h., tapered cylindrical form w/raised rim in a matte green glazes, impressed "Hampshire Pottery 106 - M (within))," early 20th c. 403
Vase, 9 1/2" h., squat body w/repeating stylized leaf design, extended neck w/flared rim, matte marbleized blue glaze, designed by Camdon Robertson, No. 124, impressed marks 978

Harker Pottery

The Harker Pottery was established in East Liverpool, Ohio, in 1840 by Benjamin Harker, Sr. In 1890 the pottery was incorporated as the Harker Pottery Company. By 1911 the company had acquired the former plant of the National China Company and in 1931

Harker purchased the closed pottery of Edwin M. Knowles in Chester, West Virginia.

Harker's earliest products were yellowware and Rockingham-glazed wares produced from local clay. After 1900 whiteware was made from imported materials. Perhaps their best-known line is Cameoware, decorated on solid glazes with white "cameos" in a silhouette fashion.

There were many other patterns and shapes created by Harker over the years. In 1972 the pottery was closed after it was purchased by the Jeanette Glass Company.

Harker Pottery Marks

BakeRite, HotOven

Casserole, cov., Red Apple I patt., Zephyr shape.. **$35**
Plate, dinner, Red Apple II patt........................ 15
Teapot, cov., Red Apple II patt., Zephyr shape... 50
Utility bowl, Red Apple I patt., Zephyr shape, 4" d. 10

Cameoware

Bowl, salad, Pear patt, Swirl shape.................... 20

Modern Age/Modern Tulip

Cookie jar, cov.. 30
Creamer, ... 10
Custard cup 5
Pie baker 15
Pitcher, cov., square, jug-type........................... 25
Plate, 6" d.. 5
Sugar bowl 10-15
Teapot, cov... 20
Utility bowl, 4" d... 8

Royal Gadroon/Chesterton (grey) or Corinthian (teal)

Bowl, cereal or soup, lug handles, Vintage patt.. 8
Cake plate, Wild Rose patt., 10" d.................... 15
Fruit dish, St. John's Wort patt. 3
Plate, 6" d., luncheon, Bermuda patt. 8
Plate, 6" d., Game Birds patt............................ 6
Plate, 9" d., dinner, Magnolia patt. 10
Plate, 9" d., dinner, Violets patt. 8
Platter, 15" l., oval, Vintage patt..................... 20
Teapot, cov., Ivy Vine patt.............................. 50

Haviland

Haviland porcelain was originated by Americans in Limoges, France, shortly before the mid-19th century and continues in production. Some Haviland was made by Theodore Haviland in the United States during the last World War. Numerous other factories also made china in Limoges. Also see LIMOGES.

Haviland Marks

Cups & saucers, Papillon butterfly handles w/Meadow Visitors decoration, six sets... **$1,320**
Fish set: 22" l. oval platter & twelve 8 1/2" d. plates; each piece w/a different fish in the center, the border in two shades of green design w/gold trim, h.p. scenes by L. Martin, mark of Theodore Haviland, 13 pcs.............................. **2,750**
Hair receiver, cov., squatty round body on three gold feet, h.p. overall w/small flowers in blues & greens w/gold trim, mark of Charles Field Haviland 150
Pitcher, 7" h., milk-type, tankard style w/tapering cylindrical white body w/a large relief-molded anchor under the heavy ropetwist loop handle, bright gold trim, old Haviland & Co. mark 175
Pitcher, 9" h., tankard-shaped lemonade-type, Ranson blank, delicate floral band around the upper body trimmed in gold, gold handle & trim bands, factory-decorated, Haviland & Co. mark 225
Plate, 6 1/2" d., bread & butter, Paisley patt., smooth blanks w/gold edge, brownish red ground w/flowers in yellow, bright blue, green & white border design w/yellow flowers & bright blue leaves, turquoise scroll trim, Haviland & Co. mark 26
Plate, 7 1/2 x 8 1/2", heart-shaped, Baltimore Rose patt...................................... 275
Punch cup, tapering scalloped pedestal foot supporting wide shallow cup bowl, decorated w/flowers in shades of green w/some pink flowers & green leaves, variation of Schleiger No. 249B on Blank 17, Haviland & Co. mark, 4" h...................... 75
Sugar bowl, cov., large cylindrical form w/small loop side handles & inset flat cover w/arched handle, white ground decorated w/sprays of pink daisies touched w/yellow & greyish brown leaves, variation of Schleiger No. 1311, 1 lb. size, Charles Field Haviland, marked "CFH/GDM"...................................... 75

Historical & Commemorative Wares

Numerous potteries, especially in England and the United States, made various porcelain and earthenware pieces to commemorate people, places and events. Scarce English historical wares with American views command highest prices. Objects are listed here alphabetically by title of view.

Most pieces listed here will date between about 1820 and 1850. The maker's name is noted at the end of each entry.

Almshouse, Boston tureen & cover, flowers within medallions border, dark blue, footed deep ovoid body w/wide angled rim, domed cover & scroll end handles, Ridgway, 12 3/4" l., 9 1/2" h. (two hairlines in base, chip on inside edge of cover) **$3,300**
Almshouse, New York platter, vine border, dark blue, 16 1/2" l. (Ridgway)............ **1,035**
Castle Garden, Battery, New York cup plate, trefoil border, dark blue, Wood, 3 3/4" d. (hairlines)............................ 138

City Hall, New York plate, flowers within medallions border, medium blue, 9 3/4" d. (Ridgway) **193**

Commodore MacDonnough's Victory plate, shell border, dark blue, 8 3/8" d., E. Wood (minor wear & knife scratches) **358**

Custom House, Philadelphia cup plate, flowers within medallions border, dark blue, Ridgway, 3 1/2" d. (short hairlines, professional repair) **275**

Dix Cove on the Gold Coast, Africa soup tureen, cov., dark blue, shell border, irregular center, pedestal base, loop end handles, 11 x 15", E. Wood (interior staining) **4,888**

East View of LaGrange, the residence of the Marquis La Fayette plate, dark blue, floral border, 9 1/4" d., E. Wood (very minor wear) **303**

Franklin (Tomb) cup & saucer, handleless, floral border, dark blue (E. & G. Phillips, Longport) **385**

Harper's Ferry, U.S. platter, flowers, shells & scrolls border, scalloped rim, red, 15 3/8" l. (Adams) **440**

Insane Asylum, New York - New York City Hall pitcher, vine border, dark blue, footed bulbous body w/high arched spout & arched handle, Stevenson, 9" h. (minor stains & wear w/some crazing in bottom).. **1,100**

Junction of the Sacandaga and Hudson Rivers platter, floral & scroll border, dark blue, 14 1/4" l. (A. Stevenson) **1,955**

Lafayette at Franklin's Tomb coffeepot, floral border, tall footed ovoid body w/flared rim & domed cover, dark blue, 113/4" h., Wood **4,888**

Landing of General Lafayette at Castle Garden, New York, 16 August 1824 pepper pot, floral & vine border, dark blue, 4 5/8" h.,Clews (shallow chip & flakes on domed top) **2,750**

Landing of General Lafayette at Castle Garden, New York, 16 August 1824 pitcher, floral & vine border, jug-type, dark blue, 6 1/4" h., Clews (stained) **1,760**

Landing of General Lafayette at Castle Garden, New York, 16 August 1824 platter, floral & vine border, dark blue, 19" l., Clews (slight scratches) **2,970**

Landing of General Lafayette at Castle Garden, New York, 16 August 1824 sauce tureen, cover & underplate, floral & vine border, dark blue, tureen 8 3/8" l., undertray 9 7/8" l., Clews, the set **1,955**

Landing of General Lafayette at Castle Garden, New York, 16 August 1824 sugar bowl & cover, floral & vine border, dark blue, deep boat-shaped form w/flared rim & domed cover, 6 1/4" h. Clews (chips on rim & cover) **605**

Landing of General Lafayette at Castle Garden, New York, 16 August 1824 tureen, cover & ladle, floral & vine border, dark blue, 11" l., 10" h., Clews (damage).. **5,175**

Marine Hospital, Louisville, Kentucky plate, dark blue, shell border, irregular center, 9 1/4" d., E. Wood (stains, crazing, short internal hairline) **330**

Pass in the Catskill Mountains undertray, shell border, circular center, dark blue, E. Wood, 8" l. (minor scratches, edge roughness) **440**

Peace and Plenty plate, cov., dark blue, wide band of fruit & flowers border, 8 7/8" d., Clews (glaze flakes) **330**

Peace and Plenty plate, fruit & flowers border, dark blue, 10 1/4" d., Clews (minor knife scratches) **330**

Peace & Plenty vegetable dish, cov., dark blue, wide band of fruit & flowers border, oblong w/flanged rim, 6 1/2 x 12 1/2", Clews (minute chip under end handle) **1,725**

Quebec vegetable dish, cov., shell border, footed square form w/domed cover & floriform finial, dark blue, 9 1/2" w. (E. Wood) **2,185**

Tappen Zee from Greensburg, New York vegetable bowl, oblong, shell border, dark blue, 8" l. (E. Wood) **935**

West Point Military Academy basket & undertray, reticulated basket & undertray, fruit & flowers border, Celtic China, dark blue, undertray 11 1/2" l., 2 pcs. (E. Wood) **3,738**

Hull

This pottery was made by the Hull Pottery Company, Crooksville, Ohio, beginning in 1905. Art Pottery was made until 1950 when the company was converted to utilitarian wares. All production ceased in 1985.

Reference books for collectors include Roberts' Ultimate Encyclopedia of Hull Pottery *by Brenda Roberts (Walsworth Publishing Company, 1992), and* Collector's Guide to Hull Pottery - The Dinnerware Lines *by Barbara Loveless Gick-Burke (Collector Books, 1993).*

Hull Marks

Bank, sitting pig, House 'N Garden line, Mirror Brown, No. 196 .... $75

Basket, hanging-type, Sun Glow patt., No. 99, 6" h. 65

Cookie jar, House 'N Garden line, Mirror Brown, 8" h. 275

Cruets, House 'N Garden line, w/"Vinegar" & "Oil," Mirror Brown, 6 1/2" h., pr. 40

Flowerpot w/attached saucer, Woodland patt., No. W11, 5 1/2" h. 150-175

Garlic pot, House 'N Garden line, Mirror Brown 30

Pie plate, House 'N Garden line, Mirror Brown, 9 1/4" d. 25

Salt & pepper shakers, mushroom-shaped, House 'N Garden line, Mirror Brown, 3 3/4" h., pr. 20

Salt & pepper shakers w/cork stoppers, bulbous semi-ovoid shape, House 'N Garden line, Mirror Brown, 3 1/2" h. 20

Vase, 5 1/2" h., Wildflower patt., No. W1-5 1/2" 50

Vase, 6 1/2" h., Water Lily patt., No. L6-6 1/2" 70

Hummel Figurines & Collectibles

The Goebel Company of Oeslau, Germany, first produced these porcelain figurines in 1934 having obtained the rights to adapt the beautiful pastel sketches of children by Sister Maria Innocentia (Berta) Hummel. Every design by the Goebel artisans was approved by the nun until her death in 1946. Though not antique, these figurines with the "M.I. Hummel" signature, especially those bearing the Goebel Company factory mark used from 1934 and into the early 1940s, are being sought by collectors though interest may have peaked some years ago.

Hummel Marks

School Boys

School Boys, 10 1/4" h., Trademark 3 (ILLUS.) **2,250**

Congratulations

Congratulations, 8 1/4" h, Trademark 1 (ILLUS.).. **$8,000**

Singing Lesson

Singing Lesson, 2 3/4" h., Trademark 1 (ILLUS.) **500**

Puppy Love

Puppy Love, 5" h., Trademark 1 (ILLUS.)......... **950**

Sister

Sister, 5 3/4" h., Trademark 1 (ILLUS.) **700**

Star Gazer

Star Gazer, 4 3/4" h., Trademark 1(ILLUS.)...... **800**

Stormy Weather

Stormy Weather, 6 1/4" h., Trademark 1
(ILLUS.).. **1,350**

Telling Her Secret

Telling Her Secret, 5 1/4" h., Trademark 2
(ILLUS.)... **725**

Hutschenreuther

*The Hutschenreuther family name is associated with
fine German porcelains. Carl Magnus Hutschenreuther
established a factory at Hohenberg, Bavaria and was
succeeded in this business by his widow and sons, Christian and Lorenz. Lorenz later established a factory in
Selb, Bavaria (1857) which was managed by Christian
and his son, Albert. The family later purchased factories
near Carlsbad (1909), Altwasser, Silesia (1918) and
Arzberg, Bavaria and between 1917 and 1927, acquired
at least two additional factories. The firm, noted for the
fine quality wares produced, united all these branches in
1969 and continues in production today.*

Figure group, two cupids dancing, signed
"Tutter," marked "U.S. Zone Germany,"
4" h. **$225**
Plaque, oval, finely painted w/a bust-length
portrait of a blue-eyed beauty turned to
the right & looking at the viewer, her long
brown hair tied w/a red ribbon, late 19th -
early 20th c., impressed monogram
mark, artist-signed, giltwood frame,
5 1/4 x 6 3/4"... **2,070**
Plate, 9 1/2" d., Royal Vienna-style, the
center finely painted w/a bust portrait of
Rosalie, Fulie von Bonar after F. Stieler,
the wide border w/elaborate gold banding, the edge enameled w/blue & red
'jewels' interrupted by gilt diamonds, titled on the back, impressed shield mark,
artist-signed, late 19th c........................... **1,380**
Plate, 9 5/8" d., Royal Vienna-style, a jeweled blue ground wide border heavily
trimmed w/gilt scrolling foliage & applied
w/turquoise & pearl 'jewels,' the center
finely painted w/a three-quarter length
portrait of a brunette beauty dressed in a
red classical gown & w/long brown hair,
standing & leaning against the landing of
a large temple, artist-signed, late 19th -
early 20th c., blue Beehive mark, im-
pressed & incised numbers **1,725**
Plates, 9 1/2" d., a wide iridescent green
ground border decorated w/a gilt Greek
key & berried laurel design, the center of
each painted in color w/a different Napoleonic scene, each titled on the reverse,
late 19th - early 20th c., impressed shield
mark, artist-signed, set of 8 .... **10,350**

Ironstone

*The first successful ironstone was patented in 1813
by C. J. Mason in England. The body contains iron slag
incorporated with the clay. Other potters imitated
Mason's ware and today much hard, thick ware is
lumped under the term ironstone. Earlier it was called
by various names, including graniteware. Both plain
white and decorated wares were made throughout the
19th century. Tea Leaf Lustre ironstone was made by
several firms.*

General
Cups & saucers, handleless, "gaudy"
Blackberry patt. in underglaze-blue
trimmed w/yellow & orange enamel &
lustre, E. Walley mark, ca. 1850, some
variation, set of 10.................................... **$1,375**

Dessert service: 10 5/8" l. shaped dish, 5 3/4" h. open compote, four 10" l. leaf-shaped dishes & fourteen 9 1/4" d. plates; Imari-style designs w/shaped edges & deep green borders, Mason's, mid-19th c., the set **3,680**
Gravy boat, Long Octagon shape, all-white, ca. 1847, T.J. & J. Mayer **125-140**
Mug, Gothic patt., all-white, ca. 1840s, James Edwards **120-130**

Mayer Table-type Pitcher

Pitcher, 9" h., table-type, Full-Panelled Gothic shape, all-white, ca. 1847, T.J. & J. Mayer (ILLUS.) **175-185**
Pitcher, 9 3/4" h., footed wide squatty bulbous body molded w/wide ribs & tapering to a wide mouth w/arched spout, high arched C-scroll handle, transfer decoration of birds in flowering trees & foliage w/polychrome enamel, mark of Ashworth Brow., England, ca. 1890 .... **303**
Pitcher, 9 3/4" h., table-type, Grape Octagon shape, all-white, Pearson & Hancock **120-130**
Plate, 8" d., twelve-sided, "gaudy" Bittersweet patt. w/underglaze flow blue & copper luster, impressed "Real Ironstone," (light stains).............................. **83**
Plate, 8 3/8" w., paneled shape, "gaudy" free-hand Strawberry patt., underglaze-blue w/green & two shades of red enamel & copper lustre trim, mid-19th c. **385**
Plate, 8 1/2" d., "gaudy" decoration, vintage grape vine design painted in underglaze-blue, black, ochre & two shades of green (wear, crazing) **110**
Plate, 8 1/2" d., "gaudy" style, center w/urn in flow blue w/pink & red flowers & copper lustre highlights (stains) **110**
Plate, 8 3/4" w., "gaudy" Strawberry patt., paneled shape w/underglaze-blue trimmed w/red, pink, green & copper lustre, impressed mark, mid-19th c. **138**
Plate, 9 1/4" w., paneled shape, "gaudy" free-hand Morning Glory patt., underglaze-blue trimmed w/two shades of green, red & black enamel, mid-19th c. **303**
Plate, 9 1/2" d., Bordered Hyacinth/Lily shape, all-white, ca. 1860, W. & E. Corn... **25-28**
Plate, 9 1/2" w., paneled sides, "gaudy" Floral Urn free-hand patt., underglaze-blue

& green & trimmed w/two shades of red enamel & copper lustre, mid-19th c. (light stains, tiny enamel flake) **330**
Plate, 9 5/8" d., "gaudy" Blackberry patt., underglaze-blue & black trimmed w/red, yellow & copper lustre, impressed "E. Walley - Niagara Shape," 1850s................... **193**
Plate, 10 1/4" d., New York shape, all-white, ca. 1858, J. Clementson.................. **35-40**
Plate, 10 1/4" d., twelve-sided "gaudy" style w/strawberries, pink flowers & underglaze flow blue leaves **248**
Plate, 10 1/2" d., Fig shape, all-white, ca. 1856, Davenport/Wedgwood **50-70**
Plates, 8 1/2" d., decorated w/floral motif in blue & rust, marked "Ashworth Brothers Hanley," England, ca. 1890, set of 9........... **134**
Plates, 9 5/8" d., paneled edge, central transfer-printed garden landscape w/urn of flowers, flower & scroll border, Florilla patt., purple highlighted w/yellow, green, blue & red enamel, mid-19th c., set of 6 (stains) **138**
Plates, 10 1/2" d., scalloped flanged rim, overall Imari-style transfer decoration in polychrome trimmed w/gold, mid-19th c., pr.. **303**
Platter, oval, 10" l., President shape, all-white, John Edwards **30-40**

Strawberry Pattern Platter

Platter, 13 1/2" l., octagonal, "gaudy" Strawberry patt., underglaze-blue w/red, pink & green enamel & luster trim, wear, stains & some enamel flaking **770**
Platter, 13 1/2" l., rectangular w/cut corners, "gaudy" free-hand Morning Glory patt., underglaze-blue trimmed w/two shades of green, red & black, mid-19th c. (old red flaking, minor stains) **385**
Platter, 11 3/8 x 14 1/8", rectangular, romantic transfer scene of a lakeside cabin w/boaters, marked "Cat, Albion" & "Turnbull, Stepney," light blue, mid-19th c................. **121**
Platter, 14 3/4" oval, "gaudy," blue transfer-printed War Bonnet patt. trimmed in red, orange & yellow, marked "Ironstone China," mid-19th c. (wear, scratches) **165**
Platter, 15 3/4" l., rectangular w/cut corners, Florentine patt., light blue, T. Mayer, mid-19th c. (internal hairline)................... **110**
Platter, oval, 16" l., Corn & Oats shape, all-white, Davenport/Wedgwood **65-75**
Platter, oval, 16" l., Rolling Star shape, all-white, James Edwards **70-80**

Platter, 16 1/4" l., oval w/lightly scalloped rim, "gaudy" free-hand Strawberry patt., underglaze black, mid-19th c. (small chips on one corner) **413**

Platter, 18 1/2" l., Indiana patt., ca. 1880, Wedgwood **196**

Platter, 16 x 21", well-and-tree-type, oval, Rural Scenery patt., broad floral border surrounding a meadow landscape w/figures & animals, Davewell & Goodfellow, England (chips on foot, hairline) **440**

Platter, 21 1/4" l., oval w/flanged rim, the center transfer-printed w/a large landscape scene of a dog holding a stick on the bank of a river w/figures rowing a boat, the river flanked by trees & a country house in the distance, wide floral border, blue & white, back w/printed mark of a ribbon-tied banner inscribed "British Views," mid-19th c. **1,265**

Platter, 22" l., oval, polychrome floral decoration w/gilt trim, Stokes Works mark on base, 19th c. **863**

Punch bowl, footed deep rounded bowl, floral embellishments around the rim & base, twig urn w/flowers & bird at center & sides, in shades of cobalt blue, yellow, pink, orange & green w/gilt highlights, mid-19th c., 14 1/4" d., 6 1/2" h. **1,035**

Relish dish, 1851 Shell shape, all-white, ca. 1851, T. & R. Boote **90-100**

Relish dish, Berlin Swirl, all-white, ca. 1856, Mayer & Elliot **65-75**

Relish dish, plain, oval w/two tab handles, all-white, ca. 1870s, Wood, Son & Co. **20-30**

Various Red Cliff Pieces

Salt & pepper shakers, Boote's 1851 shape, all-white, ca. 1960s, Red Cliff, 4" h., pr. (ILLUS. far right & far left) **30-40**

Sauce tureen, cov., oblong form, decorated in color w/the Japanese Garden patt., molded butterfly handles & finial, England, 19th c., 5 3/4" h.............................. **173**

Soap box, cover & liner, plain oval, all-white, ca. 1872-87, Thomas Elsmore & Son, 3 pcs. **40-45**

Soap box, cover & liner, President shape, all-white, John Edwards, 3 pcs. **120-130**

Soap dish, open, plain hollow rectangular body w/drain holes in well & one on side for cleaning, all-white, various potters **20-30**

Soup plate, flanged paneled rim, Paradise patt., purple floral transfer design w/polychrome trim, mid-19th c., 10 1/2" w.................. **83**

Soup plate, Sharon Arch shape, all-white, Davenport, 9 1/2" d. **28-35**

Soup tureen, cover, ladle & underplate, Stafford shape, all-white, ca. 1854, S. Alcock & Co., 4 pcs. **750-800**

Soup tureen, undertray, cover & ladle, Vista England patt., footed deep tureen, grape leaf & vine border, cranberry, tray 14 3/4" l., tureen 10 1/2" h., the set............... **605**

Teapot, cov., "gaudy" strawberry design, paneled body w/a domed cover w/blossom finial, decorated w/blue flowers, red & green strawberries & gilt trim, ca. 1850, 9 3/4" h. (nick).. **2,300**

Teapot, cov., Memnon shape, six panels w/branch handle & bud finial, all-white, ca. 1850s, John Meir & Son, 8 3/4" h. **150-165**

Teapot, cov., tall tapering paneled form w/angled handle & inset high domed cover w/florette finial, "gaudy" Strawberry patt. w/large blossoms highlighted w/flowing blue & copper lustre, mid-19th c., 9" h. (minor flake on spout, reglued finial).. **1,375**

Vegetable dish, cov., Scotia (Poppy) shape, oval, all-white, ca. 1870, F. Jones & Co., 9" l. **85-95**

Wash bowl & pitcher, miniature, Classic Gothic shape, all-white, Red Cliff, ca. 1960s, overall 4 1/2" h. (ILLUS. second from right w/salt & pepper shakers) **30-45**

Wash bowl & pitcher, miniature, Fig (registered Union shape), all-white, Red Cliff, ca. 1960s, overall 3 1/2" h. (ILLUS. second from left w/salt & pepper shakers).. **30-45**

Wash bowl & pitcher, miniature, Sydenham shape, all-white, Red Cliff, ca. 1960s, overall 4 1/2" h. (ILLUS. center w/salt & pepper shakers) **30-45**

Wash bowl & pitcher, "Tudor" patt., transfer-printed overall w/stylized floral medallions, branches & berries in lilac on an ivory ground, William Brownfield & Sons, 1871-91, bowl 15" d., overall 10" h., 2 pcs. **287**

Tea Leaf Ironstone

Pitcher, 10" h., water-type, Chelsea patt., Johnson Bros., 3 1/2 qt. **425**

Vegetable dish, cov., Square Ridged patt., Mellor, Taylor & Co., 12" l................................. **70**

Jasper Ware (Non-Wedgwood)

Jasper ware is fine-grained exceedingly hard stoneware made by including barium sulphate in the clay and was first devised by Josiah Wedgwood, who utilized it for the body of many of his fine cameo blue-and-white and green-and-white pieces. It was subsequently produced by other potters in England and Germany, notably William Adams & Sons, and is in production at the present. Also see WEDGWOOD - JASPER.

Cheese dish, cov., high cylindrical cover & matching round dished base, dark blue applied w/white relief classical figures & oak leaves, England, mid-19th c., 9 1/2" h.. **$516**

Cheese dish, cov., very tall cylindrical cover w/flat top centered by an acorn finial, on a fitted base w/wide angled rim band, black ground w/the rim of the base & lower edge of the cover decorated in white relief w/a wide band of oak leaves & acorns, the cover w/a very wide band of white relief classical figures & trees, a white relief radiating pattern of spearpoints & leaves around the finial, England, 19th c., unmarked, 11 1/4" h. 863

German Jasper Ware Hair Receiver

Hair receiver, cov., white relief figures of three Grecian ladies around sides, one looking in mirror, one taking jewels from box & one holding a bird, white relief-molded figures of cupids on lid, blue ground, Germany, 3 1/4" d., 4" h. (ILLUS.)... **95**

Pitcher, 5 3/4" h., jug-form, wide ovoid body w/a cylindrical neck w/a long pointed spout, angled & pointed handle from rim to shoulder, solid blue ground applied w/white relief classical figures & foliate bands, impressed Adams & Co. mark, England, late 18th c. (restoration to handle & tip of spout) **920**

Plaque, pierced to hang, scrolled free-form design w/scalloped rim, green ground decorated in white relief w/animals & female figures, Germany, ca. 1900, 12 1/2" l. **316**

Plaque, round, pierced to hang, green ground w/white relief blossom & leaf decorated border around center scene depicting white relief figures of a fisherman w/his arm around the shoulder of his lover, 6" d. **22**

Sugar bowl, cov., oval, a solid blue ground applied w/white relief classical figures & foliate designs, swan finial on cover, engine-turned band at the foot, impressed Adams mark, late 18th c., England, 4 1/2" h. (slight rim chip on bowl & interior collar of cover) **1,495**

Sugar bowl, cov., oval cylindrical body w/small loop end handles, dark blue ground decorated around the base in white relief w/a central continuous band of classical figures w/a large leafy flowering vine border around the bottom & a smaller similar border around the rim, the inset cover w/a raised central upright band decorated in white relief w/palmettes & centering a figural white swan finial, England, possibly Adams, early 19th c., 6 1/8" l. **1,610**

Vase, 17 3/4" h., cov., three-color, the classical form w/a light blue ground applied in white relief w/fruiting grapevine festoons & oval portrait medallions w/a lavender ground, impressed mark of Adams and Bromley, England, ca. 1880 (cover restored, inner lid missing) **690**

Vases, 7" h., handled, white relief figure of Victorian lady, green ground, Germany, pr. **44**

Kay Finch Ceramics

In 1930, Katherine Finch and her husband, Braden, whom she had met at Ward Belmont College moved to Corona del Mar, California. Katherine went to college to study with William Manker. After taking a worldwide trip, Katherine was certain that she should follow her instincts to work in ceramics. In 1939, Braden left his job and he and Katherine opened Kay Finch Ceramics.

From its beginning, animals were the mainstay and remained so through the twenty-five years Kay Finch Ceramics was in business. Kay created many pig figures and banks and, just a few years later, began creating wonderfully realistic dogs. Cheerfully whimsical characteristics abound on items such as skunks, donkeys, snails, elephants, and so on giving them an animated appearance.

California Country is a breakfast line including a plate, cup, saucer, cream and sugar. All the pieces in this line had a pink body with hand-decorated flower patterns of either Briar Rose, cherry blossoms or shaggy daisies. Items can be found as small as 2" or as large as 50". George, the Finch's son, received credit for planters, bowls, bath accessories, ashtrays and vases that, today, have a following of their own.

When Braden died in 1963, Kay channeled her energies toward dog breeding shows. However, in the mid-1970s, Freeman-McFarlin, another California company, hired Kay to create a set of dog figurines which were manufactured in Freeman-McFarlin glazes. Those dogs were not as well-received by collectors as Kay Finch's own products. Kay Finch died at the age of eighty-nine in June, 1993.

KFinch Kay Finch
Calif.   CALIFORNIA

Kay Finch Marks

Bank, model of Swiss Chalet, two story w/pastels & brown, Model No. 4628, 6" h. ... **$450**

Kay Finch Shell-Shaped Bowl

Bowl, 4" l., 2 3/4" h. shell-shaped, three feet, scalloped rim, ivory exterior, dark green interior, ca. 1939-1945, stamp mark "Kay Finch California," Model No. 510 (ILLUS.).. **$95**

Bowl, swan-shaped, chartreuse glaze, No. 4956.. **190**

Candleholder, figure of "Scandie" girl w/round candle support on her head, pale pink body, light blue accents & trim, 5 1/4" h... **175**

Cup, child's, figural cat's head **110**

Kay Finch Bride & Groom Figures

Figure of a bride, black hair w/pink flower, head bent downward, white swirling long dress w/pink accents, blue & pink flowers bouquet w/three blue ribbons trailing down the gown, elbow length white gloves, Model No. 201, 6 1/2" h. (ILLUS. right) **300**

Figure of a child, "P.J.," standing, brown hair in pigtails tied w/big bows, head slightly tilted to left, white ground w/blue accents, Model No. 5002, 5" h................... **220**

Figure of a "Godey" woman, standing, head w/hat slightly turned & lowered to left, cape across shoulders, hands just below waist & in a muff, basic glazes of white, green, pink, rose & grey, Model No. 122, 9 1/2" h.. **160**

Figure of a groom, standing w/legs slightly apart, black hair, mustache, shoes & jacket w/flower in lapel, grey trousers, Model No. 204, 6 1/2" h. (ILLUS. left) **300**

Figure of a "Scandie" girl, standing in long white dress w/blue apron & scarf tied around her blonde hair, Model No. 126, 5 1/4" h... **155**

Figures of Sage & Maiden, each on a base, Model No. 4852-55, pr......................... **275**

Model of bear, No. 4847, 5" h....................... **250**

Model of bird, "Mrs. Dove," gold-leaf treatment, Freeman-McFarlin item introduced in 1977, Model No. 804, 8 1/2" l., 5 1/2" l....... **200**

Model of cat, "Ambrosia," seated on back legs w/front legs straight & together, Model No. 155, pink & white, 10" h. **775**

Model of cat, "Hannibal," standing w/tail up, angry look, pastels, Model No. 180, 10 1/4" h... **775**

Model of dog, Pekingese reclining w/head up, white fur, Model No. 154, 14" l. **700**

Model of dog, Shih Tzu, gold-leaf treatment, marked w/block letters, Freeman-McFarlin piece, Model No. 837, 10" h. **500**

Model of dog, Yorky standing w/right front leg up, white w/pink fur, Model No. 170, 5" h. **285**

Model of elephant, "Popcorn," Model No. 192, 6 3/4" h... **385**

Model of elephant, seated, white w/pink inside ears, Model No. 4804, 4 1/2" h. **230**

Model of elephant, "Violet," walking position, pastels & flowers, Model No. 190, 17" h.. **2,900**

Model of fountain w/attached bird on edge, pink w/white bird, Model No. 5388, 6" h. **175**

Model of hen, yellow & green **200**

Model of hippo, standing w/head up & mouth open, bow tied around neck, pink body w/polka dots & pastel accents, Model No. 5019, 5 3/4" h. **475**

Model of lamb, kneeling, ears out, pink body, white & dark pink accents, Model No. 136, 2 1/2" l., 2 1/4" h..................... **95**

Model of Mr. Bird, matte teakwood, Model No. 454 .... **135**

Model of Mrs. Bird, matte teakwood, Model No. 453 .... **120**

Model of owl, "Hoot," standing, ears up, ruffled feathers, pastel green & lilac on pink body, black eyes & nose, Model No. 187, 8 1/2" h... **150**

Model of owl, "Toot," standing, ears up, ruffled feathers, pastel green & tan over white body, Model No. 188, companion piece to "Hoot," 6 3/4" h. **125**

Model of penguin, "Polly," white body w/pastel blue, green & yellow w/darker green, Model No. 467, 4 3/4" h. **250**

Model of pig, "Winkie," pink w/blossom decoration, Model No. 185, 3 3/4" h. **140**

Model of rabbit, "Cottontail," Model No. 152, 2 1/2" h.. **150**

Models of lambs, kneeling, Model No. 136, 2 1/4" h., pr.. **155**

Models of rooster & hen, Butch & Biddy, Model Nos. 176 & 177, pr............................. **300**

Mug, figural Missouri Mule, yellow glaze, 5" h. **350**

Nativity group, iridescent barn w/gold trim outside, green gloss on inside bottom, brown gloss straw & blue sky, Model No. 4952, can also be hung as a wall display, marked underglaze, "Kay Finch California," iridescent white w/gold trim, Jesus in a manger w/gold trim on top of manger, iridescent kneeling angel in prayer, iridescent standing white angel w/gold trim, barn, 6" l., 6 1/2" h., Jesus in manger, 1 1/4" h., kneeling angel, 1 1/2"., standing angel, 2 1/4" h., set of 4 .... **310**

Planter, "Baby book," pink baby in diaper w/left leg & arm raised & leaning against an open book, relief flower decoration on book, marked "Baby's First from California," Model No. B5143, 6 1/2" h................... **125**

Planter, baby's block, Baby's First from California line, 6 1/2" h. **165**

Kay Finch Bear Planter

Planter, model of a bear seated, white gloss w/pink ears, eyes & paws, Model No. 4906, 5 3/4" h. (ILLUS.).................................... **300**

Trinket box, heart-shaped, bird perched on lid, deep green box w/royal blue bird, Model No. B5051, 2 1/2" h............................. **135**

Vase, 7 1/4" h., 5 1/4" w., straight sides, light & dark green & light & dark brown leaves overall except plain green on recessed 3/4" base, marked "Kay Fiinch California".. **100**

Wall plaque/ashtray, figural, boxer dog, rounded corners, one of many from the Parade of Champions set, Model No. 4955, 4 3/4" sq.................................... **95**

Wall pocket, Santa face, white beard, red mouth, pink cheeks, black eyes & red cap on right side extending to tip of beard, holly sprig on forehead at edge of cap, Model No. 5373, 9 1/2" h........................ **425**

Wall pocket, Santa face, white beard, red mouth, pink cheeks, black eyes & red cap on right side extending to tip of beard, holly sprig on forehead at edge of cap, w/"Merry Xmas" in gold script at bottom center of beard, Model No. 5373, 9 1/2" h.. **450**

Lefton

The Lefton China Company was the creation of Mr. George Zoltan Lefton who migrated to the United States from Hungary in 1939. In 1941 he embarked on a new career and began shaping a business that sprang from his passion for collecting fine china and porcelains. Though his funds were very limited, his vision was to develop a source from which to obtain fine porcelains by reviving the postwar Japanese ceramic industry, which dated back to antiquity. As a trailblazer, George Zoltan Lefton soon earned the reputation as "The China King".

Counted among the most desirable and sought after collectibles of today, Lefton items such as Bluebirds, Miss Priss, Angels, all types of dinnerware and tea-related items are eagerly acquired by collectors. As is true with any antique or collectible, prices may vary, depending on location, condition and availability.

For additional information on the history of Lefton China, its factories, marks, products and values, readers should consult Collector's Encyclopedia of Lefton China, Books I and II *and* The Lefton Price Guide *by Loretta DeLozier.*

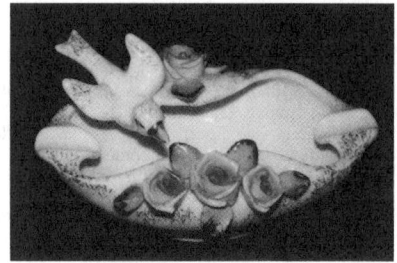

Ashtray with Figural Bird

Ashtray, oval, white w/figural bird on rim, applied pink roses & green leaves, No. 465, 5 1/2" (ILLUS.).. **$45**

Bank, model of a pig w/flowers, No. 379, pink or white, each.............................. **52**

Bank, model of a lion, wearing glasses, No. 13384, 6" h... **55**

Bank, model of an owl, bisque, No. 479, 6 1/2" h... **25**

Box, cov., candy, Blue Paisley patt., No. 2142 .... **50**

Covered Egg Box with Chick

Box, cov., footed, model of egg w/chick & floral decoration, No. 5549, 3 1/2" h. (ILLUS.) **12**

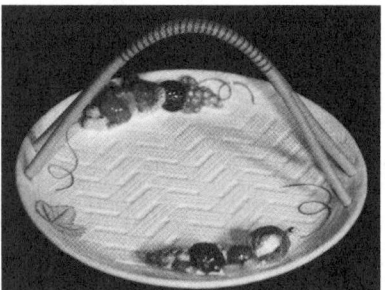

Fruit Basket Cake Plate

Cake plate, handled, Fruit Basket patt., No. 1893, 9" d. (ILLUS.)................................ **45**

Coffeepot, cov., Cosmos patt., No. 1077 .... **125**

Magnolia Pattern Coffeepot

Coffeepot, cov., Magnolia patt., No. 2518
(ILLUS.).. **175**
Coffeepot, cov., Sweet Violets patt., No.
2842, 7 1/4" h.. **75**
Cookie Jar, cov., head of girl w/bandanna,
No. 397, 8" h. **250**
Cookie jar, cov., Panda bear w/honeypot,
No. 7794, 11" h.. **175**

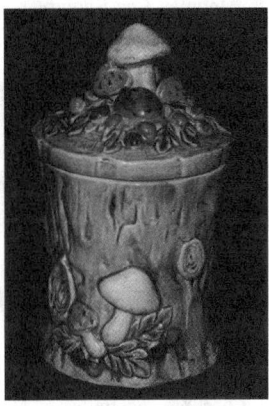

Mushroom Forest Cookie Jar

Cookie Jar, cov., Mushroom Forest, No.
6352, 11 1/2" h. (ILLUS.) **40**
Creamer & cov. sugar bowl, Festival patt.,
No. 2615, pr. **45**
Creamer & cov. sugar bowl, Fruits of Italy
patt., No. 1177, pr. **18**
Creamer & cov. sugar bowl, stacking-
type, violet decoration, No. 058, the set **95**

Thumbelina Creamer & Sugar Bowl

Creamer & cov. sugar bowl, Thumbelina,
No. 1708, pr. (ILLUS.) **50**

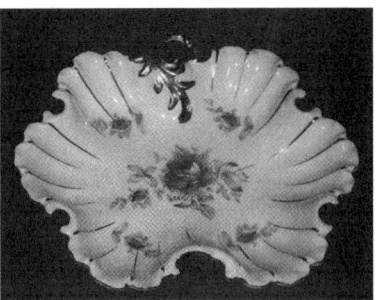

Elegant Rose Dish

Dish, Elegant Rose patt., white, scalloped
rim, gold trim, No. 2334 (ILLUS.)..................... **48**
Dish, two-compartment, Fruits of Italy patt.,
No. 1178.. **15**

Classic Elegance Dish

Dish, Classic Elegance patt., No. 4808,
8 1/2" d. (ILLUS.)...................................... **38**

Ewer with Floral Bouquet

Ewer, bisque, decorated w/applied floral
bouquet, No. 4540, 6 1/4" h. (ILLUS.) **18**
Figure group, cherub sitting on cart being
pushed by second cherub, No. 810
(ILLUS.top next page) **350**
Figure group, old man & woman w/spin-
ning wheel, No. 4146, 6 1/4" h........................ **75**
Figure group, bisque, Provincial Girl & Boy,
No. 5262, 8" h.. **130**
Figurine, angel, kissing girl, No. 02079,
3 1/2" h.. **7**

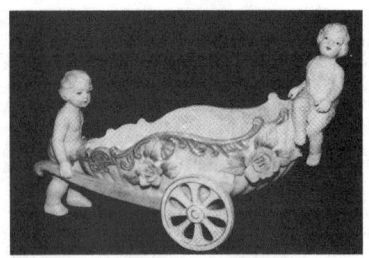

Cart with Cherubs

Figurine, Bloomer Girl, No. 1412, 4" h. **55**
Figurine, Boy w/Birdhouse, No. 3082,
4 1/2" h. **30**
Figurine, This Little Pig went to Market,
nursery rhyme, No. 1252, 5 1/2" h. **75**
Figurine, Scottish Girl, No. 3930, 6" h. **30**

Lady Fifi Figurine

Figurine, Lady Fifi, No. 5742, 7 1/2" h.
(ILLUS.)... **120**
Figurines, Colonial boy & girl, No. 1066,
12" h., pr. **400-500**
Figurines, provincial boy & girl on bench,
No. 5644, 5 3/4" h., pr. **120**
Head vase, Lady, No. 2568, 6" h. **50**
Head vase, Lady w/hat & earrings, No.
4857, 6" h. **60**
Jam jar, cov., Fruits of Italy patt., No. 623 .... **20**
Model, Country Post Office, Colonial Village
series, No. 07341 .... **65**

Model of Baltimore Oriole

Model of a bird, Baltimore Oriole, No. 465,
5 1/2" h. (ILLUS.)....................................... **35**
Model of a bird, Lark on limb, No. 440, 6" h. **40**
Model of a bird, peacock w/tail spread, No.
2330, 6" h. **55**
Model of a bird, Macaw, No. 1066, 9 1/4" h. **62**
Model of a colt, Palomino, No. 2212,
4 1/2" h. **40**
Model of a cow, Hereford, No. 451,
6 3/4" h. **35**
Model of a horse, No. 053, 5" h. **36**
Model of a raccoon, No. 4752, 5" h. **42**

Model of Red Squirrel

Model of a squirrel, bisque, red, No. 4492,
8" h. (ILLUS.) **85**

Model of a Tiger

Model of a tiger, No. 6761 (ILLUS.) **35**
Model of an eagle, No. 802, 11" h. **100**
Models of a hen & a rooster, white, No.
2396, 9" h., pr. **90**

Model of Flamingo with Baby

Models of bird, pink Flamingo w/baby, No.
504, 5 1/2" h. (ILLUS.)....................................... **75**

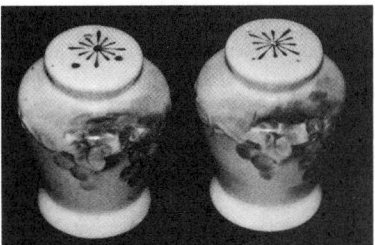

25th Anniversary Pitcher & Bowl Set

Bluebirds on Tree Branch

Models of Deer

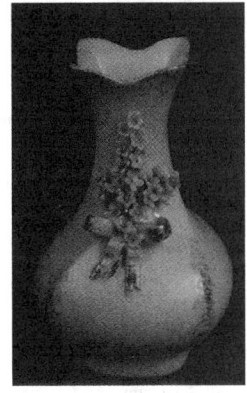

Festival Shakers

"Cuddles" Napkin Holder

Vase with Forget-Me-Nots

Vase, 5 3/4" h., decorated w/applied forget-me-not spray tied w/bow, No. 270 (ILLUS.).. **50**

Milk White Vase with Roses

Vase, 6" h., milk white china w/applied pink roses & green leaves, No. 833 (ILLUS.)......... **48**
Vase, 6 1/4" h., white w/lilacs & stones, No. 138... **45**

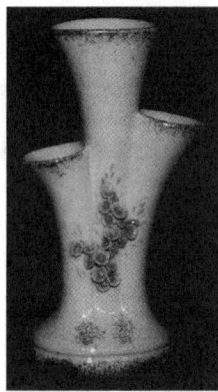

Vase with Forget-Me-Nots

Vase, 7" h., pink w/forget-me-not decoration, No. 7633 (ILLUS.)..................................... **65**
Wall plaque, round w/scalloped rim, h.p. floral decoration, No. 119, 8" d......................... **22**

Lenox

The Ceramic Art Company was established at Trenton, New Jersey, in 1889 by Jonathan Coxon and Walter Scott Lenox. In addition to true porcelain, it also made a Belleek-type ware. Renamed Lenox Company in 1906, it is still in operation today.

Lenox Mark

Busts of a man & woman, Art Deco style, the young man w/short cropped hair, a

pointed chin & long neck, the young woman w/a long face & long neck, downcast eyes, her hair in a pony tail combed to one side, each raised on a thick rectangular plinth, glossy ivory glaze, base impressed "A.B.C. O. '35" & green Lenox stamp, 8 3/4" h., pr.................................... **$220**
Figure of a young woman, Art Deco stylized standing lady w/short hair, nude except for a long drapery looped through her arms, looking down at a seated greyhound at her side, on a stepped round base, glossy ivory glaze, base impressed "Lenox - A.B.C. O. '37," 13 1/2" h.................. **468**
Figure of a young woman, Art Deco style standing lady w/her head turned to one side, holding her long flowing gown out at the sides, glossy ivory glaze, impressed on the base "Lenox - A.B.C.O. '37," 13 3/4" h. **385**
Service plates, the center painted & transfer-printed w/an urn issuing fruit, flowers & foliage within a green rim, the edge w/matching urns & floral panels flanked by scrolled foliage in blue on a cream ground, pattern number 1830/X..77.G, printed mark & mark of retailer Marshall Field & Company, Chicago, early 20th c., 10 1/2" d., set of 12...................................... **345**
Vase, 8 1/4" h., baluster-form, decorated w/applied & enameled peonies & wildflowers w/gilt trim.. **143**
Vase, 10 1/2" h., baluster-form, creamy ground decorated overall w/silver overlay in a dense vining floral design...................... **201**

Limoges

Numerous factories produced china in Limoges, France, with major production in the 19th century. Some pieces listed below are identified by the name of the maker or the mark of the factory. Although the famed Haviland Company was located in Limoges, wares bearing their marks are not included in this listing. Also see HAVILAND.

An excellent reference is The Collector's Encyclopedia of Limoges Porcelain, Second Edition, by Mary Frank Gaston (Collector Books, 1992).

Limoges Creamer & Sugar Bowl

Creamer & cov. sugar bowl, bulbous bodies decorated on front & back w/purple & lavender violets & green leaves, violet colored handles, lavish gold trim, "T & V, Limoges, France," creamer 4" d., 3 1/2" h., sugar bowl 4" d., 3 3/4" h. (Tressemann & Vogt), pr. (ILLUS.) **$110**
Lettuce bowl w/underplate, decorated w/h.p. violets, 6 1/2" d. **110**
Sweetmeat dish, cov., decorated w/roses & green leaves, gold trim, 9" w., 6" h............. **110**

Liverpool

Liverpool is most often used as a generic term for fine earthenware products, usually of creamware or pearlware, produced at numerous potteries in this English city during the late 18th and early 19th centuries. Many examples, especially pitchers, were decorated with transfer-printed patriotic designs aimed specifically at the American buying public.

Bowl, 8 3/4" d., 3 3/4" h., creamware, a wide footring below deep rounded & gently flaring sides, decorated w/black transfer-printed scene w/ships, sailor & wife reading "When this you see, remember me..." (wear & stains) **$715**

Mug, tall cylindrical form, creamware w/a black transfer-printed oval portrait medallion of "James Lawrence Esq. late of the United States Navy," scrolled handle w/foliate attachments, early 19th c., 6 1/4" h. (imperfections) **2,990**

Pitcher, milk, 5 1/2" h., Queensware, black transfer-printed oval reserve w/"Lafayette" & "Ben Franklin," eagle & reading "Republicans are not always Ungrateful, Ricd. Hall & Son" (old yellowed repairs to spout, wear & minor damage) **605**

Pitcher, 6 1/4" h., creamware, bulbous body w/wide tapering cylindrical neck & pinched spout, both sides depicting black transfer-printed decoration of an eagle, flag & two women as Peace & Plenty & a circular reserve w/the names of ten states & Boston w/the inscription "Peace, Plenty, and Independence" & under the spout "Success to the Trade of Rhode Island," restoration, minor imperfections (ILLUS. far right) **1,610**

Pitcher, 6 3/4" h., jug-form, black transfer-printed decoration of a bust of Captain Jacob Jones of the Macedonian within an oval reserve against a yellow ground w/pink lustre collar, the reverse in the same manner, early 19th c., restoration (ILLUS. far left) **1,725**

Various Liverpool Pitchers

Pitcher, 8" h., jug-form, black transfer-printed design on buff ground, one side depicts two portrait busts of John Hancock & Samuel Adams in an oval w/a beehive & horn of plenty & the inscription "The Memory of Washington and the Proscribed Patriots of America, Liberty, Virtue, Peace, Justice, and Equity to All Mankind," the reverse depicts an oval w/a military scene w/hero & cannon, w/ships & farmers plowing in the distance, inscribed "Success to America whose Militiia is better than Standing Armies. May Its Citizens Emulate Soldiers and its Soldiers Heros...," Great

Seal of the United States beneath the spout, early 19th c., restoration, chips (ILLUS. second from right) **2,300**

Pitcher, 8" h., jug-form, red transfer-printed design of an American eagle on the front & a figural panel on the reverse, early 19th c. (wear, chips, hairline in base) **978**

Washington Liverpool Pitcher

Pitcher, 8 7/8" h., jug-form, black transfer-printed scenes, one side w/"Washington in Glory America in Tears," the reverse w/"The Macedonian & The United States" & a spread eagle below the spout, minor rim nick & glaze wear, base chip, early 19th c. (ILLUS.) **2,300**

Pitcher, 10" h., jug-form, creamware, black transfer-printed scene titled "Washington in His Glory," reverse titled "America in Tears" w/eagle & ship, traces of gold trim (stains & chips) **1,705**

Pitcher, 10" h., jug-form, creamware, one side w/black transfer-printed ship flying American flag, the other side w/an oblong vine-trimmed panel filled w/Masonic emblems & "J.G.," & American eagle under the spout (chip on rim) **1,210**

Pitcher, 10 1/8" h., jug-form, one side decorated w/a black transfer-printed reserve depicting a maiden on shore waving farewell to a trio of ships, one w/American flag, captioned "Fanny's farewell. Adieu she cry'd, and waved her Lily Hand," the reverse depicts the American warship "Fanny, James Bradburn" w/polychrome decoration, Great Seal of the United States beneath the spout, early 19th c., restoration (ILLUS. second from left) **1,380**

Liverpool Pitcher

Pitcher, 10 1/2" h., jug-form, transfer-printed w/"Washington in Glory American in Tears" & on the reverse Masonic elements w/an eagle & monogram "SOS" within a Masonic reserve, below the spout, staining, old repair to handle, minor hairlines, early 19th c. (ILLUS.) **1,380**

Pitcher, 14" h., jug-form, creamware, transfer-printed w/an American eagle & monogram, the Ship America & a panel depicting George Washington as general, flanked by figures of Justice & Liberty, w/the names of fifteen states, early 19th c. **6,900**

Lustre Wares

Lustred wares in imitation of copper, gold, silver and other colors were produced in England in the early 19th century and onward. Gold, copper or platinum oxides were painted on glazed objects which were then fired, giving them a lustred effect. Various forms of lustre wares include plain lustre with the entire object coated to obtain a metallic effect, bands of lustre decoration and painted lustre designs. Particularly appealing is the pink or purple "splash lustre" sometimes referred to as "Sunderland" lustre in the mistaken belief it was confined to the production of Sunderland area potteries. Objects decorated in silver lustre by the "resist" process, wherein parts of the objects to be left free from lustre decoration were treated with wax, are referred to as "silver resist."

Wares formerly called "Canary Yellow Lustre" are now referred to as "Yellow-Glazed Earthenwares."

Copper

Copper Lustre Pitcher

Pitcher, 6 3/8" h., flared foot below globular lower section, wide flaring cylindrical neck w/long spout, C-scroll handle, a wide canary band w/white oval reserves printed in black, one w/"Lafayette," the other w/"Cornwallis," wear, interior blisters & a few exterior blisters in yellow, early 19th c. (ILLUS.) **$770**

Pitcher, 7" h., small disk foot supporting a round widely flaring rounded lower body below a short angled shoulder to the tall cylindrical neck w/a figural serpent head rim spout & angled serpent handle, the sections of the body & neck w/blue ground decorated w/applied & polychromed basket of flowers near the base & band of flowers on the neck, copper lustre bands around the foot, body & rim & copper lustre spout & handle, ca. 1840...... **413**

Copper Lustre Punch Bowl

Punch bowl, footed w/slightly flared sides, decorated w/wide white center band w/free-hand pink lustre house design, interior wear, 10 1/4" d., 4 7/8" h. (ILLUS.) **605**

Tea set: cov. 6 1/2" h. teapot, 5" h. cov. sugar bowl, 3 1/2" h. creamer; footed bulbous body, teapot w/swan's neck spout & relief-molded eagle handle, sugar bowl w/shell-shaped shoulder handles, overall copper lustre w/dark tan bands, rare, early set, 3 pcs. **280**

Silver & Silver Resist

Silver Lustre Creamer & Sugar Bowl

Creamer & cov. sugar bowl, footed, wide cylindrical body, creamer w/arched spout & D-form handle, sugar bowl w/inset cover w/blossom finial, minor stains & sugar bowl w/crow's foot hairlines, repair to scalloped lip & chips inside lid flange, 5 3/4" h., pr. (ILLUS.) **220**

Pitcher, 8 3/4" h., jug-form, wide ovoid body w/a short cylindrical neck w/a long pointed spout, C-form handle, silver resist decoration of flowers & vining leaves in silver lustre on a white ground, first half 19th c. (small chips, roughness, crow's foot in side)... **248**

Pitcher, 5 3/8" h., jug-form, bulbous ovoid body w/a short concave neck, pointed rim spout & angled loop handle, the body decorated overall in silver resist w/an ornate design of large birds perched among berry clusters, leaves & blossoms, ca. 1815...................... **575**

Pitcher, 5 1/2" h., jug-form, bulbous ovoid body w/a slightly tapering short neck, pointed rim spout & angled loop handle, the sides w/two round purple transfer-printed reserves depicting landscapes w/houses, the remainder of the body decorated in silver resist w/ornately flowering sprigs & a leaf band around the rim, ca. 1810-15 .... **460**

Sunderland Pink & Others

Frog mug, cylindrical form, two-handled, overall Sunderland pink splash lustre &

black transfer-printed inscriptions, "Sailor's Farewell" & "Sailor's Prayer," interior bottom fitted w/a small figural frog, 19th c., 5 5/8" h. (hairline) 604

Pitcher, 6 1/4" h., jug-form, pearlware, footed bulbous ovoid body tapering to a short neck w/rim spout, C-scroll handle, the sides molded w/scene of a stag, doe & fawn highlighted in pink lustre & polychrome enamel on white ground, first half 19th c. 385

Pitcher, 7 1/4" h., jug-form, decorated under the spout w/the Mariner's Arms, a ship w/two sailors, lighthouse & cannon in the background, each side w/an inspirational verse within a floral border reserve, ca. 1840 (chips) 633

Pitcher, 7 1/4" h., jug-form, transfer-printed scene of a life boat, picture of Susan & William & motto 413

Pitcher, 9" h., jug-form, wide bulbous ovoid body tapering to a short cylindrical neck w/high arched spout, C-form handle, one side w/a black transfer-printed reserve w/Masonic emblems & a verse, the rectangular reserve under the spout w/"Charlotte Todd, Born May 20th, 1825" in brick red enamel, Sunderland pink splash lustre background (wear, stains, chips) 770

Majolica

Majolica, a tin-enameled glazed pottery, has been produced for centuries. It originally took its name from the island of Majorca, a source of figuline (potter's clay). Subsequently it was widely produced in England, Europe and the United States. Etruscan majolica, now avidly sought, was made by Griffen, Smith & Hill, Phoenixville, Pa., in the last quarter of the 19th century. Most majolica advertised today is 19th or 20th century. Once scorned by most collectors, interest in this colorful ware so popular during the Victorian era has now revived and prices have risen dramatically in the past few years. Also see WEDGWOOD.

Majolica Etruscan Mark

Etruscan

Plates, 9" d., molded Maple Leaves design, white background, set of 4 (imperfections) $358

General

Cheese dish, cov., stilton-type, tall cylindrical cover molded around the side, on the rim of the base & around the cow-form knop w/a band of stiff leaves picked out in shades of green on a pink ground, the interior of the cover & underplate glazed in turquoise, George Jones, England, 1870s, 11 3/8" h. (cows' horns restored, crack in cover) 5,100

Game dish w/liner, cov., oval form molded around the sides w/leaves & ferns glazed in green on a turquoise ground within ochre rope-molded borders, the cover modeled w/a partridge resting on a bed of ferns, George Jones, England, ca. 1865, black painted "1758 111," 11" l. (minor crack to cover) 3,737

George Jones Fish & Game Tureen

Game tureen, cov., two-handled, basket-form, dark brown bamboo w/relief-molded fish & game on cover surrounded by green leaves, George Jones, England (ILLUS.) 8,250

Garden seat, "St. Louis," cylindrical lobed body molded around the sides in Japanese style w/prunus & stylized chrysanthemums in turquoise on a cream ground, impressed marks & "BGS," Wedgwood, ca. last half 19th c., 17 5/8" h. 920

Majolica Garden Seat

Garden seats, Chinese barrel-shaped, decorated w/relief-molded irises & leaves in green glazes on cream ground, ca. 1895, impressed marks, Wardle & Company, 18 1/2" h., pr. (ILLUS. of one) 4,600

Ice cream set: one round 16" d. platter & twelve 6 1/2" d. dessert plates; strawberry design on a cream ground w/bow handles, Wedgwood, late 19th c., the set (imperfections) 633

Jardiniere, figural, modeled w/an eagle w/outstretched wings perched on a branch inclined towards a rabbit crouching in the mouth of its burrow on the opposite side of a large open stump, by Brown-Westhead, Moore & Co., England, signed by painter, ca. 1880, 25" h. (ends of wings & tip of beak restored) 8,400

Jardiniere, inverted pear shape, molded w/vertical raised straps set w/lion's mask & ring handles & terminating in paw feet, blue ground, the gadrooned rim glazed in green & interior pale pink, impressed marks, Minton, England, ca. 1871, 14 1/4" h.. **2,645**

Jardiniere, flared dome foot below bulbous body w/everted rim, molded in high relief around the sides w/swags of fruit & nuts suspended from lion's masks & white puce ribbon-tied florets, turquoise ground, the stem, foot & rim molded w/bands of acanthus, pink-glazed interior, impressed marks, Minton, England, ca. 1855-60,14 1/2" h. (some restoration) **4,600**

Jardiniere & pedestal, decorated w/a cobalt blue ground & colored fish & foliage in relief, impressed mark "Modele Reserve Exclusivement Pour La France au Grand Depot 21. Rue Drouot Paris," France, 19th c., 12 1/2" h., 2 pcs. (rim & associated hairlines restored, footrim chips repaired, glaze wear on pedestal)....... **690**

Majolica Jardiniere & Stand

Jardiniere & stand, bulbous cylindrical form decorated w/relief-molded swallows swooping above sprays of white lilies on blue ground beneath a band of brown-glazed leaves, turquoise interior, the circular stand molded w/a brown-glazed Greek key border, Joseph Holdcroft, ca. 1870, impressed "8" & painted "21," stand w/painted "10," 13 3/4" h. (ILLUS.)...... **977**

Jardiniere & undertray, the deep rounded body w/gently scalloped rim & small leaf-scrolled side handles molded around the body w/a profusion of ferns, foxgloves & convolvulus on a brown ground, the interior glazed in pink, the undertray molded w/further leaves within a reeded & lobed rim, Mintons, ca. 1869, overall 15 1/2" h., 2 pcs.. **9,600**

Jardinieres, lozenge form foot supporting semi-ovoid body w/relief-molded sprays of white dog roses on brown glaze basketweave ground, relief-molded branches at rim & foot, turquoise interior, marked w/painted "2," Staffordshire, ca. 1870, 8 1/2" h., pr. **2,070**

Model of a cockatoo, naturalistically molded & colored in dark green w/a yellow crest, perched on a green tree stump above rockwork, Minton, Shape No. 1847, ca. 1900, 14 3/8" h. **633**

Oyster plates, six-well, bordered by shells & seaweed & glazed in white, alternating w/either pink, turquoise or blue about a central circular well of the same color, set of ten consisting of five turquoise, two pink & three blue, painted cross & four dots mark, English or American, after a Minton design, ca. 1880, 9 1/4" d. (four w/glaze faults or repair, one w/minor chip & one w/minor haircrack) **2,875**

Oyster plates, six-well, divided by groups of shells & seaweed, turquoise glaze, impressed "Minton 1323," 9 1/4" d., set of 6 (two w/minor bruise cracks to rim)............. **3,450**

Plant stand, model of a tree stump w/four staggered round shelves at the tops of stubby stumps w/three taller in the back & a low one in front, brown tree back decoration w/molded green leaves, late 19th c., 15 1/2" h. **743**

Marblehead

This pottery was organized in 1904 by Dr. Herbert J. Hall as a therapeutic aid to patients in a sanitarium he ran in Marblehead, Massachusetts. It was later separated from the sanitarium and directed by Arthur E. Baggs, a fine artist and designer, who bought out the factory in 1916 and operated it until its closing in 1936. Most wares were hand-thrown and decorated and carry the company mark of a stylized sailing vessel flanked by the letters "M" and "P."

Marblehead Mark

Book ends, upright square wedge-shaped design, the front of each embossed w/a different sailing ship scene in green & orange on a blue ground, stamped mark, 5 1/2" w., 5 1/2" h., pr. (some running glaze & back fleck on one, invisible restoration to corner of other) **$880**

Bowl, 4 1/8" h., tapered spherical form, dark teal blue glaze, impressed mark, early 20th c., ... **173**

Bowl, 8" d., 3 3/4" h., a small footring supporting a deep gently flaring bowl w/a widely flaring & flattened rim, lightly molded lotus design on the exterior, dark blue matte glaze on the exterior & a light blue semi-matter interior glaze, stamped mark **358**

Bowl-vase, squatty spherical form w/a closed rim, overall dark blue semi-matte glaze, impressed mark, 5" d., 3 1/4" h. **495**

Chamberstick, dished round base centered by a tall slender shaft w/a flaring cupped socket, a long loop handle from the upper shaft to the base, smooth dark green matte glaze, impressed mark, 5" d., 8 1/2" h. 550

Pitcher, 5" h., 6" d., footed bulbous shouldered body w/a short neck w/pointed spout, loop handle, embossed around the neck w/waves, the sides w/rounded medallions around galleons under sail in blue, ochre & green, the waves & handle in blue & the background in cream, semi-matte glaze, impressed ship mark 770

Vase, 4" h., 3 1/4" d., cylindrical w/a slightly rounded base, impressed around the rim w/a band of stylized flowers in red w/green leaves on a dark blue ground, impressed mark 1,980

Vase, 4 1/4" h., 4 3/4" d., bulbous ovoid body w/a flat mouth, decorated around the mouth w/red & purple stylized blossoms in a band on the semi-matte pink ground, mark under glaze 880

Vase, 4 3/4" h., swollen cylindrical form, decorated around the rim w/repeating raised flower & leaf design in faint blue, red & tan on a speckled blue matte ground, by Hannah Tutt, impressed mark & artist's initials, early 20th c. 1,610

Vase, 5" h., 3 3/4" d., tapering ovoid body w/a wide flat mouth, embossed around the rim w/a repeated band of stylized fruit & leaves in browns & blue, on a speckled grey ground, by Hannah Tuff, impressed mark.... 1,430

Vase, 5 1/2" h., ovoid body w/wide flat mouth, matte blue-grey glaze, early 20th c., impressed mark (crazing) 345

Vase, 6 1/4" h., 5 1/4" d., flaring rim over a swollen flaring body, matte blue glaze, impressed mark (minor glaze scratches) 460

Vase, 6 5/8" h., bulbous octagonal paneled body w/horizontal ribbing, wide mouth, aqua semi-gloss glaze, artist-initialed "A - B - 26," ca. 1926, impressed mark 230

Vase, 7" h., tall cylindrical form, dark matte green glaze, impressed company cipher....... 518

Vase, 8 1/2" h., 8" d., heavy bell-form body w/closed rim, unusual frothy matte bluish green glaze, incised "M" w/sea gull (repair to small drilled bottom side hole) 990

Vase, 11 3/4" h., wide slightly tapering cylindrical form w/flat rim, blue matte glaze, impressed mark (tight line at rim) 660

Wall plaque, rectangular w/profile portrait of an Egyptian in relief, glossy turquoise glaze, early 20th c., impressed mark & paper label, 7 1/2" h., 4 5/8" w. (crazing, minor wear) 546

McCoy

Collectors are now seeking the art wares of two McCoy potteries. One was founded in Roseville, Ohio, in the late 19th century as the J.W. McCoy Pottery, subsequently becoming Brush-McCoy Pottery Co., later Brush Pottery. The other was also founded in Roseville in 1910 as Nelson McCoy Sanitary Stoneware Co., later becoming Nelson McCoy Pottery. In 1967 the pottery was sold to D.T. Chase of the Mount Clemens Pottery Co. who sold his interest to the Lancaster Colony Corp. in 1974. The pottery shop closed in 1985. Cookie jars are especially collectible today.

A helpful reference book is The Collector's Encyclopedia of McCoy Pottery, *by the Huxfords (Collector Books), and* McCoy Cookie Jars From the First to the Latest, *by Harold Nichols (Nichols Publishing, 1987).*

McCoy Mark

Basket, hanging-type, Butterfly line, 6 1/2" h. $175-300

Book end/planter, model of a bird dog, ca. 1955, 5 3/4 x 6", pr. 150-200

Book ends, model of a rearing horse, 1940s, 8" h., pr. 100-125

Candleholders, Lily Bud line, 5" d., pr.......... 60-80

Antelope Centerpiece

Centerpiece, four sections w/center model of antelope, green & tan, ca. 1955, 8 1/2 x 12" (ILLUS.) 250-350

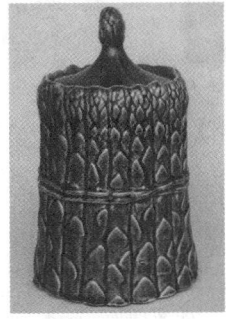

Asparagus Cookie Jar

Cookie jar, Asparagus, ca. 1977 (ILLUS.) 40-50

Davy Crockett Cookie Jar

Cookie jar, Davy Crockett head, ca. 1957
(ILLUS.)... **575-650**

Hound Dog Cookie Jar

Cookie jar, Hound Dog, ca. 1977 (ILLUS.) ... **25-35**

House Cookie Jar

Cookie jar, House, ca. 1986 (ILLUS.)........ **300-350**
Cookie jar, Love Birds: Kissing Penguins,
ca. 1946... **75-100**
Cookie jar, Pear, ca. 1952 .... **75-100**
Cookie jar, Pumpkin, ca. 1955................... **500-600**
Cookie jar, Rag Doll (Raggedy Ann)
ca. 1972... **100-125**
Cookie jar, round, Hobnail line, ca. 1940 .. **100-200**
Dog dish, embossed "Man's Best Friend,
His Dog," 7 1/2" d. **60-75**
Flower bowl ornament, model of a duck,
4" h. **75-90**
Flower holder, figural, model of a fish,
4 1/4" l. **100-200**

Chuck Wagon Food Warmer

Food warmer, model of a chuck wagon
w/brass wagon wheels & candleholder,
El Rancho line, ca. 1960, 3 qt. (ILLUS.) **225-250**
Jardiniere, Spring Wood line, ca. 1960,
10" h. **50-60**

Cameo Design Jardiniere & Pedestal

Jardiniere & pedestal base, cameo design, green, blue & ivory blended gloss
glaze, overall 21" h., 2 pcs. (ILLUS.) **250-350**
Jardiniere & pedestal base, holly design,
overall 21" h., 2 pc. **250-350**
Jardiniere & pedestal base, quilted
design, ca. 1955, overall 21" h., 2 pcs... **200-250**
Mug, relief molded scary gorilla face,
ca. 1978 .... **30-40**
Oil jar, marked "NM," 12" h. **125-200**
Pitcher, 6" h., round, Hobnail line, 48 oz..... **90-125**
Pitcher, 7 3/4" h., figural W. C. Fields head,
tan... **50-60**

Figural Fish Pitcher

Pitcher, model of a fish, ca. 1949
(ILLUS.) **500-600**
Planter, Baa Baa Black Sheep, ca. 1940s,
4 1/2" h.. **45-60**
Planter, banana boat, ca. 1959, 11" l........ **125-175**
Planter, model of alligator, ca. 1950, 10" l. ... **50-60**
Planter, model of alphabet blocks w/figural
Raggedy Ann on top, ca. 1954, 5 1/4" l... **75-100**
Planter, model of anvil, ca. 1953, 9" l. **35-50**
Planter, model of baby rattle, ca. 1954,
3 x 5 1/2"... **75-100**

Bird Dog with Pheasant Planter

Planter, model of bird dog w/pheasant, relief-molded rock base, rail fence & bush, ca. 1954, 8 1/2 x 12 1/2" (ILLUS.).. **200-250**

Grape Cluster Planter

Planter, model of cluster of grapes & leaves, 5 x 6 1/2" (ILLUS.)...................... **125-150**
Planter, model of cowboy hat, ca. 1956, 8" l... **35-50**
Planter, model of goose w/cart, 8" l............... **35-45**
Planter, model of Mary Ann-style shoe, 5" l... **25-40**
Planter, model of panda & crib, 6" l............. **75-100**
Planter, model of pheasant, ca. 1959, 6 x 7 1/2"... **60-75**
Planter, model of piano, ca. 1959, 5 x 6"... **100-150**
Planter, model of pussy at the well, ca. 1957, 7" l. **125-175**
Planter, model of quail, ca. 1955, 7 x 9" **60-75**

Rabbits & Stump Planter

Planter, model of rabbits & stump, ca. 1951, white w/brown trim, 5 1/2" h. (ILLUS.).. **60-75**
Planter, model of rocking chair, ca. 1954, 8 1/2" h.. **35-45**
Planter, model of scoop w/figural mammy seated on rim, ca. 1953, 7 1/2" h............ **150-200**

Planter, model of squirrel, ca. 1955, 4 1/2 x 5".. **25-30**
Planter, model of "stretch" pony, 3 1/2 x 5 3/8" **75-90**
Planter, model of zebra, ca. 1956, 6 1/2 x 8 1/2".. **600-700**
Porch jar, Sand Butterfly design, 20" h. **450-600**

Sand Jar with Sphinx Design

Sand jar, sphinx design, ca. 1930s,16" h. (ILLUS.) **1,000-1,400**
Spoon rest, model of a penguin, 5 x 7"..... **100-150**
Tea set: cov. teapot, creamer & open sugar bowl; oval shape w/branch handles, brown & green vine & ivy leaf decoration on white ground, 3 pcs. **90-110**
Tray, novelty, model of hands, NM mark, ca. 1940s, 8 1/2" **100-125**
TV lamp, model of a panther, ca. 1950s, 7 1/2 x 9 1/2" **65-80**

Mermaid & Shell TV Lamp

TV lamp, model of a seashell & mermaid, yellow & green, 6 x 9 3/4" (ILLUS.) **200-300**
Vase, 7 1/2" h., figural Uncle Sam head **50-60**
Vase, 8" h., figural double tulip, ca. 1948..... **75-125**
Vase, 8" h., figural hyacinth, ca. 1950 .... **100-125**
Vase, 8 1/4" h., model of a gloved hand, ca. 1940s... **150-200**

Poppy Vase

Vase, 8 1/2", figural poppy, pink, ca. 1955
(ILLUS.).. **600-800**

Ivy Decorated Vase

Vase, 9" h., footed, flaring conical body
w/brown angled branch handles, deco-
rated w/brown vines & green ivy leaves,
white ground (ILLUS.)............................... **90-100**
Vase, 9" h., petal form w/angled
handles, ca. 1955..................................... **150-175**
Vase, 9 1/2" h., model of ram's head, ... **100-150**
Vase 10" h., two-handled, Butterfly line...... **150-225**
Vase, 12" h., Harmony line, ca. 1961 .... **30-40**
Vase, 14" h., ribbed pattern......................... **200-300**
Vase, 9" h., footed, tapering body w/irregu-
lar rim, relief-molded contrasting leaf
decoration at top..................................... **100-125**

Blossomtime Wall Pocket

Wall pocket, Blossomtime line, 7 3/4" h.
(ILLUS.).. **95-130**
Wall pocket, model of a bunch of
bananas... **125-150**

Mailbox Wall Pocket

Wall pocket, model of a mailbox, 7" h.
(ILLUS.) **90-100**
Wall pocket, model of a violin, 10 1/4" h.... **100-200**
Wall pocket, model of an orange **65-80**
Wall pocket, model of an umbrella,
8 3/4" h... **60-75**

Meissen

*The secret of true hard paste porcelain, known long
before to the Chinese, was "discovered" accidentally in
Meissen, Germany by J.F. Bottger, an alchemist working
with E.W. Tschirnhausen. The first European true porcelain was made in the Meissen Porcelain Works, organized
about 1709. Meissen marks have been widely copied by
other factories. Some pieces listed here are recent.*

Meissen Mark

Beakers, covers & underplates, the tall
slightly tapering cylindrical beaker flanked
by gold loop handles, the yellow ground
decorated w/reserves of harbor scenes
w/merchants in conversation before boats
& ships within gilt quatrefoil cartouches,
the lower domed cover w/knob finial &
similar reserves, decorated gilt rim bands,
matching decor on the underplate, late
19th c., blue crossed swords mark & various incised & impressed marks, the un-
derplates 5 5/8" d., two sets **$2,300**
Candlestick, Blue Onion patt., domed
stepped foot tapering to the ringed & baluster-form standard below the cylindrical
candle socket, blue crossed swords
mark, 19th c., 9" h. **413**
Candlesticks, Rococo style, the foliate noz-
zle & drip pan on a scroll-molded stem
encrusted w/flowers & applied w/paired
putti each holding an attribute of a different season, the rocaille-molded footed
base painted w/scattered flower sprigs,
mid to late 19th c., blue crossed swords
marks, numbered, after a model by Leu-
teritz, 13 1/8" h., pr.. **2,760**

Centerpiece, Rococo-style, the deep flaring oblong bowl w/a reticulated scroll border above a wide band of encrusted floral garland in pastel colors & gilt, the bottom of the bowl molded as a shell raised on a scrolling palm tree stem similarly decorated & applied w/large figures of an amorous 18th c. couple, on a tall tapering round rocaille-molded base w/gilt trim, ca. 1850, blue crossed swords mark & numbers, modeled by Leuteritz, 19 1/8" h... **4,600**

Compote, three-tier, blue floral decorated, the figure of a female flower seller mounted at the top of the graduated dishes each w/a reticulated basketweave rim, late 19th - early 20th c., 20 3/4" h.............. **1,380**

Dishes, figural, each w/a shaped oblong base supporting a reclining male or female figure in 18th c. attire beside a fluted, flaring low oblong dish decorated in the Blue Onion patt., late 19th c., 12 1/2" l., pr............... **1,840**

Figure group, baby w/a dog, modeled as a child lying on a plaid-covered daybed holding a rattle out to a spaniel standing beside the bed, the child half-naked w/a ribbon-tied cap & shirt over the upper body, on a rectangular molded base w/canted corners & a blue & gilt rim band of egg-and-dart, late 19th - early 20th c., blue crossed swords & line mark, numbered, modeled after M.F. Acier, 7 1/2" h... **2,760**

Figure group, children in 18th c. costume at play, modeled as four children, alternating a boy & girl, playing ring-around-the-rosie about a tall leafy tree, the oval base molded w/gilt rocaille scrolls & applied w/flowers & foliage, late 19th c., blue crossed swords mark & numbers, 11 1/2" h. **3,680**

Figure group, modeled as allegorical female figures set on an oval base, one holding a ribbon at the wings of Cupid, the other feeding doves, blue crossed swords mark, 19th c., 12" h. **5,175**

Figure group, shepherd & shepherdess, seated holding hands, the shepherdess w/a ewe in her lap, another recumbent at her companion's feet, on a rocaille-molded base, late 19th - early 20th c., blue crossed swords mark & incised & impressed numbers, 8 1/2" w. **1,495**

Figure of Apollo, the god clad in a puce & gilt drapery, holding aloft his bow & w/a quiver of arrows slung across his back, seated in a chariot among grey clouds & yellow & white sunbursts, blue crossed-swords mark & incised numbers, 19th c., 8 1/4" h. (some restoration) **1,800**

Figure of Cupid, the young Cupid standing holding a broken heart, on a round socle w/marbleized decoration & gilt bands, late 19th - early 20th c., 8 1/8" h............. **1,380**

Figure of female, allegorical, seated on a high scroll-molded base wearing long loose robes & holding a script in one hand, her other arm stretched out, No. 369, late 19th - early 20th c., blue crossed swords mark, 16 1/2" h. **1,610**

Figure of hunter, standing figure w/boots, breeches & a spotted fur cloak, one hand at belt, the other arm extended, poly-

chrome decoration, blue crossed swords mark, 19th c., No. 1285, 8 3/4" h. **460**

Figures, allegorical, each a putto representing Night & Day, one in the guise of a mythological figure of Athena w/an owl, the other as Perseus w/a torch & sunflower, each on waisted faux marble & gilt-trimmed circular base, late 19th - early 20th c., blue crossed swords mark, incised & impressed numbers, 7" h., pr....... **3,220**

Figures of harvesters, one as a peasant woman walking w/a bundle of lettuce under her right arm & beside a milestone incised w/crowned crossed swords, the other a peasant man wearing long pants, a long-sleeved shirt & floral-decorated vest & carrying a scythe & a pail, on oval bases, one w/a commemorative date mark for 1710-1910, blue crossed swords marks & incised & impressed marks, 14 1/2" h., pr....... **2,300**

Fruit basket, oval form w/pierced sides, Blue Onion patt., blue crossed swords mark, late 19th c., 19 1/2" l............................... **633**

Model of Bolognese hound, seated facing left, brown fur markings, late 19th - early 20th c., blue crossed swords mark, after a model by J.J. Kandler, incised & impressed numbers, 8 3/4" h. **2,070**

Plaque, rectangular, "Feines Bouquet," a painted scene of a standing Cardinal sampling the bouquet of a white wine from a Venetian glass held in his right hand, a book in his left, in an interior rich w/pre-Renaissance Italian artifacts, late 19th - early 20th c., impressed monogram & sceptre mark, artist-signed, painted wood frame, 7 1/2 x 10" **6,900**

Platter & insert, 21 1/2" l., oval, Blue Onion patt., trimmed w/gold, early 20th c., 2 pcs. **489**

Salt dips, figural, each w/a seated child between two baskets, modeled w/foliate sprays & decorated in polychrome, late 19th c., 5 1/2" l., 5" h., pr. **2,070**

Soup tureen, cov., footed squatty bulbous oval form w/upright loop foliate end handle, high stepped & domed cover w/a putto finial, Blue Onion patt., blue crossed swords mark, late 19th - early 20th c., 14 1/4" l. **863**

Vase, 16" h., double-gourd-form, painted & trimmed in gilt in the Kakiemon style w/birds in flight & perched on flowering branches & w/butterflies, blue "AR" monogram & date mark for 1922.................. **920**

Vase, cov., 16 1/8" h., pate-sur-pate, tall baluster-form w/a ringed pedestal foot supporting the large ovoid body w/a ringed trumpet neck w/rolled rim & high domed cover w/berried finial tall scrolled lion head handles from the rim to the shoulder, cobalt blue ground w/scrolling gilt trim, the front decorated w/a large oval reserve w/a slip design of a nymph in a diaphanous drapery accompanied by Pan playing a tambourine & two frolicking putti on a celadon ground & within a gilt foliate & platinum border set w/beaded lozenges, ca. 1880, blue crossed swords mark & numbers...................................... **14,950**

Vase, 22 3/4" h., "schneeballen" type, flared baluster-form, applied overall w/mayflower blossoms in white & w/brightly plumed birds perched on green leafy branches w/large ball clusters of white blossoms, the short socle foot applied w/a nest of baby birds & eggs attended by a small yellow bird & w/green leafy vines, mid- to late 19th c., blue crossed swords marks, letters & numbers, after a model by J.J. Kandler **9,200**

Mettlach

Ceramics with the name Mettlach were produced by Villeroy & Boch and other potteries in the Mettlach area of Germany. Villeroy and Boch's finest years of production are thought to be from about 1890 to 1910.

Mettlach Mark

Plaque w/Dogs Attacking Bear

Plaque, pierced to hang, etched color scene w/hunting dogs attacking bear, signed Stocke, PUG, No. 2071, 15" d. (ILLUS.) **$525-550**

Plaque w/Hunt Scene

Plaque, pierced to hang, etched color scene w/stag & hunting dogs, No. 2070, signed Stocke, 15" d. (ILLUS.) **525**

Plaque w/Artillery Soldiers

Plaque, pierced to hang, etched color scene of artillery soldiers & horses moving cannon, signed Stocke, No. 2147, 15 1/4" d. (ILLUS.) **1,400**

Plaque w/Ulanens on Horseback

Plaque, pierced to hang, etched color scene of two Ulanens on horseback in a snow-covered field, signed Stocke, No. 2078, 15 1/4" d. (ILLUS.) **800**

Plaque w/Infantry Soldiers

Plaque, pierced to hang, etched color wooded scene of infantry soldiers w/rifles, a horse & trees, signed Stocke, No. 2146, 15 1/4" d. (ILLUS.) **700-800**

Plaque, pierced to hang, etched color scene of gnome drinking from mug & sitting in tree w/flowering branches, scrolled gold rim, signed Schlitt, No. 2113, 16" d. (ILLUS.) **1,000**

Plaque w/Greek Soldier

Plaque, pierced to hang, Etruscan style etched colored scene of a Greek soldier playing a lyre for a maiden, No. 2199, signed Schlitt, 15 1/4" d. (ILLUS.).................. **525**

Papageno Playing Flute

Plaque, pierced to hang, etched color scene of Papageno playing a flute, floral border, gold rim, No. 2149, signed Schlitt, 16 1/4" d. (ILLUS.) **1,100**

Mettlach Plaque w/Bearded Man

Plaque, pierced to hang, etched color scene of bearded man w/large feathered hat, No. 1168, gold border, 16" d. (ILLUS.).. **525**

Plaque w/Snow White & the Seven Dwarfs

Plaque, pierced to hang, etched color scene of Snow White & the seven dwarfs, floral border, gold rim, No. 2148, signed Schlitt, 16 1/4" d. (ILLUS.) ... **1,000-1,100**

Plaque w/Gnome Drinking from Mug

Woman w/Butterfly Wings

Plaque, pierced to hang, scene of woman w/butterfly wings sitting on branch, blue background, No. 1696, 16 1/4" d. (ILLUS.).. **750**

Plaque w/Woman Wearing Hat

Plaque, pierced to hang, etched color scene of woman w/fancy feathered hat, No. 1411, gold border, 16 1/2" d. (ILLUS.).. **525**

Castle Scene Plaque

Plaque, pierced to hang, etched color castle scene, No. 1108, 16 3/4" d. (ILLUS.) **450-500**

Plaque w/Castle Scene

Plaque, pierced to hang, etched color castle scene, No. 1365, gold border, 17" d. (ILLUS.).. **500**

Plaque w/Scene of Gnome in Tree

Plaque, pierced to hang, etched color scene of gnome in tree holding two large bottles, flying insects, scrolled gold rim, signed Schlitt, No. 2112, 17" d. (ILLUS.)... **1,000**

Girl Picking Fruit

Plaque, pierced to hang, etched color fall scene of young girl picking fruit from tree, bushes & fence in foreground, trees & a bench in background, gold rim, No. 2997, 17 1/2" d. (ILLUS.) **2,250**

Scenic Mettlach Plaque

Plaque, pierced to hang, etched color scene of castle on cliff, boats in water below, No. 2195, Rheinstein, 17 1/2" d. (ILLUS.) **475-500**

Plaque w/Spring Scene

Plaque, pierced to hang, etched color spring scene of young girl standing near flowering bush, trees in background, No. 2898, signed H. Gradle, 17 1/2" d. (ILLUS.)... **2,250**

Plaque w/Castle Scene

Plaque, pierced to hang, etched & colored scene of castle on cliff, No. 2196, Stolzenfels, 17 1/2" d. (ILLUS.).............. **475-525**

Phanolith Serenade Scene

Plaque, pierced to hang, phanolith, white relief-molded serenade scene, "Words of Love," No. 2795, 17 1/2" d. (ILLUS.).............. **575**

Plaque w/Summer Scene

Plaque, pierced to hang, etched & colored summer scene of young girl holding bundle of wheat, No. 2899, silver off border, retouched w/gold, 17 3/4" d. (ILLUS.)............... **1,200**

Art Nouveau Portrait Plaque

Plaque, pierced to hang, Art Nouveau etched color bust portrait of woman w/hair pulled into a bun & holding a flower, border of large flowers, gold rim, No. 2548, 18 1/4" d. (ILLUS.) **600**

Vase w/Gargoyle Handles

Vase, 11 1/2" h., flared foot below wide bulbous body w/ringed cylindrical neck flanked by gargoyle handles, polychrome & gilt decoration on beige ground, impressed mark, No. 1409 (ILLUS.).................. **220**

Mocha

Mocha decoration is found on basically utilitarian creamware or yellowware articles and is achieved by a simple chemical reaction. A color pigment of brown, blue, green or black is given an acid nature by infusion of tobacco or hops. When this acid nature colorant is applied in blobs to an alkaline ground color, it reacts by spreading in feathery seaweed designs. This type of decoration is usually accompanied by horizontal bands of light color slip. Produced in numerous Staffordshire potteries from the late 18th until the late 19th centuries, its name is derived from the similar markings found on mocha quartz. In addition to the seaweed decoration, mocha wares are also seen with Earthworm and Cat's Eye patterns or a marbleized effect.

Bowl, 4" d., 2 7/8" h., cylindrical body w/tapering sides on a thin footring, white stripes & brown band w/black seaweed decoration (hairline) **$358**

Bowl, 7 1/4" d., 4" h., bulbous cylindrical body on a thin footring, the sides tapering to flaring rim, blue, white & brown Earthworm patt. on orange ground, dark brown bands on white ground (repairs, glaze wear) **230**

Mixing bowl, footed deep round flaring form w/molded rim, yellowware w/a wide white center band w/thin brown line borders & pale blue seaweed decoration, 14 3/4" d., 7" h. (spider crack in base, flaking on interior, rim chip) **330**

Mixing bowl, footed deep round flaring form w/molded rim, yellowware w/a wide white center band w/thin brown line borders & dark green daubs of seaweed decoration, 14 3/4" d., 7" h. (rim hairline w/glaze flakes in bottom) **385**

Mixing bowl, footed w/deep rounded sides & molded rim, yellowware w/a white band w/brown line borders decorated w/a green seaweed design, 14 3/4" d., 7" h. (spider crack in base, flaking on interior, rim chip) **303**

Mixing bowl, small footring supporting a deep rounded flaring bowl w/a heavy molded rim, yellowware w/a wide central white band w/blue bands & black seaweed decoration, East Liverpool, Ohio, late 19th - early 20th c., 8 1/2" d., 4 1/4" h. **385**

Mug, cylindrical, blue, brown & cream Earthworm patt. in vertical configuration on cream & white striped ground, green impressed band, dark brown alternating stripes, white handle w/leaf-impressed ends, 4 3/8" d., 5 7/8" h. (handle & body repaired, cracks, chips) **2,760**

Mug, cylindrical body w/applied white handle w/leaf-impressed ends, decorated w/a wide band in the Open Chain patt. on pumpkin ground w/upper & lower dark brown bands & white molded base band, 19th c., 6" d., 5 3/8" h. (minor glaze imperfections, small hairline cracks) **1,955**

Mug, cylindrical, decorated w/thin black & white w/blue stripes & geometric banding, applied ribbed handle w/leaftips, early 19th c., 2 3/4" h. (stains, minor damage) **451**

Mug, cylindrical w/cream handle w/leaf-impressed ends, decorated w/a wide band

of dark brown fine wavy decoration on cream ground bordered by wide ochre bands, cream dot pattern on black stripes, blue impressed bands, late 18th - early 19th c., 3 3/8" d., 4 3/4" h. (minor glaze imperfections, minor chips) **1,150**

Mug, cylindrical w/molded base & white handle w/leaf-impressed ends, decorated w/blue & brown Earthworm patt. on olive ground, cream & ochre Sunflower patt. on dark brown ground, light blue alternating stripes, 19th c., 4 1/4" d., 5 3/4" h. (handle repaired, discoloration, cracks, minor chips) **2,415**

Mug, cylindrical w/white handle w/leaf-impressed ends, wide central band w/dark brown & white plaid geometric design, pumpkin, dark brown & cream alternating stripes, early 19th c., 3 3/8" d., 4 3/4" h. (cracks, handle repaired) **633**

Various Mocha Items

Mug, cylindrical w/narrow white & dark brown stripes, large cream band w/dark brown seaweed decoration, applied handle, chips & base hairlines, 4 5/8" h. (ILLUS. top row, left) **1,100**

Mug, cylindrical w/blue, dark brown & orange stripes, center band decorated w/white wavy lines & groups of dots in white slip, embossed green rim band & applied leaftip handle, stains, wear & surface chips, 6" h. (ILLUS. bottom row, left) **2,970**

Mug, cylindrical w/applied leaftip handle, decorated w/bands in two shades of blue w/white, yellow & black, a wide blue band w/the Cat's Eye patt. & dots in the upper & lower bands in blue & black, first half 19th c., 6 7/8" h. (damage w/hairline cracks) **1,100**

Mustard pot, cov., footed bulbous body w/C-form handle, low domed cover w/knob finial, white w/brown tooled lines, 3 3/4" h. (wear) **1,210**

Pepper pot, baluster-form body w/domed cap, decorated w/ochre, dark brown & ginger Tobacco Leaf patt. on a cream ground, first half 19th c., 4 3/8" h. (old chips, staining, crazing) **1,955**

Pepper pot, baluster-form w/domed top, decorated w/white, cinnamon & dark brown Cat's-eye patt. on blue ground, dark brown, blue & cinnamon stripes alternating on a white ground, first half 19th c., 4 3/8" h. (very minor chips) **920**

Pepper pot, baluster-form w/domed cap, white, brown & cinnamon Earthworm patt. on a blue ground, green beading impressed band, top in blue w/dark brown stripe alternating at base of dome, body & foot, first half 19th c., 4 3/4" h. (foot repaired, old chips) 805

Pepper pot, cylindrical body on a short round pedestal foot, a short tapering neck w/a fitted domed cap, decorated w/light blue, ochre & cream Cat's-eye patt. on a dark brown ground, cream & celadon green alternating stripes, domed top w/finial decorated in blue w/dark brown stripe, brown stripe on foot, first half 19th c., 4 3/4" h. (minor chips & imperfections) 1,093

Pitcher, 4 7/8" h., barrel-shaped w/arched spout & C-form handle, dark blue seaweed on burnt orange band w/black & white stripes, embossed green rim band & applied handle w/green leaftips, chips (ILLUS. bottom right) 1,870

Pitcher, 5" h., jug-form, decorated w/the Earthworm patt., a wide central tan band w/the decoration in white, pale blue & brown, thin upper & lower bands in tan & dark brown, molded leaftip handle, early 19th c. (professional repair to handle) 660

Pitcher, 5 1/2" h., 4" d., jug-form, footed ovoid body w/blue, brown & white Earthworm patt. on brown ground, brown, blue, dark brown & white alternating stripes, white handle w/leaf-impressed ends, early 19th c. (minor imperfections) .. 1,380

Pitcher, 6" h., 4" d., jug-form, footed ovoid body w/white & brown zigzag Earthworm patt. on green ground, white & brown Cat's-Eye patt. on green ground, green impressed band, dark brown & white alternating stripes, white handle w/leaf-impressed handles, early 19th c. (cracks) 1,380

Pitcher, 6" h., 4 1/2" d., blue, white & brown Cat's-Eye patt. on tan ground, blue & brown stripes on white ground, white handle w/plain impressed ends (chips to spout, imperfections) 230

Pitcher, 6 1/4" h., 4" d., jug-form, footed ovoid body decorated w/a blue, brown & white Earthworm patt. on brown ground, green impressed bands, brown & white alternating stripes, white handle w/leaf-impressed ends, early 19th c. (cracks, minor chips) 1,035

Pitcher, 6 1/4" h., 4 1/4" d., dark brown & white Cat's-Eye patt. on bright blue ground, dark brown stripes on white ground, white leaftip handle (small cracks & hairline cracks) 230

Pitcher, 6 1/2" h., jug-form, bands in two shades of blue w/white & black, a wide ochre center band decorated w/the Earthworm patt. in blue, black, white & ochre, applied leaftip handle, first half 19th c. (damage w/cracks) 688

Pitcher, 6 1/2" h., 4" d., barrel-shaped w/arched spout & leaftip handle, blue band w/dark brown stylized star decoration, dark brown & aqua bands on white ground (minor cracks & chips, imperfections) 230

Pitcher, 6 3/4" h., 4 1/4" h., barrel-shaped, brown, cream & ochre Cat's Eye patt. on blue ground, alternating w/blue, cream & dark brown Cat's Eye patt. on ochre ground, blue impressed band, dark brown & white alternating stripes, white handle w/leaf-impressed ends, early 19th c. (cracks, minor chips, staining, minor glaze imperfections) 1,495

Pitcher, 7 1/8" h., footed bulbous body tapering to flat rim, arched spout & molded leaf C-form handle, brown band w/black stripes & light blue & green bands, blue & brown Earthworm patt. (chips, stains & cracks) 770

Pitcher, 7 1/4" h., 4 3/8" d., jug-form, cream slip undulating band decoration on a dark brown ground, light blue, cream & dark brown Cat's-eye patt. on ochre ground, green impressed leaf decoration on raised shoulder, light blue & cream alternating stripes, white handle w/leaf-impressed ends, first half 19th c. (spout & neck repairs, crack on handle bottom) 3,795

Pitcher, 7 1/2" h., 5" d., blue green band w/light blue & white Earthworm patt. , dark brown & light blue bands on white ground, white leaftip handle (wear & imperfections) 805

Pitcher, 7 7/8" h., jug-form, pearlware body decorated around the sides w/pumpkin-colored bands at top & bottom w/brown geometric & line decoration on a white ground, embossed leaf decoration on handle & spout, early 19th c. (minor chips, wear, interior glaze flakes) 1,320

Shaker w/domed top, footed bulbous body w/tapered neck to the top, yellowware decorated w/stripes of blue, white & black, chips, 4 3/8" h. (ILLUS. top row, right) 578

Sugar bowl, footed wide cylindrical body w/small applied rim handles w/tooled ends, decorated w/balloons in orange, white & dark brown on deep cream ground w/dark brown & white stripes, no lid, wear & damage, 4" d., 3" h. (ILLUS. top row, center) 1,760

Waste bowl, white w/grey band & dark brown stripes, Earthworm patt. in blue & white, 4 3/4" d. 495

Moorcroft

William Moorcroft became a designer for James Macintyre & Co. in 1897 and was put in charge of their art pottery production. Moorcroft developed a number of popular designs, including Florian Ware while with Macintyre and continued with that firm until 1913 when they discontinued the production of art pottery.

After leaving Macintyre in 1913, Moorcroft set up his own pottery in Burslem and continued producing the art wares he had designed earlier as well as introducing new patterns. After William's death in 1945, the pottery was operated by his son, Walter.

MOORCROFT

Moorcroft Marks

Box, cov., Anenome patt., cylindrical w/fitted flat cover, decorated around the sides & on the cover w/large anemone blossoms in shades of mauve, blue & green against a shaded green ground, glossy glaze, impressed & painted marks, mid-20th c., 3 1/2" h. $316

Box, cov., Pansy patt., round squat form, decorated around the sides & cover w/pansies w/a glossy glaze over shades of mauve, purple & green on a cobalt blue ground, impressed marks, ca. 1930, 6" d., 4" h. 403

Box, cov., Pomegranate patt., round squat form, decorated around the sides & cover w/pomegranates under a glossy glaze, in shades of mauve, purple & green on a cobalt blue ground, impressed facsimile signature, Potter to H.M. The Queen mark & painted initials, ca. 1930, 6" d., 4" h. (small glaze flake inside bowl) 575

Compote, open, 11" d., 3 5/8" h., Wisteria patt., circular footed bowl w/flared rim, glossy glaze on a design of wisteria in yellow, green & purple on a cobalt blue ground, impressed & painted mark, ca. 1925 (minor surface scratches) 546

Vase, 3" h., miniature, Anemone patt., nearly spherical body w/a short flared rim, decorated w/two anemone blossoms in mauve & purple on a cobalt blue ground, impressed mark, mid-20th c. 230

Vase, 3 1/4" h., miniature, Anemone patt., raised rim on a bulbous body, decorated w/two anemone blossoms in mauve & purple on a cobalt blue ground, impressed facsimile William Moorcroft signature & "Potter to H.M. the Queen" mark, ca. 1947 259

Vase, 5 1/4" h., bulbous ovoid body tapering to a cylindrical neck, bluish red flowers & light green leaves on a green shading to dark blue ground, impressed mark & paper label 230

Vase, 5 1/4" h., Orchid patt., footed spherical body w/a thick molded rim, decorated w/multicolored orchid blossoms on a cobalt blue ground, impressed mark & facsimile William Moorcroft signature & initials, ca. 1930s 288

Vase, 5 1/2" h., Hibiscus patt., footed ovoid body tapering to a short flared neck, decorated w/three large hibiscus blossoms in mauve & yellow on a shaded green ground, green stamp & paper label, mid-20th c. 403

Vase, 5 3/4" h., Orchid patt., bulbous baluster-form w/a wide low molded mouth, decorated w/large orchids in shades of mauve, yellow, & blue on a shaded green to blue ground w/a glossy glaze, impressed & painted marks, ca. 1947 374

Vase, 6 1/4" h., Orchid patt., wide ovoid body w/a short flared neck, decorated w/large orchids in shades of mauve, purple, yellow & green on a cobalt blue ground w/a glossy glaze, impressed & painted marks, ca. 1947 518

Vase, 7 1/4" h., ovoid form w/a flared rim, decorated around the sides w/fish & seaweed under a glossy glaze, in shades of yellow, orange & green against a shaded orange to blue flambé ground, impressed mark & painted initials, ca. 1930 .... **3,680**

Vase, 7 3/4" h., Orchid patt., footed nearly spherical body tapering to a short cylindrical neck, decorated w/orchid & flower blossoms in mauve, purple, blue & yellow on a cobalt blue ground, impressed factory mark, painted initials of Walter Moorcroft & printed paper label, mid-20th c.......... 345

Vase, 9 3/4" h., Wisteria patt., large baluster-form body w/a short rolled neck, decorated around the sides w/purple, mauve & yellow wisteria blossoms on a cobalt blue ground, impressed factory mark & painted signature, mid-20th c....................... 431

Vase, 13" h., decorated w/pomegranates & berries among wild birds, in red, yellow & blue, impressed "Moorcroft - Made in England - WM," ca. 1930-45 977

Vase, 14 3/8" h., Palm Tree patt., tall tapered ovoid form w/flared rim, decorated in relief w/palm trees & flowers w/a body of water & rocks in the distance, glossy glaze in shades of green, brown, pink & blue, impressed marks, ca. 1997.............. 690

Morton Potteries

A total of six potteries were in operation at various times in Morton, Illinois from 1877 to 1976. All traced their origins from the Morton Brick and Tile Company begun in 1877 by six Rapp brothers who came to America in the early 1870s to escape forced military service under Kaiser Wilhelm I. Sons, nephews and cousins of the founding fathers were responsible for the continuation of the pottery industry in Morton as a result of buy-outs or the establishment of new and separate operations. The potteries are listed chronologically by beginning dates.

Morton's natural clay deposits were ideal for the Rapp's venture into pottery production. Local clay was used until it was depleted in 1940. That clay fired out to a golden ecru color. After 1940, clay was imported from South Carolina and Indiana. It fired out snow white. The differences in clay allow one to easily date production at the Morton potteries. Only a few items were marked by any of the potteries. Occasionally, paper labels were used, but most of those have long disappeared. Glaze is sometimes a determinant. Early glazes were Rockingham brown, green and cobalt blue, or transparent, to produce yellowware. In the '20s and '30s colorful drip glazes were used. In the later years solid pastel and Deco colors were in vogue.

Most of Morton's potteries were short-lived, operating for twenty years or less. Their products are elusive. However, Morton Pottery Company was in operation for fifty-four years and its products appear regularly in today's secondary market.

Rapp Brothers Brick & Tile Company & Morton Pottery Works (1877-1915) - Morton Earthenware Co. (1915-1917)

Baker, deep, yellowware, 10" d..................... $100

Morton Paperweight, Bank & Marble

Bank, figural acorn, w/advertising for "Acorn
Stove Company," green (ILLUS. center) **80**
Churn, mottled brown Rockingham glaze, 4
gal. **180**

Morton Jardiniere

Jardiniere, tapering cylindrical form, em-
bossed leaf design, green, 7" d. (ILLUS.)........ **50**
Marble, mottled brown Rockingham glaze,
4 1/2" d. (ILLUS. right with bank) **40**
Mug, yellowware, 1/2 pt. **75**
Paperweight, model of a bison, advertises
Rock Sand Company, brown Rockingham
glaze, 2 1/2" l. (ILLUS. left with bank) **70**
Pie baker, yellowware, 10" d. **125**

Morton Dutch Pitcher

Pitcher, jug-type, milk (Dutch jug), cobalt
blue, 3 1/2 pt. (ILLUS.) **90**

Pitcher with Spatter Bark Design

Pitcher, jug-type, milk, bulbous body w/re-
lief-molded tree bark design, green,
brown & yellow spatter, 1 3/4 qt. (ILLUS.) **150**
Stein, barrel-shaped w/"Trinke was klar ist
und rede was wahr ist" embossed around
rim & base, green, 1 pt. **85**
Teapot, cov., acorn-shaped, mottled brown
Rockingham glaze, 3 3/4 cup size **90**

Morton Rebecca at the Well Teapots

Teapot, cov., tapering cylindrical body
w/swan's neck spout, leaf-tip handle &
bud finial, embossed Rebecca at the
Well decoration, yellowware, 7 pt.
(ILLUS. right) **185**
Teapot, cov., tapering cylindrical body
w/swan's neck spout, leaf-tip handle &
bud finial, embossed Rebecca at the
Well decoration, mottled brown Rocking-
ham glaze, 8 1/2 pt. (ILLUS. left) **175**

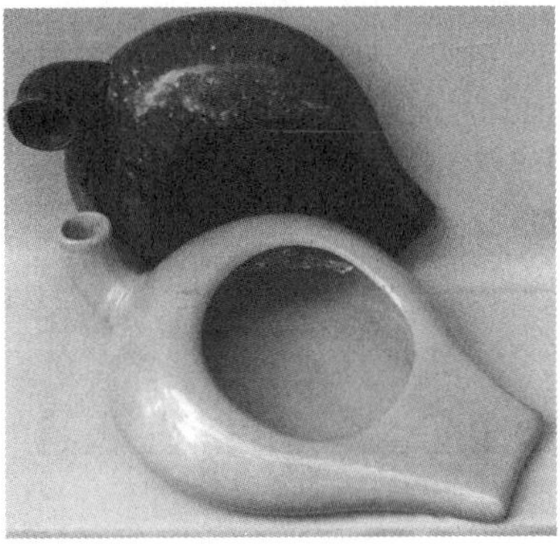

Morton Urinals

Urinal, shovel-shaped, mottled brown
Rockingham glaze (ILLUS. top) **50**
Urinal, shovel-shaped, yellowware (ILLUS.
bottom) **65**

Cliftwood Art Potteries, Inc. (1920-1940)

Dolphin-based Pieces

Compote, 5 1/4 x 8 1/2", domed base w/four figural dolphins supporting bowl w/flaring paneled sides, old rose glaze (ILLUS. top) **90**

Console bowl, rectangular w/flared rim supported by four figural dolphins on domed base, old rose glaze, 5 1/4 x 13 1/2" (ILLUS. bottom) **100**

Figural Console Set

Console set: bowl & pr. of candlesticks; figural Viking ship w/dragon head at each end, candlesticks w/cupped socket above figural dragon head w/flared base, matte ivory & turquoise glaze, the set (ILLUS.) **225**

Figural Cow Creamer

Creamer, figural cow, standing, tail forms handle, chocolate brown drip glaze, 3 3/4 x 6" (ILLUS.) **85**

Flower frog, figural turtle, holes pierced on back, herbage green, 5 1/2" l. **24**

Flower frog, figural woman, "Lorilei," blue mulberry drip glaze, 6 1/2" h. **75**

Model of a Scottie Dog

Model of dog, Scottie, standing, cobalt blue, 5 1/2 x 7 1/2" (ILLUS.) **60**

Model of elephant, grey, standing, 7 1/4 x 13 1/2" **125**

Model of lion, standing, natural color, spray glaze, 9 1/4 x 16" (ILLUS. top next column) **200**

Model of tiger, standing, natural colors, 5 x 16" **150**

Model of a Lion

Vase, 10" h., domed base w/four figural dolphins supporting tapering body w/paneled sides, fluted rim, matte ivory & turquoise, No. 224 .... **75**

Vase, 14 1/2" h., flared foot below tall tapering cylindrical body, the narrow shoulder tapering to a waisted cylindrical neck, No. 113, chocolate brown drip glaze **80**

Vase, 16" h., footed baluster-form body w/flat rim, No. 114, bluish grey drip glaze **75**

Vase, 18 1/4" h., urn-form w/figural snakes swallowing fish handles, No. 132, cobalt blue **110**

Morton Waffle Set

Waffle set: cov. batter pitcher & cov. syrup pitcher on tray; cylindrical body w/incurved side under handle, button finials, old rose drip glaze, the set (ILLUS.) **150**

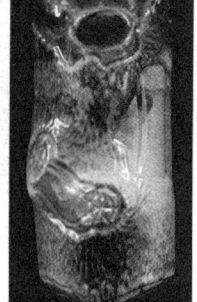

Tree Trunk Form Wall Pocket

Wall pocket, rectangular tree trunk design w/pointed base, three openings at top, chocolate drip glaze, 8" h. (ILLUS.) **80**

Morton Pottery Company (1922-1976)
Bank, acorn shape, solid bottom, brown,
3 1/4" h. **40**

A Variety of Figural Hen Pieces

Bank, figural, hen on nest, white w/red cold
painted comb, black feather detail, yellow
beak, 4" h. (ILLUS. back row, center) **50**
Bank, figural, house, shoe-shaped, yellow
w/red roof, 6 1/2" h. **30**
Bank, figural, kitten reclining, grey & white,
4 x 6" **25**
Cookie jar, cov., hen on nest, figural chick
finial, white, black trim & cold-painted red
comb (ILLUS. back row, right) **130**

Panda Bear Cookie Jar

Cookie jar, cov., panda bear, black & white
(ILLUS.) **95**
Cookie jar, cov., turkey w/poult (chick) fini-
al, brown **150**
Creamer & sugar bowl, model of chicken &
rooster, black & white w/cold-painted red
comb, pr. (ILLUS. far left & second from
left, front row) **45**

Cuspidor with Tavern Scene

Cuspidor, bulbous body w/wide flaring
neck, decorated w/embossed tavern
scene, green, 5 1/2" (ILLUS.) **35**

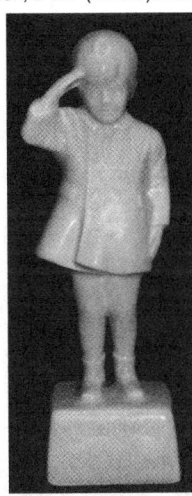

John F. Kennedy, Jr. Figure

Figure of John F. Kennedy, Jr., standing
on square base, right hand to head in sa-
lute position, grey & beige, 7" h. (ILLUS.) **95**
Grass grower, bisque, bust of soldier w/"Hi
Buddy" embossed on back of collar,
6 3/4" h. **40**
Grass grower, bisque, bust of "Paddy
O'Hair," red clay **35**
Head vase, lady w/1920s hair style, wide
brim hat, white glossy glaze **60**
Head vase, lady w/1940s hair style, pill box
hat, white matte glaze **50**
Head vase, lady w/upswept hair style, white
w/red lips, bow in hair & heart-shaped
locket **40**

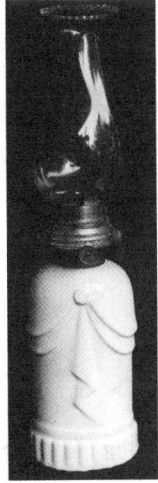

Morton Kerosene Lamp

Lamp, kerosene, brass fixture w/glass
chimney, cylindrical body w/ribbed base

& relief-molded swag design, white ground (ILLUS.) 50

Lamp base, female bunny w/umbrella, multicolored 50

Lamp base, figural Davy Crockett w/bear beside tree 125

Lamp base, male bunny in top hat, multicolored 50

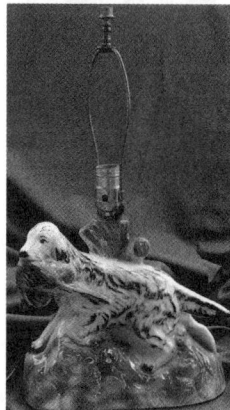

Dog with Pheasant Lamp Base

Lamp base, model of a black & white dog w/brown pheasant in mouth, relief-molded brown & green grassy base, 5 x 10", 8 1/4" h. (ILLUS.) 75

Lamp base, model of a Teddy bear, heart-shaped nose, pink or blue, each 45

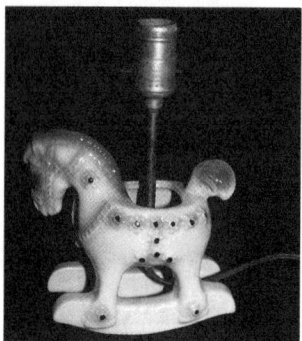

Rocking Horse Lamp/Planter

Lamp base/planter, model of rocking horse, white w/brown, pink & blue trim (ILLUS.) 40

Boston Terrier Model & Planter

Model of dog, Boston terrier, sitting, black & white, 7" h. (ILLUS. right) 40

Planter, model of Boston terrier, sitting, black & white (ILLUS. left) 30

Salt & pepper shakers, miniature, model of chick, black & white, 1 3/4" h., pr. (ILLUS. front row, right with hen pieces) 100

Toothpick holder, miniature, model of chick, black & white, 1 3/4" h. (ILLUS. front row, center with hen pieces) 50

Christmas Novelties

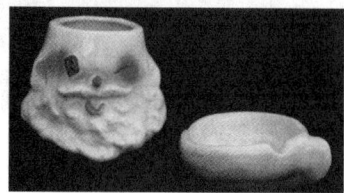

Figural Santa Claus Head Cigarette Box

Cigarette box, cov., figural Santa Claus head, hat cover becomes ashtray, cold painted red hat (ILLUS.) 40

Lollypop tree, w/holes to insert lollypops, green & white glaze, 9 1/4" h. 40

Plate, 8", figural Santa Claus face, white w/blue eyes, pink cheeks, hat cold painted red 40

Plate, 12", figural Santa Claus face, white w/blue eyes, pink cheeks, hat cold painted red 50

Figural Santa Claus Punch Set

Punch set: Punch bowl & 12 punch cups; figural Santa Claus head, white w/pink trim, 13 pcs. (ILLUS. of part) 360

Midwest Potteries, Inc. (1940-1944)

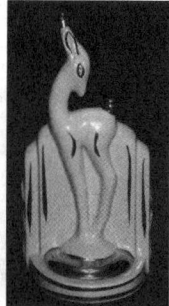

Art Deco Style Book End

Book end, Art Deco style base w/model of deer, yellow w/gold trim, 8" h. (ILLUS.) 25

Figure of baseball player, batter, grey uniform, 7 1/4" h. **300**
Figure of baseball player, catcher, white uniform, 6 3/4" h. **275**
Figure of baseball player, umpire, black suit, 6 1/4" h. **250**

Model of GOP Elephant

Model of elephant, standing, trunk raised, white w/gold trim & "GOP" in gold on side, 6 1/2" h. (ILLUS.) **30**

Model of Fish in Seaweed

Model of fish, on seaweed base, yellow & brown spray glaze, 10 1/2" h. (ILLUS.) **40**
Model of mountain goat, natural colors, spray glaze, 9 1/2". **45**

Model of Tiger

Model of tiger, stalking position w/open mouth, beige & tan w/h.p. brown stripes, 7 x 12" (ILLUS.) **50**

Figural Duck Pitcher

Pitcher, model of a duck w/cattail handle, blue & brown spray glaze, 10" h. (ILLUS.) **38**

Figural Sea Gull Planter

Planter, domed base supporting model of sea gull in flight, joined at base w/relief-molded seashell bowl, white & gold, 12" h. (ILLUS.) **40**

African Woman Wall Mask

Wall mask, African woman w/neck rings, ebony w/gold trim, 8" h. (ILLUS.) **50**

American Art Potteries (1947-1963)
Bottle, crown shape, pink & grey spray glaze, 6" h. **24**

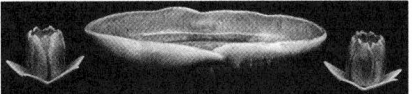

Petal-form Console Set

Console set: bowl & pr. of candleholders; shallow oblong bowl & flower-form candleholders on leaf-shaped base, grey exterior w/pink interior, 3 pcs. (ILLUS.) **30**

Vases with Ostrich Feather Decoration

Cornucopia-vase, single relief-molded ostrich feather decoration, shaded grey exterior, yellow interior spray glaze, 10 1/2" h. (ILLUS. left) **35**

Doll parts, ceramic, 7 1/2" head w/h.p. face, 4" arms & 4 1/2" legs, 5 pcs. **90**

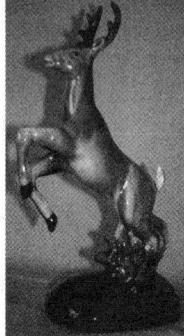

Model of Leaping Stag

Model of stag, leaping position, domed green base w/relief-molded grasses near back legs, shaded brown & white w/dark brown antlers & hooves, 12" h. (ILLUS.) **40**

Planter, model of a bunny beside log, natural colors spray glaze **20**

Jumping Horse TV Lamp

TV lamp, model of a horse jumping over wall, brown & tan spray glaze, 8" h. (ILLUS.) **40**

Afghan Hounds TV Lamp

TV lamp, model of a standing & reclining Afghan hound on oblong base, glossy black glaze, 15" h. (ILLUS.) **60**

Figural Fish Planter/TV Lamp

TV lamp/planter, model of two fish on thick rectangular base w/relief-molded shell design on front, tan, chartreuse & black spray glaze, 3 1/2 x 6 x 9" (ILLUS.) **30**

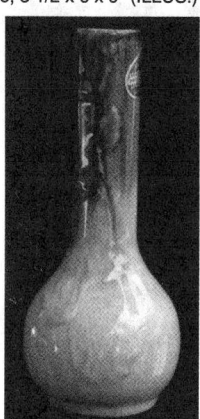

Small Morton Vase

Vase, 6" h., footed bulbous base tapering to tall slender cylindrical neck w/flat rim, decorated w/embossed leaf design, brown shading to yellow spray glaze (ILLUS.) **20**

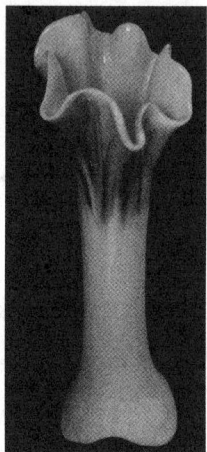

Ruffled Rim Vase

Vase, 9" h., flared footed base tapering to cylindrical body w/ruffled tulip-shaped rim, yellow, pink & mauve spray glaze (ILLUS.) **25**

Vase, 10 1/2" h., flared base w/fan-shaped body, double relief-molded ostrich feather arched end handles w/decoration extending down sides to base, brown & tan spray glaze w/yellow interior (ILLUS. right with cormucopia-vase)...................... **45**

Newcomb College Pottery

This pottery was established in the art department of Newcomb College, New Orleans, Louisiana, in 1897. Each piece was hand-thrown and bore the potter's mark & decorator's monogram on the base. It was always a studio business and never operated as a factory and its pieces are therefore scarce, with the early wares being eagerly sought. The pottery closed in 1940.

Newcomb College Pottery Mark

Pitcher, 8" h., 6" d., tall ovoid tapering to a short waisted neck w/angled handle from rim to shoulder, decorated around the neck w/a carved band of pink morning glory blossoms & green leaves on a matte dark blue ground, by Sadie Irvine, 1924, incised "NC - SI - 230 - OB69" **$3,850**

Vase, 3 5/8" h., wide shoulder tapering toward the base, a short extended rim, decorated around the rim w/leafy vines & fruit in relief, bluish green matte glaze, impressed mark & artist's initials & "EM.55," early 20th c. **920**

Small Newcomb Vase

Vase, 3 1/2" h., wide bulbous ovoid body w/narrow cylindrical neck & closed rim, incised decoration of tall trees w/Spanish moss in shades of blue against a peach sunset background (ILLUS.)........................ **1,900**

Vase, 3 7/8" h., bulbous ovoid body w/narrow molded rim, deeply carved & painted blue & green trees on matte glaze, by Anna Frances Simpson, ca. 1926, impressed w/Newcomb logo, the date, "PO60," shape number "5" & initials of potter, Joseph Meyer, incised artist's initials (two small flat chips off bottom edge)......... **1,670**

Vase, 5 1/2" h., bulbous ovoid body tapering to a short cylindrical neck, carved &

painted around the shoulder w/a narrow band of pairs of small white blossoms & green leaves & vines against a matte ground, impressed mark, "#QP91 - A.F. Simpson"... **1,320**

Vase, 5 1/2" h., footed squatty bulbous body, shoulder tapering to wide cylindrical neck w/flat rim, decorated w/abstract floral pattern in blue, green & yellow on purple ground, ca. 1922, artist-signed & impressed "NC - JM - 121 - MQ40" **1,760**

Vase, 5 1/2" h., simple ovoid form tapering to a wide flat mouth, relief-decoration w/a continuous scene of Spanish moss on live oaks under moonlight, matte glaze in shades of blue & cream, base impressed "NC - 4 SP 83" & artist's cipher, by Sadie Irvine, after 1910 .... **2,185**

Vase, 5 1/2" h., swelled cylindrical form tapering slightly to a wide flat mouth, carved & painted w/a continuous landscape of dark blue oaks hung w/green moss against a light blue sky w/a yellow moon, impressed mark, "J.M. - A.F. Simpson - #OQ81"..................................... **2,750**

Vase, 6 1/4" h., pear-shaped body w/molded rim, modeled w/leaves at base & covered in mottled matte green glaze, incised "AVL" & "JM" **1,760**

Vase, 6 1/2" h., footed wide ovoid body w/a wide shoulder sloping to a small cylindrical neck, carved & painted around the shoulder w/large stylized pale lavender rose blossoms on pale green scrolled leafy stems down the sides against a streaky blue matte ground, impressed mark, "#GC26 - M. Robertson - A.F. Simpson"..... **4,675**

Vase, 6 1/2" h., simple ovoid form tapering to a short cylindrical neck, carved & painted w/tall pointed overlapping leaves, blue, green & ivory matte glaze, impressed marks, attributed to C. Chalaron, Joseph Meyer, marked "#MZ10 - 78" **1,650**

Vase, 6 1/2" h., wide cylindrical base below bulbous body, narrow molded rim, sharply carved w/nighttime scene of live oak trees covered in Spanish moss, full moon, decorated by A.F. Simpson, ca. 1920, impressed "NC - LV31- JM - 183 - AFS".... **4,950**

Vase, 6 1/2" h., 7 1/2" d., wide bulbous body tapering to a short cylindrical base, the rounded shoulder centered by a wide, short cylindrical neck, incised & painted around the shoulder w/narcissus in pink w/yellow centers & green leaves on a dark matte blue ground, impressed marks, "A.F. Simpson - J.M. - #PO70 - G1".......... **1,980**

Vase, 7" h., 5" d., wide ovoid body w/a short cylindrical neck, decorated w/tooled stylized yellow flowers on tall stems & large pointed leaves in celadon green against an ivory ground, by Esther H. Elliott, stamped "NC - EHE - BB10 - Q - JM"..... **24,750**

Vase, 7 1/4 x 7 1/4", footed wide spherical body tapering to closed rim, incised w/an Art Deco design under a matte blue green glaze, ca. 1930s, artist's cipher **1,540**

Vase, 7 1/2" h., baluster-form body w/wide cylindrical neck & flat rim, incised lines under a semi-matte gold glaze, decorated by

Juanita Gonzales, ca. 1931, artist's cipher & impressed "NC - G71 - TC47 - JH".......... **1,210**

Vase, 7 1/2" h., footed, wide expanding cylindrical ridged body by Kenneth Smith, covered in semi-matte turquoise glaze, impressed "NC - Kenneth Smith" **605**

Vase, 7 1/2" h., 4 1/2" d., simple ovoid body w/a small tapering neck, decorated around the upper two-thirds w/a paneled band of tall incised stylized birch seed pods in bluish green against an ivory ground, a blue-washed band around the lower section, by Henrietta Bailey, 1904, marked "NC - PP71 - HBailey - JM - Q".......................... **15,400**

Vase, 8" h., slender ovoid body w/narrow shoulder tapering to wide cylindrical neck, decorated w/scene of live oaks & Spanish moss w/full moon, green tones, by Sadie Irvine, ca. 1922, impressed "NC - SI - 250 - MW7M4" **3,190**

Floral Newcomb Vase

Vase, 9" h., ovoid body, the rounded shoulder centered by small cylindrical neck w/flared rim, decorated w/ivory & yellow blossoms & leaves outlined in blue, green ground, impressed "NC - JM - N or Z," firing lines & stilt pull under base (ILLUS.) **6,600**

Vase, 9 1/2" h., bulbous w/tapering shoulder & closed rim, decorated w/incised band of stylized light blue flowers on a white ground over a dark blue band & glossy blue base, by Sabrina Wells, 1904, ink mark & "NC - S.E.WELL - SS38" (line inside rim, not through from firing) **8,250**

Vase, 9 1/2" h., tall slender waisted cylindrical body, the upper half w/an incised & finely painted band of stylized slender upright leaves & spearpoint blossoms in ivory, green & blue above the lower body w/a streaked ivory, green & blue glossy glaze, "C. Payne - J.M. - #YY29" **6,050**

Vase, 10 1/2" h., inverted trumpet-form body w/slightly flared rim, decorated w/pink berries & long green leaves on faded blue ground, by Sadie Irvine, ca. 1920, impressed "NC - KZ21 - 83 - SI" **2,750**

Vase, 12 1/4" h., tall ovoid body decorated w/moonlight scene of live oaks w/Spanish moss, by Sadie Irvine, ca. 1925, impressed "NC - SI - OX28 - JM - 117" **7,700**

Nippon

"Nippon" is a term which is used to describe a wide range of porcelain wares produced in Japan from the late 19th century until about 1921. It was in 1891 that the U.S. implemented the McKinley Tariff Act which required that all wares exported to the United States carry a marking indicating the country of origin. The Japanese chose to use "Nippon," their name for Japan. In 1921 the import laws were revised and the words "Made in" had to be added to the markings. Japan was also required to replace the "Nippon" with the English name "Japan" on all wares sent to the U.S.

Many Japanese factories produced Nippon porcelains and much of it was hand-painted with ornate floral or landscape decoration and heavy gold decoration, applied beading and slip-trailed designs referred to as "moriage." We indicate the specific marking used on a piece, when known, at the end of each listing below. Be aware that a number of Nippon markings have been reproduced and used on new porcelain wares.

Important reference books on Nippon include: The Collector's Encyclopedia of Nippon Porcelain, Series One through Three, *by Joan F. Van Patten (Collector Books, Paducah, Kentucky) and* The Wonderful World of Nippon Porcelain, 1891-1921 *by Kathy Wojciechowski (Schiffer Publishing, Ltd., Atglen, Pennsylvania).*

Nippon Vase with Molded Roses

Vase, 5 1/2" h., footed, cylindrical w/collared rim, tiny angled rim handles, decorated w/a h.p. scene of a house in a meadow, green "M" in Wreath mark (minor hairline in glaze) **$61**

Vase, 6" h., swelled cylindrical form w/an angled shoulder molded w/four deep indentations & centering a short bulbous neck, decorated w/a continuous scene of yellow geese flying against a blue sky over a meadow w/grain & a small line of dark green trees in the distance, Moriage accents (green "M" in Wreath mark) **150**

Vase, 8 1/2" h., swelled cylindrical body tapering to a tiny neck w/flared rim flanked by scrolling loop handles, the body completely decorated w/colorful large flowers in red, white & pink on a shaded green ground, the neck & handles in white on brown in the Wedgwood style (blue "Maple Leaf" mark).................................. **201**

Vase, 9" h., footed ovoid body w/incurved short neck flanked by twig handles, the sides molded in relief w/large pink roses w/green leaves & stems & trimmed in gold, on a mottled dark green & gold ground, blue "Maple Leaf" mark (ILLUS.)...... **880**

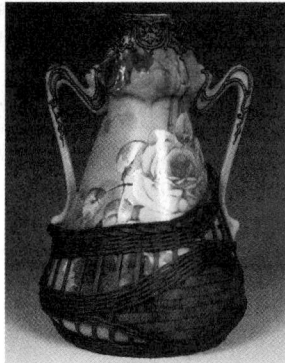

Nippon Vase with Wicker Trim

Vase, 10" h., sharply tapering conical form w/molded & bulbed neck, ornate long S-scroll side handles, decorated w/large red & pink roses & green leaves on a shaded greenish yellow ground, dark green moriage decoration on the neck & handles, the lower half wrapped in basketweave wicker, blue "Maple Leaf" mark (ILLUS.)... **550**

Noritake

Noritake china, still in production in Japan, has been exported in large quantities to this country since early in this century. Though the Noritake Company first registered in 1904, it did not use "Noritake" as part of its backstamp until 1918. Interest in Noritake has escalated as collectors now seek out pieces made between the "Nippon" era and World War II (1921-41). The Azalea pattern is also popular with collectors.

Noritake Mark

Basket, mint, "Dolly Varden"............................ **$125**
Bouillion cup & saucer, Azalea patt., No. 124.. **24**
Butter dish w/drain, open, Tree in Meadow patt.. **32**
Candy jar, cov., Tree in Meadow patt............... **325**
Cheese dish, cov., Tree in Meadow patt........... **65**
Condiment set: cov. mustard jar & pr. salt & pepper shakers on handled tray; bulbous blue lustre mustard jar w/red rose-

bud finial, green leaves, ovoid shakers w/clown head tops, red, blue, orange & white lustre, blue lustre tray, 7" l., the set (ILLUS. below)................................. **320**

Figural Condiment Set

Condiment set: cov. mustard jar & pr. salt & pepper shakers on handled tray; lustre borders & tops, 5 1/2" w. tray, the set (ILLUS.)................................ **60**
Dish, shell-shaped, three footed, Tree in Meadow patt.. **275**
Mayonnaise set, Tree in Meadow patt., 3 pcs... **48**
Platter, cold meat, 10 1/4" l., Azalea patt......... **175**
Platter, 11 1/2" l., Tree in Meadow patt. **50**
Syrup pitcher w/underplate, Azalea patt........ **110**
Vegetable bowl, open, oval, Tree in Meadow patt... **28**

North Dakota School of Mines

All pottery produced at the University of North Dakota School of Mines was made from North Dakota clay. In 1910, the University hired Margaret Kelly Cable to teach pottery making and she remained at the school until her retirement. Julia Mattson and Margaret Pachl were other instructors between 1923 and 1970. Designs and glazes varied through the years ranging from the Art Nouveau to modern styles. Pieces were marked "University of North Dakota - Grand Forks, N.D. - Made at School of Mines, N.D." within a circle and also signed by the students until 1963. Since that time, the pieces bear only the students' signatures. Items signed "Huck" are by the artist Flora Huckfield and were made between 1923 and 1949.

North Dakota School of Mines Mark

Bowl, 9" d., 4 1/4" h., narrow footring below the deep rounded upright sides, carved w/heart-shaped green leaves below a green rim band on a matte white ground, mottled glossy light blue interior, circular mark & name "Schnell"............................. **$495**
Charger, the center decorated w/a large stylized flower in polychrome cuerda seca, w/red flower petals at the dark border & centered between the five large flower petals, ink stamp & artist mark, 10" d. **770**
Pitcher, 5" h., 8 1/2" d., footed squatty bulbous body w/embossed frieze of "Red River Ox Carts" by M. Cable, glossy ivory glaze on buff clay body, die-stamped

mark, embossed signature & title & "140" (ILLUS. below) **990**

North Dakota Pitcher

Vase, 3 1/2" h., 3 1/2" d., wide bulbous body decorated overall w/painted white snowflakes on a dark blue ground, ink stamp.. **385**

Vase, miniature, 3 1/2" h., 3 3/4" d., small spherical form tapering at the base, glossy dark blue ground cut around the center w/a wide band of silhouetted coyotes against an ivory ground, circular mark & "M-298" (flat stilt pull nicks) **1,320**

Vase, 5 1/4" h., 6" d., wide bulbous ovoid form w/wide angled shoulder to flat mouth, molded around the shoulder w/rectangular panels each enclosing a bison in ochre on a brown ground, overall ochre background, by Margaret Cable, circular stamp mark & "Bison - 117A - M.Cable" **1,980**

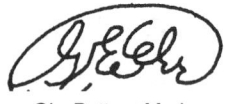

North Dakota School of Mines Vase

Vase, 5 1/2" h., ovoid body w/rolled rim, decorated w/polychrome horizontal stripes, by Julia Mattson, ink-stamped & incised mark (ILLUS.) **495**

Vase, 5 1/2" h., slender ovoid w/ringed shoulder tapering to a short cylindrical neck w/closed rim, decorated w/incised cowboys w/lassos & "Why Not Minot" under a glossy blue glaze, by Julia Mattson, ink mark & incised mark **715**

Vase, 5 1/2" h., 6" d., bulbous nearly spherical form w/a small closed rim, "Prairie Rose" patt., dark sand-colored ground decorated around the mouth w/a wide band of coral stylized roses & green leaves between thin bands, Margaret Cable, circular ink mark & "M.Cable - 131 - A - Prairie Rose" **990**

Vase, 5 3/4" h., 5 1/2" d., footed bulbous nearly spherical body w/wide raised

mouth band, carved w/a band of Indian warriors on horseback under a dark brown matte glaze, originally sold w/or without a cover, by Flora Huckfield, titled "N.D. Sioux," ink stamp mark, title & incised "151"... **1,980**

North Dakota Vase

Vase, 6 1/4" h., 7" d., spherical body w/wide shoulder band incised w/continuous scene of covered wagons pulled by oxen, shaded matte brown glaze, decorated by Margaret Cable, circular stamp & title "186, M. Cable" (ILLUS.) **2,530**

Vase, 7" h., shouldered slender ovoid body w/slightly flaring rim, decorated w/blue irises & green leaves on a shaded green ground, by Margaret Cable, ink mark & "MKC, 1916," **2,970**

Vase, 7 3/4" h., swelled cylindrical body w/narrow shoulder & wide molded rim, excised brown daffodils & leaves repeated around body on a dark brown ground, by Ruth Skyberg, 1949, ink stamp & incised signature **2,090**

Vase, 8 3/4" h., ovoid body tapering to wide cylindrical neck, large stylized excised brown daffodils & leaves on a dark brown ground, by F. Cunningham, 1950, ink stamp & incised signature.......................... **1,870**

Ohr (George) Pottery

George Ohr, the eccentric potter of Biloxi, Mississippi, worked from about 1883 to 1906. Some think him to be one of the most expert throwers the craft will ever see. The majority of his works were hand-thrown, exceedingly thin-walled items, some of which have a crushed or folded appearance. He considered himself the foremost potter in the world and declined to sell much of his production, instead accumulating a great horde to leave as a legacy to his children. In 1972 this collection was purchased for resale by an antiques dealer.

GEO. E. OHR

BILOXI, MISS.

Ohr Pottery Marks

Bowl, 2 7/8" h., flat base w/tall twisted & crumpled flared floral form, mottled green interior glaze, mottled burgundy exterior glaze, impressed "Geo. E. Ohr Biloxi Miss." **$5,520**

Inkwell, figural, a rectangular plaque back w/a high-relief molded face of a mountain lion w/a filling hole at the top of the head, shimmering dark green glaze, stamped "G.E. Ohr - Biloxi - Biloxi Welcome poem," 3 1/2 x 4 1/2" **1,320**

Inkwell, figural, model of a cabin w/a long sloping roof & stick-style chimney on one side, mottled glossy green glaze, stamped "Geo. Ohr - Biloxi, Miss.," 3 x 4 1/2" **2,310**

Pitcher, 4 1/2" h., pinched & pulled flattened rounded form w/angled integral handle, deeply scalloped & flared rim, mottled charcoal-glazed interior, dark pink glazed exterior, inscribed "G.E. Ohr".. **6,900**

Teapot, cov., footed baluster-form w/flared rim, simple strap handle & swan's-neck spout, flat inset cover w/knob finial, overall sponged design in dark brown, green & black on a khaki ground, stamped "Geo. Ohr - Biloxi, Miss.," 4" h. **6,050**

Vase, 3 3/4" h., footed squatty bulbous lower body w/folded & lobed upper body pulled together to form a narrow top opening, mottled green-flecked on yellow exterior glaze, impresed "G.E. Ohr - Biloxi, Miss. - 5" **4,370**

Vase, miniature, 3 3/4" h., 2 1/2" h., a low pedestal foot supporting a slightly tapering cylindrical body w/a deeply crumpled & twisted upper border, green & amber speckled semi-matte glaze, marked "G.E. Ohr - Biloxi, Miss." (minor rim nick).. **1,870**

Vase, 4 1/4" h., 3" d., squatty low base w/sides tapering to short wide cylindrical neck, covered in speckled green, rasberry & ochre glaze, die-stamped "G.E. OHR - BILOXI" **1,760**

Vase, 4 1/4" h., 4" d., a footring below a rounded dimpled base, gently tapering to an asymmetrically folded rim, covered in an ochre glaze w/overall green drip effect, die-stamped "G.E. OHR - Biloxi, Miss.".......... **6,050**

Vase, 4 1/4" h., 4" d., ovoid body tapering toward the foot & w/a wide gently flared rim, the waist of the body deeply twisted, matte green & light blue exterior glaze, cobalt blue & green interior glaze, script signature **4,125**

Vase, 4 1/2" h., 4" d., footed free-form shape w/collapsed body, dimpled top & torn rim, covered in green & ochre speckled glaze, die-stamped "G.E. OHR - BILOXI" **8,250**

Vase, 4 1/2" h., 4 1/4" d., ringed tapering cylindrical form w/a collapsed & folded rim, covered in a speckled caramel & mahogany glossy glaze, die-stamped "G.E. OHR - Biloxi, Miss.".............................. **3,850**

Vase, 4 1/2" h., 6" w., footed tilted free-form design w/heavily folded & pinched sides, bisque scroddled clay, incised script signature **3,575**

Vase, 4 3/4" h., squatty bulbous base w/upright dimpled neck & pinched & folded rim, covered in aventurine & black glaze, die-stamped "G.E. OHR - Biloxi, Miss." **2,750**

Vase, 5" h., free-form bisque-fired pale clay, a footring below the squatty bulbous body,

pierced & dimpled around the sides, a tall neck w/torn & folded rim, early price tag mounted w/new wire, script signature **2,310**

Vase, 5" h., 4" d., bulbous ovoid body below a twisted & crumpled shoulder & a wide upright neck w/ragged-edged torn rim, overall green, mahogany, gunmetal & ochre speckled glaze, impressed "G.E. OHR - Biloxi, Miss." **5,500**

Vase, 8 1/4" h., flaring foot below the squatty bulbous lower body tapering to a narrow waist below the tall flaring trumpet neck w/wide incurved mouth, red, purple, green, black mottled & volcanic glazes, inscribed "G.E. Ohr" **21,850**

Owens

Owens pottery was the product of the J.B. Owens Pottery Company, which operated in Ohio from 1890 to 1929. In 1891 it located in Zanesville and produced art pottery from 1896, introducing "Utopian" wares as its first art pottery. The company switched to tile after 1907. Efforts to rebuild after the factory burned in 1928 failed and the company closed in 1929.

Owens Pottery Mark

Bowl, 3 3/4" h., Lotus line, footed spherical body, the wide shoulder tapering to narrow molded rim, decorated w/a dragonfly & a few grass stalks on shaded grey ground, impressed "Owens 202" & "L" **$495**

Bowl, 6 1/8" d., 1 5/8" h., Matt Green line, low round form w/incurved shoulder w/raised lines & flat rim, impressed "Owens 330" **165**

Cruet, matt glaze in cream & grey, shape No. 1216, impressed "Owens 1216," 4 3/4" h. (fine overall crazing) **165**

Cruet, Lightweight line, footed bulbous ovoid body w/tri-point rim & C-form handle, wild rose decoration on shaded green to dark brown ground, by Cecil Excel, incised "CE" & "868," 3 1/4" h. **193**

Cruet, Lightweight line, footed bell-shaped body w/upright petal-shaped spout & loop handle, yellow nasturtium w/green leaves decoration on dark brown ground, decorated by Harry Robinson, incised "HR" & "877" w/impressed "JBO" circular logo, 5 3/8" h. (slight roughness on spout tip) **220**

Ewer, Metal Deposit line, three-footed bulbous body w/arched spout & large loop handle, electroplated copper, slip-decorated w/wild roses by Cecil Excel, marked "2 Owens 921," artist-initialed, 5 3/8" h. **385**

Jardiniere, footed cylindrical body w/scalloped rim, Majolica finish w/embossed flowers & birds in blue, white & green, marked w/raised J.B. Owens shield mark, 6 3/4' h. (small glaze flake off rim)....... **165**

Mug, Matt Green line, tapering cylindrical body w/C-form handle, decorated w/impressed combed designs & impressed "Owens 46," 3 7/8" h. 220

Paperweight, rectangular, Majolica Finish, green glossy ground w/embossed stag head & marked "Edmiston Horney Co. - Zanesville - Ohio" w/embossed scrolled border, "Made by the J.B. Owens Pottery Co." on reverse, 2 3/8 x 3 7/8" 83

Pitcher, 3 1/4" h., Embossed Lotus line, tapering cylindrical form w/incurved rim, pinched spout & C-form handle, grey ground decorated w/green & purple grape motif, impressed "Owens Lotus X 236".......... 248

Tile, Arts & Crafts style, decoration w/acorns & oak leaves in grey, green & brown on tan ground, impressed Owens," 5 3/8 x 5 7/8" 248

Umbrella stand, Henri Deux line, balusterform w/scalloped rim, portrait of woman & tan, white & light blue floral decoration on blue ground, unmarked, 22 1/4" h............ 850

Vase, 2 1/2" h., Utopian line, squatty four sided vase w/wild roses on dark brown glossy ground, by Sara Timberlake, marked "1 Owens Utopian 103," artist-initialed in slip on side... 165

Vase, 2 7/8" h., Lotus line, short wide tapering cylindrical form decorated w/a lotus blossom in white, yellow & green on dark brown ground, impressed "Owens 26".......... 303

Vase, 3" h., Utopian line, footed bulbous base & loop handles from shoulder to rim, pansy decoration on dark brown glossy ground, marked "3 J.B Owens 866" & artist mark in slip on one handle 165

Vase, 3 1/2" h., Utopian line, two-handled bulbous form w/wild rose decoration on shaded brown ground, most likely by Claude Leffler, marked "Utopian Owens 936" & artist-initialed...................................... 248

Owens Aqua Verdi Vase

Vase, 3 7/8" h., Aqua Verdi line, short wide tapering cylindrical form w/three thick loop handles from rim to base, relief-molded lizard on textured variegated light to dark green ground (ILLUS.) 650

Vase, 3 7/8" h., Utopian line, square tapering body w/short cylindrical neck, red clover decoration on shaded brown ground, possibly the work of Virginia Adams, marked "Owens Utopian 2 8 111" w/artist's initials which appears to be a conjoined VA............... 138

Vase, 4" h., Soudaneze line, footed spherical body w/molded rim, decorated w/white pansies on glossy black ground, impressed "Owens 202" (minor glaze scratches & small bruise on rim).................... 330

Vase, 4 1/4" h., two-handled, squatty bulbous body w/narrow cylindrical neck, shaded brown ground w/wild rose decoration, most likely by Martha Gray, artist-initialed & marked "J.B. Owens Utopian 980" (small nick on rim & 1/2 x 1/2" kiln kiss on back side).. 220

Vase, 4 3/8" h., Utopian line, twisted body w/floral decoration, marked "1 Owens Utopian 117" & obscure artist mark on side 165

Vase, 4 5/8" h., cylindrical w/bulbous base, raised repeating floral & leaf design, matte aqua glaze, impressed Owensart mark, ca. 1906.. 173

Vase, 4 3/4" h., Matt Utopian line, twisted body w/small cylindrical neck, pastel slip pansy decoration by Hattie Eberlein, impressed "Owens 102" & artist-initialed (some glaze discoloration & pinhead size glaze nick off base)................................... 165

Owens Onyx Line Vase

Vase, 5" h., Onyx line, footed crescent-shaped body, mottled, striated brown, tan & cream ground, unmarked, shape No. 872 (ILLUS.) 250

Vase, 5" h., Utopian line, footed bulbous body w/wide shoulder tapering to short cylindrical neck w/wide flaring rim, decorated w/orange & green leaves on dark brown glossy ground, by Virginia Adams, marked "Utopian J.B. Owens 975" w/artist's initials on side in slip 193

Vase, 5 3/8" h., Aborigine line, bulbous shouldered body tapering to wide cylindrical neck w/flat rim, light tan earthenware w/rust band & geometric decoration, chocolate brown rim & interior glaze, incised "JBO" & impressed "Owens 29" 165

Vase, 5 1/2" h., Feroza line, bulbous ovoid body w/tapering shoulder flanked by large loop handles, closed mouth, uneven molded ground in iridescent mottled brownish black, shape No. 1090 450

Vase, 5 1/2" h., Utopian line, bulbous ovoid body tapering to short cylindrical neck w/molded rim, decorated w/colorful Autumn leaves on dark brown glossy ground, marked "Owens Utopian 1048" (minor scratches & small glaze nick off high spot near base) 165

Vase, 5 5/8" h., Majolica finish, bulbous base tapering to cylindrical neck w/flat rim, shape No. 27, impressed "Owens 27"... 83

Vase, 5 3/4" h., Art Vellum line, tapering square form w/small molded rim, yellow & orange floral decoration on brown ground, shape No. 112, mark No. 13 .... **350**

Vase, 5 3/4" h., Utopian line, twisted base tapering to square neck w/molded rim, wild rose decoration on shaded brown ground, impressed "2 Owens Utopian 115" **138**

Vase, 5 7/8" h., Matt Green line, four buttressed feet support the spherical shouldered body tapering to short cylindrical neck w/molded rim, impressed "Owens 1155" (minor glaze nick off one foot) **275**

Vase, 6" h., bulbous body w/molded rim, green Arts & Crafts style rectangular designs encircling body, impressed "Owens 218" **358**

Vase, 6" h., Embossed Lotus line, wide ovoid body w/molded rim, dark brown ground w/cream band near rim decoration w/embossed & slip-painted berries & leaves, marked "Lotus," shape No. X218, mark No. 10 .... **400**

Vase, 6" h., Lotus line, waisted cylindrical body w/wide shoulder & flat mouth, decorated w/mushrooms painted by Frank Ferrell, shaded grey to cream ground, artist-initialed, impressed w/"Owensart" torch logo & shape No. 1236 (minor glaze nicks on bottom edge **468**

Owens Cyrano Line Vase

Vase, 6 1/4" h., Cyrano line, compressed base tapering to wide slightly waisted cylindrical body flanked by large loop handles, decorated w/squeeze bag applied filigree lacy & floral design in white & tan w/beading at the base & rim, dark green glossy ground, unmarked, shape No. 357 (ILLUS.) **850**

Vase, 6 3/8" h., Oriental line, three-footed ovoid body, band of white lacy squeeze bag design near top & small beads below rim, dark brown ground **300**

Vase, 6 3/8" h., Utopian Ware, flared rim on a tapered ovoid body, decorated w/rose blossoms & leaves in cream & brown on a shaded brown ground w/a glossy glaze, ornate silver overlay decoration, overlay impressed "Utopian J.B. Owens 923 - Phee F.N. Silver Co." (crazing, scratches, nicks) **288**

Vase, 6 3/4" h., Utopian line, waisted cylindrical form decorated w/detailed pansy blossoms, base impressed "Utopian J.B. Owens" **138**

Vase, 6 7/8" h., Art Nouveau line, slender baluster-form body, orange circular decoration on dark brown ground **150**

Vase, 6 7/8" h., Lightweight line, footed baluster-form body w/slightly flared rim, jonquil decoration by former Rookwood artist, Charles J. Dibowski, dark brown glossy glaze ground, incised artist's initials & "846," impressed "JBO" circular logo **358**

Vase, 8 1/2" h., Utopian line, bulbous ovoid base tapering slightly to wide cylindrical neck, nicely detailed ear of corn in yellow w/green husk done in heavy slip, impressed "Owens Utopian 223" (glaze scratches) **330**

Vase, 8 3/4" h., Henri Deux line, compressed bulbous base below tapering cylindrical neck w/closed rim, incised base & yellow floral decoration on dark brown ground, shape No. 1307, mark No. 10 .... **250**

Vase, 8 3/4" h., slightly swelled cylindrical body, Embossed Lotus line, dark brown ground decorated w/embossed & slip-painted berries & leaves, marked "Lotus," shape No. X220, mark No. 10 .... **600**

Vase, 9" h., Utopian line, footed tapering ovoid body w/flared rim, "First of Three Pharaoh's Horses," decorated by Hattie Eberlein, impressed Owens Utopian logo, artist's monogram in white slip on foot, shape No. 982, (some evidence of slightly cupped glaze) **358**

Vase, 9 7/8" h., Malachite Opalesce Inlaid line, footed bulbous ovoid body tapering to narrow cylindrical neck w/flared rim, Art Nouveau style metallic floral decoration (possibly a few missing beads at rim) . **1,650**

Vase, 10" h., Opalesce line, footed bulbous ovoid body tapering to tall slender cylindrical neck w/flared rim, decorated w/Art Nouveau style metallic florals, marked "Owens," shape No. 1124 .... **850**

Vase, 10 1/4" h., Utopian Ware, bottle-shaped, coated w/gold & overlaid w/small coral-like beads, underglaze decoration of a rose branch in shades of green, rust & brown, impressed mark & No. 1010, ca. 1905 .... **345**

Vase, 10 3/4" h., Mission line, cylindrical body w/rounded shoulder to the tiny molded mouth, decorated w/a scene of a mission w/notation on side, "Bells of San Gabriel Mission California," & "312 F Mission Pottery" on base (minor paint loss) **523**

Owens Aborigine Line Vase

Vase, 8 3/4 x 11", Aborigine line, bulbous shouldered body tapering to wide cylindrical neck w/flat rim, light tan earthenware w/rust band & geometric decoration, chocolate brown rim & interior glaze, incised "JBO" (ILLUS.) **600**

Vase, 11 1/4" h., Oriental line, waisted cylindrical form w/rows of white & tan beading at rim & base & center band of lacy squeeze bag design in white & tan, dark brown ground, unmarked, shape No. 863...... **350**

Vase, 13 1/2" h., Lotus line, ovoid body w/short wide cylindrical neck, decorated w/blue & white iris & green leaves on greyish green ground, by Walter Denny, impressed "Owens 1245" & "Denny" in light brown slip (minor color spots in flowers) **935**

Vase, Art Vellum line, footed bulbous body tapering to wide cylindrical neck, decorated w/scene of harbor w/boats, houses & trees, most likely by C. Minnie Terry, impressed w/Owens torch mark & shape No. 1039, artist-initialed in brown slip (base chip repaired)...................... **1,045**

Oyster Plates

Oyster plates intrigue a few collectors. Oysters were shucked and the meat served in wells of these attractive plates specifically designed to serve oysters. During the late 19th century they were made of fine china and majolica. Some plates were decorated in the realistic "trompe l'oeil" technique while others simply matched the pattern of a dinner service.

China, five-well, ivory ground w/white seaweed & gilt trim, one w/white ground & gilt seaweed, marked "Brownfields China for Tiffany and Co.," 9 1/4" d., set of 6 .... **$726**

Majolica, four-well, fan-shaped, turquoise w/pink & white wells, mark of George Jones & stamped "J.W. Boteler - June 16, 1874," collection label, 8 1/2 x 9 1/4" (minor glaze loss at rim)............................ **3,740**

Majolica, six-well, yellow, pink & green ground w/pink & white wells & cobalt blue center sauce dish, glazed double X mark, 19th c., 10" d. (hairline) **314**

Group of Victorian Oyster Plates

Majolica, six-well, one well molded as a large fish head, the others as fat oblong fish, round central well, brown & yellow w/green fish, England, 19th c., 9 3/4 x 10 1/4", pr. (ILLUS. back right)...................... **1,540**

Majolica, six-well, ring of turquoise blue wells separated by molded brown & green seaweed w/a central shell-shaped sauce dish, George Jones, England,

19th c., repair to sauce dish, 10 1/2" d., pr. (ILLUS. back left).................................. **2,860**

Majolica, twelve-well, round w/brown wells in the center surrounded by a flanged rim w/a green ground & relief decoration of seaweed & shells, blue trim, Longchamp mark, France, late 19th c., minor flakes, 8 1/2" d. (ILLUS. front left) **495**

Majolica, twelve-well, turquoise ground w/ivory wells around the border & green leaves around the central well, probably French, 19th c., 14 3/4" d. (ILLUS. back center) **660**

Majolica, twelve-well, oval w/brown ground & turquoise & pink wells, trimmed w/green dolphins, white shells & yellow border, shell feet, Chantilly, France, 19th c., 15" l. (hairline, chip on underside)............. **935**

Majolica, twenty-seven-well, lazy-Susan type, cobalt blue & mottled yellow w/molded green seaweed, three entwined fish finial, incised Mintons mark, England, 19th c., 10 x 12" (restoration to well rims)............. **13,200**

Porcelain, five-well, ivory ground w/gilt border, Limoges, France, late 19th - early 20th c., 7 1/2" d., set of 4 .... **220**

Porcelain, five-well, blue & white floral decoration w/gilt trim, Limoges, France, late 19th - early 20th c., 7 1/2" d., set of 6 (minor flakes) **396**

Porcelain, five-well, octagonal, multicolored ground w/h.p. seaweed & shells, marked "Oscar Gutherz - Limoges," France, late 19th - early 20th c., 7 3/4" w., set of 7 .... **1,155**

Porcelain, five-well, white ground w/pink floral decoration, marked "Karlsbad - Austria," late 19th - early 20th c., 8 1/4" d., set of 7 (minor gilt loss) **424**

Porcelain, five-well, crescent-shaped, bluish ground w/brown trim, 8 3/4" l., set of 4........... **198**

Porcelain, five-well, floral sprigs on a white ground, gilt border, L. Sazerat, Limoges, France, late 19th -early 20th c., 9" d., set of 6... **528**

Porcelain, five-well, various shell & seaweed designs, Limoges, France, late 19th - early 20th c., 9" d., set of 6.................. **528**

Porcelain, five-well, large shell form w/five oyster shell-shaped wells w/a small central well, each well decorated w/colorful scenes of birds & flowers w/gilt trim, artist-signed, Kutani ware, Japan, late 19th c., 9 1/4" d. (ILLUS. front right) **825**

Porcelain, six-well, multicolored wells w/relief-molded decoration & gilt trim, unmarked, 8" d., set of 4 .... **220**

Porcelain, six-well, floral decoration on a white ground, green borders & gilt trim, Austria, late 19th - early 20th c., 8 1/2" d., set of 5 (minor flakes)............................ **330**

Porcelain, six-well, each deep well w/a floral design on a white ground, marked "Karlsbad -Austria," 8 1/2" d., set of 6 (one w/hairline).. **462**

Porcelain, six-well, pink & yellow w/shell decorations, trimmed in brown, unmarked, 9" d., set of 4 .... **220**

Porcelain, six-well, floral-decorated wells on a green ground, incised "Karlsbad - Austria," late 19th - early 20th c., 9" d., set of 5 .... **4,125**

Porcelain, six-well, solid white ground w/shells & basketweave in relief, marked "Longchamp - France," late 19th - early 20th c., 9 1/4" d., set of 6 (two chipped) **198**
Porcelain, six-well, fan-form w/painted polychrome flowers & gilt trim, monogrammed w/seal "Spernit Pericula Virtus," K.P.M. blue sceptre mark & transfer on base, 9 1/4 x 10 1/2" **770**

Parian

Parian is unglazed porcelain in the biscuit stage, and takes its name from its resemblance to Parian marble used for statuary. Parian wares were made in this country and abroad through much of the last century and continue to be made.

Parian Bust of Captain Matthew Webb

Bust of Captain Matthew Webb, figure shown displaying sporting medals for swimming across the English Channel in 1875, bolted to a Parian pedestal base inscribed on reverse "Published as the Act directs by J.S. Crapper of Hanley & C. Marsh of Wolston, by special consent and assistance of Captain Matthew Webb. December 6th, 1875," 19th c., 25" h. (ILLUS.) **$460**
Bust of Charles Dickens, mounted on a waisted circular socle, England, 19th c., 15 1/2" h. **575**
Figure group, Naomi and Her Daughter, modeled on an oval base, attributed to John Bell, England, impressed title, no factory mark, 1865, 12 3/4" h. (hand restored, nick to bag, slight loss to ribbon) **57**

Figure Group of Civil War Soldiers

Figure group, based on Rogers Group entitled "One More Shot," attributed to Copeland, two Civil War soldiers, one standing & one wounded & wrapping a bandage on his leg, set on a festooned circular base, unmarked, ca. 1865, 20 1/2" h. (ILLUS.) **5,175**

Figure of William Shakespeare

Figure of William Shakespeare, full-bodied figure modeled in traditional pose, standing & resting his right elbow on a pile of books & a script atop a column molded in relief w/theatrical emblems, all on a shaped rectangular base, ca. 1850, minor chips to bows of shoes, 16 3/4" h. (ILLUS.) **575**
Figures, each molded as a child in a different pose, each seated on a trunk, England, 19th c., 13 1/4" h., pr. **1,265**

Paris & Old Paris

China known by the generic name of Paris and Old Paris was made by several Parisian factories from the 18th through the 19th century; some of it is marked and some is not. Much of it was handsomely decorated.

Cachepot, cov., tapering cylindrical form w/parcel-gilt & polychrome floral decoration surrounding landscape vignette cartouches, 19th c., 7 3/4" h. **$488**
Cachepots, tapering cylindrical body, lion's mask handles & decorated w/gilt floral scrollwork & cartouches on green & white ground, ca. 1840, 7 1/4" d., 8 3/8" h., pr. . **1,400**

Paris Scenic Cachpot

Cachepots, footed, tapering cylindrical body w/enamel decorated landscape scene of children, 19th c., green ground, 7 3/4" d., 7 1/2" h., pr. (ILLUS. of one).......... **805**

Paris Figural Centerpiece

Centerpiece, round scrolled foot below fan-shaped gilt ground foliate molded body w/scalloped rim & loop end handles, decorated in relief w/male & female figures in a landscape setting, 19th c., 19" w., 11 3/4" h. (ILLUS.)....................................... **1,265**
Sweetmeat baskets, reticulated body & out-curving rim, decorated w/floral sprays, 19th c., 4 1/4" d., pr............................. **126**
Urns, pedestal foot, two-handled, flared rim, decorated w/floral cartouches, 19th c., 5" d., 6 3/4" h., pr. **475**
Vase, 14 3/8" h., tall slender baluster-form body on a slender pedestal base & w/a tall slender trumpet neck, the body w/overall gold trellis & dot design above a band of tulips & stiff leaf-tips at the body, the shoulders w/upright winged Minerva bust-length handles suspending white bisque floral swags down the sides, ca. 1820.. **3,680**
Vases, 7 7/8" h., a short round pedestal foot supporting a tall ovoid body tapering slightly to the wide short flaring mouth, a platinum silvery ground w/the mouth rim & foot chased w/gilt diaper bands, one painted in color w/a country maid before an arbor w/a blindfolded Cupid led by a small dog, the reverse w/beehives, the other w/a similar maiden beside a gate accompanied by Cupid offering a bouquet, the reverse w/an open barrel, ca. 1880, the pair.. **2,300**

Pate-Sur-Pate

Taking its name from the French phrase meaning "paste on paste," this type of ware features designs in relief, obtained by successive layers of thin pottery paste, painted one on top of the other. Much of this work was done in France and England, and perhaps the best-known wares of this type from England are those made by Minton.

Vase, flask-form centering a figural rondel depicting putti in white slip on brown ground, the oval base pierced w/Chinese motifs, impressed Minton marks & crowned Minton globe mark, late 19th c. (ILLUS. top next column) **$3,450**

Minton Pate-sur-pate Vase

Vase, 9 1/2" h., Art Nouveau style, baluster-form body w/narrow shoulder tapering to short wide cylindrical neck flanked by loop handles, bust portrait of woman on central mauve ground & teal blue ground w/relief-molded cherub, gilt banded borders & foliate relief, late 19th c., France....... **460**
Vases, 7 1/2" h., slender ovoid form, decorated in white pate-sur-pate on an olive green ground w/different scenes of Diana assisting Cupid in the firing of an arrow, beneath a gilt foliate band at the shoulder, the reverse w/either a group of trophies or a heart pierced by two arrows, decorated by A. Birks, Minton marks & numbers, ca. 1900, pr. **8,400**

Paul Revere Pottery

This pottery was established in Boston, Massachusetts, in 1906, by a group of philanthropists seeking to establish better conditions for underprivileged young girls of the area. Edith Brown served as supervisor of the small "Saturday Evening Girls Club" pottery operation which was moved, in 1912, to a house close to the Old North Church where Paul Revere's signal lanterns had been placed. The wares were mostly hand decorated in mineral colors and both sgraffito and molded decorations were employed. Although it became popular, it was never a profitable operation and always depended on financial contributions to operate. After the death of Edith Brown in 1932, the pottery foundered and finally closed in 1942.

Paul Revere Mark

Bowl, 5 3/8" d., 2 1/4" h., round, a border of repeating incised rim decoration depicting three running rabbits in cream white against a blue ground, early 20th c. (hairline, glaze imperfections) **$805**

Bowl, 6 3/4" d., 3 1/4" h., deep rounded sides decorated around the rim w/a cuerda seca band w/clusters of green trees against a blue sky & brown earth, the background in moss green matte glaze, marked "S.E.G. - 4-15 - S.G." (crazing lines to rim) **2,970**

Bowl, 8 1/2" d., 2 3/4" h., a wide shallow round form w/upright sides, decorated around the interior rim w/a cuerda seca broad band w/intricate white orchids & green leaves on a two-tone blue & beige ground, the center bottom & exterior in dark blue, signed "S.E.G." & illegible initials (short tight hairline) **2,200**

Bowl, 8 1/2" d., 2 3/4" h., round w/tapering sides, matte brown exterior, tan interior, signed "S.E.G.," early 20th c. **173**

Bowl, 10 3/4" d., 4 1/4" h., a small footring supporting a deep flaring round bowl w/a wide flattened flared rim, solid white ground decorated around the inner rim w/a band of white orchids & green leaves on a dark blue band, marked "PR - 11-26"..... **880**

Bowl-vase, wide bulbous form w/a wide closed rim, decorated around the rim w/a cuerda seca band of stylized white flowers & green leaves on beige & celadon green, the lower body w/a bluish grey glaze, signed "S.E.G. 339-12-11 - S.G.," 6" d., 4" h. **4,125**

Breakfast set, child's: cereal bowl, small plate, cup & milk pitcher; each w/a bright yellow ground decorated w/a round central reserve w/a polychrome decoration of chicks or rabbits, a cream-colored rim band on each inscribed "Ellen-Louisa," black outlining, marked "PRP" in ink, 1941, plate 6 1/4" d., the set...................... **1,540**

Center bowl, decorated w/white geese in cuerda seca against a band of yellow & brown, white interior w/matte green exterior, ca. 1912, ink mark, SACB paper label, SEG Bowl Shop label & ink mark, 4 1/2 x 11 3/4" (tight hairline from rim)....... **4,950**

Cereal bowl, dark blue ground w/a white interior center & an interior cuerda seca rim band inscribed "Robert Bernard Hagan - His Bowl," ink mark "SEG - 251-12-11 - F.L.," 10 1/2" d., 4 1/2" h. (restoration to lines & chips)........................... **165**

Paperweight, low flat octagonal shape, decorated on the top in cuerda seca w/a green & brown tree on green grass w/a blue sky, marked in ink "S.E.G. - R.B.," 2 1/2" w. **440**

Pitcher, 4 1/4" h., milk-type, gently flaring cylindrical form w/a pinched rim spout & loop handle, a bluish grey ground decorated around the rim w/a cuerda seca band showing a tortoise & a hare in white, black & green w/the motto "Slow but Sure," ink mark.................... **1,650**

Paul Revere Plate w/Camel Border

Plate, decorated around the rim w/camel design, marked "S.E.G." (ILLUS.) **1,870**

Plate, 6 1/2" d., border decorated w/h.p. pine cones in brown & green, white matte ground, ink mark "SEG - 8.17"...................... **165**

Tumbler, 3 1/4" d., tapering cylindrical form, decorated below rim w/h.p. frieze of squirrels in blue on white crackled ground, ca. 1912, ink mark "SEG - 91.7.12" (two nicks to rim) **468**

Vase, 6" h., bulbous body tapering to small flared rim, matte drip glaze in shades of blue & green, early 20th c., SEG (minor flakes edge of base) **259**

Vase, 4 1/4" h., 3 3/4" d., ovoid body w/a closed rim, dark bluish grey ground, decorated around the upper half w/a landscape in shades of blue outlined in black, stamped circular Paul Revere mark & "5-25 - E.M.," 1925...................... **935**

Peters & Reed

In 1897 John D. Peters and Adam Reed formed a partnership to produce flowerpots in Zanesville, Ohio. Formally incorporated as Peters and Reed in 1901, this type of production was the mainstay until after 1907 when they gradually expanded into the art pottery field. Frank Ferrell, a former designer at the Weller Pottery, developed the "Moss Aztec" line while associated with Peters and Reed and other art lines followed. Though unmarked, attribution is not difficult once familiar with the various lines. In 1921, Peters and Reed became Zane Pottery which continued in production until 1941.

Peters & Reed Mark

Vase, 8 3/8" h., footed bulbous base tapering to slightly flared rim, decorated w/high glaze Chromal landscape scene in rich shades of blue, rust, cream, green & cobalt, unmarked...................... **$440**

drippy semi-matte glaze, stamped mark, paper label...................... 660

Vase, 5" h., 5" d., a cylindrical foot supporting a wide short flaring cylindrical body w/a wide shoulder tapering sharply to a short flared neck, overall purple mirror glaze, impressed circular mark..................... 770

Vase, 5 1/2" h., 5 1/2" d., bulbous ovoid body w/a rounded shoulder tapering to a wide short flaring neck, overall streaky turquoise & taupe lustred glaze, impressed circular mark................................. 715

Vase, 7" h., 5 1/4" d., flaring cylindrical body w/a wide angled shoulder centering a narrow neck w/molded rim, unusual brown, green & blue dripping matte glaze, stamped mark (reglued chip on base) 660

Vase, 8" h., 6" d., baluster-form w/the wide shoulder tapering to a short rolled neck, overall lustered dark blue glaze, impressed mark... 825

Moss Aztec Vase & Wall Pocket

Vase, 9 3/4" h., Moss Aztec line, tapering cylindrical body decorated w/relief-molded pine cone decoration on matte brown ground w/green tinting, unmarked (ILLUS. right)... 330

Wall pocket, conical, decorated at the top w/band of relief-molded Art Nouveau style poppies, matte brown ground w/green tinting, designed by Frank Ferrell & artist-signed, 9 1/4" h. (ILLUS. left) 138

Pewabic

Mary Chase Perry (Stratton) and Horace J. Caulkins were partners in this Detroit, Michigan pottery. Established in 1903, Pewabic Pottery evolved from their Revelation Pottery, "Pewabic" meaning "clay with copper color" in the language of Michigan's Chippewa Indians. Caulkins attended to the clay formulas and Mary Perry Stratton was artistic creator of forms & glaze formulas, eventually developing a wide range of colors for her finely textured glazes. The pottery's reputation for fine wares and architectural tiles enabled it to survive the depression years of the 1930s. After Caulkins died in 1923, Mrs. Stratton continued to be active in the pottery until her death, at age ninety-four, in 1961. Her contributions to the art pottery field are numerous.

Pewabic Pottery Mark

Box, cov., rectangular w/flat corners, center of lid w/relief-molded antelope, iridescent cream, yellow & green glaze, impressed "Pewabic Detroit," 4 3/4" w., 1 7/8" h. $358

Vase, 3 1/2" h., 5 1/4" d., wide bulbous ovoid body w/a wide shoulder tapering to a wide flat molded rim, black, green & lavender lustred glaze, impressed circular mark.. 495

Vase, 3 3/4" h., 5" d., wide squatty bulbous form w/a wide rounded shoulder centering a short tapering cylindrical neck, overall unusual blue, green & mauve

Pisgah Forest Pottery

Walter Stephen experimented with making pottery shortly after 1900 with his parents in Tennessee. After their deaths in 1910, he eventually moved to the foot of Mt. Pisgah in North Carolina where he became a partner of C.P. Ryman. Together they built a kiln and a shop but this partnership was dissolved in 1916. During 1920 Stephen again began to experiment with pottery and by 1926 had his own pottery and equipment. Pieces are usually marked and may also be signed "W. Stephen" and dated. Walter Stephen died in 1961 but work at the pottery still continues, although on a part-time basis.

Pisgah Forest Marks

Bowl, 5 1/4" d., Cameo Ware, round, slightly curved sides, covered wagon scene in white on matte olive green ground, decorated by Walter Stephen, ca. 1953, marked "1953 Cameo Stephen Longpine Ardenne" on base & "Stephen" in white slip on side, 5 1/4" d., 2 1/4" h. $138

Creamer, Cameo Ware, bulbous shape w/small pinched spout & C-form handle, scene of covered wagon pulled by oxen on matte olive green ground, decorated by Walter Stephen, ca. 1953, Longpine Ardenne mark, artist's name in white slip, paper label from Allanstand Mountain Crafts, Asheville, N.C. on bottom, 3 1/8" h.. 220

Teapot, cov., Cameo Ware, bulbous body w/inset lid w/button finial, short spout & C-form handle, pioneer family & cov. wagon scene in heavy white slip on medium blue ground, decorated by Walter Stephen, ca. 1953, Longpine Ardenne mark & date on bottom, artist's name on side, 5" h.. 303

Vase, 4" h., 5 1/2" d., wide squatty bulbous body w/the shoulder sloping to a low molded wide mouth, overall streaky white & blue crystalline exterior glaze, raised potter's mark, 1948 605

Vase, 4 1/2" h., 6" d., wide bulbous form w/a wide, short flat neck, overall white crystalline exterior glaze, raised potter's mark, 1942 330

Vase, 5" h., broad ovoid form tapering to a wide flat mouth flanked by strap shoulder handles, glossy soft green & blue glaze, raised mark, 1932 115

Vase, 7 1/4" h., wide shoulder tapering to the base, extended neck, crystallized blue glaze over a mustard yellow ground, raised mark 546

Vase, 7 3/4" h., 4 1/4" d., baluster-form w/flared neck, overall streaky blue, green & white crystalline glaze, raised potter's mark, 1949 495

Quimper

This French earthenware pottery has been made in France since the end of the 17th century and is still in production today. Because the colorful decoration on this ware, predominantly of Breton peasant figures, is all hand-painted and each piece is unique, it has become increasingly popular with collectors in recent years. Most pieces offered today date from about the mid-19th century to the present. Modern potteries continue to operate today and contemporary examples are available in gift shops.

Quimper Marks

Advertising Plaque & Pot de Creme Set

Advertising plaque, w/bracket support, for Grande Maison, "HB QUIMPER Decor Main" in bold blue letters,5 1/2" l., 4" h., mint (ILLUS. far right) $185

Bank, figural, Modern Movement, modeled as lady holding her pocketbook & umbrella, original metal closure on bottom, Henriot Quimper France, 5" h., mint.............. 200

Bell, w/original unglazed clapper, depicting traditional peasant man w/greenery to either side, reverse decorated w/floral spray, HB Quimper xxo, 4" h., 3 1/2" w., mint.. 175

Bouillon, cov., traditional peasant man on lid, lady decorates the bowl's interior, rose pink florals, HB Quimper France 179 P.u., 7" d. handle to handle, mint.............. 35

Bowl, salad, 10 1/2" d., 3" h., scalloped rim, pierced for hanging, decorated w/peasant lady w/floral sprays to either side & encirled by a floral garland, Henriot Quimper France 143, excellent (very minor glaze wear on rim)................................... 145

Butter tub, cov., "Croisille" patt., lid w/cartouche of seated man playing flute, encircled by alternating panels of blue lattice work & stylized dogwood blossoms, Henriot Quimper 14, 6 1/2", excellent (two minor chips under lid) 250

Calottes Plates

Calottes (flat European soup plates), one w/detailed peasant man playing flute, framed by a border of alternating red lattice & yellow wild gorse flowers, the other features a lady holding a flower w/matching border, Hb Quimper 222, 9 1/2" d., pr., mint (ILLUS.)... 600

Candlestick, octagonal base, peasant man w/florals, alternating panels of blue lattice work & flowers, Henriot Quimper France 78, 8" h. (broken in half & reglued)................. 80

Chamberstick, leaf-shaped w/ring handle, peasant lady w/floral garland border, Henriot Quimper France, 6 1/2" l., excellent (small professional mend on rim).......... 235

"Broderie Bretonne" Pattern Charger

Charger, "Broderie Bretonne" patt., bust portrait of elderly peasant woman encircled by raised enamel work resembling Breton embroidery on a navy background glaze, HB Quimper A 64, chip on underside of rim, 12 5/8" d., excellent (ILLUS.) 500

Cornucopia-vase, bud, 4 3/4" h., oval base, peasant lady w/florals, "Souvenir Quimper" written on base, HR Quimper, mint.. **225**

Cornucopia-vase, triple, traditional peasant lady on one compartment, flower sprays adorning the other two, 11" h., very good (two small chips on base)............. **125**

"Broderie" Cup & Saucer & Pitcher

Cup & saucer, "Broderie" patt., black background glaze w/wide yellow banded rim, applied raised enamel stylized heart design, HB Quimper d.306 f.436 P, mint, the set (ILLUS. left)............................... **25**

Cup & saucer, green dolphin handle, cup w/peasant man & floral garland border, floral garland on saucer, Henriot Quimper France, cup 5" lip to handle tip, saucer 6" d., pr., excellent **60**

Cup & saucer, hexagonal w/wishbone handle, facing peasant couple on two panels, floral sprays on the other four, Henriot Quimper France 74 & 76, pr., very good **60**

Dish, almond-shaped w/shallow flared sides & loop end handles, a leafy scroll border around a central polychrome scene of two men w/bagpipes & a horn, mark on the front "HB Quimper O," marked on back "HB," 14" l............................ **550**

Dish, model of a squatty bulbous cloth bag w/upright flared & scalloped opening w/drawstring, polychrome decoration of a standing peasant woman flanked by bands of flowers, marked "H.R. Quimper," 5 1/2" d. (chips on bottom from kiln adhesion, minor edge damage)...... **385**

Dish, child's, Modern Movement, geometric decoration in colors w/stylized star pattern, Henriot Quimper L.C., 2" d., mint............. **35**

Dish, child's, Modern Movement, geometric decoration in colors w/stylized flower blossom pattern, Henriot Quimper, 3" d., mint................. **30**

Dish, pierced for hanging, shell-shaped, "Soleil" patt., traditional scene of peasant man w/florals, H.B. Quimper France 119, 7 1/4" h. mint.. **60**

Egg cup, figural swan, blue feathers, spotted breast & striped neck, Henriot Quimper, 2 " h., 3 1/4" l., mint **85**

Figure group, St. Anne, wearing a bright yellow robe covered w/black ermine tails, reading scripture from a scroll to the child Mary, Henriot Quimper, 12" h., very good (flat chip off base)............................. **200**

Figure of a peasant man, standing in native costume & playing a bagpipe, polychrome decoration, marked "Yann - H. Quimper 23," 3 3/4" h. (edge flakes)............. **330**

Hors d'oeuvre dish, three-section w/figural swan handle, "Ivoire corbeille" patt. w/portrait busts of a peasant man & lady in each of the two compartments, floral decoration in third section, Henriot Quimper France 115, 11 1/2" d., mint.......... **300**

Inkwell, cov., low tapering square form w/scalloped bottom edges, the top centered by a round cover w/knob finial, the sides painted in polychrome w/flowers on three sides & a seated boy playing a flute on the other, marked "Henriot Quimper France," 3 3/4" w. **275**

Inkwell, double, cov. w/inserts, man w/flute posed between two wells, floral garlands on base & backstand, small seashell on top, Henriot Quimper France, 4" h., 7" l., mint... **775**

"Decor riche" Pattern Jardiniere

Jardiniere, "Decor riche" patt., center cartouche w/Crest of Brittany w/ermine tails, flanked by seated peasants resting beneath trees, Henriot Quimper 11, 9 1/2" h., 12 1/2" l., mint (ILLUS.).............. **1,050**

Knife rest, figural, Modern Movement, reclining sailor resting on his back w/head cupped by his folded hands, by C. Maillard, Henriot Quimper, C. Maillard, 4 1/4" l., mint **150**

Quimper Figural Lamp Base

Lamp base, figural, Modern Movement, peasant girl resting a basket on her shoulder at the water's edge, a pair of mallard ducks rest beside her feet on one side & a pair of mottled hens rest at the other, by C. Maillard, Henriot Quimper, C. Maillard, 10" h., 7" w., mint (ILLUS.)........ **650**

Match holder, traditional peasant lady w/blue lattice work on outer edges of compartment, yellow glaze, Henriot Quimper France 109, 3" h., mint **175**

Meat platter, 11 x 17" oval, "suject ordinaire" patt., peasant lady flanked w/flower branches & framed by concentric blue & yellow band border, Henriot Quimper France 457, mint **275**

"Decor riche" Pattern Melonniere

Melonniere, "Decor riche" patt., full-figure Breton couple surrounded by blue acanthus border w/Crest of Brittany above the scene & seashells adorning the handles, Henriot Quimper in blue, 10 3/4" d. handle to handle (ILLUS.) **950**

Pipe rack, hanging-type, w/raised crown above a shield at the top & impressed seashell on base, peasant lady framed within the shield, outlined by floral sprays, holds five pipes, Henriot Quimper France 505, 6 1/2" h., 11" l., excellent (chip on back where hung on wall) **275**

Pitcher, 5" h., classically-shaped, "Broderie" patt., black background glaze w/wide yellow bands compliment the stylized heart pattern executed in raised enamel work, HB Quimper f.295 d.306 Pi., mint (ILLUS. right with cup & saucer) **25**

Pitcher, 6 1/4" h., "biberon," gresware w/geometric pattern in navy, black, dark brown & cream, HB Quimper Odetta v., mint **500**

Pitcher, 8" h., bulbous, traditional peasant man & florals, concentric bands of blue & yellow encircling the base & neck, "Henriot Quimper France 198" signed beneath handle, mint **225**

Pitcher, 8" h., figural, Modern Movement, Breton lady's head, ribbons from her coif form the handle & spout is formed by tip of her coif, HB Quimper 228, mint **150**

Plate, 7" d., decorated w/bust portrait of peasant lady, gresware w/deep brown, tan, black & white glazes, HB Quimper, Odella 176, mint **300**

Plate, 9 1/2" d., dinner, traditional peasant lady decoration in center surrounded by a garland border w/rose pink florals, HB Quimper 176 PE, mint **35**

Plate, 9 3/4" d., Modern Movement, "La Mer" patt., conch shells surrounded by fine green striped border, by Mathurin Meheut, Henriot Quimper w/"MM" in circle, slight rim wear, very good **275**

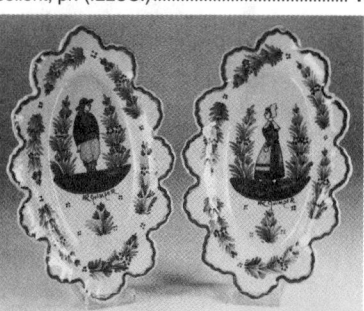

Quimper Floral Plates

Plates, 8 1/4" d., floral decoration w/concentric yellow & blue banded border, Henriot Quimper France 40 in blue, excellent, pr. (ILLUS.) **150**

Quimper Plates with Peasant Figures

Plates, 6 3/4 x 10 1/2" oval, pierced for hanging, scalloped rim, "Demi-fantasie" patt., facing w/three quarter peasant man on one, the other w/peasant woman w/hand in apron pocket, HR Quimper, pr. mint **900**

Quimper Platter with Peasant

Platter, 7 1/4 x 11 3/4", oval, "faience populaire" patt. w/scalloped rim, white ground decorated in the center w/a standing peasant man w/walking stick flanked by brush stroke flowers, garland border trim, mid 19th c., unsigned, mint (ILLUS.) **160**

Unusual Quimper Platter

Platter, 10 x 13 3/4" l. oval, peasant man executed in an artistic manner seated beneath a tree & pouring cider from a Quimper pitcher into a cup, yellow glaze, HB Quimper O & R, mint............................ **1,300**

"Decor riche" Pattern Platter

Platter, 10 1/2 x 14" rectangular w/cut corners, "Decor riche" patt., facing peasant couple, she is knitting, he is smoking a pipe, blue acanthus work border outlined w/a small orange stripe, HB Quimper on front & back, excellent (ILLUS.) **1,000**

Pot de creme set, four pots & covers w/octagonal open handled tray w/scalloped rim; "Fleuri Royale" patt., bold pink daisy design, HB Quimper France CP 199, tray 9 x 11 1/2", the set, mint (ILLUS. left & center back w/advertising plaque) **300**

Salt basket, double-type w/connecting handle in the yellow glaze "Soleil" patt., floral decoration w/blue forget-me-nots on both chambers, HB Quimper France, 122..L, 4" l., 2 1/2" h., mint **75**

Salt shaker, figural, Modern Movement, Breton sailor's head wearing blue beret w/rose colored pompom, HB Quimper p 18 _a 53, 4" h., mint **175**

Snuff bottle, figural, model of a bagpipe, decorated w/a peasant lady w/flowers to either side & a spray of flowers on the reverse, 19th c., bold HR mark, 3" l., excellent **275**

Snuff bottle, heart-shaped, pansy flower w/blue sponged edges, reverse w/peasant lady decoration, unsigned, 3" l., mint **275**

"Ivoire Corbeille" Soup Tureen

Soup tureen, cov., "Ivoire Corbeille" patt. footed bulbous form w/slightly domed lid w/blue finial, blue shoulder handles, bowl w/bust of peasant man surrounded by half sunflowers, scalloped design on lid w/half sunflowers & small flower buds, Henriot Quimper 118, 13 1/2" d. handle to handle, 8" h., mint (ILLUS.) **550**

"Fruits de la Mer" Pattern Teapot

Teapot, cov., "Fruits de la Mer" patt., black glaze ground w/conch shells & seaweed decoration, by Guy Trevoux, Henriot Quimper, 9 1/2" h., mint (ILLUS.) **300**

Tiles, "suject ordinaire" patt., peasant man & woman framed by concentric yellow & blue banded border, Herriot Quimper France 498, 4 5/8" sq., matching pr., mint **200**

Tray, round, "Croisille" patt., peasant man smoking pipe w/lady balancing milk pail on her head, alternating panels of blue lattice work & stylized dogwood blossoms form border, Henriot Quimper 143, 9 1/2" d., mint **425**

Bagpipe-shaped Tray

Tray, bagpipe-shaped, center w/traditional peasant couple, plants & tree, surrounded by sprigs of blue forget-me-nots, pale blue glaze w/dark blue ribbon & bow trimmed border, HB Quimper on front beneath figures, 12 1/2 x 16 1/4", mint (ILLUS.).. **775**

"Decor Henriot" Tray

Tray, octagonal, "Decor Henriot" patt., large D-form blue end handles, center decoration of facing peasant couple, flanked by tall floral sprays & surrounded by narrow concentric blue bands w/yellow border, HB-Henriot stamped mark (recent production), couple of spots retouched before firing at factory -factory second, 11 x 18 1/2', mint (ILLUS.) **80**

Vase with Courting Scene

Vase, 10 1/4" h., ovoid body w/short tapering cylindrical neck, "Broderie Bretonne" patt., scene of courting Breton couple, he offers her a flower, she is knitting, raised enamel work resembling Breton embroidery, navy ground glaze, HB Quimper 510, mint (ILLUS.) **425**

Vases, 12" h., "Demi-fantasie" patt., trumpet-shape w/scrolled blue tripod base, each depicting a peasant figure w/florals, HR Quimper, professional restoration to mouth of each, very good, pr. (ILLUS. top next column) **1,250**

Wall piece, scalloped rim & small loop at top, traditional peasant man w/fir tree & greens to either side, encircled by blue brush stroke border, HB Quimper D. M BREST 1972, 5 1/4" d., mint **45**

"Demi-Fantasie" Pattern Vases

Wall pocket, bagpipe-shaped, "Demi-fantasie" patt., three quarter portrait of portly peasant man smoking pipe, flanked w/flowers, blue bow at top & bottom w/red "S" link chain on outer edges, Henriot Quimper France 73, 7 1/2" l., excellent **325**

Redware

Red earthenware pottery was made in the American colonies from the late 1600s. Bowls, crocks and all types of utilitarian wares were turned out in great abundance to supplement the pewter and handmade treenware. The ready availability of the clay, the same used in making bricks and roof tiles, accounted for the vast production. The lead-glazed redware retained its reddish color though a variety of colors could be obtained by adding various metals to the glaze. Interesting effects occurred accidentally through unsuspected impurities in the clay or uneven temperatures in the firing kiln which sometimes resulted in streaks or mottled splotches.

Redware pottery was seldom marked by the maker.

Bowl, 10 3/4" d., 4 3/4" h., upright slightly flared sides w/molded rim, brown sponge decoration around the rim & in lines down the sides, 19th c. (hairlines in base, rim flakes) **$303**

Bowl, 7" d., 3 1/4" h., flat bottom, flat flaring deep sides & molded rim, dark brown sponging on a deep orange ground **440**

Chamber pot, footed deep rounded form w/a flat wide rim & applied strap handle, incised line decoration, New Hampshire, 19th c., 5 1/2" h. (glaze chips) **690**

Crock, tapered ovoid body w/incised lines around the shoulder, transparent glaze w/touches of green, New Hampshire, 19th c., 15 1/2" h. (chips, cracks) **920**

Dish, round shallow form, brown sponging on an orange ground, 4 3/8" d. (minor chips) **330**

Food mold, deep rounded exterior w/central shaft on interior surrounded by spiraled flutes below the scalloped rim, brown sponging on a pinkish amber ground, 8" d. (wear, slight hairline) **138**

Food mold, Turk's turban-form, mottled brown glaze on the exterior, impressed "John Bell," Pennsylvania, 6 3/8" d., 3 3/4" h. (hairlines, small chip on base) **275**

Jar, cov., large bulbous ovoid form tapering to a short rolled neck w/an inset flat cover, overall mottled & spotted green & tan-spotted slip glaze, a miniature jar forming the finial on the cover & glazed in dark brown splashes on tan slip, decorated on the shoulder w/a comical figure waving a banner w/the initials "S.A.B.," the base inscribed "Made in the year 1829 in June the 16th day on Sunday morning," part of the inscription nearly obliterated, Massachusetts or Rhode Island, 16" h. (edge chips) **63,000**

Jar, cylindrical body tapering to molded rim, tooled lines at shoulder rim, glazed base, green & red mottled glaze w/orange spots, Galena, Illinois-type, 5" d., 6" h. (rim flakes) **330**

Jar, wide ovoid form w/molded flared rim & small applied strap handle at rim, mottled brown glaze, 4 5/8" d., 5 1/8" h. (wear at rim) **330**

Jar, wide ovoid form w/wide cylindrical neck & eared shoulder handles, tooled lines, dark brown glaze w/brown flecks, 12 1/2" h. **176**

Jug, globular w/strap handle rising from midsection to rim, dark ivory glaze over red glaze, sgraffito designs include chains around shoulder & applied handle, man w/top hat, coat & breeches & carrying a shovel beside a dog & farm w/"Samuel Mellvill" above "Always this full of good Whiskey" & a heart w/banner reading "SM, JM, 1816," 7 1/8" h. (flaking glaze & handle crack) **3,850**

Jug, sharply tapering ovoid form w/a thin footring & small ringed mouth, applied strap handle, dark brown glaze w/black running spots around the shoulder & handle, 8" h. (old edge chips) **550**

Jug, small ovoid form decorated w/dark brown splotches, Maine, 19th c., 7 1/2" h. (chips) **633**

Milk bowl, round w/deep flat slightly flaring sides & molded rim, daubs of brown glaze on an orange ground, 13" d., 5 1/2" h. (wear) **715**

Milk bowl, unglazed exterior w/a flared rim & tapered sides, glazed interior w/small brown running streaks, found in Virginia, 18" d. (old chips) **248**

Model of a dog, reclining figure w/forlorn expression & head on paws, hand-molded & tooled w/dark brown glaze, 8 7/8" l., 3 1/8" h. **110**

Model of a rooster, stylized bird in a prancing pose w/head raised for crowing w/beak open, molded high arched tail feather, molded legs part of the molded base, mottled greenish glaze, incised label "R.R. Stahl 11-4-50," Stahl Pottery, Powder Valley, Pennsylvania, 4 1/4" h. **220**

Mug, footed squatty bulbous body w/a wide flat flaring rim, applied C-form handle, dark brown splotches on a burnt orange ground, 3 1/2" h. (edge wear, chips) **138**

Pie plate, coggled rim, green wavy daubing, 7 1/8" d. **605**

Pie plate, coggled rim, shiny glaze w/a burnt orange color, 10 1/2" d. (wear) **165**

Pitcher, 5 3/4" h., cov., bulbous body w/applied handle, dark brown sponged vertical lines (rim flakes) **660**

Pitcher, 7" h., bulbous body w/pinched spout, D-form handle, mottled green, brown & ivory glaze, possibly Shenandoah Valley (wear & some flaking) **2,035**

Pitcher, 7 1/8" h., 5 1/8" d., bulbous ovoid body w/applied ribbed strap handle, running brown glaze **385**

Pitcher, 8" h., ovoid w/molded lines at the rim, shoulder & handle, mottled pale green, yellow & brown drip glaze, New England, early 19th c. (spout & rim chips, glaze loss on handle) **1,495**

Pitcher, 9 1/4" h., bulbous w/flared rim & applied handle, light brown & green glaze w/dark brown splotches (edge chips & a firing separation at foot) **880**

Pitcher, 11" h., ovoid body w/ribbed strap handle & molded lip, dark brown splotches on an orange ground w/glossy glaze (chips, short hairline at rim) **495**

Preserving jar, cylindrical w/molded rim, green & orange glaze w/orange & yellow spots, Galena, Illinois-type, 5" d., 7 3/4" h. (minor roughness) **578**

Preserving jar, cylindrical w/tapering neck & flared rim, eared shoulder handles, greenish cream-colored slip w/reddish tan mottled glaze w/vertical brown squiggle bands, paper label reads "George McKearin Collection of American Pottery," 8" h. (chips) **2,860**

Whistle, figural, model of a bird w/a bulbous ovoid body w/a flat bottom, a short neck w/head & straight angle cylindrical tail forming whistle opening, mottled black & speckled glaze, 3 1/4" d., 2 1/2" h. **385**

Ridgways

There were numerous Ridgways among English potters. The firm J. & W. Ridgway operated in Shelton from 1814 to 1930 and produced many pieces with scenes of historical interest. William Ridgway operated in Shelton from 1830 to 1865. Most wares marked Ridgway that have been offered in this country were made by one of these two firms, or by Ridgway Potteries, Ltd., still in operation.

Also see HISTORICAL & COMMEMORATIVE WARES.

Ridgways Mark

Platter, 15" l., oval, Oriental patt., center landscape scene w/castle & figures, floral border w/temple cartouche, blue, 15" l. **$220**

Platter, 15" l., oval, Oriental patt., central landscape scene w/castle & figures, border w/alternating cartouches of flowers & temples, blue.. **440**
Vegetable dish, cov., oblong, Oriental patt., decroated w/scenes of temples, trees & flowers, blue, 10 1/2" l. (minor hairline) **825**

Rockingham Wares

The Marquis of Rockingham first established an earthenware pottery in the Yorkshire district of England around 1745 and it was occupied afterwards by various potters. The well-known mottled brown Rockingham glaze was introduced about 1788 by the Brameld Brothers and became immediately popular. 'It was during the 1820s that the production of true porcelain began at the factory and continued to be made until the firm closed in 1842. Since that time the so-called Rockingham glaze has been used by various potters in England and the United States, including some famous wares produced in Bennington, Vermont. However, very similar glazes were also used by potteries in other areas of the United States including Ohio and Indiana and only wares specifically attributed to Bennington should use that name. The following listings will include mainly wares featuring the dark brown mottled glaze produced at various sites here and abroad.

Cuspidor, footed round squatty bulbous paneled shape w/rolled & scalloped rim, dark brown running glaze w/bluish green spots on top, 9" d. **$110**
Flask, model of potato w/small molded mouth, mottled dark brown glaze, 5 1/4" h... **275**
Food mold, Turk's turban-form, interior w/molded swirled ribs & scalloped rim, mottled brown glaze, 9 5/8" d., 3 1/2" h. (minor roughness)..................................... **72**
Hot plate, round w/ridged edge, three small feet, center w/molded eagle surrounded by four urns, mottled dark brown glaze, 7 3/8" d. **550**
Loving cup, two-handled, cylindrical w/applied scenes of men w/a lantern, dogs & a man seated at a table holding a pitcher, raised leaves around the rim, mottled dark brown glaze, 12" d. at handles, 7" h. (glaze bubbles burst on interior & table ring).. **358**
Model of a dog, seated Spaniel on a thick rectangular base, free-standing front legs, mottled dark brown glaze, 10 3/4" h. (chips on base)......................... **330**
Pitcher, 8 5/8" h., footed, squatty bulbous base tapering slightly to wide cylindrical neck w/slightly flared rim, pinched spout & C-form applied strap handle, mottled brown glaze (flake on end of handle)........... **303**
Platter, octagonal, 9 3/8 x 12 1/2", large splotched glaze design, impressed mark on back (minor firing flaw)........................... **715**
Toby jug, tall bust portrait of a military man w/a tricorner hat & wearing a uniform, wide band around the base embossed "Duke of Wellington - born 1st May 1769 - Died 14th Sept. 1859," base impressed "Thompson," 8" h. (glaze chip on hat rim partially ground)................................,........... **193**

Rookwood

Considered America's foremost art pottery, the Rookwood Pottery Company was established in Cincinnati, Ohio in 1880, by Mrs. Maria Nichols Longworth Storer. To accurately record its development, each piece carried the Rookwood insignia, or mark, was dated, and, if individually decorated, was usually signed by the artist. The pottery remained in Cincinnati until 1959 when it was sold to Herschede Hall Clock Company and moved to Starkville, Mississippi, where it continued in operation until 1967.

A private company is now producing a limited variety of pieces using original Rookwood molds.

Rookwood Mark

Ewer, tall slender ovoid body tapering to a rolled rim w/pinched spout, applied shoulder strap handle, decorated w/pale orange chrysanthemum blossoms & green leaves on a warm brown ground, Standard glaze, No. 433, 1888, Harriet Elizabeth Wilcox, 7" h................................. **$748**
Plaque, rectangular, decorated w/an unusual pastoral landscape w/a path & large trees in the foreground & a misty valley in the distance, in soft tones of blue, green, mauve & pink, Vellum glaze, in original wide molded giltwood frame, date obscured, Frederick Rothenbusch, tile 8 1/2 x 11".. **6,600**
Plaque, rectangular, wooded riverside scene w/tall trees on the left river bank, shades of blue, green & peach, Vellum glaze, 1917, Elizabeth McDermott, in original wide flat wood frame w/scroll-molded border band, 6 1/4 x 8 1/4"............ **3,680**
Plaque, rectangular, a landscape of trees by a path at dusk, Vellum glaze, 1927, Fred Rothenbusch, framed, 14 x 16"....... **19,550**
Plaque, rectangular, cameo-style scene of relief-molded figures of men & women in Roman style, semi-gloss cream against a blue Matte glaze, in Arts & Crafts oak frame, 19" l., 8" h. (minor chips to edges) **550**
Plate, 6 1/2" d., Limoges-style decoration w/center scene of water bird in black w/black reeds & gold highlights, scalloped rim w/gold trim, No. 87, 1882, N.J. Hirschfeld (minor flakes) **198**
Plate, 12" d., decorated w/daisies on a sienna ground, Cameo glaze, No. 520, 1890, Harriet E. Wilcox.. **575**
Vase, 4 1/2" h., simple ovoid form w/slightly flared wide mouth, a border of raised berry decoration, blue Matte drip glaze w/a slight crystalline effect, No. 212, 1928.......... **288**
Vase, 5 3/4" h., 4 1/2" d., bulbous ovoid body tapering to a short wide neck, decorated around the shoulder w/a wide band of large yellow roses & green

leaves on a pale butter yellow ground, Vellum glaze, No. 1914, 1927, Lenora Asbury **880**

Vase, 5 7/8" h., simple ovoid form w/the flat mouth flanked by small angled shoulder handles, decorated w/honeysuckle blossoms on a shaded gold & brown ground, Standard glaze, 1900, Adeliza Drake Sehon (crazing, minor scratches) **489**

Vase, 6 1/2" h., bulbous ovoid w/closed rim, decorated w/carved & painted white & brown geese feeding at edge of pond, green grass in background shading from grey to yellow to green, Vellum glaze, No. 938D, incised signature & "V," 1907, Edith Noonan **2,420**

Vase, 6 1/2" h., footed squatty bulbous base w/the rounded shoulder tapering to a wide cylindrical neck w/flared rim, decorated w/a large yellow iris blossom & green leaves on a golden, green & brown ground, Standard glaze, 1889, Amelia Browne Sprague **575**

Vase, 6 1/2" h., tapering cylindrical body w/slightly flared rim, band near bottom decorated w/scene of boats in cobalt blue against a cream sea & sky, cobalt blue Vellum glaze, incised initials, incised "GV," No. 1658F, 1912, Lenore Asbury **1,320**

Vase, 6 1/2" h., tapering cylindrical form w/a flattened closed rim, molded around the shoulder w/a repeating design of dragonflies, Matte turquoise glaze, 1927 .... **403**

Vase, 6 1/2" h., 3 1/2" d., simple ovoid form w/molded rim, scenic decoration of a snowy landscape in green, purple & ivory, Vellum glaze, No. 913E, 1918, Elizabeth McDermott **1,100**

Vase, 6 3/4" h., swelled cylindrical form, decorated w/a waterside landscape in greens, blues & browns against a summer sky of peach, pale green & lavender, Vellum glaze, No. 551, 1921, Fred Rothenbush **1,495**

Vase, 7" h., tapering cylindrical body w/flat rim, scene of bluish green fish swimming against a pink shaded to green ground, Iris glaze, No. 1358E, 1911, Lenore Asbury **1,540**

Vase, 7 1/2" h., tapering cylindrical body w/wide flat rim, decorated w/painted & carved mushrooms in peach & white outlined in black against a light lavender ground, Vellum glaze, No. 2066, 1916, impressed "V" & incised unknown artist signature **1,210**

Vase, 7 1/2" h., 3 3/4" d., slightly swelled cylindrical form w/a tapering shoulder to the molded rim, scenic design of tall slender trees in a misty landscape in shades of grey, blue & purple, Vellum glaze, No. 2001, 1914, C. J. McLaughlin (minor pitting) **935**

Vase, 8" h., tall slender slightly waisted cylindrical body on four small tab feet, embossed around the lower half w/curling fern fronds, deep rose shaded to dusty green Matte glaze, No. 1374, 1903, K. Shirayamadani **495**

Vase, 9 1/8" h., wide ovoid body tapering to a wide flat rim flanked by small angled handles, decorated in low-relief w/dark orange poppies & green leaves on a shaded olive green & brown ground, Standard glaze, No. 604C, Kataro Shirayamadani **1,840**

Vase, 9 1/2" h., 5" d., gently flaring cylindrical form w/rounded shoulder tapering to a short molded neck, decorated w/large pink & yellow roses & green leafy stems on a shaded pink to green ground, Iris glaze, No. 943C, 1904, Ed Diers (slight crazing) **2,200**

Vase, 9 1/2" h., 6 1/4" d., Jewel Porcelain, bulbous ovoid body tapering to a wide narrow molded rim, decorated w/large pink & blue magnolia blossoms on a brown ground, drilled base, No. 5184, date obscured, K. Shirayamadani **2,310**

Vase, 9 5/8" h., bulbous nearly spherical body tapering to a tall slender trumpet neck w/wide ruffled rim, decorated w/holly & berries in autumn colors on a shaded yellow, dark green & brown ground, overlaid around the upper neck & bottom w/ornate meandering foliate silver overlay marked "Gorham Mfg. Co. R 727," Standard glaze, No. 614, 1892, indistinct artist's mark **1,840**

Vase, 9 3/4" h., 6" d., Jewel Porcelain, bulbous ovoid body w/a wide narrow molded rim, decorated w/a stylized bison in brown, black & bone, No. 6184C, 1944, Jens Jensen **2,860**

Vase, 10" h., 6 1/2" d., footed bulbous ovoid body w/a rounded shoulder tapering to a short rolled neck, finely painted w/goldenrod on leafy green stalks against a shaded grey ground, Iris glaze, No. 814A, 1902, Rose Fescheimer **4,400**

Vase, 11" h., 5 1/2" d., Jewel Porcelain, swelled cylindrical form w/short rolled neck, decorated w/a continuous wooded landscape w/blue & green trees on a shaded dark blue, white & light blue ground, No.892B, 1940, M.H. McDonald .. **3,190**

Vase, 11 " h., 5 1/2" d., tall ovoid form tapering to a short rolled neck, decorated w/large shaded blue & purple irises & bluish green leaves on a mottled blue ground, Wax Matte glaze, No. 614, 1929, Jens Jensen **2,420**

Vase, 12 1/2" h., 4 1/2" d., tall swelled cylindrical form w/a narrow tapering shoulder & rolled neck, decorated w/large pink & white magnolia blossoms on a shaded blue to white ground, Vellum glaze, No. 904C, 1930, Lenore Asbury **7,150**

Rose Medallion & Rose Canton

The lovely Chinese ware known as Rose Medallion was made through the past century and into the present one. It features alternating panels of people and flowers or insects with most pieces having four medallions with a central rose or peony medallion. The ware is called Rose Canton if florals and birds or insects fill all the panels. Unless otherwise noted, our listing is for Rose Medallion ware.

Bottle w/cover & basin, Rose Mandarin variant, 19th c., bottle 16" h., basin 15 7/8" d., 4 7/8" h. (chips, minor wear) .. **$1,840**

Bowl, shaped low oval form, 19th c. **288**

Bowl, cov., 5 7/8" d., Rose Mandarin variant, footed deep rounded sides w/C-scroll side handles, mistmatched low domed cover w/fruit finial w/underglaze-blue foliage & gilded fruit, the sides of the bowl decorated w/bands of Chinese figures........... **358**

Bowl, 8 3/8" d., Rose Mandarin variant, shallow round form w/tightly scalloped rim, the interior decorated w/four alternating reserves of figures or florals, the exterior decorated w/15 figures, orange peel glaze, 19th c. **523**

Bowl, 10" d., 4 7/8" h., Rose Mandarin variant, four-lobed rounded sides w/notched & down-curved rims, orange peel glaze, 19th c. **1,540**

Bowl, 10 5/8" d., 4" h., shallow w/scalloped sides, 19th c. (minor gilt & enamel wear, minute rim chips) **575**

Brush box, cov., rectangular w/interior divider, late 19th c., 3 3/4 x 7 1/2" **633**

Cake stand, a wide cylindrical foot supporting a wide shallow dished top decorated on the interior w/alternating floral & figural reserves, 19th c., 8 5/8" d., 3 3/4" h. (minor edge flakes) **468**

Candlesticks, cylindrical shaft above a flaring round foot, 19th c., 7" h., pr. (minor glaze wear) **1,495**

Candlesticks, tall slender cylindrical shaft flared at the base & w/a flared, flattened socket rim, 19th c., 9 1/4" h., pr. (minor chips) **1,035**

Charger, round, 12" d., 19th c. (minor glaze wear) **374**

Charger, ca. 1860, 14 1/2" d **728**

Cider jug, cov., Rose Mandarin patt., w/woven double strap applied handle, lid w/foo dog finial, 19th c., 9 1/2" (glaze wear, finial imperfections) **2,990**

Compote, 9 1/2" d., 3 1/2" h., 19th c. **288**

Compote, 11 x 14", 3" h., rounded diamond shape shallow bowl on a low flaring matching foot, 19th c. (imperfections) **748**

Dish, round w/scalloped edges, 19th c., 8" d. (minor gilt wear) **316**

Dish, Rose Mandarin variant, rectangular w/notched rounded corners & incurved shallow sides, central panel w/figures, orange peel glaze, 19th c., 9" l. **660**

Dish, Rose Mandarin variant, oblong gently lobed form, figural scene in the center, butterflies around the rim, orange peel glaze, 19th c., 10 3/4" l. (chip on table ring)........................... **605**

Dishes, almond-shaped, each shallow oblong piece decorated w/alternating figural & floral reserves, orange peel glaze, heavy gilt trim, 19th c., 10 3/4" l., pr. **660**

Fruit basket, oval w/deep gently flaring reticulated sides w/gilt leaf-form handles, 19th c., 8 1/2 x 10", 4" h. (minor gilt wear) **403**

Fruit basket, reticulated basket with undertray, 19th c. (glaze wear) **748**

Fruit basket & undertray, oval reticulated basket on matching oval undertray, China, 19th c., 8 3/4 x 10", overall 14 1/4" h. . **1,610**

Garden seat, barrel-form, paneled decoration of alternating court scenes & floral designs, 19th c., 18" h. (minor glaze wear) **1,380**

Garden seat, barrel-form, three rows of colorfully painted panels separated by bands of gilt bosses, 19th c., 18 1/2" h. (minor gilt wear)........................... **2,300**

Garden seat, paneled barrel-form w/alternating designs of court scenes & floral designs, China, 19th c., 18" h. (minor glaze wear)........................... **1,725**

Garden seat, Rose Mandarin variant, barrel-form body, decorated w/a court scene surrounding the central body w/upper & lower bands of butterflies & floral designs, China, 19th c., 18 1/2" h. (chips at interior bottom edge, minor glaze wear).... **2,645**

Mug, Rose Mandarin variant, tall cylindrical form w/decorated rim band above a band of three standing figures, entwined arched strap handle, 19th c., 4 7/8" h........... **550**

Plates: four 9 5/8" d. dinner plates, eight 8 1/2" d. luncheon plates, eight 6" d. bread & butter plates; 19th c., the set (minor chips, glaze wear) **920**

Plates, 8" d., luncheon, 19th c., set of 6 (minor glaze wear) **230**

Plates, 8 1/8" d., typical color palette, 19th c., set of 12 (minor rim chips, gilt & enamel wear)........................... **431**

Plates, 10" d., dinner, 19th c., one marked "Made in China," set of 6 (edge chips) **345**

Platter, 11 5/8" l., oval, Rose Mandarin variant, wide dished & flanged rim around the figural center scene, 19th c **660**

Platter, 15 3/4" l., oval, Rose Mandarin variant, 19th c. (gilt & enamel wear, minor chips)........................... **1,093**

Platter, 16 3/4" l., oval, Rose Mandarin variant **880**

Platter, 18" l., oval, 19th c. (minor glaze wear) **489**

Rose Mandarin Punch Bowl

Punch bowl, Rose Mandarin variant, deep rounded sides, interior & exterior decorated w/colorful panels of figures, florals & birds, 19th c., minor base chips, scratches, glaze loss, 13 1/2" d. (ILLUS.) . **1,495**

Punch bowl, Rose Mandarin variant, 19th c., 14 3/4" d. (glaze wear)........................... **2,645**

Salt dips, low oval waisted cylindrical base supporting an oval dished top, 19th c., 3 1/4 x 4 1/2", 1 1/2" h., pr. (minor imperfections) **1,725**

Serving bowl, shaped edges, 19th c., 9 1/2" d., 4 7/8" h. (very minor chips to base)... **1,093**

Serving dish, shallow lobed oval form, 19th c., 8 1/2 x 10 1/8", 1 3/4" h. (wear)................. **173**

Shrimp dish, irregular shallow rounded form w/a slightly scalloped long floral-decorated flange handle along one side, four panels on the interior, 19th c., 9 1/2 x 10" (glaze wear) **460**

Shrimp dishes, Rose Mandarin variant, shield form, one w/orange & gilt border, the other w/a floral border, 19th c., 9 3/4" d., 10" d., both (minor glaze wear) **978**

Tazza, shallow diamond-shaped bowl w/rounded corners raised on a deep conforming base w/decorative border band, 19th c., 14 1/8" l., 3 1/2" h. (minor gilt & enamel wear) **805**

Tea set: cov. 4 1/2" h. teapot, sugar, creamer, four cups w/saucers; late 19th c. (restoration to teapot spout, glaze wear)............. **805**

Teapot, cov., Rose Mandarin variant, gilt decorated spout & handle, 19th c., 8 1/4" h. (minor chips, glaze losses) **1,265**

Trembleuses, 19th c., 8 1/4" d., set of 8 (minor glaze wear) **316**

Urn, cov., Rose Mandarin variant, baluster-form w/a rounded domed cover w/a gilt seated Foo dog finial, gilt Foo dog mask shoulder handles, 19th c., 16" h. (minor glaze wear).. **1,380**

Vase, 17" h., Rose Mandarin variant, baluster-form w/flattened ruffled rim, the neck mounted w/facing pairs of recumbent gilt Foo dogs & kylins in gilt, 19th c. (minor glaze wear).. **1,495**

Vases, 9 1/4" h., baluster-form w/applied kylins & foo dogs, 19th c., pr. (minor gilt & enamel wear) **633**

Rose Mandarin Ku-form Vase

Vases, 12 3/8" h., 7 3/4" d., Ku-form w/raised acanthus leaf ribbing & gilt archaic dragon design on blue ground, first half 19th c., pr.(ILLUS. of one).................. **3,335**

Vases 15" h., baluster-form, the wide cylindrical neck w/a flaring rim & flanked by a

pair of molded foo dog handles, decorated w/panels of Oriental figures, birds & insects, ca. 1850, pr. **2,912**

Rose Medallion Covered Vases

Vases cov., 18 1/2" h., footed wide ovoid body tapering slightly to cylindrical neck flanked by figural handles, domed cover w/bud finial, on hardwood stands, gilt & enamel wear, minor chips to one lid, 19th c., pr. (ILLUS.) **2,860**

Vases 24" h., ovoid body tapering to tall cylindrical neck w/flaring rim, decorated around the neck w/applied kylins & foo dogs, 19th c., minor gilt & enamel wear, on hardwood stands, pr. **2,300**

Vegetable dish, cov., oval shaped form w/strap handles, 19th c., 6 1/4 x 10", 4" h. (minor glaze wear) **460**

Vegetable dish, cov., rectangular w/shaped corner & flanged rim, interior decoration, 19th c., 7 x 8", 4 3/4" h. (minor glaze wear)... **316**

Rose Medallion Wash Bowl & Pitcher

Wash bowl & pitcher, 14 3/4" h. bulbous ovoid body w/long slender angled handle, paneled decoration, 16" d. bowl w/deep rounded sides & flared rim, interior & rim w/matching decoration, 19th c., the set (ILLUS.) **633**

Water bottle, cov., 19th c., 14 1/2" h. (hairline, minute lid chip, minor gilt & enamel wear) **431**

Rose Medallion Water Bottle

Water bottle, cov., bulbous base w/tall slender cylindrical neck, small domed cover w/blossom finial, on hardwood stand, 19th, minor chips to lid, minor gilt & enamel wear, 15" h. (ILLUS.) 805

Roseville

Roseville Pottery Company operated in Zanesville, Ohio, from 1898 to 1954 after having been in business for six years prior to that in Muskingum County, Ohio. Art wares similar to those of Owens and Weller Potteries were produced. Items listed here are by patterns or lines.

Roseville

Roseville Mark

Apple Blossom (1948)
White apple blossoms in relief on blue, green or pink ground; brown tree branch handles.

Basket, hanging-type, green ground, 8" **$220**
Basket, hanging-type, pink ground, 8" **245**
Basket w/low overhead handle, blue ground, No. 310-10", 10" h. **280-285**
Basket w/low overhead handle, green ground, No. 310-10", 10" h. **300-350**
Basket w/overhead handle, blue ground, No. 309-8", 8" h. **315**
Basket w/overhead handle, green ground, No. 309-8", 8" h. **150-200**
Basket w/overhead handle, pink ground, No. 309-8", 8" h. **140**
Book ends, green ground, No. 359, pr. **198**
Book ends, pink ground, No. 359, pr. **260**
Bowl, 6 1/2" d., 2 1/2" h., flat handles, green ground, No. 326-6" **145**
Bowl, 8" d., blue ground, No. 328-8" **125**
Bowl, 8" d., green ground, No. 328-8" **83**
Candlesticks, pink ground, No. 351-2", 2" h., pr. **117**

Candlesticks, blue ground, No. 352-4 1/2", 4 1/2" h., pr. **350**
Console bowl, pink ground, No. 330-10", 10" l. **195**
Console bowl, blue ground, No. 331-12", 12" l. **195**
Console bowl, pink ground, No. 331-12", 12" l. **175**
Console bowl, green ground, No. 333-14", 14" l. **175-200**
Console bowl, pink ground, No. 333-14", 14" l. **175**
Cornucopia-vase, blue ground, No. 321-6", 6" h. **60**
Cornucopia-vase, green ground, No. 321-6", 6 " h. **68**
Cornucopia-vase, blue ground, No. 323-8", 8" h. **160**
Ewer, ovoid, pink ground, No. 316-8", 8" h. **143**
Flowerpot & saucer, pink ground, No. 356-5", 2 pcs. **170**
Jardiniere, blue ground, No. 300-4", 4" h. **140**
Jardiniere, green ground, No. 300-4", 4" h. **135**
Jardiniere, pink ground, No. 300-4", 4" h. **135**
Jardiniere, pink ground, No. 301-6", 6" h. **225**
Jardiniere & pedestal base, pink ground, No. 303-10", overall 31" h., 2 pcs. **1,250**
Teapot, cov., blue ground, No. 371-P **295**
Teapot, cov., pink ground, No. 371-P **260**
Vase, 6" h., two-handled, squatty base, long cylindrical neck, green ground, No. 381-6" **70**
Vase, 7" h., asymmetrical rim & handles, blue ground, No. 373-7" **225**

Apple Blossom Vase

Vase, 7" h., asymmetrical rim & handles, green ground, No. 373-7" (ILLUS.) **135**
Vase, 7" h., asymmetrical rim & handles, pink ground, No. 373-7" **195**
Vase, 7" h., flaring foot w/tapering cylindrical body, asymmetrical rim & handles, pink ground, No. 382-7" **90-100**
Vase, 7" h., flaring foot w/tapering cylindrical body, asymmetrical rim & handles, blue ground, No. 382-7" **130**
Vase, 8 1/4" h., flaring foot w/ovoid body & wide flaring rim, pointed handles from shoulder to middle of neck, blue ground, No. 385-8" **150-175**

Vase, 8 1/4" h., flaring foot w/ovoid body & wide flaring rim, pointed handles from shoulder to middle of neck, pink ground, No. 385-8" **185**

Vase, 9 1/2" h., 5" d., asymmetrical handles, cylindrical w/disc base, green ground, No. 387-9" **213**

Vase, 10" h., wide flaring foot w/base handles, trumpet-form body, blue ground, No. 388-10" **175-250**

Vase, 10" h., wide flaring foot w/base handles, trumpet-form body, green ground, No. 388-10" **297**

Vase, 10" h., wide flaring foot w/base handles, trumpet-form body, pink ground, No. 388-10" **350-400**

Vase, 10" h., swelled cylindrical body w/shaped rim, base handles, green ground, No. 389-10" **187**

Vase, 10" h., swelled cylindrical body w/shaped rim, base handles, pink ground, No. 389-10" **185**

Vase, 12 1/2" h., base handles, pink ground, No. 390-12" **295**

Vase, 15" h., floor-type, double base handles, short globular base, long cylindrical neck, pink ground, No. 392-15" **512**

Vases, 6" h., two-handled, squatty base, long cylindrical neck, blue ground, No. 381-6" **200**

Wall pocket, conical w/overhead handle, blue ground, No. 366-8", 8" h. **288**

Wall pocket, conical w/overhead handle, brown ground, No. 366-8", 8" h. **190**

Wall pocket, conical w/overhead handle, green ground, No. 366-8", 8" h. **185**

Window box, end handles, blue ground, No. 368-8", 2 1/2 x 10 1/2" **185**

Window box, rectangular, blue ground, No. 369-12", 12" l. **195**

Window box, rectangular, green ground, No. 369-12", 12" l. **160**

Bittersweet (1940)
Orange bittersweet pods and green leaves on a grey blending to rose, yellow with terra cotta, rose with green or solid green bark-textured ground; brown branch handles.

Bowl, 7" d., green ground, No. 842-7" **225**
Urn, green ground, No. 842-7", 7" h. **150**
Vase, 7" h., base handles, squared form w/flaring rim, yellow ground, No. 874-7" **138**
Vase, 7" h., yellow ground, No. 879-7" **138**
Vase, 10" h., handles at midsection, scalloped rim, green ground, No. 885-10" **165**
Vase, 10" h., handles at midsection, scalloped rim, grey ground, No. 885-10" **193**

Blackberry (1933)
Band of relief clusters of blackberries with vines and ivory leaves accented in green and terra cotta on a green textured ground.

Console bowl, rectangular w/small handles, No. 228-10", 3 1/2 x 13" **432**
Jardiniere, two-handled, No. 623-5", 5" h. **358**
Vase, 4" h., 6" d., squatty bulbous form w/small angled shoulder handles, No. 568-4" **467**

Vase, 5" h., loop handles at midsection, bulbous base tapering to wide cylindrical neck, No. 570-5" **482**
Vase, 6" h., No. 572-6" **595**

Bleeding Heart (1938)
Pink blossoms and green leaves on shaded blue, green or pink ground.

Jardiniere, small pointed shoulder handles, blue ground, No. 651-3", 3" h. **100**
Jardiniere, small pointed shoulder handles, green ground, No. 651-3", 3" h. **110**
Wall pocket, conical w/pointed overhead handle, blue ground, No. 1287-8", 8 1/2" h. (minor crazing) **619**

Burmese (1950s)
Oriental faces featured on pieces such as wall plaques, book ends, candleholders and console bowls. Some plain pieces also included. Comes in green, black and white.

Candleholders-book end combination, woman & man, green glaze, Nos. 80-B & 70-B, pr. **350**
Candleholders-book end combination, woman & man, white glaze, Nos. 80-B & 70-B, pr. **138**
Planter, green ground, No. 908-10", 10" **100**

Bushberry (1948)
Berries and leaves on blue, green or russet bark-textured ground; brown or green branch handles.

Console bowl, end handles, blue ground, No. 385-10", 13" l. **154**
Jardiniere & pedestal base, two-handled, green ground, No. 657-10", 2 pcs. (chip to rim, sm. chip to base & one handle of pedestal) **1,045**
Vase, 7" h., footed cylindrical body w/asymmetrical handles, blue ground, No. 32-7" **235**
Vase, 9" h., footed cylindrical body w/small angled handles near rim, green ground, No. 36-9" **225**
Vase, 12 1/2" h., large asymmetrical side handles, bulging cylinder w/flaring foot, russet ground, No. 38-12" **345**
Vase, 14 1/2" h., blue ground, No. 39-14" **605**
Vase, 18" h., floor-type, blue ground, No. 41-18" (short tight line to rim, restoration to one handle) **550**
Vase, 18" h., floor-type, green ground, No. 41-18" (grinding chips to base) **880**

Carnelian II (1915)
Intermingled colors, some with a drip effect.

Console bowl, stepped base, flaring octagonal shape, mottled mauve, grey, cream & black glaze, 9 5/8" l., 3 5/8" h. **220**
Vase, 5" h., footed, fan-shaped body w/shaped rim, small handles base handles, mottled grey, green & pink glaze, No. 351-5 .... **110**
Vase, 7" h., footed, wide cylindrical body tapering slightly to rolled rim, gloopy pink, mauve, green, black & cream matte glaze (small base chip professionally repaired) **165**

Vase, 9" h., ovoid w/short collared mouth, intermingled shades of pink, purple, green & tan, unmarked **399**

Clematis (1944)
Clematis blossoms and heart-shaped green leaves against a vertically textured ground — white blossoms on blue, rose-pink blossoms on green and ivory blossoms on golden brown.

Basket, hanging-type, blue ground, No. 470-5", 5" h. **225**
Basket w/overhead handle, pedestal base, blue ground, No. 389-10", 10" h. **195**
Candleholders, bulbous w/tiny pointed handles, green ground, No. 1158-2", 2" h., pr. **165**
Console bowl, blue ground, No. 461-14", 14" l. **200**
Cookie jar, cov., blue ground, No. 3-8", 8" h. **400**
Cornucopia-vase, blue ground, No. 193-6", 6" h. **85**
Creamer, blue ground, No. 5C **80**
Creamer, green ground, No. 5C **75**
Ewer, green ground, No. 16-6", 6" h. **145**
Flowerpot w/saucer, blue ground, No. 668-5", 5 1/2" h. **120-140**
Teapot, cov., green ground, No. 5 .... **200**
Vase, 6" h., two-handled, green ground, No. 102-6". **55**
Vase, 6" h., two-handled, blue ground, No. 103-6". **110**
Vase, 6" h., two-handled, brown ground, No. 103-6". **85**
Vase, 6" h., two-handled, urn-form, blue ground, No. 188-6". **95**
Vase, 7" h., blue ground, No. 105-7" **110**
Vase, 9" h., blue ground, No. 109-9" **225**
Wall pocket, angular side handles, green ground, No. 1295-8", 8 1/2" h. **150**

Columbine (1940s)
Columbine blossoms and foliage on shaded ground — yellow blossoms on blue, pink blossoms on pink shaded to green and blue blossoms on tan shaded to green.

Basket, elaborate handle rising from midsection, blue ground, No. 365-7", 7" h. **250**
Basket, blue ground, No. 366-8", 8" h. **225**
Basket, asymmetrical overhead handle, tan ground, No. 367-10", 10" h. **230**
Basket, pointed handle rising from flat base, ovoid w/boat-shaped top w/shaped rim, blue ground, No. 368-12", 12" h. **450**
Book end planters, blue ground, No. 8, 5" h., pr. **295**
Bowl, 8" d., tan ground, No. 402-8" **125**
Console bowl, stepped handles rising from rim, tan ground, No. 404-10" **135**
Console bowl, pink shading to green ground, No. 404-10", 10" l. **150**
Ewer, sharply angled handle, pink ground, No. 18-7", 7" h. **190**
Jardiniere, squatty w/small handles at shoulder, blue ground, No. 655-3", 3" h. **120**
Jardiniere, squatty w/small handles at shoulder, pink ground, No. 655-3", 3" h. **140-150**
Jardiniere & pedestal base, two-handled, tan ground, No. 655-10", 10" h., 2 pcs **1,800**

Urn-vase, pink ground, No. 150-6", 6" h. **155**
Vase, 6" h., pink shaded to green ground, No. 13-6" **125**
Vase, 7" h., tan ground, No. 16-7" **133**
Vase, 8" h., handles rising from base, blue ground, No. 19-8" **125**
Vase, 16" h., floor-type, footed slender ovoid body tapering to a slightly flared & shaped rim, pointed angular shoulder handles, blue ground, No. 27-16" **585**

Corinthian (1923)
Deeply fluted ivory and green body below a continuous band of molded grapevine, fruit, foliage and florals in naturalistic colors, narrow ivory and green molded border at the rim.

Jardiniere, 9" h., No. 601-9" **185**
Vase, 6" h., semi-ovoid **193**
Vase, 8 1/2" h. **90**
Wall pocket, No. 1232-8", 8" h. **275**

Cosmos (1940)
Embossed blossoms against a wavy horizontal ridged band on a textured ground — ivory band with yellow and orchid blossoms on blue, blue band with white and orchid blossoms on green or tan.

Basket, hanging-type, handles rising from midsection to rim, blue ground, No. 361-5", 7" h. **295**
Basket w/pointed overhead handle, pedestal base, blue ground, No. 358-12", 12" h. **485**
Candlesticks, loop handles rising from disc base, slightly tapering candle nozzle, green ground, No. 1137-4 1/2", 4 1/2" h., pr. **303**
Flower frogs, pierced globular body w/asymmetrical overhead handle, blue ground, No. 39, 3 1/2" h., pr. **248**
Urn-vase, blue ground, No. 135-8", 8" h. **275**
Vase, 7" h., handles at base, trumpet-form body, green ground, No. 949-7" (small chip off bottom of rim) **83**
Vase, bud, 7" h., slender, slightly tapering cylinder w/large loop handles at base, green ground, No. 959-7" **248**
Vase, 8" h., footed bulbous base w/wide cylindrical neck w/scalloped rim, large loop handles, No. 135-8" **248**
Vase, 9" h., handles rising from midsection of ovoid body to neck, tan ground, No. 952-9". **175**
Vase, 9" h., tapering cylinder w/shaped flaring mouth, curved handles at midsection, green ground, No. 953-9" **250**
Window box, tan ground, No. 381-9 x 3 x 3 1/2", 9" l. **242**

Crystalis, Rozane (ca. 1905)
A delicate use of a glazing process that left a crystallized matt finish flowing over thickly applied layers of dripping glazes, both a matt and high gloss glaze. Shapes looked similar to Egypto.

Vase, 6" h., 8" d., wide flared foot tapering to cylindrical body w/squatty compressed top supported on three buttressed handles, wide slightly flared rim covered in fine microcrystalline mottled green & amber glaze, unmarked **2,640**

Vase, 11" h., baluster-form body w/wide shoulder tapering to short cylindrical neck w/flared rim, green & blue, unmarked (glaze burn to shoulder, chip under rim) **605**

Vase, 15" h., 4 1/2" d., footed squatty bulbous base w/shoulder tapering sharply to tall cylindrical neck w/three relief-molded monk heads near rim, olive & blue crystalline glaze, Rozane wafer mark (some bubbles to rim & stilt-pull chip inside bottle ring **2,090**

Ferella (1931)

Impressed shell design alternating with small cutouts at top and base; mottled brown or turquoise and red glaze.

Urn-vase, compressed globular form w/tiny handles at midsection, reticulated foot & rim, turquoise & red glaze, No. 505-6", 6" h. **468**

Vase, 5" h., footed wide ovoid form w/flaring rim, long side handles, turquoise & red glaze, No. 500-5" **523**

Vase, 10" h., 6" 1/4" d., ovoid body on flaring foot & tapering to a widely flaring mouth, low angular handles down the sides, the foot pierced w/a band of small squares, the mouth pierced w/two bands of small rectangles, brown glaze, No. 511-10" **935**

Vase, 10" h., 6" 1/4" d., ovoid body on flaring foot & tapering to a widely flaring mouth, low angular handles down the sides, the foot pierced w/a band of small squares, the mouth pierced w/two bands of small rectangles, turquoise & red glaze, No. 511-10" **1,650**

Foxglove (1940s)

Sprays of pink and white blossoms embossed against a shaded matte-finish ground.

Ewer, blue ground, No. 5-10", 10" h. **270**

Jardiniere, two-handled, pink ground, No. 659-3", 3" h. **83**

Model of a conch shell, blue ground, No. 426-6", 6" h. **220**

Freesia (1945)

Trumpet-shaped blossoms and long slender green leaves against wavy impressed lines — white and lavender blossoms on blended green; white and yellow blossoms on shaded blue or terra cotta and brown.

Ewer, terra cotta ground, No. 20-10", 10" h. **325**

Urn-vase, two-handled, green ground, No. 463-5", 5" h. **220**

Fuchsia (1939)

Coral pink fuchsia blossoms and green leaves against a background of blue shading to yellow, green shading to terra cotta or terra cotta shading to gold.

Basket, a short pedestal foot supports a wide squatty half-round body w/small half-round tabs on two sides of the incurved rim, a high round handle joins the two other edges, terra cotta ground, No. 350-8", 8" h. **358**

Basket, w/overhead handle, blue ground, No. 351-10", 10" h **248**

Basket, w/overhead handle, terra cotta ground, No. 351-10", 10" h. **220**

Basket w/flower frog, a short pedestal foot supports a wide squatty half-round body w/small half-round tabs on two sides of the incurved rim, a high round handle joins the two other edges, blue ground, No. 350-8", 8" h. **534**

Bowl, urn-form, two-handled, blue ground, No. 346-4", 4" h. **253**

Bowl, 6" d., footed bulbous body w/wide flat rim, loop shoulder handles, green ground, No. 347-6" **280**

Candleholders, two handles rising from disc base, green ground, No. 1132-2", 2" h., pr. **193**

Console bowl, footed low oblong boat-shaped w/under-rim end loop handles, blue ground, No. 353-14", 15 1/2" l. **220**

Cornucopia-vase, terra cotta ground, No. 129-6", 6" h. **200**

Flowerpot, blue ground, No. 646-5", 5" h. **303**

Jardiniere, two-handled, blue ground, No. 645-4" 4" h. **253**

Jardiniere, two-handled, green ground, No. 645-6", 6" h. **193**

Jardiniere, two-handled, blue ground, No. 645-8", 8" h. **715**

Pitcher w/ice lip, 8" h., terra cotta ground, No. 1322-8" **358**

Vase, 6" h., footed spherical body w/a ringed cylindrical neck w/a flaring rim, long C-form handles from center of the neck to the center of the body, blue ground, No. 891-6" **250**

Vase, 6" h., footed spherical body w/a ringed cylindrical neck w/a flaring rim, long C-form handles from center of the neck to the center of the body, terra cotta ground, No. 891-6" **253**

Vase, 6" h., footed swelled cylindrical body w/long loop handles, terra cotta ground, No. 893-6" **180**

Vase, 7" h., bulbous base tapering to flaring rim, large loop handles from shoulder to below rim, blue ground, No. 895-7" **275**

Vase, 8" h., wide ovoid body w/handles rising from flat base to shoulder, blue ground, No. 897-8" **385**

Vase, 8" h., footed bulbous body tapering slightly to a wide gently tapering cylindrical neck w/a rolled rim, long curved handles from just under the rim to the mid-body, blue ground, No. 898-8" **350-400**

Vase, 12" h., cylindrical body w/slightly flared neck, two handles rising from above base to neck, terra cotta ground, No. 903-12" **400**

Vase, 12" h., cylindrical body w/slightly flared neck, two handles rising from above base to neck, green ground, No. 903-12" **627**

Vase, 18" h., 10" d., floor-type, a disk foot supports a tall baluster-form body w/long low C-form handles down the sides, green ground, No. 905-18" **1,500**

Vase, 18" h., 10" d., floor-type, a disk foot supports a tall baluster-form body w/long low C-form handles down the sides, terra cotta ground, No. 905-18"................... **1,200**

Wall pocket, green ground **850**

Good Night Candleholder

Good Night candleholder, unmarked, 7" h....... **715**

Iris (1938)

White or yellow blossoms and green leaves on rose blending with green, light blue deepening to a darker blue or tan shading to green or brown.

Ewer, bulbous body, cut-out rim, blue ground, No. 926-10", gold foil label, 10" h............ **440**

Pedestal base, rose blending w/green ground, unmarked, 16" h............... **715**

Vase, 6 1/2" h., two handles rising from shoulder of globular base to midsection of wide neck, rose ground, No. 917-6" **140**

Vase, 6 1/2" h., two handles rising from shoulder of globular base to midsection of wide neck, tan shading to brown ground, No. 917-6".............. **225**

Ixia (1930s)

Embossed spray of tiny bell-shaped flowers and slender leaves — white blossoms on pink ground; lavender blossoms on green or yellow ground.

Candleholders, double, pink ground, No. 1127, 3" h., pr. **138**

Console bowl, green ground, No. 330-7", 10 1/2" l., 3 1/2" h............. **135**

Console bowl, pink ground, No. 332-12", 12" l............ **300**

Console set: 9" l. console bowl, & pr. of 3" h. double candleholders; green ground, Nos. 330-9" & 1127-3" **303**

Jardiniere, yellow ground, No. 640-4", 4" h....... **95**

Jardiniere, pink ground, No. 640-7", 7" h. (tight 1" crack to rim)................. **220**

Vase, 7" h., closed handles rising from midsection to rim, expanding cylindrical body, pink ground, No. 854-7"............ **160**

Vase, 8" h., cylindrical shape tapering slightly to disk foot, buttressed handles from base to midsection, yellow ground, No. 856-8"............... **220**

Vase, 12" h., closed handles, cylindrical, pink ground, No. 864-12" **385**

Jonquil (1931)

White jonquil blossoms and green leaves in relief against textured tan ground; green lining.

Bowl, 4 x 12"............... **145**

Vase, 4 1/2 h., two-handled, No. 539-4"............. **110**

Vase, 7" h., bulbous base tapering slightly to flat mouth, No. 527-7" **413**

Vase, 9 1/2" h., bulbous base tapering slightly to wide cylindrical neck, loop handles at midsection, No. 544-9" **550**

Juvenile (1916 on)

Transfer-printed and painted on creamware with nursery rhyme characters, cute animals and other motifs appealing to children.

Feeding dish w/rolled edge, dogs, 8" d. **187**

Pitcher, 3 1/2" h., chicks.................... **286**

Pitcher, rabbit design, 3 1/2" h........... **413**

Lotus (1952)

Pointed spires of stylized leaves surround each piece. High-gloss glaze in combinations of maroon with beige, brown with beige, and turquoise with beige.

Bowl, 3 1/2 x 11", 3" h., blue & white high-gloss finish, No. L7-10".................... **330**

Vase, 10" h., cylindrical, yellow & blue high-gloss finish, No. L3-10"............... **275**

Vase, pillow-type, 10 1/2" h., blue & ivory, No. L4-10"....... **253**

Luffa (1934)

Relief-molded ivy leaves and blossoms on shaded brown or green wavy horizontal ridges.

Bowl-vase, bulbous body tapering to wide closed mouth, small angled shoulder handles, green ground, No. 255-6", 6" h. **303**

Candlesticks, two-handled, bell-shaped base, brown ground, No. 1097-4 1/2", 4 1/2" h., pr........ **330**

Jardiniere, green ground, No. 631-4", 4" h....... **440**

Lamp base, 9" h., bulbous body tapering to wide flat rim flanked by small angled handles, brown & blue ground w/metal fixture, No. 690-9"............ **715**

Lamp base, 9" h., bulbous body tapering to wide flat rim flanked by small angled handles, brown ground w/metal fixture, No. 690-9"............ **605**

Mayfair (late 1940s)

Utilitarian line with various embossed designs; glossy glaze.

Ewer, footed cylindrical form w/ornate handle, green ground, No. 1107-12", 12" h........ **121**

Jardiniere, greenish tan ground, four low tab feet supporting a round widely flaring body below a wide low shoulder centered by a wide low notched neck, No. 1109-4", 4" h........... **50**

Pitcher, 8" h., footed bulbous swirled rib-molded body below a plain wide low neck w/high arched spout & C-scroll handle, greenish tan ground, No. 1105-8" **115**

Mock Orange (1950)

Small cluster of white blossoms and green leaves on backgrounds of pink, yellow, or mint green.

Basket w/overhead handle, rose ground, No. 908-6", 6" h....... **198**

Cornucopia-vase, green ground, No. 922-8", 8" h............ **109**

Ewer, pink ground, No. 918-16", 16" h............. **308**

Moderne (1930s)

Art Deco-style rounded and angular shapes trimmed with an embossed panel of vertical lines and modified swirls and circles, white trimmed with terra cotta, medium blue with white and turquoise with a burnished antique gold.

Bowl, 7 x 11", 4" h., pleated body, turquoise, No. 301-10"....... **210**

Candleholders, triple, blue ground, No. 1112-5 1/2", 5 1/2" h., pr. (fleck to rim of one) **440**

Compote, blue ground, No. 297-6", 6" h. **440**
Compote, 5" h., open stem, white & tan,
No. 295-6 .... **177**
Console bowl, blue ground, No. 302-14",
14" l. **450**
Vase, 6" h., a round foot tapering to a nar-
row short stem supporting a tall conical
body, two small curved handles from foot
to lower body, turquoise & gold ground,
No. 788-6" **385**

Montacello (1931)

*White stylized trumpet flowers with black accents on
a terra cotta band, light terra cotta mottled in blue, or
light green mottled and blended with blue backgrounds.*

Basket, bulbous base w/wide neck & flaring
rim, a long curved upright handle from
shoulder to shoulder coming to a point
above the neck, green ground, No. 333-
6", 6" h. (handle repaired) **358**
Console bowl, low squatty bulbous oblong
form w/flat rim & small round end han-
dles, blue ground, No. 225-9", 13" l., 3" h. **385**
Jardiniere, two-handled, terra cotta ground,
No. 559-5", 5" h. **537**
Vase, 4" h., two-handled, terra cotta
ground, black paper label, No. 555-4"
(rough drill hole in bottom) **235**
Vase, 5" h., two handles at mid-section,
blue ground, No. 556-5" (small chip to
bottom ring) **303**
Vase, 5" h., two handles at mid-section, ter-
ra cotta ground, No. 556-5" **358**
Vase, 5 1/4" h., raised rim on an ovoid body
w/two handles, decorated w/stylized
fleur-de-lis design in cream within a
brown band, dark blue ovals on a
streaked light green & tan ground **431**
Vase, 6" h., ovoid w/large ring shoulder
handles, terra cotta ground, No. 560-6" **413**
Vase, 8 1/2" h., small loop handles at shoulder, cylindrical w/flared lip, terra cotta
ground, No. 563-8" **495**
Vase, 10" h., footed trumpet-form w/base
handles, terra cotta ground, No. 565-10" .. **1,760**

Moss (1930s)

*Green moss hanging over brown branch with green
leaves; backgrounds are pink, ivory or tan shading to
blue.*

Vase, triple bud, pink ground, No. 1108,
7" h. **358**
Vase, 8 1/2" h., flared foot, bulbous body
w/wide flaring rim, tan & green, No. 779-
8" **358**
Wall pocket, elongated side handles, flar-
ing rim, blue ground, No. 1278-8",
8 1/2" h. **660**

Pine Cone (1931)

*Realistic embossed brown pine cones and green pine
needles on shaded blue, brown or green ground. (Pink is
extremely rare.)*

Bowl, 6 1/2" d., 3 1/4" h., round, blue
ground, No. 426-6" **259**
Candlestick, triple, brown ground, No.
1106-5 1/2", 5 1/2" h. **413**
Flowerpot, blue ground, No. 633-5", 5" h. **319**

Jardiniere, green ground, No. 632-9", 9" h. **187**
Vase, 6" h., footed ovoid body w/flat rim,
brown ground, No. 748-6" **325**
Vase, 8" h., wide bulbous body w/asymmet-
rical branch handles, blue ground, gold
foil label, No. 114-8" (one handle re-
paired) **715**
Vase, 14" h., footed, two-handled, baluster
form w/wide cylindrical neck & slightly
flared rim, blue ground, unmarked, No.
713-14" (professional repair to base
chips) **1,210**

Poppy (1930s)

*Shaded backgrounds of blue or pink with decoration
of poppy flower and green leaves.*

Bowl, 6", pink ground, No. 335-6" **123**
Console bowl, green ground, No. 340-14",
14" l. **228**
Flower frog, pink ground, No. 35, 3 1/2" h. **110**
Jardiniere, blue ground, No. 642-6", 6" h. **220**
Jardiniere & pedestal base, green ground,
No. 642-8", 8" h., 2 pcs. (spider line to
base of jardiniere, not through, couple of
nicks & one shallow bruise to petals,
small flat chip to bottom ring, hairline to
edge of pedestal) **440**
Vase, 6" h., footed trumpet-form w/base
handles, green ground, No. 866-6" **132**
Vase, 9" h., bulbous base w/wide cylindrical
neck, small scrolled handles, pink
ground, No. 873-9" **300**
Vase, 9" h., bulbous base w/wide cylindrical
neck, small scrolled handles, green
ground, No. 873-9" **303**

Primrose (1932)

*Cluster of single blossoms on tall stems, low pad-like
leaves; backgrounds are blue, tan, or pink.*

Basket, hanging-type, pink ground, No.
354-6", 6" h. **275**
Cornucopia-vase, pink ground, No. 125-6",
6" h. **168**
Jardiniere, blue ground, No. 634-5", 5" d. **193**
Jardiniere, blue ground, No. 634-6", 6" d. **225**
Umbrella stand, tan ground, No. 773-21",
21" h. **1,320**
Vase, 6 1/2" h., ovoid body w/angled han-
dles, blue ground, No. 761-6" **128**
Vase, 7" h., two-handled, blue ground, No.
762-7" **143**
Vase, 7 1/2" h., tan ground, No. 763-7"
(minute flake to handle) **165**
Wall pocket, angular side handles, tan
ground, No. 1277-8", 8 1/2" **660**
Window box, tan ground, No. 381-10",
12 1/2" l., 6 1/2" h. **440**

Rosecraft Hexagon (1924)

*Shapes are six-sided, simple medallion design with
long slender stylized leaf extending downward. Colors
are dark green, brown with orange; catalogue also
shows blue.*

Bowl w/flower frog, 5" d., dark green, No.
136-5" **220**
Vase, 4" h., brown, No. 266-4" **284**
Vase, 5" h., dark brown, No. 267-5" **286**
Vase, 5" h., dark green, No. 267-5" **372**

Vase, 6" h., brown ground, No. 269-6" 385
Vase, 8" h., green ground, No. 270-8"............... 385
Vase, 8 1/2" h., No. 271-8", brown 495

Rosecraft Panel (1920)
Jar, cov., dark brown ground w/embossed
dandelion decoration, No. 295-9, 9" h. 523
Vase, 6" h., fan-shaped body w/wide disk
foot, brown ground w/nude decoration in
orange on either side, unmarked (very
minor glaze inconsistencies) 660

Silhouette (1952)
*Recessed area silhouettes nature study or female
nudes. Colors are rose, turquoise, tan and white with
turquoise.*

Cornucopia-vase, rose ground, No. 722-
6", 6" h.. 178
Vase, 7" h., fan-shaped, nude lady, rose
ground, No. 783-7" (small rim chip pro-
fessionally repaired)....................................... 383
Vase, 10" h., small open handles between
square base & waisted cylindrical body,
shaped rim, female nudes, white ground
No. 787-10" 248
Vase, 10" h., small open handles between
square base & waisted cylindrical body,
shaped rim, female nudes, rose ground,
No. 787-10" (one corner of base profes-
sionally repaired) 330

Teasel (1936)
*Embossed decorations of long-stems gracefully curv-
ing with delicate spider-like pods. Colors and glaze
treatments vary from monochrome matte to crystalline.
Colors are beige to tan, medium bue highlighted with
gold, pale blue and deep rose (possibly others).*

Jardiniere, footed squatty bulbous body
w/a wide cylindrical neck, small angled
shoulder handles, rust ground w/green
flowers, No. 644-4", 4" h. (small glaze
flake off one handle) 83
Vase, 9" h., closed handles at base, flaring
mouth, deep rose, No. 886-9" 110

Thorn Apple (1930s)
*White trumpet flower with leaves reverses to thorny pod
with leaves. Colors are shaded blue, brown and pink.*

Bowl, 8" d., pointed handles, shaded pink
ground, No. 309-8"... 275
Ewer, shaded pink & green ground, No.
825-15", 15" h. (small bruise & flat chip to
base)... 770
Flowerpot, shaded blue ground, No. 639-
5", 5" h. (spider line to base of pot does
not go through) 220
Jardiniere, spherical form w/three openings
& buttressed handles, shaded brown
ground, No. 305-6" (minor nick to one
corner, short tight line to rim)........................ 165
Vase, 4" h., jug-form, shaded pink ground,
No. 808-4".. 138
Vase, 6" h., shaded blue ground, No. 810-6"...... 165
Vase, 6" h., shaded brown ground, No. 810-
6".. 175
Vase, 6" h., shaded brown ground, No. 811-
6" 132
Vase, 10" h., footed, bulbous body tapering
to flaring rim, angled shoulder handles,
shaded brown ground, No. 821-10" 275

Vase, 12" h., footed, bulbous base w/small
tab handles, horizontal rings below large
wide trumpet-form neck, shaded brown
ground, No. 774-8 x 12 (restoration to
two small rim chips & two small base
chips).. 413

Topeo (1934)
*Simple forms decorated with four vertical evenly
spaced cascades of leaves in high relief at their origin,
tapering downward to a point. A light green crystalline
glaze shades to a mottled medium blue, with cascades in
alternating green and pink. A second type is done completely in a high-gloss dark red.*

Bowl, 9" d., sharply canted sides, red
ground, silver label, No. 246-3".................... 231
Vase, 6 3/4" h., ovoid body w/short wide cylindrical neck w/flat rim, red ground, No.
657-6 3/4" 220

Velmoss (1935)
*Characterized by three horizontal wavy lines around
the top from which long, blade-like leaves extend downward. Colors are green, blue, tan and pink.*

Vase, 6" h., swelled cylindrical body
w/pointed shoulder handles, mottled tan
& green crystalline glaze, No. 714-6",
gold foil label... 358
Vase, bud, 7" h., rose ground, No. 115-7" 154
Wall pocket, double, mottled green crystalline glaze, No. 1274-8", 8 1/2" h. **3,190**

Wincraft (1948)
*Revived shapes from older lines such as Pine Cone,
Bushberry, Cremona, Primrose and others. Vases with
animal motifs, contemporary shapes in high gloss of
blue, tan, lime and green.*

Cigarette box, cov., rectangular, glossy
chartreuse, No. 240, 4 1/2" l...................... 165
Vase, 10" h., cylindrical, tab handles, black
panther & green palm trees in relief on
glossy shaded tan ground, No. 290-10"
(1/4" dark line at rim) 550

Royal Bonn & Bonn

*Bonn and subsequently Royal Bonn china were pro-
duced in Bonn, Germany, in a manufactory established
in 1755. Later wares made there are often marked
Mehlem or bear the initials FM or a castle mark. Most
wares were of the hand-painted type. Clock cases were
also made in Bonn.*

Royal Bonn & Bonn Mark

Ewer, earthenware 'aesthetic movement,'
pear-form body & attenuated gently
curved spout painted w/finch perched on
a flowering orchid plant w/gilt clouds &
moon in distance on a cream ground,
shoulders applied w/angular gilt handle,

red printed & impressed factory marks, painted numeral 1807/4, late 19th c., 12" h. **$115**

Urn, tall classical form w/gilt mask-form handles, the body painted w/a floral still life, on paw feet resting on a shaped base, ca. 1900, 15 1/2" h. 316

Vase, 11 1/2" h., two-handled, ivory ground w/gilt & enameled flower garden scenes, late 19th c. 115

Ornate Royal Bonn Vase

Vase, 14" h., baluster-form w/a wide shoulder below the short flaring neck, bright pink ground decorated on the front w/an oval reserve w/a color bust portrait of a lovely long-haired lady, the back w/another reserve w/a landscape, ornate gold banding & scrolls highlighted w/green leafy vines & yellow sprigs (ILLUS.) **1,200-1,300**

Royal Copenhagen

This porcelain has been made in Copenhagen, Denmark, since 1715. The ware is hard paste.

Royal Copenhagen Mark

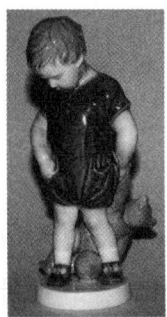

Boy with Teddy Bear Figure Group

Figure group, boy & Teddy bear, toddler standing wearing blue romper, holding tan bear behind him, No. 3468, 3 1/2" w., 7" h. (ILLUS.) 225

Girl Feeding Calf Figure Group

Figure group, girl feeding calf, a farm girl bending over to feed a calf from a pail, green oblong base, No. 779, 6 1/2" l., 6 1/2" h. (ILLUS.) 300

Hans Clodhopper Figure Group

Figure group, Hans Clodhopper, boy seated astride a billy goat, No. 1228, 5 1/2" l., 6 3/4" h. (ILLUS.) 300

Royal Copenhagen Harvest Group

Figure group, Harvest Group, young farmer & farm girl standing close together, each leaning on a hoe, No. 1300, small, 4" w., 7 1/2" h. (ILLUS.) 400

Shepherd Boy and Dog

Figure group, shepherd boy w/dog, standing boy wearing cap & long blanket cloak, No. 782, 3 1/2" w., 7 1/2" h. (ILLUS.)............. **250**

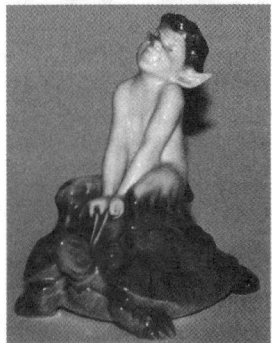

Faun on Tortoise Figure Group

Figure group, young faun seated astride a large tortoise, No. 858, 3 1/2" l., 4" h. (ILLUS.)... **175**

Young Children & Puppy Figure Group

Figure group, young girl & boy hugging brown puppy, No. 707, 5 1/2" l., 5 3/4" h. (ILLUS.).. **325**

Figure of a boy, February Boy Juggler, standing wearing a top hat & holding a baton to juggle, No. 4524, 6 1/2" h. (ILLUS. top next column) **175**

February Boy Juggler Figure

Royal Copenhagen Sandman Figure

Figure of boy, Sandman (Wee-Willie-Winkie,) standing wearing a long white nightgown & pointed blue cap, a closed umbrella under one arm, opening a brown vial in his hands, No. 1145, 6 3/4" h. (ILLUS.) **125**

Figure of Young Man Eating Lunch

Figure of young man eating lunch, reclining position earting from a lunch box, No. 865, 7" l., 4" h. (ILLUS.) **225**

Model of a Fat Robin

Model of bird, Fat Robin, rounded baby robin in blue, white & rust red, No. 2266, 3" h. (ILLUS.) **65**

Royal Copenhagen Model of a Grebe

Model of bird, Grebe, handsome swimming bird w/blue crest & grey & white body, No. 3263, 7" l., 4" h. (ILLUS.) **135**

Royal Copenhagen Icelandic Falcon

Model of bird, Icelandic Falcon, large bird w/speckled bluish grey & white feathers, No. 263, 8 1/2" l., 11" h. (ILLUS.) **375**

Model of Finches

Model of birds, pair of blue, white & grey finches perched close together, No. 1189, 5" l., 2" h. (ILLUS.) **80**

Royal Copenhagen Great Dane

Model of dog, Great Dane, large recumbent dog in tan w/black striping, No. 1679, 9" l., 4" h. (ILLUS.) **275**

Royal Copenhagen Elephant

Model of elephant, walking w/head & trunk raised & mouth open, No. 2998, small size, 6" l., 5" h. (ILLUS.) **120**

Royal Copenhagen Lioness

Model of lioness, recumbent animal, No. 804, 12" l., 6 1/2" h. (ILLUS.) **375**

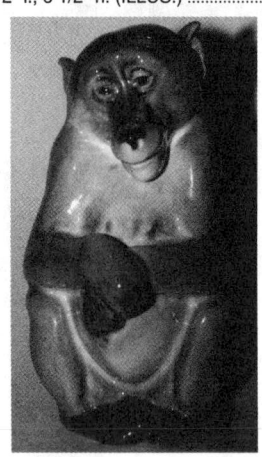

Royal Copenhagen Monkey Figure

Model of monkey, seated animal w/head tilted to side, No. 1444, 3" w., 5" h. (ILLUS.) **125**

Mouse on Ear of Corn Figure

Model of mouse, white & pink mouse perched on a ear of brown corn, No. 512, 5" l., 2" h. (ILLUS.) **65**

Royal Copenhagen Panda Figure

Model of Panda, seated eating bamboo, No. 662, 5 1/2" w., 7" h. (ILLUS.) **350**

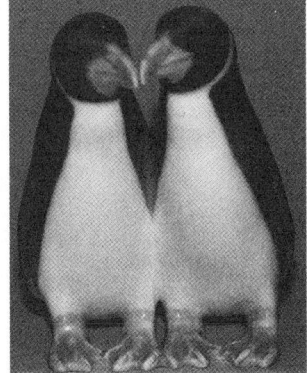

Royal Copenhagen Penguins

Model of penguins, two birds seated side by side, No. 1190, 4" h. (ILLUS.) **100**

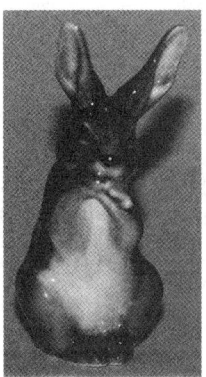

Small Royal Copenhagen Rabbit

Model of rabbit, seated upright eating leaf, No. 1019, small size, 3 1/2" h. (ILLUS.) **65**

Royal Copenhagen Rose Bowl

Rose bowl, squatty spherical form w/wide flat mouth, dark blue ground painted w/large white blossoms & green leaves, No. 424, 8" d., 6" h. (ILLUS.) **200**

Royal Vienna

The second factory in Europe to make hard paste porcelain was established in Vienna in 1719 by Claud Innocentius de Paquier. The factory underwent various changes of administration through the years and finally closed in 1865. Since then, however, the porcelain has been reproduced by various factories in Austria and Germany, many of which have also reproduced the early beehive mark. Early pieces, naturally, bring far higher prices than the later ones or the reproductions.

Royal Vienna Mark

Baskets & underplates, a deep rounded flaring bowl-form basket w/reticulated rim band & reticulated latticework sides raised on a reticulated flaring round pedestal, trimmed overall w/heavy gilt, set in a matching round dished & reticulated underplate w/gold trim, blue shield marks & dated 1812, 10 1/2" d., two sets........... **$1,955**

Charger, round, colorful scene depicting the Death of Siegfried, paneled gilt foliate border band, ca. 1890, 13 1/2" d. **1,380**

Charger, round, pink & claret ground finely painted w/a central square reserve of a mythological scene emblematic of the Arts & Sciences, named on the reverse, within an elaborately paneled round w/gilt scroll trim & small diamond-shaped reserves w/gilt florals or birds all on a claret, pale pink or lavender ground, mid-19th c., blue beehive mark, artist-signed, 16 7/8" d. **6,325**

Coffeepot, cover & underplate, the footed coffepot w/a tall tapering cylindrical body w/a scroll-molded long rim spout in gold & a pointed loop handle in gold, fitted w/a stepped domed cover w/urn-form gold finial, the body & cover w/paneled designs on a pale blue ground w/pink reserves on the neck & cover & maroon & white banding, the body painted w/a gold-bordered reserve of putti in gardens, the panels ornately trimmed w/gilt arabesques, leaf-tips & beaded chain, the wide round dished underplate w/matching decoration, late 19th c., blue beehive mark & other marks, 8 1/2" h., the set **2,530**

Plate, 9 5/8" d., painted in the center in color w/a scene of a nymph seated w/flowers in her long blonde hair & being kissed by a winged Eros, a fountain & field in the distance, within an elaborate paneled border band of stylized leaf-tips & gilt flowers, earely 20th c., crowned beehive & D mark, artist-signed............................ **1,265**

Stein, cov., cylindrical w/hinged gilt-metal low domed cover, the front finely painted in color w/a scene of a scantily clad Venus teasing Cupid in a forest glen within a gilt rectangular surround, the burgundy ground trimmed w/gilt scrolling foliage, 19th c., blue beehive mark & iron-red number, 6 1/4" h. **2,990**

Vase, cov., 11" h., slightly tapering cylindrical form w/large molded lion masks w/ring handles near the top & molded gilt scrolls & paw feet supporting the base, the low domed cover w/a gilt blossom finial, a cobalt blue ground, the body decorated on one side w/a large ornate gilt oval reserve w/a right-facing bust portrait of a lightly clad maiden w/a large flower in her long dark hair, printed & incised marks, late 19th c...................................... **1,265**

Vases, cov., 26" h., tapering pedestal round base supporting a tall slender ovoid body w/a short rolled neck & high domed cover w/double-knop finial, arched gilt leafy scroll shoulder handles down the sides, chestnut brown ground finely painted on the front & back w/putti representing the Seasons within molded & gilt ribbon-tied branches, above a band of molded gilt-

trimmed flutes & conforming gilt-trimmed base, the neck w/molded stiff-leaf tips, blue beehive mark, late 19th c., pr............ **6,325**

Royal Worcester

This porcelain has been made by the Royal Worcester Porcelain Co. at Worcester, England, from 1862 to the present. Royal Worcester is distinguished from wares made at Worcester between 1751 and 1862 that are referred to as only Worcester by collectors.

Royal Worcester Marks

Ewer, footed wide bulbous body w/a wide rounded shoulder centering a short ringed neck & high arched spout w/shaped rim, high arched & scrolled beaded gold handle from rim to shoulder, creamy ground decorated w/large sprays of ferns, late 19th c., Shape No. 1227, 10 1/4" h. **$748**

Ewer, "Patent Metallic" type, raised gold-trimmed foot supporting a bulbous ovoid body tapering sharply to a slender neck w/a large pierced bulbed ring w/gold swirled ribs below the high arched spout, long angled gilt handle from the rim to the lower body, creamy ground decorated w/delicate floral sprigs, 19th c., 13 1/8" h. **633**

Pitcher, 7 1/8" h., lobed melon-form w/vine handle, bronzed & gilt-decorated, Shape 1111, ca. 1888.............................. **345**

Service plates, round, painted in the center w/colorful summer flowers, surrounded by the blue cavetto gilded w/runs & scrolling foliage continuing around the wide flanged rim, printed factory marks, artist-signed, 10 1/2" d., set of 12 .... **2,300**

Taperstick, lotus-form w/a frog mounted on the leaf-form base, Shape No. 687, ca. 1879, 7 3/8" h. **403**

Vase, 11 3/4" h., a wide bulbous spherical body raised on a short flaring round ringed foot, a short tapering flute-molded neck supporting a reticulated cupped rim, small looped shoulder handles, the ivory ground decorated w/overall enameled ferns w/gilt trim & gilt banding on the neck & base, Shape 1109, ca. 1889, printed mark **633**

Vase, cov., 13 1/4" h., classical bottle-form, a ringed round disk foot below a short ringed & swirled fluted pedestal supporting a large squatty bulbous body w/a wide ringed shoulder centering a tall fluted & waisted neck w/a rolled rim & pierced domed cover & pointed button finial, full relief satyr head handles, molded drapery swags around the edge of the shoulder, the body & neck decorated w/raised gilt foliate designs, gilt banding & trim, Shape 1408, printed mark, late 19th c. (slight gilt loss at rim)..................... **1,035**

Royal Worcester Sabrina Ware Vases

Vases, 4 1/4" h., 3" d., Sabrina Ware, in-verted pear-shaped body, decorated w/fish & seaweed in light blue on deep blue ground, ca. 1909, pr. (ILLUS.) **375**
Vases, 6 1/4" h., bud-type, bottle-form w/gilt & enameled foliate designs on an ivory ground, Shape 854, printed mark, ca. 1888, pr. (gilt wear) **316**
Vases, 6 7/8" h., bud-type, a ringed & domed round foot w/a beaded net deco-ration below the short beaded ring stem below the tall slender cylindrical body w/a flared, swirled scroll-molded scalloped rim, ornate scrolling foliate gilt handles at the lower body, a pink shaded to yellow ground w/delicate floral decoration & gilt trim, ca. 1900, pr. (slight rim chip re-stored) **690**
Vases, 7 1/4" h., figural, one modeled as a boy & girl w/a waterpot, the other w/a boy playing a horn as a girl looks on, artist-signed, impressed marks, ca. 1880, pr. (gilt wear) **1,035**

Sascha Brastoff

Sascha Brastoff dedicated his life to creating works with a flair all his own. He was a costume designer for major movie studios, a dancer, a window dresser and a talented painter. The creator in Sascha put him on the path to ceramics early in life when he was awarded a scholarship to the Cleveland Art School; however, he also worked with watercolors, charcoals, pastels, resin, fabrics, ceramics and metal sculptures, and enamels. Nelson Rockefeller, Brastoff's friend, understood the uniqueness of his talents and, in 1953, he built a complex in Los Angeles, California to house the many creations Sascha was able to produce.

A full line of hand-painted china with names such as Allegro, La Jolla, Roman Coin and Night Song was cre-ated. Surf Ballet was a popular dinnerware line and was achieved by dipping pieces of blue, pink or yellow into real gold or platinum. Also highly popular was Sascha's line of enamels on copper. Many collectors do not know that Sascha dabbled in textiles. A yard of cloth in good condition might command several hundred dollars on today's market. His artware items included pieces such as Star Steed, a leaping-fantasy horse and Roof-tops, a series of houses where the roofs somehow seemed to be the prominent feature. Even then, as well as today, these pieces were and are, two of the most highly collect-ible Sascha artware patterns.

Sascha Brastoff also created a line of Alaskan-motif items. Many collectors confuse Matthew Adams pieces

with those of Sascha. Even though Adams worked for Brastoff for a period of time, his pieces are not nearly as sought after as those that Sascha created.

Brastoff's crystal ball served him well during his life-time. In the late 1940s and early 1950s he created a series of Western motif cachepots which excites any col-lectors when found today. Almost a decade before the poodle craze in the 1950s, Sascha created a line of poo-dle products. In the 1950s, cigarette smoking was at an all-time high and Sascha was there with smoking acces-sories.

From 1947-1952 pieces were signed "Sascha B." or with the full signature, "Sasha Brastoff." After 1953 and before 1962, during the years of his factory-studio, pieces done by his employees showed "Sascha B." and more often than not, also included the chanticleer back stamp. Caution should be taken to understand that the chanticleer with the full name "Sascha Brastoff" below it is not the "full signature" mark that elevates pieces to substantial prices. The chanticleer mark is usually in gold and will incorporate Sascha's work name in the same color. Sascha's personal full signauture is the one commanding the high prices.

Health problems forced Sascha to leave his company in 1963. After 1962 pieces were marked "Sascha B." and also included the 'R' in a circle trademark. Ten years later the business closed.

Sascha Brastoff died on Feburary 4, 1993. The pass-ing of this flamboyant artist, whose special character was well reflected in his work, means that similar cre-ations will probably never be achieved again.

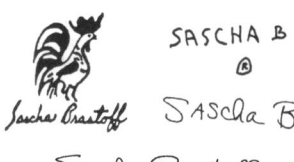

Sascha Brastoff Marks

Ashtray, floral decoration, No. 110AC **$45**
Ashtray, round, leaf decoration, full signa-ture, large **350**
Ashtray, Western scene w/covered wagon, rare promotional piece, 14" w. **175**
Bowl, 8" d., footed, abstract design **38**
Box, cov., Jewel Bird decoration, No. 020 .... **70**
Candleholder, resin, green or blue, 6" h., each **65**
Cigarette box, cov., Rooftops patt., No. 021, 8" l. **70**
Cigarette box, cov., "Star Steed" decora-tion **145**
Compote, polar bear decoration, No. 085 .... **65**
Dish, horse decoration on green ground, 6 1/2" sq. **30**
Dish, three-footed, fish-shaped (flounder), house decoration, 8 1/4 x 8 1/2" **90**
Lamp base, mosaic tile, 27" h. **210**
Model of polar bear, blue resin, 10" h. **400**
Model of rooster, mosaic design, 15" h. **515**
Plate, square, vegetable decoration, full sig-nature **275**
Plate, 9" d., Merbaby patt. **65**

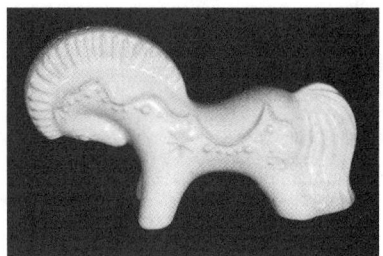

Sascha Brastoff Horse Salt Shaker

Salt shaker, model of a horse, white, produced in 1947-1948, 5 1/4" l, 3 1/4" h. (ILLUS.).. **85**
Tray, floral decoration, marked "Sample" under glaze, 7" sq. **95**
Vase, 5" h., Provincial Rooster patt., No. F20... **400**
Wall pocket, Rooftops patt., No. 031, 20" h. **415**

Schafer & Vater

Founded in Rudolstadt, Thuringia, Germany in 1890, the Schafer and Vater Porcelain Factory specialized in decorative pieces of porcelain usually in white or colored bisque. They produced many novelty figural items such as creamers, toothpick holders, boxes and hatpin holders and also produced a line of jasper ware with white relief decoration in imitation of the famous Wedgwood jasper wares. The firm also decorated whiteware blanks.

The company ceased production in 1962 and collectors now seek out their charming pieces which may be marked with a crown over a starburst containing the script letter "R."

Schafer & Vater Mark

Schafer & Vater Ashtray

Ashtray, figural, little boy in white & little girl in dark blue w/green hair ribbon, white rabbits on one corner, white doves on other, inscribed on front "Everybody's doing it," unmarked, 2 1/2 x 3 1/2", 3 3/4" h. (ILLUS.) **$145**
Toothpick holder, figural, model of a human skull **25**

Sèvres & Sèvres-Style

Some of the most desirable porcelain ever produced was made at the Sèvres factory, originally established at Vincennes, France, and transferred, through permission of Madame de Pompadour, to Sèvres as the Royal Manufactory about the middle of the 18th century. King Louis XV took sole responsibility for the works in 1759 when production of hard paste wares began. Between 1850 and 1900, many biscuit and soft-paste pieces were made again. Fine early pieces are scarce and high-priced. Many of those available today are late productions. The various Sèvres marks have been copied and pieces listed as "Sèvres-Style" are similar to actual Sèvres wares, but not necessarily from that factory. Three of the many Sèvres marks are illustrated below.

Sevres marks

Busts of the Duc & Duchesse D'Angouleme, bisque, modeled after Baron Francois Joseph Bosio, she wearing an Empire style gown, her hair in tight curls, he wearing a Napoleonic military uniform, each on a cobalt blue & gold-banded socle, dated January 10, 1821 & October 3, 1823 respectively, blue printed interlaced L's marks, artist & other marks, 10 1/4" h., pr. **$2,760**

Sevres Bisque Figure of Boy & Goat

Figure group, bisque, a bust portrait of a youth holding a kid goat draped around his shoulders, incised factory mark, early 20th c., 15" h. (ILLUS.).................................. **805**

Figure group, bisque, 'Le Triomphe de Bacchus,' modeled w/the figure of a nude Bacchus seated in an ermine drapery flanked by two nymphs, wrestling putti at his feet, another putto & lioness at the back, the rockwork base w/applied trophies, vases & fruits, after the model by Taraval, impressed marks, dated 1913, 15" h. **2,990**

Jewelry box, cov., cartouche-shaped w/concave sides & a low domed cover, the hinged cover painted w/a large reserve of 18th c. ladies in an interior reading a letter surrounded by a cobalt blue ground decorated w/a wide leafy scroll gilt band, the sides each w/a paneled reserve of a landscape within scrolling gilt borders on a cobalt blue ground, the interior painted w/flowers, late 19th - early 20th c., blue crowned wreath & "S" mark, artist-signed, overall 17" l. **8,050**

Pedestals, slightly tapering columnar form w/a gilt-bronze foot & capital, fitted on a square white onyx base & w/a thin square white onyx top, the porcelain column w/dark blue scalloped bands around the top & bottom edged in gold, a central gilt-bronze band dividing the column into two white panels decorated w/light blue figural scenes, late 19th c., top 11 1/2" sq., 44 1/2" h., pr. **20,300**

Pitcher, 7 7/8" h., jug-form, tapering ovoid body w/a short wide neck w/dished spout & notched back edge issuing a high arched gilt loop shoulder handle, the shoulder painted w/a garland of flowers on a yellow band, the lower body w/gilt arches & a band of grapevine on dark blue, mid-19th c. **173**

Plate, 9 1/4" d., the center painted w/flowers, the sky blue rim reserved w/three gilt cartouches centering a pair of exotic birds, painted interlaced L's mark w/crown, number 2,000 & "Trianon," late 18th c. **632**

Urns, cov., tall gilt-bronze mounted baluster-form, a stepped squared bronze foot below a short porcelain waisted pedestal w/a bronze connector to the tall ovoid body tapering to a waisted neck & domed cover, fiited w/angular bronze shoulder handles & a figural putto finial, the body w/a central reserve w/a figural color scene of 18th century country figures w/horses, ornate gilt border on a white ground, the reverse w/a landscape reserve, late 19th c., 45" h., pr. **55,375**

Vase, cov., 34 1/4" h., the tall ovoid body w/a cobalt blue ground, the trumpet-form neck supporting a domed cover w/pod finial, the body raised on a ormolu & porcelain ringed pedestal on a squared ormolu plinth base, the shoulders mounted w/upright ormolu acanthus & bracket ring handles suspending berried laurel, the front painted w/an oval reserve w/a color scene of an amorous couple & an interloper all within a gilt oval band w/scrolling gilt trim, further gilt trim on the cover, neck & base, ca. 1880, artist-signed **9,775**

Vases, 4 7/8" h., an inverted pear-shaped body raised on a small slender pedestal on a square plinth, the short waisted neck w/scalloped rim & gilt fluted panels, the body in dark blue applied w/gilt oak garlands from the shoulder down across the body, gilt base trim, 19th c., pr. **575**

Vases, cov., 22" h., the drum-shaped body w/a rounded bottom raised on a slender pedestal base, the shoulder tapering to a tall waisted neck fitted w/a domed cover w/pine cone finial, the pink ground decorated on the neck & around the mid-body w/oblong reserves w/color scenes of 18th century figures in landscapes within gold border w/scrolling gilt trim, gilt banding on the cover, body & base, late 19th c., spurious blue interlaced L's marks, the pair............................. **3,680**

Shelley China

Members of the Shelley family were in the pottery business in England as early as the 18th century. In 1872 Joseph Shelley formed a partnership with James Wileman of Wileman & Co. who operated the Foley China Works. The Wileman & Co. name was used for the firm for the next fifty years, and between 1890 and 1910 the words "The Foley" appeared above conjoined "WC" initials.

Beginning in 1910 the Shelley family name in a shield appeared on wares, although the firm's official name was still Wileman & Co. The company's name was finally changed to Shelley in 1925 and then Shelley China Ltd. after 1965. The firm changed hands in the 1960s and became part of the Doulton Group in 1971.

At first only average quality earthenwares were produced but in the late 1890s new shapes and better quality decorations were used.

Bone china was introduced at Shelley before World War I and these fine dinnerwares became very popular in the United States and are increasingly popular today with collectors. Thin "eggshell china" teawares, miniatures and souvenir items were widely marketed during the 1920s and 1930s and are sought-after today.

Shelley Mark

Cup & saucer, Morning Glory patt. **$62**
Cup & saucer, Polka Dot Black patt., Henley shape **135**
Cup & saucer, Polka Dot patt. **58**
Cup & saucer, Primrose patt., various Chintz shapes, each **120**
Cup & saucer, Regency patt., Dainty shape **60**
Cup & saucer, Rock Garden patt., footed Oleander shape....................................... **170**
Cup & saucer, Roses patt., Dainty shape.......... **70**
Cup & saucer, Stocks patt.................................. **65**
Cup & saucer, Stocks patt., Stratford shape **60**
Luncheon set (trio): cup, saucer & plate: Japan patt., Fairy shape, Wileman & Co., the set (ILLUS. top next page) **200**

Japan Pattern Luncheon Set

Luncheon set (trio): cup, saucer & plate: Japan patt., Queen Anne shape, Wileman & Co., the set 175
Luncheon set (trio): cup, saucer & plate: Lines & Shades patt., Eve (Art Deco style) shape, the set.......................... 250
Luncheon set (trio): cup, saucer & plate: Mandarin patt., Kenneth shape, the set........ 125

Red Blocks Art Deco Tea Set

Tea set, Red Blocks patt., Mode (Art Deco style) shape, teapot & 22 pcs. (ILLUS. of part) **3,200**

Slipware

This term refers to ceramics, primarily redware, decorated by the application of slip, or semi-liquid paste made of clay. Such wares were made for decades in England and Germany and elsewhere on the Continent, and in the Pennsylvania Dutch country and elsewhere in the United States. Today, contemporary copies of early Slipware items are featured in numerous decorator magazines and offered for sale in gift catalogs.

Bowl, 8" d., flat bottom w/upright sides, the inside center decorated w/a thin yellow slip wavy cross w/a dot between each arm (wear, edge chip).......................... $303
Bowl, 9" d., 1 7/8" h., wide shallow form, redware w/yellow slip squiggled cross design in the center, 19th c. 495
Bowl, 11 1/2" d., wide round shallow form w/the wide flanged sides decorated w/three squiggled rows of yellow slip on the redware ground, 19th c. (hairline, glaze flakes).......................... 2,634
Bowl, 12 1/4 x 15 1/2, oblong redware w/coggled edges, decorated w/three bands of triple wavy yellow slip bands, 19th c. (imperfections).......................... 605
Dish, coggle rim, brown slip stylized wide diamond-form veined leaf design across the interior on an amber ground, 5 1/2" d. (old chips).......................... 413

Dish, shallow round form, a two-line yellow slip band across the center flanked by short two-line bands above & below, 7 1/2" d. (minor wear, crazing).......................... 468
Loaf dish, oblong, coggled edge, redware yellow slip tree design, wavy lines at top & sides, 10 1/4 x 14", 2 1/2" h. (wear, glaze flake & some old restoration to rim) . 6,600
Loaf dish, redware, oblong w/coggled edge, three-line yellow slip band around the borders & across the center, 11 1/2 x 15 1/2", 3 1/4" h. (chips, hairlines, flaking).......................... 220
Loaf dish, redware, rectangular w/coggle wheel rim, yellow three-line wavy decoration on two sides & three treble clef designs in center, 17" l. (wear, hairline & chips).......................... 715
Milk bowl, flaring rounded sides, interior glaze w/floral decoration in yellow, green & brown slip, 8 1/2" d., 2 3/4" h. (wear, chips, hairline).......................... 193
Pie plate, coggled rim, wide three-line yellow slip band across the middle, 7" d. (minor chips).......................... 220
Pie plate, round, redware w/three yellow slip double wavy bands across the center, 7 1/2" d., 1 1/2" h. (shallow rim flakes).......................... 468
Pie plate, round, redware w/coggled edges, decorated w/four squiggled lines in yellow & green slip, 8" d. (imperfections).......... 330
Pie plate, coggled rim, a bold yellow slip sweeping monogram w/a "W" across the center, 9" d. (chips, minor flaking w/hairline).......................... 935
Pie plate, round slightly dished form, redware w/overall yellow slip S-scrolls & looped squiggles, 9" d., 1 7/8" h. (edge wear, flakes).......................... 330
Pie plate, redware w/coggled rim, yellow triple-quill slip decoration, 10" d. 468
Pie plate, round, redware w/coggled edges, decorated w/large "ABC" above a wavy line & flourish all in yellow slip, 10 1/8" d. (flaking & hairline).......................... 825
Pie plate, round, redware w/coggled rim, decorated w/yellow slip wavy lines in center & triple yellow slip squiggled bands at top & bottom, 10 3/4" d. (minor flaking).......................... 715
Pie plate, coggled rim, bold wavy three-line band of yellow slip across the center w/slightly wavy bands of slip above & below, 11" d. (glaze & edge chips) 715
Pie plate, redware w/coggle wheel rim, two-line yellow slip decoration, 11" d. (slip is worn & chipped, old chips.).......................... 193
Pie plate, round w/tooled rim, redware w/bold "ABC" in yellow slip, old black on back, 11 1/4" d. (chips).......................... 1,073
Pie plate, coggled rim, scattered dashes of three-line yellow slip around the top, 11 3/8" d. (edge chips, interior wear, rim hairline).......................... 413
Pie plate, coggled rim, unusual band of three-line green slip decoration, 11 3/4" d. (shallow rim chips, interior glaze wear).......................... 880

Plate, 8 1/4" d., coggled rim, a yellow slip three-line band across the center w/three three-line dashes above & below (shallow rim chips, hairline) **495**

Plate, 9" d., round w/textured rim, yellow twist slip decoration on redware, 19th c. (hairline, rim chips) **805**

Plate, 10" d., round w/coggled edge, decorated w/five wavy yellow slip lines across the center, 19th c. (surface wear, chips) **275**

Platter, 11 1/4 x 13 1/2", oval, shallow form w/notched rim, redware w/zig-zag & yellow slip serpentine designs, 19th c. (wear, glaze loss) **518**

Tray, rectangular w/rounded corners, redware w/coggled edges, decorated w/four bands of triple yellow slip wavy lines, 19th c. (surface wear, chips) **715**

Spatterware

This ceramic ware takes its name from the "spattered" decoration, in various colors, generally used to trim pieces hand-painted with rustic center designs of flowers, birds, houses, etc. Popular in the early 19th century, most was imported from England.

Related wares, called "stick spatter," had free-hand designs applied with pieces of cut sponge attached to sticks, hence the name. Examples date from the 19th and early 20th century and were produced in England, Europe and America.

Some early spatter-decorated wares were marked by the manufacturers, but not many. 20th century reproductions are also sometimes marked, including those produced by Boleslaw Cybis.

Bowl, 4 3/4" d., 2 1/2" h., footed, flared sides, yellow w/Tulip patt. in red & green (hairlines & light stain) **$2,310**

Creamer, tapering octagonal form w/wide spout & angled handle, Fort patt., red, black, green & yellow building, blue spatter background, 5 5/8" h. (hairline in handle, small chips) **990**

Cup, miniature, handleless, Rainbow spatter, bands of blue, red & green (small rim flakes) **440**

Cup, miniature, handleless, Rooster patt., yellow, blue, black & red rooster, blue spatter rim (rim flakes) **605**

Cup & saucer, handleless, Rainbow spatter border alternating blue & purple stripes **385**

Cup & saucer, handleless, Star patt. in red, green & dark yellow, blue spatter border, impressed "R" **1,210**

Cup & saucer, Peafowl patt., red spatter border, cup 2 1/2" h., saucer 5 1/2" d. **523**

Cup & saucer, handleless, Cock's Comb patt., red, green & black stylized flower, dark blue spatter border **1,155**

Cup & saucer, handleless, miniature, Rose patt., red, green & black flower w/blue spatter background, colors vary slightly (pinpoint flakes) **330**

Cup & saucer, handleless, Peafowl on Branch patt., blue, red, yellow & black bird on a blue spatter ground, impressed mark "B. and T. Stoneware" (pinpoint flakes on cup) **715**

Cup & saucer, handleless, Peafowl patt., blue, yellow, black & green bird on a red spatter ground **825-875**

Cup & saucer, handleless, Rainbow spatter, each piece banded w/alternating stripes of purple & black spatter **578**

Cup & saucer, handleless, Rose patt., red, green & black flower, blue spatter border, impressed Adams mark (minor roughness on cup rim) **605**

Cup & saucer, handleless, Thistle patt., red, green & black thistle, yellow spatter borders (pinpoint rim flake on cup) **3,410**

Dish, rectangular w/cut corners, Peafowl patt., yellow, red, black & green bird against a blue spatter center ground & a blue spatter border band, 6 x 8 1/4" (minor glaze flakes on rim, yellow glaze flakes on bird) **2,035**

Pitcher, 6 1/4" h., squatty bulbous hexagonal body tapering toward the base & to the neck w/a high arched spout, angled scroll handle, Peafowl patt. in red, yellow, green & black, blue spatter background (hairlines in base, wear, stains) **743**

Plate, 8 1/4" d., Peafowl patt., blue spatter border **413**

Plate, 7 1/4" d., underglaze blue w/red, green & yellow Tulip patt., blue spatter paneled border **825**

Plate, 8 1/4" d., Thistle patt., red & green center design, red spatter border (three small flakes on feather-molded rim) **1,155**

Plate, 8 1/2" d., Cockscomb patt., red & green center design w/a wide blue spatter border (wear, stains, small flakes) **908**

Plate, 9 1/4" d., Peafowl patt., light blue, yellow, green & black bird against a red spatter ground (minor pinpoint flakes on rim, shallow chip on table ring) **715**

Plate, 9 3/8" d., plain white center w/a wide Rainbow spatter border w/alternating bands of red, blue & green spatter, impressed Adams mark, first half 19th c. (minor wear) **605**

Plate, 9 3/8" d., white star reserve in center w/dark blue, green & red, blue spatter paneled border **935**

Plate, 9 1/2" d., Peafowl patt., free-hand bird in blue, red, green & black, red spatter backtground **1,265**

Plate, 9 1/2" d., Rainbow spatter, plain center w/alternating border bands in red, blue & green spatter, scalloped rim.............. **495**

Plate, 9 1/2" d., Star patt. in red, green & blue, blue spatter border **1,073**

Plate, 10" d., round w/Tulip patt. in red & green, red paneled border (edge wear & stains) **743**

Platter, 15 3/4" l., rectangular w/wide cut corners, overall dark blue spatter (wear, stains) **330**

Platter, 13 3/4 x 17 1/2", rectangular w/angled corners, Castle patt., free-handle red & yellow castle w/green trees & grassy field in the center, wide blue spatter border, ca. 1840 (minor discoloration, crazing) **5,462**

Sugar bowl, cov., footed squatty bulbous form w/rolled rim & inset cover, Fort patt. in black, grey, red & green, blue spatter background, 4 1/4" h. (one small chip & pinpoint flake on base, glazed-over flake on inside flange) **770**

Sugar bowl, cov., Schoolhouse patt., green spatter border, 4 1/2" h. (hairline on rim)... **2,475**

Teapot, cov., miniature, four-footed, bulbous body w/molded C-form handle, swan's neck spout, green w/Peafowl patt., free-hand bird in blue, red & yellow on one side, tree on the other, 6" l., 4 1/4" h. (minor roughness on lid edge) **605**

Teapot, cov., octagonal baluster-form w/domed cover, C-scroll handle & swan's-neck spout, Peafowl patt., red, blue, black & green bird on a red spatter ground, 9" h. (very minor flakes) **2,420**

Wash bowl & pitcher set, Adam's Rose patt. in red, green & black, dark blue spatter background on pitcher & band around the bowl, tall paneled tapering pitcher w/high arched spout & long angled handle, footed flaring bowl w/three roses in panels around the interior, bowl 13 1/2" d., 4 1/2" h., pitcher, 12" h., pr. (hairlines in pitcher, professional restoration on bowl) **2,090**

Stick or Cut-Sponge Spatter

Charger, decorated w/large flow blue foliage w/red & green sprig & flower designs, 12 1/4" d. (minor edge wear & light crazing) **165**

Charger, ironstone w/"gaudy" polychrome cut sponge decoration in red & green in center, border w/transfer rabbit decoration alternating w/frogs, 13" d. (overall light crazing)....................................... **1,100**

Cup & saucer, pale blue spatter decorated w/stick spatter cranberry flowers & green leaves (minor flakes)........................... **330**

Plate, 9 1/8" d., center decorated w/stick spatter red fruit w/green leaves, blue rim w/red stripes (bruise & rim flake) **193**

Plate, 9 1/4" d., ironstone, center round brown transfer-printed scene of three rabbits & a frog, a wide border of small cut-sponge blue blossoms w/free-hand green leaves & large trumpet-form red blossoms, brown & yellow trim **413**

Plate, 9 3/8" d., ironstone w/a gaudy design, the center w/stick spatter red, blue & green flowers, black transfer border w/rabbits, frogs & trees, yellow & green enamel **468**

Plate, 9 3/4" d., a wide border band of cut-sponge green blossom heads between thin red stripes around the central free-hand design of columbine w/a rosebud & thistle in green, blue, red, black & purple (minor wear & stains)............................. **275**

Plate, 10" d., red stick spatter border & leaves w/flow blue stripes & flowers............. **275**

Plates, 10" d., ironstone china w/a gaudy design, the center w/a central bull's-eye w/cut-sponge ring of blossoms surrounded by a wide band of brightly colored stylized leaves & flowers, the rim band w/fur-

ther cut-sponge flowerheads, cobalt blue, green & red, set of 8 (minor edge flakes, one w/hairline, one badly damaged).. **1,650**

Platter, 10 1/4 x 14 1/2" oval, ironstone china w/a gaudy design, center w/brown transfer of rabbits & frog in fenced field, yellow enamel field & green frog, border w/red, green & blue stick spatter flowers (minor enamel wear on edge)..................... **1,100**

Sugar bowl, cov., bulbous ovoid body w/a wide low rolled neck, flared footring, inset cover w/button finial, decorated w/spaced vertical stripes alternating w/looped & flowerhead designs in blue, green & red trimmed w/blue stripes, 5" d., 5" h. (minor roughness inside flange) **275**

Spongeware

Spongeware's designs were spattered, sponged or daubed on in colors, sometimes with a piece of cloth. Blue on white was the most common type, but mottled tans, browns and greens on yellowware were also popular. Spongeware generally has an overall pattern with a coarser look than Spatterwares, to which it is loosely related. These wares were extensively produced in England and America well into the 20th century.

Bowl, 7 5/8" d., 3 1/4" h., deep rounded sides tapering to a small footring, a central dark blue band flanked by white bands w/outer bands of blue sponging on white (minor wear) **$110**

Bowl, 9 1/4" d., 4" h., tapering round sides w/molded scalloped panels & a molded rim band, blue sponging on white (glaze wear on bottom, rim hairline)...................... **165**

Bowl, 11 1/2" d., wide shallow form w/flanged rim, large dots of green & brown sponging on a white-glazed ground (glaze flakes) **330**

Bowl, 12" d., 5 1/2" h., deep gently flaring rounded sides w/molded arched panels & a molded rim band, wide upper & lower bands of scalloped blue sponging on white **275**

Bowl, 12 1/4" d., 5 7/8" h., deep slightly rounded flaring sides w/a molded rim, wide bands of blue sponging on white w/scalloped edges around the top & base **385**

Crock, cov., cylindrical w/molded rim, inset flat cover, front marked "Butter," overall blue sponging on white, wood & wire bail handle, 5 3/4" d., 3 3/4" h. plus handle......... **193**

Crock, cov., cylindrical w/molded rim, inset flat cover, overall blue sponging on white, 6 1/2" d., 6 3/4" h. (chips on cover).............. **220**

Jug, cylindrical w/domed top, small cylindrical neck & strap shoulder handle, yellowware w/overall dark blue sponging, 10 1/2" h. **523**

Pitcher, 7 1/2" h., wide cylindrical form w/small rim spout & squared loop handle, overall design of large circles of blue sponging on white **495**

Pitcher, tankard, 8 7/8" h., tall slightly tapering cylindrical form, C-form handle, overall wide bands of stylized blossom-like sponging in blue on white (small flakes)....... **550**

Pitcher, 9" h., tall cylindrical form w/rim spout & low strap handle, overall light blue sponging on white.................................. 495

Pitcher, 10 3/4" h., bulbous body tapering to a tall flaring neck w/a high arched spout, C-scroll handle, decorated down the sides w/banded blue sponging on white, a painted wide blue band flanked by thin blue bands near the bottom............... 303

Pitcher, 11 1/2" h., wide bulbous ovoid body tapering to a waisted neck w/wide arched spout, arched loop handle, the body molded w/ribbons & bows & decorated overall w/wide bands of ovals in blue sponging on white (rim chips)................. 990

Soap dish, stoneware, blue sponging on white, 3 1/4 x 4 5/8"...................................... 110

Staffordshire Figures

Small figures and groups made of pottery were produced by the majority of the Staffordshire, England potters in the 19th century and were used as mantel decorations or "chimney ornaments," as they were sometimes called. Pairs of dogs were favorites and were turned out by the carload, and 19th century pieces are still available. Well-painted reproductions also abound and collectors are urged to exercise caution before investing.

Bear & dog, pearlware, bear-baiting group, modeled w/a chained bear standing four-square on a high rectangular base, a snarling dog at his side, all covered in a thin beige slip, the bear's fur, the dog's spots & the base colored in a watery green glaze, the base edged w/narrow underglaze-blue borders, ca. 1820, 8 1/2" l. (bear's head & edge of base repaired, chain a restoration)...................... **$1,380**

Cats, seated on cobalt blue pillows, looking right & left, w/yellow & black mottled decoration, 4" h., pr................................. 468

Cats, seated on cobalt blue pillows, looking right & left, yellow & black mottled decoration, 7 1/2" h., pr................................ 523

Dogs, black & white dogs seated on yellow, blue & green pillows, 4 1/2" h., pr........... 1,540

Dogs, dalmatians w/gold chains, on green base, 5" h., pr... 495

Dogs, poodles looking right & left, standing on footed pedestals w/pink & green accents, 4" h., pr.. 605

Dogs, poodles seated & looking right & left, white w/sanded coats & black muzzles, yellow eyes & gilt collars w/locks, 4 5/8" h., pr... 413

Dogs, seated dogs looking right & left, brown decoration & yellow collars, 4 1/2" h., pr... 468

Dogs, seated dogs looking right & left, rust colored decoration, 9" h., pr. 660

Dogs, Spaniels in seated position, white w/copper lustre spots, ears, neck chain & lock, yellow eyes, black nose, green highlights, open front legs, second half 19th c., 9 1/2" h., pr. (small hairlines)............ 413

Dogs, Whippets lying on a bed of grass, looking right & left, on raised platform, 4" l., pr. (loss to one tail)........................... 385

Eggs on nest, a large pile of white eggs in green grass molded to form the cover, oval yellow basket base, impressed "S. & S.," 19th c., 10" l................................. 440

Equestrian group, a man on horseback w/a basket of fruit, polychrome trim, 19th c., 9 1/2" h. 303

Figure group, "Heenan-Savers," two dark-haired male figures boxing, one wearing yellow pants w/blue belt, the other w/pink pants & orange belt, oval base w/rectangular panel in background, 9 1/4" h. (minor flakes on hair) 440

Figure group, "Uncle Tom," a tall seated black man w/a little white girl standing on one knee, polychrome decoration, ca. 1860, 10 3/4" h. (crazing)........................ 440

Figure group, "Uncle Tom," Uncle Tom seated w/Little Eva on his knee, polychrome decoration, 19th c., 10 1/4" h............ 770

Figure of Scotsman w/rifle, standing wearing kilt & leaning against a low wall, polychrome decoration, oblong base, 7 3/8" h. (minor wear)..................................... 275

Vase, spill-type, 5 3/4" h., figural model of elephant standing on oval base in front of slender coleslaw tree w/molded leaves, shaded grey w/pink & green blanket, 5 3/4" h. (minor enamel wear & one leg w/in-the-making hairline) 550

Watch hutch, figural, a man & a woman in Victorian peasant dress standing on each side of a central round watch opening below a smaller top opening flanked by figural peacocks, the holes framed by painted ivy vines, bright polychrome decoration, mid-19th c., 10 3/4" h. (hairlines, chip at back)..................................... 330

Zebra, a prancing horse-like animal w/painted stripes on body & tail, black mane, wearing reins, on an oval base w/molded shrub under the animal, polychrome trimj, 19th c., 8 3/4" h. (wear, crazing).......... 495

Zebras, a prancing horse-like animal w/painted stripes on body & tail, looking right & left, on grassy base w/stump, 4 1/2" h., pr.. 468

Staffordshire Transfer Wares

The process of transfer-printing designs on earthenwares developed in England in the late 18th century and by the mid-19th century most common ceramic wares were decorated in this manner, most often with romantic European or Oriental landscape scenes, animals or flowers. The earliest such wares were printed in dark blue but a little later light blue, pink, purple, red, black, green and brown were used. A majority of these wares were produced at various English potteries right up till the turn of the century but French and other European firms also made similar pieces and all are quite collectible. The best reference on this area is Petra Williams' book Staffordshire Romantic Transfer Patterns - Cup Plates and Early Victorian China *(Fountain House East, 1978).*

Bowl, 10" d., blue w/pastoral landscape......... **$220**

Cake stand, footed, Wild Rose patt., blue on white, mid-19th c., 12" d., 2 1/2" h. (crazing)... 403

Staffordshire Chamber Pitcher

Chamber pitcher, wide cylindrical body decorated on both sides w/green transfer-printed vignette of a steam packet in choppy seas above an Irish patriotic emblem titled "City of Dublin Steam Packet Company," floral device under the spout, handle & border, minor crazing & wear, 8" d., 8 1/2" h. (ILLUS.) **978**

Coffeepot, cov., a central reserve depicting a harbor scene w/castle buildings on the heights, surrounded by floral & grapevine transfers, the cover w/a beehive finial, blue, early 19th c., 11 1/2" h. (cover flange broken) **1,035**

Cup & saucer, handleless, central scene of a young couple in a forest setting, floral & scallop border, dark blue, marked "Clews," ca. 1830 (minor wear) **204**

Cup & saucer, handleless, scene of horse-drawn sleigh, dark blue, ca. 1830 (some edge glaze flakes) **275**

Cup & saucer, handleless, white ground w/dark blue floral pattern, Enoch Wood & Sons, Burslem, cup 2 1/2" h., saucer 5 3/4" d. **165**

Ladle, scene of a woman & child by a cottage inside the bowl, dark blue, ca. 1830, 7 1/2" l. **605**

Loving cup, wide cylindrical body w/three loop handles, black transfer-printed medallions trimmed in polychrome, one titled "Autumn," one w/the farmer's arms & the third w/"Industry Produceth Wealth," early 19th c., 6" h. (stains, light crazing, spider crack in bottom) **220**

Pepper shaker, baluster-form w/domed cap, floral transfer w/an English landscape scene w/a church & fisherman, dark blue, ca. 1830, 4 5/8" h. (chips on cap) **385**

Pitcher, 7 1/2" h., bulbous ovoid body w/a shoulder tapering to a short wide flaring cupped neck w/high arched rim spout, C-scroll handle, decorated w/haying scenes, green, impressed "Adams," ca. 1840 .... **385**

Plate, 9" d., center scene of two hunters & hounds w/game, wide floral border, dark blue, ca. 1830 (minor wear) **220**

Plate, 9" d. Cupid & Psyche patt., scalloped edge w/floral border, impressed Adams mark, dark blue, ca. 1830 (slight scratches) **275**

Plate, 10" d., decorated w/an English landscape scene, dark blue, ca. 1830 (pinpoint flakes on table ring) **149**

Platter, 11 5/8" l., oval, floral border w/fruit center, dark blue (light crazing, surface flake) **495**

Platter, 12 3/4" l., oval, floral border w/central scene of East Indian scenery w/elephant, dark blue, impressed "Rogers," ca. 1830 (pinpoint edge flakes) **385**

Platter, 13 1/2 x 15 1/2", oval w/gently scalloped rim, central scene of a group of deer standing in a wooded clearing, vintage border design, marked by Adams, early 19th c. (minor wear) **1,100**

Platter, 17 1/2" l., oval, medium blue transfer-printed center scene of fleet of ships, wide border decorated w/shells & seaweed, John Rogers & Sons (wear & scratches, small rim chips) **1,650**

Platter, 15 1/8 x 17 1/2", wide oval shape w/a gently scalloped rim, the center w/a scene of a man herding cattle, a wide flower & foliage border, dark blue, ca. 1830 (wear) **990**

Platter, 18 1/2" l., oblong, decorated w/figures, animals, etc., by a country house, blue, Adams, ca. 1830 .... **575**

Platter, 14 1/2 x 19", decorated w/a landscape w/sheep & cows in the foreground & ruins in the distance, blue on white, mid-19th c. (glaze imperfection) **575**

Platter, 15 1/4 x 19 1/4", oval, Palestine patt., central harbor scene w/willow trees & pagodas, geometric foliate border design on the wide scalloped rim, dark blue, R. Stevenson, ca. 1830 (knife scratches) **523**

Platter, 14 3/4 x 19 1/2", oval, a central Oriental landscape design w/two people on a hill w/a house, palm trees & a palm border, scalloped rim, blue (stains, glaze wear on underside) **275**

Platter, 20 1/2" l., oval, center reserve w/fruits, wide floral border, dark blue, impressed "Stubbs" (wear w/stains & scratches) **1,430**

Platter, 24" l., oval, Dagger Border patt., blue bands at inner & outer borders w/quatrefoil & dagger designs, by Minton & Boyle, 19th c. **413**

Teapot, cov., creamware, globular form w/leaf-molded handle & spout printed in black on one side w/a scene titled "Harlequin and Columbine Discovered in an Arbor by Pierrot," the reverse w/animals in a barnyard scene, England, ca. 1770, 5" h. (chips on spout, teapot & cover rims) **633**

Teapot, cov., scene of an early train, the reverse w/rail splitters, floral border & cover, blue, early 19th c., 7 1/2" h. (cracks).... **1,093**

Toddy plate, a central scene of a young woman playing a harp in a landscape, a large manor house in the background, flower & leaf border, medium blue, ca. 1830, 4 3/4" d. **105**

Toddy plate, center scene of a house in the woods, floral border, dark blue, marked "Wood," ca. 1830, 5 3/4" d. **138**

Tray, handle, oblong, Japan Flowers patt., Ridgway, Morley, Wear & Co., England, 1836-42. blue, 10 x 14 1/2".............. **275**

Undertray, wide rounded form w/gently shaped flanged rim w/molded open oak branch handles, Seashell patt., cluster of shells in the center w/a wide fruit & leaf design border, impressed Stubbs mark, dark blue, ca. 1830, 11 x 15" (roughness on handles)..................................... **1,320**

Wall plaque, pearlware, oval, a black border trim around oval transfer scene of woman on hillside w/tambourine, above inscription "Come and trip it as you go - On the light fantastic toe," England, early 19th c., 6 1/2 x 8 1/2"................. **431**

Washbowl & pitcher, tall ovoid jug-form pitcher w/tall flared neck w/scalloped rim & wide spout, arched loop handle, wide bowl w/scalloped rim, Aladdin patt., light blue, mid-19th c., bowl 13" d., pitcher 11" h., 2 pcs. **220**

Stangl Pottery

Johann Martin Stangl, who first came to work for the Fulper Pottery in 1910 as a ceramic chemist and plant superintendent, acquired a financial interest and became president of the company in 1926. The name of the firm was changed to Stangl Pottery in 1929 and at that time much of the production was devoted to a high grade dinnerware to enable the company to survive the Depression years. One of the earliest solid-color dinnerware patterns was their Colonial line, introduced in 1926. In the 1930s it was joined by their Americana pattern. After 1942 these early patterns were followed by a wide range of hand-decorated patterns featuring flowers and fruits with a few decorated with animals or human figures.

Around 1940 a very limited edition of porcelain birds, patterned after the illustrations in John James Audubon's "Birds of America," was issued. Stangl subsequently began production of less expensive ceramic birds and these proved to be popular during the war years, 1940-46. Each bird was handpainted and each was well marked with impressed, painted or stamped numerals which indicated the species and the size.

All operations ceased at the Trenton, New Jersey plant in 1978.

Two reference books which collectors will find helpful are The Collectors Handbook of Stangl Pottery *by Norma Rehl (The Democrat Press, 1979), and* Stangl Pottery *by Harvey Duke (Wallace-Homestead, 1994).*

Stangl Mark

Birds

Audubon Warbler, pair, No. 3756-D, 7 3/4" h.. **$425**

Bluebird, No. 3276-S, 5" h................................. **125**

Bluebirds, (Double), No. 3276-D, 8 1/2" h....... **250**

Bobolink, No. 3595, 4 3/4" h. **300**

Canary, Blue Flower, No. 3747, 6 1/4" h. **210**

Cardinal, pine cones, (female), No. 3444, 6" h. **125**

Chat, (Carolina Wren), No. 3590, 4 1/4" h. **260**

Cliff Swallow, No. 3852, 3 1/4" h. **150**

Cockatoo, large, No. 3584, 11 3/8" h. **395**

Duck, flying, No. 3443, 9"................................... **331**

Hummingbirds, No. 3599D, 3 x 10 1/2", pr. **300**

Parakeets, No. 3582D, blue/green, 7" h., pr. **325**

Red-Headed Woodpecker, pair, No. 3752-D, 7 3/4" h. **495**

Redstarts, pair, No. 3490-D, 9" h. **325**

Rooster, No. 3445, 9" h.................................... **250**

Rufous Hummingbird, No. 3585, 3" h.............. **75**

Scissor-Tailed Flycatcher, No. 3757, 11" h... **895**

Wilson Warbler, No. 3597, 3 1/2" h. **60**

Wren, pair, No. 3401-D, 8" **75**

Dinnerwares & Artwares

Stangl Beverage Set

Beverage set w/stand: two qt. ribbed spherical pitcher & six handleless mugs; pitcher in matte cream glaze, mugs in matte aqua glaze, nested in conforming aluminum stand, 9 1/2" h., 21" l., impressed maker's mark on base, mid-20th c., one mug w/nick, one w/hairline, minor crazing (ILLUS.)... **115**

Stoneware

Stoneware is essentially a vitreous pottery, impervious to water even in its unglazed state, that has been produced by potteries all over the world for centuries. Utilitarian wares such as crocks, jugs, churns and the like, were the most common productions in the numerous potteries that sprang into existence in the United States during the 19th century. These items were often enhanced by the application of a cobalt blue oxide decoration. In addition to the coarse, primarily salt-glazed stonewares, there are other categories of stoneware known by such special names as basalt, jasper and others.

Batter jug, ovoid body tapering to a molded rim, angled cylindrical spout at the front, small shoulder loops anchoring the wire bail handle w/wooden grip, brushed cobalt blue large crescent-form blossom on the lower front, impressed label of Evan B. Jones, Pittston, Pennsylvania, 19th c., 10" h. (tin lid missing) **$468**

Churn, tall slightly waisted cylindrical form w/molded rim & eared handles, brushed cobalt blue crude three-leaf sprig w/two blossoms below a "4," 2nd half 19th c., 4 gal., 16 1/4" h. **358**

Crock, cylindrical w/molded rim & eared handles, brushed cobalt blue large leafy vine up the front w/an impressed "3," 3 gal., 19th c., 11 1/2" h. (small chips).......... **440**

Jar, ovoid body w/a wide flat mouth, eared handles, brushed cobalt blue band of vining florals around the middle, impressed "4," mid-19th c., 4 gal., 12 3/4" h. (small chips, minor hairlines).................................... **303**

Jar, slightly ovoid w/molded rim & eared handles, light blue & free-hand label w/tulips & leafy vine above "Excelsior Works, Isaac Hewitt, Jr. Rices Landing, Pa. 3," impressed "3," 19th c., 3 gal., 14" h. (minor chips)...................................... **660**

Jar, tall wide cylindrical body tapering slightly to the deep ringed molded mouth flanked by eared handles, upper half w/brushed cobalt blue wide undulating leafy vine w/large blossoms above a central brushed narrow band of scrolled leaves, the bottom w/the blue stenciled label "Hamilton & Jones, Greensboro, PA - 15," 19th c., 15 gal., 24 1/2" h. (hairlines)............................ **1,980**

Jug, semi-ovoid, brushed cobalt blue stylized floral design, 11 1/2" h. **468**

Jug, semi-ovoid w/"All Right" blue slip-quilled, ca. 1880, 1 gal., 11 1/2" h., unsigned, (quarter size base chip on side, kiln burns & dry glaze in making, glaze separation lines in handles & at base in back) **330**

Jug, sharply ovoid form w/molded lip & strap shoulder handle, impressed label "S. Purdy" splashed in blue, Tuscarawas County, Ohio, 19th c., 11 1/2" h............. **633**

Jug, ovoid w/brushed decoration, "D. Roberts & Co., Utica," ca. 1828, 2 gal., 12" h. (overall staining & glaze spiders at spout)...... **330**

Jug, ovoid w/brushed cobalt blue flower design, "N. White Utica," ca. 1840, 2 gal., 13" h. (glaze burn & stack marks in making)...... **275**

Jug, bulbous ovoid body w/applied strap handle, cobalt blue brushed foliage decoration, impressed label "G. Heiser, Buffalo, N.Y. 2.," 14" h. (stains & minor chips on base).. **440**

Jug, semi-ovoid w/cobalt blue slip-quilled bird on foliage, scrolls, impressed "Lack & Van Arsdale, Cornwall, C-2," 14" h. (minor chips, stains) **385**

Jug, ovoid w/small molded neck & strap handle, brushed cobalt blue large tulip blossom on a slender leafy stem, impressed label "T. Reed 2," Tuscarawas County, Ohio, 19th c., 2 gal., 14 1/4" h...... **1,870**

Jug, ovoid, impressed w/a spread-winged eagle atop a cannon & "Charlestown," Charlestown, Massachusetts, 19th c., 14 1/2" h. (chips, kiln burns) **374**

Jug, semi-ovoid w/flat base, molded mouth & strap handle, brushed cobalt blue slender bird on a flowering branch, impressed label "Charlestown 2" brushed w/blue, 2 gal., 14 1/2" h...................................... **545**

Jug, semi-ovoid w/small molded mouth & applied handle, cobalt blue brushed floral design & impressed label "Cowden & Wilcox, Harrisburg Pa 3," 3 gal., 14 3/4" h. (minor lip chips) **275**

Jug, ovoid body w/molded lip & strap handle, brushed cobalt blue leafy floral sprig decoration & "2" on shoulder, impressed label of J. Maxfield, Milwaukee, mid-19th c., 2 gal., 15" h. (rim chips, stains) **495**

Milk bowl, flat bottom w/deep flared sides & molded top w/rim spout, brushed cobalt blue sprigs of leaves around the sides, impressed "1" in a circle, 11 1/2" d., 4 1/2" h. (small flakes)..................................... **440**

Pitcher, 6" h., bulbous ovoid body tapering to a wide cylindrical neck w/a pinched spout & applied ribbed strap handle, brushed cobalt blue wide floral & leaf band around the body & the neck (rim & spout chips).. **495**

Pitcher, 10 1/2" h., wide ovoid body tapering to a wide cylindrical neck w/pinched spout & molded rim, strap handle, brushed cobalt blue leaf band around the neck & body (spout chip, stains, some discoloration)... **605**

Preserving jar, semi-ovoid, molded mouth, brushed cobalt blue leafy vine w/two blossoms above three graduated bands, impressed mark of Offord & Federer, West Brownsville, Pennsylvania, 19th c., 10 1/2" h. (chips on lip)............................... **605**

Water cooler, tall domed beehive-form w/small neck flanked by loop shoulder handles, bung hole w/wooden spigot at the bottom, brushed cobalt blue "6" & a flourish on the shoulder, 18 1/2" h................. **220**

Teco Pottery

Teco Pottery was actually the line of art pottery introduced by the American Terra Cotta and Ceramic Company of Terra Cotta (Crystal Lake), Illinois in 1902. Founded by William D. Gates in 1881, American Terra Cotta originally produced only bricks and drain tile. Because of superior facilities for experimentation, including a chemical laboratory, the company was able to develop an art pottery line, favoring a matte green glaze in the earlier years but eventually achieving a wide range of colors including a metallic lustre glaze and a crystalline glaze. Though some hand-thrown pottery was made, Gates favored a molded ware because it was less expensive to produce. By 1923, Teco Pottery was no longer being made and in 1930 American Terra Cotta and Ceramic Company was sold. A book on the topic is Teco: Art Pottery of the Prairie School, by Sharon S. Darling (Erie Art Museum, 1990).

Teco Mark

Vase, 4" h., 4" d., squatty bulbous ovoid body tapering to a small flared neck, smooth matte green glaze, stamped mark **$2,640**

Vase, 4 3/4" h., compressed bulbous base w/wide horizontally ribbed cylindrical neck & flat rim, green matte glaze, marked twice on base **495**

Vase, 6 1/2" h., 5 1/2" d., bulbous ovoid gourd-form w/four slight lobes defined by upright scroll bands, four short buttress handles issue from the top & attach to an upper band w/a pierced Oriental design around the closed rim, handles form open loops at the shoulder also w/pierced openings, matte green glaze, stamped "Teco -113" **2,420**

Vase, 7 1/4" h., tall tapering cylindrical form w/flared & molded rim, four squared buttress handles from the rim to the edge of the base, seafoam green glaze, impressed twice w/mark, ca. 1910 .... **1,840**

Vase, 8" h., 5 1/2" d., low footring below the wide ovoid body tapering to a cylindrical neck w/flared rim, long squared handles from the rim down the sides, smooth matte green glaze, stamped mark **2,640**

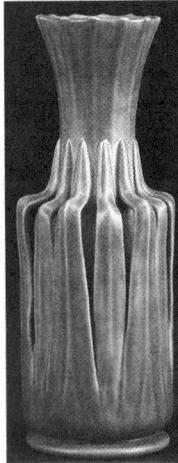

Tall Teco Vase w/Leaves

Vase, 11 3/4" h., footed wide cylindrical body w/trumpet-form neck, body covered w/relief-molded narrow leaves & forming handles, smooth matte green glaze, stamped "TECO" (ILLUS.) **16,500**

Vase, 12 1/2" h., 10 1/2" d., large spherical body tapering to a short wide neck w/molded rim, the body raised on four squared short buttress feet, matte green glaze, stamped "Teco - 339" (restoration to two small chips, hairline at rim, two small chips on one foot) **7,700**

Vase, 13" h., 6 1/4" d., footed swelled cylindrical body w/a narrow shoulder to the short flaring neck, smooth matte green glaze, impressed mark **1,100**

Teplitz - Amphora

In the late 19th and early 20th centuries numerous potteries operated in the vicinity of Teplitz in the Bohemian region of what was Austria but is now the Czech Republic. They included Amphora, RStK, Stellmacher, Ernst Wahliss, Paul Dachsel, Imperial and lesser-known potteries such as Johanne Maresh, Julius Dressler, Bernard Bloch and Heliosine.

The number of collectors in this category is growing while availability of better or rarer pieces is shrinking.

Consequently, prices for all pieces are appreciating, while those for better and/or rarer pieces, including restored rare pieces, are soaring.

The price ranges presented here are retail. They presume mint or near mint condition or, in the case of very rare damaged pieces, proper restoration. They reflect such variables as rarity, design, quality of glaze, size and the intangible "in-vogue factor." They are the prices that knowledgeable sellers will charge and knowledgeable collectors will pay.

Teplitz-Amphora Marks

Ewer, a bulbous Austrian form tapering to a narrow top w/a handle extending vertically several inches & then horizontally across the ewer to the spout, cascades of more than 150 pearl-like 'jewels' adorn the sides, handle, spout & top, finished in a mottled soft grey & soft tan w/undertones of gold, impressed "Amphora" in an oval & crown, & "3969 - 51- 5," also impressed circle w/factory logo "Amphora - Faience," 11 1/4" h.......................... **$1,500-2,000**

Vase, 7 1/4" h., a wide squatty bulbous body tapering sharply to a small neck w/a bulbed rim, Art Nouveau whiplash leaf handles from the rim & down the sides, large lily pad-like leaves swirled around the lower sides, gilt-trimmed leaves on a cream ground, Impressed Amphora & R. St. K. marks, early 20th c................................ **518**

Vase, 7 3/4" h., round bulbous shape, decorated w/a profile of a young girl w/long flowing brownish hair full of numerous multicolored high-glazed flowers w/gold touches, all surrounded by a brownish tan forest scene, finely executed, impressed "Amphora - 663", overglaze red mark "RStK - Turn - Teplitz - Made in Austria"... **1,700-2,200**

Vase, 7 7/8" h., a swollen form w/slender neck & flared rim, decorated about the shoulder w/raised outlines of stylized blossoms w/stems extending down to the base, glazed in matte teal blue against a shaded olive green ground w/gilt rim, impressed "Amphora - 863".............................. **805**

Vase, 8" h., two-handled form almost literally a golden jewel because of the overall gold high-glazed finish w/just a touch of red on one handle & a portion of the bottom, randomly covered w/a multitude of 'jewels' varying in size & color, jewel upon jewel, impressed ovals w/"Amphora" & "Austria" w/a crown, illegible numbers.. **2,200-2,700**

Vase, 8 1/2" h., portrait-type, flat shape w/narrow base, a front facing Mucha-style Art Nouveau portrait of a lady w/golden brown hair full of white flowers against a brownish white forest scene, lovely but lacks some of the elaborate gold decorations, multi-colors & 'jewels' of higher quality pieces, impressed "576" & "Amphora - Turn" enclosed in a large heart, red "RStK" stamp & artist mark "HH" in gold over glaze........................ **900-1,300**

Vase, 8 3/4" h., a restrained Edda piece exhibiting the wonderful 'drip' design characteristic of Edda without appliques of leaves & fruit, etc., which can mar the fabulous designs, a green metallic glaze w/twelve open "portholes" around the bottom, free-form shape, marked w/a raised "Edda" & swastika in a raised triangle, impressed in oval "Amphora," & "3622 - 1C," ink over glaze "22"....... **1,200-1,500**

Vase, 9" h., a bulbous Paul Dachsel forest scene w/reticulated gold top & varied reddish mushrooms in high-relief encircling the bottom, a production mold but hand-painted to produce a uniquely different forest scene, stamped over the glaze w/intertwined "PD - Turn - Teplitz," impressed "1106 -2," blue overglaze "094".. **3,000-4,000**

Vase, 9" h., three-legged triangular-shaped piece consisting of an indented top composed of three leaves w/Art Nouveau stems extending down the sides & then away from the body to form legs, the stems divide the body into panels which contain abstract Art Nouveau-Art Deco designs from the rim to base, greenish metallic glaze, Heliosine Ware, a line growing in popularity, marked "Heliosine Ware - Made in Austria - 21048 - 1 - PP" **500-1,000**

Rare Amphora Cat Head Vase

Vase, 9" h., wide bulbous tapering form, rare form suggesting an inverted Tiffany lamp shade, four large Persian cat heads molded in full relief & projecting from the sides w/a forest of abstract trees w/160-170 opal-like translucent 'jewels' symbolizing fruits, the jewels in various sizes & shades of opal blue mounted in gold surrounds, heavy gold rim, the tree branches extending to the jewels on a background of Klimt-like subtle gold circles, holes behind the jewels permit candlelight or an electric bulb to illuminate the jewels, cat heads finished in a soft pinkish gold w/traces of green & gold highlights on the ears, impressed "Amphora -

Austria" in a lozenge, a crown & "8183 - 28" (ILLUS.).................................... **12,000-14,000**

Vase, 9 3/4" h., an organic piece consisting of a large frog perched on the top & side of the body w/one leg partially extended, his main body 4" l. w/his partially extended leg reaching over 7" l., finely detailed w/a realistic appearance, natural-looking bluish green & tan colors, rare form, impressed "Amphora" & "Turn" in oval, illegible numbers **2,000-2,500**

Vase, 9 7/8" h., a Paul Dachsel abstract design w/a reticulated geometric top & a reticulated handle within a reticulated handle sweeping in an arc from the top to the bottom w/abstract tendrils extending around the bottom of the body & back of the handles, several high-glazed green pods resembling teardrops of various sizes hang from the abstract handle, vines & a center funnel, the top rim & top of handle finished in gold, rare, stamped over glaze w/intertwined "PD - Turn - Teplitz" **3,500-4,000**

Vase, 10" h., a Paul Dachsel abstract architectural style w/a geometric design consisting of a rounded bottom from which four handles begin flush & extend to the top of the rim where they flare open, each handle suggests an abstract candelabrum w/charcoal flames rising from each, finished in iridescent gunmetal grey w/charcoal black sheen touches, gold wash on top, moderne in all respects even though produced in the 1904-10 period, rare form, stamped over glaze w/intertwined "PD - Turn - Teplitz," impressed "1049"... **4,500-5,500**

Vase, 16" h., tall elegant Heliosine ware piece w/a striking Art Nouveau design, two curved slender handles swoop gracefully from the top rim to the bottom w/a slender central shaft, a wide array of iridescent metallic glazes, an increasingly popular line, marked "Heliosine Ware - Austria" & impressed "21020 -D" **1,000-1,500**

Vase, 16 1/4" h., finely executed dragon design by Johanne Maresh, the dragon's body swirls around the base from the broad bottom to the top of the neck & down to the middle of the vase where the head is well defined, detailed feet grip the front & back, the main body of the piece suggests ocean waves, the dragon finished in soft mustard tan shades w/orangy highlights, the waves in lighter mustard tan, the neck in dark gunmetal green, increasingly sought-after & values rising, impressed "JM - 1614," handwritten over glaze "716.20" **1,200-1,800**

Vase, 16 1/2" h., a massive fantasy piece w/a large golden iridescent octopus around the bottom, its tentacles extending around the sides & up to the top where they grab a large swimming sea horse, a particularly rare style of octopus w/only one known at present, impressed "Amphora" & "Austria" in ovals, a crown & "4597 - 50" (ILLUS. top next page)... **6,000-7,000**

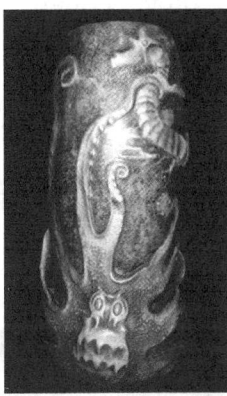

Rare Amphora Octopus Vase

Vase, 16 1/2" h., fine Paul Dachsel creation in an undulating free-form design consisting of several abstract trees extending from the bottom to the top where a branch wraps around the top & then down dividing into other branches w/a series of red-glazed leaves, numerous white 'jewels' suggesting seeds & seed pods attached to the branches & trunks, red leaves w/gold-tinged ends, very rare form, stamped over the glaze w/intertwined "PD - Turn - Teplitz," impressed "1115" **5,000-6,000**

Vase, 16 1/2" h., tall bulbous pot-form divided into four panels by raised free-form gold-finished lines extending from the bottom to the top & ending in a series of concentric circular forms, each panel contains a spider web, one panel w/a larger spider web w/an entrapped dragonfly, tan to cream w/a gold-finished top & base, exudes a sense of reality & age, rare w/many hand-finished details, impressed "Amphora" & "Austria" in ovals, red "RStK Austria" mark over the glaze, impressed hand-etched heart-shaped artist mark, "9029" in ink over the glaze **5,000-7,000**

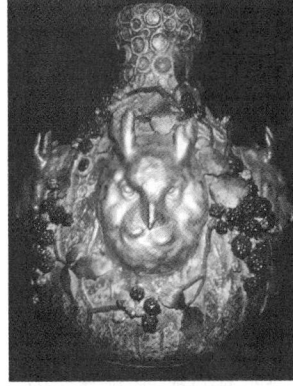

Rare Owl Head Vase

Vase, 17" h.. massive bulbous bottle-form w/four finely detailed gold-finished owl heads projecting from the sides surrounded by brambles, leaves & many clusters of berries & numerous 'jewels' of various sizes & colors interspersed among the brambles, unusual & complicated design, some similar pieces w/other animal heads exist but few survive intact, rare, impressed "Amphora" in oval, a crown & "8160" (ILLUS.) **8,500-9,500**

Vase, 17 1/8" h., tall Art Nouveau form gradually tapering to a narrower top, the bottom w/seven delicate female heads w/long flowing hair emerging from a swirling ocean, tan w/highlights of gold & green, a similar example found in a Berlin museum, marks include a raised Art Nouveau girl's head & "Amphora" in a raised rectangle, red "RStK Austria" mark over the glaze, impressed illegible numbers, handwritten "1081 - L - 372" over the glaze **2,000-3,000**

Rare Reticulated Amphora Vase

Vase, 17 1/2" h., an important reticulated piece composed of a basket-like vase within a vase elaborately entwined w/swooping gold handles joined in the middle, numerous varied colored 'jewels' around the sides, viewed through the reticulation a high-glazed blue swirly design w/gold highlights is seen, the exterior w/a metallic bluish green w/gold wash & gold highlights, high-glazed gold rim, only one known so far, impressed "Amphora" & "Austria" in ovals, a crown & "3791 -45" (ILLUS.) **12,000-14,000**

Vase, 17 3/4" h., figural, an Art Nouveau woman finished in gold w/soft rose highlights & draped around the bottom portion of the tall form w/a flowing leaf growing out of the bottom & extending to the top, mottled greens, blues, creams w/a gold wash, impressed "Amphora" & "Austria" in ovals, Imperial circle mark & "824 - 30," later Czechoslovakian versions w/lesser glazes bring about half the value **3,000-4,000**

Vase, 20 1/4" h., squatty bulbous base tapering to cylindrical neck w/flat rim, relief-molded mermaid clinging to side along w/clusters of blackberries & blackberry vines, glaze on body & mermaid give the impression of a gold doré finish on bronze, impressed "Amphora" inside an oval on bottom (restoration to several leaves & vines & also to one of the mermaid's arms & end of tail) **3,080**

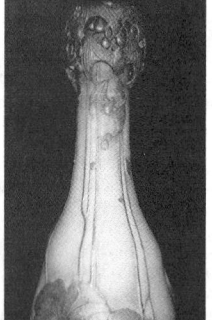

Tall Amphora Vase with Bats

Vase, 21 1/2" h., tall bottle-form w/swarms of gold bats feeding on golden fruits around the reticulated top, they are about to be joined by other bats flying up the sides, tall graceful form w/the rounded base encircled by golden lily pad leaves w/the stems extending up the sides on an eggshell off-white ground, impressed "Amphora" in oval, red "Austria RStK" mark over glaze, impressed "41 - 668" & "750 - 1029" in ink (ILLUS.) **7,000-9,000**

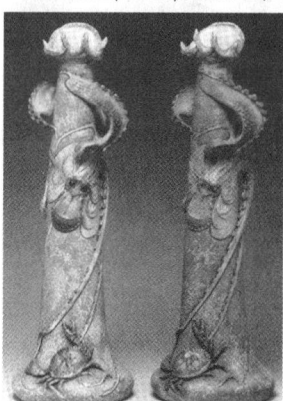

Amphora Sea Life Vases

Vases, 19 1/2" h., tapering cylindrical form w/cushion foot & spiky rim, applied w/a realistically modeled octopus capturing a crab, covered in a sponged blue, white & yellow glaze, the creatures in beige & burnt orange, printed in blue "AMPHORA - Made in Czecho-Slovakia" & impressed numbers, pr. (ILLUS.) **2,875**

Tiffany Pottery

In 1902 Louis C. Tiffany expanded Tiffany Studios to include ceramics, enamels, gold, silver and gemstones. Tiffany pottery was usually molded rather than wheel-thrown, but it was carefully finished by hand. A limited amount was produced until about 1914. It is scarce.

Tiffany Pottery Mark

Tiffany Pottery Vase

Vase, 6" h., bulbous base w/shoulder tapering to short wide cylindrical neck w/flat rim, molded w/stylized leaves & berries, covered in a mottled sea green & cobalt glaze, ca. 1910, unsigned (ILLUS.) **$3,450**

Tiffany Pottery Vase

Vase, 8 3/4" h., cylindrical body w/flared foot & slightly swelled top, decorated w/molded & reticulated arrowroot plants under blue & green lustered glaze, irregular rim formed by leaftips & blossoms, three very short, very tight hairlines from rim, incised "LCT - acid-etched L.C. Tiffany - Favrile Pottery" (ILLUS.) **15,400**

Tiles

Tiles have been made by potteries in the United States and abroad for many years. Apart from small tea tiles used on tables, there are also decorative tiles for fireplaces, floors and walls and this is where present collector interest lies, especially in the late 19th century American-made art pottery tiles.

Grueby Pottery, Boston, Massachusetts, square, decorated in cuenca depicting a cherub w/a cornucopia in matte oatmeal glaze on a grey-blue ground, design by Addison Le Boutillier, Boston, early 20th c., illegible impressed number on side, 6" d. (glaze bursts, minor edge chips) **$173**

Grueby Pottery, Boston, Massachusetts, square, decorated w/grapevine cluster & leaves in relief in green, brown & dark blue against a tan ground, impressed mark & number 4085A, 6" sq. **748**

Low Art Pottery, Chelsea, Massachusetts, square, depicting a profile of a child's head in relief, dark bluish green glossy glaze, impressed marks, early 20th c., 6" sq. (small glaze abrasion) **115**

Rookwood Pottery, Cincinnati, Ohio, square, a raised decoration of a Dutch mother holding a baby & little girl at her side by the shore w/a windmill, Matte glaze, shades of blue, green, pink & tan, 1924, 5 3/4" w. **316**

Wedgwood (Josiah), England, majolica, square w/large embossed & swirled oak leaves surrounded w/round reserve enclosing a fox head, impressed mark, ca. 1873, 8" sq., pr. (each w/restored rim chip)... **345**

Wedgwood (Josiah), England, square earthenware, decorated in crimson lustre w/floral & scrolled foliage designs in four panels, attributed to the William de Morgan workshop, raised factory mark, ca. 1900, 8" sq. **259**

Torquay Pottery

In the second half of the 19th century several art potteries were established in the South Devon region of England to take advantage of a belt of fine red clay. The coastal town of Torquay gives its name to this range of wares which often featured incised sgraffito decoration or colorful country-style decoration with mottos.

The most notable potteries operating in the Torquay area were the Watcombe Pottery, The Torquay Terracotta Company and the Aller Vale Art Pottery, which merged with Watcombe Pottery in 1901 and continued production until 1962. Other firms whose wares are collectible include Longpark Pottery and The Devonmoor Art Pottery.

Early wares feature unglazed terra cotta items in the Victorian taste including classical busts, statuary and vases and some painted and glazed wares including examples with a celeste blue interior or highlights. In addition to sgraffito designs other decorations included flowers, Barbotine glazes, Devon pixies framed in leafy scrolls and grotesque figures of cats, dogs and other fanciful animals produced in the 1890s.

The dozen or so potteries flourishing in the region at the turn of the 20th century introduced their most popu-

lar product, motto wares, which became the bread and butter line of the local industry. The most popular patterns in this line included Cottage, Black and Colored Cockerels and Scandy, based on Scandinavian rosemaling designs. Most of the mottoes were written in English with a few in Welsh. On early examples the sayings were often in Devonian dialect. These motto wares were sold for years at area seaside resorts and other tourist areas with some pieces exported to Australia, Canada and, to a lesser extent, the U.S.A. In addition to standard size teawares and novelties some miniatures and even oversized pieces were offered.

Production at the potteries stopped during World War II and some of the plants were destroyed in enemy raids. The Watcombe Pottery became Royal Watcombe after the war and Longpark also started up again, but produced simpler patterns. The Dartmouth Pottery started in 1947 and produced cottages similar to those made at Watcombe and also developed a line of figural animals, banks and novelty jugs. The Babbacombe Pottery (1950-59) and St. Marychurch Pottery (ca. 1962-69) were the last two firms to turn out motto wares but these later designs were painted on and the pieces were lighter in color with less detailing.

Many books on the various potteries are available and information can be obtained from the products manager of the North American Torquay Society.

Torquay Pottery Marks

Dresser tray, Motto Ware, Cottage patt., Devon dialect, "Dinna lie in yer bed an lippen tae yer neebor," Watcombe, 1920s, 7 1/2 x 10 3/4" (restored) **$210**

Egg cup, Motto Ware, Cottage patt., "Fresh today," Longpark Torquay, ca. 1930, 2 1/2" h. **53**

Egg cup, Motto Ware, Cottage patt., "New laid," Royal Watcombe, ca. 1950, 2 3/4" h. **42**

Egg cup, Motto Ware, Cottage patt., "Waste not - Want not," Watcombe, ca. 1950, 2 3/4" h. **45**

Torquay Egg Cup

Egg cup, Motto Ware, Black Cockerel patt., inscribed "Just laid," 1 1/2" d., 1 3/4" h. (ILLUS.) **45**

Torquay Cottage Pattern Mustard Pot

Mustard pot, cov., Motto Ware, Cottage patt., "Soft words win hard hearts," 2 1/2" d., 3" h. (ILLUS.) 55

Pin tray, Motto Ware, Cottage patt., "Don't Grouse - Work like Helen B. Merry - Ilfracombe," Watcombe, ca. 1901-10 mark, 3 1/4" sq. 52

Pin tray, Motto Ware, Scandy patt., "Tell truth and shame the Devil - Port Arthur Canada," Watcombe, ca. 1910-27, 3 1/4 x 5" 56

Pitcher, 1 3/4" h., miniature, Motto Ware, Cottage patt., "Little and good - Brixham," Royal Watcombe 55

Pitcher, 2" h., miniature, Motto Ware, Cottage patt., "For my Dolly," Royal Watcombe 62

Pitcher, 2" h., miniature, Motto Ware, Scandy patt., "Thumbs Up," Royal Watcombe 55

Pitcher, 2 1/2" h., miniature, Motto Ware, Scandy patt., "Demsher Craim tak an try it," Aller Vale 60

Pitcher, 2 7/8" h., front pouring spout, Motto Ware, Scandy patt., "The red kine bathing in the stream," Aller Vale H.H. & Co., ca. 1897-1902 mark 80

Pitcher, 4 1/2" h., Sgraffito patt., band of leafy scrolls & flowers on glazed terra cotta, Q1 pattern code, Aller Vale, 1890s 88

Torquay Cottage Pattern Pitcher

Pitcher, 5" h., 4" d., Motto Ware, Cottage patt., bulbous body w/tall cylindrical neck, "If you can't be aisy Be as aisy as you can" (ILLUS.) 110

Pitcher, 5 3/4" h., Motto Ware, Forget-me-not patt., "From Launceston," white script on dark blue, light blue forget-me-nots on white band w/trellis, Exeter, 1920 123

Pitcher, 6" h., Motto Ware, Black Cockerel patt., "It's an ill wind that blows nobody good," Longpark, ca. 1918-30 142

Pitcher, 6" h., Motto Ware, Scandy patt., "There's a saying old and musty - yet it is ever new...," Aller Vale, ca. 1891-1910 116

Pitcher, 6" h., slim shape, Scroll patt., colored scrolls on a green ground, Watcombe 72

Small Torquay Sugar Bowl

Sugar bowl, open, round tapering sides, Mottto Ware, Black Cockerel patt., "Be aisy with tha sugar," 3 1/4" d., 1 3/4" h. (ILLUS.) 65

Uhl Pottery

Original production of utilitarian wares began at Evansville, Indiana in the 1850s and consisted mostly of jugs, jars, crocks and pieces for food preparation and preservation. In 1909, production was moved to Huntingburg, Indiana where a more extensive variety of items was eventually produced including many novelty and advertising items that have become highly collectible. Following labor difficulties, the Uhl Pottery closed in 1944.

Unless it is marked or stamped, Uhl is difficult to identify except by someone with considerable experience. Marked pieces can have several styles of ink stamps and/or an incised number under glaze on the bottom. These numbers are die-cut and impressed in the glazed bottom. Some original molds were acquired by other potteries. Some production exists and should not be considered as Uhl. These may have numbers inscribed by hand with a stylus and are usually not glazed on the bottom.

Many examples have no mark or stamp and may not be bottom-glazed. This is especially true of many of the miniature pieces. If a piece has a 'Meier's Wine' paper label, it was probably made by Uhl.

While many color variations exist, there are about nine basic colors including blue, white, black, rose or pink, yellow, teal, purple, pumpkin and browns/tans. Blue, pink, teal and purple are currently the most sought after colors. Animal planters, vases, liquor/wine containers, pitchers, mugs, banks, kitchenware, bakeware, gardenware and custom-made advertising pieces exist.

Similar pieces by other manufacturers do exist. When placed side by side, a seasoned collector can recognize an authentic example of Uhl Pottery.

Miscellaneous Pitchers

Uhl Creamer & Pitchers

Creamer, Lincoln profile, blue glaze (ILLUS. center row, left) 190
Pitcher, barrel-shaped, blue glaze (ILLUS. top) 60
Pitcher, bulbous body, blue glaze (ILLUS. far right) 90-120

Miscellaneous Uhl Pitchers

Pitcher, Egyptian jug-type, black glaze (ILLUS. top left) 30-60
Pitcher, jug-type, "Creme De Coffee," blue glaze (ILLUS. bottom) 35
Pitcher, miniature Egyptian jug-type, yellow glaze (ILLUS. center, third from left with creamer) 30-40
Pitcher, miniature, jug-type, brown & white glaze, 1" h. (ILLUS. center, second from right with creamer) 75-100
Pitcher, miniature modified Egyptian jug-type, yellow glaze (ILLUS. center, far right with creamer) 30-40
Pitcher, modified Egyptian jug-type, black or red glaze, each (ILLUS. right top & bottom) 30-60
Pitcher, cov., Egyptian jug-type, blue glaze (ILLUS. bottom left) 30-60

Van Briggle

The Van Briggle Pottery was established by Artus Van Briggle, who formerly worked for Rookwood Pottery, in Colorado Springs, Colorado at the turn of the century. He died in 1904 but the pottery was carried on by his widow and others. From 1900 until 1920, the pieces were dated. It remains in production today, specializing in Art Pottery.

Early Van Briggle Pottery Mark

Bowl-vase, spherical w/a low molded mouth, matte brown glaze, Shape No. 200, 1906, 6" h. (staining) **$489**
Bowl-vase, wide bulbous body tapering slightly at the top to a wide flat mouth, embossed around the rim w/a band of large stylized morning glory blossoms & leaves atop tall slender stems down the sides, feathered blue & green glaze, Shape No. 284, 1905, 7 1/2" d., 6 1/2" h. ... **1,540**
Candlesticks, a wide seven-sided tapering foot below the tall tapering paneled shaft w/a paneled bulbous socket, matte green over brown glaze, ca. 1920, 10" h., pr. **633**
Lamp, table model, figural, the base w/a Lady of the Lake design of a maiden kneeling at one end of a shallow oblong pool-form bowl w/incurved sides, the electric lamp fitting behind her supporting the original tapering cylindrical laminated butterfly & dry grass paper shade, base in deep rose glaze w/dark highlights, ca. 1920s, 21" h. **385**
Vase, 3 3/4" h., 4" d., flat-bottomed squatty bulbous form w/a small flat mouth, molded around the sides w/crocus blossoms & leaves, leathery matte brown glaze, 1903 .... **1,430**
Vase, 5 1/4" h., 3" d., swelled cylindrical form w/a narrow angled shoulder centering a short neck, molded around the shoulder w/tulip blossoms on slender stems down the sides, thick, frothy & sheer rose & beige matte glaze w/clay showing through, Shape No. 187, 1903.... **2,200**
Vase, 7" h., cylindrical form w/swelled shoulder & short molded rim, relief-molded poppy pod decoration cov. w/maroon matte glaze w/green highlights, incised marks & "Colo. Spgs.,"K" & "7," shape No. 694, 1907-12 (nearly invisible glaze skip on base) **1,210**
Vase, 7" h., wide ovoid base, sharply tapering sloping shoulder w/wide cylindrical neck & flat rim, matte green glaze, Shape No. 415, 1906 .... **523**
Vase, 7" h., 3 1/2" d., slender cylindrical form w/a swelled shoulder & short tapering neck, embossed around the top w/jonquils on tall stems, dark purple dead-matte glaze, incised mark & dated 1902 .... **2,750**

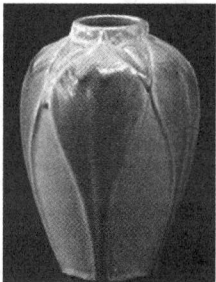

Van Briggle Vase

Vase, 7 1/2" h., bulbous ovoid body w/a narrow cylindrical neck & flat rim, embossed w/wide triangular ribbed leaves w/ruffled edges & flowers, the leaves covered in an unusual brown matte glaze against a robin's-egg blue ground, Shape No. 797, 1907-11 (ILLUS.).. **1,430**

Vase, 8" h., footed spherical body tapering to tall cylindrical neck w/flat rim, base embossed w/wide triangular leaves against a burgundy ground, incised "AA -19??," dating to the teens.................................... **715**

Vase, 8 1/2" h., 7" d., bulbous ovoid body tapering to a flat-rimmed neck, embossed around the neck & shoulder w/green-washed leaves & red berries w/an overall rich matte raspberry glaze, incised mark, Shape No. 164, dated 1904.. **3,300**

Vase, 9" h., bulbous base tapering to a tall cylindrical neck, molded around the neck w/flower blossoms on tall stems down the neck & wide pointed leaves around the bottom, two-tone blue shaded to dark green matte glaze, incised marks, ca. 1907-12 .... **770**

Vase, 9" h., wide bulbous ovoid body w/short incurved cylindrical neck, decorated w/large relief-molded daisies & leaves & covered w/rich mulberry & blue glaze, incised mark, ca. 1918 (1/4" glaze nick off rim)...................................... **468**

Vase, 9" h., 4 1/2" d., footed baluster-form w/a small molded mouth, embosed around the neck & shoulder w/large arrowroot leaves w/slender stems down the sides, fine frothy matte green glaze, Shape No. 357, 1905.............................. **2,970**

Early Rare Van Briggle Vase

Vase, 9" h., 6" d., wide tapering cylindrical body w/a bulbous swelled shoulder tapering slightly to an incurved rim, decorated around the shoulder w/embossed poppy pods & leaves on long stems, covered in a mottled red, blue & mauve matte glaze w/the brown clay body showing through, incised "AA VAN BRIGGLE - 1902 - III" (ILLUS.)............................ **15,600**

Vase, 10" h., tall slender ovoid form w/a flared foot & closed rim, molded around the shoulder w/a repeating design of tulip blossoms on tall leafy stems, dark maroon matte glaze, second quarter 20th c...... **259**

Vase, 10 3/4" h., 4" d., tall slightly tapering cylindrical form molded in relief around

the base w/large spread-winged bats, smooth speckled brown matte glaze, Shape No. 191 (4), ca. 1914 .... **4,400**

Vase, 13" h., 6 1/4" d., tall ovoid form w/four small pierced loop handles around the shoulder & below the short tapering neck, a stylized peacock feather molded between each handle, Persian Rose glaze, Shape No. 119, ca. 1917 .... **990**

Warwick

Numerous collectors have turned their attention to the productions of the Warwick China Manufacturing Company that operated in Wheeling, West Virginia, from 1887 until 1951. Prime interest would seem to lie in items produced before 1914 that were decorated with decal portraits of beautiful women, monks and Indians. Fraternal Order items, as well as floral and fruit decorated items, are also popular with collectors.

Warwick Mark

Pitcher, 6 1/2" h., Tobio #3, brown shaded to brown ground, decorated w/color portrait of Native American, A-12 .... **$300**

Pitcher, 7" h., Tobio #2, overall white ground, color bird decoration, D-1 .... **230**

Pitcher, 7 3/4" h., Tobio #1 shape, overall red ground w/color portrait of fisherman in yellow slicker, No. E-3............................. **225**

Vase, 4" h., Pansy shape, yellow shading to green ground, color portrait of Anna Potaka, K-1 .... **200**

Violet Vase with Beechnut

Vase, 4" h., Violet shape, brown shading to tan ground, color beechnut decoration, matte finish, M-2.................................. **140**

Vase, 4" h., Violet shape, overall charcoal ground, color floral decoration, C-6............... **150**

Vase, 7" h., Albany shape, tan shading to tan ground, color nut decoration, matte finish, M-64... **200**

Vase, 7 1/4" h., Cuba shape, brown shading to brown ground, color pine cone decoration, A-64 .... **295**

Vase, 8" h., Duchess shape, brown shading
to brown ground, color floral decoration,
A-27 195
Vase, 8" h., Duchess shape, overall white
ground w/color bird decoration, D-1 210
Vase, 8" h., Grecian shape, brown shading
to brown ground, color floral decoration,
A-6 230
Vase, 11" h., Oriental shape, brown shading
to brown ground, color floral decoration,
A-21 275
Vase, 11 1/2" h., Regency shape, brown
shading to brown ground, color floral
decoration, A-40 290
Vase, 11 1/2" h., Roman shape, overall
white ground, color bird decoration, D-1 285
Vase, 11 1/2" h., Senator #3 shape, brown
shading to brown ground, color floral
decoration, A-6 245

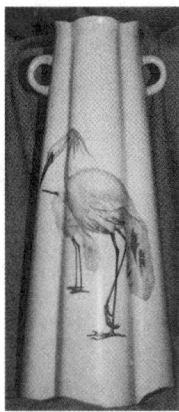

Verona Shape Vase with Bird

Vase, 11 3/4" h., Verona shape, overall
white ground, color bird decoration, D-1
(ILLUS.) 245
Vase, 11 7/8" h., Nasturtium shape, brown
shading to brown ground, color floral
decoration, A-40 265
Vase, 12" h., Gem shape, brown shading to
brown ground, color floral decoration, A-
16 220
Vase, 12" h., Helene shape, color portrait of
woman w/large hat, matte finish, M-1 255
Vase, 12 1/2" h., Alexandria shape, brown
shaded to brown ground w/color floral
decoration, No. A-40 300
Vase, 13 1/2" h., Chrysanthemum #2
shape, overall charcoal ground decorat-
ed w/colored florals, No. C-6 185
Vase, 13 1/2" h., Senator #2 shape, tan
shading to brown ground, color portrait of
a gypsy wearing scarf, matte finish, M-1 245
Vase, 15" h., A Beauty shape, brown shaded to brown ground w/red rose (Ameri-
can Beauty) decoration, No. A-20 300
Vase, 15" h., Princess shape, brown shad-
ing to brown ground, color floral decora-
tion, A-27 350
Vase, 15" h., Senator #1 shape, green
shading to green ground, color acorn
decoration, matte finish, M-4 200

Dinnerwares

Cup & saucer, Pattern No. B-9551 20
Gravy boat w/underplate, Pattern No.
B-9289 30
Plate, 6 1/2" d., bread & butter, Pattern No.
D-9351, platinum bands 20
Plate, 6 1/2" d., bread & butter, Pattern No.
E-9450 15
Plate, 9" d., Pattern No. B-9059 15
Plate, 9" d., Pattern No. C-9295, Bird of
Paradise decoration w/two birds 12
Platter, 13" l., Pattern No. B-9272, coin gold
trim 40

Add-ons

Bowl, oval, Pattern No. 2000 25
Vegetable bowl, handled, Pattern No. 2062 30

Commercial China

Bowl, 4 1/4 x 10 1/4" oval, white ironstone
w/green band, "Osiris" emblem 20
Bowl, 5" d., white w/bands, star emblem
w/"Bethleham Chapter No. 14 O.E.S." 20
Butter pat, white w/"The Brass Rail" logo,
3" 20

Warwick "Sumter Hospital" Creamer

Creamer, white w/two green bands &
"Sumter Hospital" logo, 2 1/2" h. 22
Cup & saucer, white w/"Liggett's" logo 35
Cup & saucer, white w/"St. Gregory's" logo 22
Mug, white w/green drape & emblem, "The
Security Benefit Assoc.," 3 1/2" h. 25
Plate, 6 1/4" d., white w/one green band,
double headed eagle emblem w/"AASR
32" & "Valley of Wheeling" 24
Plate, 9" d., white w/"Hotel Anthony" logo 18
Plate, 9" d., white w/black & red bands,
"Masonic Temple of Austin" emblem 18
Plate, 10" d., white w/"compliments of Dine
Furniture Company" 40
Plate, 10" d., white w/gold band, "Souvenir
of Pleasanton" decal 25
Plate, 10 1/4" d., white w/"The Washington
Duke" logo 35

Warwick "Sumter Hospital" Sugar Bowl

Sugar bowl, cov., white w/two green bands, "Sumter Hospital" logo, 3 3/4" h. 25
Tray, oval, white w/"The Washington" logo, 3 1/2 x 9 3/4" 30

Wedgwood

Reference here is to the famous pottery established by Josiah Wedgwood in 1759 in England. Numerous types of wares have been produced through the years to the present.

WEDGWOOD

Early Wedgwood Mark

Basalt

Basalt Crocus Pot

Crocus pot & undertray, domed woven basketweave beehive-form top w/loop handle pierced overall w/holes, resting on a dished matching tray, impressed mark, early 19th c., 7 1/4" h. (ILLUS.) **$1,265**
Figure of Aphrodite, nude young woman seated atop a wave-crested base & gazing up at a small seashell she holds in one hand, impressed title & mark, late 19th c., 10 3/8" h. 920
Figure of Hope, scantily clad female figure reclining on a draped rock w/an anchor by her side, impressed title & mark, 19th c., 9 3/8" h. 978

Basalt Figure of Mercury

Figure of Mercury, the naked youth standing wearing his winged helmet, leaning against a tall tree stump, round base, impressed mark & title, 19th c., 12 1/2" h. (ILLUS.) **2,070**
Figure of Oliver Cromwell, standing man modeled as a Cavalier, set on a circular base, impressed title & mark, early 20th c., 6 1/2" h. 690
Figure of Summer, allegorical style modeled as a scantily clad young maiden standing beside a slender tree stump, round base, 19th c., 10 1/8" h. 633
Figure of "The Potter," seated worker, from the Skills of the Nation series by Colin Melbourne, No. 334 of 1000, printed & impressed marks, ca. 1980, 9 1/2" h. 518
Medallion, oval, embossed bust profile portrait of Benjamin Franklin, titled & impressed mark of Wedgwood & Bentley, ca. 1780, 1 3/4 x 2" **1,035**

Basalt Plaque with Classical Scene

Plaque, oval, molded in relief w/figures of a classical lady carrying stems of poppies, a cupid walking in front, titled "Night Shedding Poppies," impressed mark of Wedgwood & Bentley, ca. 1777, hairline, 13 1/4 x 17 3/4" (ILLUS.) **6,038**
Plaque, rectangular, embossed scene titled "Beloved of the Great Enchantress," gilt-decorated, No. 31 of a limited edition of 250, 1973, impressed mark, 8 x 8 1/2" 345
Plaque, rectangular, molded w/a classical scene of Vulcan forging armor for Achilles, impressed mark, 19th c., in wide flat oak gilt-lined frame w/brass presentation plaque at the bottom, 6 x 9 1/2" 1,265
Vase, cov., classical urn-form, the tall ovoid body w/an angled shoulder tapering to a cylindrical neck w/rolled rim, small domed cover w/knob finial, bacchus head handles from rim to side of shoulder, slender waisted pedestal on a square plinth foot, the sides w/oval relief-molded medallions of classical figures, impressed lozenge mark of Wedgwood & Bentley, shape No. 1, ca. 1775, handles restored, replaced cover, 10 1/4" h. (ILLUS. top next page) **1,725**

Classical Basalt Covered Vase

Vase, 5" h., disk foot & short stem below the bulbous ovoid body tapering slightly to a wide, short rolled neck, the side cast in relief w/a continuous scene of bacchanalian boys at play, 19th c., impressed mark..... **575**

Vase, 7" h., classical form, a square plinth supporting a short waisted pedestal & the wide squatty bulbous body w/a wide shoulder centered by a short trumpet neck, molded bands of laurel leaves on rim & shoulder & molded drapery swags around the shoulder, impressed wafer mark of Wedgwood & Bentley, ca. 1775 (edge nick, cover missing) **863**

Vase, 9 1/4" h., classical urn-form, a square plinth below the short small pedestal supporting the large tall urn-form body w/a wide shoulder centering the waisted neck w/rolled rim, arched loop handles from the rim to the shoulder & ending in bacchus heads, plain body & base, Shape 1, impressed lozenge mark of Wedgwood & Bentley, ca. 1775 (missing cover) **978**

Vase, cov., 11 1/2" h., classical urn-form, a square plinth w/patterned edges supporting the short waisted pedestal below the tall urn-form body w/a narrow shoulder centering a wide short waisted neck & low domed cover w/seated sibyl finial, figural sphinx head handles atop the shoulder, the body cast w/long laurel leaf swags centered by an oval medallion of the "Three Graces," impressed mark of Wedgwood & Bentley, ca. 1775 (chips on socle footrim)... **4,025**

Vases, 3 7/8" h., cylindrical, each w/a ring band of children at play in relief above engine-turning, creamware slip interior, impressed mark, late 18th c., pr. (small rim chips) **1,093**

Vases, 11 1/2" h., trumpet-form, stepped scalloped foot, molded w/overall foliate decorations, impressed marks, early 20th c., pr.. **546**

Caneware

Creamer, molded w/bamboo leaves, enamel-decorated, impressed lower case mark, 18th c., 2 1/2" h. **1,265**

Game dish, cov., low oval form w/insert ring, piecrust-molded rim, low domed cover w/applied radiating acanthus leaves & zigzag & loop border bands, short cylindrical small opening at center of cover, impressed mark, early 19th c., 14" l. (stains, rim chips to ring)..................... **920**

Game dish & cover, oval form, the high cylindrical cover molded in relief around the sides w/leafy vines & dead game, a figural recumbent hare finial, impressed mark, ca. 1871, 7" l. (missing insert dish) **575**

Inkstand, modeled as a long narrow boat-form basket w/molded basketweave exterior & central arched handle, applied rosso antico foliate trim, molded wells at each end & holding two covered cylindrical pots w/further trim, impressed mark, late 18th c., overall 8 3/4" l., the set (inkwell stained, interior collar rim chip on one cover, slight rim lines on pots)............ **2,645**

Pie dish, cov., oval, the cover decorated w/pastry strapwork & a twig knop w/leaves & berries, impressed mark, early 19th c., 8 1/2" l. (rim nicks on cover, rim chip & hairlines in dish)............................ **690**

Teapot, cov., spherical bamboo-molded body w/a bamboo-molded spout & loop handle, domed cover w/bamboo twig handle, trimmed w/dark blue banding & dots, impressed lower case mark, 18th c., 4 1/4" h. (chips on spout).............. **2,760**

Vase, 7" h., trumpet-form w/flared foot & ringed & widely flaring mouth, applied black classical figures in relief between floral & leaf w/berry bands, impressed mark, early 19th c. (disk lid missing)............. **690**

Creamware

Condiment set: cov. jug raised on a stand w/two fixed cov. barrel form pots & filled w/a cov. pepper pot, all supported on a larger circular footed tray; each piece finely painted in brown monochrome w/various gardening implements beneath or within a border of pink thistles edged w/narrow blue enamel bands, ca. 1800, impressed Wedgwood upper & lower case marks, 8 3/4" h. (one cover restored, one cover w/minor crack)........... **8,050**

Jelly mold, conical, painted w/two groups of colorful flowers above a band of flower swags tied w/blue ribbon & a wreath of flowers on the flat circular base pierced w/four apertures, the rims & tip of the mold edged in brown, impressed mark & "D," 9" h. (minor chips to rim of base) **2,587**

Jelly mold, wedge-shaped, finely painted on each side w/two swags of flowers pendant from a red ribbon, each end painted w/colorful blue & red flower vines, raised on a canted rectangular base pierced w/four apertures, the rims picked out in brown enamel, ca. 1800, impressed "WEDGWOOD L L," 8 1/2" l (small chips to edge of base) **2,875**

Punch pot, cov., bulbous ovoid body, printed in grey & black w/two oval panels of Aurora & Apollo racing across the sky in their respective chariots, within either a border of intertwined husk & laurel garlands enclosing signs of the Zodiac or a border of triangular panels alternating w/groups of instruments & trophies, leaf-molded spout & handle, the slightly domed cover printed w/a garland of flowers about the ovoid knop, ca. 1770-80, impressed mark, 9 5/8" h. (minor restoration to inner flange of cover) **2,185**

Teapot, cov., wide ovoid body w/painted landscape scene & building on each side, entwined loop handle & foliate molded spout, the cover w/flower knop, ca. 1768, 5 3/4" h. (crack, flaked enamels on body & cover restored) **345**

Jasper Ware

Miniature Jasper Ware Busts

Busts of Pindar & Aristophanes, solid white, each on a waisted circular socle, impressed marks & titles, Wedgwood & Bentley, ca. 1775, one w/footrim chip, 4" h., pr. (ILLUS.) **3,335**

Candlesticks, cylindrical shaft w/a widely flaring base & topped by a swelled ring below the tall tulip-form candle socket, yellow ground decorated w/black relief classical figures & arabesque scroll border on the shaft & leaf bands on the socket, impressed mark, ca. 1930, 6" h., pr. **690**

Candlesticks light blue ground decorated w/white relief classical figures & foliate trim, impressed marks, ca. 1863, 10" h., pr. **460**

Candlesticks, simple columnar form w/wide flaring round foot & socket rim, dark blue ground w/simple white relief ring bands around the foot, rim & sides, impressed mark, 19th c., 6" h., pr **431**

Clock, table model, an upright disk ring in light green jasper ware surrounding the round clockworks w/dial w/Arabic numerals, raised on a waisted pedestal on a wide round foot, a pointed finial at the top, applied white relief leaf band around the dial & two further bands around the foot, impressed mark, ca. 1900, 7 7/8" h...... **403**

Clock, table model, circular form, light blue ground decorated in white relief on either side w/an oval medallion w/a classical figure, no visible mark, 20th c., 5 5/8" h. **115**

Clock, table model, upright rectangular case w/a stepped base & slightly overhanging stepped & domed top w/a pointed finial, white enameled dial w/Arabic numerals & brass bezel, dark blue ground decorated w/small white relief classic figures below the dial, ornate white scrolls at upper front, lattice or ropetwist white bands around the base & top, impressed mark, ca. 1900, 6 3/4" h....... **633**

Clock case, rectangular w/dark blue ground decorated w/white relief classical figures & foliate designs, impressed mark, ca. 1900, 6" h.. **173**

Three-Color Jasper Coffee Mug & Saucer

Coffee mug & saucer, cylindrical w/loop handle, deep dished saucer, white relief Diceware design & yellow quatrefoils on a black ground, impressed mark, mid-19th c., saucer 5 1/4" d. (ILLUS.) **2,530**

Yellow Jasper Cracker Jar

Cracker jar, cov., cylindrical w/flaring base band, black relief classical figure & fruiting grapevine garlands ending at lion mask & ring terminals, silver plate rim, flat cover w/urn finials & angled bail handle, impressed mark, ca. 1930, 5 3/4" h. (ILLUS.) **748**

Cracker jar, cov., footed wide waisted cylindrical form w/upright scroll handles at the sides, low domed cover w/pointed knob finial, the body w/white relief classical figures representing Dancing Hours w/floral swags around the rim & on the cover, geometric relief bands at the bottom & around the foot, on a green ground, impressed factory mark & "McVitie and Price 1906," handle restored, 8" h. (ILLUS. top next page) **633**

Cracker Jar with Dancing Hours

Cracker jar, cov., swelled barrel shape w/narrow shoulder, light blue decorated in white relief w/oval classical cartouches framed within acanthus leaves, trophies & fruiting grapevine borders, silver plate rim, flat cover w/acorn finial & swing bail handle, impressed mark, 19th c., 6" h. **489**

Cracker jar, cov., three-color, cylindrical body w/flared base in green w/applied yellow lattice w/white florettes in panels formed by white relief foliate & scroll frames, brass rim, cover & swing bail handle, impressed mark, late 19th c., 4 1/4" h. (slight relief loss to footrim) **575**

Cracker jar, cover & underplate, cylindrical, black ground decorated w/white relief classical figures & foliate bands, impressed mark, ca. 1876, 7 3/4" h., the set **633**

Jasper Flowerpot with Cherubs

Flowerpot & cover, drum-form w/flaring rim, inset flat cover pierced w/holes, the sides w/white relief classical figures of cherubs, narrow border bands, on light blue, surface crazing, firing lines in body, cover restored, impressed mark, ca. 1800, 11 1/2" d. (ILLUS.) **1,955**

Jardiniere, cylindrical sides in black decorated w/a white relief band of classical figures below fruiting grapevines terminating in lions' heads & ring mask handles, impressed mark, 19th c., 6 1/2" h. (lines under base) **431**

Jardiniere, footed wide cylindrical form w/a flat rim, lilac ground decorated w/white relief lion masks & rings connected by grapevine swags over classical figures, impressed mark, ca. 1876, 5 3/8" h. (spider cracks in base) **805**

Small Jasper Jardiniere & Undertray

Jardiniere & undertray, cylindrical pot w/flaring rim molded in white relief w/classical figures on a crimson ground, matching dished undertray w/white relief floral band, impressed mark, ca. 1920, 3 1/2" h. (ILLUS.) **1,840**

Fine Jasper Ware Kerosene Lamp

Lamp, kerosene table model, the large baluster-form base w/white relief classical figures alternating w/upright scrolls over a band of tall acanthus leaves on a dark blue ground, fitted on a gilt brass footed base, brass collar & burner supporting a large spherical glass shade decorated w/a dark blue ground & white classical swags & ribbons, ca. 1900, electrified, overall 22 1/2" h. (ILLUS.) **1,955**

Mustard jar, cov., rounded form in yellow applied w/black fruiting grapevine festoons terminating in lion mask, silver cover, impressed mark, 20th c., 3 3/8" h., ... **316**

Oil lamp, table model, brass-mounted w/white marble plinth, dark blue ground decorated w/white relief scene of the Four Seasons, no visible mark, 20th c., 12 1/4" h. **173**

Pedestal, rectangular form, paneled sides in light green applied w/white relief allegorical figures of the Seasons, bellflower & foliate borders, impressed mark, late 19th c, 5" h. **345**

Pedestal, upright square form w/paneled sides & slightly stepped-out base, light blue decorated w/classical swag & leaf bands, the oval recessed panels w/white relief bust portraits of Mrs. Elizabeth Montagu & Jean-Jacques Rousseau, impressed mark, 19th c., 3 5/8" h. **259**

Pen tray, narrow thin rectangular wood base w/a beaded ormolu border band & scrolled upright pen rests, the center set w/a rectangular medallion in light blue w/white relief classical scene of the marriage of Cupid & Psyche, a metal-framed round jasper medallion w/classical figures on each side, late 19th c., overall 8 1/4" l. **575**

Perfume bottle w/cap, flattened oval form, white relief classical figures on a green ground, hinged silver neck & cap, unmarked, early 19th c., 4 5/8" l. (ILLUS. right) **920**

Wedgwood Jasper Perfume Bottles

Perfume bottle w/cap, flattened teardrop-form, a white relief classical figural scene in a lilac medallion on a light blue ground, silver rim & cap, 19th c., chip to rim of screw thread, 3" l. (ILLUS. left) **863**

Perfume bottle w/stopper, blue ground applied w/white relief floral festoons framing portraits possibly depicting Frederick I & Richard Molesworth, jasper stopper & silver screw lid, unmarked, late 18th c., 2 1/2" l. **805**

Pitcher, cov., 8 5/8" h., jug-form, lobed body w/two rows of white relief classical figures arranged in the lobes, domed cover, C-scroll handle, impressed mark, 18th c., rim chips under cover edge **920**

Pitcher w/hinged pewter cover, 6 1/8" h., three-color, cylindrical w/ropetwist handle, dark blue ground w/relief-molded yellow trellis & white foliate banding, impressed mark, mid-19th c. (minor relief loss) **633**

Plaque, oval, white relief scene of Bacchanalian Boys after a design by Lady Diana Beauclerk, on a dark blue ground, impressed mark, matted & framed, 19th c., 3 3/4 x 5 3/4" **748**

Plaque, oval, light blue ground decorated w/a white relief figure of a prancing satyr playing a goat horn pipe, impressed mark, narrow frame, 19th c., 6 x 10" **518**

Plaques, oval, dark blue ground applied in white relief w/classical figural scenes, one depicting The Marriage of Cupid and Psyche, the other The Sacrifice to Hymen, impressed marks, 19th c., matted & framed, 6 1/2 x 9 3/4", pr. (surface chip on one) **2,530**

Plaques, oval, solid light blue ground decorated w/white relief figures of Muses, impressed mark, late 19th c., 3 x 4", pr. **489**

Tray, oval, black ground decorated w/white relief classical figures & designs, impressed mark, framed, late 19th c., 6 3/8 x 9 1/4" **863**

Urn, cov., crimson ground w/white relief decoration, a wide cylindrical pedestal base decorated w/swags of grapevines & oval medallions above the acanthus leaf lower border, supporting a short ringed pedestal below the bulbous ovoid body w/matching swag & medallion decoration & short flared neck, low domed cover w/knob finial, Wedgwood only mark, late 19th c., 16" h. **2,970**

Vase, 3" h., trumpet-form w/loop handles, brown ground decorated w/white relief classical figures & foliate bands, impressed mark, late 19th c. **978**

Vase, cov., 7" h., trumpet-form, the large flaring bowl on a slender flaring pedestal base, dark blue ground w/the bowl decorated w/a white relief band of large scrolling arabesque florals & foliage over a wide band of delicate leafage, white interior, impressed mark, late 18th - early 19th c. (interior damage, shallow chips on pierced cover) **633**

Vase, 8" h., baluster-form, short pedestal w/round foot supporting tall ovoid body tapering to a short waisted neck w/rolled rim, black ground decorated in white relief w/large figures of classical Muses around the sides w/a foliate rim & foot band & further hanging leaf band around the base of the neck, lion mask shoulder handles, impressed mark, mid-19th c. **863**

Vase, 8 1/4" h., footed triangular form w/rounded bottom corners & side tapering to a short flared neck, light blue ground decorated in white relief w/groups of classical putti w/fern leaves at the bottom & small starbursts & a leaf band around the neck, impressed mark, mid-19th c. **575**

Vase, 9" h., bottle-form, footed ovoid body tapering to a trumpet neck, dark blue ground decorated in white relief w/central oval medallions of Cupid & Psyche below large floral & ribbon festoon, band of smaller panels w/white relief objects around the bottom, impressed mark, 19th c. **575**

Vase, 14 3/4" h., trophy-style, classical urn-form on a domed round foot, the waisted neck w/a rolled rim, arched handles from side of neck to shoulder, dark blue ground w/white relief classical figures

around the body w/ribbons & trophies around the neck & foliate borders around the shoulder & base, impressed mark, ca. 1900 .... **978**
Vase, 5 3/8" h., yellow ground decorated w/dark blue relief classical figures & foliate & fruiting grapevines, impressed mark, 19th c. (missing cover) **748**
Vases, 4 7/8" h., tapering cylindrical form w/rolled rim & flared foot, black ground decorated w/white relief panels of floral festoons & classical medallions framed within columns, lion mask & ring handles, impressed marks, early 20th c., pr. **1,150**

Jasper Vase with Festoons

Vases, 5 7/8" h., footed baluster-form w/loop shoulder handle, white relief floral festoons down the sides, on dark blue, impressed mark, ca. 1862 (ILLUS. of one) **978**

Miscellaneous
Bowl, 8 1/2" d., "Fairyland Lustre," Kang Hsi-style, the interior decorated w/"Woodland Elves I - Striped Pants" design, the exterior w/"Woodland Elves V - Woodland Bridge variation II" design on a black background, gold printed mark, Pattern No. Z4968, ca. 1920s **4,500**
Bowl, 8 3/4" d., Amherst Pheasant Imperial Lustre, a thick footring supporting a deep rounded bowl, banded exterior design w/colorful pheasants against a light ground flanked by dark bands, a bird in a hoop interior design on a mottled orange & red ground, Pattern Z5264, "KR" monogram w/horseshoe, printed mark, ca. 1920 (slight interior glaze scratches) **2,300**
Bowl, 8 3/4" w., Fairyland Lustre, deep rounded octagonal body, the exterior w/"Leapfrogging Elves" against a night sky, the interior w/"Fairy in a Cage" against a daylight sky, Pattern Z4968, printed mark, ca. 1920 (interior glaze wear) **4,600**
Bowl, 10 1/2" d., Dragon Lustre, deep rounded upright sides on a thin footring,

the mottled ruby red & blue exterior w/gilt dragons, the mottled mother-of-pearl interior w/butterflies surrounding a central floral medallion, printed mark, ca. 1920 .... **1,265**
Bowl, 10 1/2" d., Fairyland Lustre, Lahore design, a thick footring supporting deep rounded sides, Pattern Z5266, printed mark, ca. 1920 (light interior glaze scratches) **6,325**

Wedgwood Majolica Center Bowl

Center bowl, majolica, a large oval openwork basket w/laurel leaf drapery around the base supported on each end by a kneeling figure of a putto resting on a oval platform w/block & scroll-molded feet, impressed mark, ca. 1874, restorations, 19 1/2" l. (ILLUS.) **2,415**

Wedgwood Majolica Cracker Jar

Cracker jar, cov., majolica, barrel-shaped, silver plated bands around the sides on the marbleized glazed ground, silver plate rim, domed cover & angular swing bail handle, impressed mark, ca. 1878, 6 1/2" h. (ILLUS.) **288**

Glazed Stoneware Crocus Pot

Crocus pot & undertray, stoneware, blue
smear glaze, domed basketweave beehive-form, the top pierced overall w/large
holes, matching dished round tray, impressed mark, mid-19th c., 6 1/2" h.,
2 pcs. (ILLUS.) 575

Wedgwood Partial Dessert Set

Dessert set: a low rectangular compote, pair
of chamfered rectangular serving dishes
(one w/repaired corner), pair of oblong
serving dishes (one w/long chip to foot rim),
four hexagonal serving dishes (two repaired), & twelve 8" d. dessert plates (five
w/hairline cracks), each painted w/a border
of yellow & white flower sprigs w/green foliage reserved on a lavender ground within
a black banded rim, late 18th - early 19th c.,
some rim chips & minor surface wear, impressed "WEDGWOOD" & black painted
pattern number "No. 1205," the set
(ILLUS. of part) 3,737
Dish, bone china, Chantilly patt., deep
round sides w/scallops, enamel-decorated w/a swirled border & floral center &
rim, the brass-mounted edge in a
scrolled foliate design, pseudo-Chantilly
& printed factory mark, late 19th c.,
8 1/2" d. 259
Figure group, Carrara Ware, all-white, titled
"The Interpretation" & also called Joseph
Before the Pharaoh, the Pharaoh, a female
by his side & young Joseph standing before him on an oval base, modeled by William Beattie, impressed mark, ca. 1860,
19 1/2" h. (chip on underside & footrim,
restoration to Joseph's neck & one hand &
lower body of Pharaoh) 1,725
Figure group, Carrara Ware, "Poor Maria,"
a seated young woman wearing classical
attire, her hair hanging loose, leaning on
a tree stump & looking down at a small
dog, impressed mark, mouthpiece of
horn damaged, second half 19th c.,
11 1/2" h. (ILLUS. top next column) 1,495
Figure of a Bacchanalian boy, shown
clutching a foliate-decorated vase, cobalt
blue glaze, impressed mark, ca. 1871,
8 1/4" h. (restored chips) 431
Figures of Cupid & Psyche, earthenware
w/turquoise enamel glaze, each modeled
seated on a raised rocky base, im-
pressed mark, ca. 1860, 7 3/4" h., pr. 1,093

Carrara "Poor Maria" Figure Group

Jar, cov., ovoid body w/a domed cover,
'Lahore' patt., decorated around the
sides w/figures & animals behind a bal-
ustrade beneath brightly enameled
swags of fabric around the shoulder, the
cover decorated w/multicolored swirling
designs, designed by Daisy Makeig-
Jones, Pattern No. Z5266, ca. 1920s,
9 1/2" h. 5,100
Lily tray, "Fairyland Lustre," round shallow
bowl-form w/a wide flanged rim, decorated inside with the 'Fairy Gondola' design,
the exterior printed in gilding w/birds on a
mottled greenish black ground, gold
printed mark, ca. 1920s, 13" d. (some
wear & scratching in the center) 4,500
Lithophanes, bone china, brass-framed
oval forms w/a black-glazed surface revealing white classical relief designs,
printed mark, late 19th c., 3 5/8" l., pr.
(one w/hairline) 288
Loving cup, bone china, three-handled
bowl on a pedestal foot, white decorated
w/cobalt blue-framed panels of colored
enameled flowers heavily trimmed in
gold, artist-signed by J. Bond, printed
mark, 20th c., 8 1/2" h. 748
Malfrey pot, cov., Butterfly Lustre, a wide
squatty bulbous body w/a low domed
cover, mother-of-pearl exterior w/butter-
flies, mottled orange interior w/ornamen-
tal center, printed mark, ca. 1920,
3 1/2" h. 748
Match holder, majolica, figural, model of a
high-topped man's shoe w/a brown
glaze, impressed mark, ca. 1882,
2 5/8" h. 978
Medallion, stoneware, oval, molded profile
bust portrait of George Washington,
white ground, titled & w/impressed mark
of Wedgwood & Bentley, ca. 1777, slight
rim nicks & at neckline of portrait,
2 3/4 x 3 3/8" 1,955

Fine Earthenware Pedestal

Pedestal, earthenware, tall cylindrical form w/a stepped round foot & top, enamel-decorated overall w/large blossoms on tall leafy stalks, impressed mark, surface wear, ca. 1862, 35" h. (ILLUS.)` **1,840**

Bird & Fan Majolica Pitcher

Pitcher, 6 3/8" h., jug-form, majolica, footed tapering cylindrical form in Bird & Fan patt., twig handle, argenta ground, impressed mark, ca. 1878 (ILLUS.) **345**

Pitcher, 7 1/4" h., jug-type, Cane-glazed earthenware, rounded tapering cylindrical sides w/a ropetwist molded band at the base of the short flared cylindrical neck round bamboo-form handle, U.S. Centennial model, decorated w/brown transfer printed scenes of the Philadelphia Exhibition on each side, one showing Independence Hall, the other Memorial Hall, molded narrow star band around the mouth, impressed mark, ca. 1876 .... **345**

Pitcher, 7 1/2" h., majolica, Caterer model, tankard-type w/tall slightly tapering cylindrical body w/a rim spout & C-form handle w/top tab near the rim, the body molded w/narrow bands of a motto separated by three wide bands w/almond-shaped devices enclosing oval jewels, inscribed under the base w/the monogram of F.B. Russel, impressed mark, ca. 1868 .... **374**

Pitcher, cov., 10" h., majolica, tapering cylindrical form w/impressed flowerheads on a drab body, silver plated rim & cover, impressed mark, ca. 1873 .... **460**

Pitcher, cov., 10 3/4" h., tapering cylindrical form, mottled brown, blue & black glazes, silver plated banding, spout, hinged cover & handle, impressed mark, ca. 1880 .... **460**

Plaque, "Fairyland Lustre," rectangular, decorated w/a version of 'Picnic by a River,' orange sky, green river, crimson & purple grass & black & green trees, within a checkered border, together w/its original ebonized wood frame, gold printed mark, Pattern No. Z5279, ca. 1920s, 10 7/8" l., 2 pcs. **6,000**

Plates, 8 5/8" d., majolica, round w/openwork border & mottled enamel colors in the center, impressed mark, ca. 1872, pr. **173**

Plates, 10 5/8" d., bone china, sporting designs, each w/a powder green border around enamel-painted subjects of a golfer & a tennis player, printed marks, mid-20th c., pr. **230**

Modern Wedgwood Bone China Plates

Plates, 10 5/8" d., modernistic geometric designs, limited edition series titled "Variations on a Geometric Theme," printed marks, complete w/original lucite box, Paolozzi-designed, limited edition of 200, ca. 1987, set of 6 (ILLUS. of part) **2,530**

Glazed Portland Vase

Portland Vase, glazed ware, classic form w/cobalt blue ground w/white relief classical scenes, glossy glaze, impressed mark, shallow footrim chip, 10" h. (ILLUS.) **2,990**

Potpourri, cov., miniature, Drabware, footed bowl-form body w/upturned rim loop handles, applied w/classical figures & foliage in blue relief, the domed cover pierced w/overall round holes below the button finial, impressed mark, mid-19th c., 2 3/8" h. **690**

Punch bowl, 'Butterfly Lustre,' printed on the exterior & foot w/butterflies in gilding on a ruby red & blue ground, the interior similarly decorated on a mottled pale blue & green ground beneath a gold printed Chinoiserie border at the rim, designed by Daisy Makeig-Jones, ca. 1920s, gold printed Portland Vase mark, England & painted pattern number Z4827, 11" d. **690**

Wedgwood Victoria Ware Pieces

Spill vase, Victoria Ware, footed slightly flaring cyindrical form, gilt-trimmed iron-red ground w/white relief classical drapery framing blue ground oval portrait medallions, impressed mark, ca. 1880, 2 3/4" h. (ILLUS. right)..................................... **374**

Wedgwood Bone China Tea Set

Tea set: cov. teapot, cov. sugar bowl, cov. creamer, a single-cup cov. teapot, three cups & saucers & a 20" l. handled oval tray; bone china, serving pieces of squatty bulbous form, each piece decorated w/green transfer-printed panels of flowers & fruit, printed marks, late 19th c., teapot 4 1/2" h., the set (ILLUS.) **863**

Vase, 5" h., bone china, figural, modeled as two lady's hands w/ruffled cuffs tying the lace on a high-topped shoe, on a rectangular platform base w/gilt & enamel floral decoration, printed mark, ca. 1900................ **690**

Vase, 5 3/8" h., Fish Lustre, a short pedestal w/round foot supporting a rounded trumpet-form body, mottled blue exterior decorated w/fish, mother-of-pearl interior, Pattern Z4920, printed mark, ca. 1920 ..... **863**

Vase, 6 1/2" h., wide sharply tapering ovoid body w/a wide angled & ringed shoulder centering a low cylindrical mouth, overall green glaze, Keith Murray design, printed & impressed marks, ca. 1940......................... **863**

Wedgwood Veronese Ware Vase

Vase, 8 1/2" h., Veronese Ware, footed tapering ovoid body w/a flared rim, green ground w/overall silver lustre stylized floral design w/band of lustre ribbing around the neck, impressed mark, ca. 1935 (ILLUS.) **144**

Vase, 9" h., bone china, a square foot w/notched corners below a slender pedestal supporting a wide bulbous inverted pear-form body topped by a tall, slender trumpet neck, gilt upright scroll shoulder handles, the cream-colored ground decorated w/cobalt blue trim & enameled floral panels within raised gilt frames, printed mark, late 19th c. **489**

Vase, 9 3/4" h., majolica, figural, modeled as three stepped stalks of bamboo, atop a foliate-molded base, impressed mark, ca. 1874... **1,380**

Vase, 10 1/4" h., stoneware, a simple ovoid body tapering to a flaring trumpet neck, the body in matte brown w/a mottled brown & green glossy glaze on the neck, impressed mark, ca. 1877 .... **863**

Vases, 7 3/4" h., Fairyland Lustre, Butterfly Women patt., trumpet-form w/stepped round foot, black background w/mother-of-pearl overlay, mother-of-pearl interior w/floating fairies, Shape No. 2810, No. Z4968, printed marks, ca. 1920 (ILLUS. of one top next page)................................. **11,500**

Vases, 7 3/4" h., Victoria Ware, tall baluster-form vase raised on a simple tall cylindrical plinth, gilt-trimmed iron-red & teal blue ground w/applied white relief classical swags, classical design bands & leaves w/oval medallions on the sides, impressed mark, ca. 1880, gilt wear, pr. (ILLUS. of one, left w/spill vase) **1,725**

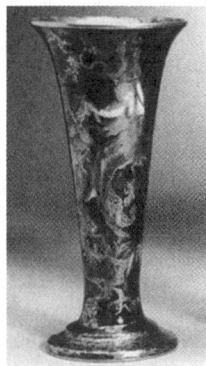

Fairyland Lustre Trumpet-form Vase

Vases, 8" h., Ivory Vellum ware, ovoid body tapering to a tall slender flaring neck, the ivory ground decorated w/colored enamel & gilt-trimmed birds perched on branches, a dark brown band w/gilt around the bottom, printed & impressed marks, late 19th c., pr. (light gilt wear).......... 546

Vases, 8 5/8" h., bone china, short pedestal base below the swelled trumpet-form body, gilt-trimmed & enamel-decorated w/cherubs & fruiting grapevine border, artist-signed by James Hodgkiss, printed mark of retailer T. Goode & Co. & factory mark, ca. 1910, pr. 633

Fine Early Wedgwood Porphyry Vase

Vases, cov., 18" h., Porphyry Ware, classic urn-form on a square plinth, creamware body w/mottled greenish blue & brown glossy glaze, high-relief oval classical medallions between drapery swags, acanthus leaf footrim, mounted on a square black basalt plinth, pierced cover w/acorn finial, raised lozenge mark of Wedgwood & Bentley, covers restored, one w/chip restored on footrim, chip & edge nicks on plinth, other w/restoration to top rim & socle, edge nicks on plinth, each w/firing lines in relief, ca. 1770, pr. (ILLUS. of one) **9,200**

Weller

This pottery was made from 1872 to 1945 at a pottery established originally by Samuel A. Weller at Fulton-ham, Ohio, and moved in 1882 to Zanesville. Numerous lines were produced and listings below are by the pattern or lines.

Reference books on Weller include The Collectors Encyclopedia of Weller Pottery *by Sharon & Bob Huxford (Collector Books, 1979) and* All About Weller *by Ann Gilbert McDonald (Antique Publications, 1989). ALSO SEE Antique Trader Books Pottery and Porcelain - Ceramics Price Guide, 3rd Edition.*

WELLER

Weller Marks

Alvin (1928)
Various shapes with molded fruits, branches or vines with a matte glaze

Vase, 12" h., tall slender tree trunk form w/small loop branch handles near the top suspending molded fruit on a pastel yellow ground.. **$77**

Ardsley (1928)
Various shapes molded as cattails among rushes with water lilies at the bottom. Matte glaze.

Bulb bowl, lobed blossom form base w/leaf-form openwork top, half kiln ink stamp logo, 4 7/8" h.. 110

Candleholders, lily pad & blossom disk base centered by a flaring blossom-form socket, half kiln ink stamp logo & old sales tag, one w/original "Weller Ardsley Ware" paper label, 2 3/4" h., pr. (minor glaze inconsistencies) 138

Vase, 19" h., floor-type, compressed domed base w/lotus blossom & tall trumpet-form body embossed w/cattails & leaves, marked w/full circle kiln ink stamp logo.. **1,210**

Aurelian (1898-1910)
Duplicate of Louwelsa except for the background which has been sponged on and gives the illusion of a distant forest fire. High-gloss brown ware. Early period.

Lamp, oil, bell-shaped body on small knob feet, decorated w/two medallions of ivory roses, by C. Mitchell, complete w/oil font, artist-signed & stamped "K116," 10 1/2 x 11" 605

Mug, tapering cylindrical body w/C-form handle, decorated w/cherry decoration, by Charles Chilcote, ca. 1900, impressed w/circular "Aurelian Weller" logo & incised shape number "435" w/"Chil" painted on side near bottom of handle, 6 1/8" h.. 275

Umbrella stand, decorated w/bright yellow irises, late 19th c., unmarked, removable galvanized sheet metal insert, 23 7/8" h. .. **1,650**

Baldin (about 1915-20)
Rustic designs with relief-molded apples and leaves on branches wrapped around each piece.

Vase, 5 1/2" h., spherical body tapering to slightly flared rim, impressed "Weller" in large block letters **275**

Vase, 10 5/8" h., bulbous base w/slightly tapering wide cylindrical neck & flat rim, unmarked **303**

Blue & Decorated Hudson (1919)

Hand-painted lifelike sprays of fruit blossoms and flowers in shades of pink and blue on a rich dark blue ground.

Vase, 9 1/8" h., ovoid body w/rolled rim, decorated near top w/bright orange & yellow flowers painted by Hester Pillsbury, unmarked, artist-initialed among flowers (4" crack descending from rim) **193**

Vase, 10" h., slender cylindrical body flaring at base & tapering to small flat rim, center of body decorated w/a band of brightly colored flowers & impressed "Weller" in large block letters **248**

Blue Louwelsa (ca. 1905)

A high-gloss line shading from medium blue to cobalt blue with underglaze slip decorations of fruits & florals and sometimes portraits. Decorated in shades of white, cobalt and light blue slip. Since few pieces were made, they are rare and sought after today.

Vase, 5 3/8" h., pillow-form w/nasturtium decoration, unmarked (1/4" chip off left edge of rim) **523**

Vase, 7" h., bottle-shaped, decorated w/honeysuckle blossoms & leaves on shaded cobalt ground **825**

Chase (late 1920s)

White relief fox hunt scenes usually on a deep blue ground.

Vase, 7 5/8" h., footed baluster-form w/rolled rim, dark blue ground w/white hunt scene, incised "Weller Pottery" on bottom **248**

Vase, 8 7/8" h., ovoid form w/flat rim, mottled blue matte ground decorated w/applied silver overlay hunt scene, marked "Sterling" & impressed "Weller Pottery" in script **358**

Claywood (ca. 1910)

Etched designs against a light tan ground, divided by dark brown bands. Matte glaze.

Jardiniere, bulbous ovoid body divided into panels by dark brown bands, the creamy panels w/floral decoration outlined in brown, unmarked, 3 1/2" h. **28**

Vase, 8" h., tapering cylindrical body w/compressed base, the sides divided into tall panels by dark brown bands, each panel etched w/a grape cluster on leafy vines in creamy white outlined in brown **55**

Coppertone (late 1920s)

Various shapes with an overall mottled bright green glaze on a "copper" glaze base. Some pieces with figural frog or fish handles. Models of frogs also included.

Flower frog, model of lily pad bloom w/seated frog, 3 7/8" h. (small chip inside edge of one petal) **168**

Pitcher, 7 5/8" h., bulbous ovoid body w/arched spout, figural fish handle, marked w/half kiln ink stamp logo (dorsal fin on handle broken & repaired) **1,183**

Vase, 5 3/4" h., wide tapering cylindrical body w/rolled rim, marked in script "Weller Hand Made"................................... **358**

Vase, 8" h., bulbous ovoid body w/molded rim, figural frog shoulder handles, ink kiln mark (short tight line to rim)....................... **1,540**

Vase, 8 3/8" h., bulbous base w/trumpetform neck, scrolled handles from base to below rim, incised "Weller Hand Made" on bottom (three small burst bubbles on back side of vase) **220**

Eocean and Eocean Rose (1898-1925)

Early art line with various hand-painted flowers on shaded grounds, usually with a clear glossy glaze. Quality of artwork varies greatly.

Mug, tapering cylindrical body w/C-form handle, wild rose decoration on shaded green ground, 4 7/8" h............................. **138**

Vase, 4 7/8" h., pillow-form, wild rose decoration on shaded green ground, unmarked (glaze on four stubby feet a bit gritty in the making) **193**

Vase, 5 3/4" h., corseted form w/pink Nasturtium on shaded grey ground, decorated by Mary Pierce, incised "Eocean-Weller 890 6" & artist-signed "MP".............. **303**

Vase, 6" h., 5" d., swelled cylindrical body w/a wide flat shoulder to the short cylindrical neck, decorated w/wild roses in ivory & red on shaded grey ground, incised "Eocean-Rose Weller 9061"................. **358**

Vase, bud, 6 5/8" h., decorated w/daisies, impressed "Weller" in large block letters **193**

Vase, 8 1/2" h., slender ovoid body decorated w/Virginia creeper against a shaded dark green to cream ground, by William Stemm, incised "Eocean Weller" "F." artist-initlaed on side below leaves **660**

Vase, 10 1/2" h., squared shape w/pink thistle decoration on dark green shaded to cream ground, incised "Eocean Rose Weller" & "S" on bottom & impressed "447" & "4" (pinhead glaze nick on top of rim).......... **440**

Vase, bulbous ovoid tapering to rolled rim, decorated a/portrait of a spaniel w/brown eyes, shaded grey ground, incised "Eocean Weller S" & impressed "2"........... **1,540**

Ethel (about 1915)

Profile of Ethel Weller, in a circle, sniffing a rose. Cream color. Matt finish

Vase, 6 1/4" h., footed fan shape w/retriculated rim & applied ring handles, floral decoration... **110**

Vase, 11 1/4" h., disk foot w/tapering cylindrical body, applied ring handles & reticulated rim w/profile of young woman on each side, incised "Weller" **330**

Glendale (early to late 1920s)

Various relief-molded birds in their natural habitats, lifelike coloring.

Console bowl w/flower frog, round w/wide flared rim, decorated w/nesting birds w/eggs, 15 1/2" d. bowl marked "Weller" in black slip, frog impressed "Weller" in large block letters 770

Vase, 12 7/8" h., ovoid body w/short cylindrical neck, w/scene of nesting bird w/eggs in a swampy, cattail-filled area, impressed "Weller" in large block letters ... **1,925**

Hudson (1917-34)

Underglaze slip-painted decoration, "parchment-vellum" transparent glaze.

Vase, 6 7/8" h., ovoid body w/wide flat rim, blue pansy decoration by Edith Hood, pink shaded to green ground, marked w/full kiln "Weller Pottery" ink stamp logo (tight line at rim).. 220

Vase, 7 1/2" h., octagonal ovoid body w/flat rim, pastel orange & yellow wild rose decoration around top, grey shading to light green ground, faintly impressed "Weller" in small block letters (some dirty crazing especially on interior)................................ 303

Vase, 8 1/4" h., baluster-form w/flaring rim, decorated w/blue flowers & green leaves on green shaded to pink ground, by Naomi Walch, marked w/half kiln ink stamp logo & artist-signed 715

Vase, 8 1/4" h., 3" d., cylindrical, decorated w/large blue & yellow iris on a pale yellow to pale sage green ground, matte glaze, artist-signed.. 495

Vase, 8 5/8" h., ovoid body, top decorated w/wild roses & green leaves on green shaded to pink ground, by Sarah Timberlake, impressed "Weller" in large block letters, artist-initialed........................... 413

Vase, 9 3/8" h., footed cylindrical body w/flat rim, decorated w/blue & yellow irises in very heavy slip by Mae Timberlake, shaded green to yellow ground, artist-signed (professional repair of two cracks at rim) 605

Vase, 10 1/4" h., footed bulbous base tapering to cylindrical neck w/flat rim, white dogwood decoration by Hester Pillsbury, grey shading to pink ground, impressed "Weller" in script & artist-initialed 770

Vase, bud, 10 1/4" h., slender waisted cylinder w/flaring base, decorated w/pink & white poppies on trailing stems in stylish Art Nouveau manner, glossy tan ground w/dark band at rim, impressed "Weller" in large block letters 770

Vase, 10 5/8" h., cylindrical body w/short slightly flared rim, blackberry decoration in pastel colors on light grey shading to yellow ground, impressed "Weller" in small block letters.. 440

L'Art Nouveau (1903-04)

Various figural and floral-embossed Art Nouveau designs.

Vase, 10 1/4" h., slender four-sided body w/embossed panels of flowers & Art Nouveau woman, impressed "Weller" in small block letters... 358

Vase, 11 1/4" h., waisted cylindrical body w/four-lobed base & molded florals at top, impressed "Weller" in small block let-

ters (very minor glaze rubs on one side at bottom).. 440

Louwelsa (1896-1924)

Hand-painted underglaze slip decoration on dark brown shading to yellow ground; glossy yellow glaze.

Clock, curvilinear stylized five-point star-shaped case decorated w/chrysanthemum blossoms in orange & yellow on standard glaze brown ground, artist-initialed "ER" on side, round white enamel clock face w/black Roman numerals, impressed "Louwelsa Weller," early 20th c., 10" h. (minor foot chip).................................. 863

Clock, mantel-type, scalloped case w/orange nasturtiums, Gilbert clock works, stamped "Louwelsa Weller 706," 4 x 10 1/2 x 12 1/2" (colored-in chip to side & a few glaze flakes & chip to base)...... 523

Cruet, bulbous body decorated w/palm fronds, by Mary Gillie, impressed "Louwelsa Weller," artist-initialed, 4 3/8" h............. 83

Ewer, squatty bulbous body decorated w/cherry blossoms, impressed "Louwelsa Weller," 6 1/2" h. 165

Jardiniere, wide flaring waisted cylindrical body w/a wide molded rim, decorated w/a large yellow iris among green leaves on a shaded brown & ochre ground, glossy glaze, impressed mark, 9" h. (glaze scratches)... 288

Pitcher, 4 1/8" h., tapering cylindrical body w/pinched spout & C-form handle, decorated w/palm fronds, by William F. Hall, impressed "Louwelsa Weller" & "X 215 11" (small rim chips) 83

Planter, cylindrical tree trunk form w/three small foxes peeking out at side, 4 1/2" h....... 330

Vase, 5" h., pillow-form, decorated w/wild roses, impressed "Louwelsa Weller" on bottom (minor scratches) 83

Vase, 7" h., pillow-form, decorated w/scene of a small house at end of a dirt path w/scruffy plants in foreground & cloudy sky in background, impressed "Louwelsa Weller 41 0" 1,100

Vase, 9" h., tapering cylindrical form w/wild rose decoration, unmarked, (very minor scratches & glaze inconsistencies) 193

Vase, 9 1/4" h., bottle-shaped body w/flaring ruffled neck, decorated w/yellow nasturtiums, stamped mark (small bruise & nick to rim).. 303

Vase, 10 1/2" h., ovoid form w/flaring rim, decorated w/wild roses, incised artist's initials on side (professional repair to rim, area of loose glaze on shoulder) 193

Vase, 10 1/2" h., wide cylindrical body decorated w/bright red wild roses, possibly by Albert Haubich, impressed on bottom, "Louwelsa Weller 602 5" & artist initialed "A.H." on side (glaze scratches) 358

Vase, 18 1/2" h., slightly tapering cylindrical shouldered body w/small flaring neck, decorated w/lifelike red & purple grapes hanging from finely detailed vine, by Frank Ferrell, impressed "Louwelsa Weller" logo & "200" & "55" (professional repair of small base chip) 1,540

Marbleized (Bo Marblo, 1915)

Simple shapes with swirled "marbleized" clays, usually in browns and blues.

Vase, 11 1/4" h., square slightly flared base tapering to flat rim, swirled colors of brown, rust, cream & black, impressed "Weller" in small block letters & incised "Weller" directly over impressed mark (very minor glaze nicks on underside of base) 110

Vase, 12 1/2" h., waisted cylindrical body w/swirled colors of tan, brown, maroon, black & grey, impressed "Weller" in small block letters (1/4" chip edge of base) 110

Muskota (1915 - late 1920s)

Figural pieces with human figures, birds, animals or frogs. Matte glaze.

Centerpiece, disk base w/two figural baby chicks on grassy mound, unmarked, 5" h. (repair to beaks of both birds) 165

Flower frog, Fishing Boy, boy seated on rockwork w/original "Weller Muskota Ware" paper label, 6 7/8" h. 330

Garden ornament, Fishing Boy, boy standing on round base, brown pants w/one leg rolled up to knee, light blue shirt & black hat, marked w/half-kiln ink stamp logo, 20 5/8" h. (two unobtrusive glazed over chips on base)................................. 6,325

Perfecto (early 1900s)

Predominantly sea green, blending into a delicate pink matte finish unglazed painted decoration.

Vase, 7 5/8" h., slender ovoid body w/flat rim, embossed scene of nude sitting on a rock, seagulls overhead, impressed "Weller" in large block letters & signed "Timberlake" on side near base (tight short line at rim) 2,750

Vase, 9 1/2" h., footed cylindrical body tapering to short wide rim, rare carved scene depicting small brown bird perched in a tree of ripe cherries, the background cut back to resemble weathered wood, by Sarah Reid McLaughlin, impressed "Weller" in large block letters & signed "SMcL" on side in black slip 3,300

Roma (1912-late '20s)

Cream-colored ground decorated with embossed floral swags, bands or fruit clusters.

Vase, 6 7/8" h., footed tapering cylinder w/molded ring rim, floral decoration, impressed "Weller" in large block letters 55

Vase, 12 3/8" h., tapering cylindrical body w/four panels of stylized roses, unmarked... 248

Wall pocket, conical, incised vertical lines & decorated w/roses & grape cluster near top, green leaves w/yellow center at base, cream ground, marked "28" in blue slip on back, 8 1/4" h. (very minor staining from use & small bruise on one horizontal band at mid body)................................ 165

Sicardo (1902-07)

Various shapes with iridescent glaze of metallic shadings in greens, blues, crimson, purple or coppertone decorated with vines, flowers, stars or free-form geometric lines.

Vase, 5 1/2" h., waisted cylindrical body w/swelled shoulder tapering to small flat rim, cloud-like decoration, iridescent blue, green & burgundy glaze, unmarked 605

Vase, 9 1/4" h., expanding cylinder w/rounded shoulders & rolled rim, decorated w/wild violets, iridescent gold, burgundy & green glaze, signed "Weller Sicard" & impressed "6" 935

Silvertone (1928)

Various flowers, fruits or butterflies molded on a pale purple-blue matte pebbled ground.

Vase, 6" h., footed squatty bulbous body w/wide flaring rim, decorated w/embossed pink roses & green leaves against a purple ground, ink mark................. 330

Vase, 8 1/4" h., 7 3/4" d., footed, spherical body w/scalloped rim, C-form shoulder handles, embossed w/pink poppies on lavender "hammered" ground....................... 275

Woodcraft (1917)

Rustic designs simulating the appearance of stumps, logs and tree trunks. Some pieces are adorned with owls, squirrels, dogs and other animals. Matte finish.

Bowl, 4 1/2" h., shallow bulbous form w/oak leaves & acorns around the rim & figural squirrel seated on rim eating a nut, unmarked (repair to oak leaves on rim opposite squirrel) 193

Bowl, 5 7/8" d., 2 7/8" h., footed round body w/flared sides & scalloped rim, decorated w/embossed squirrels & trees, unmarked 166

Jardiniere, log form w/woodpecker on side, impressed "Weller" in large block letters on bottom, 6" h. (short tight line at rim) 358

Planter, log-form w/three embossed foxes on front, crossed branch handles across top, impressed "Weller" in large block letters, 5 3/4" h. 220

Vase, bud, 8 1/4" h., cylindrical tree trunk form w/relief-molded branch, apple & leaves down the front, "Weller Woodcraft Ware" paper label............................. 165

Vase, bud, 10 1/4" h., cylindrical tree trunk form, hollow branch opening in front, flared base & molded apples, branches & leaves, impressed "Weller" in large block letters 124

Wall pocket, relief-molded log w/flowers & berries, marked "Weller" in large block letters on back, 9" h. (minor glaze flakes) 193

Zona (about 1920)

Umbrella stand, tapering cylindrical body w/embossed figures of ladies holding flower garlands, unmarked, 10 " d., 20" h. (three small chips to base & some glaze misses & glazed over chips)............. 1,540

Wheatley Pottery

Thomas J. Wheatley was one of the original founders of the art pottery movement in Cincinnati, Ohio in the early 1880s. In 1879 the Cincinnati Art Pottery was formed and after some legal problems it operated under the name T.J. Wheatley & Company. Their production featured Limoges-style hand-painted decorations and most pieces were carefully marked and often dated.

In 1882 Wheatley disassociated himself from the Cincinnati Art Pottery and opened another pottery which was destroyed by fire in 1884. Around 1900 Wheatley finally resumed making art pottery in Cincinnati and in 1903 he founded the Wheatley Pottery Company with a new partner, Isaac Kahn.

The new pottery from this company featured colored matte glazes over relief work designs and green, yellow and blue were the most often used colors. There were imitations of the well-known Grueby Pottery wares as well as artware, garden pottery and architectural pieces. Artwork was apparently not made much after 1907. This plant was destroyed by fire in 1910 but was rebuilt and run by Wheatley until his death in 1917. Wheatley artware was generally unmarked except for a paper label.

Wheatley Marks

Bowl, 6" d., 2 1/2" h., low upright corseted sides w/a wide incurved rim, embossed around the sides w/a band of short upright pointed wide leaves, thick matte green glaze, illegible mark **$165**
Vase, 5 1/2" h., 7" d., wide bulbous form w/a wide rounded shoulder centered by a wide flat molded mouth, deeply embossed w/a band of wide ribbed upright leaves alternating w/small buds, thick & frothy matte green glaze, incised "W-685" **1,320**

Willow Wares

This pseudo-Chinese pattern has been used by numerous firms throughout the years. The original design is attributed to Thomas Minton about 1780 and Thomas Turner is believed to have first produced the ware during his tenure at the Caughley works. The blue underglaze transfer print pattern has never been out of production since that time. An Oriental landscape incorporating a bridge, pagoda, trees, figures and birds, supposedly tells the story of lovers fleeing a cruel father who wished to prevent their marriage. The gods, having pity on them, changed them into birds enabling them to fly away and seek their happiness together.

Blue

Bowl, 12 1/4" d., serving-type w/beaded rim (small flake on table ring) **$50**
Bowl, cereal, Royal China Co. 11
Bowl, soup w/flanged rim, 8 1/4" d., Royal China Co. 10

Bowls, 8", 9 1/4" & 10 1/2" l., rectangular, stacking-type, Ridgways, set of 3 .... **325**
Butter dish, drain & cover, Ridgways, 3 pcs. **225**
Plate, child's, 4 1/2" d., Japan **10-15**
Plate, dinner, Booth's, England **40-45**
Trivet, scalloped foot, Moriyama, 6" (very rare) **225**
Warmer, round, holds candle, Japan **58**

Yellowware

Yellowware is a form of utilitarian pottery produced in the United States and England from the early 19th century onward. Its body texture is less dense and vitreous (impervious to water) than stoneware. Most, but not all, yellowware is unmarked and its color varies from deep yellow to pale buff. In the late 19th and early 20th centuries bowls in graduated sizes were widely advertised. Still in production, yellowware is plentiful and still reasonably priced.

Bottle, toby-type, the upper half molded as a figure of a smiling man wearing a top hat & playing a fiddle, hat forms bottle cap, 19th c., crazing, chip on hat brim, 8 1/2" h. (ILLUS. right) **$715**
Crock, cov., short cylindrical sides w/heavy molded rim & inset cover, the center decorated w/a wide band composed of thin & wider blue bands, 7" d., 3 1/2" h. (crazing, stains) **220**

Yellowware Flask & Toby Bottle

Flask, flattened ovoid sides w/impressed edge bands, one side molded in relief w/an American eagle above flags draped on horizontal poles, the other side molded w/morning glories, 19th c., chips, 7 3/8" h. (ILLUS. left) **1,210**
Model of a dog, seated Spaniel w/well-molded fur & facial details, on a thick rectangular base w/cut corners & overall crosshatched design, overall running brown glaze, signed on the base "Geo. Diehl, Jul. 9th 1870," near Bucks County, Pennsylvania, 7 5/8" h. (minor glaze flakes on base) **4,400**
Pitcher, 5" h., jug-form, bulbous baluster-form w/rim spout w/strainer & C-form handle, four thin blue stripes around the body, first half 19th c. (flakes) **578**

Pitcher, 5 1/2" h., footed baluster-form w/rim spout & C-form handle, decorated w/two wide white bands each edged by thin brown stripes, 19th c. **550**

Pitcher, 6 1/8" h., jug-form, baluster-form body w/rim spout & C-form handle, two white bands each divided by four thin black stripes, 19th c. **688**

Pitcher, 7 3/4" h., jug-form, ovoid body w/a rim spout & C-form handle, decorated w/white bands w/dark blue pinstripe borders (minor base flakes) **743**

Soap dish, shallow round form w/a large pierced hole in the center bottom surrounded by six small holes, 5 5/8" d. (some wear) **550**

Zsolnay

This pottery was made in Pecs, Hungary, in a factory founded in 1862 by Vilmos Zsolnay. Utilitarian earthenware was originally produced but by the turn of the century ornamental Art Nouveau style wares with bright colors and lustre decoration were produced and these wares are especially sought today. Currently Zsolnay pieces are being made in a new factory.

Zsolnay Marks

Bowl-vase, round footring below the squatty rounded body w/incurved sides pinched in at the rim on one side & molded in relief w/a large moth in iridescent green, gold, purple & blue on a deep red glossy ground, molded factory mark & "6383 - M" on the base, ca. 1901, 3" h. **$1,610**

Centerpiece, figural, boat-shaped, a reticulated floral border on a boat-shaped vessel decorated w/stylized Oriental flowers in pink, teal & gold tones w/gilt highlights, mounted in an ormolu base w/patinated metal cherubs riding atop wave-like formations & driving a bridled swan at the front, w/seashell feet, impressed "Zsolnay 1211" & blue stamp marks, late 19th c., 13 1/2" l. (hairline) **1,150**

Figure of a woman, seated cloaked woman beside a large low tapering vessel, iridescent gold glaze, gilt stamp mark, early 20th c., 5 1/4" h. (minor glaze wear) **374**

CHALKWARE

So-called chalkware available today is actually made of plaster of Paris, much of it decorated in color and primarily in the form of busts, figurines and ornaments. It was produced through most of the 19th century and the majority of pieces were originally quite inexpensive when made. Today even 20th century "carnival" pieces are collectible.

Bank, model of a perched dove, the high domed base molded w/branches &

leaves in brown & green, brown-painted wings, eyes & beak, 19th c., 11 1/8" h. (minor scratches & paint wear, air bubble at edge of one leaf) **$330**

Bank, model of a recumbent cat on a rectangular base, green polychrome body w/red bow around the neck, brown highlights, holding a mouse in its mouth, 7 3/4" l., 6" h. (edge chips on base) **220**

Bird on base, long-necked bird w/long wings perched on a bulbous knob above a half-round flaring pedestal, worn original black & goldenrod paint, 6 1/2" h. **880**

Cat, seated, oval bottom, worn original red, black & yellow paint, 5 1/8" h. (wear, edge damage) **385**

Cat, seated animal facing the viewer, on a squared base, grinning facial expression, worn black spots, mustard yellow collar & green base, 3 1/4" l., 6" h. (wear, glued base repair) **550**

Cat, seated calico cat w/brown spots & red collar, on a green & red-striped pedestal w/incised zigzag decoration, 19th c., 6" h. (minor chips, paint wear) **2,875**

Seated Chalkware Cat

Cat, seated animal w/rounded body & head on an oval base, yellow & black stripes w/touches of red on ears, nose & mouth, yellow base, repaired, 19th c., 10" h. (ILLUS.) **4,600**

Scarce Early Chalkware Cat

Cat, seated animal w/rounded body & head, on a round base, yellow & black-striped decoration w/touches of red on ears & mouth, a black & red spotted collar, American, 19th c., imperfections, 10 1/4" h. (ILLUS.)..................... **10,350**

Dog, seated on molded base, molded head & body detail w/worn original red, black & yellow paint, 5 3/4" h. (wear, base chips, hole between legs w/some damage) **385**

Dog, seated Spaniel facing the viewer, on a rectangular base, an opening between the front legs & body, molded fur, green & red stripes on the base & dotted collar, light brown ears & facial features, 4 1/8" l., 6 1/8" h. (minor wear, edge flakes).................. **275**

Dog, seated Spaniel holding a basket in its mouth, on a stepped square base, molded fur around the head, shoulders & front legs, green ears & tail w/red & green stripes on the basket, eyes & claws in black, green stripe on base, lighter blue appears under the green, 19th c., 4 7/8" l., 6" h..................................... **605**

Dog, standing Spaniel-like animal facing viewer, crudely cast features & curled tail, molded fur & tail, brown tail & ears, yellow eyes & daubs of red, olive green, yellow & brown around the shoulders, green rectangular base, 19th c., 6" l., 7 5/8" h. (few areas of surface damage) **935**

Figure of girl, standing, long dark hair, wearing white pantaloons & yellow dress w/red stripes, matching large brim hat, 9 1/2" h. (minor wear) **1,155**

Lamb, recumbent, molded oblong base & curly wool, white body w/red & black facial details, worn light olive green paint on base, 19th c., 5" l., 3 3/4" h. (minor wear)........ **275**

Love birds, two kissing birds w/yellow bodies, red breasts & green wings, round raised base, 5 1/4" h. (wear & one w/repaired wing).. **165**

Mantel garniture, model of an urn w/molded floral & gadroon decoration raised on a square plinth & piled high w/various fruits, decorated in red, yellow, green & tan paint, 19th c., 16" h. (repair) **2,185**

Mantel ornament, a large urn of fruit, a square plinth in brown supporting a short pedestal & large flaring white urn piled high w/various fruits painted red, yellow & green, 19th c., 16" h. (repair).................. **2,185**

Mantel ornaments, urn of fruit, a square plinth in brown supporting a short pedestal & large flaring white urn piled high w/various fruits painted red, yellow & green, 19th c., minor paint loss, 11 1/2" h., pr. (ILLUS. top next column) ... **1,840**

Poodle, standing animal on oval base, molded coat & ears w/dark green base, black tail, muzzle & collar w/black & red ears, 4 3/4" l., 7 1/4" h. (chips on back of base, touch up on some paint)....................... **468**

Poodle, standing animal w/large head & rounded body on a thick rectangular base, old black repaint on body w/red base & tail, 3 x 5 3/4", 7 5/8" h. (roughness around base) **303**

Chalkware Mantel Ornaments

Poodles, standing stylized dogs on rectangular bases, some molded detail around neck & polychrome trim including a floral garland around the necks, mid-19th c., 6" l., 7" h., pr. (minor paint loss).................... **690**

Rabbit, seated, stylized animal on a thin oblong base, worn original red, yellow & black paint, 5 1/4" h. **578**

Rooster, decorated in shades of dark red, mustard yellow, black & green, 19th c. (wear).. **920**

Rooster, stylized bird w/upright head & high arched tail, perched on a tall conical base, worn original red, green & black paint, 5 1/2" h... **358**

Squirrel, sitting on round base, holding a nut, grey wash & tail w/red details, 7 1/8" h. (wear)... **264**

Stag, recumbent animal w/one front leg raised, brown spots & collar w/red & black ears & green mottled oval base, 8 1/8" l., 8 3/4" h. (some wear, glued antler tip) **660**

Stag, seated animal w/polychrome decoration, mid-19th c., 8 1/2" h. (repair, paint loss).. **1,093**

CHARACTER, RADIO & TELEVISION COLLECTIBLES

"Astronut and the Flying Bus"

Numerous objects made in the likeness of or named after comic strip and comic book personalities or characters abounded from the 1920s to the present. Scores of these are now being eagerly collected and prices still vary widely. Also see: Antique Trader Toy Price Guide.

Archie LP record, "Everything's Archie," The Archies, Calendar/Kirshner, 1969..... **$15-25**
Archie LP record, "Jingle Jangle," The Archies, Kirshner, 1969.................................. **15-25**
Archie lunch kit, The Archies, steel box, plastic bottle, Aladdin, 1969...................... **75-110**
Archie paper dolls, Whitman, 1969.............. **25-40**
Astronut book, "Astronut and the Flying Bus," Wonder Book, #853, 1965 (ILLUS.).... **8-12**
Astronut coloring book, Treasure, 1963..... **20-30**
Batfink costume, Collegeville, 1965............. **60-100**
Batfink pinback button, "Batfink is My Hero," 3 colors, Hal Seeger, 1967, 3" d......... **50-75**

Batfink Slide Puzzle

Batfink slide puzzle, Roalex, 1960s (ILLUS.)... **20-30**
Beany boat, "Leakin' Lena," plastic & wood, Irwin, 1962... **100-150**
Beany book, "Beany: Cecil Captured for the Zoo," Tell-A-Tale Book, Whitman, 1954.. **12-20**
Beany book, "Beany Goes To Sea," Little Golden Book, #537, 1963 .... **8-12**

Beany-Copter Cap

Beany cap, "Beany-Copter" cap w/flying propeller, Mattel, 1961 (ILLUS.).............. **125-200**
Beany carrying case, round, vinyl, w/strap, 1960s, 9" d.. **50-75**
Beany colorforms, Beany & Cecil Cartoon Kit, early 1960s..................................... **60-100**
Beany coloring book, Whitman, 1960s........ **30-50**

Beany disguise kit, plush Cecil, boxed w/disguises, Mattel, 1962, 17" Cecil **75-125**
Beany game, "Beany and Cecil Match It," Mattel, 1960s **30-50**
Beany lunch kit, vinyl w/metal bottle, King Seeley Thermos, 1963 .... **350-500**

Beany Talking Plush Doll

Beany plush doll, Beany, Mattel, 1963 (ILLUS.) **75-125**
Beany plush doll, talking, Mattel, 1963, 17" **80-130**
Beany puzzle, wooden frame tray puzzle, Playskool, 1961 .... **35-55**
Beany record player, Beany & Cecil & their pals, nice graphics on case, Vanity Fair, 1961 .... **150-250**
Bullwinkle LP record, "Rocky & His Friends," 1961...................................... **25-35**
Bullwinkle lunch box, Bullwinkle & Rocky, steel box, Universal, 1962 .... **150-200**
Bullwinkle lunch kit, blue vinyl w/metal bottle, King Seeley Thermos, 1963 .... **500-750**
Bullwinkle lunch kit, yellow vinyl w/generic metal bottle, King Seeley Thermos, 1963 ... **300-500**
Bullwinkle lunch kit thermos, Bullwinkle & Rocky, metal, Universal, 1962 .... **150-200**
Bullwinkle magic slate, 1963........................ **40-65**
Bullwinkle photo, original press photo from ABC-TV, 1964.. **40-50**

Rocky & Bullwinkle Puzzle

Bullwinkle puzzle, Rocky & Bullwinkle w/aliens, Jr. Jigsaw Puzzle, 63 pcs., Whitman, 1950s-60s (ILLUS.) **25-40**
Bullwinkle spelling card, Rocky & friends, 1969, 8 1/2 x 11" **15-25**
Bullwinkle toy, Bullwinkle in car, tin wind-up, tin & vinyl, KO/Flare Import, Japan, 1962 .... **300-500**
Bullwinkle trash can, several characters, metal litho, 1961, 11" **45-60**

Captain Midnight Premium Ring

Captain Midnight Mystic Sungod ring, premium ring, gold colored wide band w/ornate circumscribed designs w/a sliding "ruby" which opens a secret compartment, together w/all papers & original mailing envelope, 1941 (ILLUS.) **690**
Cecil (Beany & Cecil) soap bottle, figural, Cecil's head & neck, Roclar Dist., 1950s-60s, 8" **30-50**
Cecil (Beany & Cecil) toy, jack-in-the-box, w/Cecil in the music box, Mattel, 1961 .. **200-300**
Daffy Duck animation cel, Daffy w/milk bottle, 1950s, 4 1/4 x 3" **350-400**

Daffy Duck Bank

Daffy Duck bank, metal, Daffy w/barrel on base, 1940s, 5 1/2" (ILLUS.) **75-125**

"Will the Real Gigantor Stand Up" Video

Daffy Duck bobbing head doll, composition, 1960s **200-300**
Gigantor record/story book set, Asahi Sonorama, Japan, 1964, 14 pp. booklet **75-125**
Gigantor toy, battery-op, plastic head, rubber nose, flashing eyes, Nomura Roy, 1960s **600-1,000**
Gigantor toy, Gigantor w/Jimmy Sparks, tin litho & celluloid, boxed, Nomura Toy, 1950s **3,000-4,000**
Gigantor video, "Will the Real Gigantor Stand Up," b&w, 30 minutes, Star Classics (1964), 1987 (ILLUS. bottom previous column) **10-18**

Hawaii Five-O Badge

Hawaii Five-O badge, heavy gold tone metal prop used on the popular 1970s TV show, features the state crest & motto of Hawaii, COA from Whiz Bang, 2 1/2 x 3 1/2" (ILLUS.) **4,905**
Huckleberry Hound bank/soap bottle, figural, plastic, Knickerbocker, 1960s, 9 1/2" **15-25**
Huckleberry Hound bath soap, Huckleberry Hound & Yogi Bear soap, MIB, 1961 .... **30-40**
Huckleberry Hound book, w/cut-out figures of Pixie, Dixie & Mr. Jinks, Golden Books, #456, 1961 .... **20-30**
Huckleberry Hound bowl, cereal, plastic, tan w/blue relief of Huck in rocket, 1960s, F&F Mold **12-15**
Huckleberry Hound card game, "Huckleberry Hound Card Game," Ed-U-Cards, w/box, 1961 .... **8-12**
Huckleberry Hound charm bracelet, Huckleberry Hound & friends, MOC, 1959 .... **25-35**
Huckleberry Hound coloring book, Whitman, 1959 .... **20-30**

Pixie & Dixie Ceramic Figure

Huckleberry Hound figure, Pixie & Dixie, ceramic, Ideas Inc., Des Moines, Iowa, early-mid 1960s, 3 3/4" (ILLUS.).............. **75-125**

Huckleberry Hound Giant Story Book

Huckleberry Hound giant story book, hardcover, Whitman, 1961, 192 pp. (ILLUS.)......................... **20-30**

Huckleberry Hound toy, bop-bop bag wPixie & Dixie, Air-line inflatable toy, MIB, 1960s, 14" h...................... **12-20**

Jetsons game, "Jetsons Fun Pad Game," Milton Bradley, 1963.................................. **60-90**

Jetsons game, "Jetsons Out of This World," board-type, Transogram, 1963 . **100-150**

"Rosey the Robot Game"

Jetsons game, "Rosey the Robot Game w/Astro the Space Dog," Transogram, 1962 (ILLUS.)............................ **65-95**

Jetsons hand puppet, Rosey, cloth & rubber, Knickerbocker, 1960s....................... **75-125**

Jetsons lunch box, steel dome, Aladdin, 1963...................... **600-800**

Jetsons lunch kit thermos, metal, Aladdin, 1963....................... **150-250**

Jetsons pull toy, Astro, hollow plastic, Transogram, early 1960s....................... **125-200**

Jetsons puzzle, Elroy at computer/George in tube, frame tray, Whitman, 1960s......... **20-30**

Jetsons puzzle, jigsaw-type, 70 pcs., Whitman, 1962..................... **30-50**

Jetsons record, "The Jetsons: First Family on the Moon," 1960s.................................. **12-20**

Jetsons toy, Astro & George, ramp walker, painted plastic, Marx, early 1960s, 3"........ **50-80**

Jetsons toy, Astro & Rosey, ramp walker, painted plastic, Marx, early 1960s, 3"........ **60-80**

Jetsons toy, "Hopping Astro," tin windup, Marx/Line-Mar, early 1960s, 4".............. **100-150**

Jetsons toy, "Hopping George," tin windup, Marx/Line-Mar, early 1960s, 4".............. **100-150**

Jetsons toy, "Hopping Rosey," tin windup, Marx/Line-Mar, early 1960s, 4"............... **200-300**

Linus the Lionhearted book, "Linus: A Smile for Grouse," Tell-a-Tale book, Whitman, 1966 .... **10-15**

Linus the Lionhearted comic book, one issue produced, Gold Key, 1965 .... **10-18**

Linus the Lionhearted doll, talking-type, Mattel, 1966, 21"....................................... **40-60**

Linus the Lionhearted game, "Linus the Lionhearted Uproarious Game," Transogram, 1965... **75-125**

Linus the Lionhearted Talking Hand Puppet

Linus the Lionhearted hand puppet, talking-type, Mattel, 1965, 14" (ILLUS.)........... **40-60**

Linus the Lionhearted LP record, voices of Sheldon Leonard & Carl Reiner, General Foods/Premier Albums, 1964............. **15-25**

Linus the Lionhearted lunch kit, vinyl w/metal bottle, Aladdin, 1965................. **350-500**

Linus the Lionhearted plush toy, cereal mail-away, 1960s **50-75**

Magilla Gorilla game, board-type, Ideal, 1964 .... **45-75**

Magilla Gorilla game, "Mushmouse and Punkin Puss," board-type, Ideal, 1964 ...... **45-75**

Magilla Gorilla puppet, hand-type, w/vinyl head, Ideal, 1960s **60-100**

Magilla Gorilla slide puzzle, various characters, Roalex, 1960s.............................. **20-30**

Magilla Gorilla Inflatable Squeak Toy

Magilla Gorilla toy, inflatable, squeak-type, Ideal, 1960s, 9" (ILLUS.) **20-30**

"Milton the Monster Game"

Milton the Monster game, board-type, Milton Bradley, 1966 (ILLUS.) **25-40**

Mr. Magoo bubble bath bottle, figural, Soaky, Colgate/Palmolive, 1960s, 10"....... **30-50**

Mr. Magoo coloring book, cut-out type, Golden, 1961 .... **20-30**

Mr. Magoo comic book, #3, Dell, 1963 .... **10-18**

Mr. Magoo doll, cloth & vinyl, Ideal, 1961, 16".. **50-75**

Mr. Magoo doll, plush cloth w/vinyl head, Ideal, 1962, 5"... **75-125**

Mr. Magoo game, "Mr. Magoo Visits the Zoo," board-type, Lowell, 1961 .... **40-65**

Mr. Magoo Sparkle paints, used, w/box, Kenner, 1963 .... **30-40**

Mr. Magoo Battery-Op Car

Mr. Magoo toy, battery-operated, tin car, Hubley, #952, 1961, 9" l. (ILLUS.).......... **150-250**

Mr. Magoo tumbler, glass, scene riding horse, 1962 .... **20-30**

Mr. Magoo tumbler, glass, scene skiing, 1963, 5 1/2"... **20-30**

Mushmouth (Moon Mullins comics) figure, bisque, nodder-type, African-American comic chef, color trim, ca. 1932, 3 3/8" h... **115**

Orphan Annie & Sandy Store Display

Mutt & Jeff figures, bisque, nodder-type, painted details, ca. 1932, 2 1/8" & 2 5/8" h., pr.. **230**

Orphan Annie puzzles, 1930s, mint in box, set of 3 .... **25**

Orphan Annie & Sandy store display, plaster, figure of Annie standing w/her hands on her hips, her dog, Sandy, standing next to her, base w/"copyright 1973, mfg. by ESCO New York News, Inc.," minor paint loss, 14 3/4" h. (ILLUS. bottom previous column) **144**

"Peter Potamus" Book

Peter Potamus book, "Peter Potamus," Little Golden Book, #556, Hanna-Barbera, 1964 (ILLUS.) **10-18**

Peter Potamus book, "Peter Potamus Meets the Black Knight," Tell-a-Tale Book, Whitman, 1965 .... **8-12**

Peter Potamus bubble bath bottle, figural, Purex, 1960s, 10 1/2"................................... **35-55**

Peter Potamus comic book, one issue produced, Gold Key, 1965........................ **10-18**

Peter Potamus doll, cloth & vinyl, Ideal, 1964, 8"... **75-125**

Peter Potamus game, board-type, Ideal, 1964 .... **50-75**

Popeye pinback button, advertising-type, image of Popeye walking in the center surrounded by wording "Popeye The Sailor - A Paramount Picture - Member Capitol Theatre Popeye Club," 1935 copyright **50**

Space Ghost animation cel, shows all Space Ghost members, handpainted, 1966 .... **225-275**

"The Sorceress of Cyba-3" Book

Space Ghost book, "The Sorceress of Cyba-3," Big Little Book, #2016, Whitman, 1968 (ILLUS.)...................................... 15-25
Space Ghost coloring book, Whitman, 1960s...................... 20-30
Space Ghost comic book, one issue produced, Gold Key, 1967............................. 50-75
Space Ghost costume, Ben Cooper, 1966.. 40-65
Space Ghost puzzle, 100 pcs., Whitman, 1968...................... 22-30
Space Ghost puzzles, four frame tray puzzles in boxed set, Whitman, 1967.............. 20-30
Space Ghost sticker book, 1968 25-35
Supercar book, "Supercar," Little Golden Book, 1962 15-25
Supercar game, "Road Race Game," Standard Toykrafts, MIB, 1963 90-120
Supercar game, "Supercar Road Race," board-type, Standard Toykraft, 1962 75-125
Supercar game, "Supercar to the Rescue," board-type, Milton Bradley, 1962, w/box. 60-100

Supercar Lunch Box

Supercar lunch box, steel, Universal, 1962 (ILLUS.)........................ 150-225
Supercar lunch kit thermos, steel & glass, Universal, 1962.......................... 50-80
Supercar Sun-Eze, Mike Mercury in Supercar, 1962............................. 12-16
Superman comic book, "Superman No. 2," fall 1939 issue, red & yellow ground w/blue title & color cartoon image of Superman flying, very good condition (spine separated, some paper loss, chip off bottom right corner) 1,190
Supermen of America ring, rare original contest ring offered as a prize to Supermen of America Club members soon after Superman's introduction, metal w/machine-painted inlaid red paint, excellent unrestored condition, center w/half-length picture of Superman, National Periodical Publications, 1940, 3/4 x 3/4 x 1/2" 6,900
Tillie the Toiler puzzles, 1930s, mint in box, set of 3.............................. 25
Touché Turtle book, "Touché Turtle and the Fire Dog," Top Tales, Whitman, 1960s...................... 10-18
Touché Turtle book, "Touché Turtle," Little Golden Book, 1962 12-20
Touché Turtle coloring book, rare, Whitman, #1185, 1960s 50-75
Touché Turtle game, board-type, Ideal, 1964........................ 200-300
Touché Turtle soap bottle, figural plastic, Bubble Club, Purex, 1960s, 10 1/2" 10-18

Touche Turtle Plush Puppet

Touché Turtle toy, push puppet, wearing large brimmed hat w/feather & holding sword in right hand, Kohner, 1960s, 4" (ILLUS.) 100-120

Mother Goose Collectibles

The Mother Goose theme is such a favorite with both children and adults that it has been featured in and on many items from long ago to the present. Few people grow up without having at least one favorite Mother Goose Rhyme. It is possible to amass a collection centering on one's single choice if that choice is a popular one such as Little Boy Blue or Mary Had a Little Lamb.

ABC plate, Mary Had a Little Lamb, tin, 8" d. 135
Bank, Humpty Dumpty, mechanical, edition of 20, 1975 1,250
Bank, Humpty Dumpty, tin, Chein, 6" h. 275
Bank, Mary & the Little Lambs, mechanical, edition of 20, 1974 850
Bank, Simple Simon, mechanical, edition of 10, 1975............................. 925
Book, "A Mother Goose ABC in a Pumpkin Shell," by Joan Walsh Anglund, Harcourt Brace, 1960......................... 20
Book, "A Pocket Full of Posies," by Marguerite de Angeli, Doubleday, 1954, 1961 18
Book, "Adventures of Little Fingers in Mother Goose Land," for piano teaching, illustrated by Nina Wright, G. Schirmer, Inc., black & white, 1923.......................... 5
Book, "Mother Goose ABC," Kinuko Craft, Platt & Munk, 1977.......................... 12
Book, "Mother Goose," by Eileen Fox Vaughn, Whitman, 1949 10-12
Book, "Mother Goose," by Esther Friend, first cover with children in pumpkin shell, Rand McNally Elf Book, 1947 15
Book, "Mother Goose," by Gertrude Elliott, Little Golden Book, first edition, 1942............ 40
Book, "Mother Goose," by Joseph Hirsch, Wonder Book, 1946................... 15

"Mother Goose"

Book, "Mother Goose," linette, Whitman, 1941 (ILLUS.).. **12-18**
Book, "Mother Goose Nursery Rhymes," Hurst & Co., ca. late 1800s........................ **40-50**

"Mother Goose Pictures and Rhymes"

Book, "Mother Goose Pictures and Rhymes," by Ruth Newton, large size, linette, Whitman, 1934 (ILLUS.)....................... **45**
Book, "Mother Goose," Volland edition, cloth over board, full-color illustrations by Frederick Richardson, 1915 .... **250-300**
Book, "Old Mother Hubbard," linette, Sam'l Gabriel Sons **30**
Book, "Ring O' Roses," Warne, illustrated by Leslie L. Brooke, no date............................ **65**
Book, "The Children's Mother Goose," by William Donahey, Reilly & Lee, 1921............. **125**

"The Metropolitan Mother Goose"

Booklet, "The Metropolitan Mother Goose," advertising type, by Watson & Clark, 1920s (ILLUS.) **15**
Carpet sweeper, Mother Goose, toy-type, metal & wood, Susy Goose by Kiddie Brush & Toy Company, 1948-50 .... **22**
Clock, Hickory Dickory Dock, tin, wind-up, Mattel **20-40**
Cookbook, "Polly Put the Kettle On," Jello, illustrated by Maxfield Parrish, 1923 .... **65**
Cookie jar, Humpty Dumpty, Abingdon **300-500**
Cookie jar, Humpty Dumpty, Metlox **500-1000**
Cookie jar, Mother Goose, Gilner Pottery ... **300-400**
Cookie jar, Old King Cole, Robinson Ransbottom **600-700**
Cup, Nursery Rhymes, milk glass...................... **22**
Curtains, Mother Goose rhyme pattern, very colorful, handmade, 1950s, pr................. **15**
Cut-out dolls, Mother Goose, life-like stand-up, Whitman, #987, 1937, each...... **15-25**
Dishes, Mother Goose, toy-type, tin, complete set in box **50-60**
Doll, bisque, Nancy Ann Storybook, 1930s, 5 1/2-7" h., each **300**
Doll, composition, Nancy Ann Storybook, 1940s, each... **60**
Doll, hard plastic, Nancy Ann Storybook, 1950s, each... **45**

Mother Hubbard Doll

Doll, Mother Hubbard, vinyl, Ideal, storybook series, early 1980s, 8" h. (ILLUS.).... **20-35**

Stuff & Sew Humpty Dumpty Doll

Doll, Stuff & Sew Humpty Dumpty, 1980s (ILLUS.) **12-15**
Doll cards, Peter Piper & My Pretty Maid, Hallmark, 1947 (ILLUS.), each................... **10-12**
Dolls, composition, Arranbee, storybook, 1930s, 9-10" h., each **150**
Dolls, composition, Madame Alexander, storybook dolls w/Mother Goose theme, 1930s-40s, 7-9" h., each............... **200**

Dolls, From the Land of Mother Goose, Platt & Munk, #221, boxed set, 1920s **25**

Dolls, vinyl, Effanbee Storybook Series, late 1970s, 11" h., each.................................... **40**

Game, Jack & Jill, board-type, Milton Bradley, 1909 .... **100**

Game, Little Bo Peep, board-type, McLoughlin Bros., 1890 .... **150**

Game, Mother Goose, board-type, 1971............. **25**

American Greetings Card w/Song Booklet

Greeting card, American Greetings, w/song booklet insert, 1949, 4 x 5", each (ILLUS.)... **5-10**

Guitar, Mother Goose, toy-type, Mattel, 1970, mint... **40**

Cream of Wheat Advertisement

Magazine ad, "Fee! Fi! Fo! Fum!," featuring Jack the Giant Killer, Cream of Wheat, full page, 1909 (ILLUS.) **18**

Magazines, Humpty Dumpty, 1950s, each........ **2-5**

Music box, "Farmer in the Dell," tin, turn crank, Mattel, 1951, 7" h. **150-300**

Nodder figure, Mother Goose, papier-maché, late 1800s..................................... **3,950**

Ornament, Mother Goose, Hallmark Keepsake, wings move, 1992......................... **199-235**

Paper doll, Children in the Shoe, by Charlot Byj, Merrill, #1562-15, 1949............................. **30**

Mother Goose Paper Doll

Paper doll, Mother Goose, probably by Dorothy Mager, Saalfield, #13318 (ILLUS.) **20**

Party dolls, Nursery Rhyme, in costume, McLoughlin, no date, each **50**

Picture, Nursery Rhyme, framed by Fern Bisel Peat, 1930s, 9 1/2 x 13"......................... **45**

Picture book, Mother Goose, cut-out type, National Art Company, no date.................. **30-40**

Plate, Little Bo Peep, Royal Doulton, 8" d. **48**

Humpty Dumpty Pull-toy

Pull-toy, Humpty Dumpty, plastic, arms spin when pulled, Fisher-Price, 1970s-80s (ILLUS.)... **12-15**

Puppet, Little Boy Blue, composition, Hazelle, 800 series **135**

Mother Goose Puzzles

Puzzles, Mother Goose characters, wooden, for pre-schoolers, several makers, each (ILLUS.).. **10-20**

Radio, Baa-Baa Black Sheep, music-box type, Fisher-Price, 1967.................................. **50**

Radio, Little Boy Blue, music-box type, Fisher-Price, 1967.. **50**

Radio, Ten Little Indians, music-box type, Fisher-Price, 1961.. **15**

Ramp Walker, Mother Goose, toy-type **55**

Sand pail, Mother Goose, tin, 9" h. (including handle)... **25**

Sheet music, Humpty Dumpty, by Charles Straight, cover art by Detakacs, 1914............. **20**

Shoe Box w/Mother Goose Characters

Shoe box, Mother Goose characters, Mother Goose Shoes, many rhymes depicted in color, mid- 1960s (ILLUS.).............................. 25
Spinning tops, Mother Goose character, tin, various manufacturers 25-75
Teapot, Nursery Rhyme Scenes, Germany, 4 1/2" h.. 40
Toy, Liddle Middle Muffet, Mattel 30
Toy, Mother Goose, battery-operated, Cragstan/Japan, 1950, excellent 100

Mother Goose-in-a-Box Toy

Toy, Mother Goose-in-a-Box, tin, crank handle, Mattel (ILLUS.) 75

Musical Old Woman In a Shoe Toy

Toy, Old Woman Who L-Price, 1964, mint in box (ILLUS.).. 110
Trading card, Mother Goose, Lion Coffee, die-cut... 15
Trading card, Mother Hubbard Soap, stock card... 6
Trading card, Old King Cole, Lion Coffee, die-cut... 10
Trading card, "The Old Woman in the Shoe," Nestle's Milk Good 10
Trading card, "The Queen of Hearts," Ceresota Flour, Northwestern Milling.............. 12
Trading card, "What Made the Lamb Love Mary So?," Soapine Soap.............................. 25

Tumbler, Hey Diddle Diddle, Royal Doulton, 3 3/4" h. 65
Wooden pull-toy, Humpty Dumpty, Fisher-Price, 1957 20-40

Peter Pumpkin Eater & Wife Stationery

Writing papers, Peter Pumpkin Eater & Wife, boxed for children, 18 sheet, 12 envelopes, 1950s (ILLUS.) 5-7
Xylophone, "Tunes from Mother Goose - The Nursery Pianette," toy-type, Schoenhut, mint in box 55

CHILDREN'S BOOKS
Miscellaneous

A Book of Old Fables in New Dresses, by Bigham, 1906.. $35
Doctor Doolittle's Circus, by Hugh Lofting, 1924 35
Easy Steps in Sewing for Big & Little Girls, Jane Eayre Fryer, 1913, sample of cooking book included.................................... 75
Hajji Baba of Ispahan, by Morier, illustrated by Baldridge, 1937, Random House 25
Henner's Lydia, by Marguerite DeAngeli, 1936, Doubleday 65
Old Mother Westwind, by Burgess, 1918 30
Peter Pan and Wendy, by James Barrie, retold by Byron, illustrated by Mabel Attwell 20
Raggedy Ann's Wishing Pebble, 1925 40
Rhymes for Kindley Children, by Fairmont Snyder, illustrated by Johnny Gruelle, originally published 1916, 36th edition 30
Storybook, "Streamline," Merrill Publishing Co., 1935, 11x13" 17
The Night Before Christmas, die-cut color illustrations, 1917, Price.............................. 55
Tick Tock Tales, by Watty Piper, illustrated by Eulalie & Lenski, 1931, Platt & Munk......... 25
Tim Tyler in the Jungle, pop-up type, 1935 275
Wizard of Oz, 1957 22
Wonder Stories, Hans Christian Andersen, 1881 85

1900-1920

Children's books of the 20th century are collected today for many reasons - probably the main reasons are for their illustrations and the memories they bring. This price section focuses on popular subjects and illustrators from approximately 1900-1920. Books listed are for good to very good condition and without dust covers. Prices are for a center of range depending on condition and desirability

1900-1920 - The Golden Age of children's book illustration - Maxfield Parrish, Arthur Rackham, N. N. Wyeth, Jesse Wilcox Smith and many other brilliant illustrators were drawn to the field of children's books

Art Nouveau illustration ruled through this time period. The classic image of a fairy in flowing gown with wings was used most often. Anthropomorphic animals are still very popular. Many reprints of fairy tales from Grimm and Anderson were available. Series books were very popular, particularly with adolescents. Large Victorian anthologies like St. Nicholas stayed popular throughout the era, but disappeared by the '20s. Most interesting in this era were the many fantasy books inspired by the success of the Wizard of Oz, which first appeared in 1900, and the perennial reprinting of Alice in Wonderland. Collectors look for titles like The Golden Goblin, Yama Yama Land and Bobbie in Bugaboo Land.

Books were printed in black and white with full color plates, two-color or simply black and white. High quality books and the first smaller size books became available. The overwhelming popularity of color Sunday Comics sections in newspapers created reprints in various book forms, though aimed at adults. Characters like Little Nemo in Slumberland, Alley Oop, Krazy Kat and Buster Brown captured the attention of children.

Beautifully illustrated dust jackets appeared for the first time, replacing the gilded and embossed covers of old.

The dates listed below are for the edition as it appears in the book, the copyright date or in lieu of that, any date found on the book or sometimes the book is undated but the illustrations are dated.

At the Back of the North Wind, George McDonald, color illustrations by Jesse Wilcox Smith, 1919, Davis McKay Pub. **50**

Behind the Garden Wall, Robert Wallace, b/w illustrations by Elsinore Robinson Crowell, 1913, Paul Elder & Co. **15**

Bible Stories and Poems, Wilbur F. Crafts, b/w & color illustrations by James Tissot, ca. 1915, illustrations Bible Selections Commission **15**

Bobby in Bugaboo Land, Curtis Dunham, b/w & color illustrations by George F. Kerr, 1907, Bobbs-Merrill Co. **30**

Chinese Fables and Folk Stories, Mary Hayes Davis, b/w illustrations, ca. 1908, American Book Co. **10**

Crab Cottage, Raymond Jacberns, b/w illustrations by J. Menzies, ca. 1905, Chambers Pub. Co. **20**

Dickie Delightful in Rainbowland, James Ball Naylor, b/w illustrations/color frontpiece, ca. 1909, Saalfield Publishing Co. **20**

English Fairy Tales, Ernest & Grace Rhys, illustrations by Herbert Cole & R. Anning Bell, ca. 1910, J.M. Dent & Sons Ltd. (ILLUS. top next column) **25**

Fairy Frolics, Enos B. Comstock, color & b/w illustrations by Frances Bassett Comstock, ca. 1913, Rand McNally & Co. **75**

Illustration from English Fairy Tales

Granny's Stories, compilation, b/w & color illustrations by Mable Lucie Atwell, ca. 1909, Raphael Tuck & Sons **30**

Heroes of the Golden Age, James Baldwin, b/w illustrations by Howard Pyle, ca. 1891, Scribners **30**

House of the Misty Star, Frances Little, b/w illustrations by Arthur Becker, ca. 1915, Century Publishing **20**

Jackieboy in Rainbowland, William L. Hill, color illustrations by Fanny Y. Cory, ca. 1911, Rand McNally **50**

Johnny Appleseed, Eleanor Atkinson, b/w illustrations by Frank T. Merrill, ca. 1915, Grosset-Dunlap **15**

Illustration - Old Mother Goose Nursery Rhymes

Old Mother Goose Nursery Rhymes, b/w & color illustrations by E. Stuart Hardy, ca. 1920, E P Dutton (ILLUS.) **30**

Illustration from Our Baby Bunnies

Our Baby Bunnies, a Linenette Book, color illustrations, ca. 1900, Sam Gabriel & Sons (ILLUS.) **15**

Ozma

Ozma of Oz, L. Frank Baum, b/w & color illustrations by John R. Neill, ca. 1907, Reilly & Lee Co. (ILLUS.) **100**

Painting Pastimes for Young Artists, Gerald Chapman, b/w illustrations by Edith O. Donnell, ca. 1905, Thompson & Thomas **20**

Pepper & Salt, Howard Pyle, b/w illustrations by Howard Pyle, ca. 1913, Harper & Bros. **75**

Peter Rabbit and His Ma, Louise A. Field, b/w illustrations by Virginia Albert, ca. 1917, Saalfield Pub. Co. **15**

Illustration from Puss and Boots in New Mother Goose Land

Puss and Boots in New Mother Goose Land, David Cory, b/w illustrations by E.J. Babcock, ca. 1919, Grosset & Dunlap (ILLUS.) **12**

Queen Tiny's Little People, Mildred L. Bailey, b/w & color illustrations by Theresa A. Jones, ca. 1914, McCauley Co. **50**

Riley's Songs of Home, b/w & color illustrations by Will Vawter, ca. 1910, Grosset & Dunlap **30**

Robin Hood, Henry Gilbert, b/w illustrations by Francis Brundage, ca. 1910, Saalfield Pub. Co. **30**

Stories from Anderson, Hans Christian Anderson, color illustrations by Edmund Dulac, ca. 1910, George H. Doran Co. **125**

Stories of Wagner's Operas Told for Children, Elizabeth M. Wheelock, b/w frontpiece, ca. 1907 .... **10**

Stories the Iroquois Tell Their Children, Mabel Powers, b/w illustrations by W. Fletcher White, ca. 1917, American Book Co. **15**

Swanhilde, Carrie Norris Horowitz, b/w illustrations by L.J. Bridgeman, ca. 1890, D. Lothrop Co. **12**

The Adventures of Prickly Porky, Thornton W. Burgess, color illustrations by Harrison Cady, 1920, Little, Brown & Co. **25**

The Best Loved Poems of James Whitcomb Riley, illustrations by Ethel Franklin Betts, 1920, Blue Ribbon Books, New York **25**

The Book of Saints and Friendly Beasts, Abbie Farwell, b/w illustrations by Fanny Cory **40**

Illustration - The Book of Wonder Voyages

The Book of Wonder Voyages, Joseph Jacobs (ed.), b/w illustrations by John Batten, 1919, G.P. Putnam & Sons (ILLUS.) **20**

The First Christmas Tree, Henry Van Dyke, b/w frontpiece, ca. 1917, Charles Scribner Sons **12**

The Glittering Festival, Edith Ogden Harrison, b/w & color illustrations by Clara Powers Wilson, ca. 1911, A.A. McClure Co. **60**

Illustration from The Golden Goblin

The Golden Goblin, Curtis Dunham, b/w & color illustrations by George F. Kerr, ca. 1905, Bobbs Merrill Co. (ILLUS.) 50

Illustration from The Goose Girl

The Goose Girl, The Cozy Hour Series, color illustrations by Kubel, ca. 1900, The John C. Winston Co. (ILLUS.) 25

The Happy Prince and Other Stories, Oscar Wilde, color illustrations by Spenser Bard Nichols, ca. 1913, The Frederick A. Stokes Co. 30

The Japanese Twins, Lucy Fitch Perkins, b/w illustrations by author, ca. 1912, Houghton Mifflin Co. 10

The Legend of Sleepy Hollow, Washington Irving, b/w & color illustrations by Arthur Rackham, ca. 1910, David McKay & Co. 100

The Little Green Goblin, James Ball Naylor, b/w illustrations by Miller, ca. 1907 Saalfield Pub. Co. 15

The Palace Made of Music

The Palace Made of Music, Raymond Alden, b/w illustrations by Mayo Bunker, ca. 1910, Bobbs Merrill Co. (ILLUS.) 20

The Pansy Wedding

The Pansy Wedding, Sara Tawney Lefferts, b/w and two color illustrations, ca. 1903 (ILLUS.) 25

The Real Mother Goose, b/w & color illustrations by Blanche Fisher Wright, ca. 1919, Rand McNally & Co. 50

The Red Fairy Book, Andrew Lang, b/w illustrations by H.J. Ford & Lancelot Speed, ca. 1900, McLoughlin Bros. 15

The Sleepy King, A Fairy Tale, Aubrey Hopwood & Seymour Hicks, b/w illustrations by Maud Trelawny, illustrations dated 1898, A.L. Burt, Publisher 15

Illustration - The Night Before Christmas

The Night Before Christmas, color illustrations by Alice Hirschberg, Hayes Lithographic Co. (ILLUS.) 40

Illustration from The Water Babies

The Water Babies, Charles Kingsley, b/w illustrations, 1899, Henry Altemus Co. (ILLUS.)............ 20
TobyTown, Chandler Oakes, b/w illustrations by George Carlson, ca. 1920, Sully & Kleinteich 25

Illustration from Treasure Island

Treasure Island, Robert Louis Stevenson, b/w illustrations by Wal Paget, ca. 1900, Charles Scribner's Sons (ILLUS.)............ 35
Wild Flower Children, Elizabeth Gordon, b/w & color illustrations by Janet Laura Scott, ca. 1918, P.F. Volland Co. 40

1920s

A Child's Garden of Verses

This price section focuses on popular subjects and illustrators from the 1920s. Books listed are for good to very good condition and without dust covers. Prices are for a center of range depending on condition and desirability. First editions bring high values and unless noted in listing, mentioned here are for later editions

Golden Age illustrators are still going strong. Arthur Rackham, Edmund Dulac, Willy Pogany and other illustrators' styles simplify as they mature. Maxfield Parrish's high end gift book Knave of Hearts (1925) is published - Parrish's last book. Style transition between Art Nouveau and Deco. "Delicate Deco" illustrations in color are best exemplified by the P. F. Volland Company, who offer beautifully illustrated books in a '20s Kate Greenaway style. Color in illustrations is vibrant and experimental. Fantasy themes are still popular, but more books appear about home life and the child's world, including books set in urban areas or with city themes. Sunday comics are increasingly popular and offer more characters. The first American animation appears, with the popularity of Gertie the Dinosaur by Windsor McKay (creator of Little Nemo in Slumberland), having a large appeal to children

Full color books are now becoming less expensive to produce, though many black and white books still appeared. High end "gift books" reach their zenith. These larger format books come boxed, well designed, with glued in ("tipped in") color plates. Though not genre specific, many children's books are produced in gift book form

My Book House series is introduced. Its theme-oriented layout sets the standard for book sets such as Book of Knowledge, replacing the older St. Nicholas style of anthology.

A Child's Garden of Verses, Robert Louis Stevenson, b/w & color illus., ca. 1920, Henry Altemus Co. (ILLUS.)............ $25

Alice in Orchestralia

Alice in Orchestralia, Ernest La Prade, b/w illus. by Carroll C. Snell, 1925, Doubleday, Doran & Co. (ILLUS.)............ 12

Alice's Adventures in Wonderland

Alice's Adventures in Wonderland, Lewis Carroll, b/w illus. by Willy Pogany, 1929, E.P. Dutton & Co. (ILLUS.)............ 35
Around an Iroquois Story Fire, Mabel Powers, b/w illus. by R. Emmett Owen, 1923, Frederick A. Stokes Co. 15
Captain January, Laura E. Richards, b/w illus. by Frank Merrill, 1927 ed., C.H. Simonds Co. 20
Champions of the Round Table, Howard Pyle, b/w illus. by the author, Charles Scribner & Sons 40
Davy and the Goblin, Charles E. Carryl, b/w illus. by E.B. Bensell, color plates by Herman Bacharach, 1928, Houghton Mifflin Co. (ILLUS.)............ 15

Davy and the Goblin

Doctor Dolittle in the Moon, Hugh Lofting, b/w illus. by the author, 1928, J.B. Lipincott **15**

Grimm's Fairy Tales

Grimm's Fairy Tales, b/w illus., color plates by Edwin John Prittie, 1924, John C. Winston Co. (ILLUS.) **20**

Happy Home Children

Happy Home Children, Elizabeth Gordon, color illus. by Marion Foster, 1924, P.F. Volland Co. (ILLUS.) **20**
In Toyland, Iris Hunter, color illus. by Gaba, 1928, The Childrens Press **25**
John Martin's Big Book #10, b/w & two color illus. by various artists, 1926, John Martin Book House **15**

Just So Stories, Rudyard Kipling, b/w illus. by Gleeson, 1925, Doubleday & Page **12**
Magic Journeys, Mary Graham Bonner, two color illus. by Luxor Price, 1928, Macmillan & Co. **20**

Millions of Cats

Millions of Cats, Wanda Gag, b/w illus., 1928, Cowan-McCann, Inc. (ILLUS.) **15**

My Bookhouse

My Bookhouse, six-book series, Olive Beaupre Miller, three-color illus. by various artists, 1928 edition, The Bookhouse for Children, for the series (ILLUS.) **100**
Myths and Enchantment Tales, Margaret Evans Price, color illus. by author, 1924, Rand McNally **35**
Nick and Nancy in the Land of Near-by, Olive Roberts Barton, b/w illus. by E.R. Higgins, 1921, George H. Doran Co. **10**
Pinocchio, C. Collodi, b/w & color illus. by Violet Moore Higgins, 1926, Albert Whitman & Co. **20**
Rachel & The Seven Wonders, Netta Syrett, b/w & color plates by Joyce Mercer, ca. 1920, Frederick Stokes Co. **15**

Raggedy Andy Stories

Raggedy Andy Stories, Johnny Gruelle, b/w & color illus. by the author, 1920, P.F. Volland Co. (ILLUS.)............................ 50
Riley Fairy Tales, James Whitcomb Riley, b/w & color illus. by Will Vawter, 1923, Bobbs-Merrill Co.................................... 25
Sails of Gold, Lady Cynthia Asquith ed., color plates by A.H. Watson, 1927, Charles Scribner & Sons..................... 25
Shoes and Ships and Sealing Wax, Ethel Glere Chamberlin, color illus. by Janet Laura Scott, 1928, Saalfield Publishing.......... 20
Spiderwebs & Sunflowers, Mary Geisler Philips, b/w illus. by Blanche Greer, 1928, Macrae Smith Co. 15

Stories from Andersen

Stories from Andersen, color plates by Edmund Dulac, ca. 1920, George H. Doran Co. (ILLUS.) 125
Sunbeams, Hazel Julia Fristad, b/w illus. by Solveg Hazel Fristad, 1928, Press Printing & Binding House 12
Tales of Toyland, Enid Blyton, b/w illus. by various artists, ca. late '20s, Dean & Son Ltd.. 12
Tales Told in Holland, Olive Beaupre Miller, color illus. by Maude & Miska Peter-

sham, 1926, The Book House for Children 50
Taxis and Toadstools, Rachel Field, b/w & color illus. by the author, 1926, Doubleday, Doran & Co....................................... 15
The Arabian Nights, b/w illus. by Adelaide Bell & Rene Bull, 1924, John C. Winston Co. 12
The Beloved Vagabond, William J. Locke, b/w illus. by Jean Dulac, 1922, John Lane 25
The Book of Courage, Herman Hagedorn, b/w illus. by Frank Godwin, 1929, John C. Winston Co.. 20
The Children's Bluebird, Georgette Lablanc, b/w & color illus. by Herbert Paus, 1928, Dodd, Mead & Co. 30
The Cruise of Noah's Ark, David Cory, b/w illus. by H.S. Barbour, 1922, Grosset & Dunlap... 10

The House at Pooh Corner

The House at Pooh Corner, A.A. Milne, b/w illus. by Ernest H. Shepard, 1928, E.P. Dutton & Co. (ILLUS.)................. 20

The Jolly Old Shadow Man

The Jolly Old Shadow Man, Gertrude Alice Kay, color illus. by the author, 1920, P.F. Volland Co. (ILLUS.).......................... 30
The Little Tailor of Winding Way, Gertrude Crownfield, b/w illus. by Willy Pogany, 1926, MacMillan & Co. 15
The Mermaid & Other Stories, Hans Christian Anderson, b/w & color illus. by Dugald Stewart Walker, 1923, Doubleday Page & Co...................................... 25
The Pied Piper of Pudding Lane, Sarah Addington, color illus. by Gertrude Kay, 1923, Atlantic Monthly Press.......................... 30

The Pirate's Treasure

The Pirate's Treasure, Edward A. Wilson, color illus. by the author, 1926, P.F. Volland Co. (ILLUS.)... 25

The Poetry Book, Miriam & Herbert Bruner, b/w & color illus. by Marjorie Hartwell, 1927, Rand McNally & Co. 20

The Rusted Knight & Other Stories

The Rusted Knight and Other Stories, Richard Von Volkmann, b/w silhouettes by Marte Landsberger, ca. 1929, Bruce Humphries Inc. (ILLUS.)..................................... 15

The Story of a Bad Boy, Thomas Bailey Aldrich, color plates by Edwin John Prittie, 1927, John C. Winston Co................................. 15

The Wishing Fairy's Animal Friends, Corinne Ingraham, b/w & color illus. by Dugald Stewart Walker, 1921, Bretano's 35

Treasure Island, Robert Louis Stevenson, color plates by Edmund Dulac, ca. mid-'20s, Doran.. 50

Tyltyl, Maurice Maeterlinck, color illus. by Herbert Paus, 1920, Dodd, Mead & Co........... 75

White Tail the Deer, George Walsh, color illus. by Edwin John Prittie, 1922, John C. Winston Co... 15

Winnie the Pooh, A.A. Milne, b/w illus. by Ernest Shepard, 1926, E.P. Dutton Co............ 35

Wooden Willie, Johnny Gruelle, color illus. by the author, 1928, M.A. Donahue & Co......... 50

1930s

This price section focuses on popular subjects and illustrators from the 1930s. Books listed are for good to very good condition and without dust covers. Prices are for a center of range depending on condition and desirability. First Editions bring high values and unless noted in listing, books mentioned here are for later editions.

The Great Depression has enormous effect on society as well as children's books. High end gift books and more lavish productions give way to simplification. Competition to traditional children's books comes in the form of less expensive coloring books, paper doll books, the famous Big Little Books and ultimately, the comic book.

Popular culture influences subjects and art. Art Deco and modernistic design are very popular. Color combinations in illustrations become toned down from the '20s.

The movement in the fine art world of Regionalism produces numerous children's books on American life, history and mythology illustrated in a realistic style of drawing. Charcoal, litho crayon and pastel as well as the printing forms of lithography and silk screen are employed.

Animated cartoons become extremely popular. Though not specifically aimed at children, Disney, Warner Bros. and others find that Mickey Mouse, Bugs Bunny and Betty Boop have a greater following among children than anticipated. Traditional children's books see more "cartoon-like" illustrations.

A Head for Happy, Helen Sewell, b/w illus. by the author, 1931, MacMillan Co. 15

A Merry-Go-Round of Modern Tales, Caroline D. Emerson, b/w illus. by Lois Lenski, 1938 ed., E.P. Dutton................................. 20

Bible Picture ABC Book

Bible Picture ABC Book, Elsie E. Egermeier, color illus. by various artists, 1939, Warner Press (ILLUS.)..................................... 12

Blaze and the Gypsies, C.W. Anderson, b/w illus. by the author, 1939, MacMillan Co. 20

Driscoll's Book of Pirates, Charles Driscoll, b/w illus. by Montfort Amory, 1934, David McKay Co. 25

Eight Nursery Tales

Fun-Time Dot Pictures

John Martin's Big Book No. 5

THE PIGS

Manners Can be Fun

Mary Poppins Comes Back

No-Sitch: The Hound

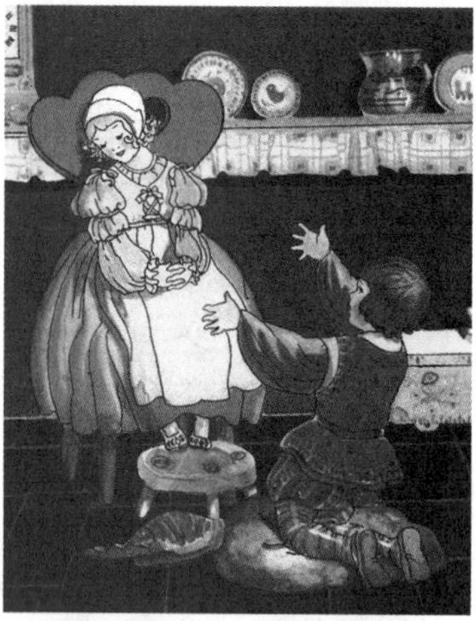

No-Sitch: The Hound, Phil Strong, b/w & color illus. by Kurt Wiese, 1936, Dodd Mead & Co. (ILLUS.) **20**

Paul Bunyan and His Big Blue Ox, R.D. Handy, b/w by the author, 1937, Rand McNally & Co. **15**

Picture Book of Mother Goose

Picture Book of Mother Goose, b/w & color illus. by Berta & Elmer Hader, 1930, Coward McCann (ILLUS.) **20**

Pinocchio, Collodi, color illus. by the Disney Studios, 1939, Random House **50**

Rewards and Fairies, Rudyard Kipling, b/w illus. by Charles Brock, 1930 ed., MacMillan & Co. **20**

Rhymes for Kindly Children, Ethel Fairmont, color illus. by Johnny Gurelle, 1937, Wise Parslow Co. **25**

Taming the Barbary Pirates, John DeMorgan, b/w illus. by E.B. Comstock, 1933, McLoughlin Bros. **20**

The ABC Bunny, Wanda Gag, b/w illus. by the author, 1933, Coward McCann Inc. **25**

The Animal Way

The Animal Way, Jean Broadhurst, color illus. by Dorothy Doubble, 3rd ed., 1930, The Cleanliness Institute (ILLUS.) **12**

The Big Show

The Big Show, Mary Baskerville, color illus. by John Dukes McKee, 1932, Rand McNally (ILLUS.) **25**

The Book of Cowboys

The Book of Cowboys, Holling C. Holling, b/w & color illus. by H.C. & Lucille Holling, 1936, Platt & Munk Co. (ILLUS.) **45**

The Children's Bluebird, Georgette LaBlanc, b/w & color illus. by Doris & Marian Henderson, 1939 ed., Grosset & Dunlap **25**

The Christ Child, b/w & color illus. by Maude & Miska Petersham, 1931, Doubleday, Doran & Co. **60**

The Five Chinese Brothers, Claire Huchet Bishop, 2 color illus. by Kurt Wiese, 1938, Cowan-McCann **20**

The Flop-Eared Hound, Ellis Credle, b/w photos by Charles Townsend, 1938, Oxford Press **30**

The Great March, Rose G. Lurie, b/w illus. by Todros Geller, 1931, Dept. of Synagogue & School Extension **30**

The Gypsy Story Teller, Cora Morris, illus. by Frank Dobias, 1931, The Jr. Literary Guild **12**

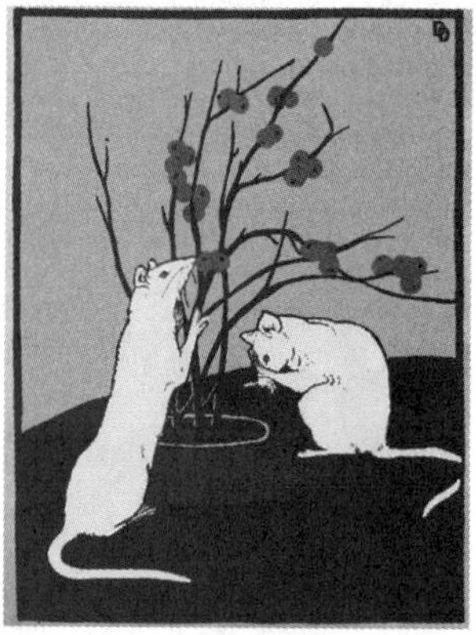

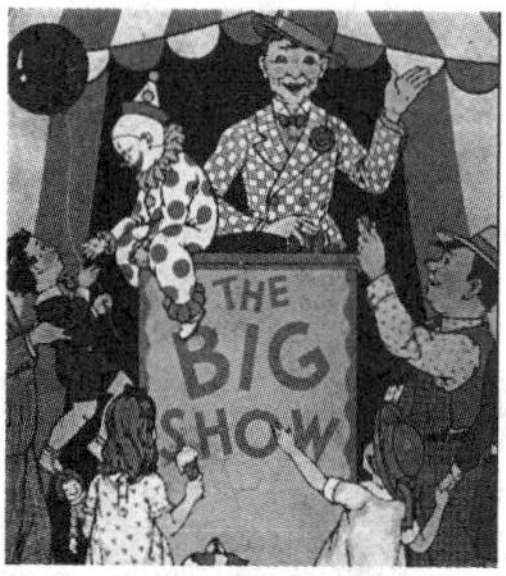

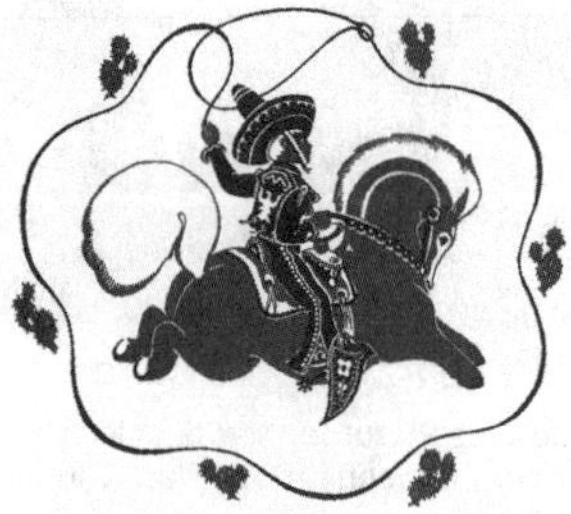

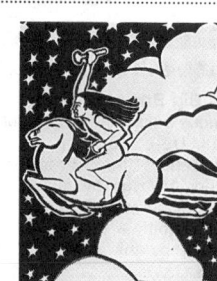

The Hurricane's Children

The Hurricane's Children, Carl Carmer, b/w illus. by Elisabeth Carmer, 1937, Farrar & Rinehart Inc. (ILLUS.) **12**

The Little Engine That Could

The Little Engine That Could, Watty Piper, color illus. by George & Doris Hauman, 1930, Platt & Munk (ILLUS.)............................ **20**

The Little Shepherd of Kingdom Come, John Fox, Jr., color illus. by N.C. Wyeth, 1931 ed., Charles Scribner Sons..................... **45**

The Magic Loaves, Hope Brister adapted, b/w illus. by Harold Minton, 1931, MacMillan & Co. **12**

The Patchwork Girl of Oz, L. Frank Baum, b/w & color illus. by John R. Neill, junior edition, 1939, Reilly & Lee **35**

The Pet's Doctor

The Pet's Doctor, June Head, color illus. by Ida Bohatta Morpurgo, 1935, Joseph Mueller Pub. (ILLUS.) **15**

The Picture Story Book of Peter Pan, J.M. Barrie, color illus. by Roy Best, 1931, Whitman Pub. Co. **50**

The Pied Piper of Hamelin, Robert Browning, b/w & color illus. by Hope Dunlop, 1934, Rand McNally **25**

The Story Book of Corn

The Story Book of Corn, Maude & Miska Petersham, color illus. by the authors, 1936, John C. Winston (ILLUS.)...................... **15**

The Story of Ferdinand

The Story of Ferdinand, Munro Leaf, b/w illus. by Robert Lawson, 1938, the Viking Press (ILLUS.) **25**

The Wizard of Oz, L. Frank Baum, color illus. by W.W. Denslow, 1939 ed., has stills from movie on inside covers, Bobbs Merrill **40**

1940s

This price section focuses on popular subjects and illustrators from the 1940s. Books listed are for good to very good condition and without dust covers. Prices are for a center of range depending on condition and desirability. First Editions bring high values and unless noted in listing, books mentioned here are for later editions.

World War II creates paper shortages, simpler books, patriotic themes and propaganda images in children's books. American folk tales and stories are revived and classics illustrated by N.C. Wyeth are reprinted

Women illustrators increase - Margaret Evans Price, Bessy Pease Guttman, Ethel Hays et al create charming illustrations in an evocative style. Regional style continues with talented illustrators like George Carlson, Robert Lawson and Henry Pitz.

The introduction of Little Golden Books changes concept of children's books. Animated cartoon characters such as Bugs Bunny, Tom & Jerry, and Woody Woodpecker can be seen more and more in children's literature. Comic books aimed specifically at children appear and compete with standard children's books

European titles and classics are released (or re-released) in America after the war.

1001 Riddles for Children

1001 Riddles for Children, George Carlson, b/w illus. by the author, 1949, Platt & Munk (ILLUS.)................................. 25

A Book for Jennifer, Alice Dalgliesh, color illus. by Katherine Milhous, 1940, Charles Scribners................................. 15

A Book of Toys, Gwen White, color illus. by the author, 1946, King Penguin Book............. 10

Airplane Andy, Sanford Tousey, two-color illus. by the author 1942, Doubleday.............. 10

An American ABC, Maud & Miska Petersham, two-color & full color illus. by the authors, 1941, MacMillan Co. 35

Bridles with Rainbows, poetry, Sarah & John E. Brewton, b/w illus. by Vera Block, 1949, the MacMillan Co. 12

Faust

Faust, Robert Lawrence adapted, b/w & color illus. by Paul Kinnear, 1943, Grosset & Dunlap (ILLUS.)..................................... 20

Five Golden Wrens

Five Golden Wrens, Private Hugh Troy, b/w illus. by the author, 1943, Oxford University Press (ILLUS.) 20

Growing Pains, religious, Florence M. Taylor, b/w & color illus. by Lucile Patterson Marsh, The Westminster Press 10

Homer Price

Homer Price, Robert McCloskey, b/w illus. by the author, 1945, the Viking Press (ILLUS.) 25

In Animal Town

In Animal Town, color illus. by M.H. & R.T.D., 1943, Platt & Munk Co. (ILLUS.) 15

Jewish Fairy Tales and Legends, Aunt Naomi, b/w illus. by Sol Aronson, 1949, Block Publishing Co.. 10

Kiddieland Rub a Pencil, color cover, b/w illus., 1944, Saalfield Pub. Co. 20

Little Town on the Prairie, Laura Ingalls Wilder, b/w illus. by Helen Sewell, 1941, Harper Bros.. 25

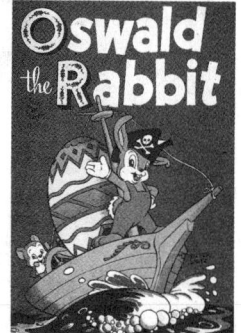

Oswald the Rabbit Comics Magazine No. 102

Oswald the Rabbit Comics Magazine No. 102, Walter Lantz, 1946, Dell Publishing Co. (ILLUS.) 25

Other Lands and Other People, Mary G. Kelty, b/w & color illus. by Herbert Paus, 1942, Gim & Co. 10

Peer Gynt, E.V. Sandys, b/w illus. by Fritz Eichenberg, 1941, Thomas Cromwell Co. 12

Peter and the Wolf, Golden Book, color illus. by Disney Studios, 1946 15

Peter Churchmouse, Margot Austin, b/w illus. by the author, 1941, E.P. Dutton 25

Pinocchio, Collodi, b/w illus. by Fritz Kredel, 1946, Grosset & Dunlap 15

Pippi Longstocking

Pippi Longstocking, Astrid Lindgren, b/w illus. by the author, 1954 ed., Oxford University Press (ILLUS.)...................................... 15

Pow Wow Stories, Freda Collins, b/w illus. by Helen Jacobs, 1948, Univ. of London Press 10

Prayer for a Child

Prayer for a Child, Rachel Field, color illus. by Elizabeth Orton Jones, 1944, MacMillan Co. (ILLUS.)...................................... 30

Presto Magic for Boys and Girls

Presto Magic for Boys and Girls, color illus., 1945, John Martin's House (ILLUS.) 15

Rabbit Hill, Robert Lawson, b/w illus. by the author, 1944, Viking Press 20

Raggedy Ann & Andy & the Fat Policeman, Johnny Gruelle, b/w & color illus. by Worth Gruelle, 1942, J. Gruelle Co. 25

Robin Hood

Robin Hood, Saul Lancourt, b/w & color illus. by Sheilah Beckett, 1940, Garden City Pub. (ILLUS.)...................................... 20

Save With the Duckbill Family, coin book, S.J. Michelson, color illus. by George Hollrock, 1942...................................... 20

Seabird, Holling Clancy Holling, b/w illus. by the author, 1948, Houghton Mifflin............. 15

Sir Hokus Pokus & Junior, Louis Ferstadt, two-color illus. by the author, 1946, Louis Ferstadt Prod. 15

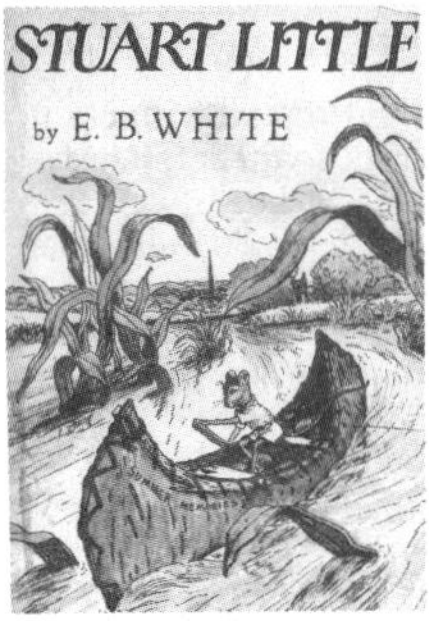

Stuart Little

Stuart Little, E.B. White, b/w illus. by Garth Williams, 1945, Harper & Rowe (ILLUS.)........ 20

Tales of Fantasy, Thomas Bailey Aldrich, various illus., 1944 ed., Auxiliary Ed. League 15

Taps for Private Tussie, Jesse Stuart, two-color illus. by Thomas Hart Benton, 1944, E.P. Dutton.. 50

The Adventures of Peter Pupp

The Children's Hour with Uncle Arthur

Treasure Island

1950s

Charlotte's Web

This price section focuses on popular subjects and illustrators from the 1950s. Books listed are for good to very good condition and without dust covers. Prices are for a center of range depending on condition and desirability. First Editions bring high values and unless noted in listing, books mentioned here are for later editions.

Postwar Baby Boom creates enormous demand for children's literature. Central theme of nuclear family is very popular subject. Grandmother types with magical properties like Mrs. Piggle-Wiggle are popular as well.

Influence of TV on children's literature explodes and comic books arrive in full force and take their place among the ranks of children's literature amid constant controversy - introducing scores of characters that find their way into children's literature (e.g. Howdy Doody, Yogi Bear). Outer space and Western themes increase in popularity, as do educational books and themes not dealt with before (My First Book of Negroes).

Black and white pen and ink style becomes popular again as seen in the styles of Maurice Sendak and Dr. Seuss. "Modern" and "abstract" art influences illustrators towards a more loose, simpler style with less detail, moving swiftly away from the highly objective style that dominated most of the 20th century.

Airplane Stories, Marian Conger, b/w illus. by Harlow Rockwell, 1951, Simon & Schuster...... **10**

Aquarian Age Stories for Children, b/w illus., 1958, Rosicrucian Fellowship **15**

Captain Kangaroo's Surprise Party, Little Golden Book, Barbara Lindsay, color illus. by Edwin Schmidt, 1958, Golden Press **12**

Charlotte's Web, E.B. White, b/w illus. by Garth Williams, 1952, Harper Bros. (ILLUS.)...... **20**

Cowboy Sam & the Rustlers

Cowboy Sam & the Rustlers, Edna Walker Chandler, two-color & b/w illus. by Jack Merryweather, 1952, Beckley-Cardy Co. (ILLUS.)...... **12**

Curious George Rides a Bike

Curious George Rides a Bike, H.A. Rey, color illus. by the author, 1952, Houghton Mifflin Co. (ILLUS.)...... **20**

Dale Evans and the Lost Goldmine, Little Golden Book, Monica Hill, color illus. by Mel Crawford, 1954, Golden Press **20**

Emil & the Detectives, Erich Kastner, b/w illus. by Walter Trier, 1950 ed., Doubleday **15**

Felix the Cat Comics

Felix the Cat Comics, Vol. 1, No. 39, 1953, Toby Press, cover shows Mouse playing a prank on Felix (ILLUS.)...... **10**

Frosty the Snowman, Little Golden Book, color illus. by Corinne Malvern, 1950, Simon & Schuster...... **10**

Harry the Dirty Dog, Gene Zion, three-color illus. by Margaret Bloy Graham, 1956, Harper & Rowe...... **15**

Hello Mrs. Piggle-Wiggle, Betty MacDonald, b/w illus. by Hilary Knight, 1957, J.B. Lippincott...... **15**

How Do We Know?, primer, color illus., 1950, Scott, Foresman & Co......

Howdy Doody Comics, Vol. 1, No. 22, 1953, Dell Comics, cover shows Howdy catching butterflies...... **20**

I Want to be a Restaurant Owner, Carla Greene, two-color illus. by Carol Rogers, 1959, Childrens Press...... **20**

Illustrated Treasury of Children's Literature, anthology, various artists, 1955, Grosset & Dunlap...... **40**

Let the Moon Go By, Emma Sterne, b/w illus. by L.F. Bjorklund, 1955, Aladdin Books...... **10**

Life-Spark Stories, R.K., b/w illus. by Henry Rox, ca. 1950...... **5**

Mighty Mouse Comics #55

Mighty Mouse Comics, #55, Paul Terry Studios, 1954, St. John Publishing (ILLUS.)...... **15**

Miss Pickerell Goes to Mars, Ellen MacGregor, b/w illus. by Paul Galdone, 1951, McGraw-Hill...... **10**

Miss Pickett's Secret, Nancy R. Julian, b/w illus. by Donald E. Cooke, 1952, John C. Winston Co...... **10**

Mrs. Piggle-Wiggle's Magic

Mrs. Piggle-Wiggle's Magic, Betty Mac-Donald, b/w illus. by Hilary Knight, 1957, J.B. Lippincott (ILLUS.) **15**

Mrs. Roo and the Bunnies, Rachel Learned, b/w & color illus. by Tom Funk, 1953, Riverside Press **14**

Once Round the Sun

Once Round the Sun, Elsa-Brita Titchnell, b/w & color illus. by Justin C. Gruelle, 1950, Theosophical University Press (ILLUS.).. **25**

Picture Cross-Word Puzzles, George Carlson, b/w illus. by the author, 1958, Platt & Munk Co. **20**

Pillow-Time Tales, Annmary Willard, color illus. by Dorcas Couri, 1954, Rand Mc-Nally.. **20**

Prince Caspian

Prince Caspian, C.S. Lewis, b/w illus. by Pauline Baynes, 1951, MacMillan Co. (ILLUS.)... **15**

Red Rooster, Edna Boutwell, b/w & three-color illus. by Bernard Garbutt, 1950, Aladdin Books **10**

Rootabaga Stories, Carl Sandburg, b/w illus. by Maude & Miska Petersham, 1951, Harcourt, Brace & World **40**

Rootie Kazootie Detective, Little Golden Book, Steve Carlin, color illus. by Mel Crawford, 1953, Golden Press......................... **20**

Rusty's Space Ship

Rusty's Space Ship, Evelyn Sibley Lampman, b/w illus. by Bernard Krigstein, 1957, Doubleday & Co. (ILLUS.)..................... **12**

Strange Sea Stories, Marie A. Lawson, b/w illus., 1955, The Viking Press.......................... **12**

The Adventures of Nicholas, James Mitchell Clark, b/w & color illus. by Paul & Golden Whitman, 1955, California State Series... **15**

The Arrow Book of Crossword Puzzles

The Arrow Book of Crossword Puzzles, Murray Rockowitz, two-color illus. by George Wilde, 1959, Scholastic Book Services (ILLUS.)... **6**

The Cat in the Hat

The Cat in the Hat, Dr. Seuss, color illus. by the author, 1957, Random House (ILLUS.) **15**

The Children's Hour - 1st Story Book, Marjorie Barrows ed., b/w & color illus. by various artists, 1953, Spencer Press **15**

The First Book of Negroes

The First Book of Negroes, Langston
Hughes, b/w & color illus. by Ursula Ko-
ering, 1952, Franklin Watts **40**
The Giant Golden Book of Elves & Fair-
ies, Jane Werner ed., color illus. by Garth
Williams, 1951, Simon & Schuster **25**

The Golden Book of Words

The Golden Book of Words, Jane Werner,
color illus. by Cornelius DeWitt, 1950,
Simon & Schuster (ILLUS.) **20**

The Great Wheel

The Great Wheel, Robert Lawson, b/w illus.
by Robert Lawson, 1957, the Viking
Press (ILLUS.) **20**
The Iliad and the Odyssey, Giant Golden
Book, color illus. by Alice & Martin Prov-
ensen, 1956, Simon & Schuster **25**
The Little Sailboat, Lois Lenski, color illus.
by the author, 1958 ed., Henry Z. Walck
Inc. **20**

The Pogo Stepmother Goose

The Pogo Stepmother Goose, Walt Kelly,
b/w illus. by the author, 1954, Simon &
Schuster (ILLUS.) **50**

The Stars, H.A. Rey, b/w illus. by the au-
thor, 1952, Houghton Mifflin Co. **25**
The Story of Sigfried, James Baldwin, b/w
illus. by Peter Hurd, 1959, Charles Scrib-
ner **25**
This is our Valley, religious, Sister M. Mar-
guerite, color illus. by Charlotte Ware,
1953, Ginn & Co. **20**
Told Under the Blue Umbrella, anthology,
b/w illus. by Marguerite Davis, 1951,
MacMillan Co. **15**
Tom Corbett - Danger in Deep Space,
Carey Rockwell, b/w illus., 1953, Grosset
& Dunlap **12**

You Will Go to the Moon

You Will Go to the Moon, Mae & Ira Freeman, color illus. by Robert Patterson,
1959, Random House (ILLUS.) **12**

Little Golden

*One of the most popular categories in children's
book collecting today are Little Golden Books. When
they appeared in 1942 (the first series had 12 titles) they
were an instant success. The appeal of these books can
be summed up in a statement by the publisher, Western
Publishing Company, "Little Golden Books revolutionized the children's book industry and put Western Publishing on the map; but a more important testimonial is
that Little Golden Books made book ownership afford-
able, brought the joys of reading to countless children
and created priceless memories on the way. 'I grew up
with Golden Books' is a phrase heard from generation to
generation." These children have now grown up and a
steady interest in collecting Little Golden Books has
grown along with them.*

*The Disney Golden Books are the most sought after
by collectors. Disney was Western Publishing's first
licensor of characters and they go all the way back to the
beginning of the books. Other licensed characters and
figures from television, movies and the toy industry followed and are also highly prized. Collectors are now
focusing on the other Golden Books - ones about a
child's life, learning, fables and animal stories. The artists who illustrated these books are becoming recognized
in their own right and some of the better illustrated
books are seeing prices rise. There are also miscellaneous merchandising items put out in conjunction with
Little Golden Books. Collectors search for Little Golden
records, toys and children's accessories. Little Golden
Books and related merchandise are still being made. The
listings and photographs in this section cover ONLY the
early Little Golden Books - approximately 1942-1960.
This listing does not include the same-sized Little
Golden Activity Books or the oversized Golden Books
made from 1942-1960. All prices below are for early or*

first editions of these vintage books (many were
reprinted for years). All prices are quoted for books in
very good to excellent condition.
    Finally, to get a more comprehensive understanding
of the scope of Little Golden Books, I strongly recom-
mend obtaining Collecting Little Golden Books, by Steve
Santi, published by Books Americana.

"A Year on the Farm," 1948, illustrations
    by Richard Floethe..................................... **10-15**
"Airplanes," 1953, illustrations by Lenora &
    Herbert Combes **4-8**

"Bugs Bunny at the Country Fair"

"Bugs Bunny at the Country Fair," 1948,
    illustrations by Warner Bros. (ILLUS.) **8-12**
"Bugs Bunny Gets a Job," 1952, illustra-
    tions by Tony Strobel................................... **5-10**

"Bunny Book"

"Bunny Book," 1951, illustrations by Dis-
    ney Studios (ILLUS.).................................... **5-10**
"Captain Kangaroo," 1955, illustrations by
    Art Seiden.. **10-15**
"Dale Evans and the Lost Gold Mine,"
    1954, illustrations by Mel Crawford **15-20**

"Davy Crockett"

"Davy Crockett," 1955, illustrations by Dis-
    ney Studios (ILLUS.).................................... **10-15**

"Dinosaurs," 1959, illustrations by William
    De Rutherford **4-8**
"Disneyland on the Air," 1955, illustra-
    tions by Samuel Armstrong **10-15**

"Doctor Dan the Bandage Man"

"Doctor Dan the Bandage Man," 1950, il-
    lustrations by Corrine Malvern, six band
    aids came w/this book & must still be at-
    tached to command top price (ILLUS.)...... **15-30**
"Doctor Dan the Bandage Man," 1950, il-
    lustrations by Corrine Malvern, without
    band aids.. **10**

"Dumbo"

"Dumbo," 1947, illustrations by Disney Stu-
    dios (ILLUS.).. **20-30**
"Farm Stamps," 1957, illustrations by Adri-
    ana Saviozzi, a Golden Activity Books
    with stamps **15**
"Five Little Firemen," 1948, illustrations by
    Tibor Gergely **15**

"Frosty the Snowman"

"Frosty the Snowman," 1950, illustrations
    by Corinne Malvern (ILLUS.)........................ **5-10**
"Gaston and Josephine," 1949, illustra-
    tions by Fedor Rajankvosky **10-15**

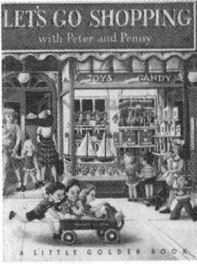

"Let's Go Shopping with Peter and Penny"

"Little Black Sambo"

"Little Lulu"

"New Brother, New Sister"

"Nursery Songs"

"Peter and the Wolf"

"Peter and the Wolf," 1946, illustrations by Disney Studios (ILLUS.).............................. **10-15**

"Prayers for Children"

"Prayers for Children," 1952, illustrations by Eloise Wilkin (ILLUS.) **4-8**

"Rocky and His Friends"

"Rocky and His Friends," 1960, illustrations by Ben de Nunez & Al White (ILLUS.)... **10-15**
"Roy Rogers and the New Cowboy," 1953, illustrations by Mel Crawford **15-20**
"Scruffy the Tugboat," 1946, illustrations by Tibor Gergely **15-20**

"Smokey the Bear"

"Smokey the Bear," 1955, illustrations by Richard Scarry (ILLUS.)............................. **10-15**
"Snow White," 1948, illustrations by Ken O'Brien, an early Disney Golden Book...... **18-20**

"The Brave Little Tailor"

"The Brave Little Tailor," 1953, illustrations by J.P. Miller (ILLUS.)............................. **4-8**

"The Color Kittens"

"The Color Kittens," 1949, illustrations by Alice & Martin Provinsin (ILLUS.) **10-12**

"The Emerald City of Oz"

"The Emerald City of Oz," 1952, illustrations by Harry McNaught, based on the Oz book (ILLUS.) **25-30**
"The Flintstones," 1961, illustrated by Mel Crawford.. **12-15**
"The Golden Book of Flowers," 1943, illustrations by Hershberger **15-20**
"The Happy Family," 1955, illustrations by Corinne Malvern..................................... **10-12**
"The Happy Man and His Dump Truck," 1950, illustrations by Tibor Gergely........... **10-12**

"The Jolly Barnyard"

"The Jolly Barnyard," 1950, illustrations
by Tibor Gergely (ILLUS.).............................. 5-10
"The New House in the Forest," 1946, illustrations by Eloise Wilkin 10-20

"The Poky Little Puppy"

"The Poky Little Puppy," 1942, illustrations by Gustaf Tenggren, from the origi-
nal 12 titles (ILLUS.) 15-20
"The Saggy Baggy Elephant," 1947, illus-
trations by Gustaf Tenggren 10-15

"The Taxi That Hurried"

"The Taxi That Hurried," 1946, illustrations by Tibor Gergely (ILLUS.) 15-20
"Three Little Kittens," 1942, illustrations
by Masha 15-25
"Through the Picture Frame," 1944, illus-
trations by Disney Studios, based on
Hans Christian Andersen fairy tale, a rare
& unusual Golden 35-40
"Tom and Jerry's Party," 1955, illustra-
tions by M-G-M Studios (ILLUS. top next
column) 4-8
"Uncle Mistletoe," 1953, illustrations by
Corinne Malvern 15-20

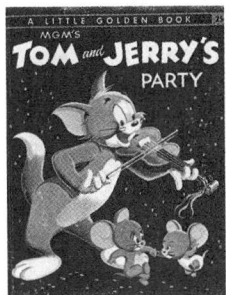

"Tom and Jerry's Party"

"Walt Disney's Old Yeller," 1957, illustrations by Edwin Schmidt.............................. 10-15
**"Walt Disney's Peter Pan and the Indi-
ans,"** 1952, illustrations by Brice Mack..... 12-15
"Winky Dink," 1956, illustrations by Richard Scarry, based on the '50s TV show 10-12
"Woody Woodpecker," 1952, illustrations
by Riley Thompson 8-12
"Zorro and the Secret Plan," 1958, illustrations by Hamilton Greene...................... 10-15

School Primers - 20th Century

Children's school books & primers have until recently been overlooked in the field of children's books collecting. But within their tattered pages are glorious memories of childhood and school days, often beautifully illustrated. Whether or not you liked school, when you find a copy of the book you read in grade school, a certain feeling hits you.

The illustrations and contents in primers and school books changed with the decades. Early decade books were in black and white or two-color, often relying on delicate Nouveau-like line work and the stories heavy on fables and animal tales. The 1930s brought Dick and Jane (and Spot and Puff), full-color illustrations and Art Deco touches; the 1940s and '50s brought still more brother and sister acts like the Alice and Jerry series, more family and religious-oriented books and an exquisite watercolor style that is instantly recognizable to most baby boomers. The 1960s brought experimentation in illustration styles from Pop Art to paper cutouts. The '60s also ended the "picket fence - all white" world of Dick and Jane with African-American and Asian characters being represented in the illustrations. In the 1970s sexist stereotyping in children's school books came under attack and the traditional Dick and Jane was put to bed forever.

A primer is a first reader or early reader. The basic "See Dick, See Dick Run..." books are sometimes called pre-primers and are softbound. This price guide offers listings for primers and pre-primers as well as upper grade school books, poetry books, science, history, art and music books. These books were handled almost daily by children so any book found in good to excellent condition is of higher value. Beautiful or unusual illustrations command more, as do illustrations by famous illustrators. Look for names like Maude and Miska Petersham, Fredrick Richardson, Milo Winter, Miriam Story Hurford, Charlotte Ware, Herbert Paus, Guy Wiser Brown and others.

Two-color usually indicates one color & black were used in the illustrations. Three-color means two colors (often a turquoise blue and some shade of orange or brown were favorites) and black were combined to produce an interesting array of shades. Most books are hardbound unless otherwise noted. Prices are for books in relatively good to excellent condition. The covers are usually not that appealing so in most instances an illustration from the book is shown here to represent the book.

Alice and Jerry Series
Published by Rowe, Peterson & Company and beautifully illustrated in full-color watercolors by Florence and Margaret Hoopes, hardbound.

Day In & Day Out, 1941 edition, 156 pp....... **10-20**
Friendly Village, 1936................................... **10-20**
New Anything Can Happen (The), 1951 edition, illustrated by Dorothy Todd, 192 pp. **8-12**

The New Day In & Day Out Cover

New Day In & Day Out (The), 1950 edition, 160 pp. (ILLUS.) **8-12**
New Down the River Road (The), 1951 edition, 160 pp. **10-15**
New Friendly Village (The), 1954 edition...... **8-12**
New If I Were Going (The), 1948 edition, 340 pp. **10-15**

California State Series
Published in Sacramento, often used innovative and stylized illustrations like the works of Guy Wiser Brown.

"The Space Child's Mother Goose" from Aboard The Story Rocket

Aboard The Story Rocket, 1961 edition, two-color & full-color by various illustrators (ILLUS.)... **8-12**
Adventures of Nicolas (The), 1955, Lyons & Carnahan, color & b&w illustrations by Paul & Colden Whitman **8-12**

Blue Sky Book (The), 1951 edition, color illustrations by Guy Wiser Brown............... **10-20**
Days of Fun, Reading for Living Series, 1954, color illustrations by Miriam Story Hurford... **5-10**

"Balder the Beautiful" - The Fire Light Book

Fire Light Book (The), 1951 edition, color illustrations by Guy Wiser Brown (ILLUS.).. **10-20**
Fun With Us, third level pre-primer, 1954, color illustrations by Miriam & A.F. Hurford, softbound.. **5-15**
Merry Hearts & Bold, 1954 edition, full-color & b&w illustrations by Fritz Kredel........ **10-20**
Music Hour (The), 1931, three-color illustrations by Shirley Kite............................... **10-15**

"The Scrapbook" from Neighbors & Helpers

Neighbors & Helpers, 1938, full-color illustrations by various artists (ILLUS.)............ **10-15**
Seasons Pass (The), 1938, full-color illustrations by Guy Wiser Brown...................... **15-20**
Story of America (The), 1936, three-color by various illustrators **10-15**

"Flowers" from We See

We See, 1944, full-color illustrations by Guy Wiser Brown, softbound (ILLUS.).............. **10-15**

Faith & Freedom Series

Catholic School series published by Ginn & Company, beautiful full-color illustrations by many popular illustrators, hardbound.

"The Good Shepherd" - These Are Our People

These Are Our People, 1943; b&w illustrations by Corrine Malvern & Herbt Paus, full-color illustrations by Dale Nicols (ILLUS.)... **15-20**

Title Page from This Is Our Family

This Is Our Family, 1942, full-color illustrations by Charlotte Ware (ILLUS.)............... **15-20**
This Is Our Town, 1953 edition, full-color illustrations by Charlotte Ware, Ruth Steed & John Shepherd............................. **10-15**
This Is Our Valley, New Edition, 1953 edition, full-color illustrations by Charlotte Ware **10-12**

Miscellaneous

Title Page Illustration - Adventures in English

Adventures in English, Grade 4, 1945, Allyn & Bacon, b&w illustrations by various artists (ILLUS.).. **6-8**

"Birds & Squirrels" - The Aldine Readers Primer

Aldine Readers Primer (The), 1907, Newson & Co., two-color illustrations by Margaret Ely Webb (ILLUS.)............................ **15-25**

"Oh, I can draw a spotted pig" from Art Stories

Art Stories, S.F.&.C. Co., 1929, full-color & two-color illustrations by various artists (ILLUS.) **10-15**
At The Lake, 1951, McMillan Co., color illustrations by various artists........................... **6-8**
Billy Bang Book (The), 1927, McMillan Co., two-color illustrations by Maude & Miska Petersham **20-25**
Days & Deeds, Child's Story Program, 1936, Lyons & Carnahan, color illustrations by various artists............................... **10-12**
Dick & Jane, 1930, Scott, Foresman & Co., color illustrations, softbound....................... **15-25**
Down the Road, Basic Reading Program, 1945, Silver Burdett Co., color illustrations by Corrine Malvern, Priscilla Pointer & Sally Tate.. **10-12**
Elson Readers (The), Book Two, 1927, three-color illustrations by LKD.................... **5-10**
Enchanted Isles, 1960 edition, Charles E. Merrill Books, full color & b&w by various illustrators .... **6-8Firemen,** Unit Study Books No. 103, 1934, Educational Printing House, b&w photos, softbound (ILLUS. top next page) **5-10**
First Reader (A), 1906, Newson & Co., two-color illustrations by Margaret Ely Webb.... **20-30**

Cover from Firemen

Five in the Family, 1954 edition, Scott, Foresman & Co., color illustrations by Miriam Story Hurford.................................... **10-15**

Founder Of Our United States, 1946, Noble & Noble, two-color illustrations by George M. Richards.................................... **4-8**

Friends & Neighbors, Basic Reader, 1941, Scott, Foresman & Co., color illustrations by Ellen Segner & Keith Ward.................. **15-20**

Friends & Neighbors, Cathedral Reader (Catholic), 1942, Scott, Foresman & Co., color illustrations by Ellen Segner, Keith Ward & Miriam Story Hurford **20-25**

Good Companions, Our Pets, 1933, Newson & Co., three-color illustrations by Margaret Mary Kearney **6-8**

Good Friends, A First Reader, 1935, Johnson & Co., full-color illustrations by Rhoda Chase **5-10**

Good Stories, First Reader, Level Two, 1930, John C. Winston Co., color illustrations by Erick Berry & Fredrick T. Chapman.. **10-15**

Good Time Book (The), 1933 edition, McMillan Co., two-color illustrations by Gladys Peck **8-12**

"A Toy City" from Good Times Together

Good Times Together, Guidance In Reading Series, 1936, Lyons & Carnahan, full-

color illustrations by Vera Stone Norman (ILLUS.) **5-10**

Growing Up, New Silent Readers, 1931, John C. Winston Co., three-color illustrations by Eunice Stephenson...................... **10-20**

"See the boat," said Tad, from Here We Play

Here We Play, 1950 edition, Bobbs Merrill Co., full-color illustrations by Miriam Story Hurford, softbound (ILLUS.)..................... **5-10**

How It Is Nowadays, 1969, Ginn & Co., full-color by various illustrators **6-8**

I Wonder Why?, Science Stories for Young Children, 1934 edition, Reilly & Lee Co., three-color illustrations by Donn P. Crane, Miriam Story Hurford & Edmund Burroughs.. **10-20**

It Happened One Day, The Wonder Story Books, 1956 edition, Rowe, Peterson & Co., full-color illustrations by May Royt **8-12**

"Come, South Wind..." from John & Jean

John & Jean, 1932, American Book Co., three-color illustrations (ILLUS.) **10-15**

"Billy's Puppy" from More Power

More Power, Scott, Foresman & Co., 1968 edition, full-color by various illustrators (ILLUS.).. **6-8**
New American Readers, 1929, two-color illustrations **8-12**
New Friends & Neighbors, Basic Reader, 1949, Scott, Foresman & Co., color illustrations by various artists **10-15**
New Friends & Places, 1955, McMillan Co., color illustrations by various artists **4-8**
Nip & Tuck, Child's Story Program, 1936, Lyons & Carnahan, color illustrations by Vera Stone Norman **10-20**

"Grandfather & Grandmother"
from On The Way To Storyland

On The Way To Storyland, 1933, Laidlaw Bros., color illustrations by Milo Winter (ILLUS.).. **10-15**
Other Lands & Other Times, 1951 edition, Ginn & Co., full-color & b&w illustrations by Herbert Paus..................................... **6-12**
Our First Music, A Singing School, Volume 1, 1938, two-color illustrations...................... **6-8**
Our Songs, A Singing School, Volume 2, 1939, two-color illustrations......................... **6-8**
Peter's Family, A Study in Home Life, 1949 edition, Scott, Foresman & Co., color illustrations by Charlotte Becker & Ellen Segner.. **5-10**
Poetry Book (The), Number 4, 1933, Rand McNally & Co., two-color illustrations by Marjorie Hartwell **4-8**
Primer (The), Reading Literature, 1910, Rowe & Peterson Co., three-color illustrations by Fredrick Richardson **25-50**

"Tiger, Suzanne & Black Toes"
from Read A New Story Now

Read A New Story Now, 1935, Beckley & Cardy Co., three-color illustrations by Keith Ward (ILLUS.)..................................... **10-20**
Right Word (The), The Pupil's Word Book for Creative Writing, 1937 edition, Allyn & Bacon, b&w silhouettes (ILLUS. top next column) **5-10**

"The Letter R" from The Right Word

School History of the United States (A), 1898, University Publishing Co., b&w illustrations **20-40**
Some Merry Adventures of Robin Hood, Scribner's Series for School Reading, 1911, b&w illustrations by Howard Pyle **20-30**
Standard Bible Story Readers, Book One, 1947 edition, full-color & b&w illustrations by various artists **6-8**
Standard Bible Story Readers, Book Two, 1947 edition, full-color & b&w illustrations by various artists **4-8**
Stone's Silent Reader, Book 4, 1927, Houghton Mifflin, two-color illustrations by Ruth Sutherland **5-10**

Cover from The Story Road

Story Road (The), Level Two, 1947 edition, John C. Winston Co., full-color illustrations by Jacob Bates Abbott & Anne Fleur (ILLUS.)... **5-10**
Sunshine & Rain, Scientific Learning Series, 1949 edition, L. W. Singer Co., full-color illustrations by Guy Wiser Brown **10-15**

"Foods which contain Vitamin C" from
Superstition Or Science?

Superstition Or Science?, Basic Science Education Series, 1948 edition, Rowe,

Peterson & Co., full-color, softbound
(ILLUS.) **3-6**

• BOOK HOUSES •

"Book Houses" from Voices of Verse

Voices of Verse, 1933, Lyons & Carnahan,
b&w illustrations by Marion Humphreys
Machett (ILLUS.) **5-10**
Voyages in English, 1958, Loyola Univer-
sity Press, b&w illustrations **3-5**
Why We Celebrate Our Holidays, 1924,
full-color illustrations by Jewel Morrison **5-10**
Wings of Adventure, Book 8, 1931, John
C. Winston Co., two-color illustrations by
Maude & Miska Petersham **15-20**

Title Page Illustration from The Winston Reader

Winston Reader (The), Second Reader,
1918, John C. Winston Co., three-color
illustrations by Frederick Richardson
(ILLUS.) **15-25**

CHRISTMAS COLLECTIBLES

*Starting in the mid 19th Century more and more
items began to be manufactured to decorate the home,
office or commercial business to celebrate the Christmas
season.*

*In the 20th century the trend increased. Companies
such as Coca-Cola, Sears and others began to employ
specially produced Christmas items. The inexpensive
glass then plastic Christmas tree decoration began to
reach into almost every home. With the end of World
War II the toy market moved into the picture with annual
Santa Claus parades and the children's visit to Santa to
leave Christmas wish lists.*

*As the 21st Century approaches this trend will con-
tinue and material from earlier Christmas seasons will
climb in value.*

Christmas Tree Lights

Figural Bulbs

Baby, dressed in red snowsuit, milk glass,
painted, Japan, ca. 1930-50s, 3" h. **$22**
Boy playing accordion, milk glass, paint-
ed, Japan, ca. 1930-50s, 3 3/4" h. **35**
Doll in red stocking, milk glass, painted,
Japan, ca. 1930-50s, 3 1/4" h. **25**
Donald Duck, milk glass, painted, Disney,
Japan, ca. 1930-50s, 3" h. **30**
Humpty Dumpty, milk glass, painted,
Japan, ca. 1930-50s, 3" h. **30**
Jack-O-Lantern, milk glass, painted,
Japan, ca. 1930-50s, 1 1/2" h. **30**
Parakeet, milk glass, painted, Japan,
ca. 1930-50s, 3 3/4" h. **15**
Santa, double-faced, milk glass, painted,
Japan, ca. 1930-50s, 2 1/2" h. **14**
Santa, double-sided, blinker, Japan,
ca. 1930-50s, " h. **15**

Skull & Crossbones Light Bulb

Skull & crossbones, milk glass, round,
painted, Japan, ca. 1930-50s, 2 1/4" d.
(ILLUS.) **38**
St. Nicholas, milk glass, painted,
Japan, ca. 1930-50s, 3 1/4" h. **22**

Sets

Bubble lights, in original box, U.S.A., set of
eight **85**
Cartoon characters, including Orphan An-
nie, Sandy, Moon Mullins, Kayo, Betty
Boop, Smitty, Dick Tracy, Andy Gump,
boxed, Japan, 1930s, each 2 3/4" l., the
set (Andy Gump damaged) **259**
Noma, eight in the set, 1920s, the type of
light that when one went out, the entire
set was turned off **25**

Tree Ornaments

Kugel, cobalt blue w/embossed brass
hanger, 4 3/8" d. (slight discoloration) **138**
Kugel, silver, 7" d. (brass hanger reat-
tached, minor flaking) **121**

Miscellaneous

Victorian Die-cut Santa Advertisement

Advertisement, die-cut cardboard, standing figure of old-fashioned Santa w/blue pants, green fur-trimmed coat & red cap carrying packages on his back, next to a red & gold sleigh filled w/more packets, red wording across the bottom "Ayer's Cherry Pectoral - The Best Gift to a Friend," ca. 1890s (ILLUS.) **1,155**

Candy container, figure of Santa Claus standing in a boot holding a slender tree, made of foil, flocked paper, painted bisque head w/cotton wool beard & a pipe cleaner tree, marked "Japan," ca. 1930s, 6" h. **61**

Candy container, figure of Santa Claus standing w/a tree over one shoulder, a painted bisque head, papier-maché body, dressed in red & blue felt w/white flannel & fur, separates at the waist, paper label on one boot "Made in Germany," 10 1/2" h. (some wear & damage) **330**

Candy container, papier-maché, figural, a standing young girl wearing a hood, long coat & a muff, silver-flecked white coat trimmed in faded blue piping, early 20th c., 5 3/4" h. (minor wear, small hole) **193**

Christmas tree fence, cast iron, an openwork design of a diamond band flanked by bands of arches between the upper & lower rails, rod ends on each section w/tiny ball finials, tiny scallop fans along the top rail, green & gold paint, seven sections & a two-part gate, late 19th - early 20th c., largest section 12" l., 4 3/4" h., the set (wear, minor edge damage) **242**

Cookie cutter, oval w/multiple Christmas cut-outs, including tree, Santa, angels, deer & hearts, 7 1/2 x 11 1/4" **193**

Figure of Belsnickle, papier-maché, standing figure in costume w/a painted face & black base & white mica-flecked robe, carrying a worn feather tree, Germany, 10" h. **550**

Figure of Belsnickle, composition, orange robe w/gold glitter, black base & boots & green feather tree, 8" h. **330**

Figure of Belsnickle, composition, white robe & base w/mica flecks & green glitter trim, red pipe cleaner trim & black boots, green feather tree, 9 1/8" h. (minor edge damage) **660**

Belsnickle Santa Figure

Figure of Belsnickle, composition, white robe w/mica flecks, black boots & base, red pipe cleaner trim & remnants of a green feather tree, wear on base,11 1/4" h. (ILLUS.) **825**

Ice cream mold, pewter, standing Santa Claus, hinged two-part style marked "E & Co.," 4 5/8" h. **248**

Santa figure, papier-maché, red felt coat w/white wool trim, rabbit fur beard, blue felt pants & black painted boots, probably held a feather tree, 13 3/4" h. **825**

Santa figure sitting on polar bear, papier-maché, white w/red trim, 8 1/2" l., 9 3/4" h. (minor damage) **132**

Tree stand, cast iron, flared base w/openwork stars & plumes & two scenes of St. Nicholas leading a horse & knocking on windows w/German verses above each scene, conical tree trunk insert w/ornate tightening screws, green paint w/gold trim, 10" d., 4 7/8" h. (wear to paint) **55**

CLOCKS

Banjo clock, Elnathan Taber, Roxbury, Massachusetts, the round brass bezel w/a tall gilt metal pointed finial at the top & enclosing a painted white dial inscribed "E. Taber" & an eight-day brass weight-driven movement above the trapezoidal églomisé throat glass w/urn & flowering vine flanked by long slender curved & pierced brass mounts, inscribed "Patent" above the pendulum box w/an églomisé sea battle scene, throat & lower case w/half-round narrow moldings, ca. 1820, 33 1/4" h. (replaced tablets) **$5,750**

Calendar wall clock, "Waterbury Clock Company, Waterbury, Connecticut," oak, double-dial type, a large molded round upper frame enclosing the clock dial w/Roman numerals above a mid-band w/small carved roundels above the smaller molded lower frame enclosing the calendar movement, brass works w/pendulum & double, paper label also reads "Patented July 30th, 1889 - Calendar No. 34," w/instructions, 29" h. (repairs).. **908**

Carriage clock, brass & glass, upright rectangular glass-sided case w/large round dial w/Roman numerals above a mercury-filled glass pendulum, rectangular platform base, dial marked by the Ansonia Clock Company, time & strike movement, w/key, late 19th c., 9 3/4" h. **275**

French Cartel Wall Clock

Cartel wall clock, Louis XVI-Style, gilt bronze, an ornate openwork works, ribbon & vine top suspending the round enameled dial w/Roman & Arabic numerals surrounded by large scrolling leaf & flower cornucopia borders, a twisted ribbon pendent base drop, two train chiming movement, France, early 20th c.,14" w., 35" h. (ILLUS.) **3,105**

Dwarf Grandfather Clock

Dwarf grandfather, attributed to Noah Ranlet, Gilmanton, New Hampshire, Federal style, pine case, broken-scroll pediment w/three brass urn finials above a molded cornice above the round molded circle around the painted dial w/Roman numerals above another molded crestrail above the waist w/a narrow short door w/an oval opening flanked by small pilasters, stepped-out lower case on simple French feet, eight-day weight-driven movement, old refinish, replaced dial, early 19th c., 48" h. (ILLUS.) **6,325**

French Gothic Style Grandfather Clock

Grandfather, Bentejec, France, oak Gothic Revival style tall case, the ornate Gothic arch-carved top enclosing the signed round steel dial w/Arabic numerals above the tall narrow case w/a two-panel Gothic arch & linenfold-carved narrow door flanked by quarter-round ropetwist edge bands, the stepped out base section w/a carved linenfold panel above the flared rectangular foot, late 19th c., 12 x 22", 95" h. (ILLUS.) **8,050**

American Gothic Grandfather Clock

Grandfather, Blunt & Co., New York, New York, Gothic Revival style, mahogany & mahogany veneer, the hood w/molded Gothic arched cornice w/central plinth & spire flanked by smaller spires above a round molded brass bezel enclosing a round engraved silver regulator dial w/Arabic numerals & signed by the maker, the waist w/a tall glazed Gothic arch door framed by crossbanding above a crossbanded rectangular panel flanked by lambrequin corners over the tall base section w/slender cut-out feet, eight-day weight-driven movement, old finish, ca. 1840, minor imperfections, 94 1/2" h. (ILLUS.).. **12,650**

Fine Tiffany "Elite" Grandfather Clock

Grandfather, Colonial Revival style, Tiffany & Co. "Elite" model, dark carved oak case, a high broken-scroll front pediment w/a large central carved urn finial & smaller corner urn finials w/smaller broken-scroll pediments & finials at the sides of the top, an arched glazed top door over the arched dial w/moon phase movement over the brass filigree-trimmed dial w/brass Arabic numerals, the tall waist w/rows of small raised square panels at each side & a glazed tall front door opening to the large weights & flanked by quarter-round columns at the sides, the stepped-out bombé base section w/a lappet-carved band above wide bands of scroll carving, on carved paw feet, nine-tube three-weight movement, late 19th - early 20th c. (ILLUS.).............. **14,850**

Grandfather, Elliott of London, England, Renaissance-Style carved oak case, the arched pediment mounted w/a pair of winged griffins flanking a central shield above a panel of acanthus leaf carving over another arched panel of leaf carving above the ornate filigree dial w/Arabic numerals & a moon phase action flanked by columns over a scroll-carved band above the tall waist w/a paneled door

Renaissance-Style Grandfather Clock

finely carved w/delicate fruit & flower vines flanked by reeded columns, the stepped-out base w/a gadrooned band around the top above leafy scroll & shield-carved panels above the flared stepped base on paw feet, two-train quarter striking movement on gongs, ca. 1890, 104" h. (ILLUS.) **13,800**

Hersheide Gothic Grandfather Clock

Grandfather, Hersheide Clock Co., Cincinnati, Ohio, Gothic Revival style mahogany & mahogany veneer case, pointed arch crest w/wide molding above a tall arch-topped door w/the upper section covering the steel dial w/Arabic numerals below a moon phase movement, the lower door w/Gothic arch glazing opening to the large weights & large pendulum, long pilasters down the sides of the case, octagonal block front feet, early 20th c. (ILLUS.) **3,650**

Grandfather, John J. Krause, Northampton, Pennsylvania, Federal cherry case, the broken swan's-neck pediment terminating in carved rosettes & centering a reeded plinth over a glazed tombstone door opening to a white enamel dial w/Arabic numerals centering a calendar aperture & signed "John Krause - Northhampton," & decorated w/fruit & flowers in the spandrels & arch, all flanked by ring-turned free-standing columns over the tall case fitted w/a double-arch tall door flanked by slender quarter-round reeded columns above the square base w/similar columns, on short French feet, old surface, 30-day weight-driven movement, early 19th c., 10 1/2 x 19 1/2", 83 1/2" h. (imperfections).......................... **4,888**

Fine Durfee Grandfather Clock

Grandfather, Walter Durfee, Providence, Rhode Island, Colonial Revival-style walnut case, a high broken-scroll pediment centering a large carved pineapple finial above the swag- and ribbon-carved frieze band above the arched glazed door opening to a steel dial w/brass Arabic numerals below the moon phase dial all flanked by free-standing colonettes & cloth-lined latticework sides on a projecting cornice over the waist section topped by a band of leafy swag carving above an arched, geometrically-glazed front door flanked by columns & w/glazed sides, the projecting base section w/shaped panels centering swagged leaf & blossom carving, carved base band above scroll-carved feet, tube striking movement, retailed by Tiffany & Co., New York, late 19th - early 20th c., 102" h. (ILLUS.)........ **20,000**

English Renaissance Style Clock

Grandfather, Whitehurst, Derby, England, Renaissance-Style oak case, a broken-scroll crest w/three brass ball finials over the scroll-carved frieze & arched glazed door flanked by elongated scroll carvings & opening to the metal dial w/Roman numerals & a moon phase & date crest above the narrow case w/narrow front panel carved w/scrolls above a full-length carved figure of a standing medieval king over a grotesque mask panel, all flanked by slender carved Gothic-style side caryatids, the lower case w/a scroll-carved panel flanked by carved mask & scroll corner bands over the deep scroll-carved apron, two-train chiming movement, late 19th c., 9 5/8 x 18 1/4", 92 1/2" h. (ILLUS.)... **2,645**

Grandfather, William Cummens, Boston or Roxbury, Massachusetts, Federal mahogany & mahogany veneer case, the arched top w/a pierced fretwork & three plinths each w/a brass ball finial, over a molded arched crest & glazed tombstone door opening to a gilt & polychrome floral-decorated white enamel dial w/Roman numbers & Arabic numeral chapter ring & centering a calendar aperture & inscription "warrented by Wm. Cummens," all flanked by free-standing columns w/brass capital & bases over the tall waist section w/a molded tall door flanked by quarter-engaged fluted columns on the box-form base w/a molded panel, on French feet, old refinish, ca. 1800, 9 x 17 1/4", 86" h. (repair to dial) **10,350**

Grandfather, William Cummens, Roxbury, Massachusetts, Federal inlaid mahogany case, the hood w/a pierced fretwork joining three inlaid plinths above the arched cornice molding & glazed tombstone inlaid door enclosing a white-painted gilt-decorated dial w/Roman numerals & a rocking ship flying an American flag in the concave arch, seconds hand & calendar aperture inscribed "Warranted by Wm. Cummens," housing an eight-day brass weight-driven movement, all flanked by brass stop-fluted free-standing columns, the waist w/molded rectangular door inlaid w/cross-banding & stringing flanked by brass stop-fluted quarter columns on conformingly inlaid base on flaring French feet, ca. 1790, 97" h. (refinished, minor restoration, imperfections) **27,600**

Rare Southern Grandfather Clock

Grandfather, William Herwick, North Carolina, Federal style inlaid mahogany case, the molded broken-scroll pediment above an arched frieze band w/line inlay over the set-back arched door opening to a painted dial w/Roman numerals & a moon phase dial & flanked by slender colonettes, the tall waist w/decorative band inlay flanking the tall door w/corner fan inlay & a central oval inlaid band, the stepped-out lower case w/further decorative inlay banding & an inlaid central circle, on small French feet, signed indistinctly, untouched & unrestored, early 19th c. (ILLUS.) **8,750**

Lantern clock, John Cotsworth, London, England, brass, the brass dial w/engraved chapter ring & alarm mechanism engraved w/the maker's name "John Cotsworth Londini," the brass weight-driven movement housed in an iron & brass four-column case w/cross arched bell at the top w/an urn-form finial, the clock set in an oak wall shelf, ca. 1670, 15" h. (restorations) **5,175**

Lyre wall clock, Abiel Chandler, Concord, New Hampshire, carved mahogany, a pointed brass ball finial above a narrow round molded frame enclosing the dial w/Roman numerals above a tall carved lyre-form throat w/pairs of large leafy scrolls up the front above a gadroon-carved band over a lower paneled box over a reverse-stepped & tapering base w/a half-round pointed drop finial, 1825, 43" h. (imperfections) **17,250**

Lyre wall clock, Sawin and Dyer, Boston, giltwood, a gilt figural eagle finial above a round leaf-carved frame enclosing a dial w/Roman numerals above a large lyre-form throat w/bold carved leafy scrolls flanking an églomisé panel painted w/a tall leafy scroll design in red, green & gold on a white ground, the lower case w/a molded small rectangular box section w/an églomisé panel painted w/classical scrolls & trophies in green, red & gold on white, a scrolled cartouche base drop, ca. 1820s, 40" h. (imperfections).... **13,800**

Mantel or shelf clock, Eli Terry & Sons, pillar-and-scroll style, mahogany veneer, the broken-scroll crest fitted w/three replaced brass urn finials above the case w/two slender colonettes flanking the two-panel glazed door over the upper dial w/Arabic numerals, the lower short glazed panel w/worn reverse-painting, molded base on scalloped apron & small French feet, original paper label on interior, w/weights, key & pendulum, early 19th c., 32" h. (refinished, professional restoration) **1,430**

Scarce Early Mirror Wall Clock

Mirror wall clock, attributed to Benjamin Morrill, Boscawen, New Hampshire, Classical style, the rectangular frame case w/a hinged split-baluster border in gilt & black w/the stenciled dial tablet framing the white-painted dial w/Roman numerals, a rectangular mirror in the lower door, w/a brass 'wheelbarrow' weight-driven movement, minor imperfections, ca. 1830, 4 x 14", 30" h. (ILLUS.) **5,175**

Unique French Novelty Bell Clock

Novelty, French shelf or mantel clock, cast brass frame, a large bell w/ornate cast designs centered by an enameled dial w/Roman numerals & enclosing the clock works suspended from a Gothic arch-form framework w/four open arches joined at the top by a temple & urn-form finial & each resting on an ornate colum-nar leg on a wooden platform base, late 19th - early 20th c. (ILLUS.) **1,350**

Chauncey Jerome Schoolhouse Clock

Schoolhouse wall clock, Chauncey Jer-ome, New Haven, Connecticut, mahoga-ny & mahogany veneer, the octagonal top case w/wide veneer border around a round glazed door over the large dial w/Roman numerals, a short rectangular drop compartment w/angled lower edge & centered by a small decorated glass panel over the short pendulum, ca. 1850, 5 x 17", 22" h. (ILLUS.)................................ **2,520**

Rare Early Aaron Willard Mantel Clock

Shelf or mantel, Aaron Willard, Boston, Massachusetts, Federal style mahogany & mahogany veneer case, a broken-scroll crest centering a large pointed gilt finial above a tall rectangular églomisé door w/a gold-ground border w/red & gold ovals & scrolls in each corner above a lower white band w/gilt scrolls & a cen-tral red oval inscribed "Aaron Willard - Boston," the door opening to the dished white enamel dial w/Roman numerals, the stepped-out lower case w/a large square églomisé panel w/a gold border band & gilt leaftip border around a central panel w/a gilt scene of Father Time, a narrow serpentine apron on French feet, ca. 1805, wear to églomisé, 5 3/4 x 12 3/4", 36 1/2" h. (ILLUS.) **23,000**

Ansonia-Royal Bonn China Clock

Shelf or mantel, Ansonia Clock Co., Anso-nia, Connecticut, china case w/arched pierced scroll crest w/large scrolled leaf finial & scroll-molded sides & ornate scroll-molded apron on small block feet, decorated around the dial w/stylized water liles in pink & yellow on a turquoise shaded ground w/gilt trim, stamped brass bezel around the dial w/Arabic numerals, Royal Bonn china case marked "La Bretagne," ca, 1900, minor imperfections, 15" h. (ILLUS.)..................................... **1,320**

Fine Pewter Art Nouveau Style Clock

Shelf or mantel, Archibald Knox, England, Art Nouveau style, enameled pewter upright rectangular case w/a projecting flat border of stylized leafy vines around the large round dial w/brass Arabic numerals against a dark blue enameled ground center w/a stylized shield design in red, gold & green, produced by Liberty & Company, England & marked "English Pewter - Made for Liberty & Co. - Rd. 46801-0609," ca. 1902-05, 8 1/4" h. (ILLUS.) **11,500**

Shelf or mantel, Bartholomew (Eli) & Co., Bristol, Connecticut, Classical style, carved mahogany & mahogany veneer, a high crest boldy carved w/a large stylized blossom & curled leaves flanked by corner blocks above the case w/leaf-, blossoms & column-carved pilasters flanking a two-pane glazed door, the upper pane over the dial w/Roman numerals, scroll-painted spandrels & a circle of pink roses around the center, the tall lower pane reverse-painted w/a landscape scene w/a large white building on the left & a large tree on the right, an oval pendulum window in the center, flat molded base, ca. 1820, 5 x 17", 34" h. **1,680**

Shelf or mantel, Birge and Fuller, Bristol, Connecticut, double-steeple style, mahogany & mahogany veneer, the peaked case w/pointed corner finials & half-round columns flanking the peaked door over the dial w/Roman numerals & a small reverse-painted lower glazed panel flanked by another pair of pointed finials above the stepped-out lower case w/a single long rectangular glazed door reverse-painted w/a bunch of fruits & leaves, on small button feet, eight-day 'wagon spring' driven movement, minor imperfections, 1840s, 4 x 13 1/8", 27" h. (ILLUS. top next column) **3,105**

Early Double-Steeple Mantel Clock

Shelf or mantel, Birge & Fuller, Bristol, Connecticut, steeple-on-steeple style, mahogany veneer, the upper section w/a pointed pedimented door flanked by pointed spires & rounded columns over a dial w/Roman numerals over a lower reverse-painted glass panel w/stylized white & orange florals, the stepped-out lower case w/pointed spires flanking the case above the lower case w/a long rectangular glazed door reverse-painted w/stylized florette in white & orange within a narrow blue border band, ca. 1830s, 4 x 13", 26" h.. **2,688**

Shelf or mantel, Eli Terry & Son, Plymouth, Connecticut, Classical style carved mahogany case, a large carved spread-winged eagle & leaves cornice flanked by corner blocks above half-round acanthus leaf-carved & ring-turned columns flanking a two two-panel door, the upper panel over the dial w/Arabic numerals & painted flowers in the spandrels, time & strike movement, the lower door panel reverse-painted w/a landscape w/a large white building & trees framed w/a black geometric border band, an oval pendulum window above the building, on small paw front feet, ca. 1830s, 4 x 18", 31" h. **2,240**

Fine Cast Bronze French Clock

Shelf or mantel, French, figural cast bronze, the top of the low rectangular body cast w/an ornate hunting scene of a hunter on horseback blowing a horn w/a racing hound beside him & a small tree & fallen stag in front, the platform case cast w/drapery swags flanking the white porcelain dial w/Roman numerals, on a heavy stepped molded base w/ornately scroll-cast feet, late 19th c. (ILLUS.)......... **3,850**

French Porcelain & Bronze Clock

Shelf or mantel, gilt-bronze & porcelain, an upright rectangular case, the temple-form gilt-bronze framework enclosing painted porcelain plaques at the front & sides, each decorated w/romantic scenes, the front w/the raised metal bezel directly over the plaque w/the scene showing through the Arabic dial numerals, heavy base, artist-signed plaques, Monti Works, France, late 19th c., 7 3/4" w., 14" h. (ILLUS.)............................. **1,955**

Rare Lalique Glass Clock

Shelf or mantel, Lalique glass, "Le Jour et La Nuit," a large front greyish blue disk set upright on a high flaring wood base, the wide side molded on one side of the wide dial w/a nude male representing Day and on the other w/a nude female representing Night, the black central dial w/white Roman numerals, introduced in 1926, inscribed "R. Lalique France," 14 7/8" h. (ILLUS.)..................................... **46,000**

Clock with Limoges China Case

Shelf or mantel, Limoges china case, slender upright form w/an ornate scroll-molded top surrounding the dial w/Arabic numerals & a seconds dial above the narrow waist w/molded columns flanking a center panel painted w/a classical maiden reaching up to a flower branch, scroll- and leaf-molded platform base, gilt trim, France, early 20th c., 12 1/2" h. (ILLUS.)................ **1,210**

Shelf or mantel, New Haven Clock Company, New Haven, Connecticut, an upright oak framework w/stamped repeating scroll band border design & small block-footed base, the sides & front inset w/pottery tiles embossed w/flying putti under a maroon glossy glaze, the top also inset w/a scroll-molded tile, the front w/a round porcelain dial w/Arabic numerals & a brass bezel, tiles by the J. and J.G. Low Company, designed by Arthur Osborn, late 19th - early 20th c., 6 x 9", 12 1/4" h. (works reconditioned, hairline in front tile, hairlines in dial)... **6,050**

Shelf or mantel, Seth Thomas Clock Co., Thomaston, Connecticut, Art Nouveau style, gilt-metal, figural, a female figure in a flowing gown resting on a foliate-form standard w/round clock face, white enameled dial w/black numerals, Seth Thomas works, early 20th c., 10 3/4" h. (minor spotting & gilt wear)........................... **173**

Shelf or mantel, Terry (Eli) and Sons, Plymouth, Connecticut, pillar-and-scroll mahogany veneer case, the scrolled pediment w/three small brass urn-form finials above a wide two-pane glazed door opening to a white dial w/Roman numerals above a lower églomisé panel decorated w/a landscape of a small white house by a road w/trees & an oval central pendulum window, flanked by slender colonettes, on a narrow molded base & serpentine apron w/slender French feet, wooden thirty-hour movement, paper

label, ca. 1810-15, 31 1/4" h. (some res-
toration) **1,955**

Gothic Revival Shelf Clock

Shelf or mantel, Victorian Gothic Revival
style, carved mahogany, the case carved
in the form of a Gothic arch w/three
spires enclosing a glazed arch door over
the engraved silver dial w/Roman numerals & a small seconds dial, blocked base,
French two-train half-strike movement,
retailed by Shreve, Crump & Low, late
19th c., 19 1/2" h. (ILLUS.) **805**

Ansonia Swinging Arm Clock

Swinging arm, Ansonia Clock Company,
Ansonia, Connecticut, figural, a tall
bronzed metal figure of a classical maid-
en on a socle base holding aloft in one
hand the clock w/a brass bezel & ribbon
crest over the round dial w/Arabic numerals suspending the bar-form pedulum
w/stamped brass bob, clock & works
swings w/the pendulum, ca. 1880s,
28" h. (ILLUS.) **3,640**

French Swinging Arm Clock

Swinging arm, patinated metal, figural, a tall
classical maiden holding one arm out &
grasping small wreathes & holding the
other arm aloft supporting the orbed clock
dial & movement w/a long pendulum, figure after a work by Auguste Moreau, on a
socle base, France, late 19th - early
20th c., restorations (ILLUS.) **1,955**

Vienna Regulator with Eagle Crest

Vienna Regulator wall clock, walnut, the
high arched crest centered by a carved
relief eagle above a flaring stepped cornice above the tall case w/a glazed front
panel over the round dial w/Arabic numerals & the long two-weight pendulum
w/large brass bob, the panel flanked by
columnar sides w/urn-turned supports on
blocks, molded base w/tapering ogee
paneled drop w/finial, Austria, ca. 1880,
6 x 16 1/4", 46" h. (ILLUS.)............................ **840**

Vienna Regulator Wall Clock

Vienna Regulator wall clock, walnut, the high scroll-cut crest w/a flat top over a shell carving flanked by corner blocks w/turned urn finials above a molded cornice over a long glazed panel showing the round dial w/Roman numerals & the long wooden pendulum w/large brass bob, the side columns w/ring- and knob-turned top & bottom sections centered by a narrow reeded colonette, ogee molded fluted base drop w/finial flanked by corner drop finials, Austria, ca. 1880, 7 x 16 1/2", 48" h. (ILLUS.) **728**

Ornate German Wall Clock

Wall clock, German, walnut Renaissance-style case, a high arched & petal-carved crest above a blocked & scroll-carved rail w/a small turned knob (one missing) above a cornice overhanging the round dial w/Arabic numerals flanked by leaf carvings & heavy turned column supports above a lower compartment w/column supports flanking a spindled gallery, scroll- and block-carved base section w/turned drops, late 19th c. (ILLUS.) **1,550**

Ansonia Wall Regulator No. 4

Wall regulator, Ansonia Clock Company, Ansonia, Connecticut, Regulator No. 4, walnut Renaissance Revival-style long case, the broken arch pediment w/a large turned central urn finial & smaller turned corner finials above an arched glazed front over a large round dial w/wide brass bezel & Roman numerals suspending a large brass pendulum w/a band of thin strings continuing into a lyre design above the large brass disk pendulum bob, molded base w/pointed scalloped apron & turned corner drops, ca. 1880 (ILLUS.) **5,880**

Gilbert Wall Regulator No. 16

Wall regulator, Gilbert Mfg. Company, Winsted, Connecticut, Regulator No. 16, walnut Renaissance Revival style long case, the high pediment top centered by an arched plaque w/bobbin-turned trim around a relief-carved mask & above a carved dentil band, a wide frieze band over the case w/a long narrow glazed door w/arched top flanked by incised & scroll-cut side pendants & opening to a dial w/Roman numerals suspending a long pendulum w/mercury weights, scroll-carved detail on lower sides of case & drop cornice at bottom w/detailing similar to the top, ca. 1875-85 (ILLUS.)... **12,320**

Wall regulator, Waterbury Clock Co., Waterbury, Connecticut, jeweler's-type, walnut & walnut veneer case, a flat flaring & stepped cornice above a floral vine-carved frieze band over a narrow carved band over reeded blocks above an upper panel enclosing the round dial w/Roman numerals & brass bezel above a long glazed window over the large brass pendulum flanked by narrow burl side panels centered by a diamond design, a molded & reeded base over blocks flanking a bottom panel w/fan carving, late 19th - early 20th c., 10 x 25", 75" h. **6,720**

Wall regulator, Waterbury Clock Co., Waterbury, Connecticut, oak, a large round molded top section w/conforming door opening to the large white dial w/black Roman numerals, time & strike movement, a tall rectangular lower case w/a narrow band of beads above & below the tall rectangular glass front over the wood & brass pendulum, Model No. 66, late 19th - early 20th c., 7 x 26", 58" h. **1,064**

CLOISONNÉ & RELATED WARES

Cloisonné

Card case, upright rectangular form w/hinged cover, the front depicting the Jack of Clubs within stylized floral & scroll border, the sides & cover w/stylized floral & foliate scrolls, the cover w/an empty oval silver-gilt cartouche, on a pale green ground, the 11th Moscow Artel, Moscow, Russia, 1908-17, 3 7/8" h. **$9,775**

Russian Cloisonné Cigarette Case

Cigarette case, flattened rectangular form, overall ornate design of scrolling foliage, flowers, birds & butterflies on a gold-washed stippled ground, gold-washed in-

terior, Russian inscription & dated 1899, Russia, 3 x 4" (ILLUS.)................................ **1,265**

Cigarette case, rectangular w/rounded corners, each side enameled w/vari-colored bird design & floral scrolls within white pellet border, on a stippled ground, Moscow, Russia, ca. 1880, 4 1/2" l.................. **1,725**

Creamer, open sugar bowl & tongs, baluster-shaped creamer & squatty bulbous sugar w/two side handles, all enameled w/stylized varicolor flowerheads, floral & foliate scrolls on a stippled gilt & dark colored ground, creamer & sugar w/angular stylized raised handles, partially erased initials of Ferodor Ruckert, Moscow, Russia, 1908-17, creamer 5 3/4" h., the set **8,050**

Salt cellar, footed squatty bulbous round form, the sides decorated overall w/vari-colored blossoms & foliate scrolls on red, green & blue ground, Cyrillic initials of Ferodor Ruckert, Moscow, Russia, 1896-1908, 3" d. **3,290**

Japanese Floral Cloisonné Vase

Vase, lobed baluster-form, a black ground decorated overall w/large multicolored blossoms, silver wires, late 19th c., Japan, 3" d., 6 3/4" h. (ILLUS.) **235**

Japanese Cloisonné Vase with Bird

Vase, small oval foot supported wide flattened ovoid body tapering to a small, short flared neck, one side w/a large oval reserve w/a light background & a bird perched on a blossoming branch down one side, the reverse w/a design of foliage, Japan, early 20th c., 13 1/2" h. (ILLUS.) 1,265

Related Wares

French Champlevé Box

Champlevé box, hexagonal, the low raised cover decorated in the center w/a pinwheel design w/delicate florals in blue & red on alternating black & white stripes all within a beveled border band w/red, white, green, yellow & light blue cartouche designs on a blue ground, the conforming base w/matching paneled cartouche & scroll designs, raised on six small brass bun feet, France, 19th c., 7" w., 3" h. (ILLUS.) 280

Champlevé coffee & tea service: cov. coffeepot, cov. teapot, double-handled sugar bowl, similar creamer, round waste bowl, & an open sugar basket w/swing handle, a tea strainer, sugar tongs , shovel & 11 teaspoons; all decorated w/stylized multicolored birds & butterflies, flowers & foliage on a black ground, between decorative borders of geometric designs, pots, creamer & sugar w/tapering cylindrical sides & angled handles, mark of P. Ovchinnikov w/Imperial warrant, Moscow, Russia, 1881-83, coffeepot 5 7/8" h., the set 21,150

Plique-a-jour box, openwork circular form w/filigree rim, the cover w/flower finial, cover & body w/polychrome enamel inlay, Europe, late 19th - early 20th c., 1 3/4" d., 1" h. 403

CLOTHING

Sequined 1940s Bathing Suit

Bathing suit, strapless style w/heart-shaped neckline, royal blue sequined design in elasticized fabric, labeled "Cole of California Original" at back zipper, 1940s, size 4-6 (ILLUS.) $316

Boa, muff & capelet, cockateel feather, black layered feathers, the capelet w/black satin lining & silk cord tie, muff w/ivory satin lining & white feather trim at sides, round neckpiece, early 20th c., boa 80" l., the set 690

Coat, lady's, red & grey plaid tweed, knee-length single-breasted design w/fitted silhouette, labeled "Harris Tweed" inside front button closure, size 6, 1960s 230

Cocktail dress, below-the-knee length silver lamé dress w/sleeveless, fitted bodice w/round neckline & natural waist, wide belt beaded w/silver & gold bugle beads, tassels, faux pearls, diamantes & filigree, full skirt w/wide band of gold & silver bugle beads at hem, labeled "Sara Fredericks Palm Beach Boston Swampscott," size 6-8, late 1950s 173

Cocktail dress, flesh-colored & metallic gold lace dress embroidered w/gold sequins in overall floral design, bodice w/scalloped neckline, open back, full below-the-knee length skirt w/scalloped hemline & interior crinoline, labeled "Bill Blass for Maurice Rentner" at back zipper closure, size 4-6, late 1950s 518

Cocktail dress, rose-patterned red & black silk taffeta below-the-knee length dress w/fitted camisole bodice, full skirt w/modified panniers & full pleated back, black taffeta lining, labeled "Scaasi" at back, size 8, ca. 1959 431

Cocktail dress & cape, pale blue dress w/silver lame zigzag brocade, below-the-knee length, A-line, empire-waist dress w/center front bow, low square neckline, matching cape w/wide pale blue fox fur collar, labeled "Tissus Haute Couture Paris" at cape side seam, size 8, 1960s, 2 pcs. 173

Cocktail dress & coat, red, black & green rose-patterned silk taffeta dress w/sleeveless bodice, fine pleating at waist, full knee-length bubble skirt, black silk lining, matching grosgrain coat w/fitted bodice, full skirt & attached belt, rose-patterned silk taffeta lining, labeled "Galanos" at coat side seam, size 4, ca. 1959, 2 pcs. 2,415

Cocktail ensemble, black wool crepe dress w/fitted, sleeveless bodice & slightly flared knee-length skirt, matching hip-length jacket w/Peter Pan collar & large rhinestone buttons, labeled "Norell" at neckline, size 10, 1960s, 2 pcs. 518

Cocktail ensemble, blue silk sleeveless mini-shift w/band of silver rhinestones, sequins & metallic thread, Eastern-inspired embroidery at neck, matching knee-length coat w/Nehru collar, large rhinestone button closure & 8" w. band of matching embroidery around cuffs, slightly flared skirt, satin linings, labeled "Christian Dior - New York" at neckline, size 10, 1960s, 2 pcs. 1,035

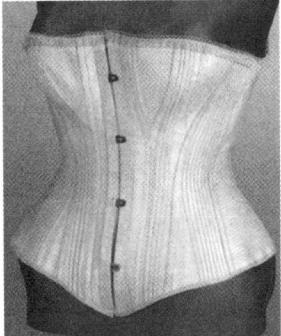

Victorian Lady's Corset

Corset, linen w/coraline boning, back lacing
& front clasp closure, labeled "Dr. Warner's Coraline Health - Patented July 3rd
1877 (re-issue)," ca. 1881, bust 32"
(ILLUS.)... **460**

English Embroidered Court Coat

Court coat, gentleman's, navy blue wool
velveteen embroidered across the lapels,
cuffs, collar & tails w/green silk oak
leaves & silver thead leaves & acorns
w/overall green & silver piping, red satin
lining & brass shield accent buttons, En-
gland, late 18th - early 19th c. (ILLUS.)......... **546**
Dress, black wool crepe sleeveless dress
w/empire waist, front slash pockets &
knee-length, slightly A-line skirt, labeled
"Norman Norell New York - 15512-504-
10" at side seams, size 8-10, 1960s **259**
Dress, grey pinstriped paper taffeta below-
the-knee length style w/fitted button-up
bodice w/taffeta rose at neckline & puffed
elbow-length sleeves, full skirt, labeled
"Pauline Trigère," 1950s, size 8 (ILLUS.
top next column)... **518**

1950s Striped Taffeta Dress

Dress, long-sleeved w/a double ruffled
matching petticoat, blue & white cotton
sateen print, the bodice & sleeves embroidered & w/cut-work trim in khaki
green ground, dark red & white, back
w/room under ruffles & flounces for a full
bustle, late 19th c... **275**
Dress, 'New Look' style, paper black silk
dress w/fitted bodice w/button detail, fitted sleeves w/wrist tie, fitted waist & vo-
luminous below-the-knee length skirt,
large patch pockets at sides of skirt, labeled "Christian Dior Paris" at neckline,
size 6, 1949.. **1,955**
Dress, pale pink, yellow, salmon & white
patterned empire-style bodice w/low V-
neck & long sleeves, solid pink skirt
w/12" wide fringed hem, designed by
Emilio Pucci, size 4-6, 1970s **690**
Dress, paper, "Campbell's Soup," sleeve-
less A-line shift w/overall design of bands
of Campbell's Soup labels, based on
Andy Warhol design.................................... **2,300**
Dress, printed cotton long-sleeved w/long
skirt, navy blue background w/red & light
green paisley print & flowers, brown &
white dots, blue & white decorative braid,
tucked bodice, flounces & ruffles for a
small bustle, late 19th c. **193**
Dress, shirtwaist-style, black silk faille
w/long sleeves, center front closure,
gathered dropped waistline w/center
front satin bow & straight skirt, labeled
"Balenciaga - Avenue Georges V Paris,"
& "101360" stamped in ink, size 10, late
1950s **374**
Dress, white knife-pleated silk w/printed
red, pink & green rose pattern, wrapped
strapless bodice & full pleated skirt, labeled "Christian Dior Made in England -
03440," size 6-8, 1950s.................................. **489**
Dress & coat, Op-Art style, black & white
wool crepe w/geometric pattern, sleeveless knee-length dress w/fitted bodice &
bell-shaped skirt, matching knee-length

long-sleeved coat w/center front button closure, follows silhouette of dress, black silk lining, size 6, 1960s, 2 pcs..................... **259**

Evening coat, ivory pleated silk organdy coat w/short sleeves & stand-up collar, silk gazar lining, labeled "Bill Blass" at back neckline, size 6-8, 1960s....................... **173**

Evening coat, knee-length satin-weave fabric printed w/Eastern-inspired pattern in pale aqua, blue & ornage, narrow silhouette w/Nehru collar, long fitted sleeves & center front closure, pale aqua lining, labeled "Christian Dior - New York" near closure, size 8, 1960s........................... **288**

Evening coat, metallic gold, brown & grey floral three-quarter length coat w/fitted silhouette, three-quarter length sleeves & notched lapel, brown silk lining, labeled "Galanos" at back neckline, size 8, 1950s...... **316**

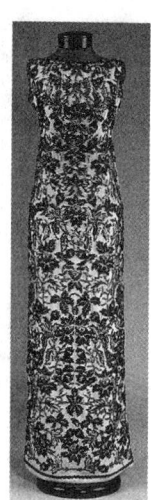

Evening Dress for Inaugural Ball

Evening dress, ivory silk crepe sleeveless sheath w/overall floral beading in silver & shades of red in faux pearls, sequins & crystal seed beads, white silk lining, labeled "Pedro Rodriguez, Madrid - Barcelona - S. Sebastian," worn to 1968 Nixon Inaugural Ball, size 6 (ILLUS.)....................... **633**

Evening dress, ivory silk Grecian-style halter top dress gathered across waist & w/full skirt falling from knife pleats at waist, hemmed, ivory silk lining, labeled "Norman Norell New York" at skirt side seam, size 4-6, 1950s **518**

Evening dress, pale pink chiffon ankle-length dress w/sleeveless, fitted bodice embroidered w/clear bugle & seed beads in wave & vermicelli design, full multi-layered skirt, fully lined, size 8, 1950s **259**

Evening dress, peach satin floor-length dress w/fitted, sleeveless bodice w/jewel neckline that wraps around to back, slight A-line skirt, pink chiffon lining & slip, labeled "Mollie Parnis" on waist tape, late 1950s, size 6... **230**

Evening gown, forest green taffeta & black velvet floor-length gown, fitted black velvet bodice w/taffeta ruffle at round neckline & cuffs, asymmetric skirt w/wide ruffle at hem, matching green taffeta sash, labeled ""Yves St. Laurent Rive Gauche" at back of neckline, size 6-8, 1976................ **460**

Evening gown, gold beaded floor-length dress, upper bodice w/high band collar, padded shoulders & bugle bead fringed yoke, flesh-colored mid-section w/rhinestones in diamond pattern, bugle bead fringe at hem, labeled "Bob Mackie" at back bodice, w/matching sequined 6 1/2" d. bag w/chain shoulder strap, size 6, 1960s, 2 pcs. **920**

Evening skirt, ankle-length taffeta skirt in olive green, red, yellow & aqua plaid, full silhouette w/one red plaid sash & one aqua plaid sash attached to waist, la-

Fitted 1930s Evening Dress

Evening dress, fitted full-length brown silk & metallic gold striped dress w/silk roses & flowers adorning neckline, spaghetti strap bodice & bias-cut skirt flaring at hem, matching waist-length jacket w/fitted waist & padded shoulders, Callot Soeurs, early 1930s, size 6 (ILLUS.) **690**

Evening dress, flesh-colored silk chiffon floor-length dress, fitted sleeveless bodice w/gold & crystal beading, empire waist & full, flowing chiffon skirt, labeled "Malcom Starr New York" at back seam, size 6, late 1960s **460**

Evening dress, floor-length dress of silk gauze covered w/teardrop shaped pieces of black plastic, V-neck, fitted silhouette, crystal & rhinestone beaded band at waistline, black silk lining, size 6, 1960s **575**

Evening dress, gray silk sheath w/blue, dark blue & silver bugle beads embroidered in overall zigzag design, 1920s, size 10... **173**

beled "Oscar de la Renta" at waistband, size 6, 1960s **288**

Evening top & matching cardigan, white net tank-style top w/overall faux pearl & bugle bead floral embroidery, matching cardigan w/zipper front, size 8-10, late 1950s, 2 pcs. **109**

Girdle, white Playtex "Mold 'n Hold" zipper model, in original blue metallic tube, medium size, 1950s **52**

Halter top & capelet, pale yellow satin wrap halter top w/black soutache & jet embroidery, reversible black velvet capelet w/matching embroidery on satin interior, late 1940s, size 6, 2 pcs. **374**

Hat, lady's, fitted form composed of large red teardrop faux gemstones, green plastic leaves & red net, labeled "Bes Ben Made in Chicago" on underside, 1940s **345**

Hat, lady's, fitted style consisting of faux pearls, gold-painted faux shells & leaves & gold net, labeled "Bes Ben Made in Chicago," attached label w/"109" written in ink, 1940s **173**

Bes Ben Surreal Hat

Hat, lady's, Surreal-style, white satin modeled in the shape of arched clasped hands w/red-painted fingernails, w/a large goldtone faux pearl & rhinestone cocktail ring & holding a long cigarette holder, labeled "Bes Ben Made in Chicago," 1940s (ILLUS.) **2,530**

Overcoat, lady's, printed leopard pattern silk satin below-the-knee length coat w/black silk trim at collar, closure, front patch pockets & cuffs, labeled "Lilli Ann San Francisco" at neckline, size 6-8, 1950s **345**

Pantsuit, lady's, pink, blue, orange, black & white, short-sleeved silk top w/round neckline, matching slim pants, labeled "Emilio Pucci" at neckline, 1970s **288**

Poke bonnet, silk, brown & light blue w/ruffle at the lower back edge, machine-sewn quilting, attributed to Zoar, Ohio (very worn in some areas) **61**

Rain hat, black patent leather hat w/high crown, wide brim & green lining, labeled "Sally Victor Boutique New York," 1950s **58**

Scarf, "Isola di Capri" pattern, black w/yellow, white, maroon, orange & green print of the Isle of Capri, printed in corner "Designed by Emilio - executed by Guido Ravasi," 1950s, 34" sq. **201**

Edwardian Tea Gown

Tea gown, ivory printed silk w/pink, lavender, green & yellow floral design, empirewaisted bodice w/sheer lace over heartshaped bodice, square neckline w/layered lace & silk sleeves, copper-colored seed beads adorn neckline & sleeves, metallic gold braided self-tie belt w/pendent tassels, asymmetrically cut skirt wraps around to proper right, short train trimmed w/silk shirred flowers & metallic braid at hem, labeled "Glover Manteaux Robes, Louisville, KY," 1911, size 2 (ILLUS.) **518**

Early English Embroidered Waistcoat

Waistcoat, gentleman's, embroidered on the front w/a feather & boat design w/a floral & dotted border, the buttons embroidered w/floral sprigs, England, 18th c. (ILLUS.) **546**

COCA-COLA ITEMS

Coca-Cola promotion has been achieved through the issuance of scores of small objects through the years. These, together with trays, signs and other articles bearing the name of this soft drink, are now sought by many collectors. The major reference in this field is Petretti's Coca-Cola Collectibles Price Guide, 10th Edition, *by* Allan Petretti *(Antique Trader Books) and* Antique Trader Advertising Price Guide. *An asterisk (*) indicates a piece which has been reproduced.*

Ashtray, clear glass, six-sided w/cigarette rest at each side, round red center w/logo & advertiser's name, ca. 1950s...................... **$20**

Bank, plastic, vending machine-shaped, marked "Drink Coca-Cola - Work refreshed - Ice Cold," 1950s, 5 1/2" h. **125**

Banner, cloth, bottle on blanket of snow & covered by icicles, 1950, 18 1/2 x 56"......... **425**

Baseball bat, aluminum, marked "Coca-Cola Baseball Bat," 1970s **60**

Book ends, bronze, bottle-shaped, ca. 1963, pr... **275**

Box, 1996, featuring 1962 Santa Claus by Haddon Sundblom, playing with Lionel Santa Fe train set while drinking a Coke, w/24 cans inside, price for box **25**

Calendar, 1923, "Flapper Girl," beautiful smiling woman w/short dark hair, wearing blue dress & white fringed stole, holding glass, 12 x 24".............................. **1,000**

Calendar, 1937, "Fishin Hole," depicting young barefoot boy w/fishing pole on his shoulder & carrying two bottles, his dog running at his side, by N.C. Wyeth, full pad w/cover sheet & metal strip, matted & framed under glass **2,200**

Can, large white diamond design, 1960 .... **175**

Can, red & white diamond design, 1960s **25**

Car key, metal, on key ring, ca. 1959................. **50**

Cigarette lighter, red & white diamond design, 1960s.. **30**

Clicker, tin, marked w/logo, 1940s..................... **125**

Coca-Cola "Contessa" Clock

Clock, "Contessa," anniversary-type, glass dome & wood base, two figural bottles form rotary pendulum, 1950s, 3 1/2 x 5" (ILLUS.)... **750**

Cuff links, celluloid, round, red w/white logo, 1920s, pr.. **75**

Dart board, center marked "Drink Coca-Cola," 1940s-50s **125**

Coca-Cola Doll

Doll, stuffed cloth, painted smiling face, blue & white striped outfit, blue socks & white shoes, red & white striped stocking hat, band marked "Coca-Cola," 1969, 14" h. (ILLUS.)... **100**

Door push, aluminum, marked "Ice Cold Coca-Cola in Bottles," 1950s **425**

Earrings, sterling silver, figural bottle, screw-on, ca. 1960s, pr................................. **35**

Fan, wicker, heart-shaped, 1950s....................... **65**

Coca-Cola Festoon

Festoon, "Chinese Lanterns," center w/young woman wearing hat & glasses & holding glass, 1920s (ILLUS.) **5,000**

Festoon, "Swans," four swans swimming among lily pads & flowers, late 1930s **1,000**

Game, board-type, Chinese Checkers, 1940s **125**

Tick-Tac-Toe Game

Game, Tick-Tac-Toe, wood w/figural bottle pieces, 1940s-1950s, Milton Bradley (ILLUS.).. **185**

Glass, bell-shaped, marked "Coca-Cola" w/trademark in tail of first C, 1929-1940 .... **40**

Glass, flared w/syrup w/syrup line, marked "Coca-Cols," 1904.. **450**

Golf ball, marked w/logo, ca. 1950s 20
Hatpin, cloisonné, oval w/logo, ca. 1930s,
1 1/2 x 2" 350
Ice bucket, cov., brass finish, barrel-
shaped, two-handled, 1950s, 10" h. 400
Ice tongs, aluminum, 1940s, 9" l. 250
Knife, pocket-type, stainless steel, one
blade & nail file, various logo designs &
manufacturers, 1950-1970 35-50
License plate, metal, red w/white lettering
"Drink Coca-Cola," 1960s-70s 40
License plate holder, metal, marked "Drink
Coca-Cola in Bottles," Dura Products
Mfg. Co., Canton, Ohio, 1940s-1950s 425

Rare Coca-Cola Lunch Box

Lunch box, tin, rectangular, red w/white let-
tering & handle, marked "Drink Coca-
Cola - Trade Mark Regd - Comeonin
Coke," 1970s, rare (ILLUS.) 200
Matchbook, white w/green oval showing
girl holding bottle, ca. 1914 750

1901 Coca-Cola Menu

Menu, 1901, featuring Hilda Clark on front
marked "What shall we Drink?" & back
w/floral spray & red circle marked "Drink
Coca-Cola 5¢," some light stains, minor
wear, light edge wear, 4 x 11 3/4" unfold-
ed (ILLUS.) 1,485
Menu board, plastic, rectangular w/clock on
left side, 1960s 200

Coca-Cola Model Kit

Model kit, plastic, Model T delivery van,
1970s (ILLUS.) 60

Cooler Music Box

Music box, doll on round disk marked
"Have Plenty on Hand for Family and
Friends," above figural cooler marked
"Drink Coca-Cola - Ice Cold," 1950s, rare
(ILLUS. of one version) 2,000
Note pad, celluloid, shows Hilda Clark hold-
ing glass, top marked "Compliments of
The Coca-Cola Company" & marked at
bottom "Atlanta - Philadephia, Chicago,
Los Angeles, Dallas, New York, Boston,
Baltimore," 1903, 2 1/2 x 5" 600
Opener, metal, bottle-shaped, Glascock,
ca. 1930 100
Opener, metal, "Key Ring," w/cigar box cut-
ter & nail puller plus square hole,
ca. 1905-15 50
Opener, metal "Shoe Horn," 1930-40 250
Paper dolls, "The Coke Crowd," cutout
book, four male & four female figures
w/various outfits, printed by Merrill Co.,
Publishers, Chicago, Illinois, 1946 185
Pillow, cloth, bottle-shaped, 1950 125
Pin, brass, routeman's, figural bottle, Imdia-
napolis Bottling Co., ca. 1930, 2 1/2" h. 150

Anniversary Plaque

Plaque, pressed metal, round, marked
"50th Anniversary - Coca-Cola - 1886-
1936," red, gold & white w/chain hanger,
1936, 16" d. (ILLUS.) 1,250
Radio, figural cooler marked "Drink Coca-
Cola - Ice Cold," 1950s, 7 x 9 1/2 x 12" 750

Radio, vending machine-shaped, 1970s............ **135**
Riding toy, plastic, "Kiddy-Car," figural can
on wheels, 1970s **85**
Rocking horse, wood, giveaway item from
the Salem Hew Hampshire Coca-Cola
Bottling Co. & Rockingham Park race-
track, 1960s.. **200**

Sandwich Plate

Sandwich plate, china, white w/scroll & flo-
ral design, center w/bottle & glass shown
half full, border at top & bottom reads
"Drink Coca-Cola," the sides marked
"Refresh Yourself," E. M. Knowles China
Company, 1931, 7 1/4" d. (ILLUS.) **300**

Coca-Cola Sign with Jean Harlow

Sign, cardboard cut-out, figure of Jean Harlow in bathing suit, holding glass, 1932
(ILLUS.).. **6,000**
Sign, cardboard cut-out, large glass resting
in snow, bottom of sign marked "Served
Here - Ice Cold," 1937, 19 x 25 1/2"............... **500**
Sign, cardboard cut-out, large platter of
snacks centered by a container of ice &
bottles, floral bouquet at top corner near
sign marked "Good with Food", bottle at
lower corner, 1950s, 20 x 21 1/2" **185**

Coca-Cola 1949 Cut-out Sign

Sign, cardboard cut-out, woman w/bouquet
of daisies, daisies in her hair, holding
glass, 1949, 14 x 18" (ILLUS.) **750**

Christmas Sign

Sign, cardboard, decorated Christmas tree
below ribbon banner reading "Host for
the Holidays," Santa shown at top hold-
ing bottle, 1952, 8 x 17 1/2" (ILLUS.)............. **350**
Sign, cardboard, marked "Drink Coca-Cola
in Bottles 5¢," score board below, 1920s **575**

Coca-Cola Die-cut Tin Sign

Sign, die-cut tin depicting 12-pack of bottles, 1955, 13 x 20" (ILLUS.) **3,150**
Sign, neon, "Drink Coca-Cola," late 1940s,
18 x 28".. **1,800**

Sign, plastic & tin, light-up type, lantern shape w/"Better with Coke" on one side & "Have Coke Here" on the reverse, 1960s...... **135**

Radiator Plate Sign

Sign, radiator plate, chrome, "Coca-Cola In Bottles" in script, 1920s, 17" (ILLUS.)........... **585**

Sign, rectangular, white w/logo at top & six-pack of bottles pictured, red & gold highlights, marked "Take home a carton - Big King Size," 1961, 20 x 28" (light wear, few very shallow dents, few light scratches)...... **1,210**

Sign, reverse glass, shows tilted bottle in center & reading "Pause... Delicious and Refreshing - Drink Coca-Cola in Bottles," foil back, metal frame, 1937, 10 x 12"....... **4,000**

Coca-Cola Syrup Bottle

Syrup bottle w/original metal top, marked w/"Drink Coca-Cola" surrounded by wreath w/bow, ca. 1910 (ILLUS.) **500**

Thermometer, round, glass front, red banner in center w/"Coca-Cola" in white lettering, black letters above & below read "Drink - Be Really Refreshed," 1960s (minor light scratches on glass, light soiling)...... **935**

Figural Bottle Thermometer

Thermometer, tin, figural bottle, 1958, 30" h. (ILLUS.).................................... **150**

1950s Coca-Cola Delivery Truck

Toy truck, battery-operated, route delivery-type, yellow & white w/red lettering1950s, Sanyo, w/original box (ILLUS.).................... **1,265**

Toy truck, metal, delivery-type, ca. 1960, Matchbox.. **55**

Toy wagon, wood & metal, 1960....................... **125**

1907 Coca-Cola Trade Card

Trade card, open shows young waitress serving drinks to two gentlemen seated at a table, marked "Drink Coca-Cola - When thirsty, tired or head-achey, or after a night out try a Coca-Cola High Ball - it hits the spot," closed reads "Appearances are sometimes deceiving but Coca-Cola can always be relied on as nourishing, refreshing and exhilerating" 1907 (ILLUS. open & closed) **850**

Coca-Cola 1942 Tray

Tray, 1942, rectangular, "Two Girls at Car," features two girls enjoying bottles of Coca-Cola, one standing & leaning on the door of a convertible where the other woman is sitting, unused condition, 10 1/2 x 13 1/4" (ILLUS.)................................ **605**

Coca-Cola Trolley Sign

Trolley sign, cardboard, girl w/glass peeking over top of lacy open fan marked "Drink Coca-Cola," shaded pink background marked "Delicious - Refreshing," 1914, 11 x 20 1/2" (ILLUS.) **6,000**

Umbrella, six panels, alternating white marked "Drink Coca-Cola" & red w/bottle, 1920s.. **900**

Yo-Yo, bottle-cap shaped, 1960s **12**

COMIC BOOKS

Comic books, especially first or early issues of a series, are avidly collected today. Prices for some of the scarce ones have reached extremely high levels. Prices listed below are for copies in fine to mint condition.

All Star Comics No. 3

All Star Comics, National Periodical Publications, No. 3, Winter 1940, origin & first appearance of The Justic League of America, very good plus (ILLUS.)............. **$5,750**

All Star Comics, National Periodical Publications, No. 33, February-March 1947, extremely sharp unrestored copy **1,725**

All Star Comics, National Periodical Publications, No. 4, March-April 1941, fine unrestored... **1,265**

All Star Comics, National Periodical Publications, No. 7, October-November 1941, fine unrestored... **1,035**

All Winners Comics, Timely Publications, Summer 1941, featuring Captain America, Human Torch, Sub-Mariner & others, fine... **7,200**

Rare Original Spider Man Comic

Amazing Fantasy, Marvel Comics, No. 15, August 1962, "Introducing Spider Man," origin & first appearance of Spider Man, near mint (ILLUS.)................................... **55,375**

Amazing Spider-Man (The), No. 14, Marvel Comics Group, July 1964, near perfect.. **2,875**

Avengers (The), No. 1, Marvel Comics Group, September 1963, brilliant unrestored **2,875**

Detective Comics No. 27 with Batman

Detective Comics, National Periodical Publications, No. 27, May 1939, first appearance of The Batman, limited restoration, fine condition (ILLUS.) **37,550**

Detective Comics, National Periodical Publications, No. 33, November 1939, Batman (restored, spine roll removed, tears on back sealed) **4,025**

Detective Comics, National Periodical Publications, No. 39, May 1940, Batman & Robin featured, consultant grade........... **2,300**

Detective Comics, National Periodical Publications, No. 40, June 1940, Batman & Robin w/origin & first appearance of Clayface, first cover appearance of The Joker, consultant grade.............................. **3,450**

Detective Comics, National Periodical Publications, No. 45, November 1940, Batman & Robin w/first Joker story, consultant grade **1,495**

Journey Into Mystery, No. 83, Marvel Comics Group, August 1961, very fine unrestored **1,150**

More Fun Comics with The Spectre

More Fun Comics, National Periodical Publications, No. 52, February 1940, first appearance of The Spectre, unrestored, very fine (ILLUS.) **25,300**

More Fun Comics, National Periodical Publications, No. 65, March 1941, The Spectre, very fine unrestored condition **6,325**

More Fun Comics, National Periodical Publications, No. 71, September 1941, Dr. Fate, bright clean tight copy **1,725**

New York World's Fair Comics, DC Comics, 1939, featuring Superman, Sandman, Zatara, Slam Bradley, etc., very good to fine... **3,300**

New York World's Fair Comics, DC Comics, 1940, second issue of New York World's Fair, features Superman, Batman & Robin, Sandman, Slam Bradley, etc., fine to very fine..................................... **3,900**

Superman No. 2, DC Comics, Fall 1939, fine plus... **3,900**

Superman No. 3, DC Comics, Winter 1939, fine plus... **4,500**

World's Best Comics No. 1

World's Best Comics, DC Comics, No. 1, Spring 1941, sharp unrestored condition, fine to very fine (ILLUS.) **4,500**

Wow Comics No. 1

Wow Comics, Fawcett Publications, No. 1, Winter 1940, removed from bound set, very limited restoration to spine, very good plus (ILLUS.)... **690**

X-Men (The), No. 1, double cover, Marvel Comics Group, September 1961, excellent unrestored... **7,475**

COMPACTS & VANITY CASES

A lady's powder compact is a small portable cosmetic make-up box that contains powder, a mirror and puff. Eventually, the more elaborate compact, the "vanity case," evolved, containing a mirror, puffs and compartments for powder, rouge and/or lipstick. Compacts made prior to the 1960s when women opted for the "au natural" look are considered vintage. These vintage compacts were made in a variety of shapes, sizes, combinations, styles and in every conceivable natural or man-made material. Figural, enamel, premium, commemorative, patriotic, Art Deco and souvenir compacts were designed as a reflection of the times and are very desirable. The vintage compacts that are multipurpose, combined with another accessory—the compact/watch, compact/music box, compact/fan, compact/purse, compact/perfumer, compact/lighter, compact/cane, compact/hatpin—are but a few of the combination compacts that are not only sought after by the compact collector but also appeal to collectors of the secondary accessory.

Today vintage compacts and vanity cases are very desirable collectibles. There are compacts and vanities to suit every taste and purse. The "old" compacts are the "new" collectibles. Compacts have come into their own as collectibles. They are listed as a separate category in price guides, sold in prestigious auction houses, displayed in museums, and several books and many articles on the collectible compact have been written. There is also a newsletter, Powder Puff, *written by and for compact collectors. The beauty and intricate workmanship of the vintage compacts make them works of fantasy and art in miniature.*

Black composition, round, the lid applied w/a faux ivory fan, 4 1/2" d. **$45**

Black enameled metal, square, w/tandem lipstick, the lid decorated w/applied gold-tone decoration, push tube on back to open compact, K & K, compact 2 1/8" w., lipstick 2 7/8" **55**

Brass, oblong, the lid decorated w/an engraved King of Hearts, when drawer tassel pulled beveled mirror pops up revealing powder well & metal sifter, Japan, 1 5/8 x 2 7/8" **125**

Elgin American Football Compact

Brown leather, oval, designed to resemble a football, Elgin American, 2 x 3" (ILLUS.)... **55**

Brushed goldtone, round, "Jeweled Powder," the lid set w/a round mabe pearl framed by pronged faceted turquoise stones, twist closures, powder compartment, Germaine Monteil, 1 3/4" d.................... **45**

Brushed goldtone, round, "October Angel," the lid decorated w/angel holding crystal-studded mirror, crystal thumb-piece, one of a series of twelve birth month angel compacts, Estee lauder, 2 1/2" d... **75**

Brushed goldtone, round, "Pepsi-Cola" engraved on the lid, upper rim decorated w/polished goldtone design, Stratton, England, 3 1/4" d.............................. **75**

Lauder "Starry Nights" Compact

Brushed goldtone, round, "Starry Nights," cobalt blue enameled lid decorated w/rhinestone stars & a cosmic band, Estee Lauder, 2 1/4" d. (ILLUS.) **175**

Brushed goldtone, round, the lid decorated w/a beautiful crystal poodle dog, Atomette, 2 3/4" d................................ **120**

Brushed goldtone, square, the lid decorated w/an engraved goldtone frame on easel centered by a relief ice wagon enameled in black & red, Volupte, 3" w. (ILLUS. top next column) **75**

Brushed goldtone, square, w/matching lipstick, the lid decorated w/rhinestone poodle, matching rhinestone poodle head decorates lipstick, complete w/black silk fitted carrying case, Ciner, 2 1/2" w.............. **175**

Volupte Compact with Ice Wagon

Celluloid, round, black, the lid decorated w/a lovely Art Deco woman's face, hand-engraved & hand-painted, Antonin of France, 3" d... **150**

Cork, round, goldtone lid decorated w/a blue & orange abstract enamel design, rare, 3" d.. **55**

Enameled goldtone, round, "Boutique," light blue & cobalt enamel centered on the lid by a turquoise blue cabochon stone, Estee Lauder, 1 1/2" d........................ **25**

Enameled goldtone, round, "Good Fortune," red enamel w/the lid decorated w/goldtone Chinese good luck symbols, red tassel, inspired by Mrs. Evelyn Lauder's design concept, Estee Lauder, 2 1/4" d.. **75**

Enameled metal, oval, an Art Deco design in green & blue enamel, w/tango-chain matching lipstick, interior reveals beveled mirror, powder & rouge compartments w/puffs, compact 1 1/2 x 2 3/4", lipstick 2 1/4" **275**

Art Deco Enameled Compact/Lipstick

Enameled silvertone, octagonal, an Art Deco design in yellow & black enamel, w/tango chain matching lipstick connected from finger ring by yellow enameled chain, compact 2 1/8" w., lipstick 2 1/8" (ILLUS.) **275**

Gold (18k yellow) compact, circular-shaped, woven textured design decorated w/"W" in diamonds, diamond-set thumb piece, numbered & signed "Van Cleef & Arpels" (ILLUS. top next page)..... **4,600**

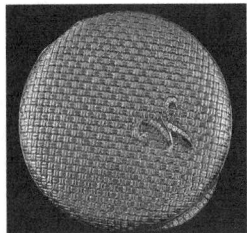

Attractive Gold Compact

Goldtone, oblong, compact, comb & lipstick, enhanced w/crystals, complete w/carrying case, Volupte, 2 1/4 x 3 1/8" **115**

Goldtone, round, coin-style w/a helmeted profile in relief on the lid, the reverse w/an eagle in relief, Elgin-American, 3" d. **65**

Goldtone, round, highly engraved basket w/swinging handle, a white duck revealed under a plastic dome on the lid, plastic interior, Kigu, England, 2 1/8" d., 1 1/2" h. **225**

Goldtone, round, lid decorated w/enameled red, white & blue stars & stripes, centered by "Roosevelt" in blue enamel, Volupte, 3" d. **225**

Goldtone, round, the lid decorated w/dimensional fish & centered w/a cabochon green stone, Max Factor, 2" d. **75**

Melissa Compact with Goldfish

Goldtone, round, the lid decorated w/enameled goldfish under a plastic dome, Melissa, England, 2 3/4" d. (ILLUS.)...................... **75**

Goldtone, round, the lid decorated w/fine prong-set multi-shaped colored stones, unmarked, 3 1/4" d... **75**

Goldtone, round, the lid decorated w/three couples in the rain underneath umbrellas on a white enamel disk in the center, 3 1/8" d... **55**

Goldtone, round, the lid features a photo of The Beatles, unmarked, desirable, 2 7/8" d.. **375**

Princess Borghese Compact

Goldtone, square, the lid decorated w/red & blue enamel hearts, framed interior mirror & puff, Princess Marcella Borghese, 2" w. (ILLUS.)... **55**

Goldtone & black enamel, bolster-shaped vanity, decorated w/applied goldtone leaves, opens to reveal powder well & pill compartment, compartment for cigarettes behind swinging center mirror, rigid handle, 3 1/2" l., 1 3/4" h. **125**

Goldtone & enamel, piano-shaped, "Grand Piano," fine lid decoration highlighted w/crystals, Estee Lauder, 2 1/2 x 2 1/2" **150**

Lancome "Le Cherubin" Compact

Goldtone & enamel, square, "Le Cherubin" limited edition, black enamel lid decorated w/a goldtone angel head, Lancome, 2 1/4" w. (ILLUS.).. **50**

Goldtone & enamel, square, the lid decorated w/a red, white & blue enameled Union Jack flag, applied goldtone royal emblem w/"Dieu Et Mon Droit" centered on lid, Evans, 2 1/2" w..................................... **75**

Goldtone & silvertone, round, "Big Weave," basketweave design, interior reveals a mirror & powder well, in original beautiful blue presentation box w/tassel, Estee Lauder, 4" d. **125**

Pewtertone, heart-shaped, "In Love Again," barely discernible Yves Saint Laurent signature underneath the red plastic disk on the lid, reverse w/name of line, complete w/a red pouch & box, 2 x 2 3/8" **160**

Plastic, round, black w/the lid centered by an applied goldtone sunburst medallion, Roger & Gallet, 3" d. **65**

Plastic, round, blue 'Love Pat' composition compact, the lid decorated w/white daisies & a girl w/a blonde bouffant hairdo, Revlon, 4 1/4" d. **35**

Polished goldtone, round, the lid decorated w/a Blackamoor elaborately decorated w/rhinestones & blue crystals, background shows polished goldtone shadows of the Blackamoor decorated w/red enamel circles, Columbia Fifth Ave., 4" d. **125**

Polished goldtone, square, an elaborately framed round mirror centered on the lid, Wadsworth, 3" w... **45**

Silvertone, miniature, "Compact Kisses," the lid decorated w/two red hearts & two silvertone Xs, complete w/grey moiré red-lined drawstring pouch, Clinique, 1 3/4" sq.. **35**

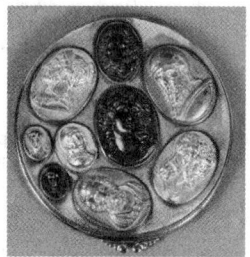

Compact with Profile Disks

Silvertone, round, the lid decorated w/gold-tone, silvertone & bronze Neoclassical high-relief profile disks, 4" d. (ILLUS.) 175

Silvertone, round, the lid designed to resemble a shell of a turtle, Polly Bergen, 1 1/2" d... 35

Silvertone, square, "Triple Compact," complete w/two lipsticks, one for daytime & one for the evening, either one can be snapped tandem to the compact, lid centered w/a family picture, interior metal mirror separates rouge from powder compartment, Yardley, compact 1 7/8" sq., w/tandem lipstick 2 1/4" 125

White enameled metal, round, the lid decorated w/a baseball, bats, an Oriole bird & the word "Orioles," 3" d................................ 65

COOKBOOKS

There was a time when most cookbook collectors were dedicated cooks buying instructions for their favorite pastime. And there was a time when the "cookbook" section of bookstores was quite small if it existed at all. Forget that time!!! The news is out, the price guides are on the bookshelves and cookbooks are a hot item.

"150 Rec. Casserole Cookery," Tracey, 1943, 154 pp. $2

"600 Recipes," by J. Marquart, 1890, 311 pp. 17

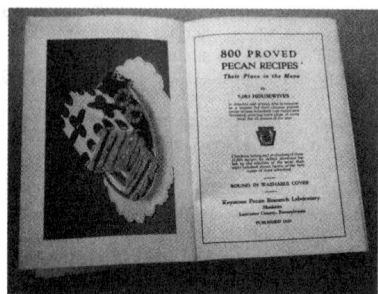

"800 Proved Pecan Recipes"

"800 Proved Pecan Recipes," by 5,083 housewives, Keystone Pecan Research Laboratory, 1925, 393 pp. (ILLUS.)................. 16

"A Date with a Dish, American Negro Recipes," by deKnight, 1948, 426 pp. 20

"A World of Good Eating," by Jack Frost, 1951, 128 pp. 10

"All About Home Baking," 1937, 144 pp........... 5

"All American Cookbook," Favorite Recipes of Famous Persons, 1954, 106 pp. 8

"America's Cookbook," Home Institute, NY, 1937, 1006 pp. 14

"Angie Earl's Treasured Lion House Recipes"

"Angie Earl's Treasured Lion House Recipes," 95 recipes, Bookcraft, Inc., Salt Lake City, 1947 (ILLUS.).................................... 6

"Aunt Caroline's Dixieland Recipes," by E. McKinley, 1922 25

"Better Homes & Garden Lifetime Cookbook," 1935.. 25

"Better Homes New Cook Book"

"Better Homes New Cook Book," tabbed w/much color, Meredith Publishing, 1953, 416 pp. (ILLUS.).................................... 18

"Betty Crocker's New Picture Cook Book"

"Esquire Cook Book"

"Foodarama Party Book"

German & Viennese Cookbook

Home Comfort Cook Book

"Joy of Cooking"

"Joy of Cooking," by Irma Rombauer, 1943, 884 pp. (ILLUS.) **22**

"Leftovers"

"Leftovers," 500 recipes, Consolidated Book, Chicago, 1954 (ILLUS.) **6**
"Let's Cook It Right," by A. Davis, 1947, 626 pp. **10**

"Lily Wallace New American Cook Book"

"Lily Wallace New American Cook Book," recipes, menu planning & table setting, color, Books, Inc., New York, 1946, 931 pp. (ILLUS.) **14**
"Low Calorie Cookbook," 1951, 253 pp. **2**
"Mary Frances' First Cookbook," by M. Hays, 1912, 175 pp. **25**
"Mary Jane's Cookbook," 1916, 307 pp. **12**
"Mary Meades Country Cookbook," by Ruth Ellen Church, Rand McNally, 1964, 376 pp. **10**
"Mastering the Art of French Cooking," by R. Church, 1964, 556 pp. **15**

"McNess Cook Book"

"McNess Cook Book," priced at Florida antique mall, no date (ILLUS.) **5**

"Meta Givens Modern Encyclopedia of Cooking" Volume I

"Meta Givens Modern Encyclopedia of Cooking," includes foreign foods & diets, Volume I, Ferguson & Associates, 1955, pp. 1-736 (ILLUS.) **22**
"Meta Givens Modern Encyclopedia of Cooking," includes foreign foods & diets, Volume II, Ferguson & Associates, 1956, pp. 737-1502 .... **22**
"Mrs. Ma's Cookbook," by N. Ma, 1966, 178 pp. **15**

"Nyal Cookbook"

"Nyal Cookbook," sold at Nyal Quality Drugstores, 1916 (ILLUS.)................................... **3**
"Praktische Konditorei-hunst," by J. Werber, German, 4th edition, 1921 .... **300**
"Querulous Cook," by D. Vanetti, 1963, 291 pp. **6**
"Rumford Complete Cookbook," black & white photos, by Lily Wallace, Rumford Chemical Works, 1946, 213 pp.......................... **7**
"Rumford Complete Cookbook," no photos, by Lily Wallace, Rumford Chemical Works, 1934, 231 pp. **12**
"Salads, Br. Lunch, Canned Meals," Chicago Press, 1933, 400 pp................................ **16**
"Standard Family Cookbook," by G. Wilkinson, 1959, 640 pp.................................... **5**
"The Chinese Cook Book," by Mr. M. Sing Au, Culinary Arts, 1936 .... **3**
"The Scandinavian Cookbook," 159 recipes, Culinary Arts Institute, 1956...................... **3**

"The WISE Encyclopedia of Cookery"

CORKSCREWS

Advertising Type Corkscrew

Advertising type, can opener, "Yankee," w/cap lifter & folding corkscrew, rounded handle end, "The Goebel Brewing Co., Brewers & Bottlers," American patent 839,229 issued to Charles G. Taylor, December 25, 1906 .... **$30-60**

Advertising type, cap lifter, key shape, w/concealed corkscrew **50-60**

Advertising type, cap lifter w/wire breaker & corkscrew, wooden sheath to protect worm is also handle of ice pick, "Cataract Brewing Co., Niagara Falls, N.Y., Cataract Beer," pr. (ILLUS.) **25-50**

Advertising type, cap lifter/corkscrew w/bell, wooden sleeve protects worm **75-100**

Advertising type, collapsing corkscrew w/hinges in four places allows the user to fully close for storage or fully open to use the case as a handle, advertises "Pabst

Collapsing Corkscrew

Milwaukee." A 1913 catalog from Lewis Brothers of Montreal, a hardware wholesaler, offered this corkscrew as the "Telescope." They sold them for $2.70 per dozen, American patent 447,185 issued to Carl Hollweg, February 24, 1891 (ILLUS.) **75-100**

Advertising type, "Duplex Power Cork Screw," advertises "Anheuser Busch," American patent 172,868 issued to William R. Clough, February 1, 1876 .... **40-100**

Advertising type, open frame corkscrew w/locking handle & two cap lifters, marked "Froediert" **150-200**

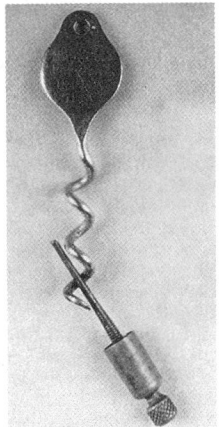

Peg & Worm Corkscrew

Advertising type, peg & worm corkscrew, peg is stored in center of worm & removed & inserted into a hole at top of worm for use; in this type the peg threads into the hole, American patent 611,046 issued to Edwin Walker, September 20, 1898 ILLUS.) **150-250**

Advertising type, picnic type corkscrew w/cap lifter, "For Genuine Satisfaction as to your Individual Taste – Drink..." & "No. 19Y Cork Screw & Bottle Opener" **100-125**

Advertising type, picnic type corkscrew, "Williamson's Power Pocket Corkscrew," double twisted wire screw, advertises "Anheuser Busch," some marked "Williamson," some have left-hand worms, C.T. Williamson Wire Novelty Co., Newark, New Jersey, sheath 2 3/4" x 7 1/16" **50-125**

Advertising type, plastic handle, wire breaker & cap lifter are part of cast bell, Anheuser-Busch eagle-in-a medallion in handle, part of a set which includes a cap lifter & can piercer, Williamson **35-50**

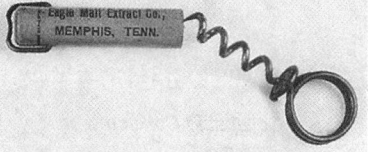

Single/Double Ring Corkscrew

Advertising type, single/double ring, "Decapitator," w/wire handle, "Eagle Malt Extract Co., Memphis, Tenn.," an interesting advertisement on this type was "The one thing finished in this nasty world is P.B. Ale" (ILLUS.) **10-30**

Sterling Silver Corkscrew

Advertising type, sterling silver, magnificently decorated, silver applied to an ivory handle w/ornate floral design caps added to the end, fine detailing on all sections wrapping the handle, silver embossed with "Compliments Rochester Brewery" & hand holding a glass of beer, marked "STERLING 5827" without a maker's mark, patented in 1886 by Edward Thiery & Charles Croselmire, Rochester Brewery, Kansas City, Missouri, c. 1900 (ILLUS.) **600-800**
Advertising type, the "Bottle-Boy" waiter's friend, corkscrew & cap lifter, "A.J., U.S.A." & "Latz Milwaukee" **20-25**

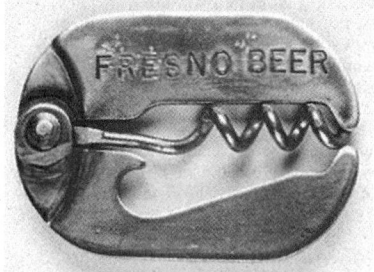

"Tip Top" Corkscrew

Advertising type, "Tip Top," advertises "Fresno Beer," a packaging card for this

corkscrew proclaims "Lies flat in your vest pocket," Williamson, Newark, New Jersey (ILLUS.) **125-150**
Advertising type, twisted wire corkscrew, single helix, stopper button, wire loops around wooden handle **40-50**
Advertising type, w/cast bell, wood handle, "J.D. Iler Brewing Co., Kansas City, Mo.," American patent 501,975 issued to Edwin Walker, July 25, 1893 .... **15-50**
Advertising type, waiter's friend corkscrew w/cap lifter on neck stand, foil cutter **75-100**
Advertising type, waiter's friend corkscrew w/cap lifter, "The Detroit pat. July 10, '94," American patent 522,672 issued to Charles Puddefoot, July 10, 1894 .... **100-200**
Advertising type, waiter's friend corkscrew w/round cap lifter & neck stand w/cap lifter, plastic handle, "Oldenberg" **5-10**
Advertising type, wood handle, cast-iron crown cap lifter in handle, "Chattanooga Brewing Co., Chattanooga, Tenn.," Walker, 1893 patent **25-60**
Advertising type, wood handle w/"Decapitator," wood sheath protects worm, "J.C. Helb ...," American patent 950,509 issued to William R. Clough, March 1, 1910 .... **25-50**
Bar mounted, "Champion," hold bottle in clamp & move handle from back to front to insert worm & extract cork, American patent 589,574 & design patent 25,607 issued to Michael Redlinger, September 7, 1897 & June 9, 1896, Arcade Manufacturing Co., Freeport, Illinois **500-700**
Bar mounted, "Rapid," crank handle to insert screw into cork & to extract, American patent 450,957 issued to Harry J. Williams, April 21, 1891 .... **500-700**
Bar mounted, rotate top handle to enter cork, pull lever to extract cork, American patent 377,790 issued to Edwin Walker, February 14, 1888 .... **600-800**

"Shomee" Bar Mounted Corkscrew

Bar mounted, "Shomee," crank handle to insert screw into cork & to extract, American patent 675,032 issued to Albert Baumgarten, May 28, 1901 (ILLUS.) **500-700**
Bar mounted, the "Quick & Easy," screws to bar top, four different versions w/four different design marks inside the handle: 1893, 1895, 1896, 1897 design, crank

handle to insert screw into cork & to extract, embossed w/"Golden Grain Belt Beers, Minneapolis Brewing Co.," Walker **500-650**

Bar Mounted Corkscrew

Bar mounted, w/crank handle to insert worm into cork, lift lever to extract, embossed w/"Albany Steam Bottling Works, Hinckel Brewing Co's Lager Beer," American patent 452,625 issued to Edwin Walker, May 19, 1891(ILLUS.) **500-700**

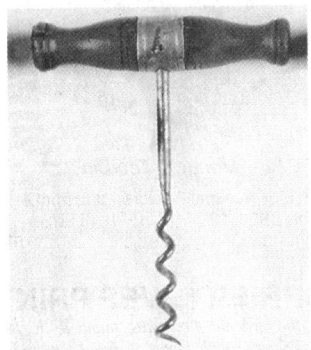

Corkscrew w/Brass Band Around Handle

Corkscrew, w/brass band around handle, American patents 315,773 & 317,123 issued to Edward P. Haff, April 14 & May 4, 1885 (ILLUS.)............................... **50-75**

Novelty, knife w/master blade, corkscrew & pen blade, celluloid handles, "Christians Solingen Germany/Rostfrei" & "Compliments Stroh's Extra Detroit" **100-150**

Novelty, knife w/master blade, foil cutter & corkscrew, mother-of-pearl handles, advertises "Schlitz Beer," Wester Brothers, Solingen, Germany **125-150**

Novelty, knife w/master blade, foil cutter & corkscrew, plain metal handles **150-200**

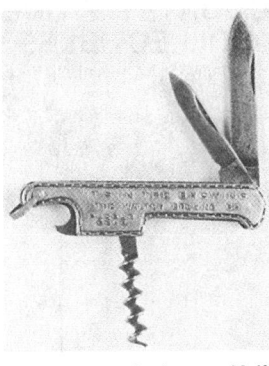

Novelty Type Corkscrew Knife

Novelty, knife w/master blade & pen blade, cap lifter formed in handle, marked "...The Walter Brewing Co.," Imperial Knife Co., Providence, Rhode Island (ILLUS.) **20-50**

Novelty, knife w/master blade used to cut cigars, file blade, wire/foil cutter & corkscrew, plain metal handles, "Toniga" on blade **125-150**

Bottle-shaped Single Blade Knife

Novelty, knife w/single blade, cap lifter & corkscrew, bottle-shaped, steel handles (ILLUS.) **150-200**

Novelty, knife w/single blade, cap lifter & corkscrew, ornate handles, "C. Pfeiffer Brewg Co." **125-250**

Novelty, knife w/two blades, corkscrew & leather case, mother-of-pearl handles, "J.A. Henckels, Solingen," "A.B.C." on handle **250-300**

Novelty, knife w/two blades, wire/foil cutter & corkscrew, "Dick & Bros.".................... **150-250**

Novelty, Swiss Army knife w/corkscrew, "Victorinox Switzerland Stainless Rostfrei, Officier Suis" **20-25**

Wall mounted, "Yankee No. 1," marked the cork puller as "a household necessity," advertising copy says: "Should be in every home. Don't let any woman struggle with a corkscrew to open tightly corked catsup, olive, pickle, medicine or any other bottle. The Yankee is screwed against any upright surface: Icebox, Sideboard, Door Frame or Wall. It's always there. No hunting for a corkscrew, always ready to draw the tightest cork from any bottle," American patent 857,992 issued to Raymond B. Gilchrist, June 25, 1907 .... **500-700**

COUNTRY STORE COLLECTIBLES

Also see: Antique Trader Advertising Price Guide.

Occident Flour Advertising Floor Stand

Floor stand, Occident Flour, advertising-type, for bread, tin litho advertising panel, 34" h. (ILLUS.) **$150-225**

"Ideal" Fountain Pen Case

Fountain pen case, "Ideal," oak & glass, holds two trays of pens, applied transfer lettering inside door, ca. 1910, 8 1/2" x 17 3/4", 7 1/2" h. (ILLUS.) **375-425**

Buckeye Root Beer Syrup Dispenser

Syrup dispenser, Buckeye Root Beer, The Cleveland Fruit Juice Co., Cleveland, Ohio, ca. 1910, 14" h. (ILLUS.) **1,700-2,200**

Cherry Chic Syrup Dispenser

Syrup dispenser, Cherry Chic, ceramic, ca. 1910, 12" h. (ILLUS.) .. **4,500-6,500**

Monarch Tea Bin

Tea bin, Monarch, multi-colored litho front & top, ca. 1900, 12" x 13", 15" h. (ILLUS.) **575-700**

CURRIER & IVES PRINTS

This lithographic firm was founded in 1835 by Nathaniel Currier with James M. Ives becoming a partner in 1857. Current events of the day were portrayed in the early days and the prints were hand-colored. Landscapes, vessels, sport and hunting scenes of the West all became popular subjects. The firm was in existence until 1906. All prints listed are hand-colored unless otherwise noted. Numbers at the end of the listings refer to those used in Currier & Ives Prints-An Illustrated Checklist, *by Frederick A. Conningham (Crown Publishers).*

Ambuscade (The), medium folio, undated, framed, 95 (pale staining, surface soil).... **$1,150**
American Autumn Fruits, large folio, 1865, framed, 106 (margins slightly trimmed, minor stains) **935**
American Express Train, small folio, 1853, framed, 128 (margins slightly trimmed) **3,190**

American Farm Scenes - No. 4 (Winter), large folio, 1853, N. Currier, framed, 136 (foxing, staining & toning) **5,463**

American Forest Scene - Maple Sugaring, large folio, 1856, N. Currier, framed, 157 (foxing, minute nicks & tears to edges) **19,550**

American Hunting Scenes - A Good Chance, large folio, 1863, framed, 174 (staining & fox marks, thin spots on reverse) **6,900**

American Hunting Scenes - An Early Start, large folio, 1863, framed, 173 (staining & toning, minor nicks to edges, repair of tear to upper left corner) **8,625**

American Railroad Scene - "Snowbound," small folio, 1871, framed, 187, (pale staining, occasional foxing) **5,175**

Arguing the Point, large folio, 1855, N. Currier, unframed, 265, (pale foxing & staining, minor creases & losses to edges, possible retouch to sky) **3,335**

Autumn in New England - Cider Making, large folio, 1866, framed, 322, (minor light-stain, faint discoloration at edges) **8,338**

Battle of Gettysburg, Pa., July 3, 1863 (The), small folio, undated, 407, early frame (edge damage & stains) **248**

Bombardment of Fort Sumter, Charleston Harbor, From Fort Moultrie, small folio, undated, framed, 597 .... **330**

Brook Trout Fishing - An Anxious Moment, large folio, 1862, framed, 703 .... **14,950**

Cares of a Family (The), large folio, 1856, N. Currier, framed, 814, (light- & mat stain, discoloration at edges) **2,645**

Clipper Ship Dreadnought Off Tuskar Light, large folio, 1856, N. Currier, framed, 1144 (fox marks, several repaired vertical creases, minor paper loss) .. **3,450**

Darktown Fire Brigade (The) - A Prize Squirt, small folio, 1885, matted & framed, 1386 (minor stains & edge damage) **248**

Darktown Fire Brigade (The) - Saved, small folio, 1885, matted & framed, 1391 (some edge damage) **358**

Deacon's Mare (The), small folio, 1879, 1465 (light water stain at bottom) **248**

El Capitan - From Mariposa Trail, small folio, undated, framed, 1681 (stains, minor damage) **275**

First Bird of the Season (The), small folio, 1879, framed, 1959 .... **385**

Four Seasons of Life - Childhood (The), large folio, 1868, framed, 2096 (light- & mat stain, foxing & tape on back) **1,955**

Futurity Race at Sheepshead Bay (The), large folio, 1889, framed, 2209 (slight lightstain, minor rubbing upper right) **3,163**

General Z. Taylor - "Rough and Ready," small folio, 1846, N. Currier, framed, 2330 (light stains) **303**

Great Fire of Boston (The) - November 9th & 10th, 1872, small folio, 1872, framed, 2614 (soiling & staining in margins, scattered pale foxing) **316**

Great West (The), small folio, 1870, laid down on card, 2658 (overall slight soiling,

few abrasions, small hole upper left, repaired tear lower right) **575**

Home to Thanksgiving

Home to Thanksgiving, large folio, 1867, framed, 2882, toning & staining, scattered fox marks, minor nicks, tears & losses to edges, some repaired (ILLUS.) **11,500**

Lady Moscow, Rocket, and Brown Dick, large folio, 1857, N. Currier, framed, 3383 (light- & mat stain, few tears in margin, discoloration on edges) **1,035**

Lady Washington, small folio, undated, N. Currier, three-quarters length portrait of young Martha standing under a tree, in period beveled veneer framed **275**

Life in the Country - The Morning Ride, large folio, 1859, framed, 3512 (foxing) **7,475**

Life of a Fireman (The) - The Metropolitan System, large folio, 1866, unframed, 3516, (staining, soiling on reverse) **4,888**

Life on the Prairie - The Buffalo Hunt, large folio, 1862, framed, 3527 (repaired tears & losses at edges & corners, discoloration on verso) **7,475**

Life on the Prairie - The Trappers Defence - "Fire Fight Fire," large folio, 1862, framed, 3528 (overall staining, masking tape at margins) **1,725**

Little Snowbird, small folio, undated, framed, 3719 (minor stains) **352**

Mansion of the Olden Time (A), small folio, undated, framed, 3969 (minor stains, white painted spot on top margin) **138**

Maple Sugaring Print

Maple Sugaring - Early Spring in the Northern Woods, medium folio, 1872, framed, 3975, toning & staining, glue or tape residue to reverse (ILLUS.) **2,300**

Maple Sugaring - Early Spring in the Northern Woods, small folio, 1872, framed, 3975 (some mat staining, skillfully remargined).. **1,265**

Midnight Race on the Mississippi (A), large folio, 1860, 4116 (repaired tears in outer image, tiny scuff in sky at right) **9,200**

New England Winter Scene, large folio, 1861, framed, clouds in sky, 4420, framed **7,200**

New England Winter Scene, large folio, 1861, framed, no clouds in sky, 4420 (tears, title trimmed from sheet)................. **3,680**

Old Farm House (The), medium folio, 1872, framed, 4557 (staining, prevalent toning) **489**

Old Farm House (The), small folio, 1872, framed, 4557 (staining, few specks of foxing).. **460**

Old Mill-Dam (The) - At Sleepy Hollow, small folio, undated, framed, 4572 (very minor stains & edge damage) **275**

Old Oaken Bucket (The), large folio, 1864, unframed, 4576 (minute nicks to upper edge, few scattered fox marks)................. **1,610**

Pigeon Shooting - Playing the Decoy, large folio, 1862, unframed, 4780 (toning, tape residue & annotations on reverse)..... **4,888**

Preparing for Market, large folio, 1856, N. Currier, framed, 4872 (toning, staining & fox marks)... **3,450**

Pride of the Garden (The), small folio, 1873, framed, 4914 (stain in upper right, some flowers uncolored).............................. **110**

The Road - Winter

Road (The) - Winter, large folio, N. Currier, 1853, framed, 5171, staining, fox marks (ILLUS.)... **52,900**

Saratoga Springs, N.Y., small folio, undated, framed, 5398 (staining, minor paper loss & tear, soiling)..................................... **460**

Siege of Charleston (The), small folio, undated, 5508, framed (minor stains & edge damage, margins trimmed)................. **220**

Snowed Up - Ruffed Grouse in Winter, large folio, 1867, framed, 5581 (light water stains, vertical stain from backboard, margins trimmed) **10,175**

Snowy Morning, medium folio, 1864, unframed, 5582 (minor tear, toning & foxing).. **2,415**

Spill Out on the Snow (A), large folio, 1870, framed, 5651 (staining, scattered foxing).. **5,463**

Splendid Naval Triumph on the Mississippi, April 24, 1862 (The), large folio,

1862, framed, 5659 (light stains, minor edge damage)... **1,320**

State Street, Boston, Massachusetts, medium folio, 1849, N. Currier, framed, 5714 (toning & staining, foxing to reverse) **460**

Steamship Bothnia of the Cunard Line (The), small folio, undated, framed, 5750 (minor damage & taped repair)................... **303**

"Stopping Place" on the Road (A) - The Horse Shed large folio, 1868, framed, 5821, (waterstains & other defects in margins, some spotting & foxing in image) **1,926**

Summer Landscape (A) - Haymaking, large folio, 1869, framed, 5867 (margins slightly trimmed, very minor stains & tape repair).. **358**

Summer Scenes in New York Harbor, large folio, 1863, framed, 5876 (light- & mat stain, mottled discoloration & few nicks & tears at edges)............................ **9,200**

Sunny Side - The Residence of the Late Washington Irving Near Tarrytown, N.Y., large folio, undated, framed, 5892 (staining, linen tape at margins, areas of foxing) **345**

Tomb of Washington (The), large folio, undated, 6111, framed (minor soiling in margins, small losses at corners)................. **201**

Trotting Cracks at the Forge, large folio, 1869, framed, 6169 (toning & staining, scattered fox marks) **8,050**

U.S. Frigate Cumberland, 54 guns - The Flag Ship of the Gulf Squadron, Comm. Perry - #607, small folio, 1848, Nathaniel Currier, 6306, framed (minor wear, edge damage & some stains, margins trimmed) **275**

View of Harper's Ferry, Va. - From the Potomac Side, large folio, undated, framed, 6395 (some minor corner damage) **550**

Washington's Reception by the Ladies..., small folio, N. Currier, 1845, in period beveled frame, 6557 (minor margin tears).. **193**

Whale Fishery, (The) - Sperm Whale "In a Flurry," medium folio, 1852, N. Currier, framed, 5648 (unobtrusive staining, annotations on reverse)................................... **1,093**

Wild Duck Shooting - A Good Day's Sport

Wild Duck Shooting - A Good Day's Sport, large folio, 1854, N. Currier,

framed, 6670, toning, margin staining & minor margin loss (ILLUS.)........................ **13,800**
Winter in the Country - The Old Grist Mill, large folio, 1864, framed (staining in margins, a few pin holes)................................... **7,150**
Winter Morning, medium folio, 1861, framed, 6740 (pale damp stain left margin, minor discoloration in margins, slightly rippled)....................................... **1,783**
Winter Morning, Feeding the Chickens, large folio, 1863, framed, 6741 (toning, slight staining).. **2,530**
Winter Pastime, medium folio, 1870, framed, 6744 (staining & foxing, annotations to reverse)..................................... **5,750**
Wonderful Maud S. (The) Record 2:10 1/4..., small folio, 1881, framed (stains)......... **440**

DECOYS

Decoys have been utilized for years to lure flying water fowl into target range. They have been made of carved and turned wood, papier-mâché, canvas and metal, and some are in the category of outstanding folk art and command high prices.

Black Duck, by A. Elmer Crowell, East Harwich, Massachusetts, carved wood w/original paint, oval name brand on bottom, 17 1/2" l., 6 1/2" h. (minor paint loss, repairs)........................ **$1,380**
Black Duck, hollow-carved wood w/bill delineation, original paint w/minor wear, Delaware River area, first quarter 20th c. (numerous small dents, body seam slightly separated, small crack under tail, several small stress cracks at body seam).. **3,450**
Bluebill Drake, carved wood & cork, old worn working repaint, glass eyes, old label attributes it to Jim Foote, Pte. Mouille, Michigan, 14" l. **165**
Bluebill Drake, carved wood w/original black, white & grey paint & glass eyes, Mason factory, 13 3/4" l. (minor wear, professional repair to tip of tail, neck puttied)... **248**
Brandt Goose, carved wood w/old paint & glass eyes,17 1/2" l. (paint wear, age crack in block, damage to bill)...................... **248**
Brant, by William McClellan, Eureka, California, carved wood w/near mint original paint, second quarter 20th c. (weight missing, two tiny cracks at top of tail)........ **4,312**
Bufflehead Hen, by Eric V. Nelson, carved wood w/relief-carved feathers, original paint & glass eyes, signed & w/incised initials "EVN '81," modern, 9 1/2" l.................. **358**
Canada Goose, block-form waxed canvas-covered hollow body painted black & white w/a tall carved wood neck & head w/glass eyes, 15 1/2" h. **303**
Canada Goose, by A. Elmer Crowell, East Harwich, Massachusetts, carved wood w/original paint, rectangular name stamp on bottom, 23 1/2" l., 11" h. (repairs, age split on underside)....................................... **3,450**
Canada Goose, old waxed canvas-covered hollow body w/carved wood tall neck & head w/old paint, glass eyes, 15 1/2" h. **220**

Canada Goose, primitive carved wood w/old worn & weathered black & white paint, glass eyes, 22 1/2" l., 14 1/2" h. **220**
Canvasback Drake, attributed to Clifford Moody Lind, Freemont, Wisconsin, hollow-carved wood body w/old black, red & white paint, 18 1/2" l. (cracks in head, minor edge wear) **220**
Canvasback Drake, by Harry Fennimore, Bordentown, New Jersey, hollow-carved wood w/bill delineation, original paint w/very minor wear, second quarter 20th c. (string marks on back & sides, several tiny dents).. **5,750**
Canvasback Drake, carved wood w/original paint, replaced glass eyes, 17 1/4" l. (minor age cracks) **110**
Canvasback Drake & Hen, by R. Madison Mitchell, carved wood w/good repaint, signed "R. Madison Mitchell, 1945," 16" & 16 1/2" l., pr. (hen w/crack in neck).............. **825**
Fish, carved wood, long narrow fish decorated in gold w/black & white stripes & a red head, metal fins & tack eyes, 9" l. **193**
Fish, carved wood, long slender body in silver repaint w/overall tiny brown dots & small metal rounded rounded bottom fins & a small dorsel fin, 11" l. **110**

McCoy Goldeneye Drake

Goldeneye Drake, attributed to Charles McCoy, Tuckerton, New Jersey, hollow-carved wood w/traditional Delaware River weight, original paint w/minor discoloration & wear, crack in neck, several tiny dents, first quarter 20th c. (ILLUS.) **5,462**
Mallard Drake, by John Blair, Sr., Philadelphia, Pennsylvania, swimming pose, hollow-carved wood w/tack eyes & fine paint detail, body halves joined by two wooden dowels, stamped "G. Banes" several times on base, original paint w/minor wear, thrid quarter 19th c. (several small dents) **60,250**
Mallard Drake, carved & painted old factory decoy, good old repaint, glass eyes, 16" l. (edge damage, age cracks)................... **116**
Mallard Drake, carved wood w/early repaint, glass eyes, Mason factory, 15 1/2" l. (small chip on end of bill, thin piece missing at neck)................................... **220**
Mallard Hen, carved wood in sleeper pose, original paint, probably made in Maryland, 14 1/2" l. (minor paint wear, chip on tail)... **385**
Merganser Drake, by Richard C. Watson, Fair Haven, Michigan, swimming pose, carved wood w/good detail on feathers &

wings, original paint & glass eyes, contemporary, 23" l. (small edge chips) **385**
Merganser Drake, carved wood w/glass eyes, worn old working repaint, 14 3/4" l. (age cracks, old puttied repair) **220**
Old Squaw Drake, by Orlando Sylvester Bibber, South Harpswell, Maine, carved wood w/head turned, bill slightly hooked, original paint w/minor wear, Starr Collection stamp on base (small knot hole in one side, small wood defect in lower edge) **17,250**
Pintail Hen, by John English, Florence, New Jersey, hollow-carved wood w/traditional Delaware River raised V wing tip carving & fluted tail, good feather detail, original paint w/very minor wear, late quarter 19th c. (minor discoloration & wear, several tiny dents) **18,400**
Red Breasted Merganser Drake, by A. Elmer Crowell, East Harwich, Massachusetts, carved wood w/original paint, oval brand mark on base, 19 1/2" l., 5 1/2" h. (horizontal age split through one eye, minor paint loss) **8,625**

English Redhead Drake

Redhead Drake, by John English, Florence, New Jersey, last quarter 19th c., hollow-carved wood w/fine feather paint detail & good patina, painted by John Dawson, Trenton, New Jersey, first quarter 20th c., paint surface w/very slight wear, several tiny dents, Mackey stamp on underside (ILLUS.) **35,650**
Redhead Drake, carved wood w/flat bottom, good old repaint, good detail, glass eyes, 14 1/2" l. (head loose) **303**
Sanderling or "peep," attributed to Dave "Umbrella" Watson, Chincoteaque, Virginia, solid construction w/inserted & splined hardwood bill & relief-carved wings, original paint w/minor wear, first quarter 20th c. (two minor shot marks) **7,475**

Large Early Swan Decoy

Swan, carved wood, two-piece hollow body w/solid neck & head, worn white paint, late 19th c., wood loss, early repair (ILLUS.) **4,888**

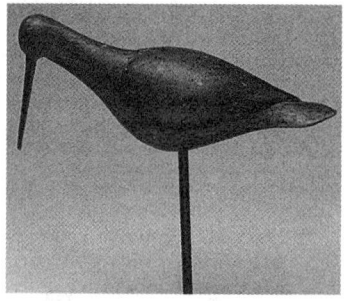

Whistling Swan Decoy

Whistling Swan, hollow-carved wood w/glass eyes, old repaint by Charles Bergman, Astoria, Oregon, professional repair to bill, several small dents, ca. 1905 (ILLUS.) **35,650**
Widgeon Drake, by John Blair, Sr., Philadelphia, Pennsylvania, hollow-carved wood body w/original weight, original paint w/minor flaking & wear, branded "D. Speckles," third quarter 19th c. (several tiny dents, professional repair to part of bill) **29,900**

Matthews Yellowleg Decoy

Yellowleg, attributed to William Matthews, Chincoteaque, Virginia, solid construction w/inserted & splined hardwood bill, carved eyes & stylized characteristic wing carving, original paint w/minor wear, one or two light shot marks, last quarter 19th c. (ILLUS.) **5,462**

DISNEY COLLECTIBLES

Scores of objects ranging from watches to dolls have been created showing Walt Disney's copyrighted animated cartoon characters, and an increasing number of collectors now are seeking these, made primarily by licensed manufacturers.
ALSO SEE Antique Trader Toy Price Guide.

Animation Cels

Baby Pegasus (Fantasia) movie cel, gouache on partial celluloid to a Courvoisier airbrush background, Baby Pegasus flying over water, 1940, 5 1/2" **$800**

Bambi drawings, graphite & color pencil on paper, deer in forest, a concept drawing together w/a training model sheet of Bambi & a publicity drawing w/Thumper, Bambi & butterfly, unframed, 1942, 9 x 12" & smaller, set of three **1,400**

Bambi & Thumper (Bambi) movie cel, gouache on trimmed celluloid applied to a Courvoisier airbrush background, Bambi & Thumper ice skating, "Walt Disney Productions" stamp on lower right corner, 1942, 6 x 7 1/2" **2,800**

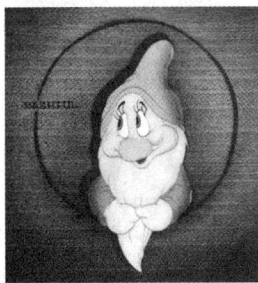

Bashful Movie Cel

Bashful (Snow White & the Seven Dwarfs) movie cel, gouache on trimmed celluloid applied to Courvoisier wood veneer background, painting of Bashful within circle, labeled "Bashful", 1937, 7 x 7" (ILLUS.) **3,000**

Big Bad Wolf movie cel, gouache on two full celluloids applied to a production background, Wolf riding machine labeled "Wolf Pacifier," 1936, 10 x 13" **2,000**

Doc (Snow White & the Seven Dwarfs) animation drawing, graphite on paper, original rough drawing of Doc, 1937, 8 x 9" **450**

Donald Duck animation drawing, graphite on paper, Donald Duck, Laurel & Cantor, unframed, ca. 1940's, 9 x 10", set of four **190**

Donald Duck (Hockey Champ) animation drawing, graphite on paper, Donald Duck trapped in birdcage suspended on bent-over limb struggling to free himself, 1939, 8 x 9" **200**

Donald Duck (Mickey's Circus) animation drawing, graphite on paper, Donald Duck wearing drum major uniform sitting in puddle of water w/fish in his mouth, 1936, 7 x 9 1/4" **280**

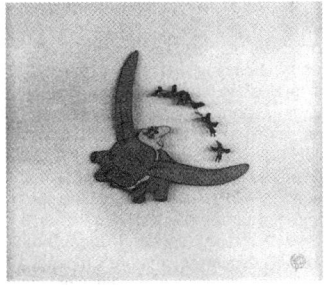

Dumbo Movie Cel

Dumbo movie cel, gouache on partial celluloid applied to a Courvoisier airbrush background, Dumbo wearing yellow hat flying in air w/crows following, "Walt Disney Productions" seal on lower right corner & Courvoisier sticker on reverse, 1941, 5 x 6" (ILLUS.) **2,200**

Dwarfs (Snow White & the Seven Dwarfs) animation drawings, graphite on paper, Dopey, Doc, Sneezy & Bashful, 1937, 11 1/2 x 13" & smaller, set of two **850**

Dwarfs (Snow White & the Seven Dwarfs) movie cel, gouache on trimmed celluloid applied to Courvoisier wood veneer background, four Dwarfs standing w/Dopey sitting on floor, all are laughing, 1937, 9 1/4 x 11" **9,000**

Fantasia concept drawings, pastel & graphite on paper, from the Nutcracker Suite, unframed, 1940, 10 x 12" & smaller, set of three **950**

Fantasia movie cel, gouache on partial celluloid applied to a Courvoisier airbrush background, three dancing mushrooms w/stars & bubbles overhead, "Walt Disney Productions" stamp on lower left corner, 1940, 6 x 7" **3,500**

Fantasia movie cel, pastel on paper, four figures playing flutes dancing in a circle around four sleeping unicorns, a concept art, 1940, 10 x 13" **1,500**

Figaro & Cleo Movie Cell

Figaro & Cleo (Pinocchio) movie cell, gouache on trimmed celluloid applied to a Courvoisier airbrush background, Cleo looks at Figaro through his fish bowl, Courvoisier Galleries sticker on reverse, 1940, 3 1/2 x 5 1/2" (ILLUS.) **2,000**

Figaro & Butterfly Movie Cel

Figaro (Pinocchio) movie cel, gouache on trimmed celluloid applied to a Courvoisier airbrush background, Figaro walking toward butterfly, 1940, 3 1/4 x 4 1/4" (ILLUS.) **1,300**

Figaro (Pinocchio) movie cell, gouache on trimmed celluloid applied to a Courvoisier airbrush background, Figaro w/head turned looking back, Gepetto's slippered foot in background, 1940, 4 1/4 x 6".. **3,500**

Goofy Movie Animation Drawing

Goofy (Clock Cleaners) animation drawing, graphite on paper, Goofy bending over to run fingers through puddle of water that he is standing in, original, 1937, 8 x 9" (ILLUS.) **100**

Goofy (How to Ride a Horse) movie cel, gouache on full celluloid applied to a Courvoisier airbrush background, Goofy trying to mount horse w/one foot in stirrup while holding onto horse's ear & tail, unframed, 1941, 9 x 11" **1,000**

Jiminy Cricket Movie Cel

Jiminy Crickett (Pinocchio) movie cell, gouache on trimmed celluloid applied to a Courvoisier airbrush background, Jiminy Cricket pointing w/his umbrella, Couvoisier Galleries sticker on reverse, 1940, 3 1/2 x 3 1/2" (ILLUS.) **1,500**

Malificent & Crow (Sleeping Beauty) movie cel, gouache on partial celluloid applied to Disneyland print background, Malificent w/staff in hand & crow on shoulder, 1959, 71/2 x 10 1/2" **1,400**

Malificent & Crow Movie Cel

Malificent & Crow (Sleeping Beauty) movie cel, gouache on partial celluloid applied to Disneyland print background, Malificent w/staff in one hand & crow in other, 1959, 8 1/2 x 10" (ILLUS.) **4,500**

Mickey Mouse animation drawings, graphite on paper, Mickey Mouse drawing w/training model sheet, unframed, 1930s, 10 x 12" & smaller, set of two............ **900**

Mickey Mouse Movie Cel

Mickey Mouse (Canine Caddy) movie cel, gouache on partial celluloid applied to a watercolor production background, Mickey Mouse holding golf club searching for ball in sand trap, 1941, 8 x 15" (ILLUS.) ... **8,500**

Mickey Mouse (Mickey's Parrot) animation drawing, graphite & color on paper, Mickey Mouse walking in stocking feet w/shoes slung over shoulder carrying a rifle, original, 1938, 8 x 9" **600**

Mickey Mouse (Society Dog Show) animation drawing, graphite on paper, Mickey Mouse pushing backside of dog that is wearing roller skates, original, 1939, 8 1/2 x 10" **1,200**

Mickey Mouse Movie Cel

Mickey Mouse (The Pointer) movie cel, gouache on trimmed celluloid applied to a Courvoisier airbrush background, Mickey Mouse sitting on log in front of pup tent holding book in hand & talking to dog, outdoor scene, Courvoisier Galleries sticker on reverse, 1939, 7 1/2 x 10 1/2" (ILLUS.) **6,500**

Peter Pan movie cel, gouache on partial celluloid, Peter Pan w/hand cupped around ear, unframed, 1953, 8 x 10" **1,500**

Pinocchio & Jiminy Cricket (Pinocchio) animation drawings, graphite on paper, unframed, Pinocchio & Jiminy Cricket, 1940, 6 1/2 x 9 1/2" & smaller, set of two...... **380**

Snow White Movie Cel

Snow White movie cel, gouache on trimmed celluloid applied to a wood veneer background, Snow White sitting on floor w/knees drawn up to chest & arms around legs, 1937, 9 x 12" (ILLUS.) **7,000**

Snow White, the Prince & Dwarfs Movie Cel

Snow White & the Seven Dwarfs movie cel, gouache applied to a Courvoisier airbrush background, Snow White sitting on horse talking to the Prince & four dwarfs, unframed, 1937, 8 1/2 x 8 1/2" (ILLUS.).. **11,000**

Snow White & the Seven Dwarfs movie cel, gouache on partial celluloid applied to a Courvoisier airbrush background, Snow White sitting on ground petting a deer & a rabbit w/chipmunks vying for her attention, 1937, 7 x 7" **5,500**

Snow White & the Seven Dwarfs movie cel, gouache on partial celluloid applied to a Courvoisier airbrush background, Snow White retrieving bucket from well surrounded by doves, 1937, 8 x 10" **13,000**

Snow White & the Seven Dwarfs movie cel, gouache on partial celluloid applied to a Courvoisier airbrush background, Snow White bends to kiss Bashful on top of head, doorway in background, 1937, 8 1/4 x 9" **16,000**

Snow White & the Seven Dwarfs movie cel, gouache on trimmed celluloid applied to a Courvoisier wood veneer background, Snow White dancing w/the dwarfs, 1937, 10 x 13" **9,000**

The Witch (Snow White & the Seven Dwarfs) animation drawing, graphite on paper, rough drawing of The Witch, 1937, 8 x 9" **650**

Thumper Movie Cel

Thumper (Bambi) movie cel, gouache on partial celluloid applied to a Courvoisier airbrush background, Thumper doubled over w/laughter among flowers, "Walt Disney Productions" seal on lower left corner & Couvoisier sticker on reverse, 1942, 5 x 6" (ILLUS.) **1,200**

Thumper (Bambi) movie cel, gouache on trimmed celluloid applied to a Courvoisier airbrush background, Thumper standing in grass, 1942, 7 1/2 x 9" **2,000**

DOG COLLECTIBLES

Dog collectibles come in all shapes, sizes and types, from paper to postcards to prints to porcelain. Canine collectors' interests vary widely. Some collect all types of items portraying one breed only; some collect figurines of all breeds, but from a certain manufacturer only; others might collect whatever dog items strikes his or her fancy. This price list concentrates on figurines with a few exceptions. Measurements are all listed with width first, then height (width x height). Figurines are all porcelain except where noted.

Figurines

Basset Hound, No. 6398, "Morning Delivery," standing puppy w/a newspaper in its mouth, Lladro, Spain, 1997, 6 3/4 x 5" .. **$175**

Beagle

Beagle, sitting, Morten Studio, Chicago, 1940s (ILLUS.) **65**

Boston Terrier

Boston Terrier, sitting, typical marking of a mask, white mantle & white feet, this dog was spotted on an episode of the television program, "Dharma and Greg," Japan, 5 1/2 x 5 1/2" (ILLUS.) **35**

Boston Terrier

Boston Terrier, standing, Morton Studio, Chicago, 1940s, 6 x 5 3/4" (ILLUS.) **125**

Boxer Puppy

Boxer, puppy, fawn, sitting, Morten Studio, Chicago, 1940s, 2 1/4 x 3 3/4" (ILLUS.) **35**
Boxers, Classic Rose series, standing in show stance, Rosenthal, 7 1/8" h. **350**
Boxers, Classic Rose series, standing in show stance, Rosenthal, 8 1/4" h. **350**
Bulldog & kitten, No. 6417, "Unlikely Friends," sleeping, Lladro, Spain, 1997, 6 1/4 x 2" **130**

Chihuahua

Chihuahua, standing, black w/tan points, Morten Studio, Chicago, 1940s, 5 x 6" (ILLUS.) **150**

Cocker Spaniel

Cocker Spaniel, No. Stae 16 in series of 22 porcelain figures of Cocker Spaniel named Butch, sitting, black & white Butch w/tan & white son between his front legs, figurine by artist Albert Staehle, Goebel, West Germany, 3 1/2 x 3 1/4" (ILLUS.) **275**

Cocker Spaniel Puppy

Cocker Spaniel, sitting, small, puppy, buff w/tan spots, Morten Studio, Chicago, 1940s, 3 1/2 x 3" (ILLUS.) **35**
Collie, No. 6459, large, reclining, rough Collie w/puppy playing on its back, Lladro, Spain, 1997, 11 x 9" **300**
Dachshund, standing w/tail up, Hutschenreuther, ca. 1940s, 5 x 3 1/4" **225**

Doberman Pincher

Doberman Pincher, sitting, black & tan, Morten Studio, Chicago, 1940s, 5 1/2 x 5 3/4" (ILLUS.) **95**

Fox Terrier

Fox Terrier, character type, white w/tan face marking & black body spot, sitting holding a bone in its mouth, reproduction of a Royal Doulton dog, Japan, reproductions can be found on all the Royal Doulton character dogs, 3 1/2 x 3 3/4" (ILLUS.) **35**

Fox Terrier

Fox Terrier, sitting, white w/tan & black spots, red painted collar, Hutschenreuther, Germany, 5 1/2 x 5 3/4" (ILLUS.).............. **245**

German Shepherd, No. 6454, large, reclining, w/one puppy laying over its front paws & another puppy standing on its hind legs looking into mom's face, Lladro, Spain, 1997, 13 x 9" **500**

German Shepherd Puppy

German Shepherd, sitting, small, puppy, Morten Studio, Chicago, 1940s, 3 x 3 1/2" (ILLUS.)... **35**

German Shepherd

German Shepherd, standing, large, Morten Studio, Chicago, 1940s, 7 x 8 1/2" (ILLUS.) **85**

German Shepherd, standing, mounted on walnut base, G. Armani, 1987, 9 1/2" h........ **350**

Gort Spaniel

Gort Spaniel, white w/black markings, 2 1/2 x 3 3/4" (ILLUS.) **45**

Great Dane, No. 6558, sitting, harlequin, Lladro, Spain, 1997, 11 x 19"......................... **900**

Greyhound

Greyhound, metal, brass plated, reclining, has collar w/loop for chain attachment, 1910, 2 1/2 x 5 1/4" (ILLUS.) **45**

King Charles Spaniel, Cavalier, brown & white, mounted on base, by MacAlliter, Border Fine Arts, Scotland, 1986, 4" h. **85**

Pointer Puppy

Pointer, No. 269, sitting, puppy, white w/grey Boston-type face mask, Royal Copenhagen, Denmark, 6 x 8" (ILLUS.)........ **265**

Pointer on Base

Pointer, solid bronze, on base, Calvano, by S.C. Tarrant Co., New York, 5 x 11" (ILLUS.).. **650**

Poodle, No. 6337, lying, Lladro, Spain, 1997, 6 3/4 x 4".. **160**

Poodle, No. 6557, standing, white, playing w/ball, Lladro, Spain, 1997, 12 x 9"............... **550**

Poodle

Poodle, standing, large, white, in show trim, Morten Studio, Chicago, 1940s, 5 x 5 1/2" (ILLUS.)... **125**

Pug, No. 258, standing, by Jan Allen, ca. 1940s, 5 1/4" h. **350**

Saint Bernard

Saint Bernard, wood, hand carved, hand-tinted w/tan body spots, black collar w/neck flask, Switzerland, 6 1/2 x 4" (ILLUS.) **65**

Schnauzer

Schnauzer, sitting, grey w/tan points, Goebel, West Germany, 3 x 4 3/4" (ILLUS.) **65**

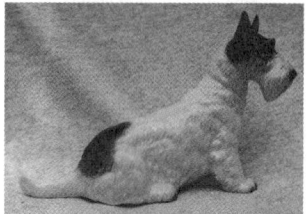

Scottish Terrier

Scottish Terrier, sitting, white w/black, tan & white face & black spot on rump, this dog is unusual in its coloration which is typical of a Fox Terrier not a Scottie, Rosenthal, Bavaria, 5 1/2 x 8 1/2" (ILLUS.) **325**

Skye Terrier

Skye Terrier, sitting, white w/grey markings & pink collar, Lladro, Spain, 1977, 6 x 6" (ILLUS.).. **350**

Smooth Dachshund Puppy

Smooth Dachshund, sitting, puppy, brown w/black points, one of a series in different poses, Rosenthal, Bavaria, 3 3/4 x 4 1/4" (ILLUS.).. **225**

Smooth Dachshund

Smooth Dachshund, standing, black & tan, Lefton, Japan, 1950s, 6 x 4" (ILLUS.)............. **45**

Smooth Fox Terrier

Smooth Fox Terrier, HN2513, this model was painted in two coat patterns, the version pictured, white w/black ears, is painted to resemble Ch. Chosen Don of Notts, comes in three sizes, pictured is the medium size, Royal Doulton, England, 7 x 6" (ILLUS.).............................. **1,200**

Smooth Fox Terrier

Smooth Fox Terrier, sitting, panting, white w/black body spots, pink tongue, Erphila, Germany, 1950s, 6 x 6" (ILLUS.) **85**

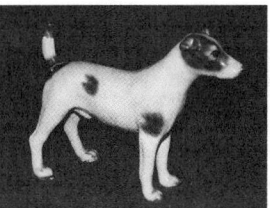

Smooth Fox Terrier

Smooth Fox Terrier, standing, small, cream w/blackish markings, this figure is more uncommon than the large 5" dog, Morten Studio, Chicago, 1930s, 3 3/4 x 4 1/2" (ILLUS.).................................... **125**

Smooth Fox Terrier

Smooth Fox Terrier, white w/dark brown face mask & spot at base of tail, standing on white plinth, small, Rosenthal, Bavaria, 4 1/2 x 3 3/4" (ILLUS.)................................ **450**

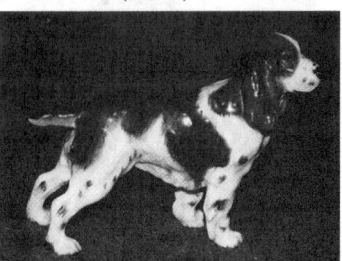

Spaniel

Spaniel, HN 2587, white w/tan markings, Royal Doulton, England, 3 3/4 x 5" (ILLUS.) **125**

Spaniel

Spaniel, white w/black markings & spaghetti-type furnishings, unsigned in style of Hardi-Arnita, figure would triple in value were it signed by Hardi-Arnita, 4 3/4 x 6 1/4" (ILLUS.) **45**

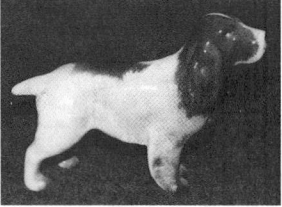

Spaniel

Spaniel, white w/tan markings, Beswick, England, 3 x 4" (ILLUS.)..................................... **45**

Terrier

Terrier, large, chalkware, white w/black face mask & body spots, Sealyham, 1940s, 10 x 7" (ILLUS.) **55**

Visla w/Red Collar

Visla, on green-tinted plinth, red collar, Hungary, 6 1/2 x 7 1/2" (ILLUS.)..................... **125**

West Highland Terrier

West Highland Terrier, white, playing w/a green slipper, Royal Copenhagen, Denmark, 3 x 5" (ILLUS.) **85**

Wire Fox Terrier Puppy

Wire Fox Terrier, character type, a running puppy w/a yellow & red ball in its mouth, Royal Doulton, England, 5 x 2 1/4" (ILLUS.) **95**

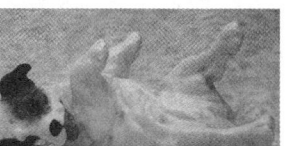

Wire Fox Terrier Puppy

Wire Fox Terrier, character type, white w/black & tan marked face & pink tongue, a puppy rolling on its back, Royal Doulton, England, 4 1/2 x 2" (ILLUS.)..................... **95**

Wire Fox Terrier

Wire Fox Terrier, plaster, cream w/tan markings, early primitive Morten Studio, Chicago, 1930s, 3 1/4 x 3 1/2" (ILLUS.).......... **95**
Wire Fox Terrier, standing, Goebel, West Germany, 5 x 4 1/2".. **65**

Wire Fox Terrier

Wire Fox Terrier, white w/black & tan markings, standing on green-tinted plinth, Rosenthal, Bavaria, 6 1/2 x 5" (ILLUS.)......... **275**

Wire Fox Terrier

Wire Fox Terrier, white w/dark brown face mask & spot at base of tail, standing on white plinth, small, Rosenthal, Bavaria, 3 1/2 x 3 1/2" (ILLUS.) **450**
Yorkshire Terrier, No. 6469, "Our Cozy Home," basket w/Terrier & puppy inside, Lladro, Spain, 1997, 6 x 5" **200**

Miscellaneous

Setter Book End

Book ends, bronze, depicting a Setter on point, base detailed w/foliage, pr. 5 1/2 x 8 1/2" (ILLUS. of one) **65**

Figural Dog Book Ends

Book ends, plaster, figural dog, Staffordshire-style, white w/black ears & black body spots, gold collar w/gold-painted tag, 1950s, pr. (ILLUS.) **65**

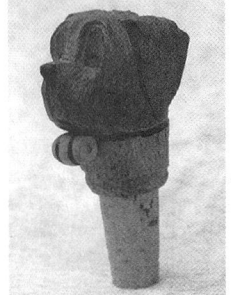

Saint Bernard Bottle Stopper

Bottle stopper on cork, Saint Bernard, carved wood, painted black eyes, nose & collar w/carved wooden flask, 3 1/2" h. (ILLUS.) **35**

Scottish Terriers Decanter

Decanter, clear glass w/red banding, decorated w/three Scottish Terriers w/"Three Canny Scots" underneath, Cambridge Glass Co., 3 1/2 x 10" (ILLUS.) **200**

English Setter Decanter

Decanter, ceramic, English Setter, S.N. 8, on a brown & green base w/pheasant in its mouth, inscribed "No. 100" on base, Ezra Brooks, Frankfort, Kentucky, Heritage China, 1970, 7 x 9 1/2" (ILLUS.) **65**

Cocker Spaniel Door Bell

Door bell, iron w/Cocker Spaniel, wall mounted, new reproduction, U.S.A. (ILLUS.) **45**

Wire Fox Terrier Door Knocker

Door knocker, brass, figural Wire Fox Terrier, back plate depicts a dog collar w/attached leash, 2 x 4" (ILLUS.) **65**

Boxer or Mastiff Doorstop/Book End

Doorstop/book end, iron, Boxer or Mastiff wearing collar, some may be painted depicting brindle body markings & white chest & mask, Bradley & Hubbard, marked w/B backstamp, 2 3/4 x 5 x 5 1/4" (ILLUS.) **85**

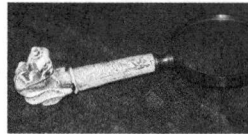

Magnifying Glass w/Dog Head Handle

Magnifiying glass, w/ivory dog head handle, 9" (ILLUS.) **75**

Mastiff Pen Holder

Pen holder, model of Mastiff, plaster, white, reclining, on a base w/black plastic pen holder, 4 1/2 x 7 1/2" (ILLUS.) **125**

Brass Plate w/Embossed Aztec Dog Figure

Plate, brass, embossed w/Aztec dog figure, inscribed "Federacion Canofila Mexicana A.C.," Mexico, 6 1/4" d. (ILLUS.) **35**

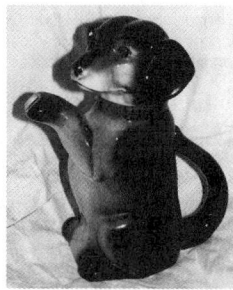

Figural Smooth Dachshund Teapot

Teapot, cov., figural Smooth Dachshund, No. 07038, black & tan w/cream highlights & red collar, Erphila, Germany, 5 x 8" (ILLUS.) **65**

DOLL FURNITURE & ACCESSORIES

Bed, cast iron, the high arched head- and footboard cast w/scrollwork & birds, the wide side rails cast w/scrolls, lions' heads & a pair of boys blowing trumpets, old white & blue repaint, late 19th - early 20th c., 16 1/2 x 22", 12 1/2" h. (glued crack in one end) **$220**

Victorian Doll Murphy Bed

Bed, Murphy-style, Victorian Eastlake design, painted black wood w/gilt trim in an Oriental design, closes to resemble a wardrobe, includes a feather mattress & pillows, late 19th c., small crack on top of drawer, 26" h. (ILLUS.).................................... **525**

Cradle, birch, the three-panel hood above a pierced, scrolled & dovetail-constructed cradle w/canted sides, the cornice w/inlaid oval panel, on rockers, old finish, northern New England, 1820, 8 x 21", 11 1/2" h.. **2,185**

Cradle, painted pine, the faceted chamfered hood on arched supports over the dovetailed box w/canted sides, molded baseboard on short shaped rockers, overall red & black paint simulating figured mahogany, probably Pennsylvania, first half 19th c. **1,020**

Doll carriage, painted wood & metal, a curved shallow sleigh-form wooden seat w/original yellow & orange paint w/blue, white & red striping, fitted in a metal frame w/folding sunscreen, two large wooden-spoked back wheels & two small wooden-spoked front wheels, all w/metal rims, late 19th c., 34" l. 26" h. (old leatherized cloth in top very worn) **330**

Doll cart, wood & wicker, a square wooden seat w/a round back fitted w/conforming woven wicker arched back curving down to form sides, a long upturned wooden pull handle at the front, fitted w/leather straps, on hard rubber-rimmed wire tires, wood painted red, wicker in natural, late 19th c., 28 1/2" l., 15" h. **480**

Dollhouse, Dutch Colonial, painted wood & fiberboard w/pressed cardboard window frames & shutters, off-white exterior w/green gambrel roof embossed in tile pattern, two stories, three rooms, opening back, A. Schoenhut, Philadelphia, Pennsylvania, ca. 1931, 15 1/4 x 22", 20" h. **1,000-1,200**

Dollhouse, Elegant Suburban Home, No. 575, lithographed paper over wood, marked "R. Bliss" on door, two stories, two rooms, opens from front, wraparound porch w/lathe-turned posts, three dormers w/lithographed sunburst designs projecting from steeply pitched roof, R. Bliss, Pawtucket, Rhode Island, ca. 1901, 10 x 18", 20 1/2" h.

.... **2,500-4,000**

Dollhouse, Flat Roof, lithographed US Gypsum hardboard w/plastic windows, Art Moderne-style w/flat roof, bay window & second story sun porch, two stories, four rooms, Rich, Clinton, Iowa, ca. 1936, 11 1/2 x 23", 15" h........................ **150-200**

Dollhouse, Flat Roof, No. 35, printed cardboard, die-cut & slotted for assembly, Art Moderne-style, two stories, three rooms w/awning covered patio, Built-Rite, Warren Paper Products, Lafayette, Indiana, ca. 1930s, 10 x 14 1/4", 11" h. (ILLUS. top next column) **100-125**

Flat Roof Dollhouse

Dollhouse, Flat Roof, No. 51, wood w/metal window, Art Moderne-style, two stories, five rooms plus two hallways, garage & sunroom, front opens in two sections, suntrap missing from roof, Tri-ang (Lines Brothers), England, ca. 1939, 11 x 26 1/2", 14" h.. **750-850**

Dollhouse, Folding Dollhouse, lithographed paper over wood & cardboard, marked under base w/company date & "Patent applied for," porch w/lathe-turned posts & lithographed railing, balcony extends across front of second story, Mosher, USA, ca. 1920s, 9 x 11 1/2", 16" h.... **1,200-1,400**

Dollhouse, Kiddie's Bungalow, lightweight cardboard, slot & tab assembly, Craftsman-style w/massive front porch & printed, exposed rafters, separate cardboard fence printed w/bricks & shrubbery, USA, ca. 1930s, 11 x 13", 8 1/2" h. **35-50**

Dollhouse, Kum-A-Part, pressed wood w/printed exterior & plain interior, doors & windows printed on & non-operable, two stories, four rooms, back-opening, Donna Lee, Woodburn, Manufacturing Co., Chicago, Illinois, ca. 1944, 8 x 21", 15" h. **75-100**

Dollhouse, Mansion, cardboard, Spanish-style w/faux tile roof & stucco exterior, two story main section w/one story wing, eight rooms, Tootsietoy (Dowst), Chicago, Illinois, ca. 1930, 18 x 27", 20" h...... **700-800**

Dollhouse, Midget Manor, No. 95, metal, lithographed inside & out, two stories, four rooms, Ohio Art, Bryan, Ohio, ca. 1949, boxed set includes 28 pieces of plastic furniture, 6 x 2", 4 1/4" h..................... **250**

Two-Room Colonial Dollhouse

Dollhouse, No. 14, wood w/metal non-opening windows, opens in two sections, two stories plus attic, six rooms plus central hallway w/staircase, original fireplaces, interior repapered, Tri-ang (Lines Brothers), England, ca. 1924, 20 x 55", 48" h. **1,800-2,000**

Dollhouse, No. 200, lithographed paper over wood, unmarked, two stories, two rooms, front opening, all details lithographed w/no cut-out windows or opening door, R. Bliss, Pawtucket, Rhode Island, ca. 1911, 4 x 7 3/4", 10" h. **600-750**

Dollhouse, No. 204, two-room colonial, lithographed paper over wood, unmarked, one story, two rooms, front opening, gambrel roof, two columns on front porch, opening double doors in center, R. Bliss, Pawtucket, Rhode Island, ca. 1911, 15 x 19 1/2", 17 1/2" h. (ILLUS. bottom previous page) **2,000-2.500**

Dollhouse, No. 462, Masonite, printed exterior & floors, two stories, four rooms, Jayline, Egg Harbor, New Jersey, ca. 1945, 8 x 19", 15" h. **75-100**

Dollhouse, No. 570, lithographed paper over wood, marked "R. Bliss" over door, two stories, two rooms, front opening. R. Bliss, Pawtucket, Rhode Island, ca. 1901, 4 x 7", 9 1/2" h. **700-800**

Dollhouse, No. 58, printed Masonite w/wood frame & metal windows, unmarked except for number above door, printed Tudor-style timbering on second story, two stories, four rooms, unprinted interior, Keystone, Boston, Massachusetts, ca. 1942, 9 x 26", 16 1/2" h. (corner of roof chipped) **75-95**

Dollhouse, Playhouse, heavy-weight laminated cardboard, shipped flat, customer assembly, two stories, six rooms, step-back design, open-fronted, printed interior depicts draped windows, book shelves, pictures, clocks, Strombecker, Moline, Illinois, ca. 1938, 14 1/2 x 26", 16 1/2" h. **200-250**

Dollhouse, Playsteel Colonial, steel lithographed inside & out, two stories, six rooms, no opening doors or windows, open-backed, National Can Corporation, New York, New York, ca. 1948, 12 x 22", 19" h. **75-100**

Doll-sized Painted Dry Sink

Dry sink, painted pine, a rectangular top w/a low splashback above the well & a work shelf at one end above a small drawer over a pair of flat cupboard doors

w/exposed hinges, simple bracket feet, white porcelain knobs, old brown over tan comb graining, 8 x 13 1/2", 13 1/4" h. (ILLUS.) **825**

Washboard, wooden frame w/top rectangular wooden panel above the molded redware pottery brown-glazed insert, 6 5/8" w., 13 3/8" h. (top backboard replaced) **578**

DOLLS

Also see: BARBIE DOLLS & COLLECTIBLES & STEIFF TOYS & DOLLS.

A.B.G. (Alt, Beck & Gottschalck) bisque solid dome shoulder head lady, marked "912 - No 4," large oval brown eyes, multi-stroke brows, open-closed mouth w/white space & accent lines between lips, original blonde mohair wig, cloth body w/leather arms, individually stitched fingers, red lower legs w/leather boots, nicely dressed in peach two-piece outfit, matching bonnet, antique underclothing, 16 1/2" (upper torso & arms recovered) **$725**

A.B.G. bisque socket head girl, marked "ABG - 1362 - Made in Germany - 2 1/2 - 10," set blue eyes w/real lashes, feathered brows, open mouth w/four upper teeth, pierced ears, synthetic blonde wig, jointed wood & composition body w/stamped mark, wearing white lace-trimmed dress, underclothing, cotton socks, old leather shoes, bonnet, 21" (eyes replaced, body repainted) **275**

A.M. (Armand Marseille) bisque socket head girl, marked "A 15 M," blue sleep eyes, feathered brows, open mouth w/accent lips, original blonde mohair wig, jointed wood & composition body, wearing pink nylon dotted Swiss dress w/attached slip, pants, original socks & pink cloth shoes, 33" (tiny chip at inner right eye, right eyeball cracked) **550**

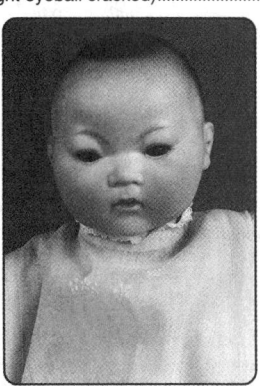

Armand Marseille Oriental Baby Doll

A.M. bisque flange head Oriental baby, marked "A.M. - Germany - 353- 4," solid dome head, dark brown sleep eyes, softly brushed brows, painted black hair, closed mouth, cloth body w/"frog" legs, celluloid hands, wearing old blue embroidered baby dress, matching slip, undershirt, diaper & blue booties, general soil & aging on body w/restitching around neck, 15" (ILLUS.) **760**

A.M. bisque socket head baby, marked "Armand Marseille - Germany - 992 - A. 12. M.," blue sleep eyes w/real lashes, feathered brows, open mouth w/accented lips & two upper teeth, old brown h.h. wig, composition baby body, wearing new mint green baby dress trimmed w/lace, underclothing, old green silk booties, 22" (light face rubs, body repainted, repair to one toe) **260**

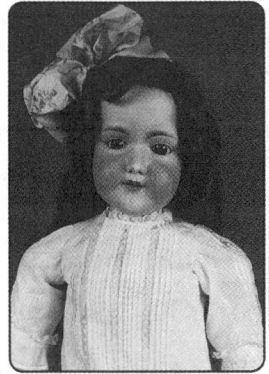

Large Armand Marseille Girl Doll

A.M. bisque socket head girl, marked "A 20 M - Germany," blue sleep eyes, feathered brows, open mouth w/well outlined lips & four upper teeth, replaced h.h. brown wig, jointed wood & composition body, wearing antique white child's dress, underclothing, socks, corduroy shoes, firing lines above ears, body repainted, upper torso repaired, left hand fingers cracked, 42" (ILLUS.) **800**

A.M. bisque socket head girl, marked "Made in Germany - Armand Marseille - 390n - A. 13. M.," brown sleep eyes w/real lashes, molded & feathered brows, open mouth w/accented lips & four upper teeth, original dark brown h.h. wig w/long curls, jointed wood & composition Heinrich Handwerck-marked body, wearing white factory chemise, underclothing, original socks & pink high button boots, 30 1/2" (inherent discoloration flaw in one ear, eyes loose) **525**

A.M. bisque socket head "googlie" girl, marked "Germany 323 - A. 6/0 M.," large blue sleep eyes to side, single-stroke brows, closed smiling mouth, original blonde mohair wig in original curls, five-piece composition chubby body, wearing possibly original white dress, antique underclothing, old socks & new leather shoes, fine pink ribbon-trimmed cape & matching hat, very faint hairline from outside corners of left eye, body repainted, 9" (ILLUS. top next column) **1,000**

Armand Marseille "Googlie" Girl

Alexander (Madame) baby, marked "Alexander" on head, also marked on various tags, vinyl head w/large painted blue eyes, multi-stroke brows, molded & painted brown hair, unjointed latex baby body, wearing original pink organdy dress, matching bonnet & underclothing, rayon socks & pink side snap shoes, w/aged box, 10" **475**

Alexander (Madame) "Binnie Walker," hard plastic head w/blue sleep eyes & real lashes, single-stroke brows, eye shadow, closed mouth, original auburn saran wig, hard plastic body w/jointed knees, not removed from trunk to check markings, wearing original tagged black leotard w/felt flower appliques, pink felt skirt w/black braid trim, socks & white skates, in original wooden trunk w/white metal covering & original wardrobe & accessories, mint, 15" **4,600**

Madame Alexander Cissy Doll

Alexander (Madame) "Cissy," marked on dress tag "'Cissy' by Madame Alexander," hard plastic head, blue sleep eyes w/real lashes, closed mouth, original blonde wig in original set, hard plastic fashion-type body jointed at knees, vinyl arms joined at elbows, high heel feet, wearing original turquoise taffeta dress, black suede jacket, pink taffeta panties &

matching half slip, stockings, black high heels w/elastic straps, black flowered hat w/veil, missing afternoon bag, 21" (ILLUS.).. **850**

Alexander (Madame) Emelie Dionne toddler, marked on back & on clothing tag, composition head, brown sleep eyes w/real lashes, feathered brows, closed mouth, molded & painted brown hair, composition five-piece toddler body, wearing original lavender romper, tagged lavender snowsuit w/pants, coat & bonnet, replaced shoes, 14" (minor craze lines)... **425**

Alexander (Madame) Glamour Girl Victorian, marked on dress tag, hard plastic head w/blue sleep eyes w/real lashes, multi-stroke brows, closed mouth, original blonde wig in original set, hard plastic body jointed at shoulders & hips, walking mechanism, wearing original pink taffeta dress w/black velvet bodice, matching hoop slip & panties, net stockings, original black strap shoes, black hat trimmed w/flowers & tulle ties, flower bouquet accent at wrist, w/Madame Alexander hat box, 18" **1,900**

Fine Madame Alexander Judy Doll

Alexander (Madame) "Judy," marked "Alexander" on back, also marked on foil wrist tag & tag on slip, composition head, amber sleep eyes w/real lashes, mauve eye shadow, closed mouth, original elaborate brown mohair wig w/flower decorations, composition five-piece body, wearing elaborate peach taffeta dress w/pinch-pleated insets at bottom, pink half slip & matching panties, pink satin shoes, flower bouquet, face has crazing & fine cracks in finish, top layer of composition cracked & lifted on back of head under wig, heavy crazing on body, 21" (ILLUS.).. **2,500**

Alexander (Madame) "McGuffey Ana," marked "Princess Elizabeth - Alexander Doll Co.," composition head, brown sleep eyes w/real lashes, feathered brows, open mouth w/four upper teeth, original blonde h.h. wig in braids & bangs in curls, five-piece composition body, wearing original tagged red & white dotted

Swiss dress w/rickrack trim & red taffeta jacket, original underclothing, socks & two snap shoes, straw hat w/red cherries, in original marked box, 19" **1,075**

Alexander (Madame) "Pamela," marked "Alexander 19©63," also marked tag, vinyl head, blue sleep eyes w/molded lashes, feathered brows, closed mouth, original blonde wig attached w/velcro, five-piece hard plastic body, wearing original pink tutu, stockings, ballet shoes & contained in original wardrobe case w/two extra dresses, black apron, flowers, two wigs attached to lid, pantaloons, slip, blue dress, socks & shoes, curlers, yellow nightgown attached to cardboard insert in bottom of case, unplayed with, 12", the set **650**

Alexander (Madame) "Scarlett," marked on dress tag, composition head, green sleep eyes w/real lashes, eye shadow, feathered brows, closed mouth, original black h.h. wig in original set, five-piece composition body, wearing original dress w/flower print & striped skirt, green velvet bodice, matching green velvet bonnet w/plume, original hoop slip & matching pantalettes, socks & green leatherette snap shoes, 17" (eyes are cloudy) **1,050**

Madame Alexander Sonja Henie Doll

Alexander (Madame) "Sonja Henie," marked "Madame Alexander - Sonja Henie" on back of head, also marked on dress tag, composition head w/brown sleep eyes & real lashes, single-stroke brow, open mouth w/six upper teeth, original blonde h.h. wig in original set, five-piece composition body, wearing original red skating dress w/white bodice, red taffeta panties, white skates, some light fading, few tiny flakes off lip, 17" (ILLUS.) **625**

All-bisque boy, illegible mark, bisque socket head w/set dark pupiless eyes, feathered brows, closed mouth w/accent line between lips, original blond mohair wig, five-piece all-bisque body jointed at shoulders & hips, molded & painted socks & one-strap shoes, in knitted outfit w/cap, 7" **825**

All-bisque girl, marked "1" on head, bisque head w/stiff neck, blue sleep eyes, feathered brows, open smiling mouth w/accent line on lips & four upper teeth, original brown mohair wig, all-bisque body jointed at shoulders & hips, molded & painted socks & black one-strap shoes, wearing antique white dress w/lace inserts, slip, old straw bonnet, 7 1/2" (tiny flake on lower rim of one eye, few small chips at leg opening)...................................... 450

All-bisque swivel-neck girl, marked "1" on head & limbs, brown sleep eyes, closed somber mouth, blonde mohair wig, loop strung jointed shoulder & hips, wearing long black stockings & blue dress, 6 1/2" (small chip top edge right leg) 690

All-china jointed lady, painted features w/blue eyes, red line above eyes, molded black center part hair w/short vertical curls, head & torso one-piece, slant-sided peg-jointed china limbs, bare feet, wearing period hand-made white kid boots, aqua silk taffeta & silk dress, white cotton underclothing, mid-19th c. (surface chips on feet & top of limbs, minor speckling, glaze roughness on right arm) 4,025

American Character Betsy McCall, marked on box & boxes for extra outfits, hard plastic head, blue sleep eyes w/molded lashes, single-stroke brows, closed mouth, original dark wig, hard plastic child body w/jointed knees, wearing original nylon teddy, socks & shoes, contained in original box w/two booklets & two original boxed outfits, 8" 1,050

Arranbee composition girl, embossed mark on head, composition head w/brown sleep eyes, closed mouth, blonde mohair wig, jointed neck, shoulders & hips, wearing printed faille antebellum dress, hat & parasol, trimmed w/lace & velvet ribbons, organdy hoop & pantaloons, green shoes, 14 1/4" (right eye crazed, some discoloration of underclothes).. 316

Arranbee Nancy Lee, marked "R&B," hard plastic head w/blue sleep eyes & real lashes, lightly feathered brows, closed mouth, original auburn mohair wig in original set, five-piece hard plastic body, red nail polish, wearing original red plaid taffeta dress w/white sleeves & red ribbon ties, white panties, original rayon socks & red leatherette skates, plaid hair bow matches dress, unplayed-with in original labeled box w/original neck cardboard, 20" (box aged & w/some repairs & damage)... 500

Averill (Georgene) Bonnie Babe, marked "Copr. by Georgene Averill 7005 13652 - Germany" on head, also on tag on bib, solid domed bisque flange head, brown sleep eyes, softly brushed brows, open mouth w/molded tongue, lightly molded & painted brown hair, cloth body w/composition arms & legs, wearing original blue romper, tagged lace-trimmed bib &

matching bonnet, original long cotton socks & black shoes, 16" (no teeth, tongue cracked, body aged, paint flaking on arms, cracks & peeling on legs) 400

Babyland Rag Doll, brown painted eyes, distinctive mouth, blonde mohair wig, cloth body jointed at shoulders & hips, wearing a white dotted Swiss dress & lace bonnet, early 20th c., 17" (some facial wear & soil, bangs only for hair) 518

Bahr & Proschild bisque socket head baby, marked "B & P - 0 - 585 - 4 - Germany," brown sleep eyes, feathered brows, open mouth w/accented lips & two upper teeth, brown mohair wig, composition baby body, wearing antique white baby dress, slip, diaper & socks, 25" (replaced cloth tongue, general body wear, arms repainted, some repair) 325

Bed doll, molded composition shoulder head w/painted eyes & mouth & painted wood cigarette, blonde fiber wig, cloth body, composition arms & legs w/high-heeled shoes, wearing blue rayon satin & lace outfit & bonnet, 1930s, 27" (some paint wear on neck & shoulders) 403

Bed doll, dressed as a Flapper, a pressed & painted felt face w/wooden cigarette, greenish blonde silk floss wig, cloth body & limbs, wearing printed cotton sateen lounging pajamas, yellow felt shoes, 1920s, 28" h. 431

Scarce Beecher Baby Doll

Beecher Baby, stockinette head w/painted & needle-sculpted features, applied ears, looped blonde yarn hair, stockinette body jointed at shoulders, hips & knees, wearing an antique white baby dress, antique underclothing, knit wool knee-high socks, crocheted bonnet, small hole on left temple, 20" (ILLUS.)............................ 2,000

Belton-type bisque socket head girl, marked "0," head flat on top w/two stringing holes, set blue eyes, single-stroke brows, closed mouth w/accented lips, pierced ears, antique blonde mohair wig in long braids tied together at ends, jointed wood & composition French-style body w/separate ball at shoulders, elbows, hips & knees, wooden lower arms w/straight wrists, wearing pale pink French-style dress trimmed w/lace & ribbon, matching hat, underclothing, socks & new leather shoes, 9" (head sits low in neck opening, wear on finish) **1,075**

Bergmann (C.M.) bisque socket head baby, marked "C.M. - Bergmann - 2," blue sleep eyes w/real lashes, feathered brows, open mouth w/two upper teeth & tongue on eye weight, composition baby body, wearing a white romper trimmed w/red, socks & red leatherette shoes, 12" h. (body poorly repainted) **175**

Bergmann Bisque Head Girl

Bergmann (C.M.) bisque socket head girl, marked "C.M. Bergmann - Waltershausen - 1916 - 9," brown sleep eyes w/real lashes, feathered brows, open mouth w/four upper teeth, original brown mohair wig, jointed wood & composition body, wearing ecru antique-style dress, underclothing, new cotton socks, old cloth shoes, right little finger missing, tape residue around neck & on body, 25" (ILLUS.).. **250**

Fine Circle-Dot Bru Lady

Bru bisque swivel head lady, impressed w/circle on back of neck & "Depose" on front shoulder plate & "Bte. SGDG" on front crown, named "Zepherine," deep blue-lined paperweight eyes, open-closed mouth, pierced ears, shoulder plates w/classic molded breasts, synthetic blonde wig, kid body, remains of Bru

paper label, early Bru bisque hands, wearing period cotton lawn summer dress & new handmade dress, fine dark firing imperfection along crease of chin, body repairs, hands repaired & over-painted, 15" (ILLUS.)................................ **9,775**

Bru bisque swivel shoulder head lady, marked "E," blue paperweight eyes, closed smiling mouth, pierced ears, light brown h.h. wig, fully-articulated Bru wooden body, wearing period oversized gunmetal & cream woven silk taffeta dress, 15" (missing thumbs)...................... **4,025**

Bru bisque swivel shoulder head lady, marked "Depose" on forehead & "E" on back of head, tri-color eyes, closed smiling mouth, pierced ears, original dark blonde mohair wig, firmly stuffed ungussetted cloth body w/kid arms, wearing a period blue & red woven cotton outfit w/long train, white underclothing, late 19th c., 16" (tiny ear flakes)...................... **3,738**

Bye-Lo Baby, marked "Copr. by Grace S. Putnam," also stamped on body & w/original button, solid dome bisque flange head w/blue sleep eyes, softly brushed brows, closed mouth w/accent line between lips, lightly molded & painted hair, cloth body w/'frog' legs, celluloid hands, wearing old white baby dress, matching slip, old knee-high booties, lovely crocheted bonnet, 20" **600**

Bye-Lo Baby, all-bisque, marked "20-12" on back, label on chest w/"Bye-Lo Baby © Germany - G.S. Putnam," bisque head w/stiff neck & painted blue eyes, soft brows indicated, closed mouth, lightly molded & painted hair, bisque baby body jointed at shoulder & hips, probably original handmade clothing, 5"........................... **400**

Bye-Lo Baby, marked "Copr. by Grace S. Putnam - Made in Germany," also stamped on right front torso, bisque solid domed flange head w/blue sleep eyes, softly brushed brows, closed mouth, lightly molded & painted brown hair, cloth body w/celluloid hands & "frog" legs, wearing original dress & slip, 14" (minor inherent roughness at top of head, body slightly aged, shoulders restitched around neck) **425**

Cameo Kewpie, marked "Kewpie - Designed and Copyright by Rose O'Neill - A Cameo Doll" on paper wrist tag, composition head w/painted side-glancing eyes, molded & painted dash brows, closed smiling mouth, molded & painted tufts of hair, five-piece chubby composition body w/starfish hands, wearing original blue check sunsuit, original socks & shoes, contained in original marked & illustrated box, 12" (unplayed-with, some overall crazing) **175**

Celluloid boy toddler, marked "Schutz Marke (heart) - 42 - Germany," & "Made in Germany" on back, celluloid socket head w/painted blue eyes, feathered brows, open-closed mouth w/two upper teeth, molded & painted brown hair, fully jointed celluloid toddler body w/diagonal hip joints, wearing a two-piece boy's suit, argyle socks, brown imitation leather shoes, 16".......................... 295

China 'flat-top' lady, stamped "7" on back, china shoulder head w/painted blue eyes w/red accent line, single-stroke brows, closed mouth w/accent line between lips, molded & painted center part blonde hair w/vertical curls, cloth body w/kid lower arms, wearing possibly original beige silk dress w/lace trim, antique underclothing, socks & newly made shoes, 24" (body aged & soiled, glued splits in kid) 450

China 'flat-top' lady, china shoulder head w/painted blue eyes w/red accent line, single-stroke brows, closed mouth w/accent line between lips, molded & painted black hair w/white center part & vertical curls, Goldsmith cloth body w/red corset as part of body, red lower legs w/red leather boots made as feet, wearing antique beige & white striped dressing gown, antique underclothing, 25" (body aged & soiled, some wear, upper arms replaced).. 375

China 'flat-top' shoulder head lady, black center part hairdo w/curls, blue painted eyes, cloth body, kid lower arms, wearing period white cotton undergarments, Germany, late 19th c., 27"...................................... 374

Fine Large China Head Lady

China shoulder head 'covered wagon' lady, unmarked, head w/pink tint, painted brown eyes w/red accent line, single-stroke brows, closed mouth, molded & painted center pair hair w/vertical side curls, cloth body w/leather lower arms, joints at hips & knees, wearing rose print two-piece outfit, antique underclothing, socks & black leather shoes, minor rubs, mended areas on torso & legs, new upper arms, 30" (ILLUS.)................................. 1,350

China shoulder head 'covered wagon' lady, pink tinted head w/black center part hairdo, blue painted eyes, shaded eyebrows, cloth body w/long china arms, wearing a period bronze silk brocade dress & original white cotton undergarments, mid-19th c., 22" 748

China shoulder head girl, marked "3," African-American w/ethnic facial features & tightly curled black hair, painted eyes

w/unglazed white, brown cloth body, wearing period yellow cotton print dress, white cotton undergarments, late 19th c., 16" 920

Door of Hope bride, marked "Made in China" on wrist tag, carved wood head, painted dark eyes, single-stroke brows, closed mouth, painted black hair w/carved braided bun, carved & painted flowers around bun, cloth body, carved wooden hands, wearing orignal red embroidered bride's outfit w/beaded head piece, long tassels on sides, original underclothing, embroidered slippers, 11" 1,350

Door of Hope groom, marked "Made in China" on wrist tag, carved wooden head, painted dark eyes, single-stroke brows, closed mouth, painted black hair w/side part, cloth body w/carved wood hands, wearing original deep purple robe w/embroidered square on front, matching hat, original underclothing, black cloth high boots, 11" h. (deep blue of underclothing faded to beige where it is exposed, light aging on facial coloring)......... 1,100

Door of Hope male mourner, marked "Made in China" on paper tag, "Kimport Dolls, Independence, MO, This Doll Was Made in China" on tag on clothing, carved wooden head w/painted eyes, single-stroke brows, closed mouth, painted black hair w/side part, cloth body w/carved wooden hands, wearing original clothing made of coarse fabric tied w/reed belt, linen underclothing, hat & shoes, wooden stick w/strips of fabric in right hand, 11 1/2"....................................... 1,425

Door of Hope widow, marked "Made in China" on paper tag, carved wooden head, painted eyes, single-stroke brows, closed mouth, painted black hair w/carved bun, cloth body w/carved wooden hands, wearing original clothing made of coarse fabric tied w/reed belt, linen underclothing, hood partially covering face, & shoes, 11"................................... 1,400

E.D. Open Mouth Girl

E.D. bisque socket head girl, marked "E 8 D - Depose," set brown eyes, feathered brows, open mouth w/accented lips & six upper teeth, pierced ears, original brown h.h. wig, jointed wood & composition French body w/jointed wrists, wearing lace & ribbon-trimmed factory chemise, pink crocheted socks, old cloth shoes, minor repairs on knees, 19" (ILLUS.).. 800

Effanbee Baby Grumpy, marked "Effanbee Dolls, Walk - Talk - Sleep," also tag on shorts, composition shoulder head, painted blue eyes to side, single-stroke brows, closed pouty mouth, molded & painted blond hair, cloth body w/composition arms & legs from above the knee, wearing original tagged tan felt shorts, multicolored shirt w/felt trim, original socks & shoes & Effanbee heart button, 14" (flaking & touch up on back of head, other light flaking, left eye touched up).......... 300

Effanbee Baby Tinyette Quintuplets, marked "Effanbee" on back of head, "Effanbee Baby Tinyette" on backs, also marked tags, each w/a composition head w/painted brown eyes, single-stroke brows, closed mouths, molded & painted brown hair, composition bent-limb baby body, wearing original long white organdy baby dresses, slips, diapers, organdy lace-trimmed bonnets, each w/original glass bottle w/black rubber nipple & pink ribbon, contained in original case w/tray & pink & white blanket trimmed w/pink ribbon rosettes, 7", the set......................... 1,200

Effanbee Betty Bounce, marked "Effanbee 'Patsy-Ann' © #1283558" on body, marked bracelet, composition head w/green sleep eyes & real lashes, feathered brows, open mouth w/two upper & two lower teeth, molded tongue, original blonde skin wig, five-piece composition child body w/bent right arm, wearing original red & white dress w/large white collar, original underclothing, socks & leatherette shoes, red felt coat & tam, 18"............. 375

Effanbee Patseyette, marked "Effanbee - Patsyette Doll" on back, tagged dress, bracelet & wrist tag, composition head, painted brown eyes to side, painted upper lashes, closed mouth, molded & painted brown hair, five-piece composition body w/bent right arms, wearing tagged original red dress, matching romper, original socks & red tie leatherette shoes, red hair ribbon, in original Pastyette box, 9" (brows missing, light crazing on hair, minor flakes, some damage on box) 500

Effanbee Patsy Ann, marked "Effanbee - "Patsy Ann" © Pat. #1283558," composition head, green sleep eyes w/real lashes, single-stroke brows, closed mouth, molded & painted brown hair, five-piece composition child body w/bent right arm, wearing original red & white organdy dress w/embroidered silk collar, white two-piece organdy underclothing, original socks w/red trim, red side snap shoes, 19" (very light crazing, minor finger flakes).. 500

Effanbee Patsy Lou Doll

Effanbee Patsy Lou, marked "Effanbee Patsy Lou" on back, also marked on bracelet & dress tag, composition head w/brown sleep eyes w/real lashes, feathered brows, closed mouth, molded hair under brown mohair wig, five-piece composition child body, wearing tagged white organdy dress, underwear & hat w/blue polka dots, rayon socks, black snap shoes, light face crazing, eyes cloudy, light body wear & flakes, 22" (ILLUS.).......... 675

Effanbee Patsy Ruth Doll

Effanbee Patsy Ruth, marked "Effanbee Patsy Ruth" on head, also marked on shoulder plate & metal heart bracelet, composition head on composition shoulder plate, green sleep eyes w/real lashes, feathered brows, closed mouth, brown mohair wig, cloth mama doll body w/composition arms & lower legs, nicely redressed in blue organdy copy of original dress, replaced underclothing, new socks & shoes, light crazing on face & body, 26" (ILLUS.)... 900

Effanbee Skippy, marked "Effanbee Skippy © P.L. Crosby," composition head w/wooden neck plug, painted blue eyes to side, peaked brown painted upper lashes, closed mouth, molded & painted brown hair, cloth body w/composition arms & black painted legs w/molded socks & shoes, wearing original soldier uniform, belt & hat, 14" (eyes touched-up, light rubs & edge flaking, missing shirt & tie & piece of leather belt) **525**

French bisque head Fashion Lady, blue paperweight eyes, closed mouth w/smile, pierced ears, original blonde mohair wig, fine long bisque arms, kid over wood upper arms jointed at shoulder, kid body w/stamp on front for Paris shop of Simonne, original commerical couturier costume of bluish green striped sheer cotton w/long train, blue leather boots, 17 1/2" (shoulder plate broken, boots missing soles) **4,025**

Frozen Charlie, china head w/blue painted eyes, black side part hair w/curls & brush marks, stiff neck on finely detailed china body w/hands outstretched, marked "10" on sole of foot, 10 1/4" (finger missing, chip on right hand) **1,093**

Frozen Charlie, china head w/pink tint, painted blue eyes, two-tone brows, closed mouth w/accent line, lightly molded & painted blond hair, unjointed pink tint china body w/arms extended, well defined finger & toenails, 11" **550**

Frozen Charlie, pink tint china head w/stiff neck, painted blue eyes, heavy black shading on lids, closed mouth w/accent line, molded & painted blond hair, unjointed china body w/arms held out, hands closed in fists, finger & toe nails outlined, wearing knit one-piece underwear, 15 1/2" **525**

Fulper bisque socket head baby, marked "Fulper - Made In - U.S.A. - A 11," set brown eyes, feathered brows, open mouth w/accented lips & two upper teeth, antique blonde h.h. wig, composition baby body, wearing old white baby dress w/smocking around top, underclothing, socks & shoes, 19" (head coloring uneven, some rubs, body repainted & flaking, crack on one leg) **225**

Gaultier (F.) bisque socket head Fashion Lady, marked "8" on head & "F.G." on left shoulder, bisque shoulder plate, bisque paperweight eyes, heavy feathered brows, closed mouth w/accented lips & accent line, pierced ears, coarse brown h.h. wig, kid fashion body w/gussets at elbows, hips & knees, inidividually stitched fingers & toes, wearing factory chemise trimmed in lace & maroon ribbon, antique underclothing, antique teal blue fashion outfit w/skirt, jacket trimmed w/black velvet ribbon & quilted cape also trimmed w/black velvet ribbon, stockings & antique leather high-button boots, 26" (some tiny inherent red lines, tiny split on inside foot seam, sawdust settled in hip gussets) **2,300**

Greiner papier-maché head lady, marked w/1858 label, black center part hair, exposed ears, painted blue eyes, cloth body, brown kid arms, wearing period brown wool dress, green & black leather child's shoes, 22" (nose & upper lip chips, wear to hair, head loose, one arm detached) **431**

H. Handwerck Large Bisque Head Girl

Handwerck (Heinrich) bisque socket head girl, marked "109-12 - DEP. Germany," body also marked, brown sleep eyes, heavy feathered brows, open mouth w/accent lips & four upper teeth, pierced ears, original blonde mohair wig, jointed wood & composition body, wearing probably original ecru silk dress w/ruffles & ribbon trim, antique underclothing, socks & high button shoes, 22" (ILLUS.) **875**

Heinrich Handwerck Girl Doll

Handwerck (Heinrich) bisque socket head girl, marked "69-6 - Germany (upside down) - Handwerck," also marked on right hip, blue sleep eyes, heavy feathered brows, open mouth w/shaded & accented lips, four upper teeth, pierced ears, original blonde mohair wig in ringlets, jointed wood & composition body, wearing probably original blue polka dot dress w/lace trim, underclothing, old socks & black leather shoes, 15 1/2" (ILLUS.) **625**

Handwerck (Heinrich) bisque socket head girl, marked "Germany - Heinrich - Handwerck - Simon & Halbig - 0 1/2," brown head w/brown sleep eyes, feathered brows, open mouth w/four upper teeth, black mohair wig, brown wood & composition body w/original finish, re-dressed in ecru French-style dress w/matching bonnet, new underclothing, stockings & shoes, 16 1/2" (left knee ball replaced)...... **800**

Handwerck (Heinrich) bisque socket head girl, marked "109 - 10 1/2x - Germany - Handwerck - 2 1/4," brown sleep eyes, feathered brows, open mouth w/distinct modeling, accented lips & four upper teeth, pierced ears, original blonde mohair wig, jointed wood & composition body, wearing antique white embroidered dress, antique underclothing, new replaced socks & shoes, feather-trimmed bonnet, 19" **450**

Handwerck (Heinrich) bisque socket head girl, marked "Germany - Heinrich Handwerck - Simon & Halbig - 5" & "Excelsior Germany 6" on lower back, brown sleep eyes, molded & feathered brows, open mouth w/accented lips & four upper teeth, pierced ears, original brown h.h. wig, jointed wood & composition body, wearing an antique white dress, antique underclothing, replaced socks & shoes, 28" (tiny rub on nose, tiny flake on each earring hole, arms repainted, missing left index finger, left fingers reglued) **425**

Handwerck (Max) bisque socket head girl, marked "421 - 7 - Germany - Handwerck 1," blue sleep eyes, feathered brows, open mouth w/well accented lips, four upper teeth, pierced ears, original blonde mohair wig, jointed wood & composition body, nicely dressed in antique white dress w/lacy ruffle around neck, underclothing, socks & old shoes, red straw bonnet, 17" (teeth replaced, hands repainted) **300**

Hertel, Schwab & Co. bisque socket head toddler, marked "made in Germany - 152 - 5," pale blue sleep eyes, feathered brows, open mouth w/accented lips & two upper teeth, original short blonde mohair wig, jointed composition toddler body w/joints at shoulders, elbows, wrists & diagonal hip joints & knees, wearing antique white baby dress, off-white jacket trimmed in light blue, knit underclothing, socks & oilcloth shoes, 14" (body repainted)...... **340**

Hertel, Schwab & Co. bisque solid dome socket head baby, marked "151 - 2," blue sleep eyes, feathered brows, open mouth w/two upper teeth, lightly molded & brush-stroked brown hair, bent-limb composition baby body, wearing bluish green lace-trimmed romper, rayon socks, new shoes, 11" (worn body finish looks washed, cracks on back of body, minor body damage)...... **400**

Heubach (Ernst) bisque socket head baby, marked "Heubach - Koppelsdorf - 399 - D.R.G.M. - Germany," painted brown solid dome head w/dark pupiless sleep eyes, molded & indicated brows, closed mouth, pierced ears, painted

black hair, brown composition baby body, wearing old red wool felt skirt & jacket w/embroidered numbers "13," white lace shirt front only, slip, 13" (flaking around neck & back of head, some touch-up) **275**

Heubach (Ernst) bisque socket head baby, marked "Heubach - 300-3 - Germany," blue sleep eyes w/real lashes, feathered brows, open mouth w/accented lips & four upper teeth, original brown mohair wig, composition bent-limb baby body, wearing fragile antique white baby dress trimmed w/lace, matching bonnet, slip & booties, 17" **250**

Heubach (Gebruder) bisque socket head girl, marked "8192 - Germany - Gebruder Heubach (sunburst) - G. - 2/0 1/2 H," set brown eyes, feathered brows, open mouth w/four upper teeth, replaced brown synthetic wig, jointed wood & composition body, wearing antique white dress, white pinafore, antique underclothing, new socks, black oilcloth shoes, 14 1/2" (body repainted w/some flaking & cracks) **300**

Heubach (Gebruder) Dolly Dimple, marked "6 - Heubach (in square) Germany," bisque shoulder head w/brown sleep eyes, feathered brows, open mouth w/four upper teeth, old brown replacement wig, kid body w/rivet joints at elbows, composition lower arms, wearing antique white organdy dress, underclothing, old black socks, new shoes, body labeled "American Beauty - Copyright by Sears, Roebuck and Co. - Germany," 17 1/2" (body aged & soiled, arms probably old replacements) **375**

Heubach (Gebruder) "googlie" girl, marked "10342 - 4 - 0 - Heubach (in square) Germany," bisque socket head w/blue sleep eyes to side, single-stroke brows, closed mouth, mohair blonde wig, five-piece composition body w/molded & painted yellow socks & brown one-strap shoes, wearing antique white dress & slip, panties & straw hat, 7 1/2" (arms probably replaced) **700**

Huret china shoulder-head man, marked "Brevet D'Inv: S.G.D.G. Maison Huret, Boulevard Montmartre, 11 Paris: Exposition Universelle de 1855, Napoleon III Empereur," painted blue eyes w/lightly molded eyelids, multi-stroke brows, closed mouth w/accented lips & accent line between lips, original blond skin wig, rare gutta percha body jointed at shoulders, elbows, hips & knees, wearing probably original shirt-type chemise, vest & straw hat, brown suit made from antique fabric, replaced socks & old shoes, 17" (general body repairs & repaint) **17,500**

Huret china shoulder-head woman, illegible stamp on kid attaching head to body, painted blue eyes w/lightly molded eyelids, multi-stroke brows, closed mouth w/accented lips & accent line between lips, antique brown mohair wig, wooden body jointed at shoulders, elbows, wrists, hips & knees, swivel joints in upper arms & legs, wearing antique black & white two-piece outfit, antique underclothing, socks & boots, black straw hat, 17" (inherent flaw high on forehead, flakes off painted body, pieces broken off knee & right elbows, toes broken off) **7,000**

Fine All-Original Betsy McCall Doll

Ideal Betsy McCall, marked "McCall Corp." on head & "Ideal Doll - P-90" on back, also marked wrist tag w/original attached curlers, vinyl head w/brown sleep eyes w/real lashes, feathered brows, closed smiling mouth, original brunette saran wig, five-piece hard plastic child body, wearing original red cotton dress trimmed w/white, attached half slip, matching panties, original socks, black vinyl shoes, in original labeled box w/wrist tag, curlers, McCall's pattern for apron, unplayed-with, 14" (ILLUS.) **725**

Ideal Toni, marked "Ideal Doll - Made in U.S.A." on head, marked tag on dress, hard plastic head, blue sleep eyes w/real lashes, feathered brows, eye shadow, closed mouth, original blonde nylon wig in original set, five-piece hard plastic body w/vinyl arms, wearing original pink & white pique dress, original panties, socks & shoes, contained in apparently original shipping box w/cardboard inserts & booklet, 14" **925**

Jerri Lee Cowboy Doll

Jerri Lee cowboy, marked "Terri Lee - Pat. Pending," a Gene Autry tag on pants & Terri Lee tag on pants & vest, hard plastic head, large painted brown eyes, single-stroke brows, closed mouth, original brown skin wig, five-piece hard plastic body, wearing original cowboy outfit w/tagged Gene Autry gold satin shirt trimmed w/silver piping, tagged blue pants, brown oilcloth boots, tagged brown leather vest, brown leather chaps w/beige leather fringe, brown leather cuffs w/leather fringe, leather holster w/silver buckle, gold plastic gun in holster, large red felt cowboy hat, leather on one cuff deteriorated, shirt slightly soiled, gun probably replaced, 16"(ILLUS.) **600**

Jumeau (E.) bisque head girl, marked "Depose Tete Jumeau - Bte. S.G.D.G. - 5," cork pate, blonde wig, blue paperweight eyes, pierced ears, outlined closed mouth, on compostion jointed body w/straight wrists, body stamped "Jumeau - Medaille d'Or - Paris," wearing a red velvet silk dress w/matching bonnet, 14" **2,875**

Jumeau (E.) bisque socket head girl, marked "Depose - Tete Jumeau - Bte. S.G.D.G. 7" on head & "Jumeau - Medaille d-Or Paris" on lower back, bulbous blue paperweight eyes, feathered brows, closed mouth w/accented lips, pierced ears, blonde mohair wig, jointed wood & composition body w/straight wrists, separate balls at shoulders, elbows, hips & knees, wearing fine antique blue dress w/ribbon trim, antique underclothing, black lace stockings, antique leather shoes, 16 1/2" (touch-up or repaint on body, repair of touch-up around neck socket) **3,950**

Jumeau (E.) bisque socket head girl, marked "E. 6 D. - (artist marks)," blue paperweight eyes, heavy feathered brows, closed mouth w/accented lips, pierced ears, auburn mohair wig, marked Jumeau jointed wood & composition body w/jointed wrists, redressed in elaborate peach silk dress & bonnet trimmed w/much lace & ribbons, underclothing, socks & shoes, 16 1/2" (inherent dark flaw in upper left forehead, some touch-up on body) **2,500**

Jumeau (E.) bisque socket head girl, marked "758 - 7," blue sleep eyes, heavy feathered brows, open mouth w/outlined lips & six upper teeth, pierced ears, brown h.h. wig, jointed wood & composition marked Jumeau body w/jointed wrists, non-working or missing voice box, wearing a green silk dress w/net overlay, matching bonnet, underclothing, socks & antique cloth shoes, 17" (upper lashes missing, some flaking & wear on body) **875**

Jumeau (E.) bisque socket head girl, marked "Depose E. 8 J. - H," stamped blue mark on lower body, bulbous blue paperweight eyes, feathered brows, closed mouth w/white space between accented lips, pierced ears, brown h.h. wig, jointed composition body w/straight wrists & working mama/papa pull string crier, wearing fine antique embroidered white dress, antique underclothing, socks & shoes, bonnet w/flower decorations, two small firing lines in left ear, body well refinished, 19" (ILLUS. below)... **4,900**

Lovely Jumeau Girl

Jumeau (E.) bisque socket head girl, marked "Depose - Tete Jumeau Bte. - S.G.D.G. - 9," blue paperweight eyes, heavy feathered brows, closed mouth w/white space between lips & accent lines, pierced ears, brown h.h. wig, jointed wood & composition body w/jointed wrists & Jumeau mark, redressed in beige & red sailor-type dress, antique underclothing, original socks & marked shoes, beige & red striped bow in hair, 20" **4,300**

Jumeau Girl in Original Dress

Jumeau (E.) bisque socket head girl, marked "Depose - Tete Jumeau - 10," marked on lower back & shoes also, large blue paperweight eyes, heavy

feathered brows, long painted upper & lower lashes, closed mouth w/accented lips, pierced ears, original blonde mohair wig, jointed wood & composition Jumeau body w/jointed wrists, wearing original flowered factory dress, antique underclothing, antique blue socks, marked Jumeau shoes, small inherent firing crack at rim of left ear, several areas of touch-up on body, flaking on arms, hands mostly repainted, 21 1/2" (ILLUS.)` **3,300**

K (star) R (Kammer & Reinhardt) bisque socket head baby, marked "n K*R - Simon & Halbig - 126 - Germany," blue sleep eyes, feathered brows, open mouth w/two upper teeth & spring tongue, original blond mohair wig, composition bent-limb baby body, wearing a yellow & white knit romper, replaced socks & shoes, 10" (minor inherent roughness on seam below ear, fine cracks in finish, arms may be slightly larger than body) **410**

K (star) R bisque socket head baby, marked "K*R - Simon & Halbig - 126/11 - Germany," brown flirty eyes w/tin lid & real lashes, feathered brows, open mouth w/two upper teeth & molded tongue, synthetic wig, composition bent-limb baby body, well dressed in lace-trimmed baby dress & bonnet, antique underclothing, socks & booties, 24" (left middle finger replaced).................................... **675**

K (star) R bisque socket head baby, marked "K*R - Simon & Halbig - 126 - 62," blue flirty eyes w/tin lids, feathered brows, open mouth w/two upper teeth & spring tongue, mohair blonde wig, composition bent-limb baby body, wearing antique white baby dress & cape & slip, 24" (very minor damages & wear)................. **375**

*K*R Bisque Head Girl*

K (star) R bisque socket head girl, marked "K*R 101 -34," painted blue eyes w/lightly molded eyelids, single-stroke brows, closed pouty mouth, original blonde mohair wig, jointed wood & composition Kammer & Reinhardt body, wearing possibly original white lace-

trimmed dress, pink slip, antique underclothing, antique socks & shoes, antique
bonnet, 13 1/2" (ILLUS.)............................ **2,500**
K (star) R bisque socket head girl,
marked "K*R - Simon & Halbig - 76," blue
sleep eyes w/real lashes, molded &
feathered brows, open mouth w/accent-
ed lips & four upper teeth, pierced ears,
replaced blonde wig, jointed wood &
composition body, nicely redressed in
lavish pale blue silk dress w/lace, ribbons
& flowers, matching bonnet, new underclothing, socks & shoes, 29" (general
body wear, repairs or touch-ups at joints,
lower arms & hands repainted) **600**
K (star) R bisque socket head girl,
marked "Simon & Halbig - K*R 85," blue
sleep eyes w/remnants of real lashes,
molded & feathered brows, open mouth
w/accented lips & four upper teeth,
pierced ears, original brown mohair wig,
jointed wood & composition Kammer &
Reinhardt body, wearing an antique
white dress w/eyelet trim, antique underclothing, original pink socks, no shoes,
33" (minor firing line behind ears, general
body wear).. **1,450**
K (star) R bisque socket head girl,
marked "Simon & Halbig - K*R - 85," set
blue eyes, molded & feathered brows,
open mouth w/four upper teeth, pierced
ears, antique brown h.h. wig, jointed
composition body, wearing antique white
child's dress, antique underclothing,
socks & newer black one-strap shoes,
33" (finish on arms, legs & around neck
socket very worn, hands repainted) **1,000**
**K (star) R bisque socket head girl tod-
dler,** marked "K*R - Simon & Halbig - 126
- Germany -32," brown flirty sleep eyes
w/tin lids, feathered brows, open mouth
w/two upper teeth & spring tongue, original brown mohair wig, five-piece toddler
body w/diagonal hip joints, working crier,
wearing antique organdy baby dress, underwear combination, new socks &
shoes, 13" **600**
K (star) R bisque solid dome baby,
marked "K*R 100 - 50," brushed brown
hair, painted blue eyes w/molded lids,
single-stroke brows, open-closed mouth,
bent-limb composition baby body, well
dressed in antique long embroidered
baby dress, slip & undershirt, 19" (tiny
flake on right side of neck opening) **550**
Kamkins cloth swivel head girl, marked
"Kamkins - A Dolly Made to Love - Patented by L.R. Kampes - Atlantic City
N.J.," painted blue eyes, single-stroke
brows, closed mouth, original brown mohair wig, cloth body tab jointed at shoulders, stitch-jointed hips, wearing blue &
white flowered dress, matching romper,
cotton sockets, replaced leather shoes,
gold coat & matching hat, 19" (overall
wear to finish, soil & aging on body, part
of left hip restitched) **575**

Kathe Kruse Boy Doll

Kathe Kruse boy, IX Deutsches Kind, partial
mark on left foot "Kathe Kruse - 031836,"
oil-painted cloth swivel head, painted
brown eyes, single-stroke brows, closed
mouth, h.h. blond wig, cloth body jointed
at shoulders & hips, wearing original red
print top w/red collar & pockets, red
shorts, replaced socks, blue leather tie
shoes, touch-up around left eye & on face,
water stain on right arm, 14" (ILLUS.) **200**
Kestner (J.D.) all-bisque "googlie" girl,
marked "112 -1," blue glass sleeping
eyes to right, watermelon smiling mouth,
original brown mohair wig, bisque limbs
jointed at shoulders, elbows & hips,
brown molded shoes, w/three outfits including white wool flannel coat & tam, 5" . **3,220**
Kestner (J.D.) Baby Jean, marked "J.D.K.
- made in 6 Germany," & "Made in Germany" on neck, solid dome bisque socket
head w/brown sleep eyes w/real lashes,
feathered brows, open mouth w/two upper teeth & molded tongue, lightly molded & brush-stroked hair, composition
bent-limb Kestner baby body, wearing
new white romper & two-piece outfit
w/pants & tunic-type top, 11" (left big toe
damaged) **675**
Kestner (J.D.) bisque flange head baby,
marked "A.M. Germany - 518 - 5 - 1/2 K,"
solid dome head w/brown sleep eyes,
softly brushed brows, open mouth w/two
upper teeth, lightly molded & painted
hair, composition baby body, wearing antique baby dress, slip, diaper, socks &
booties, 16" **340**
**Kestner (J.D.) bisque shoulder head Gib-
son Girl,** uplifted head w/brown sleep
eyes w/real lashes, single-stroke brows,
closed mouth w/accent line between lips,
original blonde mohair wig over plaster
pate, kid body w/rivet joints at elbows,
hips & knees, bisque lower arms, wearing antique eyelet blouse, white skirt,
black velvet ribbon at waist, slip, pants,
socks & antique black leather shoes,
black hat w/glass fruit decoration, 20"
(short inherent line at side of nose, wig
sparse, wear & mending on body)............. **1,400**
Kestner (J.D.) bisque shoulder head girl,
marked "Dep 19 (?) - 154," brown sleep

eyes, molded & feathered brows, open mouth w/accent lines on lips & four upper teeth, original h.h. brown wig, kid body w/jointed wood & composition arms, rivet joints at hips & knees, wearing lovely antique white dress trimmed w/lace & tucks, antique underclothing, black socks & new leather black shoes, 22 1/2" (real lashes missing on left eye, body aged & slightly soiled) **300**

Kestner (J.D.) bisque shoulder head girl, marked "Dep 154. 13" on back of head & "J.D.K. Germany 1/2 Cork Stuffed" on front of torso, blue sleep eyes, heavy feathered brows, open mouth w/accented lips & four upper teeth, original blonde mohair wig, kid body w/wooden & composition arms, rivet joints at hips & knees, finely dressed in antique white dress trimmed w/lace & tucks, antique underclothing, socks & brown high-button shoes, 26" (body lightly soiled & aged, minor hip repair) **400**

Kestner (J.D.) bisque socket head baby, marked "K. made in Germany - 14 - 211 - J.D.K.," brown sleep eyes, feathered brows, open-closed mouth, brown mohair wig, bent-limb baby body, wearing a long white antique baby dress, antique underclothing, newer bonnet, 18" (minor inherent lines, old body repaint, repair & touch-up around neck socket) **325**

Kestner (J.D.) bisque socket head baby, marked "J.D.K. - 20," solid dome head w/blue sleep eyes, feathered brows, open mouth w/accented lips & two lower teeth, lightly molded & brush-stroked hair, composition Kestner baby body, wearing antique white lace-trimmed baby dress, slip, diaper & booties, 25" (minor damages & repairs).. **575**

Kestner "Hilda" Baby

Kestner (J.D.) bisque socket head baby "Hilda," marked "H. made in 12 - Germany - 245 - J.D.K. jr. - 1914 - © - Hilda - ges. gesch. N. 1070," brown sleep eyes, feathered brows, open mouth w/accented lips & two upper teeth & tongue, blonde h.h. wig, composition Kestner baby body, wearing antique white baby dress w/pink & blue smocking, slip, diaper, new booties, old knit bonnet, faint

hairline from crown in front, right little finger repaired, touch-up, 16" (ILLUS.)......... **1,600**

Fine Kestner Boy Toddler Doll

Kestner (J.D.) bisque socket head boy toddler, marked "A. made in Germany 5 - 211 - J.D.K.," blue sleep eyes, feathered brows, open-closed mouth w/accented lips & shading, original blond mohair wig, fully-jointed toddler body does not have diagonal hip joints, wearing a two-piece outfit tagged by Helen Huchison 1953, cotton socks, tie leatherette shoes, replaced right knee ball, 11" (ILLUS.) **950**

Kestner (J.D.) bisque socket head girl, marked "made in Germany C 160 - 7 - Dep.," brown sleep eyes, feathered brows, open mouth w/lightly accented lips, four upper teeth, h.h. blonde wig, jointed wood & composition body, wearing fine antique red low-waisted dress, antique underclothing, replaced socks & shoes, red straw hat w/flower trim, 16" (sleep eyes loose in sockets, touch-ups on body, hand & feet repainted) **750**

Kestner No. 128 Girl Doll

Kestner (J.D.) bisque socket head girl, marked "H. made in Germany 12 - 128," set brown eyes, feathered brows, closed mouth w/accent line between lips, auburn mohair wig, jointed composition body w/separate balls at shoulders, elbows, hips & knees, straight wrists, wearing antique white dress w/lace trim, antique underclothing, old replaced socks & shoes, repair at neck edge, few cracks on torso finish, 19" (ILLUS.)........................ **2,100**

Kestner (J.D.) bisque socket head girl, marked "L 1/2 made in Germany 15 1/2 - 146," brown sleep eyes, heavy feathered brows, open mouth w/shapely modeling & outlined lips, four upper teeth, brown h.h. wig, jointed wood & composition marked Kestner body, wearing antique blue print dress, antique underclothing, new black socks & shoes, 28" **725**

Kestner (J.D.) bisque socket head girl, marked "L made in Germany 15 - 146," brown sleep eyes, feathered brows, open mouth w/accented lips & four upper teeth, synthetic brown wig, jointed wood & composition body, wearing antique white dress, antique underclothing, socks & old shoes, 28" (finger repairs, finish cracking on a seam, repair on right torso) **500**

Kestner (J.D.) bisque socket head girl, marked "M made in Germany - 16 - 171 - 6 1/4," painted brown head, brown sleep eyes w/real lashes, feathered brows, open mouth w/six upper teeth, replaced black wig, painted brown wood & composition body, wearing gold silk bead-trimmed dress, pale yellow underclothing, fine antique socks & brown leather shoes, 28" (teeth replaced, slight color wear)... **450**

Kestner (J.D.) bisque socket head girl, marked "M made in Germany - 16 - 164," brown sleep eyes w/real lashes, heavy feathered brows, open mouth w/finely accented lips, four upper teeth, brown synthetic wig, jointed wood & composition body, dressed in an antique white dress trimmed w/lace & tucks, antique underclothing, socks & old baby shoes, 30" h. (minor inherent firing line behind ear, finish on body is washed & pale, hands repainted, minor repair at hip joints) **900**

Kestner (J.D.) bisque socket-head girl, marked "M 1/2 - 16 1/2 - 146," blue sleep eyes, open mouth, blonde mohair wig, fully articulated composition Kestner body, wearing a Victorian child's printed pink striped cotton pouf-sleeved dress, white underclothing, 31"........................... **1,093**

Kestner (J.D.) bisque solid dome socket head baby, marked "made in Germany 19," & "Made in Germany" stamped on rear torso, brushed light brown hair, set brown eyes, feathered brows, open mouth w/two upper teeth & molded tongue, lightly molded hair, composition bent-limb baby body, wearing antique pink baby romper, undershirt, 25" (rubs on cheeks & top lip, body repainted w/cracks)... **400**

Kestner (J.D.) Century Baby, marked "Century Doll Co. Kestner Germany," solid dome bisque flange head w/blue sleep eyes, softly brushed brows, open-closed

mouth w/two upper teeth & molded tongue, lightly molded & painted brown hair, cloth body w/non-working crier, composition hands, disk-jointed hips, wearing possibly original pink organdy dress & matching bonnet, diaper, booties, w/three extra handmade dresses, sweater & matching bonnet, bib & two blankets, 16" (overall body soil & wear at neck edge)... **500**

Kley & Hahn bisque socket head baby, marked "K & H (in banner) 525 - 4," & "Germany" on left shoulder, solid dome head w/blue intaglio eyes w/molded lids, feathered brows, open-closed mouth, lightly molded & brush-stroked blond hair, composition bent-limb baby body, wearing pink knit outfit w/matching bonnet, 12" (fine inherent line above upper lip, light overall body wear, repair at right leg at hip)... **300**

Kley & Hahn Walkure bisque socket head girl, marked "250 - K.H. - Walkure - 4 3/4 - Germany," brown sleep eyes w/real lashes, molded & feathered brows, open mouth w/accented lips & four upper teeth, replaced brown wig, jointed wood & composition body, wearing a white dress w/pale blue print, antique underclothing, socks & antique brown leather shoes, 25" (general wear on body, repairs at joints & finger)..................................... **375**

Konig & Wernicke Character Girl

Konig & Wernicke bisque socket head character girl, marked "K&W - 9," blue sleep eyes w/real lashes, feathered brows, open mouth w/outlined lips, two upper teeth & tongue, brown h.h. wig, jointed composition body w/straight wrists, wearing fine antique white dress w/tucks & lace inserts, antique underclothing, new socks & shoes, upper arms & legs replaced w/old parts, repair on both knee joints, 20" (ILLUS.) **650**

Kuhnlenz (Gebruder) bisque shoulder head girl, marked "G.K. 10-27," blue stationary eyes, closed mouth, Belton-type solid crown, pierced ears, new brown h.h. wig, kid body, bisque hands, wearing period maroon cotton satin dress, white cotton underclothing, 18 1/2"... **460**

Kuhnlenz (Gebruder) bisque socket head girl, marked "41-22," set brown eyes, heavy feathered brows, open mouth w/two molded upper teeth, pierced ears, mohair wig, jointed wood & composition body, wearing a factory chemise, underclothing, new socks & shoes, 12" (rub on nose, tiny flake at earring hole, body lightly touched-up).. **420**

Kuhnlenz (Gebruder) bisque socket head girl, marked "30,5 - Gbr. 165 K - 9 - Germany - 9," blue sleep eyes w/real lashes, molded & feathered brows, open mouth w/accent lips & four upper teeth, replaced brown synthetic wig, jointed wood & composition child body, wearing antique white dress w/tucks, blue print pinafore, antique underclothing, socks & white leather shoes, 27" (light wear to finish, repairs at knee sockets & right heel) **375**

Lenci boy, all-felt body jointed at neck, shoulders & hips, felt head w/painted brown eyes, light brown rooted mohair wig, wearing original felt shirt & shorts, knitted sweater & leg warmers w/black kid shoes, marked on bottom of left foot, 1920s, 17" (slight discoloration on exposed felt).. **460**

Lenci boy mannequin, marked "Lenci - Turin - Italy" on wooden base of torso & "Kirsch & Reale Inc. - 167 Madison Ave. - New York City," pressed felt swivel head, painted brown side-glancing eyes, multi-stroke brows, closed mouth, applied felt ears, brown mohair rooted hair, felt-covered wooden torso, felt-covered metal or wooden arms & legs, metal ball attachment at shoulders, metal assembly allows for posing, wearing antique shirt w/wide eyelet collar & cuffs, checkered two-piece suit w/short pants, socks & leather one-strap shoes, 38" (rather faded, few tiny moth holes, fingers repaired).. **1,650**

Lenci "Modestina" Girl

Lenci "Modestina" girl, illegible marks on feet, pressed felt swivel head, large surprised-looking eyes to the side, molded & lightly feathered brows, painted upper lashes, open-closed two-tone mouth, original curly brown mohair wig, five-piece body w/cloth torso, upper torso felt-covered, felt arms & legs, wearing original felt dress w/colorful plaid skirt, felt-trimmed organdy sleeves & bloomers w/ruffles, gold felt flower-trimmed bonnet, underclothing, white cotton socks & green felt shoes, light aging & slight discoloring, 20" (ILLUS.) **1,000**

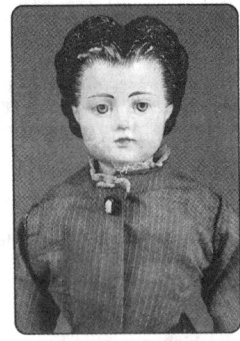

M & S. Superior Papier-maché Lady

Papier-maché head lady, marked "2018 - M & S - Superior," painted blue eyes, multi-stroke brows, closed mouth w/accent line between lips, molded & painted black hair w/brush strokes around face, cloth body w/leather lower arms, red & white striped lower legs, red leather boots, wearing original green dress trimmed w/brown, old underclothing, some wear, touch up & minor repair on shoulder plate, 18" (ILLUS.) **425**

Papier-maché milliner's model, papier-maché shoulder head w/painted brown eyes, single-stroke brows, closed mouth, molded & painted center part black hair w/wavy sides brought back into braided bun, wearing old pink print dress & pants, 13 1/2" (light wear, crack on side of shoulder plate)... **475**

Papier-maché shoulder head lady, a delicate face w/black pupiless glass eyes, brown h.h. wig over black-painted solid crown, kid body & limbs, wearing a period Empire white cotton dress & undergarments, early 19th c., 28" (damage, head repainted) **489**

Papier-maché shoulder head man, a small head w/short black male hairstyle, brown painted eyes, cloth body & limbs, period brown pants, cotton shirt & red leather shoes, Germany, 1840s, 21" (some paint loss to eyes, wear on face & hair, body leaking sawdust)........................... **748**

Parian head lady, unmarked lightly tinted bisque socket head, glass eyes, feathered brows, closed mouth, molded & painted café au lait hair w/black bow & jewelry tiara, kid body w/bisque lower arms & cloth lower legs, gussets at hips & knees, wearing white-trimmed blouse, antique white & blue skirt, underclothing, old socks & white leather tie-up shoes, 19" (ILLUS. top next page) **1,425**

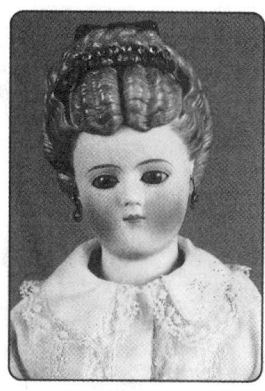

Parian-head Lady Doll

Parian shoulder head boy, molded & painted hair & features, cloth body & legs, kid hands, wearing handmade wool & cotton dress, 15" **403**

Patty Jo Doll by Terri Lee

Patty Jo hard plastic girl, marked "Terri Lee - Pat. Pending," brown hard plastic head, large side-glancing painted brown eyes, heavy arched brows, closed mouth, original coarse black wig, five-piece brown hard plastic body, wearing black polished cotton dress, tagged Terri Lee slip, cotton panties, rayon socks, white tie leatherette shoes, minor wear, 16" (ILLUS.) **1,150**

Poupee Peau bisque head straight-necked lady, marked "1," bisque shoulder plate w/wooden plug & kid lining to accommodate neck, pale blue paperweight eyes, multi-stroke brows, painted upper & lower lashes, closed mouth w/accented lips, pierced ears, replaced short blonde wig, kid fashion-type body w/individually stitched fingers, gussets at hip & knees, dressed in mid-calf beige plaid dress w/wide ruffle around bottom

of skirt, gold braid trim, antique underclothing & socks, no shoes, 13 1/2" (head color different than shoulder plate, chip back of one earring hole, general wear & soil on body) **1,550**

Poupee Peau bisque socket head lady, marked "3" on back of head, bisque shoulder plate, set light blue eyes, multi-stroke brows, closed mouth w/accented lips, pierced ears, original blonde mohair wig, kid fashion-style body w/gussets at elbows, hips & knees, individually stitched fingers, wearing fine olive green & gold striped silk two-piece outfit, antique underclothing, high button boots, 17" (body may be later, mend on right wrist seam) **3,000**

R & B Littlest Angel Doll

R & B vinyl head girl, marked "R & B Doll Co." on back, wrist tag marked "R & B Littlest Angel, Kneels, Walks, Sits, Stands, Turns Her Head, R & B Doll Co. Inc., New York City" on wrist tag, vinyl head w/blue sleep eyes w/molded lashes, single-stroke brows, closed mouth, rooted blonde saran hair, hard plastic body w/jointed knees, wearing original panties, socks & shoes, in original box w/two booklets & wrist tag, original price tag, boxed outfit including red & white play outfit, matching hat, socks & black shoes, near mint, 10 1/2" (ILLUS.) **300**

Revalo bisque socket head boy toddler, marked "Germany - Revalo - 22-7," blue sleep eyes w/real lashes, feathered brows, open-closed mouth w/two lower teeth, blond mohair wig, jointed wood & composition toddler body w/straight legs & diagonal hip joints, wearing clothing of antique fabric, antique underclothing, replaced socks & shoes, 16 1/2" (tiny hairline just over edge of rim, body repainted, light cracking in finish of legs & torso) **350**

Revalo by Ohlhaver bisque socket head girl, marked "8 Revalo 3 - Germany," blue sleep eyes w/real lashes, feathered brows, open mouth w/four upper teeth,

Revalo Bisque Head Girl

replaced blonde h.h. wig, jointed wood & composition body, redressed in maroon flowered dress, new underclothing, socks & shoes, slight wear, 24 1/2" (ILLUS.)... **625**

S.F.B.J. bisque head girl toddler, marked "S.F.B.J. 236 - Paris -4," blue sleep eyes w/real lashes, feathered brows, open-closed mouth w/two upper teeth, h.h. wig, jointed wood & composition toddler body w/diagonal hip joints, wearing replaced red lace-trimmed nylon dress, underclothing, red corduroy coat & hat, new socks & shoes, 13" (small hairline from firing line in left crown, touch-up on body, some body chips) **400**

S.F.B.J. bisque socket head girl, marked "S.F.B.J. - 301 - Paris - 9," & paper label on back, set blue eyes, molded & feathered brows, open mouth w/accented lips & four upper teeth, replaced black wig, jointed wood & composition French body, wearing white organdy lace-trimmed dress, underclothing, new socks & white leather shoes, 22" (three small flakes at neck socket, real lashes missing, some body flaking)... **375**

S.F.B.J. bisque socket head girl, marked "SFBJ - 301 - Paris - 10," set blue eyes w/real lashes, molded & feathered brows, open mouth w/accented lips & six upper teeth, pierced ears, blonde h.h. wig, jointed wood & composition French body w/jointed wrists, wearing new pink ribbon-trimmed dress, antique underclothing, socks, marked antique shoes, & French-style bonnet, 23" (very minor damages)... **600**

S.F.B.J. bisque socket head girl walker, marked "25 - France - S.F.B.J. - 301 - Paris - 10," head attached to walking mechanism, blue sleep eyes w/real lashes, molded & feathered brows, open mouth w/four upper teeth, pierced ears, replaced brown wig, jointed wood & composition walking, kiss-throwing body, redressed in light blue French-style dress, antique underclothes, new black socks & shoes, 22 1/2" (ILLUS. top next column)....... **525**

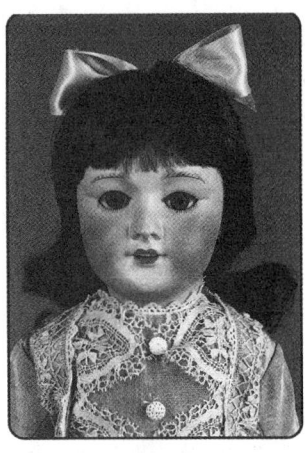

S.F.B.J. Girl Walker

S.F.B.J. Jumeau mold bisque socket head girl, marked "21 - S.F.B.J. - 301 - Paris" & "Tete Jumeau - 11" label on back of head, blue sleep eyes w/real lashes, molded & feathered brows, open mouth w/accented lips & six upper teeth, pierced ears, h.h. brown wig, jointed wood & composition marked Jumeau body w/jointed wrists, wearing new pink lace-trimmed dress, underclothing, possibly original socks, old shoes, 24" (two minor neck flakes, minor earring hole flake, lower legs repainted, some flaking) **550**

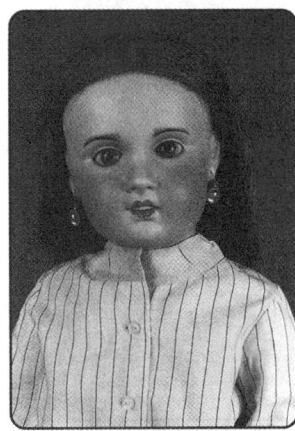

S.F.B.J. Jumeau Mold Girl

S.F.B.J. Jumeau mold bisque socket head girl, marked "21 - S.F.B.J. - Paris - 13," blue sleep eyes, feathered brows, open mouth w/accented lips & six upper teeth, pierced ears, brown h.h. wig, jointed wood & composition French body, wearing antique two-piece striped outfit, underclothing, new black socks & shoes, flakes at earring holes, real lashes missing, some body flaking & touch-up, 28" (ILLUS.) **750**

Bruno Schmidt Toddler Boy

Schmidt (Bruno) bisque socket head boy toddler, marked " & P 0" & "BSW (in heart) 2072 - 5" on back of head, brown sleep eyes, feathered brows, closed mouth w/accented lips & dark area between lips, original brown mohair wig, fully-jointed wood & composition toddler body w/diagonal hip joints, wearing fine old knit outfit w/knit top, sweater, pants, & cap, socks & replacement shoes, two small flakes off eye liner, hands may be old replacements, some wear, old repaint & finish chips, 19 1/2" (ILLUS.) **750**

Schmidt (Franz) bisque socket head baby, marked "F.S. & Co. - 1271-35 - Z - Deponiert," solid domed head w/blue sleep eyes, single-stroke brows, open-closed mouth w/two upper teeth, lightly molded & brush-stroked hair, composition baby body, wearing lovely antique white long baby dress trimmed w/lace & tucks, 14" (tiny fleck near rear neck, body crazed, hip sockets damaged from stringing) **375**

Schoenau & Hoffmeister bisque socket head girl, marked "5 - Germany - S PB (in star) H - 1906 - No. 11," brown sleep eyes w/real lashes, molded & feathered brows, open mouth w/accented lips, four upper teeth, replaced brown wig, jointed wood & composition body, redressed in new white antique-style dress trimmed w/lace & tucks, new underclothing, new socks & high button boots, 28 1/2" (upper legs repainted, minor finish crack, flakes & touch-ups) **325**

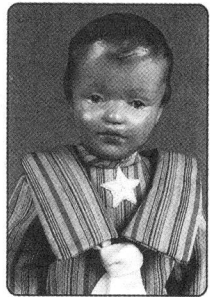

Carved Wood Schoenhut Boy

Schoenhut boy, marked "Schoenhut Doll - U.S.A." on partial label, carved wooden head w/molded & carved hair, brown intaglio eyes, feathered brows, closed mouth, painted brown hair, spring-jointed wooden body w/joints at shoulders, elbows, wrists, hips, knees & ankles, redressed in blue striped two-piece sailor-type suit, old blue cotton socks & white leatherette shoes, slight touch up, hands & feet very worn, 14" (ILLUS.) **800**

Schoenhut Toddler Boy Walker

Schoenhut boy toddler walker, labeled on head & back, wooden socket head, painted blue eyes, single-stroke brows, closed mouth, original blond mohair wig, wooden toddler body jointed at shoulders & hips w/construction for walking, wearing possibly original navy two-piece dress & jacket, lace-trimmed cotton underclothing, old replaced socks & shoes, very light discoloration, rubs, light wear, 14" (ILLUS.) **575**

Schoenhut character girl, impressed mark on back, carved wood head w/molded hair parted in middle w/braids around head held w/blue bow at back, blue painted intaglio eyes, open-closed somber mouth, wearing period pink & white cotton dress & slip, original Schoenhut tan stockings & kid boots, w/provenance, ca. 1911, 16" (painted chips on hair, bow, face, neck front & right hand) **690**

Schoenhut Girl with Pouty Mouth

Schoenhut girl, incised on back "Schoenhut Doll - Pat. Jan. 17, 11, U.S.A. - & Foreign Countries," wooden socket head w/brown intaglio eyes, faded brows, closed pouty mouth, blonde mohair wig, spring-jointed wooden body w/joints at shoulders, elbows, wrists, hips, knees & ankles, redressed in blue & white check dress, slip, lace-trimmed knit union suit, original cotton socks w/bound hole in bottom, white leather shoes w/holes for stand, w/round metal stand, few minor craze lines in face, 19" (ILLUS.) 900

Schoenhut Carved Wood Girl

Schoenhut girl, marked on back "Schoenhut Doll - Pat Jan. 17, '11 U.S.A. - & Foreign Countries," wooden socket head w/brown intaglio eyes, multi-stroke brows, closed mouth, carved & painted brown hair w/carved pink ribbon, spring-jointed wooden body, redressed in Schoenhut-style dress, slip, knit union suit, socks & shoes, small touch-up, light wear, left little finger missing, 16" (ILLUS.)... 900

Fine All-Original Shirley Temple Doll

Shirley Temple, marked "Cop. Ideal - N & T Co.," composition head w/hazel sleep eyes w/real lashes, feathered brows, open mouth w/six upper teeth, original blonde mohair wig in original set, five-piece composition child body, wearing original blue organdy pleated dress w/pink ribbons & NRA tag & Shirley Temple button, original underwear combination, socks & center snap shoes, in original box w/photo of Shirley Temple holding a Shirley doll, unplayed-with, general light crazing, 20" (ILLUS.) 1,700

Shirley Temple, marked "Ideal Doll - ST - 12," vinyl head, hazel eyes w/molded lashes, single-stroke brows, open-closed mouth w/six upper teeth, rooted blonde hair in original set, five-piece vinyl marked body, wearing tagged black velvet dress w/white nylon sleeves & neck, pink taffeta slip & panties, original socks & black plastic shoes, w/seven extra outfits, 1957, 12" (slightly yellowed, stain around waist from elastic)................................ 475

Simon & Halbig bisque socket head girl, marked "550 Germany - G - Simon & Halbig - S&H," brown sleep eyes, feathered brows, open mouth w/full lips & four upper teeth, synthetic blonde wig, jointed wood & composition body stamped "Gimbel Bros., Germany" on right hip, wearing lace-trimmed blue dress w/white dots, underclothing, new white socks & white leather shoes, 22" (repair & touch-up on hip joints) 400

Simon & Halbig bisque socket head girl, marked "570 - Germany. Halbig - S&H," brown sleep eyes, feathered brows, open mouth w/four upper teeth, original blonde mohair wig, jointed wood & composition body, wearing antique maroon two-piece outfit, lace-trimmed blouse, antique underclothing, socks & shoes, 23" (tiny inherent line under one ear, hands repainted) 500

Simon & Halbig bisque socket head girl, marked "S & H 1079 - DEP - Germany - 13 1/2," dark brown sleep eyes, feathered brows, open mouth w/accented lips & four upper teeth, pierced ears, replaced dark brown wig, jointed wood & composition body, nicely redressed in new sailor outfit w/white top trimmed in red, navy blue pleated skirt, antique underclothing, replaced shoes, 27" (minor inherent firing line above ear, body repair around neck socket, minor repairs at hip joints)... 700

Simon & Halbig bisque socket head girl, marked "1079 S & H DEP - 16 - B - Germany," brown sleep eyes, molded & feathered brows, open mouth w/accented lips & four upper teeth, pierced ears, original dark brown h.h. wig, jointed wood & composition body, wearing ecru antique silk child's dress, antique underclothing, old cotton socks, old leather child's shoes, 34" (reglued ring finger, some finish wear on body)......................... 1,300

Steiner Le Parisien Girl

Simon & Halbig Lady Doll

Simon & Halbig bisque socket head shoulder plate lady, marked "SH 1039 - 4 DEP," set dark brown eyes, feathered brows, open mouth w/four upper teeth, pierced ears, original brown mohair wig, cloth body w/bisque lower arms, stitch-jointed hips & knees, wearing original ethnic-style outfit, original underclothing, black socks & shoes, 16" (ILLUS.) **650**

Steiner bisque socket head Le Parisien girl, marked "A-9 - Le Parisien, Bte. S.G.D.G. - A 9," stamped mark on body, brown paperweight eyes, feathered brows, closed mouth, pierced ears, brown h.h. wig, jointed light-weight composition body, wearing antique clothing, underclothing, socks & shoes & newer bonnet, fleck near inside corner one eye, tiny flake at one earring hole, two fingers reglued, 16 1/2" (ILLUS.) **3,400**

Steiner Figure A Girl

Vogue Ginny Walker with Box

Steiner bisque socket head Figure A girl, marked "Steiner - Paris - Fre A-14," fine blue paperweight eyes, feathered brows, closed mouth w/nicely accented lips, pierced ears, replaced blonde h.h. wig, jointed composition Steiner body w/jointed wrists & slender fingers, wearing antique white dress trimmed w/tucks on the bodice & at the hem, new underclothing, socks & antique leather shoes, 22" (ILLUS.) **3,100**

Vogue "Ginny," marked "Ginny - Vogue Dolls - Inc. - Pat. No. 2887954 - Made in U.S.A.," Vogue tag on dress, hard plastic head, blue sleep eyes w/molded lashes, single-stroke brows, closed mouth, original brown wig in braids, hard plastic body w/straight legs & walking mechanism, wearing tagged Tiny Miss #42 outfit from 1955, in original box w/blue taffeta panties, blue socks & extra marked blue Ginny shoes, near mint, 7" (ILLUS.) **375**

Large Wax Over Composition Lady

Wax over composition lady, unmarked, wax over composition shoulder head, set blue eyes, single-stroke brows, closed mouth, original blonde mohair wig, cloth body w/kid lower arms, individually stitched fingers, jointed at shoulders, hips & knees, wearing possibly original white blouse trimmed w/eyelet & tucks, blue plaid silk jumper, antique underclothing, antique socks & red leather shoes, lace & flower-trimmed bonnet, flake of wax off chin, circular crack & discoloration on one cheek, wig sparse, one finger seam split, 26" (ILLUS.) **750**

Wax over papier-maché shoulder head lady, blue painted eyes, pink painted mouth, molded hat w/feather & flowers, blonde mohair wig w/snood, cloth body, composition limbs, lower edge of shoulder plate finished as white molded chemise edged in lace, blue molded heeled boots, white gloves, wearing period cotton flower print dress & white underclothing, 15" (minor paint loss on eyes, wax loss to hat) **863**

Wax shoulder head lady, tiny glass eyes, single-stroke brows, closed mouth, molded & painted brown hair, cloth body w/wax lower arms & lower legs w/molded & painted black shoes, wearing original green & white dress w/white bodice & sleeves, original underclothing, ribbon-trimmed bonnet, mid-19th c., unplayed-with, 5 1/4" **775**

Rare Vogue Hawaiian Ginny

Vogue "Ginny," marked "Vogue Doll," brown hard plastic head, brown sleep eyes, single-stroke brows, closed mouth, original brown wig, brown five-piece hard plastic body wearing original Hawaiian-style clothing w/print top, 'grass' skirt, panties, lei around neck, flower in hair, hair slightly mussed, 7" (ILLUS.)................ **2,900**

Vogue Toddles Draf-Tee, marked "Vogue" on head & "Doll Co." on back, composition head w/painted blue eyes to side, single-stroke brows, closed mouth, original short blond mohair wig, five-piece composition toddler body, wearing tagged original brown military uniform, brown leather belt w/small metal gun attached, matching cap, socks, brown side snap shoes, 7 1/2" **350**

Wax child, poured wax shoulder head w/set blue eyes, feathered brows, painted upper & lower lashes, closed mouth, original blonde mohair inset wig, cloth body w/poured wax lower limbs attached w/grommets, wearing original white dress trimmed w/eyelet lace & tucks, original underclothing, no socks or shoes, blue velvet ribbon at waist, 17 1/2" (repair or inherent eye flaw, grommet missing from left leg, piece out of wax, crack on shoulder plate, left wax arm reattached w/string) **400**

Wax lady, wax chubby round shoulder head w/set blue eyes, single-stroke brows, closed mouth, original blonde mohair wig in ringlets, cloth body w/wax-over-papier-maché lower arms & lower legs w/molded orange boots, wearing original uniform of water carrier in the Crimean War, 11" h. (darkening to finish, body not inspected) **225**

Rag & Cloth

When the first rag doll was made is not known. They were handmade with loving hands by mothers wanting to please their children. They have always been a favorite with little ones because they are soft and easy to cuddle. Rag dolls abound and are easy collectibles to find. A folk art popularity boom has resulted in rising prices during the past decade...especially for those that were made prior to the 1940s. Those from the 1950s through the 1970s are not so expensive, but many are much sought after.

Annalee Mobilitee dolls, 1934-present, felt dolls with painted features, their tags are the key to their dates: first tags were woven lettering on white linen tape. Second tags were made of white rayon with red embroidered letters. The third tags (around 1969) were red printing on white satin tape. The fourth tags (about 1976) had red printing on gauze-type cloth. The hair from 1934 to 1963 was made of yarn. From 1960-1963, it was made of orange or yellow chicken feathers. Since 1963, the hair has been made of synthetic fur.

Advertising premium, A.P.W. Paper Co., girl w/Dutch-cut bobbed yellow hair, checked dress, 1925, 12"................................. **$45**

Alabama Indestructible Doll, all-cloth, painted w/oils, tab-joint shoulders & hips, black, made from 1899 to 1925 by the Ella Smith Doll Company in Roanoke, Alabama, 14-19", each **6,000**

Alabama Indestructible Doll, all-cloth, painted w/oils, tab-joint shoulders & hips, made from 1899 to 1925 by the Ella Smith Doll Co. in Roanoke, Alabama, 11" **1,400-1,600**

Alabama Indestructible Doll, all-cloth, painted w/oils, tab-joint shoulders & hips, made from 1899 to 1925 by the Ella Smith Doll Company in Roanoke, Alabama, 14-15", each **1,400-1,600**

Clown Rag Doll

Annalee Mobilitee doll, clown, 1970s, 18" (ILLUS.)... **450**

Annalee Mobilitee doll, skier, 1960s, 10" **250**

Annalee Mobilitee doll, skier, 1980s, 10" **150**

Annalee Mobilitee doll, skier, synthetic fur hair, 1960s, 10"... **450**

Annalee Mobilitee doll, skier, yarn hair, white rayon w/red embroidered letters tag, 1950s, 10".. **900**

Annalee Mobilitee dolls, American Indian, 1970s, 18", each **200**

Arbuckle premium cloth dolls: Mary & her little lamb, Jack & Jill, Tom the piper's son, printed sheets of cotton to be completed at home, offered by Arbuckle Coffee in 1931,14 1/2", each **45-70**

Arnold Print Works, Little Red Riding Hood, designed by Celia & Charity Smith, 1892, 16" (ILLUS. top next column)........ **115-125**

Babyland rag, h.p. features, black, sometimes mohair wig, cloth body jointed at shoulders & hips, early 1900s, Horsman, 15"... **650-700**

Little Red Riding Hood Rag Doll

Babyland rag, h.p. features, sometimes mohair wig, cloth body jointed at shoulders & hips, early 1900s, Horsman, 13-15", each (fair condition) **400**

Babyland rag, h.p. features, sometimes mohair wig, cloth body jointed at shoulders & hips, American Indian, one of a kind, early 1900s, Horsman, 4" **525**

Babyland rag, h.p. features, sometimes mohair wig, cloth body jointed at shoulders & hips, early 1900s, Horsman, 13-15", each **800**

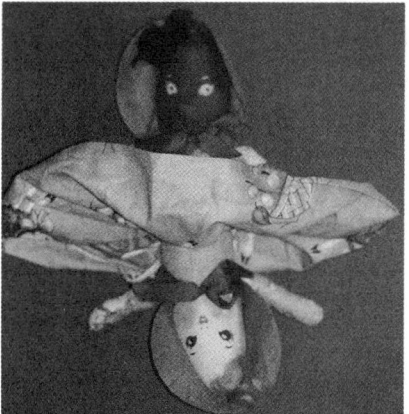

Babyland Rag Doll

Babyland rag, Topsy-Turvy, one black face/one white, early 1900s, 13-15", each (ILLUS.)... **800**

Barney Google, from the comic strip, stuffed cloth, 1930s, 12"................................. **150**

Boudoir dolls (also called bed dolls & pillow dolls), usually made w/a mask face, many companies made them, quality decides value, very good quality, 1920s-1930s, 27", each **85-125**

Boys & girls w/printed outer clothes made by several companies around 1903, 12-13", each **125-150**

Boys & girls w/printed outer clothes made by several companies around 1903, 17", each **175-200**

Brownies Rag Dolls

Brownies, designed for Arnold Print Works by Palmer Cox, one yard of material had 12 characters printed on the cloth to be cut, sewn & stuffed, copyright 1892, 8" h., each (ILLUS.)..................................... **80-90**

Buster Brown of Buster Brown Shoe fame, printed on cloth, 1912, 13"............................. **65**

Butterick, "To Teach the Future Mother to Dress the Future Child," premium offered by the Butterick Patterns in 1907, printed on cloth to be made at home, 18"........ **50**

Campbell Kids Rag Dolls

Campbell Kids, boy & girl advertising dolls, made from pattern offered as a premium in the 1980s, embroidered features, 16", each (ILLUS.) **10-20**

Campbell Kids, boy & girl advertising dolls, printed features, manufactured by Knickerbocker in 1973, 12", each........................ **12-20**

Columbian doll by Emma & Marietta Adams, all-cloth w/h.p. hair & features on flat face, appropriate old clothes, 1891-1910, 20-22", each **4,000-6,000**

Columbian Doll Rag Doll

Columbian doll by Emma & Marietta Adams, all-cloth w/h.p. hair & features on flat face, appropriate old clothes, 1891-1910, 15" (ILLUS.) **5,000**

Hallmark Rag Doll

Cut, sew & stuff doll by Hallmark, printed on cloth, uncut, early 1970s, 12" (ILLUS.) **15**

Darkey doll, 1890s, 16".................................... **250**

Dennis the Menace, stuff & lace doll, 1950s, 15" **30**

Disney Dwarf, Dopey, heavy oilcloth type mask, painted expression, body made from velveteen, large cloth ears, late 1930s - early 1940s, by the Knickerbocker Co., 11 1/2".. **115-200**

Foxy Grandpa, from comic strip that ran from 1900-1918, stuffed, early 1900s, 17" (ILLUS. top next page) **100**

Georgene Novelties, Raggedy Ann or Andy, created by Johnny Gruelle, made from 1938-1963, 15-18", each **250**

Foxy Grandpa Rag Doll

Golliwog w/clothes as part of body, felt buttons & features, mohair hair, tagged "Chad Valley," 10" **325**

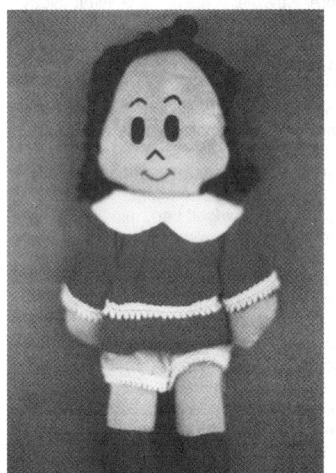

Little Lulu Rag Doll

Gund, Little Lulu, 1944, 5" (ILLUS.)...................... **25**

Raggedy Ann & Andy Rag Dolls

Hallmark, Raggedy Ann & Andy, created by Johnny Gruelle, 1972, 5", each (ILLUS.) **20-35**

Little Man Rag Doll

Handmade little man, needle sculptured features, leather hands, shoes & hat, documentation as to maker & date, Mrs. S.W. Williams, 1909, 6" (ILLUS.)............... **50-75**

Ideal Toy & Novelty Co., Scarecrow from the Wizard of Oz, pink sateen mask face, yarn hair, arms & legs sewn to white cloth body, brown flannel mitt hands w/separate thumbs, 1939, 16" **300**

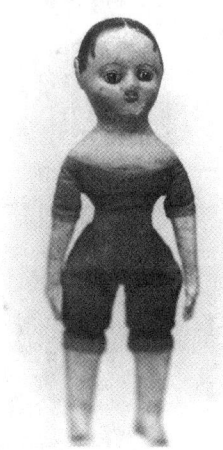

Izannah Walker Rag Doll

Izannah Walker, stockinette, molded & painted oil features, individually stitched fingers & toes, separate thumbs, usually have applied ears, made in Central Falls, Rhode Island, 1870-1880, 17-19", each (ILLUS.) **16,000-18,000**

Izannah Walker, stockinette, molded & painted oil features, individually stitched fingers & toes, separate thumbs, usually have applied ears, made in Central Falls, Rhode Island, 1870-1880, each (only fair condition) **8,500-9,500**

Izannah Walker, stockinette, molded & painted oil features, individually stitched fingers & toes, separate thumbs, usually have applied ears, made in Central Falls, Rhode Island, 1870-1880, each (very worn) **3,000-4,000**

Kathe Kruse, molded h.p. muslin head, jointed at shoulders & hips, usually marked on foot, slim hips, 1929-on, 17", each.. **3,000**

Kathe Kruse, molded h.p. muslin head, jointed at shoulders & hips, usually marked on foot, wide hips, 1920-1929, 16", each.. **4,000**

Kellogg's Goldilocks, the three bears were also made, lithographed advertising doll, she had blonde corkscrew curls tied w/a red bow, wide open blue eyes, a round mouth & rosy cheeks, uncut, 1926, 14", each **85**

Knickerbocker, Holly Hobbie, 1970s, ranged in size from 4-36", each (played with & worn)... **1-10**

Holly Hobbie Rag Dolls

Knickerbocker, Holly Hobbie, 1970s, ranged in size from 4-36", MIB, each (ILLUS.)... **10-45**

Nancy Rag Doll

Knickerbocker, Nancy, early 1970s, 5" (ILLUS.).. **25**

Wedding Couple Rag Dolls

Korean dolls, wedding couple, made for tourist trade, late 1960s, 21", pr. (ILLUS.) **50**

Kuddle Kewpie, mask face w/fat cloth body including wings & peak on head, 1930s, by Krueger Inc., New York, 10-12" each.. **215**

Lenci doll, baby, usually all-felt, sometimes cloth torso, painted features w/swivel head, jointed shoulders & hips, eyes usually glance to the side, clothes are of felt or organdy, made in Italy, 1920-on, 14-18", each................................ **2,000**

Lenci doll, boy w/golf bag, usually all-felt, sometimes cloth torso, painted features w/swivel head, jointed shoulders & hips, eyes usually glance to the side, clothes are of felt or organdy, made in Italy, 1920-on, 17", each...................................... **2,700**

Lenci doll, googlie-eyed, w/watermelon mouth, usually all-felt, sometimes cloth torso, painted features w/swivel head, jointed shoulders & hips, eyes usually glance to the side, clothes are of felt or organdy, made in Italy, 1920-on, 22" **1,600-2,000**

Lenci doll, Indian girl w/papoose, usually all-felt, sometimes cloth torso, painted features w/swivel head, jointed shoulders & hips, eyes usually glance to the side, clothes are of felt or organdy, made in Italy, 1920-on, 17"...................................... **5,000**

Lenci doll, Mozart, usually all-felt, sometimes cloth torso, painted features w/swivel head, jointed shoulders & hips, eyes usually glance to the side, clothes are of felt or organdy, made in Italy, 1920-on, 17".. **3,700**

Lenci dolls, children, usually all-felt, sometimes cloth torso, painted features w/swivel head, jointed shoulders & hips, eyes usually glance to the side, clothes are of felt or organdy, made in Italy, 1920-on, 13", each (ILLUS. top next page) **850**

Lenci dolls, ladies & long-legged novelty dolls, usually all-felt, sometimes cloth torso, painted features w/swivel head, jointed shoulders & hips, eyes usually glance to the side, clothes are of felt or organdy, made in Italy, 1920-on, 24-28", each **3,000**

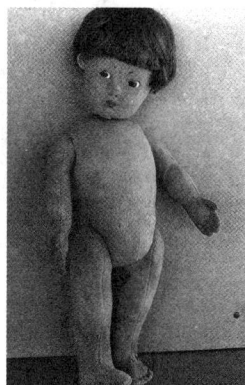

Lenci Rag Dolls

Lenci dolls, miniatures & mascots, usually all-felt, sometimes cloth torso, painted features w/swivel head, jointed shoulders & hips, eyes usually glance to the side, clothes are of felt or organdy, made in Italy, 1920-on, 8-9", each **300-350**
Little Lulu, cowgirl outfit, 1944 .... **250**
Little Lulu, molded linen face, black yarn hair, plastic purse, 1944, 15" **175**
Madame Alexander, all-cloth w/one piece arms & legs sewn on, mohair wig & molded mask face, Little Women series, 1930s, 16", each.............................. **600**
Madame Alexander, all-cloth w/one piece arms & legs sewn on, mohair wig & molded mask face, Susie Q. or Bobby Q., 1930s, 12-16", each...................... **650**
Madame Alexander, all-cloth w/one-piece arms & legs sewn on, mohair wig & molded mask face, Dionne Quintuplets, 1930s, 17", each **800**
Madame Alexander, Bunny Belle, all-cloth w/one-piece arms & legs sewn on, mohair wig & molded mask face, 1930s, 13"...... **700**

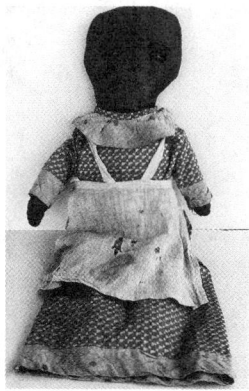

"Mammy" Rag Doll

"Mammy," handmade, embroidered features, old clothes, documentation as to maker & date, 1930s, 18" (ILLUS.) **75-125**
"Mammy Castoria," printed, stuffed advertising doll offered by Fletcher's Castoria during the 1930s, 10" **125**
Mattel, cloth talker w/pull strings to activate the talking mechanism, Shrinking Violet, 1962 .... **45**

Mrs. Beasley Cloth Talker

Mattel, cloth talker w/pull strings to activate the talking mechanism, Mrs. Beasley from the TV show Family Affair, 16" (ILLUS.) **50**
Mattel, cloth talkers w/pull strings to activate the talking mechanism, Pillow dolls, many sizes, each **3-10**
Maud Tousey Fangel, Snooks & Sweets, reproductions of Fangel drawings that appeared in the magazines across the land, the blonde is Sweets, the brunette Snooks, 12", each **500**
Miss Malto Rice, lithographed advertising doll, distributed by American Good & Manufacturing Co., New Jersey, ca. 1900, 20".................................... **55**

Missionary Ragbaby Doll

Missionary Ragbaby w/molded & painted features, looped yellow wool hair, stitched fingers & toes, the dolls originally were priced from $3-$8 & were meant to benefit a missionary fund sponsored by

the Park Congregational Church of Elmira, New York, they were made of old silk
underwear, by Julia Beecher, Elmira,
New York from 1893-1910, 20" each
(ILLUS.)... **5,000**
**Missionary Ragbaby w/molded & painted
features,** looped yellow wool hair,
stitched fingers & toes, the dolls originally
were priced from $3-$8 & were meant to
benefit a missionary fund sponsored by
the Park Congregational Church of Elmira, New York, they were made of old silk
underwear, by Julia Beecher, Elmira,
New York from 1893-1910, 21" each........ **6,000**
Molly-'es, Raggedy Ann or Andy, created
by Johnny Gruelle, 1935-1938, 18-22",
each.. **1,000**

"Nina" Rag Doll Pattern
"Nina," pattern by McCall, 1945 (ILLUS.) **10-20**

Orange Blossom Rag Doll
Orange Blossom, one of the many cloth
Strawberry Shortcake Characters from
the early 1980s (ILLUS.) **15-25**
Orphan Annie, oilcloth w/separate fabric
dress, 1930s, 17"... **300**
Poupees Gerb's, a French Company,
man, mask face dolls, h.p. features, usually little girl-type, sometimes dressed in
national costumes, bed-type doll, w/sewn
label, 1927-early 1930s, 27" (ILLUS. top
next column)... **500**

Man Bed-Type Rag Doll
Poupees Gerb's, a French Company,
Scottish girl, mask face dolls, h.p. features, usually little girl-type, 1927-early
1930s, 16" **400-450**
Rastus, advertising doll of Cream of Wheat
chef, distributed by the Cream of Wheat
Corporation, lithographed on cloth to be
cut, sewn & stuffed, he holds red & white
bowl w/Cream of Wheat printed on it,
1949 version, 18" **75**
Rastus, advertising doll of Cream of Wheat
chef, distributed by the Cream of Wheat
Corporation, lithographed on cloth to be
cut, sewn & stuffed, he holds red & white
bowl w/Cream of Wheat printed on it,
1930 version, 18-20" h., each **100**
Rastus, advertising doll of Cream of Wheat
chef, distributed by the Cream of Wheat
Corporation, lithographed on cloth to be
cut, sewn & stuffed, he holds red & white
bowl w/Cream of Wheat printed on it, as
a premium box top & 10¢, 1922,16"............. **150**
Rollinson doll, all-molded cloth w/painted
head & limbs, painted hair or human hair,
painted features, molded hair, 1916-on,
18-22", each...................................... **800-1,200**

"Roy" Scarecrow Rag Doll
Russ, Scarecrow, "Roy," 1970s, 13"
(ILLUS.) **12-20**

Santa Claus Rag Doll

Twin Sisters Rag Dolls

Santa Claus, designed by Edward Peck for the New York Stationery & Envelope Co., New York City, may have been the first commercially made doll of its kind in America, ca. 1884-1886, cut 15" (ILLUS.).. **325**

Santa Claus, designed by Edward Peck for the New York Stationery & Envelope Co., New York City, may have been the first commercially made doll of its kind in America, ca. 1884-1886, uncut 15".............. **600**

Santa Claus, mask face, red corduroy suit used as body, painted features, music box inside body, by Gund, late 1930s, 16".. **100-150**

Skeezix, painted oilcloth, 1930s, 12"................. **50**

Smitty, embroidered features, 1930s, 13".......... **50**

Snap, Crackle, & Pop of Kellogg's fame, printed on cloth to be cut, sewn & stuffed, 1954, uncut, each... **35**

Snuffy Smith, felt doll, 1930s, 17"................... **150**

Steiff, children, felt, plush, or velvet, jointed, seam down the middle of the face, button eyes, painted features, 1894-on, 11-12", each.. **900-1,250**

Steiff, children, felt, plush, or velvet, jointed, seam down the middle of the face, button eyes, painted features, 1894-on, 16-17", each.. **1,500-1,600**

Steiff, Gnome, felt, plush, or velvet, jointed, seam down the middle of the face, button eyes, painted features, 1894-on, 12"............ **900**

Storybook dolls, mask face, stuffed w/ko-pak, worsted straight hair w/bangs, name of each character printed on dress, by Ideal, 1939, 16".. **50-75**

Twin sisters, individually stitched fingers, embroidered features, old clothes, 1920s, 12", pr. (ILLUS. top next column)........ **75-100**

Unmarked Topsy-Turvy, cotton & felt, mohair, 1930s-early 1940s, 12"..................... **50-75**

Volland, Raggedy Ann or Andy, created by Johnny Gruelle, early edition w/brown yarn hair & outlined nose, each **1,600**

DOOR KNOCKERS
Cast iron unless otherwise noted.

Basket of daffodils, brown w/white back & blue bow on top, near mint, 2 1/2 x 4 1/4" .. **$660**

Bathing beauty, backing w/scrolled casting effect, Fish, pristine, 2 1/2 x 5 1/8"............ **1,760**

Birdhouse with bird, polychrome, two birds perched on exterior, excellent to pristine, 1 5/8 x 3 3/4"................................. **825**

Bunch of roses, polychrome, pink box on top of backing, near mint, 2 3/4 x 4 1/4"....... **770**

Buster Brown and Tige, Buster seated on fence w/Tige looking up, excellent, 2 1/2 x 4 3/4".. **198**

Castle, marked "#632," backing mark #630, castle on mountain top surrounded by cloud, pristine, 2 3/4 x 4".............................. **495**

Comical dog, boxed example, marked "Made in England," near mint, 1 3/4 x 3 1/4".. **770**

Eagle, spread-winged bird, American, 19th c., 8 3/4" l. (minor wear)...................... **345**

Flower basket, purple painted bow handle & purple trim backing, Hubley, #124, mint, 2 3/4 x 4"... **275**

Hanging floral basket, polychrome, marked "#205," Hubley, near mint, 2 1/8 x 3"... **275**

Hanging floral, floral & leaf backing, pristine, 3 x 3 1/4".. **440**

Large crowing rooster, oval backing featured cast leaves, excellent, 3 x 4 1/4"......... **308**

Morning glory, blue flowers w/green backing, near mint, 2 3/4 x 3 1/4"...................... **550**

Parrot in hoop, green bird, backing done in white, near mint, 2 1/4 x 3 1/4"................... **330**

Peace dove, marked "#623," backing mark #626, olive branch in beak, floral pattern trim, pristine, 2 3/4 x 4".............................. **495**

Poinsettia, marked "#627," red & green w/white backing, Hubley, mint, 3 1/2 x 2 1/2"... **495**

Rooster in ring, rooster crowing perched on green painted ring, pristine, 2 7/8 x 3 1/4".. **385**

Rose, deeply cast w/small branches & leaves, white backing w/green trim, pristine, 3 x 5 1/4"... **418**

Spider, w/fly in arms, web cast backing, rare, pristine, 1 3/4 x 3 1/2"......................... **1,100**

Vase with flowers, marked "#205," vase in green, pink backing w/gold trim, near mint, 2 1/4 x 3 3/4" **275**

Woodpecker, marked "#251," red headed bird pecking on tree trunk, Hubley, mint, 2 3/4 x 3 5/8"... **308**

Zinnia, painted in pink w/gold highlights, heavily detailed, marked "Pat. Pend. LVL," mint, 2 1/" x 3 3/4" **550**

DOORSTOPS

All doorstops listed are flat-back cast iron unless otherwise noted. Most names are taken from Doorstops— Identification & Values, *by Jeanne Bertoia (Collector Books, 1985).*

American Indian, standing wearing a tall upright feathered headdress, a long cloak & striped dress, arms across chest, on a rockwork rectangular base, old worn polychrome repaint, 13" h. **$413**

Cat, "Fireside Cat," original paint, signed Hubley (some wear & rust) **250**

Cat, "Persian Cat," full-figure, worn original light paint, Hubley, 8 1/2" h............................ **303**

Seated Cat Doorstop

Cat, seated animal on thick rectangular flaring base, original paint, 12 1/2" h. (ILLUS.)... **330**

Dog, Boston Terrier, large, original brown & white paint w/some wear, Hubley, National Foundry & others, 10" l., 10" h. **138**

Eagle, flattened spread-winged bird w/head to right, perched clutching long clusters of feathers in each talon, on a flat oval disk base, 12" l. **220**

Kitten Doorstop

Kitten, seated w/ribbon & bow around its neck, on a half-round base, old worn grey & pink w/green eyes, Hubley & National, 8" h. (ILLUS.) **248**

Fine Owl Doorstop

Owl, tall perched bird, original paint, mold No. 7797, Bradley & Hubbard, 16" h. (ILLUS.) **1,100**

Punch, old green repaint, English, 12" h. **83**

Punch & Judy Doorstop

Punch & Judy, half-round model of a large standing Judy w/bonnet holding a baby Punch, old paint in red, blue, black & white, some paint loss, 8" w., 12" h. (ILLUS.) **1,725**

Sitting Rabbit Doorstop

Rabbit, seated upright on oval molded leafy grass base, original dark brown paint & green base, Bradley & Hubbard, 15 3/8" h. (ILLUS.).. **3,300**

Rooster, full-bodied stylized slender bird w/wide rounded tail, traces of polychrome paint, 6 1/2" h. **248**

Squirrel on Log Doorstop

Squirrel, full-bodied detailed animal holding a nut, sitting on log, raised bushy tail, old grey repaint w/traces of yellow on the log, 11 1/2" h. (ILLUS.).. **908**

Gnome Warrior Doorstop

Warrior, standing gnome holding up large club on one side & duffle bag under other arm, rectangular base, original paint, Bradley & Hubbard, early 20th c., 13 1/4" h. (ILLUS.).. **550**

ENAMELS

Enamels have been used to decorate a variety of substances, particularly metals. The best-known small enameled wares such as patch and other small boxes and napkin rings, are the Battersea Enamels made by the Battersea Enamel Works in the last half of the 18th century. However, the term is often loosely applied to other English enamels. Russian enamels, usually on a

silver or gold base, are famous and expensive. Early 20th century French enamel on copper wares and those items produced in China at the turn of the century in imitation of the early Russian style are also drawing dealer and collector attention.

Box, cov., Battersea-type, oval w/metal mounts, the top decorated w/a large sailing ship titled "The Constitution," in polychrome on a white ground, mounted on a pink base, the interior w/a mirror, England, made for the American market, late 18th - early 19th c., 1 3/8 x 2", 7/8" h. (minor wear).. **$2,415**

Russian Enameled Cigarette Case

Cigarette case, flattened rectangular form, silver decorated overall w/a wavy blue guilloché enamel design, by Andre Gorianov, Russia, late 19th - early 20th c., 3 1/2" l. (ILLUS.).. **5,600**

Clock, miniature, onion-domed top above an upright rectangular case w/arched top & scroll-cast ormolu framing enclosing colored scenic panels around the sides, round dial w/Roman numerals, Vienna, Austria, late 19th c., 5 1/2" h. **1,725**

Viennese Enameled Clock

Clock, table model, a disk-shaped case decorated w/leafy scrolls around the dial w/Roman numerals & painted w/a landscape w/people, topped by an metal urnform finial & figural side handles & raised on scrolled caryatid metal supports above the oblong lobed & domed base enameled w/a tree-filled landscape w/18th c. lovers, Vienna, late 19th c., 8 1/2" h. (ILLUS.)...................................... **2,990**

Cup, cov., a domed foot supporting a ring-and knob-turned slender pedestal below the deep ovoid bowl w/a chased metal shoulder band below the short wide waisted neck, low domed cover w/standing figure finial, the foot, body & cover all enameled w/colorful classical scenes, scroll & mask designs on the pedestal & neck, Vienna, Austria, 19th c., 14" h. **4,600**

Easter egg, ovoid, red enamel stylized panel over a guilloché ground w/rose-cut diamonds in the middle interval w/stylized leaf design set w/a rose-cut diamond in the middle within white opaque enamel borders, Workmaster Michael Perchin, Fabergé, St. Petersburg, Russia, 1896-1908, 5/8" l. **9,400**

Fine Enameled Russian Small Jar

Jar, cov., tapering squatty double gourd-form body decorated w/wide bands of ornate scrolls in blues, reds, yellows & brown flanked by white dot bands, one band w/a pale green ground, the other w/a pale peach ground, the stepped domed cover w/dot band, lappet band & scrolls & a large knob finial, Russia, ca. 1900, 3 1/2" h. (ILLUS.) **2,240**

Knobs, a round brass-framed knob enclosing a brown on white depiction of "Genl. Washington," Bilston, England, late 18th - early 19th c., 2" d., pr. (one w/small chips).. **2,035**

Knobs, round brass frame enclosing an enameled black & white bust portrait of "Gen. Lafayette," wearing a red, yellow & blue uniform, Bilston, England, late 18th c., 2" d., pr. (one w/damage where post pushed into facing).. **880**

Knobs, round brass frame enclosing an enameled scene of a woman w/brown hair & purple & yellow robes holding a pink cup, an eagle beside her, Bilston, England, late 18th c., 2" d., pr....................... **578**

Knobs, round brass frame enclosing enameled polychrome scene of a young girl w/brown hair & a red & blue dress holding

a canary, Bilston, England, late 18th c., 1 7/8" d., pr.. **990**

Ornately Enameled Russian Kovsh

Kovsh, footed wide rounded boat-shaped bowl w/a wide flattened fleur-de-lis handle, pale green ground decorated w/elaborate flowering leafy scrolls in reds, blues, greens, orange & white, a golden brown walking lion in the interior bottom, crafted by Feodor Ruckert, Russia, late 19th - early 20th c., 4 1/2" l. (ILLUS.)......... **4,200**

Patch box, cov., oval, a molded pale blue base w/a white cover, the cover decorated in red & blue floral ribbons w/a black verse "Have communion with few...speak evil of none," cover interior w/a mirror, England, 18th c., 1 5/8" l. (hairlines, wear) **330**

Patch box, cov., light blue rectangular form w/concave sides, the lid w/grisaille decoration depicting a fishing scene & motto "No Toil is Pain When Love's the Gain," interior fitted w/mirror, England, early 19th c., 1 x 1 1/2", 3/4" h. (enamel damage & repair) **489**

Patch box, cov.,oval, molded pink base, the white cover w/polychrome flowers w/a bird & inscription "A Trifle from Penzance," cover interior w/a mirror, England, 18th c., 1 3/4" l................................ **358**

French Enameled Plaque

Plaque, rectangular copper plaque decorated w/the full-length figure of a standing cavalier w/sword & plumed hat, in a flat & wide oak & copper-inlaid frame, Limoges, France, ca. 1895, 4 3/4 x 8 1/4" (ILLUS.).. **633**

Large Ornate Viennese Enamel Vase

Vase, large baluster-form body, large ovoid center section divided by a raised band w/foliage & masks, a short banded & enameled pedestal w/flaring foot, trumpet-form neck w/a raised base band & rim flanked by scrolled horse-form handles, the body & shoulder w/large oval reserves painted w/Classical landscape scenes w/figures, further continuous scenes around the neck & base, Vienna, Austria, late 19th c., drilled, 13" h. (ILLUS.).. **9,775**

Small Viennese Enameled Vase

Vase, squatty bulbous body raised on a pedestal base w/wide center ring & disk

foot, a wide stamped metal shoulder band centering a knopped tall cylindrical neck w/flared rim, the body, neck & base decorated w/colorful Classical allegorical scenes, Vienna, Austria, 19th c., 7" h. (ILLUS.) **1,840**

FABERGÉ

Carl Fabergé (1846-1920) was goldsmith and jeweler to the Russian Imperial Court and his creations are recognized as the finest of their kind. He made a number of enamel fantasies, including Easter eggs, for the Imperial family and utilized precious metals and jewels in other work.

Fabergé Figural Bonbonniere

Bonbonniere, silver, figural ostrich, realistically modelled, the body of two halves of an ostrich egg, the mounts applied w/repoussé, chased & engraved wings & feathers, the curved neck & head cast & engraved, the cast legs on a circular aventurine quartz base, marked on mounts & legs "Faberge," workmaster Julius Rappoport, St. Petersburg, ca. 1890, 12 3/4" h. (ILLUS.).................... **$1,750**

Bowl, silver-gilt enamel, footed wide rounded sides w/ringed rim band, the exterior body in pale blue enamel over a guilloché ground, marked under the base, unrecorded workmaster's initials, St. Petersburg, 1896-1908, 2 7/8" d. **2,760**

Brooch, diamond & gold, lyre-shaped, the gold mount set w/old mine- and rose-cut diamonds, centered by a triangular diamond suspending a diamond teardrop, mark of unidentified workmaster, St. Petersburg, ca. 1880, scratched inventory number, 1 1/8" w. **11,500**

Casket, silver-mounted wood, rectangular, the plain wood body w/tied-reeded base band on four ball feet, the two hinged covers w/scroll-engraved borders & surmounted by two gadrooned knop finials, marked & w/the Imperial Warrant, Workmaster Anders Nevalainen, St. Petersburg, ca. 1890, 8 3/4" l.................. **10,350**

Gum-pot, cov., silver & ceramic, cylindrical green-glazed ceramic body on a silver beaded & stepped base, the fitted domed silver top w/a Greek key band, the central gum-brush handle in top w/a domed fluted finial surmounted by an egg-shaped pale blue stone, mark of unidentified workmaster, St. Petersburg, 1896-1908, w/inventory number, 3 1/2" h.................... **4,025**

Kovsh, parcel-gilt cloisonné enamel, traditional rounded boat-shape w/upright pointed prow, raised on a slightly spreading round foot, high hooked handle, enameled overall w/stylized multicolored flowerheads, foliate sprays & geometric designs on cream & dark blue grounds, gilt interior, Imperial Warrant mark, Workmaster Fedor Ruckert, Moscow, 1908-17, 5 7/8" h.. **16,100**

Kovsh, silver & enamel, triangular-shaped, the prow & sides w/a wide chased band of scrolling foliage & geometric designs in the Pan-Slavic style on a matte moss green enamel ground, the handle set w/a rouble coin depicting the profile of Catherine the Great dated 1742, marked & w/the Imperial Warrant, Moscow, 1896-1908, 4" l....................................... **5,750**

Model of a chick, gold-mounted rock crystal, clear egg-shaped chick body w/gold-mounted ruby eyes & realistic gold feet, apparently unmarked, ca. 1890, 1 1/2" l.... **8,050**

Paper knife, silver & gold-mounted gemset & bowenite, the tip of the handle w/an anthemion support below the raised reeded ovoid bowenite green handle set at each end w/a small cabochon garnet, a long slender spearpoint silver blade, mark of unidentified workmaster, St. Petersburg, ca. 1890, scratched inventory number, 10 5/8" l.................................. **11,500**

Photograph frame, gold-mounted nephrite, rectangular flat green nephrite frame w/a round narrow gold chased & engraved laurel bezel opening, w/a scrolled strut support, mark of Workmaster Henrik Wigstrom, St. Petersburg, 1896-1908, 4 1/4" h.. **32,500**

FANS

Canton Brise Lacquered Fan

Canton brise, lacquered in silver, pink, green & gold w/figures in a garden, w/po-

em & a border of birds & flowers, verso similarly painted, ca. 1820, 8" (ILLUS.) ... **$2,041**

Canton ivory brise, carved & pierced w/figures & buildings, tips of the sticks shaped as roundels, guardsticks carved in high-relief, ca. 1850, in a wooden box painted w/a view of Hong Kong, w/ships in the foreground, 9 1/2" **875**

Chromolithograhed brise card, advertising almanac fan w/calendar for July 1905 to June 1906, w/seven bathing beauties, one buoyed up by the fizz of the champagne, verso w/a giant in 18th c. dress carrying bottles of Brut Imperial & White Seal, w/miniature men at his feet w/armfuls of champagne, mounted in a temporary perspex case, Moet & Chandon White Seal, French, 1905, 10" (some wear) **437**

Chromolithographed paper, Chemins de Fer de l'Ouest, w/views of Rouen, the Casino de Dippe & Dinard, advertising cheap trips to the seaside & to London, verso w/advertisements including Agence Cook & Compagnie Generale Transatlantique w/weekly services to New York, published by J. Ganne, Paris, printed by Oberthur, Rennes - Paris, w/wooden sticks, guardsticks w/advertisements for the Casino de Dieppe & Phosphatine Falieres, ca. 1900, 13" **73**

Chromolithographed paper, two cats chasing a little boy's aeroplane, signed "Benjamin Rabier," w/wooden sticks, French, ca. 1920, 9" **554**

Conundrum, an etching w/medley of objects including Bouquet Fantasque, banner w/mirror image, inscribed "France Heureuse," two fans inscribed "to arms," verso w/Cupid & a quotation w/no vowels, published by Sarah Ashton No. 28 Little Britain, April 25th, 1791, w/wooden sticks, 1791, 10" **379**

Découpé, leaf of finely cut paper painted w/a hunting scene, w/six vignettes of mica applied w/découpé work, verso w/three port scenes in carmine, attributed to Preissler, ivory sticks carved, pierced & painted, rare, Bohemian, early 18th c., mounted slightly later, 10" (some wear) **5,831**

Gauze, embroidered w/pansies & trimmed w/sequins, horn sticks gilt w/stars, ca. 1810, 8" **277**

Gilt sequined painted silk, medallion of a woman stealing cupid's bow, gilt wire mesh leaf w/carved, pierced & polychrome sticks, displayed in a fan-shaped case, ca. 1850, 10 x 18".............................. **336**

Ivory brise, painted & lacquered w/shepherds & shepherdesses & a man playing the bagpipes, reserves w/chinoiserie, verso w/figures in a landscape, 18th c., 8".......... **729**

Ivory brise, painted w/banquet al fresco, reserve pierced & painted w/chinoiserie, verso outlined in brown w/the scene, mid-18th c., 8"....................................... **875**

Ivory brise, upper guardstick carved in high-relief w/three groups of stags in woods, German, ca. 1880, 8"...................... **583**

Lithographed paper, embossed & gilded w/hand-colored court scenes, gilded brass trim, bone ribs & oval mirror insert, 19th c., framed, 17" w. (some damage)........ **165**
Painted canepin, w/an allegory of marriage, the mother-of-pearl sticks carved w/nymphs & putti & oyster shells, signed E. Parmentier & dated 1853, French, 1853, 10 1/2"... **1,603**
Painted Canton, recto & verso w/figures on terraces, their faces of ivory, clothes of silk, w/lacquered sticks w/central vignettes, ca. 1860, in lacquer box, 11"........ **146**
Painted chickenskin, A Grand Tour w/Aldobrandini Wedding, dismounted & remounted on later sticks, leaf late 18th c., 11"... **262**

Moses in the Bullrushes Painted Fan

Painted chickenskin, Moses in the Bullrushes, verso w/lady wearing a chinoiserie hat, mother-of-pearl sticks carved, pierced, silvered, gilt & backed w/mother-of-pearl, w/a lady, musicians & putti, guardsticks w/gentleman digging, Genoese, w/French sticks, ca. 1750, 11 1/2" (ILLUS.)... **1,603**
Painted chickenskin, Narcissus looking at his reflection in a pool whilst Echo pines watched by nymphs & putti, ivory sticks carved & pierced w/a couple & Cupid, Italian, sticks possibly English, ca. 1800, 8"............................... **437**
Painted chickenskin, the departure of a hero, ivory sticks carved & pierced w/figures, painted & gilt & cloute w/mother-of-pearl, in glazed case, mid-18th c., 10"............ **36**

The Offering of Abigail Painted Fan

Painted chickenskin, The Offering of Abigail, w/Abigail offering bread to King David & his band of outlaws, verso w/walled village, mother-of-pearl sticks carved & pierced w/Apollo & Marsyas & etched w/inscription "Apollon fait ecorchee Marcias" & painted & lacquered w/shepherds & shepherdesses, Genoese w/French

sticks, ca. 1730, 11 1/2", guardsticks repaired, old repairs to leaf (ILLUS.)............. **875**

A Charming & Unusual Painted Fan

Painted paper, a couple dancing surrounded by beasts including a turkey, peacock & cattle, the verso w/a stock, butterflies & flowers, w/ivory sticks, guardsticks carved w/lady in Turkish dress, tips & handle w/mother-of-pearl filets, ca. 1730, charming & unusual, 12" (ILLUS.)............. **6,122**
Painted paper, a couple picnicking by a river & another couple dancing & a man playing a hurdy gurdy, verso w/a couple, the gentleman playing a flute, ivory sticks carved, pierced & painted w/a frieze w/houses, swan, windmill, mother-of-pearl & tortoiseshell, ca. 1730, verso probably a 19th c. pastiche, 11".................. **146**
Painted paper, chinoiserie figures in a garden, the verso w/prunus & butterflies, ivory sticks carved & pierced, guardsticks w/chinoiserie figures & etched mother-of-pearl tips & filets, edge near handle carved w/a heart on each side when closed, English, ca. 1760 - in 18th c. fan box, 10 1/2"... **437**
Painted paper, Cupid & a chariot drawn by lions, presiding over a procession of newlyweds, verso painted w/birdcatchers, mother-of-pearl sticks carved & pierced w/classical scene, silvered & gilt, French, ca. 1760, 11"...................................... **190**

Rare 17th Century Painted Fan

Painted paper, Cupid watching over series of scenes in a gentleman's life; to the left he brings flowers to a lady watching from a window, next he attends her toilette; admires a large litter of puppies; next she strokes his head as he sits on her lap; in the centre an elderly gentleman kneels before a lady holding a miniature & a fan; the gentleman wearing a muff trimmed w/red bow & talks to a lawyer; later he dances w/two ladies; to the right a gentleman in court dress has a vision of thirty virgins, verso painted w/two ladies; one playing the mandolin, two chinoiserie figures, birds & flowers, ivory sticks lacquered w/nymphs & putti, rare, ca. 1680, 11", sticks rubbed, leaf worn (ILLUS.) **5,831**

Painted paper, dancing Nymphs & Cupid riding a leopard, signed "J. Donzel fils," verso w/a landscape, ca. 1890, 8 1/2" **379**

Painted paper, dismounted leaf painted w/seven ladies in a garden, one playing a wind instrument in a kiosk, another riding a dog of foo, characters are the name of the Ming artist Qiu Ying, ca. 1495-1552, & the seal below is Shi Chuon one of Qiu Yin's other names Ten Streams, late 18th c., framed & glazed, 18" w. **1,166**

Painted paper, elegant figures watching others playing shuttlecock & battledore, bowles & gardening, verso w/elegant lady, gentleman playing bagpipes & lady w/tambourine, mother-of-pearl sticks carved & pierced w/lovers, flautist & birds & putti, silvered & gilt, French, ca. 1770, 11" **948**

Painted paper, Europa & the Bull, verso w/two ladies & a hero in classical dress, ivory sticks carved & painted w/serpentine frieze & applied w/mother-of-pearl finely carved & pierced w/musicians & putti, backed with mica, the guardsticks carved w/winged trumpeters riding winged horses & painted w/miniature chinoiserie vignettes under mica, French, ca. 1730, 11 1/2" **948**

Painted paper, figures on terraces, their faces of ivory, clothes of silk, w/a green border, verso painted w/birds & flowers against silver ground, ivory sticks carved & pierced w/figures, Macao, ca. 1850, 10" **292**

Painted paper, Judgment of Paris, verso w/a village, unusual ivory sticks carved & pierced w/a gentleman resting his horse by a well, w/three dogs, the reserves w/birds & flowers against a trellis, guardsticks w/chinoiserie figures, sticks possibly English, ca. 1750, 12" (one stick cracked, old repairs to leaf) **729**

Painted paper, Juno & Jupiter, verso w/lady in a landscape, within a garland of honeysuckle & a butterfly, mother-of-pearl sticks carved & pierced w/Bacchus & Ariadne w/leopards, painted w/Diana, Mars & Venus & decorated w/chased gold plaques & flowerheads, mid-18th century, 11" ....

Painted paper, musicians in a boat, watched by shepherdess in the foreground, verso w/a shepherdess, ivory sticks carved & pierced w/musicians, putti & beasts & painted w/fruit when closed, English, ca. 1730, 10" (guardsticks repaired) **1,458**

Painted paper, musique champetre by fountain, w/one lady playing the hurdy gurdy, verso w/a lady, ivory sticks pierced & painted w/chinoiserie figures & musical instruments, mid-18th c., 11" **146**

Painted paper, Salome offering John the Baptist's head to Herodias, verso w/a shepherd & shepherdess by a well, ivory

sticks carved & pierced w/lovers, & putti w/doves, ca. 1860, 9" **161**

The Betrothal of the Virgin Painted Fan

Painted paper, The Betrothal of the Virgin w/Joseph holding his flowering rod, the border painted w/series of miniature landscape vignettes w/figures in foreground, four of which are in tones of pink, verso painted w/ship being loaded at a port, w/fortified gatehouse, the border also painted w/15 miniature vignettes, ivory sticks carved & pierced w/figures, ca. 1730, 11" (ILLUS.)............... **1,749**

The Birth of the Infante Philip, Duke of Calabria

Painted paper, the birth of the infante Philip, Duke of Calabria, w/Queen Marie Amalia of Saxony in bed in the Palace of Portici near Naples, w/crimson canopy w/Royal arms above & lace coverlet, attended by six ladies, two carrying fans & the Duchess Miranda Caracciolo who holds the baby Prince who already bears the order of the Golden Fleece, beside the bed stands her husband King Charles III of the Two Sicilies, later to be King Charles III of Spain, & his brother the Duke of Parma, the dressing table mirror, clock, three mirrors & overdoor are all crowned, verso painted with allegories of the four continents w/children of the four continents dancing & waving blue banners inscribed "Pr & PP," Spanish scenes have a country palace in the background, Chinese scene a pagoda, the ivory sticks carved, pierced, silvered & gilt w/figures & flowers, fore-edges carved w/birds & pots of flowers, handle w/flower, a flower when closed, probably 1747, 11 1/2" (ILLUS.)............................. **26,239**

Painted paper, The Calydonian Boar Hunt, verso w/a shepherd, ivory sticks carved & pierced w/figures w/moneybags &

w/buildings, ca. 1740 - in contemporary fan box, 11" **204**

Painted paper, the King & Queen of Spain, enthroned, w/coats of arms above, chamberlain to their left, the throne room furnished w/four gilt armchairs upholstered in blue, statues, blue & white vases, two candelabra, wall sconces attached to pillars, a pier glass, the verso w/putti bearing blue banners, one blows a trumpet, the reverse with chinoiserie flowers & birds, the sticks painted w/pilasters & caryatids, ca. 1725, 11 1/2" (three sticks broken & a guardstick broken) **11,662**

Painted paper, tones of blue w/elegant figures admiring a fountain beside the statue of Neptune, in formal garden, reserves w/farming scenes w/cattle & cottages, verso w/prunus in tones of blue, ivory sticks pierced & painted w/bird & prunus in tones of blue, guardsticks carved w/chinoiserie figures, probably English, ca. 1850, 10" **3,353**

Painted paper, Venus & Apollo in their chariots, verso w/a fisherman, ivory sticks carved, pierced & gilt w/rocaille, & backed w/horn, ca. 1750, 12" **394**

Painted paper, Venus & Mars, w/putti playing w/Mar's armour, reserves w/chinoiserie figures, ivory sticks carved & pieced w/shepherd & shepherdess & putti & painted w/vignettes, English, ca. 1760, 10" (w/some overpainting) **408**

Painted paper, w/an allegory of marriage, verso w/spray of flowers, bone sticks pierced & silvered, Dutch, ca. 1780, 11" **131**

Painted Fan w/Pagoda Sticks

Painted paper, w/pagoda sticks, harvest scene, verso w/figures dancing to a fiddler & drinking, in a landscape w/fountain by a pond, w/church spire beyond, ivory sticks painted w/flowers, fruit & musical instruments, guardsticks carved w/chinoiserie figures, French, ca. 1770, 11", one stick repainted, old repairs & overpainting (ILLUS.) **1,458**

Painted silk, elegant figures in a park & two oval landscape vignettes w/monuments, ivory sticks carved, pierced & silvered, French, ca. 1775, 11" **437**

Painted silk, musique champetre after Goya inscribed Garcia-Valladolid, ivory sticks carved pierced & painted w/chinoiserie, leaf ca. 1890, sticks ca. 1750, 10" **146**

Paper, hand-painted w/a romantic scene of Roman soldiers & women celebrating, the highly carved sticks w/a walking frame of couples dancing surrounded by winged putti finely gilt & silvered, displayed in fan-shaped case, 18th c., 12 x 22" **560**

Paper, hand-painted w/elaborate garden & waterfall scenes on front & back w/couples courting, finely scrolled gilt borders, delicately carved & pierced sticks silvered & gilt, ca. 1790, displayed in fan-shaped case, 15 x 24" (one stick damaged) **560**

Paper, hand-painted w/scene of three young 18th c. couples in a park, elaborate gilt scrolling on leaf, pierced mother-of-pearl sticks w/silvered decoration, ca. 1790, displayed in fan-shaped frame, 14 x 22 1/2" (some tears) **364**

Plaited straw, handscreen or ventola, inserted in lacquered wood, w/turned bone handle, probably Venetian, 18th c., 16" **437**

Printed paper, an oval stipple engraving w/portrait of Admiral Lord Nelson, w/wreath above & poem below, w/wooden sticks, English, 1801, 7 1/2" (one stick cracked & piece missing from another stick, verso of leaf slightly torn) **1,603**

Printed paper, Moses Striking the Rock, hand-coloured etching, inscribed "published by M. Gamble...1740," with pierced ivory sticks, guardsticks carved, English, 1740 - in 18th c. fan box, 11" **408**

Printed paper, The Frost Fair, line engraving "printed upon the Ice, on the River Thames Jan. 23d 1739/40," w/wooden sticks, English, 1739, 10", rare (slight tears at some folds) **1,020**

Silk leaf, scene w/11 putti entangled in a vine, by Harry George Theaker, R.B.A., early 20th c., fan-shaped mount, framed & glazed, 18" w. (small holes) **364**

FIRE FIGHTING COLLECTIBLES

Fire bucket, painted & decorated leather, cylindrical, yellow wording on a black ground "John Cobby 1840 No. 2," green trim on rim, mid-19th c., 8" d., 16 3/4" h. (minor wear) **$3,335**

Fire bucket, painted leather, cylindrical w/replaced handle, gilt & black lettering "Protector 17" (?) on red, gilt & black bands, 19th c., 13 3/4" h. (lettering obscure) **374**

Fire bucket, painted leather, slightly tapering cylindrical body w/rim rings for strap handle, a black painted rim band above dark red sides centered by a large brown & gold spread-winged eagle w/a long scrolling banner in its beak, a green breast shield showing bootmaker's tools, draped swags below the bird, inscribed "Mechanic Fire Society - Ezra Young" & on the reverse "No. 2 1811," probably Portsmouth, New Hampshire, 12" h. (broken handle, minor paint wear) **54,675**

Fire bucket, painted leather, slightly tapering cylindrical form w/rim rings for leather strap handle, a black-painted rim band above a pale yellow-painted body w/a greenish looped ribbon over a large oval wreathed panel centering a red reserve inscribed in black & white "Leonidas H. Titcomb Jr. 1820 Bid Vulcan Yield to Neptunes Powr," 13" h. (handle replaced, paint loss) **3,220**

Fire bucket, painted leather, swelled cylindrical form w/rim rings for strap handle, a black painted rim band above yellow sides centered by a large shield cartouche framed by red drapery & gold scrolls & band, inscribed in black on white "Warren - Fire Club - J. Shove - Danvers - 1829," 12" h. (broken handles, paint wear)... **2,415**

Leather Fire Bucket

Fire bucket, painted leather, waisted cylindrical form w/leather swing handle, brass stud trim, black & red banner on front w/"Constitution" in gold lettering, old yellow paint, 8 1/2" h. (ILLUS.) **385**

Fire buckets, painted leather, gently swelled cylindrical form w/rim rings for leather strap handle, painted w/a red border band above dark green sides w/a design of clasped hands over a banner w/inscription "1833 - Mutual Fire Society - Solomon L. Dyer No.1" and "No. 2," 12 1/2" h., pr. (handles & loops repaired, paint loss) **11,500**

Parade Fire Hat

Fire hat, ceremonial parade-type, composition, painted blue w/painted red brim, front depicting a spread-winged American eagle grasping a banner in its talons, inscribed in gilded lettering "Columbia Hose Co.," the top w/initials "D.H." & the back w/a flouishing "H," probably Philadelphia, mid-19th c., minor inpainting along the cracks, new coat of varnish on crown, 8 x 13" (ILLUS.) **6,000**

Brass Fire Horn

Fire horn, brass, tapering trumpet form w/oval mouthpiece, traces of silver plate on inside of bell, minor dents, 20 1/2" l. (ILLUS.) **248**

Fire hose box, painted wood, long rectangular box w/hinged lid, chamfered front panel w/painted scene of a ship in the water near a rocky shore, top & sides painted red w/yellow decorative trim, from an early firehose wagon, 19th c., 10 x 39 1/4", 10 1/4" h. (paint wear, loose locking mechanism) **230**

Fire mark, cast lead, a green tree mounted on an oval wooden plaque w/a beveled edge, identifying information attached to the back, Philadelphia, ca. 1799, 10 1/4 x 15" (wear, age splits)................... **2,875**

Helmet, leather, painted white w/brass front plate held in place by brass eagle device & reading "HUMANE #1- POTTSVILLE PA" & "1830" painted in yellow & red paint on back brim, Cairns & Bro. of New York, 19th c. (some leather drying & cracking & weakness to brim) **550**

Painting, oil on canvas, side view of an early fire engine, four-wheeled wagon-style marked on the side "Howard - 34," shown on a cobblestone streetscape w/trees & homes in the background, initialed "T.C.E." in the lower right, 19th c., mounted on a panel, framed, 23 x 30" (scattered retouch, minor scattered losses, craquelure) **4,025**

FIREARMS

Rare Early Derringer

Derringers, finely engraved nickel silver mounts & back action locks, fine checkered grips & blued barrels, signed "J.E. Evans, Phila.," w/period mahogany case w/red wool lining, early 19th c., barrels 5" l., pr. (ILLUS. of one) **$5,500**

Fowler, two-part walnut stock w/silver pineappled trigger guard w/hallmarks of Birmingham, England, old percussion conversion lock, tang w/relief rococo carving & a chased silver thumbpiece, engraved brass butt plate w/worn silver plate, 56" l. octagonal to round barrel, England, 19th c., 71 1/2" l. (age cracks, two ramrod pipe replaced, part of side plate missing).. **1,760**

Long rifle, percussion full-stock model, curly maple stock, octagonal barrel, back-action lock marked "P.S. & J. Co.," 52" l. (small area of surface wear) **330**

Long rifle, percussion half-stock, curly maple stock, octagonal barrel, engraved signature appears to be "H. Huun," overall 57 1/4" l. (cracks in the stock) **358**

Long rifle, percussion-type, curly maple stock w/mellow finish, 40" l. octagonal barrel w/engraved brass patch box, 55" l. (pieced repairs around lock & breech).......... **990**

Long rifle, percussion-type, curly maple stock w/silver cheek piece & escutcheons, engraved brass side plate, marked "J. Chandler," refinished stock, overall 52 1/4" l. (restored wrist crack) **578**

Musket, Harpers Ferry 1841 percussion model, brass hardware including patch box, refinished walnut stock, 32" l. round barrel, 49" l. (age cracks & chips, missing ramrod).. **715**

Musket, Parker & Snow w/Miller conversion, 1861 musket w/1863 date on lock, good condition w/old dark finish, 56" l. (age cracks & chips, ramrod missing)........... **605**

Musket, percussion flintlock conversion, faint circular cartouche on the buttstock, round barrel, overall 57 3/4" l. **495**

Musket, percussion-type w/brass hardware & three steel bands, round barrel, Europe, 19th d., 56 1/2" l. (old dark finish, some pitting).. **550**

Musket, U.S. Model 1841, brass hardware including patch box, Remington Arms mark & 1853 date on lock, refinished, 48 3/4" l. (well done repairs)........................... **550**

Musket w/bayonet, flintlock, walnut stock w/an old worn dark finish, 42" l. tapered round barrel w/three bands & iron hardware, 57" l. (overall pitting, hammer appears to be a replacement)............................. **660**

Pistol, British percussion model, brass hardware & iron loop on grip cap, mark of East India Co. w/rampant lion on lock, carved markings ahead of trigger guard, overall 15 1/2" l.. **275**

Pistol, Colt Model 1911 A1 model, .45 caliber, Parkerized finish w/a blued clip, 8 1/2" l.. **440**

Pistol, flintlock, stock w/old refinishing & brass hardware, lock marked "Ketland & Co." w/crown mark & "G.R.," England, 9" tapered round barrel, overall 15" l. **935**

Pistol, flintlock, walnut stock w/a martial rammer, brass hardware & an engraved grip cap, lock engraved "Tower - G.R." & crown, cap marked "2, Husar, K.G.L.," England, overall 15 1/2" l. **990**

Pistol, percussion model, walnut stock w/age cracks & brass hardware, lock w/abbreviated stamp for Middletown, Connecticut & dated 1847, 8 1/2" l. round barrel, probably by Aston or Johnson, 14" l. (missing ramrod attachment) **440**

Pistol, Remington-Elliot pepperbox model, .32 caliber, hard rubber grips, 5" l. **193**

Pistol, Winchester Model 1873 lever-action, .44 caliber, overall very good condition w/edge wear to blue, 24" l. octagonal barrel... **1,210**

Revolver, Colt 1861 Navy model, .36 cailiber, wooden grips, overall 12 1/2" l. (two screws added in grips, one strap screw replaced) **440**

Rare "Fluck" Colt Dragoon Revolver

Revolver, Colt .44 "Fluck" pre-first Model Dragoon percussion model, sighted half-round/half-octagonal barrel marked "Address, Saml Cot New-York City," cylinder w/"Model USMR/Colt's Patent" w/Indian & Dragoon battle scene, the frame marked "Colt's - Patent - U.S." near the center, a Walker-type brass trigger guard, catouched walnut grips, marked "P" on barrel, wedge, frame, cylinder, hammer, trigger guard & backstrap, light grey patina overall, pitting on barrel, lever & cylinder, engraved scene faint, mainspring broken, lever latch a replacement, hammer screw broken, barrel w/crack at forcing comb, one of an estimated 300 produced, Serial No. 2177 for 1848, barrel 7 1/2" l. (ILLUS.)` **9,775**

Revolver, Colt Model 1860, fluted cylinder w/1850 patent date, frame marked "Colts Patent," 8" barrel w/Hartford address (overall light pitting, grip strap w/old silver finish which may not be original)............... **2,035**

Revolver, Colt New Line Model 32, areas of original case coloring on the frame, 6" l. **165**

Revolver, Remington Model 1858 percussion model, faint inspector's markings on wooden grips, 14" l... **550**

Revolver, Remington-Beals Navy Model, .36 caliber, octagonal barrel, wooden grips, 13 1/2" l. (hairline in grip) **633**

Revolver & holster, Colt Army Model, single-action, .45 caliber, antler grips, reconditioned blued barrel, cylinder & frame, grip strap, loading gate & ejector tube chrome-plated, barrel 5 1/2" l., w/an unsigned finely tooled belt & holster, 2 pcs... **935**

Rifle, flintlock long-rifle, curly maple w/old dark finish, raise-carving including C-scrolls behind the cheek piece & detail around the tang, engraved horse head patchbox w/silver star & thumbpiece inlay, 47 3/4" octagonal to round smooth bore barrel, Abraham Schweitzer, Lancaster & Chambersburg, Pennsylvania, 63" l. (Dreppert lock old replacement, forend of stock professionally ended out).. **8,525**

Rifle, flintlock long-rifle, curly maple w/old dark finish, simple raise-carving around cheek piece & comb, brass hardware w/bird's-head patch box & engraved eagle cheek piece inlay, signature appears to be D. Sheets, 62 3/4" l. (old repair at tang & lock reconverted) **3,025**

Rifle, fullstock flintlock model, curly maple w/old dark finish & over-varnish, brass hardware including a delicate four piece patch box, Golcher lock w/a double-throated hammer, unsigned but some characteristics of William or Peter Young, 39 1/4" l. octagonal barrel, overall 52 1/2" l... **2,640**

Rifle, Kentucky flintlock long-rifle, raise-carved walnut stock w/old refinishing & nine silver & brass inlays, finely carved C-scrolls on buttstock & around cheek piece & tang, checkered wrist & relief scrolling ahead of lock & side plate, signed on barrel "M. Fordney," Melchoir Fordney, Lancaster, Pennsylvania, 55" l. (reconversion to flint, patch box & trigger guard replaced, forend shortened slightly) **6,050**

Rifle, percussioin long-rifle, curly maple stock w/a beaver tail cheek piece & engraved silver eagle inlay, brass hardware including an engraved & pierced patch box, signed on barrel "A.G. Joy," 54 1/4" l. (forend restorations).................... **2,750**

Rifle, percussion long-rifle, curly maple w/good figure & patina, brass hardware including an engraved patch box & toe plate signed "S. McClain," eagle inlay over cheek piece, signed "J. Yeager," 51 1/4" l. (some wear ahead of lock)......... **1,320**

Rifle, Spencer Army Model, repeating action, .54 caliber, walnut stock stamped "J. Besse" for Sgt. John Besse, Co. G., 46th Regt. O.V.I., 30" l. barrel (forestock shortened just ahead of first band)............. **1,320**

Rifle, U.S. 1841 percussion model, brass hardware including patch box, round barrel, lock signed "E. Whitney, N. Haven - 1852," 49" l. (refinished, pieced repairs) **440**

Rifle, Winchester Model 1873, lever-action, .38 caliber, walnut stock, old finish & cleaning rod, 24" l. octagonal barrel.............. **550**

Rifle w/bayonet, Springfield trapdoor model, 45-70 cal., eagle stamp & signature on the lock, bold inspector's markings on barrel & faint marks on the stock, 48 3/4" l. (split at top of buttstock) **495**

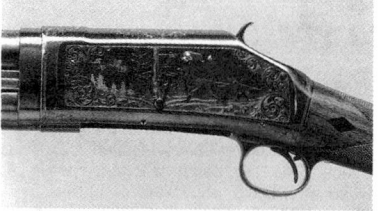

Rare Engraved Winchester Shotgun

Shotgun, Winchester 12 gauge Model 1897 Pigeon Grade Black Diamond Takedown model w/rare factory engraving, bead-signed barrel w/matted sighting plain, deluxe checkered walnut forend on take-down magazine tube, factory-engraved frame w/decorative scrollwork highlighting large panel scenes of two pointers flushing quail & four ducks taking flight, rare black diamond inlaid deluxe oil-finished walnut pistol grip stock w/checkered wrist & rare Monte-Carlo comb, mounted w/factory original "Winchester" red rubber recoil pad (tired & collapsing), together w/original leather leg-o-mutton type case w/overall wear, Serial No. E 796442, barrel 30" l. (ILLUS. of engraving)... **5,750**

FIREPLACE & HEARTH ITEMS

Fine Decorated Federal Andirons

Andirons, brass, Federal style, a large belted ball top w/a tall turned finial resting on a high square plinth engraved w/flowers & a bow-knotted wreath surrounded a monogram "B," a stylized flower on two flanking sides, on arched spurred front legs w/ball feet, attributed to R. Wittingham, New York, early 19th c., surface scratches, grime, 19 3/4" h., pr. (ILLUS.)............................... **$4,313**

Andirons, cast brass, figural, cast in the half-round as a profile of a hound seated at attention w/rear legs & tail tucked underneath hind quarters, late 19th - early 20th c., 13 1/4" h., facing pair.................... **3,220**

Andirons, cast iron, figural Scottie dogs, molded in the half-round as a dog seated on its hind legs begging, well detailed hair, eyes & nose, each facing right, stamped "JM 68," early 20th c., 16 1/4" h., pr.................................... **4,600**

Rare Painted Baseball Player Andirons

Andirons, cast iron, figural, standing facing baseball players in the half-round, one a pitcher facing a batter, wearing white uniforms w/blue socks, belts & caps, black shoes, stamped "R.B.S.- 09," early 20th c., 19 3/8" h., pr. (ILLUS.) **9,775**

Andirons, cast iron, figural swords, each cast in the round as a large sword standing on the tip of the blade, red-painted hilt & black blade, early 20th c., 23 3/4" h., pr... **1,380**

Bellows, painted & decorated wood, a gilt, green, brown & black cornucopia of fruit on a red ground, brass finial & tack decoration, early 19th c., 18" l. (leather restored).. **518**

Bellows, painted & decorated wood, flat sides free-hand painted & stenciled w/a cornucopia, fruit & foliage in black, gold, green & yellow, brass nozzle, old worn leather, 17" l. (ILLUS. top next column)..... **1,100**

Bellows, painted wood & leather, flat-sided, original yellow ground w/stenciled & free-hand painted stylized fruit & foliage designs in red, green, brown & black, brass nozzle, wear to decoration, old worn rleathering, 17 1/2" l. **605**

Bellows, painted wood & leather, flat-sided, original yellow painted w/stenciled & free-hand painted design of stylized fruit & foliage in red, green, brown & black, brass nozzle, wear to decoration, very worn old leather, 18" l. **275**

Painted Antique Bellows

Bellows, turtle-back type, painted wood & leather, old black paint ground decorated w/a large long-tailed bird w/berries in yellow, gold, green, blue, red, etc., brass nozzle,wear, very worn old leather, 17 1/2" l. **660**

Bellows, turtle-back type, painted wood & leather, old refinished surface w/painting of a bluish grey crested bird w/yellow highlights, perched on a branch, yellow striping, brass nozzle, leather worn, 19th c., 17 5/8" l. (some replaced tacks, two glued splits on backboard) **385**

Bellows, turtle-back type, painted wood & leather, old repaint w/black ground & faint gold stenciled basket of fruit, red & orange stripes, brass nozzle, 19th c., 17" l. (releathered, wear, old edge damage).. **220**

Bellows, turtle-back type, painted wood & leather, original green paint ground w/tan border & yellow stenciled design of a large fruit-filled compote, brass nozzle, old releathering, minor wear, 17" l.............. **935**

Bellows, turtle-back type, painted wood & leather, original mustard yellow paint w/flowers & foliage in shades of copper w/black accents & stripe, the back w/a starburst around the air hole, brass nozzle, 19th c., 18" l. (paint wear, releathered, added strap).. **358**

Bellows, turtle-back type, painted wood & leather, stenciled & free-hand decoration of a basket of flowers in gold & green on a red ground, stenciled gold borders, old releathering, brass nozzle, 19th c., 17 3/8" l. (wear, flaking) **110**

Bellows, turtle-back type, painted wood, original red paint w/yellow edge stripe, stenciled & free-hand decoration w/shells & foliage in black & gold, brass nozzle, old leather very worn, 18" l. **440**

Bellows, turtle-back type, painted wood, original stenciled design of a bowl of fruit & foliage in gold & green on a rosewood-grained ground w/a red border w/gold stenciling, brass nozzle, 19th c., 18 3/4" l. (poorly releathered, back handle reinforced)....................................... **209**

Fireboard, painted wood, a rectangular wide frame enclosing a latticework panel, painted dark green, 19th c., 36 3/4 x 47 1/2" (minor paint wear & losses)... **748**

Fireplace fender, brass & wire, Federal style, long low form w/curved ends, a brass top rail above scroll-decorated vertical wirework screening, America or England, late 18th - early 19th c., 15 x 49 1/2", 10" h................. **2,875**

Early Fireplace Fender

Fireplace fender, brass & wire, long slender upper & lower brass rails curving at the ends to form fender & enclosing a decorative latticework wire band above a fine wire lower vertical band interwoven w/wire scrolls, upper rail set w/three ball finials, America or England, late 18th - early 19th c., minor dents, 18 x 43 1/2", 12 1/4" h. (ILLUS.)....................................... **2,070**

Fireplace fender, brass & wire, long slender upper & lower brass rails curving at the ends to form fender & enclosing a decorative latticework wire band above a fine wire lower vertical band interwoven w/wire scrolls, America or England, late 18th - early 19th c., 15 x 49 1/2", 10" h. **2,875**

Fireplace fender, copper, Arts & Crafts style, straight-edged w/rectangular repoussé panels decorated w/an oval & foliate design, accented w/oval & heart-shaped turquoise blue stone insets, England, early 20th c., 53" l., 3 1/2" h........... **259**

Grill, cast iron, Horace Greeley-type, fan-shaped grill w/grease reservoir, raised on three legs, Campbell Foundry Co., Harrison, New Jersey, 19th c., 16 3/4 x 25", 3 1/4" h.. **230**

Hearth broom, horse hair bristles fitted in a small board w/a long center slender turned handle, original red paint w/black, yellow & gold striping & stenciled & freehand floral decoration in brown powder & black, 28" l. (wear, some paint flaking) **248**

Hearth toaster, wrought iron, rotating-type, twisted double-arch rack bars & three twisted & stylized tree designs, American, early 19th c., 14 x 15", 6 3/4" h. (corrosion) **920**

Hearth trivet, wrought iron, three tall slender legs supporting a horseshoe-shaped trivet top w/spade & scroll openwork designs, carved wooden handle extending from top, American, early 19th c., 14 1/2" l., 7 5/8" h. (corrosion, holes)............ **316**

FISHING COLLECTIBLES

Books & Paper Items

Catalog, "Heddon Deluxe Catalog," 1953, color chart for lures, 76 pp. (stains & some tears on cover)................................... **$83**

Catalog, "Shakespeare," 1927, fold-over design, illustrated, features rods, lures, accessories & reels, including the Beetzel, 88 pp., 8 x 8 1/2"................................... **138**

Catalog, "T.H. Chubb Rod Co ," illustrated rods, reels, flies & accessories & still retains two tear-out order blanks, 119 pp, 6 x 9" (minor stains on cover) **770**

Catalog, "Thomas H. Bate & Co.," 1867, large fish depicted on cover above "Needles, Fish Hooks - Fishing Rods and Tackle - of Every Design," contains line drawings of reels, hooks, lures, rod building components & floats, 32 pp, 10 1/2" x 13 1/2" (interior pages in excellent condition, cover w/light foxing & minor edge chips & tear in spine)............. **3,740**

Magazines, "Tackle," 1909, Shakespeare monthly bulletin sent to dealers, containing various articles on fishing, tackle, stories & jokes, 24 pp., Vol. 1, Nos. 3,4 & 6, the set (some foxing & staining) **303**

Lures

Braidwood Stamp Co., "Gay Lure Spoon Plug," made of genuine Catalin w/large glass eyes, No. 7 fluted spinner blade attached to back to which a large single hook is attached, long heavy wire line tie & yellow body, w/original box, Perth Amboy, New Jersey, 2" l.................................... **171**

Creek Chub, No. 100 Wiggler, glass eyes, improved lip, red head, white finish, in original box.. **154**

Creek Chub, No. 600 "Husky Musky," glass eyes, unmarked lip, through wire hook harness, finished in mullet, w/original unmarked box & fold-out flyer, 5" l. (some age lines & hook dings, good box) **220**

Geen Spiral Bait

Geen, twisted metal spiral bait w/fish-shaped tail & applied metal fins w/iridescent blue stripe finish & accented w/black rib design w/two trebles attached to twisted wire passing through body w/line tie loop, edge stamped "Geen's Patent 2103," 4" l. (ILLUS.) **138**

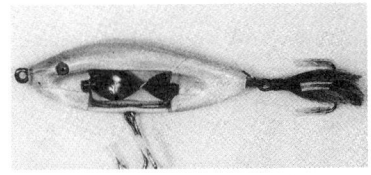

Immell Chippewa Lure

Immell Bait Co., fish-shaped Chippewa bait w/glass eyes & feathered rear treble, internal spinner w/original red paint & stamped "Pat. Nov. 1, 1910" on blade, some age cracks & darkening of finish, 3 1/2" l. (ILLUS.) **660**

"Kingfisher Wood Minnow" Lure

Pflueger, "Kingfisher Wood Minnow," three hook minnow w/glass eyes, neverfail hardware & finished in white w/green & red spots, sliding lid wooden box w/colorful red & blue label marked "Kingfisher - Wood Minnow - For Catching Game Fish" flanked by illustrations of birds & "Trade - Mark" (ILLUS.).................................. **990**

Shakespeare, fish-shaped w/two hooks & flat plate hook hanger, yellow perch scale finish, h.p. gill marks, later style props, 3" l. (some chips on belly & minor scratches) **110**

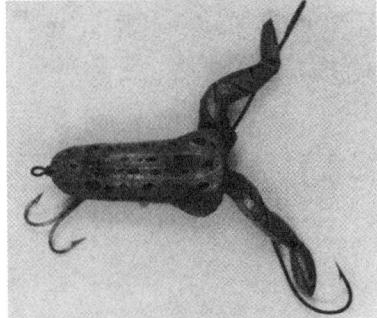

"Rhodes Mechanical Frog" Lure

Shakespeare, "Rhodes Mechanical Frog," h.p. rubber-bodied frog w/two flexible (now hardened) legs which kicked each time the line was pulled, round lead weight attached to belly, one leg broken, ca. 1910 (ILLUS.)............................... **110**

Weller, classic minnow, three-sectioned bait w/large glass eyes, finished in brown pike scale, w/original red, white & blue box marked "143" on end, with fish illustrations & flyer picturing four baits, 4 1/4" l. **110**

Winchester, "Gold Boy," marked "Winchester Trade Mark 9623" on blade, on original card (some moth damage to feathered treble & slight staining to card) **193**

Winchester, "Multi-Wobbler," fat-bodied w/green back & gold scale finish on white body, glass eyes, diving blades marked "Winchester Trade Mark Made In U.S.A. - 9201," w/original box (some varnish flaking & age lines, box w/tears on cover, end labels missing) **385**

Winchester, "Spinner," No. 9476, large spinner w/3 1/4" teardrop blade & worn feathered treble w/top & bottom portions of original card, Winchester Repeating Arms Co., New Haven, Connecticut **110**

Reels

Billinghurst Reel

Billinghurst, trout, brass, birdcage, sidemount w/folding walnut handle & rare click, marked "Billinghursts Patent, Rochester, N.Y., Aug. 9, 1859 & 1873," accepted to be nation's first patented & produced fly reel, 3 3/8" d. (ILLUS.)................ **1,430**

Handmade "Baby" Trout Reel

Bogdan, Stan, trout, silver anodized w/black plates, handmade "Baby" reel w/original leather pouch, 1" w. spool, Nashua, New Hampshire, unused, mint condition, 2 5/8" d. (ILLUS.) **1,870**

Scarce Clinton Trout Reel

Clinton, Charles M., trout, German silver w/aluminum side-mount spool, marked "C.M. Clinton, Ithaca, N.Y. - Pat. Oct. 29, 1889," features internal click & unusual self-lubricating oil reservoir, near mint condition, perhaps unfished, 2 5/8" d. (ILLUS.).. **3,850**

Hendryx, trout, nickel plated, side-mount single action safety reel, counter balance weight on spool, long smaller diameter handle, ca. 1907, 3 5/8" d., near mint **660**

Meek (Horton Mfg.), tournament casting, No. 3, handmade German silver w/aluminum handle & tournament spool, drag switch only, unpolished & shows normal age patina.. **385**

Early Meek & Milam Bait Casting Reel

Meek & Milam, bait casting reel, handmade, German silver w/three numbered screws & early two-piece seamed head cap, 2" w. spool, crank handle w/bulbous ivory handle grasp, click switch, two knurled front cap rim bands & knurled ring on back plate, marked "Meek & Milam, Frankfort, KY - No. 3," handle crank w/dings & number two screw marking somewhat faint, 2" d. (ILLUS.) **4,400**

Pflueger, trout, metal "click & drag ratchet" plate, No. 1496 1/2 Medalist, in original 1949 factory dated box w/paper & hanging tag **99**

Pflueger "Golden West," trout, No. 5092, German silver w/hard rubber & aluminum plates, black Bulldog medallion, pat. Feb. 10, 1903 & Jan. 23, 1907, 7/8" w., 2 1/2" d. **1,210**

Seamaster (McChristian), tarpon or salmon, gold anodized, anti-reverse S-handle, 1" w. spool, 3 7/8" d. (tiny pock

marks on handle & initials etched on bottom of foot) **990**

Shakespeare 1744, tournament free spool Model 26, (1926), jeweled German silver & aluminum, 100 yds., 1 1/4" w. spool w/cork arbor, click switch & rim free spool switch, 2" d. (corrosive stains to aluminum back plate) **165**

Talbot, tournament casting, custom handmade tiny jeweled German silver, serial No. 962, 1 3/8" w. spool w/opaque bearing jewels, aluminum ends & large diameter balsa wood arbor, click switch, aluminum handle w/three tiny maroon grasps, unique thumb rest & offset rounded end foot (to clear thumb rest?) stamped "Talbot Reel - Richardson, Chicago," 1 3/4" d. (two screw slots show use) **3,080**

Valentine, salt water or salmon, gold anodized anti-reverse control, 1 1/8" w. spool, unique rotating handle, marked "Valentine 400," 4" d. **220**

Vom Hofe (Edward), salmon, German silver & hard rubber, handmade Model 423, size 3/0 Restigouche, roller pillar line guides, 1 1/2" w. spool, click switch, aluminum handle, foot & spool ends w/Vom Hofe adjustable drag w/indicator dots, marked "Edward Vom Hofe & Co., Phila. - Pat. May 20, 02," 3 5/8" d. **1,375**

Vom Hofe (F.) & Son, multiplying reel, handmade German silver S-handle, marked "F. Vom Hofe & Son - Maker," 1 1/4" w. spool w/front rim push-pull button drag switch & original long thick handle w/long slightly tapered hard rubber grasp, ca. 1865, New York, very scarce, this reel spins forever, 3" d. **1,980**

Vom Hofe (Julius), trout, German silver handle, aluminum 1" w. spool reel w/brass spool shaft w/raised rear plate mounted click housing early hard rubber click button, circular pattern of pillars enclosing air drying holes in spool ends around the brass spool arbor & handle counterweight w/decorative circular dot pattern, marked "Thos. J. Conroy, NY - The Wells," ca. 1889, 3 1/4" d. (very good condition w/minimum corrosive pitting & some dings to raised housing) **1,650**

Rods

Granger (W & M) Special, fly, three-piece, two tip, appears to be unfished, mint in bag & tube, 9 1/2' l. **275**

Heddon, trout, marked, "Heddon - Featherweight - Bill Stanley's Favorite - #20 - 7 1/2' - 0 3/4 F," two-piece, two tip, 0 3/4 size ferrule, light line rod w/screw downlocking reel seat, half-Wells handle & maroon wraps, in original maroon bag w/tag & maroon tube w/label, 7 1/2' l. (some finish wear to reel seat parts) **825**

Leonard, trout, Model 371, Baby Catskill, two-piece, two tip w/tiny slide band over butternut spacer reel seat, serial No. 349, in original bag & tube, 6' l., 1 oz., mint condition **2,200**

Leonard, trout, two-piece, two tip, w/knurled slide band over tiger stiped maple spacer reel seat, original handle, serial No. 9082, 8' l., mint, unfished condition in bag & tube **1,870**

Orvis, salmon, three-piece, two tip, detachable extension butt, GAF(9) wt. line rod w/screw down-locking reel seat very near mint in original bag & labeled tube **303**

Payne, trout, Model 98, two-piece, one tip w/slide band over walnut spacer reel seat, labeled tube, in original bag, 7' l., 3 oz. **2,255**

Sewell Dunton, fly, "Angler's Choice," three-piece, two tip w/short cork extension butt, screw down-locking reel seat & super-Z type ferrules, in bag & tube, 9' l. (areas of light varnish roughness) **138**

Thomas (F.E.), trout, three-piece, two tip w/screw down-locking, over walnut spacer, reel seat in apparently unfished near mint condition in original bag w/hanging tag & labeled tube, Bangor, Maine, 8 1/2' l. **770**

Miscellaneous

Angler's knife, combination knife, priest & scale, Puma, unsharpened condition w/extremely minor wear & hardened leather thong **165**

Angler's knife, stainless steel w/serrated edge blade, disgorger, opener & ball end priest which contains a retractable 36" metal rule, marked "Luna-Italy," unsharpened excellent condition **138**

Unusual Wooden Creel

Creel, oval, wooden, lid w/center hole & wood bottom, carved sides w/brass lion head-shaped medallions w/rings attached to each side for attaching strap or harness, front w/small copper plaque w/applied & engraved brass fish, handmade, early 1900s, old white paint on interior, natural finish w/old crusty varnish on exterior, some warpage on bottom, some finish discoloration (ILLUS.)................. **660**

Rare "Carry All" Creel

Creel, woven whole willow w/leather strap lid latch, (possibly predecessor to normally found brass examples) two compartments, the upper one for lunch, tackle or gear & the lower to hold the catch, hole on lid passes down to lower compartment & hinged in center to retrieve fish, secured w/leather straps which are hardened & cracked, structure of creel is excellent w/no damage, rare early example of Hardy's "Carry All," 7 x 12", 10" h. (ILLUS.) **550**

Woven Willow Creel

Creel, woven wicker, squatty bulbous melon-shaped, French style construction, wood frame w/curved back to fit the hip, copper shield-shaped peg & loop lid latch (peg missing), small center hole, opposing screw eye hinges on curved lid, old leather shoulder strap, old green finish, light wear to finish on edges of lid & bottom (ILLUS.) **495**

Fish/eel trap, woven reed construction w/funnel-shaped 12" d. opening, interior funnel w/sharpened reeds to prevent exit of captured fish, small end w/reed cap for access, 19" l., excellent condition w/no breaks **193**

Fly box, 14 various size interior compartments & sliding celluloid lids, Hardy Neroda, 4 x 6" **303**

Handcrafted Fly Tying Chest

Fly tying chest, handcrafted wood w/eleven cedar-faced drawers w/metal pulls & two doors w/storage capability for spools, etc., folding handle for transporting & hasp on doors, 7 x 14 x 28" (ILLUS.)............. **220**

Gaff, copper & brass w/wood handle & spring-activated retractable hook guard attached to shaft w/small set screw allowing it to slide down shaft when not in use, retains old finish, 21" l............................ **165**

Net, collapsible, 12" round bent wood ring w/brass fixtures & vintage replacement bag, cane handle w/brass ferrule, refin-

ished in 1960 w/some decorative inter-
mediate wraps, marked "Woodfield &
Son Patent," very scarce, in excellent
condition **220**

Net, folding-type, triangular, brass & aluminum, 30" l. handle, brass catch & belt
clip, Hardy.. **165**

Painting, watercolor by W.J. Shaldach of a
fly-hooked leaping rainbow trout, matted
in shadow box frame above seven trout
flies, 10 x 12", framed to 20 x 22"............... **2,475**

Print, "American Brook Trout," hand-colored lithograph depicting brook trout on
bed of grass, Currier & Ives, 8 1/2 x 12"
image, period walnut veneer frame (minor foxing, edges trimmed 1 1/2" on all
sides & minor damage to corners of
frame) **330**

FOOT & BED WARMERS

Bed warmer, brass & copper pan w/hinged
lid pierced w/four small arcs of small
holes, engraved design across the center, long slender baluster- and knob-
turned wooden handle, 43" l. (old repairs)... **$220**

Bed warmer, brass pan, the hinged lid engraved w/foliate designs, long turned
wood handle, 19th c., 43 3/4" l. (minor
imperfections) **184**

Bed warmer, brass pan w/hinged brass lid
w/tooled design, long slender baluster-
and knob-turned wood handle, 40" l. **253**

Bed warmer, brass pan w/hinged cover engraved w/a large starflower & pierced
w/an outer band of small holes, long
slender turned wood handle, 42 1/2" l. **204**

Bed warmer, brass pan w/hinged cover
pierced around the edge w/small clusters
of holes & engraved w/a floral design,
long turned wood handle w/old dark fin-
ish, 11 1/2" d., handle 36" l. **220**

Bed warmer, brass pan w/hinged cover
pierced w/a ring of small holes & engraved overall w/an ornate scrolling design, long slender ring- and knob-turned
wooden handle, 42" l. (age crack in
handle) **275**

Bed warmer, brass pan w/hinged cover
pierced w/four small clusters of holes
around the rim & engraved w/an overall
floral design, long turned wood handle
w/old dark finish, pan 11 1/2" d., handle
33" l. (rim damage, handle wear).................... **220**

Bed warmer, brass pan w/hinged lid engraved w/a rosette design at center surrounded by scrolls & rope-like designs,
well-turned long slender wood handle
w/old refinishing & traces of original
paint, 44 3/4" l. (small split in pan near
hinge) **275**

Bed warmer, brass round pan w/hinged
cover w/pieced outer ring of tiny holes
around another ring of pierced clustered
holes & a third ring pierced w/small
hearts, the center pierced w/a ringed circle design, long turned wood handle,
40" l. (damage at hinge).................................. **358**

Brass Bedwarmer

Bed warmer, bright-cut brass pan w/hinged
cover pierced w/star motifs & decorated
w/flowers, scrolls & punchwork, ball finial
above a maple shaped handle & tapering
shaft, late 18th c., 43" l. (ILLUS.)............... **1,725**

Bed warmer, copper pan w/hinged cover
decorated w/floral engraving, long slender ring- and baluster-turned handle,
43" l. **220**

Bed warmer, copper pan w/tooled brass lid
w/sunburst design, long slender rod- and
knob-turned wood handle w/worn original
graining, 42" l.. **275**

Bed warmer, copper pan, brass cover
w/center flower medallion, turned wood-
en handle, 36 1/2" l. **165**

Bed warmer, brass w/pierced & floral engraved lid & turned wooden handle, old
patina, 38" l. (split in lid w/wear & batter-
ing, handle has worm holes) **165**

Bed warmer, brass pan w/hinged cover
w/floral engraved design, turned wooden
handle ended out & large brass ring
hanger added, 43" l. **220**

Bed warmer, brass pan w/hinged cover
w/tooled sunburst design, turned wooden
handle, 44" l. (split in rim at hinge)................. **193**

Foot warmer, mahogany & tin, punched
holes & punched initials "E.O.T.," old finish, 8 x 11", 6 3/4" h. (old burn in back
corner has pieced repair, minor edge
damage)... **297**

Foot warmer, painted pine, rectangular tall
box-form w/old red-painted pine top &
base w/corner posts joining the wooden
sides w/five pierced holes & a relief-
carved compass star, wire bail handle,
7 x 9", 7 1/4" h. (some edge damage,
sliding door replaced) **165**

Foot warmer, painted wood, rectangular
top & bottom w/molded edges, slender
corner posts framing the sides, pierced
overall w/designs of hearts, diamonds &
circles, wire bail handle, painted red,
19th c., 7 3/4 x 9 3/4", 7 1/4" h. (wear,
crack) **431**

Foot warmer, pine, tin & glass, a rectangular wood case w/tin back & lid baffle, glazed oval front & side panels, tin font w/whale oil burner, asbestos paper glued to inside of lid, metal handle an old addition, original dark finish w/gold-stenciled label "Patented March 14th 1865 - Manfd. by D. Dennis & Co., Cleveland, O.," 8 1/2" l. (glass replaced, damage to burner)... 330

Foot warmer, punched tin & wood, a mortised hardwood frame w/baluster-turned corner posts enclosing tin container punched w/a circle & diamond design, 8 x 8 1/2", 5 1/2" h....................................... 154

Foot warmer, punched tin & wood, a mortised wooden frame w/turned corner posts enclosing tin panels punched w/hearts in concentric circles & a compass star, an interior coal pan, wire bail handle, Pennsylvania, 19th c., 7 3/4 x 9", 5 3/4" h. (minor edge damage & rust)........... 275

Foot warmer, tin, rectangular w/pierced bands around the sides, soapstone cover w/old wire staple repair, interior w/font w/whale oil burner, 9 3/4" l............................... 110

Foot warmer, tin & wood, double-size, a mortised poplar frame w/old patina, enclosed double tin panels on the sides punched w/a circle & "V" design, wrought-iron pan, 9 1/4 x 14 3/4", 6 1/4" h.. 330

Foot warmer, tin & wood, nearly square punched tin sides decorated w/diamond designs & central round holes, poplar top & bottom boards held by wire, wrought-iron pan, 7 1/2 x 8 1/2", 5 1/2" h. (some edge damage).. 193

Foot warmer, tin & wood, square tin insert w/the sides pierced w/circle & diamond designs, framed by turned corner posts & a mortised frame, 19th c., 7 1/2 x 8 1/4", 6" h. (minor repair) 220

Foot warmer, tin & wood, tin box punched w/a design of hearts w/a Maltese cross on the door, in a mortised bird frame & turned corner posts, old dark finish, 7 3/4 x 8 1/2" (some solder repair, mismatched tin pan inside)` 303

Foot warmer, walnut, nearly square dovetailed form w/pierced designs on the sides, one side w/a pierced circle w/"L.F.," the sliding side pierced w/date "1814," wire bail handle, original finish w/scorching, 7 3/4 x 8 1/2", 6 1/2" h. (one piece of top molding an old replacement) 319

Early Walnut Foot Warmer

Foot warmer, walnut w/good old worn finish, rectangular deep box w/drilled holes in heart & butterfly designs, back w/"T.V.D.," brass reinforcing plates & handle, sliding cover, back loose, 7 3/4 x 10", 7" h. (ILLUS.) 330

Foot warmer, wood & tin, a mortised wooden frame w/turned corner posts framing the tin sides punched w/a design of hearts & circles, 7 1/2 x 9, 5 3/4" h. 193

FRAKTUR

Birth & Baptismal Certificate Fraktur

Fraktur paintings are decorative birth and marriage certificates of the 18th and 19th centuries and also include family registers and similar documents. Illuminated family documents, birth and baptismal certificates, religious texts and rewards of merit, in a particular style, are known as "fraktur" because of the similarity to the 16th century type-face of that name. Gay watercolor borders, frequently incorporating stylized birds, hand-lettered documents, which were executed by local ministers, school masters or itinerant penman. Most are of Pennsylvania Dutch origin.

Birth & baptism record, pen & ink & watercolor on paper, recording the birth of Mary Grimes, June 15, 1802, in Pikeland Township, Chester County, Pennsylvania, the center panel w/many religious verses done in print & script, the watercolor border w/a symmetrical design containiing a cherub holding horn, hex signs, parrots, flowers & vines, angels on clouds holding lyres, all done in red, yellow, blue, green, black & white, signed by Israel Grimes & dated February 28, 1823, 16 1/2 x 21" (loss throughout, needs restoration) **$4,675**

Birth & baptism record, printed & hand-colored, rectangular w/two small upper blocks of type flanking a floral design above a long rectangular central block of type flanked by large angels w/cherubs at the bottom, records a birth in 1833 in Mill Creek, Coshocton County, Ohio, printed by Peter Kaufman, Canton, Ohio, signed "Jacob Croft," good colors, modern frame, 15 x 19" (fold lines, minor stains)... **605**

Birth & baptismal record, lithograph, ink & watercolor on paper recording the birth of Catharina Nonenmacher, April 27, 1795,

Berks County, Pennsylvania, a large central heart flanked by two of smaller size surrounded by h.p. flowers & vines, late 18th c., Pennsylvania German School, framed, staining, toning, creases, tears, not examined out of frame, 12 1/2 x 15 1/2" (ILLUS.) **633**

Birth letter for George Enderlein, watercolor & pen & ink on paper, the name in large letters at the center above a lengthy script German inscription below, three circles across the center top, two facing birds on each side flanking the central one of a man in 18th c. attire shooting a bow & arrow, a large tulip flower & other blossoms issuing from a small urn up each side, Dauphin County, Pennsylvania, dated 1799-1816, framed, 12 x 17 1/2" **13,200**

Birth record, pen & ink & watercolor on laid paper, a large central heart enclosing the inscription recording an 1813 birth in North Hampton County & signed "F. Krebs," the heart flanked by a facing pair of large parrots & designs of tulips, stars & other devices in orange, brown, green & yellow, Pennsylvania, framed, overall 15 3/4 x 18 1/2" (some damage, glue stains from old rebacking) **1,100**

Birth record, pen & ink & watercolor on laid paper, rectangular, a narrow red rectangular border topped by a band of stylized tulips & other flowers in red, blue, brown & black, the border enclosing handwritten text in red & black recording an 1804 birth in Berks County, Manheim Township, Pennsylvania, by Martin Brechall, in molded modern frame, image 6 x 8" (stains, some paper damage) **715**

Birth record, pen & ink & watercolor on wove paper, a design w/four large hex signs in circles in each corner around a large central ring enclosing the text, records the birth in 1772 in Pennsylvania, orange, black & brown, in a beveled frame w/worn red graining, 14 x 18" (stains, fading & minor damage from acid ink) **880**

Birth Record Fraktur

Birth record, pen & ink & watercolor on wove paper, the text in a series of large concentric circles in the center surrounded by stylized flowers & birds & topped by two angels in the upper corners, records

the birth of Anna Metzler on July 28, 1819, the circle includes numbers corresponding to each verse from one to twelve, pious verse at the bottom w/date of June 13th, 1824, Pennsylvania, good color in shades of red, green, blue, yellow & black, framed, 10 1/2 x 12 1/2" (minor stains & paper damage) **29,700**

Birth record, watercolor, pen & ink on paper, by Martin Brechall, recording 1810 birth of Johannes Hewser, Berks County, Pennsylvania, center rectangular panel w/Pennsylvania German text bordered by five hearts w/German blessings, yellow stylized flowers in each corner w/bellflower & vine decoration throughout in yellow, red & blue, 13 x 16" (ILLUS. bottom previous column) **1,760**

Bible Book Plate

Book plate w/original bible, watercolor & ink, the rectangular triple-bordered reserve w/two conforming frames of shaded scales centering a meandering floral & foliate-decorated shaded scale-vine centered at the top by a winged angel head & inscribed at the center (trans.) "This Bible Belongs to me Johannes Schneider in Hagers County 1786" w/further inscription below, in original Bible of dark calf over beveled wooden boards, two brass clasps & catches, lacking one clasp, corners worn, scattered spotting to text, minor stains at end, the bookplate 9 x 9 3/4" (ILLUS. of bookplate) **14,950**

Bookplate, pen & ink & watercolor on wove paper, a large tulip blossom issuing from a small vase & on a slender leafy stem also issuing small blossoms, red, green & brown, framed, 5 3/4 x 7 3/4" (glued down at corners, light stains, short margin tear) **715**

Drawing, pen & ink & watercolor on laid paper, a bird perched on a scrolling leaf looking back over its shoulder to a large flying butterfly, in green & black w/thin border stripes in black, green & faded yellow, an "18" in a corner, later frame, image 2 5/8 x 3 1/8" (some wear) **413**

Drawing, pen & ink & watercolor on paper, rectangular, a pair of facing angels at the top above a starburst over a large heart enclosing a pair of birds perched on flowers in a pot, stylized flowers along the sides & two women standing at the bottom, in red, green, blue, yellow & black w/a tin whitewashed background, modern frame, 9 5/8 x 12 1/2" (minor paper edge damage) **1,100**

Pennsylvania German Fraktur

Drawing, pen & ink & watercolor on wove paper, a large heart-form border w/brown, yellow & blue half-circle design, the interior heart w/flowers & foliage & "Maria Hoffert" in yellow, white, green & brown, Pennsylvania, 6 x 7 3/4", minor stains & very small amount of flaking w/short edge tear, framed 8 1/4 x 10 1/3 (ILLUS.) **2,200**

Vorschrift, pen & ink & watercolor on paper, rectangular, very large lettered heading decorated w/colorful floral vines & sprigs above lines of small script & a musical notation for Maria, by Johan Adam Eyer, early 19th c., in early grain-painted frame, 8 x 12 1/4" **5,750**

FRAMES

Brass, figural, model of a late Victorian highwheel-style bicycle w/the oval picture opening in the large front wheel, late 19th c., 8" h. **$220**

Carved pine, draped putti holding stylized foliate crown & standing on scrolls & scrolled foliage, all surrounding an arched frame, painted gold, late 19th c., 17 x 26" (crack, repaired cracks) **518**

Cast iron, oval, the oval opening w/a beveled glass mirror, the sides cast w/bold fuchsia-like flowers w/scrolls at the bottom & a spread-winged eagle at the top, old gold repaint, 19th c., 11 1/4 x 15 1/2" **220**

Cherry, oval hand-carved design, gently rounded border w/outer & inner finely scallop-carved edges, the top relief-carved w/an American shield below the stylized head & wings of an American eagle, three carved feathered headdresses spaced around the sides & bottom, old soft finish, mid-19th c., 12 1/2 x 16 1/2" **715**

Enameled Bronze Tiffany Frame

Enameled bronze, wide flattened sides w/a narrow rim band enclosing a wide band of mottled brown enameled blocks, rectangular gilded inner opening border w/rounded corners, Tiffany Furnaces, early 20th c., 6 x 7 1/2" (ILLUS.) **1,400**

Gilt-bronze, rectangular w/flattened sides, narrow geometric border decorated w/alternating patches of black & red enamel, signed "Tiffany Studios New York 2076," early 20th c., 8 3/4 x 10 3/4" (ILLUS. right, below) **2,300**

Gilt-bronze, rectangular w/flattened sides, "Molded Design," the corners w/geometric designs, stamped "Tiffany Studios New York 1128," early 20th c., 8 3/4 x 11 1/4" **1,495**

Two Gilt-Bronze Tiffany Frames

Gilt-bronze, rectangular w/flattened sides, "Venetian" patt., the border cast w/stylized foliate designs, the base w/a band of ermine, stamped "Tiffany Studios New York 1682," early 20th c., 9 x 12" (ILLUS. left) **1,725**

Inlaid mahogany, Art Nouveau style, the arched & notch-cut crest ending in angled corners above incurved molded sides flaring down to outswept rounded base corners, the double-arch bottom w/notched foot supports, the center w/two large inverted-heart design picture openings framed by undulating light wood flowering vine inlay all around the sides, original finish, early 20th c., 13 1/2 x 22 1/2" **1,540**

Inlaid mahogany, table model, Arts & Crafts style, an upright rectangular form w/a gently arched top & slender edge buttresses, a tall oval opening above a two-color diamond-shaped inlay, original finish, early 20th c., 6" w., 9 1/2" h. **413**

Mahogany & brass, flat rectangular wood w/incurved sides, Arts & Crafts style, mounted at the corners w/pierced fanned leaf-cut brass plaques, original finish & patina, early 20th c., 7 1/2 x 10 1/2"............... **605**

Painted wood, rectangular, red & yellow sponged paint on embossed paper glued to ogee molding, containing N. Currier prints, the "Evening Prayer" & "Morning Prayer," mid-19th c., 16 x 20", pr. (minor imperfections) **3,680**

Thermoplastic, rectangular, heavy thick border molded w/ornate floral clusters in each corner w/leafy scrolls down the sides, contains a half-plate tintype of two seated gentlemen, ca. 1860, 7 x 8"............... **358**

Walnut, figured carved wood w/a large cut-out heart flanked by slender S-scrolls above a narrow diamond-form base, the heart w/a rectangular picture opening, old varnish finish, 7 1/8" h., pr...................... **385**

Walnut, rectangular shadowbox-style w/wide gilt liner, black enamel line detail, w/floral prints, third quarter 19th c., 12 1/2 x 14 1/4", pr..................... **165**

FRATERNAL ORDER COLLECTIBLES

Silk Masonic Apron

What do George Washington, Oliver Hardy and Gene Autry all have in common? They share a bond that traverses all walks of life—membership in the world's oldest fraternal organization, the Free & Accepted Masons (F&AM). Dating back to 14th century England, this organization's roots are steeped in the architectural craft guilds and operative lodges—builders, stone masons and the like. From these early members comes the elements of the Masonic emblem...a level, plumb and square, and the "G" to signify their belief in God.

Masonic ephemera, bric-a-brac and sacred books are abundant. In addition to the Masons, collectibles from sub-groups like the Order of the Eastern Star (OES), Shriners (32nd degree Masons), Scottish Rite, Knights

Templar, etc. create a wide range of memorabilia that is prized by today's collectors.

Also see: BARBERIANA

Masonic altar stand, pot metal w/brass finish, cut-out of Masonic emblem, mounted on a wood block, 2 3/4 x 9 x 12"............... **$15-20**

Masonic apron, silk w/silk embroidery of Masonic symbols including an arc, hourglass, sun, beehive & eye, paper label inscribed "Daniel McDowel, Unanimity Lodge of Edentown North Carolina, Entered June 1827, passed 1827, raised 1827," losses & staining, 15 x 15 1/2" (ILLUS.) **1,380**

Victorian Masonic Apron

Masonic apron, white silk w/a blue border w/yellow brocade, two tabs w/metallic twists, decorated w/calipers & eye & "Solon 771" in same gold metallic piping plus under flag is "Peter Vogler Jun. 15, 1885," New York origin, blue tasseled braid ties, 13 x 14 1/2" (ILLUS.)...................... **55**

Masonic apron & sash, the rectangular apron in silk w/a salmon border & black, green & gold w/red ribbons, the center printed w/various large Masonic emblems, w/a maroon velvet sash w/hand-knotted fringe, from the Harmony Lodge, New Britain, Connecticut, early 19th c., 2 pcs. (apron w/stains, fragile w/damage at fold lines) **165**

Masonic armchairs, painted & decorated wood, firehouse Windsor-style w/curved raised crestrail tapering & curving down to form arms all raised on six simple turned spindles, wide shaped plank seat on knob- and rod-turned front legs joined by double knob-turned stretchers, plain turned double side stretchers & a single back stretcher, original brown paint w/grained decoration on seats & crest, black & gold striping w/gold-stenciled calipers & square symbol in center of crest, original paper label of L.F. Wehrmann Furniture Warerooms, Cincinnati, mid-19th c., 30 1/2" h., set of 6 (areas of wear) **1,188**

Masonic ashtray, bronze w/Masonic logo in center, 3 3/4" h., 6 1/2" l. **10-15**

Masonic ashtray, ceramic, blue w/gold Masonic emblem in center, 5" d. **6-8**

Masonic Book

Masonic book, "History of Freemasonry and Concordant Orders," 1890 edition, 12 1/2 x 15" (ILLUS.) **15-20**

Masonic book, "Structure of Freemasonry" by Richard S. Biddle, copyright 1951, 12 1/2 x 15 1/2".. **15-20**

Masonic bowl, ceramic, white w/blue Masonic symbol & trim, marked "Walker China Vitrified, Bedford, Ohio, 6.44," 5" d. **12-15**

Masonic brandy set: glass, 5" h. snifter & six 2 1/4" h. matching glasses; dark blue Masonic emblem & marked "Marble Lodge," the set... **10-15**

Masonic Cigarette Box

Masonic cigarette box, cov., ceramic, square, white w/blue & gold Masonic emblem & gold trim, marked "Royal Winton, Made in England," 3 3/4 x 5 1/4" (ILLUS.)... **15**

Masonic flag pole top, cast iron, Masonic emblem on wood block, back is marked "IF © Irving Florma, MADE IN USA " **20**

Masonic ingrain carpet, red & black, a design of a sun, all-seeing eye on plinth, moon, Masonic tools, ark, hour glass, beehive, etc., within central arch, 36 1/4 x 53" (minor edge wear, loss at top).. **110**

Masonic jar, cov., china, cream w/blue & gold Masonic emblem, marked "McNicol China, W. Clarksburg, W. Va., X88," 4 1/4" d... **10-15**

Masonic Emblem Lamp

Masonic lamp, table model, pot metal w/brass wash, cut-out Masonic emblem in center, square base, marked on bottom "Rehmann," 8 3/4" w., 12 1/2" h. (ILLUS.) **25**

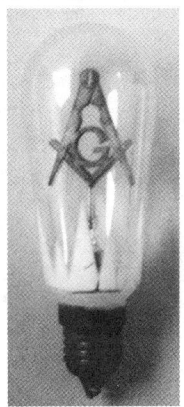

Masonic Ceremonial Light Bulb

Masonic light bulb, w/Masonic symbol inside, used on altar during ritual ceremonies, marked "Made in Germany," 100-110 volts, 2 1/2 x 6 1/4" (ILLUS.).............. **15-20**

Masonic Magazine Cover

Masonic magazine cover, "The New York Masonic Outlook," May 1928, framed, 9 3/4 x 12 3/4" (ILLUS.) **10-12**

Masonic Match Holder

Masonic match holder, metal, triangular shape w/Masonic symbol, black & gold, 3 x 3 1/4" (ILLUS.) **20-25**

Masonic medal, white metal w/red, white & blue ribbon, marked "Delegate - 29th Annual New York State Masonic Convention, Albany, N.Y., Sept. 4-5, 1911" (ILLUS. left, below) **10**

Masonic Anniversary Medals

Masonic medal, yellow metal w/blue ribbon, commemorating the "50th Anniversary of the New York State Council, Sept. 24-25, 1923" (ILLUS. right) **10**

Masonic Mirror

Masonic mirrors, carved black walnut frame w/top, bottom & sides pierced w/Masonic decoration, the molded mirror w/arched top & gold leaf liner flanked by classical columns, pedestals & globes over a base w/anchor, shield, hammer & scrolls, one frame dated w/patent label May 1st 1866, attributed to John Haley, Bellamy, Kittery Point, Maine, ca. 1860, 22 x 31", pr. (ILLUS. of one) **9,795**

Masonic motto, black & white, "The Work of a True & Loyal Mason," marked "Copyright 1938, The Buzza Company," framed in black wood, 6 1/2 x 7 1/2" **12-15**

Masonic needlework picture, needlepoint embroidery in shaded wool w/Masonic symbols including the all-seeing eye, moon, star, square & compass, pillars, trowel & others, dated 1827, framed, 11 x 13 1/4" (fading, toning, small areas of loss) **748**

Masonic Panel

Masonic panel, canvas, center w/painted yellow rayed sun face on yellow ground surrounded by three intersecting triangles of white, dark green & black, the uppermost points w/black letters, "E.A.J.J.Y.A.O.A.H." surrounded by a green serpent swallowing its tail, on red ground w/black border, late 19th - early 20th c, unsigned, America, abrasions, staining, fading, 50" sq. (ILLUS.) **920**

Masonic Picture with Roses

Masonic picture, reverse painting on glass, foil-backed, a wreath of pink & white roses w/green leaves surrounding center Masonic symbol, framed, 14 1/4 x 17 1/4" (ILLUS.) **75-95**

Masonic plaque, octagonal, pinewood w/Masonic emblem, 8" d. **15**

Masonic plaque, painted wood, rectangular board w/scribed Masonic symbols including the compass & square, three columns & various geometric designs in red, cream & black on a grey ground, framed in red & grey, from Connecticut, early 19th c., 24 1/2 x 28 1/2" (scattered staining, fading).. **9,200**

Masonic plaque, velvet, dark blue mounted w/wooden Masonic emblem, 8 1/2 x 13 1/2" **10**

Masonic plate, ceramic, white w/deep blue & gold trim, listing "National Officers for New York State Masons, 1781-1956" & marked "Syracuse China, Made in America," 8" d. **35**

Masonic plate, ceramic, white w/medium blue highlights & gold trim, commemorating Essex Lodge, 1857-1917, Elizabeth, New York, 8" d. **35-40**

Masonic plate, ceramic, Zembo Temple, Harrisburg, featuring an image of the interior of the Masonic Temple, marked "WT Wise Architect & Designer" on front, reverse marked "Tho's Maddox's Son's Co., Trenton, N.J.," 9 3/4" d. **35-45**

New York World's Fair Masonic Plate

Masonic plate, glass, rectangular multicolored scene of Masonic building & trees, marked on back "© New York World's Fair 1964-1965 Corporation, Sponsored by Grand Lodge for the World's Fair," 7 1/2 x 9" (ILLUS.) **22-25**

Masonic Print of George Washington

Masonic print, depicting George Washington, in ceremonial garb, closing the lodge after a ritual meeting, 25 1/2" w., 33 1/2" l. (ILLUS.)...................................... **50-60**

Masonic Print in Compass-shaped Frame

Masonic print, in compass-shaped mahogany frame, shows a woman hugging a man wearing a turban & reads "I love to love A MASON 'Cause a Mason Never Tells," 8 " w., 11 1/2" l. (ILLUS.).................. **12-15**

Satirical Masonic Print

Masonic print, satirical depiction of a man & a woman in formal dress sitting on a compass above "I dearly love a MASON, because a Mason's 'ON THE SQUARE'!," back is marked "Copyright 1908, The Ullman Mfg. Co., N.Y.," 9 x 11" (ILLUS.) **15**

Masonic Presidents of the United States

Masonic print, w/images of the 15 presidents who were members of the Masonic Order, late 1940s, 18 x 24" (ILLUS.) **30-40**

Framed "Masonic Parade March" Sheet Music

Masonic sheet music, "Masonic Parade March" by F.R. Kimball, McKinley Music Company, white, red & black, framed, 12 3/8 x 15 1/2" (ILLUS.) **15-25**

Shelf with Masonic Emblem & Symbols

Masonic shelf, mahogany, Masonic emblem & symbols centered in fretwork design, 6 x 10 1/2 x 18 1/4" (ILLUS.) **30-40**
Masonic thermometer, metal, shaped like square & compass, 7 1/2" h. **35**

Masonic Tool Sets

Masonic tool set, miniature, ivory, working set of the Masonic Lodge including a square, compass, trowel, gauge, gavel, level & plumb, the set (ILLUS. top right w/wood working set) **20**
Masonic tool set, woodworking tools of the Masonic Lodge including a square, compass, trowel, gauge, gavel, level & plumb, wood handles of the trowels engraved w/Masonic emblem, the set (ILLUS. w/miniature tool set) **20**

Inlaid Tray with Masonic Emblem

Masonic tray, inlaid mahogany, rectangular, full color butterfly art depicting various scenes, Masonic emblem in center, 11 x 24" (ILLUS.) **50-75**
Masonic vase, ceramic, white book-form w/The Lord's Prayer in gold, gold trim, marked "24 KT. Gold, Made in U.S.A.," 3 1/2 x 4 1/2" **15**
Masonic wall hanging, ceramic, Masonic Lord's Prayer, 4 1/8 x 6 5/8" **12-15**
Order of the Eastern Star ashtray, ceramic, round, white w/gold trim & gold stars, OES emblem in center, marked on bottom "Royal Winton, Made in England, A," 4" d. **6-8**
Order of the Eastern Star bell, ceramic, light blue w/four color OES emblem & gold trim, 5" h. **15**
Order of the Eastern Star coffeepot, ceramic, bulbous body w/swan's neck spout & C-form handle w/thumbrest, white w/four color OES emblem & gold trim, 7 1/2" h. **20-30**
Order of the Eastern Star compact, brass plated w/OES emblem in four colors & depicting a woman w/a parasol & man w/cane, w/original powder puff & marked inside "Doresett Fifth Avenue," 4" d. **20**
Order of the Eastern Star creamer & sugar bowl, ceramic, white w/four color OES emblems & gold trim, ink-marked "Lefton China, Hand Painted, Reg. U.S. Pat. Off., 2789," 2 3/8" h., 4" d. **15-20**

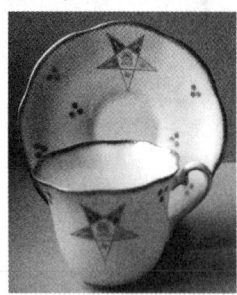

Order of the Eastern Star Cup & Saucer

Order of the Eastern Star cup & saucer, ceramic, white w/multicolored OES emblem, gold trim, bottom marked "Rosina Bone China, Made in England," 2 1/2" h. (ILLUS.).. 15

Order of the Eastern Star cup & saucer, ceramic, white w/multicolored OES emblem, gold trim, bottom marked "Bone China-Rampant House Logo, Taylor & Kent England, 7255" 3" h...................... 15

Order of the Eastern Star emblem, foil OES emblem, four color, marked "Arthur E. Cost, Emblem Jewelry-Bibles-Novelties-Gavels-Books, 29 James St., West Haven, Conn.," framed, 5 3/4" sq. 12-14

Order of the Eastern Star License Plate Attachment

Order of the Eastern Star license plate attachment, brass, round w/"Order of the Eastern Star" red lettering in white border w/center enameled multicolored OES emblem, 3 1/2" d. (ILLUS.) 15

Order of the Eastern Star motto, four color OES motto w/rose decoration around border, marked "© The Blank of Volland Co., Joliet, Illinois," 7 1/4 x 9 3/4" 12-15

Order of the Eastern Star salt & pepper shakers, ceramic, white w/four color OES emblem, sticker w/"Lefton's Exclusives, Reg. U.S. Pat. Off., Japan, Gold 103," 3" h., pr. 10

Order of the Eastern Star Teapot

Order of the Eastern Star teapot, cov., ceramic, white w/gold trim & multicolored OES emblem, marked "1725" on bottom, 5 3/4" h. (ILLUS.)... 20

Shriner ashtray w/matchbook holder, cast iron, Shriner emblem on raised back, 2 1/2 x 4 1/2 x 7 1/4" 20

Shriner decanter w/stopper, ceramic, figural Shriner wearing red Fez w/gold tassel & black suit, sticker on bottom marked "Japan," 11" h. 30

Shriner doll, composition, bobbing-head type, Shriner figure, 7 1/21" h. 20-30

Brass Shriner Symbol

Shriner emblem, brass, Shriner symbol, 3 3/4" d. (ILLUS.).. 15

FRUIT JARS

Trade Mark Advance Fruit Jar

Advance (overlaid on JW monogram below) Trade Mark - Pat. Apl'd For, ground lip w/correct glass lid marked "Trade Mark Advance," smooth base, aqua, ca. 1880, qt. (ILLUS.) **$495**

Allen's Pat. June 1871 (on base), upright rectangular w/low ground lip, glass lid & original metal strap clamp, ca. 1871-75, aqua, qt.. 231

Arthur, Burnham & Gilroy 10th & Geo. Sts. Philadelphia - R. Arthur's Patent Jany 2nd 1855, ground lip w/pressed wax sealer groove, smooth base, aqua, ca. 1860, some light outside stain, tiny bruise on side of base, qt. (ILLUS. top next page)... 523

Automatic (The) Sealer, ground lip, "Clayton Bottle Works Clayton, N.J." on smooth base, "Patd. Sept. 15. 1885" on original domed glass lid, ca. 1885-90, aqua, qt. (repro wire closure) 132

Arthur, Burnham & Gilroy Fruit Jar

Baker's (J.C.) Patent Aug. 14. 1860, smooth base, ground lip, glass lid embossed "Crown Jar - J.C. Baker's Pat. Aug, 14, 1860," metal yoke stamped "Crown Jar, J.C. Baker," bluish aqua, ca. 1860-75, 1/2 gal. (some lip roughness, minor iridescent neck bruise) 468

Baltimore Glass Works Jar & Stopple

Baltimore Glass Works, applied mouth, smooth base, original Willoughby stopple, deep bluish aqua, ca. 1865, qt. (ILLUS.)... 853

Early Canadian Fruit Jar

Beaver (below design of beaver), ground lip, smooth base, original zinc screw band lid w/clear glass insert, medium golden amber, Canada, ca. 1875, qt. (ILLUS.) 578

Bennett's No. 2, applied mouth, smooth footed base, non-original glass closure w/"A.Kline," ca. 1875-85, aqua, qt. 303

Bennett's Fruit Jar & Lid

Bennett's No. 2 (reversed 2), applied mouth, smooth base w/six raised feet, correct winged glass stopper embossed "Bennett's Patent Feb 6, 1866," aqua, ca. 1870, in-making cooling crack, qt. (ILLUS.) 1,100

Chambers (A. & D.H.) Union Fruit Jar Pittsburgh, PA, cylindrical wax sealer-type, bluish cornflower, qt. (small open bubble on inner ridge) 70

Chicago Trade - CFPJ (monogram) - Mark Fruit Jar, ground lip, smooth base, correct glass 'pickle pusher' lid & lightning-style metal closure, Australian, ca. 1880-90, aqua, 1/2 gal. (minor edge roughness) 215

Cohansey Glass Mfg. Co. Pat Mar 20 77 (on base), ringed barrel-shape, pressed-down groove ring wax sealer, smooth base, correct tin lid, ca. 1877-85, aqua, qt. 138

Dandy (The) below Trade Mark, ground lip, "Gilberds" on smooth base, original glass lid marked "Pat Oct. 13th 1885," lightning metal closure, ca. 1885-90, amber, 1/2 gal. (small chip polished out edge of lid)... 198

Electric (motif of world globe) Fruit Jar, ground lip, "Pat Apd For" on smooth base, original glass lid & metal clamp closure, ca. 1885, aqua, pt. (two small chips on top of applied ring, open bubble inside)... 275

Empire, applied mouth, smooth base, original metal stopple marked "Patented January 10, 1860 King & Co. Pittsburgh, PA. Empire," bluish aqua, ca. 1865, minor outside stain, qt. (ILLUS. top next page)... 1,485

Fahnstock Albree & Co. (on base), applied mouth, pontiled base, original stopple marked "J.D. Willoughby Patented January 4, 1859," ca. 1860, deep bluish aqua, qt... 550

Empire Jar with Original Stopple

Flaccus Bros. Steers (motif of steer's head) Head Fruit Jar, ground lip, smooth base, metal screw lid w/original milk glass insert w/eagle, ca. 1900, milk glass, pt. **176**

Flaccus Bros. Steers (motif of steer's head) Head Fruit Jar, ground lip, smooth base, original amber glass screw lid, ca. 1900, yellowish amber, pt. **523**

Flaccus (E.C.) Co. (inside banner w/stag's head), ground lip, smooth base, metal screw lid w/original domed milk glass insert marked "The E.C. Flaccus Co. (stag head) Wheeling, W. Va.," ca. 1900, milk glass, pt. (glass insert w/chipping on edge) **550**

Gilberds Improved (star) Jar, ground lip, smooth base, original glass lid w/wire closure, lid embossed "Gilberd's Improved Jar Cap Jamestown N.Y. 3 Pat July 31.83.," ca. 1890, bluish aqua, qt. **242**

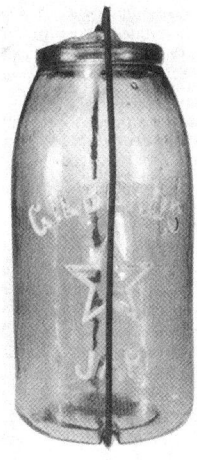

Gilberds Half-gallon Fruit Jar

Gilberds (star) Jar, ground lip, smooth base, original glass lid & wire closure, lid embossed "Gilberd's Improved Jar Cap Jamestown New York - 2 - Pat July 31.83.," bluish aqua, ca. 1885, 1/2 gal. (ILLUS.) **264**

Gilberds (star) Jar, original glass lid w/wire clamp from top to base, medium to deep aqua, qt. **275**

Haines's Improved - March 1st 1870, smooth base, applied mouth, correct glass lid marked "Patented March 1st 1870," wire closure, ca. 1870-75, bluish aqua, qt. **187**

Hartell's Glass Air Tight Cover - Patented Oct 19 1858 (on glass lid), ground lip, smooth base, original embossed glass lid, greenish aqua, 1/2 gal. **110**

Hilton's Pat Mar 10th 1868, ground lip, smooth base, original glass lid w/metal closure stamped "Hilton's Pat.," ca. 1870, aqua, qt. (chip on edge of lid, inside lip bruise) **1,595**

Improved Crown (motif of crown), smooth lip, zinc screw lid w/glass insert, Canadian, aqua, qt. **20**

Rare Indicator Jar & Closure

Indicator, ground lip, smooth base, original metal two-piece closure stamped "Patent Applied For," deep aqua, ca. 1875, qt. (ILLUS.) **2,860**

J & B (inside octagon) Fruit Jar Pat'd June 14th 1898, ground lip, smooth base, original screw-on zinc lid, ca. 1900, aqua, qt. (some lid edge deterioration) **94**

Kline's Patent Oct. 27 63 (on hollow stopper), tooled rolled lip, smooth base, ca. 1865, deep bluish aqua, qt. **77**

L & W - Manufactured For Rice & Burnett Cleveland, applied mouth, smooth base w/"L & W," original 'Kline' glass stopple, ca. 1880, bluish aqua, qt. **358**

Lafayette (below bust of Lafayette), ground lip, smooth base, original glass stopper w/two-piece metal closure, aqua. 1885-95, pt. (ILLUS. top next page) **3,410**

Lightning (below) Trade Mark, ground lip, smooth base w/"Putnam," correct yellow olive glass lid & lightning closure, ca. 1882-90, very crude, golden amber, qt. **209**

Rare Lafayette Pint Jar

Ludlow's Patent June 28 1859 & August 6 1861 (on glass lid), ground lip, smooth base, original glass lid & metal cage-like yoke, ca. 1865, aqua, qt. 165

Mason Fruit Jar, ground lip, smooth base, zinc screw lid, ca, 1875-1895, aqua, qt. 30

Mason Fruit Jar, ground lip, smooth base, zinc screw lid, ca, 1875-1895, medium amber, 1/2 gal. 210

Mason's Patent Nov 30th 1858, 'Christmas Mason,' ground lip, smooth base, zinc screw lid, ca. 1875-1895, medium to deep blue aqua, pt. 250

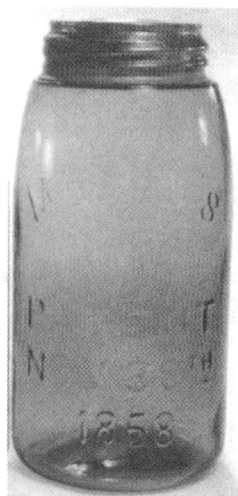

Rare Amber Mason's Jar

Mason's Patent Nov. 30th 1858, ground lip, original zinc lid, number "101" on base, golden to medium amber (ILLUS.).............. **1,000**

Mason's Patent Nov 30th 1858, ground lip, smooth base marked "1," zinc screw lid, ca. 1865-1885, apple green, qt. 90

Mason's Patent Nov 30th 1858, ground lip, smooth base marked w/a backward "9," zinc screw lid, ca. 1865-1885, deep amber, qt. **400**

Millville Atmospheric Fruit Jar - Whitall's Patent June 18th 1861, applied groove ring wax sealer, original glass lid & metal yoke, smooth base, ca. 1865-1870, aqua, 1/2 gal. (some stain in lower half)......... 80

Pet - L. & W., applied mouth, smooth base, original glass lid w/wire closure, ca. 1875-85, aqua, qt. 143

Swayzee's & Woodbury Fruit Jars

Swayzee's Improved Mason, smooth lip, original zinc lid, green, minor interior stain (ILLUS. left) 210

Woodbury, original metal band on glass lid, aqua, qt. (ILLUS. right)..................................... 50

FURNITURE

Furniture made in the United States during the 18th and 19th centuries is coveted by collectors. American antique furniture has a European background, primarily English, since the influence of the Continent usually found its way to America by way of England. If the style did not originate in England, it came to America by way of England. For this reason, some American furniture styles carry the name of an English monarch or an English designer. However, we must realize that, until recently, little research has been conducted and even less published on the Spanish and French influences in the area of the California missions and New Orleans.

After the American revolution, cabinetmakers in the United States shunned the prevailing styles in England and chose to bring the French styles of Napoleon's Empire to the United States and we have the uniquely named "American Empire" (Classical) style of furniture in a country that never had an emperor.

During the Victorian period, quality furniture began to be mass-produced in this country with its rapidly growing population. So much walnut furniture was manufactured, the vast supply of walnut was virtually depleted and it was of necessity that oak furniture became fashionable as the 19th century drew to a close.

For our purposes, the general guidelines for dating will be:

> Pilgrim Century - 1620-85
> William & Mary - 1685-1720
> Queen Anne - 1720-50
> Chippendale - 1750-85
> Federal - 1785-1820
>   Hepplewhite - 1785-1820
>   Sheraton - 1800-20
> American Empire (Classical) - 1815-40
> Victorian - 1840-1900
>   Early Victorian - 1840-50
>   Gothic Revival - 1840-90
>   Rococo (Louis XV) - 1845-70
>   Renaissance - 1860-85
>   Louis XVI - 1865-75
>   Eastlake - 1870-95
>   Jacobean & Turkish Revival - 1870-95
>   Aesthetic Movement - 1880-1900
> Art Nouveau - 1890-1918
> Turn-of-the-Century - 1895-1910
> Mission (Arts & Crafts movement) - 1900-15
> Art Deco - 1925-40

All furniture included in this listing is American unless otherwise noted.

Bedroom Suites

Louis XV-XVI-Style: double bed, a pair of five-drawer tall side cabinets, a lady's work table, a lady's dressing table, a nightstand, a guerdon, two armchairs, a side chair & footstool; bronze-mounted tulipwood, overall designed by patterned veneered panels w/gilt-bronze mounts in the form of shells, foliage, laurel branches & putto, the bed signed "Linke," France, early 20th c., the footstool associated, the set... **$29,500**

Modern style: two single beds, two wardrobes, a nightstand, a dressing table, two benches & a blanket chest; painted beech, the beds & stand w/rectangular frames enclosing vertical slats w/crossform framing, the two-door wardrobe w/one door composed of slats & the other w/a mirror above a long lower drawer, the dressing table & stool w/slatted base end sections, designed by Bruno Emmel, by A. Siegl, Vienna, early 20th c., the set **13,800**

Modern Style Bedroom Furniture

Modern-style: double bed, large & small chest of drawers & nightstand; molded plywood, each piece w/a simple rounded

box form, the chests w/flush-front drawers w/incised finger grip bands, on bentwood band supports, color-enhanced reddish brown finish, decal mark of Plymodern Furniture, Plymold Corporation, Lawrence, Massachusetts, late 1940s - early 1950s, minor wear, large chest 42" h., the set (ILLUS. of large chest & nightstand)... **805**

Aesthetic Movement Vanity

Victorian Aesthetic Movement: bed, chest of drawers w/mirror, night table, side chair, vanity & side table; ebonized & gilt-decorated, each piece w/a high rounded flat crestrail continuing to form a framework around the mirrored pieces & ornately decorated w/delicate gilt florals, the drawers & panels on each piece also decorated w/delicate gilt fern leaf or floral vine decorations, American, ca. 1875, the set (ILLUS. of vanity) **4,600**

Victorian Aesthetic Movement: double bed, chest of drawers w/mirror & washstand; cherry & mahogany, the highbacked bed w/a high, wide squared headboard w/a shaped crestrail carved w/scrolls & leaves above oblong panels w/further detailed leafy scroll carving, reeded pilaster stiles, a matching lower footboard & original siderails, the chest w/a tall superstructure frame carved to match the headboard & enclosing a large swiveling beveled mirror, the case w/a row of three small drawers over two long drawers on a molded base w/simple bracket feet, the washstand w/a door, two open side compartments & one drawer w/a mismatched, undersized marble top, ca. 1890, bed 61" w., 80" h., the set (some wear & edge damage)........ **4,125**

Unusual Victorian Faux Bamboo Bed

Victorian faux bamboo style: two twin beds, dressing table, nightstand, chest of drawers & side cabinet; pine, each piece w/peaked crestrails & side posts all w/faux bamboo turnings enclosing bamboo-bordered panels & applied trim, ca. 1890, bed 35 x 73", the set (ILLUS. of one bed)... **9,600**

Large Renaissance Revival Chest

Victorian Renaissance Revival: bed, chest of drawers w/mirror, side chest & cabinet; walnut & burl walnut, each w/a wide arched & ornately scroll-carved crestrail above a carved frieze band, the chest of drawers w/a large recangular swivel mirror w/gently arched top frame, case pieces w/rectangular pink marble tops w/serpentine fronts above conforming veneered drawers, ca. 1885, bed 63" w.,88" h., the set (ILLUS. of chest of drawers)... **17,920**

Outstanding Renaissance Revival Bed

Victorian Renaissance Revival: bed, tall chest of drawers, dressing table & bureau; gilt-incised walnut, each piece w/a massive arched crestrail centered by a large block over curved brackets & topped by a large urn-form finial, large ta-

pering turned finials at each top corner, delicate gilt-incised banding & scrolls, the tall bed w/a lower footboard w/a heavy turned crestrail over turned & reeded sideposts & a shaped rectangular panel, bed siderails w/original velvet padding, ca. 1880, bed 56 1/2 x 73", 77" h., the set (ILLUS. of bed).................. **23,750**

Victorian Renaissance Revival: double bed & chest of drawers; walnut, the chest w/a white marble top below a tall swiveling mirror w/a carved applied arched pediment, glove boxes on the top, the case w/three long drawers w/burl veneer raised panels & carved pulls, matching high back bed, ca. 1875-80, chest 21 x 44", 90" h., 2 pcs. **1,650**

Beds

Classical Country-style Painted Bed

Classical country-style low-poster bed, the wide scrolled head- and footboards flanked by ball-topped ring-turned posts ending in ring-turned tapering legs, overall graining simulating rosewood highlighted w/gilt stenciling & striping, old surface, probably northern New England, 1825-35, minor height loss, 52 1/4 x 79", 46 1/2" h. (ILLUS.) **1,495**

Classical Tiger Stripe Maple Bed

Classical country-style low-poster bed, tiger stripe maple, four boldly baluster-, ring- and urn-turned posts continuing to turned tapering legs, a scroll-cut headboard, the footboard w/a baluster- and ring-turned blanket rail above a lower flat rail, old refinish, New England, ca. 1830, side rails replaced, 52 x 81 1/2", 46" h. (ILLUS.) **1,840**

Classical country-style low-poster rope bed, curly maple, head- and footposts w/ball-turned finials above an urn over a tapering turned post continuing to a long block over the ring-turned tapering legs, a high rolled headboard w/ball terminals, the footboard w/a ball- and rod-turned blanket bar above a lower flat rail, refinished, includes original rails & bolts, first half 19th c., 54 x 72", 54" h. 935

Classical country-style rope bed, cherry, boldly turned baluster-, ring- and rod-turned head- and footposts w/large ball finials & baluster- and ring-turned legs, the wide headboard w/scrolling crest arched in the center below a turned horizontal rod w/double-ball knobs at each end, the footboard w/a narrow shaped board above the pegged rails, cleaned down to old mellow finish, found in Ohio, first half 19th c., original rails, 51 x 76 1/4", 59 3/4" h. **1,210**

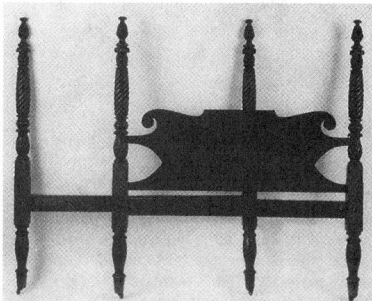

Early Classical Tall-poster Bed

Classical tall-poster bed, mahogany, the head- and footposts w/pineapple-carved finials on leaf spiral & ring-carved posts ending in vase- and ring-turned legs w/brass cuffs & casters, the headposts joined by a scrolled & shaped headboard, old refinish, New England, ca. 1820, imperfections, 49 1/4 x 72", 60" h. (ILLUS.) **2,875**

Classical 'sleigh' bed, carved mahogany, high outscrolled ends w/rosette terminals & veneered crests, reeded edges continuing to a long narrow reeded seatrail w/leaf-carved blocks above the squared acanthus leaf carved legs raised on casters, probably New England, first quarter 19th c., 59 1/2 x 102", footboard 34 3/4" h., headboard 41 1/2" h. **4,025**

Classical 'sleigh' bed, carved mahogany, twin sized, reverse-scrolling head- and footboards on flowerhead- and leaf-carved supports, joined by gadrooned wide side rails on leaf-carved paw feet, New York, first half 19th c. **5,100**

Country style rope bed, maple & curly maple, cannon ball-style, the even well-turned head- and footposts w/baluster- and ring-turnings & large ball finials, headboard w/cut-out ends w/shaped corners, footboard w/turned blanket bar, original rails 69" l., 51 1/2" w. **770**

Country-style child's bed, cherry, rectangular w/deep board sides gently down-curved between the head- and footboards w/slightly scrolled crests between turned ball corner finials w/ivory buttons, baluster- and ring-turned legs w/peg feet, pegged construction w/chip-carved detail at the posts, original finish, Zoar, Ohio, 19th c., 25 x 43", 30" h. (minor age splits) . **2,420**

Country-style low-poster bed, tiger stripe maple, ball tops above ring-turned posts which flank a shaped headboard, similar ring-turned legs on casters, old surface, side rails w/angle irons, New England, second quarter 19th c., 49 x 75 1/2", 50 1/4" h. (minor height loss) **1,610**

Country-style low-poster rope bed, painted poplar & pine, a gently arched headboard flanked by low heavy ring-turned posts w/large knob finials, a matching lower footboard, original side rails, good old red paint, 47 1/2 x 71", headboard 37" h. **358**

Federal country-style tall-poster tester bed, maple & birch, an arched tester frame above the tapering pencil headposts flanking a low arched headboard & joined by rails to reeded vase-, cup- and ring-turned footposts, on casters, New England, early 19th c., 53 1/2 x 75", overall 78 1/4" h. **1,380**

Federal country-style tall-poster tester bed, maple & poplar, tall head- and footposts w/ring-, baluster- and knob-turned top sections w/acorn finials above a long baluster-turned section over another ring-turned section over long block & baluster-turned legs w/tapering peg feet, a rectangular headboard w/incurved side cut-outs, w/a flat tester & original side rails, refinished, early 19th c., 51 1/2 x 73", 84" h. **1,650**

Federal tall-poster bed, carved mahogany, the square tapering birch headposts flank an arched pine headboard, the reeded tapering footposts w/tobacco leaf carving & reeded legs ending in turned feet, w/rails & flat tester, probably Southern U.S., early 19th c., 56 3/4 x 79 1/2", 83 1/2" h. (restoration, patches) **4,025**

Federal tall-poster bed, carved mahogany, the tapering reeded footposts w/vase- and ring-turning continuing to square tapering spade-footed legs, the simple square tapering headposts joined by a plain rectangular headboard, original side rails, probably Massachusetts, ca. 1810-15, 50 x 70", 89 1/2" h. **2,070**

Federal tall-poster bed, carved mahogany veneer, the reeded turned posts w/leaf carving above turnings punctuated w/neoclassical beading over carved Gothic arches & leaves on figured mahogany veneer dies above the ring-turned tapering legs, old refinish, Salem, Massachusetts, 1820-30, 55 3/4 x 58", 79" h. (height loss) **6,325**

Federal tall-poster tester bed, carved mahogany, the arched canopy surmounting four ring-turned & waterleaf-carved posts w/square-sectioned corner supports mounted w/ormolu medallions joined by straight rails, on ring-turned & compressed-ball legs, school of Samuel McIntire, Salem, Massachusetts, ca. 1800, 56 x 80", 80" h. **4,025**

Federal tall-poster tester bed, figured maple & pine, the arched tester above baluster-turned posts centering an arched headboard on tapering turned legs w/round spade feet, matching footposts, old dry surface, probably Massachusetts, ca. 1810, 52 x 78", 70" h. **7,800**

Federal tall-poster tester bed, mahogany veneer, the mahogany veneered flat tester w/central rectangular tablets & ovolo corners above spiral- and leaf-carved footposts & turned red-painted headposts flanking a scrolled headboard, ring- and knob-turned legs, Salem Massachusetts, early 19th c., 52 x 76 1/2", 89" h. (some old refinish & height loss) **4,888**

Federal-Style tall-poster twin beds, mahogany, the headboard w/a wide arched board between the tapering reeded posts w/a turned columnar upper section below the turned urn finial, heavy tapering turned feet, the footboard w/a reeded baluster- and knob-turned blanket rail above a lower rail & also on turned tapering feet, varnish finish, good condition, first half 20th c., 42 x 75", the pr. **660**

French Empire-Style bed, mahogany w/ormolu trim, the rectangular headboard w/flat crest & end ears above stiles w/long palmette ormolu mounts flanking the large central raised panel border, the lower footboard matching, long siderails w/downcurved top & decorated at each end w/triangular scrolling ormolu mounts, France, early 20th c., 52 x 82", 46" h. (wear, some missing pieces of ormolu) **495**

Mission-style (Arts & Crafts movement) three-quarters bed, oak, tall tapering corner posts on the head- & slightly lower footboard, each w/six vertical slats, original side rails, original finish, mark of L. & J.G. Stickley, 51 3/4 x 84 3/4", 54" h. **3,300**

Victorian Aesthetic Movement substyle bed, walnut & burl walnut, the high square headboard w/a slightly stepped crestrail w/the wider central panel carved w/a stylized blossom & leafy twigs flanked by low side panels w/a carved trellis design all above a triple-arch border over three large burl walnut rectangular panels flanked by narrow pilasters & blocks, a matching lower footboard w/a flat crestrail, ca. 1880, 67" w., 79" h. **3,360**

Victorian Renaissance Revival substyle bed, carved walnut & burl walnut, the very high headboard topped by a high central canopy-style crest w/a large carved maiden's bust above an arched & scroll-carved crestrail over a sawtooth border band over a recessed arched burl panel flanked by balusters all flanked by lower peaked side crests & blocked corners w/turned urn finials, the wide triple-panel lower section w/arched top moldings, the low arched footboard w/a molded railing over arched burl panels over a triple-arch panel & rectangular burl panels along the bottom, ca. 1875, 66" w., 96" h. **2,800**

Fine Victorian Rococo Bed

Victorian Rococo substyle, mahogany & mahogany veneer tall-poster style, monumental round headposts w/squatty flame-turned finials above the high arched headboard w/a shell- and fruit-carved crest over scrolled borders & two raised triangular panels above a large inset rectangular panel w/a rosette at each corner, gadrooned turning at the base of each post, the low footboard w/short round posts w/pointed gadrooned caps & bands above long Gothic arch panels flanking the low arched & scroll-carved footrail w/a central rosette & oval banding, old dark finish, some reconstruction, minor veneer damage, original rails, ca. 1850, 63" w., headposts 101" h. (ILLUS.) **6,875**

Large Rosewood Rococo Bed

Victorian Rococo substyle, rosewood, the very high & wide headboard w/an arched & leaf-carved crestrail above a large lacy scroll-framed cartouche over long lobed recessed panels all flanked by tall paneled headposts w/urn-turned finials, the low footboard w/matching low posts flanking an arched central panel w/a leafy scroll-carved center design, ca. 1850-60, 63" w., 87" h. (ILLUS.)........... **3,360**

Benches

Art Deco Bench

Art Deco bench, mahogany, the reeded curved backrail continuing to half arms above an upholstered oblong seat w/fluted apron raised on square tapering & slightly curved legs joined by an H-stretcher, ca. 1930, 17 x 35 1/2", 21" h. (ILLUS.)...................................... **1,680**

Arts & Crafts hall bench, oak, the high rectangular back w/a slightly arched crestrail above the inset back panel w/an arched top, flat open end arms w/rounded grips raised on rectangular stile front legs, long rectangular seat lifting to a storage compartment, medium brown finish, early 20th c., 17 3/4 x 38 1/2", 36 1/2" h. (minor abrasions & losses, newer finish, joint separations, crack)........... **403**

Bench, painted pine, the overhanging rectangular seat on shaped supports & arched cut-out feet joined by a straight skirt, vestiges of original salmon paint, probably Pennsylvania, ca. 1840, 11 3/4 x 77 3/4", 19 3/4" h. **2,760**

Bucket (or water) bench, country-style, painted, a superstructure w/a narrow shelf w/a high three-quarters gallery above a row of three small drawers w/cast-iron finger pulls, shaped tapering tall sides above the wide rectangular lower shelf over a case w/a pair of paneled cupboard doors w/cast-iron thumb latches, slender bracket feet, old yellow repaint over earlier colors, pulls overpainted, 19th c., 17 1/4 x 42", 48" h. **4,400**

Bucket (or water) bench, country-style, painted pine, a two-board rectangular top w/a rounded front corner at one end overhanging & raised on one-board ends

w/bootjack feet, joined by a lower one-board open shelf, old red paint, square nail construction, Pennsylvania, 19th c., 16 x 48", 27 1/2" h. (minor damage to foot finish) **660**

Bucket (or water) bench, country-style, painted poplar, a narrow upper shelf raised on tall shaped & incurved supports above a wide lower open shelf w/an apron & bootjack ends joined by a bead through-tenon cross stretcher, square nail construction, various colors of old paint, 37" w., 33 1/4" h. (some later round nails) **1,155**

Bucket (or water) bench, country-style, poplar, the tall superstructure w/a rectangular top above a closed back w/a single shelf above a projecting rectangular well above a long deep dovetailed drawer above the closed back & lower shelf, one-board ends, worn red finish, 19th c., 21 3/4 x 42", 59 1/2" h. (some edge damage, feet worn down & w/some dry rot)..... **2,420**

Bucket (or water) bench, painted pine, a narrow rectangular top shelf above incurved upper sides above two wider lower shelves above bootjack legs, traces of red paint, 19th c., 12 x 32", 37" h. (minor edge damage)................................. **495**

Early Painted Bucket Bench

Bucket (or water) bench, painted pine, a rectangular top w/chamfered edges above an apron w/a pair of drawers w/turned wood knobs above two long open shelves, bootjack ends, old surface w/remains of old red paint, possibly New England, early 19th c., minor imperfections, 18 x 55 1/2", 40" h. (ILLUS.)............ **4,025**

Bucket (or water) bench, painted pine, rectangular top overhanging shaped supports & cut-out arched feet joined by a shaped skirt, red wash finish, New England, early 19th c., 10 3/4 x 41", 17 3/4" h. (surface imperfections).................. **978**

Bucket (or water) bench, painted pine, the rectangular top w/beaded & shaped sides joining cut-out splayed mortised ends to the beaded front stretcher, painted blue over earlier red, probably Pennsylvania, early 19th c., 10 1/2 x 40 1/4", 16" h. **863**

Bucket (or water) bench, painted poplar, two narrow top shelves w/a closed back & low pointed crestrail & gallery above curved-out wide sides flanking two wider

open shelves w/a narrow apron across
the bottom, old red painted finish, square
nail construction, bootjack ends, 19th c.,
12 3/4 x 43 3/4", 51 1/2" h. (one thin sup-
port missing at back)................................. **2,200**

Bucket (or water) bench, painted wood, a
rectangular top on a dovetailed case
w/three mortised shelves, incised molded
ends on case & shelves, bootjack feet,
two-board back, old red wash, 19th c.,
12 1/2 x 42", 49 1/2" h. **605**

Bucket (or water) bench, painted wood,
the shallow shelf above a projecting lower shelf joined by cut-out sides & double-
arch cut-out feet, probably New England,
early 19th c., 10 1/2 x 28", 26" h. (imper-
fections) **3,738**

Cobbler's bench, painted pine, the thick
rectangular top w/a three-quarters gallery & an open compartment at one end,
the case w/a long drawer & small slot
above an enclosed kneehole opening beside a stack of three deep drawers above
an open compartment, a columnar-
turned post attached to the left end,
wooden knobs, old worn green paint,
very worn from use, late 19th c., 17 x 43",
35 1/2" h.. **550**

Cobbler's bench, pine, rectangular top w/a
large square lid over a compartment at
one end beside three small compartments w/sliding lids over shallower wells
& above a row of small square drawers
w/wood knobs along the bottom of the
case, raised on slightly outset slender
square tapering legs, w/a shoe pattern
cut-out from a newspaper dated 1829,
old refinish, 14 x 36", 20" h. **1,815**

Country-style bench, painted pine, long
rectangular plank top flanked by narrow
side aprons, raised on high shaped bootjack ends w/angled support braces to
seat, layers of old worn paint,
12 1/2 x 54", 19" h. (wear, edge damage)...... **248**

Country-style bench, painted poplar, mortised construction, long narrow board top
above narrow beaded aprons w/shaped
ends, wide shaped bootjack legs, green
repaint & scrubbed top, 19th c.,
13 1/2 x 39", 18 1/2" h. (age cracks) **358**

Country-style bench, pine, long board seat
w/rounded ends above deep side aprons
w/shaped ends, bootjack plank legs
joined by a medial shelf, refinished,
19th c., 10 1/2 x 28 3/4", 17 1/4" h. (edge
damage) **275**

Country-style bench, stained pine, long
narrow rectangular top above narrow
rounded side aprons & bootjack ends,
square nail construction, embossed "C--
an.Dom" on end, 19th c., 9 x 31 1/2",
8" h. (one later nail added) **495**

Kneeling bench, painted wood, narrow
long top on low base, grey-painted graining on a putty-colored ground, 19th c.,
6 x 28 3/4", 7 1/2" h. (wear) **1,840**

Kneeling bench, walnut, a narrow long
rectangular top above a rounded-end
apron, on short bootjack legs mortised
through the top, old patina, late 19th c.,
5 1/2 x 36".. **275**

**Mission-style (Arts & Crafts movement)
bench,** oak, rectangular bench seat
flanked by high side rails w/five narrow
slats, joined by through-tenons, lower
horizontal stretcher, medium brown finish, early 20th c., 17 x 26 3/4", 28" h.
(edge wear, scratches).................................... **575**

George Nelson Modern Style Bench

Modern-style bench, a rectangular long
seat composed of solid maple slats
raised on three ebonized wood trapezoidal open legs, designed by George Nelson, produced by Herman Miller,
ca. 1956, 72" l., 14" h. (ILLUS.) **1,568**

Koloman Moser Bench

Modern-style bench, Koloman Moser,
beechwood & bronze, arched bentwood
frame continuing to paneled sides, enclosing an upholstered seat, all raised on
bronze feet, stained brown, J. & J. Kohn,
Model No. 412, ca. 1902, 21" w., 26" h.
(ILLUS.) **5,175**

George III Window Bench

Window bench, upholstered mahogany,
the long upholstered rectangular seat
w/raised rolled end arms, raised on six
square molded legs joined by stretchers,
on casters, George III era, England, late
18th c., 18 3/4 x 51", 26" h (ILLUS.) **6,900**

Bookcases

Biedermeier bookcase, maple & part-ebonized, the later high rounded arch cresting over an open shelf & a long narrow frieze drawer above a case fitted w/two tall glazed cupboard doors flanked by freestanding columns, on a shaped plinth, Europe, ca. 1820, 19 x 45", 81" h. **4,600**

Cherry Chippendale Bookcase

Chippendale bookcase, cherry, the flat rectangular top w/a flared cornice above a pair of large 12-paned glazed cupboard doors w/molded muntins opening to four shelves above a pair of long thumb-molded drawers w/replaced butterfly brasses, molded base on scroll-cut ogee bracket feet, old refinish, New England, ca. 1790, restored, 13 x 58 1/2", 62 1/2" h. (ILLUS.).. **4,313**

Large Classical Style Bookcase

Classical bookcase, mahogany & crotchgrain mahogany veneer, two-part con-struction: the upper section w/a rectangular top w/rounded corners on the wide flaring coved cornice lifting off of the case w/a pair of tall 4-pane glazed doors w/double raised panels in the lower half, flowerheads carved at center of door mullions, opening to three shelves, on a shaped apron & bracket feet, ca. 1840, 18 x 62", 83 1/2" h. (ILLUS.)...................... **3,900**

Tall Classical Mahogany Bookcase

Classical bookcase, mahogany, three-part construction: the top section w/a rectangular top & scroll-carved crest above a plain frieze centered & flanked by inlaid retangular reserves above a conforming case fitted w/a pair of 9-pane glazed doors opening to a single shelf; the middle section w/a pair of tall 12-pane glazed cupboard doors opening to four shelves; the lower section w/a case fitted w/a pair of cockbeaded short drawers above two similar drawers over an applied reeded molding centering an incised diamond plaque above a shaped skirt, on ring- and inverted baluster-turned legs, possibly Portsmouth, New Hampshire, 1825-45, 15 1/2 x 63", 114" h. (ILLUS.) **6,900**

Country-style bookcase, decorated hardwood, a rectangular top above a tall case w/a pair of 2-pane cupboard doors w/a small pane above a tall pane, square stile legs on casters, the front frame decorated overall w/a burnt-wood narrow grapevine decoration against a checkered ground, dark red stain, late 19th - early 20th c., 16 1/2 x 40 1/2", 61" h. **495**

Gothic Revival bookcase, mahogany & mahogany veneer, the rectangular top w/rounded front corners on the deep coved cornice above a pair of tall glazed doors w/arched mullions at the top, opening to four shelves, on a shaped bracket base, ca. 1840, 15 x 52", 83" h. (ILLUS. top next column)... **5,700**

Fine Gothic Revival Bookcase

Lawyer's bookcase, stacking-type, four-section, a flat lift-off cornice w/rounded front edge above a long lift-front section w/a geometrically-leaded door above another long section w/a plain glazed lift-front door over a deeper section w/plain glazed lift-front door, the bottom projecting section much taller w/a plain glazed lift-front door, all on a ogee-front molded base, labeled "Globe Wernicke Co. Cincinnati, O.," ca. 1900, 19 x 34", 67" h. **798**

Mission Oak Bookcase

Mission-style (Arts & Crafts movement) bookcase, oak, a rectangular top on a four-shelf case, four D-shaped cut-outs on each canted side board, arched aprons at top & toe board, dark brown finish, stains, joint separation, early 20th c., 14 1/2 x 16 3/4", 43 3/4" h. (ILLUS.) **1,495**

Mission-style (Arts & Crafts movement) bookcase, oak, rectangular case w/overhanging top above double doors each w/eight small square leaded glass

panes over pairs of tall narrow panes, flanked by a column w/capital at each side, above an arched apron, designed by Harvey Ellis, partial Craftsman paper label of Gustav Stickley, Model No. 73, ca. 1904, 14 1/8 x 54", 58" h. **15,525**

Mission-style (Arts & Crafts movement) bookcase, oak, rectangular top w/corbel support over two doors w/curved shaped top of two short over two long window panels, the interior fitted w/eight half-shelves, copper ring pulls, caned panels on the lower front & side, Lifetime Furniture Co., Grand Rapids, Michigan, early 20th c., 12 1/2 x 46 1/2", 57 1/2" h. (damage to caning, wear) **1,995**

Neoclassical bookcase, kingwood & tulipwood parquetry, rectangular galleried top w/canted corners above a long drawer above a pair of tall glazed cupboard doors opening to three shelves, raised on square tapered legs ending in flattened balls, ivory pulls & escutcheons, Baltic region, first quarter 19th c., 16 1/4 x 33 1/4", 57 1/2" h. (minor losses) **2,300**

Victorian Aesthetic Substyle Bookcase

Victorian bookcase, Aesthetic Movement substyle, carved & figured walnut, the pitched pediment above a pierced gallery & a reverse-breakfront frieze on columnar supports surmounted by figural masks, centering a pair of tall glazed doors w/adjustable wooden shelves on a conformingly-shaped plinth, decorated overall w/incised gilt designs, probably New York City, ca. 1870, missing central finial, 17 x 72", 104" h. (ILLUS.) **8,400**

Victorian bookcase, Renaissance Revival substyle, walnut, a rectangular top w/a long low arched crestrail centered by a large crown cornice above a blocked panel & w/scalloped upright ears at each end, above a stepped frieze band above a pair of large two-pane glazed cupboard doors opening to four shelves & flanked by narrow paneled edges all above a slightly stepped-out lower section w/a pair of long line-incised drawers, flat molded base band, ca. 1880, 15 x 60", 93" h. **2,744**

Victorian Block-front Bookcase

Victorian Renaissance Revival bookcase, oak, a tall block-front style in three sections, the taller end sections w/rectangular tops & flared & dentil-carved cornices above tall glazed cupboard doors opening to shelves above a deep paneled drawer at the base, the protruding central section w/a scroll-cut crest above a stepped-down rectangular top w/beaded cornice above a tall glazed cupboard door above a paneled drawer, conforming blocked base w/beaded band trim, stamped brass pulls w/bails on drawers, ca. 1880-90, 16 x 75", 69" h. (ILLUS.).. **3,025**

European Victorian Bookcase

Victorian Renaissance Revival bookcase, stained walnut, two-part construction: the upper section w/a rectangular top & deep flared cornice above a pair of tall glazed cupboard doors w/molded trim opening to a shelf; the lower stepped-out section w/a molded frieze band above a pair of circular-paneled cupboard doors on a plinth base, decorated throughout w/roundels & incised designs, Europe, probably Russian, late 19th c., 23 x 57", 87" h. (ILLUS.) **2,400**

Ornate Victorian Rococo Bookcase

Victorian Rococo substyle bookcase, carved rosewood, two-part construction: the upper section w/an arched top w/a high ornate pierced, scroll-carved crest above a floral-carved frieze band & blocked corners above a pair of tall glazed arched doors w/delicate scroll-carved edging flanked by outset corner blocks w/bold leaf-, scroll- and floral carving & w/a pair of narrow drawers just below the doors; the stepped-out lower section w/conforming blocked corners & a pair of narrow drawers w/oval banding above a pair of paneled cupboard doors w/delicate scroll-trimmed edging, molded serpentine apron, leaf- and scroll-carved blocked front corners above compressed bulbous feet, ca. 1850-60, 25 x 52", 95" h. (ILLUS.) **4,140**

Late Victorian Oak Bookcase

fVictorian turn-of-the-century bookcase, oak, a rectangular top w/a narrow flared cornice above a tall case w/a pair of large glazed doors w/inset rectangular panels at the bottom above a deep molded flat base, beaded board pine back, opens to five adjustable shelves, short section of molding missing at the side, ca. 1900, 18 x 68", 83" h. (ILLUS.) **1,045**

Bureaux Plat

Unique Egyptian Revival Bureau Plat

Egyptian Revival bureau plat, parcel-gilt & ebonized wood, the rectangular top w/beveled & gilt-trimmed border above an ornate apron w/three drawers decorated w/grotesque masks, spread-winged bird & lotus motifs & raised on curved figural legs carved & decorated to resemble a pharoah's casket, legs joined by a long slender X-stretcher mounted by a pair of recumbent Egyptian figures, early 20th c., 40 x 57 1/2", 31" h. (ILLUS.) **18,000**

Rare Louis XV-Style Bureau Plat

Louis XV-Style bureau plat, gilt-bronze mounted tulipwood, the rectangular top w/ormolu edging above three frieze drawers w/ormolu banding & scrolled pulls raised on slender simple cabriole legs topped w/ormolu helmeted male busts & ending in scrolled sabot, further mounts & banding at each end, France, late 19th c., 47" l., 31" h. (ILLUS.) **11,400**

Louis XV-Style bureau plat, ormolu-mounted tulipwood parquetry, rectangular top w/rounded leaf-cast corners, surrounding top & fitted w/three drawers opposed by sham drawers, on cabriole legs, covered w/foliate & gilt mask mounts, early 20th c., 32 x 70", 30" h. **2,760**

Louis XV-Style Bureau Plat

Louis XV-Style bureau plat, tulipwood marquetry, the rectangular top w/serpentine edges w/ormolu banding above a conforming apron inlaid w/banding & veneered designs & fitted on one side w/three drawers w/scrolled ormolu pulls & corner mounts, each cabriole leg headed by a large scrolled ormolu mount & metal-capped feet, France, late 19th c. (ILLUS.) **6,000**

Fine Louis XV-Style Bureau Plat

Louis XV-Style bureau plat, gilt-bronze mounted tulipwood parquetry, the rectangular top w/a gilt-tooled leather inset writing surface framed by a gilt-bronze border above the apron w/three shaped frieze drawers w/parquetry designs & scrolling gilt-bronze mounts, the central one recessed & opposing faux drawers, the sides fitted w/bacchic masks, raised on cabriole legs headed by female busts & ending in paw-form sabots, France, late 19th c., 69" l., 31" h. (ILLUS.) **5,750**

Louis XV-Style bureau plat, gilt-bronze mounted tulipwood, the rectangular top inset w/an embossed leather writing surface above shaped metal-mounted border over an apron w/three drawers, the central drawer recessed, complete on all sides, the reverse w/false opening drawers, raised on slightly shaped cabriole legs w/soldier bust caryatids at the top & fitted w/sabots at the foot, by Conquet, France, after a model by Charles Cressent, late 19th c., 39 3/4 x 81", 31" h. **23,750**

Louis XVI-Style Bureau Plat

Louis XVI-Style bureau plat, gilt-bronze mounted mahogany, the rectangular molded top w/an inset leather writing surface above a central pull-out writing surface over the knee hole & flanked by two small paneled drawers on each side, raised on turned tapering stop-fluted legs ending in toupie feet, France, late 19th c., 25 3/4 x 43 1/2", 29 3/4" h. (ILLUS.) **2,645**

Marquetry Bureau Plat

Marquetry bureau plat, rectangular top w/tooled leather border enclosing a central writing panel inlaid in various woods w/berries & leafage, above conforming inlaid apron w/two drawers, all raised on twist-carved legs, ca. 1900, 31 1/2 x 31 1/2 x 48" (ILLUS.) **6,900**

Cabinets

Cellarette (wine cabinet), Federal, inlaid mahogany, rectangular top w/inlaid stringing & crossbanding above a shield-form inlaid keyhole escutcheon set on a molded frame above square casters, the top opening to a compartmented baize-lined interior containing eleven colorless blown glass decanters, old surface, possibly New England, ca. 1790-1810, 18 1/4" w., 22" h. (minor imperfections)..... **8,050**

Attractive Arts & Crafts China Cabinet

China cabinet, Arts & Crafts style, oak, a wide peaked crestrail flanked by open side rails on the rectangular top w/a pointed front edge above the conforming case w/a pair of tall glazed doors w/a diamond lattice panel at the top of each above a long plain glass pane, opening to five wooden shelves, matching glazed sides, peaked narrow apron & slender square tapering stile legs on small casters, ca. 1910, 15 x 37", 67" h. (ILLUS.) **952**

China cabinet, Arts & Crafts style, oak, the rectangular top w/a low arched backsplash above a pair of tall glazed cupboard doors opening to six adjustable shelves, flat apron, short stile legs, silver-washed hammered copper hardware, fine original reddish brown finish, remnants of a paper label from a Grand Rapids maker, 13 x 45 1/2", 55 1/4" h. **1,760**

Unique Arts & Crafts China Cabinet

China cabinet, Arts & Crafts style, oak, the rectangular top w/an upright stepped & paneled crestboard w/metal mounts above a case w/a pair of glazed cupboard doors w/a pair of small panes flanking a central pane overlaid w/a pierced stylized spearpoint copper ornament above two tall narrow panes all above a pair of small square paneled doors flanking a stack of four small drawers at the bottom, long spearpoint copper strap hinges & inset pulls, matching glazed sides, short stile legs joined by sleigh feet on casters, metal tag marked "From Alexander H. Revel & Co. Chicago, Ill.," Model No. 8646, Stickley Brothers, ca. 1908, 18 x 48", 75 1/4" h. (ILLUS.) **14,100**

China cabinet, Classical Revival style, oak, a low flat crestrail on the D-form top above a conforming case w/a long curved glass center door flanked by curved glass sides & opening to four wooden shelves w/the top shelf backed by a rectangular mirror, conforming base on two C-scroll front legs & two square back legs all on casters, ca. 1910, 16 x 36", 60" h. (ILLUS. top next column) **532**

Classical Revival China Cabinet

China cabinet, Federal-Style, inlaid mahogany & mahogany veneer, two-part construction: the upper section w/a rectangular top w/a molded cornice above a wide frieze band over two long 8-pane glazed doors opening to two shelves; the lower section w/a mid-molding above a case w/three long graduated drawers w/banded inlay & cast round ring pulls, shaped bracket feet, 20th c., 16 x 36", 69 1/4" h. **1,100**

China cabinet, late Victorian Classical Revival style, oak, the wide D-form top over a deep carved & molded cornice above glazed curved sides & a wide curved tall center door flanked by carved caryatids above tall blocked pilasters, molded base on four bold paw feet, mirrored interior back, four glass shelves, ca. 1890, 50" w., 66" h. **2,800**

China cabinet, Mission-style (Arts & Crafts movement), oak, a rectangular top slightly overhanging tall case w/a tall single glazed door opening to three wooden shelves, chamfered back, arched apron, hammered copper V-pull on door, fine original finish & glass, unmarked Gustav Stickley, 15 x 35 3/4", 59 3/4" h. **18,700**

Strickley Brothers China Cabinet

China cabinet, Mission-style (Arts & Crafts movement), oak, a rectangular top w/a narrow crestrail above a case w/a pair of tall glazed cupboard doors w/gently arched tops, a small panel above a tall lower panel, 3-pane glazed sides, three interior shelves w/the top shelf backed by a mirror, flat apron, square stile legs, branded mark & Quaint tag of the Stickley Brothers, ca. 1914 (ILLUS.) **2,875**

Golden Oak China Cabinet

China cabinet, Victorian Golden Oak, the high arched crestrail w/rounded corners & applied scroll trim centering an oblong mirror over the D-form top w/flattened front edge above a long flat glazed center door & curved glass sides opening to three wooden shelves, conforming base raised on four simple cabriole legs on casters, ca. 1900, 13 x 34", 72" h. (ILLUS.) **784**

Delicate Louis XV-Style Curio Cabinet

Curio cabinet, Louis XV-Style, walnut, two-part construction: the upper section w/an arched & scroll-trimmed cornice above a three-section case w/tall slender side doors w/tall oblong mirrors w/scrolled borders above a rounded scroll reserve flanking the slightly outset central cabinet section w/a glazed door w/delicate scrolling wood overlay opening to three shelves; the stepped-out lower section w/a pierced lattice & scroll-carved apron raised on four slender & gently backswept cabriole legs joined at the base w/an arched & scrolled X-stretcher, France, late 19th - early 20th c., 16 x 43", 75" h. (ILLUS.) **2,475**

Hanging wall cabinet, Victorian Aesthetic Movement substyle, cherry, the crestrail w/an arched & scroll-cut central crest flanked by pointed end crests above a narrow shelf over a small cabinet w/a beveled glass door w/a cut-out top band flanked by open side shelves w/slender columns supporting the ends of the upper shelf, the right side of cabinet shelf extended & w/a low scroll-cut back, the lower section below the cabinet w/a paneled backboard w/scalloped rim, original finish, ca. 1890, 8 x 26", 24" h. (small glued edge break) **440**

Liquor cabinet, Arts & Crafts style, oak, rectangular top w/the front half hinged to open to a copper-lined compartment over a single narrow drawer over a tall flat cupboard door opening to a shelf & fitted compartment, metal pulls, square stile legs, early 20th c., 17 1/4 x 23 1/2", 43" h. (one replaced pull) **2,415**

Decorated Arts & Crafts Cabinet

Side cabinet, Arts & Crafts style, oak, a rectangular top above a paneled long door w/a wooden latch & pyrographic picture of a peasant woman carrying a basket, each side trimmed w/three narrow slats, door opens to single shelf, square stile legs project at top corners, early 20th c., minor wear, 13 3/4 x 19 1/2", 42 1/2" h. (ILLUS.) **978**

Gothic Revival Side Cabinet

Side cabinet, Victorian Gothic Revival substyle, a rectangular white marble top w/molded edges & rounded corners above a frieze w/a pair of narrow drawers framed by Gothic arch molding above a pair of cupboard doors also w/Gothic arch molding, scalloped apron & bracket feet on casters, marble top may be of later date, stenciled mark in drawers, C.A. Baudouine, New York City, ca. 1840, 21 x 45", 36 1/2" h. (ILLUS.) **3,300**

Fine Renaissance Revival Cabinet

Side cabinet, Victorian Renaissance Revival substyle, bronze-mounted & marquetry inlaid rosewood, a small stepped platform on the long top w/projecting central section w/incurved sides above a conforming case w/an ornate inlaid frieze band above a central arch-paneled door w/ornate swags & scrolls enclosing a large round bronze plaque depicting Cupid & Psyche w/a satyr infant, the curved side panels w/ornate inlaid floral & geometric reserves, turned columnar posts at front corners & sides above the conforming plinth base on disk feet, America, ca. 1870, 20 x 56", 48" h. (ILLUS.) **5,175**

Victorian Rococo Side Cabinet

Side cabinet, Victorian Rococo substyle, carved rosewood, a white marble D-form top w/serpentined front edge above a conforming case w/a stack of four serpentine molded & fruit-carved drawers w/turned wood knobs flanked by quarter-round top drawers over quarter-round side cabinet doors w/large boldly carved fruit & nut clusters, conforming scroll- and cartouche-carved apron, New York City, ca. 1850-60, 21 x 52", 37 1/2" h. (ILLUS.) **2,530**

Smoker's cabinet, Mission-style (Arts & Crafts movement), oak, overhanging rectangular top above a single drawer & cabinet w/an arched apron, red decal mark of Gustav Stickley, Model No. 89, ca. 1910, 15 x 20 1/8", 29" h............... **3,450**

Fine Cherry Spool Cabinet

Spool cabinet, cherry, a rectangular top w/molded edges above a case of six long shallow drawers w/incised line trim & simple bail pulls, on a flat molded base, label for the Willimantic Linen Company, back displaying the original lithograph logo of a winking owl against a full moon, late 19th c., 20 x 26", 20" h. (ILLUS.)......... **1,018**

Vitrine cabinet, Empire-Style, gilt-bronze mounted mahogany, the D-form red marble top w/a flat central section above a conforming frieze band mounted w/gilt-bronze griffins, sheaves of wheat & palmettes above a conforming case w/the wide flat glazed central door opening to glass shelves & flanked by gilt-bronze-mounted flat pilasters above a wide lower panel w/a large gilt-bronze mount of Apollo driving his chariot, the curved glass sides above lower panels w/gilt-bronze wreath mounts, molded apron on short peg feet, Antoine Krieger, Paris, early 20th c., 18 1/2 x 51", 72" h................ **9,000**

Vitrine cabinet, Louis XV-Style, decorated giltwood w/ormolu trim, the oblong top w/rounded ends & peaked front corners above a conforming frame w/a wide bowed front door & curved glass ends & back enclosing two oval glass shelves, conforming narrow flared apron, on simple slender cabriole legs w/ormolu mounts at the knees & feet, original gold w/h.p. floral trim, beveled glass insert in the top, early 20th c., 21 x 27", 4' 2 1/2" h.. **1,265**

Outstanding Louis XV-Style Vitrine

Vitrine cabinet, Louis XV-Style, gilt-bronze mounted abalone & inlaid wood, two-part construction: the top section w/a high curved & arched cornice fitted w/pierced gilt-bronze scrolled crest & female terms at the corners above a curved & arched glazed cabinet door & rounded glazed sides all w/gilt-bronze trim, the conforming base w/gilt-bronze scrolls & a narrow inlaid panel; the conforming slightly stepped-out lower section w/serpentine edges above a pair of curved cupboard doors inlaid w/mother-of-pearl flowers & foliage within foliate-scrolled borders, the slender cabriole legs headed by foliate-cast female term mounts continuing down to leaf sabots & joined by a shaped stretcher shelf, France, ca. 1900, 34 1/4" w., 79" h. (ILLUS.) **10,200**

Vitrine cabinet, Louis XV-Style, simulated painted rosewood finish w/ormolu mounts, a demi-lune top w/a crestrail dramatically arched at the front & fitted w/ormolu leafy scroll edge trim & a wreath mount above the conforming case w/a curved glass center door flanked by curved glass sides all trimmed w/ormolu banding & separated by pendant ormolu drops, the lower door & side panels w/further round ormolu medallions, serpentine apron & four slender cabriole legs w/ormolu knee & foot mounts, opening to two glass shelves, early 20th c., 13 1/2 x 26 1/2", 62 1/4" h. **715**

French Vernis Martin Vitrine Cabinet

Vitrine cabinet, Louis XV-style, vernis martin decoration, the high arched crestrail centered by a gilt-bronze pierced scroll crest above a figural decorated frieze band over the tall curved-front glaze door w/a bombé base decorated w/a large vernis martin decorated figural panel, the sides w/narrow glazed panels above the bombé base panels w/further painted decoration, short outswept legs, overall gilt-bronze mounts, France, late 19th - early 20th c., 17 x 32", 75" h. (ILLUS.) **1,870**

Vitrine cabinet, Louis XV-Style, walnut, a rectangular red marble top atop the tall case w/a tall door w/a rectangular beveled glass front within a serpentine framework above a lower rectangular panel w/serpentine edges & ornate scroll carving, molded chamfered corner bands, scroll-carved serpentine apron & simple cabriole legs w/scroll carving & scroll & peg feet, France, late 19th - early 20th c., 15 1/2 x 32", 61" h... **2,310**

Chairs

Adirondack-style Painted Armchair

Adirondack-style armchairs, composed of hickory sticks, the rectangular back frame enclosing seven spindles above the open round arms on curved supports continuing down to form front legs, woven splint seat, double front & side rungs, crackled white over earlier green paint, possibly New York state, early 20th c., 38 3/4" h., pr. (ILLUS. of one) **805**

Art Deco Upholstered Armchair

Art Deco armchair, carved parcel-gilt mahogany & upholstery, the narrow gently arched gilt-trimmed crestrail above the upholstered back flanked by downswept closed upholstered arms w/carved hand rests atop tapering round front reeded legs, cushion seat, attributed to Sue et Mare, France, ca. 1925 (ILLUS.) **4,600**

French Art Deco Club-style Armchair

Art Deco armchairs, club-style, upholstered, an arched flat-topped upholstered back flanked by deep curved-top upholstered closed arms, the upholstered seat on a deep front seatrail, in Bachausen upholstery in shades of silvery taupe & black, raised on narrow Macassar ebony bases, France, ca. 1930, pr. (ILLUS. of one) **3,450**

Art Deco 'Zig-Zag' Chair

Art Deco 'Zig-Zag' chair, elm, flat boards forming an angular seat, designed by Gerrit Reitvelt in 1934, produced by De Groenekan, Holland (ILLUS.).................... **4,600**

Arts & Crafts armchair, oak, a wide gently curved crestrail above a back w/a pair of slender slats flanking a wide center slat w/two square cut-outs all resting on a lower back rail, flat open arms on flat front stile legs w/narrow tapering rectangular cut-outs, new black leather seat cushion, wide flat low stretchers, original finish, Limbert branded mark, 38 1/2" h. (small repair to rear leg) **4,675**

Arts & Crafts chairs, oak, each w/a square-topped back stile flanking a shaped crestrail pierced w/a heart flanked by scrolls above three slender slats, shaped open arms, upholstered seat, squared tapering front legs, medium brown finish, England, early 20th c., two armchairs & four side chairs, 42 1/4" h., set of 6 (some wear) **3,565**

Arts & Crafts Inlaid Rocking Chair

Arts & Crafts rocking chair w/arms, inlaid oak, a wide gently arched crestrail rail & flat lower rail flanking two plain slats & a shaped center splat w/Art Nouveau style looping foliate inlay, tapering stiles w/rounded tops, flat open arms on shaped armrests forming front legs, floral upholstered seat, flat stretchers, mortised rockers, medium brown finish, ca. 1910, 35" h. (ILLUS.) **1,035**

Arts & Crafts style side chair, ebony-inlaid oak, the arched crestrail decorated w/three ebony-inlaid squares on chair back w/a woven cane center panel, shaped back posts inlaid w/ebony squares connected w/a narrow band, woven cane seat, offset stretchers w/single slats, medium brown finish, branded Charles Limbert mark, ca. 1915, 38 1/2" h. (minor wear) **1,093**

Bentwood armchair, beech, Modern style, the U-form backrail angling down to form open arms, a rectangular upholstered back panel above the upholstered seat, slender square front & canted rear legs each w/a ball mount at the corner & connected to the U-form base, design attributed to Kolomon Moser, produced by J. & J. Kohn, Vienna, Austria, Model No. 725 BF, ca. 1902 .... **4,025**

Bentwood armchair, the U-shaped frame w/armrests centering a diamond-shaped element, the seat w/a sphere beneath each corner, U-form base rail, traces of the paper label of J. & J. Kohn, Austria, designed by Josef Hoffmann, Model No. 728/3F, ca. 1907, 30 1/2" h. **978**

Biedermeier-Style Side Chairs

Biedermeier-Style side chairs, fruitwood & part-ebonized, wide arched & shaped crest above a small ebonized wreath on a shaped lower back rail flanked by simple stiles, overupholstered seat on gently curved square tapering legs, Europe, late 19th c., 32 1/2" h., set of four (ILLUS. of two) **3,335**

Boston rocking chair w/arms, painted & decorated, the wide rounded crestrail above six tall spindles & simple turned stiles above the S-scroll arms on a spindle & turned canted arm support, deep S-scroll seat, knob- and rod-turned front legs w/a knob-turned front stretcher, plain turned side & back stretchers, worn original red & black graining w/yellow striping & stenciling w/fruit in colored bronze powder on the crest, early 19th c., 39 1/2" h. (rockers worn) **220**

Chippendale country-style corner chair, cherry, the shaped U-form crest on flat outscrolled arms on vase- and ring-turned supports flanking two pierced vasiform splats, the rush slip seat in a valanced frame joining four square beaded legs & box stretchers, refinished, probably Connecticut, ca. 1770-80, 32" h. **5,175**

Massachusetts Chippendale Chair

Chippendale side chair, carved mahogany, the bow-shaped crestrail ending in scrolled terminals above a pierced & scroll-carved splat flanked by outward flaring stiles above a trapezoidal slip seat, front cabriole legs ending in pad feet on platforms, joined by turned stretchers to the raked chamfered rear legs, old finish, Boston or Salem, Massachusetts, ca. 1770, minor imperfections, 37 3/4" h. (ILLUS.)........................ **7,475**

Chippendale side chair, carved mahogany, the serpentine crestrail w/foliatecarved scrolled ears above a piercecarved interlaced Gothic splat flanked by molded stiles over a trapezoidal seat & conforming slip-seat on cabriole front legs ending in ball-and-claw feet, Philadelphia, ca. 1770, 38 1/4" h. **8,625**

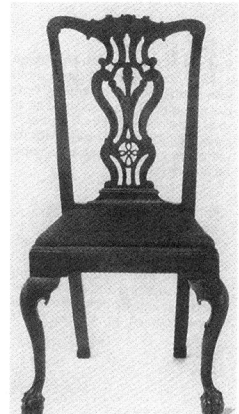

Chippendale Mahogany Side Chair

Chippendale side chairs, mahogany, a cyma-curved crestrail w/raked terminals & a central carved fan over a scroll- and bar-pierced splat on a molded shoe over the trapezoidal upholstered slip seat in molded seatrails, square front legs w/beaded edges joined by an H-stretcher & a single rear stretcher, old surface, Massachusetts, 18th c., 37 3/4" h., pr. **8,625**

Chippendale-Style chairs, carved mahogany, the scalloped crest w/shell-carved center & carved ears above a Gothic-style pierced splat, two w/S-scroll arms w/carved hand grips on incurved leafcarved supports, upholstered slip seat, arched apron on cabriole front legs w/flower- and acanthus leaf-carved knees & ending in heavy ball-and-claw feet, 20th c., two armchairs & ten side chairs, 40 1/4" h., the set (edge wear, one w/damage at knee & upholstery stain) **4,400**

Chippendale-Style child's wingchair, tall upholstered back w/arched crest above narrow curved wings over the rolled upholstered arms & overupholstered seat, square mahogany legs w/side stretchers, worn floral upholstery, early 20th c., 29" h. (cross-stretcher missing, leg chips) **660**

Chippendale-Style side chairs, mahogany, the relief-carved serpentine crestrail above a pierced looped scrolling splat flanked by molded stiles, overupholstered seat, square molded legs joined by box stretchers, varnished finish, 20th c., 36" h., set of 6 (minor foot wear)................. **1,430**

Boston Chippendale Side Chair

Chippendale side chair, mahogany, the serpentine crestrail centering a foliatecarved device & ending in scrolledcarved ears above the pierced carved intertwining splat flanked by raked stiles, trapezoidal overupholstered seat on cockbeaded square legs joined by flat stretchers, old refinish, minor imperfections, Boston, Massachusetts, ca. 1780, 37" h. (ILLUS.) **8,625**

Chippendale side chair, the serpentine crestrail w/scrolled-back ears & a central carved shell above a vasiform splat & raked stiles joined to the molded trapezoidal slip seat centering a shell-carved seatrail on front cabriole legs ending in claw-and-ball feet, old finish, Philadelphia, 1760-80, 40" h. (minor repairs, losses)... **6,325**

Chippendale side chair, walnut, the serpentine crestrail ending in shaped terminals above a heart-pierced vasiform splat, chamfered raked stiles & a trapezoidal slip seat on frontal cabriole legs ending in pad feet on platforms, Newbury, Massachusetts, ca. 1760-80, 37 1/2" h. (minor imperfections)................. **1,955**

Chippendale side chairs, carved mahogany, the serpentine crest above an ornate scroll-pierced splat & raked stiles over a trapezoidal slip seat on frontal cabriole legs w/carved scrolled returns & ending in claw-and-ball feet, raked square rear legs, old refinish, possibly North Carolina, ca. 1760-80, 40 3/4" h., pr. (ILLUS. of one, top next column)................. **5,750**

Classical country-style rocking chair w/arms, the wide crestrail w/rounded ends above a wide bootjack-form splat flanked by tapering stiles, heavy scrolled arms over a single spindle, wide shaped plank seat, turned & canted front legs joined by a turned front stretcher, on long rockers, original green paint w/black & grey striping & stenciled & free-hand floral & fruit decoration w/grapes, strawberries, etc. in black red, gold & green, gilt trim on crestrail, Pennsylvania, mid-19th c., some wear, 42 1/2" h. (ILLUS. top next page)................. **715**

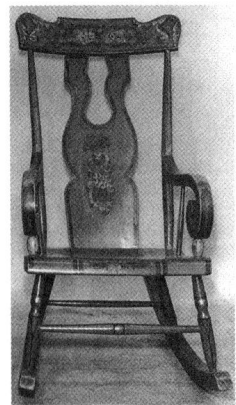

Decorated Pennsylvania Rocker

Classical side chair, carved mahogany, klismos-style, the crestrail w/a rectangular outset inlaid panel over a carved splat w/central molded medallion enclosing a carved flower further flanked by stylized flowers, pierced rings & feathers centered by outscrolling stiles over a trapezoidal seat, on klismos legs, New York, ca. 1810, 32 1/4" h. **575**

Classical side chairs, carved tiger stripe maple, the scroll & acanthus leaf carved tablet crest above a pierced acanthus leaf & scroll-carved splat & shaped stiles continuing to trapezoidal cane seats on flaring vase- and ring-turned front legs joined to the raked back legs by turned stretchers, old finish, probably New England, ca. 1825, 32 1/2" h., set of 4 .... **2,645**

Fine Boston Classical Side Chairs

Classical side chairs, mahogany & mahogany veneer, the concave veneered crestrails w/leaf-carved terminals atop shaped stiles joined by scroll-carved slats above the upholstered slip seats & molded seatrail, incurved front legs & outswept rear legs, old refinish, very minor imperfections, Boston, 1825-35, set of 4 (ILLUS. of two) **2,300**

Country style 'banister-back' armchair, painted, the carved stag horn form crestrail over four split banisters on a stayrail flanked by baluster-, knob- and rod-turned stiles w/knob finials, shaped scrolling arms on baluster-turned arm

supports over the woven rush seat on ring- and rod-turned front legs joined by two baluster-turned front stretchers & plain double side stretchers, old black paint, Portsmouth, New Hampshire area, ca. 1725-75, imperfections, 43 3/4" h. (ILLUS. below)........................... **2,990**

Early 'Banister-back' Armchair

Country-style "arrow-back" side chairs, decorated, wide crestrail above four curved arrow slats between the curved tapering stiles, shaped saddle seat on bamboo-turned legs joined by a turned front stretcher & plain turned side stretchers, original red decoration, the crestrail w/yellow & green foliage, usual stretcher wear, early 19th c., 35" h., set of 4 .... **2,970**

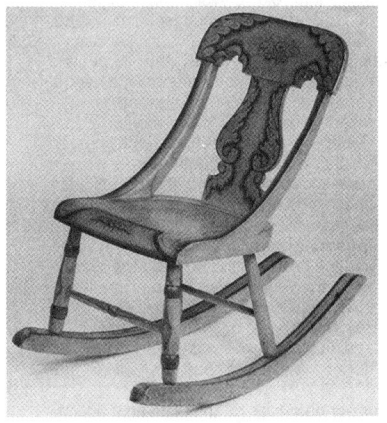

Early Painted Child's Rocker

Country-style child's armless rocking chair, painted & decorated, the wide rounded crestrail above a vasiform splat flanked by curved stiles joined to the wide plank seat, ring-turned front legs & stretcher, long rockers, a mustard yellow ground paint w/yellow, red, green & black accents & leafy scroll & floral decoration on the crestrail & splat, original surface, very minor imperfections, Pennsylvania, mid-19th c., 32" h. (ILLUS.) **748**

Country-style "ladder-back" armchair, maple, the tall turned stiles w/turned ball finials joined by reverse-graduated arched slats, shaped open arms w/scrolled handholds on baluster- and ring-turned arm supports above the rush seat, rod- and ball-turned front legs w/ball feet joined by a double ball & ring-turned front stretcher & plain turned side & back stretchers, old refinish, Delaware River Valley, 18th c., 46 1/2" h. (slight imperfections)... **9,200**

Early 18th Century Ladder-back Chair

Country-style 'ladder-back' armchair, pine & ash, the tall back w/four arched graduated slats between tall ring- and rod-turned stiles w/triple-knob finials above simple rod arms w/rod-turned front supports & button finials continuing to form front legs, woven rush seat, simple double stretchers at the front & sides, remnants of old red paint, Scituate or Marshfield, Massachusetts, early 18th c., imperfections, height loss, 43 3/4" h. (ILLUS.).. **2,875**

Country-style "ladder-back" child's rocking chair w/arms, the back w/three arched slats between simple turned stiles w/knob finials, flat shaped arms on turned arm supports continuing into the turned front legs, woven splint seat, old dry red surface, 25 1/4" h. (minor seat damage).. **275**

Country-style "ladder-back" highchair, simple turned back stiles w/vase- and ring-turned finials, the back rails composed of shaped horizontal slats, the arms fitted w/cylindrical hand-holds, the cylinder & ring-turned stiles & arm supports joined by stretchers, old surface, New England, late 18th c., 37 1/2" h. (imperfections, missing front seatrail)................ **374**

Country-style "ladder-back" weaver's chair, hardwood, the tall back w/two arched slats between slender turned stiles w/button finials, stiles continue down to form very tall back legs & matched tall front legs supporting a woven splint seat, a high simple turned front stretcher above a lower ring-turned stretcher, plain turned double side stretchers, button-and-peg feet, old natural finish, 19th c., overall 38" h. (joints need regluing)..................................... **770**

Danish Modern rocking chair w/arms, teak, a curved crestrail & arms on tapering squared stile legs joined by slender arched seatrails, on rockers, woven rust-colored back & seat cushions, foil label of M. Nissan, Denmark, 28" h............................ **173**

Early American "banister-back" armchair, painted, the double arched & scalloped crestrail flanked by ring- and baluster-turned stiles flanking four half-round banisters & attached to serpentine arms above ring-turned front legs ending in knob feet, old black paint, Connecticut, 1725-75, 49" h. (imperfections)................. **6,900**

Early American "ladder-back" child's highchair, maple, the tall back stiles forming rear legs & back & ending in turned knob finials above three arched slats in the back above serpentine open arms on baluster-turned arm supports continuing into front tall turned legs, replaced paper rush seat, front rungs worn from use, refinished, 35" h. (age cracks, chips on finial)...................................... **468**

Early American "ladder-back" side chair, painted, the tall back w/four reverse-graduated arched slats between slender ring- and rod-turned stiles w/knob finials, replaced rush seat on baluster-, knob- and rod-turned front legs joined by a double-knob turned high stretcher, plain turned double side & a single back stretcher, old black repaint, late 18th - early 19th c., 43" h. **825**

Egyptian Revival armchair, painted hardwood, the square back w/an upholstered panel below the wide rectangular crestrail decorated w/a winged half-serpent ornament & flanked by slender open arms w/carved wings & curved supports above the over-upholstered seat on a flat seatrail & turned front legs ending in carved paw feet, old worn red & green repaint w/gilding, early 20th c., 36 3/4" h. **605**

Federal side chair, mahogany, the shield-form back w/fanned & pierced splat carved at the center w/sheaf of wheat & raised above the overupholstered seat on square tapering legs, old refinishing, late 18th - early 19th c., 36 3/4" h. (minor repairs)... **495**

Federal side chairs, mahogany, arched molded crestrails continuing to shaped stiles flanking vasiform pierced carved splats over the trapezoidal slip seat, on square beaded tapering front legs joined to the raked rear legs by square stretchers, New England, ca. 1790, refinished, minor imperfections, 37 1/4" h., pr. (ILLUS. below) **2,990**

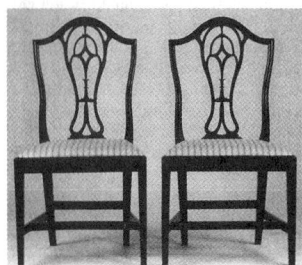

Federal Mahogany Side Chairs

Federal-Style side chair, mahogany, shield-shaped back w/a vase-form pierced splat centered by Prince of Wales Plumes, raised above an overupholstered seat w/blue needlepoint w/roses, square tapering legs joined by flat stretchers, legs w/line inlay & banded cuffs, late 19th - early 20th c., 37" h. **220**

Louis XV-Style armchair, carved hardwood, the rectangular upholstered back panel w/serpentine sides & a gently arched crestrail carved w/rococo scrolls above open shaped padded arms & raised above the over-upholstered seat w/a curved seatrail w/scroll carving & carved simple cabriole front legs ending in peg feet, antique white highlights, platinum satin upholstery w/gold bees, early 20th c., 37 1/2" h. **523**

Louis XV-Style open-arm armchair, the squared back frame w/serpentine edges & arched crest w/floral carving & molded edges enclosing a petit-point upholstery panel of a man in 18th c. attire walking in a garden, padded open molded & serpentine arms above the spring seat w/further petit-point upholstery in a floral design, serpentine front seatrail w/carved central floral reserve, molded cabriole legs w/peg feet, early 20th c., 37 1/2" h. (some stitches missing) **385**

Mission-style (Arts & Crafts movement) rocking chair w/arms, oak, a curved crestrail over five back slats, shaped arms w/through-tenons & long corbel supports, two side slats on each side, medium brown finish, spring cushion seat, early 20th c., 35" h. (needs upholstering, minor wear) **403**

Mission-style (Arts & Crafts movement) rocking chair w/arms, oak, a curved crestrail over four vertical slats, shaped flat arms over a single slat w/cut-out, arched seatrail, square legs on rockers, original finish, branded Charles Limbert mark, Model No. 644, 39" h. (no seat) **1,093**

Mission-style (Arts & Crafts movement) rocking chair w/arms, oak, double flat & gently curved crestrails above five vertical slats between the square back stiles, flat gently arched arms over rails flanking vertical slats on each side, wide flat se-

atrail, new brown leather drop-in cushion spring seat, fine original finish, unmarked Harden Co., 36" h. (shallow gouging, crack in one crestrail) **1,045**

Mission-style (Arts & Crafts movement) rocking chair without arms, oak, the tall rectangular back w/three slats below the crestrail, each inlaid w/a stylized pewter & wood floral design, raised above the drop-in leather seat above arched aprons & square legs joined by box stretchers, designed by Harvey Ellis, Gustav Stickley Model No. 337, ca. 1912, 33 3/4" h. **6,325**

Mission-style (Arts & Crafts movement) side chair, oak, a back w/tall square stiles flanking a leather-covered panel w/tack trim, raised above the leather-covered seat, square slender legs joined by a wide flat front stretcher & narrow flat side stretchers, small red decal mark of Gustav Stickley, Model No. 380, ca. 1904-07, 39 1/2" h. **2,300**

Mission-style (Arts & Crafts movement) side chairs, oak, a flat crestrail & lower rail supporting three vertical slats above the planked seat, square slender legs joined by wide flat box stretchers, L. & J.G. Stickley Model No. 940, ca. 1915, set of 8 .... **2,070**

Wright-designed Modern Armchair

Modern style armchair, wood & upholstery, deep upholstered sides w/a rolled crest & large back cushion above the wide cushion seat over a deep flat upholstered seatrail, wood base frame on short squared legs, green velvet upholstery, designed by Frank Lloyd Wright, manufactured by Heritage Henredon, Style No. 1483, ca. 1955, 29 1/2 x 33 1/2", 27" h. (ILLUS.) **748**

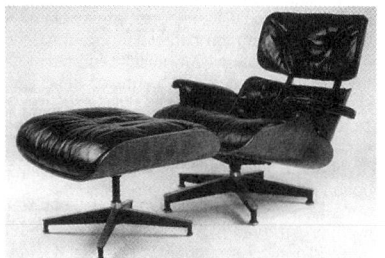

Eames Armchair & Ottoman

Modern style armchair & ottoman, molded wood & leather, the armchair w/a high wide rectangular black leather-upholstered back rest above a lower upholstered back flanked by rolled arms & a deep upholstered seat w/a molded rosewood veneer shell raised on a five-prong aluminum base, the large leather-upholstered ottoman of matching construction, designed by Charles & Ray Eames, ca. 1956, wear to leather, 33" h., 2 pcs. (ILLUS.).. **748**

Norman Cherner Plywood Chair

Modern style chairs, molded plywood, a wedge-shaped back tapering sharply & continuing to the rounded seat, raised on slender tapering legs, molded walnut arms on the armchair, designed by Norman Cherner, ca. 1960, made by Plycraft, Lawrence, Massachusetts, one armchair & three side chairs, repair to one leg, wear, nicks, 31" h., the set (ILLUS. of side chair) **920**

Saarinen "Womb" Chair & Ottoman

Modern style "Womb" armchair & ottoman, upholstered, the deep rounded & cupped form w/rolled arms enclosing two cushions raised on a tubular steel frame & legs, together w/a matching ottoman, avocado green wool upholstery, manufacturer's tag of Knoll Associates, New York, designed by Eero Saarinen, introduced in 1948, wear to upholstery edges, chair 36" h., 2 pcs. (ILLUS.)......................... **1,380**

Oriental armrchair, carved teak, the square back w/a gently arched crest above the pierce-carved panel centering a figural reserve surrounded by long dragons & clouds w/the dragon heads facing each other at the crest, heavy plain back stiles & bottom rail above pierce-carved arms above the wide seat w/curved, scroll-incised seatrail, simple cabriole front legs ending in paw feet, w/brocade cushion, China, 20th c., 42" h. **457**

Pilgrim Century "Great Chair," turned & joined oak, the flame & ring finials above turned & incised stiles centering a double-baluster & ring-turned crest over three tapering spindles, all above cylindrical open arms & bun-turned hand grips over turned front post legs over a trapezoidal rush seat, on cylindrical legs joined by double box stretchers, Plymouth County, Massachusetts, 1715-30, 38 3/4" h. **8,050**

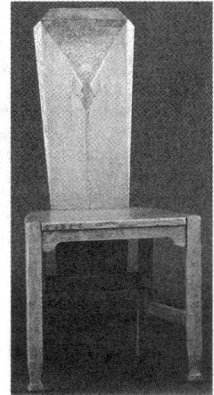

Prairie School Oak Side Chair

Prairie School side chairs, inlaid oak, a tall slender flat back w/angled top corners above an inlaid geometric design, board plank seat mortised through to the back & on square legs w/Mackmurdo feet, some veneer loss to top of one back, original finish, early 20th c., 41" h., pr. (ILLUS. of one) **1,760**

New England Queen Anne Armchair

Queen Anne armchair, maple, the yoked crestrail over a vasiform splat & molded stay-rail flanked by raked stiles joining scrolling molded arms on baluster-, block- and ring-turned supports continuing to front legs, joined by a bulbous turned front stretcher & square side & back stretchers to the raked rear legs, vestiges of old red stain, New England, ca. 1740-60, minor imperfections, 40 3/4" h. (ILLUS.) **9,200**

Queen Anne corner armchair, walnut, the low shaped crest on a U-form flattened crestrail ending in outscrolled grips on vase- and ring-turned supports flanking two vasiform splats, the slip seat on a shaped seat frame on a frontal cabriole leg ending in a pad foot, remaining simple turned legs w/tiny pad feet, all joined by block- and vase-turned cross-stretchers, old surface, Boston, ca. 1740-60 (imperfections) **6,900**

Queen Anne corner armchair, walnut, the shaped low crest continuing to scrolled hand holds above three ring- and rod-turned stiles & two vase-form splats on molded shoes, the slip compass seat on a frontal cabriole leg ending in a pad foot, three straight turned tapering back legs ending in pad feet (one damaged), all joined by cut-out seat frame above block, rod- and ring-turned cross stretchers, old surface, Boston, 1752-60, 30" h. (imperfections) **43,700**

Queen Anne country-style side chair, cherry & ash, the shaped crestrail above a vase-form splat on an arched stay rail flanked by baluster- and ring-turned stiles, the rush seat on baluster- and ring-turned tapering legs ending in pad feet on platforms, joined by bulbous turned front stretchers & plain turned double side stretchers, old refinish, attributed to Jacob Smith, New York, 18th c., 41 1/2" h. **748**

Queen Anne country-style side chair, grain-painted, the yoked crestrail above a vasiform splat & raked stiles joined by a lower rail above the woven rush seat, on block-, vase- and ring-turned front legs ending in carved Spanish feet joined by a bulbous turned front stretcher & side stretchers, old brown grained painting, New England, second half 18th c., worn, 39 3/4" h. **920**

Queen Anne country-style side chair, painted maple, the ox-yoke crest w/rounded corners above tall flat stiles flanking a vase-form splat to a lower rail, woven splint seat w/old light green paint, old dry red paint, 18th c., 42 1/4" h. **1,045**

Queen Anne country-style side chair, painted, slighted curved crestrail above tall knob- and baluster-turned stiles flanking the vasiform splat, replaced rush seat, ring- and rod-turned tapering front legs ending in raised pad feet, double-knob turned front stretcher, plain turned side & back stretchers, old alligatored red

& black repaint, attributed to Samuel Durand, Milford, Connecticut, 18th c., 40 3/4" h. **880**

Queen Anne Maple Side Chair

Queen Anne side chair, maple, the yoked crestrail over a vasiform splat & molded shoe flanked by raked & chamfered stiles, the overupholstered balloon seat on frontal cabriole legs ending in pad feet, joined to the rear shaped & raked legs by block-, baluster- and ring-turned stretchers, old refinish, Massachusetts, ca. 1740-60, minor restorations (ILLUS.) **4,313**

Queen Anne side chair, painted & carved, the yoked crestrail w/beaded edges continuing to raked beaded stiles flanking the vasiform splat over a trapezoidal needlework slip seat, scalloped front seatrail on front arris cabriole legs ending in squared arris pad feet & squared & chamfered back legs joined by block-, vase- and ring-turned H-form stretchers & swelled rear stretcher, old red stain w/black accents, Connecticut River Valley, ca. 1740-60, partial MFA exhibition label on rear leg, 41 3/4" h. (imperfections) **2,300**

Early Painted Queen Anne Chair

Queen Anne side chair, painted maple, transitional style w/a carved yoked crestrail over a vasiform splat flanked by molded raked stiles above an over-upholstered seat w/a cyma-curved skirt & a medial stretcher w/ball- and reel-turnings flanked by black- and baluster-turned front legs ending in Spanish feet, joined to the rear raked legs by square stretchers, old black paint w/gilt highlights, Portsmouth, New Hampshire, 1735-50, 40" h. (ILLUS.) **3,738**

Queen Anne side chair, painted, the yoked crestrail above a vasiform splat & raked stiles joined to the rush seat by block-, vase- and ring-turned legs on Spanish feet w/a double-knob turned front stretcher & square side stretchers, old surface, Massachusetts, 18th c., 41" h. **1,150**

Roman-Style armchair, carved mahogany, a wide arched & heavily scroll-carved back rail w/a grotesque face between blocked carved stiles w/high inscrolled ears above the open serpentine arms above the wide U-form seat raised on four S-scroll supports resting on a heavy block X-form base w/carved toes on casters, dark reddish brown original finish, paper label for Stomps - Burkhart, Dayton furniture company, early 20th c., 37 3/4" h. (crack in support board beneath the seat) **330**

Italian Baroque-Style Grotto Armchair

Victorian Baroque Revival armchair, walnut, a grotto-style chair w/the high back & wide seat carved as large shells w/figural dolphin-form arms, on curved coral-form legs, Italy, ca. 1880 (ILLUS.) **1,500**

Victorian Baroque Revival Armchair

Victorian Baroque Revival armchair, walnut, the tall back ornately pierced-carved w/an arched scroll-carved crestrail above a wide pierced scroll- and lattice-carved splat flanked by slender turned stiles above the heavy scrolled & molded arms on curved supports, wide over-upholstered seat on spiral-turned front legs joined by a high arched & pierced scrolling stretchers, turned H-stretchers joins all the legs, ca. 1900 (ILLUS.) **920**

Ornate Baroque Revival Dining Chairs

Victorian Baroque Revival dining chairs, carved hardwood, each w/a tall narrow back w/an ornately carved framework, the high arched crest centered by a carved animal head surrounded by pierced leafy scrolls & continuing down to form the carved framework around a narrow tufted upholstered back panel, flanked by spiral-turned stiles capped w/urn finials & raised above the overupholstered seat, block-, baluster- and ring-turned front legs joined by a spiral-turned front stretcher w/turned H-stretcher connecting all the legs, the armchairs w/padded rests & carved dog head hand grips, four side chairs & two armchairs, late 19th c., the set (ILLUS. of two) **6,325**

Victorian Baroque-style Morris chair, mahogany, the upright adjustable rectangular back frame above wide flat arms over boldly carved figural arm supports w/large winged griffin heads on bold scrolls & arched carved front legs ending in padded paw feet, curved back arm supports on down-scrolled back legs, upholstered back & seat cushions, on casters, ca. 1890 .... **1,904**

Victorian country-style "balloon-back" side chairs, painted & decorated, the arched rounded backrail w/a gently scalloped crest above a wide vertical splat, the shaped plank seat on slightly canted knob-turned front legs joined by a knob-turned front stretcher, original black over red ground w/white scrolled trim, fruit & foliage on crest & splat, some initialed under seat "W.F.H., Trenton, O.," restorations w/small areas of touch-up, 33" h., set of 4 .... **770**

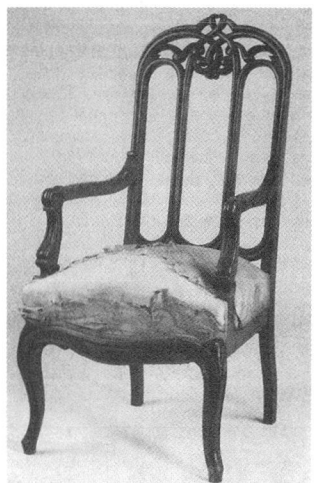

Fine Gothic Revival Armchair

Victorian Gothic Revival armchair, carved rosewood, the arched Gothic-carved crestrail above tall oblong molding flanked by open arms w/carved scrolled terminals & curved arm supports over the spring-upholstered serpentined & cyma-curved seat & seatrail, front demi-cabrole legs, 1850-60, possibly New York City, surface imperfections, 41 1/2" h. (ILLUS.)........................... **3,335**

Victorian Neo-Grec Armchair

Victorian Neo-Grec armchairs, ebonized & gilt-trimmed hardwood, the canted & back-scrolled crest w/upholstered central panel above a frame enclosing seven short turned spindles flanked by conforming gilt-incised stiles leads to downscrolling upholstered arms & arched, gilt-incised armrests over similarly incised downscrolling side rails flanking the rectangular upholstered seat, on a carved & gilt-incised cu-

rule-form base joined by a turned stretcher, on casters, American, ca. 1870, 34 1/4" h., pr. (ILLUS. of one)...................... **3,680**

Fancy Victorian Child's Rocker

Victorian Renaissance Revival child's rocker without arms, walnut, a scroll-carved crestrail w/fanned center crest above the oval caned back panel w/scroll-cut bottom frame & raised on stiles w/serpentine skirt guards flanking the rounded caned seat, ring-turned front legs & front stretcher w/plain turned side & rear stretchers, on long rockers, 30" h. (ILLUS.) **336**

Victorian Renaissance Revival Chair

Victorian Renaissance Revival side chairs, carved rosewood, the tall upholstered back w/a high scroll- and architectural carved crestrail centered by a carved maidenhead above incurved stiles over the serpentine upholstered seat on a conforming seatrail w/central carved drop, on boldly turned & tapering trumpet legs on casters, red silk upholstery, attributed to John Jelliff, ca. 1870, 38 1/2" h., pr. (ILLUS. of one) **978**

Victorian Rococo substyle side chair, carved & laminated rosewood, a tall waisted balloon back w/an arched floral-carved crest above the upholstered back panel, over-upholstered spring seat w/a serpentine finger-molded seatrail above demi-cabriole front legs on casters & outswept rear legs on casters, "Rosalie" patt. by John H. Belter, ca. 1855, 37" h. **1,680**

Victorian Rococo substyle side chairs, carved rosewood, an oval back w/a finger-carved frame w/a carved floral crest enclosing the upholstered panel, raised above the overupholstered spring seat w/a serpentine seatrail w/finger-carving continuing into demi-cabriole front legs on casters, reupholstered in red floral damask, ca. 1860, 39" h., set of 4 (repairs)...... **528**

Victorian Steer Horn Armchair

Victorian steer horn armchair, the high arched tufted upholstered back framed by curved steer horns continuing down to flank the deep upholstered seat, on arched outswept steer horn legs, original worn upholstery, on casters, ca. 1870, 36 1/2" h. (ILLUS.)...................................... **1,035**

Unique Victorian Folk Art Folding Chair

Victorian stick-style novelty folding chair, the back & front legs formed from a single forked tree branch w/the upper back squared off & fitted w/a short crossbar above etched designs of people, animals, flowers, birds & inscriptions above the small rectangular seat supported by a hinged carved third support leg, marked "Liberty Indiana, March 1892," made by Hosea Hayden, 30" h. (ILLUS.) **13,750**

Nutting-signed Child's Windsor Chair

Wallace Nutting-signed child's "fanback" Windsor armchair, the serpentine crest w/scrolled ends raised on seven tall spindles above a U-form central rail ending in shaped arms & above numerous turned swelled spindles, on baluster- and knob-turned canted arm supports, on a deeply shaped saddle seat, on canted baluster-, ring- and rod-turned legs joined by a swelled H-stretcher, labeled "Wallace Nutting, Saugus, Mass.," early 20th c., surface imperfections, dark stain, 27" h. (ILLUS.) **1,380**

Wicker corner chair, a flat rolled crestrail of tightly woven wicker above back panels w/bands of fine diamond lattice weaving above & below a narrow central band w/short vertical strips, a tightly woven cane quarter-round seat above a double band looped wicker apron, three front & one rear wrapped legs, old burgundy painted finish, early 20th c., 28" h. (minor scuffs)... **248**

Wicker rocking chair w/arms, a high rounded back w/a rolled wide tightly woven border continuing down to form rounded arms, the back w/a large woven wheel-form center panel over a lacy scroll lower section, loosely scrolled arm supports, oblong woven seat above a lattice woven front apron & double turned side & back rungs, on rockers, ca. 1890 .... **392**

Wicker rocking chair w/arms, the high arched serpentine back w/wide bands of tightly woven wicker centered by a tall tapering oblong delicately scrolled wicker central panel, the rolled crestrail continues down to form wide rolled arms over lattice panels, rounded seat over ornately scrolled apron on rockers, ca. 1880-90 .... **784**

Fancy Victorian Wicker Rocker

Wicker rocking chair w/arms, the tall back w/a tall pointed center crest composed of ornate tight cane scrolls above curved bands of lattice weaving above the ornately caned back panel, all flanked by very tall pointed stiles, ornate looping scroll arms & ornate scrolls under the back panels, later upholstered seat cushions, each leg w/ornate scrolled cane corner brackets, original natural finish, ca. 1890, 46" h. (ILLUS.) **504**

William & Mary-Style wing chair, upholstered mahogany, the tall upholstered back w/a round top flanked by tall rolled wings over the upholstered rolled arms & upholstered seat, the turnip-, block- and ball-turned front legs joined by a high, wide arched pierced scrolled front stretcher, turned H-stretcher joins the legs, dark green velvet upholstery, Kittinger, 20th c., 49 1/2" h. **715**

Windsor "arrow-back" armchair, painted, a flat curved crestrail between two tapering curved stiles flanking three curved arrow back slats, turned rod open arms w/canted bamboo-turned arm supports & a single arrow splat, wide rounded shaped plank seat, canted bamboo-turned legs joined by a flattened front stretcher & bamboo-turned side & back stretchers, old worn mustard yellow paint, first half 19th c., 32" h. **275**

Windsor "arrow-back" side chairs, painted & stenciled, each w/a gently curved rectangular crestrail between tapering curved stiles flanking four arrow slats, shaped incised plank seat on bamboo-turned splayed legs joined by a front shaped & decorated stretcher & plain round side & back stretchers, original yellow ground decorated on the crestrail w/roses & green leaves, first half 19th c., 33 3/4" h., set of 5 .... **5,750**

Windsor "birdcage" side chair, painted, the birdcage crestrail w/three short over seven long spindles flanked by turned stiles on a shaped, incised saddle seat, four splayed bamboo-turned legs joined by matching stretchers, overall old red

paint w/yellow accents & yellow seat, the stiles w/leaf decoration, New England, ca. 1810, seats repainted, 34 1/4" h., pr. (ILLUS. of one, below) **1,850**

Painted Birdcage Windsor Side Chair

Windsor "birdcage" side chairs, painted, the double bamboo-turned crestrails & curved stiles enclosing three short spindles above seven long spindles joining the shaped & incised seat on splayed bamboo-turned legs & stretchers, old brown paint, underside inscribed in chalk "N. Tuck," New England, ca. 1800, 34" h., set of 6 .... **6,325**

Windsor "bow-back" armchair, painted, the bowed crestrail above seven spindles, shaped arms on two spindles & a canted bamboo-turned arm support, slightly shaped plank seat on canted bamboo-turned legs joined by a bamboo-turned H-stretcher, old alligatored black paint over earlier colors, illegible signature, Pennsylvania, late 18th - early 19th c., 36" h. (repaired crack in seat) **935**

Windsor Child's Armchair

Windsor "bow-back" child's armchair, maple & ash, the bowed crestrail over five slender spindles & joined to shaped arms over a spindle & canted arm supports, shaped saddle seat raised on canted bamboo-turned legs joined by a bamboo-turned H-stretcher, New England, early 19th c., refinished, repairs, 22 1/3" h. (ILLUS.)...................................... **1,265**

Windsor "bow-back" side chair, a bowed & reeded back rail above nine slender swelled spindles, shaped saddle seat on canted bamboo-turned legs joined by a bamboo-turned H-stretcher, old dark finish, branded mark of Ebenezer Tracey, Lisbon, Connecticut, late 18th - early 19th c., 35 1/2" h. (well done repairs) **880**

Windsor "bow-back" side chair, painted, the bowed crestrail above eight swelled spindles & a shaped saddle seat w/a pair of swelled back brace spindles, on splayed ring- and baluster-turned legs joined by a swelled H-stretcher, old green over early dark green, New England, ca. 1780, 35 1/2" h. **748**

Windsor "bow-back" side chairs, painted, the rounded molded back rail above seven bamboo-turned spindles, shaped saddle seat on canted bamboo-turned legs joined by a bamboo-turned H-stretcher, old red repaint over white, attributed to the Boston area, late 18th - early 19th c., 37 3/4 & 38" h., pr. **1,430**

Windsor "comb-back" rocking chair w/arms, painted, a curved rectangular small crest raised on five bamboo-turned curved spindles above the plain crestrail between canted stiles & above five bamboo-turned spindles, S-scroll arms on canted, bamboo-turned arm supports, wide thick plank seat, canted bamboo-turned legs joined by stretchers, inset rockers, old dark greenish black repaint w/yellow striping & crest w/date of 1769 & a "C" on the comb, found in Vermont, late 18th - early 19th c., 44" h. **770**

Windsor "combed arrow-back" rocking chair w/arms, painted, the comb-back above the rectangular crest & four arrow-form slats flanked by raked stiles & scrolled arms on bamboo-turned supports over the shaped seat, splayed turned legs on rockers joined by stretchers, original yellow & green foliate decoration on a mottled brown & black ground, New England, ca. 1830, 38" h. (imperfections) **633**

Windsor "continuous-arm" armchairs, each w/a molded bowed back continuing down to slender shaped arms, seven slender bamboo-turned back spindles & two short spindles under each arm w/a canted baluster- and ring-turned arm support, wide shaped saddle seat on canted bamboo-turned legs joined by a swelled H-stretcher, old brown finish, size varies so possibly a lady's & gentleman's set, attributed to Connecticut, possibly by Beriah Green, Windham Country, 37" & 39 3/4" h., pr. **5,225**

Windsor "continuous-arm" brace-back armchair, painted, the incised arched crestrail curving down & ending in shaped hand grips enclosing twelve spin-

dles & two splayed rear braces, on ring- and baluster-turned canted arm supports, shaped saddle seat, canted ring-, baluster- and rod-turned legs joined by a swelled H-stretcher, painted green, late 18th c., 37" h. **633**

Windsor "fan-back" armchair, ash & maple, the shaped crestrail above eight tall spindles & a U-form central rail continuing to form shaped arms on baluster- and ring-turned arm supports & six additional short spindles, wide shaped saddle seat, splayed baluster- and ring-turned legs joined by a swelled H-stretcher, refinished, New England, ca. 1790, 46" h. **3,738**

Fine Windsor Fan-back Armchair

Windsor "fan-back" armchair, painted, a long serpentine crestrail w/scroll-carved terminals above nine tall spindles, a medial armrail ending in scrolled carved hand holds on baluster- and ring-turned arm supports, shaped saddle seat, canted baluster-, ring- and rod-turned legs joined by a swelled H-stretcher, New England, ca. 1780, 43 1/2" h. (ILLUS.) **5,463**

Windsor "fan-back" rocking armchair, serpentine crestrail w/downscrolling ear volutes above ring- and baluster-turned & blocked stiles centered by nine tapering spindles over shaped arms terminating in downscrolling knuckled hand holds above ring- and baluster-turned arm supports over a shaped plank seat, on ring- and baluster-turned legs joined by a baluster-turned H-stretcher, shaped rockers, early 19th c., 39" h. **1,610**

Windsor "fan-back" side chair, painted, a serpentine crestrail above a back w/seven slender turned spindles between canted baluster- and ring-turned stiles, shaped saddle seat w/incised band at back, on canted baluster- and ring-turned legs joined by a swelled H-stretcher, old worn black paint over traces of earlier red, attributed to Connecticut or Rhode Island, late 18th c., 33 1/4" h. (age cracks in seat) . **1,980**

Windsor "fan-back" side chair, painted, the serpentine crestrail above five slender tapering spindles flanked by baluster- and knob-turned stiles, a shaped plank seat w/pommel & bulbous turned splayed legs joined by swelled H-stretchers, original green paint, southern New Hampshire or northern Massachusetts, ca. 1790, 35 1/4" h. (minor paint loss) **2,070**

Windsor "sack-back" armchair, painted, the bowed crestrail above seven slender spindles continuing through a medial rail to form flat arms w/carved hand grips, a spindle under each arm & canted baluster- and ring-turned arm supports, wide shaped rod-turned legs joined by a swelled H-stretcher, black repaint, late 18th c., 38 1/4" h. (old break in bow crest) **2,860**

Windsor "sack-back" armchair, painted, the bowed crestrail over seven spindles joining shaped arms w/vase- and ring-turned canted supports, the shaped & incised seat on splayed vase- and ring-turned legs joined by swelled H-form stretchers, old worn black over green paint, New England, ca. 1790, 39" h. (imperfections) **14,950**

Windsor "sack-back" armchair, the arched crestrail on a U-form medial rail ending in shaped hand-holds on canted baluster-turned arm supports & nine spindles across the back, on a thick shaped seat w/incising & pommel on ring-turned splayed legs joined by swelled stretchers, old refinish, New England, 1790-1810, 38" h. **1,495**

Windsor Sack-back Armchair

Windsor 'sack-back' armchair, the bowed crestrail over seven spindles continuing through the U-form medial rail forming the arms w/scrolled hand grips above canted baluster- and ring-turned arm supports, shaped saddle seat on canted baluster- and ring-turned legs joined by a swelled H-stretcher, late 18th c. (ILLUS.).. **2,860**

Windsor-Style "birdcage" side chair, painted, double slender turned crestrails joined by three short spindles above seven long spindles between slightly canted stiles, shaped saddle seat on canted baluster- and ring-turned legs joined by a turned & swelled H-stretcher, worn yellow repaint, old but not period, laminated seat w/painted-over paper label, 35 1/2" h. **275**

Windsor-Style "bow-back" braced side chairs, painted, the bowed & molded backrail over eight slender rod-, knob- and baluster-turned spindles w/two matching brace spindles at the back, shaped saddle seat on canted baluster- and ring-turned legs joined by a swelled H-stretcher & a single swelled rear stretcher, original dark finish w/wear, labeled "Phoenix Chair Company, Sheboygan, Wisconsin," early 20th c., 36" h., set of 4 .... **495**

Chests & Chests of Drawers

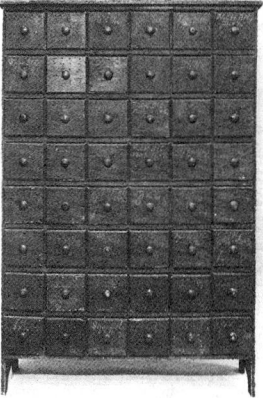

Early Apothecary-style Chest

Apothecary chest, country-style, painted pine, the rectangular top w/a high three-quarters gallery above the tall case w/rows of 49 small square drawers w/small brass pulls above a single long drawer across the bottom, bootjack feet, old penciled or ink labels, original bluish grey paint, New England, early 19th c., 9 x 37 3/4", 57 1/2" h. **24,200**

Apothecary chest, painted & decorated pine, a rectangular top on the dovetailed case enclosing 64 small square numbered drawers w/small knobs above a row of three deep drawers across the bottom, grain-painted overall in light brown on tan to resemble mahogany, probably New England, early 19th c., 14 1/4 x 43", 39" h. (imperfections) **10,925**

Apothecary chest, painted pine, a rectangular top above a short open compartment across the top of the tall case containing rows of 20 large drawers over a lower section of 16 graduated small drawers, various wood & brass knobs & remnants of labels, square nail construction, old worn brown & tan grained repaint, 19th c., 15 1/2 x 48 1/4", 66" h. **3,520**

Apothecary chest, poplar, a rectangular top above a case w/three stacks of six small rectangular drawers above a single long drawer across the bottom, square nail construction, old finish, 7 x 21", 24 1/2"h. (some damage on back boards) **1,045**

Apothecary chest, stained wood, rectangular top slightly overhanging tall case of 48 square drawers w/turned wood pulls & beveled edges, sizes & lettering on most drawers, wire nail construction, bootjack ends, old black stain, probably used by a cobbler or saddle maker, 19th c., minor edge chips, 13 x 42 1/2", 62" h. (ILLUS.) .. **4,070**

Blanket chest, country-style, painted & decorated pine, the rectangular hinged top w/molded edges opening to a well w/a lidded till, the dovetailed case w/a base molding above shaped dovetailed bracket feet, original brown over salmon squiggled band decoration w/black paint on the feet, script signature within the decoration on the front panel reads "James Mortlane, 1850," 17 1/2 x 38", 22 3/4" h. (wear, repairs to feet, hinges replaced) **715**

Blanket chest, country-style, painted & decorated poplar, a rectangular hinged top w/molded edges opening to a deep well, dovetailed case w/applied moldings & a pair of narrow bottom drawers above the narrow curved apron & bracket feet, original red paint w/black & yellow trim & gold-stenciled decoration including foliage, flowers & "Jeremias Wever, 1859, Mf. by C.C.B.," drawer divider a cut-out small panel w/heart & circles in black over yellow, old round glass drawer pulls, replaced inlaid escutcheons, Soap Hollow, Pennsylvania, 22 3/4 x 49 1/2", 28 1/2" h. (minor repairs to feet, some edge damage & wear) **11,000**

Blanket chest, country-style, painted pine, a rectangular hinged top opening to a deep well in the plain case above a flush long drawer at the bottom, arched bootjack feet, old grey paint, possibly Long Island, 18th c., 19 x 39", 33 1/2" h. **2,300**

Blanket chest, country-style, painted pine, a rectangular top w/molded edges opening to a well w/a lidded till, the front w/four small rectangular panels each centered by an applied finger-carved rectangle & all painted dark green, band of four plain square large panels painted deep red, the dividing stiles w/brown-grained yellow paint resembling curly maple, molded base band in dark green on bracket feet in dark red, found in Johnstown, Pennsylvania area, 21 x 48 1/2", 25" h. (minor edge damage, one front foot facing w/damage) **4,400**

Blanket chest, country-style, painted pine, rectangular hinged lid w/molded edges opening to a well w/a lidded till & wrought-iron strap hinges & beartrap lock

w/key, the dovetailed case decorated w/original vinegar graining faded to an olive & mustard yellow, molded base & black scroll-cut bracket feet, penciled inscription in lid, late 18th - early 19th c., 18 x 40", 22 3/4" h. **3,300**

Blanket chest, painted & decorated, a rectangular hinged top w/applied molding opening to a well w/till & a dovetailed case w/a molded base & double-scallop apron & bracket feet, overall greyish blue paint decorated w/yellow, red & blue rosettes, pinwheels & geometric designs around a double scrolling foliate vine above three painted reserve-enclosed inscriptions "DUR - MUR - 1819," Indiana, 22 3/4 x 52 1/2", 27 3/4" h. **9,200**

Blanket chest, painted & decorated pine, the rectangular one-board hinged lid w/mortise & tenon breadboard ends opening to a well w/a till & two small drawers, dovetailed case painted on the front w/three arched panels w/bold stylized bouquets of flowers on a light ground in each panel, molded base on scroll-cut bracket feet, wrought-iron hinges w/replaced screws, several old repaints, Pennsylvania, late 18th - early 19th c., 18 3/4 x 49", 24 1/4" h. (lock missing, age cracks, edge damage) **1,375**

Blanket chest, painted & decorated poplar, Sonnenberg-type, rectangular hinged top w/molded edges opening to a well w/a lidded till, dovetailed base w/bottom flat molding, simple bracket feet, decorated w/original dark red paint ground w/yellow stripe-edged reserves w/polychrome floral designs on the front panel, yellow striping & a compass star in red & yellow on the top, 19th c., 19 3/8 x 37 5/8", 23 1/4" h. **10,450**

Paint-decorated Blanket Chest

Blanket chest, painted poplar, six-board dovetailed construction, the rectangular top opening to a deep well on the dovetailed case w/a molded base & scroll-cut bracket feet, old salmon orange paint in a dappled brown pattern, probably Pennsylvania, early 19th c., paint worn, imperfections, 48" l., 24 1/2" h. (ILLUS.) **1,150**

Blanket chest, painted, six-board construction, the rectangular top w/molded edge above a well w/lidded till, on a molded base w/shaped bracket feet, original blue paint, Connecticut, late 18th c., 17 x 42", 23 1/2" h. (very minor paint wear) **2,070**

Chippendale blanket chest, walnut, rectangular hinged top w/molded edges opening to a well w/lidded till & two secret drawers, the dovetailed case w/two bottom drawers w/simple bail pulls, molded base on ogee bracket feet, old finish, original brasses, wrought-iron strap hinges, Pennsylvania, late 18th c., 23 1/2 x 51 1/2", 28" h. (lock missing, minor age cracks in top, small repairs to feet)......... **7,260**

Chippendale chest-on-chest, cherry, two-part construction: the upper section w/a deep flared molded cornice above a case w/a row of three small drawers over a pair of drawers above three long thumb-molded graduated drawers all w/butterfly pulls & keyhole escutcheons; the lower section w/a mid-molding above a case w/three long graduated drawers, both cases flanked by fluted quarter columns, on a molded base w/ogee bracket feet, Delaware River Valley, ca 1770-90, 20 1/2 x 40", 78 3/4" h. (replaced brasses, restoration, imperfections).................. **12,650**

Chippendale chest-on-chest, maple, two-part construction: the upper section w/a rectangular top w/a flaring coved cornice above a pair of thumb-molded drawers over a stack of four long graduated thumb-molded drawers; the lower section w/a mid-molding over four long graduated thumb-molded drawers, probably original brass butterfly pulls & keyhole escutcheons, molded base, tall shaped bracket feet, old refinish, possibly Torrington, Connecticut, ca. 1760-80, 17 1/4 x 36", 71" h. (imperfections) **14,950**

Chippendale country-style blanket chest, painted & decorated poplar, rectangular hinged top w/molded edges opening to a well w/a lidded till & two secret drawers, the dovetailed case w/a molded base on ogee bracket feet, original stylized painted decoration w/green swirls & a diagonal wavy band across the front on a white ground, red shows as ground under lip & small places, dark green feet, good wear, Pennsylvania, late 18th - early 19th c., 21 x 49 1/4", 28" h........... **6,050**

Chippendale country-style chest of drawers, painted & decorated pine & curly maple, rectangular top w/deep coved cornice above a case w/four long overlapping dovetailed drawers w/simple bail pulls, one-board ends, scroll-cut bracket feet, original red flame graining, backboards signed "L.L. 1807 - P.P.H.G.—(grained) 1847," replaced brasses, 22 x 39 1/4", 42 1/2" h...................................... **6,050**

Chippendale country-style chest of drawers, tiger stripe maple, rectangular top w/molded edge above a case of four long thumb-molded graduated drawers w/butterfly pulls, molded base on dovetailed bracket feet, old refinish, southern New England, ca. 1780, 38 1/2" h. (replaced brasses, minor imperfections) **2,990**

Chippendale country-style tall chest of drawers, cherry & maple, the rectangular top w/a deep coved cornice above a

case w/five long graduated thumb-molded drawers, base molding on tall bracket feet, old refinish, New England, ca. 1780, 19 3/4 x 39 1/2", 49" h. (replaced oval brasses & keyhole escutcheons, imperfections) **3,105**

Chippendale country-style tall chest of drawers, pine, the molded rectangular top above a case of three thumb-molded faux drawers & two working drawers, on bracket feet w/a central rounded drop, old refinish, replaced butterfly brasses, New England, second half 18th c., 18 1/2 x 40", 45 1/2" h. **1,840**

Chippendale "serpentine-front" chest of drawers, mahogany, the rectangular top w/serpentined sides & molded edges overhanging a conforming case w/three long cockbeaded graduated drawers w/replaced butterfly brasses & keyhole escutcheons, molded base on four scroll-cut short cabriole legs ending in ball-and-claw feet, Boston, ca. 1760-80, old refinish, 20 x 36", 32 1/4" h. **34,500**

Chippendale tall chest of drawers, cherry, a rectangular top w/a deep flaring stepped cornice above a case w/seven long graduated thumb-molded drawers w/simple bail pulls & oval keyhole escutcheons, molded base on tall bracket feet, old red-stained finish, Rhode Island, late 18th c., 19 1/2 x 36 3/4", 62 1/2" h. (minor imperfections)................................... **7,475**

Chippendale tall chest of drawers, cherry & maple, a rectangular top above a deep coved cornice over a case w/a top central deep fan-carved drawer flanked by a stack of two small drawers on each side above six long graduated drawers, molded base on tall scroll-cut bracket feet, oval brass pulls appear to be original, old finish, probably Connecticut, 18th c., added casters, 18 x 37", 62 3/4" h. (minor restoration) **46,000**

Chippendale tall chest of drawers, cherry, rectangular top w/deep flaring cornice above a row of three small drawers over a pair of drawers above five long graduated cockbeaded drawers, reeded quarter-columns down the front sides, molded base, scroll-cut tall ogee bracket feet, old replaced round brass pulls in original holes, attributed to New Jersey, late 18th - early 19th c., old refinish, 22 x 42 3/8", 5' 9 1/4" h. (minor glued breaks in some foot facings, small chips on drawer edges) **10,725**

Chippendale tall chest of drawers, cherry, rectangular top w/deep molded cornice above a case w/six long graduated thumb-molded drawers, molded base on tall scroll-cut bracket feet, round brass pulls, New England, 1770-80, 19 1/2 x 38 1/2", 56" h. **6,900**

Chippendale tall chest of drawers, maple, a rectangular top w/a coved cornice above a case of six long thumb-molded drawers w/butterfly pulls & keyhole escutcheons, molded base above scroll-carved apron w/central drop & tall bracket feet, original brasses, refinished, New Hampshire, late 18th c., 18 x 36 3/4", 58" h. (ILLUS. top next page).................... **6,613**

Chippendale Tall Chest of Drawers

Chippendale tall chest of drawers, maple, the rectangular top w/a deep flaring molded cornice above a case w/a pair of drawers over five long thumb-molded drawers all w/butterfly brasses & keyhole escutcheons, molded base on high scroll-cut bracket feet & central pendant, original brasses, old refinish, Connecticut, ca. 1760-80, 16 1/2 x 36", 58" h. (very minor imperfections) **9,200**

Chippendale tall chest of drawers, tiger stripe maple, rectangular top above a deep flaring stepped cornice over a case w/a pair of drawers above a stack of five long graduated thumb-molded drawers w/simple bail pulls & brass keyhole escutcheons, molded base raised on shaped bracket feet, original brasses, refinished, southwestern Massachusetts or Rhode Island, late 18th c., 19 1/4 x 38", 53" h. (very minor imperfections) **8,050**

Chippendale tall chest of drawers, walnut, a rectangular top w/molded flaring cornice above a case w/a row of three small drawers over a pair of drawers above four long graduated drawers all w/oval brasses, molded base on scroll-cut bracket feet, old finish, late 18th - early 19th c., 24 3/8 x 43", 58 5/8" h. (replaced brasses, some corner repair on upper drawer, some edge damage) **4,400**

Classical chest of drawers, curly maple & cherry, a rectangular cherry top over a cherry frame w/a long deep curly maple drawer flanked by inlaid curly maple side reserves & overhanging three long graduated curly maple lower drawers flanked by half-round ring- and spiral-twist-turned columns, ring- and baluster-turned legs w/button feet, replaced round brasses w/rings, signed on back "Jacob Kinney - Weston, Ohio," first half 19th c., 21 3/4 x 43 3/4", 49 7/8" h. (age cracks in top, refinished) **1,375**

Classical Child's Chest of Drawers

Classical child's country-style chest of drawers, painted & decorated, the rectangular top fitted w/an arched crestboard w/a pair of small handkerchief drawers above a long deep drawer projecting over two long drawers flanked by serpentine side pilasters & C-scroll front feet, decorated overall w/original brown & red painted w/gold & olive band linear trim, original turned wood pulls, New England, 1835-45, very minor surface imperfections, 14 1/8 x 22", 27 1/4" h. (ILLUS.) **748**

Dower chest, painted & decorated pine, the rectangular hinged white pine top w/molded edge & strap hinges opens to a well in the dovetailed case, molded base w/worn bracket feet, the front decorated w/three painted arches each w/a small urn w/a large bouquet of flowers in blue, red, yellow & brown on a white ground outlined in red, paint appears original, attributed to Christian Selzer, Lebanon County, Pennsylvania, late 18th c., 222 1/4 x 51 1/2", 23" h. (height loss, other imperfections) **6,325**

Dower chest, painted poplar, rectangular hinged top w/molded edges opening to an interior w/a till, dovetailed case w/a lower molding over two thumb-molded drawers on a molded base w/bracket feet, old light blue paint, replaced brasses, Pennsylvania, ca. 1780, 22 x 48", 26 1/2" h. (minor imperfections) **1,725**

Dower chest, walnut, a rectangular hinged top w/molded edge opening to a well w/till, dovetailed case above a heavy molding over a pair of base drawers above a molded base on scroll-cut bracket feet, old refinish, replaced brass pulls, Berks County, Pennsylvania, 1780s, 23 1/4 x 50 3/4", 31" h. (imperfections) **1,380**

Federal "bowfront" chest of drawers, mahogany, rectangular top w/a curved front edge overhanging a conforming case of four long cockbeaded graduated drawers w/round brasses, valanced skirt & tall slender flaring French feet, brasses appear to be original, old refinish, probably Massachusetts, ca. 1800, 19 3/4 x 40", 38 1/2" h. (imperfections) **3,738**

Federal chest of drawers, inlaid cherry, rectangular top w/string inlaid edges overhanging a case w/four long graduated drawers w/mahogany veneer bordered by stringing & interrupted line inlay, on tall splayed French feet joined by an inlaid valanced skirt, apparently original oval brasses, old refinish, possibly Connecticut, ca. 1800, 18 3/4 x 39 1/4", 36 3/4" h. (minor imperfections) **5,750**

Federal chest of drawers, inlaid walnut, rectangular top w/molded edge & border inlay above a case w/a pair of small drawers over four long graduated drawers each w/oval line inlay, molded base on tall scroll-cut bracket feet, old replaced oval eagle brasses, early 19th c., 21 1/4 x 37 1/2", 46" h. (refinished, edge repairs, some renailing on drawer bottoms)... **2,420**

Federal chest of drawers, mahogany & mahogany veneer, a rectangular top w/reeded edges above a case of four cockbeaded long graduated drawers w/pairs of original oval brass pulls, deeply scalloped apron raised on tall French feet, early 19th c., 20 3/8 x 41 3/4", 37 3/4" h. (age cracks in top, refinished, restorations) **1,375**

Federal chest of drawers, walnut, rectangular top w/beaded edges above a dovetailed case w/four long dovetailed overlapping drawers w/original oval brasses, molded base on tall slender French feet, attributed to Ohio, early 19th c., 20 1/2 x 38 1/2", 40 1/4" h. (some insect damage in drawers, repairs to feet) **3,300**

Federal Mahogany Chest-on-Chest

Federal chest-on-chest, inlaid mahogany & mahogany veneer, two-part construction: the upper section w/a rectangular top & widely flaring stepped cornice over a wide line-inlaid frieze band above a pair

of drawers over three long graduated drawers w/inlaid ivory diamond keyhole escutcheons & simple turned wood pulls; the lower section w/a mid-molding over a case w/three long graduated drawers matching upper drawers, curved apron & high simple bracket feet, old finish w/original painted side decoration, section of side molding missing, several veneer chips & puttied repairs, late 18th - early 19th c., 24 x 44", 80" h. (ILLUS.) **3,740**

Federal country-style chest of drawers, birch & flame-grained birch, a rectangular top w/reeded edges above a case w/four long flame birch drawers w/beaded edging & simple turned wood pulls, on ring- and baluster-turned legs, refinished, early 19th c., 18 3/4 x 41 1/4", 34 3/4" h. (minor damage to rear foot)...................... **1,320**

Federal country-style chest of drawers, cherry, rectangular top w/banded inlay around the edges above a case of four long graduated beaded drawers w/replaced round brasses, a band of inlay above the scrolled apron above ring- and baluster-turned legs, attributed to Stark County, Ohio, early 19th c., old soft finish, 19 1/4 x 41", 45 3/4" h. **3,575**

Federal country-style chest of drawers, cherry, rectangular top w/ovolo corners overhanging a case w/four long graduated scratch-beaded drawers flanked by reeded quarter engaged columns ending in turned tapering legs, original turned wooden pulls, old refinish, Massachusetts, 1820-30, 21 x 43 1/8", 39 1/4" h. **1,150**

Federal country-style chest of drawers, painted & decorated maple & birch, rectangular top above a case of four long graduated drawers w/old replaced round brasses, serpentine apron & tall bracket feet, old black & brown grain decoration over an earlier red, 17 1/2 x 37", 34 1/2" h. (minor age cracks) **1,980**

Decorated Ohio Federal Chest

Federal country-style chest of drawers, painted & decorated poplar, a low scroll-cut crestrail on the rectangular top above a narrow projecting frieze board over a long deep top drawer & three long graduated drawers all flanked by turned half-round columns, ring-turned feet, original red graining on a yellow ground w/ebonized detail, replaced oval brasses, attributed to North Jackson, Trumbull County, Ohio, early 19th c., 20 1/2 x 41 3/4", overall 53 1/2" h. (ILLUS.)............................ **7,150**

Federal Birch & Cherry Chest

Federal country-style chest of drawers, wavy birch & grained cherry, the double-arched & scroll-cut top splashboard above a rectangular top w/ovolo front corners over ring-turned colonettes flanking four long graduated drawers w/oval brass pulls, raised on ring- and baluster-turned legs w/knob feet, old refinish, North Shore, Massachusetts, early 19th c., replaced brasses, imperfections, 17 1/2 x 39 1/2", 49" h. (ILLUS.) **1,380**

Federal Cherry Sugar Chest

Federal country-style sugar chest, cherry, a rectangular hinged top w/molded edges opening to a deep divided interior well above a pair of small drawers, baluster- and ring-turned legs w/peg feet, paneled sides, oval drawer brasses, early 19th c., 16 1/2 x 35 1/2", 35" h. (ILLUS.).. **6,050**

Federal country-style tall chest of drawers, curly maple veneer & cherry, a rectangular top w/a deep coved cornice above a case w/a row of three small cockbeaded drawers above a stack of five long graduated beaded drawers, simple turned curly maple knobs, drawers w/curly maple veneer & frame & ring- and knob-turned legs in cherry, inlaid shield-shaped keyhole escutcheons replaced, refinished, early 19th c., 21 1/2 x 42 3/4", 67" h. (some edge damage, replaced knobs, minor repair) **4,345**

Federal tall chest of drawers, cherry, a rectangular top w/a deep coved cornice above a case w/a row of drawers w/two larger flanking a small central one above five long graduated drawers w/oval brasses & keyhole escutcheons. drawers flanked by reeded quarter columns down the sides, molded base on scroll-cut bracket feet, old mellow refinish, original brasses, early 19th c., top 23 x 42 1/2", 63 3/4" h. (minor edge damage) **6,050**

Federal Tall Chest of Drawers

Federal tall chest of drawers, cherry & walnut, the rectangular top w/a wide flat flaring cornice above a band of inlay over a row of three drawers over a stack of five cockbeaded graduated long drawers w/oval brasses & oval keyhole escutcheons, old finish, double-paneled sides, scroll-cut ogee bracket feet, replaced brasses, 21 1/2 x 41 1/2", 65" h. (ILLUS.) .. **6,050**

Federal tall chest of drawers, curly maple & cherry, rectangular top above a wide coved cornice over a narrow diamond-inlaid frieze band above a row of three drawers over five long graduated beaded drawers w/replaced oval eagle brasses, a wide diamond-inlaid band across the bottom, scroll-cut bracket feet, refinished, minor restorations, late 18th - early 19th c., 22 1/2 x 45 1/2", 5' 2 3/4" h. **4,400**

Federal-Style "serpentine-front" chest of drawers, inlaid mahogany, a rectangular top w/serpentine front above a conforming case w/a pull-out serving shelf above four long graduated drawers w/crotchgrain veneering & cross-banding, on a serpentine apron & bracket feet, manufacturered by Baker Furniture, 20th c., 20 3/4 x 35", 35 1/4" h. (minor wear) **1,210**

Decorative Immigrant's Chest

Immigant chest, painted & decorated, heavy rectangular slightly domed top w/braced ends opening to a deep well, deep dovetailed case decorated on the front w/red & yellow scrolls & swags with a name & date of 1828, the top w/original forest green ground w/red & black trim & polychrome florals similar to the front, scalloped wrought-iron brackets, bands & lockplate, w/partial paper label for Royal Mail Steamers, w/original key, Scandinavian, early 19th c., 20 x 40", 23" h. (ILLUS.) **770**

Modern style chest of drawers, hardwood, rectangular top over a case w/five plain graduated long drawers w/recessed handles, platform base, light finish, metal tag mark of Dunbar, Berne, Indiana, post-World War II, 18 x 28", 31 1/4" h. (scratches, wear) **863**

Heywood-Wakefield Vanity Chest

Modern style vanity chest, maple, a large, tall upright rectangular back mirror w/rounded corners at one end above a glass shelf & open compartment, a case w/three graduated drawers at the other end, each w/tapering applied finger grip

pulls, short block feet, wheat colored finish, round branded mark of Heywood-Wakefield, ca. 1950s, light wear, 13 1/4 x 53 3/4", base 24" h. (ILLUS.) **345**

Mule chest (box chest w/one or more drawers below a storage compartment), Classical country-style, painted & decorated pine, a rectangular hinged top w/molded edges opening to a deep well faced w/two false drawers above two matching working drawers all w/turned wood knobs, on bulbous baluster- and ring-turned legs, original reddish brown graining in imitation of flame figured wood w/line inlay, black feet, found in New Hampshire, first half 19th c., 18 3/4 x 40", 40" h. (minor edge damage) **1,650**

Mule chest (box chest w/one or more drawers below a storage compartment), country-style, painted & decorated pine, a rectangular hinged top opening to a very deep well above two long reverse-graduated bottom drawers, on tall bootjack legs, overall old red paint w/sponged black dot band graining, mismatched Rockingham glazed pottery drawer pulls, 17 1/4 x 38 1/4", 42 3/4" h. (old replaced hinges, batten on lid renailed) **2,090**

Mule chest (box chest w/one or more drawers below a storage compartment), country-style, painted pine, six-board construction, rectangular hinged top w/molded edges opening to a well, a long bottom nailed drawer w/round brasses, curved apron & bracket feet, original brown flame graining, 19th c., 19 1/2 x 49", 33 1/4" h. (one front foot split & nailed, edge damage) **550**

Mule chest (box chest w/one or more drawers below a storage compartment), Federal country-style, painted, a rectangular top w/molded edge lifting above a deep well faced with two mock drawers w/round metal knobs above two long working drawers w/knobs, high cut-out bracket feet, old red paint, ca. 1820, 19 x 38", 38" h. **4,888**

Mule chest (box chest w/one or more drawers below a storage compartment), Federal country-style, painted pine, a hinged rectangular top w/molded edges opening to a well w/two false long drawer fronts w/oval brasses above two long matching working drawers, original greyish blue vinegar graining on a greyish olive ground w/black & yellow edge striping, shaped apron on high tapering feet, bottom signed "Daniel," attributed to Essex, Massachusetts, early 19th c., 19 3/8 x 42 3/4", 41 3/4" h. **7,700**

Mule chest (box chest w/one or more drawers below a storage compartment), Federal country-style, painted pine, a rectangular top w/molded edges opening to a deep well w/interior compartment fitted w/iron lock & hinges, two long graduated dovetailed drawers at the bottom above the scalloped apron & high bracket feet, old red repaint, early 19th c., 17 1/2 x 36", 35 1/4" h. (replaced oval drawer brasses, minor age cracks) **2,585**

Fine Decorated Pine Mule Chest

Mule chest (box chest w/one or more drawers below a storage compartment), painted & decorated pine, a rectangular molded top opening to a deep well above two long drawers at the bottom, each w/replaced round brass pulls, high shaped bracket feet, original putty wood graining in red, green & yellow w/umber tones, very minor surface imperfections, northern New England, ca. 1830, 17 5/8 x 38", 36 1/2" h. (ILLUS.).... **16,100**

Early Pilgrim Century Joined Chest

Pilgrim Century blanket chest, oak & pine, joined construction, the overhanging thumb-molded hinged white pine top above a three-paneled front w/applied moldings over a long drawer flanked by shadow molded stiles, recessed panel sides, the drawer w/stippled inscription "1707 HI," interior open till, old dark stained surface, New Haven Colony, Connecticut, 1680-1740, minor imperfections, 19 1/4 x 43", 31 1/2" h. (ILLUS.) **9,775**

Queen Anne blanket chest over drawers, pine, rectangular hinged top w/molded edges opening to a well above a pair of faux short drawers & a long faux drawers above two lower working long drawers, all w/teardrop pulls, molded base & wide bracket feet w/valanced sides, remains of bluish green paint, Mid-Atlantic States, 14 1/2 x 21 1/2" (replaced brasses, restorations)... **2,070**

Queen Anne chest of drawers, maple, a rectangular top w/a deep molded edge above a case w/a pair of drawers above four long graduated cockbeaded drawers

each w/butterfly brasses & keyhole escutcheons, molded base on shaped bracket feet, refinished, replaced brasses, New England, late 18th c., 19 x 41", 46" h. (imperfections) **2,070**

Queen Anne Chest of Drawers

Queen Anne chest of drawers, stained wood, rectangular top above a case w/four long graduated drawers w/small turned wood pulls, molded base on high arched bracket feet, old dark brown stain, imperfections, New England, mid-18th c., 16 1/4 x 38", 40 1/2" h. (ILLUS.)................. **2,990**

Queen Anne country-style chest of drawers, cherry, rectangular top w/deep molded cornice above a case w/four long overlapping graduated dovetailed drawers w/pierced butterfly brasses & keyhole escutcheons, molded base w/apron w/central drop & high bracket feet, cleaned down to old red, attributed to Pennsylvania, 18th c., 17 3/4 x 38", 44" h. (one front foot ended out, some edge damage, minor repair to drawer lip, backboards old replacements)................... **2,255**

Queen Anne country-style chest of drawers, stained birch & butternut, rectangular top w/deep ogee cornice above a pair of thumb-molded drawers over three long drawers all w/turned wood knobs, molded base on bracket feet, old red surface, replaced pulls, Connecticut, 18th c., 18 3/4 x 36 3/4", 40 1/4" h. (minor losses)... **2,645**

Queen Anne tall chest of drawers, tiger stripe maple, the rectangular top w/a narrow flared cornice above a case w/a row of four small thumb-molded drawers over a pair of drawers above four long graduated drawers all w/butterfly brasses & keyhole escutcheons, molded base on tall bracket feet, replaced brasses, old refinish, southeastern New England, ca. 1750, 18 x 34 3/4", 49 1/2" h. (minor imperfections) **21,850**

Spice chest, country-style, oak & bird's-eye maple, rectangular top w/molded edges over a square nailed case w/two ranks of four deep drawers each w/turned wood knobs, cut-out end legs, maple drawer fronts, 7 1/2 x 14 1/2", 17 3/4" h. **385**

Sugar chest, cherry & poplar, a rectangular hinged top w/molded edges opening to a deep well above a small drawer beside a long drawer over a pair of matching drawers over a single long bottom drawer, knob-turned feet, paneled ends, refinished, found in Kentucky, 15 3/4 x 37 1/4", 29 3/4" h. (restorations, old alterations to drawers, turned pulls replaced) **2,420**

Victorian country-style child's chest of drawers, walnut, an arched & shaped splashback on the rectangular top above a case w/a pair of small drawers above two long drawers, simple turned wood knobs, scalloped apron, simple bracket feet, old varnish finish, ca. 1870, 7 1/2 x 12 3/4", 12 1/2" h. plus splashback **550**

Pine Renaissance Revival Chest

Victorian Renaissance Revival chest of drawers, pine w/walnut stain, the arched superstructure enclosing an arch-topped swiveling mirror flanked by shaped sides w/small candle shelves above small handkerchief drawers on the rectangular top w/molded edges, the case w/four long graduated drawers w/raised oval bands & carved leaf pulls, low serpentine apron & bracket feet on casters, ca. 1870, 17 x 39", 71" h. (ILLUS.) **495**

Cradles

Pilgrim Century Oak Cradle

Deep cradle on rockers, Pilgrim century, joined & paneled oak, the high paneled

headboard stepping to deep paneled sides & a paneled footboard, turned corner finials, on wide solid rockers, refinished, New England, late 17th - early 18th c., minor imperfections, 20 x 39", 30 1/2" h. (ILLUS.) **1,840**

Hooded cradle on rockers, mahogany, top board of hood w/flame veneer over the enclosed headboard & gently canted sides, shaped dovetailed footboard, Chippendale-style brasses on ends, mortised rockers w/scrolled ends, old dark finish, found in Michigan, 18 x 40", 26 1/2" h. (renailing w/veneer repair, empty holes in base) **330**

Low cradle on rockers, cherry w/soft old worn finish, rectangular w/nearly straight sides & slightly shaped top edges, corner posts w/turned acorn finials, low wide rockers, two hanging knobs on each side, heart cut-outs in head- and footboards, 16 x 35", 20" h. (some edge damage)...................................... **275**

Low cradle on rockers, painted walnut, rectangular w/slightly canted dovetailed sides & gently arched head- and footboards, the sides composed of three panels in a mortised & pinned frame, top of headboard shows holes possibly for removable hood, old worn red & black paint, 19th c., 39" l. **275**

Cupboards

Tall Slender Corner Cupboard

Chimney cupboard, poplar, rectangular flat top above a very tall narrow case w/a long two-panel door opening to four shelves above a single panel lower door opening to two shelves, dark stain on the front, unfinished on sides, 13 3/4 x 20 1/4", 92" h. **1,100**

Corner cupboard, Chippendale style, walnut, two-part construction: the upper section w/a deep stepped flaring cornice above a large 12-pane glazed cupboard door opening to three shaped shelves; the lower section w/a mid-molding over a wide four-panel hinged door raised on a molded base on ogee bracket feet, old refinish, Chester County, Pennsylvania, ca. 1780, 22 1/2 x 44", 84 1/4" h. (replaced brass H-hinges & ring pulls, minor imperfections)... **14,950**

Corner cupboard, country-style, cherry & poplar, two-piece construction: the upper section w/a stepped coved cornice above a pair of 6-pane glazed cupboard doors; the lower section w/a long center drawer above a pair of paneled cupboard doors, flat apron & simple cut-out feet, mismatched cast-iron thumb latches w/porcelain knobs, mid-19th c., refinished, 58" w., 83 1/2" h. (one end of cornice w/nailed repair) **2,640**

Corner cupboard, country-style, painted pine, one-piece construction, the top & sides framed by a wide molding flanking a tall upper geometrically-glazed cupboard door opening to three shelves above a tall double-panel cupboard door, serpentine apron, old green repaint, interior painted red, early 19th c., repairs, border molding replaced, 27" w., 87 1/2" h. (ILLUS.) **1,155**

Corner cupboard, country-style, painted poplar, one-piece construction, the flat top w/narrow molded cornice above a long cupboard door divided into a cross panel at the top above two parallel panels, a shorter two-panel lower door, scalloped apron w/bracket feet, distressed two-tone orange repaint, 19th c., 34 1/4" w., 81" h. **1,045**

Early Barrel-back Corner Cupboard

Corner cupboard, country-style, pine, barrel-back style, one-piece construction, a flat molded deep cornice above a tall raised panel cupboard door opening to three shaped shelves, a smaller raised panel cupboard door below, framed by applied moldings, original wrought-iron butterfly hinges, old natural color, minor imperfections, New England, late 18th c., 20 1/2 x 46", 93 1/2" h. (ILLUS.) **3,450**

Corner cupboard, country-style, pine, one-piece construction, the flat top w/molded edge above a central 6-pane glazed cupboard door over a four-panel cupboard door all flanked on each side by four narrow rectangular panels, flat apron & low cut-out feet, side molding at each side, old refinish, missing front bracket, New England, ca. 1800, 22 x 48", 84" h. **3,450**

Corner cupboard, country-style, poplar, one-piece construction, the flat top w/a narrow molded cornice above a tall narrow paneled door w/wood knob above a shorter paneled door, simple cut-out feet, old dark cherry finish, wide front stiles, 19th c., 45 1/2" w., 74" h. **1,210**

Corner cupboard, country-style, walnut, two-piece construction: the upper section w/a deep coved cornice above a pair of tall 8-pane glazed cupboard doors opening to three shelves; the lower section w/a mid-molding above a pair of drawers w/wooden knobs above a pair of paneled cupboard doors w/original brass thumb latches, molded base w/short bracket feet, old finish, late blue paint on the interior, 19th c., 59 1/2" w., 84" h. (feet worn down, one end of cornice incomplete, panes incomplete) **3,960**

Yellow Pine Corner Cupboard

Corner cupboard, country-style, yellow pine, one-piece construction, the flat molded cornice above an arched opening w/three shaped shelves above two raised panel cupboard doors, all framed by an applied molding, wrought-iron hinges appear to be original, blue, green & yellow wash, Shenandoah Valley, Virginia, late 18th c., repairs, 22 x 41", 89 1/2" h. (ILLUS.) **2,990**

Corner cupboard, Federal, cherry, one-piece construction, the top w/a deep ogee & molded cornice w/a dentil-carved band above a pair of tall 8-pane glazed cupboard doors flanked by reeded side panels & opening to three shelves, a wide medial band above a pair of paneled cupboard doors also flanked by reeded side panels, molded base over a small central apron scallop & tall simple bracket feet, old mellow finish, found in Ohio, early 19th c., 21 x 53", 90 1/2" h. (stress cracks in back foot w/added support, few pieces of dentil molding missing) **8,250**

Corner cupboard, Federal, cherry, one-piece construction, the top w/a deep stepped & cove-molded cornice above a case w/a tall single 12-pane glazed cupboard door w/original brass ring pull & opening to three butterfly shelves, a medial band above a pair of raised-panel cupboard doors w/a wooded knob, scalloped apron & simple bracket feet, good old dark finish, early 19th c., 22 1/2 x 46", 91 3/4" h. (some plate rails missing or replaced) **6,600**

Federal Cherry Corner Cupboard

Corner cupboard, Federal country-style, cherry, one-piece construction, the flat deep coved cornice above a pair of tall 8-pane glazed cupboard doors opening to three shelves above a pair of paneled cupboard doors, serpentine apron & simple bracket feet, old mellow refinishing, two panes cracked, back piece replaced, piece of cornice missing, early 19th c., 48" w., 80 3/4" h. (ILLUS.) **2,640**

Early Ohio Cherry Corner Cupboard

Corner cupboard, Federal country-style, cherry, one-piece construction, the flat flaring cornice above a wide 9-pane glazed cupboard door w/brass thumb latch above a mid-molding over a pair of raised-panel cupboard doors, serpentine apron & simple bracket feet, found in Ohio, early 19th c., top 44 3/4" w., 76 1/2" h. (ILLUS.) **4,620**

Painted Two-piece Corner Cupboard

Corner cupboard, Federal country-style, painted pine, two-piece construction: the upper section w/a coved cornice over a carved geometric band above reeded stiles flanking a pair of tall double-paneled cupboard doors w/a small panel over a tall panel & opening to serpentine shelves w/spoon cut-outs; the lower section w/a mid-molding over a single long drawer over a pair of paneled cupboard doors all flanked by reeded stiles, molded base & simple bracket feet, old worn dark blue repaint over earlier cream, possibly Hackensack, New Jersey area, early 19th c., top 45" w., 84 3/4" h. (ILLUS.) **15,400**

Grain-painted Corner Cupboard

Corner cupboard, Federal country-style, painted walnut, one-piece construction, a deep coved cornice above a single wide 9-pane glazed cupboard door opening to two shelves above a mid-molding over a pair of tall paneled cupboard doors, molded base on bracket feet, old brown grained repaint, brass knob on lower door may be original, early 19th c., top 25 3/4 x 48 1/4", 79" h. (ILLUS.) **4,675**

Early Dark Pine Corner Cupboard

Corner cupboard, Federal country-style, pine, one-piece construction, the deep stepped & flaring cornice above a dentil-carved band above narrow raised molding framing the single wide 9-pane glazed cupboard door opening to two shelves, a mid-molding above a pair of double-panel cupboard doors, molded base on simple bracket feet, old dark varnish finish, rose-head nail construction, hinged & back foot replaced, some renailing, pads added on front feet, late 18th - early 19th c., top 27 x 50", 81" h. (ILLUS.) **5,500**

Pennsylvania Pine Corner Cupboard

Corner cupboard, Federal country-style, pine, one-piece construction, the thick stepped cornice above a pair of tall narow 2-pane glazed cupboard doors w/early

brass latch & ring pulls & opening to shelves above a mid-molding over a pair of short paneled cupboard doors, molded base & simple bracket feet, two small sections of molding replaced, original red finish, Pennsylvania, early 19th c., top 23 1/2 x 47 1/2", 78" h. (ILLUS.) **3,300**

Corner cupboard, Federal country-style, poplar, two-piece construction: the upper section w/a high broken-arch scrolled crest w/three replaced baluster-turned finials & a center block w/rosette over a short half-round turned bar above the large arched cupboard door w/15 panes of glass opening to three shelves cut-out for spoons flanked by long half-round ring-, knob- and baluster-turned pilasters; the lower section w/a pair or drawers w/turned wood knobs above a pair of paneled cupboard doors flanked by shorter ring-, knob- and baluster-turned pilasters, molded base w/low shaped bracket feet, mellow finish, pulls replaced, minor restoration to waist molding, Pennsylvania, early 19th c., 24 x 44 1/2", 90 1/2" h. **5,610**

Corner cupboard, Federal style, cherry, two-piece construction: the upper section w/a wide flaring flat cornice above a single wide 12-pane glazed door w/three top panes rounded at the top, opening to three shelves; the lower section w/a mid-molding over a pair of drawers w/small brass knob pulls over a pair of paneled doors w/brass turnbuckle, molded base, high curved bracket feet, beaded backboards w/square nails, early 19th c., 23 x 47", 89 1/4" h.................................... **7,425**

Corner cupboard, Federal style, poplar, two-part construction: the upper section w/a deep molded cornice above a large 12-pane glazed door w/the three top panes arched, opening to three shelves; the lower section w/a mid-molding over a case w/a pair of small drawers flanking a longer center drawer all above a pair of paneled cupboard doors, flat base raised on heavy cylindrical feet, old cherry finish, early 19th c., 40 1/2" w., 80 3/4" h. (feet ended out, replaced brasses including H-hinges).................................... **2,750**

Corner cupboard, Federal, tiger stripe maple, one-piece construction, the flat top w/a molded cornice above a pair of tall 8-pane glazed cupboard doors opening to a three-shelved interior above a pair of recessed panel doors opening to a simple shelf, scalloped apron & short bracket feet, old surface, Middle Atlantic States, 1820, 54" w., 91" h. (height loss) **8,625**

Corner cupboard, Federal, walnut, one-piece construction, the top w/a deep coved cornice above a tall solid cupboard door w/a raised tombstone panel above a lower rectangular raised panel door, wrought-iron surface hinges, molded base w/bracket feet, dovetailed case w/rose-head nail construction, old finish, attributed to James Gheen, Piedmont, North Carolina, late 18th c., top 18 5/8 x 41", 83" h. (feet ended out, front bracket replaced).. **9,625**

Hanging cupboard, country-style, painted, a rectangular top w/a double-arched crestrail centered by a small point above a tall paneled door opening to three shelves & a drawer, old red paint on exterior, mustard yellow on interior, flat base, 19th c., 12 x 26", 41 1/2" h. **1,045**

Hanging cupboard, country-style, pine, a narrow rectangular top w/a peaked front edge & molded crest above a pair of canted hinged doors w/molded arched glazed panels opening to three shelves, on a conforming molded base, old refinish w/vestiges of green & red paint, probably New England, late 18th c., 7 x 25", 23" h. (imperfections) **2,645**

Hanging cupboard, painted poplar, a rectangular top w/a narrow widely flaring cornice over a dovetailed case w/a single paneled door opening to an interior fitted w/vertical pigeonholes, a narrow drawer across the bottom, flat molded base, original dark red paint, 19th c., 12 x 23", 26" h. (latch missing, old chips on top interior of cornice) **880**

Hanging wall cupboard, country-style, walnut, a rectangular top w/molded cornice over a narrow dentil-carved band over the single beaded panel cupboard door within a beaded frame, molded flat base, old finish, Ohio, early 19th c., 13 3/4 x 20 1/2", 25 3/4" h. **1,760**

Hanging wall cupboard, painted cherry & ash, a rectangular top w/molded edges above a tall single door w/two raised panels above a small set-back shelf across the bottom, dovetailed case, brass pull, old mustard yellow repaint, 19th c., 11 1/4 x 25", 42" h. (small glue repair on lower back) **990**

Hanging wall cupboard, painted pine, rectangular top w/molded border framing a hinged door w/two vertical recessed panels opening to a shelved interior, original red grain-painted surface, New England, early 19th c., 6 1/2 x 16 1/4", 23" h. (minor imperfections) **1,840**

Early Painted Hutch Cupboard

Hutch cupboard, painted pine, one-piece construction, the flat rectangular top w/a narrow front molded cornice above a large open hutch front w/two shelves flanked by wide side boards above a single flat lower door w/H-hinges opening to three shelves, old bluish grey paint, New England, late 18th - early 19th c., replaced hinges, imperfections, 18 x 47 3/4", 72 1/2" h. (ILLUS.) **2,645**

Jelly Cupboard with Tin Panels

Jelly cupboard, cherry, the rectangular top w/a low three-quarters gallery above a pair of tall two-panel cupboard doors, the upper panels fitted w/added punched tin panels, scalloped apron & slender bracket feet, refinished, first half 19th c., 20 1/4 x 41 1/4", 51" h. (ILLUS.) **880**

Jelly cupboard country-style, cherry & poplar w/flame veneer, a rectangular top above a pair of flat drawers w/flame veneer over a pair of tall paneled cupboard doors opening to three shelves, flat apron & shaped bracket feet, mid-19th c., 18 1/2 x 46 3/4", 59" h. (drawer pulls removed & holes filled in, slight warp to top, backboards renailed) **1,485**

Jelly cupboard, country-style, painted & decorated poplar & pine, a high peaked crestrail w/molded top above the rectangular top above a pair of deep drawers w/replaced porcelain knobs overhanging the lower case w/a pair of tall paneled cupboard doors, molded base & tapering ring-turned feet, old comb graining w/chamfered designs on drawers & tops & bottoms of doors, 19th c., 21 x 45", 55 3/4" h. (replaced cast-iron door latches) **1,430**

Jelly cupboard, country-style, painted pine, rectangular top w/flared, stepped cornice above a pair of tall paneled cupboard doors opening to shelves, molded base w/simple bracket feet, original reddish brown grained decoration w/crosshatch design on door & side panels, back w/'T' & rose head nails, feet w/worn black paint, one shelf missing, glued repairs on feet, early 19th c., 17 x 45", 66" h. (ILLUS. top next page) **5,390**

Old Grain-painted Jelly Cupboard

Jelly cupboard, painted, a high peaked crestboard on the rectangular top over a pair of drawers over a pair of tall paneled doors w/iron latches, simple bracket feet & bootjack ends, old dry mustard yellow paint, found in Berks County, Pennsylvania, 19th c., 17 x 44 1/2", 4' 10 1/4" h. **3,630**

Jelly cupboard, painted & decorated pine & poplar, a rectangular top w/an arched & shaped crestboard above the tall narrow case w/a single drawer w/porcelain knobs above a molding over a single tall paneled cupboard door w/a chamfered surround & opening to four shelves, small bracket feet, old mustard combed & grained decoration over early red, Pennsylvania, 21 x 25 1/2", 5' 11 1/2" h. **1,210**

Jelly cupboard, painted & decorated, rectangular top w/a thick stepped cornice above a case w/a pair of tall double-paneled cupboard doors opening to three interior shelves, original cast-iron & brass latches, old mustard yellow over tan grained repaint w/an orangish red on the cornice, Ohio, 19th c., 15 1/2 x 51", 59" h., 4' 11" h. (areas of wear, one rear foot ended out, chip on front foot) **1,650**

Jelly cupboard, painted pine & poplar, rectangular top w/high three-quarter gallery w/shaped ends, a pair of drawers w/old replaced wooden knobs above a pair of tall paneled cupboard doors w/old brass latches, one-board ends w/cut-out feet, found in Smoketown, Pennsylvania, old yellow graining over red, 19th c., 13 x 40", overall 47 1/2" h. **3,960**

Jelly cupboard, painted poplar, a rectangular top w/a low crestrail above a case w/a long drawer w/two turned wood knobs above a pair of tall paneled cupboard doors w/a turned wood knob, two punched tin panels w/a heart & leaf design on each side, scalloped apron, square stile legs, old brown repaint, attributed to Ohio, 19th c., 16 1/2 x 40 1/4", 52 1/2" h. plus crest (minor edge damage) **1,045**

Jelly cupboard, painted poplar, the rectangular top w/a low three-quarters gallery

above a case w/a pair of drawers w/porcelain knobs above a pair of tall paneled doors w/porcelain knobs & cast-iron latch, scroll-cut apron & bracket feet, yellow grained decoration over earlier red & black, square nail construction, minor edge wear, first half 19th c., 19 x 42 1/2", 51" h. (ILLUS. below) **1,540**

Painted Jelly Cupboard with Gallery

Jelly cupboard, painted walnut & poplar, the rectangular top w/a low three-quarters gallery above a pair of drawers over a pair of tall two-panel cupboard doors w/a longer panel over a shorter panel, flat apron, one-board sides, short stile legs, old red paint, 19th c., 16 x 44 1/2", 53 1/2" h. plus gallery **990**

Jelly cupboard, pine, a rectangular top fitted w/a shaped backsplash over two short drawers over a pair of paneled doors, raised on elongated tapering legs, 19th c., 22 1/2 x 51 1/2", 48 1/2" h. **1,624**

Jelly cupboard, walnut, country-style, a rectangular top w/a narrow coved cornice above a pair of tall narrow flat doors opening to five shelves, flat molded base, nice mellow color, Zoar, Ohio, 19th c., 16 x 39 1/2", 55" h. **1,210**

Early New Jersey Linen Press

Linen press, Chippendale, gumwood, two-part construction: the upper section w/a rectangular top above a narrow cornice w/a dentil-carved band above a frieze band w/blind fretwork over a pair of tall cupboard doors w/arched panels flanked by reeded pilasters & opening to three shelves; the lower section w/a mid-molding over a case w/three long graduated drawers over a molded base & simple bracket flat feet, replaced brasses, refinished, repairs, attributed to Matthew Egerton, New Brunswick, New Jersey, late 18th c., 17 3/4 x 48", 84" h. (ILLUS.).. **5,175**

Fine Classical Linen Press

Linen press, Classical, carved walnut veneer, the rectangular top above a plain frieze band over two tall recessed three-panel doors flanked by wide carved & fluted flat columns on molded bases above four front ring-turned legs w/knob feet, the front doors open to an interior of shelves & drawers, the central ones small & veneered, the recessed panel sides open to an interior w/wooden pegs, old surface, minor imperfections, probably Philadelphia, ca. 1830, 24 x 84", 87 1/2" h. (ILLUS.)...................................... **10,925**

Linen press, Federal country-style, painted & decorated pine & poplar, one-piece construction, rectangular top above a pair of tall paneled cupboard doors w/ring pulls opening to a repainted bluish grey interior w/four shelves above a stepped-out lower case w/three long graduated drawers w/ring pulls, French feet, original brown over tan grain painting w/dark brown painted border detail simulating band inlay on drawers & doors, attributed to Maine, early 19th c., base 14 3/8 x 49", 81 3/4" h. **4,400**

Linen press, Federal, mahogany, mahogany veneer & ebony inlay, three-part construction: the rectangular top w/a removable deep cornice arched at the top w/a molded cornice & ball finials at each cor-

ner, the frieze band inlaid w/ebony banding, the central section w/a pair of tall molded-panel doors opening to five pull-out shelves; the lower section w/a mid-molding above a case w/a pair of small drawers above three long graduated drawers all w/turned wood knobs, scalloped apron & tall French feet, attributed to New York, early 19th c., 22 x 48", 88" h. (repairs to cornice, center finial missing) **8,800**

Federal Mahogany Linen Press

Linen press, Federal, mahogany & mahogany veneer, two-part construction: the upper section w/a rectangular top over a flared, stepped cornice above a pair of large paneled cupboard doors opening to three adjustable shelves; the stepped-out lower section w/two long faux drawers folding down to form desk writing surface above a pair of paneled cupboard doors, molded base & scroll-cut backet feet, labeled "Thomas Burling," New York, ca. 1830-40, old refinish, replaced pulls, lower case of different origin, 23 1/2 x 49", 88 1/2" h. (ILLUS.) **1,840**

Linen press, Victorian country-style, painted walnut & pine, two-piece construction: the upper section w/a rectangular top w/a widely flaring deep cornice above a pair of tall paneled cupboard doors w/a cast-iron thumb latch opening to two shelves; the flush lower section w/a pair of drawers above two long graduated drawers all w/turned wood knobs, gently scalloped apron & low block feet, old brown over mustard yellow grained decoration, originally made as one piece, 21 x 47 1/2", 71" h. (small sections of cornice missing)..... **1,540**

Pewter cupboard, country-style, poplar, one-piece construction, a rectangular top w/a widely flaring stepped cornice above a tall beaded open hutch w/three shelves above a stepped-out lower case w/a single cupboard door w/four raised panels, old red finish, attributed to Ohio, cornice replaced, early 19th c., top 14 x 39 1/4", 79" h. (ILLUS. top next page).................... **3,960**

Early Ohio Pewter Cupboard

Pewter cupboard, painted pine, one-piece construction, a rectangular top w/a very deep flaring stepped cornice above wide side boards flanking a tall narrow open compartment w/two incurved shelves & scallop-cut sides & top above a tall narrow raised-panel lower door w/wood thumb latch, molded base w/short scroll-cut bracket feet, old red repaint on exterior, areas of old dry blue on interior, case w/wooden peg & rosehead nail construction, top 18 3/4 x 39 1/2", 79 3/4" h. (wear, age cracks, insect damage, base reshaped) **2,750**

Pie safe, hanging-type, pine & tin, a flat rectangular top above a frame of four square projecting stiles framing a single front door w/a long pierced tin panel decorated w/a central circle w/star & quarter-round circles in each corner, the door flanked by narrow side tin panels w/pierced half-circle designs, tin sides w/similar pierced designs, old red finish, 19th ., 20 x 30", 34 1/2" h. **935**

Pie safe, painted cherry, a rectangular top above a pair of dovetailed drawers over a pair of tall cupboard doors each fitted w/six side-by-side punched tin panels forming continuous patterns of central rings enclosing four hearts & half-round & quarter-round corner rings w/hearts alternating w/a large rounded pinwheel in each panel, side tin panels w/pinwheel & birds designs, a flat apron & round ring-turned legs w/knob feet, old green repaint, square nail & peg construction, 24 1/2 x 58", 64" h. (door hinges, pulls & turn buckles old replacements) **4,675**

Pie safe, painted cherry, the flat rectangular top above a single very wide door w/raised molding around two long pierced tin panels w/stars & hex signs & further decorated w/thin reeded bands, matching pierced tin side panels, heavy tapering ring-turned feet, old red paint,

probably New Jersey, early 19th c., imperfections, 31 1/4" w., 46 1/4" h. (ILLUS. below) **633**

Single-door Cherry Pie Safe

Pie safe, painted & decorated, a rectangular top w/a high triple-arched & shaped backrail, the case w/a pair of large cupboard doors w/wide bottom & top moldings enclosing screen panels & opening to two shelves, simple bracket feet, small Rockingham glazed door pulls, old brown over mustard yellow graining, 19th c., 18 x 61", 50 1/2" h. (one rear foot & shelf missing, some pieces of molding missing) **1,320**

Pie safe, painted poplar, a rectangular top above a pair of tall cupboard doors each fitted w/three panels of pierced tin panels decorated w/a large five-point star within a circle in the center against an urn device in background, two small stars in the upper panel corners & two larger ones in the lower corners, three tin panels down each side, on tall square stile legs, old black repaint, white porcelain door knob, tins mounted backward, 19th c., 17 x 41 1/2", 59" h. (one side tin starting to deteriorate, one door w/small half moon edge cut-out) **2,090**

Pie safe, painted poplar, a rectangular top w/a low three-quarters gallery above the tall case w/a pair of tall doors each w/three pierced tin panels, three matching tin panels on each side, flat apron, tall rectangular stile legs, the tin panels pierced w/a large central diamond enclosing a sunburst & w/a half-circle on each edge, old bluish green repaint, 15 1/4 x 36 1/2", 52 1/2" h. plus replaced gallery (tin panels w/some rust & damage) **743**

Pie safe, painted poplar, the flat rectangular top above a tall case w/a pair of tall three-panel cupboard doors w/three pierced tin inserts in a circle & diamond design above a central long drawer over a pair of paneled doors at the bottom, flat stile legs, old black paint, bookjack ends, light stains at sides, first half 19th c., 16 x 41 3/4", 84 1/2" h. (ILLUS. top next page) **1,980**

Tall Painted Poplar Pie Safe

Pie safe, painted poplar & walnut, a rectangular top above a tall case w/a long narrow dovetailed drawer w/small knobs above a pair of tall three-panel cupboard doors w/star pattern punched tin panels, slender stile legs, old paint w/a top layer of green, found in Missouri, 19th c., 16 1/2 x 38 1/2", 54" h. (some damage to tins) **440**

Tall Painted Walnut Stepback Pie Safe

Pie safe, painted walnut, one-piece construction, a rectangular top w/a thick molded cornice above a pair of tall three-panel cupboard doors each w/three pierced tin panels decorated w/tulips & leaves above a pair of drawers, the stepped-out lower section w/a pair of two-panel cupboard doors w/matching pierced tin panels, old light blue repaint, one-board sides, edge & rodent damage, tin rusted, holes drilled in bottom case, first half 19th c., 19 1/2 x 40", 79 1/4" h. (ILLUS.) **2,200**

Early Screened Pie Safe

Pie safe, pine, a rectangular top above a single long drawer w/two recessed panels over a pair of four-panel screened cupboard doors all flanked by reeded stiles, opening to three shelves, old refinish w/some red color remaining, New Jersey, early 19th c., imperfections, 44" w., 54" h. (ILLUS.) **2,645**

Pie safe, pine country-style, mortise & tenon construction, a flat rectangular top above a pair of tall doors each w/two upper rectangular openings for screening above a lower solid panel, matching configuration on the sides, on tall slender square tapering stile legs, mid-19th c., 17 x 45", 77" h. (screen missing in panels) **523**

Pie safe, pine & poplar, rectangular top above a single long drawer over a pair of tall doors each w/three star-punched tin panels on each side, stile legs, 19th c., 17 1/4 x 43", 57 3/4" h. (refinished) **605**

Pie safe, walnut, a rectangular top w/a flared cove-molded cornice above a mortised & pinned case w/a pair of tall three-panel doors each w/a punched tin panel decorated w/a large pinwheel & quarter-round circles in each corner, three matching panels on each side, tall simple turned legs, old gold repaint on tins, 19th c., 19 3/4 x 44 1/4", 57" h. (some damage to side tins) **1,540**

Side cupboard, cherry, a rectangular top w/chamfered front corners & narrow molded cornice above a conforming case w/a long raised panel door w/a central raised diamond, wrought-iron rattail hinges w/leaf finials, long bottom drawer w/wooden knob, molded flat base, Zoar, Ohio, early 19th c., (old mellow refinishing, missing feet, small chip off base molding, top lip of drawer damaged) **3,575**

Side cupboard, painted pine, rectangular top w/flat molded cornice above two doors w/raised panels opening to two shelves, on a flat base w/applied moldings, brasses appear to be original, old brown varnished surface, New England, early 19th c., 10 x 36", 23 1/2" h. (imperfections) 920

Step-back hutch cupboard, walnut, one-piece construction, a rectangular top w/narrow molded cornice above an open-front case w/three shelves above a stepped-out lower case w/a pair of paneled cupboard doors w/a thumblatch & porcelain knob, scalloped apron & slender bracket feet, mellow old finish, 19th c., 11 1/2 x 40 1/2" top, 76" h. **1,760**

Flame-painted Step-back Cupboard

Step-back wall cupboard, country-style, painted & decorated pine & poplar, two-piece construction: the upper section w/a rectangular top over a deep coved cornice above a pair of tall cupboard doors w/three horizontal panels over an open pie shelf w/shaped ends; the stepped-out lower section w/a rectangular top over a row of three round-fronted drawers above a pair of cupboard doors w/two horizontal panels each, flat apron & short bracket feet, one-board ends, original red flame-graining on yellow ground w/solid red door panels, mismatched latches & replaced pulls, mid-19th c., 13 x 57 3/4", 84" h. (ILLUS.) **6,875**

Step-back wall cupboard, country-style, painted & decorated walnut, two-piece construction: the upper section w/a rectangular top & deep flaring coved cornice above a pair of 3-pane glazed cupboard doors opening to two shelves above an open piece shelf w/shaped sides; the stepped-out lower case w/a pair of drawers w/turned knobs above a pair of paneled cupboard doors w/a cast-iron latch w/porcelain knob, gently scalloped apron & short bracket feet, reddish brown over tan grained repaint, 19th c., 18 1/2 x 49", 85 1/4" h. **1,925**

Step-back wall cupboard, country-style, painted pine, one-piece construction, a rectangular top w/a narrow molded cornice above a pair of long plain flush doors

opening to three shelves above three low compartments on the projecting lower case w/another pair of plain doors opening to three shelves, flat base, interior painted red, exterior painted light blue, New England, early 19th c. (surface losses & repairs) **2,990**

Step-back wall cupboard, country-style, painted pine, one-piece construction, the rectangular top w/a widely flaring coved cornice above a pair of tall paneled doors separated by a paneled center stile, the stepped-out base w/a pair of shorter paneled doors separated by a paneled center stile, molded base w/finely scroll-cut apron, old red paint w/red comb graining at one end, trim picked out in green, old replaced cast-iron thumb latches w/brass knobs, first half 19th c., 18 x 55", 75" h. **2,475**

Step-back wall cupboard, country-style, painted poplar, two-piece construction: the upper section w/a rectangular top w/a wide flat & flaring cornice over a pair of tall 2-pane glazed cupboard doors opening to two shelves; the stepped-out lower section w/a single long shallow drawer over a pair of cupboard doors, flat apron & simple cut-out bracket feet, dark red repaint w/yellow interior & yellow line banding on drawer & lower doors, 17 3/4 x 39 1/2", 81 1/2" h. **1,540**

Step-back wall cupboard, country-style, walnut, butternut & oak, two-piece construction: the upper section w/a rectangular top & deep stepped cornice above a pair of large single-pane glazed cupboard doors w/molded edging w/rounded corners, opening to two shelves & plate racks above an open pie shelf; the stepped-out lower section w/a row of three molded drawers w/cast-iron finger grip pulls above a pair of double-panel cupboard doors each w/a cast-iron thumb latch w/white porcelain knob, flat apron on slender curved bracket feet, old varnish finish, Ohio Amish, second half 19th c., 19 1/4 x 51 3/4", 80 1/2" h. **1,320**

Painted Step-back Wall Cupboard

Step-back wall cupboard, Federal country-style, painted, two-part construction: the upper section w/a flat rectangular top above a pair of tall narrow raised panel doors opening to four shelves above an open pie shelf; the stepped-out lower section w/a pair of raised panel cupboard doors opening to two shelves, small wood knobs & wood thumb latches, old blue paint, New England, early 19th c., imperfections, 17 x 36 1/2", 80 1/2" h. (ILLUS.)...................................... **7,475**

Step-back wall cupboard, Federal country-style, walnut, one-piece construction, a rectangular top w/a molded cornice above a pair of tall 4-pane glazed cupboard doors opening to two shelves above the projecting base w/a pair of paneled cupboard doors, scallop-cut apron & narrow feet, old refinish, probably Pennsylvania or Ohio, early 19th c., 16 x 35 3/4", 62" h. **2,415**

Mid-Atlantic Federal Cupboard

Step-back wall cupboard, Federal, maple, two-part construction: the upper section w/a rectangular top & deep flared cornice above two 6-pane glazed cupboard doors flanking a 3-panel central panel above a tall pie shelf w/scalloped sides; the stepped-out lower section w/a pair of narrow long drawers flanking a small central drawer over a pair of paneled cupboard doors, molded base w/serpentine apron & simple bracket feet, Mid-Atlantic States, early 19th c., H-hinges on upper doors, 17 1/2 x 57 1/2", 84" h. (ILLUS.)...................................... **6,325**

Step-back wall cupboard, Federal, pine, two-part construction: the upper section w/a rectangular top & deep flaring stepped cornice above a reeded frieze band over a pair of 6-pane glazed cupboard doors flanked by reeded pilasters & opening to shaped shelves; the stepped-out lower section w/a long central drawer w/two panels of molding flanked by small square drawers above a pair of recessed panel doors flanked by narrow molded side panels, molded base, bootjack feet at sides, old refinish, minor imperfections, Hackensack, New

Jersey, ca. 1800-10, 51" w., 84" h. (ILLUS. below)................................. **6,900**

Early Hackensack Wall Cupboard

Step-back wall cupboard, Federal style, pine, two-part construction: the upper section w/a rectangular top w/a deep stepped flaring cornice over a patterned diagonally-reeded frieze band above a pair of 6-pane glazed doors w/arched top panes & molded muntins all flanked by paneled & reeded pilasters; the lower section w/a mid-molding on the projecting top over a long molded central drawer flanked by small square end drawers above a pair of double-molded cupboard doors flanked by tall narrow molded panels, molded base on slender arched feet, old brass pulls, old refinish, probably Hackensack, New Jersey, ca. 1810, 19 x 50 3/4", 85" h................................. **10,350**

Simple Painted Pine Cupboard

Step-back wall cupboard, painted pine, one-piece construction, a rectangular top w/narrow cornice above a pair of tall flat cupboard doors opening to three shelves above a short section of three open compartments above the stepped-out lower case w/a pair of flat cupboard doors, painted light blue, interior painted red, New England, early 19th c., surface losses & repairs (ILLUS.)................................. **2,990**

Step-back wall cupboard, painted pine, one-piece construction, the rectangular flat top above a pair of narrow flat board-and-batten doors w/small wood knobs & thumbpieces, the stepped-out lower section w/a matching pair of tall narrow flat doors, flat apron w/angled cut-out feet, old apple green repaint over earlier red, found in New Hampshire, 19th c., 22 3/4 x 43", 79" h. (chip in one front foot).. **1,100**

Step-back wall cupboard, painted pine, one-piece construction, the rectangular top w/a flared molded cornice above a pair of tall paneled doors w/steel thumblatch, the stepped-out lower section w/a long nailed drawer w/iron pull above a pair of paneled cupboard doors, very narrow arched apron, old green repaint, second half 19th c., 17 3/4 x 35 3/4", 59 1/2" h. **990**

Early Pennsylvania Painted Cupboard

Step-back wall cupboard, painted pine, two-part construction: the upper section w/a rectangular top & deep flaring cornice above a pair of 6-pane glazed cupboard doors opening to three shelves w/plate grooves & spoon rack above a low open pie shelf; the stepped-out lower section w/a row of three drawers above a pair of paneled cupboard doors, molded base & simple bracket feet, later off-white paint, replaced hardware, Pennsylvania, late 18th c., imperfections, 17 1/2 x 52", 84" h. (ILLUS.) **9,775**

Painted One-piece Cupboard

Step-back wall cupboard, painted poplar, one-piece construction, the rectangular top w/a narrow flat cornice above a pair of 6-pane glazed cupboard doors opening to two shelves above a stepped-out lower section w/a pair of paneled cupboard doors, gently curved apron & angled bracket feet, old brown repaint, interior w/old worn yellow paint, first half 19th c., repairs, top 12 1/4 x 50 1/2", 76" h. (ILLUS.) **880**

Painted Step-back Wall Cupboard

Step-back wall cupboard, painted wood, two-part construction: the upper section w/a flat rectangular top above a pair of tall narrow raised paneled doors above a pie shelf; the lower stepped-out section w/a pair of raised panel cupboard doors, interior shelves, old blue paint, New England, early 19th c., imperfections, 16 x 36 1/2"., 80" h. (ILLUS.) **7,475**

Step-back wall cupboard, pine, two-part construction: the upper section w/a rectangular top w/narrow molded cornice over a pair of short paneled doors, the stepped-out lower section w/a pair of tall paneled doors, simple cut-out feet, old refinishing w/nut brown color, 19th c., 17 1/2 x 48 1/2", 75" h. **1,089**

Step-back wall cupboard, pine, two-piece construction w/dry sink base; the upper section w/a rectangular top over a deep coved cornice above a pair of tall paneled doors w/replaced brass thumb latches over a high open section w/three paneled sides; lower section w/a top dry sink well w/molded edges over a case w/three short graduated raised-panel drawers beside a small paneled door, molded base, dovetailed & nailed construction, refinished, 19th c., base 18 1/4 x 41 1/2", overall 87 1/2" h. **1,650**

Step-back wall cupboard, Victorian country-style, painted & decorated pine, two-part construction: the upper section w/a rectangular top w/a very widely flaring stepped cornice above a case w/two single-pane glazed cupboard doors w/arched tops opening to two shelves; the lower case w/a molding around the upper case & the stepped-out lower case w/a molded edge above a single drawer w/two turned wood knobs above a pair of arch-topped paneled cupboard doors, thick molded flat base, old black over brown grained decoration, mid-19th c., 17 3/4 x 35 1/2", 71 1/4" h. (edge wear, one pane cracked) .. **1,100**

Step-back wall cupboard, Victorian country-style, walnut, two-part construction: the upper section w/a rectangular top & deep flaring flat cornice above a pair of tall paneled cupboard doors w/cast-iron latches w/porcelain knobs above a pie shelf w/shaped sides; the lower stepped-out section w/a pair of drawers w/porcelain knobs over a pair of paneled cupboard doors w/cast-iron latches, simple bracket feet, mellow finish, 19th c., 18 x 45", 85 1/2" h. (one knob missing, right door swollen) **2,090**

Step-back wall cupboard, walnut, two-part construction: the upper section w/an overhanging flared & stepped cornice above a pair of 6-pane glazed cupboard doors opening to two shelves fitted w/spoon racks, flanked by wide fluted pilasters over the open pie shelf; the stepped-out lower section w/fluted side pilasters flanking a row of three small drawers each separated by a fluted block above a pair of wide paneled cupboard doors centered by another fluted pilaster, molded base on straight bracket feet, old finish, Pennsylvania, 1750-70, 19 1/2 x 63 1/2", 90" h. (patch on left side of cornice, strips added to base of upper section) **20,700**

Step-back wall cupboard, walnut & poplar, two-piece construction: the upper section w/a rectangular top over a flat angled cornice over a pair of very tall paneled doors over a low pie shelf; the lower stepped-out section w/a pair of drawers w/wooden knobs over a pair of paneled cupboard doors, simple bracket feet, bootjack sides, old refinish, mid-19th c., 19 x 45", 85 3/4" h. (chip on rear foot, one end of cornice replaced) **1,870**

Wall Cupboard with Paneled Doors

Wall cupboard, cherry, one-piece construction, a rectangular top w/a widely flaring shaped cornice above a pair of tall

double-paneled cupboard doors above a pair of drawers over another pair of shorter double-paneled cupboard doors, shaped apron & simple bracket feet, old refinishing, 19th c., 19 1/4 x 47 3/4", 80 3/4" h. (ILLUS.) **2,200**

Eighteenth Century Wall Cupboard

Wall cupboard, Chippendale country-style, painted pine, one-piece construction, a rectangular top w/narrow flared cornice above a pair of tall narrow doors each w/two narrow raised panels & mounted w/HL hinges, molded base w/short bracket feet, opens to five shelves, old tan over green paint, hinges appear to be original, probably Rhode Island, late 18th c., imperfections, 10 1/2 x 41 3/4", 75 3/4" h. (ILLUS.) **6,900**

Country Chippendale Pine Cupboard

Wall cupboard, Chippendale country-style, pine, a rectangular top w/a narrow cornice above a pair of tall cupboard doors each w/four raised panels & hung w/H-hinges, molded base & scroll-cut bracket feet, opening to three shelves, old refinish, restored, late 18th c., 20 3/4 x 42", 69" h. (ILLUS.) **2,990**

Unique Classical Open Cupboard

Wall cupboard, Classical, painted & decorated, a rectangular top w/flared & stepped cornice above a tall open compartment w/seven shelves flanked by tall tapering pilasters w/carved, scrolled Ionic capitals, painted to resemble rosewood, probably New England, ca. 1820-30, minor imperfections, 11 1/2 x 32", 65 1/2" h. (ILLUS.)...................................... **5,463**

Wall cupboard, country-style, painted pine, one-piece construction, the rectangular top w/a narrow coved cornice above a large tall door w/two raised panels, opening to five shelves w/plate grooves, simple curving cut-out front feet & cut-out side feet, original powder blue painted surface, possibly New Hampshire, early 19th c., 12 1/2 x 36 3/4", 75 1/2" h. (very minor imperfections) **34,500**

Early Pine Wall Cupboard

Wall cupboard, country-style, pine, a rectangular top w/a narrow coved cornice above a single narrow tall two-panel door flanked by wide side rails, low shaped bracket feet, shelved interior, old natural

surface, interior w/red wash, New England, early 19th c., minor imperfections, 42 x 42 3/4", 78" h. (ILLUS.)........................ **1,265**

Fancy Federal Pine Wall Cupboard

Wall cupboard, Federal, pine, one-piece construction, the rectangular top w/deep stepped cornice & blocked corners above a conforming case w/a pair of tall geometrically-glazed cupboard doors flanked by wide reeded pilasters & opening to interior reeded columns & arched top shelved unit above a mid-molding over a pair of paneled cupboard doors above further reeded pilasters ending in a blocked deep base, old mellow refinishing, base molding replaced, some height loss & restoration, early 19th c., 15 x 42 1/2", 76" h. (ILLUS.)........................ **2,750**

Wall cupboard, mahoganized poplar, a long rectangular top w/a stepped flared cornice above a case w/a pair of tall double-raised paneled doors w/H-hinges flanked by wide matching side panels, a single long drawer below the doors, molded base on simple bracket feet, appears to retain original wrought-iron hinges, Pennsylvania, second half 18th c., 20 x 61", 78" h. **1,800**

Unique Decorated Southern Cupboard

Wall cupboard, painted & decorated poplar, one-piece construction, the top w/a high upright front cornice board deeply cut in a zigzag design above molded bands over a pair of tall double-panel cupboard doors w/wide molded framing & side stiles, the top panels in blue & tan paint in a design of undulating stripes & a recumbent stag, the lower panels w/further stripes, molded base w/deep zigzag cut apron, molded block feet, framing painted black, opens to two shelves, found in Georgia, one foot replaced, 14 3/4 x 45", 84" h. (ILLUS.) **4,070**

Wall cupboard, painted & decorated, the rectangular top w/a coved molding above a pair of tall paneled doors w/knobs opening to two interior shelves above another longer pair of paneled doors opening to shelves, the molded base on ogee bracket feet, decorated overall w/burnt-orange & mustard yellow combed painted decoration, probably Pennsylvania, 19th c., 21 1/4 x 41 1/2", 72 1/2" h. **12,650**

Tall Narrow Painted Wall Cupboard

Wall cupboard, painted pine, a flat rectangular top above a single tall door w/two raised panels opening to five shelves, original bright blue paint, New England, early 19th c., some surface imperfections, 14 1/2 x 28", 79 3/4" h. (ILLUS.) **5,520**

Wall cupboard, painted pine, a rectangular thick top above a pair of tall double-panel cupboard doors opening to three shelves, deeply scalloped apron & simple bracket feet, old Spanish brown paint, New England, mid-19th c., height loss, surface imperfections, 18 x 48", 60" h. (ILLUS. top next column) **2,300**

Wall cupboard, painted pine, one-piece construction, the rectangular top w/a molded cornice above a raised-panel cupboard door above a matching door both above a long drawer at the bottom, one-board sides w/cut-out feet, cut-out front feet, old grey paint w/good history of

earlier colors, interior w/modern paint, found in Rhode Island, 21 1/2 x 38 1/2", 73" h. (rehinged w/"H" hinge & turned)...... **5,775**

Painted New England Wall Cupboard

Wall cupboard, painted pine, the rectangular top w/a peaked front crest w/molding above a tall door w/a forty-two opening lattice grill above two lower panels, wide flat front side boards & flat baseboard, opens to incomplete shelves, old worn red paint over orange, attributed to Wisconsin, 19th c., 19 x 42", 74 3/4" h. (hinge replaced, porcelain knob added, some edge damage & age cracks) **880**

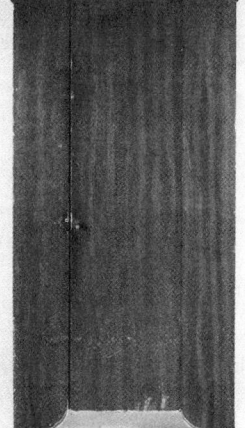

Painted Poplar Wall Cupboard

Wall cupboard, painted poplar, a flat rectangular top above a single tall narrow flat door flanked by wide side boards continuing down to form shaped bracket feet, opens to single shelf & closet, old red & grain-painted surface, probably New England, first half 19th c., base reshaped, 17 1/4 x 37", 76 1/4" h. (ILLUS.) **920**

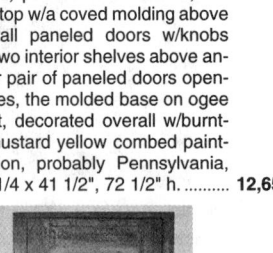

Grained Poplar Wall Cupboard

Wall cupboard, painted poplar, one-piece construction, rectangular top w/molded cornice above a stack of two paneled cupboard doors flanked by wide board side stiles forming simple bracket feet, cast-iron turn latches, worn old yellow graining, wear, one front foot w/edge damage, 19th c., 19 3/4 x 40", 72" h. (ILLUS.).. **3,080**

Simple Pine Wall Cupboard

Wall cupboard, pine, one-piece construction, rectangular top w/narrow coved cornice above a single tall narrow two-panel door flanked by wide side boards forming simple bracket feet, opening to shelves, old natural surface, interior w/red wash, New England, early 19th c., minor imperfections, 42" w., 78" h. (ILLUS.) **1,265**

Desks

Fine Art Deco Walnut Desk

Art Deco desk, walnut & ivory, the rectangular top w/rounded corners & inset front section decorated w/veneer panels & inlaid banding above the shallow case w/a pair of small drawers w/square ivory pulls on each side of a long central drawer over a thin pull-out slide, outset slender rounded tapering legs w/light stripe inlay, designed by D.I.M., France, ca. 1925, 43 1/2" l., 32" h. (ILLUS.) **14,950**

Chippendale country-style slant-front desk, birch, a narrow rectangular top above a wide hinged slant lid opening to a two-stepped interior w/open valanced compartments above smaller drawers & a central opening, all above a case of four long graduated drawers w/butterfly brasses & keyhole escutcheons, molded base on scroll-cut bracket feet, refinished, northern New England, mid- to late 18th c., 18 x 39", 43" h. (replaced brasses, imperfections) **3,105**

Chippendale country-style slant-front desk, painted maple & pine, a narrow rectangular top above the wide hinged slant front opening to an interior fitted w/four narrow drawers flanking a square center drawer over two long low arcaded slots, the case w/four long graduated drawers w/butterfly pulls, molded base on scroll-cut bracket feet, old red finish, 18th c., 18 1/2 x 37", 41 3/4" h. (replaced brasses) **12,100**

Chippendale slant-front desk, tiger stripe maple, a narrow rectangular top above a wide hinged slant front opening to a two-stepped interior of valanced compartments over small drawers, the central one flanked by document drawers & tiger stripe maple columns w/capitals & bases over a molded step above three additional small drawers over the case w/four long graduated thumb-molded drawers w/butterfly pulls, molded base w/bracket feet & central drop, old refinish, New England, mid-18th c., 19 1/2 x 34", 44 1/4" h. (some replaced brasses) **6,325**

Chippendale-Style partner's desk, walnut, the rectangular top w/molded edges above a case w/each side fitted w/a pair of long drawers over an arched kneehole opening flanked by fan-carving & a small drawer, cabriole legs ending in ball-and-claw feet, refinished, early 20th c., 27 1/2 x 48 1/2", 30" h. (base moldings replaced) **385**

Early Painted Pine Country Desk

Country-style desk, painted pine, a narrow rectangular top above an interior fitted w/stacks of 16 small & larger drawers w/porcelain knobs flanked by curved sides above the pull-out writing surface over a case w/a pair of small drawers over two long drawers, painted old red, New England, early 19th c., imperfections, 19 x 36", 48" h. (ILLUS.) **5,750**

Early New England 'Stand-up' Desk

Country-style 'stand-up' desk, stained pine, the rectangular top w/a wide slightly sloped hinged lid opening to an interior fitted w/four open compartments, raised on slender turned legs joined by a square H-stretcher, peg feet, old red stain, New England, early 19th c., surface imperfections, 17 3/4 x 30", 44" h. (ILLUS.) **1,380**

Danish Modern Teak Desk

Danish Modern desk, teak, a narrow rectangular top above a wide fall-front opening to interior compartments & two small drawers above a stepped-out lower case w/three long drawers w/wooden pulls, raised on four tapering cylindrical legs, paper label, designed by Mogensen Designs, Finland, retailed by Design Research, Cambridge, Massachusetts, late 1940s - early 1950s, 18 x 39 1/4", 47 1/2" h. (ILLUS.) **690**

Empire Revival style partner's desk, carved mahogany, a wide rectangular top w/a gadrooned border above a molded apron w/carved corner panels & each side fitted w/two long drawers, one working & one false, above small drawers flanking the kneehole opening, one drawer working & the other false, raised on pairs of heavy carved pineapple-form supports resting on rectangular blocks raised on gadrooned large paw feet joined by a turned leaf-carved heavy stretcher, old dark finish, late 19th - early 20th c., 33 x 54", 29 1/4" h. (one lock & a few brasses missing) **1,045**

Federal butler's desk, inlaid mahogany, the rectangular top w/inlaid edge of cross-banding & stringing above a cock-beaded inlaid drawer w/hinged front opening to a desk interior of four drawers & nine small valanced compartments, above a case w/three long graduated drawers all w/ring pulls, on an inlaid base of flaring French feet joined by a valanced skirt, old refinish, ca. 1800, 21 x 41", 43" h. (replaced brasses, imperfections) **2,990**

Federal country-style slant-front desk, cherry, a narrow rectangular top above the wide hinged slant front opening to a well w/four dovetailed small drawers & a hidden central compartment, the deep apron w/an inlaid diamond keyhole escutcheon at the front, on ring-, knob- and spiral-turned rod legs w/short peg feet, mellow refinishing, first half 19th c., 23 3/4 x 32 3/4", 35 1/2" h. (hinges replaced) **825**

Fine Federal Lady's Desk

Federal lady's desk, mahogany & mahogany veneer, two-part construction: the upper section w/a rectangular top w/a narrow molded cornice over a pair of beaded & veneered cupboard doors enclosing three shaped document drawers flanked by two short drawers above three valanced compartments; the lower projecting section w/a fold-out writing surface above a case w/three long cockbeaded & veneered drawers, scalloped apron & ring- and baluster-turned legs w/peg feet, old pressed glass pulls, old refinish, imperfections, Massachusetts, ca. 1810, 32 3/4 x 39 1/2", 53" h. (ILLUS.) **3,220**

Federal "oxbow" slant-front desk, mahogany & birch, a narrow top above the wide hinged slant front opening to an interior of seven small drawers w/inlaid stringing above seven valanced compartments, the cockbeaded case w/four graduated long serpentine-front drawers w/oval brasses, on a conforming base w/bracket feet, old brasses, probably Massachusetts, ca. 1780, 19 1/2 x 40", 43 1/2" h. (refinished) **4,025**

Federal slant-front desk, cherry, a narrow rectangular top above the wide hinged slant front opening to an interior fitted w/a central prospect door in front of two concave carved drawers flanked by three valanced compartments & two drawers, the lower case w/four long graduated cockbeaded drawers w/oval brasses, scalloped apron & tall flared French feet, old finish, New England, ca. 1800, 40 3/4" w., 42 3/4" h. (imperfections) **3,450**

Federal slant-front desk, mahogany & mahogany veneer, narrow rectangular top above a wide hinged slant lid opening to an interior w/seven small drawers & seven valanced compartments, the case w/four long graduated veneered drawers w/inlaid edges & oval brasses, molded base on tall inlaid bracket feet, old refinish, New England, ca. 1790, 19 x 39 3/4", 43 1/2" h. (old replaced brasses, imperfections) **2,875**

Federal-Style lady's writing desk, inlaid mahogany & flame veneer, a narrow rectangular top above an upper case w/a pair of end doors flanking a pair of small drawers over two long drawers all w/line inlay & round brass pulls, the projecting lower section w/a fold-out hinged writing surface above an apron w/pull-out supports flanking a long line-inlaid drawer w/oval brasses, slender square tapering legs joined by an H-stretcher, labeled "Williams - Kemp Furniture, Grand Rapids, Mich.," 20th c., 16 x 28", 38 3/4" h. **825**

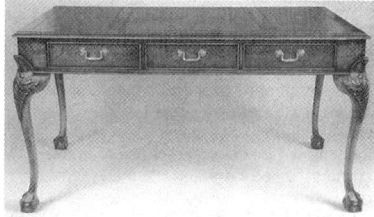

George III-Style Partner's Desk

George III-Style partner's desk, mahogany, the rectangular molded top inset w/gilt-tooled burgundy leather, above an apron fitted w/three drawers on each side, raised on cabriole legs w/scroll-carved knees & ending in claw-and-ball feet, England, early 20th c., 36 x 61 1/2", 31" h. (ILLUS.) **3,220**

Modernist Heywood-Wakefield Desk

Modern style desk, light hardwood, a rectangular top w/a gently bowed front above a single long comforming drawer over two stacks of two deep drawers flanking the kneehole opening, each drawer w/a long low arched grip pull, on small rounded block feet, Heywood-Wakefield Co., Model No. C3978W w/wheat finish, ca. 1950, 21 x 46", 30" h. (ILLUS.) **138**

Modern Style Oak Desk

Modern style desk, oak, rectangular top w/cream-colored laminated surface & curved face front w/a long center drawer flanked by a shallow & deep drawer w/curved finger grips, raised on slender square tapering gently curved legs, light finish, metal tag of Dunbar Company, Berne, Indiana, mid-20th c., wear, stains, scratches, 21 x 50", 29 1/4" h. (ILLUS.) **460**

Plantation desk, country-style, painted poplar, two-part construction: the upper section w/a rectangular top w/a flat flared cornice above a single wide 6-pane glazed cupboard door opening to a shelf above a high arched base opening; the widely stepped-out lower section w/a long front hinged drop leaf w/rounded corners, raised on square tapering legs, old worn red finish, 19th c., base 17 1/2 x 36 1/4", 66 1/2" h. **550**

Queen Anne Child's Slant-front Desk

Queen Ann child's slant-front desk, cherry & tiger stripe maple, a narrow rectangular top above the hinged slant-front opening to an interior fitted w/pigeonholes, the case w/two graduated long drawers w/butterfly pulls & keyhole escutcheons, molded base w/simple bracket feet, engraved brasses appear to be original, New England, mid-18th c., height loss, other imperfections, 19" w., 20 3/4" h. (ILLUS.).. **9,200**

Queen Anne desk, inlaid walnut, a rectangular top w/molded edges & stringed inlay outlining above a case w/a single long drawer above two banks of small square drawers flanking the kneehole opening w/a recessed raised panel door opening to a shelf & pulls forward, banded inlay in each drawer front, butterfly brasses, molded base, simple curved bracket feet, Boston, 1735-60, 31 1/2 x 33 3/4", 30 1/2" h. (repairs) **25,300**

Queen Anne slant-front desk, maple, a narrow rectangular top above a wide hinged slant lid opening to an interior of valanced compartments separated by scrolled dividers & small drawers, above a case of four long graduated thumb-molded drawers w/butterfly pulls, molded base w/short cabriole legs ending in square pad feet, original brasses, early surface, Norwich, Connecticut area, 1730-50, 18 1/4 x 33 3/4", 41" h. **6,325**

Schoolmaster's desk, country-style, walnut, a narrow top w/low three-quarters gallery above a wide hinged slant-top w/breadboard ends opening to pigeonholes, on tall square tapering legs, refinished, 19th c., 24 1/2 x 36 1/2", overall 36" h. (edges of lid & front rail ended out) **275**

Schoolmaster's desk on frame, poplar, two-part construction: the upper section w/a narrow top shelf w/a three-quarters gallery above a wide hinged sloping lid opening to the dovetailed case w/ten pigeonholes; the lower section w/a single long drawer w/two wooden knobs raised on baluster- and ring-turned legs w/knob feet joined by flat box stretchers, original red wash, 19th c., 26 1/2 x 39", 47 1/2" h. (base wobbly) **660**

Wooton Patent Cylinder Top Desk

Victorian 'patent' desk, Renaissance Revival substyle, walnut & burl walnut, a low spindled three-quarters gallery w/a central paneled crest above a sawtooth-cut frieze band over a cylinder front opening to an interior fitted w/pigeonholes & small drawers over the writing surface over a row of three narrow drawers, the lower case w/two rotary swing-out compartments fitted w/drawers & letter slots flanking the central kneehole opening, signed by The Wooton Desk Company, Indianapolis, Indiana, ca. 1875, 29 x 53", 62" h. (ILLUS.).. **15,120**

Wooton Patent Secretary-Desk

Victorian 'patent' desk, Renaissance Revival substyle, walnut & ebonized wood, the high arched & scroll-carved crest w/turned finial flanked by similar ornament above a shaped & veneered gallery over a molded shelf above an outset rectangular case w/projecting quarter-round upper section fitted w/two conforming & paneled doors embellished w/applied ornament & each w/a molded metal plaque, the first w/flip door & inscribed "Letters" & fitted on the reverse w/various shelves & the second inscribed "Manufactured by - The Wooton Desk Co. - Indianapolis Ind. - Pat. Oct. 6 1874" & fitted on the reverse w/forty small cardboard removable drawers opening to an elaborately compartmented interior comprised of variously sized pigeonholes & drawers w/fall-front & leather-lined writing surface, all above a shaped skirt, on paired downscrolling legs fitted w/casters, 31 x 42 1/2" closed, 72" h. (ILLUS.) **21,850**

Dining Room Suites

Danish Modern Dining Suite

Danish Modern: extension dining table, two armchairs & four side chairs; walnut, the oval topped table w/three leaves raised on tapering cylindrical legs, each chair w/an upholstered back panel in a simple turned walnut frame w/a cushion-form seat, all in original green upholstery, minor upholstery wear, laminate loss on skirt, Denmark, ca. 1955, chairs 30" h.,

table 42 x 60", 28 1/2" h., the set (ILLUS.) **575**
Victorian Golden Oak substyle: round-top extension dining table & six side chairs; quarter-sawn oak, the table top opening to hold four leaves above a heavy round ring-turned split pedestal w/four curved legs ending in paw feet on casters, side chairs w/flat slightly curved crestrail above a simple vase-form splat above the seat w/upholstered insert, simple cabriole front legs ending in paw feet, ca. 1900, table 48" d., 30" h., the set **1,540**

Dry Sinks

Early New England Painted Dry Sink

Painted pine, a low backsplash over the deep rectangular well over a pair of flat cupboard doors w/wood knobs, shaped bracket feet, old red paint, New England, early 19th c., imperfections, 17 1/2 x 42", 30" h. (ILLUS.) **633**
Painted pine & poplar, child's size, the superstructure w/a shaped & pointed crestboard over a narrow shelf & two short doors w/old replaced blue glass panels over a set-back narrow shelf above a rectangular well & work surface over a

Painted Child's Dry Sink

small drawer, the lower case w/a pair of paneled cupboard doors, simple bracket feet, original brown paint, wire nail construction, white porcelain pulls, late 19th c., 13 x 28", 34" h. (ILLUS.) **660**

Dry Sink with Lift-top

Painted pine & poplar, the rectangular top w/a low backsplash above a long hinged lift-top over a well on the right end next to a smaller work surface over a small drawer, two paneled cupboard doors below, on turned knob feet, old red paint, some paint touch up, door pulls & thumb latches replaced, minor repair to one foot, 19th c., top 21 1/2 x 49", 36 1/2" h. (ILLUS.).. **1,210**

Painted poplar, a shallow rectangular well beside a small rectangular working surface over a single smaller drawer w/a turned wood knob above the case w/a pair of paneled rectangular cupboard doors w/cast-iron latch, curved bracket feet, w/old zinc liner, dry-scraped to original putty-white color, 19th c., 18 3/4 x 48 1/4", 32" h. (chip on one rear foot & along top edge of drawer) **1,375**

Painted poplar & chestnut, two-piece construction: the upper section w/a rectan-

gular top over a pair of raised panel cupboard doors raised high above the lower case; the lower section w/a rectangular well w/a small work shelf at one end above a small drawer w/turned wood knob, two raised panel cupboard doors below, simple low bracket feet, old dark brown paint & brown feathering over yellow on door panels, attributed to the Ohio Amish, 19th c., base 19 1/4 x 44 1/2", 68" h. (two repairs in well) **2,200**

Painted poplar & pine, a superstructure w/a narrow rectangular top over a pair of small drawers flanking a long central compartment, the lower rectangular well above a case w/a pair of paneled cupboard doors w/cast-iron latches w/knobs, shaped bracket feet, worn comb-grained decoration, 19th c., 18 3/4 x 48", 50 1/2" h. **2,090**

Painted walnut, a long rectangular top well w/a high splashback & stepped sides above a case w/a pair of doors w/raised double panels flanking a small square central drawer over a rectangular small raised panel, shaped bracket feet, old black paint & traces of dark blue & red on splashback, 19th c., 22 1/4 x 54 1/4", 33" h. (crack in drawer front) **3,300**

Fine High-back Dry Sink

Painted walnut & ash, high-back style, the superstructure w/a high stepped crestboard w/shaped sides flanking a narrow shelf over a row of three small drawers raised above incurved sides & the long well, the base w/a pair of double-paneled cupboard doors, simple bracket feet, beaded backboards, old grey paint, chips on drawers & glued repair, 19th c., 17 3/4 x 48", 68" h. (ILLUS.)...................... **5,775**

Painted wood, rectangular top w/shallow well above a case w/a pair of shallow drawers w/turned wood knobs above a pair of paneled cupboard doors w/a cast-iron thumb latch w/porcelain knob, low arched apron, original dark brown paint, one-board ends, found in Ohio, 19th c.,

17 1/2 x 42", 33 1/2" h. (surface wear, one foot ended out).. **990**

Decorative Pine Dry Sink

Pine, a long rectangular shallow top well above a case w/beadboard paneling in the sides & forming a diagonal panel in the two doors, cast-iron latches, narrow sawtooth-cut apron, warm patina, late 19th c., 19 x 44", 32" h. (ILLUS.) **633**

Pine, the rectangular splashboard w/shelf joining molded shaped sides above a cockbeaded case & a single cupboard door w/recessed panel, on cut-out arched base, old surface w/vestiges of red paint, possibly New England, early 19th c., 25 x 44 1/2", 41" h. (replaced hinges & hardware, other imperfections)... **1,035**

Poplar, long rectangular well w/a small work shelf at one end above a smaller drawer, a wide two-panel door in the base flanked by wide side boards, square nail construction, scalloped apron, red stain finish, 19th c., 18 1/4 x 53 3/4", 34 1/2" h. (damage & repair to back feet, some edge damage)....... **688**

Red-stained softwood, a rectangular shallow dry sink well above one-board ends w/crescent cut-out feet flanking a single open shelf, 19th c., 21 x 41", 32" h............. **1,100**

Simple Soft Wood Dry Sink

Soft wood, a low three-quarters gallery above the shallow rectangular well over a pair of drawers over a pair of paneled cupboard doors, simple bracket feet, 19th c., 17 x 35 1/2", 35" h. (ILLUS.).............. **770**

Walnut & maple, a low splashback above the long rectangular well w/a small working surface at one end above a small drawer w/an oval facing & turned wood knob, two large double-paneled cupboard doors below, flat apron & short bracket feet, refinished, square nail construction, 19th c., 20 x 54 1/4", 34" h. **825**

Garden & Lawn

Cast iron unless otherwise noted.

Armchair, the arched back composed of entwined tree branches w/scattered leaves, arched twig arms, seat & legs w/twig end stretchers, dark green repaint, late 19th c., 29" h. **715**

Armchairs, the squared back w/two crossbars flanking an openwork cast design of a classical urn issuing long leafy grapevines, high shaped bar handles on incurved arm supports above the seat composed of slender crossbars, X-form arched side legs joined by two bar stretchers, old dark green repaint, 19th c., 28 1/4" h., pr. **3,025**

Planter, painted & decorated wood, a tapering square paneled form w/faceted carved finials painted in shades of green, the grain-painted sides w/green border outlined in yellow, early 19th c., 13 3/4" sq., 14" h. (minor paint wear) **4,600**

Settee, a high triple-arch back composed of pierced looping scrolling flowering leafy vines curving to form arms w/shaped bird head arm supports above the D-form geometrically-pierced seat, on cabriole legs w/pierced leafy corner brackets, dark green repaint, seat labeled "Kramer Bros., Dayton, Ohio," 33 1/2" h. (old repair on back, one screw in leg needs replacing) **990**

Settee, the arched back composed of entwined tree branches w/scattered leaves, arched twig arms, seat & legs w/twig end stretchers, dark green repaint, late 19th c., 33" h. **1,540**

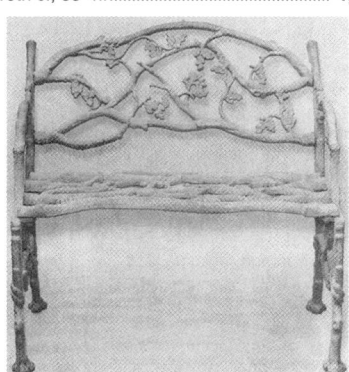

Small Branch-form Garden Settee

Settee, the arched back composed of open-work leafy entwined branches flanked by arched branch arms over the entwined branch seat, on branch-form legs joined by end stretchers, old blue repaint, 19th c., 35" l., 33" h....................................... **1,430**

Settee, the back w/an overall pierced design of scrolling fern fronds continuing to form high arms & the pierced seat, arched end legs, painted white, 19th c., 53 1/2" l... **920**

Long Branch-form Garden Settee

Settee, the long back composed of entwined leafy branches flanked by arched branch arms over the openwork entwined branch seat, branch-form legs w/looped end stretchers, painted, 19th c., 50" l. (ILLUS.).. **2,160**

Garden Settee with Figural Medallions

Settee, the long cast-iron back w/sawtooth upper & lower borders & an arched center enclosing four small round pierced medallions w/various plant designs & a large central medallion w/a pierced design of a dog among foliage, scrolled cast-iron arms w/round medallions w/birds flanking the long shaped wood plank seat, on a cast-iron trestle-form base w/arched legs, painted, ca. 1890, 50 1/2" l. (ILLUS.).. **1,265**

Settee, the serpentine crestrail cast w/ornate scrolls above the back pierced w/rows of small arches flanked by serpentine stepped arms w/upright scroll supports, scroll-pierced seat above a scroll-cast seatrail & scrolling cabriole front legs, 19th c., worn dark green paint over earlier white, 45 1/2" l., 36" h.................. **633**

Settee, the serpentine crestrail w/heavy scrolls centered by a small classical bust above a band of delicate lacy scrolls over the high back composed of a wide band of interlacing ovals flanked by outswept scrolling half-arms above the oblong scroll-pierced seat w/a serpentine seatrail above a lacy scroll apron on scroll-cast cabriole front legs, dark green repaint, 19th c., 44 1/4" l., 32 1/2" h. (repaired break on one side of front leg)........... **990**

Settee, triple-back style, a high central rectangular panel w/arched & floral scroll-pierced crest & ears above a leafy scroll-pierced panel flanked by two shorter matching panels, low rounded arms w/pierced scrolls above the pierced rectangular seat & front apron, on gently arched end legs joined by scroll stretchers, marked "Patd. May 17, 1895," old green repaint over white, 33" l., 38 1/4" h. (rust)... **605**

Settee, twig design, the gently arched back composed of entwined slender branches w/scattered leaves, arched branch arms & seat composed of straight twig branches, entwined branch legs, layers of old paint, 39" l., 32" h. **1,100**

Hall Racks & Trees

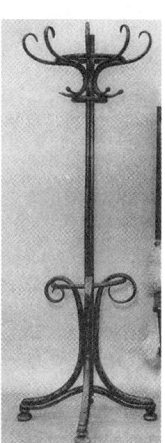

Tall Bentwood Hall Tree

Hall tree, bentwood, hickory, the top composed of a ring of long upturned S-scroll hooks joined by central rings & raised on a tall square shaft w/four long scroll braces joining the cross-form base on disk feet, worn original black paint, one hook repaired, one ball finial missing, ca. 1900, 74" h. (ILLUS.)..................................... **248**

Hall tree, Mission-style (Arts & Crafts movement), oak, the wide tall rectangular back w/a wide convex oak frame surrounding a large mirror & mounted with four ornate three-part brass coat racks w/long shaped flat backplates, all above a scroll-carved panel flanked by low shaped arms flanking a rectangular lift-top seat

Large Mission Oak Hall Tree

above the deep apron fitted w/scroll-cut applied brass corner binding, flaring molded base on bun feet, refinished, minor wear to mirror, early 20th c., 20 x 53", 92" h. (ILLUS.) **1,430**

Hall tree, turn-of-the-century, mahogany, a tall molded back w/a carved pediment centering a beveled mirror, mounted w/cast-metal coat & hat hooks, leading down to scrolling hand rests, over a hinged seat, a molded front bottom panel, ending in reeded bun feet, ca. 1890, 20 x 36 1/2", 80" h. **644**

Victorian Faux Bamboo Hall Tree

Hall tree, Victorian faux bamboo style, maple, the tall rectangular back composed of numerous turned faux bamboo crossbars joined by short turned spindles & supported by bamboo-turned side posts w/beehive-turned finials, mounted w/nine long S-scroll hat hooks & centered by a

rectangular mirror, the lower section w/a narrow rectangular umbrella rack, ca. 1880, 9 x 35", 87" h. (ILLUS.) **5,040**

Elaborate French Hall Tree

Hall tree, Victorian Rococo substyle, cast iron, the back formed as a tree wrapped w/a berried vine, the four tree branches issuing double-arm hooks, the back enclosing a hinged oval mirror, the whole topped w/three candle branches, the lower section w/branches forming an umbrella holder continuing to figures of French soldiers w/guns & a cannon, the base fitted w/removable drip trays, stamped "Alfred A. Charleville No. 29," France, third quarter 19th c., 85" h. (ILLUS.) **2,280**

Acanthus Leaf & Scroll-cast Hall Tree

Hall tree, Victorian Rococo substyle, cast iron, the tall top section composed of pierced acanthus leaf & S-scrolls w/six long scrolling coat hooks centered by a small oval mirror above a wide cast acanthus leaf-cast supported on scrolls above the oblong scroll-cast base fitted w/a drip tray, old dark finish, small break, umbrella holder ring needs to be reattached, ca. 1850, 13 x 28 1/2", 78" h. (ILLUS.) **1,100**

Fancy Victorian Cast-Iron Hall Tree

Hall tree, Victorian Rococo substyle, cast iron, the top w/an oblong lacy pierced scrolling floral design centering a small oval mirror & raised on a scroll-cast standard supporting an oblong loop for umbrellas above a leaf- and scroll-cast lower standard above the scroll-cast oblong base w/a drip tray, old black paint, signed "Greenwood Co. Patent 1852," umbrella loop w/welded break, 26" w., 74" h. (ILLUS.).. **1,760**

Highboys & Lowboys

Highboys
Chippendale "flat-top" highboy, walnut, two-part construction: the upper section w/a molded cornice above a rectangular case w/a row of three small drawers over a pair of drawers above three long graduated & thumb-molded drawers, all flanked by fluted quarter columns; the lower case w/a conforming mid-molding over a case fitted w/a long thumb-molded drawer flanked by similar fluted quarter columns above an elaborate scroll-cut apron, on shell-carved cabriole legs w/ball-and-claw feet, Pennsylvania, 1750-60, 22 1/2 x 40 1/2", 63" h. **40,250**
Queen Anne "flat-top" highboy, figured maple, two-part construction: the upper section w/a rectangular top w/deep flaring & stepped cornice above a case w/a row of three small drawers above four long graduated thumb-molded drawers w/butterfly pulls & keyhole escutcheons; the lower section w/a mid-molding above a shallow long drawer over a pair of deep drawers flanking a central shallow drawer over a large shell-carved & scalloped

apron w/acorn drops, cabriole legs w/padded disk feet, possibly by Major John Demeritt, Madbury, New Hampshire, 1770-1800, 20 1/2 x 40", 73" h. **17,250**
Queen Anne "flat-top" highboy, hardwood, two-part construction: the top section w/a rectangular top above a very deep flaring stepped cornice above a case w/a pair of dovetailed drawers over a stack of three long graduated drawers; the lower section w/a mid-molding above a pair of deep drawers flanking a shallow central drawer all above a scalloped apron w/two pointed turned drops, cabriole legs ending in pad feet, old dark red finish, old replaced batwing brasses, New England, first half 18th c., 20 x 37 1/2", 66" h. (restorations) **7,700**
Queen Anne "flat-top" highboy, maple & birch, two-part construction: the upper section w/a deep flared & molded cornice above a case w/five long graduated thumb-molded drawers w/butterfly brasses; the lower section w/a mid-molding above a long narrow drawer over a row of three deep drawers, the central one fancarved, a valanced concave apron on cabriole legs ending in pad feet, apparently original brasses, old refinish, Massachusetts, ca. 1770, 19 x 38 1/4", 73 1/4" h. (repairs) **10,350**
Queen Anne "flat-top" highboy, maple, two-part construction: the upper section w/a flat rectangular top w/a deep stepped flaring cornice above a case w/four long graduated drawers w/butterfly brasses & keyhole escutcheons; the lower section w/a mid-molding above a case w/a long narrow drawer above two deep drawers flanking a shallower central drawer w/fancarving, scalloped apron, cabriole legs ending in raised pad feet, New England, mid-18th c., 19 x 38 1/4", 71 1/2" h. **4,313**

Queen Anne Curly Maple Highboy

Queen Anne "flat-top" highboy, maple w/curly maple facade, two-part construction: the upper section w/a rectangular top above a deep flared coved cornice above a pair of drawers flanking a small square central drawer above four long thumb-molded graduated drawers w/butterfly pulls & keyhole escutcheons; the lower section w/a mid-molding above a long narrow drawer above a pair of deep drawers flanking a shallow central drawer, deeply scalloped apron, cabriole legs ending in trifid feet, refinished, original brasses, base reworked, some incomplete brass & one missing escutcheon, mid-18th c., top 20 7/8 x 39", 70 1/4" h. (ILLUS.)... **7,370**

Queen Anne "flat-top" highboy, walnut & maple, two-part construction: the upper section w/a flat high coved cornice above two short & three long thumb-molded drawers each w/butterfly pulls & keyhole escutcheons; the lower section w/a mid-molding over a narrow long drawer over a row of three deep drawers, flat apron, cabriole legs ending in pad feet on platforms, original brasses, old mellow surface, Massachusetts, ca. 1740-60, 20 x 38", 70 3/4" h. (minor imperfections) **17,250**

Queen Anne-Style "bonnet-top" highboy, mahogany & mahogany veneer, two-part construction: the upper section w/a broken-scroll bonnet top w/three urn- and flame-turned finials above a case w/a pair of small drawers flanking a deeper fan-carved center drawer over four long beaded graduated drawers w/butterfly brasses; the lower section w/a mid-molding over a case w/a long drawer over a row of three drawers, the longer center drawer w/fan-carving, scalloped apron, cabriole legs ending in raised pad feet, by Henredon, 20th c., 20 x 37", 80 1/2" h. **880**

Queen Anne-Style "bonnet-top" highboy, maple, two-part construction: the upper section w/a broken swan's-neck pediment centering & flanked by three urn-turned finials above a case fitted w/three thumb-molded short drawers, the central drawer w/carved fan, over four long graduated thumb-molded drawers; the lower section w/a mid-molding above three thumb-molded short drawers, the central one w/a carved fan, over a shaped skirt, on cabriole legs ending in padded disk feet, in the New England manner, 20th c., 19 1/2 x 36", 77" h. **920**

William & Mary 'flat-top' highboy, maple & pine, two-part construction: the upper section w/a rectangular flat top w/narrow flaring cornice over a row of three small drawers over three long graduated drawers; the lower section w/a heavy mid-molding over a case w/two deep drawers flanking a shallow central drawer over a triple-arched apron, raised on four trumpet-form front legs w/bun feet joined by flat curved stretchers, grained in the late 19th c., original brasses & keyhole es-

Rare William & Mary Highboy

cutcheons, North Shore, Massachusetts, 1700-30, minor repairs to stretchers, 22 5/8 x 44", 63 1/2" h. (ILLUS.) **34,500**

Love Seats, Sofas & Settees

Day bed, child's, country-style, painted wood, the shaped back & side panels joining four square tapering posts, old red paint, New England, early 19th c., 22 1/4 x 39 1/2", 32" h. **1,380**

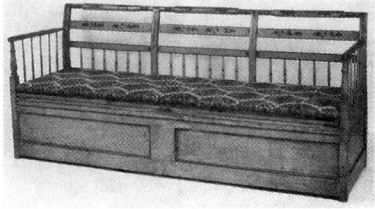

Early Decorated Federal Day Bed

Day bed, Federal country-style, painted & decorated, the triple-sectioned back w/turned top rails above a flat center rail & lower rail above rows of short spindles flanked by turned arms over spindles & w/baluster-turned arm supports, a hinged fold-out seat forming the seat w/a deep paneled apron, original yellow ground paint w/brown leaf & berry stencil decoration & striping, New England, early 19th c., replaced seat w/modern textile cover, minor surface imperfections, 18 x 84", 36 1/2" h. (ILLUS.) **4,025**

Day bed, Mission-style (Arts & Crafts movement), oak, a low slanted back w/angled sides at one end, on a rectangular seat frame w/square post legs, branded Limbert mark, Model No. 850, early 20th c., 30 1/4 x 79 1/4", 24 3/4" h. **7,050**

George Nelson Modern Day Bed

Day bed, Modern style, a rectangular seat & back frame in solid maple raised on V-form bent wire legs, fitted w/two checkered pattern rectangular back cushions & a single long seat cushion, designed by George Nelson, produced by Herman Miller, ca. 1956, 75" l., 26" h. (ILLUS.)....... **1,344**

Love seat, Art Deco, ébène-de-macasar & upholstery, the long narrow arched crestrail above a three-section upholstered back, narrow arm rails w/a raised upholstered central section above the closed arms, long cushion seat above a narrow gently curved seatrail, gently swelling arm supports continuing down to form the tapering from legs, tapering rear legs, branded mark of Emile-Jacques Ruhlmann, France, ca. 1925, 63" l. **43,125**

Mammy's bench, country-style, painted & decorated, the long rectangular crestrail above numerous simple turned back spindles flanked by turned stiles & scrolled arms raised on a spindle & baluster- and knob-turned arm supports, S-scroll long seat w/a wide rectangular upright board insert w/rounded top corners at one end, ring-, knob- and baluster-turned front legs joined by a flat stretcher & plain turned rear legs w/a flat stretcher, on rockers, old black repaint w/well done free-hand & stencilled decoration including fruit & vining on the crest, pineapple & leaves on the seat insert & yellow flourish designs on arm supports, legs & stretchers, first half 19th c., 52" l., 30 1/2" h. (repairs where legs meet rockers, one arm w/pieced repairs) **523**

Fine Classical Méridienne

Méridienne, Classical, carved mahogany, the shaped crestrail carved w/a flower-head above a conforming padded back, the outscrolled arms w/flowerhead terminals continuing to elaborately-carved flowerheads, the rectangular upholstered seat above conforming seatrail raised on legs carved w/S-scrolls, foliage & fruit & ending in paw feet, American, ca. 1820-30, 88 1/2" l. (ILLUS.) **5,520**

Belter High-backed Méridienne

Méridienne, Victorian Rococo substyle, carved & laminated rosewood, the high arched upholstered curved back at one end enclosed by a scroll-carved border w/a fruit- and flower-carved crest, the oblong serpentine upholstered seat above a conforming floral-carved seatrail, on demi-cabriole legs on casters, John H. Belter, New York, New York, ca. 1850, 42" l., 38" h. (ILLUS.)................................... **5,040**

Carved & Painted Belter Méridienne

Méridiennes, carved & painted wood, the low arched & curved upholstered back at one end enclosed by high pierce-carved C-scrolls & ornate floral carvings continuing down the molded end arm, the upholstered oblong serpentine seat on a conforming seatrail w/further ornate leafy scroll & blossom carving, on front demi-cabriole legs ending in scrolls & square rear legs all on casters, John H. Belter, ca. 1855, 25" l., pr. (ILLUS. of one) **14,950**

Recamier, Classical style, brass-mounted carved mahogany & mahogany veneer, of box form, an upright squared end w/a heavy rounded crestrail along the arm & long back & terminating at each end w/a leaf-carved scroll, the closed upholstered arm & low back panel opposite the out-scrolled end w/cornucopia-carved support, long upholstered seat on a flat seatrail, the closed arm w/a columnar arm support w/brass-mounted capital & base, on heavy short legs w/a carved acanthus leaf cluster over a bulbous reeded knob foot, New York, ca. 1815, 34 x 86", 16" h. .. **8,400**

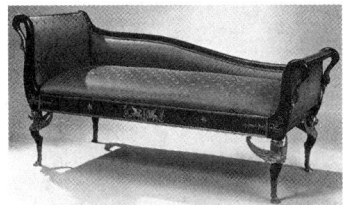

Empire-Style Recamier

Recamier, Empire-Style, gilt-bronze mounted mahogany, the low undulating back continuing to rolled arms terminating in carved swans' heads, above a simple rectangular upholstered seat w/straight seatrail mounted w/gilt-bronze winged lions, stars & scrolls, raised on figural legs headed by gilt winged lion heads & ending in paw feet, France, late 19th c., 72 1/2" l. (ILLUS.) **4,888**

English Regency Inlaid Recamier

Recamier, Regency, brass-inlaid beechwood, a long low upholstered back w/serpentine molded crestrail ending in a inlaid brass pinwheel, the curved upholstered end arm w/a carved arm support, the long oblong seat w/a wide reeded seatrail decorated w/inlaid scrolling brass plaques above the heavy carved acanthus leaf legs on reeded knob feet on casters, long seat cushion & bolster pillow, England, second quarter 19th c., 76" l. (ILLUS.) **4,600**

Scarce Child's Windsor Settee

Settee, child's Windsor arrow-back stye, painted & decorated, the wide flat crestrail over eight plain spindles alternating w/two arrow slats, simple turned end arms over the incised plank seat, on simple turned raked legs w/a rectangular front stretcher & round side & back stretchers, original red paint w/yellow striping to simulate inlay on the crest which includes yellow & black leafage & highlights, all original form & decoration, New England, early 19th c., 9 x 25 3/4", 21 3/4" h. (ILLUS.) **12,650**

Settee, Edwardian, painted satinwood, the rectangular back frame w/a raised, painted central crest panel above a long rectangular caned panel flanked by pierced panels w/forked splats centered by a decorated oval medallion, a pierced lattice band along the bottom of the back, slender open downswept arms on molded supports above the caned seat w/a loose button cushion, raised on square tapering legs ending in spade feet, painted w/flowers & classical designs, England, ca. 1900 (repairs, chips)............. **3,120**

Settee, Federal country-style "fancy" type, a long flat crestrail w/downturned scroll ends above a triple back w/three decorated slats, S-scroll arms on ring- and knob-turned arm supports, long rush seat, four canted ring-, knob- and baluster-turned front legs & plain turned rear legs joined by baluster- and ring-turned front stretchers, the front seatrail w/double-lobed pendants at the centers of each section, ground paint simulates rosewood w/gold stencil decoration of compotes of fruit & leafage on the crestrail & slats, old surface, New York, 1815-25, 76 3/4" l., 35 1/2" h. (losses, needed repairs) **920**

Settee, Federal country-style, painted & decorated, triple-back style, the long wide board crestrail divided into three sections, each w/a flat-topped center flanked by serpentine sections & ending in rounded corners, four back stiles dividing the three lower rails each above five baluster- and knob-turned short spindles, S-scroll arms on two baluster- and knob-turned spindles & a matching arm support, long shaped plank seat, four ring- and rod-turned front legs joined by simple turned stretchers, original painted decoration w/birds & fruit across the back panels in red, blue, green & tan, yellow line detail around borders, Pennsylvania, first half 19th c., 73" l., 35" h. (wear, repair to arms) **1,210**

Settee, Federal country-style, turned & painted, triple-back style w/the divided crestrail having a tablet at the center of each section above three slender cut-out medallion & urn-shaped spindles in each section joined to a lower rail & divided by four simple turned stiles, high end arms w/matching cut-out spindles above the long rush seat above eight simple turned legs, the front four joined by medallion-cut stretchers, original brown paint w/gilt, red highlighting the neoclassical elements, New England, 1810-20, 16 x 70", 33" h. (imperfections, one spindle missing) **2,070**

Settee, Louis XVI-Style, hardwood, long oval back w/gadroon-carved frame around central caning, open padded end arms w/carved incurved arm supports above the caned seat w/a fitted cushion, gadroon-carved seatrail, turned reeded legs w/peg feet, early 20th c., 46 1/2" l. **880**

Settee, Queen Anne-Style, walnut, the triple-arched crest on the paneled upholstered back w/wood end stiles above open scrolled arms & curved supports above the overupholstered seat w/scalloped edge, simple cabriole front legs w/shell-carved knees ending in raised pad feet, dark mellow finish, early 20th c., 21 x 62", 42" h. (one front leg return replaced) **330**

Fine Early Wicker Settee

Settee, wicker, ornate late Victorian style, the high serpentine back w/ornate feather-like border scrolling above a shaped delicately woven back panel flanked on one end by a rolled arm & on the other by a high flattened arm, tightly woven seat w/rolled-under end above a seat apron composed of wicker heart-form designs, raised on wrapped outswept legs joined by a cross-stretcher, original varnished rattan, Heywood Brothers & Wakefield Company, Gardner, Massachusetts, 1898-1904, 41 1/4" l., 41" h. (ILLUS.) **4,025**

Settee, Windsor "birdcage" style, maple, ash & hickory, a long double-bar crestrail joined by six short spaced out spindles above a multi-spindled lower back w/bamboo-turned spindles flanked by bamboo-turned arms on two spindles & a canted arm support, the long plank seat raised on four gently canted bamboo-turned front legs & four rear legs all joined by long bamboo-turned stretchers, old finish, New England, early 19th c., 72" l., 31 1/2" h. (imperfections) **2,415**

Windsor "Birdcage" Style Settee

Settee, Windsor "birdcage" style, maple & pine, a triple-section back w/a pair of upper crestrails in each section centered by a rectangular tablet & two tiny spindles above the lower back composed of numerous bamboo-turned spindles & bamboo-turned stiles, the bamboo-turned open arms w/two short spindles & a canted arm support above the long rectangular plank seat raised on eight bamboo-turned canted legs joined by bamboo-turned stretchers, old refinish, imperfections, New England, ca. 1810, 78" l., 33" h. (ILLUS.) **3,220**

Windsor Country Settee

Settee, Windsor country style, painted & decorated, the long flat crestrail between tapering stiles & a narrow medial rail over numerous short turned spindles, scrolled arms over turned spindles & a canted turned arm support, long plank seat raised on four canted ring-turned front legs joined by three baluster-turned front stretchers & four simple turned rear legs joined by simple turned stretchers, worn old red & brown graining w/yellow & orange striping & floral decoration on the crestrail & slat, crack in seat w/old underside bracing, repairs, early 19th c., 81" l. (ILLUS.) **880**

Settle, child's early American country-style, painted pine, the tall back w/a flat top & three rectangular banded panels flanked by tall incurved narrow arms above the lift seat opening to a compartment, the lower front w/two rectangular banded panels, mortised construction w/rosehead nails, small worn feet & low arched aprons, old comb-grained repaint, 14 x 36", 37 1/2" h. (edge wear, one seat hinge damaged) **2,475**

Settle, Jacobean, oak, the rectangular upright paneled back & scrolled open end arms above a rope seat, planked legs joined by box stretchers, England, late 17th c., 75" l., 41 1/2" h. **6,325**

Early High-back Painted Settle

Settle, painted pine, the high back constructed of beaded horizontal boards above the seat w/a hinged top over the deep straight front & cut-out feet, tall shaped arms formed by end boards, old red varnish over earlier blue paint, New England, early 19th c., imperfections, 16 x 42", 49" h. (ILLUS.) **18,400**

Early Painted Pine Settle

Settle, painted yellow pine, the low rectangular back flanked by downswept arms above a hinged long seat & straight deep apron, the sides w/exposed tenons on cutout feet, old green over earlier white paint, probably Pennsylvania, early 19th c., 18 x 60 1/2", 34 1/2" h. (ILLUS.) **2,415**

Sofa, Classical, carved mahogany, the crest-rail w/a raised central rectangular panel flanked by scroll-carved sections & decorated w/water-leaf carving & veneered crossbanding, above the upholstered back flanked by high upright outscrolled reeded arms curving down to form the seatrail w/circular bosses flanking leaf-carved panels below the upholstered seat, on frontal hairy paw feet below carved eagle head & wing supports, leaf-carved turned rear feet, old refinish, on casters, probably New York, ca. 1830, 21 1/4 x 82", 31 3/4" h. (imperfections) **1,955**

Carved Mahogany Classical Sofa

Sofa, Classical, mahogany & mahogany veneer, the raised flat crestrail w/a rod crest ending in pineapple finials above serpentine leaf-carved rails over the long upholstered back flanked by wide rolled upholstered arms w/leaf-carved arm supports continuing to the seatrail, raised on carved cornucopias above flared paw feet on casters, old finish, reupholstered in gold velvet, ca. 1830-40, 77" l., 35" h. (ILLUS.) **1,430**

Sofa, Danish Modern style, teak, a long rectangular tack back frame joined to the seat by two steel rods, slanted teak armrests similarly joined to seat, tapered legs, repeating fan design on the salmon-colored upholstered back, seat & arm cushions, Hans Wegner, Denmark, ca. 1955, 82" l., 30 1/4" h. **575**

Sofa, Federal, inlaid mahogany, the gently arched upholstered back flanked by side upholstered arms & molded armrests w/vase- and ring-turned, reeded & swelled posts, inlaid panels at the legs & arm supports, the bowed seat frame joining four front vase- and ring-turned reeded tapering legs ending in turned peg feet, old finish, probably Boston or North Shore, Massachusetts, ca. 1800-10, 25 x 80 1/2", 39" h. (imperfections) **17,250**

Massachusetts Federal Sofa

Sofa, Federal, mahogany & mahogany veneer, the narrow flat reeded crestrail above an upholstered back & downswept arm rails over closed arms & baluster-turned arm supports, a long cushion seat over the curved seatrail on four turned & tapering front legs on brass casters & four square tapering rear legs on casters, old refinish, imperfections, some height loss, Boston or North Shore, Massachusetts, ca. 1815-20, 13 x 76", 34 1/8" h. (ILLUS.) **7,475**

Sofa, Federal, mahogany veneer, the upholstered back w/a flat crest above downswept upholstered arms w/curved, reeded & baluster-turned arm supports on veneered corner blocks, over-upholstered seat, on four front tapering reeded legs w/swelled & turned feet, square rear legs, old surface, Massachusetts, ca. 1800, 76" l. (imperfections) **2,530**

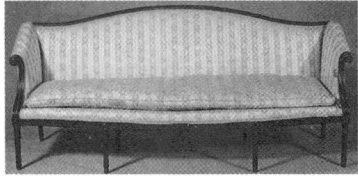

Fine Federal-Style Sofa

Sofa, Federal-Style, carved mahogany, the narrow molded serpentine crestrail above an upholstered back flanked by rolled upholstered deep arms w/molded scrolled arm supports, a long cushion seat over the serpentine seatrail w/dentil carving raised on four reeded, turned & tapering front legs, late 19th c. (ILLUS.).... **1,792**

Sofa, Mission-style (Arts & Crafts movement), oak, long crestrail w/downcurved top edge over seven wide back slats, shaped drop arms over two wide slats & long corbel supports, three-cushion seat, red decal mark of L. & J.G. Stickley, Model No. 263, ca. 1914, 69 1/2" l., 37" h. (replaced brown vinyl cushions & seat support, staining, wear, some joint separation) **6,900**

Sofa, Victorian Egyptian Revival substyle, ebonized & brass-mounted, the gently arched upholstered crest flanked by rails w/leaf-and-berry carving further flanked by brass-mounted lions' heads w/open jaws above an upholstered back over tufted arms above scrolled supports fronted by brass-mounted Egyptian busts over a partially over-upholstered triplelobed seatrail centered by a brassmounted lion's head, on sabre legs w/brass-mounted hoof feet, the mounts stamped "PS," attributed to Pottier & Stymus, New York City, ca. 1880, 72" l. **9,200**

Sofa, Victorian Renaissance Revival substyle, carved, gilt & ormolu-mounted rosewood, the carved, incised & gilt pediment crest centered w/a carved stylized palmette cartouche over a swag w/central applied ormolu rosette above an incised & gilt Greek key motif, all flanked w/acanthus leaf carving over a partitioned canted back w/ormolu rosettes heading further Greek key designs centering & flanked by the upholstered back & arms w/ormolu figural cherub head hand rests & carved & gilt-incised arm supports surrounding a trapezoidal partially over-upholstered seat w/gilt & molded front rail centered w/gilt-incised scrolldecorated pendant on Ionic gilt-incised tapering colonettes, the center ones headed w/ormolu rosettes, the side ones w/gilt triglyphs, decorated w/ormolu cuffs & fitted w/casters, New York, 1860-80, 28 1/2 x 74 1/2", 42 3/4" h. **2,990**

Fine Renaissance Revival Sofa

Sofa, Victorian Renaissance Revival substyle, mahogany & burl veneer, a triplepanel tufted upholstered back w/the central arched panel topped w/a carved figural crest & leafy & drop carved decorations on the side back panels, upholstered curved half-arms w/figural carved arm supports flanking the upholstered seat over the scalloped & carved apron w/burl panels, raised on four trumpet-turned tapering front legs on casters, burgundy velvet upholstery, ca. 1875, 81" l., 53" h. (ILLUS.)................................. **2,200**

Quality Renaissance Revival Sofa

Sofa, Victorian Renaissance Revival substyle, upholstered parcel-gilt walnut, the long back w/a low carved & scroll-ended center rail over upholstery joining high curved & upholstered end sections w/tufted upholstery backs each flanked by carved curved stiles w/large turned & carved drops flanked by low rolled upholstered arms w/wide arm supports carved as figural Grecian lady heads, the long serpentine-fronted seat above a conforming seatrail w/burl walnut panels & incised gilt trim centered by three curved center drops & raised on four boldly carved & incised front trumpet-form legs on casters, attributed to John Jelliff, ca. 1870, 81" l. (ILLUS.)............................. **2,070**

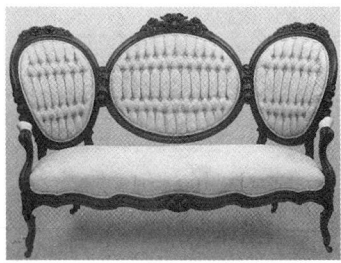

Triple-back Victorian Rococo Sofa

Sofa, Victorian Rococo substyle, walnut, triple-back style w/a large oval upholstered central panel flanked by oval upholstered panel each w/finger-carved frames & floral- and leaf-carved crests, raised above a long upholstered seat flanked by padded open arms on curved arm supports, serpentine molded & carved seatrail joined to demi-cabriole legs on casters, canted back legs w/casters, ca. 1860 (ILLUS.)... **1,680**

Renaissance Revival Rosewood Sofa

Sofas, Victorian Renaissance Revival substyle, carved rosewood, a long narrow gently arched crestrail centered by a carved cartouche w/shell & scrolls flanked by molded stiles headed by scroll-carved finials on floral-incised plinths w/carved drapery above the tufted upholstered back over padded arms on downswept arm supports above the long tufted upholstered seat w/a bowed seatrail trimmed w/raised banding centering an oval reserve above a shaped pendant, on tapering turned legs on casters, probably New York City, ca. 1875, 68 1/4" l., 44" h., pr. (ILLUS. of one) **5,750**

Early Faux Bamboo Tete-a-Tete

Tete-a-tete, early faux bamboo-style, painted wood, each corner bamboo-turned crestrail above four bamboo-turned spindles & matching lower rail, between bamboo-turned stiles continuing to form the six legs joined by double bamboo-turned stretchers, old black paint, probably Boston, early 19th c., minor imperfections, 17 1/2 x 37", 28" h. (ILLUS.)....................... **1,380**

Wagon seat, maple & hickory, double-seat type, three back stiles w/pointed turned finials each separated by two gently arched slats, simple rod open arms to heavy front leg supports w/a mushroom

grip, double woven splint seat, simple turned double rungs in front & at sides, old refinishing, pegged construction, 29 3/4" h. (some reweave & damage on seat) **550**

Wagon seat, painted pine, the rectangular seat flanked by side supports w/rounded tops & flaring bases joined by a single square stretcher, old orange wash finish, New England, early 19th c., 12 1/2 x 34 1/2", 30" h. (imperfections) **1,265**

Wagon seat, painted, two-back style, each section of the low back w/two arched slats between the three heavy turned stiles w/pointed tips, open arms on turned arm supports continuing down to form the front legs, replaced woven rush seat, double rungs at the front & sides, original green paint, found in Brewster, Massachusetts, 19th c., 19 x 34 1/2", 30 3/4" h. (back feet ended-out) **935**

Primitive Painted Wagon Seat

Wagon seat, painted wood, primitive country-style, a narrow square crestrail & matching lower rail flanked by turned tapering back leg stiles & forming a two-section back w/seven slender turned spindles in each section, open turned arms above the two-part early splint seat above six heavy turned legs, original red paint, New England, mid-19th c., imperfections, 34 1/4" l., 17" h. (ILLUS.) **460**

Mirrors

Art Nouveau wall mirror, carved hardwood, rectangular w/the wide flat crestrail centered by a large applied carved cluster of two pine cone-shaped fruits & leaves, curved sides w/pointed ears at the top & long carved vines forming the edges ending in large fruit & leaf clusters at each bottom corner, brass liner & rectangular beveled mirror, ca. 1900, 27 x 41".. **385**

Chippendale wall mirror, carved mahogany, the arched & scroll-cut pediment flanked by shaped ears above a molded frame w/cusped upper corners enclosing a rectangular mirror, a scrolled pendant base w/scrolled ears, the backboard w/printed paper label of John Elliott, Jr., Philadelphia, 1796-1803, 32 3/4 x 45"..... **12,650**

Fine Chippendale Mirror with Phoenix

Chippendale wall mirror, mahogany, the arched & scroll-cut crest centering a pierced & gilded carved phoenix flanked by scrolled ears above a rectangular & gilt-carved liner w/cusped upper corners enclosing a mirror, scroll-shaped base, American or English, late 18th c., 20 1/4 x 36 1/2" (ILLUS.).............................. **4,025**

Chippendale Mahogany Wall Mirror

Chippendale wall mirror, mahogany veneer & giltwood, the high arched scrolled & pierced crest w/a central gilded Hoho bird above a molded & parcel-gilt molding surrounding the mirror plate, deep scroll-cut pendant base, old surface, minor repairs, probably England, 18th c., 31 1/4" h. (ILLUS.).. **1,093**

Chippendale wall mirror, walnut & giltwood, the wide arched crest ornately scroll-cut & centered by a round opening enclosing a giltwood foliate device, tall

rectangular mirror plate w/rounded top corners & gilt incised liner, scroll-cut ears & apron at the bottom, old refinish, England, ca. 1750-70, 25 1/2" w., 45" h. (imperfections)... **6,900**

Chippendale-Style Wall Mirror

Chippendale-Style wall mirror, curly maple, the high & elaborately scroll-cut crest flanked by ears above a rectangular molding enclosing the mirror, deep scroll-cut base drop & ears, old mellow finish, early 20th c., one ear cracked, one small piece missing, 21 x 45" (ILLUS.) **660**

Classical overmantel mirror, gilt gesso, the egg-and-dart molded cornice above a frieze of oak leaves & acorns, the tri-part mirror glass outlined by black reeded liner w/rosettes at top frame corners, half-engaged ring-turned acanthus leaf columns, New England, ca. 1825, 55" l., 33" h. (regilding, imperfections) **1,265**

Classical Giltwood Pier Mirror

Classical pier mirror, giltwood, the rectangular divided mirror plate surrounded by flattened & partially reeded pilasters w/bold carved fleur-de-lis corner mounts, second quarter 19th c., 34 1/2 x 62" (ILLUS.) **2,300**

Classical wall mirror, painted & decorated wood, the rectangular narrow frame composed of knob- and rod-turned half-round columns painted in alternating black & gold w/corner blocks w/applied florettes, a tall rectangular mirror plate below an upper reverse-painted square glass plate decorated w/an elegant seated Empire period lady wearing a long dress, shawl & turban & framed w/large swagged draperies within a stenciled polychrome leaf border band, ca. 1830-40, 16 x 32" **578**

Early European Courting Mirror

Courting wall mirror, a wide rectangular molded frame w/a high stepped & rounded crest w/hanging hole, the framework encloses narrow panels of reverse-painted glass, the mirror plate w/a border of delicate scrolls, leaf springs & a small leaping stag at the bottom center, Northern Europe, late 18th c., imperfections, 11 1/4 x 18 1/2" (ILLUS.)............................. **3,738**

Federal country-style wall mirror, pine, molded flat top w/blocked corners above reeded side pilasters to lower corner blocks joined to a reeded lower rail, original upper reverse-painted glass panel showing the steam paddlewheeler "Ohio," good color, old refinished pine frame, early 19th c. (pieced cornice repairs)... **605**

Federal Mahogany Dressing Mirror

Federal dressing mirror, mahogany & mahogany veneer, the shield-form mirror in a conforming veneered frame w/string-inlaid edges flanked by scrolled & incised supports w/ringed bosses at the terminals, on stepped & shaped trestle feet joined by incised shaped stretcher, old finish, imperfections, label of I. Richman, New York City, late 18th - early 19th c., 8 3/4 x 14", 21 1/4" h. (ILLUS.) **1,265**

Federal Decorated Wall Mirror

Federal wall mirror, gilt gesso, the flat molded crestrail w/stepped-out block ends above a band of applied spherules above a large reverse-painted tablet showing a woman w/a spyglass surrounded by a silver & white border, the rectangular mirror below, the sides w/half-round engaged turned columns, back w/label of James Todd, Portland, Maine, ca. 1825, tablet cracked (ILLUS.)...... **920**

Federal wall mirror, giltwood, a narrow molded cornice over applied spherules & a rectangular narrow frame enclosing an upper églomisé tablet painted w/a large basket of fruit below swagged drapery above the rectangular mirror panel flanked by applied spiral rope carvings, square molded base, tablet, gilding & mirror appear to be original, Boston, 1810-20, 13 1/2 x 28 1/2" (imperfections) **1,610**

Federal wall mirror, giltwood, a narrow rectangular cornice w/stepped-out corners above a band of small spherules over an églomisé panel decorated w/a central almond-shaped reserve w/a basket of flowers surrounded by a diamond-lattice design & flanked by blocks w/small molded trophies, slender half-round pilasters down the sides flanking the mirror, narrow bottom rail w/corner blocks, probably English, early 19th c., 30 x 47"........................ **1,840**

Federal wall mirror, giltwood, a narrow rectangular projecting molded cornice w/fourteen spherules over a rectangular églomisé tablet showing an American & British ship battling within a marbleized border & above the rectangular mirror, all in a narrow molded frame flanked by ropetwist carving, old gilt surface & mirror, apparently original tablet, probably Massachusetts, ca. 1815, 21 1/4 x 32 1/4" (minor imperfections)..................................... **2,530**

Federal wall mirror, inlaid mahogany & parcel-gilt, the scrolled cresting w/rosette terminals centering an urn of flowers above an oval inlaid conch shell, the rectangular string-inlaid frame w/gilt-incised borders & flanking fillets above scrolled pendant, refinished, New York, ca. 1800, 20 x 51" (regilding, imperfections) **9,775**

Victorian cheval mirror, Aesthetic Movement substyle, oak, a tall rectangular narrow reeded mirror frame topped by a half-round high pierced crest w/a band of circles & bars set w/two green 'jewels' above an arch of four small spindles, the mirror frame w/bulbous pointed corner finials & swiveling between tall slender columns w/small urn finials, raised on a trestle base w/a wide band of spindles joining the arched legs on casters, ca. 1880-90, 26" w., 73" h. **2,408**

Victorian Faux Bamboo Cheval Mirror

Victorian faux bamboo cheval mirror, maple, a beveled tall rectangular mirror swiveling between faux bamboo stiles surmounted by a delicate pierced crest w/turned spindles centering roundels, a band of faux bamboo spindles across the bottom frame, outswept faux bamboo legs, late 19th c., 30 1/2 x 71" h. (ILLUS.).. **6,325**

Victorian pier mirror, Aesthetic Movement substyle, walnut & burl walnut, tall narrow form, the top w/a dentil rail above a pierced & leafy scroll-carved crestrail flanked by pointed finials above a coved cornice w/zigzag incised band above carved blocks & long narrow burl panels down the sides, the base w/a stepped-out central block w/square white marble top above a carved bracket panel flanked by raised panels carved w/drop clusters of leaves, molded conforming base, ca. 1890, carving picked out in gold paint, 29 3/4" w., 100" h. **660**

Fine Renaissance Revival Mirror

Victorian Renaissance Revival overmantel mirror, giltwood, the crestrail carved w/a raised central female mask on an acanthus-topped shield flanked by husk swags, blocked top corners w/palmettes above a raised frieze molding over the large gently arched mirror flanked by block & columnar sides above a molded flat base, w/a marble support shelf, third quarter 19th c., 56" w., 79" h. (ILLUS.)...... **3,335**

Renaissance Revival Wall Mirror

Victorian Renaissance Revival wall mirror, walnut, the deep molded shadowbox frame w/a wide arched top & flat base, a scroll-carved crest centered by a carved leaf & cone cluster, scroll brackets at the bottom corners, gilt liner, ca. 1870, 24" w., 48" h. (ILLUS.)..................................... **560**

Parlor Suites

Rare Art Deco Parlor Suite

Art Deco: settee & two armchairs; carved giltwood & upholstery, arched crestrail on the settee above high rolled upholstered arms w/reeded arm supports continuing to form the front legs, barrel-back armchairs w/matching legs, cushion seats, molded seatrails, attributed to Paul Follot, France, ca. 1920s, settee 62" l. (ILLUS.).. **31,625**

Art Nouveau: settee, two armchairs & two side chairs; Fougères patt., carved mahogany, each piece w/a high back w/a downcurved crestrail w/peaked corners pierce-carved w/a lattice leaf design & continuing down to form the back frame enclosing the upholstered back, the outswept closed arms w/curved lattice-carved arm supports continuing into the squared, gently curved front legs w/further carving, serpentine front seatrail, Louis Majorelle, France, ca. 1900, settee 55" l., the set **27,600**

Three-piece Thonet Bentwood Set

Bentwood: rocking chair w/arms, side chair & armchair; each w/a rounded rectangular back enclosing a horizontal backrail pierced w/circular cut-outs, above vertical slats & a D-shaped seat, the armchair & side chair branded "Thonet," Model No. 511, Austria, early 20th c., side chair 39" h., the set (ILLUS.) **2,300**

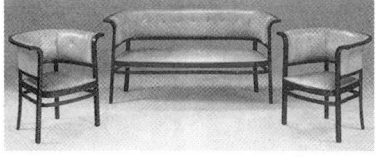

Early Bentwood Parlor Suite

Bentwood: settee & two armchairs; each w/a flared back of continuous form w/rolled crestrail, the padded bentwood frame above a cushioned seat, the legs joined by

hoop stretcher, upholstered in camel-colored leather, attributed to Marcel Kammerer, for Thonet of Austria, ca. 1906, settee 68 1/4" l., the set (ILLUS.) **5,875**

Empire-Style: settee & a pair of open-arm armchairs; ormolu-mounted mahogany, each w/an upright squared panel back w/gently rolled stiles joined by a narrow crestrail w/ormolu mounts, downswept arms w/further mounts on incurved arm supports, upholstered back panel & seat, the seatrail w/a central long leaf spring mount & corner rosettes atop the square tapering legs w/ormolu paw feet, France, ca. 1890, settee 54 1/2" l., the set **6,463**

Louis XV-Style: settee & four open-arm armchairs; giltwood, each w/a needlepoint upholstered back panel surrounded by a squared serpentine giltwood frame w/molded corner scrolls & central leafy floral bands & a central cluster, padded open arms w/leaf-molded incurved arm supports above the wide needlepoint upholstered seat, molded serpentine seat-rail w/central floral clusters & simple cabriole legs w/leafy scroll feet, France, ca. 1880, settee 67" l., the set.... **15,275**

Louis XVI-Style: settee, two open-arm armchairs, four side chairs; giltwood, each piece w/a molded oval medallion back w/a ribbon-twist design & a ribbon bow top crest upholstered in floral needlepoint & raised on short stiles above wide rounded needlepoint spring seats, the arms w/upholstered pads & downswept carved arm supports, on reeded tapering round legs ending in peg feet, needlepoint w/red, white & pink roses w/yellow tulips & leaves on a cream ground, France, late 19th - early 20th c., the set (minor wear)..................................... **2,145**

Louis XVI-Style Giltwood Parlor Suite

Louis XVI-Style: settee & two open-arm armchairs; giltwood, each w/a raised tapestry upholstered back panel w/a gently arched crestrail w/twisted ribbon band centered by a small wreath crest above matching slightly canted side stiles, padded gently curved arms on incurved leaf-carved arm supports above the wide tapestry upholstered seat, curved seatrail w/narrow roundel band, on turned & tapering reeded & carved legs, France, second half 19th c., settee 52" l., the set (ILLUS.) **8,500**

Victorian Egyptian Revival Armchair

Victorian Egyptian Revival: triple-back sofa, armchair & two side chairs; carved walnut, each gently arched crestrail set w/a patinated-metal plaque depicting classical figures & flanked by carved ears above the tapering tufted upholstered back panel, the arms terminating in carved Egyptian busts, curved seatrail centered by a half-round plaque, ring-turned & tapering front legs on casters, canted rear legs, third quarter 19th c., the set (ILLUS. of armchair) **6,038**

Victorian Golden Oak substyle: settee, low-arm chair & armchair; oak, each w/a low arched crestrail carved w/central scrolls framed by carved gadrooning above an upholstered back, shaped molded open arms ending in carved lions' heads on incurved arm supports, upholstered spring seat, flat molded seat-rail, heavy cabriole front legs ending in large paw feet on casters, reupholstered in burgundy vevlet, ca. 1900, settee 51" l., the set **1,650**

Victorian Renaissance Revival: pair of 64" l. settees, armchair, & four side chairs; walnut w/parcel-gilt & patinated metal mounts, the settee w/double oval-shaped upholstered back panels flanking a large central upright oval medallion w/a carved Grecian woman's profile, all matching frames carved w/elongated leaftips & acorn back finials, deep upholstered spring seats, tapering trumpet-form front legs on casters, incised gilt decoration, attributed to Pottier and Stymus, New York, 1865-75, the set **6,900**

Victorian Renaissance Revival: sofa, armchair & two side chairs; ormolu-mounted rosewood, the armchair w/carved & gilded crest above an upholstered back flanked by incised gilt column stiles headed by turned finials, padded arms fronted by applied ormolu putti & acanthus leaves above an over-upholstered seat, on turned tapering front legs on casters, the sofa w/a three-part upholstered back w/an arched, gilt-trimmed crestrail flanked by ormolu female busts,

side chairs similar to armchair, New York City, ca. 1880, sofa 72" l., the set **2,990**

Ornate Renaissance Revival Armchair

Victorian Renaissance Revival: sofa, gentleman's chair & lady's chair; carved & gilt-incised rosewood, oval tufted upholstered back medallions topped by a high peaked & pierce-carved crest of scrolls centering a bust, the high outswept stiles ending in ornate turned ears, curved padded open arms w/female busts carved on the arm supports, deep rounded upholstered seat on a conforming seatrail, raised on tapering ring-turned front legs on casters, canted rear legs on casters, attributed to John Jelliff, ca. 1875, the set (ILLUS. of gentleman's chair) **6,160**

Victorian Renaissance Revival: sofa & three armchairs; carved walnut, each piece w/a long narrow crestrail centered by a high arched center crest carved at the top w/a bust of a Classical woman above a roundel & flanked by curved pierced side swags, each rounded corner carved w/a down-curved projecting scroll w/drop, rectangular upholstered backs, two chairs w/lower backs & one w/a tall back, the long sofa back curving to form rolled upholstered arms w/pendant-carved arm supports, spring upholstered seats on burl-paneled seatrails, raised on turned trumpet-form front legs on casters, John Jelliff, ca. 1870, the set **3,920**

Elaborate Victorian Rococo Sofa

Victorian Rococo substyle: sofa, armchair & slipper chair; carved rosewood, the serpentine-back sofa w/a high pierce-carved crestrail of ornate fruiting grapevines centered by a large fruit cluster center crest, rounded sides continuing down to the half-arms w/molded serpentine arm supports, serpentine seatrail w/molded & leaf-carved reserves continuing into the demi-cabriole legs on casters, canted rear legs on casters, ca. 1855, 71" l., the set (ILLUS. of the sofa) **17,250**

One of a Pair of Rococo Sofas

Victorian Rococo substyle: two sofas & three chairs; carved rosewood, the triple-back sofa w/a high fruit- and flower-carved center crest & smaller carved crests at each end continuing to spiral-carved side rails above the padded half-arms w/incurved spiral-carved arm supports, serpentine seatrail w/central carved reserve, demi-cabriole front legs on casters, canted rear legs on casters, ca. 1860, the set (ILLUS. of one sofa).. **7,560**

Screens

French Art Deco Firescreen

Firescreen, Art Deco, wrought iron, an upright square frame centered by a vining flowering plant composed of tightly scrolled leafy branches ending in blos-

soms, an outer border band of thin bars accented w/small C-scrolls & w/a large flowerhead in each corner, on short curved feet, in the manner of Paul Kiss, France, ca. 1925, 34" w., 40 1/2" h. (ILLUS.) **6,900**

Fine Early Classical Firescreen

Firescreen, Classical, carved rosewood veneer & grained giltwood, a central large rectangular black ground floral needlepoint panel set in a frame w/simulated brass inlay & flanked by faux rosewood columns w/brass capitals & bases above gilded acanthus leaves on curving legs ending in brass paw feet on casters, Boston, 1815, surface imperfections, 18 x 24", 38 1/4" h. (ILLUS.)..................... **32,200**

Art Nouveau Pyrography Screen

Folding screen, three-fold, Art Nouveau, pyrographic-decorated oak, each oak-framed panel divided into three sections w/the top section pierced w/leafy landscape scenes above red, green & gilt-painted decoration of birds & cascading foliage, the reverse w/fabric, heavy wear to fabric, paint wear, American, early 20th c., 73" w., 63 1/4" h. (ILLUS.) **403**

Ornate Carved Baroque Revival Screen

Folding screen, three-fold, Baroque Revival style, walnut, the center panel pierced & carved w/a female caryatid beneath a pair of flowerheads, the lower section w/a standing female figure, all amid elaborate foliage, the side panels pierced & carved w/urns issuing flowers & foliage above the lower panel carved w/medallions, the central mythological mask-form crest flanked by cartouche crests, raised on opposing lion-form feet, late 19th c., each panel 21" w., 73 1/8" h. (ILLUS.) **3,450**

English Regency Folding Screen

Folding screen, three-fold, Regency style, walnut & ebonized wood, each walnut crossbanded & molded ebonized framework panel fitted w/a pleated green silk insert, England, second quarter 19th c., each panel 24 1/2" w., 53 1/2" h. (ILLUS.) **2,070**

Folding screen, four-fold, lacquer & cloth, each section w/a black lacquer frame w/gilt trim & a stepped crestrail above a rectangular panel painted w/a scene of an Oriental temple, each panel fitted w/printed fabric w/tall Chinese landscape scenes in browns, grey & salmon, China, late 19th - early 20th c., each panel 27" w., 74 1/2" h. **413**

Louis XVI-Style Folding Screen

Folding screen, four-fold, Louis XVI-Style, giltwood, each panel w/a carved giltwood frame w/foliate-scrolled crest & a lower floral- and scroll-decorated silk panel, France, early 20th c., each panel 19" w., 65" h. (ILLUS.) **1,380**

Piero Fornesetti Modern Screen

Folding screen, four-fold, Modern style, each panel w/a mottled cream-colored ground transfer-printed in black & white w/long detailed pendant Renaissance-style trophies, designed by Piero Fornesetti, Italy, ca. 1955, 56" w. (ILLUS.) **6,900**

Art Deco Eight-Panel Walnut Screen

Fig. 1

Fig. 2

Fig. 4

Fig. 5

Fig. 3

Fig. 6

Fig. 7

Fig. 1 Sunrise Beer serving tray $182
Courtesy of Fink's Off The Wall Auctions,
Lansdale, Pennsylvania.

Fig. 2 Congress Beer serving tray $181
Courtesy of Fink's Off The Wall Auctions,
Lansdale, Pennsylvania.

Fig. 3 Little sad iron with wooden grip,
marked with number "9" in star, J. & E.
Stevens Co., 3¼" l $80
Courtesy of Jimmy Walker, Waelder, Texas.

Fig. 4 Loyl Coffee 1 lb. screw-top
can, 4 x 6" $275
Courtesy of Past Tyme Pleasures,
San Ramon, California.

Fig. 5 Monadnock 1 lb. Peanut Butter
can with bail handle $198
Courtesy of Past Tyme Pleasures,
San Ramon, California.

Fig. 6 Little wood grip iron marked
"White City Sad Iron," 3½" l. $225
Courtesy of Jimmy Walker, Waelder, Texas.

Fig. 7 Little box iron, brass with
wooden handle, ox-tongue style,
single post, 3" l $500
Courtesy of Jimmy Walker, Waelder, Texas.

Fig. 8

Fig. 9

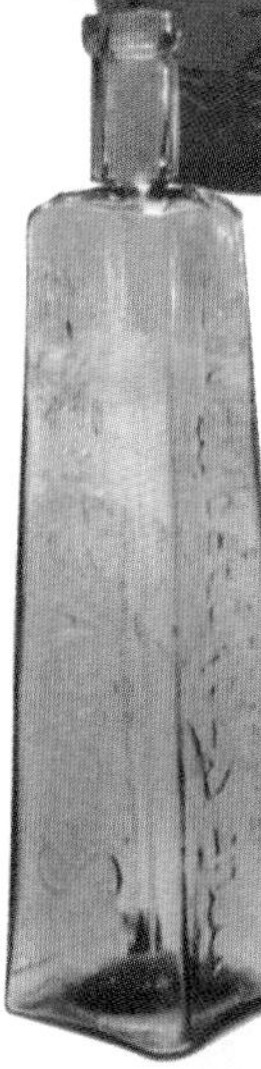

Fig. 10

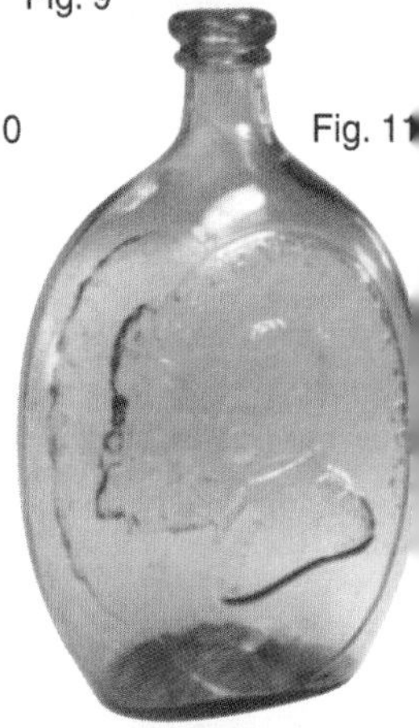

Fig. 11

Fig. 8 Left: Drake's Plantation Bitters bottle, light golden olive, D-102 . . . . . $1,200 Right: Drake's Plantation Bitters bottle, reddish amber, D-102 . . . . $120
Courtesy of Pacific Glass Auctions, Sacramento, California.

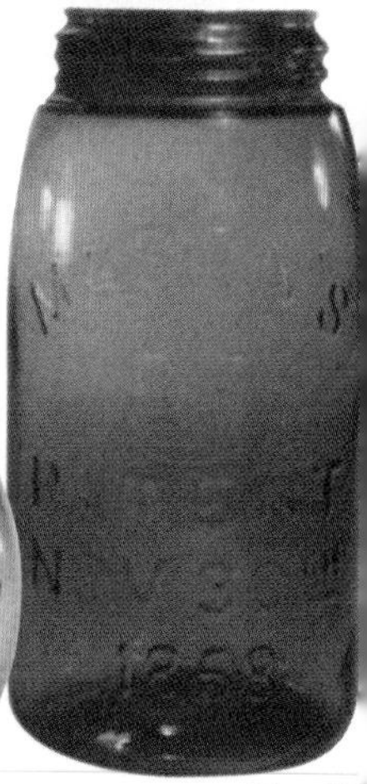

Fig. 9 Left: I. Sutton & Co Covington, KY early cobalt blue root beer bottle, ca. 1850 . . . . $500 Right: H. Nash & Co. Root Beer Cincinnati cobalt blue bottle, mid-19th c. $1,000
Courtesy of Pacific Glass Auctions, Sacramento, California.

Fig. 10 Tall tapering square yellowish green bottle for "The Sherry Iron Co. Stockton Cal Sherry & Iron - The Standard Tonic," 11¼" h. $1,300
Courtesy of Pacific Glass Auctions, Sacramento, California

Fig. 11 Washington-Taylor historical flask, brilliant emerald green, GI-42. . . . . $375
Courtesy of Pacific Glass Auctions, Sacramento, California.

Fig. 12 Emerald green Jenny Lind calabash flask, quart, GI-99 . . . . $950
Courtesy of Pacific Glass Auctions, Sacramento, California.

Fig. 13 Medium amber Mason's Patent Nov. 30th 1858 fruit jar, number "101" on base, metal lid $1,000
Courtesy of Pacific Glass Auctions, Sacramento, California

Fig. 12

Fig. 13

Fig. 14

Fig. 15

Fig. 16

Fig. 17

Fig. 18

Fig. 19

Fig. 14 China shoulder head 'covered wagon' lady doll with brown eyes & molded side curls, 30" h........... $1,350
Courtesy of McMasters Doll Auctions, Cambridge, Ohio.

Fig. 15 Madame Alexander "Sonja Henie" character doll with composition head, brown sleep eyes & original hairdo wearing original red skating dress, 17" h. $625
Courtesy of McMasters Doll Auctions, Cambridge, Ohio.

Fig. 16 Bisque socket head Steiner Le Parisien doll, 16½" h. $3,400
Courtesy of McMasters Doll Auctions, Cambridge, Ohio.

Fig. 17 Madame Alexander "Judy" doll with composition head, amber sleep eyes, original elaborate mohair wig & wearing detailed outfit, 21" h. $2,500
Courtesy of McMasters Doll Auctions, Cambridge, Ohio.

Fig. 18 Armand Marseille bisque socket head girl with replaced human hair wig, 42" h. $800
Courtesy of McMasters Doll Auctions, Cambridge, Ohio.

Fig. 19 Stockinette head "Beecher Baby" doll with painted & needle-sculptured features, 20" h......... $2,000
Courtesy of McMasters Doll Auctions, Cambridge, Ohio.

Fig. 20

Fig. 22

Fig. 21

Fig. 23

Fig. 20 Rare three-fold counter-top display for "Old Gold Cigarettes," featuring Babe Ruth batting, 38 x 52", 1930s. $32,766
Courtesy of Mastro Fine Sports Auctions, Oak Brook, Illinois.

Fig. 21 1962 Cliff Hagan All-Star Game-worn uniform $1,530
Courtesy of Leland's, New York, New York.

Fig. 22 Early 1960s Roger Maris miniature bobbing-head figure with original box, 5" h. $843
Courtesy of Leland's, New York, New York.

Fig. 23 Rare 1908 Johnson vs. Burns boxing contest program, Sydney, Australia . . $6,780
Courtesy of Mastro Fine Sports Auctions, Oak Brook, Illinois.

Fig. 24 Original 1885 advertising poster for "Spalding's Official Base Ball Guide," with large image of early batter, 17¼ x 22⅛" $5,604
Courtesy of Leland's, New York, New York.

Fig. 24

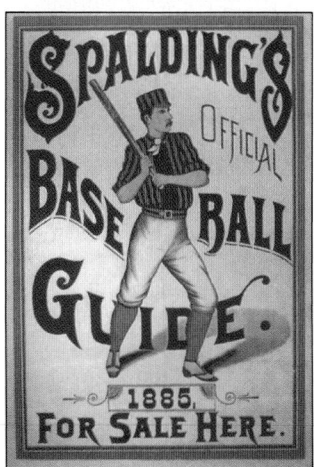

Fig. 25

Fig. 26

Fig. 27

Fig. 28

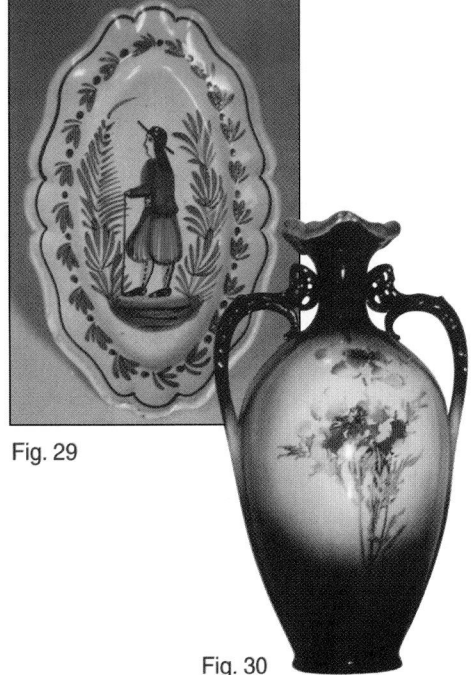

Fig. 29

Fig. 25 Royal Doulton large toby jug of
Captain Hook, D 6597 . . . . $575
Courtesy of Reg Morris, Chesterland, Ohio.

Fig. 26 Lefton China bisque finish figure
group of bluebirds on tree branch with
wooden base, No. 655, 9½" h. $110
Courtesy of Loretta DeLozier,
Knoxville, Tennessee.

Fig. 27 Lefton China figural kitten "Cuddles"
napkin holder, No. 1452, 5" h. $20
Courtesy of Loretta DeLozier,
Knoxville, Tennessee.

Fig. 28 Royal Doulton large toby jug of
George Washington/King George III,
D 6749 . . . . $175
Courtesy of Reg Morris, Chesterland, Ohio.

Fig. 29 Quimper Pottery oval platter in the
"Faience Populaire" pattern, scalloped
border, 7¼ x 11¾", unsigned, 19th c. . . $160
Courtesy of Sandra Bondhus,
Unionville, Connecticut.

Fig. 30 Warwick China ovoid vase with flared
neck & ornate scrolled handles, Bonnie
shape, color florals on a brown shading to
yellow ground, 10¼" h. $290
Courtesy of Don Hoffmann, Aurora, Illinois.

Fig. 30

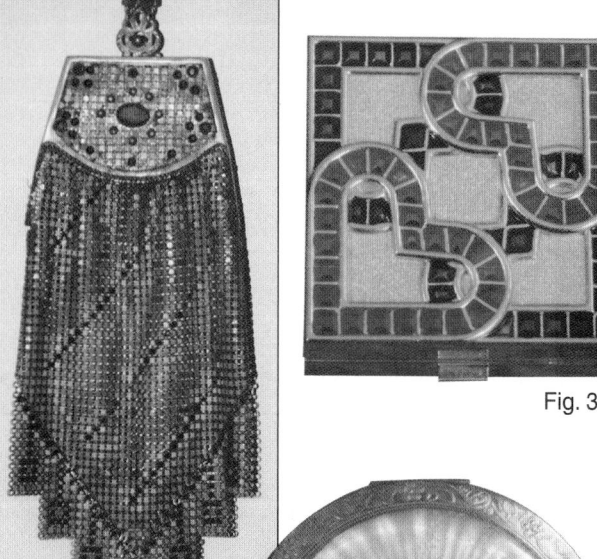

Fig. 33

Fig. 31

Fig. 32

Fig. 34

Fig. 31 Enameled mesh purse with blue & green designs on white, ornate frame with enameled medallion & two blue stones, Mandalian Mfg. Co., 4½ x 9½" $350
Courtesy of Ellen Bercovici, Bethesda, Maryland.

Fig. 32 Enameled mesh purse with compact top closure set with stones. Top opens to powder & puff compartment, unmarked $500
Courtesy of Ellen Bercovici, Bethesda, Maryland.

Fig. 33 Square goldtone metal compact with the lid decorated with red & blue enameled hearts, interior with framed mirror & puff, Princess Marcella Borghese, 2" w. $55
Courtesy of Roselyn Gerson, Lynbrook, New York.

Fig. 34 Round goldtone metal compact with the lid decorated with enameled goldfish under a plastic dome, Melissa, England, 2¾" d. $75
Courtesy of Roselyn Gerson, Lynbrook, New York.

Fig. 35 Elegant bi-colored 18k yellow & white gold handbag with fitted accessories, Italian hallmarks. . $4,600
Courtesy of Antiquorum Auctioneers, New York, New York.

Fig. 35

Fig. 37

Fig. 36

Fig. 38

Fig. 39

Fig. 40

Fig. 36 Large framed advertisement for "The Union Metallic Cartridge Co., Bridgeport, Conn., U.S.A.," illustrating their various cartridges & a naval scene, 1898, ... $4,125
Courtesy of Past Tyme Pleasures, San Ramon, California.

Fig. 37 White House Coffee flange-type tin sign, early 20th century $4,300
Courtesy of Daniel Auction Company, Sylvester, Georgia.

Fig. 38 Late 18th century pieced & quilted linsey-woolsey coverlet, 84½ x 92" $14,950
Courtesy of Skinner, Inc., Bolton, Massachusetts.

Fig. 39 Framed Ribbon Doll wearing bright yellow ribbon dress with gold threads, silk thread hair, lace pantaloons & holding a lace & velvet floral bouquet, 11½" h. $60-75
Courtesy of Bobbie Zucker Bryson, Tuckahoe, New York.

Fig. 40 Advertising cardboard die-cut of 1890s Santa Claus for "Ayer's Cherry Pectoral" $1,155
Courtesy of Past Tyme Pleasures, San Ramon, California.

Fig. 41 Early 20th century comic leather postcard $5
Courtesy of Susan Eberman, Bedford, Indiana.

Fig. 41

Fig. 43

Fig. 44

Fig. 45

Fig. 42 Original 1941 "The Maltese Falcon" movie poster featuring Humphrey Bogart & Mary Astor, one-sheet $9,183
Courtesy of Mastro Fine Sports Auctions, Oak Brook, Illinois.

Fig. 43 Tiffany "Nasturtium" table lamp with 22" d. shade, base & shade signed $72,800
Courtesy of John Fontaine Gallery, Pittsfield, Massachusetts.

Fig. 44 Victorian kerosene hanging parlor lamp by Miller, embossed brass frame, hand-painted floral-decorated shade & font, 15" d. . . . $784
Courtesy of Jackson's Auctioneers, Cedar Falls, Iowa.

Fig. 45 Handel geometric leaded glass 22" d. shade on Handel bronzed metal base $9,520
Courtesy of John Fontaine Gallery, Pittsfield, Massachusetts.

Fig. 46 Rare 1952 calendar titled "Dame & Dane" featuring Norma Jean Baker (Marilyn Monroe), 7½ x 11½" $686
Courtesy of Mastro Fine Sports Auctions, Oak Brook, Illinois.

Fig. 42

Fig. 46

Fig. 47

Fig. 48

Fig. 49

Fig. 50

Fig. 47 Elvis Presley autographed
record album for movie "Kid
Galahad," 1963, RCA/Victor $1,205
Courtesy of Leland's, New York, New York

Fig. 48 Near mint No. 1 Ponytail
Barbie with original box & outfit $8,700
Courtesy of McMasters Doll Auctions,
Cambridge, Ohio.

Fig. 49 Early Beatles felt banner
circa 1964, made in Canada, 21" l. . . . $383
Courtesy of Leland's, New York, New York.

Fig. 50 Arvin early 1950s Hopalong
Cassidy radio with red & silver front
& black case & trim, near mint $1,455
Courtesy of Leland's, New York, New York.

Fig. 51 Hopalong Cassidy movie
poster for "Forty Thieves," 1940s,
27 x 41". $616
Courtesy of Leland's, New York, New York.

Fig. 51

Fig. 55

Fig. 54

Fig. 53

Fig. 52

Fig. 52 Ceramic "Emperor" hand-made clothes sprinkler bottle by Holland Mold $150
Courtesy of Ellen Bercovici, Bethesda, Maryland.

Fig. 53 Ceramic "Merry Maid" clothes sprinkler bottle, ca. 1950s $50
Courtesy of Ellen Bercovici, Bethesda, Maryland.

Fig. 54 Halloween candy container featuring papier-mâché pumpkin man on low round base with plaid decoration, ca. 1930s, Germany $250
Courtesy of Ellen Bercovici, Bethesda, Maryland.

Fig. 56

Fig. 55 Halloween lantern, papier-mâché black cat head with green paper eye inserts & red paper mouth insert, black & orange fence-form base, ca. 1940-50, U.S.A., mint . . $300
Courtesy of Ellen Bercovici, Bethesda, Maryland.

Fig. 56 Halloween lantern, papier-mâché Jack-o'-lantern with red & black trim & paper eye, nose & mouth inserts, Germany, ca. 1920 . . $275
Courtesy of Ellen Bercovici, Bethesda, Maryland.

Fig. 57 Halloween tambourine, lithographed tin with head of scary witch, T. Cohn, U.S.A., ca. 1950s $95
Courtesy of Ellen Bercovici, Bethesda, Maryland.

Fig. 57

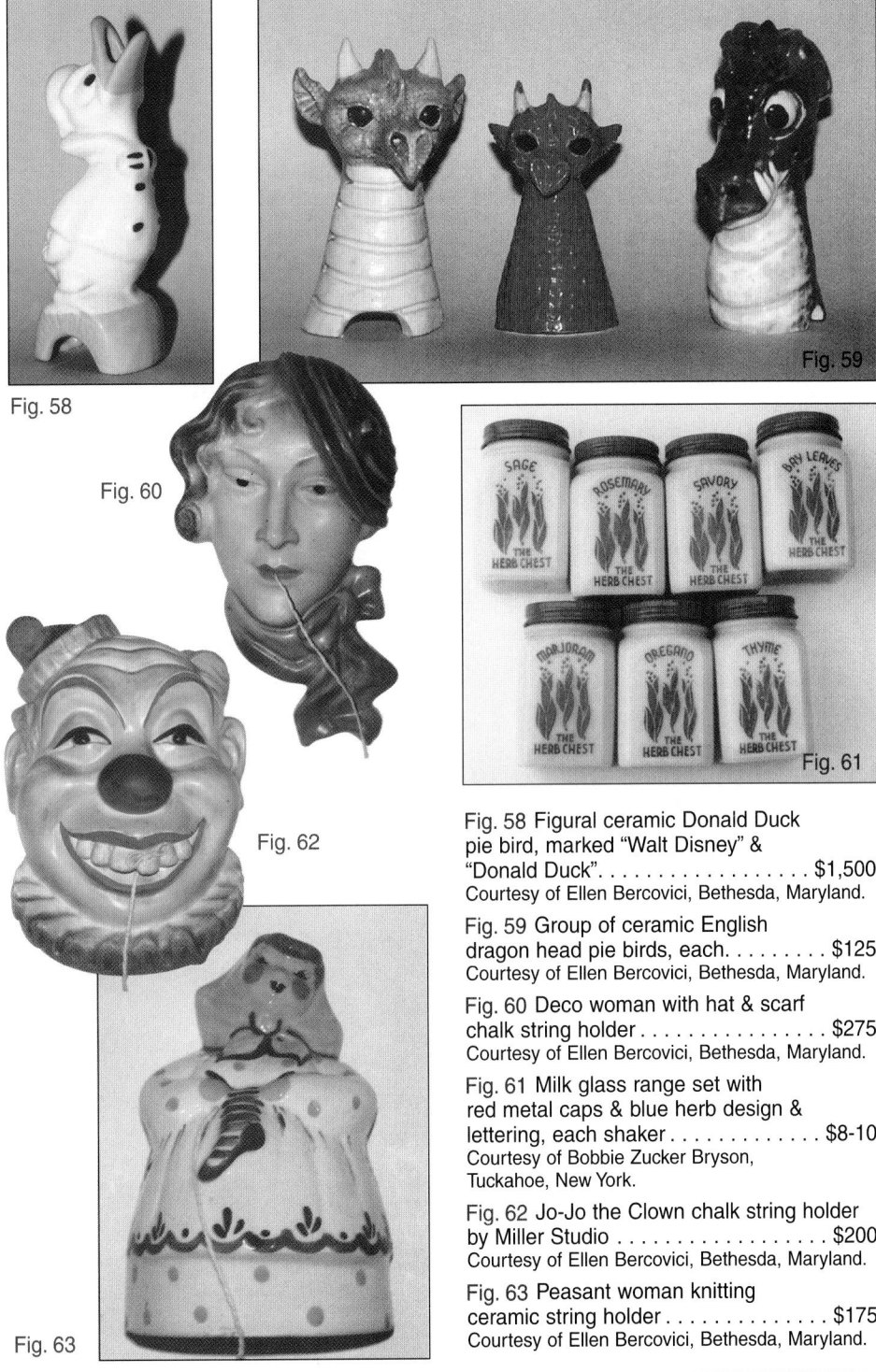

Fig. 58

Fig. 59

Fig. 60

Fig. 61

Fig. 62

Fig. 63

Fig. 58 Figural ceramic Donald Duck
pie bird, marked "Walt Disney" &
"Donald Duck". $1,500
Courtesy of Ellen Bercovici, Bethesda, Maryland.

Fig. 59 Group of ceramic English
dragon head pie birds, each. $125
Courtesy of Ellen Bercovici, Bethesda, Maryland.

Fig. 60 Deco woman with hat & scarf
chalk string holder $275
Courtesy of Ellen Bercovici, Bethesda, Maryland.

Fig. 61 Milk glass range set with
red metal caps & blue herb design &
lettering, each shaker $8-10
Courtesy of Bobbie Zucker Bryson,
Tuckahoe, New York.

Fig. 62 Jo-Jo the Clown chalk string holder
by Miller Studio $200
Courtesy of Ellen Bercovici, Bethesda, Maryland.

Fig. 63 Peasant woman knitting
ceramic string holder $175
Courtesy of Ellen Bercovici, Bethesda, Maryland.

Fig. 65

Fig. 66

Fig. 64

Fig. 64 Figural lipstick holder girl
seated at a dressing table $75
Courtesy of Ellen Bercovici, Bethesda, Maryland.

Fig. 65 Left: novelty figural ceramic
salt & pepper shakers of American
Indians in drum, nodder heads,
Japan, pr. $65
Right: novelty figural ceramic salt
& pepper shakers with mice in
cheese, nodder heads, "Say
Cheese," by Fitz & Floyd, Japan,
1980, pr. $300-350.
Courtesy of the T. Nader Collection.

Fig. 66 Half-figure girl lipstick holder
with blond hair & green gown, low
basket held in front, paper sticker
reads "M'Lady's Valet - by Enesco" $50
Courtesy of Ellen Bercovici, Bethesda, Maryland.

Fig. 67

Fig. 67 Ceramic napkin doll lady
with dark skin & wavy black hair
standing with her arms behind her
back & wearing a long light green
gown, marked "Holland Mold,"
6¾" h. $95-115
Courtesy of Bobbie Zucker Bryson,
Tuckahoe, New York.

Fig. 68 Tall ceramic napkin doll of
a woman wearing yellow gown &
holding a green toothpick tray,
Japan, 9¾" h. $75-95
Courtesy of Bobbie Zucker Bryson,
Tuckahoe, New York.

Fig. 68

Fig. 69 Figural lipstick holder girl
with black hair & wearing a peach-
colored gown with embossed flowers . . . $55
Courtesy of Ellen Bercovici, Bethesda, Maryland.

Fig. 69

Fig. 70

Fig. 71

Fig. 72

Fig. 73

Fig. 74

Fig. 75

Fig. 70 Fry opalescent glass
one-piece reamer with tab & loop
handle, 6¼" d. $20-30
Courtesy of Bobbie Zucker Bryson,
Tuckahoe, New York.

Fig. 71 Ceramic figural egg timer with
standing bears, Goebel, Germany $125
Courtesy of Ellen Bercovici, Bethesda, Maryland.

Fig. 72 Black glass wall pocket with
textured body molded with leaves,
berries & a bird painted in red,
black & gold, 7 x 7¾" $75-100
Courtesy of Bobbie Zucker Bryson,
Tuckahoe, New York.

Fig. 73 Ceramic figural clown reamer
pot with reamer cone hat, 6" h. $65-85
Courtesy of Bobbie Zucker Bryson,
Tuckahoe, New York.

Fig. 74 Amber glass wall pocket
with conical branch & leaf body &
overhead branch handle, 4 x 6½" . . . $65-95
Courtesy of Bobbie Zucker Bryson,
Tuckahoe, New York.

Fig. 75 Ceramic figural egg timer with
kneeling Native American wearing a
painted headdress & holding up timer,
marked "Germany". $125
Courtesy of Ellen Bercovici, Bethesda, Maryland.

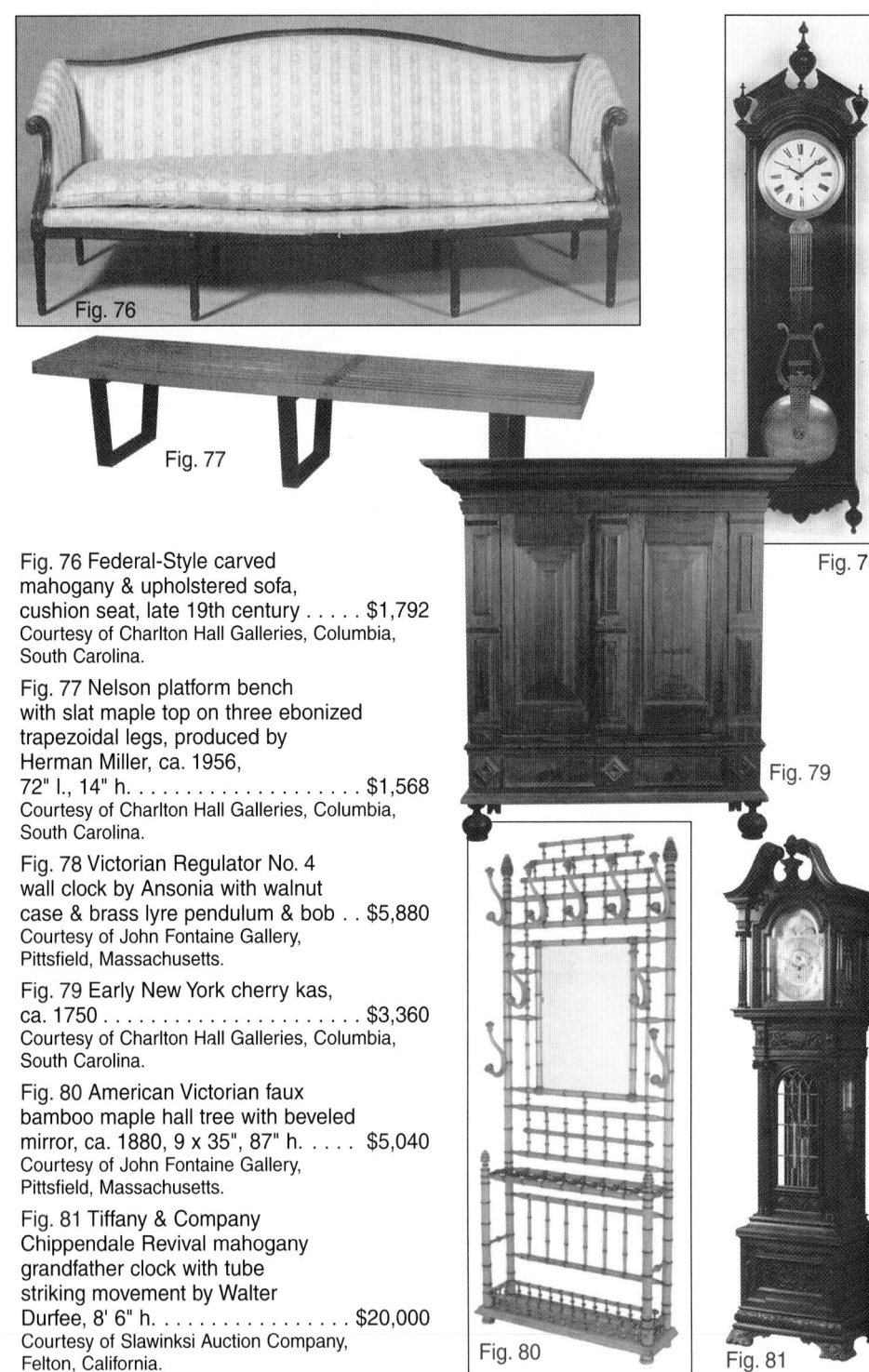

Fig. 76

Fig. 77

Fig. 78

Fig. 79

Fig. 80

Fig. 81

Fig. 76 Federal-Style carved mahogany & upholstered sofa, cushion seat, late 19th century $1,792
Courtesy of Charlton Hall Galleries, Columbia, South Carolina.

Fig. 77 Nelson platform bench with slat maple top on three ebonized trapezoidal legs, produced by Herman Miller, ca. 1956, 72" l., 14" h. $1,568
Courtesy of Charlton Hall Galleries, Columbia, South Carolina.

Fig. 78 Victorian Regulator No. 4 wall clock by Ansonia with walnut case & brass lyre pendulum & bob . . $5,880
Courtesy of John Fontaine Gallery, Pittsfield, Massachusetts.

Fig. 79 Early New York cherry kas, ca. 1750 . . . . $3,360
Courtesy of Charlton Hall Galleries, Columbia, South Carolina.

Fig. 80 American Victorian faux bamboo maple hall tree with beveled mirror, ca. 1880, 9 x 35", 87" h. $5,040
Courtesy of John Fontaine Gallery, Pittsfield, Massachusetts.

Fig. 81 Tiffany & Company Chippendale Revival mahogany grandfather clock with tube striking movement by Walter Durfee, 8' 6" h. $20,000
Courtesy of Slawinksi Auction Company, Felton, California.

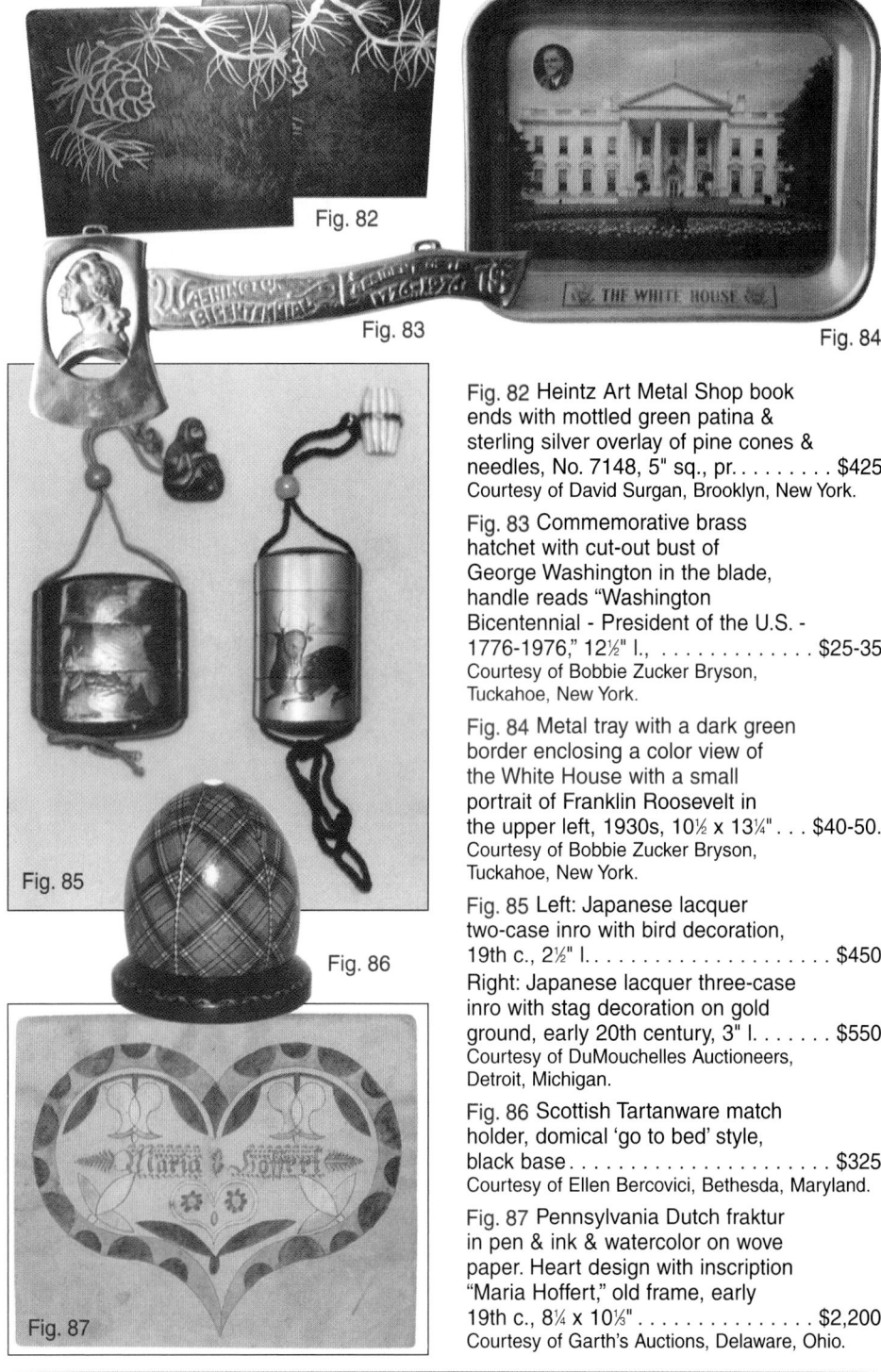

Fig. 82

Fig. 83

Fig. 84

Fig. 85

Fig. 86

Fig. 87

Fig. 82 Heintz Art Metal Shop book ends with mottled green patina & sterling silver overlay of pine cones & needles, No. 7148, 5" sq., pr. $425
Courtesy of David Surgan, Brooklyn, New York.

Fig. 83 Commemorative brass hatchet with cut-out bust of George Washington in the blade, handle reads "Washington Bicentennial - President of the U.S. - 1776-1976," 12½" l., ... $25-35
Courtesy of Bobbie Zucker Bryson, Tuckahoe, New York.

Fig. 84 Metal tray with a dark green border enclosing a color view of the White House with a small portrait of Franklin Roosevelt in the upper left, 1930s, 10½ x 13¼" . . . $40-50.
Courtesy of Bobbie Zucker Bryson, Tuckahoe, New York.

Fig. 85 Left: Japanese lacquer two-case inro with bird decoration, 19th c., 2½" l. $450
Right: Japanese lacquer three-case inro with stag decoration on gold ground, early 20th century, 3" l. $550
Courtesy of DuMouchelles Auctioneers, Detroit, Michigan.

Fig. 86 Scottish Tartanware match holder, domical 'go to bed' style, black base $325
Courtesy of Ellen Bercovici, Bethesda, Maryland.

Fig. 87 Pennsylvania Dutch fraktur in pen & ink & watercolor on wove paper. Heart design with inscription "Maria Hoffert," old frame, early 19th c., 8¼ x 10⅓" $2,200
Courtesy of Garth's Auctions, Delaware, Ohio.

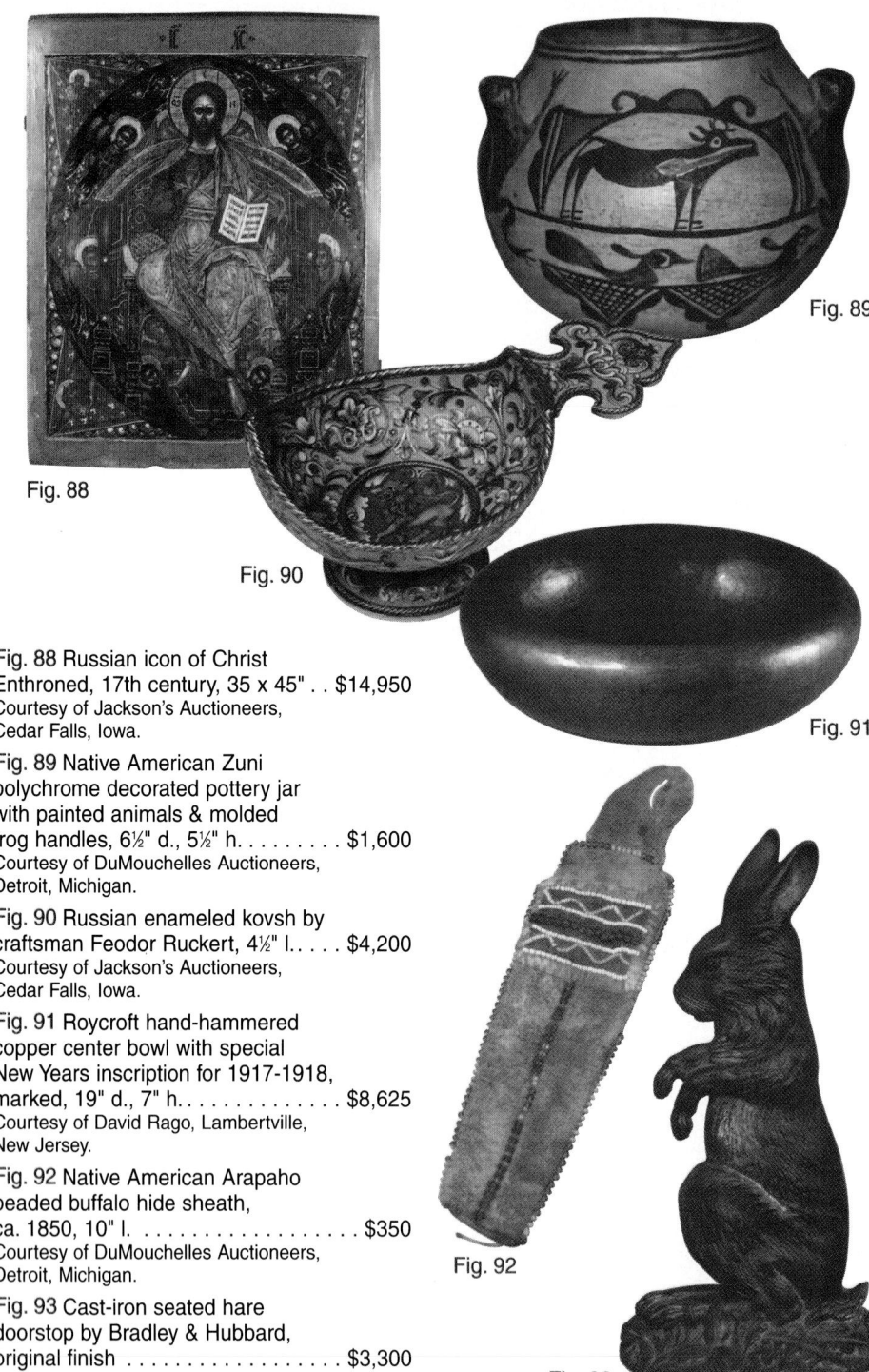

Fig. 88

Fig. 89

Fig. 90

Fig. 91

Fig. 92

Fig. 93

Fig. 88 Russian icon of Christ
Enthroned, 17th century, 35 x 45" . . $14,950
Courtesy of Jackson's Auctioneers,
Cedar Falls, Iowa.

Fig. 89 Native American Zuni
polychrome decorated pottery jar
with painted animals & molded
frog handles, 6½" d., 5½" h. $1,600
Courtesy of DuMouchelles Auctioneers,
Detroit, Michigan.

Fig. 90 Russian enameled kovsh by
craftsman Feodor Ruckert, 4½" l. $4,200
Courtesy of Jackson's Auctioneers,
Cedar Falls, Iowa.

Fig. 91 Roycroft hand-hammered
copper center bowl with special
New Years inscription for 1917-1918,
marked, 19" d., 7" h. $8,625
Courtesy of David Rago, Lambertville,
New Jersey.

Fig. 92 Native American Arapaho
beaded buffalo hide sheath,
ca. 1850, 10" l. $350
Courtesy of DuMouchelles Auctioneers,
Detroit, Michigan.

Fig. 93 Cast-iron seated hare
doorstop by Bradley & Hubbard,
original finish $3,300
Courtesy of DeFina Auctions, Austinburg, Ohio.

Folding screen, eight-fold, Art Deco style, walnut & bronze, each narrow walnut panel enclosed in a wide bronze border band, attributed to Eugene Printz, France, ca. 1928, 99" l., 67 1/2" h. (ILLUS.).. **23,000**

Secretaries

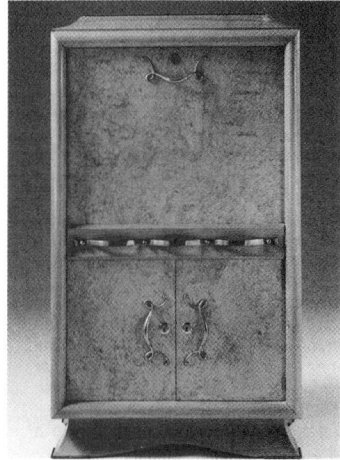

French Art Deco Secretary

Art Deco secretary, fruitwood, a rectangular mirrored top w/molded edges above a case w/a heavy rounded molding enclosing an upper wide fall-front panel opening to a fitted interior above a medial band w/an undulating brass strap band above a pair of flat cupboard doors, looped brass pulls, raised on a flared platform base, France, ca. 1940, 17 1/2 x 31 1/2", 53" h. (ILLUS.) **8,625**

Country Chippendale Secretary

Chippendale country-style secretary-bookcase, butternut, two-part construction: the upper section w/a rectangular top w/a deep stepped cornice above a pair of tombstone-arched paneled cupboard doors w/H-hinges on the sides of the case above a pair of narrow drawers; the lower section w/a hinged slant front opening to an interior of valanced pigeonholes & a row of small drawers, the lower case w/four long graduated drawers, molded base on high bracket feet, old dark red finish, brasses replaced, pigeonhole valances replaced, feet w/nailed repairs, found in Vermont, late 18th c., top 11 3/4 x 36 1/4", 78 1/2" h. (ILLUS.) **11,550**

Chippendale Cherry Secretary

Chippendale secretary-bookcase, cherry, two-part construction: the upper section w/a rectangular top over a deep flared cornice above a pair of tall paneled cupboard doors; the lower section w/a hinged slant front opening to an interior w/a central prospect door w/two faux valanced compartments & drawer & three interior drawers flanked by four valanced compartments & two interior drawers, the lower case w/four long graduated drawers w/butterfly pulls & keyhole escutcheons, molded base on scroll-cut bracket feet, southeastern New England, ca. 1780, old brasses, refinished, restored, 18 x 40 1/4", 82" h. (ILLUS.)....................... **2,760**

Classical secretary-bookcase, carved mahogany & mahogany veneer, two-part construction: the upper section w/a rectangular top w/a narrow cornice & frieze band over a pair of triple Gothic-arch glazed 6-pane doors opening to two shelves & flanked by free-standing columns; the lower section w/a wide cylinder-front opening to an interior fitted w/six small drawers over nine valanced compartments & a felt-lined writing surface above a pair of overhanging small

Fine Classical Secretary-Bookcase

drawers above two long graduated drawers flanked by short free-standing columns, original round brass & ring pulls, ring- and knob-turned feet on casters, early surface, imperfections, Baltimore, Maryland, ca. 1825-35, 24 x 46", 78 1/4" h. (ILLUS.)...................................... **2,070**

Fine Classical Secretary-Bookcase

Classical secretary-bookcase, carved mahogany & mahogany veneer, two-part construction: the upper section w/a rectangular top & narrow molded cornice over a pair of Gothic arch-glazed cupboard doors opening to two shelves & flanked by free-standing columns; the lower section w/a wide cylinder front opening to an interior w/six small drawers over nine valanced compartments & a felt-lined writing surface, all above a pair of stepped-out cockbeaded drawers

above two long set-back drawers flanked by columns above large ball feet on casters, early surface, original round brasses, Baltimore, ca. 1825-35, imperfections, 24 x 46", 78 1/4" h. (ILLUS.)............. **2,070**

Classical secretary-bookcase, carved mahogany, two-part construction: the upper section w/a rectangular top w/a deep flaring stepped cornice over a plain frieze band above a pair of tall glazed doors fitted w/scroll- and leaf-carved mullions centered by rosettes & opening to a shelved interior; the stepped-out lower section w/a rectangular fold-down writing surface opening to an interior w/a row of three small shallow drawers above the case w/a pair of drawers overhanging a pair of raised-panel cupboard doors flanked by free-standing columns w/leaf and Ionic-carved capitals above a conforming base, on double ball-turned feet, attributed to Anthony H. Jenkins, Baltimore, Maryland, ca. 1835-40, 25 1/4 x 41 1/4", 93 1/2" h. **9,200**

Country-style secretary-bookcase, painted, a rectangular top w/a narrow molded cornice above a pair of tall plain flush doors opening to a painted interior w/three fixed shelves over a lower case w/a flat hinged drop lid opening to a desk interior of open compartments above a pair of plain lower cupboard doors opening to two shelves, old dark red paint on exterior, old mustard yellow paint on interior, New England, early 19th c., 14 3/8 x 48", 84 1/2" h. (imperfections) **1,380**

Federal secretary, cherry, two-part construction: the upper section w/a rectangular top & narrow coved cornice above a pair of paneled cupboard doors opening to an interior of four drawers & five valanced compartments; the projecting lower section w/a fold-out writing surface & case of three long graduated drawers w/incised beading, curved inlaid apron & flared French feet, old finish, New England, ca. 1800-10, 22 x 42", 55" h. (replaced oval brasses, imperfections)...... **1,840**

Federal secretary, mahogany, bird's-eye maple & rosewood veneer, two-part construction: the upper section w/a rectangular top & narrow flared cornice above an inlaid three-panel frieze band above two veneered doors flanked by inlaid simulated columns; the stepped-out lower section w/a fold-out felt-lined writing surface above the case w/three long cockbeaded drawers outlined in bird's-eye maple inlay flanked by bird's-eye maple veneered edge panels over the ring-turned tapering legs w/peg feet, early surface, Gilman Clifford, Gilmanton, New Hampshire area, ca. 1810, 20 x 41 3/8", 57 1/2" h. (replaced brasses, some veneer loss) **9,775**

Federal secretary-bookcase, inlaid bird's-eye maple, two-part construction: the upper section w/a scrolled gallery centering a satinwood & cockbeaded plinth & urn foliate-carved finial, flanked by corner reeded plinths & finials, above a cove molding & a veneered frieze centering a satinwood panel, over two-pane glazed doors w/reeded muntins & arched upper panes & inlaid satinwood panels bordered by mahogany banding & opening to two shelves above two short rectangular cockbeaded doors w/bird's-eye maple veneer & mahogany cross-banded border opening to a multi-drawer, valanced & compartmented interior; the lower section w/an inlaid fold-out writing surface & a case of three long graduated cockbeaded inlaid drawers w/butterfly pulls flanked by cockbeaded panels, the scroll-cut apron centered by a cockbeaded satinwood rectangular panel, raised on tapering baluster- and ring-turned legs, old refinish, New Hampshire, early 19th c., 20 x 40", 83 3/4" h. (replaced brasses, imperfections) **10,350**

Victorian Country-style Secretary

Victorian country-style secretary-bookcase, walnut, one-piece construction, a rectangular top w/a deep flaring cornice above a pair of tall single-pane glazed doors opening to two shelves above a flat hinged fall-front opening to a writing surface & an interior fitted w/pigeonholes & two small drawers above the lower case w/a pair of paneled cupboard doors, second half 19th c., 19 x 38", 82" h. (ILLUS.)...... **660**

Victorian "cylinder-front" secretary-bookcase, Eastlake substyle, walnut, two-part construction: the upper section w/a rectangular top w/a deep flaring molded cornice above a frieze band w/incised sprigs above a pair of tall glazed doors w/incised sprigs around the edges; the lower section w/a paneled burl-veneered cylinder front opening to an interior fitted w/pigeonholes & two drawers above a long line-incised drawer w/incised leafy vines slightly overhanging two small drawers beside a small paneled door all w/line-incised bands & scrolling leafy vines, blocked & molded edges &

base, on casters, ca. 1890, 22 x 36 1/4", 85" h. **1,870**

Victorian Cylinder-front Secretary

Victorian secretary-bookcase, Renaissance Revival substyle, walnut & walnut burl veneer, two-part construction: the upper section w/a rectangular top w/a deep flared cornice over a wide frieze band w/two narrow raised burl panels flanking a center button over a pair of two tall single-pane glazed cupboard doors w/arched tops, the tops & sides trimmed w/small raised burl panels, opening to three shelves; the lower section w/a cylinder-front desk w/the two-panel lid trimmed in burl veneer & opening to an interior fitted w/pigeonholes & two small drawers all above a long slightly projecting drawer w/raised burl panels & brass ring pulls above two matching long lower drawers, molded base on casters, ca. 1880, 22 x 43", 87" h. (ILLUS.)............. **3,136**

Shelves

Early Painted Floor Shelves

Floor shelves, painted hard pine, the four long graduated open shelves w/two molded rails joining cut-out sides w/arched tops, old blue paint, possibly Pennsylvania, early 19th c., 11 x 60 3/4", 59 1/2" h. (ILLUS.)..................... **2,875**

Hanging corner shelf, painted poplar, each half ornately cut w/graduated scallops & spearpoint drops, a single quarter-round shelf above a bin w/slanted baffle, old black paint w/gold edging, 19th c., 16" w., 34" h. **330**

Hanging shelves, country-style, pine, four narrow open shelves, each joined by slender baluster- and ring-turned spindles joined to blocks at each corner, knob-turned finials & pointed knob bottom corner drops, old worn brown finish, 19th c., 6 5/8 x 28", 31 3/4" h. **1,045**

Hanging shelves, pine, long whale ends supporting two open shelves, old worn finish, found in Lancaster County, Pennsylvania, 10 x 31", 30" h.................... **660**

Hanging shelves, walnut, four long narrow graduated open shelves w/rounded front corners, joined by slender knob- and baluster-turned spindles & short turned finials at the front, the back w/a slender plain slat at each end & a wider center slat pierced & scroll-carved w/a pinwheel, star & almond shapes, old finish, 19th c., 9 3/4 x 30", 34 1/2" h. (minor edge damage)................... **330**

Hanging shelves, walnut, whale-end style w/shaped tall sides flanking three shaped & graduated open shelves above a bottom shelf over a pair of small drawers w/small wood knobs, old finish, 7 3/4 x 24 1/8", 35 3/4" h............................ **2,750**

Wall shelf, carved walnut, a shaped half-round shelf set on a detailed full-bodied spread-winged eagle above a drop w/carved leaves tapering to a point, second half 19th c., 9 3/4" w., 12 1/2" h. (minor crack near eagle) **275**

Wall shelf, painted pine, ogee molded edge on shelf w/extended backboard & box compartment, brown paint, 9 x 20", 29" h. (wear, some wood loss, age crack)...... **403**

Wall shelves, oak, chip-carved through rail joined by shaped sides, centering three graduated shelves, dark finish, late 19th c., 37 x 38"................................. **115**

Wall shelves, oak & walnut, ornately pierced & scroll-carved sides w/graduated projections flanking the four open graduated shelves, two narrow back braces, original dark finish, second half 19th c., 24" w., 39" h. (few screws missing, minor hairline)............................ **303**

Wall shelves, painted walnut, three-tier, the three graduated tiers w/rounded, chamfered & carved edges, each tier on four vase- and ring-turned baluster-form supports, all joined by two back vertical pierced hangers, old dark paint, New England, 19th c., 8 x 36", 23 1/2" h. (imperfections, medial shelf w/crack on rear right corner)................... **1,265**

Wall shelves, painted wood, the scrolled ends joining three shelves over three short drawers, painted to resemble rosewood w/pinstriped yellow scrolled foliage designs & beige painted backboard, New England, ca. 1836-40, 10 3/4 x 29 1/2", 17" h., pr. (restoration, damage)................ **2,070**

Wall shelves, painted wood, the shaped sides joining three graduated shelves w/two vertical back supports, old brown grain-painted surface, probably New England, mid-19th c., 9 1/4 x 28 1/2", 30" h. . **1,035**

Wall shelves, pine, narrow rectangular top & dovetailed frame enclosing three open shelves, old varnish finish, 19th c., 6 1/2 x 38", 30 1/2" h. **330**

Wall shelves, pine, three open shelves between deeply scallop-cut side boards, backed by a central horizontal hanging support board, old dark finish, New England, mid-19th c., 9 x 26", 28" h. **4,715**

Wall shelves, stained wood, shaped & cut-out sides w/a tall scroll-cut crestboard w/hanging holes above the top shelf, a wide space between the top & bottom shelf, red stain, 6 x 13 1/4", 18 1/2" h. **468**

Sideboards

Majorelle Art Nouveau Sideboard

Art Nouveau sideboard, carved mahogany, "La Vigne" patt., the superstructure w/a long flat crestrail over a narrow shelf supported by downswept curved supports carved w/grapevines above a paneled back & D-form top over a case w/a pair of paneled drawers above a pair of paneled doors all flanked by boldly carved bands of grapevine & curved side panels, molded serpentine base, Louis Majorelle, France, ca. 1900, 21 3/4 x 102", 72" h. (ILLUS.)....................................... **14,950**

Arts & Crafts sideboard, oak, the superstructure w/a long rectangular top above an arched mirrored back flanked by two shelves & two pedestal supports w/applied copper repoussé floral decorated hardware, the rectangular top over a case w/a pair of drawers flanked by squared cut-out corner brackets above a pair of paneled rectangular cupboard doors w/spearpoint copper & brass hardware, medium brown finish, England,

English Arts & Crafts Sideboard

early 20th c., minor wear, 23 1/2 x 60",
66" h. (ILLUS.) **2,415**

Bauhaus style sideboard, oak, flat rectangular top on a case w/three flat cupboard
doors w/ball-shaped steel pulls, the interior fitted w/four drawers on one side,
shelf & drawer on the other side, short
square legs, dark brown finish,
Germany, ca. 1927, 23 3/4 x 78 3/4",
45" h. (edge nicks, scratches) **1,150**

Chippendale-Style server, carved mahogany, the long rectangular top w/line inlay,
a gadroon-carved edge above an apron
w/a row of three drawers w/bail pulls over
a gadrooned edge band, raised on acanthus leaf-carved cabriole legs ending in
claw-and-ball feet, 20th c., 22 x 59",
30 1/4" h. **770**

Classical server, country-style, cherry &
solid curly maple, a high flat-topped crestrail w/shaped sides above the rectangular top on a case w/a row of three small
round-fronted drawers w/two wood
knobs above a deep long drawer w/beveled edges & two wood pulls overhanging the lower case w/a pair of raised-panel cupboard doors flanked by heavy freestanding turned columns, wide quarterround base molding on heavy ring-turned
tapering feet, maple facade & cherry
crestrail, ca. 1850, 23 x 44", 60 1/2" h.
(one column needs to be reattached, age
cracks in feet, chips in burl panels) **1,705**

Classical server, mahogany veneer, a rectangular top above a pair of shallow long
ogee-front drawers centered by a small
flat-fronted drawer over a deep long
drawer projecting above a pair of paneled cupboard doors flanked by flattened
columns, C-scroll front feet, replaced
wood pulls, old surface, New England,
1830s, 18 1/2 x 44", 49" h. (some veneer
loss) **978**

Simple Classical Sideboard

Classical sideboard, mahogany & mahogany veneer, a flat rectangular crestboard
flanked by end blocks above the rectangular top over two round-fronted drawers
flanking a central flat-fronted drawer all
overhanging a row of three paneled cupboard doors flanked by free-standing side
columns resting on blocks above the leaf-carved front paw feet, ring-turned tapering
rear feet, New York, ca. 1825, veneer &
other imperfections, 23 3/4 x 60 3/4",
54 3/4" h. (ILLUS.) **2,185**

Large Classical Sideboard

Classical sideboard, mahogany & mahogany veneer, the rectangular top above
two short drawers flanking a long central
drawer all w/lion mask & ring pulls projecting over a row of four paneled cupboard doors flanked by free-standing end
columns w/gilt-metal capitals, raised on
heavy double-knob turned front legs, replaced brasses, old finish, minor imperfections, Boston, ca. 1820, 22 x 59 3/4",
39 1/2" h. **4,888**

Southern Country-style Sideboard

Country-style sideboard, yellow pine, a rectangular top w/molded edges above a pair of three-panel cupboard doors w/a horizontal panel above two vertical panels, turned wood knobs, molded base raised on baluster- and knob-turned legs, old dark varnished finish, attributed to the Carolinas, early 19th c. (ILLUS.) **3,630**

Empire-Style Mahogany Sideboard

Empire-Style sideboard, gilt-bronze mounted mahogany & mahogany veneer, the superstructure w/a long low arched crestboard w/gilt-bronze winged lion mounts above a narrow rectangular shelf above the long rectangular mirrored back & four marbleized column supports on the rectangular marble top over a band of three narrow drawers w/pierced scrolling gilt-bronze mounts above three cupboard doors w/figural & wreath gilt-bronze mounts & separated by four flat columns w/gilt-bronze capitals & bases, molded base on short heavy turned feet, France, early 20th c., 24 x 77", 72" h. (ILLUS.) **8,400**

Federal country-style huntboard, walnut, a rectangular top on a deep case w/a pair of deep drawers w/simple turned wood knobs, on slender tall square tapering legs, possibly Tennessee, ca. 1830, 20 x 30", 36" h. **2,464**

Federal 'serpentine-front' sideboard, inlaid & veneered mahogany, the rectangular top w/a serpentine front & canted corners above a conforming case w/a center square door w/fan-inlaid corners flanked by a stack of three small drawers w/simple bail pulls on each end, line-inlaid side stiles & square tapering legs ending in spade feet, Maryland, 1790-1810, 21 1/2 x 53", 37 1/4" h. **20,700**

Federal sideboard, inlaid mahogany, rectangular top w/crossbanded veneer outlining the edge which overhangs the case of a stack of two cockbeaded working drawers to the right of a pair of flat central cupboard doors w/a single deep drawer on the left w/a double false-front, all w/outlined stringing & w/ovolo corners, on four very slender tapering square legs delicately outlined in stringing & ending in

cuff inlays, replaced oval brasses, old refinish, small size, Providence area, Rhode Island, 1790-1825, 21 1/2 x 50", 39" h. (minor imperfections) **20,700**

Federal sideboard & butler's desk, inlaid mahogany, the elliptical top w/an inlaid edge overhanging a case of veneered cockbeaded drawers & end cupboards outlined w/stringing & having central bone-inlaid keyhole escutcheons as well as a central hinged drawer opening to an interior of small drawers & open compartments w/a felt-lined writing surface, above a long working drawer & an arched skirt outlined w/patterned inlay, raised on square tapering legs outlined w/stringing & ending in cuff inlays, original surface, replaced oval brasses, Boston area, early 19th c., 24 x 62", 41" h. (imperfections) **14,950**

Mission-style (Arts & Crafts movement) server, oak, long coffin-shaped top overhanging long corbels joining the four tall slender square front legs & two rear legs, a wide apron w/a long single central drawer w/two metal pulls, low flat box stretchers joining the legs, Limbert paper label, 22 x 67", 31" h. (very minor finish wear) **825**

Mission-style (Arts & Crafts movement) sideboard, oak, a superstructure on the top back w/a narrow shelf & plate rail above end supports flanking three open slats on each side of a low rectangular mirror, the rectangular top on a case w/through-tenon construction, a pair of square paneled doors flanking two central graduated drawers over a large single bottom drawer, square stile legs w/through-tenon stretchers joining them across the back & sides, small square wood drawer pulls on small drawers & original hardware & metal loop pulls on doors & bottom drawer, branded Limbert mark, Model No. 1453 3/4, 19 x 52", 48" h. (skinned finish) **2,860**

Mission Oak Sideboard

Mission-style (Arts & Crafts movement) sideboard, oak, the superstructure w/a narrow shelf & flat crestrail above brackets flanking a rectangular mirror above the rectangular top over a case w/a stack of three small drawers flanked by paneled cupboard doors all above a single long base drawer, wooden pulls, paneled ends, square stile legs, veneer loss at corner, retailed by Paine Furniture, Boston, Model 5229, ca. 1915, 19 3/4 x 54", 54" h. (ILLUS.) **1,265**

Victorian sideboard, Renaissance Revival substyle, carved mahogany, the superstructure w/a long shelf w/rounded ends raised on scroll-carved end brackets & lions' head-carved front supports flanking a long low oblong mirror, the rectangular top w/wide rounded front corners above a conforming case, the curved panels carved in bold relief w/pendent fruit clusters, the front case w/three small raised panel drawers w/scroll-carved pulls above three shaped raised paneled cupboard doors each centered by a large carved bunch of pendent game, on a wide molded base, 24 1/2 x 82", 64" h. **2,300**

Fine Renaissance Revival Sideboard

Victorian sideboard, Renaissance Revival substyle, chestnut & walnut, the very tall superstructure w/a large arched & rounded central section w/a scroll-cut & fruit-carved crest on the molded crestrail terminating in upturned ring-turned finials above a long narrow shelf flanked by raised round candle shelves above the wide scroll-cut rounded side panels w/half-round small shelves flanking a long beveled oval mirror, the rectangular white marble top over a case w/two long drawers flanking a small center drawer all w/fruit- and leaf-carved pulls above a pair of large paneled cupboard doors w/oval panels centered by large carved fruit mounts & flanking a narrow rectangular recessed panel decorated w/a carved wild game mount, canted front corners & deep molded base on thin corner feet, ca. 1870, 68" w., 95" h. (ILLUS.).. **3,080**

Renaissance Revival Tall Sideboard

Victorian sideboard, Renaissance Revival substyle, walnut & burl walnut, the superstructure w/a high paneled & crown-form crestrail over a narrow shelf above a tall rectangular mirror flanked by wide burl-paneled sides fitted w/two pairs of small open shelves w/blocked support brackets above the rectangular white marble top, the lower case w/a pair of oblong-paneled drawers over a pair of cupboard doors w/large oval panels, plinth base, ca. 1875, 18 x 41", 83" h,. (ILLUS.) . **2,800**

Ornate Victorian Rococo Sideboard

Victorian sideboard, Rococo substyle, carved walnut, the high superstructure w/an arched & molded crest centered by a shield medallion above a large relief-carved wild game & fish mount, outswept leafy scroll-carved sides over a narrow rectangular shelf above an oval mirror flanked by pierced scroll-carved brackets over the rectangular white marble top w/cut front corners over a conforming case w/a pair of drawers w/recessed oval burl panels w/leaf-carved pulls above a pair of cupboard doors w/large oval burl recessed panels centered by hanging game & fish carved mounts, molded plinth base, ca. 1860-70, 20 3/4 x 54 1/2", 88" h. (ILLUS.) **5,170**

Stands

Mission Oak Bookstand

Bookstand, Mission-style (Arts & Crafts movement), oak, rectangular top w/three-quarters gallery above three open shelves flanked by three narrow side slats, square stile legs, Stickley Bros., Grand Rapids, Michigan, Model No. 4708, refinished, wear, medium brown finish, 12 x 26 3/4", 38 1/2" h. (ILLUS.) **1,035**

Mission Oak Bookstand

Bookstand, Mission-style (Arts & Crafts movement), oak, tall narrow board sides w/rounded tops flanking a slanted top

shelf over two lower open shelves w/keyed mortise & tenon joinery, medium brown finish, wear, ca. 1910, 7 3/4 x 17", 40 3/4" h. (ILLUS.) **201**

Early Candle Dipping Stand

Candle dipping stand, turned wood, a slender turned upright post w/a bulbous ball top fitted w/ten radiating turned arms each suspending a pierced disk, the post raised on a X-form base, 19th c., 46" d., 34" h. (ILLUS.) **1,495**

Candlestand, Chippendale country-style, cherry, the square top w/ovolo corners & serpentine sides on a baluster- and ring-turned pedestal on a tripod base w/cabriole legs ending in pad feet, possibly Connecticut River Valley, ca. 1770-90, 18 3/4 x 19", 27 1/2" h. (refinished) **1,035**

Chippendale Candlestand

Candlestand, Chippendale, mahogany, square top w/serpentine edges tilting above a block raised on a baluster-turned pedestal over a tripod base w/cabriole legs ending in arris pad feet, incised "I. Young," old surface, Boston or coastal Essex County, Massachusetts, 1775-1800, imperfections, 21 3/4 x 22", 29 1/2" h. (ILLUS.) **2,185**

Candlestand, Classical country-style, tiger stripe maple, a rectangular top w/canted corners on a baluster-, urn- and ring-turned pedestal on a tripod base w/flat outswept S-scroll legs, old finish, New England, ca. 1825, 16 3/4 x 21 3/4", 28 1/2" h. (ILLUS. top next page) **1,390**

Classical Country Candlestand

Candlestand, country-style, painted cherry, a round small top mounted on a rectangular post & triangular chamfered platform & three short splayed turned feet, old bluish grey paint over earlier red wash, probably New England, late 18th - early 19th c., 12 1/4" d., 24 3/4" h. (imperfections)..................... **1,150**

Candlestand, country-style, painted wood, a round top on a baluster- and ring-turned pedestal on a tapering cross-form base, original red paint, possibly Connecticut River Valley, late 18th c., 16 3/4" d., 23 1/2" h. (minor imperfections)................. **3,738**

Candlestand, Federal country-style, cherry, rectangular one-board top w/applied gallery edge on a ring- and baluster-turned birch pedestal on a tripod base w/flattened cabriole legs, good old finish, early 19th c., 16 3/8 x 19 1/8", 25 1/4" h. (repair at base of pedestal, top reattached) **770**

Candlestand, Federal country-style, painted birch, rectangular top w/deeply chamfered corners tilting above a baluster- and ring-turned pedestal on the tripod base w/spider legs, painted red, Massachusetts, ca. 1810, 16 x 23", 30" h. **4,025**

Candlestand, Federal country-style, painted hardwood, one-board rectangular top w/chamfered corners above an urn-form turned pedestal on a tripod base w/cabriole legs ending in snake feet, old black repaint w/yellow striping, earlier red shows through, late 18th - early 19th c., 15 3/4 x 22", 26 1/2" h. (age cracks in top)...................... **1,320**

Candlestand, Federal country-style, rectangular top w/notched & rounded corners above a boldly turned pedestal w/heavy ring-turnings above & below a central baluster-turned section, on a tripod base w/spider legs, old mellow finish, 16 1/4 x 19 1/2", 27 1/2" h. (one leg w/glued repair at pedestal) **935**

Candlestand, Queen Anne, mahogany, the square top w/scalloped sides & rounded corners above a ring- and urn-turned pedestal on a tripod base w/cabriole legs ending in padded snake feet, Salem, Massachusetts, 1750-80, 14 1/2 x 15 1/4", 26 3/4" h. **5,750**

Candlestand, Queen Anne, maple, round molded top on a ring- and vase-turned pedestal on a tripod base w/cabriole legs ending in snake feet, old refinish, probably New England, ca. 1740-60, 14" d., 27 1/2" h. **1,725**

Early Turned Candlestand

Candlestand, turned wood, the baluster-turned cross bar supporting two removable candle sockets, raised on a threaded & baluster-turned standard continuing to a X-form base ending in turned feet, probably New England, early 18th c., 28 3/4" h. (ILLUS.) **2,070**

Federal Mahogany Canterbury

Canterbury (music stand), Federal style, mahogany, the curved crestrails form three slots divided by flat column-like inner supports & ring- and baluster-turned corner supports above an apron w/a long cockbeaded drawer w/original turned wood pulls, raised on ring-, rod- & knob turned legs on brass casters, old refinish, minor imperfections, probably Boston, 1815-25, 12 1/2 x 18 1/8", 20 1/8" h. (ILLUS.)...................................... **4,600**

Crock stand, painted, a three-tiered half-round form w/wide stepped back & a single front brace supporting the rounded shelves, square nail construction, old mustard yellow paint, found in Pennsylvania, 19th c., 25 1/2 x 49 1/2", 36" h. (wear, age splits) **660**

Crock stand, painted poplar, rectangular narrow top shelf above narrow flat canted front legs w/notched brackets supporting two open lower shelves, slender knob-and rod-turned canted rear legs, worn red paint, 32 x 41", 49 1/2" h. **1,210**

Display stand, Arts & Crafts style, oak, a rectangular top raised on four square upright stiles above a narrow arched apron, a medial shelf above a lower case w/a pair of small drawers over two deep drawers all w/rectangular hammered copper pulls, Limbert paper label, Model No. 260, original finish, 15 1/2 x 17", 36" h. (minor buckling to veneer on sides) **3,190**

Decorative Victorian Fern Stand

Fern stand, Victorian Renaissance Revival substyle, carved walnut, a small rounded molded top w/a marble insert supported on three slender ring- and baluster-turned supports centered by a round shelf w/a carved full-figure standing stag, a central post connecting the supports & raised on a tripod base w/leaf-carved cabriole legs ending in scroll feet, brass chain swags w/four drops around the top, old varnish finish, ca. 1875, two brass drops missing, one support w/damage, 36" h. (ILLUS.) **1,045**

Magazine stand, Mission-style (Arts & Crafts movement), oak, a rectangular top w/three-quarters low gallery above slatted sides & back enclosing two lower shelves, square stile legs, original finish, unmarked Stickley Brothers, early 20th c., 12 1/4 x 16", 31 1/2" h. **880**

Magazine stand, Mission-style (Arts & Crafts movement), oak, tapered side

panels w/cut-outs at top & bottom & set w/four shelves w/through-tenon construction, early 20th c., 12 x 15 7/8", 40" h. **748**

Fine Mahogany Music Stand

Music stand, Federal, mahogany, the square top w/molded edge tilting open on a support bar & shaped rachet mechanism over a single drawer, tall slender square supports enclosing the four open lower shelves each w/a low three-quarters gallery, on casters, appears to retain original brasses, old refinish, England or America, 1800-10, repairs, imperfections, 16 x 17 3/4", 45 1/2" h. (ILLUS.) **2,875**

Classical Mahogany Nightstand

Nightstand, Classical, carved mahogany & mahogany veneer, the rectangular top w/gadrooned edges above a single long curved-front drawer w/pressed glass pulls flanked by leaf-carved panels & above a gadrooned apron band, raised on ring-and knob-turned leaf-carved supports over a medial shelf w/shaped front, on carved blocks over short turned legs w/knob feet, probably Philadelphia, ca. 1825, minor imperfections, refinished, 17 x 25", 29" h. (ILLUS.) **978**

Nightstand, Mission-style (Arts & Crafts movement), oak, a square top w/inset stile legs enclosing a case w/a pair of small drawers over two longer drawers all w/square wood knobs, a lower medial shelf, new finish, unmarked, early 20th c., 18" sq., 28 1/2" h. **1,210**

Nightstand, Mission-style (Arts & Crafts movement), oak, rectangular top above two narrow drawers w/ring pulls, on square slender legs, red decal mark & paper label of Gustav Stickley, 17 3/4 x 20", 30 1/2" h. **3,450**

Fine French Art Nouveau Nightstand

Nightstands, Art Nouveau, carved mahogany & rosewood, an arched & paneled crestboard w/pierced loops & floral-carved crest above the brown marble-inset top above a small drawer raised on molded & forked open brackets continuing to the slender square molded front supports joined by a medial shelf, solid back panels above the base shelf on a scroll-carved apron on short curved feet, possibly by Louis Majorelle, France, one w/a lower door, ca. 1900, 11 1/2 x 15", 41" h., pr. (ILLUS. of one) **8,050**

Plant stand, Modern style, stained wood, of cruciform, composed of four rectangular section holders w/pierced slatted panels & metal liners, on four post legs, Austria, early 20th c., 10 1/4 x 31 3/4", 37 3/4" h. **329**

Plant stand, painted pine, three graduated demi-lune tiers on turned supports over a base of turned posts on arched feet joined by turned stretchers, old green paint, New England, late 19th c., 18 1/2 x 37 3/4", 36" h. **748**

Plant stand, wirework, composed of two stepped & rounded tiers w/scrolling decorated sides above scrolled skirt, on four supports & casters, painted black, late 19th c., 16 1/4 x 35", 32 1/2" h. (minor imperfections) **546**

Sewing stand, Federal, inlaid mahogany, the figured mahogany rectangular top w/four turret corners topped by turned disks above colonnettes flanking two graduated cockbeaded drawers raised on a heavy ring-turned pedestal on four scrolled & curving legs ending in brass paw feet on casters, North Shore, Massachusetts, early 19th c., 17 1/4 x 19 1/2", 30 1/2" h. (replaced pulls, sun fading, minor repair) **1,610**

Mission Oak Smoker's Stand

Smoker's stand, Mission-style (Arts & Crafts movement), oak, a rectangular top overhanging a case w/a small drawer above a tall paneled door, both w/hammered copper pulls, slightly arched aprons, short square stile feet, medium brown finish, red decal mark of L. & J. G. Stickley, Model No. 26, ca. 1907, wear, 15 x 20", 29 1/4" h. (ILLUS.) **4,888**

Smoking stand, Mission-style (Arts & Crafts movement), oak, nearly square top on an upright cabinet w/chamfered case construction, through-tenon corners, a single tall paneled door opening to an interior drawer over a divided storage area w/shelf, original dark finish, unmarked Gustav Stickley, 15 x 17", 27" h. (top & front refinished) **6,050**

Telephone stand, Mission-style (Arts & Crafts movement), oak, a square top above a single drawer w/square copper knob over an open compartment above a single rectangular door w/square copper knob, paneled sides, new finish, unmarked, early 20th c., 17 1/2" sq., 36" h. .. **1,430**

Umbrella stand, Gothic-style, oak, rectangular grid top supported by four arched-top columnar legs w/recessed arch design, over rectangular base w/fitted metal tray, medium brown finish, 12 1/2 x 34", 29 1/2" h. (splitting) **518**

Classical Corner-style Washstand

Washstand, Classical country-style, corner-style, maple & bird's-eye maple veneer, a high rounded gallery over the quarter-round white marble top above a conforming deep apron w/a single drawer, on three slender ring- and baluster-turned supports to the lower section on four baluster-turned legs w/knob feet, old refinish, New England, ca. 1820s, imperfections, 19 x 27", 35 3/4" h. (ILLUS.)........ **1,380**

Classical Marble-topped Washstand

Washstand, Classical, mahogany & mahogany veneer, a molded three-quarters gallery above the rectangular white marble top over a single long drawer w/large round brass pulls, raised on four simple columnar supports over a deep lower shelf w/incurved front, raised on knob-turned feet, refinished, Maryland, ca. 1825, imperfections, 21 1/4 x 29 5/8", 33 1/2" h. (ILLUS.).. **1,495**

Massachusetts Classical Washstand

Washstand, Classical, mahogany & mahogany veneer, the top w/a high three-quarters gallery w/a raised scroll-cut center crest above the rectangular bow-fronted top w/a large bowl cut-out, the bowed apron flanked by two small square drawers, the incurved sides above a lower shelf over a single drawer w/replaced brass pulls, raised on spiral-turned legs w/knob feet, refinished, probably North Shore, Massachusetts, ca. 1825, minor imperfections, 14 1/2 x 20 1/2", 51 1/4" h. (ILLUS.)... **1,150**

Washstand, Classical, stenciled mahogany, the rectangular hinged top w/stenciled border & edges & mirrored underside opening to a basin interior above a conforming case fitted w/a short drawer w/stenciled surround over cupboard doors above a short drawer w/stenciled surround, all flanked by stenciled columns on stenciled ring-, baluster- and ball-turned feet, probably New York, ca. 1825-35, 21 x 36 1/4", 34" h. **2,070**

Washstand, Federal corner-style, mahogany, the arched, shelved superstructure above two tiers, one fitted w/a drawer, on square tapering supports w/French feet joined by a shaped undertier, 19th c., 16 x 24", 39 1/4" h...................................... **1,035**

Washstand, Federal country-style, cherry, a high serpentine splashback over the rectangular top w/a serpentined front above a conforming apron w/a single long drawer w/replaced embossed round brass pulls, ring- and rod-turned columnar supports to the wide medial shelf w/a serpentine front raised on tapering ring- and rod-turned legs w/knob feet, refinished, first half 19th c., 18 7/8 x 34 3/4", 34 1/4" h. (splashback replaced, veneer on drawer painted) **330**

Washstand, Federal country-style, cherry, a high splashback w/down-curved galleried sides on the rectangular top, apron w/a single lower dovetailed drawer w/small original brass button pulls, on double-baluster turned supports to a medial shelf w/incurved front, raised on block- and double-baluster turned legs w/peg feet, refinished, 17 1/4 x 22 1/8", 32 1/2" h. (restorations).................................... **523**

Washstand, Federal country-style, cherry, a high three-quarters gallery w/quarter-round corner shelves above the rectangular top w/a large central hole & two smaller rear holes raised on slender square tapering legs joined by a medial shelf above a narrow dovetailed drawer w/round brass knob, early 19th c., refinished, 17 3/4 x 19 1/2", overall 40 1/2" h. (pull replaced, age cracks & old repair in top, repair in shelf) **495**

Washstand, Federal country-style, cherry, rectangular top w/three-quarters dovetailed gallery over a single drawer in the apron, on turned legs joined by a medial shelf, Pennsylvania, ca. 1820-35, 15 x 28", 34" h. (replaced hardware)...................................... **1,760**

Rare Curly Maple Federal Washstand

Washstand, Federal country-style, curly maple, a high shaped backsplash flanked by stepped sides on the rectangular top w/a large central bowl cut-out, raised on ring- and baluster-turned supports above a medial shelf over a single drawer w/early pressed glass knob, on baluster- and ring-turned legs, refinished, early 19th c., 17 x 20", 33" h. (ILLUS.) **3,410**

Washstand, Federal country-style, painted & decorated, a high scroll-cut splashback & low & short scroll-cut gallery sides on the rectangular top w/a large center cut-out round hole raised on ring- and rod-turned supports to the medial shelf above a single drawer, ring- and baluster-turned legs w/knob feet, overall smoke decoration on a creamy white ground bordered w/green striping, early 19th c., 16 x 18 3/4", 28 1/2" h. (minor paint wear).............................. **770**

Washstand, Federal country-style, painted pine, a rectangular top overhanging a nar-

row apron raised on four tall simple turned supports to a medial shelf over a single drawer w/porcelain knob, block- and baluster-turned legs, old red paint over earlier mustard yellow, first half 19th c., 18 1/2 x 20", 31" h. (hairline in rear leg, chips in feet) **385**

Federal Country-style Washstand

Washstand, Federal country-style, stained hardwood, a tall three-quarters splashback w/arched back panel & rolled sides above the rectangular top, raised on simple turned supports on a medial shelf over a single drawer, raised on ring- and baluster-turned legs w/peg feet, stained, lightly cleaned old surface, New England, early 19th c., minor imperfections, 13 3/4 x 20 1/2", 35" h. (ILLUS.) **460**

Fine Inlaid Federal Corner Washstand

Washstand, Federal, inlaid mahogany, corner-style, the quarter-round top w/a large round bowl cut-out & two small round cutouts above a narrow banded inlay apron raised on three square supports to the medial shelf over an inlaid apron fitted w/three small drawers outlined w/stringing, on four square tapering legs w/banded inlay, old refinish, Charleston, South Carolina, 1790-1800, repairs, height loss, 15 x 21 1/2", 29 1/8" h. (ILLUS.) **2,990**

Washstand, Modern style, blue-painted wood, the rectangular superstructure w/graduated planes, a high rectangular backsplash w/clipped corners & ceramic tile insets decorated w/a royal blue Secessionist design, side drawer, towel rack & an open bay above a small cabinet door, together w/a matching ceramic water pitcher, wash bowl & cov. bucket, each w/matching Secessionist design, Austria, early 20th c., stand 24 1/8 x 26", 44" h., the set **2,233**

Washstand, Victorian country-style, curly maple, a rectangular top w/three-quarters gallery over a convex frieze drawer over a pair of paneled cupboard doors flanked by turned pilasters, raised on turned feet, mid-19th c., 18 1/2 x 29", 35" h. **805**

Victorian Walnut Washstand

ing drawers, low arched & cut-out apron, on casters, ca. 1870, 18 x 35", 35" h. (ILLUS.) **358**

Fine Victorian Mahogany Washstand

Decorated Victorian Washstand

Washstand, Victorian country-style, painted & decorated pine, a rectangular hinged top w/molded edges opening to a deep well above a small working drawer beside a faux drawer over a heavy mid-molding & a lower rectangular door, serpentine apron, grain-painted ground w/painted panels simulating bird's-eye maple & dark wood, fine finish, second half 19th c., 18 x 29", 31" h. (ILLUS.) **303**

Washstand, Victorian Renaissance Revival substyle, walnut, a serpentine molded splashback connected to outswept end towel bars flanking the rectangular top w/molded edges above the case w/a pair of small drawers w/oval molding & carved leaf pulls above two long match-

Washstand, Victorian Rococo substyle, mahogany & mahogany veneer, the rectangular white marble top w/a serpentine front & a three-quarters marble splashback w/small corner shelves above a conforming case w/a single long drawer w/carved acanthus leaf lock plate & corner brackets above a pair of paneled cupboard doors w/scroll-carved corner brackets above the scroll-carved apron w/simple bracket feet on casters, attributed to Prudent Mallard, New Orleans, Louisiana, mid-19th c., 18 x 40", 36" h. (ILLUS.) **1,344**

Weaver's stand, painted pine, the octagonal top on turned supports & chamfered T-form tripod base, overall old red paint, New England, early 19th c., 14 1/4 x 14 1/2", 23" h. (restored) **920**

Classical Tiger Stripe Maple Stand

Classical country-style one-drawer stand, tiger stripe maple, a square top overhanging an apron w/a single drawer raised on ring- and baluster-turned legs ending in knob feet, old refinish, New England, ca. 1830, imperfections, 19 x 20", 29" h. (ILLUS.) **2,070**

Classical Country Two-drawer Stand

Classical country-style two-drawer stand, bird's-eye maple, tiger stripe maple & cherry, the nearly square thick top slightly overhanging the deep apron w/two drawers each w/two large turned wood pulls, raised on baluster-, rod- and ring-turned legs ending in knob feet, old refinish, imperfections, possibly Pennsylvania, ca. 1825, 19 x 21 1/2", 29" h. (ILLUS.) **1,610**
Classical country-style two-drawer stand, cherry & curly maple, a rectangular top above a deep case w/a curved-front drawer over a flat drawer each w/a replaced curly maple knob, raised on bal-

uster-, ring and knob-turned legs w/peg feet, ca. 1850, 17 3/4 x 20 1/2", 29 1/2" h. (wafers added to bottom of feet, age cracks in top) **605**
Federal country-style one-drawer stand, cherry & curly maple, one-board square top above a cherry frame w/a single curly maple dovetailed drawer w/turned wooden pull, ring- and baluster-turned legs w/a long octagonal central section, knob feet, original finish w/varnish overcoat, early 19th c., 19 1/2" w., 28 1/2" h. **468**
Federal country-style one-drawer stand, cherry & curly maple, the nearly square cherry top overhanging a cherry frame w/a single narrow curly maple drawer w/clear lacy glass knob, raised on very slender rod- and ring-turned legs w/tapering peg feet, early 19th c., 17 1/2 x 18", 29 1/8" h. (minor warp in top) **935**
Federal country-style one-drawer stand, cherry, pegged construction, rectangular one-board top slightly overhanging an apron w/a single dovetailed drawer w/replaced brass bail pull, refinished, early 19th c., 18 3/4 x 24 1/4" **715**
Federal country-style one-drawer stand, cherry, square top w/ovolo corners overhanging an apron w/a single dovetailed drawer w/replaced brass knob, slender square tapering legs, old refinishing, early 19th c., 17 1/2 x 17 3/4", 27" h. **1,073**
Federal country-style one-drawer stand, child's, tiger stripe maple, square top overhangs an apron w/a single drawer, raised on ring- and baluster-turned tapering legs w/knob feet, early surface, New Hampshire, early 19th c., 14 3/4 x 16 3/4", 19 1/4" h. (replaced drawer pull, minor imperfections) **4,888**
Federal country-style one-drawer stand, curly maple, a rectangular one-board top above an apron w/a single drawer w/an opalescent lacy glass pull, slender ring-, knob and baluster-turned legs w/peg feet, refinished, good wood figure, first half 19th c., 18 1/2 x 21", 30" h. (few chips) **2,090**
Federal country-style one-drawer stand, painted & decorated cherry, a rectangular two-board top widely overhanging a deep apron w/a single drawer w/a porcelain knob, on slender knob- and rod-turned legs w/knob feet, original brown sponged vinegar graining w/gold striping & old brown overvarnish, two decal designs on the drawer, Pennsylvania, first half 19th c., 22 x 23 1/2", 30" h. **2,200**
Federal country-style one-drawer stand, painted pine & maple, nearly square top w/ovolu corners above a deep slightly canted apron w/a single conforming drawer, on splayed tapering square legs, yellow paint & scrubbed top, Pennsylvania, early 19th c., 18 1/4 x 20", 28" h. (missing drawer pull, repainted) **690**
Federal country-style two-drawer stand, birch & bird's-eye maple veneer, rectangular thin top above a deep apron w/two

dovetailed drawers w/veneer & mahogany banded inlay & diamond-shaped escutcheon inlays, on ring- and baluster-turned slender figured wood legs w/tall peg feet, early 19th c., 15 1/4 x 20", 28" h. (slight warp at back of top, chips on banded inlay) **1,210**

Federal country-style one-drawer stand, hardwood, a square top w/ovolo corners widely overhanging an apron w/a single drawer, mortised & pinned apron on tall slender square tapering legs, old dark worn finish, early 19th c., 18 x 18 1/2", 26" h. (top reattached) **1,100**

Federal one-drawer stand, cherry, rectangular top over a single drawer & straight apron on vase- and ring-turned legs ending in ball feet, brass pulls appear to be original, old refinish, southern New England, ca. 1825, 16 1/2 x 21 1/2", 28" h. **578**

Federal Mahogany One-drawer Stand

Federal one-drawer stand, mahogany, a square top overhanging an apron w/a single drawer above ring-turned & reeded legs ending in peg feet in brass casters, refinished, Massachusetts, ca. 1810-15, minor restoration, 19 x 19 1/4", 27 1/2" h. (ILLUS.) **1,840**

Federal one-drawer stand, maple & birch, a nearly square top w/ovolo corners overhanging an apron w/a single drawer w/two brass knobs, raised on swelled ring- and rod-turned legs w/long peg feet, refinished, probably New Hampshire, ca. 1820, 18 1/2 x 20 1/2", 29 1/2" h. (replaced knobs) **690**

Federal one-drawer stand, painted pine & ash, a nearly square top overhanging a thumb-molded apron w/a single drawer, raised on square chamfered tapering legs, old green paint, possibly New England, early 19th c., 18 3/4 x 19 1/2", 27 3/4" h. **1,035**

Federal two-drawer stand, cherry & mahogany veneer, rectangular top flanked by wide hinged drop leaves above a deep apron w/two paneled drawers w/mahogany veneering & beaded inner edges, raised on ring-, rod- and baluster-turned legs w/knob feet, old finish, 19 1/4 x 22" plus 9 1/4" leaves, 28 1/2" h. (replaced hinges) **468**

Federal two-drawer stand, cherry & mahogany veneer, square cherry top above a deep case w/a serpentine front w/two conforming dovetailed drawers w/applied beading & a large lacy glass pull, slender ring-, rod- and knob-turned legs w/knob & peg feet, old finish, early 19th c., 20 x 20 1/2", 28" h. (minor age cracks in top, top reattached, lock removed, one pull chipped) **1,100**

Federal two-drawer stand, mahogany & mahogany veneer, a nearly square one-board top flanked by D-form hinged drop leaves flanking the deep apron w/two narrow drawers w/crotch grain veneer & pairs of small round brass pulls, ropetwist-turned legs w/knob- and ring-turning at the top & ending in peg feet, mellow refinish, ca. 1830, 16 x 17" plus leaves, 29" h. (few hairline cracks in legs) **880**

Stools

Art Deco Cone-shaped Stool

Art Deco stool, upholstered bird's-eye maple, the inverted cone-form upholstered seat on a round maple base, 1930s, 17" d., 23" h. (ILLUS.) **300**

Fine French Art Deco Stool

Art Deco stool, upholstered mahogany, a deep round cushion top on an upholstered apron & round wood frame w/beaded edge & scroll-carved turned legs, Sue et Mare, France, ca. 1925, 27" d., 18 1/2" h. (ILLUS.) **6,325**

Bentwood stool, round seat & stretcher joined by pairs of bentwood upright supports each centering a spherical element, the padded seat upholstered in pale green suede, design attributed to Josef Hoffmann, Austria, early 20th c., 14" d., 18 1/8" h... **999**

Boston Classical Footstool

Classical footstool, carved mahogany, the rectangular overupholstered top on a cu-rule base w/leaf carvings & C-scroll feet & central concentric circles & a ring-turned medial stretcher, old surface, imperfections, Boston, 1825-35, 15 1/2 x 22 1/2", 15" h. (ILLUS.)... **1,265**

American Classical Mahogany Stool

Classical stool, upholstered mahogany, the gently bowed rectangular uphol-stered top on a deep conforming apron raised on two scrolled X-form supports trimmed w/roundels & joined by a turned stretcher, American, second quarter 19th c., 26" l. (ILLUS.) **1,495**

Country-style, poplar & hardwood, a round seat on four slender tapering ring-turned canted legs joined by plain double stretchers on each side, red stain, late 19th - early 20th c., 16" h............................... **193**

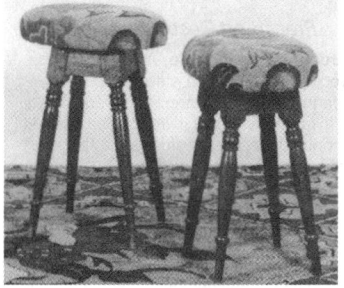

Country-style Stools with Round Tops

Country-style stools, stained wood, a round upholstered top raised on a canted apron raised on ring- and knob-turned reeded & canted legs, stained red, 19th c., pr. (ILLUS.)...................................... **1,840**

Federal Curly Maple Stool

Federal stool, curly maple, the oblong wo-ven rush seat enclosed w/a wooden framework & raised on four ring-, knob- and rod-turned tapering canted legs joined by slender double stretchers sep-arated by three spheres, early 19th c., 11 1/2 x 15", 16 1/4" h. (ILLUS.) **1,980**

Footstool, cherry, small rectangular top w/board edges angled at the ends, on scroll-cut board feet mortised through the top, old & probably original finish, 7 x 12 3/4", 7 1/4" h. **193**

Footstool, country-style, painted pine, rect-angular top over scallop-cut apron, on canted supports w/cut-out feet, worn original black & red graining, 6 x 14", 6" h. **330**

Footstool, country-style, walnut, a small rectangular board top on mortised boot-jack legs, scrubbed top, lower original fin-ish, serpentine pierced in the top, 19th c., 8 3/4 x 16", 6 5/8" h. **165**

Footstool, painted & decorated, narrow rectangular top above narrow ornately scallop-cut aprons, scalloped flat legs w/arched feet, alligatored red, yellow & green paint w/gold & black stenciled buildings, flowers & "E.H." on the top, 19th c., 6 x 14", 6 7/8" h. (minor edge wear, two scallop points missing on apron)... **770**

Footstool, painted oak, 'rolling pin'-type on four ring-turned legs, painted yellow, 19th c., 8 1/2 x 19" (paint loss) **144**

Footstool, painted poplar, rectangular top on slightly splayed turned legs w/old add-ed dowel rod rungs, old worn brown paint w/gold striping, 9 x 13 3/4", 9" h. **275**

Italian Gilt-bronze Rope Stool

Modern style stool, gilt-bronze, the rounded mesh seat enclosed w/a rope-form gilt frame continuing to four legs conjoined by a knotted rope stretcher, stamped twice "Made In Intaly," second quarter 20th c., 26" d., 14" h. (ILLUS.) **1,560**

Patented Victorian Piano Stool

Piano stool, Victorian Renaissance Revival substyle, carved walnut, Roman-style design w/a rectangular upholstered top on a narrow burl-paneled apron raised on a four-legged scissor-action base w/a threaded mechanism w/large carved rosette handles for controlling the seat height, paper label reads "The X Piano Taboret L. Postawka Co., Cambridgeport, Mass. Pat. April 4, 1871," axle caps appear absent, 16 x 20", 26" h. (ILLUS.)....... **392**

Renaissance Revival Ebonized Stool

Victorian stool, Renaissance Revival substyle, ebonized & parcel-gilt wood, the squared upholstered seat w/serpentine ends above a conforming scalloped apron w/gilt-incised line designs, raised on a heavy center post w/four radiating blocked & angled legs curving out at the bottom to form snake feet, American, ca. 1870, 18 1/2" h. (ILLUS.) **805**

Weaver's work stool, painted wood, tall w/a round hollowed seat frame w/woven leather seat on four reverse-tapering legs joined by turned stretchers, worn old red paint, New England, early 19th c., top 13 1/4 x 13 1/2", 28" h. **920**

Windsor stool, painted, a triangular top on three canted baluster- and ring-turned legs joined by swelled stretchers, old black paint, the top recovered w/worn hooked rug fragment, early 19th c., 13" h. **550**

Tables

Art Deco Glass-topped Table

Art Deco center table, the round glass top above a framework of wrought-iron calligraphic devices raised on four scrolling legs joined by a X-form looped stretcher, France, ca. 1930, 26 3/4" d., 20 3/4" h. (ILLUS.) **1,800**

Art Deco dining table, rosewood, glass & marble, the oblong green glass top w/gilt-lined decoration above a tapering oblong central pedestal raised on a conforming verte antico marble plinth, France, ca. 1940, 38 x 80", 31 1/2" h. **8,050**

French Art Deco Dressing Table

Art Deco dressing table, African Bubinga wood & rosewood, a stepped form w/an upright square cabinet at one end fitted w/a tall burled door w/rosewood trim & ebonized handle beside a rectangular top w/low rosewood crestrail & rounded end enclosing a narrow drawer w/ebonized pull above the kneehole opening & a smaller upright cabinet door at the other side, square curved front legs, France, ca. 1930, 15 3/4 x 50", 36 1/2" h. (ILLUS.) **1,150**

Art Deco typewriter table, bird's-eye maple veneer & lacquer, an oval top formed w/a half-round drop leaf at one end above an upright center board w/two half-round open shelves below the fixed half of the top, top & shelves w/black lac-

Art Deco Typewriter Table

Arts & Crafts Oak Tabouret

quered edges, on three heavy casters, America, ca. 1930, minor veneer cracks, small repair, 21 x 36", 31 1/4" h. (ILLUS.)...... **978**

Gallé-signed Art Nouveau Table

Art Nouveau side table, fruitwood marquetry, a two-tiered form w/each rectangular tier outlined w/an undulating molding enclosing the ornate floral marquetry design, loop-carved S-scroll supports below the upper tier, the lower tier w/ormolu loop edge handles, raised on simple molded cabriole legs w/carved cuffs, by Gallé, designed for the Exposition Universelle, Paris, 1900, marquetry inscription "Sicut Loitus Semer Suum germinal sic Deus germinalit Jus Ti Tiam - Gallé Exposé 1900 - IS," 26 x 37", 34" h. (ILLUS.)... **10,925**

Arts & Crafts library table, oak, rectangular top over an apron w/a single long drawer w/hammered copper pulls, lower median shelf w/through-tenons, arched side stretchers, ca. 1912, 30 1/4 x 48", 30" h. (stains, wear) **518**

Arts & Crafts tabouret, octagonal top w/corbel supports above four canted sides w/curved cut-outs & medial shelf w/deep aprons, dark brown finish, ca. 1912, minor scratches & imperfections, 17" w., 23 1/2" h. (ILLUS.) **978**

Chippendale card table, mahogany, the folding hinged overhanging top w/serpentine edges above a conforming apron w/a serpentine cockbeaded border centering a carved fan joining four square molded slightly tapering legs w/inside chamfering, old finish, probably coastal northern Massachusetts, ca. 1780, 17 3/4 x 35 1/4", 28 1/4" h. (minor imperfections) **18,400**

Chippendale card table, mahogany, the rectangular hinged top w/molded edges above a straight beaded apron on four square Marlborough legs, original surface, Massachusetts, 1760-75, 16 x 33 1/2", 29 1/4" h. (repairs)................ **1,265**

Chippendale country-style tea table, cherry, a large square top tilting diagonally above a baluster- and ring-turned pedestal on a tripod base w/cabriole legs ending in pad feet on platforms, New England, ca. 1780, 30 x 31 1/2", 28" h. (minor imperfections)................................... **1,265**

Chippendale country-style work table, maple, birch & pine, scrubbed one-board rectangular top w/breadboard ends widely overhanging the deep apron w/a single long dovetailed drawer w/brass pulls, square stile legs joined by box stretchers, original red finish, attributed to Maine, 29 3/4 x 50 1/4", 26" h. **3,300**

Chippendale dressing table, walnut, the rectangular top w/molded edge & shaped front corners overhanging a case w/a long drawer over three small lip-molded drawers, deeply scalloped apron, raised on cabriole legs ending in trifid feet, butterfly brasses, Delaware Valley, 18th c., 21 1/4 x 35 1/4", 29 1/2" h. (ILLUS. top next page) **5,175**

Chippendale Walnut Dressing Table

Chippendale Pembroke table, mahogany, rectangular top flanked by hinged rectangular drop leaves, apron w/one dovetailed end drawer w/cockbeading & original brass, square molded legs w/inside chamfer & cross-stretcher, found on Cape Cod, Massachusetts, 20 1/4 x 31 3/4" plus 10 3/4" leaves, 28 3/4" h. (added steel angle braces on underside, minor stains in top) **3,575**

Chippendale tea table, mahogany, round one-board dished top above a pedestal w/a turned columnar section above a baluster-turned lower section, on a tripod base w/cabriole legs ending in snake feet, old mellow finish, attributed to Newport, Rhode Island, 18th c., 23 1/2" d., 27 5/8" h. (restoration, pieced repairs, filled holes in top from a larger cleat) **8,575**

Chippendale-Style tea table, mahogany, the wide round top w/a carved piecrust edge tilting on a birdcage section above the columnar pedestal w/a leaf-carved baluster base resting on a tripod base w/heavy cabriole legs w/leaf-carved knees & ending in claw-and-ball feet, 20th c., 31" d., 29" h. (repairs) **495**

Chippendale-Style tea table, rosewood & walnut veneer, a round piecrust top w/molded edges tilting above a leaf-carved pedestal on a tripod base w/three cabriole legs w/leaf-carved knees & ending in paw feet, ca. 1900, 28" d., 42" h. **1,064**

Classical breakfast table, carved mahogany, the wide rectangular top flanked by wide drop leaves w/notched corners above the convex apron flanked by small rosewood panels w/brass inlaid stringing & turned pendants, raised on a heavy turned acanthus leaf-carved pedestal on four scrolled acanthus leaf-carved legs ending in hairy paw feet, old refinish, probably New York, ca. 1825, 24 3/4 x 39 1/2", 29 1/4" h. (minor imperfections) **920**

Classical card table, carved mahogany, the hinged rectangular top w/rounded corners above a conforming frame w/applied skirt on foliate-carved & ring-and ball-turned pedestal surrounded by a stylized leaf-carved ring over a square base on downswept legs w/leaf-carved knees fitted w/brass casters, probably Boston, 1810-30, closed 17 3/4 x 35 3/4", 28 1/2" h. **2,300**

Classical card table, carved mahogany veneer, a rectangular hinged fold-over top w/reeded edges & rounded corners above a conforming rounded apron, raised on a heavy gently tapering columnar pedestal on a quatrefoil platform raised on ornate S-scroll-carved feet on casters, Boston, 1815-25, 18 3/4 x 38", 30 1/2" h. (imperfections) **1,380**

Classical card table, carved mahogany veneer, rectangular top swivels above the skirt w/scrolled ends raised on a tapering rectangular pedestal w/acanthus leaf carving around the bottom raised on a long cross-form platform raised on carved paw feet on casters, old refinish, attributed to Isaac Vose and Son, Boston, ca. 1825, 17 3/4 x 36", 29" h. **3,738**

Classical card table, mahogany & mahogany crotch grain veneer, a rectangular fold-over top above a deep ogee apron raised on a heavy pedestal w/a beehive ring-turned section above a wide baluster-turned & acanthus-leaf carved lower section, raised on a long heavy rectangular plinth w/concave sides raised on four carved wing & paw feet on brass casters, old dark finish, ca. 1840, 17 1/2 x 36", 29 3/4" h. (veneer repairs, well done column repair) **1,045**

One of a Pair of Classical Card Tables

Classical card tables, carved mahogany & mahogany veneer, the rectangular hinged top w/rounded front corners above a narrow rounded skirt w/anthemion carved corners, raised on a ring-turned & acanthus leaf-carved pedestal on a shaped veneered platform above leaf-carved paw feet, old refinish, Philadelphia, 1830s, casters missing, other imperfections, 17 3/4 x 36", 28 1/4" h., pr. (ILLUS. of one) **6,325**

Classical center table, carved mahogany & mahogany veneer, the round veneered top tilting & overhanging a veneered apron above the central heavy round tapering pedestal w/a molded collar above the egg-and-dart carved base band, cen-

Classical Tilt-top Center Table

tered on the tripartite base above carved paw feet on casters, old refinish, Philadelphia, ca. 1830, imperfections, 44 3/4" d., 28 1/2" h. (ILLUS.) **4,370**

Classical Japanned Center Table

Classical center table, japanned wood, the rounded top painted w/chinoiserie decoration in gold on black, tilting above a heavy ring-turned columnar standard, on a cross-form plinth raised on tapered turned feet, New York State, ca. 1830, some losses & restoration to decoration, 34" h. (ILLUS.).................................. **2,760**

Classical console table, bird's-eye maple & mahogany, the rectangular white marble top w/a molded edge above a straight apron centering a mahogany inlaid panel w/ovolo corners, repeated on the side, flanked by square mahogany corner blocks ending in turned acorn pendants, on a heavy square tapering pedestal & concave-shaped cross-form platform on double-ball turned feet, old finish, probably Vermont, ca. 1825-30, 20 x 40", 32" h. **2,875**

Classical console table, mahogany & mahogany veneer, the long white marble top w/canted front corners above a conforming ogee apron w/crotch grain veneering raised on two heavy S-scroll front legs w/veneering resting on a rectangular plinth w/concave front, the back framework enclosing a rectangular mirror, ca. 1840, 19 1/2 x 42 1/2", 32" h. **2,990**

Classical Country-style Work Table

Classical country-style work table, bird's-eye maple, tiger stripe maple & cherry, the rectangular top above a deep case w/two drawers w/turned wood knobs, raised on knob-, ring- and rod-turned legs w/double-knob feet, old refinish, possibly Pennsylvania, ca. 1825, imperfections, 19 x 21 1/2", 29"h. (ILLUS.)......... **1,610**

Classical Mahogany Pier Table

Classical pier table, carved mahogany & mahogany veneer, a rectangular black marble top w/rounded edges above a veneered frieze w/banded edges above a pier mirror flanked by heavy scrolled & fancarved supports on a conformingly shaped platform joined by an incurved shelf, on four turned feet, original finish, Boston, ca. 1825, imperfections, 19 1/4 x 38", 33 3/4" h. (ILLUS.)....................................... **2,760**

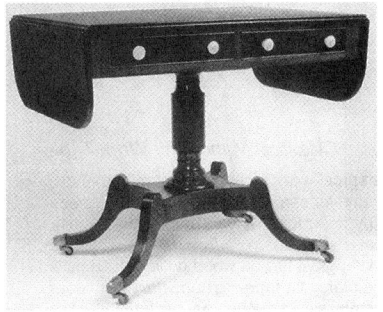

Fine Classical Sofa Table

Classical sofa table, mahogany & mahogany inlaid veneer, the rectangular overhanging reeded top w/two rounded end drop leaves above an apron w/one faux & one working cockbeaded string-inlaid drawer on each side, raised on a ring-turned pedestal & concave platform above outswept curving legs ending in cast foliate brass casters, appears to retain original ivory pulls, Rhode Island, ca. 1810-15, imperfections, open 35 1/2 x 55 1/2", 29 1/4" h. (ILLUS.) **6,900**

Classical Work Table

Classical work table, carved mahogany & mahogany veneer, the rectangular top flanked by two wide D-form drop leaves above the deep apron w/two round-fronted drawers w/simple turned wood pulls, on a heavy square tapering pedestal w/a stepped base on the cross-form platform raised on scrolled leaf carving & paw feet on casters, refinished, attributed to Isaac Vose and Son, Boston, ca. 1825, closed 21 x 22", 30 1/2" h. (ILLUS.) **2,875**

Classical Mahogany Work Table

Classical work table, mahogany & mahogany veneer, a nearly square top flanked by half-round hinged drop leaves above a deep apron w/two small drawers w/original turned wood pulls, raised on a rectangular tapering pedestal w/four concave sides above the conforming platform base on bulbous baluster-turned

feet on casters, old refinish, imperfections, Boston, 1830s, 18 1/8 x 19" plus leaves, 29 3/4" h. (ILLUS.) **1,300**

Country-style tavern table, maple, birch & pine, a rectangular one-board pine scrubbed top w/breadboard ends, on an apron w/a single dovetailed drawer w/beaded edge & brass pull, on knob- and rod-turned legs w/blocks on button feet joined by flat box stretchers, old worn red finish, New England, late 18th c., 18 1/2 x 22 1/2", 25" h. (two posts w/top age cracks w/square nails added) **4,675**

Country-style work table, painted pine, a rectangular three-board removable top overhanging a deep apron w/a pair of deep drawers w/turned wooden knobs, on ring-, knob- and baluster-turned legs w/peg feet, old worn brown paint over red, Pennsylvania, 19th c., 36 x 54", 30 1/2" h. (age cracks, chips on legs, replaced pegs in the top) **1,760**

Federal card table, inlaid mahogany & satinwood, the hinged top w/elliptical front half w/serpentine ends & dart inlaid edges above a conforming apron of satinwood panels w/edge of crossbanding & geometric inlay, inlaid dies top the reeded turned & tapering legs ending in swelled peg feet, old finish, Boston, ca. 1810, 36 1/2" w., 29" h. (minor imperfections) **17,250**

Federal country-style breakfast table, tiger stripe maple, a rectangular top flanked by drop leaves w/ovolo corners above a straight apron on four slender square tapering legs, old finish, New England, ca. 1810, 18 x 36 1/4" closed, 27 1/2" h. **3,738**

Federal country-style dining table, cherry, rectangular top flanked by wide drop leaves, on slender baluster-, ring- and rod-turned legs w/double knob feet, refinished, early 19th c., 17 1/2 x 36" plus 13" leaves, 28 1/2" h. **880**

Federal country-style dining table, curly maple & cherry, the rectangular maple top flanked by wide maple drop leaves above a maple apron, on six baluster- and ring-turned cherry legs w/knob feet, refinished, first half 19th c., 19 3/8 x 48" plus 18" leaves, 29" h. (age cracks in top, some warp) **715**

Federal country-style dining table, painted pine, rectangular top w/rounded ends flanked by two hinged half-round drop leaves, apron w/a single dovetailed end drawer, on square tapering legs, old brown graining, 19th c., found in Maine, 19 1/4 x 40 3/4" plus 10 3/4" w. leaves, 29 1/4" h. (worm holes, wear, some paint touch-up) **1,320**

Federal country-style dining table, tiger stripe maple, a narrow rectangular top w/rounded ends flanked by deep D-form drop leaves above a deep flat apron raised on tall square tapering legs, old refinish, New England, ca. 1800-10, open 41 1/2 x 41 3/4", 28 1/2" h. (ILLUS. top next page) **2,645**

Federal Country Dining Table

Federal country-style dining table, tiger stripe maple, a rectangular top flanked by wide drop leaves w/rounded corners, on plain turned legs ending in baluster-turned & peg feet, old refinish, New England, ca. 1820, open 20 x 47", 29 1/2" h. (imperfections)... **1,150**

Federal country-style dressing table, cherry, a rectangular top w/a high ornately scroll-cut three-quarters gallery above a single long dovetailed drawer, raised on ring- and rod-turned supports over a medial shelf w/concave front, on ring-turned short legs w/knob feet, refinished, first half 19th c., 16 x 30", 34 1/2" h. (glued restorations, top reset) **550**

Federal country-style dressing table, grain-painted, the high scroll-cut splashboard above a narrow rectangular top over a pair of drawers set-back on the rectangular top w/rounded edges, the apron w/a single long drawer, simple turned-wood knobs, baluster- and ring-turned legs w/peg feet, labeled "J.G. Briggs, Charlestown, New Hampshire," original black & gold graining to similuate rosewood, ca. 1830-33, 16 x 36 3/8", 39" h. (minor imperfections)............................. **920**

Federal country-style dressing table, painted & decorated, an upright flat rectangular backsplash flanked by blocked uprights above a narrow rectangular top over a pair of small drawers on a stepped-out rectangular top w/rounded edges above an apron w/a single long narrow drawer painted to resemble two small drawers, multi-ring turned legs w/knob feet, old yellow ground w/olive green & gold highlights, banding & fruit & foliage stenciled decoration on the backsplash & drawers, original round brass pulls, Newburyport, Massachusetts, ca. 1820-30, 17 1/2 x 35 3/4", 40 1/2" h. (minor surface imperfections)..................... **4,600**

Federal country-style side table, cherry & maple, the long octagonal top tilting over a baluster- and ring-turned pedestal on a tripod base w/spider legs, New England, ca. 1790, 14 3/4 x 22", 28" h. (old finish) **4,025**

Federal Country-style Tavern Table

Federal country-style tavern table, maple, the rectangular breadboard top widely overhanging an apron w/a single long drawer raised on slender square tapering legs, old surface w/vestiges of dark brown paint, possibly southeastern New England, ca. 1800, 25 x 36", 27 3/4" h. (ILLUS.) **2,875**

Federal country-style tavern table, pine, rectangular two-board removable top above a slightly canted apron on four canted square tapering legs, old red finish, Pennsylvania, early 19th c., 22 1/2 x 26 1/2", 28 3/4" h. (pins for top missing, top cleaned)......................... **990**

Federal country-style work table, birch & pine, wide one-board rectangular top overhanging the apron w/a single long dovetailed drawer w/replaced small wood turned pulls, square tapering legs, cleaned down to old red wash, pegged construction w/square nails, first half 19th c., 27 1/8 x 41 3/4", 29" h. (chips on top, areas of touch up) **550**

Federal country-style work table, walnut, rectangular three-board removable top w/underside cleats dovetailed into the top, on a deep apron w/a pair of deep dovetailed drawers w/turned wood knobs, ring- and knob-turned legs w/a long central octagonal section, knob feet, probably original finish, early 19th c., 33 3/4 x 48", 30" h. (one cleat cracked) **1,320**

Federal dining table, mahogany, a long rectangular top flanked by wide rectangular drop leaves, raised on four square double tapering legs, two swinging out for support, joined by a straight apron w/crossbanded & string inlaid edge, cuff inlaid legs, original finish, New England, ca. 1790-1800, 17 x 47", 28 1/2" h. (very minor imperfections) **2,990**

Federal dining table, mahogany & bird's-eye maple, long rectangular top flanked by D-form hinged drop leaves above a dovetailed drawer at each end w/maple veneer drawer fronts w/old brass rosette & bail pulls, on slender square tapering legs w/double line inlay, early 19th c., 18 7/8 x 44" plus 9 1/2" leaves, 27 1/2" h. (restorations)............................... **1,100**

Federal dining table, mahogany & mahogany veneer, three-part, D-form end sections on conforming aprons w/cock-beaded edges joining four vase- and ring-turned slightly swelled reeded legs topped by veneered dies & ending in applied brass ball feet, flanking a central rectangular top w/deep hinged drop leaves on a deeply recessed straight apron joining six tapering square legs, two of which swing out, old surface, Philadelphia, ca. 1810-15, open 54 x 122", 28 3/4" h. (minor repairs) **9,200**

Federal dining table, mahogany & mahogany veneer, two-part, each section w/a D-shaped top above a conforming straight apron w/cross-banded lower edges continuing around the square tapering legs, each half w/a single wide hinged rectangular drop leaf, old refinish, New England, ca. 1800, 43 x 84", 29" h. (imperfections) **2,645**

Federal dining table, mahogany veneer, three-part, the two D-form ends flanking a rectangular center section w/two hinged drop leaves, raised on square tapering legs, old surface, Virginia, early 19th c., extended 48 x 85 1/2", 28 3/4" h. (imperfections) **12,650**

Federal dining table, mahogany veneer, two-part, the two ends each rounded & w/a hinged leaf supported from beneath, above a skirt on ring-turned spiral-carved legs ending in ring-turned feet on casters, Massachusetts, 1820s, 46 x 78 3/4", 28 3/4" h. (minor surface blemishes) **1,840**

Federal Pembroke table, mahogany & mahogany veneer, rectangular top flanked by two half-round scalloped drop leaves above an apron w/a working beaded drawer at one end & a false drawer at the other, on slender reeded turned & tapering legs w/peg feet, attributed to Newburyport, Massachusetts, early 19th c., refinished top, old finish on base, closed 19 x 30 1/2", 28 1/2" h. (replaced brasses, break in one rule joint, minor restoration)........................... **2,090**

Federal Pembroke table, mahogany veneer, a rectangular top flanked by wide D-form drop leaves w/notched corners above an apron w/a working drawer at one end & a faux drawer at the other, raised on turned tapering reeded legs w/baluster- and knob-turned feet, old refinish, New York, early 19th c., 22 1/2 x 36", 28 1/8" h. (replaced drawer pull, very minor imperfections) **1,380**

Federal Pembroke table, mahogany veneer, rectangular top flanked by shaped drop leaves & two end drawers, one working, one faux, above a cockbeaded skirt & turned & reeded tapering legs on casters, old refinish, replaced brass, New York, New York, ca. 1815, 22 1/4 x 34", 29" h. (very minor imperfections)............... **3,105**

Federal Pembroke table, mahogany veneer, rectangular top flanked by wide half-round hinged leaves above an apron w/a working drawer at one end & a faux drawer at the other, cockbeaded skirt raised above spiral-turned tapering legs

ending in ring-turned peg feet, old refinish, New York, ca. 1815, 23 x 36", 27 1/2" h. (replaced brass) **1,150**

Federal-Style card table, inlaid mahogany, a fold-over D-form top w/two pointed rim sections above the conforming lower top on a deep apron w/line-inlaid panels & diamonds at the top of the four square tapering legs, rear spring legs, old dark finish, early 20th c., 18 x 35", 28 3/4" h. (veneer chips on inside of apron) **550**

Harvest table, country-style, ash, a long three-board top overhanging a deep apron, on ring-, knob- and rod-turned legs w/baluster-turned feet, old red wash, 26 x 94 3/4", 31 1/2" h. (added supports)...... **660**

Harvest table, painted pine, a very long scrubbed top flanked by hinged drop leaves, painted base w/ring- and rod-turned legs w/knob feet, early surface w/old natural color top & early olive green paint on base, New England, late 18th - early 19th c., open 39 3/4 x 102 3/4", 20 1/2" h. (imperfections)........................... **11,500**

Harvest table, painted pine, long rectangular two-board top w/breadboard ends widely overhanging a straight skirt & ring- and baluster-turned tapering legs w/ball feet, original red paint, central Massachusetts, 1820-30, 32 x 96", 29 1/4" h. (very minor imperfections) **9,775**

Early Painted Hutch Table

Hutch (or chair) table, painted & decorated pine, the rectangular overhanging top lifting above a bench seat joining cut-out ends w/recessed panels on cut-out feet, old yellow paint w/grain-painted oblong panels & black accents, possibly Upstate New York, early 19th c., imperfections, 35 3/4x 52 1/4", 30" h. (ILLUS.) **3,335**

Hutch (or chair) table, painted pine, a long wide rectangular three-board top tilting on mortised braces above wide bootjack ends flanking the wide two-board seat w/apron, old worn green repaint, 35 x 72", 28" h. (chips, age cracks)........... **3,300**

Hutch (or chair) table, painted pine, the long rectangular top lifting above a reeded bench seat joining double-demilune cut-out ends w/exposed tenons, old red paint, New Jersey, early 19th c., 35 3/4 x 76", 27" h. (minor imperfections) **9,775**

Hutch (or chair) table, painted pine, the round top attached w/dowels & tilting above the shaped arms & plank seat over shoe feet, early red paint, New England, 18th c., 48 3/4 x 54 1/4", 27 1/2" h. **6,900**

Hutch (or chair) table, pine, birch & poplar, two-board rectangular top w/breadboard ends & scrubbed finish, tilting above a mortised & pinned base w/a single drawer under the seat & raised on shoe feet, traces of old red finish, found in Vermont, 19th c., 37 3/4 x 41 3/4", 28 3/4" h. (age cracks in top).. **4,180**

Louis XV-Style Marquetry Side Table

Louis XV-Style side table, gilt-bronze mounted tulipwood marquetry, the shaped rectangular top veneered w/a flower-filled basket & sprays of flowers within a brass banding, above a single frieze drawer, the drawer & apron sides similarly inlaid w/flowers, raised on simple cabriole legs w/gilt-bronze knee mounts & sabots, France, late 19th c., 16 x 27", 28" h. (ILLUS.) **6,600**

Mission-style (Arts & Crafts movement) dining table, a narrow rectangular top w/rounded ends flanked by wide half-round drop leaves, raised on double square legs forming a trestle base & w/two swing-out support legs, branded mark of L. & J.G. Stickley, Model No. 553, ca. 1915, 42" d., 30" h. **4,935**

Mission-style (Arts & Crafts movement) library table, oak, a rectangular top slightly overhanging an apron w/a pair of drawers w/rectangular copper pulls over long corbels on the heavy square legs joined by a lower medial shelf w/through-tenons joining the end stretchers, Hand-craft decal of L. & J.G. Stickley, Model No. 522, 1906-10, 30 x 48", 30" h. **1,840**

Mission-style (Arts & Crafts movement) library table, oak, a wide rectangular top overhanging a case w/two-tiered end open shelves w/vertical slats at each end & joined by a single long drawer over a lower medial stretcher shelf, original finish, branded Charles Limbert mark, Model No. 106, ca. 1907, 29 1/2 x 48", 29 1/2" h. (ILLUS. top next column) **1,380**

Limbert Mission Oak Library Table

Mission-style (Arts & Crafts movement) library table, oak, rectangular top overhanging an apron w/a pair of drawers w/rectangular copper pulls, heavy square legs joined by medial shelf w/pegged through tenons, medium brown finish, red decal mark of Gustav Stickley, Model No. 675, 29 3/4 x 47 1/2", 30" h. (stains, scratches, joint separation)........................ **1,840**

Modern style coffee table, laminated birch, "Surfboard"-style, the top of seven-ply Baltic birch cover, long oval high-pressure laminate top & underside, raised on a wire base w/black power-coated finish, Herman Miller, ca. 1950s, 29 x 89", 10" h. **7,280**

1950s Dinette Table

Modern style dinette table, laminate & metal, the rectangular top flanked by wide D-form drop leaves all in red laminate w/black edging, raised on forked black tubular metal angled legs, National Chair Company, Whitman, Massachusetts, ca. 1955, minor surface abrasions, closed 21 3/4 x 29 3/4", 29 1/4" h. (ILLUS.) **86**

Queen Anne country-style tavern table, maple, rectangular two-board top w/notched corners cleaned & w/old finish w/stains, widely overhanging a deep flat mortised & pinned apron on turned tapered legs ending in duck feet, old red on the base, 18th c., 26 1/2 x 36", 27 1/2" h. (minor old age crack in top)........................ **5,500**

Queen Anne country-style tavern table, pine & maple, rectangular top widely overhanging a deep apron w/a single dovetailed drawer w/early peg pull, on ring-, baluster- and block-turned legs w/worn button feet, joined by worn box stretchers, mortise & peg construction, refinished, 18th c., 26 x 39", 27" h. (two glued breaks w/putty repairs in top) **2,640**

Queen Anne dining table, maple, a narrow rectangular top w/rounded ends flanked by wide D-form drop leaves on a straight apron raised on four block-turned tapering legs ending in pad feet, old refinish, Rhode Island, ca. 1750-70, 41 x 42", 26 1/2" h. (imperfections, restorations) **1,610**

Queen Anne dining table, maple, narrow rectangular top w/slightly rounded ends flanked by wide half-round hinged drop leaves above a straight apron on four block-turned tapering legs ending in pad feet, two legs swing-out for support, southeastern New England, 1740-60, refinished, 30 1/2 x 38 1/4", 26" h. (minor imperfections) **6,325**

Queen Anne dining table, Santo Domingo mahogany, rectangular narrow top flanked by deep rectangular hinged leaves overhanging the shaped apron on cabriole legs ending in pad feet on platforms, old finish, Rhode Island, ca. 1750-60, 16 1/2 x 47 3/4", 28 1/2" h. (minor imperfections) **10,925**

Queen Anne dressing table, carved cherry, rectangular thumb-molded top overhanginig the case w/a single long drawer above a row of three smaller drawers, the central one fan-carved, large ornate butterfly brasses, cyma-curved apron, four cabriole legs w/spurs & arris knees ending in high-pad feet, original brasses, old refinish, coastal Massachusetts, New Hampshire or Maine, 1750-80, 20 x 33", 30" h. (imperfections) **29,900**

Queen Anne dressing table, walnut, the rectangular top w/a molded edge & notched front corners overhanging a case w/a long thumb-molded drawer over a row of three deep drawers, the central long one w/fan carving, the apron w/flat-headed arches on cabriole legs ending in pad feet, replaced brasses, old surface, Massachusetts, 1730-50, 19 1/2 x 34 1/2", 28 1/2" h. (minor repairs & losses) **28,750**

Queen Anne tea table, cherry, the round top tilting above a birdcage platform & a vase- and ring-turned pedestal on a tripod base w/cabriole legs ending in pad feet on platforms, old surface, probably Rhode Island, late 18th c., 33" d., 29 3/4" h. (minor imperfections) **1,610**

"Sawbuck" table, country-style, painted pine, rectangular one-board top w/scrubbed & stained finish above the flat cross-legs w/flat stretchers, old yellow & brown ground repaint on base, found in New Hampshire, 26 x 50", 30" h. **550**

"Sawbuck" table, painted pine, a rectangular one-board scrubbed top on crossed end legs joined by cross stretcher of applied moldings w/beaded edges, old red paint on base w/traces of white, square nail construction, 19th c., 18 3/4 x 31 3/4", 25 1/4" h. **990**

"Sawbuck" table, painted pine, one-board rectangular top w/scrubbed finish on crossed end legs joined by flat board braces w/a removable board top forming a shallow bin, square nail construction, old bluish grey repaint, 19th c., 25 1/2 x 36 1/2", 28" h. (top age cracks, some water damage to feet) **2,420**

"Sawbuck" table, pine, rectangular top on braces over cross-form legs joined by stretchers, enclosing a V-shaped trough, bluish green paint over old red stain, New England, 19th c., 25 1/2 x 42", 30 1/2" h. (imperfections) **805**

Early New England Sawbuck Table

"Sawbuck" table, the rectangular table overhanging a trough above square tapering X-legs, original surface w/a darkened top above a red-stained base, New England, late 18th - early 19th c., minor imperfections, 23 5/8 x 34 1/2", 28 1/2" h. (ILLUS.) **2,645**

Store table, country-style, painted, a very long rectangular top widely overhanging a deep apron w/three large drawers each w/two old iron finger-grip pulls, on square tapering chamfered legs, old beige & brown grain painting, probably New England, first half 19th c. **10,925**

Tavern table, country-style, maple, poplar & pine, a rectangular one-board wide top w/scalloped corners & a single wide drop leaf at one side also w/scalloped corners, pegged apron raised on four baluster- and block-turned legs w/turned feet all joined by flat box stretchers, late 18th - early 19th c., 23 1/2 x 39 1/2", 29" h. (hinged replaced, top loose & w/age crack, feet ended out) **1,320**

Turn-of-the-century dining table, oak, round divided top resting on a columnar pedestal supported by four heavy cabriole legs ending in carved paw feet, ca. 1900, 48" d., 30 1/2" h. **588**

Turn-of-the-century library table, oak, an oblong top above a conforming apron w/a pair of drawers on one side w/bail pulls, each corner carved w/a classical female bust at the top of a cabriole leg ending in a claw-and-ball foot, a rectangular medial shelf w/serpentine sides joined w/C-scroll brackets to each leg, ca. 1890, 28 x 42", 29" h. **1,568**

Victorian Baroque Dining Table

Victorian Baroque Revival dining table, carved walnut, a rectangular draw-leaf top w/a molded & scallop-carved chamfered edge above a deep scroll-carved apron, raised on large boldly carved angled figural griffin legs joined by a cross-stretcher, late 19th c., 41 x 48", 31" h. (ILLUS.).. **1,150**

Late Victorian Round Dining Table

Victorian Baroque Revival dining table, mahogany, the round expandable top w/narrow gadrooned rim band & deep apron raised on a heavy round pedestal w/the ribbed lower section surrounded by four large carved lion's heads over leaf-carved scrolls continuing into extended legs ending in paw feet, old mellow alligatored finish, w/five leaves, minor wear, late 19th c., 59 1/2" d., 29 1/2" h. (ILLUS.).. **5,225**

Victorian Eastlake side table, walnut, a rectangular top w/molded edges above a deep apron w/a narrow central burl panel flanked by incised line bands & a scroll-cut edge band on each side, raised on a cluster of four slender flat rectangular line-incised legs flaring out at the bottom & on porcelain casters, the legs centered by a baluster- and ring-turned post joined to them by a short cross stretcher, ca. 1890, 20 1/2 x 28", 31 1/4" h..................... **358**

Victorian Eastlake Parlor Table

Victorian Eastlake substyle parlor table, walnut, a rectangular white marble top w/scalloped corners above a line-incised apron w/scallop-cut trim raised on a cluster of four squared legs curving out at the lower section & each w/cut-out bands & scallop-cut trim, the cluster joined at the center by a center ring-turned post, on casters, ca. 1885, 18 x 30", 26" h. (ILLUS.) **252**

Victorian Renaissance Revival substyle dining table, walnut, round extension top w/molded edges & a molded apron, raised on a heavy octagonal split pedestal w/four ornate molded & S-scroll legs on casters alternating w/slender tall oblong raised panels, w/three leaves, ca. 1870, 45" d. **2,520**

Victorian Renaissance Revival substyle parlor center table, walnut, a shaped wood-framed brown marble top resting on a center urn pedestal surrounded by four shaped legs w/acanthus leaf- and medallion-carvings, w/burl wood veneer panels & incised gilt carvings overall, ca. 1875, 23 1/2 x 33", 30 1/2" h. **990**

Renaissance Revival Parlor Table

Victorian Renaissance Revival substyle parlor center table, walnut & burl walnut, the rectangular top w/a wide molded edge w/chamfered corners & an inset white marble top above the deep apron w/raised burl panels & molded lower edge, raised on four slender trumpet-turned legs w/baluster-turned feet & a serpentine cross-stretcher centered by a turned urn finial, ca. 1875, 22 x 28", 35" h. (ILLUS.) **1,064**

Victorian Renaissance Revival substyle parlor center table, walnut, the rectangular top w/wide rounded ends & molded edges above a conforming apron w/panels & incised decoration flanked at each corner by a block w/a small square carved lion head, knob-, block & tapering cylindrical-turned legs w/peg feet joined by a knob- and ring-turned cross-stretcher joining incurved end stretchers, ca. 1875, 24 1/2 x 41", 29" h. **633**

Fine Victorian Rococo Console Table

Victorian Rococo substyle console table, rosewood marquetry, the bow-front white marble top w/rounded outset corners above a conforming apron w/floral marquetry above an applied scroll skirt centered w/an ormolu rosette on two scroll-carved legs headed w/stylized flower and scroll ormolu mounts & joined by a shaped arched stretcher w/a central cartouche decorated w/a rocaille mount, New York, ca. 1860, 21 3/4 x 35 1/2", 35 5/8" h. (ILLUS.).. **3,680**

Victorian Rococo Parlor Center Table

Victorian Rococo substyle parlor center table, carved rosewood, a white marble 'turtle-top' above a serpentine molded apron deeply carved on all sides w/a spray of flowers & fruit, raised on four in-

curved cabriole legs carved to match & joined by a pierced foliate-carved X-form stretcher centered by an urn filled w/nuts & w/a turned finial, on casters, ca. 1850, 30 1/2 x 42 3/4", 30" h. (ILLUS.)................ **2,880**

Victorian Rococo substyle parlor center table, rosewood, a white marble 'turtle' top above a deep conforming serpentine apron carved w/banded panels centered by a large fruit cluster on each side, raised on incurved cabriole legs w/carved knees & joined by cross-form S-scroll stretchers centered by a small turned urn, on casters, ca. 1860, 42" l., 29" h. **1,120**

Wicker tea cart, rectangular top w/deep slightly rounded tightly woven apron supporting a wicker-trimmed lift-off glass tray top, wrapped corner supports joined by a lower oak shelf w/flat braided wicker edging, front wooden-spoked wheels, upright tall S-scroll wrapped handle at the back, old brown-stained finish, early 20th c., 20 x 33 3/4", 33 1/2" h. (minor damage & small repaired break on one side of handle)... **385**

William & Mary tavern table, maple & pine, the rectangular breadboard top overhanging an apron on block-, baluster- and ring-turned splayed legs joined by box stretchers on small knob feet, old surface, 15 x 21 3/4", 25" h. (imperfections)... **2,530**

William & Mary Tavern Table

William & Mary tavern table, painted birch & pine, the oval overhanging top rests on four splayed slender baluster- and ring-turned legs continuing to turned feet & joined by a straight apron & box stretchers, painted black, probably New England, mid-18th c., imperfections, 24 x 33", 17" h. (ILLUS.) **8,050**

Windsor side table, painted pine, a scrubbed rectangular top w/breadboard ends widely overhanging four slightly canted rod- and baluster-turned legs joined by upper & lower box stretchers, legs w/red staining, top w/old natural finish, New England, early 19th c., 20 1/4 x 29 1/2", 26 1/2" h. (ILLUS. top next page) **2,415**

Early Windsor Side Table

Wardrobes & Armoires

French Art Deco Armoire

Armoire, Art Deco, mahogany veneer, a three-section curvilinear form composed of a center section w/two short open shelves above a cupboard w/hinged drop door opening to a compartment w/two drawers in shades of blond wood & three drawers below, the whole flanked by two tall flat cupboard doors w/rounded corners, one opening to three shelves, France, ca. 1930, 22 x 71", 71" h. (ILLUS.)... **1,955**

Elegant Classical Armoire

Armoire, Classical, mahogany & mahogany veneer, the rectangular top w/a widely flaring deep ogee cornice above a frieze band w/ormolu figural swan mounts above a pair of tall paneled doors flanked by half-round columns w/acanthus leaf & scroll carvings & ormolu mounts, flat rounded front feet w/mounts, early 19th c., 19 x 60", 90" h. (ILLUS.) **2,200**

French Provincial Carved Armoire

Armoire, French Provincial, oak, a rectangular top w/a widely flaring deep stepped cornice w/carved geometric frieze bands centered by pierce-carved central blocks, birds & grapevines above a pair of tall paneled doors w/grapevine carved panels at the top & base of each & long narrow brass strap hardware, a long carved pilaster between the doors, the deep scalloped apron carved w/further grapevines & a central floral medallion, short scroll front feet, France, 19th c., 18 x 72", 88" h. (ILLUS.)... **2,415**

Armoire, Louis XV Provincial-style, fruitwood, the arched molded wide cornice above a pair of paneled & scroll-carved doors, raised on short cabriole legs ending in scrolled toes, France, late 18th - early 19th c., 24 1/2 x 56", 95" h. (worming, restoration)... **1,725**

Louis XV-Style Oak Armoire

Armoire, Louis XV-Style, oak, a rectangular top w/rounded corners on the deep, widely flaring stepped cornice above a leaf-carved frieze band centered by a carved basket above a pair of tall doors w/scroll and floral vine top border over an asymmetrical glazed panel above a medial band of leafy scroll carving above the lower solid panel, the sides w/three square panels, raised on a molded plinth on square feet, w/the original oak panels for the glazed door sections, France, 19th c., 24 x 60", 87" h. (ILLUS.) **3,450**

French Provincial Hardwood Armoire

Armoire, Louis XV-Style Provincial style, hardwood, a rectangular top above a deep rounded & curved cornice above a pair of tall paneled cupboard doors w/long scroll-tipped keyhole escutcheons opening to shelves & a drawer, a deep scallop-edged front apron joining tall scrolled feet, France, 19th c., 23 x 50", 7' 6" h. (ILLUS.) **690**

Armoire, Louis XV-Style, walnut, the arched crestrail w/a high scroll- and cartouche-carved center crest above a conforming molded frieze band over the tall arched mirrored door, scroll-molded apron on short scrolled cabriole legs, overall marquetry veneer work, France, late 19th - early 20th c., 19 x 39", 99" h. .. **1,100**

Large Baroque-Style Rosewood Kas

Armoire, Louis XV-XVI Provincial-style, cherry & elm, a later rectangular molded cornice above a pair of tall paneled doors, shaped skirt, raised on short cabriole legs w/scroll feet, late 18th c., 24 1/2 x 55", 80" h. (restorations, worming) **1,150**

Kas (a version of the Netherlands Kast or wardrobe), Baroque-Style, rosewood, the large rectangular top w/a widely flaring & stepped cornice overhanging the case w/a wide frieze band above a carved figural tablet above the pair of tall paneled cupboard doors opening to shelves, on a molded plinth raised on heavy turned bun front feet, Europe, 19th c., 32 1/2 x 87", 88" h. (ILLUS. bottom previous column) **1,440**

Fine Early New York Kas

Kas (a version of the Netherlands Kast or wardrobe), cherry, a rectangular top w/a very deep & widely flaring stepped cornice above a molded frieze band over a pair of tall doors w/stepped raised panels, flanked & centered by wide vertical two-panel raised above a lower molding over a pair of deep drawers w/wooden knobs separated by three raised diamond devices, flared molded base raised on heavy turned turnip feet, top part of crown of later date, New York state, ca. 1750 (ILLUS.) **3,360**

Chippendale Gumwood Kas

Kas (a version of the Netherlands Kast or wardrobe), Chippendale, gumwood, the rectangular top w/a widely flaring deep stepped cornice above a pair of tall raised panel cupboard doors opening to three shelves, a mid-molding over a long bottom drawer on the molded base w/ogee bracket feet, cast brass hardware, New York or New Jersey, ca. 1780 (ILLUS.)... **8,400**

Early New York Kas

Kas (a version of the Netherlands Kast or wardrobe), William & Mary style, gumwood & poplar, the rectangular top w/a widely flaring deep stepped cornice above a frieze band over a pair of tall raised panel doors separated by three sections of rectangular applied molding, the interior w/two shelves, a mid-molding over a single long drawer w/the face divided w/moldings to resemble two drawers & flanked by raised diamonds, molded base on tall turnip front feet, refinished, New York, ca. 1740, imperfections, 55 1/2" w., 78" h. (ILLUS.) **13,800**

New York Stained Poplar Kas

Kas (a version of the Netherlands Kast or wardrobe), William & Mary style, stained poplar, the rectangular top w/a widely flaring deep stepped cornice above a

paneled frieze band over a pair of doors each w/two raised panels, the upper panel w/an arched top, exterior-mounted butterfly hinges, narrow vertical panels flanking the doors, a single long drawer across the bottom, deep molded base raised on large ball feet, New York state, mid-18th c., feet replaced, wear, 23 x 59", 78 3/4" h. (ILLUS.)...................... **5,175**

Art Deco Style Wardrobe

Wardrobe, Art Deco, oak, a flat rectangular top above a plain case w/a large tall flat door on the left & two shorter flat doors on the right, one side opens to a clothes rack, the two doors fitted w/four slide-out shelves, light finish, Bauhaus influenced design, Germany, ca. 1930, wear, scratches, 23 3/4 x 53", 71 1/2" h. (ILLUS.) **460**

Wardrobe, Chippendale, painted poplar, a rectangular top w/cove-molded cornice above a pair of tall cupboard doors w/two raised panels, the upper panels w/arched tops, a single long deep drawer w/molded edging at the bottom, molded base on scroll-cut bracket feet, mustard yellow repaint, late 18th - early 19th c., 20 x 45", 67" h. (replaced brass escutcheon, repaired breaks in feet)... **2,750**

Wardrobe, country corner-style, painted walnut, poplar & chestnut, flat top w/a coved cornice above a tall narrow paneled door flanked by sharply angled side boards above bootjack feet, front bracket feet, old red-painted finish, 19th c., 23 x 42", 81" h. (paint removed from framework of door, edge damage on cornice)... **3,025**

Wardrobe, country-style, painted pine & poplar, a rectangular thick top above a tall two-panel off-center door above a single bottom drawer, molded flat base, pottery knob on door, wood knobs on drawer, interior fitted w/14 small cast-iron hooks & replaced shelf, old brown repaint, 19th c., age crack in door, top 19 x 39 3/4", 83 1/2" h. (ILLUS. top next page) **523**

Painted Country-style Wardrobe

Wardrobe, country-style, painted pine, rectangular top over a single tall door opening to an interior of nine coat pegs & four short shelves, on a cut-out base joined by shaped skirt, overall original red paint, New England, early 19th c., 13 x 46 3/4", 67 1/2" h. (paint wear) **4,140**

Painted Break-down-style Wardrobe

Wardrobe, country-style, painted poplar, a rectangular top w/a deep coved cornice above a pair of tall two-panel cupboard doors opening to four added shelves & a peg rack, four wide boards across the back, well done brown over mustard yellow grained repaint, breaks down into three sections, 19th c., 17 x 59", 80" h. (ILLUS.).. **440**

Wardrobe, country-style, painted poplar, a rectangular top w/a flat flaring cornice above a pair of tall narrow double panel doors opening to eight adjustable shelves & fixed center shelf, simple low bracket feet, original brown over tan wood graining, Amish, Ohio, 19th c., 20 1/4 x 64", 93 1/4" h. (ILLUS. top next column) **990**

Ohio Amish Painted Wardrobe

Wardrobe, country-style, pine, the rectangular top w/a flaring step-down cornice above a case w/a pair of tall doors w/three raised panels each & w/rattail iron hinges, molded base & cut-out bracket feet, mortise & peg construction, raised panels down the sides, refinished, Canada, late 18th - early 19th c., 18 x 50", 76" h. (feet & small section of cornice replaced).. **1,870**

Gustav Stickley Mission Wardrobe

Wardrobe, Mission-style (Arts & Crafts movement), oak, a rectangular top above a pair of tall double-paneled doors w/a small panel over a tall panel, copper V-pulls, interior fitted w/two open compartments over four long drawers above two open shelves, gently arched apron, red decal & paper Craftsman label of Gustav Stickley, Model No. 920, ca. 1910, some wear, small losses to wood at top, 16 1/2 x 34", 59 3/4" h. (ILLUS.).............. **14,950**

Victorian Faux Bamboo Wardrobe

Wardrobe, Victorian faux bamboo-style, bird's-eye maple, the pedimented top outlined w/bamboo-turned trim forming a forked finial above a deep frieze band w/applied bamboo-turned panels over the tall mirrored door framed w/bamboo turnings & opening to shelves, flanked by bamboo-turned stiles, a bamboo-turned medial rail over the single bottom drawer w/further applied bamboo turnings, side stiles continue down to form round feet, America, second half 19th c., 17 3/4 x 40", 92" h. (ILLUS.)` **3,162**

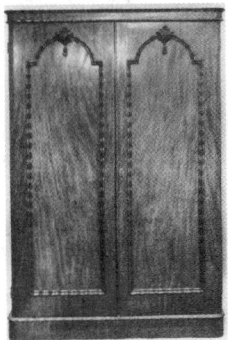

English Victorian Mahogany Wardrobe

Wardrobe, Victorian, mahogany & mahogany veneer, the rectangular top w/a narrow undulating cornice band w/rounded corners above a matching frieze band over a pair of tall arch-paneled doors w/carved scrolls at the top & further undulating molding outlining the panels, a matching base molding on the flat plinth base, brass pulls, refinished, England, mid-19th c., minor damage, 21 1/2 x 57", 82 3/4" h. (ILLUS.)...................................... **1,375**

Wardrobe, walnut, a rectangular removable top w/upright border boards centered at the front w/a long triangular pediment w/a large fan carving above a molded coved cornice above a wide frieze centered by a raised diamond above a pair of tall two-panel cupboard doors w/a small rectan-

gular panel above a tall raised rectangular lower panel, a mid-molding above the deep lower case w/molded bottom on blocked feet, original dark brown alligatored finish & black-painted detail, Zoar, Ohio, mid-19th c., 19 x 56 1/2", 83" h. (minor chips on cornice, narrow section of side molding missing) **2,750**

Whatnots & Etageres

Federal-Style Mahogany Etagere

Etagere, Federal-Style, mahogany & oak, a three-quarters gallery on the rectangular top above four tiered open rectangular shelves each w/an X-form back brace & three baluster-turned supports on each side, the bottom shelf above a single long drawer w/brass ring pulls, baluster- and ring-turned legs, turned acorn finials at the front of the two middle shelves, dark varnished finish, signed "Sahon, New York," early 20th c., 15 1/2 x 24", 64" h. (ILLUS.) **1,705**

English Regency-Style Etagere

Etagere, Regency-Style, mahogany, composed of four open graduated square shelves supported on slender ring-turned supports, the bottom shelf over a shallow drawer, slender turned legs on casters, marked by Edwards & Roberts, England, late 19th c., restorations, 21" sq., 54 1/2" h. (ILLUS.).. **4,025**

Victorian Aesthetic Corner Etagere

Etagere, Victorian Aesthetic Movement substyle, corner-style, fruitwood w/ivory inlay, the superstructure w/a scroll-cut & pierced pediment above a swag- and dentil-inlaid cornice over a scroll & floral triangular panel flanked by mirrored triangular panels over two rectangular mirrored panels above a galleried shelf above a pair of rectangular mirrors flanked by narrow inlaid side panels, the lower case w/a three-sided front above a conforming case w/a rectangular ribbon-, scroll & grotesque face panel flanked by two side shelves over a deep open lower compartment w/slender turned front supports, ca. 1870, 17 x 27 1/2", 6'10" h. (ILLUS.).. **2,300**

Etagere, Victorian Renaissance Revival substyle, carved walnut, the very high crest topped by a small arched & scroll-carved finial over a scroll-carved cartouche flanked by angled rails over raised burl panels & an arched molding w/a bold carved center cartouche flanked by turned finials, further raised burl panels above a tall arched mirror flanked by shaped sides w/three graduated quarter-round shelves on each side w/two oblong mirror panels on each side, the stepped-out base w/a shaped white marble top above a conforming plinth centered by a single drawer w/a carved ram's head pull, base molding on small block feet,

Ornate Renaissance Revival Etagere

two side scrolls missing, minor backboard replacements, ca. 1875, 17 x 43 1/4", 95 1/2" h. (ILLUS.)................ **3,850**

Ornate Rosewood Etagere

Etagere, Victorian Rococo substyle, carved rosewood, composed of three upper graduated open serpentine shelves supported by ornate S- and C-scroll brackets w/a leaf-carved top finial over looping scrolls w/pierced looping scrolls backing the lower two shelves & the large bottom shelf, a scroll-carved apron at the front, mid-19th c., 36" w., 68" h. (ILLUS.)................ **476**

Etagere, Victorian Rococo substyle, rosewood, a fretwork-carved pediment surmounting a triptych mirror w/tiered shelves, over a demi-lune marble top base w/mirrored back & tiered shelves, supported by acanthus leaf-carved cabriole legs, mid-19th c., 23 x 55", 94" h. **2,200**

GAMES & GAME BOARDS

The following listings cover Early Age American Games for the years 1744-1880. All prices are for games in very good condition. Very good condition is defined as still a collectible game, but shows strong signs of use and deterioration. A game in this condition is still considered collectible in pre-1970 games. The outside box corners have heavy wear, the edges are worn and one or two edges are torn. The box top has minor pen or pencil marks with some fading. The aprons have bowing and wear. Inside of the box is characterized by warped build ups, heavy stress at folds of the board, if this is a card game there are slight creases on the cards. The components of a game considered to be in very good condition are: if the die-cuts are punched, the implements show wear and there may be slight tears in the instructions. Some minor implements can be missing and still be considered in very good condition.

Chiromagica Board Game

A Game - Counties of the State of New York, geography card game, copyright 1849, McCleary & Pierce $350

American Revolution, military/American Revolution card game, ca. 1850s, Nora Norwood, ... 750

Anybody and Everybody; Somebody and Nobody, social card game, ca. 1875, William R. Gould.. 150

Auctioneer, economic card game, copyright D. Eckley Hunter in 1866, A. Flanagan Co. 350

Authors Improved Card Game

Authors Improved, literary card game, copyright 1872, Milton Bradley & Co. (ILLUS.).. 150

Biographer, literary card game, copyright D. Eckley Hunter in 1866, A. Flanagan Co. 350

Botanical cards, plant card game, ca. 1822-23, F. & R. Lockwood.................. 1,500

Centennial Games of the Revolution, history card game, ca. 1870s, National Art Co. 350

Chameleonoscope, strategy card game, copyright 1870, Fisher & Denison 150

Chief, card game, copyright 1851, Thomas Lawrence 500

Chiromagica, mystic board game, ca. 1879, McLoughlin Brothers (ILLUS. top next column)..................................... 450

Christmas Game of the Months, holiday card game, ca. 1853, W. & S.B. Ives............ 500

Chronicles of Uncle Sam's Family, history card game, copyright 1876, Noyes, Snow & Co. 250

Comic Game of Multiplication Table, numbers card game, copyright 1846, Richard H. Pease... 400

Comical Converse, social card games, ca. 1849, W. & S.B. Ives.............................. 400

Conversations on Love, social card game, ca. 1875, McLoughlin Brothers.......... 150

Double Snap, action card game, copyright D. Eckley Hunter in 1866, A. Flanagan Co. 250

Fashion and Famine, social card game, ca. 1875, McLoughlin Brothers.......... 200

Figurette, miscellaneous card game, copyright 1875, Goodnow Brothers....................... 200

Fireside Game, social card game, ca. 1852, W. & S.B. Ives............................... 350

Flags of Nations, geography card game, ca. 1852, W. & S.B. Ives.................... 350

French Puzzle Brain Game, puzzle card game, copyright 1851, W. & S.B. Ives.......... 300

Game of Artists, art card game, ca. 1850s, Owens & Agar...................................... 350

Game of Dr. Busby, literary card game, 1st edition, beige cover, small symbols, copyright 1843, W. & S.B. Ives 450

Game of Dr. Busby, literary card game, 3rd edition, green cover, large symbols, copyright 1843, W. & S.B. Ives 250

Game of Dr. Busby, literary card game, lady at piano cover, ca. 1840s, Henry Ives, Selchow & Righter................................. 500

Game of Dr. Busby, literary card game, lady w/child cover, ca. 1840s, S.B. Ives, M. Bradley Co....................................... 500

Game of Pinafore, literary card game, copyright 1879, Fuller, Upham & Co............. 350

Game of Pope and Pagan, strategy board game, copyright 1844, W. & S.B. Ives....... 2,000

Game of Quotations, literary card game, copyright 1878, Clay Herrick 150

Game of Railway Traffic, travel & rail board game, copyright 1870, Fisher & Denison...... 500

Game of Snip, Snap, Snorum, social card game, new & illustrated, ca. 1850s, Bence & Recother................................... 350

Game of the Races, sports & horse racing board game, ca. 1840s, C.S. Francis & Co. .. 1,800

Game of the Travellers, travel, land, sea & rail board game, copyright 1856, John M. Ives & Co. **400**

Game of the Zouave, military card game, ca. 1861, Many & Delameter.......... **1,000**

Games of Ambuscade, Bounce & Constellation

Games of Ambuscade, Bounce & Constellation, combination board game, copyright 1877, McLoughlin Brothers (ILLUS.).. **350**

Games of Bobbing Around the Circle, Tri Bang, Robbing the Miller

Games of Bobbing Around the Circle, Tri Bang, Robbing the Miller, combination board game, ca. 1870s, McLoughlin Brothers (ILLUS.) **300**

Games of History for Young and Old

Games of History for Young and Old, history card game, ca. 1829, anonymous (ILLUS.) **500**

Grandmama's Game of Useful Knowledge, history card game, ca. 1860s, McLoughlin Brothers.. **125**

Helps to History, history card game, copyright 1866, D. Eckley Hunter **250**

Instructive Game of Authors, literary card game, copyright 1873, Porter & Coates........ **150**

Interrogatory Geographical Game of the World, geography card game, W.G. Evans, copyright 1830, C.S. Francis & Co....... **500**

Laughable Game of What D'ye Buy (Professor Punch), social card game, ca. 1860s, S. Hart & Co. **400**

Le Jeu des Auteurs, literary card game, copyright 1873, Henry Holt & Co. **1,500**

Life's Mishaps, A Merry Game

Life's Mishaps - A Merry Game, social board game, copyright 1875, McLoughlin Brothers (ILLUS.) **300**

Little Corporal - The World and Its People, history card game, copyright 1854, Hoffman & Knickerbocker **450**

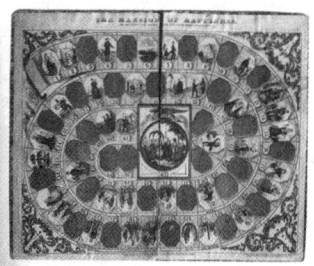

Mansion of Happiness Board Game

Mansion of Happiness, social board game, 2nd Edition, green spaces, fine engraving, copyright 1844, W. & S.B. Ives (ILLUS.).. **800**

Marque or Triple-Score, miscellaneous card game, copyright 1879, A.A. McCormick **150**

Multiplication - An Arithmetical Game, numbers card game, ca. 1850s, Charles L. Mores... **400**

Multiplication Merrily Matched, numbers card game, copyright 1846, C.S. Francis & Co.. **400**

New Game of Aesop, literary board game, copyright 1861, H.M. Francis **1,200**

New Railroad Game or Trip Around the World, travel board game, ca. 1873, A.E. Lyman & Son **900**

Old Curiosity Shop, economic card game, copyright 1869, Nora Norwood, ... **250**

Old Maid, classic card game, ca. 1860s, A.J. Fisher, Publisher **200**

Old Pampheezle and His Comical Friends, classic card game, ca. 1840, Lee & Shepard.. **500**

Old Pamphezzle and his Comical Friends, classic card game, copyright 1861, M.A. Mayhew **400**

Parlor Monuments to the Illustrious Dead, history block game, ca. 1870s, Oakley & Mason **1,500**

Patent Parlor Bagatelle Table, skill board game, pat. 1871, M. Redgrave **500**

Patriot, history card game, copyright D. Eckley Hunter in1866, A. Flanagan Co. **400**

Peter Coddle's Trip to New York, reading card game, copyright 1858, Gould & Lincoln **450**

Portfolio of Social Games, social & combination card games, copyright 1864, William H. Hill, Jr. & Co. **300**

Presidential Quartets - A New Game, politics card game, copyright 1859, D.O. Goodrich **600**

Puss in the Corner, animal board game, ca. 1860s, A.J. Fisher, Publisher.... **1,000**

Right and Wrong or The Princess Belinda, social card game, copyright 1876, Albert A. Hill.. **165**

Sabbath School Cards, religious card game, copyright 1850, A.C. Beaman **400**

Schoolmaster, education card game, copyright D. Eckley Hunter in 1866, A. Flanagan Co. **300**

Scripture cards, religious card game, copyright 1860, Henry Holt & Co. **150**

Sentiment, social card game, copyright D. Eckley Hunter in 1866, A. Flanagan Co. **250**

Shakespeare in a New Dress, literary card game, copyright 1845, C.S. Francis & Co. **500**

Sixteen Merry Face, kiddie card game, ca. 1870, M. Jacobs & Co. **150**

Snake Game, political board game, ca. 1860s, A.J. Fisher, Publisher............... **1,000**

Snap, action card game, copyright D. Eckley Hunter in 1866, A. Flanagan Co.............. **200**

Sybelline Leaves, mystic card game, copyright 1852, Lindsay & Blakiston **350**

The Bugle Horn or Robin Hood, literary & adventure card & board game, ca. 1860s, McLoughlin Brothers (ILLUS. bottom previous column)............................ **1,200**

The Checkered Game of Life Board Game

The Checkered Game of Life, board-type, red & blue squares, ca. 1870s, Milton Bradley & Co.(ILLUS.).................................... **200**

The Conquest of Nations (Game of Nations), history card game, copyright 1853, W.P. Hazard.. **500**

The Diamond Game, skill board game, ca. 1850s, Alexander S. Jorden................. **2,000**

The Expanding Fortune Teller, mystic skill game, copyright 1849, Charles T. Gill **350**

The Flower Game, plants card game, copyright 1857, D. Appleton & Co. **400**

The Game of Circles, miscellaneous card game, ca. 1852, W. & S.B. Ives..................... **400**

The Game of Miser, social card game, ca. 1840s, D.P. Ives & H.P. Ives **600**

The Game of the Gypsy Fortune Teller, mystic card game, copyright 1859, Mayhew & Baker.. **400**

The Jolly Game of Goose, religious board-type, copyright 1851, J.P. Beach.................... **400**

The Bugle Horn or Robin Hood Game

The Merry Game of Old Maid Card Game

The Merry Game of Old Maid, classic card game, ca. 1870s, McLoughlin Brothers (ILLUS.).. **200**

The New Alphabet of Nations, geography card game, ca. 1840s, A. Phelps.................... **400**

The New Military Game, military card game, copyright 1859, G.W. Fisher **1,000**

The Original Game of Letters, letters card game, copyright 1878, E.L. Horsman **150**

Comic Leaves of Fortune,
The Sibyl's Prophecy Card Game

The Sibyl's Prophecy Comic Leaves of Fortune, mystic card came, ca. 1860s, Charles Magnus and Co. (ILLUS.) **200**

Trades or Knowledge is Power Card Game

Trades or Knowledge is Power, economic card game, ca. 1850s, Richard H. Pease (ILLUS.).. **1,200**

Travels and Sojourn of Ichabod Solo, Esquire, Among the Pee-Wee Indians, social card game, copyright 1858, L.J. Hodges... **500**

Tyche: The Fireside Oracle (Author C.B.B.), mystic card game, copyright 1876, J.S. Goodman...................................... **200**

Uncle Sam's Game of American
History Card Game

Uncle Sam's Game of American History, history card game, copyright 1851, McLoughlin Brothers (ILLUS.).................... **1,250**

Visit to the Gypsies Card Game

Visit to the Gypsies, mystic card game, ca. 1870s, Milton Bradley & Co. (ILLUS.) **175**

Where's Johnny Card Game

Where's Johnny, social card game, painted cards & cover, ca. 1860s, McLoughlin Brothers (ILLUS.) **400**

Word Making & Talking, word card game, copyright 1877, Hammet & Hammet............. **150**

Yacht Race, Franklin and Great Republic, sports & sea board game, copyright 1853, A.N. Jordan-S.W. Chandler............. **2,500**

Painted

Checkerboard

Checkerboard, black & salmon painted, New England, 19th c., 15 1/4" sq. (ILLUS.).......... **2,300**

Checkerboard

Checkerboard, black & white on tan colored ground, signed "F. Smith," Pennsylvania, ca. 1870, 12 3/4 x 12 1/2" (ILLUS.).. **1,955**

Checkerboard

Checkerboard, blue & white w/yellowed varnish, New England, 19th c., 16" sq. (ILLUS.).. **3,335**

Checkerboard

Checkerboard, gilt decorated w/molded edge, reverse reading "Saco Lodge No-2," Saco, Maine, 19th c. 18 3/4 x 20" (ILLUS.).. **5,175**
Checkerboard, hunter green & iron red paint w/black frame, checkers on obverse, yellow grain paint on reverse, America, 19th c., 13 7/8 x 13 3/4" (minor paint wear).. **1,380**

Checkerboard

Checkerboard, in yellow & black w/green detailing, ca. 1880, 18 1/2" sq. (ILLUS.).... **5,463**

Checkerboard

Checkerboard, oblong form, green & yellow paint, late 19th c., paint imperfections, 10 1/2 x 19 1/2" (ILLUS.).................. **1,955**

Checkerboard

Checkerboard, painted & gilded, second half 19th c., 19 x 25" (ILLUS.) **2,300**
Checkerboard, painted pine, a central checkerboard in old red, yellow & black, a narrow rectangular compartment w/sliding lid at each end for holding wooden checkers, 21 x 31 3/8" (minor edge wear) **4,400**
Checkerboard, painted pine, original black paint border w/inner yellow band around the red & black squares, applied gallery, 14 1/4 x 14 1/2" **1,595**

Checkerboard

Checkerboard, red field w/black squares & yellow stars, all bordered in yellow & black, Ohio, ca. 1890, 18 x 17 1/4" (ILLUS.) **2,415**

Checkerboard, red & white in original cherry frame, Newburyport, Massachusetts, ca. 1850, 16 x 17 1/2" **978**

Checkerboard

Checkerboard, small, brown & white, w/sliding panel & compartment containing zinc checkers on the reverse, 19th c., 10 1/4 x 8 3/4" (ILLUS.) **2,760**

Checkerboard

Checkerboard, stamped "CA Brown 1852" on the reverse, gold, red, crimson & black paint, minor paint wear, 22 1/8 x 22 1/4" (ILLUS.) **1,380**

Game board, Backgammon & Checkers, two-sided, w/game piece compartments, polychrome decorated in apple green, black & red, America, ca. 1870-80, 17 1/4 x 23" **3,738**

Game board, carved & painted wood, the square framed board w/carved outline & polychromed Parcheesi game in green, blue, yellow & orange on a brown ground, the reverse painted w/a red & black checkerboard, 19th c., 24" sq. (wear) **1,610**

Two-sided Game Board

Game board, Checkers & Backgammon, two-sided, mustard, red & green paint, 19th c., 15 x 16" (ILLUS.) **3,335**

Game board, dark green & white, America, 19th c., 9 1/4 x 9 1/2" (repaired) **1,092**

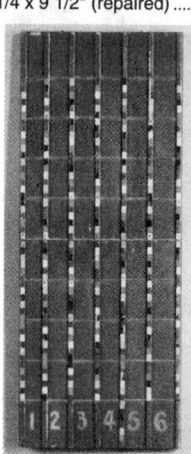

Folding Game Board

Game board, folding-type, avocado green w/colorful raised segmented tracks, opens for storage, mid-20th c., wear, 12 1/2 x 31" (ILLUS.) **575**

Game board, inlaid wood, pine w/a walnut inlaid checkerboard on one side within a border inlaid w/spaced diamonds, the reverse w/a painted backgammon game in original green, black & red paint, original mellow varnish finish, molded edges, 19th c., 17 x 17 1/8" (one small piece of inlay missing) **715**

Folding Painted Parcheesi Board

Game board, painted & decorated wood, folding-type, a hinged square board opens to a polychromed Parcheesi game in red, green, blue & yellow outlined in black, 19th c., scratches, 23 1/2 x 24" (ILLUS.) **1,955**

Game board, painted & decorated wood, one side painted w/a Parcheesi board w/white stars & dots, a checkerboard on the reverse in red & black w/white dots, molded edge, old paint, mid-19th c., 17" sq. (age splits, minor paint loss) **6,325**

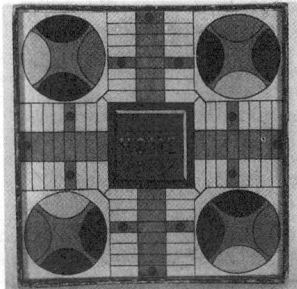

Very Fine Painted Game Board

Game board, painted wood, a square board painted w/a Parcheesi game in shades of red, blue, yellow, grey, brown & gilt on an off-white ground, a center square marked "Home," black molded frame, minor paint wear, 19th c., 18 1/4 x 18 5/8" (ILLUS.) .. **17,250**

Folding Parcheesi Game Board

Game board, Parcheesi, folding-type, w/American flag & spade, heart, diamond & club motifs, Massachusetts, ca. 1870, 18 1/2" sq. (ILLUS.)..................................... **46,000**

Game board, Parcheesi, hunter & olive green, red & yellow game on off-white ground, painted off-white on the reverse, America, 19th c., 17 3/4" sq. (minor paint loss & surface grime)................................... **1,725**

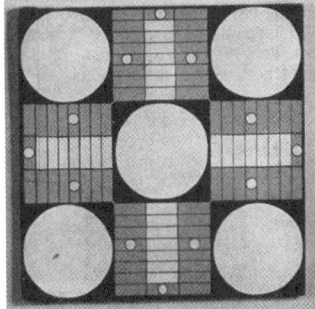

Parcheesi Game Board

Game board, Parcheesi, orange, black & cream-colored board on elaborate four-legged stand wrought to resemble twined twigs & vines, American, late 19th - early

20th c., minor paint imperfections, stand not pictured, 19 3/4 x 20", game board, 35 3/4 x 24" overall ht. (ILLUS.)...................... **575**

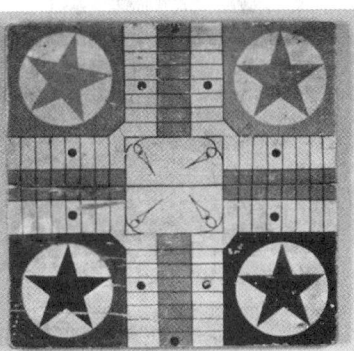

Parcheesi Game Board

Game board, Parcheesi, polychrome, red, yellow, orange & green paint, late 19th c., paint wear, 20 x 19" (ILLUS.) **1,955**

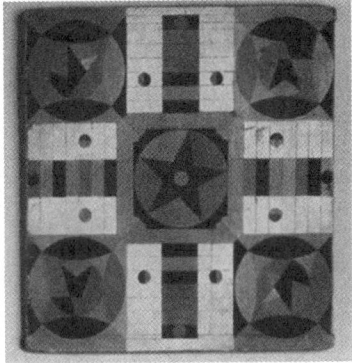

Two-sided Game Board

Game board, Parcheesi, two-sided, scribed & painted in eight colors, checkerboard on the reverse, New Hampshire, 19th c., minor wear, crack, 18 1/2 x 20" (ILLUS.) **21,850**

Parcheesi Game Board

Game board, Parcheesi, w/center rosette & bull's-eye corners, probably Maine, 19th c., wear, 24 1/2 x 25" (ILLUS.) **4,600**

Game Board w/Numbered Squares

Game board, the squares are numbered 1 to 32, New York, ca. 1870, 16 1/2 x 14 1/2" (ILLUS.)........................... **4,312**

Game board, w/Parcheesi, Checkers, Capture & Attack game motifs, two-sided, wood, w/corner carom pockets, grain painted playing area America, 20th c., 28 3/4" sq. (imperfections)........................... **575**

Child's Puzzle Board

Puzzle board, child's, old black paint, possibly New York, ca. 1890-1900, some wear, 18 1/2 x 12 1/2" (ILLUS.).................. **1,495**

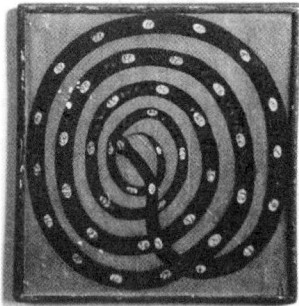

Two-sided Game Board

Two-sided game board, Checkerboard & Snake Motif game, apple green, brown & black, mid-19th c., 12 x 12 1/4" (ILLUS.) ... **36,800**

GARDEN FOUNTAINS & ORNAMENTS

Ornamental garden or yard fountains, urns and figures often enhanced the formal plantings on spacious lawns of mansion-sized dwellings during the late 19th and early 20th century. While fountains were usually reserved for the lawns of estates, even modest homes often had a latticework arbor or cast-iron urn in the yard. Today garden enthusiasts look for these ornamental pieces to lend the aura of elegance to their landscaping.

Fountain, bronze, in two sections, the cast draped female figure holding a tipped vase to her side & raised on a circular base cast w/leaftips, set on a wide ruffled shell on four opposing dolphins raised on a shaped plinth & circular base, 19th c., 51 3/4" d., 89 1/2" h. **$4,312**

Figural Swan Cast-Iron Fountain

Fountain, cast iron, figural, large of a spread-winged swinging swan w/its neck upright & beak forming fountain opening, white w/black beak, on a green cylindrical pedestal, late 19th c., wear, 17 1/2" l., 37 1/2" h. (ILLUS.) **5,750**

Fountain, cast iron, figural, three-part, the top w/a standing cherub finial on a ring-turned short pedestal centered in a wide shallow bowl w/rolled scalloped edges above a heavy pedestal cast w/lions' heads w/openings for jets of water raised on applied leaf feet & set in a very wide shallow base w/rounded & gently scalloped rim, base signed "Robert Wood & Co., Philadelphia," partial white repaint, second half 19th c., 70" d. base, 63" h. (mismatched, welded repairs)..................... **4125**

Victorian Cast-Iron Fountain

Fountain, cast iron, the wide urn-form basin cast w/a lower leafy band & rolled banded sides, raised on a tall columnar pedestal cast w/tall reeds & standing cranes, on a thick round base, old white paint, weathered, attributed to J.W. Fiske, New York, New York, late 19th c., 26" d., 46 3/4" h. (ILLUS.) 2,875

Boy on Snail Marble Fountain

Fountain, marble, figural, a boy riding astride a large snail, late 19th c., 46 1/2" h. (ILLUS.) 10,800

Garden Gate

Garden gate, 36 x 50" h. (ILLUS.) 175
Garden ornament, bird bath, fluted base & scalloped edges, 32 x 32" h. 375
Garden ornament, carved limestone baluster, removed from an old hotel in New York City, 29" t., top surface is 8" sq. 200

Gladiator Garden Ornament

Garden ornament, carved limestone gladiator, cement base, from an estate outside Philadelphia, Pennsylvania, some

repairs, missing arm, statue 48" h., base 16" h. (ILLUS.) 2,375
Garden ornament, chimney smoker, terra cotta chimney top from brownstone in Philadelphia, 26" h. 175
Garden ornament, chimney smoker, terra cotta chimney top from brownstone in Philadelphia, 38" h. 175
Garden ornament, concrete, fleur de lis design, from railing of commercial building, 33 x 23" h. 475

Boy & Serpent Garden Ornament

Garden ornament, quartz stone, boy & serpent, 30" t. (ILLUS.) 750
Garden ornament, sundial, carved sandstone, poured lead w/acorn & leaf pattern & Roman numerals, England, 18 x 44" h. 1,795
Model of a rabbit, cast iron, seated full-body form w/open front legs, old worn white repaint, 19th c., 11 /34" h. 275
Model of a stag, cast iron, standing walking animal w/raised antlered head, on a thick rectangular base, body w/worn layers of white paint, late 19th c., 62 1/4" h. 3,850

Cast-Iron Lion Ornaments

Models of lions, cast iron, recumbent animal w/mouth open, on rectangular base, painted brown, late 19th c., wear, 13 1/2 x 39", 19 1/2" h., facing pr. (ILLUS.) 6,325

Victorian Stag Garden Ornaments

Models of stags, cast iron, each standing w/head raised supporting large antlers, painted brown, possibly by J.W. Fiske, New York, New York, late 19th c., imperfections, 47" l., 62 1/4" h., pr. (ILLUS.) **6,900**

Tall Victorian Cast-Iron Planter

Planter, cast iron, a wide shallow bowl w/leaf-cast rolled & scalloped edges raised on a ribbed basin section above a square block cast w/portrait medallions above the ringed columnar pedestal & wide low domed round foot, rusted w/old white paint, 19th c. (ILLUS.) **1,568**

Planter, cast iron, footed rectangular form w/deep sides & flared rim, cast w/bands of leaf & blossom decoration w/a large central scrolled wreath, white repaint, 19th c., 14 3/4 x 30", 14 3/4" h. **385**

Urn, cast iron, a square plinth supporting a domed & banded foot w/cast designs below the short ringed pedestal, a wide shallow rounded bowl-form urn w/a wide everted rim, the sides cast w/four grotesque faces, base labeled "J.W. Fiske, Barclay St., N.Y. - Patd. June 1, 1875," 17 1/2" d., 16 1/2" h. **468**

Urn, cast iron, a wide shallow ribbed bowl w/a wide rolled lappet-cast rim, on a short ribbed pedestal on a ring-turned foot & square plinth, dark green repaint, 23" d., 17 1/4" h. **385**

Large Victorian Garden Urn

Urn, cast iron, campana-form, a wide shallow round urn w/a wide rolled egg-and-dart rim & gadrooned base band flanked by ornate scrolling grapevine handles, raised on a short flaring reeded pedestal on a tall square stepped plinth base w/a sunburst & lion mask on each side, late 19th c., 43" d., 60" h. (ILLUS.) **5,750**

Urn, cast iron, campana-form, the urn-form top w/a wide rolled & gadrooned rim, gadrooned urn base flanked by upright loop handles above the slender flaring ringed pedestal on a square plinth, old dark green repaint, late 19th c., 12 1/4" d., 14 1/2" h. **220**

Urn, cast iron, flaring deep rounded two-section top w/cast bands of scrolling leaves below the incurved rim band, high arched scroll handles from ring to center of body, raised on a short ringed pedestal w/a widely flaring round base on a square base & high stone plinth, worn layers of white paint, late 19th c., 34" h. **330**

Urns, cast iron, campana-form, a wide rolled & scalloped rim on a wide low urn w/cast scrolled heart designs, short ribbed pedestal w/round base w/square foot, raised on a high tapered square plinth, signed "Kramer Bros., Dayton," new white paint, 19th c., 22" d., 25" h., pr. **880**

Urns, cast iron, campana-form w/ foliate, reeded vine & basketweave detail on square bases, weathered old green paint, ca. 1860-80, 27 1/2" d., 21" h., pr.... **2,415**

Urns, cast iron, in two parts, the upper section w/a flared rim & large scrolled foliate-cast handles raised on a tall circular pedestal cast w/three standing herons above a stepped plinth base, American, 19th c., 52" h., pr. **5,175**

Urns, cast iron, large inverted bell-form urn w/molded foliate borders & blade-form ribbing raised on a round pedestal base set upon a tall square stepped plinth, old worn paint, late 19th c., 22" d., overall 44" h., pr. **1,725**

Urns, terra cotta, wide baluster-form body molded w/foliate scrolls & flowerheads, 25" h., pr. **690**

GLASS

ALSO SEE: Antique Trader Books Pressed Glass & Bottles Price Guide, 2nd Edition *and* American & European Decorative and Art Glass Price Guide, 2nd Edition.

Agata

Agata was patented by Joseph Locke of the New England Glass Company in 1887. The application of mineral stain left a mottled effect on the surface of the article. It was applied chiefly to the Wild Rose (Peach Blow) line but sometimes was applied as a border on a pale opaque green. In production for a short time, it is scarce. Items listed below are of the Wild Rose line unless otherwise noted.

Bowl, 5 1/2" d., 2 3/4" h., upright deeply ruffled sides **$950**

Finger bowl, deep round upright ruffled form **550**

Lemonade glass, tall slightly tapering form
w/small applied pink loop handle near the
base 688

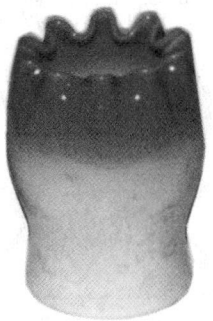

Rare Agata Spooner

Spooner, deeply ruffled lavender rim,
4 1/2" h. (ILLUS.) 1,250

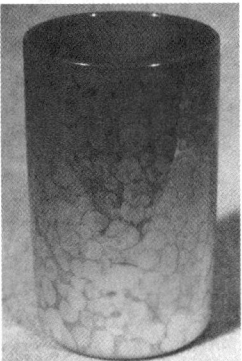

Fine Agata Tumbler

Tumbler, cylindrical, 3 3/4" h. (ILLUS.) 550-750
Tumbler, cylindrical, dark mottled & gold
tracery 800
Vase, 6 1/4" h., green opaque, fourteen-rib
gently tapering ovoid body w/flared rim,
New England Glass Co. 650

Amberina

*Amberina was developed in the late 1880s by the New
England Glass Company and a pressed version was
made by Hobbs, Brockunier & Company (under license
from the former). A similar ware, called Rose Amber,
was made by the Mt. Washington Glass Works. Ambe-
rina-Rose Amber shades from amber to deep red or
fuchsia and cut and plated (lined with creamy white)
examples were also made. The Libbey Glass Company
briefly revived blown Amberina, using modern shapes,
in 1917.*

Amberina Mark

Berry set: 9" sq., 2 1/2" h. master bowl &
six 5" sq., 1 3/8" h. sauce dishes;
pressed Daisy & Button patt., attributed
to Hobbs, Brockunier & Co., the set (mi-
nor rim chips) $650

Small Cylindrical Amberina Bowl

Bowl, 3 3/4" d., 2 3/4" h., cylindrical body
w/a deeply ruffled fuchsia rim (ILLUS.) 325
Bowl, 5 1/2" d., ruffled rim 200
Bowl, 5 1/2" d., 3" h., Reverse Amberina,
round w/irregular folded rim 110

Amberina Bowl & Barrel-shaped Mug

Bowl, 5 3/4" d., 3 3/4" h., squatty bulbous
body w/swirled molded ribbing below the
deeply ruffled & crimped rim (ILLUS.
right) 135
Bowl, 6 1/2" d., 6 3/4" h., deeply ruffled flar-
ing amber rim, applied amber handles,
applied amber base forming feet 350
Bowls, individual berry, 5" sq., pressed
Daisy & Button patt., set of 6 500
Butter dish, cov., Inverted Thumbprint
patt., 5" h. 220
Butter dish, cov., round blown cover in In-
verted Thumbprint patt., pressed Daisy &
Button underplate 275
Butter pat, square, pressed Daisy & Button
patt. 125
Castor set: four bottle w/mustard jar, shak-
er, oil & vinegar cruets & one stopper;
each bottle engraved, in a silver plate
frame, the set 985
Celery vase, Diamond Quilted patt., New
England Glass Co., 6 1/2" h. 375
Celery vase, scalloped rim, in ornate silver
plate frame marked "Pairpoint," 4" d.,
6 1/2" h. celery insert w/original Mt.
Washington Glass Co. seal, overall
11 1/4" h. 950
Cheese plate, twelve-paneled, optic de-
sign, 9 1/2" d. 315
Creamer, spherical swirled pattern-molded
body w/a wide cylindrical neck w/pinched
spout, applied angled amber handle
w/end curl, 3 1/2" d., 5" h. 175

Creamer, squatty bulbous body, Inverted Thumbprint patt., applied amber handle, 3" h. **413**

Cruet w/original stopper, bulbous body supported on a pedestal base, applied amber handle & amber facet-cut stopper, polished pontil **375**

Amberina Inverted Thumbprint Cruet

Cruet w/original stopper, spherical body in Inverted Thumbprint patt., slender cylindrical neck w/a tricorner mouth, applied amber handle, amber bubble stopper, 3 1/2" d., 6" h. (ILLUS.) **250-275**

Superb Plated Amberina Cruet

Cruet w/original stopper, Plated Amberina, spherical body w/a tall slender neck & a tricorner rim, applied amber handle, facet-cut amber stopper, superb coloring & wonderful condition, 7" h. (ILLUS.) **8,800**

Cruet w/stopper, squatty bulbous body tapering to a slender neck w/arched spout, Inverted Thumbprint patt., decorated w/delicate enameled forget-me-nots, applied amber handle & facet-cut amber stopper **1,210**

Dish, sawtooth rim, diamond-shaped, pressed Daisy & Button patt., Gillinder Glass Co., 4 1/4" w., 6 1/8" l. **375**

Finger bowl, Hobnail patt., squared rim on squatty rounded body, 4 3/8" d., 2 3/4" h. **125**

Amberina Hobnail Finger Bowls

Finger bowls, squared rim above a rounded Hobnail patt. bowl, polished pontil, 4 1/4" w., 2 7/8" h., the set (ILLUS.) **450**

Goblet, rose to amber coloring, optic ribbed design, 3 3/8" d., 6 1/8" h. **125**

Amberina Barrel-shaped Mug

Mug, barrel-shaped body, amber applied handle, Swirled Optic Rib patt., 2 7/8" d., 4 7/8" h. (ILLUS.) **58**

Mug, barrel-shaped body w/wafer foot, cranberry to golden amber, applied amber rope handle, 2 5/8" h., 4 3/4" h. **65**

Mug, barrel-shaped swirled optic-ribbed body on an applied disk foot, amber twisted rope handle w/end curl, heavily decorated w/gold flowers & leaves, 2 3/4" d., 4 5/8" h., (ILLUS. left with bowl) **150**

Amberina Tall Cylindrical Mug

Mug, tall cylindrical body swelled at the base, wide swirled ribs up the sides to a plain rim, applied amber ropetwist C-form handle, decorated w/gilt stems w/flowers & leaves, 2 1/2" d., 5 1/2" h. (ILLUS.) **165**

Perfume bottle w/stopper, disk foot below the tall slender ovoid body w/a flattened four-lobed rim, large optic ribbed ball stopper, stamped "Libbey Amberina," ca. 1917, 8 1/4" h. **2,530**

Bulbous Plated Amberina Pitcher

Pitcher, Plated Amberina, bulbous ovoid body tapering to a tricorner mouth, applied ruby handle, creamy white lining (ILLUS.).. **10,000**

Plated Amberina Tankard Pitcher

Pitcher, Plated Amberina, tankard-type, small pinched spout, applied amber handle (ILLUS.) **12,000**

Pitcher, 5" h., Inverted Honeycomb patt., bulbous body w/tricorner rim, applied amber handle **150**

Swirled Pattern Amberina Pitcher

Pitcher, 8 7/8" h., 5 1/4" d., tapering ovoid body w/a swirled rib design, wide cylindrical neck w/pinched spout, applied squared amber handle (ILLUS.) **245**

Pitcher, 9" h., melon-ribbed body w/clear applied reeded handle, decorated w/h.p. enameled flowers **550**

Pitcher & tumbler, pitcher 6 1/2" h., 2 1/2" d., the pitcher w/a footed ovoid body in the Inverted Thumbprint patt. tapering to a cylindrical neck w/a small pinched spout, applied angled amber handle, matching footed 3 3/8" h. tumbler, 2 pcs... **185**

Punch cup, Diamond Quilted patt., applied threaded handle, New England Glass Co. **150**

Punch cup, eighteen optic ribs, New England Glass Co., 2 1/2" h. **185**

Salt & pepper shakers w/original metal lids, cylindrical molded rib design, pr. **303**

Salt shaker w/original two-piece lid, Baby Thumbprint patt., bulging dual mold-blown body, 2 1/2" h. **235**

Spooner, Diamond Quilted patt., New England Glass Co., 4 1/2" h. **235**

Sugar bowl, cov., pressed Daisy & Button patt., cylindrical bucket-style w/tab rim handles & flattened fitted cover w/knob finial, base in all-amber, 5 1/4" h. (flake on cover).. **575**

Trinket dish, wide flared rim, Diamond Quilted patt., Mt. Washington Glass Co., 4 3/4" d.. **195**

Tumbler, Inverted Thumbprint patt., flat bottom, 2 3/4" d., 3 3/4" h...................................... **65**

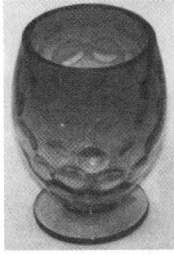

Amberina Tumbler

Tumbler, Inverted Thumbprint patt., footed, cylindrical, 2 1/2" d., 3 7/8" h. (ILLUS.) **69**

Tumbler, mold-blown, large blown-out ribs **85**

Tumbler, Reverse Amberina, Optic Rib patt. **100**

Vase, 3 1/2" h., miniature, bulbous form w/pinched neck & swirled dimpled body, applied rigaree collar **495**

Vase, 5" h., 5 3/4" w., jack-in-the-pulpit form, signed "Libbey" **1,200**

Three Amberina Vases

Vase, 6 3/8" h., 4 1/8" d., melon-lobed ovoid body tapering to a widely flaring four-ruffle neck, h.p. dainty white & yellow flowers & green leaves (ILLUS. at left) **250**

Decorated Cylindrical Amberina Vase

Vase, 6 3/4" h., 3 7/8" d., a narrow cushion foot below a wide cylindrical body w/an optic ribbed swirled design, finely enameled w/white blossoms & green leaves (ILLUS.) **195**

Vase, 7" d., trumpet-form, wafer foot **550**

Vase, 7 1/8" h., 3 3/4" d., cylindrical body w/a narrow cushion foot, pattern-molded swirled rib design, h.p. soft pink flowers & green leaves, gilt rim (ILLUS. at right w/other vases) **245**

Vase, 11 3/4" h., stick-form, swirled design from rim down the sides, Libbey, ca. 1917 .... **440**

Vase, 12" h., bud-type, disk foot supporting a very tall, slender slightly swelled cylindrical stem, signed "Libbey Amberina," ca. 1917 .... **770**

Vase, 12" h., 5 1/2" d., jack-in-the-pulpit-style, tall tapering ovoid body in the Inverted Thumbprint patt., the wide rolled rim w/a fluted edge & a pull-up back peak, on an applied amber foot (ILLUS. at center w/other vases) **245**

Amberina Water Set

Water set: 9 1/2" h., 4" d. tankard pitcher & four 3 3/4" h. tumblers; all in the Inverted Thumbprint patt., the pitcher w/a flat angle-cut rim & applied angled amber handle, the set (ILLUS.) **395**

Water set: pitcher & six tumblers; the bulbous pitcher w/a swirled Coin Spot patt. & applied reeded amber handle, matching tumblers w/optic swirled design, tumblers 3 3/4" h., pitcher 9" h., the set **715**

Art Glass Baskets

Popular novelties in the late Victorian era, these ornate baskets of glass were usually hand-crafted of free-blown or mold-blown glass. They were made in a wide spectrum of colors and shapes. Pieces were highlighted with tall applied handles and often applied feet; however, fancier ones might also carry additional appliqued trim.

Cased, white body w/amber rim band, decorated w/red cherries & multicolored leaves, 5" d., 7 1/2" h. **$143**

Colored swags, a tall slender waisted form w/a widely flaring rim pulled up on two sides & joined by a high applied clear arched handle, the sides composed of alternating dark green, gold & white swags, iridescent interior, attributed to Imperial, 9 1/2" h. **275**

Light green custard, applied floral decoration & applied green twisted handle **127**

Mother-of-pearl satin, shaded blue Diamond Quilted patt., ruffled rim, applied frosted clear handle, 4 1/2" w., 6" h. **440**

Pink opalescent, ruffled rim & applied clear twisted handle, applied white flowers, glossy finish, 4 1/2" d., 6 3/4" h. **176**

Spangled, blue cased in white w/silvery mica flecks, clear applied ruffled rim & applied rope handle, 9" d. **138**
Spangled, blue cased w/white basket w/a layer of silvery mica flecks, ruffled border, applied twisted clear handle, 6 1/2" w., 6 1/2" h. **66**
Spangled, gold cased in white body w/a layer of golden mica flecks, ribbed sides w/applied clear reeded & pointed handle, 7" d., 7" h. **88**
Spangled, pink w/overall mica flecks, ruffled rim, applied clear handle, 5 1/2" d., 5" h. **121**

Blown Three Mold

This type of glass was entirely or partially blown in a mold and was popular from about 1820 to 1840. The object was formed and the decoration impressed upon it by blowing the glass into a metal mold, usually of three—but sometimes more—sections hinged together. Mold-blown glass actually dates back to ancient times. Recent research reveals that certain geometric patterns were reproduced in the 1920s; some new pieces, usually sold through museum gift shops, are still available. Collectors are urged to read all recent information available. Reference numbers are from George L. and Helen McKearin's book, American Glass.

Pieces are clear unless otherwise noted.

Bowl, 5 1/2" d., 3 1/8" h., geometric, a deep rounded bowl w/folded rim, raised on a thick applied foot (GIII-4) **$990**
Compote, open, Baroque, a small trumpet-form body w/folded rim raised on applied ringed stem & disk foot, amethystine tint, 4" d., 4" h., GV-24 inverted variant (imperfection in bottom of bowl) **385**
Decanter w/no stopper, geometric, ovoid tapering to a tooled lip, olive green, 6 7/8" h. (GIII-16) **715**
Decanter w/original stopper, geometric, bulbous ovoid body tapering to a neck w/three applied rings, hollow ball stopper, 10 1/4" h. (GIII-5) **110**
Decanter w/original stopper, tapering cylindrical sides w/slender neck & flattened rim, hollow ball stopper, 11 1/2" h., GIII-5 (minor residue in bottom) **220**
Dish, geometric, small round center w/low widely flaring flattened sides w/folded rim, 6 1/4" d., 1 3/8" h. (GII-22) **248**
Dish, geometric, wide flat-bottomed form w/low flared sides w/a folded rim, 5 3/4" d., 1 1/2" h., GIII-20 (minor wear) **165**
Flip glass, geometric, tall slightly tapering cylindrical form, top ribs swirled to left, 5 7/8" h. (GII-25 variant) **187**
Flip glass, geometric, tall tapering cylindrical form, folded rim, amethystine tint, 4 1/2" h., GII-18 (potstone w/star crack) **110**
Pan, geometric, very wide round flat-bottomed form w/low upturned rounded sides w/folded rim, 7 7/8" d., 1 7/8" h., GIII-20 (minor wear) **275**
Pan, geometric, wide round flat-bottomed form w/shallow upright rounded sides w/folded rim, 6" d., 1 1/2" h. (GIII-24) **165**

Pitcher, miniature, 2 7/8" h., geometric, ovoid body w/flared rim & pinched spout, applied strap handle, (GIII-21) **204**

Bohemian

Decorated Cylindrical Vase

Numerous types of glass were made in the once-independent country of Bohemia and fine colored, cut and engraved glass was turned out. Flashed and other inexpensive wares also were made; many of these, including amber- and ruby-shaded glass, were exported to the United States during the 19th and 20th centuries. One favorite pattern in the late 19th and early 20th centuries was Deer & Castle. Another was Deer and Pine Tree.

Decanter w/original stopper, flashed, ruby cut to clear, flattened baluster-form w/balloon stopper, cut w/plain flutes & etched w/diapered cartouches, scrolls & birds in flight, late 19th c., 14 3/8" h. **$173**
Pokals, cov., ruby-flashed, a round disk foot & knob stem supporting a tall slightly waisted cylindrical bowl w/a high domed cover w/flanged rim & facet-cut pointed finial, each cut w/a continuous scene of dogs chasing a stag through the woods, well-detailed, late 19th - early 20th c., 16 1/2" h., pr. (flakes on bases) **715**
Salt dip, raised clear rim on a squat bulbous base of clear decorated internally w/concentric rings & arcs of millefiori canes, the base facet-cut & centered by a starburst, 19th c., 2 3/4" d., 1 7/8" h. **546**
Tumblers, cylindrical, etched, ruby-flashed etched to frosted clear w/scene of harvesters & a German inscription around rim, 19th c., 6 1/4" h., pr. (some wear) **226**
Vase, 3 7/8" h., yellowish green mold-blown form w/a flared rim over a bulbous body, enamel-decorated w/dragonflies & frogs by a pond in light blue, white, tan, red & black, early 20th c. (nicks at rim) **115**
Vase, 7" h., thick disk foot supporting a delicate crystal trumpet-form vase w/a widely flaring rim, engraved w/a figure of a young boy standing amid floral bouquets & falling rose sprigs, engraved w/the mark of Lobmeyr, attributed to Michael Powolny, ca. 1908 .... **920**

Vase, 8" h., cushion base below the tall cylindrical body, dark blue ornately enameled w/a colorful figure of a standing Harlequin against a gilt-stenciled garden terrace background, attributed to Rossler, ca. 1920 (ILLUS.) 250

Elaborate Persian-style Victorian Vase

Vase, 20" h., Persian-style, a flaring pedestal base supporting a wide squatty compressed body tapering to a tall ringed cylindrical neck, ruby w/blue & white enameled delicate birds & flowers in bands & reserves w/further gilt decoration, inscribed "Bouteille Persane en Verre Epoque Sass Anide," 19th c. (ILLUS.) **3,680**
Vase, 22 1/2" h., squatty bulbous bottom tapering sharply to a very tall slender body w/flared & ruffled rim, clear w/optic ribbing, ornately enameled w/delicate gold, green & blue leafy scrolls up the sides, ground pontil **280**
Vases, 4 5/8" h., cut-overlay, baluster-form w/trefoil rim, white cut to green w/gilt trim, late 19th c., pr. **374**

Fine Cut-overlay Bohemian Vase

Vases, 16 1/2" h., white cut to blue cut-overlay, classic baluster-form, each w/an octagonal flaring neck, the lip suspending spade-form leaves, the sides w/anthemion alternating w/stylized foliage & floral diamonds, the ground gilt overall w/scrolling foliage, on circular bases cut w/overlapping leaves, mid-19th c., pr. (ILLUS. of one) **3,450**

Bride's Baskets & Bowls

These berry or fruit bowls were popular late Victorian wedding gifts, hence the name. They were produced in a variety of quality art glasswares and sometimes were fitted in ornate silver plate holders.

Unusual Pressed Glass Basket

Blue bowl, pale blue pressed glass arched rectangular bowl w/a star in block design, bowl swinging in a metal harp above a figural brass base w/two standing cherubs, late 19th c., 5 x 7", 8 1/2" h. (ILLUS.) **$325**
Cased bowl, deep green to golden amber interior w/a deeply fluted & crimped rim, decorated w/pink-trimmed white florals on the interior, white exterior, 11" d. **112**

Bride's Basket with Figural Silver Base

Cased bowl, pink interior w/deep flaring lobed & crimped rim w/applied frosted clear band, white exterior, the interior enameled w/small maroon sprays & orange buds, ornate resilvered silver plate pedestal stand w/three figural small dolphins above a scroll- and shell-cast three-footed base, 7 1/2" d., 8 1/4" h. (ILLUS.) 325

Shaded Pink Decorated Basket

Cased bowl, shaded pink interior decorated w/large yellow & white daisy-like blossoms & greenish brown leaves, deeply ruffled & crimped rim pulled into points, white exterior, ornate silver plate frame w/looped & arched handle, 10 3/4" d., 10 3/4" h. (ILLUS.)... 395

Cased bowl, white exterior w/dark pink interior & applied amber crimped rim, two long sides turned-up & the narrow ends turned-up, in a Wilcox silver plate frame w/an ornate leaf vine around the handle & raised on pierced arched feet, 11" h. 275

Cased satin, shaded lavender interior enameled w/yellow, white & lavender florals, angular ruffled rim, 10 1/2" d., 4" h. 220

Creamy white bowl, deep waisted bowl w/six pointed rim lobes, the sides h.p. w/colorful purple hibiscus blossoms & green leafy stems, resting on an ornate, unusual Meriden silver plate frame w/a low central pedestal supporting the bowl flanked by large figural rampant lions on an oblong platform raised on shell- and scroll-cast feet... 1,045

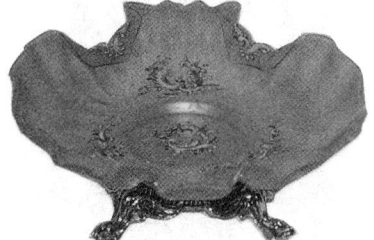

Shaded Pink Decorated Bowl

Pink shading to frosted clear bowl, wide shell-shaped form w/ruffled rim & two

turned-in edge sections, decorated w/white & pink scrolling feather-like clusters & small blue & white flowers & tiny gold flowers, gilt edge band, on a resilvered silver plate scroll-footed stand, 10 1/2" d., 4 1/4" h. (ILLUS.) 295

Burmese

Burmese is a single-layer glass that shades from pink to pale yellow. It was patented by Frederick S. Shirley and made by the Mt. Washington Glass Co. A license to produce the glass in England was granted to Thomas Webb & Sons, which called its articles Queen's Burmese. Gundersen Burmese was made briefly about the middle of the 20th century, and the Pairpoint Company is making limited quantities at the present time.

Bell, high body w/flaring base, applied amber handle, glossy finish, Thomas Webb, 6 3/4" h... $750

Bell, high domed bell w/flaring base, tall applied clear handle w/beehive form finial, glossy finish, Thomas Webb, 11 1/2" h. 750

Bowl, 4" d., 2 1/2" h., squatty bulbous body w/a wide flat rim, raised on a short foot, the sides decorated w/a blue butterfly & reddish blossoms on slender vines trimmed in gold, attributed to Webb 585

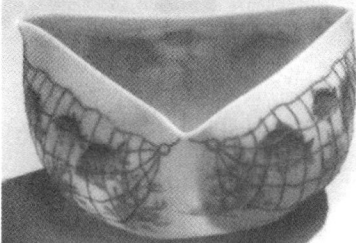

Tricorner Burmese Bowl with Fish Net

Bowl, 5" w., shallow rounded base w/an incurved tricorner rim, enameled around the sides w/an elaborate fish in net design (ILLUS.) 1,610

Bowl, 5 1/2" w., 2 1/4" h., rectangular w/slightly folded rim, polished pontil, satin finish.. 250

Bowl, 6 1/4" d., 3 3/4" h., squatty bulbous body on a footring, enameled floral decoration 1,110

Bowl, 6 1/2" widest d., 2 1/2" h., cylindrical base w/a flaring & folded over elongated oval rim, applied yellow rigaree trim on rim, Mt. Washington Glass Co. 950

Celery vase, footed, fluted rim, Mt. Washington Glass Co., 10" h. 550

Cologne bottle w/original stopper, Mt. Washington Glass Co., 4" d., 5" h. 975

Condiment set: cylindrical ribbed salt & pepper shakers & barrel-shaped ribbed mustard jar, each w/original silver plate lids, in a fitted silver plate stand w/round ruffled base, support rings & a central handle w/loop top, sterling silver mustard spoon, frame signed by Pairpoint, the set 798

Cracker jar, cov., bulbous tapering ovoid body decorated w/large enameled salmon colored blossoms on brown & green leafy stems, silver plate rim, cover & shaped bail handle, ground pontil, unmarked Webb, 7" h. **1,568**

Creamer & open sugar bowl in holder, the wide bulbous ovoid sugar bowl w/a wide upright six-sided mouth, the smaller ovoid creamer w/matching mouth & applied yellow handle, each heavily enameled w/large orangish blossoms & autumnal leaves, fitted into a silver platform w/ring supports & an arched divided central handle, unmarked, overall 7" h., the set... **1,568**

Creamer & sugar bowl, individual, satin finish, Mt. Washington Glass Co., pr............. **750**

Creamer & sugar bowl, pitcher-shaped creamer w/applied yellow handle, globular open sugar bowl, creamer 3 3/4" h., sugar bowl 3 1/2" d., 2" h., pr. **750**

Cruet w/original mushroom stopper, melon-ribbed body, Mt. Washington Glass Co., 6 3/4" h. **1,200**

Fine Mt. Washington Burmese Cruet

Cruet w/original stopper, squatty bulbous ribbed body tapering to a slender neck w/arched spout, bulbous ribbed & pointed stopper, applied yellow handle, glossy finish, Mt. Washington Glass Co., 7 1/4" h. (ILLUS.).. **1,250**

Cruet w/original stopper, squatty bulbous ribbed body w/cylindrical neck, matching ribbed stopper, applied yellow handle, Mt. Washington Glass Co., 6 3/4" h. **1,045**

Cup & saucer, conical cup w/applied angled handle, satin finish, saucer 4 3/4" d....... **550**

Cup & saucer, cylindrical cup w/applied yellow angled handle, wide & deep saucer, glossy finish **550**

Custard cup, flared rim, applied yellow handle, glossy finish, Mt. Washington Glass Co., 2 7/8" h. **450**

Dish, ruffled rim, satin finish, 4 3/4" d., 1 1/2" h. **120**

Dish, tricornered, satin finish, 5" w...................... **150**

Ewer, tall ovoid body tapering to a tall, pointed upright spout, an applied loop handle & disk foot, satin finish, Mt. Washington Glass Co., 6" h. **950**

Burmese Lamp with Flying Ibis

Lamp, kerosene table model, a gilt-metal scroll-cast base supporting the wide domed & tapering cylindrical font decorated w/a group of ibis flying over a sunrise scene of pyramids & palm trees, fitted w/a brass shoulder & burner w/wire spider supporting a high domed open-topped matching shade, Burmese glass chimney, ca. 1890s, electrified, shade 10" d., overall 20" h. (ILLUS.).................... **10,350**

Mustard pot w/silver plate hinged lid, barrel-shaped w/vertical ribbing, silver plate collar & bail handle, Mt. Washington Glass Co., 4 1/2" h... **375**

Perfume bottle & stopper, rare partial label on bottom, 5" h................................ **385**

Pitcher, 5 1/2" h., slightly tapering cylindrical body in the Hobnail patt., applied yellow handle, Mt. Washington Glass Co.......... **950**

Plate, 9" d., Mt. Washington Glass Co. **250**

Plate, 9" d., satin finish, Mt. Washington Glass Co... **225**

Miniature Burmese Rose Bowl

Rose bowl, miniature, eight-crimp rim, unsigned Webb, glossy finish, 2 1/4" d., 2 1/4" h. (ILLUS.) **225**
Rose bowl, wide squatty bulbous form w/flat rim, decorated w/h.p. blue butterfly, bittersweet blossoms & gold foliage, Thomas Webb, 4" d., 2 1/2" h. **585**
Rose bowl, ruffled rim, applied molded leaf, 4" d., 2 3/4" h. **700**

Floral-decorated Burmese Rose Bowl

Rose bowl, crimped rim, floral decoration & applied glass at rim, marked by Thomas Webb, 6 1/4" d., 3 3/4" h. (ILLUS.) **950**
Salt & pepper shakers w/original metal lids, cylindrical finely ribbed form, satin finish, pr. **413**
Sugar shaker w/original metal top, decorated w/h.p. daisies, Mt. Washington Glass Co., 4 1/4" h. **425**
Sweetmeat jar, cov., compressed globular body, decorated w/enameled flowers & foliage, silver plate rim, cover & overhead handle **375**
Tazza, bowl on short stem joined by a wafer, 7" d., 4 1/2" h. **550**
Toothpick holder, bulbous base w/square top, h.p. pine cone decoration, satin finish, Mt. Washington Glass Co. **375**
Toothpick holder, bulbous body w/six-sided collared rim, polished pontil, satin finish, 3" h. **275**
Tumbler, cylindrical, enameled yellow roses, Mt. Washington Glass Co., 3 3/4" h. **550**

Mt. Washington Burmese Tumbler

Tumbler, cylindrical, satin finish, Mt. Washington Glass Co., 3 7/8" h. (ILLUS.) **250**
Vase, 2 1/2" h., miniature, bulbous body w/a six-sided top **165**
Vase, 2 1/2" h., miniature, squatty bulbous body w/Diamond Quilted patt. **150**
Vase, 2 1/2" h., 2" d., miniature, bulbous body w/collared hexagonal top, decorated w/flowers, leaves & branches **295**
Vase, 2 1/2" h., 2 1/2" d., miniature, scalloped rim, glossy finish, marked by Webb **525**

Vase, 2 1/2" h., 3 1/2" d., miniature, squatty body below a hexagonal rim, decorated w/flowers & leaves, satin finish **225**

Spherical Burmese Vase by Webb

Vase, 3" h., 2 5/8" d., miniature, spherical body tapering to ruffled rim, satin finish, Thomas Webb (ILLUS.) **225**
Vase, 3 1/8" h., 3 1/8" d., miniature, ovoid body tapering to a flattened ruffled rim, satin finish, unsigned Webb **200**
Vase, 3 1/4" h., miniature, bulbous body w/a six-sided crimped rim, satin finish, decorated w/flowers & leaves, Thomas Webb **358**
Vase, 3 3/4" h., 2 5/8" d., bulbous base tapering to a cylindrical neck w/flaring & crimped rim, enameled w/lavender five-petal flowers & green & brown leaves, satin finish, unsigned Webb **350**

Small Ivy-Decorated Burmese Vase

Vase, 3 3/4" h., 3 1/4" d., spherical body tapering to a short hexagonal neck, the sides enameled w/green, yellow & brown ivy leaves, satin finish, attributed to Thomas Webb (ILLUS.) **395**
Vase, 3 3/4" h., 4 1/4" d., eight deep lobed sections continue to the flaring rim, decorated w/ivy in shades of green **480**
Vase, 4" h., 2 7/8" d., waisted cylindrical body w/folded-over star-shaped rim, satin finish, unsigned Webb **250**
Vase, 4 1/4" h., ribbed baluster-form w/scalloped flaring rim, glossy finish (ILLUS. top next page) **475**

Baluster-shaped Burmese Vase

Vase, 6" h., bud-type, a small disk foot & slender short pedestal supporting a slender tall cylindrical body w/a ruffled rim, decorated down the sides w/delicate colorful foliage, satin finish.................................. 495

Vase, 6 1/4" h., ovoid swirled rib body, satin finish.. 413

Vase, 6 1/2" h., lily-form w/jack-in-the-pulpit rim, Gundersen-Pairpoint.............................. 250

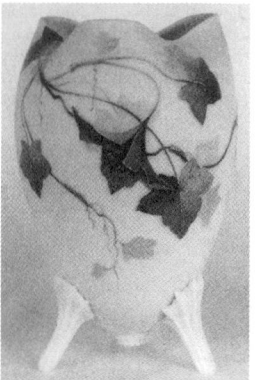

Webb Egg-shaped Burmese Vase

Vase, 7" h., tapering egg-shaped body w/three-lobed rim, raised on three ribbed & pointed legs, enameled around the sides w/large ivy leaves & vines, signed by Thomas Webb & Sons (ILLUS.)............ **1,250**

Vase, 8" h., spherical body below a tall slender 'stick' neck swelled at the base, decorated w/enameled blue & white forget-me-nots, Mt. Washington Glass Co. 575

Vase, 8 1/8" h., 3 7/8" d., ovoid body tapering to a cylindrical neck, decorated w/coral flower buds w/green & tan foliage, satin finish, unsigned Webb................................ 850

Vase, 8 1/8" h., 3 7/8" d., bulbous body on short foot tapering to thin cylindrical neck w/flat rim, decorated w/coral-colored flower buds w/green & tan foliage, unsigned Webb (ILLUS.).................................... 750

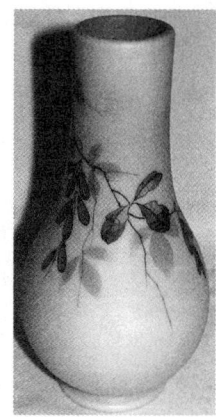

Floral-Decorated Vase by Webb

Vase, 8 1/4" h., h.p. floral decoration, in silver plate handled frame, Thomas Webb & Sons 515

Vase, 10 1/2" h., tall simple ovoid form w/a small closed mouth, finely enameled overall w/brown & green leaves & branches & yellow raised flowers & twin songbirds, marked "Queen's Burmese - Thomas Webb & Sons"................................ **3,575**

Vase, 10 1/2" h., trumpet-form w/jack-in-the-pulpit tightly ruffled rim, satin finish 650

Vase, 12" h., trumpet-form w/crimped jack-in-the-pulpit rim, overall finely painted pointillist-style large flowers in gold on slender leafy vining stems down the sides & around the foot, Thomas Webb's Queen's Burmese **2,750**

Vases, 12" h., swelled cylindrical form w/flaring neck & footring, decorated w/flowering vines & two small birds on each, pr.. **5,030**

Whiskey taster, satin finish, probably Webb, 2 1/2" d., 2 7/8" h. 150

Cambridge

The Cambridge Glass Company was founded in Ohio in 1901. Numerous pieces are now sought, especially those designed by Arthur J. Bennett, including Crown Tuscan. Other productions included crystal animals, "Black Amethyst," "blanc opaque," and other types of colored glass. The firm was finally closed in 1954. It should not be confused with the New England Glass Co., Cambridge, Massachusetts.

NEAR CUT

Cambridge Marks

Almond dish, individual, etched Cleo patt., pink, 2 1/2" **$64**

Ashtray, triangular, pressed Caprice patt., No. 206, Moonlight Blue.................................... 12

Basket, footed, two-handled, etched Diane patt., Crystal, 6" h.. 26

Bitters bottle, etched Elaine patt., No.
1212, Crystal **295**

Bonbon, footed, two handled, etched Candlelight patt., Crystal **42**

Bonbon, 6" sq., low, footed, pressed Ca-
price patt., Moonlight Blue **65**

Bouillion w/liner, Decagon line, pink **25**

Bowl, almond, 4" d., four-footed, pressed
Caprice patt., No. 95, Crystal **25**

Bowl, almond, footed, Decagon line, No.
611, Amber **16**

Bowl, almond, footed, Decagon line, No.
611, pink **20**

Bowl, cream soup, Decagon line, pink **22**

Bowl, cream soup, Decagon line, Willow
Blue **22**

Bowl, ruffled, pressed Caprice patt., No. 61,
Moonlight Blue **125**

Bowl, cranberry-type, 3", etched Apple
Blossom patt., No. 3400/71, Topaz **65**

Bowl, 5" d., flanged rim, Decagon line, pink **18**

Bowl, fruit, crimped, 5" d., pressed Caprice
patt., Moonlight Blue **75**

Bowl, 10 1/2" d., pressed Caprice patt., No.
53, Moonlight Blue **110**

Bowl, 8 1/2" sq., four-footed, pressed Caprice patt., No. 50, Moonlight Blue **137**

Bowl, 10", etched Wildflower patt., No.
3900/54, three-footed, Crystal **55**

Bowl, 11 1/2" d., footed, etched Chantilly
patt., No. 3900/28, Crystal **85**

Bowl, 11 1/2" d., footed, low, pressed Caprice patt., Moonlight Blue **85**

Bowl, 12" d., Decagon line, No. 842, Willow
Blue **60**

Bowl, 12" d., etched Wildflower patt., No.
3400/4, four-footed, flared, gold-encrust-
ed clear **115**

Butter dish, cov., etched Wildflower patt.,
No. 506, Crystal **195**

Cake plate, etched Elaine patt., No. 170,
Crystal **210**

Candleholder, etched Chantilly patt., No.
P500, Crystal **100**

Candlestick, three-light, Cambridge Arms
patt., Crystal, 5 1/4" h. **42**

Candlestick, three-light, keyhole shape,
pressed Caprice patt., Crystal **35**

Candlesticks, etched Wildflower patt., No.
3900/68, Crystal, pr. **110**

Candlesticks, two-light, pressed Caprice
patt., Moonlight Blue, pr. **550**

Candlesticks, pressed Caprice patt.,
Moonlight Blue, 7" h., pr. **160**

Celery dish, etched Chantilly patt., No.
P246, Crystal **50**

Champagne, Decagon line, Amethyst **22**

Champagne, etched Apple Blossom patt.,
No. 3130, Topaz **28**

Cheese & cracker dish, Decagon line,
Willow Blue **60**

Cheese stand, pressed Caprice patt.,
Moonlight Blue **350**

Cigarette box, cov., etched Elaine patt.,
No. 615, Crystal **165**

Cigarette box, cov., footed, etched Gloria
patt., gold encrusted Crown Tuscan **220**

Cigarette urn, etched Diane patt., Crystal **38**

Coaster, pressed Caprice patt., No. 13,
pink **55**

Comport, two-handled, Mt. Vernon line,
Emerald green **65**

Compote, open, cheese, Decagon line,
Willow Blue **30**

Cordial, pressed Cambridge Square patt.,
Crystal, 2 1/8" h. **28**

Cordial, pressed Caprice patt., Moonlight
Blue, 4 1/2" h. **115**

Cordial, pressed Pristine patt., No. 1936,
Crystal, 4 1/2" h. **52**

Cordial, Tally-Ho line, Forest green, 5" h. **74**

Creamer, flat, Decagon line, pink **15**

Creamer & sugar bowl, English Hobnail
patt., Crystal, pr. **32**

Creamer, sugar bowl & cover, individual,
etched Wildflower patt., No. 3900/40,
Crystal, pr. **45**

Cup & saucer, Decagon line, Willow Blue,
pr. **14**

Cup & saucer, etched Wildflower patt., No.
3400, Crystal, pr. **45**

Cup & saucer, pressed Caprice patt.,
Midnight Blue **44**

Cup & saucer, pressed Cascade patt.,
Crystal **22**

Cup & saucer, Tally-Ho line, Royal/cobalt
blue **64**

Decanter w/stopper, etched Portia patt.,
No. 1321, clear, 28 oz. **325**

Figural flower frog/holder, "Draped Lady,"
Crystal, 13" h. **125**

Figure flower frog/holder, "Bashful Charlotte," Emerald green, 13" h. **295**

Finger bowl, etched Apple Blossom patt.,
No. 3130, Crystal **95**

Finger bowl & liner, pressed Caprice patt.,
No. 16, Moonlight Blue **110**

Goblet, etched Candlelight patt., Crystal,
6 1/4" h. **58**

Goblet, water, Cambridge Square patt.,
Crystal, 5" h. **26**

Goblet, water, Decagon line, Royal Blue **30**

Goblet, water, Decagon line, Willow Blue **32**

Goblet, water, Gadroon (No. 3500 line),
Royal/cobalt blue, 8 3/8" h. **49**

Goblet, water, hand blown Caprice patt.,
Crystal, 5 7/8" h. **34**

Goblet, water, pressed Caprice patt.,
Crystal, 6 3/4" h. **30**

Goblet, water, pressed Caprice patt.,
Midnight Blue, 6 1/2" h. **48**

Goblet, water, pressed Cascade patt.,
Crystal, 5 1/2" h. **18**

Goblet, sherry, etched Portia patt., No.
7966, Crystal, 2 oz. **45**

Ice bucket, cov., Amethyst body in Farber-
ware metal holder **200**

Ice bucket, etched Candlelight patt., No.
3900, Crystal **135**

Ice tub, etched Chantilly patt., No. P671,
Crystal **145**

Martini jug, etched Apple Blossom patt.,
No. 1408, Crystal, 60 oz. **950**

Martini jug, etched Chantilly patt., No.
P100, Crystal w/metal base **175**

Mayonnaise bowl, pedestal base, divided,
pressed Caprice patt., Moonlight Blue **75**

Mayonnaise dish, Decagon line, No. 873,
Willow Blue **45**

Nut bowl, individual, pressed Caprice patt.,
No. 93, Moonlight Blue **60**
Nut dish, pressed Caprice patt., yellow **38**
Parfait, pressed Caprice patt., Midnight
Blue, 6 1/2" h.. **154**
Pickle dish, pressed Caprice patt., Moon-
light Blue, 9" **60**
Pitcher, etched Elaine patt., No. 3400/141,
Doulton jug-form, Crystal **350**
Pitcher, etched Wildflower patt., No.
3400/38, ball-shaped, Crystal **265**
Pitcher, etched Chantilly patt., Crystal
w/metal base, 20 oz.. **300**
Plate, dinner, pressed Caprice patt., Crystal....... **40**
Plate, 7 1/2" d., etched Elaine patt., No.
3400/176, Crystal **22**
Plate, 8 1/4" d., low, footed, Decagon line,
pink **8**
Plate, 8 1/4" d., off-center indent, Decagon
line, pink **28**
Plate, 8 1/2" d., Everglade patt., Crystal **36**
Plate, 8 1/2" d., low, footed, pressed
Caprice patt., No. 131, Moonlight Blue........... **35**
Relish dish, etched Elaine patt., No.
3500/152, four-part, Crystal **85**
Relish dish, etched Elaine patt., No.
3500/71, center handle, three-part,
Crystal... **125**
Relish dish, etched Portia patt., No. 862,
four-part w/center handle, Crystal **95**
Relish dish, three-part, etched Candlelight
patt., No. 3400, Crystal, 8".............................. **38**
Relish dish, etched Wildflower patt., No.
3400/88, two-part, Crystal, 8 3/4" **55**

Caprice Rose Bowl

Rose bowl, pressed Caprice patt., Moon-
light Blue, large (ILLUS.) **125-160**
Salt & pepper shakers, footed, etched
Chantilly patt., Crystal, pr................................. **36**
Sherbet, Decagon line, Willow Blue, low **22**
Sherbet, etched Chantilly patt., No. 3779,
Crystal, tall **25**
Sherbet, pressed Caprice patt., Midnight
Blue, 4 1/2" h.. **38**
Sherbet, pressed Caprice patt., No. 301,
Crystal, 4 1/4" h.. **12**
Sherbet, pressed Caprice patt., No. 301,
Crystal, 5 3/4" h.. **18**
Sherbet, blown Caprice patt., No. 300,
Moonlight Blue, 6 oz. **32**
Tumbler, etched Cleo patt., Amber, 8 oz............ **22**
Tumbler, footed, pressed Cascade patt.,
Crystal, 5 1/8" h.. **20**
Tumbler, iced tea, Caprice patt., No. 300,
Crystal, 6 1/8" h.. **36**

Tumbler, juice, Cambridge Square patt.,
Crystal, 4" h.. **14**
Tumbler, juice, Decagon line, Royal Blue **25**
Tumbler, pressed Caprice patt., No. 188,
Crystal, 2 oz. **32**
Tumbler, whiskey, footed, etched Apple
Blossom patt., green, 2 oz................................. **85**
Tumbler, whiskey, footed, etched Apple
Blossom patt., Topaz, 2 oz................................ **65**
Tumbler, etched Apple Blossom patt., No.
3130, Crystal, 3 oz. **30**
Tumbler, footed, pressed Caprice patt.,
Moonlight Blue, No. 12, 3 oz. **95**
Tumbler, footed, pressed Caprice patt., No.
11, Moonlight Blue, 5 oz. **45**
Tumbler, footed, pressed Caprice patt., No.
180, Moonlight Blue, 5 oz. **55**
Tumbler, juice, pressed Caprice patt., No.
310, Moonlight Blue, 5 oz. **105**
Tumbler, pressed Caprice patt., No. 300,
footed, Crystal, 10 oz. **18**
Tumbler, etched Portia patt., No. 3400/38,
Crystal, 12 oz.. **45**
Tumbler, Old Fashioned, pressed Caprice
patt., No. 310, Moonlight Blue.......................... **125**
Vase, Amethyst body in Farberware metal
holder **350**
Vase, bud, 6" h., etched Elaine patt., No.
6004, Crystal... **60**
Vase, 6" h., etched Apple Blossom patt.,
No. 3400/103, Topaz **150**
Vase, 6" h., etched Wildflower patt., No.
1620, Crystal... **300**
Vase, bud, 6" h., pressed Caprice patt.,
Midnight Blue **68**
Vase, 9" h., etched Candlelight patt., key-
hole shape, Crystal **74**
Vase, 10" h., etched Gloria patt., No. 1242,
Crystal... **250**
Vase, bud, 10" h., etched Chantilly patt.,
No. 1528, Crystal **125**
Vase, bud, 10" h., etched Wildflower patt.,
No. 1528, Crystal **165**
Vase, 11" h., etched Cleo patt., Emerald
green **130**
Wine, Decagon line, pink **30**
Wine, pressed Caprice patt., Crystal **38**
Wine, pressed Caprice patt., No. 300,
Crystal, 4 1/2" h.. **44**
Wine, pressed Caprice patt., No. 302,
Crystal, 5 5/8" h.. **21**
Wine, Tally-Ho line, No. 1420, Crystal,
4 1/2" h.. **58**
Wine, pressed Caprice patt., No. 6,
Moonlight Blue, 3 oz. **195**

Etched Rose Point Pattern

Ashtray, clear, 4 1/2" **59**
Bell, clear **148**
Butter dish, cov., round, clear, 5 1/2"............... **200**
Cake plate, handled, No. 3500, clear,
13 1/2" d. **74**
Cake plate, handled, No. 3900, clear, 14" d. **89**
Candlestick, single-light, No. 3400, clear,
5 1/4" h.. **42**
Candlestick, single-light, No. 3900, clear,
4 1/2" h.. **37**
Candlestick, two-light, No. 3400, clear............... **59**
Candy dish, cov., No. 3500/57, clear **125**
Celery tray, No. 3500, clear, 11 1/2" l................ **54**

Champagne, No. 3121, clear 27
Cordial, clear, 5 1/2" h. 82
Cordial, No. 3106, clear.. 250
Cordial, No. 7966, clear.. 165
Cup & saucer, No. 3400, clear............................. 48
Cup & saucer, No. 3900, clear............................. 42
Decanter w/stopper, No. 1320, clear 410
Goblet, water, clear, 8 3/4" h. 48
Lamp globe, hurricane-type, clear, 6" h. 190
Mayonnaise bowl, ladle & underplate,
No. 3400, clear, the set 70
Nappy, No. 3500, 6 3/4" d. 39
Oyster cocktail, No. 3121, clear......................... 65
Pitcher, 7" h., No. 3400, clear 420
Pitcher, 8" h., No. 3400, Doulton-style,
clear.. 290
Plate, 8 1/2" d., No. 3500, clear........................... 27
Plate, 9 1/2" d., No. 3400, clear........................... 48
Plate, 10 1/4" d., No. 3400, clear 160
Plate, 10 1/2" d., No. 3900, clear 174
Relish dish, No. 3400, clear, 8" 56
Relish dish, two-part, No. 3500, clear,
8 1/2"... 48
Salt & pepper shakers, No. 3400, clear, pr........ 68
Tumbler, flat, No. 3400, clear, 2" h. 100
Tumbler, flat, No. 3400, clear, 4" h..................... 68
Tumbler, footed, clear, 7" h. 29
Tumbler, iced tea, clear, 7 1/2" h........................ 36
Tumbler, No. 497, clear, 8 oz. 125
Tumbler, No. 3400/38, clear, 12 oz. 85
Vase, bud, 8 1/2" h., clear.................................... 64
Wine, clear, 5 7/8" h. 94
Wine, clear, 6 1/4" h. 115

Car Vases

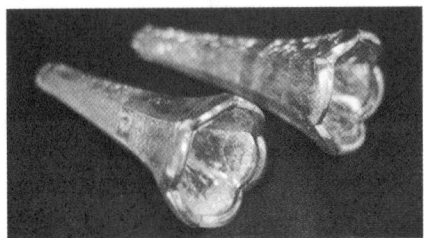

Carnival Six-sided Car Vases

Carnival, marigold, six-sided trumpet-form
w/scalloped rim, 7 1/4" l., pr. (ILLUS.) $155

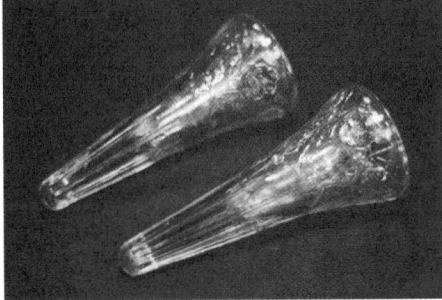

Blossoms & Band Pattern Car Vases

Carnival, marigold, trumpet-form, Blos-
soms & Band patt., 7 1/2" l., pr. (ILLUS.) 185

Eight-sided Clear Car Vase

Clear, trumpet-form, eight-sided w/wide
flared & scalloped mouth, sterling silver
tip, 8 1/2" l. (ILLUS.) 105

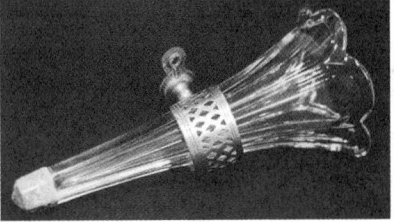

Clear Crystal Six-sided Car Vase

Clear, trumpet-form, six-sided w/scalloped
rim & sterling silver tip, Model T fitting,
8 1/2" l. (ILLUS.).. 85

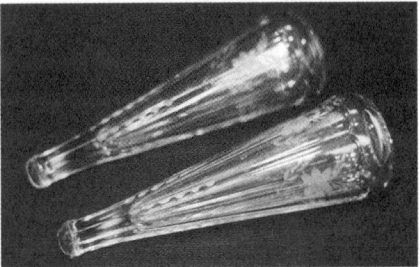

Clear Car Vases w/Floral & Fern Etching

Clear, trumpet-form w/incurved mouth, Floral & Fern etching, 7 1/2" l., pr. (ILLUS.) 175

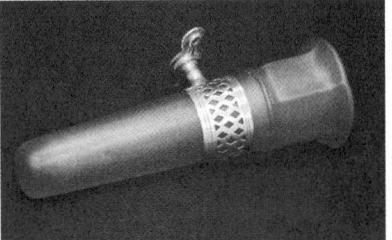

Green Car Vase w/Model T Fitting

Frosted green, trumpet-form w/flared
mouth & Model T fitting, 8" l. (ILLUS.) 135

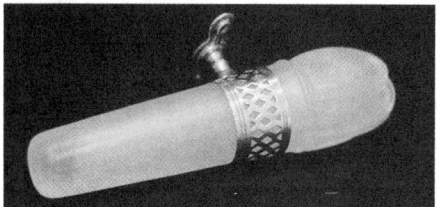

Frosted Yellow Tulip Style Car Vase

Frosted yellow, tulip style w/Model T fitting,
8 1/4" l. (ILLUS.) **135**

Carnival

Earlier called Taffeta glass, the Carnival glass now being collected was introduced early in this century. Its producers gave it an iridescence that attempted to imitate that of some Tiffany glass. Collectors will find available books by leading authorities Donald E. Moore, Sherman Hand, Marion T. Hartung, Rose M. Presznick, and Bill Edwards.

Acorn Burrs (Northwood)
Berry set: master bowl & 4 sauce dishes;
purple, 5 pcs. **$395-425**
Berry set: master bowl & 6 sauce dishes;
marigold, 7 pcs. **250-260**
Butter dish, cov., green............................ **750**
Butter dish, cov., marigold **150**

Acorn Burrs Butter Dish

Butter dish, cov., purple (ILLUS.).............. **350-400**
Creamer, marigold.................................... **150**
Creamer, purple... **150**
Pitcher, water, green................................. **400**
Pitcher, water, marigold............................ **425**
Pitcher, water, purple................................ **425-500**
Punch bowl base, green............................ **125**
Punch cup, green....................................... **55-60**
Punch cup, ice green................................. **100-150**
Punch cup, marigold.................................. **35**
Punch cup, purple...................................... **45**
Punch set: bowl, base & 6 cups; purple,
8 pcs. **1,250-1,400**
Sauce dish, green **60**
Sauce dish, marigold.................................. **30**
Sauce dish, purple **40-50**
Spooner, green **170-180**
Spooner, marigold...................................... **100**
Spooner, purple.. **255**
Sugar bowl, cov., marigold **160**
Sugar bowl, cov., purple............................ **290**
Sugar bowl, open, purple........................... **220**
Tumbler, green **60**

Tumbler, marigold **45-50**
Tumbler, purple **80**
Water set: pitcher & 6 tumblers; purple, 7
pcs. **955-975**

Advertising & Souvenir Items
Basket, "Feldman Bros. Furniture, Salisbury, Md.," open edge, marigold..................... **68**
Basket, "Miller's Furniture," marigold **88**
Bell, souvenir, BPOE Elks, "Atlantic City,
1911," blue **2,200**
Bell, souvenir, BPOE Elks, "Parkersburg,
1914," blue **2,000**
Bowl, "E. A. Hudson Furniture Co.," ruffled,
purple **850**
Bowl, "Gervitz Bros.," ruffled, purple (Northwood) **500**

"Great House of Isaac Benesch" Bowl

Bowl, "Isaac Benesch," 6 1/4" d., purple,
Millersburg (ILLUS.)..................................... **325**
Bowl, "H. Mayday & Co., 1910," 8 1/2" d.,
Wild Blackberry patt., purple **190-350**
Bowl, "Dreibus Parfait Sweets," smoky lavender, ruffled.................................... **567**
Bowl, "Horlacher," green, Peacock Tail patt.
.... **100-115**
Bowl, "Horlacher," green, Thistle patt. **175**
Bowl, "Horlacher," marigold, Vintage patt. **120**
Bowl, "Morris Smith," purple, ruffled.............. **1,250**
Bowl, souvenir, BPOE Elks, "Atlantic City,
1911," blue, one-eyed Elk.......................... **1,298**
Bowl, souvenir, BPOE Elks, "Detroit, 1910,"
blue, one-eyed Elk **900**
Bowl, souvenir, BPOE Elks, "Detroit, 1910,"
green, one-eyed Elk................................. **1,250**
Bowl, souvenir, BPOE Elks, "Detroit, 1910"
purple, one-eyed Elk................................ **600**
Bowl, souvenir, BPOE Elks, "Detroit, 1910,"
purple, two-eyed Elk (Millersburg)............. **1,900**
Bowl, souvenir, "Brooklyn Bridge," marigold
.... **250-350**
Bowl, souvenir, "Millersburg Courthouse,"
purple **850**
Bowl, souvenir, "Millersburg Courthouse,"
purple, unlettered **2,000-2,500**
Card tray, "Fern Brand Chocolates,"
turned-up sides, purple, 6 1/4" d. **600**
Card tray, "Isaac Benesch," marigold, Holly
Whirl patt. **106**
Hat, "Miller's Furniture - Harrisburg," marigold, basketweave **125**
Paperweight, souvenir, BPOE Elks, green... **3,500**
Plate, "Brazier Candies," w/handgrip, 6" d.,
purple **1,050**
Plate, "Central Shoe," purple, flat................. **1,200**

Plate, "Davidson Chocolate Society,"
6 1/4" d., purple 1,100
Plate, "Dreibus Parfait Sweets," 6 1/4" d.,
purple 385-400
Plate, "Fern Brand Chocolates," 6" d., pur-
ple 700
Plate, "Gervitz Bros., Furniture & Clothing,"
w/handgrip, 6" d., purple 1,690
Plate, "Hudson, E. A.," w/handgrip, purple 1,450
Plate, "Old Rose Distillery," green, Grape &
Cable patt., stippled, 9" d. 614
Plate, "Season's Greetings - Eat Paradise
Soda Candies," 6" d., purple 500
Plate, souvenir, BPOE Elks, "Atlantic City,
1911," blue 1,600
Plate, souvenir, BPOE Elks, "Parkersburg,
1914," 7 1/2" d., blue.............................. 1,225
Plate, "Spector's Department Store," mari-
gold, Heart & Vine patt., 9" d.................... 1,000

Basket (Fenton's Open Edge)
Amber 200-250
Aqua 125
Aqua, two sides turned up........................ 110
Aqua, w/two rows, jack-in-the-pulpit shape
.... 100-125
Aqua, w/two rows, two sides turned up............. 110
Black amethyst, two sides turned up 175-185
Blue 70
Blue, jack-in-the-pulpit shape 78
Blue, w/two rows...................................... 45
Celeste blue 250
Green, four sides turned up........................ 225
Green, jack-in-the-pulpit shape................. 200-300
Ice blue, w/three rows................................. 560-575
Ice blue, w/two rows, open edge, six ruffled...... 270
Ice green 200-225
Ice green, w/three rows 300-325
Ice green, w/two rows, two sides up, small 350
Lavender 118
Marigold 35-40
Marigold, hat-shaped................................. 30
Marigold, jack-in-the-pulpit shape 31
Marigold, w/two rows................................... 30-35
Purple 93
Red 428
Red, hat shape 275-300
Red, jack-in-the-pulpit shape............................ 400
Red, w/two rows, small................................ 300-350
Vaseline 85
Vaseline, jack-in-the-pulpit shape, small 115
Vaseline, plain interior 95
Vaseline, w/marigold overlay, small 95
Vaseline, w/two rows, large 65-75
White, 6"... 220-230
White, square 125
White, w/two rows..................................... 175
White, w/two rows, four sides turned up 100-110

Basket or Bushel Basket (Northwood)
Aqua, 4 1/2" d., 4 3/4" h............................... 800-850
Aqua opalescent, 4 1/2" d., 4 3/4" h.................. 375
Blue 123
Blue opalescent 220
Green 375-400
Horehound, variant................................... 650
Horehound, variant 525-625
Ice blue, ... 450
Ice green 175
Lavender, ... 250

Lavender 340
Lime green, ... 438
Lime green 450
Lime green opalescent 1,825

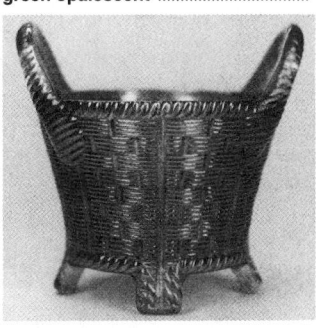

Marigold Basket

Marigold (ILLUS.)....................................... 165-185
Purple 95
Sapphire blue 1,700
Smoky 800
White 225-350

Big Fish Bowl (Millersburg)
Green 675
Green, ice cream shape 1,000
Green, square 900-1,000
Marigold 625
Marigold, ice cream shape 800

Big Fish Bowl

Marigold, ruffled (ILLUS.) 550
Marigold, square 1,500
Purple, ice cream shape 900
Purple, ruffled.. 535
Purple, square... 1,200

Butterfly (Northwood)

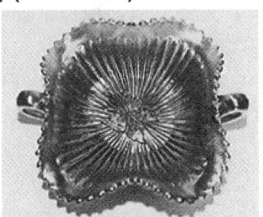

Butterfly Bonbon

Bonbon, blue, threaded exterior (ILLUS.)
.... 250-270
Bonbon, blue w/electric iridescence, threaded exterior 450-500
Bonbon, emerald green, threaded exterior 575
Bonbon, green 125-150
Bonbon, ice blue, threaded exterior 2,850
Bonbon, marigold 48
Bonbon, purple 67
Bonbon, purple, threaded exterior 200-250

Butterfly & Tulip
Bowl, square, marigold 275

Butterfly & Tulip Bowl

Bowl, 9" w., 5 1/2" h., marigold, footed (ILLUS.).. 275-350
Bowl, 10 1/2", marigold, square flat shape, footed 275
Bowl, 10 1/2", purple, square flat shape, footed 1,900
Bowl, 12" d., marigold, upturned sides, footed 354

Cherry or Hanging Cherries (Millersburg)
Banana compote (whimsey), purple 2,700
Berry set: master bowl & 4 sauce dishes; purple, 5 pcs. 750
Bowl, 5" d., blue 825
Bowl, 5" d., green satin, ruffled 145
Bowl, 5" d., marigold satin, ruffled 130
Bowl, 6" d., purple, crimped 190
Bowl, 7" d., ice cream shape, green 140
Bowl, 7" d., lavender 450
Bowl, 7" d., marigold 175
Bowl, 7" d., marigold, ice cream shape 125-150
Bowl, 8" to 9" d., purple 98
Bowl, 10" d., green, ice cream shape 450
Bowl, 10" d., green, ruffled, Wide Panel exterior 125
Bowl, 10" d., marigold, ice cream shape 150
Bowl, 10" d., marigold, ruffled, Hobnail exterior 650-750
Bowl, 10" d., marigold, three-in-one rim............ 195
Bowl, 10" d., purple, ice cream shape............... 275
Bowl, 10" d., purple, ruffled, Hobnail exterior.. 875
Bowl, 10 1/2" d., white, ruffled 125
Butter dish, cov., purple............................ 200-225
Compote, purple.. 3,500
Creamer, green.. 100-125
Creamer, marigold....................................... 100-125
Creamer, purple... 100-125
Pitcher, water, green.................................... 500-600
Pitcher, water, purple.................................... 600-650
Spooner, green... 77
Spooner, marigold.. 65

Spooner, pastel marigold................................... 100
Spooner, purple... 100-125
Sugar bowl, cov., green...................................... 95
Sugar bowl, cov., marigold.................................. 85
Table set, marigold, 4 pcs................................ 415

Cherry Pitcher & Tumbler

Water set: pitcher & 4 tumblers; marigold, 5 pcs. (ILLUS. of part) 950

Chrysanthemum or Windmill & Mums
Bowl, 8" to 9" d., blue, three-footed................... 145
Bowl, 9" d., blue, ruffled.................................... 113
Bowl, 9" d., green, ruffled.................................. 100
Bowl, 9" d., marigold, ruffled............................... 58
Bowl, 9" d., purple, ruffled................................. 150
Bowl, 9" d., red w/amber center.......... 1,500-2,500
Bowl, 9" d., ruffled, red 4,500
Bowl, 10" d., blue, three-footed......................... 210
Bowl, 10" d., green, three-footed...................... 350

Chrysanthemum Bowl

Bowl, 10" d., marigold, three-footed(ILLUS)
.... 80-100
Bowl, 10" d., red, collared base 2,000-2,500
Bowl, 11" d., blue, ice cream shape, footed..... 120
Bowl, 11" d., blue, three-footed......................... 220
Bowl, 11" d., marigold, three-footed................... 55
Bowl, 11" d., purple, three-footed...................... 250
Bowl, marigold, collared base 63

Coin Dot
Bowl, 6" d., green 48
Bowl, 6" d., red, ice cream shape 1,000-1,500
Bowl, 6 1/2" d., purple, stippled.......................... 50
Bowl, 7" d., green 50

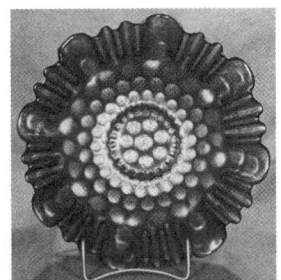

Coin Dot Bowl

Bowl, 7" d., green, candy ribbon edge
(ILLUS.).. 50
Bowl, 7" d., purple, candy ribbon edge 35
Bowl, 7" d., red... 1,450
Bowl, 7 1/2" d., blue 55
Bowl, 8" d., purple, pie crust rim 20
Bowl, 8" to 9" d., green 25-50
Bowl, 8" to 9" d., green, stippled......................... 25
Bowl, 8" to 9" d., marigold 35-40
Bowl, 8" to 9" d., peach opalescent.................. 149
Bowl, 8" to 9" d., purple 43
Bowl, 9" d., purple, three-in-one edge................ 97
Bowl, 9 1/2" d., purple, ruffled 60-65
Bowl 10" d., peach opalescent, ruffled.............. 158
Bowl, green.. 70
Bowl, marigold, ruffled 15
Bowl, purple.. 77
Compote, celeste blue opalescent 850
Compote, purple... 60
Rose bowl, green 70-75
Rose bowl, marigold 45
Rose bowl, marigold, stippled 60
Rose bowl, purple, stippled 65-70
Rose bowl, vaseline... 100

Dragon & Strawberry Bowl/Dragon & Berry (Fenton)
Bowl, 9" d., blue.. 850
Bowl, 9" d., marigold 425
Bowl, 9" d., purple 2,500-3,000
Bowl, footed, marigold 750

Embroidered Mums (Northwood)

Embroidered Mums Bowl

Bonbon, white, stemmed 1,025-1,075
Bowl, 8" to 9" d., blue.. 495
Bowl, 8" to 9" d., blue, ruffled 1,000
Bowl, 8" to 9" d., blue w/electric iridescence...... 612
Bowl, 8" to 9" d., ice blue.................................... 785
Bowl, 8" to 9" d., ice green................................. 875
Bowl, 8" to 9" d., marigold 475-500

Bowl, 8" to 9" d., marigold, ruffled..................... 285
Bowl, 8" to 9" d., purple (ILLUS.)....................... 400
Bowl, lavender 975-1,000
Bowl, purple, ruffled 275
Bowl, purple, ruffled, ribbed exterior 612
Bowl, sapphire blue, piecrust rim.................. 2,850
Plate, ice green 3,100

Fanciful (Dugan)
Bowl, ice cream shape, marigold....................... 130

Farmyard (Dugan)

Farmyard Bowl

Bowl, purple, candy ribbon edge (ILLUS.)
.... 4,000-4,500
Bowl, three-in-one edge, purple..................... 7,000

Fashion (Imperial)
Bowl, 9" d., clambroth.. 40
Bowl, 9" d., marigold 25
Bowl, 9" d., smoky, ruffled................................. 175
Breakfast set: small size creamer & sugar
bowl, smoky, pr. 175
Creamer, purple, breakfast size 225
Creamer, smoky 85

Fashion Pitcher

Pitcher, water, marigold (ILLUS.) 100-125
Pitcher, water, purple............................... 900-1,000
Punch bowl & base, marigold, 12" d.,
2 pcs.. 125-150
Punch cup, marigold 21
Punch cup, smoky 40
Rose bowl, purple, large 2,050
Sugar bowl, smoky 90
Tumbler, marigold 30
Tumbler, purple 200
Tumbler, smoky 95-115

Fenton's Flowers Rose Bowl - See Orange Tree Pattern

Fentonia

Berry set: master bowl & 4 sauce dishes; marigold, 5 pcs. 145-165
Bowl, master berry, blue....................................... 263
Bowl, master berry, marigold.............................. 55
Butter dish, cov., blue, footed.................... 150-200
Butter dish, cov., marigold, footed.................... 350
Creamer, blue.. 100
Creamer, marigold... 60
Pitcher, water, blue 695
Sauce dish, blue, claw feet.................................... 35
Sauce dish, marigold, claw feet........................... 22
Spooner, marigold.. 75-100
Tumbler, blue 60-65
Tumbler, marigold 47

Fentonia Water Set

Water set: pitcher & 6 tumblers; marigold, 7 pcs. (ILLUS.)... 500

Fisherman's Mug

Marigold 300
Pastel marigold 200-250
Peach opalescent 600-800

Fisherman's Mug

Purple (ILLUS.) 105
Purple, w/advertising.................................... 150-175

Fluffy Peacock - See Peacock, Fluffy Pattern (Fenton)

Garden Path

Bowl, 8" to 9" d., marigold.................................... 68
Bowl, 9" d., marigold, ice cream shape............... 75

Bowl, 9" d., marigold, variant, Soda Gold exterior.. 35-45
Bowl, 9" d., purple, ice cream shape................. 750
Bowl, 10" d., marigold, ruffled.............................. 95
Bowl, 10" d., purple, ice cream shape 1,300
Bowl, 10" d., white, ruffled......................... 300-325
Hatpin, purple... 150
Plate, 6" d., white, variant................................... 525
Plate, 6 1/2" d., white 375

Garden Path Plate

Plate, chop, 11" d., purple (ILLUS.) 6,250

Greek Key (Northwood)

Bowl, 8" to 9" d., blue... 255
Bowl, 8" to 9" d., green, fluted............................ 275
Bowl, 8" to 9" d., marigold, ruffled.............. 150-200
Bowl, 8" to 9" d., purple.. 325
Bowl, 8" to 9" d., purple, ruffled........................ 145
Bowl, blue, ribbed exterior 700
Bowl, green, dome-footed...................................... 75
Bowl, green, piecrust rim...................................... 900
Bowl, purple, piecrust rim................................... 200
Pitcher, water, green 1,300-1,350
Pitcher, water, marigold 750

Greek Key Plate

Plate, 9" d., green (ILLUS.) 475
Plate, 9" d., marigold... 525
Tumbler, green 145
Tumbler, marigold 90-100
Tumbler, purple 120-140

Heavy Grape (Imperial)

Bowl, 4" d., purple 45
Bowl, 5" d., green 19
Bowl, 5" d., purple 150
Bowl, 5" d., 2" h., marigold.................................. 30
Bowl, 5" d., 2" h., purple...................................... 26
Bowl, 6" d., green 25-35
Bowl, 7" d., green, fluted 40

Bowl, 7" d., purple 60-70
Bowl, 8" to 9" d., amber 175
Bowl, 8" to 9" d., light blue w/marigold overlay 125
Bowl, 8" to 9" d., marigold 45
Bowl, 8" to 9" d., purple 75-85
Bowl, 9" d., aqua 150
Bowl, 9" d., ruffled, smoky 225
Bowl, 10" d., purple 335
Bowl, 12" d., marigold 135
Nut bowl, six-footed, purple 75
Plate, 7" to 8" d., amber 175-200
Plate, 7" to 8" d., green 50-75
Plate, 7" to 8" d., marigold 50-60
Plate, 7" to 8" d., purple 145
Plate, 9 1/2" d., stippled, marigold 50

Heavy Grape Chop Plate

Plate, chop, 11" d., amber (ILLUS.) 255
Plate, chop, 11" d., green 240-250
Plate, chop, 11" d., lavender 410
Plate, chop, 11" d., marigold 195
Plate, chop, 11" d., purple 295
Plate, chop, 11" d., smoky 500
Punch bowl, marigold 140
Punch bowl & base, marigold, 2 pcs 400
Punch cup, amber 50
Punch cup, green 55
Punch cup, marigold 20
Punch cup, purple 45

Holly, Holly Berries & Carnival Holly (Fenton)

Holly Bowl

Bonbon, green, two-handled 55
Bonbon, marigold, two-handled 110

Bonbon, purple, two-handled 65
Bowl, 5" d., marigold 28
Bowl, 6 1/2" d., crimped edge, red 425
Bowl, 8" d., black amethyst 225
Bowl, 8" to 9" d., amber 150
Bowl, 8" to 9" d., aqua 550
Bowl, 8" to 9" d., blue 75-100
Bowl, 8" to 9" d., green 70
Bowl, 8" to 9" d., light blue w/marigold overlay 180
Bowl, 8" to 9" d., marigold 70-80
Bowl, 8" to 9" d., purple (ILLUS) 130
Bowl, 8" to 9" d., red 1,500-1,550
Bowl, 8" to 9" d., white 100-125
Bowl, 8" to 9" d., candy ribbon edge, blue 50-55
Bowl, 8" to 9" d., candy ribbon edge, green 150-175
Bowl, 8" to 9" d., candy ribbon edge, marigold 65
Bowl, 8" to 9" d., candy ribbon edge, pastel green 550
Bowl, 8" to 9" d., candy ribbon edge, purple 100-125
Bowl, 8" to 9" d., ice cream shape, blue 75-100,00
Bowl, 8" to 9" d., ice cream shape, celeste blue 1,500-2,000
Bowl, 8" to 9" d., ice cream shape, green 122
Bowl, 8" to 9" d., ice cream shape, ice green 2,700
Bowl, 8" to 9" d., ice cream shape, marigold . 55-75
Bowl, 8" to 9" d., ice cream shape, purple 80
Bowl, 8" to 9" d., ice cream shape, red 2,000-2,500
Bowl, 8" to 9" d., ice cream shape, white .. 135-140
Bowl, 8" to 9" d., ruffled, blue 113
Bowl, 8" to 9" d., ruffled, blue opalescent 1,350
Bowl, 8" to 9" d., ruffled, emerald green 300
Bowl, 8" to 9" d., ruffled, green 160
Bowl, 8" to 9" d., ruffled, lime green 225
Bowl, 8" to 9" d., ruffled, marigold 63
Bowl, 8" to 9" d., ruffled, peach opalescent 48
Bowl, 8" to 9" d., ruffled, purple 165
Bowl, 8" to 9" d., ruffled, red 1,300-1,475
Bowl, 8" to 9" d., ruffled, vaseline 165
Bowl, 8" to 9" d., ruffled, white 100-150
Bowl, three-in-one edge, blue 50
Compote, lime green w/marigold overlay 85
Compote, small, Amberina 650
Compote, small, aqua w/marigold overlay 138
Compote, small, blue 105
Compote, small, green 125-150
Compote, small, purple 75
Compote, small, red 800-1,000
Compote, small, vaseline 95
Dish, hat-shaped, Amberina 400-425
Dish, hat-shaped, aqua, 5 3/4" 75-85
Dish, hat-shaped, blue, 5 3/4" 35-45
Dish, hat-shaped, marigold, 5 3/4" 35-40
Dish, hat-shaped, purple, 5 3/4" 40-45
Dish, hat-shaped, red, 5 3/4" 450-500
Dish, hat-shaped, vaseline, 5 3/4" 80-90
Goblet, blue 45
Goblet, marigold 39
Plate, 9" to 10" d., blue 375
Plate, 9" to 10" d., green 1,025
Plate, 9" to 10" d., marigold 175-200
Plate, 9" to 10" d., pastel marigold 175
Plate, 9" to 10" d., purple 700-1,000
Plate, 9" to 10" d., white 200

Sauceboat, peach opalescent, handled 85
Sherbet, green 28
Sherbet, marigold 26
Violet bowl, marigold 17

Holly Star Paneled or Holly Star (Northwood)
Bonbon, green 70

Horse Heads or Horse Medallions (Fenton)
Bowl, 5" d., footed, marigold 57
Bowl, 7" d., ice cream shape, marigold 155
Bowl, 7" to 8" d., blue 220
Bowl, 7" to 8" d., green 250-300

Horse Head Medallions Bowl

Bowl, 7" to 8" d., marigold (ILLUS) 100-150
Bowl, 7" to 8" d., red 1,250-1,500
Bowl, footed, green 395
Bowl, footed, purple 325
Bowl, footed, ruffled, marigold 175
Bowl, jack-in-the-pulpit shaped, blue 225-300
Bowl, jack-in-the-pulpit shaped, lime green 300
Bowl, jack-in-the-pulpit shaped, marigold 75
Nut bowl, three-footed, amethyst 225
Nut bowl, three-footed, aqua 1,800
Nut bowl, three-footed, blue 195
Nut bowl, three-footed, green 145
Nut bowl, three-footed, marigold 68
Nut bowl, three-footed, red 1,200
Nut bowl, three-footed, smoky 500-525
Nut bowl, three-footed, vaseline 475
Plate, 7" to 8" d., blue 1,050-1,075
Plate, 7" to 8" d., marigold 220
Rose bowl, blue 315
Rose bowl, marigold 150-200
Rose bowl, marigold, giant 500
Rose bowl, vaseline 650

Imperial Grape (Imperial)
Basket, marigold 75
Basket, purple 60
Berry set: master bowl & 4 sauce dishes;
    green, 5 pcs. 125-150
Berry set: master bowl & 4 sauce dishes;
    purple, 5 pcs. 285
Berry set: master bowl & 6 sauce dishes;
    marigold, 7 pcs. 150-200
Bowl, 6" d., marigold 35
Bowl, 6" d., ruffled, purple 75
Bowl, 8" to 9" d., aqua 75
Bowl, 8" to 9" d., marigold 35-45
Bowl, 8" to 9" d., purple 140
Bowl, 9" d., low, amber 400
Bowl, 9" d., ruffled, amber 150
Bowl, 10" d., green 60-70

Bowl, 10" d., marigold 40
Bowl, 10" d., purple 185
Bowl, 10" d., smoky 45
Bowl, 11" d., ruffled, purple 145-165
Compote, marigold 38
Compote, smoky, made from goblet 350
Cup & saucer, marigold 75-80
Decanter w/stopper, green 125-150
Decanter w/stopper, marigold 95-100
Decanter w/stopper, purple 200-250
Goblet, amber 45
Goblet, marigold 36
Goblet, purple 125
Goblet, smoky 75-100
Pitcher, water, amber 650
Pitcher, water, marigold 77
Pitcher, water, purple 350-400
Pitcher, water, smoky 300-400
Plate, 6" d., amber 140-150
Plate, 6" d., green 74
Plate, 6" d., marigold 55
Plate, 6" d., purple 150
Plate, 7" d., green 75
Plate, 7" d., marigold 50-75
Plate, 8" d., clambroth, stippled 75
Plate, 8" d., green 63
Plate, 9" d., green, flat 75
Plate, 9" d., green, ruffled 156
Plate, 9" d., marigold, flat 85-100
Plate, 9" d., marigold, ruffled 65-75
Plate, 9" d., purple, ruffled 1,500
Plate, 9" d., white, ruffled 55
Rose bowl, purple 68
Sauce dish, amber 40-45
Sauce dish, marigold, ruffled 20
Sauce dish, purple 35
Tray, center handle, amber 30
Tray, center handle, clambroth 45
Tray, center handle, marigold 63
Tray, center handle, smoky 65
Tumbler, emerald green 210
Tumbler, green 29
Tumbler, marigold 15-20
Tumbler, purple 40-50
Tumbler, smoky 90-100
Water bottle, green 100-125
Water bottle, marigold 135-175

Imperial Grape Water Bottle

Water bottle, purple (ILLUS.) 200-225
Water bottle, smoky 525

Water set: pitcher & 6 tumblers; marigold,
7 pcs. 195-225
Water set: pitcher & 6 tumblers; purple,
7 pcs. 625-675
Wine, green 25-30
Wine, lime green 40
Wine, marigold 30-40
Wine, purple 35-45
Wine, smoky 50

Kittens (Fenton)
Bowl, cereal, aqua 725
Bowl, cereal, blue 425-475
Bowl, cereal, marigold 200
Bowl, four-sided, marigold, ruffled 185-200
Bowl, ruffled, marigold 125
Bowl, ruffled, purple 200
Bowl, six-sided, marigold, ruffled 250-300
Cup, blue 550
Cup, marigold 125
Cup & saucer, marigold 200-250

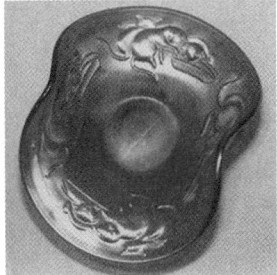

Kittens Dish

Dish, turned-up sides, marigold (ILLUS.)... 145-165
Dish, turned-up sides, purple 450-500
Plate, 4 1/2" d., marigold 150-200
Saucer, marigold 140
Toothpick holder, blue 450-500
Toothpick holder, marigold 150
Vase, marigold 179
Vase, marigold, child's, ruffled 143

Leaf & Beads (Northwood)
Candy bowl, footed, aqua opalescent 500
Nut bowl, green, handled, w/interior pattern 175

Leaf & Beads Rose Bowl

Rose bowl, aqua opalescent (ILLUS) 400
Rose bowl, blue 225
Rose bowl, blue w/electric iridescence 300-500
Rose bowl, green 130-150
Rose bowl, ice blue 1,400

Rose bowl, ice green opalescent 3,000
Rose bowl, marigold 95-100
Rose bowl, marigold, souvenir 125

Lion (Fenton)
Bowl, 6" d., blue 250-350
Bowl, 6" d., marigold 100-125
Bowl, 7" d., blue 335
Bowl, 7" d., ice cream shape, blue 300-315

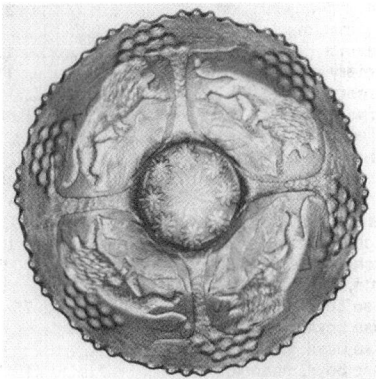

Lion Bowl

Bowl, 7" d., ice cream shape, marigold
(ILLUS.) 175
Bowl, 7" d., ruffled, blue 275-300
Bowl, 7" d., ruffled, marigold 130

Loving Cup (Fenton) - See Orange Tree Pattern

Lustre Rose (Imperial)

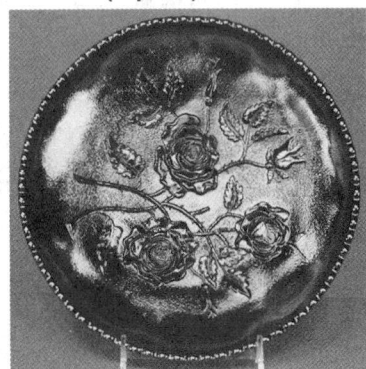

Lustre Rose Fernery

Bowl, 6 1/2" d., amber 100
Bowl, 6 1/2" d., stippled, marigold 65
Bowl, 7" d., three-footed, amber 35
Bowl, 7" d., three-footed, green 40
Bowl, 7" d., three-footed, marigold 40-45
Bowl, 8" to 9" d., three-footed, amber 83
Bowl, 8" to 9" d., three-footed, clambroth 56
Bowl, 8" to 9" d., three-footed, green 45
Bowl, 8" to 9" d., three-footed, marigold 38
Bowl, 8" to 9" d., three-footed, olive green 75
Bowl, 8" to 9" d., three-footed, purple 110
Bowl, fruit, 10" d., amber 275
Bowl, 10 1/2" d., three-footed, marigold 35

Bowl, 10 1/2 d ., three-footed, purple 350
Bowl, 10 1/2" d., three-footed, smoky 67
Bowl, 11" d., ruffled, collared base, green 75
Bowl, 11" d., ruffled, footed, marigold 43
Bowl, 11" d., ruffled, footed, smoky 95
Bowl, fruit, red 2,500-3,000
Bowl, ruffled, amber 60
Bowl, whimsey, centerpiece, amber 150-175
Butter dish, cov., marigold 75-100
Butter dish, cov., purple 250
Creamer, marigold 37
Creamer, purple 125
Fernery, amber 115
Fernery, blue 110
Fernery, green, 7 1/2" d., 4" h. 60
Fernery, marigold 35
Fernery, olive 85
Fernery, purple (ILLUS.) 93
Fernery, smoky 110
Pitcher, water, amber 200
Pitcher, water, clambroth 105
Pitcher, water, marigold 65
Plate, 9" d., marigold 55
Rose bowl, amber 75-80
Rose bowl, clambroth 50
Rose bowl, green 45
Rose bowl, marigold 43
Sauce dish, clambroth 30
Sauce dish, green 24
Sauce dish, smoky 50
Spooner, amber 50
Spooner, green 40
Spooner, marigold 35
Spooner, purple 150
Sugar bowl, cov., marigold 40
Tumbler, green 25
Tumbler, marigold 25
Tumbler, pastel marigold variant 100
Tumbler, purple 69
Water set: pitcher & 6 tumblers; marigold,
  7 pcs. 200-225

Maple Leaf (Dugan)

Bowl, 6" d., small berry, purple 35
Bowl, ice cream, footed, purple, large 110
Bowl, master berry or fruit, purple 135
Butter dish, cov., marigold 120

Maple Leaf Butter Dish & Spooner

Butter dish, cov., purple (ILLUS.) 145
Creamer, blue 60
Creamer, marigold 48

Creamer, purple 58
Pitcher, water, marigold 250
Pitcher, water, purple 245
Spooner, blue 70
Spooner, marigold 40
Spooner, purple (ILLUS. w/butter dish) 60
Sugar bowl, cov., marigold 48
Sugar bowl, cov., purple 95
Table set: cov. sugar bowl, creamer &
  spooner; purple, 3 pcs. 200-225
Table set, blue, 4 pcs. 300-350
Tumbler, blue 65
Tumbler, marigold 29
Tumbler, purple 38
Water set: pitcher & 4 tumblers; purple,
  5 pcs. 425-475

Millersburg Trout & Fly - See Trout & Fly Pattern

Nu-Art Homestead Plate (Imperial)

Amber 1,950
Green 675-750
Purple 975-1,050

Orange Tree (Fenton)

Berry set: master bowl & 6 sauce dishes;
  blue, 7 pcs. 300-375
Bowl, 8" to 9" d., blue 90-100
Bowl, 8" to 9" d., green 225-275
Bowl, 8" to 9" d., marigold 55-60
Bowl, 8" to 9" d., purple 195
Bowl, 8" to 9" d., white 100-125
Bowl, 10" d., three-footed, blue 250-325
Bowl, 10" d., three-footed, green 235

Large Orange Tree Bowl

Bowl, 10" d., three-footed, marigold
  (ILLUS.) 175
Bowl, 10" d., three-footed, purple 325
Bowl, 10" d., three-footed, white 200
Bowl, ice cream shape, blue 300
Bowl, ice cream shape, blue, w/trunk center 230
Bowl, ice cream shape, green 300
Bowl, ice cream shape, marigold 85
Bowl, ice cream shape, purple 250-300
Bowl, ice cream shape, red 2,100
Bowl, ice cream shape, white 125
Bowl, milk white w/marigold overlay 1,150-1,250
Bowl, peach opalescent 1,900
Bowl, ruffled, amber 275-300
Bowl, three-in-one edge, marigold 85-90
Breakfast set: individual size creamer &
  cov. sugar bowl; marigold, pr. 195
Breakfast set: individual size creamer &
  cov. sugar bowl; purple, pr. 239
Breakfast set: individual size creamer &
  cov. sugar bowl; white, pr. 150-200

Butter dish, cov., blue 375
Butter dish, cov., marigold 350
Centerpiece bowl, footed, purple, 12" d.,
     4" h. 1,000-1,500
Compote, 5" d., blue 50
Compote, 5" d., green.. 85
Compote, 5" d., marigold 35-45
Creamer, footed, blue 80
Creamer, footed, marigold........................... 47
Creamer, footed, purple................................ 50
Creamer, footed, white................................ 125-175
Creamer, marigold, individual size...................... 37
Creamer, purple, individual size........................ 45
Creamer & sugar bowl, blue, footed, pr. 100
Dish, blue, ice cream, footed 38
Dish, marigold, ice cream, footed.................. 30-40
Goblet, aqua.. 110
Goblet, blue 55
Goblet, marigold 57
Hatpin holder, blue................................... 300-350
Hatpin holder, marigold.......................... 300-325
Loving cup, aqua opalescent..................... 15,000
Loving cup, blue... 225
Loving cup, green............................... 400-475
Loving cup, marigold................................ 325
Loving cup, purple.. 400
Loving cup, white... 150
Mug, amber.. 89
Mug, Amberina.. 385
Mug, blue.. 65-75
Mug, green.. 875-900
Mug, lavender... 180
Mug, lime green.. 500
Mug, marigold.. 45
Mug, purple... 80-100
Mug, red.. 500
Mug, vaseline.. 100-150
Mug, white... 948
Pitcher, water, blue 325
Pitcher, water, marigold.................................... 275
Plate, 9" d., flat, blue 400
Plate, 9" d., flat, clambroth 300-350
Plate, 9" d., flat, green................................. 3,000
Plate, 9" d., flat, marigold 250-350
Plate, 9" d., flat, pastel marigold................. 175-200
Plate, 9" d., flat, purple............................... 600
Plate, 9" d., flat, teal blue.................... 1,000-1,500
Plate, 9" d., flat, white.................................. 180
Plate, 9 1/2" d., trunk center, Beaded Berry
     exterior, clambroth 250
Plate, 9" d., flat, Beaded Berry exterior, blue...... 550
Plate, 9" d., trunk center, flat, Beaded Berry
     exterior, marigold....................................... 200
Plate, 9" d., trunk center, white.................... 275
Plate, 9" d., Blackberry exterior, "Souvenir
     of Hershey," blue...................................... 335
Powder jar, cov., blue 150-175
Powder jar, cov., green 400-500
Powder jar, cov., marigold 75-100
Punch bowl & base, blue, 2 pcs. 275-300
Punch bowl & base, marigold, 2 pcs........ 185-195
Punch bowl & base, white, 2 pcs................ 595
Punch cup, blue 32
Punch cup, white... 50
Punch cups, marigold, set of 6 125-150
Punch set: bowl, base & 6 cups; marigold,
     8 pcs.. 330
Punch set: bowl, base & 6 cups; white,
     8 pcs.. 900

Punch set: bowl, base & 10 cups; blue,
     12 pcs. 650
Rose bowl, blue.. 85
Rose bowl, clambroth.. 90
Rose bowl, green....................................... 100-125
Rose bowl, purple..................................... 100-125
Rose bowl, white...................................... 200-225
Sauce dish, footed, white 100-125
Shaving mug, blue.. 50
Shaving mug, green.. 875
Shaving mug, marigold...................................... 50
Shaving mug, marigold, large.................. 100-125
Shaving mug, olive green................................ 975
Shaving mug, purple... 195
Shaving mug, red 600-650
Spooner, blue 60-70
Spooner, marigold.. 50
Sugar bowl, cov., blue.................................... 60
Sugar bowl, cov., marigold............................ 98
Sugar bowl, cov., white................................. 100
Tumbler, blue.. 60
Tumbler, marigold... 40
Tumbler, white... 100
Wine, green.. 225
Wine, marigold.. 25

Panther (Fenton)
Berry set: master bowl & 5 sauce dishes;
     marigold, 6 pcs..................................... 200-375
Berry set: master bowl & 6 sauce dishes;
     marigold, 7 pcs..................................... 350-375
Bowl, 5" d., footed, aqua 275
Bowl, 5" d., footed, blue................................ 175
Bowl, 5" d., footed, clambroth.......................... 35
Bowl, 5" d., footed, green........................... 90-100
Bowl, 5" d., footed, marigold...................... 45-55

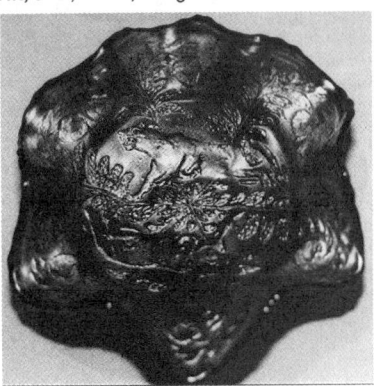

Panther Bowl

Bowl, 5" d., footed, red (ILLUS.) 675-750
Bowl, 5" d., footed, white............................. 475
Bowl, 9" d., claw-footed, green................. 625-675
Bowl, 9" d., claw-footed, marigold 195-225
Bowl, 9" d., claw-footed, purple................. 395-500
Bowl, 9" d., claw-footed, white 750-1,000
Bowl, low, marigold.................................. 100-125
Centerpiece bowl, marigold...................... 575-600

Peacock at Fountain (Northwood)
Berry set: master bowl & 4 sauce dishes;
     purple, 5 pcs. 450
Bowl, berry, green... 375
Butter dish, cov., marigold 175-225

Butter dish, cov., purple 250-300
Compote, blue 2,500
Compote, ice blue 1,325
Compote, purple 750
Compote, white 305
Creamer, purple 100-125
Pitcher, water, blue 400-450
Pitcher, water, marigold 375
Pitcher, water, purple 400
Pitcher, water, white 1,000-1,025
Punch bowl & base, blue, 2 pcs. 3,000
Punch bowl & base, ice green, 2 pcs. 9,500
Punch bowl & base, marigold, 2 pcs. 500
Punch bowl & base, purple, 2 pcs. 1,400-1,425
Punch cup, ice green 525
Punch cup, marigold 40
Punch cup, purple 40-45
Punch cup, white 90
Punch set: bowl, base & 5 cups; purple,
    7 pcs. 1,900
Punch set: bowl, base & 6 cups; marigold,
    8 pcs. 750
Sauce dish, green 25
Sauce dish, ice blue 100-110
Sauce dish, marigold 30
Sauce dish, purple 45
Sauce dish, teal blue 75
Sauce dish, white 70-80
Spooner, blue 150
Spooner, blue w/electric iridescence 250
Spooner, green 185
Spooner, ice blue 280
Spooner, purple 100-120
Spooner, white 183
Sugar bowl, cov., ice blue 375-400
Sugar bowl, cov., purple 115
Tumbler, blue 60-70
Tumbler, green 325
Tumbler, ice blue 325
Tumbler, marigold 45
Tumbler, purple 65-70
Tumbler, white 225-250
Water set: pitcher & 3 tumblers; purple,
    4 pcs. 600-625

Peacock, Fluffy (Fenton)
Pitcher, water, green 650-700
Pitcher, water, marigold 450-500

Peacock, Fluffy Pitcher

Pitcher, water, purple (ILLUS) 575-600
Tumbler, purple 45-50
Water set: pitcher & 4 tumblers; marigold,
    5 pcs. 500

Water set: pitcher & 5 tumblers; purple,
    6 pcs. 750-800

Persian Medallion (Fenton)
Bonbon, two-handled, aqua 250-300
Bonbon, two-handled, green 80
Bonbon, two-handled, marigold 50-60
Bonbon, two-handled, purple 60-70
Bonbon, two-handled, red 860
Bonbon, two-handled, vaseline 130
Bowl, 5" d., aqua 125-150
Bowl, 5" d., blue 55
Bowl, 5" d., marigold 30-35
Bowl, 5" d., purple 67
Bowl, 6" d., ruffled, marigold 30-40
Bowl, 7" d., purple, candy ribbon edge 85-95
Bowl, 8" to 9" d., blue, fluted 100-125
Bowl, 8" to 9" d., green, ice cream shape 155
Bowl, 8" to 9" d., marigold 55-65
Bowl, 8" to 9" d., purple, candy ribbon edge
    100-125
Bowl, 9" d., green, ruffled 75
Bowl, 9 1/2" d., blue, footed, Grape & Cable
    exterior 325-375
Bowl, 10" d., purple 295
Bowl, fruit, purple, Grape & Cable exterior 275
Bowl, ice cream shape, blue 65
Bowl, salad shape, large, blue 400-425
Bowl, three-in-one edge, blue 100
Compote, blue, 6 1/2" d., 6 1/2" h. 110
Compote, green, 6 1/2" d., 6 1/2" h. 225-300
Compote, marigold, 6 1/2" d., 6 1/2" h. 115
Compote, purple, 6 1/2" d., 6 1/2" h. 140
Compote, candy ribbon edge, cobalt blue
    200-250
Hair receiver, blue 165-195
Hair receiver, marigold 70
Hair receiver, white 125
Plate, 6 1/2" d., blue 125-150
Plate, 6 1/2" d., green 160
Plate, 6 1/2" d., marigold 75-100
Plate, 7" d., marigold 110-125
Plate, 7 3/4" d., blue 300
Plate, 9" d., blue 275

Persian Medallion Chop Plate

Plate, chop, 10 1/2" d., blue (ILLUS.) 650
Rose bowl, blue 185
Rose bowl, marigold 75-100
Rose bowl, purple 350
Rose bowl, white 125-135

Poinsettia (Imperial)
Pitcher, milk, blue opalescent 260
Pitcher, milk, green 220-225

Poinsettia Milk Pitcher

Pitcher, milk, marigold (ILLUS.) **90-100**
Pitcher, milk, purple **2,100**
Pitcher, milk, smoky **200-250**

Poppy Show (Northwood)
Bowl, 7" d., purple **65**
Bowl, 7 1/2" d., marigold, ruffled **30**
Bowl, 8" to 9" d., blue w/electric iridescence
.... **1,125**
Bowl, 8" to 9" d., clambroth................................ **190**
Bowl, 8" to 9" d., ice blue............................... **1,425**
Bowl, 8" to 9" d., ice green **2,013**
Bowl, 8" to 9" d., marigold **535**
Bowl, 8" to 9" d., pastel marigold **760**
Bowl, 8" to 9" d., purple **1,100**
Bowl, 8" to 9" d., white **450**
Plate, blue **3,600**
Plate, blue w/electric iridescence **2,650**

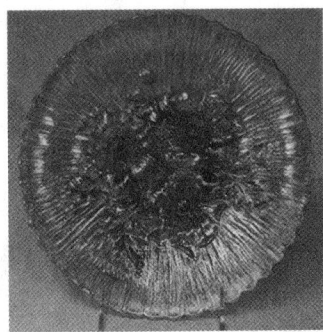

Poppy Show Plate

Plate, green (ILLUS.).. **4,050**
Plate, ice blue **2,700**
Plate, ice green **3,900-4,000**
Plate, marigold... **1,400**
Plate, pastel marigold....................................... **2,700**
Plate, purple **1,000**
Plate, white... **500**

Question Marks
Bonbon, two-handled, white, 5 1/2" sq. **94**
Bonbon, footed, peach opalescent, 6" d.,
3 3/4" h.. **65**
Bonbon, footed, purple, 6" d., 3 3/4" h............... **50**
Bonbon, footed, purple, Georgia Belle exte-
rior, 6" d., 3 3/4" h. **155**
Bonbon, stemmed, marigold **50**

Bonbon, stemmed, peach opalescent **48**
Bonbon, stemmed, purple **90-125**
Bonbon, stemmed, white **65-75**
Compote, crimped edge, marigold **55**
Compote, crimped edge, peach opalescent **92**
Plate, candy ribbon edge, footed, peach
opalescent **150**
Plate, dome-footed, white.................................. **225**
Plate, stemmed, marigold.................................. **110**
Plate, stemmed, white....................................... **280**

Ripple Vase
Amber, 6" h.. **95**
Amber, 7 1/2" h.. **77**
Amber, 9" h... **175**
Amber, 10" h.. **95-100**
Amber, 11 1/2" h... **125**
Aqua, 10" h... **125**
Aqua, 11" h... **300**
Aqua **145-150**
Blue, 9" h.. **350**
Clambroth, 10" h. **75**
Clambroth, funeral, 15 1/2" h. **225**
Green, 8 1/4" h... **55**
Green, 9 1/2" h... **85**
Green, 10" h.. **40-50**
Green, 11" h... **38**
Green, 12 1/2" h... **95**
Green, 13" h... **93**
Green, 15 1/2" h.. **100-125**
Green, funeral, mid-size **175**
Ice green, 14 1/2" h.................................... **200-245**
Lavender, 7 1/2" h... **115**
Lavender, 14" h... **135**
Marigold, 5" h.. **210**
Marigold, 6" h.. **100-150**
Marigold, 6 1/2" h.. **45-55**
Marigold, 8" h.. **30**
Marigold, 9 1/2" h.. **25-30**
Marigold, 10 1/2" h.. **40**
Marigold, 12" h.. **78**
Marigold, 16 1/2" h., funeral **58**
Marigold, 17" h.. **65**
Marigold, funeral, 17 1/2" h. **248**
Marigold, funeral, 19" h...................................... **175**

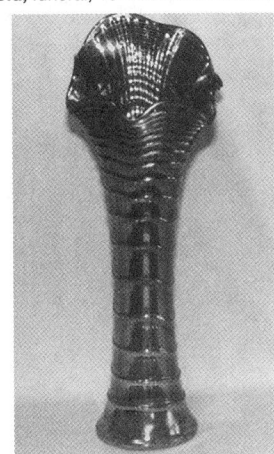

Ripple Vase

Marigold, 20" h. (ILLUS.) **150-200**
Purple, 8" h.. **85**

Purple, 10" h. 143
Purple, 11" h. 250
Purple, 11 1/2" h. 175
Purple, 12" h. 100-125
Purple, 13" h. 208
Smoky, 12" h. 86
Smoky, 15 1/2" h. 250
Teal blue, 11 1/2" h. 350
White, 9" h. 100-125
White, 9 1/2" h. 175-200

Rococo
Bowl, 5" d., ruffled, marigold 35
Bowl, ruffled, low, smoky 60
Vase, marigold 100-120
Vase, purple 160
Vase, smoky 215

Round Up (Dugan)
Bowl, ice cream shape, marigold 85
Bowl, ice cream shape, peach opalescent 275
Bowl, ice cream shape, white 178
Bowl, three-in-one edge, peach opalescent 150
Plate, 9" d., blue, flat 475

Round Up Plate

Plate, 9" d., blue (ILLUS.) 350-400
Plate, 9" d., marigold, ruffled 100-125
Plate, 9" d., peach opalescent, flat 700-750
Plate, 9" d., peach opalescent, ruffled 200-275
Plate, 9" d., purple, flat 350-400
Plate, 9" d., purple, ruffled 325-350

Rustic Vase

Rustic Vase

Blue, 7" to 12" h. 35-55
Blue, 15" h. 105
Blue, 16" h. 100-125
Blue, funeral, 18" h., 5" base 900-1,000
Blue, 19" h. 165
Blue, funeral, 19 1/2" h. 900-1,000
Blue, funeral, 23 1/2" h., w/plunger base,
    blue 1,300
Green 6" h. to 10 1/2" h. 75
Green 16" h. 100-125
Green funeral, 19" h. 1,400-2,000
Marigold, 6" to 10 1/2" h. (ILLUS.) 35
Marigold, 11" h. 35
Marigold, 15" h. 100-125
Marigold, 16" to 21 1/2" h., 5 1/2" base 100-125
Marigold, funeral, 16" h. 385
Marigold, funeral, 19" h., marigold 650-675
Purple, 6" to 10 1/2" h. 50
Purple, 11" h. 44
Purple, funeral, 12" h. 175
Purple, 15" h. 160
Purple, 16" h. 255
Purple, 16 3/4" h. 88
Purple, 18 1/2" h. 750-1,000
Purple, funeral, 19" h. 1,050
Purple, funeral, 20" h. 1,250
Purple, funeral, 5" base 1,350
Red, 6" to 10 1/2" h., crimped top 2,900
Vaseline, funeral 3,500
White, 6" to 12 1/2" h. 175
White, funeral, 15" h. 250
White funeral, 18" h. 850

Sailboats (Fenton)
Bowl, 5" d., aqua 90-100
Bowl, 5" d., blue, ruffled 44
Bowl, 5" d., marigold 40
Bowl, 5" d., marigold, ice cream shape 40
Bowl, 5" d., purple 95
Bowl, 5" d., red, ruffled 525
Bowl, 5" d., vaseline 200-225
Bowl, 6" d., blue 75

Sailboats Bowl

Bowl, 6" d., marigold, Orange Tree exterior
    (ILLUS.) 60
Bowl, 6" d., marigold, ruffled 30-40
Bowl, vaseline, ice cream shape 475
Compote, marigold 85-90
Goblet, water, green 260-275
Goblet, water, marigold 100-125
Goblet, water, purple 225-275
Plate, 6" d., blue 548

Plate, 6" d., marigold 400-425
Wine, blue 85
Wine, marigold.. 30-35

Singing Birds (Northwood)
Berry set: master bowl & 6 sauce dishes;
    green, 7 pcs. 400-450
Bowl, master berry, green........................... 250-275
Bowl, master berry, marigold.............................. 75
Bowl, master berry, purple 90
Butter dish, cov., marigold 295
Butter dish, cov., purple................................... 400
Creamer, green... 150
Creamer, marigold....................................... 65-75
Creamer, purple.. 125-150
Mug, aqua opalescent................................. 1,150
Mug, blue... 180
Mug, blue, stippled.. 675
Mug, blue w/electric iridescence................. 200-250
Mug, green.. 250-275
Mug, green, stippled.................................. 400-450
Mug, ice blue 700-750
Mug, lavender.. 250-300
Mug, marigold.. 60-70
Mug, marigold, stippled.............................. 140-150
Mug, purple 95-125
Mug, purple, w/advertising, "Amazon Hotel"
    175-200
Mug, Renniger blue, stippled 1,500
Mug, white... 600-625
Pitcher, green.. 625
Pitcher, marigold.. 350
Pitcher, purple... 450
Sauce dish, marigold 55
Sauce dish, purple 45
Spooner, green.. 150
Spooner, marigold.. 56
Spooner, purple 100-125
Sugar bowl, cov., marigold........................... 90-110
Table set: cov. sugar bowl, creamer &
    spooner; marigold, 3 pcs.............................. 225
Table set, purple, 4 pcs. 750
Water set: pitcher & 4 tumblers; green,
    5 pcs... 850

Singing Birds Water Set

Water set: pitcher & 4 tumblers; purple,
    5 pcs. (ILLUS. of part) 575-675

Stag & Holly (Fenton)
Bowl, 7" d., spatula-footed, blue 200-275
Bowl, 8" d., footed, ice cream shape, blue 184
Bowl, 8" d., footed, ice cream shape, green...... 200
Bowl, 8" d., footed, ice cream shape, mari-
    gold.. 100-125

Bowl, 8" d., footed, ice cream shape, purple
    250-275
Bowl, 8" to 9" d., footed, ice cream shape,
    lavender.. 185
Bowl, 8" to 9" d., spatula-footed, green 228
Bowl, 8" to 9" d., spatula-footed, marigold 105
Bowl, 8" to 9" d., spatula-footed, purple..... 175-200
Bowl, 10" to 11" d., three-footed, blue 450
Bowl, 10" to 11" d., three-footed, green........ 1,050
Bowl, 10" to 11" d., three-footed, marigold
    150-200

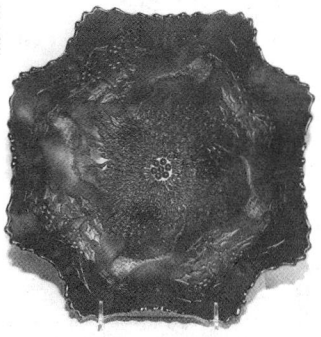

Stag & Holly Bowl

Bowl, 10" to 11" d., three-footed, purple
    (ILLUS.) 425
Bowl, 10" to 11" d., three-footed, vaseline
    300-400
Bowl, 10 3/4" d., footed, ice cream shape,
    marigold... 150
Bowl, 11" d., flat, amber 750
Bowl, 11" d., ruffled, blue 250
Bowl, 12" d., ice cream shape, blue 300-325
Bowl, 12" d., ice cream shape, green 900
Bowl, 12" d., ice cream shape, marigold ... 125-150
Bowl, spatula-footed, red 1,750
Plate, 9" d., spatula-footed, marigold 800-825
Plate, chop, 12" d., three-footed, marigold
    700-800
Plate, chop, 13" d., three-footed, marigold 1,400
Rose bowl, blue, large................................ 1,665
Rose bowl, marigold, large................................ 150
Rose bowl, marigold, giant 375-400

Star of David (Imperial)
Bowl, 7" d., ruffled, purple..................................... 270

Star of David Bowl

Bowl, 8" to 9" d., collared base, green
    (ILLUS.) 100-125

Bowl, 8" to 9" d., collared base, marigold **160**
Bowl, 9" d., flat, ruffled, purple **125-150**

Strawberry (Northwood)
Bowl, 5" d., purple, fluted **40**
Bowl, 6" d., green **65**
Bowl, 7" d., marigold **45**
Bowl, 8" to 9" d., blue, stippled **1,000**
Bowl, 8" to 9" d., blue, stippled, piecrust rim **425**
Bowl, 8" to 9" d., blue, stippled, ruffled,
   Basketweave exterior **500-525**
Bowl, 8" to 9" d., green, ruffled,
   Basketweave exterior **145**
Bowl, 8" to 9" d., green, stippled, piecrust
   rim **700**
Bowl, 8" to 9" d., marigold **55**
Bowl, 8" to 9" d., marigold, ruffled,
   Basketweave exterior **55-60**
Bowl, 8" to 9" d., marigold, stippled,
   piecrust rim **450**
Bowl, 8" to 9" d., purple **145**
Bowl, 8" to 9" d., purple, ruffled,
   Basketweave exterior **100-125**
Bowl, 8" to 9" d., smoky, piecrust rim **900**
Bowl, 8" to 9" d., stippled, ruffled, purple **425**
Bowl, 8 1/2" d., green, three-in-one edge **350**
Bowl, 9" d., marigold, piecrust rim **80**
Bowl, 9" d., marigold, stippled, ribbed exte-
   rior **150**
Bowl, 9" d., ruffled, Basketweave exterior,
   piecrust rim, purple **275**
Bowl, 10" d., green, Basketweave exterior **125-150**
Bowl, 10" d., ice green **1,900**
Bowl, 10" d., marigold, Basketweave exteri-
   or **110**
Bowl, 10" d., purple, Basketweave exterior **173**
Bowl, horehound, stippled, ruffled **800**
Plate, 6" to 7" d., w/handgrip, green **205**
Plate, 9" d., Basketweave exterior, marigold **265**

Northwood Strawberry Plate

Plate, 9" d., Basketweave exterior, purple
   (ILLUS.) **250-375**
Plate, 9" d., marigold **140**
Plate, 9" d., purple **185**
Plate, Basketweave exterior, green **200-275**
Plate, stippled, marigold **800-1,000**

Tornado Vase (Northwood)
Marigold **375**
Marigold, small, ribbed **700**

Tornado Vase

Purple, ribbed (ILLUS.) **475**

Trout & Fly (Millersburg)
Bowl, ice cream shape, green **710**
Bowl, ice cream shape, marigold **450-500**
Bowl, ice cream shape, purple **575-600**
Bowl, ribbon candy rim, lavender **1,050**
Bowl, ribbon candy rim, marigold **350**
Bowl, ribbon candy rim, purple **575**
Bowl, ruffled, green **425**
Bowl, ruffled, marigold **350**
Bowl, square, green **1,140**

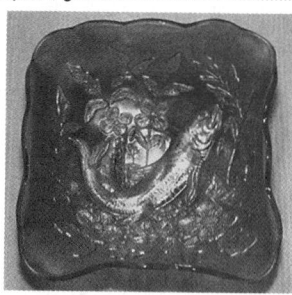

Trout & Fly Square Bowl

Bowl, square, marigold (ILLUS.) **675**
Bowl, square, purple **950-975**
Bowl, 8 1/2" d., marigold **325**

Venetian Giant Rose Bowl (Cambridge)

Venetian Giant Rose Bowl

Green (ILLUS.) **1,100**
Marigold **1,300**

Vintage or Vintage Grape

Bonbon, two-handled, blue (Fenton)............. 45-55
Bonbon, two-handled, purple (Fenton)............... 35
Bowl, 5" d., purple 28
Bowl, 6" d., blue (Fenton)................................ 40
Bowl, 6" d., celeste blue, ruffled...................... 1,100
Bowl, 6" d., green (Fenton).................................. 38
Bowl, 6" d., purple (Fenton) 25-35
Bowl, 6" d., red (small flake) 2,000
Bowl, 6" d., vaseline, ruffled............................... 120
Bowl, 6 1/2" d., ice cream shape, green............. 43
Bowl, 7" d., fluted, blue.. 42
Bowl, 7" d., fluted, green (Fenton) 33
Bowl, 7" d., green 70-75
Bowl, 7" d., purple (Millersburg) 75
Bowl, 7" d., ruffled, vaseline........................ 115-125
Bowl, 7 1/2" d., ice cream shape, blue................ 55
Bowl, 8" d., piecrust rim, blue 110
Bowl, 8" d., ribbon candy rim, aqua opales-
cent... 1,700-1,900
Bowl, 8" d., ribbon candy rim, blue 95-100
Bowl, 8" d., ribbon candy rim, blue, Wide
Panel exterior 55
Bowl, 8" d., ribbon candy rim, green................. 100
Bowl, 8" to 9" d., aqua opalescent....... 1,000-1,200
Bowl, 8" to 9" d., blue, footed (Fenton) 40-45
Bowl, 8" to 9" d., blue, ruffled 70
Bowl, 8" to 9" d., green (Fenton)........................ 49
Bowl, 8" to 9" d., green (Millersburg).................. 39
Bowl, 8" to 9" d., marigold (Fenton).................... 35
Bowl, 8" to 9" d., purple, footed (Fenton)............ 38
Bowl, 8" to 9" d., purple, ruffled, footed 40-45
Bowl, 8" to 9" d., red, ruffled 2,800-3,000
Bowl, 8" to 9" d., teal blue, fluted 75
Bowl, 8" to 9" d., vaseline................................. 200
Bowl, 9" d., green, three-in-one edge.................. 65
Bowl, 9" d., purple 100
Bowl, 9" d., purple, ruffled (Fenton) 90
Bowl, 9 1/2" d., green.. 85
Bowl, 9 1/2" d., marigold, ruffled, dome-
footed 70
Bowl, 10" d., blue.. 55-75
Bowl, 10" d., Hobnail exterior, green (Mill-
ersburg)... 1,175
Bowl, 10" d., ice cream shape, blue 200
Bowl, 10" d., ice cream shape, red (Fenton)
.... 2,500-3,500
Bowl, 10" d., ice cream shape, vaseline
(Fenton) 225
Bowl, 10" d., ruffled, green................................. 65
Bowl, 10" d., ruffled, purple................................ 50
Bowl, 10" d., ruffled, vaseline w/marigold
overlay... 110
Bowl, 11" d., ice cream shape, marigold 200
Bowl, dome-footed, marigold.............................. 48
Bowl, three-in-one edge, red 4,500
Compote, 7" d., blue (Fenton).......................... 90
Compote, 7" d., green, fluted (Fenton) 75
Compote, 7" d., marigold (Fenton) 67
Compote, 7" d., purple (Fenton) 75
Epergne, blue (Fenton)..................................... 165
Epergne, green (Fenton) 150
Epergne, green, large 225-250
Epergne, marigold (Fenton)......................... 250-300
Epergne, purple, small....................................... 95
Fernery, footed, blue (Fenton) 75-100
Fernery, footed, green (Fenton) 60-70
Fernery, footed, marigold (Fenton)................ 35-45
Fernery, footed, purple (Fenton) 57

Ice cream set: master ice cream bowl &
four 6" d. bowls; cobalt blue, 5 pcs. 575
Nut dish, footed, blue, 6" d. (Fenton)............. 80-90
Nut dish, footed, green, 6" d. (Fenton) 100
Nut dish, footed, red 450-500

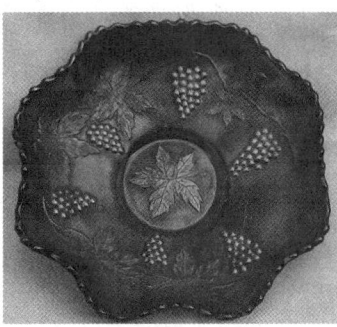

Vintage Plate

Plate, 7" d., blue, Millersburg (ILLUS.)
.... 1,000-1,500
Plate, 7" d., green (Fenton)......................... 225-250
Plate, 7" d., marigold (Fenton)........................... 150
Plate, 7" d., purple (Fenton) 250-350
Plate, 8" d., blue.. 128
Plate, 8" d., green 150-175
Plate, 9" d., flat, purple................................. 4,500
Plate, lavender 900
Powder jar, cov., marigold 85
Powder jar, cov., marigold (Fenton).............. 80-85
Powder jar, cov., purple (Fenton) 150-175
Sandwich tray, handled, aqua opalescent 90
Sandwich tray, handled, clambroth 30-35
Sandwich tray, handled, marigold 35
Sauce dish, blue.. 30
Sauce dish, blue, ice cream shape 32
Sauce dish, green 27
Sauce dish, marigold (Fenton)........................... 20
Wine, marigold (Fenton) 28
Wine, purple (Fenton) 35-45

Wishbone (Northwood)

Bowl, 7" d., three-footed, ruffled rim, mari-
gold.. 65-75
Bowl, 7 1/2" d., three-footed, ruffled rim,
purple.. 120-130
Bowl, 8" to 9" d., footed, blue 450
Bowl, 8" to 9" d., footed, green 375
Bowl, 8" to 9" d., footed, ice blue 1,700
Bowl, 8" to 9" d., footed, ice green 1,600-1,675
Bowl, 8" to 9" d., footed, marigold 125-150
Bowl, 8" to 9" d., footed, pastel marigold........... 125
Bowl, 8" to 9" d., footed, purple 122
Bowl, 8" to 9" d., footed, white.................... 450-500
Bowl, 10" d., footed, blue 600
Bowl, 10" d., footed, ruffled, purple 165
Bowl, 10" d., footed, ruffled, stippled, purple 850
Bowl, 10" d., piecrust rim, blue w/electric
iridescence 2,000
Bowl, 10" d., piecrust rim, green 275-300
Bowl, 10" d., piecrust rim, green,
Basketweave exterior 900-975
Bowl, 10" d., piecrust rim, lavender w/mari-
gold overlay... 500
Bowl, 10" d., piecrust rim, marigold 150-200
Bowl, 10" d., piecrust rim, marigold,
Basketweave exterior 183

Bowl, 10" d., piecrust rim, pastel marigold 425
Bowl, 10" d., ruffled, green........................... 250-350
Bowl, 10" d., ruffled, marigold...................... 145-150
Bowl, footed, ruffled, horehound 650
Bowl, footed, ruffled, ice blue 1,800-1,900
Bowl, footed, ruffled, lime green.................... 1,200
Bowl, footed, ruffled, marigold........................... 200
Bowl, footed, ruffled, white.............................. 800
Bowl, footed, tri-cornered, purple................... 1,400
Bowl, large, Basketweave exterior, emerald
green 325
Bowl, Rings & Roses exterior, purple................. 210
Bowl, 10" d., piecrust rim, footed, white..... 475-500
Epergne, green 975-1,200
Epergne, marigold 500-525
Epergne, purple 750
Epergne, white 1,725-1,850
Pitcher, water, green............................... 1,800
Pitcher, water, marigold................................. 1,500
Pitcher, water, purple....................................... 900
Plate, 8 1/2" d., footed, marigold 475-500

Wishbone Plate

Plate, 8 1/2" d., footed, purple (ILLUS.) 325
Plate, 8 1/2" w., footed, tricornered, green 1,200
Plate, 8 1/2" w., footed, tricornered, purple 400
Plate, chop, 11" d., green 3,000
Plate, chop, 11" d., marigold 1,200
Plate, chop, 11" d., purple 1,500-2,000
Tumbler, marigold 95-100
Tumbler, purple... 135-145

Chocolate

Tall Cat on Hamper Animal Dish

This glass is often called Caramel Slag. It was made by the Indiana Tumbler and Goblet Company of Greentown, Indiana, and other glasshouses, beginning at the turn of the 20th century. Various patterns were produced, highly popular among them being Cactus and Leaf Bracket.

Animal covered dish, Cat on Hamper, low-
style $900
Animal covered dish, Cat on Hamper, tall-
style (ILLUS.) 650

Chocolate Hen Covered Dish

Animal covered dish, Hen (ILLUS.)................. 750
Animal covered dish, Rabbit............................ 675
Bowl, master berry, Leaf Bracket patt................ 90
Bowl, master berry, Wild Rose with Bow-
knot patt.. 160
Butter dish, cov., Cactus patt. 375

Chrysanthemum Leaf Chocolate Butter

Butter dish, cov., Chrysanthemum Leaf
patt. (ILLUS.)... 1,200
Celery holder, Fleur-de-lis patt., two han-
dles 250

Melrose Chocolate Compote

Compote, open, 7 1/2" d., Melrose patt.
(ILLUS.) 325
Cracker jar, cov., Cactus patt., Greentown....... 250
Creamer, cov., Cactus patt., Greentown 95

Creamer, Dewey patt., no cover............................ **75**
Creamer, Leaf Bracket patt................................. **125**
Creamer, Wild Rose with Bowknot patt. **145**

Cactus Covered Creamer

Creamer w/Dewey cover, Cactus patt.
   (ILLUS.).. **185**
Cruet w/original stopper, Cactus patt.,
   Greentown... **350**

Chocolate Chrysanthemum Leaf Cruet

Cruet w/original stopper, Chrysanthemum
   Leaf patt. (ILLUS.).. **1,250**
Cruet w/original stopper, Dewey patt. **1,100**
Cruet w/original stopper, Wild Rose with
   Bowknot patt. **750**

Wild Rose with Festoon Lamp

Lamp, kerosene table model, Wild Rose
   with Festoon patt. (ILLUS.)............................. **850**

Outdoor Drinking Scene Mug

Mug w/metal cap, Outdoor Drinking Scene
   patt. (ILLUS.)... **175**
Pitcher, water, Cactus patt. **475**
Sauce dish, Leaf Bracket patt............................. **45**
Sauce dish, Wild Rose with Bowknot patt. **80**
Spooner, Wild Rose with Bowknot patt. **130**
Sugar bowl, cov., Dewey patt., small **110**
Sugar bowl, cov., Leaf Bracket patt.................. **175**
Toothpick holder, Cactus patt., Greentown **63**

Chocolate Uneeda Biscuit Tumbler

Tumbler, Uneeda Biscuit advertising, tall
   (ILLUS.) **125**

Coralene

*Coralene is a method of decorating glass, usually
satin glass, with the use of beaded-type decoration cus-
tomarily applied to the glass with the use of enamels,
which were melted. Coralene decoration has been faked
with the use of glue.*

Pitcher, 7 1/2" h.,. bulbous body w/a cylindrical neck & small pinched spout, cased
   orange over white w/a swirled ground
   decorated w/yellow "seaweed" coralene
   beading, applied clear reeded handle,
   late 19th c... **$258**

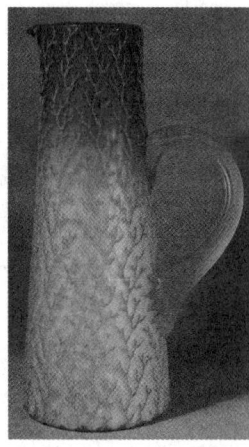

Fine Coralene Tankard Pitcher

Pitcher, 12" h., tankard-type, tall slender tapering cylindrical form in shaded pink mother-of-pearl satin Diamond Quilted patt., decorated w/yellow "seaweed" coralene beading (ILLUS.) **1,200-1,500**

Vase, 4 1/2" h., bulbous form in blue satin mother-of-pearl decorated w/opal "snowflake" coralene beading.................................. **193**

Cranberry

Gold was added to glass batches to give this glass its color on reheating. It has been made by numerous glasshouses for years and is currently being reproduced. Both blown and molded articles were produced. A less expensive type of cranberry was made with the substitution of copper for gold.

Bell, cranberry bell w/applied clear handle, England, late 19th c., 11" h. **$94**

Bell, cranberry body w/applied crystal handle & original cranberry clapper, 13 1/4" h.. **248**

Celery vase, cylindrical tapered sides, Inverted Thumbprint patt., enameled w/forget-me-nots, 7" h. **110**

Cracker jar, cov., cylindrical w/rounded base & shoulder, Inverted Thumbprint patt. w/large enameled blue & white blossoms on green leafy stems, silver plate rim, domed cover & bail handle, 11" h. **280**

Cruet w/original stopper, bulbous Inverted Thumbprint patt. body, applied clear reeded handle & clear facet-cut stopper, 8 1/2" h... **149**

Cruet w/stopper, optic ribbed body w/an applied clear handle & stopper, 9" h. **135**

Cruet w/stopper, squatty bulbous body tapering to a slender neck w/arched spout, Inverted Thumbprint patt., decorated overall w/enameled brown floral pods joined by slender stems, applied clear reeded handle, clear bubble stopper, 6 1/2" h.. **341**

Decanter w/original stopper, ovoid body tapering to a tall slender neck w/a tricorner rim, the front panel decorated w/two ducks partially hidden among rushes, applied angled clear handle, clear facet-cut stopper, 12 1/4" h... **210**

Decanter w/stopper, bulbous ovoid optic ribbed body tapering to a slender neck w/tricorner rim, enameled w/sprigs of lily-of-the-valley, clear bubble stopper & applied handle, 9 3/4" h...................................... **193**

Finger bowl, ruffled rim w/clear applied rigaree around the base, Inverted Thumbprint patt., decorated w/multicolored enameled flowers, England, late 19th c., 4 1/2" d. **66**

Loving cup, handled, applied threading & gilt decoration, applied clear foot, 11 1/4" h. **88**

Pickle castor, cylindrical Inverted Thumbprint insert enameled w/delicate flowers, in an ornate footed silver plate frame w/domed cover, upright handle & tongs........ **495**

Pitcher, water, 7" h., bulbous body in Inverted Thumbprint patt., applied clear reeded handle **88**

Pitcher, 7 3/4" h., ribbed bulbous body w/squared top, applied clear rope handle **160**

Pitcher, 8" h., tankard-form, applied clear handle, England **220**

Pitcher, 8 1/2" h., Inverted Thumbprint patt., large spherical body w/a cylindrical neck & pinched spout, applied clear reeded handle, the sides elaborately enameled overall w/delicate blue flowers & a gold rim... **853**

Salt & pepper shakers, ovoid body w/optic design & enameled w/dainty white daisies, in a fitted silver plate footed stand w/upright central handle w/loop finial, late 19th c., 6" h., the set................................. **220**

Tumbler, squared ovoid form w/Inverted Thumbprint design & pinched-in sides, overall enameled dainty flowers, 4" h. **286**

Vases, 10 1/2" h., optic ribbed body tapering to a small neck decorated w/enameled white & pink blossoms, applied enameled buds, attributed to Moser, pr........ **330**

Crown Milano

This glass, produced by Mt. Washington Glass Company late in the 19th century, is opal glass decorated by painting and enameling. It appears identical to a ware termed Albertine, also made by Mt. Washington.

Printed Crown Milano Mark

Atomizer, swirled body, trumpet vine decoration, 6 1/2" h. **$595**

Bowl, 9 1/2" w., 3 1/4" h., tricorner-form w/rolled-under sides, yellowish green ground decorated w/pansies, roses & forget-me-nots, purple "CM" & crown mark (some interior stain) **1,200**

Box, cov., w/tiny applied feet, melon-ribbed, decorated overall w/enameled pansies & gold accents, 3 1/2" d., 2 1/2" h. **350**

Cracker jar, cov., barrel-shaped, creamy Burmese-colored decorated w/a cluster of large exotic blossoms on a branch, all trimmed in gilt, silver plate cover, rim & swing bail handle, silver impressed "MW," "CM" crown mark on base, 7 1/4" h. **1,200**

Fine Crown Milano Cracker Jar

Cracker jar, cov., squatty bulbous body decorated w/gold & orange roses & leaves on a white ground, ornate silver plate rim w/ruffled edge, shaped bail handle & cover w/figural turtle finial (ILLUS.) .. **1,200**
Creamer, square, applied ribbed handle, gold enameled flowers, berries & leaves **275**
Creamer & cov. sugar bowl, creamy satin ground decorated w/h.p. lavender violets framed by pink blush edging & gold trim, paper label, creamer 3 12" h., sugar bowl, 4 1/4" h., pr. **1,250**

Crown Milano Decorated Sugar Bowl

Creamer & open sugar bowl, squatty bulbous body tapering to a high arched spout on the creamer & a flared ruffled rim on the sugar, applied handle on creamer, each decorated w/purple & blue pansies & stems on a yellow shaded to white ground, gilt trim on rims, signed, sugar 4" d., creamer 3 1/2" h., pr. (ILLUS. of sugar) **900**
Creamer & open sugar bowl, white satin ground decorated w/blush pink around the edge, lavender violets & gold trim, w/paper label, sugar bowl 4 1/4" d., creamer 3 1/2" h., pr. **1,250**
Dish, triangular w/two rolled-in edges, decorated w/multicolored flowers & heavy gold trim, signed **475**

Fine Crown Milano Covered Jar

Jar, cov., bulbous ovoid body tapering to a small domed cover w/a ribbed & pointed finial, creamy white ground ornately decorated w/ivy leaves & vine in heavy green & brown enamel outlined in gold w/light brown scrolls outlined in gold around the base & cover, unmarked, 10 1/2" h. (ILLUS.) **2,750**
Jardiniere, bulbous body decorated w/ten pansies w/ten medallions in violet, yellow & tan, heavy gold trim around the neck, signed on the bottom, 9 1/4" d., 7" h. **1,250**
Jardiniere, squatty bulbous body w/a wide flat bottom, short & wide cylindrical neck, gold-outlined large autumn leaf decoration, purple "CM" crown & "598" mark, 8 1/4" d., 6" h. **1,275**
Pickle castor, cov., a wide swelled cylindrical body w/scattered small embossed four-arm crosses, shaded peach to pale yellow ground decorated w/colorful flowers, fitted in an ornate footed silver plate frame w/silver plate rim, domed cover & high arched handle & tongs, silver marked by the Knickerbocker Silver Co. **1,100**
Rose bowl, decorated overall w/h.p. daisies & roses on a soft ivory ground, 3 1/2 x 4 1/2" **350**
Rose bowl, spherical, decorated w/ten pansies h.p. in pastel shades of purple, blue, brown & white & highlighted w/delicate gold foliage, three gold blossoms & randomly placed gold embellishments, 5 1/8" d. **675**
Rose bowl, spherical, eight-crimp rim, yellow beige satin ground decorated w/blue & lavender pansies, purple crown mark, 5" h. **750**
Salt dip, master size, enameled w/pink & mauve floral decoration **150**
Spooner, embossed diamond quilted body decorated w/chrysanthemums & gold trim **550**
Sweetmeat jar, cov., creamy satin ground decorated w/enameled gold designs, silver plate rim, cover & bail handle, cover marked "M.W." & numbered **450**
Sweetmeat jar, cov., melon-ribbed body, pink shaded to opaque white body deco-

rated w/ornate gold scrolling on upper portion & multicolored flowers on the lower sections, ornate silver plate cover, rim & bail handle, marked, 5 1/4" d., 4 " h. **950**

Fine Crown Milano Syrup Pitcher

Syrup pitcher w/original top, melon-ribbed body, decorated w/enameled gold flowers & leaves & hundreds of blue, white, black, coral & turquoise enamel dottings on a soft butter cream ground, embossed silver plate rim, hinged domed cover & arched twisted handle (ILLUS.).... **1,500**

Syrup pitcher w/original top, white ground shaded to deep orange, decorated w/a blue daisy, green leaves & foliage & a large gold butterfly above the flower, dated "1884," 7 1/2" h. **650**

Vase, 5" h., footed bulbous ovoid body tapering to a tiny short neck w/a flared four-ruffle rim, creamy ground decorated w/gold ferns & shadow leaves trimmed w/gold **440**

Vase, 5 3/4" h., wide squatty bulbous body below a squatty bulbous short neck, heavy gilt enameled overall leaf design over a gold & pink scrolling & double eagle medallion ground, unsigned **750**

Vase, 6 1/4" h., spherical body w/a tiny cylindrical neck, decorated overall w/blue-centered pink & white blossoms on a pastel beige & yellow foliate background, unsigned **550**

Vase, 7" h., baluster-form body w/a narrow neck & widely flaring flattened rim, the body lightly molded w/swirled ribs & decorated w/large white blossoms & buds outlined in gold against a ground of blue scrolls, label on base reads "M & W G Co. Crown Milano" **1,100**

Scenic Crown Milano Vase

Vase, 7" h., 6 3/4" d., squatty bulbous swirl-molded body tapering to a short neck flaring into four fluted lobes, decorated w/dahlia flowers in yellow & burgundy, the leaves & stems w/heavy gold trim, tan shadow leaves in the background, gold trim on foot & rim, unmarked (ILLUS.)....... **1,750**

Vase, 8" h., tall cylindrical body w/flat rim, decorated in pastel coloring w/a distant desert city, palm trees & birches in foreground, dotted & gold rim border, unsigned, some dots missing (ILLUS.) **900**

Vase, 8" h., wide ovoid body tapering sharply to a small flat mouth, decorated w/large branches of gold & silver enamel apple blossoms & leaves w/applied bead 'jewels' in the blossom centers, against a pastel yellow & pink floral background, unsigned (gilt worn at rim) **950**

Vase, 10" h., footed large spherical body centered by a ring below the slightly flaring cylindrical neck, shadow background blending blue, green, turquoise, opal & lavender creating an ocean wave effect, decorated w/raised gold, multi-jeweled starfish, finely painted w/two swimming fish & nautilus w/heavy gold trim, original paper label from the C.E. Selzer Store...... **7,975**

Vase, 14" h., tall slender ovoid body w/a very slender & slightly flaring tall neck, decorated w/lilacs highlighted w/heavy matte gold scrolls & a cross design on the neck.. **2,800**

Cruets

Amber, bulbous body w/applied runny white overlay covering the sides, applied reeded amber handle, hollow amber stopper, 7 3/4" h... **$165**

Amber, bulbous optic ribbed body, applied blue handle & blue stopper, 7 3/4" h............. **110**

Blue, bulbous optic ribbed body w/applied clear reeded handle & clear facet-cut stopper, 7 1/4" h. **110**

Floral-decorated Crown Milano Vase

Decorated Lime Green Cruet

Lime green, footed tapering cylindrical body w/optic ribbing, shouldered cylindrical neck w/pinched spout, applied green handle, tall green teardrop stopper, enameled w/large pink & white blossoms & blue leafy sprigs, 3 1/2" d., 9 3/4" h. (ILLUS.).. **145**

Sapphire Blue Decorated Cruet

Sapphire blue, barrel-shaped w/three raised body bands around optic ribbed form tapering to a short cylindrical neck w/a wide arched spout, applied blue handle, bulbous beehive stopper, the body decorated w/bands of white blossoms & leaf swags, 2 3/4" d., 6" h. (ILLUS.) **125**

Satin glass, shaded blue mother-of-pearl Diamond Quilted patt., squatty bulbous body tapering to a slender neck w/tricorner rim, applied frosted clear reeded handle & frosted clear ovoid stopper, finely enameled w/a bird, 7 1/4" h............................ **330**

Satin glass, shaded blue mother-of-pearl Herringbone patt., squatty bulbous body tapering to a slender neck w/wide tricorner rim, applied frosted clear handle, frosted clear optic ribbed teardrop stopper, 6" h. **550**

Satin glass, shaded butterscotch mother-of-pearl Diamond Quilted patt., ovoid body tapering to a flat base, slender neck w/arched spout, clear frosted applied

thorn handle, clear frosted facet-cut stopper, 6 1/2" h... **605**

Satin glass, shaded pink mother-of-pearl Diamond Quilted patt., bulbous body w/applied frosted clear reeded handle & frosted clear stopper, 7 1/2" h. **770**

Cut

Cut glass most eagerly sought by collectors is American glass produced during the so-called "Brilliant Period" from 1880 to about 1915. Pieces listed below are by type of article in alphabetical order.

Hawkes, Hoare, Libbey and Straus Marks

This mold-blown, two-layer glassware is usually lined in white with a colored exterior with a molded pattern. Pieces have a satiny finish, giving them a 'velvety' appearance. The Mt. Washington Glass Company was one of several firms which produced this glass.

Baskets

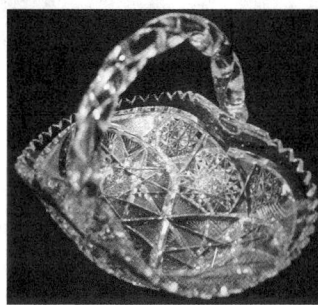

Meriden Cut Glass Basket

Meriden-signed, wide shallow form w/two sides turned-up, hobstars, large stars & fans, heavy applied rope twist handle (ILLUS.) **$895**

Bowls

Large Centerpiece Fruit Bowl

Centerpiece fruit bowl, Meriden-signed, oblong form cut w/panels of cane design alternating w/large & small hobstars & fans, scalloped & notched rim, 10 1/2" l. (ILLUS.) **1,250**

Bowl with Clusters of Hobstars

Clusters of hobstars, six-sided form w/each side cut w/clusters of small hobstars, large hobstar in the bottom, 9 1/4" d. (ILLUS.)... **475**

Libbey-signed Fruit Bowl

Fruit bowl, Libbey-signed, hobstars alternating w/stars & panels of crosshatched cutting w/a large square of crosshatch cutting in the bottom, 10" d., 4" h. (ILLUS.)... **570**

Hoare Marquis Pattern Bowl

Hoare-signed, Marquis patt., Napoleon's hat form, band of hobstars above cane band & triangles w/cane cutting (ILLUS.).. **1,550**

Hobstar & Tusk Cut bowl

Hobstars, large hobstars around the scalloped rim above alternating hobstar clusters & plain tusk designs, hobstar in bottom, 9 1/4" d., 4" h. (ILLUS.) **385**

Wheeler Pattern Bowl

Orange bowl, Mt. Washington's Wheeler patt., large oval boat-shaped from, cut w/bands of strawberry diamond & crosshatching w/fans around the rim, 8" l., 4 1/2" h. (ILLUS.).. **385**

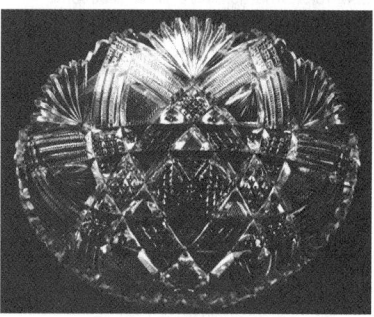

Bowl with Zipper-cut Bands

Zipper-cut bands, shallow form w/long curved bands w/rows of zipper cutting alternating w/small panels of block cutting, fans around the rim, 9" d. (ILLUS.)................ **395**

Boxes

Zipper-cut Dresser Box

Dresser box, spherical w/overall zipper-cut bands, sterling silver domed cover, 5" d. (ILLUS.) **125**

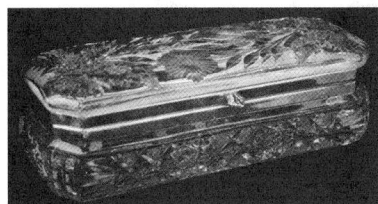

Floral-etched Glove Box

Glove box w/hinged cover, long narrow rectangular form w/notched corners, the top w/etched floral designs, the base cut w/hobstars, crosshatching & fans (ILLUS.).. **1,350**

Butter Dishes & Tubs

Propeller Pattern Butter Dish

Covered dish, Propeller patt., cut w/hobstars framed by cane cutting & divided by almond-shaped vesicas, facet-cut finial (ILLUS.).. **565**

Candlesticks & Candleholders

Russian & Swirl Pattern Candlesticks

Hawkes-signed, baluster-form swirl design stem w/an ovoid Russian cut socket & disk foot, 10" h., pr. (ILLUS.) **2,150**

Cheese Dishes

North Star Pattern Cheese Dish

Clark-signed, North Star patt., diamond-shaped hobstar panels alternating w/large blazing stars & small cane panels, facet-cut finial, 8 1/2" d., 7" h. (ILLUS.) **695**

Creamers & Sugar Bowls

Harvard Pattern Creamer & Sugar

Libbey-signed, Harvard patt., square form cut w/panels of strawberry diamond & crosshatching w/fans around the rim, angled handle on creamer, pr. (ILLUS.) **350**

Dishes, Miscellaneous

Wheat Pattern Bonbon Dish

Bonbon, Wheat patt. by J. Hoare, round swirled design w/Russian cut panels alternating w/wheat head panels, 6" d. (ILLUS.) **325**

Diamond Dish from a Bridge Set

Bridge dish, Newark Cut Glass Co., diamond-shaped, cut w/hobstars in pointed reserves centered by a cane-cut center, one of a set of four (ILLUS.) **115**

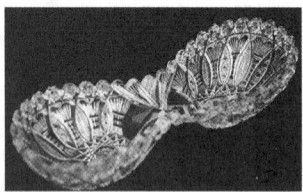

Unusual Peru Pattern Candy Dish

Candy dish, Peru patt. by Pairpoint, barbell-shaped w/a narrow center & deep oblong ends cut w/alternating vesicas & fan panels, small hobstars around the rim, 8 3/4" l. (ILLUS.) **650**

Hawkes-signed Serving Dish

Serving dish, Hawkes-signed, blown-out blank w/eight-petal pinwheel form, alternating petals of hobstars & fans & zipper cutting, 10" d. (ILLUS.) **1,285**

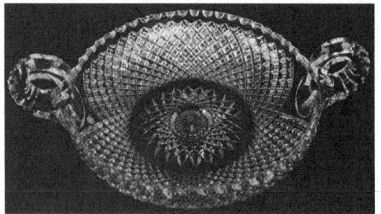

Strawberry Diamond Serving Dish

Serving dish, round w/overall strawberry diamond cutting, hobstar in the center, two applied notched handles, 8 1/4" d. plus handles (ILLUS.) **385**

Flower Centers

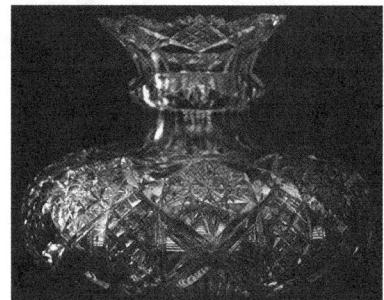

Empress Pattern Flower Center

Empress patt. by Libbey, the body cut w/hobstars above cross-cutting alternating w/strawberry diamond panels, facet-cut ringed neck w/diamond-cut rim, 10" d. (ILLUS.) **1,100**

Flower Center with Hobstars & Fans

Hobstars & fans, squatty bulbous body cut w/large hobstars alternating w/large fans below the ring-cut shoulder & short neck w/flared & scalloped rim (ILLUS.) **495**

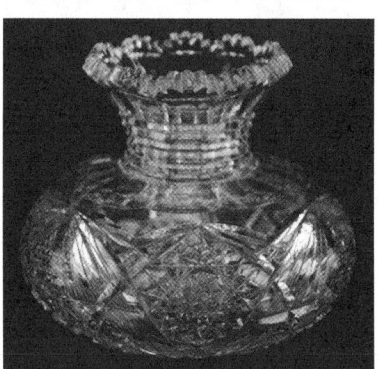

Flower Center with Varied Motifs

Hobstars, fans, cane & strawberry diamonds, squatty bulbous base cut w/large hobstars & fans combined w/other motifs, short flaring ring-cut neck w/notched & scalloped rim, 7 1/2" d., 6 1/4" h. (ILLUS.) **465**

Ice Tubs & Buckets

Venetian Pattern Ice Tub

Hawkes-signed, Venetian patt., bulbous form cut w/large hobstars in diamonds alternating w/fans, large blossom-form cutting in the bottom, silver plate rim & bail handle (ILLUS.) **475**

Ice Tub with Hobstar Design

Hobstars, round w/tab handles, large hobstars alternating w/angular cut panels, tab handles w/blazing stars (ILLUS.) **350**

Jars

Greek Key Pattern Tobacco Jar

Tobacco, Greek Key patt. by Meriden, vertical bands of hobstars alternating w/cane-cut bands below the Greek Key cut shoulder, 9 1/2" h. (ILLUS.) **4,650**

Two Marlboro Pattern Humidors

Tobacco, Marlboro patt. by Dorflinger, overall cutting w/small hobstars, fans & diamonds w/crosshatching (ILLUS. left) **1,250**

Tobacco, Marlboro patt. by Dorflinger, overall cutting w/small hobstars, fans & diamonds w/crosshatching (ILLUS. right) **1,450**

Knife Rests

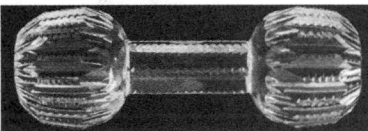

Notched Prism-cut Knife Rest

Barbell-shaped, notched prism-cut knob ends, zipper cut crossbar, 5" l. (ILLUS.) **55**

Knife Rest with Pointed Knob Ends

Barbell-shaped, pointed knob ends cut w/strawberry diamond & pointed bands, zipper-cut crossbar, 5" l. (ILLUS.) **100**

Miscellaneous Items

Cut Glass Cup & Saucer

Cup & saucer, cut w/hobstars & fans, applied handle on cup, saucer 4 3/4" d., cup 2 3/4" d., 2 1/4" h. (ILLUS.)............................ **235**

Cut & Engraved Lady's Cuspidor

Cuspidor, lady's, Sinclaire-signed, wide ovoid form w/widely rolled finely cut rim, delicate floral engraving around the body, 8" d., 6 1/2" h. (ILLUS.)......................... **395**

Rare Hawkes Epergne

Epergne, St. Regis patt. by Hawkes, four-lily, the wide dished conical base w/fan-cut upturned edges, metal top fitting supports a tall central trumpet surrounded by three curved smaller lilies all cut w/star-bursts & fans, 18 1/2" h. (ILLUS.) **5,850**

Russian Cut Juice Set

Juice set, pitcher & four tumblers, bulbous pitcher w/overall Russian cut design & panel-cut neck, applied notched handle,

four matching tapering cylindrical tumblers, the set (ILLUS.) **850**

Brunswick Rose Bowl by Hawkes

Rose bowl, Brunswick patt. by Hawkes, pedestal base below large spherical bowl cut w/long ribbon and zipper-cut bands w/bands of small hobstars around the rim & bottom, 6" h. (ILLUS.) **1,095**

Navarre Pattern Rose Bowl

Rose bowl, Navarre patt. by Hawkes, spherical, cut w/hobstars & punties alternating w/wide zipper-cut bands & fans, 6" d. (ILLUS.) **475**

Nappies

Fine Rex Variation Pattern Nappy

Rex Variation patt., round shallow form cut w/a band of small hobstars centered by a large blossom-form design, applied notched rim handle, 6 1/2" d. (ILLUS.) **425**

Plates

Mt. Washington Cut Plate

6 1/2" d., Mt. Washington Glass Co., a large hobstar in center framed by panel cutting & hobstars & fans, smooth rim (ILLUS.) **110**

Arcadia Plate by Sterling

7" d., Arcadia patt. by Sterling, large hobstars alternating w/crosshatched panels around the rim, inner band of small hobstars enclosing another band of hobstars & a large central hobstar (ILLUS.) **250**

Hawkes' Centauri Pattern Plate

7" d., Hawkes' Centauri patt., central large star within a star-form w/small hobstars framed by fan-cut small panels & dia-

mond-form reserves cut w/alternating sizes of hobstars, notched & scalloped rim (ILLUS.) **210**

Hawkes-signed Plate

7" d., Hawkes-signed, elaborate design of hobstars in diamond panels alternating w/crosshatched panels & centered by a large star (ILLUS.) **165**

Plate with Hobstars & Prism Cutting

7" d., hobstars alternating w/wide panels of prism cutting, crossed diamond panels centering a large hobstar in the middle (ILLUS.) **210**

Plate with Large Hobstars

7" d., hobstars within teardrop panels separated by six rayed cut arms (ILLUS.) **225**

7" **d.,** Libbey's Kenmore patt., a central eight-point star motif composed of points w/hobstars & vesicas around a central hobstar, starburst-cut scallops around the rim **295**

Neola Pattern Plate by Libbey

7" **d.,** Neola patt. by Libbey, hobstars alternating w/blazing crosses w/a large star in the center (ILLUS.).. **415**

Stars & Pillars Plate by Sinclaire

7" **d.,** Sinclaire's Stars & Pillars patt., cut around the border w/large hobstars in diamonds, inner band of pillar-cutting surrounding a central hobstar (ILLUS.) **450**

Salt Dips

Canoe-shaped Salt Dip

Canoe-shaped, cut w/small hobstars & fans, 1 1/2" l. (ILLUS.) **45**
Round, diamonds w/crosshatching alternating w/pointed panels, 1 1/4" d. (ILLUS. right) **35**

Two Round Salt Dips

Round, Pine Tree patt., slash-cut paneled sides, 1" d. (ILLUS. left) **20**

Salt Dip with Hobstars & Panels

Round, small hobstars alternating w/pointed cut panels, hobstar in bottom, 1 1/2" d. (ILLUS.)... **35**

Trays

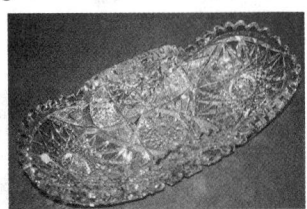

Sultana Asparagus Tray

Asparagus, Libbey's Sultana patt., oblong, large hobstars at each end w/a cluster of hobstars & diamonds centering the middle hobstar, 12" l. (ILLUS.) **445**

Hunt's Aldine Pattern Tray

Hunt's Aldine patt., oblong, cut w/large round clusters of small hobstars alternating w/larger hobstars, 14" l. (ILLUS.)............. **475**

Vases

Large Urn-form Vase

Hobstars, large ovoid urn-form body cut w/overall hobstars, cane-cut panels & crosshatched blocks, paneled & prism-cut neck flanked by applied notched angled handles (ILLUS.) **1,550**

Vase in Jewel's Aberdeen Pattern

Jewel's Aberdeen patt., campana-form, the wide flaring urn-form bowl w/an upright cut rim band above panel-cut sides above a lower hobstar-cut border, raised on a plain applied pedestal & square foot, 12" h. (ILLUS.) **3,950**

Vase, 6 1/4" h., ovoid w/ruffled fold-over top, pink Swirl patt. **121**

Vase, 9" h., ruffled rim, pale yellow Diamond Quilted patt. **138**

Daum Nancy

This fine glass, much of it cameo, was made by Auguste and Antonin Daum, who founded a factory in 1875 in Nancy, France. Most of their cameo and enameled glass was made from the 1890s into the early 20th century.

Daum Nancy Marks

Etched & Enameled Daum Box

Box, cov., squatty bulbous tapering form w/a wide shoulder centered by a fitted domed cover, rose etched & enameled in pastel tones to depict floral sprays w/gilt accents, the cover w/a butterfly & dragonfly, gilt signature, 2 1/8" h. (ILLUS.) **$3,680**

Cameo bowl-vase, squatty bulbous oblong form tapering to a wide flat rim, mottled frosted white ground overlaid w/green & maroon & cut w/rose blossoms on leafy stems, ca. 1910, 4 1/4" h. **6,900**

Cameo bowl-vase, wide flat rim on deep rounded sides set on a small cushion foot, grey opalescent body, the lower section mottled w/lime green & cut w/large iris blossoms & leaves, the blossoms in lavender & finely wheel-carved, signed in cameo "DAUM - NANCY" w/cross of Lorraine, ca. 1900, 6 1/4" h. **3,737**

Cameo lamp, table model, the 16" d. cameo shade in a disk form w/a wide angled border centered by an inset dome, in swirled & mottled amber & yellow overlaid w/mottled brown & black & cut w/large horse chestnut leaves, raised on a Louis Majorelle gilt-bronze base w/pierced scrolling arms & a ribbed vine-like standard w/inwardly scrolling loops at the base, signed in cameo, ca. 1900, overall 26" h. **25,300**

Cameo vase, 6 3/8" h., cushion foot & shoulder pedestal base supporting a bulbous ovoid body tapering to a short wide flared neck, frosted white ground overlaid w/mottled rust, brown & green & cut w/leafy stems, signed in intaglio, ca. 1910 .... **4,600**

Rare Martelé Cameo Daum Vase

Cameo vase, 9 1/4" h., four-sided baluster-form w/flared neck & applied foot, martelé (hammered) clear ground overlaid in white & carved from the base upward w/slender thorny blossom branches supporting a spiderweb, signed in intaglio, ca. 1900 (ILLUS.) **11,500**

Cameo vase, 11 1/4" h., tall swelled cylindrical form w/a narrow shoulder & short flaring neck, shaded dark blue to white to mottled orange to dark purple ground, overlaid & blown-out w/thick dark purple plant stems w/blossomheads around the shoulder, signed in gilt intaglio **13,800**

Cameo vase, 18 1/2" h., a cushion foot below a slender pedestal continuing to a bulbous lower body tapering to a very tall, slender & slightly flaring neck, three applied loop handles around the lower body, shaded from mottled white to yellow & overlaid w/mottled green to light rose & cut w/a slender blossom stem rising from green foliage at the base, signed in intaglio, ca. 1904 .... **14,950**

Large Cameo Vase with Grapes

Cameo vase, 24 1/2" h., tall slender baluster-form w/a short flared neck, grey internally shaded w/lemon yellow & mottled w/orange, overlaid in green & black & cut w/grape clusters on vines, signed in cameo, ca. 1900 .... **9,475**

Centerpiece, a stepped rounded dark brown foot supporting a deep very long boat-form bowl pulled into sharp points at the end & pulled into four short points around the gently arched rim, frosted & mottled white & yellow overlaid w/green & cut w/stylized leafy stems & blossoms, signed in intaglio, ca. 1910, 15" l., 5 1/2" h. **9,775**

Cordials, cylindrical, various background colors, each etched w/a different landscape & enameled w/naturalistic colors, signed, w/original silk-lined presentation box, each 1 7/8" h., set of 6 .... **8,050**

Fine Daum Nancy Creamer

Creamer, wide ovoid body tapering to a wide mouth w/pinched spout, applied frosted amber handle, the speckled rose body shading to mint green, etched &

enameled w/a meadow landscape dotted w/wild flowers, tree-bordered pond & distant village en grisaille, gilt trim & signature, 5 3/4" h. (ILLUS.) **8,050**

Vase, 3" h., miniature, flattened form in fiery yellowish amber etched w/scrolling stylized hops decoration painted in black & gold, marked on base "Daum (cross) Nancy" (chip on base) **1,380**

Vase, 6 3/4" h., bulbous ovoid body tapering to a molded flat rim, shaded blue to frosted clear decorated w/a vitrified enamel spring landscape w/stylized dark brown trees w/reddish leafage above mottled green & yellow enameled grass, signed in intaglio **9,775**

Vase, 8" h., the lower body round & gently flaring below the very irregular rim which is high & arched on one side w/a sharp drop to the stepped lower half, clear frosted ground w/an enameled landscape in pale green & lavender w/a very large leafy green tree on the tall half, signed in enamel **6,900**

Daum Acid-etched Vase

Vase, 8 1/4" h., bulbous ovoid body w/a flat molded rim, light blue deeply etched w/three rows of rectangles separated by horizontal bands, signed, drilled near base & filled, ca. 1925 (ILLUS.) **1,380**

Vase, 8 1/2" h., coupe-form, small pedestal foot below the deep cup-form body w/applied dark loop rim handles, mottled dark brown, orange, pale yellow & amber w/gold foil inclusions, signed, ca. 1925 ..... **4,600**

Rare Vitrified Enamel Daum Vase

Vase, 9" h., simple baluster-form w/a flaring neck & molded rim, mottled blue to greenish amber ground enameled w/a vitrified spring landscape of styliized greenish brown trees w/reddish brown leafage, dark greenish black foot, signed in intaglio, ca. 1906 (ILLUS.) **11,500**

Vase, 11 3/4" h., Art Deco style, tall ovoid body tapering to a short tapered neck, mottled amber & clear w/pronounced ribs & textured panels up the sides, acid signature, ca. 1930 .... **920**

Vase, 17 1/2" h., a cushion foot tapering to a tall slender trumpet-form body, salmon & yellow streaked ground etched & enameled w/thistles & foliage w/gilt accents, etched mark...................................... **3,220**

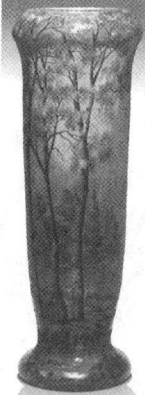

Daum Nancy Vase w/Fall Landscape

Vase, 18 3/4" h., cushion foot below the gently swelled cylindrical body w/a incurved mouth, etched & enameled around the sides w/an autumnal landscape w/tall trees in the foreground, signed (ILLUS.).. **7,763**

Vase, 19 1/2" h., very tall slender waisted trumpet-form body, mottled pumpkin orange shading to yellow, etched & enameled w/a snowy winter landscape, in brown, white, charcoal & grisaille, signed in enamel **7,475**

Vase, 21" h., a cushion foot & short pedestal below the tall slender slightly flaring cylindrical body, clear internally decorated w/charteuse, yellow & raspberry streaks, etched to depict thorny branches & blackberries, enameled in amber, purple & rust, cameo signature **4,600**

Depression

The phrase "Depression Glass" is used by collectors to denote a specific kind of transparent glass produced primarily as tablewares, in crystal, amber, blue, green, pink, milky-white, etc., during the late 1920s and 1930s when this country was in the midst of a financial depression. Made to sell inexpensively, it was turned out by such producers as Jeannette, Hocking, Westmoreland, Indiana and other glass companies. We compile prices on all the major Depression Glass patterns. Collectors should consult Depression Glass references for information on those patterns and pieces which have been reproduced.

Aunt Polly, U.S. Glass Co., late 1920s (Press-mold)

Bowl, 4 3/4" d., berry, blue.............................. **$18**
Bowl, 4 3/4" d., berry, green **7**
Bowl, 7 1/4" d., oval, handled pickle, blue........... **30**
Bowl, 7 1/4" d., oval, handled pickle, green **10**
Bowl, 7 7/8" d., large berry, blue....................... **43**
Bowl, 7 7/8" d., large berry, green **16**
Butter dish, cov., blue..................................... **233**
Butter dish, cov., green **240**
Candy dish, footed, two-handled, blue.............. **50**
Candy dish, footed, two-handled, green **22**
Creamer, blue **50**
Pitcher, 8" h., 48 oz., blue................................ **200**
Plate, 6" d., sherbet, blue **14**
Plate, 6" d., sherbet, iridescent........................... **13**
Sherbet, blue **14**
Sherbet, green **11**
Sherbet, iridescent **6**
Sugar bowl, cov., blue..................................... **210**
Sugar bowl, cov., iridescent.............................. **65**
Tumbler, water, blue, 3 5/8" h., 8 oz. **36**
Vase, 6 1/2" h., blue **61**

Bubble, Bullseye or Provincial, Anchor-Hocking Glass Co., 1940-65 (Press-mold)

Berry set: master bowl & 4 sauce dishes: clear, 5 pcs. **7**
Berry set: master bowl & 6 sauce dishes: blue, 7 pcs. **33**
Berry set: master bowl & 6 sauce dishes: milk white, 7 pcs. **13**
Berry set: master bowl & 8 sauce dishes; clear, 9 pcs. **18**
Bowl, 4" d., berry, blue................................... **21**
Bowl, 4" d., berry, clear **6**
Bowl, 4" d., berry, green **10**
Bowl, 4" d., berry, milk white............................... **4**
Bowl, 4" d., berry, pink................................... **15**
Bowl, 4 1/2" d., fruit, blue **13**
Bowl, 4 1/2" d., fruit, clear **6**
Bowl, 4 1/2" d., fruit, green................................. **9**
Bowl, 4 1/2" d., fruit, milk white **4**
Bowl, 4 1/2" d., fruit, ruby red **11**
Bowl, 5 1/4" d., cereal, blue **14**
Bowl, 5 1/4" d., cereal, clear................................. **6**
Bowl, 5 1/4" d., cereal, green **18**
Bowl, 7 3/4" d., soup, blue **13**
Bowl, 7 3/4" d., soup, clear **5**
Bowl, 7 3/4" d., soup, pink.................................. **9**
Bowl, 8 3/8" d., blue...................................... **17**
Bowl, 8 3/8" d., clear...................................... **14**
Bowl, 8 3/8" d., green..................................... **26**
Bowl, 8 3/8" d., milk white **5**
Bowl, 8 3/8" d., pink...................................... **11**
Bowl, 8 3/8" d., ruby red **19**
Bowl, 9" d., flanged, blue................................ **18**
Candlesticks, clear, pr. **17**
Creamer, blue **37**
Creamer, clear **6**
Creamer, green **15**
Creamer, milk white **3**
Cup, blue.. **3**
Cup, clear.. **4**
Cup, green **9**
Cup, ruby red **10**

Cup & saucer, blue 25
Cup & saucer, clear.. 6
Cup & saucer, green 15
Cup & saucer, milk white 3
Cup & saucer, ruby red 15
Lamp, clear 34
Lamps, clear (electric), pr.................................... 56
Pitcher w/ice lip, 64 oz., clear 65

Bubble Pitcher w/Ice Lip

Pitcher w/ice lip, 64 oz., ruby red (ILLUS.) 61
Plate, 6 3/4" d., bread & butter, blue..................... 4
Plate, 6 3/4" d., bread & butter, green 9
Plate, 9 3/8" d., dinner, blue 8
Plate, 9 3/8" d., dinner, clear 7
Plate, 9 3/8" d., dinner, green 26
Plate, 9 3/8" d., dinner, ruby red 27
Plate, 9 3/8" d., grill, blue 22
Platter, 12" oval, blue... 14
Saucer, blue.. 3
Saucer, ruby red 4
Sugar bowl, open, blue 22
Sugar bowl, open, clear.. 9
Sugar bowl, open, green.. 14
Sugar bowl, open, milk white 5
Tumbler, juice, green, 6 oz. 13
Tumbler, juice, ruby red, 6 oz............................... 10
Tumbler, old fashioned, ruby red, 3 1/4" h.,
   8 oz.. 16
Tumbler, water, ruby red, 9 oz. 12
Tumbler, iced tea, clear, 4 1/2" h., 12 oz............. 15
Tumbler, iced tea, ruby red, 4 1/2" h.,
   12 oz.. 14
Tumbler, lemonade, ruby red, 5 7/8" h.,
   16 oz.. 17

Cloverleaf, Hazel Atlas Glass Co., 1931-35 (Process-etched)

Bowl, 5" d., cereal, green 27
Bowl, 7" d., salad, deep, green 42
Bowl, 7" d., salad, deep, yellow............................ 69
Candy dish, cov., green 69
Candy dish, cov., yellow 124
Creamer, footed, black, 3 5/8" h........................... 20
Creamer, footed, green, 3 5/8" h........................... 10
Creamer, footed, yellow, 3 5/8" h.......................... 16
Cup & saucer, black 25
Cup & saucer, green 11
Cup & saucer, pink 12
Cup & saucer, yellow.. 14

Dinner service: eight each 9" d. plates,
   8" d. plates, 6" d. plates, 3 1/2" h. footed
   juice tumblers, 4 3/4" h. footed water
   tumblers, cups & saucers, sherbets to-
   gether w/cov. sugar bowl, creamer, the
   set 1,050
Plate, 6" d., sherbet, black.................................... 38
Plate, 6" d., sherbet, yellow.................................... 8
Plate, 8" d., luncheon, black................................. 17
Plate, 8" d., luncheon, clear 5
Plate, 8" d., luncheon, green................................ 10
Plate, 8" d., luncheon, pink................................... 11
Plate, 8" d., luncheon, yellow............................... 14
Plate, 10 1/4" d., grill, green................................. 25
Plate, 10 1/4" d., grill, yellow................................ 25
Salt & pepper shakers, black, pr. 95
Salt & pepper shakers, green, pr. 36
Salt & pepper shakers, yellow, pr. 100
Sherbet, footed, black, 3" h. 21
Sherbet, footed, green, 3" h. 11
Sherbet, footed, pink, 3" h. 8
Sherbet, footed, yellow, 3" h................................ 11
Sugar bowl, open, footed, black, 3 5/8" h. 19

CloverLeaf Sugar Bowl

Sugar bowl, open, footed, green, 3 5/8" h.
   (ILLUS.) 10
Sugar bowl, open, footed, yellow, 3 5/8" h. 19
Tumbler, flared, green, 3 3/4" h., 10 oz. 40
Tumbler, flared, pink, 3 3/4" h., 10 oz.................. 26
Tumbler, footed, green, 5 3/4" h., 10 oz.............. 28
Tumbler, footed, yellow, 5 3/4" h., 10 oz. 37

Diamond Quilted or Flat Diamond, Imperial Glass Company, late 1920s-early 1930s (Press-mold)

Bowl, 4 3/4" d., cream soup, black 18
Bowl, 4 3/4" d., cream soup, blue 18
Bowl, 4 3/4" d., cream soup, green 13
Bowl, 4 3/4" d., cream soup, pink 9
Bowl, 5 1/2" d., single handle, black.................... 16
Bowl, 5 1/2" d., single handle, blue 18
Bowl, 5 1/2" d., single handle, green.................... 12
Bowl, 5 1/2" d., single handle, pink 8
Bowl, 7" d., crimped rim, black............................. 21
Bowl, 7" d., crimped rim, blue............................... 19
Bowl, 7" d., crimped rim, pink............................... 11
Candlesticks, flat or domed base, black, pr. 37
Candlesticks, flat or domed base, blue, pr......... 43
Candlesticks, flat or domed base, green,
   pr. 25
Candlesticks, flat or domed base, pink, pr. 22
Candy jar, cov., footed, pink............................... 135
Compote, open, 7 1/4" d., 6" h., green 40
Console bowl, rolled edge, pink........................... 33
Creamer, black... 16

Creamer, blue 15
Creamer, green 10
Creamer, pink 8
Cup, black 15
Cup, blue 17
Cup, green 11
Cup, pink 9
Cup & saucer, amber 8
Cup & saucer, black 20
Cup & saucer, green 12
Cup & saucer, pink 17
Ice bucket, blue 64
Plate, 6" d., sherbet, black 5
Plate, 6" d., sherbet, blue 6
Plate, 6" d., sherbet, green 4
Plate, 6" d., sherbet, pink 5
Plate, 8" d., luncheon, black 13
Plate, 8" d., luncheon, blue 15
Plate, 8" d., luncheon, green 9
Plate, 8" d., luncheon, pink 5
Sherbet, blue 12
Sherbet, green 7
Sherbet, pink 7
Sugar bowl, open, amber 8
Sugar bowl, open, black 17
Sugar bowl, open, blue 18
Sugar bowl, open, green 10
Sugar bowl, open, pink 8
Tumbler, whiskey, green, 1 1/2 oz. 7

Doric, Jeannette Glass Co., 1935-48 (Press-mold)

Bowl, 4 1/2" d., berry, green 11
Bowl, 4 1/2" d., berry, pink 11
Bowl, 5 1/2" d., cereal, green 68
Bowl, 5 1/2" d., cereal, pink 85
Bowl, 8 1/4" d., large berry, green 32
Bowl, 8 1/4" d., large berry, pink 24
Bowl, 9" d., two-handled, pink 16
Bowl, 9" oval vegetable, green 36
Bowl, 9" oval vegetable, pink 39
Butter dish, cov., green 85
Butter dish, cov., pink 80
Cake plate, three-footed, green, 10" d. 24
Cake plate, three-footed, pink, 10" d. 30
Candy dish, three-section, Delphite, 6" 8
Candy dish, three-section, green, 6" 11
Candy dish, three-section, pink, 6" 9
Candy jar, cov., green, 8" h. 43
Candy jar, cov., pink, 8" h. 49
Coaster, green, 3" d. 19
Coaster, pink, 3" d. 19
Creamer, green, 4" h. 13
Creamer, pink, 4" h. 15
Cup, green 12
Cup, pink 11
Cup & saucer, green 17
Cup & saucer, pink 14
Pitcher, 5 1/2" h., 32 oz., green 44
Pitcher, 5 1/2" h., 32 oz., pink 45
Pitcher, 7 1/2" h., 48 oz., footed, pink 750
Plate, 6" d., sherbet, green 5
Plate, 6" d., sherbet, pink 6
Plate, 7" d., salad, green 21
Plate, 7" d., salad, pink 17
Plate, 9" d., dinner, green 20
Plate, 9" d., dinner, pink 19
Plate, 9", grill, pink 24
Platter, 12" oval, green 35

Platter, 12" oval, pink 32
Relish, square inserts in metal holder, pink 48
Relish or serving tray, green, 8" x 8" 21
Relish or serving tray, pink, 8" x 8" 24
Relish tray, green, 4" x 4" 7
Relish tray, pink, 4" x 4" 16
Relish tray, green, 4" x 8" 20
Relish tray, pink, 4" x 8" 21
Salt & pepper shakers, green, pr. 38
Sandwich tray, handled, green, 10" d. 18

Doric Sandwich Tray

Sandwich tray, handled, pink, 10" d.
  (ILLUS.) 17
Saucer, green 5
Saucer, pink 5
Sherbet, footed, Delphite 7
Sherbet, footed, green 17
Sherbet, footed, pink 14
Sugar bowl, cov., green 35
Sugar bowl, cov., pink 28
Tumbler, pink, 4 1/2" h., 9 oz. 83
Tumbler, footed, pink, 4" h., 10 oz. 67
Tumbler, footed, pink, 5" h., 12 oz. 82

Floral or Poinsettia, Jeannette Glass Co., 1931-35 (Process-etched)

Bowl, 4" d., berry, green 24
Bowl, 4" d., berry, pink 24
Bowl, 7 1/2" d., salad, green 25
Bowl, 7 1/2" d., salad, pink 32
Bowl, 8" d., cov. vegetable, green 54
Bowl, 9" oval vegetable, green 26
Bowl, 9" oval vegetable, pink 22
Butter dish, cov., green 110
Butter dish, cov., pink 109
Candlesticks, green, 4" h., pr. 101
Candy jar, cov., green 41
Candy jar, cov., pink 42
Coaster, green, 3 1/4" d. 13
Coaster, pink, 3 1/4" d. 15
Creamer, green 17
Creamer, pink 19
Cup, green 14
Cup, pink 13
Cup & saucer, green 26
Cup & saucer, pink 26
Lamp, green 478
Pitcher, 5 1/2" h., 24 oz., green 638
Pitcher, 8" h., 32 oz., cone-shaped, pink 40
Pitcher, 8" h., 32 oz., cone-shaped, pink 42
Pitcher, lemonade, 10 1/4" h., 48 oz., green 325
Pitcher, lemonade, 10 1/4" h., 48 oz., pink 347
Plate, 6" d., sherbet, green 10
Plate, 6" d., sherbet, pink 7

Plate, 8" d., salad, green.. 15
Plate, 8" d., salad, pink 18
Plate, 9" d., dinner, green.. 23
Plate, 9" d., dinner, pink.. 24
Platter, 10 3/4" oval, green....................................... 22
Platter, 10 3/4" oval, pink 21
Platter, 11" oval, scalloped edge, pink.............. 140
Relish, two-part, oval, green................................... 24
Relish, two-part, oval, pink...................................... 18
Salt & pepper shakers, footed, green,
    4" h., pr. 55
Salt & pepper shakers, flat, pink, 6" h., pr. 50
Saucer, pink... 12
Sherbet, green 20
Sugar bowl, cov., green.. 28
Sugar bowl, cov., pink.. 28
Sugar bowl, open, green.. 15
Sugar bowl, open, pink.. 12
Tray, closed handles, pink, 6" sq. 25
Tumbler, juice, footed, green, 4" h., 5 oz. 27
Tumbler, juice, footed, pink, 4" h., 5 oz. 21
Tumbler, water, footed, green, 4 3/4" h.,
    7 oz. 24
Tumbler, water, footed, pink, 4 3/4" h., 7 oz........ 21
Tumbler, green, 4 1/2" h., 9 oz......................... 230
Tumbler, lemonade, footed, green,
    5 1/4" h., 9 oz. 57
Vase, 6 7/8" h., octagonal, clear...................... 298

Lorain or Basket or Number 615, Indiana Glass Co., 1929-32 (Process-etched)

Bowl, 9 3/4" oval vegetable, green 44
Bowl, 9 3/4" oval vegetable, yellow 68
Creamer, footed, green.. 16
Creamer, footed, yellow.. 28
Cup & saucer, clear... 15

Lorain Cup & Saucer

Cup & saucer, yellow (ILLUS.)............................ 21
Plate, 5 1/2", sherbet, green.................................... 7
Plate, 5 1/2", sherbet, yellow................................ 12
Plate, 7 3/4", salad, clear...................................... 10
Plate, 7 3/4", salad, green 12
Plate, 7 3/4", salad, yellow 16
Plate, 8 3/8", luncheon, green............................... 20
Plate, 8 3/8", luncheon, yellow............................. 30
Plate, 10 1/4", dinner, clear.................................. 36
Plate, 10 1/4", dinner, green.................................. 65
Plate, 10 1/4", dinner, yellow................................ 77
Platter, 11 1/2", green.. 33
Platter, 11 1/2", yellow... 48
Relish, four-part, clear, 8"...................................... 16
Relish, four-part, green, 8" 20
Relish, four-part, yellow, 8" 37
Sherbet, footed, green 21
Sherbet, footed, yellow 31
Sugar bowl, open, footed, green 15
Sugar bowl, open, footed, yellow 28
Tumbler, footed, green, 4 3/4" h., 9 oz. 27
Tumbler, footed, yellow, 4 3/4" h., 9 oz. 34

Moderntone, Hazel Atlas Glass Co., 1934-42, late 1940s & early 1950s (Press-mold)

Ashtray w/match holder, cobalt blue,
    7 3/4" d.. 185
Ashtray w/match holder, pink, 7 3/4" d............... 62
Bowl, 4 3/4" d., cream soup, amethyst 18
Bowl, 4 3/4" d., cream soup, cobalt blue 25
Bowl, 4 3/4" d., cream soup, platonite 12
Bowl, 5" d., berry, amethyst................................. 25
Bowl, 5" d., berry, cobalt blue.............................. 30
Bowl, 5" d., cream soup w/ruffled rim,
    cobalt blue... 66
Bowl, 5" d., cream soup w/ruffled rim,
    platonite 7
Bowl, 6 1/2" d., cereal, cobalt blue 117
Bowl, 7 1/2" d., soup, cobalt blue 187
Bowl, 8 3/4" d., large berry, amethyst 46
Bowl, 8 3/4" d., large berry, cobalt blue............. 56
Butter dish w/metal lid, cobalt blue 100
Cheese dish w/metal lid, cobalt blue, 7" d. 433
Creamer, amethyst... 11

Moderntone Pieces

Creamer, cobalt blue (ILLUS.)............................. 11
Cup, amethyst 12
Cup, cobalt blue 11
Custard cup, amethyst.. 14
Custard cup, cobalt blue....................................... 20
Plate, 5 7/8" d., sherbet, amethyst........................ 5
Plate, 5 7/8" d., sherbet, cobalt blue..................... 6
Plate, 6 3/4" d., salad, cobalt blue...................... 13
Plate, 7 3/4" d., luncheon, amethyst..................... 9
Plate, 7 3/4" d., luncheon, cobalt blue................ 13
Plate, 8 7/8" d., dinner, amethyst 11
Plate, 8 7/8" d., dinner, cobalt blue 21
Plate, 10 1/2" d., sandwich, amethyst 39
Plate, 10 1/2" d., sandwich, platonite 20
Platter, 11" oval, cobalt blue 46
Platter, 12" oval, amethyst 51
Platter, 12" oval, cobalt blue.............................. 128
Salt & pepper shakers, amethyst, pr. 43
Salt & pepper shakers, cobalt blue, pr.
    (ILLUS. w/sugar and creamer)......................... 43
Salt & pepper shakers, platonite, pr. 25
Saucer, amethyst... 4
Saucer, cobalt blue.. 5
Saucer, platonite.. 5
Sherbet, amethyst.. 12
Sherbet, cobalt blue 14
Sugar bowl, open, amethyst 12
Sugar bowl, open, cobalt blue (ILLUS.
    w/creamer) 11
Tumbler, whiskey, cobalt blue, 1 1/2 oz. 41
Tumbler, water, cobalt blue, 4" h., 9 oz. 41

Little Hostess Party Set

Moderntone, Hazel Atlas Glass Co., 1934-42, late 1940s & early 1950s (Press-mold)

Creamer, 1 3/4" h., dark 14
Creamer, 1 3/4" h., pastel 17

Cup, 1 3/4" h., dark.. 12
Cup & saucer, dark.. 17
Plate, 5 1/4" d., dark.. 13
Plate, 5 1/4" d., pastel 10
Saucer, 3 7/8" d., dark 9
Saucer, 3 7/8" d., pastel 8
Sugar bowl, 1 3/4" h., dark.................................. 14
Sugar bowl, 1 3/4" h., pastel 15
Tea set, dark, 16 pcs.. 295
Tea set, pastel, 16 pcs... 257
Teapot, cov., 3 1/2" h., dark............................... 110

Moroccan Amethyst, Hazel Ware, Division of Continental Can, 1960s (Early 1960s - not true Depression)

Ashtray, 3 3/4" triangle 7
Ashtray, 6 7/8" triangle 10
Bowl, 4 3/4" w. octagonal, fruit............................. 9
Bowl, 5 3/4" sq., cereal, deep.............................. 11
Bowl, 6" d... 11
Bowl, 7 3/4" oval... 15
Bowl, 7 3/4" rectangle... 15
Bowl, 10 3/4" 31
Candy jar, cov., short.. 33
Candy jar, cov., tall... 37
Chip & dip set, w/metal holder (5 3/4" &
    10 3/4" bowls) 41

Moroccan Amethyst Cup & Saucer

Cup & saucer (ILLUS.).. 9
Goblet, wine, 4" h., 4 1/2 oz................................ 11
Goblet, juice, 4 3/8" h., 5 1/2 oz. 10
Goblet, water, 5 1/2" h., 10 oz. 13
Plate, 5 3/4" w. octagonal 5
Plate, 7 1/4" w., salad... 8
Plate, 9 3/4" w., dinner 8
Sandwich server, w/metal center handle,
    12".. 19
Tumbler, juice, 2 1/2" h., 4 oz.............................. 8
Tumbler, Old Fashioned, 3 1/4" h., 8 oz............. 14
Tumbler, water, crinkled bottom, 4 1/4" h.,
    11 oz... 11
Tumbler, water, 4 5/8" h., 11 oz.......................... 11
Tumbler, iced tea, 6 1/2" h., 16 oz...................... 15
Vase, 8 1/2" h., ruffled... 38

Number 612 or Horseshoe, Indiana Glass Co., 1930-33 (Process-etched)

Bowl, 6 1/2" d., cereal, yellow............................. 48
Bowl, 7 1/2" d., salad, yellow............................... 28
Bowl, 9 1/2" d., large berry, green 49
Bowl, 9 1/2" d., large berry, yellow 50
Cup, green 13
Cup & saucer, green 17
Cup & saucer, yellow 20

Pitcher, 8 1/2" h., 64 oz., yellow 375
Plate, 6" d., sherbet, green................................. 9
Plate, 6" d., sherbet, yellow................................ 8
Plate, 8 3/8" d., salad, yellow............................ 11
Plate, 9 3/8" d., luncheon, green 14
Plate, 11 1/2" d., sandwich, green 24
Plate, 11 1/2" d., sandwich, yellow 24
Platter, 10 3/4" oval, green 60
Platter, 10 3/4" oval, yellow................................ 32
Relish, three-part, footed, yellow 23
Saucer, green... 5
Sherbet, green.. 15
Sherbet, yellow 16
Sugar bowl, open, footed, green 17
Tumbler, footed, green, 9 oz. 27
Tumbler, footed, yellow, 9 oz. 28

Parrot or Sylvan, Federal Glass Co., 1931-32 (Process-etched)

Bowl, 5" sq., berry, amber................................. 21
Bowl, 5" sq., berry, green 25
Bowl, 7" sq., soup, amber.................................. 32
Bowl, 7" sq., soup, green 58
Bowl, 10" oval vegetable, green 65

Parrot Butter Dish

Butter dish, cov., green (ILLUS.) 433
Creamer, footed, green 54
Cup & saucer, green 64
Hot plate, green, scalloped edge........................ 888
Jam dish, amber, 7" sq. 34
Plate, 5 3/4" sq., sherbet, amber........................ 26
Plate, 5 3/4" sq., sherbet, green 28
Plate, 7 1/2" sq., salad, green............................ 38
Plate, 9" sq., dinner, amber................................ 40
Plate, 9" sq., dinner, green................................. 55
Plate, 10 1/2" d., grill, green............................... 45
Plate, 10 1/2" sq., grill, amber............................ 30
Platter, 11 1/4" oblong, green............................. 59
Salt & pepper shakers, green, pr. 288
Sherbet, footed, cone-shaped, amber 23
Sugar bowl, cov., green 225
Sugar bowl, open, green 40

Petalware, MacBeth-Evans Glass Co., 1930-40 (Press-mold)

Bowl, 4 1/2" d., cream soup, clear........................ 6
Bowl, 4 1/2" d., cream soup, decorated
    Cremax or Monax.. 12
Bowl, 4 1/2" d., cream soup, pink 18
Bowl, 4 1/2" d., cream soup, plain Cremax
    or Monax.. 14
Bowl, 5 3/4" d., cereal, clear................................ 4
Bowl, 5 3/4" d., cereal, Florette.......................... 13
Bowl, 5 3/4" d., cereal, pink 11

Bowl, 5 3/4" d., cereal, plain Cremax or Monax.. 5
Bowl, 5 3/4" d., cereal, Red Trim Floral 42
Bowl, 7" d., soup, plain Cremax or Monax 70
Bowl, 9" d., large berry, clear 6
Bowl, 9" d., large berry, decorated Cremax or Monax... 32
Bowl, 9" d., large berry, pink................................ 23
Bowl, 9" d., large berry, plain Cremax or Monax.. 13
Creamer, footed, clear... 4
Creamer, footed, decorated Cremax or Monax.. 14
Creamer, footed, plain Cremax or Monax 6
Creamer, footed, Red Trim Floral 33
Cup & saucer, clear 4
Cup & saucer, decorated Cremax or Monax.. 9
Cup & saucer, Florette 13
Cup & saucer, pink 10
Cup & saucer, plain Cremax or Monax 7
Lamp shade, Monax, 6" h. 15
Lamp shade, Cremax, 9" h. 17
Lamp shade, Monax, 11" h. 18
Lamp shade, pink, 12" h. 21
Mustard jar, w/metal cover, cobalt blue............... 15
Plate, 6" d., sherbet, clear 2
Plate, 6" d., sherbet, Florette 6
Plate, 6" d., sherbet, pink 4
Plate, 6" d., sherbet, plain Cremax or Monax.. 3
Plate, 6" d., sherbet, Red Trim Floral 22
Plate, 8" d., salad, clear... 2
Plate, 8" d., salad, decorated Cremax or Monax.. 8
Plate, 8" d., salad, Florette 10
Plate, 8" d., salad, pink 6
Plate, 8" d., salad, plain Cremax or Monax 4
Plate, 9" d., dinner, clear....................................... 6
Plate, 9" d., dinner, decorated Cremax or Monax.. 12
Plate, 9" d., dinner, Florette................................... 15
Plate, 9" d., dinner, pink 21
Plate, 11" d., salver, decorated Cremax or Monax.. 17
Plate, 11" d., salver, Florette................................. 17
Plate, 11" d., salver, pink 18
Plate, 11" d., salver, plain Cremax or Monax........ 8
Plate, 12" d., salver, Florette................................. 18
Plate, 12" d., salver, Red Trim Floral.................... 44
Platter, 13" oval, pink... 22
Platter, 13" oval, plain Cremax or Monax 13
Sugar bowl, open, footed, clear............................. 5
Sugar bowl, open, footed, decorated Cremax or Monax.. 11
Sugar bowl, open, footed, Florette....................... 11
Sugar bowl, open, footed, plain Cremax or Monax.. 6

Royal Ruby, Anchor Hocking Glass Co., 1939-60s (Press-mold)

Ashtray, 4 1/2" sq.. 8
Bowl, 4 1/4" d., berry... 10
Bowl, 7 1/2" d., soup 15
Bowl, 8" oval vegetable 38
Bowl, 8 1/2" d., berry... 19
Bowl, 10" d., popcorn, deep.................................... 43
Bowl, 11 1/2" d., salad 38
Creamer, flat 10

Creamer, footed.. 8
Cup, round 6
Cup & saucer, round 7
Goblet, ball stem... 15
Lamp 46
Pitcher, 3 qt., tilted or upright 43
Plate, 6 1/2" d., sherbet 4
Plate, 7" d., salad 8
Plate, 7 3/4" d., luncheon 6
Plate, 9" d., dinner 12
Playing card or cigarette box, divided, clear base 64
Popcorn set, 10" d. serving bowl & six 5 1/4" d. bowls, 7 pcs. 125
Punch bowl 38
Punch cup 3
Punch set, punch bowl, base & 8 cups, 10 pcs. 110
Sherbet, footed 7
Sugar bowl, flat 7
Sugar bowl, w/slotted lid, footed 17
Tumbler, juice, 5 oz. 8
Tumbler, water, 9 oz... 8
Tumbler, water, 10 oz... 4
Vase, various styles, large...................................... 15
Vase, 4" h., ball-shaped 5

Sailboats or Ships or Sportsman Series, Hazel Atlas Glass Co., late 1930s

Cocktail mixer w/stirrer 28
Cup (plain) "Moderntone" & saucer 30
Ice bowl 34
Pitcher w/ice lip, 86 oz. 73
Pitcher without ice lip, 82 oz. 62
Saucer 22
Tumbler, juice, 3 3/4" h., 5 oz. 14
Tumbler, roly poly, 6 oz. 13
Tumbler, Old Fashioned, 3 3/8" h., 8 oz. 22
Tumbler, water, straight sides, 3 3/4" h., 9 oz... 16
Tumbler, water, 4 5/8" h., 9 oz. 13
Tumbler, iced tea, 4 7/8" h., 10 1/2 oz................... 17
Tumbler, iced tea, 12 oz. 21

Spiral, Hocking Glass Co., 1928-30 (Press-mold)

Spiral Pitcher

Bowl, 4 3/4" d., berry, green 5
Bowl, 8" d., berry, green.. 13
Creamer, flat or footed, green 8
Cup, green 5

Cup & saucer, green 7
Ice or butter tub, green 27
Pitcher, 7 5/8" h., 58 oz., green (ILLUS.) 32
Plate, 6" d., sherbet, green 2
Plate, 8" d., luncheon, green 4
Sandwich server, w/center handle, green 33
Sherbet, green 5
Sugar bowl, flat or footed, green 7

Swanky Swigs, early 1930s to early 1940s (Kraft cheese glasses)

Band No. 1 4
Band No. 2 5
Bustlin' Betsy, blue, brown, green,
orange, red or yellow 7
Carnival, yellow 6
Checkerboard, green & white 25
Circles & Dot, blue or green 7
Daisy (or Bachelor Button), green, red or
white 4
Forget-Me-Not, dark, blue, light blue, red or
yellow 4
Kiddy Kup, black, blue, brown, green,
orange or red 6
Posy - Cornflower No. 1, 3 1/2" h. 5
Posy - Cornflower No. 1, 4 1/2" h. 15
Posy - Cornflower No. 2, dark blue, light
blue, red or yellow 4
Posy - Jonquil 5
Posy - Tulip 4
Posy - Violet 5
Sailboat No. 1 (3 boats), blue 11
Stars No. 1, black, blue, green, red or
yellow 7
Tulip No. 1, black, dark blue, green or red,
3 1/2" h. 3

Waterford or Waffle, Hocking Glass Co., 1938-44- (Press-mold)

Ashtray, clear, 4" 8
Bowl, 4 3/4" d., berry, pink 18
Bowl, 5 1/4" d., cereal, pink 35
Bowl, 8 1/4" d., berry, clear 11
Butter dish, cov., clear 27
Butter dish, cov., pink 220
Cake plate, handled, clear, 10 1/4" d. 11
Pitcher, juice, 42 oz., tilt-type, clear 23
Pitcher w/ice lip, 80 oz., clear 35
Pitcher w/ice lip, 80 oz., pink 173
Plate, 6" d., sherbet, pink 7

Waterford Plates

Plate, 7 1/2" d., salad, clear (ILLUS. left) 7
Plate, 9 5/8" d., dinner, clear 10
Plate, 13 3/4" d., sandwich, clear
(ILLUS. right) 10
Plate, 13 3/4" d., sandwich, pink 30
Salt & pepper shakers, clear, short, pr 8
Sherbet, footed, clear 4
Sherbet, footed, pink 15
Sugar bowl, cov., oval, clear 10
Tumbler, footed, clear, 5" h., 10 oz. 13
Tumbler, footed, pink, 5" h., 10 oz. 27

Dugan-Diamond

The Dugan and Diamond Glass factories operated in Indiana, Pennsylvania between 1904 and 1931. Thomas E.A. Dugan and Alfred Dugan, cousins of Harry Northwood, reopened the former Northwood factory in that city in 1904 and operated as the Dugan Glass Company until 1913. After 1913 and until the factory's destruction by fire in 1931, it was known as the Diamond Glass Company.

Both companies produced decorative pressed glasswares similar to lines being produced by the Northwood factory during those years including opalescent glass, colored and decorated wares and Carnival and Stretch glass. The Dugan's "Diamond-D" trademark was introduced in late 1906.

Dugan's Diamond-D" trademark, introduced in late 1906.

Diamond Glass-ware Company Patterns

Dugan Patterns

AEarly Colored and Opalescent Lines

Beaded Ovals in Sand (Erie) pitcher, water, green $175
Beaded Ovals in Sand spooner, light green 100
Beaded Ovals in Sand toothpick holder,,
light green 250

Clubs & Spades Tumbler

Clubs & Spades tumbler, green w/gold
trim (ILLUS.) 50

Cornflower Pitcher & Tumbler

Cornflower pitcher, emerald green & gold
(ILLUS. left) **275**
Cornflower tumbler, emerald green & gold
(ILLUS. right) **45**
Fan bowl, master berry, custard **125**
Fan butter dish, cov., green **185**

Fan Creamer

Fan creamer, dark blue w/gold, "Diamond-
D" mark, ca. 1907 (ILLUS.) **175**
Fan creamer, green **100**

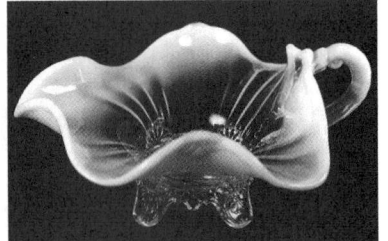

Fan Gravy Boat

Fan gravy boat, clear opalescent, "Dia-
mond-D" mark (ILLUS.) **90**
Fan pitcher, water, custard **250**
Fan sugar bowl, cov., blue w/gold **175**
Fan sugar bowl, cov., green **135**
Inverted Fan & Feather butter dish, cov.,
blue opalescent **450**

Inverted Fan & Feather Creamer

Inverted Fan & Feather creamer, blue
opalescent w/gold trim (ILLUS.) **145**

Inverted Fan & Feather Creamer

Inverted Fan & Feather creamer, green
w/gold (ILLUS.) **125**
Inverted Fan & Feather pitcher, water,
green w/gold **175**
Inverted Fan & Feather sauce dish, green
w/gold **50**

Inverted Fan & Feather Sauce Dish

Inverted Fan & Feather sauce dish, pink
slag (ILLUS.) **225**
Inverted Fan & Feather spooner, blue
opalescent w/gold **200**
Inverted Fan & Feather spooner, green
w/gold **100**
Maple Leaf butter dish, cov., custard **350**

Maple Leaf creamer, blue w/gold 150

Maple Leaf Creamer

Maple Leaf creamer, dark cobalt blue w/gold trim, D-in-diamond mark (ILLUS.) 275

Maple Leaf Salt Shaker

Maple Leaf salt shaker, custard (ILLUS.) 375
Maple Leaf sugar bowl, cov., blue w/gold 175

Maple Leaf Sugar Bowl

Maple Leaf sugar bowl, cov., dark cobalt blue w/gold trim, D-in-diamond mark (ILLUS.) 250
Nestor compote, open, jelly, blue 75
Nestor cruet w/original stopper, amethyst 250
Nestor pitcher, water, amethyst 175

Nestor Salt Shaker

Nestor salt shaker w/original lid, amethyst w/gold & white trim, ca. 1905 (ILLUS.) 110
New York (Beaded Shell) bowl, master berry, blue opalescent 160
New York butter dish, cov., light green 400

New York Creamer

New York creamer, green w/gold trim (ILLUS.) 100
New York creamer, light green 125
New York pitcher, water, light green 450
New York sugar bowl, cov., light green 250
New York tumbler, light green 65

Quill Tumbler

Quill tumbler, ruby w/gold trim (ILLUS.) 125
S-Repeat goblet, blue 75
S-Repeat (National) cruet w/original stopper, blue 250
S-Repeat pitcher, water, purple 175
S-Repeat punch cup, purple 50
S-Repeat syrup jug w/original metal lid, light green 450
S-Repeat tumbler, blue 50
S-Repeat wine, purple w/gold (ILLUS. left) 75

S-Repeat Decanter & Wine

S-Repeat wine decanter w/original stopper, purple w/gold trim, top of photo cropped (ILLUS. right) 175

Venetian or Japanese Striped Vase

Venetian or Japanese vase, light blue green w/amber stripes (ILLUS.) 95

Venetian or Japanese Vase

Venetian or Japanese Vase, twisted, light blue green w/amber stripes (ILLUS.) 110

Victor Salt Shaker

Victor (Jewelled Heart) salt shaker w/original top, blue (ILLUS.) 110
Victor pitcher, water, light green 150

Victor spooner, clear opalescent 75
Victor sugar shaker w/original metal lid, blue 300
Victor syrup jug w/original metal lid, blue, ca. 1905 450
Victor tumbler, green opalescent 60
Victor tumbler, light green 30

"Goofus" Lines

Cherry Compote

Cherry compote, open, ruffled sides, hexagonal base (ILLUS.) 55

Holly Bowl

Holly bowl, smooth rim (ILLUS.) 50

Carnival Glass Lines

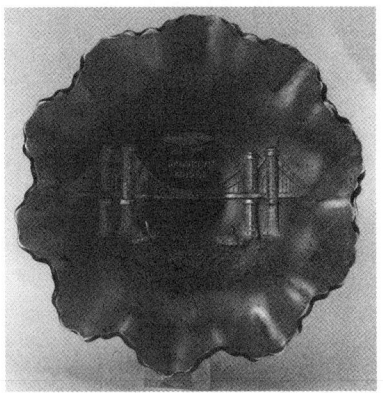

Brooklyn Bridge Bowl

Brooklyn Bridge bowl, marigold (ILLUS.).......... **60**

Butterfly & Tulip Bowl

Butterfly & Tulip bowl, Feather Scroll exterior, marigold (ILLUS.) **200**

Grape & Cable Perfume Bottle

Grape & Cable perfume bottle w/stopper, purple (ILLUS.) **650**

Grape Delight Bowl

Grape Delight bowl, purple (ILLUS.)........... **80-100**

Lattice & Daisy Pitcher

Lattice & Daisy pitcher, tankard-type, marigold (ILLUS.)... **225**

Stippled Petals Bowl

Stippled Petals bowl, peach opal w/h.p. lily of the valley decoration inside (ILLUS.)..... **195 +**

Diamond Glass-ware Company Patterns

Black Glass

Candleholder

Candleholder, hexagonal socket & round foot, "Jack and the Bean Stalk" decoration, ca. 1928 (ILLUS.) **25**

Console Bowl & Base

Console bowl & base, gold band decoration, ca. 1924-28 (ILLUS.) **45**

Tall Vase

Vase, tall ovoid body w/short cylindrical neck, "hammered gold" band decoration (ILLUS.).. **145**

Clear Decorated Items

Decorated Tankard Pitcher

Pitcher, tall footed tankard-style w/ruffled rim, applied angled handle, h.p. decorat-

ed bands around the middle, ca. 1920 (ILLUS.) **75**

Blue Bird Tumblers

Tumblers, Blue Bird decoration, ca. 1916, each (ILLUS.).. **25**

Wine Decanter

Wine decanter w/bulbous stopper, h.p. w/large daisy-like blossoms, leaves & bands (ILLUS.) **65**

Cut Pieces

Diamond Cut Basket

Basket, shallow upturned sides, applied center handle, cut flowers around the sides (ILLUS.).. **65**

Vase with Swags & Berries

Vase, wide slightly flaring cylindrical iridescent blue body w/swelled, closed mouth, cut w/stylized swags & berries (ILLUS.) **100**

Stretch Glass

Console Bowl

Console bowl, shallow widely flaring sides, blue stretch, on a separate black glass base, ca. 1924 (ILLUS.) **60**

"Adam's Rib" Pattern Pitcher

Pitcher, tankard-type, "Adam's Rib" patt., blue stretch (ILLUS.) **600**

Sandwich Server

Sandwich server w/central handle, green stretch, ca. 1927 (ILLUS.) **75**

Sherbet

Sherbet, footed, blue stretch (ILLUS.) **25**

Other Lines

Candleholder with Flared Base

Candleholder, green w/fluted base, ca. 1928 (ILLUS.) **20**

Green Candlestick

Candlestick, iridescent green w/white trim (ILLUS.) **50**

Candlestick w/Geometric Decoration

Candlestick, satin-finished blue w/h.p. geo-
metric decoration (ILLUS.) **60**

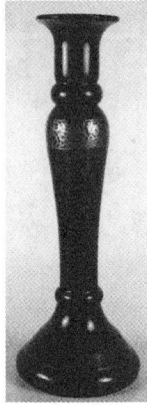

Cobalt Blue Candlestick/Vase

Candlestick/vase, blown, cobalt blue
w/gold trim (ILLUS.) **55**

Covered Candy Jar

Candy jar, cov., iridescent blue (ILLUS.) **85**

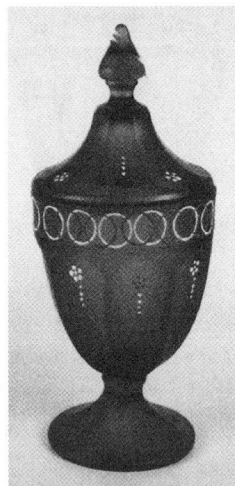

Candy Jar w/Geometric Decoration

Candy jar, cov., satin-finished blue w/h.p.
geometric decoration (ILLUS.) **100**

Vanity Set

Vanity set: a pair of tall bottles, cov. powder
dish & oblong tray; rose-pink, gold band
trim, the set (ILLUS.) **125**

"Barcelona" Line Vase

Vase, "Barcelona" line, black glass w/twist-
ed body & flared rim (ILLUS.) **125**

Durand

Fine decorative glass similar to that made by Tiffany and other outstanding glasshouses of its day was made by the Vineland Flint Glass Works Co. in Vineland, New Jersey, first headed by Victor Durand, Sr., and subsequently by his son Victor Durand, Jr., in the 1920s.

Bowl, 6" d., shallow cased bowl w/a wide flattened & gently ruffled rim, overall gold iridescence, signed "V. Durand" **$450**

Center bowl, blue iridescence, signed, 14" w. **1,500**

Center bowl, low wide flat-bottomed form w/a wide rolled rim, overall butterscotch iridescence, signed & numbered 2605, 14" d., 2 1/2" h. **385**

Center bowl, ruffled rim, red crackle iridescent exterior, stretch iridescent interior, 11" d. **650**

Ginger jar, cov., wide ovoid body fitted w/a domed cover, overall dark blue iridescence decorated w/overall dark blue random threading, a small yellow reeded florette finial on the cover, 8 1/4" d., 9" h. (slight threading loss) **1,650**

Ice bucket, cut-overlay, cylindrical form in blue cut to clear w/a design of honeycomb vesicas connected by crosshatched diamonds, silver plate rim & bail handle, 6" h. (short crack in base) **248**

Jar, cov., wide tapering ovoid body w/a domed cover centered on the shouldered top, overall green & opal white swirled & 'crackled' surface, berry finial on the cover, overall iridescent finish, unsigned, 10" h. **1,500**

Lamp base, "King Tut" patt., simple ovoid body tapering to a trumpet neck, mounted on an octagonal gilt-metal base, gilt-metal electric fittings at the top w/two sockets, the body of golden orange iridescence w/dark olive green pulled coils & swirls, glass 12" h., overall 20" h. **750**

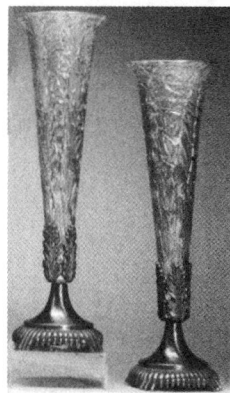

Egyptian Crackle Durand Torcheres

Torcheres, tall slender trumpet-form in green & white striated design w/iridescent gold "Egyptian crackle" decoration, mounted in a bronze acanthus leaf electrified base, ca. 1926, overall 15 1/2" h., pr. (ILLUS.) **1,725**

Vase, 4 1/2" h., gold iridescence, signed **450**

Vase, 4 1/2" h., waisted short cylindrical body w/a widely flaring & ruffled rim, the exterior w/blue hanging heart & vine design over gold iridescent ground, gold iridescent interior, unsigned **604**

Vase, 6 3/4" h., baluster-form body w/cushion foot & short flaring neck, gold iridescent ground decorated w/five pulled feathers in yellow & white w/blue outlining, base center inscribed "Durand" in silver script (some interior stain) **750**

Two Durand "King Tut" Vases

Vase, 7" h., baluster-form body w/a flaring trumpet neck, "King Tut" patt., white pulled & hooked design over the iridescent blue ground, unsigned (ILLUS. left) **1,200**

Vase, 7" h., "King Tut" patt., the shouldered ovoid body in brilliant amber iridescence decorated w/bluish green iridescent scrolls & trailings, inscribed "Durand," ca. 1925 .... **750**

Vase, 8 1/4" h., wide bulbous baluster-form w/flattened flaring rim, "King Tut" patt., iridescent green hooked & pulled swirls on a golden orange cased to opal ground, signed "Durand" across the pontil (ILLUS. right) **1,750**

Graceful Blue Durand Vase

Vase, 8 1/2" h., footed tall ovoid body w/a wide flaring short neck, body in overall dark blue iridescence, disk foot w/golden iridescence (ILLUS.) **1,000**

Vase, 9 3/4" h., baluster-form w/a cushion foot, the rounded shoulder w/a small trumpet neck, overall blue iridescence, foot signed "Durand V113" **990**

Vase, 9 3/4" h., tall wide waisted cylindrical form swelled at the base & w/a wide stepped shoulder to the wide flat mouth, golden iridescent ground decorated over-all w/cascading dark blue iridescent vines & heart-shaped leaves, signed "Durand - 1969-10" **1,375**

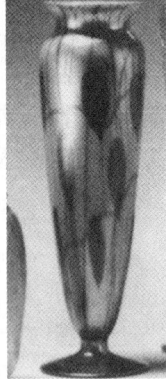

Tall Decorated Durand Vase

Vase, 12 1/8" h., tall ovoid body w/waisted neck & flaring lip, brilliant amber-orange iridescence decorated w/green heart-shaped leafage & trailings, inscribed "Du-rand - 2011 - 12," ca. 1925 (ILLUS.) **1,200**

Vase, 16 1/4" h., globular body tapering to a tall trumpet neck, brilliant blue shading to purple iridescence, signed "Durand - 1716.16," ca. 1900 .... **1,750**

Findlay Onyx & Floradine

In January, 1889, the glass firm of Dalzell, Gilmore & Leighton Co. of Findlay, Ohio began production of these scarce glass lines. Onyx ware was a white-lined glass produced mainly in onyx (creamy yellowish white) but also in bronze and ruby shades sometimes called cin-namon, rose or raspberry. Pieces featured raised flow-ers and leaves that are silver-colored or, less often, bronze. By contrast the Floradine line was produced in ruby and autumn leaf (gold) with opalescent flowers and leaves. It is not lined.

Celery vase, creamy white w/silver flowers & leaves **$495**

Findlay Onyx Creamer

Creamer, bulbous ovoid body w/an upright ribbed neck, applied handle, creamy white w/silver flowers & leaves, 3" h. (ILLUS.) **485**

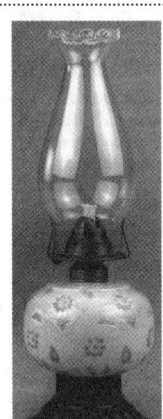

Extremely Rare Findlay Onyx Lamp

Lamp, kerosene table model, black opaque glass base w/flaring ruffled foot & wide short cylindrical shaft supporting the squatty bulbous Findlay Onyx font w/brass collar, burner & chimney, piece of base rim reglued, overall to burner 7 1/4" h. (ILLUS.) **7,150**

Findlay Onyx Spooner

Spooner, bulbous tapering to an upright ribbed neck, creamy white w/silver blos-soms & leaves, 4 1/4" h. (ILLUS.) **375**

Floradine Sugar Bowl

Sugar shaker w/original lid,   Floradine, cranberry (ILLUS.) **800**

Fostoria

Fostoria Glass company, founded in 1887, produced numerous types of fine glassware over the years. Their factory in Moundsville, West Virginia closed in 1986.

Fostoria Label

Appetizer set, American patt., clear, 7 pcs.... **$325**
Ashtray, Coin patt., ruby, 5 1/2" 34
Banana split dish, American patt., clear,
  3 1/2" w., 9" l. 1,200
Beer mug, American patt., clear, 12 oz.,
  4 1/2" h. 88
Bonbon, three-footed, American patt., am-
  ber, 7" d. 125
Bonbon, three-footed, American patt., blue,
  7" d. 175
Bonbon, three-toed, Baroque patt., clear,
  7 3/8" 95
Bonbon, three-toed, Chintz etching, No.
  2496/137, clear...................................... 35
Bonbon, three-footed, American patt., red,
  7" d. 125
Bottle w/original stopper, catsup, Ameri-
  can patt., crystal, 6 3/4" h. 160
Bowl, desert, two-handled, June etching,
  azure, large 140
Bowl, 9" oval, Coin patt., ruby 46
Bowl, 9 3/8" w., 4" h., Colony patt., clear........... 85
Butter dish, cov., Colony patt., No. 2412,
  clear, 1/4 lb. 38
Butter dish, cov., round, American patt.,
  clear.. 100
Cake salver, American patt., clear, 10" sq. 250
Cake stand, Coin patt., amber 140
Cake stand, Coin patt., clear, 10" d.................. 78
Candlestick, Coin patt., ruby, 4 1/2" h. 46
Candlestick, Colony patt., No. 2412, clear,
  7" h. 30
Candlestick, two-light, Flame patt., clear........... 80
Candlestick, Baroque patt., clear w/Lido
  etching, 4" h. 32
Candlestick, Colony patt., No. 2412, clear,
  7" h. 30

Baroque Two-light Candlestick

Candlestick, two-light, Baroque patt., clear
  (ILLUS.).. 24
Candlesticks, June etching, topaz, pr. 2" h. 45
Candlesticks, three-light, Chintz etching,
  No. 2496, clear, pr. 95
Candy dish, cov., Coin patt., ruby, 4 1/4" 42
Candy dish, cov., Coin patt., ruby, 6" 58

Candy dish, cov., American patt., "wedding
  bowl," milk glass, 8" h........................... 125
Celery dish, Chintz etching, clear 40
Cigarette box, cov., Baroque patt., No.
  2496, clear.. 38
Cologne bottle w/original stopper, Amer-
  ican patt., clear 100
Compote, 8", Lucere No. 1515, blue milk
  glass 75
Condiment tray, cloverleaf-shaped, Ameri-
  can patt., clear 250
Cordial, Colonial Dame patt., clear,
  3 1/2" h. 42
Cordial, Colonial Dame patt., green bowl,
  clear foot & stem, 3 1/2" h. 46
Cordial, Mayflower etching, clear, 3 3/4" h. 44
Cordial, June etching, Topaz, 3 7/8" h. 98
Cordial, Lido etching, clear, 4" h. 34
Creamer & open sugar bowl, footed,
  Chintz etching, clear, pr. 35
Creamer & open sugar bowl, individual,
  Chintz etching, clear, pr. 40
Cruet w/original stopper, Baroque patt.,
  Topaz, 3 1/2 oz.. 295
Cruet w/original stopper, Coin patt., clear,
  6" h. 42
Cup & saucer, Baroque patt., clear................... 12
Cup & saucer, Colony patt., clear 10
Cup & saucer, Kashmir etching, blue 56
Decanter w/original stopper, Coin patt.,
  clear.. 94
Figure of Madonna, clear, 10" h. 45
Figure of Madonna & Child, clear,
  13 1/2" h. 95
Goblet, American Lady patt., cobalt blue,
  10 oz., 6 1/8" h. 80
Goblet, American patt., clear, 5 1/2" h. 14
Goblet, American patt., clear, 6 7/8" h. 26
Goblet, Colonial Dame patt., clear,
  6 1/2" h. 22
Goblet, Colonial Dame patt., green bowl,
  clear stem & foot, 6 1/2" h. 26
Goblet, Jamestown patt., blue, 6" h. 14
Goblet, Jamestown patt., green, 6" h. 14
Goblet, Jamestown patt., pink, 6" h. 22
Goblet, June etching, azure, 10 oz..................... 75

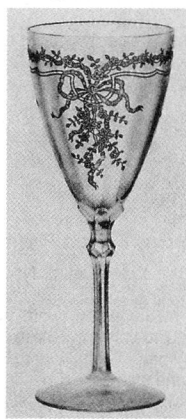

June Etched Goblet

Goblet, June etching, clear, 8 1/4" h.
  (ILLUS.) 46

Goblet, June etching, pink, 8 1/4" h...................... 94
Goblet, Lido etching, clear, 7 1/2" h. 21
Goblet, Navarre etching, clear, 7 5/8" oz. 52
Goblet, Navarre etching, pink, 7 5/8" oz. 72
Goblet, Sunray patt., clear, 5 3/4" h. 22
Goblet, wine, June etching, topaz...................... 50
Goblet, Chintz etching, No. 6026, short
stem, clear, 6 1/8" h., 9 oz. 27
Gravy boat w/undertray, Chintz etching,
clear, 2 pcs. 75
Hairpin box, cov., American patt., clear,
1 1/2 x 1 2/4", 3 1/2" l. 2,000
Ice bowl, Colony patt., footed, clear 200
Ice bucket w/metal handle, Baroque patt.,
Topaz 85
Ice tub, American patt., clear, 5 5/8" d.,
3 3/4" h... 98
Ice tub w/underplate, cov., American patt.,
clear... 200
Jam jar, cov., American patt., clear..................... 60
Mug, Bicentennial, No. 2493/705, clear,
15 oz.. 24
Mustard jar, cover & spoon, American
patt., clear, 3 pcs. 50
Napkin ring, American patt., clear, 2"................. 50
Nappy, handled, flared, Baroque patt.,
clear, 5" d... 15
Oyster cocktail, Chintz etching, clear................ 25
Parfait, June etching, blue, 5 1/2" h. 94
Pickle dish, Colony patt., clear 25
Pitcher, 5 3/5" h., single serving, American
patt., clear... 55
Pitcher, Jamestown patt., pink, 7 1/2" h. 137
Pitcher, 6 1/2" h., American patt., clear,
3 pt... 75
Pitcher, American patt., clear, 1 pt. 40
Pitcher, 5 3/8" h., Coin patt., ruby...................... 140
Pitcher, 6 1/2" h., Coin patt., clear...................... 89

Colony Pattern Pitcher

Pitcher, 7 3/4" h., Colony patt., No. 2412,
clear (ILLUS.).. 80
Pitcher, 7 1/2" h., Jamestown patt., pink 120
Pitcher, Jenny Lind patt., milk glass.................... 95
Pitcher, Sunray patt., frosted clear, 2 qt. 58
Plate lemon, June etching, azure 30
Plate, 7 3/8" d., Kashmir etching, blue 38
Plate, 8 3/4" d., June etching, azure.................... 25
Plate, 9 1/2" d., Colony patt., clear...................... 34
Plate, torte, 18" d., American patt., clear 90
Plate, dinner, Chintz etching, clear 75

Preserve dish, cov., two-handled, Ameri-
can patt., clear, 5 3/4" d., 4 1/4" h................. 100
Puff box, cov., American patt., clear,
1 1/2" d.. 725
Punch bowl, Tom & Jerry-type, pedestal
footed, American patt., clear, 12" d............... 193
Relish dish, two-part, Chintz etching, clear 38
Relish dish, three-part, American patt.,
clear, 9 1/2" l... 45
Relish dish, three-part, Baroque patt.,
Topaz, 10" l. 28
Relish dish, three-part, two-handled, Colo-
ny patt., clear, 13"... 24
Relish dish, four-part, American patt.,
clear, 10" sq.. 170
Ring holder, American patt., clear 750

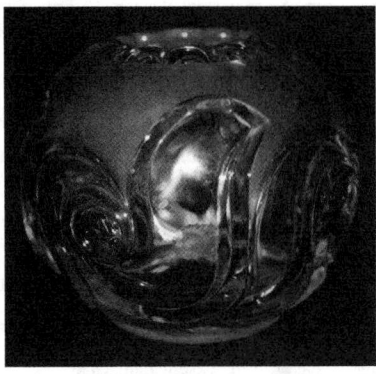

Victoria Pattern Rose Bowl

Rose bowl, Victoria patt., clear w/satin fin-
ish (ILLUS.) 100-150
Salt dip, American patt., clear 12
Salt & pepper shakers Coin patt., ruby, pr. 52
Salt & pepper shakers, Mesa patt., No.
4186, ruby, pr. 28
Sherbet, American Lady patt., burgundy
bowl w/clear stem, 5 1/2 oz., 4 1/8" h............. 16
Sherbet, American Lady patt., cobalt blue,
5 1/2 oz., 4 1/8" h.. 60
Sherbet, American patt., footed, handled,
clear, 4 1/2 oz... 145
Sherbet, Baroque patt., clear, 5 oz...................... 10
Sherbet, Coin patt., clear, 5 1/8" h. 26
Sweetmeat dish, cov., Baroque patt., clear....... 175
Syrup pitcher, cov., American patt., clear,
5 1/4" h.. 120
Syrup pitcher, cov., Dripcut, American
patt., crystal, 6 1/2" oz....................................... 45
Tom & Jerry Mug, American patt., clear............. 50
Toothpick holder, Priscilla patt., No. 676,
clear... 23
Tray, five-part, American patt., clear
w/frame 160
Tray, handled, Chintz etching, clear, 10 1/2" 45
Tray, tidbit, Colony patt., clear w/patterned
top 85
Tray, tidbit, Colony patt., three-toed, clear,
7 1/2"... 18
Tray, rectangular, American patt., clear,
7 1/2 x 10 1/2".. 100
Tray for creamer & sugar bowl, Colony
patt., clear.. 15
Tumbler, Colony patt., clear, 4" h........................ 22

Tumbler, footed, Kashmir etching, green,
5" h. **42**
Tumbler, footed, Line 4020, black foot,
clear bowl.. **32**
Tumbler, ice tea, footed, American Lady
patt., clear, 5 1/2" h., 12 oz. **18**

American Pattern Iced Tea Tumbler

Tumbler, iced tea, American patt., clear,
12 oz., 5 3/4" h. (ILLUS.).................................. **21**
Tumbler, iced tea, Coin patt., ruby, 5 1/2" h......... **95**
Tumbler, iced tea, June etching, Topaz **58**
Tumbler, Jamestown patt., green, 5 1/4" h. **28**
Tumbler, juice, Jamestown patt., ruby,
4 3/4" h. **22**
Tumbler, juice, Mayflower etching, clear,
4 7/8" h. **19**
Tumbler, June etching, azure, 9 oz. **50**
Urn, cov., Colony patt., clear w/patterned
base... **85**
Vase, 9 1/2" h., flared rim, American patt.,
clear.. **175**
Vase, 10" h., flared, American patt., clear........... **90**
Vase, 12" h., Colony patt., clear **275**
Vase, 12" h., straight sides, American patt.,
clear.. **150**
Vase, 13" h., Lotus patt., amber **220**
Vase, 14" h., Colony patt., clear **550**
Vase, 18" h., Heirloom patt. No. 5056, blue
opalescent **74**
Vase, bud, Coin patt., clear **32**
Vase, bud, Coin patt., ruby **38**
Vase, Coin patt., clear **34**
Wedding bowl, American patt., clear, small...... **125**
Wedding bowl, cov., American patt., milk
glass, 6 1/2".. **105**
Wine, Colonial Dame patt., green bowl,
clear foot & stem, 4 3/4" h................................ **36**
Wine, June etching, pink, 5 3/8" h....................... **112**
Wine, Navarre etching, clear, 6 1/2" h................. **90**
Wine, Navarre etching, clear, 7 1/4" h................. **150**
Wine, Navarre etching, pink, 6 1/2" h.................. **82**
Wine, Sunray patt., clear, 4 7/8" h. **32**
Youth set, mug & bowl, American patt.,
clear, 2 pcs.. **75**

Fry

*Numerous types of glass were made by the H.C. Fry
Company, Rochester, Pennsylvania. One of its art lines*

*was called Foval and was blown in 1926-27. Cheaper
was its milky-opalescent ovenware (Pearl Oven Ware)
made for utilitarian purposes but also now being collected. The company also made fine cut glass.*

*Collectors of Fry Glass will be interested in the
recent publication of a good reference book, The Collector's Encyclopedia of Fry Glassware, by The H.C. Fry
Glass Society (Collector Books, 1990).*

Candlesticks, Foval, opalescent wide disc
foot w/a blue connector to the tall slender
cylindrical white shaft wrapped w/a thin
thread of blue below a translucent blue
bobeche supporting the pearl white cylindrical socket w/gently flared rim, ca.
1926, one w/faint Fry Shield acid stamp,
10 3/8" h., pr. **$345**

Gallé

*Gallé glass was made in Nancy, France, by Emile
Gallé, a founder of the Nancy School and a leader in the
Art Nouveau movement in France. Much of his glass, both
enameled and cameo, is decorated with naturalistic motifs.
The finest pieces were made in the last two decades of the
19th century and the opening years of the 20th.*

*Pieces marked with a star preceding the name were
made between 1904, the year of Gallé's death, and 1914.*

Various Gallé Marks

Cameo box, cov., wide squatty bulbous
base w/wide low domed cover, deep orange overlaid in burgundy, the top &
sides cut w/encircling bands of vines &
flowers, signed in cameo, 6 1/2" d.,
2 3/4" h.. **$990**
Cameo lamp, table model, 10 1/2" d. domi-
cal shade in golden amber overlay
w/deep maroon & cut w/large stylized
leaves & blossoms, supported on bronze
spider arms above the slender baluster-
form matching base cut w/a matching design, base & shade signed, ca.1900,
overall 20 1/2" h. **16,100**

Fine Gallé Cameo Table Lamp

Cameo lamp, table model, 7 1/2" w. domed squared shade in deep golden amber overlaid in deep maroon & cut w/large leafy branches of fuchsia blossoms, supported above a matching ovoid base, shade & base signed in cameo, overall 11" h. (ILLUS.) **12,650**

Cameo vase, 5 1/8" h., flattened spherical vessel w/short cylindrical neck & molded rim, applied loop handles, grey & pale yellow layered in burnt orange & etched & engraved w/primroses, cameo signature (star), polished pontil, ca. 1905 .... **1,495**

Cameo vase, 8" h., bulbous tapering ovoid body w/a slender trumpet neck, light blue overlaid w/dark blue & cut w/morning glories & vines, fire polished, signed **1,610**

Cameo vase, 8" h., flattened spherical form in golden yellow overlaid w/brown & cut w/grapevines & leaves & mold-blown grape clusters, signed (cut down).............. **1,840**

Cameo vase, 11 3/8" h., footed tapering cylindrical form w/a short cylindrical neck, shaded deep golden amber ground overlaid w/deep purple cut as pendent leafy stems suspending 'blown-out' clusters of pale blue cherries, signed in cameo, ca. 1925 .... **8,050**

Molded Mountain Laurel Gallé Vase

Cameo vase, 11 3/8" h., footed tapering ovoid body w/a short tapering cylindrical neck, grey infused w/lemon yellow, overlaid in pale blue & purple & molded in medium-relief w/pendent clusters of mountain laurel berries & serrated leaves, signed, ca. 1925 (ILLUS.) **5,750**

Cameo vase, 13" h., footed slender flattened ovoid body tapering to a small flared rim, pink shading to white & overlaid in dark blue, cut w/a landscape of tall trees in the foreground & a fence & shorter trees near a river in the distance............ **2,990**

Cameo vase, 15" h., yellow ground overlaid & mold-blown in very dark green, cut w/large stylized palm trees & molded w/a parade of walking elephants around the middle, signed in cameo, ca. 1925........... **57,500**

Cameo vase, 15 3/4" h., footed tall flaring cylindrical form w/a tapering shoulder to the cylindrical neck, yellow ground overlaid w/deep purple & 'blown-out' clusters

of pendent plums & cut leafy vines, signed in cameo, ca. 1925........................ **16,100**

Finely Decorated Gallé Center Bowl

Center bowl, wide shallow form w/tri-lobed upturned & incurved sides, decorated w/internal decorations, applied, enameled & wheel-carved designs on the clear frosted & mottled amber ground, decorated w/slender leafy stems w/large rounded blossoms, signed in enamel "Emile Gallé - fecit," ca.1900, 9 3/4" w., 3 1/4" h. (ILLUS.) **5,750**

Vase, 6 1/8" h., Islamic-style, round foot below the squatty bulbous tapering body below the tall conical neck, clear ground ornately enameled around the neck w/gilt florets enclosing different animals & around the body w/gilt horses & riders, a finely enameled background of arabesques & scrolling lines in black & gold, signed, ca. 1890 .... **16,100**

Rare Gallé Exposition Vase

Vase, 6 1/2" h., classic wide baluster-form, clear swirled w/dark blue & golden amber internally decorated, faceted & enameled on the exterior w/a large exotic bird & Oriental-style white & gold blossoms around the sides, designed for the Exposition Universelle, Paris, 1889, signed in gilt intaglio "Emile Gallé - Nancy - Paris Exposition 1889" (ILLUS.)................................... **48,875**

Greentown

Greentown glass was made in Greentown, Indiana, by the Indiana Tumbler & Goblet Co. from 1894 until 1903. In addition to its famed Chocolate and Holly Amber glass, it produced other types of clear and colored glass. Miscellaneous pieces are listed here. Also see PATTERN GLASS.

Rare Fighting Cocks Animal Dish

Animal covered dish, Fighting Cocks, green (ILLUS.) **$1,750**

Greentown Amber Hen on Nest Dish

Animal covered dish, Hen on Nest, amber (ILLUS.) **200**

Herringbone Buttress Berry Bowl

Bowl, master berry, Herringbone Buttress patt., amber (ILLUS.) **400**

Cord Drapery Amber Compote

Compote, open, ruffled rim, Cord Drapery patt., amber (ILLUS.) **450**

Green Austrian Pattern Creamer

Creamer, Austrian patt., dark emerald green, 4" h. (ILLUS.) **225**

Herringbone Buttress Creamer

Creamer, Herringbone Buttress patt., green w/gold trim (ILLUS.) **275**

Herringbone Buttress Green Cruet

Cruet w/original stopper, Herringbone Buttress patt., green (ILLUS.) **550**

Blue Dewey Pattern Mug

Mug, Dewey patt., blue (ILLUS.) **325**

Greentown Amber Corn Vase

Novelty, Corn vase, amber (ILLUS.) **125**

Greentown Buffalo Paperweight

Paperweight, figural, Buffalo, opaque Nile
Green (ILLUS.) **1,250**

Austrian Pitcher in Canary

Pitcher, water, Austrian patt., canary
(ILLUS.) **650**

Brazen Shield Pitcher & Tumbler

Pitcher, water, Brazen Shield patt., blue
(ILLUS. right).. **250**

Green Dewey Pitcher with Gold Trim

Pitcher, water, Dewey patt., emerald green
w/gold decoration (ILLUS.) **275**

Dewey Pattern Green Salt Shaker

Salt shaker w/metal lid, Dewey patt., em-
erald green (ILLUS.) **85**

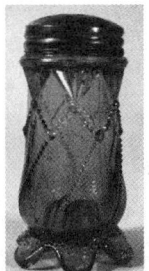

Cord Drapery Salt Shaker

Salt shaker w/metal top, Cord Drapery patt., amber (ILLUS.) **275**

Herringbone Buttress Green Spooner

Spooner, Herringbone Buttress patt., green w/gold trim (ILLUS.) **250**

Opaque White Cord Drapery Sugar

Sugar bowl, cov., Cord Drapery patt., opaque white (ILLUS.) **500**
Tumbler, Brazen Shield patt., blue (ILLUS. left w/pitcher) **45**

Herringbone Buttress Green Tumbler

Tumbler, Herringbone Buttress patt., green (ILLUS.) **240**

Cord Drapery Handled Tumbler

Tumbler w/applied handle, Cord Drapery patt., blue (ILLUS.) **650**

Herringbone Buttress Amber Wine

Wine, Herringbone Buttress patt., amber (ILLUS.) **450**

Heisey

Numerous types of fine glass were made by A.H. Heisey & Co., Newark, Ohio, from 1895. The company's trademark, an H enclosed within a diamond, has become known to most glass collectors. The company's name and molds were acquired by Imperial Glass Co., Bellaire, Ohio, in 1958, and some pieces have been reissued. The glass listed below consists of miscellaneous pieces and types. Also see PATTERN GLASS.

Heisey Diamond "H" Mark

Bowl, 7" oval, combination, Orchid etching, clear **$45**
Bowl, 11" d., two-handled, Lariat patt., clear **30**
Cake plate, Rose etching, low pedestal, clear, 14" **310**
Champagne, Rose etching, clear **27**

Cigarette holder, Orchid etching, footed,
clear... 165
Cocktail, Rosalie etching, No. 4092, 3 oz. 10
Cocktail, Rose etching, clear................................ 33
Cordial, Rose etching, clear 150
Cruet w/original stopper, oil-type, Yeo-
man patt., Moongleam, 2 oz. (ILLUS.)... 100-125
Goblet, Plantation patt., pressed........................... 55
Goblet, Rose etching, clear, 9 oz......................... 42
Mayonnaise set, Rose etching, clear,
3 pcs. 135
Plate, 7" d., Empress patt., Moongleam............. 175
Plate, 7" d., Orchid etching, clear.......................... 18
Punch bowl base, Greek Key patt., clear. 80
Relish dish, Lariat patt., three-part, clear,
10 1/2".. 24
Salt & pepper shakers, Rose etching,
clear, pr.. 120
Sherbet, Colonial patt., clear 10
Toothpick holder, Prison Stripe patt.,
marked.. 295
Toothpick holder, Sunburst patt., marked........ 125
Tray, Plantation patt., clear, 8 1/2"..................... 100
Tumbler, iced tea, Plantation patt., footed,
pressed, clear 90
Vase, 4" h., Orchid etching, clear 135

Imperial

*Imperial Glass Company, Bellaire, Ohio was orga-
nized in 1901 and was in continuous production, except
for very brief periods, until its closing in June 1984. It
had been a major producer of Carnival Glass earlier in
this century and also produced other types of glass,
including an art glass line called "Free Hand Ware"
during the 1920s and its "Jewels" about 1916. The company acquired a number of molds of other earlier factories, including the Cambridge and A.H. Heisey
Companies, and reissued numerous items through the
years. Also see CARNIVAL GLASS.*

Imperial Nucut Mark   Later Imperial Marks

Early Imperial Cross Mark

Candlewick
Ashtray, heart-shaped, clear, 4" $10
Ashtray, clear, No. 400/133, 5" d........................... 8
Ashtray, No. 400/60, clear, 6" 150
Ashtray, w/embossed eagle center, No.
1776/1, clear, 6 1/2"... 70
Ashtray, No. 400/118, clear................................ 12
Ashtray set, nested, round, No. 400/450,
clear, 3 pcs.. 50
Baked apple dish, No. 400/53X, blue,
6 1/2".. 85

Baked apple dish, No. 400/53X, clear,
6 1/2".. 25
Basket, No. 400/40/0, clear, 6 1/2" h. 36
Basket, No. 400/40/0, clear w/gold beads,
6 1/2" h. 60
Basket, No. 400/73/0, clear, 11" 255

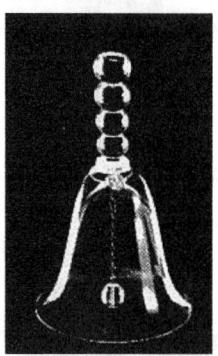

Candlewick Bell

Bell, No. 400/108, clear, 5" h. (ILLUS.)............... 95
Bitters bottle, No. 400/117, 4 oz., clear............ 100
Bonbon, heart-shaped, handled, clear, 5" 24
Bonbon bowl, handled, No. 400/40H,
clear, 5"... 25
Bonbon bowl, handled, No. 400/51H,
clear, 6".. 36
Bonbon bowl, heart-shaped, No. 400/174,
clear, 6 1/2" 22
Bowl, 5", heart-shaped, clear 18
Bowl, 5", heart-shaped, No. 400/49H, clear...... 175
Bowl, 5" sq., No. 400/231, clear........................ 150
Bowl, 5 1/2", heart-shaped, No. 500/53H,
clear.. 45
Bowl, cream soup, 5 1/2" d., No. 400/50,
clear.. 50
Bowl, 6" d., clear, No. 400/3F............................. 12
Bowl, 6" h., No. 400/182, three-toed, clear 73
Bowl, 7" sq., No. 400/233, clear........................ 160
Bowl, 8-8 1/2" d., No. 400/74B, clear............... 110
Bowl, 8-8 1/2" d., No. 400/74B, ruby................. 450
Bowl, 8 1/2" d., handled, No. 400/72B,
clear.. 39
Bowl, 8 1/2" d., No. 400/69, clear w/cutting 55
Bowl, 9" sq., No. 400/74SC, four-toed,
crimped, ribbed, black w/flower 550
Bowl, 9-10", heart-shaped, No. 400/73H,
clear.. 55
Bowl, 10" d., fruit, footed, No. 400/103C,
clear.. 185
Bowl, 10-11", No. 400/75F, float-type, clear 45
Bowl, salad, 10" d., No. 400/75B, clear 50
Bowl, 10 1/2" d., bell-shaped, No. 400/63B,
clear 55
Bowl, 10 1/2" d., No. 400/63B, clear 55
Bowl, 11" l, oval, divided, No. 400/125A,
clear.. 550
Bowl w/underplate, 8" d., two-handled
w/10" underplate, bowl No. 400/4272B,
underplate No. 400/4272D, clear, the set 55
Butter dish, cov., No. 400/144, clear,
5 1/2" d... 30
Butter dish, cov., No. 400/276, clear................. 140
Butter dish, cov., round, clear 64

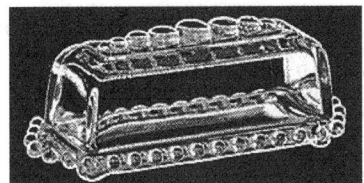

Candlewick Butter Dish

Butter dish, cov., w/beaded top, No. 400/161, clear, 1/4 lb. (ILLUS.) 33
Butter & jam dish, No. 400/262, three-part, clear, 10 1/2" 193
Cake plate, 71 birthday candle holes, clear, 13" 340
Cake plate, No. 400/160, clear w/swirl center, 72 candle holes in rim, 13-14" d. 390
Cake plate, two-handled, clear, 13" d. 75
Cake stand, No. 400/67D, low-footed, clear, 10" d. 68
Canape set, plate No. 400/36 & 3 1/2 oz. tumbler, No. 400/142, clear, 2 pcs. 60
Candle/flower holder, No. 400/40C, clear, 5" h. 47
Candleholder, three-way, No. 400/115, clear 300
Candleholders, No. 400/100, clear, pr. 55
Candleholders, No. 400/147, clear, pr. 72
Candleholders, No. 400/207, 4 1/2" h., clear, pr. 250
Candleholders, No. 400/224, beaded stem, clear, 5 1/2" h., pr. 475
Candleholders, No. 400/40/HC, clear, pr. 250
Candleholders, No. 400/79R, clear, pr. 27
Candleholders, No. 400/81, 3 1/2" h., clear, pr. 112
Candleholders, No. 400/86, clear, pr. 84
Candlestick, single light chamberstick w/handle, clear 52
Candlestick, single light, Eagle, clear 85
Candlestick, single light, mushroom form, clear 28
Candlestick, three-light, clear 78
Candy box, cov., No. 400/59, clear, 5 1/2-6 1/2" 55
Candy box, cov., No. 400/260, clear, 7" 223
Candy box, cov., three-part, No. 400/110, clear, 7" d. 172
Candy dish, cov., No. 400/245, clear, 6 1/2" sq. 450
Candy dish, No. 400/51C, clear, 6" d. 65
Celery tray, oval, handled, No. 400/105, clear, 13 1/2" l. 42
Center bowl, No. 100/13B, Viennese Blue, 11" d. 150
Center bowl, No. 400/131B, oval, flat, clear, 14" 450
Champagne/sherbet, No. 3400, saucer-type, clear, 6 oz. 17
Cheese & cracker set, No. 400/88, clear, 10" d., 2 pc. 65
Cigarette box, cov., clear, 3" 28
Coaster, No. 400/78, clear, 4" d. 6
Cocktail, No. 3400, clear, 4 oz. 16
Compote, 4 1/2", clear 26
Compote, 4 1/2" h., No. 400/63B, no bead stem, clear 32
Compote, 5" h., No. 400/220, clear 148

Compote, 5 1/2" h., No. 400/66B, two-bead stem, clear 30

Imperial Compote with Rose Decoration

Compote, 10" h., crimped, three-bead stem, No. 400/103F, clear w/h.p. pink roses & blue ribbons (ILLUS.) **260-400**
Compote, 10" h., fruit, No. 400/103C, clear 275
Compote, 10" h., No. 400/103F, clear w/sterling silver base 325
Compote, 10 1/2" h., No. 400/63B, clear 33
Console bowl, three-toed, No. 400/205, clear, 10" l. 33
Cordial, No. 3400, clear, 1 oz. 48
Cordial, ruby, 4 1/2" h. 95
Cordial decanter, applied handle, No. 400/82, clear etched (top chip) 495
Creamer, clear 16
Creamer, individual, No. 400/96, clear 7
Creamer & sugar bowl, beaded handle, No. 400/30, clear, pr. 15
Creamer & sugar bowl, individual, No. 400/122, clear, pr. 21
Creamer, sugar bowl & undertray, clear, the set 42
Cruet w/original stopper, handled, clear 48
Cruet w/original stopper, No. 400/119, clear 25
Cruet w/original stopper, No. 400/275, clear, 6 oz. 75
Cruet w/original stopper, No. 400/278, handled, clear, 4 oz. 95
Cruet w/original stopper, No. 500/121/O, clear 75
Cup, coffee, No. 400/37, clear 8
Cup, tea, No. 400/35, clear 8
Cup & saucer, demitasse, No. 400/77AD, clear 30
Cup & saucer, No. 400/35, clear 13
Cup & saucer, No. 400/37, clear 14
Decanter w/original stopper, No. 400/163, clear, 26 oz. 875
Epergne set, No. 400/196, clear, 2 pc. 295
Goblet, cocktail, No. 400/190, clear, 3 1/2-4 oz. 19
Goblet, No. 3400, water, black, 7 1/2" h. 200
Goblet, No. 3400, water, clear, 7 1/2" h. 22
Goblet, No. 3400, water, ruby, 7 1/2" h. 118
Goblet, No. 3400, wine, clear, 4 oz. 28

Goblet, No. 400/19, clear, 4 3/4 h....................... **14**
Goblet, No. 400/190, water, clear, 10 oz. **25**
Gravy boat, No. 100/169, clear.......................... **185**
Honey dish, clear, 4 3/4"................................... **119**
Hurricane candle lamp, No. 400/79, clear,
2 pcs.. **165**
Ice tub, No. 400/168, tab-handled, clear, 7"...... **173**
Icer, No. 400/53C, clear, 6" **75**
Icer & liner, No. 400/53, clear **135**
Jelly/ashtray, No. 400/33, clear, 4"..................... **14**
Knife, No. 4000, clear **550**
Marmalade set, No. 400/8918, clear, 3 pcs....... **110**
Mayonnaise bowl & underplate, No.
400/23, clear, 2 pcs. **34**
Mayonnaise set: divided bowl & under-
plate; No. 400/84, clear, 2 pcs. **80**
Mint bowl, ring-handled, No. 400/51F,
clear, 6"... **28**
Mustard jar, cov., footed, No. 400/156,
clear... **26**
Mustard jar, cover & spoon, clear, 3 pcs. **58**
Nappy, fruit, No. 400/1F, blue, 5"........................ **45**
Nappy, handled, No. 400/51, clear, 6" **16**
Pastry tray, No. 400/68D, clear, 11 1/2" d. ... **60-70**
Pickle/celery dish, No. 400/57, clear,
7 1/2".. **32**
Pitcher, juice/cocktail, No. 400/19, clear,
40 oz. **325**
Pitcher, No. 400/16, clear, pint.......................... **275**
Pitcher, No. 400/18, clear, 40 oz. **275**
Pitcher, No. 400/19, Liliputian, clear, 16 oz....... **350**
Plate, 4 1/2" d., No. 400/34, clear **9**
Plate, bread & butter, 6" d., two-handled,
No. 400/1D, clear **6**
Plate, canapé, 6" d., w/off-center indenta-
tion, No. 400/36, clear **16**
Plate, 7" d., No. 400/52E, two-handled,
black... **375**
Plate, salad, 7" d., No. 400/3D, clear.................... **9**
Plate, luncheon, 9" d., No. 400/7D, clear............ **15**
Plate, dinner, 10 1/2" d., No. 400/10D,
clear... **44**
Plate, 11" d., No. 400/145D, two-handled,
clear... **30**
Plate, torte, 12 1/2" d., cupped edge, No.
400/75V, clear **33**
Plate torte, 13", No. 400/75V, rolled edge,
clear... **58**
Plate, 14" d., No. 400/92D, clear **35**
Plate, torte, 17" d., clear **34**
Plate, torte, 17" d., cupped edge, No.
400/20V, clear **72**
Platter, 16" l., oval, two-handled, No.
400/131D, clear **234**
Punch set: 13" d. punch bowl, 17" d.
cupped-edge underplate, 12 cups & la-
dle; No. 400/20, clear, 15 pcs. **260**
Punch set: punch bowl, ladle, underplate &
12 punch cups; clear, 15 pcs. **190**
Relish dish No. 400/54, clear, 6 1/2" **20**
Relish dish, two-part, handled, clear, 6 1/2"....... **12**
Relish dish, two-part, No. 400/84, clear,
6 1/2"... **22**
Relish dish, two-part, No. 400/234, clear,
7" sq. **140**
Relish dish, two-part, oval, No.400/268,
clear, 8" l. **31**
Relish dish, two-part, No. 400/52, clear **25**
Relish dish, cov., three-part, rectangular,
No. 400/216, clear, 10" l.............................. **1,250**

Relish dish, three-part, three-toed, No.
400/208, clear **127**
Relish dish, four-part, No.400/112, clear,
10 1/2" l. **33**
Relish tray, three-part, handled, No.
400/213, clear, 10" l. **74**
Relish tray, five-part, No. 400/104, clear **65**
Relish tray, five-part, five-handled, No.
400/56, clear, 10 1/2" l. **55**
Relish tray, five-part, No. 3900/120, clear,
13" **65**
Salad fork, No. 400/75, clear **15**
Salad serving set, fork & spoon, No. 475,
clear, 9 1/2" l., the set...................................... **46**
Salt dip, No. 400/61, clear, 2"............................. **12**
Salt & pepper shakers, amethyst, pr. **110**
Salt & pepper shakers, individual, No.
400/109, clear, pr. **20**
Salt & pepper shakers w/chrome tops,
No. 400/190, footed, clear, pr. **100**

Candlewick No. 400/247 Shakers

Salt & pepper shakers w/chrome tops,
No. 400/247, clear, pr. (ILLUS.)....................... **45**
Salt shaker w/chrome top, No. 400/96,
clear... **8**
Seafood cocktail, No. 400/190, clear,
3 1/2-4 oz. **93**
Sherbet, tall, No. 400/190, clear, 5 oz. **18**
Sugar bowl, clear **12**
Tray, lemon, center-handled, No. 400/221,
clear, 5 3/4" **42**
Tray, mint, center-handled, No. 400/149D,
clear, 9" d. **36**
Tray, No. 400/159, clear, 9" l. **29**
Tray, No. 400/72C, two-handled, crimped,
clear, 10"... **30**
Tumbler, No. 400/15, footed beaded base,
clear, 10 oz.. **235**
Tumbler, No. 400/15, footed beaded base,
clear, 6 oz.. **200**
Tumbler, water, No. 3400, clear, 10 oz. **12**
Tumbler, juice, No. 400/19, clear, 4" h.,
5 oz. **6**
Tumbler, flat, No. 400/19, clear, 5 1/2" h. **14**
Tumbler, iced tea, footed, No. 400/19,
clear, 6" h., 12 oz. **26**
Tumbler, iced tea, No. 3400, clear, 6 1/2" h. **22**
Tumbler, water, No. 400/19, clear, 10 oz........... **15**
Tumblers, iced tea, footed, No. 400/19,
clear, 12 oz., set of 6 .... **77**
Vase, bud, 7" h., domed foot, No. 400/186,
clear.. **450**
Vase, 8" h., fan-shaped w/beaded handles,
No. 400/87F, blue.. **121**
Vase, 8" h., fluted rim w/beaded handles,
No. 400/87C, clear.. **44**

Vase, 8 1/2" h., No. 400/21, flared rim, clear...... 413
Vase, Peachblow, cased heat sensitive red
over white 180
Vase, two open beaded arms, crimped top,
clear 38
Vegetable bowl, No. 400/69B, clear w/cut-
ting, 8 1/2" d. 55
Wine, No. 3400, clear, 4 oz. 16

Cape Cod
Ashtray, clear... 10
Baked apple dish, clear, 5 3/4" 12
Bar bottle, clear 150
Basket, clear, 11" h. 195
Basket, No. 160/73/0, clear............................... 350
Book end, Lu-tung/Mandarin, No. 5030,
jade.. 85
Bowl, spider, 4 1/2" d., handled, No.
160/180, clear 25
Bowl, 5" w., heart-shaped, No. 160/49H,
clear 20
Bowl, spider, 6 1/2" d., divided, handled,
No. 160/187, clear 32
Bowl, 8 1/2" d., low, clear................................... 34
Bowl, 11" oval, clear 90
Butter dish, cov., clear, 1/4 lb. 42
Butter dish, cov., round, clear............................. 52
Cake stand, No. 160/103D, clear, 11" d. 115
Cake stand, footed, clear, 12" d. 94
Candlestick, single light, clear, 3" h. 22
Candlestick, single light, clear, 5" h. 24
Candy jar, cov., bamboo handle, clear 74
Center bowl, No. 160/75L, ruffled edge,
clear.. 65
Cigarette box, cov., clear.................................... 38
Cigarette lighter, stemmed, purple slag............. 40
Coaster, clear, 3" sq... 10
Coaster, No. 160/78, clear 10

Cape Cod Cocktail

Cocktail, No. 1602, clear, 3 1/2 oz. (ILLUS.)........ 10
Compote, 7" d., No. 160/48B, clear 28
Cookie jar, cov., clear....................................... 110
Cordial, clear, 3 3/4" h. 12
Cordial, No. 1602, milk white, 1 1/2 oz. 15
Creamer, clear, 3" sq.. 38
Creamer, clear, 4 1/2" h....................................... 10
Creamer & open sugar bowl, No. 160/30,
clear, pr. 24
Cruet w/original stopper, No. 160/119,
amber, 4 oz. 28
Cruet w/original stopper, No. 160/119,
Verde green, 4 oz. 45
Cruet w/original stopper, blown, No.
160/70, clear, 5 oz. 60

Cruet w/original stopper, No. 160/70,
clear, 5 oz. 27
Cruet w/original stopper, No. 160/241,
clear, 6 oz. 55
Cup & saucer, clear.. 12
Decanter w/original stopper, clear,
8 1/2" h.. 124
Decanter w/original stopper, clear,
9 3/4" h.. 89
Decanter w/original stopper, ruby-
stained, 9 3/4" h. 119
Decanter w/original stopper, clear, 13" h. 142
Decanter w/original stopper, No. 160/163,
clear, 30 oz. 75
Decanter w/original stopper, square-
shaped, No. 160/212, clear, 24 oz. 80
Decanters w/original stoppers, square-
shaped, clear, in chrome rack w/lock, the
set.. 225
Egg cup, No. 160/225, clear................................ 32
Epergne, bowl w/trumpet, clear 78
Goblet, water, clear, 5 1/2" h. 10
Goblet, water, pink, 6 1/4" h. 28
Goblet, water, amber, 6 1/2" h. 10
Goblet, water, clear, 6 1/2" h. 14
Goblet, magnum, No. 160, clear, 14 oz. 28
Goblet, water, No. 1600, clear, 10 oz. 15
Goblet, water, No. 1602, Verde green,
9 oz. 8
Lamp, hurricane-type, clear, 12" h...................... 96
Mayonnaise bowl, ladle & underplate,
clear, 3 pcs. 36
Mug, clear, 4 3/4" h. 42
Mug, clear, 12 oz. 58
Mustard jar, cover & spoon, clear, 3 pcs. 22
Oyster cocktail, No. 1602, clear 9
Perfume bottle w/original stopper, round,
clear... 48
Pitcher, 8 1/2" h., clear....................................... 94
Pitcher, 10" h., clear.. 240
Pitcher, milk, No. 160/240, clear, 16 oz.............. 50
Plate, 8 1/2" d., amber 8
Plate, 8 1/2" d., pink 19
Plate, 9" d., clear.. 26

Cape Cod Dinner Plate

Plate, dinner, 10" d., No. 160/10D, clear
(ILLUS.) 58
Plate, torte, 13 1/2" d., clear................................ 32
Punch bowl & base, clear, 2 pcs. 125
Relish dish, three-part, oval, No. 160/55,
clear, 9 1/2" l. 18

Relish dish, three-part, No. 160/1602, clear...... 150
Salad serving set, fork & spoon, clear,
9 1/2" l., the set... 28
Salt dip, clear, 2 1/4" d. 16
Salt & pepper mill, amber, pr. 55
Salt & pepper shakers w/original tops,
individual, No. 160/251, clear, pr. 18
Salt & pepper shakers w/original tops,
individual, original factory label, No.
160/251, clear, pr. 25
Salt & pepper shakers w/original tops,
Verde green, pr.. 40
**Salt & pepper shakers w/original tops &
undertray,** clear, the set.................................. 42
Sherbet, No. 1600, clear, 6 oz.............................. 7
Sherbet, tall, No. 1602, Verde green, 6 oz. 15
Sugar bowl, clear, 4 1/4" h. 10
Tray, for creamer & sugar, No. 160/29,
clear, 7" l. 15
Tumbler, flat, clear, 3 3/4" h., 6 oz. 20
Tumbler, flat, clear, 6 1/2" h., 14 oz. 22
Tumbler, iced tea, flat, clear, 5 1/2" h. 18
Tumbler, iced tea, amber, 6" h............................ 12
Tumbler, iced tea, clear, 6" h. 16
Tumbler, iced tea, pink, 6" h. 34
Tumbler, juice, footed, No. 1602, clear,
6 oz. 12
Tumbler, juice, footed, No. 1602, Verde
green, 6 oz. 15
Tumbler, juice, No. 1600, clear, 5 1/4" h.,
6 oz. 12
Tumbler, water, footed, No. 1602, clear, 10
oz. 9
Tumbler, water, No. 160, clear, 10 oz. 12
Vegetable bowl, divided, oval, clear, 11" l. 79
Whiskey set w/metal rack, No. 160/260,
clear bottles w/raised letters "Bourbon,"
"Rye" & "Scotch," the set 650
Wine, clear, 4" h. 6

Free-Hand Ware

Candlestick, slender baluster-form stem
w/cushion foot in clear w/white heart &
vine decoration, a tall cylindrical iridescent dark blue socket, original paper la-
bel, 10" h... 440
Vase, 6 1/2" h., Mosaic design, deep cobalt
blue body shaded & swirled w/opal &
lined in iridescent orange.............................. 489
Vase, 8" h., small swelled base below the
tall slightly flaring cylindrical body w/a
widely flaring flattened & deeply ruffled
rim, iridescent metallic hues of purple,
green & blue in a wavy random design 121
Vase, 8 1/2" h., cylindrical, iridescent green
heart & vine design on a white ground,
marigold lining w/some wear 385
Vase, 8 1/2" h., decorated w/a dark blue
drapery design on a marigold iridescent
ground.. 275
Vase, 8 1/2" h., simple cylindrical form, or-
ange iridescent ground decorated w/blue
hanging heart design, cased over white,
rim possibly ground... 575
Vase, 8 3/4" h., green heart & vine decora-
tion on opaque white body w/iridescent
lustre overall.. 690
Vase, 9 1/2" h., bulbous base w/a wide
flared neck, white cased to a cobalt blue
exterior, interior of rim flashed in brilliant

iridescent orange, polished pontil, early
20th c. 575
Vase, 10" h., bulbous ovoid bottom below a
tall trumpet neck, exterior in a mottled taffeta w/amber shoulder band, slate blue
interior 220
Vase, 10" h., tall slender form, iridescent or-
ange exterior w/deep orange throat 193
Vase, 10 1/2" h., jack-in-the-pulpit-form,
wide flared mouth of opaque white w/or-
ange stretch iridescence, raised on an
elongated stem w/blue pulled loops, on a
blue disk foot w/overall orange & gold iridescence on exterior, polished pontil
w/gold foil label, ca. 1925 1,610
Vase, 10 1/2" h., tall body w/flaring rim, a
white swagged design on an iridescent
ground, stretched multi-hued design at
the rim 523
Vase, 10 3/4" h., very slender baluster-form
body w/flaring short neck, overall orange
iridescence w/a blue pulled drapery de-
sign cased on milk glass 748
Vase, 11" h., slender swelled cylindrical
body w/short rolled neck, overall orange
lustre over a milk glass body, ground
pontil... 98

Miscellaneous Patterns & Lines

Animal covered dish, Atterbury lion, purple
slag 90
Basket, Daisy patt., marigold carnival,
marked "IG" 42
Basket, Daisy patt., marigold carnival, un-
marked.. 48
Basket w/arched overhead handle, Monti-
cello patt., No. 698, clear, 10" h..................... 42
Bowl, pearl amethyst iridescent stretch
glass, Iron Cross mark 100
Bowl-vase, Free-Hand ware, a wide waist-
ed cylindrical body w/a widely flaring six-
ruffle rim, marigold iridescent exterior
decorated w/light blue vines & heart-
shaped leaves, blue rim band, marigold
iridescent interior, original Imperial Free-
Hand label, 7 1/4" d., 5" h. 1,320
Box, cov., model of duck on nest, jade
green slag.. 46
Candlestick, single light, No. 3130, spiral,
green, 3 1/2" h. 24
Candlestick, single light, Packard patt. No.
320, vaseline, 8 1/2" h...................................... 54
Candy box, cov., Zodiac patt., No. 619,
azure blue, carnival.. 54
Compote, No. 3297, shell bowl w/dolphin
stem, black w/gold decoration........................ 140
Creamer & sugar bowl, owl form, red slag,
pr... 60
Cup & saucer, Grape patt., No. 473, rubi-
gold & marigold carnival................................. 62
Decanter w/original stopper, Grape patt.,
marigold carnival, marked "IG"....................... 64
Decanter w/original stopper, Grape patt.,
marigold carnival, unmarked 95
Ivy ball, Hobnail patt., No. 742, black 68
Lamp, Zipper Loop patt., marigold carnival,
8" h. 400
Paperweight, model of a tiger, Heisey
mold, amber & caramel slag........................... 100

Pitcher, crackle Tree of Life, marigold carnival **40**
Pitcher, No. 701, green w/clear reeded applied handle **80**
Pitcher, Windmill patt., marigold carnival, unmarked **70**
Plate, 8" d., Spun patt., reeded, clear **8**
Plate, 8" d., Spun patt., reeded, red **38**

Molly Rose Bowl w/Silver Deposit

Rose bowl, Molly line, black w/silver deposit floral decoration, 5" h. (ILLUS.) **40-50**
Tumbler, crackle Tree of Life, marigold carnival **8**
Tumbler, Hobnail patt., No. 742, clear **14**
Tumbler, Windmill patt., carnival, unmarked **18**
Vase, 4 5/8" h., 7 7/8" d., Free-Hand ware,
a blue rim wrap on a broad & ruffled rim
of opal glass decorated w/mottled blue
hearts on a trailing vine, the interior & exterior flashed orange, polished pontil
w/gold foil Imperial Free Hand label,
ca. 1924 (minor wear) **374**
Vase, Hobnail patt., No. 742, flip, amber **38**
Vase, Loganberry patt., ball top, purple carnival **2,200**
Vase, bud, 5" h., Spun patt., reeded, amber **28**
Vase, 6 1/2" h., Free-Hand ware, wide
ovoid body w/a short trumpet neck, overall marigold iridescence on interior & exterior **138**
Vase, 7 1/2" h., Free-Hand ware, bulbous
ovoid body tapering to a widely flaring
trumpet neck, white opal ground decorated w/wide dark blue swagged bands,
orange iridescent interior **935**
Vase, 8 3/4" h., Free-Hand ware, tall slender cylindrical form w/a slightly flared
base & rim, white opal exterior decorated
w/looped green heart & vine decoration,
gold iridescent interior **495**
Vase, 10" h., Hanging Vine & Heart, white
cased w/orange **450**
Vase, 10" h., Loganberry patt., marigold
carnival **240**
Vase, 10 3/4" h., Free-Hand ware, tall slender baluster-form w/cushion foot & short
flared neck, cobalt blue ground decorated w/overall light blue looping vines &
large opal white heart-shaped leaves **1,595**
Vase, 11 1/2" h., Free-Hand ware, a tall
slender baluster-form body w/a bulbed
neck flared at the top & pulled into three
downward curled loops attaching to the

upper neck, iridescent opal surface decorated overall w/light blue entwining
vines & heart-shaped leaves, iridescent
marigold interior **1,595**
Vase, 12" h., Poppy Show patt., Helios
green carnival **1,050**
Vase, 12" h., Poppy Show patt., marigold
carnival **600**
Vase, fan-shaped, clear **84**
Vase, three looped feet, orange w/blue
Hanging Vine & Heart **650**
Wine, Old Williamsburg patt., amber **18**
Wine, Old Williamsburg patt., Azalea **18**

Kelva

*Kelva was made early in the 20th century by the C.F.
Monroe Co., Meriden, Connecticut, and was a type of
decorated opal glass very like the same company's Wave
Crest and Nakara wares. This type of glass was produced until about the time of the first World War. Also
see NAKARA and WAVE CREST.*

Box w/hinged lid, pink flowers on blue
ground, 6" d., 3 1/2" h. **$775**

Kelva Hexagonal Box

Box w/hinged lid, Hexagonal mold, lid decorated w/a molded yellow rose on a mottled green ground, 3 3/4" d., 2 1/2" h.
(ILLUS.) **750**
Box w/hinged lid, Octagonal mold, lid
enameled w/pink & white flowers on a
mottled green ground, 4" w., 3 3/4" h. **350**
Box w/hinged lid, round, lid decorated
w/pink flowers on a mottled bluish grey
ground, mirror inside the lid, 4 1/2" d. **750**

Kelva Rose Ground Box

Box w/hinged lid, round, lid decorated
w/white flowers & green leaves on a mottled rose ground, 4 1/2" d., 2 1/2" h.
(ILLUS.) **550**

Box w/hinged lid, heavy gold floral decoration on a dark green ground, 5 1/2" d., 5" h. 475

Box w/hinged lid, round, bluish grey flowers on a red ground, 6" d., 3 1/2" h. 750

Humidor w/hinged cover, mottled blue ground, "Cigars" in gold across the front, 5" d. 900

Jewelry dish, dainty pink flowers on a mottled green ground, ornate ormolu handles & rim, signed, overall 4 1/2" w. 200

Watch box, cov., green mottled ground w/dusty rose floral & beige ribbon, heavy beading on cover, ornate ormolu fittings (one bead missing) 600

Kew Blas

In the 1890s the Union Glass Works, Somerville, Massachusetts, produced a line of iridescent glasswares closely resembling Louis Tiffany's wares. The name was derived from an anagram of the name of the factory's manager, William S. Blake.

Kew Blas Candlestick

Candlestick, cylindrical socket w/flattened wide rim raised on a swirled balusterform shaft on a round foot, overall gold iridescence, inscribed mark, 8 1/4" h. (ILLUS.).. $450

Tumbler, cylindrical pinch-sided form, overall gold iridescence, 3 1/4" h........................... 303

Vase, 7" h., elongated ovoid w/flaring rim, gold iridescent & green diagonally striped large fishscale design, engraved mark 900

Vase, 9" h., waisted cylindrical body w/scalloped rim, overall gold iridescence w/carved bees.. 950

Vase, 10" h., cylindrical w/flared base, rim w/alternating peaks & lower scallops, iridescent gold body w/repeating green pulled leaf decoration, inscribed mark 750

Lalique

Fine glass, which includes numerous extraordinary molded articles, has been made by the glasshouse established by René Lalique early in the 20th century in France. The firm was carried on by his son, Marc, until his death in 1977 and is now headed by Marc's daughter, Marie-Claude. All Lalique glass is marked, usually on, or near, the bottom with either an engraved or molded signature. Unless otherwise noted, we list only those pieces marked "R. Lalique" produced before the death of René Lalique in 1945.

Lalique Marks

Ashtray, "Faune," a shallow round clear dish centered by a vertical round clear & frosted disk molded w/a dancing satyr, grey stain, introduced in 1931, 4 1/8" d., 3 3/4" h... $1,035

Ashtray, "Sirènes," a clear & frosted round dish w/raised sides & a wide central knob molded at the top w/two intertwined female figures, blue stain, introduced in 1920, 4 1/2" d. 863

Bowl, 9 3/8" d., "Poissons No. 1," deep rounded sides w/wide flat rim, clear opalescent w/molded spiral design of stylized slender fish, introduced in 1921................. 1,035

Lalique Perruches Bowl

Bowl, 9 3/4" d., "Perruches," round w/upright gently curved sides, clear & frosted opalescent molded w/a band of large parakeets, green stain, introduced in 1931 (ILLUS.) 3,220

Bowl, 12" d., "Tournon," deep rounded flaring form in clear opalescent molded in bold relief w/bouquets of flowers, introduced in 1928 2,300

Candy Box with Molded Roses

Candy box, cov., "Roses en Relief," low wide oblong base w/a wide low domed cover, frosted pink patina, molded across the cover & down the sides w/bands of molded rose blossoms & vines, base molded "Lalique," introduced in 1914, 7" l., 1 3/4" h. (ILLUS.)................................ 13,800

Champagne glasses, "Strasbourg," clear & frosted, each stem molded w/two male grape pressers, introduced in 1926, set of 6.. 1,035

Clock, table model, "Deux Figurines," arched clear glass plate molded w/two frosted classical standing maidens on either side of & supporting a floral wreath surrounding the round dial w/Arabic numerals, mounted on a narrow rectangular tapering patinated bronze base w/small knob feet, introduced in 1926, 15 1/8" h.. **16,100**

Decanter w/stopper, "Reine Marguerite," large rounded base w/two flattened sides molded as large flowerheads, tapering plain neck fitted w/a wide low domed stopper, clear & frosted w/brown enamel detail & stain, 10 3/4" h. **2,300**

Figurine, "Été Surtout Quatre Saisons," clear & frosted figure of a kneeling stylized nude female surrounded w/wheat, representing Summer, introduced in 1939, 7 3/4" h.. **1,955**

Model of a bird, "Pigeon Bruges," clear & frosted large plumb pigeon on a rounded foot, introduced in 1911, 10 1/2" l. **748**

Perfume bottle & stopper, "Au Coeur des Calices," for Coty, tapering domical frosted pale blue base molded w/tiered flower petals, the small molded mouth fitted w/a figural bee stopper, signed "Lalique," 2 5/8" h.. **5,175**

Perfume bottle & stopper, "Bouchon Figurines," upright flattened square bottle in grey & frosted, centered w/an oval reserve w/two back-to-back nude figures holding up & separated by flowering branches, the small cylindrical neck fitted w/an openwork stopper cast as two nude females leaning back & holding up floral garlands, signed "R. Lalique - No. 490," introduced in 1912, 5 1/4" h........................ **8,050**

Lalique Two Pigeons Platter

Platter, 14 3/4" d., "Deux Pigeons," flat round clear disk enameled in black w/two large pigeons perched among curved branches of tiny blossoms, signed, ca. 1920 (ILLUS.) **4,887**

Vase, 4 1/2" h., "Grenade," footed spherical body tapering to a short rolled neck, clear & frosted, molded w/overall bands of stylized rounded flower petals, blue stain, introduced in 1930... **1,380**

Vase, 5 1/4" h., "Canards," tapering ovoid body w/flared neck, clear & frosted decorated w/spiraling bands of stylized ducks

up around the sides, black enamel detail, introduced in 1931 .... **1,610**

Lalique "Pigeons" Vase

Vase, 5 1/4" h., "Pigeons," No. 939, wide ovoid body w/short cylindrical neck, pale blue molded in low relief w/pigeons amidst branches, original white patina, introduced in 1924, inscribed "R. LALIQUE" (ILLUS.) **6,900**

Vase, 6" h., "Fougères," bulbous frosted blue form tapering to a small flared neck, molded w/tiered rows of stylized long leaves w/molded knob buds, white stain, introduced in 1912 .... **5,750**

Vase, 6 3/4" h., "Bagatelles," small cylindrical foot below the wide swelled cylindrical body w/a wide short cylindrical neck, the clear & frosted sides molded in bold relief w/plump birds among foliage, blue stain, introduced in 1939............................ **1,955**

Vase, 7" h., "Dordogne," wide squatty bulbous frosted opalescent body w/a narrow shoulder below the short neck w/wide flattened rim, molded in bold relief around the middle w/two rows of pointed shell-like spirals, blue stain, introduced in 1927 .... **4,600**

Vase, 7" h., "Saint-Francois," frosted trumpet-form w/widely flaring rim, molded in high-relief w/chickadees perched on leafy stems, acid-stamped "R. LALIQUE," introduced in 1930 .... **1,092**

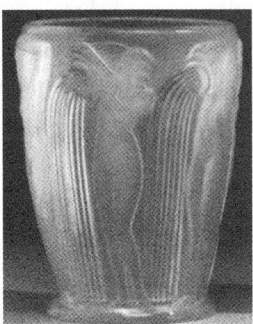

Lalique "Danaides" Vase

Vase, 7 1/8" h., "Danaides," molded foot below the wide gently flaring cylindrical body w/a wide flat mouth, clear & frosted opalescent molded w/full-length figures of female nudes pouring cascades of water from jugs on their shoulders, introduced in 1926 (ILLUS.) **5,750**

Vase, 9" h., "Monnaie du Pape," footed swelled cylindrical body w/short cylindrical neck, clear & frosted deep amber molded overall w/silver dollar plants, introduced in 1914 .... **6,325**

Vase, 9 1/8" h., "Ronces," simple ovoid form tapering to a tiny cylindrical neck, opalescent amber cased over white, molded overall w/intertwining thorny branches, molded "R. LALIQUE," inscribed later "Lalique," introduced in 1921 .... **3,162**

Vase, 10 1/4" h., "Sophora," large wide spherical body w/a wide shoulder centered by a short trumpet neck w/flattened rim, clear & frosted molded w/vertical bands of stylized leafy branches, green stain, introduced in 1926 .... **4,600**

Fine Lalique "Baies" Vase

Vase, 10 1/2" h., "Baies," spherical body w/a small short cylindrical neck, clear & frosted molded overall w/interlacing budding thorny branches, black enamel trim, introduced in 1924 (ILLUS.) **13,800**

Vase, 11" h., "Davos," swelled wide cylindrical body w/a short cylindrical wide mouth, clear plum brown molded overall w/variously sized bubble-like scales forming a geometric design, introduced in 1932 .... **5,463**

Vase, 11 1/4" h., "Acanthes," large ovoid body tapering to a tiny flared mouth, cased deep amber orange, molded w/an overall design of acanthus leaves, signed, introduced in 1921 .... **18,400**

Le Verre Francais

Glassware carrying this marking was produced at the French glass factory founded by Charles Schneider in 1908. A great deal of cameo glass was exported to the United States early in the 20th century and much of it was marketed through Ovingtons in New York City.

Various Le Verre Francais Marks

Le Verre Francais Cameo Vase

Cameo vase, 4 1/8" h., squatty spherical body tapering to a short wide rolled neck, mottled yellow & peach ground overlaid in mottled aubergine & etched around the shoulder w/a band of cats at play above a geometric lower band, engraved signature (ILLUS.) **$1,955**

Cameo vase, 10" h., a bulbous cushion foot & short stem supporting a tall slender swelled cylindrical body, pink overlaid w/dark red shading to dark purple & cameo cut in the "Garance" patt. w/stylized florals, signed **990**

Cameo vase, 13 3/4" h., tapering cylindrical body on a cushion foot, grey mottled w/yellow, overlaid w/pink shading to purple & cut w/three stylized leaves, signed, ca. 1925 .... **805**

Cameo vase, 15 1/4" h., tall tapering cylindrical form w/rounded base & short flared neck, grey w/yellow mottling overlaid w/green infused orange cut w/an Art Deco design of fruits & leaves, apparently unmarked **1,344**

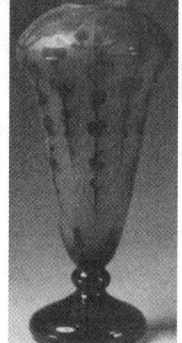

Le Verre Francais Cameo Vase

Cameo vase, 19 1/4" h., tapering ovoid body on a knopped stem & cushion foot, grey internally decorated w/pink, overlaid w/mottled pink & purple & cut w/stylized flowers & tendrils of berries above a brickwork border, signed (ILLUS.) **2,185**

Cameo vase, 19 3/4" h., tall swelled & tapering cylindrical body on a cushion foot, lemon yellow internally decorated w/purple spots, overlaid w/orange & cut w/stylized poppies, signed, ca. 1925 .... **2,300**

Three Tall Le Verre Francais Vases

Cameo vase, 23 3/8" h., cushion foot taper-ing to a tall slender ovoid body w/a flat mouth, mottled yellow & orange overlaid w/orange shading to brown & cut w/a garden of stylized peonies above a leaft-ip border, signed in cameo "Charder" & inscribed "Le Verre Francais," ca. 1928 (ILLUS. right) **2,415**

Cameo vase, 25" h., cushion foot support-ing a bulbous lower body tapering sharp-ly to a tall slender slightly waisted cyindri-cal neck w/flared rim, grey mottled w/pink & overlaid w/purple & cut w/stylized dahl-ias, signed, ca. 1925-27 (ILLUS. center)... **2,760**

Cameo vase, 25" h., tall tapering ovoid body w/a cushion foot & small domed mouth, grey mottled w/pale yellow shad-ing to blue, overlaid w/yellow shading to orange & cut w/stylized palm trees, signed in cameo "Charder," inscribed "Le Verre Francais," ca. 1925 .... **4,600**

Cameo vase, 26 1/2" h., thick cushion foot tapering to a knopped stem below the tall slender ovoid body tapering to a small flared rim, grey overlaid w/tangerine shading to red & traces of violet & cut w/four vertical bands each decorated w/six stylized flowerheads, signed in cameo "Charder," inscribed "Le Verre Francais," ca. 1928 (ILLUS. left) **2,587**

Legras

Cameo and enameled glass somewhat similar to that made by Gallé, Daum Nancy and other factories of the period was made at the Legras works in Saint Denis, France, late last century and until the outbreak of World War I.

Typical Legras Mark

Cameo vase, 13 3/4" h., tall slender cylin-drical body tapering slightly to a bulbed neck w/flat rim, grey w/citrine shading & internal blue & green mottling overlaid in powder blue opalescent & cut w/apple blossoms & branches enameled in light green, brown & amber, signed in cameo **$2,016**

Vase, 7 1/4" h., dimpled ovoid body, etched & painted w/sea fauna, signed **460**

Vase, 8 1/4" h., swelled cylindrical form w/a short closed neck, heavy walled olive green acid-etched w/fruit-laden branches on a textured ground & then decorated w/gilt & enamel highlights in ochre & grey, incised signature, ca. 1920 (enam-el wear) **460**

Libbey

Libbey Silhouette Elephant Compote

In 1878, William L. Libbey obtained a lease on the New England Glass Company of Cambridge, Massachu-setts, changing the name to the New England Glass Works, W.L. Libbey and Son, Proprietors. After his death in 1883, his son, Edward D. Libbey, continued to operate the company at Cambridge until 1888 when the factory was closed. Edward Libbey moved to Toledo, Ohio, and set up the company subsequently known as Libbey Glass Co. During the 1880s, the firm's master technician, Joseph Locke, developed the now much desired colored art glass lines of Agata, Amberina, Peach Blow and Pomona. Renowned for its Cut Glass of the Brilliant Period (see CUT GLASS), the company continues in operation today as Libbey Glassware, a division of Owens-Illinois, Inc.

Bowl, 5 1/2" d., 2 1/2" h., Amberina, bul-bous base w/rectangular rim, ribbed pat-tern **$300**

Bowl, 6" d., Peking patt., pink, scalloped edge, Libbey-Nash series **125**

Bowl, 6" d., 4" h., Amberina, paneled optic design w/ruffled rim, signed **595**

Candlesticks, pedestal foot supporting a bulbous base tapering to a tall cylindrical neck, intaglio-cut floral design, 12" h., pr. **550**

Champagne, Silhouette patt., clear bowl, opalescent figural squirrel stem **163**

Claret, Silhouette patt., clear bowl, opales-cent figural bear stem, Libby-Nash series **225**

Cocktail, Silhouette patt., clear bowl, frost-ed figural bear stem **95**

Cocktail, Silhouette patt., clear bowl, opalescent figural kangaroo stem, signed, 6" h. **100-125**

Cocktail, Silhouette patt., clear bowl, opalescent figural squirrel stem, signed, 6" h........ **95**

Compote, open, 7 1/2" d., 3 1/4" h., Amberina, a flattened & widely flaring rim on a rounded bowl raised on a short knop stem w/a round foot, marked "Amberina" & "Libbey" in a circle, ca. 1917...................... **550**

Compote, open, 11" d., 7 1/2" h., Silhouette patt., wide crystal bowl on an opalescent figural elephant stem, signed (ILLUS.) **750**

Console set: bowl & 12" h., candlesticks; cobalt blue over clear, polished pontils, 3 pcs... **750**

Cordial, Silhouette patt., clear bowl, opalescent figural greyhound stem **175**

Cordial, Silhouette patt., figural kangaroo stem.. **110**

Cordial, Silhouette patt., figural monkey stem.. **150**

Cornucopia-vases, heavy clear crystal cornucopias w/a bold twist in the body & upright trumpet ends, w/a pair of ball supports, marked, 1940s, 12" l., 6 1/2" h., pr. (wear, some scratches).................................. **275**

Maize Celery Vase

Maize celery vase, clear w/amber iridescent kernels & blue husks (ILLUS.)............... **225**

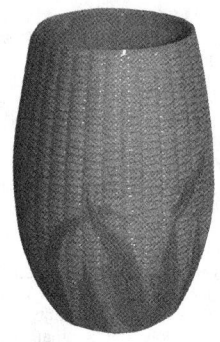

Maize Celery with Yellow Husks

Maize celery vase, creamy white ground w/yellow husks, 6 1/2" h. (ILLUS.)................ **225**

Maize salt shaker, original top, condiment size, creamy opaque **125**

Maize sugar shaker w/original lid, creamy opaque w/green husks **325-375**

Maize sugar shaker w/original top, creamy opaque w/blue husks......................... **325**

Model of a shoe, embossed florals on the toe, peach shoe w/black heel........................ **175**

Punch cup, pressed clear petal-form marked "World's Fair 1893," impressed "Libbey Glass Co., Toledo, Ohio - World's Fair" inside **75**

Rose bowl, round w/eight-crimp rim, pink w/light ribbing in white, glossy finish, probably produced at the 1893 Columbian Exposition **330**

Sherbet, low, Silhouette patt., clear bowl, opalescent figural rabbit stem, Libby-Nash series **75-100**

Tumblers, Currier & Ives Classics Collection, 12 oz.., set of 4, mint in original box........ **75**

Vase, 8" h., clear pedestal base, white opal ground w/pink pulled feather design, signed in pontil... **750**

Vase, 9" h., two applied handles, fuchsia flower etching on a clear ground, signed **150**

Vase, 10" h., turquoise zipper pattern on a clear ground, signed **475**

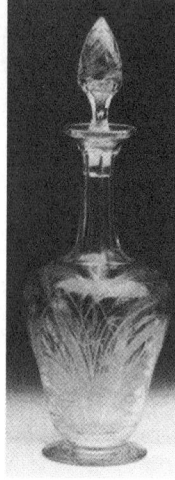

Engraved Libbey Decanter

Decanter w/pointed teardrop stopper, the clear footed inverted pear-form body tapering to a slender panel-cut neck w/flared rim, the body engraved w/a design of long-stemmed wheat & grain grasses w/an elaborate monogram, the stopper also engraved, signed, 13" h. (ILLUS.)... **650**

Dinner bell, etched "1893 World's Fair" & molded w/"1893 World's Columbian Xposition (sic)," frosted glass handle & metal clapper, 5 3/4" h. **285**

Goblet, Silhouette patt., clear bowl, opalescent figural monkey stem.............................. **175**

Goblet, water, Silhouette patt., clear bowl, opalescent figural cat stem............................ **225**

Vase, 11" h., Amberina, #3304, ca. 1917.......... **750**
Vase, 15" h., lily-shaped, Amberina, signed, ca. 1917 .... **1,200**
Wine, Silhouette patt., black figural polar bear stem, signed, 6" h. **125**
Wine, Silhouette patt., opalescent figural kangaroo stem, signed, 6" h. **135**
Wine, Silhouette patt., opalescent figural monkey stem, signed, 6" h. **125**

Loetz

Iridescent glass, some of it somewhat resembling that of Tiffany and other contemporary glasshouses, was produced by the Bohemian firm of J. Loetz Witwe of Klostermule and is referred to as Loetz. Some cameo pieces were also made. Not all pieces are marked.

Loetz Mark

Bowl, 6 3/4" d., 2 1/2" h., ruffled sides, blue oil spotting on a gold iridescent ground, blue iridescent interior **$275**
Cameo bowl, 5" d., 3" h., a deep wide cupped form raised on three ball feet, white cased in amethyst & cut vining leaf & blossom design around the sides **660**

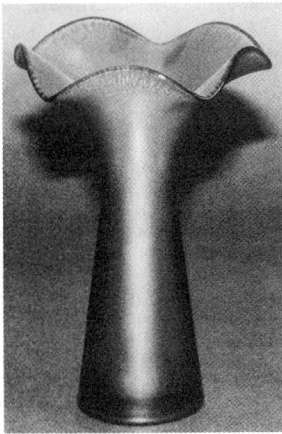

Simple Loetz Iridescent Vase

Vase, slightly tapering cylindrical body w/a widely flaring six-ruffle rim, dark golden iridescence w/blue highlights, signed (ILLUS.).. **275**
Vase, 1 3/4" h., 1 3/4" d., miniature, small spherical body w/a small flared neck, loop handles from rim to shoulder, overall gold iridescence w/oil spotting **468**
Vase, 2" h., miniature, footed simple ovoid body w/a short flared neck, overall golden iridescence w/bluish highlights & oil spotting **303**
Vase, 3 1/8" h., miniature, a tricorner rim on a pinched ovoid body, ambergris deco-

rated w/foliate silver overlay over a light blue iridescent surface, silver marked "Sterling" w/a faint hallmark, polished pontil, late 19th c. (irregular edges on overlay) **748**
Vase, 5 1/8" h., footed spherical body w/a flaring cylindrical neck, applied scrolled loop handles from side of neck to shoulder, iridescent pale green ground decorated w/an iridescent blue oil spot design, silver overlay cast in a scrolling foliate design in bands down the sides & the handles encased in silver **2,530**
Vase, 5 1/4" h., bulbous ovoid body w/dimpled rounded shoulder & widely flaring three-lobed neck, gold iridescent body w/overall small dimples **220**
Vase, 5 3/4" h., large ovoid body w/dimpled sides & a short tri-lobed rolled neck, iridescent green ground decorated w/large scattered dark blue oil spots.......................... **798**

Loetz Vase with Floral Silver Overlay

Vase, 6 1/2" h., sharply tapering cylindrical form, swirled iridescent green rising to pearly blue, silver overlay Art Nouveau looping vines & blossoms, polished pontil, rubbed marks on silver, ca. 1905 (ILLUS.) **748**
Vase, 8 1/4" h., a thick cushion foot supporting a very slender baluster-form body w/a short flared neck, amber w/overall blue wavy iridescent finish & applied w/amber tendrils twisting down the sides, signed, based on drawing No. 1/65, ca. 1900....... **6,325**
Vase, 11 1/4" h., bottle-form, a bulbous ovoid body w/a wide rounded shoulder centered by a tall slender waisted neck, amber w/overall wavy blue iridescence, encased overall w/silver overlay in a delicate scrolling Art Nouveau design, unsigned, ca. 1900.................................... **3,162**
Vase, 11 1/2" h., baluster-form w/a short crimped & flared rim, citrine shaded w/cranberry mottling & pulled green leaves under an iridescent finish, ground pontil, unmarked... **1,232**
Vase, 15" h., round cushion foot below the tall slightly flaring cylindrical body

w/pinched-in designs up the sides, overall blue & gold iridescence, engraved sig-
nature **2,640**
Vase, 18" h., squatty bulbous wide base
centered by a tall slender & slightly flaring
neck w/a flared & crimped rim, green iridescent ground decorated w/a blue pap-
illon finish of iridescent oil spots **3,850**

Lustres

Lustres were Victorian glass vase-like decorative objects often hung around the rim with prisms. They were generally sold as matched pairs to be displayed on fireplace mantels. A wide range of colored glasswares were used in producing lustres and pieces were often highlighted with colored enameled decoration.

Fine Bristol Glass Decorated Lustre

Bristol, milky white w/a wide squatty bulbous top bowl w/a high four-lobed rolled
& crimped rim & a ringed base raised on
a slender ringed pedestal above the
stepped cushion foot, the top bowl finely
enameled w/delicate florals, the base of
the bowl hung w/two rows of long facet-
cut triangular prisms in two sizes,
16 1/2" h., pr. (ILLUS. of one) **$1,320**
Cut overlay, cranberry cut to clear, the wide
round bowl-form top w/ruffled, flared rim
cut w/a leafy vine design, raised on a
slender slightly tapering standard on a
round domed foot with further cut panels
& gilt band trim, hung w/large triangular
cut spearpoint prisms, 13" h. **550**
Cut-overlay, white cut to emerald green, a
slender trumpet-form bowl w/a curved
crown-form pointed notch rim, each point
cut w/an oblong panel, the sides of the
bowl w/further long slender oblong panels, the flaring domed foot cut w/spear-
point panels, fine gilt floral trim, each suspending ten long cut spearpoint crystal
prisms, 19th c., 10" h., pr. (some prism
chips) **798**

Deep Green Mantel Lustre

Deep green, the wide paneled socket-form
top w/flared rim above a shallow round
mid drip pan raised on a ringed paneled
shaft w/a ringed botton on the paneled
foot, the pan hung w/clear facet-cut
prisms, 10" h., pr. (ILLUS. of one) **518**
Ruby, a squatty bulbous round top bowl w/a
high flared & crown-cut top rim, raised on
a slender baluster-form pedestal & round
stepped foot, the bowl enameled in white
w/daisy-like blossoms & leaves, white
dot trim, long facet-cut triangular prisms
suspended from base of bowl, deep col-
or, 10 1/2" h., pr. **420**

Milk Glass

Opaque white glass, or "opal," has been called "milk-white glass" perhaps to distinguish it from transparent or "clear-white glass." Resembling fine white porcelain, it was viewed as an inexpensive substitute. Opacity is obtained by adding bone ash or oxide of tin to clear molten glass. By the addition of various coloring agents, the opaque mixture can be turned into blue milk glass, or pink, yellow, green, caramel, even black milk glass. Collectors of milk glass now accept not only the white variety but virtually any opaque color and color mixtures, including slag or marbled glass. It has been made in numerous forms and shapes in this country and abroad from about the first quarter of the 19th century. Many of the items listed here were also made in colored opaque glass which collectors call blue or green or black 'milk glass.' It is still being produced, and there are many reproductions of earlier pieces. Pieces are all-white unless otherwise noted. Also see PATTERN GLASS and WESTMORELAND.

Chicks on Round Basket Dish

Animal covered dish, Chicks on Round Basket, Westmoreland Specialty Company, old paint, early 20th c., 4 1/2" w., 3" h. (ILLUS.) **$95**

Plaque, Lincoln, Westmoreland, rare original, excellent, 8 1/4" l. **305**

Plaque, Madonna, relief-molded three dimensional design, 5 1/4" l. (small chip on back edge) **50**

Plaque, Sunken Rabbit with Clover, some paint, very good, 5 1/2" l. **370**

Plate, 6 1/4" d., Mother Goose patt., w/bunnies in relief **125**

Plate, 6 3/8" d., "Easter Lay," chicks w/floral banner w/musical note, White, excellent **90**

Plate, 7 1/4" d., "Easter," chick & basket of eggs, excellent paint, very good **50**

Plate, 7 1/4" d., "Easter," Chicks, leaf & loop border, gold, yellow & green paint, Westmoreland, excellent **25**

Plate, 7 1/4" d., "Easter," Setting Hen and Chicks, slight gold paint **45**

Plate, 7 1/4" d., Pussy Cat, good paint, excellent **470**

Plate, 7 1/4" d., Queen Victoria profile w/some gilding, club & fan border (age cracks in bowl of plate) **210**

Plate, 7 1/4" d., sunken Rabbitt **45-55**

Plate, 7 1/4" d., Taft Campaign **60**

Plate, 7 1/4" d., Wm. McKinley & Wife & their home in Canton, Ohio w/"IT IS GOD'S WAY HIS WILL BE DONE," **125**

Plate, 7 1/2" d., "Easter Opening," two chicks emerging from eggs & lily-of-the-valley, excellent paint, very good **70-95**

Plate, 7 1/2" d., Easter Sermon, no paint, very good **160**

Fishnet & Poppies Syrup Pitcher

Syrup pitcher w/original top, Fishnet & Poppies patt. (ILLUS.) **175**

Moser

Ludwig Moser opened his first glass shop in 1857 in Karlsbad, Bohemia (now Karlovy Vary, in the former Czechoslovakia). Here he engraved and decorated fine glasswares especially to appeal to rich visitors to the local health spa. Later other shops were opened in various cities and throughout the 19th and early 20th century lovely, colorful glasswares, many beautifully enameled, were produced by Moser's shops and reached a wide market in Europe and America. Ludwig died in 1916 and the firm continued under his sons. They were forced to merge with the Meyer's Nephews glass factory after World War I. The glassworks were sold out of the Moser family in 1933.

Bowl, 7 1/2" d., 5" h., rounded w/a fold-over top edge, decorated in enameled colorful flowers on a blue ground on the orange body, applied amber feet **$330**

Cameo vase, 8" h., 7" d., wide bulbous ovoid body tapering slightly to the wide flared rim, deep amethyst cut to deep amber & decorated w/a continuous tropical landscape of elephants feeding among palm trees, trimmed w/white & gold enameling, gold lines around the rim & base, signed in raised gold "Moser - Karlsbad" & "R.W." as well as a script signature on the base **3,575**

Cruet w/stopper, bulbous amethyst body shading to clear, decorated w/multicolored enameled flowers, applied handle, 7 3/4" h. **550**

Ewers, bulbous cobalt blue body trimmed in gold & encrusted w/gold & white enameled flowers, 13 1/2" h., pr. **385**

Moser Flashed Finger Bowl & Plate

Finger bowl & underplate, dark green flashed on clear, a deep rounded bowl w/scalloped rim on a matching underplate, each etched w/paneled scenes of pairs of birds in clear between etched green trees & ground, bowl 4 1/2" d., plate 7" d., pr. (ILLUS.) **400**

Goblet, Middle Eastern-style decoration enameled in blues, reds, green & yellow on a white ground w/gold borders, 5 3/4" h. **385**

Moser Cranberry & Clear Stemware

Stemware set: six wines, six tumblers & four cordials; the wines w/deep rounded ruby bowls ornately enameled in gilt & raised on a finely ringed trumpet stem, slender slightly tapering cylindrical ruby tumblers w/ornate enameling & four ruby-bowled cordials on clear stems w/ornate enameling, the set (ILLUS.) 500

Vase, 6 1/4" h., hexagonal faceted form, heavy walled clear w/a classical gilt frieze band of Amazon women, acid stamped mark, ca. 1925.................... 144

Vase, 8 1/2" h., Alexandrite, spherical, lavender w/acid-etched & wheel-cut tropical fish & sea horses in an underwater scene, acid-stamped "Moser - MM," designed ca. 1930s......................... 2,012

Vase, 10" h., flared cylindrical form, heavy walls in smoky grey, facet-cut panels in four horizontal bands, unsigned, ca. 1925 (minute nicks)......................... 259

Mt. Washington

A wide diversity of glass was made by the Mt. Washington Glass Company of New Bedford, Massachusetts, between 1869 and 1900. It was succeeded in 1900 by the Pairpoint Corporation. Miscellaneous types are listed below.

Bell, white satin enameled w/pink florals & gold trim, original clapper, 5" h..................... $150

Boudoir bottles w/original blown stoppers, decorated w/large shaded yellow roses, 9 1/4" h., pr..................... 145

Bowl, 4 1/2 x 4 1/2", pillow-shaped, satin Diamond Quilted patt., creamy white ground decorated w/pink enameled florals & a yellow rim.......................... 275

Bowl, 8 1/2" d., 3 1/2" h., "Napoli," clear ground, interior decorated w/h.p. flowers & exterior decorated w/gold outlining of the flowers, signed.......................... 750

Box w/hinged cover, colorless frosted rounded & molded swirl design decorated in the Royal Flemish manner w/yellow blossoms on leafy branches, central enamel outlined cartouche w/single red bead, gilt-metal hinged rims, 7" d., 4" h. (wear, no lining).......................... 2,645

Box w/hinged cover, round, squatty bulbous base w/low domed cover joined by fancy gold-washed silver plate rim & hinge, the cover decorated w/a scene of a monk drinking a glass of red wine, shaded green ground on cover & base, artist-signed, original satin lining, 5 1/4" d., 3 1/4" h.......................... 750

Bride's basket, cased bowl w/pointed & ruffled rim, shaded rose interior, white exterior, ornate footed silver plate frame w/scrolling handle, 10 1/4" d. bowl, framed 12" w., 12 1/4" h.......................... 550

Bride's basket, pink shaded to white satin Hobnail patt., w/applied blue rim, on a tall footed Barbour silver plate frame w/large parrots on the handles, bowl, 9" d., 4 3/4" h., overall 13 1/2" d.......................... 950

Celery tray w/original silver plate holder, acid-etched deep cranberry to clear floral

design, patent dated Aug. 22, 1893, holder marked "Pairpoint," 2 pcs.......................... **425**

Collars & cuffs box, cov., white opal wide short cylindrical box in the form of two collars w/a big bow in the front, the cover decorated w/Oriental poppies in shades of pink & orange w/a silver poppy finial w/gold trim, the sides of the base also w/Oriental poppies & gold trim, the bow at the bottom front in bright blue w/white polka dots & a buckle at the back, signed on the base "Patent applied for April 10, 1894," large.......................... **950**

Compote, open, 9 1/2" h., "Napoli," clear w/disk foot & tall slender stem supporting a low widely flaring ruffled bowl, enameled in the bowl w/blue, yellow, purple & red blossoms & green leaves, further leafage down the stem, traces of gilt outlining, unmarked.......................... **308**

Condiment set: salt & pepper shakers, cov. mustard pot & holder; robin's egg blue ground decorated w/daisies, silver plate holder w/swan-shaped feet & center ring handle signed "Wilcox," 4 pcs.......................... **275**

Melon-form Crown Milano Cracker Jar

Cracker jar, cov., melon-ribbed squatty white opal body decorated w/blackberries & green leaves, silver plate rim, domed cover & scroll-trimmed bail handle, silver marked w/Pairpoint logo, 5" h. (ILLUS.).......................... 750

Creamer & cov. sugar bowl, "Albertine," deeply ribbed milk white body w/gold trim, silver plate cover marked "MW," creamer & sugar bowl signed w/Wreath & Crown, pr.......................... 900

Cruet w/original thorn stopper, applied frosted twig handle, apricot Diamond Quilted satin ground (chip on stopper) 450

Dresser box, cov., round footed silver plate box w/a hinged lid inset w/a round opal glass disk h.p. w/delicate flower clusters, satin-lined, base w/the Pairpoint mark, 4 1/2" d., 1 3/4" h. (silver & satin worn)......... 275

Dresser tray, free-form shape w/three turned-in scallops, h.p. purple irises & green leaves on a white satin ground, 8 x 8".......................... 275

Flower bowl, raised satin Diamond Quilted patt., decorated w/a soft pink rim & enameled bouquets of yellow & white forget-me-nots, 4 x 4 1/2", 3 1/4" h. 350

Rare Colonial Ware Lamp

Lamp, banquet-style, Colonial Ware, spherical ball shade on a metal ring & burner above a small squatty bulbous font w/ribbed scroll upturned handles above the tall slender shaft flaring to a wide squatty bulbous base, shiny opaque ground decorated down the side of the base w/a wide gilded ribbon of glass & h.p. on the shade w/a gilt lattice background at the lower section of the base, marked, all original, 38" h. (ILLUS.) **12,650**

Mustard pot, cov., bulbous ribbed body, decorated w/florals, silver plate rim & cover... 325

Photo box, decorated overall w/gold scrolls & enameled blue forget-me-nots, satin finish, 3 3/4 x 5" 135

Pitcher, 4 1/4" h., bulbous ribbed body in light blue shaded to white w/a satin finish, robin's egg blue interior...................................... 94

Pitcher, 8 3/4" h., shaded pink mother-of-pearl satin Diamond Quilted patt., wide ovoid body tapering to a wide neck w/a tricorner rim w/crimping at the back & a wide smooth spout at the front, the sides enameled w/large white stylized flowers, applied clear reeded handle 880

Powder box, cov., round, h.p. violets on base & cover 75

Rare Mt. Washington Punch Bowl

Punch bowl on stand, decorated in the Royal Flemish manner, deep rounded bowl w/a flaring & notched rim, domed base, the bowl decorated w/three reserves of Palmer Cox Brownies in comic scenes involving a keg of ale, gilt scrolling trim, some gold loss, chip on base insert edge, 16" d., 13 1/2" h. (ILLUS.)....... **20,000**

Ring holder, saucer base supports a beaded ring-stick, satin white ground enameled w/blue forget-me-nots............................... 85

Rose bowl, bulbous base w/rim flaring to twelve protruding "fingers," white satin ground decorated w/lavender pansies & yellow rim, 4" d., 3" h. 375

Rose bowl, crystal w/optic ribbing, the rim highlighted in gold, green ivy leaf decoration w/rust-colored stems w/petite pink & yellow blossoms 485

Salt dip, individual, ribbed opal ground decorated w/a beaded gold rim & colored florals 110

Salt & pepper shakers w/original lids, cylindrical w/vertical ribbing, floral decoration, resilvered handled frame, the set 325

Salt & pepper shakers w/original lids, bulbous blue optic ribbed form enameled w/colorful florals, fitted in a marked Pairpoint silver plate footed stand w/central loop handle, 4 3/4" h., the set 770

Salt, Pepper & Sugar Shakers

Salt & pepper shakers w/original metal lids, egg-shaped, one decorated w/fuschia blossoms & the other w/a band of ivy, 2 1/2" h., pr. (ILLUS. left & right) 325

Salt & pepper shakers w/original tops, egg-shaped, reclining-type, souvenir of "Columbian 1893 Exposition," pr. 375

Salt & pepper shakers w/original tops, fig-shaped, white opal, pr................................ 450

Salt & pepper shakers w/original tops, ribbed pillar-form, white opal, in a resilvered silver plate frame, the set..................... 425

Salt & pepper shakers w/original tops, ribbed white ground, one decorated w/oak leaves & cobalt blue dotting, the other w/oak leaves & cobalt blue dotted flowers, in a fancy footed & handled silver plate holder, the set................................. 375

Salt shaker w/original top, egg-shaped, decorated w/a band of red berries & green leaves 110

Salt shaker w/original top, egg-shaped, decorated w/enameled Shasta daisies & leaves, shaded pink ground 85

Salt shaker w/original top, egg-shaped, embossed "Egg in Blossom" & trimmed in gold... 110

Salt shaker w/original top, figural cockle shell, decorated w/blue & yellow florals on a white satin ground................................. 750

Sugar shaker w/original metal lid, fig-shaped, shaded pale yellow to creamy opal, enameled w/dainty flowers & foliage, 3 3/4" h.. **2,310**

Sugar shaker w/original metal lid, egg-shaped, white satiny ground decorated w/a band of pink apple blossoms & green leaves, 4 1/4" h. (ILLUS. center w/salt & peppers).......................... 375

Sugar shaker w/original metal lid, egg-shaped, clear cut glass in an overall fan design, 4 1/2" h.. 1,045

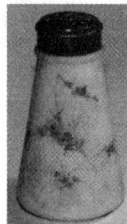

Tapering Cylindrical Sugar Shaker

Sugar shaker w/original metal lid, tapering cylindrical form, satin white ground decorated overall w/delicate stems of blue forget-me-nots, 4 3/4" h. (ILLUS.)......... 400

Sugar shaker w/original top, egg-shaped, white opal w/shaded yellow satin ground h.p. w/pink wild roses & green shadow leaves.............................. 350

Syrup pitcher w/original top, cannon ball-shaped, h.p. roses & foliage on a white opal ground, 5 3/4" h. 275

Tazza, cornflower blue bowl w/engraved floral decoration, silver plate pedestal base w/three dolphin-shaped feet, signed............. 450

Toothpick holder, bulbous melon-lobed body, decorated w/h.p. blue florals on a shaded yellow to white ground...................... 150

Vase, 5 1/2" h., melon-ribbed body w/ruffled rim, apricot mother-of-pearl satin Rain-drop patt., white lining................................... 250

Rare Mt. Washington "Lava" Vase

Vase, 6" h., "Lava," wide ovoid body tapering to a trumpet neck, applied reeded black ring shoulder handles (ILLUS.) 2,000-2,800

Vase, 6" h., 5 3/4" d., footed squatty bulbous body tapering to a short cylindrical neck flaring to a four-fold rim, twenty-four swirling molded ribs in body, decorated w/blue & white forget-me-nots, signed....... 1,200

Vase, 9" h., 5 1/2" w., footed bottle form w/tall cylindrical neck, "Pairpoint Delft" opal white ground decorated in pink w/a scene of a windmill in a landscape w/a small figure, gold trim on the base & top 375

Vase, 10 5/8" h., slender cylindrical base flaring to a fluted rim, rim applied w/wide clear edging, pale water green satin ground decorated w/floral designs in heavy raised enamels 550

Vase, 11 1/2" h., decorated w/enameled spider mums & leaves & heavy gold branches, signed.. 950

Vase, 13 1/2" h., pinched-form, white opal ground decorated w/enameled flowers in pink, gold & brown, marked at the base w/numbers & letter "P".. 550

Vase, 14" h., ruffled rim, Delft blue h.p. windmill scene on white ground...................... 375

Nakara

Like Kelva, Nakara was made early in this century by the C.F. Monroe Company. For details see WAVE CREST.

Box w/hinged cover, decorated w/h.p. cupids on a blue ground, 3" d............................ $425

Small Nakara Box with Flowers

Box w/hinged cover, Hexagonal mold, the top w/wide shaded pink angled panels decorated w/large daisy-like blossoms alternating w/tan panels w/white beading, the base w/a shaded pink ground decorated w/large white blossoms, signed, 3 1/4" w., 3" h. (ILLUS.)..................... 375

Box w/hinged cover, Hexagonal mold, green ground w/pink roses on the top & base, 4" w... 425

Box w/hinged cover, h.p. pink daisies decoration on a blue ground, 4" d., 2 3/4" h....... 325

Box w/hinged cover, Octagonal mold, lemon yellow shaded to deep peach ground decorated w/h.p. orchid-like blossoms in shades of orchid w/green foliage & white beading, 6" w. 550

Nakara Box with Portrait Decoration

Box w/hinged cover, round, Burmese coloring w/18th century courting couple on the cover, 6" d. (ILLUS.) **1,250**

Box w/hinged cover, yellow shaded to green ground decorated w/pink & white flowers outlined in gold, white beading on cover, 6" d. **875**

Box w/hinged cover, Crown mold, cover decorated w/five h.p. roses on an olive green ground, sides w/similar decoration, 8" d., 5" h. **1,750**

Cigar humidor, cov., blue mottled ground decorated w/h.p. pink flowers, "Cigars" in gold on the side **950**

Dresser box w/hinged cover, Bishop's Hat mold, blue ground finely decorated w/purple violets, original lining, wide gilt-metal rim fittings & base band w/pierced scroll feet, 4 3/4" w., 4 3/4" h. **798**

Dresser box w/hinged cover, Crown mold, shaded dark gold ground decorated w/h.p. large white & blue daisies, original lining & interior mirror, 8 1/2" w. **2,090**

Fernery, deep wide cylindrical form w/rounded rims & a gilt-metal rim band, a dark green washed ground enameled w/large pink blossoms on scrolling stems trimmed w/white beading, marked, 8" d. **644**

Humidor, cov., decorated w/an owl sitting in a tree, metal lid **1,500**

Salt shaker w/original metal top, concave bulb shape, decorated w/a transfer scene of Niagara Falls applied over a tan painted background, 2 5/8" h. **175**

Vase, 8" h., squatty bulbous base tapering to a tall cylindrical neck, h.p. florals & white beaded decoration on a blue shaded to yellow ground, w/decorative footed ormolu base **375**

Vase, 13 1/2" h., footed, burnt orange ground decorated w/purple irises **1,500**

Tall Nakara Vase

Vase, 15 3/4" h., tall slender baluster-form body w/a wide flaring mouth, decorated w/large pink & white flowers on a shaded pale green ground (ILLUS.) **2,000**

New Martinsville

The New Martinsville Glass Mfg. Co. opened in New Martinsville, West Virginia in 1901 and during its first period of production came out with a number of colored *opaque pressed glass patterns. They also developed an art glass line they named "Muranese," which collectors refer to as "New Martinsville Peach Blow." The factory burned in 1907 but reopened later that year and began focusing on production of various clear pressed glass patterns, many of which were then decorated with gold or ruby staining or enameled decoration. After going through receivership in 1937, the factory again changed the focus of its production to more contemporary glass lines and figural animals. The firm was purchased in 1944 by The Viking Glass Company (later Dalzell-Viking).*

Covered Batter Jug

Batter jug, cov., dark green (ILLUS.) **$95**

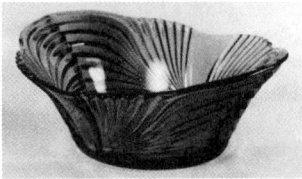

No. 18 Bowl

Bowl, 15" oval, No. 18, amber (ILLUS.) **90**

Bride's basket, Muranese, vivid gold iridescence in ornate silver-plated holder, 9" **400**

Butter dish, cov., Carnation patt. (No. 88 Line), clear w/ruby-stain & gold decoration **275**

Modernistic Candleholders

Candleholders, Modernistic patt. (No. 33 Line), light green w/cut decoration, pr. (ILLUS.) **125**

Candy box, cov., Janice patt. (No. 45 Line), light blue **125**

Candy box, cov., Modernistic patt. (No. 33 Line), black w/traces of silver overlay **90**

Celery vase, Rock Crystal patt. (No. 49 Line), overall gold decorated **160**

Moondrops Comport & Sherbet

Comport, 4" d., stemmed, Moondrops patt.
(No. 37 Line), cobalt blue (ILLUS. left) **40**
Comport, No. 35 (Statesman), jade green,
small **45-50**

Rock Crystal Child's Creamer

Creamer, child's, Rock Crystal patt. (No. 49
Line), overall gold decorated (ILLUS.) **125**
Creamer, Klear-Kut (No. 705 Line), clear
w/ruby-stain... **185**
Creamer, Old Glory patt. (No. 719 Line),
clear w/gold decoration **75**
Creamer & sugar bowl, Modernistic patt.
(No. 33 Line), green satin finish, pr. **110**

Silver Overlay Creamer & Sugar Bowl

Creamer & sugar bowl, Modernistic patt.
(No. 33 Line), opaque jade green w/Call
of the Wild silver overlay, pr (ILLUS.) **200**
Creamer & sugar bowl, Moondrops patt.
(No. 37 Line), amber, pr. **45**
Cup & saucer, No. 34 (Addie), ruby, pr. **20**

No. 35 Cup & Saucer

Cup & saucer, No. 35 (Statesman), jade
green, pr. (ILLUS.) **25**
Finger bowl, Rock Crystal patt. (No. 49
Line), overall gold decorated **100**
Flower bowl, Janice patt. (No. 45 Line),
crimped rim, light blue **95**
Goblet, luncheon, Janice patt. (No. 45
Line), light blue **35**
Ivy vase, Janice patt. (No. 45 Line), light
blue **65**
Mug, handled, Moondrops patt. (No. 37 Line),
amber, large (ILLUS. top next column)............... **60**
Night lamp, miniature, By-the-Sea patt.,
opaque pink.. **425**

Moondrops Mug

Pitcher, Celtic patt. (No. 100 Line), clear
w/gold decoration **85**
Pitcher, Klear-Kut (No. 705 Line), clear
w/ruby-stain.. **325**
Pitcher, Rock Crystal patt. (No. 49 Line),
overall gold decorated **225**
Powder box, cov., Martha Washington
patt., pink satin finish **145**
Punch bowl w/underplate & ladle, Radi-
ance patt. (No. 42 Line), ruby, the set **450**
Salt & Pepper shakers w/original tops,
Radiance patt. (No. 42 Line), ruby, pr. **100**
Sandwich tray, No. 34 (Addie), black........... **75-80**
Sandwich tray, No. 34 (Addie), jade green **90**
Sandwich tray, No. 35 (Statesman), jade
green **80**
Sherbet, stemmed, Moondrops patt. (No.
37 Line), cobalt blue (ILLUS. right
w/comport)... **50**

New Martinsville Smoking Set

Smoking set, two ashtrays & cigarette pack
holder on rectangular tray, amethyst, the
set (ILLUS.).. **275**
Spooner, Carnation patt. (No. 88 Line),
clear w/ruby-stain & gold decoration............. **125**
Spooner, Old Glory patt. (No. 719 Line),
clear w/gold decoration **80**
Sugar bowl, cov., Carnation patt. (No. 88
Line), clear w/ruby-stain & gold decora-
tion **200**

Klear-Kut Sugar Bowl

Sugar bowl, cov., Klear-Kut (No. 705 Line),
clear w/ruby-stain (ILLUS.) **225**
Sugar bowl, cov., Old Glory patt. (No. 719
Line), clear w/gold decoration **90**
Tumbler, Celtic patt. (No. 100 Line), clear
w/gold decoration **20**
Tumbler, Klear-Kut (No. 705 Line), clear
w/ruby-stain **85**

Moondrops Tumbler

Tumbler, Moondrops patt. (No. 37 Line),
amethyst, 12 oz. (ILLUS.) **22**
Tumbler, water, Rock Crystal patt. (No. 49
Line), overall gold decorated **45**
Vase, 8" h., Janice patt. (No. 45 Line), flared
rim, light blue **200**

Modernistic Vase

Vase, Modernistic patt. (No. 33 Line), black
(ILLUS.) **100**
Vase, Modernistic patt. (No. 33 Line), blue
satin finish **80**

Northwood

*Harry Northwood (1860-1919) was born in England,
the son of noted glass artist John Northwood. Brought
up in the glass business, Harry immigrated to the United
States in 1881 and shortly thereafter became manager of
the La Belle Glass Company, Bridgeport, Ohio. Here he
was responsible for many innovations in colored and
blown glass. After leaving La Belle in 1887 he opened
The Northwood Glass Company in Martins Ferry, Ohio
in 1888. The company moved to Ellwood City, Pennsylvania in 1892 and Northwood moved again to take over
a glass plant in Indiana, Pennsylvania in 1896. One of
his major lines made at the Indiana, Pennsylvania plant
was Custard glass (which he called "ivory"). It was
made in several patterns and some pieces were marked
on the base with "Northwood" in script.*

*Harry and his family moved back to England in 1899
but returned to the U.S. in 1902 at which time he opened
another glass factory in Wheeling, West Virginia. Here
he was able to put his full talents to work and under his
guidance the firm manufactured many notable glass*

*lines including opalescent wares, colored and clear
pressed tablewares, various novelties and probably best
known of all, Carnival glass. Around 1906 Harry introduced his famous "N" in circle trade-mark which can be
found on the base of many, but not all, pieces made at his
factory. The factory closed in 1925.*

*In this listing we are including only the clear and col-
ored tablewares produced at Northwood factories. Specialized lines such as Custard glass, Carnival and
Opalescent wares are listed under their own headings in
our Glass category.*

Northwood

Northwood Signature Mark, ca. 1898

Northwood "N" in Circle Mark, ca. 1906

Berry set: master bowl & six sauce dishes;
Regal patt., clear opalescent, Wheeling,
West Virginia factory, 7 pcs. **$225**

No. 643 Covered Bonbon

Bonbon, cov., footed, No. 643, Rosita Amber, Wheeling, West Virginia factory
(ILLUS.) **60**

Stretch Bowl

Bowl, deep lobed sides, on square flaring
foot, pearl Stretch glass, Wheeling, West
Virginia factory (ILLUS.) **60**

Bowl, master berry, Chrysanthemum Swirl patt., clear opalescent, Martins Ferry, Ohio factory 70

Posies & Pods Master Berry Bowl

Bowl, master berry, Posies and Pods patt., green w/gold trim, Wheeling, West Virginia factory (ILLUS.) 85

Butter dish, cov., Alaska patt., blue opalescent w/h.p. decoration, Indiana, Pennsylvania factory 300

Butter dish, cov., Peach patt., clear, Wheeling West Virginia factory 75

Celery tray, Alaska patt., blue opalescent, Indiana, Pennsylvania factory 375

Celery vase, Cherry Thumbprint patt., clear, Wheeling West Virginia factory 95

Brecciated Marble Compote

Compote, open, Brecciated Marble glass, Wheeling, West Virginia factory (ILLUS.) 400

Northwood Stretch Compote

Compote, open, deep flaring bowl on a tall stem w/double knobs, round foot, blue, Wheeling West Virginia factory (ILLUS.) 75

Iceland Poppy Compote

Compote, open, Iceland Poppy patt., "Verre D'or" decoration on dark blue, Wheeling, West Virginia factory (ILLUS.) 125

Console set: footed compote & pair of 9 1/2" h. candlesticks; Chinese Coral, 3 pcs., Wheeling West Virginia factory 85

Cherry & Cable Color-stained Creamer

Creamer, Cherry & Cable patt., color-stained trim, Wheeling, West Virginia factory (ILLUS.) 40

Creamer, Cherry Thumbprint patt., clear, Wheeling, West Virginia factory 35

Creamer, Intaglio patt., blue opalescent, Indiana, Pennsylvania factory 95

Creamer, Klondyke (Fluted Scrolls) patt., blue opalescent, Indiana, Pennsylvania factory 95

Leaf Medallion Green Creamer

Creamer, Leaf Medallion (Regent) patt., green w/gold, Wheeling, West Virginia factory (ILLUS.) **145**

Leaf Umbrella Creamer and Pitcher

Creamer, Leaf Umbrella patt., Rose du Barry, Martins Ferry, Ohio factory (ILLUS. left)... **375**

Creamer, Lustre Flute patt., blue opalescent, Wheeling, West Virginia factory **90**

Panelled Holly Creamer

Creamer, Panelled Holly patt., blue opalescent w/gold trim (ILLUS.) **200**

Creamer, Peach patt., clear w/gold & red trim, Wheeling, West Virginia factory **72**

Scroll with Acanthus Creamer

Creamer, Scroll with Acanthus patt., "Mosaic," (slag) glass, Wheeling, West Virginia factory (ILLUS.) **100**

Chrysanthemum Swirl Cruets

Cruet w/original faceted stopper, Chrysanthemum Swirl patt., cranberry opalescent, note difference in stripe widths, Martins Ferry, Ohio factory, each (ILLUS.) **200-250**

Cruet w/original stopper, Leaf Umbrella patt., cased blue w/clear facet-cut stopper, Martins Ferry, Ohio factory, 7" h. **275**

Cruet w/original stopper, Regal patt., blue opalescent, Wheeling, West Virginia factory... **750**

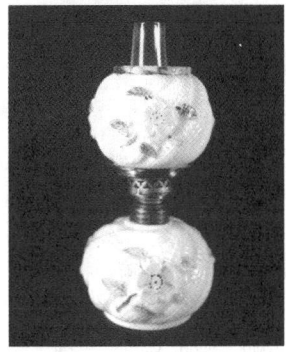

Leaf Umbrella Pattern Cruet

Cruet w/replaced stopper, Leaf Umbrella patt., crystal w/a frosted smoky finish, Martins Ferry, Ohio factory (ILLUS.) **100**

Sunflower Dish

Dish, Sunflower patt., rolled rim, clear, Wheeling West Virginia factory (ILLUS.) **30**

Decorated Apple Blossom Fairy Lamp

Fairy lamp, Apple Blossom patt., opaque white w/h.p. decoration, Indiana, Pennsylvania factory (ILLUS.) **500**

Singing Birds Mug

Mug, Singing Birds patt., blue opalescent, Wheeling, West Virginia factory (ILLUS.) **75**

Blue Covered Pitcher w/Iridescence

Pitcher, cov., footed ovoid body, blue w/light iridescence, Wheeling, West Virginia factory (ILLUS.) **600**

Pitcher, milk, Leaf Umbrella patt., blue w/milk glass lining, Martins Ferry, Ohio factory (ILLUS. right w/creamer) **500**

Rare Opalescent Royal Oak Pitcher

Pitcher, Royal Oak patt., cranberry opalescent Swirl design, Martins Ferry, Ohio factory (ILLUS.) **1,200**

Rubina Jewel Pattern Pitcher

Pitcher, water, Jewel patt., rubina, Martins Ferry, Ohio factory (ILLUS.) **350**

Pump Novelty

Pump & Trough, white opalescent, 2 pcs., Ellwood City, Pennsylvania factory (ILLUS.) **100**

Salt & pepper shakers w/original metal tops, Apple Blossom patt., opaque white w/h.p. decoration, Indiana, Pennsylvania factory, the pair **325**

Salt & pepper shakers w/original tops, Paneled Sprig patt., milk white w/color trim, Indiana, Pennsylvania factory, pr. **150**

Bow and Tassel Blue Salt Shaker

Salt shaker w/original top, Bow and Tassel patt., opaque blue, Ellwood City, Pennsylvania factory (ILLUS.)........................... 50

Salt shaker w/original top, Cactus patt., cranberry opalescent, Ellwood City, Pennsylvania factory...................................... 325

Salt shaker w/original top, Leaf Umbrella patt., cased blue, Martins Ferry, Ohio factory.. 75

Salt shaker w/original top, Parian Swirl patt., milk glass w/floral decoration, Martins Ferry, Ohio factory 125

Parian Swirl Salt Shaker

Salt shaker w/original top, Parian Swirl patt., opaque blue w/h.p. decoration, Martins Ferry, Ohio factory (ILLUS.) 145

Northwood Luna Ivory Shade

Shade, domed Luna Ivory glass w/embossed scroll design trimmed w/nutmeg brown stain, Wheeling, West Virginia factory (ILLUS.).. 100

Trumpet-shaped Shades

Shades, trumpet-shaped w/molded ribs, marigold Carnival finish, Wheeling, West Virginia factory, each (ILLUS.) **60-75**

Spooner, Cherry Thumbprint patt., clear, Wheeling, West Virginia factory....................... 55

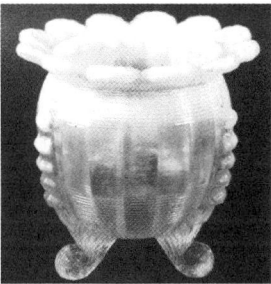

Klondyke Opalescent Spooner

Spooner, Klondyke (Fluted Scrolls) patt., topaz opalescent, Indiana, Pennsylvania factory (ILLUS.) 110

Spooner, Plums & Cherries patt., clear w/ruby & gold trim, Wheeling, West Virginia factory... 75

Belladonna Sugar Bowl

Sugar bowl, cov., Belladonna patt., clear w/enameled trim, Wheeling, West Virginia factory (ILLUS.) 50

Sugar bowl, cov., Cherry thumbprint patt., clear, Wheeling, West Virginia factory........... 100

Regal Sugar Bowl

Sugar bowl, cov., Regal patt., emerald green w/gold trim, Wheeling, West Virginia factory (ILLUS.) **95**

Decorated Venetian Sugar Bowl

Sugar bowl, cov., Venetian patt. opaque white w/h.p. scenic decoration, Indiana, Pennsylvania factory (ILLUS.) **175**

Daisy & Fern Sugar Shaker

Sugar shaker w/original top, Daisy & Fern patt., Parian Swirl mold, clear opalescent, Ellwood City, Pennsylvania factory (ILLUS.) **100**
Sugar shaker w/original top, Leaf Umbrella patt., cased crystal, Martins Ferry, Ohio factory **295**

Flat Flower Syrup Jug

Syrup jug w/original top, Flat Flower patt., opaque green, Ellwood City, Pennsylvania factory (ILLUS.) .... **: 400**

Grape & Leaf Blue Syrup Jug

Syrup jug w/original top, Grape and Leaf patt., opaque blue, Indiana, Pennsylvania factory (ILLUS.) **350**

Swirl & Leaf Toothpick Holder

Toothpick holder, Swirl & Leaf patt., opaque pink, Ellwood City, Pennsylvania factory (ILLUS.) **60-75**
Tumbler, Daffodil patt., cranberry opalescent, Wheeling, West Virginia factory **500**

Gold Rose Tumbler

Tumbler, Gold Rose patt., green, Wheeling, West Virginia factory (ILLUS.) **50**

Tumbler, Paneled Cherry patt., clear, Wheeling, West Virginia factory 30

Northwood Enameled Floral Tumblers

Tumbler, plain design, blue Carnival finish w/enameled florals, Wheeling, West Virginia factory (ILLUS. left) 30-35

Tumbler, plain design, green w/enameled flower, Wheeling, West Virginia factory (ILLUS. right) 25-30

Northwood Etruscan Vase

Vase, ovoid w/short flared neck, Etruscan line (note brown streaked decoration), Wheeling, West Virginia factory (ILLUS.) 450

Water set: pitcher & three tumblers; Intaglio patt., green w/gold trim, Wheeling, West Virginia factory, 4 pcs. 300

Peach Pattern Water Set

Water set: pitcher & four tumblers; Peach patt., green w/gold trim, Wheeling, West Virginia factory, 5 pcs. (ILLUS. of part) 300

Water set: pitcher & six tumblers; Barbella patt., cobalt blue w/gold trim, Wheeling, West Virginia factory, 7 pcs. 350

Water set: pitcher & six tumblers; Cherry Thumbprint patt., clear, Wheeling, West Virginia factory, 7 pcs. 225

Water set: pitcher & six tumblers; Plums & Cherries patt., clear w/ruby & gold trim, Wheeling, West Virginia factory, 7 pcs. 350

Opalescent

Presently, this is one of the most popular areas of glass collecting. The opalescent effect was attained by adding bone ash chemicals to areas of an item while still hot and refiring the object at tremendous heat. Both pressed and mold-blown patterns are available to collectors and we distinguish the types in our listing below. Opalescent Glass from A to Z *by the late William Heacock is the definitive reference book for collectors.*

Mold-blown Opalescent Patterns

Coin Spot
Pitcher, 8 1/2" h., blue, ovoid w/ruffled rim & applied clear blue handle $105

Daisy & Fern
Cruet w/original stopper, blue, Ellwood City, Pennsylvania factory 225

Cruet w/original stopper, blue, swirled rib body, applied blue handle, facet-cut stopper, 6 3/4" h. 175-225

Cruet w/original stopper, clear, Ellwood City, Pennsylvania factory 110

Finger bowl, cranberry, satin finish, Ellwood City, Pennsylvania factory 150

Pitcher, clear, Ellwood City, Pennsylvania factory 140

Tumbler, cranberry, Ellwood City, Pennsylvania factory 75

Hobnail, Hobbs
Water set: pitcher & four tumblers; cranberry, applied clear handle on pitcher, bulbous w/squared mouth, pitcher 8" h., the set 605

Poinsettia
Syrup pitcher w/original metal lid, blue 900

Ribbed Opal Lattice
Sugar shaker w/original lid, cranberry 330

Spanish Lace
Pickle castor, cov., cranberry cylindrical insert, ornate Meriden silver plate frame w/floral decoration, cover & tongs, overall 12 1/4" h. 440

Pitcher, water, cranberry 900

Spanish Lace Opalescent Rose Bowl

Rose bowl, white (ILLUS.) 90
Tumbler, cranberry, Ellwood City, Pennsyl-
 vania factory.. 55

Pressed Opalescent Patterns

Diamond Spearhead
Cruet w/original stopper, canary 325
Toothpick holder, cobalt blue............................ 200

Honeycomb & Clover
Pitcher, green.. 325
Tumbler, blue 100
Tumbler, green 110

Iris with Meander
Butter dish, cov., blue 275
Creamer, green... 85
Spooner, white.. 50
Sugar bowl, cov., blue.. 180

Jewel & Flower
Cruet w/original stopper, blue........................... 750

Jeweled Heart
Tumbler, green 65

Ribbed Spiral
Butter dish, cov., white 275
Compote, jelly, white.. 100
Creamer, white 180
Sugar bowl, cov., white....................................... 225
Vase, swung-type, white, 14" h............................ 60

Sunburst-on-Shield

Blue Sunburst-on-Shield Cruet

Cruet w/original stopper, blue (ILLUS.)........... 450

Swag with Brackets
Butter dish, cov., green....................................... 250
Compote, jelly, green.. 60
Pitcher, green... 325

Tokyo
Butter dish, cov., green 175
Creamer, blue 95
Spooner, white.. 65
Sugar bowl, cov., blue.. 160

Water Lily & Cattails
Bowl, master berry, purple................................... 95
Creamer, purple.. 140
Sauce dish, small, purple 45

Wild Bouquet
Sauce dish, blue.. 60

Wreath & Shell
Butter dish, cov., blue... 275
Cracker jar, cov., canary, h.p. decoration 250
Creamer, blue 175
Spooner, canary 250
Toothpick holder, canary 310

L.G. Wright Copies

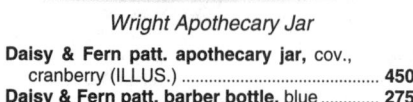

Wright Apothecary Jar

Daisy & Fern patt. apothecary jar, cov.,
 cranberry (ILLUS.) 450
Daisy & Fern patt. barber bottle, blue 275

Wright Daisy & Fern Finger Bowl

Daisy & Fern patt. finger bowl, green
 (ILLUS.) 125
Daisy & Fern patt. pitcher, reeded handle,
 canary 375

Wright Dot & Mitre Milk Pitcher

Dot & Mitre pitcher, milk, cranberry
(ILLUS.).. **600**
Moon & Star patt. goblet, canary **75**
Panel Grape patt. sauce dish, blue **25**

Wright Stars & Stripes Cruet

Stars & Stripes patt. cruet, no stopper,
cranberry (ILLUS.).. **300**

Miscellaneous Pressed Novelties

Cashews Bowl

Cashews bowl, ruffled, white (ILLUS.) **65**
Dew Drop candleholders, square, canary,
pr. **60**
Dew Drop creamer & open sugar bowl,
canary, pr. **40**

Frosted Leaf & Basketweave Spooner

Frosted Leaf & Basketweave spooner,
blue (ILLUS.) **100**

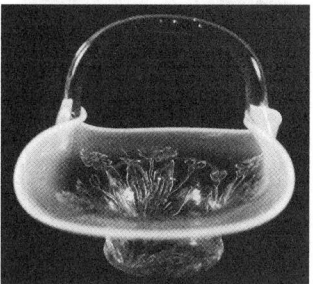

Dugan Intaglio Pattern Basket

Intaglio (Dugan's) basket, applied handle,
white w/goofus decoration (ILLUS.) **60**
Jackson (Klondyke) creamer, blue, deco-
rated **145**
Lace Edge vase, blue.. **30**
Lace Edge vase, green **35**
Peacocks on the Fence bowl, ruffled,
green **145**
Pump & Trough, white, 2 pcs. **195**
Trailing Vine bowls, scalloped edges, var-
ious shapes, blue, each **110-150**
Trailing Vine butter dish, cov., canary............. **225**
Twist child's table set: creamer, cov. sug-
ar, cov. butter & spooner; canary, 4 pcs. **450**
Waffle & Vine compote, open, green............... **500**

Orrefors

*This Swedish glasshouse, founded in 1898 for pro-
duction of tablewares, has made decorative wares as
well since 1915. By 1925, Orrefors had achieved an
international reputation for its Graal glass, an engraved
art glass developed by master glassblower Knut Berquist
and artist-designers Simon Gate and Edward Hald. Ariel
glass, recognized by a design of controlled air traps and
the heavy Ravenna glass, usually tinted, were both
developed in the 1930s. While all Orrrefors glass is collectible, pieces signed by early designers and artists are
now bringing high prices.*

Orrefors Mark

Bowl, 6" d., 2 1/4" h., "Graal," a deep round-ed & gently flaring bowl w/flattened rim raised on a thick disk foot, blue internally decorated w/colorless loops, foot inscribed "Orrefors Graal 2109-E6 Edvard Hald," ca. 1940 .... $1,380

Bowl-vase, "Ariel," deep rounded thick-walled vessel in clear infused w/vertical bands of controlled air bubbles, designed by Edvin Ohrstrom, inscribed "Orrefors Sweden - Ariel - No. 520 - E. Ohrstrom," ca. 1960s, 6 5/8" d., 3 1/4" h. 402

Vase, 5 1/4" h., "Graal," heavy walled tear-shaped clear body, internally decorated w/fish swimming among aquatic plants in greenish brown, base inscribed "Orrefors Sweden Graal 2775D Edward Hald," mid-20th c. (light wear)..................................... 489

Orrefors Fish Graal Vase

Vase, 5 1/2" h., "Graal," heavy walled tear-drop-shaped form, clear internally decorated w/fish among seaweed in brownish green, base signed "Orrefors Graal No. 95216 II Hald," designed by Edvard Hald, ca. 1940 (ILLUS.).................................. 920

Vase, 6 7/8" h., "Ariel," cylindrical w/slightly flaring rim, internally decorated w/'Pro-files' patt., deep purple & white stylized human profiles in a clear ground, designed by Ingeborg Lundin, signed "Orre-fors Ariel No. 236 - E9 - Ingeborg Lundin" 6,325

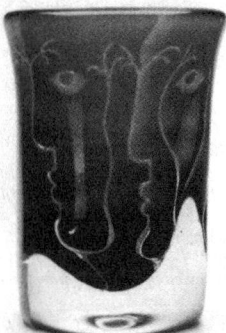

Orrefors 'Profiles' Pattern Vase

Vase, 7 1/2" h., "Ariel," cylindrical w/slightly flaring rim, internally decorated w/'Pro-files' patt., shaded moss green w/stylized

human profiles in a clear ground, de-signed by Ingeborg Lundin, signed "Orre-fors Ariel No. 556. G - Ingeborg Lundin" (ILLUS.) 6,325

Pate de Verre

Pate de Verre, or "paste of glass," was molded by very few artisans. In the pate de verre technique, powdered glass is mixed with a liquid to make a paste which is then placed in a mold and baked at a high temperature. These articles have a finely-pitted or matte finish and are easily distinguished from blown glass. Duplicate pieces are possible with this technique.

Pate De Verre Marks

Pate-de-Verre Bowl & Bowl-Vase

Bowl, 3 1/8" h., "Ceres," footed squatty spherical form w/a wide flat mouth, trian-gular panels w/diamond lattice alternat-ing w/triangular panels of wheat heads in shades of brown, gold & black, G. Argy-Rousseau, ca. 1926 (ILLUS. right).......... $5,175

Bowl-vase, flared inverted bell-form w/rounded bottom, textured clear ground w/a band of stylized deep ruby leaping gazelles above a ruby & black base bor-der & upright scrolled flowers, G. Argy-Rousseau, ca. 1928, 3 3/4" h. (ILLUS. left w/bowl) 11,500

Box, cov., slightly swelled cylindrical sides w/a fitted domed cover, mottled frosted white & lavender, molded around the body w/large red roses on brown stems, a rose blossom on the cover, G. Argy-Rousseau, ca. 1920, 3" h. 5,750

Pate de Verre Clock - Vide Poche

Clock case - vide poche, an upright square back w/rounded corners centered by the round clock dial w/Arabic numerals above a narrow rectangular dished front base, yellow shading to butterscotch ground molded w/green & rose budded stems up the sides w/a black bee at the center bottom, signed in the mold "A. Walter Nancy - H. Berge Sc.," designed by Henri Berge for A. Walter, 4 5/8" h. (ILLUS.)... **3,450**

Coupe, round stepped foot tapering to cylindrical pedestal flaring into a deep rounded cup w/a wide flat rim, lemon yellow above mottled brown molded on the side w/a large insect, signed by Henri Bergé, molded "AWalter - Nancy - HBergé - sculp," ca. 1925, 6 1/2" h. **5,750**

Dish, round w/shallow incurved sides, greenish yellow frosted ground decorated on the interior w/a pair of large red fruits on brown stems w/green leaves, signed "Decorchement," 6 1/2" d. **2,750**

Figure, "Danseuse," an Art Deco style dancing lady nude except for a long drapery over one uplifted leg & wrapped around her back & help by her two hands, her head turned looking over her back, a fan-shaped backing behind her lower legs, posed on a deep rectangular block-form base, mottled dark golden amber & black, designed by Marcel Bouraine for G. Argy-Rousseau, molded "Pâte de Cristal D'Argy-Rousseau, 18 Bouraine," France, ca. 1928, 11 5/8" h. **35,250**

Vase, 3 5/8" h., "Vase à décor de gazelles et de fleurs," gently flaring cup-form in frosted clear & mottled yellow cast around the base w/a dark orange band & around the sides w/a band of leaping orange gazelles & stylized brown stems w/yellow blossoms, G. Argy-Rousseau, ca. 1928 .... **10,350**

Vase, 5 7/8" h., "Rayons de Soleil," a swelled cylindrical form w/a wide flat rim, cast around the base & rim w/gadrooned bands, cast just below the rim w/a wide band of stylized deep reddish daisy-like blossoms on mottled yellow heavy stems & leaves all against a blackish ground, molded "G. Argy-Rousseau - France," ca. 1926 .... **9,400**

Vase, 10 1/4" h., "Vase à décor de danseuses grecques à robe longue," simple ovoid form w/flaring neck, the upper half molded w/panels w/deep reddish amber dancing Greek figures separated by dark brown geometric bands & herringbone-style bands in yellow & orangish brown, all on a mottled brownish yellow ground, G. Argy-Rousseau, ca. 1930 .... **23,000**

Vase, 12" h, "Libations," ovoid mottled white & amethyst body cast around the center w/a wide dark amethyst band composed of bands of wheel-like devices separating large rectangular relief-cast panels w/a half-length figure of an ancient water carrier w/a jug on the shoulder in shades of dark reddish amber & amethyst, G. Argy-Rousseau, ca. 1924 .... **68,500**

Rare "Fleurs de Perse" Vase

Vase, 12 1/8" h., "Fleurs de Perse," tall ovoid body w/wide mouth, pale amber mottled w/purple, orange & yellow, molded in medium-relief around the shoulder w/two rows of flowerheads in orange within scrolling enclosures in mottled charcoal, G. Argy-Rousseau, ca. 1924 (ILLUS.) **10,350**

Veilleuse (night light), "Faun and Nymphs," tall gently swelled cylindrical shade w/wide flat mouth, molded near the top w/a wide band depicting a nymph, a fawn & a satyr amid foliage in red, yellowish green & yellow w/an upper band & the lower body in purple & charcoal molded w/stylized morning glories, signed in the mold "G. Argy-Rousseau," on a cushion-form gilt-metal base, 10 1/8" h. **3,450**

Pattern

Though it has never been ascertained whether glass was first pressed in the United States or abroad, the development of the glass pressing machine revolutionized the glass industry in the United States and this country receives the credit for improving the method to make this process feasible. The first wares pressed were probably small flat plates of the type now referred to as "lacy," the intricacy of the design concealing flaws.

In 1827, both the New England Glass Co., Cambridge, Mass. and Bakewell & Co., Pittsburgh, took out patents for pressing glass furniture knobs and soon other pieces followed. This early pressed glass contained red lead which made it clear and resonant when tapped (flint.) Made primarily in clear, it is rarer in blue, amethyst, olive green and yellow.

By the 1840s, early simple patterns such as Ashburton, Argus and Excelsior appeared. Ribbed Bellflower seems to have been one of the earliest patterns to have had complete sets. By the 1860s, a wide range of patterns was available.

In 1864, William Leighton of Hobbs, Brockunier & Co., Wheeling, West Virginia, developed a formula for "soda lime" glass which did not require the expensive red lead for clarity. Although "soda lime" glass did not have the brilliance of the earlier flint glass, the formula came into widespread use because glass could be produced cheaply.

An asterisk (*) indicates a piece which has been reproduced.

Actress
Bowl, 8" d., Adelaide Neilson $65

Bread tray, Miss Neilson, 12 1/2" l., frosted...... 110
Cake stand, frosted stem 150-165
Celery vase, Pinafore scene.............................. 160
Celery vase, frosted rim, stem & foot, 9" h........ 220
Cheese dish, cov., "Lone Fisherman" on
   cover, "The Two Dromios" on under-
   plate... 225-250
Cologne bottle w/original stopper, 11" h............. 90
Compote, cov., 6" d., 10" h................................ 95

Actress Compote

Compote, cov., 10" d., 14 1/2" h., Fanny
   Davenport & Maggie Mitchell (ILLUS.) 200
Compote, open, 6" d., 3" h.................................. 55
Compote, open, 8" d., 5" h............................. 65-70
Creamer, clear.. 75
Creamer, frosted... 100
Creamer, Miss Neilson & Fanny Davenport...... 110
Dresser box, cov. 3 1/2" d. 60
Dresser box, cov., footed, 2 1/2 x 6" oval 75
Egg cup 70
Goblet, clear bowl, frosted stem 135
Goblet, frosted bowl 125
Mug, Pinafore scene.. 50
Pitcher, water, 9" h., Miss Neilson & Mag-
   gie Mitchell.. 350
Platter, 7 x 11 1/2", Pinafore scene.................... 125
Relish, Maude Granger, 5 x 9" 63
Salt & pepper shakers w/original tops, pr....... 100
Salt shaker w/original pewter top 85
Sauce dish, Maggie Mitchell & Fanny Dav-
   enport, 4 1/2" d., 2 1/4" h. 20
Sauce dish, clear, footed 16
Spooner, frosted.. 68
Sugar bowl, cov., Lotta Crabtree & Kate
   Claxton.. 130
Table set, creamer, cov. sugar bowl, cov.
   butter dish, spooner, 4 pcs. 275

Art (Job's Tears)
Banana stand 85-95
Bowl, 7" d., flared rim, footed............................. 25
Bowl, 8" sq., shallow... 33
Butter dish, cov., clear.. 60
Butter dish, cov., ruby-stained 100
Cake stand, 9" to 10 1/2" d. 68
Celery vase 55
Compote, cov., 7" d. 80
Compote, cov., 9" d. 60
Compote, open, 7" d. 57
Compote, open, 9" d., 7 1/4" h. 48
Cracker jar, cov., 7" d., 8" h. to top of finial....... 150
Creamer 49
Cruet w/original stopper, ruby-stained 175

Art Goblet

Goblet (ILLUS.).. 55-65
Mug 50
Pitcher, milk, clear.. 100
Pitcher, water, bulbous... 83
Punch cup 20
Salt shaker w/original top 25
Sauce dish, flat or footed, each.......................... 15
Sugar bowl, cov., engraved 44
Sugar bowl, cov., plain.. 45
Sugar bowl, open.. 28
Toothpick holder 30
Vinegar jug 45
Wine 110

Ashburton
Ale glass, flint, 6 1/2" h...................................... 130
Celery vase, plain rim, flint 140
Celery vase, scalloped rim, canary yellow,
   flint 775
Celery vase, scalloped rim, clear, flint.............. 108
Champagne, flint... 65-75
Claret, flint, 5 1/4" h. 65
Cordial, flint, 4 1/4" h. 65
Cordial, non-flint 85
Creamer, applied handle, flint........................... 175
Decanter, bar lip & facet-cut neck, clear,
   flint, qt. 75
Egg cup, clear, flint 25-30
Egg cup, double 95
Goblet, barrel-shaped, flint 105
Goblet, flared, flint, clear 38
Goblet, short, flint 45
Honey dish, 3 1/2" d. 8
Mug, applied handle, 4 3/4" h. 88
Pitcher, water, applied hollow handle, flint....... 425
Sauce dish, flint.. 8
Sugar bowl, cov., fiery opalescent, flint......... 1,650

Ashburton Sugar Bowl

Sugar bowl, cov., flint (ILLUS.) 102
Tumbler, bar, flint 65-70
Tumbler, water, footed... 93
Tumbler, whiskey, applied handle, flint............. 135
Vase, 10 1/2" h., scallop rim........................ 140-150
Wine, clear, flint.. 40
Wine, non-flint.. 35

Atlanta (Lion or Square Lion's Head)
Butter dish, cov... 105
Cake stand 110
Cake stand, frosted, 9" w., 5 3/4" h. 320
Celery vase 88
Compote, cov., 5" sq., 6" h. 123
Compote, cov., 7" sq., high stand..................... 188
Compote, cov., 7" sq., low stand 110-150
Compote, cov., 9" sq., 13" h.............................. 175
Compote, open, 6" sq., 7 1/2" h. 80
Creamer 60
Cruet w/original stopper 125
Cruet w/original stopper, engraved................. 290

Atlanta Goblet

*Goblet (ILLUS.) 60-70
Mustard jar 750
Relish, boat-shaped... 28
Salt dip, master size.. 117
Sauce dish 25-35
Spooner 60
Spooner, ruby-stained.. 75
Sugar bowl, cov., engraved............................... 160
Sugar bowl, cov., plain.................................... 90-95
Toothpick holder, clear & frosted satin milk
    glass 35-75
Tumbler, engraved.. 60
Tumbler, plain 45
Tumbler, ruby-stained.. 80
Wine 85-110

Balder - See Pennsylvania Pattern

Bamboo - see U.S. Glass Co. Broken Column Pattern

Banded Portland (Portland w/Diamond Point Band, Virginia (States series), Portland Maiden Blush (when pink-stained)
Berry set: master bowl & 4 sauce dishes;
    pink-stained, 5 pcs. 175
Bowl, 6" d., open, deep, straight-sided,
    clear.. 25
Bowl, 6" d., open, deep, straight-sided,
    pink-stained... 40

Butter dish, cov., pink-stained.......................... 173
Celery tray, pink-stained, 10" oval 75
Celery tray, clear, 5 x 12"................................... 28
Celery vase, clear 33
Cologne bottle w/original stopper, clear,
    large 49
Cologne bottle w/original stopper, clear,
    small 35
Cologne bottle w/original stopper, pink-
    stained, small.. 65
Compote, cov., 8" d., high stand....................... 105
Compote, open, jelly.. 25
Compote, open, 7" d.. 30
Compote, open, 8 1/4" d., 8" h., scalloped
    rim.. 38
Creamer, pink-stained 50
Creamer, individual size, clear 35
Creamer, individual size, pink-stained 45
Cruet w/original stopper, clear............................ 60
Cruet w/original stopper, pink-stained............. 175
Dresser jar, cov., clear, 3 1/2" d. 36
Goblet, clear.. 45
Goblet, pink-stained... 55
Goblet, yellow-stained.. 85
Pickle dish, 4 x 6".. 20
Pin tray, souvenir, pink-stained........................... 25
Pitcher, water, 9 1/2" h., clear............................. 95
Pitcher, water, 9 1/2" h., pink-stained 135
Pitcher, tankard, 11" h., pink-stained 238
Pomade jar, cov. 28
Punch cup, clear 11
Punch cup, pink-stained 35
Ring tree, gold-stained 75
Ring tree, pink-stained 125
Salt & pepper shakers w/original tops,
    clear, pr.. 45
Salt & pepper shakers w/original tops,
    pink-stained, pr. 84
Salt shaker w/original top, clear 20
Salt shaker w/original top, pink-stained 50
Sauce dish, clear, 4 1/2" d................................... 15

![Banded Portland Sauce Dish]

Banded Portland Sauce Dish

Sauce dish, pink-stained, 4 1/2" d. (ILLUS.) 21
Sauce dish, boat-shaped, clear, 4 3/4" l. 10
Sugar bowl, cov., clear 45
Sugar bowl, cov., gold-stained 80
Sugar bowl, individual size, clear........................ 24
Sugar bowl, individual size, pink-stained 35
Sugar shaker w/original top, clear 50
Sugar shaker w/original top, pink-stained 135
Sugar shaker w/original top, vaseline-
    stained 60
Syrup jug w/original top, pink-stained 250
Toothpick holder, clear 41
Toothpick holder, pink-stained 45-60
Tumbler, clear... 20-25
Tumbler, pink-stained 44
Vase, 6" h., flared, clear...................................... 32
Vase, 6" h., flared, pink-stained.......................... 35

Vase, 9" h., clear 42
Wine, blue-stained 45
Wine, clear 20
Wine, clear w/gold trim 42
Wine, pink-stained 60

Beaded Dewdrop - see Wisconsin Pattern

Beaded Loop (Oregon, U.S. Glass Co.)

Bowl, berry, 7" d. 17
Bowl, 8 1/4" d. 20
Bowl, berry, 9 1/2" l., 6 3/4" w. oval, clear 25
Bowl, berry, 9 1/2" l., 6 3/4" w. oval, ruby-
   stained.. 35
Bread platter 35
Bread tray 35
Butter dish, cov., clear 70
Butter dish, cov., ruby-stained.......................... 125
Cake stand, 8" d., 5" h. 50
Cake stand, 9" to 10 1/2" d. 56
Carafe, individual size 30
Celery vase, clear, 7" h. 30
Compote, cov., 6" d., 10" h. 95
Compote, cov., 7" d. 80
Compote, cov., 11".. 125
Compote, open, jelly, clear 31
Compote, open, 5 1/4" d., 4 1/2" h., clear 20
Compote, open, 6 1/2" d., clear 20
Compote, open, 7" d., clear 27
Compote, open, 7 1/2" d., low stand, clear 38
Creamer, clear.. 40
Creamer, ruby-stained 70
Cruet w/faceted stopper, clear 35
Cruet w/faceted stopper, ruby-stained.............. 75
Goblet, clear w/gold trim.................................. 50

Beaded Loop Goblet

*Goblet (ILLUS.) 49
Mug, footed, clear 40
Mug, ruby-stained 55
Pitcher, pint, 7" h. 44
Pitcher, milk, 8 1/2" h...................................... 55
Pitcher, water, tankard..................................... 60
Salt & pepper shakers w/original tops, pr......... 43
Sauce dish, flat or footed, each 13
Spooner, clear.. 28
Spooner, ruby-stained 55
*Sugar bowl, cov., clear................................... 39
Sugar bowl, cov., ruby-stained 55
Toothpick holder 48

Tumbler, clear.. 49
Tumbler, ruby-stained 35
Vase, small... 43
Wine 65-70

Bearded Head - see Viking Pattern

Bellflower

Bowl, 6" d., 1 3/4" h., single vine....................... 150
Bowl, 8" d., 2" h., round, single vine, scallop
   & point rim, plain polished base..................... 180
Butter dish, cov... 167
Castor set, 4-bottle, w/pewter stand 400
Castor set, 5-bottle, single vine, w/pewter
   stand.. 558
Celery vase, w/cut bellflowers.......................... 313
Champagne, fine rib, double vine, w/cut
   bellflowers, 5" h. 450
Champagne, barrel-shaped, fine rib, single
   vine, knob stem, rayed base, 5 1/4" h. 96
Cologne bottle w/stopper, clambroth.............. 425
Compote, open, 7" d., 5" h., fine rib, double
   vine 90-100
Compote, open, 8" d. 85
Compote, open, 8" d., high stand 190
Compote, open, coarse rib, single vine, low
   foot w/scallop rim, 8" d., 5" h. 250
Cordial, barrel-shaped, knob stem, rayed
   base.. 165
Cordial, fine rib, single vine, knob stem............. 150
Cordial, fine rib, single vine, plain stem..... 120-125
Creamer, fine rib, single vine, applied handle 325

Bellflower Decanter

Decanter, double vine, flint, qt., no stopper
   (ILLUS.) 110
Decanter w/bar lip, cut shoulder, single
   vine, w/stopper 550
Decanter w/bar lip, double vine, qt.................. 208
Decanter w/bar lip, single vine, qt. 207
Egg cup, coarse rib.. 28
Egg cup, double vine, w/cut bellflowers 75
Egg cup, fine rib, single vine 44
Goblet, barrel-shaped, fine rib, single vine,
   knob stem, rayed base 56
*Goblet, barrel-shaped, fine rib, single vine,
   plain stem 35
Goblet, coarse rib, flared top 60
Goblet, fine rib, double vine, w/cut bellflowers 425
Goblet, fine rib, single vine, w/cut bellflow-
   ers, 5 1/2" h... 2,050

Goblet, single vine w/cut bellflowers, 6 1/4" h... **400**
Honey dish, scalloped rim, star base, 3" d. **100**
Lamp, whale oil, pattern on inside of font, top of ribs scalloped, scalloped base, 9" h. (replaced collar, hard to see internal line under collar, probably factory flaw) **650**
Lamp, whale oil, brass stem, marble base **300**
Pitcher, double vine, straight sides, 1 pt., 6 1/4" h... **1,800**
Pitcher, milk, double vine, 7" h.................... **2,000**
Pitcher, milk, single vine, 7 1/2" h................. **1,750**
Pitcher, water, 8 3/4" h., coarse rib, double vine... **463**
Sauce dish, single vine **16**
Spooner, low foot, double vine.......................... **97**
Spooner, scalloped rim, single vine.................... **66**
Sugar bowl, cov., double vine.......................... **137**
Sugar bowl, cov., single vine **300**
Sugar bowl, cov., octagonal, domed lid, 8" h.. **1,450**
Syrup pitcher w/original top, applied handle, fine rib, single vine, clear...................... **894**
Syrup pitcher w/original top, applied handle, milk white **1,233**
Tumbler, bar, fine rib, single vine.................... **113**
Tumbler, whiskey, single vine, 2 7/8" h. **230**
Tumbler, double vine, w/cut bellflowers, 3 1/2" h.. **400**
Tumbler, fine rib, double vine, 4 7/8" h. **275**
Wine, barrel-shaped, knob stem, fine rib, single vine... **60**
Wine, barrel-shaped, knob stem, fine rib, single vine, rayed base.................................. **108**
Wine, double vine w/cut bellflowers, 4" h......... **250**
Wine, fine-rib, single vine, straight sides, 4" h. **63**

Bow Tie
Bowl, 6" d... **20-25**
Bowl, berry, 8" d. **32**
Compote, cov., 7" d. **165**
Compote, open, 6 1/2" d., low stand **40**
Compote, open, 8 1/4" d., high stand................. **53**
Goblet **54**
Pitcher, milk **58**
Pitcher, water.. **85-90**
Punch bowl **125**
Salt dip, master size... **95**
Salt & pepper shakers w/original tops, pr........ **70**
Salt shaker w/original top **45**
Spooner **35**

Broken Column (Irish Column, Notched Rib or Bamboo)
Banana stand **195**
Bowl, 7" d... **40**
Bowl, 9" d... **32**
Bowl, cov., vegetable... **95**
Butter dish, cov. **115**
Celery tray, 5 x 10", w/red notches **65**
Celery vase, clear... **73**
Celery vase, ruby-stained................................. **155**
Compote, cov., 5" d., high stand, clear............... **70**
Compote, cov., 5" d., high stand w/red notches **225**
Compote, cov., 7" d., high stand.............. **175-200**
Compote, cov., 8" d., high stand....................... **175**
Compote, cov., 8" d., high stand w/red notches **525**
Compote, open, 6" d., high stand **35**

Compote, open, 7" d., low stand.......................... **50**
Compote, open, 8" d., high stand, ruby-stained **350**
Compote, open, 8" d., low stand......................... **63**
Compote, open, 9" d., 7 1/2" h., clear................. **75**
Compote, open, 9" d., 7 1/2" h. w/red notches **175**
***Creamer,** clear... **35-40**
Creamer, w/red notches **250**
Cruet w/original stopper, w/red notches **525**
Decanter w/original stopper, 10 1/2" h............. **85**

Broken Column Goblet

***Goblet,** clear (ILLUS.) **60**
Pickle castor, cov., clear, original ornate frame.. **238**
Pickle castor, ruby-stained, w/frame & tongs.. **413**
***Pitcher,** water, clear **123**
Pitcher, water, w/red notches........................... **450**
Relish, 3 3/4 x 5".. **13**
Relish, 6 1/2" l. **18**
Relish, clear, 9" l., 5" w. **25-30**
Relish, w/red notches, 9" l., 5" w. **78**
Salt & pepper shakers w/original tops, pr. **85**
Salt shaker w/original top, w/red notches......... **75**
Sauce dish, w/red notches **32**
***Spooner,** clear... **32**
Spooner, w/red notches **125**
***Sugar bowl,** clear **72**
Sugar bowl, cov., w/red notches **150**
Sugar bowl, open, clear...................................... **30**
Sugar bowl, open, w/red notches........................ **73**
Sugar shaker w/metal top **110**
Sugar shaker w/metal top, w/red notches **450-500**
Syrup pitcher w/metal top, clear.............. **175-200**
Syrup pitcher w/metal top, w/red notches **405**
Tumbler, clear... **48**
Tumbler, w/red notches.............................. **75-100**
***Wine** **85**

Cabbage Rose
Bitters bottle, 6 1/2" h.. **180**
Cake stand, 9 1/2" to 12 1/2" d. **65**
Celery vase **50**
Champagne **75**
Compote, cov., 7 1/2" d., high stand **90-100**
Compote, cov., 8 1/2" d., high stand................... **95**
Compote, open, 7" d., low stand.......................... **30**

Compote, open, 8 1/2" d., high stand.................. 80
Compote, open, 9 1/2" d., high stand............... 100
Compote, open, 9 1/2" d., low stand................... 90
Cordial 50
Egg cup 45
*Goblet 35-45
Mug, child's 65

Cabbage Rose Pickle Dish

Pickle or relish, 7 1/2" to 8 1/2" l. (ILLUS.)......... 18
Pitcher, milk, qt. 125
Pitcher, water, 1/2 gal.. 100
Pitcher, 3 pint 165
Sauce dish 11
*Spooner 30-35
Sugar bowl, cov... 63
Sugar bowl, open 40
Tumbler, ... 30-40
Tumbler, bar 44
Wine 45

Diamond Quilted
Butter dish, cov., canary....................................... 75
Celery vase, blue... 50
Celery vase, deep amethyst................................... 68
Champagne, clear... 22
Claret, clear 40
Compote, cov., 7" d., low stand, blue................... 65
Compote, cov., 8" d., 13" h., amber 95
Compote, cov., 8" d., 13" h., clear...................... 75
Compote, open, 8" d., low stand, canary............. 52
Compote, open, 9" d., low stand, blue 40
Compote, open, 9" d., low stand, canary............. 37
Cordial, amber 33
Creamer, amber 38
Creamer, amethyst... 40
Creamer, turquoise blue 68
*Goblet, amber.. 48
*Goblet, amethyst.. 30-35
*Goblet, blue... 37
*Goblet, canary 33
*Goblet, clear.. 28
Mug, amber... 20
Mug, amethyst 30
Mug, clear 15
Pickle castor, w/silver plate frame, cover &
   tongs... 225
Pitcher, water, amber.. 54
Pitcher, water, blue 80
Pitcher, water, canary... 75
*Salt dip, amber, master size, rectangular 32
Sauce dish, amber, flat or footed, each.............. 12
Sauce dish, amethyst, flat or footed, each......... 18
Sauce dish, canary, flat or footed, each............. 10
Sauce dish, turquoise blue, flat or footed,
   each.. 11
Spooner, amethyst... 38
Spooner, canary 37
Sugar bowl, cov., amber....................................... 68
Sugar bowl, cov., amethyst................................... 85
Sugar bowl, cov., blue..................................... 35-40

Sugar bowl, cov., canary 55
Tray, water, cloverleaf-shaped, amber,
   10 x 12"... 30-40
Tray, water, cloverleaf-shaped, canary,
   10 x 12"... 30-35
*Tumbler, amethyst.. 40
*Tumbler, canary... 25-30
*Tumbler, clear 25
Waste bowl, blue, 4 1/2" d................................... 38
*Wine, amethyst 42
Wine, clear 17

Emerald Green Herringbone - see Paneled Herringbone Pattern

Florida - see Paneled Herringbone Pattern

Hand (Pennsylvania, Early)
Celery vase 35-40
Cordial 85
Creamer 30-40
Cruet w/original stopper, applied handle 60-65

Hand Goblet

Goblet (ILLUS.).. 50-55
Marmalade jar, cov. 40
Mug 45-50
Pitcher, water.. 100
Salt dip, master size 35-40
Salt shaker w/original top, 4" h. (single)...... 25-30
Sugar bowl, cov. 55-60
Syrup pitcher w/original top, 4" h. 140-150
*Tumbler, juice... 35
*Tumbler, water.. 50
*Tumbler, whiskey.. 25
Wine, clear 45-55

Jacob's Ladder (Maltese)
Celery vase (ILLUS. top next page)..................... 85
Compote, cov., 9 1/2" d., high stand............... 165
Compote, open, dolphin stem, smooth rim,
   high stand 425
Compote, open, 9 1/2" d., high stand 45-68
Compote, open, 10" d., 5" h. 30-35
Compote, open, 13 1/2" d., high stand 75
*Creamer 32
Goblet 65
Marmalade jar, cov. 125-135
Pickle castor, complete w/stand 175-200
Pitcher, milk.. 150-175
Pitcher, water, applied handle........................... 175
Plate, 6" d., amber 125
Plate, 9" d... 60
Salt dip, master size, footed 30-35
Spooner 25-30

Jacob's Ladder Celery Vase

Tumbler,	**85-90**
Tumbler, bar	**75**
Wine	**40-45**

Jewel & Dewdrop - see Kansas Pattern

Job's Tears - see Art Patter

Kansas (Jewel & Dewdrop)
Bowl, 5 x 7" oval	**30**
Bread tray, "Our Daily Bread," 10 1/2" oval	**47**
Butter dish, cov.	**70**
Cake stand, 8" to 10" d.	**55-60**
Celery vase	**75**
Compote, open, 7" d., high stand	**88**
Compote, open, 8" d., high stand	**60-65**
Creamer	**50**
Goblet	**49**

Small Kansas Mug

Mug, small, 3 1/2" h. (ILLUS.)	**35-45**
Mug, large	**55-60**
Relish, 8 1/2" oval	**26**
Salt shaker w/original top	**60**
Sauce dish, 4" d.	**16**
Spooner	**75**
Sugar bowl, cov.	**100**
Sugar bowl, open	**55**
Syrup jug w/original top	**175-190**
Toothpick holder	**40**
Tumbler, water, footed	**57**
Wine, clear	**40-50**

King's Crown (Also see Ruby Thumbprint)
Celery vase, plain	**62**
Champagne, clear	**30**
*Compote, cov., 5" d., 5 1/2" h., engraved	**33**
Compote, cov., 8" d., 12" h.	**61**
Compote, open, 7 1/2" d., high stand	**41**

Creamer, w/green thumbprints	**75**
*Creamer, individual size, clear	**19**
Ice cream tray	**40**
Nappy, handled, 5" d.	**20-25**
Pitcher, tankard, 8 1/2" h.	**65**
Relish, 7 1/2 x 10 1/2" oval	**24**
Spooner	**39**
Toothpick holder, rose stain, souvenir	**30-35**
*Tumbler, clear	**22**

Liberty Bell
Bowl, 6" d., footed	**60-65**
Bowl, berry or fruit, 8" d., footed	**95-100**
Bread platter, w/thirteen original states, twig handles, 8 1/4 x 13"	**70**
*Bread platter, "Signer's," twig handles	**120-130**
Butter dish, cov.	**125**
Butter dish, cov., miniature	**143**
Compote, open, 6" d.	**95**
Creamer, applied handle	**75**
Creamer, miniature	**88**
Creamer & cov. sugar bowl, pr.	**150-175**

Liberty Bell Goblet

*Goblet (ILLUS.)	**30**
Mug, miniature, 2" h.	**175**
Pitcher, water	**750**
Plate, 6" d., no states, dated	**55-65**
Relish, shell handles, 7 x 11 1/4"	**59**
Salt shaker w/original pewter top	**130**
Sauce dish	**20-25**
Spooner	**50-60**
Sugar bowl, cov.	**110**
Sugar bowl, cov., miniature	**163**
Sugar bowl, open	**25-30**
Syrup pitcher w/original top	**90**

Loop with Stippled Panels - see Texas Pattern

Magnet & Grape
Butter dish, cov., frosted leaf, flint	**185**
Champagne, frosted leaf, flint	**190-200**
Champagne, stippled leaf, non-flint	**55-60**
Compote, open, stippled leaf, 7 1/4" d., high stand, non-flint	**50**
Egg cup, frosted leaf, flint	**75-80**
Goblet, clear leaf, non-flint	**35-40**
*Goblet, frosted leaf, flint (ILLUS. top next page)	**80**
Goblet, stippled leaf, non-flint	**35-40**
Salt dip, frosted leaf, flint	**65-70**
Salt dip, master size, frosted leaf, flint	**80-85**
Salt dip, stippled leaf, non-flint	**15-20**

Magnet & Grape Goblet

Spooner, frosted leaf, flint **90-95**
Sugar bowl, open, frosted leaf, flint **35-40**
Sugar bowl, open, stippled leaf, non-flint **25-30**
Syrup pitcher w/spring lid, stippled leaf,
   non-flint **175-200**
*Tumbler,** frosted leaf, flint **110-120**
Tumbler, stippled leaf, non-flint **35-40**
*Wine,** frosted leaf, flint **100-110**
Wine cooler, frosted leaf, flint .... **2,500+**

Maltese - see Jacob's Ladder Pattern

Minnesota
Banana bowl, flat **50-55**
Basket w/applied reeded handle **75**
Bowl, 6" sq. **32**
Bowl, 7 1/2 x 10 1/2" **38**
Bowl, 7 1/2 x 10 1/2", ruby-stained **375**
Bowl, 8" sq. **32**
Bowl, 8 1/2" d., clear **40**
Bowl, 8 1/2" d., ruby-stained **70**
Carafe **48**
Celery tray, 13" l. **34**
Cheese dish, cov. **58**
Cracker jar, cov. **85-100**
Creamer, clear w/gold **50**
Creamer, clear, 3 1/2" h. **36**
Cruet w/original stopper **55-65**
Doughnut stand **40-45**
Goblet, clear **30**

Minnesota Goblet

Goblet clear w/gold (ILLUS.) **35**
Mug **25**
Spooner, clear **35**

Spooner, clear w/gold **53**
Sugar bowl, cov. **37**
Syrup pitcher w/original top **65**
Toothpick holder, three-handled, clear **25-30**
Toothpick holder, three-handled, green **115**
Tumbler **18**
Wine **15-20**

Moon & Star
Bowl, cov., 6" d. **26**
*Bowl,** cov., 7" d. **34**
Bowl, 7" d., footed **25**
*Bowl,** 9" d., flat **40**
Bread tray, scalloped rim, 6 1/2 x 10 3/4" **60-65**
Cake stand, 10" d. **95**
Carafe, water **40**
Celery vase **45**
*Compote,** cov., 6" d., high stand **75**
Compote, cov., 8" d., 12" h. **55-65**
Compote, cov., 10" d., high stand **93**
Compote, cov., 10 1/2" d., 16 1/4" h. **218**
Compote, open, 6" d., high stand **28**
Compote, open, 8" d., 8" h. **44**

Moon & Star Compote

Compote, open, 9" d., 6 1/2 h. (ILLUS.) **35**
Compote, open, 10" d., high stand **100-125**
*Egg cup** **40**
*Goblet** **35-40**
Lamp, kerosene-type, table model, clear
   font, milk white base, 15" h. **100-110**
*Pitcher,** water, 9 1/4" h., applied rope
   handle **155-175**
Relish, oblong **20**
Salt dip, individual size, footed **32**
*Salt dip,** master size **20-25**
*Spooner** **45**
*Sugar bowl,** cov. **65**
*Syrup pitcher w/original top** **125**
*Tumbler,** flat **40**
*Wine** **43**

New England Pineapple

New England Pineapple Egg Cup

Bar bottle, qt. **275**

Cake stand 150-160
Castor set, 2 castor bottles & 2 mustard jars
  in frame, set 175-220
Champagne 175-210
Compote, open, 8" d., 5" h. 150-200
Compote, open, 8" d., 7" h. 97
Compote, open, 9" d. 145
*Cordial, 4" h. 119
Creamer, applied handle 150-175
Decanter w/original stopper, qt. 250-275
Egg cup (ILLUS.) 50-55
*Goblet 65
Goblet, lady's 125-130
Goblets, set of 5 425-450
Pitcher, milk, 1 qt. 650
Pitcher, water 725
Spooner 65-70
Sugar bowl, cov. 140-145
Sugar bowl, open 25-30
Tumbler, water 91
Tumbler, water, extra large 125-130
Tumbler, whiskey, applied handle 180-190
*Wine 143
Wines, set of 3 480-500

Old Man of the Mountain - see Viking Pattern

Oregon No. 1 - see Beaded Loop Pattern

Paneled Herringbone (Emerald Green Herringbone or Florida)

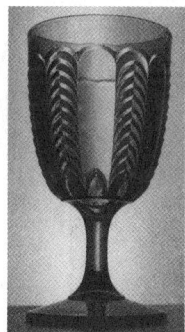

Paneled Herringbone Goblet

Banana bowl, folded-up sides, green 60-65
Berry set: 9" d. master bowl & 8 sauce dishes; green, 9 pcs. 100
Bowl, cov., 8" d., green 35
Bowl, 6" d., clear 20
Bowl, 6" d., green 40
Bowl, 7 1/2" d., green 55
Bowl, master berry, 9" sq., green 35
Bowl, master berry, 10 3/4" sq., green 37
Bowl, oval vegetable, green, medium 30
Bowl, oval vegetable, green, large 35
Bread tray, green 40-45
Butter dish, cov., green 80-85
Cake stand, clear 45
Cake stand, green 80
Celery vase, green 55
Compote, open, jelly, 5 1/2" sq., green 30
Cordial, green 40
Creamer, clear 20
Creamer, green 45-50
Cruet w/original stopper, green 65-70

*Goblet, clear 30
*Goblet, green (ILLUS.) 38
Marmalade jar, green 45
Pickle dish, green 23
Pitcher, milk 45
Pitcher, milk, green 55-65
Pitcher, water, clear 50
*Plate, 9" sq., clear 28
*Plate, 9" sq., green 35
Relish, 4 1/2 x 8" oval, green 14
Spooner, green w/gold 75
Sugar bowl, cov., green 50
Sugar bowl, open, green 28
Syrup pitcher w/original top, clear 175
Tumbler, clear 20
Tumbler, green 30

Pennsylvania (Balder or Kamoni)

Pennsylvania Wine

Bowl, berry or fruit, 8 1/2" d., clear w/gold
  trim 30
Butter dish, cov., clear 54
Carafe 47
Celery vase 28-35
Champagne 35
Cheese dish, cov. 65-70
Compote, open, 5" h., child's 15-20
Cracker jar, cov. 42
Creamer, child's 60-65
Creamer, 3" h., clear w/gold trim, individual 35
Creamer, 3" h., green w/gold trim, individual 55
Creamer, 4" h., table size 35
Creamer 6 1/2" h. 45
Decanter w/original stopper, handleless,
  10 3/4" h. 110
Decanter w/original stopper, handled,
  10 3/4" h. 90
Goblet, clear 24
Goblet, clear w/gold 35-38
Pitcher, water 65
Plate, 8" d. 30
Punch bowl, 10" d., 5" h., on 6" h. pedestal
  base 150-160
Salt shaker w/original top 25-30
Sauce dish, boat-shaped 22
Sauce dish, round or square 12
Spooner, child's 24
Sugar bowl, cov., child's, clear w/gold trim 35
Sugar bowl, cov., child's, green w/gold trim 160
Sugar bowl, cov., clear 45
Sugar bowl, cov., ruby-stained 75-80

Sugar bowl, open, individual size, clear
  w/gold trim **25-28**
Syrup pitcher w/original top **70-75**
Toothpick holder, clear **30-40**
Toothpick holder, clear w/gold...................... **40-45**
Toothpick holder, green................................... **143**
Tumbler, juice, clear....................................... **12**
Tumbler, juice, green **21**
Whiskey shot glass, clear.................................. **13**
Wine, clear (ILLUS.) **10-15**
Wine, green... **35**
Wine, ruby-stained, souvenir............................ **45-50**

Pennsylvania, Early - see Hand Pattern

Polar Bear
*Goblet, clear.. **100-125**
Goblet, clear & frosted.............................. **145-175**
Goblet, flared rim, frosted **125-150**
Pitcher, water, clear **525-550**
Pitcher, water, frosted................................... **1,050**
Tray, water, frosted, 16" l........................... **225-250**

Polar Bear Waste Bowl

Waste bowl, frosted (ILLUS.) **115**

Red Block
Berry set, master bowl & 10 sauce dishes,
  11 pcs... **235**
Bowl, berry or fruit, 8" d... **85**
Butter dish, cov.. **70**
Celery vase, 6 1/2" h. **160-175**
Creamer, large **65-70**
Creamer, small, applied handle........................... **45**
Decanter, whiskey, w/original stopper,
  12" h... **133**
*Goblet **40**
Pitcher, 8" h., bulbous.. **210**
Pitcher, tankard, 8" h. **160**
Salt & pepper shakers w/original tops, pr....... **150**
Spooner **32**
Sugar bowl, cov.. **50-70**
Sugar bowl, open **45**
Table set, creamer, sugar bowl & spooner,
  3 pcs... **150**
Tumbler **40**
*Wine **33**

Rose Sprig
Bowl, 5 x 8", canary.. **48**
Bowl, 6 x 9" oblong, canary **51**
Cake stand, clear, 9" octagon, 6 1/2" h. **70**
Celery vase, amber....................................... **45-50**
Celery vase, canary **135**
Celery vase, clear.. **45**
Compote, cov., high stand, large, clear **75**
*Goblet, blue.. **68**
*Goblet, clear (ILLUS. top next column) **30-35**
Pitcher, milk, clear.. **65**

Rose Sprig Goblet

Pitcher, water, amber **60**
Pitcher, water, canary... **60**
Plate, 6" sq., canary **48**
Punch bowl, footed, clear................................... **345**
*Whimsey, sleigh (salt dip), clear, 4 x 4 x 6" **110**
Whimsey, sitz bath-shaped bowl, blue,
  7 x 10"... **80**
Wine, canary... **65**
Wine, clear.. **45-50**

Ruby Thumbprint

Ruby Thumbprint Pitcher

Bowl, master berry or fruit, 8" l., boat-
  shaped, engraved **145**
Bowl, master berry or fruit, 10" l., boat-
  shaped **145**
Castor set, 4-bottle, in clear glass frame .. **365-425**
Celery vase **75**
*Claret **75**
Compote, open, jelly, 5 1/4" h. **95**
Compote, open, 7" d., engraved **170**
Compote, open, 7" d., plain **130**
Compote, open, 8 1/2" d., 7 1/2" h., scal-
  loped rim.. **220**
*Cordial, plain **24**
Creamer, engraved **68**
*Creamer, plain **45-50**
Creamer, individual size **28**

*Cup, plain.. 24
Cup & saucer, engraved............................... 60-65
*Cup & saucer, plain..................................... 57
Goblet, engraved vintage band 70
*Goblet, plain.. 50
Pitcher, milk, 7 1/2" h., bulbous.................... 100
Pitcher, milk, tankard, 8 3/8" h. 145
Pitcher, water, tankard, 11" d., w/engraved
    leaf band (ILLUS.)................................... 325
Pitcher, water, bulbous, large....................... 250
*Plate, 8 1/4" d.. 20
Salt & pepper shakers w/original tops, pr........ 90
Sauce dish, boat-shaped.............................. 45
Sauce dish, round, engraved 48
*Sherbet 18
Spooner 70
Sugar bowl, open, individual size, 2 1/2" h....... 31
Toothpick holder, engraved 45
Toothpick holder, plain................................. 31
Tumbler, engraved....................................... 61
*Tumbler, plain... 38
Water set, tankard pitcher & 6 tumblers,
    7 pcs... 385
*Wine 38
Wine, engraved... 35

Shell & Tassel
Bowl, 10" oval, clear..................................... 59
Bowl, 8" d., cov., canary, collared base............ 120
Bride's basket, 8" oval blue bowl in silver
    plate frame 320-350
Butter dish, cov., round, dog finial 151
Cake stand, shell corners, 9" sq. 94
Cake stand, shell corners, 10" sq. 100-125
Celery vase, round, handled.......................... 80
Compote, open, 6 1/2" sq., 6 1/2" h. 50

Shell & Tassel Compote

Compote, open, 8 1/2" sq., 8" h. (ILLUS.)..... 50-55
Creamer, round................................... 35-45
Creamer, square..................................... 60
*Goblet, round, knob stem 45-55
Mug, miniature, blue.................................... 145
Oyster plate, 9 1/2" d.................................... 250
Pitcher, water, round.................................... 150
Pitcher, water, square................................... 110
Platter, 8 x 11" oblong.................................. 54
Platter, 9 x 13" oval 51
Relish, amber, 5 x 8".................................... 95
Relish, blue, 5 x 8"..................................... 100-110
Relish, canary, 5 x 8"................................... 125

Salt dip, shell-shaped 17
Salt shaker w/original top 110
Sauce dish, flat or footed, 4" to 5" d., each........ 15
Spooner, round... 40
Spooner, square.. 52
Sugar bowl, cov., round, dog finial.................... 128
Table set, 4 pcs. 398
Tray, ice cream 125
Tumbler, clear.. 40
Vase 175

Texas (Loop with Stippled Panels)
Bowl, 7" d. 15
Bowl, 8" oval.. 35-45
Butter dish, cov., clear.................................. 113
Butter dish, cov., ruby-stained........................ 165
Cake stand, 9 1/2" to 10 3/4" d. 145
Compote, open, jelly 90-95
Compote, cov., 6" d., 11" h............................. 195
Compote, cov., 7" d., high stand 125
Creamer 51
*Creamer, individual size............................... 30
Cruet w/original stopper, clear........................ 108
Goblet, clear.. 95-100
Pitcher, water, 8 1/2" h.................................. 225
Pitcher, water, straight-sided w/inverted de-
    sign, 3 pt. 145-150
Plate, 8 3/4" d. 63
Relish, handled, ruby stained, 8 1/2" l. 55
Sauce dish, flat or footed, each 15
Spooner 53
Spooner, ruby-stained................................... 115
Sugar bowl, cov. 85

Texas Toothpick Holder

Toothpick holder, clear (ILLUS.) 25-30
Toothpick holder, clear w/gold 30
Toothpick holder, ruby-stained........................ 175
Tumbler 58
Vase, bud, 8" h... 35
Vase, 9" h.. 35
*Wine, clear... 100
Wine, ruby-stained..................................... 120-125

Three Face
*Butter dish, cov., plain................................. 190
*Cake stand, 8" to 10 1/2" d. 175-250
*Champagne 245
Champagne, hollow stem, 3 1/2" d., 4" h...... 4,600
*Compote, cov., 6" d., high stand (ILLUS.
    top next page).................................... 150-175
Compote, cov., 7" d., high stand..................... 285
Compote, cov., 8" d., high stand..................... 295
Compote, cov., 10" d., high stand 275

Three Face Compote

Compote, open, 8 1/2" d., high stand........... **90-100**
Compote, open, 9 1/2" d., high stand, en-
graved **375**
Compote, open, 9 1/2" d., high stand, plain..... **168**
*Cracker jar, cov.. **1,475**
Creamer **85-90**
*Goblet, engraved.. **105**
*Goblet, plain.. **50**
*Lamp, kerosene-type, pedestal base,
8" h. **200-250**
Marmalade jar, cov. **325**
Pitcher, milk.. **750**
Pitcher, water **575**
*Salt dip, individual... **43**
*Salt shaker w/original top **65**
*Sauce dish, 4" d.. **35**
*Spooner, engraved **120-125**
*Spooner, plain **70**
*Sugar bowl, cov. **125-150**
Table set, 4 pcs. **500**
*Wine **208**
*Wine etched **300**

U.S. Coin
Bowl, berry, 6" d., clear coins, plain rim............. **500**
*Bowl, berry, 6" d., frosted coins, plain rim........ **475**
Bowl, berry, 7" d., clear quarters, plain rim **425**
Bowl, berry, 8" d., clear half dollars, plain
rim.. **450**
Bowl, berry, 8" d., frosted half dollars, plain
rim.. **400**
Bowl, berry, 9" d., clear dollars, plain rim **1,100**
Bowl, berry, 9" d., frosted dollars, plain rim...... **800**
Bowl, berry, 6" d., clear coins, scalloped rim...... **900**
Bowl, berry, 6" d., frosted coins, scalloped
rim.. **1,175**
Bowl, berry, 7" d., clear quarters, scalloped
rim.. **900**
Bowl, berry, 7" d., frosted quarters, scal-
loped rim **1,067**
Bowl, berry, 8" d., clear half dollars, scal-
loped rim **900-1,000**
Bowl, berry, 8" d., frosted half dollars, scal-
loped rim **1,000-1,150**

Bowl, berry, 9" d., clear dollars, scalloped
rim... **1,350**
Bowl, berry, 9" d., frosted dollars, scalloped
rim.. **1,500-1,600**
Bowl, cov., 6" d., frosted quarters...................... **650**
Bowl, cov., 7" d., frosted quarters...................... **600**
Bowl, cov., 8" d., frosted half dollars **600**
Bowl, cov., 9" d., frosted dollars..................... **1,500**
*Bread tray, frosted dollars & half dollars.. **350-385**
Butter dish, cov., clear dollars & half dollars **450**
Butter dish, cov., frosted dollars & half
dollars.. **350-450**
Cake plate, clear dollars & quarters, 7" d........ **450**
Cake plate, frosted dollars & quarters, 7" d. **400**
Cake stand, clear dollars, 10" d. **375-385**
Cake stand, frosted dollars, 10" d. **425**
Celery tray, clear quarters **300**
Celery tray, frosted quarters.............................. **325**
Celery vase, frosted quarters **330-350**
Champagne, flared rim, clear half dimes **1,000**
Champagne, flared rim, frosted half dimes..... **900-
1,000**
Claret, flared rim, clear half dimes..................... **800**
Claret, flared rim, frosted half dimes **700**
Claret, straight rim, clear half dimes.................. **800**
Claret, straight rim, frosted half dimes **700**
Compote, cov., 6" d., high stand, clear
dimes & quarters **450**
*Compote, cov., 6" d., high stand, frosted
dimes & quarters **400-450**

U.S. Coin Compote

Compote, cov., 7" d., high stand, frosted
dimes & quarters (ILLUS.) **600-700**
Compote, cov., 8" d., high stand, clear
quarters & half dollars **550**
Compote, cov., 8" d., high stand, frosted
quarters & half dollars **550**
Compote, cov., 9" d., high stand, clear dol-
lars.. **3,000**
Compote, cov., 9" d., high stand, frosted
dollars & quarters **1,500-2,000**
Compote, cov., 6" d., low stand, clear twen-
ty cent pieces & quarters **650-700**
Compote, cov., 6" d., low stand, frosted
twenty cent pieces & quarters................. **600-650**

Compote, open, 7" d., high stand, flared rim, clear dimes & quarters............................ **450**

Compote, open, 7" d., high stand, flared rim, frosted dimes & quarters **450**

Compote, open, 7 1/4" d., high stand, straight rim, clear dimes & quarters **450-500**

Compote, open, 7 1/4" d., high stand, straight rim, frosted dimes & quarters **300**

Compote, open, 7 1/4" h., high stand, flared & scalloped rim, clear dimes & quarters **900**

Compote, open, 7 1/4" h., high stand, flared & scalloped rim, frosted dimes & quarters **800**

Compote, open, 8 1/4" d., high stand, flared rim, clear dimes & quarters **450-500**

Compote, open, 8 1/4" d., high stand, flared rim, frosted dimes & quarters **500**

Compote, open, 8 1/4" d., high stand, scalloped rim, clear quarters & dimes **1,000**

Compote, open, 8 1/4" d., high stand, scalloped rim, frosted quarters & dimes **1,000-1,200**

Compote, open, 8 1/4" d., high stand, straight rim, clear dimes & quarters **500**

Compote, open, 8 1/2" d., high stand, straight rim, frosted dimes & quarters **475**

Compote, open, 9 1/4" d., high stand, scalloped rim, clear quarters & dimes **1,200**

Compote, open, 9 1/4" d., high stand, scalloped rim, frosted quarters & half dollars... **1,200**

Compote, open, 9 1/2" d., high stand, flared rim, clear quarters & half dollars **850**

Compote, open, 9 1/2" d., high stand, flared rim, frosted quarters & half dollars **900-1,200**

Compote, open, 9 3/4" d., high stand, straight rim, clear quarters & half dollars **500**

Compote, open, 9 3/4" d., high stand, straight rim, frosted quarters & half dollars **500**

Compote, open, 10 1/4" d., high stand, scalloped rim, clear quarters & half dollars **1,500**

Compote, open, 10 1/4" d., high stand, scalloped rim, frosted quarters & half dollars **1,500-1,800**

Compote, open, 10 1/2" d., high stand, flared rim, clear quarters & half dollars **1,000**

Compote, open, 10 1/2" d., high stand, flared rim, frosted quarters & half dollars.. **1,200-1,500**

Compote, open, 10 1/2" d., high stand, straight rim, clear quarters & half dollars **700**

Compote, open, 10 1/2" d., high stand, straight rim, frosted quarters & half dollars **600**

Compote, open, 6" d., low stand, flared & scalloped rim, frosted twenty cent pieces **800-900**

Compote, open, 6" d., low stand, straight top w/scalloped rim, clear twenty cent pieces **1,000**

Compote, open, 7" d., low stand, flared & scalloped rim, frosted twenty cent pieces...... **900**

Compote, open, 7" d., low stand, straight top w/scalloped rim, frosted twenty cent pieces **800**

*Creamer, frosted quarters............................... **800**

Cruet w/original stopper, frosted quarters, 5 1/2" h.. **800**

Epergne, frosted quarters & dollars................... **900**

Finger bowl, flared rim, clear coins **800**

Finger bowl, flared rim, frosted coins **750**

Finger bowl, straight rim, clear coins................ **800**

Finger bowl, straight rim, frosted coins **700-750**

Goblet, straight top, clear dimes, 6 1/2" h. **300**

Goblet, straight top, frosted dimes, 6 1/2" h. **300**

Goblet, flared top, clear half dollars, 7" h. **900**

Goblet, flared top, frosted half dollars, 7" h. **500-700**

Goblet, straight top, clear half dollars, 7" h. **900**

Goblet, straight top, frosted half dollars, 7" h. **500**

Lamp, kerosene-type, flaring font, frosted half dollars, 11" h. **1,000**

Lamp, kerosene-type, flaring font, frosted half dollars, 11 1/2" h.................................. **1,000**

Lamp, kerosene-type, flaring font, frosted quarters, 8 1/2" h............................. **800-900**

Lamp, kerosene-type, flaring font, frosted quarters, 9 1/2" h............................. **900-950**

Lamp, kerosene-type, flaring font, frosted quarters, 10" h. **900-950**

Lamp, kerosene-type, handled, clear twenty cent pieces, 5" h. **825**

Lamp, kerosene-type, handled, clear quarters, 5" h. **800-900**

Lamp, kerosene-type, round font, clear quarters, 8" h. **850**

Lamp, kerosene-type, round font, frosted quarters, 8" h. **825**

Lamp, kerosene-type, round font, frosted quarters, 8 1/2" h....................................... **750**

Lamp, kerosene-type, round font, clear half dollars, 9 1/2" h....................................... **850**

Lamp, kerosene-type, round font, frosted half dollars, 9 1/2" h. **800**

Lamp, kerosene-type, round font, clear half dollars, 10" h....................................... **850**

Lamp, kerosene-type, round font, frosted half dollars, 10" h. **800**

Lamp, kerosene-type, round font, frosted half dollars, 10 1/2" h.................................. **850**

Lamp, kerosene-type, round font, clear dollars, 11 1/2" h. **900**

Lamp, kerosene-type, round font, frosted dollars, 11 1/2" h. **750-850**

Lamp, kerosene-type, round font, frosted half dollars, 11 1/2" h.................................. **875**

Lamp, kerosene-type, square font, clear quarters & half dollars, 8 1/2" h. **850**

Lamp, kerosene-type, square font, frosted quarters & half dollars, 8 1/2" h. **800-900**

Lamp, kerosene-type, square font, clear quarters & dollars, 9 1/2" h............................. **850**

Lamp, kerosene-type, square font, frosted quarters & dollars, 9 1/2" h. **800-850**

Lamp, kerosene-type, square font, frosted half dollars & dollars, 10 1/4" h. **825**

Lamp, kerosene-type, square font, frosted half dollars & dollars, 11" h. **900**

Lamp, kerosene-type, square font, clear dollars, 11 1/2" h. **925**

Lamp, kerosene-type, square font, frosted half dollars & dollars, 11 1/2" h. **875**

Mug, frosted dollars... **450**

Pickle dish, clear half dollars, 3 3/4 x 7 1/2" **250**

Pickle dish, frosted half dollars, 3 3/4 x 7 1/2" **250**

Pitcher, milk, clear half dollars **800**

Pitcher, milk, frosted half dollars........................ **800**

Pitcher, water, frosted dollars............................. **700**

Preserve dish, frosted half dollars in rim, dollars in base, 5 x 8" **350**

Salt & pepper shakers w/original tops,
clear coins 375
Salt & pepper shakers w/original tops,
frosted coins, pr.. 375
Salt shaker w/original top, frosted coins 175
Sauce dish, flat, plain rim, clear quarters,
3 3/4" d.. 300
Sauce dish, flat, plain rim, frosted quarters,
3 3/4" d.. 300
Sauce dish, flat, plain rim, clear quarters,
4 1/4" d.. 175
Sauce dish, flat, plain rim, frosted quarters,
4 1/4" d.. 200-250
Sauce Dish, flat, scalloped rim, frosted
quarters, 4" d... 350
Sauce dish, flat, scalloped rim, clear quar-
ters, 4 1/2" d... 125
Sauce dish, flat, scalloped rim, frosted
quarters, 4 1/2" d.. 475
Sauce dish, footed, plain top, clear quarters...... 100
Sauce dish, footed, plain top, frosted quar-
ters.. 125-135
Sauce dish, footed, scalloped rim, frosted
quarters.. 375
Spooner, clear quarters..................................... 225
***Spooner,** frosted quarters................................ 250
Sugar bowl, cov., clear quarters & half dol-
lars... 350
***Sugar bowl,** cov., frosted quarters & half
dollars.. 400-450
Syrup jug w/original dated pewter top,
clear coins 600
Syrup jug w/original dated pewter top,
frosted coins.. 630
Toothpick holder, clear dollars 176
Toothpick holder, clear w/ruby-stain, clear
dollars.. 2,000
***Toothpick holder,** frosted dollars 150
Tumbler, clear dime on side 300
Tumbler, dollar in base, clear sides w/clear
1879 coin 100-125
Tumbler, dollar in base, clear sides w/frost-
ed 1882 coin.. 200
Tumbler, dollar in base, paneled sides
w/clear 1878 coin 150
Water tray, frosted coins 800
Wine, frosted half dimes 700-800

Viking (Bearded Head or Old Man of the Mountain)

Viking Sugar Bowl

Apothecary jar w/original stopper 120-125
Bowl, cov., 8" oval 100
Bowl, 8" sq... 45

Butter dish, cov., clear 115
Celery vase 50-55
Compote, cov., 9" d., low stand 170
Compote, cov., 12" h. 135-145
Compote, open, 8" d., high stand 63
Creamer 65
Mug, applied handle 63
Pickle dish, 7" l.. 45
Pitcher, water, 8 3/4" h., clear 110-115
Pitcher, water, 8 3/4" h., clear & frosted 240-250
Salt dip, master size 40-45
Sauce dish, footed 17
Sugar bowl, cov. (ILLUS.) 73

Virginia - see Banded Portland Pattern

Washington Centennial
Bowl, 8 1/2" oval... 21

Washington Centennial Bread Platter

Bread platter, Carpenter's Hall center
(ILLUS.) 100-115
Bread platter, George Washington center,
frosted 100-115
Bread platter, Independence Hall center........... 85
Cake stand, 8 1/2" to 11 1/2" d. 55-75
Celery vase 57
Goblet 40-45
Pitcher, milk.. 350
Pitcher, water.. 155-225
Relish, bear paw handles, dated 1876 45
Sauce dish, flat or footed, each 10

Wildflower

Wildflower Creamer

Basket, cake, oblong w/metal handle 130
Bowl, 5 3/4" sq., canary 33
Bowl, 5 3/4" sq., clear 20
Bowl, 6 1/2" sq., amber 30
Butter dish, cov., apple green, footed 95
Butter dish, cov., canary, collared base 75
Celery vase, canary 80
Celery vase, clear 31
*Champagne, amber 55-65
Compote, cov., 7" d., canary 80
Compote, cov., 8" d., blue, high stand 125
Compote, open, 7" d., low stand, blue 39
*Creamer, amber 30
*Creamer, clear (ILLUS.) 35-45
*Goblet, apple green 30-40
*Goblet, blue 30
*Goblet, canary 40
Pitcher, water, amber 55
Pitcher, water, apple green 135
Pitcher, water, clear 38
Plate, 10" sq., amber 40
Plate, 10" sq., apple green 33
Plate, 10" sq., canary 27
Relish, apple green 22
*Salt dip, turtle-shaped, apple green 128
Salt & pepper shakers w/original tops,
   blue, pr. 80-90
Salt & pepper shakers w/original tops,
   canary, pr. 130
*Salt shaker w/orginal top, amber 35
*Salt shaker w/orginal top, apple green 45-55
*Sauce dish, blue, flat or footed, each 15
Spooner, canary 40
*Sugar bowl, cov., blue 50
Syrup pitcher w/original top, canary 265-275
Tumbler, amber 31
Tumbler, apple green 45
Tumbler, blue 40

Wisconsin (Beaded Dewdrop)

Wisconsin Wine

Bowl, 8" d. 36
Bowl, 8 1/2" oblong 35
Butter dish, cov. 79
Cake stand, 8 1/4" d., 4 3/4" h. 58
Cake stand, 9 3/4" d. 85
Celery tray, flat, 5 x 10" 36
Celery vase 35-40
Compote, open, 6 1/2" d., 6 1/2" h. 45
Compote, open, 7 1/2" d., 5 1/2" h. 50
Cruet w/original stopper 45
Cup & saucer 40
Dish, cov., oval 36
Doughnut stand, 6" d. 45

Goblet 100-125
Marmalade jar, cov. 175
Mug, 3 1/2" h. 50-55
Mustard jar, cov., bulbous 60
Nappy, handled, 4" d. 34
Pitcher, milk. 55-60
Plate, 5" sq. 20
Sauce dish 12
Spooner 33
Sugar shaker w/original top 126
Wine (ILLUS.) 75

Peach Blow

Several types of glass lumped together by collectors as Peach Blow were produced by half a dozen glasshouses. Hobbs, Brockunier & Co., Wheeling, West Virginia, made Peach Blow as a plated ware that shaded from red at the top to yellow at the bottom and is referred to as Wheeling Peach Blow. Mt. Washington Glass Works produced an homogeneous Peach Blow shading from a rose color at the top to pale blue in the lower portion. The New England Glass Works' Peach Blow, called Wild Rose, shaded from rose at the top to white. Gunderson-Pairpoint Co. also reproduced some of the Mt. Washington Peach Blow in the early 1950s and some glass of a somewhat similar type was made by Steuben Glass Works, Thomas Webb & Sons and Stevens & Williams of England. New England Peach Blow is one-layered glass and the English is two-layered.

Another single layered shaded art glass was produced early in this century by the New Martinsville Glass Mfg. Co. Originally called "Muranese," collectors today refer to it as "New Martinsville Peach Blow."

Gundersen - Pairpoint

Bowl, footed, 5" d., 3 1/2" h. $250
Champagne, 4 1/4" d., 5 1/2" h. 350
Compote, open, 4 1/2" d., 3" h., paper label 198
Compote, open, 6 1/2" d., 4 3/4" h. 350
Compote, open, 10" d., 5" h., ruffled rim,
   signed 425
Compote, open, 10" d., 7" h., pulled-up rim,
   signed 600
Cup & saucer, glossy finish 250

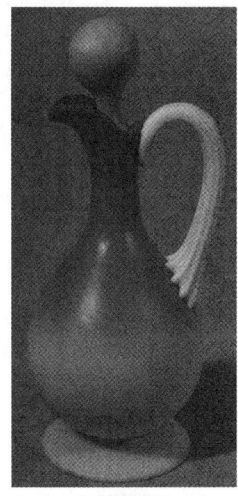

Gundersen Peach Blow Decanter

Decanter w/original stopper, footed ovoid body tapering to an arched spout, pink ball stopper, applied reeded white handle, satin finish (ILLUS.) **750-1,000**
Nappy, triangular shape, w/applied milky white handle **175**
Vase, 7" h., lily-form **193**
Vase, cornucopia-type, 7" h., ruffled rim, satin finish.. **450**
Vase, 7 1/2" h., jack-in-the-pulpit shape, enameled decoration **375**
Vase, 9" h., lily-form... **300**

Mt. Washington
Tumbler, satin finish, 4" h. **2,000**
Vase, 7" h., glossy finish................................. **1,500**
Vase, 7" h., satin finish.................................... **1,500**

New England
Bowl, 5 1/4" d., 2 1/2" h., scalloped rim **300**
Bowl, 9 1/2" d. **250**
Bride's basket, the wide deep rounded bowl w/a widely flaring ruffled rim, set into an ornate silver plate frame w/high scroll-pierced legs below a plain base ring centered by a small embossed cylindrical ring holding the bowl, a wide curved upright handle trimmed along the top w/berries & leaf sprigs, frame marked by the Derby Silver Plate Co., bowl 10" d., overall 12 3/4" h.`` **840**
Celery vase, bulging cylindrical form w/piecrust crimped rim, 3 1/2" d..................... **650**
Creamer, 2 1/2" h. **225**
Creamer, squatty bulbous form w/lightly ribbed sides, applied white handle, 3 1/2" d., 2 3/4" h...................................... **300-400**

Peach Blow Creamer & Sugar Bowl

Creamer & open sugar bowl, lightly molded ribs, satin finish, applied satin handles, one of the items sold at the Libbey exhibit at the 1893 Columbian Exposition, sugar bowl bears faint trace of that decoration, 2 1/2" h., pr. (ILLUS.) **950**
Cuspidor, lady's, bulbous base narrowing in the middle then flaring to a wavy rim **750**
Dish, leaf-shaped w/applied handle, 6 1/2" d.. **350**
Pitcher, 4 1/2" h., squatty bulbous body w/tri-corner rim, satin finish, applied crystal reeded handle.. **865**
Rose bowl, bulbous, seven-crimp top, satin finish, 2 3/4" d., 2 5/8" h. **350**
Rose bowl, round w/crimped rim, satin finish, 3 1/2" h. **275**

New England Peach Blow Tumbler

Tumbler, cylindrical, satin finish, 3 3/4" h. (ILLUS.) **425-475**
Tumbler, glossy finish, 4" h. **450**
Vase, square rim, two applied handles, glossy finish... **450**
Vase, 7" h., squatty bulbous base tapering to a tall slender 'stick' neck............................ **650**
Vase, 8 1/4" h., lily-form...................................... **633**

Webb
Bowl, 4" d., 2 1/4" h., decorated w/gold prunus blossoms & pine needles & gold trim, white lining, satin finish **325**
Cracker jar, cov., barrel-shaped, decorated w/daisies in light blue & white, matching glass cover w/metal finial, white interior, 7 3/4" h.. **830**

Webb Peach Blow Finger Bowl

Finger bowl, three-lobed rim, gold prunus blossom decoration on three sides w/small butterfly in each corner, 4 1/2" d., 2 3/4" h. (ILLUS.).. **325**
Finger bowl w/underplate, round bowl w/a tightly crimped rim, ruffled underplate, bowl shaded both inside & out w/creamy opaque layer between, underplate w/typical coloring on top, creamy color on bottom, glossy finish, decorated w/gold prunus flowers & butterflies, plate 6 1/4" d., bowl 4 1/4" d., 2 3/4" h., pr. **600**
Jar w/sterling silver cover, spherical squared body w/pinched-in sides, decorated w/a gilt floral sprig, hallmarked silver rim, inset cover & bail handle, 4 1/2" h... **173**
Pitcher, tankard, 9" h., signed **385**
Pitcher, 11" h., bulbous body w/a tricorner mouth, applied clear frosted handle, trimmed in gold... **193**
Rose bowl, miniature, decorated w/gold flowers & butterfly, 2 1/4" d............................. **425**

Webb Decorated Peach Blow Vases

Vase, 3 1/4" h., 2 3/4" d., baluster-form, decorated w/gold prunus & branches, creamy white lining (ILLUS. right).................. 400

Vase, 3 3/8" h., 2 5/8" d., pedestal footed squatty bulbous body w/short flaring rim, heavy gold florals & branches on front, gold butterfly on reverse, creamy white lining, satin finish 365

Vase, 3 1/2" h., 4" d., spherical form w/short cylindrical neck, decorated w/heavy gold prunus blossoms & leaves, gold butterfly on back side, gold band around top 345

Vase, 3 3/4" h., 2 3/4" d., ovoid body w/short flared neck, gold prunus blossom decoration, white lining, glossy finish............. 275

Vase, 3 3/4" h., 3 1/4" d., ovoid form tapering to a short neck w/flaring rim, decorated w/silver flowers & heavy gold leaves, glossy finish 325

Vase, 5" h., 3 1/2" d., ovoid body tapering to a short cylindrical neck, decorated w/enameled branches of white flowers, gold leaves, two birds on branches in brown, yellow & orange, white lining, glossy finish... 495

Vase, 5 1/8" h., 3 1/4" d., ovoid body tapering to a small flared neck, decorated w/heavy gold leaves & silver flowers, creamy white lining (ILLUS. left with small vase) 295

Vase, 5 3/8" h., 3 1/4" d., spherical body tapering to a flaring, ruffled neck, decorated w/enameled white flowers & green & brown leaves, creamy white lining, glossy finish.. 225

Vase, 5 7/8" h., 3" d., tapering ovoid body w/a wide cylindrical neck, decorated w/heavy gilt leaves & vining blossoms & an insect highlighted w/white enamel, white interior.. 295

Vase, 6 3/8" h., 3" d., bottle-form bulbous body tapering to a 'stick' neck, enameled w/gold leaves & branches & silver flowers, glossy finish, creamy white interior........ 245

Vase, 8 1/4" h., pinch-sided bulbous body w/'stick' neck 300

Vases, 5" h., 2" d., cylindrical, applied creamy blackthorn flowers, applied clear frosted leaves & clear frosted thorny base, creamy white lining, pr.......................... 750

Vases, 8 1/2" h., 4" d., tapering cylindrical body w/short neck, applied creamy white wafer foot, creamy white interior, pr.............. 395

Vases, 10" h., bottle-form, bulbous base w/tall 'stick' neck, decorated w/applied raised flowers & pears in gold & silver, pr. 775

Wheeling

Claret jug w/stopper, large spherical body flattened on two sides, a slender cylindrical neck w/pinched spout, applied reeded amber handle & amber facet-cut stopper, 9" h. 1,430

Wheeling Peach Blow Creamer

Creamer, globular w/tricorner top, applied amber handle, glossy finish, 4 1/4" h. (ILLUS.) 785

Creamer, tapering ovoid body w/a flared rim & pinched spout, satin finish, applied frosted pink handle, 5 1/2" h............................ 330

Flask, tooled lip, glossy finish, 4 1/2" widest, 7" h... 750

Mustard jar, cov., footed spherical body, fitted w/a silver plate rim, hinged lid w/spoon hole & angular handle, glossy finish, 2 1/2" h.. 476

Pitcher, 4 1/4" h., bulbous ovoid body tapering to a flaring tricorner rim, applied amber handle, glossy finish............................. 950

Pitcher, 6" h., footed squatty bulbous body w/a short squared flaring neck, molded Drape patt., applied clear reeded handle, glossy finish (four potstone blemishes) 450

Pitcher, 7 1/4" h., bulbous body w/quatrefoil rim, applied amber handle, deep red shading to pale green, white lining, polished pontil (small factory imperfection bottom of handle) 795

Pitcher, claret, 9 3/4" h., tall conical body tapering to a short cylindrical neck w/a pinched spout, an applied amber reeded angled handle attached to a band of applied amber rigaree at the base of the neck (small scratch at side)......................... 2,200

Salt & pepper shakers w/lids, spherical, one engraved "M.E. Gaslin 1887," glossy finish, pr (one w/replaced old pewter lid)....... 550

Salt shaker w/original metal top, spherical footed shape, glossy finish, 2 3/4" h. 460

Tumbler, cylindrical, glossy finish, 3 3/4" h.. 400-450

Tumbler, cylindrical, molded Drape patt., 3 1/2" h... 275

Tumblers, cylindrical, molded Drape patt., two w/satin & one w/glossy finish, 3 3/4" h., group of 3.. **450**

Vase, baluster-form w/a short flaring neck, Shape No. 6 .... **400-500**

Vase, 3 1/2" h., miniature, spherical body w/a small short cylindrical neck, satin finish **440**

Vase, 3 3/4" h., 1 3/8" d., bulbous body tapering to a short cylindrical neck **250**

Vase, 6 1/2" h., 6 1/2" d., bulbous, glossy finish **850**

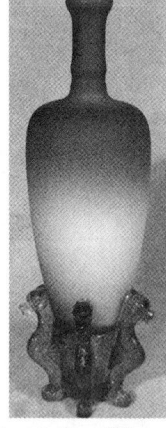

Satin Peach Blow "Morgan Vase"

Vase, 8" h., "Morgan Vase," satin finish, in original glossy amber gargoyle base, 2 pcs. (ILLUS.) **2,200-2,800**

Vase, 8 1/2" h., ovoid body tapering to a slender 'stick' neck, satin finish **825**

Pomona

First produced by the New England Glass Company under a patent received by Joseph Locke in 1885, Pomona has a frosted ground on clear glass decorated with mineral stains, most frequently amber-yellow, sometimes pale blue. Some pieces bore smooth etched floral decorations highlighted with staining. Two types of Pomona were made. The first Locke patent covered a technique whereby the piece was first covered with an acid resistant coating which was then needle-carved with thousands of minute criss-crossing lines. The piece was then dipped into acid which cut into the etched lines giving the finished piece a notable "brilliance."

A cheaper method, covered by a second Locke patent on June 15, 1886, was accomplished by rolling the glass piece in particles of acid-resistant material which were picked up by it. The glass was then etched by acid which attacked areas not protected by the resistant particles. A favorite design on Pomona was the cornflower.

Berry set: 8" d. master berry bowl & eight 4" d. sauce dishes; Inverted Thumbprint patt. w/turned-in scalloped amber rims, 2nd patent, 9 pcs.. **$275**

Bowl, 10" d., 4 1/4" h., upright crimped sides, pansy & blue butterfly design, 2nd patent **375**

Butter dish, cov., lid w/acanthus leaf decoration, 1st patent, 8" d., 4" h. **750**

Celery vase, ruffled rim, applied clear handle, blue cornflower decoration, 1st patent, 6 1/4" h. **375**

Celery vase, ruffled rim, clear applied base, 1st patent, 6 1/4" h... **370**

Champagne, amber-stained rim, 2nd patent **325**

Rare Pomona Cracker Jar

Cracker jar, cov., large ovoid body w/a fitted domed cover w/an applied amber-stained crown finial w/clear ball knop, Acanthus Leaf patt., 1st patent (ILLUS.) **1,200-1,500**

Pomona Cornflower Cruet

Cruet w/original bubble stopper, spherical body on applied crimped foot, applied handle, blue cornflower decoration, 2nd patent (ILLUS.) **700**

Finger bowl, ruffled rim, 1st patent, 5 1/2" d., 1 3/4" h... **220**

Goblets, 2nd patent, set of 6 .... **900**

Pitcher, 7" h., blue cornflower decoration, 1st patent... **750**

Pitcher, tankard, 12 1/4" h., blue butterflies & gold grasses, 1st patent.............................. **750**

Punch cup, blue cornflower decoration, 1st patent **150-175**

Tumbler, blueberry decoration, 2nd patent **200**

Pomona Cornflower Tumbler

Tumbler, cylindrical, blue cornflower decoration, 2nd patent, 2 1/2" d., 3 1/2" h. (ILLUS.).. **145**

Unusual Pomona Vase-Planter

Vase, 5 1/2" h., 5 1/2" d., planter-form, cylindrical w/upright crimped rim, three applied peg feet, blue cornflower patt., 1st patent (ILLUS.) **546**

Vase, 5 3/4" h., 4 1/2" d., crimped rim & ruffled foot, blue cornflower decoration, 2nd patent **500**

Vase, 9" h., lily-form, tri-cornered top, Diamond Quilted patt., 2nd patent........................ **225**

Quezal

In 1901, Martin Bach and Thomas Johnson, who had worked for Louis Tiffany, opened a competing glassworks in Brooklyn, New York. The Quezal Art Glass and Decorating Co. produced wares closely resembling those of Tiffany until the plant's closing in 1925.

Quezal

Quezal Mark

Center bowl, deep flaring wide-ribbed bowl on a ribbed funnel base, blue shading to purple w/overall golden iridescence, signed, ca. 1900, 13 1/8" d. **$1,200**

Compote, open, 5 1/4" d., 4 1/2" h., a disk foot & short ringed pedestal in bluish gold iridescence supporting a wide squatty bulbous bowl tapering below the wide flaring rim, bowl w/marigold iridescent exterior & gold iridescent interior, signed **550**

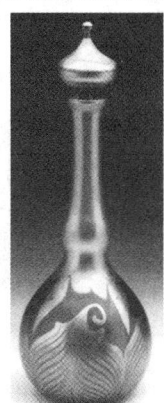

Rare Quezal Decanter

Decanter w/original pointed mushroom stopper, bulbous base tapering to a tall 'stick' neck w/flared rim, green & gold double-hooked feather designs on green, gold iridescent neck & stopper, designed by Martin Bach, signed, 11 1/2" h. (ILLUS.) **4,750**

Lamp, table model, two-light, the balusterform body in cased white decorated w/feathered trailings in blue & iridescent silver & in iridescent gold, w/reeded & foliate-cast metal mounts, two curving arms fitted w/a pair of paneled opalescent floriform shades w/iridescent gold interiors & gold feathering on the exterior, each side signed, ca. 1925, overall 25 3/4" h. **750**

Plate, 6 1/2" d., gold iridescence w/purple highlights **225**

Taster, squared sides w/pinched dimples, gold iridescent interior & exterior, signed "Quezal" on base, 2 3/4" h............................. **175**

Bulbous Quezal Pulled-Feather Vase

Vase, bulbous ovoid body tapering to a short rolled neck, bold gold pulled-feather & scroll designs on a dark colored ground w/white around the shoulder & neck, gold iridescent interior (ILLUS.)........ **2,800**

Vase, floriform, a decorated cushion foot supporting a slender stem to the widely flaring ruffled top, iridescent gold ground decorated w/white pulled-feather design... **2,750**

Vase, 3 3/4" h., miniature, bulbous squatty form, overall gold iridescence, signed **440**

Vase, 4" h., simple ovoid form w/flaring trumpet neck, green pulled-feathers extending down from the gold iridescent pulled upper band all on an opal ground, signed "Quezal H 319" **2,915**

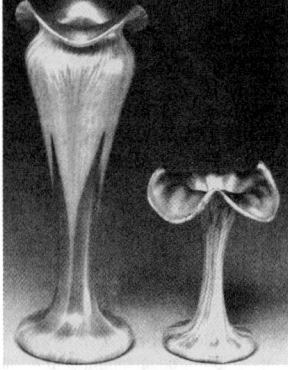

Quezal Floriform Vases

Vase, 4 1/4" h., floriform, cushion foot below tapering to a slender ribbed body w/a trefoil floriform lip, white w/green trailings & pink & amber iridescence, signed "Quezal - 167" centering a "T" (ILLUS. right) **920**

Vase, 4 1/2" h., ruffled rim, gold iridescent pulled-feather decoration, signed **550**

Short and Tall Quezal Vases

Vase, 5 1/8" h., wide ovoid body tapering to a tiny short neck, deep reddish amber w/silvery blue & gold iridescence, overlaid w/silver depictions of flowers & wispy foliage, signed "Quezal - D1150" (ILLUS. left).. **1,380**

Vase, 6" h., "Agate," ovoid body tapering to a tall trumpet neck, opaque greyish brown w/agate-like streaks of amber, blue, aqua, green & black at the rim, signed on the base..................................... **2,500**

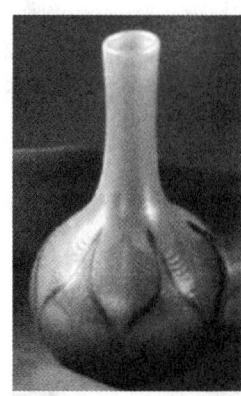

Fine Pulled-Feather Quezal Vase

Vase, 6" h., bottle-form, spherical base tapering to a tall slender 'stick' neck, yellow opal ground in iridescent gold w/a pulled-feather band around the base trimmed in dark green, signed on the pontil (ILLUS.) . **2,090**

Vase, 6" h., floriform, a round thin cushion foot tapering to a short slender stem supporting the cupped bowl w/a high wide six-lobe flaring rim, green pulled-feather design from the foot up halfway on the opal body, gold iridescent interior, signed "Quezal 8".. **3,080**

Vase, 6 3/16" h., floriform body on a low domed foot, opalescent decorated w/pulled green feathering w/amber iridescent interior, inscribed "Quezal - R - 858," ca. 1900.. **1,500**

Vase, 6 1/4" h., bulbous ovoid body w/a rounded shoulder to the cylindrical neck w/a flared ruffled rim, amber iridescent ground overlaid around the neck & shoulder w/stylized interlacing sterling silver design, inscribed mark, ca. 1920............... **1,500**

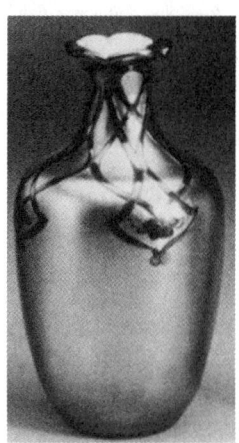

Quezal Vase with Silver Overlay

Vase, 6 1/2" h., ovoid body w/a broad shoulder tapering to a short cyindrical neck w/a flaring crimped rim, amber w/gold iridescence, overlaid around the neck & shoulder w/silver Art Nouveau floral & vine designs, glass stressed at rim silver attachment, signed "Quezal - D 1193" (ILLUS.).. **1,035**

Vase, 7 1/2" h., floriform, the opalescent sides decorated w/green striated feathering, the foot further decorated w/amber iridescent feathering, the interior in amber iridescence, inscribed "Quezal," ca. 1925 .... **1,550**

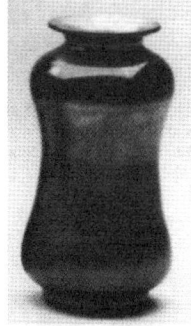

Blue Iridescent Quezal Vase

Vase, 8" h., footed double-bulbed cylindrical body w/a short flaring neck, blue iridescent exterior, signed (ILLUS.) **750**

Vase, 8" h., ovoid body w/a slender neck w/everted rim, overall gold iridescence, signed.. **483**

Vase, 8" h., swelled cylindrical shouldered body tapering to a trumpet-form neck, silvery & bluish green gold iridescent finish, signed on base **750**

Vase, 8" h., tall ovoid body w/a short flaring neck, overall gold iridescence, signed **578**

Vase, 8 1/4" h., floriform, slender baluster-form body w/a trefoil lip & cushion foot, white w/green pulled-leaf decoration & gold trailings w/pink iridescence, very small internal crack under foot, signed "Quezal - 794" surrounding an O (ILLUS. left with small floriform vase) **1,035**

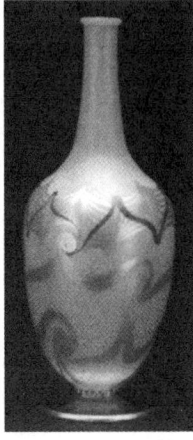

Fine Decorated Quezal Vase

Vase, 9" h., footed ovoid body tapering to a slender 'stick' neck, Egyptian Revival style w/a creamy white body decorated w/a green zigzag shoulder design above gold iridescent double hooked & pulled-feather design, by Martin Bach, foot inscribed "Quezal N.Y." (ILLUS.) **4,000**

Vase, 9 3/8" h., slender footed ovoid body w/constricting neck & flaring lip, amber iridescence shading to yellow & violet, pontil signed, ca. 1920 .... **750**

Vase, 9 1/2" h., flared rounded base tapering gently to a tall cylindrical body w/a flat rim, amber w/golden crimson iridescence, signed "Quezal - D1203" (ILLUS. right with silver-decorated vase) **546**

Vase, 9 3/4" h., a cushion foot supporting a slender trumpet-form body w/a widely flaring & ruffled rim, opaque white ground decorated on the exterior w/green & gold pulled-feather designs & a band of gold iridescent hearts around the neck, etched "Quezal 6"... **2,750**

Vase, 9 7/8" h., bulbous ovoid base tapering to a tall slender & slightly flaring 'stick' neck, amber iridescence overlaid in sterling silver & cut w/blossoms, leaves & whiplash strapwork, signed on pontil, ca. 1910 .... **1,600**

Vase, 10 1/2" h., baluster-form w/a cushion foot, the rounded shoulder w/a small widely flaring trumpet neck, overall blue iridescence, signed **1,210**

Vase, 10 3/4" h., jack-in-the-pulpit-form, green pulled-feather design tipped in iridescent gold stretch from base to top, iridescent gold interior **3,300**

Vase, 12 1/4" h., jack-in-the-pulpit form w/cushion foot, slender cylindrical body & wide rolled rim, purplish blue shading to golden iridescence, silver feathering on the foot extending into the body, signed.... **2,750**

Vase, 12 3/4" h., bulbous cushion foot tapering to a tall slightly flaring cylindrical body w/a widely flaring six-ruffle rim, overall gold iridescence, signed................. **1,568**

Vase, 12 3/4" h., tall baluster-form body swelled at the top & w/a short cylindrical neck, opalescent decorated w/pulled green & gold iridescent leafage & applied w/reeded gold medallions w/tendrils down the sides, unsigned, ca. 1910 .... **4,500**

Vase, 13 1/8" h., jack-in-the-pulpit form, the widely flaring ruffled rim above a slender stem & bulbous base in opalescent decorated w/finely pulled feathering in mint green & amber iridescence, the interior in amber iridescence, signed, ca. 1920 .... **5,750**

Vase, 13 1/2" h., jack-in-the-pulpit form, widely flaring top above a slender stem & squatty bulbous base, overall amber iridescence w/the top tinged w/rings of pink & green, signed "Quezal - G646," ca. 1920 .... **5,750**

Vase, 16" h., jack-in-the-pulpit form, the broad undulating mouth w/crackled gold iridescence, issuing from a slender stem & bulbous cushion foot, elaborately decorated w/gold & green pulled-feather & swirled designs, signed "Quezal M 702" ... **6,500**

Rose Bowls

These decorative small bowls were widely popular in the late 19th and early 20th centuries. Produced in various types of glass, they are most common in satin glass or spatter glass. They are generally a spherical shape with an incurved crimped rim, but ovoid or egg-shaped examples were also popular.

Their name derives from their reported use, to hold dried rose petal potpourri or small fresh-cut roses.

Miniature Amethyst Rose Bowl

Amethyst, miniature, six-crimp rim, enameled w/white & rust blossoms & green leaves, 2" h. (ILLUS.).................................. **$250**

Two Intaglio Engraved Rose Bowls

Amethyst, six-crimp rim, deep color w/intaglio floral engraving, attributed to Moser, ca. 1910, 2 1/2" h. (ILLUS. right).. **300-350**

Two "Jewell" Glass Rose Bowls

Blue, eight-crimp rim, threaded body w/overall thumbprints, Stevens & Williams "Jewell" glass, 2 1/4" h. (ILLUS. right) **125-175**

Reproduction Maize Rose Bowl

Cased, golden amber cased in white, Libbey's Maize patt. reproduced by L.G. Wright Glass Co., ca. 1970, 4 1/2" h. (ILLUS.) **85-125**

Two Thomas Webb Satin Rose Bowls

Cased satin, eight-crimp rim, blue shaded to pale blue, decorated w/heavy gilt prunus blossoms, decorated by Jules Barbe for Thomas Webb & Sons, 2 1/4" h. (ILLUS. left).. **250-325**

Floral Embossed Rose Bowl

Cased satin, eight-crimp rim, dark green shaded to pale green, Floral Embossed patt., ca. 1890s, 3 1/2" h. (ILLUS.)......... **125-175**

Cased satin, eight-crimp rim, deep red shaded to soft orange, decorated w/heavy gold prunus blossoms, a butterfly on the reverse, decorated by Jules Barbe for Thomas Webb & Sons, 3" h. (ILLUS. right with blue bowl) **400-600**

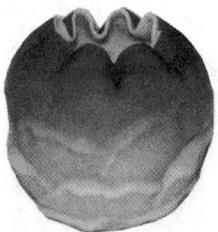

Cabbage Pattern Satin Rose Bowl

Cased satin, eight-crimp rim, deep rose pink shaded to creamy white, Cabbage patt., white lining, 4 1/2" d., 4 1/2" h. (ILLUS.) **165**

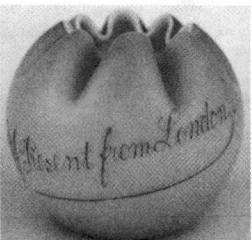

Souvenir Satin Rose Bowl

Cased satin, eight-crimp rim, peach shaded to creamy white, inscribed in yellow enamel "A Present from London," marked on base "Made in Bohemia," 3 1/2" h. (ILLUS.).................................... **125-175**

Mother-of-Pearl Satin Rose Bowl

Cased satin, eight-crimp rim, shaded blue mother-of-pearl Diamond Quilted patt., probably Webb, 3 3/4" h. (ILLUS.)......... **275-325**

Shell & Seaweed Pattern Rose Bowl

Cased satin, eight-crimp rim, Shell & Seaweed molded patt., deep pink shaded to pale pink, enameled around the top w/orange leaves & white blossoms, orange dots on the shells, ca. 1880s, 5" h. (ILLUS.).. **125-175**

Cased satin, eight-crimp rim, spherical, shadow dark brown to cream enameled w/gold foliage w/a butterfly on the reverse, attributed to Webb, 3 1/4" d., 3" h....... **468**

Box-pleated Satin Rose Bowl

Cased satin, six-crimp box-pleated rim, brown shaded to creamy white, Stevens & Williams, 4 3/4" h. (ILLUS.)................. **200-250**

Cased satin, six-crimp rim, miniature, plum shaded to light plum, heavy gilt prunus blossoms decoration, creamy lining, Thomas Webb, 3 1/2" d., 2 1/2" h. (ILLUS. top next column).. **245**

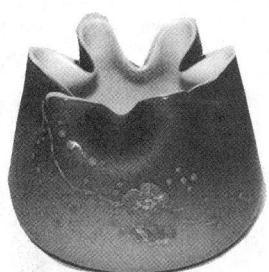

Plum Satin with Prunus Rose Bowl

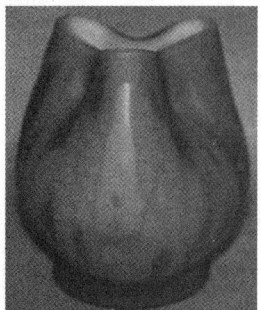

Mother-of-Pearl Stripe Rose Bowl

Cased satin, three-crimp rim, miniature, green mother-of-pearl Stripe patt., Thomas Webb, 2 1/2" h. (ILLUS.) **150-200**

Satin Rose Bowl with Acorns

Creamy white, four-crimp rim, miniature, satin ground decorated overall w/orange acorns on green stems, 2 3/4" h. (ILLUS.) **85-110**

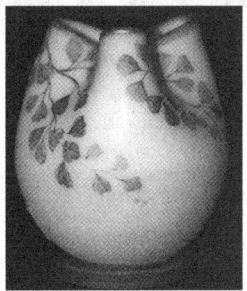

Decorated Satin Rose Bowl

Creamy white, three-crimp rim, footed satin decorated w/light green & brown gingko branches, Thomas Webb, 2 3/4" h. (ILLUS.).. **225-275**

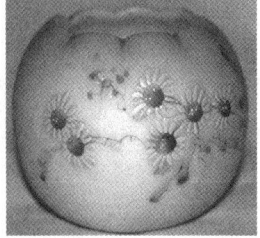

Miniature Rose Bowl with Daisies

Crown Milano, eight-crimp rim, miniature, pale blue shaded to creamy white, boldly enameled w/large yellow & purple daisies w/green leafy stems, 2 3/4" h. (ILLUS.)... **400**

Pale Green Decorated Rose Bowl

Green, six-crimp rim, miniature, pale optic-ribbed form w/gilt decoration around the rim, 2" h. (ILLUS.)...................................... **75-100**
Green shaded to clear, six-crimp rim, intaglio etched w/a large blossom, attributed to Moser, ca. 1910, 2" h. (ILLUS. left w/amethyst intaglio bowl)........................ **250-300**
Olive green, eight-crimp rim, threaded body w/overall thumbprints, Stevens & Williams "Jewell" glass, 2 1/4" h. (ILLUS. left w/blue "Jewell" bowl) **125-175**

Porcelain Souvenir Rose Bowl

Porcelain, six-crimp rim, miniature, souvenir-type, cobalt blue ground w/a round gold-trimmed reserve w/a color transfer scene of the "National Cash Register Co., Dayton, Ohio," 2" h. (ILLUS.) **35-55**
Spangled, eight-crimp rim, reddish orange cased in white spatter w/silver mica flecks throughout, 3 1/2" h. (ILLUS. top next column).. **100-150**

Spangled Glass Rose Bowl

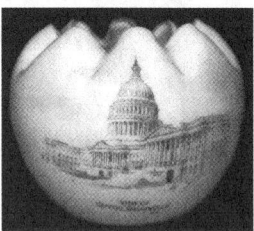

White Satin Souvenir Rose Bowl

White, eight-crimp rim, souvenir-type, satin ground decorated w/a black transfer of the U.S. Capitol, made in Austria, 4 1/2" d., 3 3/4" h. (ILLUS.).................... **100-150**

Yellowish Green Optic Ribbed Bowl

Yellowish green, eight-crimp rim, optic ribbed design, 5" h. (ILLUS.) **45-50**

Royal Flemish

Royal Flemish Cracker Jar

This ware, made by Mt. Washington Glass Co., is characterized by very heavy enameled gold lines dividing the surface into separate areas or sections. The body, with a matte finish, is variously decorated.

Cracker jar, cov., barrel-shaped, gold Roman Coin decoration on a ground of brown & tan random panels outlined in heavy gold lines, ornate silver plate rim, cover & bail handle, signed (ILLUS.)... **$1,800-2,200**

Cracker jar, cov., ovoid body, overall decoration of large Roman coins on stained panels divided by heavy gold lines, ornate silver plate cover, rim & bail handle, original paper label w/"Mt. W. G. Co. Royal Flemish," 8" h.................................... **2,200**

Cracker jar, cov., wide bulbous form w/molded scallop bands around the shoulder & base decorated in gold, the body enameled w/large yellow & white mums & leaves, silver plate scroll-molded cover, 5 1/4" h. **825**

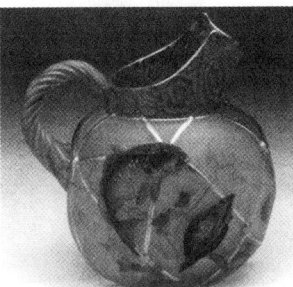

Rare Royal Flemish Pitcher

Pitcher, 8 5/8" h., bulbous body w/a low cylindrical neck w/angled rim, applied ropetwist handle, acid-finished, enameled w/two small fish swimming against a background of shells & marine plants in various shades of lavender puce, deep emerald green, Chinese red, chocolate brown & lemon yellow w/heavy gilt trim, reserved against a ground formed of irregular panels enameled in lavender & pale yellow between raised gold borders conjoined by raised balls, the neck enameled w/scrolling coral edged in gilt & reserved against a strawberry ground, original paper label (ILLUS.)...................... **9,000**

Vase, 4" h., gold enameled griffin & scrolling against an orangish amber stained glass window ground... **1,250**

Vase, 4" h., 4 3/4" d. footed wide squatty bulbous body w/the wide shoulder centered by a tiny cylindrical neck, decorated w/panels of tan, brown & rust separated by heavy gilt bands & decorated w/a large gilt griffin **715**

Vase, 6" h., double gourd-form, decorated w/colorful pansies & gold enameling on a frosted ground... **1,500**

Satin

Satin glass was a popular decorative glass developed in the late 19th century. Most pieces were composed of

two layers of glass with the exterior layer usually in a shaded pastel color. The name derives from the soft matte finish, caused by exposure to acid fumes, which gave the surface a "satiny" feel. Mother-of-pearl satin glass was a specialized variety wherein air trapped between the layers of glass provided subtle surface patterns such as Herringbone and Diamond Quilted. A majority of satin glass was produced in England, Bohemia and America, but collectors should be aware that reproductions have been produced for many years.

Celery vase, cylindrical, shaded blue mother-of-pearl Diamond Quilted patt., 6 1/2" h.. **$165**

Rare Satin Creamer & Sugar Bowl

Creamer & open sugar bowl, each footed w/a melon-lobed body tapering to a upright crimped rim, nearly translucent opal to rose to blue mother-of-pearl Herringbone patt., applied frosted clear handle on creamer, sugar 3 1/2" h., creamer 5" h., pr. (ILLUS.) **5,060**

Creamer & open sugar bowl, footed bulbous form in blue mother-of-pearl Ribbon patt., the sugar w/a three-lobed form, the creamer w/one side pinched to form the spout, applied clear frosted handle & bases, creamer 2 1/8" h., sugar 2 3/8" h., pr. **325**

Cruet w/original stopper, shaded pink mother-of-pearl Diamond Quilted patt., squatty bulbous body tapering to a slender neck & tricorner rim, decorated w/finely enameled blue forget-me-nots & white daisies & leaves, applied frosted clear reeded handle, clear frosted facet-cut stopper, 8" h. **990**

Cruet w/original stopper, shaded pink mother-of-pearl Herringbone patt., bulbous tapering to a tricorner rim, clear frosted stopper & applied handle, 5 1/4" h.. **330**

Decorated Pink Satin Ewer

Ewer, a cushion foot supporting a squatty tapering bulbous melon-lobed body below a tall slender gently flaring neck w/a tricorner wide rim, shaded pink decorated w/large white & tan flowers w/yellow centers & blue & yellow stems, applied frosted slender handle, 3 3/4" d., 10" h. (ILLUS.).. **165**

Ewer, ovoid body w/small neck tapering to a ruffled top, shaded yellow mother-of-pearl Herringbone patt., applied amber thorn handle, 7 1/4" h. **220**

Ewer, shaded pink mother-of-pearl Herringbone patt., bulbous base w/slender neck to a ruffled spout, applied frosted clear handle, 6 3/4" h... **105**

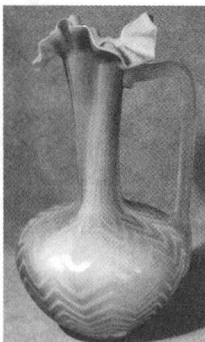

Rainbow Mother-of-Pearl Satin Ewer

Ewer, squatty bulbous base w/a wide shoulder centering a tall gently flaring neck w/a tricorner ruffled rim, Rainbow mother-of-pearl Herringbone patt., applied angular clear frosted handle, 10 1/2" h. (ILLUS.)................... **1,500-2,000**

Mustard pot, cov., ovoid shaded pink mother-of-pearl Raindrop patt., silver plate rim, cover & bail handle, 3" h. **303**

Pitcher, 8 1/2" h., bulbous ovoid body tapering to a short neck w/a crimped & ruffled rim at the back of the wide smooth spout, shaded pink mother-of-pearl Raindrop patt., applied frosted clear reeded handle **385**

Pitcher, 9" h., shaded golden brown to white mother-of-pearl Coin Dot patt., bulbous body w/pinched indentations around the sides, cylindrical neck, applied handle... **330**

Decorated Blue Herringbone Vase

Vase, 6 1/2" h., 4" d., wide tapering ovoid body w/a wide shoulder centering a short trumpet neck, shaded blue mother-of-pearl Herringbone patt., decorated w/stripes of gilt leaf sprigs, white lining (ILLUS.) **225**

Blue Diamond Quilted Satin Vase

Vase, 7 3/4" h., 4" d., simple ovoid form tapering to a cyindrical neck w/a widely flaring rolled three-lobe rim, blue mother-of-pearl Diamond Quilted patt., applied frosted clear rim (ILLUS.)................................. **225**

Seneca

Seneca operated from 1891 until 1983. Starting in Ohio it soon relocated to Morgantown, West Virginia where it gained a world class reputation for high quality lead cut crystal. Seneca glass was exported as early as the late 1890s and would be commissioned by U.S. embassies, presidential palaces and dignitaries. While known for colorless crystal, the period of the 1920s through the 1940s and the 1970s and '80s saw major production in a rainbow of colors. Colored patterns by Seneca were produced in a variety of shapes and forms making it a good collectible.

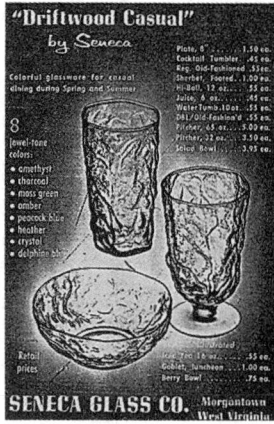

Seneca "Drfitwood" Advertisement

Bell, classic, cut 1450, 3" h. **$65**
Bell, moss green, 3" h. 32
Bell, ruby, 4" h. 42
Bell, hanging-type, Christmas 1978 18
Bell, Liberty w/pewter & wood stand, etched
    1976, signed "Seneca" 85
Bowl, 4 1/2" d., Cascade, cobalt blue 32
Bowl, fruit/sauce, Candlewick etching, ruby
    foot & stem, clear bowl 32
Bowl, fruit/sauce, Driftwood, plum 12
Candlestick, No. 4 clear, cut 853, 10" h. 98
Candlestick, mushroom shape No. 30,
    clear w/cut 900 48
Candlestick, mushroom shape No. 30,
    ruby w/clear foot 120
Candy jar, cov., stemmed cutting 778, clear 90
Compote, 7" d., clear line No. 449, cut 597 68
Compote, Driftwood, Apple green 24
Cordial, clear Majestic cut, 5 1/8" h. 58
Cordial, square clear foot, cobalt bowl 64
Creamer & sugar bowl, No. 1934,
    stemmed clear cut, pr. 189
Goblet, water, Cascade, ruby w/clear foot,
    6" h. 32
Goblet, water, cut 1445 Heritage, 8 1/2" h. 54
Goblet, water, airtwist stem cut 795 125
Goblet, water, Artichoke, clear w/black foot 28
Goblet, water, Artichoke, Delphine blue 22
Goblet, water, Candlewick etching, depres-
    sion green stem & foot, clear bowl 38
Goblet, water, Candlewick etching, ruby
    foot & stem, clear bowl 45
Goblet, water, Driftwood, Apple green 19
Goblet, water, Driftwood, Avocado green 8
Goblet, water, Driftwood, clear 9
Goblet, water, Driftwood, cobalt blue 24
Goblet, water, Driftwood, ruby 28
Goblet, water, Estes etching, platinum rim
    line 499 65
Goblet, water, No. 903, Naomi platinum en-
    crusted band, cobalt bowl, square foot
    line 903 48
Goblet, water, No. 903, square foot,
    opaque green/jade optic bowl 125
Parfait, Driftwood, pink, 5" 18
Pitcher, Driftwood, plum, 32 oz. 48
Pitcher, Cascade, cobalt blue, 40 oz. 74
Pitcher, Driftwood, Apple green, 66 oz. 58
Pitcher, Driftwood, ruby, 66 oz. 89
Plate, 8" d., clear cut 779 48
Plate, 8" d., Sang Blue etch, clear 42
Plate, Driftwood, Apple green 14
Plate, Driftwood, cobalt blue 21
Punch bowl & ladle, clear cut 326, 2 pcs. 480
Roly poly, Driftwood, Avocado green 44
Tree, stackable four-piece box, moss green 58
Tree, stackable four-piece box, ruby
    w/drape optic 120
Tumbler, highball, Driftood, pink, 5" h. 14
Tumbler, iced tea, Driftwood, gray 9
Tumbler, iced tea, Driftwood, yellow 12
Tumbler, juice, flat, Driftwood, cobalt blue 14
Tumbler, footed, Driftwood, Apple green 10
Vase, 1 1/2" h., Driftwood, ruby 32
Vase, 7 1/2" h., Driftwood, amber 18

Silver Deposit - Silver Overlay

Silver Deposit and Silver Overlay have been made
commercially since the last quarter of the 19th century.
Silver is deposited on the glass by various means, most
commonly by utilizing an electric current. The glass was

very popular during the first three decades of this cen-
tury, and some pieces are still being produced. During
the late 1970s, silver commanded exceptionally high
prices and this was reflected in a surge of interest in sil-
ver overlay glass, especially in pieces marked "Sterling"
or "925" on the heavy silver overlay.

Basket, lime green, a tall slender waisted
form w/a widely flaring rim w/two sides
turned up & joined by a tall pointed handle,
decorated overall w/silver overlay of roses
& foliate border, silvered handle & berry
prunts at handle, silver mark of the La
Pierre Mfg. Co., polished pontil, early
20th c., 11 3/4" h. (minor repair to silver)... **$2,415**

Three Silver-Overlay Decanters

Decanter w/stopper, wide squatty bulbous
clear form w/the wide shoulder centering
a short cylindrical neck w/a high arched
spout, flat-topped bubble stopper & applied silver-encased handle, the body &
stopper overlaid w/ornate scrolled foliage
designs, late 19th - early 20th c., 6 3/4" h.
(ILLUS. right front) 748
Decanter w/stopper, a wide domed form
w/a flat base, short cylindrical neck
w/spout & loop handle, clear decorated
overall w/an elaborate silver overall vining floral design, monogrammed,
8 1/2" h. 715
Decanter w/stopper, squared tapering
clear body w/a narrow shoulder & short
paneled neck w/flat rim, faceted clear
stopper, decorated overall w/large silver
overlay blossoms & scrolling leafy stems,
late 19th - early 20th c., 9" h. (ILLUS. left
front 690
Decanter w/stopper, bulbous teardrop-
form w/fitted silver stopper, clear w/or-
nate silver oak leaf design centered by a
scrolling silver monogram & a date on the
collar, marked by Gorham Mfg. Co.,
Providence, Rhode Island, late 19th -
early 20th c., 9 1/2" h. (ILLUS. center
back) 863
Decanter w/original stopper, bulbous
clear shape w/octagonal neck, decorated
w/engraved grape & vine silver overlay
w/a central cartouche, the base w/a cut
sunburst design, w/matching faceted silver overlay stopper, Alvin Silver Co.,

Providence, Rhode Island, early 20th c.,
8 1/4" h... **403**

Silver Overlay Perfume Bottle

Perfume bottle w/original stopper, clear
squatty tapering lobed form w/a short cylindrical neck & flattened rim, tall pointed
& lobed stopper, decorated overall w/sil-
ver overlay scrolling design w/inscription
dated 1913, 4 3/4" h. (ILLUS.) **305**

Perfume bottle w/stopper, clear squat
pear-shaped body w/flared rim, plain ball
stopper, the body w/scrolling silver over-
lay decoration, late 19th c., 3" h. **86**

Perfume bottles w/original stoppers,
squat cone shape w/flared lip & bulbous
stopper, clear w/overall engraved foliate
design in silver overlay, polished pontil,
Alvin Silver Co., Providence, Rhode Is-
land, early 20th c., 3 3/4" h., pr. **575**

Pitcher, 9 1/4" h., tankard-type, a swelled
base tapering to a tall cylindrical body,
clear completely encased in a silver overlay scrolling design of grapevines, silver-
overlaid handle, marked "Sterling - 33" **825**

Ornate Silver Deposit Vase

Vase, 12 1/2" h., squatty wide base w/a
wide shoulder centered by a gently flaring cylindrical body w/a bulbed shoulder
below the short cylindrical neck, clear
w/smoky iridescence & an overall silver
deposit design of scrolling leafy stems &
carnation blossoms, ca. 1920s (ILLUS.) **700**

Smith Brothers

*Originally established as a decorating department of
the Mt. Washington Glass Company in the 1870s, the
firm later was an independent business in New Bedford,*

*Massachusetts. Beautifully decorated opal white glass
was their hallmark but they also did glass cutting. Some
examples carry their lion-in-the-shield mark.*

Smith Brothers Vase with Stork

Smith Brothers Mark

Bowl, 5 1/4" d., 2 1/2" h., melon-ribbed
body, decorated w/purple violets **$100**

Bowl-vase, wide squatty bulbous body w/a
wide short cylindrical neck, ivory ground
decorated w/yellow daises & green
stems, enameled dots around rim,
stamped Lion trademark, 5 1/2" d.,
3 3/4" h. (four rim dots missing) **220**

Box w/hinged lid, melon-ribbed body,
white decorated w/h.p. pansies, 5 1/2" d. **450**

Cracker jar, cov., barrel-shaped, creamy
white ground decorated w/h.p. daisies,
silver plate rim, cover & bail handle,
signed... **575**

Cracker jar, cov., melon-ribbed body, h.p.
pansies outlined in gold on a peach
ground, silver plate cover, marked,
6 1/2" d., 6 1/2" h... **550**

Pitcher, 8" h., decorated w/gold floral
branch on glossy white ground **198**

Powder box, cov., enameled floral decora-
tion w/beaded trim, lion mark **275**

Sugar bowl, cov., squatty bulbous body in
opal decorated w/daisies & leaves, silver
plate rim, low domed cover & twisted bail
handle, marked... **413**

Sugar shaker w/original metal lid, cylindrical finely ribbed body, decorated
w/delicate daisy blossoms on a satin
white ground, 5 3/4" h. **440**

Sweetmeat jar, cov., opaque white squatty
melon-ribbed body & cover, decorated
overall w/h.p. tiny blue flowers, silver
plate rim & ball handle, signed, 5 1/2" d.,
5 1/2" h. to top of handle **750**

Vase, 3 3/4" h., acorn-shaped melon-ribbed
body, decorated w/enameled florals &
leaves w/enameled beading on rim.............. **145**

Vase, 4 1/2" h., bulbous satin ivory body w/four indentations around the sides, the shoulder centered by a tiny flared neck, decorated w/yellow daisies & green stems, an enamel dotted rim, red lion trademark.. **358**

Vase, 5 1/2" h., 3 3/4" d., narrow squatty base tapering to cylindrical sides, h.p. decoration of a stork standing amid grasses, pale pink background (ILLUS.) **250-300**

Vase, 6 1/4" h., baluster-form, embossed rope decoration around rim, decorated w/delicate daisies & leaves & heavy gold trim, rampant lion mark.................................... **275**

Rare Smith Brothers Canteen Vase

Vase, 8 1/2" h., double canteen-form, two flattened disk form vases conjoined & decorated w/lovely wisteria blossoms & vines on a creamy ground, signed (ILLUS.).. **2,000-2,500**

Spatter

This variegated-color ware is similar to Spangled glass but does not contain metallic flakes. The various colors are applied on a clear, opaque white or colored body. Much of it was made in Europe and England. It is sometimes called "End Of Day."

Floral-decorated Spatter Cruet

Cruet w/stopper, squatty bulbous body tapering to a cylindrical neck w/arched spout, deep maroon, red & white spatter in clear, enameled w/a sprig of small blue flowers on green & yellow leafy stem, ap-

plied clear handle, facet-cut clear stopper, 3 1/2" d., 5 1/2" h. (ILLUS.).................. **$245**

Cruet w/stopper, melon-lobed body, shades of amber spatter, applied clear handle & facet-cut stopper, 6 3/4" h.............. **110**

Pitcher, 8 1/4" h., water, spherical body w/square top & applied reeded handle, mottled wine red & white in clear...................... **94**

Decorated Spatter Vase

Vase, 7" h., 4 1/2" d., footed bulbous body w/a rounded shoulder centering a ringed trumpet neck, yellow cased w/white spatter, enamel-decorated w/a large flowering branch w/a bird in purple, white, green, brown & black, applied angled clear shoulder handles (ILLUS.)...................... **165**

Water set: pitcher & one tumbler; bulbous pitcher w/a clover-form rim, decorated w/amber tones of spatter & enameled w/colorful spring blossoms, matching tumbler, pitcher 8 1/2" h., the set.................. **110**

Water set: pitcher & six tumblers; bulbous pitcher w/squared mouth, Inverted Thumbprint patt. w/white & cranberry splashes in clear, applied clear handle, matching tumblers, pitcher 8 1/2" h., the set (one tumbler w/small chip) **193**

Steuben

Most of the Steuben glass listed below was made at the Steuben Glass Works, now a division of Corning Glass, between 1903 and about 1933. The factory was organized by T.G. Hawkes, noted glass designer, Frederick Carder, and others. Mr. Carder devised many types of glass and revived many old techniques.

Steuben Marks

Acid Cut-back

Vase, 8 3/4" h, round Alabaster foot below the wide bulbous body w/the shoulder centered by a wide low rolled neck, Green Jade cut to a textured Alabaster ground w/a scalloped green band around the neck & shoulder & a wide band of large stylized round blossoms on angular stems around the center **$1,595**

Alabaster
Bowl, 7 7/8" d., 4 3/4" h., small foot on a wide rounded base w/tall upright & gently flared sides w/broad lightly molded pillars, Shape No. 6415 variant, ca. 1925 ..... **1,495**
Urn, cov., pedestal foot below the wide ovoid body tapering to a fitted domed cover, decorated around the bottom of the body w/a wide band of blue & iridescent gold leaf devices, similar design radiating from the center of the cover, acorn finial, 6 3/4" h. (small flake on finial) **1,925**

Aquamarine
Perfume bottle & stopper, footed tall slender swelled cylindrical body w/a short neck & flattened rim, tall pointed stopper, Shape No. 1988, 8" h. **330**

Aurene
Bowl, 6" d., shallow round form w/wide flattened & ruffled rim, overall blue iridescence, pontil marked "Aurene Haviland" (minor nick on edge of pontil) **460**
Bowl, 6" d., 2 1/4" h., deep rounded flaring sides, overall gold iridescence, signed "F. Carder Aurene" on base............................ **518**
Candlesticks, wide disk foot below the slender standard swelled & twisted near the top below the cylindrical candle socket w/flattened rim, overall gold iridescence, Shape No. 686, signed, 10" h., pr... **1,430**
Console bowl, wide rounded form on three applied prunt feet, Shape No. 2586, signed, 10" d. **330**
Darning egg, spherical head on a tapering rounded handle, overall blue iridescence, 7" l. **308**
Finger bowl & underplate, round bowl on matching wide underplate, overall gold iridescence, bowl signed "Steuben Aurene 2889," underplate signed "Steuben Aurene 2028," bowl 4 3/4" d., plate 8 1/4" d., the set... **523**
Pitcher, 5" h., bulbous cylindrical form w/applied handle, blue dusted w/a silvery blue iridescence, signed "aurene - 3064," ca. 1920... **977**
Vase, 5 3/4" h., bottle-form, spherical body w/a tall slender 'stick' neck bulbed at the base & flared at the top, fine ribbing on the shoulder & up the neck, overall gold iridescence, Shape No. 240, signed **1,100**
Vase, 6 1/4" h., double-gourd form, the body composed of two squatty bulbous sections below the very wide flaring trumpet neck, spaced ribbing up the sides & neck, dark blue iridescence, signed.............. **935**
Vase, 6 1/2" h., "tree-trunk" form, three staggered thorny cylindrical holders on a round foot, deep blue iridescence, inscribed "STEUBEN Aurene 2744," ca. 1910-20 .... **990**
Vase, 6 1/2" h., trumpet-form w/widely flaring six-ruffle rim, overall gold iridescence

w/stretched effect at the rim, Shape No. 346, signed.. **880**
Vase, 8 1/4" h., bulbous ovoid body w/a wide rounded shoulder centered by a wide short rolled neck, overall fine gold iridescence, Shape No. 2412, signed **825**

Aurene Acid-etched Vase

Vase, 8 3/8" h., bulbous ovoid body tapering to a short widely rolled neck, iridescent gold acid-cut w/a band of leafy vines laden w/grape clusters, the shoulder & base cut w/palm fronds, against a mirror black ground, ca. 1925 (ILLUS.)................ **4,025**
Vase, 10" h., flaring foot below the tall swelled cylindrical body w/a narrow shoulder to the lower trumpet neck, overall blue iridescence, Shape No. 2908, signed.. **1,183**
Vase, 10" h., 10" d., trumpet-form w/a footed slender stem below the wide bulbous shoulder below a wide squatty bulbous neck & wide flattened rim, overall blue iridescence, Shape No. 2684, signed **1,980**

Feather-decorated Aurene Vase

Vase, 12" h., slender baluster-form w/cylindrical neck, organic green leaf forms pulled into Alabaster white decorated w/gold Aurene peacock feathers centering four gold hearts w/green peacock eyes, signed "Aurene - 535," short shallow scratch on side (ILLUS.) **3,910**

Vase, 12" h., wide bulbous ovoid body w/a short flared neck, amber w/overall strong gold iridescence, Shape No. 2683, signed (minor scratches) **3,738**

Bristol Yellow
Urn, cov., a cylindrical body w/swirled optic ribbing raised on a domed optic pedestal foot w/foled rim, the high domed cover w/a tall pointed green finial, rough pontil, signed near edge, 4" d., 9" h. **259**

Vase, 7" h., 6 3/4" d., a thick footring below the wide cylindrical optic swirled body flaring at the rim, polished pontil, signed **173**

Calcite
Candlestick, flaring pedestal base supporting a cylindrical socket w/a domed & widely flaring rim lined in gold Aurene, signed, Shape No. 3581, 6 1/2" h. **385**

Vase, 8" h., trumpet-form w/a widely flaring six-lobed ruffled rim, iridescent gold Aurene interior **495**

Cintra

Steuben Cintra Bowl

Bowl, 7 1/4" d., 6" h., amethyst quartz-type, deep rounded cup-form w/undulating rim, mottled & crackled pink, blue & frosted colorless body w/three applied leafing branches connecting to the looped branch feet, Shape No. 6856, small chips (ILLUS.) **1,150**

Cluthra

Steuben Cluthra Wall Pocket

Vase, 4 3/4" h., 6 7/8" d., wide squatty form w/flat angled lower body w/wide inwarded angled flat upper body, bubbly glass shading from green to white, signed on base **690**

Vase, 10 1/4" h., wide bulbous ovoid shouldered form w/a short small rolled neck, lime green w/overall white bubbled mottling, Shape No. 2683, signed **2,640**

Wall pocket, half-round flared bowl of black & white Cluthra cut & mounted in a foliate gilt-metal framework, polished pontil, slight corrosion to metal, ca. 1930, 15 1/2" w., 8" h. (ILLUS.) **489**

Ivrene
Center bowl, wide w/ruffled rim, Shape No. 7423, 12" d., 4 3/4" h. **248**

Console set, deep rounded bowl w/deeply ruffled flaring sides & a pair of cornucopia vases on trumpet bases, bowl signed, bowl 12" l., vases 6" h., 3 pcs. **1,456**

Epergne, a wide round low domed foot supporting a tall slender central trumpet vase w/wide rim flanked by a pair of jack-in-the-pulpit vases w/high pointed pulled-up back edges attached to the central vase & rolled edges & front, Shape No. 7566, signed, 12 1/4" h. **1,100**

Vase, 5" h., 5" d., footed squatty bulbous base below the wide tall trumpet-form body w/slightly ruffled rim, signed in script on base "F. Carder Steuben" **345**

Vase, 8" h., wide ovoid body w/the wide shoulder centered by a short rolled neck, faint iridescent sheen, Shape No. 8453, ca. 1920, later signature **805**

Ivrene Baluster-form Vase

Vase, 11 1/4" h., wide baluster-form body w/wide ribbing, lightly iridized finish, three applied aqua Cintra shoulder handles, thin brush line of opaque white around the shoulder, signed, Shape No. 7568 (ILLUS.) **1,380**

Ivrene Jack-in-the-Pulpit Vase

Vase, 12 1/2" h., jack-in-the-pulpit-type, disk foot below the swirled trumpet-form body w/crimped & pulled-up rim (ILLUS.).. **1,200**

Vases, 5 1/2" h., ribbed morning glory-form bodies, Shape No. 813, pr. **220**

Jade

Fine Yellow Jade & Aurene Lamp

Bowl, 4 5/8" d., 2 1/2" h., small flat bottom on deep upright sides w/a widely flaring flat rim, Yellow Jade, polished pontil **345**

Bowl, 11 1/4" d., 4" h., small cushion foot below the wide rounded body w/upright sides below the wide flat rim, Green Jade, signed on base (base wear) **518**

Center bowl, wide shallow round form w/incurved sides, Blue Jade, Shape No. 5019, 10" d. **440**

Center bowl, wide shallow round form w/incurved sides, Yellow Jade, Shape No. 5019, 10" d. **495**

Compote, open, 7" d., 2 3/4" h., a wide shallow flat-rimmed Jade Green bowl raised on a short plain Alabaster stem & round foot, polished pontil w/edge roughness **259**

Console bowl, wide round form, Mirror Black Jade, Shape No. 5019, 12" d. **220**

Lamp base, baluster-form, the Yellow Jade body w/a speckled ground decorated w/an applied dripping shoulder band of iridescent blue Aurene, on a fitted gilt-metal base w/figural sphinx & paw feet, gilt-metal collar around the neck, ca. 1920, overall 27" h. (ILLUS.) **6,000**

Plum Jade Steuben Lamp Base

Lamp base, bulbous double gourd-form body in Plum Jade cased w/an Alabaster interior & overlaid w/amethyst, cameo-etched in a Chinese design & double-etched w/scrolling design, mounted in gilt-metal fittings w/three scroll arms, shallow chip under fixture, repair to one scroll arm, glass 13" h., overall 28" h. (ILLUS.) **1,840**

Green Jade & Aurene Lamp Base

Lamp base, flattened round flask-form in Green Jade cameo-etched w/stylized blossom forms below an applied gold Aurene dripping border incorporated into the acid-cut design, mounted on a scroll-pierced gilt-metal footed base & w/a pierced gilt-metal collar, possibly the Marlene patt., Shape No. 8492, glass 10" h. (ILLUS.) **3,450**

Perfume bottle & stopper, footed tall slender swelled cylindrical body w/a short neck & flattened rim, tall pointed stopper, Green Jade w/Alabaster foot, Shape No. 1988, 8" h. **467**

Vase, 6" h., fan-type, the flattened swirled rib Green Jade vase on an Alabaster knopped & ringed pedestal base w/disk foot, variant Shape No. 6287, ca. 1920 (dark inclusions) **805**

Vase, 6 7/8" h., 6 7/8" d., thick footring supporting the wide cylindrical body flaring gently at the rim, Green Jade w/a swirled design, polished pontil, signed **374**

Rare Jade & Aurene Vase

Vase, 8" h., broad bulbous ovoid body w/a wide shoulder centered by a short cylindrical neck w/a flared & flattened rim, Yellow Jade body cameo-etched overall w/a blanket of flowers design, the neck & shoulder w/an applied dripping band of blue Aurene, Shape No. 7014 (ILLUS.)..... **9,775**

Rosaline
Console set: bowl & pair of candlesticks; the Rosaline bowl in a wide flaring form w/a flattened rim scalloped around the edge, raised on a funnel-form Alabaster pedestal base, each candlestick w/a domed Rosaline foot below the ringed Alabaster stem & tall bulbed Rosaline candle socket w/a flattened rim scalloped around the edge, all marked, the set **2,415**
Perfume bottle & stopper, footed tall slender swelled cylindrical body w/a short neck & flattened rim, tall pointed Alabaster stopper & foot, Shape No. 1988, 8" h....... **550**

Silverina
Compote, open, 7" d., 5" h., the wide very shallow gently ruffled amethyst bowl raised on a slender ring matching stem on the domed round foot w/folded rim, bowl & foot w/mica flecks enclosed in diamond-shaped air traps, rough pontil, signed, ca. 1925 .... **805**

Threaded
Bowl, 5 3/8" h., a flat bottom below the wide flat sharply flaring sides in clear w/a diamond quilted optic design, applied random dark blue threading around the upper half, variation of No. 6778, ca. 1920, signed.. **230**
Compote, open, 7" h., a wide shallow bowl in blue raised on a very tall slender tapering blue stem on a dished blue disk foot, yellow threading applied under edge of the bowl... **201**
Vase, 7 1/2" h., 5" d., a thin cushion foot below the wide slightly tapering cylindrical body in clear w/a diamond quilted optic design, applied around the upper third w/random black threading, signed on base.. **144**

Verre de Soie
Perfume bottle & stopper, squatty bulbous onion-form lobed body tapering to a short neck w/flared rim, Celeste Blue flame stopper, Shape No. 1455, 4 3/4" h. **523**
Vase, 3 1/4" h., miniature, fluted top, Shape No. 1945 .... **110**
Vase, 7 7/8" h., 4" d., baluster-form w/a wide upper body w/short flat molded mouth, copper wheel engraved floral design around the sides **460**
Vase, 8" h., waisted trumpet-form body w/a wide gently ruffled rim, Diamond Quilted patt. w/random red threading around the rim, Shape No. 6813, ca. 1925 .... **259**
Vase, 8 3/8" h., small flared base tapering to tall flaring cylindrical sides w/an angled shoulder tapering to a short neck w/molded rim, copper wheel engraved w/floral bands around the body.................................... **489**

Miscellaneous Wares

Large Steuben Crystal Bowl

Bowl, 9 1/4" d., deep crystal rounded vessel on a ring-form base applied w/six scroll feet, designed by John Dreves, 1942, signed (ILLUS.) **632**
Bowl, 10" d., slightly tricornered bowl on a trillium-shaped foot, signed, design created in 1958 .... **345**
Bowl, 10" d., 4 1/2" h., flared bowl in crystal raised on four scrolled feet on a disk base, base signed, design created in 1940 .... **259**

Steuben Excalibur Paperweight

Paperweight, Excalibur, a faceted hand-polished solid crystal block embedded w/a removable sterling silver sword w/18k gold scabbard, designed by James Houston in 1963, signed, sword 8 1/2" l. (ILLUS.)... **1,955**

Steuben Heavy Cut Lion Vase

Vase, 12 1/2" h., 9" d., footed bulbous ovoid body tapering to a short trumpet neck, heavy cut smoky amber w/a relief design of walking lions around the center, a band of large diamond panels around the base & cut scrolls around the shoulder, Shape No. 6680 (ILLUS.)............................. **2,750**

Tiffany

This glassware, covering a wide diversity of types, was produced in glasshouses operated by Louis Comfort Tiffany, America's outstanding glass designer of the Art Nouveau period, from the last quarter of the 19th century until the early 1930s. Tiffany revived early techniques and devised many new ones.

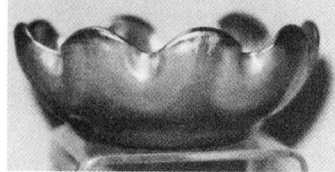

Various Tiffany Marks & Labels

Tiffany Spiral Candlestick

Candlesticks, tapering spirally-molded stem on a cushion foot & supporting a cupped ribbed socket, amber w/pink & silvery blue iridescence, signed & w/original paper label, 9" h., pr. (ILLUS. of one)......... **1,610**

Candy dish, footed pointed leaf-shaped dish w/incurved rolled sides & back, applied finger handle w/thumbrest at the back, overall gold iridescence, signed "525274G LCT Favrile," 4" w., 5" l. **990**

Compote, open, 5 1/2" d., 3 3/8" h., optic ribbed oval form w/wide flared rim raised on stem & circular foot, pale yellow, stretched iridescence at rim, ca. 1920, inscribed "1893 L.C.T. Favrile O" around polished pontil.. **690**

Compote, open, 8" d., 2 1/8" h., two-color, a wide low domed foot supporting a widely flaring shallow bowl, cobalt blue w/golden iridescent rim, signed **1,495**

Cordials, disk foot & slender tall stem supporting a bell-form bowl, overall gold iridescence, signed, 4 1/2" h., pr. **476**

Decanter w/original stopper, footed bulbous ovoid body w/a wide rounded shoulder centering a tall slender neck w/flared rim, fitted w/double-knop bulbed stopper, iridescent light gold, modeled around the shoulder & down the sides w/applied "pig tails," signed "L.C.T. M9342," 10 1/2" h.................................... **1,265**

Finger bowl, optic ribbed bowl w/flared rim, colorless w/pastel aqua & stetched iridescence at rim, opalescent ribs, early 20th c., base inscribed "1777 L.C.T. Favrile," 5" d., 1 7/8" h................................... **690**

Tiffany Favrile Bonbon Dish

Bonbon dish, small round form w/upright sides & a deeply scalloped rim, overall gold iridescence, ca. 1903, 4" d., 1 1/2" h. (ILLUS.)... **$600**

Bowl, 7 1/4" d., 2 1/2" d., stepped foot below ten-ribbed lobed shallow gold iridescent form w/pronounced scalloped rim, early 20th c., base inscribed "X-129 L.C.T. Favrile".. **489**

Bowl w/overhead handle, 10 1/4" d., 8" h., raised bronze handle w/mottled green enameled channel decoration on a rust brown stained ground, on a bronze rim encircling a green & opalescent deep widely flaring bowl w/pulled feather decoration & stretched iridescence at the rim, underside of bronze rim signed "Louis C. tiffany Furnaces Inc. Favrile 307" & Tiffany monogram, early 20th c. **2,415**

Bowl-vase, spherical w/wide molded flat mouth, overall gold iridescent ground decorated w/green leaves & entwined vines, signed "1036-6525M L.C. Tiffany Inc. Favrile," 3" d., 2 1/2" h. **2,365**

Bowl-vase, wide squatty bulbous form sharply tapering at the base, wide shoulder w/a low rolled rim flanked by tiny S-scroll applied handles, iridescent gold decorated w/caramel, cream & silver trailings, signed "9899 J L.C. Tiffany Favrile," 6 1/4" d., 2 3/4" h. **3,680**

Fine Tiffany Perfume Bottle

Perfume bottle w/stopper, footed bulbous spherical body w/a short cylindrical neck & flattened rim, in dark blue iridescence w/overall green heart-shaped leaves & vines, matching ball stopper, ca. 1912, 5 1/4" h. (ILLUS.).. **2,900**

Plate, 8" d., slightly scalloped broad rim on a fourteen-ribbed dish of opalescent & colorless glass w/stretched green iridescence at the rim, signed "1775 L.C.T. Favrile"... **633**

Salt dip, round w/ruffled rim, overall blue iridescence, signed, 2 1/2" d............................ **413**

Toothpick holder, slightly flared rim over four pinched-in sides, light amber w/overall gold iridescence, signed w/initials, 2" h. **316**

Tumbler, a bulbed base below gently flaring cylindrical sides, overall gold iridescence w/bluish highlights, signed, 3 3/4" h. **248**

Vase, 2 1/4" h., miniature, bulbous lobed body w/a row of smaller lobes below the larger lobes w/an appied shoulder & tiny cylindrical neck, overall gold iridescence, signed "L.C. Tiffany - Favrile X 44" **1,035**

Vase, 3 5/8" h., miniature, simple ovoid form w/eight pinched ribs, amber w/overall gold iridescence, signed "L.C.T. M 6734" (light wear) **374**

Vase, 5" h., bottle-form, spherical base w/a tall slender 'stick' neck, wavy gold iridescent peacock feather design on a bluish gold iridescent ground, signed "LCT 5177".. **1,210**

Vase, 5 1/2" h., footed bulbous base below a tall wide cylindrical neck, overall ruby red, signed "5949 N L.C. Tiffany Favrile" .. **4,070**

Vase, 8 3/4" h., disk foot below a tall slender knopped stem continuing to a tall slender bulbed body w/a wide flat mouth, iridescent blue w/green trailings & heart-shaped leaves, engraved "3930 G L.C. Tiffany - Favrile"...................................... **3,680**

Vase, 10 1/2" h., tall slender ovoid body w/a bulbed tall neck tapering to a small mouth, white opaque decorated w/feathering in gold at the collar, a gold zipper decoration running vertically from top to bottom, signed "LCT H1218"...................... **3,575**

Vase, 11 1/2" h., floriform, an iridescent amber base & extended slender stem w/green pulled-feather design against a clear ground, rising to a bulbous iridescent opal bowl, gold iridescent interior, signed "8194M LC Tiffany Favrile" **5,060**

Vase, 12 1/8" h., slender blossom-form w/a long bulbous top w/a small flattened mouth, slender knopped stem on a disk foot, overall dark blue iridescence w/a band of yellow heart-shaped leaves around the upper body, ca. 1915, engraved "3465 J.L.C. Tiffany-Favrile".......... **5,875**

Vase, 12 3/8" h., paperweight-type, a flared base below the tall waisted cylindrical body below the wide squatty bulbous bulbed top w/a closed rim, the upper rim w/a wide band of bright yellow stylized daffodils w/green centers raised on tall dark green stems & leaves all cased in clear, signed "2502 G L.C. Tiffany-Favrile," ca. 1912 .... **37,600**

Vase, 13 3/4" h., glass & patinated bronze, trumpet-form, the flaring glass trumpet in pink & opalescent striped glass w/a scalloped rim, mounted in a bronze upright foliate mount above the flaring round ribbed foot, base impressed "Louis C. Tiffany Furnaces, Inc. - 158A" w/monogram, 1918-28 .... **1,495**

Vase, 16 3/8" h., floriform, an upright bowl w/a crimped & ruffled rim, raised on a tall slender swelled stem on a domed optic-ribbed foot, pale green opalescent w/an amber foot, signed "L.C.T. R9652," ca. 1902 .... **9,200**

Monumental Tiffany Vase in Stand

Vase, 21 1/4" h., tall slender baluster-form w/a short slightly flared neck, tall peacock feather design around the sides in dark blue & silvery iridescence against a feathered iridescent ground w/green & lavender highlights, fitted in a bronze support w/thin upright tabs on a disk base w/beaded rim band, signed "L.C.T. F1978" (ILLUS.).. **25,300**

Venetian

Venetian glass has been made for six centuries on the island of Murano, where it continues to be produced. The skilled glass artisans developed numerous techniques, subsequently imitated elsewhere.

Venetian "Sidereo" Bowl

Bowl, 9" d., 3 7/8" h., "sidereo," footed wide rounded form in clear, the exterior w/randomly applied hollow cane sections in clear & deep violet, applied foot, unsigned Barovier & Toso, designed by Ercole Barovier, ca. 1966 (ILLUS.) **$1,840**

Figures of dancing man & woman, each a tall slender figure cased in deep red, he wearing tight pants in red threaded in white around the calves, his jacket trimmed w/clear rigaree, white face & arms, wearing a tall shaped red top hat, she wearing a long bell-form gown w/white threading around the bottom, red jacket w/applied clear rigaree, white arms & face, a large red picture hat, mid-20th c., 11 1/2" h., pr. **280**

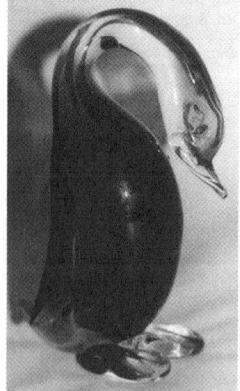

Blown Amber Venetian Duck

Model of a duck, free-blown bird standing upright w/its neck bent down over its breast, large applied feet, deep amber cased in heavy crystal, mid-20th c., 7" h. (ILLUS.).. **35**

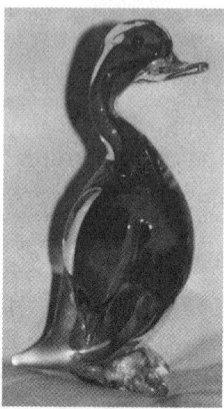

Deep Cranberry Venetian Duck

Model of a duck, free-blown bird standing w/head raised, large applied feet, deep cranberry red cased in heavy crystal, applied bill & feet w/gold inclusions, applied black bead eyes, 6" h. (ILLUS.) **100**

Models of pheasants, large cobalt blue blown body w/long curled-under tail, applied closed wings, applied clear w/gold crest & beak, perched on a tall curved clear pedestal w/gold inclusions, mid-20th c., 12" h., pr. **224**

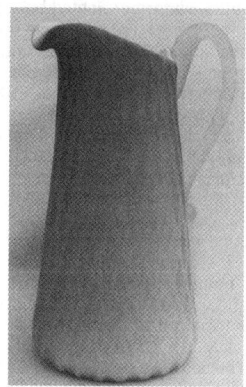

Reproduction Satin Glass Pitcher

Pitcher, 9" h., tankard-type, reproduction shaded blue mother-of-pearl satin in the Diamond Quilted patt., tapering cylindrical body w/curled spout & applied frosted handle, mid-20th c. (ILLUS.) **90**

Fine Venetian "Intarsio" Vase

Vase, 6 3/4" h., "intarsio," deep gently flaring bowl-form w/flat rim, composed of triangular inlays in bright red, amber, pale lavender & cobalt blue, alternating w/patches of clear bullicante glass, unsigned Barovier & Toso, designed by Ercole Barovier, original foil label "Made in Italy - For Gumps," ca. 1961-63 (ILLUS.) **7,187**

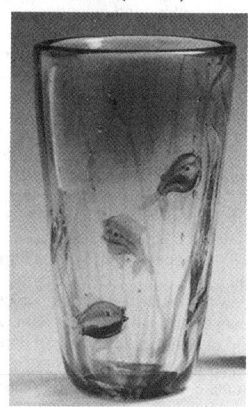

Venetian Aquarium Vase

Vase, 11 1/2" h., flaring cylindrical form w/thick walls shading from emerald green to pale green, enclosing fish w/white, maroon & orange canes, silver foil inclusions, unsigned Cenedese, 1950s (ILLUS.).. **2,760**

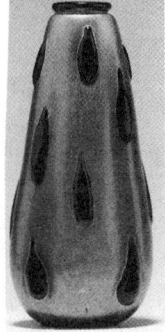

Tall Fratelli Toso Vase

Vase, 11 1/2" h., tall flattened teardrop-form in emerald green overlaid w/gold foil, further decorated w/applied green glass drops, unsigned Fratelli Toso, ca. 1950s (ILLUS.).. **1,495**

Venetian "Intarsio" Vase

Vase, 12" h., "intarsio," bulbous teardrop-form, composed of red & clear patches each enclosing tiny controlled bubbles, by Ercole Barovier for Barovier & Toso (ILLUS.).. **4,025**

Cenedese "La Fornace" Vase

Vase, 12" h., 8" w., "La Fornace," thick cylindrical form cast in low-relief w/two glass artisans at work, in shades of tan, orange, red, green & blue, designed by Napoleone Martinuzzi, by Cenedese, 1953-58 (ILLUS.)... **5,175**

Striped Seguso Studio Vase

Vase, 13 1/2" h., tapered ovoid heavy walled colorless form internally decorated w/transparent vertical stripes & an asymmetric opaque grey band about the body, signed "Desl. Seguso," 1975 (ILLUS.) **748**

Vase, 19 1/2" h., studio-type, tall wide square form in cobalt blue w/each side bearing etched & enameled designs in the manner of Miro, J. Arp, Modigliani & K. Appel, in red, green, yellow & white, base inscribed "Aureliano Toso Murano," 20th c. (tiny rim chip) **1,610**

Vases, 9" h., "Mezza Filigrana," elongated neck on flattened spherical body, translucent white w/spiral canes alternating pastel green & turquoise blue cased in clear, turquoise rim, polished pontil, mid-20th c., pr. (slight cloudy staining) **345**

Victorian Colored Glass

There are, of course, many types of colored glassware of the Victorian era and we cover a great variety of these in our various glass categories. However, there are some pieces of pressed, mold-blown and free-blown Victorian colored glass which don't fit well into other specific listings, so we have chosen to include a selection of them here.

Gilt-decorated Sapphire Blue Bottle

Bottle w/original stopper, tall squared form w/incurved ribbed sides below the sharply tapering paneled shoulder & ringed neck w/flared rim, panel-cut mushroom stopper, sapphire blue, the body decorated w/scalloped gold grape clusters & leafy scrolls, 2 3/4" w., 8 1/8" h. (ILLUS.)............................ **$160**

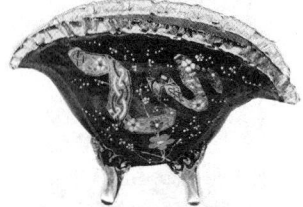

Decorated Blue Fanned Bowl

Bowl, 12" w., 8" h., deep form pulled up on two sides & fanned out, sapphire blue w/an applied crimped clear rim band & four applied clear peg feet, ornately enameled w/colorful banner & dotted blossoms (ILLUS.).. **275**

Enameled Blue Compote

Compote, open, 5 3/4" d., 7 1/8" h., deep rounded wide optic ribbed sapphire blue bowl raised on a hollow tapering stem & cushion foot, the exterior of the bowl delicately enameled w/small yellow & white flowers w/gold branches & leaves (ILLUS.)....... **145**

Berry-decorated Blue Decanter

Decanter w/original stopper, footed ovoid sapphire blue body tapering to a tall slender cylindrical neck w/a tricorner rim, decorated down the sides w/an ornate thorny branch w/red berries, green & yel-

low leaves & pink blossoms, applied clear handle & tall pointed facet-cut clear stopper, 4 1/2" d., 13" h. (ILLUS.) **225**

Ruby Jar with Gold Filigree

Jar, cov., cylindrical deep ruby base w/a high domed cover w/knob finial, cover & base encased in lacy gold filigree metal on small ball feet, 3" d., 5 1/4" h. (ILLUS.) **165**

Ornate Blue Covered Pitcher

Pitcher, cov., 6" h., 4" d., footed bulbous sapphire blue optic-ribbed body tapering to a wide cylindrical neck & applied blue handle fitted w/a hinged flat pewter cover w/thumbrest, the body ornately enameled w/gilt arches & scrolls alternating w/gold & white floral clusters, gilt script wording "Lamalou-les-Bains" (ILLUS.) **135**

Decorated Lobed & Enameled Vase

Vase, 8 1/4" h., 5 1/2" d., footed ovoid melon-lobed body tapering to a flaring lobed neck, deep amethyst enameled w/large branches of pink & cream blossoms & green leaves w/rust colored buds ILLUS.) **245**

Brightly Decorated Amethyst Vase

Vase, 10 3/4" h., 4" d., slightly flared cylindrical dark amethyst body w/a rounded shoulder & short, wide cylindrical neck w/cupped rim, brightly enameled w/a large cluster of green leaves, yellow & white blossoms, yellow fruit & blue buds w/a blue butterfly nearby (ILLUS.) **225**

Wall Pocket Vases

Textured Amber Wall Pocket Vase

Amber, conical form, textured body w/branch form overhead handle, 4 x 6 1/2" (ILLUS.) **$65-95**

Ribbed Amber Wall Pocket Vase

Amber, tapering deeply ribbed form, 8 x 10 1/2" (ILLUS.) **75-100**

Crackle Finish Wall Pocket Vases

Black, conical form, crackle finish w/wide band across top, 5 3/8 x 5 7/8" (ILLUS. left) **25-35**

Wall Pocket with Bird & Grapevine

Black, flaring conical form, textured body w/relief-molded black & red bird on vine w/clusters of black & red grapes & gold leaves, 7 x 7 3/4" (ILLUS.) **75-100**

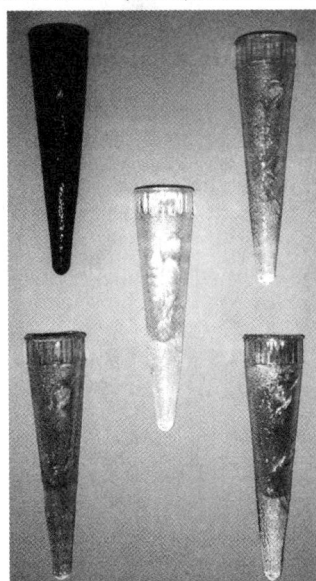

Variety of Northwood/Dugan/Diamond Glass Ware Company Wall Pockets

Black, slender conical shape w/embossed woodpecker design & pebble finish, Northwood/Dugan/Diamond Glass Ware Company, 8 1/2" l. (ILLUS. top left) **60-70**

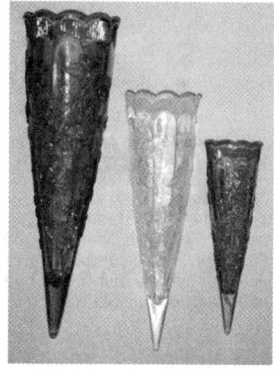

Anniversary Pattern Wall Pocket Vases

Crystal, ribbed conical form w/pointed end finial, Anniversary patt., No. 2930, by Jeannette Glass Co., 3 1/2 x 6 1/2" (ILLUS. center) **15-20**

Wall Pocket Vase with Owl

Black amethyst, swelled cylindrical form w/relief-molded owl w/yellow eyes on tree branch, w/green leaves, 4 x 6 1/2" (ILLUS.).. **85-125**

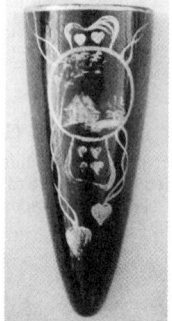

Cobalt Blue & Silver Wall Pocket Vase

Cobalt blue, conical form, decorated w/silver hearts & ribbons w/round center medallion scene of house & trees, 3 3/8 x 7 5/8" (ILLUS.) **100-125**

Beaded Grape Pattern Wall Pocket Vases

Crystal, slender conical form w/pointed end finial, Beaded Grape patt., U.S. Glass Co., 8" l. (ILLUS. center) **50-65**

Crystal, slender conical shape w/embossed woodpecker design & pebble finish, Northwood/Dugan/Diamond Glass Ware Company, 8 1/2" l. (ILLUS. center w/black vase) . **40-50**

Jack-in-the-Pulpit Form Wall Pocket Vase

Crystal, white & green, jack-in-the-pulpit form, handblown, crystal base w/ball-shaped end finial, applied green spiral trim, opaque white top trimmed w/green edge & top ring, 6 3/4" l. (ILLUS.).......... **100-125**

Handpainted Crystal Wall Pocket Vase

Crystal, cylindrical w/rounded base, decorated w/h.p. pink & white roses, green leaves & blue bands, two loop handles, 3 3/8 x 8" (ILLUS.).. **50-65**

Hand-painted Wall Pocket Vases

Green, conical, hand-blown, decorated w/h.p. white daisies w/yellow centers & slender green leaves, made in Czechoslovakia, 4 3/4 x 7 3/4" (ILLUS. left) **95-125**

Wall Pocket Vase with Masonic Emblem

Green, conical w/pointed base, decorated w/gold leaf Masonic emblem & gold trim, Style No. 1881, Fostoria Glass Company, 3 x 8 1/4" (ILLUS.) **165-185**
Green, slender conical form w/pointed end finial, Beaded Grape patt., U.S. Glass Co., 6" l. (ILLUS. right w/crystal vase) **40-60**
Green, slender conical form w/pointed end finial, Beaded Grape patt., U.S. Glass Co., 10" l. (ILLUS. left w/crystal vase) **75-100**
Green, slender conical shape w/embossed woodpecker design & pebble finish, Northwood/Dugan/Diamond Glass Ware Company, 8 1/2" l. (ILLUS. bottom left w/black vase) **50-65**

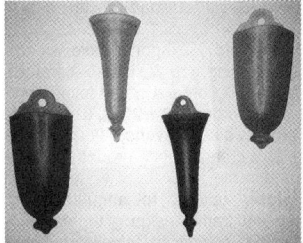

Blue Tiffin Wallpocket Vases

Jasper blue, conical form w/spearpoint end finial, rounded top w/hanging hole, satin finish, Style No. 320, Tiffin Glass Co., 3 3/8 x 9 1/8" (ILLUS. bottom right) **75-95**
Jasper blue, swelled tapering cylindrical form w/pointed button end finial, scalloped top w/hanging hole, satin finish,

Style No. 16258, Tiffin Glass Co., 3 7/8 x 9 1/4" (ILLUS. bottom left) **95-125**
Light blue, conical form w/spearpoint end finial, rounded top w/hanging hole, satin finish, Style No. 320, Tiffin Glass Co., 3 3/8 x 9 1/8" (ILLUS. top left) **75-95**
Light blue, swelled tapering cylindrical form w/pointed button end finial, satin finish, scalloped top w/hanging hole, satin finish, Style No. 16258, Tiffin Glass Co., 3 3/8 x 9 1/8" (ILLUS. top right) **95-125**
Marigold carnival, conical form w/crackle finish & wide band across top, 5 3/8 x 5 7/8" (ILLUS. right w/black crackle vase) **25-35**
Marigold carnival, slender conical shape w/embossed woodpecker design & pebble finish, Northwood/Dugan/Diamond Glass Ware Company, 8 1/2" l. (ILLUS. bottom right w/black vase) **20-30**
Milk glass, wide conical form w/flaring rim, relief-molded zig zag design in blue on lower body & ringed base, the upper portion decorated w/gold bands & h.p. blue flowers, 4 3/4 x 6 1/8" (ILLUS. right w/green h.p. vase) **50-60**

Czechoslovakian Wall Pocket Vase

Orange, conical form w/black trim, Czechoslovakia, 4 x 7 1/8" (ILLUS.) **50-75**
Pink, ribbed conical form w/pointed end finial, Anniversary patt., No. 2930, by Jeannette Glass Co., 3 1/2 x 6 1/2" (ILLUS. left with crystal Anniversary vase) **30-40**
Pink, slender conical shape w/embossed woodpecker design & pebble finish, Northwood/Dugan/Diamond Glass Ware Company, 8 1/2" l. (ILLUS. top right w/black vase) **50-65**
Red flashed crystal, ribbed conical form w/pointed end finial, Anniversary patt., No. 2930, by Jeannette Glass Co., 3 1/2 x 6 1/2" (ILLUS. right w/crystal Anniversary vase) **15-25**

Wave Crest

Now much sought after, Wave Crest was produced by the C.F. Monroe Co., Meriden, Connecticut, in the late 19th and early 20th centuries from opaque white glass blown into molds.

It was then hand-decorated in enamels and metal trim was often added. Boudoir accessories such as jewel boxes, hair receivers, etc., were predominant.

WAVE CREST WARE

Wave Crest Mark

Ash receiver, squared body w/slight ribbing, floral decoration on a creamy white
background, applied gilt-metal rim band,
pierced handles, 5" d. **$495**

Bonbon, cov., Rococo mold, metal rim &
twisted bail handle, 8" d. **925**

Bonbon w/silver bail handle, decorated
w/a network of vines, leaves & blue flowers, deep lemon yellow at top shading to
white, original label **595**

Box w/hinged lid, Double Shell mold, top &
sides decorated w/tiny blue & yellow
flowers & green leaves on an opaque
white ground, 3" d. **225**

Box w/hinged lid, Egg Crate mold, decorated w/red clover blossoms, 3" sq. **195**

Box w/hinged lid, Embossed Rococo
mold, decorated w/pink & white roses,
original lining, 5" sq., 2 1/2" h. **425**

Box w/hinged lid, Baroque Shell mold,
scene of Niagara Falls bordered by white
enamel dots & blue forget-me-nots,
cream background, 5 1/4" d. **790**

Box w/hinged lid, Baroque Shell mold,
decorated w/clover blossoms on white
ground, 5 1/2" h. **225**

Box w/hinged lid, embossed scrolling top
& sides, decorated w/roses on a blue
background, 5 1/2" oval **550**

Box w/hinged lid, Egg Crate mold,
enameled h.p. sprays of small pink &
white flowers & green leaves, blue trim
on a white ground, 3 x 5 1/2" rectangle,
3" h. **525**

Helmschmied Swirl Box

Box w/hinged lid, Helmschmied Swirl
mold, lid decorated w/dainty pink & gold
flowers & green leaves, shaded blue to
white ground, unmarked, no lining,
5 1/2" d., 3 1/2" h. (ILLUS.)............................. **400**

Box w/hinged lid, wide spiral panels on
base & edge of lid, center of lid w/a large
oval reserve decorated w/a row of dancing storks, panels alternating pink &
green w/dainty florals & scrolls, gilt-metal
fittings, unsigned, 5 1/2" d., 3 1/2" h. **1,500**

Box w/hinged lid, Egg Crate mold, enameled floral decoration on lid & "Collars &
Cuffs" on side, 6" w. (ILLUS. top next
column) **950-1,200**

Wave Crest "Collars & Cuffs" Box

Box w/hinged lid, round, the top decorated
w/a courting couple in period costume,
6" d., 4 1/2" h. **950**

Box w/hinged lid, Embossed Rococo
mold, h.p. blue flowers on a pink ground,
raised on an ornate gilt-metal footed
base, 5" w., 6" l. **875**

Box w/hinged lid, Helmschmied Swirl
mold, lid w/h.p. peach, pink & white as-
ters & moss green leaves, opaque white
ground, ornate footed gilt-metal base,
7" d., 6 1/2" h. **1,100**

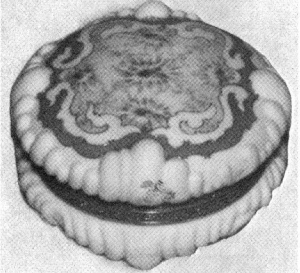

Baroque Shell Box

Box w/hinged lid, Baroque Shell mold,
decorated on top w/pink daisies bordered
by sky blue & all outlined in lavender,
7 1/4" d. (ILLUS.)... **765**

Box w/hinged lid, Baroque Shell mold,
decorated w/pink daisies bordered by
sky blue & all outlined in lavender,
7 1/4" d. **765**

Box w/hinged lid, Hexagonal mold w/em-
bossed scrolling, top & sides decorated
w/shaded pink florals & green foliage on
a soft green ground, 8 1/2" w., 6" h. **1,500**

Broom holder, blue & lavender floral decoration on a creamy white ground, ornate
gilt-metal frame... **1,795**

Card holder, upright rectangular form
w/embossed frame design, gilt-metal rim,
cloth lining, decorated w/delicate pink
flowers & a blue border **375**

Card holder, upright rectangular form
w/embossed frame design, gilt-metal rim,
cloth lining, decorated w/h.p. blue flowers
& pink border... **425**

Card holder w/gilt-metal insert, narrow
upright rectangular form w/oblong scalloped side panels, pink floral decoration
in scroll on creamy white background............ **450**

Cigar holder, plain cylindrical body decorated w/h.p. florals, gilt-metal handled rim & scroll-footed base 550

Cigar humidor, cov., cylindrical, the white opal body molded w/florals & h.p. w/"Cigars" in pink on the side over blue enameled forget-me-nots, the domed cover decorated w/an Indian on horseback, gilt-metal hinged mounts, red flag mark on base 750

Cologne bottles w/original stoppers, cylindrical body w/deep scroll-molded shoulder, a short cylindrical neck w/a flaring rim, enameled w/dainty blue flowers, green leaves & foliage & heavy gold scrolling on the creamy white ground, stoppers scroll-molded creamy white, pr....... 925

Cracker jar, cov., barrel-shaped, Egg Crate mold, h.p. flowers on robin's-egg blue ground, silver plate rim, cover & bail handle, overall 10 1/4" h. 885

Wave Crest Cracker Jar

Cracker jar w/metal lid, smooth tapering cylindrical body decorated w/a large white & purple iris & green leaves on a cream ground bordered by scrolled panels of pale tan, silver plate rim & twisted bail handle, unmarked (ILLUS.) 450

Creamer, Helmschmied Swirl mold, decorated w/blue forget-me-nots, 3 1/4" h............. 116

Creamer, Helmschmied Swirl mold, mushroom garden decoration 75

Creamer & cov. sugar bowl, decorated w/h.p. cupids & whimsical scrolling, creamer w/gilt-metal lipped rim & handle, sugar bowl w/gilt-metal rim, cover & bail handle, pr.. 100

Creamer & cov. sugar bowl, Helmschmied Swirl mold, lower portion in solid beige separated by enamel beading from the upper section w/pink roses, pr. 630

Creamer & cov.sugar bowl, smooth body, squatty bulbous form decorated w/cupid amid floral scrolls, sugar w/silver plated rim, cover & twisted bail handle, ring finial, creamer w/silver plate rim & bail handle, pr 475

Deck of cards holder, turquoise ground w/enameled large pink rosebud, white dotting on the front & back & similar decoration on both sides 450

Dresser box w/hinged cover, ornate scroll-molded body decorated in light green w/dainty pink roses, 7 3/4" d. 440

Wave Crest Humidor

Humidor w/original brass cover & finial, cream & brown bulbous cylindrical body decorated w/three bulldog heads & "Three Guardsmen," unmarked, 5 1/8" d., 6 1/2" h. (ILLUS.) 525

Jardiniere, bulbous body tapering to a short cylindrical rim, body decorated w/h.p. mums & foliage, gold lacy trim on the rim, 9" d., 8" h. 600-800

Jardiniere, bulbous nearly spherical body w/a wide short cylindrical neck, the sides molded w/delicate scroll-bordered cartouches decorated w/h.p. flowers, all on a pink ground, raised on a gilt-metal base w/scroll feet, 6 1/2" h. 895

Salt & pepper shakers w/original tops, Helmschmied Swirl mold, opaque white ground decorated w/delicate white flowers w/yellow centers & green foliage, pr. 485

Salt & pepper shakers w/original tops, hexagonal, Embossed Rococo mold, decorated w/h.p. florals, pr. 145

Salt shaker w/original metal top, Scroll Wave mold, pink to white ground w/blue flowers... 75

Salt shaker w/original top, embossed beaded foot, squatty bulbous body tapering to a cylindrical neck w/embossed beaded ring below the lid, decorated w/embossed scrolling & enameled w/two red-headed birds sitting side-by-side among yellow & brown foliage, 2 1/4" h. 75

Spooner w/silver plate rim & loop handles, cylindrical paneled rib shape, decorated w/floral transfer...................................... 285

Sugar bowl, cov., Helmschmied Swirl mold, decorated w/flowers & three mushrooms on each side, silver plate cover & two-handled rim, unsigned 175

Sugar shaker w/original top, Helmschmied Swirl mold, alternating panels of blue scrolls & yellow flowers......................... 650

Sugar shaker w/original top, tapering cylindrical form, decorated w/h.p. daisies on front & back 195

Syrup pitcher w/original hinged silver plate top & handle, Helmschmied Swirl mold, lovely floral decoration.......................... 395

Vase, 7 1/2" h., footed, bulbous body w/long cylindrical neck, embossed scrolling, decorated w/small red flowers......................... 425

Vase, 8" h., bottle-form, spherical footed body tapering to a tall 'stick' neck flared at the rim, gilt-metal feet, dark green free-form lines, blue forget-me-nots & pink scrolls filled w/tiny white dots 495

Vase, 8 3/4" h., squatty bulbous base tapering to a tall cylindrical neck, dark green lines bordering areas of pink covered w/white dots & winding over a background of blue forget-me-nots, on a gilt-metal base w/small scroll feet 670

Large Fine Wave Crest Vase

Vase, 11 1/2" h., large ovoid body w/a wide flat mouth, fitted w/a gilt-metal rim band, ornate scrolling handles & a footed base, decorated w/scattered Wedgwood blue cartouches painted w/white daisies against a white ground w/clusters of small pink blossoms on slender leafy stems, signed (ILLUS.)...................... 1,500-2,000

Vase, 12 1/4" h., footed tapering bulbous body, Rococo mold w/gilt-metal fittings, daisies on a shaded rust background, olive green flare around the bottom.............. 1,850

Webb

This glass is made by Thomas Webb & Sons of Stourbridge, one of England's most prolific glasshouses. Numerous types of glass, including cameo, have been produced by this firm through the years. The company also produced various types of novelty and "art" glass during the late Victorian period. Also see BURMESE, ROSE BOWLS, and SATIN.

Rare Webb Gem Cameo Bowl-Vase

Cameo bowl-vase, footed wide squatty bulbous form tapering to a wide upright rim band, white cut to blue, the neck w/band enclosing reserves of an exotic bird perched on flowering branches alternating w/scale-form panels w/quatrefoils, the body cut w/a continuous exotic scene of small birds flying amid delicate leafy branches & large flowering plants, Gem Cameo, 9" d., 7" h. (ILLUS.)................... $28,000

Cameo cologne bottle w/stopper, flat-bottomed domed cylindrical form w/a small cylindrical neck & ball stopper, white cut to ruby red, the sides divided into three arched panels each featuring a different flower bloom, a band of small daisies around the neck & a narrow ribbed band around the stopper, acid-stamped mark "Thomas Webb and Sons Gem Cameo," 5" h. 4,510

Cameo vase, 5 1/2" h., footed ovoid body w/a cupped neck, white cut to dark blue, the sides decorated w/large leaves, buds & a flower w/a butterfly on the reverse, the cupped neck cut w/delicate elaborate geometric bands 4,950

Cameo vase, 6" h., footed ovoid body w/the rounded shoulder centered by a short cylindrical neck, white cut to a frosted deep raisin amber ground & decorated w/sunflowers on leafy stems & a butterfly, white bands around the neck & foot 4,125

Cameo vase, 6 1/4" h., footed ovoid baluster-form w/a low wide flattened rim, white cut to dark blue w/a design of large pendent leafy gingko branches........................ 1,980

Cameo vase, 8 3/4" h., 2 1/2" d., tall cylindrical bamboo-ringed form in white satin cased in red & cameo cut overall w/vines of raspberries... 2,035

Cameo vase, 10 1/2" h., footed bottle-form w/tall slender 'stick' neck, ivory ground overlaid in white & cameo cut w/tall foxglove blossoms & leaves w/brown tinting, signed... 1,375

Westmoreland

Westmoreland Specialty Company was founded in East Liverpool, Ohio in 1889 and relocated in 1890 to Grapeville, Pennsylvania where it remained until its closing in 1985.

During its early years Westmoreland specialized in glass food containers and novelties but by the turn of the century they had a large line of milk white items and clear tableware patterns. In 1925 the company name was shortened to The Westmoreland Glass Company and it was during that decade that more colored glasswares entered their line-up. When Victorian-style milk glass again became popular in the 1940s and 1950s, Westmoreland produced extensive amounts in several patterns which closely resemble late 19th century wares. These and their figural animal dishes in milk white and colors are widely collected today but buyers should not confuse them for the antique originals. Watch for Westmoreland's "WG" mark on some pieces. A majority of our listings are products from the 1940s through the 1970s. Earlier pieces will be indicated.

Early Westmoreland Label & Mark

Animal covered dish, Camel, amber satin, Humphrey **$48**

Animal covered dish, Duck, rimmed base, blue milk glass **45**

Animal covered dish, Eagle, two-part, w/added eyes, milk white **85**

Animal covered dish, Hen on Nest, looking left, green slag **58**

Animal covered dish, Hen on Nest, looking left, milk white, red decoration **38**

Basket, No. 752, ruby-stained ribs w/h.p. floral medallion **52**

Basket, oval, American Hobnail patt., lilac opalescent, small **32**

Basket, Pansy patt., two handles meet from sides, amber **12**

Bell, No. 1902, blue satin w/Mary Gregory decoration **28**

Bell, No. 1902, green satin w/h.p. white daisy **18**

Box, cov., Rabbit on eggs, milk white w/painted eggs, 7" **55**

Box, cov., Santa in Sleigh, milk white w/painted decoration **34**

Butter dish, cov., American Hobnail, milk white **38**

Cake stand, Beaded Grape patt., footed, milk white, 11" sq. **108**

Candle lamp, two-part, milk white stemmed base, blue satin shade w/Mary Gregory decoration **55**

Candlestick, single light, Beaded Grape patt., milk white, 4" h. **16**

Lotus Single Candlestick

Candlestick, single light, Lotus patt., green, 9" h. (ILLUS.) **40**

Candlestick, single light, Spiral wrap around square base, black, 7" h. **32**

Candlestick, single light, two-handled, Mission patt., No. 1015, clear, 7" h. **28**

Candlestick, three-light, Lotus patt., green satin **56**

Candy container, novelty, model of clock, green **15**

Candy dish, cov., Della Robbia patt., No. DR-17, pastel stained fruit **32**

Candy dish, cov., English Hobnail patt., green **38**

Cordial, English Hobnail, square base, clear, 3 3/4" h. **12**

Creamer & open sugar bowl, Maple Leaf (Bramble) patt., milk white, pr. **28**

Creamer & sugar bowl, American Hobnail patt., milk white, pr. **26**

Cup & saucer American Hobnail patt., milk white **18**

Cup & saucer, English Hobnail patt., milk white **16**

Decanter w/stopper, American Hobnail, milk white **42**

Egg cup, American Hobnail, clear, 4 1/2" h. **42**

Fairy lamp, two-part, Thousand Eye patt., Brandywine blue **28**

Goblet, American Hobnail patt., clear, 6" h. **16**

Goblet, American Hobnail patt., milk whhite, 6" h. **9**

Goblet, Beaded Grape patt., round, footed, clear, 8 oz. **24**

Goblet, Della Robbia patt., stained dark colors, 6" h. **48**

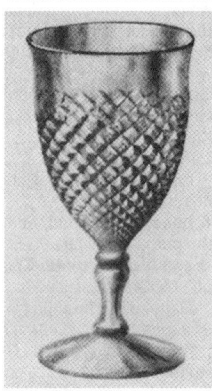

English Hobnail Goblet

Goblet, English Hobnail patt., round base, clear, 6" h. (ILLUS.) **12**

Goblet, English Hobnail patt., square base, clear, 6" h. **9**

Goblet, Paneled Grape patt., clear, 6" h. **19**

Goblet, Paneled Grape patt., ruby, 6" h. **29**

Goblet, wine, Della Robbia patt., milk white, 4 3/4" h. **16**

Goblet, wine, Della Robbia patt., stained dark colors, 4 3/4" h. **52**

Goblet, wine, Paneled Grape patt., clear, 4" h. **18**

Goblet, wine, Paneled Grape patt., ruby, 4" h. **29**

Model of butterfly, No. 2, green satin, small **18**

Model of owl, on two stacked books, cobalt carnival, 3 1/2" h. **26**

Model of sleigh, milk white w/holly decoration, No. 1872 .... **30**

Model of slipper, grandma's, blue satin w/white decoration **18**

Novelty, model of a straw hat, milk white w/decoration, 4 1/2" **38**

Pitcher, 7 1/4" h., American Hobnail, milk white **68**

Pitcher, 8 1/2" h., Old Quilt patt., ruby carnival........ 89

Rocker Pattern Covered Pitcher

Pitcher, cov., Rocker patt., No. 101, clear
(ILLUS.)... 80
Pitcher, water, 8 1/2" h., Old Quilt patt., milk
white 38
Plate, 10 1/2" d., English Hobnail patt.,
green 28
Plate, 8 1/2" d., round, English Hobnail
patt., milk white 10
Plate, 8" d., English Hobnail patt., green 12
Plate, dinner, 10 1/2" d., Beaded Grape
patt., milk white 22
Plate, lattice border, black w/white enamel
Mary Gregory decoration 38
Plate, Three Kittens, milk white 45
Plate, Three Owls, milk white............................... 48
Punch bowl & base, bell-shaped, Princess
Feather patt., clear.. 280
Punch bowl & base, bell-shaped, Princess
Feather patt., purple carnival.......................... 450
Punch bowl, base & underplate, Colonial
Paneled patt., black 340
Punch cup, Paneled Grape patt., milk
white, 2 1/2" h. 19
Relish dish, three-part, Beaded Grape
patt., milk white, 9 1/2" d. 58
Salt & pepper shakers, footed, Princess
Feather patt., clear, pr. 28
Sherbet, American Hobnail patt., milk
white, 3 3/4"... 14
Tumbler, iced tea, Della Robbia patt.,
stained dark colors, 6" h..................................... 24
Tumbler, iced tea, English Hobnail patt.,
round base, clear, 6" h. 14
Tumbler, juice, Paneled Grape, clear,
4 3/4" h.. 24
Vase, bud, American Hobnail, lilac opales-
cent.. 28
Vase, miniature, jack-in-the-pulpit shape,
pink satin w/white "snow flower" decora-
tion 22
Wedding bowl, Beaded Grape patt., Roses
& Bows decoration, milk white, 9 1/2" d. 75

Wright (L.G.) Glass Company

*This firm, operating from 1938 until its liquidation in
1999, was a wholesaler of reproductions of Victorian-
era glass and pressed pattern glass and novelty items
such as covered animal dishes. Wright owned some original moulds, but the vast majority of the glass was produced for Wright by Fenton, Viking or Westmoreland
from new moulds commissioned by Wright. A recent
book,* The L.G. Wright Glass Company, *by Measell and
Roetteis, provides a comprehensive history of the company and its products and also pictures more than 1900
pieces of Wright glass in color.*

Animal covered dish, Frog, blue $45
Animal covered dish, Horse, amber................. 35
Animal covered dish, Rooster, Amberina......... 45

Wright Turkey Covered Dish

Animal covered dish, Turkey, purple slag
(ILLUS.) 55

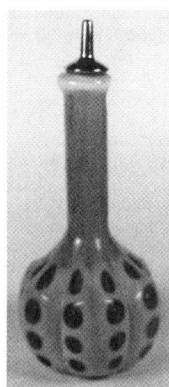

Wright Coin Spot Barber Bottle

Barber bottle, fluted form, cranberry opalescent Coin Spot patt. (ILLUS.).................... 225
Barber bottle, fluted form, cranberry opal-
escent Fern patt. 165
Basket, Panel Grape patt., blue opalescent
w/crystal handle... 195
Butter dish, cov., Argonaut patt., blue opal-
escent... 100

Wright Chocolate Argonaut Butter Dish

Butter dish, cov., Chocolate glass, Argo-
naut patt. (ILLUS.).. 125

Butter dish, cov., Eye-Winker patt., ruby 75
Compote, cov., Eye-Winker patt., green,
    large.. 75
Compote, cov., Stipple Star patt., amber,
    large.. 95
Compote, open, crimped rim, Princess
    Feather patt., blue 35
Compote, open, Eye-Winker patt., amber,
    large.. 60
Creamer, Argonaut patt., blue opalescent........... 45

Cranberry Beaded Curtain Creamer

Creamer, Beaded Curtain patt., cranberry
    w/crystal handle (ILLUS.)................................. 145

Wright Cherry Decorated Creamer

Creamer, Cherry patt., red, green & gold
    decoration (ILLUS.)... 25

Opalescent Coin Dot Creamer

Creamer, cranberry opalescent Coin Dot
    patt. (ILLUS.)... 110
Creamer & cov. sugar bowl, Stipple Star
    patt., ruby, pr... 120

Moon and Star Wright Cruet

Cruet w/original stopper, Moon and Star
    patt., amber, crystal stopper (ILLUS.)............ 135

Opalescent Coin Dot Finger Bowl

Finger bowl, crimped edge, cranberry opal-
    escent Coin Dot patt. (ILLUS.)......................... 95
Goblet, Eye-Winker patt., amber 25

Wright Herringbone Goblet

Goblet, Herringbone patt., ruby (ILLUS.)............. 40
Goblet, Mirror and Rose patt., ruby 40
Goblet, Panel Grape patt., blue opalescent........ 40

Wright Princess Feather Goblet

Goblet, Princess Feather patt., amber
(ILLUS.).. **30**
Goblet, Princess Feather patt., blue..................... **28**

Wright Sawtooth Pink Goblet

Goblet, Sawtooth patt., pink (ILLUS.)................... **25**
Novelty, hand vase, amber.................................. **145**

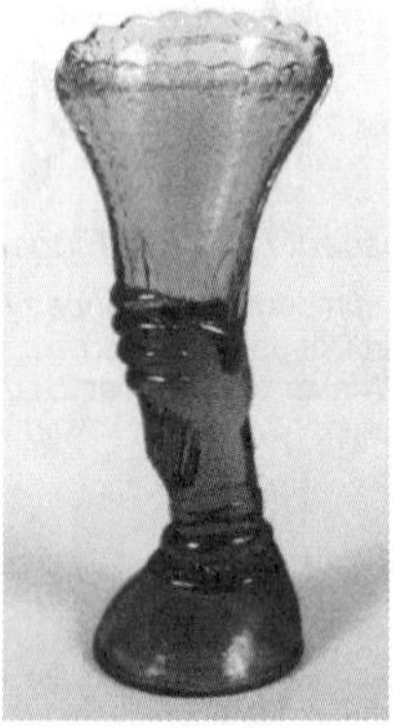

L.G. Wright Hand Vase Novelty

Novelty, hand vase, emerald green
(ILLUS.).. **125**
Pitcher, Carnival glass, God & Home patt.,
purple **175**
Pitcher, Eye-Winker patt., ruby **85**

Wright Inverted Thumbprint Pitcher

Pitcher, milk, amethyst Inverted Thumb-
print patt. (ILLUS.).. **100**

Opalescent Drapery Pattern Pitcher

Pitcher, milk, cranberry opalescent Drapery
patt. (ILLUS.)... **300**

Opalescent Spiral Pattern Pitcher

Pitcher, milk, cranberry opalescent Spiral
patt. (ILLUS.)... **275**
Pitcher, Panel Grape patt., blue opalescent **145**
Pitcher, tankard, Beaded Curtain patt., milk
glass w/green interior **550**

Rare Sample Coin Dot Pitcher

Pitcher, Topaz opalescent Coin Dot patt.,
appljed crystal handle, sample item only
(ILLUS.) **650**
Salt shaker w/metal lid, Argonaut patt.,
blue opalescent **25**
Salt shaker w/metal lid, Mirror and Rose
patt., green.. **30**
Sauce dish, Eye-Winker patt., blue
(ILLUS. top next page) **20**

Eye-Winker Sauce Dish

Spooner, Argonaut patt., blue opalescent.......... **40**

Beaded Curtain Peach Blow Spooner

Spooner, Beaded Curtain patt., peach blow
(ILLUS.)... **90**

Wright Cranberry Sugar Shaker

Sugar shaker w/metal lid, cranberry Inverted Thumbprint patt. (ILLUS.) **125**

Carnival God & Home Tumbler

Tumbler, Carnival glass, God & Home patt.,
purple (ILLUS.) **55**

Mirror and Rose Pattern Wine

Wine, Mirror and Rose patt., emerald green
(ILLUS.) **40**
Wine, Mirror and Rose patt., pink......................... **30**

Moon and Star Opalescent Wine

Wine, Moon and Star patt., flared rim, Topaz opalescent (ILLUS.) **125**
Wine, Stipple Star patt., amethyst........................ **25**

Wright Stipple Star Wine

Wine, Stipple Star patt., blue (ILLUS.)................. 25

Panel Grape Blue Wine

Wine glass, Panel Grape patt., blue
(ILLUS.)... 30

GLOBE MAPS

Celestial globe, globe mounted in a mahogany Regency-style framework
w/curved reeded supports & molded ring
w/a worn paper zodiac label & red paint
around outer ring, raised on a ring-turned
pedestal w/a tripod base of outswept tapered saber legs w/cast brass paw feet
w/casters & relief-carved acanthus
leaves on the knees, old finish, globe
signed "J. Wilson & Sons, 1826, Albany
St. N.Y.," early 19th c., 35" h. (few small
cracks in globe, formerly had support un-
derneath the legs) **$11,275**

Cary Globe Map

Celestial & terrestrial globes, on stands,
the terrestrial globe corrected to January
1, 1825, the celestial corrected to January 1, 1800, both w/brass meridian engraved w/degrees & quadrants w/horizon
bars showing degrees, compass points,
zodiacal signs & months, the mahogany
stands w/tripod bases w/cabriole legs

ending in pointed pad feet, made & sold
by G. J. Cary, London, England, globe
12" d., overall 24" h., pr. (ILLUS. of one) **16,100**

Celestial & terrestrial globes, the celestial
globe corrected to 1810, the terrestrial to
1816 & includes a chart for the location of
the sun, each w/brass meridian & compass, set on ebonized wood stands, each
w/four ring-turned legs joined by turned
cross-stretchers, by Newton's of Chan-
cery Lane, London, first quarter 19th c.,
globe 12" d., stand 19" h., pr. (daily lack-
ing pointers) **8,625**

HARDWARE

Fine Irish Setter Doorknob

Doorknob, bronze, cast w/the head of an
Irish Setter, introduced by Russel & Erwin in 1891, complete w/straight step-
down shank & original spindle, possibly
polished at one time, good color & detail
(ILLUS.) **$860**

Doorknob, bronze, entry-type, drum-form,
fleur-de-lis design on a hash-marked
ground w/four shamrocks included, Chi-
cago-style shank, made by Chicago
Hardware Co., ca. 1895, excellent w/rich
mellow color 60

Doorknob, bronze, passage-type, bold ea-
gle design, fine quality...................................... 160

Doorknob, cast iron, features a lady's profile, the top cast w/two pins extended
through the melon-form reverse side
then hammered flat to connect the two
pieces, American-made, 1860s 35

"Flying M" Cast-iron Doorknob

Doorknob, cast iron, "Flying M" design,
from an athletic club, faintly marked by
Russell & Erwin, ca. 1900 (ILLUS.)................. 45

Doorknob, glass & brass 'fisheye' style,
passage-type, decorated w/flowers printed on a paper disk set beneath a concave 'fisheye' lens, American-made,
ca. 1900... 220

Scarce Bennington Pottery Doorknob

Doorknob, pottery, octagonal on a brass step-down shank, mottled brown Rockingham glaze, from Bennington, Vermont, ca. 1860s (ILLUS.)................................ **95**

Fine Mercury Glass Doorknob

Doorknob, silvered (mercury) glass, a Dewdrop design knob on a bronze shank, created by Nashua Hardware, 1860s (ILLUS.)... **100**

Doorknob & back plate, bronze, entry-type, dramatic custom-made design, architect-design & signed by George Arcularius, 1970s, attached to orginal mahogany display plinth, knob about 2 3/4" d., circular plate 4" d., the set **85**

Doorknob & back plate, bronze, passage-type, transitional design of the late 1870s - early 1880s, by H&D, great old patina.......... **55**

Doorknob with Japanese Motif

Doorknob & rosette, bronze, part of a Japanese design collection produced by Russell & Erwin, features a floral design w/other Oriental motifs, the original rosette w/a Greek Key design, the knob w/a beaded band edging, late 19th c. (ILLUS.).. **225**

Doorknob & rosette, bronze, passage-type, fleur-de-lis & sunbursts design, knob design elements contrast w/darkened, rusticated background, Mallory Wheeler Company, a later design **35**

Doorknob & rosette, walnut, a detailed cameo-style bust of a warrior showing

chinstrap & fancy helmet, rosette w/bronze ferrule & beaded border, perfect **95**

Doorknob, rosette & back plate, bronze, a Victorian Aesthetic Movement design featuring a sunflower, sunrise & a spiky-leaved 'mystery' flower, by Sargent, late 1880s, fine old patina, the set **20**

Doorknobs, porcelain, passage-type, h.p. floral decorations & gilt trim, Limoges, France, 19th c., pr.. **30**

Door pull, bronze, Masonic design w/the Masonic crest w/square, calipers & a capital "G," marked "Sargent" on the back & dated 1895, 4 x 16"``` **65**

Doorbell, brass & iron, clockwork-type, iron housing w/a nickel-plated bell, fancy thumb-twist in brass, marked by Russell & Erwin, dated 1893, thumb-twist 4 3/4" l., fine working order, bell 4 1/2" d........ **75**

Doorbell buttons, bronze, larger one includes original button & electrical contact plate w/old green patina, ca. 1890, smaller cast bronze one from mid-1880s marked "WE Co.," smaller 2 1/4" d., large 2 1/4 x 5", the two **30**

Doorbell pulls, various materials, one porcelain & one silvered (mercury) glass w/original threaded back plates, one bronze w/a miniature "starburst" design of the 1870s by Russell & Erwin & a fourth in pressed glass w/original wire & interior wall lever, all 1870s or earlier, the group (pressed glass one w/a couple of dings, silver glass one w/some deterioration).. **80**

Hardware set, brass-plated cast iron, a group of 105 pieces marked "Chatham," a Russell & Erwin pattern, includes 62 passage knobs, 39 passage back plates w/a single keyhole & four mortise pulls for pocket doors, need cleaning, ca. 1900, the set **400**

Scarce Keyhole Escutcheon & Cover

Keyhole escutcheon, bronze, 'Rorschach' type w/an elaborate leafy scroll & blossom design, perfect & complete w/original swing cover, scarce, Russell & Erwin, late 19th c., 2 1/2 x 3 1/2" (ILLUS.) **160**

Early Letter Slot Cover

Letter slot cover, bronze, long rectangular form w/lobed tab ends, never used, 1870s, 2 x 7" (ILLUS.) **25**

Pocket door pulls, one gold-plated, Art Nouveau design w/flowers & leaves, possibly the "Anemona" patt. in the Corbin catalog of 1905, 2 x 10", the other in copper-plated cast iron, a medievel design w/neo-classical details, marked "Ideal," dates about 1890, 2 x 7 1/2", the two **65**

Push plates & keyhole covers, porcelain, decorated w/transfer-printed hunt scenes, plates marked "1971 BLD," keyhole covers marked "England," mid-to-late 20th c., covers 3/4 x 2 1/2", plates 3 x 11", the set **60**

Cast-iron Window Sash Lifts

Window sash lifts, cast iron, Greek Key border & Aesthetic style interior florets, probably early 1880s, 1 3/4 x 3 1/4", set of 4 (ILLUS.) **30**

Window sash lifts, four in bronze dated 1871, 1 1/2 x 2" & four in cast iron w/Victorian Aesthetic designs, 1880s, group of 8 .... **45**

HEINTZ ART METAL SHOP WARES

Secessionist-style Book Ends

Otto Heintz (Buffalo, N.Y., 1877-1918) changed the name of his Art Crafts Shop to Heintz Art Metal Shop in 1906 as he shifted his focus from copper to machine-formed bronze bodies and from colored enamels to sterling silver overlays as decoration. A patent for the solderless application of the overlays was awarded in 1912

and the diamond mark enclosing the conjoined letters "HAMS" came into use. A series of sophisticated chemical patinas and plated finishes was developed for a line of vases, bowls and book ends. Otto died suddenly in 1918, but the company struggled through the Depression until the end came on Feb. 11, 1930. Values are a function of form, rarity, overlay and originality of patina.

Ashtrays, brown patina, a nest of five w/attached matchsafe, Arts & Crafts design silver overlay, outer tray 4" d......................... **$95**

Book ends, brown patina, upright square backs w/an arched top, sterling silver overlay in a linear Vienna Secessionist style, No. 7145, 5" sq., pr. (ILLUS.) **390**

Book ends, French Grey finish, sterling silver date palm overlay, No. 7090, 3 x 5", pr. **395**

Heintz Book Ends with Pine Cones

Book ends, mottled green patina, upright square back decorated w/sterling silver overlaid pine cones & pine needles, No. 7148, 5" sq., pr. (ILLUS.) **425**

Bowl, brown patina, sterling silver stylized floral overlay, No. 3665, 9 1/4" d., 3" h. **450**

Jonquil Bowl & Candlesticks

Bowl, brown patina, wide rounded flat-rimmed bowl w/angular handles from the rim to center of the bottom, raised on a short pedestal w/a wide flaring round stepped foot, sterling silver overlay of jonquils, No. 1868, 9 1/4" d., 5 1/2" h. (ILLUS. center) **350**

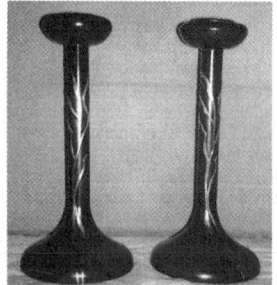

Tall Heintz Art Metal Candlesticks

Candlesticks, brown patina, a cupped mushroom-form candle socket atop a tall slender cylindrical shaft w/sterling silver overlay of grass continuing across the flaring round base, No. 3107, 10" h., pr. (ILLUS.) **850**

Candlesticks, brown patina, a flaring bell-form socket w/removable bobehe on a wide round flaring base w/sterling silver overlay of jonquils, No. 3128, 5 1/2" d., 5" h., pr. (ILLUS. left & right with bowl) **650**

Cigar ashtray, brown patina, shallow round dished form w/three cigar rests on the rim, Art Nouveau style sterling silver overlay on rim, No. 2641, 8" d. **275**

Cigar humidor, cov., brown patina, cylindrical, sterling silver overlay of two peacocks, No. 2539, 4" d., 8" h. **500**

Cigar humidor, cov., green patina, cylindrical w/Arts & Crafts style sterling silver overlay, No. 2647, 5 1/2" d. base, 7" h. **680**

Cigarette box, cov., brown patina, rectangular w/sterling silver overlay of birds in flight, cedar-lined, 3 x 4", 1" h. **300**

Desk set: inkwell on tray, calendar frame - letter rack combination, 11 x 19" blotter pad w/four metal corners, letter knife, rocker blotter; all w/an acid-etched silver finish w/sterling silver water lily overlay, the set **350**

Heintz Metal Lamp with Cut-out Shade

Lamp, boudoir, green patina, a conical 9" d. metal frame w/delicate panels of grapevine cut-outs & lined w/parchment, raised on a trumpet-form base w/sterling silver grapevine overlay around the rim, overall 10" h. (ILLUS.) **2,100**

Heintz Bamboo-decorated Desk Lamp

Lamp, desk, brown patina, 6" d. domed helmet shade decorated w/sterling silver bamboo & mounted between curved harp supports above the slender base w/flaring foot also decorated w/bamboo overlay, overall 10" h. (ILLUS.) **900**

Letter opener, brown patina, Art Nouveau style silver overlay on the handle, 9" l. **160**

Notepad holder, brown patina, hinged top, Arts & Crafts design sterling silver overlay, holds about 50 sheets of paper, 4 x 6" **275**

Heintz Art Metal Picture Frame

Picture frame, brown patina, rectangular w/large oval picture opening, the sides w/heavy sterling silver stylized flower & leaf designs, hinged easel back, No. 2124, 5 x 7" (ILLUS.) **850**

Stamp box, cov., French Grey finish, round w/sterling silver overlay of coneflowers accented w/a turquoise jewel on the hinged cover, 2 1/2" d. **145**

Trophy, brown patina, classical urn-form, Arts & Crafts sterling silver overlay on each side, from a 1920 tennis tournament, polished liner, No. 6545, 7" h. **255**

Heintz Vase with Cherry Blossoms

Vase, ovoid body tapering to a short wide neck w/flat rim, green patina, sterling silver overlay of branches of cherry blossoms, No. 3582, 6" h. (ILLUS.) **500**

Vase, cylindrical, brown patina, sterling silver floral overlay, No. 3668, 2" d., 6" h. **335**

Vase, tall slender cylindrical form w/rolled-in rim, green patina, sterling silver overlay of cattails, No. 3608, 10" h. **750**

Vase, cylindrical stick-form, brown patina, sterling silver mistletoe overlay on base & shaft, No. 3684, 12" h. **400**

Vase, slender cylindrical 'stick-form' w/disk foot, green patina, sterling silver overlay of pussy willows, No. 3705, 3 1/2" d. base, 12" h. **400**

Vase, chalice-form, brown patina, sterling silver overlay of irises, No. 3722, 14" h. **900**

HOLIDAY COLLECTIBLES

Halloween

Although Halloween is an American tradition and holiday, we must credit the Scottish for bringing it to the United States. The earliest symbols of Halloween appeared around the turn of the 20th century. During Victorian times, Halloween parties became popular in the United States. Decorations were seasonal products, such as pumpkins, cornstalks, vegetables, etc. Many early decorations were imported from Germany, only to be followed by their demand in the United States during WW I, when German imports ceased.

Today Halloween collectibles are second only to Christmas collectibles. Remembering the excitement one felt as a child dressing up in costume, going treat or treating, carving pumpkins, bobbing for apples, etc., the colors of orange and black bring back the nostalgia of youth for many of us.

The variety of Halloween collectibles is immense. Whether it be noisemakers, jack o' lanterns, candy containers, paper or plastic goods, candy molds or costumes, with the availability, the choice is yours.

Remember to buy the best, be it the very old or not so old. Search those antiques shops, flea markets and house sales.

Hat-shaped Candy Container

Candy container, cardboard hat shape covered w/black crepe paper, orange band of crepe paper above brim, orange jack-o'-lantern decoration, ca. 1940s-50s (ILLUS.)... **$50**

Pumpkin Man Candy Container

Candy container, composition figure w/pumpkin head, dressed in yellow, yellow hat, black shoes, standing on round cardboard container, ca. 1920, Germany (ILLUS.) **175**

Candy container, composition jack-o'-lantern stein w/excellent painted details, marked "Germany" **660**

Candy container, glass, smiling face jack-o'-lantern w/screw top **286**

Candy container, glass, smiling face jack-o'-lantern w/witch's hat, screw top................. **275**

Candy container, hard plastic, figural pumpkin carriage w/four green wheels & a cat & a witch, Kokomold, Inc., Indiana **550**

Candy container, jack-o'-lantern head, 3 1/2" h.. **297**

Luggage-shaped Candy Container

Candy container, paper-covered pressed board, luggage-shaped, yellow jack-o'-lantern face w/strap, ca. 1916, Germany (ILLUS.) **150**

Black Cat Candy Container

Candy container, papier-mâché, black cat w/yellow eyes, arched back, ca. 1940-50 (ILLUS.) **95**

Witch on Pumpkin Candy Container

Candy container, papier-mâché, figure of witch dressed in black & sitting on top of orange pumpkin, ca. 1940s-50s, USA (ILLUS.) **250**

German Pumpkin Man on Candy Container

Candy container, papier-mâché, ginger-bread man-type figure w/pumpkin head on round cardboard container w/plaid decoration, ca. 1930s, Germany (ILLUS.)... **250**

Jack-O'-Lantern Man Candy Container

Candy container, papier-mâché, orange figure w/jack-o'-lantern head, yellow mouth, nose & eyes, black shoes & tie, ca. 1940s-50s, USA (ILLUS.) **400**

Candle on Candy Container

Candy container, pressed board covered w/crepe paper, white candle figure w/eyes & mouth, fuzzy wick as hair on top of round red & black striped container, ca. 1920, Germany (ILLUS.)........... **95**

Candy container, w/nodding black cat head, Germany... **231**

Lithographed Tin Clickers

Clickers, lithographed tin, black & orange Halloween scenes, ca. 1950s, each (ILLUS. of two)... **25**

Die-cut Cat

Die-cut, black cat, w/tissue inserts at eyes & mouth, unmarked (ILLUS.) **75**

Skull & Crossbones Die-cut

Die-cut, skull & crossbones w/tissue inserts for nose & eyes, by H.L. Luhrs, ca. 1935, 10" h. (ILLUS.).. **50**

Figure, hard plastic witch riding a motorcy-cle w/jack-o'-lantern **495**

Figure, "Squash Body Bird Man," w/jack-o'-lantern head & top hat...................................... **248**

Jack-o'-lantern, painted tin, two molded ro-tating half-spheres on a heavy wire central shaft w/wooden knob at the top, wound at the bottom to hold a pole, cut-out features w/black trim, 19th c., 6 1/2" d., 9 1/4" h. (scattered paint wear) .. **2,530**

Jack-o'-lantern, papier-mâché, bulbous tapering molded form w/smiling cut-out mouth & eyes w/a paper insert w/rows of teeth & side-glancing eyes, orange w/green lower section, early 20th c., 6 1/2" w., 5" h. (minor wear) **138**

Jack-o'-lantern, pressed, formed paperboard w/tissue insert, 5" **385**

German Cardboard Jack-O'-Lantern

Lantern, cardboard, orange, black, red & green JOL (jack-o'-lantern) w/paper inserts for eyes, nose & mouth, ca. 1920s, Germany (ILLUS.) **225**

Glass & Tin Jack-O'-Lantern

Lantern, glass & tin, JOL, orange & black, battery-operated, ca. 1960, made in Hong Kong, 6" h. (ILLUS.) **65**

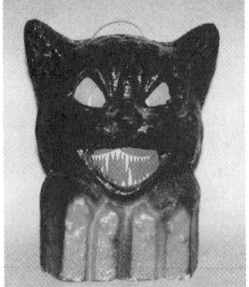

Cat on Fence Lantern

Lantern, papier-mâché, black cat w/paper inserts, green eyes, red mouth w/pointed white teeth, on black & orange fence-form base, ca. 1940s-50s, USA, mint condition (ILLUS.) **300**

Black Cat Lantern

Lantern, papier-mâché, heavy, black cat w/yellow eyes, crepe paper accordian neck, ca. 1920s, Germany, if in mint condition (ILLUS.) **400**

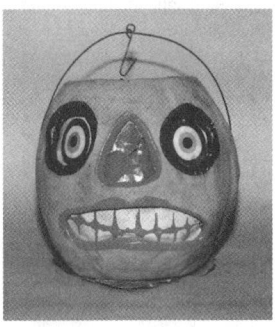

Early German Jack-O'-Lantern

Lantern, papier-mâché, heavy, orange, red & black JOL w/paper inserts at eyes, nose & mouth, ca. 1920, Germany (ILLUS.) **275**

Orange Cat Lantern

Lantern, papier-mâché, orange cat w/green paper eye inserts, red paper mouth insert w/sharp white teeth, 1940s-50s, USA (ILLUS.) **275**

Jack-O'-Lantern with Stem

Lantern, papier-mâché, orange & green JOL w/closed top & stem, blue, white, yellow & red paper inserts, ca. 1940s, USA (ILLUS.) **250**

Papier-mâché Jack-O'-Lantern

Lantern, papier-mâché, orange JOL w/paper inserts, USA (ILLUS.) **175**
Lantern, papier-mâché w/printed tissue insert, black cat, 6 1/2" h. **490**
Lantern, papier-mâché w/tissue insert, black cat... **358**

Model of Owl

Model of owl, papier-mâché, black w/yellow eyes (ILLUS.) **150**

Pair of Owls on Branch

Models of owl, crepe paper, grey & black w/feather detail, perched on branch, pr. (ILLUS.)... **95**

German Nodder Figure

Nodder, papier-mâché, figure of man in blue, green & yellow w/green cap on orange head, ca. 1920s, Germany (ILLUS.) **195**
Nodder, papier-mâché, gentleman w/jack-o'-lantern head w/black top hat, spring-mounted on wax body, felt tie & shoes, Germany.. **413**

Pipe-shaped Horn Noisemaker

Noisemaker, cardboard horn w/wooden mouthpiece, pipe-shaped, covered w/Halloween motif paper, ca. 1920, Germany (ILLUS.).. **125**
Noisemaker, composition figure of a goblin...... **220**

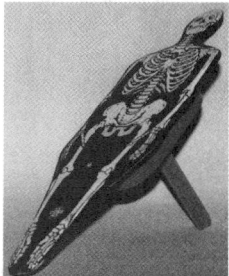

Skeleton Noisemaker

Noisemaker, metal, wood & plastic, skeleton, ca. 1950s, USA, unmarked, rare (ILLUS.) **95**

Tin Noisemaker with Wooden Handle

Noisemaker, tin w/wooden handle, circular-shaped, orange w/black & white lithographed scene of a jack-o'-lantern, witch w/broom, cat, demon & bat, ca. 1925 (ILLUS.)... **65**

Halloween Nut Cup

Nut cup, cardboard & crepe paper, w/orange & black twisted overhead handle, orange w/black bow around middle section, ca. 1950s (ILLUS.) **15**

Party Hat

Party hat, cardboard, orange & black w/cat decoration, 1950s (ILLUS.)................................ **15**

Tambourine with Witch

Tambourine, tin w/lithograph of witch's head w/long hair, hoop earrings, large hat w/small broom trim, orange, black & yellow, ca. 1950s, USA, T. Cohn (ILLUS.) **95**

Tea Bag Can with Halloween Decoration

Tea bag container, cov., metal, round, black decorated on lid w/scene of young girl wearing mask, a yellow dress & long green ruffled cape & pointed hat holding a broom w/jack-o'-lantern on top, ca. 1940s (ILLUS.) **95**

HORSE & BUGGY COLLECTIBLES

Hitching post, cast iron, figural African-American stable boy w/ragged shirt & pants standing & holding a square lantern w/green & white slag glass panels, on a high square base, old green repaint, late 19th - early 20th c., 44" h. (areas of rewelding at joints)....................................... **$880**

Hitching post, cast iron, model of a large horse head w/a ring in its mouth, raised on a tall columnar base, old bluish green worn repaint, 70 1/4" h. (rusted) **1,100**

Figural Hitching Post

Hitching post, cast iron, standing figure of an African-American stable boy wearing green & white shirt & pants, raised on a square pedestal, molded "JW FISKE NY," 19th c., 46" h. (ILLUS.)........................ **7,475**

Hitching post, cast iron, figural, a standing jockey holding one arm out w/ring, wearing riding boots, pants, vest & cap, white-painted face & hands, tall platform base marked "Champion Iron Fence Co., Kenton, Ohio," red, white & black repaint, late 19th c., 50 1/4" h. **578**

Hitching post, granite, an iron ring on the dome-topped elongated square stone post, New England, 19th c., 6 1/2" d., 30 1/2" h. **920**

Tree Trunk-form Hitching Posts

Hitching posts, cast iron, tree trunk-form w/looped branches at top, late 19th c., America, one painted black, one w/seam separation, breakage & loss, 46 1/4" h., pr. (ILLUS.) **690**

ICE SKATING COLLECTIBLES

Autographs

Captioned Photo of Michelle Kwan

Autographs are available in a variety of forms, from signed photos to autographed ice skates. If possible, try to obtain your autographs directly from the skater so you know where it came from. Most dealers in autographs will supply a COA, a Certificate of Authenticity, with a signed photograph. But even a COA does not guarantee the autograph is genuine since many dealers get their *autographs from a variety of sources and some are, unfortunately, forgeries. Also make sure the autograph is signed on the surface of the print, not imprinted in the photograph, which means it is printed, not signed.*

Dick Button, photo, 8 x 10 .... **$15**
Ekaterina Gordeeva, photo, "Discover Stars on Ice," 8 x 10 .... **20**
Kristi Yamaguchi, autographed skate **53**
Michelle Kwan, autographed skate, signed shortly after winning the Olympic Silver Medal for Ladies Figure Skating in 1998 .... **543**
Michelle Kwan, color, photo, captioned "Michelle Kwan-World Champion," 1990s, 8 x 10" (ILLUS.) **25-55**

Color Photo of Michelle Kwan

Michelle Kwan photo, signed, color, silver medalist at the 1998 Nagano Olympics, 8 x 10" (ILLUS.) **45-65**
Nancy Kerrigan, color photo, signed w/blue marker, 8 x 10" **25**
Nancy Kerrigan, Olympics, 1st Day Issue Postcard, 8 x 10" **31**
Nicole Bobek, autographed skate, white **40**
Oksana Baiul, Tara Lipinski, Katarina Witt & Kristi Yamaguchi, autographed skate **202**
Peggy Fleming, color photo, imprinted "1968 Olympics," 8 x 10" **22**
Peggy Fleming, color photo, posed in skating rink, 8 x 10" **25**

Photo of Peggy Fleming

Peggy Fleming photo, signed, b&w, signed in gold felt-tipped marker "Peggy Fleming, 1968 Olympian" (ILLUS.).................. 45

Scott Hamilton, color photo, signed after performance at Madison Square Garden, 8 x 10".. 34

Sonja Henie, program cover, inscribed "To Nanette Wersman, Best Wishes, Sonja Henie," 1950s.. 41

Tara Lipinski, autographed skate, signed shortly after winning Olympic Gold Medal for Ladies Figure Skating.............................. 720

Tara Lipinski, autographed skate, w/black Sharpie.. 103

Tara Lipinski, color photo, signed before winning Olympics, 6 x 9"................................. 25

Tenley Albright, Sports Illustrated, inscribed w/blue marker "Very Best Wishes! Tenley Albright".. 22

Tia Babalonia & Randy Gardner, photo, b&w, posed studio shot, signed by both, ca. 1980s, 8 x 10"................................ 48

Books

Brokaw, "The Art of Skating," w/13 chapters on figure skating w/many photos, chapters include "History of Skating," "Skating for Women," "Pair Skating," etc., hard cover, 1st Edition, published by American Sports Publishing Company, NY, 1915... 65

Browne, George H., "A Handbook of Figure Skating," an extensive handbook of figure skating patterns & techniques, w/handwritten field notes from 1917 on back inside flap, published by Barney & Berry, Springfield, MA, 223 pp., 3 1/2 x 6 1/4".. 38

"Hans Brinker or The Silver Skates" Book

Dodge, Mary Mapes, "Hans Brinker or The Silver Skates," illustrated by Arthur Jameson, Whitman Publishing Co., Racine, WI, 1945, in original dust jacket, 6 x 8 1/4" (ILLUS.)...................................... 12-18

Henie, Sonja, "Wings on My Feet," inscribed on title page: "With Best Wishes, Sonja Henie," w/original dust jacket

(worn), some foxing & yellowing, 1940, 1st Edition, 177 pp. **65-95**

Lewis, John F., "Skating & the Philadelphia Skating Club," describing the history of the club, no illustrations, Philadelphia, 1895, some fading 40

Dolls

"Dream Skater," "Spins, goes forwards, and backwards just like a ice skating star," Tomy, 1985, in original box, a very funny & entertaining skating toy....................... 15

Sonja Henie Doll

Sonja Henie, plastic, w/silver outfit & skates, ca. 1940s, 8 1/2" tall (ILLUS.) 17

Figurines, Sculptures & Ceramics

Ceramics, tile, artwork of skating couple in circular design, marked "Winter" on top, "Minton's China Works, Stoke on Trent," ca. 1900, one of four seasons tiles, 4 x 4", ... 80

Statue of Sonja Henie

Figurine, chalkware, full color, painted, Sonja Henie statue, stylized figure skater, ca. 1940s, 12 1/4" tall (ILLUS.) **75**

Statue of Kristi Yamaguchi

Figurine, molded plastic, Kristi Yamaguchi statue, Limited Edition, hand-painted & numbered, w/embossed "Kristi" signature, by Gartlan, 4 1/2" h., 2 1/2" d. base (ILLUS.)... **35-60**

Figurine, porcelain, sitting female skater, w/blue Lomonosov mark, ca. 1955-65, 6 1/2" h., 6 1/2" base **55-70**

Miscellaneous

Advertising tray, Coca Cola, female skater sitting & enjoying a Coke on ice, ca. 1940s, 10 1/2 x 13 1/4" **285**

Whitman's Chocolate Box

Chocolate box, Whitman, marked "Whitman's Choice candies for children," probably later used as a crayon box—someone has written in pencil "Wonder Box," 5 1/2 x 7 1/2 x 1/2" (ILLUS.) **12**

Chocolate mold, tin, three skaters, ca. 1910, 2 1/2 x 4 1/4".................................... **45**

Printing press block, two skaters, on metal print plate attached to a wooden base, 1940s, 1 5/8 x 1 1/8 x 7/8" **18**

Silhouette, framed skaters, ca. 1920, 5 x 10" **62**

Skater's lantern, brass, ca. 1890s, small dent in top section of lamp, 7" h. **85**

Skater's lantern, brass, w/cobalt globe, marked "#2," very rare colored glass, 7" h. **430**

Snow globe, skating pair, Norman Rockwell, Limited Edition, 1990s, from "Rockwell's Winter Wonderland Collection" **49**

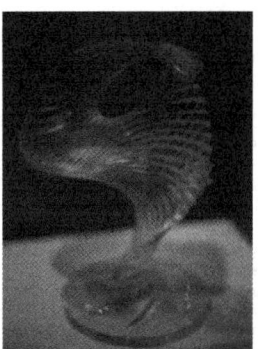

Lalique Glass Trophy

Trophy, glass, w/design of ice skater in motion, Lalique, France, approx. 12" (ILLUS.) **4,000-6,000**

Trophy, skating trophy in shape of metal skate, brass finish, ca. 1910-1930, approx. 12" l. **100-350**

Paper

Finding postcards with skating images is difficult. Most are available at specialty Internet auctions or at postcard conventions. Their rarity makes them highly collectible and they bring high prices. Skating shows have toured the world for many years. The programs from these shows are still plentiful and offer an interesting variety for the collector to choose from. The cover art on these is very collectible and is often framed. Sonja Henie's programs bring the highest prices. Collectible programs of the future will be those featuring the most popular stars of today. Unlike football and baseball trading cards, figure skating cards really never took off. A number of companies produced them in the early 1980s, but because the response was weak, they were discontinued. This actually makes them quite rare, and for that reason, they realize good prices.

"Alfred's Ice King" Catalog

Book illustration, wood engraving, Skater w/Sails, 1902, 8 1/2 x 11" **12-18**

Card Set, Ladies Olympic Champs, 13 different views, each card pictures an Olympic Gold Medalist: Sonja Henie,

Tenley Albright, Peggy Fleming, Dorothy Hamill, Katarina Witt, Oksana Baiul, Kristi Yamaguchi, etc., brands include Topps, Sports Illustrated & Sportscaster, 1983-1997 .... **55**

Catalog, "Alfred's Ice King," w/skates, shoe outfits & sharpeners, distributed by Hennepin Hardware Catalog, Minneapolis, Minnesota, 1929, 32 pp., 3 1/2 x 6 1/2" (ILLUS.)... **15-20**

Die-cut, full color, three Victorian children wearing ice skates, ca. 1890, 3 1/2 x 4" **38**

Display, store photo, full color, 1984 Olympics, Kodak cardboard tabletop film display w/female ice skater on backboard, 15 x 20" **15**

Illustration of Skaters

Illustration, almanac page, Dec. 1868, w/skaters, lists tides & celestial phenomena, 7 1/2 x 10 1/2" (ILLUS.) **16**

"All American Girl" Illustration

Illustration, calendar, "All American Girl," signed Buell, ca. 1940s-50s, 7 1/2 x 9 1/2" (ILLUS.) **18**

Illustration, poster, watercolor, "Skate America," pairs skaters performing lift, Lake Placid, 1981, 23 x 35" **25**

Letter & skating ticket, handwritten letter w/account of skating mentioned & orange ticket for Baltimore Skating Club, ca. 1860s, 2 1/2 x 5 1/2" letter & 2 x 3 3/4" ticket (ILLUS. top next column)........ **55**

Letter & Skating Ticket

Lithograph, "Flavio and Hilaria," from Goethe's "Wilhelm Meister," lovers skating in moonlight, 1892, 5 x 8" on sheet size of 8 1/2" x 11 1/2" **37**

"Skating Scene—Moonlight"

Lithograph, "Skating Scene - Moonlight," Currier & Ives, 1940s, copy of 1870s original, 9 x 12" (ILLUS.)..................................... **10-20**

Boston Sunday Post

Magazine, Boston Sunday Post, 1913, artist-signed - Valentine Andberg, young woman w/furs skates across river, edge damage, 10 1/2 x 14 1/2" (ILLUS.)............ **10-15**

Magazine, "Disadvantageous Knowledge," 1890s romantic skating scene, illustrated by "Harrison Fisher," one page color lithograph, Puck, 1898, 10 x 13 1/4" 41

Harper's Bazaar Magazine

Magazine, Harper's Bazaar cover, Feb. 1914, full color, Art Nouveau style illustration of a graceful skater w/a flowing scarf & elaborate costume, w/artist's initials "S.S.S.W.," w/light creases & slight pencil erasure, 9 1/2 x 13 3/4" (ILLUS.) **55**

Life Magazine Cover

Magazine, Life, female figure skater Gretchen Merrill on cover, Mar. 4, 1946, two-color, 10 1/2 x 14" (ILLUS.) **10-25**

Literary Digest Cover

Magazine, Literary Digest, February 13, 1937, female skater in "flying pose" on cover, slight wear, 8 1/2 x 11 3/4" (ILLUS.) **18**

Look Magazine Cover

Magazine, Look, Dec. 7, 1948, figure skater on cover in three animated poses, two-color, 10 1/2 x 13" (ILLUS.) **9**

Magazine, New Yorker, 1950, skating illustration on cover, full color, 8 1/2 x 11" **13**

Sports Illustrated Cover w/Peggy Fleming

Magazine, Sports Illustrated, w/cover titled: "Olympic Champion Peggy Fleming," Feb. 19, 1968 (ILLUS.) **15-25**

Good Literature Newspaper Cover

Newspaper cover, Good LIterature, 1901, romantic cover illustration of man helping Victorian woman w/her skates, two-color, wear & tear damage, 11 x 16" (ILLUS.)............ **8**

The Illustrated London News

Newspaper cover, Illustrated London News (The), 1895, w/illustration of skaters at an indoor rink (ILLUS.) **29**

"Skating Sketches" Paperback Book

Paperback book, "Skating Sketches - Notes on Skating - Strictly Personal," 1866, w/12 sketches of various skating scenes, blue covers w/people on the ice forming the title words, printed by Rivingtons, London, Oxford & Cambridge, 7 3/4 x 9 3/8" (ILLUS.) **70**

Tenley Albright Photo

Photo, press release-type, Tenley Albright, the first American woman to win the Gold Medal in Figure Skating at the 1956 Winter Olympics, restored, 13 3/4 x 17" (ILLUS.) **35**

Photogravure of "The Skating Party"

Photogravure, "The Skating Party," by L. Doucet, 1893, published by Appleton & Co., NY, 10 1/2 x 14 1/2" (ILLUS.) **35**

"Amish Skaters" Postcard

Postcard, "Amish Skaters," ca. 1950s-60s, unused, captioned on reverse: "Two Amish youths head for the frozen farm pond to enjoy an afternoon of ice skating," 3 1/2 x 5 1/2" (ILLUS.) **5**

Young Girl Skating w/Christmas Tree

Postcard, Christmas illustration of young girl skating w/Christmas tree, inscribed on back "To Nellie Ewing, Jackson, O, 12/24/12, Merry Xmas! Cousin Thelma," embossed, 3 1/2 x 5 1/2" (ILLUS.) **15-25**

Postcard w/Couple Skating & Kissing

Postcard, couple skating & kissing,
ca. 1910, unmarked but probably Euro-
pean origin, 3 1/2 x 5 1/2" (ILLUS.) **12**

Postcard w/Man Lacing Woman's Skates

Postcard, man lacing woman's skates on
beautiful frozen lake, Norway, post-
marked 1908, 3 1/2 x 5 1/2" (ILLUS.) **16**

"Love Laughs At Winter" Postcard

Postcard, man skating w/woman w/flowing
scarf, captioned "Love Laughs at
Winter," ca. 1910, Austria, 3 1/2 x 5 1/2"
(ILLUS.)... **12**

Girls Skate Down River Postcard

Postcard, photo-type, four college girls
skate down river, Massachusetts, 1906
postmark, 3 1/2 x 5 1/2" (ILLUS.) **10-20**
Postcard, real photo, 1933 Century of
Progress, Ohio man w/his collection of
ice skates in basement, 3 1/2 x 5" **20**
Postcard, real photo, skaters near Washington D. C. Monument, ca. 1929,
3 1/2 x 5 1/2".. **13**

Postcard w/Skating Couple

Postcard, skating couple w/cupid in
tree, ca. 1910, Germany, unused, em-
bossed, 3 1/2 x 5 1/2" (ILLUS.)......................... **9**

Feb. 1921 Postcard Calendar

Postcard calendar, Feb. 1921, female skater posed in winter scene w/calendar & advertisement for "Richards-Wilcox Mfg. Co.," Aurora, Illinois, 3 1/2 x 5 1/2" (ILLUS.) **22**

Postcards, 3 different views, 3 boys skating on pond, w/Gold Leaf borders, color illustrations by same artist **36**

Poster, LeRoy Neiman, signed, action illustration of female figure skater **100-150**

Poster, stamp-type, from Bulgaria, to honor 1988 Olympics, photo of Katarina Witt w/block of four (mint) Winter skating stamps mounted in upper left corner of poster, 10 x 13" **7-12**

Print, wood engraving bookplate, Skaters w/Boston Terrier, "The Glory of a Winter's Day," by A.B. Frost, 1904, 10 3/4 x 15 1/8" **28**

"Skating" Print

Print, wood engraving, hand-colored, "Skating," a famous scene at Central Park, NY, where thousands of skaters gathered for Winter entertainment, by Winslow Homer, framed later copy, 16" x 22 1/2", print in 20 x 26" frame original $9,000.00-18,000.00, copy (ILLUS. of copy) **85**

Program, Ice Capades, 1945, w/"Orcadette" cover, painted by Petty, WWII ad on back cover for War Bonds, 8 1/4 x 11".. **35-45**

1949 Ice Capades Program

Program, Ice Capades, 1949, features for the first time "Snow White & the Seven Dwarfs, Mickey & Goofy," 10 pp., 8 x 10 1/2" (ILLUS.) **10-15**

Program, Ice Capades, 1950, produced in exclusive management w/"Walt Disney Products & starring Bobby Specht, Eric Waite, Mary Lou Landreville, Helen Davidson, Alan Conrad, Mary Lela Wood & many others!," very good condition, 8 x 10 1/2" **10-15**

Program, Ice Capades, 1959-61, 20th Birthday Edition presented by John Harris, includes "Blue Danube, Babes in Toyland, etc.," good condition, minor wear on edges, staples rusted, 9 x 12" **6-10**

1951 Ice Follies Program

Program, Ice Follies, 1951, 15th Anniversary Edition, produced by Oscar Johnson, Eddie & Roy Shipstad, featuring an imaginary trip to Mexico, a New Year's Eve party, a supper club & bakery & umbrella land where it has rained 1,000 years, 8 1/2 x 11" (ILLUS.) **15-20**

Program, Ice Follies of 1943, Shipstads & Johnson, features "Indian Legend, Enchanted Lake, Arabian Nights & Sunday Go to Meeting," WWII ad on back cover for U. S. Savings Bonds, 8 1/2 x 11" **10-15**

Program, Ice Vogues, 1950, cover illustration by Ross, 16 pp. **14**

Program from 1954 Ice Follies

Program, Shipstads & Johnson Ice Follies of 1954, w/back cover advertisement for "Stereo Realist" camera w/ice skaters, 9 x 12" (ILLUS. of back cover) **45-55**

Sonja Henie Ice Revue Program

Program, Sonja Henie, 1943-44, "Hollywood Ice Revue," red felt cover w/gilt lettering, 16 pp., light wear, very collectible, 9 x 12" (ILLUS.) **35-60**
Program, Sonja Henie, 1948, "Icetime of 1948 w/Sonja Henie & Arthur M. Wirtz, at Rockefeller Center" **16-20**
Program, Sonja Henie, 1953 "Ice Review," good condition, cover wear & scuffs, spine tear, yellowing, 20 pp. **13-18**

Sonja Henie & 1953 Ice Revue Program

Program & real photo, original airbrushed press photo of Sonja Henie used as the source for the accompanying program cover design for the 1953 Ice Revue, 9 x 12" & 8 x 10" (ILLUS.) **55-75**

Greeting Cards Scrapbook

Scrapbook, greeting cards w/skating designs, about 200 cards, some signed by famous skaters of the time, particularly from "Ice Follies" & "Ice Capades" shows, 1930s-1940s, 11 x 14" (ILLUS.) **100-200**

Scrapbook Card -Victorian Couple On Ice

Scrapbook card, romantic Victorian couple on ice w/woman tossing out mistletoe, marked in grey outer mat "with best wishes—Christmas," ca. 1900, 4 1/2 x 6 1/2" (ILLUS.) **9**

Scrapbook Card w/Victorian Skater

Scrapbook card, Victorian skater in rural setting, ca. 1910, tear damage, 4 1/2 x 6 1/2" (ILLUS.) **8-12**

"Love and Folly" Sheet Music

Sheet music, "Love and Folly," woman on ice w/skaters in background, full color, ca. 1910, 9 1/4 x 12" (ILLUS.) **12**

"Winter" Sheet Music

Sheet music, "Winter," Victorian couple skating in snowfall, by Alfred Bryans & Albert Gumble, published by Jerome H. Remick & Co., Detroit, NY, ca. 1910, 10 3/4 x 13 1/2" (ILLUS.) **18**

Tobacco card, titled "Winter Scenes - A Series of 48 - No. 29 The Figure Skater," inscribed "Light as thistledown, her every action expressing the very poetry of motion, the skater is an entrancing sight," Senior Service Cigarettes, by J. A. Pattreiouex, 1937 .... **6-10**

Die-Cut Valentine w/Skaters

Valentine, die-cut design of male & female skaters, ca. 1920s-30s, inscribed "In February, well you know, the world is wrapped in ice & snow. But warm within my heart so true, a place is waiting for you," (folded) approximately 3 x 5" (ILLUS.).. **4-8**

Engraving-"Skating Carnival in Brooklyn"

Wood engraving, from Harper's Weekly, Feb. 10, 1862, "Skating Carnival in Brooklyn," amazing scene of hundreds of skaters on the ice during the Civil War wearing costumes, men in hoop dresses, devils, animals, etc., 7 1/2 x 10 1/2" (ILLUS.).. **12-25**

"The Skater" Wood Engraving

Wood engraving, "The Skater," early image of male skater w/curled prow skates leisurely skating along, ca. 1840-70, 4 x 6" image size (ILLUS.) **20-35**

Photographs

Photographs of skaters are more readily available than you would think. Who hasn't gone figure skating on a pond or river or at the local rink as a child? Mom are Dad were usually there with their camera capturing the moment. Older photos are more rare, of course, and command high prices. Celebrity photographs of well-known skaters are sure to be the collectibles of the future.

Victorian Era Skater Cabinet Card

Cabinet card, female Victorian era skater posed in studio w/winter scene backdrop, marked "William Notman, Montreal, 'Photographer to the Queen,' branches at Ottawa, Toronto & Halifax," ca. 1880s, rare, 4 x 6" (ILLUS.)...................................... **125**

Cabinet card, Norwegian skater Axel Paulson posed in studio w/medals, Axel invented the 1 1/2 rotation jump that bears his name & was first introduced in Vienna, Austria in 1882, ca. 1880s, 4 x 6" **78**

Skaters Cabinet Card

Cabinet card, oversized, group of skaters in studio setting w/one man tying woman's skates, marked "Pearson, East Des Moines," ca. 1890s, minor stains on mount, 8 x 10" (ILLUS.)...................................... **50**

Russian Skater Cabinet Card

Cabinet card, Russian skater wearing skates w/curved prow blades, Russian photographer, ca. 1880s, 4 x 6" (ILLUS.)........ **40**

Cabinet card, skater in long coat w/skates around his neck, ca. 1890, 4 x 6" **86**

"Winter Sport" Photo Illustration

Carte de visite, "Winter Sport," photo illustration of a female skater w/curved prow skates, New York Photographic Co., ca. 1850s-60s, vertical crease, 2 3/8 x 4" (ILLUS.).. **11**

1985 News Photo

Photo, 1985 news photo, Torville & Dean w/Lady Diana, caption on reverse "Wearing a white evening gown, Princess Diana watched Jayne Torville & Christopher Dean begin their world tour at Wembley yesterday...," 6 x 8" (ILLUS.) **58**

Mounted Photo of Skaters

Photo, group of skaters in a studio setting, Maine, ca. 1890s, stained, 6 x 8" mounted on a 11 x 14" board (ILLUS.) **28**

"Central Park, American Views" Stereoview

Stereoview, "Central Park, American Views," on curved yellow card, 1860s, 3 1/2 x 7" (ILLUS.)... **12**

Stereoview, "Skating Central Park, NY, City Winter 1866," marked "E & HT Anthony & Co.," 3 1/2 x 7" **50-75**

Tintype Antique Photograph

Tintype, young boy holding skates in photographic studio, slightly tinted, excellent tones & detail, ca. 1870s, rare, minor wear on edges, 2 3/8 x 3 5/8" (ILLUS.) ... **75-150**

Skates

The most popular figure skates for collectors are early ones with the curly toe. Early wooden straight skates are also collected, and are hung on the wall as ornaments. Interior decorators are discovering all types of skates for use as decorating accents.

English, wood & brass, marked "Corporate Mark," w/dog hallmark, "Marsden Brothers Manufacturers," "By Special Appointment to Her Majesty & The Royal Family Sheffield," 1800s **524**

German, Hudora, 30/32, marked "Eis-Zepp, Hudora & Laufbahn Gehartet," 1920s, mint in original blue box **35-50**

Ice Skate Sharpener

Sharpener, "Berghman Skate Sharpener," River Forest, IL, 1920s, w/instructions & original box, 1 1/2 x 3 1/4 x 3 3/4" (ILLUS.) **10-15**

Union Hardware Metal Skates

United States, metal, Union Hardware, ca. 1915, w/original box, skate key & Union Hardware catalog, red cover w/small hole on key, catalog lists screw-clamp & full strap skates, parts list & telegraph code, 32 pp., 3 1/2 x 6" (ILLUS.) **110**

United States, metal, w/large leather heel straps, ca. 1890s, blades rusted, 10 1/2" l. **35-65**

Woman's Skates

United States, woman's, white, size 9 1/4, marked "Arnold Glove Grip Shoes," w/Barnard wood (maple) guards, St. Paul, 1940s-50s (ILLUS.) **35**

Child's Wooden Skates w/Curved Toe

United States, wooden, child's, w/slightly curved toe, leather straps, ca. mid 1800s, worn condition, 12" l. (ILLUS.) **50-85**

Stamps & Coins, Medals & Pins

Stamps, coins and medals are a unique area of skating collectibles. They not only hold value for their skating imagery, but are also very collectible as investments by the general public. Consult specialty price guides for stamps and coins to establish prices. For medals, see Olympic guides or get personal appraisals from other collectors.

Coin, 100 Dinara Silver Proof, 1984 Yugoslavia Olympics **34**

100 Dinara Silver Proof Coin

Coin, 100 Dinara Silver Proof, 1984 Yugoslavia Olympics w/Figure Skating Pairs (ILLUS.) **48**

Lake Placid Olympic Coin

Coin, Chinese, commemorating Lake Placid Olympics, embossed design of female skater, 1 1/4" d. (ILLUS.) **14**

1968 Grenoble Olympic Games Coin

Coin, premium made for Coca-Cola commemorating 1968 Grenoble Olympic Games, obverse features embossed design of Peggy Fleming, reverse tells of her accomplishments, aluminum, 1 5/8" d. (ILLUS.)...................................... **18-32**

"1921 Skating Carnival" Medal

Medal, "1921 Skating Carnival," w/popular design motif of wingfooted skate, no location, mark on reverse "T.D. Gard Co., Worcester, Mass," blue cloth by pin is torn (ILLUS.)...................................... **12**

Medal, "C.Y.O. 1936" on front w/winged human foot, green & white satin fabric, vibrant color, medal 1 1/4" d. **18**

Medal & pin collection, 1940s-50s, group of Ice Capades pins, medals, tie tacks & key chains, some designed by Petty, brass, sterling & celluloid, rare...................... **500**

"Alfred's" Skate Pin

Pin, "Alfred's" skate pin w/wingfooted skate, gold finish, w/some of the gold worn off exposing actual metal, probably an advertising pin for Alfred Johnson Skate Company, 1" l. (ILLUS.) **10**

Pin, "Ice Capades," souvenir pin of female skater design, gold finish, design of skater w/blue ruffled skirt, holding a scarf w/motto over her head, w/safety clasp, 1950s-60s, 1 3/8 x 2 3/4" **20**

Pin, Minute Maid, 1998 Nagano Olympics, 1 x 1" **20**

Female Skater Pin

Pin, stick-type, w/design of female skater jumping, marked 3x "Sjoukje, Gould, 1964" (ILLUS.) **8**

Worldwide Skating Stamps

Stamps, 100 Worldwide skating stamps, circulated, variety of artwork on stamps with skating as the theme (ILLUS.) **5-20**

Paraguay Stamps with Peggy Fleming

Stamps, Republic of Paraguay, commemorative set of 9 stamps creating filmstrip animation of Peggy Fleming in motion during the 1968 Olympics, 7 x 9 3/4" (ILLUS.) **18**

Russian Pairs Skating Stamps

Stamps, Russian Pairs skating stamp, diagonal design, full sheet, 1980 (ILLUS.)........ **10-15**

Stamps, Vietnam, seven different pairs figure skaters.. **3**

ICONS

Icon is the Greek word meaning likeness or image and is applied to small pictures meant to be hung on the iconostasis, a screen dividing the sanctuary from the main body of Eastern Orthodox churches. Examples may be found all over Europe. The Greek, Russian and other Orthodox churches developed their own styles, but the Russian contribution to this form of art is considered outstanding.

Annunciation (The), the Archangel Gabriel on the left announces the birth of Christ to Mary on the right, image overlaid w/a fine heavy repoussé & chased gilded silver riza w/attached haloes, God the Father at the top center, on the top border a church title, mark of Tikhon Zalesove, St. Petersburg, Russia, mid-19th c., 10 x 12 1/4" **$2,688**

Annunciation (The), traditional rendering w/the Archangel Gabriel on the left before the Virgin seated & studying the scriptures, his outstretched hand holds a lily, at top center a hand appears from heaven, overlaid w/a later 19th c. fine repoussé & engraved silver-gilt riza w/multicolored enameled halos, Russia, icon 18th c., 10 1/2 x 12 1/2" **2,520**

Icon of Archangel Michael

Archangel Michael, Russia, ca. 1800, 20 x 42" (ILLUS.) **12,096**

Archangel Raphael (The), Raphael holds a scepter representing his authority & in his left hand he holds a disk w/an abbreviated inscription for Jesus Christ, goldleaf ground heavily incised w/scrolling foliage, Ural region, Russia, ca. 1850, 15 1/4 x 18 3/4" **1,344**

Baptism of Christ (The), Christ stands in the Jordan River as John the Forerunner baptizes him, the Holy Spirit descends from heaven as a dove in an aureole of light, three angels attend Christ, titled, Russia, ca. 1890, 10 1/2 x 12 1/4" **1,456**

Christ Enthroned, large central scene of seated Christ holding open Gospels, surrounded by angles & saints, Russia, 17th c., 34 x 45" (ILLUS. top next column) **14,950**

Early Russian Icon of Christ

Deisis (The), fully painted & detailed w/Christ enthroned in the center w/Mary on his right & John on his left, Christ holds the Gospels, Mary & John hold scrolls, overlaid w/a fine repoussé & chased gilt-silver riza hallmarked from Moscow, 1847, Russia, mid-19th c., 10 1/2 x 12 1/2" **1,940**

Descent of the Holy Spirit (The), shows twelve Apostles together w/the Mother of God in a room, Holy Spirit in form of dove descends & leaves flame atop each one, image overlaid w/outstanding heavily repoussé & chased gilded silver riza w/applied halo & dove, Kursk hallmark dated 1823 w/maker's initials, Russia, 10 1/2 x 12 3/4" **2,016**

Entrance Into Jerusalem (The), Christ upon an ass entering through the gates of the city in the company of his disciples as a crowd holding palms looks on, borders w/faux enameling, top inscription, in the Mstera style, Russia, 10 1/2 x 12 1/4" . **2,240**

Holy Apostle and Evangelist St. Matthew (The), large & ornate depiction of Matthew seated at a table inside a room beginning his Gospel, his symbol, a winged man, in the background, the uniquely decorated kovcheg suggests it was produced in the village of Mstera, Russia, abbreviated inscription across the top, 19th c., 14 x 17 1/4" **1,120**

Holy Prince Vladimir (The), Vladimir shown w/his left hand to his heart, a cross in his right hand & wearing a crown & royal garments, overlaid w/brilliant two-tone silver & gilt riza w/elaborate repoussé work & engraving, engraved nameplate at the lower margin, riza w/Moscow hallmark, ca. 1899, 9 x 10 3/4" **3,640**

John the Forerunner, John shown wearing a hair shirt & holding a scroll w/inscription, Moscow Armory School influence, overlaid w/later rare silver filigree riza, Moscow hallmark & dated 1818, 10 2/3 x 13" **7,000**

Lord Almight (The), bust portrait of Christ in the 17th c. style, painted on a dark caramel ground w/gold hatched halo &

highlights, overlaid w/fine silver repoussé & chased riza, maker's mark of Maxim Fontikov, Moscow, dated 1848, 10 1/2 x 12 1/4" 1,680

Mother of God Joy To All Who Sorrow with Saints (The), unique rendering of Mary & the Infant Christ surrounded by a throng of needy humans, below is the image of the "Not Made by Human Hands" image of Christ, central motifs flanked by a gathering of 15 saints, fine detail atop goldleaf & applied silver-gilt haloes, title inscribed on top margin in Slavonic, late Yaroslavi style, Russia, 18th c., 11 1/4 x 12 1/4" 3,360

Mother of God of the Passion (The), Mary looks tenderly on her infant son, Christ looks up at two descending angels, overlaid w/a silver-gilt, repoussé & chased riza w/shaded enamel haloes & corner plaques, also painted porcelain title plaques, Cyrillic maker's mark probably of Andre Alexandrov, Moscow, Russia, ca. 1908, 10 3/4 x 12 3/4" 3,920

New Testament Trinity (The), painted showing the three persons of the Trinity, Christ seated at the left holding the Gospels & delivering a blessing, God the Father on the right & a dove between them, both Father & Son seated on red six-winged seraphim, saints in upper corners, overlaid w/a fine silver-gilt repoussé & chased riza, Russia, ca. 1882, 10 1/4 x 12 1/4" 3,080

Old Testament Trinity (The), three angels at the center, perhaps representing the Trinity, on the left the Prophet Abraham, on the right his wife Sarah, overlaid w/a fine repoussé & chased gilt silver riza hallmarked Kaluga, 1794, Russia, 18th c., 10 1/2 x 12" 7,280

Resurrection (The), at the center the resurrected Christ stands triumphant over death atop his empty tomb, below two angels look on, the head of Christ encircled w/the cross-form halo & the goldleaf ground incised w/rays emanating from the head of Christ, borders ornately incised & colorfully decorated, inscription along the base, Moscow, Russia, ca. 1890, 10 1/2 x 12 1/2" 896

Resurrection (The), sixteenth century style w/scene of Christ's descent into hell to free the Old Testament righteous men & women, Christ shown at center atop fallen gates of hell, he grasps the hands of Adam & Eve kneeling at his feet, behind them are others identified w/inscriptions, Russia, ca. 1900, 10 1/2 x 12 1/2" 672

Resurrection with Feasts (The), colorful & complex scene w/central image showing the subject of the Resurrection, both Eastern & Western versions, central icon surrounded by the twelve major church festivals, outer margins in faux enamel, image laid down on a goldleaf ground, Russia, ca. 1890, 12 1/4 x 14" 2,688

Saint John the Divine in Silence, John contemplates writing his Gospel, which he reads as he receives devine inspiration in the form of an angel whispering in

his ear, colorfully painted on a heavily incised & decorated goldleaf ground, the left border w/St. Sergiy of Radonezh & on the right the Holy Martyr Maris, inscription along the top, Russia, probably Palekh, ca. 1900, 10 1/4 x 12 1/4" 1,064

Smolensk Mother of God (The), Mary holds the infant Jesus who delivers a blessing, overlaid w/a two-tone silver-gilt riza w/multicolored enamel halo & enamel title plaques, Moscow hallmark, 19th c., 10 1/2 x 12 1/4" 3,640

Icon of St. John the Baptist

St. John the Baptist, large standing angel in the center surrounded by vignette scenes of the saint's life, Russia, late 18th - early 19th c., 10 1/4 x 12 1/2" (ILLUS.) 863

St. Nicholas, less frequently encountered bust portrait of the saint, borders w/the Guardian Angel & a male martyr, Russia, 19th c., 12 x 14" 896

Tikhvin Mother of God (The), the Virgin & Child depicted in realistic manner, overlaid w/a multiple piece silver-gilt riza w/applied shaded enamel halo & their garments overlaid in ornately fashioned silver filigree, chip-carved liner & beveled glass hinged door, Russia, ca. 1900, 8 1/4 x 9 1/2" 5,600

Vladimir Mother of God (The), finely detailed painting on goldleaf ground of Mary & Child Jesus in a cheek to cheek embrace, left border w/a guardian angel, on the right the female martyr Fotinna, overlaid w/a gilded, repoussé & chased riza, the gown of Mary & Jesus covered w/a riza sewn w/a profusion of seed pearls, paste gemstones & beads, Russia, 19th c., 10 3/4 x 12 3/4" 5,040

INDIAN ARTIFACTS & JEWELRY

Arm bands, Sioux, beaded & quilled leather, the leather strands decorated w/red, white & purple quillwork & beaded disks of white, translucent blue, white heart red & faceted silver, leather attachments wrapped in red & green quills w/yellow feathers & tin cone dangles, ca. 1910, 18 1/2" l., pr. (wear, quill loss) **$825**

Awl case, Sioux, beaded leather, the leather wrapped in pink, green & dark blue beads, flap cover, leather thong hanger & tin cone dangles, 9" l. **193**

Basket, California Mission, bowl-shaped w/a simple design in dyed & natural juncus & sumac, attached tag reads "'Conejo' made by Mrs. Lorenzo La Chappa, 1914" written in ballpoint pen, 5" d., 3 1/2" h. **193**

Basket, California Mission, shallow coiled bowl-form w/a frieze of three stepped design areas, dyed juncus & natural juncus body, 8 1/4" d., 2 1/2" h. (missing three rim stitches at coil end) **468**

Basket, Paiute, coiled & beaded, small rounded form w/geometric polychrome netted beading in a typical serrated design covering the coiled structure, 4 1/2" d. **220**

Basket, Pima, woven willow, bowl-shaped, a stepped key design in dark martynia, whipped rim stitch, 5 1/2" d., 2 1/2" h. **193**

Basket, Tlinglit, woven 'Yakutat' berry basket w/a rectangular & a diamond eye design in bear grass & bracken fern root on a spruce body, old tag reads "grass utility basket, Yucatat, Alaska," 4 3/4" d., 4" h. (some rim wear) **358**

Belt, Crow, beaded woman's, leather w/a geometric design in pink, white, red, green & dark blue on a sky blue ground, interspersed w/brass tack decoration, metal buckle, long end folds over to show geometric tack design on the back end, overall 66" l. (missing tack, some bead loss) **990**

Bowl, Papago, woven martynia & willow, wide round shallow form, decorated w/four Gans-type figures around the sides separated by pairs of small diamond devices, 10 1/4" d., 3 1/4" h. (some rim stitches missing) **523**

Cap, Sioux, child's, grey cloth w/beaded geometric designs in pink, dark blue & white heart red on a yellow ground, orange print calico lining, ca. 1910-20, 8" l. **715**

Carrying container, Ojibwa, birch bark-covered, rectangular base w/slight tapering bark sides & narrow bentwood rim & flat cover, splint laced seams dyed red & black, leather carrying thong, 8 1/2 x 9 3/4", 7 1/2" h. (minor wear) **413**

Doll, Navajo, cloth body w/inked facial features & black hair wig, red velvet dress w/petticoats & beaded boots, stamped tin, tack & yellow & blue beaded jewelry, rubber hands, ca. 1920, 13" h. **495**

Gauntlets, Woodlands, moose hide w/beaded floral designs in faceted beads of red, blue, gold & translucent pink, green, white & clear, worn seal skin edging & red cloth lining, 16 1/2" l., pr. **550**

Hair ornament, Sioux, leather w/beading & quillwork, the quillwork in red, green & orange, opaque pale green beaded trim,

leather attachments w/worn red, orange & purple quill wrapping, tin cone dangles & remnants of white & purple feathers, partial horsehair attachment at back, ca. 1910, 17 1/2" l. **468**

Jar, California Mission, basketry, a netted design overall in dyed juncus w/a mottled juncus body over grass, 3 3/4" d., 3 1/4" h. **248**

Zuni Polychrome Jar

Jar, Zuni, pottery, bulbous form w/flat rim, mottled tan w/reddish brown & black geometric & animal designs, painted lizards on shoulder, heads form handles, 6 1/2" d., 5 1/2" h. (ILLUS.) **1,600**

Arapaho Beaded Sheath

Knife sheath, Arapaho, buffalo hide w/design of red, white & brown beads across top, a line of beads down the front w/border of blue & red beads along the top & sides, ca. 1850, 10" l.(ILLUS.) **350**

Knife sheath, Arapaho Sioux, beaded leather, the beading in a geometric design in green, blue & white heart red beads on a white ground, traces of hide on interior, inked note on back from collection, Prussian knife included, 10 1/2" l. **605**

Leggings, Crow, beaded leather, cuffs w/bands of white, dark blue & yellow & translucent red & green beads on a pale blue ground, attached to later red wool trade cloth, round brass buttons, ca. 1920, 17 1/2" l. (minor stains, old stitched repair) **880**

Leggings, Flathead, red wool trade cloth w/black stripes, sky blue, dark blue, pink, green & translucent red beaded stripes, twisted leather fringe w/yellow stain, ca. 1880-90, 29" l. (very minor wear & bead loss) **990**

Mirror case, Apache, beaded deerskin, polychrome beading w/designs of morning stars, turtle & dragonflies, white, green, faceted silver, pale blue & assorted translucent beads, beaded edging & long fringe, ca. 1890-1910, 6 1/4 x 10" (old leather patches & some bead loss) **880**

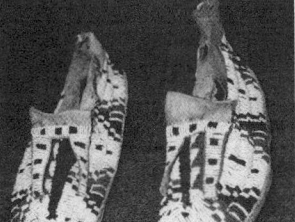

Sioux Beaded Moccasins

Moccasins, Sioux, fully beaded w/red, green & blue design on white beaded background, ca. 1840 (ILLUS.) **560**

Necklace, Navajo, silver & turquoise, a string of heavy silver beads suspending a small crescent-shaped pendant w/ropetwist detail & silver beads, each end & the center w/a single turquoise stone, 23" l. **193**

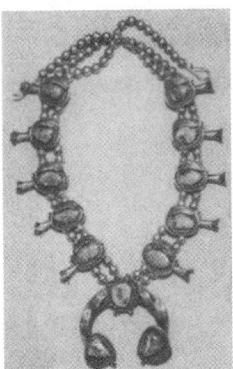

Squash Blossom Necklace

Necklace, Navajo, squash blossom-type, thirteen blossoms set w/light blue turquoise on double strands of silver beads, rope twist & applied leaf details, 26 1/2" l. (ILLUS.)... **220**

Olla, California Mission, basketry, a globular shape w/a short neck decorated in natural & dyed juncus w/grass, boldly woven w/"April 1, 1907" framed by large floral designs, chickens & birds separated by vertical leafy bands, probably Dieguno, stitches missing at rim & spots on body, juncus pale & indistinct, 16" d., 17" h. (ILLUS. top next column) **8,250**

Pipe-tomahawk head, possibly Great Lakes region, brass w/good dark patina, engraved bear on one side & Indian head on the other, 7" l. **715**

Rare Boldly Dated Basketry Olla

Pot, Santa Clara Pueblo, pottery, ovoid form w/closed rim, highly polished blackware glaze w/a carved Avanyu (water serpent) design on a recessed matte ground, signed "Donna Tafoya, Santa Clara Pueblo," 20th c., 6" d., 6" h. **330**

Pouch, Apache, beaded leather, beaded designs on both sides w/circles, triangles & stepped diamonds, shades of blue, yellow, green, white & translucent red, leather string tie, 7 1/2" l. **990**

Pouch, Apache, beaded leather, both sides w/beadwork including borders, triangles & diamonds in solid & translucent shades of red, white, pink, blue, green & yellow, leather fringe & tie string, pre-1920, 8 3/4" l. plus fringe **715**

Rug, Navaho, Crystal area, rectangular, centered w/two stepped diamonds in brownish black & natural carded white on a grey ground, each diamond w/tan geometric elements outlined in orange w/feathers, sides have feathers throughout w/Nahokas, white & brownish black border, 1920s, 38 x 61"................................. **880**

Rug, Navajo, transitional type w/simple stripe & corner fringe, central red area w/small orange & yellow diagonal figured stripes, grey strip & red ends, early 20th c., 36 x 52" (loss at one end, repair, some damage)................................. **523**

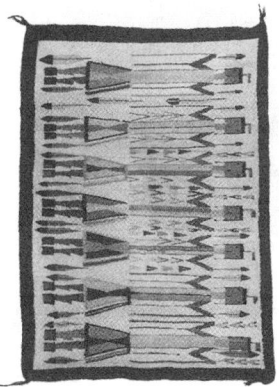

Navajo Yei Rug

Rug, Navajo, early design w/some natural colored dye on natural background, seven Yei figures w/aniline red border, hand-carded & spun wool, minor edge damage, 2' 4" x 3' 2" (ILLUS.) 880

Rug, Navajo, Ganado area, red, white & black stylized geometric design on a carded grey wool ground w/black & white border, 38 x 53" 440

Rug, Navajo, Crystal area, looped terrace & diamond design in brown, gold & red on a natural white & carded tan ground, 49 x 86" (some stains, bleeding to red & gold) 660

Navaho Saddle Blanket

Saddle blanket, Navaho, large serrated "X" design of adjoining strips of bright Germantown yarn in maroon, gold, faded purple, red, faded evergreen & white, whipped Red Germantown selvage & remnant fringe in red, green, gold & white, late 19th c. (approx. 1885), selvage yarn break at one end, damage to selvage on one edge & slight color bleeding, 2' 1" x 2' 9" (ILLUS.) 2,420

Saddle blanket, Navajo, double-type, carded tan central field, small nahokas figures in corners & border w/red band, orange, natural & dark brown stepped fret border, ca. 1910, 31 x 55" (minor color bleeding & stains) 495

Strike a light pouch, Cheyenne, beaded leather, tanned leather w/beaded geometric designs on both sides in dark blue, yellow, white heart red & translucent pale blue, attached leather fringe w/tin cone dangles, ca. 1880, 5 1/4" l. plus fringe (minor bead loss) 1,265

Tray, Hopi Second Mesa, coiled basketry, geometric design elements of rain clouds in browns & tans, closed gate rim finish, fine sheen, 18 3/4" d. 880

Tray, Pima, basketry, woven dark martynia (devil's claw) & willow, wide round shallow form, a design of interlocking whirling fret over the flat base, braided rim finish, 8" d., 2" h. 330

Woven panel, Navaho, rectangular panel w/three female Yei figures alternating w/tall corn stalks surrounded by the Rainbow God on three sides, mainly in red, green & yellow accents on grey & tan carded figures on a natural white ground, 34 x 56" 1,210

IVORY

Angel & Child Ivory Figure Group

Beaker, footed cylindrical body w/a slightly flared rim, the sides carved in high-relief w/a continuous intricate classical battle scene, Europe, 19th c., 3 7/8" h. **$1,380**

Box, cov., oval, the slightly domed hinged cover carved in relief w/a large cluster of flowers, the sides carved w/a continuous band of leafy vining blossoms, France, late 19th c., 3 3/4" l., 2" h. 690

Figure group, a courting couple, a young cavalier & a lady in 17th c. costume, he standing beside & slightly behind her poised to give a kiss, on a tall turned ivory socle pedestal, Europe, late 19th c., 9" h. . **2,300**

Figure group, an angel flying & holding a young child, intricately pierced-carved above a large knob on a turned disk & tall waisted pedestal base, Europe, late 19th c., restorations, 9" h. (ILLUS.) **2,760**

Tall Carved Ivory Chinese Beauty

Figure of a nude bather, the standing young female w/her head turned to one side & one arm arched above her head, the other arm across her waist holding a draped towel in front, on an ebony paneled socle, France, second half 19th c., 10 3/4" h. **2,857**

Figure of a nude holding a rose, the standing young woman looking up at a rose blossom she holds aloft in one hand, the other arm to her side, w/a band of beads & swagged drapery around her waist, leafy plants at her feet, on a tall tapering columnar ivory base w/scrolls entitled "Erste Rose," France, late 19th c., signed illegibly on the base, 16 3/4" h. (cracking) **3,738**

Figure of a Viking, standing warrior w/helmet, body armor & a draped cloak leaning against a shield, on a tall tapering columnar ivory base, France, late 19th c., 8 3/4" h. (shrinkage cracks) **1,725**

Figure of Chinese beauty, tall intricately carved figure of a beautiful Chinese woman wearing a tall feathery headdress & holding a tall intricate bouquet of flowers, on a wooden stand, face & hair highlighted in black, late 19th - early 20th c. (ILLUS. bottom previous page) **4,000**

Ivory Chinese Empress Figure

Figures of Emperor & Empress, intricately carved details overall, China, late 19th - early 20th c., 14" h., pr. (ILLUS. of Empress) **3,520**

Carved Ivory Page Turner

Page turner, long flattened blade, the handle end carved w/a delicate band of grapevine below a bust of Dionysus set among acanthus leaves, Europe, second half 19th c., 14 1/4" l. (ILLUS. of handle) . **1,265**

Parasol handle, the top of the tapering handle w/a carved continuous floral garland against a carved wood-grained ground, Europe, late 19th c., overall 23 1/4" l **259**

Plaque, oval, relief-carved profile bust of a fashionable 17th c. gentleman w/long curly wig, carved on the back "I. Cavalier" & dated 1685, in a pierced leafy scrolled oval frame, Europe, plaque 3 1/4 x 3 7/8" (shrinkage cracks) **978**

Tankard, cov., tall slightly tapering form w/stepped cover, the cover w/a figural finial of a seated bacchante, the body carved in high-relief w/a continuous mythological scene above a band of grotesque masks, the double-scroll handle w/a carved herm, Europe, 19th c., 4 3/4" h. **2,070**

French Figure of a Lady & Parasol

Figure of lady w/parasol, titled "Merveilleuse," a fantastically costumed lady w/puffed & ruched gown w/laced bodice & a tall bonnet, holding a lace-edged parasol, also holding a reticule, on a turned ivory socle, France, late 19th c., 7 3/4" h. (ILLUS.) **1,380**

Figure of Marie de Bourgogne, standing lady in medieval costume wearing a pointed hat & long fur-trimmed robes, holding a hawk perched on one hand, on a low wooden socle, France, late 19th c., 12" h. **2,645**

Figure of St. Sebastian, stylized figure of a young man tied to a tree trunk wearing only a loincloth, pierced w/several arrow holes, Europe, late 18th - early 19th c., 8 3/4" h. **1,150**

Tusk, commemorative, slightly curved section carved in bold relief w/the British royal arms on one side & a cartouche portrait of King George I on the other, England, 18th c., 6 3/4" h. (losses, restoration) **748**

JAPANESE WOODBLOCK PRINTS

Chikanobu, oban tate-e, "Bijin and Her Dog," dated Meiji 31 (1897), fine impression, condition & color **$500-700**

"Bijin and Keo"

Chikanobu, oban tate-e triptych, "Bijin and Keo," dated Meiji 29 (1896), very fine impression, color & condition (ILLUS.) **1,800-2,300**

Hasui Kawase, oban tate-e, "Ueno Park, Tokyo," dated Showa 23 (1948), published by Watanabe, fine impression, color & condition **900-1,200**

"Zojo-ji Temple, Shiba"

Hasui Kawase, oban tate-e, "Zojo-ji Temple, Shiba," dated Taisho 14 (1925), printed 1931, published by Watanabe, fine impression, color & condition (ILLUS.) **5,500-7,500**

Hiroaki Takahashi (Takahashi Shotei), oban yoko-e, "Mt. Fuji in the Moonlight," published by Fusui Gabo (ca. 1930s, early edition, fine impression, color & condition, 10 1/4 x 15 1/2" **1,000-1,500**

Hiroaki Takahashi (Takahashi Shotei), tanzanku, "Daikon Vender," ca. 1920, fine color, impression & condition (ILLUS. top next column) **775-975**

"Daikon Vender"

Hiroshige, oban tate-e, "Hirikiri no Hanashobu," (Iris Flowers at Horikiri), from the series Edo Meisho Hyakkei, (One Hundred Views of Famous Places in Edo), signed "Hiroshige ga," published by Uyoa Eikichi, fine impression, very good color, some stains & soiling, 10 x 15" **3,000-4,000**

"Kameido Tenjin Shrine"

Hiroshige, oban tate-e, "Kameido Tenjin Shrine," Snake 5 (1857), from the series Meisho Edo Hyakkei, (One Hundred Views of Famous Places in Edo), signed "Hiroshige ga," published by Uoya Eikichi, fine impression, very good color, binding hole in right margin (ILLUS.).............. **6,000-9,000**

"Volcano"

Hiroshige II, oban tate-e, "Volcano," from the series Shokoku Meisho Hyakkei (One Hundred Famous Views of the Province), publisher Uoei (Uoya Eikichi), fine impression, very good color & condition (ILLUS.) **300-4,500**

Hiroshige II (Shigenobu), oban yoko-e, 1855 (Year of the Hare) from the series Chushingura, very good impression, color & condition.................................... **900-1,200**

"Les Jades, Chinoise"

Jacoulet, Paul, dai oban tate-e, "Les Jades, Chinoise," (Jade Lady, Chinese), dated 1940, boat seal, from an edition of 250, fine condition, color & impression (ILLUS.)... **2,500-4,500**

"The Great Lantern at the Asakusa Kannodo"

Kasamatsu Shiro, oban tate-e, "The Great Lantern at the Asakusa Kannodo," published by Watanabe, dated Showa 9 (1934), early edition, excellent impression, condition & color (ILLUS.) **2,000-3,000**

Kasamatsu Shiro, oban tate-e, "The Suwa Shrine at Nippori at Sunset," published by Watanabe, 6mm seal, fine impression, color & condition **800-1,200**

Katshira Tokushi, oban yoko-e, dated Showa 14 (1939), signed & sealed w/images in lower left, signed & sealed in left margin, self carved, self printed, fine condition, impression & color.................. **3,500-5,500**

"Night Festival"

Kiyochika, oban yoko-e, "Night Festival," signed "Kiyochika hitsu," published by Fukuda Kumanjiro, dated Meiji 10 (1877), very good impression, color & condition (ILLUS.) **3,500-4,500**

Kiyokata, Kaburagi, an album of 12 prints, dated Meiji 34 (1901), fine condition, impressions & color (album), 7 x 9 1/2" **4,000-6,500**

Woodblock Illustration for Romantic Novel

Kiyokata Kaburagi, Eisen Tomioka, Kiuochika Kobayashi, Hanko Kajita, Kason Suzuki, Keishu Takeuchi, Chikanobu Yoshu, Toshimine Tsutsui, Toshikata Mizuno, oban yoke-e, (Keishu Takeuchi), 24 woodblock illustrations for romantic novels, late Meiji period ca. 1900, fine impressions, very good color & condition, gauffrage, 8 1/2 x 11 1/2" (ILLUS.).................... **2,500-4,500**

Koitsu Tsuchiya, oban tate-e, "Bridge in Rain," dated Showa 8 (1933), published by Doi, early edition, fine impression, color & condition............................... **1,200-1,800**

"Mt. Fuji at Sunset"

Koitsu Tsuchiya, oban yoko-e, "Mt. Fuji at Sunset," dated Showa 13 (1938), early edition, fine impression, color & condition, 10 1/2 x 15 1/2" (ILLUS.) **1,500-2,200**

"Duck Underwater"

Koson Ohara, shishiban, "Duck Underwater," ca. 1920s, original folio w/states on the back "Imported Japanese Prints Made By Hand From Cherrywood Blocks On Mulberry Paper," published by Shima Art Company Inc., New York & Tokyo, Print #21, fine condition, color & impression (ILLUS.) **475-675**

Kotondo Torii, dai oban, "Bijin Adjusting Hairpin," from a limited edition, fine impression, color & condition.......... **12,000-18,000**

Kotozuka Eiichi, oban tate-e, "The Children on Festival," ca. 1955, early edition, published by Uchida, fine impression, color & condition, 11 1/2 x 17 1/2" **375-500**

From Tale of Genji

Kunichika, oban tate-e, from Tale of Genji chapter 28 Nowaki, ca. 1880, fine impression, color & condition, 9 1/2 x 14 3/4" (ILLUS.)............................ **675-975**

Kunichika, Shunga (erotica), signed & sealed within image, fine impression, condition & color, 7 x 10" **700-900**

"Gototei Kunisada"

Kunisada, surimono, three actors, one w/a long pipe, one w/a short pipe, two engaged in playing go, signed "Gototei Kunisada," c. 1829-1842, fine impression, very good color, slightly rubbed (ILLUS.) **2,500-3,500**

Kunisada II, oban tate-e, Genji, fine impression, very good color, trimmed left & right margins **300-500**

From the Series Hyakunin Isshu Kaisho

Kunisada (Toyokuni III), oban tate-e, a beauty holding a lantern, w/playing cards on the left, from the series Hyakunin Isshu Kaisho, (a selection of pictures matched to one hundred poems, one by each poet), signed "Kunisada aratame nidaimi Toyokuni ga," w/Toshidama seal, Kiwame seal, published by Sanoya Kihei (this print dates 1844 & has both names - Kunisada & Toyokuni III), very good impression, condition & color (ILLUS.).................... **900-1,500**

"Taibeiki Yeiyu Den"

Kuniyoshi, oban tate-e, "Taibeiki Yeiyu Den," (Heroic Stories of the Taibeki, the Taikeiki is "Chronicle of Great Peace"), ca. 1848-49, Shimura Masazo Katsutoyo seated & stripped to his loin-cloth, a kimono over one shoulder, his swords, a bucket of water & paper towels behind, Yamamota-ya Heikichi publisher, censor Mura-Murata, fine impression, condition & color (ILLUS.) **1,000-1,800**

Lum, Bertha, "Baby," signed in pencil & sealed, fine impression, condition & color **1,500-1,800**

"Little Sisters"

Lum, Bertha, "Little Sisters," signed & sealed, 1912, fine impression, color & condition, 7 x 12" (ILLUS.) **1,500-2,500**

Maekawa Senpan, dai oban, woman w/red kerchief, signed & sealed, ca. 1950, very good impression, color & condition . **3,500-5,500**

"Camilla"

Ohno Bakufu, oban tate-e, "Camilla," printed by Kyoto Hanga-In, 1950, fine color, impression & condition (ILLUS.) **375-550**

"Night View of Mt. Fuji"

Okada Koichi, oban tate-e, "Night View of Mt. Fuji," from the series 12 Views of Japan, published by Unsodo, dated Showa 21 (1956), signed in pencil "Koichi Okada" in lower right margin, signed & sealed in lower left within image, fine impression, color & condition, paper slightly toned, 10 3/4 x 16" (ILLUS.) **1,800-2,500**

Okuyama Gilhachiro, oban tate-e, ca. 1950, signed & sealed lower right within the image, published by Kyoto Hanga In, fine impression, color & condition, 11 1/4 x 16 1/4" **700-950**

Saito Kiyoshi, oban tate-e, "Boy with Butterflies," ca. 1960, very good condition, color & impression, 11 1/2 x 17" **450-600**

Saito Kiyoshi, oban tate-e, "Girl with Butterflies," ca. 1960, very good condition, color & impression, 11 1/2 x 17"..... **450-600**

"Maiko"

Saito Kiyoshi, oban tate-e, "Maiko," ca. 1960, signed & sealed Saito, fine impression, color & condition, 11 1/2 x 17" (ILLUS.)... **1,000-1,500**

Saito Kiyoshi, oban tate-e, "Maiko," ca. 1960, signed & sealed Saito, fine impression, color & condition, 11 1/2 x 17" **1,000-1,500**

Shinsui Ito, oban tate-e, woman applying lipstick, signed "Shinsui ga," dated Taisho 11 (1922), published by Watanabe, fine impression, color & condition.. **9,000-15,000**

"Beauty With Fan"

Shuho Yamakawa, oban tate-e, "Beauty With Fan," signed "Shuho," above leaf pattern seal, dated Showa 3 (1928), publisher Bijutsusha, fine impression, color & condition (ILLUS.) **1,200-1,800**

Sozan Ito, tanzaku, "Parrots," artist signed & sealed, published by Watanabe, ca. 1927, fine impression, color & condition (ILLUS. top next column).................. **775-975**

"Parrots"

Takagi Shiro, from an edition of 200, dated 1972, signed in pencil on bottom margin "S. Takagi," very good condition, 11 3/4 x 17 1/4" **300-475**

Takuriki Tomikichiro, shishiban, "Torii Gate," published by Uchida, from a set of 15 Views of Japan, ca. 1955, very good condition, color & impression **100-150**

Terauchi Manjiro, oban tate-e, "Sailboat," signed in white in lower left within image, published Kyoto Hanga-In, ca. 1950, fine condition, color & impression, 11 3/4 x 15 3/4" **700-950**

Tetauchi Manjiro, oban tate-e, "Riverscape," published by Kyoto Hanga-In, ca. 1950, fine impression, color & condition **700-950**

Toshikata Mizuno, kuchi-e, ca. 1903, fine impression & color, 9 x 12" (slightly soiled, crease) **300-475**

Wada Sanzo, oban yoko-e, "The Fortune Teller," ca. 1952, signed & sealed lower right within image, published by Kyoto Hanga-In, fine condition, color & impression, 11 1/2 x 16"...................................... **375-575**

"Sarusawa Pond (in Nara)"

Yoshida Hiroshi, oban tate-e, "Sarusawa Pond (in Nara)," dated Showa 8 (1933), signed & sealed, Jizuri seal, very good impression, color & condition (ILLUS.).. **1,200-1,800**

"Yomei Gate"

Yoshida Hiroshi, oban tate-e, "Yomei Gate," dated Showa 12 (1937), Jizuri seal, fine condition, color & impression (ILLUS.)... **1,200-1,800**

Yoshida Hiroshi, oban yoko-e, "Usendake," dated Showa 2 (1927), Jizuri seal, fine condition, color & impression **1,500-1,800**

"Moon at Ogurusu: The Ambush of Akechi Mitsuhide by Moonlight"

Yoshitoshi, oban tate-e, "Moon at Ogurusu: The Ambush of Akechi Mitsuhide by Moonlight," from the series The 100 Aspects of the Moon, signed "Yoshitoshi," Taiso seal, published by Akiyama, carver Enkatsu, dated Meiji 19 (1886), fine impression, color & condition (ILLUS.).. **900-1,200**

Yoshitoshi, oban tate-e, "The Moon of Sumiyoshi," from the series The 100 Aspects of the Moon, dated Meiji 20 (1887), 6th month 23rd day (June 23), signed "Yoshitoshi," Taiso seal, published by Akiyama Buemon, carver Yamamoto, fine impression, color & condition **800-1,200**

"Bejin With Telephone"

Yukawa Shodo, oban, "Bijin With Telephone," from the series One Hundred Beauties, Past and Present, signed & sealed "Shodo," dated 1903, mica, hand-painted embellishment, fine impression, condition & color (ILLUS.)................ **1,500-2,000**

JEWELRY

Also see: Antique Trader Jewelry Price Guide

Antique (1800-1920)

Fine Micromosaic Brooch/Pendant

Brooch/pendant, micromosaic, an oval form w/a black onyx ground inlaid w/the image of a walking peasant lady in a red & white dress & shawl, in a 14k gold ropetwist border mount, ca. 1850 (ILLUS.) **$1,064**

Pendant/brooch, platinum, diamond & sapphire, the modified rectangular shaped plaque of openwork design, set w/two old European-cut diamonds accented w/two curving bands set w/20 French-cut sapphires, cornered by four single-cut diamonds, mounted in platinum, completed by a delicate white gold chain, ca. 1920, 17 1/4" l. **1,610**

Pin, gold, enamel & diamond, designed as a crescent moon decorated w/light blue enamel flowers w/white enameled leaves, framing a flowerhead w/applied purple & greenish yellow enamel petals, set w/one old mine-cut diamond, mounted in gold, ca. 1890. .... **373**

Ring, gold, diamond & green hardstone, crossover design, set w/one old European-cut diamond & one round green hardstone, mounted in gold, ca. 1900 .... **805**

Ring, gold, diamond & split pearl, alternately set w/three split pearls & two old mine-cut diamonds within an incised openwork mounting, ca. 1900 .... **460**

Ring, gold, opal & diamond, the lozenge-shaped mounting centering one oval opal, set throughout w/20 rose-cut diamonds, engraving along the inside of the shank, mounted in gold, ca. 1900. .... **431**

Modern (1920-1960s)

Lily of the Valley Brooch

Bracelet, silver & sodalite, an oval cabochon stone set in silver, marked "Mexico Sancho," mid-20th c., 8" l. **115**

Bracelet, sterling silver, cuff-type, a spiral form w/rows of lapped leaves highlighted w/beaded decoration, impressed mark "HL 925 Sterling Mexico - Taxco" w/an eagle & 3, 2 1/4" d. **173**

Bracelet, sterling silver & shell, cuff-style, two ridged bands of silver surrounding a leaf-shaped insert of dark brown shell, decorated w/nine silver rivets, impressed "WS" script hallmark & 925, Spratling, Mexico, design created in 1958, 2 1/2" l. **1,840**

Brooch, jade, diamond & quartz, lily of the valley design w/carved jade leaf, flowers of carved quartz suspending prong-set round diamonds, 14k gold mount, marked "Made in Austria" (ILLUS.). **1,495**

Brooch, sterling silver, model of a deer decorated w/an ivy vine, signed "Georg Jensen, No. 311" (ILLUS. top next column) **489**

Sterling Silver Deer Brooch

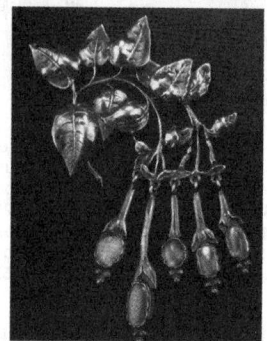

Silver & Moonstone Fuchsia Brooch

Brooch, sterling silver & moonstone, the fuchsia flower designed w/five flexibly set cabochon moonstone drops, signed "Sterling by Cini" (ILLUS.). **748**

JUKE BOXES

Rock-Ola Model 1428 Juke Box

AMI Continental I, 1960, professionally reconditioned **$2,200**

AMI Model C, 1949, professionally reconditioned **2,000**

AMI Model E120, 1953, professionally reconditioned **1,800**

AMI Model G 120, 1955, professionally reconditioned **1,600**
Evans, 1952, professionally reconditioned **750**
Gabel, 1935, professionally reconditioned **2,500**
Gabel Charme, 1936, professionally reconditioned **2,500**
Rock-Ola (Fireball) Model 1436, 1952, professionally reconditioned **2,000**
Rock-Ola Model 1428, restored (ILLUS.) **6,000**
Rock-Ola Model 1454, 1956, professionally reconditioned **2,600**
Rock-Ola Regular 1936, professionally reconditioned **1,000**
Seeburg Model 100C, 1952, professionally reconditioned **3,200**
Seeburg Model 100R, 1954, professionally reconditioned **3,200**
Seeburg Model 222, 1959, professionally reconditioned **3,200**
Seeburg Model AY-100, 1961, professionally reconditioned **1,000**
Seeburg Model "B," 1950, professionally reconditioned **2,200**
Seeburg Model KD 200, 1957, professionally reconditioned **4,500**
Seeburg Model KD200, 1956, professionally reconditioned **5,500**
Seeburg Model V-200, 1955, professionally reconditioned **2,800**
Wurlitzer, 1941, professionally reconditioned... **6,500**

KEWPIE COLLECTIBLES

Rose O'Neill's Kewpies were so popular in their heyday that numerous objects depicting them were produced and are now collectible. The following represents a sampling.

In recent years a number of older Kewpie dolls and figurines have been reissued. The German Doll Company has a number of figurines currently available. Jesco Dolls, R. John Wright Dolls and Effanbee also have been producing modern Kewpie dolls.

Dish, bisque, figural, model of a rectangular 'postcard' w/gently curved up sides, a figure of a seated Kewpie at one end holding a large fountain pen & writing "With Kewpish Love from Rose O'Neill," also shows a copy of a canceled stamp in one corner, card 2 3/4 x 4 1/2", 2 3/4" h. (base possibly reattached).......................... **$476**

Original Kewpie Doll in Box

Doll, bisque, all-bisque w/jointed arms, heart sticker on chest, round sticker on back, impressed "O'Neill," Germany, 1913, in original box, 7" h. (ILLUS.) **450-500**
Doll, bisque head w/flirty glass eyes on a toddler composition body, J.D. Kestner, Germany, marked "Ges.gesch., O'Neill J.D.K.," 10-14" each **3,500-6,500**

Kewpie Doll

Doll, cloth "Cuddle Kewpie," pink sateen cloth head w/unjointed neck, cloth mask face, large side-glancing eyes, dash brows, tiny painted upper lashes, lightly molded & painted button nose, closed smiling mouth, pink cheeks, molded tufts on top & sides of head, pink sateen unjointed body w/mitten hands, knee & ankle joints indicated w/modeling, original pink ribbon around neck, coloring of mask face shows slight aging, condition & color of sateen are near mint w/only slightest hint of aging, 13" h. (ILLUS.) **320**
Doll, molded hard plastic standing Kewpie, fully jointed, painted features, embossed "KEWPIE © by Rose O'Neill" on back, 1950s, 13" h. **400-500**
Doll, molded hard plastic standing Kewpie w/jointed arms, painted features, embossed "KEWPIE © by Rose O'Neill" on back, 1950s, 8" h. **100-150**
Doll, quality vinyl, finely dressed & boxed, Jesco Dolls, 1983-mid-1990s, 8-24", each.. **35-75**

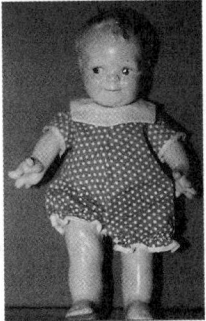
Original "Scootles" Doll

Doll, "Scootles," composition, jointed arms & hips, original clothes, Cameo Doll Co., 1925, 15" h. (ILLUS.) **700**

Doll, vinyl, dressed standing Kewpie, Cameo Dolls, 1960s-70s, allow extra for all-original in boxes or wrap, 12-13", each ... **75-110**

Doll, vinyl, dressed standing Kewpie, Cameo Dolls, 1960s-70s, allow extra for all-original in boxes or wrap, 16", each **125-165**

Figure group, bisque, a Kewpie standing w/valise & black umbrella, 3 3/8" h. **288**

Figure group, bisque, action Kewpie, Kewpie sitting w/cat on foot, 3 1/2" h. **550-650**

Figurine, bisque, action Kewpie, dressed as a bellhop, green or red uniform, 4" h. **1,000-1,700**

Figurine, bisque, action Kewpie, dressed as sitting soldier, 3 1/2" h. **1,000-1,500**

Figurine, bisque, action Kewpie, dressed as standing soldier, 5-6" h. **900-1,250**

Action Kewpie with Pen

Figurine, bisque, action Kewpie, seated holding a fountain pen, Germany, 1913, 3" h. (ILLUS.) **450-475**

Figurine, bisque, action Kewpie, shown riding a rabbit, goat, hobby horse or other animal, 4 1/2" h., each **2,500-5,300**

Kewpie Figurine with Guitar

Figurine, bisque, action Kewpie, standing playing guitar, sticker on side, Germany, 1913, 3 1/2" h. (ILLUS.) **400-450**

Figurine, bisque, action Kewpie, "Traveler" standing w/closed umbrella & suitcase, 3 1/2" h. **325-500**

Figurine, bisque, action Kewpie, tumbling "Blunderboo" Kewpie, 3" h. **550-625**

Newer Kewpie from Original Mold

Figurine, bisque, Kewpie dressed as bellhop, marked on bottom of foot "Made in Germany," produced from original molds, German Doll Co., 1990s, 4" h. (ILLUS.) **154**

Figurine, bisque, seated Kewpie w/legs pulled up to body & head resting on knees, incised mark on the base, 5" h. **246**

Figurine, bisque, standing Kewpie w/jointed arms, painted features, "O'Neill" mark under foot, heart sticker on chest or back, Germany, 1913-16, 2 1/2" h. **100-125**

Figurine, bisque, standing Kewpie w/jointed arms, painted features, "O'Neill" mark under foot, heart sticker on chest or back, Germany, 1913-16, 4" h. **145-155**

Figurine, bisque, standing Kewpie w/jointed arms, painted features, "O'Neill" mark under foot, heart sticker on chest or back, Germany, 1913-16, 5" h. **175-185**

Figurine, bisque, standing Kewpie w/jointed arms, painted features, "O'Neill" mark under foot, heart sticker on chest or back, Germany, 1913-16, 6" h. **225-240**

Figurine, bisque, standing Kewpie w/jointed arms, painted features, "O'Neill" mark under foot, heart sticker on chest or back, Germany, 1913-16, 7" h. **300-350**

Figurine, bisque, standing Kewpie w/jointed arms, painted features, "O'Neill" mark under foot, heart sticker on chest or back, Germany, 1913-16, 8" h. **400-500**

Figurine, bisque, standing Kewpie w/jointed arms, painted features, "O'Neill" mark under foot, heart sticker on chest or back, Germany, 1913-16, 9" h. **550-700**

Figurine, bisque, standing Kewpie w/jointed arms, painted features, "O'Neill" mark under foot, heart sticker on chest or back, Germany, 1913-16, 10" h. **750-850**

Figurine, bisque, standing Kewpie w/jointed arms, painted features, "O'Neill" mark

under foot, heart sticker on chest or back,
Germany, 1913-16, 11" h................. **1,000-1,500**
Figurine, celluloid, standing frozen pose
w/jointed arms, by Karl Standfuss,
Germany, 2 1/2" h. **25-50**
Figurine, celluloid, standing frozen pose
w/jointed arms, by Karl Standfuss,
Germany, 5" h.. **75-100**
Figurine, celluloid, standing frozen pose
w/jointed arms, by Karl Standfuss,
Germany, 8" h.................................... **150-225.0**
Figurine, celluloid, standing frozen pose
w/jointed arms, by Karl Standfuss,
Germany, 12" h... **250-350**
Figurine, celluloid, standing frozen pose
w/jointed arms, by Karl Standfuss,
Germany, 22" h... **450-600**

Newer Kewpie Figurine

Figurine, Kewpie in car, stamped "c. Jesco
1993" on bottom, Enesco, 3" l. (ILLUS.).......... **20**

KITCHENWARES

Cast-iron Items

*During the 19th century, several foundries in the
United States produced cast-iron kitchenware, prized for
its durability and, in the case of cookware, even heat dis-
tribution when used on wood stoves. Some of today's
most popular collectible items were produced by the
Griswold Mfg. Co. of Erie, Pa. and the Wagner Co. of
Sidney, Ohio, during the mid-19th and early 20th centuries. Most cast-iron cookware from that period is
marked with its maker's name and a style number.*

Apple parer, Goodell, 1898 .... **$60-70**
Apple peeler, Reading Hardware Co.................. **90**

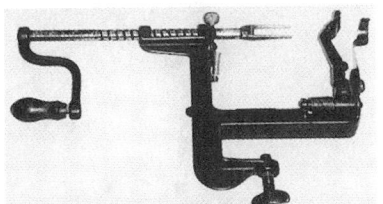

Apple Peeler

Apple peeler, unmarked (ILLUS.).................. **30-35**
Ashtray, Griswold #770, square, has
matchbook holder on end, 3 3/8 x 6 1/2"
(ILLUS. top next column) **15**
Ashtray, Wagner #1050E, round, 6 1/4" d. **8-10**

Ashtray

Bean pot, Blue Valley Co., Kansas City,
Mo.. **100**
Bread pan, Griswold #2, two loaf...................... **600**
Bread stick pan, Griswold #6, pattern #23........ **85**
Brownie pan, Griswold #9, pattern #947,
7 x 10 3/8 x 1" deep...................................... **145**
Bundt pan, Griswold #965 .... **950-1000**
Cake mold, Griswold #866, lamb................. **90-100**
Cake mold, Griswold, rabbit **750**
Can opener, Blue Streak, clamp-on.................... **85**
Can opener, World's Best, Dillsburg, Pa............. **40**
Cherry seeder, Enterprise, 1903................... **70-75**
Cherry seeder, "Family Cherrystoner"................. **40**
Corn bread pan, Griswold, Model F, pat-
tern #955, 7 1/2 x 14" **75**

"Crispy Corn Stick" Pan

Corn stick pan, "Crispy Corn Stick," Gris-
wold #273, 5 3/4 x 12 1/2" (ILLUS.) **25-35**
Corn stick pan, Griswold #262,
8 1/2 x 4 1/2 x 3/4" **85**
Corn stick pan, Griswold #280, 7 alternat-
ing ears **500**
Corn stick pan, Wagner, "Junior Krusty
Korn Kobs," #1319, July 6, 1920 .... **18-20**
Corn stick pan, Wagner, "Krusty Korn
Kobs," #1318, July 6, 1920, 15"................. **25-28**

Dutch Oven

Dutch oven, Griswold #8, "Tite-Top," 6 quart capacity, w/lid, handle, trivet (ILLUS.)... **50-75**
Dutch oven, Wagner, #1268E............................... **50**
Food press, Sensible, 2 quart............................. **135**

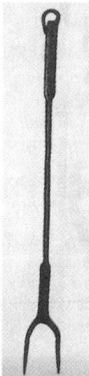

Fork

Fork, two prongs, wrought iron, 19" (ILLUS.)... **18-22**
Griddle, Griswold #7, rectangular, 7 x 16 1/2".. **40**
Griddle, Griswold #9, rectangular, 9 1/2 x 21"... **40-45**
Griddle, Wagner #9 (1109E)........................... **45-55**
Grill, Wagner #8, utility grill **60**
Ice shredder, Griswold, ca. 1900...................... **75**
Iron, "Geneva Fluting Iron," two pieces, bottom 2 1/2 x 5" **45-50**
Iron, Ober #6, 5 3/4" l................................... **25**
Kettle, Griswold #8, flat bottom, 7 quart........ **40-50**

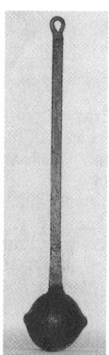

Ladle

Ladle, two pouring "lips," 22" (ILLUS.) **20**
Lemon squeezer, hinged, two handles, 7 1/2" **40**

Meat Tenderizer

Meat tenderizer, single edge & square grid for tenderizing, 7 1/2" (ILLUS.) **10**
Mold, Turk's Head, Griswold #140.................... **200**

Mortar & Pestle

Mortar & pestle, unmarked, 19th c., 8" h. mortar (ILLUS.).. **35-40**
Muffin pan, Griswold #10...................................... **20**
Muffin pan, Griswold #17...................................... **75**

Nutcracker

Nutcracker, eagle head, four-legged base (ILLUS.) **75-85**
Patty mold, Griswold #72 .... **50**
Popover pan, Griswold #10, 7 5/8 x 11" **35-40**
Roaster, Griswold #5, oval.................................. **120**
Roaster, Wagner #3, oval **185**
Roll pan, Griswold #11 .... **45**
Skillet, Eagle Stove Works #12.......................... **300**

Griswold Skillet

Skillet, Griswold #3, 6 1/2" (ILLUS.)............... **10-15**
Skillet, Griswold #8, "Odorless," pat. Oct. 17, 1898, 14" d. **35-40**
Skillet, Griswold, square egg skillet, 4 3/4" sq. **45**

Skillet, Wagner #3, 6" d............................ **10-12.50**
Skillet, Wagner #6, 9" d.................................. **20-25**
Stove lid lifter, "Jewel," ca. 1890......................... **15**
Sugar nippers, two handles, hinged, 9" **35**

"Thayer's Household Combination" Tool

"Thayer's Household Combination" tool,
#83, used for stove, pot or lid lifter, meat
tenderizer, trivet, pat. 1881 (ILLUS.)............... **35**
Waffle iron, Griswold #8, 1901, black iron
w/wooden handles **20**
Waffle iron, Wagner #9 .... **75**

Wick Trimmer

Wick trimmer, scissors w/design in handle,
attached "box" to hold trimmed wicks, 6"
(ILLUS.).. **25**

Coffee Mills

Coffee mills, commonly called grinders, are perfectly collectible for many people. They are appealing to the eye and are frequently coveted by interior decorators and today's coffee-consuming homeowners. Compact, intricate, unique, ornate, and rooted in early Americana, coffee mills are intriguing to everyone and are rich and colorful.

Coffee milling devices have been available for hundreds of years. The Greeks and Romans used rotating millstones for grinding coffee and grain. Turkish coffee mills with their familiar cylindrical brass shells appeared in the 15th century, and perhaps a century or two later came the earliest spice and coffee mills in Europe. Primitive mills were handmade in this country by blacksmiths and carpenters in the late 1700s and the first half of the 19th century. These were followed by a host of commercially-produced mills which included wood-backed side mills and numerous kinds of box mills, many with machined dovetails or fingerjoints. Characterized by the birth of upright cast-iron coffee mills, so beautiful with their magnificent colors and fly wheels, the period of coffee mill proliferation began around 1870. The next 50 years saw a staggering number of large and small manufacturers struggling to corner the popular home market for box and canister-type coffee mills. After that, the advent of electricity and other major advances in coffee grinding and packaging technology hastened the decline in popularity of small coffee mills.

Value-added features to look for when purchasing old coffee grinders include:

•*good working order and no missing, broken, or obviously replaced parts*
• *original paint*
• *attractive identifying markings, label or brass emblem*
• *uncommon mill, rarely seen, or appealing unique characteristics*
• *high quality restoration, if not original.*
—*Mike White*

Box Mills

Landers, Frary & Clark Coffee Mill

Box mill, decorative bronzed black iron box
w/open hopper, twist-off circular base
catches ground coffee, unique patented
grind adjuster, crank embossed
"Landers, Frary & Clark," 5" h. (ILLUS.) **550**

No. 1 Crown Coffee Mill

Box mill, tin w/recessed hopper & domed
tin cover, black w/red & gold decal reading "No. 1 Crown Coffee Mill, Made By
Landers, Frary & Clark," fair to good condition (ILLUS.).. **140**

Brighton No. 1180 Coffee Mill

Box mill, w/lift-up iron cap on top & iron handle on side, distinctive iron crank embossed "Logan & Strobridge," Brighton No. 1180, 1 lb. (ILLUS.) **175**

Waddel Coffee Mill

Box mill, w/sunken hopper, decorative iron cover & handle, crank embossed w/Waddel's 1888 patent date, side-opening door w/tin cup & written grinding instructions inside, made by Sun Mfg. Co. (ILLUS.)... **140**

Arcade Telephone Mill

Box mill, wood, dovetailed, w/bronzed & attractively embossed iron front, marked "Telephone Mill, Arcade Mfg. Co., Freeport Ill" & patent dates, crank w/wooden knob on front, tin catch cup underneath, about 13" h., excellent condition (ILLUS.) **800**

American No. 14 Coffee Mill

Box mill, wooden w/raised retinned hopper & bronzing, wingnut grind adjusters on top, paper label reads "American No. 14 Coffee Mill, Wrightsville, Hardware Co." (ILLUS.) **70**

Primitive Coffee Mills

European Coffee Mill

Box mill, hand-carved w/brass wire inlay & brass hopper, folding crank, 18th c., Europe, overall 6" h. (ILLUS.) **800**

French Coffee Mill

Box mill, post-mounted, wooden w/embedded metal blades on grinding drum, four wood screws to remove back, another screw on back for grind adjustment, 6" hopper, ca. mid-18th c., France (ILLUS.) **1,100**

Adams Coffee Mill

Box mill, raised iron hopper & large drawer, Adams, well-used condition (ILLUS.)............. **100**

Side Mills

E. Nagle Coffee Mill

Box mill, w/Moravian base & pewter hopper, handmade dovetails, signed by "E. Nagle, maker," 6 x 7", 5" h. (ILLUS.) **240**

Arcade Favorite No. 17 Coffee Mill

Side mill, all iron w/wood back, hopper & lid 4" w., Arcade Favorite No. 17 (ILLUS.) **110**

Iron Coffee Mill

Iron mill, post-mounted blacksmith's-type, 6" hopper, forged crank on right side, cylindrical drum grinding arrangement, late 1700s (ILLUS.)... **450**

Simmons Delmar S10 Coffee Mill

Side mill, bronzed cast iron, rounded hopper w/lid & knurled adjusting nut in front, wood back, Simmons Hardware Co.'s Delmar S10 (ILLUS.) **200**

Peckham Iron Coffee Mill

Iron mill, wall or post-mounted, 4" wide hopper & grind adjusting knob at bottom, Peckham (ILLUS.)... **350**

Dr. Edwards Coffee Mill

Side mill, cast iron w/wood back, hopper embossed w/Dr. Edwards' name & 1859 patent date (ILLUS.) **300**

Parker Eagle No. 70 Coffee Mill

Side mill, w/backing board, wingnut for grind adjustment in front, tin hopper & lid, brass emblem, Parker Eagle No. 70 (ILLUS.).. **120**

Upright Mills

Elgin National No. 10 Coffee Mill

Upright mill, cast iron, Elgin National No. 10 floor model w/double 28" wheels & nickel-plated copper hopper, made by C.H. Woodruff & Co., complete & very good original condition (ILLUS.) **1,800**

Enterprise No. 14 Coffee Mill

Upright mill, cast iron, Enterprise No. 14 large countertop mill w/nickel-plated brass hopper & tin catch can, double 25" wheels, original paint & flower decals, iron nameplate on front marked "No. 14" (ILLUS.)... **1,600**

Peugeot Freres 2A Coffee Mill

Upright mill, cast iron, single 13" wheel mill w/gears, raised iron hopper w/tin dome, wooden drawer inside iron box, original green paint w/gold trim, Peugeot Freres 2A (ILLUS.) **550**

No. 20 Crown Coffee Mill

Upright mill, cast iron, two 8 3/4" wheels, pivoting cover on cast iron hopper, original black paint & decals, Landers, Frary & Clark No. 20 Crown, very good condition (ILLUS.).. **1,000**

1898 Enterprise Coffee Mill

Upright mill, cast iron, two 8 3/4" wheels, pivoting cover on hopper, original red paint, decals & pin striping, 1898 patent date marked on grinding burrs, very good condition (ILLUS.) **1,150**

ELMA Coffee Mill

Upright mill, cast iron w/crank & gears (no wheels), raised hopper w/tin dome, wood drawer, original red paint, made by ELMA, Spain, about 13" h. (ILLUS.) **225**

Upright mill, counter-type, cast iron, two-wheel, cast-iron drawer at bottom on a wooden base, worn original black paint w/red & gold trim & decals, marked "Land" 12" h... **660**

Wall Canister Mills

German Ceramic Coffee Mill

Wall canister mill, ceramic canister decorated w/Dutch scenes, wooden lid, rectangular glass receiver, small metal tag on mounting board marked "Gebr. Roittner, Salzburg," made by R. Zassenhaus, Germany (ILLUS.) **225**

Parker Co. Coffee Mill

Wall canister mill, cylindrical black tin canister & lid, eagle decal, iron grinding body embossed "The Chas. Parker Co., Meriden, Conn.," attached metal glass holder below, also marked "Eagle No. 044" & "Pat. Applied For" (ILLUS.) **275**

Lightning No. 23 Coffee Mill

Wall canister mill, cylindrical tin canister, green & white litho-printed "Lightning No. 23 Coffee Mill, Belmont Hardware Co.," angled mounting bracket, tin receiving cup hangs below (ILLUS.) **325**

Arcade Jewel Coffee Mill

Wall canister mill, w/decorative rectangular glass canister & tin lid, tin receiving cup below rests on iron holder, gold paint on metal parts, canister marked "Jewel, Arcade Mfg. Co.," 14" h. (ILLUS.).................. **400**

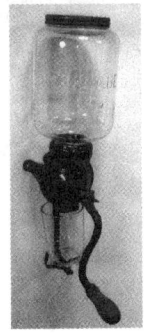

Arcade 25 Coffee Mill

Wall canister mill, w/glass jar embossed "Arcade 25," tin lid & iron grinding body also marked w/Arcade name, glass receiver not original, 15" h. (ILLUS.).................. **150**

Miscellaneous

"Queen" Arcade Coffee Mill

Box mill, child's, wooden w/gold painted decorative metal parts, removable drawer w/metal front, paper label marked "Queen," Model No. 9 in series of children's mills made by Arcade, 2 1/2 x 2 1/2" (ILLUS.) **150**

Enterprise No. 650 Coffee/Corn Mill

Iron mill, wall-mounted corn & coffee mill, 19" wheel, black w/gold trim & lettering, Enterprise No. 650, excellent original condition (ILLUS.) **325**

Iron "Steamship" Coffee Mill

Iron mill, wall-mounted, "steamship" mill, crank in front w/gear arrangement, grind adjusting screw below, about 6" h. (ILLUS.) **150**

Enterprise No. 00 Coffee Mill

Iron mill, wall-mounted w/open hopper & hanging iron cup, original black paint & decals, Enterprise No. 00, 9" h. (ILLUS.) **350**

Cookie Cutters

General

Amish Horse & Buggy Cookie Cutter

Amish horse & buggy, by Eugene Valasek, Canton, Ohio (ILLUS.) **20-25**

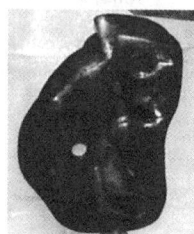

Beelzebub Cookie Cutter

Beelzebub, tin, replica of an antique cutter, made to look old (ILLUS.) **10-20**

Bird Cookie Cutter

Bird, tin, outline of bird, narrow (ILLUS.)........ **10-20**

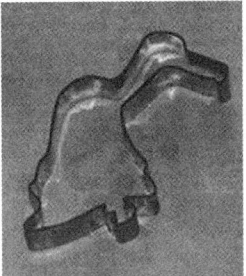

Buzzard Cookie Cutter

Buzzard, by Little Fox Factory, Bucyrus,
Ohio (ILLUS.) **5**

Cathedral Window Cookie Cutter

Cathedral window, by Eugene Valasek,
Canton, Ohio (ILLUS.) **20-25**

Cattoline Shortening Cookie Cutter

Cattoline Shortening, tin, w/fold down handle, given by companies in the early
1900s (ILLUS.).. **25-35**

Crinkled Circle Cookie Cutter

Circle, crinkled edges, early 1900s (ILLUS.).. **25-35**

Circle Cookie Cutter

Circle, used for several purposes such as
apple corer, funnel, donut cutter or cook-
ie cutter, early 1900s (ILLUS.) **50-75**

Cookie cutter, tin, a large heart w/a backplate pierced w/two holes, applied back
handle, 8 1/4" l.. **50**

Cookie cutter, tin, stylized design of a running rabbit, w/backplate pierced w/two
holes, applied back handle, 7 1/4" l. **50**

Cookie cutter, tin, stylized figure representing Santa Claus, w/a rectangular backplate w/hole, marked "Cake Art Germany," 4 1/2 x 11 1/2" (soldered seam
loose) **138**

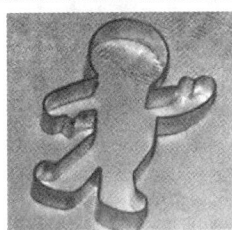

Waving Gingerbread Boy Cookie Cutter

Gingerbread boy, outline, waving, by Little
Fox Factory, Bucyrus, Ohio (ILLUS.)................ **5**

Gingerbread Boy Cookie Cutter

Gingerbread boy, tin, w/handles, signed E.
Valasek, 1979, Canton, Ohio (ILLUS.) **15-20**

Gingerbread Girl Cookie Cutter

Gingerbread girl, heavy tin, no signature
(ILLUS.).. **20-30**

Signed Gingerbread Girl Cookie Cutter

Gingerbread girl, tin, w/handles, signed
Gene Valasek, 1980, Canton, Ohio
(ILLUS.).. **15-20**

Gingerbread Man Cookie Cutter

Gingerbread man, tin, flat back, signed B.
Cukla, Hammer Song, Boonsboro, Mary-
land (ILLUS.).. **10-15**

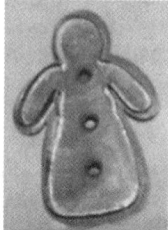

Gingerbread Woman Cookie Cutter

Gingerbread woman, galvanized metal,
flat back handle w/edges turned under,
no signature on cutter, Baxter Oberlin,
Angola, Indiana (ILLUS.)............................ **10-15**

Tin Gingerbread Woman Cookie Cutter

Gingerbread woman, heavy tin, large, edges & corners turned in, no signature
(ILLUS.).. **20-30**

Hansel & Gretel Set of Cookie Cutters

Hansel & Gretel set: Hansel, Gretel, witch,
tree, gingerbread house; first boxed set,
plastic, w/recipes & story of Hansel &
Gretel, Educational Products, 1947, front
of box features Mr. Meiro, owner of E.P.
Co., wife & two daughters, set of six cut-
ters in original box (ILLUS.)........................... **150**

Heart Cookie Cutter

Heart, w/Gingerbread boy & girl inside, has
a crinkled edge handle w/edge folded to
outside, signed inside of heart B. Cukla©,
Hammer Song, Boonsboro, Maryland
(ILLUS.) **15-20**

Outhouse Cookie Cutter

Outhouse, by Eugene Valasek, Canton,
Ohio (ILLUS.)... **25-35**

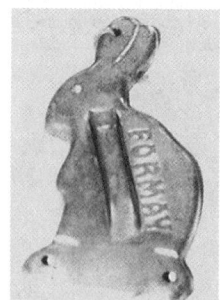

Rabbit Cookie Cutter

Rabbit, tin, standard self handle, sold on
West Coast, Formay, Swift & Co.,
3 x 8 1/8" (ILLUS.)....................................... **25-50**

6-Sided Cookie Cutter

Six-Sided, replica of a cutter a roving tin-smith would have made in the late 1800s or early 1900s (ILLUS.) **10-20**

Snowman Cookie Cutter

Snowman, galvanized metal, flat back handle w/edges turned under, no signature on cutter, Baxter Oberlin, Angola, Indiana (ILLUS.).. **10-15**
Soldier on horseback, figural, soldier wearing plumed helmet, 9" l., 10" h. (some rust & a loose seam).......................... **935**

Swiss Cheese Slice Cookie Cutter

Swiss cheese slice, small "Ohio" in upper left hand corner, by Stan Baker, Dover, Ohio (ILLUS.)... **20**

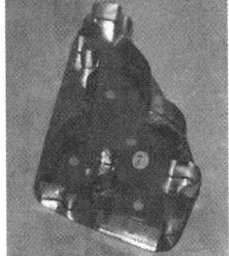

Woman on Pot Cookie Cutter

Woman on pot, replica of a cutter in the Historical Society Collection at Lewiston, Pennsylvania, by Bob Jones, Allen Park, Michigan (ILLUS.) **25-50**

Cookie Cutters - Hallmark

Hallmark began producing cookie cutters in the 1960s. These were of a translucent plastic and came on greeting cards. Few and far between, they were basically overlooked as far as collectors were concerned. Cookie cutter collectors were interested in the cutters used by their grandmothers and great-grandmothers. However, Hallmark began cookie cutter production in a big way in the early 1970s. Following their emphasis on seasonal/holiday items, these products were colorful and well-made. Most collectors of Hallmark are not only interested in the Christmas ornament line, but in everything from Hallmark. That includes the cookie cutters, which have steadily climbed in value – somewhat surprisingly for small items of plastic and vinyl. (If not specified, all cutters are marked Hallmark.)

Fire Chief badge, soft vinyl, yellow, 1978, 4 1/2" **$3-5**
Fozzie Bear, hard plastic, brown, white & lavender, signed H.A., 1980, 4 1/2" **10-12**
Gingerbread boy or girl, either hard plastic or soft vinyl, brown, 1977 .... **7-12**
Good luck, hard plastic, yellow & red, this cutter is mint in package but cellophane packages don't inflate value, 1979, 2 3/4" **5**
Goofy in space helmet, soft vinyl, blue, 1979, signed WDP, 3 1/2" **10-15**
Ice cream cone, soft vinyl, orange, 1980, 5" ... **8-10**
Joan Walsh Anglund, reissued in pink, signed Wolfpit Enterprises, Inc., 1980, 4 1/2" **7-10**
Joan Walsh Anglund, soft vinyl, orange, signed Wolfpit Enterprises, Inc., 1978, 4 1/2" **10-12**
Peanuts characters, first Peanuts set featuring Linus, Lucy, Snoopy & Charlie Brown, hard plastic w/curved handles, colors varied but for the set to be complete each cutter must be a different color - blue, orange, red, green or white, signed United Features Syndicate, 1971, all about 4 3/4", set of 4 .... **85-125**
Raggedy Ann & Andy, hard plastic, one red, one blue, signed BM for Bobbs Merrill, the company that held the copyright at the time, originally sold for 75¢, 1972, 4 3/4", pr. **40-60**

Holiday

Painted Reindeer from 1979

Christmas, angel w/lute, soft vinyl, blue, 1979, 4".. **4-6**
Christmas, candy cane, soft vinyl, red, 1979, 3".. **3-5**

Christmas, gingerbread man, soft vinyl, brown, 1981, 2 1/4" **4-6**

Christmas, holly leaves, soft vinyl, green, 1979, 2 1/2" **2-5**

Christmas, "JOY" ornament, soft vinyl, red, 1979, 2 3/4" **3-6**

Christmas, kneeling angel, soft vinyl, yellow, 1982, 2 1/2" **1-3**

Christmas, Peanuts characters Charlie Brown, Linus, Snoopy & Lucy, hard plastic, various colors, white, red, blue & green, to be complete set each cutter must be a different color, signed United Features Syndicate, 1972, 3 1/2" to 4 1/2", set of 4 .... **85**

Christmas, printed "HOHOHO," soft vinyl, green, 1984, 3 3/4" **2-3**

Christmas, reindeer, hard plastic, brown, red, white & green, painted, hard to find, 1979, 4 1/2" (ILLUS.) **15-20**

Christmas, rocking horse, hard plastic, white, gold, red, green & brown, dated 1981, 4" **25**

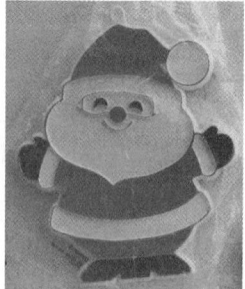

Santa from 1982

Christmas, Santa, hard plastic, white, red, black & gold, 1982, 4 1/2" (ILLUS.) **8-10**

Christmas, Santa head, hard plastic, red or green, 1974, 5" **40**

Christmas, Santa sleigh, hard plastic, brown, red, white & green, 1979, 3" **10-12**

Christmas, Santa w/candy cane, soft vinyl, red, 1981, 4 1/4" **4**

Christmas, Santa w/sack on back, soft vinyl, red, 1979, 4" **5-8**

Christmas, snowflake, soft vinyl, white, 1980, 2 1/2" **3-5**

Christmas, snowman, angel, tree, Santa, hard plastic, red or green, 4 1/4", 1973, set of 4 .... **60**

Christmas, snowman head, hard plastic, red or green, 1974, 5 1/4" **45**

Christmas, snowman w/bird, soft vinyl, white, 1981, 4 1/2" **5**

Christmas, snowman w/broom, soft, white, 1979, 2 1/2" **4-8**

Christmas, star, hard plastic, red or green, 1977, 2 1/2" **5-7**

Christmas, Teddy bear, soft vinyl, tan, 1983, 2 1/4" **2**

Christmas, toy soldier, 1983, soft vinyl, red, 4 1/4" **5**

Christmas, tree, hard plastic, green, gold, red & white, 1980, 4 1/2" (ILLUS. top next column) **12**

Tree from 1980

Christmas, wreath, soft vinyl, green, 1980, 3 1/4" **3-5**

Easter, acorn, hard plastic or soft vinyl, brown or golden, 1976, 4" **10**

Easter, apple, soft vinyl, red, 1981, 3 1/2" **2-3**

Easter, Barnaby Bunny, hard plastic or soft vinyl, yellow, blue or pink, 1978, 5" **12-22**

Easter, bunny, hard plastic, white, blue, yellow & pink, 1982, 4 3/4" **10-12**

Easter, bunny head, soft vinyl, blue, 1980, 4" **4-6**

Easter, bunny w/basket, hard plastic, white, pink, blue, yellow & brown, 1979, 4 1/4" ... **10-12**

Chickery Chick

Easter, Chickery Chick, hard plastic or soft vinyl, yellow, blue or pink, 1978, 5" (ILLUS.) **12-22**

Easter, duck, soft vinyl, yellow, 1982, 4" **2-4**

Duck w/Daisy

Easter, duck w/daisy, hard plastic, white, yellow, green, orange & brown, 1979, 4 1/4" (ILLUS.) **10-12**

Easter, egg decorated w/flowers, hard plastic, lavender, 1984, 2 3/4" **1-4**

Easter, egg, hard plastic, blue, white, green & lavender, 1981, 4 1/4".............................. **10-12**

Easter, flower, hard plastic, white, green, orange & pink, 1980, 4 1/4" **10-12**

Easter, football helmet, soft vinyl, red, 1978, 4".. **3-6**

Easter, football player, soft vinyl, gold, 1983, 4 1/2"... **1-2**

Easter, football, soft vinyl, brown, 1978, 4 1/2".. **5-7**

Easter, lamb, soft vinyl, white, 1980, 4" **2-5**

Easter, leaf, hard plastic or soft vinyl, brown or yellow, 1976, 4".. **10**

Easter, maple leaf, soft vinyl, rust, 1981, 3 3/4".. **1-2**

Easter, owl, soft vinyl, gold, 1980, 3 3/4".......... **3-5**

Easter, scarecrow, soft vinyl, orange, 1984, 4 3/4".. **2-5**

Easter, smiling egg, soft vinyl, blue, 1981, 4".. **2-4**

Easter, squirrel, soft vinyl, orange, 1980, 4 1/4".. **2-4**

Easter, tee-shirt, soft vinyl, blue, 1984, 3 1/2".. **1-2**

Easter, tulip, soft vinyl, blue, 1982, 4" **2-4**

Easter set: egg, rabbit, boy & girl, hard plastic, varied colors, lime green, blue, yellow & pink, to be a complete set must be one of each color, originally sold for $1.50, 1974, 3 3/4" to 4 1/2", set of 4......... **60-90**

Halloween, bat, soft vinyl, black, 1982, 2 1/2".. **1-3**

Halloween, "BOO" ghost, soft vinyl, white, 1981, 3 1/4".. **5-7**

Halloween, cat w/tail up over back, soft vinyl, black, 1979, 4 1/4" **6-7**

Halloween, crouching cat, hard plastic or soft vinyl, black or orange, 1976, 2 3/4" **10-15**

Halloween Ghost

Halloween, ghost, hard plastic or soft vinyl, white or orange, 1976, 3 1/2" (ILLUS.) **10-15**

Halloween, jack-o'-lantern, hard plastic, orange, 1976, 3"... **20**

Halloween, scarecrow, hard plastic, yellow, green, orange & black, 1979, 4 1/4" **15-20**

Halloween, skull, soft vinyl, white, 1980, 4 1/4".. **2-4**

Halloween, Snoopy on pumpkin, hard plastic, orange, signed United Features Syndicate, has sold for over $100, original price 75¢, 1974, 6 1/2" (ILLUS. top next column) .... **60-80 +**

Snoopy on Pumpkin

Halloween, spider, hard plastic, black, orange, gold, green, yellow & white, 1981, 3 1/2"... **10-12**

Halloween, standing witch w/pointed hat, soft vinyl, orange, 1979, 4" **4-6**

Halloween, super bat, hard plastic, purple, black, white & red, 1980, 3"............................ **15**

Vampire

Halloween, vampire, hard plastic, blue, black, yellow, red & white, 1979, 4 1/4" (ILLUS.) **10-12**

Halloween, witch, side view, hard plastic or soft vinyl, orange, 1976, 3 1/2" **12-15**

Halloween, witch, soft vinyl, purple, 1983, 4 1/4".. **1-3**

Halloween set: owl, witch head, pumpkin & cat head, hard plastic, orange, 1973, 3 1/2", set of 4... **80-100**

Beer Mug from 1985

St. Patrick's Day, beer mug, soft vinyl, green, 1985, 4 1/4" (ILLUS.) **1-3**

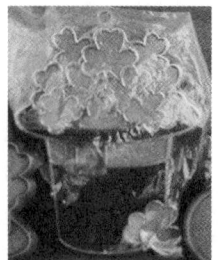

Hat w/Shamrocks from 1981

St. Patrick's Day, hat w/shamrocks, hard plastic, greens & gold, hats a' plenty for the luck of the Irish, 1981, 4 1/2" (ILLUS.)........ **10**

St. Patrick's Day, Kermit, soft vinyl, lime green, signed "H.A.," 1982, 3 1/2"................. **4-7**

St. Patrick's Day, large shamrock, soft vinyl, green, 1980, 3 1/4" **4-6**

Painted Leprechaun w/Matching Merry Miniature Figure

St. Patrick's Day, leprechaun, hard plastic, greens, tan, brown & black, painted, 1979, 5" (ILLUS.)... **10-15**

Leprechaun of 1981

St. Patrick's Day, Leprechaun, soft vinyl, translucent green, 1981, 4 1/4" (ILLUS.)....... **1-4**

St. Patrick's Day, puppy w/shamrock, soft vinyl, green, 1984, 3 3/4" **2-4**

Round Derby from 1980

St. Patrick's Day, round derby, soft vinyl, green, hats a' plenty for the luck of the Irish, 1980, 3" (ILLUS.).................................... **4-6**

St. Patrick's Day, small shamrock, hard plastic, green, 1977, 2 3/4" **10**

St. Patrick's Day, square derby, hard plastic, green, 1977, 2 3/4" **10-12**

Thanksgiving, cornucopia, soft vinyl, gold, 1978, 3"... **2-3**

Miniature Pilgrim

Thanksgiving, mini Pilgrim boy or girl, 1976, hard plastic, orange, tan or brown, 1976, 2 3/4" (ILLUS.).................................... **10-15**

Pilgrim Bird from 1980

Thanksgiving, Pilgrim bird, soft vinyl, brown, 1980, 4 1/4" (ILLUS.)........................... **2-4**

Pilgrim Boy's Head

Thanksgiving, Pilgrim boy's head, soft vinyl, orange, 1978, 4 1/2" (ILLUS.).................. **2-4**

Thanksgiving, printed "GOBBLE," soft vinyl, orange, 1984, 2".. **1-2**

Thanksgiving, turkey, hard plastic, orange, tan or brown, 1976, 2 3/4" **4-7**

Thanksgiving set: Pilgrim boy & girl, leaf & turkey, hard plastic, various colors, red, green, orange & tan, to be complete set each cutter must be a different color, turkey will sell for $20, 1974, 3 1/2" to 5 1/4", set of 4 (ILLUS. of turkey top next column) **60-90**

Turkey from Thanksgiving Set

Valentine's Day, charmer girl, soft vinyl, red, 1984, 3 3/4" **3-6**

Cupid

Valentine's Day, Cupid, hard plastic, flesh, white, yellow & brown, 1979, 3 1/2" (ILLUS.)... **10**

Valentine's Day, Cupid, soft vinyl, pink, 1981, 4 1/4" **4-6**

Dove from 1979

Valentine's Day, dove, hard plastic, pinks, gold & white, all of the Hallmark cutters of this type are called "painted" by collectors, 3 1/4" **10**

Valentine's Day, hard plastic, solid red, pink, lavender or yellow, hearts said "Love Ya" or "Hi Cutie," 1977, 2 3/4" **5-9**

Valentine's Day, heart & Cupid set, hard plastic, red, 1974, heart 3 1/4", Cupid 3 3/4", pr. **50-60**

Valentine's Day, Hug Bug heart, soft vinyl, red, 1980, 3" **3-7**

Valentine's Day, Kermit, hard plastic, greens, red, gold, white & black, w/a cheery smile & a "Be Mine" heart, Hallmark loved to use Jim Henson's muppets & Kermit was one of their favorite characters, signed "H.A.," 1981, 4 1/2" (ILLUS. top next column) **8-10**

Kermit w/"Be Mine" Heart

Valentine's Day, koala bear, soft vinyl, red, 1981, 3 1/2".. **2-5**

Valentine's Day, Mickey Mouse heart, soft vinyl, red, signed WDP, 1980...................... **12-15**

Valentine's Day, printed "LOVE," hard plastic, red, pink, lavender & yellow, 1977, 2 1/4" **15-20**

Script "Love" from 1981

Valentine's Day, script "Love," hard plastic, white, pink, red & gold, 1981, 3" (ILLUS.) **10**

Valentine's Day, smiling heart, soft vinyl, red, 1982, 3".. **3-6**

Cow Creamers

These silver or earthenware cream jugs were modeled in the form of that beautiful bovine animal, the original source of their intended contents. The most desirable versions are the early silver and Dutch Delft faience creations turned out in the 18th century. However, traditional style cow creamers, made in the late 19th or in the 20th centuries, are also deemed collectible.

Bennington Pottery Cow Creamer

Bennington pottery, platform-type, Rockingham glaze, rare, missing lid, chip on one horn, tail repair, expect damage as this creamer is a rare find in any condition, 5 x 7" (ILLUS.)................................... **450-550**

Bisque Cow Creamer

Bisque porcelain, highly textured bisque body, black spots, pink bow, w/yellow bell at neck, all glazed, "Japan" paper label, 4 1/4 x 5 3/4" (ILLUS.)......................... **20-24**

Black Ceramic Cow Creamer

Ceramic, black high-gloss glaze over red clay pottery, highly detailed, cold-painted features, maker unknown, 5 x 5 1/2" (ILLUS.)... **39-44**

Blue Painted Japanese Cow Creamer

Ceramic, blue painted flowers on both sides, molded green bell around neck, flowers in various colors, ink stamped "Japan" on bottom, 5 1/4 x 7 3/4" (ILLUS).. **32-35**

Blue Polka-dotted Cow Creamer

Ceramic, blue polka-dots on white glazed pottery, molded bell at neck, eyes accented w/long lashes, unmarked, maker unknown, 5 1/2 x 5 3/4" (ILLUS.)............... **49-55**

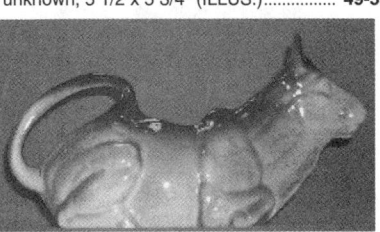

Brahma Cow Creamer

Ceramic, Brahma, laying down, black at top, graduating to reddish brown over cream pottery, highly glazed, unglazed bottom, very unusual, maker unknown, 3 3/4 x 8 3/4" (ILLUS.)................................. **39-45**

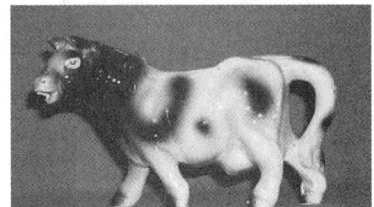

Brown & White Cow Creamer

Ceramic, brown markings on white glazed ceramic, hand-painted eyes, tail curls down & connects to back hind leg forming handle, unmarked, 4 x 7" (ILLUS.)....... **21-24**

Common Cow Creamer

Ceramic, brown markings over highly glazed white ceramic, ink stamped number "B544" underneath, common, 3 1/2 x 5 3/4" (ILLUS.) **22-26**

Ceramic, bull, brown & white, grey hooves & facial shading, tail curls under to form handle, ink stamped "K393," maker unknown, 4 1/2 x 7 3/4" **29-35**

Grouping of Bull Creamers

Ceramic, bull creamers, also found w/matching salt & pepper shakers, stamped "Made in Japan," also "Occupied Japan," 3 x 3", each (ILLUS.) **19-24**

Ceramic, bull creamers, also found w/matching salt & pepper shakers, stamped "Made in Japan," also "Occupied Japan," larger sizes, each **24-35**

Cow Creamer Bust

Ceramic, bust-form, brown markings on white w/pink ears, cheeks & mouth, bulging eyes, yellow horns & bell at neck, commonly found in various other animal shapes, hand-painted, marked "Japan," 4 x 4" (ILLUS.) **24-28**

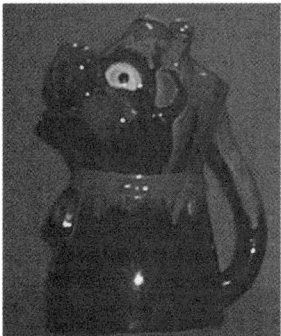

Artmark Originals Cow Creamer

Ceramic, bust-form, dark brown w/lighter brown paint-dripping effects, gold highlights on tips of horns, lashes & bell, bottom red & gold foil paper label, hand-painted, "Artmark Originals, Japan," 3 1/2 x 5 3/4" (ILLUS.) **25-29**

Smiling Cow Creamer

Ceramic, bust-form, golden ringlets & horns at crown, molded blue bell about the neck, black markings, highly detailed smiling features, ink stamped "M6149 Japan," original price 49 cents, 4 x 4 1/4" (ILLUS.) **49-55**

Comical Cow Creamer

Ceramic, comical, pink on white, ink stamped "Japan" on bottom, original ink stamp price of 19 cents on bottom of hoof, 4 x 5" (ILLUS.) **19-24**

Ceramic, dark brown over red clay, highly glazed, w/gold accents about the feet & eyes, light brown drippings of paint at opening, missing paper label, Japan, 4 1/2 x 5 1/2" **19-23**

Ceramic, dark green shamrocks on white glaze, tail curls underneath to form handle, marked "Cream" on front side, unmarked, 5 x 8" **40-45**

Blue Floral Cow Creamer

Ceramic, dark & light blue flowers on white glaze, w/blue nose & ears, tail curled up over back to form handle, "Cream" stamped on one side, bottom ink stamp "E-3801," 4 1/4 x 7" (ILLUS.) **39-46**

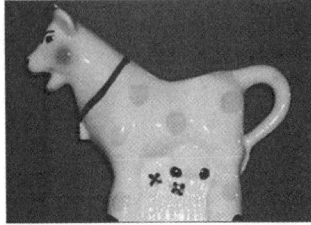

Flat-Bottomed Cow Creamer

Ceramic, flat bottom, turquoise spots on cream glazed pottery w/brown accents, molded bell at neck, rouge painted jaw area, unmarked, unglazed bottom, 5 1/2 x 7" (ILLUS.).. **65-69**

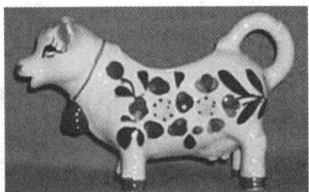

Hand-Painted Cow Creamer

Ceramic, hand-painted floral on white, molded bell at neck, many found with "Souvenir" label from places visited, Japan, 3 1/4 x 5 1/4" (ILLUS.) **14-19**

Holly Ross Cow Creamer

Ceramic, hand-painted flower on one side, bud on reverse, facial features, hooves & ribbon in gold, w/gold under glaze bottom marks, artist signed "Holly Ross, LaAnna, PA. Made in the Poconos," 5 x 7 1/2" (ILLUS.)... **39-45**

Otagiri Cow Creamer

Ceramic, hand-painted, w/gold foil label "M O C Japan, Otagiri 1981," embossed underneath, foil label on side, "Hand-painted," still being produced, common, by Otagiri, 3 x 5 1/2" (ILLUS.)........................... **12-15**

Black Cow Creamer

Ceramic, highly-glazed black over red clay, cold-painted features in pink, blue & gold, pottery bell w/painted flower attached by metal chain, original lid w/tip of tail ornamental to top, unmarked, 5 1/2 x 6" (ILLUS.) **34-39**

Calico Cow Creamer

Ceramic, laying down, dark blue on white, "Milk" stamped on one side, bottom ink stamp "Calico Burleigh Staffordshire England," new, still in production, 3 x 7 1/4" (ILLUS.) **35-39**

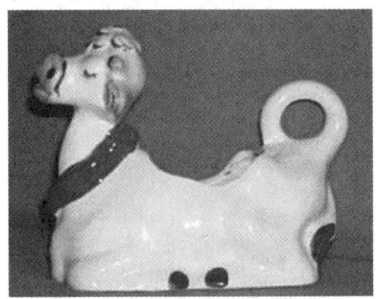

Cow Creamer w/Eyes Shut

Ceramic, laying down, eyes shut, yellow crown, pink nose, highlighted in brown on white glazed pottery, tail curled up to form handle loop over rear, impressed branding iron marking, "R" within a "G" on back side, unglazed pottery bottom, maker unknown, 5 x 6 1/2" (ILLUS.)................. **42-45**

Ceramic, laying down, feet tucked under, lustreware w/black spots & gold accented horns, red ink stamp "Made in Japan," 4 x 6" **27-32**

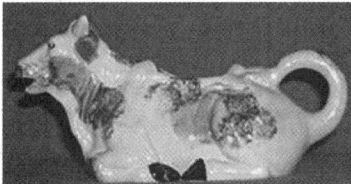

Sponged Design Cow Creamer

Ceramic, laying down, legs tucked underneath, dark green sponging over brown, yellow & cream glazed pottery, "Made in Japan" bottom ink stamp, rare sponged design, 3 1/2 x 7 1/4" (ILLUS.) **95-100**

Hand-painted Japanese Cow Creamer

Ceramic, laying down, red dotted flowers on white w/dark green tail, hooves & crest, pink nose & ribbon, bottom marking "Hand Painted Japan," 1950-60, 4 x 6 1/2" (ILLUS.) **24-29**

Brown & White Cow Creamer

Ceramic, light brown over white, sometimes mistaken as the popular "Elsie" creamer, hand-painted dark green garland at neck & bow on tail, black hooves, eyes shut w/fine lashes, unmarked, 6 x 6" (ILLUS.) **25-29**

Tan & White Japanese Cow Creamer

Ceramic, light tan over white, high glaze, large black painted eyes & hooves, bot-

tom ink stamp "B588," "Japan," 3 3/4 x 5 3/4" (ILLUS.) **14-19**

Miniature Japanese Cow Creamer

Ceramic, miniature, hand-painted flower on each side, stamped "Japan" on front hooves, 2 1/4 x 3 1/2" (ILLUS.) **16-20**

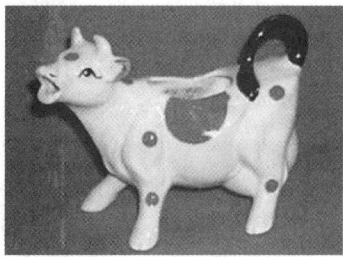

Orange & White Cow Creamer

Ceramic, orange spots on both sides over white, black tail & facial features, unmarked, 1960 (ILLUS.) **19-24**

Petite Cow Creamer

Ceramic, petite, decorated w/flowers on white glaze, molded bell at neck, unmarked, Japan, 4 1/2 x 4 3/4" (ILLUS.) **16-19**
Ceramic, pink mottled high glaze, grey base, horns & tail, black ink stamp "Made in Japan" w/flower in middle, very unusual, 4 1/2 x 6 1/4" **49-55**

Cow Creamer Pitcher w/Gold Accents

Ceramic, pitcher, black high gloss w/22 kt. gold detailed accents, bottom stamped in gold "Pearl China Co., hand decorated, 22 kt. Gold, U.S.A.," impressed "#635," larger than usual cow creamer, 6 1/2 x 6 1/2" (ILLUS.) **29-35**

Kenmar Purple Cow Creamer

Ceramic, purple glazed, small tin bell attached at neck w/fine wire, gold foil label marked "Kenmar, Japan," various colors, common, mint w/bell, 4 1/2 x 6 1/2" (ILLUS.)... **25-29**

Cow Creamer w/Pink Flowers

Ceramic, reddish brown on cream, pink flowers at base, unmarked, w/flat bottom base, 1950-60, 3 3/4 x 5 1/2" (ILLUS.) **19-25**

Common Japanese Cow Creamer

Ceramic, reddish brown over cream, Japanese, mass-produced before, during & after the war, found in many sizes, color & various markings, common, 3 1/2 x 5 1/4" (ILLUS.) **25-28**

Ceramic, set: cow creamer & cov. sugar, brown markings over white, large prominent eyes, molded bells at neck, standing cow creamer, laying down sugar w/lid, tail curls up to form handle on lid of sugar, unmarked, 1950, creamer 5 1/4 x 5 1/2" h., sugar 4 3/4 x 6", the set (ILLUS.) **42-49**

Purple Cow Creamer & Sugar Set

Ceramic, set: cow creamer & cov. sugar, purple accents on white, sugar has satin ribbon on head, sold by Norcrest China Co., unmarked, "Japan," common, also found w/matching salt & pepper shakers, creamer 6 x 4 3/4" h., sugar 3 x 4 3/4", the complete set (ILLUS.) **29-35**

Cow Creamer & Sugar

Ceramic, set: cow creamer, cov. sugar, salt & pepper, grey & black markings on white, highly glazed, removable salt & pepper heads, warehouse find, "Japan" stamped, mint in box, 5 x 5", the set (ILLUS. of part w/creamer on right)............ **39-44**

Hand-painted Creamer & Sugar Set

Ceramic, set: creamer & cov. sugar, purple over white glaze, large pink flared nostrils, yellow horns, hooves & tails, tails curl up over backs to form handles, ink stamp "52/270" under glaze, foil gold & black paper stickers "Made in Japan," marked "Thames, Hand-painted," found w/matching salt & pepper, complete, mint, creamer 5 x 5 1/2", sugar 4 1/2 x 6", the set (ILLUS.) **45-49**

Ceramic, set: creamer & matching cov. sugar, purple over white glaze, yellow horns & molded bell at neck, "Japan" paper label, 1950-60, both 5 x 5", the set **29-32**

Brown Cow Creamer & Sugar Set

Blue Tulip Decorated Cow Creamer

Ceramic, sitting, blue tulips on white glaze,
bottom ink stamp "Japan" under glaze,
1950-60, common, 3 3/4 x 4" (ILLUS.) **14-19**

Kent Ceramic Cow Creamer

Ceramic, sitting, brown w/white spots, gold
molded bell around neck, tail curled up
connecting at back of neck to form handle, bottom impressed stamp "Kent,"
5 1/4 x 6" (ILLUS.) **24-29**

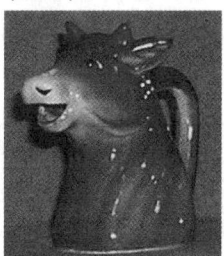

Sitting Bust Cow Creamer

Ceramic, sitting bust, reddish brown, bottom ink stamp "Made in Japan,"
3 1/2 x 3 3/4" (ILLUS.) **29-35**

Sitting Cow Creamer w/Flowers

Ceramic, sitting, flowers on both sides over
deep yellow chrome, enhanced gold
highlights around features, no bottom
markings, 4 3/4 x 6 1/2" (ILLUS.) **39-45**

Sitting Cow Creamer

Ceramic, sitting, mottled brown on white
pottery, yellow tail forming handle, found
w/many other color variations, top of
head is both opening & pouring vessel,
unmarked (ILLUS.)...................................... **14-19**

Japanese Ceramic Cow Creamer

Ceramic, small, blue, w/molded green bell
around neck, "Made in Japan" ink stamp
underneath, 3 1/2 x 5" (ILLUS.) **30-35**

Nashville Souvenir Cow Creamer

Ceramic, souvenir-type from Nashville,
Tennessee, Music City, U.S.A., usually
gold in color, found w/all states printed on
side, paper label "Made in Japan," com-
mon, 3 1/2 x 5" (ILLUS.)............................. **14-19**

Early 1940s Cow Creamer

Ceramic, two large black spots on cream w/black hooves, unmarked, early 1940s, formerly used as a planter, also found in brown on cream, 5 1/2 x 7" (ILLUS.).......... **39-45**

Ceramic, very simple in form & markings w/five light spots about body, horns & hooves highlighted in brown, paper label missing, 4 1/4 x 5 3/4" **24-29**

Cow Creamer w/Pink & Grey Transfers

Ceramic, w/pink & grey flower transfer on both sides & gold hooves, found in various floral designs, unmarked, 5 1/2 x 7" (ILLUS.)...................... **39-45**

Czechoslovakian pottery, sitting, orange spots on white porcelain, black tail, circle black ink stamp "Made in Czechoslovakia," 4 3/4 x 5 3/4" **75-78**

Czechoslovakian Cow Creamer

Czechoslovakian pottery, sitting, orange w/black ears & tail, dime size circle black ink stamp "Made in Czechoslovakia," minor paint wear, 4 3/4 x 5 3/4" (ILLUS.) **59-65**

Delft Faience Cow Creamer

Delft faience, exceptional blue coloring, windmill scene on front side, unmarked, 4 1/4 x 6 1/2" (ILLUS.)............................. **124-130**

Delft Pottery Cow Creamer

Delft pottery, hand-painted, light blue w/darker blue accents, signed by the artist, lidded opening, unusual that tail doesn't form handle, bottom marking under glaze "Made in Holland," mint, 3 3/4 x 6" (ILLUS.)................................... **129-135**

Delft pottery, painted & lightly glazed porcelain, cow dressed in assorted men's clothing, either sitting or standing, rare & very desirable **165-179**

Standing Cow Creamer w/Infant

German china, standing in upright position, reddish brown cow wearing a white & blue dress, holding an infant in a blanket, bottom circular ink stamp "Made in Germany," rare, 3 3/4" w., 5 3/4" h. (ILLUS.) **400-475**

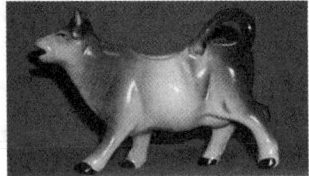

German Porcelain Cow Creamer

German porcelain, brown markings over white, black highlights on tail, hooves & horns, unmarked, 4 1/2 x 5 1/2" (ILLUS.).... **48-52**

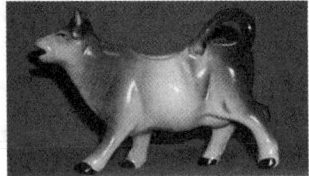

Brown & Cream German Cow Creamer

German porcelain, brown on cream porcelain, black accented tail, horns & hooves,
red ink stamped "Germany," 3 1/2 x 5"
(ILLUS.)... **55-59**
German porcelain, laying, w/tail curled up
to form handle, impressed "Germany
1391" on back side, unusual light green
color, mint, 3 1/2 x 7 1/2" **114-120**

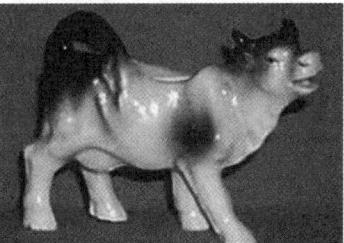

Miniature German Cow Creamer

German porcelain, miniature, grey/black
on fine white porcelain, impressed on
back "Germany," 2 5/8 x 3 5/8" (ILLUS.) ... **45-55**
German porcelain, reddish brown graduat-
ing to white on softly glazed fine porcelain, extremely detailed features, impressed on reverse side "Germany
8610," 7 1/2" h., 4 3/4" l. **75-82**

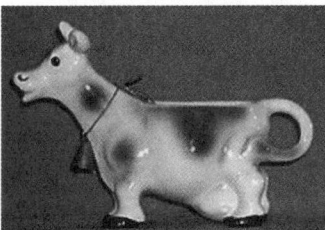

Goebel China Cow Creamer

Goebel china, brown markings on cream
glazed ceramic, tin gold bell on string, tail
curls under to form handle, unmarked,
opening 2 1/4", 3 3/4 x 5 3/4" (ILLUS.) **32-36**
Goebel china, brown markings on white,
original tin bell on cord, full "Bee" blue ink
stamp, "Germany," 5 x 7 1/2" **74-79**

Ironstone China Cow Creamer

Ironstone china, laying, w/legs tucked under, burgundy floral transfer on both
sides, backstamp reads "Charlotte Royal
Crownford Ironstone England," commonly found mold w/markings of different
companies in various colors, marked
"Made in England," 3 1/2 x 7" (ILLUS.)...... **39-45**

Black Platform-Style Cow Creamer

Jackfield pottery, high-gloss black glaze
over red clay w/gold trim, on platform
w/lid, Shropshire, England, 4 1/2 x 6 1/4"
(ILLUS.) **139-145**

Jackfield Cow Creamer

Jackfield pottery, platform base, high-
gloss black glaze over red clay, gold details, w/original lid, Shropshire, England,
5 x 7 1/4" (ILLUS.).................................... **195-225**

Limoges Porcelain Cow Creamer

Limoges porcelain, solid white, highly
glazed, stamped in green ink inside top
opening "Limoges, France," common
mold, used for some souvenir items,
4 1/2 x 6 1/2" (ILLUS.)................................ **25-29**

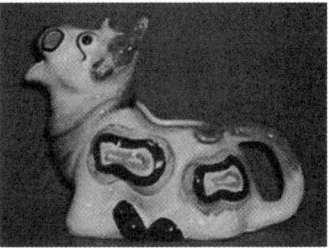

Rare Occupied Japan Cow Creamer

Occupied Japan china, lying down, legs folded underneath, irregular spots, graduating colors of greens & brown on cream, ink stamped "Made in Occupied Japan," rare, mint, 5 1/4 x 7" (ILLUS.) **69-75**

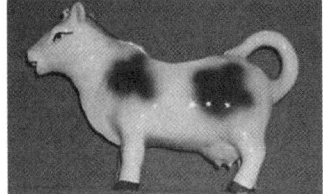

Occupied Japan Cow Creamer

Occupied Japan china, various dark brown markings, white background, glazed, tail curls up to form handle, found w/many different Japan stamps, common, prices depend on bottom markings, largest size 5 x 8" (ILLUS.) **35-39**

Japanese Cow Creamer w/Lacy Collar

Porcelain, grey on white w/gold accents, very delicate & lacy collar around neck w/bell attached, eyes shut, red ink stamp "Japan" on hoof, 3 3/4 x 4 1/2" (ILLUS.).... **21-24**

German Porcelain Cow Creamer

Porcelain, white, tail & horns, missing black cold-paint due to wear, "Germany" impressed on back underneath side, 4 3/4 x 7" (ILLUS.)...................................... **64-69**

Brown Pottery Cow Creamer

Pottery, medium brown sponged markings, blue molded bell at neck, unmarked, 1970-80, 4 1/2 x 6" (ILLUS.)...................... **12-17**

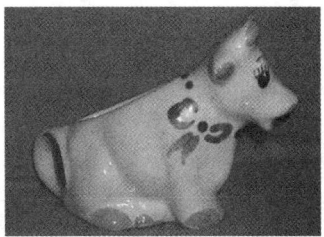

Pottery Cow Creamer

Pottery, pink accents on cream, green dots around neck forming a bow, lock handle tail, unmarked, 3 1/2 x 5" (ILLUS.) **14-19**

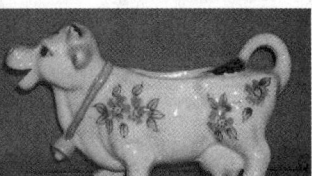

Staffordshire Cow Creamer

Staffordshire pottery, pink floral transfer on white, w/yellow bell at neck, unmarked, 5 x 8" (ILLUS.).............................. **80-95**

Staffordshire pottery, platform-type, reddish brown spots over white, embossed green flower on platform, w/original lid, early, dates from 1870, minor paint loss to be expected, 4 1/2 x 6 1/2" **225-250**

Staffordshire pottery, platform-type, w/lid, sponged dark brown & orange over white pottery, milkmaid seated on green base, facing forward, ca. 1810-20, 6 1/2" l. **1,200-1,400**

Staffordshire pottery, standing, sponged in manganese & yellow, milkmaid seated performing her task at oblong platform base, facing left, lidded opening, ca. 1780, repair, 6 3/4" l. **1,400-1,800**

Staffordshire pottery, w/lid, sponged purple lustre over cream, glazed pottery, orange backstamp "Old Staffordshire Ware, England," 1910-20, small chip on ear, 6 1/2" l. **165-179**

Staffordshire solid agate, cov., her body, two of her legs & the suckling calf w/brown & ochre striations, the group modeled standing on a domed rectangular plain creamware base, the cover applied w/a creamware flower-form knop, ca. 1775, 8" l. (restoration front of base, cover, calf's legs, horns & tail, tiny glaze chips) **2,875**

Sterling silver, ornate flowers around lid w/fly perched on top, marks "R C" w/"M" in a shield, lion w/raised paw facing left, leopard's head, letter "e," English, ca. 1960, still being produced, expect to pay more for earlier versions, weight is 5.2 oz., 4 x 6".. **500-700**

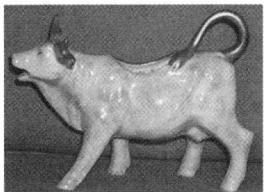

White Lusterware Cow Creamer

White lustreware china, w/gold horns & tail, opening highlighted in gold, unmarked, mint, 4 3/4 x 6 1/2" (ILLUS.)......... **74-79**

Yellowware pottery, standing on a platform, lid w/little or no repair, similar to the Bennington cow creamer, very rare
.... **1,500-2,000**

Egg Timers

Egg timers had long been considered an essential kitchen tool until in the 1920s and 1930s a German pottery company, W. Goebel, introduced figural egg timers. Goebel crafted miniature china figurines with attached glass vials. After the Great Depression, Japanese companies introduced less detailed timers. The Goebel figural egg timers are set apart by their trademark, delicate painting and distinctive clothes. It is best to purchase egg timers with their original tube, but the condition of the figure is most important in setting prices.

Goebel Bears Egg Timer

Bears, ceramic, brown & tan, white base, Goebel (ILLUS.).. **125**

Bellhop, ceramic, Oriental, wearing red outfit, marked "Germany".................................... **65-85**

Bird, ceramic, sitting on nest, wearing white bonnet w/green ribbon, Josef Originals sticker.. **25-45**

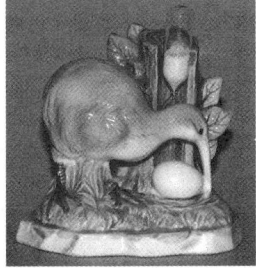

Bird & Egg Near Stump Egg Timer

Bird, ceramic, standing next to stump w/egg at base, shades of brown w/green grassy base & leaves on stump, Japan (ILLUS.)........ **95**

Boy, ceramic, holding rifle, marked "Germany" **65-85**

Boy, ceramic, skiing, marked "Germany" **75**

Boy, ceramic, wearing Swiss outfit, marked "Germany" **75-95**

Wooden Cat Egg Timer

Cat, wooden, black cat w/yellow eyes & red collar on domed yellow base, timer lifts out of back (ILLUS.)... **40**

Chef, ceramic, holding blue spoon, marked "Germany" **65-85**

Chef, ceramic, winking, white w/black shoes & trim, turn on head to activate sand.. **60**

Chef, composition board, black chef holding platter of chicken, w/potholder hooks **75-95**

Egg Timer with Chef Holding Egg

Chef, porcelain, white & blue, holding reddish orange egg, supporting timer, Germany (ILLUS.)... **75**

Chef, wood, "Time Your Egg" **25-45**

Chick, ceramic, white, yellow & purple chick, marked "Japan" **65-85**

Chicken, ceramic, white w/black wings & tail feathers, marked "Germany"................. **75-95**

Chimney sweep, ceramic, wearing black outfit w/top hat, carrying ladder, Germany **75-95**

Clown on phone, ceramic, standing, full figure, Japan, 3 3/4" h. **75**

Colonial man, ceramic, yellow & white, Japan... **45-65**
Dog, ceramic, Dachshund, red w/hole in back for timer, label on back reads "Shorty Timer".. **35-65**
Dog, ceramic, Pekingese, standing brown & white dog, marked "Germany".................... **75-95**

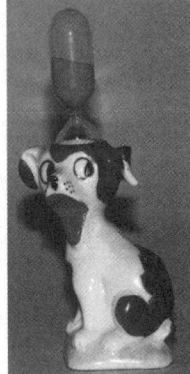

Dog Egg Timer

Dog, ceramic, sitting, white w/brown tail & ears, timer in head, Germany (ILLUS.)............ **65**
Dogs, ceramic, scotties, brown, standing facing each other holding timer in paws, marked "Germany".. **75-95**
Duck, wood, hanging-type, duck sitting on green egg, marked "Germany".................. **25-45**
Dutch boy, ceramic, wearing blue & white sailor outfit, Germany, small **65-85**
Dutch boy, ceramic, yellow pants, brown shoes, hat, scarf, Japan **45-65**

Dutch Boy Egg Timer

Dutch boy, composition, blue pants & hat, red shirt, white tie w/blue polka dots, Germany (ILLUS.).. **50**
Dutch boy & girl, ceramic, double-type, unknown modeler, timer marked w/3-, 4- & 5-minute intervals, Goebel, Germany, 1953... **125**
Dutch girl, ceramic, talking on telephone, Japan... **45-65**
Dutch girl, ceramic, w/red heart on apron, Germany **65-85**

Elephant, ceramic, white, sitting w/timer in upraised trunk, marked "Germany" **65-85**

English Bobby Egg Timer

English Bobby, ceramic, blue uniform & hat, black shoes, Japan (ILLUS.) **95**

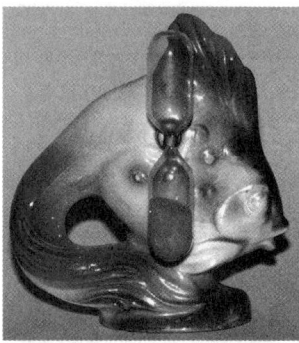

Lustreware Fish Egg Timer

Fish, ceramic, lustreware, burgundy, yellow & green, Germany (ILLUS.)............................... **95**

Fisherman Egg Timer

Fisherman, ceramic, standing, brown jacket & hat, tall black boots, carrying a large white fish on his shoulders, timer attached to mouth of fish, Germany (ILLUS.) **95**

Frog, ceramic, multicolored frog sitting on egg, marked "Japan"..................................... **45-75**

Golliwog, ceramic, character-type, marked "FOREIGN".. **150-200**

Happy the dwarf, ceramic, from "Snow White & the Seven Dwarfs," Maw Co., England.. **125-150**

Honey bear, ceramic, brown & white, w/timer in mouth made to resemble milk bottle, Cardinal China Co., No. 1152 .... **65-95**

Humpty Dumpty, ceramic, wearing hat & bow tie, turn on head to activate sand, marked "California Cleminsons" **45-75**

Indian Egg Timer

Indian, ceramic, kneeling, white wearing headdress w/red, blue & green feathers, holding timer in one hand, marked "Germany," rare (ILLUS.) **125**

Leprechaun, glazed chalkware, sitting on wishing well, "Porkush" on front base, marked "Manorware," England **35-65**

Mammy, tin lithographed, mammy cooking on gas stove, w/potholder hooks **145**

Minuteman, ceramic, holding rifle & leaning against stone wall, "Kitchen Independence" on front base, marked "Enesco" & "Japan"... **25-35**

Mouse Chef Egg Timer

Mouse, ceramic, sitting & holding timer, brown w/white apron marked "Chef" in red letters, Josef Originals (ILLUS.) **50**

Oliver Twist, ceramic, wearing red pants & vest, brown jacket, black hat, marked "Germany" **95-125**

Penguin, glazed chalkware, standing on green & white base w/"Bagnor Regis" painted on front, marked "Manorware, England" **75**

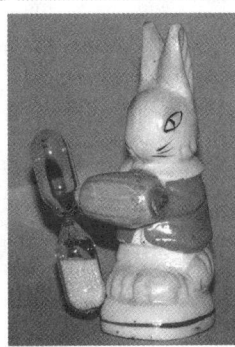

Rabbit with Carrot Egg Timer

Rabbit, ceramic, sitting, white w/red jacket, holding carrot which supports the timer, Germany (ILLUS.).. **75**

Rooster, wood, multicolored, standing on thick base **25-45**

Sailboat Egg Timer

Sailboat, ceramic, lustreware, tan boat w/white sails, Germany (ILLUS.) **75**

Santa Claus, ceramic, sitting, unmarked....... **50-75**

Seagull Egg Timer with Bottle Opener

Sea gull, iron, white & tan bird w/red beak & legs, on black & white branch which is also a bottle opener (ILLUS.) **35**

Swiss woman, ceramic, w/multicolored striped apron, marked "Germany" **65-85**

Waiter Egg Timer

Waiter, ceramic, standing next to ovoid holder for timer, black & white, Germany (ILLUS.)... **75**

Glass - Miscellaneous

Fire-King
Batter bowl, Jadeite, w/spout & handle, 1" w. rim band **45**

Fire-King Jadeite Batter Bowl

Batter bowl, Jadeite, w/spout & handle, 3/4" w. rim band (ILLUS.).................... **35**

Berry bowl, Jane Ray patt., Jadeite..................... **12**

Charm Pattern Jadeite Berry Bowl

Berry or dessert bowl, Charm patt., Jadeite (ILLUS.) **11**

Bowl, 5 3/8" d., Philbe patt., Sapphire Blue **18**

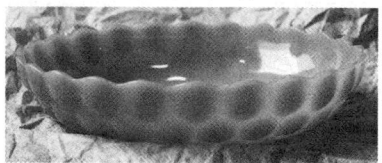

Jadeite Bubble Pattern Bowl

Bowl, 8 1/2" l., Bubble patt., shallow oblong form (ILLUS.) **22**

Fire-King Casserole & Table Protector

Casserole w/knob-handled cover, Philbe patt., Sapphire Blue (ILLUS.) **22**

Creamer, Jane Ray patt., Jadeite **20**

Charm Pattern Cup & Saucer

Cup & saucer, Charm patt., Azurite blue (ILLUS.) **7**

Cup & saucer, Jane Ray patt., Jadeite.................. **9**

Cup & saucer, Restaurant Ware, Jadeite, G319 & G295.. **15**

Jadeite Double Egg Cup

Egg cup, double, Jadeite, part of breakfast
set (ILLUS.) **45**

Philbe Sapphire Blue Loaf Pan

Loaf pan, Philbe patt., Sapphire Blue
(ILLUS.).. **18**

Fire-King Commemorative

Measuring cup, commemorative, crystal
w/red wording, "Commemorating 50
Years - Fire-King," 1992, 2 cup (ILLUS.)... **14-18**

Pint Swedish Modern Mixing Bowl

Mixing bowl, Swedish Modern patt.,
Jadeite, 1 pt., 5 3/4" l. (ILLUS.) **45**
Mixing bowl, Swedish Modern patt.,
Jadeite, 1 qt., 6 1/4" l. **85**

Swedish Modern 2 Quart Mixing Bowl

Mixing bowl, Swedish Modern patt.,
Jadeite, 2 qt., 7 1/4" l., (ILLUS.)..................... **110**
Mixing bowl, Swedish Modern patt.,
Jadeite, 3 qt., 8 3/4" l. **135**

Ivory Swirl Pattern Mixing Bowls

Mixing bowl, Swirl patt., Ivory, 6" d.
(ILLUS. left) **7**
Mixing bowl, Swirl patt., Ivory, 7" d. **8**
Mixing bowl, Swirl patt., Ivory, 8" d.
(ILLUS. top right)... **13**
Mixing bowl, Swirl patt., Ivory, 9" d.
(ILLUS. bottom right) **15**

Boxed Set of Fire-King Mixing Bowls

Mixing bowls, four graduated sizes, fired-
on colors, 1 pt., 1 qt., 1 1/2 qt. & 2 1/2 qt.,
boxed set (ILLUS.) **25**

Sapphire Blue Mixing-Measuring Bowl

Mixing-measuring bowl, Sapphire Blue,
two handles, two spouts (ILLUS.).................... **30**
Mug, Jadeite, "D" handle **13**

Jadeite Restaurant Ware Mug

Mug, Restaurant Ware, Jadeite, 6 oz.
(ILLUS.)... **9**

Turquoise Blue Fire-King Mug

Mug, Turquoise Blue, w/"D" handle (ILLUS.)........ **10**
Oatmeal bowl, Jane Ray patt., Jadeite................. **12**
Pie pan, crystal, 1960s label **8**

Beads & Bars Pattern Milk Pitcher

Pitcher, milk, Beads & Bars patt., crystal,
part of breakfast set, 20 oz. (ILLUS.) **10**

Jadeite Restaurant Ware Dinner Plate

Plate, dinner, 9" d., Restaurant Ware, Jade-
ite (ILLUS.) **23**
Plate, dinner, Jane Ray patt., Jadeite................... **15**
Plate, luncheon, Jane Ray patt., Jadeite **10**
Platter, 9 3/4" l., 'football'-style, Restaurant
Ware, Jadeite.. **55**
Platter, oval, Jane Ray patt., Jadeite.................... **35**

Jadeite Single-Spout Skillet

Skillet, Jadeite, single-spout, handled
(ILLUS.) **90**
Soup bowl, flat-style, Restaurant Ware,
Jadeite, 9 1/4" d. **125**

Jane Ray Pattern Soup Plate

Soup plate, Jane Ray patt., Jadeite
(ILLUS.) **30**

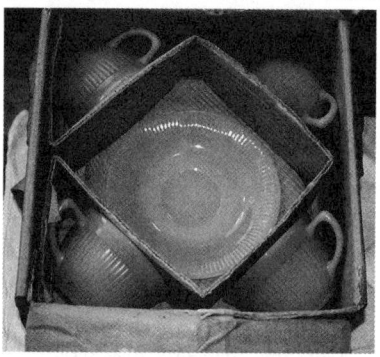

Jane Ray Boxed Starter Set

Starter set, Jane Ray patt., Jadeite, in orig-
inal box, the set (ILLUS.) **175**
Sugar bowl, cov., Jane Ray patt., Jadeite **30**

Pink Swirl Pattern Open Sugar Bowl

Sugar bowl, open, pink Swirl patt., tab han-
dles (ILLUS.) **9**

Sugar bowl cover, for pink Swirl patt. sugar bowl **12**
Table protector, round w/scroll handles, Philbe patt., Sapphire Blue (ILLUS. with casserole) **20**
Tea cup, Swirl patt., Jadeite................................... **16**

Jane Ray Jadeite Vegetable Bowl

Vegetable bowl, Jane Ray patt., Jadeite (ILLUS.).. **25**

Pyrex

Pyrex "Arsenic" Yellow Casserole

Casserole, cov., oval, "Arsenic" yellow (ILLUS.)... **10-12**

Canadian Pyrex Piecrust Creamer

Creamer, footed, Piecrust patt., Canadian blue (ILLUS.).. **10-13**
Custard cups, six in original box, the set............ **15**

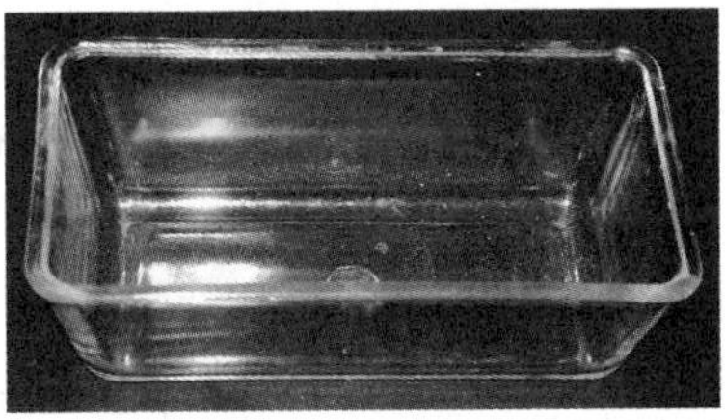

Pyrex "Arsenic" Yellow Loaf Pan

Loaf pan, old "Arsenic" yellow (ILLUS.) **8-10**

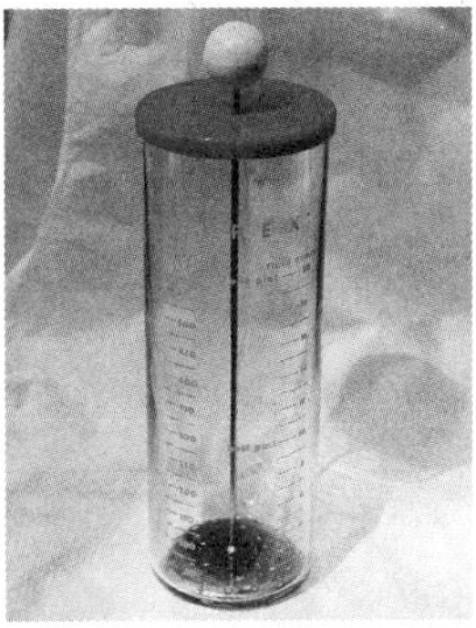

Pyrex Mayonnaise Maker

Mayonnaise maker, cylindrical w/yellow wording, red plastic cover & yellow knob on plunger (ILLUS.) **8-10**
Refrigerator dish, cov., Delphite Blue w/Delphite Blue cover, 1 1/2 cup **45**

Canadian Pyrex Blue Piecrust Sherbet

Sherbet, footed, Piecrust patt., Canadian blue (ILLUS.)... **5-8**

Pyrex Teapot w/Blue Handle

Teapot, cov., crystal, w/blue glass handle (ILLUS.) **30-45**

Kitchen Utensils

Apple corer/parer, commercial size, 1889 Rival No. 2, Rochester, NY, 16" h., 28" l. **275**
Apple parer, cast iron, clamp-on type, Domestic.. **195**
Apple parer, cast iron, clamp-on type, Hudson, 1868... **175**
Bacon greaser, wire, used w/removable cloths to grease bottom of pans........................ **25**
Biscuit cutter, tin, egg-shaped handle above small round biscuit cutter marked "Egg Baking Powder".. **275**

Cake or pie divider, wire, marks cake or pie
into six equal segments.................................... **25**

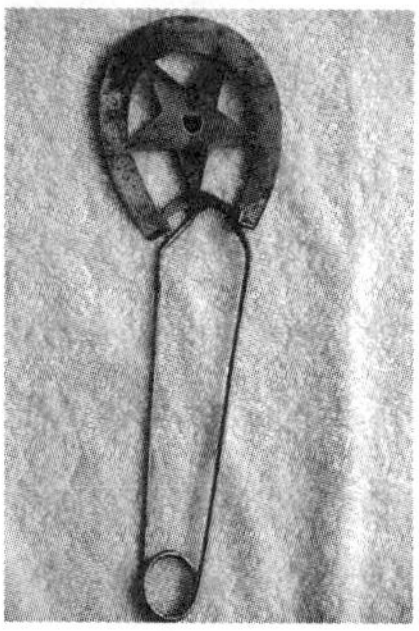

Horseshoe & Star Cake Turner

Cake turner, tin, horseshoe-shaped w/star
marked "M.C.W. Cake Turner, Pat. Apr.
2. 07," wire handle flips it (ILLUS.) **115**

Melco Kut-Rite Can Opener

Can opener, metal, Kut-Rite, Melco Mfg.
Co., St. Louis, Missouri (ILLUS.) **125**

Cast Iron Cherry Pitter

Cherry pitter, cast iron w/three legs,
marked "Pat'd Nov. 17, 1863" (ILLUS.) **145**

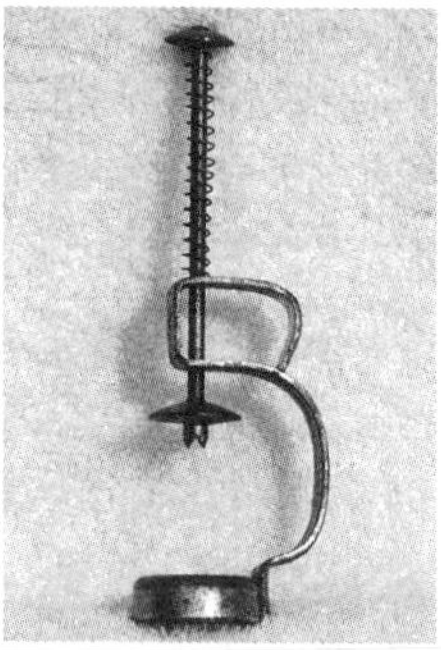

Single Cherry Pitter

Cherry pitter, tin, single pitter, no markings
(ILLUS.) **30**

Metal Chopper

Chopper, cast iron handle w/two metal
blades, handle marked "Pat'd. May 2, 93
No. 20 Croton, NY" (ILLUS.) **45**
Coffee measure, tin, small cup w/flat han-
dle advertising ice cream **14**

Universal Coffee Mill

Coffee mill, cast iron, clamp-on type, original label marked "Universal #010 Coffee
Mill" Pat'd Feb. 14, 1905 (ILLUS.) **95**
Coffee mill, miniature, child's, box-type
w/drawer, paper label marked "DAISY" **95**
Combination tool, tin, flat w/apple corer
w/apple peeler & grater at end, 8 1/2" l. **20**
Combination tool, tin, funnel-shaped, can
be used as funnel, apple corer, cookie
cutter, pie crimper or grater for corn or
horseradish, patented in 1868 (beware of
reproductions).. **175**
Cookie or cake cutter, tin, handmade bul-
bous short squatty heart design w/back
cut close to design, 3 1/2" w., 3" h. **45**
Cookie or cake cutter, tin, handmade ele-
phant form, no handle **175**
Corn cutter, tin, marked "Corn Cutter Pat.
Applied For Nesco" **65**
Corn sheller, cast iron, hand-held, tri-fold
sections, marked "C.M. O'Hara" **210**
Corn sheller, cast iron w/wood handle,
hand-held, marked "The Bird Pat July 6
1869, Springfield Ohio" **585**
Cutters, miniature, eleven various tin de-
signs in cov. 3 1/2' d. round tin container,
the set (ILLUS. top next page) **95**
Dish protector, wire screen dome, edge
banded in tin, wooden knob on top, used
as food protector from insects, 7" d. **45**

Miniature Cutters & Container

Doughnut cutter, wood, round w/wood insert & handle 35

Egg beater, wheel marked "Holt's Egg Beater & Cream Whip, Pat Aug 22, 99 Apr 3, 00 USA," 11".. 45

Egg beater w/stand, metal w/removable beater, Speedy Chef.................................... 145

Egg beater w/syllabub, tin, lightly stamped "The Wonder Cream Whip & Egg Beater Absolutely Unequalled" 75

Egg separator, ceramic, yellowware, English, 4" d. 55

Egg separator, plastic, red w/advertising for Maytag... 10

Egg separator, tin, Rumford advertising 45

Flour sifter, tin, divided w/lids on both ends, marked "Bromwells Multiple"............................ 28

Flour sifter/scoop, tin w/half round wire mesh scoop & removable screwed-on long handle, marked "Pillsbury's Flour Universal Scoop with Flour Attachment" 110

Food chopper, iron & wood, the wide flat blade w/rounded shoulders flanking a large inverted heart cut-out below the pointed baluster-turned wood handle w/a brass ferule, 19th c., 10 3/4" l......................... 275

Fork, three-prong, green handled w/cream stripe on end, 14" l. 14

Funnel cake pourer, tin, handmade, long handle w/funnel attached to end...................... 35

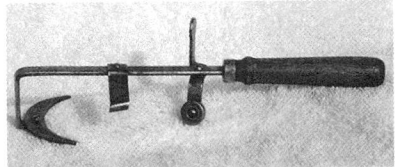

W. Fabrick Jar Sealer

Jar sealer, metal w/wooden handle, marked "W. Fabrick, Elgin, Ill." (ILLUS.).......... 45

Lemon squeezer, cast iron, w/decorated porcelain insert, marked "The Arcade No 2 Lemon Squeezer" 30

Lunch pail, tin, rectangular, no tray.................... 65

Milk bucket, wood w/wire banding & bail, top 12" d., 10" h. 45

Mold, cast iron, curved fish design..................... 145

Mold, tin w/tube in center, marked "Silvers Pudding Mold Brooklyn, NY," 5" h., 3 1/2" d. base.. 50

Muffin pan, tin, 12-cup size, plain........................ 12

Muffin pan, tin, six-cup size w/three different designs... 35

Rare Francis Nutmeg Grater

Nutmeg grater, cast iron, marked "Francis Grater Pat'd," rare (ILLUS.) .... 1,000+

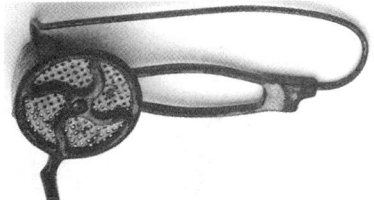

Church Nutmeg Grater

Nutmeg grater, cast iron, tin & wire, patented by Church in 1886, 7" l. (ILLUS.) 375

"The Gem" Nutmeg Grater

Nutmeg grater, cast iron, tin & wood, "The Gem" (ILLUS.) 85

Nutmeg grater, plated metal, marked "MTV," common type, 4" l. 65

Nutmeg grater, tin, cylindrical pocket-type, hinged lid folds down to reveal grater, 1" d., 2 1/2" h. (traces of japanning).............. 110

Rare Carsley Nutmeg Grater

Nutmeg grater, tin, marked "H. Carsley, Patented Nov. 20, 1855, Lynn, Mass," rare (ILLUS.) 975

Triangular Nutmeg Grater with Plunger

Nutmeg grater, tin, triangular w/wood plunger, stamped "Patented Oct. 13th 1857," remnants of blue japanning (ILLUS.).. 550

Tin Nutmeg Grater with Plunger

Nutmeg grater, tin w/wood plunger, known by patentee Hughes, sometimes stamped Pat. Feb. 27, 1877, 3 3/4" h. (ILLUS.).. 425
Nutmeg grater, wooden w/nicely turned handle, paper label reads "Champion Grater Co. Boston," brass cap marked "Patent Apr 2 1867".. 575
Pastry blender, wire, green handle..................... 12
Pea sheller, cast iron, clamp-on type, marked "Gem Pea Sheller Pat'd July 1866"... 335
Pie board, pine, round, cleated boards w/short tapered handle, 26 1/2" l............... 85
Pie lifter, tin, flat plate w/green handle, two flat metal arms above plate 55
Pie pan, tin, impressed "Crusty Pie" w/sun rays extending from center, 9 1/2" d. 15
Pie rack, wall-hung, fancy cast-iron wall bracket w/six folding wire pie holders, stamped "Patented," 15 1/2" l......................... 350
Pie rack, wire, tiered rack holds six pies............ 120
Popcorn popper, mechanical, wire box cage operated by egg beater-type crank handle, Quincy, IL, mint condition 650
Pot scraper, chain linked w/metal scraper as part of handle... 25
Potato ricer, metal w/red handle 15
Raisin seeder, cast iron, clamp-on type, long goose neck, marked "The Crown, Pat. Applied For," 6" h. 85
Rolling pin, wood cylinder w/green handles........ 18
Scoop, tin, flour scoop w/advertising for Neyhart Hardware Co., Williamsport, PA 20
Sifter, tin, child's version, marked "Hunter-toy-Sifter; Pat. May 16.71 - Apr. 7.74 Buy A Large One," approximately 2" h. 350
Skimmer, tin, 5 3/4" d. bowl w/punched six-pointed star, w/handle 13" l. 65

Slaw board, wood w/old red paint, hand wrought blade & early ram's horn fastener, 7 1/2" w., 18 1/2" l. 75
Spatula, flat green handle, marked "Daisy Kitchen Spatula".. 15
Spice box, round wooden box w/tin top & bottom rim, contains eight individual tin banded wood spice containers, each stamped w/different spice, 9 1/4" d. 350
Spice set, tin, six round japanned containers in japanned handled tray, tray 4 1/2" w., 7" l., the set.. 45
Spoon, tin w/wood handle, one side of spoon has rolled edge w/jagged teeth, patented in 1901, no markings...................... 65
Toaster, two long wires culminating in circular designs extend from end of wood handle, complete w/tension producing sliding ring 45
Trivet, cast iron, designed w/a four-pointed star in center & four Duchy hearts in between points, 6 1/4" d. 235
Whisk, coiled wire in egg shape w/wire handle, 9" l. 10

Napkin Dolls

During the period immediately following World War II colorful, decorative and functional were the key characteristics of popular household accessories. Imported novelty items like figural salt and pepper shakers, vases in the shapes of people and animals and children's toothbrush holders lined the shelves of variety and department stores. And if you were a housewife during the late 1940s through the 1950s, chances are a napkin doll sat on your kitchen counter waiting for your next party buffet.

Today, napkin dolls have regained their position in the kitchen as well as the display cabinets and shelves in many collectors' homes. Ranging from the individualistic charm of those made in ceramics classes to jeweled Japanese models, and the wide variety of wooden examples, these hot items are no longer mistaken for planters or miniature dress forms. In the past two years, the napkin doll has risen to the top of the collecting ladder as the craze for "stuff" from the 1930s, 1940s and 1950s has reached an all time high.

Ceramic, figure of angel holding a bouquet, pink & white, slits in rear & shoulders for wings, Japan paper sticker, 5 3/8" h. **100-115**

Deco Woman Napkin Holder

Ceramic, figure of Art Deco-looking woman w/black hair, hands on her hips, pink & white, 9 1/4" h. (ILLUS.) **65-85**

Ceramic, figure of genie, white w/gold trim, holding a lantern, wearing tag, "Genie At Your Service", Enesco, 8" h. **100-135**

Girl with Gold Bow Trim Napkin Doll

Ceramic, figure of girl w/black hair, beige lustre finish dress w/gold bow trim & large gold bow in back, 7 1/2" h. (ILLUS.)........... **75-85**

Oriental Woman Ceramic Napkin Doll

Ceramic, figure of Oriental woman in beige w/gold yoke across shoulders, carrying salt & pepper shaker buckets on her hips, candleholder in her coolie hat, toothpick holes below her waist & back, paper label on bottom w/"Hachiya Brothers, No. 81435, Made in Japan," 10 1/4" h. (ILLUS.)................................... **125-150**

Ceramic, figure of Spanish dancer holding tambourine, blue & white dress, marked "#460 California Originals USA," 15" h. . **135-150**

Napkin Doll Holding Bird & Tray

Ceramic, figure of woman, green & white lustre dress, flowers on front, holding a pink bird on out-stretched hand & a toothpick tray on her head w/other hand, 9 1/2" h. (ILLUS.).. **75-95**

Woman with Tray Napkin Doll

Ceramic, figure of woman holding a green toothpick tray, in yellow dress w/painted flowers on bottom of skirt, made in Japan, 9 3/4" h. (ILLUS.) **75-95**

Ceramic, figure of woman holding a muff, pink & jewel-decorated, hat masks candleholder, marked "Kreiss and Co.," 10 1/4" h. **95-110**

Napkin Doll with Pink Hat

Ceramic, figure of woman, in white w/pink trim, hands clasped behind back, dark brown face, 12" h. (ILLUS.) **70-90**

Napkin Doll with Toothpick Bowl on Head

Ceramic, figure of woman on base, white w/black hair, molded blue lustre apron, toothpick bowl on head, by Marcia of California, 13" h. (ILLUS.) **95-110**

Napkin Doll with Large Yellow Hat

Ceramic, figure of woman, pink & yellow dress, blue shawl, holding her hand on a floppy yellow hat, stamped "Japan" on bottom, 8 1/2" h. (ILLUS.) **65-85**

Woman w/Braids Napkin Doll

Ceramic, figure of woman w/braids, red, white & green, kitchen mitts on hands & holding turkey on tray w/toothpick holes, 9 3/4" h. (ILLUS.).. **75-95**
Ceramic, figure of woman w/braids, red, white & green, matching salt & pepper shakers available, 3 3/8" h. **25-35**

Napkin Doll with Picture Hat

Ceramic, figure of woman w/green & white dress, black hair, holding a picture hat behind her back, bottom marked "Holland Mold," 6 3/4" h. (ILLUS.) **95-115**

White & Yellow Ceramic Napkin Doll

Ceramic, figure of woman w/red hair, wearing white & yellow dress w/full skirt, 9" d. base, 9" h. (ILLUS.) **85-110**

Napkin Doll with Candleholder

Ceramic, figure of woman wearing off-the-shoulder green & yellow dress w/flowers on front, wide-brimmed hat w/candle-holder, stamped "Kreiss and Company," 8 1/2" h. (ILLUS.).. **45-65**

Napkin Doll with Large Red Hat

Ceramic, figure of woman, white skirt & jacket w/red & blue trim, red picture hat, hands held behind her back, 12 3/4" h. (ILLUS.).. **75-95**

Figural Woman Napkin Doll

Ceramic, figure of woman, white w/blue lustre molded-on apron, base & toothpick bowl on head, ca. 1958, 12 3/4" h. (ILLUS.).. **75-95**

Ceramic, figure of woman, yellow, holding a green toothpick tray, 9 1/4" **65-95**

Ceramic Rooster Napkin Doll

Ceramic, model of rooster, black w/red & yellow trim, 10 1/4" h. (ILLUS.) **35-45**

Ceramic, model of rooster, black w/red & yellow trim, matching shakers available, 6" h. **10-20**

Ceramic, Sunbonnet Miss, pink dress, white gloves & black hat, marked "Holt Howard 1958," 5" h. **100-125**

Lady Baker Napkin Doll

Ceramic & metal, half figure of lady baker w/wire bottom, blue dress w/white apron & hat, yellow hair, holding loaf of bread in one hand, pie in the other, both w/toothpick holes, 7" h. (ILLUS.) **95-110**

Brown Rooster with Wire Tail Napkin Holder

Ceramic & metal, model of rooster, brown w/wire tail, marked "T.C., U.S.A.," 6 1/4" h. (ILLUS.) **15-25**

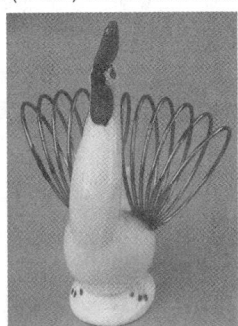

Rooster with Napkin Holder Tail

Ceramic & metal, model of rooster, white w/red comb & waddle, yellow feet, wire tail w/"Our Own Imports" gold foil label, 7" h. (ILLUS.) **15-25**

Mexican Woman Napklin Holder

Ceramic, metal & wood, half figure of Mexican woman w/yellow blouse & hat w/red trim, multicolor striped scarf on shoulder, wooden base w/wire napkin holder, 9" h. (ILLUS.) **175-195**

Dutch Girl on Wooden Base Napkin Holder

Ceramic, metal & wood, half-figure of
Dutch girl wearing white cap & blouse,
blue skirt & scarf, on wooden base w/wire
napking holder (ILLUS.) **150-175**

Napkin Holder Woman with Tray of Fruit

Wood, figure of black native girl, pink dress,
basket of fruit on head w/moveable arms,
6 3/4" h. (ILLUS.)... **65-85**
Wood, figure of woman, yellow, ca. 1949,
Finland, 10 1/2" h. **40-50**

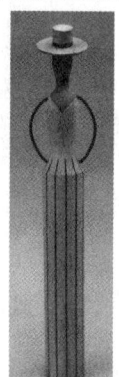

Stylized Wooden Figure Napkin Doll

Wood & metal, stylized slender figure,
wearing wide-brimmed hat, wires for
arms. Finland, 10 1/2" h. (ILLUS.) **40-50**

Pie Birds

*A pie bird can be described as a small, hollow device
usually between 3-1/2" to 6" long, glazed inside and
vented from the top. Its function is to raise the crust of a
pie to allow steam to escape, thus preventing juices from
bubbling over onto the oven floor while providing a
flaky, dry crust. Originally, in the 1880s, pie birds were
funnel-shaped vents used by the English for their meat
pies. Not until the turn of the century did figurals
appear, first in the form of birds, followed by elephants,
chefs, etc. By the 1930s, many shapes were found in
America. Today the market is flooded with many reproductions and newly created pie birds, usually in many
whimsical shapes and subjects. It is best to purchase
from knowledgeable dealers and fellow collectors.*

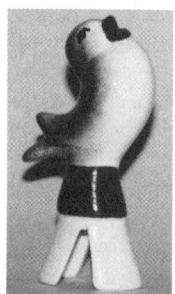

Puff-chested Bird Pie Bird

Bird, ceramic, brown & lavender trim, puff-
chested, ca. 1940s (ILLUS.)........................... **450**

Rowe Pottery Pie Bird

Bird, ceramic, two-piece w/detachable
base, 1992, Rowe Pottery (ILLUS.) **25**
Bird, on nest w/babies, Artissian Pottery,
USA **750**

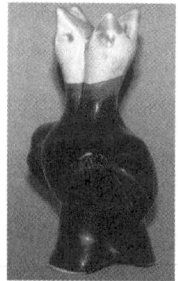

Two-headed Pie Bird

Bird, two-headed, Barn Pottery, Devon,
England (ILLUS.) **125**

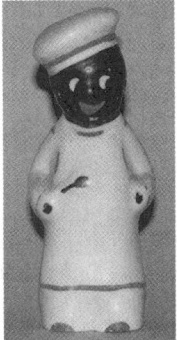

Black Chef w/Gold Spoon Pie Bird

Black chef, ceramic, w/gold spoon, white
w/red trim (ILLUS.) **200**

Black Chef with Blue Smock

Black Chef, full-figured, blue smock, "Pie-
Aire," USA (ILLUS.) **185**
Chef, "Benny the Baker," w/tools & box,
Cardinal China, New Jersey, USA **175**
Chef, ceramic, "Servex Oven China, Bohe-
mia, Guaranteed Heatproof, RD 17494
Aus., RD 4098 N.Z.," Australia, 4 5/8" h. **175**

Holland Servex Chef Pie Bird

Chef, ceramic, white w/black buttons, "The
Servex Chef" in black letters on hat,
marked "Holland" inside (ILLUS.) **175**

Donald Duck Pie Bird

Donald Duck, ceramic, "Walt Disney"
marked on one side & "Donald Duck" on
the other, rare **1,500**
Dragon, ceramic, Creiciau Pottery, Wales,
United Kingdom **225**

English Dragon Pie Birds

Dragons, ceramic, various shapes & colors,
1980s-1990s, England, each (ILLUS. of
three) **125**
Duck, ceramic, full-bodied, pink, yellow or
blue, USA **85**

Dutch Girl Multipurpose Pie Bird

Dutch girl, ceramic, doubles as pie vent,
measuring spoon holder and/or recepta-
cles for scouring pads & soap, rare
(ILLUS.) **250**

Nutbrown, England Elephant

Elephant, all-grey w/trunk up, ca. 1930s, Nutbrown, England (ILLUS. right).................. **250**
Elephant, all-white w/trunk up, Nutbrown, England (ILLUS. left) **80**

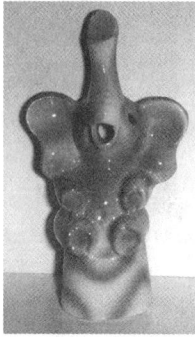

Elephant Pie Bird

Elephant, ceramic, grey & pink w/swirled pink base, Cardinal China Co., USA (ILLUS.).. **350**

"Fred the Flour Grader" Pie Bird

"Fred the Flour Grader," ceramic, black & white, from Homepride Flour, ca. 1978 (ILLUS.).. **125**

Charles & Diana Funnel-shaped Pie Bird

Funnel-shaped, ceramic, white w/blue transfer-printed image of Prince Charles & Princess Diana above "Charles and Diana 1981" (ILLUS.).. **75**

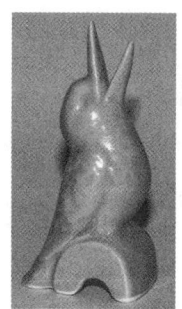

Kookaburra Pie Bird

Kookaburra, ceramic, light blue, Australia (ILLUS.) **250**

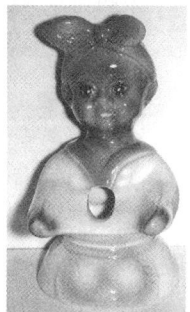

Mammy Pie Bird

Mammy, ceramic, outstretched arms, USA (ILLUS.) **100**

Mushroom Pie Bird

Mushroom, ceramic, white w/brown & green trim, designed by Clarice Cliff, ca. 1930s, England (ILLUS.) **150**

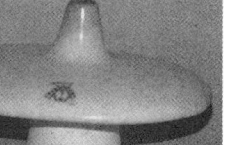

Mushroom-shaped Pie Bird

Mushroom-shaped, ceramic, England (ILLUS.) **350**

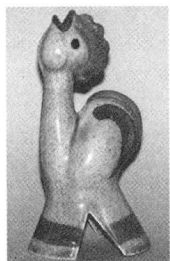

Rare Brown "Patrick" Pie Bird

"Patrick," ceramic, tan w/brown trim, California Cleminson, USA, rare (ILLUS.)............ **250**

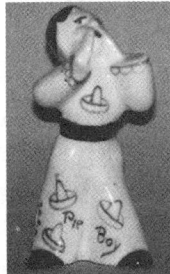

Pie Boy Pie Bird

"Pie Boy," ceramic, white w/black & green trim, Squire Pottery of California, USA (ILLUS.).. **650**

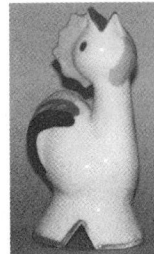

Cleminsons Rooster Pie Bird

Rooster, ceramic, white w/pink & burgundy trim, thin line around base, California Cleminsons, rare (ILLUS.) **125**

Thistle-shaped Pie Bird

Thistle-shaped, ceramic, blue, England (ILLUS.).. **250**

Reamers

The reamer's origin dates back to 18th century Europe where they were invented as a means for extracting citrus juice for medicinal purposes. By the late 1800s the reamer appeared in the United States and, thanks to the California Fruit Growers Association, by the roaring '20s glass juice squeezers were a fixture in the American kitchen. Today reamers rank as one of the hottest collectibles in the market place.

Ceramic, clown head in saucer, orange & white, Germany, 5" d. **250-300**

Chef Reamer

Ceramic, figure of black chef lying on his back, white w/blue trim, 2 3/4" h. (ILLUS.) **200-275**

Clown Reamer

Ceramic, figure of clown, light brown body & cone hat, blue buttons & collar, 6" h. (ILLUS.) **65-85**

Reamer Clown Salt & Pepper Shakers

Ceramic, figure of clown, reamer salt & pepper shakers, white w/red trim & red & blue dots, 3 1/4" h., pr. (ILLUS.) **30-40**

Ceramic, figure of clown w/pig head top, tan & light green body, yellow hat cone, marked "Hand Painted Made in Japan," 5" h. 175-250

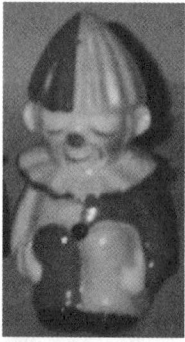

Yellow & Orange Clown Reamer Shaker

Ceramic, figure of clowns, reamer salt & pepper shakers, yellow & orange w/black trim, 2 3/4" h., pr. (ILLUS. of one).............. 25-35

Ceramic, figure of dog, yellow w/red & black trim, marked "Made in Japan," 8" h. 250-325

Ceramic, figure of woman's head w/black hair, sitting in white lustre saucer, 3 1/4" h. 325-400

Ceramic, green & cream, Hall China, 6" h.
.... 500-600

Ceramic, Jiffy Juicer, yellow, marked "US Pat. 2130,755, Sept. 20, 1938," 5 1/4" h. .. 75-95

Bear Reamer

Ceramic, model of bear, orange, marked "Foreign," 4 1/2" h. (ILLUS.) 325-400

Bird Reamer

Ceramic, model of bird, red w/grey beak & green wings, 4 3/4" h. (ILLUS.).............. 400-500

Ceramic, model of camel, kneeling, beige lustre w/light green top, 4 1/4" h. 225-250

Ceramic, model of lime, two-handled, marked "Orange For Baby" on front & "Handpainted" on bottom, 4 3/8" h. 75-85

Ceramic, model of orange w/white top & cone, painted smiling face, marked "Florida" on the front, 3 1/2" h. 45-55

Ceramic, model of red strawberry w/green leaves, marked "401 Beswick England," 4" h. 85-100

Ceramic, model of three-piece pear, orange w/gold trim & green stem, marked "Handpainted Made in Japan," 4" h. 60-75

Ceramic, model of three-piece pear, white w/black & gold trim, marked "Handpainted Made in Japan," 4" h. 55-65

Pitcher Reamer

Ceramic, pitcher, beige w/red & yellow flowers & black trim, bottom marked "Japan," together w/four matching 3" h. juice glasses, pitcher 8 1/2" h., the set (ILLUS. of pitcher).. 60-75

Pitcher Reamer and Juice Cup

Ceramic, pitcher, green w/blue & brown flowers, green leaves & brown trim, marked "Hand Painted Japan K," together w/four matching 3" juice cups, pitcher 8 1/2" h., the set (ILLUS. of part)............... 60-75

Ceramic, pitcher w/clown head top, bottom decorated w/yellow & purple flowers, yellow cone & lustre trim, marked "Made in Japan," 6" h. 75-95

Sauceboat-shaped Reamer

Ceramic, sauceboat-shaped, beige decorated w/orange fruit & green leaves, blue & white pedestal base, black handle & trim, marked "Made in Japan," 3" h. (ILLUS.) **65-85**

Ceramic, saucer shape, cream & tan w/maroon & blue trim, marked "A Present From Framington," "Made In England," 3 1/4" d. **125-150**

Ceramic, saucer shape, green & yellow w/red & tan trim, Dutch boy on one side & windmill on other, marked "A Present from Newport IOW, Made in England," 5 1/4" d. **100-135**

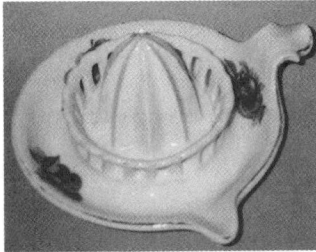

Reamer w/Lattice Edging

Ceramic, saucer shape, w/lattice edging, white w/red cherries, green leaves & gold trim, 5 1/2" d. (ILLUS.) **75-95**

Floral Decorated Reamer

Ceramic, saucer shape white w/light & dark pink roses, green leaves & gold & dark blue trim, 4 1/2" d. (ILLUS.) **125-150**

Ceramic, turquoise, marked "U.S.A. Zippy Trademark Patent Applied For Wolverine Products Inc., Detroit, Mich.," 3 1/4" h., 6 1/2" d. **85-115**

Ceramic, two-piece cream pitcher w/red & black cattail design, marked "Universal Cambridge, Ovenproof Made in USA," 9" h. **135-165**

Reamer with Kitten Decoration

Ceramic, two-piece, green w/white kitten in yellow pajamas on front, yellow, green, pink & white top, marked "Made in Japan 429," 4" h. (ILLUS.) **65-80**

Reamer with Roses

Ceramic, two-piece, light green w/pink roses, yellow highlights & gold handle, marked "Germany" on bottom, 3 1/8" h. (ILLUS.) **85-115**

Flowerpot Reamers

Ceramic, two-piece, tan lustre w/red & yellow flowers in pots, 2 1/4" h. (ILLUS. left) **100-125**

Ceramic, two-piece, tan lustre w/red & yellow flowers in pots, flanked by blue fence, 2" h. (ILLUS. right) **100-125**

Ceramic & metal, white bowl on green base, Presto Juicer National Electric Appliance Corp., Bridgeport, Connecticut, 7 5/8" h. **85-125**

Ceramic & wood, blue & white cone w/wood handle, 10 1/8" l. **150-175**

Glass, Chalaine Blue, embossed "Sunkist," marked "Pat. No. 18764 Made in USA," McKee Glass Co., 6" d. **175-225**

Jeannette Glass Reamer with Measure

Glass, Jade-ite, two-piece, two-cup measure, Jeannette Glass Co., 6 1/4" h. (ILLUS.).. **55-65**

Federal Glass Reamer

Glass, one-piece, amber w/tab handle, ribbed sides, Federal Glass Company, 5 1/4" d. (ILLUS.)....................................... **20-25**

White Milk Glass Reamer

Glass, one-piece, white milk glass, 3 1/4" h. (ILLUS.)..................................... **85-125**

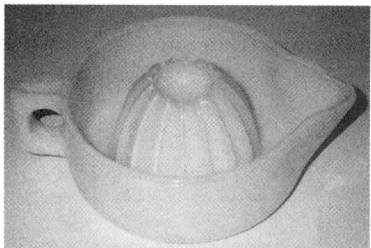

Yellow Milk Glass Grapefruit Reamer

Glass, one-piece, yellow milk glass, grapefruit, McKee Glass Company, 6" d. (ILLUS.).. **225-275**

McKee Saucer-type Reamer

Glass, saucer shape, Skokie Green on base, loop handle, McKee Glass Company, 5 1/2" d. (ILLUS.)................................... **50-60**

Opalescent Reamer

Glass, opalescent, one-piece, tab/loop handle, Fry Heat Resisting Glass, 6 1/4" d. (ILLUS.)....................................... **20-30**
Glass, two-piece, pink "Party Line Measuring Set," four-cup measure on one side, etched flowers on other, Paden City Glass Co., 8 3/4" h. **150-175**

Metal & Wood Reamer

Metal, one-piece w/hinged top & green wooden handle, marked "Kwik Way Products Inc., Pat No. 1743661," 7 1/2" l. (ILLUS.) **14-18**

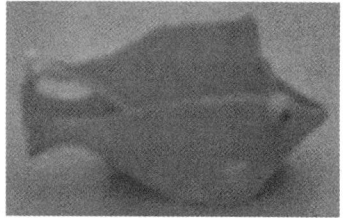

Fish-shaped Reamer

Plastic, model of fish, yellow w/red eye, marked "SQUEEZEIT CORP., Morris

Heights 53, N.Y.C., Pat. Pend.," 4" l.
(ILLUS.)... **8-12**
Silver plate, sauceboat-shaped, gold-plat-
ed exterior, silver plate interior, Lyn-Sil-
versmith, 4" d. **95-125**

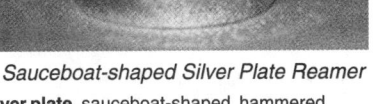

Sauceboat-shaped Silver Plate Reamer

Silver plate, sauceboat-shaped, hammered
finish, marked "T&t, ns, 30 66, Hand
Hammered," 5 1/8" d. (ILLUS.) **100-125**

Silver Plate Reamer

Silver plate, spiral handle, 10" l. (ILLUS.) **55-75**

Salt & Pepper Shakers

Indians & Mice Salt & Peppers

American Indians in drum, ceramic, nod-
der-type, Japan (ILLUS. left) **65**

Cartoon Character Shaker Sets

Astro Boy & Astro Girl, ceramic, cartoon
character-type, Japan, 1980s   (ILLUS.
right) **150**

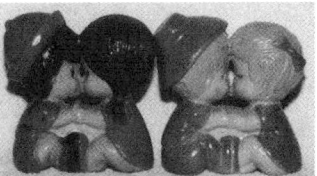

Plastic One-piece Shaker Sets

Boy & girl kissing, plastic, one-piece,
Hong Kong, each (ILLUS. of two)...................... **5**

Various Plastic Shaker Sets

Croquet set, plastic, USA (ILLUS. right) **40**

Anthropomorphic Style Shaker Sets

Dust Pan Head ladies, ceramic, anthropomorphic-style, PY Japan (ILLUS. left)............. **85**
Flowers & flowerpot, plastic, USA (ILLUS.
center with croquet set)............................... **18-20**

Various Advertising Shakers

"Happy Homer," ceramic, advertising-type,
for Staggs-Bilt Homes, Phoenix, Arizona,
1,000 sets made, Japan, 1950s (ILLUS.
far left).. **225+**

Fairy Tale Salt & Pepper Sets

Humpty Dumpty, ceramics, fairy tale theme, eggs sit on low wall, Japan (ILLUS. left) **20**

Idaho "Spud" Heads, ceramic, anthropomorphic-style, Japan (ILLUS. center with Dust Pan Head ladies) **65**

Jonah & the Whale, ceramic, story theme, Japan (ILLUS. right with Humpty Dumpty) **25**

Ketchup bottles, plastic, advertising-type, "Heinz Tomato Ketchup," red w/yellow cap & black & white label, Hong Kong (ILLUS. center back with Happy Homer) **10**

Mice in cheese, ceramics, nodder-type, "Say Cheese," Fitz & Floyd, Japan, 1980 (ILLUS. right with Indians) **300-350**

Old fashioned sewing machine, plastic, w/movable parts (ILLUS. left with croquet set) **40**

Pillsbury doughboy & cupcake, ceramic, advertising-type, "Funfettie" (ILLUS. front right with Happy Homer) **35**

Pixie and Dixie, ceramic, cartoon character-type, Japan (ILLUS. center with Astro Boy & Girl) **50**

Popeye & Olive Oyl, ceramic, cartoon character-type, Vandor (ILLUS. left with Astro Boy & Girl) **125**

Twin Winton Squirrel Shakers

Squirrels, ceramic, Twin Winton, USA (ILLUS.) **25**

Three Men in a Tub, ceramic, fairy tale theme, shaker & sugar bowl, the set (ILLUS. center with Humpty Dumpty) **65**

Tomato Head Kids, ceramic, anthropomorphic-style, Japan (ILLUS. right with Dust Pan Head ladies) **20-25**

Range Shaker Sets

Range Shaker Set in Metal Holder

Salt, pepper, flour & sugar shakers, milk glass w/flower basket design on front w/blue metal caps, marked "Tipp USA," in matching metal holder, 2 3/4" h., the set (ILLUS.) **30-40**

Range Shaker Set w/Scroll Design

Salt, pepper, flour & sugar shakers, milk glass w/green scroll design above & below "Sugar," "Salt," "Pepper" & "Flour," black metal caps, 3 3/4 to 4 1/2" h., the set (ILLUS.) **45-65**

Milk Glass Shaker Set w/Cherry Design

Salt, pepper, flour & sugar shakers, milk glass w/red cherry design, red metal caps, marked "Tipp USA," in black metal holder, 3 3/4" h., the set (ILLUS.) **30-40**

Jadite Salt & Pepper Shakers

Salt & pepper shakers, Jadite, Roman Arch style, metal caps, McKee, 4 1/4" h., each (ILLUS.) **65-85**

Shakers w/Scene of Woman Churning Butter

Salt & pepper shakers, milk glass w/aluminum caps, pepper w/red & salt w/blue design of woman churning butter on front, 3 1/2" h., pr. (ILLUS.) **15-20**

Tappan Chef Salt & Pepper Shakers

Salt & pepper shakers, milk glass w/fired on blue & yellow, figure of Tappan chef on front, black plastic caps, 3 3/4" h., each (ILLUS.) **10-12**

Milk Glass Shakers with Tulips

Salt & pepper shakers, milk glass w/red & yellow tulip design on front, white plastic caps, marked "Made in USA," 3 3/8" h., pr. (ILLUS.) **15-20**

McKee Roman Arch Style Shakers

Salt & pepper shakers, Roman Arch style, fired-on red, McKee, 3 1/2" h., pr. (ILLUS.) **18-25**

Variety of Salt Shakers

Salt shaker, black milk glass w/ "S" on front, aluminum cap, marked "Pat. Appld. For" on bottom, 4 1/4" h. (ILLUS. center) **15-20**
Salt shaker, milk glass w/"Salt" in green on front, aluminum cap, Hocking Glass Co., 4 1/2" h. (ILLUS. right) **10-12**

Salt shaker, milk glass w/black bird on green-leaved branch on front, aluminum cap, 5" h. (ILLUS. left) **10-15**

"The Herb Chest" Spice Shakers

Spice shakers, milk glass w/red metal caps, blue herb designs on front, marked "The Herb Chest" & "Sage," "Rosemary," "Savory," "Bay Leaves," "Marjoram," "Oregano" & "Thyme," 3 3/16" h., each (ILLUS.) **8-10**

Spice Shakers with Dutch Scenes

Spice shakers, milk glass w/various blue Dutch scenes on front, red metal caps, paper labels on reverse, red star & name of spice in red letters above scene, 3 1/4" h., each (ILLUS.) **8-10**

String Holders

String Holders were standard equipment for general stores, bakeries and homes before the use of paper bags, tape and staples became prevalent. Decorative string holders, mostly chalkware, first became popular during the late 1930s and 1940s. They were mass-produced and sold in five-and-dime stores like Woolworth's and Kresge's. Ceramic string holders became available in the late 1940s through the 1950s. It is much more difficult to find a chalkware string holder in excellent condition, while the sturdier ceramics maintain a higher quality over time.

Apple with berries, chalkware, common **35**

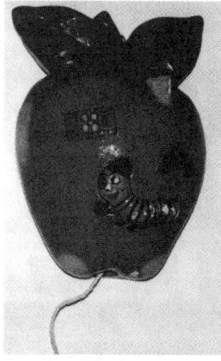

Apple with Worm String Holder

Apple with worm, chalkware, "Willie the Worm," ca. 1948, Miller Studio (ILLUS.).......... **65**

Art Deco Woman String Holder

Art Deco woman, chalkware, green beret & scarf (ILLUS.)... **275**
Balloon, ceramic, variety of colors, each **75**
Bird, ceramic, yellow bird on green nest, embossed "String Nest Pull," Cardinal China, U.S.A. **50**
Bird, chalkware, peeking out of birdhouse **175**
Boy, w/top hat and pipe, eyes to side, chalkware... **65**
Butler, ceramic, black man w/white lips & eyebrows .... **350+**

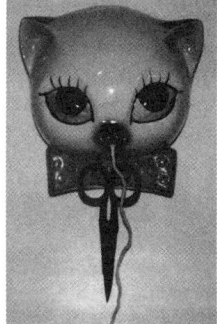

Cat Face String Holder

Cat, ceramic, white, w/large green eyes, scissors hang on bow (ILLUS.) **65**

Cat on Ball of String String Holder

Cat, chalkware, grinning, on a ball of string, Miller Studio, 1952 (ILLUS.) **60**

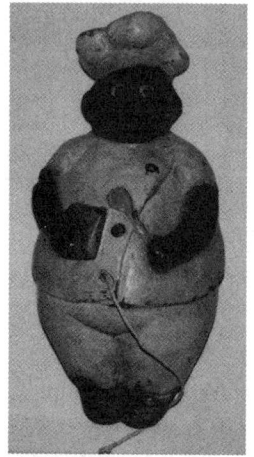

Chef w/Spoon & Box String Holder

Chef, chalkware, full-figured black chef w/spoon & blue box (ILLUS.) **275**

Chef w/Bottle & Glass String Holder

Chef w/bottle & glass, ceramic, full-figured, Japan (ILLUS.) **175**

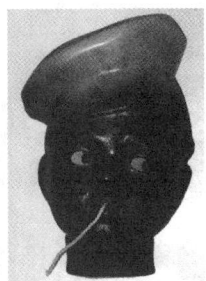

Black Chef's Face String Holder

Chef's head, chalkware, black face, white hat (ILLUS.) **200**

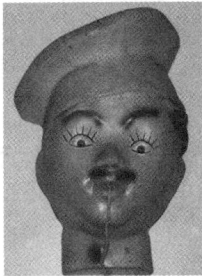

Chalkware Chef's Head String Holder

Chef's head, chalkware, common (ILLUS.) **60**

Chipmunk String Holder

Chipmunk's head, ceramic, white & brown, red & white striped hat & bow, bow holds scissors, Japan (ILLUS.) **55**

Clown, ceramic, full-figured, "Pierrot," hand holds scissors **85**

Jo-Jo the Clown String Holder

Clown, chalkware, "Jo-Jo," ca. 1948, Miller Studio (ILLUS.) **200**

Stoneware Crock String Holder

Crock, stoneware, tan, marked "Kitchen String," string hole in top along w/slot for holding scissors, England (ILLUS.) **75**

"The Darned String Caddy"

"Darned String Caddy" (The), ceramic, marked "Fitz & Floyd, MCMLXXVI" (ILLUS.) **55**

Delicious apple, chalkware, w/stem & leaves.. **25-50**

Dog, ceramic, "Bonzo" w/bee on chest **175**

Dog, ceramic, Boxer.. **135**

Dog String Holder

Dog, ceramic (ILLUS.) **175**

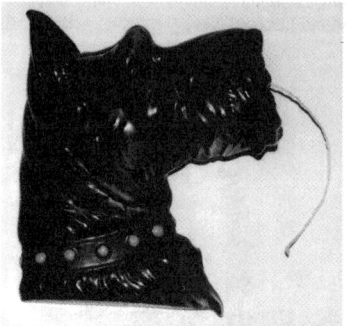

Scottie String Holder

Dog, ceramic, Scottie, marked "Royal Trico,
Japan" (ILLUS.) 135
Dog, ceramic, w/diamond shaped eyes **85-100**
Dog, ceramic, w/puffed cheeks........................ **35-55**
Dog, ceramic, w/scissors as glasses,
marked "Babbacombe Pottery, England" .. **45-65**
Dog, chalkware, w/chef's hat, "Conovers
Original" 275
Dutch Boy, chalkware, w/cap........................... 125

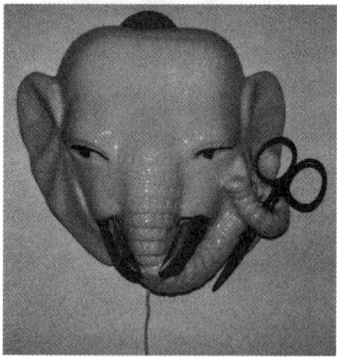

Elephant w/Pincushion String Holder

Elephant, ceramic, white w/gold tusks, pincushion on head, Japan (ILLUS.) **75**

Father Christmas String Holder

Father Christmas, ceramic, Japan
(ILLUS.) 175

Flowerpot & Spoon Holder String Holder

Flowerpot, ceramic, yellow w/measuring
spoon holder (ILLUS.) 95

Granny String Holder

Granny, ceramic, full-figured, top of nose
holds scissors that look like glasses
(ILLUS.) 50

Granny in Rocking Chair String Holder

Granny in rocking chair, ceramic, marked
"PY," Japan (ILLUS.)...................................... 125
Heart, ceramic, puffed, California Clemin-
son 75

Puffed Heart String Holder

Heart, ceramic, puffed, heart reads "You'll always have a 'pull' with me!" California Cleminsons (ILLUS.)... **95**

Humpty Dumpty String Holder

Humpty Dumpty, ceramic, sitting on wall, white & yellow (ILLUS.) **125**

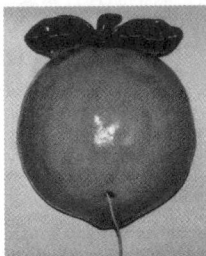

Lemon String Holder

Lemon, ceramic, Japan (ILLUS.) **95**

Little Bo Peep String Holder

Little Bo Peep, ceramic, white w/red & blue trim, marked "Japan" (ILLUS.) **175**

Mammy w/Plaid & Polka Dot Dress String Holder

Mammy, ceramic, full-figured, plaid & polka dot dress, Japan (ILLUS.)............................... **125**

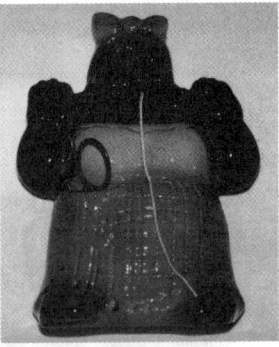

Mammy String Holder

Mammy, ceramic, full-figured, w/arms up & scissors in pocket (ILLUS.)............................. **225**
Man, ceramic, head only, drunk, designed by & marked "Elsa" on back, Pfaltzgraff, York, Pennsylvania **125**
Mexican woman, chalkware, head only, w/braids & sombrero....................................... **150**
Owl, ceramic, full-figured, Josef Originals **65**

Peasant Woman Knitting String Holder

Peasant woman, ceramic, full-figured, knitting sock, sticker reads "Wayne of Hollywood" (ILLUS.).. **175**

Penguin, ceramic, full-figured w/scissors holder in beak, marked "Arthur Wood, England" **85**

Floral Decorated Pig String Holder

Pig, ceramic, white w/red & yellow flowers & green leaves decoration, scissors holder on back near tail, Arthur Wood, England (ILLUS.).. **75**

Pineapple, chalkware, "Prince Pineapple," by Miller Studio **250**

Prayer lady, ceramic, by Enesco **300**

Sailor Boy, chalkware................................ **150**

Sailor Girl (Rosie the Riveter), chalkware...... **225**

Snail String Holder

Snail, ceramic, dark brown (ILLUS.).................. **65**

Southern Gentleman with ladies, ceramic...... **125**

Strawberry, chalkware, w/white flower, green leaves & no stem **55**

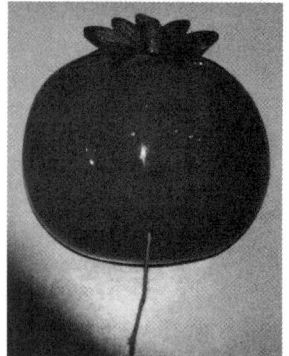

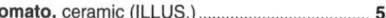

Tomato String Holder

Tomato, ceramic (ILLUS.)................................ **55**

Woman in Flowered Dress String Holder

Woman, ceramic, full-figured, blue dress w/white & red flowers, Japan (ILLUS.) **125**

Woman, ceramic, head only, arched eyebrows.. **175**

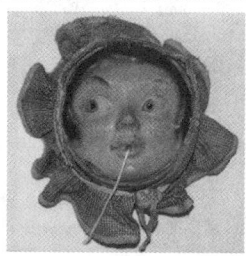

Chalkware, Cardboard & Cloth String Holder

Woman's face, chalkware on cardboard box w/cloth bonnet (ILLUS.) **150**

LACQUER

Most desirable of the lacquer articles available for collectors are those of Japanese and Chinese origin, and the finest of these were produced during the Ming and Ching dynasties, although the Chinese knew the art of fashioning articles of lacquer centuries before. Cinnabar is carved red lacquer.

Inro (small Japanese storage box), three-case style, gold ground painted w/a recumbent stag, w/cord, bead & netsuke, Japan, early 20th c., 3" l. (ILLUS. right)...... **$550**

Two Japanese Lacquer Inro

Inro (small Japanese storage box), two-case style, ground ground decorated w/gilt bird, w/cord, bead & netsuke, Japan, 19th c., 2 1/2" l. (ILLUS. left) **450**

Sewing box, cov., rectangular casket-form w/angled convex corners on short scroll feet, slightly domed cover, black ground decorated overall w/gilt Chinese landscape scenes framed by leafy vines, the interior fitted w/ivory sewing implements above a single drawer fitted w/compartments, Chinese Export, 19th c., 10 x 14", 6 1/2" h. (minor cracks, replaced hinges).. **1,610**

Table, round top on a cluster of short pedestals on a square block above the baluster-turned shaft over a tripod base w/ornately carved arched legs ending in beast heads, black decorated w/gilt landscapes on the top & shaft, Chinese Export, mid-19th c., 36" h., 31 1/2" h. **2,530**

Tea caddy, cov., deep casket-form w/angled corners, conforming domed cover, raised on gilt carved paw feet, red ground decorated w/gilt scenes of figures, dragons & foliage, the interior w/two lidded pewter canisters, w/key, Chinese Export, 19th c. **2,185**

LAUNDRY ROOM ITEMS

Clothes Sprinkler Bottles

Hand-decorated Glass Sprinkler Bottle

Bottle, glass, two-handled, green w/hand-decorated scene of two swans & lily plants (ILLUS.) **$10-20**

Cat, ceramic, black, handmade **350**

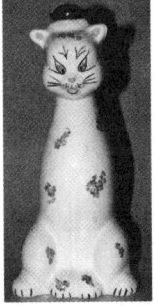

Hand-decorated Cat Sprinkler Bottle

Cat, ceramic, hand-decorated, variety of colors & designs, each (ILLUS. of one) **135**

Chinese Man Sprinkler Bottle

Chinese Man, ceramic, marked "104" on bottom, handmade, all colors, each (ILLUS. of one) **50-100**

Chinese Man w/Removable Head

Chinese man, ceramic, w/removable head (ILLUS.) **500**

Chinese Man Holding Towel

Chinese man, ceramic, white w/green collar, holding towel (ILLUS.) **500**

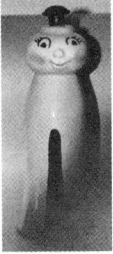

Cardinal China Clothespin Sprinkler Bottle

Clothespin, ceramic, green & white w/h.p. face, Cardinal China, rare (ILLUS.) **400**

Clothespin, ceramic, w/smiley face **250**

Plastic Clothespin Sprinkler Bottle

Clothespin, plastic, orange w/flower decoration (ILLUS.) **45**

Dearie is Weary, ceramic, Enesco **400**

Dutch Girl, ceramic **350**

Dutch Girl, ceramic, wetter-downer.................. **250**

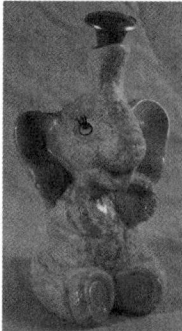

Pink & White Elephant Sprinkler Bottle

Elephant, ceramic, handmade w/rough finish, pink & white (ILLUS.)............................... **125**

Elephant, ceramic, pink & grey, trunk up, Cardinal China Co... **75**

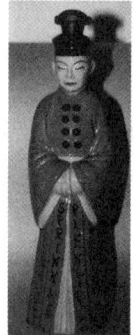

Emperor Sprinkler Bottle

Emperor, ceramic, "Sprinkle Plenty," variety of colors & designs, Holland Mold, handmade, each (ILLUS. of one) **150**

Fireman, ceramic, California Cleminsons, rare **1,500**

Iron with Embossed Rooster

Iron, ceramic, white w/embossed rooster (ILLUS.) **150**

Plastic Iron Sprinkler Bottle

Iron, plastic, green w/paper label which reads "Laundry Sprinkler also used for Watering Plants" (ILLUS.)................................ **45**

Vintage Merry Maid Sprinkler Bottle

Merry Maid, ceramic, vintage, pink, white & black, red hair (ILLUS.) **50**

Peasant Woman Sprinkler Bottle

Peasant Woman, ceramic, white, green & yellow, red hair, Provincial Pottery, California (ILLUS.) **400**

Rooster Sprinkler Bottle

Rooster, ceramic, red, white & green
(ILLUS.).. **135**

Irons

Fancy Lift Gate Box Iron

Box iron, brass & iron, fancy cut-out lift gate
(ILLUS.)... **1,200**

Lyre Lift Gate Box Iron

Box iron, brass & steel, Lyre lift gate
(ILLUS.)... **1,500**

Asbestos Boxed Iron Set

Boxed set, four bases w/one hood, one
tourist iron, one toy iron, Asbestos, the
set (ILLUS.)... **800**

Acme Carbon Iron

Charcoal iron, "Acme Carbon Iron," U.S.A.,
Pat. Mar. 15, 1910 (ILLUS.) **100**

Polish Charcoal Iron

Charcoal iron, Josef Rubin Brezezan,
Poland (ILLUS.).. **800**

Combination Reversible Iron

Combination reversible iron, marked
"Family Laundry Iron" (ILLUS.) **1,500**

Howell Detachable Handle Iron

Detachable handle iron, Howell Co.,
Geneva, Illinois (ILLUS.) **45**

Ober Detachable Handle Iron

Detachable handle iron, Ober (ILLUS.).............. **65**

Ober Detachable Handle Iron Set

Detachable handle iron, w/three bases, Ober, the set **100**

Asbestos Detachable Handle Irons

Detachable handle iron set, three bases, one hood, trivet & box, Asbestos, the set (ILLUS.).. **160**

Early Electric Iron

Electric iron, early GE F14 type (ILLUS.) **45**

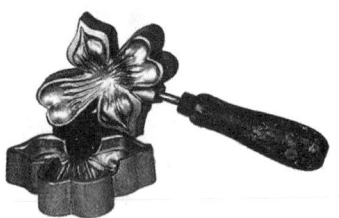

Flower Iron

Flower iron, brass, for making silk flowers (ILLUS.) **100**

"Indicator" Hand Fluter with Stand

Fluter, hand-type, "Indicator," w/separate stand, manufactured by Van Gumster & Trueman, Ilion, N.Y., Ilion Herkemer Co. NY (ILLUS.).. **1,200**

Fluter with Separate Stand

Fluter, hand-type, non-indicator w/separate stand, manufactured by Pat. Sad Iron Co., Ilion, N.Y. (ILLUS.)................................... **800**

Ribbon Crimper Fluter

Fluter, hand-type, ribbon crimper (ILLUS.)........ **325**

Coleman Fuel Iron

Fuel iron, petroleum, Coleman 4A w/accessories, blue (ILLUS.).. **150**

"Imperial" Fuel Iron

Fuel iron, petroleum, "Imperial" (ILLUS.).......... **100**

"Jubilee" Fuel Iron

Fuel iron, petroleum, "Jubilee" No. 9
(ILLUS.).. **250**

Serpent Upright Goffering Iron

Goffering iron, brass & steel, serpent up-
right (ILLUS.).. **1,500**

"Giraffe" Goffering Iron

Goffering iron, "Giraffe" (ILLUS.) **700**

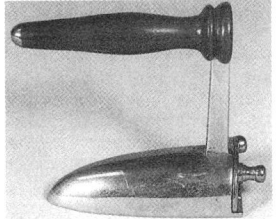

Little Box Iron

Little box iron, brass, single post, ox
tongue-style, 3" l. (ILLUS.).............................. **500**

J&E Stevens Co. Little Iron

Little iron w/wood grip, "No. 9" in star, J&E
Stevens Co., 3 1/4 l." (ILLUS.) **80**

"White City Sad Iron" Little Iron

Little iron w/wood grip, "White City Sad
Iron" on face, 3 1/2 l." (ILLUS.) **225**

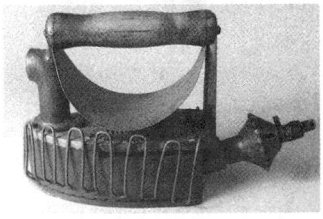

"Jewel Diamond" Gas Iron

Natural gas iron, "Jewel Diamond" w/guard
& wire shield (ILLUS.) **270**

Primitive Iron

Primitive, serpent grip (ILLUS.) **175**

"Slave" Iron with Bell in Handle

Primitive, "Slave" iron, bell in handle
(ILLUS.) **175**

French Porcelain Sadiron

Sadiron, blue porcelain, "UNIC" on face, France (ILLUS.) **100**

"Indicator" Sadiron

Sadiron, "Indicator Ilion NY, Pat'd June 4, 1878" (ILLUS.) **650**

Asbestos Sleeve Iron

Sleeve iron, nickel plated, marked "Pat. May 22, 1900," Asbestos (ILLUS.) **100**

"The Sweeney Iron"

Sleeve iron, "The Sweeney Iron - Pat. Nov. 17, 96," nickel plated (ILLUS.) **275**

Miscellaneous

Bank, "Flatiron" building, 8 1/4" h. (ILLUS. top next column) **3,200**

"Flatiron" Building Bank

Ironing board, painted wood, the scrubbed top on a folding blue-painted base w/shaped support, New England, late 19th c., 16 x 51 1/2", 29 3/4" h. **345**

LIGHTING DEVICES

Handel Lamps

The Handel Company of Meriden, Connecticut (1885-1936) began as a glass and lamp shade decorating company. Following World War I they became a major producer of decorative lamps which have become very collectible today.

Handel Lily-form Boudoir Lamp

Boudoir lamp, a bronzed metal lily pad-form rounded base w/turned up edges centering two naturalistic upright stems, the taller stem ending in a large floriform slag glass shade w/overlapping green & white slag petals, the shorter stem ending in a green slag bud, base w/brown patina, raised mark on base illegible, ca. 1903, 13" h. (ILLUS.) **$460**
Boudoir lamp, 7" d. domical reverse-painted shade decorated w/a desert scene of silhouetted camel riders & walkers against a pale yellow & gold background w/pyramids & mountains, artist-signed, No. 6557, on a slender simple bronzed metal Handel base w/gently lobed foot...... **3,304**
Boudoir lamp, 7" d. domical reverse-painted shade decorated w/scattered clusters of pink blossoms & green leaves on a frosted paneled ground, No. 6834, on a

painted white slender reeded Handel metal base **2,800**

Boudoir lamp, 7" w. molded domical squared reverse-painted shade w/a lightly scalloped rim, decorated w/a wide band of rust & yellow roses & green & grey leaves around the lower border, creamy frosted white upper section, raised on a slender ribbed standard w/an Oriental-style pierced round Handel base in grey, shade No. 6698, artist-signed **2,800**

Boudoir lamp, 8" d. domical hexagonal reverse-painted shade, decorated w/overall scattered pink & yellow roses on leafy stems w/small butterflies scattered between on a frosted ground, on a frosted glass simple pedestal Handel base w/round foot & metal banding **2,576**

Boudoir lamp, 8" d. domical reverse-painted shade decorated w/a continuous band of large & small pink rose blossoms & leaves around the lower border against a shaded grey to white front & lightly ribbed ground, on a metal Handel slender ribbed pedestal on a round Chinese-style pierced round foot, shade No. 6918, artist-signed **2,744**

Floor lamp, 24" d. conical shade w/lobed rim, decorated w/panels of intricate metal filigree in a palm tree design over panels of mottled orange, yellow & red slag glass representing a sunset skyline, on a tall bronzed metal Handel base w/a slender reeded shaft & a waisted & lobed heavy foot **11,200**

Floor lamp, 9 7/8" d. domical reverse-painted shade w/a chipped ice exterior finish, painted w/a stylized grape & vine border in purple, black, spring & moss green, against a speckled turquoise blue & rose ground, signed "Handel 734-6849," suspended from a wide bronze harp above a slender bronze standard w/a round dished foot w/knob-cast border band, overall 56 1/2" h.. **6,815**

Hall Light Decorated with Parrot

Hall light, 6" d. spherical shade w/textured amber exterior painted on the exterior w/a green & blue parrot & leafy grapevines, a round stepped bronze-patinated ceiling plaque w/a gadrooned rim above a chain & shade mount, tassel base drop, shaded signed "Handel 7006 RA" on rim, minor rim nicks, overall 28" h. (ILLUS.) **2,530**

Handel Spherical Hall Light

Hall light, spherical shade w/chipped ice finish, the exterior painted w/a highly stylized floral & geometric design in yellow, green & salmon, the patinated metal mount terminating w/a faux tassel drop, shade 9 5/8" d., overall 29" h. (ILLUS.) **764**

Handel Slag Glass Piano Lamp

Piano lamp, 6 1/8" w. tapering square slag glass shade w/four mottled green & amber panels w/striated yellow border within a metal diamond design overlay, on a single-socket base w/slender arched reeded arms attached to a round domed weighted base, impressed mark on base, metal tag on shade, cracks, 7 1/2" h. (ILLUS.) **1,380**

Table lamp, wide low conical leaded glass shade composed of a lapped arch design frame enclosing striated greenish amber & white slag glass segments, raised on a slender five-socket standard w/swelled base & round disk foot, raised mark on base, patination wear, two panels cracked, ca. 1907, 30" h. (ILLUS. top next page) **9,200**

Simple Slag Glass Handel Lamp

Table lamp, 14" d. domical reverse-painted shade decorated w/geraniums in green & reddish orange on a yellow ground, chipped ice exterior finish, on a baluster-turned patinated metal base, shade signed "Handel GC 6588," 20" h. (flake on shade rim) **1,980**

Table lamp, 15" d. conical shade decorated on the exterior w/a continuous heavily wooded landscape w/a stream in the foreground, on a slender bronzed metal Handel base w/round paneled foot, No. 5942 .... **5,600**

Table lamp, 15" d. conical shade decorated on the exterior w/overall delicate vines w/clusters of long green leaves, painted on the interior w/tall slender trees along a hillside, on a slender flaring ribbed bronze metal Handel base, No. 6411 .... **6,720**

Handel Lamp with Dutch Landscape

Table lamp, 15" d. domical reverse-painted shade, chipped ice exterior finish, interior painted w/silhouetted Dutch landscape in brown w/light pink & green, patinated metal base w/slender ribbed standard on a flaring ribbed foot, signed three times, 22 1/2" h. (ILLUS.) **3,300**

Table lamp, 16" d. domical shade w/an etched wide border band of pine needles

& a brownish red mosserine finish on the upper shade, on a slender ribbed bronzed metal Handel standard w/a flaring ribbed foot **4,480**

Handel Lamp with Chinese-style Base

Table lamp, 16 1/2" d. reverse-painted shade w/a blue textured ground trimmed w/a wide polychrome floral border, raised on a Chinese style rouleau base incised w/a band of fretwork above a textured body w/flaring foot, shade No. 6747, base & shade signed, 23 1/2" h. (ILLUS.) . **7,700**

Table lamp, 18" d. domical eight-lobed shade painted on the exterior w/a continuous landscape of slender trees w/delicate green leaves & flying birds, No. 6868, artist-signed, on a bronze metal bulbous ribbed urn-form Handel base w/a rectangular foot, ... **8,400**

Table lamp, 18" d. domical reverse-painted 'Rose Blossom' patt. shade, decorated overall w/large clusters of red, pink, purple & white rose blossoms & green foliage w/yellow & pink butterflies flying between, on a slender bronzed metal lobed standard w/a squared lobed foot, shade signed "Handel 6688 R," base w/impressed mark **23,520**

Handel Lamp with Cabin Scene Shade

Table lamp, 18" d. domical reverse-painted shade decorated w/a cabin perched on a rocky shoreline at sunset in shades of brown, yellow & purple, partial paper label, raised on a two-socket base in patinated metal w/a pod shape w/ribs & molded leaves & on four small feet, woven label on base, overall 18 3/4" h. (ILLUS.).. **2,875**

Table lamp, 18" d. domical reverse-painted shade, decorated w/a mound of trees surrounded by choppy water forming waves in the background, shades of green, pale yellow, rose red, white & maroon, raised on a bronzed metal slender urn-form standard w/a scroll-embossed rim band & a wide low-domed foot, shade & base signed **6,440**

Handel 'Treasure Island' Lamp

Table lamp, 18" d. domical reverse-painted shade decorated w/a Treasure Island design w/sailing ship & tropical isle in naturalistic colors, raised on a dark cast bronze slender waisted standard w/thick round foot (ILLUS.) **10,000**

Rose & Butterfly Shaded Handel Lamp

Table lamp, 18" d. domical reverse-painted shade decorated w/an overall design of multicolored small roses & butterflies on a pale yellow ground, raised on a slender metal urn-form base w/ribbed, domed foot, shade signed "Handel 7032," base depatinated, 24" h. (ILLUS.)...................... **8,625**

Table lamp, 18" d. domical reverse-painted shade, 'Exotic Bird' patt., decorated w/large colorful flying exotic birds against a background of dark blue, green & pale yellow foliage & clusters of large red & pink blossoms w/green leaves, raised on a slender bronzed metal tapering baluster paneled standard on a matching wide round foot, shade signed "Handel 7125 Bedique," base w/impressed mark **17,360**

Table lamp, 18" d. domical reverse-painted shade in the Jungle Bird patt., decorated w/a pair & a single large colorful macaw perched on jungle branches w/colorful leafy & flowering jungle foliage in the background, on a polychromed metal Handel base w/a vase-form shaft in tan shaded to cream & painted w/delicate white blossoms & green leafy vines, a brown lobed bottom disk above the domed & green-trimmed reeded base band, shade No. 6874 .... **21,840**

Table lamp, 18" d. domical reverse-painted shade in the Parrot & Floral patt., molded w/eight vertical lobes & decorated w/a colorful parrot perched on branches amid pink & red rose blossoms & green leaves against a deep turquoise background w/black tree trunks & branches, on a bronzed metal Handel base w/a leaf-case ring- and knob- pedestal on a round disk foot w/leaf-cast border band, shade No. 7028, artist-signed **44,800**

Handel Lamp with Banded Shade

Table lamp, 18" d. domical reverse-painted shade w/a chipped ice exterior, the interior decorated w/a wide border of repeating flowers, birds & scrolls in shades of brownish green, blue, pink & yellow on a mottled amber ground, raised on a bronze base w/three flattened scroll supports resting on a stepped round base, impressed "Handel Lamps" on top shade rim, felted base w/"Handel Lamps" woven cloth label, base patination loss, early 20th c., 24 1/2" h. (ILLUS.) **4,888**

Handel Tapestry Border Shade Lamp

Table lamp, 18" d. domical reverse-painted shade w/a chipped ice exterior, interior decorated w/a floral tapestry border in shades of green, amber, blue & red on a burnt orange ground, signed "Handel Co. S 6750," raised on a three-socket Chinese design patinated bronze wide baluster-form base w/pierced & scrolled disk foot, base unmarked, 24" h. (ILLUS.) **6,900**

Table lamp, 18" d. domical shade decorated on the exterior in opal w/overall colorful blossoms in yellow, pink & blue against tall dark brown leaves & stems, No. 6931, raised on a bronze metal base w/a vase-form shaft upon a stepped Oriental-style foot w/curved pierced-scroll design.. **8,400**

Handel Lamp with Leaded Shade

Table lamp, 18 1/2" d. conical leaded glass shade w/a wide drop apron, a top geometric border of bluish green glass over radiating panels of light green glass, the

drop apron w/a paneled border of diamond-shaped segments in bluish green & opalescent white on a light green ground, raised on a bronzed metal base w/a slender waisted standard & flaring base w/shaped feet, base marked (ILLUS.) **1,725**

Handel Bent Panel Slag Glass Lamp

Table lamp, 19 1/2" d. domical slag glass shade w/eight bent panels of amber slag glass overlaid w/a linear Art Nouveau metal design & green painted highlights, on a three-socket baluster-form patinated metal base molded w/serpentine decoration over four squared bracket feet, raised marks on shade rim & base, painted decoration possibly retouched, replaced handle, 27" h. (ILLUS.).................... **4,313**

Table lamp, 20" d. umbrella-form leaded glass shade w/a domed center & wide rounded shoulder above a wide vertical border w/pointed rim, composed of an overall floral design w/mottled green leaves in the top center w/a shoulder band of mottled yellow & white large blossoms & a border band of large orange blossoms against a green leafy ground, on a bronzed metal tapering & finely ribbed Handel base **5,600**

Handel Geometric Overlay Lamp

Table lamp, 22" d. Geometric Overlay domical leaded glass shade w/radiating bands enclosing graduated green tiles streaked w/yellow & white above a paneled drop border of yellow & white Greek key design, raised on a slender embossed bronzed standard w/rounded scrolled panel design & low feet (ILLUS.)... 9,520

Handel Lily-form Wall Sconce

Wall sconces, leaded glass, a rounded naturalistic lily-form shape on vine support joining the lily pad form wall mount of bronze metal, shade composed of overlapping green & white slag glass petals & two green slag glass buds, mount w/rich reddish brown patina, raised signature, ca. 1903, one screw missing for shade, 10" h., pr. (ILLUS. of one)............................ 1,380

Pairpoint Lamps

Well known as a producer of fine Victorian art glass and silver plate wares between 1907 and 1929, the Pairpoint Corporation of New Bedford, Massachusetts also produced a wide range of decorative lamps.

Boudoir lamp, 5" d. "Puffy" bonnet-shaped 'Four Color Rose' patt. shade, decorated w/large rose blossoms in red, pink, yellow & white, raised on a bronze metal Pairpoint base w/a reeded stem standard above a lily pad cluster foot, shade signed.. 8,960
Boudoir lamp, 5" d. "Puffy" domed & lobed 'Lilac' patt. shade, deep pink & red lilac blossoms w/green foliage & yellow & black butterflies, turquoise edge band, raised on a signed bronze Pairpoint tree trunk base.. 16,240
Boudoir lamp, 8 1/2" d. reverse-painted 'Exeter' shade decorated w/a continuous landscape of slender leafy trees in shades of green, rust & gold above butterflies & wild flowers, raised on a polished copper slender ringed & knobbed shaft on a heavy stepped foot, base marked, 15 1/2" h. 2,035

Boudoir lamp, 9" d. "Puffy" reverse-painted 'Dogwood Blossom Stratford' flat-topped domical shade decorated w/pairs of large lavender & pink roses & green leaves around the rim against a frosted clear ground w/a white lacy lattice design, raised on a patinated metal slender standard cast w/overlapping pointed leaves above the lobed & leaf-cast foot, shade & base signed, overall 14 1/2" h..................... 3,850
Boudoir lamp, 9" d. "Puffy" reverse-painted 'Papillon' shade, flat-topped domical form w/straight sides molded w/large pairs of rose blossoms & butterflies around the sides in shades of rose, red, green & creamy yellow on a creamy ground, a molded blossom at the center of the closed top, raised on a patinated metal base w/a slender paneled trumpet-form standard on a domed flaring paneled foot, base & shade signed, ca. 1915, 14" h.. 6,900
Candle lamps, each w/a mold-blown "Puffy" shade reverse-painted to depict pansies, in shades of burgundy, yellow, mauve, green, orange & white, stamped company mark, on wooden bases, 7 3/4" h., pr.. 2,233
Table lamp, 12" d. bulbous mushroom-shaped reverse-painted 'Venice' patt. shade, decorated w/pointed oval panels of stylized tulip blossoms in deep pink & white alternating w/wide bands of wavy light green & yellow bands & pale white-striped panels w/bands of small yellow ovals enclosing colorful flower clusters, raised on a Pairpoint silvered metal base w/a flattened four-lobed base w/a reeded edge, base & shade signed 7,840
Table lamp, 14" d. domed straight-sided 'Palm' shade w/a scalloped rim reverse-painted w/a countryside landscape w/tall trees in autumn colors, raised on a cast bronze metal tree trunk Pairpoint base...... 7,840
Table lamp, 14" d. domical "Puffy" reverse-painted 'Papillon' patt. shade, decorated w/colorful red & pink roses around the edge w/large flying yellow butterflies, white green-streaked background, on a slender bronzed metal square standard above a rectangular plaque foot, base signed... 13,440
Table lamp, 14" d. "Puffy" domed shade in the 'Lilac' patt., vibrant colors of purple, deep red, gold, yellow, black & green w/butterflies among lilac blossoms & leaves, on bronze Pairpoint tree trunk base... 145,600
Table lamp, 14" d. "Puffy" domical flat-topped reverse-painted 'Stratford' patt. shade, reverse-painted w/multicolored roses at the border & hummingbirds in flight against a mottled mauve & black background, shade signed, on a slender swelled bronzed metal shaft w/a wide round foot decorated w/ribbing & lappets, base signed "Pairpoint Mfg." 7,280

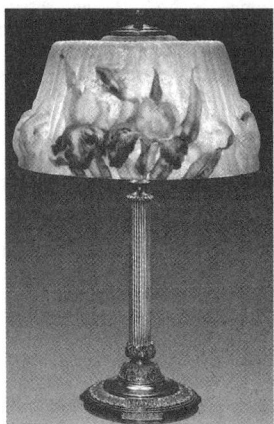

Puffy Pairpoint Lamp with Irises

Table lamp, 14" d. "Puffy" domical flat-topped reverse-painted 'Stratford' patt. shade, decorated w/blossoming irises & leaves against a blue & yellow speckled ground, in shades of yellow, purple, orange, blue & amber, marked, on a slender silvered-metal base w/reeded standard on domed leaf-banded footed base, base marked, 13 7/8" h. (ILLUS.) **8,225**

Puffy Pairpoint with Roses Border

Table lamp, 14" d. "Puffy" domical flat-topped reverse-painted 'Stratford' patt. shade, decorated w/molded border of large roses & flying hummingbirds in shades of deep rose, purple & yellow on a white linen-fold ground w/thin yellow bands, raised on a slender patinated metal base w/impressed leaf design on standard & domed ribbed foot, base impressed "Pairpoint C 3066," 21" h. (ILLUS.) **9,775**

Table lamp, 14" d. reverse-painted 'Palermo' patt. shade, open-topped, decorated w/wide bands & stripes alternating w/baroque scrolls or leafy floral scrolls in shades of pink, green, white, gold & black, in a worn silvered metal base w/a square slender shaft w/a bulbed section above the wide hexagonal foot **4,200**

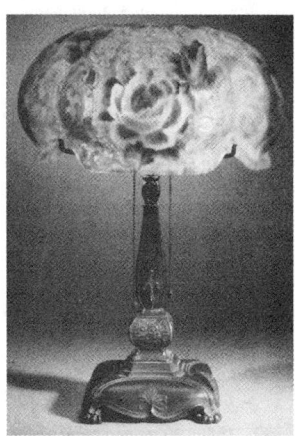

Pairpoint Lamp with Venice Shade

Table lamp, 14 1/2" d. mushroom-shaped reverse-painted 'Venice' shade decorated w/the Rose Tapestry patt., the ribbed rust background w/scrolling leaves & flowers, each panel decorated w/large rose blossoms in shades of pink & green, a central rose medallion at the closed top, on a patinated metal two-socket base w/a squared baluster-form standard w/raised flower & fleur-de-lis designs above the squared domed base, base w/impressed Pairpoint mark & "83058," patina wear, 20" h. (ILLUS.) **6,325**

Table lamp, 16" d. reverse-painted 'Bombay' shade decorated w/a continuous autumn landscape scene w/figures by a lake, raised on a patinated metal tall urn-form base w/arched side handles on a disk foot, shade & base marked, overall 22" h. **2,875**

Pairpoint Lamp with Landscape Shade

Table lamp, 16 1/2" d. domical reverse-painted shade w/a textured exterior surface, decorated w/a continuous landscape of birch trees near water w/boats & mountains in the background, naturalistic colors, raised on a three-socket patinated metal baluster-shaped ribbed knopped base, shade unsigned, base w/impressed Pairpoint mark & "D 3063," minor chips to top rim, 22 1/4" h. (ILLUS.)................................. **2,530**

Pairpoint Lamp with Exeter Shade

Table lamp, 16 1/2" d. reverse-painted 'Exeter' shade decorated w/a pastoral scene of trees & grassy hillside against a shaded blue sky, a decorative yellow band around the shoulder painted w/a repeating windmill design in brown, signed "C. Durand," raised on a gilt-metal urn supported by a double-baluster central column flanked by three scroll supports resting on a tripartite foot, base impressed "Pairpoint - D 3070" & company trademark, gilt wear, early 20th c., 23" h. (ILLUS.)` **2,990**

Table lamp, 19 3/4" d. domical reverse-painted 'Copley' shade in the Sea Gull patt., a seascape w/birds in shades of dark blue, brown, tan & white, raised on a matching baluster-form glass internally-lit base on a mahogany disk foot, artist-signed & marked, ca. 1915, overall 25 " h. **10,925**

Unique Pairpoint Urn-form Table Lamp

Table lamp, wide urn-form reverse-painted glass body decorated w/an elaborate ribbon & floral garland design in shades of blue, yellow, green, orange, charcoal, rose & eggshell white, the exterior w/gilt highlights, fitted in a gilt-metal round & band frame w/cast griffin heads atop the incurved reeded supports above the square cross-form base, 18" h. (ILLUS.)... **3,525**

Tiffany Lamps

Floor lamp, 24 1/2" d. domical leaded glass shape w/a perforated serpentine cap, composed of brickwork tiles in mottled shades of amber over a stylized geometric border finished w/a deep drop apron of amber & opalescent, rippled, vertical rectangular glass tiles, six-socket gilt-bronze standard on a cushion-shaped base, shade tag marked "Tiffany Studios New York 1616," base impressed "Tiffany Studios New York 87," 78" h. (some cracked segments, wear & spotting on bronze) **74,000**

Rare Tiffany Hydrangea Floor Lamp

Floor lamp, "Hydrangea," a 24 1/2" d. high domed leaded glass shade composed of small dark blue, dark green, mottled green & yellow & yellow petals at the top above a wide lower border of large mottled yellow, pale blue, dark blue & mottled green petals w/an uneven rim, raised on a tall slender bronze base, shade signed "Tiffany Studios - New York - 1533-21," base marked "Tiffany Studios - New York - 376," replacement metal finial, 78" h. (ILLUS. of shade) **159,750**

Tiffany Student Lamp & Favrile Shade

Student lamp, a 10" d. domical open-topped Favrile glass shade w/a ribbed design in opal white w/a wavy iridescent gold exterior decoration, fitted on a ring above the long burner supported on an arm extending from an adjustable ball joint also fitted w/a tall cylindrical fuel canister w/applied scrolled wire decoration, all raised on a domed metal base w/applied pebbled texture, shade marked "S2881," base stamped "1539," electrified, small nick on rim of shade, 24 5/8" h. (ILLUS.).. **9,775**

Table lamp, "Apple Blossom," a 16" d. domical leaded glass shade composed of overall large mottled pink & white blossoms & green leaves above a narrow dark amber border band, raised on a bronze bulbous amphora-style base w/a low domed top issuing curved shade supports above a bulbous body tapering sharply to a pointed base & held suspended in a slender tripod framework above a wide slightly dished disk foot, brown patina, shade signed, base marked "Tiffany Studios - New York - 29940," 26" h... **29,500**

Tiffany Arrowroot Table Lamp

Table lamp, "Arrowroot," 14" d. conical leaded glass shade composed of stylized arrowroot leaves & blossoms in mottled blue & green w/white opalescent blossoms, an upper & lower border of green & white tiles, rare bronze base w/pierced fern fiddlehead design in various stages of opening on a round foot, shade & base signed (ILLUS.).. **57,120**

Table lamp, "Clematis," an 18" d. wide & sharply tapering conical leaded glass shade composed of large purple, mottled red & dark blue blossoms against a mottled white & mottled green ground, a narrow flat border band of pale yellow mottled blocks, raised on a jeweled bronze base w/a bulbous jeweled knob at the top above a very slender slightly swelled standard on a domed ribbed foot w/flanged rim, shade signed, base marked "Tiffany Studios - New York - 10926," 24 1/2" h...................................... **55,375**

Table lamp, "Daffodil," 19 1/2" d. domical open-topped leaded glass shade w/cascades of yellow daffodil blossoms & green leaves issuing from the top & ending in wide border bands of mottled blue, green & yellow blocks, raised on an ornate gilt-bronze base w/a slender tapering standard pieced w/small almond-shaped openings above the lobed round foot w/large pierced leaf-form panels above small penny feet, shade marked "Tiffany Studios - New York - 1919," base impressed "Tiffany Studios - New York - 397," 26" h................................. **75,500**

Table lamp, "Dogwood," 18" d. domical leaded glass shade w/an overall design of mottled pink & white blossoms w/green highlights above a border band of matching petal & leaf-form blocks between two narrow bands of mottled green blocks, raised on a brownish green patinated bronze base w/a slender knopped & ribbed standard continuing to a round foot w/radiating raised bands of tight small scrolls ending in small scroll feet, w/pierced shade finial, base marked "Tiffany Studios - New York - 543," 24 1/4" h. **69,758**

Table lamp, "Dragonfly," 17" d. wide conical leaded glass shade w/an even bottom edge, composed of a band of large dragonflies below an upper band of yellow & reddish yellow flame-form panels & a double narrow border band of deep reddish & mottled green blocks, on a simple non-Tiffany patinated metal pedestal base, shade signed, 22 1/4" h. **20,300**

Table lamp, "Lily," seven-light, seven gold iridescent ribbed long trumpet-form shades mounted on arched or twisted bronze stems issuing from a large lily pad cluster base, shades signed, base marked "Tiffany Studios - New York - 385," 19" h. (one shade replaced w/reproduction, one shade repaired, one stem re-configured)................................... **12,600**

Table lamp, "Lily," ten-light, ten long iridescent gold ribbed trumpet-form shades attached to tall upright stems arched at the top & issuing from a large lily pad cluster base, each shade signed & base marked "Tiffany Studios - New York - 381," 20 1/2" h. **30,650**

Table lamp, "Nasturtium," 22" d. domical leaded glass shade w/overall scattered blossoms in orange, red & pink on a mottled green & translucent pink ground w/brownish stems, apron & border rows of green rectangles mottled w/reddish brown, bronze base w/slender reeded standard above a domed leaf-embossed border & small scroll feet, shade & base signed (ILLUS. top next page) **72,800**

Tiffany Nasturtium Table Lamp

Table lamp, "Peacock Feather," a 16" d. high domed leaded glass shade composed of large peacock feather tips w/reddish-orange & mottled blue 'eyes' surrounded by dark blue shaded to green & mottled greenish yellow feathers w/a mottled pale orange & green bottom border, raised on a brownish green bronze base w/a slender waisted standard above a domed, ribbed foot, shade & base signed, 22" h. **64,000**

Tiffany Pomegranate Table Lamp

Table lamp, "Pomegranate," 18" d. domical leaded glass shade composed of radiating mottled amber & green tile segments & a border of mottled orange & amber pomegranates, metal rim tag reads "Tiffany Studios New York 1457," raised on a three-socket fixture over a slightly swollen slender paneled bronze shaft w/a flar-

ing round foot, dark brown patina, base stamped "Tiffany Studios New York 534," minor spotting on base, 22 1/4" h. (ILLUS.) **14,950**

Table lamp, "Poppy," 20" d. conical leaded glass shade w/an overall design of poppy blossoms in shades of red & violet opalescent, the centers overlaid w/bronze filigree, the leafage in shades of mottled blue & green & overlaid around the lower border w/bronze filigree, the background in mottled striated blue & white, the apron & upper border in a colorful rippled glass, on a twisted vine bronze base w/wide round swirled foot, base & shade signed.. **123,200**

Table lamp, "Swirling Lemon Leaf," 18" d. domical leaded glass shade composed of upper & lower sections of small mottled green & yellow tiles flanking a narrow band of swirled yellow & dark green leaves, on a tall bronze base w/a bulbed top above a flaring reeded shaft & wide cushion foot, shade signed & base marked "Tiffany Studios - New York - 28642," 25 1/2" h....................................... **18,000**

Tiffany Tulip Pattern Lamp

Table lamp, "Tulip," 16" domical leaded glass shade w/a design of tulip blossoms & leaves in shades of yellow, violet & green, foliage in rippled glass, raised on a heavy bronze urn-form base w/slender strap supports to round foot, shade & base signed (ILLUS.)................................. **41,440**

Lamps, Miscellaneous

Czechoslovakia art glass boudoir lamp, a high mushroom-form shade in spatter glass in yellow, blue, aqua & green, raised on a matching slender baluster-form base, chased metal three-arm mount, ca. 1930, rim chip, 13 1/4" h. (ILLUS. top next page) **460**

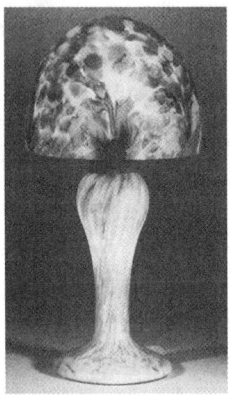

Czechoslovakian Boudoir Lamp

Daum Nancy table lamp, Art Nouveau style, a cameo glass tulip blossom-form shade in yellow overlaid in peach & cut w/petals, mounted on gilt-bronze base in the form of a tall slender curved leafy stem on a fanned scroll-cast foot, shade unsigned, base signed "L. Majorelle - Nancy," France, ca. 1900, overall 20 1/2" h.. **46,000**

Rare Dirk Van Erp Table Lamp

Dirk Van Erp table lamp, Arts & Crafts style, the wide conical shade composed of tapering mica panels between hammered copper framework, raised on four spider arms above the hammered copper tapering bulbous ovoid base, early 20th c. (ILLUS.) **60,500**

Emeralite desk lamp, a flared amber glass shade w/floral-textured surface, reverse-painted w/scrolling twig & floral border, amber glass panel light diffuser set in shade, raised on an adjustable square standard over a domed square patinated metal base, metal manufacturer's tag, H.G. McFaddon and Co., New York, ca. 1916, 8 3/4" l., 12 3/4" h. **1,380**

Jefferson table lamp, 16" d. domical reverse-painted shade decorated w/a caramel ground w/scattered dark pink wild rose blossoms w/green leaves above a two inch wide wine-colored band near

the rim also decorated w/the wild roses, raised on a bronze-patinated slender baluster-form metal base w/dished & ribbed foot, signed.. **16,500**

Early English Argand Lamp

Argand lamps, bronze & glass, double-arm, a central upright lobed urn-form font above turned cross arms ending in burners supporting frosted & etched tulip-form glass shades, raised on a squared, stepped pedestal & square foot, labeled "Messenger & Sons," England, manufactured for Alfred Welles, Boston, early 19th c., surface wear, soiling, 20" h., pr. (ILLUS. of one) **2,185**

Art Deco table lamp, figural, a partially draped gilt-metal seated female nude, her outstretched hand resting on her knee holding a petal-form alabaster shade, the figure raised on a rectangular alabaster base, ca. 1930, 5 1/2 x 14", 12 1/4" h. (gilt wear, minor edge chips) **460**

Arts & Crafts Wood & Slag Glass Lamp

Arts & Crafts table lamp, slag glass & oak, a 17 1/2" w. square tapering open-topped shade w/an oak frame, each panel w/slag glass fan & geometric designs in pink, green & red on a striated caramel ground, the scalloped wood apron w/round cut-outs, raised on a pedestal composed of four square columns over a square footed base, early 20th c., a few cracked glass segments, 27" h. (ILLUS.) **978**

Astral table lamp, a large spherical open-topped frosted & etched glass shade w/a Gothic panel design, fitted on a wide brass ring suspending long triangular prisms above the gilt-bronze pedestal base w/a baluster-form stem above four cast dolphins above the domed & squared rococo-style footed base, elec-trified, mid-19th c., 23" h. **1,840**

Chicago Mosaic table lamp, 18" d. domi-cal leaded glass shade, composed of scattered pink rose blossoms & buds & green leaves against an amber ground, uneven border, on a Chicago Mosaic gilt-metal base w/a slender urn-form handled shaft above a ribbed & lobed round foot ... **3,360**

Duffner & Kimberly table lamp, a 19" d. domical leaded glass shade w/a large shell & medallion design above an un-even lower border, a bright striated sky blue & multi-hued background w/shells & medallions in vermillon & orange & en-closed w/mottled green leafy scrolls, on a bronze metal Duffner base w/a slender ribbed baluster-form shaft on a round knobbed foot w/greenish verdigris patina

.... **22,400**

Lithophane & Ruby-Flashed Hall Lamp

Hall hanging lamp, lithophane & ruby-flashed glass, an upright square form w/beveled corners, each side panel set w/a white porcelain lithophane plaque above a narrow leaf - and flower-en-graved ruby-flashed panel all framed in brass, narrow ruby-flashed engraved

panels also at each corner, late 19th - early 20th c., 9 1/2" h. (ILLUS.)................... **1,495**

Jefferson Table Lamp

Jefferson table lamp, 18" d. domical re-verse-painted shade, painted w/a land-scape of a lake & woodland in naturalistic tones, two-socket fixture on a tapered five-sided standard w/a flaring foot, dark green patinated metal, shade indistinctly signed "Jefferson Co. WJS," minor shade imperfections, early 20th c., 22 3/4" h. (ILLUS.) **2,645**

Kerosene hanging parlor lamp, a high domed open-topped milk glass shade decorated w/a colorful transfer-printed scene of Kate Greenaway-style Victorian children relaxing on the grass under a large leafy tree, a squatty bulbous milk glass font w/matching decoration, ornate stamped brass cap ring & support ring for the shade w/brass suspension chains, stamped brass fittings around the font w/delicate scrolling brasswork connect-ing the shade ring & font & continuing into a scrolling base drop, the shade ring hung w/numerous faceted prisms, ca. 1890, overall 32" h..................................... **770**

Victorian Hanging Parlor Lamp

Kerosene hanging parlor lamp, original embossed brass frame supporting a green & red floral-decorated milk glass domed shade & matching bulbous font, ornate scrolling brass lower frame, cut crystal prisms, original smoke bell & match holder, removable electric socket, chain mechanism complete, Miller Co., ca. 1890s, 15" d. (ILLUS.) **784**

Kerosene table lamp, cut-overlay glass, the bulbous inverted pear-shaped font in white cut to cranberry w/ovals, stars & quatrefoils, w/a brass collar & raised on a reeded brass columnar standard on a stepped painted white marble square base w/an embossed brass band, mid-19th c., 15" h. (minor chips on base) **920**

Kerosene table lamp, cut-overlay glass, the inverted bell-form font & slender waisted standard in cranberry cut to white cut to clear w/ovals, loops, quatrefoils & circles, a brass collar & connector between the font & standard & a flaring ringed brass foot raised on a painted black marble stepped square base w/embossed sheet brass band, mid-19th c., 17" h. (chips to base)................................... **4,600**

Kerosene table lamp, Ripley double Marriage lamp, pressed glass w/stepped squared milk glass base w/brass connnector to a white clambroth upper section w/top center well flanked by blue clambroth fonts w/brass collars, marked "D.C. Ripley, Pat. Pending," ca. 1880s, 12 1/8" h. (minor roughness on base)........... **770**

Ripley "Marriage" Lamp

Kerosene table lamp, Ripley "Marriage" lamp, double bulbous blue fonts w/burner rings flank a clambroth match holder & harp-form support joined by a brass collar to the milk glass pedestal base w/stepped squared & scrolled foot, marked w/1870 patent date, D.C. Ripley and Company, very minor base chips, 12 3/4" h. (ILLUS.)...................................... **1,265**

Pan lamp, wrought iron, an arched tripod base w/scalloped collar fitted above the legs centering a tall slender iron rod w/a

small round open fluid pan on adjustable bracket, ring finial at the top, old dark pitted finish, 24 3/4" h. **605**

Reverse-Painted Table Lamp

Reverse-painted table lamp, 19" d. reverse-painted shade composed of six wide tapering ribbed glass panels mounted in a metal framework & painted w/a continuous desert landscape w/palm trees, lakes & mountains, on a tall tapering cylindrical glass paneled base w/matching decoration & mounted in a scrolled & pierced gilt-metal framework on a egg-and-dart embossed foot rim, unsigned, early 20th c., 23" h. (ILLUS.)......... **990**

Fine Victorian Sinumbra Lamp

Sinumbra table lamp, gilt-brass & glass, a slender columnar standard raised on a petal-molded square base, the squatty wide clear frosted & engraved shade w/a tall flaring central opening decorated w/flowers & baskets, the shade ring hung w/cut prisms, mid-19th c., 31" h. (ILLUS.) **2,875**

Slag Glass Lamp with Flat Panels

Slag glass table lamp, 17 1/2" d. eight-paneled shade composed of flat caramel slag glass panels overlaid w/a lattice & urn design patinated metal frame, raised on a two-socket slender reeded & leaf-embossed standard on a round leaf-embossed foot, base marked "EM & Co.," some glass panels replaced, early 20th c., 26" h. (ILLUS.) **863**

Ornate Slag & Filigree Table Lamp

Slag glass table lamp, 17 1/2" w. paneled pyramidal shape w/striated green & white slag glass panels completely overlaid w/an ornate pierced metal filigree of leaves on trailing vines, beaded & braided trim, raised on a matching tapering paneled standard w/flaring base of matching overlaid slag glass, on four paw feet, four-socket fixture w/wiring for illuminating the base, attributed to Riviere Studios, early 20th c., wear, minor repairs, 26 12" h. (ILLUS.) **2,300**

Slag glass table lamp, 19" d. domical caramel slag paneled shade w/floral filigree overlay, supported on a conforming cast-metal base, early 20th c., 24" h. **880**

Slag glass table lamp, 19" d. domical shade composed of six amber slag glass bent panels fitted w/a repainted cast-metal framework, raised on a tapering cylindrical base w/inset amber slag glass panels fitted in the pierced metal framework, early 20th c., 21" h. **688**

Slag Glass Lamp with Ornate Overlay

Slag glass table lamp, deep domical shade composed of wide bent panels of slag glass overlaid w/an ornate openwork metal overlay w/a landscape of tall trees & woodland meadows, on a slender brass-plated reeded standard above the scalloped & scrolled foot all cast w/leaves & beading, signed "Royal Art Glass Co. - 1912," shade metal w/gold repaint, 24" h. (ILLUS.).................................... **715**

Post & Company Student Lamp

Student lamp, brass, double burner, a rounded domed foot supporting a slender standard w/large cylindrical font & arched loop upright handle, the font issuing straight arms ending in slender cylindrical burner supports & shade rings, original domed open-topped milk glass shades w/clear chimneys, stamped mark "Post & Co.'s American Student Lamp, Cincinnati," about 24" h. (ILLUS.) **2,090**

Student lamp, brass, single-light, a round domed foot centered by a tall slender rod w/top ring, an adjustable cross arm w/an upright cylindrical font opposite a slender cylindrical burner support fitted w/a slender clear glass chimney & a milk glass ball shade, ring beneath burner marked "Cleveland Safety Library Lamp," never electrified, last quarter 19th c., 20 7/8" h. **440**

Wilkinson & Suess Table Lamp

Wilkinson & Suess table lamp, 19 1/2" d. parasol-shaped leaded glass shade composed of radiating panels of caramel & light green glass segments, drop apron w/square opalescent & red triangular shaped jewels, raised on a slender reeded three-socket standard w/a flaring scroll- and foliate-embossed footed Suess base, early 20th c., some cracked segments, 24" h. (ILLUS.) **2,070**

Wilkinson table lamp, 20" d. conical leaded glass shade composed of radiating bands of large & small mottled yellowish amber blocks above a wide border band of nasturtium blossoms in shades of pink, red, green & yellow, serpentine border, on a Wilkinson bronzed metal base w/a slender ribbed shaft above a scroll-cast domed & four-footed base **8,120**

Other Lighting Devices

Chandeliers

Arts & Crafts, leaded glass, petal-form shade of radiating bent glass panels of red & amber slag, highlighted by a border of diamond-shaped green glass segments, suspended from patinated metal chains, early 20th c., shade 14" d., pr. **805**

Blued Steel Chandelier

Blued steel, six-light, Louis XVI-Style ormolu, ribbon-tied corona supporting a central stem & quiver of arrows mounted w/Bacchic masks, supporting acanthus-sheathed reeded branches, each mounted w/a bird & terminating in a ram's mask, electrified, in the manner of Pierre Gouthiere, 20th c., 33 1/2" h. (ILLUS.) **5,500**

Brass, w/five Steuben art glass shades, domed brass ceiling mount terminating w/a hook, chain drop supporting fixture w/raised leaf decorations & five shade mounts & bell-form gold lustre glass shades w/gold hearts & threading & gold Aurene interiors, silver fleur-de-lis acid stamp, Corning, New York, drop 39 1/2", 19" d., chips to some top rims (ILLUS. below)... **1,265**

Brass Chandelier

Brass, w/six Steuben art glass shades, circular domed ceiling mount w/three chain drops, supporting round domed fixture w/etched curvilinear & floral motifs & extensions suspending six bell-form glass shades w/ruffled rims, creamy white lustre & pulled gold Aurene striations on rims, gold Aurene interiors, shape No. 2282, silver fleur-de-lis acid stamp, drop 23", 20 1/2" d., dents on shade mounts **6,325**

Bronze, w/alabaster panels, inscribed "Albert Cheuret," ca. 1925, 24" h. **94,000**

Fine Classical Solar Chandelier

Classical style, brass & cast gilt-metal, four-light Solar model, the leaf- and grape-cast scalloped corona above a flared reeded standard, enclosed by four leaf scroll chains leading to a circular pan issuing leaf-cast S-scrolled arms supporting tapering fonts w/globular frosted glass & wheel-cut shades, a central leafy base drop, electrified, mid-19th c., 33" w., 36" h. (ILLUS.) **10,200**

Cut Glass Chandelier

Cut glass, eighteen-light, Neoclassic style ormolu, w/domed acanthus-cast corona, above a band set w/square lozenges & hung w/drop festoons, above spreading drop chains supporting a similar central band surmounted by anthemion-crested drop-set laurel wreaths, above ten graduated tiers of drops, w/faceted ball terminal, ca. 1900, 70" h. (ILLUS.) **7,500**

Cut Glass Chandelier

Cut glass, fifteen-light, Neoclassic style ormolu, the scrolled acanthus-cast corona above husk & glass drop chains supporting a band alternately cast w/acanthus-flanked baskets of flowers & flambeaux flanked by adorsed dolphins, above tapering husk-cast straps & further glass drop chains, w/fruit terminal, electrified, ca. 1900, 51 1/2" h. (ILLUS.) **5,500**

Cut Glass Chandelier

Cut glass, ten-light, the scrolled corona above husk & bead chains, supporting a central foliate-pierced band hung w/ribbon-tied lights & pendant drops, w/further bead chains below, electrified, ca. 1900, 39 1/2" h. (ILLUS.) **4,500**

Cut Glass Chandelier

Cut glass, thirty-six-light, Rococo style ormolu, of cage form, hung throughout w/flowerhead, star & lozenge-shaped drops, ca. 1900, 54" h. (ILLUS.) **11,000**

Baccarat Glass Chandelier

Cut glass, twenty-five-light, Rococo style ormolu, hung throughout w/pear & lozenge-shaped drops & prisms, the central baluster stem supporting an upper tier of scrolled arms & a lower tier mounted w/obelisks on star-shaped bases, above two tiers of lights, each w/spirally-fluted drip-pan & urn-shaped sconce, w/faceted spheroid terminal, the glass stamped throughout "BACCARAT/DEPOSE," Baccarat, Paris, electrified, ca. 1900, 53" h., 44 1/2" d. (ILLUS.) **18,000**

Cut glass, twenty-one-light, Neoclassic style ormolu, the acanthus corona above a domed reeded strapwork top hung w/floral swags, above tapering drop & husk pendant chains, terminating in eight down-turned trumpet-shaped lights joined by floral swags, above a guilloché-cast band supporting ten tiers of drops, ca. 1900, 62 1/4" h. (ILLUS. top next column).. **9,000**

Cut Glass Chandelier

Empire-Style, gilt- and patinated bronze, twelve-light, a large round central patinated bronze disk w/a conical top & a slightly round bottom centered by a pineapple drop, the edge band mounted w/four large figural spread-winged gilt-bronze swans each supporting three candle sockets, suspended from four chains composed of metal disks, rods & classical masks hung from the upper small round support ring w/gilt acanthus finials, Europe, 19th c., 36" h. **7,200**

Gilt Metal & Cut Glass Chandelier

Gilt metal & cut glass, twenty-four-light, Italian Baroque style, lace work, hung throughout w/beaded drops & flowerheads, w/beaded corona above latticed cage-form upper section, the central upright supporting an upper tier of eight beaded branches & a lower tier of sixteen, each w/circular drip-pan & cylindrical sconce, terminating in a spheroid finial, electrified, ca. 1880, 51" h., 43" d. (ILLUS.) **19,000**

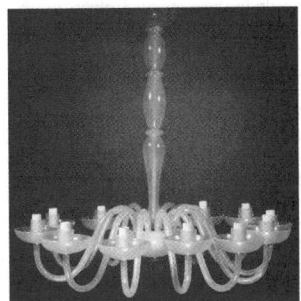

Czechoslovakian Glass Chandelier

Glass, twelve-light, Czechoslovakian, painted metal ceiling mount suspending a yellow-green glass standard w/alabaster bulbed segments, supporting twelve yellow-green curved arms each fitted w/shallow bobeche, ca. 1930, drop 23, dia. 28 1/2" sight (ILLUS.)............................... **748**

Lalique Molded Glass Chandelier

Lalique-signed, molded glass, "Fougeres," Rene Lalique, designed in 1924, 33" h., 31 1/2" d. (ILLUS.)...................................... **17,625**

Lalique Opalescent Glass Plafonnier

Lalique-signed, opalescent glass plafonnier, "Deux Sirenes," molded R. LALIQUE, Rene Lalique, designed in 1921, 15 1/2" d. (ILLUS.)...................................... **14,100**

Leaded Glass Chandelier

Leaded glass, Greek key shade, domed shade composed of radiating geometric segments of striated caramel & white glass, lower cobalt blue glass Greek key pattern border, early 20th c., America, shade 11 3/4" h., 24 1/2" d., hardware not original (ILLUS.).. **173**

French Rococo Style Ormolu

Ormolu, thirty-three-light, French Rococo style, the pierced corona hung w/fruit & floral pendants, above a central palm trunk upright flanked by scrolled acanthus volutes, supporting an upper tier mounted by three music-making putti & w/three lights, above a lower tier of six acanthus branches each supporting five naturalistically-cast lights, w/acanthus & fruit terminal, ca. 1880, 46" h. (ILLUS.) ... **32,000**

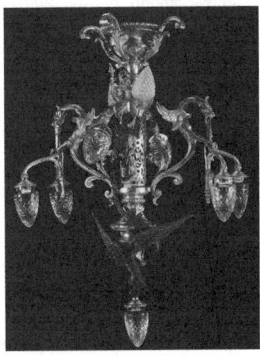

Patinated Bronze Chandelier

Patinated bronze, eight-light, French ormolu, the scrolled acanthus corona above a pierced barrel upright mounted w/a pair of satyrs supporting flambeaux & grotesque beast branches, w/a further pair of dragon branches each terminating in two lights, the lower section cast w/a coiled dragon, w/cut & frosted glass shades, possibly by Ferdinand Barbedienne, Paris, ca. 1880, 43 1/2" h. (ILLUS.)...................... **18,000**

Silvered Bronze & Alabaster Chandelier

Silvered bronze, w/alabaster panels, inscribed "Albert Cheuret," ca. 1925, 23" h., approx. 19" w. (ILLUS.)................ **22,325**

Tiffany-signed, "Black-eyed Susan," a 29" d. sharply tapering open-topped leaded glass shade composed of large swirled pale yellow & shaded dark gold & brown blossoms above dark green, mottled green & pale yellow leaves & stems, dark amber narrow border band w/a finely beaded metal edging, suspended from long chains **64,000**

Tin, six-light, a round flat band fitted w/six candle cups w/drip trays suspended from three chains of linked metal rods joined to a small top disk, 19th c., 26" h. (wear) .. **1,725**

Wood & tin, twelve-light, country-style, a slender central ring- and rod-turned shaft issuing twelve slender iron wire arched & upturned arms each supporting a tiny candle cup w/crimped edges, 20th c., 24" h. **550**

Wrought iron, eight-light, a central shaft w/hook at each end w/eight curved arms which extend to form candle sockets, American, early 19th c., 23" d., drop 25"... **2,875**

Wrought iron, six-light, a wide central ring w/six incurved scrolled iron drops & six S-scroll iron bar arms around the top each ending in a candle socket, three shaped short iron bars for the three hanging chains, blacksmith-made, probably 19th c., 22 1/2" d., overall 38" h..................... **770**

Lanterns

Barn candle lantern, wood & glass, an upright mortised wood framework w/corner posts, four glass panels, tin top & wire bail handle, 10" h. (one pane cracked) **275**

Barn candle lantern, wood & glass, an upright mortised wood framework w/corner posts mortised through top & base & held w/pegs, tin candle socket & lined air hole in top, wire hinges, latch & handle, 9 3/4" h. plus handle (minor edge damage & burned hole in top) **523**

Candle lantern, painted pine, cherry & glass, the upright rectangular dovetailed frame w/chamfered & pierced top & wrought-iron handle above four scratch-beaded sides w/diamond glazed & pierced panels, one panel forming a hinged door opening to a candle socket & pierced tin reflector, original bluish green paint, New England, early 19th c............. **25,300**

Candle lantern, pierced tin Revere-type, cylindrical w/hinged doors & conical top w/ring strap handle, pierced designs w/the initials "N.A." in the door, 13 1/2" h. plus handle (some battering & repair)........... **303**

Candle lantern, sheet copper, Arts & Crafts style, an upright square form w/one side forming a hinged door, each side pierced through w/banded designs w/three starbursts in vertical allignment, each centered by a colored glass jewel, a low pointed four-sided top, original dark patina, Bradley & Hubbard, early 20th c., stamped mark, 7" sq., 12" h. **385**

Candle lantern, tin & glass, a small cylindrical tin font base supporting a large round clear blown glass globe w/a cylindrical cap & conical pierced top w/ring strap handle, traces of old dark japanning w/light rust, 10" h. plus handle (candle socket replaces font) **385**

Candle lantern, tin & glass, hexagonal, tall upright form w/six vertical glass panels each w/vertical wire guards & two forming the door, tall crimped conical vented cap w/ring handle, single candle socket inside, New England, early 19th c., 15 1/2" h. (minor corrosion, electrified)......... **805**

Candle lantern, tin & glass, upright rectangular form w/tin frame w/four glass sides, one forming sliding door, pyramidal top w/a chamfered design & large ring handle, wire loop side protectors, 12 1/2" h. plus ring handle (one old glass panel) **165**

Candle lantern, tin, hanging-type, eight-sided tapered glass globe w/a tin font, base & top, mushroom top w/ring handle, top & base w/star & diamond-shaped piercings, 10" h. plus ring handle (brass burner appears to be old replacement) **330**

Candle lantern, tin, hanging-type, three glass panels w/a tin sliding back panel, mushroom top w/ring handle, 19th c., 14 1/2" h. (corrosion, one broken glass panel) **115**

Candle lantern, tin, upright square form w/the sides composed of vertical tin strips originally enclosing three panes of glass, square tin base & top w/pierced conical cap & large ring handle, 19th c. (glass missing).. **165**

Candle lantern, tin w/glass sides, domed top w/two vents, punched leaf & star designs & ornate pierced top, double fluted candle sockets w/snuffer (now attached to base), one side panel opens, yellow repaint w/red striping, 4 3/4 x 9 1/8", 15 3/4" h. (minor wear to paint) 358

Candle lantern, tin w/three glass sides w/wire guards, pointed top w/punched star design & ring handle, back marked "Parker's Patent, Boston, 1853," 11" h. plus ring handle 385

Fluid lantern, blown glass & tin, a short cylindrical tin font w/brass collar below the squatty onion-form clear glass globe topped by a cylindrical top w/pointed cap & large ring handle, the top w/star & diamond pierced designs, old pitted finish, mid-19th c., 10" h. plus handle 440

Fluid lantern, tin & glass, a short cylindrical tin font supporting a cobalt blue blown glass ovoid globe topped by a cylindrical cap w/pierced design air vents & wire bail handle, 19th c., 10 1/2" h. (small chips on top edge of cap, brass burner replaced) 578

Early Footman's Lantern

Footman's lantern, wood & glass, a rectangular wood-framed box-form w/a lift-top w/arched bail handle, three sides w/glass pane w/wire guards, back w/punched tin plate, frame painted dark green w/h.p. red border designs & porcelain buttons, top w/yellow stenciled label "H.B. Ost... Manufacturer, Angola, N.Y....," inside of top w/floral felt panel, hook damaged, minor wear, 19th c., 5 1/4 x 7 3/4", 6 1/4" h. plus handle (ILLUS.) 220

Hall lantern, Arts & Crafts style, slag glass, a slightly tapering upright square form w/a wide four-sided tapering top w/electric fitting, the sides composed of narrow & slightly wider stripes of varied caramel slag glass, the sides of the top w/light caramel slag panels, fitted in a metal framework w/worn patina, early 20th c., 8" w., 13" h. 880

Kerosene lantern, bull's-eye style, japanned bull & glass, cylindrical w/sliding door at the back opposite the clear thick glass convex hinged front lens, tiered pointed & ruffled vented top, double wire handles & belt clip, late 19th - early 20th c., 7 1/2" h. (wear) 248

Kerosene lantern, tin, brass & glass, a round slightly domed foot centered by a short cylindrical font w/air holes around

the top & fitted w/a brass double spout burner, clear glass pear-shaped globe within wire cage, cylindrical cap w/pierced air holes & a wire bail handle, removed base marked "Pat. Sep. 14. 78," late 19th c., 9 1/2" h. (some resoldering) 83

Skater's lantern, brass, tin & glass, a domed & ringed font base supporting a round burner fitted w/an emerald green glass baluster-form globe, pierced domed cap w/a wire bail handle, 7" h. 468

Skater's lantern, tin & glass, a domed font base supporting a round burner fitted w/a clear pressed glass globe, pierced domed cap w/a wire bail handle, "Perko Wonder Junior," 6 7/8" h. plus handle 72

Traveler's lantern, tole & glass, square scalloped frame, collapsible w/mica panels, brown japanning w/yellow stenciling & label "Minor's Patent, Jan 24th 1865," 5 1/8" h. (minor wear) 385

Whale oil lantern, tin & glass, a round tin base w/flared foot supporting the clear blown glass pear-shaped globe, cylindrical cap w/conical top w/pierced designs & large ring handle, removable font w/whale oil burner, worn original brown japanning, probably New England Glass Co., first half 19th c., 11" h. plus handle........ 358

Whale oil lantern, tin & glass, a short cylindrical tin font w/flattened flaring foot supporting a single wick burner enclosed by a clear blown glass squatty onion-form globe within a wire guard, the cylindrical cap pierced w/vent holes below the conical top w/strap ring handle, 19th c., 9" h. plus handle (some resoldering) 385

Shades

Fine Bigelow and Kennard Shade

Bigelow and Kennard-signed, domical leaded glass shade composed of rose blossoms in reddish orange undulating glass segments, rippled green leaves within a striated green & red ground, irregular border, two metal rim tags, one impressed "Bigelow Studios," the other "Bigelow, Kennard & Co., Boston," early 20th c., some cracked segments, 21 1/2" d., 9 1/4" h. (ILLUS.) 20,700

Handel, 20" d. umbrella-form nine-paneled shade w/bent slag glass panels in striated tones of rose & yellow above a border band of green slag glass, the upper panels w/a patinated overlay of tropical trees, the border band w/undulated overlay design, scalloped rim, joints reinforced, early 20th c. (ILLUS. top next page) 7,475

Handel Bent Panel Slag Glass Shade

Leaded glass, 22 1/2" d. domical leaded glass w/a brown slag ground & colored floral border band in rose & yellow, early 20th c. **880**

Lustre Art-signed, bell-form, amber lustre glass w/five pulled white feathers on an iridescent gold ground, ca. 1920, each signed "Lustre Art," 2 1/2" d., 5" h., pr. **403**

Quezal Bell-form Shade

Quezal-signed, tall ribbed bell-form w/overall gold iridescence w/magenta highlights, 5 1/4"h., pr. (ILLUS. of one) **275**

Quezal Tulip-shaped Shades

Quezal-signed, wide tulip-shaped shade w/gently flared & ruffled rim, sixteen lightly molded ribs, overall gold iridescence, signed on base flange, 5 1/4" h., pr. (ILLUS.). **330**

Steuben-signed, tapering cylindrical form w/the rim opening band narrower than the body, Ivrene w/slight iridescence & acid-etched w/a medallion & swag design, 3 1/2" d., 4 1/2" h. **86**

Tiffany-signed, 15 5/8" d. domical leaded glass Fleur-de-lis shade w/a design of radiating mottled green glass tiles w/a band of mottled greenish amber fleur-de-lis, rim impressed "Tiffany Studios New York 1437-5," 6 1/2" h. (out of round, cracked segments) **6,038**

Tiffany Leaded Glass Acorn Shade

Tiffany-signed, Acorn patt., 14" d. domical leaded glass shade composed of mottled green segments w/a band of mottled amber & green acorns, stamped rim tag, early 20th c., 5 3/4" h. (ILLUS.)................. **7,475**

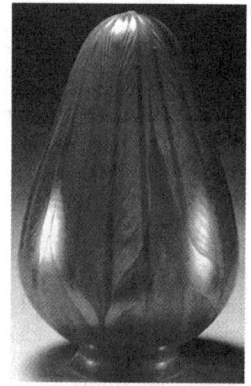

Tiffany-signed Favrile Shade

Tiffany-signed, oblong bullet-form, iridescent gold cased over white & decorated w/a pulled green feather design, signed, w/replacement bronze hardware, 7" d., 11 1/4" h. (ILLUS.) **8,400**

Wedgwood China Lithophane Shade

Wedgwood-signed, bone china lithophane-type, a wide shallow dished form, pale yellow ground w/intaglio design of Dancing Hours design surrounding a central ring of radiating acanthus leaf & bellflower design, 20th c., printed mark, 13 7/8" d. (ILLUS.) **1,265**

LIPSTICK HOLDER LADIES

Collecting items for the woman's vanity has gained much popularity in recent times. There has always been a need to organize all her paraphernalia, whether it be jewelry, perfume, hair accessories or makeup. Everyone knows that the right color lipstick is essential to the outfit one wears. Where do we keep all these different shades of lipstick? In the 1940s through the 1960s the lipstick "lady" seemed to be the answer. What a cute way to have your lipsticks right at hand. These adorable ladies, usually made from some type of ceramic material, seem to have gotten the job done well. Keeping them within reach at your dressing table kept them readily available.

Lipstick ladies are not easy to find. Because of their fragile nature, many were relegated to the trash can after use or damage.

Josef Originals Lipstick Holder Lady

Figure of a girl, brown hair pulled up at top, short torso on wide domed pale blue skirt w/lipstick holders, by Josef Originals (ILLUS.) **45**

Standing Girl with Flower Bouquet

Figure of a girl, black hair pulled up, standing w/arms to side & a small bouquet of yellow & green flowers, widely flaring ruffled golden yellow gown (ILLUS.) **$50**

Holt Howard "Daisy Dorable" Girl

Figure of a girl, "Daisy Dorable," cute stylized small girl w/blonde hair in pony tail & holding a large blossom to her face, standing at the center of a lobed petalform holder base trimmed in violet, Holt Howard (ILLUS.)... **75**

Girl Holding Sides of Gown Holder

Figure of a girl, black hair pulled up & tied w/pink bow, standing holding out the sides of her peach-colored gown w/embossed flowers (ILLUS.).................................... **55**

Flower Child Lipstick Holder

Figure of a girl, Flower Child, a young girl w/long blonde hair, arms crossed on her chest holding pink blossoms, flaring white base decorated w/pink blossoms & green leafy stems (ILLUS.)............................... **75**

Mod Girl Lipstick Holder Lady

Figure of a girl, Mod Girl, large head w/green bouffant hairdo, heavy blue eyeliner, seated wearing short, off-the-shoulder dress, yellow cushion-form base, paper sticker reads "Our Own Imports" (ILLUS.).. **55**

Josef Originals Valentine Girl

Figure of a girl, Valentine Girl, blonde hair, holding a Valentine in one hand, wide squatty domed pink gown decorated w/hearts & gold trim, Josef Originals (ILLUS.).. **75**

Lipstick Holder Lady Beside Mirror

Figure of a girl seated beside mirror, girl w/brown hair applying lipstick, a wide round frame encloses a mirror above the four lipstock holders, pink gown & applied pink blossoms (ILLUS.)............................ **50**

Lady with Mask Lipstick Holder

Figure of a lady, blonde hair piled high, arms away from body w/a mask in one hand, wearing a wide squatty pink gown w/straight edge, ornate ruffles trimmed in gold (ILLUS.)... **50**

Lipstick Lady from Chadwick of Japan

Figure of a lady, brown hair in a pony tail, arms away from body, wearing a long gown w/short sleeves, peplum & lower ruffles forming pockets for lipstick, gown in pale yellow w/rust & gold trim, made by Chadwick, Japan, common (ILLUS.) **28**

Home-made Lipstick Holder Lady

Figure of a lady, home-made, brown hair w/curls to one side, crudely painted facial features, wearing a wide squatty domed purple gown w/white ruffle (ILLUS.) **10-20**

Kneeling Lipstick Holder Lady

Figure of a lady, kneeling w/her deep rose-colored gown flared out around her forming compartments, brown hair, holding a small bouquet of flowers w/other blossoms scattered around the gown (ILLUS.) **50**

"Miss Pretty Face" Lipstick Holder Lady

Figure of a lady, "Miss Pretty Face," brown hair w/large pink blossom, hands together near face, ruffled blue & white gown w/large pink blossoms forming the lipstick compartments (ILLUS.) **55**

Lady in 18th Century Costume

Figure of a lady, standing wearing 18th c. costume, her grey hair pulled up into a

bun, white swagged gown trimmed w/gold bands & specks (ILLUS.) **50**

Lipstick Holder Lady with Purse

Figure of a lady, standing wearing a deep pink gown, blonde hair piled high w/long side curls, arms away from body at front w/a small purse over one arm, looped ribbon in white w/applied pink roses forms lipstick compartments on gown (ILLUS.)........ **65**

Rare Two-Piece Lipstick Holder Lady

Figure of a lady, two-piece, standing lady in fancy 18th c. gown, holding a mirror in one hand, white w/gilt trim, top lifts off base w/four lipstick wells, rare (ILLUS.) **75**

Lipstick Lady in Deep Rose Gown

Figure of a lady, w/brown hair piled in a beehive hairdo, arms away from body at front, wearing a wide squatty deep rose gown trimmed w/pink blossoms (ILLUS.)........ **50**

Lipstick Holder Lady with Baskets

Figure of a lady, wearing a long flaring full gown, holding a fan in one hand, a large basket w/two lipstick compartments each over her arms, all in white w/heavy gold trim except her face & arms (ILLUS.).............. **75**

Lady in Front of Large Mirror & Holders

Figure of a lady in front of large mirror, blonde hair, standing applying lipstick, wearing a long gown applied w/lacy trim, a large round mirror behind her w/lipstick compartments in front beside her, white w/gold trim (ILLUS.) **35**

Girl at Dressing Table Lipstick Holder

Figure of girl seated at a dressing table, girl w/brown hair & pink gown seated powdering her nose in front of a dressing table w/round mirror, on an oblong base w/two cylindrical lipstick compartments behind her (ILLUS.) **75**

Enesco Lipstick Holder Lady

Half-figure of a girl, finely detailed head & shoulders of a girl, blonde hair pulled up, well-painted face, off-the-shoulder green gown w/deep shoulder swags, arms hold low basket at the front, silver paper sticker reads "M'Lady's Valet - by Enesco" (ILLUS.) **50**

MARDI GRAS MEMORABILIA

Admission card, 1891, Rex Krewe, color one side, 4 x 5"... **$125**
Admission card, 1931, Rex Krewe, color one side, 3 1/2 x 6" **75**
Admission card, Comos Krewe, color one side, 2 1/2 x 4 1/2" **75**

Admittance Card

Admittance card, paper, Rex Krewe, color both sides, 1883, 3 3/4 x 5" (ILLUS.)............ **125**
Ball invitation, 1875, Feb. 9, Rex Krewe, color one side, 6 x 9 1/2" **600**
Ball invitation, 1880, Feb. 5, Knights of Momus Krewe, two color, both sides, oval shape, 6 x 7 1/2" **425**
Ball invitation, 1884, Feb. 26, Comus Krewe, two color, one side, 6 x 10".............. **425**
Ball invitation, 1893, Feb. 14, Comus Krewe, two color, one side, 5 x 11"............... **350**
Ball invitation, 1897, Feb. 15, Nereus Krewe, color one side, diamond-shaped, 7 x 10" **375**

Ball invitation, 1901, Feb. 14, Knights of Momus Krewe, one color, one side, 5 1/2 x 6 3/4" **200**

Ball invitation, 1902, Feb. 11, Comus Krewe, color both sides, fold-out type, 8 1/2 x 15 1/2" **400**

Ball invitation, paper, Comus Krewe, color both sides, four folds, 1897, 13 3/4" sq. **500**

Ball Invitation

Ball invitation, paper, Comus Krewe, color one side, 1861, 6 x 9" (ILLUS.) **600**

Ball Invitation

Ball invitation, paper, Comus Krewe, two color, one side, 1877, 8 1/4 x 8 1/2" (ILLUS.) **350**

Ball Invitation

Ball invitation, paper, Knights of Momus, color both sides, single fold, 1878, 7 3/4 x 9" (ILLUS.) **500**

Ball Invitation

Ball invitation, paper, Krewe of Proteus, color both sides, 1883, 8 x 9" (ILLUS.) **500**

Ball Invitation

Ball invitation, paper, Krewe of Proteus, color one side, 1882, 5 x 11" (ILLUS.) **400**

Ball Invitation

Ball invitation, paper, Krewe of Proteus, tri-fold, 1905, open 8 3/4 x 16 1/2" (ILLUS.) **250**

Ball Invitation

Ball invitation, paper, Phunny Phorty Phellows, color both sides, four folds, 1883, 11 1/2 x 18 3/4" (ILLUS.) **400**

Ball Invitation

Ball invitation, paper, Phunny Phorty Phellows, color both sides, tri-fold, 1896, 11 3/4 x 17 1/2" (ILLUS.) **500**

Ball Invitation

Ball invitation, paper, Rex Krewe, color both sides, 1884, eight pieces fold into 3 x 9" circle (ILLUS.) **600**

Ball Invitation

Ball invitation, paper, Rex Krewe, color both sides, 1888, 9 x 11" (ILLUS.) **500**

Ball Invitation

Ball invitation, paper, Rex Krewe, color both sides, four pieces that slide inside each other, 1896, 10 1/2 x 13" (ILLUS.) **500**

Ball Invitation

Ball invitation, paper, Rex Krewe, color one side, 1891, 15 x 20 1/2" (ILLUS.) **500**

Ball invitation, paper, Rex Krewe, five piece fold-out fan, color both sides, 1890, 9 1/4 x 15 1/4" **750**

Ball Invitation

Ball invitation, paper, Rex Krewe, twelve artichoke leaves peel back to reveal Rex, color both sides, 1892, 12.15" side at all points (ILLUS.) **750**
Ball invitation, paper, Twelfth Night Revelers, color one side, 1872, 7 1/2 x 10" **350**

Ball Invitation

Ball invitation, Rex Krewe, tri-fold, color both sides, 1898, open 7 1/2 x 12 3/4" (ILLUS.) **450**
Book, "Carnival and Mardi Gras in New Orleans," by Perry Young, 1939, printed in New Orleans, soft cover, 82 pp, 5 1/2 x 8" **100**
Book, Knights of Babylon Krewe, "The Arts," 1947, printed in New Orleans, 17 float illustrations & ads, 48 pp, 8 1/4 x 10 3/4" **75**

Knights of Hermes Krewe Book

Book, Knights of Hermes Krewe, ads, 1937, printed in New Orleans, soft cover, 164 pp, seven float illustrations (ILLUS.) **75**
Book, Krewe of Carrollton, "Holidays Around the World," 1949, printed in New Orleans, 16 float illustrations & ads, 16 pp, 8 1/4 x 10 3/4" **75**
Book, Krewe of Comus, "Feathered Fantasies," 1933, printed in New Orleans, 20 float illustrations & ads, 24 pp, 7 x 11" **100**

Book, Krewe of Mid-City, "Academy Awards," 1941, printed in New Orleans, three float illustrations & ads, 64 pp, 15 1/4 x 8 1/2" **75**

Book, Krewe of Venus, "Goddesses," 1941, printed in New Orleans, 12 float illustrations & ads, 24 pp, 8 1/2 x 5 1/2" **100**

Book, "Mardi Gras Day," by Ralph Wickiser, Caroline Durieux & John McCrady, 1948, series of 31 drawings, history of Mardi Gras, Henry Holt & Co., Inc., hard cover, dust jacket, 92 pp, 7 x 10" **50**

Book, "New Orleans Masquerade," by Arthur Lacour, 1952, printed in New Orleans, profusely illustrated, hard cover, 232 pp, dust jacket, 7 3/4 x 10" **250**

Book, "Our Creole Carnivals 1830-1890," by T.C. DeLeon, 1890, printed in Mobile, soft cover, 40 pp, 5 x 9" **300**

Book, "The Mistick Krewe," by Perry Young, 1931, printed in New Orleans, hard cover, 268 pp, 30 full-color plates, 7 x 10" **400**

Bulletin, 1882, Proteus Krewe, Ancient Egyptian Mythology, chromolithographs, folded type, depicts the floats in parade, ads & parade information on reverse in black & white, open 28 x 42" **700**

Bulletin, 1884, Comus Krewe, illustrated Ireland, chromolithographs, folded type, depicts the floats in parade, ads & parade information on reverse in black & white, open 28 x 42" **600**

Bulletin, 1888, Rex Krewe, Ivanhoe, chromolithographs, folded type, depicts the floats in parade, ads & parade information on reverse in black & white, open 28 x 42" **600**

Bulletin, 1900, Comus Krewe, stories of the Golden Age, chromolithographs, folded type, depicts the floats in parade, ads & parade information on reverse in black & white, open 28 x 42" **400**

Bulletin, 1900, Nereus Krewe, The Christian Era, chromolithographs, folded type, depicts the floats in parade, ads & parade information on reverse in black & white, open 28 x 42" **500**

Bulletin, 1905, Rex Krewe, Idealistic Queens, chromolithographs, folded type, depicts the floats in parade, ads & parade information on reverse in black & white, open 28 x 42" **400**

Bulletin, 1923, Momus Krewe, Alice's Adventures, chromolithographs, folded type, depicts the floats in parade, ads & parade information on reverse in black & white, open 28 x 42" **300**

Bulletin, 1936, Comus Krewe, The Beautiful, chromolithographs, folded type, depicts the floats in parade, ads & parade information on reverse in black & white, open 28 x 42" **250**

Bulletin, 1940, Rex Krewe, A Fantasy of the Alphabet, chromolithographs, folded type, depicts the floats in parade, ads & parade information on reverse in black & white, open 28 x 42" **250**

Bulletin, 1951, Carrollton Krewe, Scenes of Beauty, chromolithographs, folded type, depicts the floats in parade, ads & parade information on reverse in black & white, open 28 x 42" **75**

Rex Krewe Carnival Bulletin

Carnival bulletin, paper, Rex Krewe, full color, reverse features float description & advertising in black & white, printed in New Orleans by T. Fitzwilliam, 28 x 42" (ILLUS.) **600**

Dance card, paper, Comsus, dances listed inside, color two sides, 1902 3 x 5" (ILLUS.) **100**

Dance Card

Dance card, paper, Comus Krewe, reverse lists 12 dances, 1899, 5 x 6 1/4" (ILLUS.) **175**

Five Dance Cards

Dance card, paper, High Priests of Mithras, dances listed inside, color two sides, 1899, 3 x 5" (ILLUS.) **100**

Dance card, paper, Knights of Momus, dances listed inside, color two sides, 1911, 3 x 5" (ILLUS.) **100**

Dance card, paper, Phunny Phorty Phellows, dances listed inside, color two sides, 1897, 3 x 5" (ILLUS.) 100

Dance card, paper, Proteus, dances listed inside, color two sides, 1899, 3 x 5" (ILLUS.) 100

Illustration of Comus Krewe

Illustration, 1858 May 8 Illustrated London News, paper, Comus Krewe, parade, hand-colored, 6 1/2 x 9 1/2" (ILLUS.) 100

Illustration, 1867 April 6 Frank Leslie's Illustrated Newspaper Mardi Gras Celebration in New Orleans, Tuesday, March 6 Procession of Mistick Krewe of Comus, 11 x 16" 75

Illustration, 1872 March 9 Frank Leslie's Illustrated Newspaper Louisiana - The Carnival in New Orleans - The Torchlight Procession of Maskers Passing Before The Grand Duke Alexis at the City Hall, 11 x 16" 75

Illustration, 1873 March 29 Harper's Weekly, Mardi Gras in New Orleans - Grand Tableau of the "Mistick Krewe," 11 x 16" 75

Illustration, 1878 March 16 Frank Leslie's Illustrated Newspaper, three scenes, Louisiana - The Mystic Krewe of Komus (sic) - Preparation, in New Orleans, For the Masquerade Procession of March 5th, 11 x 22" 125

Illustration, 1878 March 23 Frank Leslie's Illustrated Newspaper Louisiana Grand Masquerade Mardi Gras Procession Through the Streets of New Orleans, 11 x 22" 100

Illustration, 1879 March 22 Frank Leslie's Illustrated Newspaper, two scenes, Louisiana - Arrival & Reception of King Carnival at New Orleans, February 24, 11 x 16" 125

Illustration, 1883 Feb. 24 Harper's Weekly, seven scenes, New Orleans in Carnival Garb, 11 x 22" 100

Illustration, 1884 March 8 Harper's Weekly, In Carnival Time - New Orleans, 11 x 16" 75

Illustration, 1885 March 7 Harper's Weekly, The Carnival at New Orleans, 8 x 11" 50

Illustration, 1892 March 19 Harper's Weekly, seven scenes, The New Orleans Mardi Gras - The Red Procession, 11 x 16" 75

Illustration, 1893 March 2 Frank Leslie's Illustrated Newspaper, four scenes, New Orleans Great Annual Fete - The Mardi Gras Celebration, 11 x 16" 75

Illustration, 1898 March 12 Harper's Weekly, The New Orleans Mardi Gras Carnival - The Rex Pageant, 11 x 22" 100

Illustration, 1899 March 4 Harper's Weekly, New Orleans - The Mardi Gras Carnival Celebration, 1899, six photographs, 11 x 16" 75

Illustration, 1899 March 4 Harper's Weekly, The Mardi Gras Carnival at New Orleans - Maskers on the Street, 11 x 16" 75

Illustration, 1903 Feb. 14 Harper's Weekly, The Day Before Lent in New Orleans, 8 1/2 x 13" 75

Paper dolls, Mardi Gras King & Queen statuette dolls and costumes, Saalfield Publishing Co., 1956, 10 x 12" 40

Playing cards, New Orleans Carnival cards, face cards: Rex, Comus, Momus, Proteus, copyright Mary Wallace, New Orleans, ca. 1925, 2 1/4 x 3 1/4" 75

Postcard, panoramic view, Mardi Gras Pageant N.O., Raphael Tuck & Sons, Series No. 2442, color, tri-fold, copyright 1904, photo by John Teunisson, published by F.F. Hansell & Bros. Ltd., printed in Germany, 3 1/2 x 16 1/2" 50

Postcards, "Carnival Postcards," Series 6, ca. 1905, published by Raphael Tuck & Sons, Series No. 2468, depicting Rex, Comus, Proteus, Momus & two versions of Carnival flag, lithography by F.F. Hansel & Bros., Ltd., New Orleans, printed in Germany, each 25

Postcards, Rex parade of 1908, series of 20 cards, published by Adolph Seliege Publishing Co., St. Louis, issued as a set & as individual cards, single cards 25

Postcards, Rex parade of 1908, series of 20 cards, published by Adolph Seliege Publishing Co., St. Louis, issued as a set & as individual cards, fold-out set 100

Proclamation

Proclamation, paper, Rex Krewe, full color, blank on back, printed by Walle & Co., New Orleans, 1924, 28 x 42" (ILLUS.) 500

Souvenir Program

Souvenir program, paper, New Orleans Mardi Gras, printed in New Orleans, 1946, 56 pages, 8 x 10 3/4" (ILLUS.) 50

METALS

Aluminum

Floor lamp, single-socket fixture on a tall cylindrical standard ending in an urn-shaped device on a square platform w/four disk-shaped feet, designed & built by Otto Schricker, University of California, Santa Barbara, 1947, impressed marks, 55" h. **$230**

Table lamp, single-socket fixture on an urn-form cylindrical standard over a similar urn-shaped element on a square platform base, designed & built by Otto Schricker, University of California at Santa Barbara, 1947, impressed marks, 21" h. **374**

Brass

Hat rack, wall-type, Arts & Crafts style, square form w/embossed oak leaves & acorns on a textured ground, three iron double hooks, fitted w/a mirror, early 20th c., 20 1/2" w. **316**

Kettle, cylindrical spun form w/wrought-iron bail handle, marked "Hayden's Patent," 19th c., 24 1/2" d., 18" h. **193**

Pitcher, cov., Art Nouveau style, floral decorated cone-shaped body w/a simple scrolling handle, rounded molded base, cover w/spade-shaped finial, ca. 1890, 14" h. **146**

Samovar, footed bulbous urn-form w/flaring neck, including chimney & underliner, Russia, late 19th c., 20 1/2" h. **230**

Skimmer, round pierced brass bowl w/a long wrought-iron handle, 19th c., 18 1/2" l. **99**

Trivet, long slender spade form w/hearts & diamond cut-outs, 10" l. **110**

Trivet, slender spade-form w/a heart-shaped handle w/heart opening above a diamond opening & a large central heart opening, on three peg feet, 9 5/8" l. **138**

Wine cooler, deep ovoid form w/wide gadrooned band below the flaring ribbed neck, lion mask & ring end handles, raised on four paw feet, Holland, early 19th c., 8 1/4 x 12", 6 1/4" h. (ILLUS. top next column) **715**

Dutch Brass Wine Cooler

Bronze

Box, cov., Arts & Crafts style, rectangular w/a hinged lid decorated w/an etched central six-sided oval reserve flanked by scroll designs & geometric outlining, mottled texture on recessed areas, wood-lined interior, impressed marks of Silver Crest, early 20th c., 3 5/8 x 6 1/4", 1 1/2" h. **40**

Dish, shallow round form w/a foliate border, textured surface, stamped "Tiffany Studios New York 1677," early 20th c., 6 1/2" d. (minor spotting) **144**

Ewers, hammered body cast & applied w/an animal-form spout & foliate handle, Dutch, 18th c., 16" h., pr. **1,955**

Magazine rack, bronze, upright circular sides w/an openwork design of a greyhound in stride, scrolling leaf border, American-made, ca. 1930, 4 1/2 x 11 7/8", 12" h. **374**

European Neoclassical Bronze Urn

Urns, cov., Neoclassical style, ovoid body tapering to a wide cylindrical neck, raised on a ringed pedestal & square foot, the body w/leaf-cast handles & overall bands of flowers, grapes, scrolls & gadrooning, the low domed cover w/cast foliage & an acorn finial, Europe, 19th c., 50" h., pr. (ILLUS. of one) **4,025**

Vase, footed slender ovoid form tapering to a short neck w/flat rim, etched overall, the textured surface decorated around the shoulder w/drooping polished slender stylized vines, impressed mark of Silver Crest, early 20th c., 7" h. (some discoloration) **230**

Chrome

Manning-Bowman Chrome Set

Beverage set: cov. pitcher, six glasses & tray; Art Deco style, footed conical-form bodies, the pitcher w/a short capped rim spout, stepped & domed cover & angular Bakelite handle, the oval tray w/marbleized green & yellow Bakelite handles & surface, Manning-Bowman Co., ca. 1930, minor corrosion, tray 9 x 18 1/4", pitcher 13 1/4" h., the set (ILLUS.) **575**

Store display, figural, tubular metal outline of a woman's head & elongated neck curving down to spiral base, 20th c., 19 1/2" h. (minor chrome loss) **230**

Copper

Bowl, 10 3/8 x 14 7/8", 5 1/2" h., repoussé, Arts & Crafts style, four raised incurved corners on a quatreform body, the center w/raised horse chestnut decoration centered by a green ceramic disk, dark brown patina, unmarked, early 20th c. (minor spotting & dents) **374**

Early Copper Candy Kettle

Candy kettle, deep half-round form w/rolled rim & wrought steel loop ring handles, dovetailed construction, stamped label, polished, 19th c., 13" d., 6 1/2" h. (ILLUS.) **193**

Candy kettle, deep rounded sides w/rolled rim & sturdy cast-iron rim handles, dovetailed construction, 17 1/2" d., 7 1/2" h. **248**

Chamberstick, Arts & Crafts style, hand-hammered, a round deeply dished base

centered by a tall slender cylindrical shaft w/a wide flared socket rim, a riveted loop strap handle down one side of shaft, cleaned patina, Als Ik Kan mark of Gustav Stickley, 6 3/4" d., 8 3/4" h. **605**

Charger, Arts & Crafts style, hand-hammered, round w/the center embossed w/a writhing large dragon, the wide flanged rim, embossed w/a repeating band of large carp, by J.D. Mackenzie & P. Hodder, fine original dark patina, Newlyn Industrial Class, England, stamped & signed, early 20th c., 12 1/2" d. **2,200**

Charger, Arts & Crafts style, round w/wide hand-hammered center & a flanged rim embossed w/a repeating wave pattern, fine original patina, England, early 20th c., unmarked, 21" d. **1,540**

Charger, large round form w/dished center & wide flanged rim, the center hammered w/an embossed design of three writhing sea serpents, the wide border embossed w/long leafy vines & salamanders, John Pearson, England, fine dark original patina, 1901, signed "J.P. 1901 - 2726," 24" d. **5,225**

Early Copper Chestnut Roaster

Chestnut roaster, cov., bed warmer-form, round pan w/pierced cover engraved w/tulip designs, a long ring- and baluster-turned wood handle, dents in base, 36" l. (ILLUS.) **358**

Gustav Stickley Copper Coal Scuttle

Coal scuttle, Arts & Crafts style, a flared round foot below the gently flaring cylindrical body w/a wide rounded upright spout, high wrought-iron top swing handle & small loop grip at lower back, Gustav Stickley, 19" h. (ILLUS.) **5,775**

Dipper, round copper bowl w/flared sides, wrought-iron handle w/applied brass cartouche inscribed "John F. Stratton, New York," 19th c., 22 1/2" l. **358**

Dish, Arts & Crafts style, hand-hammered, a wide shallow bowl raised on a small cylindrical reticulated base w/a loop design, fine original patina, closed box mark of Dirk Van Erp, 9 1/2" d., 2 3/4" h. **1,100**

Dresser set: rectangular pen tray, letter holder & letter opener; hand-hammered, each piece w/handles or rim tabs w/a reticulated branching tree lunette, medium patina on opener & tray, dark patina on letter holder, open box mark of Dirk Van Erp on two pieces, the set **1,650**

Jardiniere, Arts & Crafts style, hand-hammered, a flaring foot riveted to a tall flaring cylindrical body w/a wide rim band w/a row of large embossed ovals, cast riveted loop handle on each side, fine original patina, unmarked, attributed to Gustav Stickley or Benedict Studios, early 20th c., 11 1/2" d., 12" h. (minor dents).. **2,090**

Stickley Bros. Copper Jardiniere

Jardiniere, Arts & Crafts style, hand-hammered, deep slightly tapering rounded form w/closed rim, heavily embossed around the sides w/stylized grape clusters, fine original patina, few small dents, Stickley Brothers, early 20th c., stamped "302," 13" d., 8" h. (ILLUS.) **2,420**

Jardinieres, modern style, oblong twolobed boat-form w/the ends pulled into curved points, the bowl resting on a cross-form platform w/tightly scrolled-under feet, each w/a liner, by Marie Zimmermann, ca. 1920, stamped "M. Zimmermann Maker" w/monogram, 13 1/2" l., 4 1/2" h., pr. **15,275**

Early Dovetailed Copper Jug

Jug, hand-hammered, dovetailed construction, flat-bottomed gently flaring cylindrical form w/wide rounded shoulder centered by a small tapering cylindrical neck, arched strap shoulder handle, 9 1/2" h. (ILLUS.) **550**

Measure, haystack-form, dovetailed construction, wide flared foot below the wide sharply tapering cylindrical sides w/a deep flared spout neck, large D-form handle from rim to shoulder, embossed crown mark on interior of rim, exterior marked "Gallon," England, late 19th - early 20th c., 11" h. **275**

Measure, haystack-form w/pouring spout & hollow handle, 1/2 gal., 7 1/4" h. (dented) **330**

Sauce pan, cov., deep flat-bottomed round tapering cylindrical body w/a molded rim & low domed fitted cover w/small arched strap handle, a high arched swing strap handle from rim to rim stamped "I. Witman," Jonathan Witman, Pennsylvania, ca. 1805, 6 1/2" d., 11" h. **9,600**

Sauce pans, cov., each cylindrical w/dovetailed construction & cast-iron handles extending from rim, stamped "H.P." & "Harrods Stores, Ltd., London," tinwashed interiors, England, graduated set of 6, 4 3/4" d. to 8 3/4" d., the set (smallest missing cover) **1,100**

Early Signed Copper Teakettle

Teakettle, cov., dovetailed construction, flat-bottomed bulbous form w/wide rounded shoulder centering a low-domed fitted cover, angled swan's-neck spout, high arched strap swing handle stamped "I. Roberts Phila.," Israel Roberts, Philadelphia, early 19th c. (ILLUS.) **1,800**

Teakettle, cov., dovetailed construction, wide flat bottom & swelled cylindrical sides below a flat shoulder centered by a short cylindrical neck w/a fitted domed cover w/scroll finial, short swan's-neck spout w/end flap, high swing bail handle stamped "C.A. Bayard," 7" h. **220**

Teakettle, cov., dovetailed, cylindrical bottom for insetting into stove top, swelled short wide cylindrical body w/flat shoulder centered by a short cylindrical neck w/low domed cover, short swan's-neck spout w/hinged end cover, high arched swing handle stamped "A.F.B. - G.B.," 10" h. **165**

Teakettle, cov., flat-bottomed squatty bulbous form w/a wide rounded shoulder centering a domed cover w/small finial, angled gooseneck spout, arched strap swing handle stamped "W. Heiss No. 23 North Phila.," 1809-36, 11" d., 10 1/2" h.... **1,320**

Teakettle, cov., hand-hammered, dovetailed, wide flat-bottomed rounded form w/narrow shoulder & fitted domed cover w/ring finial, angled spout, swing overhead strap handle w/beveled edges, 10 3/4" h. (dents)... **165**

Teakettle, cov., large bulbous form w/swing handle & lidded spout, a retardant interior lining, early 19th c., 15 1/2" d., 14 1/2" h. (minor wear & corrosion)................................. **403**

Teakettle, cov., wide flat bottom on a nearly cylindrical body w/a rounded shoulder centering a domed cover w/a brass ball finial, arched strap swing handle stamped "D: Price," angled gooseneck spout, David Price, Philadelphia or North Carolina, 1793-1820, 11" d., 11" h. **3,600**

Tray, Arts & Crafts style, hand-hammered, round w/a wide flanged rim embossed w/four elongated heart designs alternating w/slightly arched oval cut-outs, Craftsman stamp of Gustav Stickley, early 20th c., 19 3/4" d. (minor patina cleaning)... **990**

Tray, hand-hammered, Arts & Crafts style, elongated oval form w/fold-over rim, strap handles riveted at each end, medium brown patina, stamped w/joiner's compass mark of Gustav Stickley, Model No. 355, ca. 1910, 11 1/8 x 23 1/8" (scattered spotting, dent)... **489**

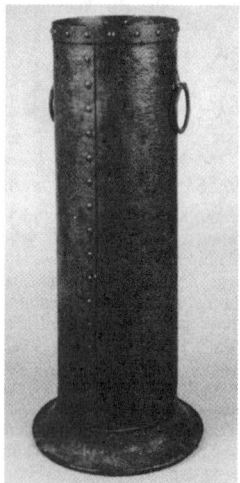

Arts & Crafts Umbrella Stand

Umbrella stand, hand-hammered, Arts & Crafts style, flaring round foot riveted to the tall cylindrical riveted body w/a riveted rim band, two loose swing handles at sides, dark patina, America, early 20th c., some wear & discoloration, 11" d., 26 1/2" h. (ILLUS.)... **288**

Vase, Arts & Crafts style, hand-hammered, bulbous ribbed form tapering to a scalloped everted rim w/embossed pine cone, scallop & stylized floral decoration, unmarked, early 20th c., 8 1/2" h. (polished patina) **403**

Vase, Arts & Crafts style, hand-hammered w/an overall warty finish, bulbous ovoid form w/a narrow shoulder & wide flat mouth, open box mark of Dirk Van Erp, 7" d., 7" h. (some restoration to patina)..... **2,530**

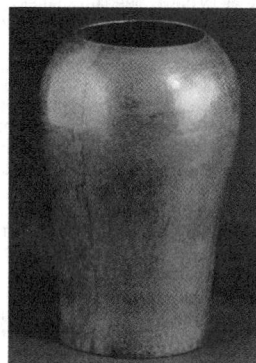

Dirk Van Erp Copper Vase

Vase, hand-hammered, Arts & Crafts style, gently swelling cylindrical form w/bulbed top & closed rim, excellent original patina, closed box mark of Dirk Van Erp, San Francisco, early 20th c., 6" d., 10" h. (ILLUS.) **5,500**

Iron

Bird roaster, hand-wrought, an arched tripod base w/penny feet centering a tall slender rod w/a small turned finial & fitted w/a flattened open bell-form bracket w/hooks for attaching the bird, 23 1/2" h. **396**

Boot scraper, cast, a heavy squared pan w/canted corners & wide rolled sides supporting two upright dolphins joined by a central shell design below the top crossbar, good detail, late 19th - early 20th c., 12 1/2 x 15 1/2", 10" h. (pitted) **193**

Boot scraper, cast, a round shallow dish base w/low flared & ruffled edges, a center crossbar supporting brackets fitted w/brushes below a high rounded arch centered by a figural seated African-American boy, black repaint, late 19th c., 12 1/2" h. (base restorations)......................... **248**

Boot scraper, cast, model of an elongated dachshund dog, head up w/mouth open, tail curled into a large loop, old black paint, 21 1/2" l.. **193**

Boot scraper, hand-wrought, a side-wall type w/twisted supporting braces, 18th c., 10" l., 12 1/2" h. (wear) **230**

Boot scraper, hand-wrought, side-wall type w/scrolled end, early 19th c. (wear) **144**

Cookie board, cast, almond-shaped, cast w/a bird on a branch framed by a border of dots, 5 1/4" l... **165**

Cookie board, cast, oblong, cast w/a large acorn below a pair of large leaves, beaded border, 5 3/4" l. 193

Cookie board, cast, oval flat form cast w/a large basket of flowers, 5 1/2" l. 138

Cookie board, cast, rectangular, the surface cast as twelve small blocks each w/a different design including birds, animals, buildings, etc., 5 1/4 x 7 3/4" 220

Cuspidor, cast, large model of a top hat, old black repaint, 7 1/4" h. 220

Door latch, hand-wrought, the double-cusp latch w/large spearpoint ends & arched grip, impressed maker's mark & date, M. Aling, Housitonic Valley, Connecticut, 1822, 17 1/2" l. (reinforced hardware) **1,840**

Dough scraper, hand-wrought, a twisted curved handle, 19th c. 55

Fire carrier, cov., hand-wrought, a narrow long rectangular box tray w/a hinged flat cover controlled by a top bar w/scrolled finger loop on the long slender bar handle w/an end loop, faintly marked on the cover "Pat. applied for," 24 1/4" l. 550

Early Cast-Iron Fireplace Insert

Fireplace insert, cast, a bowfront flat base w/a small raised lip, scalloped side panels w/relief-cast fans & faces, biscuit corners on the top w/circular & oval fans, original seamed brass finials, signed "Wyer & Noble," early 19th c., originally had feet, back plate cracked, base 22 3/4" w., 28" h. (ILLUS.) 330

Food mold, round domed shape cast in the form of a pig head, small loop handles at the round base rim, 9" d. 303

Hanging bar, hand-wrought, thin narrow bar w/two curved hooks & three raised brass knobs w/escutcheons, background engraved w/primitive tulips, 21 3/4" l. (some wear) 550

Herb crusher, cast, the elongated oval trough impressed w/the name "C.B. Ro_s," turned wooden handle on rolling disk blade, American, early 19th c., 18 1/4" l., 3 3/4" h. **1,150**

Herb grinder, cast, two-piece implement, iron disk blade w/wooden handles & elongated oval slant-sided trough, 19th c., 15" l., 6 3/4" h., 2 pcs. 920

Kettle shelf, hand-wrought, a rectangular top w/crossbars & an arched apron w/support bar raised on front cabriole legs, 15 5/8 x 17 1/2", 11 3/8" h. 110

Kettle shelf, hand-wrought, the rectangular top & front apron w/decorative pierced designs, cabriole front legs & straight rear legs, England, 11 x 13", 13" h. 165

Kettle stand, hand-wrought, a flat ring top w/a small center ring connected by three flat spokes, raised on three slender cabriole legs joined by forked twisted bar stretchers in the center, penny feet, 12" h. 193

Lawn sprinkler, cast, figural, model of a wood duck w/old yellow, green & red paint, the turning sprinkler head atop the duck's head, some wear, good detail, 13 1/2" h. 660

Mirror, cast, table model, a large oval top frame cast as grapevine enclosing a mirror, raised on a short openwork vine shaft above the wide openwork looping grapevine base, mirror w/adjustable back, marked "Chinnock's Pat. 1830," green repaint, 19th c., 25" h. 358

Victorian Cast-Iron Table Mirror

Mirror, table model, cast, the oval mirror swiveling on a frame cast w/flags beneath a crown, oak leaves & acorns, set on two suits of armor raised on a base pierced w/a military trophy & shield-form feet, cold-painted, mid-19th c., 19 3/4" h. (ILLUS.) 747

Model of a rooster, cast, large lawn ornament in the form of a crowing rooster, rounded base, 19" h. (rusted finish) 578

Model of an eagle, cast in two sections w/hollow body, perched on a rock w/widely spread wings w/detailed feathers, green paint w/two mounting brackets on base, 10 x 30 1/4", 13 1/2" h. 330

Nutcracker, cast, model of a seated squirrel on an oval base, curved tail forms handle, old finish, marked "Patented May 28, 1879," 8 1/2" h. (some minor pitting, one ear w/old smooth chip, replaced wood base) 413

Nutcracker, cast, model of an alligator, 13 1/4" l. 83

Oven peel, hand-wrought, a flat tapering rectangular blade w/a very long slender bar handle, 45 1/2" l 55

Oven peel, hand-wrought, a squared blade w/a long thin handle w/a heart-shaped scroll finial, impressed "1831," American, 45 1/2" l. (loss) 460

Pipe tongs, hand-wrought, an acorn-tipped hanging hook, decorative bronze inlay, England, 18th c., 17" l. 1,840

Skewer rack & skewers, hand-wrought, a small round hanging hole at the end of the long flat handle above two spurred skewer supports, handle stamped "C.J. DeWitt," w/four skewers, English or American, late 18th - early 19th c., the group 720

Early American Iron Stove Plate

Stove plate, cast, rectangular form, the top w/two arched reserves separated w/spiral columns, one side w/a man on horseback, the other w/an urn of vining flowers, embossed wording "Shfarwell Furnace in Oly - Dieter Weiker," Friedensburg, Bucks County, Pennsylvania, 19 x 22" (ILLUS.) 605

Teakettle, cov., cast, cylindrical body w/narrow angled shoulder to the wide mouth w/low domed tin cover w/brass knob, high looped wrought-iron handle, swan's-neck spout, cover w/labeled escutcheon marked "J. & J. Siddons West Bromwich," England, 19th c., 10" h. 110

Early Wrought Iron Trammel

Trammel, hand-wrought, scalloped & scrolled finials on top, side bar & catch, engraved detail w/a cross & "1809," adjusts from 43" to 60" (ILLUS.)........................... 495

Trivet, hand-wrought, heart-shaped flat top on three shoulder legs w/penny feet, 19th c., 7 3/4" l. (some damage on feet) 303

Finely Detailed Iron Utensil Rack

Utensil rack, hand-wrought, a flattened bar w/double scrolls at each end, an upright center flat bar w/pairs of small scrolls below the large forked curled-under top scrolls, 28" l., 14 1/2" h. (ILLUS.)............... 1,980

Wafer iron, scissor-form, long slender handles, opening to reveal rectangular panels decorated w/incised suns, flowers, birds, hearts & other designs, initials "IA," Pennsylvania, 1737, panels 10" w., overall 38 1/2" l.. 2,700

Waffle iron, a round hinged end w/a heart design, long rod handles w/ring ends, 19th c., end 8 1/2" d., 22 3/4" l........................ 165

Pewter

Basin, eagle touch of Samuel Pierce, Greenfield, Massachusetts, 1792-1830, 13 1/4" d. (edge damage, wear w/dents & pitting).. 220

Basin, round, faint eagle touch, possibly Gershom Jones, Providence, Rhode Island, late 18th - early 19th c., 7 3/4" d........... 275

Basin, round w/flanged rim, touch marks of Townsend & Compton, England, late 18th - early 19th c., 9 1/8" d. (wear, pitting)... 165

Basin, round w/upright sides & narrow flanged rim, Richard Lee (senior or junior), New England, late 18th - early 19th c., 8 3/4" d., 2" h. (polished)................................. 578

Basin, round w/upright sides, Thomas D. Boardman, Hartford, Connecticut, 1805-50, 9 1/4" d. (minor pitting, scratches).......... 489

Basin, round w/wide flanged rim, eagle touch of Ashbil Griswold, Meriden, Connecticut, 1807-15, 13 1/8" d. (wear, scratches)... 495

Basin, w/flanged rim, partial eagle touch of Samuel Kilbourne, Baltimore, Maryland, 1814-39, 12" d. (dents)................................ 468

Basin, wide flattened bottom, low sides w/molded rim, hammered bouge, partial London touchmark, 13" d., 3 1/4" h. (areas of pitting) 248

Candlestick, round domed foot w/a ring-and knob-turned shaft below the cylindrical socket w/flattened rim, mark of Rufus

Dunham, Westbrook, Maine, 1837-61, 6" h. (edges a bit battered) **165**

Charger, flanged rim, touch mark "B.L.," 13 1/4" d. (wear, pitting) **193**

Charger, round w/flanged rim, Frederick Bassett, New York & Hartford, 1761-99, 16" d. **7,800**

Charger, shallow round form w/flanged rim, unmarked, England, late 18th - early 19th c., 16 1/4" d. (wear, pitting) **275**

Coffee & tea service: cov. coffepot, cov. teapot, cov. sugar bowl, creamer & shaped oval tray; Art Nouveau style, the footed ovoid hollowware pieces w/angular handles & raised oblong panels of stylized flowers & leaves, an engraved initial on each piece, raised or impressed marks for Kayserzinn, Germany, late 19th - early 20th c., tray 20" l., coffeepot 10" h., the set **345**

Coffeepot, cov., tall lighthouse-form, hinged domed cover w/knopped finial, tapering body w/multiple encircling rings, molded S-shaped handle, William Calder, Providence, Rhode Island, 1817-56, 11 1/4" h. **1,150**

Communion flagon, cov., flared round base w/tall cylindrical gently tapering body w/a medial band, stepped domed hinged cover w/thumbrest, simple C-scroll handle, rim spout, Reed & Barton, mid-19th c., 11 1/4" h. **220**

Dish, deep dished center w/wide flanged rim, Samuel Hamlin, Sr. or Jr., Providence, Rhode Island, late 18th - early 19th c., 13 3/4" d. **2,280**

Dish, deep dished round center w/flanged rim, Peter Young, New York or Albany, 1775-95, 13 3/4" d. **480**

Flagon, cov., flaring stepped round base, tall cylindrical body w/double rings around the center, flared rim w/hinged stepped, domed cover, short curved rim spout, long C-scroll handle, Smith, Sheldon & James Feltman, Jr., New York, 1847-48, 10 5/8" h. **385**

Sheldon and Feltman Flagon

Flagon, cov., flaring stepped round base, tall cylindrical body w/double rings around the center, flared rim w/hinged stepped, domed cover, short curved rim spout, long C-scroll handle, Smith, Sheldon & James Feltman, Jr., New York, 1847-48, area of pitting on base, dents, 10 5/8" h. (ILLUS.) **385**

Flagon, cov., tall tapering cylindrical body w/flared ringed base & mid-body ring, flared rim w/arched rim spout, hinged domed cover w/thumbrest, long S-scroll handle w/flat terminal, Reed and Barton, mid-19th c., 9 5/8" h. (minor pitting on handle) **440**

Flagon, cov., tall tapering cylindrical sides on a flaring domed round base, stepped domed hinged cover w/beehive finial, double scroll handle, Samuel Danforth, Hartford, Connecticut, 1795-1816, 6 1/4" d., 13 1/2" h. **14,400**

Lamp, a dished tray base w/loop edge handle, centered by an acorn-form font w/whale oil burner, Henry Hopper, New York City, 1842-47, 5" h. (polished) **193**

Lamp, fluid-burning, a domed round foot & ringed stem supporting a slightly flaring cylindrical font w/domed top fitted w/a camphene burner, mark of Eben Smith, Beverly, Massachusetts, 1813-56, 6 7/8" h. (no snuffer) **413**

Lamps, whale oil, ovoid-shaped font w/double burner raised on a tall conical pedestal base w/tooled rings, unsigned, 8" h., pr. (minor dents in base) **248**

Mug, straight-sided w/low fillet-molded foot, ball terminal & C-scroll handle, Samuel Hamlin, Providence, Rhode Island, 1801-56, quart, 4 7/8" d., 6" h. **5,700**

Mug, straight-sided w/molded foot & ball terminal C-scroll handle, William Will, Philadelphia, 1764-98, quart, 4 5/8" d., 5 1/2" h. **9,000**

Mug, tapering cylindrical form w/heavy C-form handle, Jacob Whitmore, Middletown, Connecticut, 1758-90, 4 1/2" h. (polished, wear, small scratches, handle w/possible repair at top) **4,015**

Pitcher, long flaring neck on a bulbous base w/raised oak leaves & acorns, raised mark for Kayserzinn, Germany, early 20th c., 11" h. (wear) **316**

Plate, flanged rim & hammered bouge, William Will, Philadelphia, 1764-1798, 8" d.... **1,200**

Plate, flanged rim, double touch w/eagle & initials of Blakslee Barns, Philadelphia, Pennsylvania, 1812-17, 7 3/4" d. (minor rim dents & wear) **385**

Plate, flanged rim, eagle touch of Thomas Danforth III, Phildelphia, 1777-1818, 7 3/4" d. **385**

Plate, flanged rim, mark, of Samuel Ellis, London, England, late 18th c., scratch-engraved initials on rim "H.L.," 7 3/4" d. (some wear & scratches) **110**

Plate, flanged rim, touch of Samuel Kilbourn, Baltimore, Maryland, ca. 1820, 7 3/4" d. (wear, scratches) **275**

Plate, flanged rim, eagle touch of William Danforth, Middletown, Connecticut, 1792-1820, 8" d. (wear, scratches) **275**

Plate, flanged rim, eagle touch of Thomas Badger, Boston, 1787-1815, 8 1/2" d. bottom pitted & worn) **248**

Plate, flanged rim, eagle touch of George Lightner, Baltimore, Maryland, 1806-15, 8 3/4" d. (minor rim dents) **358**

Plate, flanged rim, eagle touch & marks of Nathaniel Austin, Charlestown, Massachusetts, 1763-1800, 9 1/2" d. (battered, rim repair) 220

Porringer, round w/cast pierced crown handle, unmarked, 5 1/2" d. 193

Porringer, round w/plain rounded tab handle w/hanging hole, attributed to Pennsylvania, 5 1/4" d. plus handle, 2" h. (polished, small rim split near handle) 440

Porringer, small round bowl w/scroll-pierced pointed tab handle, Richard Lee (senior or junior), New England, late 18th - early 19th c., 3 3/4" d. (polished) 1,183

Soup plate, flanged rim, thistle touch mark, England, rim engraved w/initials, 9 3/4" d. 138

Rare American Pewter Sugar Bowl

Sugar bowl, cov., round slightly domed foot below the stepped tapering rounded body w/a beaded rim band, the stepped, domed cover w/a beaded rim band & urn-form finial, attributed to Parks Boyd, Philadelphia, ca. 1800, finial & bowl slightly bent, 5" d., 4 1/2" h. (ILLUS.) 6,900

Tankard, Art Nouveau style, cylindrical w/C-form handle, decorated w/raised stylized fruiting branch flanking the handle & extending around the body, impressed marks of Liberty & Co., England, early 20th c., 5 3/8" h. (dents, minor pitting & corrosion) 201

Tankard, cov., flared ringed base & gently tapering cylindrical sides, hinged stepped domed cover w/scrolled "ram's horn" thumbrest, S-scroll handle w/fish tail terminal, Frederick Bassett, New York or Hartford, Connecticut, 1761-99, quarter, 5" d., 7" h. 30,650

Rare Early American Pewter Tankard

Tankard, cov., slightly tapering cylindrical form w/ringed base, the flat-topped domed cover w/a crenate lip & 'chair back' thumbpiece, the hollow scroll handle w/a ball terminal, John Will, New York City, 1752-74, 4 5/8" d., 5 1/2" h. (ILLUS.) 38,125

Tazza, Arts & Crafts style, a wide shallow rounded bowl w/incurved sides flanked by pierced gryphon handles, raised on a slender stem w/a flaring round foot, hammered surface w/a row of small embossed beads around the top of the bowl & around the foot, impressed mark "W & Co. English Pewter - Hand-beaten - Homeland," early 20th c., 11" d., 10" h. (minor surface wear) 173

Teapot, cov., bulbous pear-shaped body tapering to a high domed cover w/pointed finial w/ivory wafer, swan's-neck paneled spout, arched C-scroll handle, Thomas D. & Sherman Boardman, Hartford, Connecticut, 1810-30, 8" h. (polished) 880

Teapot, cov., flared pedestal base below the squatty bulbous body w/a stepped shoulder to the short flaring neck, hinged pointed domed cover, C-scroll handle, swan's-neck spout, J.D. Locke, New York City, 1835-60, 9" h. 413

Teapot, cov., footed squatty bulbous body tapering to a short flared neck, hinged domed cover w/wooden finial, swan's-neck spout, pointed arched scroll handle w/black paint, J.W. Cahill & Co., ca. 1830s, 7" h. (polished) 358

Teapot, cov., footed squatty bulbous body w/a short flaring neck, hinged pointed domed cover, swan's-neck spout & ornate scroll handle, mark of Smith & Co., Boston, Massachusetts, 1847-49, 6 3/4" h. 303

Teapot, cov., footed tall baluster-form body w/a domed hinged lid w/finial, swan's-neck spout & angled scroll handle, Roswell Gleason, Dorchester, Massachusetts, 1822-71 (minor pitting, finial incomplete) 413

Teapot, cov., Queen Anne-style, squatty bulbous pear-shaped body w/a pointed domed hinged lid, shaped spout & arched C-scroll handle, Israel Trask, Beverly, Massachusetts, 1807-56 (pitting, wear, old repair) 715

Teapot, cov., round flaring foot below the rounded bulbous lower body w/an incurved shoulder band below the tall waisted upper body w/a flaring rim, hinged stepped & domed cover w/finial, swan's-neck spout, ornate scroll metal handle, eagle touch probably of Luther Boardman, South Reading, Massachusetts, 1836-42, 10 3/4" h. 468

Teapot, cov., round short pedestal foot below the wide squatty bulbous body w/angled shoulders to the short flaring neck, hinged domed cover, paneled spout, angled C-scroll handle, eagle touch of Ashbil Griswold, Meriden, Connecticut, 1802-42, 8 1/4" h. (small hole in handle, repaired hinge, splits in bottom) 248

Teapot, cov., short pedestal base & bulbous ovoid body tapering to a flaring neck, hinged pointed domed cover, swan's-neck spout & C-scroll metal handle, tooled lines around body, probably Joshua B. Graves, Middletown, Connecticut, ca. 1850, 9" h. (minor dents) **292**

Teapot, cov., tall lighthouse-form, flared & ringed base below the tapering cylindrical sides w/a raised center band, pointed domed hinged cover w/finial, ornate C-scroll handle, swan's-neck spout, John H. Whitlock, Troy, New York, 1836-44, 11 1/4" (areas of pitting, well done repair)...... **330**

American Lighthouse-form Teapot

Teapot, cov., tall lighthouse-shape, flared ringed base on the tall gently tapering body w/a flared rim & high domed cover w/finial, swan's-neck spout & ornate C-scroll black-painted metal handle, John Munson, Yalesville, Connecticut, 1846-52, 11" h. (ILLUS.)...................................... **605**

Teapot, cov., tall lighthouse-shaped, flared base & tall gently tapering body w/domed cover, ornate C-scroll handle & swan's-neck spout, Freeman Porter, Westbrook, Maine, 1835-60s, 10 3/4" h. **468**

Teapot, cov., tall pigeon-breasted form, a paneled domed pedestal base supporting a wide squatty bulbous paneled body tapering to a flaring paneled neck, hinged domed paneled cover & fluted spout, scrolled wooden handle, Roswell Gleason, Dorchester, Massachusetts, 1822-71, 10" h... **303**

Teapot, cov., tall ring-footed baluster-form w/hinged domed cover w/button finial, ornate C-scroll black-painted metal handle, swan's-neck spout, eagle touch of Ashbil Griswold, Meriden, Connecticut, 1802-42, 11 1/2" h. (foot restoration) **303**

Vases, slender trumpet form tapering to a stepped round base, decorated w/raised & stylized vertical branches bearing fruit, impressed Tudric marks of Liberty & Co., England, early 20th c., 11" h., pr. (wear)....... **230**

Sheffield Plate

Basket, a high oval footring w/a narrow band of rectangular piercing, the long boat-form basket w/a similar pierced band near the rim, tapering forked central

swing handle, engraved heraldic device in the interior, early 19th c., 13 1/4" l. **374**

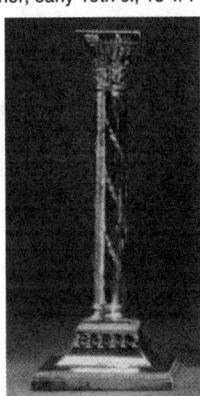

One of a Set of Sheffield Candlesticks

Candlesticks, on a square weighted base beaded at the top & bottom rim & engraved w/a band of husk drops, columnar standard engraved w/spiraling band of husks, a flat leaf capital w/a square beaded socket rim, 19th c., 11" h., set of 4 (ILLUS. of one) **1,955**

Fine Sheffield Coffee Urn

Coffee urn, cov., wide tapering ovoid body raised on a ringed pedestal & flaring ringed domed foot, a short wide rolled neck w/gadrooned rim, stepped domed cover w/pointed acanthus leaf finial, scrolled spigot at base w/scrolled loop handle, chased lion head handles w/rings at the sides, early 19th c., minor dents, 26 1/2" h. (ILLUS.) **1,760**

Epergne, Classical style, the oval stand w/gadrooned rim, supported by four reeded column legs w/paw feet, the four reeded branches supported by a central boss w/cast lions' masks, below a reeded boss topped by a cast acorn finial, w/five cut glass inserts, Matthew Boulton, Birmingham, England, late 18th - early 19th c., 10 7/8" l., 12 1/4" h. (losses) **1,840**

Classical Sheffield Hot Water Urn

Hot water urn, cov., classical urn-form, the deep body w/the lower half decorated w/repoussé spiral gadrooning & the flaring upper half w/an everted repoussé foliate gadrooned rim, raised on a ringed pedestal w/band of gadrooning on a square base raised on paw feet, the wide domed cover w/a gadrooned band & reeded foliate finial, first half 19th c., 18" h. (ILLUS.) **1,035**

Teakettle, cover & stand, plain inverted pear-form, the rim beaded, the cover w/repoussé engraved leaves & urn finial, w/serpentine spout, resting on a pierced circular stand w/bright-cut & engraved foliates, on three footed scroll legs, Wilkinson & Co., Sheffield, England, last quarter 18th c., stand 14 1/4" l., the set................ **690**

Teakettle, cover & stand, the bulbous lobed pot w/a domed chased & engraved cover w/cast foliate finial, the body w/repoussé & engraved flowers, on four scroll & shell feet, w/a shaped rectangular stand w/cast scroll sides w/lion & horse terminals, on four foliate feet, Elkington & Co., mid-19th c., 12" h., the set...................... **431**

Warming dishes, liners & covers, rectangular, surrounded by gadrooned borders & rims, applied w/reeded foliate handles & knop, raised on scrolled feet headed by foliage, early 19th c., 14 1/4" l., pr. **1,725**

Wine coasters, rounded form w/everted gadrooned rims, wood bases, England, mid-19th c., 6" d., pr.. **230**

Wine coolers, cylindrical footed form, the side engraved w/an armorial & mounted w/a pair of ring handles near the top, fitted w/a liner, collar & pierced gallery, early 19th c., 7" h., pr. **5,175**

Sheffield Handled Wine Coolers

Wine coolers, cylindrical w/a wide gadrooned rim over applied looped foliate-cast handles, embossed cartouche on the front, complete w/liner & collar, overall 10" w., 4 3/4" h., pr. (ILLUS.) **3,450**

Wine coolers, urn-form, leaf-capped reeded handles, engraved w/a crest above a monogram, gadrooned rim, fitted w/collar & liner, early 19th c., 9 1/2" h., pr. **2,587**

Silver

American (Sterling & Coin)

Basket, coin, oval boat-shape, the shaped rim & base w/molded scrolling, cast loop end rim handles, the sides embossed overall w/flowers, on four cast acanthus leaf feet, engraved presentation in center, S. Kirk & Son., Baltimore, 1846-61, 6 3/4 x 9 5/8" excluding handles................ **1,610**

Alvin Sterling Flower Basket

Basket, flower-type, a round stepped foot below the tall slender trumpet body w/a wide cupped rim w/four applied floral roundels flanked by engraved floral sprays & linked by husk swags, the foot engraved w/floral sprays & swags & the sides engraved w/floral drops & lappets, the shaped rim centered by a high upright arched handle pierced w/flat leaves & bat's wing fluted roundels, Alvin Silver Co., early 20th c., 22 1/2" h. (ILLUS.)........ **1,035**

Frank W. Smith Decorative Basket

Basket, oblong form w/two upturned sides, a wide looped reticulated border band w/a fleur-de-lis design above lattice-pierced sides w/central reserves, a high center reeded swing handle, by Frank W. Smith Silver Co. for Bailey, Banks & Biddle, 11 1/2" h. (ILLUS.) **468**

Basket, oval shape w/fixed upright handle, chased medallion & swag design, pierced sides, inscribed w/presentation dates of 1893-1918, a long list of names under the base, Whiting Mfg. Co., 7 1/2" h. **330**

Basket, the pierced basket applied w/floral sprays on the shaped edge, w/tapered upright handle, monogrammed on interior, stepped oval foot, Tiffany & Co., 1902-07, 9" h. **978**

Beaker, coin, slightly tapering cylindrical form w/a reeded top & base rim, marked by E. & D. Kinsey, Cincinnati, Ohio, 1840-61, 3 1/2" h. **403**

Beaker, coin, tapering cylindrical form w/molded rim, engraved w/a contemporary foliate cypher sprouting flowers, on a rim foot, Myer Myers, New York, ca. 1775, 3 7/8" h. **14,400**

Bowl, a wide everted rim around the center stamped w/lobing centered by floral sprays, J.E. Caldwell & Co., Philadelphia, early 20th c., 10" d. **173**

Bowl, footed w/deep upright sides, overall fine repoussé decoration of roses & leaves, Jacobi & Jenkins, Baltimore, 1894-1908 .... **770**

Bowl, oval on a stepped conforming foot, the shallow lobed bowl w/broad border of stylized fruit & flowers & reeded rim, Gorham Mfg. Co., Providence, Rhode Island, ca. 1930, 13 3/4" l. **1,610**

Bowl, round, the shaped rim reticulated w/embossed foliates, S-scrolls & husk swags w/six cartouches surrounding embossed bouquets, the interior w/a central monogram, the flared sides w/C-scroll & foliate chasing, on a banded spreading foot, Bailey, Banks & Biddle Co., first quarter 20th c., 10 3/4" d. **546**

Bowl, round w/a ruffled everted rim, embossed gadrooning & raised & engraved band, the sides w/repoussé reeding, Black, Starr & Frost, late 19th - early 20th c., 12" d. **259**

Bread tray, oval w/ornate scalloped & molded scroll rim w/reticulated scrolling rolled sides w/molded foliate swags, Graff, Washbourne & Dunn, New York, New York, early 20th c., 8 1/4 x 12 3/4" **633**

Breakfast set: child's bowl & underplate; the deep round bowl w/acid-etched acorn branches on the rim & cut cardwork squirrels around the sides w/a lower portion w/engraved stylized cobblestones, the round dished plate w/an identical rim band, Tiffany & Co., early 20th c., bowl 5 1/8" d., plate 7 1/2" d., 2 pcs. (ILLUS. top next column) **2,185**

Sterling Child's Breakfast Set

Cake plate, round w/a shaped reticulated rim w/embossed swags & foliate-centered cartouches, the center w/engraved foliage, on a circular molded foot, Shreve, Crump & Low, Boston, early 20th c., 10 1/2" d. **546**

Cake plate, the waved rim w/molded scallop shell decoration, the face w/openwork engraved band, on a reticulated & engraved trumpet-form base, monogrammed in the center, Tiffany & Co., New York, 1907-47, 12 1/2" d., 5 3/4" h. ... **2,185**

Cann, coin, footed plain baluster-form body w/a capped double-scroll handle, one side engraved w/a script monogram, the other w/another monogram & "A Gift," Elias Pelletreau, Southampton, New York, ca. 1770, 6 1/8" h. **13,200**

Cann, coin, molded foot below the tapering cylindrical body w/slightly everted rim, scroll handle w/acanthus grip, marked by Myer Myers, New York, ca. 1750, 4 1/2" h. **21,850**

Ornate Kirk & Son Center Bowl

Center bowl, a low oval pedestal foot supporting a long oval boat-shaped bowl w/high incurved ends topped by large figural butterfly handles, the foot & side ornately decorated w/repoussé designs of leafy fruits & flowers, S. Kirk & Son, late 19th c., 13" l. (ILLUS.) **2,530**

Center bowl, in the Rococo taste, w/four reserves each depicting different flower species, S. Kirk & Son, 19th c., 10 1/4" l. **633**

Gorham Sterling Center Bowl

Center bowl, round w/deep rolled rim w/molded scroll edge & embossed & engraved foliate & scroll decoration, on a stepped round base, Gorham Mfg. Co., Providence, Rhode Island, ca. 1910, 14 1/4" d. (ILLUS.)............................... **1,870**

Center bowl, round w/everted rim, engraved w/scrolls, bellflowers & floral drops, offset w/four scroll-reticulated cartouches, engraved & dated 1925 in the center, Whiting Mfg. Co., 10" d. **201**

Centerpiece, a large hemispherical bowl w/a shaped interior & wide rolled rectangular lappet rim, raised on a base composed of four cast dolphins separated by shells, Black, Starr & Frost, New York, early 20th c., marked & numbered, 12 1/2" d.. **3,600**

Centerpiece, sterling, oval w/a wide interior border engraved w/scrolling foliage, the wide everted rim pierced & applied w/foliage & scrolls, retailed by J.E. Caldwell & Co., late 19th c., 16" l. **1,380**

Charger, Martelé line, hammered round form w/shaped & waved rim w/chased lobing, each lobe w/an embossed leaf & buds, embossed monogram in one lobe, on a domed foot, Gorham Mfg. Co., Providence, Rhode Island, ca. 1900, 13" d....... **5,463**

Child's set: a 5 1/2" d., 2 3/8" h. bowl w/rolled flared rim, the exterior w/a central band of embossed children's toys, the matching plate w/a rolled rim & similar band, Gorham Mfg. Co., Providence, Rhode Island, ca. 1910, 2 pcs. **1,725**

Cigarette case, rectangular w/engraved diagonal lines on front & back, the gilt interior monogrammed, Tiffany & Co., New York, early 20th c. **144**

Cocktail shaker, cov., hand-hammered, tall slightly ovoid form w/a lift off top, a diamond-shaped applique on the side, the cylindrical cap w/a pointed spout, stamped w/the Gorham trademark & "Sterling - A10059 - 1," ca. 1920s, 4" d., 10" h. (three minor dents) **220**

Coffeepot, cov., coin, of large partly fluted, oval vase-form, w/urn finial & swan's-neck spout, engraved w/contemporary foliate cyphers on both sides, conforming pedestal foot, Joel Syre, New York, New York, ca. 1805, 13 1/2" h............................. **5,175**

Coffeepot, cov., coin, urn-form, round foot on a square thin platform, tapering pedestal to the tall body w/beaded rims & waisted shoulder, hinged domed cover surmounted by an urn-form finial, leaf-capped wood scroll handle & beaded scroll spout, body engraved w/a monogram, marked by Joseph Shoemaker, Philadelphia, ca. 1795, 15 1/2" h............. **10,350**

Coffeepot, cov., slightly tapering cylindrical form, chased overall w/various blossoms on a stippled ground, the angular handle cast w/a ram's head, S. Kirk & Son Co., early 20th c., 8 1/2" h................................... **1,610**

Rare Early American Coffeepot

Coffeepot, cov., coin, tall inverted pear-form engraved on one side w/later arms in 18th c. style, the domed foot w/embossed beaded border repeated on the rim of the domed cover w/a wrythen urn finial, a shell-decorated swan's-neck spout, the leaf-capped carved wood handle rising from a cast shell upper terminal, double stamped mark of Joseph & Nathaniel Richardson, Philadelphia, ca. 1780, 12 7/8" h. (ILLUS.) **30,650**

Communion cup, coin, the straight-sided bowl above a rounded foot w/applied disk, the bowl engraved w/a church presentation inscription dated 1802 within a bright-cut swag, Boston, early 19th c., 6 1/4" h. **1,380**

Compote, open, round w/a molded rim w/embossed beaded foliate band, the body w/engraved band w/central cartouches, cast loop handles, on a trumpet-form base w/embossed band, monogrammed, Gorham Mfg. Co., Providence, Rhode Island, 1874, 8" d., 5 3/4" h.. **546**

Compote, open, round w/raised reticulated rim, the center monogrammed w/an engraved foliate border, on a molded round foot, Dominick & Haff, New York, New York, early 20th c., 8" d. **173**

Compote, open, the bowl w/a wide band of floral repoussé, on a trumpet foot w/repoussé, Baltimore Sterling Silver Co., late 19th c., 2 3/4" h............................ **173**

Compotes, open, round w/molded everted rim w/openwork foliate designs & scrolls, on similarly decorated domed base, monogrammed in the center, one w/engraved date on the base, Graff, Washbourne & Dunn, New York, New York, early 20th c., 10 1/2" d., pr.......................... **1,725**

Creamer, coin, classic urn-form w/high arched spout, tall looped handle down the side & a domed pedestal foot, beading at the girdle & rim, engraved w/a name under the spout, Harding & Co., Boston, mid-19th c., 8 1/4" h. **201**

Creamer, coin, Classical style, a round domed foot w/applied floral edge banding supporting a wide bulbous lobed lower body tapering to an applied floral shoulder band below the short waisted neck & high arched spout, ornate C-scroll handle, monogrammed, Geradus Boyce, New York City, ca. 1830-40, 6 1/2" h. **460**

Creamer, coin, tall helmet shape, a wide arched spout & high loop handle from rim to base of tapering body, raised on a short pedestal over a square foot, engraved w/a monogram, molded rim around top, marked on the foot rim by Paul Revere, Jr., Boston, ca. 1790, 6 1/2" h. **7,200**

Creamer, covered sugar bowl & undertray, Arts & Crafts style w/a hammered surface, impressed mark "Hand Wrought - at the Kalo Shop - 158," Chicago, New York, ca. 1920, undertray 9 3/4" d., creamer 3 3/4" h., 3 pcs. **345**

Creamer, open sugar bowl & undertray, each pear-shaped on a domed foot, serpentine handles & stamped w/a band of C-scrolls & flowerheads at the girdle, oval tray w/matching stamped edge, Gorham Mfg. Co., Providence, Rhode Island, ca. 1951, tray 9 3/4" l., creamer 4" h., the set **173**

Ewer, coin, classical-form, footed large ovoid body w/a tall waisted neck & wide arched spout, high arched S-scroll plain handle, the body w/a large engraved coat-of-arms, Obadiah Rich, Boston, mid-19th c., 12 1/2" h. **920**

Tall Kirk & Son Sterling Ewer

Ewer, cov., coin, a round disk foot & slender pedestal supporting a tall slender ovoid body tapering to a tall neck w/high arched rim spout & tall squared loop handle, the shaped rim w/molded scrolls, the hinged domed cover w/embossed & engraved acanthus leaves w/grape cluster finial, the handle w/a ram's head mount, the body embossed overall w/foliate designs surrounding architectural scenes on a matte ground, the pedestal w/acanthus leaves & the foot w/embossed foliage, w/an engraved crest, S. Kirk & Son, Baltimore, probably 1846-61, 18 1/4" h., (ILLUS.) **7,475**

Fish knife, the back tipt handle w/a bright-cut border & engraved crest, the blade w/bright-cut foliate designs, Shreve, Crump & Low, Boston, late 19th c., 12 3/8" l. **143**

Flask, ovoid, chased & embossed on each side w/scenes of monks in the wine cellar, hinged lid w/locking collar, engraved on top of lid, R. Wallace & Sons, early 20th c., 5 1/2" l. **690**

Fruit bowl, Francis I patt., lobed quadrangular form, the shaped rim everted, w/embossed scrolls & fruit, Reed and Barton, Taunton, Massachusetts, 20th c., 11 1/2" d. **546**

Fruit bowl, round w/shaped flared rim w/foliate engraved band, the body w/overall foliate engraving w/a central cartouche, on a circular molded foot, Gorham Mfg. Co., Providence, Rhode Island, late 19th - early 20th c., 11" d....................................... **345**

Goblet, coin, deep bowl w/fluted lower half, on a stem w/flaring round foot, beaded edge molding, mark of Richard Humphries, Philadelphia, ca. 1780, 6" h. **10,925**

Jar, cov., cubical, the square cover w/molded scroll rim & embossed foliate top, the body w/embossed foliate designs between molded scroll bands at the shoulder & base, monogrammed on the base, Duhme & Co., Cincinnati, Ohio, late 19th - early 20th c., 3 3/4" h. **690**

Julep cup, coin, slightly tapering cylindrical form, tooled rings at rim & base, mark of Edward & David Kensey, Newport, Kentucky & Cincinnati, Ohio, 1836-50, 3 3/8" h... **413**

Ladle, Medallion patt., the handle w/a profile medallion of a classical woman, ovoid bowl w/regilded interior, Gorham Mfg. Co., Providence, Rhode Island, retailed by Tiffany & Co., New York, late 19th c., 12 1/2" l. **690**

Loving cup, three-handled, the bombé vase-form embossed & chased w/grapevine, matching cast base rim & capped handles, Theodore B. Starr, New York, New York, ca. 1910, 11 5/8" h. **6,325**

Mug, child's, coin, octagonal w/a molded rim band & double base bands, C-scroll handle, the body engraved w/a scroll design, inscribed on the front & base, Bailey & Kitchen, Philadelphia, 1832-48, 3 3/8" h... **288**

Early Victorian Coin Silver Mug

Mug, coin, octagonal, each panel chased & embossed w/floral sprays & C-scrolls, a plain central cartouche, reeded rim & base band, angled loop handle, J.E. Caldwell & Co., Philadelphia, mid-19th c., 3 1/2" h. (ILLUS.)............................ 230

Mug, coin, presentation-type, hexagonal baluster-form w/gently flared top, handle w/foliate decoration above a hexagonal molded flaring base, long inscription dated 1852, Geradus Boyce, New York, New York, 5 1/4" h. (minor dents)................... 863

Mug, Colonial Revival style, pear-shaped w/a banded rim & scroll handle, on a molded round base, monogrammed, James Woolley, Boston, early 20th c., 5 1/4" h................................ 546

Napkin rings, Art Nouveau style, each w/a band of slender entwined flowers, monogrammed, Gorham Mfg. Co., Providence, Rhode Island, late 19th c., 1 1/2" w., pr. 460

Pitcher, baluster-form, on four paw feet w/shell & floral cartouche joins, the body chased w/a guilloché band enclosing flowerheads, the scroll handle w/foliate joins, the everted rim w/acanthus scroll band, marked by Tiffany & Co., New York, 1895-1902, 10 1/4" h......................... 4,025

Tiffany Chrysanthemum Pitcher

Pitcher, "Chrysanthemum" patt., bulbous lower body w/a wide swelled cylindrical neck w/a wide rim spout, hollow loop handle, repoussé & engraved flowers & scrolls, Tiffany & Co., ca. 1880, 9 1/4" h. (ILLUS.).. 4,025

Pitcher, coin, classical style w/a round foot w/applied floral banding & a short pedes-tal supporting the squatty bulbous lobed body flaring to a medial applied floral band below the high arched wide spout & rim w/another applied floral band, large S-scroll handle, monogrammed, Geradus Boyce, New York, New York, 1820-57, 6 1/2" h. 460

Pitcher, cov., coin, jug-form, baluster-shaped, the shaped rim beaded, domed cover w/cast swan finial, ear-shaped handle, on a beaded molded foot, monogrammed & dated in the center, Bigelow Bros. & Kennard, Boston, ca. 1860, 8 3/4" h. 518

Pitcher, squat baluster-form, the domed foot chased & embossed w/shells & seaweed, the body partially fluted w/overhanging girdle chased & embossed w/shells & dolphins on a stippled ground engraved w/cattails, foliate ear handle, rim rolled at spout & everted at sides w/half leaves, Tiffany & Co., New York, late 19th c., 10 3/4" h................................... 4,025

Pitcher, squat fluted form, the shaped rim & base w/molded scrolling, serpentine handle, monogrammed on one side, Smith Co., Denver, Colorado, ca. 1900, 5 3/4" h. 518

Pitcher, vasiform, the shaped molded rim on a beaded & banded neck w/engine-turned decoration, the handle w/cast stag's head thumbrest, on a domed foot, w/presentation & date inscribed on front, Gorham Mfg. Co., Providence, Rhode Island, third quarter 19th c., 7 5/8" h. 920

Pitcher, water, Japanese-style decoration, flared ringed base below the tall cylindrical body applied w/die-rolled bands, engraved w/aquatic plants & applied w/swimming fish, small rim spout, angled curved handle, marked & numbered, Tiffany & Co., New York, ca. 1880, 9 1/8" h. . 9,000

Pitcher, ovoid body, the center chased w/a band of figures in a village scene, centered by two registers of foliage, the spout w/a beaded mask, mounted w/a leaf-capped scroll handle & on a flared foot, S. Kirk & Sons Co., early 20th c., 12 1/2" h. 3,450

One of Two Gorham Sterling Pitchers

Pitchers, footed baluster-form w/upright rounded spout & C-scroll handle, the body chased & embossed around the lower section w/dense floral sprays, a plain cartouche on one side, a monogrammed cartouche on the other side, the handle w/flat leaves at the top & base, Gorham Mfg. Co., Providence, Rhode Island, late 19th c., 7 3/4" h., pr. (ILLUS. of one) **1,610**

Plate, plain round form w/a rolled rim, decorated w/repoussé clusters of grapes & engraved leaves, Wallace Silver Co., Connecticut, early 20th c., 10 1/2" d. **230**

Plates, bread & butter, silver-gilt, round, the center of each engraved w/a monogram, the border pierced & chased w/paterae & swags, Durgin for Gorham Mfg. Co., 20th c., 6 1/4" d., set of 12 (gilt wear) **747**

Platter, George III-Style, round, engraved w/a trophy, the shaped border & body raised on scrolled foliate-capped feet, dated 1929, 20 1/4" d. **1,092**

Early American Silver Porringer

Porringer, coin, low rounded form w/a scroll-pierced tab handle w/monogram, by Henrick Boelen, New York City, mid-18th c., 7" l. (ILLUS.).................................... **1,035**

Early Boston Porringer & Tankard

Porringer, coin, shallow rounded form w/ornate scroll-pierced tab handle w/monogram, handle stamped twice w/mark of Benjamin Burt, Boston, 18th c., repair to the rim at handle, minor dents, 5 1/4" d. (ILLUS. left) **1,265**

Porringer, ovoid bowl w/shaped & pierced handle w/engraved detailing, Tiffany & Co., 1902-07, overall 7 1/4" l. **403**

Presentation cup, raised on a high domed & scalloped reticulated foot w/diapering, rocaille scrolls & roses, the ovoid body w/a gently ruffled rim, two curved horn handles set in stylized horn sockets, engraved on one side w/initials & dated 1899, Bigelow, Kennard & Co., 12" w. w/handles, 11 1/2" h. (ILLUS. top next column) **3,105**

Fine Sterling Presentation Cup

Punch bowl, Japanese-style, deep footed bowl etched w/a scene of fish swimming among waterlilies & reeds below an embossed rim of churning waves, spot-hammered foot, Gorham Mfg. Co., Providence, Rhode Island, 1886, 13 1/4" d. **6,900**

Rare Gorham Martelé Punch Bowl

Punch bowl, Martelé line, a shaped round wavy foot, the deep lobed body deeply repoussé & chased w/large dandelions & lilies, deeply scalloped everted rim, Gorham Mfg. Co., Providence, Rhode Island, 1898, 10 3/4" d. (ILLUS.) **25,300**

Punch bowl & ladle, deep rounded bowl embossed & chased w/scrolling grapevine below an applied band of scrolling classical foliage, waved rim, beaded foot, the gilt interior w/engraved monogram, raised on a low round pedestal foot w/beaded edge, the ladle w/matching waved rim, the handle applied w/three-dimensional cast grapevine, engraved on reverse "1868 - S - 1893," both marked & numbered, Gorham Mfg. Co., Providence, Rhode Island, ca. 1893, bowl 13 1/2" d., 2 pcs. **6,600**

Punch ladle, coin, elliptical bowl w/fiddle handle, engraved "James Johnson to Mary B. Dale, May 20, 1840," Davis, Palmer & Co., Boston, 12" l. (minor pitting).. **230**

Sauceboat, coin, a punched beaded rim & leaf-capped flying multiple-scroll handle, pedestal foot w/beaded borders, engraved w/a contemporary monogram, Abraham Dubois, Philadelphia, ca. 1790, 6 3/4" l. **8,050**

Serving bowl, rectangular w/lobed molded rim w/reeded scroll decoration, the reticulated sides w/molded floral swags & scallop shells within roundels, on four pad feet, Frank Herschede Company, Cincinnati, Ohio, 20th c., 11 1/2 x 14"....... **1,495**

Soup tureen, cov., coin, oval bombé form, the four paw-and-ball feet headed by acanthus, the everted rim applied w/dense band of flowers, leaves & scrolls, the two bracket handles cast & chased as grapevine capped by a rose, the domed cover w/an acanthus calux surmounted by a floral ring finial, each side of the body engraved w/a coat-of-arms, crest & motto, the cover engraved w/crests, marked by Frederick Marquand, New York, New York, ca. 1830, overall 15 3/4" l. **12,650**

Sugar urn, cov., coin, urn-form w/circular foot on a square pedestal, beaded rims & pierced gallery, the conical cover w/urn-form finial, the body engraved w/a monogram, marked by Charles Moore & John Ferguson, Philadelphia, ca. 1801-05, 11" h. **3,680**

Sugar urn, cov., coin, urn-shaped body on a flaring pedestal & square foot, a stepped spire-form cover w/an urn finial, row of chased beadwork above the body, monogrammed, A.W. Robinson, Philadelphia, 1795-98, 10 3/4" h. **1,495**

Tankard, cov., coin, tapered cylindrical body w/a hinged stepped & domed cover w/flame finial & scrolled thumbrest, S-scroll handle w/terminal in the form of a Queen Anne coin, body w/mid-19th c, arms & initial, handle engraved w/initials, cover of later origin, George Hanners, Boston, ca. 1740, 8 3/4" h. **3,600**

Tankard, cov., coin, tapering cylindrical body w/ringed base & medial ring, stepped & ringed domed hinged cover w/scrolled thumbrest, C-scroll handle, John Coney, Boston, ca. 1721, early engraved initials & later script inscription dated 1854, 4 3/4" d., 8" h. (cover of later origin) **9,200**

Tankard, cov., coin, tapering cylindrical body w/flaring ringed base, medial ring & flared ringed rim, the stepped & domed hinged cover w/an urn & flame finial, hollow scrolled handle w/scrolled thumbpiece & convex tip, monogrammed, a spout added later & removed, some restoration, Benjamin Burt, Boston, 18th c., 9" h. (ILLUS. right with porringer) **7,475**

Tazza, the bowl w/chased & embossed rim & shaped edge, on a trumpet foot partially chased & embossed w/flowers on a stippled ground, S. Kirk & Son Co., early 20th c., 6 1/2" d., 3 1/4" h., pr......................... **633**

Tea & coffee service: cov. coffeepot, cov. teapot, cov. sugar bowl, creamer & waste bowl; sterling, the urn-form coffeepot on four paw feet w/leaf joins, the cross-supports centering a paterae, the body w/dentilated & paterae shoulder, the hinged domed cover w/urn finial, the scroll handle w/ivory insulators, other pieces matching, each marked w/retailer's mark & mark of the Gorham Mfg. Co., Providence, Rhode Island, w/an oval mahogany tray w/paterae inlay & silver gallery w/bracket end handles, 1919, coffeepot 9 3/4" h., the set........................... **3,680**

Tea & coffee set: cov. coffeepot, cov. teapot, creamer, cov. sugar bowl & waste bowl; Art Nouveau style, upright baluster-form bodies w/an undulating foot & a flaring rim w/wide sawtooth border, simple loop handle, the domed covers w/a cast flower finial, applied monograms, Tiffany & Co., New York, 1891-1902, coffeepot 12" h., the set... **2,875**

Tea & coffee set: cov. coffeepot, cov. teapot, creamer & open sugar bowl; each of urn-form w/shaped embossed foliate rims, the pots w/waisted domed cover w/repoussé engraved swags w/urn finials, the bodies fluted w/repoussé engraved foliate swags & chased reeding on domed & embossed bases, monogrammed on the base, Shreve, Crump & Low, Boston, early 20th c., teapot 9 3/4" h., the set **3,105**

Tea service: cov. teapot, cov. sugar bowl, creamer & waste bowl; coin, Classical-style, each shaped rectangular bombé form, on a conforming base w/four leaf-capped paw feet, scroll handles, the teapot w/ivory insulators, the domed covers w/a star calyx & acorn finial, each engraved on one side "JAK," marked by Alcock & Allen, New York, New York, ca. 1820, teapot 13" l., the set **4,025**

Tea set: cov. teapot, cov. coffeepot, cov. handled sugar bowl & creamer; coin, each of oval form, the domed covers w/urn-form finials & borders of bright-cutting, the oval body w/a shield-shaped crest, the front depicting an eagle w/brood in a nest, the back w/a monogram w/floral, foliate & geometric bright-cut decoration, molded rim & base, angular reeded handles on sugar & creamer, angular ebonized wood handles on pots, Hugh Wishart, New York, New York, ca. 1784, coffeepot 8 1/2" h., the set (minor repair, dents)... **3,738**

Tea set: cov. teapot, cov. sugar bowl & creamer; coin, Classical style, the oval teapot w/straight sides & concave rim, w/wood scroll handle & straight spout, the hinged domed cover w/a pineapple finial, the sugar & creamer each of urn-form on square pedestal foot, all w/beaded rims & bright-cut engraving on both sides w/floral garlands & a shield centering a monogram, teapot marked by Gerrit Schanck, New York, the creamer & sugar marked by John Schanck, New York, ca. 1795, teapot overall 12" l., the set **8,625**

Tea set: cov. teapot, creamer & cov. sugar bowl; Colonial Revival style, baluster-form bodies, domed covers w/reeded urn finials, molded rims gadrooned, on stepped round bases, Gorham Mfg. Co.,

Providence, Rhode Island, 1950, teapot
9" h., the set **690**

Tea set: tete-a-tete-style w/a cov. teapot,
cov. sugar bowl, creamer & cov. teakettle
on stand; each w/a squat bulbous body
w/engine-turned central band of Greek
key, angular handles & knob finials, the
stand w/a pointed reticulated lappet panel, on tall slender squared legs w/ivy leaf
knees & scroll feet, monogrammed on
both sides, Tiffany & Co., New York,
ca. 1865-70, kettle 9 1/4" h., the set **2,185**

Tea tray, coin, oval, two-handled, molded
rim & loop handles, the center engraved
w/flowers & rococo scrolls, marked by
Platt & Brother, New York, New York,
1825-34, 31 1/4" l. **4,600**

Tray, coin, oval, a gadrooned border enclosing an engraved design of flanking
vases containing floral & foliate scrolls,
on four scrolled feet, monogram, Gorham
& Company, 1848-65, 8 3/4 x 12" **374**

Tray, coin, oval w/gadrooned border enclosing an engraved design of flanking
vases containing floral & foliate scrolls,
on four scrolled feet, monogrammed,
Gorham and Co., Providence, Rhode Is-
land, 1848-65, 8 3/4 x 12".............................. **374**

Tray, coin, round w/beaded border enclosing an engraved scrolled foliate design,
raised on three scrolled feet, monogrammed, Jones, Shreve, Brown & Co.,
Boston, 1854, 10" d. (slightly misshapen)...... **489**

Tray, round w/molded rim w/foliate & scroll
designs, the sides w/embossed foliate
decoration & castles on a matte background, the face w/engine-turned decoration surrounding an engraved roundel,
monogrammed in the center, Loring An-
drews Co., Cincinnati, Ohio, 20th c., 9" d...... **489**

Tumbler, coin, slightly tapering cylindrical
form w/ring bands at the rim & base,
marked by E. & D. Kinsey, Cincinnati,
Ohio, 1840-61, 3 1/2" h. **403**

Tureen, cov., the oval body & domed cover
chased overall w/blossoms on a stippled
ground, mounted w/leaf-capped scroll
handles, the base engraved w/a scrolling
monogram, made & retailed by Bailey,
Banks & Biddle, late 19th c., overall 13" l... **3,450**

Vase, Martelé line, the hammered bulbous
body w/flared shaped & waved rim, the
rim w/embossed leaves, the lobed body
w/embossed daffodils, on a shaped
domed foot w/embossed buds & leaves,
w/embossed monogram, Gorham Mfg.
Co., Providence, Rhode Island, ca. 1900,
8" h. **5,463**

Vase, the body vertically paneled w/foliate
designs & scrolls & acanthus leaf decoration around the bottom, a molded, reeded
rim above a repoussé frieze, a knopped
stem above a repoussé foot w/molded
bands, Gorham Mfg. Co., Providence,
Rhode Island, early 20th c., 10 1/8" h........... **978**

Vase, baluster-form, on a spreading foot
w/an openwork cornucopia & scroll rim,
the flared neck w/a border of openwork
cornucopiae, scrolls & acanthus leaves,

marked by Dominick & Haff, New York,
New York, ca. 1895, 11 1/4" h. **3,450**

Vase, Martelé line, inverted baluster-form
w/spot-hammered surface, the domed
lobed base & body repoussé & chased
w/berries & leaves, w/everted wavy &
lobed rim, marked by the Gorham Mfg.
Co., Providence, Rhode Island, ca. 1902,
14" h... **10,925**

Vases, 7" h., bud-type, Arts & Crafts style,
flared rolled rim on cylindrical body tapering to a round disk base, hammered surface, impressed "Sterling Kalo 377G" on
base, Chicago, early 20th c., pr................. **1,840**

English & Others

Apostle spoon, the handle w/molded lamb,
cross & winged cherub head w/a cast
apostle terminal, engraved "St. Bartho-
lomew" on the back, London, 1856, 9" l. **115**

Beaker, slightly tapering cylindrical form on
a bulbous squat foot, chased & em-
bossed w/stylized rocaille, the sides
chased & embossed w/eagles on pediments bearing floral swags & sprays,
w/two rococo cartouches centered by engraved crosshatching & fishscaling, Mos-
cow, Russia, early 19th c., 6" h. **805**

Bowl, broad body banded at the high waist
w/an ovolo band, the rims applied w/ga-
drooned bands, St. Petersburg, Russia,
1841, 8 1/8" d. **575**

Bowl, round, chased & repoussé w/scrolling
flowers, thistles, grapes, foliage, C-
scrolls & diaperwork on a matte ground,
one cartouche engraved w/a crest & motto, the other side monogrammed & dated
1858, George IV period, George McHat-
tie, Edinburgh, 1826-27, 10 3/4" d. **2,185**

Cake basket, oval shape w/embossed leaf
& bud rim, the openwork swing handle
w/beaded S-scrolls, chased beaded
band & chased spiral reeded, on a reticulated oval base w/a twisted wire foot,
marks of William Plummer, London,
1766, 13" l. **2,070**

Center bowl, cov., oval, the raised rim
w/openwork design, gilt openwork insert,
resting on an oval base w/similar decoration, Oporto, Portugal, 20th c.,
7 5/8 x 13 3/8".. **201**

Cigar case, hinged four-finger style, presentation initials engraved on the lid &
dated 1889, gold-washed interior, Lon-
don, 1886, 3 1/8 x 5 1/4".................................. **518**

Coffeepot, cov., footed tall tapering cylindrical form w/a stepped domed hinged cov-
er w/tall button finial, swan's-neck spout
& ornate C-scroll wooden handle, engraved w/a crest, George III period, Lon-
don, England, 1781, 9 1/2" h...................... **2,185**

Coffeepot, cov., ovoid body raised on a flaring ringed round foot, the body repoussé
& chased w/scrolls, flowers & rocaille, the
ivory handle & scroll spout w/foliate joins,
the hinged domed cover w/similar decoration & surmounted by a baluster finial,
Lisbon, Portugal, 1770-1804, 11 3/4" h...... **4,600**

Coffeepot, cov., Rococo-style, pyriform, on
three paw feet headed by scrolls & car-

touches, the swirled lobed body w/wood scroll handle, the spout w/rocaille, shell & floral join, the hinged high-domed cover surmounted by a leaf & bud finial, Mons, Belgium, 1762, 13 1/2" h. **9,775**

Coffeepot, cover & stand, the pot of a lobed pear shape, on a domed foot w/shaded edge, scroll handle w/ivory heat stops, serpentine spout, domed cover w/a flower finial, the stand raised on four scroll legs mounted w/carved ivory flattened ball feet, w/an unmarked burner, Holland, the pot 1876, the stand 1863, the pot 9 1/2" h., the set **633**

Creamer, fluted helmet-form w/wide arched spout & beaded rim w/engraved band, high arched reeded handle, engraved overall w/foliates & scrolls, on an engraved round foot above a horizontally reeded octagonal plinth, monogrammed, Hester Bateman, London, 1789, 6 1/4" h. **489**

Early Russian Silver Creamer

Creamer, footed ovoid boat-form w/a lobed lower body below an applied floral shoulder band below the finely beaded rim w/wide arched spout, carved ivory C-form handle w/ear, gold-washed interior, Russia, 1829, 4 3/4" h. (ILLUS.) **374**

Ladle, ovoid bowl w/gold-washed interior, shaped stem & long carved ivory handle, Europe, 19th c., 15 1/2" l. **86**

Ladle, ovoid bowl w/tapered back tipt stem, mongrammed, Dublin, Ireland, 1762, 13" l. **316**

Monteith, the domed circular foot chased w/sprays of blossoms, the circular bowl chased w/C-scrolls alternating w/sprays of foliage, the shaped border flat-chased w/a scroll rim, rubbed mark of maker, Birmingham, England, 1853, 6 1/2" d. **546**

Pitcher, cov., figural, circular base supporting the leafy head of a tall inverted turnip w/a hinged top & slender loop vine handle down the side, Koch & Bergfeld, Bremen, ca. 1890, retailed by Gotting, 17 1/2" h. **2,300**

Pitcher, tapered vasiform body, vertical reeding around body w/high spout, fluted round pedestal foot, cast S-scroll handle, Russia, 19th c., 8 1/2" h. **1,150**

French Neoclassical Planter

Planter, Neoclassical design, oval form w/the sides chased & embossed w/husk swags on a pierced guilloché ground, a ribbon-tied undulating rim, two cast scroll rim handles, on pierced scroll & shell feet, w/fitted metal liner, France, late 18th - early 19th c., 14" l., 5 1/2" h. (ILLUS.) **1,725**

Plates, round w/a shaped border, engraved w/a mottoed crest below a coronet, w/a banded rim, maker's mark M&K, Vienna, Austria, 1846, 10" d., set of 6 .... **2,645**

Punch bowl, deep wide ovoid bowl w/flared rim & round spreading foot, the bowl chased & embossed overall w/scenes of village revelry, gold-washed interior, Paul Storr, London, 1827 opposed by an engraved heraldic device, further marked by John Samuel Hunt, 1852, 12 1/8" d., 5 3/4" h. **8,050**

Punch bowl, footed, circular form w/repoussé flower garlands around the sides, later engraved monogram, raised on a molded gadrooned foot, George IV period, William Eaton, London, 1825, 12 1/4" d. **1,725**

Punch ladle, the twisted handle knopped w/molded foliates & acanthus leaves, w/ivory end, the oval bowl reeded w/a scalloped rim, rubbed marks, France, .950 standard, second half 19th c., 17 14" l. **173**

Sake set: 8 3/4" d., 4 3/4" h. bowl & five 1 1/4" h. sake cups; the bowl on a trumpet foot w/hammered surface & w/curved optical ribbing on the exterior, each cup on a low footring w/slightly flared rim, Japan, 20th c., the set **460**

Salver, in the Georgian style, the shaped border applied w/a scroll rim, on three leaf-capped scroll feet, London, England, 1904, 14" d. **1,150**

Sauce tureen, boat-shaped on an oval beaded foot, beaded edge & loop handles, engraved on one side w/heraldic crest over husk swag w/coat of arms on the other side, John Schofield, London, England, 1784, 10 3/8" l., 5 3/4" h. **1,265**

English Georgian Sauce Tureen

Sauce tureen, cov., deep oblong body engraved on one side w/a heraldic device, w/applied rim cast as a stylized continuous hunting scene featuring stags & hunting dogs, raised on four hairy paw feet topped by rocaille shells flanked by acanthus, two acanthus loop end handles centered by shells, domed cover w/a band of vertical reeding & a finial formed as entwined snakes on a leafy ground, George III era, Jos. Craddock & William Reid, London, 1819, 9" l. plus handles, 6 1/4" h. (ILLUS.).. **2,070**

Sauceboat, boat-form w/a shaped molded rim, two loop side handles, on a domed round base attached to a circular underplate w/shaped edge, maker's mark "KK," Hungary, .800 standard, 20th c., 7 3/4" d., 4" h. **460**

Sauceboat & underplate, oblong boat-shaped w/serpentine molded rim w/scroll decoration, the body w/embossed rococo-style cartouches flanked cattails, a bunch of cattails below the cast ear handle, the oval molded foot resting on an underplate w/shaped rim & scroll decoration, monogrammed, Europe, probably Germany, 19th c., 8 7/8" l., 6 1/4" h., 2 pcs.. **1,265**

Soup ladle, tapered handle w/engraved foliates, the terminal w/engraved crest within a cartouche, the reeded bowl w/repoussé beading, a chased eagle on the reverse, possibly Alexander Richards, Dublin, Ireland, 1766, 14 1/8" l.................... **1,093**

Sugar box, cov., squatty oval bombé form, on four splayed scroll feet, the fluted body engraved w/rocaille cartouches, the stepped hinged cover centered by an engraved eagle within a rocaille cartouche, mark w/the Cyrillic initials of Aleksei Vasil'ev Polozov, Moscow, Russia, 1764, 4 3/8" h... **2,760**

Sugar caster, fluted tapered cylinder, the domed top w/pierced repoussé foliate decoration, knob finial, the rim beaded, the body w/repoussé acanthus leaves, on a molded shaped foot w/floral decoration, Henry Wilkinson & Co., Sheffield, England, 1851, 5 1/4" h.................................. **201**

Tankard, cov., baluster-form w/a low wide round foot, open scrollwork thumbpiece to the stepped, domed cover, double C-scroll handle w/heart-shaped terminal, engraved w/initials, mark of a London silversmith, dated 1776, 8 3/4" h. **3,900**

Early English Sterling Tankard

Tankard, cov., slightly tapering cylindrical body w/a flaring ringed base, medial ring & rim band, hinged stepped domed cover w/volute thumbpiece, hollow scroll handle, front w/an engraved plain rococo cartouche, George I era, Thomas Tearle, London, 1725, 7 1/2" h. (ILLUS.)............... **3,220**

Tazza, figural, an allegory of Autumn, a child holding aloft a cornucopia, draped & seated on a plough w/a chain resting on sheaves of corn on a naturalistic ground, on a circular stepped base engraved w/a crowned cypher, a later glass dish, marked by Sazikov w/the Imperial Warrant, St. Petersburg, Russia, 1867, 28" h. **16,100**

Tazza, ringed flaring round base w/gadrooned band between bands of palmettes, rising to a fluted knopped baluster stem, the circular dish chased w/elongated gadroons at intervals around the rim, marked by Assay Master Lourenco Ribeiro da Rocha, Bahia, Brazil, early 18th c., 13 1/4" d., 7" h. **8,050**

Tea caddy, cov., ovoid form, the body reeded on lower section, engraved on the front w/heraldic crest, the flush hinged cover w/carved ivory egg-shaped finial, Thomas Robins, London, England, 1794, 4 3/4" h... **1,495**

Tea caddy, cylindrical w/large squatty bulbous cover, the body w/overall repoussé band of genre scenes within C-scrolls & foliate designs, Germany, early 20th c., 5" h.` **345**

Tea & coffee service: cov. teapot, cov. coffeepot, open sugar bowl & creamer; Islamic-style, each of baluster-form on a rounded beaded flaring foot, the body chased & repoussé overall w/lobes & scrolls against a matted ground, one side w/vacant cartouche, the scroll handle w/ivory insulators & similar decoration, surmounted by a hinged domed cover w/a baluster finial, Robert Hennell III, London, England, 1870, coffeepot 11" h., the set **4,600**

Tea service: cov. teapot, water jug, milk jug & cov. sugar bowl; 'trompe l'oeil' style, each piece imitating the shape of an embroidered saddle bag cloth w/stylized scrolling foliage within a leaf border, the high domed caps joined to the bodies by link chains, the spouts w/stopper spouts joined by similar chains, each marked under the base "Made for Tiffany & Co.," engraved "D.G.C.," marked w/Cyrillac initials of Nikolai Vasil'evich Nemirov-Kolodkin, Moscow, Russia, 1896-1908, teapot 8 1/4" h., the set **6,325**

Tea tray, oval w/pierced foliate scroll gallery, beaded rim & cut-out end handles, the field engraved w/bright-cut border, Diederik Willem Rethmeyer, Amsterdam, Holland, 1797, 26" l. **5,750**

Teapot, cov., globular hexagonal form on a conforming rim foot, the sides cast & chased w/relief panels of Chinese scenes, the angular handle w/ivory insulators, the conforming cover surmounted by a Chinaman finial, John Lias, London, England, 1816, 5 1/2" h............................. **3,220**

Teapot, cov., melon-shaped w/beaded openwork rim, the domed cover w/repoussé scrolls & urn finial, the body w/repoussé genre scenes within scrolls, upright cast handle w/embossed medallion heads, on a spreading circular base w/beaded edges, monogrammed, Holland, 19th c., .833 standard, 6 3/4" h............ **460**

English Victorian Sterling Teapot

Teapot, cov., Neoclassical-style, scalloped oval body engraved w/a plain foliate roundel on each side, a rim band w/a floral vine, a short serpentine spout, flat-topped ear handle, slightly domed hinged cover w/mushroom finial, Jas. Dixon & Sons, Sheffield, England, 1869, 6" h. (ILLUS.)... **575**

Teapot, cov., pear-shaped w/molded rim, the domed cover w/everted gadrooned rim & reeded bud finial, on a circular molded base w/repoussé gadrooned band, possibly Lewis Harmon or Lewis Herne, London, England, 1768, 10" h........... **920**

Teapot, cover & stand, octagonal form, the domed lid w/an engraved rim & wooden mushroom finial, the body w/bands of engraved foliates w/central cartouches, w/a similarly engraved & banded stand w/molded octagonal rim, on four reeded pedestal feet, Hester Bateman, London, 1788, 7" h. **4,888**

Tray, rectangular, the shaped molded rim beaded, the face w/bands of engraved decoration, a central monogrammed oval, marked "Tizaine," France, mid-19th c., 11 1/8 x 13 3/4"............................ **546**

Vegetable dishes, cov., shaped oblong form, the lobed body w/everted rim applied w/foliated scrolls, the conforming cover surmounted by a removable foliate ring-form handle, Robinson, Edkins & Aston, Birmingham, England, 1840, 13 1/2" l., pr. **3,680**

Wine coolers, urn-form, on four openwork foliate scroll feet under a cast circular rim w/anthemion & Bacchic panther heads, the fluted body w/two bracket handles entwined w/grapevine, the everted rim w/gadrooned border w/shells & foliage at intervals, engraved under the base w/inscribed marks, Pierre-Francois-Augustin Turquet, Paris, France, 1844-55, 10" h., pr. **35,650**

Silver Plate (Hollowware)

Basket, shaped body decorated w/a grapevine design, hinged swirl handle, on a pedestal base, ca. 1850, 12" d., 9 1/2" h. **280**

Candelabra, five-branch, a central stem decorated w/pressed foliage design & scrollwork bands, supporting four scrolling arms each ending in a decorated socket & flanking a central socket, ca. 1895, 18" w., 19" h., pr. **252**

Candelabra, three-light, Art Nouveau style, a slender stem-form central shaft issuing from a bulbed openwork cluster of long leaves & supporting a blossom-form socket w/rolled edges, two further up-curved side arms w/matching candle sockets all above a slender lower standard issuing from a round pierced loop foot, Georges de Feure, France, ca. 1900, 13 3/8" h., pr. **5,640**

Candlestick, typical form, the stem w/engraved knops, the stepped circular base w/engraved bands, monogrammed, Europe, late 19th c., 8 3/4" h......................... **115**

English Silver Plate Candlesticks

Candlesticks, a square molded base stamped w/a band of flowers & scrolls, the baluster-form stem w/four panels stamped w/flower sprigs, a shaped square floral knop above & below, a plain socket w/removable floral-stamped shaped square bobeche, England, 20th c., 12" h., pr. (ILLUS.)............................. **403**

Art Deco Silver Plate Cocktail Set

Cocktail set: cocktail shaker, six glasses & serving tray; Art Deco style, the shaker w/a tall ovoid body w/cylindrical neck fitted w/a mushroom domed cover, short angled shoulder spout & long angled handle, each conical cup on a flared foot, all pieces decorated w/an applied anchor & rope design, impressed maker's mark, retailed by Bernard Rice & Sons, ca. 1930, tray 2 3/4 x 9 1/2", shaker 13 1/4" h., the set (ILLUS.) **575**

Coffee urn, cov., tall ovoid urn-form body tapering to a short flared rim w/domed cover, long loop side handles, slender base w/loop-handled spigot above high scroll-cast legs supporting the burner, cast vintage details & engraved Neoclassical designs w/a relief-cast Minerva head medallion on the back, marked "Rogers, Smith & Co., New Haven, Conn.," late 19th - early 20th c., 17 3/4" h. **385**

Egg server, comprising six egg cups w/reticulated bands, on banded circular feet, & a stand w/shaped rim, the central handle above twisted wire decoration, on four ball feet, England, late 19th - early 20th c., the set **230**

Hot water urn, cov., urn-form body flanked by loop handles & fitted w/a warmer below, overall decoration of grapevines, American-made, ca. 1885, 10" d., 15" h. **280**

Hot water urn, cov., urn-form body flanked by two lion mask handles, raised on elongated shells, beadwork legs ending in claw feet, shaped cover, fitted on a round base w/warmer, American-made, ca. 1880, overall 17" h. **420**

Mirror plateau, tapered cylindrical sides raised on three large scroll feet w/maiden head knees, the rolled rim w/embossed grape decoration, the base w/beading, probably England, late 19th c., 17 1/4" d., 4 1/2" h. **575**

Pitchers, water, bulbous form, engraved w/foliage & flowerheads, cast w/a ruffled C-scroll spout & leaf-capped C-scroll handle, the domed cover w/a swirled knop, Toronto & Co., Canada, 10 1/2" h., pr. **373**

Platter, oval, the shaped rim gadrooned , w/an engraved crest & coat-of-arms, probably England, late 19th - early 20th c., 12 3/4 x 17 1/2" **144**

Platter, round w/shaped rim embossed w/foliate & scroll designs w/devil's head medallions, central foliate designs surrounding an engraved coat of arms, on three embossed foliate feet, Ellis-Barker, Birmingham, England, late 19th c. **690**

Sauceboats, oval foot w/gadrooned bands supporting the oval boat-shaped bowl w/high, wide arched spout & high looped handle, decorated in the late Georgian taste w/overall repoussé flowers & shellwork, Tiffany & Co., New York, late 19th c., 7 3/4" l., pr. **748**

Tea & coffee service: cov. coffeepot, cov. teapot, cov. sugar bowl, creamer & related tray; each piece of a simple classical tall urn-form w/domed cover & button finial, swan's-neck spout & high angled handles, oblong tray w/cast loop end handles, American-made, 20th c., coffeepot 10 5/8" h., the set **220**

Tea & coffee service: cov. teapot, cov. coffeepot, creamer, handled cov. sugar bowl, waste bowl & oval tray; each piece of flaring chamfered rectangular section w/pendent bellflowers at each corner, the shaped tray w/cut-out handles at each end, engraved w/a monogram, Gorham Mfg. Co., Providence, Rhode Island, 20th c., tray 23" l., the set **345**

Tea set: cov. teapot, cov. coffeepot, open sugar & creamer w/large similar oval tray; each piece w/a bulbous ovoid body raised on a short pedestal base, coffeepot & creamer w/tall trumpet necks, each piece w/high upright loop handles, ornately engraved rococo designs, marked "J.B. & S. - EP - H.W.," probably English, ca. 1855, the set **1,100**

Tea tray, rectangular, repoussé border, w/end handles, 19th c., overall 31 3/4" l. **345**

Tea tray, scalloped molded rim w/reticulated sides, the interior engraved w/foliate & scroll designs, Germany, 19th c., 18 3/4 x 23" **230**

Teakettle on stand, squat bulbous body w/beaded rim & flower finial on the cover, an upright scroll handle, a plain body, the stand w/cast foliate swags & four scroll legs w/shell feet, Shreve, Stanwood & Co., Boston, 1860-69, 11" h., the set **288**

Tray, oval, handled, a gallery rim w/end handles & pierce work, geometric designs on the top, on four compressed ball feet, silver over copper, mark of Ellis-Barker Silver Companies, late 19th - early 20th c., 14 1/2 x 22" **358**

Tray, oval w/an applied grapevine border w/etched scrolling floral & foliate designs in the center, loop end handles & short scrolling feet, American-made, late 19th - early 20th c., 17 1/2 x 26 1/2" **280**

Tray, rectangular w/rounded corners, pierced sides, engraved scroll & floral design in center w/monogrammed cartouche, end handles, Wilcox Silver Plate Company, 20th c., 9 x 20" **132**

Tray, round w/scalloped scrolling foliate slightly raised rim, centering a round center heavily engraved w/floral & foliate designs, raised on four scrolling feet, ca. 1900, 7 1/4" d., 1 3/4" h. **224**

Tureen, cov., classical urn-form body w/loop end handles, raised on a pedestal base, domed cover w/finial, Gorham Mfg. Co., dated 1910, 8 x 14 1/2", 11" h. **420**

Tureens, cov., in the late Georgian taste, oval footed base w/gadrooned bands below the wide squatty bulbous oval lobed base w/reeded loop end handles, the domed, stepped cover decorated overall w/repoussé flowers & shellwork, Tiffany & Co., New York, late 19th c., overall 13" l., pr. **1,725**

Vegetable dish, cov., deep round form w/a gadrooned rim & cover, the cover w/a central rosette surmounted by a cast silver & wood finial, the upright S-scroll handles w/wood grips, probably England, late 19th - early 20th c., 8 3/4" d. **259**

Vegetable dish, cov., urn-form body w/double handles, repoussé & chased floral & C-scroll decoration, marked by "L & WS," 16" l., 9" h. **275**

One of Two Fine English Wine Coolers

Wine coolers, classical ovoid body on a short lobed stem w/a stepped round foot, a wide short everted rim, ornate ram's head shoulder handles, the body w/a central foliate & scroll engraving around a roundel, engraved Greek key bands around the shoulder & bottom, Mappin & Co., England, late 19th c., 12 1/4" h., pr. (ILLUS. of one) **2,760**

Tin & Tole

Candle mold, tin, eight-tube, a rectangular frame w/loop strap handle at the top, the tubes tapering down to a domed base w/four curved legs, 11" h................................ **385**

Candle mold, tin, round flared base & top w/a ring of twelve tall candle tubes, small strap handles flank the top rim, 9" d., 11 1/2" h. (some rust) **550**

Candle sconce, tin, the wide slightly peaked oval backplate w/a narrow crimped edge & top hanging hole, above an oblong projecting tray w/crimped edges & holding three cylindrical candle sockets, old yellow paint, American, 19th c., 9" w., 8 1/2" h. (minor corrosion) **4,025**

Candle sconces, tin, a large oval tin reflector w/crimped edges on a reeded strap above the flaring crimped pan centered by a candle socket, old but not mid-19th c., 8" h., pr. (some resoldering) **1,320**

Candlestand, tin, oval fluted-edge drip pan w/three candle sockets adjusting on a slender metal shaft on a conical sand-weighted base, early 19th c., 34 1/2" h. (corrosion) **2,415**

Chamberstick, tin, a round deep dished base w/flaring sides & one side continuing up & tapering into a high C-scroll handle also serving as a holder for the conical snuffer, cylindrical candle socket w/flattened rim, 9" l. **605**

Coffeepot, cov., punched tin, a flared foot below the flat flaring lower body & tapering upper body, fitted low domed cover, arched wide spout & strap handle, the side punched w/a design of hearts &

flowers, unusual V-shaped spout, 19th c., 10" h. **550**

Scarce Punched Tin Coffeepot

Coffeepot, cov., tin, the angled ovoid body decorated on each side w/wrigglework flowers in two-handled pots & four spiral-twisted punchwork lower bands, the hinged domed cover w/a turned finial, angled gooseneck spout, strap handle w/grip impressed "J. Ketterer" for John B. Ketterer, Pennsylvania, mid-19th c., 11 1/2" h. (ILLUS.) **3,300**

Tole Coffeepot and Mug

Coffeepot, cov., tole, flared foot on a tall gently tapering cylindrical body, angled gooseneck spout, strap handle w/grip, domed cover w/small finial, old polychrome floral decoration w/bands on a dark brown ground, in white, green, yellow & red w/some touch-up, early 19th c., 10 1/2" h. (ILLUS. left with mug) **523**

Coffeepot, cov., tole, lighthouse-style, a flared base & tall gently tapering cylindrical sides w/a hinged domed cover w/small finial, loop strap handle & angled tall spout, japanned finish decorated w/painted bright red & yellow flowers on light green panels within a circle of yellow brush marks on each side, yellow leaves around the base & cover, 19th c., 11" h. (repair to bend in spout) **1,210**

Coffeepot, cov., tole, tapering cylindrical form w/gooseneck spout & strap handle, hinged domed cover w/scrolled finial, decorated w/fruit & leaves in a diamond formation in shades of orange, yellow & green on a black ground, wear, small hole, first half 19th c., 10 1/4" h. (ILLUS. right with document box top next page) **863**

Early Tole Coffeepot & Document Box

Document box, cov., tole, deep rectangular form w/hinged gently arched cover w/loop bail handle, decorated w/flowers & fruit in red, yellow & green on a black ground, wear, small dents, early 19th c., 4 3/4 x 10", 6 1/2" h. (ILLUS. left with coffeepot) **403**

Fine Tole Decorated Document Box

Document box, cov., tole, rectangular w/a gently domed hinged cover w/wire loop handle, the front decorated w/two birds & leafy branches of fruit, the sides w/a band of leaves in orange, green, yellow & white on a black ground, attributed to Mercy North, Flycreek, New York, late 18th - early 19th c., wear, 6 1/2 x 9 5/8", 7 1/4" h. (ILLUS.) **1,150**

Flower holder, tin, four-tier w/graduating shallow round containers on a conical base, painted dark green, American, second quarter 19th c., 6 1/4" d., 14 1/2" h. (paint wear) **345**

Knife & fork, tin, anniversary-type, oversized set w/diagonal ribbed handles, 13" & 22" l., pr. (wear, dents) **633**

Mantel decorations, tin, cut & molded flower blossoms & leaves, some painted putty w/orange highlights, raised on slender rod shaft on a round, turned wooden base, American, 19th c., 9" w., 21 1/2" h., pr. (paint losses) **1,955**

Mug, tole, cylindrical form w/strap handle, original floral decoration in red & yellow on a worn dark ground, early 19th c., 5 3/4" h. (ILLUS. right with coffeepot) **248**

Sieve, tin, heart-shaped, the top pierced w/a central sunburst surrounded by diamond-form bands, on three feet, w/wire loop hanger, 5 3/4 x 6", 3 1/4" h. **193**

Sieve, tin, heart-shaped w/shallow sides & a small loop strap handle at the top end, the top side pierced w/bands of holes &

fitted w/three small feet, 3 5/8 x 4 1/2" (minor rust) **303**

Sieve, tin, large heart shape w/three large deep round indentations pierced w/circles compass star designs, three feet on the back & ring hanger, old black patina, 19th c., 13 1/2 x 14 1/2" **633**

Spice box w/nutmeg grater, shallow rectangular form on tiny round strap feet, the hinged lid punched w/a fish, the interior w/four compartments around a center that holds the grater, includes a second nutmeg grater, 19th c., 3 5/8 x 5 7/8", 2 7/8" h. (replaced tin hasp incomplete) **303**

Spoon, tin, anniversary-type, long ribbed handle w/bent rod hanger, 19th c., 41" l. (corrosion) **374**

Tea caddy, tole, cylindrical w/angled shoulder to a small cylindrical neck w/domed cap, black ground w/yellow stripes & yellow, red & green floral decoration, 7" h. (repainted, few dents & chips) **193**

English Victorian Tole Tea Canister

Tea canisters, cov., cylindrical form w/rounded shoulder & short cylindrical neck, dark green ground decorated in gilt w/Chinese characters, applied label reading "Parnall & Sons Ltd. Manufacturer - Complete Shop Fitters for all Trades - Narrow Wine St. Bristol," England, 19th c., now mounted as lamps, pr. (ILLUS. of one) **1,610**

Tinder box, cov., tin, short wide cylindrical form w/flat fitted cover centered by a cylindrical candle socket, interior compartment w/removable damper, old dark finish, 19th c., 3 1/4" h. (minor base dent) **303**

Tray, tole, round, a repeating heart-shaped pierced rim, the center w/a floral bouquet & floral border in shades of red, yellow, blue & green on a red ground, England or America, 19th c., 26 1/2" d. (wear) **805**

Tray, tole, rectangular w/rounded flared ends, incurved sides, japanned ground w/yellow stripe & red & green daubing, white edge on ends w/red & green fruit decoration, some wear, 8 x 14" (ILLUS. top next page) **385**

Tole Tray

Tray on stand, tole rectangular tray w/rounded corners & flanged rim, black ground decorated w/Chinoiserie figures within a river landscape, raised on a faux bamboo wood stand w/slender legs joined by a cross-stretcher, England, 19th c., 21 1/4 x 26 1/4", overall 18" h., 2 pcs. **1,610**

MILITARIA & WARTIME MEMORABILIA

Since the early 19th century, every war that America has fought has been commemorated with a variety of war-related memorabilia often in the form of propaganda items produced during the conflict or as memorial pieces made after the war ended. These materials are today quite collectible and increasingly important for the historic insights they provide. Most common are items dating from World War I and II.

Civil War (1861-65)

Ambrotype of Seated Confederate

Ambrotype, a close-up half-length portrait of a young Confederate solider w/a goatee & parted hair combed to one side, facing the viewer head on & wearing a high-collared military jacket w/gilt buttons, pencil inscription on paper inside the back gives his name & the Tennessee unit he belonged to, embossed leather case w/taped hinge, 2 3/4 x 3 1/4" (liner damaged) **$715**

Ambrotype, a young Confederate soldier shown from the waist up, lean face w/a goatee, wearing a long military coat & kepi, brown gutta percha case molded in relief w/fruit, 2 x 2 1/2" (some crazing) **550**

Ambrotype, Confederate soldier seated next to a table w/long tablecloth, wearing a shell jacket w/vest & checked shirt, his hat & books on the table, embossed leather-covered case w/narrow metal frame & mat w/oval opening, slight halo next to gilt liner, small chip in emulsion, 3 1/4 x 4 1/4" (ILLUS.) **770**

Ambrotype, full-view of a Confederate soldier seated next to a table w/legs crossed & one elbow on the table, wearing a slouch hat & shell jacket, embossed metal liner in a leather-covered case, 2 3/4 x 3 1/4" (halo along edge of liner in image) **660**

Ambrotype of Young Union Soldier

Ambrotype, sixth plate, standing slender serious looking Union soldier holding a rifle w/other equipment around his waist including a long knife w/an ornate handle, Ohio Volunteer Militia belt buckle visible, slight edge halo, stamped brass mat, in case (ILLUS.) **743**

Broadside, printed in black on white, rectangular, reading "Now is the Time to Serve Your Country. - Volunteeers - Wanted - for The 2d Massachusetts - Heavy Artillery! - A Bounty of $150.00...," followed by address of enlisting sergeant, printed in Gloucester, Massachusetts, ca. 1861-62, 18 1/4 x 23 1/4" (creases, staining, toning) **748**

Calvary sword & scabbard, brass knuckle bow & hilt w/brass wire wrapping & leather grip, marked "US ADK 1860," imported, the set (throat guide missing) **476**

Carte de visite, photo of a seated officer holding a map w/a teenaged black orderly in uniform standing to his left, Guay & Co., New Orleans (light soil, small ink spots along bottom, light spotting) **545**

Officer's side knife, Confederate, stag antler grip, brass hilt, engraved blade w/"CS," illegible mark, ca. 1865 .... **784**

Officer's sword, fancy brass knuckle bow & hilt, brass wire-wrapped & leather grip, engraved blade marked "Wm. Horstman and Sons, Philadelphia," w/king's head punch, ca. 1850 .... **504**

Photograph of Robert E. Lee, signed in pencil, ca. 1863, 3 x 4 1/2"......................... **1,680**

Sax horn, brass, over-the-shoulder model, reinforced bell w/original mouthpiece, unmarked, 47" l. (denting, few small cracks, evidence of early repairs & soldering) **1,815**

Sheet music, "Milwaukee Light Guard Quick Step," illustrated cover, music copyrighted 1859, cover copyrighted 1866 (cover separated) **55**

Tintype, full-plate, a Civil War Union soldier wearing a kepi, hand-painted detail & background, old backing included & signed "L.H. Newell, Philadelphia," 6 1/2 x 8 5/8" **220**

Tintype, half-plate, a view of a standing Union soldier beside a small side chair, wearing a tinted blue coat & painted w/high boots & a forage cap, in thermoplastic case w/molded oval panels & flowers, sharp image, 4 x 4 7/8"..................... **385**

Tintype, image of a standing Union soldier in uniform wearing a kepi & holding his rifle & bayonet to his side, identified as Enoch Bailey, light blue tint on pants, in full case, 2 1/2 x 3 3/4" (few minor flecks, case spine repaired) **352**

World War II

World War II Propaganda Poster

Poster, propaganda, "Our Carelessness - Their Secret Weapon - Prevent Forest Fires," at top above raging forest fire, printed in dark red, black & white, small tear in white border, 22 x 28" (ILLUS.)........... **746**

German/Italian Aviator's Watch

Wrist watch, German/Italian aviator's model, over-sized Chronograph type w/luminous double dial, case w/grey mat military finish & a brown leather over-sized

band w/brass findings, case marked on side rim w/numbers, contained in original box w/front label "Laco, Lacher & Co., Inh Ludwig Hummel Urhn and Gehausef Abrik Pforzheim, Golden Medaille Paris 1937," also a postal label dated "3.9.42," end of box also marked, ca. 1940, mint (ILLUS.) **2,240**

MINIATURES (PAINTINGS)

Bust portrait of a lady, facing right, her dark hair pulled up into a bun at the top above tight curls, wearing a black dress & light shawl, blue sky & white cloud background, thin oval engraved brass frame w/small ring handle, from the Cook Family of Connecticut, 2 18 x 2 5/8" **$605**

Bust portrait of a lady, seated facing the viewer head-on, a close-fitting bonnet around her center-parted hair & decorated w/pink flowers & a wide lavender sash, wearing a dark colored cloak over her dress w/a lacy collar w/jewelry shown, in a molded gilt-brass oval frame, ca. 1850, 3 x 3 7/8"............................. **688**

Bust portrait of a lady, watercolor on ivory, an 18th c. lady facing left w/her hair in a high period style & wearing a low-cut gown, identified as Mary McCall Cadwalader, Philadelphia, attributed to John Ramage, 18th c., in an oval pendant frame, 1 1/4 x 1 1/2" **6,325**

Bust portrait of a military man, a young man facing right w/short dark hair, wearing a high-collared red uniform w/gold braid trim, flat rectangular black lacquer frame w/brass-lined oval opening, early 19th c., 5 x 6 1/4" (some wear, especially to gold) **220**

Bust portrait of a young man, facing left, his short hair combed forward, wearing a high-collared white shirt w/narrow black tie & a high-collared blue frock coat w/yellow waistcoat, rectangular black lacquered frame w/oval gilded brass liner & fittings, early 19th c., 4 3/8 x 5 1/2" **2,310**

Miniature of a Young Man

Bust portrait of a young man, on ivory, facing right, his round head w/short brown hair, wearing a high-collared ruffled-front shirt & a high-collared button-trimmed dark blue frock coat, white waistcoat w/blue polka dots, round rose gold-colored case w/beveled edge lens front & back, back w/faded pink silk embroidered "B," in a folding leatherized case, first half 19th c., 2" d. (ILLUS.) **660**

Bust portrait of a young man, watercolor on ivory, facing right, short brown hair, wearing a high cravat collar, light vest & high-collared navy blue coat w/brass buttons, identified as Richard or Archibald McCall, American, early 19th c., in an oval pendant frame, unsigned, 2 3/4 x 3 1/2" (pigment loss, foxing).......... **2,415**

Bust portrait of George Washington, watercolor on ivory, shown facing left wearing a high-collared brown frock coat & ruffled cravat, in a Stuart-style pose, rectangular black lacquered frame w/oval brass liner & brass acorn & leaf hanging clip, early 19th c., 5 x 5 5/8"........................ **1,100**

Bust portraits of a gentleman & lady, watercolor on ivory, he facing left, his dark hair combed forward, wearing a high-collared shirt & cravat & high-collared jacket, she facing right, her dark hair curled atop her head, wearing a wide bertha collar over a dark dress, old back papers signed "By S. Broadbent, Novem. 15, 1831," later backing paper w/names of sitters, "Francis Ely - Mrs. Francis Ely," ebonized shadowbox frames w/oval gilt liners, 4 3/8 x 5", pr. (side edges of ivory are straight & not completely covered, crack in background of lady) **3,300**

Portraits of a Husband & Wife

Bust portraits of husband & wife, watercolor on paper trimmed w/gum arabic, the couple facing each other, he w/parted hair & a short beard wearing a long jacket, she w/her hair pulled to the back wearing a high-waisted puffed-sleeve dress w/wide lacy collar, identified as Mr. & Mrs. E.F. Wade of East Avon, New York, 1848, each 2 5/8 x 3 1/4", in common beveled frame, unsigned, minor pigment loss, paper glued to back (ILLUS.) ... **2,185**

Bust profile portrait of a young man, watercolor on paper, facing left w/side-parted hair & curled sideburns, wearing a high-collared shirt, cravat & high-collared black jacket, unsigned, first half 19th c., inlaid wooden beveled frame, toning, minor staining, 3 x 3 3/4" (ILLUS. top next column) **1,035**

Bust Portrait of a Young Man

Figure group, painted on ivory, four classical maidens seated or standing close together in an interior, Europe, 19th c., matted & framed, 2 1/2" d............................... **316**

Half-length portrait of a baby, wearing a white dress & bonnet w/blue ribbon, yellow background, paper backing w/label reattached reading "Painted by White Ivory 1833," rectangular flat black lacquer frame w/oval opening & brass fittings, 4 1/8 x 4 3/4" (colors faded, frame worn) **248**

Half-length portrait of a gentleman, seated facing left, wearing a high-collared black frock coat, white vest & black cravat, behind him to the right is a column w/a drapery, pen inscription on the back "William Crum, March 1833, J. Eastin...," gilt mat & narrow molded gilt frame, 7 x 8 1/2" (minor stains) **330**

Half-length portrait of a young boy, watercolor on ivory, standing facing left, wearing a blue coat w/brass buttons & a narrow white ruffled collar, standing in a landscape w/trees in the background, paper backing inscribed "Charles Hulse, Nottingham, May 1815, Born 9th Jan. 1810, on Ivory," Pennsylvania, black lacquered rectangular frame w/rectangular gilded brass liner & fittings, 4 5/8 x 5 3/8" . **2,310**

Cased Portrait on Ivory of a Young Lady

Half-length portrait of a young woman, painted on ivory, seated facing forward, her brown curly hair piled on her head, wearing an off-the-shoulder white Empire gown w/puffed sleeves, initialed "S.H.B.," in a folding leatherized case, 2 1/2 x 3 5/8" (ILLUS.) **798**

Half-length portrait of a young woman, watercolor on paper, standing facing right, her dark hair pulled back w/curls at the back & around her face, wearing a delicate grey Empire gown w/white lace collar, good details, first quarter 19th c., narrow giltwood frame w/dark inner frame w/narrow brass oval liner, 4 3/4 x 5 1/4" (edge chips on inner frame) **880**

Half-length portrait of an elderly man, pen & ink on paper, shown facing the viewer wearing a high-collared coat, vest & cravat, labeled on the back "A rough sketch of my father, W.W. --- taken at the age of 92 by W. Mathews of --- 1843," black lacquered frame w/oval opening & brass liner, 4 5/8 x 5 1/2" h. (glued down w/some stains, damaged corner on frame) **83**

Three-quarters length portrait of a young girl, painted on tin, seated in a bowback chair facing the viewer, short dark hair, wearing a white dress w/wide blue sash, holding flowers, in a large oval locket-type case w/brass back & domed glass front, late 18th - early 19th c., 4 1/8 x 6 1/4" (minor flaking) **468**

MINIATURES (REPLICAS)

Armoire, Louis XV-Style, figured walnut veneers, rectangular top above a long door w/inset rectangular mirror w/rounded corners & ormolu mounts at each corner flanked by beveled front stiles w/ormolu mounts, a long bottom drawer w/further mounts above a scalloped apron w/ormolu mounts, added interior shelves, late 19th - early 20th c., 7 x 12 1/2", 18 1/2" h. (minor chips & repairs to veneer) **$660**

Basket, "buttocks"-type, woven splint, 22-rib construction, deep rounded sides & wrapped rim, bentwood handle, 5 1/2 x 5 3/4", 3 1/2" h. plus handle **149**

Blanket chest, country-style, painted pine, rectangular hinged top w/molded edges opening to a well, heavy applied base moldings, lock, high bootjack feet, old worn dark green over lighter green, penciled inscription inside lid "Ernest E. Olin," 6 1/2 x 14", 10" h. **605**

Blanket chest, Federal country-style, curly maple, cherry & walnut, the rectangular top w/molded edges opening to a well w/a lidded till, the sides w/rectangular raised panels framed by curly maple framing, inlaid keyhole escutcheon, oval end brasses w/thistles added, early 19th c., 12 x 19 3/4", 14 1/2" h. (repairs) **1,155**

Blanket chest, painted pine, Chippendale style, a rectangular hinged top w/molded edges opening to a well w/till, dovetailed case w/a pair of drawers at the bottom, molded base on scroll-cut ogee bracket feet, old crusty grey paint w/black daubed graining, 18th c., 9 3/4 x 17 5/8", 11" h. (old repair to hinge rail of lid) **24,200**

Bucket, cov., wooden, slightly flared cylindrical form w/flat turned cover, two brass bands & wire bail handle w/wood grip, original orangish red paint, pencil inscription on the bottom, 4" h. (wear, fading, minor age cracks) **220**

Chest of drawers, Classical style, mahogany & mahogany veneer, a rectangular top above a single long deep drawer overhanging two long graduated drawers all w/small brass knobs, the lower case w/ring-turned pilasters at each side, baluster- and knob-turned legs, good old finish, ca. 1830-40, 9 3/8 x 14 1/8", 15" h. (one pull replaced, minor veneer chips & wear) **1,540**

Chest of drawers, Classical style, walnut, a rectangular top above a case w/a long top round-fronted drawer w/two wood knobs over three long slightly set-back flat-front drawers w/knobs, shaped front stiles & C-scroll front feet, old varnish finish, ca. 1850, 8 x 12 1/4", 11 5/8" h. **468**

Chest of drawers, mahogany, a rectangular top w/chamfered front corners & molded edges above a case w/three long graduated drawers w/pairs of tiny turned wood knobs flanked by chamfered front sides, molded plinth base on tiny block feet, refinished, wire nail construction, Europe, 19th c., 7 x 14 1/8", 10" h. **413**

Miniature Eastlake Chest of Drawers

Chest of drawers, Victorian Eastlake substyle, walnut, the superstructure w/a pediment to above shaped sides w/candle shelves framing a tall rectangular mirror, the case w/rectangular top above three long drawers each w/cross-carved black & gold details, third quarter 19th c., 6 x 12 1/2", 22 3/4" h. (ILLUS.) **248**

Cupboard, step-back wall-style, painted poplar, a rectangular top above a pair of cupboard doors w/molded trim & tiny wood knobs above an open pie shelf, the stepped-out lower section w/a pair of cupboard doors w/molded trim & tiny knobs, gently arched apron, old dark red repaint, square & round nail construction, 8 5/8 x 12 1/2", 24" h. (end sections of cornice replaced) 880

Desk, William & Mary slant-front style, cherry, a narrow rectangular top above the hinged slant lid opening to a compartmented interior over a case w/three long drawers w/butterfly pulls, molded base on ball-turned feet, probably 19th c., 15 3/8 x 22 1/2", 24 5/8" h. (feet later) **9,200**

Food mold, redware, Turk's turban-style, round domed shape w/molded interior flutes, rim w/dark sponging on a deep orange ground, 4 3/8" d. (minor chips, wear) **116**

Porringer, pewter, small round dish w/pierced scroll crown-type handle, stamped "R.G.," probably for Roswell Gleason, Dorchester, Massachusetts, 1822-71, 2" d **468**

Side cupboard, butternut & walnut, a rectangular top above a case w/a long dovetailed drawer w/two wood knobs slightly overhanging a pair of paneled cupboard doors, molded base, mellow refinishing, square nail construction, 19th c., 7 1/2 x 10 3/4", 11" h. (small section of backboard missing) **413**

Early Classical Style Sideboard

Sideboard, Classical style, mahogany & mahogany veneer, the top w/two raised convex small drawers above the rectangular top over a pair of convex drawers over a pair of cupboard doors w/Gothic arch panels flanked by S-scroll pilasters above C-scroll feet, flat apron, ca. 1840, 11 x 18", 16 1/2" h. (ILLUS.) **1,725**

Stove, cast iron "Eclipse," painted silver, floral scrollwork decoration, shelves & accessories including teapot & coal hod, 8 1/2 x 13 1/2", 16 1/2" h. **715**

Teakettle, cov., copper, dovetailed construction, flat-bottomed squatty bulbous form w/rounded shoulder & fitted domed cover w/button finial, looped strap handle, swan's-neck spout, 5 3/4" h. **220**

Trunk, dome-top, painted & decorated pine, original mustard yellow, green, orange, black, white & blue polychrome decoration w/pairs of large stylized blossoms on

the top & front divided into two panels by a spiral-twist central band, bottom & interior of top painted light green, small open till inside, steel ring handles at each end, old dark putty filler near hinges on top, wire nail construction, 19th c., 5 1/8 x 8 5/8", 5 1/2" h. **743**

Trunk, hinged lift-top w/simulated black leather covering, brass nailhead trim, leather handle, the interior lined w/marbleized paper & manufacturer's label "Theodore Kellogg No. 56 Hanover St. Boston...," late 19th c., 5 1/2 x 8", 4 1/4" h. (wear, damage) **144**

Work table, Classical style, mahogany, the rectangular top w/rounded front corners above a conforming case w/two long graduated drawers w/pairs of small round brass pulls, squared baluster-form pedestal on a cross-form platform raised on C-scroll feet, ca. 1840, 9 1/2" w., 12" h. **403**

MOLDS - CANDY, FOOD & MISCELLANEOUS

Candle mold, thirty-six tube, a rectangular walnut framework enclosing the rows of tin candle tubes, old finish on wood, bootjack ends on base, square nail construction, 19th c., 7 3/4 x 16", 12 3/4" h. **$825**

Candle mold, twelve-tube, a rectangular pine framework enclosing the rows of pewter candle tubes, high feet w/scalloped ends & cross pieces dovetailed at ends w/square nails & some added screws, old refinish on wood, 8 5/8 x 15", 17 1/4" h. (age cracks) **688**

Candy, figural comic character smoking large cigar, tin, marked "H. Walter Berlin," 6 1/4" l. **61**

Chocolate, rabbit, cast iron, seated full-bodied animal, two-part, marked "Griswold Mfg. Co., Erie, Pa.," 10" l., 11" h. **143**

Chocolate, sheep, cast iron, recumbent animal, two-part, 10 1/2" l., 7" h. (some rust) **83**

Food, lamb, cast iron, recumbent pose, two-part w/front & back loop handles, 14 1/2" l. **110**

Ice cream, baby, pewter, hinged two-part, marked "E. & Co. N.Y. 1020," 4 3/4" l. (ILLUS. right) **50**

Ice cream, large heart, pewter, two-part, hinged, marked "E. & Co. N.Y. 902," 4 1/8" l. **39**

Two Figural Ice Cream Molds

Ice cream, Santa Claus, pewter, hinged two-part, hinges worn thing & looses, 4 3/8" h. (ILLUS. left) **176**

MOVIE MEMORABILIA
Costumes

Al Pacino, "Godfather II," 1974, two-piece checkered suit, pants w/Western Costume Company tag & typed actor's name, accompanied by letter of provenance.. **$10,575**

Bert Lahr, "The Wizard of Oz," 1939, pawstyle shoe made of African lion w/attached claws & rubber sole on verso, mounted in a forest-inspired Lucite presentation case w/engraved plaque reading "The Cowardly Lion's paw worn by actor Bert Lahr in 'The Wizard of Oz,' Metro Goldwyn-Mayer, 1939".................. **25,850**

Charlton Heston, "Ben Hur," 1959, wheat-colored caftan w/elaborate gold threading & detailing around an elongated V-neck opening w/pronounced vertical gold stripes throughout, together w/vintage color lobby card from the movie **5,875**

James Caan Movie Shirt

James Caan, "Honeymoon in Vegas," loud Hawaiian print shirt, w/original prop tag attached, framed in plexiglass w/a still from the movie (ILLUS.) **383**

John Wayne, "How The West Was Won," 1962, uniform jacket & vest, the navy blue cavalry-style jacket w/gold eagle buttons, the vest w/"Western Costume" label & Wayne's name typed on it, accompanied by black & white photograph of Wayne wearing the costume, the set **8,225**

Judy Garland, "The Wizard of Oz," 1939, "Ruby Slippers," spool-heeled shoes of red silk faille, overlaid w/hand-sequinned georgette, flat jeweled bows applied at the toes, the soles painted red w/red/orange felt affixed, the white kid leather lining stamped "6B E 58 68," w/"double" handwritten & cloth label sewn to inner sole of right shoe reading "Innes Shoe Co. Los Angeles, Hollywood Pasadena" **666,000**

Lobby Cards

"Bambi," insert card, Disney, 1942, folded, 14 x 36", B **750**

"Dinner at 8" Lobby Card

"Dinner at 8," MGM, 1933, Jean Harlow, John Barrymore, the only card of the set showing Harlow, 11 x 14", A- (ILLUS.) **1,000**

"Dishonored" Lobby Card

"Dishonored," Paramount, 1931, Victor McLaglen, Marlene Dietrich, 11 x 14", A- (ILLUS.) **600**

"Gold Diggers of 1933" Window Card

"Gold Diggers of 1933," window card, Warner Brothers, 1933, 14 x 22", B+ (ILLUS.) **900**

"King Kong" Lobby Card

"King Kong," RKO, 1933, lobby card, framed, linen backed, 11 x 14", B+ (ILLUS.).. **1,000**

"Saboteur," insert card, Universal, 1942, Priscilla Lane, Robert Cummings, 14 x 36", B+.. **450**

"The Buccaneer," insert card, Paramount, 1938, folded, 14 x 36", B................................ **400**

"The Gay Divorcee," insert card, RKO, 1934, Fred Astaire, Ginger Rogers, 14 x 36", A-.. **1,000**

"The Masquerader," insert card, United Artists, 1933, Elissa Landi, 14 x 36", B.......... **500**

"Way Out West," insert card, MGM, 1937, Stan Laurel, Oliver Hardy, paper backed, 14 x 36", A.. **2,200**

Posters

"Adventures of Sherlock Holmes" Poster

"Adventures of Sherlock Holmes," 1939, Basil Rathbone, Ida Lupino, France, linen-backed, 31 x 47", A- (ILLUS.)........... **3,000**

"Beyond Bengal," Style B, Showman's Pictures, 1934, one of those great posters for a film very few have seen, w/literature: Reel Art; Rebello & Allen, folded, one-sheet, 27 x 41".................................... **350**

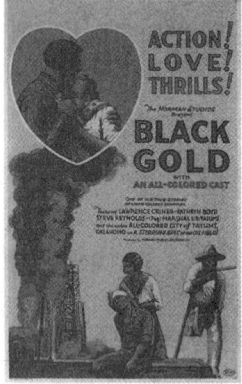

"Black Gold" Poster

"Black Gold," Norman, 1928, "all-colored cast," w/literature: Separate Cinema, rolled, one-sheet, 27 x 41", A- (ILLUS.)........ **700**

"Bright Lights or the Lure of Broadway" Poster

"Bright Lights or the Lure of Broadway," Triangle Keystone, 1916, Roscoe Arbuckle, Mabel Normand, linen-backed, one-sheet, 27 x 38", B+ (ILLUS.)............... **2,600**

"Crossfire" Poster

"Crossfire," Style A, RKO Radio, 1947, Robert Young, Robert Mitchum, linen-backed, one-sheet, 27 x 41", A- (ILLUS.) **600**

"Down to Earth," style A, Columbia, 1946, Rita Hayworth, Larry Parks, linen-backed, one-sheet, 27 x 41", A- **950**

"Fatty and Mabel Adrift," Triangle Keystone, 1916, Roscoe Arbuckle, Mabel Normand, this is a printer's progressive proof, one of the stones was incompletely inked, linen-backed, one-sheet, 28 x 41", A-.. **1,500**

"Fatty and Mabel at the San Diego Exposition," Keystone/Mutual, 1915, linen-backed, three-sheet, 36 1/2 x 74 1/2", B+ **5,500**

*"Gone With the Wind/Autane en
Emporte Le Vent" Poster*

**"Gone With the Wind/Autane en Emporte
Le Vent,"** 1940s, Clark Gable, Vivien
Leigh, this was the poster for the original
release of the film in post-war France,
artist Soubie, linen-backed, France,
Grande, 47 x 63" (ILLUS.) **4,200**

"Grand Hotel" Poster

"Grand Hotel," MGM, 1932, Greta Garbo,
John Barrymore, the only known U.S.
poster for this title to have appeared at
auction, linen backed, Tooker Litho, NY,
one-sheet, 27 x 41", A- (ILLUS.).............. **42,000**

Early Paul Muni Movie Poster

"I Am A Fugitive From A Chain Gang,"
Warner Bros., 1932, starring Paul Muni,
Glenda Farreel, Preston Foster & Helen
Vinson, dark green, black & white w/dark
pink-tinted head of the lead character at
lower right, couple of minor tears,
22 x 30" (ILLUS.)... **739**

"Jour de Fete," Discina, 1948, a larger than
life French film that has a poster to match
it in size & quality, artist Jacquelin, linen-
backed, France, 63 x 94", A-...................... **3,000**

"La Grande Illusion," RAC, re-release,
1945, Jean Gabin, Eric von Stroheim,
this is one of those rare occasions when
the re-release is a more desirable poster
than the one from the original year of release, France, linen-backed, rolled, artist
Bernard Lancy, 23 x 33".............................. **4,000**

"Lawrence of Arabia" Promo Poster

"Lawrence of Arabia," British, 1962, large
central hooded bust drawing of
Lawrence, promotional wording about &
below image reads "Arrange A Party to
go to Toronto to see -- Lawrence of Arabia -- Gray Coach Lines - Odeon-Carlton
- Reserved Seats - Go By Bus...," yellow
& pink background, 22 x 30" (ILLUS.) **127**

"Le Sheik/Le Cheik" Poster

"Le Sheik/Le Cheik," Paramount, 1921, Agnes Ayres, Rudolph Valentino, artist Gottlob, France, Grande, 47 x 63", A- (ILLUS.).. **2,500**

"Lifeboat," 20th Century Fox, 1943, Tullulah Bankhead, William Bendix, w/literature: Nourmand Hitchcock, folded, one-sheet, 27 x 41", A-.. **1,300**

Hayworth "Louisiana Gal" Poster

"Louisiana Gal," Century Picture, 1940s, starring Rita Hayworth, sultry bust image of the star on a day-glo lavender & pink ground w/black & white lettering, 22 x 30" (ILLUS.)... **380**

"Meet John Doe," Warner Brothers, 1941, Gary Cooper, Barbara Stanwyck, paper backed, 14 x 36", A-.................................... **450**

"Montana," Warner Bros., 1950, starring Errol Flynn, color image of Flynn above large title, one-sheet, near mint **575**

"Now, Voyager," Warner Brothers, 1942, Bette Davis, Paul Henreid, linen-backed, one-sheet, 27 x 41", A **1,600**

"Orphee," 1950, Jean Marais, Francois Perier, framed, Belgium, 14 x 22", A-............ **600**

"Plan 9 From Outer Space" Poster

"Plan 9 From Outer Space," 20th Century Fox, 1959, starring Bela Lugosi, Vampira & Lyle Talbot, considered to be the worst movie ever made, some light creasing & staining, 27 x 41" (ILLUS.) **1,628**

"Rainbow Valley," Monogram, 1935, John Wayne, George Hayes, linen-backed, one-sheet, 27 x 41", A **2,600**

"Safety Last," Hal Roach Studios, 1923, attributed to Jeorgii & Vladimer Stenhart, Russia, linen-backed, 28 x 42", A- **1,500**

"Sahara," Columbia, 1943, starring Humphrey Bogart, color one-sheet (restoration to folds, whitewashing on some borders) **843**

"Shanghai Gesture," United Artists, 1942, Gene Tierney, Victor Mature, linen-backed, one-sheet, 27 x 41", A- **500**

"Snow White and the Seven Dwarfs" Poster

"Snow White and the Seven Dwarfs," Style A, Disney, RKO, 1937, folded, one-sheet, 27 x 41" (ILLUS.).................................... **950**

"Spellbound" Poster

"Spellbound," Selznick, 1945, Ingrid Bergman, Gregory Peck, paper-backed, half-sheet, 22 x 28", A- (ILLUS.)............................ **450**

"Sunset Boulevard/Viale Del Tramonto" Poster

"Sunset Boulevard/Viale Del Tramonto," 1950, Italy, Quattro, artist Ercole Brini, linen-backed, 55 x 79" (ILLUS.)................. **5,500**

"**The Cowboy Millionaire,**" Selig, 1910, period cloth backing, the backing on this poster is similar to that of carnival & sideshow posters from the same period, it was obviously displayed at a variety of venues, one-sheet, 29 1/2 x 40", B **2,000**

"**The Eagle,**" United Artists, 1925, Rudolph Valentino, paper-backed, half-sheet, 22 x 28", A.. **650**

"**The General Died at Dawn/L'Oro Della Cina,**" Paramount, 1936, paper-backed, Italy, 28 x 39", B+ **1,600**

"**The Grapes of Wrath,**" Style B, 20th Century Fox, 1939, folded, one-sheet, 27 x 41", A-.. **600**

"The Milky Waif" Poster

"**The Milky Waif,**" MGM, 1946, cartoon, linen-backed, one-sheet, 27 x 41", A- (ILLUS.).. **1,200**

"**The Other Man,**" Triangle Keystone, 1916, Roscoe Arbuckle, w/Keystone Players, one-sheet, 28 x 41", folded, A-.... **1,400**

"**The Passionate Plumber,**" MGM, 1932, Buster Keaton, Jimmy Durante, linen-backed, one-sheet, 27 x 41", A................ **800**

"**The Rounders,**" Keystone/Mutual, 1914, this is the earliest known poster for a Chaplin film, linen-backed, one-sheet, 27 x 41", B+.. **6,000**

"The Sisters" Poster

"**The Sisters,**" Warner Brothers, 1938, Errol Flynn, Bette Davis, linen-backed, one-sheet, 27 x 41", A- (ILLUS.)........................ **2,200**

"Three Musketeers" Poster

"**The Three Musketeers,**" United Artists, 1921, Douglas Fairbanks, half-sheet, 22 x 28", B (ILLUS.)................................... **1,000**

"**The Treasure of the Sierra Madre,**" 1948, Humphrey Bogart, Walter Huston, artist Rene Peron, France, Grande, linen-backed, 47 x 63"..................................... **2,000**

"Too Hot to Handle" Poster

"**Too Hot to Handle,**" Style C, MGM, 1938, Clark Gable, Myrna Loy, folded, one-sheet, 27 x 41", A- (ILLUS.)............................ **450**

"**Under Two Flags,**" 20th Century Fox, 1936, Ronald Colman, Claudette Colbert, folded, one-sheet, 27 x 41", B............... **600**

"**Virtuous Husband,**" Universal, 1931, folded, one-sheet, 27 x 41", B+ **400**

"**You Know Me, Charlie Chaplin,**" Essanay, ca. 1915, this poster was issued when Chaplin joined Essanay in 1915, this is one of three lots showing different color or typeface variations, Hennegan & Co., Cincinnati, linen-backed, one-sheet, 27 x 41", A- **900**

"Zombies of the Stratosphere" Poster

"**Zombies of the Stratosphere,**" Republic, 1952 twelve-part serial, garrish color design w/various characters & rocket ships, folded, some minor edge wear, one-sheet (ILLUS.) **231**

Miscellaneous

Book, "Gone With The Wind," by Margaret Mitchell, 1939 motion picture edition **55**

Early Norma Jean Baker Calendar

Calendar, 1952, "Dame and Dane," a color photo of Norma Jean Baker (pre-Marilyn Monroe) in front of a Great Dane dog, full calender pad, 7 1/2 x 11 1/2", framed (ILLUS.) **686**

Check, cancelled Gary Cooper check, signed & dated November 1, 1940 in the amount of $500 .... **505**

Comic cards, color-printed card stock, "Film Funnies" series, each printed w/a comic scene featuring 1930s movie stars in various poses & asking questions, the answers listed on the card reverse, from Gum, Inc., excellent to near mint, set of 24 .... **1,627**

Magazine, "Life," June 1964, Marilyn Monroe **20**

Magazine, "Life," September 1972, Marilyn Monroe **15**

"Ten Commandments" Movie Standee

Movie theater standee figure, "Ten Commandments (The)," Paramount, 1956, life-sized color image of Yul Brynner in costume as the pharoah, heavy cardboard, some wear & restoration, 6' h. (ILLUS.) **506**

Photograph, black & white half-length portrait of Sidney Greenstreet, inscribed "Best Wishes Bob, Sidney Greenstreet," near mint, 5 x 7" **207**

Early Signed Fatty Arbuckle Photo

Photograph, sepia tone half-length shot of Fatty Arbuckle, silent film comedian, smiling portrait w/blue ink inscription dated June 1915, 8 x 10" (ILLUS.) **1,235**

MUCHA (ALPHONSE) ARTWORK

Fine Alphonse Mucha Poster

A leader in the Art Nouveau movement, Alphonse Maria Mucha was born in Moravia (which was part of Czechoslovakia) in 1860. Displaying considerable artistic talent as a child, he began formal studies locally, later continuing his work in Munich and then Paris, where it became necessary for him to undertake commercial art-

work. In 1894, the renowned actress Sarah Bernhardt commissioned Mucha to create a poster for her play "Gismonda" and this opportunity proved to be the turning point in his career. While continuing his association with Bernhardt, he began creating numerous advertising posters, packaging designs, book and magazine illustrations and "panneaux decoratifs" (decorative pictures).

Poster, "Biscuits Champagne Lefevre-Utile," lithographed in color, a colorful turn-of-the-20th century interior scene w/two elegant ladies & a monocled gentleman having champagne & crackers, F. Champenois, Paris, 1896, signed in the plate, framed, 14 1/8 x 20 3/4" (ILLUS.).. **$8,050**

Print, color lithograph depicting a nude maiden w/long reddish hair partially wrapped in a pinkish orange drapery on a green ground, titled w/the letters "Vient de Paraitre - Decoratifs de A. M. Mucha," matted & framed, 6 x 15 1/4" **1,380**

Print, "Irises," a tall narrow rectangular form, a design of an Art Nouveau maiden w/blonde hair standing among towering light purple iris w/green stems & leaves against a pale cream & blue ground, signed in the plate, ca. 1897, framed, 17 3/8 x 41 1/4" **1,763**

Print, "Lilies," tall narrow rectangular form, an Art Nouveau maiden standing amoung white lilies which wrap around her body & head, in white & shades of pale green & blue, printed in color by F. Champenois, Paris, ca. 1897, framed, 17 1/4 x 40 5/8" **3,290**

Prints, "Flowers," lithographed in color, each w/a full-length portrait of an Art Nouveau maiden standing amid a background of flowers, one each w/carnations, lilies, roses & iris, signed in the plate, 1898, each 18 3/4 x 42 1/2", the set of 4 .... **6,900**

Prints, "The Four Seasons," lithographs printed in color, by F. Champenois, Paris, each w/an outdoor scene w/an Art Nouveau maiden representing one of the four seasons, laid down on linen, silk-matframed, signed in the plate, 1896, each 21 5/8 x 41", set of 4 (repairs, minor losses, bullet hole in one) **24,150**

MUSIC BOXES
Automatons

The general term "music box" is used to describe all automatic music playing machines. The three types covered here are cylinder, disk and automaton.

Music is generated in a cylinder music box by a cylinder of metal spiked with nubs. As the cylinder rotates, one or more metal combs placed near the cylinder strike the nubs, creating the sound. The disk-type music box works in much the same way. A flat disk of metal spiked with nubs rotates and metal combs striking it again produce the sound.

Musical automatons are mechanical creations meant to imitate the motions of humans or animals playing or moving to music. The automatons can be made of wood, metal or porcelain, and generally are dressed in costumes of the era.

Barn Dance Automata Diorama

Automata diorama, "Great Racket," scene of a barn dance in a shadowbox frame, w/a chromolithographed background of a barn interior & eight moving & partially moving African-American figures, wood frame w/gilt gesso liner, instruction label on the back from The Parisian Importing Co., 33" w. (ILLUS.) **$3,450**

Singing Bird Automaton

Bird automaton on box, a small tortoiseshell bird within an oval compartment w/an engraved bronzed lid & rear compartment, the bird w/moving perch, wings & ivory beak, on a rectangular box base, 3 3/4" l. (ILLUS.) **2,185**

Birds in Birdcage Automaton

Birds in birdcage automaton, three birds w/moving heads, beaks & tails enclosed in a wire domed cage on a gilt gesso rectangular platform base w/canted corners, 22" h. (ILLUS.) **6,325**

Bontems Bocage Automaton

Bontems bocage automaton, a tall leafy tree w/eight birds, one w/flapping wings, two flying between limbs, one drinking, one on a spring & two static, above a glass rod waterfall & two-train clock w/white enamel dial, on an oblong ebonized base, signed "Bontems, Paris," bird song weak, lacking dome & pendulum, 26" h. (ILLUS.) **4,600**

Gothic Castle Clock Automaton

Clock & building automaton diorama, a silvered & gilt-metal large Gothic castle-like structure on a high rocky base, a central clock tower w/bell turret containing a working clapper, two-train movement, further two w/working see-saw action semaphore signal, the rocky outcrop w/two early-style railway trains on contra-rotating bands passing between two tunnels, on a deep rectangular inlaid rosewood base w/rounded corners & containing a replacement two-air movement, 25" h. (ILLUS.) **9,200**

French Barrel Organ Automaton

French barrel organ, the rectangular top w/two seated monkey violinists w/moving heads, opening mouths & moving arms, on a 17-note organ w/six-air barrel in a grained & rosewood veneered rectangular footed case, 27" h. (ILLUS.).................. **6,325**

Old Lady Manivelle Automaton

German Manivelle figural automaton, an old lady seated in a high-back chair holding a coffee grinder in her lap, carved & painted head, moving eyes, opening mouth & turning hand, on a paper-covered rectangular wood base, 14" h. (ILLUS.) **1,093**

German Manivelle Tableau

German Manivelle tableau, two bisque head musicians under vine-draped arches seated behind three small dancers at the front, on a paper-covered wood rectangular base, containing a single-air movement (ILLUS.)...................................... **2,875**

Jardiniere & Bird Automaton

Jardiniere w/flowers & bird automaton, the bird perched atop a tall bouquet of flowers within a squared gilt gesso jardiniere-form base w/a porcelain plaque on the front w/a Watteauesque scene, 20 1/2" h. (ILLUS.)... **6,325**

Lambert clown automaton, large clown seated on a chair, moving composition head & tongue, strumming a mandolin, bending forward & lifting his leg, on a rectangular cloth-covered wood base w/a two-air movement & tune card, 23" h. (redressed) **5,175**

Manivelle String Duet Automaton

Manivelle string duet automaton, two seated men in 18th c. attire, in a three-walled room setting, one playing the violin, the other a cello, painted composition heads & moving hands, on a rectangular wood base containing a damaged single-air movement, 16" w. (ILLUS.) **1,380**

Monkey Musical Trio Automaton

Monkey musical trio automaton, seated figures of a violinist, harpist & cellist under a floral arbor, w/moving heads & playing arms, on an ebonized plinth w/a one-air movement, 25" h. (ILLUS.)............. **6,900**

Renou Little Girl Automaton

Renou Little Girl automaton, seated girl holding birdcage w/bird, bisque head & hands, waving her stick & opening the cage to let the bird come out & go back in, on a velvet-covered rectangular base w/drawer, hat replaced, 20" h. (ILLUS.) **5,175**

Rocking Ship Automaton

Rocking ship automaton, a tall landscape backdrop w/village buildings & a large clock tower to the front sides centering a sailing ship being tossed on stormy waters in the foreground, two-train movement w/action in the clock, ship, train, water wheel & windmill, two-air movement, under a repaired tall painted glass dome, 24 1/2" h. (ILLUS.) **2,070**

Rocking ship automaton, small size w/ship & moving water wheel, two-air movement, under a painted glass dome, 13 1/2" h. **1,035**

Roulet & Decamp Chef Automaton

Roulet & Decamp Chef automaton, standing figure keeping time by banging his pan w/a pair of tongs, his head turning & his cup raising, composition head, bisque hands & original costume on a velvet-covered base, 22" h. (ILLUS.) **5,175**

Singing birdcage automaton, round brass cage containing a singing bird, 11" h. **345**

Singing birdcage automaton, the bird w/moving head, beak & tail enclosed in a brass birdcage on an embossed round base, 20 1/2" h. **1,840**

Vichy Japanese Mask-Seller

Vichy figural automaton, standing Japanese lady mask-seller, turning composition head, opening & closing eyelids, moving composition arms, mask in right hand, parasol mechanism, key & two-air movement, on a circular ebonized base w/Geo. Baker & Co., Geneva, retailer label, lacking kimono, parasol, mask tray & knob, 32 1/2" h. (ILLUS.) **11,500**

Williams Rocking Ship Automaton

Williams rocking ship automaton, painted harbor background w/a Gothic clock tower in the front right & a water wheel & windmill at the front left side, a sailing ship tossed on stormy waters in the foreground, moving procession, windmill, water wheel & ship, single train timepiece, signed "Williams Paris," under a painted glass dome, 20 1/2" h. (ILLUS.) **2,645**

Cylinder Music Boxes

Ami Rivenc "Buffet" Music Box

Ami Rivenc "Buffet" cylinder music box, an 11" l., 2 1/2" d. twelve-air cylinder, zither attachment, in upright walnut veneered case w/double doors, 23" l. (ILLUS.) **2,530**

Ami Rivenc cylinder music box, 6 1/4" l. eight-air cylinder, in a grained wood case, No. 34548, 14" l. **460**

Ami Rivenc cylinder music box, a 6" l. four-air cylinder, w/tune card, in grained wood case, No. 34997, 14" l. **805**

Baker Sublime Harmony Music Box

Baker Sublime Harmony Interchangeable cylinder music box, w/four 13" l. six-air cylinders, double-spring nickeled motor, tune indicator & selector, zither attachment & speed control, in a veneered & cross-banded case w/drawer in base, case exterior stained, 34" l. (ILLUS.) **4,025**

Bremond Jeu de Flutes cylinder music box, a 14" l. eight-air & 17-note cylinder playing operatic & other airs, in grained wood case w/grille behind the movement, tune card & veneered & inlaid front & lid, No. 9071, 23 1/2" l. **1,495**

Bremond six-bell cylinder music box, a 13" l. eight-air cylinder, numbered on the lever 6816, in grained wood case w/veneered & inlaid front & lid, 22" l. **1,610**

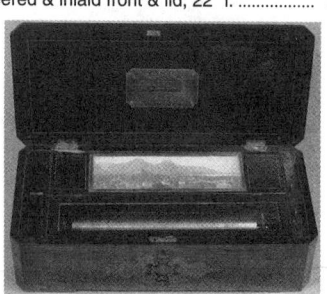

Cylinder Music Box with Landscape

Cylinder music box, a 13" l. eight-air cylinder playing operatic & other tunes, engraved brass tune card, view of Interlachen behind the movement & engraved brass control panel, in grained wood case w/canted corners & veneered & inlaid front & lid, one tooth replaced, No. 14561, 21" l. (ILLUS.)............................ **1,840**

Cylinder music box, a 13" l. ten-air cylinder playing operatic & other tunes, tune card w/partial Paillard retailer's label, in grained wood case w/inlaid lid, No. 8090, 20 1/2" l. **805**

Cylinder music box, a 9 1/2" l. eight-air cylinder playing dance & popular tunes, silver-painted bedplate & tune indicator, in a grained wood case w/tune card & inlaid lid, 18" l. **920**

Cylinder music box, a 9 1/4" l. six-air cylinder, in a grained case w/inlaid lid & tune card, 18" l. **1,725**

Cylinder music box, four-bell & drum attachments w/a 7 1/4" l. eight-air cylinder, in a grained wood case w/tune card & inlaid lid, No. 25399, 19 1/4" l. **863**

Cylinder music box, key-wind mechanism, 9 1/4" l. cylinder playing six operatic & other airs, in a grained wood case w/end flap & blue tune card, Model No. 2581, 15 1/4" l. **632**

Cylinder music box, key-wind mechanism, a 13" l. eight-air cylinder playing dances by Strauss & others, in grained wood case w/end flap & inlaid lid, No. 11979, 21 1/2" l. **1,150**

Small Cylinder Music Box

Cylinder music box, key-wind movement, 8" l. four-air cylinder, square-headed comb bolts, in replacement oak case w/exposed controls, No. 32, 13 1/4" l. (ILLUS.)... **1,035**

Ducommun-Girod cylinder music box, an 8" l. six-air cylinder, in a grained wood case w/end flap, inlaid lid & fruitwood handled winding key, No. 33672, 16" l. **518**

"Expressif" Cylinder Music Box

Ducommun-Girod cylinder music box, key-wind mechanism, a 10 3/4" l. six-air cylinder, in grained wood case, tune card & end flap, No. 30592, 17 1/2" l. **920**

Ducommun-Girod cylinder music box, key-wind mechanism, a 7 3/4" l. four-air cylinder, fruitwood case w/exposed controls, No. 10993, 13" l. **1,150**

"Expressif" cylinder music box, an 11" eight-air cylinder playing operatic & dance airs by Strauss, Offenbach, Verdi & others, in a grained wood case w/tune card & inlaid lid, 20" l. (ILLUS. bottom previous column)... **1,150**

Interchangeable Cylinder Music Box

Interchangeable cylinder music box, two 13" l. eight-air cylinders w/popular & operatic airs, two-piece comb, nickeled double-spring, zither attachment & twin-tune cards w/images of musical putto, in a veneered & cross-banded case w/inlaid front & lid & end carrying handles, 33" l. (ILLUS.) **3,335**

L'Epee cylinder music box, 8 1/4" l. six-air cylinder playing dance tunes, in a maple case, No. 40494, 16 1/2" l. **1,035**

L'Epee Six-air Cylinder Music Box

L'Epee cylinder music box, an 8 1/4" l. six-air cylinder, in a plain case w/brass-inlaid lid & enamel & mother-of-pearl, No. 21915, 16" l. (ILLUS.)................................... **805**

L'Epee Seven-Bell Music Box

L'Epee seven-bell cylinder music box, a 9 1/4" l. six-air cylinder, bell control, A Woog stamp on bedplate, in grained wood case w/veneered front & inlaid lid, No. 38489, 19" l. (ILLUS.) **2,300**

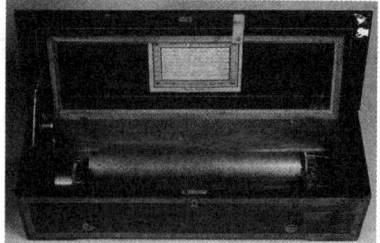

Langdorf Forte Piano Music Box

Langdorf Forte Piano cylinder music box, a 15 1/4" l. eight-air cylinder playing operatic & other tunes, in grained wood case w/tune card, veneered front & inlaid lid, No. 15712, 24 1/2" l. (ILLUS.) **2,530**

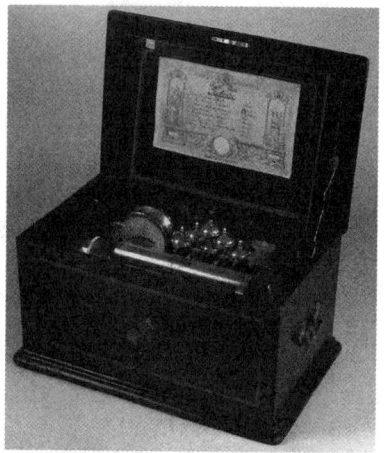

Langdorf Orchestral Music Box

Langdorf Orchestral cylinder music box, a 13" l. eight-air cylinder playing operatic & dance tunes, accompanied by a 15-note organ & optional drum, castanets & six bells w/bee strikers, in a grained wood case w/tune card & indicator, carrying end handles & veneered & inlaid front & lid, 26 1/2" l. (ILLUS.) **3,220**

Lecoultre - Berens, Blumberg & Co. cylinder music box, key-wind movement, 11" l. six-air cylinder, in veneered case w/tune card & end flap, No. 21573, 18" l. **863**

Lecoultre cylinder music box, lever-wind movement, a 13 1/4" l. eight-air cylinder, in grained wood case, No. 30178, 20 1/2" l. **978**

Mandolin cylinder music box, 13" l. six-air large cylinder, approximately two-thirds in mandolin, the case w/a flared veneered front & lid, 24" l. **2,645**

Mandolin cylinder music box, an 11" l. six-air cylinder w/zither attachment, in a

grained wood case w/inlaid lid, No. 5570, 20" l. **1,495**

Mandoline Expressive cylinder music box, a 13" l. eight-air cylinder including the song "Dixie," a two-piece comb, zither attachment & massive double-spring motor, in grained wood case w/tune card, veneered & cross-banded front & inlaid lid, No. 10537, 26" l. **1,495**

Mermod cylinder music box, an 11 1/2" l. eight-air cylinder, crank-wind motor, tune indicator, zither attachment & speed control, in grained wood case w/inlaid lid, No. 93148, 25" l. **805**

Nicole Freres cylinder music box, a 13" l. eight-air cylinder, in a grained wood case, the lid w/simulated marble & wood inlay, No. 39974, 20 1/2" l. **2,070**

Nicole Freres Eight-Air Music Box

Nicole Freres cylinder music box, early lever-wind movement, a 13" l. eight-air cylinder playing hymns, in grained wood case w/inlaid lid, No. 41706, 20 3/4" l. (ILLUS.) **1,610**

Nicole Freres cylinder music box, key-wind mechanism, w/an 8 1/4" l. four-air cylinder, in a light fruitwood case w/stringing & Cox Savory, London, England, tune card, No. 34471, 15" l. **1,955**

Nicole Freres cylinder music box, key-wind movement, a 13" l. eight-air cylinder, in grained wood case w/end flap & inlaid lid, No. 27972, 20" l. **1,495**

Nicole Freres Cylinder Music Box

Nicole Freres Forte Piano cylinder music box, a 13" l., 3" d. twelve-air cylinder playing mostly operatic tunes, in a grained case w/inlaid front & lid, six piano teeth replaced, now w/a reproduction tune card, No. 43379, 23" l. (ILLUS.) **3,105**

Nicole Freres "Hire" cylinder music box, an 8 1/2" l. six-air cylinder playing operatic & dance tunes, the comb signed "F. Nicole," in grained wood case w/inlaid lid, end flap, removable glass inner lid locked from the rear & Spiers and Son, Oxford, England, tune card No. S.12 w/printed instructions & advertisements, No. 21863, 16 3/4" l. **4,313**

Fine Nicole Freres 12-Air Music Box

Nicole Freres two-per-turn Mandoline cylinder music box, 12" l., 3" d. 12-air cylinder w/operatic airs by Verdi, Rossini, Bellini & others, cylinder two-thirds - three-quarters mandolin, & Wales & McCulloch, London, England, tune card, in veneered & cross-banded case w/canted corners, the lid & front inlaid w/reclining classical figures, No. 43273, 22" l. (ILLUS.) **5,463**

Paillard "Expressive" Music Box

Paillard "Expressive" (Mandoline) cylinder music box, a 13" l., 3" d. six-air cylinder playing operatic tunes, cylinder approximately three-quarters in mandolin, tune card w/W. Mitchell McAlister, Philadelphia, Pennsylvania, retailer's label, in case w/veneered, cross-banded & inlaid front & lid, 25" l. (ILLUS.) **4,025**

Paillard, Vaucher & Fils Mandoline Expressive zither cylinder music box, a 13" l. cylinder playing six operatic & dance airs, approximately two-thirds of cylinder in mandolin, w/zither attachment & tune card, in amboyna veneered case w/cross-banding, diamond inlay on front, lid & carrying handles, No. 13787, 22 1/2" l. (two treble teeth replaced) **2,760**

Two-per-turn cylinder music box, a 7 1/2" l., 2 3/4" d. twenty-air cylinder, tune indicator, zither attachment & tune card, grained wood case w/carrying end handles & transfer-decorated lid, 24" l. **1,265**

Disk Music Boxes

Harmonia disk music box, walnut case w/monochrome print in lid, twin-comb movement, plays 9 7/8" d. disks, No. 1824, w/14 projectionless disks **1,380**

Harmonia disk music box, walnut case w/paneled lid, single-comb movement, plays 16 1/2" d. disks, No. 107, w/three projectionless zinc disks, 24 1/2" w **1,610**

Kalliope Disk Music Box

Kalliope disk music box, walnut rectangular case w/colored print inside the lid, single-comb top-wind motor & ten optional bells, plays 13 1/4" disks, w/approximately twenty disks (ILLUS.) **2,990**

Polyphon (Polyphon Musikwerke, Leipzig, Germany) disk music box, grained wood case w/transfer-decorated lid, single-comb rachet-wind movement, six optional bells, plays 9 5/8" d. disks, No. 160210, w/twelve disks **2,990**

Polyphon Music Box in Walnut Case

Polyphon (Polyphon Musikwerke, Leipzig, Germany) disk music box, quarter-veneered walnut case w/monochrome print inside the lid, Nicole Freres, London, England, retailer's label, egg-and-dart molded plinth & inlaid lid, plays 15 1/2" d. disks, No. 120656, w/ten disks, winder replaced (ILLUS.) **2,645**

Fine Polyphon Disk Music Box

Polyphon (Polyphon Musikwerke, Leipzig, Germany) disk music box, typical upright walnut case w/scrolled panels above the arched glass front flanked by half-round turned pilasters, a drawer at the bottom, twin-comb movement w/coin mechanism for a British penny, a single/double play selector, plays 19 5/8" d. disks, w/ten disks, lacking pediment, 36 1/2" h. (ILLUS.).............................. **4,600**

Polyphon (Polyphon Musikwerke, Leipzig, Germany) disk music box, walnut case w/monochrome print inside the lid, engaged corner columns, astragal & acanthus leaf moldings & inlaid lid, twin-comb movement, plays 15 1/2" d. disks, w/ten disks (winder replaced) **4,313**

Rare Polyphon Floor Model

Polyphon (Polyphon Musikwerke, Leipzig, Germany) floor model disk music box, upright Art Nouveau-style walnut case on knob feet, twin-comb coil-spring auto-change movement, disk lifting mechanisms, disk-selector & ten-disk magazine, plays 19 5/8" d. disks, No. 591, coin drawer & part of back replaced, 56" h. (ILLUS.).. **14,950**

Polyphon Coin-Op Disk Music Box

Polyphon (Polyphon Musikwerke, Leizig, Germany) disk music box, upright walnut case w/lyre fretwork on the door flanked by half-round knob- and ring-turned pilasters, on bun feet, twin-comb top-wind coin-operated movement, plays 11" d. disks, w/twelve disks, missing pediment, nameplate replaced, No. 62431 (ILLUS.) **2,185**

Regina Disk Music Box

Regina disk music box, rectangular oak case w/serpentine sides, name panel inside the lid, plays 12" disks, No. 7200083, w/one disk (ILLUS.).................... **3,220**

Symphonion Disk Music Box & Base

Symphonion disk music box, a walnut case w/monochrome print, glass inner lid, corner columns & inlaid paneled lid, on a matching stand w/central shelf, paneled back & disk storage below, twin-comb movement, plays 11 7/8" d. disks, No. 329526, w/approximately 30 disks, 41 1/2" h. (ILLUS.)...................................... **6,325**

Symphonion disk music box, ebonized wood case w/transfer-decorated lid, diagonally-mounted twin-combs, ratchet-wind motor, numbered comb-plate & bedplate, w/tri-lingual instructions **518**

Symphonion disk music box, in associated English Renaissance Revival cabinet, twin-comb coin-operated movement, plays 19 1/8" d. disks, w/seven disks, 51 1/2" h... **2,760**

Upright Symphonion Disk Music Box

Symphonion disk music box, typical upright walnut case w/scrolled panels

above the arched glass front flanked by half-round turned drops, a drawer at the bottom, twin-comb movement w/coin mechanism for a British penny, plays 19 1/8" d. disks, w/ten disks, 35 1/2" h. (ILLUS.) **4,600**

Symphonion disk music box, walnut case w/canted corners, monochrome print inside paneled lid & W.J.H. Swan, Lynn retailer's label, plays 13 1/2" disks, No. 345298, w/23 disks **2,415**

Wurlitzer disk music box, mahogany case w/molded base, figural color print mounted inside the lid, side crank, w/18 disks, case 17 3/4 x 19 3/4", 9" h. (some edge damage).. **3,135**

MUSICAL INSTRUMENTS

Fife, tiger stripe maple w/brass ferrules, six-hole model, Revolutionary War era, w/19th century note on provenance, 17" l. **$1,100**

Steinway Baby Grand Piano

Piano, baby grand, Steinway & Sons, ebonized case, Serial No. 322896/M, stenciled "N.A. /A1875," scratches, small chips, 65" l. (ILLUS.)................................. **$12,000**

Steinway Model S with Bench

Piano, baby grand, Steinway & Sons, Model S, ebonized case, Serial No. 32918, 48" l. ivory keyboard, excellent original condition, w/matching bench, case 56 x 62" (ILLUS.).. **14,000**

Fine French Grand Piano

Piano, grand, A. Guillot, Paris, France, Louis XVI-Style gilt-bronze mounted tulipwood marquetry satinwood inlaid case, typical form, veneered on the sides & top w/roundels & fitted w/gilt-bronze mounts, raised on octagonal legs, stamped mark, 78" l. (ILLUS.)... **21,450**

American Violin and Case

Violin, tiger stripe maple case w/carved whale bone fittings, decorated w/red, white & blue patriotic symbols, in a grain-painted wood case, mid-19th c., imperfections, case 23 1/4 x 30 1/4" (ILLUS.).... **2,070**

NAUTICAL ITEMS

Model of the Warship "Victory"

The romantic lure of the sea, and of ships in general, has opened up a new area of collector interest. Nautical gear, especially items made of brass or with brass trim, is sought out for its decorative appeal. Virtually all items that can be associated with older ships, along with items used or made by sailors, are now considered collectible, for technological advances have rendered them obsolete. Listed below are but a few of the numerous nautical items sold in recent months.

Broadside, printed paper, black & white, announcing the Steam Packet General Lincoln to leave Borston & Hingham at

her usual hours accompanied by the Boston Brigade Band, dated July 25, 1833, J. Farmer, print, Hingham, Massachusetts, framed, 9 1/2 x 11 1/2" (toning, staining, probably laid down)......................... **$920**

Ship model, carved & painted wood, model of Admiral Nelson's flagship "Victory," three-masted warship w/detailed deck planking, pulleys, rigging, cannons & other details, polychromed in shades of blue, black, tan, red & green, mounted on an inlaid mahogany base in a paneled glass case, 19th c., 34 1/2" l., 23" h. (ILLUS.) **1,955**

Ship Model in Frame

Ship model, carved & painted wooden half-hull of sailing vessel, painted white above & green below water line, mounted in frame w/ochre ground, black frame, late 19th c., America, 6 1/2 x 29" (ILLUS.) **2,875**

Ship's logbook, from the U.S.S. North Carolina for voyages from 1837-1839, details weather, shipboard occurrences & various other events, pen & ink on paper, 74 pp. (possible loss of several pages in the back) **1,870**

Ship's stern board, painted wood, curved oblong form, relief-carved "AID" in a cartouche flanked by foliate scrolls, painted yellow on a black ground w/traces of gilt, American, 19th c., 9 1/2 x 48 1/2" (wear) **978**

Spy glass, silver & leather, Naval model, engraved French inscription dated 1861, in a fitted wooden case, France, mid-19th c., 24 1/2" l. (minor wear to leather)................. **2,070**

Stern board, carved & painted, a long narrow arched board, the black asphaltum ground w/molded top edge, lettered in gilt "William West," signed "C.L. Bedell, Painters" on each end in a conforming enclosure w/red & black trim, edged in gilt on a dark blue ground, original paint, Essex, Massachusetts, 1869, 15 x 103", 6" h. (wear)... **1,725**

NUTCRACKERS

Although primitive people probably cracked the hard shells of nuts between two stones, more advanced societies developed a wide variety of functional tools with fanciful designs that today's collectors appreciate for their beauty and ingenuity. Nutcrackers can be classified into three basic styles: the "percussion" type in which a nut is placed on a sturdy base then struck with a hammer, the "screw" type in which a nut is placed between two flat surfaces that create a vise, and the "pressure" or "lever" type in which a nut is held between two moving parts of a lever. Most nutcrackers are made of metal or wood or a combination of these materials. The painted, figural, wooden nutcrackers from the Erzgebirge region of Germany are prized for their decorative function, but are rarely used to crack nuts.

For more information on nutcrackers, the author suggests the following: Ornamental & Figural Nutcrack-

ers *by Judith A. Rittenhouse (Collector Books, 1993),* American Nutcrackers: A Patent History and Value Guide *by James Rollbland (Off Beat Books, 1345 Poplar Avenue, Sunnyvale, California 94087-3770).(Newsletter) Susan Otto, 12204 Fox Fun Dr., Chesterland, Ohio 44026, Phone (440) 729-2686.*

Admiral Count Von Luckner, painted wood, Steinbach, 15 1/2" h....................... **$75-85**
Alligator, brass, 9" l. **20-25**

Alligator Nutcracker

Alligator, bronze, mounted on wood, 1864, 12" l. (ILLUS.).. **150-160**
Alligator, cast aluminum, John Wright, 1960s, 13" l. **30-40**
Alligator, cast iron, 12" **40-50**
Antelope head, carved wood, lever type, glass eyes, 8 1/8" h................................ **175-200**
Bear, wood, seated, glass eyes, 19th c., 3 3/4 x 8 3/4" **175-200**

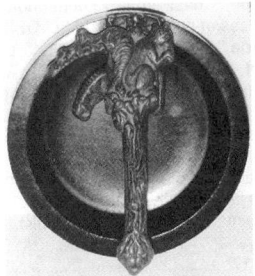

Bowl Nutcracker

Bowl, w/raised design of squirrel & nut on metal handle, 4 x 8 1/2" (ILLUS.)............ **175-200**

Bowl Nutcracker

Bowl, wood base & handle, iron lever, 1919, 9 x 10 1/2" (ILLUS.).................................... **35-45**
Bowl, wood w/raised center to hold nut, bark around edges, wooden hammer w/metal striker... **10-12**

Bowl, wood w/screw type nutcracker in center, A.H. Kolker, 1917 .... **30**
Box, birds eye maple, two nutcrackers & six picks, 6 x 8", set **20-25**

Cannon Nutcracker

Cannon, bronze, base resembles cannon shell, 5 x 6" (ILLUS.)................................ **125-135**

Chimney Sweep Nutcracker

Chimney sweep, Erzgebirge region of Germany, 5 1/2 x 14 5/8" (ILLUS.)................ **135-145**
"Clamp-on style," cast iron, Enterprise, 1914 .... **30**
"Clamp-type," Squirrel brand, Woldert Co., Tyler, Texas, 11" **10-15**
Clown, brass, double-faced, England, 1 1/2 x 5 1/4"...................................... **75-85**
Dog, aluminum, curly tail, marked "Crack Your Nuts Here" **50-60**
Dog, brass, 1930s, 4 x 9" **70-80**

Dog Nutcracker

Dog, bronze, base decorated w/embossed flowers & shells, 5 1/2 x 12" (ILLUS.) **45-50**
Dog, cast iron, painted black, Harper Supply Co., 13" l... **90-100**
Dog head, carved wood, glass eyes, 7 7/8" h... **440**
Dragon, cast iron, gold paint, ca. 1900, 3 1/2 x 5 1/2 x 14" **275-350**

Duck head, carved wood, orange beak,
8 1/2" h. **250**
Eagle head, carved wood, glass eyes, han-
dles open & close beak, 8 1/4" l. **480**
Eagle head, cast iron, a long feather-form
lever handle issuing from the back of the
head & operating the beak as the crack-
er, traces of red paint on eyes, 10 1/4" l. **138**
Eagle head, cast iron, ca. 1860, 4 x 10" **125**
Eagle head, cast iron, wood base, 6 1/2" l. **175**
Elephant, brass, w/rider, 1930s, 2 x 6 5/8" **45**
Elephant, cast iron, painted, flattened body,
trunk forms handle, 4 5/8 x 9 3/4" **150-175**

Elf Nutcracker

Elf, carved wood, handle in back, 6" h.
(ILLUS.) **50-65**
Elf, cast iron, w/beard, 10" **285**
Elf, wood, Norwegian, red hat **65**
Fish, cast iron, nickel plated, glass eyes,
England, 1930, 2 1/4 x 8 1/2" **150-175**
Fish, olive wood, Greek, 1950s, 2 1/4 x 8" .. **75-100**
Frog, iron, glass eyes, Germany, 6 x 8" **250-300**
Hand, wood, screw-type, handle twists to
crush nut held in hand, 19th c., 9" l. **135-140**

Horse Nutcracker

Horse, bronze-plated iron, stylized, molded
letters on head, 4 x 7" (ILLUS.) **185**
Indian head, carved wood, feather head-
dress, painted, glass eyes, rests on wood
base, 2 3/4 x 8 1/2" **400-425**
Kangaroo, "Nestor," England, ca. 1930,
4 1/2 x 5 1/2" **150-175**

"Knee-Warmer" Nutcracker

"Knee-warmer," cast iron, fits over knee,
2 1/2 x 4 x 5" (ILLUS.) **50-65**

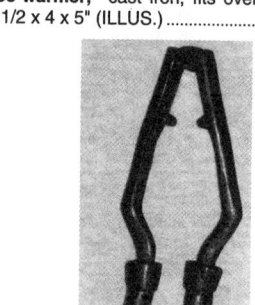

Legs With Boots Nutcracker

Legs, w/boots, brass, 4 1/2" h. **85-100**

"Lever-Type" Nutcracker

"Lever-type," cast iron, accommodates
three sizes of nuts, 1 1/2 x 7" (ILLUS.) **45-50**
"Lever-type," metal, on stand, Clark, L.A.
Co., pat. Jan. 24, 1860 .... **150**
Man, full figure, hinged jaw, carved wood,
Black Forest region, 9" h. **400-435**
Man's head, carved wood, "Oberammer-
gau," man wears hat **120**
Man's head, cast aluminum, handles close
to open jaw, 8" h. **65-75**
Merlin, painted wood, Steinbach, dist. by
Kurt Adler, New York, ca. 1990,
5 1/4 x 17" **165-175**
Mermaid, brass, England, ca. 1930, 1 x 5"
.... **100-125**
"Miller Cracker," aluminum, Ft. Worth,
Texas, 1976, 3 x 7 1/2" **25-35**

"Moon Man" Brass Nutcracker

"Moon Man," brass, hinged jaw, 4 x 5"
(ILLUS.).. **50-65**

"Moon Man" Wooden Nutcracker

"Moon Man," wood, hinged jaw, 4 x 5"
(ILLUS.)... **900-1000**

Naked Woman Nutcracker

Naked woman, brass, full figure, 6 1/2" h.
(ILLUS.).. **55-75**

Oriental Man Nutcracker

Oriental man, brass, handle in back opens
jaw, 8" h. (ILLUS.) **150-165**

Owl Head Nutcracker

Owl head, carved wood, glass eyes, 8" h.
(ILLUS.) **125-135**
Parrot, painted aluminum, green & gold,
5 1/4 x 10" **75-85**

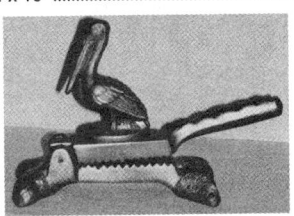

Pelican on Lever Type Nutcracker

Pelican, brass, lever type, base decorated
w/four different kinds of nuts, 4 1/2 x 8"
(ILLUS.) **35-45**
"Pliers-type," brass, embossed designs on
handles, 5 3/4" l. **45-50**
"Pliers-type," cast iron, hinged, two serrat-
ed spaces for small or large nuts, 5" l......... **8-10**
"Pliers-type," w/pick, silver plated, Wallace
Bros., 5 3/4" l. **35-40**
"Pliers-type," w/six picks, steel, double-
hinged, "HMQ," Quackenbush Company,
Pennsylvania, Aug. 10, 1909 .... **10-15**

"Press-Type" Nutcracker

"Press-type," case iron, w/walnuts deco-
rating handle, 4 1/2 x 4 1/2" (ILLUS.)............. **100**
Punch and Judy, brass, two-sided,
England, 4 3/4" **65-75**

Puppeteer Nutcracker

Puppeteer, Erzgebirge region of Germany,
5 1/2 x 14 5/8" (ILLUS.)............................. **155-165**
Rabbit head, carved wood, glass eyes,
8 1/2" l. **125-135**

Rabbit Head Nutcracker

Rabbit head, carved wood, glass eyes, 8" h. (ILLUS.) **100-125**
Ram's head, carved wood, 2 1/2 x 9" **200-225**

Rocking Horse Soldier Nutcracker

Rocking horse soldier, painted wood, German, 1989, 6 1/2 x 7 3/4" (ILLUS.) **55-65**
Sailor, "Tough Nut," England, ca. 1897, 4 3/4 x 7 3/4" **650-800**
"Screw-type," cast iron, clamps on table, Perfection, pat. Nov. 17, 1914, Waco, Texas... **50-65**
"Screw-type," metal, mounted in center of wood bowl, Labelle pat. pend., 9 1/2" d..... **12-15**
Shakespeare, brass, cottage on obverse, 5" l.. **85-110**
Skull and Crossbones, cast iron, nickel plated, England, 1928, 2 x 6" **80-100**
Soldier, cast iron, painted, 1940s, 10" h....... **40-45**
Soldier, painted wood, contemporary, China, 5 1/4 x 15 1/2" **15-20**

Soldier Nutcracker

Soldier, tri-corn hat & flag, Erzgebirge region of Germany, 5 x 14" (ILLUS.) **125-135**
Soldier, wood, painted, red coat, Black Forest, Germany, label "GDR," 26" h. **45-50**

Soldier "King" Nutcracker

Soldier "King," painted wood, German, red jacket, 14 1/2" h. (ILLUS.)........................... **75-85**

Squirrel Nutcracker

Squirrel, bronze, 5 1/2 x 8" (ILLUS.) **35-40**
Squirrel, bronze, 5 x 9"...................................... **200**
Squirrel, mahogany, wood screw in belly, 7 1/8" l... **115-125**

Turtle Nutcracker

Turtle, painted wood, wooden handle & iron screw, 6 x 6" (ILLUS.).................................. **75-85**
"Twist action-type," wood frame, four wood columns crack nut, USA, 1990, 3 3/4 x 9"... **5-10**
Whale, brass, hand-wrought, 1 1/2 x 6 1/4" **110-125**
Wolf head, chrome, wooden base, pat. June 1920, 5 x 10" **125-150**
Woman's legs, brass, 4 1/2" l. **35-40**

NUTTING (WALLACE) COLLECTIBLES

In 1898, Wallace Nutting published his first hand-tinted pictures and these were popular for more than 20 years. An "assembly line" subsequently colored and placed a signature and (sometimes) a title on the mat of these copyrighted photographs. Interior scenes featuring Early American furniture are considered the most collectible of these photographs.**Nutting's photographically illustrated travel books and early editions of his antiques reference books are also highly collectible.

Furniture

Armchair, country Dutch-style, maple, No. 461	$400
Armchair, New England ladderback, No. 492	770
Armchair, Pilgrim, No. 493	1,050
Bed, maple, No. 809	600
Candlestand, cross-braced, No. 22	525
Chair, New England ladderback, No. 490	825
Chair, side, Pilgrim, No. 393	425
Chair, side, Wild Rose, No. 365	440
Chair, side, Windsor-Style, No. 326	850
Footstool, No. 292	275
Side chair, maple ladderback, No. 392	350
Table, butterfly, No. 625	2,200
Table, ogee top, No. 609	625

Prints

Across the Charles, 11 x 14"	175
Across the Meadows, 10 x 16"	105
Afternoon Tea (An), 13 x 16"	45
All the News - and More, 18 x 22"	210
Arbor Arch (An), 13 x 16"	440
At Sunset, 12 x 16"	115
At the Fender, 13 x 16"	330
Autumn Grotto, 16 x 20"	175
Berkshire Brook (A), 10 x 16"	110
Blossom Valley, 8 x 13"	65
Blossoms at the Bend, 10 x 13"	110
Blossoms on the Housatonic, 11 x 17"	120
Book by the Window (A), 13 x 17"	660
Boys at Positano, 13 x 15"	770
Bride's Door, 13 x 16"	465
Bridesmaid's Procession (The), 10 x 12"	110
Bridesmaid's Procession (The), 12 x 16"	105
By the Wayside, 11 x 17"	525
Canopied Road (A), 13 x 16"	145
Charms of Home (The), 11 x 14"	175
Clarinda at Home, 17 x 21"	110
Clogheen Bridge (A), 13 x 16"	715
Coming Out of Rosa (The), 12 x 14"	230
Concord Banks, 11 x 14"	145
Cottage Beautiful (The), 11 x 13"	210
Crawford Notch Cascade, 10 x 12"	120
Cup that Cheers (The), 11 x 14"	105
Dainty China, 13 x 16"	100
Decked as a Bride, 16 x 20"	170
Delicate Stitch (A), 8 x 11"	120
Dell Dale Shadows, 13 x 16"	121
Disappearing in Blooms, 13 x 17"	145

Dog-On-It

Dog-On-It, 7 x 11" (ILLUS.)	3,960
Donjon, Chenanceau (The), 14 x 17"	735
Double Drawing Room (A), 11 x 17"	100
Dream and Reality, 10 x 16"	120
Dykeside Blossoms, 10 x 12"	165
Elm Birch Arch (An), 18 x 22"	50
Flowering Time, 11 x 14"	80
Flume Falls, 11 x 14"	160
Formal Call (A), 16 x 20"	200
Garden Landing (A), 9 x 11"	300
Garden of Larkspur (A), 13 x 16"	100
Going Forth of Betty (The), 13 x 16"	220
Grace, 12 x 15"	155
Grandmother's Garden, 11 x 14"	85
Green Mountain Range (The), 13 x 22"	110
Highland Vale (A), 11 x 17"	410
Hollyhock Cottage, 17 x 22"	155
Home Hearth (The), 10 x 16"	195
Honeymoon Stroll, 10 x 12"	80
Interrupted Letter (An), 14 x 17"	75
Is the Fire Ready?, 13 x 16"	70
Ivy and Rose Cloister, 16 x 20"	385
La Jolla, 13 x 15"	155
Laggard in Love (A), 18 x 22"	220
Larkspur, 15 x 19"	165
Litchfield Minster, 10 x 12"	200
Little Dutch Cove (A), 14 x 17"	880
Little River (A), 20 x 30"	200
Locust Cottage, 16 x 20"	175
Maiden Reveries, 14 x 17"	250
Mary's Little Lamb, 11 x 14"	275
Meadow Lilies, 13 x 16"	1,980
Meeting of the Ways (The), 14 x 17"	130
Morning Among the Birches, 16 x 20"	210
Morning Duties, 10 x 12"	155
Mossy Logs, 16 x 20"	208
Nap Time Stories, 10 x 12"	410
New Hampshire Drive (A), 16 x 20"	55
New Hampshire Home Room (A), 8 x 10"	165
New Hampshire in June, 13 x 16"	175
New Hampshire Roadside (A), 11 x 13"	95
Newton Broads, 10 x 16"	140
Nutting Garden Corner (The), 9 x 11"	320
Old Drawing Room (An), 14 x 17"	185
Old Pasture (The), 9 x 14"	465
Old Round House (An), 13 x 16"	275
On the Heights, 9 x 15"	740
Orchard in the Hills (An), 13 x 15"	155
Paradise Portal, 9 x 11"	190
Parlor Mantel, Keim House, 13 x 16"	1,650
Patriarch in Bloom (A), 13 x 16"	140
Peep at the Hills (A), 11 x 14"	130
Pergola, Amalfi (The), 14 x 17"	464
Petersham Banks, 13 x 16"	190
Pilgrim Hollyhocks, 9 x 11"	195
Ponti Fabrico, 10 x 12"	185
Pool of Delights (A), 9 x 11"	125
Positano, 16 x 20"	385
Preparing an "At Home," 11 x 17"	165

Reading from Arabian Nights, 14 x 17"....... **2,200**
Riot of Bloom (A), 13 x 15".................................. **70**
Rocks Off Portland, 11 x 14" **140**
Rose Gate, 8 x 10" **275**
Roses and a Bud, 12 x 14" **685**
Russet and Gold, 16 x20" **175**
Salisbury Shadows, 10 x 14" **285**
Salt Foam, 12 x 15"... **275**
Scotland Beautiful, 11 x 13"............................ **175**
Sea Capn's Daughter (The), 13 x 15".............. **300**
Sea Ledges, 16 x 20"....................................... **410**
Sea Song (A), 13 x 16" **220**
Sheltered Road (A), 11 x 17"............................. **70**
Silver White, 7 x 11" **70**
Smothered in Flowers, 13 x 16" **330**
Southern Colonial Room (A), 13 x 17" **265**
Spinning at 84, 14 x 14"................................... **355**
Spring in the Dell, 12 x 14" **185**
Stirring Scene (A), 18 x 22" **287**
Stony Brook Drive, 11 x 14" **105**
Summer Stream (A), 18 x 22"............................ **145**
Sunshine and Music, 10 x 16" **215**
Swimming Pool (The), 20 x 28" **95**
Swirling Seas, 20 x 30"..................................... **210**
Tea for Two, 10 x 12" **2,145**
The Breakfast Hour, 3 x 12" **195**
Three Chums, 10 x 12" **385**
Token in Remembrance (A), 13 x 16" **440**
Tranquil Vale (The), 13 x 22"............................ **295**
Under the Blossoms, 13 x 16"............................ **285**
Venice's Chief Glory, 14 x 17" **1,485**
Vermont Road (A), 11 x 14"............................. **100**
Village End, 14 x 20" **275**
Virginia Reel (A), 13 x 17" **320**
Warm Spring Day (A), 11 x 17"........................ **240**
Wavering Footsteps, 12 x 15"........................... **320**
Way It Begins (The), 13 x 15"............................ **465**
Way Through the Orchard (The), 12 x 15"........ **75**
Wealth of October (The), 11 x 13".................... **115**
Westfield Water, 10 x 16"................................. **155**
Westmore Drive, 17 x 21" **210**
White Way (A), 13 x 16".................................... **190**
Willow Pastoral (A), 13 x 17".......................... **825**
Wissahickon Decorations, 13 x 16" **300**
Worcester Byway (A), 13 x 16"........................... **65**
World in Tune (A), 8 x 10".................................. **70**

OLYMPIC COLLECTIBLES

1983 Special Olympics Signed Lithos

1983 Special Olympics Signed Lithos,
executed in 1983 for the 15th anniversary of the Special Olympics, dubbed "Spirit of Sport," lithos feature landscapes meant to represent six great athletes, each signed by both the athlete & Robert Peak in pencil, athletes include Joe DiMaggio, Wilt Chamberlain, Pele, Jack Nicklaus, Frank Gifford & Chris Evert Lloyd, mint condition w/signatures grading "10," set of 6 (ILLUS.)............................ **$1,021**

Torches

1960 Squaw Valley Winter Olympic Torch

1960 Squaw Valley, VIII Winter Olympics, steel, features a 14" steel shaft crowned by a 6 1/2" torch, intricately engraved w/Olympic rings, Squaw Valley logo & words "VIII Olympic Winter Games 1960" & "To Squaw Valley Olympiad," number "18" stamped on bottom, w/copy of citation awarded w/the torch to Don Merry & signed by 1960 Olympic's Chairman of Pageantry - Walt Disney, exceptionally rare, charred but intact wick (ILLUS.) **15,830**

1968 Mexico City Summer Olympic Torch

1968 Mexico City, Summer Olympics, one of original relay torches, w/leather handle, cut out metal casting, over a foot long (ILLUS.) **3,573**

1984 Los Angeles Summer Olympic Torch

1984 Los Angeles, Summer Olympics, one of original relay torches w/two-piece torch carrier's uniform, aluminum & bronze, leather handle, engraved Olympic rings & motto "Olympiad, Los Angeles, 1984," w/original carrying case & instruction booklet, near mint condition, 22" l. (ILLUS.)... **5,244**

1996 Atlanta Summer Olympic Torch

1996 Atlanta, Summer Olympics, cylindrical shape, composed of aluminum "reeds" on top & bottom separated by wooden handle, top brass "band" engraved w/Atlanta Olympic Torch logo & the Quilt of Leaves, bottom engraved w/the names of the 22 cities which have hosted the Olympic Games, signed by Muhammad Ali in black Sharpie pen on handle, w/letter of authenticity & picture of Ali signing the torch, near mint condition (ILLUS.)... **4,478**

PAPER COLLECTIBLES

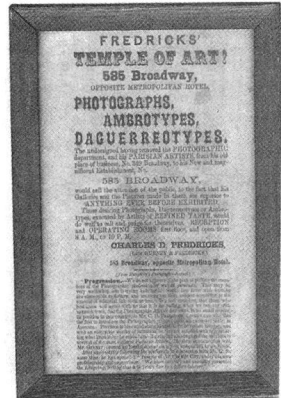

Photographic Advertising Broadside

Also see: BLACK AMERICANA, CHARACTER COLLECTIBLES, FIRE FIGHTING COLLECTIBLES, FRATERNAL ORDER ITEMS, MAGAZINES, MUCHA ARTWORK, POLITICAL ITEMS, POP CULTURE COLLECTIBLES, POSTERS, SIGNS & SIGNBOARDS, TOBACCIANA, VALENTINES and WESTERN CHARACTER COLLECTIBLES.

Anniversary memorial, pen & ink on paper, a tall document in red & brown ink w/penciled leaves & diamond detail, reading "June 10, 1884 - Ninety-third Anniversary - Miss Eleanor Bright - Born on June 10, 1791 - Married June 1817 to Mr. Jacob Pealer," professionally framed in period frame w/gilt liner, 20 x 28 1/2" (minor stains, fold lines)................................... **$330**

Bond, issued by the State of Massachusetts Bay, details loan of 13 pounds 1 shilling by Samuel Mossmon to the state of Massachusetts, dated December 1, 1777, 6 x 9 1/2"... **143**

Broadside, "Fredricks's Temple of Art - 585 Broadway, New York," photographic advertising, ca. 1850s, mounted in later frame, broadside 5 x 7 1/2" (ILLUS.) **495**

Early Woman Suffrage Calendar

Calendar, "The Woman Suffrage Calendar - 1910," light blue & grey on cream paper covers, each day w/a quotation on women's rights or related theme, punched at top w/two metal rings, published by Collegiate Equal Suffrage League of New York state, light soil on covers, some wear & light damage, 53 pp., 7 x 11" (ILLUS.) **3,465**

Calligraphic drawing, pen & ink on paper, a flying eagle in Spencerian penwork, signature card in corner in black & colored ink w/glitter "J.W. Hough, The Automatic Penman, Plain, Ohio," framed, 18 x 23 1/4".. **110**

Family record, pen & ink & watercolor on paper, a design w/a top central heart w/the names of the parents above a ring of large round stylized blossoms each inscribed w/the dates of a child, the center filled w/three large three-petal plants w/similar plants in each corner, for the Decost Family, in a grain-painted frame, 19th c., 13 x 15 3/4" **2,300**

Indenture, hand-written, between Griffith Jones & William Davis, in Philadelphia, dated November 23, 1691, signed by

Davis Lloyd, w/a wax seal tab, 10 1/2 x 23" **193**

Ledger book page, for John Ross, first husband of Betsy Ross, lists 15 entries of various amounts owed to John Ross, late 18th c., conserved by backing & fronting w/tissue, 6 x 7 1/2" **55**

Newspaper, "The Pittsburgh Gazette," September 6, 1794, story on Alexander Addison, President of the Court delivering charge to Grand Jury of Allegheny County calling for submission & peace during the Whiskey Rebellion in that region, 4 pp., 10 1/2 x 17 1/2" (slight browning, fold w/split, through stain) **121**

Paper cut-out birth record, a large rectangular piece w/a latticework cut-out border w/leaves & tulips on top & bottom w/cut-out text "Jannens Stratingh, Ge Boren Den 4 October, 1812," & two other names w/leaf dividers, early flat mahogany veneer frame, overall 21 x 25 3/4" (margin stains) **1,320**

Pay certificate, Revolutionary War, for Ralph Pomeroy in the amount of 10 pounds, from the State of Connecticut, dated October 9, 1781, uncancelled **81**

Property indenture, for land in Northern Liberties, Pennsylvania being sold to John Browne, goldsmith, dated May 1, 1763, 23 x 24" (some fold splitting) **83**

Reward of merit, watercolor on paper, inscribed "Susan P. Merriam, Orange," presented to Miss Irene Bachelder by her teacher, depicting a wreath of sweet briar, early 19th c., framed, 6 x 7" (small tear, creases, foxing, toning) **1,380**

Shipping bill, steamboat-type w/top vignette of a steamboat, lists materials shipped on the steamboat Fulton from Pittsburgh to St. Louis, dated March 9, 1839, 8 x 10" **33**

Stock note, prnted, between Philip Hord & the Free Society of Traders, signed & dated August 17, 1683, note for 50 pounds, society's seal in lower right, 2 1/2 x 7 1/2" **3,575**

PAPERWEIGHTS

Baccarat "Double Garland" Weight

Baccarat "Double Garland" weight, w/double trefoil garland of red & white canes centered by a ring of blue canes & a pink, white & green cane, 19th c., France, minor wear, 3" d., 2" h. (ILLUS.) ... **$489**

Clichy Chequer weight, complex millefiori canes centered by a pink & green Clichy rose all divided by white latticinio twists, 19th c., 2 3/4" d. **1,265**

Clichy Garland weight, a trefoil of purple millefiori canes w/seven complex canes interspersed including a pink & green Clichy rose, all set on a crystal ground, 19th c., 2 1/2" d. (minor wear)....................... **633**

Clichy Millefiori weight, complex millefiori canes set concentrically on a white lace ground, 19th c., 2 1/2" d. (inclusions, minor wear) **863**

Clichy Millefiori weight, complex millefiori centered by a pink & green Clichy rose set concentrically on a green moss ground, 19th c., 2 3/4" d. (minor wear) **13,800**

New England Glass Company Millefiori weight, concentric rings of white & alternating turquoise, red & blue canes centered by a yellow cane & set on a white latticinio cushion, Massachusetts, 19th c., 2 1/4" d. (inclusions, minor wear)..................... **259**

New England Glass Pear Weight

New England Glass Company pear weight, figural pear in chartreuse w/light blush color laying on its side on a colorless cookie glass base, late 19th c., Massachusetts, 3" d., 2 1/4" h. (ILLUS.) **690**

New England Pink Flower weight, a striated pink five-petal flower w/millefiori cane center & pink bud on a deep green leafy stem on a white latticinio bed, Massachusetts, 19th c., 2 1/4" d. (minor wear) **690**

Sandwich Dahlia weight, a white flower highlighted w/trapped air bubbles & centered by a complex cane of red, yellow & blue, two green leaves & stem, Massachusetts, ca. 1875, 3" d. (minor wear) **1,265**

Sandwich Flower weight, a poinsettia-type flower in cobalt blue highlighted w/trapped air bubbles, centered by a white rose-style cane & w/five light green leaves & stem, Massachusetts, ca. 1875, 2 3/4" d. (minor wear) **690**

Stankard (Paul) Jack-in-the-Pulpit weight, central green & maroon-throated jack-in-the-pulpit over blueberries, flanked by four yellow flowers & a pink blossom, all in moss enclosing spirits & word canes, signature in cane, 1996, 2 3/4" d. **2,300**

Tarsitano (Debbie) Pansy weight, two central blue & yellow pansies flanked by three rose pink blossoms & three yellow blossoms, all on green leafy stems, signature cane, late 20th c., 3 1/4" d. **920**

PAPIER-MACHÉ

Various objects, including decorative adjuncts, were made of papier-maché, which is a substance made of pulped paper mixed with glue and other materials, or layers of paper glued and pressed and then molded.

Candy container, model of a seated cat, grey & white painted w/pink neck ribbon & glass eyes, 3 3/4" h. (touch-up repair) **$275**

Candy container, model of a standing boy cat wearing overalls & long-sleeved shirt, polychrome paint & glass eyes, 5" h. (some wear, glued repair to feet) **275**

Candy container, model of a standing fat pig, worn & soiled pink flocking, head forms cap, early 20th c., 5 5/8" l. (some edge damage) **165**

Rare Decorated Papier-Maché Case

Case, painted & leather-sided, flattened form w/rounded ends, central panel on top painted in color w/a battle scene, the black rounded ends inscribed in gold "The Battle - Of Palo Alto," Mexican-American War era, 3 x 5 1/2" (ILLUS.) **2,400**

Letter holder, Moorish-arch form, paint-decorated w/stylized scrolls & griffins, a central female nude, 19th c., 7 1/4" l., 9 1/4" h. **374**

Milliner's model, bust of a woman covered in kidskin & decorated w/white paint & colored facial features, includes two early cotton bonnets, early 19th c., 15" h. (wear) **2,185**

Papier-maché Hen on Nest

Model of a hen on nest, soft colors of brown, beige, red & green, glass bead eyes, labeled "Drake Process - Patented May 29, 1919 - Copyright 1924 - F.N. Burt Co. Ltd. Buffalo, N.Y.," some base damage, 7" l. (ILLUS.) **165**

Model of an Easter rabbit, seated carrying a pack on its back, upright tall ears, old white paint w/later pink & green trim, glass eyes, 12 1/2" h. **138**

Snuff box, cov., round, the flat cover w/a black lithographed bust portrait of Andrew Jackson titled "Major Genl. Andrew Jackson," early 19th c., 3 1/2" d. (wear).... **1,430**

Tray, oval w/flanged rim, black ground w/central gold castle scene titled "Hurst-monceux Castle," gold rim bands, 29 1/4" l. (edge repair, resurfaced) **314**

Fine Victorian Papier-maché Tray

Tray, rectangular w/scalloped rim, black lacquer w/parcel-gilt & mother-of-pearl inlaid border w/urns issuing flowers, an exotic bird & C-scrolls hung w/vines & tassels, mid-19th c., Victorian, 23 1/2 x 31" (ILLUS.) **1,495**

PERFUME, SCENT & COLOGNE BOTTLES

Clear Ribbed Seahorse Scent

Blown glass, seahorse-style scent bottle, clear w/26 ribs swirled to the right, tightly curled end & sheared lip, applied clear rigaree trim, American, ca. 1830-50, 3 3/8" l. (ILLUS.) **$110**

Blown glass, seahorse-style scent bottle, clear w/red, white & blue spiral striping formed into a tight curl w/a sheared lip, applied cobalt blue rigaree trim, American, ca. 1830-50, 2 5/8" l. **358**

Blown glass, seahorse-style scent bottle, clear w/white striping formed into a tight curl w/a sheared lip, applied cobalt blue rigaree trim, American, ca. 1830-50, 2 3/8" l. (ILLUS. top next page)..................... **132**

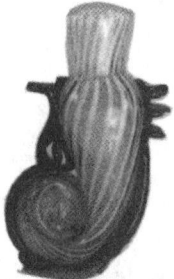

Seahorse Scent Bottle with Blue Trim

Czechoslovakian glass, a curvilinear etched clear glass stopper on a diagonally faceted red glass bottle, ca. 1925, 6 1/4" h. (minor staining) **403**

Green Czech Glass Perfume Bottle

Czechoslovakian glass, candy apple green, pressed w/a tall arched pierced shield-form stopper on a pyramidal notched base, 2 1/4" w., 4 1/2" h. (ILLUS.)... **165**

Torch & Leafy Scroll Cologne

Mold-blown glass, clear, upright rectangular flattened cologne embossed around the sides w/a torch & scrolled leaf design, shoulder tapering to a ringed & bulbed neck w/rolled lip, pontiled base, ca. 1850, 8" h. (ILLUS.) **143**

Mold-blown glass, deep cobalt blue, "Bunker Hill Monument" cologne, tall slender tapering square form molded to resemble a monument, smooth base, rolled lip, ca. 1870, 8 1/8" h. **468**

Unusual Tall Cologne Bottle

Mold-blown glass, medium turquoise blue, tall squared cologne w/slightly tapering side molded w/thumbprints & a herringbone design, smooth base, rolled lip, some light inside haze, American, ca. 1855-70, 9" h. (ILLUS.)............................ **523**

Mold-blown glass, opalescent milk glass, tall slender tapering rounded cologne w/molded stripes of beads & flutes, smooth base, tooled lip, American, ca. 1855-70, 5 3/4" h. **61**

PHONOGRAPHS

Edison Cylinder Phonographs

Amberola 1A, inside horn, fancy floor model, same motor as Opera **$3,000**

Amberola 30, No. 103228, w/Diamond C reproducer, oak case.................................... **432**

Home, Model A, No. H 54047, now w/combination gearing, early C reproducer, recorder, New Style oak case, two brass horns 14" & 31", & approx. 80 cylinders.... **1,035**

Home, Model A, No. H132692, now w/combination attachment, C & reproduction H reproducers, oak case, 30" brass horn & crane **547**

Home, Model A, No. H79657, now w/combination gearing, H reproducer, oak New Style case, 35" brass horn (winder replaced) **547**

Home, Model A, No. H98461, w/C reproducer, New Style oak case, brass horn (lacking winder) **518**

Home, Model B, No. 314497, now w/combination gearing, C & H reproducers, instructions in lid, oak case, 36" witches' hat horn.. **518**

Home, Model D. No. 400932, w/combination gearing, Diamond B. Model H & Model C reproducers, oak case, instructions in lid, No. 10 cygnet horn, repainted gold, w/back-bracket & scratch-built crane **805**

Home, Model F, No. 408205F, combination gearing, Diamond B reproducer, oak case, cygnet horn neck w/scratch-built bell & crane **633**

Home, w/banner decal & large black "witches' hat" horn **700**

Home, w/cygnet question mark shaped black horn **1,200**

Home, w/Edison "signature" decal & large black "witches' hat" horn **675**

Home, without horn **450**

Edison Opera Phonograph

Opera, w/large wood horn, ca. 1912 (ILLUS.)... **6,000**

Standard, early Model B, No. S261373, w/C-reproducer, oak case............................... **288**

Standard, Model B, No. 360058, w/C reproducer, oak case, witches' hat horn, approx. 20 cylinders **432**

Standard, Model B, No. 554376, w/combination attachment, C & H reproducers, oak case, 30" witches hat horn **547**

Standard, No. 638048, w/C reproducer, two-minute gearing, Model B style case but Model C style bedplate, Model D instructions in lid, crane & part Standard horn... **374**

Standard, w/large cygnet black metal horn .. **1,050**

Standard AA, open works & black front mount horn **675**

Standard Model A, table model, without horn, ca. 1901-5 .... **380**

Standard Model C, w/reproduction 14" black & brass bell horn, ca. 1908-9.............. **410**

Standard/I.C.S. phonograph, Model C, No. 782302, w/C reproducer, repeater, oak case **432**

Standard/I.C.S. phonograph, Model C, No. 789039, w/C reproducer, repeater, earphones, a quantity of I.C.S. instructions & correspondence, approx. 35 music cylinders.. **518**

Triumph, large colored horn, w/flowers painted inside **1,150**

Triumph, table model, without horn................... **825**

Victor Disc Phonographs

Victor D, fancy case D, w/large black & brass bell horn **2,800**

Victor D, fancy case D, w/oak spear tip wood horn.. **5,200**

Victor E (Monarch Jr.), table model w/oak case, disc player, pre-dog logo tag, medium size black metal & brass bell horn, ca. 1910... **1,400**

Victor II Humpback w/Oak Horn

Victor II, "humpback," has corner columns, back is raised where bracket attaches, w/smooth oak horn (ILLUS.)...................... **1,300**

Victor III, table model, 78 record player, w/large black & brass bell-metal horn **1,400**

Victor III w/Oak "Spear Tip" Horn

Victor III, w/large oak "spear tip" horn (ILLUS.) **2,900**

Victor M (Monarch), ridged arm, tone arm looks like a straight pipe & is not tapered.. **2,900**

Victor MS (Monarch Special), medium size black & brass bell horn......................... **1,520**

Victor V, w/large black metal horn................. **1,600**

Victor VI, w/large black & brass bell-metal horn **4,500**

Victor Victrolas and Other Models

Army Navy, WWII, 78 phonograph, 7" h., 25 lbs... **130**

Army Navy Edison, WWI, 78 phonograph, 12 1/2" h., 100 lbs. **1,500**

Bing Pigmyphone, 6" x 6" colorful tin case, wind-up toy, made in Germany....................... **285**

Brunswick, floor model, simple case................ **245**

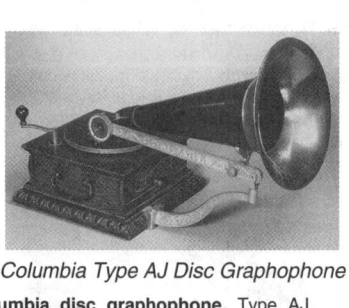

Columbia Type AJ Disc Graphophone

Columbia disc graphophone, Type AJ, top-wind motor, oak case w/rope-twist & egg-&-dart moldings, aluminum extension & traveling arms, brass-belled black horn (ILLUS.) **2,300**

Columbia Type AK Disc Graphophone

Columbia disc graphophone, Type AK, w/wood traveling & aluminum extension arms, 7" turntable, single-spring motor, cast top plate, oak case w/wavy molding, brass-belled black horn (ILLUS.) **1,725**

Columbia Type BI Disc Graphophone

Columbia disc graphophone, Type BI, w/Dolcher soundbox, 10" turntable w/guard, double-spring motor, paneled oak case w/Chicago retailer's label, oak flower horn, 22" d. (ILLUS.) **3,335**

Columbia Grafonola, floor model, inside horn, 78 player **325**

Columbia Grafonola, Model 25, hornless, oak case, 30" witches' hat horn **173**

Columbia Grafonola, table top, inside horn, 78 player, louver front **280**

Columbia Grafonola, Type C, w/louvers, Denholm & McKay, Worcester retailer's label, oak case **259**

Columbia graphophone, Type BE, No. 793, w/Lyric reproducer, nickeled bed-

plate, serpentine case w/fluted corner columns, reproduced witches' hat horn **863**

Columbia Type BG Graphophone

Columbia graphophone, Type BG, w/four-spring motor, 6" mandrel, nickeled mechanism, mahogany case w/corner columns & crane, lacking reproducer & horn (ILLUS.) **805**

Columbia graphophone, Type Q, w/floating reproducer, black base w/gilt decoration, conical horn (key replaced) **230**

Columbia Regent Grafonola

Columbia Regent Grafonola, mahogany desk-form cabinet, w/turntable compartment under lid, detached No. 6 soundbox, 12" turntable, used needle chute, the right side w/twin record cupboards & accessories drawer, the left side w/internal horn w/grille & double doors, the front & rear each w/single record cupboards, rear w/dividers, on paw feet, w/replacement No. 6 soundbox, Victrola No. 2 & a RCA, 46" w. (ILLUS.) **575**

Edison, talking doll, w/mechanism & box **7,000**

Edison, talking doll, without mechanism **2,900**

Pathe Model X disc phonograph, No. 61068, w/dual Concert soundbox, internal horn covered by grille, "butterfly" volume control & record cupboard, oak cabinet, 44" h. **288**

Pooley mahogany disc record cabinet, w/outswept sides, double-doors, pull-out shelf, top is 18 x 20" **87**

U.S. Army Special Services portable phonograph, by Waters Conley, in olive-green wood case **144**

Victor 6 Phonograph

Victor 6, No. 2757, w/triple-spring motor, 12" turntable, gilt fittings, mahogany case w/corner columns, Hawthorne & Sheble flower horn, now w/gilt Orthophonic soundbox, horn repainted, 19" d. (ILLUS.)... **3,795**

Victor E/Monarch Phonograph

Victor E/Monarch, No. 29995, 7" turntable, double-spring motor, Exhibition sound-box, metal extension & traveling arms, oak case w/fluted corner pilasters, brass-belled black horn (ILLUS.) **1,380**

Victor Electrola 10-70E

Victor Electrola 10-70E, No. 1858, w/auto-matic record changing mechanism, elec-tric pick-up, speaker, radio switch & eight record boxes, Italianate style cabinet, w/large quantity of records, 51" h. (ILLUS.)... **1,610**

Victor IV Phonograph

Victor IV, No. 46620-A, w/Exhibition sound-box, 10" turntable, double-spring motor, mahogany case w/corner pilasters, fluted mahogany horn, 21 1/2" d. (ILLUS.) **3,450**

Victor P2 Phonograph

Victor P2, No. 692, w/oxidized top-plate, Exhibition soundbox, wood traveling arm, oak case, 14" witches' hat horn, exten-sion arm replaced (ILLUS.)............................ **920**

Victor VV-XVIII, fancy floor model w/bowed sides **2,900**

Victrola IX, No. 3080076, w/Exhibition soundbox, mahogany case w/bracket feet... **259**

Victrola Model 240, No. 52841, No. 2 soundbox, mahogany console cabinet, A-F record albums, 32" w. **173**

Victrola portable phonograph, Model 50, No. 105066, mahogany case (soundbox replaced).. **173**

Victrola X Phonograph

Victrola X, w/No. 2 soundbox, mahogany case, cabriole legs w/ shelf, quantity of records, motor defective (ILLUS.).................. **575**
Victrola XIV, No. 150833, w/No. 2 soundbox, mahogany cabinet w/record cupboard, 45" h.. **173**
Watchtower, small inside horn, leatherette case, wind-up.. **400**
Zonophone, small case w/bevel glass sides & small front mount horn **5,000**
Zonophone, wood case, rear mount blue or red horn.. **950**

Zonophone Grand Opera Phonograph

Zonophone Grand Opera phonograph, No. 10003, w/V Concert soundbox, metal traveling & foliate extension arms, ornately cast top plate, 9" turntable, oak case w/beveled glass panel & turned corner columns, 24" brass horn & elbow (ILLUS.).. **4,370**

PHOTOGRAPHIC ITEMS

Winter Logging Scene

Albumen print, an Infantry Officer, shown from the knees up, wearing a kepi w/halfmoon & "I" insignia, frock coat, sash, sword belt & ornate sword, good image, blind stamp mark "E. J. Jacobs, Cap St. N.O.," framed, 14 1/8 x 16".......................... **$413**
Albumen print, Class of 1862 from Rutger's College, showing a group of 33 men in front of building, oval image, mounted on larger board, 6 x 8" image **143**
Albumen print, large format, exterior view of a Philadelphia street scene, mounted on larger board, blindstamped by photographer McClees, ca. 1860-70, image 9 x 11".. **138**
Albumen print, lumber mill scene, the mill on the right side w/a large group of workers & piles of lumber on the left, unidenti-

fied but found in Maine, late 19th - early 20th c., image 6 x 8 1/2", mat 8 x 10" **25**
Albumen print, winter logging scene, a large horse-drawn sled piled high w/large logs, four men standing on the pile, snow on the ground, late 19th c., image size 6 x 8", mat size 8 x 10" (ILLUS.)...................... **33**
Ambrotype, half plate, image of three children, two boys & one girl, girl standing in center & boys seated on either side, shown from the knees up, housed in push-button case.. **165**

Ambrotype of Early Storefront

Ambrotype, quarter plate, building exterior, large classical-style storefront w/sign reading "H.A. Murdock, Merchant Taylor," Wincester, New Hampshire, fullframe view w/boy in front of stoore, black cloth backing, full case w/spine split (ILLUS.) **207**

Ambrotype of Two Children

Ambrotype, quarter plate, children standing on either side of a draped table, a young girl in a floral print dress & earrings on the left & a young boy wearing a bow tie & dress jacket on the right, ca. 1850s, gilt liner w/half case (ILLUS.) **220**
Ambrotype, quarter plate, family group w/parents & two grown daughters seated around a table on which sits a small dark puppy above two curled up cats, in a half case w/stamped metal liner w/oval opening, ca. 1850s (few small scratches) **330**

Ambrotype of Ladies in Landscape

Ambrotype, quarter plate, ladies in outdoor scene, one lady rides side saddle on a horse, the other stands & watches, rail fence & fields in the background, few tiny blemishes, full case w/split spine, ca. 1850s (ILLUS.) **248**

Ambrotype, quarter plate, two cute young girls standing side by side & wearing identical off-the-shoulder knee-length dresses w/petticoats & pantaloons, also each w/a locket & chain around her neck, in full case w/metal mat w/oval opening, ca. 1850s.. **363**

Ambrotype, sixth plate, half-length portrait of a man & woman seated side-by-side, brass liner & open thermoplastic rectangular frame molded w/scrolling flowers & leafy vines, ca. 1855, 4 1/4 x 4 3/4" (some flaking on image)................................. **165**

Ambrotype, sixth plate, ruby ambrotype of a Civil War Zouave soldier seated & shown from the knees up, wearing Zouave tunic & tasseled fez, image tinted, housed in a leatherette case w/split hinge (image dark) **275**

Boudoir cabinet photo, a view of Manitou Springs, Colorado by W.E. Hook, reverse w/advertisements for local businesses, ca. 1880s... **55**

Cabinet Photo of a Young Mark Twain

Cabinet photo, bust portrait of a young Mark Twain, hand-written identification on front & information on Twain on the back, period copy print on ivory mount, very slight soiling (ILLUS.) **323**

Carte-de-visite, Bishop Matthew Simpson, by Hallet & Bro., New York, Simpson gave the funeral oration at Lincoln's funeral (trimming on bottom edge) **50**

Carte-de-visite, exterior view of Dunlap's Photographic Gallery of Salem, Ohio, studio backmark on reverse (minor edge bumping & trims) **220**

Unusual Exterior View Daguerreotype

Daguerreotype, family in exterior scene, the family group standing in front of a carriage & horse w/a Greek Revival house in the background, ca. 1850s, in thermoplastic case w/gilt metal liner, damage around edges of image, 3 1/4 x 3 3/4" (ILLUS.) **2,990**

Daguerreotype, half plate, an older woman seated & shown waist up, wearing a bonnet, old collection tag on glass, image resealed, housed in leatherette case w/detached hinge, ca. 1840s.................................. **94**

Daguerreotype, half plate, portrait of a woman & young boy, posed next to each other w/the woman seated & the boy standing, shown knees up, by Root's Gallery of Philadelphia, identified in ink on a pad, resealed & housed in leatherette case, ca. 1840s.................................... **413**

Daguerreotype, half plate, two boys posed next to each other, one seated, one standing, shown from the knees up, image by Whitehurst, still sealed (dirt under glass)... **385**

Daguerreotype of Militia Officer

Daguerreotype, officer in uniform of the New York Militia, seated in ornate uniform holding a dress sword, tinted highlights, pressed leather & velvet case

w/metal liner, damage & wear to
case, ca. 1840s, 4 3/4 x 6" (ILLUS.) **3,450**
Daguerreotype, quarter plate, a portrait
sketch of Josiah Quincy, 1772-1864,
probably a working sketch of the portrait
of Quincy by Gilbert Stuart which hangs
in the Museum of Fine Arts in Boston,
contained in a half photo case,
3 3/4 x 4 5/8" **575**
Daguerreotype, quarter plate, group of
three adults, two women & one man, all
seated & shown from knees up, by
Chase, resealed, in leatherette case
w/detached hinge, ca. 1840s.......................... **132**
Daguerreotype, quarter plate, half-length
portrait of a gentleman wearing a high-
collared shirt, cravat, vest & frock coat,
in an open rectangular thermoplastic
frame molded w/fruits, flowers &
beading, ca. 1855, 5 1/4 x 6 1/4" (slight
halo on image near liner) **248**
Daguerreotype, quarter plate, portrait of
an older woman, seated shown from
knees up, by Root's Gallery of Philadelphia, resealed, housed in leatherette
case, ca. 1840s (minor case damage) **165**
Daguerreotype, sixth plate, a young boy
shown standing from the knees up, wearing a plaid jacket w/wide buckle belt, image
by Wm. Stroud, Norristown, Pennsylvania,
original seal, housed in leatherette case
w/detached hinge, ca. 1850s........................... **105**

Rare Winter Outdoor Scene

Daguerreotype, sixth plate, close-up exteri-
or view, a man in top hat seated in one-
horse sleigh in foreground w/a standing
group of men & boys on the porch of a
large building just behind him, possibly
Chester County, Pennsylvania, full
case, ca. 1850s (ILLUS.) **4,992**
Daguerreotype, sixth plate, occupational-
type, a young man seated, shown waist
up wearing a straw hat, at a table working
on a side-armature sewing machine,
tools resting around the bottom of the
machine, by Ennis Gallery, 106 Chestnut
Street, Philadelphia, accompanied w/lat-
er note naming sitter & dating image
about 1848, ca. 1840s (probably
cleaned, resealed)...................................... **19,250**
Daguerreotype, sixth plate, portrait of a
young girl seated in a Gothic Revival side
chair, shown waist up holding a china

head doll, housed in a leatherette case
w/detached hinge, original seal,
ca. 1850s... **440**
Daguerreotype, sixth plate, portrait of a
young girl, standing & shown from the
knees up, her hair in pigtails, wearing an
off-the-shoulder blouse, resealed, in
leatherette case, ca. 1840s (split hinge)........ **220**
Daguerreotype, sixth plate, portrait of a
young woman seated & shown from the
knees up, holding a book & wearing a
fine dress, by Wm. Stroud of Norristown,
scratched photographer's name & date
on reverse, original seal, in half Union
case w/molded grape & leaf design, 1854 ..... **165**

1864 Fire Department Photograph

Photograph, printed on oval metal plate,
scene of engine house & U.S. Fire department in Alexandria, Virginia,
ca. 1864 (ILLUS.) **375**

Early Curtis Native American Portrait

Photogravure, portrait of "Middle Calf-Pie-
gan," Native American sepia portrait by
E.S. Curtis, Plate No. 202, ca. 1900, mat-
ted, 11 1/2 x 15 1/2" (ILLUS.)......................... **550**
Salt print, exterior view of the Hancock
House in Boston, Massachusetts, mounted to larger board as used in illustration
for a book, ca. 1853, image 4 x 5".................. **77**
Tintype, full plate, showing a group of men
outside a building with a barrel-loaded
wagon drawn by a six-mule/horse team,
uncased **77**
Tintype, group shot of milliners & seam-
stresses, five Victorian ladies with four

standing behind a small table & the fifth seated beside it, holding various hats & needlework, scarce female occupational shot, ca. 1880s, 4 x 5" (light plate wear, focus a bit soft) **466**

Tintype, half plate, children w/a goat cart, a Victorian boy standing beside a small cart pulled by a small goat, a young girl in a long white dress standing ahead of the goat, a house porch in the immediate background, late 19th c., in a full case (few tiny blemishes, case spine split)............ **200**

Tintype, sixth plate, a seated young girl wearing a dark dotted dress, her hair pulled back, pets the head of a large sleeping dog on the bench beside her, in a full case, slightly dark image, mid-19th c. **133**

Tintype, sixth plate, occupational-type, showing a bricklayer seated, from the knees up, holding a trowel in his right hand & brick in his left, wearing a vest, broad-brimmed hat & smoking a cigar, tinted image, in leatherette half case, ca. 1860s **303**

Union case, ninth plate, molded on the front w/a bust portrait of an American Indian chief facing right, holds a tintype of a child (minor case chipping) **94**

PINBACK BUTTONS

"Rockaways' Playland - Member of Jo-Jo Club" Pin

Pinback buttons or pinbacks, have been around since the dawn of the 20th century. For most of the century pinbacks were strictly utilitarian in purpose. Their many uses included political, commemorative, holiday, advertising or simply as badges. During World War I and II, pinbacks helped the war effort(s). In the 1950s and '60s, pinbacks with teen idols, TV personalities and cartoon characters appeared.The pinback button was still strictly utilitarian by the mid-1960s when they became the rage as a means of personal expression. You could not only convey your political beliefs, but your spiritual, sexual and personal points-of-view as well. The "message" button craze lasted into the early '70s, with the smiley face button being the last gasp of the fad. Pinback buttons settled back into utilitarian use – t-shirts and bumper stickers had become the accepted mode of self-expression. The Punk/New Wave movement of the late '70s reintroduced "message" buttons to popular culture, whose popularity continued well into the '80s.

Pinback buttons are almost always round and made of metal. Some buttons have the image screen-printed right on the metal. More common are the paper printed ones – the printed image covers the metal button and is sealed in the back by a metal insert. Printed paper but-

tons are usually gloss-coated. Sizes range from a tiny 1/2" in diameter to a pretentious 4". Some older buttons have the dreaded hatpin-type pin that jutted out dangerously. Most have the shorter pin with a catch. Sometimes, you will find manufacturer's information on the rim if you look on the button's side. The buttons listed here are from the 1900 to 1970s.

Advertising

"Freshie and the Southern Baker," yellow & blue cartoon faces of a chef & an imp, 1940s, 1"... **$3-6**

"Join the American Party," red, white & blue image of 1940s man w/Amoco sign, 1940s, 1".. **4-8**

"Rockaways' Playland - Member of Jo-Jo Club," white w/red & blue image of Jo-Jos face, 1900-1930s, 1 3/4" (ILLUS.)............ **10**

"You Can't Keep a Squirrel on the Ground," premium for Hassam Cigarettes, full color litho of squirrel in tree, 1900-1930s, 1" **10-15**

Commemorative

"Boys Week 1928," blue, boy's face, 1900-1930s, 3/4".. **5-10**

"Cardinal Spellman" Pin

"Cardinal Spellman," photo, 1950s, 1 1/4" (ILLUS.) **3-6**

"Souvenir Los Angeles County Fair Pomona Calif.," white w/red & blue cartoon pig w/suitcase, 1950s, 1 1/4".................. **3-6**

"Souvenir Royal Visit 1959" Pin

"Souvenir Royal Visit 1959," yellow background, photo of Queen Elizabeth & Prince Philip, 1950s, 2" (ILLUS.) **10-20**

"Welcome Back to Earth, Glenn" Pin

"Welcome Back to Earth, Glenn," white w/blue photo of John Glenn, attached ribbon, 1960s, 1 3/4" (ILLUS.) **10-20**

Holiday

"Count Your Blessings - Loyalty Day May 1st 1929," white w/blue lettering, 1900-1930s, 1 1/4" **4-8**

"Easter," full color litho of Easter lilies & cross, 1900-1930s, 1/2" **5-10**

"Mothers Day 1917," green w/white carnation, 3/4" **5-10**

Miscellaneous

"Alienation Can Be Fun," yellow & black, 1960s, 1 1/4" **5-10**

"Archie Bunker for President," red, white & blue, 1970s, variations on theme e.g. Another Meathead for Bunker, To the Rear March with Bunker, 1", set of 12 .... **25**

"Ban Buttons," yellow & black, 1960s, 1 1/4" **5-10**

"Closets Are For Clothes," blue w/white lettering, 1970s, 1 1/2" **5-10**

"Does Mama Know Your Out" Pin

"Does Mama Know Your Out," red & blue, 1950s, 1" (ILLUS.) **5-10**

"Don't Monkey With Me," white & blue image of cartoon monkey, 1950s, 1" **5-10**

"Draft Beer Not Students" Pin

"Draft Beer Not Students," white & blue, 1960s, 1 1/4" (ILLUS.) **5-10**

"End the War in Vietnam," silver & black, 1960s, 1 1/2" **5-10**

"End War Taxes April 15," blue & white Dove of Peace, 1960s, 1 1/2" **20-30**

Farrah Fawcett, photo, 1970s, 3" **5-10**

"Flower Power," black & orange image of gun shooting flowers, 1960s, 1 3/4" **10-20**

"Fonzie is Cool," image of Fonzie from Happy Days, 1970s, 3" **5-10**

"Foxy," white w/red lettering, 1970s, 1" **3-6**

"Funky But Chic," 1970s, 1 1/4" **3-6**

"Gene Autry," photo of Gene Autry, 1950s, 1 1/4" **10-20**

"I Had a Computer Date - Now I'll Try People," white & blue, 1960s, 1 1/4" **5-10**

Ivory Soap box, depicted w/Marilyn Chambers as mother on box holding baby, 1970s, 1" **10-20**

"Jesus Wore Long Hair" Pin

"Jesus Wore Long Hair," dayglo orange & black, 1960s, 1 1/4" (ILLUS.) **5**

"Kiss Me I'm Jewish" Pin

"Kiss Me I'm Jewish," blue & white, 1960s, 1 1/4" (ILLUS.) **5-10**

"LSD Not LBJ" Pin

"LSD Not LBJ," white & black, 1960s, 1 1/2" (ILLUS.) **5-10**

"Make Love Not War," image of red peace sign, 1960s, 1 1/4" **10-20**

"Man, I Mean Like You Fell For It!" Pin

"Man, I Mean Like You Fell For It!," red & white, 1950s, 1" (ILLUS.) **5-10**

"Mary Poppins is a Junkie" Pin

"Mary Poppins is a Junkie," yellow & orange, 1960s, 1 1/2" (ILLUS.) **10-20**

"Meat is Murder," white w/brown image of soldier, 1970s, 1" **5-10**

"My Button Loves Your Button," black w/silver lettering, 1960s, 1 1/4" **5-10**

Rosie the Riveter in front of factory, signed ©Trina marked on side produced by "Pinback Jack," 1970s, 2 1/4" **10-15**

"Souvenir of the Circus," blue w/clown face, 1900-1930s, 1 3/4" **5-10**

"Star Trek 1974" Pin

"Star Trek 1974," tan w/black image of Mr. Spock, Star Trek Convention, 1970s, 2" (ILLUS.) **20-25**

"The Lone Ranger" Pin

"The Lone Ranger," illustration of the Lone Ranger & Silver, 1950s, 1 1/4" (ILLUS.) **10-20**

Peace Sign Pin

U.S. Capitol, in background w/large hand flashing the two-finger peace sign in foreground, marked "National Mobilization Committee 1970," 1960s, 2 1/2" (ILLUS.) . **15-25**

"Wars Will Cease When Men Refuse to Fight," white w/red & blue psychedelic design & lettering, 1960s, 1 1/2" **5-10**

"White Punks on Dope," purple w/white lettering, 1970s, 1" **4-8**

"Woodstock Music and Art Fair" Pin

"Woodstock Music and Art Fair," red, white & blue logo of fair, 1960s, 1 1/4" (ILLUS.) **20-30**

"XRay Spex.," new wave graphics in black w/orange lettering, 1970s, 2 1/2" **5-10**

Music

"All Possible Love to the Rolling Stones," blue & yellow, 1960s, 1 1/4" **10-20**

"Blondie is a Group," white w/red lettering, 1970s, 1 1/2" **4-8**

Blues Brothers, white w/black image, marked "©1978 Phantom Ent.," 1970s, 1 1/2" **4-8**

"Disco Sucks," orange w/white lettering, 1970s, 1" **5-10**

Grateful Dead Pin

Grateful Dead Teddy bear, white, holding red rose, 1970s, 1 1/2" (ILLUS.) **3-5**

Harry Belafonte Pin

Harry Belafonte, photo, 1960s, 1 1/2" (ILLUS.) **5-10**

"I Like Elvis," red & white w/blue lettering, 1950s, 1 3/4" **10-15**

John Lennon, black & white image of former Beatle, holding a wrench, 1960s, 1" **5-10**

"Let's Twist," black w/silly lettering, 1960s, 1" **5-10**

"Oakridge Boys Have Arrived 1979," blue w/green lettering, 1970s, 3" **4-8**

"Paul Anka" Pin

"Paul Anka," red background face & signature, 1950s, 1 3/4" (ILLUS.) **10-12**

"Rock n Roll," gold w/silhouettes of teenagers dancing, 1950s, 1" **10-15**

Rolling Stones tongue & lips logo, 1970s, 1" **5-10**

Political

"For Governor Edwin Warfield," shows photo of man, 1900-1930s, 1" **10-20**

"I Like Ike" Pin

"I Like Ike," red, white & blue, 1950s, 1" (ILLUS.) **10-15**

"Iran Sucks," white w/black lettering, 1970s, 2" **10-15**

"McGovern President '72," dark blue w/white lettering, 1970s, 1 1/4" **4-8**

"Nazis Are No Fun - Rock Against Racism," black & green, 1970s, 1" **10-15**

"Nixon's the One" Pin

"Nixon's the One," white w/red lettering, 1970s, 1 1/2" (ILLUS.) **5-10**

"Republican Parity & Prosperity," gold & dark blue w/image of American flag, 1900-1930s, 1/2" **10-20**

"Screw Our Political Enemies - Watergate," white w/blue lettering, 1970s, 1 1/2" **5-10**

"We Mourn Our Loss" Pin

"We Mourn Our Loss," white photo of FDR, 1940s, 1 3/4" (ILLUS.) **15-25**

"WIN, Whip Inflation Now," white w/red, 1970s **4-8**

Sports

"Philadelphia Phillies" Pin

"Philadelphia Phillies," screened-on-metal, red, white & blue graphics, 1940s, 1" (ILLUS.) **10-15**

"YMCA Knot Hole Gang Minneapolis," red & blue image, 1900-1930s, 1 1/4" **10-15**

Wartime

"Hello Gobs - We're Glad to See You Back" Pin

"Hello Gobs - We're Glad to See You Back," yellow & black face of cartoon sailor, 1940s, 1 1/4" (ILLUS.) **10-15**

"I'm Chinese," worn by Chinese during World War II to ward off hysterical anti-Japanese sentiment, white w/black letters, 1940s, 1 1/2" **25-50**

"Keep 'Em Flying," blue w/plane, 1940s, 1" **10-20**

PLANT WATERERS

Ceramic plant waterers were designed in a variety of shapes, ranging from obvious forms like watering cans to animals (such as birds, cats, owls & frogs), flowers, people & an assortment of whimsical creations. While

*size may vary, the majority usually range from 4" to 6".
The top has a hole that is filled with water (typically a
seven day supply) which seeps through the pointy porous
stem into the planter or flowerpot. This ingenuous invention allowed the homeowner to leave town without fear
that their plants would die of thirst.*

*Plant waterers continue to be made today in both
ceramic & terra cotta. However, except for a few of
newer vintage that are worth noting, most of these listed
are from the 1950s-60s.*

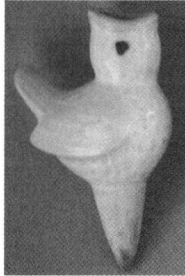

Bird Plant Waterer

Ceramic, bird, white w/yellow beak,
    4 1/8" h. (ILLUS.).. **$6-10**
Ceramic, cabin, light brown, 5 3/4" h................ **6-12**

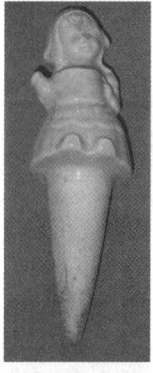

Dutch Girl Plant Waterer

Ceramic, Dutch girl, yellow, 6" h. (ILLUS.) **8-12**
Ceramic, fish, Shawnee, marked "USA,"
    5" h. **35-50**

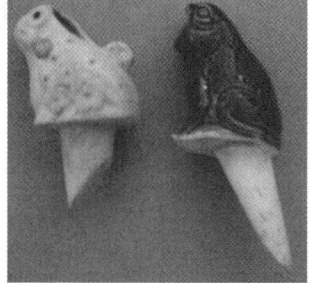

Frog Plant Waterers

Ceramic, frog, green w/black & tan spots,
    6 1/8" h. (ILLUS. right).................................... **6-10**

Frog on Bird Bath Plant Waterer

Ceramic, frog, perched on bird bath edge,
    marked "Korea" on sticker, 4 1/2"
    (ILLUS.) **18-25**
Ceramic, frog, white w/yellow flowers &
    green dots, 4 1/8" h. (ILLUS. left)................ **6-10**

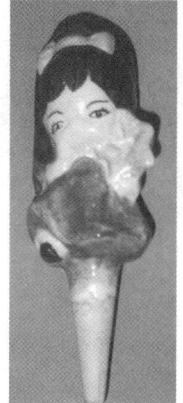

Girl with Bouquet Plant Waterer

Ceramic, girl, holding bouquet, handmade
    & signed by artist, 5 1/4" h. (ILLUS.)......... **20-25**

Josef Originals Girl Plant Waterer

Ceramic, girl in pink bonnet & dress, hold-
    ing a watering can, Josef Originals, 6" h.
    (ILLUS.) **45-60**

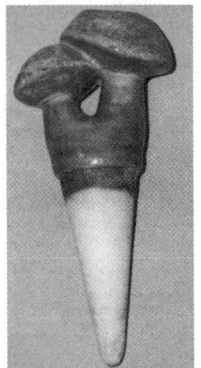

Double Mushroom Plant Waterer

Ceramic, mushroom, double, light brown,
4 1/2" (ILLUS.) **8-12**
Ceramic, pump, water, red, 5" h. **15-25**
Ceramic, pump, water, red, 7 1/2" h. **10-18**
Ceramic, rose, yellow, 5 1/4" h. **15-20**

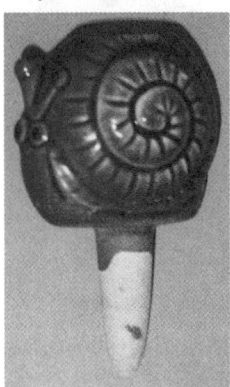

Snail Plant Waterer

Ceramic, snail, brown, 4 1/2" h. (ILLUS.) **8-12**

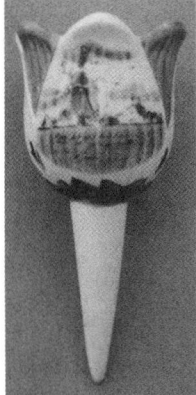

Tulip Plant Waterer

Ceramic, tulip, blue & white "Delft" pattern,
6" h. (ILLUS.) **18-25**

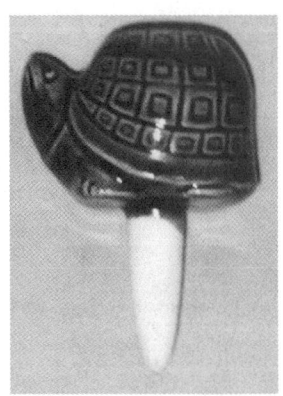

Turtle Plant Waterer

Ceramic, turtle, green, 4" h. (ILLUS.) **8-12**
Ceramic, windmill w/flowers at base, light
blue, 6" h. **8-15**

POLITICAL & CAMPAIGN ITEMS

Campaign

Dewey-Bricker Armband

Armband, 1944 campaign, worn by female
campaign workers, marked "Dewey-
Bricker, Liberty Belle," w/image of a bell,
3 3/4" w, 14" l. (ILLUS.) **$25-35**

1912 Roosevelt Campaign Bandanna

Bandanna, 1912 campaign, Theodore
Roosevelt & Bull Moose (Progressive)
party, red cloth printed in white w/a center oval portrait of Roosevelt below "Progressive" & above "Roosevelt - 1912 -
Battle Flag," checked block background
design, framed, 20" sq. (ILLUS.) **151**

Wendell Willkie Banner

Banner, 1940 campaign, silk, "Win With Willkie - For President," 5 x 7" (ILLUS.)..... **15-20**

1976 Campaign Buttons

Buttons, 1976 campaign, Carter-Mondale, Rosalyn & Jimmy Carter, Gerald Ford & Gerald Ford - Robert Dole, 2" d., the set of 4 (ILLUS.).. **20-25**

Franklin Roosevelt Inaugural Program

Inaugural program, Franklin Delano Roosevelt & Henry A. Wallace, January 20, 1941, framed, 8 3/4 x 10 3/4" (ILLUS.)... **50-60**

Willkie License Plate Attachment

License plate attachment, 1940 campaign, marked "Willkie" flanked by stars (ILLUS.) **75-90**
License plate attachment, 1940 campaign, half-round metal printed in red, white & blue w/wording "The Hope of Our Country - Willkie," locally produced in Elwood, Illinois for the Steel Workers Organizing Committee, never used, 6 1/2 x 11" (few scuffs & dings) **36**
Magazine, 1946 Congressional campaign, John F. Kennedy's first campaign, "PIC - The Magazine for Young Men," November 1946 issue w/cover photo of standing John F. Kennedy smiling w/his campaign poster in the background (worn spine w/chips).. **47**

GOP National Convention Pennant

Pennant, 1968 campaign, red felt w/white elephant marked "GOP" & white lettering reading "Republican National Convention Miami Beach, Fla.," 10" l. (ILLUS.) **15-18**
Pinback button, 1896 campaign, celluloid jugate-type, William McKinley & Garret Hobart, bust portraits of the facing candidates in brown & white, excellent condition **18**
Pinback button, 1896 campaign, celluloid, William J. Bryan, a bust portrait of the Democratic candidate w/wording "Victory 1896 - W.J. Bryan," printed in red, white & black (red slightly faded) **19**
Pinback button, 1908 campaign, William Howard Taft, color bust photo of the Republican candidate within a color border w/a small shield at the top, Whitehead and Hoag, 1 1/4" d. (small spot above head) **55**

Large Stevenson Photo Button

Pinback button, 1952 campaign, Adlai Stevenson, large button w/photo portrait of Stevenson framed in red, white & blue by stars & wreaths w/shield at top center, reads "Stevenson - Vote Democratic," some light yellowing, 9" d. (ILLUS.) **33**

Eisenhower-Nixon Jugate Button

Pinback button, 1952 campaign, Eisenhower & Nixon, jugate portraits of candidates on red, white & blue ground, reads "Vote - Ike - Nixon - Republican," small crimps at edges, 3 1/2" d. (ILLUS.) **22**

Pinback button, 1992 campaign, Bill Clinton & Al Gore, "Steelworkers - Clinton - Gore - '92," multicolored w/photos of each candidate & the steelworker's union logo, 3" d. **11**

Pitcher, 1840 campaign, pottery, a bulbous hexagonal baluster-form w/a wide arched spout & ornate C-scroll handle, transfer-printed in four panels in black w/a scene of a log cabin above a laurel wreath enclosing a bust of William Henry Harrison over an American eagle w/shield, marked below each cabin "The Ohio Farmer" & below each portrait "W.H. Harrison," American Pottery Mfg. Company, Jersey City, New Jersey, 12" h. (general discoloration, old cracks) **33,350**

Postcard, 1952 campaign, Adlai Stevenson, printed typed message w/a small bust photo of the candidate in the upper right corner, mentions "get a fresh new administration..., dedicated to highest ethical and executive standards...," printed in blue (light soil) **23**

Smith-Robinson 1928 Poster

Poster, 1928 campaign, Alfred E. Smith & Joe T. Robinson, jugate paper poster in brown on white w/large oval portraits of Democratic candidates, reads "Democratic Nominations - For President - Alfred E. Smith - of New York - for Vice-President - Joe T. Robinson - of Arkansas," folded, light soiling, 19 x 25" (ILLUS.)............................ **75**

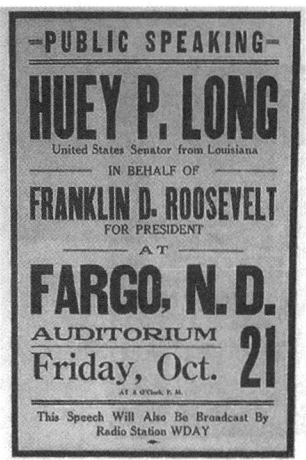

1932 Huey Long & Roosevelt Poster

Poster, 1932 campaign, heavy card stock, for Franklin D. Roosevelt, reads "Public Speaking - Huey P. Long - United States Senator from Louisiana - in Behalf of - Franklin D. Roosevelt - for President - at - Fargo, N.D. - Auditorium - Friday, Oct. 21...," matted, 11 x 17" (ILLUS.)................... **880**

Poster, 1948 campaign, Harry S Truman & Alben Barkley, large facing photo bust portraits of the two candidates below "Beat High Prices," under the photos "Elect Harry S. (sic) Truman, President - Alben W. Barkley - Vice-President," red, blue & white w/black & white photos, 20 x 27" (heavy crinkles & folds) **28**

Poster, 1956 campaign, Adlai Stevenson & Estes Kefauver, red bands at top & bottom edges with blue letter on bands & white center area, the top band w/a bust portrait of Stevenson & "Vote For Stevenson and Democratic Candidates" w/lower bands listing the other Democratic candidates from Pennsylvania, folded, scarce, 28 x 42" **91**

Robert F. Kennedy Poster

Poster, 1956 campaign, Dwight Eisenhower & Richard Nixon, a red & blue band at the top w/photos of Eisenhower & Nixon & "Back Ike's Team," lower section in white w/listing of Republican slate for Pittsburgh, Pennsylvania, 28 x 44" (pieces missing at bottom corners, tack holes at top & center edges, 28 x 44")......................... 54

Poster, 1960 campaign, John F. Kennedy & Lyndon Johnson, blue & red letters on white, photo of Kennedy at the top right, top section reads "Mark X on First Line of Ballot to Vote Straight Democratic - Insure Leadership for the 60's," next section listed Kennedy & Johnson w/lower bands listing the Democratic slate of candidates in Pittsburgh, Pennsylvania, 28 x 44" (tack holes in corners, scuff at bottom, wrinkle at bottom, folded) 77

Poster, 1968 campaign, comical scene of Robert F. Kennedy holding a tennis racket & a football, featuring images of the Capitol, a donkey & several children, 18 1/4 x 24" (ILLUS. bottom previous column) **25-35**

1856 Fremont Campaign Ribbon

Ribbon, 1856 campaign, Fremont & Dayton, printed on blue silk w/large oval reserve w/portrait of Fremont on horseback w/"Pathfinder" behind him, printed at top "Fremont & Dayton," printed at bottom "Free Soil - Free Press - Free Speech - Fremont.," slight water stain at his head, 2 3/8 x 4 3/4" (ILLUS.) 163

Ribbon, 1880 campaign, James Garfield & Chester Arthur, pink silk printed in blue "Assistant Marshal - Business Men's - Garfield and Arthur - Parade - Oct. 27, 1880," 2 1/4 x 6 1/2" (top soil, back w/residue from paper hanger, creases).......... 33

Ribbon, 1884 campaign, Cleveland & Hendricks, woven silk w/portraits of Democrat Cleveland & his running mate Hendricks, a four-color American eagle w/the portraits, manufactured by Schweizer-Katz, 3 x 5 1/4" (some staining) 110

Ribbon, 1900 campaign, William McKinley & Theodore Roosevelt, gold printed on white silk w/U.S. flag & bow at the top above "McKinley & Roosevelt - Union League - Nov 6th 1900 - Special Aid," 2 x 6 1/2"... 83

Ribbon, 1908 campaign, William Howard Taft & James Sherman, white silk printed in red, blue & black, jugate-type w/a round bust photo of Taft at the top & Sherman at the bottom w/a large draped American flag & eagle between them, 5" l... 83

Ribbon, 1952 campaign, Dwight Eisenhower & Richard Nixon, blue cloth printed in gold "Eisenhower Guest - Ike and Dick - They're for You - Hunt Armory - Oct. 27, 1952," 6" l. 25

Smock, 1968 campaign, white cotton smock-mini-dress w/self-tie neckline, wide blue band trim at half-length sleeves & hem, "Nixon" printed in large block letters down one side of the front.......... 86

Stickpin, 1868 campaign, small rectangular brass frame w/oval opening holding an albumen bust photo of Ulysses S. Grant, very choice condition, 3/4 x 1" 191

Non-Campaign

Albumen print, from the series "President Arthur's Journey through Wyoming," shows horse-drawn wagons w/tents in the background, supply wagons, etc., printed stamp of F.J. Haynes & Fargo, 6 3/8 x 8 7/8" (light stains along margin, small chip in mount).. 110

Franklin D. Roosevelt Silk Banner

Banner, silk, shield-form white background w/image of Franklin D. Roosevelt in blue, flanked by blue stars w/"America Demands" above the portrait & "Franklin D. Roosevelt " in red letters below, framed, 6 3/4 x 7 3/4" (ILLUS.) **15-20**

President Arthur Cabinet Photo

Cabinet photo, bust portrait of President Chester A. Arthur, by New York City photographer Sarony, ca. 1881, slight foxing in background (ILLUS.) **51**

Calligraphic memorial drawing, "General Grant in Memoriam," pen & red & brown ink, a large spread-winged eagle w/a banner in its beak above three wide inscribed columns, inscribed "designed and written for J.A. Throckmorton, Esq. by the author, Barnegat N.J., July 23rd, 1886," signed "William Erickson," framed, 21 1/2 x 27 1/2" (minor foxing, soiling, fading) **1,035**

Franklin Roosevelt Figural Clock

Clock, metal, shelf or mantel, figure of Franklin Delano Roosevelt standing at the wheel of a ship, the base marked "FDR The Man Of The Hour," United Electric, 13" w., 15" h. (ILLUS.) **150-175**

Drawing, pen & ink on paper, a large scene of a soldier on a prancing horse below a pair of facing spread-winged eagles holding a banner reading "The Hero of Bueno Vista," represents General Zachary Taylor, later President of the United States, in shades of brown, ca. 1848, framed, 20 3/4 x 25 3/4" (minor stains, a repair) **1,045**

Handkerchief, cotton, printed w/a central pictorial oval depicting the deceased George Washington on his deathbed attended by physicians & Mrs. Washington, surrounded by six bordered reserves of printed tributes, dark brown print on white ground, early 19th c., framed, 18 1/4 x 20 1/2" (fabric loss, staining, repairs) **1,093**

Handkerchief, cotton, the upper half w/scene of George Washington & the cherry tree w/the fable printed below, banners at top reading "The Love of Truth, Mark the Boy," blue & white, framed, old note & photographs on back pertaining to first owner, 12 3/4" sq. (minor stains, small holes & short tear in upper left) **385**

Bicentennial Hatchet

Hatchet, brass, blade w/cut-out bust of George Washington, handle marked "Washington Bicentennial - President of the US - 1776-1976," 12 1/2" l. (ILLUS.) ... **25-35**

Inauguration press badge, 1953 inauguration, celluloid button in blue on white w/black lettering reading in part "Working Press - 380 - 1953 Inaugural Committee," on original paper hanger authorizing bearer to cross Pennsylvania Avenue on January 20, 1953, button 3 1/2" d. **110**

Letter, concerning release of George Washington's slaves, from John Butcher to Sarah Horner, conveys information concerning the possible release of Washington's slaves & related information, dated Alexandria, Virginia, January 4, 1800, 1 pg. **3,850**

Newsweek Cover with Harry S Truman

Magazine cover, Newsweek, November 8, 1948, Harry S Truman, framed, 10" w., 13" l. (ILLUS.) **30-35**

Mourning ribbon, printed silk in gold on black w/a small tintype bust portrait of Abraham Lincoln in a brass frame, attached ribbon reads "We Mourn Our Fallen Chief - U.S. Mint," ca. 1865, 1 1/2 x 7" (tintype dark, fraying at top & bottom of ribbon) **358**

Presidents of the United States Paint Book

Paint book, "Mr. Peanut Presents a Historical and Educational Paint Book - Presidents of the United States of America," center view of the White House flanked by portraits of George Washington & Dwight Eisenhower, issued by Planters Nut and Chocolate Co., 1953, 7 3/4 x 10 1/2" (ILLUS.) **12-15**

Pitcher with Portraits of Presidents

Pitcher, ceramic, squatty bulbous body w/ornate handle & scalloped rim w/pinched spout, decorated w/presidential eagle & bust portraits of Presidents George Washington to Lyndon B. Johnson, gold trim, marked on bottom "© Chadwick Miller Importers 1965 Japan," 6" h. (ILLUS.) **30-40**

George Washington Plaque

Plaque, brass, profile of George Washington, border marked "First in the Heart's of His Countrymen - 1732-1932," 8" d. (ILLUS.)..... **15-20**

Franklin D. Roosevelt Plaque

Plaque, celluloid, image of Franklin Delano Roosevelt, 9" d. (ILLUS.) **100-125**

William H. Taft Plate

Plate, ceramic, center w/sepia tone bust of President William H. Taft, border w/green iridescent trim, 6 7/8" d. (ILLUS.) **28-35**

Plate with Taft & Sherman

Plate, ceramic, centered by bust portraits of President William H. Taft & Vice President James Sherman, eagle below & flanked by flags, 7 1/4" d. (ILLUS.)............. **45-50**

Plate w/White House & Presidents

Plate, ceramic, features an image of the White House surrounded by bust portraits of the Presidents from George Washington to Woodrow Wilson, 9 3/8" d. (ILLUS.)... **45-50**

Polk Presidential China Plate

Plate, porcelain, dessert plate from the James K. Polk presidential china service, gilt relief border & lobed cavetto, apple green rim band w/cartouche containing colorful U.S. shield & scrolling ribbon w/U.S. motto, h.p. floral spray in the center, manufactured by Eduoard Honoré, France, 1846, 9 1/8" d. (ILLUS.) **3,738**

"Stars and Stripes Forever" Print

Print, "Stars and Stripes Forever," features Presidents Wilson, Lincoln & Washington below crossed flags, framed, 17" w., 21" l. (ILLUS.).. **45-50**

Abraham Lincoln Ribbon

Ribbon, silk, Stevengraph-type, center oval medallion w/portrait of Abraham Lincoln below shield & eagle w/banner & surrounded by circle of stars, reading at top "Assassinated At Washington - 14 April 1865" & "I have said nothing but what I am willing to live by, and if it be the pleasure of Almighty God, to die by. - (A. Lincoln)," reading under the portrait & above two flags, "The Late Lamented President Lincoln," white, black, blue & purple thread, minor wear & stains w/pinhole in top, 2 1/4 x 9 1/2", w/gilt frame 5 1/4 x 11 1/2" (ILLUS.) **578**

"Roosevelt March" Sheet Music

Sheet music, "Roosevelt March - A Tribute to the Memory of Col. Theodore Roosevelt" by F.Carl Jahn, w/photo of the President, framed, 7 3/4 x 12 3/4" (ILLUS.) **35-40**

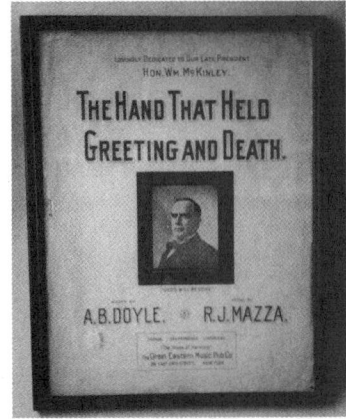

"The Hand that Held Greeting and Death" Sheet Music

Sheet music, "The Hand that Held Greeting and Death" marked "Lovingly Dedicated to Our Late President Hon. Wm. McKinley - God's Will Be Done" by A.B. Doyle & R.J. Mazza, framed, 8 x 12 3/4" (ILLUS.)............ **35-40**

Stereoview card, bust photo portrait of Abraham Lincoln, reprint of the famous Anthony view, w/a Lincoln biography on the reverse written by Carl Sandburg w/facsimile signature, Keystone view No. 28016 .... **303**

Textile, printed cotton, rectangular form w/an elaborate design centered by an oval bust portrait of George Washington below crossed flags & a spread-winged eagle, flanked by numerous flowers & fruits on each side, printed in blue, green, tan & brown, semi-regular design of dark brown specks, framed, early 19th c., 16 x 27" (minor fading, small holes) **330**

Textile, printed silk, a small central bust of George Washington in a small medallion flanked by crossed flags, bugles, oak leaves, acorns & a spread-winged eagle below "First in War, First in Peace...," a wide border band printed w/a naval battle scene, in black, olive green, mustard yellow & red, early 19th c., framed, 24 3/4 x 29 1/2" (minor stains) **1,430**

Woodrow Wilson Tile

Tile, Wedgwood blue w/white bust profile of President Woodrow Wilson, back marked "The Mosaic Tile Company, Zanesville Ohio, New York N.Y.," 3 1/2" d. (ILLUS.) **50-65**

"The White House" Tray

Tray, metal, features photo of the White House w/flowers in front, image of Franklin Roosevelt in upper left corner, dark green border & gold trim, titled "The White House," 10 1/2 x 13 1/4" (ILLUS.) ... **40-50**

Walking stick, wooden twig shaft mounted w/a sterling silver cap inscribed "HENRY CLAY 1832 To Gen. Harrison To Wm. Harrell 1840," given by Clay to William Henry Harrison & then to Wm. Harrell, 33" l. **1,495**

POP CULTURE COLLECTIBLES

Beatles cartoon cel, title cel from 1966 Beatles animated weekly cartoon series, shows the four band members w/facsimile signatures, three-layer, excellent condition, framed, 10 x 13 1/2" (some tape on edges) **$3,061**

Beatles concert program, "The Beatles Show," British publication w/photos & biographical information on the band, includes a 6 x 8" photo from the press kit mailed w/the program, 1963, 16 pp., excellent condition **230**

Beatles concert ticket, full ticket for August 20, 1965 concert at White Sox Park, Chicago, lavender w/black printing, near mint **827**

Beatles Bobbing Head Figures

Beatles figures, bobbing head-type, each on square base w/name written on front, wearing matching green nehru jackets & trousers, bowl-cut hair, playing guitars & drum, near mint condition, ca. 1964, the set (ILLUS.) **1,224**

Beatles Mug

Beatles mug, porcelain, slightly tapering cylindrical shape w/C-form handle, marked in black "The Beatles" w/portraits & names in black on white, "England" stamped on bottom, ca. 1963, 4" h. (ILLUS.) **230**

Rare Beatles Pennant

Beatles pennant, w/original tassels & metal grommets, depicts Beatles w/"Yeah, Yeah, Yeah" slogan, white, red & blue, Canada, ca. 1964, 21" l. (ILLUS.) **383**

Beatles Record Player

Beatles record player, four-speed record player, blue case featuring paper label picturing the Beatles on front & large image on inside lid, perfect working condition, minor deterioration to fuzz circling the plate of the turntable, small dings in blue coating outside front, ca. 1964, 6 x 10 x 17 1/2" (ILLUS.) **8,891**

Beatles talcum powder, cylindrical tin container w/original top & contents intact, depicts the four singers w/"With The Beatles" at top & "Talc - Margo of Mayfair" at bottom, "Made in England" stamped on bottom, 1963 .... **616**

Bon Jovi platinum record, for "Slippery When Wet," commemorating the total of nine million records sold, mounted in a display frame w/a note from the band, 1987, near mint, 20 x 31" **259**

Brian Jones letter, hand-written letter by Brian Jones, one-page note to a fan, near mint w/original mailing envelope, 1964 .... **611**

Bruce Springsteen photograph, famous color image of Springsteen preforming before a large American flag, from his "Born in the U.S.A." period, signed during a rehearsal, w/authentication, near mint, 10 x 13" **259**

Elvis Presley Autographed Album

Elvis Presley autographed album, 45 r.p.m. soundtrack album for "Kid Galahad," sleeve inscribed in near mint blue ink "To Laura, Happy Valentine's Day, Elvis Presley," 1963, wear to sleeve, record near mint (ILLUS.) **1,205**

Elvis Presley Book Ends

Elvis Presley book ends, plaster, bone colored half-length finely detailed figure of Elvis holding guitar, "Elvis Presley" on front is incised facsimile signature, verso of each reads "Copyright 1964 By Elvis Presley Enterprises All Right Reserved," 1964, near mint condition, 8" h., pr. (ILLUS.) **927.00**

Elvis Presley Wallet

Elvis Presley wallet, vinyl, brown w/image of Elvis holding guitar w/record image in background surrounded w/musical notes, his name & the names of some of his recordings, opens to reveal change purse & clear plastic photo section, marked on back "1956 Elvis Presley Enterprises All Rights Reserved," minor chip top front border (ILLUS.) **348**

Elvis & Priscilla Presley contract, sales contract from Elvis & Priscilla Presley, for the sale of their Beverly Hills home in December 1971, framed w/pictures of each **3,716**

Grateful Dead Poster

Grateful Dead poster, center portrait of grinning Jerry Garcia, two-night concert engagement of band at the Fillmore in San Francisco, ca. 1966, near mint condition, 13 1/2 x 22" (ILLUS.)............................. **904**

Janis Joplin letter, hand-written by Janis Joplin, five-page letter to a friend, 1965, w/original mailing envelope **2,464**

"New Year Bash" Concert Poster

Jefferson Airplane/Grateful Dead poster, advertising "New Year Bash" at Fillmore West, San Francisco, classic '60s psychedelic artwork, 1966, near mint condition, 14 x 24" (ILLUS.) **348**

Jim Morrison check, endorsed on the back by Morrison, $100 drawn from the Johnson and Harband Management Account, dated September 26, 1969 .... **1,668**

Jimi Hendrix clothes hanger, die-cut cardboard, a black & white head & shoulder cut-out of Hendrix, two-sided, late 1960s **201**

Led Zeppelin poster, for a performance at Fillmore West in 1969, a pink, blue & white image w/a large central rear view of a zeppelin, the name of the band at the top, near mint, 14 x 21" **994**

The Who poster, for a 1969 performance at Fillmore East, titled "The Who Perform Their Entire Rock-Opera 'Tommy,'" dark rose, dark blue & white, near mint, 23 x 37" **679**

POSTCARDS

Common Easter Postcard

Easter, large white cross w/blue violets printed over pink blossoms on a blue ground, "A Happy Easter" at the bottom (ILLUS.) **$3**

Early Leather Postcard

Leather, center scene of laughing man reading large open book titled "Pickwick Papers - Dickens," printed at sides "Why The (Dickens) Don't You Write?," marked "Copyrighted W.S. Heal" at bottom right, early 20th c. (ILLUS.).. **5**

Real photo, "Cutting Fruit - Reedley, Calif.," California fruit packers working in an open-sided shed, female occupational, well-lighted, clear image, by Besaw, ca. 1910 .... **55**

Real Photo Card with Farm Scene

Real photo, exterior scene of farm wagon w/two-horse team, farmer seated on one horse, small boy standing in bed of wagon, early 20th c. (ILLUS.)................................. **35**

Real photo, Mississippi steamboats going through locks, two large vessels in close-up view in the locks, oversized, 1913, 6 x 9" **110**

Real photo, schoolhouse construction, a small frame country schoolhouse w/a bell tower being finished w/group of workmen in front, early 20th c. (creases & wear in corners, clear image)....................................... **39**

Early Vegetable Vendor Photo Card

Real photo, vegetable vendor, exterior scene of horse-drawn vegetable wagon w/vendor standing near rear, baskets & scales visible, appears to have been mounted, paper residue at leaf, post-marked 1910 (ILLUS.) **88**

Real photo, view of the House of David miniature railroad, a row of five miniature train engines each w/a driver, House of David w/a utopian sect that supported it-self was amusement park & fielding a traveling baseball team, early 20th c. **21**

Bernhardt Wall Suffrage Postcard

Suffrage, Bernhardt Wall artwork, cartoon scene of young girl wearing large hat & scolding boy in overalls, reads "Votes For Women - For the work of a day, - For the taxes we pay, - For the Laws we obey, - We want something to say.", early 20th c. (ILLUS.).. **25**

Suffrage, "Her First Vote," half-length color portrait of a seated elegant young lady wearing a very large feathered hat, drawn by Clarence Underwood, ca. 1910-15 .... **88**

Suffrage, "Votes For Women - The Spirit of 1776 (crossed out) To-Day" at top, "No Taxation Without Representation," at bottom, a cute Wall card w/a color drawing of a young girl wearing a cockcade hat & holding a long sword (discoloration at right)... **33**

Rare Suffrage-Valentine Postcard

Suffrage Valentine, artwork by E. Clapsad-dle, colorful scene of a young girl in Colo-nial attire wearing ribbon reading "Votes For Women," printed above & below "To My Valentine - Love me - Love my Vote," wear at bottom, clean (ILLUS.) **200**

Early Tuck Valentine Postcard

Valentine, one of "Poster Girls" series by Raphael Tuck, England, smiling young lady in elaborate wrap w/huge feathered hat, reads at top "Valentine Remem-brance," No. 231 in series (ILLUS.)................. **15**

POSTERS

Pearl Harbor Remembrance Poster

World War II, "Avenge December 7," large image of fist-shaking sailor at the top w/exploding ship at the bottom, red letter-ing across center on brownish back-ground, folds, matted, 21 x 26" (ILLUS.) **$248**

World War II, "Back the Attack! - Buy War Bonds," colorful image of a landed para-trooper w/other troops parachuting be-hind him, grey band at bottom, original folds, never used, 1943, 20 x 28" **87**

World War II, "'Deliver us from evil' - Buy War Bonds," black, white & blue, central bust portrait of frightened young girl against a large swastika & clouded sky, U.S. Treasury issue for September 1943,

Dramatic War Bonds Poster

also w/an eight-page tabloid booklet titled "Complete & Official Instructions on
the 3rd War Loan" showing other available posters, poster 22 x 28", 2 pcs.
(ILLUS. of poster) **806**
World War II, "Enlist in a Proud Profession
- Join the U.S. Cadet Nurse Corps," colorful bust portrait of pretty young nurse in
uniform, original folds, 14 x 20" (brown-
ing around border) **83**
World War II, "I'll Carry Mine, Too!," show-
ing a half-length portrait of a housewife
carrying groceries w/shadows of soldiers
up behind her, signed by artist Sarra
(some weakness at folds) **83**
World War II, "Keep Him Flying - Buy War
Bonds," colorful image of a pilot getting
seated in the cockpit of his fighter, original folds, w/original mailing envelope,
1943, 28 x 40" **101**
World War II, "Save waste fats for explo-
sives - Take them to your meat dealer,"
dramatic color image of a hand holding a
frying pan & pouring grease which produces a large batch of bombs & torpedos
flying toward the viewer, original folds,
artist H. Koerner, 1943, unused, 20 x 28" **356**

POWDER HORNS & FLASKS

Rare Early Decorated Powder Flask

Flask, decorated horn, a two-piece pressed
horn body retained by a molded copper
strap mounted w/four hanging rings &
copper throat ferrule, bearing the polychrome painted images of an officer on
horseback marked "GOVr TOMPKINS" &
surmounted by an American Eagle surrounded by 18 stars & a scrolling red &
green floral arrangement on each side,
section of copper strap missing, spout
missing, cracks in horn at base, early
19th c., 3 1/2 x 6 1/2" (ILLUS.) **$3,450**
Horn, engraved "Jacob Spilman - April the
18 - 1845. Scipio, Meigs Co. Ohio," relief-
carved ring w/chip-carving & a flat wood-
en plug w/square nails, good patina, 9" l. . **1,100**
Horn, engraved w/a coat-of-arms w/drag-
ons & crowns, a soldier w/kilt & feathers
in helmet, an officer tipping his hat, etc.,
good patina, 19th c., overall 16 1/2" l.
(plug missing) **660**

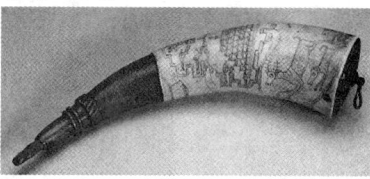

Engraved Powder Horn with Map

Horn, engraved w/a map of a fort & the
roads leading to it, also a stag hunt
scene, plug engraved "JR," 18th c., very
minor loss to plug, 10 1/2" l. (ILLUS.) **2,760**

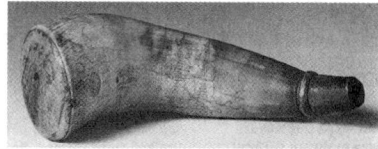

Horn Engraved with Sailing Ship

Horn, engraved w/a ship under full sail
w/American flag & American eagle
w/shield under the phrase "Success to
the American eagle, Who with an air of
disdain, spit on the crown of Great Britain" & "Imortality (sic.) to Washington,"
wood plug held in place w/small square-
head metal nails, signed "G. Swartnout"
& dated "Sept 9th 1820," America,
9 1/2" l. (ILLUS.) **1,265**
Horn, incised w/two rows of geometric de-
vices around the bottom, carved & incised lines at the spout, a long signed &
dated inscription, dome-shaped wooden
plug, 1785, 18" l. (small age crack, wear) . **1,610**
Horn, ornately inscribed & incised w/overall
decoration, central section w/"Gideon
Booth his horn made at Winter Hill Decm:
1775," contained in an ornamented cartouche, "Ozias Prentis" beneath cartouche flanked on the right by the British coat
of arms w/banner inscribed "success to
America," on the left w/elaborate floral
scrolls, decorated w/a scene of dueling
soliders w/swords, a mermaid, deer,

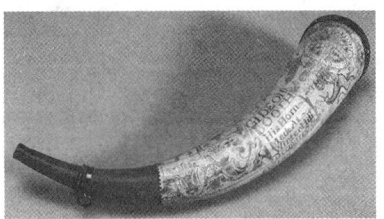

Early Ornate Powder Horn

dogs, trees, a cannon & other designs, mounted w/later sterling silver fittings marked "Tiffany and Co., Union Square," the end engraved "Martin Dymond. Myra Dymond," signed "By J. Gay," attributed to Jacob Gay, late 18th c., crack at plug end, four age splits at top, several small insect holes, overall 15" l. (ILLUS.) **34,500**

PRINT ARTISTS - EARLY 20TH CENTURY

Bessie Pease Gutmann

Awakening, 14 x 21"	**$120**
Butterfly (The), 14 x 18"	**160**
Come Play With Me, 3 x 5"	**55**
Daddy's Coming, 14 x 18"	**440**
Double Blessing (A), 14 x 18"	**1,045**
Friendly Enemies, 11 x 14"	**155**
Guest's Candle (The), 14 x 18"	**255**
Home Builders, 14 x 17"	**110**
In Disgrace, 14 x 18"	**230**
Little Bit of Heaven (A), 14 x 14"	**115**

Lorelei

Lorelei, 14 x 17" (ILLUS.)	**1,650**
Message of the Roses (The), 14 x 20"	**360**
Mighty Like a Rose, 14 x 18"	**155**
Nitey Nite, 14 x 18"	**95**
On Dreamland's Border, 14 x 14"	**165**
On the Up and Up, 14 x 18"	**140**
Our Alarm Clock, 14 x 20"	**220**
Popularity Halts Disadvantages, 14 x 21"	**170**
Postcard group, "The Five Senses," 8 x 22	**360**
Postcard group, "Woman," 8 x 22	**525**

Seeing, 11 x 14"	**250**
Snowbird, 14 x 18"	**380**
Winged Aureole (The), 14 x 18"	**375**

Maxfield Parrish

Advertisement, Edison Mazda, "Dawn," 4 x 8"	**40**
Advertising print, The Broadmoor Hotel, 4 x 5"	**45**
Book, The Arabian Nights, Wiggins & Smith, 1909	**130**
Calendar of Sunshine, 1920, 6 x 8	**45**

The Canyon

Canyon (The), 12 x 15" (ILLUS.)	**275**
Christmas Eve, 8 x 11"	**525**
Circe's Palace, 10 x 12"	**175**
Daybreak, 6 x 10"	**110**
Garden of Allah (The), 15 x 30"	**275**
Hilltop, 18 x 30"	**715**
Lantern Bearers (The), 9 x 11"	**550**
Magazine cover, Collier's, August 5, 1905	**20**
Magazine cover, Collier's, December 2, 1905	**45**
Magazine cover, Collier's, January 6, 1906	**140**
Magazine cover, Collier's, September 12, 1908, "School Days"	**200**
Magazine cover, Ladies' Home Journal, July 1912, "A Shower of Fragrence" from the Florentine Fete murals	**115**
Magazine cover, Ladies' Home Journal, May 1913, "Buds Below the Roses" from the Florentine Fete murals	**30**
Magazine cover, Life, January 5, 1922, "A Man of Letters"	**210**
Menu, Broadmoor Hotel, late 1950s - early 1960s, 10 x 14"	**175**
Page (The), 10 x 12"	**175**
Postcard, Broadmoor Hotel, 1920s, 3 x 5"	**50**
Postcard, The Pied Piper, 1915	**100**
Prince (The), 10 x 12"	**185**
Valley of Enchantment, 5 x 6"	**85**

R. Atkinson Fox

Approaching Storm (An), 9 x 12"	**110**
Dawn, 10 x 18"	**95**
Down by the Bridge calendar, 1933	**55**
Dreamland, 14 x 20"	**95**
Flowerland, 18 x 30"	**205**
Garden of Contentment, 10 x 18"	**70**
Garden of Happiness, 10 x 18"	**85**

Garden of Hope, 10 x 12".................................. 145
Glories of Autumn (The), 10 x 24" 105
Good Ship Adventure, 10 x 16"............................ 90
Heart's Desire, 12 x 18"..................................... 185
Home Sweet Home, 16 x 20".............................. 75
Indian Summer, 18 x 30"..................................... 100
Land Where Shamrock Grows, 14 x 22".......... 45
Moonlight and Roses, 14 x 18" 90
Nature's Beauty, 14 x 22".................................. 95
Nature's Grandeur, 14 x 22"............................. 115
Nature's Sublime Grandeur, 16 x 20" 65
Nature's Treasures, 18 x 30".............................. 100
Old Fashioned Garden (An), 14 x 20 45
Old Oak (An), 10 x 12" 95
Poppies, 18 x 30"... 250
Romance Canyon wood box, 9 x 12"............... 95
Russet Gems, 16 x 20"....................................... 145
Shower of Daisies, 10 x 24" 195
Spirit of Youth, 10 x 18"..................................... 100
Stately Sentinels, 14 x 22"................................. 85
Sunny South (The), 10 x 18" 140
Sunset Dreams, 18 x 30".................................... 120
Waiting For Their Master, 6 1/2 x 8".................. 95

Other Photographers

David Davidson
Beckoning Trail, 7 x 9" 60
Berkshire Jewel (A), 13 x 16 145
Berkshire Jewels, 5 x 7"..................................... 50
Berkshire Sunset, 13 x 20"................................. 130
Birches and Reflections, 9 x 15"........................ 50
Brook's Mirror (The), 12 x 16"............................ 120
Canoeist's Delight (The), 13 x 16" 65
Deacon's Parlor, 14 x 16".................................. 105
Forest Lake, 12 x 14" 65
Gay Head, 13 x 15" 100
Grandpa's Marquerites, 7 x 9".......................... 100
Heart's Desire Facsimile, 12 x 16".................... 40
In the Making, 8 x 10"... 70
Jack Frost Palette, 10 x 12"............................... 60
Lambs May Feast (The), 5 x 7" 120
Lover's Lane, 9 x 16".. 85
Match Makers (The), 13 x 16"............................ 125
Meeting House Lane, 7 x 9" 80
Neighbors, 10 x 13".. 300
Pergola Gate (The), 13 x 15" 95
Profile Water Hazard, 12 x 15"........................... 105
Queen (The), 10 x 12".. 60
Snow Bound Brook, 10 x 12".............................. 70
Spent Wave (The), 5 x 7" 65
Stone Arch, 8 x 10"... 70
Vacation Seat (A), 12 x 16"................................ 85

Fred Thompson
Apple Tree Road, 11 x 17" 60
Birch Road, 8 x 16"... 40
Birthday Card, 4 x 6"... 45
Bridal Blossoms, 7 x 14"..................................... 35
Colonial Baby, 13 x 15" 155
Deep Hole Brook, 10 x 15".................................. 80
Flower Maid, 8 x 15".. 60
Gay Head, 10 x 15".. 300
Gay Head Cliffs, 10 x 15" 120
Hazy Morn, 7 x 9"... 160
Learning to Sew, 7 x 9" 60
Miniature Interior, 3 x 4".................................... 60
Mirror with Interior Scene, 4 x 13"..................... 60
Oceanside, 14 x 16".. 120

Old-Time Flowers, 7 x 9".................................... 60
Outlet (The), 7 x 9"... 40
Paring Apples, 7 x 9" 60
Pond Cove, 7 x 11".. 60
Portland Head, 8 x 13".. 90
Portland Head Light, 11 x 13"............................. 65
Roses and Reading, 8 x 16"................................ 85
Stony Brook, 9 x 15".. 30
Sunbonnet Days, 7 x 9"....................................... 175
Tray with American Flag, 3 x 4".......................... 55
Tray with Interior Scene, 2 x 3".......................... 40
Tray with Interior Scene, 3 x 4".......................... 60
Untitled Interior, 5 x 7"....................................... 40
Whittier's Home, 8 x 13"..................................... 230

Sawyer
Afterglow (The), 9 x 11"...................................... 50
Along the Heights, 7 x 9" 60
Among the Frost Flowers 120
At the Bend of the Road, 7 x 9 45
At the Water's Edge, 7 x 9"................................. 90
Ausable Chasm, 6 x 8"....................................... 60
Bit of Mackerel Cove, 9 x 15"............................. 275
Bridge of Flowers, 10 x 13"................................. 175
Cathedral Mountain, 7 x 9"................................. 85
Chapel Isle of Shoals Card, 4 x 5"..................... 65
Clear Water Pond, 7 x 11".................................... 175
Crawford Notch in Box, 6 x 8"............................ 155
Echo Lake, 16 x 20".. 70
Echo Lake, 8 x 10".. 35
Elk of the Mohawk Trail, 7 x 9".......................... 155
Flume Falls, 10 x 12".. 55
Flume (The), 5 x 7".. 50
Franconia Notch, 8 x 13" 60
Gates of Yosemite, 13 x 15"............................... 265
Jackson Falls, 14 x 16"....................................... 85
Jordan Pond Road, 5 x 7".................................... 40
Joseph Lincoln's Garden, 4 x 5"........................ 105
Mt. Lafayette, 7 x 8".. 85
Newfound Lake, 4 x 5".. 65
Old Man of the Mountains, 7 x 9" 90
Original Denison Plant (The), 14 x 17"............. 145
Paradise Falls, 7 x 9".. 45
Pool (The), Ausable Chasm, 8 x 10" 85
Rainbow & Horseshoe Falls, 8 x 10" 120
Rose Cottage (A), Cape Cod, 4 x 5"................. 220
Sunset on Rangely Lake, 6 x 7"........................ 100
Up Thro' Dixville Notch, 13 x 16".................... 250
Which Way?, 14 x 16"... 80

Lesser-known Photographers

Bicknell (J. Carleton)
Double Head, 8 x 12".. 30
Mirror with Exterior Scene, 8 x 11" 85
Sourduahump, 8 x 10"... 45

Burrowes
Country Road (A), 8 x 10"................................... 35
Natural Bridge of Virginia, 8 x 12".................... 20
Untitled Natural Bridge, 5 x 7"........................... 65

Carlock (Royal)
Washington DC card, 4 x 5"................................ 15
Washington DC Monument, 5 x 7" 30

Edson (Norman)
Mt. Elephantic, 8 x 10".. 45

Gardiner (H. Marshall)
Bermuda, 12 x 15".. 65
Bermuda, 7 x 9".. 45
Bermuda, 8 x 10".. 45
Bermuda, 8 x 10".. 120

Gibson
Rustic Bridge (A), 11 x 14" 30

Gourley
Rose Cloister, San Fernando, 8 x 10" 65

Harris
Approach to Limekiln Lake, 11 x 14"............. 155
City Gates, St. Augustine, 11 x 14"................. 40
Florida Wilds, 10 x 13"..................................... 65
Moss and Hyacinth, Florida, 11 x 14".............. 90
Mt. Lake Sanctuary, 11 x 14" 30
Natural Bridge, Virginia, 12 x 22" 90
St. Augustine, 9 x 16".................................... 75
St. Augustine City Gates, 8 x 10" 45

Haynes
Yellowstone Triptych, 10 x 23"....................... 45

Higgins (Charles)
Birch Ladies, 10 x 13"..................................... 60
Christmas card, 3 x 8" (rare) 65
Fireside Reflections, 7 x 11" 80
Untitled Girl by Tree, 11 x 14"......................... 145

Hodges
Untitled Exterior, 11 x 13"............................... 40

Lamson,
Apple Blossom Time, 8 x 10".......................... 35
Golden Hour, 7 x 11"....................................... 60
Willow Road, 8 x 15".. 60

LeBusch
Country Road (A), 11 x 13"............................... 25

Martin (Fred)
Spanish Mission, 6 x 11"................................. 85

McLeod (N.)
Cabot Trail, Cape Breton, 10 x 16".................. 45
Lake O'Law, Cape Breton, 10 x 16"................. 40

Meiers (J.W.)
Sunset on Flathead Lake, 11 x 15".................. 65

Moosilauke Studio
Echo Lake, black & white, 8 x 10"..................... 25

Moran
In the Garden, 12 x 14"..................................... 10

Neville
Sunset glow, 14 x 16" 10

Payne
Cavern Cascade, 8 x 14".................................. 60

Petty (George B.)
Favorite Walk (A), 11 x 14" 35

Rogers (Stanley)
Gay Head Cliffs, 8 x 18".................................... 120
Gay Head Cliffs, 9 x 12".................................... 135

Sanger
Contemplative, 18 x 22"................................... 80

Sawyer's
Timberline Lodge, Mt. Hood, 5 x 6"................. 30

Smith
Nature's Mirror, 11 x 14" 25

Sunsene
Along Florida Coast, 10 x 12"........................... 25
Storks, 7 x 9"... 35

Thompson (Florence)
Canyon (The), 6 x 12" 40
June Blossoms, 7 x 11" 20
Six Master, 7 x 11".. 320

Tillinghast
Untitled Cows, 9 x 11" 40

Underhill (Nelson)
Unframed pictures, pr. 45

Vannatta
Singing Tower, Florida, 11 x 14"....................... 25

Villar
Steps to the Road (The), 11 x 14"..................... 90

Winslow (R.)
Outer Shore (The), Cape Cod, 11 x 14"............. 75

Woolford (J.P.)
Sentinel Pines, 14 x 16" 65

Unknown Photographers
Child at Cradle, 10 x 12"................................... 25
Close-Framed Fisherman, 8 x 10"..................... 40
Cordova, Alaska, 14 x 20" 60
Crater Lake, Oregon 5
Exterior Triptych, 7 x 15".................................. 75
Exterior Triptych, 7 x 15".................................. 85
Florida, 8 x 10"... 15
Florida Bigononias, 8 x 10"............................... 15
German Photo - Nazi Flag, 9 x 11" 50
Grand Canyon, in original box, 4 x 5"............... 30
Japanese Village, 14 x 24" 50
Japanese Village, 14 x 24" 65
Lake George, 12 x 16"...................................... 25
Men by Arches, 13 x 17" 10
Mirror with Canoe in Lake, 8 x 10".................. 70
Old Spanish Quarter, Florida, 7 x 9"................. 20
Schooner, 7 x 9"... 60
Tall Building, 6 x 7"... 10
Untitled Railroad Tracks, 16 x 19"..................... 160
Washington, DC, 4 x 6"..................................... 10
Washington, DC, 5 x 7"..................................... 15
Watkins Glen, New York, 6 x 8".......................... 30

PURSES & BAGS
Alligator, brown ark-shaped handbag
w/flap closure, goldtone hardware, short
hand strap & two compartments, 1940s,
7 x 12".. $173
Beaded, hand-beaded rectangular bag
w/decorative silver frame & silvertone
link strap, glass beads on linen in a floral
pattern in red, pink, blue, lilac, black,

green, clear, gold & purple, gold metallic fringe at bottom, linen lining, hallmark on frame "1K - 13," matching purse inside w/similar patterning w/"Sophie Beck" beaded around perimeter, 1846, small purse 3 1/4 x 4", larger bag 7 x 9", 2 pcs....... **109**

Black suede, pouch-shaped shoulder bag type, leather trim, goldtone hardware & wide leather strap, hardware stamped "Gucci," 1980s, 4 x 11 1/2 x 12"...................... **288**

Brown leather, handbag w/round handle & goldtone hardware, stamped "Christian Dior Made in France," w/matching sunglasses w/3" d. lenses, stamped "Christian Dior" on interior arm, purse 2 x 8 x 10 1/2", 2 pcs. **460**

Camel suede, large rectangular shoulder bag w/darker camel overall Gucci logo "G" print, camel leather trim & piping, stamped "Made in Italy by Gucci 14" on leather lining, 1970s, 13 x 14"...................... **575**

Canvaswork, pocketbook-style, worked in Irish stitch w/wool yarn in a diamond design, silk lining w/four interior pockets, initialed "IK" & dated 1759, American, 18th c., 3 1/2 x 6 1/2" (minor losses).......... **1,955**

Crocodile, brown framed handbag w/darker brown crocodile stripe at center, goldtone hardware, short handle, stamped "Lucile de Paris" on leather lining, 1950s, 2 3/4 x 7 1/2 x 9 1/2"...................................... **288**

Cut steel, silvertone & goldtone cut steel bag w/geometric patterning & goldtone hardware, clasp & short handle, ivory satin lining labeled "Hand made in France," 1940s, 6 x 8 1/4".............................. **144**

Embroidered silk, rectangular evening clutch-style of taupe Chinese embroidered silk, two front flaps reveal two compartments, one holding matching compact, cigarette case & satin pocket, the other holding satin change purse, lining stamped "George Jensen, Inc. New York" & "Azka Paris - New York," 1950s, 5 1/4 x 10".. **86**

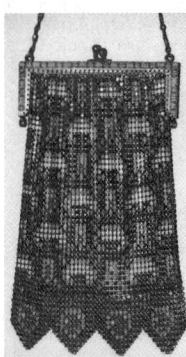

Decorative Whiting & Davis Purse

Enameled mesh, a narrow squared delicately enameled frame, the purse elaborately enameled w/repeating checked Art Deco design in white, black, blue, orange & red, Whiting & Davis, 1920-40, 4 x 7 1/4" (ILLUS.).. **150**

Rare Mesh Purse & Compact

Enameled mesh, "Delysia" purse & compact model, decorative metal mounts w/wide hinged center bands, blue & white enameled decoration on the mesh, ball & mesh base tassel, Whiting & Davis, interior w/rouge & powder compartments, very rare, 1920s, 4 x 6 1/2" (ILLUS.) **750**

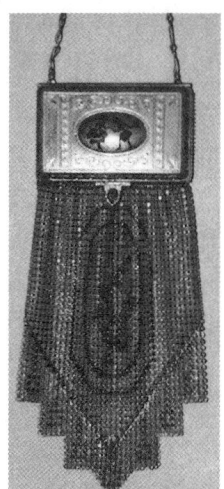

Fine Purse & Compact Combination

Enameled mesh, "El-sah" model, purse & compact combination, a rectangular giltmetal compact at the top w/a central oval w/black silhouette figures of an 18th c. lady & gentleman, the mesh purse in dark green w/a black-bordered center oval enclosing a blue & black flower, Whiting & Davis, 1920s, 3 x 7 1/2" (ILLUS.) **350**

Rose-decorated Enameled Purse

Enameled mesh, green ground painted w/a large center red rose & green leaves w/smaller roses in each corner & stylized blossoms along the scalloped bottom border, Whiting & Davis, ca. 1920-40, 5 1/2 x 9 1/2" (ILLUS.) **450**

Ornate Mandalian Mesh Purse

Enameled mesh, long mesh purse w/a white ground enameled w/light blue panels at the top & base trimmed w/bands of pink blossoms & green leaves, ornate metal frame set w/a small oval enamel panel flanked by small blue stones, Mandalian Mfg. Co., fine chain base fringe, 1920-40, 4 1/2 x 9 1/2" (ILLUS.) **350**

Mesh Purse Decorated with Oranges

Enameled mesh, ornate frame enameled w/a band of oranges & blossoms, the fine mesh w/a green ground w/stylized oranges in each corner & a center oval floral medallion, Whiting & Davis, 5 x 7 1/2" (ILLUS.) **300**

Rare Mesh Purse & Compact

Enameled mesh, purse & compact combination, the frame top opens to a powder & puff compartment, frame decorated w/delicate colored enamel metal set w/small colored stones, the purse enameled w/slashed bands in shades of gold, red, black, yellow, pink & blue w/a blue border & notched fringe in blue, black & red designs, unmarked, rare, 1920-40 (ILLUS.) **500**

Gold fabric, rectangular, clutch-style, 18k woven basketweave design, signed "Tiffany & Co." **4,025**

Gold mesh, 14k gold, Art Nouveau design w/engraved foliate frame, hallmark for Carter, Howe & Gough & Co......................... **403**

Gold mesh, 14k gold, the top pierced & engraved w/chimera, scroll & bellflower motifs, trace link chain handle, European hallmark **863**

Gold Mesh Evening Bag

Gold mesh, 14k yellow gold, elongated, stylized bell-shaped form suspending a gold tassel, both sides centrally decorated w/a lozenge-shaped palladium mesh design, the front set w/four old European-cut diamonds & four round, faceted emeralds, the rigid engraved frame topped w/a round, cabochon-cut emerald push piece & a small pivoting gold frame to which is attached the fine mesh handle (ILLUS.)... **1,495**

Gold mesh, 18k, evening bag supported by a shaped frame & trace link handle, thumbpiece set w/two cabochon blue stones, Swiss assay mark **1,150**

Gold mesh, 18k gold, drawstring style, accented w/a black cord closure & tassel, by Elsa Peretti for Tiffany & Co...................... **920**

Diamond & White Gold Handbag & Accessories

Gold mesh, 18k white gold, curved, rigid clutch w/woven, textured finish, the front undulating edge decorated w/a row of 84 round, single-cut diamonds, fitted beveled mirror & four matching accessories consisting of a key case, lipstick holder, cigarette case & compact w/a diamond-set push piece, w/Italian hallmarks, the set (ILLUS.) **6,900**

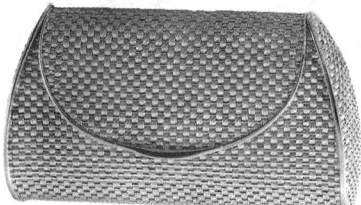

Gold Mesh Clutch Purse

Gold mesh, 18k yellow gold, curved rigid clutch w/textured woven design, interior w/fitted beveled mirror (ILLUS.) **2,760**

Fine Gold Mesh Handbag

Gold mesh, 18k yellow gold, rectangular form w/fine woven V-shaped geometric pattern, a rigid frame w/a cross-over type catch topped w/cabochon-cut sapphires, open link chain handle, English hallmarks, ca. 1908 (ILLUS.)...................... **1,265**

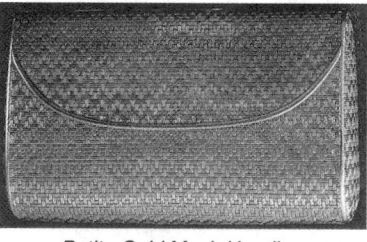

Petite Gold Mesh Handbag

Gold mesh, 18k yellow gold, rigid clutch of interwoven design w/pressure release flap, the inside fitted w/a beveled mirror, w/maker's mark (ILLUS.) **1,610**

Elegant Bi-colored Gold Handbag

Gold mesh, 18k yellow & white gold, curved rigid clutch w/a woven, lozenge-shaped design, the front lip decorated w/a row of round, brilliant-cut diamonds, a spring-loaded front panel, the interior decorated w/a fitted beveled mirror (ILLUS.)............... **4,025**

Gold mesh, 18k yellow & white gold, rectangular w/woven, lozenge-shaped pattern, w/fitted beveled mirror & fitted compartments on a spring-loaded front for the matching compact, lipstick holder & comb, w/Italian hallmarks, the set (ILLUS. top next page) **4,600**

Gold Mesh Purse w/Fitted Accessories

Gold mesh, Art Deco style, cathedral frame engraved in a foliate design w/seed pearl tassel pendant, a gold mesh cord handle accented w/four cabochon sapphires, cabochon sapphire closure, 14k yellow gold, hallmark, 105.8 dwt. **805**

Gold mesh, top engraved w/floral & geometric motifs, bag decorated w/two platinum mesh stripes, cabochon blue stone clasp, trace & baton link chain, dated "March 1920" (some damage to mesh) **690**

Leather, pale yellow two-compartment handbag w/goldtone hardware, clasp & thick chain handle, yellow, aqua, brown & cranberry-striped cotton lining, small plaque stamped "Bonnie Cashin" attached to lining, 1960s, 5 1/2 x 8" **144**

Leather & metal disk, taupe leather clutch-style w/flap closure, w/goldtone disk sides & trim, labeled "paco rabanne - paris - production - RICAF - Italy," & on interior flap "Model Deposé," 1960s, 1 1/2 x 7 x 8" **173**

Lucite, pouch-shaped Lucite handbag w/brushed green & gold pattern, top closure & turned handle, 1950s, 4 x 6 1/4 x 7 3/4" **144**

Metallic embroidery, large flat round handbag w/bronze, silver & gold metallic embroidery & metal fringe, braided metallic strap w/decorative tassels, purple silk lining, ca. 1911, 10 x 11" **316**

Navy & ivory fabric, barrel-style bag, woven Dior logo, navy blue leather corners, handle & lining, Christian Dior, 1980s, 7 x 10 x 13" **173**

Needlepoint, drawstring-type, bargello stitch in a geometric design in red, yellow, blue & green, striped silk ribbon trim at top, linen lining, late 18th - early 19th c., 7 1/4 x 8" (wear, losses to silk ribbon) **230**

Needlework, multicolored floral decoration work in petit-point stitch in shades of red, yellow, greens & blue on a light blue ground, bound in silk, pink silk-lined interior w/two pockets, England or America, late 18th - early 19th c., 2 1/4 x 6 1/4" (imperfections) **1,380**

Plastic, geometric marbleized brown handbag w/top flap w/decorative closure & turned handle, interior hardware stamped "Wilardy," 1940s, 3 3/4 x 6 x 6" **173**

Red plastic, rectangular clutch-type, composed of beveled plastic rectangles, top zipper closure w/wooden tassel, plaid lining w/attached change purse, 1940s, 8 x 12 1/2" **92**

Silk, telescoping neck suspending a floral silk bag layered by trace links & freshwater pearl accents, rope link handle, 14k yellow gold, Edwardian **690**

Silver mesh, mesh silver strap w/engraved findings attached to silver mesh bands inlaid w/blue sapphire stones, opening to fitted compartments w/money compartment & mirrored compact, ending in a silver mesh tassel, ca. 1900 .... **252**

Snakeskin, large shoulder bag in camel snakeskin w/darker brown snakeskin piping & goldtone shoulder strap, beige leather lining, labeled "Judith Leiber" on interior goldtone plate, 1970s, 14 1/2 x 15" **460**

Suede, small handbag in black printed w/rose design in pink, green & blue, black satin lining, labeled "Rosita Montenegro - Plaza Hotel - Fifth Avenue at 59th Street - New York," 1940s, 8" sq. **98**

Theorem-decorated velvet, reticule-type, ivory velvet ground decorated on the obverse w/a central floral bouquet flanked by strawberries & carnations, the reverse w/a cornucopia of fruit, iridescent green silk lining, the top finished w/pink ribbon casing & drawstrings, early 19th c., 6 3/4 x 8 3/4" (staining, minor losses) **1,150**

Velvet, Art Nouveau style, round, black velvet bag w/center sterling monogram & leather interior, the top chased & engraved w/Greek motifs, suspended from a clip of similar design, hallmark for Gorham, date symbol for 1901 .... **201**

RADIOS & ACCESSORIES

A.C. Dayton, Model R-12, large wooden set w/Bakelite panel, mid-1920s **$100**

Rare Addison Model 2A

Addison, Model 2A, yellow & burgundy Bakelite, Art Deco design (ILLUS.) **2,000**

Admiral, Model 34F5, portable, leatherette case w/decorative grill, 1940s **25**

Admiral, Model 4x11, plastic portable model, 1950s **40**

Admiral, Model 5A32, clock radio, brown or white, each **30**

Admiral, Model 5Y22, oversized radio-phonograph tabletop model in brown Bakelite **30**

Air Chief, Model 4-A-24, simple wooden tabletop model w/AM-FM, 1940s **30**

Air King, Model 52, classic "skyscraper" style in white Bakelite, 1933 .... **3,500**

Air King, Model A-510, portable, leatherette case **25**

Amrad Neutrodyne, crystal set, wooden case, five or seven tubes, 1920, each **150**

Arvin, Model 302A, streamlined painted Bakelite radio-phonograph, 1940s **45**

Arvin, Model 441-T, Hopalong Cassidy metal table model in red & silver.................... **650**

Arvin, Model 532, maroon Catalin w/yellow trim, 1930s... **2,000**

Atwater Kent, Kiel table-model, on six legs, top exposes radio inside **350**

Early Atwater Kent Crystal Set

Atwater Kent, Model 10, breadboard-style crystal set, exposed controls & tubes (ILLUS.).. **1,250**

Atwater Kent, Model 20C, crystal set, simple wide wooden tabletop model, 1920s **75**

Atwater Kent, Model 441, simple metal table top model, late 1920s.................................. **85**

Belmont, Model 6D128, streamlined painted Bakelite case **135**

Bendix, Model 0526C, green Catalin case w/black trim, no cracks **850**

Bendix, Model 0526C, thin plastic tan & brown case **250**

Capehart, Model 1P55, plastic portable style w/handle **20**

Channel Master Model 6506

Channel Master, Model 6506, small tabletop radio (ILLUS.)... **45**

Colonial, New World Globe model, novelty Bakelite style, 1930s..................................... **850**

Early Crosley Model 50 Radio

Crosley, Model 50, early two-tube radio (ILLUS.).. **175**

Crosley, Model 51, crystal set, two-tube style, early 1920s.. **250**

Crosley, Model 9-102, simple Bakelite tabletop model **30**

Crosley, Model 9-214, AM/FM console model w/phonograph...................................... **45**

Crosley, Model F-5 "Musical Chief" model, plastic.. **35**

Crosley Pup Model Metal Set

Crosley, Pup model, small square metal case w/tube in top (ILLUS.) **250**

DeWald, Model 502-A, tabletop model w/clock, yellow Catalin case.......................... **550**

DeWald, Model A-501, brown Catalin case, late 1930s.. **650**

Emerson, Model 410, wooden case w/Mickey Mouse character decoration, 1930s **2,000**

Emerson, Model 427, large portable style, cloth-covered w/handle, early 1940s **60**

Emerson, Model AU-190, tabletop style, blue Catalin case...................................... **3,500**

Emerson, Model AX-235, small green Catalin case.. **2,500**

FADA, Model 10, wide wooden tabletop model, late 1920s...................................... **100**

FADA, Model 1000, Bullet-style, all-yellow or pumpkin Catalin case, each...................... **950**

FADA, Model 189, Bullet-style in red, white & blue, all original & mint **4,000**

FADA, Model 5F-50, small tabletop model in yellow Catalin **1,000**

FADA Model 5F-50

FADA, Model 5F-50, yellow Catalin case, square dial (ILLUS.)................................... **1,000**

FADA, Model 652, Temple-style tabletop model in blue Catalin, mint condition **1,850**

FADA, Model P-80, cloth-covered portable, late 1940s.. **75**

General Electric, Model 50B, plastic clock radio, unbroken... **45**

General Electric, Model 605, simple plastic
portable model **40**
General Electric, Model H-87, Art Deco-
style console model, 1939 .... **150**
Kadette, Junior model, tall brown Bakelite
case, two-tube portable model, 1930s **375**
Kadette, Model K15, green classic over-
sized table model **1,000**
Kadette, Model L25, Topper Bakelite set
w/unusual round grille at top, mint................. **850**

Motorola Circle Grille Catalin Radio

Motorola, Model 50XC2, "Circle Grille" Cat-
alin case in turquoise blue w/yellow trim
(ILLUS.)... **3,000**
Motorola, Model 51X16, "S-Grille" Catalin
case in yellow w/green trim **2,500**
Motorola, Model 58F1, wooden tabletop
model w/phonograph **65**
Motorola, Model 5C1, plastic clock radio **40**
Motorola, Model 67F14, large wooden con-
sole w/radio & phonograph............................... **75**
RCA, Aeriola Senior (usually marked West-
inghouse), one-tube crystal set, 1920s.......... **250**

RCA Model 1-BT-2 Portable Radio

RCA, Model 1-BT-2, tabletop plastic porta-
ble w/charger (ILLUS.) **85**
RCA, Model 66BX, plastic portable w/alumi-
num trim **65**
RCA, Model 8T10, black case w/tubular
chrome frame, 1930s................................... **2,500**
RCA, Model 9X571, Bakelite tabletop mod-
el, late 1940s... **45**
RCA, Radiola Model 18, wide wooden case,
late 1920s **65**
Sparton, Model 1039, simply stylized radio-
phonograph, 1940s.. **45**
Sparton, Model 121, simple wooden table-
top model.. **30**
Sparton, Model 506, "Bluebird" circular blue
mirror-front model... **2,500**
Sparton, Model 557, three-knob tabletop
model w/blue mirror & chrome trim **2,500**

Standard Pocket-sized Radio

Standard, Model SR-H436, pocket-size,
chrome & black case (ILLUS.) **70**

Toshiba Transistor Radio

Toshiba, Model 6TP-385, transister-type
w/chrome grill (ILLUS.)..................................... **40**
Zenith, Model 5D011, square wooden table-
top model, mid-1940s.. **25**
Zenith, Model 6D311, Wavemagnet
Bakelite tabletop model, late 1930s **175**
Zenith, Model 6G001, Trans-Oceanic mod-
el in cloth-covered case, mid-1940s, av-
erage condition.. **95**

Zenith Royal 755 Portable Radio

Zenith, Royal Model 755, leatherette-cov-
ered portable (ILLUS.)....................................... **30**

RAGGEDY ANN & ANDY COLLECTIBLES

Say the names Raggedy Ann and Andy and visions of red yarn hair, floppy stripped legs, and friendly smiling faces come to mind. Without a doubt, they are the most famous rag dolls of all time. Books that feature the famous duo and dolls number high in this collectible field. Other Raggedy Ann and Andy items have always been out there, but not in the numbers they appeared in the early 1970s when there was a new found interest in these lovable characters.

Ball, musical roly-poly, 1974 .... **$55**

Vinyl Raggedy Ann Bank

Bank, Raggedy Ann, vinyl, 1972, 11"
(ILLUS.).. **12-22**
Bedspread, 1970s... **50**

"Beloved Belindy"

Book, "Beloved Belindy," 1926, Volland edition (ILLUS.) **160**

"Raggedy Andy Goes Sailing"

Book, "Raggedy Andy Goes Sailing," 1943, McLoughlin, the "Westfield Classics" series (ILLUS.) **40**
Book, "Raggedy Andy Stories," 1920, Volland... **150**
Book, "Raggedy Andy's Treasure Hunt," 1973, Tell-a-Tale **5**
Book, "Raggedy Ann and Andy and the Camel with the Wrinkled Knees," 1924, Donohue **85**
Book, "Raggedy Ann and Andy and the Nice Fat Policeman," 1942, illustrations by Worth Gruelle **40**
Book, "Raggedy Ann and Fido," 1969, Little Golden Book **7**
Book, "Raggedy Ann and Marcella's First Day at School," 1952, Wonder Book (ILLUS. top next column) **25**
Book, "Raggedy Ann and the Cookie Snatcher," 1972, Little Golden Book **8**

"Raggedy Ann and Marcella's First Day at School"

Book, "Raggedy Ann and the Left-Handed Safety Pin," 1935, Whitman............................. **45**
Book, "Raggedy Ann Helps Grandpa Hoppergrass," 1943, McLoughlin, "Westfield Classic" **40**

"Raggedy Ann in Cookie Land"

Book, "Raggedy Ann in Cookie Land," pop-up book w/record by Hallmark, 1974 (ILLUS.) **25**
Book, "Raggedy Ann Stories," 1918, Volland edition.. **150**
Book, "Raggedy Ann's Friendly Fairies," 1919, Donohue... **60**
Book, "Raggedy Ann's Lucky Pennies," 1932, Donohue... **55**
Book, "Raggedy Ann's Lucky Pennies," dust jacket, 1932, Volland............................... **210**

"Raggedy Ann's Sunny Songs"

Book, "Raggedy Ann's Sunny Songs,"
1930, Miller Music (ILLUS.) 70
Book ends, ceramic, figural, 1970s, pr. 70
Bowl, Ware by Crooksville, 1941, 9" 27
Can, Raggedy Ann spray starch, large can,
full, 1967 55

Animation Cel

Cel, original animation cel (ILLUS.) 45
Chair, metal & vinyl, folding chair & table,
1960s, 34" 100

Clock

Clock, album talking w/figures of Ann, Andy
& Arthur, 1972 (ILLUS.) 60
Colorforms, Ann & Andy dress-up kit, 1967 25
Coloring book, unused, Whitman, 1976 35

Cookie Cutter

Cookie cutter, marked Bobbs Merrill, Hall-
mark, 1972, 5" (ILLUS.) 15
Cookie jar, ceramic, Ann or Andy, Bobbs
Merrill, 1977 each 50
Cup, plastic 5
Cup, Ware pottery, 1941 32
Cup & saucer, ceramic 18
Curtains, 1970s 50

Ann and Andy Dolls

Doll, Ann or Andy, Knickerbocker, 12-15",
each (ILLUS.) 60
Doll, Ann or Andy, Knickerbocker, 6", each 18
Doll, Ann or Andy, Molly-'es, 1935-38, 18-
22", each 1,000

Raggedy Ann Doll

Doll, Ann or Andy, original clothes, good
condition, marked "Patented Sept. 7,
1915," Volland, 23-24", each (ILLUS. of
Ann) 2,500
Doll, Ann or Andy, talking, Knickerbocker,
1974, 12", each 50
Doll, Ann, original clothes, good condition,
marked "Patented Sept. 7, 1915," Vol-
land, 16" 1,300-1,500
Doll, Ann, sleeps on one side, awake on the
other, Georgene, 13-14" 450
Doll, Beloved Belindy, Knickerbocker,
1965, 15" 600

Beloved Belindy Doll

Game, Raggedy Ann, Milton Bradley, 1954 .... **45**

Beloved Belindy Greeting Card

Greeting card, Beloved Belindy card/book-let, Hallmark, 1974 (ILLUS.) **25**
Hand puppet, mint in package, 1973.................. **45**

Aladdin Lunch Box

Lunch box, metal w/thermos, unused, Al-addin, 1973 (ILLUS.)... **90**

Magnets

Magnets, Magnetics, 1978, 4", ea. (ILLUS.).......... **2**
Metal tray, features Ann & Andy, 1970s.............. **15**
Music box, ceramic, revolving, 1950s................. **40**
Music box, Schmidt, Japan, 1971 .... **75**
Music box, w/stuffed felt figures, 1972 .... **55**
Nightlight, figural Ann, Bobbs Merrill, 1976........ **65**
Ornament, Christmas, handcrafted Ann or Andy, Hallmark, 1975, each **300-350**
Ornament, Christmas, satin ball, Hallmark, 1975... **50**

Paper doll, Raggedy Ann cut-out dolls w/dresses, Milton Bradley, 1941...................... **55**
Paper dolls, Raggedy Ann & Andy, boxed set, 1975.. **7-10**
Paper dolls, Raggedy Ann & Andy, circus, Whitman, 1974 .... **10-15**

Raggedy Ann & Andy Paper Dolls

Paper dolls, Raggedy Ann & Andy, Ethel Hays Simms, uncut, Saalfield, 1945 (ILLUS.) **65**
Paper dolls, Raggedy Ann & Andy, Flip a Page, Change An Outfit, Whitman, 1967.. **12-20**
Paper dolls, Raggedy Ann & Andy, Fun Fashions, Whitman, 1974............................. **9-15**

Raggedy Ann & Andy Paper Dolls

Paper dolls, Raggedy Ann & Andy, Whit-man, 1935 (ILLUS.) **75-150**

Raggedy Ann & Andy Paper Dolls

Paper dolls, Raggedy Ann & Andy, Whit-man, 1966 (ILLUS.) **15-25**

Record w/Pop-Up Book

Record, w/pop-up book, Hallmark, 1974
(ILLUS.)... **25**
Record player, heart-shaped **90**
Sand pail, metal, 1940s... **70**

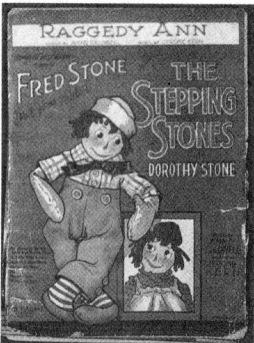

Sheet Music

Sheet music, large format, 1923 (ILLUS.) **25**
Stationery, kiddie, boxed, 1960s **20**
Tea set, tin, mint in box, 1940s............................ **100**
Thimble, pewter, Ann or Andy, each.................... **12**
Toy house, furniture & miniature Ann &
Andy, 1970s **45**

RECORDS

British Invasion - 45s

It started with the Beatles. Once they had conquered America, the invasion began in earnest. In its few brief years of frenzy – from 1964 to 1966 – the British Invasion of musical groups dominated and ultimately altered the popular music scene in America. The British Invasion can be characterized as male-dominated music groups (also called combos at the time) who sang and performed popular music. These were usually quartets (Beatles, Kinks, Who) or quintets (Dave Clark Five, Yardbirds, Rolling Stones). Duos like Chad and Jeremy or Peter and Gordon also were popular, as were solo female artists like Petula Clark, Lulu and Dusty Springfield. Until the Beatles' success, American teenagers' music was all American-made and produced – Elvis, rock 'n roll and surf music. As carefully planned as the Beatles Invasion of America had been, their phenomenal success took the music industry by surprise. The British Invasion consisted of this flood of groups and talent from England – some superb and some mediocre – which hit America starting in 1964 – all hoping to be "the next Beatles." The peak years for the British Invasion were 1964 and 1965. By 1967, popular music was changing. Many British Invasion artists adapted to the "psyche-

delic" and "rock" music of the times and competition from a second wave of British Groups (Procol Harum, Pink Floyd). A fair amount of early British Invasion groups and performers continued on with successful music careers, while others became memories by 1969. In the earliest phase, British Invasion groups wore matching outfits a la the Beatles. But by 1965, hair was getting longer and many groups appeared more informal and a little rougher. This also was reflected in their music. In an ironic twist, British Invasion music was heavily influenced by American rhythm and blues and rock and roll. Every group did numerous "cover" versions of American music. Despite this, British Invasion music had its own "sound." It could be cute and sappy (Herman's Hermits, Freddie and the Dreamers) or rough and bluesy (Animals, Rolling Stones). Listed here are 45 rpms – the teenagers' plastic-of-choice for almost 30 years until its demise in the 1980s. Since promotion was very important, images of the groups flooded the teenage market and all early releases of a 45 record came in a picture sleeve. Picture sleeves alone are worth quite a bit. Records listed here with picture sleeves (ps) are priced accordingly. Prices are based on values quoted in Goldmine Price Guide to 45 rpm Records and are priced between the very good and very good+ condition range as devised in the price guide. Picture sleeves not from the author's collection were loaned by Crossroads Music in Portland, Oregon. Unsleeved British Invasion-era 45s can still be found at garage sales and in thrift stores, but their condition is usually highly compromised. PRICE GUIDE: (ps) - Picture Sleeve; b/w - the other side of the record; EP - extended play, 45 size usually with four cuts.

Animals - House of the Rising Sun

Animals, House of the Rising Sun, b/w,
Talkin' 'bout You, ps, MGM (ILLUS.) **$10**
Animals, See See Rider, b/w, She'll Return
It, MGM **4**

Beatles - Help!/I'm Down

Hullaballoos - Beware

Kinks, Dead End Street, b/w, Big Black
 Smoke, Reprise **15**
Lulu, Shout, b/w, Forget Me Baby, Parrot **8**
Manfred Mann, Come Tomorrow, b/w,
 What Did I Do Wrong?, ps, Ascot **10**
Manfred Mann, Just Like a Woman, b/w, I
 Wanna Be Rich, Mercury **4**

Manfred Mann - Sha La La!

Manfred Mann, Sha La La!, b/w, John Har-
 dy, ps, Ascot (LLUS.) **10**
Mercybeats, Mr. Moonlight, b/w, Think of
 You, Fontana **6**
Merseys, Sorrow, b/w, Some Other Day,
 Mercury **8**
Mindbenders, Game of Love, b/w, Since
 You've Been Gone, Fontana **6**
Peter Best, Boys, b/w, Kansas City, Cameo **30**
Rolling Stones, 19th Nervous Breakdown,
 b/w, Sad Day, ps, London **15**
Rolling Stones, As Tears Go By, b/w, Gotta
 Get Away, London **5**

Rolling Stones - Have You Seen Your Mother?

Rolling Stones, Have You Seen Your
 Mother?, b/w, Who's Driving my Plane?,
 ps, London (ILLUS.) **15**

Rolling Stones - It's All Over Now

Rolling Stones, It's All Over Now, b/w,
 Good Times, Bad Times, ps, London
 (ILLUS.) **35**
Searchers, Love Potion Number Nine, b/w,
 Hi-Heel Sneakers, Kapp **4**

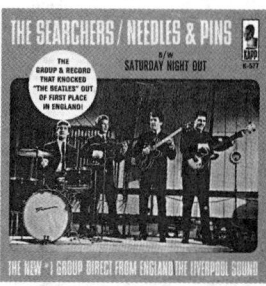

Searchers - Needles & Pins

Searchers, Needles & Pins, b/w, Saturday
 Night Out, ps, Kapp (ILLUS.) **12**
Small Faces, She-La-La-La-Lee, b/w, Grow
 Your Own, Press **5**
Small Faces, Tin Soldier, b/w, Feel Much
 Better, ps, Immediate **10**
Spencer Davis Group, Gimme Some Lov-
 in', b/w, Blues in F, United Artists **5**
Them, Here Comes the Night, b/w, All by
 Myself, Parrot **5**
Walker Brothers, Doin' the Jerk, b/w, Pret-
 ty Girls Everywhere, Smash **5**
Who, Happy Jack, b/w, Whiskey Man, ps,
 Decca **12**
Who, Substitute, b/w, Waltz for a Pig, Atco **18**
Who, The Kids Are Alright, b/w, A Legal
 Matter, Decca **12**

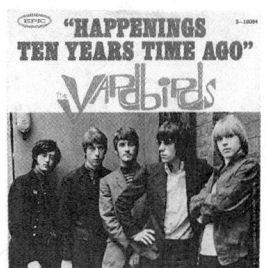

Yardbirds - Happenings Ten Years Ago

Yardbirds, Happenings Ten Years Ago,
 b/w, The Nazz are Blue, ps, Epic (ILLUS.) **15**

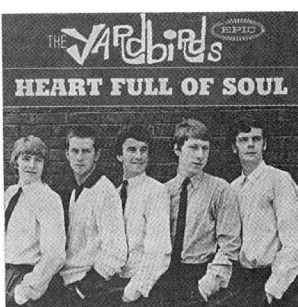

Yardbirds - Heart Full of Soul

Yardbirds, Heart Full of Soul, b/w, Steeled Blues, ps, Epic (ILLUS.) **20**

Zombies - Tell Her No

Zombies, Tell Her No, b/w, Leave Me Be, ps, Parrot (ILLUS.) **20**

REVERSE PAINTINGS ON GLASS

George Washington Painting

Basket of fruit, various fruits in a basket w/a red drapery, early 19th c., mahogany veneer frame, American, 9 1/2 x 11 1/2" (paint loss) **$690**

Bust portrait of gentleman, half-length stylized portrait of a balding middle-aged man facing left wearing a high-collared shirt & cravat & dark blue coat, brown ground, labeled "M. Van Buren," Martin Van Buren, President of the United States, 1837-41, in original narrow wood frame, 9 1/4 x 12" (background flaked) **550**

Bust portrait of gentleman, tall slender half-figure facing left, dark hair & long sideburns, wearing a high-collared shirt & vest w/cravat & a high-collared blue frock coat, rectangular portrait w/a white liner titled "Leop Koi v. Belgien," original molded wood frame, first half 19th c., 10 3/8 x 13 3/8" (flaking, especially in white border) **248**

Bust portrait of George Washington, shown facing forward, wearing dark jacket, shirt w/ruffled front, dark background, 19th c., Chinese Export, framed, 18 x 24" (ILLUS.) **978**

Bust portrait of lady, a young woman seated facing right, wearing a blue dress, red cape w/gold trim & a green, blue & red hat w/a white feather, shaded ground, titled "Eleanor," early 19th c., framed, 9 x 11 5/8" (some wear) **440**

Bust portrait of lady, shown facing right w/head turned, wearing a large colorful turban & a green dress w/a wide white ruffled collar & a blue scarf, brown background, titled "Pungdrugterin," Europe, first half 19th c., old narrow giltwood frame, 11 1/4 x 14 1/4" (flecking) **242**

Bust portrait of man, a half-length portrait of a young man w/dark hair & long sideburns facing right, wearing a high-collared blue jacket w/gold detail, a red vest & a high-collared white shirt, shaded bluish green background, framed, early 19th c., image 7 1/2 x 10" **220**

Bust portrait of Napoleon, shown facing left wearing a military uniform, within a round opening w/a floral band across the top & his name & slender scroll bands at the bottom on the white ground, old narrow molded wood frame, early 19th c., 9 1/4 x 11 1/4" (some flaking, touch-up repair)... **220**

Compote of fruit, a large shallow oval gadrooned bowl filled to overflowing w/various fruits against a dark background & within a trompe l'oeil frame surrounded w/a projecting small shelf at the foot of the compote in the picture, unsigned, Chinese School, 19th c., original frame, 7 5/8 x 9 1/2" (minor paint loss) **3,105**

Half-length portrait of a lady, facing right, her dark hair pulled up into a large topknot tied w/a large red ribbon, wearing a low-cut balloon-sleeved yellow Empire gown, against a brown ground, thin old giltwood frame, ca. 1830, 8 1/2 x 10 7/8" (minor wear).. **220**

Half-length portrait of a military figure, a standing young man w/dark hair facing left w/arms crossed, wearing a long white coat w/blue collar & red sash at waist, medals on his chest, titled "F. Napoleon," brown background, original narrow molded wood frame, first half 19th c., 9 1/8 x 11 7/8" (flaking on white title strip).. **495**

Reverse-Painted Genre Scenes

Interior scenes, one scene w/young father greeting his newborn child w/his wife in bed in background, titled "The First Pledge of Love," the second scene of the same family group showing the young toddler taking its first steps, titled "Going Alone," Chinese School, ca. 1810, early Chinese carved frames, based on unknown European prints, very minute losses, frames repainted, each 13 x 15 1/2", pr. (ILLUS.) **8,625**

Reverse-Painted Washington Portrait

Portrait of George Washington, half-length portrait shown facing left, wearing full uniform w/sword, brick red ground w/good color portrait, white border w/"Washington" at bottom, minor wear, one area of touch-up, molded old black-painted frame, early 19th c., 9 3/8 x 12 1/16" (ILLUS.) **1,265**

Portrait Painting

Portrait of woman & child, the woman w/dark hair facing front, wearing an off-the-shoulder dress w/long full sleeves, seated in a chair holding a small white dog, a young girl standing beside her mother, blue oval background w/marble-ized spandrels, under a clear sheet of glass, old gilded frame, some minor wear & flaking, one corner damaged, 12" w., 14" h. (ILLUS.) **330**

RIBBON DOLLS

Long before women were a dominant force in the work-place their days were spent taking care of the household chores, reading the latest novels and honing their needle-work talents. One way these ladies could demonstrate their skilled handiwork was by making ribbon dolls or ribbon pictures. Some of these ladies were completely homemade projects, from the actual design of the paper figure, to all the lace, ribbon and trims that went into her ensemble. Others were purchased in kit form, complete with paper doll, ribbon supplies and the actual frame and glass. You could also purchase a paper pattern for a mere ten cents and add the necessary dress materials.

Ladies in hoop skirts, large hats and carrying bou-quets or parasols were the most common subjects. Brides were also a popular design and often given to a young woman as a gift on her wedding day. Today col-lectors are particularly interested in ladies in unusual poses, pictured in a unique setting, or the hard-to-find male examples.

Ribbon Doll with Real Hair Braid

Girl, blue ribbon dress w/black sash, blue bonnet, real brown hair braid, holding bouquet of orange & yellow flowers, 10 7/8" h. (ILLUS.) **$45-65**

Ribbon Doll in Pink Dress & Bonnet

Girl, wearing a pale pink dress & hat w/lace trim, black velvet sash, gold shoes, carrying a velvet floral bouquet encircled by lace, 11" h. (ILLUS.)..................................... **45-60**

Ribbon Doll with Lacy Parasol

Lady, in pale blue dress w/lace collar & hat brim, decorated w/dark peach velvet flowers, holding a lace parasol trimmed w/peach flowers, 10 1/4" h. (ILLUS.).......... **45-60**

Ribbon Doll with Colonial-style Hat

Lady, rosy-cheeks, dressed in light blue ribbon dress w/large lace collar & Colonial-style hat, standing on her toes & carrying a parasol, 9 1/4" h. (ILLUS.) **60-75**

Ribbon Doll in Pink with Pastel Bouquet

Lady, wearing pale pink ribbon dress w/ecru lace trim & carrying a pastel ribbon

flower bouquet, lace pantaloons, lace trimmed bonnet w/flat top, 11" h. (ILLUS.) **50-65**

Ribbon Doll Pattern

Pattern, bride, black & white, ca. 1950 (ILLUS.) **3-6**

Bride and Bridesmaid Ribbon Dolls

Set: bride in beige dress, flowing veil together w/bridesmaid in orange dress & bonnet, both holding pastel colored bouquets, 13 x 16 3/4" (ILLUS.) **125-175**

Bride Ribbon Doll

Woman, bride, off-white ribbon & veil, holding bouquet w/ribbon streamers, marked on back "A friend made for my wedding, September 15, 1928, Anna M. Koopmans & Chas. Kuelhas," 11 5/8" h. (ILLUS.) **85-100**

Ballerina Ribbon Doll

Woman, in short orange ribbon dress w/lace trim, wearing orange ballet slippers & carrying a matching parasol over her shoulder, 10 5/8" h. (ILLUS.) **75-100**

Woman, in yellow satin ribbon dress w/black lace cuffs, holding a matching open parasol & large ribbon & lace bouquet, background decorated w/painted & ribbon flowers.. **100-135**

Woman in Blue Ribbon Doll

Woman, w/flowing real dark brown hair, medium blue ribbon & white lace dress, lace pantaloons, wearing a flower-decorated hat, carrying a flower & lace bouquet, 12 1/4" h. (ILLUS.)................................ **40-55**

Woman Holding Feather Ribbon Doll

Woman, w/long blonde curls, dressed in pink satin w/dark lace trim & ribbon rosettes & pink bonnet w/long ribbon ties, holding a feather, 9 1/2" h. (ILLUS.)......... **85-125**

Woman with Red Curls Ribbon Doll

Woman, w/red curls wearing a pale green dress w/black velvet sash, large brimmed bonnet decorated w/lavendar flowers & carrying a multicolor rose bouquet surrounded by lace, 12 3/4" h. (ILLUS.).......... **50-75**

Ribbon Doll with Floral Lace Dress

Woman, wearing a lace dress & deep lavendar embroidery hat decorated w/gold ribbon, holding bouquet of gold & pale lavendar ribbon rosettes w/trailing gold ribbon, 9" h. (ILLUS.) **45-60**

Ribbon Doll in Yellow Dress

Woman, wearing bright yellow ribbon dress w/gold threads, sash tied into large bow, silk thread red hair, lace pantaloons, holding a lace & velvet flower bouquet, 11 1/2" h. (ILLUS.) **60-75**

ROYCROFT ITEMS

Elbert Hubbard, eccentric entrepreneur of the late 19th century, founded Roycroft Shops and established a craft community in East Aurora, New York in 1895. Individuals were trained in the trades of bookbinding, leather tooling and printing. Craft-style furniture in the manner of Gustav Stickley and known as "Aurora Colonial" furniture was produced. A copper workshop, begun in 1908, turned out numerous items. All of these, along with those pieces of Buffalo Pottery china which were produced exclusively for use at the Roycroft Inn and carry the Roycroft symbol, constitute a special category associated with the Arts and Crafts movement.

Book ends, hand-hammered copper, tall rectangular uprights w/a bold relief design of a thick knobby tree trunk issuing slender branches at the top, grass & flowers below, fine original dark patina, early mark, 4" w., 6 1/2" h., pr. **$8,250**

Bowl, cov., hand-hammered copper, wide low form w/upright sides, nearly flat fitted cover w/small knob finial, original dark patina, unmarked, 6" d., 2 1/2" h. **413**

Candelabra, hand-hammered copper w/brass wash, a tall slender central shaft topped by a flat-rimmed candle socket, a pair of slender S-scroll upright arms flanking the central shaft & topped by matching sockets, the lower section of the central shaft w/twist above the wide disk foot, normal wear, marked, 20" h., pr. **1,430**

Custom-made Copper Center Bowl

Center bowl, hand-hammered copper, custom-made, wide low rounded sides w/incurved rim, inscribed "PAOWNYC - New Years Houseparty - 1917-18," made to serve popcorn, excellent new patina, stamped mark, 19" d., 7" h. (ILLUS.) **8,625**

Dining armchair, oak, from the Grove Park Inn, a flat crestrail w/the incised initials "GPI" above a wide vertical slat & square stiles flanked by open shaped flat arms on outswept arm supports above the tack-on leather seat, square legs joined by box stretchers, orb & cross mark, 40 3/4" h. (seat cover replaced, refinished) **3,738**

Dinner bell, hand-hammered copper, small pointed conical form w/angled tab handle at the top, fine original dark patina, marked, 1 3/4" d., 3" h. **495**

Dish, hand-hammered copper, round w/slightly dished edges, narrow tooled border band of ivy leaves, fine original dark patina, early mark, 5 3/4" d. **523**

Jardiniere, hand-hammered copper, small peg feet below the wide squatty bulbous lower body below a riveted medial band & wide tall cylindrical sides w/a flared rim, stamped mark, ca. 1915, 10 7/8" d., 10 3/4" h. **5,750**

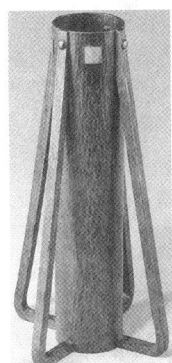

Small Roycroft Table Lamp

Lamp, table model, brass-washed hammered copper, a domed helmet-form shade raised on an electric socket above a slender ringed shaft above the flaring round foot, orb & cross mark, 6" d., 14" h. (ILLUS.) **1,870**

Letter box, oak, low rectangular open box w/half-round cut-out at each end, fine original finish, marked, possibly from the Roycroft Inn, 10 x 13", 3 1/4" h. **1,320**

Nut bowl, hand-hammered copper, wide low round form w/incurved sides & molded rim band, on small tab feet, fine original patina, marked, 10" d., 4" h. (normal scratches at rim) **990**

Purse, woman's, hand-tooled leather, squared flat form w/leather strap handle, long rectangular stylized embossed floral design down the front, marked, 6 x 7 1/2" (minor strap wear) **660**

Roycroft "Egyptian" Vase

Vase, hand-hammered copper, "Egyptian" model, a tall slender cylindrical body w/applied German silver square near the rim alternating w/four long square buttress handles extending from the rim to the base, original patina, orb & cross mark, 7 7/8" h. (ILLUS.)............... **5,175**

Vase, miniature, hand-hammered copper, swelled cylindrical form tapering to a trumpet rim, fine original patina, marked, 2 1/4" d., 4 1/4" h.............................. **413**

Vase, hand-hammered copper, a wide shallow cushion-form body centered by a short waisted neck, fine original medium-dark patina, marked, 4 1/4" h., 6 1/2" d. **880**

Vase, hand-hammered copper, cylindrical w/closed rim, decorated near the rim w/a polychrome verdigris band of stylized quatrefoils, original patina, marked, 2 1/2" d., 5" h. (small dent at rim, few scratches) **385**

Vase, hand-hammered copper, bulbous ovoid form w/closed rim, original patina, marked, 4 1/2" d., 5" h. (minor patina wear, few shallow dents & scratches on shoulder).. **358**

Vase, hand-hammered copper, cylindrical w/closed rim, decorated w/a double band w/pointed drops inlaid in nickel silver around the top, fine original patina, marked, 3" h., 6 1/4" h. **1,980**

Vase, hand-hammered copper, cylindrical, embossed w/a band of stylized lozenge-shaped flowers on tall stems, trimmed w/green patina & finely hammered finish, stamped mark, 7" h........................... **1,955**

Vase, hand-hammered copper, simple cylindrical form w/a rim band of stamped diamonds enclosing stylized florettes & each on a thin upright stripe, the band w/polychrome trim, original patina, early mark, 2 1/2" d., 7" h. (slight patina wear) .. **1,980**

RUGS - HOOKED & OTHER
Hooked

Bowl of Flowers Hooked Rug

Baskets of flowers w/birds, rectangular, a large flared basket w/arched rim & high arched handle overflowing w/large colorful flower blossoms, a large bird perched on each end of the handle, bright multicolored yarns, 33 x 51"................................ **$825**

Bird & berries, a flying bird w/a sprig of three berries in its beak, other sprigs of white & red berries flanking the bird & a chain link border along top & bottom edge, corner scrolls, worked in shades of brown, red, tan & green on a black ground, late 19th c., 19 x 33 1/4" (repairs, fading) **2,185**

Block design, alternating blocks of thin stripes & a cross device worked in grey, salmon, black & multicolored stripes, 35 x 60" (wear) **248**

Bowl of flowers, rectangular, a footed, flaring lobed bowl issuing large stylized flowers enclosed in scalloped border, worked in wool, cotton, silk yarn & ribbons in shades of red, blue & green, outlined in black on ochre ground, meandering borders of purple, cream & shades of brown & ochre, mounted on a frame, late 19th c., America, minor imperfections, 31 1/2 x 55 1/2" (ILLUS.) **5,175**

Hooked Rag Rug

Checkerboard design, rectangular rag rug composed of colorful stripes in an alternating checkerboard pattern, minor edge wear, 36 x 62" (ILLUS of part)...................... **275**

Child & dog, rectangular, the rectangular center reserve w/a scene of a young child in a blue dress & w/shoe button eyes kneeling beside a large seated black dog, a wide flowering vine border w/"Baby Dog" at the bottom, worked in pink, red, ochre, cream, orange, green & black, 19th c., 34 x 44 1/2" (minor imperfections, one eye missing) **2,530**

Diamonds, a long rectangular form composed of bands of striped diamonds w/striped corner blocks, multicolored w/black diamond grid, 23 x 68" (wear).......... **248**

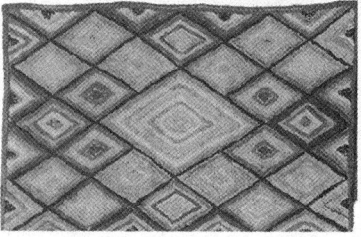

Diamond Pattern Hooked Rug

Diamonds, rectangular, overall design of diamonds forming diamonds all centered by a large diamond, worked in beige, yellow, green & rust w/black outlines, late

19th c., minor wear, 26 x 41 1/2"
(ILLUS.).. **690**

Dog, a large animal in variegated shades of brown, oak leaves at each corner, on a tan ground w/a braided border, late 19th c., 32 x 42" (repairs, minor staining) **2,875**

Dog, rectangular, a large recumbent dog facing right, within a rectangular inner leaf band border, double dark outer border bands, worked in brown & green w/maroon & black borders, 39 x 55" (well done repairs, minor wear) **385**

Dog, Chickens & Ducks Hooked Rug

Dog, chickens & ducks, rectangular w/a design of a small seated black & white dog watching over black & white hens, chicks & ducks, red highlights on tan ground w/two black border bands, hooked in various fabrics & yarn, mounted on a frame, minor imperfections, late 19th c., 28 x 43 1/2" (ILLUS.) **863**

Floral spray, a central floral spray in red, purple, brown & tan on a mottled tan & light blue ground framed by a scalloped leafy border worked in shades of red, blue, brown & tan, late 19th - early 20th c., 58 x 78" (wear) **690**

![Hooked Rug with Tree and Stags]

Hooked Rug with Tree and Stags

Flowering tree, stags & horses, rectangular, a central reserve w/a pair of leaping stags flanking a large potted flowering tree, the geometric wide border band w/a horse in each corner, mounted on a frame, 19th c., minor imperfections, 41 1/2 x 48" (ILLUS.) **5,463**

Flowers, rectangular w/a central oval bouquet of colorful tulips, daffodils, lilies & irises against a central white ground, wide border w/further clusters of the flowers against a grey border, 35 x 54" **358**

Horse, brown animal w/red tail standing on green grass, light brown ground w/red & black border, late 19th c., 25 x 35" (losses, fading).. **1,610**

Horse, carriage & people, rectangular w/rectangular central silhouetted scene of a Victorian gentleman helping a lady down from an open carriage, in black, olive green & grey against a beige striped ground, dark scalloped border band, 24 1/2 x 45 1/2" (wear, damage, edges rebound) **275**

Kitten, a white kitten w/a black spot on a light brown ground w/red, white & brown scalloped designs at each end, bound w/floral fabric, late 19th - early 20th c., 22 x 39 1/2" (staining, fading) **5,750**

Hooked Rug with Lions

Lions, long rectangular form w/a scene of a large resting lion in foreground & smaller standing lion in background, flanked by flowers & surrounded by a green & beige striped border, worked in cotton & wool in red, green, blue, beige & black, late 19th - early 20th c., America, 31 1/4 x 60 1/4" (ILLUS.) **8,050**

![Hooked Rug with Mill Scene]

Hooked Rug with Mill Scene

Mill in landscape, rectangular, a brown water mill building w/paddlewheel within a landscape w/flowers in the foreground, hills & trees in the distance, worked in naturalistic tones, late 19th c., minor wear, 22 x 36" (ILLUS.).................................. **920**

Oak leaves & acorns, runner-type, a multicolored narrow striped hit-or-miss center band bordered along each side by a wide band of oak leaves & acorns in shades of green & brown on a tan ground, dark brown narrow border band, Massachusetts, ca. 1930, 23" x 256" (wear, some reinforcements) **3,738**

Rabbit, rectangular, a stylized large animal in tan & brown, light & dark grey background follows the silhouette of the rabbit radiating outward, large red stars in each corner, 24 x 40" (minor wear, small holes, mounted on stretcher) **550**

Rooster Hooked Rug

Rooster, rectangular, a center scene of a large rooster w/a small tree at the left & a flower at the right, a checkered border band, worked in red, shades of brown w/black highlights on an oatmeal-colored ground, mounted on a frame, late 19th - early 20th c., 24 x 41" (ILLUS.) **1,495**

Shells, rectangular, repeating design of overlapping shells worked predominantly in reds, pinks & purples w/black outlines, 19th c., 27 1/2 x 46 1/4" (minor wear).......... **201**

Snowy Landscape w/Dog Sled Hooked Rug

Sled & dog team, rectangular, scene of a five-dog team pulling a sled w/two seated hooded figures across a field of snow near a body of water, mountains in background, worked in wool & cotton in shades of brown, cream, taupe, teal & black, Grenfell, Newfoundland, early 20th c., 26 3/4 x 39 5/8" (ILLUS.) **5,175**

Stag in winter landscape, a large stag standing in snow in the foreground w/two fallen trees & a bare tree w/an owl perched on a branch, fir trees & a mountain in the distance, in shades of white, grey, black, tan & yellow, on an undersized stretcher, 34 1/2 x 36 1/2" **1,155**

Swirl Design Hooked Rug

Swirl design, rectangular w/rounded corners, large center cartouche, banded & repeating half circle border, in multiple shades of green, turquoise & black, late 19th - early 20th c., America, minor losses, patch wear, 8' 3 1/2" x 10' 9 1/2" (ILLUS.) **5,463**

Vase of flowers, a tall waisted vase in magenta w/a black base band & black scrolled rim band, holds a large arched & vining bouquet of flower & leaf branches in tones of red, rose, tan, blue, green & black, on a grey & black ground, black, tan, brown, magenta & grey borders, late 19th c., 27 x 38 1/2" (backed w/burlap, edge losses, fading)..................... **1,840**

Winter landscape, rectangular, a winter scene w/two men, a dog sled & a team in shades of brown, beige, green, pink & black w/grey borders, Grenfell, Newfoundland or Labrador, Canada, early 20th c., traces of fabric label, 26 x 44 1/4" (fading).. **978**

Other

Penny rug, all-wool, hexagonal, composed of bands of appliqued circles in multicolors on a brown ground, 45 x 50" (wear) **358**

Penny rug, composed of rows of multicolored woven fabric disks within a border of leaf shapes embroidered onto linen toweling, mid-19th c., 28 1/2 x 52" (minor repair) **431**

Penny rug, rectangular w/long pointed ends, composed of colored disks w/darker bands at each end & along the sides & lighter disks in the center section w/diamond- and triangular-shaped designs in darker colors, worked in dark green, tan, light green, orange & blue on a tan ground, 19 1/4 x 33" (staining, minor damage)... **220**

Penny rug, rectangular w/pointed ends, composed of small circles in shades of dark green, tan, light green, orange & blue on a tan ground, black border, 19 1/4 x 33" (staining & minor damage) **198**

Woven rag, room-sized, striped design in wool w/multicolored narrow stripes, woven on a large loom & no seams, 100 x 156" **1,320**

Woven rag runner, varied stripes in red, green, white & black, Pennsylvania, 33 x 120"... **220**

SCALES

Balance scale, brass, analytical-type, enclosed in a mahogany glass-sided case w/narrow bottom drawer w/ivory knobs, scale labeled "Becker's & Sons Rotterdam," case labeled "E.H. Sargent & Co. Chicago," weights in bottom drawer, late 19th - early 20th c., 9 x 16 3/4", 18 1/4" h. **$220**

Early New England Balance Scale

Balance scale, brass & wood, two brass pans suspended from a painted tin arm, two paper & tin registers, enclosed in a red grain-painted pine case w/a glazed door & narrow single lower drawer, pedimented top back, salmon-colored interior, New England, 19th c., minor paint wear, 12 1/2 x 18" (ILLUS.) **1,265**

Gold scales, wrought-iron & brass, w/nine weights, in a fitted mahogany case w/partial label of Freeman, London, England, faint carved initials, 6" h. **660**

SCHOOLHOUSE COLLECTIBLES

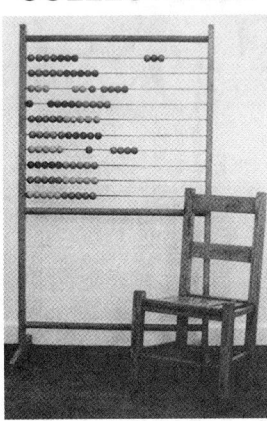

Oak Frame Abacus & Oak Child's Chair

Schooling began in America during the 1600s with private instruction in reading, writing and religion. To be American, you were to follow the rules and not deviate from the chosen way. School materials were considered a way to unify and give children a sense of their nation's greatness.

Massachusetts was the first state to have a state board of education, paving the way for other states to follow. The year was 1837. By 1852, the same state passed the first compulsory school-attendance law in the United States. By 1918, every state had enacted their own compulsory education laws.

Not as varied as some areas of collecting, there is still much to choose from in the "schoolhouse" field.

Abacus, large oak frame w/wooden balls (ILLUS.) **$45-60**

1890s Alphabet Book

Alphabet book, w/school theme, 1890s (ILLUS.) **18-30**

1880s Autograph Book

Autograph book, 1887 (ILLUS.) **35-55**
Autograph book, 1956 .... **5**
Banner, FFA (Future Farmer's of America) **50**

Brass School Bell

Bell, brass, wooden handle, 1890s, 5" (ILLUS.) **48**
Blocks, American spelling blocks, 64 blocks in wooden case **90**

Alice & Jerry School Books

Book, Alice & Jerry reader (ILLUS.) **15-35**
Book, Eclectic Geography, 1888 10
Book, high school dictionary, 1868 10

Sally, Dick & Jane Reader

Book, Sally, Dick & Jane Reader, hardback
books that followed in this series
(ILLUS.) **25-50**
Book, Sally, Dick & Jane Reader, paper-
back primer **40-60**
Book cards, Sally, Dick & Jane, 19 x 20",
18 pp. 195
Books, small books such as the "Little Gold-
en" series w/school theme 2-15
Bulletin board cut-outs, 1940s 2-5
Chair, oak, child's (ILLUS. w/abacus) **20-40**
Chalk holder, wooden 10
Clock, Stromberg master regulator, 1915,
60" 575

Composition Books

Composition books, early 1900s-1940s,
each (ILLUS.) **2-10**
Desk, schoolmaster's, cherry, 32 x 39 x 30" **525**

Slant Top School Desk

Desk, w/slant lid, pegged, 36 x 30 x 24"
(ILLUS.) 195
Diploma, ornate letter, 1930 18
Doll, Ginny by Vogue, Kinder Crowd series,
1950s **145-175**

Kimberly Dolls

Dolls, Kimberly by Tomy, 1981-84 (ILLUS.) **60**

Boy & School Marm Framed Print

Framed print, 1930, Boy & School Marm
(ILLUS.) 45
Game, Alphabok, 1968 20
Game, Geography Lotto, 1956 25
Game, Go To The Head Of The Class, 1955 20
Globe, floor standing, w/mahogany stand 225

Globe by Chein

Globe, tin, by Chein, 1930s (ILLUS.)............. **35-50**
Ink jar, Sanford's ceramic w/wire lock............... **125**
Lab manual, zoology, 1940 .... **10**
Lunch box, pail type **20**

Signed Twelvetrees Magazine Cover

Magazine cover signed Twelvetrees, boy
w/chalk in front of blackboard, April 1925
(ILLUS.).. **30**

Magazine Paper Doll Sheet

Magazine paper doll sheet, w/school
theme, October 1923 (ILLUS.)................... **12-20**
Map, pull-down canvas, Universal, New
York **25**
Paper dolls, "School Days," by Gabriel &
Sons **47**
Paper dolls, "School Mates," by Gabriel &
Sons **35**
Pencil box, double-level, wooden, 1901............. **50**
Pencil box, tin, Jackie Coogan............................ **40**

Pencil box, tin, Red Goose Shoes **45**
Pencil sharpener, Scottie dog, celluloid **35**

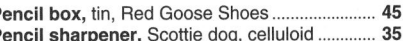

Penmanship Tablets

Penmanship tablets (ILLUS.)............................ **4-8**

Photo Postcards of School Groups

Postcards, photocard showing school
groups, 1920s to 1930s, each (ILLUS.)............. **5**
Poster, Schools at War... **100**
School war bond card **20**
Schoolhouse, Fisher-Price, w/Little People . **40-60**
Sheet music, "School Bells," 1919...................... **10**
Sheet music, "School Days," 1936 .... **10**
Slate, wood frame, 11 x 8" **60**
Teacher Barbie, MIB **30-45**
Teacher valentine, 1920s..................................... **12**

Teacher Valentine

Teacher valentine, folded card, 1930s
(ILLUS.)... **5**
Trade card, "Henderson School Shoes,"
1880s... **15**
Water-colors, tin container, Milton Bradley....... **18**
Yearbook, photos taken & pasted in by stu-
dents, 1930s.. **75**

SCOTTISH TARTANWARE

Small wooden snuff & trinket boxes, hand-decorated with pen & ink scenes or portraits, were made in Scotland in the early 19th century and are the forerunner to Mauchline wares. Named after the Scottish village of Mauchline where numerous small sycamore boxes & souvenirs of excellent quality were produced, its production was not limited to that particular town. The "tartan" wares, first produced about 1820, originally were hand painted with the famed tartan plaids. A less expensive method that allowed for transfer printing directly to the wood was introduced later & by the late 19th century transfer-printed tartan paper or scenes were glued to the wood & varnished over. This latter type of ware, primarily with plaid decoration, is what the collector will most frequently encounter today.The Mauchline firm of W. & A. Smith, & their descendants, turned out enormous quantities of the ware until their boxworks was destroyed by fire in 1933.

Tartanware Double-ended Emery

Emery, double-ended, cylindrical body
(ILLUS.).. **$150**

Tartanware Eraser

Eraser, Tartanware holder w/extended
eraser ends (ILLUS.) **95**

Tartanware Game Box

Game box, cov., rectangular, hinged w/peg
holes on top, complete w/pegs (ILLUS.) **150**

Tartanware Decorated Hairpin Box

Hairpin box, long rectangular form, the top
w/a rectangular plaque illustrated w/a
portrait on an easel at one end & a scene
of peasants in color (ILLUS.)......................... **250**

Cylindrical Match Holder

Match holder, cylindrical, "Go to bed" type,
black base (ILLUS.) **225**

Tartanware Match Holder

Match holder, domical "Go to bed" style,
black base (ILLUS.) **325**

Novelty Tartanware Cauldron

Model of a cauldron, novelty, w/string han-
dle (ILLUS.).. **225**

Tartanware Needle Box

Needle box, upright square form w/sharply
angled top (ILLUS.)... **175**

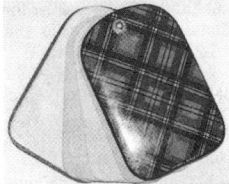

Tartanware Note Pad

Note pad, pivoting Tartanware covers &
celluloid pages (ILLUS.)................................... **350**

Tartanware Pincushion

Pincushion, purple velvet sliding pincushion top on small rectangular Tartanware
box (ILLUS.).. **175**

Tartanware Ruler

Ruler, cylindrical case w/black knob end
handles (ILLUS.) **300**

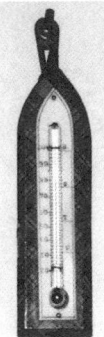

Rare Tartanware Thermometer

Thermometer, hanging-type, narrow rectangular tartan framework w/pointed top,
celluloid insert, very rare (ILLUS.)................. **500**

Star-shaped Thread Winder

Thread winder, star-shaped, rare (ILLUS.) **225**

Rare Tartanware Whistle

Whistle, tapering cylindrical form w/turned
black knob top & black mouth end
(ILLUS.) **350**

SCOUTING ITEMS

Air Scouting/Air Exploring

Handbook, Air Scout Manual, H.W. Hunt,
Lorne W. Barclay, ed. 2 pre-proof edi-
tions, 1942.. **$50-60**

Air Scout Manual, 1942-43

Handbook, Air Scout Manual, H.W. Hunt,
Lorne W. Barclay, ed. 6 printings, 1942-
43 (ILLUS.).. **40-60**
Merit badge, Aerodynamics, blue border &
background, 1942-52................................... **75-150**
Merit badge, Aeronautics, blue border &
background, 1942-49................................... **75-150**
Merit badge, Airplane Design, blue border
& background, 1942-49.............................. **75-150**

Merit badge, Airplane Structure, blue border & background, 1942-49 .... **75-150**

Position badge, Tenderfoot emblem above rectangle w/2 blue bars, gold wings at sides, 1942-49 .... **25-40**

Rank badge, Air Explorer Ace, four-motor plane, w/Air Scout & FDL below, 1949-54 .. **15-25**

Air Explorer Ace Medal Badge, 1949-54

Rank badge, Air Explorer Ace Medal, wings up-stretched, four-motor plane & Tenderfoot emblem below compass in back, red-blue-red ribbon of equal widths, 1949-54 (ILLUS.) **1,200-1,500**

Rank badge, Air Explorer Apprentice, single-engine plane, w/Air Scout & FDL below, 1949-52 .... **15-25**

Rank badge, Air Explorer Craftsman, trimotor plane, w/Air Scout & FDL below, 1949-54 .... **15-25**

Rank badge, Air Explorer Observer, twin-engine plane, w/Air Scout & FDL below, 1949-52 .... **15-25**

Rank badge, Air Scout Ace, four-motor plane w/Air Scout & FDL below, 1942-49 .. **25-40**

Rank badge, Air Scout Apprentice, single-engine plane w/Air Scout & FDL below, 1942-49 .... **25-40**

Rank badge, Air Scout Craftsman, tri-motor plane w/Air Scout & FDL below, 1942-49 .. **25-40**

Rank badge, Air Scout Observer, twin-engine plane w/Air Scout & FDL below, 1942-49 .... **25-40**

Rank badge, First Class Air Scout Candidate, four-blade prop. in blue on tan or khaki cut twill, 1942-49 .... **20-30**

Rank badge, Second Class Air Scout Candidate, triple-blade prop. in blue on tan or khaki cut twill, 1942-49 .... **20-30**

Rank badge, Specialist Rating, Ace Airman, 1947-49 .... **10-15**

Rank badge, Tenderfoot Air Scout Candidate, twin-blade prop. in blue on tan or khaki cut twill, 1942-49 .... **20-30**

Rank badges, Specialist Rating, Ace Navigator, 1947-49 .... **10-15**

Uniform, Air Scout Hat Patch, gold Tenderfoot emblem on silver wings, 1942-49 .... **20-30**

Uniform, Air Scout Universal Wings, type 1, Tenderfoot emblem w/silver wings, 1942-49 .... **40-50**

Uniform, Community Strip, dark blue embroidery on light blue twill, 1942-49 .... **20-30**

Uniform, Squadron Numerals, 0-9, royal blue embroidery on light blue felt, 1942-49 .... **10-20**

Boy Scout Memorabilia

Badge, Bugler, green First Class, gold thread bugle on tan cloth, 1917-25 .... **600-850**

Badge, Bugler, Second Class, gold thread bugle on tan cloth, 1917-25 .... **600-850**

Badge, Bugler, Tenderfoot, gold thread bugle on tan cloth, 1917-25 .... **600-850**

Badge, Patrol Leader Bugler, silver thread Second Class & bugle on tan cloth, 1917-25 .... **350-400**

Badge, Patrol Leader Bugler, silver thread tenderfoot & bugle on tan cloth, 1917-25 .... **800-1,000**

Badge, Patrol Leader Scribe, silver thread Second Class & crossed quills on tan cloth, 1916-25 .... **600-850**

Badge, Patrol Leader Scribe, silver thread tenderfoot & crossed quills on tan cloth, 1916-25 .... **600-850**

Badge, Patrol Leader, silver thread Second Class on tan cloth, 1915-25 .... **500-750**

Badge, Patrol Leader, silver thread tenderfoot on tan cloth, 1921-25 .... **500-750**

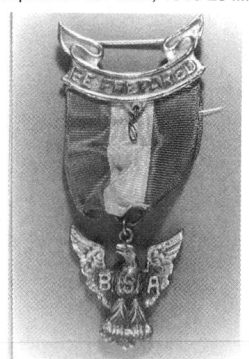

Green First Class Scribe Badge

Badge, Scribe, green First Class, gold thread crossed quills on tan cloth (ILLUS.) **500-750**

Badge, Scribe, Second Class, gold thread crossed quills on tan cloth, 1916-25 ...... **500-750**

Badge, Scribe, Tenderfoot, gold thread crossed quills on tan cloth, 1916-25 ...... **500-750**

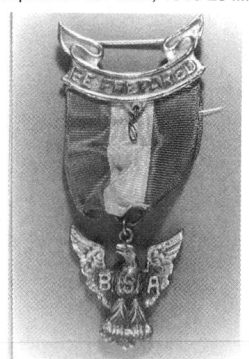

Closed Beak Eagle Scout Award

Eagle Scout award, closed beak, BSA, feathered but flatter back, 1970-78 (ILLUS.).. **60-85**

Eagle Scout award, closed beak, BSA is high, A hangs over edge, 1930.............. **250-300**

Eagle Scout award, closed beak, no BSA, flat back, 1955-69....................................... **60-85**

Eagle Scout award, closed beak, no BSA, full back, 1933-54.................................... **100-150**

Eagle Scout award, closed beak, where body & tail feathers meet on back form "W." 1925-26.. **200-300**

Eagle Scout award, finely engraved feathers, centered BSA, back feathers form a body-ridge as V for a smooth transition, 1930-33.. **150-200**

Eagle Scout award, open beak, flat line notch on back where body meets tail feathers, 1926-30 .... **200-250**

Handbook for Boys

Handbook, BSA, Handbook for Boys, green cover, twenty-third edition, 1921, 488 pp. (ILLUS.) **100-150**

Handbook, BSA, Handbook for Boys, light gray cover, Morse Code Signal Flags, square center., no knot on First Class badge, eleventh-twelfth edition, 1914-15, 472 pp. **150-250**

Handbook, BSA, Handbook for Boys, light gray cover, Morse Code Signal Flags, square center., no knot on First Class badge, thirteenth edition, 1915-16, 464 pp. **150-250**

Handbook, BSA, Handbook for Boys, red or green cover, scout signals letter "L," knot on First Class badge, fourteenth-eighteenth edition, 1916-18, 498 pp. **150-250**

Handbook, BSA, Handbook for Boys, scout striding, raising hat in air, maroon cover, fourth edition, 1913-14, 416 pp. **200-400**

Handbook, BSA, Handbook for Boys, scout striding, raising hat in air, maroon cover, 1914, 440 pp. **200-400**

Handbook, BSA, Handbook for Boys, scout striding, raising hat in air, olive-drab or maroon cover, proof copy, first edition, 1911, 320 or 400 pp................................. **500-750**

Handbook, BSA, Handbook for Boys, scout striding, raising hat in air, olive-drab or

maroon cover, second edition, 1-5 printing, some marked fourth edition, 1911-13, 404 pp. **400-600**

Handbook, BSA, Official Handbook, red leather-bound, gilt imprint, Baden-Powell & Seaton, 1910, 192 pp. **2,500-3,500**

Handbook, BSA, Official Handbook, tan-yellow w/brown imprint or green w/light green imprint, Baden-Powell & Seaton, 1910, 192 pp....................................... **800-1200**

Handbook, BSA, Official Manual or Handbook, cloth cover, Seaton, 1910, 192 pp. **1,750-2,250**

Medallion, Alpha Phi-Omega, 25th Anniversary National Convention, silver, 1950, 28mm **15-25**

Medallion, Bruder Dairy, Cleveland, OH, good luck piece, aluminum, 1959, 32mm **10-17.50**

Medallion, Dodge City Land Rush, District 4, Detroit, MI, aluminum, 1950, 33mm **15-25**

Medallion, Kansas City, MO, First National Camporee, Honor Camper, brass, 1933, 30mm **60-80**

Medallion, Nassau County Council, National Scout Jamboree, copper, 1937, 22mm . **20-30**

Medallion, Piase Bird Council, National Scout Jamboree, brass, 1937, 25mm....... **20-30**

Medallion, Region 9, BSA encased buffalo nickel, aluminum, 1949, 39mm **50-80**

Salt Lake Council

Medallion, Salt Lake Council, Do a good turn daily, steer's skull, brass, 1935, 26mm (ILLUS.) **30-50**

Medallion, Silver Lake Scout Booster, encased cent, aluminum, 1937, 34mm **5-10**

Medallion, Troop 2, Wilkinsburg, PA 25th Anniv., white metal, 1937, 36mm **30-50**

Medallion, World's Fair Greetings, Scout saluting w/Trylon & Perisphere in background, elongated Lincoln cent, Indian cent, large cent, two-cent piece, & various foreign coins & tokens, 1939 .... **20-35**

Youth of the Scouting World Medallion

Medallion, Youth of the Scouting World, Society of Medalists issue #46, eagle breaking chains, reverse scouts signaling & receiving, silver, 1952, 72mm (ILLUS.)... **150-200**

Medallion, Youth of the Scouting World, Society of Medalists issue #46, eagle breaking chains, reverse scouts signaling & receiving, bronze, 1952, 72mm **75-100**

1944-48 Membership Card

Membership Card, bi-fold, Cub, Boy Scout & Sea Scout walking left, 1944-48 (ILLUS.)... **10-15**

Membership Card, bi-fold, flag exterior, Cub, Tenderfoot & Explorer E emblems inside, 1983-84 .... **.50-1**

Membership Card, bi-fold, flag exterior, Diamond Jubilee emblem inside, 1985-86..... **.50-1**

Membership Card, single, Bicentennial motif, 1975-77 .... **.50-1**

1952-56 Membership Card

Membership Card, single, Cub, Boy Scout & Explorer Scout walking forward, Liberty Bell in background, forward on Liberty's Team legend, 1952-56 (ILLUS.) **5-7.50**

1946-49 Membership Card

Membership Card, single, Cub, Boy Scout & Sea Scout walking left, red banner at bottom, 1946-49 (ILLUS.) **5-7.50**

1957-60 Membership Card

Membership Card, single, Cub, Explorer & Scout looking upward, Washington in prayer in background, 1957-60 (ILLUS.)........ **4-6**

1965-72 Membership Card

Membership Card, single, First Class emblem & patrol hiking, 1965-72 (ILLUS.) **2-4**

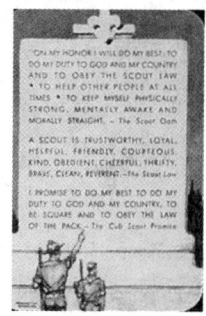

1955-58 Membership Card

Membership Card, single, Leader & Scout looking up at tablet w/Oath, Law & Cub Promise, scout oath & Tenderfoot emblem on blue background, 1955-58 (ILLUS.) **4-6**

1942-45 Membership Card

Membership Card, single, scout leader &
boy within archway on top, olive-black
color, 1942-45 (ILLUS.) **5-7.50**
Membership Card, single, scout oath &
Tenderfoot emblem on blue background,
50th Anniversary emblem added, 1960 .... **3-5**
Membership Card, single, Scouting the
Better Life slogan, 1981-83 .... **.50-1**
Membership Card, single, Scouting's 70th,
Cub Scouts' 50th Anniversaries, 1979-81 ... **.50-1**
Membership card, single, Tenderfoot em-
blem on green background, 1972-76 .... **.50-1**

Neckerchief w/Tenderfoot Badge

Neckerchief, full square, combination of
two colors, Tenderfoot badge within diamond, 14 colors available, 1932, 30 x 30"
(ILLUS.) **5-7.50**
Neckerchief, full square, solid color, eight
colors available, 1914-15, 28", w/official
badge 6 1/2 x 11" **20-25**

First Class Badge Neckerchief

Neckerchief, full square, solid color, First
Class badge within circle, 17 colors avail-
able, 1926-31, 28 x 32" (ILLUS.) **5-7.50**
Neckerchief, full square, solid color, Tenderfoot badge within diamond, 13 colors
available, 1932, 30 x 30" **5-7.50**
Neckerchief, full square, solid colors Tenderfoot badge within diamond, 15 colors
available, 1933-47, 32 x 32" **4-7.50**
Patrol medallion, colored, 1972-89 .... **.50-1**

Patrol Medallion, 1927-33

Patrol medallion, red felt circle, black im-
age, 1927-33 (ILLUS.) **10-25**

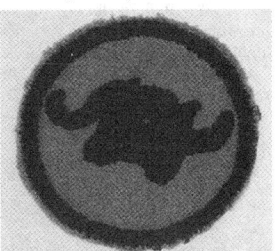

Patrol Medallion, 1933-52

Patrol medallion, red felt circle, black image w/BSA below, 1933-52 (ILLUS.) **3-7.50**
Patrol medallion, red felt square, black im-
age, 1926 .... **40-75**

Patrol Medallion, 1953-65

Patrol medallion, red twill circle, gauze
back, 1953-65 (ILLUS.) **1-2**
Patrol medallion, red twill circle, plastic
back, 1965-72 .... **1-2**

Anniversary Week Pinback Button

Pinback button, Anniversary Week, Feb.
7-13, scout bust, 1930, 7/8" (ILLUS.) **15-20**
Pinback button, Ben Alexander Says,
"Scott of the Scouts, a Rayart Serial
Play," scout saluting, 1915-25, 7/8" **20-25**
Pinback button, Boy Scout Guide, First
Class emblem, 1935-45, 1 3/4" **10-15**

Boy Scout Pinback Button

Pinback button, Boy Scout, scout standing w/Morse signal flags, 1 1/8" shield-shaped fold tab, 1915-25 (ILLUS.) **25-35**

Pinback button, Bucks County Council, scouting booster, 1936, 2 1/4" **10-15**

Pinback button, Camden County Boy Scouts, scout saluting, 1920, 7/8" **15-20**

Camp Ki-Shau-Wau Pinback Button

Pinback button, Camp Ki-Shau-Wau, First Class emblem, 1940-50, 1" (ILLUS.) **10-15**

Camp Migration of '37 Pinback Button

Pinback button, Camp Migration of '37, BSA & arrowhead, 1937, 1 1/4" (ILLUS.).. **15-20**

Pinback button, Camp Rush of '36, Wagon Boss, BSA & nugget, 1936, 1 1/4" **20-25**

Pinback button, Chicago Boy Scout Camps, Paul Bunyan's Crew, Paul & the blue ox, 1935, 1 1/4" **15-20**

Dad Scout Pinback Button

Pinback button, Dad Scout, Dan Beard seated talking w/scout, 1935-45, 1 1/2" (ILLUS.)... **20-25**

Official Pinback Button

Pinback button, Official BSA, 1960, 2 1/2" (ILLUS.) **3-5**

Uniform, BSA in blue felt circle, sweater patch, 1924-41.. **15-20**

Lone Scouts of America

Award medal, Merit Award, first prize, gilt, red-blue ribbon, 1916-30............................ **50-75**

Award medal, Merit Award, second prize, silvered metal, red-blue ribbon, 1916-30... **50-75**

Award medal, Merit Award, third prize, bronze, red-blue ribbon, 1925-30 .... **50-75**

Award medal, Merit Award, third prize, literary achievement, bronze, red-blue ribbon, 1925-30.. **50-75**

Flag, LSA in circle in red, blue field, 1918-20 .... **100-150**

Fifth Degree, Totem Pole Lodge Handbook

Handbook, Fifth Degree, Totem Pole Lodge, variety w/or w/o BSA paper street address label, post 1925, 1920-30 (ILLUS.) **20-30**

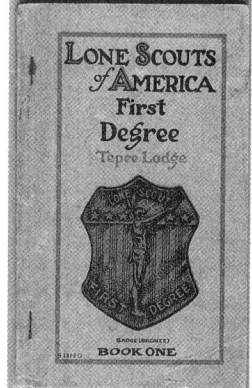

First Degree, Tepee Lodge Handbook

Handbook, First Degree, Tepee Lodge, 1920-30 (ILLUS.)... **20-30**

Handbook, Lone Scouts of America, Indian striding right w/arms outstretched, 1920-21 .... **30-50**

Second Degree, Tepee Lodge Handbook

Handbook, Second Degree, Tepee Lodge, 1920-30 (ILLUS.) **20-30**

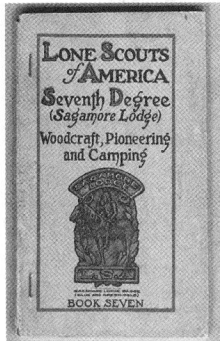

Seventh Degree, Sagamore Lodge Handbook

Handbook, Seventh Degree, Sagamore Lodge, woodcraft, pioneering & camping, varieties w/or w/o BSA address, post 1925, 1920-50 (ILLUS.) **20-30**
Key chain, Indian on horseback, within inverted triangle, LSA on shield, DAUNTED below, bronze or silvered, 1917-21 ... **80-100**

Lone Scout Magazine

Magazine, Lone Scout, weekly 10/1915-12/1920, then monthly to 4/1924, 1915-1924 (ILLUS.) **10-15**

Pin, LSA Helping to Win the War, bronze, scene of planes above fields & glass preservers, 1918, 1 5/16" **25-40**

LSS & BSA in Red Circle Position Badge

Position badge, LSS & BSA in red circle, standing Indian, full square, 1933-50 (ILLUS.) **20-30**
Postcard, 1918 Lone Scout magazine cover **10-20**
Rank badge, arrowhead in circle, "Lone Scout Do a Useful Thing Each Day" on arrowhead, bronze, 1916-21, 3/4" **20-30**
Rank badge, First Degree, Indian Brave striding right w/arms extended on shield, bronze, pin back or lapel clasp, 1916-28, 5/8" **40-60**
Rank badge, Fourth-Sixth Degree, Totem Pole Lodge, LSA on scroll, head & hands at top, gilt bronze, enamel, 1916-28 .... **80-100**
Rank badge, membership pin, celluloid, 1915-16, 7/8" **15-25**
Rank badge, Sagamore Lodge, Indian on horseback within wreath, gilt bronze, enamel, 1917-28 .... **100-125**
Rank badge, Second Degree, campfire within triangle on shield, bronze, 1916-28, 11/16" **40-60**
Rank badge, Third Degree, eagle in flight on shield, nickel silver, 1916-28, 5/8" **40-60**
Ring, LCD & BSA w/Indian striding left on round top, sides w/shield & First Class badge, 1927-30 .... **100-125**
Service bar, LSA on silvered bar, one year membership, 1919-26, 1 5/16" l **50-75**
Sweater, LSA monogram in red on blue circle, 1917-21 .... **80-100**
Watch fob, Indian on horseback within inverted triangle, LSA on shield, DAUNTED below, bronze or silvered, on leather strap, 1917-21 .... **150-200**

Sea Scouting/Sea Exploring

Handbook, Cruising for Sea Scouts, Carey, A.A., three printings, 1912-14 .... **45-60**
Handbook, Sea Scouting and Seamanship for Boys, Baden-Powell, Warrington, The English Sea Scout Manual used in the U.S., 1911 .... **100-150**
Handbook, The Sea Scout Manual, Capt. Felix Riesenberg, ed. 14 printings, 1925-38 (ILLUS. top next page) **35-45**

The Sea Scout Manual

Handbook, The Sea Scout Manual, J.A. Wilder, ed. five printings, 1919-23 .... **45-60**

Position badge, Assistant Crew Leader, anchor behind First Class emblem, one split chevron behind, 1949 .... **5-10**

Position badge, Boatswain, anchor behind First Class emblem, two split & one full chevron behind, star below, 1949 .... **5-10**

Position badge, Boatswain's Mate, anchor behind First Class emblem, two split & one full chevron behind, 1949 .... **5-10**

Position badge, Cabin Boy, anchor on blue background within gold oval border, tan cut cloth, 1924-35 .... **40-60**

Position badge, Crew Leader, anchor behind First Class emblem, two split chevrons behind, 1949 .... **5-10**

Position badge, Sea Explorer Purser, crossed keys behind anchor & First Class emblem, 1949 .... **5-10**

Position badge, Sea Explorer Quartermaster, anchor behind First Class emblem, 1949 .... **5-10**

Position badge, Sea Explorer Specialist, title below anchor & First Class emblem, 1949 .... **5-10**

Position badge, Sea Explorer Storekeeper, crossed oars behind open book, 1949 .... **5-10**

Position badge, Sea Scout Boatswain, anchor behind First Class emblem, three felt chevrons, 1918-49 .... **5-10**

Position badge, Sea Scout Boatswain's Mate, anchor behind First Class emblem, two felt chevrons, 1918-49 .... **5-10**

Position badge, Sea Scout Boatswain's Mate, anchor behind First Class emblem, two twill chevrons, 1918-49 .... **5-10**

Position badge, Sea Scout Coxswain, anchor behind First Class emblem, one twill chevron, 1918-49 .... **5-10**

Position badge, Sea Scout Coxwain, anchor behind First Class emblem, one felt chevron, 1918-49 .... **5-10**

Position badge, Sea Scout Yeoman, crossed quills, 1941-49 .... **10-15**

Position badge, Sea Scouter Bugler, bugle, 1941-49 .... **10-15**

Position badge - leader, Local Council Staff, anchor behind First Class emblem, two stars below, 1949 .... **10-15**

Position badge - leader, Sea Scout, anchor behind First Class emblem, one stripe below, 1918-41 .... **20-25**

Position badge - leader, Ship Committee, anchor behind First Class emblem, all within rope oval, one & one half stripes below, 1918-41 .... **20-25**

Rank badge, Eagle Scout, blue felt, full wording in silk thread, 1933-55 .... **40-60**

Rank badge, Life Scout, white twill, knot under heart, gold-lettered motto, 1925-42 ..... **25-35**

Rank badge, Sea Scout Able, anchor behind First Class emblem, 3 bars below, 1924 .... **5**

Sea Scout Apprentice Badge

Rank badge, Sea Scout Apprentice, anchor behind First Class emblem, 1 bar below, 1924-49 (ILLUS.) **5-10**

Rank badge, Sea Scout Apprentice, anchor behind First Class emblem, 1 bar below, 1924 .... **5**

Rank badge, Sea Scout Ordinary, anchor behind First Class emblem, 2 bars below, 1924 .... **5**

Rank badge, Star Scout, blue felt, single knot below, 1925-42 .... **25-35**

Quartermaster Award Medal

Rank medal, Quartermaster Award Medal, anchor behind First Class emblem on compass & ship's wheel, blue ribbon, enamel on silver pendant, Sea Scouting's highest honor, 1937-69 (ILLUS.).. **175-200**

Uniform, Council Strip, blue on white twill on blue felt **15-20**

Uniform, Flagship Flotilla Rating, anchor behind First Class emblem at center, red & blue fully-embroidered background patch, 1941-47 .... **10-15**

Uniform, State Strip, blue on white twill or white on blue felt, 1924 .... **3-5**

SCRIMSHAW

Scrimshaw is a folk art by-product of the 19th century American whaling industry. Intricately carved and engraved pieces of whalebone, whale's teeth and walrus tusks were produced by whalers during their spare time at sea. In recent years numerous fine grade hard plastic reproductions have appeared on the market so the novice collector must use caution to distinguish these from the rare originals.

Corset busk, engraved w/a scene of a small country house w/trees flanked by geometric designs, one w/a heart & initials "S.M.T.," w/a checkered border, 19th c., 12 3/4" l. **$1,035**

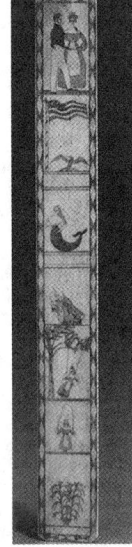

Fine Engraved Scrimshaw Busk

Corset busk, engraved whalebone, long flat strip w/squared ends, a narrow diamond design border band, engraved w/a row of panels w/various designs including a romantic couple, an eagle & flag, a mermaid, a ship, a girl on a swing, a girl w/jump rope & a potted plant, highlighted in red & blue, 19th c., 13 1/4" l. (ILLUS.) ... **3,335**

Corset busk, whalebone, narrow flat form w/rounded tip & double round tab top, scratch-carved w/vining leaves & divided images of canopy bed, star, clipper ship & geometric designs, finely done w/red & black ink highlights, 19th c., 13 3/4" l. **4,950**

Jagging wheel, whale ivory, a two-tined crimper, a baleen spacer & a figural serpent handle, 19th c., 5 1/4" l. (repair) **1,725**

Snuff box, horn, book-shaped, scratch-carved w/foliage designs on top, cover & sides, the back w/a great scene of carpenters at work w/the tools of their trade, cover dated "1828" & attached w/copper & brass wires over an hourglass-shaped opening, highlighted in red, yellow & black, 2 1/8 x 3", 7/8" h. (minor insect damage) **1,045**

Engraved Walrus Tusk

Walrus tusk, black inked engravings on one side of a woman wearing a lace-trimmed dress, a young girl w/a flower, a mermaid w/harp & a deer, hole drilled in one end, 19th c., 18 1/8" l. (ILLUS.) **770**

Walrus tusk, engraved w/a woman wearing a hat, a two-masted fishing ship, two husky dogs & a man sluicing for gold, inscribed "Nome Alaska 1901," the back showing the S.S. Oregon, early 20th c., 15 1/2" l. (age cracks) **575**

Whale's teeth, engraved w/a fashion portrait of a Victorian lady, one holding a flower sprig, the other a bouquet, mid-19th c., 4 1/8" h., pr. (age cracks) **1,265**

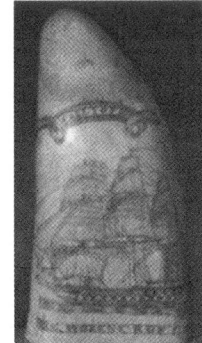

Engraved Whale's Tooth with Ships

Whale's tooth, engraved on both sides, depicting the British ship "Calliope" at sea w/flags flying, one side w/"G. Wozencroft" inscribed below & "Calliope" in a banner above, the reverse w/"Calliope" in an oval above the ship, 19th c., touches of red sealing wax, 5 3/4" l. (ILLUS.) **3,450**

Whale's tooth, engraved on one side w/a scene of an eagle & shield over a cannon barrel, surrounded by a flowering vine &

a butterfly, the reverse decorated w/a rooster, 19th c., 5 1/2" l. (age cracks) **2,415**

Whale's tooth, engraved & polychromed, one side w/a native woman picking fruit from a tree, a hut, palm trees & mountains, the other side w/a lady, anchor & trees on shore, a marine scene in the distance, 19th c., 8" h. (minor age cracks) **2,300**

Whale's tooth, engraved & polychromed, one side w/a woman wearing a cape & hat & holding flowers & a basket in yellow, red & brown, the other side w/a parrot in a tree w/red & yellow highlights, 19th c., 4 1/4" h. (minor chips on edge, age cracks) **863**

Whale's tooth, engraved & polychromed w/one side featuring a seated woman in a red & yellow dress playing a guitar, the other side w/a town scene w/a clock tower & other buildings w/red & brown highlights, 19th c., 4 5/8" h. (minor age cracks) **920**

Whale's tooth, engraved w/a lady in mid-19th century costume & bonnet, 6" l. (age crack, chip) **920**

Whale's tooth, engraved w/a scene of an American three-masted sailing ship w/intaglio-cut hull, reverse faintly inscribed, depicting a two-masted sailing ship w/a lighthouse in the background beneath an eagle, 19th c., 6 1/4" h. (surface imperfections) **2,070**

Whale's tooth, engraved w/an American eagle & shield w/banner above a man & woman on horseback, mounted on a round wooden pedestal, 19th c., 5 1/8" h. **748**

Scrimshaw Whale's Tooth

Whale's tooth, engraved w/various figures including a woman seated on a sea serpent & a banner inscribed "The Queen of the Sea," a woman wearing mid-19th c. dress & a costumed man & woman holding a flag stating "United States Secret Service," mid-19th c., age cracks, 6" l. (ILLUS.) **2,415**

Whale's tooth, one side etched w/a scene of a ship flying the American flag, the other side w/a whaling scene w/a ship in the background & men in rowboats harpooning whales in the foreground, highlighted in black w/some red, 5 1/4" h. **3,410**

Whale's tooth, scratch-carved w/an American ship sailing near a French fort on a hillside on one side, the other side w/two women picking flowers, shown in an oval w/geometric border resembling inlay, 6" h. (age cracks, minor edge damage) **5,500**

SEWING ADJUNCTS

With sewing tools and accessories so popular, collectors in the United States, Canada and England actively search for these small antiques. The wide variety available gives buyers a good selection from which to choose - and allows for plenty of different price ranges too. Be cautious of reproductions - Victorian and Georgian styled sterling thimbles and needlecases marked "Thailand" are found frequently and new pewter thimble holders are sometimes sold as old. A good reference book on sewing tools and accessories is Gay Ann Rogers' An Illustrated History of Needlework Tools, which can be found in many bookstores. All items listed below are in good condition, minor wear and with no missing parts.

Bodkin, bone, America, 2" l. **$10**

Bodkin, brass w/engraved decoration, 19th c. **22**

Chatelaine, cut steel, w/thimbleholder, scissors holder, needleholder, pin disc, 19th c., England **795**

Chatelaine, cut steel, w/thimbleholder, scissors holder, scent bottle, pin disc & buttonhook, mermaids & cherubs design, 19th c., England **695**

Clamp, ivory w/winding wheel on top, 19th c., England **395**

Crochet hook, bone, turned end handle, 19th c., America, 6" l. **18**

Crochet hooks, bone, turned handles, 19th c., America, matching set of 4 .... **49**

Darner, black wood w/Art Nouveau style sterling handle, early 20th c. **85**

Darner, glass, blue **165**

Darner, sterling silver w/double ends for darning gloves, America **145**

Emery, Mauchline stickware, double-ended, 19th c., England **140**

Emery, satin, figural white strawberry w/stitched seeds, 19th c., America **110**

Emery, velvet, figural red strawberry w/sterling cap, 19th c., America **135**

Hemming clamp, carved ivory & whale baleen, decorated w/two contrasting ivory triangles & polka dots, turned wooden screw, 19th c., 5 3/4" h. (age cracks) **633**

Knitting needle guards, simple bone, no design, 19th c., England **110**

Knitting needle guards, sterling silver w/chain, twist design, 19th c., England, 1 1/2" l. **185**

Lace bobbin, bone w/dots, marked "Sally," 19th c. **140**

Lace bobbin, bone w/pewter, Leopard & Tiger, 19th c. **135**

Lace bobbin, bone w/pewter, marked "May," 19th c. **125**

Lace bobbin winder, walnut w/bobbin drawer, mid-19th c., England **385**

Lace making pillow, w/24 wood bobbins & lace pattern, mid-19th c., England, 5 x 11 x 13", the set **225**

Thimbles

Blush ivory porcelain, the sides painted w/a bird on a foliate branch, a foliate spray on the reserve, Worcester, late 19th c. **407**

Brass, Prudential Insurance................................. **12**

Gold, 10k, decorated w/scene of sailboats & mountains, unmarked **185**

Gold, 14k, floral pattern, monogrammed **175**

Gold, 9k, "Dorcas," marked "Charles Horner," 19th c., England **180**

Gold, indented all over, English, probably late 18th c. **2,407**

Gold, the body enameled overall w/birds, foliage & flowers in shades of red, blue, green & white, w/blue enameled rim, Indian (Jaipur Region), probably early 19th c. **241**

Gold, the body w/applied three-colored gold flowers & foliage & a shield-shaped cartouche w/engraved initials, set w/a stone top, English, late 18th - early 19th c. **407**

Gold, the border diagonally fluted & w/vacant shaped cartouche, each flute w/applied alternate split pearls & turquoise, Ketcham & McDougall, American, late 19th c. **778**

Gold, the border w/applied two-color gold flowers & foliage on a raised matte ground, the body w/applied vacant shield-shaped cartouche, French, late 19th c. **315**

Gold, the plain sides w/engraved initials within raised milled borders, South American, 19th c. **648**

Enameled Gold Thimble

Gold, the raised border decorated w/enameled flowers & foliage, possibly English, late 19th c. (ILLUS.) **519**

Foliage & Flowers Design Thimble

Gold, the sides cast overall w/scrolled foliage & flowers on a matte ground above a waved rim, Indian, late 19th c. (ILLUS.) **352**

Gold, the sides w/three heavily cast floral & foliate friezes enclosing the phrase "Pastora M Mora," South American, mid-19th c. **407**

Enameled Thimble w/Pearl Set Rim

Gold, the wide border decorated w/bands of white, dark & light blue enamel, the dark blue band highlighting the phrase, "Profitez Du Temps," an oval cartouche engraved w/the word "Vous," w/split pearl-set rim, French, mid-19th c. (ILLUS.)......... **1,018**

Gold, the wide border depicting a panoramic architectural study and the legend, "Worlds Columbian Exposition, 1492-1892," Simons Bros., late 19th c. **241**

Flower and Foliage Border Thimble

Gold, the wide border w/applied cloisonné enameled flowers & foliage in shades of blue, green, red & yellow, supporting a cartouche engraved w/initials, possibly American, late 19th c. (ILLUS.)...................... **444**

Gold, the wide border w/applied two-color gold flowers & foliage & a shaped vacant cartouche, some flowerheads set w/turquoise or split pearls, inset w/stone top, probably Continental, late 19th c. **278**

English Gold Thimble

Gold, the wide border w/applied two-color gold flowers & trailing foliage on a matte ground & w/applied shaped vacant cartouche, above a bright-cut floral rim, English, late 19th c. (ILLUS.) **241**

Gold, w/plain border, the rim w/an applied frieze of contrasting color gold rising stiff foliage, French, late 18th c. **1,203**

Enameled Geometric Thimble

Gold combination thimble & scent bottle,
the thimble border w/blue enameled geometric frieze, unscrewing to reveal a
clear glass scent bottle & stopper, the
base engraved w/initials, probably
English, ca. 1850 (ILLUS.)............................ 278

Golden Spike Thimble

Gold "Golden Spike," the border chased
w/a train, wagons, a hunting scene, a
cartouche engraved w/initials, & the
words "Official 1904" bordering the cartouche, Simons Bros., early 20th c.
(ILLUS.).. 2,037
**Gold-topped Piercy's patent tor-
toiseshell,** the body w/applied gold tip &
rim & the Royal Coat of Arms supported
by a scroll engraved w/the legend,
"Piercy's Patent," English, ca. 1825 240
Sterling, amethyst top, 19th c., England,
w/original leather case.................................. 135
Sterling, heavily decorated band w/oval de-
signs, scalloped edge, Simons 120
Sterling, turquoise cabochons around rim 165
Sterling over steel, "Dorcas," plain style,
Charles Horner, late 19th c., England 65
Sterling silver, Dogwood patt., Waite,
Thresher Co. 87

SHAKER ITEMS

*The Shakers, a religious sect founded by Ann Lee,
first settled in this country at Watervliet, New York, near
Albany, in 1774. By 1880 there were nine settlements in
America. Workmanship in Shaker crafts is an extension
of their religious beliefs and features plain and simple
designs reflecting a chaste elegance that is now much in
demand though relatively few early items are common.*

Basket, woven splint, round w/carved rigid
bentwood handle, double-laced rim,
19th c., 14" d., 14" h. $805
Basket, woven splint, wide shallow round
form w/single wrap over shaped rims, upright alternating cut-out & turned-down
on outside, painted light greenish blue,
14 1/2" d., 5 1/2" h. (minor wear).............. 2,990

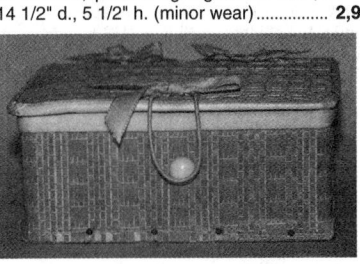

Basketweave Shaker Box

Box, cov. woven poplar splint, rectangular
w/flat cover trimmed w/pink bows, probably Enfield, New Hampshire or Sabbathday Lake, Maine, 2 1/2 x 4 1/2", 2" h.
(ILLUS.) 100
Butter churn, painted pine, the rectangular
shaped wash receptacle w/square sides,
a turned handle at the side, fitted lid
w/slotted bar seal, all resting on a wood-
en stand w/canted braced legs, blue
paint, 8 x 19", 38" h. (minor wood loss)........ 403
Carrier, oval bentwood, maple & pine w/ash
handle, two finger lappets, painted blue,
8 1/4 x 11 1/4", 7 1/2" h. (wear) 1,035
Carrier, round bentwood, two-finger construction w/copper tacks, two splints,
5 1/4" d., 2 1/4" h. plus handle 330
Dining chair, low-back production model,
the tapering stiles w/ball-top finials joined
by two turned horizontal spindles over a
tape seat on tapering turned legs joined
by double stretchers, left back leg
marked "Shaker's No. 4 Trademark
Mount Lebanon" w/gold lettered decal,
old dark brown varnished stain, New
York, late 19th - early 20th c., 28" h.............. 518
Dustpan, sheet metal pan w/rolled top rim,
finely turned wood handle w/scribe lines
& small knob at end, 7 3/8 x 15 1/2"
(wear, rust) 920
Footbench, maple, production model, a
square top on a slanted stool raised on
turned & incised legs, dark brown varnish
finish, decal mark, Model No. 0, Mt. Lebanon, New York, ca. 1875, 11 1/2" sq.,
6 1/2" h.. 230
Footstool, maple, production model, the
four turned tapering posts joined by a
tape seat & turned stretchers, marked
"Shaker's No. 1 Trademark Mount Lebanon, NY" w/gold stenciled decal, old
brown stain, late 19th - early 20th c.,
9 1/2 x 12 3/4", 9 1/2" h..................................... 489
Harness rack, painted wood, six tapering
pegs tenoned through a rectangular
board w/chamfered edge & original blue
paint, 4 1/2 x 62" (minor paint loss on
pegs) 1,150

Early Shaker Oxen Muzzles

Oxen muzzles, woven splint, deep cylindrical loosely woven form w/rounded bottom & wide wrapped rim, New England,
mid-19th c., 14" d., 14 1/2" h., pr.
(ILLUS.) 2,875
Pail, painted & stenciled wood, pine staves
& bottom, iron hoops, grain-painted exterior w/stenciled gilt floral reserves & rim
band, interior painted white, hardwood

handle & coffin-shaped bail plates, 8 3/4" d., 7" h. (wear) **978**

Pail, painted wood, cylindrical turned maple w/ears & bail handle w/four scribe lines encircling the body, brass disk w/the number "43" on the base, painted blue w/black trim, 8 1/2" d., 12" h. (repaint, wear) **1,380**

Rocking chair w/arms, tall turned stiles w/pointed finials & a blue & ivory woven tape back above turned open arms w/mushroom hand rests on baluster-turned arm supports, blue & ivory woven tape seat, turned legs joined by double front & side rungs & a single rear rung, worn original finish, stenciled label, #5 size, Mount Lebanon, New York, 37 3/4" h. (woven tape an old replacement) **715**

Rocking chair with arms, painted, the tall back w/round stiles & ovoid finials flanking the four arched & graduated splats flanked by shaped arms w/down-turned terminals above turned & tapering arm supports flanking an old taped seat, turned stretchers, on rockers, early black paint, Canterbury, New Hampshire, ca. 1840, 45 1/4" h. (minor repairs) **2,185**

Rocking chair without arms, maple production model, the tall turned stiles surmounted by acorn finials joined by a taped back, the taped seat over turned double-stretchers & turned front legs on rockers, old finish, Model No. 7, Mount Lebanon, New York, late 19th - early 20th c., 42" h. (imperfections) **575**

Seed box, cov., shallow rectangular form, divided interior w/chromolithograph fruit labels on front, marked "Shaker Seeds, Mt. Lebanon, N.Y." & "Shaker Seed Co.," top w/worn brownish red finish, 12 x 23 1/2", 3 1/2" h. (worn w/traces of old label along edges, cracks) **193**

Shaker Bentwood Sewing Box

Sewing box, cov., round bentwood w/copper tacks, bentwood swing handle, interior trimmed in pink silk & pink ribbons around outside, holds a tomato-shaped pincushion, needle wax, strawberry emery & needle felt, probably Sabbathday Lake, Maine, 5 1/2" d., 5 1/2" h. (ILLUS.) **600**

Sewing box, hardwood, two-tiered style w/round pincushion at top center, small tapering spires at each top corner, top section w/interior posts for thread w/holes in sides for feeding out thread, drawer w/wooden knob below, on tapering peg feet, 5 x 7", 5 1/2" h. (ILLUS. top next column) **250**

Shaker Tiered Sewing Box

Sewing carrier, cov., oval bentwood, three finger lappets w/a bentwood swing handle, the interior lined w/royal blue silk & fitted w/a straw pin keep & needle book, a fabric pincushion, emery & wax block, includes a group of eight postcards w/scenes of the Community at East Canterbury, New Hampshire, mid-20th c., 3 1/2 x 9 1/2" **690**

Sewing desk, butternut & chestnut, the top gallery divided into thirds by a frame & panel-constructed small door flanked by stacks of three small drawers w/large turned wood knobs, the stepped-out base w/four graduated drawers on the right side, the lowest w/a lock, in the front a sliding work surface above two recessed horizontal panels next to a door of frame & panel construction, the left side w/two horizontal recessed panels, all above ring-turned tapering legs, refinished, Canterbury, New Hampshire community, 1860s, 22 x 29", 38 1/4" h. **17,250**

Shaker Sewing Pouch

Sewing pouch, cloth & leather, brown cloth & black leather trimmed w/brown silk ribbon, leather flap lifts to hold needles, interior to hold thread, 6" l. (ILLUS.) **75**

Sewing steps, painted pine, nailed five-board construction, overhanging top, semi-circular cut-out ends, bottom step set into dado in sides, painted light green, 8 1/4 x 15", 9 3/4" h. (minor paint wear) **518**

Side chair, maple-stained, the three arched back slats flanked by lightly tapering stiles above a taped seat & turned legs & double stretchers, rear tilters refinished, Watervliet, New York, ca. 1850, 41" h. (minor imperfections) **920**

Side chair, the three arched slats joining turned stiles to the tape seat, on turned legs joined by stretchers, old red paint, Massachusetts, possibly Harvard, Massachusetts, early 19th c., 40" h. **460**

Side chairs, cherry & maple, ladder-back style, tall turned stiles w/elongated ovoid finials above three arched beveled slats, woven tape seat, simple turned legs & double front & side stretchers, rear legs w/wooden tilters, Watervliet, New York community, ca. 1840, 41 1/2" h., pr. (refinished, replaced seat tape) **2,185**

Shaker Spool Holder - Pincushion

Spool holder - pincushion, wooden round base w/wire posts for spools of thread, turned center shaft topped by a round pincushion (ILLUS.) **150**

Storage box, cov., bentwood, oval, three finger lappets on the base w/copper tacks, a single lappet on the flat, fitted cover, slightly worn old finish, 11 3/8" l., 4 3/4" h. **479**

Storage box, cov., oval bentwood, painted maple & pine, three finger lappets on the base & one on the fitted flat cover, 8 1/2 x 12", 4 3/4" h. (stress cracks, abrasion, wear) **863**

Storage box, cov., oval bentwood, painted maple & pine, three finger lappets on the base & one on the fitted flat cover, grey paint, 8 x 11 1/2", 4 3/4" h. **1,265**

Storage box, cov., oval bentwood, painted maple & pine, two finger lappets on the base & one on the cover, chrome yellow paint, 19th c., 4 3/8 x 6 1/4", 2" h. (wear) .. **2,645**

Storage box, oval bentwood, two finger lappets on the base & one on the fitted flat lid, w/copper tacks, old worn varnish finish w/good patina, 5 7/8" l. (some edge damage) **275**

Wall cupboard, painted poplar, a rectangular top on a tall case w/a pair of drawers above a pair of very tall, narrow paneled cupboard doors opening to a four-shelved interior, arched base, old light grey paint, Mt. Lebanon, New York community, 1850-60, 16 1/2 x 36 3/4", 73" h. (paint surface imperfections) **2,760**

Early Shaker Washstand

Washstand, painted hardwood, double-size, the tall backsplash w/a narrow open shelf above ogee-shaped sides flanking the rectangular work surface above a pair of tall paneled cupboard doors w/thumb latches opening to two shelves, flat base, old light brown paint, shoft shelf & top crestrail later additions, surface imperfections, probably Enfield, Connecticut, 1820-30, 18 x 38 1/2", overall 41 1/4" h. (ILLUS.) **4,600**

Work table, cherry & pine, large rectangular pine top w/breadboard ends widely overhangs the apron w/a single long drawer w/two turned wood knobs, slender turned tapering legs w/'boots,' New Lebanon, New York, mid-19th c., 27 3/4 x 58", 30 3/4" h. **3,335**

SIGNS & SIGNBOARDS

Also see Antique Trader Advertising Price Guide.

Automobile, "Buick," one-sided porcelain, round, dark blue outer ring w/"Authorized Service" in white surrounding inner "Buick" logo in blue & white, ca. 1930s, 42" d. (one edge chip w/a few other small rim chips) **$660**

Automobile, "Rambler," two-sided tin, round w/red wide border ring & crossbar printed in white "Rambler - Parts - Service," 1950s, 22" d. **523**

Bootmaker, carved & painted model of a high-topped boot, white repaint w/black detail of straps & lacing over earlier gilding, on a modern steel stand, late 19th c., 25 1/2" h. (age cracks) **385**

Bootmaker, cast zinc model of a large man's boot, suspended from a wrought-iron angled bracket, boot painted golden brown, impressed "570," paint loss, 19th c., 22 1/2" h. (ILLUS. top next page) **1,380**

Bread, "Merita Bread," embossed tin, tall rectangular form, a red ground w/a color embossed loaf of bread flanked by the wording "Buy Enriched Merita Bread - Always Fresh!," wording in red, yellow & white, 1940-50, 18 x 54" (some mild discoloration, light edge wear) **633**

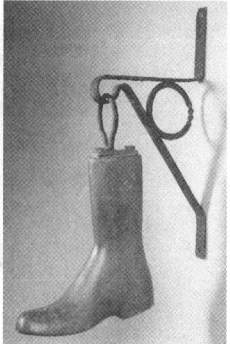

Cast Zinc Bootmaker Trade Sign

Bread, "Sunbeam Bread," embossed tin, long narrow rectangular form w/narrow dark green border band w/a half-length color portrait of the Sunbeam girl in a blue dress at the left, red background w/yellow & white wording to the right "Reach For... Sunbeam - Energy-Packed Bread," 1950s, 19 x 55" (some tiny dark spots, near perfect) **688**

Chiseled Brass Butcher's Sign

Butcher, "J.W. Goatcher - Butcher," chiseled black wording on a rectangular brass ground, ca. 1900, 4 1/2 x 16" (ILLUS.).. **77**

Butcher shop, painted cast iron, full-bodied model of a standing bull, overall worn gold paint, late 19th - early 20th c., 11 1/2" h.. **4,830**

Catsup, "Snider's Catsup," embossed diecut cardboard, dark red border w/white center reserve printed in color w/a large bottle of the product w/tomato plants & a black & white center banner w/"Snider's," ca. 1930s, 11 x 17" (edge wear, some light rubbing & medium wear at top, few light bends) **523**

Chewing gum, "Oh Boy Gum," tin, narrow vertical rectangle, black ground w/a color half-length image of a smiling boy w/an elf whispering in his ear, the boy holds four large, colorful packages of the gum, printed in yellow at the bottom "1¢ - It's Pure!," 1930s, framed w/no glass, 7 1/2 x 16" (light wear & edge bends) **688**

Cigars, "Admiration Cigars," embossed & colored chalkware, rectangular, a large boldly embossed man in the moon w/a cigar in his mouth at the center flanked by brown cigars & tobacco leaf, black ground w/white wording at top & bottom "Admiration Cigars - Mild and Mellow to the Last Inch," ca. 1930s, 11 x 15" (light soiling, very few nicks & wear) **633**

White House Coffee Flange Sign

Coffee, "White House Coffee," tin flange-type, a large hand holding up a large can reading "White House Coffee - 1 lb. - Net - Dwinell-Wright Co. - Boston Chicago," printed above hand "None Better at any Price," early 20th c. (ILLUS.)...................... **4,300**

Insurance, "American Eagle Fire Insurance," black & white porcelain, large spread-winged eagle at top above wording "American Eagle Fire Insurance Company - New York," ca. 1930s, 14 1/2 x 15" (small corner chip & few small edge chips, mior warping) **88**

Magician, "Carter the Great," poster paper mounted on linen, the eight sheets forming a full-color image w/a spirit leaving the body of a hanging man w/the man's bust portrait to the right above a crowd of pointing on-lookers, name at the top & white wording across the bottom reads "Carter Condemned to Death for Witchcraft Cheats the Gallows," ca. 1920s, 7 x 9' (few minor wrinkles) **633**

Simple Notary Public Sign

Notary public, "Notary Public," narrow long porcelain rectangle, large wording in blue block letters, red sunburst in center, early 20th c., 3 x 15" (ILLUS.)...................................... **44**

Neon Optometrist Sign

Optometrist, neon, large bluish white spectacles in the center w/reddish orange wording above & below "Glasses On Credit - Easy Terms," mid-20th c. (ILLUS.).. **250**

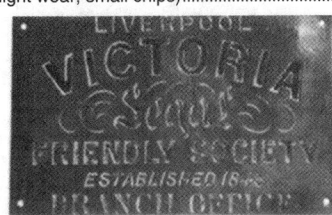

Early Optometrist Trade Sign

Optometrist, trade-type, painted cast iron & zinc, double-sided large molded spectacles w/colored eyes in center, black wording on white "Glasses Fitted - Eyes Tested," late 19th c., wear, old paint retouches, 26 1/4" l., 11 1/2" h. (ILLUS.) **4,313**

Overalls, "Smith's Overalls," tin, narrow rectangular form, yellow ground w/dark blue & white wording "Smith's Overalls - Trademark," 1930s, 2 1/2 x 7"........................ **248**

Paint, "Sherwin Williams," convex porcelain, colorful design of a yellow & red paint can marked "SWP" pouring red paint over a green globe w/white wording "Cover The Earth," ca. 1940-60, 18 x 34" (light wear, small chips).................................... **550**

Brass Sign for a Private Club

Private club, "Victoria Legal Friendly Society," heavy brass w/chiseled wording, rectangular, reads "Liverpool - Victoria - Legal - Friendly Society - Established 1848 - Branch Office," 19th c., 8 x 13" (ILLUS.).. **66**

Carborundum Scythe Stones Sign

Scythe stones, "Carborundum Scythe Stones," long rectangular lithographed cardboard, a narrow black border around a red ground w/a round color logo of a Native American chief's head, large wording in white, string-hung, early 20th c., 3 1/2 x 12" (ILLUS.) **149**

Shoe shop, large wooden model of a lady's high-heeled slipper, laminated construction w/worn & weathered yellow, blue & salmon paint, early 20th c., 25" l............ **2,365**

Shoes, "Buster Brown Shoes," porcelain & neon, nearly square form w/a red, yellow,

blue & pink image of Buster Brown & Tige all outlined in yellow or white neon above a bottom red band w/"Buster Brown Shoes" in yellow w/yellow neon, ca. 1950s, 54 x 55" (some later tube repair, some minor surface wear, light stains, small chips, mounted on deep wooden frame).. **1,540**

Soap, "Ivory Soap," paper lithograph titled "A Busy Day" by Maud Humphrey, artist-signed, gesso frame, 10" w., 22 1/2" h. **259**

Soft drink, "7Up," embossed tin, long rectangular vertical form, a large green pop bottle against a white ground w/"'Fresh up' with" at the top in red & black, 1962, 18 x 48" (light edge wear & scratches, small chip upper right).................................... **418**

Early 7Up Flange Sign

Soft drink, "7Up," tin flange-type, a stylized arm & hand holding a round tray w/a bottle of 7Up & a red & white logo box reading "We Proudly Serve 7Up," early 20th c. (ILLUS.) **2,300**

Soft drink, "Whistle," embossed tin, rectangular, narrow yellow border around a dark blue ground w/a large angled orange bottle of pop w/white wording "thisty? - just - (Whistle) - Demand the Genuine," orange & blue Whistle logo in lower right, 1930s, 6 1/2 x 9 1/2" (very light edge wear, minor paint chipping) **660**

Telephone, "Bell Telephone," rectangular porcelain two-sided flange-type, dark blue ground w/"Telephone" above round white & blue Bell logo w/"The Bell Telephone Company of Canada," ca. 1940-60 (large chip at top of flange) **220**

Tires, "Goodyear," die-cut molded tin flange-type, a large narrow white & blue tire w/name imprinted under a dark blue bar w/"Goodyear" in gold over the red winged sandal logo, made in Germany, ca. 1930s, 22 x 34" (some light stains & edge chipping w/light wear & surface marks, small tip bend) **1,485**

Tobacco, "Edgeworth Smoking Tobacco," rectangular tin over cardboard, color image of large open tin of tobacco beside a pocket tin of tobacco behind a pipe in an ashtray, red rectangular bar at top w/white wording reads "Edgeworth Smoking Tobacco - Extra High Grade," ca. 1930-50, 9 x 11" (dent in upper left, few minor crimps, light overall wear, small paint chips & nicks).................... **248**

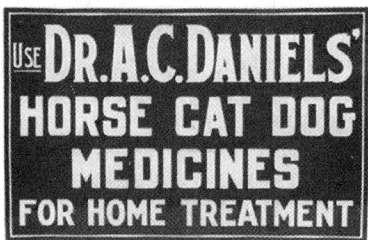

Veternary Medicines Sign

Veternary medicines, "Dr. A.C. Daniels' Horse Cat Dog Medicines," rectangular embossed tin, black ground w/bold white wording "Use Dr. A.C. Daniels' Horse Cat Dog - Medicines - For Home Treatment," unused, early 20th c., 17 1/2 x 28" (ILLUS.).. **231**

SILHOUETTES

These cut-out paper portraits in profile were named after Etienne de Silhouette, Louis XV's unpopular minister of finance and an amateur profile cutter. As originally applied, the term was synonymous with cheapness, or anything reduced to its simplest state. These substitutes for the more expensive oil painting or miniatures were popular from about 1770 until 1850 when daguerreotype images replaced the vogue. Silhouettes may be either hollow-cut, with the head cut away leaving the white paper frame for mounting against a dark background, or the profile itself may be cut from black paper and pasted to a light background.

Bust of a young boy, hollow-cut, facing right, details showing short hair & bow at his neck, high-collared jacket, old ink inscription w/sitter's name, partial Peale embossed mark at bottom, black cloth backing, early beveled mahogany veneer frame, first half 19th c., 6 x 7" (margin stains, chips to frame veneer) **$385**

Bust portrait of a gentleman, hollow-cut, facing left, his short hair combed back, wearing a high-collared jacket w/a string bow tie showing, faint embossed mark of the Peale Museum, black cloth backing, framed, 5 x 6 1/4"... **358**

Bust portrait of a woman, cut paper, facing right, her hair piled high & held w/a large comb, wide-collared dress, stenciled back label reads "Gallery of Cuttings, Cut by Master Hankes with Common Scissors," rectangular embossed brass on wood frame, 4 3/4 x 5 1/2"............................. **495**

Bust portrait of a woman, hollow-cut, facing left, wearing a large bonnet w/a wide front brim, black cloth backing, erased pencil inscription & old backing labeled "Mrs. Nicholas Johnson," old molded wood black frame, first half 19th c., 5 1/2 x 6 3/4"... **248**

Bust portrait of a young girl, hollow-cut, facing left, her head w/short hair, a slender neck above a round ruffled collar, cut

& penciled detail, black cloth backing, old pen & ink label on back "Sally Tilton 5 years old, 1822," old molded frame w/black repaint, 4 1/4 x 5 1/4" **358**

Bust portrait of a young man, hollow-cut, facing left, wearing a high-collared shirt & vest w/high collared jacket, black ink detail, sawtooth cut borders, small tin frame, early 19th c., 3 x 3 7/8" **440**

Bust portrait of a young woman, hollow-cut, facing right, her hair pulled up in back & held w/a tall comb, wearing a ruffled high collar, early 19th c., black cloth backing, possibly Peale Museum, old molded black wood frame, 5 1/4 x 6 7/8" (added oval mat) **193**

Bust portraits of a gentleman & lady, black paper, half-length view of a middle aged stocky gentleman seated in a chair facing right, gilded detail showing his hair combed forward & wearing a high-collared shirt & jacket w/buttons, the slender lady shown half-length facing left, decorated w/gilded trim showing her hair arranged w/sausage curls at the sides & a braided bun at the back, a high-collared dress w/a pleated front, in similar beveled curly maple frames w/gilded liners, ca. 1840, 6 x 7 1/4", pr. **440**

Double Silhouette & Lady & Man

Bust portraits of a lady & gentleman, hollow cut, she facing right w/her curly hair pulled to the back & wearing a high lacy collar, he facing left w/curly hair & wearing a high-collar jacket w/ruffled cravat, pen & ink detail, each in an octagonal opening in a black mat w/gilt stars in the corners, framed together in a narrow gilt frame, early 19th c., 5 1/2 x 8 5/8" (ILLUS.) **330**

Family group, figures in an interior, two women facing each other, one holding a baby, on the left, two gentleman shaking hands, one wearing a top hat, on the right, small dog at the far right, cut black paper w/white details, on a brushed ink interior in black & white, signed "Weston of New York 1840," back w/original paper label w/"Weston Profiles, 149 1/2 Bowery, New York" as well as pen & ink names of the gentlemen shown, original beveled maple veneer frame, 17 x 19 3/4" (stains wear, frame worn & delaminating) **1,210**

Fine August Edouart Silhouette

Figure of a standing youth, full-cut figure facing left & wearing a dress suit & holding his hat in one hand, his other hand on his hip, on a lithographed exterior background, named as Charles Burrall Hoffman, signed in lower left corner by August Edouart, 1837, framed, 8 x 11" (ILLUS.).. **1,265**

Full-length portrait of a woman, hollow-cut, standing facing left, wearing a wide long dress & holding a bouqet of flowers, her hair pulled up & back, traces of green watercolor on the bouquet, mid-19th c., worn giltwood narrow frame, 4 3/8 x 6 1/4" (stains)... **248**

SPICE CABINETS & BOXES

Cabinet, black walnut, a narrow rectangular top above a case w/three stacks of five small graduated dovetailed drawers w/original white porcelain pulls, molded base & thin molded cornice, Ohio, 19th c., refinished, 7 1/8 x 18 1/2", 14 3/4" h...... **$715**

Cabinet, decorated pine & poplar, a narrow rectangular top w/a high arched crestrail w/hanging hole above a case w/three rows of five drawers each, each drawer w/a large wooden knob, mustard yellow paint w/sponge decoration, wire nail construction, 4 x 11", 18 1/2" h...................... **2,200**

Cabinet, hanging-type, oak, a high arched crestboard w/rounded corners & two hanging holes above a case w/two stacks of four square drawers each, small inset drawer knobs, flat base, old finish, crest marked "Spice Cabinet," old advertising on back w/"May & Company, Ohio," late 19th - early 20th c., 5 1/4 x 10 3/4", 16 3/4" h. (age cracks in back)... **523**

Cabinet, hanging-type, pine, an arched crest w/two hanging holes above a case w/two ranks of four small drawers each w/inset round knobs, flat base, old finish,

wire nail construction, 5 x 10", 17 1/2" h. (damage, some replaced knobs)................... **220**

Cabinet, hanging-type, poplar & ash, high arched crestboard w/hanging hole above a case w/nine small square drawers over two long bottom drawers, all w/porcelain knobs, pressed label on each drawer, old finish, attributed to Cincinnati, Ohio, 4 1/2 x 10", 25" h.. **303**

Cabinet, oak, hanging-type, an arched crest above a narrow case w/six square drawers w/impressed labels & white porcelain pulls, original varnish finish, stamped advertising "Pure Food Co., Cincinnati, Ohio," late 19th - early 20th c., 4 1/2 x 8 1/4", 12 1/2" h................................ **303**

Cabinet, oak, rectangular top above a case w/five long drawers w/oval notched finger grip pulls, dark gold & black stenciling drawer fronts read "The Frank Tea and Spice Co., Cincinnati," names of various spices on drawers, molded base, paneled ends, original finish, late 19th - early 20th c., 19 1/4 x 25", 25 3/4" h. (wear on top)........... **1,750**

SPINNING WHEELS

Flax wheel, carved & painted wood, small size, the molded wheel w/six baluster-turned spindles on a slanted top board w/a swelled, turned end handle, the upright yarn holder finely turned but missing the distaff, raised on three canted baluster- and ring-turned legs joined by a pedal platform base, old black paint, impressed "N. Wolf T," 19th c., 21 1/2" h. **$220**

Flax wheel, oak, grooved wheel w/ten slender turned spindles, supported by ring-turned posts on a slanted thick board w/ring-turned bobbin & distaff, on three canted ring-turned legs w/pedal base, natural brown patina, orange & black striping, branded "B. Green," 19th c., 34" h. (bobbin & distaff damaged & incomplete)... **248**

Flax wheel, turned & painted wood, the wheel painted black w/salmon red & blue trim, inscribed in yellow "Anna Grettta M.D.S. 1859," Pennsylvania German, 21 x 39", 38" h. (imperfections, incomplete)... **345**

Flax wheel, various hardwoods, grooved wheel w/fourteen simple turned spindles supported between simple turned uprights on a slanted platform w/turned end handle, simple turned distaff & bobbin, simple turned canted feet joined by treadle, old dark brown finish, Shaker-made, stamped "SR. AL.," 19th c., 33 1/2" h. (two pieces of distaff replaced)...................... **330**

Flax wheel, walnut, oak & hardwood, ring-turned wheel w/twelve turned spindles mounted between heavy baluster- and ring-turned supports on a slanted plank w/ring-turned end upright & crossbar, on three canted ring- and baluster-turned legs joined by treadle, complete w/distaff & bobbin, old dark brown patina, 19th c., 36" h. **220**

SPORTS MEMORABILIA
Basketball

Cincinnati Royals Team-signed Ball

Basketball, 1965 Cincinnati Royal team-signed model, Jerry Lucas official model, signed in black marker by a dozen members of the team, near mint (ILLUS.).......... **$560**
Basketball, 1979 Seattle Supersonics team-signed official Wilson model, w/a dozen signatures of players from the World Champion team, near mint................. **345**
Basketball card, Wilt Chamberlain, 1961 Fleer series, No. 8, mint........................... **15,988**

1970-71 Topps Basketball Set

Painting, acrylic half-length portrait of Michael Jordan in uniform drinking Gatorade, by Jay Stewart, signed by Jordan in silver ink & w/his added "#23," w/letters of authenticity, 20 x 24".................................. **2,596**
Pinback button, promotional-type from a bread bakery, printed in red & blue on white, a center head portrait of Bob Cousy above his name, wording around the top "Reach for Town Talk," late 1950s, 1"d. (some rust on back)................... **115**

Indiana Pacers Championship Ring

Ring, 1973 Indiana Pacers ABA championship model, the oblong top set w/three diamonds surrounded by raised wording "ABA - World Champions - ABA," shanks feature Pacers logo "Freeman" & number "13" as well as an engraved Pacer going for a dunk w/the ABA logo, 10k gold, awarded to Donnie Freeman, pristine (ILLUS.) **3,701**

Chamberlain-signed Topps Card

Basketball card, Wilt Chamberlain, 1970 Topps 'tall boy' version No. 1, signed by Chamberlain in black marker, near mint (ILLUS.).. **463**
Basketball card set, 1970-71 Topps series, complete set of 175 cards, excellent to near mint, the set (ILLUS. of part top next column).. **1,444**
Championship ring, 1960 Boston Celtic World Championship type, gold, a round top centered by a three-leaf green-enameled clover centered by a diamond, raised lettering in border ring reads "Boston Celtics - 1960 World Champions," 10k, size 10 .... **2,037**

Jordan Game-used Shoes

Shoes, Michael Jordan game-used white & red Nike Air sneakers, worn during his first championship season of 1990-91, autographed in blue Sharpie on right shoe, show use, pr. (ILLUS.) **2,464**

Original Boston Gardens Seats

Stadium seats, double seat removed from Boston Garden stadium before its demolition, left seat autographed by Larry Bird, affixed plaque reads "Genuine Artifact from the Boston Gardens, Home of the Boston Bruins 1923-1995 - Boston Celtics 1946-1995" (ILLUS.) **1,457**

Cliff Hagan Game-worn Uniform

Uniform, Cliff Hagan 1962 All-Star game-worn uniform, creamy white jersey w/red name, number & stars & matching satin shorts, "Rawlings 36" & washing instructions on waistband, very fine condition, the set (ILLUS.) **1,530**

Uniform, Larry Costello All-Star game-worn uniform, dark blue cotton w/red & white banding & red stars around the number "7" on the jersey, Wlson, size 44, 1950s **996**

Boxing

Boxing card set, Leaf 1948-49 complete 50 card set including rare No. 50 Rocky Graziano card, most cards near mint to mint, the set **20,873**

Cabinet photograph, John L. Sullivan & his family, studio shot, ca. 1890, framed, 18 x 21" (very light foxing at edges) **1,082**

Figure group, Staffordshire pottery, two bare-knuckled boxers punching each other, standing on an oval base embossed "Heenan - Sayers," commemo-

rates a great English fight of the bare-knuckle era, ca. 1860, 9 1/2" h. **696**

Magazine, "Life," March 6, 1964, Cassius Clay cover & story **30**

Rare James Corbett Movie Poster

Movie poster, "The Eye of Death," starring James J. Corbett, full-color three-sheet poster showing three main characters above the credits & title, restored & linen-backed, ca. 1910, 41 x 81" (ILLUS.) **1,093**

Movie poster, "The Prizefighter and The Lady," MGM, 1933 window card, rectangular, starring Myna Loy, Max Baer, Primo Carnera & Jack Dempsey, color images of the stars against a black & yellow ground w/bright pink highlights, trimmed, 14 x 18" **511**

Pennant, black felt w/white lettering, two figures of boxers at wide end, tapering white lettering reads "Worlds Heavyweight Championship - Dempsey - Carpentier - Jersey City July 2, 1921," near mint **3,123**

Photograph, full-length black & white photo of Cassius Clay (Mohammed Ali) wearing white trunks, signed "From Cassius Clay," typed along the bottom edge "Cassius Clay - I am the Greatest," near mint, 3 x 7" **2,406**

Photograph, signed black & white Jack Dempsey full-length photo, shown in boxing stance, by Apeda, personally inscribed & signed by Dempsey, jumbo 11 x 14" **895**

Pinback button, celluloid w/half-length black & white photo of Joe Louis w/his name above, 1940s, near mint, 1 3/4" d. **285**

Joe Louis Political Campaign Button

Pinback button, "Joe Louis Wants Willkie," black & white, Joe Louis endorsement of 1940 Republican presidential candidate Wendall Willkie, 1 3/4" d. (ILLUS.) **173**

Rare Johnson vs Burns Fight Program

Program, 1908 Burns vs Johnson program, color cover in red, black, blue & white w/black & white photos of the two boxers at the bottom, reads "Souvenir of the Tommy Burns - Jack Johnson - Boxing Contest - The Stadium, Sydney - For The Championship of the World," held in Australia, minor restoration (ILLUS.) **6,780**

Program, 1924 Carpentier vs Gibbons match, cover printed in shades of brown & orange w/black lettering, dated May 31, 1924, includes photos and measurements, 20 pp., near mint (heavy vertical crease) **285**

Ring, premium-type, Lucite-like plastic w/domed top over a rectangular black & photo of Joe Louis in a boxing pose, late 1930s - early 1940s **447**

Robe, green polyester & white satin, white name on the back "Roberto Duran," signed by Duran in black Sharpie, w/photo of Duran signing the robe, fight-worn **2,021**

Robe, green velour w/black trim & lettering, exhibition fight model used by Muhammed Ali, his name on the back, Everlast label inside the collar, w/letter of authenticity signed by Ali **11,163**

Sheet music, "Knock Him Down Whiskey," black & white cover photo of Sugar Ray Robinson wearing a sports jacket & bow tie, 1953, near mint **422**

Shoes, Muhammad Ali fight-worn shoes, high-top white shoes by Everlast, w/a red, white & blue lightning bolt-style letter "E" logo, each shoe signed & personalized by Ali & dated 1972, size 13, show heavy use, pr. (ILLUS. top next column) **25,850**

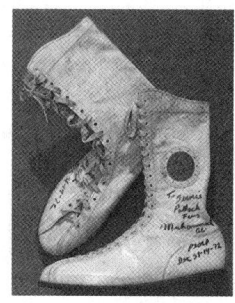

Rare Muhammad Ali Fight Shoes

Silkscreen, bust portrait of Muhammed Ali by Andry Warhol, in shades of purple, green & black, signed & numbered by the artist, signed & dated by Ali in 1990 on the reverse, framed, 40 x 50" **8,625**

Statue, cast brass w/bronzed finish, realistic rendition of an early boxer in an action pose, good detail, oblong domed base, ca. 1900, 10" h........................ **505**

Ticket, Demsey vs Tunney full ticket for the September 22, 1927 bout, yellow w/red & black printing, near mint (invisible tape at left & right edges, minor paper loss on back)... **616**

Ticket, full ticket for Joe Louis' first title fight, Chicago Tribune's 1932 Golden Gloves Tournament, dated March 1, 1932, near mint... **173**

Ticket, full-ticket for Joe Louis vs Jim Braddock championship bout on June 22, 1937, excellent to mint **900**

Rare Sullivan-Dempsey Fight Ticket

Ticket, John L. Sullivan vs Jack (Nonpariel) Dempsey fight ticket, printed in black "LaGrande Skating Rink - North Clark St. - Grand Sparring Contest - Sullivan vs Dempsey - Monday Evening, May 31st, 1886. - 2548 - Admission ..$1.00," reverse w/pencil notation of donor of this complimentary ticket, fight held in Chicago, fair condition (ILLUS.) **1,668**

Football

Book ends, cast brass w/bronzed finish, figural bust of a smiling Knute Rockne, stamped "Copyright Oct. 30, 1930," pr. **285**

Broadside, printed cardboard, promotional-type for the Cleveland Browns, printed in black, white & red, shows a player in action on the left, titled "Best Show in Football" above list of scheduled games, 1950s, near mint, 13 1/2 x 20" **285**

Check, personal check signed by John Heisman, dated April 20, 1912, w/attached receipt, fine signature **2,444**

Buddy Lee Football Player Doll

Doll, Buddy Lee composition doll, dressed as a football player w/original leather helmet, red football sweater & canvas gridiron pants w/white sewn-on reeded design, some minor crazing, 1930s (ILLUS.).. **2,406**

Football, leather, 1964 New York Giants team-signed model, non-official ball w/70 near mint ballpoint team signatures, near mint... **904**

Football, official National Football League white leather style w/black bands & dark blue lettering, game-used, 1950s **812**

Football card, Bob Waterfield, 1948 Bowman series, No. 26, near mint **886**

Football card, Norm VanBrocklin, 1952 Bowman large series, No. 1, in color, near mint.. **4,807**

Helmet, 1944-46 Notre Dame game-worn model, leather, worn by Mike Ganey, gold coloring still visible.............................. **1,834**

Helmet, 1972 Miami Dolphin team-signed model, white printed in dark green & red, signed at the silver anniversary reunion party by 40 members of the undefeated World Champions, black Sharpie signatures... **2,325**

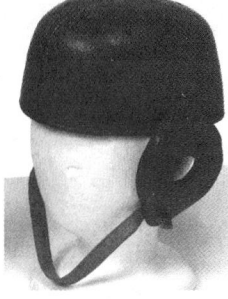

Rare Early Leather Football Helmet

Helmet, leather, Double Head Harness No. 60 model by Spalding Sporting Goods, patented March 11, 1902, original strap, near mint (ILLUS.)...................................... **4,339**

Helmet, Princeton-style, leather, flat-topped design w/two leather pieces sewn together & lined w/wool batting, top section w/scalloped edges painted yellow above black lower section w/rounded ear guards, ca. 1910, excellent condition **3,874**

Jersey, Michigan Wolverines jersey worn by Norm Daniels, ca. 1930, large sewn-on "32" on the front, size 42 tag, w/ 5 x 7" photo of the team w/Daniels wearing the jersey, 2 pcs.. **927**

Letter, typed & hand-signed letter by Knute Rockne to a former player, written three days before he was killed in a plane crash, dated March 31, 1931, signed "K.K. Rockne" (two vertical & one center fold).. **1,834**

Nose guard, early rubber 'batwing' style, hard rubber w/molded dome for nose pieced w/air holes, flaring rounded 'batwing' sides, bite plate for mouth, original head strap, by Victor Sporting Goods, 1890s, near mint............................ **1,302**

Photograph, black & white magazine page showing half-length portrait of Vince Lombardi, signed by Lombardi in black ink, 1960s, 7 1/2 x 9" (some creasing, very minor paper loss)...................................... **190**

Photograph, promotional-type, bust portrait of a smiling Red Grange, facsimile signature & title "One Minute To Play," his only motion picture appearance, excellent condition, 8 x 10"... **173**

Rare 1942 Rose Bowl Program

Program, 1942 Rose Bowl program, game moved to North Carolina because of outbreak of World War II, cover printed in red, white & blue w/gold, a large central oval reserve showing a young football player, Duke vs Oregon State game, January 4, 1942, near mint (ILLUS.).......... **1,323**

Rare Jim Thorpe Football Program

Program, Brown vs Carlisle, the final college game of Jim Thorpe, cover printed in orange & black on white w/two full-length black & white photos of the two team captains, Thorpe & Ashbaugh, cover reads "Football - Brown vs Carlisle - Andrews Field - Thursday, November 28, 1912," 16 pp., neatly repaired interior edge tear, some small corner & edge stains (ILLUS.).. **2,686**

Unusual Football-shaped Radio

Radio, ceramic model of a football in brown & white houses a fully functional radio, speaker & controls behind white laces, base reads "Gridiron Radio," 1930s, near mint, 15" l. (ILLUS.)................................... **928**

Ring, 1958 Baltimore Colts N.F.L. Championship model, 14k gold, the oval top centered by a diamond surrounded by a laurel wreath within a border band w/raised wording "Baltimore Colts - World Champions," left side w/a horseshoe enclosing bucking horse & w/wording "1958 World Champions," right side w/matching design by wording "Colts 23 - Giants 17," owner's name engraved inside, by Balfour, size 10.. **13,559**

Sign, counter display type, die-cut color-printed cardboard w/easel back, for Old Gold Cigarettes, large image of a young football player charging forward carrying the ball, large red wording across the top "Old Gold Cigarettes" above "Scored...with Natural Goodness," color picture of pack in lower right, printed across the bottom "Not A Cough In A Carload," 1930s, excellent condition, 37 x 50".. **1,357**

Sweater, letterman's, blue wool V-neck style, worn by Earl Brown of Notre Dame, large dark gold "ND" patch on front, 1937, large, near mint..................................... **812**

Ticket stub, from Red Grange's last college game, Illinois vs Ohio at Ohio Stadium, dated November 21, 1925, printed in

dark blue & red on white, mint front (some paper loss on base)............................. **222**

Vest, heavy duck material, sleeveless w/lace-up front, made by A.G. Spalding & Bros., ca. 1890 .... **2,308**

STATUARY - BRONZE, MARBLE & OTHER

Bronzes and other statuary are increasingly popular with today's collectors. Particularly appealing are works by "Les Animaliers," the 19th-century French school of sculptors who turned to animals for their subject matter. These, together with figures in the Art Deco and Art Nouveau taste, are common in a wide price range.

Bronze

Aizelin, Eugene, figure of a young peasant girl, seated on a bench w/a lute at her feet, titled "Mignon," signed "Ene Aizelin 1880" w/a Barbedienne foundry mark, France, 26 1/2" h.. **$7,050**

Bonheur, Rosa, model of a bull, standing on an oblong base, inscribed "R. Bonheur" & w/a Peyrol foundry stamp, France, ca. 1880, 10 1/2" l., 6 3/4" h. **5,288**

Figure Group of Baccante & Herm

Carrier-Belleuse, Albert-Ernest, figure group of a baccante & herm, the nude maiden w/only a small drapery at her waist standing beside a tall square pedestal supporting a bust of Bacchus, she raises a cup & cluster of grapes above his head, signed & w/a foundry mark, gilt finish, France, ca. 1880, 26 3/4" h. (ILLUS.) **7,050**

Colombo, Renzo, bust of Napoleon, wearing his cockade hat & high-collared overcoat, on a shaped marble plinth above a marble-topped quadruple-legged wood pedestal, Italy, ca. 1890, bronze 21" h. **9,400**

Dubois, Paul, figure group, "Charity," a young seated maiden holding a young boy & girl in her lap & suckling the boy, signed & w/a Barbedienne foundry stamp, France, ca. 1880, 18 3/4" h. **3,055**

Falconnier, Leon, figure group, Abraham Lincoln standing over a kneeling black slave, dual-patinated, commemorating the Emancipation Proclamation, signed, France, ca. 1870, 21 1/2" h. **3,760**

Fremiet, Emmanuel, model of a nanny goat & kid, goat standing over the curled up kid, on a thin oblong base, signed, France, ca. 1880, 6 3/4" h........................... **1,763**

Gratchev, Vassily, equestrian group, a mounted Cossack lifting his wife up in his arms to give her a goodbye kiss, signed in cyrillic & w/foundry mark, Russia, ca. 1880, 9 3/4" h... **2,350**

Keyser, Ephraim, figure of a Renaissance lady w/a falcon, standing wearing a heavily pleated gown, a large feathered hat & holding the falcon aloft in one hand, signed "E. Keyser fec. Rome 1879" & "A. Cav. Nelli Fuse Roma," dark brown patina, 56" h... **16,800**

Kuhne, August, figure of a woman, a young lady standing wearing a long Empire era gown, her hair in short curls, one arm across her shoulder, the other holding up the front of her gown, signed "A. Kuhne 1889" w/a stamped foundry mark, brown patina, 43" h. **8,400**

Lanceray "Cossack Plunder" Bronze

Lanceray, Eugene, "Cossack Plunder," figure group w/a Cossack on horseback holding the reins of a second horse loaded w/plunder, blackish patina, ca. 1874, 19" l., 19" h. (ILLUS.) **6,900**

Le Faguays, Pierre, Femme, a standing stylized Art Deco woman, half-naked but wearing a skullcap & a long draped wraparound skirt patinated in black & damascened w/a gilt stylized floral decoration, her body w/a silver finish, signed, 26" h. **13,800**

Levasseur, Henri Louis, figure group, titled "Gloire au Travail," a young seated laborer w/his tools looking up at a tall figure of a female Glory holding a palm leaf above his head & a torch aloft in her other hand, signed & w/Austrian foundry mark, ca. 1890, 28 1/4" h. (ILLUS. top next column) **1,880**

Figure Group by Levasseur

Mene, Pierre-Jules, model of a stallion, standing on a thin rectangular base, titled "Arabe," France, ca. 1870, 7 3/4" h. **3,290**

Moreau, Mathurin, figure of an Art Nouveau maiden, standing w/arms uplifted, one hand swirling a long veil over her head, the other holding a rose blossom, on a domed base w/paneled plinth mounted w/a plaque inscribed "Le Rosée Par M Moureau Medaille d'Honneur au Salon," brown patina, signed "Math. Moreau," early 20th c., 26 1/2" h. **2,700**

Omerth, Georges, figure of a Crusader, chryelephantine-type, standing medieval soldier w/an ivory face, holding his sword point down in one hand, leaning on his shield w/the other, gilt trim, signed, France, ca. 1900, 15 1/2" h. **1,998**

Pascual, Manolo, figure of a young girl in a loose sheath seated on a log, dark brown patina, France, early 20th c., 10" h. **431**

Pinedo, Emile, figure of an Arab peasant, walking wearing a turban & short robes, carrying a staff across his shoulders, titled on the base front "Arabe en Marche," signed, France, ca. 1890, 13" h. **1,175**

Figure of Young Girl by Prost

Prost, Louis, figure of a young girl, seated atop a rocky crag, nude except for a drapery across her lap, turning her head down & tying a bandage around one upper arm, France, ca. 1910, 27 1/2" h. (ILLUS.).. **5,875**

Rheinhold, Hugo Wolfgang, model of a chimpanzee seated atop a book & contemplating a human skull, titled "The Origin of the Species," on a verde antico marble plinth, signed, Germany, ca. 1880, 11 3/4" h. **5,288**

Saulo, Georges Ernest, figure of Joan of Arc, chryelephantine-type w/silvered & gilt decoration, she w/ivory head & hands standing wearing armor & holding a sword, on a square pink marble base, artist-signed, inscribed on the front base "Dieu et La France," France, ca. 1900, 11 3/8" h... **3,525**

Bronze Group of Young Girls Reading

Seifert, Prof. Victor Heinrich, figure group, two young girls seated side by side reading a book, on a thick rectangular base w/beveled corners titled at the front "Marchen," Germany, ca. 1920, 15 1/4" h. (ILLUS.) **2,820**

Spagagna, P., figure of a North African man, shown walking wearing a turban & short loose smock, a rifle & large jug across his back, a bowl in one hand & a small bulbous jug in the other, brownish green patina, signed, late 19th c., 32" h. .. **7,200**

Tegner, Rudolph Christopher, Diana The Huntress, Art Deco-style figure of the naked Diana in an action pose w/arms raised ready to throw a long spear, standing on an arch above a gently sloped block base, green patina, signed "R. Tegner - Premiere Epreuve" w/Colin, Paris foundry mark, 38" h. **31,625**

Van der Straeten, Georges, bust of a young woman representing January, reddish brown patina, on a red marble socle, France, late 19th c., 8 3/4" h. **690**

Vannetti, Antonio, Napoleon on horseback, wearing a long windswept jacket, his head slightly bowed, on a rectangular base, brown & green patina, ca. 1900, 27 1/2" h....................................... **7,800**

Marble

Batelli, H., figure of Venus, standing nude except for a diaphonus drapery around her waist, posed in a large scalloped half shell on a scroll-carved tall base, late 19th c., 41" h................................ **9,600**

Battelli, R., bust of a young maiden, her long hair parted in the center & her head tilted slightly forward, wearing a low-draped robe w/one bossom exposed, on a waisted pedestal w/a round plaque at the front, late 19th c., 24" h. **5,700**

Marble Figure of Brother & Sister

Carpeaux, Jean-Baptiste, figure group of a youthful girl holding a crying boy, titled "Frere et Soeur" (Brother & Sister), inscribed "J.B. Carpeaux," France, ca. 1880, 25" h. (ILLUS.) **7,050**

Marble Bust of a Young Woman

Cipriani, A., bust of a young woman in Classical garb, her curled hair piled high on her head & tied w/a wide band, wearing a square-necked gown & swagged shawl, on a marble pedestal, late 19th c., 29 1/2" h. (ILLUS.) **4,800**

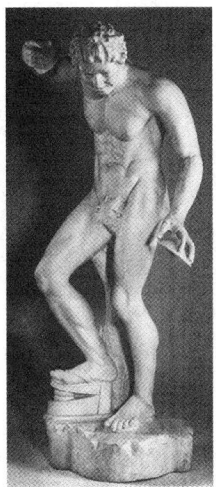

Faun with Cymbals Marble Statue

Faun with cymbals, standing faun nude except for a fig leaf, holding a cymbal in each hand & operating a foot pipe, near life-sized, after the antique, titled "Invitation to the Dance," late 19th - early 20th c., 59 1/2" h. (ILLUS.) **6,900**

Magni Marble Bust of a Young Woman

Magni, Pietro, bust of a young woman, a long scarf at the back of her head, wearing a necklace & fringed shawl, signed "Pro Pietro Magni Fe 1871 Milano," Italy, 29 1/2" h. (ILLUS.)...................................... **3,900**

Peyre, Charles Raphael, figure group of Venus & Cupid, she standing nude & leaning against a tall square column draped w/flowers, the young cupid w/large wings leaning down from the top to kiss her forehead, France, ca. 1885, 35 3/4" h...................................... **14,100**

Marble Bust of Young Victorian Girl

Stevenson, D.W., busts of a young boy & young girl, wearing mid-Victorian dress, signed "D.W. Stevenson A.R.S.A. 1884," 21" h., facing pr. (ILLUS. of girl) **3,600**

Other

Alabaster allegorical figure, a standing young maiden representing 'Night,' slightly curved pose, nude except for a light shear veil about her waist which she pulls up over her head, a nude putto at her feet, both resting on a high domed rockwork base, late 19th c., 39 1/2" h....... **9,000**

Alabaster, bust of a classical woman w/her hair pulled up & back & held w/a headband, looking to the right, bare chested, on socle base, late 19th c., 18" h. **440**

Alabaster, bust of a Neoclassical beauty, carved w/upswept hair w/chignon held w/a circlet, on a green marble socle, Italy, 20th c., 15" h.. **316**

Alabaster, figure of a woman, wreathed at the base w/flowers, Italy, 19th c., 23" h..... **2,070**

Terra Cotta Bust of Smiling Woman

Terra cotta, bust of a smiling young woman w/roses in her fair, facing right, titled "La

Rieuse aux Roses," by Jean-Baptiste Carpeaux, signed "J Bt Carpeaux," dated 1874, also signed "Atelier & Depot - 71 Rue Boileau - Auteuil - Paris," 21 1/2" h. (ILLUS.)...................... **3,290**

Terra cotta, figure group of a Bacchante & a putto, she standing carrying a putto w/dove under one arm & a basket of flowers in the other hand, on a round base, in the manner of Clodion, France, ca. 1880, 15 7/8" h....................... **1,880**

STEIFF TOYS & DOLLS

From a felt pincushion in the shape of an elephant, a world-famous toy company emerged. Margarete Steiff (1847-1909), a polio victim as a child and confined to a wheelchair, planned a career as a seamstress and opened a shop in the family home. However, her plans were dramatically changed when she made the first stuffed elephant in 1880. By 1886 she was producing stuffed felt monkeys, donkeys, horses and other animal forms. In 1893 an agent sold her toys at the Leipzig Fair. This venture was so successful that a catalog was printed and a salesman hired. Magarete's nephews and nieces became involved in the business, assisting in its management and the design of new items.

Through the years, the Steiff Company has produced a varied line including felt or plush animals, Teddy Bears, gnomes, elves, felt dolls with celluloid heads, Kewpie dolls and even radiator caps with animals or dolls attached as decoration. Descendants of the original family members continue to be active in the management of the company still adhering to Margarete's motto "For our children, the best is just good enough."

Bear, "Zotty" bear, curly mohair, fully jointed, glass eyes, embroidered nose, open mouth, shaved muzzle, tan pads, excelsior stuffing, 1950s, 11" h. **$173**

Boxer dog, cream mohair, a sitting pose, excelsior stuffing, shoe button eyes, black embroidered nose, mouth & claws, tan left ear & black right eye, ear button, ca. 1913, 8" h. (very minor fiber loss)............................... **345**

Camel, standing, ivory wool w/gold velvet legs & face, pale brown eyes, 13" h.............. **110**

Cat on wheels, plush grey-striped tabby, standing w/tail out at back, light green glass eyes, pink neck ribbon w/bell, button in ear, early 20th c., 10" l., 6 1/2" h. (minor wear, one wheel crooked)............... **1,210**

Chimpanzee, brown mohair w/white chin & felt face, orange glass eyes, feet & hands, jointed, ear button w/tag & name tag "Jocko," seated 10" h. **165**

Cocker Spaniel dog, mohair, excelsior stuffing, jointed head, black & white w/freckles, novelty glass eyes, embroidered nose & claws, 1930s, 12 3/4" l. (some spotty fur loss) **173**

Doe on wheels, mohair w/excelsior stuffing, unjointed, glass eyes, ear button, cast-iron spoke wheels, ca. 1913, 9" l. (remnants of black embroidered muzzle, traces of fur) **259**

Giraffe, ivory mohair w/orange spots, blue glass eyes, ear button, 13 1/4" h. **55**

Lamb on wheels, white curly wool body, white felt face, ears & legs, black bead

eyes, red ribbon w/bell around neck, steel frame on small cast-iron wheels, ca. 1918, 6 1/2" l. (bell dented, button missing, some spotty fur loss) **1,035**

Steiff Leopard & Lion

Leopard, ivory & tan mohair w/dark brown spots, embroidered nose, mouth & paws, green glass eyesm, 9" l. plus tail (ILLUS. right) **165**

Lion, tan & brown mohair w/dark brown mane & tail, embroidered nose, mouth & paws, orange glass eyes, "Leo" name tag, 15" l. plus tail (ILLUS. left) **220**

Lion & lioness, mohair, fully-jointed, glass eyes, excelsior stuffing, raspberry red embroidered nose, black mouth & claws, ear buttons, ca. 1925, each 12" l., pr. (claws missing on lion, general fur loss, lion repaired at neck joint)............................... **288**

Mountain goat, ivory mohair w/light brown felt horns, green glass eyes, ear button & remaining string from name tag, 7 1/2" l., 9 1/4" h.. **165**

Poodle dog, "Snobby," greyish tan mohair, black button nose & brown glass eyes, jointed head & legs, ear button, 8" l., 8 1/2" h... **83**

Rabbit, platinum mohair, standing up w/long ears, glass eyes, embroidered nose & mouth, ear button, 28" h. (squeak box not working) **1,265**

Rabbit skittle toy, cream velveteen, rust-colored markings, black bead eyes, on a half-round wooden base, ca. 1900, 5 3/4" h. (button missing, cloth somewhat soiled) **690**

Ram, white mohair body w/black mohair legs, tail & face, felt horns & ears, green glass eyes, holes in ear for button, 9" l., 8 1/4" h... **220**

Rhinoceros, "Nosy," brown velvet w/grey details, felt ears & horn, ear button w/tag & name tag, 13" l.................................. **105**

Scotch Terrier dog, standing, black mohair w/brown & white glass eyes, jointed head, ear button & piece of "Scotty" name tag on red collar w/bell, 5 3/4" l. **110**

Shetland pony, white darlon w/brown spots & yellow mane & tail, brown glass eyes, ear button & name tag marked "Sheddy," 10 2/4" l., 9 1/2" h............................. **193**

Snail, "Nelly," vinyl & velveteen plush, tags & button, ca. 1962, 5 3/4" l. (fading).............. **201**

Squirrel, ivory & brown mohair w/felt paws holding velvet nut, dark glass eyes, ear button w/name tag "Perri, Copyright Walt Disney Productions," 5 1/2" h. (minor wear) **193**

Teddy bear, ginger mohair, excelsior stuffing, fully jointed, glass eyes, embroidered nose & mouth, pad-less style, ca. 1910, 5 1/4" h. (remnants of fur) **374**

Teddy bear, light brown mohair & velvet paw pads, black bead eyes & embroidered nose, ear button, 9" l. (minor wear)...... **165**

Teddy bear, light yellow mohair, excelsior stuffing, fully jointed, black shoe button eyes, black embroidered nose, mouth & claws, tan felt pads, shaved muzzle, ca. 1915, 16" h. (spotty fur loss on front, extensive loss on back) **1,093**

Teddy bear, miniature, beige mohair, excelsior stuffing, black steel eyes, embroidered nose & mouth, fully jointed, no pad style, ear button, ca. 1910, 5 1/4" h. **863**

Teddy bear, tan mohair, excelsior stuffing, fully jointed, black steel eyes, black embroidered nose, mouth & claws, pad-less style, ca. 1905, 7 1/4" h. (spotty fur loss) **518**

Teddy bear, yellow mohair, excelsior stuffing, fully jointed, black metal eyes, embroidered black nose, mouth & claws, peach felt pads, ear button, ca. 1907, 25" h. (spotty fur loss, slight moth damage on pads) **3,795**

Teddy bear, yellow mohair, fully jointed, black steel eyes, black embroidered nose & mouth, pad-less style, ear button, ca. 1905, 5" h. (some spotty fur loss)... **1,093**

Teddy bear, golden mohair, jointed limbs, glass eyes, felt paw pads, embroidered nose & mouth, button in ear & cloth label, working voice box, 29" h. **935**

Turtle, "Slo," tan mohair w/pale underneath, felt claws, rubber shell & dark blue glass eyes, button & name tag, 7 1/4" l. **55**

Walrus, "Paddy," brown spotted mohair w/blue glass eyes & white rubber tusks, name tag, 5" h.. **55**

STEINS

Earthenware, cylindrical w/domed pewter cover w/ball thumbrest & flaring pewter base band, tin-glazed polychrome h.p. decoration of a horse in a landscape, Germany, late 18th c., 8" h. **$1,150**

Earthenware, cylindrical w/pewter domed cover w/ovoid thumbrest & pewter base band, polychrome h.p. decoration of a bird perched on a branch, Germany, 19th c., illegible impressed mark, 7 7/8" h... **690**

Mettlach Stein with Cavalier Portrait

Mettlach, No. 1078 (1526), PUG (print underglaze), decorated w/a large bust portrait of a cavalier wearing wide ruffled collar & w/pipe, stein, dice & cards, signed "Schlitt," domed pewter lid, 1/2 liter, 6 1/2" h. (ILLUS.)... **288**

Mettlach with Etched Cavalier Scene

Mettlach, No. 1796, etched decorated w/a main panel of a drinking, frolicking cavalier, inlaid pewter lid, signed "Warth," 1/2 liter, 8 7/8" h. (ILLUS.)..................................... **403**

Mettlach with King Gambrinus Scene

Mettlach, No. 2107, etched design of King Gambrinus on his throne holding a large stein, jeweled base, inlaid pewter lid, signed "Schlitt," 1 1/2 liter, 13 5/8" h. (ILLUS.) **805**

Mettlach Occupational Stein

Mettlach, No. 2719, etched occupational-style w/a large crest of bakers featuring a large pretzel, inlaid pewter lid, 1/2 liter, 7 3/4" h. (ILLUS.)... **1,150**

Mettlach, No. 966 (2184), PUG, scene of gnomes drinking & dancing, raised molded bands, domed pewter lid, 1/3 liter **248**

Mettlach, No. 2134, etched, scene of a gnome seated in a nest & holding two steins, inlaid lid, 1/2 liter, 7" h. **1,610**

Porcelain, cylindrical body molded w/raised bands of flowers flanking a central scrolled foliate band, blue glaze, hinged pewter cover w/ball thumbrest, K.P.M. mark, Germany 19th c., 6 1/4" h. **230**

STEREOSCOPES & STEREO VIEWS

Hand stereoscope viewers with an adjustable slide may be found at $30.00 to $50.00 each in good condition. Elaborate table models are priced much higher. Prices of view cards depend on the subject material and range from less than $1.00 to $10.00 or more.

Stereo Views

Civil war scenes, part of "War Views" series, titled "Lt. Gen. Grant at his headquarters" w/Brady standing at corner, "Ft. Corcoran, Va.," & "Signal Corp. Cobbs Hill," by E. & H.T. Anthony, group of 3 (very minor stains, Grant is light) **$330**

Jackson Iron Furnace, Michigan, No. 149 of a series "Gems of Lake Superior Scenery" by C.R. Brubaker, Marquette, Michigan, shows beehive ovens on the left, furnace in the background along the lakefront, town now a ghost town preserved by the State of Michigan, late 19th c. (some soil in lake area) **111**

Klondyke Goldrush Stereo Card

Klondyke scene, "Prospectors on the Allenkaket River," an animated view of miners pulling sleds, orange mat, Whiting, No. 1366, ca. 1900 .... **40**

Los Angeles, California, panoramic early view of the city, inscribed below image "View fr. High School - Los Angeles, Cal.," T.E. Stanton, photographer, ca. 1880, scarce **94**

"Maple Sugaring in Vermont," woodland scene w/open fire & boiling equipment shown w/workers, E. Anthoney, 308 Broadway, New York, New York, No. 193, pre-1859... **39**

Mining scene, "Drills at Work 1000 Feet under Butte," close-up view of hard rock miners w/large power drills, by N.A. Forsythe, Butte, Montana, ca. 1908 .... **61**

Pennsylvania Coal Miners, "Coal Mine No. 8," No. 164 of a series of views along the line of the Lehigh Valley Railroad, photo-

graphed & published by M.A. Kleckner, Bethlehem, Pennsylvania, eight miners sit & crouch at the low entrance to a mine, penciled on reverse "Purchased at Munch Chunck, August 28, 1871," ca. 1860s............... **55**

Santa Claus at fireplace, mid-Victorian Santa arranges a mountain of toys in front of fireplace, hand-tinted, grey square-cornered mount, marked on back "Christmas Series - #284. A bunch of toys he had flung on his back - And he looked like a peddler (sic) just opening his pack.," label on back "James Cremer's Stereoscopic Emporium, Phil." pasted over publisher's name on original label, ca. 1861, 3 1/3 x 6 3/4"......................... **74**

Rare Stereoscope Factory View

Stereoscope factory, interior view of a worker in apron in front of a large machine, labeled in period in on the back "Stereoscope works, Bennington, Vt.," yellow mount, rare subject, ca. 1868, corners worn (ILLUS.)... **232**

Early Smoky View of Pittsburgh

View from Pittsburgh's Point, panoramic view w/people on a rocky outcrop on the right overlooking a smoky view of Pittsburgh & the Ohio River, Keystone View Co. No. 23099, ca. 1900 (ILLUS.)................... **69**

TEDDY BEAR COLLECTIBLES

Theodore (Teddy) Roosevelt had become a national hero during the Spanish-American War by leading his "Rough Riders" to victory at San Juan Hill in 1898. He became the 26th president of the United States in 1901 when President McKinley was assassinated. The gregarious Roosevelt was fond of the outdoors and hunting. Legend has it that while on a hunting trip, soon after becoming President, he refused to shoot a bear cub because it was so small and helpless. The story was picked up by a political cartoonist who depicted President Roosevelt, attired in hunting garb, turning away and refusing to shoot a small bear cub. Shortly thereafter, toy plush bears began appearing in department stores labeled "Teddy's Bear" and they became an immediate success. Books on the adventures of "The Roosevelt Bears" were written and illustrated by Paul

Piper under the pseudonym of Seymour Eaton and this version of the Teddy Bear became a popular decoration on children's dishes.

Teddy bear, blond mohair plush w/swivel head, jointed limbs, black shoe button eyes, black floss mouth & nose w/horizontal stitching, felt paw pads w/five black floss claws, wears crocheted lace collar tied w/a ribbon, unmarked, 13" h. (nose possibly restitched, light wear on nose) **$600**

Teddy bear, cream mohair, excelsior stuffing, fully jointed, black shoe button eyes, brown embroidered nose, mouth & claws, tan felt pads, shaved muzzle, Ideal, ca. 1915, 13" h. (spotty fur loss, fiber damage on muzzle, chest, left leg & pads) **230**

Teddy bear, golden mohair plush w/excelsior stuffing, swivel head & jointed limbs, amber glass eyes, shaved muzzle w/floss nose & mouth, shaved mohair paw pads, non-working squeaker, unmarked, 13" h. (bottom of torso mended, mohair somewhat thin, small tear on one ankle)................... **170**

Teddy bear, light gold mohair, excelsior stuffing, fully jointed, glass eyes, remnants of nose, mouth & claw embroidery, beige felt pads, late 1920s - early 1930s, 19" h. (fur loss back of head, back & ears, fiber damage at neck edge & top of head)............... **259**

Teddy bear, yellow mohair, excelsior stuffing, fully jointed, glass eyes, traces of embroidered features, original cotton romper suit, Ideal, ca. 1920, 17" h. (fur loss, pads damaged) **230**

Teddy bear, golden mohair, jointed limbs, glass eyes, felt paw pads & embroidered nose & mouth, probably Steiff, 21 1/2" h. (minor wear).. **275**

Teddy bear on wheels, ginger mohair, excelsior stuffing, yes-no style, embroidered nose & mouth, felt pads, on thin steel frame & small solid metal wheels, Schuco, 1920s, 11 1/2" l., 9 1/2" h. (eyes missing, spotty overall fur loss, no fur on tail)................ **374**

TELEVISION SETS

Admiral 10" Bakelite Table Model

Admiral, 10" Bakelite tabletop model, late 1940s, unbroken (ILLUS.)............................ **$125**

Admiral 19T1, 7" Bakelite tabletop model, 1948... **150**

Admiral 20X122, 10" Bakelite console model, no cracks **350**

Andrea 1-F-5, tabletop model w/5" CRT, 1938 .... **4,000**

Andrea CO-VK15, console w/15" picture tube, late 1940s... **100**

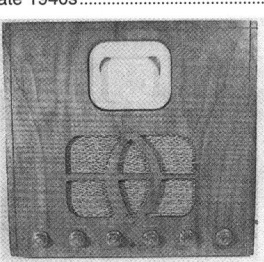

Andrea 1939 Kit Television

Andrea KTE-5, kit television w/5" tube, 1939 (ILLUS.) **3,500**

Automatic TV-490, cloth-covered 7" portable w/built-in magnifier...................................... **500**

Automatic TV-707, 7" blonde wooden set, unusual **400**

Automatic TV-710, 7" console model, rare style **750**

CBS Columbia 12CC2, experimental color-drum set, ca. 1951, very rare .... **4,500+**

CBS Columbia 205C1, color set w/19" round CRT, 1955... **550**

CBS Columbia 22C05, black & white console w/21" picture tube, 1955...................... **55**

DuMont 183, pre-war w/14" CRT & four-channel tuner, 1937, rare.......................... **5,500**

DuMont RA-102, Clifton 12" console, 1947, unusual **850**

DuMont Chatham Table Model

DuMont RA-103, Chatham tabletop model w/trapezoidal case (ILLUS.) **350**

DuMont RA-103 D3, square version of 12" tabletop model **75**

DuMont RA-109, large screen console model, typical **75**

DuMont RA-119, Royal Sovereign 30" console, good CRT, 1952 .... **750**

Emerson 571 Wooden Tabletop

Emerson 571, wooden 10" tabletop model
(ILLUS.).. **100**
Emerson 608, console style w/pop-up 16"
screen... **550**

FADA 880 Projection Television

FADA 880, unusual projection TV
w/stepped top (ILLUS.)..................................... **450**

General Electric No. 800 Model

General Electric 800, Bakelite 10" tabletop
model, streamlined case, unusual
(ILLUS.)... **400**
General Electric 802, 10" console, screen
& large AM dial, 1947 .... **175**
General Electric 806, 10" tabletop model,
tall w/glass front plate.................................... **100**
General Electric 901, very large & heavy
projection set, 1947, complete **550**
General Electric HM-171, 5" tabletop mod-
el, 1938.. **4,500**
General Electric Hotpoint, painted metal
case, various nice colors, clean, mid-
1950s, each **85**
Jenkins Model 100, 1932 scanning disc
TV, complete... **3,500**
Jenkins Model R-400, scanning disc TV
w/lens projecting image................................. **4,500**
JVC 3100D, Video Capsule, pyramid-
shaped set, 1970s.. **400**
JVC 3240, Video Sphere, ball-shaped............... **200**
Motorola 14K1, simple style console set,
mid-1950s... **50**
Motorola 19P1, early, large portable tran-
sistor TV, 1954... **125**
Motorola VT-105, 10" wooden tabletop
model, stepped top, 1948 .... **450**

Motorola VT-73 Table Model Set

Motorola VT-73, 7" table model set, 1947
(ILLUS.) **150**

Panasonic TR-005 TV

Panasonic TR-005, flying saucer-shaped
table model, 1970s, mint (ILLUS.)................. **500**
Philco 48-1000, unusual stepped-top 10"
table model.. **650**

Philco 50-700 Tabletop Model

Philco 50-700, wide wooden case 7" table-
top model (ILLUS.)... **450**
Philco 50-701, Bakelite tabletop model w/7"
screen, very clean.. **350**
Philco Predicta, blonde barber pole-style
console model, mint.. **750**
Philco Predicta, tabletop model, metal
case, working condition.................................. **400**
Philco Predicta, Tandem model, two-piece
set, 21" CRT on a long white cord, as
found... **400**
Philco Safari, Model H2010, first transistor
television... **200**
RCA 630-TS, 10" tabletop model, RCA's
first tabletop, 1946 .... **300**

RCA 721 Wooden Tabletop Model

RCA 721, 10" wooden tabletop model
(ILLUS.)... **150**
RCA 8PC41, pop-up screen projection set,
1948... **300**
RCA 8PT, small metal portable set **200**
RCA 8T244, wooden 10" tabletop model
w/sliding doors **175**
RCA CT-100, color set w/15" CRT, picture
tube works, 1954 .... **750**

1939 RCA TRK-12 Console TV

RCA TRK-12, Art Deco-style wooden con-
sole w/mirror in lift lid, 1939 (ILLUS.) **4,500**
RCA TRK-9, console set w/five-channel
tuner, 1939 .... **5,000**

Sentinel Portable Wooden Set

Sentinel, 7" portable wooden set, ca. 1949
(ILLUS.)... **175**

Zenith Blonde Porthole Console TV

Zenith, blonde porthole style console set
(ILLUS.) **400**
Zenith H2229, 17" rectangular screen set **65**
Zenith Jackson, G2437, 16" porthole con-
sole model **350**
Zenith Marlborough, huge combination
w/12" porthole screen **650**

TEXTILES

Bedspreads

Cotton, white candlewicked design, rectangular form composed of three panels
stitched together centering an elaborately worked Tree of Life design originating
from a double-handled pot, surrounded
by a border of undulating grape leaves &
vines, swags & floral designs, made by
Martha Dabney Chisholm, probably
Charleston, South Carolina, ca. 1814,
160 x 192" (light staining, several re-
paired areas)... **$4,600**

Early Cotton Chintz Bedspread

Cotton chintz, whole-cloth coverlet-type, in
shades of brown & red on a natural
ground, hand-quilted, constructed of
three panels w/designs of large urns
w/birds surrounded by flowering vines,
mid-19th c., minor stain, 79 x 90 3/4"
(ILLUS.) **2,070**

Early Candlewicked Bedspread

Embroidered candlewick, white on white embroidered decoration, a central cartouche w/floral urn, medallion above w/name & date surrounded by grapevine border, further framed by grapevine & tulip border & center floral urn, by Eliza Spink, Auburn, New York, 1829, small holes, light staining, repairs, 108 x 112" (ILLUS.).. **1,840**

Early Glazed Chintz Bedspread

Glazed chintz, block-printed Palm & Pheasant design printed at Bannister Hall, England in shades of madder, green, ivory & brown, backed w/brown striped fabric & finished w/woven twill binding, very minor fading & staining, early 19th c., 11 x 114 1/2" (ILLUS. of part) **2,070**

Coverlets

Jacquard, double woven, one-piece, a central design of graduated leafy scrolling rings surrounded by spread-winged eagles w/banners, scrolls & domed buildings in border, flower-like sun corner blocks, dated 1857, navy blue & natural white, minor stains, 86 x 94" (ILLUS. top next column)....................................... **715**

Jacquard Coverlet w/Eagles & Rings

Jacquard, double woven, one-piece, the center w/bands of slender stems & blossoms w/pairs of arched leaves on each, pairs of facing birds & cherry sprigs around the borders, corners labeled "1839 Ohio," navy blue & natural white, attributed to Abram Allen, Wilmington, Ohio, 78" sq. (minor wear & stains) **2,475**

Coverlet with Blocks & Floral Borders

Jacquard, double woven, two-piece, a central design of nine square medallions & herringbone bands framed by double borders w/pots of flowers & single borders w/flowers & foliage, flying pheasants in corners, tomato red & natural white, 90" sq. (ILLUS.) **715**

Floral Medallion Coverlet Dated 1841

Jacquard, double woven, two-piece, central design of rows of large floral medallions alternating w/smaller flowerheads, birds & tree borders, corners labeled "Made by P.H. For Mary S. Hixson, U.M.T. - Bethel 1841," navy blue & natural white, minor stains, wear, fringe on end only, 76 x 86" (ILLUS.)............................. 660

Jacquard, double woven, two-piece, large delicate floral medallions w/slender leafy scroll borders, spread-winged eagle & Masonic borders, corners labeled "Agriculture & Manufactures Are the Foundation of Our Independence," navy blue & natural white (no fringe, minor damage w/wear & some repair, both ends turned & whip-stitched) 622

Floral Medallions & Eagles Coverlets

Jacquard, double woven, two-piece, overall center design w/rows of large stylized floral medallions alternating w/small diamond designs, eagle & tree borders, corners labeled "M. Sharp - W.C.N.J. - L.M.T. Bethel Philla - RD. 1835," navy blue & natural white, wear, minor edge damage, worn fringe, 78 x 88" (ILLUS.) 770

Coverlet with Unusual Border Designs

Jacquard, double woven, two-piece, overall center rows of large four-rose clusters on leafy stems, vining flowers on side borders & spread-winged eagles above cats & dogs on end borders, corners labeled

"E. Willse 1831," navy blue & natural white, very worn w/repair & replaced fringe, 69 x 83" (ILLUS.).......................... 660

Jacquard, double woven, two-piece, rose & floral medallions in the center, bird & rose borders, corners labeled "G. Stich - Newark - Ohio - 1838," tomato red, navy blue & natural white, 73 x 83" (stains, wear, damage, fringe incomplete) 440

Jacquard, double woven, two-piece, the field w/various shaped foliate medallions on a figured striped background, geometric scrolled & stylized flower border, fringed on three sides, dark blue, magenta, gold & white, mid-19th c., 85 x 97" 230

Jacquard, single weave, one-piece, large central floral medallion w/large eagles in each corner above corner pineapple & scrolling leafy border, bottom edge labeled "Manufactured by H.F. Stager & Son - Fast Colors - Mount Joy, Lancaster County, Penn.," bright colors of red, green, navy blue & natural white, 80 x 84" (worn sewn-on bottom fringe).......... 440

Jacquard, single weave, one-piece, rows of large star medallions within leafy rings, building borders & birds, trees & roses borders, corners labeled "Daniel Bury, New Portage, Ohio, 1846," red, navy blue & natural white, old note attached, 76 x 90" (minor stains, little fringe wear) 880

Jacquard, single weave, two-piece, floral & star medallions in rows w/bird & rose tree borders, corners labeled "Gabriel Rausher, Delaware County, Ohio 1845," navy blue, light blue, red & natural white, 72 x 83 (wear, stains, repair)........................ 385

Jacquard, single weave, two-piece, four-rose medallions w/a vintage border, corners labeled "CHS. Heily, Wayne County, Ohio," navy blue & natural white, 72 x 83" (stains, wear, some damage) 330

Jacquard, single weave, two-piece, large floral border w/eagle corners labeled "Bellville, Ohio 1850," tomato red, royal blue & natural white, 75 x 82" (minor wear, slight moth damage) 660

Jacquard, single weave, two-piece, rows of large floral medallions in the center, vintage vine border, corners labeled "F.J. Scholl - Uniontown - Stark Co. - Ohio 1848," navy blue, deep salmon & natural white, 68 x 84" 468

Jacquard, single weave, two-piece, rows of large starburst medallions alternating w/smaller geometric floral medallions, facing birds or buildings borders, corners labeled "Sidney, Shelby County, Ohio," navy blue, tomato red, dark greyish blue & natural white, 68 x 92" (minor stains)......... 935

Jacquard, two-piece, large flower & leaf medallions w/a starburst center, pairs of birds & roses borders, corners labeled "Gabriel Rausher, May 10, Delaware, Ohio 1855," red, blue & natural white, 43 x 72" (wear, edge damage, fringe incomplete).................... 385

Jacquard, two-piece, rows of starbursts centering large flower & leaf clusters, double bird & flowering tree border, corner blocks signed "C. Lochman Hamburg, Berks County 1835," tomato red & natural white, 80 x 98" (few stains, stitched repair, small hole) **413**

Jacquard, single weave, one-piece, bands w/blocks of 24 scrolled leaf clusters w/tiny blossoms, flowering plant border, star corner blocks signed "E.K." & "1845," green, gold, navy blue & tomato red, 82 x 96" (wear, stains) **303**

Linsey-woolsey, overall gold quilted w/diamond blocks set in diagonal rows flanked by scrolling feather designs on a ground of diagonal lines, American, early 19th c., 98 x 99" (minor staining, holes) **4,888**

Early Linsey-Woolsey Coverlet

Linsey-woolsey, the center constructed of a glazed brown & tan woven fabric in a leafy design, the salmon-colored wide border decorated w/a crewelwork multicolored floral vine, mustard-colored backing, quilted in diamond designs, a paper tag identfies maker as "Annie Brown, ca. 1780," minor losses, 84 1/2 x 92" (ILLUS.) **14,950**

Overshot, double woven, two-piece, summer-winter style, Snowball & Nine Patch pattern w/pine tree borders, navy blue, red & natural white, 64 x 90" (minor wear, some fringe damage) **605**

Overshot, double woven, two-piece, summer-winter type, geometric, dark navy blue & natural white, 74 x 96" (minor wear) **358**

Overshot, double woven, two-piece, summer-winter type, snowflake design divided by double-band blocks, tomato red, dark navy blue & natural white, 80 x 100" (top edge w/tattered brown print binding) **220**

Overshot, two-piece, Optic design in blocks & bars, navy blue, red & natural white, w/fringe, 78 x 92" **303**

Overshot, two-piece, Optical patt., navy blue & natural white, fringe on one end, 70 x 86" (minor wear) **193**

Linens & Needlework

American flag, fifteen-star, hand-sewn wool w/cotton stars, fourteen cut-out & overcast, one double-faced, hand-sewn

grommets, 19th c., 30 x 66" (soiled, minor fading, fabric loss) **2,990**

Early Hand-sewn American Flag

American flag, hand-sewn homespun cotton, double-faced w/sixteen six-point stars on an indigo field, rope grommets, fading, ca. 1800, 37 x 66" (ILLUS.) **4,600**

American flag, thirteen-star, handsewn wool w/double appliqued cotton stars, canvas hoist w/pierced holes, mid-19th c., 60 x 100" (soiled, fabric loss) . **2,185**

American flag, twenty-star, hand-sewn cotton w/double-faced stars, reinforced w/machine stitching, four cotton double-faced grommets, early 19th c., 38 1/2 x 53 1/2" (minor stains, small tears) **4,313**

Bell pull, pettit point, a floral design in pinks, golds, blues & greens on an ivory ground, w/a large tassel w/floral medallions, good condition, 19th c., 59" l. **220**

Blanket, homespun wool, a navy blue & natural white checkered design, two-piece construction, 70 x 84" (small holes, wear) **165**

Blanket, homespun wool, natural white w/a black pinstripe grid design, 56" sq. (holes) **94**

Blanket, homespun wool, overall tiny white checks w/thin black borders, two-piece construction, 68 x 76" (wear, holes) **330**

Blanket, homespun wool, plaid blue & tomato red design, two-piece construction, 72 x 78" (small holes, repairs) **193**

Blanket, homespun wool, two-piece construction, fringe at one end, plaid design in tomato red & medium blue, 80 x 88" **528**

Blanket, wool, two-piece, woven in a checked design of butternut & rust w/a striped border, early 19th c., 79 x 82" (minor loss, repair) **1,150**

Blanket, woven all-wool, two-piece, plaid design in tomato red, navy blue & green, 68 x 80" (overall & fringe wear, small holes) **220**

Blanket, woven wool, a red & white plaid design, hand-sewn w/two-panel construction, fringe at one end, American, mid-19th c., 80 x 96" (minor losses) **374**

Blanket, woven wool, plaid design in red, blue & off white, hand-sewn in two-panel construction, American, early 19th c., 68 x 83 1/2" (minor losses) **259**

Bolster cover, homespun linen w/an overall small blue & white check design, hand-sewn seams, 18 x 55" (some seams loose) **138**

Chair seat cover fragment, crewelwork, an overall multicolored floral design on a blue ground, worked in wool yarn on toweling, 19th c., 21 x 25 1/2" (minor losses to edges) **4,600**

Dresser scarf, drawnwork edging, technique covers the exposed threads with a dense pattern, making the drawnwork both beautiful & reasonably durable, good quality, small holes in the cloth detract from the value, 24 x 38"...................... **25-45**

Dresser scarf, drawnwork w/an unusual geometric design, 22 x 42" **75-85**

Early Pennsylvania Family Register

Family register, needlework on linen, a central small square register w/family names & dates surrounded by a wide border w/foliate, bird & geometric designs above inspirational verses near the bottom above a lower panel of various animals amid trees, meandering & geometric floral borders, framed, signed "Elizabeth H. Kay's Work, 1809," Pennsylvania, toning, scattered staining, fading, 21 5/8 x 22 3/4" (ILLUS.) **3,738**

Lap robe, velvet & silk-embroidered, pieced in a Windmill Blades variant, the centers w/embroidered flora & fauna, the border w/padded silk roses & chenille embroidered leaves, pieced scalloped edge w/silk embroidered fans & tassels, decorative embroidery throughout, backed w/olive green velvet, dated & initialed "1885 CLH," 56 x 58 1/2" (minor losses) ... **4,313**

Mattress cover, homespun cotton, an overall delicate blue & white check pattern, machine-sewn, 19th c., 68 x 73" (small holes)... **165**

Show towel, homespun linen, long rectangular form, embroidered w/pink & blue diamonds, trees, urns of flowers, crowns & hearts, six embroidered line dividers beneath w/triple fringed bottom, dated "1806," 17 5/8 x 61" (several small holes, minor stains).. **193**

Show towel, homespun linen, long rectangular form w/embroidered hearts in stars, pots of flowers, ladies & birds, bottom fringe, signed & dated "1848 with Seaver," 15 x 72" (staining) **248**

Early American Silk Embroidery

Silk embroidery, a central large cornucopia filled w/flowers surrounded by scattered blossoms & two butterflies all within an oval floral wreath border, worked in mulitcolored silk threads on beige silk ground, signed "Polly Chapin 1792," New England, framed, toning, fading, 17 1/4 x 20 3/4" (ILLUS.) **690**

Arts & Crafts Table Centerpiece

Table centerpiece, embroidered linen, Arts & Crafts style w/scalloped rim & wide border band w/curved designs in pastel colors, early 20th c., 28" d. (ILLUS.) **585**

Table mat, appliqued, a whimsical design of various symbols & designs including hearts, on a tan cotton ground w/black sawtooth border, late 19th - early 20th c., 39 1/2 x 67" (staining, losses) **3,450**

Table mat, appliqued & embroidered, multicolored woolen fabric floral sprays appliqued to a black ground in a block design w/meandering border, late 19th c., 30 1/2 x 47 1/2" (losses) **1,840**

Tablecloth, crocheted, many produced by homemakers in the U.S. using patterns typical of Eastern European designs, early to mid-20th c. **50-150**

Tablecloth, linen, two-tone grey & natural woven design w/a chain & lattice design w/ivy leaves, 82 x 116"...................................... **121**

Tablecloth, linen w/white on white cut-out & embroidery in a floral & vintage grape design, scalloped edge, 72 x 113" **220**

Tablecloth, white linen w/overall cut-work flowers in the center, machine chain-stitch embroidery, early 20th c., 80 x 106" **165**

Textile fragment, woven wool in a plaid design in brown w/salmon, bluish green & black threads, 19th c., about 38 x 300" **575**

Textile fragment, woven wool in a plaid design in red, orange, olive green & dark brown, 19th c., 33 1/2 x 36" (minor losses) **431**

Needlework Pictures

American eagle, silk on silk, the large bird w/raised wings stands on a large American shield, the tops of three flags & poles above the head & a narrow arched banner above the bird inscribed "E Pluribus Unum," on a mauve ground, possibly China Trade, early 19th c., in a narrow early worn giltwood frame, picture 21 x 23" **715**

Buildings in Landscape Needlework

Buildings in landscape, silk embroidery depicting a large church on the left & a large Federal house flanked by trees on the right, fenced garden, duck pond & gentleman walking his dog in the foreground, wide vining floral border, signed "by Anna Margaret Houghtaling aged 9 years 1835," America, unfinished, toning, fading, 16 1/2" sq. (ILLUS.) **2,875**

English Needlepoint of Children

Children in landscape, silk embroidery of two young girls w/a pet bird, birdcage & dog in a landscape w/a large tree on the left & cottage in the right background, worked in silk & chenille threads, watercolor on ivory portraits, paper hands & arms, in an églomisé mat, framed, England, early 19th c., fading, staining, minor losses, 10 1/4 x 14" (ILLUS.)............... **1,610**

Fishing Couple in Landscape

Figures in landscape, silk embroidery titled at the bottom "The Anglers Delight," a standing man & woman in 18th c. attire at the center in front of a large tree, he holding a long fishing rod & their catch, a dog & basket in the foreground, a man w/a fishing net by a river in the left background w/a cottage beyond, watercolor features, horizon & sky, solidly stitched silk threads in shades of green, gold & blue w/an oval floral in foliate border, black églomisé mat w/corner florettes, framed, America or England, early 19th c., minor toning & fading, 13 x 15 1/2" (ILLUS.) **2,875**

Lady Elizabeth Gray & King Edward IV, silk on silk, a large exterior scene w/a number of men, women & children in front of a low trellis wall w/a Gothic tower in center background, inscribed along the bottom on a black mat "Lady Elizabeth Gray Petitioning King Edward IV for the Restoration of her husband's lands," painted & embroidered in tones of brown, tan & blue, in probably original giltwood & gesso frame, Philadelphia, ca. 1820, 28 x 30" (mat glass replaced by title original).. **21,450**

Landscape, silk thread on silk, a broad landscape view w/a young lady gathering roses beside a lake in the foreground w/large ruins across the lake & a large structure shown in the distance, solidly stitched w/watercolor features & sky, in an oval format w/églomisé mat, framed, England, 19th c., 6 1/4 x 9 1/4" (losses to silk, toning, mat restored) **403**

Landscape scene on silk, a pensive young lady & her black & white dog seated in a landscape, solidly stitched in silk threads, watercolor features & sky, worked in an oval format, tacked to a padded backing, in an églomisé tablet, framed, England or America, early 19th c., 6 1/2 x 9" (minor toning, tablet restored) **460**

Landscape scene on silk, depicting a pensive young woman seated w/her brown dog in a landscape, solidly stitched silk threads, fabric costume, watercolor features & sky, in an oval format, églomisé mat, framed, England, 19th c., 9 1/2 x 11 1/2" (minor staining, mat restored) **546**

Landscape w/people, a round image w/a close-up view of a young couple in classical dress w/a child under a grape arbor, silk thread on a silk ground highlighted w/hand-painted features & sky, surrounded by a wide églomisé tablet trimmed w/floral clusters & inscribed "Wrought by Dorothy Harris at Mrs. Saunders & Miss Beach's Academy Dorchester, 1809," Massachusetts, in an early narrow giltwood frame, image 9 1/2" d. (damage to tablet) **4,025**

Map of the world, silk on satin, central view of two halves of the globe labeled "The World with all the Modern Discoveries," the hemispheres & famous sea voyages worked in black thread, ink & floss, a continuous wide floral border in satin stitch colors of blues, browns, gold, green, etc., floral work incomplete w/some flowers only in ink outline, narrow black églomisé mat & molded giltwood frame, early 19th c., 24 x 28 1/2" (wear, fading, damage to satin) **1,045**

Elaborate Memorial Embroidery

Memorial scene, silk needlework depicting three Neoclassical urn-form memorials w/flanking willows & weeping figures beside them, each memorial embroidered w/names & dates, Rehobeth, Massachusetts, early 19th c., framed, toning, fading, small tears, fabric loss, 18 x 21 1/4" (ILLUS.) **3,450**

Mourning scene, silk embroidery scene of a young woman leaning against a tall monument inscribed "Betsy H. Wallace," the whole within a black glass mat w/gilded trumpeting angels & flowerheads in corners, worked in greens, gold, brown & blue threads, painted highlights, worked by Mary Wallace, probably Boston, dated 1799, framed, 15 1/2 x 19" (ILLUS. top next column) **9,775**

Fine American Mourning Picture

Quilts

Applique 'broderie perse' design, appliqued w/a large & elegantly wrought tree of life w/spade-shaped leaves & flowering blossoms, birds perched on the trunk & on the boughs, the whole mounted on a linen ground heightened w/diagonal line & outline quilting, within printed feather-patterned chintz, probably Southern, late 18th - early 19th c., 92 x 100" (some staining & discoloration) **7,800**

Appliqued Album quilt, rectangular, worked in various red, blue, green, yellow, orange, beige & purple cottons & calicos in sixteen squares of pieced & appliqued berried floral wreaths, urns issuing flowers, Odd Fellows emblems, stars & a spreadwing eagle clutching crossed American flags & an inscription "Grand. Lodge - of Maryland," w/red sashing & red sawtooth double border, channel, diamond, foliate & meandering channel quilting, Baltimore, Maryland, dated 1848, 80 1/4 x 82 1/2" **7,475**

Appliqued American Eagle Quilt

Appliqued American Eagle patt., composed of red 'stencil-cut' American eagles grasping arrows & an oak leaf below tulips & rainbows of red & yellow, mounted on a white cotton ground w/diagonal line quilting, probably Pennsylvania, mid-19th c., 89 x 92" (ILLUS.) **6,600**

Appliqued California Rose patt., worked in pink, green & yellow & pink calicos, w/stylized flowers flanked by leaves & issuing leafy stems w/further flowers on a white ground quilted w/Princess Feather wreaths centering diamond quilting, all framed w/a meandering pink & calico scalloped border issuing stylized tulips & Princess Feather quilting, bound in dark & light pink & green, together w/a ca. 1858 award medal in leather case, by Rhoda Beatty Whitcomb, ca. 1853, 72 3/4 x 91 1/2" **1,495**

Eagle & Flowering Vines Quilt

Appliqued Eagle & Vining Flowers patt., decorated at the center w/a large spread-winged eagle trimmed w/stars & holding flowers all within an oval reserve of vining tulips & red-petaled flowers framed by a narrow rectangular inner border surrounded by vining tulips & blossoms within a narrow outer border, hand-stitched in red, yellow & green on a natural white ground, ca. 1930, some stains, 82 x 100" (ILLUS.) **1,375**

Floral Vines Appliqued Quilt

Appliqued Floral Vines & Vases patt., overall flowering leafy vines w/a star-like formation in the center & vines issuing from vases around the border, worked in green & red on a white ground w/trapunto in applied pieces, 19th c., minor restoration, 77 x 84" (ILLUS.) **1,045**

Appliqued Hawaiian-style Quilt

Appliqued Hawaiian-style patt., composed of nine large blocks w/large leafy starbursts in each in red on a white ground bordered by red sashing, white backing, conforming quilted design, mid-19th c., minor staining, 84" sq. (ILLUS.) **546**

Appliqued Leaves Pattern Quilt

Appliqued Leaves patt., composed of an overall design of bands of moss blue leaves within a matching border all on a white ground, hand-stitched, minor stains, 78 x 80" (ILLUS.) **275**

Appliqued Lyre patt., composed of 20 large lyres in green & goldrod w/a heart design in the base of each, on a well-quilted white ground, machine-sewn knit binding, 82 x 86" (minor stains, some greens slightly faded) **715**

Appliqued North Carolina Lily patt., worked in yellow, red & green cotton & calico, the design centering 16 floral blocks set w/alternating diamonds all in a red Flying Geese inner border framed by a white-on-white outer border w/Princess

Feather, channel & scroll quilting, all bound in red, 19th c., 76 3/4 x 77 1/2"....... **1,380**

Appliqued Oak Leaf Medallion patt., composed of ten oak leaf medallions in red & green & all but two w/yellow centers, on a white quilted background, one leaf w/a printed label, 64 x 82" (replaced binding, minor stains).. **385**

Appliqued Occupational design, composed of a variety of red, yellow, blue, green & white printed & solid calico patches arranged in a series of 42 squares, appliqued & pieced w/symbols of a variety of occupations including winemaker, dressmaker, a Zoave, blacksmith, mason, carpenter & more, each square w/an inscribed name of the maker, also a square w/an appliqued black silk horse entitled "Father's Dolly," each within calico sashings on a white cotton ground w/outline quilting, probably New York, dated 1861-63, 80 x 99" (some minor breaks & discoloration)......................... **7,200**

Appliqued Peony variant patt., stylized peony flowers in red & green calico machine-stitched to pieced white blocks, quilted in a square grid design, white backing bound w/green print cloth, 19th c., 74 x 89".. **460**

Pinwheel & Flowers Quilt

Appliqued Pinwheel patt., composed of four large Princess Feather pinwheel designs w/red & green alternating arms & an orange center, the border w/large bouquets of flowers w/peacocks, flying doves & spread-winged eagles all worked w/button hole stitches & reverse applique on a white ground worked w/floral, wreath & linear quilting, crossstitched owner's label on the back signed "Mary Price died Age 87 - Grandmother's work in 1850 - Keepsake for Francis Fowlar - Barnsville. O - J.B. 1916," 80 x 96" (ILLUS.).. **3,450**

Appliqued Pinwheel patt., composed of nine large stylized pinwheels in red & green calico on a white ground well-quilted w/feather circles, old typewritten label noted it was made by Diana Wolf in the 1850s, 90 x 94" (minor stains)................... **1,265**

Red & White Princess Feather Quilt

Appliqued Princess Feather patt., a large spiraling Princess Feather starburst in the center surrounded by pairs of curled Princess Feather patches alternating w/smaller stars, bright red pieces w/channel quilting on a white ground w/diamond quilting, red binding, Cincinnati, Ohio, late 19th c., 84 x 86 1/2" (ILLUS.) **4,370**

Appliqued Princess Feather Quilt

Appliqued Princess Feather patt., four large swirled Princess Feather clusters around a small center star & within a narrow outer border of triangles, handstitched in red & green, minor stains, 78 x 80" (ILLUS.).. **660**

Appliqued Sunflower Medallion patt., composed of ten round goldenrod & green sunflower blossoms scattered on a white quilted ground framed by a swag & heart border, flowers w/hooked black centers, natural ground, unwashed, 76 x 88" (minor stains) **468**

Tulip & Floral Wreath Quilt

Appliqued Tulip & Flower Wreath patt., composed of nine wreaths of tulip & floral blossoms & leaves alternating w/pairs of tulip blossoms & florettes, a floral stem in each corner & sawtooth border band, worked in red, green & yellow calico on a white quilted ground, red border, stains, 19th c., 93" sq. (ILLUS.) **1,760**

Tulip Medallions Appliqued Quilt

Appliqued Tulip Medallions patt., composed of nine radiating tulip medallions in green, red & goldenrod w/four small red squares around the center, a red border & binding, finely quilted w/floral scrolls & braided bands on border, original pencil marks, minor stains, 19th c., 78 x 80" (ILLUS.).. **880**

Appliqued Quilt with Tulips

Appliqued Tulip patt., composed of rows of 16 tulip blooms on leafy stems in red & yellow w/green print leaves & stems, on a finely quilted background including meandering feathers design, narrow inner & outer green sawtooth borders, minor stains & wear, 92" sq. (ILLUS.) **1,540**

Vintage Pattern Appliqued Quilt

Appliqued Vintage patt., composed of nine vining grapevine blocks within a wide border w/grapevines & large scrolled leaves, worked in green & red w/puffed grapes, white ground w/fine princess feather & tulip quilting, original pencil lines, red edging, 19th c., minor stains, 92 x 94" (ILLUS.) **2,310**

Unusual Elaborate Crazy Quilt

Crazy quilt, composed of 16 blocks of green, blue, pink, yellow, red, brown & beige silk patches arranged in the blocks, each w/a soldier in dress uniform displaying his country's flag, each square embellished w/raised work embroidery of floral sprays, the whole surrounded by a yellow border, together w/two pillow shams each decorated w/a central medallion embroidered w/a Colonial scene, late 19th c., 77 x 78" quilt, the set (ILLUS. of quilt) **4,025**

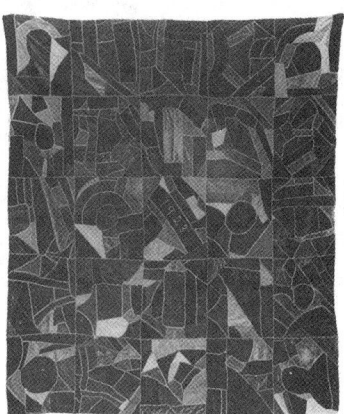

1920s Dated Crazy Quilt

Crazy quilt, composed of 25 blocks composed of random patches mostly in velvet, corduroy & some felt in blues, purples, red, browns, greens, black & grey, stitched date of 1923, blue backing w/printed flowers, minor wear, 72 x 82" (ILLUS.) **248**

Fine Appliqued Crib Quilt

Crib quilt, appliqued designs of a large leafy floral wreath enclosing four seated cats & a center flowerhead, a rooster in each corner, worked in blue, red, mustard brown & grey solid cotton & calico fabric, cats w/embroidered ears, eyes, brown whiskers & nose, all on a white ground, roosters w/embroidered legs & feet, quilted overall w/floral rosettes & leaves, bound in blue calico, early 20th c., 32 3/4 x 33 3/4" (ILLUS.) **2,760**

Crib quilt, pieced Bow Ties patt., worked in red, white & variously printed blue cottons, centering twenty alternating bow tie squares, the whole framed by a conforming triple border of red, white & blue, overall channel, shell, leaf & double-diamond quilting & self-bound in red, Pennsylvania, 1920-30, 31 x 32" **2,530**

Dolly Madison Workbox Crib Quilt

Crib quilt, pieced Dolly Madison Workbox variant, composed of 16 squares of pattern divided by bands all within a triangular block border, in shades of red, brown, cream & violet on a natural ground, minor stains & edge wear, 42" sq. (ILLUS.) **248**

Crib quilt, pieced Nine Patch patt., composed of black sateen w/patches in solid colors of brown, red, blue & green, Amish, Ohio, 39 1/2 x 47 3/4" **440**

Crib quilt, pieced Robbing Peter to Pay Paul patt., composed of red & white blocks w/green border, hand-stitched, ready to hang, 37 x 43" **275**

Crib quilt, pieced Lone Star patt., composed of multicolored patches on a pink calico ground, 39 x 52" (overall wear) **275**

Linsey-woolsey, deep indigo blue w/olive green wool w/some other fabrics used for backing, 82 x 92" (wear, holes, patches) .. **1,678**

Pieced Bar patt., composed of maroon & slate blue wool flannel & cotton patches, the field w/finely stitched feather, diamond & sunflower quilting, the back w/grey & white printed cotton, Amish, probably Lancaster, Pennsylvania, late 19th c., 76 x 84" **3,900**

Pieced Bar patt., composed of three wide green central stripes within a red frame w/purple block corners, in flannel, the border stitched w/stylized baskets & stars, Amish, probably Lancaster County, Pennsylvania, ca. 1910, 70 x 81" **4,800**

Pieced Barn Raising patt., composed of brown & blue print blocks on a white ground w/feather quilting, 82 x 85" (very minor wear) **825**

Pieced Bars and Nine Patch patt., worked in green, crimson, turquoise, black & blue wool twill centering the combined pattern w/a dark green border, the Bars w/rope & channel quilting, surrounded by an inner border of rosette quilting w/a scallop-quilted edge, an outer border of diamond-patterned basket, heart & rosette quilting, centered by turquoise binding, Amish, Lancaster County, Pennsylvania, ca. 1910, 75 3/8 x 76" **14,950**

Pieced Basket patt., rows of blue & white baskets w/blue border, 72 x 75" (stains & minor damage) **330**

Pieced Basket patt., worked in grey against a black ground w/checkered quilting within a grey border enclosed within a black border w/foliate quilting surrounded by grey binding, late 19th - early 20th c., 77 x 84" **805**

Pieced Basket patt., composed of navy polka dot blocks on white, sawtooth inner border, 63 x 74" (stains) **550**

Pieced Baskets in Diamonds patt., composed of various patterned fabrics arranged as large baskets within diamond blocks on a white ground, green bands, hand-stitched, 90" sq. (minor stains) **220**

Pieced Chinese Coins patt., rectangular form worked w/six narrow bands in various red, blue, green, yellow, brown & grey wools on a grey wool ground w/brown binding, Amish, Lancaster County, Pennsylvania, 1920-30, 48 3/8 x 60" (ILLUS. top next page) **6,900**

Pieced Cross & Crown variant patt., composed of blocks of calico prints in green, brick red & yellow, bars pattern backing, 77 x 84" **330**

Amish Chinese Coins Pieced Quilt

Pieced Diamond-in-the-Square patt., worked in blue, lavender & burgundy cotton & wool, the blue diamond w/star quilting enclosed by Princess Feather wreath & tulip quilting surrounded by a lavender floral vine-quilted inner border w/burgundy corner blocks, all within a scrolling vine-quilted blue outer border w/similarly quilted red corner blocks, lavender binding, Amish, Lancaster County, Pennsylvania, ca. 1930, 80 x 81 1/4" **4,600**

Dove of Peace Pieced Quilt

Pieced Dove of Peace patt., composed of nine blocks each w/a flying white dove, each dove surrounded by leaves, w/a reverse-appliqued & embroidered eye & a leaf in its beak, the square separated w/white channel and diamond-quilted sashing joined by squares centering a machine-appliqued circle, in red, green & orange cotton & all surrounded by a white square-quilted inner border & a red quilted outer border, orange binding, Pennsylvania, ca. 1890, 77 1/2 x 80" (ILLUS.).. **3,680**

Pieced Eastern Star Masonic patt., worked in yellow, green, red, blue & orange cotton centered by the star design on a white ground w/diamond-pieced medial rays, the whole set in a Princess Feather quilted circle, w/diamond, Prin-

cess Feather, rope & Masonic emblem quilting, bound in white, Maryland, ca. 1910-30, 72 1/2 x 74"............................ **1,840**

Pieced Fan patt., composed of blocks w/large fans in striped & checked cloth w/some floral pieces on a burgundy calico ground, maroon, grey, green & white striped cotton backing, hand-stitched, 67 1/4 x 68" **220**

Feathered Star Quilt

Pieced Feathered Star patt., worked in double calico pinks on a white ground, composed of nine large blocks & four small blocks all within a Flying Geese border band, hand-stitched, stains, 76 x 80" (ILLUS.)... **330**

Pieced Flying Geese & Stars Borders patt., worked in various polychrome calicos, the central broderie perse square enclosed by a chintz & calico border surrounded by alternating chintz & calico pattern borders with a chintz frame, self-bound, Easton, Pennsylvania, late 19th - early 19th c., 105 1/8 x 107 5/8"................ **7,475**

Pieced Irish Chain patt., composed of medium blue & mauve blocks alternating on a white ground, wide white border w/feather quilting, initials "KR," Pennsylvania, 84" sq. (minor stains).......................... **468**

Pieced Joseph's Coat patt., worked in cream, yellow, orange, red, tan, blue & green, diamond quilting at the center within a border of alternating diagonal bands w/Princess Feather quiltings, all enclosed within a red binding, late 19th - early 20th c., 82 x 83"................................ **2,070**

Pieced Log Cabin patt., intricate hand-sewn design in assorted fabrics, shades of brown, ivory, red, blue, yellow & orange, machine-sewn red wool scalloped edge border w/embroidered flowers, backing light brown felt w/tied yarn, 71 x 80" (holes & some patches, mostly in border) **935**

Pieced Log Cabin patt., worked in red, green & blue wool, the whole channel-quilted, w/red, green & blue channel-quilted borders w/red binding, Amish, Pennsylvania, ca. 1940, 84 3/4 x 87 3/4" **3,220**

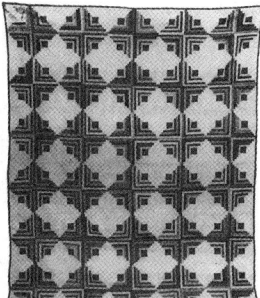

Log Cabin Variant Pieced Quilt

Pieced Log Cabin variant patt., composed of 36 blocks of Log Cabin patt. in multicolored calicos & solids alternating w/white blocks, homespun backing, applied paper label on one corner signed "Mrs. C.E. Johnson, made by Grandmother about 1829," 76 x 90" (ILLUS.) **468**

Fine Lone Star Pieced Quilt

Pieced Lone Star patt., the large eight-point star composed of diamond patches in blues, burgundy, pinks, green, goldenrod, etc. on a white ground w/small starbursts in each corner, a light blue border w/pink diamond patches, well-quilted w/meandering feathering, 88" sq. (ILLUS.) **1,100**
Pieced Lone Star patt., composed of blue & white diamond-shaped patches on a well-quilted white ground, machine-sewn binding, 72 x 84" (minor overall wear) **303**
Pieced Mariner's Compass patt., composed of brown on brown & white blocks separated by black & white printed grid forming the border, backed w/brown & white checked cotton, late 19th - early 20th c., 76 x 77 1/2" (minor staining) **546**
Pieced Monkey Wrench patt., the design in blue calico on white squares w/varying black polka dots, blue border band w/white polka dots, light stains, 68 x 80" (ILLUS. top next column) **468**
Pieced Nine Patch Irish Chain variant patt., composed of red printed & white fabrics w/a triple border of rose pink & green, mid-19th c., 74 1/2 x 87 1/4" (minor staining) **345**

Pieced Monkey Wrench Quilt

Pieced Nine Patch patt., composed of red & white tiny polka dot blocks alternating w/yellow calico blocks & sawtooth inner & outer borders, red & white homespun backing, machine-sewn binding, 76 x 80" **550**
Pieced Nine-Patch patt., worked in blue, purple, brown & green cotton, the channel-quilted blocks on a ground w/interlaced-circle & scalloped quiltings, enclosed by a diamond-quilted border surrounded w/stylized leaf-and-vine quilting, green binding, initialed "L.A.Y.," Amish, Mifflin County, Pennsylvania, 1910-30, 71 x 73 1/4" **5,175**
Pieced Pine Tree patt., composed of overall tightly spaced blocks of green trees on a white ground, wide green border, 77 x 101" (minor stains) **330**
Pieced Pine Tree patt., composed of 25 blocks w/green & white trees within a green inner border, white ground w/good quilting & meandering borders & round medallions, 19th c., 80" sq. (some fading to greens) **1,705**
Pieced Rob Peter to Pay Paul patt., composed of indigo print blocks & white blocks, Pennsylvania, 73 x 74" **440**

Schoolhouse Pieced Quilt

Pieced Schoolhouse patt., the buildings composed of red patches on a white ground w/a wide red scalloped border band, nicely quilted, minor overall wear, 71 x 72" (ILLUS.) **1,430**

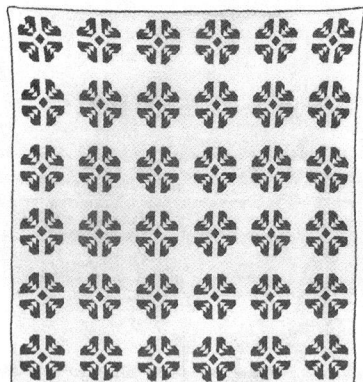

Pieced Snowflake Pattern Quilt

Pieced Snowflake patt., composed of 36 blocks of red & white snowflakes on a white ground w/red piping border, minor stains, 75 x 78" (ILLUS.) **385**

Pieced Stained Glass Window patt., composed of blocks of solid & printed fabric, diagonal red lattice w/solid blue, pink, white print & plaid triangles within, narrow inner border, wide blue print outer border, Berks County, Pennsylvania, ca. 1885, 70 1/2 x 71" (minor fading) **345**

Pieced Stars Pattern Quilt

Pieced Stars patt., composed of nine blocks each w/a multicolored eight-point star in green, yellow & pink calico w/red on a white ground, green calico grid & pink binding, diamond & stripes quilting, light stains & some wear, 72" sq. (ILLUS.).. **385**

Pieced Sunset over the Mountain patt., composed of multicolored print blocks w/black & white gingham & double wide pink calico border, Pennsylvania, 65 x 84" (some wear & stains) **330**

Pieced Sunshine & Shadow patt., a Log Cabin variant composed of patches in reds, blues, greens, oranges & browns, chevron design border band, plaid backing, hand- and machine-quilting, late 19th - early 20th c., 80 x 82" (ILLUS. top next column)... **1,485**

Sunshine & Shadow Pieced Quilt

Pieced Sunshine & Shadow patt., worked in wool, cotton & synthetic fiber blends in polychromatic squares, within a pink border headed by rose blocks w/diagonal & rosette quilting, all enclosed within a purple border headed by rose blocks surrounded by cranberry binding, Lancaster County, Pennsylvania, ca. 1925, 83 x 84"... **2,300**

Pieced Triple Irish Chain patt., composed of red & white cotton blocks, white on white fern quilting, signed in center "Jennie S. Boggs," 84" sq...................................... **880**

Pieced Triple Irish Chain patt., worked in red & green against a purple ground w/Princess Feather wreath centering diamond quilting within a purple border headed by red blocks w/Princess Feather quilting, all enclosed within a red rayon binding, early 20th c., 74 x 75".................. **2,760**

Pieced Tumbling Block patt., composed of red, light mustard yellow & white blocks, inner red & outer white border, quilted clam shell border, ca. 1900, 82 1/2" sq. (minor staining)............................ **403**

Pieced Tumbling Block patt., composed of red, light mustard yellow & white blocks, inner red & outer white border, quilted clam shell border, ca. 1900, 82 1/2" sq. (minor staining)............................ **403**

Fine Washington's March Quilt

Pieced Washington's March patt., composed of small patches of green & red on white, appliqued vining berries border, well quilted w/diagonal stripes on the border & small diamond design elsewhere, tiny stains, 81 x 84" (ILLUS.) **2,035**

Elaborate Whig's Defeat Quilt

Pieced Whig's Defeat patt., worked in blue & red cotton featuring ten blue diamonds w/scalloped tips overlaid on red squares & alternating w/white squares, the border appliqued w/white diamonds flanked by a red & blue sawtooth border, princess feather & heart quilting, bound in blue, Kansas, ca. 1866, 68 1/4 x 84 3/4" (ILLUS.) **3,450**

Pierced Flying Geese variation patt., composed of red & white patches, handstitched except for the binding, 76 x 82" (very minor stains & edge wear, overall yellowing) **358**

Sunshine and Shadow patt., log cabin, assorted fabrics, including wool, in shades of black, grey, brown, blue & ivory, chintz backing w/red rose print, 88 x 90" **715**

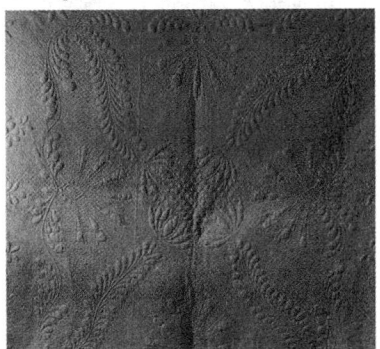

Ornate Early Trapunto Quilt

Trapunto quilt, white on white w/a detailed design, the center w/a rounded cluster of leaf sprigs, long feather leaves extending from the corners to the center & alternat-

ing w/fanned leaf sprays, vining feathered leaf border, applied woven fringe, stains, burn mark, 82 x 86" (ILLUS.) **2,530**

Samplers

Very Rare Early American Sampler

Alphabets & numerals, a central rectangular reserve w/letters & numbers above a pastoral landscape scene w/a shepherdess tending her flock, inscribed below "Marcy Hay - Her Sample-r - Aged 11 1777," all within a wide crewel embroidered border of climbing vines w/buds & blossoms, worked in a variety of pink, green, yellow & blue stitches on a canvas ground, probably Boston, some discoloration, 9 1/2 x 12 1/2" (ILLUS.) **18,400**

Alphabets, numerals & geometric bands, worked on linen w/the bands of small alphabets & numerals alternating w/geometric bands, a small flowering tree w/bird in the center bottom w/a pious verse on the left, inscribed "Catherine Walton Born July 5, 1784 - Wrought This Sampler," within a meandering floral vine border, Massachusetts, late 18th c., unframed, 21 x 21 1/2" (general toning, fading, small losses) **1,495**

Neatly Done Signed & Dated Sampler

Alphabets, numerals & pious verse, the rows of numbers & letters across the upper half above a central pious verse over a delicate scroll border enclosing the signature "Martha Mary Miller Newport Augst 25 1823," all within a vining floral border, minor toning, framed, 17 1/4" sq. (ILLUS.)... **1,955**

Floral Silk Embroidered Sampler

Alphabets & pious verse, a central square w/rows of letters above a pious verse above the inscription "Elizabeth Miller Aged 12 1820," a large basket full of flowers at the bottom center & tall sprays of flowers up the sides w/a leafy grapevine across the top, silk on linen homespun in satin stitch in shades of yellow, olive, blue, green, etc., attributed to New England, framed, 22 5/8 x 23 3/4" (ILLUS.).. **2,090**

Alphabets, pious verse & baskets of flowers, needlework on linen, rows of alphabets across the top above a large floral wreath enclosing a long pious verse flanked on each side by a stack of two baskets of flowers & fruits above a central floral cartouche w/signature flanked by pairs of cornucopias w/flowers, birds & hearts, all within a floral vining border, signed "Betsey J Conklin August the 9th 1835," framed, 16 1/4 x 17" (overall even toning) **1,840**

Alphabets, pious verse & floral bands, silk on homespun linen, narrow bands of alphabets alternating w/stylized vining floral bands on the upper half, the lower half w/a large central pious verse & lower inscription flanked by baskets of flowers, birds & trees, inscribed "Elizabeth Bennett, Her work, Sept. 1845," worked in shades of brown, blue & green, unframed 12 x 12 1/4" (small areas of missing floss, light stains, holes in border) **880**

Alphabets, pious verse & landscape, an upper block enclosing rows of alphabets above an inscription & pious verse, the bottom w/a full-width landscape w/a fruiting tree on one side & a vase of vining flowers on the other flanking a scene w/four fig-

ures, a large basket & various animals & birds, signed "Nabey Bradley born December 23 in the year of our Lord 1785. This wrought in the 10 year...," Essex County, Massachusetts, 1795, 12 1/2 x 15" (toning, some silk thread loss) **18,400**

Early Dated Ohio Sampler

Alphabets & pious verses, a pious verse at the top above rows of letters above another verse & inscription, a two-story house at the bottom flanked by a slender leafy tree & large urn of flowers, stylized leafy vine border on three sides, signed "Eleanor Wilson aged 8 years April 9th 1829 Xenia," worked in gold, yellow, white & tan silk on homespun linen, Ohio, framed w/old preparer's label, 16 3/4 x 17 3/4" (ILLUS.) **7,700**

Pious verse, building & varied plants & animals, a wide border band w/floral vine enclosing a two-column lengthy pious verse above a large & very wide building w/five towers & numerous windows representing Solomon's Temple, the lower panels w/the name & date of the maker above bands of stylized trees, baskets of flowers, urns, various animals & a shepherd & shepherdess, inscribed "Sarah Jubb Aged 9 Dec 4, 1809," framed, 18 x 20" (toning, staining, scattered fabric loss).. **690**

Tapestries

Brussels Verdure, depicting a wooded landscape w/parrot perched in tree, eagle attacking a dog, w/river & castle in background, 17th - 18th c., 90 x 100 .... **9,200**

Brussels Verdure, wool, long rectangular form, woven w/a scene depicting two mythical beasts frolicking in a forest landscape w/a town scene in the distance, a wide fruit & foliate border, 17th c., 122 x 202" (some re-weave) **13,800**

Flemish, large central scene w/figures including a king being attacked by soldiers, a landscape background, a wide border w/female figures in each corner & florals & landscape scenes along the sides, 16th c., 8' 4" x 9' 10" (ILLUS. top next page) **12,000**

Large Flemish Battle Scene Tapestry

Flemish, rectangular, depicting a heavily wooded landscape w/milkmaids & a herder in the foreground, w/birds & flowers & a Palladian folly by a stream w/fountain garden in the background, a pair of swans below, bi-color border, backed on muslin, first half 18th c., 9 x 15'.. **9,775**

Flemish Baroque, large rectangular panel depicting two large standing allegorical figures centering a shield inscribed "Libertas," beneath a pair of putti supporting a crown inscribed "Libertas," all within a berried laurel wreath border, 17th c., 78 1/2 x 111" (restored, torn).................... **14,950**

Flemish Verdure, rectangular, depicting in the center a wooded landscape w/thistles & hydrangeas & a pair of fowl by a stream, flower-filled wide border band, 17th - 18th c., 104-x 135" (separation, thread weakness) **9,775**

THEOREMS

Theorem w/Fruit in Basket & Bowls

During the 19th century, a popular pastime for some ladies was theorem painting, or stencil painting. Paint was allowed to penetrate through hollow-cut patterns

placed on paper or cotton velvet. Still life compositions, such as bowls of fruit or vases of flowers, were the favorite themes, but landscapes and religious scenes found favor among amateur artists who were limited in their ability and unable to do freehand painting. Today these colorful pictures, with their charming arrangements, are highly regarded by collectors.

Basket & bowls of fruit, watercolor on velvet, an oval bowl, decorated around the rim holding peaches & a footed decorated round bowl w/flaring sides filled w/berries, together w/wicker basket overflowing w/clusters of red & green grapes, all surrounded w/various other fruits, including a pineapple, melons & apples, unsigned, 19th c., America, framed, minor staining & toning, 21 x 24 1/2" (ILLUS.).................... **$12,650**

Basket of fruit, watercolor on velvet, a flaring wicker basket w/high central handle filled to overflowing w/various fruits & leafy blossoms, by William Rank, 20th century Pennsylvania folk painter, in red-grained frame, 17 1/4 x 19 1/2"...................... **440**

Basket of fruit, watercolor on velvet, a large wicker yellow & brown basket w/loop end handles piled high w/colorful fruits including peaches, pears, a melon, grapes, cherries & strawberries, resting on a mound of green grass, molded gilt-wood period frame, first half 19th c., 17 3/4 x 20 1/4" (background staining)...... **2,090**

Fruit Basket Theorem

Basket of fruit, watercolor on velvet, wicker basket w/side scrolled handles on a fringed mat, overflowing w/colorful array of fruits, including a melon, clusters of grapes, pears, lemons & berries, worked in shades of dark blue, green & mustard, New England, early 19th c., unsigned, framed, minor staining, toning, 14 x 17 3/4" (ILLUS.) **7,475**

Basket of fruit & flowers w/a bird, watercolor on velvet, large low basket piled high w/fruit & flowers, signed "W. Rank," William Rank, 20th c. Pennsylvania artist, original grained frame, 20 1/2 x 21 1/2" **523**

Basket of fruit on velvet, a large oval latticework basket w/a large mound of fruits & foliage in soft colors of green, blue, yellow & brown,w/a scrap of paper giving provenance & dated 1862, unframed,

16 x 20 1/4" (damage to selvage, wear, minor stains)...................................... **3,630**

Basket of fruit with parrot, watercolor on velvet, decorated in shades of gold, green & brown, unsigned, early 19th c., framed, 13 x 17" (heavy toning)................ **2,070**

Bird & nest on paper, pen & ink & watercolor on paper, a bird looking over its shoulder perched on the edge of its nest w/eggs, leaves & cherries on branch, in shades of green, brown, red & blue, signed in pencil "L. Lewis," old molded frame w/red & yellow sponged repaint, image 5 3/4 x 7" (reds a bit faded)................ **358**

Bouquet of flowers, watercolor on velvet, a tall bouquet of roses & other flowers in shades of rose, blue, green & rust, framed, 19th c., 14 1/4 x 18 3/4" (minor foxing, fabric abrasions)................................. **460**

Bouquet of flowers in vase, watercolor on paper, mixed flowers in shades of pink, yellow, blue & green foliage in a brown vase, unsigned, oval format, framed, 19th c., 10 x 12 1/2" (minor toning, staining)... **489**

Bouquet of flowers on velvet, magnolia & lilies w/foliage in colors of blue, burgundy, teal & green, narrow wood frame w/repainted black & gold reverse-painted border w/crazing, 12 7/8 x 14 3/8" (stains).. **523**

Bouquet of flowers w/insects & shells, watercolor on paper, a tall grouping of flowers including tulips as well as dragonflies, shells, a lady bug & peacock feather, in bright colors of yellow, blue, green, white, brown & tan, in period beveled walnut veneer frame w/gilt liner, framed 21 1/8 x 22 1/4" (light water stains w/foxing in margins, minor corner damage)... **1,760**

Bowl w/Flowers & Fruit Theorem

Bowl with flowers & fruit, watercolor on paper, a footed flaring bowl in shades of brown on a dark green mat & holding a large light green & yellow melon, red berries, clusters of purple grapes, a bright yellow lemon together w/flowers in white & maroon, green vines & leaves, American, 19th c., in what appears to be the original frame under the original glass, 14 x 18 3/4" (ILLUS.)................................ **20,700**

Flowers in vase, watercolor on paper, mixed flowers in shades of pink, yellow, blue & green in a brown vase, in oval format, framed, 19th c., 10 x 12 1/2" (minor toning & staining)... **489**

Fruit still life, watercolor on velvet, various fruits in shades of green, yellow & dark blue, framed, unsigned, 7 x 9 1/2" (foxing, fabric abrasions)..................................... **920**

Mourning picture, watercolor on velvet, a scene of a woman in mourning placing flowers on a monument among trees w/a church in the background, in shades of black & grey, by Sarah C. Wyer, Nantucket, Massachusetts, 1825, 13 x 17" (toning)... **2,070**

Over-turned bowl of fruit on velvet, a still life w/an upturned Canton china bowl spilling & surrounded by various fruits atop a marble-topped table, nice old colors of red, blue, green, brown & yellow, old narrow frame, 18 1/2 x 22 1/2" (some wear, minor stains).................................... **2,860**

Rose bouquet, watercolor on velvet, in shades of red, pink, green & white, old molded giltwood frame, 15 3/4" sq. (some frame damage)................................... **138**

Vase of flowers, watercolor on paper, a footed gently flaring cylindrical vase filled w/a huge bouquet of flowers in old soft colors of blue, pink, green, yellow & brown, old narrow giltwood frame, 17 3/4 x 22 1/2" (minor stains)................... **1,650**

Vase of flowers, watercolor on paper, footed chalice form grey vase filled w/pink & red roses, buds & carnations, bird & bee in upper corners, signed in ink "Eliza A. Horan May 1st, 1848," pine frame, 12 3/8 x 15 3/8" (fold lines & few tears, top corners glued down & 1" of bottom folded under)... **303**

TOBACCIANA

Although the smoking of cigarettes, cigars & pipes is controversial today, the artifacts of smoking related items pipes, cigar & tobacco humidors, cigar & cigarette lighters and, of course, the huge range of advertising materials are much sought after. Unusual examples, especially fine Victorian pieces, can bring high prices. Below we list a cross section of Tobacciana pieces.
Also see: Antique Trader Advertising Price Guide.

Cigar & Cigarette Cases & Holders

Cigarette holder, 14k yellow gold, collapsible & cylindrical hinged lid, both stamped "14K," the case marked "64"....................... **$154**

Match Holders & Safes

Carved & painted wood safe, model of a squirrel carved peering into an ear of corn mounted on a round wooden base, shaded ochre paint, traces of gilt, 19th c. (small losses, paint wear).............................. **460**

Painted wood holder, barrel-form container w/brown & tan sponge-painted exterior, 19th c., 2 1/8" h.. **115**

Snuff Bottles & Boxes

Snuff box, burl w/tortoiseshell liner, small
round disk-form w/a round glass lens in
the center of the lid over a brass repoussé portrait medallion of "General
Washington," early 19th c., 2" d. (age
crack, liner damage) **165**
Snuff box, deer's hoof, mounted in silver
plate w/a pattern of thistle set w/pink
paste, England, 19th c., 4 3/4" h. **316**
Snuff box, horn, gild hinge & inlay-decorat-
ed, carved w/a bust on a textured
ground, Europe, 19th c., 1 1/2 x 2 1/4"
(losses, cracks) **173**
Snuff box, leather, model of a man's shoe,
19th c., 4" l., 2 1/8" h. (wear, loss) **115**

Miscellaneous

Cigar box, cov., parcel-gilt silver, shallow
rectangular form, the hinged flat cover &
sides chased & engraved to simulate
wood grain & tax bands, gilt interior, unrecorded maker's mark, St. Petersburg,
Russia, 1886, 7 5/8" l. **4,830**
Cigar cutter, rose gold-filled w/scrolled re-
poussé decoration & white gold suit of armour helmet w/grid work, monogrammed
on one side **55**

Unique Ram's Horn Pipe Rack

Pipe rack, Sheffield plate-mounted ram's
horn, the long curled horn mounted w/a
silver top w/a circle of 12 loops for holding pipes & two match wells below a
waisted cylindrical compartment w/a
hinged top w/a horse-form finial, late 19th
- early 20th c., 17" l., 11" h. (ILLUS.) **748**

Unique Figural Tobacco Cutter

Tobacco cutter, wooden bellows-shaped
base w/ring turned handle & carved tulip,
blade is cut-out horse silhouette w/en-
graved face, bridle, mane & tail, ferule
loose, worm holes, 13 1/2" l., 7" h.
(ILLUS.) **660**

TOOLS

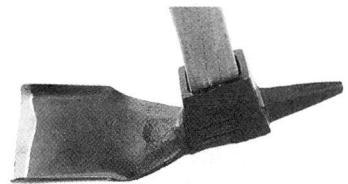

Plumb Lipped Carpenter's Adze

Adze, Fayette R. Plumb, Philadelphia,
Pennsylvania, lipped carpenter's style,
unused condition, 32 1/2" l. (ILLUS.) **$125**
Adze, Robert Sorby, Sheffield, England,
Model No. 1, polled carpenter's type,
marked, ca. 1820s, 20 1/2" l. **75**

Minnesota-made Axe

Axe, Kelley-How-Thomson Co., Duluth,
Minnesota, "Hickory" embossed logo,
36" l. (ILLUS.) **145**
Axe, Kelly Axe & Tool Works, Charleston,
South Carolina, felling axe, emossed "Oil
Whetted & Hand Honed," rare, 7" l. **345**
Bevel, Stanley Rule & Level No. 18 adjust-
able model, cast iron, basically unused,
8" l. **35**

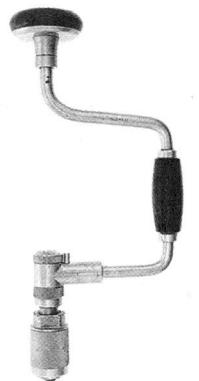

Stanley Tools No. 2101 Brace

Brace, Stanley Tools No. 2101 A model,
"Yankee" heavy duty type, 10" sweep, af-
ter 1946, 13 1/2" l. (ILLUS.) **75**

Victorian Figural Caliper

Caliper, early full-body female figural-style, anatomically correct, unmarked, Victorian, 6 1/2" l. (ILLUS.) **1,175**

Carpenter's slick, Buck Bros., Millbury, Massachussetts, 3" l. blade w/turned mahogany handle, 32" l. **185**

Chisel, Buck Bros., Millbury, Massachusetts, crank neck chisel, 1/8" type, original fruitwood handle, 11 3/4" l. **55**

Chisel, Wm. Marples & Son., Sheffield, England, lock mortise chisel, 1/2" size, original decal on side, 18" l. **75**

Chisel grinder, Stanley Rule & Level No. 200 model, adjustable, patented in 1912, near new condition, 7" l. **95**

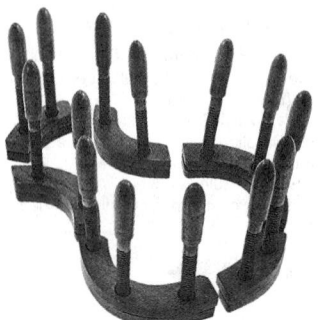

Early Violin Maker's Clamps

Clamps, violin maker's, wooden, six-part full working set, early, unmarked, 8" l., the set (ILLUS.) **245**

Mathieson & Son Rosewood Gauge

Gauge, Mathieson & Son, Glasgow, Scotland, rosewood & brass marking gauge, screw adjusting scribe, scarce maker, 6 3/4" l. (ILLUS.) **175**

Gauge, Robert Sorby, Sheffield, England, rosewood mortise & marking gauge, original decal mark, nearly new condition, 8" l. **85**

Figural Goat-head Bronze Hammer

Hammer, figural goat-head, bronze, Mitteldorfer Straus ceremonial-type, patented in 1928, 8 1/2" l. (ILLUS.) **345**

Hammer, Stanley Rule & Level No. RG 1 1/2, rare rubber grip model, 16 oz. size, 13" l. **145**

Level, Davis Level & Tool Company, Springfield, Massachusetts, cast iron, inclinometer-type, patented September 17, 1867, original pinstriping & lacquer on the brass parts, 12" l. **1,175**

Hibbard, Spencer & Bartlett Level

Level, Hibbard, Spencer & Bartlett Co. No. 100 model, solid rosewood, "Our Very Best" line, 26" l. (ILLUS.) **225**

Level, Stanley Rule & Level No. 31 hexagonal machinist's level, ca. 1910, 3 1/2" l. (slight split in body) **45**

Micrometer, Brown & Sharpe Mfg. Co. No. 25 patent 'Digital' model, patented in 1911, w/original case, 6" l. **875**

Rare Chelor-made 18th Century Plane

Plane, Cesar Chelor-made & marked bead molding plane, yellow birch w/replaced wedge, Chelor was a freed African-American slave working in the 18th c., 10" l. (ILLUS.) **1,395**

Plane, Ja. Campbell-marked ogee & astragal molding plane, yellow birch body, American, 18th c., 10 1/4" l. **1,475**

Rare Ohio Tool No. 111 Plow Plane

Plane, Ohio Tool Co. No. 111 ivory tip plow plane, w/centerwheel, Columbus, Ohio, 19th c., rare, 11 1/2" l. (ILLUS.) **18,975**

Spiers, Stewart Stuffed Panel Plane

Plane, Spiers, Stewart, Ayr, Scotland, stuffed panel metallic model, Herring & Sons iron, rosewood handle, 14" l. (ILLUS.) **645**

Stanley No. 2 Smooth Plane

Plane, Stanley Rule & Level No. 2 smooth plane, prelateral-type, cast iron, early 7" l. (ILLUS.) **775**
Plane, Stanley Rule & Level No. 20 "Victor" compass plane, full nickel plating, "Pat. '92" trademark, 9 1/2" l. **265**

Stanley No. 42 Miller Patent Plane

Plane, Stanley Rule & Level No. 42, Miller Patent plow plane, patented in 1870, nearly new condition, 9" l. (ILLUS.) **7,450**

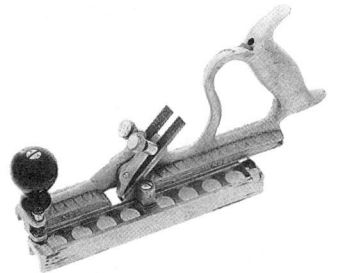

Stanley No. 48 Tongue & Groove Plane

Plane, Stanley Rule & Level No. 48 tongue & groove plane, swinging fence-style, apparently unused, 10 1/2" l. (ILLUS.) **225**

Stanley No. 164 Block Plane

Plate, Stanley Rule & Level No. 64 low angle block plane, patented in 1927, 9" l. (ILLUS.) **6,450**
Plumb bob, Stanley Rule & Level No. 1, brass retractable reel model, patented in 1874, 4" l. **195**

Stanley No. 2 Plumb Bob

Plumb bob, Stanley Rule & Level No. 2 retractable reel model, brass body & reel, w/Stanley mark, 4" l. (ILLUS.) **245**
Plumb bob, turned wood early turnip-shaped type w/knurled cap, excellent patina, unmarked, 4" l. **265**

Rabone & Sons Ivory Folding Rule

Rule, Rabone & Sons, Birmingham, England, ivory architect's folding rule, early style, ca. 1880s, 24" l. (ILLUS.) **545**

Saw, Atkins & Co., Indianapolis, Indiana, 8" dovetail saw, marked w/company logo, overall 13" l. **75**

Saw, Moses True, Oakfield, New York, model w/multiple adjustments, patented in 1874, 11 1/2" l. **95**

Keen Kutter No. 88 Saw

Saw, Simmons Hardware Co. No. 88 "Keen Kutter" saw, 5 1/2 point rip, all-original, carved applewood handle, 29 1/2" l. (ILLUS.) **145**

Rare Winchester "Plumber's" Saw

Saw, Winchester Repeating Arms Co., nested "plumber's" saw, w/four original blades, nearly new condition, rare, 20" l. (ILLUS.) **1,850**

Rare Early Screwdriver

Screwdriver, early turned ivory handle model, capped w/a mahogany pad & ornamented w/an ivory shaft buttressed by a pair of brass ferrules, unmarked, 4" l. (ILLUS.) **445**

Screwdriver, Iriwn Auger Bit Company, "Perfect Handle" model, square shank blade, apparently unused, ca. 1950, 9 1/2" l. **45**

Keuffel & Esser Slide Rule

Slide rule, Keuffel & Esser Co., New York, No. 4092-3 double cursor model, patented in 1908, w/original case, 10" l. (ILLUS.) **145**

Tape measure, Stanley Rule & Level No. 1260 "Defiance" automatic model, 1950s, 72" l. **25**

Trammels, Stanley Rule & Level No. 1, bronze metal, smallest size, w/pencil clip, 3" l. **115**

Stanley No. 14 Try Square

Try square, , adjustable model, early japanned finish, patented in 1882, 4" l. (ILLUS.) **135**

Billings & Spencer Bicycle Wrench

Wrench, Billings & Spencer Co. bicycle wrench, side-adjusting model, made for Pope Mfg. Co., patented in 1895, 5 1/2" l. (ILLUS.) **265**

Wrench, Ellis nickel-plated nut wrench w/pivot head, patented in 1903, 6" l. **365**

TOOTHPICK HOLDERS
China, Glass, Metal

Personal hygiene was not a high priority with our Victorian ancestors. However, the more elite often carried a personal toothpick. This was typically a small slender case that held the "pick" which would be exposed for use by either sliding it out of the casing or twisting a portion of the case. Many of these were made of gold or silver and some were adorned with a gemstone. By the late Victorian years it had become fashionable to have a toothpick holder as part of the table setting. Wooden toothpicks would be passed around the table following the meal and the guests would use them discretely hidden behind their linen napkin. These are the items that have become such a popular collectible.

Toothpick holders were made from a wide variety of materials, but the most popular with collectors are of china, glass, or metal. Toothpick holder shapes are often confused with match holders, open sugars, and small vases. Match holders typically include a rough or ridged area for striking matches. Vases will typically be smaller around the neck to support the flowers with a larger area for the water reservoir.

Toothpick holders have been widely reproduced and some have been "faked" by having the Heisey mark added to them or by having references to other glass manufacturers written on the ruby stained area.

Art Glass
Alexandrite, honeycomb, ruffled top **$2,000**
Amberina, Diamond Quilted patt., piecrust
   rim **475**
Amberina, Diamond Quilted patt., square
   top **275**

Amberina Toothpick Holder

Amberina, Inverted Thumbprint patt., ruffled top (ILLUS.) **500**
Burmese, Diamond Quilted patt., tri-corner,
   glossy, no decoration **450**

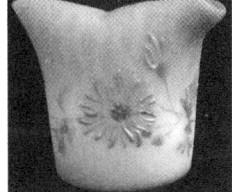

Burmese Toothpick Holder

Burmese, Diamond Quilted patt., tri-corner,
   satin finish w/decoration (ILLUS.) **575**
Pomona, square top w/decoration **350**

China

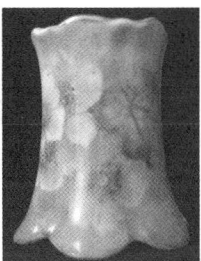

Bavarian Toothpick Holder

Bavaria, Madeleine, handpainted floral
   (ILLUS.) **35**

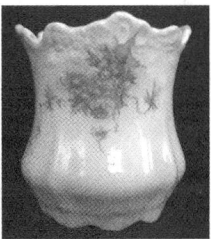

Eglantine Shape Toothpick Holder

Germany, Eglantine shape, unknown pattern (ILLUS.) **65**

German Toothpick Holder

Germany, marked 'D' crossed pipes,
   church scene (ILLUS.) **65**
Germany, marked 'D' crossed pipes, sailboats **65**
Germany, swirled mold, floral **35**
Royal Bayreuth, three-handled, girl
   w/geese **145**
Royal Bayreuth, triangular, Sunbonnet Babies **475**

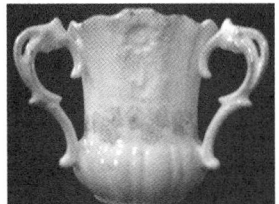

R.S. Prussia Toothpick Holder

R.S. Prussia, three-handled, blue base
   (ILLUS.) **185**

Glass

Alabama Toothpick Holder

Alabama, clear (ILLUS.) **65**
Alabama, ruby-stained **275**

Beatty Ribbed Opal Toothpick Holder

Beatty Ribbed Opal, opalescent (ILLUS.) **35**

Brittanic Toothpick Holder

Brittanic, amber-stained, McKee (ILLUS.) **185**
Brittanic, clear, McKee **75**
Brittanic, ruby-stained, McKee **145**

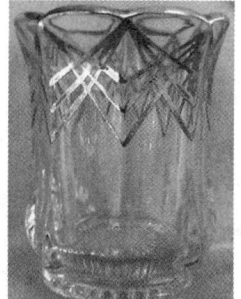

Chippendale Toothpick Holder

Chippendale, w/silver overlay, Jefferson
(ILLUS.) **50**

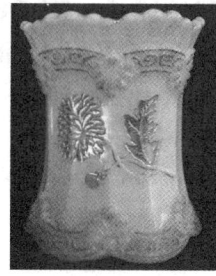

Chrysanthemum Sprig Toothpick Holder

Chrysanthemum Sprig, custard, decorat-
ed, signed Northwood, beware of recent
reproductions (ILLUS.) **290**
Cordova, clear, O'Hara **20**
Cordova, green, O'Hara **30**
Cordova, ruby-stained, O'Hara **55**

Cut Block Toothpick Holder

Cut Block, ruby-stained, Heisey (ILLUS.) **180**
Delaware, clear w/ruby stain, U.S. Glass **95**
Delaware, green w/gold, U.S. Glass **80**
Diamond Spearhead, blue opalescent............... **85**
Diamond Spearhead, green opalescent............. **85**

Flute Toothpick Holder

Flute, marigold carnival (ILLUS.) **75**
Georgia Gem, custard, Tarentum........................ **65**

Georgia Gem Toothpick Holder

Georgia Gem, green opaque, Tarentum
(ILLUS.).. **75**
Kentucky, clear, U.S. Glass **85**
Kentucky, green, U.S. Glass............................. **120**

Manhattan Toothpick Holder

Manhattan, w/gold trim (ILLUS.) **40**

New Era Toothpick Holder

New Era, blue (ILLUS.) **95**
New Era, clear.. **45**
Orinda, clear, Lancaster **65**
Orinda, milk glass, Lancaster **65**

Orinda Toothpick Holder

Orinda, ruby-stained, Lancaster (ILLUS.).......... **240**

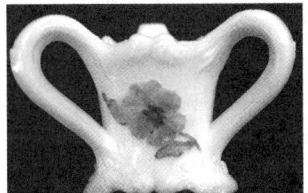

Pansy Toothpick Holder

Pansy, milk glass, handpainted, Kemple
(ILLUS.).. **35**
Pleating, clear, Bryce.. **45**

Pleating Toothpick Holder

Pleating, ruby-stained w/grape pattern,
Bryce (ILLUS.) **96**

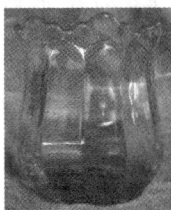

Pressed Optic Toothpick Holder

Pressed Optic, vaseline (ILLUS.)........................ **75**
Ruby Thumbprint, ruby-stained, souvenir.......... **35**

1893 World's Fair Toothpick Holder

Ruby Thumbprint, ruby-stained, World's
Fair 1893 (ILLUS.) **65**

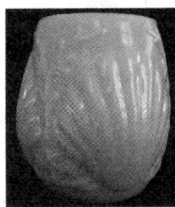

Shell & Seaweed Toothpick Holder

Shell & Seaweed, blue opaque, Consoli-
dated (ILLUS.) **85**

Shrine Toothpick Holder

Shrine, clear (ILLUS.) 95

Spearpoint Band Toothpick Holder

Spearpoint Band, clear, Duncan (ILLUS.).......... 35
Sunbeam, blue, McKee 135
Sunbeam, clear, McKee 45
Sunbeam, green, McKee 75
Sunbeam, ruby-stained 240
X-Ray, green w/gold, Riverside 65
Zipper Slash, amber-stained, Duncan................. 95
Zipper Slash, clear, Duncan................................. 35
Zipper Slash, enamel decoration, Duncan.......... 55
Zipper Slash, ruby-stained, Duncan 50

Metal

Adelphia, quadruple plate, band of re-
poussé flowers, ruffled rim............................... 45
Derby, quadruple plate, bulbous, large
strawberry & leaf, ruffled rim 65
Derby, quadruple plate, repoussé floral de-
sign, ruffled rim 55
Meriden, quadruple plate, squirrel playing
horn, ruffled top 110
Middletown, white metal, overall floral
w/firefly attached 75

New Amsterdam Toothpick Holder

New Amsterdam, quadruple plate, three-
footed, beaded rim, etched heart design
(ILLUS.)... 55
Osborn, quadruple plate, square w/ball
feet, open work on top half 55
Victor, quadruple plate, bulbous body, single rose design, horse mark 40

Wilcox Toothpick Holder w/Ruffled Rim

Wilcox, quadruple plate, snail-like pattern
on base, ruffled rim, crossed hammers
mark (ILLUS.) 45
Wilcox, quadruple plate., violin & top hat at-
tached 145

Floral Wilcox Toothpick Holder

Wilcox, quadruple plate, repoussé floral
over entire body, ruffled rim, crossed
hammers mark (ILLUS.)..................................... 50

TOYS

Also see Antique Trader Toys Price Guide.

African Chief, Teddy Roosevelt Adventure
in Africa Series, jointed wood, wearing a
top hat, coat, vest, houndstooth pants,
Schoenhut, ca. 1912, 9" h. (some holes
& restitching on coat, top hat a bit worn).... **$575**
Airplane, cast iron, tri-motor monoplane,
finished in grey w/red stars in circles
flanking "America" across the top of the
wing, featuring an elaborate pulley system that connects the propellers to the
wheels, when rolled forward all three aluminum propellers whirl & the plane
makes a clicking sound, w/cast pilot & co-
pilot in cockpit, Hubley, ca. 1930, 14" l.,
17" w. (some light wear, tiny hairline near
tail, wheels missing)..................................... 3,737

Steelcraft Army Scout Plane

Airplane, pressed steel, tri-motor Army
Scout Plane, silver w/red trim & rubber-
rimmed metal tires, Steelcraft, late 1920s
(ILLUS.) 2,475

Marx U.S. Army Bomber

Airplane, windup tin, U.S. Army Bomber, dark green w/yellow, red, white & blue trim, metal wheels, Marx, ca. 1940, 18" wingspan (ILLUS.).. **281**

Airport, "City Airport," lithographed metal, small scale, part of "bluebird" series, metal gas pump, straight runway in front, Marx, 7 x 12", 3 1/2" h. **125-150**

Airport, "City Airport," lithographed metal w/round central control tower flanked by two open bays, part of "gull" series, revolving search light on top, large base w/runways, three metal planes, Marx, ca. 1937, base is 11 x 17".......................... **350-400**

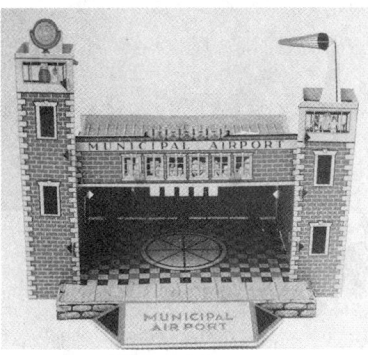

"Municipal Airport"

Airport, "Municipal Airport," set No. 18, heavy printed cardboard, assembled w/slots & tabs, box becomes foundation, open front, Built-Rite, ca. 1935, 12 x 15", 11" h. (ILLUS.) **200-250**

Alice Cooper Action Figure

Alice Cooper action figure, plastic, Alice w/14-piece diorama, Todd McFarlane, 2000, 6" h. (ILLUS.) **14-20**

Alice Cooper model kit, resin, unlicensed, unmarked, 1990s, box 10 1/2" l. (ILLUS. top next column) **30-50**

Alice Cooper Model Kit

Automatic parking garage, No. 213, printed Tekwood & wood, two opening garage doors, knob on roof moves turntable inside, ticket window in front, Keystone, ca. 1955, 11 3/4 x 12", 4" h. **150-175**

Hubley Town Car Coupe

Automobile, cast iron, Town Car Coupe, worn light blue painted body, white hard rubber tires & spare, Hubley, 1930s (ILLUS.) **523**

Kingsbury Pressed Steel Sedan

Automobile, pressed steel, sedan, black body w/orange bands, white rubber tires w/orange hubs, Kingsbury, ca. 1929, 14" l. (ILLUS.) **605**

LaSalle Auto & Trailer by Wyandotte

Automobile & trailer, pressed steel, long red LaSalle w/white rubber tires & matching two-wheeled trailer, Wyandotte, 1930s, 2 pcs. (ILLUS.)..................................... **550**

Barn, lithographed wood w/one sliding door, gambrel roof, outbuildings w/printed interiors, color lithographed cardboard animals w/wood stands, Anchor Toys, ca. 1934, 8 x 13", 9" h. **150-250**

Kenton Hardware Double-Decker Bus

Bus, cast iron, double-decker w/seven riders on top, bright red & green paint, white rubber tires, Kenton Hardware, 1930s, 12" l. (ILLUS.).. **1,485**

Bus terminal, marked, lithographed Masonite, large driveway in front for plastic bus, clock on roof, plastic stop light, Keystone, ca. 1950s, 18 x 24", 6" h. **200-250**

Marx "Bus Terminal"

Bus terminal, small scale, lithographed metal, "bluebird style," names of cities printed around exterior, large parking area in front for buses, missing gas pumps, signs & bus, Marx, ca. 1938, 6 3/4 x 12", 3 1/2" h. (ILLUS.)................... **75-100**

Nichols Stallion 45 Cap Pistol

Cap pistol, cast metal & plastic, Nichols Stallion 45 Six Shooter Cap Pistol, 1950, complete in box (ILLUS.) **275**

Church, "Church and Sunday School Blocks," marked, lithographed paper over wood building blocks, box forms main part of building, tall steeple w/conical turret, lathe-turned finials, Bliss, ca. 1895, 8 1/2 x 8 1/2", 20 1/5" h. (ILLUS. top next column) **1,200-1,500**

Church, "Reed's Sunday Toy," marked, printed wood blocks, Bible verse printed on interior, ca. 1880s, 11 x 11", 15 1/2" h... **1,000-1,200**

"Church and Sunday School Blocks"

Circus band wagon, cast iron, "Overland Circus," consisting of two white horses w/outriders pulling a high wagon w/a driver & a six-member band, polychrome paint, Kenton Hardware Co., 15 3/4" l. (edge wear, peg holding wagon chipped) **715**

Britains Mammoth Circus Set

Circus set, cast lead, Britains Mammoth Circus, 21 figures & animals w/circus ring tied in original cardboard box, issued in 1945, the set (ILLUS.) **1,500**

Circus wagon, cast iron, Overland Circus Calliope wagon, original paint, Kenton Hardware **688**

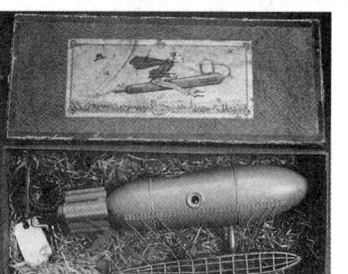

Very Rare Ernst Plank Airship

Clockwork airship, a shaded mustard-colored superstructure & tubular fins, twin-bladed celluloid propeller, each embossed w/E.P. trademark, steel-blue colored gondola w/a captain holding telescope, airman standing by the engine, ventilator, rubber & tinplate forward propeller, w/cloth-covered suspension wire & cast-metal winding key, Ernst Plank, Germany, early 20th c., w/excelsior-filled maker's carton w/lithographed comic label, torn triangular label, dent & chipping around suspension eyelet, chip to nose & rear propeller shaft, motor shifted within body, damages to box (ILLUS.) **23,000**

Clockwork gig, horse-drawn, featuring an American tin white horse pulling a composition-headed girl doll on a small cart housing the clockwork mechanism, possibly by Althof Bergmann, ca. 1880 (coat replaced, restoration to clockwork housing)... **2,300**

Early Carrette Limosine

Clockwork limosine, lithographed tin, open cab w/driver, closed rear, original dark green body w/red & yellow trim, metal & hard rubber tires, Carrette, Germany, early 20th c. (ILLUS.) **4,950**

Gunthermann Clockwork Windmill

Clockwork windmill, lithographed tin, tall upright open-sided mill on a round stepped base, yellow & red printed decoration, Gunthermann, Germany, early 20th c., 14 1/2" h. (ILLUS.) **303**

Drum, child's size, wooden bentwood top & base hoops flank the brass-plated sides in blue enamel w/a lacquered finish, relief-molded stars all around the body, stenciled designs on the wooden hoops, includes sticks, 19th c., 10" d., 8" h. (few small areas of rust) **385**

Arcade Baby Dump Truck

Dump truck, cast iron, "Baby Dump Truck No. 2," metal wheels, original worn red paint, worn white decal on cab door, Arcade, 1920s (ILLUS.)...................................... **457**

Buddy L Dump Truck

Dump truck, pressed steel, open cab, old worn black & red paint, worn label, Buddy L, some repair, 1930s, 24" l. (ILLUS.) **660**

Farm set, "Honor Bilt Farm," Tekwood, printed inside & outside, outbuildings of lithographed wood, large opening in front w/no doors, color printed animals w/stands, Sears, ca. 1937, 9 x 17", 10 1/2" h. **100-125**

Rare Coaster Fire Patrol Wagon

Fire patrol wagon, coaster-type, painted wood, rectangular painted red platform w/side rails & front seat marked along sides in large letters "Fire Patrol," two large & two smaller wooden wheels w/iron rims, w/auxillary set of sled runners, late 19th - early 20th c. (ILLUS.)....... **2,090**

Fire station, "Fire Company No. 9," painted wood w/brick paper, two opening doors in front, bell on side, pressed fiberboard roof, Schoenhut, ca. 1933, 8 x 8", 8 1/2" h... **300-350**

Fire station, "Hometown Fire Department," marked, lithographed metal box w/floor & three walls, clock & two trucks printed on back wall, two metal trucks, two metal fire fighters, metal telephone booth, Marx, ca. 1931, 2 3/4 x 5", 3 1/4" h. **250-300**

Arcade Fire Pumper Truck

Fire truck, cast iron, fire pumper in red w/six cast blue & red firemen, rubber tires, Arcade, 1930s,13" l. (ILLUS.)..............................**770**

Fire truck, cast iron, Mack-model hook & ladder truck, red finish w/black & gold accents, nickel-plated driver, ladder hooks & hose reel, w/six removable extension ladders, bell on spring undercarriage that rings when the truck rolls, Arcade, ca. 1930, retains original decal (one ladder support broken, another replaced) **1,035**

Kenton Fire Wagon Set

Fire wagon, cast iron, horse-drawn, a black & a white horse on a single small wheel pulling a fire wagon filled w/seven firemen, red wagon embossed "Fire Patrol," worn yellow wheels, Kenton Hardware Co., 1920s (ILLUS.) **440**

Early French Flip-toy

Flip-toy, lithographed paper on wood, four blocks forming figure of Napoleon III of France, each block double-sided, the Emperor in two naval uniforms, w/turned wood handle, w/torn slipcase, ca. 1850, 7 1/4" h. (ILLUS.)...**690**

Bliss Fort

Fort, No. 530, small scale, lithographed paper over wood, hinged front, round tower on right side, Bliss, 4 1/2 x 8 3/4", 8 3/4" h. (ILLUS.)...............................**1,500-1,800**

Gottschalk Fort

Fort, No. 5730, German, painted wood & fiberboard, buildings can be stored in base, ramp in front w/trap door, Gottschalk, ca. 1920s, 13 x 17", 13" h. (ILLUS.) **450-600**

Freight terminal, lithographed metal w/loading platform, storage areas & ramp, green roof, Marx, ca. 1957, 10 3/4 x 28", 8 1/2" h. **100-125**

Hot Wheels, Beatnik Bandit, No. 6217, ca. 1968, mint in mint blister............................ **150**

Hot Wheels, Custom Barracuda, No. 6211, purple, ca. 1968, near mint loose................ **760**

Hot Wheels, Custom Corvette, No. 6215, orange, ca. 1968, mint in good blister........... **410**

Hot Wheels, Custom Mustang, No. 6206, light green, ca. 1968, cut blister..................... **235**

Hot Wheels, Deora, No. 6210, dark green, ca. 1968, mint in blister................... **2,050**

Hot Wheels, Hot Heap, No. 6219, pink, ca. 1968, mint loose.. **250**

Hot Wheels, Python, No. 6216, pink, ca. 1968, mint loose... **405**

"Friendly Folks Motel"

Motel, "Friendly Folks Motel," No. 777, marked, lithographed metal, two motel rooms flanking central office, parking area in front, metal sign, plastic furniture, people, car & accessories, original box, Kiddie Brush & Toy Co., ca. 1954, 18 x 32", 15" h. (ILLUS.) **450-500**

Police Motorcycle with Sidecar

Motorcycle, cast iron, police motorcycle w/sidecar, red paint, rubber tires, driver replaced, Hubley, 1930s (ILLUS.) **715**

Early Noah's Ark Pull Toy

Noah's Ark, lithographed paper on wood, building-shaped w/colored panels around the sides of animals & plants, narrow board base pointed at each end on small wooden wheels, ca. 1900 (ILLUS.) **495**
Pedal car, fire chief's, Gendron, restored, ca. 1927, 50" l. **5,200**
Pedal car, Lincoln Tandem, "Skippy Line," American National, 1935, 66" l. **5,500**
Pedal car, Lincoln Zephyr, Garton Toy Co., restored, 1937, 45" l. **4,500**

Late 1930s Pedal Car

Pedal car, pressed steel body w/rubber tires & chrome hubcaps, original red paint, unmarked, late 1930s, 16 x 38", 22" h. (ILLUS.) **900**
Pedal car, "Race Car #6," Gendron, ca. 1924, 53" l. **4,000**
Pedal car, race car, Bugatti-type Grand Prix, aluminum body, 1/2 h.p., ex-Harrah collection, 80" l. **6,000**
Pedal car, roadster, 1920s Cadillac, American National, ca. 1920, 48" l. **6,500**
Pedal car, roadster, Auburn, American National, 1935, 66" l. **5,500**
Pedal car, roadster, Chrysler Air Flow, American National, ca. 1935, 51" l. **12,500**
Pedal car, roadster, Pierce Arrow, Steelcraft, integral headlights, restored, ca. 1935, 43" l. **4,200**

Pedal car, roadster, Stutz, Garton, ca. 1934, 47" l. **4,200**
Pedal car, sedan, Pontiac, Gendron "Skippy Line," ca. 1935, 45" l. **4,000**
Pedal car, yellow cab, 1920s model, contemporary by Greg Schneider, 1990, 86" l. **9,000**
Pedal vehicle, airplane, "Skylark," highwing, probably American National, ca. 1928, 46" l. w/23" wingspan................. **3,000**
Pedal vehicle, airplane, "Spirit of St. Louis," trimotor bi-wing, American National, ca. 1932, restored, 63" l. w/36" wingspan... **5,000**

"Coast-to-Coast" Bus

Pedal vehicle, bus, "Coast-to-Coast," Keystone w/decal, late 1920s, 31 1/4" l. (ILLUS.) **4,000**
Pedal vehicle, fire truck w/hose reel, American National, two passenger, fire boots & helmet, restored, ca. 1935, 70" l. **4,400**
Pedal vehicle, locomotive, "Fast Mail," Toledo Wheel Goods, original paint & stenciling, 1920s, 42 1/2" l. **3,500**
Pedal vehicle, truck, American Express Delivery, Steelcraft, screened back panels, restored, 64" l. **6,000**
Pedal vehicle, truck, "Fire Pumper #6," Toledo, nickel-plated radiator band & boiler, 1924, 63" l. **8,500**

Early German Penny Toy

Penny toy, lithographed tin, motorcycle w/side car & two figures, Germany, early 20th c. (ILLUS.) **633**

Early Pond Yacht Toy

Pond yacht, wood & canvas, model of a single-masted sailboat w/wooden hull & canvas, string & brass rigging, worn paint, late 19th c., 64" l., 80" h. (ILLUS.) **880**

Wolverine Post Office

Post office, lithographed metal, three folding sections w/floor, cut out service windows, paper accessories, Wolverine, ca. 1940, courtesy of Gail Carey, 11 1/2 x 22 1/2", 12" h. (ILLUS.) **300-350**

Pull toy, Barky Buddy, Fisher-Price #150, dog w/oilcloth ears & military hat, 1934 .... **600**

Pull toy, Big Performing Circus, Fisher-Price #250, circus wagon w/eight animals, ladder, clown, ball & accessories, 1932 .... **950**

Pull toy, Blackie Drummer, Fisher-Price #785, circus bear playing drum, 1939 .... **625**

Pull toy, Bouncing Bunny Cart, Fisher-Price #723, w/hopping action, 1936 .... **400**

Pull toy, camel on wheels, stuffed gold mohair w/red felt saddle blanket between the double humps, black button eyes, metal rod & spoke wheels, base w/worn gold paint, early 20th c., 17" l., 12 3/4" h. (wear) **495**

Pull toy, Chubby Chief, Fisher-Price #110, elephant w/oilcloth hat & nickel plated bell, 1932 .... **700**

Circus

Pull toy, circus, Fisher-Price #900, came w/30 pieces including circus wagon, 1962 (ILLUS.) **250**

Pull toy, Circus Wagon, Fisher-Price #156, band wagon, band leaders arms move up & down, 1942 .... **425**

Pull toy, concrete-mixer truck, Fisher-Price #926, complete w/rotating corn-popper mixer drum, 1959 .... **250**

Pull toy, Ding Dong Ducky, Fisher-Price #724, hidden piano wires play a tune while duck's head turns from side to side when pulled, 1949 .... **225**

Pull toy, Doc & Dopey Dwarfs, Fisher-Price #770, playing drum, 1938 .... **1,000**

Pull toy, Doggy Racer, Fisher-Price #7, dog drives race car, felt arms, 1942 .... **200**

Pull toy, Drummer Bear, Fisher-Price #102, white bear w/black top hat, 1931 .... **700**

Pull toy, Ducky Daddles, Fisher-Price #148, true to life waddle, feet move & head goes from side to side, 1942 .... **225**

Pull toy, Easter Bunny, Fisher-Price #490, pink & white, 1936 .... **225**

Pull toy, Farm Truck, Fisher-Price #845, driven by a Campbell Kid, came w/a full color folder of vegetable cut-outs, 1954 .... **280**

Pull toy, Gabby Duck, Fisher-Price #190, bill that opens & closes, quacking noise, 1939 .... **350**

Gabby Goofies

Pull toy, Gabby Goofies, Fisher-Price #775, the first of three such duck families, this one has dad pulling three wobbling baby ducks all w/twirling acetate wings, 1956 (ILLUS.) **55**

Pull toy, Granny Doodle & Family, Fisher-Price #101, mother duck w/oilcloth bonnet followed by two attached ducklings, 1933 .... **600**

Pull toy, Hot Dog Wagon, Fisher-Price #750, dog drives & rings bell, 1938 .... **435**

Pull toy, Humpty Dumpty, Fisher-Price #757, rolls on his roller type arms, tummy & feet, smiling face on one side, crying on the other, movable eyes on both sides, two bells on his arms, 1957 .... **285**

Pull toy, Ice Cream Wagon, Fisher-Price #778, dog driver ringing bell, 1940 .... **350**

Jolly Jalopy

Pull toy, Jolly Jalopy, Fisher-Price #724, was made from 1965-78 (ILLUS.) **10**

Pull toy, Lookee Monk, Fisher-Price #104, felt hat & tassel w/pipe cleaner tail, 1931 ...... **650**

Pull toy, Puppy Back-Up, Fisher-Price #365, wind-up black & white dog, 1932 .... **800**

Pull toy, Pushy Pat, Fisher-Price #515, engineer dog in train engine w/"pushy" stick, 1933 .... **600**

Pull toy, Raggedy Ann & Andy, Fisher-Price #711, playing drum, 1941 .... **925**

Pull toy, Rooster Cart, Fisher-Price #469, rooster on platform w/container decorated w/chicks, 1938 .... **225**

Snoopy Sniffer

Pull toy, Snoopy Sniffer, Fisher-Price #180, this well known canine remained in the Fisher-Price line for more than 40 years, the original version had oilcloth ears, four rubber feet & a spring & ball tail, 1938 (ILLUS.) **225**

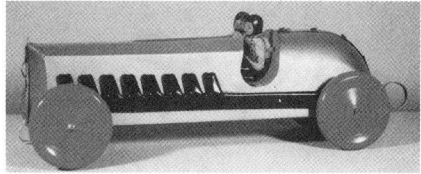

Teddy Bear Parade Pull Toy

Pull toy, Teddy Bear Parade, Fisher-Price #195, lithographed paper on wood, 1938 (ILLUS.) **891**

Pull toy, Tiny Ding-Dong, Fisher-Price #767, elephant engineer driving engine & ringing bell, 1940 .... **400**

Pull toy, Woofy Wowser, Fisher-Price #700, dachshund, 1940 .... **400**

Pull toys, Fido Zilo, Fisher-Price #707, dog playing xylophone, 1955 .... **125**

Rare Victorian Push Toy Cabriolet

Push toy, cabriolet & horse, the small hide-covered horse w/mane & tail above a small front wire-spoked wheel attached

to rails supporting the seat w/low back w/turned spindles above two large wire-spoked wheels, upright curled iron bars w/turned wood handle at the back, late 19th c. (ILLUS.) **2,750**

Early Child's Push Toy

Push toy, steel & wood, "Trot-a-way King," jointed wood dappled horse w/mane & tail raised on large red metal wheel w/rubber rim w/metal seat platform & smaller wheels at the back, patent-dated 1889 (ILLUS.) **1,100**

Restored Silver Dash Racer

Race car, pressed steel, sleek silver body w/large red metal wheels, two drivers, Silver Dash Racer, Buffalo Toys, 1925, restored, 13 3/4" l. (ILLUS.) **226**

Railroad station, "Talking Railroad Station," No. 418, printed Masonite, speaker unit on left, cut out windows, hipped roof, Keystone, ca. 1952, 7 1/2 x 17", 6" h..... **200-250**

Restaurant, "Bar B-Q," printed Masonite, open-backed, opening door, four stools at service windows, "curb service" marked on front, Rich Toys, ca. 1950s, 11 1/4 x 21", 12 1/2" h. **175-200**

Rocking horse on platform, painted wood, the body w/original white paint w/smoke decoration & a stenciled red platform base w/iron rods supporting the body, original cloth & velvet saddle w/cast bit & glass eyes, 19th c., 36" l., 28" h. (stirrups missing, some wear, mounting bars replaced) **880**

Rocking horse on rockers, carved & painted wood, a primitively carved horse w/small head & straight blocky canted legs, decorated w/worn original white paint w/black sponging, worn oilcloth saddle & leather straps, remnants of hair mane, long curved rockers w/end stretchers & center platform painted burgundy w/red line detail, the platform decorated w/a primitive lake scene w/sailboats, 19th c., 56" l., 29 1/2" h. (nailed repair on one runner) **688**

School, "Little Red School House," #1200, folding cardboard w/cut out windows, side opening, four plastic school desks, teacher's desk & chair, original box, Renwal, ca. 1947, 8 1/2 x 14", 10 1/2" h. **300-350**

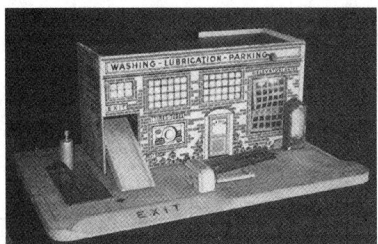

Wooden Service Station Set

Service station, lithographed paper on wood, rectangular building in red & white w/black & green trim, w/chute opening, car rack & air pump all on rectangular base, ca. 1940, unmarked (ILLUS.) **180**

DeLuxe Service Station

Service station, marked, printed Tekwood w/plastic window, opening garage door, plastic pumps, DeLuxe Game Corp., ca. 1948, 6 x 15", 5 1/2" h. (ILLUS.)....... **100-125**

Service station, "Sky-View Service Station," lithographed metal, parking on roof w/elevator, plastic gas pumps, people, vehicles & accessories, original box, Marx, ca. 1950, 14 3/4 x 26", 11" h. **350**

Sled, child's, decorated wood, the long platform incurved at the front & rounded at the back, painted red w/a black transfer of a running horse, red & black striping, long wooden runners w/wrought-iron bands, runners labeled "PMC," old varnish, late 19th - early 20th c., 10 1/2 x 37 1/4"... **358**

Sled, child's, painted wood, the long platform incurved at the front & rounded at the back, decorated w/an old repaint of a running horse, red striping & scrollwork on a greenish grey ground, black wooden runners w/red striping & the word "Pony," late 19th - early 20th c., 10 x 21" **550**

Sled, child's, painted wooden platform repainted in old dark blue w/gold scrolls, stencilled medallion in yellow & white w/small stars & edge striping, slender curved iron runners, late 19th c., 13 1/2 x 29", 8 3/4" h. **413**

Sled, child's, the long wooden platform decorated in old yellow, black & red repaint w/the name "Chester," wooden rungs w/beveled supports & detail, late 19th c., 16 x 34 1/2", 14" h. (age cracks).................... **605**

Sled, painted wood, wide curved-tip runners w/iron blades, the scallop-edged top platform painted red w/a center reserve w/floral sprays of roses & leaves, the initials "F.C.W." & a banner stating "Flora Temple - 1877" in shades of red, yellow & green against a black ground, black & gold outlining & decorative scrollwork on the runners, 15 x 55 1/4", 6 1/4" h. (wear, paint restoration) **1,955**

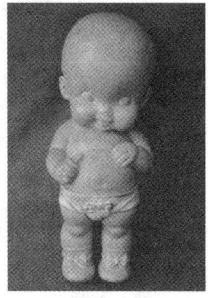

Baby with Pacifier by Sun Rubber

Squeeze toy, baby holding molded pacifier w/molded shoes & diaper, Sun Rubber/Ruth Newton mark, 1950s, 8" (ILLUS.) **40-55**

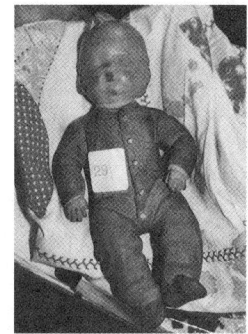

Sleeping Baby Squeeze Toy

Squeeze toy, baby, rubber, sleeping, closed-eye type, no marks, 1940s, sold at auction in 1999, 8" h. (ILLUS.) **48**

Large Ball

Squeeze toy, ball, large, w/"Mittens" the cat molded on one side & "Woofie" the dog on the other, Edward Mobley Co., dated 1958 (ILLUS. both sides) **35**

Squeeze toy, boy wearing swimsuit, early thin rubber, Bye Bye Baby stamp on toy **55**

Squeeze toy, bunny, rubber, Rempel Enterprises, 1940s, 12"...................................... **85-120**

Squeeze toy, clown, rubber, Roly Poly type, no mark, 1950s, 7".. **35**

Squeeze toy, cowboy, rubber, Future Products, 1940s, 8" h.. **150**

Squeeze toy, elephant, rubber, w/trunk raised, walking, Rempel, 1950s, 4"................ **125**

Elephant w/Circus Decoration on Head

Squeeze toy, elephant w/circus decoration on head, vinyl, head turns, The Sun Rubber Co. mark, dated 1961, 10" h. (ILLUS.)................ **100**

Squeeze toy, "Froggy," rubber, from the Andy Devine TV show, Rempel, 1950s, 5"............... **150-175**

Squeeze toy, girl, plastic head & vinyl squeaky body, head is rattle, no marks, 1940s, 6".. **75-90**

Squeeze toy, Indian w/tomahawk, vinyl, Rempel, late 1940s, 6" h............................. **85-90**

Squeeze toy, kangaroo w/baby in pouch, rubber, stamped Formulette Co. Inc., Design, 8"... **35-45**

Kitten by Sun Rubber

Squeeze toy, kitten, early vinyl, Sun Rubber, late 1940s, 3" (ILLUS.)............................. **15**

Squeeze toy, Mugger the monkey, rubber, Rempel, 1950s, 12" h..................................... **150**

Poodle

Squeeze toy, poodle, vinyl, Sun Rubber, 1961, 12" h. (ILLUS.)................................. **30-35**

Squeeze toy, rooster, rubber, Rempel, 1940s, 10" h.. **130**

Santa

Squeeze toy, Santa, rubber, Edward Mobley, 1950s, 8" (ILLUS.)................................. **65-85**

Squeeze toy, Snap, Crackle & Pop, vinyl, from Kellogg Co., marked Kellogg, 1960s, 7" h., ea. **65**

Squeeze toy, Sweetie doll, premium offered in the November 1917 "Ladies Home Journal," Faultless Wearever Rubber Goods, 3 3/4" t.................................... **100-125**

Squeeze toy, Teddy bear, sitting w/red circus hat & bow tie, Arrow Rubber stamped on toy, 8" h. **18-22**

Squeeze toy, toy soldier standing at attention, rubber, Alan Jay Charolyte Company, late 1940s, 8 1/2" h. **25**

Gottschalk Stable

Stable, No. 4423, German, lithographed paper over wood w/paper on roof, stable on right w/living quarters on left, non-accessible loft, Gottschalk, 8 x 12 1/2", 11" h. (ILLUS.) **1,200-1,600**

Store, "Corner Grocer," No. 182, lithographed metal w/three folding sections, metal counter & accessories, cardboard food products, original box, Wolverine, ca. 1937, 11 x 31", 14 1/2" h. **750-900**

Store, "Grocery Store," No. 347, lithographed paper over wood, open front, shed dormers on side of gabled roof, opening door, fair condition, Bliss, ca. 1896, 6 1/2 x 8 1/4", 9 1/2" h. **450-600**

Theater, "Home Town Movie Theater," marked, lithographed metal w/rolling paper "movie," wood knobs, cut-out for movie screen, Marx, ca. 1931, 2 3/4 x 5", 3 1/4" h. **175-250**

Theater, plastic projection building w/large screen, parking area for cars, six filmstrips, original box, Remco, ca. 1959, 7 x 14", 9 1/2" h. **175-250**

Auburn Trench Mortar Soldier

Toy soldiers, Auburn, hard rubber, trench mortar soldier, 1930s (ILLUS.) **20-45**

Authenticast British Desert Troops Set

Toy soldiers, Authenticast of Ireland, metal, British Desert Troops of World War II, 1960s, boxed set (ILLUS.) **15-25**

Authenticast Box

Toy soldiers, Authenticast of Ireland, original box for "History in Miniatures" set, red, white & blue (ILLUS.) **5-15**

Barclay Motorcycle with Gunner

Toy soldiers, Barclay, cast-metal, motorcycle w/driver & sidecar w/gunner, 1930s, 3" l. (ILLUS.) **25-45**

Barclay Soldier with "Pod Feet"

Toy soldiers, Barclay, cast-metal, walking soldier w/"pod feet," 1950s, 2 1/2" h. (ILLUS.) **8-12**

Beton Five-and-Dime Plastic Soldier

Toy soldiers, Beton (Bergen Toy and Novelty Company), plastic, five-and-dimestore soldier, standing holding rifle, 1950s, 2 3/4" h. (ILLUS.) **3-5**

Toy soldiers, Beton (Bergen Toy and Novelty Company), plastic, five-and-dimestore soldier, machine gunner or ammo carrier, 1940s, 2 3/4" h., each.............. **3-5**

Britains German Infantry Soldiers

Toy soldiers, Britains, cast lead, "Armies of the World - German Infantry," ca. 1940, set of 20 (ILLUS. of part)................................ **300**

British Soldiers by Britains

Toy soldiers, Britains, cast lead, British soldiers, various sets, ca. 1940, group of 20 (ILLUS. of part) **250**

Toy soldiers, Britains, cast lead, "Types of U.S.A. Forces," "Marines" & "West Point Cadets - Summer Dress," ca. 1940, group of 16 .... **225**

Britains Queen Elizabeth on Horse

Toy soldiers, Britains, cast-metal, Queen Elizabeth II on horseback, "British-Regiments" series, No. 7230, 1970s, boxed (ILLUS.)... **40-75**

Britains Stretcher Carriers Set

Toy soldiers, Britains, cast-metal, stretcher carriers, 1940, three-piece set (ILLUS.) **20-30**

Toy soldiers, Britains, original catalog of products, 1972 .... **20-50**

Elastolin 1930s German Soldier

Toy soldiers, Elastolin, cast-metal, German soldier charging, 1930s, 2 3/4" h. (ILLUS.)... **35-60**

German-made Flat Civil War Soldiers

Toy soldiers, German-made, flat-style cast-metal, soldiers of the American Civil War, 1960s, boxed set of 10 (ILLUS.) **10-20**

Japanese-made West Point Cadet

Toy soldiers, Japanese-made, cast-metal, West Point Cadet, copy of American piece, 1930s, 3" h. (ILLUS.) **10-25**

Toy soldiers, Kellogg's Sugar Smacks premiums, plastic soldiers, 1951, 2 1/4" h., each.. **10-20**

Lineol Horse-Drawn Wagon & Driver

Toy soldiers, Lineol, cast-metal, horse-pulled wagon & driver, Germany, 1930s, overall 10" l., the set (ILLUS.) **100-250**

Marx Plastic Russian Soldier

Toy soldiers, Marx, plastic, Russian soldier, standing holding rifle, 1963, 6" h. (ILLUS.) **5-7**

Minot of France Cavalry Figure

Toy soldiers, Minot of France, 1914 Dragoon Cavalry figure on horseback (ILLUS.) **100-150**

Toy soldiers, Minot of France, complete boxed sets **300-700**

Reliable of Canada Toy Soldier

Toy soldiers, Reliable of Canada, soldiers, 1950s, 2 3/4" h., each (ILLUS. of one) **3-5**

Silk Mortar Soldier

Toy soldiers, Silk of Lansing, Iowa, composition, Korean War mortar soldier, 1952, 5" h. (ILLUS.) **25-50**

Rare Lionel Santa Car

Train car, "Lionel Santa Car," Santa pumping handcar w/Christmas tree at opposite end, Mickey Mouse in Santa's backpack, mint in box, 1930s (ILLUS.) **2,310**

Ives No. 1122 Locomotive & Tender

Train engine, Ives No. 1122 steam locomotive & tender, original black paint, tag on tender reads "The Ives Railway Lines," ca. 1920-30 (ILLUS.) **385**

Buddy L Truck with Steam Shovel

Truck, pressed steel, flatbed truck w/steam shovel in back, dark blue, orange & grey paint, Buddy L, original labels, rubber wheels, 1930s (ILLUS.) **1,100**

Truck, pressed steel, Ford dump truck, open cab, working steering wheel w/short dump bed activated by small hand lever on side, hinged tailgate, on red-spoked metal & rubber wheels, red paint, retains partial label under steering wheel, Buddy L, Model 211A, w/original canvas-covered bale, ca. 1927 (some wear & corrosion) **920**

Heinz Delivery Truck by Metalcraft

Truck, pressed steel, Heinz delivery truck, white w/closed cab & slatted back, rubber wheels, original labels on the back, Metalcraft, ca. 1930s (ILLUS.) **440**

Sheffield Farms Milk Truck

Truck, pressed steel, milk truck w/stake back, red body w/rubber wheels on yellow hubs, printed on cab door "Sheffield Farms Company" & labeled on back "Sheffield Farms Sealect Milk," w/four original metal milk cans, late 1920s - early 1930s (ILLUS.) **2,200**

Buddy L Junior Tank Truck

Truck, pressed steel, tank truck, flattened green tank on red rack, black cab, rubber-rimmed red wheels, decal on tank, Buddy L Junior, 1930 (ILLUS.)................... **1,320**

Arcade Auto Carrier & Four Autos

Truck set, cast iron, auto carrier & four autos including three coupes & one sedan, green truck cab & autos in red or blue, metal wheels, Arcade, late 1920s, the set (ILLUS.)... **3,520**

Schoenhut Truck Terminal

Truck terminal, marked, embossed cardboard & wood, glass windows w/silk screened grill, opening doors, Schoenhut, ca. 1920s, 12 1/2 x 17", 12" h. (ILLUS.) **650-900**

Wheelbarrow, painted wood, dark green-painted exterior, red-painted interior, wheels & handle tops, w/stenciled horses & flowers at the sides & linear decoration, 12 3/4 x 46", 13" h. (wear, paint loss) **575**

Girard Fire Chief Siren Coupe

Windup tin automobile, "Fire Chief Siren Coupe," red body w/decal on door, Girard, ca. 1940, battery conversion, 14 1/2" l. (ILLUS.)... **450**

Windup tin "Bunny Express," a windup lithographed tin rabbit w/pink eyes & blue bow at neck placed on track & pulling three gondola cars brightly lithographed w/fluffy yellow chicks & ducklings in pastel green, blue & purple w/pink interiors, w/original box & cover, L. Marx, ca. 1935, overall 24" l. (some scuffs, some stains on box) **1,955**

Marx Coo Coo Car Windup Toy

Windup tin "Coo Coo Car," red crazy car w/black & white driver, w/original color box, L. Marx, ca. 1930s (ILLUS.)................... **605**

Strauss "Dizzie Lizzie" Car

Windup tin "Dizzie Lizzie," black sedan w/various slang slogans of the 1920s written in white around the body, metal wheels, w/driver, Strauss, 1926, 8" l. (ILLUS.) **330**

G.I. Joe & K-9 Pups Windup Toy

Windup tin "G.I. Joe & the K-9 Pups," light green w/red & yellow trim, Unique Art Mfg. Co., ca. 1930s, 9" h. (ILLUS.) .. **175-225**

Marx Knockout Champs Toy

Windup tin "Knockout Champs," tin & celluloid, raised square platform w/printed figures supports two celluloid boxers, Marx, ca. 1940 (ILLUS.) **413**

Marx Motorcycle Cop Windup

Windup tin motorcycle, police officer in white & red uniform on a yellow cycle, black windup button on side, L. Marx, ca. 1930s, slight wear (ILLUS.)...................... **209**

"Quack Quack" Windup toy

Windup tin "Quack Quack," mother duck pulling basket cart w/three ducklings, good color, Lehmann, Germany, early 20th c. (ILLUS.) **413**

TRADE CARDS

The Victorian trade card evolved from informal calling cards and hand-decorated notes. From the 1850s through the 1890s, the American home was saturated with these black and white and chromolithographed advertising cards given away with various products.

Cologne, E. W. Hoyt, scene of young girl in blue dress & cap, marked at the top "Ladies Perfumed Calendar - 1893" w/"Compliments of E. W. Hoyt & Co. Lowell, Mass - Proprietors of Hoyt's German Cologne - also Rubifoam for the Teeth," 3 1/2 x 5 1/2" **$33**

Chicago Corset Company Trade Card

Corset, "Chicago Corset Company," oval w/bust of woman wearing blue dress w/lacy white collar, dark hair swept up in back, flowers & scrolls at bottom flanking paper scroll w/illegible message, 3 x 4 1/2" (ILLUS.)............................... **44**

Cutlery Trade Card

Cutlery, "Will & Finck, San Francisco," scene of African Americans & cabin, reverse w/1884 address, list of products & 3/4" round sticker (loose), 3 x 4 3/4" (ILLUS.) **523**

Mechanical bank, "Bear Hunt" bank, J. & E. Stevens Co., early 20th c. (small tear in upper right corner) **58**

Hires Root Beer Trade Card

Soda, "Hires Root Beer," scene of small child in red w/white bib, empty glass on table, reads "Say Mama, I want another glass of Hires Root Beer," by Knapp Litho, N.Y., dated 1891, 3 x 5" (ILLUS.) **44**

Ritter & Hubbell Stove Trade Card

Stove, "Ritter & Hubbell, Boscobel, Wis.," brightly colored scene of young girl standing near small baby on floor by round black heating stove, 3 1/2 x 5 1/2" (ILLUS.) **33**

Stoves, Gold Coin & Gold Medal Stoves & Ranges, depicts an Arctic scene w/rainbow in the sky, a seal on the ground next to a stove radiating heat, marked at bottom "Chicago Stove Works, Chicago, ILL," litho by Mayer, Merkel, New York, 3 1/2 x 6".. 33

Tea, The Great Atlantic & Pacific Tea Co., colorful die-cut style w/a Victorian man riding his highwheel bicycle w/a young lady standing on the back bar w/her arms around his neck, the wheel spokes list various store addresses, dated 1883............ 110

Yeast, "Fleischmanns," scene of smartly dressed African American couple, reverse w/recipes, dated 1877, 2 1/2 x 4 3/4".. 44

TRAMP ART

Tramp art flourished in the United States from about 1875 into the 1930s. These chip-carved woodenwares, mostly in the form of boxes or other useful items, were made mainly from old cigar boxes although fruit and vegetable crates were also used. The wood is predominately edge-carved and subsequently layered to create a unique effect. Completed items were given an overall stained finish which was sometimes further enhanced with painted highlights. Though there seems to be no written record of the artists, many of whom were itinerants, there is a growing interest in collecting this ware.

Tramp Art Decorative Box

Box, rectangular w/hinged cover, a pair of inset stepped small pyramids centered on the cover & surrounded by wide stepped notch cutting, the sides w/bands of small stepped pyramids, 8 1/2 x 11", 7" h. (ILLUS.) **$125**

Rare Elaborate Tramp Art Cabinet

Cabinet, pine, upright rectangular form w/a pair of tall sunflower-encrusted cupboard doors made from cigar boxes &

opening to two shelves, the base w/two short drawers, the front & sides w/layered pyramids of chip-carved decorations in the form of zigzags, scallops, triangles & diamonds w/gold-painted accents on a blue ground, double arch crest w/chip-carved upright balls flanking an upright almond finial, old crazed surface, on crate understructure, ca. 1900, 21" w., 42" h. (ILLUS.)............ **29,900**

Dresser box, deep rectangular casket-form w/the deep hinged lid w/tapering chip-carved tiers & acorns & a medallion on the top, the front & sides w/large tiered diamonds w/the front diamond enclosing "Andenkin, B.B.," lion pulls on each end, brass paw feet, the velvet-lined interior w/a lift-out divided tray & a mirror, the back dated 1893, 6 1/2 x 10", 6 1/4" h. (edge chips, one small piece missing).......... **358**

Frame, rectangular w/pointed crestrail decorated w/a raised central heart flanked by smaller raised knobs & flanked by rounded corners w/larger knobs, 16 1/4 x 23 1/2" **193**

Tramp Art Frame with Tulips

Frame, tall narrow rectangular two-part form, each corner w/a chip-carved tulip blossom, the sides w/stylized chip-carved points & balls, the crossbar w/chip-carved diamond, probably Pennsylvania, ca. 1900, 22 x 46" (ILLUS.) **6,900**

Picture frame, a thick tapered pine block base supporting large upright rectangular frame of numerous interlocking pointed sections forming an overall finely pointed design w/a pointed arch crest flanked by small spire corner blocks, the crest w/three carved applied small stars, 28 x 44" (few broken points & one finial missing) **440**

Picture frame, oval, the sides composed of graduated tiers of wood w/chip-carved designs & deep grooves separating the sections around the sides, mellow dark finish, late 19th - early 20th c., 21 1/2 x 27" (some insect damage) **413**

Picture frame, rectangular, the borders applied w/tiered blocks w/notch-carved edges, long blocks at the top & bottom & two long blocks flanking a small block on each side, square corner blocks w/a cross design on top, old varnish finish, 8 x 10 1/2" (one small piece missing) **165**

Picture frame, rectangular, the borders of graduated strips of wood stacked & chip carved, old gold & silver repaint on inner liners & outer border w/dark original finish in between, 21 x 23" (minor wear)........... **495**

Picture frame, rectangular w/a double band border backed by red, white & blue bunting under glass, the top centered by a large carved eagle in flight, stylized tulip blossoms at each corner, hearts at top & bottom center, borders further carved w/circles & 'paisley' designs, old stain w/heavy crazing, probably Midwestern, 1875-1890, 29 1/2 x 38 " **6,325**

Ornate Painted Tramp Art Sewing Box

Sewing box, rectangular, the top w/two rectangular pyramids flanking a large square pyramid topped by a fabric pincushion, each side w/a long rectangular stepped pyramid, on short pyramidal feet, painted w/alternating bands of red, white & blue, interior lined w/woven wool tape, last quarter 19th c., 15" l., 10" h. (ILLUS.).. **9,200**

Large Tramp Art Wall Cabinet

Wall cabinet, a wide oblong undulating flat border frame w/pointed top decorated w/chip-carved circles, stars in circles & hex signs alternating w/sections of triangular chip-carving, the upper section w/a cabinet w/a hinged mirrored door & fall-front compartment, frame fitted w/a razor holder, comb box & pincushion, late 19th - early 20th c., loss to comb holder, 23" w., 45" h. (ILLUS.) **825**

TRAYS - SERVING & CHANGE

Both serving and change trays once used in taverns, cafes and the like and usually bearing advertising for a beverage maker are now being widely collected. All trays listed are heavy tin serving trays, unless otherwise noted.

Also see Antique Trader Advertising Price Guide.

Arrow Beer tray, lithographed tin, 13 1/4" h. **$44**

Buffalo Brewing Co. tip tray, round, metal, colorful court scene of woman on steps flanked by attendants, border reads "Buffalo Brewing Co. - Sacramento, California," litho by Kaufman & Straus, N.Y., 4 1/2" d. **275**

Columbia Ice Cream Tray

Columbia Ice Cream tray, round oval, tin w/lithograph showing a young woman petting her dog, a horse grazing in the background, scratches, stains & dents, 16" l. (ILLUS.) **130**

Deer Run Whiskey Tray

Deer Run Whiskey tray, round, metal, lake & mountain scene w/impressive elk in foreground, black border w/gold lettering reading "Deer Run Whiskey - Aug. Baetzhold's Sons, Buffalo, NY," litho by Haeusermanns, New York, 12" d. (ILLUS.) **275**

Eversweet Deodorant tip tray, rectangular, tin w/lithograph of dark-haired woman wearing long white dress, arms over her head holding floral spray, border w/geometric designs on sides, marked "Eversweet" at top & "A Toilet Necessity for Refined People" at the bottom, 5" h.

(few small spots & light stains, soiling & wear).. **495**

Fro-Joy Ice Cream tray, lithographed tin, 13 3/4" l. (minor scratches)............................... **28**

Stagg Company Whiskey Tray

George T. Stagg Co. O.F.C. Bourbon tray, round, metal, image of stag w/trees & sunset in background, red border reading "The George T. Stagg Company - Frankford, KY," edge scuffs & minor crazing, 12" d. (ILLUS.).................................. **220**

Hoffman's Ice Cream tray, lithographed tin, 15 1/4" h. (flaking & scratches).................. **77**

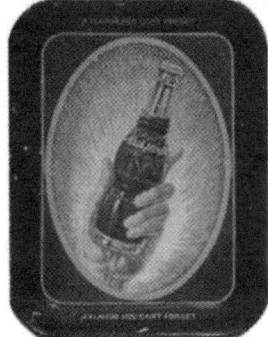

Nugrape Serving Tray

Nugrape tray, rectangular, metal, center oval depicts hand holding bottle, black border w/yellow lettering at top & bottom reading "A Flavor You Can't Forget," litho by American Art Works, Coshocton, Ohio, rim chips & minor scratches, 10 1/2 x 13" (ILLUS.)....................................... **99**

Olympia Beer Tray

Olympia Beer tip tray, round, metal, black & white, image of man dressed as a musketeer holding a bottle, glass on table before him, marked "Olympia Beer - It's the Water," minor crazing, 4 1/4" d. (ILLUS.)........ **55**

Red Raven tray, round metal, lithograph scene of small nude boy w/one foot on a box & reaching up onto a cabinet for a bottle, large red bird on box next to him, border reads "Red Raven - Ask the Man," ca. 1910 (light scratches, overall wear, minor dents) **1,265**

Resinol Soap and Ointment Tip Tray

Resinol Soap and Ointment tip tray, round, metal, center bust portrait of beautiful woman w/long brown hair, low cut dress w/red flower decoration, red flowers in hair, black border w/gold lettering reading "Resinol Soap and Ointment - For All Skin Diseases - At All Drug Stores," 4 1/4" d. (ILLUS.) **165**

Star Brewery Tray

Star Brewery tray, round, metal w/center image of three white horse heads, gold lettering reads "Star Brewery - Brewers of the Famous Hop-Gold," Star Brewery, Vancouver, Washington, few minor scrapes, 12" d. (ILLUS.)................................. **523**

Wolverine Toys tray, lithographed tin, 6 1/2" l. (minor dents & scratches) **77**

TRIVETS

During the late 19th and early 20th centuries, cast-iron trivets were produced in great quantities by American and Canadian foundries. The most common trivets measured 4 x 6" and were "spade shaped" in order to accommodate the bottom of household irons and protect surfaces from the heat they generated. Other shapes included squares, circles, rectangles and ovals. Trivets often carried advertising slogans, symbols or initials of the foundries that produced them. Small trivets – from 2 to 5 inches in length – were made for children who used them to press doll clothes or handkerchiefs. Oversized trivets – 7 inches and longer – were made to support commercial laundry irons. The production of trivets declined when electricity became readily available in the early years of the 20th century; few were produced after 1920. Many of the earlier trivets have been reproduced. Many new designs appeared during the later years of the 20th century and some are still being manufactured and imported today. However, trivets produced after 1920 are usually marked on the back by the name of the manufacturer along with a number that identifies the design. American trivets made before the 1920s have no marks on the reverse; some Canadian trivets have the name of the foundry embossed on the reverse side. Dick Hankenson photographed and cataloged more than 500 trivets in two books: Trivets (1963) and Trivets: Old and Re-Pro (1968). The names and numbers refer to his books which, although now out of print, may sometimes be purchased from used book dealers.

* All trivets are cast iron unless otherwise noted.

"1894," #25, Bk 1, "Cathedral" design w/"1894" in bottom scroll, handle, 3 3/4 x 9" **$25**

"A in S" Trivet

"A in S," #135, Bk 1, spade shape, large "S," small "A" in center, 4 x 6 3/4" (ILLUS.).. **15-20**

"AF" Trivet

"AF," #136, Bk 1, "American Foundry & Mfg. Co., St. Louis, MO" embossed in panel, 4 x 6" (ILLUS.) **20-22**

"B" Trivet

"B," #113, Bk 2, spade shape, large "B" in center, 4 1/4 x 6" (ILLUS.) **10-15**
"B & D," #134, Bk 1, cut-out letters in opening, plain panel, 4 x 6" **18-20**
"Banded Sheath," #139, Bk 2, child's trivet, oval w/handle, wheat design in center, 1 7/8 x 5 3/8"... **25-28.50**
"Bar and Holes," #93, Bk 1, 14 holes in side panels, vertical bar in center, 4 x 6"......... **10**
"C," #138, Bk 1, scroll letter "C" in center, plain panel, 4 x 6"....................................... **10-12**
"Canadian Daisy," #142, Bk 2, center is round w/petal design, irregular border, 1 3/4 x 2 5/16".. **20-22.50**

"Canadian Spider Web" Trivet

"Canadian Spider Web," #73, Bk 2, manufactured by Jas. Smart Mfg. Co., Brockville, Canada (on reverse), 4 x 5 3/8" (ILLUS.) **15-18**

Cathedral #5 Trivet

Cathedral #5, #36, Bk 1, large, scrollwork in center, handle 3 3/4 x 8 1/2" (ILLUS.)........ **15-18**

"Cathedral Variation" Trivet

"Cathedral Variation," teardrop shape, center scrolls & handle 3 3/4 x 9 1/2" (ILLUS.).. **12.50-15**

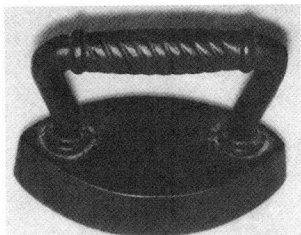

Child's Iron

Child's iron, rope design on handle, 2 1/4 x 4 1/4 x 3 1/4" h. (ILLUS.) **28**

"Colebrookdale Crown & Maltese Cross," #119, Bk 1, "Colebrookdale Iron Co., Pottstown, PA" embossed in panel, 4 1/4 x 6"... **25**

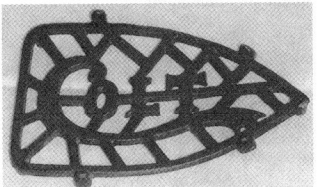

"Colt" Advertising Trivet

"Colt," #130, Bk 1, advertising type, Colt name in center, 4 legs, 4 x 6 1/2" (ILLUS.)... **30-45**

"Dubuque Potts," #108, Bk 1, oval, vertical bars impressed w/name, 4 x 7 1/2" **20-25**

"E. Ketcham & Co., NY," round, four "paw" legs, cut out letters in center, border of circles, 5 3/8" d. **30**

"Enterprise E," #114, Bk 1, scroll "E" in center, Enterprise Mfg. Co., Phila., USA in panels, 4 x 6" **10**

"Ferrosteel Urn," #121, Bk 1, "Ferrosteel, Cleveland" embossed around panel, outline of urn in center, 4 x 6" (ILLUS. top next column).. **20**

"Ferrosteel Urn" Trivet

"Five Point Star in Circle," #31, Bk 1, star in center of circle, handle, 5 1/4 x 7 3/4" ... **25-30**

"Four Stars" Trivet

"Four Stars," #37, Bk 1, heart shape w/one large & three small stars in center, handle, 3 1/2 x 8 1/4" (ILLUS.) **15-18**

"G" in Diamond Trivet

"G" in diamond, spade shape, w/diamond center, "Smart, Brockville" on back, Canadian, 4 1/2 x 7 1/2" (ILLUS.)................... **15-20**

"Geometric #1," #34, Bk 1, pattern of circles within larger circle, handle 3 1/4 x 4 1/2"... **15-20**

"Geometric #3," #86, Bk 1, fleur-de-lis in center, plain panels, 4 x 6" **15**

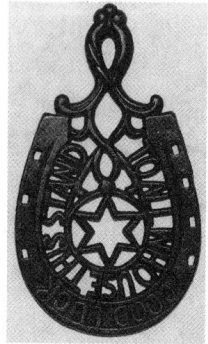

"Good Luck to All Who Use This Stand" Trivet

"Good Luck to All Who Use This Stand," #35, Bk 1, horseshoe shape w/handle, star in center, motto around panel & center, 4 1/2 x 7 3/4" (ILLUS.) **20-25**

"H Co.," #124, Bk 1, "W.H. Howell Co., Geneva, IL, USA," embossed in panels, logo in center, 4 x 6" **8-10**

"H2H General Specialty," #63, Bk 2, oval, "Humphrey Gas Iron, General Specialty Company" embossed in panels, 4 x 7 3/4".. **20-25**

"Handled Geometric" Trivet

"Handled Geometric," child's trivet, spade shape w/handle, 2 3/8 x 5 3/4" (ILLUS.).... **15-18**

"Handled M," #140, Bk 2, oval w/handle, scroll "M" in center, 2 x 5 1/2"........................... **40**

"Heart with D," #54, Bk 1, two hearts & circle enclose sideways letter "D," handle, 3 3/4 x 8".. **20-25**

"Heart with W," #53, Bk 1, two hearts & circle enclose letter "W," handle, 4 x 8 1/2"......... **20**

"Howell H," spade shape, "Howell Co., Geneva, ILL" embossed in panel.......... **10-12.50**

"Howell Plain H," #125, Bk 1, spade shape, scrolled "H" in center, wide panel, 4 3/8 x 5 7/8" (ILLUS. top next column)... **10-12.50**

"Imperial," oval, "Consolidated Gas Iron Co., NY" impressed in panel, 4 3/4 x 8 1/4".. **25-30**

"Irregular Spider Web," #82, Bk 1, "spider web" design enclosed in concave bands, 3 1/2 x 5".. **15-20**

"Howell Plain H" Trivet

"Iwantu, Double Point," #149, Bk 1, oval, flat ends, iron in center, "Strause Gas Iron Co., Phila., Pa.," in panels, 4 x 7 1/2" . **35-40**

"Iwantu, Spade," #148, Bk 1, spade shape, iron in center, "Strause Gas Iron Co., Phila., Pa.," in panels, 4 x 6 1/2" **35-40**

"J.E. Lewis," spade shape, crossed bars in center, made in Hamilton, Ontario, 4 x 6" . **15-20**

"J.R. Clark" Trivet

"J.R. Clark," #106, Bk 1, oval, "The J.R. Clark Co., Minneapolis" in panel, 3 7/8 x 7" (ILLUS.).. **35-45**

"Lacy" Trivet

"Lacy," #49, Bk 1, floral design in "spade" outline & on handle, 3 1/2 x 8" (ILLUS.) **10-12.50**

"Lacy Double Point," #155, Bk 1, child's iron, oval w/scrolls in center, 1 3/4 x 3 1/2".. **15-20**

"Lacy Double Point No. 2," #155, Bk 1, 1 1/4 x 4 3/4"... **25-28**

"Lady Urn," #87, Bk 1, shade shape, flat top, urn in center, pattern of holes in panels, 4 1/2 x 5 3/4".................................... **15-20**

"Oblong Waffle," #75, Bk 1, rectangular w/crisscrossed bars inside making 12 smaller rectangles, 3 3/8 x 4 1/2" **12-15**
"Ocean Waves," #84, Bk 1, three wavy lines running vertically in center opening, 4 x 6 1/2" **15**

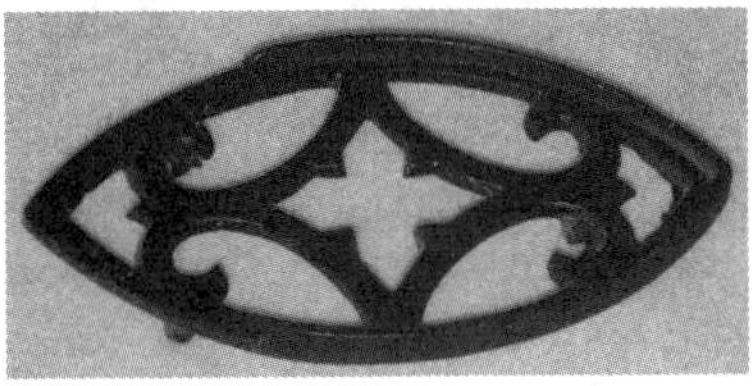

"Oval" Trivet

"Oval," #164, Bk 1, oval trivet w/half rail, 2 1/4 x 4 3/4" (ILLUS.) **15-18**
"Roman Key," #68, Bk 1, spade shape w/open center, geometric design cut out of panel, raised key design, 4 x 6" **15-20**
"Round Lattice," #62, Bk 1, pattern of 8 fleur-de-lis enclosed in four bars, four plain legs, 5" d. **15**
"Round Petal," #61, Bk 1, floral design w/10 open-work petals, inside edge of border is scalloped, 5" d. **15-20**

"Sensible" Trivet

"Sensible," #129, Bk 1, name die-cut in center, six holes & rectangular opening in one end, 4 x 5" (ILLUS.) **20-28**

"Spider Web" Trivet
"Spider Web," #90, Bk 1, 4 x 6" (ILLUS.) **8-10**

"Spider Web," #90, Bk 1, design of criss-crossed lines resembles a web, many variants were made, 4 x 6" **10**

Spider Web Variant Trivet
"Spider Web," variant, 4 x 6" (ILLUS.) **10**

"Spider Web" Variant Trivet

"Spider Web," variant, "spider web" design in center, bordered by "Enterprise Mfg. Co., Philadelphia," 4 x 6" (ILLUS.) **10-15**
"Star & Sunburst," #122, Bk 1, six pointed star over a saw-toothed "sunburst," Cleveland Foundry Co., 4 1/4 x 6" **10-15**
"Star with Holes," #53, Bk 1, child's, star in center, surrounded by holes, handle, 2 5/8 x 5 3/4" **25**
"T in Diamond," same as trivet in illus. but w/single letter T **15**
"Target," #55, Bk 1, spade shape w/open work in center, handle, 3 3/4 x 7 1/2" **10-12**

"TF in Diamond" Trivet

"TF in Diamond," diamond shape, letter T w/bar for "F" on vertical line, 4 x 7" (ILLUS.) **18**

"Tree of Life" Trivet

"Tree of Life," #33, Bk 1, heart shape w/swirls radiating from center, handle, 4 1/2 x 8" (ILLUS.).. **10-15**

"Two Hearts" Trivet

"Two Hearts," #161, Bk 1, oval trivet w/double heart design, 2 1/4 x 5" (ILLUS.)... **25-28**

"Uneedit" Trivet

"Uneedit," #147, Bk 1, iron in center, embossed letters: "Uneedit Gas Iron, Rosenbaum Mfg. Co., NY," 4 x 7" (ILLUS.)............... **30**

"Waffle," #95, Bk 1, crisscrossed lines make center design, plain panel, 4 x 6".......... **10**

TRUNKS

Dome-top, painted & decorated basswood w/original brown, green & black vinegar decoration, black border detail covers a line of sponging & appears to be a period repaint, 15 3/4 x 30 1/4", 12 3/8" h. **$1,650**

Dome-top, painted & decorated poplar, the hinged top & sides w/old red paint background decorated w/borders of scallops

& a leaf in each corner on each side in black & yellow, early 19th c., 24 1/2" l. (wear, age cracks, hasp incomplete) **715**

Early Grain-painted Dome-top Trunk

Dome-top, painted & decorated wood, overall salmon color graining highlighted w/yellow striping in simulated inlaid stringing, original surface & hardware, New England, early 19th c., 13 1/2 x 26 3/4", 11 1/4" h. (ILLUS.) **1,150**

Flat-top, leather-board, rectangular w/decorative brass tack trim all around the edges of the lid & sides w/swags & round drops flanking the front wrought-iron lock w/hasp & brass escutcheon, brass plaque engraved "VFC," worn, 19th c., 14 x 24", 11 1/2" h............................... **468**

Flat-top, leather-bound camphor wood, brass tack trim around the top & around the sides w/a long swag across the front, brass bail handles at each end, 19th c., 15 1/2 x 30 1/2", 13 3/4" h. (binding missing in areas, leather damage) **220**

Tack-decorated Leather-bound Trunk

Flat-top, leather-bound wood, rectangular, the black leather w/tooled line decoration & brass tacks around the lid & on the front & sides forming swags & diamonds w/the initials "G.T.," the top w/a padded leather seat, interior lined w/cloth in an acorn design, wear, leather damage, early 19th c., 15 1/4 x 30 1/4", 16" h. (ILLUS.) **330**

VALENTINES

Cut paper, round, folded & delicately cutout w/hearts, verse & endearments in pen & ink, inscribed "To Miss Elizabeth Girtz from William Robinson," on a red cloth ground, attributed to the Mennonites, narrow giltwood frame, valentine 13 1/4" d. (damage to frame) **$468**

Sailor's Valentine

Sailor's valentine, double-hinged octagonal wood box, one side w/center heart surrounded by shell designs of alternating colors & bordered by a band overlapping shells, the other side w/"Forget Me Not" in center w/circles of overlapping shells flanking a band of shells set in a floral design, late 19th c., 9 x 9" (ILLUS.) .. **2,990**

Children's

The lacy frills and layered look of antique valentines had become a thing of the past by the 1920s. Larger and larger numbers of valentines were being printed expressly for children. Big eyes, cute kiddies and animals became the illustrated favorites. The Valentine box appeared in every grammar school room across the land. Children's valentines had become big business!

Art Deco, little girl & boy around valentine tree, USA, 4 x 5" **5**
Beatnick, U.S.A., 1960s, 2 x 8".......................... **1-4**
Big band & radio broadcasting, USA, 1940s, 6 x 7 1/2".. **15**
Booklet, Mary Had a Little Lamb, 1940s **15**

Boy in Barrel Valentine

Boy in barrel, "Campbell Kid" look, 1930s, 4 x 7" (ILLUS.) **20**
Boy painting girl's portrait, USA, 1930s, 4 x 6" **4**
Boy & Teddy bear walking, w/movable eyes, Germany, 3 x 5" **2-6**
Card, gift-giving card w/lollipop, 1930s, 5 x 5" **25**
Cat w/fishing pole, w/movable ears, Germany, 3 x 6" **10**
Charlie Chaplin, caricature, feet turn into easel base, 4 1/2 x 6" **50**

Chocolate Soldier

Chocolate soldier, USA, 1950s, 3 x 8" (ILLUS.) **8**

Disney Valentine

Clarabell cow, Disney, 1938, 2 x 6" (ILLUS.) **75**
Cowboy stick person, USA, 1940s, 4 1/2 x 5 1/2" **10**
Die-cut, girl & boy in boat on waves, USA, 1930s, 4 x 5" **4-7**
Die-cut & folded, child mailing valentine, 1930s, 3 x 4" **8**
Dimensional, Collie & doghouse/chain, USA, 6 x 6" **40**

Double-Glo Valentines

Doubl-Glo, make your own valentine book, complete w/envelopes, 1940s, 100 pcs., makes 50 valentines (ILLUS.) **10-20**
Flat, Bull Terrier, USA, 1940s, 4 1/4 x 9 1/2"........ **35**

Fold-out Valentine

Fold-out type, big-eyed girl w/honeycomb tissue skirt, 1930s, Germany, 8" (ILLUS.).. **15-25**
Fold-out type, w/honeycomb heart wheelbarrow being pushed by squirrel, printed in Germany, 1930s, 6 x 7" **15**
Fold-out type, w/honeycomb tissue, boy & girl exchanging valentines, 1930s, 3 x 4" **15**

Fold-out Valentine

Fold-out type, w/honeycomb tissue, cat looking in fish bowl, Germany, 1930s, 6 x 10" (ILLUS.) **35-45**
Fold-out type, w/honeycomb tissue, children on phone, 1930s, Germany, 6 x 8".......... **25**

Fold-out Valentine

Fold-out type, w/honeycomb tissue heart, nude little boy in big sombrero, Germany (ILLUS.) **12-20**
Fold-out type, w/honeycomb tissue, sailor, World War II, USA, 1940s, 4 x 5" **30**
Folded paper, African American girl in bubble, USA, 1940s, 2 1/2 x 3 1/2" **15**
Folded paper, die-cut, boy w/valentine, bashful girl, Raphael Tuck Co., 1920, 4 x 5 1/2"... **20**

Folded Paper Valentine

Folded paper, for "teacher," duck standing at easel painting the valentine with brush, 1940s, 3 x 4" (ILLUS.) **3-5**

Folded Paper Valentine

Folded paper, free-standing, girl & boy w/school books, For My Teacher, USA, 1940s, 4 x 5" (ILLUS.) **2-3**

Folded Paper Valentine

Folded paper, girl in tub, folds down to reveal message, USA, 1930s (ILLUS.) **7-10**
Folded paper, little girl by desk & blackboard, for teacher, free-standing, 1930s, 3 x 3" (ILLUS. top next page)........................... **4-6**

Folded Paper Valentine

Folded paper, Little Red Riding Hood, windows open revealing secret messages, Germany, 1930s, 4 x 4".............................. **12-15**

Folded Paper Valentine

Folded paper, thin paper, tied w/ribbon, young girl w/arms full of flowers, USA, 3 x 5" (ILLUS.) **3**
Girl, inserted into heart forming an easel, 1930s, 4 x 6" **5**
Girl, sewing doll dress, USA, 1940s, 4 x 5"....... **3-5**
Girl troll, 1960s, 3 x 5"... **15**

A-MERI-CARD Valentine

Little boy, carrying valentine for teacher, orange & grey colors, by A-MERI-CARD, 2 x 4" (ILLUS.) **2-5**
Little girl w/wooden duck, possibly an unsigned Charles Twelvetrees design, Germany, 1930s, 3 x 4" (ILLUS. top next column) **12**

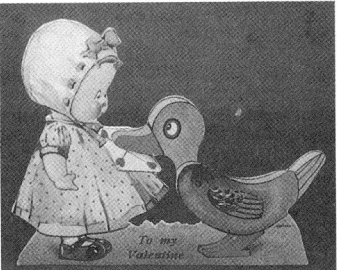

Little Girl with Wooden Duck Valentine

Love-Line bus, unsigned Charles Twelvetrees, USA, 1920s, 1 3/4 x 8"............................ **15**
Mechanical, boy & girl on motorcycle, printed in Germany, 1930s, 6 1/2 x 7" **12**

Mechanical Valentine

Mechanical, boy in car, opens up to reveal message, USA, 1930s, 3 x 5" (ILLUS.) **12**
Mechanical, boy playing piano, girl on piano, 1950s, 8 x 10" **10**
Mechanical, Boy Scout, USA, 1940s, 4 x 6" **25**
Mechanical, boy w/three legs that simulate running, 1930s, 3 x 4" **7**

Mechanical Valentine

Mechanical, bumble bee boy inserted in heart, moves from side to side, 1930s, 8 x 10" (ILLUS.) **15**
Mechanical, child w/barrel that slides up & down on body, 1930s, 4 x 5" **7**
Mechanical, clown on dog, rocks back & forth revealing message, 1930s, Germany, 5 x 7"... **35**

Mechanical Valentine

Mechanical, magician pulling rabbit out of hat, die-cut, 1940s, 4 x 5" (ILLUS.) **6**

Mechanical, monkey w/lobster, 1940s, 5 x 7" **35**

Mechanical, pull-the-string type, squirrel runs up a tree while children watch, Germany, 1930s, 3 x 7"................................ **35-40**

Mechanical, Skippy, USA, 1930s, 6 1/2 x 7".. **25**

Mechanical, soldier looking at his sweetheart, printed in USA, 1940s, 8 1/2 x 9" **50**

Mechanical Valentine

Mechanical, World War II ambulance, 1940s, 4 x 5" (ILLUS.) **15-18**

Mechanical, young man presenting a pot of flowers, 1920s, 2 1/2 x 5 1/2" **15**

Novelty Valentine

Novelty, chicken cracking egg, front attached to back by spring causing a wiggle effect, USA, late 1940s-early 1950s, 4 x 6" (ILLUS.) **10**

Paper Dolls Valentines

Paper dolls, boy & girl, w/one outfit to be punched out, 1940s, 3 x 5", each (ILLUS.) **6-8**

Pink Panther, sheet of valentines from Crush, give-a-way, 12 per sheet........................ **20**

Policeman, Carrington Co., 1930s, 5 x 7".......... **25**

Pop-up type, Googly-eyed children, 1920s, 9 1/2"... **358**

Pop-up type, pilot flies up to meet his lady love when opened, 1920s, 4 x 5" **20-25**

Pop-up type, ship w/boy & girl, 1920s, Germany, 12".. **207**

Pull-out type, girl waving goodbye w/plane overhead, printed in Germany, 1930s, 7x11" **35**

"Punch & Judy," puppet theater, 1920s, 2 x 5" **35**

Rocker-type Valentine

Rocker-type, girl riding donkey, valentine actually rocks, Germany, 1930s, 3 x 5" (ILLUS.) **10-12**

Self-standing type, Cinderella, dimensional, Germany, 1930s **10**

Self-standing type, embossed, die-cut & folded, 1920s, 3 x 3".. **10**

Stand-up type, Little Lulu & Tubby, 8"................ **20**

WATCHES

Also see Antique Trader Jewelry Price Guide.

Pocket watch, hunting case, lady's, Empress JMG Co., pendent-type, gold-filled case w/floral-engraved outer case w/engraved scalloped edge, monogrammed inside & dated 1911, enameled dial w/seconds hand, case marked by the Ideal Watch Case Co., 15 jewels **$280**

Fine American Waltham Pocket Watch

Pocket watch, hunting case, man's, American Waltham, 14k gold case, 17 jewels adjustable, shield engraving on the case, works marked by P.S. Barlett, Waltham, Massachusetts, ca. 1906 (ILLUS.) **952**

Pocket watch, hunting case, man's, American Waltham Co., P.S. Bartlett, white enameled dial & small second, blued steel hands, Roman numerals, movement #1331680, patent pinion, 14k yellow gold case w/engine-turned design & monogrammed crest **743**

Pocket watch, hunting case, man's, American Waltham Watch Co., white enameled dial & small seconds, Roman numerals & red Arabic seconds numerals, blued steel Brequet-style hands, movement #5150465, safety pinion, coin silver case w/chased decoration, sterling watch chain **154**

Pocket watch, hunting case, man's, Elgin National Watch Co., 14k mixed-color gold ornately engraved case w/floral yellow, green & rose gold engraving surrounding a repoussé engraving of a deer in rose gold, the reverse engraved w/a center shield of rose gold surrounded by floral designs in yellow, white, green & rose gold bordered w/scalloped edge front & back, 17 jewels, ca. 1924 .... **3,360**

Pocket watch, hunting case, man's, Elgin National Watch Co., G.M. Wheeler, white enameled dial & small second, blued steel hands, Roman numerals, movement #278696, patent pinion, gold-filled case w/chased scrollwork & shield & engine-turned background, w/key & gold-filled T-bar chain **248**

Pocket watch, hunting case, man's, Hampton Watch Co., Springfield, Massachusetts, white enameled dial w/small second & blued steel hands, Roman numerals, movement #475644, gold-filled case w/floral chased decoration & horse head on one cover, gold-filled socket chain w/rose gold-filled baby fob engraved on one side w/"BABY BORN June 13th 1900 CARRIE May 23rd 1873" & the reverse w/"BABY DIED November 23rd 1900 CARRIE DIED March 31st 1901" **242**

Pocket watch, hunting case, man's, Illinois Watch Co., Springfield, Illinois, patent pinion, gilt dial w/small seconds hand & raised Roman numerals, movement #654721, center scene of buildings, gold-filled case w/interior engraved "Jan 27, 1900" & exterior floral & scroll chase decorated w/one bowl depicting buildings, w/key & gold-filled T-bar chain **275**

Pocket watch, hunting case, man's, Illinois Watch Co., Springfield, Illinois, white enameled dial & small seconds, blued steel hands, Roman numerals, movement #740317, ornate gold-filled case w/chased design of building & flowers **286**

Pocket watch, hunting case, man's, Illinois Watch Company Bunn model, Springfield, Illinois, 18k yellow gold engraved case, 21 ruby jewels, adjusted temperature, five positions, Isochronison, double rolled, working, ca. 1910 .... **532**

Pocket watch, hunting case, man's, U.S. Watch Co., Waltham, Massachusetts, white enameled dial & small seconds decorated w/mauve & gilt flowers, each Arabic numeral surrounded by a pink circle, movement #20811, smooth gold-filled case w/floral etched edge **330**

Pocket watch, hunting case, man's, Zenith, 14k gold engraved case, ca. 1900, mint condition **1,568**

Rare Waltham Chronograph Watch

Pocket watch, open face, man's, Waltham Chronograph, 14k gold case, works marked "Pat. Sept. 28.80 Eng Pat No 3224 Ser. #3127188 AW Co. Waltham, Mass," fine condition w/slight dial crazing, ca. 1880 (ILLUS.) **1,176**

Pocket watch, open-face, man's, American Watch Co., Keller & Bros., Allentown, Pennsylvania, white enameled dial & small seconds, Roman numerals, movement #2751998, safety pinion, gold-filled case w/engine-turned cover & chased floral work on rim **220**

Pocket watch, open-face, man's, Appleton, Tracy & Co., Waltham, Massachusetts, 17-jewel movement, white enameled dial w/small seconds hand, Arabic numerals, blued steel hands, gold-filled smooth case, gold-filled chain & small pocket knife, signed **193**

Pocket watch, open-face, man's, Tiffany & Company, New York, 18k yellow gold case w/21 jewel Swiss movement, works marked "AG Agassiz W. Co.," w/a 14k yellow gold watch chain, ca. 1900, the set **1,512**

Wristwatch, gold (14k), 17 jewels, double teardrop lugs, ca. 1945, Driva **125-200**

Wristwatch, gold (18k), 17 jewels, chronological by Venius W. Co., Hilton W. Co. **300-400**

WEATHERVANES

Boy with hoop & running dog, cut sheet metal, silhouetted form of a young boy running w/hoop & stick preceded by a running dog, weathered to an overall verdigris, mounted on a rod on a black metal base, ca. 1930, 55 1/2" l., 43" h. **$7,800**

Cod fish, carved & painted wood, full-bodied form w/scales, tail, mouth & eyes & inset carved dorsal & pectoral fins, mounted to an iron rod & rectangular modern base, gold paint, late 19th - early 20th c., 33" l., 17" h. **2,990**

Cow, gilt copper, flattened full-bodied animal, attributed to Cushing and White, late 19th c., 24 3/4" l., 13 1/2" h. (seam split on muzzle, gilt loss to upper back & head) **6,325**

Cow, molded copper & zinc, full-bodied form w/zinc head & udder, depicted standing, w/horns & outstretched ears, late 19th - early 20th c., 24" l., 15 3/8" h. .. **6,325**

Eagle, copper & cast zinc, hollow body w/good cast & embossed details, upraised wings, perched on a ball above an arrow directional, worn old gilding & green patina, late 19th c., on modern stand, 17" w., 16" h. **3,850**

Fish, painted zinc, flat sheet metal figure w/applied fins & green glass eyes, gilt finish, 19th c., 16" l, 13 3/4" h. (gilt loss, glass eye cracked) **1,035**

Flying goose, carved wood, w/an articulated bill, eyes & feather edging, extended neck & downswept wings, on a cylindrical metal support w/modern base, early 20th c., 27" l., 22" h. **5,750**

Sailing Galleon Weathervane

Galleon, gilt-copper & iron, molded deep keeled sailing vessel w/two sails & a large banner at the top of the mast, w/three directionals, from Gloucester, Massachu-

setts area, late 19th c., gilt loss, imperfections, 25" l., 32" h. (ILLUS.) **2,300**

Unusual Grasshopper Weathervane

Grasshopper, cast iron, long full-bodied insect retaining some original gilding & polychrome decoration, mounted on a black metal base, late 19th - early 20th c., 31 1/2" l., 24" h. (ILLUS.) **23,000**

Prancing Horse Weathervane

Horse, copper, swell-bodied prancing animal w/raised fore and back legs, molded tail, spike mane & sheet copper ears, on a rod in a black metal base, traces of old gilding, late 19th c., 54" l., 43 3/4" h. (ILLUS.)......... **11,500**

Horse, molded & gillded copper & zinc, small scale 'Index' type, the swell-bodied animal w/cast zinc forequarters, molded & gilded 'crinkled' cut sheet copper mane & tail, molded copper legs & applied sheet copper ears, J. Howard & Co., Massachusetts, third quarter 19th c., 17" l. 16" h. **13,800**

Horse, running, molded gilt copper, tail out behind, ribs showing on body, w/directionals, late 19th c., 24 1/2" l., 15 1/4" h. (dents, gilt loss, seam separation)............. **2,530**

Horse & jockey, gilt copper, full-bodied running animal w/a bobbed tail, 19th c., 31 1/2" l., 18" h. (regilded) **4,600**

Horse & jockey, molded copper & cast zinc, the swell-bodied figure of a running horse w/a cast zinc jockey, surface weathered to an overall verdigris w/remains of old gilding, third quarter 19th c., 30 1/2" l., 18 1/2" h. **21,450**

Horse & sulky, molded copper & zinc, full-bodied galloping animal w/molded articulated eyes, flowing mane, nostrils, mouth & tail, pulling a rider w/hat, coat, pants, boots & whip on a seat flanked by large wheels, 19th c., 33 3/4" l., 18 1/2" h........ **12,650**

Rooster, cast iron, well-detailed body w/a gilt sheet-iron tail, traces of gilt on the body, above a ball over scroll-trimmed directionals, attributed to the Rochester Iron Works, 19th c. (partial foot missing, repairs) 4,313

Rooster, gilt molded copper, full-bodied bird w/small high, wide breast & large arched tail, on an arrow directional, late 19th c., 38" l., 39 1/2" h. (minor gilt loss). 12,650

Rooster, painted sheet iron, silhouetted form painted yellow, 19th c., 24" l., 27 1/2" h. (wear, rust) 2,415

Rooster, sheet metal, hollow body of two pieces w/raised wings, eyes & open beak, tapering sharply to a pedestal base w/tall arched detailed tail feathers cut from one piece of metal, alligatored brown repaint, mounted on a later wooden base, 18 1/4" w., 22 1/2" h. (one bullet hole, bent feather) 2,640

Merino Sheep Weathervane

Sheep, copper, standing Merino sheep w/flattened full body, w/large & small copper spheres & iron directionals, solder repairs, possibly L.W. Cushing and Sons, Waltham, Massachusetts, 28 1/2" l., 21 1/2" h. (ILLUS.) 9,775

Tandem bicycle, cut sheet metal, silhouetted figures of a man smoking a pipe & wearing a bowler hat & a woman wearing a hat & a mutton-sleeved dress riding a tandem bicycle w/moving rear wheel, mounted on a rod continuing to a large sheet metal arrow, directionals below, ca. 1930, 44" l., 28 1/2" h. 1,800

Rare Tennis Player Weathervane

Tennis player, copper, swell-bodied full figure of a young female tennis player in an action pose & wearing a long skirt & cap, good naturally patinated surface retaining traces of original gilding, some splitting in foot, late 19th c., 19 1/4" w., 31" h. (ILLUS.) 23,000

WESTERN AMERICANA

Bit, iron, Canon City curb-style, the cheekpiece silver inlaid w/S-shaped panels engraved w/the vine & leaf design, the middle of the cheek adorned w/round conchas inscribed "US," by Robert Baldwin, early 20th c., 8" l. **$518**

Bit, iron, U.S. Cavalry ring-type, the cheeks decorated w/standard brass ornaments showing the initials "U.S.," marked on the outside cheekpiece "Barclay," late 19th c., 7 1/2" l. 437

Bit, silver-overlaid steel, the cheekpieces designed in the Santa Maria style & overlaid w/silver deeply engraved w/a foliate design, the mouthpiece in the Mona Lisa style, hallmarked "A Tietjen Reno, Nev," late 20th c., 8" l. 115

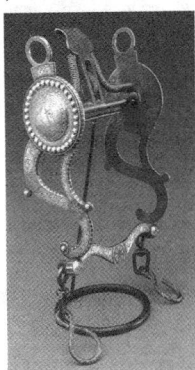

Finely Engraved Spade Bit

Bit, spade-style, iron, classic style engraving illustrates skills of artist John Estrada, the cheekpieces overlaid in silver & engraved w/scrollwork featuring a foliate design, the 3 1/4" d. conchas engraved to depict Estrada's exquisite horseheads surrounded w/a berry design border, hallmarked "G.S.S. Co. Winnemucca Nev." & "J.E.", by Goldberg and Staunton Company, bit 8 3/4" l. (ILLUS.) 6,670

Book, "Bank and Train Robbers of the West," by Belford, Clark & Co., two-parts, first part on the James Brothers, w/details on their career & a portrait of Robert Ford, the second part about the Younger Brothers, printed by Donohue & Henneberry, Chicago, ca. 1882, 486 pp. 403

Bridle, hitched horsehair, Deer Lodge Prison model, intricately hitched w/seven different colors including green, yellow, red, purple, pink & black on a natural background, colors create a striking diamond design throughout the headstall & a barber pole spiral design on the throat latch & reins, white tassels adorn the headstall & reins, the glass rosettes w/images of horse & dogs, early 20th c. (ILLUS.)......... **3,450**

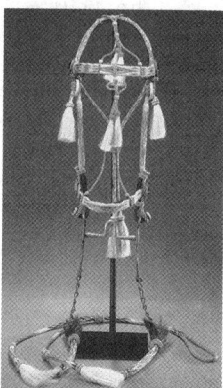

Deer Lodge Prison Horsehair Bridle

Chaps, shotgun-style, brown leather, legs embellished w/spaghetti-style fringe, the pockets w/leather knotted buttons, marked twice on either side of the billet "J.S. Collins Cheyenne, Wyo.," late 19th c., pr..................................... **3,450**

Chaps, shotgun-style, brown leather, the legs adorned w/spaghetti fringe & the pockets w/snap closures, marked "Victor Marden Maker The Dalles, Or.," late 19th c., pr... **978**

Cowboy boots, black leather w/leather pulls, late 19th c., 20" h., pr. **322**

Cowboy hat, black felt, by J.B. Stetson, w/original box, ca. 1930s **322**

Cowboy hat, Tom Mix-style, silver belly felt, by J.B. Stetson, size 4X, 1950s **368**

Letter, hand-written two-page document from lawman Pat Garrett to his wife & signed "P.F. Garrett," dated Roswell, New Mexico, 16 July 1893, pale ink, w/original postmarked envelope in Garrett's hand, the group.................................. **1,495**

Annie Oakley-signed Photograph

Photograph, albumen portrait view of Annie Oakley, the international sharp-shooting star of Buffalo Bill Cody's Wild West, signed on the lower mount "Annie Oakley," by Baker's Art Gallery, Columbus, Ohio, late 19th c., 4 x 6 1/2" (ILLUS.).................... **4,025**

Photograph, albumen print, portrait of Oglala Sioux Chief Red Cloud wearing a full eagle headdress & a breastplate composed of bone 'hair pipe' beads, by Barry, 6 1/2 x 8 1/2" **1,955**

Photograph, gelatin silver print, imperial size studio view of legendary Buck Taylor, wearing impressive leopard chaps, sporting his six-shooter, Taylor known as "The King of the Cow-Boys" & starred in Buffalo Bill's Wild West for nearly ten seasons, by Gilbert & Bacon, 10 x 16"...... **5,175**

Photograph, gelatin silver print of Buffalo Bill Cody & Chief Joseph shaking hands, w/teepees in the background, 5 x 7 1/2" ... **5,520**

Photograph, gelatin silver print of twenty-nine members of Buffalo Bill Cody's band, led by William Sweeney, newspaper article attached to the back describes band, by Stacy, 6 x 8"................................ **2,300**

Photograph, gelatin silver print, studio view titled "Bear Ranchers in the West," shows Yellowstone Kelly, John Howard & Mountain Charlie wearing beaded & fringed jackets & sporting their firearms, one standing in back, one seated & third reclining in front, by Maul, 6 x 8 1/4"......... **2,185**

Early Photograph of Geronimo

Photograph, gold-tone platinum print of Geronimo, a studio view of the subject wearing a ribbon & medal pinned to his jacket, by F.A. Rinehart, copyright 1898, 7 1/4 x 9 1/4" (ILLUS.)................................ **2,760**

Pocket Watch of Bat Masterson

Pocket watch, gold, owned by Bat Masterson, an octagonal 14k gold open-faced case equipped w/an opera movement surrounded by silver filigree designed by the Waltham Watch Co. of Waltham, Massachusetts, movement marked "A.W.W.C.O. Ruby 19113096," case marked "J. Depollier & Son 14k 3426," the inside of the back engraved "To Bat Masterson From Freddie Welsh Xmas 1915" (ILLUS.) **6,670**

Buffalo Bill's Cased Colt Revolver

Revolver, Colt Frontier six shooter 'etched panel' model, owned & used by Buffalo Bill Cody, w/Cody's customized stippled grip straps, marked "O3/ICP" on both sides of the walnut grips, presented in its original factory deluxe mahogany case lined in royal purple velour & equipped w/a mahogany block for 50 cartridges contoured for the revolver, Serial No. 77234 for 1882, descended in the family, 7 1/2" barrel, the set (ILLUS.)................... **36,800**

Riata, braided rawhide, four-strand w/a leather-covered honda, fine patina, early 20th c., 50' l. **115**

Saddle, brown leather, full-seat model, fully adorned w/an early basket stamp design inset w/floral tooling on the corners of the skirts & at the center of the jockeys, hallmarked "RT Frazier Maker Pueblo, Colo." at front of seat & also "RT Frazier R'G'D. Trade Mark" inside a cartouche on the cantle, early 20th c., seat 15".......... **1,308**

Saddle, brown leather, square skirts, fully carved in a floral design, hallmarked in a silver plaque mounted on the front of the seat, the horn mounted w/a silver horn cap adorned w/a gold longhorn steer head, intricately engraved in floral & foliate designs, the back of the cantle w/a silver plate engraved w/three names of owners, marked "Makers Nolte Olson San Francisco, Calif.," 1937-41, seat 15" **1,610**

Saddle, brown leather, the entire front as well as the cantle edge adorned w/beautifully engraved heavy sterling silver, the back of the cantle board fully silver-mounted & intricately engraved, inscribed w/the owner's name, the saddle profusely adorned w/fine California Poppy conchas & smaller intricate No. 484 spots, the saddle deeply hand-carved w/a floral & foliate design matching the theme of the conchas, hallmarked on an early silver plaque "Edward H Bohlin Hollywood California Made for Fred W. Bergman," advertised in the Bohlin catalog as the "Bohlin Special Saddle," mid-20th c., seat 15".. **13,800**

Saddle, full seat model, black leather, early basket stamp design adorns the swells, skirts, jockeys, seat & stirrup leathers, nickel-covered brass spot decoratively placed behind the fork binding, hallmarked on both side jockeys "J H Hanes and Sons Makers Omaha NEBR.," early 20th c., seat 16".. **805**

Saddle, full seat model, brown leather, adorned w/a combination of early basket stamping inset w/carving in a foliate & floral design on the seat, skirts, jockeys & fenders, hallmarked "E C Lee Pierce, So. Dak.," early 20th c., seat 16" **1,610**

Saddle, full seat model, brown leather, classic style tooled w/border designs along the perimeters of the skirts, side jockeys & the stirrup leathers, the seat & gullet decorated w/a scalloped tooled edge, hallmarked "F.A. Meanea maker Cheyenne, WYO" & model "14P," early 20th c., seat 15"... **1,150**

Saddle, lady's astride model, brown leather, decorated w/border stamping, the seat tooled in floral & foliate designs, hallmarked in a circular cartouche on the seat "F.A. Meanea maker Cheyenne, Wyo," early 20th c., seat 15" **1,093**

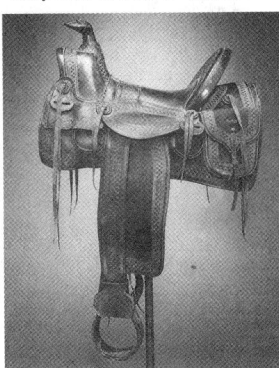

Scarce Robbins & Lenoir Saddle

Saddle, loop seat-style, brown leather, adorned w/a bold basketweave design on the perimeters of the fork, gullet, skirts, jockeys, fenders, stirrup leathers & saddle bags, the inside of the cantle exquisitely carved w/a foliate & floral design, marked "Robbins and Lenoir Miles City Mont," 1891-94, seat 16" (ILLUS.) ... **12,650**

Saddle, loop seat-style, brown leather, entirely hand-carved w/a foliate & floral design, the fork binding laced w/brown leather buckstitching, front of seat hallmarked "F. Ringe Yreka," late 19th c., seat 15"... **1,725**

Saddle, martingale & bridle, silver-mounted parade-style, a 'San Gabriel' model classic black leather saddle deeply carved w/small intricate scroll & floral designs, the entire front & cantle board completely covered w/finely engraved

Bohlin Silver-mounted Parade Outfit

heavy sterling silver, the horn neck & front of the gullet adorned w/special sterling rope roll design, other ornamentation includes conchas mounted alternatively w/figures in silver of buffalos, bucking broncos, steer heads, horse heads & eagles, the exquisite tapaderos, breast collar & bridle elaborately embellished w/matching sterling silver conchas, the back of the cantle inscribed "Margaret Rowe El Rancho Margarita Yearington Neveda," made by Edward H. Bohlin, seat 15", the set (ILLUS.).......................... **17,250**

Saddle, martingale, bridle & sarape, parade-type, silver-mounted black leather, custom-made, the entire front of the saddle as well as the cantle board, skirts, back jockeys, fenders & tapaderos completely embellished w/silver engraved w/cowboys & American Indians, the gullet, cantle binding & horn neck w/special sterling rope roll, the border ornamentation composed of conchas w/bucking horses & American Indian head designs, matching ornamentation on all pieces, made by Edward H. Bohlin, worn in 35 Tournament of Roses parades, cantle inscribed "W.H.B.," mid-20th c., the set **40,250**

Fine Silver-mounted Parade Saddle

Saddle, martingale, bridle & sarape, silver-mounted parade-type, the black leather saddle deeping hand-carved w/an intricate floral & foliate design by H.H. Heiser,

the silver work commissioned by Keyston Bros. of San Francisco, the heavy solid sterling silver elaborately adorns the entire horn, swells, cantle edge & board, skirts & tapaderos, the swells covered w/silver engraved in a foliate design & decorated w/large Indian heads raised in high-relief, the saddle's horn w/matching gold Indian head figure in high-relief, the cantle binding decorated w/a sterling silver rope roll & the cantle board completely silver mounted, the skirts entirely embellished w/conchas in an interlocking diamond design & each concha adorned w/Indian heads, the sarape elaborately adorned w/interlocking diamond conchas bordered by square conchas alternately mounted w/gold Indian heads & round conchas, the matching matingale & bridge also fully mounted w/interlocking silver squares & adorned w/engraving in a foliate design & Indian heads, silver plate on back of cantle engraved "A.W. Frederick," saddle hallmarked "H.H. Heiser" on the seat, Keyston stamp found on conchas, buckles & tips, mid-20th c., the set (ILLUS. of saddle) **9,200**

Vintage Carved Wood Saloon Doors

Saloon doors, carved walnut, the top of the doors adorned w/a scrolling foliate design & the centers are inset w/beveled glass mirrors, the bottoms constructed w/a band of short wooden carved dowels, late 19th c., each 25 x 44 1/2", pr. (ILLUS.) **1,840**

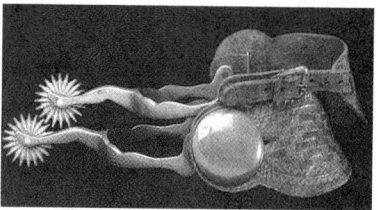

Double Gal Leg-Style Spurs

Spurs, bronze, double gal leg-style, one piece, the heel bands & shanks formed w/the shape of a woman's leg & ornately chased to depict her boots, stockings & garter, a twenty-point rowel, hallmarked w/a star & "Hercules," by North and Judd, early 20th c., spur 6" l., pr. (ILLUS.).............. **690**

Spurs, cast silver, Navajo, two-piece, the heel bands adorned w/large scalloped conchas & a linear design continued on through the shanks, chap guards & rowels, the spur strap conchas & buckles created in the same fashion together w/carved leather straps depicting a road runner, early 20th c., spur 8" l., pr. **2,990**

Spurs, iron, California-style, single-mounted one-piece, heel bands nickel inlaid w/the chevron design, the spur shank designed w/a bird's head & an impressive thirty-point rowel, hallmarked "C H Ketchum" beside the fixed button on each spur, 20th c., spur 7" l., pr. **1,495**

Spurs, iron, California-style, two-piece double-mounted, the heel bands designed w/scalloped edges & inlaid w/silver hearts opposing a central concha adorned w/engraving & dot punching, the reverse heel bands inlaid w/silver in a linear design, the wide shanks constructed w/silver-inlaid barrel chap guards & eight-point rowels, late 19th c., 7 1/2" l., pr. **2,070**

Spurs, iron, California-style, two-piece double-mounted, the heel bands inlaid w/silver in an early 'target' design, the center concha & surrounding outside edge adorned w/filigree work & decorated w/wiggle line & dot punch engraving, the offside heel band beveled & inlaid w/silver forming a linear design, the shank features silver inlay on the chap guard continuing down the shank, ten-point rowel, late 19th c., 8" l., pr. **4,140**

Spurs, iron, Colorado-style, one-piece single-mounted, heel bands adorned w/nickel silver overlaid panels & engraved w/a foliate design, the shanks w/rectangular nickel panels & nine-point rowels, heel band hallmarked "Crockett," early 20th c., spur 6" l., pr. **863**

Spurs, iron, double gal leg-style, double-mounted one-piece, heel bands overlaid w/silver, brass & copper in rectangular designs, the offside overlaid w/nickel-silver in a tapering form & incised w/typical Texas-style engraving, the shanks constructed to form ladies' legs & adorned w/silver overlay engraved to depict a garter, stockings & lace-up boots, hallmarked "G.A. Bischoff & Co.," early 20th c., spur 6 1/4" l., pr. **6,900**

Spurs, iron, Spanish Colonial-type, one-piece double-mounted w/ornately chased & inlaid heel bands, the shanks designed w/open filigree work depicting dogs as the chap guards, equipped w/chased jinglebobs & eight-point rowels, mid-18th c., 8" l., pr. **1,955**

Texas-style Overlaid Iron Spurs

Spurs, iron, Texas-style, double-mounted one-piece, heel bands overlaid w/copper & decorated w/nickel silver hearts, the reverse heel band mounted w/nickel silver in an elongated diamond, the shanks mounted w/alternating copper & nickel silver overlay & ten-point rowels, inside of heel band hallmarked "K B & P" for Kelly Brothers & Parker, early 20th c., spur 7" l., pr. (ILLUS.) **920**

Wyoming-Style Decorated Spurs

Spurs, iron, Wyoming-style, two-piece double-mounted, the heel bands inlaid w/silver depicting the name "Frank," the offside heel band inlaid w/silver engraved in a floral & foliate design, the chap guards & shanks fully inlaid w/silver in a linear design, the rowels adorned w/engraved silver rowel covers, hallmarked "GS Garcia Elko Nev.," early 20th c., spur 7 1/2" l., pr. (ILLUS.) **6,900**

Stationery cabinet, hardwood, a narrow rectangular top above an upright case w/a wide two-panel door opening to an interior fitted w/rows of pigeonholes over letter slots w/a small drawer at the bottom, flat molded base, original black stenciled marking on the door "Wells Fargo & Co. Express," original paper label on top reads "Wells Fargo & Co. Express From Supply Department Chicago" w/an agent's signature, late 19th c., 10 1/2 x 22", 30" h. **978**

Stevensgraph, woven silk picture w/portraits of Mr. Nate Salsbury, Good Eagle, Moccasin Top, Little Chief, Flies Above, Blue Horse, Little Bull, Red Shirt & Buffalo Bill Cody, the lower section adorned w/crossed American flags & a golden eagle, England, late 19th c., 3 1/2 x 5 1/2".... **1,840**

WESTERN CHARACTER COLLECTIBLES

Since the closing of the Western frontier in the late 19th century the myth of the American cowboy has loomed large in popular fiction. With the growth of the motion picture industry early in this century, cowboy heroes became a mainstay of the entertainment industry. By the 1920s major Western heroes were a big draw at the box office and this popularity continued with the dawning of the TV age in the 1950s. We list here a variety of collectibles relating to all American Western personalities popular this century.

Gene Autry Jigsaw Puzzle

Gene Autry jigsaw puzzle, Gene Autry color photo, frame tray-type, Gene nailing up wanted sign, Whitman No. 2628, 1950s (ILLUS.).. **$25-35**

Gene Autry lunch box & thermos, steel, Melody Ranch design, Universal, 1950s.. **300-350**

Gene Autry toy, Magic Slate, "Gene Autry's Champion Slate," Lowe Co., 1950s **30-40**

Hopalong Cassidy billfold, brown leather, Hoppy riding Topper, w/zipper, 1950........ **50-90**

Hopalong Cassidy billfold, head shots of Hoppy & Topper, black w/zipper, 1950...... **40-80**

Hopalong Cassidy & Topper Binoculars

Hopalong Cassidy binoculars, silvered metal w/yellow decal of Hoppy & Topper, flaring red plastic eye sockets (ILLUS.) ... **75-100**

Hopalong Cassidy domino set, Milton Bradley, 1950... **150-200**

Hopalong Cassidy figures, hard plastic, Hoppy on Topper, chain reins, Ideal, 1950s, boxed, 5" h., 2 pcs. **125-200**

Hopalong Cassidy game, "Hopalong Cassidy Lasso Game," Transogram, 1950s... **125-175**

Hopalong Cassidy jigsaw puzzle, Hopalong Cassidy frame tray-type, photo of Hoppy & Topper, Whitman, 1950 .... **20-35**

Hopalong Cassidy lunch box & thermos, steel, Hoppy riding Topper, Aladdin, 1954.. **225-300**

Hopalong Cassidy movie poster, "Forty Thieves," starring William Boyd as Hopalong Cassidy, 1940s, one-sheet, 27 x 41" (ILLUS. top next column)................. **616**

Hopalong Cassidy Movie Poster

Hopalong Cassidy on Topper, windup tin, rocking base motion, colorfully lithographed, Marx, 1946, 11" l. **450-750**

Hopalong Cassidy Felt Pennant

Hopalong Cassidy pennant, triangular felt, black w/picture of Hoppy & Topper & a rope-style Hopalong facsimile signature, Casey Premium Merchandise Company, Chicago, mint (ILLUS.)................................ **30-45**

Hopalong Cassidy Radio

Hopalong Cassidy radio, black case w/red & silver front, Arvin, 1950, near mint (ILLUS.).. **1,455**

Hopalong Cassidy rocking chair, child size, chrome & vinyl, scene of Hoppy & Topper, Comfort Lines, 1950s **100-175**

Hoppy Wave-lid Aladdin Thermos

Hopalong Cassidy thermos, steel, yellow ground w/red lettering, color scene of Hoppy standing beside Topper, wave design red lid, Aladdin, 1950-52 (ILLUS.)...... **40-60**

Hopalong Cassidy toy, inflatable Topper figure, barrel-shaped body w/painted legs, early 1950s, 19" h........................ **100-150**

Hopalong Cassidy View-Master reel, scenes of Hoppy & Topper, 1950s.............. **8-12**

Lone Ranger billfold, Lone Ranger sign & "Hi-Yo Silver," brown vinyl, color artwork, 1953....................... **65-95**

Lone Ranger card game, Parker Bros., 1938, box 3 1/2 x 5"........................ **87**

Lone Ranger coloring book, Hi-Yo Silver, Whitman, 1955, 6 1/2 x 7 1/2"........ **20-30**

Lone Ranger figure, chalkware carnival-type, Lone Ranger on Silver, 1940s, 11" h........................... **75-125**

Lone Ranger game, board-type, "Lone Ranger Game - Hi-Yooo Silver!," Parker Bros., 1938..................... **60-85**

Lone Ranger game, "Lone Ranger and the Silver Bullets," 1956, box 13 1/2 x 16"....... **60-80**

Lone Ranger game, target-type, square color cardboard target, Marx, 1946......... **90-160**

Lone Ranger game, target-type, tin stand-up Silver & Lone Ranger, Marx, 1938, box 9 1/2" sq. **225-300**

Lone Ranger guitar, pressed wood, reads "Hi-Yo Silver - Lone Ranger," Superior Musical Instruments, 1940s................. **150-200**

Lone Ranger jigaw puzzles, Lone Ranger set of three puzzles, Puzzle Craft, 1945, boxed, the set **100-150**

Lone Ranger jigsaw puzzle, Lone Ranger frame tray-type, Lone Ranger rides Silver across the desert, Whitman, 1950s, 11 x 15"........................ **25-35**

Lone Ranger jigsaw puzzle, Lone Ranger frame tray-type, Lone Ranger & Silver & Tonto & Scout, Whitman, 1954.................. **25-35**

Lone Ranger jigsaw puzzle, Lone Ranger, photo with Silver in foreground w/the Lone Ranger & Tonto, 1978 .... **12-20**

Reproduction Lone Ranger Lunch Box

Lone Ranger lunch box, steel, scene of Lone Ranger riding Silver, red sides, 1990s reproduction by G Whiz (ILLUS.).... **20-30**

Lone Ranger lunch box, steel, scene of Lone Ranger & Silver, reads "Hi-Yo Silver," blue sides version, ADCO Liberty, 1954........................ **250-400**

Lone Ranger lunch box, steel, scene of Lone Ranger & Silver, reads "Hi-Yo Silver," red sides version, ADCO Liberty, 1954 .... **200-300**

Legend of the Lone Ranger Set

Lone Ranger lunch box & thermos, steel, color scene of Lone Ranger on Silver & Tonto on Scout, black trim, marked "The Legend of the Lone Ranger," Aladdin, 1980 (ILLUS.) **30-55**

Lone Ranger model kit, plastic, Lone Ranger on a rearing Silver, 1/10 scale, Aurora, 1967 .... **20-150**

Lone Ranger 1974 Model Kit

Lone Ranger model kit, plastic, Lone Ranger on a rearing Silver, comic scenes series, re-release of 1967 kit, Aurora, 1974 (ILLUS.) **20-25**

Lone Ranger paint book, scene of Lone Ranger w/"Hi-Yo Silver," Whitman, 1938, 11 x 14"........................ **65-95**

Lone Ranger paint box, lithographed tin w/paints inside, Milton Bradley, 1950s **35-60**

Lone Ranger picture printing kit, rubber stamps & booklet, Staperkraft, 1939, the set........................ **80-120**

Lone Ranger push puppet, Lone Ranger on Silver, 1968, on a 2" d. round base **40-65**

Lone Ranger rocking horse, painted wood, Lone Ranger & Silver w/"Hi-Yo Silver," 1940s, 21" h. **250-350**

Lone Ranger & Silver figures, articulated plastic figures w/accessories, Gabriel, 1977, 12" h., 2 pcs. (ILLUS. top next page) **40-75**

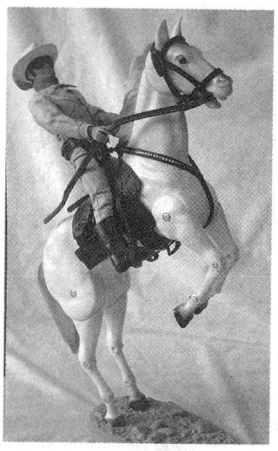

Gabriel Lone Ranger & Silver Figures

Lone Ranger & Silver figures, hard plastic, half-rearing pose, Hartland, 1950s, boxed, 9 1/2" h., pr.................................. **150-250**

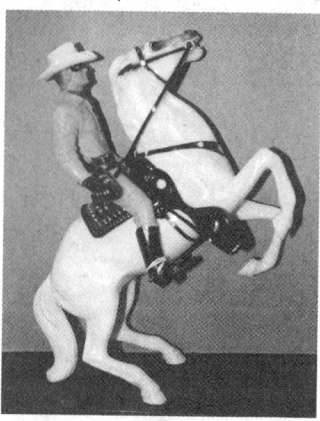

Hartland Lone Ranger & Silver

Lone Ranger & Silver figures, hard plastic, rearing horse, Hartland, 1954, boxed, 9 1/2" h., pr. (ILLUS.).............................. **200-300**

Lone Ranger & Silver figures, hard plastic, standing pose, Hartland, 1950s, boxed, 9 1/2" h., pr.................................. **200-300**

Lone Ranger & Silver toy, windup tin, the Lone Ranger riding a rearing Silver, a lariat in one hand, L. Marx, 1938, boxed, 7" l.. **350-700**

Lone Ranger tattoo transfers, sold w/bubble gum, Swell, 1970s **12-20**

Lone Ranger toy, paddle-ball, Hi-Yo Silver Lone Ranger Bat-O-Ball, from Tom's Toasted Peanuts, 1939 .... **100-150**

Lone Ranger View-Master packet, The Legend of the Lone Ranger, three-reel set, 1981.. **10-15**

Lone Ranger View-Master packet, The Lone Ranger, three-reel set, GAF, 1956... **25-35**

Lone Ranger playset, "Lone Ranger Rodeo," Marx, 1950, box 13 x 15".............. **150-250**

Roy Rogers Camera

Roy Rogers camera, black plastic & silver metal, scene of Roy & Trigger on front w/their names, late 1940s, boxed, 4" h. (ILLUS.) **100-200**

Roy & Dale with Pets Lunch Box

Roy Rogers & Dale Evans lunch box & thermos, steel, names in oval center reserve surrounded by color scene of Roy & Dale w/various pets, yellow border, 1950s (ILLUS.) **150-250**

Roy & Dale at Ranch Lunch Box

Roy Rogers & Dale Evans lunch box & thermos, steel, Roy riding Trigger w/Dale standing in background near gateway to the ranch, wood grain backing, 1953 (ILLUS.).................................... **150-250**

Roy Rogers Rodeo Game

Roy Rogers game, "Roy Rogers Rodeo Game," Dee McCann, 1939 (ILLUS.)..... **100-150**

Roy Rogers Guitar

Roy Rogers guitar, cardboard & wood, bust portrait of Roy & Trigger, Range Rhythm Toys, 1950s, 28" l. (ILLUS.)........ **75-175**

Roy Rogers jigsaw puzzle, frame tray-type, Roy on Trigger, w/cover photo to frame, 1950 .... **30-55**

Roy Rogers jigsaw puzzle, frame tray-type, Roy & Trigger stand together, Whitman, 1948...................................... **30-50**

Roy Rogers on Trigger pull toy, wood & metal, musical-type, late 1940s, 8 1/2" l. **125-175**

Roy Rogers playing cards, marked "Happy Trails," Victorville, California, in plastic box, the deck................................... **8-15**

Cardboard Roy Rogers Playset

Roy Rogers playset, cardboard fold-out type, shows Roy Rogers Double R Bar Ranch, 1950s (ILLUS.)........................... **100-175**

Roy Rogers playset, plastic, Roy Rogers Double R Bar Ranch, w/figures, Marx, 1950s, 24" l. box, the set........................ **250-350**

Roy Rogers playset, plastic, Roy Rogers Rodeo, w/figures, Marx, early 1950s, 15" l. box, the set.................................... **250-350**

Roy Rogers riding toy, plastic on metal base w/wheels, skinny model of Trigger, 1950s, 18 1/2" h. **150-225**

Roy Rogers riding toy, plush on metal base w/wheels, model of Trigger, early 1950s, 18" h. **200-300**

Roy Rogers toy, horse trailer & jeep w/figures of Roy, Trigger & Pat, Ideal, 1950s, box 15" l., the set..................................... **200-300**

Roy Rogers Semi-Truck & Trailer

Roy Rogers toy, semi-truck & trailer, lithographed tin, yellow, red & blue w/Roy on rearing Trigger & "Roy Rogers - Trigger - Trigger Jr. - King of the Cowboys - Smartest Horses in the Movies" on the side, holds figures, early 1950s, the set (ILLUS.) **250-350**

Roy Rogers & Trigger figures, hard plastic, small size on card, Hartland, late 1950s **60-100**

Roy Rogers & Trigger Figures

Roy Rogers & Trigger figures, hard plastic, Trigger standing, half-rearing or rearing, Hartland, 1950s, each pr. (ILLUS. of one) **150-250**

Roy & Standing Trigger Figures

Roy Rogers & Trigger figures, hard plastic, Trigger standing, Hartland, late 1950s, boxed w/tag (ILLUS.)................... **125-250**

Roy Rogers yo-yo, plastic, photo of Roy & Trigger on the side, Western Plastics, 1950s......... **15-25**

Silver Figure Sealed on Card

Silver (Lone Ranger's horse) figure, plastic, jointed legs, from "The Legend of the Lone Ranger" movie, sealed on original card, Gabriel, 1979 (ILLUS.) **30-45**

Tom Mix booklets, a set of card-sized eight-page paper booklets w/two-color cover featuring a sketched scene w/Tom Mix, issued by National Chicle, 1934, excellent to near mint, set of 48 ...... **3,687**

Tonto & Scout figures, hard plastic, Hartland, boxed, 1954, 9 1/2" h., pr...... **100-250**

Tonto & Scout figures, hard plastic, semi-rearing pose, Hartland, boxed, 1954, 9 1/2" h., pr...... **200-350**

Gabriel Tonto & Scout Figures

Tonto & Scout figures, plastic w/articulated limbs, Gabriel, 1977, 12 " h., 2 pcs. (ILLUS.)...... **40-75**

Topper (Hopalong Cassidy's horse) rocking horse, plastic & wood, Rich Toys, early 1950s, 27" h. **200-250**

Trigger (Roy Rogers' horse) lunch box & thermos, steel, picture of Trigger, American Thermos, 1956 ...... **175-300**

Wagon Train playset, based on TV series, Marx, No. 4888, 1950s...... **300-1,700**

WIENER WERKSTATTE

The Wiener Werkstatte (Vienna Workshops) were co-founded in 1903 in Vienna, Austria by Josef Hoffmann and Koloman Moser. An offshoot of the Vienna Secession movement, closely related to the Art Nouveau and Arts and Crafts movements elsewhere, this studio was established to design and produce unique and high-quality pieces covering all aspects of the fine arts. Hoffmann and Moser were the first artistic directors and oversaw the work of up to 100 workers, including thirty-seven masters who signed their work. Bookbinding, leatherwork, gold, silver and lacquer pieces as well as enamels and furniture all originated from these shops over a period of nearly thirty years. The finest pieces from the Wiener Werkstatte are now bringing tremendous prices.

Basket, painted metal, of octagonal form w/a widely flaring rim & upright rectangular pierced strap handle, two sides w/a panel of pierced small quatrefoils in rectangles, painted white, w/glass liner, designed by Josef Hoffmann, printed "WIENER - WERKSTATTE," ca. 1905, 6 7/8" h...... **$1,380**

Finely Enameled Glass Beaker

Beaker, clear enameled glass, large inverted bell-form bowl raised on a gently flared trumpet base, decorated w/stylized flowers & foliage on the clear ground w/bubbles, enameled monogram "WW," early 20th c., 7 3/4" h. (ILLUS.)...... **2,760**

Figure of a nude woman, ceramic, stylized seated figure w/long hair, mounted on a square marble block base, designed by Susi Singer, ca. 1927, 3 x 3", 8" h. (base not original) **413**

WOOD SCULPTURES

American folk sculpture is an important part of the American art scene today. Skilled wood carvers turned out ship's figureheads, cigar store figures, plaques and carousel animals of stylized beauty and great appeal. The wooden shipbuilding industry, which had originally nourished this folk art, declined after the Civil War and the talented carvers then turned to producing figures for tobacconist's shops, carousel animals and show figures for circuses. These figures and other early ornamental carvings that have survived the elements and years are eagerly sought.

American eagle, carved & painted, the stylized spread-winged bird w/a shield on the breast & resting on an angled pole w/a long banner reading "Dum Vivimus Vivamus," polychrome paint, attributed to John H. Bellamy, 25 1/2" l., 8 1/4" h. (minor paint abrasions) **$23,000**

American elk, carved & stained pine, very realistic standing stag w/his head raised calling, finely carved & detailed w/wide spread antlers, standing on a stepped rockwork oblong base w/small tree stump, Northeastern Seaboard, late 19th c., 14" l., 20 1/4" h. **8,400**

Cigar store Indian Chief, carved & painted pine, the free-standing full figure Chief wearing powerfully carved feathered headdress & a bearskin cloak over a skirted garment, one arm raised & holding a tomahawk, the figure mounted on a rolling wood & concrete base, John L. Cromwell, New York, ca. 1850, overall 70" h. (nose & chin broken & repaired, numerous age cracks in headdress, arms, hands & body).................................. **69,750**

Cigar store Indian Princess, full-length standing figure wearing a feathered headdress & red costume w/green cloak, the right arm raised grasping a bunch of tobacco leaves, mounted on a brown-painted rectangular platform base, third-quarter 19th c., repainted, 61 1/4" h. **4,200**

Eagle, carved & gilded, a large perched spread-winged eagle w/high arched wings, perched on a rocky formation on a rectangular wooden base, gilt over black paint, 19th c., 27 x 41", 23 1/2" h. (gilt wear)... **2,645**

Eagle, carved & painted, the spread-winged bird in a downward swooping pose w/the head lowered, glass eyes, painted dark red w/gilt highlights, American, 19th c., 46 3/4" w., 34" h. (imperfections)................ **3,105**

Horse, well-detailed animal w/head & ears erect in a prancing pose, a bobbed tail, old black paint, later thin rectangular base, 7" h.. **880**

British Officer Band Organ Figure

Lion, the large recumbent animal w/head turned facing the viewer, well-detailed head & mane, dark weathered surface w/old gold repaint, 29" l................................... **880**

Military figure, carved & painted band organ figure depicting a British officer in uniform w/an articulated arm dressed in a blue & white uniform, a shako w/red plume & black boots, orginal paint, loss to base, paint wear, late 19th c., 31" h. (ILLUS. bottom previous column).............. **5,750**

Victorian Ship's Figurehead

Ship's figurehead, carved & painted pine, three-quarters length portrait of a young lady wearing a blue dress, w/braided reddish brown hair parted in the center, probably New England, ca. 1850, 24" h. (ILLUS.) **7,200**

Fine Carved Swan Figure

Swan, carved & painted, flattened full-bodied bird painted white w/black & yellow features, mounted on a carved oblong base painted blue & white, crackles, small losses on wings, 19th c., 16 3/4" l., 13" h. (ILLUS.) **14,950**

Urn finials, carved pine, a tall classical ribbed urn carved w/swagging drapery below the top rim, wide tapering cover w/a large flame finial, the tall pedestal base composed of tiered rings, Federal era, probably New England, ca. 1800, 8" d., 24" h., pr. **5,400**

Whirligig, African-American man & woman, he standing & jointed to pump a pump handle while she stands & bends to do wash in front of the pump, on a board w/a wide finned tail & a four-blade front propeller, red, white & blue stars on ends of propeller blades, white stars along the base board w/compass stars on the directional, 26 1/2" l. (glued age cracks, other minor age cracks w/wear & weathering) **1,073**

Unusual Whirlgig Figure of Man

Whirligig, carved & painted stylized figure of man w/pot belly, large hooked nose & pointed chin, face painted red & white, wearing a black top hat & shoes w/curled toes, the arm baffles wind activated, mounted on a rod standard in a wood base, white & red paint shows under black on body, wear, age cracks, some damage to arm, one is replacement, 19th c., America, 11 3/4" h. plus base (ILLUS.) **3,300**

WOODENWARES

The patina and mellow coloring, along with the lightness and smoothness that come only with age and wear, attract collectors to old woodenwares. The earliest forms were the simplest and the shapes of items whittled out in the late 19th century varied little in form from those turned out in the American colonies two centuries earlier. A burl is a growth, or wart, on some trees in which the grain of the wood is twisted and turned in a manner which strengthens the fibers and causes a beautiful pattern to be formed. Treenware is simply a term for utilitarian items made from "treen," another word for wood. While maple was the primary wood used for these items, they are also abundant in pine, ash, oak, walnut, and other woods. "Lignum Vitae" is a species of wood from the West Indies that can always be identified by the contrasting colors of dark heartwood and light sapwood and by its heavy weight, which caused it to sink in water.
Also see KITCHENWARES.

Barrel, cov., all-wood stave construction, four finger-lappet bands, flat cover w/low arched handle, old red finish, 30" h. **$2,008**

Basket, stave construction, rounded w/upright sides & bentwood lappet rim, bentwood swivel handle, old reddish brown paint, 1/2 bushel, 15" d., 8 3/4" h. plus handle **138**

Ash Burl Bowl

Bowl, burl ash, deep rounded sides, old soft patina, good wear, 14" d., 4 1/2" h. (ILLUS.) **1,430**

Bowl, burl, small shallow rounded form w/good figure & dark patina, turned footring & rim ring, natural imperfections at rim, 5" d., 1 5/8" h. **385**

Bowl, cov., turned ash burl, wide bulbous base tapering toward the bottom, fitted low domed cover w/disk finial, good figure, mellow finish, 5 3/4" d., 4 1/2" h. (exterior crack in bottom) **1,650**

Bowl, ash burl, deep rounded gently flaring sides w/molded rim, wide band turned near the foot, good figure, refinished, 14" d., 6" h. **1,650**

Bowl, ash burl, round w/sharply angled widely flaring sides, thinly turned w/raised rim & turned foot, good patina, 7 1/4" d., 2 1/2" h. (rim cracks) **385**

Bowl, burl, wide shallow rounded form w/well-turned decorative rings, good figure & color, 7 3/4" d., 2 1/2" h. **660**

Bowl, burl, small flat round base below steep deep gently rounded sides, good figure & color, turned foot & rim, soft patina w/interior wear, natural imperfections, 7 3/4" d., 3" h. (scorch mark) **605**

Rare Handled Burl Ash Bowl

Bowl, burl ash, small flat base below wide sloping sides w/two rectangular cut-out rim handles, small rim split, one handle w/glued repair, 16 1/2 x 19 1/2", 7 3/4" h. (ILLUS.) **7,700**

Bowl, ash burl, small flat bottom below deep steeply angled sides & flat rim, worn dark finish partially removed, 8" d., 3 1/2" h. (age crack in rim) **220**

Early Burl Bowl with Handles

Bowl, burl, a flat bottom below deep widely flaring elliptical sides w/rounded ends & cut-out handles, American, 18th c., minor age cracks, 20" l., 8" h. (ILLUS.)................ **2,760**

Bowl, burl, wide round form w/low upright sides w/a raised ring around the center of the sides, old dark finish, 9" d. **715**

Bowl, burl, a small flat base below deep flaring & gently rounded sides, old nut brown finish, good figure, incised line in body & shallow spiral-carved grooves around rim, 11 3/8" d., 3 1/2" h................... **1,430**

Bowl, turned curly maple, wide shallow round form w/raised ring around rim, good figure, 12 7/8" d. **275**

Bowl, turned, deep rounded form w/molded rim, the exterior w/dark red, the interior w/wear & a dark patina from use, 13 5/8" d., 4 1/8" h............................. **605**

Bowl, burl, round w/tapering sides, 19th c., 14" d., 5 1/2" h. (wear, losses around rim).. **978**

Bowl, turned & painted, round shallow form w/yellow paint, 19th c., 14 1/4" d., 3 1/2" h. (minor wear) **633**

Bowl, bird's-eye maple, wide shallow form w/molded rim, good color, some wear, 15" d., 4 1/4" h. **220**

Bowl, ash burl, flat base w/steeply angled flat sides, good figure, soft old scrubbed finish, 15 3/4" d., 5" h. (some natural age cracks, old putty-filled imperfections)......... **1,100**

Bowl, curly maple, a small base w/wide deep rounded sides, varnished finish, slightly oval, 14 3/4 x 15 3/4", 5" h. **248**

Bowl, turned ash burl, widely flaring sides w/a wide rim ring, old scrubbed surface, 16 3/4" d., 5" h. (early rim chips)..................... **715**

Bowl, ash burl, deep rounded sides w/faint turning rings & a wide molded rim, dense figure, heavy varnish, 16 3/4" d., 5 3/4" h. (some old putty-filled repairs) **1,100**

Bowl, ash burl, flat bottom w/wide rounded & flaring sides w/molded flat rim, good figure, old worn patina, 17" d., 6 1/4" h. (pieced repair in bottom) **1,100**

Bowl, ash burl, wide rounded sides w/molded rim, good figure, traces of red paint, detailed foot, 18" d., 5 1/2" h. (minor age cracks, edge wear)....................... **1,980**

Bowl, bird's-eye maple, deep wide rounded sides w/wide rim band, worn mellow varnish finish, good color, 19 1/2" d., 6 3/8" h., light stains on exterior) **468**

Bowl, almond-shaped, wide low angled sides, good old dark patina w/good wear, leather thong for hanging, attributed to Zoar, Ohio, 12 5/8 x 20 1/4", 4 1/2" h............ **495**

Bowl, ash burl, a small turned footring below the very deep & wide rounded sides w/a wide turned rim band, scrubbed finish, 19th c., 21" d., 8 1/2" h. (two age cracks w/old putty repair, wear) **1,650**

Bowl, turned poplar, wide rounded form w/molded rim band, red-stained exterior, varnished interior, 22" d., 7" h. **330**

Bucket, stave construction, wide cylindrical form w/two staves extending to form side rim handles, two wide finger-lappet bands, original bluish green paint w/cream-colored interior, 10" d., 8 1/2" h. at handles... **2,970**

Bucket, stave construction, wide tapering cylindrical form w/two steel bands & a wire bail handle w/turned wood grip, old bluish green paint, 12 1/2" d., 10 1/2" h. **330**

Bucket, stave construction, wide cylindrical form w/three wide finger-lappet bands, pegged bentwood swing handle, old black repaint w/gold line borders, 11 1/4" d., 13 3/4" h. (minor wear & chips)... **578**

Bucket, tapering cylindrical stave construction w/lapped wooden bands, curved swing handle w/pegged joinery, old bluish green paint, 19th c., 14 1/4" h.............. **1,150**

Butter churn, miniature dasher-type, stave construction, tapering sides, light natural finish, mostly copper tacks on hoops, small raised medallion handle on rim, embossed signature on base for "Fearing, Hingham," 9 3/4" h., w/dasher 20" h. **605**

Butter churn, painted pine, stave construction, tapering cylindrical form w/two lapped hickory bands & one iron band, old green paint, wooden dasher & inset oak lid, 19th c., 16 3/4" h. (base warped & loose).. **165**

Early Painted Butter Churn

Butter churn, stave construction, slightly tapering cylindrical form w/steel bands signed "John Bradley & Co. Stourbridge," w/lid & dasher, original red paint on exterior & yellow on interior, churn 18 1/2" h. (ILLUS.) **440**

Butter paddle, burl, large shallow rounded bowl w/an upright S-scroll handle w/finely scrolled handle terminal & carved fluting where handle joins bowl, good dark patina, 7 3/4" l. (few scorch marks) **2,530**

Butter paddle, burl, wide rounded shallow bowl & nearly upright angled rounded handle w/large ring opening at the tip, good figure & color, 9" l............................. **2,035**

Butter paddle, bird's eye maple, wide rounded shallow bowl w/tapering cylindrical handle, soft finish, 9 1/8" l. (age cracks) **55**

Butter paddle, burl, the wide shallow rounded bowl w/a slightly curved side handle carved w/a horse head terminal, fine burl, 9 1/4" l. **825**

Butter paddle, curly maple, wide gently curved oblong paddle w/a long narrow rounded end handle w/hook end, 9 5/8" l. (wear, short age crack).................................... **110**

Butter paddle, burl, an oblong bowl w/a sharply angled rounded long handle w/stylized bird head end terminal, 11 1/8" l. **715**

Carrier, cov., round bentwood, lapped seams w/copper tacks, fitted flat cover & bentwood swing handle, good old patina, 15" d., 7" h. plus handle **468**

Carrier, cov., round bentwood, deep cylindrical sides w/flat fitted cover & bentwood swing handle, old green paint, impressed label on cover "Robert Hyde, Winchendon," Massachusetts, 12" d., 7 1/4" h. **550**

Charger, turned wood w/decorative rings on both sides, 19 3/4 x 21" **193**

Churn, stave construction, oak, tall gently swelled barrel shape w/flared top, old red paint w/seven black metal bands, w/lid & dasher, Pennsylvania, 19th c., 27 1/2" h. plus dasher.. **330**

Cookie board, carved mahogany, rectangular board carved on one side w/a large almond-shaped reserve enclosing a spread-winged American eagle & shield, the other side w/a basket of flowers in a circle & a cornucopia in an almond reserve, attributed to Conger of New York, old dark worn patina, early 19th c., 7 1/4" h. **4,840**

Cookie board, rectangular, three carved roses w/vine border within a carved heart shape, dark refinishing, 6 3/4" w., 7 3/4" h. (age cracks & minor insect damage w/putty filler) **440**

Cookie board, pine w/old patina, a stylized silhouetted figure of a Native American leaning on a long rifle all within a narrow ring, carved pineapple on the reverse, 5 x 8" **825**

Finely Carved Cookie Board

Cookie board, carved mahogany, rectangular w/a large carved central circle w/finely detailed relief carving of a large spread-winged American eagle & shield

w/banner in its beak reading "E Pluribus Unum" above a central figure of George Washington standing & flanked by allegorical figures of Lady Liberty & Harvest Goddess, upright fruit-filled cornucopias at outer sides & a band of stars below, 19th c., 8 x 11 7/8" (ILLUS.) **4,620**

Cookie board, rectangular w/designs on both sides, one w/a woman w/a chicken in a basket on her back & wearing a long dress, the other side w/a man wearing a long coat & holding a chicken by its feet, 7 1/2 x 15" (age cracks in ends, iron staple hanger added).. **165**

Cookie board, carved, one side w/a full-length portrait of a man in 17th c. costume w/a knee-length jacket w/wide cuffs, long curled hair & hat, the other side w/a full-length portrait of a matching lady in a long dress, 6 1/2 x 18"..................... **440**

Cutlery tray, cherry, rectangular w/low canted sides, arched center divided w/oval cut-out grip flanked by small scrolls, old mellow finish, 8 7/8 x 14 3/4", 5 5/8" h. (old break at tip of one scroll) **303**

Dough box, cov., painted poplar & pine, canted sides on flat bottom, board top w/two top cleats, old mustard yellow paint over earlier red, Newsom-Berdan area, Pennsylvania, 19th c., 16 1/4 x 34", 12 1/2" h. (one top cleat repositioned, section of side molding missing).................... **330**

Dough box on stand, softwood, a flat board top on a dovetailed box w/canted sides, resting on a base w/a deep arched apron above four canted square tapering legs, 19th c., 18 x 40 1/2", 29 1/2" h. **550**

Dough box on stand, poplar, a rectangular two-board top w/brace battens lifting above a deep dovetailed well w/canted sides, raised on a rectangular frame on ring- and baluster-turned legs w/knob feet, scrubbed interior, dark refinishing, 19th c., 20 x 38 3/4", 30" h. (battens reset, age crack in top) **385**

Early Dough Trough on Stand

Dough trough on stand, poplar & pine, a long rectangular top w/breadboard ends lifting off a deep dovetailed dough box w/canted sides, set on a stand w/canted apron above canted ring- and ring-turned legs, refinished, pieced restorations, 19th c., top 29 1/2 x 55", 30" h. (ILLUS.) **770**

Drying rack, pine, hinged two-section type, each section w/three flat racks, old black finish, mortised & pinned construction, 50" w., 35" h. **121**

Drying rack, painted, folding-type, the center section composed of two square posts w/rounded tops on shaped arched feet joined by square rails, the two extendable conforming end sections swinging out from the center, old brown paint, New England, 19th c., 43" w., 36" h.............. **978**

Flax hatchel, a hardwood long flat board tapered toward each end & w/small holes there, a central large round nest of long spikes, the surface of the board scratch-carved w/various geometric designs highlighted in old red & black, 19th c., 30" l. (spikes deteriorating, some loose) **330**

Grain bin, painted pine, the rectangular molded overhanging lift top opening to an interior well, on cut-out feet, painted blue, New England, 19th c., 21 x 31 1/4", 30 1/2" h.............. **978**

Grain bin, painted wood, wide poplar boards w/original chocolate brown paint, shaped bracket base w/an applied molding, slant front w/large iron hinges, square nail construction, 22 x 49 1/2", 39" h. (cracks in front feet & minor edge wear)............. **413**

Jar, cov., a small high flaring turned foot below the bulbous ring-turned body tapering to a short flared neck & w/fitted domed cover w/pointed knob finial, wire bail handle w/wood grip, faint pencil inscription on base, soft worn finish, attributed to Pease of Ohio, 4" h. **385**

Jar, cov., turned, a short flaring foot below the bulbous turned body tapering to a short neck & fitted low-domed cover w/pointed knob finial, attributed to Pease of Ohio, lightly worn patina, 5" d., 6 1/2" h.............. **605**

Jar, cov., short flaring foot below the bulbous body tapering to a short neck & fitted low-domed cover w/conical knob finial, reddish brown w/yellowish sponging & dots, 6 5/8" d., 7 1/2" h. **1,073**

Jar, cov., short flaring foot below the bulbous body tapering to a short neck & fitted low-domed cover w/knob finial, brown graining w/yellow sponged tree or feather-like designs, 6" d., 8" h. (some wear, edge damage & age cracks)............ **1,430**

Jar, cov., painted poplar, flared foot on bulbous barrel-shaped body w/a raised ring around the top, low domed cover w/turned button finial, original reddish brown vinegar decoration over a yellow base coat, 19th c., 9 1/4" d., 12" h. (minor grain separation on interior of cover, couple of base chips)................... **3,850**

Jar, cov., wide cylindrical body, raised rings around the slightly tapering top & base, slightly domed top w/turned finial, original red vinegar decoration over yellow ground, some wear but 95% paint remaining, 13 1/4" d., 12 1/4" h. (ILLUS.)..... **5,280**

Keg, stave construction, six finger-lappets, carved bung & stopper, leather carrying strap, painted grey, early 19th c., 5 1/2 x 8 3/4" (wear) **489**

Kraut cutter, curly maple, rectangular board w/molded sides & arched crest w/a heart cut-out, inset w/an angled blade, old worn finish, 19 1/2" l. (nail hole, age cracks) **495**

Kraut cutter, walnut, rectangular board w/molded edges, inset w/an angled metal blade, the heart-shaped crest w/a small heart cut-out, old finish, 19th. c., 20 1/2" l. (age crack in crest)........................ **550**

Kraut cutter, curly maple, long rectangular board w/molded sides & an inset angled metal blade, a round projection at the top w/a hanging hole, arched cut-out at the bottom, old soft finish, 19th c., 8 x 25 1/2" **330**

Ladle, burl, hand-hewn w/a large wide rounded cupped bowl & squared straight handle, incised decoration of line & star on handle, mellow finish, 11 1/2" l. (filled knot holes)........................ **440**

Ladle, curly maple, a small deep round bowl w/a long gently arched rounded handle, good patina, 13 1/4" l. **330**

Mortar & pestle, burl, footed mortar, 19th c., mortar, 5" d., 6" h., pestle 9 1/4" l., 2 pcs. **193**

Mortar & pestle, turned hardwood, the mortar w/a turned short pedestal base below the barrel-form bowl, old red finish, 7 1/4" h., 2 pcs. (minor age cracks) **275**

Mortar & pestle, turned poplar, the mortar w/a heavy turned flared foot supporting a swelled cylindrical bowl, bulbous pestle w/slender handle, old red finish, 19th c., 7 1/2" h., 2 pcs. **275**

Oven peel, long handle w/a round plate end, handle end pierced for hanging, 18th c., 56 1/2" l. (wear)...................... **374**

Pantry box, cov., round bentwood, deep cylindrical sides w/fitted flat cover w/large knob finial, lapped construction w/steel tacks, old green & red painted finish, 12" d., 10 1/4" h.............................. **633**

Large Decorated Jar   *English Oak & Brass Pitcher*

Pitcher, stave-constructed oak, flat-bottomed ovoid form bound w/five brass bands & fitted w/a flared brass rim w/long spout & rounded copper arched handle, England, 19th c., 21 1/2" h. (ILLUS.) **3,795**

Plate, curly maple, wide flat bottom w/low canted sides, incised rings around top & under rim, old mellow finish, 9 1/8" d. **468**

Quilt rack, painted, the tapering chamfered square posts on trestle feet joined by two rails, old salmon paint, New England, 19th c., 48" l., 48" h. **920**

Scoop, wide rectangular form w/round double butterprint handle, flower on one side, floral medallion on the other, good patina on handle, 11 7/8" l. (worm holes) **248**

Smoothing board, painted, a long narrow rectangular board w/molded edges & stylized horse-form upright handle near one end, original green, red & black paint, the top w/incised compass stars & chip carving & hearts within star, incised "K.A.D. 1833," old reddish brown paint on handle, probably Scandinavian, 24" l. (handle head old replacement) **605**

Spice container, decorated, round w/turned foot & rim w/raised ring around the center, original reddish brown vinegar decoration over mustard yellow w/"Spice" in gold, 7" d., 4" h. (glued crack in one side, rim chips, may have had a cover) **193**

Early Painted Spoon Rack

Spoon rack, painted ash, a pedimented top w/angled cornices flanking a scalloped center section w/hanging hole, the long board fitted w/three pierced racks above the scalloped base, rose head nail construction, old red repaint, 8 3/4" w., 17 1/4" h. (ILLUS. w/separate spoons) **660**

Spoon rack, painted pine, the high backboard w/a stepped cut-out pointed top fitted w/two narrow spoon holding bands above an open rectangular bottom box, painted dark green, 18th c., 6 1/2 x 12", 20" h. (wear, minor loss) **7,475**

Storage barrel, stave construction, slightly tapering wide cylindrical form w/fitted flat cover, three metal bands around the body & single finger lappet on the cover, painted red, 19th c., wear, loose rims, 21 1/2" h. (ILLUS.) **1,150**

Stave-constructed Storage Barrel

Storage bin, painted poplar, a wide hinged slant top w/molded edges above a deep dovetailed case w/wide bootjack feet, old worn grey repaint over yellow, late 19th c., 20 1/2 x 37 1/4", 37 1/2" h. **220**

Early Painted Storage Box

Storage box, painted pine, tall rectangular slightly tapering dovetailed case w/a rectangular hinged & sloped top opening to shallow & deep compartments, molded base on simple bracket feet, old greyish blue paint, possibly Ohio, early 19th c., 22 x 47 3/4", 46 1/2" h. (ILLUS.) **3,450**

Sugar bowl, cov., burl, wide rounded form w/flat bottom & wide flat mouth fitted w/a domed cover & button finial, incised linear decoration, American, ca. 1800, 7" d., 6 1/4" h. **17,250**

Sugar bucket, cov., stave construction, slightly tapering cylindrical form w/two finger-lappet bands on body w/steel tacks, single lappet on flat fitted cover, wire bail handle w/wood grip, worn original olive green paint, 6 7/8" h. **523**

Sugar bucket, cov., stave construction, two finger-lappet bands on base w/copper tacks, single lappet on the fitted flat cover, pale yellow repaint over ivory, cover stamped "Wilder P. Clark," 10 1/8" d., 9 3/4" h. (paint wear, glued split in cover) **330**

Sugar bucket, cov., stave construction, tall tapering cylindrical sides w/two single lappet base bands & a single band at the rim, fitted flat cover w/single lappet, bentwood swing handle, old worn blue repaint over lighter blue, impressed label on cover "So. Hingham, Mass.," 9 1/4" d., 10" h. . **1,265**

Sugar bucket, cov., stave construction, tall tapering cylindrical sides w/two single lappet base bands & a single band at the rim, fitted flat cover w/single lappet, steel tacks on bucket & copper tacks on lid, bentwood swing handle, old grey paint w/partial label reading "Apple Butter, 1883, 1889" & stenciled "P.S." on lid, 14" h. (wear) 440

Sugar bucket, cov., stave construction, tapering cylindrical form w/two single lappet bands & fitted flat cover w/single lappet, old green paint, impressed label on cover "C. Wilson & Son, Hingham, Mass.," 14" d., 15" h. plus bentwood swing handle 605

Tankard, cov., stave & loop construction, tapering cylindrical form w/ring loops near the rim & base, carved cover & angular handle, England, 17th c., 7 3/4" h. (hoops loosened).. **2,415**

Tape loom, painted hardwood, a wide rectangular board w/a rounded top, pierced w/two bands of long narrow slits, a small inverted-heart cut-out at the top, old slate blue paint w/red decorations w/initials & a date of 1817, 9 1/2 x 14 1/2" **2,970**

Tazza, tiger stripe maple, a concave round shallow bowl on a turned baluster-form standard, dark finish, 19th c., 9 1/2" d., 7 1/4" h. (wear, scratches)........................... **1,380**

Trencher, hand-hewn oblong boat-form w/widely angled ends, old red painted exterior & rim, good color, 13 3/8 x 22 1/2", 4 1/4" h. (minor wear, age crack & chip at one end)... 440

Trough, hand-chiseled, rectangular, w/a reinforcing strip at each end on the top edge, 19th c., 21 1/2 x 45", 8 1/2" h. (age split) 115

Tub, cedar, alternating light & dark wood, stave construction w/extended cut-out rim handles secured w/metal bands, oval paper label reads "Cedar Ware, Manufactured by Joseph H. Clark, Andover, Mass," 19th c., 6 1/4" d., 5 1/4" h. (wear, loose band)... 173

Tub, stave-constructed w/two longer side staves extended for handles w/heart cutouts, wrapped w/two steel bands, old red & green paint, 9 1/4" d................................... 303

Early Pine Wall Box

Wall box, pine, a rounded top on the tapered crestboard w/hanging hole above a dovetailed box w/a hinged slant lid, original surface-mounted brass hinges, original dark finish, 19th c., 11 x 11 5/8", 17" h. (ILLUS.) 990

Watch hutch, carved mahogany, scalloped shaped top on hutch w/chip-carved decoration w/diamond, heart & snowflake designs, 19th c., 2 1/4 x 11 1/2", 6 1/2" h. (minor wear, loss to backboard) 748

Watch hutch, carved, model of a miniature grandfather clock case, the molded hood w/carved scrolls & spire finials, dentil molding above & below the rectangular dial opening, thin beaded columns flank dial opening & the arched central door & stepped-out base, molded center rosette in base over an arched apron, painted dark brown, 19th c., 3 x 4 3/4", 17 1/4" h. . **1,265**

Water keg, barrel shape w/old stopper, stave constructed, worn original red paint w/steel nails, 8 3/4" d...................................... 275

WRITING ACCESSORIES

Inkwells & Stands

Tiffany Favrile Glass Inkwell

Blown glass well, squatty bulbous eight-sided body w/dimpled sides & heavy ring around the shoulder below the short cylindrical neck, fitted w/a hinged bronze cap w/raised scroll decoration, the body in cobalt blue decorated w/swirled blue & silvery blue iridescence, glass well inside, polished pontil, circular paper label of Tiffany Studios, minor wear, late 19th c., 5 1/2" h. (ILLUS.) **$8,050**

Blown glass well, squatty bulbous form in colorless glass w/a spiral air trap pattern, sterling silver hinged cap w/monogram, polished pontil, silver marked "Sterling 2246," possibly Pairpoint Glass Co., early 20th c., 3" h. 374

Bronze stand, figural, a figure of Cupid kneeling beside the well, Europe, ca. 1900, 4 3/8" l. 345

Bronze well, figural, a bust of a satyr w/hinged mask lid, raised on a flat leaf standard, on tripartite base w/scroll legs ending in hoof feet, late 19th - early 20th c., 10 1/4" h. 288

Figural Fish Inkwell

Cast metal well, figural, modeled as a fish w/large front fins used as supports, hinged head & gills open to a clear glass well, 80% original paint, late 19th c., 5" l., 2 3/8" h. (ILLUS.)... **187**

Ornate Gilt-brass Inkstand

Gilt-brass stand, a pair of footed nearly spherical inkwells cast in relief w/classical bust portraits & scrolls & w/a lid topped by a winged griffin finial, the pair set onto a rectangular tray w/an ornate leafy scroll design & cast center medallion surrounded by a wide raised border band w/gadrooned edging, a loop handle at each end, raised on four scroll feet, Europe, 19th c., tray 8 x 11", inkwells 4" h., the set (ILLUS.) **220**
Gilt-bronze well, figural, in the form of a small barrel of fish surrounded by an anchor & ropes on a rocky base, barrel forms the well, on an oval stepped green marble base, France, late 19th c., 5" l. **345**
Gilt-metal stand, figural, model of a stag's head w/antlers forming pen rest on a rectangular base raised on trefoil feet & w/a border of leaves, head flanked by two pressed glass inkwells, Bradley and Hubbard, late 19th c., 5 x 10".......................... **345**
Pewter stand, Art Nouveau style, a narrow rectangular tray on thin disk foot fitted at each end w/a square clear glass inkwell w/hinged metal cap, decorated w/a raised vine & leaf design, impressed marks "English Pewter 2 - 0715 - Made in England," early 20th c., 3 1/2 x 10 1/4", 2 5/8" h... **374**

Decorated Porcelain Inkwell

Porcelain well, square form w/a flattened shoulder centering a brass collar & hinged porcelain button-form lid, white ground decorated w/bands of light blue alternating w/white bands decorated w/colorful florals, ca. 1900, 3 1/8" h. (ILLUS.) **303**

Rockingham-glazed Dog Inkwell

Pottery inkwell, figural, modeled as a recumbent long-haired dog on an oblong base, single pen hole in front, overall mottled brown Rockingham glaze, late 19th c., 6 1/8" l., 3 7/8" h. (ILLUS.)................ **385**
Wood well, waisted cylindrical form, brown & yellow sponge decoration w/gilt stenciling, glass insert, paper label on bottom w/"Manufactured by S. Silliman & Co....Conn.," 4 1/4" d., 2 1/2" h. (wear to top) **193**

Lap Desks & Writing Boxes

Ornate Chinese Export Lap Desk

Black lacquer, the hinged rectangular case in black lacquer decorated around the front & sides w/gilt Chinese landscape scenes w/figures incised w/wide floral & leaf borders, end ring handles, opening to a row of pigeonholes & opening again to a two-section velvet-lined writing slide, the lower section opening to storage, the second to storage w/further pigeonholes, spring mechanism secret panel opening to small drawers, Chinese Export, late 19th c. (ILLUS.) **1,093**
Burl w/a chestnut bottom, wide hinged slant lid above a low compartment, dovetailed construction, good old finish, 15 1/2 x 21 1/2", 9 1/2" h. (repairs) **1,320**
Exotic wood & satinwood veneer, rectangular w/hinged lid, satinwood trim, diamond-shaped inlay on center of lid & escutcheon, the fitted velvet-lined interior w/two glass ink bottles, pen tray & com-

partment fitted w/five drawers, 19th c., 9 x 17 3/4", 6 7/8" h. (minor cracks) **633**

English Mahogany Lap Desk

Mahogany, a narrow rectangular top above a wide hinged slanted lid serving as writing surface & opening to a fitted interior, very small square drawer at top of one end w/longer drawer at the bottom of that end, brass shield-shaped keyhole escutcheon on the front, England, 19th c., 10 x 14", 9" h. (ILLUS.).................................... **350**

Mahogany, rectangular hinged form w/brass strapping to corners, plain brass plaque on lid, opening to compartments w/inkwells, the lid interior w/a document folio, further opening to baize writing surface w/storage flaps, England, late 18th - early 19th c., 9 3/4 x 14", 4 3/4" h................... **345**

Rosewood, rectangular, brass edging, flush brass handles, inlaid escutcheon & cartouche on lid, opening to lined writing slide & storage compartments, 19th c., 11 x 19 3/8", 7" h. **345**

Miscellaneous

Letter opener, bronze, designed w/two relief-molded dachshund heads, early 20th c., 10" l. **173**

Stamp box, cov., bronze, Zodiac patt., small rectangular form w/hinged cover w/zodiac design, three stamp compartments inside, brownish green patina, base stamped "Tiffany Studios New York 802," early 20th c., 2 x 3 1/2", 1" h. **374**

YARN LONG PRINTS

Pompeian Beauty Yard Long

These out of proportion colorful prints were fashionable wall decorations in the waning years of the 19th century and early in the 20th century. They come in both vertical and horizontal format. A wide variety of subjects is available to collectors.

All listed are framed unless otherwise noted.

Advertising, Pompeian Beauty, titled "Absence Cannot Hearts Divide," featuring movie star Margarite Clark wearing ankle-length peach colored gown, 1921, litho by Forbes, minor creases top & bottom band (ILLUS.)... **$66**

Variety of Yard Long Prints

Advertising, Pabst Co., beautiful woman w/dark upswept hair w/red flower band, wearing long red dress trimmed in black & holding bouquet of yellow flowers, double-sided, framed under glass (ILLUS. center right)....................................... **350**

Advertising, Pompeian Beauty, lovely lady in long pink dress w/sheer overskirt holding a letter, minor tears, framed under glass (ILLUS. center left) **220**

Flapper woman, signed "Alfred Everett Orr, 1914," stains (ILLUS. far left) **66**

Mary Pickford, standing on a step, holding a floral spray, wearing light peach colored long ruffled tiered dress, her blond hair pulled back w/long sausage curls on her shoulders, signed at bottom "Sincerely Mary Pickford," tears & stains (ILLUS. far right)................................. **55**

YARN WINDERS

Floor model reel, maple & other hardwood w/a curly maple cross-form base, a small upper crossbar & a large flat & shaped lower crossbar joined by double spindles at each side, a small turned cup at the top center, the slender tapering central shaft fitted into the thick heavy cross-form base, old patina, 19th c., 43" h. **$110**

Floor model reel, pine & hardwood, three turned & canted legs supporting a round turned base centered by a large ring-and baluster-turned post w/six long bars extending around the revolving top, each arm w/adjustable upright pegs, light natural finish, attributed to the Shakers,

19th c., 32" h. (repaired age crack in base, two spindles of darker color)................. **330**

Niddy-noddy, carved walnut, detailed chip-carved decoration, initialed "O.P." & dated 1798, 14 1/4 x 17 1/2" (small age splits)................. **403**

Niddy-noddy, carved wood, the crossed bars carved w/polyhedron intervals, incised heart & zig-zag decoration, 19th c., 14 1/2 x 18"................. **633**

Swift, brass & steel, brass pin cup w/steel slats, shaft & clamp, tied w/red silk ribbons, 22 1/2" h. (minor corrosion, lacking two silk ribbon ties)................. **489**

Swift, painted wood, red-painted cup w/flower at center, green & black painted shaft w/natural wood expanding slats, the turned wooden clamp painted yellow w/red & blue painted flowers, 19th c., 22 1/2" h. (minor wear)................. **575**

Table model reel, hardwood, the reel w/four T-form blades joining a bobbin-turned cross stretcher between turned uprights w/a long handle on one side & a geared mechanism on the other, a lower turned stretcher & a trestle-style turned rail base frame, old patina, chip-carved detail, 19th c., 17" h. (repairs, worm holes)................. **193**

Index